# 1890
# CIVIL WAR
# VETERANS CENSUS:
# TENNESSEE

*Transcribed by*
**BYRON SISTLER**
*and*
**BARBARA SISTLER**

JANAWAY PUBLISHING, INC.
Santa Maria, California

## Notice

In many older books, foxing (or discoloration) occurs and, in some instances, print lightens with wear and age. Reprinted books, such as this, often duplicate these flaws, notwithstanding efforts to reduce or eliminate them. The pages of this reprint have been digitally enhanced and, where possible, the flaws eliminated in order to provide clarity of content and a pleasant reading experience.

Copyright © 1978, Byron Sistler

Originally published:
Evanston, Illinois
1978

Reprinted by:

Janaway Publishing, Inc.
732 Kelsey Ct.
Santa Maria, California 93454
(805) 925-1038
www.janawaygenealogy.com

2014

ISBN: 978-1-59641-334-4

*Made in the United States of America*

# EXPLANATION

At the time of the 1890 U.S. census the Census Office undertook an enumeration of all veterans who had served in the Union forces during the Civil War. In addition to names of the veterans (and their widows, if deceased) the schedules were to include branch of service and unit served with, dates of enlistment and discharge, current post office address, disability incurred, plus "other information necessary for a complete statement of the veteran's term of service." Persons who served under assumed names were to be listed under their real names followed by their aliases.

Unfortunately the schedules as ultimately rendered were far from complete. More often than not some of the requested information was omitted, and in many cases we are able to learn only the name of the veteran, branch of service, county of residence and Civil District number. Nevertheless, since practically all the 1890 census other than the veterans census was lost or destroyed, even this sketchy information is valuable to genealogical researchers.

That the Census Office failed to produce complete schedules was not from lack of trying. In addition to the customary house-to-house effort by enumerators (completed during the month of June, 1890), records of the Pension Office were examined, Grand Army of the Republic post rosters procured, and requests were made for State rosters, adjutant generals' reports, and similar documents. "Many thousands of letters were written to veterans to obtain information not obtained by the enumerators, and inquiries were published in about 500 newspapers throughout the country in order to elicit responses from veterans overlooked in the enumeration." (National Archives: Introduction to Schedules)

Some of the enumerators seem to have been quite conscientious in their efforts to complete the requested information, but faced many obstacles. As one reported:

> "It is difficult to get near to parts. In some instances the person is absent and others have but little interest in giving the items desired. I have taken great pains to have the schedule correctly reported but have fallen short."
> (A. J. Greer, C1-58-3)

This book lists in alphabetical order the names of about 26,000 Tennessee men who served in some branch of service during the Civil War. While as noted above the intent was to cover only Union servicemen, we discovered that about 10% of those included were Confederates. Several hundred more, not so identified, were probably Confederates, judging from the unit numbers.

It has been our intent to include virtually all data shown on the schedules, including some that appears to have no importance and some that, to us at least, makes no sense. We did not copy the information of "yrs mos days of service" except where it seemed pertinent since the "dates of enlistment and discharge" column was sufficient in our view.

Where the words "no" or "none" appeared on the schedule we would usually omit this as being of little or no value.

A substantial number of blacks served with the Union Army'. Usually they are identified in the transcription by the letters "Col." Sometimes one can determine the color only by the unit served with, or by the fact. most of the blacks enlisted fairly late in the war and often remained with the army a year or more after the war ended. Their units were segregated and were entirely officered by whites.

Regarding "Colored" soldiers--while the vast bulk of them enlisted in the Union Army late in the war, it appears some were serving as early as August 1862. On August 1, 1862, a Federal official in South Carolina announced the issuance of papers indicating their freedom to Negro soldiers, not yet legally enlisted.
Occasionally in this volume you will observe the curious phenomenon of a black man listed as a Confederate. This was not necessarily an error. A few did so serve, probably without exception in return for a promise of freedom from slavery. This procedure was indeed made official by the Confederate Congress on March 13, 1865, and late that month "Negro soldiers were seen in Richmond." (The Civil War Day by Day, E. B. Long, 1971)

We have identified Confederates with the letters CONF at the end of an entry.

It should be remembered that by no means all veterans listed in the special census were residents of Tennessee at the time of the war. Many Northerners moved to Tennessee in the 1870s and 1880s, usually for the purpose of working in the new factories which were springing up in the larger cities of Knoxville, Nashville, Chattanooga and Memphis.

The order in which we have recorded the entries is as follows;

> name of veteran
> symbol for county of residence, enumeration district and
> page number
> (for identification on the microfilm, where a second
> page number
> appears in parentheses it signifies that the pagination
> as shown
> by the enumerator was in error)
> name of widow, if any
> veteran's alias, if any
> rank and unit
> dates of enlistment and discharge
> post office address
> disability incurred
> remarks

Where a person whose surname differed from that of a veteran (including aliases) appears in an entry, this is cross referenced in the appropriate alphabetical location.

One does not have to read far in this book to wonder at the strange variety of spellings encountered. Spelling in most of Tennessee in 1890 was about where it was 100 years before in parts of the country where people were better educated. Keep in mind that within the memory of living man there were many parts of the South where "book learning" was considered dangerous and evil. So forgive us for not trying to make corrections in spelling--we can visualize a game developing where the winner is the one who can figure out the most ways to spell "diarrhea" in 1890.

In trying to interpret the listings regarding military units in the various entries it is well to remember that the basic "unit" was the regiment. Where the unit is identified only by number it can be assumed it was a regiment, and if the state was omitted it almost always was a Tennessee unit.

Except where an unidentifiable abbreviation of a state was indicated by the enumerator, we have supplied our own abbreviations, and these are the standard two-letter state abbreviations now approved by the U.S. Post Office.

A fairly serious problem we encountered in transcribing this material was the occasional difficulty of determining which were first names and which last. Some of the enumerators were not consistent in placing given or surnames first on the schedule. While we used special care, we feel sure that some of the names are reversed. Please keep this in mind while searching for a specific name.

You will note in perusing the volume that considerable attention was given by the enumerators to "prisons" where prisoners of war were confined. Anyone who has read details about the notorious Andersonville and who realizes that some other prisons, North and South, might not be far behind in unpleasantries, must understand that there was a real reason for dwelling on the prisons and how long a given soldier was incarcerated.

The primitive nature of medicine, even in 1890, is appalling. The description of disabilities as reported by the enumerators often defies the imagination.

We have personally found this project the most interesting and rewarding of all those we have undertaken in this field. We hope you will as well, and that you will not stop examining when you have extracted the information you are interested in. Certainly the Civil War has come alive for us in a way we never found in the history books.

Byron Sistler  
Barbara Sistler  
Evanston, IL  
February, 1978

## ARCHAIC AND UNUSUAL MEDICAL TERMS

Preparation of the following list was aided by use of <u>Our Family Physician</u> (Henderson & Smith, 1885), a book, we are happy to report, that is long out of print. How it was possible for anyone, treated by the antidotes found therein, to survive to adulthood is one of the mysteries of life.

AFFECTION, a general term indicating a disease or ailment
ANASARCA--generalized edema or dropsy
APOPLEXY--sudden loss, more or less complete, of consciousness and voluntary
    motion, without the circulation or breathing being suspended. It is pro-
    duced by pressure on the brain
CATARRH--inflamation of mucous membrane, especially of the nose or throat
CHILLBLAINS--painful swelling or inflamed sore on the feet or hands, caused by
    exposure to cold
CHOLERA MORBUS--a disease characterized by vomiting, purging, violent gripings
    coldness and cramps of the extremities. This was probably appendicitis
COLA--apparently an inflamation of the colon
CONSUMPTION--tuberculosis
CYANOSIS--bluish coloration of the skin due to lack of oxygen
DENTITION--teething
DROPSY--an accumulation of serum or watery fluid in cavities or tissues of the
    body
DYSPEPSIA--indigestion or heartburn
ERYSIPELAS--an acute infectious disease of the skin or mucous membranes, also
    known as St. Anthony's fire
GRAVEL--kidney stone or stone in the bladder
FLUX (or bloody flux)--dysentery
HYDROCELE--a collection of watery fluid in a cavity of the body, especially in the
    scrotum or along the spermatic cord
INANITION--exhaustion from lack of food or inability to absorb and digest food
INFORMATION OF _____ --an inflamation
JANDERS--jaundice
LOCKJAW--tetanus
MARASMUS--atrophy; progressive emaciation
NEURALGIA--pain in a nerve. In late 19th century the term was used quite frequently,
    and apparently in many cases for distress that had little to do with the
    nervous system. For example, there was "neuralgia of the heart" which,
    judging from the symptoms, was either heart attack or angina. "Neuralgia
    of the stomach" seems to have been what we call heartburn. "Neuralgia of
    the head" was simply a headache
PARTURITION--labor and childbirth
PHTHISIS (phthisis pulmonalis)--a wasting away of the body, particularly from
    tuberculosis
PILES--hemorrhoids
PROLAPSIS--the falling or slipping out of place of an organ
PUTRID SORE THROAT--general infection of mouth and throat area
REMITTING (or intermittent) FEVER--symptoms suggesting malaria
RISING--a morbid swelling
ST. ANTHONY'S FIRE--see "erysipelas"
SCARLETINA--scarlet fever
SCROFULA--enlargement of one or more glands, particularly of the neck; goiter was
    considered scrofula
SPINA BITHIDA (bifida)--birth defect involving spinal column
TABES MESENTERICA--a type of tuberculosis
TERTIARY--a stage in the development of syphilis
THRUSH--ulcerative sore throat
TRICHINIA--apparently trichinosis
TRISMUS NASCENTIUM--tetanus
VARICOCELE--a varicose vein in the scrotum

CORRECTION

In our book <u>1890 Civil War Veterans Census--Tennessee</u> the county symbol Cr was inadvertently used for both Carroll and Crockett counties. To determine which county applies where this symbol appears, note that the following are the Crockett County entries:

Acuff, Richard W.
Allen, Sam
Andrews, C. P.
Ausment, Calvin J.
Baird, George W.
Ballard, Thos. A.
Barnes, Benjamin F.
Beliford, Charley
Best, Jno. C.
Blackwell, Alford
Bleadson, Jos. M.
Bowen, Reece
Bradley, Joseph B.
Branch, K.
Brandburg, Dave M.
Bridger, Richard C.
Briggs, Stephen M.
Britton, Benjamin F.
Burrow, Newt
Campbell, W. W.
Carr, Allen
Carr, Lucitta
Chaney, E. J.
Chrisman, Atlantic M.
Cleek, Shad R.
Cochran, J. M.
Cofer, John H.
Conyers, T. F.
Cook, Alford
Cousins, Robt. T.
Craiglow, Daniel
Crews, Gordon N.
Curtis, Charley F.
Daniel, Lewis W.
Dean, George W.
Edwards, Joseph J.
Fielder, William
George, B. F.

Gibson, Thomas F.
Gooch, Willice C.
Green, Ike
Harbert, J. W.
Hart, James K.
Haynes, Joe A.
Hess, Nelson J.
Hicks, Erasmus F.
Hicks, James N.
Hicks, John W.
Hiter, William Y.
Hodge, Charley H.
Holt, Jacob
Hopkins, Samuel J.
Jackson, William
Jacox, Augustus
Jenkins, Jas. W.
Jetton, Robert
Johnson, Chas. R.
Johnson, Edd
Jones, Henry
Kelly, James
Kenner, Thomas H.
Kirkpatrick, Thos. C.
Lacy, Sam
Lawson, William P.
Lowry, Robert W.
Lovelace, Simon
Lytle, Gardner
Mason, Lee H.
Mays, William T.
McClanahan, James R.
McKelvey, John W.
Mitchell, James
Moore, Charles N.
Moss, George N.
Norvill, William H.
Pate, William N.
Patrick, William

Payne, James K.
Perry, Simon
Phelps, David R.
Phillips, James E.
Phillips, William R.
Pitner, Robert M.
Pratt, Willis V.
Prescott, William
Richardson, Daniel
Sandling, Orman
Sherrod, William N.
Smith, J. T.
Smith, John H.
Spence, Joseph S.
Spinks, J. H.
Stamps, J. T.
Stevens, Wm. J.
Stine, Chas. L.
Taylor, David H.
Taylor, James N.
Thomas, Wesley
Trimer, Andrew J.
Tucker, James
Turner, Ben F.
Turner, John B.
Turner, William N.
Vaughan, William
Wade, Osias H.
Webb, Willie K.
Weddle, John B.
White, Robt. K.
Williams, John W.
Williams, R. L.
Williams, Solomon G.
Witzgan, John
Wood, Francis J.
Wray, William E.
Young, Moody

## KEY TO COUNTY SYMBOLS

| | | | | | |
|---|---|---|---|---|---|
| A | Anderson | Ha | Hancock | Moo | Moore |
| B | Bedford | Hr | Hardeman | Mg | Morgan |
| Be | Benton | Hd | Hardin | O | Obion |
| Bl | Bledsoe | Hm | Hamblen | Ov | Overton |
| Bo | Blount | Hw | Hawkins | P | Perry |
| Br | Bradley | Hy | Haywood | Pi | Pickett |
| C | Campbell | He | Henderson | Po | Polk |
| Ca | Cannon | Hn | Henry | Pu | Putnam |
| Cr | Carroll | Hi | Hickman | R | Rhea |
| Ct | Carter | Ho | Houston | Ro | Roane |
| Ce | Cheatham | Hu | Humphreys | Rb | Robertson |
| Ch | Chester | J | Jackson | Ru | Rutherford |
| Cl | Claiborne | Ja | James* | S | Scott |
| Cy | Clay | Je | Jefferson | Se | Sevier |
| Co | Cocke | Jo | Johnson | Sq | Sequatchie |
| Cf | Coffee | K | Knox | Sh | Shelby |
| Cc | Crockett | L | Lauderdale | Sm | Smith |
| Cu | Cumberland | La | Lawrence | St | Stewart |
| D | Davidson | Le | Lewis | Su | Sullivan |
| De | Decatur | Lk | Lake | Sn | Sumner |
| Dk | DeKalb | Li | Lincoln | T | Tipton |
| Di | Dickson | Lo | Loudon | Tr | Trousdale |
| Dy | Dyer | M | Macon | U | Unicoi |
| F | Fayette | Ma | Madison | Un | Union |
| Fe | Fentress | Mr | Marion | V | Van Buren |
| Fr | Franklin | Ms | Marshall | W | Warren |
| G | Gibson | Mu | Maury | Wa | Washington |
| Gi | Giles | Mc | McMinn | Wy | Wayne |
| Gr | Grainger | Mn | McNairy | We | Weakley |
| Ge | Greene | Me | Meigs | Wh | White |
| Gu | Grundy | Mo | Monroe | Wi | Williamson |
| H | Hamilton | Mt | Montgomery | Wl | Wilson |

*James Co. does not appear on modern maps. This county was formed out of part of Hamilton Co. in 1870, and was reunited with Hamilton in 1919.

AABNY, Henri, Ge-93-1; Lucinda Snyder widow US Sol; PO omitted
AARONS, Robert, Pu-146-2; Permelia widow of; Cpl B Co 1st TN Mtd Inf Vol; 11-22-64 to 4-14-65; Ai PO
ABANATHY, Charles H., Rb-228-2; Pvt; 61 to __ (1 yr); Springfield PO; CONF
ABANATHY, Dan, We-220-2; Pvt A Co TN State Troop; Oct 14 64 to Apr 14 65; PO omitted
ABBET, Isaac, Se-220-1; Elizabeth E. widow of; Pvt A Co 2nd TN Cav; Emurts Cave PO
ABBEY, Charles, K-180-2; Pvt H Co 103rd OH Vol Inf; 9 Aug 62 to 23 Jun 65; Bearden PO
ABBEY, Frank, Sh-158-2; Pvt A Co 55th Col Inf; 62 to 14 Aug 64; Memphis PO; eyes badly injured by powder and palpitation of heart, a badly used up man; discharge papers in Washington and has pension of 7? per month
ABBOTT, Abner T., Mc-109-2; Mary widow of; Regret PO; failed to find discharge
ABBOTT, Abner W., K-166-1; Pvt A Co 3rd TN Inf; 26 Feb 62 to __; Knoxville PO; piles, diarrhea, deaf, kidney trouble
ABBOTT, Franklin, Bo-20-1; Pvt B Co 6th TN Inf; 3-8-62 to 4-21-65; Bank PO
ABBOTT, John, Bo-23-1; Winnie widow of; Cpl B Co 6th TN Inf; 3-8-62 to __-4-63; Lyon Springs PO; discharged on sur(geon's?) certificat, now dead
ABBOTT, Martin L., R-157-2; Sol; 12th Dist, Grand View PO
ABBOTT, Melvin M., Wh-182-1; Sol; 3rd Dist
ABBOTT, Noah, Bo-20-1; Cpl E Co 9th TN Cav; 10-1-63 to 9-11-65; Bank PO; cronic diarhia & rumatism, in the invalid corps
ABEL, Almon, D-44-3; M Co 2nd IA Cav; 9-28-61 to 8-74; Nashville PO
ABEL, George, Ro-209-1; Pvt E Co 1st TN Inf; 23 Jul 61 to 10 Aug 65; Glen Alice PO
ABEL, James, Ro-209-1; Pvt E Co 1st TN Inf; 23 Jul 61 to Aug 65; Kings Creek PO
ABEL, William, Ro-209-1; Pvt E Co 1st TN Inf; 23 Jul 61 to Sep 65; Glen Alice PO
ABERNATHA, James, D-92-1; US Sol; Davidson Co. PO
ABERNATHA, James, D-92-2; Nashville PO
ABERNATHY, J. R., Hd-48-1; Pvt F Co TN Inf; Aug 3 63 to Jun 29 65; Savannah PO
ABERNATHY, James E., Gi-133-1; Capt 1st TN; Dec 61 to Dec 63; Bufords PO; CONF
ABERNATHY, James T., R-159-2; Col 10th TN Cav; 10-62 to 8-1-65; Rhea Springs PO; diseased in body
ABERNATHY, John H., Gi-127-5; Pvt E Co 12th US Col Inf; 8-1-63 to 1-16-66; Pulaski PO
ABERNATHY, Lewis, Gi-128-1; Pvt G Co 111th TN Inf; 63 to 65; 8th Civil Dist
ABERNATHY, Monroe, Gi-132-2; Pvt F Co 110th USCV; Dec 6 63 to Feb 6 66; DeRay PO
ABERNATHY, Rheubin, Gi-128-1; Pvt G Co 111th TN Inf; 63 to 65; 8th Civil Dist
ABERNATHY, Thomas, Col, Gi-133-1; Pvt F Co 110th TN; 64 to 66; Bufords PO
ABERNATHY, William, Gi-127-8; Silvester widow of; Pulaski PO; dates & particulars not known
ABINGTON, Matthew, Sh-152-1; Collierville PO; lost left eye
ABLE, James, Mr-95-2; Pvt A Co 9th TN Cav; 9-1-63 to 9-13-65; Victoria PO
ABLE, Joseph C., Sq-164-5(1); Pvt A Co 9th TN Cav; 9-1-63 to 8-11-65; Brock PO
ABLES, John D., H-50-1; Pvt K Co 4th R TN Cav; 1-28-64 to 7-12-65; Daisy PO; relapse of measles
ABNEY, Jacob, Sh-161-1; US Sol; 16th Dist
ABRAMS, William C., Mr-99-2; discharge lost, no details on unit or dates; Jasper PO
ABRAMS, William F., Hd-49-2; Pvt D Co 2nd TN Mtd Inf; Sep 1 63 to Feb 1 65; Gillis Mills PO; rumatism, lung & kidney & piles
ABRETUN, Alfred, Je-141-2; Pvt F & M Cos 1st TN Cav; 1 Nov 62 to 25 Jun 65; Mossy Creek PO
ABSTON, Byrd, Ro-210-7; Louiza Newson formerly widow of; Pvt 1st TN Inf; Rockwood PO
ACHESON, Isaac, Sh-167-1; Pvt K Co Morgans Cav; 12 Jul 61 to 65; CONF
ACKER, Benjamin F., D-92-1; Pvt I Co 132nd IN Inf; 63 to 65; West Nashville PO; rheumatism
ACKERSON, Thomas, Sh-183-1; Pvt B Co 7th Ch; 10-29-62 to 9-6-65; Memphis PO; wound hand, foot and back

ACKISON, David, Br-12-1; Charleston PO
ACKLEY, Patrick, Ma-125-1; Jackson PO
ACKLIN, Dave, H-62-1; Lucy widow of; 303 West Sixth, Chattanooga PO
ACKLIN, Joseph (see Robinson, Joseph)
ACREE, John, Ov-136-1; Pvt G Co 9th TN Cav; 4-9-63 to 9-11-65; Livingston PO; measles & cold settling on lungs
ACTON, Morton, Co-66-1; Pvt B Co 26th TN Inf; 15 Nov 62 to 1 Sep 63; Birdsville PO; rheumatism; CONF
ACUFF, Cannon, Je-141-3; Pvt B Co 8th TN Cav; 1 May 63 to 65; Mill Springs PO
ACUFF, Coram, Un-250-2; Pvt D Co 1st TN Inf; 26 Jul 62 to 26 Jul 65; Maynardville PO; diarhea resulted in chronic gastritus or indigestion incured in service
ACUFF, David M., Ro-205-1; Sgt E Co 1st TN Inf; 20 Aug 61 to 17 Sep 65; Rockwood PO
ACUFF, Howard, Un-253-3; US Sol; 4th Civil Dist
ACUFF, James, Bl-3-3; Pvt F Co 2nd TN Cav; 10-62 to 1-63; Billingsly PO; CONF
ACUFF, Joel, Je-145-2; Pvt E Co 3rd TN Cav; Dec 62 to Sep 63; Dumplin PO
ACUFF, Joel R., Gr-81-3(1); Cpl A Co 2nd TN Cav; 1 Aug 62 to 5 Jul 65; Clear Spring PO; lungs & stomach, partly disabled
ACUFF, Nathaniel F., Un-253-2; Sgt B Co 8th TN Cav; 23 Apr 63 to 11 Sep 65; Lorenaton PO; shot through right leg
ACUFF Peter, Gr-82-1; Pvt D Co 1st TN Inf; 4 Jul 62 to 17 Sep 64; Powder Spring PO; eyes, exposure
ACUFF, Richard W., Cr-4-5; Pvt A Co 1st TN Cav; 61 to 65; Bells Depot PO; CONF
ADAIR, Robert A., K-174-1; Pvt K Co 1st TN Cav; 1 Apr 62 to 6 Apr 65; Church Grove PO; gun shot wound, all most disable from labor
ADAIR, William C., Mc-111-2; Pvt B Co 7th TN Mtd Inf; 9-24-64 to 7-27-65; Athens PO
ADAMER, James A., H-51-4; Pvt A Co 6th TN Inf; 8-2-64 to 7-26-65; Hill City PO
ADAMS, Abe, Ce-30-1; Bettie widow of; Pvt 12th TN Inf; 63 to 65; Pegrams PO; rheumatism
ADAMS, Abraham E., Jo-249-2; Pvt H Co 4th TN Inf; 10 Apr 65 to 2 Aug 65; Mountain City PO; dirrhea & neuralgia
ADAMS, Charles R., Ro-210-1; Pvt M Co 3rd US Art; 2 May 63 to 2 May 66; Rockwood PO
ADAMS, Charley, H-51-7; Pvt E Co 29th NC Inf; 8-1-61 to 11-1-64; Fairmount PO
ADAMS, Edwin S., Sn-262-3(2); Pvt 3rd Col Inf; 62 to 65; Fountain Head PO; all the information I could get
ADAMS, Felix, Gi-134-1; Dist 14
ADAMS, Francis O., M-107-6; 7th Civil Dist
ADAMS, George, Sn-255-1; Cpl D Co 16th TN Inf; 1-1-63 to 5-1-63 (sic) (8 mos); Worsham PO; shot in neck, can't stoop or bend over
ADAMS, Geo., Hd-54-2; Sgt C Co 6th TN Cav; 18 Jan 64 to 26 Jul __ (1 yr 4 mos 8 days); Saltillo PO; right testacle mashed, draws pension
ADAMS, George Jr., H-62-2; Drummer B Co 128th OH Inf; 2-28-65 to 7-13-65; Chestnut, Chattanooga PO
ADAMS, Giles, H-74-1; Quartermaster Sgt G Co 12th TN Cav; 10-63 to 10-65; 711 Montgomery Ave, Chattanooga PO
ADAMS, Gillispie, Lo-192-2; 4th TN; 63 to 65; Meadow PO; eyes effected & rheumatism, discharge lost
ADAMS, Hamilton, H-49-1; Susan widow of; Pvt A Co 16th TN Mtd Inf; 8-2-64 to 6-30-65; Brown's Chapel PO
ADAMS, Henry, Sh-183-2; Pvt G Co 8th TN Cav; Memphis PO; papers lost
ADAMS, Henry, Ro-202-2; Elizabeth widow of; Pvt I Co 1st TN Inf; 9 Aug 61 to 17 Sep 64; PO omitted
ADAMS, Ike, Hy-76-2; US Sol; Stanton Depot PO
ADAMS, J. W., L-108-1; Cherey widow of; Pvt I Co 36th US Inf; Glimpville PO
ADAMS, James, Ge-88-2; Pvt F Co 1st TN Lt Art; 2 Oct 63 to 3 Aug 65; Bulls Gap PO; wound in side & blind in right eye
ADAMS, James, Di-31-1; Pvt G Co 12th TN Cav; 12-29-63 to 10-7-65; Dickson PO

ADAMS, James B., Cy-27-1; Pvt 18th IN Bat; 9-12-64 to 6-30-65; Clementsville PO
ADAMS, James H., Ro-203-1; Pvt K Co 5th TN Inf; 9 May 62 to 19 May 65; Guenther PO; injury from relapse of measles
ADAMS, Jessee, Ru-245-1; PVt A Co 3rd US Vol; 10-15-64 to 11-29-65; Readville PO
ADAMS, John, K-185-2; Pvt; Scaggston PO
ADAMS, John C., Sh-178-2; Pvt K Co 16th IL; 63 to 65; rear 303 Monroe, Memphis PO; wounded in left leg
ADAMS, John I., A-5-3; Jane widow of; Pvt I Co 1st TN Inf; Aug 6_ to _; Clinton PO
ADAMS, Joseph, Hy-75-2; Pvt; Koko PO
ADAMS, Joseph, Mt-148-1; Pvt I Co 101st TN Mtd Inf; 10-1-64 to 1-21-66; Orgains X Roads PO; hernia, double injured
ADAMS, Luman (see Fuller, Luman)
ADAMS, Mary J., T-213-2; widow; PO omitted; CONF
ADAMS, Mathew, Sh-184-1; US Sol; 194 Poplar, Memphis PO
ADAMS, McKimey Sr., H-49-4; Pvt A Co 6th TN Mtd Inf; 8-2-64 to 6-30-65; Lake Side PO
ADAMS, McKinney Jr., H-49-1; Pvt A Co 6th TN Cav; 8-2-64 to 6-30-65; Lake Side PO
ADAMS, Samuel J., H-74-1; Cpl H Co 195th OH; 5-4-65 to 12-18-65; 817 11th St, Chattanooga PO
ADAMS, Sandy, Ru-241-4; Sarah widow of; Pvt TN Inf; 61 to 65; Murfreesboro PO; killed at Nashville
ADAMS, Tennessee, U-245-1; Pvt M Co 8th TN Cav; 27 Aug 63 to 4 Aug 64; Okolona PO (Carter Co.); in prison
ADAMS, William, T-218-1; Pvt A Co 11th TN Inf; 9 Mar 64 to 20 Feb 65; Covington PO
ADAMS, William C., He-67-1; Pvt C Co 6th TN Cav; 62 to no discharge, left on furlow, never returned; Sardis PO; hemorhoids, rheumatism
ADAMS, William H., Sh-174-1; Pvt B Co 83rd OH Vol Inf; B Co 48th OH V V Inf; 8-21-64 to 7-24-65; Memphis? PO; chronic diarrhoea
ADAMS, William M., Di-40-1; Tennessee D. wife of; Lt G Co 12th TN Cav; 7-20-64 to 10-20-65; Edgewood PO
ADAMSON, Christerford E., Dk-33-3; Pvt K Co 5th TN Cav; 5-13-63 to 8-14-65; Halesville PO; crippled in left leg by hosen? in service
ADAMSON, James E., D-45-2; Pvt I & A Cos 5th TN Cav; 11-29-62 to 8-14-65; Nashville PO; hurt by horse falling on him causing loss of right eye
ADAMSON, William, D-45-3; Pvt F Co 4th TN Inf; 9-22-64 to 8-25-65; Nashville PO
ADCOCK, Akin L., K-184-3; Pvt B Co 6th TN Cav; 62 to 65; Thorn Grove PO
ADCOCK, Archibald, Mg-196-2; Cpl H Co 3rd TN Inf; 10 Feb 62 to 23 Feb 65; Coalfield PO
ADCOCK, Lessee A., Di-30-1; Sgt K Co 11th TN Inf; 5-23-61 to 5-65; Dickson PO; CONF
ADDCOCK, Charles M., B-15-1; Pvt C Co 5th TN Cav; 7-61 to 70; Shelbyville PO; gun shot right foot
ADEN, Simion, We-220-2; Lydia widow of; Pvt; PO omitted
ADISON, Dean, Sm-168-1; Emiline widow of; 61 to 64; Difficult PO; died
ADKIN, Ephram, Sh-157-4; Cpl G Co; 63 to 65; PO omitted
ADKINS, Allen A., Me-89-1; Eviline widow of; Pvt A Co 8th TN Cav; 63 to 64; Big Spring PO
ADKINS, Arthur, S-215-1; Goodman, Lewis for widow of; Jeffers PO; died from consumption caused by exp.
ADKINS, Benjamin F., Mg-198-3; Pvt F Co 2nd TN Inf; 23 Sep 61 to 14 Mar 65; Herburtsburgh PO; kidney affection
ADKINS, Berry, Rb-221-2; Pvt; Adams Station PO
ADKINS, Brock, S-212-1; Pvt I Co 9th KY; 15 Oct 62 to 8 Oct 63; Onida PO; right arm off
ADKINS, Charles, A-2-3; Elizabeth widow of; Pvt C Co 2nd TN Inf; 8-7-61 to 2-8-65; Hinds Creek PO; in Belle Isle and Andersonville 13 mos
ADKINS, Charles T., Ro-211-1; Mary J. widow of; Pvt K Co 1st TN Inf; 9 Aug 61 to 17 Sep 64; Webster PO
ADKINS, Elijah W., K-159-1; Quartermaster Sgt 3rd TN Inf; 10 Feb 62 to 23 Feb 65; Knoxville; lost right eye in service, pentioned $8 per mo

ADKINS, George, Hd-51-1; Pvt D Co 4th TN Inf; 1 Aug 61 to Nov 61; Pickens PO
ADKINS, J. R., A-1-3; Talittro widow of; Pvt C Co 2nd TN Inf; 8-6-61 to 7-28-64; Andersonville PO
ADKINS, James C., We-223-1; Pvt H Co 38th VA Inf; Jul 61 to 66; Palmersville PO: CONF
ADKINS, John, D-67-3; Pvt Col Inf; Nashville PO
ADKINS, John, H-49-2; Polly widow of; Pvt K Co 1st US Hvy Art; Lake Side PO; rheumatism
ADKINS, John, A-2-1; Pvt B Co 3rd TN Inf; Twinville PO (Knox Co.); captured & paroled 9-27-62 and never returned
ADKINS, John K., Hd-54-1; Pvt I Co 136th IL Inf; 20 May 64 to 22 Oct 64; Saltillo PO
ADKINS, John T., C-26-1; Cpl A Co 1st TN Inf; 8-2-61 to 9-17-64; Jacksboro PO
ADKINS, Joshua F., C-26-2; Pvt F Co 7th TN Inf; 11-8-64 to 7-30-65; Caryville PO
ADKINS, Louis, C-25-3; Pvt A Co 1st TN Inf; 8-1-61 to 9-17-64; Coal Creek PO
ADKINS, Louis, C-26-1; Pvt A Co 1st TN Inf; 8-1-61 to 9-17-64; Coal Creek PO
ADKINS, Mack, Mt-149-1; Pvt A Co 13th US Col Hvy Art; 10-26-64 to 11-18-65; Palmyra PO; sunstroke and measles
ADKINS, Morris, Ro-204-4; Mariah widow of; Elverton PO; no disch., died in army
ADKINS, Parniah, A-4-6(2); Lt C Co 2nd TN Inf; 8-6-61 to 3-8-65; Coal Creek PO; breast infected
ADKINS, Rufus, H-60-5(2); Sgt K Co 16th US CI (Col Inf)?; Chattanooga PO; wounded in back
ADKINS, Sherwood, S-215-2; Pvt, Cpl H Co 2nd TN Inf; 15 Nov 61 to 25 Nov 64; Jeffers PO; lung disease c. cold in prison 4½ mos
ADKINS, William L., C-27-1; PVt A Co 1st TN Inf; 7-63 to 10-63; Jacksboro PO
ADKINSON, W. S., Cr-13-2; US Sol; Pvt; 20th Civil Dist
ADKISON, I. S., De-22-2; Pvt A Co 51st TN Inf; 1 Oct 62 to 1 Oct 63; Dunbar PO; CONF
ADKISON, Joseph F., T-211-1; Pvt G Co 52nd IN; 12 Dec 62 to 10 Sep 65; Tipton PO
ADKISON, Wilkinson B., Ro-211-4; Sgt H Co 3rd TN Inf; 10 Feb 62 to 23 Feb 65; Kingston PO; wounded
ADKISSON, Green, Mu-213-1; Pvt B Co 18th MO Inf; Aug 61 to Apr 65; Glenns Store PO
ADKISSON, James W., Ro-206-1; Elizabeth N. widow of; Capt H Co 3rd TN Inf; Feb 62 to Jul 62; Kingston PO
ADRIAN, James, D-63-2; PVt 4th OH Cav; Nashville PO
ADSON, John, Cl-46-1; Pvt C Co 1st TN Inf; 8-16-61 to 6-4-62; Clairfield PO; rumatism and sight
ADWAY, Thomas, Sh-290-1; Mandy widow of; 653 Shelby in rear, Memphis PO
AFRED, Wiley (see Robertson, Alfred)
AGEE, Genmioh, Sm-172-3(1); Pvt G Co 4th TN Inf; 11-1-64 to 8-25-65; Hickman PO
AGEE, James H., C-27-3; Sgt I Co 143rd IN Inf; 1-24-65 to 10-17-65; Jacksboro PO
AGEE, John D., Sm-172-3(1); Pvt G Co 4th TN Inf; 11-1-64 to 8-25-65; Hickman PO
AGEE, Thom, Bl-3-2; Sarah widow of; Pvt; was in Cav; Orones Store PO; CONF
AGEE, William B., Sm-172-3(1); Pvt G Co 4th TN Mtd Inf; 11-1-64 to 8-25-64 (sic); Brush Creek PO
AGEW, William H., K-172-2; 14th Dist; wife dont know
AGNEW, James N., Sm-174-2; Pvt H Co 5th OH Art; 9-10-61 to 9-11-64; Grant PO; US Regulars soldier
AGY, Joshua H., Ho-96-1; Pvt L Co 5th IA Cav; Oct 25 61 to _; Tennessee Ridge PO; bayonet wound in arm; discharge now in Washington, could not get length of service
AIKEN, William M., Lo-195-3(1); Pvt F Co 3rd TN Inf; 11 Feb 62 to 23 Feb 65; Loudon PO; rheumatism of the heart
AIKIN, David C., Wa-274-3; Pvt Battery 22 OH Lt Art; 21 Sep 64 to 13 Jul 65; Jonesboro PO
AIKIN, Robert, C-33-3; Pvt I Co 9th TN Cav; 3-28-62 to 9-65; Newcomb PO
AIKIN, William, K-159-2; Martha O. widow of; Chapl. 8th PA Reserve; 61 to 64; Knoxville PO

AIKMAN, William F. M., Mc-92-4(1); 1st Sgt D Co 7th TN Mtd Inf; 11-64 to 7-65; Pin Hook PO; foot mashed & hands burned
AILS, John W., Cl-58-1; Pvt I Co 3rd TN Inf; 4-62 to __ (3 yrs 3 mos); Tazewell PO; shot in face, left leg, left foot
AILSHIRE, George W., Ge-86-2; Pvt B Co 8th TN Inf; 15 Dec 62 to 30 Jun 65; Thula PO
AKIN, Ephraim P., Cu-16-1; Pvt D Co 4th TN Inf; 3-22-65 to 8-65; Wine Sap PO; diarrhea
AKIN, Francis M., G-67-1; Cpl M Co 6th TN Cav; 11 Aug 62 to 26 Jul 65; Treynant? PO; diarrhea & bronchitis
AKIN, George W., G-67-2; Sallie M. widow of; Cpl; 62 to __; Bradford PO; three ribs broken; Sallie M. widow of George W. Akin has forgotten all about the name of the regiment and date of discharge yet she is a pensioner of the government
AKIN, James M., G-67-1; Cpl M Co 6th TN Cav; 11 Aug 62 to 26 Jul 65; Treynant? PO; kidney disease
AKIN, John F., De-23-1; Lt I Co 52nd TN Inf; 63 to 63; Bath Springs PO; CONF
AKIN, Jos. H., Dy-27-3; Pvt TN; 61 to 65; Tatemville PO; CONF
AKIN, William H., Tr-269-2; Pvt H Co 30th KY? Inf; Mar 64 to Oct 65; John PO
AKINS, Robbert, Mu-210-1; Addie G. widow of; Sprin Hill PO; CONF
AKISON, John, T-212-1; Pvt G Co 52nd IN Inf; 15 May 63 to 16 Sep 65; Atoka PO; rhumatism, hart dis.
AKRIDGE, James C., K-183-1; Pvt L Co 3rd TN Cav; 10 Oct 63 to __; Riverdale PO
AKRIDGE, William, K-179-4; Pvt 6th TN Inf; PO omitted
ALAMUTH, Sandberg, Cr-8-1; Cpl B Co 1st IL? Inf; 7-11-61 to 5-14-65; Maury City PO; CONF
ALAXANDER, William J., H-50-1; 1st Sgt L Co 9th TN Cav; 9-15-63 to 9-11-65; Daisy PO; chronic rheumatism, also relapse of measles
ALBERT, Andrew J., K-155-2(1); Drugest Navy Indianola; Aug 61 to 1 M__ 63; Knoxville PO
ALBERT, Jacob H., A-4-6(2); Pvt L Co 2nd OH Hvy Art; 6-16-63 to 6-24-65; Coal Creek PO
ALBRIGHT, Susan, Ha-111-2; Susan Ford formerlly Albright widow; Upper Clinch PO
ALBRITON, David W., Dy-21-1; 2nd Lt E Co 47th TN Inf; 8 Dec 62 to 63 (6 mos); Chestnut Bluff PO; CONF
ALCORN, Nelson, W-196-1; 15th Civil Dist
ALDER, Mark A., Mr-97-1; Pvt B Co TN Cav; 7-25-62 to 6-25-65; Victoria PO
ALDER, Wiley, Mr-96-1; Pvt C Co 6th TN Mtd Inf; 9-12-62 to 6-13-65; Whitwell PO; piles
ALDRICH, Alden, Ma-119-1; Pvt B Co 151st NY Inf; Aug 19 62 to Jul 2 65; Malesus PO
ALDRIDGE, Henry, Ms-175-1; Pvt I Co 5th TN Cav; 24 Dec 62 to 17 Aug 65; Reeds Store PO (Williamson Co.)
ALDRIDGE, Isaac H., Dy-25-2; Pvt; 3 yrs; Newbern PO; CONF
ALDRIDGE, Thomas, Sn-262-1; Pvt A Co 16th TN Inf; 63 to 65; Fountain Head PO; CONF
ALDWORTH, Fred, Sh-158-5(1); alias Williams; Pvt A Co 63rd US Col Inf; 64 to 9 Jan 66; Memphis PO; discharged at the close of the war with discharge papers
ALEN, James, Sh-188-1 US Col; Haynes Alley, Memphis PO
ALEXANDER, Andrew, A-4-3; Pvt H Co 119th VA Inf; 4-14-65 to 4-14-66; Coal Creek PO; bronchitis
ALEXANDER, Andrew P., Lo-192-2; Cpl G Co 9th TN Inf; 10 FEb 62 to 15 Mar 65; Griffits PO; shot in ankle but well now
ALEXANDER, Andrew J., Ge-91-1; Non C E Co 4th TN Inf; Mar 25 63 to Aug 2 65; Greeneville PO; lungs & liver & general disability
ALEXANDER, Andrew M., We-224-4; 6th Dist
ALEXANDER, Anthony, Wl-300-2; 16th Dist
ALEXANDER, Benjamin F., Ha-54-2; Sgt C Co 6th TN Cav; 18 Sep 62 to 26 Jul 65; Saltillo PO
ALEXANDER, Chas. C., Hd-54-2; PVt TN; 61 to __ (30 days); Saltillo PO; data forgotten
ALEXANDER, Charley, Ru-231-1; Pvt F Co 72nd IN Vol; 63 to 65; Lamar PO; paralysis side & eye & effects cold from exp.

ALEXANDER, Columbus B., Ro-204-3; Elverton PO; discharge lost
ALEXANDER, Daniel J., Ja-85-1; Sgt E Co 5th TN Mtd Inf; Thatchers Landing PO
ALEXANDER, Elisiah, Ma-128-2; Pvt C Co 2nd TN Mtd Inf; Feb 16 64 to May 13 65; Jackson PO; thrown from mule, right knee injured
ALEXANDER, Frances A., We-222-2; Elizabeth C. widow of; Pvt 13th TN; Gardner PO
ALEXANDER, Francis M., Lo-192-2; PVat A Co 3rd TN; Feb 62 to Feb 65; Meadow PO; heart & liver disease, gun shot wound
ALEXANDER, Henry C., Ca-20-1; Pvt E Co 1st MO Inf; 8-7-63 to 8-7-64; Woodbury PO
ALEXANDER, Jacob, Mu-197-2; Elsie widow of; Pvt B Co 101st TN; 62 to 65; Columbia PO
ALEXANDER, James, La-115-1; Pvt K Co 48th TN Inf; 30 Mar 63 to 24 Dec 63; Henryville PO; CONF
ALEXANDER, James, alias James Harvy; Pvt F Co 3rd US Col; 62 to May 64; Piperton PO
ALEXANDER, James C., Sh-169-1; Pvt A Co 4th TN Inf; May 61 to Oct 64; Memphis PO
ALEXANDER, James K., We-229-1; Pvt I Co 5th TN Regt; 20 May 61 to 20 May 65; Gleason PO; shot through bowels; CONF
ALEXANDER, Jas. M., R-163-3; Sgt A Co 6th TN Mtd Inf; 8-20-64 to 6-30-65; Graysville PO; shot through right hand, caused arm to be amputated
ALEXANDER, James N., Hd-45-1; Pvt F Co 6th TN Cav; 9-21-62 to 5-14-65; Whiton PO; cronic diarrhoea, 1st & 2nd index fingers shot off on right hand
ALEXANDER, John, G-57-3; Yorkville PO; CONF
ALEXANDER, John, Lo-192-3; Pvt E Co 3rd TN; 13 Jul 64 to 13 Nov 64; Coytee PO
ALEXANDER, John, H-67-1; Pvt A Co 45th OH Hvy Art; 62 to 3-65; Chattanooga PO
ALEXANDER, John E., F-44-3; Pvt C Co 35th AL; 61 to close 65; PO omitted; CONF
ALEXANDER, John M., Ru-245-1; Pvt D Co 4th TN Mtd Inf; 10-11-64 to 7-25-65; Porterfield PO; disabled in left shoulder
ALEXANDER, John W., K-164-3; Pvt H Co 4th TN Cav; Jun 63 to 10 Aug 65; PO omitted (Knoxville)
ALEXANDER, Joseph W., Mu-210-1; Pvt E Co 3rd TN Inf; 4-61 to 4-65; Spring Hill PO; shot through right lung; CONF
ALEXANDER, Martin, Mc-113-1; Pvt 4th TN Inf; Goodfield PO; no disability, discharge misplaced, cant find dates
ALEXANDER, Mary (see Hasty, Benjamin F.)
ALEXANDER, Melinda J., Wa-260-2; widow US Sol; 1st Civil Dist
ALEXANDER, Miltie, H-73-5(3); widow US Sol; Chattanooga PO
ALEXANDER, Paton S., O-134-2; Lucinda widow of; Cpl 13th __; Hornbeak PO
ALEXANDER, R. H., G-57-5(3); Pvt; 61 to 64; Yorkville PO; CONF
ALEXANDER, Rhoda (see Mull, Sam1.)
ALEXANDER, Robert, Gi-122-8; Pvt K Co 110th TN Inf; Mar 3 63 to 65; Lester Sta. PO
ALEXANDER, Robert L. P., Hd-53-2; Pvt C Co 6th TN Cav; 11 Sep 62 to 26 Jul 65; Morris Chapel PO
ALEXANDER, Robert M., Hd-49-2; Pvt F Co 6th TN V; Sep 21 62 to 5 Aug 65; Martins Mills PO; ruptur, by fall of hors in action at Lenndon, TN
ALEXANDER, Samuel D., Ja-84-2; Cpl E Co 5th TN Mtd Inf; 9-19-64 to 6-26-65; Harrison PO
ALEXANDER, Samuel A., Cl-48-3; Pvt D Co 2nd TN Cav; 64 to 65 (8 mos); Compensation PO; dont remember date of enlisment; CONF
ALEXANDER, Sanford D., Wy-173-1; Pvt H Co 6th TN Cav; 9-18-62 to 7-25-65; Lutts PO
ALEXANDER, Thadeus A., Sh-159-3; PVt C Co 12th TN Cav; Nov 63 to May 65; Memphis PO; CONF
ALEXANDER, Thomas, Sh-186-1; Lt 34th KY; 8-62 to 5-64; Memphis PO
ALEXANDER, Thomas, Wl-294-1; Pvt K Co 5th TN Cav; Feb 22 63 to Aug 14 65; Tuckers X Roads PO; hemorrhoids 15 yrs, generally able to work
ALEXANDER, William, H-57-2; Pvt D Co 15th TN Col; 63 to 65; Orchard Knob PO
ALEXANDER, William (see Mahone, William)
ALEXANDER, William, K-161-5(6); Emaline widow of; Knoxville PO

ALEXANDER, William S., Br-9-1; Callie P. widow of; Sgt G Co 2nd IN Cav; 10-12-61 to 1-3-65; Cleveland PO
ALEXANDER, William T., Ca-20-1; Pvt E Co 14th NY Inf; 8-7-63 to 8-8-64; Woodbury PO
ALEXANDER, Winston, Sh-150-1; PVt A Co 4th US Inf; 2 yrs 6 mos; Bonds PO; discharged on account of rheumatism
ALEXANDRA, Anderson, Wl-300-1; Pvt 17th KY Inf; Sep 64 to Sep 65; Cherry Valley PO
ALEXIUS, Edmund (see McCarmel, Edmund)
ALFERD, Wallace K., Gi-122-2; Pvt G Co 50th NC Inf; Jan 1 64 to 1 Sep 64; Prospect Sta. PO; CONF
ALFORD, Byron C., Co-63-4; Musician, E Co 197th OH V Inf; 15 Mar 65 to 31 Jul 65; Newport PO
ALFORD, John, Ru-241-2(1); Pvt M Co 17th TN Inf; Mar 62 to Jun 66; Murfreesboro PO; shot in the leg
ALFORD, Josep, H-54-2(3); Sgt E Co 25th WI Inf; 8-9-62 to 6-27-65; Sherman Heights PO
ALFORD, Nancy M. (see Fortner, Joab)
ALFORD, Patrick, D-68-3; Pvt A Co 13th USC Inf; 24 Sep 63 to 10 Jan 66; 19 S. Sycamore St, Nashville PO; rheumatism contracted in the army
ALFORD, Wm. H., Cl-48-3; Pvt A Co 32nd IL Inf; 8-27-61 to 1-1-64; Pleasant PO; was reenlisted
ALGEO, Susania, Sh-178-3; widow US; rear 313 Union St, Memphis PO
ALIN, Bunk (see Malone, James)
ALISON, Preston, Hd-50-2; Elizabeth widow; Savannah PO
ALKINGS, J. N., He-57-2; Pvt D Co 12th KY Cav; 10-1-63 to 11-1-64; Juno PO; also spelled Elkings; CONF
ALLAN, Isaac, Sh-162-1; Pvt L Co 3rd Hvy Art; 63 to 65; Bings Town PO
ALLAN, William, Br-14-3; Mary J. widow of; Pvt G Co 5th TN Inf; 4-11-62 to 7-4-62; McDonald PO; died in army in 1862
ALLBRIGHT, Daniel, Un-256-2; Pvt D Co 1st TN Inf; 9 Aug 61 to 17 Sep 64; Rule PO; measels & taken a relapse
ALLCOCK, James, Mg-296-2; Margarette widow of; Pvt E Co 1st TN Inf; 20 Aug 61 to Sep 64; Welstone PO; wounded by kick from mule
ALLDRIDGE, Thomas, Ma-123-1; Pvt M Co 7th TN Cav; Aug 4 63 to Jun 14 65; Jackson PO; left eye out and scurvey in mouth
ALLEAN, Hirran G., Hm-33(103)-1; Pvt; 64 to __ (1 yr 6 mos); Dyersburg PO; in rite arm, acurred in Georgia while scout
ALLEN, Annie E. (see Davis, Thomas J.)
ALLEN, Benjamine F., Sm-174-1; Pvt G Co 4th TN Inf; 1-1-65 to __ -25-65 (9 mos 25 days); New Middleton PO
ALLEN, Calvin, S-216-1; Pvt G Co 49th KY; 1 Jun 64 to 26 Dec 64; Cheftsheene PO; rhumats contracted in war
ALLEN, Catherine W., H-74-2; widow US Soldier; Chattanooga PO
ALLEN, Charles, Sh-144-1; Pvt P Co at first, 2nd TN, 61st US Cav; 23 Aug 63 to 30 Dec 65; Tipton St, Memphis PO
ALLEN, Charles, O-136-1; Pvt E Co 4th IL Inf; May 25 61 to Oct 26 65; Terrill PO
ALLEN, Charles, Sh-157-2; Sallie Jacob formerly a widow of; Memphis, 322 Trent? St PO
ALLEN, Charles, D-72-3; Pvt K Co 13th TN Inf; Nov 8 63 to Apr 16 66; Nashville PO
ALLEN, Chas. J., D-50-2; Pvt E Co 137th PA Inf-- Aug 8 63 to Jan 1 63; Pvt C Co 143rd PA Inf-- Sep 7 63 to Jan 6 65; 1021 N. Summer, Nashville PO
ALLEN, Daniel, Se-225-1; Pvt K Co 3rd TN Cav; 3 Oct 63 to 10 Jun 65; Allensville PO; chronic dyspepsia, scurvey, skin and heart disease 25 yrs, kidney trobble
ALLEN, Daniel, Sh-189-3; Drummer K Co 17th US Col Inf; 12-63 to 4-15-66; Broadway, Memphis PO
ALLEN, Daniel S N., Ct-40-5; Pvt A Co 13th TN Cav; 9-22-63 to 9-5-65; Elizabethton PO
ALLEN, David E., La-115-2; Pvt H Co 2nd MI Cav; 19 Dec 63 to 4 May 66; Henryville PO
ALLEN, Earnest, Je-146-1; Pvt C Co 1st US Col Hvy Art; 1 Feb 64 to __ (6 mos); Leadvale PO; never got a discharge
ALLEN, Edgar M., Dy-25-6(2); Newbern PO; CONF

ALLEN, Francis, Dk-32-2; Pvt K Co 5th TN Cav; 12-6-62 to 8-14-65; Alexandria PO
ALLEN, Franklin C., Sm-174-1; Pvt G Co 4th TN Inf; 11-1-64 to 8-25-65; New Middleton PO
ALLEN, Fredrick, Sh-192-1; Pvt C Co 61st US Col Inf; __ to 65; Memphis PO
ALLEN, George, Hm-103-3; Abbie widow of; Pvt; Morristown PO
ALLEN, Harry, F-37-2; Pvt C Co 61st US Col _ol Inf; May 1 65 to Dec 30 65; Somerville PO
ALLEN, Henry, H-68-2; Pvt; Chattanooga PO
ALLEN, Henry, Hu-99-1; Pvt D Co 41st US Col Inf; Sep 63 to Jun 65; Johnsonville PO
ALLEN, Henry, Sh-173-2; 197 Monroe St, Memphis PO
ALLEN, Ike, F-38-2; Pvt I Co 61st US Inf; 63 to 65; Lambert PO
ALLEN, Isaac D., H-69-1; 1st Lt G Co 9th GA Inf; 6-12-61 to 6-14-65; Chattanooga PO; CONF
ALLEN, Isaac W., Mc-112-6; Margaret I. widow of; Pvt B Co 14th TN Inf; 3-62 to 8-65; Athens PO; fever settled in left shoulder
ALLEN, Jackson C., T-206-2; Pvt H Co 25th MI; Sep 29 63 to Jun 5 66; Rialto PO
ALLEN, James, Sh-152-1; Pvt B Co 59th TN Inf; 63 to 65; Collierville PO; rheumatism
ALLEN, James, H-51-5; Elizabeth widow of; Cpl H Co 4th TN Cav; 8-62 to 7-65; Hill City PO
ALLEN, James, Co-69-2; Pvt A Co 5th TN Cav; 1 Oct 61 to 1 May 65; Rankin PO; CONF
ALLEN, James, Co-63-3; Louisa widow of; Pvt D Co 9th TN Cav; Oct 63 to __ (1 yr 6 mos); Newport PO; died during service
ALLEN, James, Ro-202-3(1); Catharine widow of; Pvt I Co 1st TN Inf; 9 Aug 61 to 17 Sep 64; Kingston PO; lung trouble
ALLEN, James, Mg-197-2; Mary L. widow of; Pvt 11th TN Cav; Crooked Fork PO
ALLEN, James C., Ja-85-5; Cpl H Co 4th TN Cav; 8-5-63 to 7-12-65; Long Savannah PO
ALLEN, James L., Mc-111-3; Lucy widow of; Pvt M Co 4th TN Cav; 4-64 to 7-65; Mortimer PO
ALLEN, James R., Jo-152-3; Pvt D Co 13th TN Cav; 24 Sep 63 to 5 Sep 65; Butler PO; breast & lung disease
ALLEN, James W., Dk-34-2; Pvt I Co 4th TN Inf; 2-1-65 to 2-25-65; Dowelltown PO; rheumatism
ALLEN, Jesse C., Po-148-2; Sgt C Co 5th TN Mtd Inf; 8-5-64 to 7-18-65; Benton PO
ALLEN, Jessie, Sh-191-3; Mary widow of; Memphis PO; records no were seen
ALLEN, John, D-50-4; Maria widow of; Pvt; 209 Jackson, Nashville PO; wounded in face, has no record
ALLEN, John, Je-142-2; Cpl K Co 1st US CA Hvy; 1 Nov 64 to 31 Mar 66; New Market PO; inflammatory rheumatism
ALLEN, John, Ha-116-1; US Sol; 13th Dist
ALLEN, John, Je-136-2; Pvt F Co 9th TN Cav; 24 Jul 63 to 20 Sep 65; no PO
ALLEN, John B., Br-12-5; McPherson PO; CONF
ALLEN, John J., Co-87-1; Pvt I Co 62nd TN Inf; 25 Oct 62 to Jul 63; Bison PO; CONF
ALLEN, John M., Bo-13-2; Sgt C Co 4th TN Inf; 4-63 to 8-65; Maryville PO
ALLEN, John P., J-82-2; Pvt K Co 4th TN Mtd Inf; 11-1-64 to 8-30-__ (9 mos 29 days); Bloomington PO; disease eyes result small pox
ALLEN, John R., He-67-1; Mary A. widow of; Pvt C Co 6th TN Cav; Sardis PO; dead
ALLEN, John T., Co-67-2; Pvt I Co 62nd TN Inf; 25 Oct 62 to Jul 63; Cosby PO; CONF
ALLEN, John W., St-163-1; US Sol; Dover PO
ALLEN, John W., K-167-4; Pvt E Co 9th TN Cav; 63 to 65; Knoxville PO; rheumatism, gets pension
ALLEN, Joiner, Mt-148-1; Pvt I Co 101st TN Cav; __ to 2-65; Orgains X Roads PO; hernia
ALLEN, Joseph, K-154-1; Knoxville PO
ALLEN, Joseph D., Sh-204-1; Cenie widow of; Pvt G Co 11th TN Inf; 62 to 64; Bethel Avenue, Memphis PO; could not remember dates
ALLEN, King S. (see Hayes, King S.)
ALLEN, Lenna, D-99-2; widow of Sol; Davidson Co. Poor House PO
ALLEN, Lotta, Sh-179-2; Browne Ave, Memphis PO
ALLEN, Mack, Je-146-1; Pvt C Co 1st US Col Hvy Art; 10 Dec 64 to __ (1 yr); Leadvale PO; sayes he lost discharge

ALLEN, Moses, Se-221-1; Pvt B Co 8th TN Inf; 3 Nov 62 to 30 Jun 65; Fair Garden PO
ALLEN, Nancy P., Hu-105-1; widow of US Sol; PO omitted
ALLEN, Oragon H., Hn-69-1; Pvt K Co 2nd TN Mtd Inf; 18 Mar 62 to 27 Jun 65; Paris PO; disease of kidney & blader & liver
ALLEN, Robert, T-215-2; US Sol; Mason PO
ALLEN, Robert, Gr-79-3; Pvt C Co 12th Batt; 62 to ___; Thorn Hill PO; CONF
ALLEN, Robt. H., Mo-119-2; Pvt A Co 1st TN Mtd Inf; Sweetwater PO
ALLEN, Sam (see Lacy, Sam)
ALLEN, Thomas, H-67-3; Sol US; Chattanooga PO
ALLEN, Thomas, Cf-35-1; Pvt B Co 37th TN Inf; Jul 61 to May 65; Normandy PO; CONF
ALLEN, Thos. J., Wi-274-1; Pvt D Co 63rd OH Inf; 22 Aug 62 to 8 Jul 65; West Harpet PO
ALLEN, Thomas M., D-69-1; Bugler Kirgatlette? 27th M; Jul 63 to 65; Third? & Davidsson Street, Nashville PO; in good health, discharge lost
ALLEN, Thomas W., Mu-213-1; Pvt H Co 4th US Mtd Inf TN; Jan 64 to Feb 65; Glenns Store PO
ALLEN, William C., Ge-98-4; Capt A Co 4th TN Cav; 61 to Aug 65 (2 yrs 11 days); no PO; brochal disease of throat
ALLEN, William, Co-66-2(1); Pvt I Co 62nd TN Inf; 15 Oct 62 to 1 Feb 65; English PO; shot in the side; CONF
ALLEN, William, C-27-4; Pvt A Co 1st TN Inf; 12-10-62 to 4-7-65; Jacksboro PO
ALLEN, William, Me-90-2(1); Pvt B Co 7th TN Mtd Inf; 10-64 to 7-26-65; Big Springs PO; shot in right side 3 in. above nipple
ALLEN, William P., P-156-2; Martha J. widow of; Pvt H Co; Lobelville PO; CONF
ALLEN, Wm., Mo-119-2; Pvt; Sweetwater PO; shot in back and hearing defective
ALLEN, William, Ma-124-1; Pvt F Co; Jackson PO
ALLEN, William, Hy-84-3(5); alias William Edwards; Pvt C Co 61st Inf; Jul 62 to May 65; Forkeddeer PO; wound on ankle & hand, discharge misplace-
ALLEN, William J., Ch-17-2; Pvt B Co 49th IL Inf; 7-1-63 to 9-9-65; Masseyville PO
ALLEN, William L., Se-221-1; Elisabeth Thurman formerly widow of; Pvt B Co 2nd TN Cav; ___ to 16 May 63; Shrader PO; can't get correct dates
ALLEN, William N., Wi-276-1; Pvt D Co 10th TN Cav; May 62 to 9 May 65; Beechville PO; prisoner at Camp Morton 18 mos; CONF
ALLEN, William T., W-195-1; Pvt G Co 4th TN Vol Mtd ___; 11-1-64 to 8-25-65; 12th Dist; now a farmer
ALLENSON?, John, Ma-125-1; Mary A. widow of; Pvt C Co 55th AL; ___ to 65; Jackson PO
ALLERS, Samuel, Mc-109-6; Dicy widow of; Pvt H Co 9th TN Cav; 7-21-63 to 9-11-65; Regret PO; soldier dead, widow totally blind
ALLEY, Andrew D., K-171-1; Sgt A Co 6th NC Cav; Aug 62 to Apr 65; Knoxville PO; CONF
ALLEY, Pleasant M., We-221-1(4); Pvt E Co 46th TN Inf; Oct 62 to Apr 65; Martin PO; wounded in left leg; CONF
ALLGOOD, Alex, Sn-252-1; Pvt A Co 42nd TN Inf; 4-4-63 to 4-29-65; Gallatin PO
ALLISON, Alec, Ms-171-1; Teamster I Co 4th TN Inf; 10 Jan 64 to 65; Belfast PO
ALLISON, Andrew K., Hd-47-2; Seaman Gunboat Exchange; Jun 63 to Jun 64; 4th Civil Dist
ALLISON, Chester, Wa-274-2; Pvt D Co 8th TN Cav; 11 Nov 64 to 11 Sep 65; Jonesboro PO; disease of lungs & diarhoea
ALLISON, G. A., Hd-48-2; Pvt B Co 24th IL Inf; Savannah PO
ALLISON, Hickerson, Sh-177-1; 555 Shelby St, Memphis PO
ALLISON, Joe, T-216-2; 11th Civil Dist
ALLISON, John B., Ov-137-1; 1st Sgt A Co 5th TN Cav; 9-10-63 to 8-10-65; Nettle Carrier PO; lung and liver diseases
ALLISON, John H., H-54-6; Pvt C Co 1st Battalion PA Vol; 6-64 to 64 (5 mos); Sherman Heights PO; contracted spinal trouble by over heat and exertion, also heart disease
ALLISON, Robert, Bl-4-3; Melvina widow of; Pvt Mexican War; 46 to 48; Pikeville PO; breast injured; died 1877

ALLISON, Samuel, D-86-1; Brentwood PO
ALLISON, William, Bo-11-7; Pvt M Co 9th TN Cav; 8-15-64 to 9-11-65; Houk PO; rhumatism
ALLMAN, Benjamin C., B-18-1; Pvt M Co 4th E TN; 8-10-64 to 65; Flat Creek PO
ALLMAN, James W., We-224-3(1); Pvt D Co 45th TN Inf; Nov 61 to Apr 62; Como PO (Henry Co.); parolled at Sumpterville, AL; CONF
ALLMAN, John A., Sm-172-3(1); Pvt A Co 9th TN Cav; 7-1-63 to 9-1-65; Gordonsville PO
ALLMAN, John F., We-224-3(1); Sgt I Co 6th TN Cav; 22 Jan 62 to 8 Jul 65; Como PO (Henry Co.); wounded in left arm and left side, so feble minded that he cannot give any particulars
ALLRED, Anthony C., Fe-42-3; Pvt Capt. David Beaty's Co. TN Ind. Scouts; Boatland PO
ALLSUP, Henry, Col, Gr-76-2(1); Pvt B Co 1st TN Inf; 14 Feb 64 to 31 Mar 66; Tampico PO; injury to left hip
ALLUM, David C., He-61-3; Pvt G Co 7th TN Cav; 5 Aug 62 to 25 Oct 63; 15th Civil Dist
ALLUMN, William C., A-3-1; Wi-na A. widow of; Pvt C Co 2nd TN Cav; 62 to 63; Wilson PO
ALMEN, Arin G., O-141-2; Lt K Co 6th TN Vol Cav; Aug 7 62 to Jul 26 65; Union City PO
ALRED, Calvin, Hd-46-1; Pvt A Co 3rd IA Bat; Oct 10 61 to Jul 10 65; Economy PO
ALSHIRE, Ezechial, Hw-130-1; Pvt E Co 43rd TN Inf; 15 Sep 62 to 65; Lee Valley PO; lung disease; CONF
ALSTON, Ben, T-209-2; Sol; PO omitted
ALSTON, Ch___lie, Wi-287-1; Pvt B Co 44th TN Inf; 2 yrs 8 mos; Civ Dist #18
ALSTON, William, T-208-1; Pvt M Co 4th Col; 63 to 65; Burleson PO; loss of slight (sic), now blind
ALSUP, Elizabeth, Be-6-2; widow of US Sol; Pvt; 8th Dist
ALSUP, Martha, Ru-238-2; widow; Murfreesboro PO
ALSUP, Riley, D-64-1; Pvt E Co 14th TN Col Inf; Sep 61 to Mar 64; Nashville PO
ALTON, Abraham, K-177-3; Sol US; PO omitted
ALTON, Maggie M. (see Hill, John H.)
ALVERSON, Andrew J., Wh-182-1; Pertima A. widow of; Pvt C Co 3rd KY Inf; 3-25-64 to 6-9-76; Doyle's Sta. PO
ALVERSON, John R., A-5-1; Lt F Co 26th MO Cav; 62 to 10-25-64; Clinton PO; rheumatism
ALVIS, Robert G., Sm-173-2; Sgt B Co 5th TN Cav; 8-9-62 to 6-25-65; Brush Creek PO
ALVIS, William N., Hw-119-3(1); Pvt K Co 13th TN Cav; Jan 64 to ___ (5 mos); Alum Well PO
AMANNS, Charles, K-186-2; Pvt C Co 138th OH Inf; 2 May 64 to 1 Sep 64; Beaver Ridge PO; chronic diareaha
AMANNS, George, K-186-2; Pvt H Co 12th IN Inf; 8 Aug 62 to 13 Jun 65; Beaver Ridge PO; scurvey
AMBROES, George W., Gr-73-1; Pvt M Co 1st TN Cav; 63 to 65; Turley's PO
AMBROS, David C., Lo-188-3; Pvt F Co 2nd TN Cav; 1 Aug 63 to 3 Aug 65; Sweetwater PO
AMBROSE, Hays, L-109-1; Sarah widow of; Musician KY Inf; 61 to 65; Lightfoot PO
AMBROSE, James, Ro-205-2; Pvt G Co 4th TN Inf; 15 Mar 63 to 2 Aug 65; Hatch PO
AMBURN, Joseph, Bo-12-3(1); Sol US; 17th Dist
AMBURN, Samuel, Po-152-5(1); Pvt I Co 10th TN Cav; 3-1-64 to 8-1-65; Ducktown PO; rheumatism and lung disease
AMENT, Joseph P., Wh-187-1; Pvt TN Cav; 61 to 65; Sparta PO; shot in right arm
AMEY, Alfred J., Jo-151-2; Pvt B Co 4th TN Inf; Mar 63 to Sep 65; Bakers Gap PO; mump, measles, results, paralyzed in right side
AMI, Virginia (see Rogers, Coleman)
AMICK, Columbus, Mu-209-4; Pvt G Co 17th TN Inf; May 15 61 to May 30 62; Columbia PO; CONF
AMIS, Charles, Hm-103-2; Lucinda widow of; Pvt; Morristown PO
AMIS, Samuel, Mu-196-2; Sgt 110th Reg Inf; Columbia PO; right thumb shot off in service
AMMONS, William, We-274-1; Pvt C Co 3rd TN Inf; 7-26-64 to 12-25-64; Sweetwater PO; gravel and weak lung from exposure
AMMONS, Wm., Sh-173-2; 197 Monroe St, Memphis PO
AMON, Martague, Ho-95-1; Pvt A Co 3rd MO Inf; Jun 1 61 to Jul 15 65; McKinnon PO

AMOS, Henry S., Hw-131-1; Martha E., widow of; Pvt L Co 9th TN Cav; 30 Sep 63 to 13 Jul 65; PO omitted
AMOS, James B., Hm-109-3; Pvt A Co 12th TN Cav; 20 Nov 62 to 7 Oct 65; Russellville PO; heornea
AMOS, Joseph, Mu-205-1; Mary widow of; Sgt A Co 14th TN Inf; May 62 to May 65; Williamsport PO; left hip & right ankle wounded
AMROS, David C., Lo-188-1; Pvt F Co 2nd TN Inf; 1 Aug 63 to 3 Aug 65; Sweetwater PO
AMUS, Frank, D-63-1; Pvt I Co 17th US Col?; Nashville PO
AMY, Edmund, Mu-192-1; Pvt A Co 110th __; 62 to 66; Bigbyville PO; not wounded
AMYS, Riley, Hw-130-1; Pvt C Co 7th KY Inf; 18 Aug 61 to 5 Oct 65; Lee Valley PO; heart disease
ANDERS, Elizia (see Cottral, George)
ANDERSON, Alexander, Sh-201-4; Pvt B Co 3rd TN Hvy Art; 9 May 63 to 15 Jul 65; Memphis PO
ANDERSON, Allen, Rb-230-1; alias William, Allen; Pvt E Co 15th TN Inf; Oct 64 to Feb 65; Springfield PO
ANDERSON, Amos J., Lizzie Davis formerly widow of; Pvt L Co 8th TN Cav; 10 Dec 63 to __; Alum Well PO; died with yellow fever
ANDERSON, Andrew, G-64-1; Pvt M Co 61st TN; Feb 1 61 to 64; Bradford PO
ANDERSON, Andrew, Sn-260-6; Pvt A Co 1st TN Mtd Inf; 12-18-63 to 1-30-65; Westmoreland PO; reenlisted 3-17-65
ANDERSON, Andrew J., Fe-44-1; Pvt G Co 8th TN Inf; 1-1-63 to 6-30-65; Jamestown PO; heart disease and rheumatism
ANDERSON, Andy, T-214-1; Pvt G Co 3rd US Art; May 62 to May 64; Dist 9
ANDERSON, Benjamin F., Fr-112-3; Pvt B Co 1st TN Inf; 4-61 to 3-65; Elk River PO; CONF
ANDERSON, Buford, Gi-131-1; Pvt B Co 110th Col Inf; Nov 18 63 to Feb 8 66; Sumac PO
ANDERSON, David B., H-63-3; Anna widow of; Pvt 1st Col Hvy Art; 813 Pine, Chattanooga PO
ANDERSON, David M., Fr-112-3; Pvt; 64 to 65 (4 mos); Elk River PO; CONF
ANDERSON, David N., Fe-44-1; Pvt I Co 152nd IL Inf; 2-18-65 to 9-11-65; Jamestown PO; rheumatism and paralysis, right leg paralyzed
ANDERSON, Edward H., F-42-1; Pvt Forrests Cav; 3 yrs; Collierville PO; wife can't give particulars; CONF
ANDERSON, Francis, Lo-194-2; Pvt; Oct 1 62 to Mar 65; Muddy Creek PO; CONF
ANDERSON, Francis M., J-82-1; Capt C Co 1st TN Mtd Inf; 7-1-63 to 10-4-64; Bloomington PO; disease bladder
ANDERSON, George, Hw-126-1; Pvt F? Co 47th KY Inf; 18 Jun 63 to 26 Dec 64; Fishers Creek PO
ANDERSON, George, H-73-4(2); Chattanooga PO
ANDERSON, George B., S-215-2; Pvt; Norma PO
ANDERSON, George H., Ha-113-1; Pvt Potomac Fleet; 1 yr 8 mos; Sneedville PO; could not give vessel or dates
ANDERSON, George J., D-96-1; Pvt 23rd IN Art; 11 Jun 63 to 3 Jul 65; Nashville PO; invalid
ANDERSON, George R., Hm-105-1; Pvt G Co 9th TN Cav; 22 Dec 63 to 11 Sep 65; Jarnagan PO
ANDERSON, George S., De-26-2; C Co 12th TN; Nov 63 to __ (1 yr 10 mos); Bible Hill PO
ANDERSON, Geo. W., Hd-54-2; Sgt C Co 6th TN Cav; Sep 62 to 64; Saltillo PO; no discharge
ANDERSON, George W., Ja-85-3; Sgt E Co 4th TN Cav; 12-22-62 to 7-12-65; Georgetown PO
ANDERSON, Green, Ru-232-1; Pvt TN Inf; Aug 64 to __ (1 yr 6 mos); 3rd Civil Dist
ANDERSON, Henry, Sh-151-1; Brunswick PO
ANDERSON, J. G., He-57-2; Pvt E Co 17th TN Inf; 7-2-64 to 4-15-65; Law PO; CONF
ANDERSON, J. P., Gi-139-1; Pvt C Co 3rd TN Inf; 11-19-62 to 12-20-64; Campbellville PO; CONF
ANDERSON, Jacob, Hu-99-1; Pvt E Co 13th Col US Inf; 11 Jun 64 to 10 Jun 66; Johnsonville PO
ANDERSON, Jacob D., Sh-157-1; Pvt B Co 1st AR Inf; Jan 62 to May 65; PO omitted
ANDERSON, Jas., D-50-2; Isabella widow of; Pvt; 2 yrs 6 mos; Nashville PO
ANDERSON, James, K-172-2; Cpl E Co 3rd TN Cav; 30 Nov 62 to 10 Jun 65?; Knoxville PO
ANDERSON, James, Je-146-4; Pvt E Co 1st US Art; 1 Aug 62 to 31 Mar 66; White Pine PO; not at home, wife don't know
ANDERSON, James, Sh-152-1; 1st Sgt L Co 3rd AR Inf; 63 to 65; Collierville PO; prisoner in Washington DC 3 mos, prisoner Point Lookout 2 mos
ANDERSON, James, Col, Moo-217-1; Pvt I Co 40th TN; Jun 1 63 to 1 Sep 64; Stonesboro PO
ANDERSON, James, Mu-188-1; Pvt C Co 13th TN Inf; Parks Station PO
ANDERSON, James (see Feeds, James)
ANDERSON, James B., Fr-112-3; Pvt; 9-64 to 1-65; Elk River PO; don't remember regiment; CONF
ANDERSON, James F., Bl-5-3; Cpl D Co 6th TN Mtd Inf; 9-12-64 to 6-30-65; Pitts X Roads PO
ANDERSON, James M., D-77-2; Harriet widow of; Colonel 12th WI Bat; May 64 to May 65; Nashville PO
ANDERSON, James P., K-181-5(2); Pvt A Co 6th TN Inf; 28 Nov 62 to 24 May 65; Knoxville PO
ANDERSON, James P., Hm-107-3; Cpl C Co 8th TN Cav; 4 Ma__ to 11 Sep 65; Witts Foundry PO; drugs of measles 25 yrs
ANDERSON, James R., Cu-16-3; Pvt D Co 4th TN Mtd Inf; 3-23-65 to 8-25-65; Pleasant Hill PO; relapse measles
ANDERSON, James R., Ct-43-2; Pvt B Co 13th TN Cav; 9-22-63 to 9-5-65; Carter Furnace PO
ANDERSON, James T., K-166-5; Central Ave, N. Knoxville PO
ANDERSON, Jefferson, Hw-119-4(1); Mollie L. widow of; Gillenwater PO
ANDERSON, John, S-217-2; Cpl G Co 4th TN Cav; 62 to 65; Winfield PO
ANDERSON, John, Mc-109-5; 1st Lt K Co 10th TN Cav; 64 to 7-31-65; Sweetwater PO (Monroe Co.); enlisted in 2nd TN Cav & transferred
ANDERSON, John, Sm-172-4; Pvt K Co 5th TN Cav; 5-13-63 to 13-8-65; Hickman PO; disabled by horse falling on him
ANDERSON, Jno., Sh-183-1; Mary widow of; Memphis PO
ANDERSON, John M., Ru-13-3; Pvt; Murfreesboro PO
ANDERSON, John W., Sn-262-3(2); Pvt B Co 52nd KY Inf; 18 Aug 63 to 17 Jan 65; Sulphuria PO; general healt impared and ankle thrown out of place
ANDERSON, Joseph, Gr-27-1; Pvt C Co; Y.Z. PO; piles
ANDERSON, Joseph, Col, Ma-128-1; Pvt; 63 to 64; Jackson PO; right eye shot out, could not see Joseph Anderson
ANDERSON, Josiah, Mr-96-2; Pvt 6th TN Mtd Inf; 64 to 65; Whitwell PO
ANDERSON, King D., Bo-12-1; Pvt A Co 3rd TN Inf; 12-18-62 to 8-2-65; Houk PO; vertigo in head partialy deaf from service of sixty three
ANDERSON, Larkin, H-67-1; Larkin Fennel alias; Pvt F Co 17th US Col; 11-63 to 5-65; Chattanooga PO; weakened spine from lifting heavy timbers
ANDERSON, Lindsy, Sh-190-2; 196 Carolina St, Memphis PO
ANDERSON, Martin, Hw-124-1; Pvt K Co 13th TN Cav; 1 Oct 63 to 5 Sep 65; New Canton PO
ANDERSON, Mary E. (see Fergerson, Isaac H.)
ANDERSON, Mathew N., K-172-4; 1st Lt I Co 3rd TN Cav; Dec 62 to May 65; PO omitted
ANDERSON, Nicholas, K-172-4; Pvt E Co 3rd TN Cav; Knoxville PO; doubtful whether a soldier or not
ANDERSON, Obe B., Hn-70-1; Pvt A Co 1st TN Mtd Inf; 4 May 64 to 7 Jul 65; Paris PO
ANDERSON, Overton B., Sm-170-3; Pvt D Co 7th TN Inf; 10-8-63 to 4-65; Maggart PO; colored
ANDERSON, Peter, Gu-48-1; Pvt 5th TN Inf; 6-2-62 to 6-23-65; Tracy City PO
ANDERSON, Peter, D-60-1; alley back of McCrairy, Nashville PO; colored
ANDERSON, Pleasant, K-171-3(2); Pvt G Co 4th TN Cav; 2 Jan 62 to 20 Jun 65; Knoxville PO
ANDERSON, R. J., Gi-139-2; Pvt E Co 11th TN Inf; 5-63 to 11-65; Campbellsville PO; CONF
ANDERSON, Richard, Ct-42-1; Susan W. widow of; Pvt A Co 13th TN Cav; Watauga PO
ANDERSON, Robert, K-167-2; 1st Hvy __; 62 to 65; Knoxville PO
ANDERSON, Robert, H-50-5; Martha A. widow of; 1st Lt F Co 6th R TN Mtd Inf; 7-12-64 to __; Soddy PO
ANDERSON, Samuel, K-167-2; 1st Hvy __; 62 to 65; Knoxville PO

ANDERSON, Samuel, Mc-109-5; Pvt K Co 10th TN Cav; 2-64 to 7-31-63; Sweetwater PO (Monroe Co.); left shoulder broken
ANDERSON, Samuel, Tr-266-1(2); Pvt H Co 3rd TN Cav; Apr 61 to May 18 63; Hartsville PO; CONF
ANDERSON, Samuel H., De-26-2; C Co 12th TN ___; 15 Oct 63 to Nov 27 64; Bible Hill PO
ANDERSON, Thomas, Ha-117-3; Pvt A Co 1st TN Cav; Dec 62 to 15 Jan 65; Sneedville PO; measles
ANDERSON, Thomas, Lo-191-3; Sgt F Co 2nd TN Vols Cav; 1 Aug 62 to 5 Jul 65; Morganton PO
ANDERSON, Thomas A., Pu-145-3(4); Silver Point PO; discharge not at home
ANDERSON, Thomas B., H-66-2; Pvt G Co 18th OH Inf; 1-23-65 to 10-9-65; Chattanooga PO
ANDERSON, Thomas J., Ho-96-2; US Sol; PO omitted
ANDERSON, Thomas L., Hm-107-1; Pvt C Co 8th TN Cav; 4 May 63 to ___ ; Witts Foundry PO; diarrhea
ANDERSON, Thomas M., K-168-1; Pvt D Co 1st TN Lt Art; 19 Sep 63 to 25 Jul 65; Knoxville PO; lungs diseased
ANDERSON, Thomas R., H-51-2(1); Pvt A Co 2nd TN Inf; 8-10-61 to 10-10-64; Hill City PO
ANDERSON, Tolbert, Wl-302-1; Pvt C Co 5th WI Art; 1 Aug 63 to 20 May 66; no PO
ANDERSON, William, H-67-1; Ed Anderson alias; Pvt D Co 42nd US Col Inf; 8-63 to 66; Chattanooga PO
ANDERSON, William, Co-64-1; Mary widow of; Pvt M Co 8th TN Cav; 8 Oct 63 to 11 Sep 65; PO omitted (Newport?)
ANDERSON, William, K-156-4; Easter widow of; Pvt K Co 1st TN Hvy ARt; 24 Jul 64 to 21 Jul 66; 5 Crozier St, Knoxville PO
ANDERSON, William, Sh-149-3; Pvt M Co 3rd US Art; 22 Dec 63 to 30 Aug 66; Raleigh PO
ANDERSON, William, F-35-1; Sgt I Co 10th Reg Cav; 17 Feb 64 to Aug 65; Ina PO
ANDERSON, William, Gi-127-7; Maria widow of; Pulaski PO; papers misplaced
ANDERSON, William, Sh-189-1; Bugler A Co 121st IN Vol; 10-2-63 to 7-6-65; La. Ave, Memphis PO
ANDERSON, William A., Ct-43-2; Dicey Garland formerly widow of; Pvt B Co 13th TN Cav; 9-22-63 to ___ ; Carter Furnace PO; died Camp Nelson, KY, Dec 1864
ANDERSON, William A., K-170-2; Pvt C Co 6th TN Inf; 18 Apr 62 to 30 Jun 65; Knoxville PO; catarrh of head 14 yrs
ANDERSON, William F., Ja-85-6; Sgt E Co 4th TN Cav; 1-10-63 to 7-12-65; Long Savannah PO
ANDERSON, William G., Rb-219-2; Pvt H Co 2nd TN Reg; May 61 to Apr 2 65; Orlinda PO
ANDERSON, William H., Lo-192-1; Pvt H Co 5th TN; 9 Apr 62 to 16 May 65; Morganton PO
ANDERSON, Wm. J., B-4-1; Pvt C Co 2nd Reg Vol US; 9-63 to 11-65; Bell Buckle PO; eyes week, eyes affected by small pox
ANDERSON, William L., G-71-3; Spicy A. widow of; Pvt G Co 15th TN Inf; 15 May 61 to 15 Jul 63; PO omitted; CONF
ANDERSON, William P., We-225-2(1); Pvt C Co 8th TN Cav; Mar 12 65 to Aug 17 65; Dresden PO; bad hearing by cannon
ANDERSON, William T., Rb-221-1; Pvt D Co Art; May 1 61 to Jun 1 63; Cedar Hill PO; CONF
ANDES, Adam W., Ge-96-1; Pvt I Co 3rd TN Cav; 1 Sep 62 to 1 Jun 65; Jockey PO; nervousness
ANDES, Isaac, Se-224-1; Sgt K Co 2nd TN Cav; 16 Oct 62 to 6 Jul 65; Waldens Creek PO; partial deafness
ANDES, John W., Se-223-4; Lt K Co 2nd TN Cav; 16 Oct 62 to 6 Jul 65; Sevierville PO
ANDES, Rily H., Se-223-4; Lt F S Co 2nd TN Cav; 8 Nov 62 to 6 Jul 65; Sevierville PO
ANDIES, A. C. (see Johnson, Marry J.)
ANDRESS, Henry A., La-117-4; Pvt; 15th Dist
ANDREW, Robert, Sh-149-1; Pvt H Co US Cav; 15 Feb 63 to 25 Jan 66; National Cemetery PO
ANDREWS, Bruce, Sh-190-1; Pvt K Co 14th IL Inf; 5-11-61 to 6-25-64; 809 Main St, Memphis PO
ANDREWS, Burton S., Cu-17-3; Pvt C Co 3rd MN Inf; 12-64 to 6-65; Grassy Cove PO
ANDREWS, C. P., Cr-4-2; Pvt H Co 50th TN Inf; Oct 61 to Feb 65; Bells Depot PO; CONF
ANDREWS, Charles, Hr-96-1; Cpl B Co 4th KY Cav; Feb 61 to 65; Pinstop PO; injured in mouth, arm

ANDREWS, Charles, D-68-1; Pvt D Co 13th USC Inf; Oct 63 to 10 Jan 66; 86 Green St, Nashville PO; rheumatism and 2 ribs broken in the army
ANDREWS, Charles H., H-73-5(3); Pvt; Chattanooga PO
ANDREWS, Elbert G., Rb-219-1; Pvt A Co TN Reg; Feb 62 to Sep 62; Orlinda PO; infantry service; CONF
ANDREWS, Henry H., M-106-1; Pvt B Co 8th TN Inf; 3-22-65 to 8-7-65; Union Camp PO
ANDREWS, James (see Stanley, James)
ANDREWS, Joseph A., A-4-5; Pvt C Co 2nd TN Inf; 11-1-61 to 11-5-64; Coal Creek PO; heart trouble
ANDREW, Napolian, Wl-293-2; Pvt L Co 5th TN Cav; Apr 27 63 to Aug 14 65; Buhler PO
ANDREWS, Orville T., R-161-4; Nancy P. Hashbarg formerly widow of; 1st Lt 9th OH Cav; 1862 to close of war; Dayton PO; right leg shot off at knee in Battle of Shiloh; papers all destroyed by fire
ANDREWS, Peter, Mu-213-1; Jane Graham formerly widow of; Pvt; 62 to ___; Glenns Store PO; died from sickness
ANDREWS, William H., Co-64-2; Pvt I Co 5th TN Inf; Sep 61 to Jun 65; Philips PO; shot in boath legs; CONF
ANDREWUS, John P., Rb-226-1; Pvt A Co 38th WI Inf; 3 Sep 64 to 2 Jun 65; Greenbrier PO; rheumatism since 1865
ANDRISE?, Henry A., La-117-3; 15th Dist; CONF
ANESLY, John, Sh-188-2; Pvt E Co 64th US Col; 63 to 65; Dunlap St, Memphis PO
ANFRY?, Thomas D., H-73-1; Recruiting Office K Co 42nd IA; 6-62 to 2-63; Chattanooga PO
ANGEL, Dick, R-162-5; Clementine widow of; Dayton PO
ANGEL, George, Cf-35-2; Pvt D Co 23rd TN Inf; 2 Nov 62 to 22 Dec 64; Tullahoma PO
ANGEL, Jas. R., Wa-267-3; Sgt G Co 13th TN Cav; 11 Sep 63 to 5 Sep 65; Johnson City PO; chrc. rheumatism
ANGEL, Lorina (see Smith, Findley)
ANGEL, Newton J., Sm-166-3(1); Pvt A Co 1st TN Inf; 1-20-64 to 1-30-65; Monoville PO
ANGEL, Samuel, H-51-5; Pvt E Co 14th TN Inf; 10-15-63 to 3-26-65; Hill City PO
ANGEL, Samuel P., K-160-4; 4th Ave, Knoxville PO
ANGLE, Abraham, Col, Br-10-1; Pvt F Co 40th TN Inf; 4-7-65 to 4-25-66; Cleveland PO
ANGLE, John, Sn-261-3(2); Pvt B Co 3rd KY Mtd Inf; 4-64 to 64 (4 mos); Brackentown PO; CONF
ANGLIN, William, He-67-3; Pvt D Co 6th TN Cav; Oct 21 62 to Jul 26 65; Scotts Hill PO; chronic bronchitis 28 yrs
ANGLING, R. A., He-57-1; Sgt I Co 8th TN Inf; 3-15-62 to 7-1-65; Juno PO; wound in the hip at Shylo
ANKENY, Tolbert C., Di-34-4; 2nd Lt I Co 1st WI Cav; 11-18-61 to 8-12-63; Dickson PO; physical disability, discharge on accout of
ANN, Roberta (see Pool, Alexander)
ANNEY?, Joel, Se-220-3; US Sol; Emerts Cave PO
ANTHONEY, Willey, H-69-3; Martha widow of; Cpl D Co 14th TN Inf; Chattanooga PO
ANTHONY, Bob, Sh-153-2; Pvt E Co 61st USC Inf; 15 Jul 63 to 30 Dec 65; Collierville PO
ANTHONY, Ely, Hy-78-1; Sgt C Co 1st US Inf; Jan 63 to 65; Jones PO
ANTHONY, J. F., G-57-5(3); Pvt C Co 32nd TN Inf; 18 Aug 62 to 18 Dec 64; Yorkville PO; CONF
ANTHONY, Sameul T., F-42-1(3); Morgans Command; 62 to 64; Collierville PO; cant give particulars; CONF
ANTRIKN, John, Ha-116-1; US Sol; 13th Dist
APPLEGATE, W. T., La-117-2; Lt B Co 28th KY Inf; Oct 61 to Oct 62; 15th Dist
ARBINSPECK?, David K., Wi-270-1; Pvt B Co 113th PA Inf; 24 Sep 61 to 25 Jun 65; Gingo PO
ARBIST, Jackson, C-33-1; Blacksmith E Co 2nd KY Cav; 2-6-64 to 7-17-65; Newcomb PO
ARBUCKLE, E., Hn-77-1; F. widdow of; Capt A Co 13th TN Cav; PO omitted
ARCHER, Drury J., Mn-122-1; Cpl A Co 6th TN Cav; 8-11-62 to 7-26-65; Bethel Springs PO; disease of heart, discharged by GO No. 12
ARCHER, John, Co-63-3; Pvt A Co 4th TN Mtd Inf; 62 to 65 (1 yr 6 mos); Newport PO
ARCHER, Richard, T-206-1; Covington PO

ARCHER, Smith, Ct-45-2; Nancy A. widow of; Pvt B Co 13th TN Cav; 8-5-63 to __; Carter Furnace PO; killed at Indian Creek, TN, shot February 1865
ARCHER, Watkins, Wi-274-1; 1st Sgt D Co 13th TN Inf; 6 Oct 63 to 12 Jan 66; Franklin PO; now partially deaf
ARCHER, William A., Hn-71-1; 1st Lt K Co 12th KY; Jan 29 64 to Aug 23 65; Spring Hill Academy PO; hurt in left shoulder, Mr Archer received the injury refered to by falling from horse on march from Greensboro to Asheville, NC
ARCHIE, John, Sh-145-3; alias Morgan, John; Pvt D Co 3rd US Hvy Art; Dec 64 to Jan 66; Millington PO; Capt Ward
ARDEFFER, Elihu W., Ct-43-1; Pvt L Co 13th TN Cav; 9-22-63 to 9-5-65; Carter Furnace PO; urinary trouble, thrown by a horse in USS(ervice) April 1864
ARDEFFER, Isaac, Ct-43-3; Ast. Fireman US Steamer Briliant; 7-64 to 65; Watauga PO
ARDEFFER, William D., Ct-43-1; Pvt C Co 13th TN Cav; 9-22-63 to 9-5-65; Carter Furnace PO; neuralgia and rhumatism, 3 mos in Danville Prison, VA
ARDWAY, Allin, Gi-136-2; Cpl B Co 101st TN Inf; 2-1-62 to 11-1-65; Redell PO; wounded in left hip
ARGENBRIGHT, James M., Wa-262-1; Pvt I & M Cos 1st TN Cav; 1 Dec 62 to Jun 19 65; Washington College PO; right leg & left side
ARGENBRIGHT, William H., Ge-95-2; Pvt M Co 1st TN Cav; 1 Dec 62 to 19 Jun 65; Rheatown PO
ARGUBRIGHT, Comodore, A-5-1; Pvt C Co 2nd TN Inf; 3-18-62 to 4-15-65; Clinton PO; rheumatism
ARLIS, Haywood, Ma-128-2; Jane widow of; 5th Civil Dist
ARM, Thomas J., De-22-2; Pvt A Co 52nd TN Inf; 25 Nov 61 to 14 Apr 62; Dunbar PO; CONF
ARMBUSTER, John A., Bo-21-2; Ellijay PO; could not get to see
ARMENTROAT?, Fredrick V., Ge-96-2; Cpl B Co 12th TN Cav; 22 Jul 63 to 27 Oct 65; Jockey PO; liver disease, lung truble
ARMER, Sabert T., A-9-2; Druse widow of; Pvt; 8-15-62 to 4-14-65; Podopholine PO; CONF
ARMITAGE, George, Ge-93-4(2); Sgt I Co 1st TN Cav; 1 Dec 62 to Jun 65; Albany PO
ARMITAGE, Isaac A., Ge-93-4(1); 1st Sgt A Co 4th TN Inf; 6 Apr 63 to 15 Aug 65; Greeneville PO
ARMITAGE, John, Ge-90-1; Pvt I Co 7th TN Cav; 8 Dec 62 to 19 Jun 65; Greenville PO; defected eyes by camp life, cause by exposure
ARMS, George W., Un-253-1; Cpl F Co 3rd TN Inf; 10 Feb 62 to 23 Feb 65; New Flat Creek PO; piles, rupture, hurt brest
ARMS, John, K-183-2; Sgt B Co 6th TN Inf; 8 Mar 62 to Apr 65; High Point PO
ARMSTEAD, Hamlin H., Sh-159-7; Pvt C Co 61st US Col Inf; 17 Jan 64 to 30 Dec 65; Memphis PO
ARMSTEAD, Spencer, D-49-3; he was away and his wife only knew he was a soldier; Nashville PO
ARMSTEAD, Wiliam, Wl-295-1; Pvt 101st TN Inf; 63 to 65; Lebanon PO
ARMSTRONG, Alexander, Ge-98-1; Roda widow of; Pvt C Co 4th TN Vol; PO omitted
ARMSTRONG, Andrew J., Mc-116-2; Pvt A Co 5th TN Mtd Inf; 9-1-64 to 6-26-65; Longs Mills PO; disability diareah
ARMSTRONG, Author, Su-243-1; Harriate widow of; Pvt TN; __ to 64 (6 mos); Bristol PO; fever
ARMSTRONG, Benjamin, Mu-205-2; Pvt A Co 13th TN Inf; 12 Aug 62 to May 65; Williamsport PO; right thumb & arm injured by RR train
ARMSTRONG, Berry, D-91-1; Catherine widow of; Pvt A Co 13th TN Cav; 63 to 66; Union Stock Yards, Nashville PO
ARMSTRONG, Doubling, Mu-199-2; Pvt A Co 13th TN Inf; Southport PO
ARMSTRONG, E. W., K-183-1; Maj. 9th TN Vol Cav; Asbury PO
ARMSTRONG, Hugh, Ru-238-1; Pvt B Co 1st US Art; 15 Mar 63 to Apr 65; Murfreesboro PO
ARMSTRONG, J. M., K-183-1; Capt B Co 6th TN Inf; 8 Mar 62 to 66; Asbury PO
ARMSTRONG, James, Bo-11-7; Pvt E Co 3rd TN Mtd Inf; 7-15-64 to 11-30-64; Big Gulley PO
ARMSTRONG, James, H-62-4; Amanda widow of; Pvt 1st US Hvy Art; 138 Chestnut, Chattanooga PO
ARMSTRONG, James, K-183-2; Pvt D Co 1st US Col Art; 17 Mar 64 to Mar 66; Riverdale PO
ARMSTRONG, James H., St-161-1; Pvt F Co 48th KY Inf; Aug 63 to Dec 64; Dist 5
ARMSTRONG, Jasper N., Dy-29-4; Pvt 29th MS; 61 to 65; Trimble PO; CONF
ARMSTRONG, Joe, Mu-197-1; Pvt B Co 14th US; 3 yrs; Columbia PO; shot on the knee & abdomen, now crippled
ARMSTRONG, John, B-14-1; Pvt C Co 4th TN Inf; 12-2-63 to 8-25-65; Brandville PO
ARMSTRONG, John B., K-183-1; Pvt B Co 6th TN Inf; Asbury PO
ARMSTRONG, John F., Wa-273-2; Pvt G Co 8th TN Cav; 63 to 65; Locust Mt. PO; gunshot and rheumatism, seems to know but little about his case, papers lost
ARMSTRONG, John P., He-60-1; Pvt I Co 3rd RI; 7-62 to 8-64; Lexington PO
ARMSTRONG, Luke T., D-64-1; Capt E Co 8th TN Inf; May 61 to __; Nashville PO; CONF
ARMSTRONG, Moses A., K-184-1; Pvt B Co 6th TN Inf; 14 Apr 62 to 5 May 65; PO omitted
ARMSTRONG, Oscar, K-183-3; US Sol; 23rd Dist
ARMSTRONG, R. L., Bo-11-7; Pvt E Co 3rd TN Mtd Inf; 7-15-64 to 11-30-64; Big Gulley PO
ARMSTRONG, Richard, Ge-92-2; Pvt D Co 12th TN Cav; 28 Apr 64 to 7 Oct 65; Romeo PO; liver and kiney troble, rheumatism in sholders
ARMSTRONG, Thomas T., Ro-210-2; Pvt; Rockwood PO; captured; CONF
ARMSTRONG, W. A., Bo-11-2; Pvt A Co 3rd TN Inf; 2-10-62 to 2-23-65; Houk PO; piles
ARMSTRONG, Wm. L., Hw-125-2; Inf G Co 3rd TN; 61 to May 65; Stony Point PO; CONF
ARMSTRONG, ____, Emily E. widow of; H-54-6; Sherman Heights PO
ARN, John, Sh-162-1; Annie widow of; E Co 88th Cav; Bings Town PO
ARNELL, Robert Jane, Mu-189-1; Pvt 44th TN Inf; Hurricane Switch PO
ARNETT, Joseph W., Dy-25-7(3); Pvt G Co 20th TN Cav; Apr 64 to Jul 64; Newbern PO; wounded in leg & hip; CONF
ARNIS, Simeon B., Mt-145-1; Pvt B Co 22nd KY Inf; 1 Jan 61 to 16 Jul 65; Clarksville PO
ARNOLD, Alexander, Jo-151-4; Pvt F Co 13th TN Cav; 22 Sep 63 to 5 Sep 65; Bakers Gap PO; lung disease
ARNOLD, Alexander, Je-142-1; Pvt B Co 6th TN Inf; 8 Mar 62 to 27 Apr 65; Lucilla PO; falling back of mumps and contraction of spinal muscles
ARNOLD, Anthony, H-64-3; Pvt B Co 27th OH Inf; 7-11-61 to 11-25-64; Chattanooga PO
ARNOLD, Aquilla, Jo-151-2; Pvt M Co 13th TN Cav; 2 Feb 64 to 5 Sep 65; Bakers Gap PO; injury to head and right side resulting in catarrh
ARNOLD, Arthur, Su-241-1; Pvt H Co 1st TN Cav; 1 Sep 62 to 15 Jun 65; Blairs Gap PO; exposure
ARNOLD, Baker, Hw-121-3(2); Pvt K Co 29th TN Inf; 1 Oct 62 to 15 Apr 65; New Hope PO; none in war; CONF
ARNOLD, Benjamin, Wa-268-1; discharge away from home; Johnson City PO; rheumatism
ARNOLD, Calvin M., Jo-149-3; 1st Lt D Co 13th TN Cav; 24 Sep 63 to Aug 65; Edom PO; dirrhera resulting piles
ARNOLD, Demsy B., We-228-1(9); Pvt K Co 6th TN Cav; 15 Aug 62 to 18 Jul 65; Dresden PO; kidney affection, still kidney affected
ARNOLD, John, Wa-266-2; Martha A. widow of; Pvt 8th TN Cav; Fall Branch PO
ARNOLD, John, Jo-151-4; Rachel widow of; Pvt F Co 13th TN Cav; 22 Sep 63 to 5 Sep 65; Bakers Gap PO; died, brain fever, 1874
ARNOLD, John, Hw-119-2(1); Sgt E Co 1st TN Cav; 17 Mar 62 to 11 Apr 65; Alum Well PO; rheumatism
ARNOLD, John A., Hw-125-2; C? A Co 18th TN Inf; 16 Feb 64 to 65; Stony Point PO; CONF
ARNOLD, Michael, Ro-203-1; Sarah widow of; Pvt; Wheat PO; CONF
ARNOLD, Powel, Ct-45-1; Rebecca Estep formerly widow of; Pvt B Co 4th TN Inf; 5-63 to __; Stony Creek PO; shot at Richmond, VA, 10-63; prisoner

ARNOLD, Samuel B. Sr., Me-89-2; Pvt M Co 9th TN Cav; 9-1-63 to 9-11-65; Maloney PO
ARNOLD, Seth, Hw-122-1; Pvt D Co 4th TN Inf; 15 Oct 63 to 2 Aug 65; New Canton PO; piles, suffers considerably (at times)
ARNOLD, William, P-156-2; Elizabeth widow of; Pvt; Lobelville PO; wound in right leg; CONF
ARNOLD, William, Je-142-2; Malinda widow of; Pvt B Co 6th TN Cav; died in service; New Market PO
ARNOLD, William, Hw-123-1; Sarah widow of; PVt; Solitude PO
ARNOLD, Wm. B., Dy-27-3; Cpl C Co 47th TN Inf; 61 to Jun 65; Tatemville PO; CONF
ARNOLD, William C., Ct-44-1; Eca E. widow of; Sgt F Co 13th TN Cav; 9-22-63 to 9-5-65; PO omitted
ARNOLD, William M., Dk-35-4(2); Pvt A Co 5th TN Cav; 8-27-63 to 8-14-65; Cav; 8-27-63 to 8-14-65; Capling PO; crushed by horse falling
ARNOTT, Augustus, Hw-132-2; Sgt G Co 5th TN Cav; 63 to 5 May 65; Persia PO; CONF
ARNOTT, Hardin M., Hw-132-2; Pvt B Co 60th TN Inf; Oct 62 to 64; Persia PO; CONF
ARNOTT, James, Hw-131-1; Jane widow of; Pvt; PO omitted; heart disease, not discharged
ARNWINE, Alfred, Mc-110-1; Amanda widow of; Mt. Vesa PO; discharge lost
ARONWOOD, William, Co-65-2; Pvt; 15th Dist
ARP, Alfred C., Mo-130-3; Pvt D Co 3rd TN Mtd Inf; 7-25-64 to 11-30-64; Ballplay PO
ARP, Benjaman, Mo-130-2; Pvt D Co 3rd TN Mtd Inf; 7-12-64 to 12-25-64; Ballplay PO
ARRENDELL, Melvin, Jo-150-3; Pvt I Co 13th TN Cav; 15 Jan 64 to 5 Sep 65; Key Station PO
ARRENDELL, William, Jo-150-1; Lt I Co 13th TN Cav; 12 Apr 64 to 9 Sep 65; Osborn PO; no record found
ARRINGTON, Leroy, Ha-111-3; Pvt E Co 1st TN Cav; 17 Mar 62 to 11 Apr 65; PO omitted
ARRONDER, Clark P., D-67-2; alias Palamore; Pvt F Co 42nd Col Inf; Nov 1 64 to Feb 12 66; Nashville PO
ARRONS, Frank, Ma-125-2; US Sol; Chester St, Jackson PO
ARROWSMITH, Westley, Cf-40-1; Susan W. widow of; Sgt D Co 12th US Reg; Apr 62 to Apr 65; Tullahoma PO; shot in arm
ARTHUR, Silas, C-28-2(1); Pvt G Co 8th IN Inf; 8-16-62 to ___; Fincastle PO; lung trouble
ARWOOD, Henly N., Co-59-2; US Sol; 1st Dist
ARWOOD, James, Co-67-5; Pvt A Co 2nd NC Inf; 15 Sep 63 to 16 Aug 65; Naillon PO
ARWOOD, John, Se-231-1; Rebeca A. widow of; Pvt K Co 13th TN Cav; 22 Sep 63 to 5 Sep 65; Boyds Creek PO
ARWOOD, John H., Co-61-2(1); Pvt C Co 2nd NC Mtd Inf; 16 Jun 61 to 1 Jun 63; Parrotsville PO
ASBERRY, Henry, Cy-27-4(2); Pvt A Co 7th TN Inf; 11-62 to 7-65; Miles Cross Roads PO
ASBERRY, Whitley, Be-7-1; Pvt G Co 48th MO Inf; 29 Jan 65 to 29 Jun 65; Enlow, Cape Deralio PO
ASBURRY, Denlly E., Hn-68-1; Sgt Maj 101st US CI; 4 Oct 64 to 5 Oct 65; Paris PO
ASBURY, George W., Ov-150-1; Pvt 5th KY Cav; Eagle Creek PO
ASBURY, James A., Wh-183-1; Pvt A Co 1st KY Cav; 10 Jun 62 to 65; Quebeck PO; no disability incurred, discharge burned in house
ASHBUN, James, We-221-1(4); Pvt D Co 51st IL Inf; 1 Jul 61 to 1 Apr 64; Martin PO; ruptured, caused by strain
ASHCRAFT, Jno. W., Dy-27-3; Pvt I Co 1st TN Cav; Feb 62 to Apr 65; Newbern PO; CONF
ASHFORD, Charles, Gi-122-5; Pvt A Co 110th TN Inf; 3 Aug 62 to 6 Feb 66; Aspen Hill PO; hurt back
ASHFORD, John, Dk-33-2; Pvt A Co 5th TN Cav; 11-10-63 to 8-14-65; Gasaway PO; sight, powder burns in service
ASHLEY, Benjamin F., G-57-4(1); Pvt C Co 12th TN Inf; 6-1-61 to 1-1-62; Yorkville PO; CONF
ASHLEY, George R., H-49-4; Cpl C Co 32nd KY Inf; 12-5-62 to 8-10-63; Pvt A Co 4th TN Cav; 12-15-63 to 7-1-65; Lake Side PO; contracted rheumatism & diarheoa, enlisted twice
ASHLEY, James K., F-35-1; Pvt K Co 9th Cav; 2 Oct 63 to Sep 11 65; Ina PO; cold from measles settle on lungs
ASHLEY, Joe, We-221-3; Cassie L. widow of; Cpl B Co 12th TN Inf; May 6 61 to Dec 24 61; Martin PO; contracted death; CONF
ASHLEY, Joshua F., Cr-20-3; Rebecca widow of; Pvt B Co 7th TN Cav; Hollow Rock PO
ASHLEY, Josiah, Mg-196-2; Sarah A. widow of; Pvt B Co 2nd TN Inf; 61 to ___; Hunnicutt PO; died in prison
ASHLEY, Stephen K., W-189-3(2); Pvt A Co 19th KY Inf; 10-7-61 to 4-12-63; McMinnville PO; lung disease & rheumatism
ASHLEY, Wm., G-57-4(1); Pvt A Co 15th TN Cav; 7-1-61 to 7-1-65; Yorkville PO; CONF
ASHLEY, ___, Be-1-1; Veuona E. widow of; Sol; 1st Dist
ASHTON, Lucretia A., Mn-129-2; widow; no PO
ASHWORTH, Benjamin, D-68-3; Pvt G Co 14th USC Inf; 5 Dec 63 to Mar 66; 13 S. Sycamore St, Nashville PO; hearing injured
ASKEW, Henry H., Sm-172-1 (see Askew, William F.)
ASKEW, William F., Sm-172-1 (Henry H. Askew on same line); Pvt F Co 4th TN Inf; 10-64 to 8-27-65; Gordonville PO; chronic sore eyes, now blind; CONF
ASKEW, Winfield S., Pu-146-1; Pvt I Co 4th TN Mtd Inf W(hite?); 1-1-65 to 8-25-65; Buffalo Valley PO
ASKEW, Wylie, Sh-150-1; Wylie Roberson on same line; Cpl G Co 61st W TN Inf; 2 yrs 6 mos; Bartlett PO; shot in left knee
ASKINS, Emaline (see Snider, Peter)
ASKINS, William, Di-34-2; Pvt D Co 13th OH Cav; 4-10-64 to 8-19-65; Dickson PO; discharged in hospital Petersburg, VA
ASKYS, John J., Ma-114-2; Pvt I Co 26th TX Cav; Feb 62 to May 65; Pinson PO; CONF
ASLINGER, Joshua, Ja-85-2; Missouria widow of; Pvt E Co 5th TN Inf; 3-2-62 to 4-5-65; Birchwood PO
ATCHELY, Isaac, K-181-6(3); Pvt M Co 2nd TN Cav; Oct 62 to 10 Jun 65; Knoxville PO
ATCHISON, James H., Cf-40-1; Artificer F Co 1st NY Eng; 8 Mar 65 to 18 Jun 65; Tullahoma PO; went north in 61, joined the US army
ATCHLEY, James, Me-89-1; Cpl H Co 3rd TN Cav; 6-25-63 to 6-4-65; Big Spring PO; rheumatism
ATCHLEY, John D., Br-14-1; Sgt A Co 1st MD Inf; 3-64 to 7-65; Cleveland PO; disease of the eyes
ATCHLEY, Noah, Se-226-1; Sgt M Co 2nd TN Cav; 8 Nov 62 to 6 Jul 65; Straw Plains PO; chronic diarrhoea & rheu.
ATCHLEY, Pleasant L., Se-225-2; Cpl K Co 3rd TN Cav?; 5 Nov 63 to 10 Jun 65; Trotters Store PO; rheumatism and piles 25 yrs
ATCHLEY, Sampson, Me-92-4(1); Pvt I Co 9th TN Cav; 5-16-63 to 9-11-65; Pin Hook PO; eye sight affected
ATCHLEY, William D., Se-225-3; 2nd Lt? B Co 8th TN Inf; 8 Mar 62 to 27 Apr 65; Colletsburg PO; diarrhoea result in piles 25 yrs, shot through right hip
ATCHLY, Jessee, Se-223-5(1); Pvt E Co 1st TN Lt Art; 14 Sep 63 to 20 Sep 65; Sevierville PO
ATHENS, Edward G., Un-254-2; Pvt A Co 2nd TN Inf; Paulett PO; captured during service
ATHY, James W., Ma-126-1; Pvt F Co 153rd OH Inf; 2 May 64 to 10 Sep 64; Jackson PO
ATKERTON, John, Hn-73-1; Cpl Co I 25th NY; 61 to 63; Como PO; discharged on account of sickes
ATKIN, Calvin, Co-69-6(1); Pvt D Co 4th TN Inf; Jan 62 to Apr 65; Driskill PO; don't remember dates correct
ATKINS, Anderson W. (see Watkins, Anderson)
ATKINS, Archable, Gr-80-1; Pvt G Co 47th KY Inf; 62 to 63 (1 yr 4 mos); Thorn Hill PO; joined & served 1 year, discharged & joined & served 4 mos 4 days
ATKINS, Benjamin F., Mc-116-1; Pvt F Co 17th IN Mtd (Inf?); 10-8-64 to 8-65; Riceville PO
ATKINS, Daniel H., Gr-80-1; Pvt G Co 47th KY Inf; 29 Aug 63 to 26 Dec 64; Thorn Hill PO; chronic diarrhea; for God's sake help this soldier
ATKINS, G. A., Gr-80-1; Pvt G Co 47th KY Inf; 1 Aug 63 to Oct 63; Thorn Hill PO; nervous debility
ATKINS, James, Gi-135-1; Pvt A Co 3rd TN Inf; 2-62 to 63; Lynnville PO

ATKINS, James C., Wy-173-1; Pvt A Co 10th TN Inf; 4-16-62 to 5-23-65; Lutts PO
ATKINS, John T-206-2; Pvt B Co 9th OH Cav; Dec 62 to __; Covington PO
ATKINS, Joseph W., Ro-210-9; Pvt; Rockwood PO; CONF
ATKINS, Levi, K-167-5; Pvt D Co 4th Cav; 61 to 65; Knoxville PO
ATKINS, Thomas J., We-223-2; Sgt B Co 7th TN Cav; Jun 63 to 5 Aug 65; Palmersville PO
ATKINS, William, D-72-6; Pvt KY Inf; 64 to 65; Nashville PO
ATKINS, William, K-160-2; Pvt B Co 23rd KY Vol; 63 to 31 Dec 65; Knoxville PO
ATKINSON, Henry, H-69-4; Pvt A Co 101st TN Col Inf; 2-26-64 to 1-26-66; Chattanooga PO
ATKINSON, James J., K-158-1; Mareret widow of; 1st Lt E Co 1st TN Art; 62 to 65; Knoxville, 80 Fauche St PO; shot in hand
ATKINSON, John G., Gi-122-1; Fannie widow of; Pvt A Co 53rd TN Reg; 1 Nov 61 to 2 Nov 62; Prospect Sta. PO; died of sickness in 2 Nov 1862; CONF
ATKINSON, Marion, We-225-3(2); Marttey widow of; Pvt K Co 6th TN Cav; Aug 62 to 64; Dresden PO; cronic diareas?, discharged for phisical disability
ATKINSON, Nuneul N., Hd-50-3; Pvt A Co 10th TN Inf; Apr 9 62 to May 25 65; Lowervyille PO
ATKINSON, Spencer, Mc-112-3; Pvt G Co 7th TN Mtd Inf; 62 to 66 (3 yrs 3 mos); Athens PO; bloody piles
ATKINSON, William C., Hm-109-5; USS; PO omitted
ATKINSON, William C., K-166-3; Pvt C Co 4th TN Inf; 1 Jul 63 to 2 Aug 65; Knoxville PO; chronic diarrhea
ATKINSON, William M., Wy-178-1; Pvt B Co 2nd IL Art; 1-9-65 to 7-15-65; PO omitted
ATTAM, Joel H., De-23-2; Pvt F Co; Aug 61 to Oct? 61; Bath Springs PO; CONF
ATWELL, Abidah H., B-18-1; Pvt I Co 1st US; 12-15-62 to 10-1-63; Flat Creek PO
ATWELL, Henry C., B-18-1; G Co 29th MI Inf; 9-3-64 to 4-27-65; Flat Creek PO
ATWOOD, James N., Sm-173-2; Elizabeth widow of; Pvt G Co 5th TN Cav; 9-27-62 to 8-14-65; Brush Creek PO
ATWOOD, John W., Sm-173-3; Ord Sgt D Co 4th TN Mtd Inf; 7-25-64 to 8-25-65; Brush Creek PO
AULEY, Madison, We-220-2; Pvt C Co 1st TN State Troop; Oct 18 63 to Mar? 65; 4th Civil Dist
AURIN, Gustive W., C-33-2; Martha J. widow of; Pvt B Co 2nd TN Inf; 7-63 to 66; Jellico PO
AUSMENT, Calvin J., Cr-4-4; Pvt C Co 16th TN Cav; 9-1-62 to 9-1-65; Bells Depot PO
AUSMUS, Henry, Cl-47-1; Teamster E Co 6th TN Inf; 3-6-62 to 4-65; Speedwell PO
AUSMUS, Joseph, Cl-47-2; Pvt A Co 1st TN Inf; 6-30-63 to 8-3-65; Speedwell PO; rheumatism 1864
AUSMUS, William, Cl-47-3; Capt E Co 6th TN Inf; 9-19-61 to 9-15-64; Compensation PO
AUSTIN, Augustus, Hd-50-3; Pvt C Co D 2nd TN Mtd Inf; Mar 1 64 to May 13 65; Lowervyille PO
AUSTIN, Carie, Hy-83-1; alias Ray Bailey; Pvt F Co W? L? Cav; Aug 27 63 to Feb 25 65; Brownsville PO
AUSTIN, Francis M., Wi-276-2; Pvt D Co 2nd OH Art; 63 to 65; Beechville PO
AUSTIN, Goodman M., Br-9-4; C Bugler B Co 10th TN Cav; 9-15-63 to 8-1-65; Cleveland OP
AUSTIN, Hariet, K-185-3; widow; River Dale PO
AUSTIN, Henry, D-63-3; on same line name Lewis; Pvt I Co 14th TN Inf; Nov 16 63 to Mar 66; Nashville PO
AUSTIN, James, Sm-171-1; Melvina J. widow of; Pvt C Co 8th TN Mtd Inf; 2-20-65 to 8-25-65; Chestnut Mound PO
AUSTIN, James F., Ch-12-3; Pvt C Co NC Bat; 7-5-62 to 4-28-65; Wild Goose PO; CONF
AUSTIN, John, Hd-50-3; Walnut Grove PO
AUSTIN, John E., D-84-1; Pvt C Co 4th TN Inf; Sep 63 to Aug 65; Antioch PO
AUSTIN, John J., De-22-2; Pvt F Co 9th TN Cav; 1 Sep 62 to 8 May 65; Dunbar PO; shot in right arm; CONF
AUSTIN, John W., M-107-1; Martha widow of; Pvt A Co 9th KY Inf; 9-61 to __; Red Boiling Springs PO; chronic diarrhea
AUSTIN, Luisa, Hd-50-6; Sol US; 6th Civil Dist
AUSTIN, Melvin, Cl-58-3; Tazewell PO
AUSTIN, Patan, Sh-160-2; Pvt 9th TN Hvy Art; __ to 65; Memphis PO
AUSTIN, Ross, Sh-193-1; Pvt; Memphis PO; have lost all papers
AUSTIN, Shederic T., Tr-265-1; Pvt A Co 14th KY Cav; 12 Apr 65 to 20 Oct 65; Hartsville PO
AUSTIN, William, He-67-3; Pvt H Co 6th TN Cav; Mar 64 to Jul 25 65; Scotts Hill PO; palpatation of hart 26 yrs
AUSTIN, William, Dk-39-5(1); Pvt C Co 4th TN Mtd Inf; Laurel Hill PO
AUSTON, Willis, Sh-158-5(1); Pvt G Co 11th US Hvy Art; 11 Feb 63 to 12 Jan 66; Memphis PO; discharged at close of the war with discharge papers
AUTHERFORD, Abner D., C-28-2(1); Pvt F Co 6th TN Inf; 3-10-62 to __ (4 mos 2 days); Big Creek Gap PO; kidney disease
AUTHOR, Howard, C-72-3; Pvt E Co 101st TN Col Inf; Apr 16 __ to Jun 22 65; Nashville PO
AUTRY, Dirgon, We-225-3(2); Susan widow of; Pvt E Co 7th TN Cav; Jul 61 to 65; Dresden PO; scurvy in prison, died at Annapolis, MD
AUTRY, John P., Ma-126-1; Pvt C Co 7th TN Cav; 28 Aug 62 to 9 Aug 65; Jackson PO
AUTRY, Liza (W), Be-2-1; Pvt E Co 7th TN Cav; 60 to 64; Holladay PO
AVANTS, James T., O-138-1; Pvt A Co 2nd Mis (C); 1 Apr 61 to 17 Jan 65; Lanes PO; CONF
AVERELL, Robert, Tr-268-2 (Col); Pvt A Co 14th US Inf; Dec 62 to Oct 66; Hartsville PO; chronic diarhea, not able to work
AVERETT, William O., P-151-3; 1st Sgt E Co 6th TN Cav; Linden PO
AVERY, Jessey D., R-161-2; Pvt D Co 2nd OH Inf; 1 yr 6 mos; Dayton PO; discharge in N. Carolina
AVINGTON, Nelson, We-221-7; Pvt TN Inf; 62 to 64; Martin PO
AWOOD, James, Ch-12-1; Lorind L. Gourly widow of; Pvt 13th TN Cav; 11-12-63 to 4-15-65; Wild Goose PO
AXLEY, Elija L., Mo-122-2; Martha J. widow of; Pvt A Co 62nd TN Inf; 11-24-62 to 3-19-63; Dancing Branch PO; CONF
AXLEY, James W., Mo-122-2; Pvt A Co 62nd TN Inf; 3-20-63 to 7-4-63; Dancing Branch PO; CONF
AYERS, C. B., Su-234-1; Lucinda widow of; 13th TN Cav; 4th Civil Dist
AYERS, Mary A., Wy-175-2; widow; Pvt; 10th Civil Dist
AYERS, William, Ov-134-1; Sgt M Co 13th TN Cav; 2-2-63 to 9-8-65; Hilham PO; had measles and resulted in diarrhea, lung trouble & heart disease, is still affected
AYLES, Alfred C., Cu-17-4; 4th Sgt E Co 1st TN Inf; 8-20-61 to 2-15-65; Crab Orchard PO; liver disease--dyspepsia, piles, promoted to Capt Co C, 2-25-63
AYLES, Elisabeth A. (see Hamby, James H.)
AYLOR, Joseph S., We-229-1; Pvt D Co 18th TN Inf; 15 May 61 to 20 Sep 64; Gleason PO
AYRES, Charles V., Mu-209-7; Adjutant C Co 9th Bat Cav; 5-61 to 5-65; Columbia PO; CONF
AYRES, Robert O., Mc-112-10; Pvt A Co 60th OH Inf; 10-1-61 to 9-10-62; Athens PO; dates lost
AYTSE, A. C., Fe-42-2; Loretta Reed formerly widow of; Capt 2nd TN; Jamestown PO
AYTSE, Julius, Mc-112-7; Capt B Co 1st TN Inf; 8-6-61 to 11-29-64; Athens PO; shell wound
BABASIAN, Cael, F-35-1; widow; 2nd Dist
BABB, Abraham, Ro-202-2; Menirva widow of; Pvt D Co 5th TN Inf; 7 Mar 62 to 14 Oct 63; Union X Roads PO; strangury
BABB, Alexander F., Ge-93-1; Pvt E Co 4th TN Inf; 15 Mar 63 to 2 Aug 65; Greeneville PO
BABB, Alford, Ge-97-4; Sol US; 20th Civil Dist
BABB, Barnet, Ge-97-4; Sol US; 20th Civil Dist
BABB, Caleb, We-274-3; Pvt Battery 23 IN Lt Art; 11 Jun 63 to 9 Sep 63; Jonesboro PO
BABB, Isaac, Ro-202-2; Pvt H Co 5th TN Inf; 7 Mar 62 to 14 Oct 63; Oral PO; heart disease 30 yrs
BABB, Isaac N., Wa-274-3; Armors Mate Crystom Shanty; Jan 64 to Feb 65; Jonesboro PO

BABB, John, Mr-98-2(5); Kizziah widow of; Pvt; Whiteside PO
BABB, Loyd A., Ge-89-4; Pvt O Co 7th KY Inf; 19 Aug 62 to 18 Jul 65; Marvin PO; in eyes, cron. diarhea & back
BABB, Samuel, Ge-99-2; Pvt H Co 8th TN Inf; 25 Jul 63 to __; Cedar Creek PO; janders, didn't get any discharge
BABB, William L., Ge-91-3; Pvt E Co 1st TN Art; 23 Nov 63 to 1 Aug 65; Greeneville PO; indigestion, piles & deafness
BABBITT, H. H., We-229-2; "found while examining work"; 11th Civil Dist
BABCOCK, George W., Mg-200-2; Pvt F Co 19th NY Cav; Aug 62 to Jun 65; Skene PO; gunshot left hip
BABCOCK, Orlow, Mg-200-2; Phenis C. widow of; Pvt A Co 108th NY Inf; 21 Jul 62 to 28 May 65; Skene PO
BABLE, Abner, Ge-97-2; Pvt G Co 4th TN Inf; 5 Apr 63 to 2 Aug 65; Upchurch PO; rheumatism, lungs & piles
BACHMAN, James, Sh-176-1; Elizabeth widow of; Capt C Co 12th IN Reg; 5-6-62 to 63; 95 St. Martin St., Memphis PO
BACKLEY, John, Co-69-7(3); Pvt B Co 8th TN Inf; 15 Dec 62 to 15 Jun 65; Rankin PO; mumps, dirhea; Lexton KY PO
BACKNER, Lewis, D-46-1; Pvt A Co 17th US Col; 4-28-64 to 4-25-66; Nashville PO
BACON, Adam, Wa-272-2; Pvt I Co 8th TN Cav; 25 Sep 63 to 11 Sep 65; Morning Star PO; rheumatism, chr. diarrhoea, resulting disease of heart
BACON, Allen S., Lo-195-2(1); Cpl A Co 2nd TN Inf; 10 Aug 61 to 6 Oct 64; Oral PO (Roane Co.); rheumatism
BACON, Drewe A., A-9-5(3); Nancy J. widow of; Sgt A Co 2nd TN Inf; 5-8-63 to 8-3-65; Dossetts PO
BACON, Elbert, Mc-114-1; Pvt 6th TN Inf; 4-10-62 to 6-30-65; Folger PO
BACON, James, Ge-85-3; Pvt I Co 8th TN Cav; Cavey Branch PO; heart disease caused from fever while in the army
BACON, James, Je-146-2; Pvt C Co 1st TN Cav; White Pine PO; soldier not at home, wife cant give dates
BACON, James M., Ge-85-1; 2nd Lt M Co 9th TN Cav; 1 Jun 63 to 11 Sep 65; Cavey Branch PO; kidney affection
BACON, Joseph C., Wa-266-2; Pvt 8th TN Cav; Fall Branch PO
BACON, Martin K., Wa-273-2; Pvt I Co 8th TN Cav; 9 Jun 63 to 11 Nov 65; Crookshanks PO; rheumatism
BACON, Samuel H., Lo-187-4; Pvt L Co 1st US Col Hvy Art; 64 to 31 Mar 66; Loudon PO; rheumatism
BACON, William A., Ro-201-1; Amelia J. widow of; 1st Lt 5th TN Inf; 25 Feb 62 to 29 Mar 65; Kingston PO
BACON, William H. H., Br-9-1; Mary J. widow of; Sgt L Co 1st TN Cav; 3-20-62 to 3-31-65; Cleveland PO
BADGETT, B. N., Bo-19-3; Pvt G Co 3rd TN Cav; 62 to 63; Rockford PO; diseased hip; CONF
BADGETT, Benjamin, H-72-1; Ellen J. widow of; Pvt H Co US Inf; Chattanooga PO
BADGETT, Harison, Bo-19-3; Pvt A Co 1st US Art; 2-8-64 to 3-21-66; Rockford PO
BADGETT, Rich, Bo-19-3; Pvt H Co 1st US Inf; 2-8-64 to 3-21-66; Rockford PO; deafness
BADGETT, S. H., Bo-19-3; 1st Sgt L Co 3rd TN Cav; 10-10-63 to 6-10-65; Rockford PO
BADGETT, Thomas, K-171-2; US Sol (Col); 12th Civil Dist
BADEF, Daniel, Sh-178-3; US Sol; 64 Wellingston St, Memphis PO
BADER, Herman, D-45-2; Capt F Co 29th MO Inf; 7-18-62 to 3-15-65; Nashville PO
BAGBY, James L., He-67-3; Pvt G Co 6th TN Cav; Sep 18 62 to Jul 26 65; Scotts Hill PO; chronic bronchitis 26 yr-
BAGGETT, Dinah (see Gray, Benjamon)
BAGWELL, Hiram, Jo-149-1; Pvt G Co 4th TN Inf; 15 Aug 62 to 7 Jul 65; Mountain City PO; rupture disease of side, piles

BAIER, John, D-45-3; Pvt C Co 32nd IN Inf; 8-62 to 63; Nashville PO
BAILESS, Hiram, D-102-1; Pvt E Co 6th IN Cav; 11 Jun 62 to 20 Jul 65; Jordonia PO
BAILEY, All M., Mu-210-7; Pvt TN Inf; May 61 to May 64; Spring Hill PO; shot through left arm; CONF
BAILEY, Charly, Wl-292-1; Pvt F Co 101st Col Inf; Oct 63 to Jun 65; Lebanon PO
BAILEY, Danial, Hw-121-3(2); Nancy widow of; Pvt B Co 3rd TN Mtd Inf; 30 Jun 62 to 3 Nov 64; Fry PO
BAILEY, Dave, Mu-210-2; 1 yr; Spring Hill PO
BAILEY, David, Hw-133-1; Mary widow of; Hewells Batery Lt Art; 1 Feb 63 to Nov 63; Beurams Store PO; killed in battle; CONF
BAILEY, George W., Mu-209-7; Pvt G Co 1st MO; 61 to 64; Columbia PO; CONF
BAILEY, George W., Mu-209-6; Pvt; Columbia PO; CONF
BAILEY, Henry, A-4-1; Pvt D Co 5th TN Inf; 2-26-62 to 3-30-65; Coal Creek PO; spinal affection
BAILEY, Henry F., Wa-261-2; on same line with Sturart, George G., can't tell which man the following data belongs to: Pvt G Co 63rd TN Inf; 63 to 30 Jul 65; Nola Chuckey PO; CONF
BAILEY, Isaac, Hd-47-2; Salina widow of; Pvt C Co 55th US Col Inf; 63 to 65; Savannah PO
BAILEY, James, Sh-163-1; Pvt B Co 12th NY Cav; 62 to 65; Memphis PO; 12 days in Libby Prison, in Shelby County Poor House
BAILEY, James, Sh-159-4; Pvt Inf; Memphis PO
BAILEY, James, Ja-86-1; Pvt B Co 4th TN Cav; Snowhill PO; piles
BAILEY, James, C-8-1; Pvt H Co 2nd TN Inf; 3-9-62 to 8-20-62; Well Spring PO; rheumatism, don't get pension
BAILEY, James H., Bo-19-2; Pvt C Co 3rd TN Cav; 61 to __; South Rockford PO; CONF
BAILEY, James W., A-4-1; Cpl J Co 7th TN Inf; 11-8-64 to 7-27-65; Coal Creek PO; spinal affection and piles
BAILEY, Jasper, Ge-92-3; Pvt H Co 8th TN Inf; 8 Jun 63 to __; Laurel Gap PO
BAILEY, Jessee, Hw-125-2; Pvt TN Inf; 62 to 65; Surgoinsville PO; CONF
BAILEY, John, Un-252-2; Pvt A Co 1st KY Inf; Apr 62 to Apr 65; Haynes PO; rheumatism
BAILEY, Jno. (see Oliver, Jno.)
BAILEY, John B., Ha-111-4(1); Pvt B Co 3rd TN Inf; Jul 64 to Mar 65; Upper Clinch PO
BAILEY, John E., Ro-201-6; Sarah F. widow of; Pvt C Co 30th TN Inf; Kingston PO
BAILEY, Joseph (see Beard, Joseph)
BAILEY, Levy, Mr-102-1; Pvt; South Pittsburg? PO
BAILEY, Martin, G-51-2; US Sol; Baker in US Army; 3rd Civil Dist
BAILEY, Perry, Cl-48-1; Pvt D Co 17th VA Inf; 64 to 65 (11 mos); Culberson PO (Larence Co. OH); measels & chronic diarea
BAILEY, Peter, Wl-294-1; Pvt K Co 17th TN Inf; Jan 63 to May 65; Tuckers X Roads PO; contracted rheumatism, but able to work
BAILEY, Ray (see Austin, Carie)
BAILEY, Richard N., Hw-133-3; Pvt; 12 May 61 to 12 May 65; Sigornsville PO; CONF
BAILEY, Sallie, Sh-173-1; 196½ Beale St, Memphis PO
BAILEY, Shervood W., Tr-268-1; Pvt F Co 1st TN Inf; 28 Jan 64 to 15 Apr 65; Hartsville PO; broken shoulder, filled out term of service
BAILEY, Virgil V., H-69-4; Pvt G Co 40th GA Inf; 62 to 64; Chattanooga PO; hand shot off at the seige of Vicksburg; CONF
BAILEY, William, Hw-133-3; Martha widow of; Pvt; Sigornsville PO
BAILEY, William E., H-58-1; Cpl B Co 50th OH Inf; 7-26-62 to 6-26-65; Sale Creek PO
BAILEY, William K., Se-226-6; Pvt; Henrys X Roads PO
BAILEY, William W., D-64-4; Cpl K Co 47th KY Inf; 61 to 61; Nashville PO; rheumatism
BAILEY, __, Hw-125-4; Nancy widow of; Pvt C Co; 64 to 65; Surgoinsville PO; shot 3 times
BAILIFF, Columbus A., Dk-31-2; Sgt I Co 4th TN Mtd Inf; 1-30-65 to 8-25-65; Alexandria PO
BAILLY, Polode, Gi-129-1; Pvt K Co 110th TN Inf; 15 Dec 63 to 6 Feb 66; Conway PO

BAILS, John M., Ge-96-4; Pvt I Co 8th TN Cav; 25 Sep 63 to 65; Rheatown PO; kidneys affected, heart truble, cant get dates
BAILY, A., Sh-190-2; Emma widow of; Pvt K Co 63rd US Inf; 63 to 66; 193 Carolina St, Memphis PO; face powder burned
BAILY, Armsted, Sh-195-2; US Sol; Memphis PO
BAILY, Carter, Rb-223-3(5); Pvt I Co 15th TN Inf; 64 to 65; 9th Dist
BAILY, James A., Je-136-3; Pvt M Co 1st US Hvy Art; 11 Oct 64 to 6 Apr 66; PO omitted
BAILY, John, Ja-84-1; Rebeca A.J. Thompson formerly widow of; Pvt; Harrison PO
BAILY, Rufus, Wa-268-3; Virginie L. widow of; Johnson City PO
BAILY, Sarah (see Wright, William)
BAIN, Lucien, Gu-48-2; Pvt B Co 1st IN Cav; 8-1-63 to 6-16-65; Tracy City PO; thrown from horse, lame in back ever since
BAIN, Mrs. Mary M., La-111-2; widow of Sol?; Pvt I Co 1st AL Cav; 7-61 to __ (6 mos); Pleasant Point PO; died with diarrhoea
BAIN, William, D-98-1; Pvt D Co 4th TN; Nov 25 64 to Aug 30 65; 19th Civil Dist
BAIN, Widow, Wa-261-1; Pvt TN Inf; Sep 62 to Apr 63; Cankling PO; lungs; CONF
BAINES, Thomas, D-45-3; Margret widow of; Pvt B Co 10th TN Inf; 4-14-62 to 5-25-66; Nashville PO
BAIRD, Andrew, C-34-1; Martha J. Lay widow of; Pvt A Co 1st TN Inf; 8-6-61 to __ (killed); Elk Valley PO
BAIRD, George W., Cr-8-1; Sgt B Co 9th TN; 6-25-61 to 8-15-63; Gates PO; shot through right leg
BAIRD, Hiram, C-34-4; 11th Civil Dist
BAIRD, J.M., G-65-1; Julis F. widow of; Pvt; Dist 15
BAIRD, James, C-33-1; Pvt 6th TN Inf; 62 to 65; Newcomb PO
BAIRD, Lewis, C-34-1; Pvt G Co 7th TN Mtd Inf; 11-8-64 to 7-28-65; Elk Valley PO
BAIRD, Prier P., C-32-2; Pvt A Co 1st TN Inf; 8-2-61 to 10-10-64; Pine Mountain PO; runites & hart diseas 26 yrs
BAIRD, Richard, Hd-51-2; US Sol; 9th Civil Dist
BAIRD, Samuel C., C-27-3; Pvt A Co 1st TN Inf; 8-2-61 to 9-17-65; Jacksboro PO
BAIRD, Y. D., C-34-1; Pvt A Co 1st TN Inf; 8-1-64 to 9-17-64; Elk Valley PO
BAKER, Alfred, K-179-4; Pvt K Co 3rd TN Cav; 25 Jul 63 to 3 Aug 65; PO omitted
BAKER, Benjamin, St-162-1; Pvt D Co 8th KY; 1 Jul __ to Mar __; Cumberland City PO; rheumatism
BAKER, Benjamin, C-33-3; Wagoner I Co 2nd TN; 62 to 65; Newcomb PO
BAKER, Benjamin W., T-206-2; Cpl G Co 6th TN Cav; Aug 18 62 to Jul 26 65; Covington PO
BAKER, Butler, K-171-5(4); Pvt C Co 2nd TN Cav; Oct 62 to 7 Jul 65; Knoxville PO
BAKER, Calloway, K-156-4; Pvt G Co 4th TN Cav; 13 Sep 61 to 15 Aug 65; 88 State St, Knoxville PO; CONF
BAKER, Calvin C., Cy-27-4(2); Pvt F Co 1st TN Mtd Inf; 3-8-64 to 5-18-65; Spivey PO
BAKER, Charles C., Di-34-1; Pvt 1st OH Lt Art; 10-61 to 6-62; Dickson PO
BAKER, Clarence W., H-51-2(1); Capt US Troops; 11-1-63 to 3-26-66; Hill City PO
BAKER, Clement, Sh-196-2; Mary P. Malone formerly widow of; Hospital Stewart 22nd PA Inf; 1-12-64 to 10-16-65; 120 Dunlap St, Memphis PO
BAKER, Clever, Ja-85-2; Pvt G Co 3rd TN Cav; 8-21-63 to 6-8-65; Birchwood PO; chronic diarrhoea
BAKER, Curtis?, Su-240-3; Pvt A Co 63rd TN Inf; 62 to 65; Kindricks Creek PO; eyes, no discharge; CONF
BAKER, Daniel B., Jo-151-1; Pvt G Co 13th TN Cav; 22 Sep 63 to 5 Sep 65; Casper PO; deafness, diarrhoia, piles
BAKER, David A., Ro-204-3; Pvt F Co 2nd TN Inf; 29 Aug 61 to 25 Jul 65; Elverton PO; kidney disease
BAKER, Elisha L., Ge-96-4; Pvt F Co 8th TN Cav; 19 Oct 64 to 11 Sep 65; Rheatown PO; rupture, chronic diareah
BAKER, Esquire, D-66-2; Pvt I Co 17th US C Inf; 1 Nov 63 to 22 Sep 66; Nashville, 144 S. Front PO; wounded in back & right shoulder, is feeble from his wounds
BAKER, Ezekiel, U-246-1; Pvt H Co 8th TN Cav; 15 Sep 63 to 11 Sep 65; Limonite PO
BAKER, Ezra, Lk-113-3; Pvt F Co 189th OH; Feb 17 65 to Sep 18 65; Dist 5
BAKER, George C., Wh-187-3; Pvt K Co TN Cav; 7-64 to __ (1 yr); Key PO; contracted fever
BAKER, German, B-20-1; Pvt H Co 5th TN Cav; 10-62 to 8-14-65; Bedford PO
BAKER, Henry, Je-143-1; Pvt promoted to Capt K Co 1st US Art; 3 Aug 64 to 31 Mar 66; Mossy Creek PO; rheumatism
BAKER, Hugh B., Se-224-1; Pvt M Co 2nd TN Cav; 2 Nov 62 to 5 Jul 65; Waldens Creek PO; chronic diarrhea
BAKER, Jacob, Je-137-2; Pvt F Co 9th TN Cav; 24 Jul 63 to Sep 65; Hickory Ridge PO
BAKER, Jacob F., Wl-294-1; Sgt F Co 11th KY Inf; Oct 61 to Dec 9 64; Tuckers X Roads PO; rheumatism 28 yrs, wholly disabled
BAKER, James, Sm-174-1; Pvt B Co 5th TN Cav; __ to 8-14-65 (2 yrs 11 mos); Gordonsville PO
BAKER, James P., D-58-1; Pvt I Co 50th IN Inf; 62 to Jan 65; Nashville PO; made deaf at Moble
BAKER, James W., Bo-21-1; Cpl B Co 3rd TN Cav; 10-13-62 to 6-12-65; Veeba PO
BAKER, James W., Ma-121-1; Mrs. Nancy widow of; Pvt B Co 7th TN Cav; Apr 6 63 to May 15 65; Medina PO; Mr. James M. Baker was not wounded in the war but he was constantly suffering from white swelling from his youth until his death, his leg was amputated some months before his death. The widow has boys, but they are quite poor. She has had quite a drs. bill to pay for her husband since his death.
BAKER, Jefferson C., Hw-119-2(1); Capt 8th TN Cav; 63 to __; Lee Valley PO
BAKER, Jessee W., Hw-120-1; Pvt K Co 13th TN Cav; 10 Sep 63 to 5 Sep 65; War Gap PO; disease of legs
BAKER, John, D-49-2; Pvt; Nashville PO; could not get particulars
BAKER, John, Br-12-4; Pvt G Co 3rd TN Cav; 8-21-63 to 6-10-65; Etola PO; eyes affected
BAKER, John, K-167-4; Mary Gibbs widow; Pvt; 62 to Jun 65; Knoxville PO
BAKER, John Ge-96-3; Pvt H Co 4th TN Cav; 29 Jul 63 to 12 Jul 65; Rheatown PO
BAKER, John G., Hu-103-2; Pvt E Co TN Cav; 10 Aug 61 to 28 Dec 61; PO omitted
BAKER, John H., Dy-25-3; Pvt; 4 yrs; Newbern PO; CONF
BAKER, John H., Hn-73-1; Pvt I Co 6th TN; Como PO; chronic piles; honable discharge
BAKER, John H., Se-226-3; S Sgt K Co 3rd TN Cav; 25 Jul 63 to 3 Aug 65; Henrys X Roads PO
BAKER, John H., K-181-2; Pvt B Co 3rd TN Cav; 28 Nov 62 to 27 Jun 65; Knoxville PO; diarie
BAKER, John P., Sh-189-6; Pvt B Co; can't get other information; Carolina Ave, Memphis PO
BAKER, John R., Ha-117-1; Pvt E Co 43rd TN Inf; 13 Oct 63 to 65 (3 mos 6 days--sic); Kyle's Ford PO; CONF
BAKER, John S., Mc-118-1; Nuscis widow of; Pvt A Co 5th TN Mtd Inf; 9-1-64 to 6-29-65; Cogshill PO
BAKER, John W., Mr-95-1; Pvt A Co 123rd OH Inf; 61 to 62; Victoria PO
BAKER, Jonathan N., Ma-265-1; Cpl R Co 126th OH Inf; 13 Sep 62 to 2 Jul 65; Chuckey Valley PO; bronchitis
BAKER, Joseph J. W., Br-6-3; Pvt A Co 10th TN Cav --12-62-3 to __; Lt A Co 10th TN Cav--64 to __; Dare PO; gunshot wound and hemerage stomach
BAKER, Joseph R., Ha-117-2; Pvt E Co 8th TN Cav; 23 Sep 63 to 11 Sep 65; Kyle's Ford PO; disease breast & lungs
BAKER, Josiah F., F-40-2; Pvt I Co 38th TN Inf; 10 Mar 62 to 25 Apr 65; Oakland PO; CONF
BAKER, Newton G., Hd-50-1; Ordily F Co 13th IL Cav; Dec 1 63 to May 1 65; Savannah PO
BAKER, Nickolas, Di-40-1; Arbella wife of; Pvt H Co 3rd US; 7-17-63 to 7-67; Edgewood PO
BAKER, P. S., Hu-103-4; Pvt E Co 10th TN Cav; 10 Aug 64 to 12 May 65; PO omitted

BAKER, Phillip J., Sm-174-1; Pvt G Co 4th TN Inf; 11-1-64 to 8-25-65; New Middleton PO
BAKER, Pinkney A., Sh-145-3; Sarah J. widow of; Pvt F Co 47th MO Inf; 1 Sep 64 to 29 Mar 65; Kerrville PO; Cap. W. P. Adair
BAKER, Robert N., A-9-3(1); 2nd Sgt E Co 3rd TN Inf; 8-18-62 to __; transferred to 4th TN Inf a 1st Sgt in H Co on 4-7-65 to 6-26-65; Lowes Sulphur Springs PO
BAKER, Ruben, Mg-199-1; Capt F Co 17th IL Cav; 22 Jan 64 to 18 Dec 65; Sunbright PO
BAKER, Russell, Co-67-1; Pvt TN; 26 Aug 61 to 20 Feb 62; Bison PO; CONF
BAKER, Samuel, Sh-174-1; Ruth widow of; Memphis? PO; discharge lost
BAKER, Squire, D-64-6; Back 314 S. High, Nashville PO
BAKER, Sterling J., Un-250-2; Martha J. widow of; Pvt G Co 2nd TN Cav; 1 Oct 62 to died Mar 63; Have? Hill PO
BAKER, Thomas, Di-30-2; Pvt E Co 10th TN Art?; 7-12-63 to 5-8-65; Dickson PO; CONF
BAKER, Thomas, Lo-193-2; Pvt H Co 1st US Hvy Art; 10 Jun 64 to __ (21 days); Unitia PO; did not receive any discharge
BAKER, Thomas J., Cl-50-1; Rebeca Wolf widow of; Pvt A Co 63rd TN Inf; 4-5-62 to 4-28-65; Cedarford PO; CONF
BAKER, Thomas M., Ct-44-1; Pvt E Co 3rd G.C.? Inf; 10-63 to ?; Hampton PO; discharge lost
BAKER, W. H. H., Br-6-3; Pvt A Co 10th TN Cav; 8-12-63 to 7-8-65; Dare PO; rheumatism and nephritis & gun shot wound
BAKER, Wade, Wl-308-1; Capt F Co 28th TN; Sep 18 61 to May 18 62; Rural Hill PO; CONF
BAKER, Wallen W., Ha-112-1; Pvt G Co 19th KY Inf; 1 Nov 61 to 14 Sep 62; Sneedville PO
BAKER, Wesley, D-46-2; Pvt G Co 12th US Col; 8-12-63 to 1-16-66; Nashville PO
BAKER, Wiley, W-189-1; Ellen widow of; Pvt E Co 15th KS Cav; 10-11-64 to 10-19-65; McMinnville PO
BAKER, William, K-171-1; Pvt D Co 6th tN Inf; 18 Apr 62 to 27 Apr 65; Bearden PO
BAKER, William, Se-228-1(2); Pvt B Co 3rd TN Cav; 62 to 65; New Knob Creek PO
BAKER, William H., Ja-85-1; Pvt G Co 3rd TN Cav; 8-21-63 to 6-12-65; Birchwood PO
BAKER, William M., K-184-1; Pvt H Co 3rd TN Cav; 3 Oct 63 to 3 Aug 65; Riverdale PO
BAKER, William M., U-245-2; Pvt B Co 12th TN Cav; 1 Jan 63 to 5 Jun 65; Limestone Cove PO; Tavern, TN in 1864
BAKER, William P., G-67-2; Pvt M Co 6th TN Cav; 1 Sep 62 to 4 Mar 64; Bradford PO
BAKER, William R., Je-136-1; Pvt C Co 1st TN Lt Art; 1 May 64 to 1 Aug 65; Dandridge PO
BAKER, William W., Pu-144-2; Pvt; Bloomington PO
BAKER, Wilson, Me-92-4(1); Pvt D Co 7th TN Mtd Inf; 11-2-64 to 7-27-65; Pin Hook PO; hurting in breast & lungs, not really able to work ½ time
BALCH, Rueben E., H-53-4; Sgt C Co 4th OH Cav; 9-16-61 to 8-9-65; Chattanooga PO; wounded face
BALCOMB, Isaac W., H-56-4; Pvt G Co 7th MI Inf; 61 to 63; St. Elmo PO
BALDEN, James, Cl-54-2; Pvt E Co 8th TN Cav; Tazewell PO; cant get date of his enlistment nor discharge
BALDEN, Scugay?, Col, Sh-146-2; Pvt D Co 59th; Woodstock PO
BALDEWIN, George A., H-69-3; Pvt I Co 68th IL Inf; 6-62 to 62 (3 mos); Chattanooga PO
BALDIN, Wyatt, Cr-20-1; Pvt C Co 1st TN Inf; 8-8-63 to 12-13-64; Proffit PO; rheumatism
BALDRIDGE, Daniel, Dy-32-1; Pvt F Co 106th OH Inf; Nov 5 61 to May 1 62; Trimble PO
BALDWIN, Drewry P., Bo-13-1; Pvt H Co 3rd TN Inf; 12-10-63 to 9-65; Freindsville PO
BALDWIN, George R., R-159-2; Pvt C Co 8th TN Inf; 3-30-63 to 8-17-65; Spring City PO; rheumatims, brought on by exposure
BALDWIN, Hugh C., Br-11-1; Deborah L. widow of; Sgt I Co 10th TN Cav; 3-4-64 to 8-5-65; Chatala PO
BALDWIN, J. W. H., Lo-188-2; Lucinda widow of; Sgt A Co 5th TN Inf; 26 Feb 62 to 4 Apr 65; Stockton PO
BALDWIN, John, Wa-264-1; Pvt A Co 2nd TN Cav; 1 Jul 62 to 1 Apr 63; Jonesboro PO; shot through left thigh & in l. knee
BALDWIN, William H., C-30-2; Pvt C Co 1st TN Inf; 8-9-61 to 9-17-64; Stockville PO
BALEN, Pleasant, Ca-22-2; Pvt B Co 1st TN Lt Art; 62 to 6-20-65; Burt PO
BALENTINE, Dundridge, Gl-125-2; Pvt C Co 7th IA Inf; Jan 63 to 65; Wales PO
BALER, George H., Br-11-1; Lacah? A. widow of; Sgt G Co 12th TN Inf; 62 to 65; Chatala PO; CONF?
BALES, Donel M., Mc-109-2; Pvt B Co 7th TN Inf; 9-17-64 to 7-27-65; Chuckaluck PO; heart disease & results, died 6-4-1890
BALES, Edward, La-115-1; Pvt C Co 120th IN Inf; 6 Dec 64 to 6 Dec 65; Henryville PO
BALES, Harvey, Je-140-1; Pvt M Co 1st TN Cav; 1 Apr 63 to 22 Jun 65; Lucilla PO; injury right rist
BALES, Jacob, Wa-275-1; Elizabeth widow of; Pvt K Co 1st TN Cav; Pettibone PO
BALES, Jacob, K-183-2; Pvt B Co 6th TN Inf; Riverdale PO
BALES, Joseph N., H-53-7; Pvt K Co 10th TN Cav; 2-28-64 to 8-1-65; Chattanooga PO; horse fell on him, hurt hip
BALES, Mary A. (see Saffels, Harl)
BALES, Robert F., Fe-42-3; Pvt Capt David Beaty's Co TN Ind Scouts; Boatland PO
BALES, Sam, K-167-3; Fannee widow of; Pvt 2nd TN Inf; 61 to 65; Knoxville PO
BALES, Samuel, Se-226-2; Pvt C Co 9th TN Cav; Jul 62 to 13 Sep 65; Sinking Springs PO; chronic diarrhoea
BALES, Samuel, K-154-4; Knoxville PO
BALES, William M., Pi-156-2; Pvt B Co 15th KY Cav; 10-10-61 to 13-10-65; Travisville PO; blind in right eye
BALEW, John, C-24-4(3); Pvt K Co 14th IN Inf; 5-16-61 to 6-16-64; Forkvale PO; bronchitus & affection of heart & back
BALEY, Andrew J., K-172-3; Pvt; PO omitted; CONF
BALEY, John, Ct-35-2; Pvt 13th TN Cav; Butler PO (Johnson Co.); in US Army; soldier not at home and discharge not to be found
BALEY, John, Un-253-2; Pvt D Co 10th MI Cav; 10 Aug 63 to __ (3 yrs); Meltabarger PO; catarrh
BALEY, John W., K-177-6; Pvt D Co 1st TN Inf; Jul 61 to 64; Powells Station PO; CONF
BALEY, Louis, Sm-174-1; Pvt F Co 101st Inf Vol; 9-28-64 to 1-31-66; New Middleton PO
BALEY, William, Ma-125-1; Sgt F Co 100th KY; 63 to 65; Jackson PO; shot in right arm, healthy & well
BALEY, William, A-7-3; PVt J Co 9th __; 9-10-63 to 9-15-65; Robertsville PO
BALEY, William H., Co-63-1; alias Balypaw, William H.; Pvt K Co 8th TN Inf; 3 Jan 63 to 30 Jun 65; Newport PO; bayonet through thigh
BALL, Alford, Co-65-1; Pvt I Co 2nd TN Cav; 22 Sep 62 to 5 Jul 65; Wilton Springs PO; ruptured, not pensioned
BALL, Charles H., Hu-106-1; Waverly PO; Chief of Scouts Army; Cumberland PO
BALL, Ebenezer L., Br-8-2; Pvt H Co 23rd MI Inf; 8-11-62 to 8-12-65; Cleveland PO; rheumatism, chronic diarhea
BALL, Fredric, K-170-2; Pvt E Co 42nd US Art; 1 Dec 63 to 1 Nov 66; Knoxville PO; blind
BALL, George, Mu-205-1; Wag. Wheeler Com. Neylers?; 62 to 65; Water Valley PO; stunned by cannon ball striking him, six months wagon in CONF, captured at Murfreesboro, 6 mos. wagoner in US
BALL, George, Wa-265-1; US Sol; Emberville PO
BALL, George W., Mc-109-1; Cpl D Co 7th TN Inf; 12-4-64 to 7-27-65; Sewee PO (Meigs Co.)
BALL, John, Co-67-6; Pvt F Co 8th TN Cav; 11 Aug 63 to __; PO omitted
BALL, Rail, Co-68-1; Pvt I Co 2nd TN Cav; 62 to 65; Costner PO
BALL, Wesley, Hw-121-1; Pvt K Co 19th TN Inf; 20 Dec 62 to 4 Jun 65; Lucas PO
BALL, William, L-105-1; Mary E. widow of; Pvt K Co 14th IL Cav; Mar 13 65 to Jul 31 65; Edeth PO; widow has the discharge

BALL, William H., Hy-84-1; Pvt A Co 6th TN; 1 May 61 to __ (1 yr); Gates PO
BALL, William J., Me-92-3; Pvt H Co 5th TN Inf; 3-21-62 to 5-16-65; Hester Mills PO; eyes affected, also liver & kidney disease
BALLARD, Anthoney, Sm-174-2; Pvt H Co 1st TN Art; Grant PO; discharge lost
BALLARD, James, Sh-188-2; US Col; 212 Short Saffron St, Memphis PO
BALLARD, Jell, K-156-6; Easter widow of; Lithgoe St. 12, Knoxville PO
BALLARD, John, C-25-1; Pvt F Co 6th TN Inf; 3-10-62 to 3-28-65; Agee PO; hear diseas and lame leg
BALLARD, John, Mo-120-1; Cpl C Co 44th US Col Inf; 11-17-64 to 4-30-66; Glenloch PO
BALLARD, John, Co-61-6(2); Pvt C Co 4th TN Cav; 19 May 64 to 12 Jul 65; Bridgeport PO
BALLARD, Judge, H-63-4; Pvt 15th KY Inf; 61 to 64; 827 Broad St, Chattanooga PO
BALLARD, Levi G., Sol MS?, Hd-50-6; 6th Civil Dist; crippled in war
BALLARD, M. L., Bo-19-1; Pvt C Co 6th TN Inf; 9-1-62 to 6-10-65; South Rockford PO; mashed on RR wreck
BALLARD, Preston, H-75-2; Pvt L Co; Chattanooga PO; papers lost
BALLARD, Thos. A., Cr-4-1; Pvt N Co 9th TN Inf; May 61 to Mar 65; Bells Depot PO; wounded, head; CONF
BALLARD, William H., Hw-131-4; PO omitted; CONF
BALLARD, _____, Mn-126-1; Delila widow of; Purdy PO
BALLENGER, Frank, Hu-106-2; Pvt K Co 44th MO Cav; Waverly PO
BALLENTINE, Anthony, Gi-127-8; Pulaski PO; dates lost
BALLENTINE, Simon, Gi-131-1; Pvt G Co 111th Col Inf; Feb 62 to 65; Sumac PO; shot in right leg and left foot, is now lame, KuKlux destroyed discharge
BALLER, Claiborn W., Ha-117-2; Pvt E Co 8th TN Cav; 23 Sep 63 to 11 Sep 65; Kyle's Ford PO; jaundice (3W), no disability
BALLER, Joseph W., Ha-117-2; Pvt E Co 8th TN Cav; 23 Sep 63 to 11 Sep 65; Kyle's Ford PO; fever settled lower limbs & _____ r. testicle
BALLET, John, H-69-5; Pvt; Chattanooga PO
BALLEW, George, Ro-210-9; Pvt; Rockwood PO; CONF
BALLEW, John D., Ro-203-6; Pvt K Co 1st TN Inf; 9 Aug 61 to 17 Sep 64; Union Cross Roads PO; shell shock & chronic diarrhea
BALLINGER, Elkanah, Je-141-2; Pvt D Co 1st TN Art; Oct 62 to 64; Mill Springs PO
BALLINGER, Francis M., Hm-104-1; Anna widow of; Pvt M Co 1st TN Cav; 1 Sep 62 to 5 Jun 65; Talbotts PO (Jefferson Co.)
BALLINGER, Henry, Je-141-2; Mill Springs PO
BALLINGER, John, L-104-1; Pvt C Co 7th TN; Aug 8 64 to Jun 26 65; Ripley PO
BALLINGER, P. M., Je-141-3; Pvt F Co 9th TN Cav; 13 Oct 63 to 11 Sep 65; Mill Springs PO
BALLINGER, Wm., Je-141-2; Pvt F Co 1st TN Cav; 62 to 64; Mill Spring PO
BALLUE, _____, H-70-4(1); Rosa widow of; Pvt; Chattanooga PO
BALTIMORE, Charles, D-93-1; Pvt B Co 13th TN Inf; Nov 63 to 10 Jan 66; Belleview PO; wound in right hand
BALYPAW, Mathew, Co-63-1; Pvt K Co 8th TN Inf; 3 Jan 63 to 30 Jun 65; Newport PO; measels settled in eyes & back
BALYPAW, William H. (see Baley, William H.)
BAMAR, Bettie, B-6-1; widow; PO omitted
BAMES, William B., Dk-36-1; Pvt H Co 4th TN Mtd Inf; 9-25-64 to 8-25-65; Smithville PO
BAMESTER, Louisa, H-57-2; widow; Pvt H Co 16th US Col; 63 to 65; Orchard Knob PO
BANCHER, William M., Fr-115-1; Pvt I Co 6th MO Inf; 11-16-64 to 8-17-65; Cowan PO
BANDIGRIFF, John, Dk-34-3; Pvt D Co 4th tN Inf; 9-13-64 to 8-25-65; Dowelltown PO; heart disease
BANDY, Alfred, Hw-125-6; Pvt I Co 4th NC Inf; 6 Jan 65 to 15 Apr 65; Amis PO; CONF
BANDY, H. I., Hw-125-1; Pvt H Co 18th NC Cav; Aug 62 to Apr 65; Surgoinsville PO; CONF

BANDY, James C., Ce-20-2; Sgt C Co 7th US Inf; 5-28-60 to 8-8-64; Ashland City PO
BANDY, John T., M-108-5; Pvt I Co 5th KY Inf; 12-2-61 to __; Haysville PO; chronic dierhea & rheumatism, never received any discharge
BANDY, Joseph P., Sn-256-1; Zurelda widow of; Pvt A Co 9th KY Reg; 61 to __; Worsham PO; said to have been killed by gerrilla in the neighborhood, family knows nothing
BANDY, Lewis R., M-108-4; Cpl & Pvt E Co 1st TN Mtd Inf; 1-9-64 to 1-22-65; Lafayette PO; wound left arm
BANE, Stephen, Dk-33-4; Delia widow of; Pvt G Co 1st TN Inf; 8-16-64 to 8-25-65; Dowelltown PO
BANHAM, James S., K-165-4; Capt E Co 1st TN Inf; 10 Dec 63 to 5 Sep 65; Knoxville PO
BANK, John, Sh-203-1; Colored Pvt C Co 3rd Art; Memphis PO
BANKER, Thomas C., Sh-201-2; Mamie V. widow of; Memphis PO
BANKES, Alexander, Hr-89-1; Pvt H Co 61st TN; 62 to 65; Whiteville PO
BANKETT, Henry, Sh-174-4; Pvt K Co 3rd US Hvy Art; 63 to 66; 44 Hadden Ave, Memphis PO; discharge destroyed by fire in the riot of 1866 (Memphis)
BANKS, Adam, We-223-4; served in KY Col, Conall; Palmersville PO
BANKS, David, Hy-83-1; Pvt B Co 55th TN Cav; Oct 25 61 to 65; Brownsville PO; hurt in back, insurable, lost discharge
BANKS, Ervin, S-217-2; Pvt G Co; Feb 65 to Oct 66; Oneida PO
BANKS, G. T., Sh-157-5; Lt K Co 9th MS; Feb 61 to May 65; PO omitted; CONF
BANKS, George W. J., Ge-99-1; Pvt C Co 3rd NC; __ to 8 Aug 65; Limestone Springs PO; rheumatism, could not get date enlistment
BANKS, Henry, Co-64-1; Pvt B Co 39th NC Inf; Newport PO; wounded in right arm; CONF
BANKS, James M., Hd-50-5; Pvt E Co 8th TN Mtd Inf; 3-11-65 to 9-1-65; Nixon PO
BANKS, Jefferson J., Hd-49-3; US Sol; 4th Civil Dist
BANKS, John, D-75-3; Pvt L Co 14th KY Cav; 15 Dec 62 to 1 Ma__ 64; Stewarts Ferry PO
BANKS, Robert J., He-60-2; Lexington PO
BANKS, Simson, Sh-203-1; Pvt H Co 88th Regt; __ to 65 (10 mos); Memphis PO
BANKS, Thomas S., K-177-5; Pvt I Co 62nd TN Inf; Sep 63 to 4 Jul 64; Powells Station PO; constitution impaired
BANKS, William J., R-161-1; Cpl I Co 11th TN Cav; 10-63 to 65; Dayton PO; piles from direa
BANKS, Z. W., Mc-115-1; Pvt I Co 11th TN Cav; 6-63 to 65; Riceville PO; heart diarhea liver & kidney trouble, spinal trouble
BANKSTON, John H., H-61-2; Ord Cpl A Co 1st TN Reg; 4-61 to 4-65; Chattanooga PO; CONF
BANNAN, Frank D., Sh-188-1; Capt 115th NY; 6-61 to 4-65; Kerr St, Memphis PO
BANNAN, Thomas J., Ge-83-2; Pvt E Co 4th TN Inf; 22 Jul 63 to 2 Aug 65; Horse Creek PO; chronic diorrheal
BANNUM, Peter, Po-151-1; Pvt G Co; Serville PO
BANYON, Marth (see Thomas, Alfred)
BARBEE, Gus, Rb-223-1; Pvt D Co 15th TN Inf; Aug 64 to 65; Springfield PO
BARBEE, George Y., M-108-5; Pvt; Hayesville PO; not at home & discharge not at hand
BARBEE, John B., Sm-174-1; Sgt G Co 4th TN Inf; 12-1-64 to 8-25-65; Grant PO
BARBEE, Lewis, Ja-84-2; Pvt E Co 4th TN Cav; Snow? Hill PO; rheumatism
BARBEE, Y. G., Ma-108-5; Pvt G Co 37th KY Mtd Inf; 63 to 64 (1 yr 3 mos); Lafayette PO; diabetes, discharge not at hand
BARBER, Daniel, P-157-1; Pvt H Co 3rd US Inf; 10-1-64 to 11-29-65; Theodore PO
BARBER, Edward H., Bl-4-2; 2nd Lt D Co 7th IL Inf; 5-2-62 to 3-1-63; Pikeville PO; wounded at Murfreesborough, TN, crippled for life, pensioner resigned
BARBER, Elam A., Dk-31-1; Cpl H Co 4th TN Mtd Inf; 2-1-65 to 8-25-65; Alexandria PO
BARBER, J. H., Gi-139-3; Pvt C Co 48th TN Inf; 61 to 12-65; Wales Sta. PO; CONF

BARBER, James A., P-157-1; Pvt F Co 2nd TN Inf; 10-20-64 to 3-4-65; Linden PO
BARBER, John R., Sq-165-2; Nancy M. widow of; Pvt I Co 10th TN Inf; 2 yrs 11 mos 7 days; Sunnyside PO; received an honorable disc.
BARBER, Jonas T., R-106-1; Pvt; 5th Civil Dist
BARBER, Stephen J., Hd-54-1; Pvt D Co 6th TN Cav; 24 Dec 62 to 26 Jul 65 (Jul-Aug); Saltillo PO; chest disease
BARBER, Washington, H-63-4; Pvt D Co 1st OH Inf; 9-61 to 11-61; Cor Chestnut & Broad, Chattanooga PO
BARBER, William A., Sn-261-3(2); Cpl I Co 30th TN Inf; 10-61 to 8-63; Brackentown PO; came home on discharge 8-63; CONF
BARBER, Wm. F., Hd-54-1; Pvt D Co 6th TN Cav; 24 Dec 62 to 26 Jul 65; Saltillo PO; from small pox
BARBER, William M., Hi-92-1; Pvt D Co 12th TN Cav; Oct 26 63 to Oct 11 65; Aetna PO
BARBETT, J. T., F-44-2; L. O? widow of; Pvt; 62 to 65; PO omitted; CONF
BARBOUR, Sarah A., D-66-1; widow; Pvt 11th IL Inf; Nashville, 710 S. Colleg PO; his wife did not know what had become of his papers
BARBRA, William E., Bo-21-4; Pvt B Co 3rd TN Cav; 9-18-62 to 7-6-65; PO omitted
BARDEN, Charles H., Mg-199-2; Pvt E Co 23rd NY Inf; 6 May 61 to 22 May 63; Sunbright PO; catarrh & rheumatism
BARDILL, John, Mg-197-4; Pvt F Co 1st TN Inf; 9 Aug 61 to 17 Sep 64; Wartburg PO; rheumatism
BARDILL, Martin, K-160-3; Pvt 3rd Inf; 11 Aug 63 to 3 Aug 65; Knoxville PO
BARDWELL, Thomas E., J-82-2; Pvt C Co 8th TN Mtd Inf; 3-16-65 to 8-17-65; Bloomington PO; disease lungs & eyes
BARE, George W., Hw-129-2; Pvt; Mooresburg PO; hip & side & hearing
BAREL, Jacob, Bo-23-1; Pvt 19th TX Cav; 62 to 65; Tuckaleechee Cove PO; crippled in knee, now hail an harty; CONF
BARFIELD, Mills T., We-223-3; Pvt C Co 67th NC Inf; May 62 to May 65; wounded in left breast; CONF
BARGER, George, K-164-2; Pvt A Co 1st US Col Hvy Art; 26 Jan 64 to 31 Mar 66; PO omitted (Knoxville?)
BARGER, Julian, Ro-204-1; Pvt A Co 11th TN Cav; 20 Jul 63 to 15 Sep 65; Elverton PO; throat disease
BARGER, Robt. H., R-163-1; Cpl B Co 6th TN Mtd Inf; 8-15-64 to 6-30-65; Graysville PO
BARGER, William O., Hn-77-3(1); Pvt F Co 6th TN Cav; __ to 8-65; Baris PO; not at home day examination
BARGER, William T., R-163-1; Pvt E Co 4th TN Cav; 11-11-61 to 7-12-65; Graysville PO
BARHAM, Alexander B., Ge-95-1; Pvt K Co 13th TN Cav; 20 Sep 63 to 5 Sep 65; Upchurch PO
BARHAM, Davies, Ge-95-2; Elizabeth widow of; Cpl A Co 3rd TN Mtd Inf; 13 Jun 64 to 13 Nov 64; Home PO
BARHAM, John, Ge-91-5; Pvt A Co 3rd TN Inf; 30 Jun 64 to 30 Nov 64; Greeneville PO; rupture & rheumatism
BARKER, Alferd H., Mc-116-2; Pvt A Co 5th TN Mtd Inf; 8-31-64 to 6-26-65; Athens PO; heart disease contracted while in service
BARKER, C., K-166-5; Pvt 2nd TN Inf; Aug 61 to Oct 64; Knoxville PO
BARKER, Charles W., K-166-2; Pvt 2nd TN Inf; Knoxville PO; rheumatism, deaf, neuralgia
BARKER, Harriet, Wi-278-1; widow; Cameron St, Franklin? PO
BARKER, Howell, H-49-3; Pvt D Co 6th TN Mtd Inf; 8-2-64 to 6-30-65; Lake Side PO
BARKER, Isaac L., K-166-2; Pvt H Co 26th KY Inf; 19 Sep 64 to 30 Jun 65; Knoxville PO
BARKER, Jack, Gi-122-5; Sinda Murry widow of; Pvt H Co 110th AL Inf; 63 to __; Prospect Sta. PO; killed at Mobile, AL; CONF
BARKER, James M., Se-225-2; Pvt K Co 5th TN Cav; Millican PO; chronic piles till death two years ago
BARKER, Jim H., Sn-153-1; Pvt A Co 26th OH Inf; 7-27-61 to 12-31-63; No. One PO; sun stroke, also gunshot wound
BARKER, Joel W., Hw-49-1; 2nd Cpl F Co 6th TN Mtd Inf; 9-12-64 to 65 (9 mos); Falling Water PO; dyspepsia & piles following fever had during war, was sick when command was discharged
BARKER, L. P. (see Love, Littleton P.)
BARKER, Paul, K-180-3; Marinda widow of; Pvt; Ebenezer PO
BARKER, Rufus G., Ma-121-1; St? 7th TN Cav; Sep 20 62 to Aug 65; Jackson PO; could not tell but little, he was out of humor, rheumatism & scurvy
BARKER, Rolly W., Dy-25-5(1); Pvt G Co 47th TN Inf; Sep 61 to 26 Apr 65; Newbern PO; CONF
BARKER, Samiel A., He-66-1; Cpl H Co 7th TN Cav; Aug 2 62 to Jun 16 __ (2 yrs 10 mos 14 days); Lexington PO
BARKER, Watson, Mt-149-1; Pvt A Co 13th US Inf; 62 to 65; Carbondale PO
BARKER, William, Hw-119-2(1); Sarah J. widow of; Pvt G Co 8th TN Inf; 3 yrs; Hales Springs PO; lost hearing right ear, now dead disease heart & liver
BARKER, William, Un-259-1; Sgt E Co 2nd TN Inf; 9 Aug 61 to 6 Oct 64; Rhodelia PO; dir. bowels, hydrocele & ruptured
BARKER, William F., Gi-131-1; Pvt E Co 40th TN Inf; 62 to 65; Redell PO; left arm injured
BARKLEY, Henry B., Ru-13-1; Sgt E Co 46th TN Inf; Nov 61 to 1 May 65; Murfreesboro PO; CONF
BARKLEY, J. T., G-57-7(4); Lt C Co 2nd TN Cav; 1 Dec 61 to 5 Apr 65; Yorkville PO; CONF
BARKLEY, William B., Wa-276-2; Pvt 2nd OH Battery; 63 to __ (11 mos); Leesburg PO; no discharge
BARKSDALE, William, Tr-269-2; Pvt F Co 14th TN Inf; Oct 62 to Mar 65; Caruthers PO; shot in left hip & head
BARLEY, Benjamin J., Mr-96-2; Pvt E Co 6th TN Inf Mtd; 2 Sep 64 to 13 Jun 65; Whitwell PO
BARLEY, George P., C-32-2; Pvt G Co 1st TN Inf; 8-9-61 to 9-17-64; Pine Mountain PO
BARLEY, Nelson, Gi-136-1; Pvt A Co 111th TN Inf; 1-1-63 to 11-1-65; Buford Station PO; shot in right hips & left leg, not able to work
BARLEY, Thomas, Wl-297-1; Col; Pvt F Co 101st US Inf; 28 Sep 64 to 21 Jan 66; Commerce PO
BARLOW, George, Gi-127-3; Pvt I Co 13th US C Inf; Oct 1 63 to Jan 10 66; Pulaski PO; injured health
BARLOW, George W., Ov-134-1; Pvt C Co 27th KY Inf; 10-12-61 to 1-22-64; Hilham PO; wounded in head
BARLOW, John W., D-62-1; Sol; 1509 McGavock St, Nashville PO
BARLOW, Joseph, Hm-106-1; Pvt G Co 64th TN Inf; PO omitted; CONF
BARLOWE, Ira W., H-63-4; Sgt A Co 15th IN Inf; 4-23-61 to 8-29-65; 707 Market St, Chattanooga PO
BARMAN, Charles, D-43-1; Margrett widow of; Pvt F Co NY; 4 yrs; Nashville PO
BARN, Delila, Be-6-2; widow of US Sol; Pvt; 18th Dist
BARNARD, Elvis, Sn-261-2(1); Pvt I Co 30th TN Inf; 10-19-61 to 10-19-62; Brackentown PO; prisoner Camp Butler 4 mos, parroled; CONF
BARNARD, King, D-87-2; 9th Dist
BARNARD, Wiley M., Hw-121-5(4); Pvt K Co 19th TN Inf; 20 Dec 62 to 13 Aug 65; Chimney Top PO; pneumonia, tifoid; CONF
BARNERD, Simpson, La-117-2; Pvt F Co 12th IN Inf; Nov 18 64 to Nov 17 65; 15th Dist
BARNES, Allen L., Wa-269-1; Pvt B Co 4th TN Inf; 24 Nov 62 to 2 Aug 65; Carters Depot PO (Carter Co.); rheumatism
BARNES, Benjamin F., Cr-4-3; Pvt E Co 1st TN Inf; Jun 61 to Apr 65; Bells Depot PO; CONF
BARNES, Charles, Sh-152-3; alias Hooker, Charles; Pvt B Co 64th IL Inf; Jan 63 to Jan 66; Collierville PO
BARNES, Charles E., Ce-30-1; Sgt G Co 11th ME Inf; Oct 15 61 to Feb 2 66; PO omitted
BARNES, Chupley, Cu-15-1; Louisa C. Watson widow of; Pvt E Co 1st TN Inf; 8-20-61 to died 9-28-61; Hebbertsburg, TN PO; cause of death, measeles, died while in army

BARNES, David G. W., Jun., Wa-272-2; Cpl I Co 8th TN Cav; 5 Sep 63 to 11 Sep 65; Clara PO; chronic diarrhoea
BARNES, George, Sh-198-1; George Bond alias; Pvt C Co 3rd Col Hvy Art; 6-5-63 to 4-30-66; Memphis PO; has his discharge
BARNES, George A., H-53-6; Cpl C Co 16th MA Inf; 61 to 10-10-62 (1 yr 6 mos); Ridgedale PO; wounded left foot, enlisted in 15th, changed to 16th
BARNES, James, Ja-86-4; Pvt E Co 5th TN Mtd Inf; 9-64 to 6-29-65; Apison PO; cold
BARNES, James H., Wa-272-3; Pvt B Co 4th TN Inf; 12 Sep 63 to 2 Aug 65; Clara PO; results of measles
BARNES, James H., Be-2-2; Pvt C Co 7th nN Cav; Jan 1 65 to Aug __ (7 mos 8 days); Holladay PO
BARNES, Joel H., Mc-116-2; Cpl E Co 6th TN Mtd Inf; 63 to 6-65 (1 yr 4 mos); Athens PO; heart & kidney disease; contracted while in service
BARNES, Joel S., Mg-200-3; Jennie widow of; Cpl F Co 1st KY Inf; 61 to 63; Tinah? (Tinch?) PO
BARNES, John, Pu-143-1; Jeremiah PO
BARNES, John H., H-69-2; Pvt; __ to 65; Chattanooga PO; CONF
BARNES, Joseph S., Wa-261-1; Pvt I Co TN Cav; 25 Dec 62 to 9 May 65; Cankling PO; diseas of leg
BARNES, Joshua, La-116-1; Strathmore PO
BARNES, Madison M., Wa-269-1; Pvt B Co 4th TN Inf; 24 Nov 62 to 2 Aug 65; Carters Depot PO; Brights disease
BARNES, Martin L., Cu-15-1; Pvt E Co 1st TN Inf; 8-31-61 to __ (4 mos 28 days); Craborchard PO; diarhea and lef leg swolen, I lef without leave and aimed to return when I regained health
BARNES, Nancy, Gr-82-2; 13th Dist
BARNES, Robert S., H-53-3; Pvt D Co 92nd OH Inf; 8-62 to 6-65; Chattanooga PO
BARNES, Samuel H., Mr-102-1; 1st Lt E Co 106th NY Inf; 8-9-62 to 1-9-64; South Pittsburg PO
BARNES, William H., A-4-4; Pvt C Co 2nd TN Inf; 11-11-61 to 11-25-64; Coal Creek PO; ruptured
BARNET, James, L-103-2; alias Barnet, Conner; Pvt 57th IN? Inf; 62 to 65; Plum Point PO; infantry 1 yr, navy 1 yr
BARNET, Zackaria, Ge-91-2; Pvt A Co 2nd NC Inf; 15 Sep 63 to 16 Aug 65; Greeneville PO; rheumatism & heart disease
BARNETT, Dannill W., Hd-50-4; Nixon PO
BARNETT, Eli, Ct-41-4; Permelia widow of; Pvt E Co 11th TN Inf; Keensburgh PO; CONF
BARNETT, Elisha, Mr-99-4; Sol US; Jasper PO
BARNETT, Frank, Mr-96-2; Nancy widow of; Pvt; Whitwell PO
BARNETT, James, Gu-48-3; 2nd Lt A Co 3rd MD Inf; 6-15-61 to 65; Tracy City PO; record of discharge lost
BARNETT, James, Mc-114-5; Sarah A. widow of; Pvt; Santfordville PO; in prison at Atlanta, GA
BARNETT, James F., Sm-174-1; Mary J. widow of; Pvt C Co 136th IN Vol; 5-11-64 to 9-2-64; New Middleton PO
BARNETT, James M., Mo-127-1; Elizabith widow of; Pvt K Co; 10-61 to 64 (3 yrs 6 mos); Povo PO
BARNETT, James T., A-2-3; Nancy C. widow of; no data on organization or term svce; Hinds Creek PO
BARNETT, Jasper N., Mc-111-1; Pvt G Co 3rd TN Mtd Inf; 8-8-64 to 12-24-65; Mortimer PO
BARNETT, Jefferson P., O-134-2; Cpl C Co 2nd TN Cav; Jan 5 64 to Feb 6 65; Hornbeak PO; poisined while in service
BARNETT, John, Gu-45-2; Manerva widow of; Pvt E Co 1st TN Cav Vidette; 63 to 64 (8 mos); Altamont PO; dead
BARNETT, Louis W., K-161-2; Capt K Co 1st KY Cav; 61 to 65; Knoxville PO; wounded in left hand
BARNETT, M___, F-42-1(3); Mollie widow of; Colliersville PO; cant give any particulars whatever; CONF
BARNETT, Simon, Wa-274-1; Susannah widow of; Pvt B Co 13th TN Cav; Jonesboro PO
BARNETT, William R. D., Wy-172-1; Sgt H Co 2nd TN Mtd Inf; 12-15-63 to 1-21-65; Waynesboro PO
BARNETTE, Jesse J., St-160-2; Pvt E Co 14th TN Inf; May 14 61 to Nov 62; Big Rock PO; CONF
BARNETTE, Sameul, Cl-52-1; Marthy widow of; Pvt E Co 8th IN Inf; 12-10-61 to 4-2-62; Quarter PO
BARNHART, Jacob D., Cr-20-3; Pvt I Co 7th TN Cav; Sep 15 63 to Aug 9 65; Hollow Rock PO; scurvey in the service
BARNHILL, J. N., Hi-85-1; Elizabeth widow of; Pvt IL Inf; 3-1-65 to 3-65; Litter Lot PO; took the measles and died
BARNHILL, Terrence C., K-179-5; Cpl D Co 3rd TN Inf; 10 Feb 62 to 23 Feb 65; Concord PO; rheumatism & heart disease
BARNNETT, Jobe, Hd-53-3; Susan Huyes widow; Cpl C Co 1st AL Cav; 20 Feb 63 to died 64; Morris Chapel PO; remarried to W. C. Hughes (he is dead)
BARNS, David G. W., Sen., Wa-272-2; Saraphina widow; Pvt I? Co 8th TN Cav; 5 Sep 63 to 11 Sep 65; Clara PO
BARNS, Jasper P., Mg-196-2; Pvt; Hunnicutt PO
BARNUM, Frank D., Sh-198-2; Capt I Co 47th NY Inf; 115th NY Inf; about 7-61 to about 6 or 7-65; Memphis PO; has his discharge
BARNWELL, Isaac, Ro-201-5(3); Elizabeth widow of; Sgt B Co 5th TN Inf; 21 Feb 62 to 30 Mar 65; Kingston PO
BARNWELL, W. G., K-163-1; Sol B Co 5th TN Reg; Feb 62 to 65; Knoxville PO; Haryman Farm? PO; his back and kidneys injured
BARR, Henry C., K-154-6(3); Knoxville PO; catarrh
BARR, Jacob C., Pu-145-2; Pvt C Co 1st Mtd Inf; 10-21-63 to 12-13-64; Burton PO
BARR, Robert N., H-61-6; Sarah F. widow of; Sgt 136th OH Vol; 5-62 to 4-9-65; Chattanooga PO
BARRAN, J. M., Hd-56-1; Sgt A Co 1st AL Cav; 10-1-63 to 10-1-64; Adamsville PO; abdominal dropsey
BARRET, Campbell, Wa-266-1; Pvt G Co 8th TN Inf; 1 Mar 63 to 30 Jun 65; Lovelace PO
BARRET, James K., Wi-281-2; Pvt D Co 4th OH; 62 to 65; College Grove PO; lose health in prison, Macon, GA
BARRET, Plese, T-214-1; Pvt B Co US Inf; 62 to 65; Dist 9
BARRETT, Clinton S., H-63-2; Capt H Co 15th MO Inf; 11-61 to 4-65; 610 Cypress, Chattanooga PO
BARRETT, David F., Cf-42-1; Pvt G Co 11th MI Inf; 2-19-62 to 7-11-65; Hickerson PO
BARRETT, Elizabeth, Ja-86-4; widow US Sol; 5th Dist
BARRETT, Hillery, Br-12-1; Pvt D Co 42nd TN Inf; 7-63 to 3-65; Charleston PO
BARRETT, James, Li-165-1; Pvt C Co 64th IL Inf; Mar 21 64 to Jul 11 65; Elora PO; bone broken in right foot
BARRETT, James B., Ge-95-3; Pvt M Co 1st TN Cav; 19 Jan 63 to 19 Jun 65; Home PO
BARRETT, John C., D-68-1; Pvt E Co 3rd KY Inf--61 to 64; Pvt A Co 1st KY Lt Art--1 Jan 64 to 5 Jul 65; 175 Fillmore, Nashville PO; gunshot in right hand
BARRETT, Joseph, Sh-179-3(1); Memphis PO
BARRETT, Nancy R., T-213-2; widow; 8th Civil Dist
BARRETT, Obeydiah, Dk-33-3; Pvt I Co 5th TN Cav; 11-30-62 to 8-14-65; Halesville PO; rheumatism
BARRETT, Taylor H., Mc-112-6; Pvt E Co 7th TN Mtd Inf; 11-1-64 to 7-27-65; Athen PO; rheumatism
BARRETT, W. P., W-194-1; Nancy widow of; Pvt B Co 5th TN Cav; 8-61 to 1-65; Davenport PO
BARRETT, Wells, Dk-33-3; Cpl K Co 5th TN Cav; 3-5-63 to 8-14-65; Halesville PO; dislocated ankle
BARRETTE, Lafaette, Ca-23-3; Sarah A. widow of; Pvt M Co 5th TN Cav; Leoni PO; husband died in war
BARRON, Madison, Ma-263-4; Pvt; Alfred PO; CONF
BARRON, N. C., H-54-2(3); Sherman Heights PO
BARRON, Nick P., H-69-5; Sgt B Co 17th TN Inf; 61 to 65; Chattanooga PO; CONF
BARRONEY, Nannie E., He-58-2; widow of Soldier; 7th Civil Dist
BARROW, Mahala, Ms-180-1; widow; 14th Dist
BARRY, Henry C., Dk-31-1; Sgt G Co 4th TN Mtd Inf; 11-4-64 to 8-31-65; Alexandria PO
BARRY, Henry C., K-156-2; Pvt B Co 1st TN Hvy Art; 15 Mar 62 to 16 Mar 65; 4 Lee St, Knoxville PO; CONF

BARRY, James H., Sm-173-2; Delila E. widow of; Pvt B Co 5th TN Cav; 6-4-63 to 6-25-65; Brush Creek PO
BARRY, James H., U-246-2; Mary E. widow of; Sgt E Co 13th TN Cav; 24 Sep 63 to 5 Sep 65; Limonite PO
BARRY, Peter T., U-246-2; 2nd Lt E Co 13th TN Cav; 18 Oct 65 to 5 Sep 65; Limonite PO
BARRY, Thomas H., Dk-34-3; Sgt B Co 5th TN Cav; 8-2-62 to 8-25-65; Dowelltown PO; rheumatism
BARRY, Thomas J., Jo-149-1; Capt E Co 13th TN Cav; 24 Sep 63 to 8 Sep 65; Mountain City PO; disease liver
BARRY, William M., Jo-153-2; Sgt E Co 13th TN Cav; 24 Sep 63 to 5 Sep 65; Shady PO; injury to back by kick of horse
BARSTOW, Isaac L., R-163-4; Sgt N Co 11th PA Cav; 7-1-61 to 8-25-64; Ogden PO; shot in side; received enlargement--varicose veins
BARTEE, James, We-225-2(1); alias James Kenham; Mary A. widow of; Pvt L Co 6th TN Cav; Jul 7 62 to Jul 26 65; Dresden PO; leg broke, died in 1872
BARTHOLAMEW, Silas, Sh-172-1; Pvt H Co 11th OH Inf; 6-1-61 to 2-13-64; 386 Main St, Memphis PO; Pvt 31st OH Inf; 2-14-64 to 7-20-65
BARTHOLOMEW, Alfred B., Sh-201-3; Cpl H Co 11th IA Inf; 27 Feb 64 to 15 Jul 65; Memphis PO
BARTHOLOMEW, Milton B., He-60-2; Pvt A Co 7th TN Reg; Aug 62 to 65; about 3 yrs; Lexington PO
BARTHOLOMEW, Thomas P., He-60-1; Permelia A. widow of; Co Commisary Sgt A Co 7th TN Cav; 8-62 to 65 (about 3 yrs); Lexington PO; lost his life in Camp Chase, OH
BARTLETT, Alexander L., Rb-221-1; Pvt F Co 11th TN; Apr 1 62 to Apr 1 65; Cedar Hill PO; broken arm; CONF
BARTLEY, Hart B., Ge-95-2; Pvt 5? Co 1st TN Hvy Art; Chucky City PO; chronic diarrhea
BARTLEY, John L., Ge-84-2; Cpl C Co 2nd NC Inf; 26 Sep 63 to 15 Aug 65; Greeneville PO; dis. spinel kidney
BARTON, Lewis, D-102-1; Pvt A Co 14th TN Inf; 27 Sep 63 to 26 Mar 66; Jordonia PO
BARTON, Starns W., Cf-35-2; Pvt D Co 23rd TN Inf; 2 Nov 62 to 22 Dec 64; Normandy PO; CONF
BARTON, William (see Harrass, William)
BARTLOW, Samuel, Cr-21-1; Pvt A Co 6th TN Cav; Apr 61 to __; Tryevant PO; Samuel Bartow says he enlisted for 5 yrs, he has a discharged dated 65; he was paroled, did not do any service and dont know how to fill out his name, he also was in the Mexican War
BARTT, Eliga L., D-72-1; Pvt M Co 5th TN Cav; Jun 28 64 to Aug 14 65; Nashville PO
BARTTEL, James M., D-43-1; Nashville PO
BASEMOORE, Anthony, Sh-195-1; Pvt A Co 14th Col Inf; Memphis PO
BASFORD, Louisa (see Paschal, John R.)
BASFORD, Louisa J., Ce-23-2; widow Sol; Thomasville PO
BASHAM, Hardy, Gi-131-1; Sarah widow of; Cpl A Co 111th Col Inf; 63 to 65; Pulaski PO; died at Murfresboro, TN, of smallpox
BASHAM, Willis, Gi-123-1; Pvt A Co 111th TN Col Inf; Jan 63 to Apr 65; Bethel PO
BASHAN, J. Peter, Wl-308-1; Cpl I Co 7th TN; May 20 61 to __; 3-10-20; Mount Juliet PO; shot with shell in head & through right leg; CONF
BASHART, James D., Hd-49-2; Pvt A Co US 2nd IL Inf; Jan 13 64 to Jun 6 65; Gillis Mills PO; rheumatism, this man was not mustered out
BASHEARS, Lorenzo, Ro-206-3; Martha J. widow of; Pvt B Co 5th TN Inf; 25 Feb 62 to 30 Mar 65; Emory Gap PO
BASHETT, John E., R-162-1; Pvt G Co 1st TN Inf; 8-9-61 to 9-17-64; Dayton PO
BASHMERLE, John, Mc-112-9; Pvt I Co 4th OH Vol Cav; 9-3-62 to 6-29-65; Athens PO
BASHOR, Benjamin F., K-168-3; Adair's Creek PO
BASKET, George W., Ge-98-2; 2nd Lt B Co 4th TN Cav; 11 Sep 62 to 12 Jul 65; Lovelace PO; catarrh of head
BASKET, Johnathan H., Ge-96-1; Pvt D Co 8th TN Cav; 1 Sep 63 to 28 Sep 65; Hascue PO; chronic diareah, gun shot
BASKET, Richard, Wa-275-1; PVt D Co 8th TN Cav; 28 Sep 63 to 11 Sep 65; Pettibone PO; nearly totally deaf, same as Richard H. Basket
BASKET, Richard H., Wa-275-1; Pvt F Co 3rd TN Mtd Inf; 1 Jul 64 to 30 Dec 64; Pettibone PO; partially deaf; same as Basket, Richard
BASKINS, Maxan?, O-136-1; Pvt E Co 2nd TN Cav; Jan 4 64 to Jul 4 65; Terrill PO
BASS, Ben, Wl-300-1; Pvt B Co 14th US Inf; Watertown PO
BASS, Dave, Col, Wl-297-1; Pvt G Co 40th US Col Inf; Nov 10 64 to 25 Aug 66; Watertown PO
BASS, Edward, Hw-125-1; Capt A Co 8th TN Cav; 11 Jun 63 to 11 Sep 65; Blevins PO; shot in the left leg
BASS, Ezekile W., Dk-34-5(4); Pvt I Co 5th TN Cav--12-24-62 to 12-26-64; 2nd Lt I Co 5th TN Cav--2-22-63 to __; Capt K Co 5th TN Cav--8-6-63 to __; Dowelltown PO; kidney disease & piles
BASS, Jane, Wl-302-2; widow; PO omitted
BASS, Josephine, Sh-178-4; widow; rear 263 Monroe, Memphis PO
BASS, Lamuel, D-69-3; 15 Lewis St, Nashville PO
BASS, Martin, Hw-134-1; Pvt B Co 49th IN V Inf; 30 Sep 64 to 15 Jul 65; Rogersville PO; rheumatims
BASS, Thomas, Gi-129-2; Emma widow of; Pvt 111th TN Inf; 10 Jan 64 to 24 Oct 65; Elkton PO
BASS, Thomas W., Mr-102-1; Pvt H Co 1st AL & TN Cav; 1-26-64 to 6-16-64; South Pittsburg PO
BASS, Wm., Hw-125-5; 19th TN Inf; 63 to 65; Surgoinsville PO
BASSETT, Henry D., Fr-112-1; Pvt M Co 1st MI Engineers; Oct 22 63 to Sep 22 65; Tullahoma PO; contracted chronic diarrhoea
BASTIN, Adley O., P-157-1; Pvt F Co 6th TN Inf; 2-20-64 to 3-4-65; Farmers Valley PO
BATE, Edmund, G-68-1; US Sol; PO omitted
BATE, H. H., Sn-250-1; Pvt K Co 2nd __; 5-3-61 to __ (4 yrs); Castalian Springs PO; CONF
BATE, James H., Sn-250-2; Pvt K Co 2nd __; 5-3-6? to __ (4 yrs); Castalian Springs PO; CONF
BATEMAN, Charles, Sh-146-1; Missy widow of; PO omitted
BATEMAN, Iby I., Ch-17-3; widow US Sol; 7th Dist; this entry crossed out
BATEMAN, Willis (see Gordon, Jeff)
BATES, Adam, Gr-70-1; Pvt D Co 4th TN Inf; 1 Feb 63 to 3 Aug 65; Doyal PO; rheumatism &c
BATES, Chambers S., La-113-3; Cpl C Co 83rd PA Inf; 18 Apr 61 to 18 Nov 65; Ethridge PO; paralysed & general disability
BATES, Charles, Ru-241-2(1); Jane widow of; Pvt 14th Inf; 3 yrs 6 mos; Murfreesboro PO
BATES, David O., H-51-2(1); Pvt K Co 10th MI Inf; 2-14-61 to 12-5-62; Hill City PO
BATES, Franklin B., Mr-98-2(5); Mary widow of; Pvt; Whiteside PO
BATES, George W., Ms-183-1; Pvt A Co 110th US Col Inf; 11-20-64 to 2-6-66; Comenville PO; rheumatism & other affliction, not able to do hard labor
BATES, Henry M., D-57-4; Pvt C Co 67th IL Inf; Apr 62 to Jan 63; Nashville PO; trans. to 14th MO Cav as Lt
BATES, John, Gr-70-3; Pvt D Co 4th TN Inf; 1 Feb 63 to 11 Aug 65; Doyal PO; strained abdomen
BATES, John R., P-156-1; Ord Sgt F Co 53rd TN Inf; 4-15-62 to 10-5-65; Lobelville PO; CONF
BATES, Joseph, Un-254-3; Pvt B Co 50th TN Inf; Gravestown PO
BATES, Lorenzo D., Un-254-2; Pvt D Co 3rd TN Inf; 12 Feb 62 to 12 Feb 65; Gravestown PO
BATES, Major, L-101-2; alias Majr. Gilderland; Capt B Co 4th Hvy Art; Aug 6 63 to Feb 25 66; Henning PO
BATES, Martin, Po-148-3; Pvt F Co 101st IL Inf; 65 to 65 (3 mos); Benton PO discharge misplaced
BATES, Morris, Sn-254-1; Pvt B Co 40th US Col Inf; Hendersonville PO; chronic dyerahea, lame in back & hips
BATES, Pleasant P., Je-141-1; Pvt F Co 1st TN Cav; 1 Mar 62 to 30 Mar 65; New Market PO
BATES, Thomas, D-49-2; Julia widow of; Nashville PO
BATES, William M., Cf-39-1; Pvt K Co 173rd OH Inf; 25 Aug 64 to 26 Jun 65; Hillsborro PO; rheumatism & chronic diarrhoea

BATES, William T., Pu-146-1; Pvt G Co 1st US TN Col Mtd Inf; 2-14-64 to 4-21-65; Buffalo Valley PO
BATHMAN, Chris, H-60-2; Pvt 44th NY Inf; Chattanooga PO
BATMAN, J. J., Cr-15-1; Pvt K Co 2nd TN Inf; Jan 20 63 to Apr 20 65; Maple Creek PO
BATTLE, Andrew, D-100-1; Sarah Butter widow of; Pvt D Co 7th TN Inf; Nashville PO; totally deaf and dumb by jar of canon; Battle died in Dec 1889 & his wife is weak minded & cannot obtain dates correctly
BATY, Willis, Ru-241-5; Pvt I Co 107th TN Inf; 64 to 66; Murfreesboro PO
BAUCOM, Joseph F., Hy-84-1; Sgt L Co 7th TN; 14 Apr 62 to 25 Aug 64; Gates PO; CONF
BAUER, Henry C., U-247-1; Pvt A Co 3rd NC Mtd Inf; 15 Aug 64 to 8 Aug 65; Erwin PO; measles resulting in lung diseas, heart disease & diarhoe
BAUER, Melinda (see Wells, Ellison)
BAUER, William, Se-231-2; Mary E. widow of; Pvt B Co 8th TN Cav; discharg lost; Arther PO
BAUERS, Wm., Sh-173-1; Manerva widow of; Pvt B Co 64th MS Inf; 1-26-64 to 2-3-66; Memphis PO
BAUGH, Elishia, Hr-86-1; Pvt F Co 5th KY Cav; Sep 28 61 to Mar 4 64; Grand Junction PO; bed sores, partally paralysed
BAUGH, Mack, Gi-129-2; Patsey widow of; PVt 111th TN Inf; Conway PO
BAUGHMAN, Robert, Hw-125-6; Blevins PO
BAUGHN, Squire, D-60-2; Pvt 13th Reg Inf; 306 McNairy St, Nashville PO; black
BAUGUS, George W., P-156-3; Pvt A Co 10th TN Cav; 12-62 to 12-65; Lobelville PO; general health injured by exposure; CONF
BAUMAN, Darins, Ro-207-2; Sarah widow of; Pvt; Fossil PO; died
BAUMGARDNER, Cooper, Bo-14-5; Pvt L Co 2nd TN Cav; 9-27-63 to 7-6-65; Mint PO; shot in left arm; discharge lost, had guess at time
BAW, Jacob, Sm-173-3(1); Pvt I Co 5th TN Cav; 1-25-62 to 8-1-65; Gordonsville PO
BAXTER, Green B., Wa-266-1; Pvt F Co 3rd TN Mtd Inf; 16 Jul 64 to __; Lovelace PO
BAXTER, Hugh, He-57-2; Pvt F Co 2nd TN Inf; 4-25-61 to 7-25-6? (4 yrs 2 mos); Speim PO; leaders cut under right thigh; CONF?
BAXTER, James L., H-51-5; Pvt I Co 18th OH Inf; 2-12-64 to 9-26-65; Stanley PO
BAXTER, Joseph H., Cf-35-1; Capt D Co 23rd TN Inf; 2 Nov 62 to 22 Dec 64; Tullahoma PO; CONF
BAXTER, Levi W., Ge-98-2; Louiza widow of; Pvt C Co 4th TN Inf; Cedarlane PO
BAXTER, Samuel, Co-66-3(1); Pvt C Co 26th TN Inf; 24 Nov 62 to 15 Sep 63; English PO
BAYATT, Andy, S-212-2; Pvt G Co 30th KY Inf; 2 Feb 64 to 18 Apr 65; Onida PO; feet froze
BAYER, Creed F., Co-63-4; Pvt A Co 3rd TN Mtd Inf; __ Jul 65 to 16 Dec 64 (6 mos); Newport PO
BAYER, Miles, Ge-95-1; Pvt A Co Bat MN Cav; 11 Jul 63 to 1 May 65; Home PO
BAYER, Richard, De-24-1; Pvt L Co 17th KY Cav; 1 Oct 64 to 15 May 65; Decaturville PO
BAYGAN, William H., De-23-1; Pvt H Co 31st TN; Nov 61 to 65; Bath Springs PO; bronchitus, prisoner Jeffersonvill, IN; CONF
BAYLESS, Anderson, Sh-160-1; Liza widow of; Pvt F Co Hvy Art; 62 to 65; Memphis, Poplar St. (126 to 130) PO; middle and third finger lost
BAYLESS, Daniel B., Cl-47-3; Pvt A Co 1st TN Inf; 7-10-63 to 8-3-65; Compensation PO; gone from home
BAYLESS, David W., Wa-261-2; Pvt H Co 5th TN Cav; 21 Oct 61 to 20 Apr? 65; Nola Chuckey PO; CONF
BAYLESS, Houston, Hw-125-5; 1st TN Lt Art?; Surgoinsville PO
BAYLESS, Jacob A., Wa-274-3; Pvt A Co 2nd OH Col Cav; Feb 62 to 64; Jonesboro; gunshot in right leg
BAYLESS, James H., Je-144-2; Pvt L Co 1st TN Cav; 1 Apr 63 to 19 Jun 63; Talbotts PO; spine injured, throat?; discharge close war
BAYLESS, John C., K-176-2; Pvt I Co 9th TN Inf; 62 to 65; Halls X Roads PO
BAYLESS, Robert, Wa-270-2; Pvt I Co 60th TN Inf; 61 to 65; Johnson City PO
BAYLESS, William B., K-161-3; Knoxville PO
BAYLESS, William M., Wa-263-3; Pvt & Ord Sgt A Co 20th TN Vol Inf; Jun 61 to 62; Garbers Mills PO; CONF
BAYLIS, Bruce, Hd-48-1; Pvt A Co Crawley Batery; Jun 64 to musterd out 64 (6 mos); Pvt H Co 11th KY Reg; Jun 64 to Dec 14 64; Savannch PO; shoulder dislocated, rheumatism, indigestion & piles
BAYLOCK, Allison, H-56-3; St. Elmo PO
BAYSBY, James, Wi-281-2; Pvt H Co 5th TN; Jul 25 63 to Aug 25 66; Allisona PO; feet frost bit, piles
BAZEMORE, Jesse, Sh-152-3; Dexter PO
BAZEUL?, George W., Lk-113-2; Drummer G Co 18th IL; Feb 27 65 to Dec 16 65; Civil Dist 6
BAZZEL, Thomas, Mc-116-3; Pvt E Co 9th TN Cav; 9-28-63 to 9-11-65; Williamsburg PO
BEACH, John L., Ge-100-1; Asst? Sgt B Co 8th TN Inf; 17 Dec 62 to 4 Mar 65; Midway PO
BEACH, Marshall, Sh-169-2; US Sol; 9 Jefferson St, Memphis PO
BEADLE, James H., Cu-17-1; Sgt C Co 12th US Inf; 12-22-61 to 3-27-65; Crossville PO; asthma, dropsey, eye trouble suffering
BEADLES, Thomas, Wl-299-1; Pvt E Co 4th TN Inf; 20 Oct 64 to 20 Aug 65; Statesville PO
BEAL, Dickson, Sm-166-3(1); Cpl A Co 1st TN Inf; 12-63 to 2-65; Monoville PO
BEAL, Elias, Hw-127-3; Capt H Co 8th TN Inf; 25 Jul 63 to Jun 65; Rogersville PO; confined 11 different prisons, wounded in hip
BEAL, George W., K-183-3; Cpl A Co 3rd TN Cav; 15 Oct 62 to 13 Jun 65; High Point PO
BEAL, James H., Hm-109-2; Pvt D Co 3rd TN Inf; 1 Nov 63 to 30 Jun 65; Whitesburg PO
BEAL, Joseph J., Hw-127-1; Sarah M. widow of; Sgt G Co 1st TN Cav; 1 Apr 63 to 20 May 65; Austins Mill PO; shot in left shoulder, died from effect of wound
BEAL, Newton T., Hw-127-3; 2nd Lt G Co 1st TN Cav; 1 Aug 62 to 5 Jun 65; Rogersville PO; bronchitis & rheumatism
BEAL, Robt., K-183-3; Pvt B Co 12th TN Cav; Lyonton PO
BEALS, Francis, Lo-191-3; Sadie L. widow of; Morganton PO
BEALS, Henderson, Ge-97-3; P-t K Co 1st TN Cav; 12 Jul 62 to 5 Jun 65; Home PO; nazel cattarrh
BEALS, Henry A., Ge-95-1; Pvt E Co 4th TN Inf; 15 Ma_ to 2 Aug 65; Home PO
BEALS, Joseph M., Wa-265-1; Sgt H Co 8th TN Cav; 18 Sep 63 to 11 Sep 65; Trump PO; chronic direhea
BEALS, Lewis R., Ge-95-1; Cpl M Co 1st TN Cav; 2 Apr 63 to 19 Jun 65; Home PO
BEALS, Nancy E. (see Haws, John S.)
BEALS, Thomas J., Bo-13-3(1); Pvt I Co 1st TN Cav; 11-14-61 to 4-7-65; Freindsville PO; injured in stomach & back by horse falling on him while in battle
BEAMAN, Terdinan C., K-167-6; Capt G Co 98th MY? Inf; Nov 61 to May 65; Knoxville PO
BEAN, Baxter, Hm-109-4; Sgt L Co 13th TN Cav; 16 Oct 64 to 8 Sep 65; Whiteburg PO
BEAN, Chas. F., R-163-1; Pvt B Co 6th TN Mtd Inf; 9-12-64 to 6-30-65; Graysville PO; since suffering--liver disease
BEAN, Elexander, Hw-118-1; Cpl K Co 8th TN Cav; 8 Sep 63 to 11 Sep 65; St. Clair PO; cattarrh
BEAN, Jacob C., R-163-3; Pvt G Co 5th TN Inf; 11-11-61 to 5-12-65; Graysville PO; disease of heart
BEAN, James, M-107-2; Pvt D Co 9th KY Inf; 9-20-61 to 1-8-65; Red Boiling Springs PO; rheumatism & paralysis of legs
BEAN, James K. P., K-173-1; Pvt I Co 3rd TN Cav; 16 Sep 63 to 10 Jun 66; Caswell PO; lame back
BEAN, James Wm., H-49-9; Amanda Gann formerly widow of; Pvt A Co 6th TN Mtd Inf; 8-2-64 to 6-30-65; Igon's Ferry PO; got leg hurt which finally killed him
BEAN, Jerrymiah, M-107-2; Pvt D Co 9th KY Inf; 9-20-61 to 12-15-64; Red Boiling Springs PO; disease of lungs & paralysis

BEAN, John, D-66-2; Pvt E Co 81st IN Inf; 21 Jul 62 to 14 May 65; Nashville, Water Works St.; left arm shot off during action, is pensioned
BEAN, Sim, F-20-3; Pvt F Co 61st TN Inf; Apr 65 to Dec 65; Hickory Withe PO
BEAN, Thomas, Cy-27-5(3); Pvt D Co 9th KY Inf; 9-61 to 12-64; Red Springs PO (Macon Co.)
BEAN, William H., H-49-8; Pvt I Co 2nd TN Inf; 1-20-62 to 6-26-62; Maj 6th TN Inf; 10-6-64 to 6-30-65; PO omitted
BEAN, Wm. M., R-163-1; Pvt G Co 5th TN Inf; 6-24-62 to 6-12-65; Graysville PO; served in Co G Dis. K
BEAN, William M., K-164-1; Pvt C Co 6th TN Vol; 18 Apr 62 to 27 Apr 65; PO omitted (Knoxville?)
BEANCA, Madison, Sh-178-3; US Sol; 26 Marshall, Memphis PO
BEANE, William, K-165-3; Pvt C Co 6th TN Inf; 13 Apr 60 to 27 Apr 65; 25 Lenore St, Knoxville PO
BEANY, Ellis (see Gooch, Ellis)
BEAR, Alfred, Gr-79-4; Pvt Co 9th TN Cav; 62 to 65; Ball Point PO; piles
BEAR, John, Su-239-2; Pvt 4th TN Cav; PO omitted
BEARD, George T. P., Wi-270-1; Tabitha widow of; Pvt I Co 2nd TN Inf; 13 Oct 64 to 7 Nov 65; Union Valley PO
BEARD, Jackson, Sh-159-1; Pvt TN; 62 to __; Memphis PO
BEARD, Jacob, D-54-2; Pvt; Nashville PO; wounded in hip, away from home & impossible to get record
BEARD, Joseph, D-64-5; alias Bailey, Joseph; Nashville PO
BEARD, Major, Sm-173-2; Sgt E Co 17th US Col Inf; 1-21-64 to 4-25-66; Alexandria PO (Dekalb Co.)
BEARD, Stephen, Br-9-1; Mahala B. widow of; Lt Cav? 5th MD Inf; 1-31-65 to __; Cleveland PO; discharge at Washington
BEARDEN, Aaron J., A-8-3; Cpl K Co 1st TN Inf; 8-9-61 to 9-17-64; Scarborough PO; contracted measels 9-61
BEARDEN, Andy, K-171-3(2); Pvt H 1st Col US Hvy Art; 2 Feb 64 to 31 Mar 66; Knoxville PO
BEARDEN, Lawson, Fr-105-1; Pvt F Co 5th TN Cav; 6 Sep 62 to 25 Jun 65; Winchester PO
BEARDEN, Capt. M. D., K-171-3(2); Dicy widow of; Capt D Co 6th TN Inf; Apr 62 to Apr 65; Bearden PO
BEARDEN, William E., B-18-1; Sgt F Co 5th TN Cav; 9-6-62 to 6-25-65; Flat Creek PO
BEARDSLEY, Sh-167-3; Pvt 12th OH; 26 Feb 64 to 10 Jul 65; PO omitted
BEARY, James H., Fe-41-2; Pvt H Co 30th KY Inf; 64 to 65; Fitz PO
BEARY, Jemirah, Fe-41-2; Pvt H Co 1st KY Cav; 62 to 65; Travisville PO
BEASLEY, Calvin, Sm-166-3(1); Pvt L Co 5th TN Cav; 8-7-63 to 8-14-65; Pleasant Shade PO
BEASLEY, Caroline, D-66-2; Nashville, S. Chery St. PO
BEASLEY, Charlie, D-64-6; 110 S. Sumner, Nashville PO
BEASLEY, Isaac J., Sm-169-3(5); Pvt; Defeated PO; CONF
BEASLEY, Jesse, M-107-3; Pvt A Co 1st TN Mtd Inf; Walnut Shade PO; spinal irritation & __ heart
BEASLEY, Joseph, Mc-118-2; Sarah widow of; Pvt K Co 4th TN Cav; 12-20-62 to died 4-6-64; Cogshill PO
BEASLEY, Rufus, Sm-168-2; Pvt F Co 5th TN Cav; 8-7-63 to 8-14-65; Pleasant Shade PO; heart disease and bronchitis
BEASLY, Alford, K-184-2; Pvt H Co 16th KY? Cav; 2 yrs 6 mos; Thorn Grove PO
BEASLY, James R., Hu-103-2; Pvt E Co 10th TN Inf; 10 Aug 61 to 28 Dec 64; PO omitted
BEASLY, Nelson, Gi-133-1; Township 13
BEASON, James, Cl-47-3; Pvt 2nd TN Inf; 62 to 65; Cappford PO
BEATTY, Franklin, Hd-52-2; Pvt M Co 7th TN; Jul 6 62 to May 65; Hurley PO
BEATTY, James S., H-53-2; Pvt A Co 93rd OH Inf; 8-7-62 to 5-20-65; Chattanooga PO; prisoner Libby 14 months, also Belle Isle--Andersonville 6 mos, prisoner at Danville, wounded in arm

BEATY, Andrew J., Fe-40-2(1); Didama A. widow of; Pvt D Co 1st TN Mtd Inf; 1-25-64 to 4-25-65; Moodyville PO
BEATY, Claiborn, Fe-42-2; Lt Capt David Beaty's Co TN Ind Scouts; Allerdt PO
BEATY, George, Fe-41-4; Zilpphia A. widow of; Pvt Capt. Beaty's Co. Indpt. TN Scouts; Boat Land PO; died in prison at Saulsbury Prison
BEATY, James, Fe-41-3(1); Ellenger J. Stephens formerly widow of; 1st Lt Capt Beaty's Co. Indept. Scouts of TN; 61 to Spring 65; Boat Land PO
BEATY, James K., Fe-40-2(1); Pvt D Co 1st TN Mtd Inf; 1-25-64 to 4-25-65; Moodyville PO; back injured by a horse
BEATY, John, Br-13-3; Pvt G Co 5th TN Inf; 4-11-62 to 5-15-65; Cleveland PO
BEATY, Johnathan A., Fe-42-3; Pvt B Co 2nd TN; Boatland PO
BEATY, Thomas, Br-13-3; Pvt G Co 5th TN Inf; 4-11-62 to 5-15-65; Cleveland PO; chronic bronchitis
BEATY, William, Gr-74-1; Ann J. widow of; May Spring PO; CONF
BEATY, Zilpha, Pi-156-3; widow of US Sol; 8th Civil Dist
BEAUCHAMP, Jno. A., D-99-5; Asst Surgeon 1st MO Art; Sep 61 to May 65; Nashville, Central Hos. for Insane PO; CONF
BEAUMONT, Alexander, Sh-171-1; Col; Pvt B Co 14th Reg; Memphis PO
BEAUMONT, Henry, Sh-189-5; Pvt A Co 3rd US Col Hvy Art; 1-5-63 to 4-30-66; Penn. Ave, Memphis PO
BEAVER, John, C-33-4; Pvt B Co Lt Art; 62 to 64 (2 yrs 6 mos); Jellico PO
BEAVER, William H., Hw-132-4; Maj C Co 58th NC Inf; 28 Apr 62 to Feb 65; Otes PO; broken down constitution; CONF
BEAVERS, Sarah J. (see Edmondson, Ambrose)
BECK, David M., Gi-139-3; Pvt G Co 6th TN Cav; 8-62 to 9-64; Campbellsville PO; died 2-7-65; C. C. Beck wife of D. M. Beck; CONF
BECK, Ephraim, Me-90-2(1); Pvt C Co 8th TN Cav; 2-11-64 to 9-16-65; Pine Land PO
BECK, Jacob, Sh-199-1; 45 Larose St, Memphis PO
BECK, Jacob S., K-154-3; Pvt F Co 2nd KY; 1 Feb 62 to Jan 65; Knoxville PO
BECKER, Robt. M., Sh-176-1; found while examining population schedules; 86-88 Vance, Memphis PO
BECKHAM, Gorges, Hd-44-2; Charity A. widow of; Pvt 8th TN Mtd Inf; PO omitted
BECKHAM, Thomas J., Wy-173-2; Pvt B Co 2nd TN Mtd Inf; 63 to 64; Houston PO
BECKURN, Mary E. (see Hensley, Daniel)
BECKWITH, Alexander W., Mu-210-1; 1st Lt A Co 27th AL Inf; 3-61 to 63 (3 yrs--sic); Spring Hill PO; CONF
BECKWITH, Mary (see Bell, Sam)
BECKWITH, Pleasant, Gi-136-1; Pvt A Co 44th TN Inf; 6-1-62 to 1-9-65; Lynnville PO; slightly wounded in head
BECTON, Mike (see Hunter, Mike)
BECTON, Samuel, Sh-150-1; Pvt D Co 11th US Inf; 3 yrs 1 mo; Bonds PO
BEDDOW, Thomas, Sh-167-2; Pvt K Co 1st NJ; 5 Jan 64 to 29 Jun 65; no PO; blow one eye, gun shot l. arm
BEDWELL, Andrew J., Bl-4-3; Pvt F Co 3rd TN Cav; 4-12-63 to 5-9-65; Pikeville PO
BEDWELL, Hiram, Br-12-2; Nancy widow of; Charleston PO; died in hospital; CONF
BEDWELL, John, Rb-226-1; Pvt C Co 4th TN Cav; 4 May 63 to 12 Jul 65; Greenbrier PO; sun stroke and frost bite, still getting worse since discharge
BEDWELL, William, Mc-118-5; Pvt C Co 10th TN Cav; 10-1-63 to 8-2-65; Calhoun PO
BEECH, Cincinattus, Dy-25-8(4); Newbern PO; CONF
BEECH, David G., Dy-25-8(4); Pvt B Co 1st TN Cav; 61 to 61 (7 mos); Newbern PO; contracted rheumatism; CONF
BEECH, Ferd B., Dy-25-7(3); Pvt; Newbern PO; in prison 1 yr; CONF
BEECHAM, George W., He-64-3; Pvt A Co 8th TN Cav; 1 Jul 61 6o 8 Apr 65; Reagan PO; flesh wound in left thigh; CONF

BEECHER, Lina?, Cu-17-1; Capt A Co 3rd NY Cav; 1-13-61 to 11-14-64; Crossville PO; wounded 3 times
BEEL, Alexand, Co-69-7(3); May widow of; Pvt A Co 31st TN Inf; 28 Dec 61 to 28 Dec 62; Leadvale PO; deseas not non; CONF
BEEL, James W., Sq-165-2; Sunnyside PO; died in service in 1865
BEELER, Danil, Un-255-2; Mary widow of; Pvt A Co 12th E TN Cav; 8 Ju_ 63 to 20 May 65; Warwicks X Roads PO
BEELER, David R., Un-257-1; Pvt C Co 8th TN Inf; 1 Feb 63 to Jun 30 65; New Prospect PO; eyes & rupture
BEELER, G. M., Br-11-1; Laura A. widow of; Sgt C Co 12th KY Inf; 62 to 65; Chatala PO; gunshot wound in foot
BEELER, Henry, Un-250-1; Pvt A Co 12th TN Cav; 8 Jul 63 to 12 Oct 65; Maynardville PO; chronic diarhea, disease of head & brest, incured while in service
BEELER, Isaac, Gr-81-4(2); Pvt A Co 12th TN Cav; 8 Jun 63 to 28 Oct 65; Oleot PO; eyes and gen. disibility, now feble
BEELER, John, Gr-81-5(3); Pvt A Co 12th TN Cav; 28 Jun 63 to 7 Oct 65; Liberty Hill PO; disabled in right leg and hip
BEELER, Joseph, Gr-81-4(2); Pvt D Co 5th TN Cav; 10 Nov 62 to 13 Jul 65; Oleot PO; chron. dyrhie, partly disabled
BEELER, William, Cl-56-1; Pvt M Co 9th TN Cav; 5-1-64 to 9-14-65; Seartlick PO
BEELS, Wiley, A-2-1; Pvt J Co 7th TN Mtd Inf; 11-8-64 to 7-27-65; Hynds Creek PO (Anderson Co.)
BEERS, Theoder, Sh-167-2; Pvt I Co 1st MI Cav; 23 Oct 61 to 30 Oct 64; PO omitted
BEETS, Calaway, Un-255-2; Rachel widow of; 63 to 65; PO omitted
BEETS, Caleway, Un-256-2; Rachel widow of; Pvt B Co 3rd TN Inf; Duk PO; contracted mumps
BEETS, George W., A-3-3; Clinton PO
BEETS, Isaac, Gr-82-2; 13th Dist
BEETS, Mary A. (see Nelson, William)
BEEVER, Hosie A., Mo-122-3(1); Pvt B Co 65th GA Inf; 4-62 to 3-25-65; Hiwassee College PO; CONF
BEGGARLY, Thomas A., D-75-3; Sgt I Co 5th TN Cav; 16 Nov 62 to 25 Aug 65; Stewarts Ferry PO
BEGGARS, Edward S., We-223-1; Pvt I Co 6th TN Cav; 5 Jun 62 to 24 Jun 65; Palmersville PO; severe deafness in r. ear
BEGLEY, George, Ha-111-1; Cpl E Co 1st TN Cav; 15 Apr 62 to 15 Apr 65; Upper Clinch PO
BEGLEY, James, Ha-111-4(1); Pvt F Co 16th TN Cav; 65 to 65 (4 mos); Upper Clinch PO; CONF
BEGLY, Thomas, S-213-2; Pvt K Co 30th KY Inf; 2 Feb 64 to 18 Apr 65; New River PO; piles
BEISLEY, William, Ov-138-1; Pvt G Co 4th TN Inf; 1-1-65 to 10-1-65; 5th Civil Dist
BELCHER, Caroline, D-71-1; US; Nashville PO
BELCHER, James M., Tr-269-1; Pvt A Co 23rd TN Inf; 19 Jan 61 to 17 Mar 65; John PO
BELE, Harriet, Sh-146-4; widow Sol; 3rd Civ Dist
BELEU, William W., J-77-1; Rebecca W. widow of; Pvt 13th KY Cav; 63 to 65; Celina PO
BELEW, John G., Cr-14-1; Pvt G Co 7th TN Cav; 5 Aug 62 to 25 Oct 65; Clarksburg PO; heart affection
BELEW, Rainey M., La-111-1; Pvt TN Cav; 4-10-62 to 65; Pleasant Point PO; CONF
BELEW, William James, La-111-1; Pvt C Co 32nd KY Inf; Jul 7 61 to ___ (4 yrs); Pinkeney PO; died, measles; CONF
BELIFORD, Charley, Cr-3-1; Pvt G Co 110th US Inf; Nov 62 to 64; Gadsden PO
BELKNAP, Augustus J., Mg-199-1; Sgt C Co 8th IA Cav; 15 Aug 63 to 13 Aug 65; Sunbright PO; wounded in face by piece of shell
BELL, Anderson, L-101-2; Pvt F Co 17th C Inf; Nov 30 62 to Apr 25 66; Henning PO; small pox, fell in legs, suffering from rheumatism veneral
BELL, Asa, Mn-126-3; Sgt Maj 6th TN Cav; 9-1-62 to 7-26-65; Bethel Springs PO
BELL, Athea, We-225-4(3); Sol; Dresden PO
BELL, Ben B., H-60-5(2); Pvt H Co 36th IN Inf; 3-18-62 to 3-18-65; Chattanooga PO

BELL, Benjamin, T-206-1; Pvt G Co 61st TN Inf; Feb 15 64 to Dec 65; Covington PO; Buton Rout?
BELL, Charley, H-73-4(2); Chattanooga PO
BELL, Charley, Sh-149-2; Pvt I Co 61st Lt Art; Nov 64 to ___; Raleigh PO
BELL, Dr. David, U-245-2; Sgt B Co 13th TN Cav; 63 to 64; Limestone Cove PO; wound in left leg in 1864, he lost his speech, criple in wright and cant wright to give information
BELL, Easter (see McLaurine, Anthony D.)
BELL, Edward, Mt-148-1; Cpl L Co 13th TN Mtd Inf; 10-63 to 1-15-66; Orgains X Roads PO
BELL, Elial, Di-41-1; alias Eli Roberson; Pvt G Co; White Bluff PO
BELL, Francis M., Po-152-2; Margret J. formerly widow of; Pvt L Co 10th TN Cav; Ducktown PO
BELL, George W., Wa-260-1; Pvt B Co 12th Reg Cav; Oct 1 63 to Sep 19 65; Clarkson PO; insanity
BELL, H. G.?, Hn-74-1; Susan widow of; Pvt I Co 6th TN Cav; 63 to ___; Gleason PO
BELL, Harris, Hw-127-2; Pvt E Co 8th TN Cav; 22 Jun 63 to 11 Sep 65; Rogersville PO; bronchitis, wounded in left foot
BELL, Henderson, G-57-4(1); Pvt C Co 13th TN Inf; 7-12-61 to 8-1-63; Yorkville PO
BELL, Henry, Lo-189-3(1); H Co 2nd OH Hvy Art; 18 Aug 63 to 29 Aug 65; Philadelphia PO; ruptured by fallin on ice hauling water
BELL, Isaac, D-77-3; Pvt E Co 3rd KY Vol Inf--Aug 61 to Aug 64; Pvt 1st KY Lt Art--Aug 64 to Dec 65; Nashville PO
BELL, James, Wl-297-1; Pvt H Co 4th TN Mtd Inf; 1 Dec 64 to 25 Aug 65; Commerce PO
BELL, James H., Cl-52-1; Pvt F Co 9th TN Cav; 10-1-63 to 9-1-65; Quarter PO; shot in side
BELL, James H., Hm-104-4(2); Pvt C Co 4th TN Inf; 62 to ___; Morristown PO; taken prisoner at evacuation _____ KY, no discharge
BELL, James S., Su-242-1; Cpl H Co 13th TN Cav; 24 Sep __ to Jul 20 65 (3 yrs 9 mos 26 days); Bluff City PO; foot off 3 inches above ankle joint, right foot gunshot wound. Comrade? shell wounded in the Bulls Gap fight, 64, and leg was amputated, rct. of pension 20/mo?
BELL, James T., Wa-276-1; Pvt B Co 12th TN Cav; Oct 1 63 to Jun 8 65; Lees Burg PO; pleuracy & bronchitis
BELL, James W., R-158-1; Pvt E Co 7th Mtd Cav; 12-18-64 to 7-27-65; Lucknow PO; no disability
BELL, James W., M-107-1; Cpl H Co 5th KY Cav; 12-4-61 to 5-13-65; Red Boiling Springs PO; disease of lungs ___ & chronic rheumatism
BELL, James W., K-155-1; Pvt 3rd TN Cav; 14 Mar 62 to 66; Knoxville PO
BELL, Job, Ch-16-1; Sgt 6th TN Cav; 10-62 to 3-65; Henderson PO
BELL, John, Gi-127-1; Sgt F Co 111th TN USC Inf; Jan 6 64 to Apr 30 66; Pulaski PO
BELL, John, Po-150-1; 5th Civil Dist
BELL, John, Col, De-22-1; Musician A Co 40th US Col Inf; 1 Jan 63 to 1 May 65; Clifton PO
BELL, John H., Mt-141-1; Dist 11; colored vol. of TN
BELL, John H., M-107-1; Pvt D Co 9th KY Inf; 9-20-61 to 12-15-64; Red Boiling Springs PO; gunshot of right arm
BELL, John W., P-156-2; Pvt 10th TN Cav; 3-63 to 65; Lobelville PO; CONF
BELL, Joseph B., Gi-122-7; Pvt V? Co AL Bat; 10 Dec 62 to 15 May 65; Prospect Sta. PO
BELL, Joshua, O-140-1; Union City PO; couldn't find man
BELL, Lucy, Hw-134-2; widow; 20th Civil Dist
BELL, Mathew, Mg-199-1; Mary widow of; Pvt KY Inf; Sunbright PO
BELL, Ninian O., Rb-221-3; Pvt F Co 8th & 12th KY; 1 Oct 64 to 15 ___ 65 (6 mos 15 days); Adams Station P_; CONF
BELL, Perndilla M. (see Chitwood, Shadrach)
BELL, Pinkney M., Po-162-1; Pvt L Co 10th TN Cav; 3-2-64 to 8-7-65; liver and lung disease and injury to breast
BELL, Robert, Gi-128-1; Pvt G Co 111th TN Inf; 63 to 65; 8th Civil Dist
BELL, Robert, R-158-1; Pvt E Co 10th TN Cav; 1-15-64 to 8-1-65; Rhea Springs PO; spinal trouble --injury in shoulders, arm and head

BELL, Sam, Dy-25-6(2); Mary Beckwith widow of; Pvt; 2 yrs 6 mos; Newbern PO; CONF
BELL, Samuel M., K-177-2; Sol US; PO omitted
BELL, Sandy, O-136-1; Elizabeth widow of; Pvt B Co 61st TN Inf; Feb 20 62 to Aug 20 65; Terrill PO
BELL, Solomon, Ja-86-4; Pvt 7th TN Inf; 63 to 64 (1 yr 6 mos); Apison PO; splen in side & piles
BELL, T. F., G-57-5(3); Pvt D Co 13th TN Inf; 10-1-61 to 8-1-62; Yorkville PO; CONF
BELL, Thomas I., Wl-297-2; Pvt H Co 4th TN Mtd Inf; 20 Oct 64 to 25 Aug 65; Commerce PO
BELL, W. J., A-1-1; Pvt E Co 2nd TN Inf; 11-1-62 to 6-30-65; Andersonville PO
BELL, William, R-158-1; Pvt E Co 10th TN Cav; 1-15-64 to 8-1-65; Rhea Springs PO; lung disease and sore eyes
BELL, William, D-57-1; Pvt 4th AL Cav; 61 to __; PO omitted, 8th Ward; shot in hand and cut
BELL, William, Mn-126-1; Margret widow of; Pvt A Co 6th TN Cav; 9-1-62 to 7-26-65; Purdy PO
BELL, Wm. F., Br-6-1; Pvt F Co 1st TN Cav; 3-1-62 to 6-14-65; Chatala PO; rheumatism and dizzy to scrotum
BELL, William H., Li-144-1; Pvt B Co 98th OH Inf; 8-6-62 to 6-1-65; Flintville PO; right eye out 24 yrs
BELL, William S., Ha-117-3; Caroline widow of; Pvt 1st TN Cav; 62 to __; Sneedville PO
BELL, Wilson, Mt-148-1; Pvt C Co 40th US Col Inf; 8-18-64 to 4-25-66; Orgains X Roads PO
BELLANFANTE, Peter, Mu-191-1; 7th Dist
BELLANFONT, Jane, Mu-209-7; Pvt; Columbia PO
BELLAH, William P., H-61-2; 1st Lt G Co 41st GA Inf; 8-61 to 9-63; Chattanooga PO; wounded 10-8-62; CONF
BELLE, John M., D-72-3; Pvt B Co TN Inf; Oct 22 61 to May 15 65; Nashville PO; CONF
BELLENFONT, W., Wi-281-2; Miry widow of; College Grove PO; could not ascertain other particulars
BELLEW, Isaac J., Gu-48-4(1); Pvt C Co 25th KY Cav; Mount Ary PO (Habersham Co., GA); shot through both thighs, no record of discharge
BELLOWS, John H., D-99-3; Sgt H Co 4th OH Cav; 6 Oct 62 to 10 Jul 65; State Penitentiary PO; shot wound in leg & hit in head
BELLS, Martin V., Cr-4-1; Sgt G Co 15th TN Cav; Dec 63 to May 65; Bells Depot PO; wounded, right side; CONF
BELOATE, Samuel H., L-108-2; Pvt; 10th Civil Dist
BELT, Cardinnan, Bo-11-2; Temperence widow of; Pvt A Co 3rd TN Inf; 2-1-62 to died in service; Houk PO; canot give length of service
BELT, Jeremiah, Sn-259-1; Pvt; 62 to 65; Bransford PO
BELT, Robert, Lo-191-2; Betsey J. Lambert widow of; Pvt B Co 4th TN Inf; 1 May 63 to 2 Aug 65; Greenback PO
BELVIN, James, Ja-87-1; Pvt E Co 4th TN Cav; 12-5-62 to 7-12-65; Apison PO; scurvy, rheumatism & heart disease
BELVIN, John A., He-66-1; Pvt F Co 1st US Cav; Feb 26 64 to __ (1 yr 5 mos 1 day); Life PO
BENCH, William B., Cl-50-1; Cpl G Co 1st TN Cav; 7-1-62 to 6-5-65; Tazewell PO; about 8-15-62
BENDALL, Francis M., Mn-120-1; Pvt G Co 1st AL Cav; Jan 63 to Jan 4 64; Pocahontas PO
BENDOFF, Joseph R., Sh-159-1; Lt D Co VA Cav; 60 to 65; Memphis PO; cold caught; CONF
BENEDICT, A. B., D-79-1; 17th CT Vol Inf; Aug 22 62 to Jul 6 65; Nashville, Meridian & Berry PO
BENEDICT, James M., Mr-99-2; Pvt A Co 17th IN Inf; 5-22-61 to 6-19-65; Jasper PO; disabled in back by train leaving track
BENFIELD, Absolum E., Po-152-2; Pvt L Co 12th TN Cav; 5-64 to 12-65; Ducktown PO; captured
BENFIELD, Noah H., Po-152-2; Pvt L Co 12th TN Cav; 5-64 to 12-64; Ducktown PO; loss of eye and gun shot wound of thigh; captured
BENGE, Thos. H., H-61-2; Pvt M Co 5th TN Cav; 9-62 to 5-65; Chattanooga, rear of Burk's Alley PO; wounded in face
BENNET, Fred J., H-56-2; East End PO
BENNETT, Caleb L., H-61-3; Mary J. widow of; Sgt Maj. 24th OH Lt Art; 63 to 4-9-65; Chattanooga PO

BENNETT, Christopher C., Su-238-1; Sgt B Co 13th TN Cav; 23 Sep 63 to 15 Sep 65; Piney Flats PO; rheumatism
BENNETT, Dock F., G-55-1; Pvt D Co 111th Col Inf; 64 to 66; Trenton PO; wound in neck; lost discharge and dont recollect dates
BENNETT, George, Sm-166-2; Lonnie Young formerly widow of; Pvt; she did not know anything about his service; Carthage PO
BENNETT, Henery S., D-47-2; Pvt 150th OH G Co; 5-5-64 to 10-1-64; Fisk University, Nashville PO
BENNETT, Henry, Col, Lo-192-2; Pvt; Greenback PO; gunshot in hand; off on Rail R, can't find out the co.
BENNETT, Henry C., Wl-298-1; Pvt E Co 4th TN Mtd Inf; 29 Sep 64 to 25 Aug 65; Round Top PO
BENNETT, James, Dk-32-4; Pvt K Co 5th TN Cav; 2-5-63 to 8-14-65; Doneltown PO; ruptured
BENNETT, James, Ro-211-1; Martha J. widow of; Pvt H Co 3rd TN Inf; 10 Feb 62 to died in army; Webster PO
BENNETT, James J., Dk-36-2; Pvt B Co 4th TN Mtd Inf; 9-25-64 to 8-25-65; Smithville PO
BENNETT, Jessee, Rb-228-1; Pvt G Co 10th TN Inf; 28 Jun 62 to Jun 65; Crunk PO; prisoner at Knoxville 9 mos
BENNETT, John, D-73-1; Pvt 13th TN; Olympic St, Nashville PO
BENNETT, John, H-72-1; Marshie formerly widow of; Pvt H Co 16th US Col Inf; __ to 4-30-66 (3 yrs); Chattanooga PO
BENNETT, John, K-183-1; Pvt B Co 3rd TN Cav; 10 Oct 63 to 8 Mar 65; Riverdale PO
BENNETT, Jollas?, D-57-1; Pvt G Co 15th US Inf; 64 to Apr 66; PO omitted, 8th Ward
BENNETT, Louis P., Dk-33-1; Pvt F Co 11th OH Cav; 6-3-63 to 5-1-66; Dowellton PO
BENNETT, March, Gi-140-1; Dist 20
BENNETT, Rufus M., K-180-2; Capt C Co 6th TN Inf; 18 Apr 62 to 1 Mar 63; Bearden PO; bronchitis and rheumatism
BENNETT, Samuel H., Cr-19-1; Pvt F Co 7th TN Cav; 63 to 64; Huntington PO
BENNETT, Thomas E., Dk-35-2; Pvt B Co 17th KY Cav; 10-1-64 to 9-20-65; Temperance Hall PO; eye and heart affection
BENNETT, William, Cr-20-2; Martha A. widow of; Pvt B Co 7th TN Cav; Aug 15 62 to __; Hollow Rock PO
BENNETTE, Alex, Wi-282-1; Pvt A Co 9th TN Reg; May 63 to Aug 65; Peytonsville PO; rheumatism
BENNETTE, Wm., Wi-282-1; Pvt A Co 9th TN Reg; May 63 to Aug 65; Peytonsville PO; rheumatism
BENNITT, Benjamon F., Dk-31-3; Pvt L Co 5th TN Cav; 4-8-63 to 8-14-65; Alexandria PO; rheumatism & nuralgia 4 yrs
BENSON, Abraham, Gi-129-2; Pvt F Co 110th TN Inf; __ to 66; Elkton PO
BENSON, Benjamin F., Se-225-1; Cpl I Co 2nd TN Cav; 22 Oct 62 to 6 Jul 65; heart disease, hurt of breast and testacle, injuries done by a horse
BENSON, Jesse C., T-214-1; Pvt E Co 13th OH Cav; Feb 63 to Jun 65; Mason Depot PO; rheumatism, other injured
BENSON, John W., Se-224-2; Pvt H Co 9th TN Cav; 1 Oct 63 to Apr 65; Wears Valley PO; diarrhea
BENSON, Riley A., Mo-119-2; Cpl D Co 5th TN Mtd Inf; Sweetwater PO
BENSON, Thomas, Gi-129-2; Pvt B Co 12th TN Inf; Oct 63 to Mar 66; Elkton PO
BENSON, William, Se-223-2; Ord Sgt E Co 2nd TN Cav; 15 Sep 62 to 6 Jul 65; Pigeon Forge PO; chronic diarrhea, kidney disease
BENSON, William B., R-161-5; Cpl G Co 2nd TN Inf; 11-5-61 to 11-5-64; Dayton PO
BENTLEY, Calbe, K-165-3; C Co 1st TN Inf; 10 May 63 to 23 Feb 65; 45 Hauer Ave, Knoxville PO
BENTLEY, James A., Sh-160-2; Pvt; 15th Dist
BENTLEY, John, Un-252-1; Judy A. widow of; Pvt A Co 6th TN Inf; 63 to Sep 65; Acuff PO
BENTLEY, John, D-45-1; Capt K Co 10th OH Inf; 4-12-61 to 3-16-63; Nashville PO; shot in left foot
BENTLEY, Thomas H., Sn-250-1; Pvt C Co 2nd __; 5-16-62 to __-20-65; Castalian Springs PO; CONF

BENTON, Charles, D-68-1; Color Sgt A Co 7th US Inf; 7 Dec 61 to 7 Dec 66; 276 Fillmore, Nashville PO; gunshot in arm and body in the year 1863
BENTON, Christifer, Be-7-1; Pvt A Co 7th TN Cav; 13 Jan 64 to 9 Aug 65; PO omitted
BENTON, George, La-112-2; Pvt F Co 5th TN Cav; 2-5-64 to 8-14-65; Chisem PO
BENTON, Thomas, Sh-150-3; Pvt C Co 59th TN Inf; 2 yrs; Bartlett PO
BENTON, Thomas R., He-64-2; Pvt C Co 1st TN Gd; 10 Jun 63 to 10 Jul 63; Center Point PO; discharged at Nash.
BENTON, Warren, K-161-5(6); Knoxville PO; wounded in hip
BERDEN, Peter, Wh-180-1; Pvt K Co 4th TN Inf; 3-15-63 to 8-30-65; Sparta PO; no disease
BERGER, Fredrick E., D-99-1; Poorhouse; Pvt A Co 9th IN Inf; 62 to 65; Nashville PO; feeble minded
BERKLIN, Alexander, Mr-98-1; Pvt D Co 5th TN Inf; to 2-65; Oat's Island PO
BERNARD, Abe (present name), Sh-195-2; Albert Bernard, sol. name; Pvt 11th Hvy Art; Memphis PO
BERNARD, Albert, D-63-2; Pvt I Co 17th TN; Nashville PO
BERNARD, Thomas M., Hw-13-14; Cpl E Co 1st TN Cav; 1 Apr 62 to 11 Apr 65; Otes PO; piles chronic
BERREY, Driver, Dk-32-4; Catherine widow of; Pvt E Co 4th TN Mtd Inf; 10-1-64 to 8-25-65; Liberty PO; contracted consumption
BERREY, Nathaniel M., K-181-5(2); Pvt C Co 6th TN Inf; Apr 63 to 30 Jun 65; Knoxville PO; rheumatism 25 yrs
BERRY, Alford, Hw-131-2; Susan W. widow of; Pvt A Co; White Horn PO
BERRY, Arch, R-158-2; Pvt A Co 7th TN Mtd Inf; ___ to 65; Carp PO
BERRY, Chas. S., D-103-1; Mrs. M. J. widow of; Pvt E Co 4th TN Cav; Oct 1 61 to Oct 1 62; Joelton PO; stricture
BERRY, Cleon, Hw-131-3; 3rd Sgt B Co 3rd TN Inf; 23 Jun 64 to 19 Nov 64; Otes PO; horse thrown, in Co D from Aug 62 to Dec 63
BERRY, David, D-63-2; Pvt ___; Nashville PO
BERRY, David, Ha-115-2; Elizabeth widow of; Pvt A Co 1st TN Cav; 5 Apr 62 to 5 Apr 65; Alanthers Hill PO; shot through thigh; killed since '65 by Revenue Officers
BERRY, Franklin, Hw-131-3; Recruiting Off B Co 3rd ___; Otes PO; gunshot in left hand
BERRY, Franklin K., Mo-121-2; Hos Stew 9th TN Cav; 8-7-63 to 9-11-65; Philadelphia PO; pluntic adhesion
BERRY, Geo. W., Mg-200-2; Pvt B Co 46th MA Inf; 22 Aug 62 to 29 Jul 63; Rugby PO; chronic diarrhoea
BERRY, Green, Hd-55-1; Pvt F Co 6th TN Cav; 15 Oct 62 to 6 Jul 65; Olive Hill PO; rheumatism and piles
BERRY, Jackson, Wy-173-1; Sarah widow of; Pvt B Co 1st AL Cav; 1-20-63 to 1-22-64; Lutts PO
BERRY, James, La-111-3; Pvt G Co 10th TN Inf; 62 to 9-64; PO omitted
BERRY, Joahson?, Hw-131-3; 3rd Sgt B Co 3rd TN Inf; 29 Jun 64 to 28 May 65; Otes PO
BERRY, John U., Wl-300-2; Manda widow of; Pvt H Co 4th TN Inf; 24 Oct 64 to 25 Aug 65; Cherry Valley PO
BERRY, Josep, Wl-300-1; Pvt B Co 5th TN Cav; 28 Jul 62 to ___; Cherry Valley PO
BERRY, Lenard P., K-181-5(2); Pvt C Co 6th TN Inf; 18 Apr 62 to 27 Apr 65; Knoxville PO; fever settled head and side, rheumatism & ruptur
BERRY, Marry, K-181-6(3); widow of; Pvt C Co 6th TN Inf; Nov 63 to ___; Knoxville PO
BERRY, P. L., Cf-47-1; Malinda Sinth Jones widow of; Pvt 2nd TN Inf; Speedwell PO
BERRY, Pleasant, Hw-131-2; Mariam J. familly widow of; Pvt D Co 8th TN Inf; 15 Mar 63 to 30 Jun 65; White Horn PO
BERRY, Robert, Sh-196-2; Pvt L Co 3rd US Hvy Art; 1-20-65 to 4-30-66; 120 Dunlap St, Memphis PO; ankle injured
BERRY, Robert H., Cf-40-1; Mamgrum, Louiza widow of; Pvt; Nov 61 to ___; Tullahoma PO
BERRY, Samuel, F-45-1; Pvt 136th GA; 63 to 65; Moscow PO; I ___ n Berry, statement to be truthful that he was a soldier for 2 yrs
BERRY, Samuel C., Wa-263-5; Pvt A Co 3rd NC Inf; 18 Aug 64 to 65; May Day PO
BERRY, Simon, We-221-1(4); Pvt D Co 5th LA Inf; 15 Sep 63 to 25 Oct 64; Martin PO
BERRY, Spencer, D-87-1; Jennie widow of; Pvt 12th TN Inf; Nashville PO
BERRY, Thomas, Hw-130-2; Nancy J. widow of; Pvt A Co Cav; Lee Valley PO
BERRY, William, Hw-118-1; Pvt B Co 8th TN Inf; 15 Nov 62 to 2 Jul 65; St. Clair PO; back & hips
BERRY, William A., Wy-173-4; Pvt B Co 2nd TN Mtd Inf; 10-16-63 to 10-17-64; Victory PO
BERRYHILL, Eveline, We-229-2; found while examining work; 11th Civil Dist
BERRYHILL, J. D., La-117-1; Harriet F. widow of; Pvt A Co 118th TN Cav; Jan 12 61 to ___ (3 mos 12 days); West Point PO; shot through thigh; CONF
BERRYMAN, Sanford A., Un-252-1; Pvt F Co 1st NC Cav; 64 to 65; Haynes PO
BARTON, John, Hw-130-1; Francis M. widow of; Pvt B Co 1st TN Cav; 4 Mar 62 to 4 Feb 63; Lee Valley PO
BERY, Docker M., La-108-1; US Sol; 1st Civil Dist
BESO, John, W-192-1; Pvt A Co; 6-17-63 to 65; Steppsville PO
BESS, Henry, Dk-33-1; Pvt E Co 4th TN Inf; 9-27-64 to 8-25-65; 4th Civil Dist; rheumatism
BESS, William S., Wl-299-2; 15th Civil Dist
BEST, Daniel, Bo-11-2; Pvt; 61 to 62; Brick Mill PO; couldent get dates
BEST, F. D., Bo-11-3; Pvt F Co 2nd TN Cav; 1-1-63 to 7-6-64; Hout PO
BEST, J. F., Bo-11-7; Pvt A Co 3rd TN Inf; 2-10-62 to 2-23-65; Houk PO; rhumatism
BEST, James M., Bo-12-4; Sol US; 17th Dist
BEST, Jno. C., Cr-4-1; Pvt G Co 27th TN Inf; 61 to 65; Bells Depot PO; wounded arm, leg; CONF
BEST, Johnston, Di-34-2; Pvt A Co 2nd DC Inf; 10-16-62 to 7-23-63; Dickson PO; transferred to 2 Regt Dist Columbia, unatached PA Militia
BEST, M. V., Bo-11-3; Pvt D Co 2nd TN Cav; 9-1-62 to 7-7-65; Houk PO
BEST, Samuel P., Bo-12-1; Pvt H Co 3rd TN Inf; 9-20-64 to 11-30-64; Houk PO; injured back caused by
BEST, W. R., Bo-11-2; 1st Lt K Co 5th TN Inf; 2-25-62 to 5-17-65; Houk PO; bronchitis
BEST, Wm., F-39-1; I Co 51st OH Inf; Galloway PO; discharge misplace
BEST, William H., T-208-1; Pvt K Co 17th IN; 61 to 65; Garland PO
BETS, Booker, Hw-127-1; Carrie widow of Booker Hill, alias; Rogersville PO; kidny & gravill trouble
BETTIS, Alexander, Ja-85-5; Pvt A Co 4th TN Cav; 25 62 to 7-12-65 (2 yrs 8 mos 17 days); Georgetown PO
BETTIS, James D., Je-143-1; Cpl D Co 9th TN Cav; 11 Sep 63 to 11 Sep 65; Mossy Creek PO; injury to hip, rheumatism & heart disease
BETTIS, James M., Ja-85-5; Cpl A Co 4th TN Cav; 10-25-62 to 7-12-65; Long Savannah PO
BETTIS, P. C., Je-135-2; Pvt B Co 9th TN Cav; 14 Nov 64 to 11 Sep 65; Piedmont PO
BETTIS, Samuel H., Ja-86-3; Rebecca J. widow of; Long Savannah PO
BETTNER, Fred, La-115-3; Sol US; Summertown PO
BETTS, Daniel, T-216-3; 14th Civil Dist
BETTS, Seldon W., Hw-74-1; Pvt I Co 6th TN Cav; Jun 62 to 26 Jul 65; McKenzie PO; discharged on special order
BETTY, Si, Mu-198-2; 10th Dist
BETZ, Golled, Bo-14-3; Pvt G Co 11th MO Cav; 4-30-63 to 7-27-65; Montval PO; chronic diarrhea
BEUZER, Lemuel, Je-137-2; Pvt M Co 2nd TN Cav; 63 to 65; Hickory Ridge PO
BEVANS, Robert, Sh-195-1; Pvt E Co 56th PA; 63 to 64; Memphis PO
BEVELEY, Frances J. (should be Francis?), H-58-1; Pvt B Co 6th TN Mtd Inf; 9-12-64 to 6-30-65; Sale Creek PO
BEVERLY, George W., Hr-86-1; Pvt Sanitary Commison; 65 to 66; Grand Junction PO; rheumatism; Dr. McDonald was captain
BEVIL, Rebecca, G-51-2; widow US Sol; Humboldt PO

BEVINS, John, Br-6-3; Pvt L Co 9th TN Cav; 10-1-63 to 65; Grief PO
BEVINS, Saml. S., Hd-54-3; US Sol; PO omitted
BEWLEY, Jacob A., Hm-108-1; Pvt F Co 9th TX Inf; 61 to 64; Russellville PO; wounded in L. S.; CONF
BEWLEY, Jacob M., Hm-108-2(1); 2nd Lt B Co 1st TN Lt Art; 20 Dec 62 to 16 Jan 65; Russellville PO; lung disease
BEWLEY, Josiah B., Ge-86-2; Pvt A Co 2nd TN Cav; 1 Sep 63 to 6 Jul 65; Pates Hill PO; blood poison or scrofulah
BEWLEY, William S. (Resque), Hm-104-3(1); Capt C Co 8th TN Inf; 14 Dec 62 to resign Nov 63; Vally Home PO; rheumatism, resigned as Capt Co C
BEYAN, Stephen, D-99-1; Poorhouse; Pvt K Co 12th KY Cav; 63 to 65; Nashville PO; wounded once slightly, old and crippled
BEYER, Philip, Cu-16-1; Pvt D Co 111th PA Inf; 9-20-61 to 7-19-65; Crossville PO; partial paralysis and deafness, reenlisted veteran
BIAS, Henry, Ca-20-1; Pvt G Co 1st MO Inf; 3-10-62 to 11-10-63; Braxton PO
BIBB, Henry, Ge-100-1; Pvt & Cpl A Co 8th TN Cav; 11 Jun 63 to 11 Sep 65; Mohawk PO
BIBB, Isaac, Col, D-62-1; Nashville, 1300 Damonbreim PO; paralysed
BIBB, Levi B., Ge-100-2; Pvt A Co 7th IN Cav; Aug 62 to Apr 65; Midway PO
BIBB, Sam, Ru-231-1; Pvt H Co 17th TN (Col?); May 63 to Apr 65; Lamar PO
BIBB, William H., Ge-100-2; Pvt A Co 8th TN Cav; 11 Jun 63 to 11 Sep 65; Midway PO
BIBEE, William W., Co-63-4; Pvt C Co 8th TN Cav; 1 Oct 63 to 11 Sep 65; Newport PO; soriasis
BIBLE, Addison J., Ge-90-2; Pvt I Co 7th TN Cav; 7 Aug 62 to 5 Jun 65; Greeneville PO; bronchitus, measles the cause
BIBLE, Charles, Ge-89-1; Pvt I Co 1st TN Cav; 1 Aug 62 to 5 Jun 65; Mosheim PO
BIBLE, Christain, Ge-90-1; Pvt F Co 4th TN Inf; Apr 63 to Jun 65; Greeneville PO; chronic bronchitus, exposure
BIBLE, Christian W., Ge-94-1; Tusculum PO
BIBLE, Ellent, Co-62-1; Ordly Sgt D Co 8th TN Inf; 18 Mar 63 to 9 Jan 64; Help PO
BIBLE, Ezra, Co-61-4(1); Pvt D Co 8th TN Inf; 10 Mar 63 to 20 Jun 65; Parrottsville PO
BIBLE, Frank C., Ge-90-2; Pvt A Co 12th TN Cav; 62 to __ (2 yrs); Greeneville PO; measels caus deafness, exsposure
BIBLE, Jacob, Co-59-2; US Sol; 1st Dist
BIBLE, Jacob, Ge-90-1; Pvt D Co 4th TN Inf; Apr 63 to Jun 65; Greeneville PO
BIBLE, John C., Ge-87-3; Capt G Co 8th TN Cav; 11 Jun 63 to 11 Sep 65; Pates Hill PO; 1 Pvt Sgt to Jun 64, 2nd Lt to 18 Mar 65; Capt to 11 Sep 65
BIBLE, John M., Co-62-4; USS; 4th Dist
BIBLE, Lemuel, Co-62-1; Lt E Co 8th TN Inf; 28 Mar 63 to 1 Sep 65; Help PO; shot in hip
BIBLE, Prestin, Co-62-1; Pvt C Co 8th TN Inf; 1 Dec 62 to 27 May 65; Help PO
BIBLE, Thomas, Ge-86-1; Capt C Co 8th TN Inf; 2 Dec 62 to 30 Jun 65; Warrensburgh PO; bronchitis
BIBLE, William, K-161-6; Pvt B? Co 8th TN Inf; PO omitted; died at Andersonville
BICH, George W., Pi-155-2; 2nd Sgt G Co 9th TN Cav; 6-6-62 to 7-6-65; Byrdstown PO; right testicle mashed
BICKEL, Amos, Cf-41-1; Holly PO; absent, could not learn his co & reg
BICKNELL, Thomas S., Ov-137-1; Margaret C. widow of; Pvt H Co 3rd KY Inf; Nettle Carrier PO; widow can give no further information
BICKWUTH, William C., Wl-299-2; 15th Civil Dist
BIDDILL, John M., Ge-91-2; Pvt D Co 9th TN Cav; 29 Jul 64 to 11 Sep 65; PO omitted
BIDDIN, Samuel W., Mg-196-4; US Sol; 10th Dist
BIDDLE, Robert F., K-156-5; Pvt F Co 1st E TN Inf?; Apr 63 to May 65; 14 W. Church St, Knoxville PO; CONF
BIDDLY, Columbus A., Je-146-5; Pvt D Co 9th TN Cav; 10 Sep 63 to 11 Sep 65; White Pine PO; rheumatism

BIDWELL, Daniel, Me-91-1; Pvt G Co 30th IN Inf; 9-24-61 to 9-27-64; Bonham PO; defness
BIEN, Reubin, Cl-47-1; Pvt C Co 1st TN Inf; 63 to 65; Speedwell PO
BIESE, Charles W., H-62-4; Lt A Co 16th IL Cav--7-61 to 7-62; 524 West Fifth, Chattanooga PO; Lt B Co 82nd IL Inf--8-62 to 1-65; rheumatism and heart disease, wounded in hand
BIEVIERLIN, John, D-43-1; Pvt; Nashville PO
BIFORD, James, Dk-33-2; Virginia widow of; Pvt F Co 4th TN Inf; 10-16-64 to 8-25-65; Dowelltown PO; disease of lungs
BIGELOW, James, H-72-3(2); Cornelia widow of; 1st Sgt G Co 88th IN Inf; 8-15-62 to 7-2-64; PO omitted; killed at Mt. Kenesaw
BIGGER, G. Columbus, Ms-175-1; Pvt H Co 5th TN Cav; Sunns Store PO; left leg 10th day Sep 64
BIGGERT, John, Sh-157-4; Pvt F Co 20th OH; Nov 17 61 to Jul 20 65; Dist 13
BIGGERTS, John, Sh-157-3; __ to 65; Memphis PO
BIGGINS, Mary, St-164-2; widow US Sol; Civic Dist No 11
BIGGS, Jennie, D-91-4; Davidson PO
BIGGS, Shederit, Sh-152-2; Pvt D Co; Nov 63 to __ (1 yr); Collierville PO; captured and not discharged
BIGGS, Stephen, Sh-196-2; Pvt I Co 11th TN Bat; 62 to 65; Memphis PO; wounded in one leg; served also as a corporal
BIGGS, William L., Je-138-2; Sgt A Co 9th TN Cav; Sep 63 to 12 Sep 66; Mount Hareb PO
BIGGS, Wilson, Cl-52-2; Chaney widow of; Pvt A Co 1st TN Cav; 7-1-62 to __; Quarter PO; died at Nashville
BIGHANS, Asbarry, Br-6-3; Pvt A Co 11th TN Cav; 64 to (captured and was never discharged); Grief PO; injury to right eye; captured prisoner war
BIGINS, John J., Mo-130-3; Pvt D Co 3rd TN Mtd Inf; 7-25-64 to 11-30-64; Ballplay PO
BILBERRY, Chame, Pi-153-3; Pvt G Co 9th TN Cav; 6-6-61 to 7-9-65; Apurnier PO
BILBRO, Jefferson, Ru-241-3; Mary widow of; Pvt E Co 17th TN Inf; Oct 61 to 66; Murfreesboro PO
BILES, Stephen J., Gi-122-4; Pvt A Co 3rd TN Inf; 2 Oct 61 to 29 May 65; Prospect Sta. PO; slight wound in arm, prison 7 mos; CONF
BILES, Thomas H., H-59-3; Lt OH Cav; 63 to 65; Chattanooga PO
BILHHAM, Joel G., Hd-49-2; Pvt A Co 2nd TN Mtd Inf; Oct 2 63 to Oct 14 64; Smiths Ford PO; rheumatism indicated? by L. D. Hager, M. D., Sgt of 2nd TN Mtd Inf
BILL, Giles, Mu-189-2; Pvt A Co 101st TN Inf; 2 yrs 6 mos; Hurrican Switch PO
BILLINGS, George W., Mo-110-3(1); Pvt A Co 11th TN Cav; 5-62 to 4-65; Mouse Creek PO; discharge not at home
BILLINGS, Jasper, Lo-188-3; Eliza J. widow of; Pvt A Co 5th TN Inf; 25 Feb 62 to 4 Apr 65; Erie PO
BILLINGS, John, Cy-29-1; Pvt C Co 11th KY Inf; 61 to 12-19-64; Speck PO
BILLINGS, John, Mc-109-6; Pvt D Co 11th TN Cav; 4-1-63 to 11-64; Mouse Creek PO; measles & results, no discharge
BILLINGSLEY, James L., Ro-203-7; Pvt B Co 63rd TN Inf; Vancouver PO; gunshot wound; CONF
BILLINGSLEY, John J., Cy-27-2; Pvt I Co 1st TN Mtd Inf; 3-64 to 7-65; Boles PO (Monroe Co. KY)
BILLINGSLY, Leander, Bl-3-4; Cpl F Co 2nd TN Cav; 1-12-61 to 1-63; Billingsly PO; CONF
BILLINGTON, William (see Grant, William)
BILLUPS, Jerry, H-61-3; Evaline Outen formerly widow of; Sgt I Co 44th Inf; 4-62 to 4-9-65; Chattanooga, Burk's Alley PO
BILYEN, Andrew J., Ov-134-1; Hilham PO; Civil Dist #3
BILYEN, William, Ov-134-1; Civil Dist #3
BINDERMAN, Midlton, Mu-191-1; Cpl G Co 13th Vol TN; 63 to 66; Bigbyville PO
BINGHAM, Benjamin, Bo-14-3; Capt H Co 8th TN Inf; 2-10-62 to 2-23-65; Mint PO
BINGHAM, Elkana D., Mo-124-1; 9th Civil Dist
BINGHAM, John H., Mo-129-2; Pvt I Co 5th TN Cav; 9-1-63 to 6-30-65; Four Mile Branch PO
BINGHAM, L. E., De-22-3; Pvt F Co 27th TN Inf; 1 Aug 61 to __; Dunbar PO; CONF

BINGHAM, Thomas J., Wl-293-2; Pvt; 62 to 63; Lockport PO; CONF
BINKLEY, Ben F., D-71-1; 909 Summer, Nashville PO
BINKLEY, James J., Rb-228-2; Pvt F Co TN Cav; __ to 64; Crunk PO; CONF
BINKLY, Franklin, Ce-20-2; Pvt D Co 17th KY Cav; 8-10-64 to 9-20-65; PO omitted; fistiles
BINSEN, Andy G., K-156-2; Diana widow of; Pvt; 132 Kennedy St, Knoxville PO
BIRCHEL, James M., Hm-108-4(3); Pvt D Co 1st TN Cav; 15 Apr 62 to 15 Apr 65; Trentham PO; heart disease & 20 yr
BIRCHETT, Daniel A., D-68-3; 1st Asst Engineer Shaddell US Navy; Fall of 62 to captured 63 (3 mos); 32 S. Sycamore St, Nashville PO; general debility, hearing injured in the Mexican War
BIRCHFIELD, Burton, Bo-23-1; Pvt H Co Hurn? Legion; 7-15-62 to 65; PO omitted; CONF
BIRCHFIELD, Charles, Ct-36-2; Sgt B Co 12th TN Cav; 6-18-6? to __ (3 yrs); Roan Mt. PO
BIRCHFIELD, James N., Ct-36-2; Sgt B Co 12th TN Cav; Roan Mt. PO
BIRCHFIELD, John, Br-8-3(1); Pvt D Co 4th TN Cav; 10-1-62 to 3-26-64; Cleo PO; lame
BIRCHFIELD, John, Ro-210-2; Mary E. widow of; Sgt F Co 12th KY Inf; 12 Feb 63 to 11 Jul 65; Rockwood PO
BIRCHFIELD, John P., Bo-15-2; Maery widow of; Pvt C Co 4th IL Inf; 61 to 62; Blockhouse PO
BIRCHFIELD, Joseph C., Mo-130-1; Pvt D Co 3rd TN Mtd Inf; 7-12-64 to 12-23-64; Povo PO; lungs & rheumatism
BIRD, Abraham, Gr-74-2; Pvt B Co 9th TN Cav; 4 Nov 64 to 11 Sep 65; May Spring PO; partial deafness, cause small pox
BIRD, Adam, Ge-94-1; Pvt C Co 10th Cav; Home PO
BIRD, Bengiman M., H-69-1; Mary widow of; Pvt I Co 21st GA Cav; 9-10-61 to 5-10-65; Chattanooga PO; CONF
BIRD, Benjamin, Sh-158-2; Sgt K Co 3rd Cold. Cav; 21 Oct 64 to 26 Jan 66; Memphis PO; gun shot wound in right shoulder, weakening arm. Bird says he was first enlisted in IL & served as cook 2 yrs for Co B 4th IL Cav
BIRD, Benjamin, Lo-191-4; Hannah Norwood widow of; Pvt A Co 7th TN Inf; 13 Aug 64 to 27 Jul 65; Trigonia PO
BIRD, Caledonia, B-3-2; widow; Wartrace PO
BIRD, David A., Ge-84-3; Pvt E Co 4th TN Inf; 5 Jan 63 to 2 Aug 65; Greenville PO; chronic dis. heart, lung
BIRD, Elbert, Pi-156-1; Pvt K Co 4th TN Cav; 11-1-64 to 8-21-65; Permelia PO; lumbago in back, not able to do general labor
BIRD, Elder, H-69-2; Pvt 19th MO Inf; 62 to 66; Chattanooga PO
BIRD, Francis M., Gr-73-1; Pvt D Co 4th TN Cav; 17 Feb 63 to 2 Aug 65; Heltonville PO
BIRD, Hiram W., H-73-4(2); Chattanooga PO
BIRD, Jacob W., Gr-73-2; Cpl D Co 4th TN Inf; 7 Feb 63 to 2 Aug 65; Turley's Mills PO; spinal iritation, mumps while in service
BIRD, James, Pi-153-2; Pvt A Co 13th KY Cav; 1-1-63 to 1-10-65; Byrdstown PO
BIRD, James, Se-221-3; Pvt F Co 9th TN Cav; 1 Oct 63 to 11 Sep 65; Fox PO
BIRD, John A., Mu-195-2; Sol; Columbia PO
BIRD, John L., D-89-1; Pvt F Co 3rd TN; Jul 64 to Apr 65; Buchville PO; papers allright, just rec'd pay
BIRD, Michael, Se-221-1; Pvt F Co 9th TN Cav; 18 Sep 63 to 11 Sep 65; Fox PO
BIRD, Peter, C-34-2; Comfort widow of; Pvt 2nd TN Inf; 61 to __ (served about 10 mos); Buckeye PO
BIRD, Simon A., Se-221-2; Com Sgt F Co 9th TN Cav; 13 Sep 63 to 25 Mar 65; Fox PO
BIRD, William, F-39-1; Pvt K Co 3rd US Col Cav; Nov 64 to Jan 66; Braden PO
BIRD, William, Sq-164-2(1); Pvt E Co 3rd TN Mtd Inf; 7-15-64 to 11-30-64; Dunlap PO; rheumatism 26 yrs
BIRD, William A., Se-225-2; Cpl F Co 9th TN Cav?; 18 Sep 63 to 17 Sep 65; Cottettsburg PO; rheumatism and piles 25 yrs
BIRD(ER?), Baxter, U-244-1; Pvt D Co 8th TN Cav; 28 Sep 63 to 11 Sep 65; Loganton PO; diarrheaer & piles
BIRDSONG, Allen, Gi-129-1; Pvt D Co 111th TN Inf; Conway PO; eyes burnt and almost blind
BIRDSONG, K. L., Gi-122-5; Pvt B Co 32nd TN Inf; Sep 61 to May 65; Prospect Sta. PO; shot in thigh; CONF
BIRDWELL, Albert H., Cr-17-1; Pvt D Co 7th TN Reg; 8(7?)-14-62 to 10-25-63; Buena Vista PO; rheumatism, not pentioned
BIRDWELL, Sellers, Bo-14-1; Darel A. widow of; Pvt; Clover Hill PO; captured and died in prison
BIRDWELL, William, Cy-27-2; Pvt 1st TN Mtd Inf; 64 to 65; Clementsville PO
BIRK, Dick, G-64-1; Pvt; 62 to 63; Bradford PO
BIS, Robt., Fr-115-2; Pvt I Co 36th WI; 2-25-62 to 7-12-65; PO omitted
BISCO, Elijah, Hr-92-1; Pvt H Co 188th PA; 7-10-62 to 4-1-64; Bolivar PO; wounded in hip, side & neck
BISEN, Joseph, La-113-3; Pvt F Co 2nd MO Inf; 1 Aug 61 to 19 Jan 65; Ethridge PO; one shot left shoulder and right side, prisner 14 mos Andersonville
BISHOP, Alfred M., Mu-210-2; Pvt I Co 6th KY Cav; 5-14-62 to 6-29-65; Spring Hill PO; gun shot through body
BISHOP, Archie H., Sh-163-1; Pvt A Co 59th IL Inf; Sep 61 to May 65; Memphis PO; was a Mexican Veteran, in Shelby Co. Poorhouse
BISHOP, Ed P., D-72-4; Helen widow of; Lt K Co 19th MA? Inf; Aug 16 61 to __; Nashville PO; lost his papers
BISHOP, Frank M., Mu-201-1; Sol; 13th Civil Dist
BISHOP, James F., Ch-14-2; Mary E. widow of; Pvt; PO omitted; CONF
BISHOP, John, Ct-42-1; Margaret widow of; Pvt A Co 13th TN Cav; Watauga PO
BISHOP, Jonathan, K-175-1; Pvt D Co 1st TN Inf; 18 Aug 62 to 18 Aug 65; Bullrun PO
BISHOP, Richard, Gr-71-1; Mahala widow of; Tate Spring PO; discharge misplaced and know not
BISHOP, Sampson, Ms-171-1; Sgt I Co 111th TN Inf; 1 Feb 64 to 30 Apr 66; Belfast PO
BISHOP, Samuell, Ct-41-1; Pvt F Co 2nd TN Inf; 7-22-62 to 6-18-65; Elizabethton PO; rhumatism and dyareer
BISHOP, Sevester, Br-12-6; Charleston PO; CONF
BISHOP, Simpson J., Ch-14-1; Pvt F Co 52nd TN Cav; 7-25-63 to 12-20-65; Wild Goose PO; CONF
BISHOP, William H., Hm-104-1; Martha mother of; Pvt G Co 4th TN Cav; Alpha PO; full with nervesnes, on the pensin rolls for loss of son
BISHOP, William M., Ct-40-2; Pvt G Co 13th TN Cav; 9-24-63 to 9-5-65; Elizabethton PO; hernia
BISHOP, William M., Ch-12-1; Mary J. widow of; Pvt 21st TN Cav; 10-1-62 to __ (2 yrs); Wild Goose PO; CONF
BISHOP, William P., K-177-4; Pvt D Co 6th TN Inf; 1 Oct 62 to 25 Jul 65; Powells Station PO; lung diseas
BITTICK, John R., Gi-133-2; Pvt C Co 9th TN; 62 to 64; Bufords PO
BITTNER, Fred, La-115-1; Pvt K Co 6th MS Inf; 27 Dec 64 to 8 Aug 65; Summertown PO; CONF
BIVANS, Dannel E., Mc-114-5; Pvt F Co 5th TN Inf; 9-1-64 to 6-26-65; Santfordville PO; eyes affected--caused by neuralgia
BIVINS, Banister, Mo-130-3; Pvt D Co 11th TN Cav; Ballplay PO
BIVINS, James P., Ro-207-2; Pvt C Co 7th TN Mtd Inf; 20 Aug 64 to 27 Jun 65; 17th Dist
BIZZLE, Nancy S., Wi-281-2; 22nd Dist
BLACK, Adeline (see Stephens, Noah)
BLACK, Benjamin, Gi-127-6; Pvt F Co 111th US Col Inf; Jan 2 64 to Apr 3 66; Pulaski PO
BLACK, David H., Gi-125-1; Pvt 110th US Col Inf; 23 Dec 63 to 64; Weakly PO
BLACK, Elizabeth, Ge-100-3; Midway PO
BLACK, George, Ru-241-5; Margaret widow of; Cpl 119th KY Inf; 64 to 66; Murfreesboro PO
BLACK, George W., A-4-1; Cpl F Co 1st TN Cav; 3-1-62 to 3-30-65; Coal Creek PO; paralysis, was shot shoulder & foot
BLACK, Isaac, A-4-3; Pvt B Co 1st TN Inf; 8-1-61 to 9-17-64; Coal Creek PO; cut by bayonet

BLACK, Jacob, Gi-136-1; Pvt A Co 2nd TN Lt Art; 8-15-63 to 4-15-65; Buford Station PO
BLACK, James, Mr-102-2; Mary widow of; Pvt A Co 116th OH Inf; 8-7-62 to 6-22-65; South Pittsburg PO
BLACK, James E., A-3-2; Pvt I Co 7th TN Inf; 11-1-64 to 7-6-65; Wilson PO; catarrh
BLACK, Jesse L., Mo-120-2; Pvt G Co 3rd NC Inf; 1-1-65 to 8-65; Glenloch PO
BLACK, John, Co-67-4; Sgt H Co 1st TN Cav; 15 Jul 62 to 5 Jul 65; Naillon PO; hemorrage of lungs
BLACK, John, Ro-201-5(3); Pvt F Co 1st TN Hvy Art; 17 Sep 64 to 31 Mar 66; Kingston PO
BLACK, John W., C-27-3; Pvt B Co 1st TN Inf; 8-1-61 to 9-17-64; Jacksboro PO
BLACK, L. W., Mu-194-1; Columbia PO; this man is away & I can't get dates
BLACK, Lewis, Col, D-62-1; Pvt C Co 10th US Col; Aug 22 64 to 7 Nov 65; Nashville, Cor. Broad & McNairy PO
BLACK, Peyton, D-77-1; Pvt C Co 111th US Inf; Nashville PO
BLACK, Reubin, Gi-123-2; Cinthy? widow of; Pvt F Co 111th TN Col Inf; Oncaster? PO
BLACK, Robert (see Hoover, Robert)
BLACK, Samuel, A-8-3; 1st Lt C Co 3rd TN Inf; 2-12-62 to 2-22-65; Scarborough PO
BLACK, Solomon, Co-59-1; Pvt Co A 8th TN Inf; 63 to 65; Del Rio PO; rheumathism
BLACK, Thomas, A-4-6(2); Cpl K Co 11th USC Inf; 6-17-65 to 1-3-66; Coal Creek PO; bronchitus
BLACK, Tillman, Col, Li-154-1; Pvt E Co US Inf; 1-64 to 3-10-65; Cyruston PO; had small pox in army, has no discharge but served
BLACK, William, Wa-263-5; Pvt D Co 61st TN Inf; Sep 63 to 25 Dec 63; Conkling PO; deserted CONF army and joined US; Pvt K Co 4th TN Cav; 3 May 64 to 12 Jul 65
BLACK, William H., A-4-3; Pvt F Co 1st TN Cav; 4-12-62 to 4-14-65; Coal Creek PO; deafness
BLACKBURN, Fernie, Sh-189-3; Memphis PO
BLACKBURN, Gidion H., A-4-2; Pvt Linches Batty 1st TN Cav; 11-18-61 to 4-8-65; Coal Creek PO; CONF
BLACKBURN, Ivison B., H-75-1; Pvt A Co 44th VA Art; 62 to 65; Chattanooga PO; papers lost
BLACKBURN, James H., Dk-34-2; Pvt A Co 5th TN Cav --7-28-62 to 10-26-64; 1st Lt D Co 4th TN Mtd Inf--10-26-64 to 8-25-65; Dowelltown PO; face & eyes powder burnt
BLACKBURN, John A., Gr-82-1; Rebeca widow of; Cpl A Co 12th TN Cav; 8 Jul 63 to 7 Oct 65; Powder Springs PO
BLACKBURN, Joseph H., Dk-34-2; Capt A Co 5th TN Cav--8-30-62 to 6-2-64; Lt Col 4th TN Mtd Inf --8-4-64 to 8-25-65; Dowelltown PO; gun shot & hernia
BLACKBURN, Julius, Sh-169-1; Sgt D Co 6th IN? Inf; 62 to 64; Memphis PO
BLACKBURN, Larkin P., Jo-150-3; Trade PO
BLACKBURN, Milton E., Ca-23-2; Pvt D Co 5th TN Inf; 7-64 to 6-65; Leoni PO; injured by frost bite
BLACKBURN, Richard W., Jo-152-1; Sgt H Co 4th TN Inf; Jan 1 65 to 2 Aug 65; Doeville PO; kidney & liver disease
BLACKBURN, Thomas, G-57-5(3); Pvt; 61 to 65; Yorkville PO; CONF
BLACKBURN, William, D-100-1; Pvt G Co 17th TN Inf; Oct 12 62 to Apr 15 65; Nashville PO; he has a letter from 2nd auditors office showing that his discharge certificate was returned to Nashville
BLACKBURN, William T., Dk-34-1; Pvt D Co 4th TN Inf; 9-22-64 to 8-25-65; Dowelltown PO; lame in left leg & eye sight damaged, now very feeble
BLACKBURN, William W., Je-138-2; 1st Lt B.C.S. 9th TN Cav; 6 May 63 to 11 Sep 65; Dandridge PO; chronic diarrhea
BLACKHEART, Ben, F-35-1; 6 mos; New Castle PO (Hardeman Co)
BLACKMAN, Luther M., Mo-121-2; Maj 4th TN Cav; 8-8-62 to 7-12-65; Eve Mills PO
BLACKNAL, Thomas Y., Hn-69-1; Nancy H. widow of; Pvt L Co 7th TN Cav; 4 Dec 63 to died in prison Sep 64; Paris PO; died in Andersonville
BLACKNALL, John F. M., We-225-1; Martha J. widow of; Pvt K Co 6th TN Cav; Dresden PO
BLACKSHIRE, Wiliam S., Hn-74-2; PO omitted
BLACKWELL, Alford, Cr-1-2(1); Sgt K Co 3rd Hvy Art; 62 to 65; Gadsden PO
BLACKWELL, Charles H., H-56-2; East End PO
BLACKWELL, Faviny I., We-231-1; #13 Weakley PO
BLACKWELL, Jackson M., Po-151-1; Bettie J. widow of; Pvt; Servilla PO
BLACKWELL, John, Mu-210-7; Pvt; PO omitted
BLACKWELL, John, Be-8-1; Bugler M Co 12th TN Cav; 12 Aug 64 to 25 Oct 65; Spring Creek PO; Bugler G Co 2nd TN Inf--6 Jan 64 to 12 Aug 64
BLACKWELL, John H., Sh-144-1; Pvt B Co 61st US Col; Jan 16 64 to 13 Dec 65; Brunswick PO
BLACKWELL, Peter, F-37-1; Nancy widow of; Pvt 88th US Col Inf; Taylors Chapel PO
BLACKWELL, Stephen, K-161-5(6); Knoxville PO
BLACKWELL, Susie (see Hollaway, John)
BLACKWELL, Thomas, Rb-221-1; Pvt 13th GA; May 1 61 to May 1 65; Cedar Hill PO; CONF
BLACKWILL, Henry, D-69-2; US Sol; 57 Mury St, Nashville PO; discharge lost
BLAGG, Jeffres, S-213-1; Pvt F Co 7th TN Inf; Dec 64 to Sep 65; Huntsville PO; from measels in army
BLAIR, Adam, Br-13-2; Sgt C Co 72nd OH Inf; 64 to 65; Ora PO
BLAIR, Charles, C-33-4; Jellico PO
BLAIR, Charley, Se-223-4; Pvt G Co 1st TN Bat; Sevierville PO
BLAIR, George, Bo-12-2(1); Pvt D Co 1st TN LAL (Lt Art Legion?); 9-10-63 to 7-65; Rasor PO
BLAIR, George, Sh-153-3; (Bettis B.)?; Collierville PO; no disability as far as a know
BLAIR, James A., La-113-3; Pvt A Co 14th TN Inf; Ethridge PO; herenah; re-enlisted veteran
BLAIR, James A., La-117-1; Pvt B Co 23rd TN Inf; Jul 9 61 to ___ (4 yrs); 15th Dist; CONF
BLAIR, Jerry, Lo-120-1; Pvt H Co 1st TN Inf; 15 Jun 64 to 65; Loudon PO
BLAIR, John, K-166-2; Pvt A Co 8th TN Cav; 12 Apr 62 to Apr 65; Knoxville PO; hand injured, gravel, hip injured
BLAIR, John C., Sm-170-3; Pvt G Co 28th TN Inf; 10-15-62 to 1-23-65; Chestnut Mound PO; CONF
BLAIR, Robert, Ho-96-2; Pvt E Co 6th NY Hvy Art; Dec 25 63 to Jan 1 65; Erin PO; shot through thighs & foot, so he stated
BLAIR, Robert C., La-117-1; Sgt B Co 23rd TN Inf; Jul 9 61 to ___; West Point PO; shot through right leg; CONF
BLAIR, Samuel, Mo-131-1; Pvt D Co 2nd TN Cav; 9-1-62 to 6-9-65; Chilhowee PO
BLAIR?, Wade H., K-156-1; Anna M. widow of; Pvt; Patton 46, Knoxville PO
BLAIR, William, Bo-23-2; Pvt B Co 6th TN Inf; 3-8-62 to 4-27-65; PO omitted (Cades Cove?)
BLAIR, William C., Cr-19-2; Pvt G Co 2nd TN Inf; 11-11-63 to 12-28-64; Buxter PO
BLAIR, William R., Fe-44-2; Pvt; Allardt PO; rheumatism
BLAK, James, H-63-3; Pvt; 811 Pine, Chattanooga PO
BLAKE, Charles N., Wh-180-1; Sparta PO; gone from the state
BLAKE, Ely, Mg-198-3; Pvt K Co 11th TN Inf; 20 Aug 63 to 20 Dec 63; Rockwood PO; dropsy
BLAKE, J. B., K-167-1; 1st Hvy TN; 63 to 65; Knoxville PO; shot in left knee
BLAKE, Louis A., R-163-2; Pvt C Co 13th VA Vol Inf; 8-15-62 to 6-22-65; Graysville PO
BLAKE, Orestus W., H-61-4; Pvt H Co 28th MI Inf; 4-63 to 6-5-66; Chattanooga PO
BLAKE, Richard, Dk-33-2; Pvt D Co 7th TN Inf; 10-8-62 to 4-3-65; Maggart PO; left side & breast injured by horse falling on him; CONF
BLAKELY, Auston, L-100-1; Pvt H Co 8th TN Cav; 62 to 62; Ripley PO; cannot give dates
BLAKELY, Harriet, Mu-192-1; widow; 8th Civil Dist
BLAKEMAN, John, Sh-191-3; Memphis PO; records not seen
BLAKEMAN, Mason A., La-115-1; Pvt; Henryville PO
BLAKEMORE, John (see Smith, John, T-214-1)
BLAKEMORE, Stephen, Sh-150-3; Pvt 55th Inf; 1 yr; Bartlett PO
BLAKEMORE, William, Hy-74-1; alias Miller; Pvt D Co Art; 63 to 65; Dancyville PO; this soldier has lost his discharge; he can't give anything more than I have put down

BLAKENEY, Benjamin, Cr-17-2; Martha widow of; Pvt E Co 7th TN Cav; 8-62 to died 9-6-64; Buena Vista PO; have no means of getting date of enlistment as have died

BLAKESLE, Henry M., La-115-3; Sol US; Summertown PO

BLAKLEY, William A., Su-241-1; Pvt A Co 1st TN Cav; 20 Mar 62 to 4 Apr 65; Clover Bottom PO; exposure, mash by wagon

BLALOCK, Abijah, Se-230-2; 1st Lt I Co 2nd TN Cav; 22 Oct 62 to 29 Mar 63; Pokeberry PO; liver & rheumatic dis.

BLALOCK, Enock F., Ms-176-1; Pvt D Co 13th TN; 9-10-64 to 6-1-65; Caney Springs PO

BLALOCK, Thomas F., Bl-2-2(1); Nancy widow of; Pvt K Co 4th TN Cav; 62 to 65; Farmingdale PO; affected health by relapse of measles

BLANCED, Jordan J., Ru-13-2; Pvt; Secret Service 18th? Army CL; Apr 1 63 to 65; PO omitted

BLAND, John, Ce-21-1; Cpl D Co 10th TN Inf; 5-1-62 to 1-10-65; Hoffas Wells PO; rumatism

BLANDELL, Martin, La-117-3; Pvt; 61 to 65; 15th Dist; CONF

BLANGUM, Benjamin, Hd-50-6; US Sol; 6th Civil Dist; catarrh in head

BLANKBLEWHICKER, James M., Ro-210-11; Pvt F Co 3rd TN Cav; 12 Apr 65 to 10 Jun 65; Post Oak Springs PO; deaftened

BLANKENSHIP, Asa, M-108-4; Pvt I Co 5th KY Inf; 12-1-61 to 2-65; Lafayette PO; gunshot wound, discharge not at hand

BLANKENSHIP, Calab F., He-61-3; Elizabeth widow of; Pvt A Co 7th TN Cav; 8 Aug 62 to Diey? Jun 65; 15th Civil Dist

BLANKENSHIP, Chas. W., Lo-191-1; Mary E. widow of; Pvt; Morganton PO

BLANKENSHIP, Danial S., He-62-3; Pvt Co D 7th TN Cav; Sep 63 to 64 (4 mos); Darden PO

BLANKENSHIP, James A., Po-149-2(1); Pvt F Co 5th TN Mtd Inf; 10-17-64 to 7-17-65; Conasauga PO; Mtd Inf one yr

BLANEKNSHIP, John R., Dk-37-1; Cpl G Co 5th TN Cav; 10-1-62 to 8-4-65; Cullenville PO

BLANKENSHIP, John R., Dk-36-3; Cpl G Co 5th TN Cav; 10-1-62 to 8-14-65; Cullenville PO

BLANKENSHIP, Robert S., D-85-1(2); Nancey E. widow of; B Co 1st AL Inf; 61 to __; Wilkerson PO

BLANKENSHIP, Sarah J., He-61-2; widow Sol; 15th Civil Dist

BLANKENSHIP, T. C., T-208-1; Mary C. widow of; Cpl E Co 1st TN Bat; 62 to 65; Brighton PO; died with hart disease in 64?

BLANKINBECKLIR, Jackson M., Jo-149-2; Pvt D Co 13th TN Cav; 2 Feb 64 to 5 Sep 65; Mountain City PO; liver, bronkitis, eyes

BLANKINGHIP, Andrew, Ho-95-1; Pvt H Co 1st US Inf; Sep 27 62 to Jun 29 65; McKinnon PO

BLANKINSHIP, Isaac, Mc-112-8; 2nd Sgt A Co 5th TN Mtd Inf; 10-4-64 to 7-17-65; Athens PO

BLANKINSHIP, Samuel S. M., M-108-4; Pvt I Co 9th KY Inf; 12-1-61 to 1-28-65; Lafayette PO; struck on foot by cannon ball

BLANTON, Margaret (see _____ Claburn)

BLANTON, Vincent L., Cf-40-3; Pvt G Co 4th TN Vol; 20 May 62 to 23 Jun 65; Tullahoma PO

BLARE, Thommas J., Se-231-1; Pvt A Co 9th TN Cav; 18 Oct 62 to lost discharge; Boyds Creek PO

BLARNSET?, William M., Mr-99-2; Eliz. widow of; Pvt C Co Smith TN Inf; 9-7-64 to 6-30-65; Jasper PO

BLASSINGER, Jeff, Col, Ma-119-1; Cook Pvt A Co 2nd CT?; 62 to 65; Jackson PO

BLATHERWICK, Wilfred, H-54-2(3); Pvt H Co 183rd OH Inf; Sherman Heights PO

BLAZER, Christopher, Co-61-1; Pvt B Co 8th TN Inf; 2-14-63 to 6-30-65; Ottinger PO

BLAZER, Franklin, Co-60-2; E Co 8th TN Inf; 4-19-64 to 6-30-65; Caney Branch PO; defected loungs

BLAZER, George M., Se-221-3; Cpl M Co 2nd TN Cav; 8 Nov 62 to 6 Jun 65; Fair Garden PO

BLAZER, Henry, Co-60-2; B Co 8th TN Inf; 7-1-63 to 6-13-65; Salem PO; pneummonia fever

BLAZER, Iranious, Co-61-1; Pvt A Co 4th TN Inf; 13 Dec 62 to 2 Aug 65; Ottinger PO; rumatism

BLAZER, Martha (see Webb, George)

BLAZER, Phillip, Co-60-2; A Co 4th TN Inf; 4-20-63 to 8-2-65; Salem PO; chills & fever

BLAZER, Samuel, Co-61-1; Sarah A. widow of; Pvt A Co 4th TN Inf; 12-13-63 to 8-2-65; Salem PO

BLAZER, Tilghman, Co-60-2; Sgt K Co 8th TN Inf; 7-1-63 to 5-19-65; Salem PO; rheumatism

BLEADSON, Jos. M., Cr-3-1; Gadsden PO; smallpox

BLEDSAW, Isaac, Cl-50-2(1); B Co 1st TN Art Bat; 64 to 7-65; Hoop PO; cant give the date of discharge

BLEDSOE, Allen M., Mg-198-1; Pvt E Co 1st TN Inf; 14 Aug 61 to 17 Sep 64; Lavender PO; diarhoe

BLEDSOE, Charles T., Ov-136-1; Margaret widow of; Cpl E Co 10th IL Cav; 4-11-64 to 11-22-65; Livingston PO

BLEDSOE, Dick, Gi-127-7; Pulaski PO; papers & dates lost

BLEDSOE, James, Sh-152-3; Diana widow; Dexter PO

BLEDSOE, John, Gi-129-2; Pvt A Co 111th TN Inf; Elkton PO

BLEDSOE, Toliver, Gi-129-3; Pvt A Co 111th TN Inf; Jan 63 to __; Elkton PO

BLEVINS, Allen, Ct-39-2; Pvt B Co 4th TN Inf; 12-62 to 8-65; Happy Valley PO; wound inflicted during war

BLEVINS, Daniel, S-212-1; Pvt D Co 30th KY; 15 Jan 64 to 18 Apr 65; Porchcorn PO; rigt leg spraned

BLEVINS, Dillard, Ct-42-2; Pvt F Co 13th TN Cav; 11-29-63 to 9-5-65; Watauga PO

BLEVINS, James P., Ct-45-1; Pvt H Co 4th TN Inf; 5-3-63 to 8-2-65; Stony Creek PO; Nashville 1863 measles

BLEVINS, John, Ct-43-1; Addaline Taylor formly widow of; Pvt K Co 23rd MD Inf--6-27-63 to 11-12-64; Pvt F Co 13th TN Cav--11-28-64 to 9-5-65; Carter Furnace PO; neuralgia & rheumatism, died in 1880, rheumatism

BLEVINS, John, Bo-15-1; Pvt D Co 1st TN Lt Art; 9-20-63 to 7-20-65; Mountvale PO; dislocation of shoulder

BLEVINS, John N., Su-234-1; Pvt C Co 13th TN Cav; 27 Jan 64 to 5 Sep 65; Blountville PO; December 1864 took cold on Itonea? raid resulting in rheumatism

BLEVINS, Luna, Ct-45-2; Pvt H Co 4th TN Inf; 63 to 8-2-65; Stony Creek PO

BLEVINS, Nathan, A-2-1; Pvt J Co 1st OH Cav; 64 to 65; Hynds Creek PO; piles, formerly of Co F, 71st OH Inf

BLEVINS, Ruben B., Ct-43-2; Pvt F Co 13th TN Cav; 9-23-64 to 9-5-65; Carter Furnace PO; shot through left hand in NC

BLEVINS, Thomas C., A-10-1; Pvt G Co 8th TN Inf; 1-22-63 to 6-30-65; Briceville PO; bronchitis

BLEVINS, William H., Su-232-1; Pvt H Co 4th TN Inf; 29 Apr 64 to Jul 65; Ruthton PO

BLIVENS, Henry, Bo-14-3; Pvt H Co 3rd TN Inf; 12-18-62 to 8-2-65; Ellworth PO; chronic catarrh, transferred from Co H to B aft to A

BLIVENS, Luna, Bo-14-3; Pvt D Co 1st TN Art; 9-24-63 to 7-65; Ellsworth PO

BLIZARD, Leonadus, Mc-112-11; Cpl L Co 4th TN Cav; 11-25-62 to 7-12-65; Athens PO

BLOCK, George, K-169-2; Jennie widow of; QOS? 1st TN Inf; Jul 62 to Mar 65; Knoxville PO

BLOCK, Marx, H-60-4; Capt Surgeon 114th US Col; 63 to 65; Chattanooga PO

BLODDWORTH, John J., Rb-219-2; Pvt C Co 14th TN Reg; Apr 61 to Aug 22 62; Black Jack PO; CONF

BLOOM, Robert V., H-56-1; Pvt B Co 147th IN Inf; 1-24-65 to 8-4-65; St. Elm(o) PO

BLOOMFIELD, Samuel, O-138-3; Pvt E Co 12th & 125th IL; 1 Sep 62 to __; 15 Dec 61 to about Jul 65; Minnick Box PO

BLUEROCK, Henry, Ho-96-2; Pvt D Co 6th PA Hvy Art; Sep 1 64 to Jun 13 65; Erin PO; had ribs broken and did not receive discharge

BLUFORD, James, Mo-124-1; Pvt; Brakebille PO; somewhat deficient in sight, went to his house but could not see him

BLUING, John, D-49-4; Pvt H Co 40th __; we state all he can remember, he has no papers; Nashville PO

BLUNDELL, Edward R., T-217-1(39?); Pvt B Co 138th OH Inf; May 64 to 64 (100 days); Covington PO; original Reg 7th N. Guards

BLUNT, Edmon J., Be-7-1; Pvt F Co 29th IL Inf; 10 Aug 62 to 13 Jun 65; Big Sandy PO
BLYTHE, Alexander, Wl-303-1; Martha F. widow of; Pvt E Co 4th TN Mtd Inf; Nov 10 64 to 25 Aug 65; Bairds Mills PO; reenlisted veteran
BLYTHE, Claley G., La-113-1; Pvt Bat 8; 1 Nov 62 to 15 Jul 65; Lawrenceburg; all the information could get
BLYTHE, F. M., La-117-3; Pvt 48th TN Inf; Jan 2 62 to May 65; 15th Dist; CONF
BLYTHE, James B., Dk-32-3; Pvt A Co 5th TN Cav; 7-28-62 to 6-25-65; Liberty PO
BLYTHE, Nathaniel, Wl-300-2; Pvt; 20 Aug 63 to Aug 65; Cherry Valley PO
BOALS, Nelson, F-39-2(1); Sgt A Co 59th US Col Inf; 1 Jun 63 to 31 Jan 66; PO omitted
BOATMAN?, James L. W., Mn-120-1; Capt D Co 6th TN Cav; Sep 25 62 to Jul 26 65; Falcon PO
BOATMAN, Nathan A., Bo-14-1; Pvt H Co 4th TN Inf; 1-25-63 to 6-23-65; Cliff PO
BOAZ, Abraham, D-99-2; Pvt F Co 115th KY Inf; Sep 6 64 to Feb 10 66; Edgefield PO
BOAZ, Bengamin, D-99-2; Cyrildan Hope widow of; Pvt F Co 115th KY Inf; Sep 6 64 to Feb 10 66; Edgefield Junction PO
BOAZ, William N., We-221-5(2); Sgt D Co 2nd KY Inf; 13 Jul 61 to 1 May 61; Martin PO; CONF
BODDY, Hilliard, Sh-189-4; Ester mother of; Memphis PO; CONF?
BODDY, William, W-189-1; Sgt A Co 92nd IL Mtd Inf; 8-9-62 to 7-15-65; McMinnville PO
BOFORD, Ed., F-43-2; Pvt E Co; 63 to __; Piperton PO; partie cannot furnish any information
BOGARD, ____, Lk-112-2; Corn. B. widow of; Tiptonville PO; Bogard was killed about 2 yrs ago in a drunken brawn and I could not get the facts--he had drawn a pension
BOGART, George W., Mc-111-2; Pvt A Co 7th TN Mtd Inf; 8-27-64 to 7-27-65; Mortimer PO
BOGART, Jeremiah, U-247-2; Pvt A Co 3rd NC Mtd Inf; 3 Sep 64 to 8 Aug 65; Erwin PO; phthisic & diarrhoea
BOGART, John D., Sh-201-1; Sarah S. widow of; Pvt; Memphis PO; CONF
BOGART, William W., Wa-265-1; Susan M. widow of; Pvt G Co 4th TN Inf; 25 Nov 62 to 2 Aug 65; Trump PO; died chronic diarhia
BOGLE, Erastus H., Lo-189-1; Pvt F Co 46th VA Inf; Jan 61 to 9 Apr 65; Philadelphia PO; gun shot wound in right foot; CONF
BOGLE, Newton M., Ca-19-1; Pvt K Co 4th TN Cav; 12-2-64 to 9-25-65; Auburn PO
BOHANAN, Horatio B., Se-223-2; Pvt E Co 9th TN Cav; 1 Oct 63 to 11 Sep 65; Pigeon Forge PO; chronic diarrhea &c
BOHANAN, James, J-78-2; Pvt K Co 7th TN Inf; 12-1-64 to 8-23-65; Rough Point PO; lungs
BOHANAN, John, Se-230-1; Pvt 9th TN Cav; 3 yrs; Stinnett PO; shot, close enogh to injure hearing
BOHANAN, Louis W., Be-2-1; Pvt M Co 6th Reg; Oct 62 to Jun 64; Rockport PO
BOHANNON, Iven, Se-219-1; Martha widow of; East York PO
BOHANNON, John, Ge-90-1; Cpl A Co 4th TN Inf; 7 Jan 63 to 2 Aug 65; Greeneville PO; rumatism & truble of head
BOHANNON, William E., Ge-91-3; Cpl K Co 119th IL Inf; 9 Aug 62 to 9 Sep 65; Greeneville PO; rhumatism, diarhea
BOHN, Jarrett S., We-220-3; 1st Civil Dist
BOHV, Charles A., H-59-2; Pvt OH Cav; Chattanooga PO
BOICE, Leonard, H-70-2(1); Pvt; Chattanooga (Walnut) PO; out of town & couldn't find out about him
BOLDEN, Ellen, G-51-1; widow US Sol; 3rd Civil Div
BOLDEN, Wilburn, Lo-190-1; Pvt L Co 16th NC Inf; May 62 to __; Loudon PO; CONF
BOLDEN, William, Hm-107-5; Pvt C Co 8th TN Inf; 1 Jan 63 to __; Morristown PO; injury of hip & back from fall
BOLDER, Ruben, Sh-189-6; Sol US; Va. Ave, Memphis PO
BOLDON, Samuel, Sh-157-2; Pvt A Co 55th USC Inf; Jun 62 to 65; Memphis, 470 Main St, right hip shot; I am very much disable

BOLE, William L., We-229-1; Pvt E Co 8th IN Inf; 5 Sep 61 to 5 Sep 64; Gleason PO; piles from service
BOLEN, Thomas, K-177-5; Pvt I Co 2nd TN Inf; 63 to 10 Aug 65; Powells Station PO; over heat & pneumonia fever
BOLER, Ren, F-37-1; Pvt D Co 119th US Col Inf; Mar 64 to Feb 65; Stanton Depot PO (Haywood Co.); discharged on account of sickness
BOLES, Danial, Ge-89-3; Pvt M Co 1st TN Cav; 29 Mar 63 to 19 Jun 65; Marvin PO; cattarrh & liver
BOLES, George, Pi-153-3; Pvt TN Cav; 62 to 65; West Fork PO
BOLES, John, Pi-153-3; Matilda widow of; Capt D Co 2nd TN Inf; 9-61 to 9-63; West Fork PO
BOLIC, Henry J., Dk-37-1; Pvt C Co 1st KY Cav; 62 to 10-65; Kellanburgh PO; gun shot in left arm
BOLIN, Barnett, We-220-1; Sgt C Co 1st KY Inf; May 20 64 to Feb 28 65; Palmersville PO
BOLING, Mitchell, We-228-1(2); Pvt G Co TN Cav; Oct 62 to Dec 63; Cox PO; wounded in right leg; was conscripted
BOLINGER, Benjamin, Cl-47-2; Sgt E Co 6th TN Inf; 3-25-62 to 4-27-65; Pleasant PO; nervious affections
BOLLINGER, Oliver, Sh-145-3; Pvt G Co 120th IL Inf; 22 Aug 62 to 10 Sep 66; Quito PO (Tipton Co.); chronic diarhea & piles & rhumatism; Cap. James H. McSpain, veteran
BOLT, James R., W-193-1; Pvt G Co US Inf; 10-6-64 to 11-7-66; Smartt PO; enlisted out of a rebel prison
BOLTON, David A., H-74-5(3); Pvt 25th IN; Chattanooga PO
BOLTON, David S., H-58-6; Pvt B Co 6th TN Mtd Inf; 8-15-64 to 6-30-65; Retro PO; lung trouble
BOLTON, Henry R., D-79-1; 6th Cpl C Co 6th WI Inf; Apr 13 61 to Apr 20 65; Nashville, N. 2nd PO; 3 wounds, once in each ankle, once in face, still painful
BOLTON, James, Sh-146-3; Feranna widow of; Pvt "A" Pioneers; 62 to 65; Millington PO; this woman can give me no information except that her husband was a soldier in Georgia
BOLTON, James H., Ge-98-4; Pvt I Co 1st TN Cav; 21 Sep 62 to 5 Jun 65; PO omitted; disease of legs and chronic diarhea
BOLTON, John H., Ge-84-2; Sgt C Co 8th TN Inf; 15 Jun 63 to 21 May 65; Greenville PO; dis. wound piles
BOLTON, Joseph S., Wa-273-1; Pvt B Co 8th TN Cav; Jun 63 to Sep 65; Locust Mt. PO; disease of lungs
BOLTON, Robert N., H-58-2; Pvt B Co 5th TN Mtd Inf; __ to 6-30-65; Coulterville PO; measles settled on lungs
BOLTON, Thomas J., Wa-276-1; PVt B Co 12th TN Cav; Nov 20 63 to Oct 20 65; Limestone PO; crippled ankle, not certain as to dates
BOLTON, Whit (see Champion, Whit)
BOLTON, William H. C., Ge-96-3; Pvt B Co 12th TN Cav; 19 Nov 63 to 27 Oct 65; Limestone PO; chronic diareah, liver trouble
BOMAN, George W., Ro-208-1; Malinda C. widow of; Pvt B Co 5th US TN Inf; 13 Feb 62 to 30 Mar 65; Barnardsville PO; rheumatism
BOMAN, Josire, Ov-139-1; Nancy B. widow of; Pvt K Co; Lovejoy PO
BOMAN, William, Sh-188-2; US Col; Maxwell St, Memphis PO; could get no further information
BOMAN, William, Ov-139-2; Pvt D Co 1st TN Inf; 10-12-63 to 4-25-65; Qualls PO
BOMER, Richard E., Be-7-1; US Sol; Enlow PO; deseas of I.
BOND, Abraham, Hy-79-1; Pvt; Brownsville PO
BOND, Blount, Hy-85-1; Pvt C Co 64th MS; 62 to 65; Nut Bush PO
BOND, Elzia, Rb-219-2; Pvt E Co 5th KY Cav; Oct 4 61 to Jan 24 64; Price's Mill, KY PO; rail road accident, hurt in chest, cavalry service
BOND, George (see Barnes, George)
BOND, Haywood, Hy-81-1; 7th Civil Dist
BOND, John B., Sh-175-1; Cpl G Co __ Inf; 63 to 66; Memphis PO
BOND, Retta, Hy-85-1; widow; Nut Bush PO

BOND, William E., W1-301-1; Pvt H Co 4th TN Mtd Inf; Nov 1 64 to Aug 25 65; Simmons Bluff PO; feet frost bitten
BOND, William L., Ru-235-1; Pvt 61st IL Inf; Dec 63 to 28 Feb 65; Jefferson PO
BONDS, Andrew J., Cr-17-1; Elizabeth widow of; Pvt B Co 7th TN Cav; 63 to 6-11-64 (died); Buena Vista PO; certificated can't give date of enlistment
BONDS, Wesley, G-51-2; US Sol; Humboldt PO
BONDS, Willia (sic), Mu-193-2; Pvt D Co 100th OH Inf; 9-15-62 to 3-15-63; PO omitted
BONDS, Zachariah M., O-130-1; Catherine widow of; Pvt B Co 24th MO Inf; 20 Aug 61 to 19 Apr 66; Jordan PO (Fulton Co. KY); heart disease & deafness, reenlisted veteran
BONDURANT, Church E., We-223-3; Stuart L Co 6th TN Cav; Aug 62 to Jul 65; Cottage Grove PO; chronick diareah
BONDURANT, John W., F-40-1; Pvt C Co 13th TN Inf; 20 Mar 62 to 15 Apr 65; Hickory Withe PO; CONF
BONE, Baley P., P-156-3; Cpl F Co 63rd TN Inf; 12-25-62 to 8-6-63; Lobelville PO
BONGIVER?, Joseph, Ge-83-3; Pvt F Co 4th TN Inf; 24 Mar 63 to 2 Aug 65; Painters PO; chronic diarrhea
BONHAM, Romulus C., K-179-5; 2nd Lt K Co 1st TN Inf; 2 Nov 61 to 17 Sep 64; Concord PO
BONHAM, William T., Gi-125-1; Pvt I Co; Dec 63 to 10 May 65; Weakly PO
BONIGN, William M., Mc-112-9; Pvt D Co 11th TN Cav; 5-1-63 to ___; Athens PO
BONING, Isaac R., Bo-12-4; Sol US; 3rd Dist
BONING, J. P., Bo-22-2; Pvt H Co 2nd TN Cav; 9-62 to ___; Seaton PO; has no discharge; can't get the date
BONNER, Abram, T-210-1; G Co 9th IL; 63 to 65; Richardson Ldg PO
BONNER, Charles, Col, Cf-40-3; Pvt C Co 14th US Col Inf; 1 Nov 63 to 28 Mar 66; Tullahoma PO
BONNER, Harry, W-189-3(2); US Sol; McMinnville PO
BONNER, Henry, Li-149-1; Teamster C Co 5th TN Cav; 8-63 to 8-65; Fayetteville PO
BONNER, Howard, Me-90-1; Pvt K Co 1st Hvy Art; Magellan PO
BONNER, James, Li-149-2; Pvt K Co 110th US Col Inf; 1-13-64 to 12-15-66; Fayetteville PO
BONNER, James, Li-161-1; Pvt K Co 160th TN; 62 to Jul 65; Fayetville PO
BONNER, William, Sh-197-1; Pvt L Co 3rd Col Art; 2-8-65 to 4-13-66; Memphis PO; chronic piles
BONNER, Woodfin, Li-143-1; Pvt F Co 111th US Inf; 62 to 64; Rowell PO; prisoner at Andersonville 8 mos
BONNETT, Edmund, Sh-157-5; Pvt C Co 55th; May 1 63 to Dec 25 65; Memphis, Salm Baptist Church PO; right thumb shot in a ___
BONNING, Absolm, Bo-12-2(1); Pvt L Co 2nd TN Cav; 9-8-63 to 11-30-64; reenlisted 7-13-64 Co C 3rd TN Mtd Inf; Rasor PO
BOO, John H., Mn-122-1; Pvt B Co 6th TN Cav; 8-25-62 to 7-26-65; McNairy PO; discharged genl OWB
BOOK, Samuel J., Cf-40-2; 2nd Lt E Co 100th PA Inf; 27 Aug 61 to 1 Mar 63; Tullahoma PO; shell and minnie ball
BOOKER, Benjamin F., Un-253-2; Pvt G Co 2nd TN Cav; 7 Sep 62 to 7 Jul 65; Lorenaton PO; wounded breast
BOOKER, Charles, H-72-2(1); Annie formerly widow of; Pvt; Chattanooga PO
BOOKER, Green, D-64-3; Emmaline Harris widow of; Pvt D Co 44th TN Inf; Nashville PO; killed
BOOKER, John, K-173-3; Cpl E (G?) Co 2nd TN Cav; 1 Oct 62 to 1 Jul 65; McMillen PO
BOOKER, Lemuel, Mu-196-2; Cpl C Co 40th ___; 2 yrs 2 mos; Columbia PO
BOOKER, Lige, Mu-189-1; Pvt 7th TN Cav; Hurricane Switch PO
BOOKER, Peter, Ov-137-2; Tennessee widow of; Pvt H Co 3rd kY Inf; 12-11-61 to 65; Monroe PO; this soldier died 11 Feb 1888, camp cough
BOOKER, Prior, Un-253-2; Cpl G Co 2nd TN Cav; 1 Sep 62 to 6 Jul 65; Meltabarger PO
BOOKER, William H., Ov-137-1; Pvt H Co 3rd KY Inf; 12-11-61 to 65; Nettle Carrier PO; rheumatism & lung disease, wounded at Resacca, GA, 14 May 64
BOOKET, John B., Ge-98-1; 1st Sgt B Co 4th TN Cav; 8 Sep 62 to 13 Jul 65; PO omitted; invalid disability
BOON, Dock, Sh-147-1; Pvt A Co 17th IA Inf; 15 Jul 63 to 30 Apr 66; Cuba PO
BOON, Israel J., Br-8-3(1); Pvt E Co 4th TN Cav; Red Clay, GA PO; hearing--rheumatism
BOON, John, Sh-158-4; Pvt H Co 59th Col Inf; Jun 63 to May 65; Memphis PO; rheumatism in right shoulder & arm 25 yrs; discharge in hands of Moyers & Deadrick
BOON, Perly, Sh-190-2; widow of Sol; 182 Kansas Ave, Memphis PO
BOON, Wesly, Hr-94-1; Anna widow of; Musician D Co 59th TN Inf; Saulsbury PO
BOORD?, Dr. Richard D., O-134-1; Pvt L Co 1st TN Cav; May 16 61 to 12 May 65; Hornbeak PO; wounded five times; CONF
BOOTH, Ebenezer, Wa-263-3; Lt B Co 12th TN Cav; Jul 22 63 to Aug 12 64; May Day PO
BOOTH, James W., Wa-263-4; Mary E. widow of; Pvt B Co 12th TN Cav; Jul 22 63 to May 20 65; May Day PO; rheumatism
BOOTH, Jeremiah, Wa-263-4; Pvt B Co 12th TN Cav; Jul 22 63 to Oct 7 65; May Day PO; reumatism
BOOTH, John, L-106-1; US Sol; 8th Dist
BOOTH, Jnot., Sh-189-4; Pvt MS Reg--could not get record; Memphis PO; CONF
BOOTH, Joseph, Wa-263-3; 1st Sgt B Co 12th TN Cav; Jul 22 63 to Aug 8 65; May Day PO; rheumatism & bronchitis 1864
BOOTH, Mary Ann (see Weston, Richd)
BOOTH, Nancy, Ha-116-2; widow US Sol; Dist No 13
BOOTHE, Hiram, U-246-1; Sgt B Co 12th TN Cav; 14 Jun 63 to 24 Oct 65; Erwin PO
BORDEN, John, M-107-4; Pvt D Co 9th KY Inf; 9-61 to ___; Red Boiling Spring PO
BORDEN, Nathaniel, M-107-2; Rhoda A. Hawkins former widow of; Pvt D Co 9th KY Inf; 9-61 to ___; Red Boiling Springs PO; chronic diareah, died in Chattanooga hospital
BORDON, Ned D., T-216-1; Pvt A Co 25th OH Inf; 23 Feb 62 to 16 Apr 65; Corona PO
BOREN, David C., Ct-39-1; Pvt 13th TN Cav; 9-63 to 9-65; Davidson County PO; rheumatism chronic diarrea bowel trouble
BOREN, Lawson B., He-62-1; Sgt Co C 7th TN Cav; Aug 62 to Jun 65; Darden PO; chronic diarhea and scurvy
BOREN, William F., G-64-1; Pvt A Co; May 62 to 65; Bradford PO
BORENES, William, Sh-183-1; Pvt C Co MO; 61 to 63; Memphis PO
BORGER, John C., Ro-210-5; Pvt D Co 2nd TN Inf; 9 Mar 62 to Aug 64; Rockwood PO; blood ruptured
BORGER, Lemuel, Dk-34-2; Sgt G Co 1st TN Inf; 3-1-64 to 4-21-65; Dowelltown PO; rheumatism & eye sight, disfigured by small pox
BORGER, Richard, Mc-114-2; Sarah Dooly widow of; Pvt; Magellan PO
BORING, David, Ho-96-2; Foster, George alias; Pvt K Co 56th OH Inf; Dec 10 61 to Dec 23 64; Erin PO; crippled feet & eyes affected from small pox
BORING, John W., Wa-267-2; 2nd Lt G Co 4th TN Inf; 22 Sep 62 to 11 Oct 65; Febuary PO; enlarged ankle joint
BORING, Joseph A., K-179-2; Cpl G Co 3rd TN Inf; 10 Feb 62 to 23 Feb 65; Campbell PO; g.s. wound left heel
BORING?, Joshua, Wa-268-3; discharge away from home; Johnson City PO
BORING, William, Bo-23-2; Cpl L Co 2nd TN Cav; 9-8-63 to 7-6-65; Cades Cove PO; piles
BORNSTEIN, Albert, D-96-1; Pvt D Co 10th TN Inf; 1 Jan 64 to 24 Jun 65; Nashville PO; invalid
BORRIFF, Valentine, Un-257-1; Serene widow of; Pvt; New Prospect PO
BORTHICK, William S., Rb-218-1; Pvt B Co 26th KY Inf; 10 Dec 61 to 15 Jun 65; Franklin PO (Simpson Co., KY)
BORUF?, Authur, Un-258-2(1); Pvt K Co 7th KY Inf; 14 Feb 62 to 29 Feb 64; Rhodelia PO; shot in the neck

BORUFF, William C., Un-258-2(1); Pvt E Co 6th TN Inf; 6 May 62 to 27 Apr 65; Longhollow PO
BORUM, Henry H., Wl-300-1; Pvt 4th TN Cav; Feb 64 to Feb 65; Watertown PO; shot in the leg
BORUM, Thomas, Wl-297-2; Pvt B Co 5th TN Cav; 12 Aug 62 to 25 Jul 65; Commerce PO
BOSHEL?, James W., Mn-121-4; Elisibeth J. Johnson formerly widow of; Pvt B Co 6th TN Cav; __ to 7-26-65; Bethel Springs PO
BOSLEY, William, D-47-1; Pvt G Co 12th US Col Inf; 8-12-63 to 1-16-66; Jackson St., Nashville PO
BOSS, Edward T., Sh-201-2; Henrietta widow of; Pvt B Co 1st IL Lt Art; 13 Jul 61 to 20 Jul 63; Memphis PO
BOSS, Thomas B., Po-148-2; PVt A Co 3rd TN Inf; 2-10-62 to 2-23-65; Benton PO
BOSS, Thomas W., Ma-126-2; Cpl E Co 32nd WI Inf; 4 Jul 62 to Jun 65; Jackson PO (at present); dont recollect exact date of discharge
BOSS, William C., Sh-168-1; Sgt I Co 129th OH Inf; 62 to 64; 136 Hind St, Memphis PO
BOSSHAM, Eli F., Mn-121-1; Pvt B Co 6th tN Cav; 25 Aug 62 to 17 Jul 65; Bethel Springs PO; cronic sore eyes & longs
BOSTICK, Burton, Ru-239-1; Fireman Bragg; Jan 1 63 to Sep 65; Overall PO
BOSTICK, Charles R., Hn-77-1; Pvt K Co 6th TN Cav; 1 Jan 64 to 10 Aug 65; PO omitted
BOSTICK, Edmon D., De-26-3; 1st Sgt D Co 7th TN; 24 Sep 62 to 25 Oct 63; Poplar Springs PO
BOSTON, David C., D-99-2; Pvt B Co 8th TN Mtd Inf; Feb 25 65 to Aug 17 65; PO omitted
BOSWELL, S., He-57-1; Pvt I Co 21st TN Cav; 7-1-62 to 5-1-65; Juno PO; CONF
BOTAN, Ben, Fr-47-3; Pvt B Co 14th MO Cav; 3-62 to 12-63; Medina PO
BOTTELS, Lusein, Wa-261-1; Capt TN Inf; 10 May 61 to 26 Oct 63; Washington Colleg PO; died from wound; CONF
BOTTS, Hook P., Ro-210-9; Pvt; 1st NC Inf; Rockwood PO; CONF
BOTTS, William F., Dk-31-1; Cpl D Co 4th TN Mtd Inf; 9-23-64 to 8-25-65; Alexandria PO; suffering with Brights disease
BOUDEN, John A., Hm-104-3(1); Pvt B Co 8th TN Cav (2nd NC transferred); 63 to 65; Alpha PO
BOUGH, Anthony, G-66-1; Fireman 35th Reindeer; 15 Nov 63 to 15 Nov 64; Trenton PO; no disability
BOULEN, Daniel, D-58-2; Julia Ward formerly widow of; Pvt E Co; Nashville PO
BOULTON, Napoleon B., Wl-295-2; Pvt G Co 4th Reg Cav; Feb 64 to Aug 25 65; Lebanon PO
BOUMAN, Chares, K-182-2; Sgt K Co 13th TN Cav; Aug 63 to Jun 65; Nast PO; left hand broke, rupture
BOUNDS, Daniel F., K-168-1; Pvt B Co 6th TN Inf; 30 Mar 62 to 27 Apr 65; Knoxville PO
BOUNDS, Elbert S., K-168-2; Pvt B? Co 6th TN Inf; 8 Mar 62 to 27 Apr 65; Knoxville PO
BOUNDS, Thomas J., K-173-1; Sgt B Co 6th TN Inf; 2 Nov 62 to 30 Jun 65; Caswell PO; asthma & lung trouble
BOUSE, Please, Sh-157-3; Pvt K Co 61st US Hvy; 63 to 66; Memphis, Main St. 407 PO
BOUTH, S. H., Gr-81-1; Pvt A Co 2nd TN Cav; 1 Sep 62 to 1 Jul 65; Clear Spring PO; defective in cits
BOUTON, George H., Sm-170-1; Pvt H Co 81st TN Inf; 9-10-62 to 5-15-63; Elmwood PO
BOVILES, Elbert, Br-6-1; Pvt I Co 10th TN Cav; 2-3-64 to 8-18-65; Grief PO; diarrhoea & deafness
BOWAN, James A., Cy-28-1; Pvt J Co 1st KY Cav; 8-8-61 to 2-15-65; Celina PO
BOWDEN, Barley O., Ov-137-1; 1st Sgt A Co 122nd IL Inf; 8-9-62 to 7-15-65; Nettle Carrier PO; sun stroke, recd bayonet wound in face and gunshot wound in head at Tupelo, MS
BOWDEN, Morgan, O-136-1; Pvt A Co 21st TN Inf; 63 to 66; Crocket Sta? PO; shot in left leg and has since been cut off
BOWDON, Prior, Ms-171-1; Pvt B Co 111th nN Inf; 1 Dec 63 to 3 Aug 65; Belfast PO
BOWEN, John T., H-61-4; Pvt F Co 8th GA Inf; 4-61 to 6-63; Chattanooga PO; Sgt F Co 8th GA Inf --6-63 to 4-9-65; CONF
BOWEN, Lee, K-161-3; Mary Montgomery widow of; __ 1st US Hvy Art; Knoxville PO; died of small pox
BOWEN, Reece, Cr-4-1; Lou E. widow of; Pvt G Co 46th TN Cav; 1 Jun 61 to 62; Bells Depot PO; eyes damaged; CONF
BOWEN, William H., Ha-111-2; Pvt A Co 1st TN Lt Art; 1 Mar 64 to 8 Aug 65; Kyle's Ford PO
BOWER, Anthony, Ge-85-2; Pvt A Co 10th MI Cav; Cavey Branch PO; dont remember date
BOWER, Newton M., Ja-85-2; Pvt E Co 5th TN Inf; 3-2-62 to 4-4-65; Birchwood PO; left arm shot off
BOWERMAN, Mary A., Po-149-2(1); widow of US Sol; 3rd Dist
BOWERS, Augustus C., Wa-271-1; Cpl H Co 8th TN Cav; 1 Nov 63 to 11 Sep 65; Boones Creek PO; disease of throught & lungs & wounded in left hand, rumatism
BOWERS, Bailey T., Rb-221-3; Sgt C Co 14th TN ; Apr 1 61 to Apr 1 65; Holmansville PO; flesh wound; CONF
BOWERS, David, D-99-1; Pvt G Co 13th TN Inf; Oct 10 63 to Jan 10 66; Bakers PO; wounded in right arm
BOWERS, David A., Wa-271-1; Sgt H Co 8th TN Cav; Aug 63 to 11 Sep 65; Boones Creek PO; heart trouble
BOWERS, David G., Ro-205-1; Maj A Co 5th TN Inf; 22 Feb 62 to 22 Apr 65; Post Oak Springs PO; sound bodied
BOWERS, Ed., D-49-4; Nashville PO
BOWERS, Isaac, Sn-252-1; Pvt D Co 14th TN Inf; 10-15-63 to 3-26-66; Gallatin PO
BOWERS, James, D-97-1; Pvt A Co 19th NC Inf; Sep 15 61 to 64; Nashville PO; CONF
BOWERS, James N., Se-228-3; Pvt A Co 6th TN Inf; 8 Mar 62 to 18 Mar 65; Cox PO
BOWERS, Jefferson, K-170-1; Pvt K Co 85th IL Inf; 18 Jul 62 to 6 Mar 63; Knoxville PO; gun shot in left thigh; discharged on account disability
BOWERS, John, D-71-2; Nashville PO
BOWERS, Jno. F. M., We-225-1; Sgt K Co 6th TN Cav; 20 Jul 62 to 26 Jul 65; Dresden PO
BOWERS, John J., D-54-3; Pvt; Nashville PO
BOWERS, Joseph P., Ct-42-3; Emeline widow of; Pvt A Co 8th TN Cav; Watauga PO
BOWERS, Lee L., D-70-2; 139 Maple St, Nashville PO
BOWERS, Leonard, Su-242-1; widow of; Regt. Clk. F Co 13th TN Inf; 16 Sep 63 to died 11 Jun 64; Bluff City PO; typhoid fever, remarried--comrade Peters, March 16, 1866
BOWERS, Levi, Lo-192-1; Pvt A Co NC; 61 to 63; Griffitts PO; CONF
BOWERS, Owen, F-36-1; Pvt A Co 61st __; 62 to 65; Brinkley PO
BOWERS, Rachel (see Carriger, Chrisley C.)
BOWERS, Reuben, Ge-87-2; Pvt A Co 8th TN Cav; 11 Jun 63 to 11 Sep 65; Timberridge PO; chronic diarrhea &c
BOWERS, Rufus, Ge-87-1; Sgt A Co 8th TN Cav; 11 Jan 63 to 20 May 65; Little Chucky PO
BOWERS, Samuel, Ro-204-3; Rebecah J. widow of; Elverton PO; discharge no found
BOWERS, Tetter N., Ct-42-1; Pvt A Co 13th TN Cav; 9-2-63 to 5-22-65; Watauga PO; neuralgia, discharged on surgeon's list
BOWERS, William, O-136-2; Pvt G Co 1st TN Cav; Mar 1 63 to Oct 1 65; PO omitted
BOWERS, William A., Se-223-5(1); Serena C. widow of; Pvt B Co 3rd TN Cav; Sep 62 to 4 Jan 63; Sevierville PO; died January 4th 1868
BOWERS, William M., Ct-36-1; Pvt I Co 3rd NC Inf; 1-15-63 to 8-10-65; Roan Mt. PO
BOWMAN, Andrew, Bl-1-2; Pvt D Co 5th TN Inf; 8-16-64 to 6-30-65; Stevens Chapel PO; chronic rheumatism & dyspepsia
BOWMAN, Andrew, Ge-102-2; Pvt E Co 4th TN Inf; 63 to 65; Whig PO
BOWMAN, Andrew J., Wa-274-1; Sarah widow of; Pvt A Co 13th TN Vol; Jonesboro PO
BOWMAN, Andy, Col, Lo-192-3; Pvt L Co 1st TN; Mar 64 to 65; Griffitts PO; rheumatism & black tongue fever
BOWMAN, Blunt, Col, Me-89-1; Pvt I Co 1st US Art; 4-26-64 to 3-31-66; Big Spring PO

BOWMAN, Charlie, Sm-166-3(1); Pvt D Co 8th TN Cav; 2-6-65 to 4-31-65; Monoville PO
BOWMAN, Cyrus S., Gi-127-1; Sgt E Co 3rd US Hvy Art; Sep 16 64 to Apr 30 66; Pulaski PO
BOWMAN, Daniel, Bl-1-2; 2nd Lt D Co 6th TN Inf; 10-26-64 to 6-30-65; Stevens Chapel PO; chronic asthma and sight
BOWMAN, Elijah K., Bl-5-2; Pvt D Co 5th TN Mtd Inf; to 65; Bitts X Roads? PO
BOWMAN, Henry, Bl-5-1; Pvt D Co 6th TN Mtd Inf; 10-22-64 to 6-30-65; Retro PO (Hamilton Co.)
BOWMAN, Hyram, J-77-2; Pvt D Co 8th TN Cav; 2-1-65 to 8-21-65; Gainesboro PO
BOWMAN, Jake T., Br-10-1; Pvt; Cleveland PO
BOWMAN, James, U-245-1; Pvt 13th __; PO omitted
BOWMAN, James, K-161-5(6); Knoxville PO
BOWMAN, James, Ro-202-4; Pvt I Co 1st TN Inf; Oct 62 to Sep 63; Cave Creek PO; gun shot wound
BOWMAN, James W., De-26-1; A Co 7th __; __ to 7 Aug 65; Bible Hill PO
BOWMAN, Jane, G-51-1; widow US Sol; Humboldt PO
BOWMAN, John, Sh-172-2; 55 Union St, Memphis PO; out of city
BOWMAN, John, Un-251-2; Pvt; 2nd Dist
BOWMAN, John, Pu-144-3; Pvt B Co 1st TN Mtd Inf; 12-29-63 to 4-14-65; Hudgins PO; hurt in groin by lifting
BOWMAN, John C., Wa-270-2; Pvt I Co 60th TN Inf; Nov 63 to 65; Austins Springs PO
BOWMAN, John W., Ro-205-4; Col A Co 2nd TN Cav; 20 Aug 61 to __; Kingston PO; rheumatism
BOWMAN, Jonathan, H-49-6; Pvt C Co 1st E TN Lt Art; 6-10-62 to 10-65; PO omitted
BOWMAN, Joseph, Ge-102-1; Pvt E Co 4th TN Inf; Nov 61 to Jul 65; Henshaw PO; chronic diarear; now lame in hip
BOWMAN, Joseph, Bo-19-1; Pvt C Co 6th TN Cav?; 4-4-62 to 65; Rockford PO
BOWMAN, Laura J., De-26-3; widow of US Sol; Poplar Springs PO
BOWMAN, Mahaley, Cr-13-2; widow of US Sol; Pvt; Atwood PO
BOWMAN, Mary J. (see Bullman, Eziekel)
BOWMAN, Richard, Wa-270-2; Pvt I Co 33rd TN Inf; 10 Feb 62 to Apr 65; Austin's Springs PO
BOWMAN, Samuel, Wa-272-3; Pvt I Co 8th TN Cav; 63 to 11 Sep 65; Nellie PO; rheumatism, injury to eyes
BOWMAN, Samuel G., K-182-3; Riverdale PO; CONF
BOWMAN, Sparling, Ge-102-1; Pvt E Co 4th TN Inf; 15 Nov 61 to 7 Jul 65; Camp Creek PO; breast disease
BOWMAN, Sparling, Ge-94-1; Catherine A. widow of; Pvt E Co 4th TN Inf; 18 Nov 61 to 7 Jul 65; Tusculum PO
BOWMAN, Steven, Sh-173-1; Sgt E Co 3rd Hvy Art; Memphis PO
BOWMAN, Theodore, Su-237-1; Margaret E. widow of; Sgt I Co 8th TN Cav; 20 Nov 63 to 11 Sep 65; Boring PO
BOWMAN, Thomas, Fr-112-1; Mary E. widow of; Pvt 7th IN Inf; Tullahoma PO; ruptured by being run over by horse, died suddenly in 1886
BOWMAN, Thos. J., Lo-188-2; Martha P. widow of; 1st Lt A Co 2nd TN Cav; 10 Aug 61 to 6 Oct 64; Erie PO
BOWMAN, William, De-26-1; 2nd Cpl C Co 7th TN Cav; 22 Aug 62 to 65; Genett PO
BOWMAN, William, Sq-164-2(1); Pvt Dunlap PO
BOWMAN, William, Sq-165-1; Pvt; 61 to 62; Delphi PO
BOWMAN, William B., Wa-271-1; Boones Creek PO
BOYER, Lafayett, Br-6-2; Pvt A Co 10th TN Cav; 8-12-63 to 8-1-65; Chutala PO; disease of stomach, indigestion
BOWING, Isaac R., Bo-12-3(1); listed as Joseph D. Cooper on regular census schedule; Pvt L Co 2nd TN Cav; 9-8-63 to 7-6-65; Chilhowee PO
BOWLEN, John W., He-59-1; Sol US; PO omitted
BOWLER, Darus S., R-160-1; Pvt H Co 150th OH; 5-2-64 to 8-22-64; 6th Civil Dist
BOWLER, Jesse, R-162-4; Pvt H Co 13th TN Inf; 6-1-64 to 9-5-65; Dayton PO; had lug fever while in service which effected lungs
BOWLIN, Asa, Ge-98-4; Mary A. widow of; Pvt C Co 4th TN Inf; PO omitted; consumption
BOWLIN, Britton, Ha-117-1; Pvt A Co 10th TN Inf; Jun 63 to Nov 63; Kyle's Ford PO
BOWLIN, James W., Hd-44-1; Pvt H Co 6th TN Cav; 12-12-62 to 7-26-65; Clifton PO (Wayne Co.)
BOWLIN, William, Sq-164-3(1); Nancy widow of; Pvt 4th TN Cav; Dunlap PO
BOWLIN, William F., Ro-205-3; Pvt A Co 2nd TN Inf; 10 Aug 61 to 6 Oct 64; Hatch PO; kidneys affected
BOWLING, Ephraim, A-5-4; alias Jacson, Ephraim; Pvt M Co 1st TN Hvy Art; 9-19-64 to 3-31-66; Clinton PO
BOWLING, Geo. W., Rb-221-3; Pvt D Co 40th TN; Oct 1 64 to Apr 25 66; Adams Station PO
BOWLING, Hawood, F-43-2; Pvt A Co 2nd MI? Cav; 63 to Jan 66; Piperton PO
BOWLING, James, Cl-53-1; Pvt B Co 1st KY Cav; 8-62 to 10-65; Springdale PO; injured by horse falling on him
BOWLING, James P., Hm-109-3; Pvt M Co 1st TN Cav; 22 Jul 63 to 5 Dec 65; Russelville PO
BOWLING, William, Ct-40-5; Pvt F Co 64th VA Cav; __ to 65; Elizabethton PO; CONF
BOWRS, Nicholas, K-186-5; Beaver Ridge PO
BOWSER, Thomas J., Wa-273-1; Pvt B Co 4th TN Cav; 1 Dec 62 to 18 Jul 65; Morning Star PO; lung disease, blind in one eye, a physical wreck
BOYSURELL, Andrew J., Bo-12-1; Pvt H Co 10th TN Cav; 3-7-64 to 8-2-65; Alleghaney Springs PO; shoulder dislocated
BOX, George, Lk-112-1; Pvt C Co 15th TN Inf; 64 to 65; Tiptonville PO; bronchitis, so stated by said Box
BOX, James A., We-227-1; Pvt C Co 7th TN Cav; 10 Aug 63 to 9 Aug 65; Greenfield PO
BOXLEY, Chas., D-58-1; Pvt A Co 15th TN US; __ to 65; Nashville PO
BOYCE, ____, Sh-159-7; Lucinda widow of; Pvt TN; 62 to __ (3 yrs); Memphis (Collins Chapple) PO; wounded and lost health
BOYD, Andrew W., Su-232-1; Pvt B Co 13th TN Cav; 1 Jan 65 to 5 Sep 65; Bridleman's PO; palpatation of heart and rheumatism
BOYD, Charles, Sh-159-7; Pvt; Memphis PO
BOYD, Charles, Hm-103-5; Sgt; Morristown PO; crippled back
BOYD, Christopher A., T-219-1; alias Christopher Hunt; Cpl G Co 4th Hvy Art; 13 Oct 63 to 25 Feb 66; Phelan PO
BOYD, Columbus, Gi-135-2; Pvt; Lynnville PO
BOYD, David, Co-63-2; Cpl K Co 8th TN Cav; 6 Oct 63 to 11 Sep 65; Newport PO; pleurasy & sore eyes from measles
BOYD, David L., Mc-115-1; Pvt I Co 11th TN Cav; 8-7-63 to 9-11-65; Riceville PO; rheumatism & heart trouble
BOYD, Elliot H., Mr-99-2; Pvt G Co 6th TN Mtd Inf; 2-20-65 to 6-30-65; Jasper PO
BOYD, George, K-161-3; Knoxville PO
BOYD, George A., T-214-1; Pvt C Co 88th US Inf; Jan 64 to Jan 65; Dist 9
BOYD, George M., Mc-110-2(1); Pvt F Co 4th TN Cav; 5-63 to 65; Mouse Creek PO; discharge lost
BOYD, George M., Mc-109-6; US Sol; 2nd Civil Dist
BOYD, Gilbert (see McCarroll, Gilbert)
BOYD, J. W., Wl-308-1; Pvt Art TN; Sep 15 61 to May 1 62; Rural Hill PO; CONF
BOYD, James J. R., Ct-40-5; Capt B Co 4th TN Inf; 5-11-63 to __; Elizabethton PO
BOYD, James K., Mc-111-3; Sgt D Co 4th TN Cav; 12-10-62 to 7-18-65; Athens PO
BOYD, John A., Sn-256-1; Soldier; 8th Civil Dist
BOYD, John R., Co-63-2; Blacksmith B Co 9th MI Cav; Newport PO
BOYD, John T., Mc-111-2; Mary T. widow of; Pvt D Co 4th TN Cav; 12-10-62 to 7-12-65; Athens PO
BOYD, John W., Su-240-3; Sgt K Co 8th TN Cav; 11 Oct 63 to 11 Sep 65; Slawghter PO; chronic spinal epochor?
BOYD, John W., Dy-32-1; US Sol; Trimble PO
BOYD, JOhn W., D-46-2; Sol US; Nashville PO
BOYD, Joseph, Ru-13-3; Leana widow of; PVt C Co 111th Reg Inf; 61 to Mar 65; Murfreesboro PO; wounded in leg & shoulder
BOYD, Joshua, C-33-5; Pvt A Co 10th LA Art; Newcomb PO
BOYD, Mannerva, D-71-2; Nashville PO

BOYD, Marquis D., W-191-1; Cpl G Co 6th TN Mtd Inf; 1-65 to 6-6? (6 mos); Safley PO; lost his discharge
BOYD, Peter, Gi-123-1; alias Peter Brown; Pvt F Co 12th TN Col Inf; 2 Aug 63 to Feb 65; Bethel PO
BOYD, Ransum, Gi-135-2; Pvt; Lynnville PO
BOYD, Robert T., Cr-17-1; Pvt B Co 7th TN Cav Reg; 8-21-62 to 6-16-65; Buena Vista PO; scurvy and weakness of eyes
BOYD, Samuel, K-155-1; Pvt M Co 1st Col Hvy Art; Knoxville PO; frost bitten feet
BOYD, Solomon, Sh-173-1; Pvt G Co 59th TN Inf; 7-63 to 6-65; Memphis PO
BOYD, Tate, D-89-1; Pvt P Co 15th TN; Jan 62 to 65; Nashville PO
BOYD, Walter E., T-216-2; 14th Civil Dist
BOYD, William, D-59-1; 6th OH; 1706 Hays St, Nashville PO
BOYD, William, H-65-1; US Sol; Carter Bayce and Leonard Sts, Chattanooga PO
BOYD, William C., Bo-15-4; 1st Sgt A Co 3rd TN Inf; 2-10-62 to 2-23-65; Corn PO; shocked with a shell
BOYD, William Franklin, La-11-2; Mrs. Boyd widow of; Pvt; 62 to 65; Lawrenceburg PO; wounded
BOYDAN, John, H-63-1; Jennie Briggs formerly wife of; Cpl D Co 40th Col Inf; 64 to 65; 707 Cypress, Chattanooga PO
BOYERS, Cassie, Sn-252-3; Gallatin PO
BOYLE, Harry, Sh-161-2; US Sol; 16th Dist
BOYLE, William, Sh-186-1; dead, no papers; Memphis PO; wounded in shoulder, died 1880
BOYNTON, Susan C., K-155-2(1); widow Sol; 90 West Cumberland, Knoxville PO
BOYSAN, Daniel, Rb-223-3(5); Pvt D Co 16th TN Inf; Mar 65 to Apr 65; 9th Dist
BOZARTH, Joseph, Pu-145-4(5); Cpl C Co 1st Mtd Inf; 10-21-63 to 12-13-64; Silver Point PO
BOZARTH, Phineas, Dk-39-1; Pvt A Co 5th TN Cav; 12-18-63 to 8-22-65; Bozarth PO; liver disease & general debility
BOZEMAN, William L., K-154-2; Knoxville PO; CONF
BRABSON, Samuel, Se-223-4; Pvt I Co 1st TN Bat; 10 Jul 64 to 31 Mar 66; Sevierville PO
BRABSON, William P., Se-226-6; Pvt A Co 1st US Hvy Art; 30 Jan 64 to 31 Mar 66; Henrys X Roads PO
BRABSTON, David, Se-226-6; Pvt B Co 1st US Col Hvy Art; 30 Jan 64 to 31 Mar 66; Sinking Springs PO
BRACHRAGLE, William, Sh-189-6; Theresa widow of; Pvt B Co 2nd IL Cav; 8-12-61 to 10-64; Ark & Carolina Sts, Memphis PO
BRACKET, John, Sh-188-2; US Col; Saffron St, Memphis PO
BRACKET, Ruffus M., Ro-205-1; Pvt F Co 2nd TN Inf; 27 Jan 62 to 7 Feb 65; Rockwood PO; rheumatism 20 yrs
BRACKETT, James K., Po-149-1; Seaman Oshtaw; 7-25-64 to 8-23-65; Old Fort PO
BRACKETT, John, Ro-205-3; Hoods Landing PO; CONF
BRACKETT, Thomas, Lo-188-2; Pvt A Co 5th TN Inf; 25 Feb 62 to 4 Apr 65; Stockton PO
BRACKIN, Samuell, Hm-106-1; Pvt G Co 64th NC Inf; Hanible PO; CONF
BRACKIN, Thomas, Hy-74-1; 1st Civil Dist
BRADBERN, James, Bo-15-2; Catherain widow of; Pvt H Co 2nd TN Cav; 10-10-62 to 1-63; Blockhouse PO
BRADBERRY, John H., We-228-1(9); Cpl H Co 6th TN Cav; 22 Aug 62 to 26 Jul 65; Dresden PO; gun shot wound in l. shoulder
BRADBURY, Edward, Lo-191-3; 1st Lt I Co 31st VA Hvy Inf; May 61 to Mar 64; Trigonia PO; gunshot wound--ball passed through nasal bone, nose, frontal articulation, ranged downward through inf. max. cavity open
BRADDOCK, Francis M., Cu-15-2; Pvt F Co 88th IN Inf; 8-7-62 to 6-7-65; Crossville PO
BRADEN, Andrew J., Gi-135-1; Cpl E Co 110th TN Inf; 12-63 to 2-6? (2 yrs 2 mos); Lynnville PO
BRADEN, Bluford, Mg-196-2; Pvt TN Inf; Oliver Springs PO; shot through the left leg
BRADEN, Elizabeth, S-216-2; widow of Sol; 6th & 7th Dist
BRADEN, Granville, S-217-1; PVt F Co 7th TN; 8 Nov 64 to 27 Jul 65; PO omitted
BRADEN, John, D-70-2; Maple St, Nashville PO
BRADEN, Jordon, Gi-135-2; Pvt; Lynnville PO
BRADEN, Joseph, Gi-132-2; Pvt E Co 110th USCV; Pulaski PO
BRADEN, Len, A-6-3(1); Sarah widow of; Pvt J Co 9th TN Cav; 9-63 to 9-65; Olivers PO
BRADEN, Wiley, A-5-2; Pvt J Co 9th TN Cav; 8-1-63 to 9-11-65; Clinton PO
BRADEN, William W., Un-258-1; Pvt C Co 1st TN Inf; 18 Aug 61 to 17 Sep 64; Phebe PO
BRADFIELD, Elgah, He-61-3; Elizabeth widow of; C Co 7th TN Cav; 8 Aug 62 to died; 15th Civil Dist
BRADFORD, Chas., D-99-5; Pvt D Co 15th TN Inf; Jul 64 to May 26 66; Nashville PO; Central Hos. for Insane PO
BRADFORD, Crofford, Ch-17-1; Mahalia L. widow of; Henderson PO; killed Memphis, TN
BRADFORD, David A., H-56-6; Pvt HO Inf; 64 to 65; St. Elmo PO
BRADFORD, Isam, D-90-1; Fifer Pvt E Co 15th TN Col; 2 yrs; Nashville PO; not cripple
BRADFORD, James, K-161-3; Mary widow of; Pvt E Co 1st US Hvy Art; Knoxville PO
BRADFORD, John, D-69-1; Pvt C Co 54th R US Col Inf; May 63 to 27 Aug 66; Nashville PO; had his writ sprined
BRADFORD, Leeroy, Hi-85-1; Pvt D Co 56th IL Inf; 1-16-64 to 8-12-65; Naomi PO
BRADFORD, Mack, L-108-2; Pvt; 10th Civil Dist
BRADFORD, Marion, Ha-114-1; Pvt C Co 2nd NC Inf; 1 Oct 63 to 1 Aug 65; Xenophon PO
BRADFORD, Mary J. (see Clark, Ben)
BRADFORD, N. B., Mc-114-6; Mollie widow of; Pvt; Santfordville PO
BRADFORD, Nathaniel, Mu-200-1; Teamster TN Inf; Apr 63 to Oct 64; Mt. Pleasant PO
BRADFORD, Nina, Wl-308-2; Stewart Ferry PO (Davidson Co.); captured; CONF
BRADFORD, William F., H-61-2; Col 31st TN Reg; 2-62 to 5-65; Chattanooga PO; CONF
BRADFUTE, Hazel A. C., Br-7-3; Pvt D Co 12th TN Cav; 9-23-63 to 9-5-65; Stamper PO; bronchial affection
BRADLEY, Benjamin, Sm-173-1; PVt G Co 4th TN Mtd Inf; 11-1-64 to 8-25-65; Brush Creek PO; hydra seal
BRADLEY, Charles, Hw-123-2; Rotherwood PO
BRADLEY, Daniel, Di-37-1; 1st Sgt K Co 12th TN Inf; 8-12-63 to 1-16-66; Cumberland Furnace PO
BRADLEY, Edward L., Dk-32-1; Pvt G Co 11th KY Cav; 1-14-63 to 10-1-63; Liberty PO
BRADLEY, Frank, Sh-169-2; US Sol; 9 Jefferson St, Memphis PO
BRADLEY, Harrison, D-77-4; 8th St, Nashville PO
BRADLEY, Henery, D-47-1; Sgt D Co 8th US Inf; 3-62 to 6-65; Jackson St, Nashville PO
BRADLEY, John, Mo-130-2; Pvt D Co 8th TN Mtd Inf; 7-12-64 to 12-25-64; Ballplay PO
BRADLEY, John K., Ge-92-2; Sibby widow of; __ K Co 1st TN Cav; 12 Jul 62 to 5 Jun 65; Laurel Gap PO
BRADLEY, John W., We-223-1; Pvt F Co 154th S TN Cav; Apr 61 to Dec 63; Palmersville PO; wounded in right elbow; CONF
BRADLEY, Joseph B., Cr-4-4; Pvt C Co; Bells Depot PO; wounded left leg; CONF
BRADLEY, Milton, K-161-2; Knoxville PO
BRADLEY, Napolion, Dk-33-1; Pvt G Co 1st TN Inf; 2-5-64 to 4-27-65; 4th Civil Dist; lungs & ruptured
BRADLEY, Richard, Hw-123-2; alias Phipps, Richard; Cpl A Co US Cav; 1 Sep 65 to 24 Mar 66; Solitude PO
BRADLEY, W. M., G-57-3; Yorkville PO; CONF
BRADLEY, William, Ha-111-2; Pvt A Co 64th TN Inf; 62 to Apr 65; Upper Clinch PO; CONF
BRADLEY, William A., K-177-6; Pvt F Co 3rd TN Inf; 11 Feb 62 to 23 Feb 65; Powells Station PO; diarrhoea & rheumatism since 1862
BRADLEY, William T., K-186-1; Pvt G Co 6th TN Inf; 18 Apr 66 to 17 May 66; Chumlea PO; rheumatism, at home unable to work
BRADLEY, Wilson, Co-69-7(3); Pvt F Co 16th NC Inf; 1 May 63 to 1 May 65; Rankin PO; CONF

BRADLY, Lewis, Hw-123-1; Pvt 9th tN Cav; 64 to 65; Rotherwood PO
BRADLY, Matthew, K-176-2; Pvt G Co 7th TN Cav; 62 to 65; Halls X Roads PO
BRADLY, Solomon, Hw-123-1; Pvt E Co 10th MI Cav; 63 to 65; Solitude PO
BRADSHAW, Anderson, Sh-150-3; (Anderson Jackson); Marine Silver Lake 23; 63 to 64; Bartlett PO
BRADSHAW, Arch., Cr-13-1; Pvt C Co 40th TN Inf; Jul 62 to Apr 65; Atwood PO; wounded at Chatanooga PO
BRADSHAW, George, Sh-178-4; US Sol; 338 Union, Memphis PO
BRADSHAW, George, Sh-178-2; Edward Isaac alias; Artificer M Co 3rd US; 12-22-63 to __; Pvt E Co 46th US--1-64 to 1-30-66; 338 Union St, Memphis PO
BRADSHAW, Hannah, Cf-38-1; widow; 10th Civil Dist
BRADSHAW, Hudson, D-94-1; Pvt C Co 40th TN Inf; Aug 17 64 to Apr 25 66; c/o G. M. Campbell, Nashville PO; 1 eye out from military service, pension applied for
BRADSHAW, Jacob, Sh-198-1; PVt D Co 106th Col Inf & 40th Col Inf; 5-63 to 5-66; Memphis PO; discharge stolen from him in a hand satchel with his clothing
BRADSHAW, James E., O-138-2; Pvt G Co 15th TN (C); 20 Dec 61 to 20 Dec 64; Lanes PO; CONF
BRADSHAW, Jason A., Wa-262-1; Maj 12th TN Cav; 26 Dec 62 to Oct 24 65; Telfords PO; cron. dirrhea & spine affection
BRADSHAW, John, Je-141-1; Pvt D Co 3rd TN Inf; Jan 64 to Jan 65; New Market PO
BRADSHAW, John H., Ro-210-8; Mary C. widow of; Pvt; Rockwood PO
BRADSHAW, Peter C., O-138-1; Pvt A Co 1st? TN; 20 Sep 62 to 25 Dec 62; Elbridge PO; CONF
BRADSHAW, Solomon, Sh-159-4; Sgt B Co; 30 Apr 66 to 30 Apr 65 (sic); Memphis PO
BRADSHAW, William, A-9-5(3); Pvt __ Co 3rd TN Inf; Dutch Valley PO; rheumatism, discharge in hands of pension attorney
BRADSTON, Samuel C., Mg-197-3; Cpl B Co 2nd TN Inf; 10 Aug 61 to 6 Oct 64; Crooked Ford PO; a fall injuring hip, back & head
BRADY, Braxton, Mo-130-3; Pvt B Co; Ballplay PO
BRADY, George, Co-69-5; Deda widow of; Pvt C Co 2nd NC Cal; Dec 61 to Aug 65; PO omitted
BRADY, Hugh J., V-178-1; Col 206th PA Inf; 11-1-62 to 6-26-65; Meade PO
BRADY, James, Hy-178-1; Pvt I Co 17th MS? Inf; 9 May 61 to 3 Aug 64; Jones PO
BRADY, John, K-183-3; Pvt H Co 8th TN Cav; Thorn Grove PO
BRADY, Mitchell, Sn-253-1; Pvt K Co 168th OH Inf; 5-2-64 to 9-8-64; No. One PO
BRADY, Nathan, D-45-3; Pvt D Co 4th TN Cav; 9-22-64 to 8-25-65; Nashville PO
BRADY, Simon C., K-161-1; Belle widow of; Pvt D Co 8th TN Inf; 28 Mar 63 to 30 Jun 65; Knoxville PO
BRAGG, Elmore, We-221-6(2); Pvt TN Cav; Apr 64 to May 64; Martin PO; CONF
BRAGG, George W., Su-241-1; Pvt B Co (and E) 8th TN Cav; 23 Jul 63 to 17 May 64; Clover Bottoms PO; in head and whole body
BRAGG, Jacson (see Glays, Jacson)
BRAGG, Nich, Je-138-2; US Sol; 4th Civil Dist
BRAIKBILL, John, K-156-5; Pvt A Co 3rd TN Cav; 15 Sep 62 to 3 Aug 65; 102 State St, Knoxville PO
BRALEY, David K., Hm-109-1; Pvt F Co 68th OH Inf; 1 Nov 61 to 11 Jan 65; Russelville PO; gunshot wound
BRAMBLE, Robert A., T-217-1(39); Pvt B Co 136th IL Inf; 16 May 64 to 22 Oct 64; Bride PO
BRAMEL, John P., S-214-1; Carrilla J. widow of; Pvt A Co 10th KY Cav; Sep 61 to Sep 62; Robbins PO
BRAMER, Deadrick, Je-143-2; Maria wife of; Quartermaster Sgt D Co 1st KY Hvy Art; 4 Mar 64 to 31 Mar 66; Mossy Green PO
bramer, Georg (see Rice, George)
BRAMLETT, Gilbert, Gi-132-4; Pvt F Co 111th USCV; Sep 63 to __; Wales PO; deserted
BRANAM, Andrew J., L-105-1; Pvt; 64 to 65; Curve PO; does not remember the dates

BRANAM, Beverage, Je-147-1; Wagoner I Co 2nd TN Cav; 22 Sep 62 to Jul 65; Shady Grove PO
BRANAN, John, H-66-2; Pvt 10th OH Inf; Chattanooga PO
BRANCH, Andrew, Mo-110-3(1); Eliza widow of; Pvt A Co 5th TN Inf; Mouse Creek PO; died with small pox in camp
BRANCH, Calline, Dy-29-1; widow US Sol; 9th Civil Dist
BRANCH, Henry, T-206-1; Pvt I Co 138th GA Inf; Sep to __; Covington PO
BRANCH, J. J., He-57-2; Pvt F Co 7th TN Cav; 8-3-62 to 10-25-63; Peaele Grove PO; vaccination, final enlisted A Co 7th TN Inf
BRANCH, John W., K-176-3; Capt G Co 59th IN Inf; 11 Oct 61 to 1 Apr 65; Halls X Roads PO
BRANCH, K., Cr-8-2; A Co 12th TN Cav; 12 Jan 61 to May 65; Maury City PO; CONF
BRANCH, Martin V., Be-1-1; 13th Dist
BRANCH, Randall, Sh-157-4; Nelly widow; White Haven PO; killed in battle, he is suposed to have been kill in the battle of Vicksburg, MS
BRANDBURG, Dave M., Cr-3-1; Pvt L Co 1st MD; Apr 6 64 to Jul 65; Gadsden PO
BRANDETT, Robert, Gi-127-6; Pvt F Co 111th TN Col Inf; Pulaski PO; papers lost
BRANDFORD, John, J-82-1; Pvt 1st TN Mtd Inf; Bloomington PO
BRANDON, Allen H., Cr-19-1; Pvt G Co 2nd TN Cav; 12-29-63 to 2-7-65; Buxter PO
BRANDON, Chronicle S., Be-1-5; Pvt; Coxburg PO; discharge lost
BRANDON, Harrison E., Ro-210-6; Harriet A. widow of; Pvt F Co 2nd TN Cav; 1 Aug 62 to 6 Aug 65; Rockwood PO; loss left eye
BRANDON, Harrison S., Cr-14-1; Pvt G Co 7th TN Cav; 5 Aug 62 to 25 Oct 63; Clarksburg PO
BRANDON, James M., Cr-14-1; Pvt C Co 7th TN Cav; 6 Aug 63 to 22 Nov 63; PO omitted
BRANDON, Jerry, Gi-128-2; Pvt I Co 12th TN Cav; Feb 10 64 to May 28 65; Pulaski PO
BRANDON, John D., Cr-14-1; Cpl G Co 7th TN Cav; 5 Aug 62 to 25 Oct 63; Clarksburg PO; reenlisted veteran, Hardies Batalion
BRANDON, John H. Sr., Ge-98-5; Pvt H Co 4th TN Cav; 4 Mar 63 to 12 Jul 65; Jeroldstown PO; disease of lungs & heart and chronic diarhea
BRANDON, Lewis C., Hd-54-1; Sgt D Co 5th TN Cav; 1 Oct 63 to 26 Jul 65; Saltillo PO
BRANDON, Margaret (see McCory, John R.)
BRANDON, Mary A., Hd-44-1; widow of Sol; no PO
BRANDON, William, K-169-2; D Co 3rd TN Inf; 10 Feb 62 to 23 Feb 65; Knoxville PO
BRANDT, Gilbert S., Hu-106-1; Pvt PA Art; Waverly PO
BRANHAM, Andrew, Br-12-4; Pvt E Co 5th tN Inf; Etola PO; frost bit feet
BRANHAM, John, Sn-264-2; Portland PO
BRANHAM, Pete, O-141-1; Union City PO; sold discharge, forgot dates
BRANHAM, Sturlin, Br-7-4; Pvt E Co 7th TN Mtd Inf; 12-3-64 to 7-27-65; Cleveland PO; blind
BRANHANBURG, Abram, C-32-2; Pvt D Co 8th KY Inf; 9-1-61 to __; Pine Mountain? PO
BRANNAJAN, Pat, La-117-1; Pvt D Co 69th NY Inf; Jun 14 64 to __ (1 yr 8 mos); 15th Dist
BRANNAM, John W., Cr-20-2; Sgt A Co 15th TN Cav; 62 to 65; PO omitted; CONF
BRANNAN, Sarah, Bo-12-4; Sarah widow US Sol; 17th Dist
BRANNANS, James, Se-220-1; Catharine widow of; Pvt I Co 2nd TN Cav; PO omitted; died at Richmond VA
BRANNOCK, Adolphus, Sh-198-2; Pvt M Co 3rd Col Hvy Art; 11-15-65 to 4-30-66; Memphis PO; has his discharge
BRANNUM, Sol G., K-156-5; Pvt B Co 6th AL Art; 21 Apr 61 to 1 Jan 65; 5 W. Cumberland St, Knoxville PO; CONF
BRANNUM, William M., K-166-2; Pvt I Co 2nd TN Cav; 22 Sep 62 to 6 Jul 65; Knoxville PO; wounded through right chest
BRANSCOMB, Alex, F-46-2; Cpl D Co 59th TN; 63 to 66; LaGrange PO; arm injured by shell, Alex is needy
BRANSFORD, Ellen, O-141-1; Union City PO; discharge lost (widow)

BRANSON, Alexander, Hd-50-2; Cpl F Co 10th TN Mtd Inf; May 6 62 to Nov 6 62; Walnut Grove PO
BRANSON, Alford, Gr-82-1; Cpl M Co 1st TN Cav; 1 Nov 62 to 19 Jan 65; Ambro PO
BRANSON, Frank M., Ge-91-2; Cpl E Co 1st TN Art; 9 Oct 63 to Apr-Aug 65; Greeneville PO; catarrh & several others
BRANSON, David, Gr-81-3(1); Pvt H Co 1st TN Cav; 15 Jul 62 to 15 Jan 64; Clear Spring PO; menter defect, disabled at times
BRANSON, Eli M., Un-251-2; Pvt H Co 26th TN Inf; 2 Oct 62 to 25 May 65; Esco PO; kidney disease
BRANSON, Gains, Gr-81-3(1); Cpl G Co 8th TN Cav; 6 Aug 63 to 19 Sep 65; Clear Spring PO; rheumatism, disabled partly
BRANSON, Henry, Ro-201-5(3); Mary Wells widow of; Pvt D Co 5th TN Inf; 27 Feb 62 to died in the army; Kingston PO
BRANSON, Huston, Gr-81-3(1); Eliza J. widow of; Pvt C Co 1st TN Malisha; 66 to __ (3 mos); Clear Spring PO; deraingment stummach, disabled at times
BRANSON, James W., Un-250-1; Capt D Co 1st TN Inf; 9 Aug 61 to 17 Sep 64; Maynardville PO; chronic stricture of blader
BRANSON, Newton, Gr-82-1; Pvt H Co 1st TN Cav; 1 Nov 62 to 19 Jun 65; Ambro PO
BRANSON, Thomas L., Un-252-3; Pvt B Co 1st TN Inf; 9 Aug 61 to 17 Sep 64; Nave Hill PO
BRANTLEY, John, M-57-3; Pvt 4th MI Cav; 62 to 65; Orchard Knob PO
BRANUM, Hilory F., C-32-1; Pvt F Co 6th TN Inf; 2-63 to 6-10-65; Pine Mountain PO; rupture 26 yrs
BRANUM, James, C-32-1; Pvt H Co 148th IN Inf; 6-10-64 to 5-10-65; Newcomb PO; kidney & lunges 25 yrs
BRANUM, William R., C-32-1; Pvt C Co 49th KY Inf; 8-10-63 to 6-65; Pine Mountain PO; by reaper of measels. 25 yrs
BRANUM, William T., R-161-2; Pvt B Co 5th TN Inf; 10-12-63 to 6-31-65; Dayton PO; (later) discharged from co I
BRASEL, Levi, Mg-197-3; Pvt G Co 8th tN Cav; 26 Jul 63 to 19 Sep 65; Crooked Fork PO; chronic rheumatism __ in heart
BRASHEARS, John E., A-4-3; Pvt J Co 1st TN Inf; 11-2-61 to 11-3-64; Coal Creek PO; eyes injured, discharge lost
BRASHEARS, John H., Ro-204-1; Pvt E Co 1st TN Inf; 20 Aug 61 to 17 Oct 64; Elverton PO
BRASHEARS, Samuel, Ro-204-4; Pvt G Co 1st TN Inf; 9 Aug 61 to 17 Sep 64; Kreis PO; lung dis. & varicose veins
BRASHEARS, W. J., Gi-139-3; Pvt K Co 18th MO Inf; 9-63 to 6-65; Campbellsville PO; sore eyes & piles
BRASHEARS, William, Ro-211-2; Drummer H Co 3rd TN Inf; 10 Feb 62 to 23 Feb 65; Webster PO; disabled by measles
BRASSELL, James R., Pu-144-2; Double Springs PO
BRASSELL, William, Pu-144-3; Pvt I Co 5th TN Mtd Inf; 5-11-64 to 7-22-65; Ai PO; mumps
BRASSWELL, Alexander D., Sn-260-6; Pvt; 61 to 64; Pondville PO; 14 mos in prison; CONF
BRASSWELL, John T., F-40-2; Pvt B Co 12th TN Cav; 1 Sep 62 to 7 Sep 64; Hickory Withe PO; CONF
BRASWELL, E. L., Sn-260-7; Cpl C Co 13th KY Cav; 8-25-63 to 1-10-65; A.B.C. PO; rheumatism spine & lung disease. Mr. Ellison L. Braswell is applicant for a pension, much of his time he is confined to his bed with rheumatism
BRASWELL, James M., Dk-33-1; Pvt A Co 5th TN Cav; 1-1-64 to 8-14-65; Dowelltown PO
BRASWELL, Peter, Dk-33-2; Pvt A Co 5th TN Cav; 12-21-63 to 8-14-65; Dowelltown PO; prualicious in both legs
BRATCHER, William W., Un-257-1; Pvt C Co 4th TN Cav; 17 Jul 62 to 12 Jul 65; New Prospect PO; chills & fever settled on head
BRATEN, Elijah J., W1-300-1; Matilda A. widow of; Pvt A Co 5th TN Cav; Oct 62 to 4 Dec 64; Watertown PO
BRATSCHI, John H., Ho-97-1; Pvt D Co 74th PA Inf; 10 Sep 61 to 17 Aug 62; Erin PO; verycose vaines both legs

BRATTEN, J. F. (see Jackson, Jacob)
BRATTEN, Paten, Di-30-1; Pvt A Co 12th TN Cav; 9-63 to 64 (1 yr); Dickson PO
BRATTON, Joseph M., Fr-112-3; Lt D Co 44th TN Inf; 11-1-60 to 5-11-61; Decherd PO; CONF
BRATTON, Thomas E., Dk-34-4; Sgt A Co 5th TN Cav; 7-30-62 to 8-15-65; Dowelltown PO; left leg hurt by horse falling
BRATTON, William, H-76-2; Pvt F Co 40th TN Inf; Chattanooga PO
BRAUGHMAN, Alice (see Hays, George)
BRAUN, Mena (see Frank, Augustus)
BRAUNER, Frank, K-161-5(6); alias Frank Brown; Pvt G Co 1st US Hvy Art; 22 May 64 to 31 Mar 66; Knoxville PO
BRAUNER, Rolack L., O-140-1; Pvt E Co 20th KY Inf; 12 Oct 61 to 22 Jan 64; Union City PO
BRAUNER, Yillie L., O-140-1; Cpl E Co 20th KY Inf; 12 Oct 61 to Jun 62; Union City PO; bronchitus effects of exposure caused death
BRAWNER, Harrison, M-108-4; Susanah widow of; Pvt A Co 5th KY Inf; 61 to 64; S. Hayesville PO; discharge lost
BRAWNER, Jeremiah, M-106-1; Pvt I Co 9th KY Vol Inf; 11-61 to __; Lafayette PO; sent home sick and never got a discharge
BRAXTON, Eward D., Ro-201-3(1); Sgt K Co 1st TN Hvy Art; 1 Aug 64 to 31 Mar 66; Kingston PO
BRAXTON, Henry, Sh-179-2; 361 Beal St, Memphis PO
BRAXTON, Thomas, Ro-201-6; Amanda widow of; Pvt K Co 1st TN Hvy Art; 1 Aug 64 to 31 Mar 66; Kingston PO
BRAY, Fidello L., Hw-127-1; Pvt L Co 8th TN Cav; 17 Sep 63 to 19 Sep 65; Rogersville PO; disease of eyes, stomach, kidney &c
BRAY, John, A-9-2; Pvt G Co 2nd TN Inf; 6-1-63 to 8-3-65; Podopholine PO; measles resulting in disease of head & lungs
BRAY, John Br., A-2-2; Pvt 7th TN Inf; 64 to 65; Bull Run PO (Knox Co.); formerly Co H 102nd TN Inf
BRAY, Joshua, A-2-2; Pvt 7th TN Inf; 64 to 65; Bull Run PO (Knox Co.); formerly Co H 102nd TN Inf
BRAY, McHenry, Ha-116-1; Pvt I Co 8th TN Inf; 1 Jul 63 to May? 65; Bray's PO
BRAY, Patrick, Hw-119-1; Sgt 1st TN Cav; 62 to 65; Lee Valley PO; urine affection, died Jun 4, 1880
BRAY, Perry, A-6-3(1); Pvt G Co 7th TN Inf; 4-64 to 3-65; Olivers PO
BRAY, Thomas, Hw-119-3(1); Pvt B Co 4th TN Cav; 22 Dec 62 to 12 Jul 65; Rogersville PO; sun stroke
BRAY, Thomas P., K-184-1; Pvt B Co 1st TN Cav; 10 Oct 62 to 10 Apr 65; Riverdale PO
BRAY, Wiley, Ca-25-1; Martha widow of; Shoat? Mountain PO
BRAY, William R., Wa-268-2; Nancy A. widow of; Johnson City PO
BRAY, Wilson, M-107-3; Pvt F Co 1st TN Mtd Inf; 1-18-64 to 5-3-65; Gamaliel PO (Monroe Co. KY); kidney disease
BRAYLER, Thomas, Ge-83-3; Mary widow of; Pvt E Co 4th TN Inf; 4 Apr 63 to 2 Aug 65; Painters PO; abses of liver & side
BRAZEAL, John G., Lo-195-2(1); Pvt D Co 5th TN Inf; 26 Feb 62 to 30 Mar 65; Oral PO (Roane Co.); piles
BRAZEAL, Willis L., Ro-210-1; Pvt I Co 1st TN Inf; 9 Aug 61 to 12 Aug 63; Rockwood PO; stomach disease
BRAZEE, George A., H-54-4; Pvt I Co 3rd CT Inf; 4-61 to 61 (3 mos); Pvt D Co 150th NY Inf; East Chattanooga PO
BRAZEL, Jefferson, Dk-35-2; Pvt I Co 1st TN Mtd Inf; 9-25-64 to 7-22-65; Temperance Hall PO
BRAZELTON, Isaac, Je-143-1; Sgt L Co 1st US CA Hvy; 11 Aug 64 to 31 Mar 66; Mossy Creek PO; diareah; the exact day of enlistment not known
BRAZELTON, Laban, D-63-3; Pvt US Col; Nashville PO
BRAZIEL, Thomas, Lo-194-2; PO omitted; CONF
BRAZIER, Jerry, W-189-3(2); Lt G Co 47th OH Inf; 9-61 to 4-64; McMinnville PO
BRAZZELL, Green B., J-77-1; Pvt B Co 8th TN Cav; 1-15-65 to 8-17-65; Gainesboro PO; fever & fell on left leg

BRAZZELL, James, Di-30-2; Pvt K Co 11th TN Inf; 5-25-61 to 7-1-64; Dickson PO; CONF
BRAZZLETON, Andrew, Je-142-2; Leanna widow of; Sgt L Co 1st Col Inf; New Market PO
BRAZZLETON, Cyrus, Je-142-2; Mariah widow of; Pvt L Co 1st USCA Hvy; 11 Aug 64 to 31 Mar 66; New Market PO
BRAZZLETON, John, Lo-189-1; alias John Dick; Pvt; Philadelphia PO; discharge lost, no information
BREAZEAL, James, Ro-202-5; Susan E. Hinds widow of; Pvt I Co 1st TN Inf; 9 Aug 61 to 4 Aug 64; Cave Creek PO; deafness, this widow has married
BREAZEALE, William K?, Ro-201-5(3); Elizabeth E. widow of; Cpl I Co 1st TN Inf; 9 Aug 61 to died in the army; Kingston PO
BRECKEEN, Levi R., Ms-180-1; Sgt F Co 1st TN Cav; 8-27-63 to 6-16-64; Lewisburg PO; rheumatism, he is getting old
BREDEN, George, Bo-21-3; Mary A. widow of; Pvt C Co 8th TN Cav; 10-1-63 to 9-11-65; Veeba PO
BREEDEN, Bryant, Se-219-3; Pvt C Co 8th TN Cav; 1 Oct 63 to 11 Sep 65; Jones Cave PO
BREEDEN, Fransis M., Mo-127-2; Pvt D Co 11th TN Cav; 63 to 65; Notchy PO
BREEDEN, Mathew, Se-223-2; Pvt I Co 2nd TN Cav; 2 Aug 63 to 6 Jul 65; Henderson Springs PO; diarrhea & piles
BREEDEN, Rufus G., Lo-189-2; Orderly F Co 62nd TN Inf; 15 Sep 62 to ___; Philadelphia PO; paroled at Vicksburg, not rejoined?
BREEDIN, Marrell, Se-219-1; Pvt I Co 2nd TN Cav; 22 Sep 62 to Jul 65; East York PO; maimed in left foot
BREEDLOVE, Joseph, We-220-2; Mary widow of; Pvt C Co 8th TN; 64 to Feb 10 66; 1st Civil Dist
BREES, Danel, Ro-209-3; Pvt B Co 10th TN Inf; 61 to 15 Aug 65; Glen Alice PO; CONF
BREES, Jack, Ro-209-3; Pvt A Co; Glen Alice PO; CONF
BREN?, Rulen, Bl-3-2; Martha E. widow of; Pvt F Co 2nd TN Cav; 6-61 to 64; Orones Store PO
BRENAN, Thomas, Mo-120-3(1); Sgt G Co 93rd OH Inf; 8-12-62 to 5-16-65; Sweetwater PO; wounded at Chickamauga and Nashville
BRENNER, John, Sh-167-1; Pvt LPC Co 4th LA; 28 Apr 61 to 15 Jul 62; PO omitted; CONF
BRENT, James, Dk-32-2; Pvt K Co 5th TN Cav; 5-20-63 to 8-14-65; Temperance Hall PO; rheumatism
BRENTZ, Mingo, Ms-171-2; Belfast PO
BRESLER, Dave W., H-60-4; Pvt & Cpl C Co 137th PA Inf; 8-5-62 to 6-6-63; Chattanooga PO
BRESNAN, Thomas, Sh-179-3(1); Pvt B Co 3rd US Cav; 4-13-58 to 4-13-63; Memphis PO
BRETTON, William R., Dk-32-5; Cpl A Co 5th TN Cav; 7-8-62 to 6-25-65; Liberty PO; rheumatism caused by measles
BREWER, Ambros, Ha-114-1; Pvt C Co 3rd TN Cav; 2 Mar 61 to 3 Apr 65; Xenophon PO; CONF
BREWER, Daniel, K-171-5(4); Pvt; 65 to 65 (3 mos); Bearden PO
BREWER, Daniel C., H-53-4; Bugler D Co TN Inf; 61 to 65; Ridgedale PO; fell--hurt his hip
BREWER, Edmon, Be-6-1; Pvt; Big Sandy PO
BREWER, Edmond, Rb-219-2; Pvt E Co 17th KY Reg; 63 to 64; Orlinda PO; Cavalry
BREWER, Edmond, Rb-219-2; Pvt D Co 52nd KY Reg; Sep 61 to 63; Orlinda PO; mounted infantry
BREWER, Ellen, He-59-1; widow of US Sol; PO omitted
BREWER, Ezra, K-166-3; Rhoda B. widow of; Pvt E Co 8th TN Cav; 10 Oct 63 to 7 Jun 65; Knoxville PO
BREWER, George, G-57-3; 8th Dist
BREWER, George, G-57-1; 61 to 65; Yorkville PO; CONF
BREWER, George, Sh-145-1; Cpl I Co 59th US Col Inf; 27 Mar 63 to 31 Jan 66; Millington PO; Cap. A. J. Henderson, Co I
BREWER, George W., Mr-99-2; Pvt K Co 10th TN Col; 9-13-64 to 8-1-65; Jasper PO
BREWER, George W., K-154-4; Knoxville PO; CONF
BREWER, J. C., Bo-11-4; Pvt D Co 2nd TN Cav; 9-1-62 to 7-7-65; Brick Mill PO
BREWER, James S., Mc-118-1; Cpl A Co 5th TN Mtd Inf; 9-1-64 to 6-26-65; Cogshill PO; rheumatism 25 yrs

BREWER, Jane, Wy-171-3; widow of US Sol; 5th Civil Dist
BREWER, John, K-171-5(4); Pvt; 65 to 65 (3 mos); Bearden PO
BREWER, John J., Pu-143-1; Sgt D Co 2nd TN Inf; 9-1-61 to 9-18-63; Cookville PO
BREWER, John O., Sh-201-3; Pvt M Co 5th MO Cav; 61 to 66; Memphis PO
BREWER, John S., K-179-3; Sgt D Co 3rd TN Inf; 10 Feb 62 to 28 Feb 65; Rodelin PO
BREWER, Joseph, Lo-189-3(1); Pvt A Co 5th TN Inf; 25 Feb 62 to 4 Apr 65; Philadelphia PO
BREWER, Joseph C., Hw-127-3; Pvt B Co 8th TN Inf; 1 Mar 63 to 30 Jun 65; Rogersville PO; measles settled on lungs
BREWER, Josiah, De-26-3; D Co 61st TN; 7 mos; Poplar Springs PO; CONF
BREWER, P. B., Cr-15-1; Pvt D Co 7th TN Cav; 25 Oct 63 to 25 Jan 65; PO omitted
BREWER, Pleasant B., Cu-16-1; Pvt G Co 6th TN Inf; 3-25-65 to 6-30-65; Wine Sap PO; lungs affected
BREWER, Riley, Ma-129-1; Hannah widow of; Pvt A Co; Jun 62 to died 62 (4 mos); Jackson PO
BREWER, Thomas J., Je-137-1; Sgt F Co 9th TN Cav; 14 Jul 63 to 22 Mar 65; Hickory Ridge PO
BREWER, William, Lo-189-2; Mary J. widow of; Cpl I Co 5th TN Inf; Oct 62 to 27 Jan 64; Philadelphia PO; died of smallpox
BREWER, Wm., Bo-11-3; Sgt D Co 2nd TN Cav; 9-1-62 to 7-7-65; Brick Mill PO
BREWER, William B., Cu-16-1; Pvt D Co 2nd TN Inf; 9-1-61 to 10-6-64; Wine Sap PO; rheumatism
BREWER?, William T., Be-6-1; Julia A. widow of; Pvt D Co 7th TN Cav; Jan 64 to ___; Big Sandy PO; captured & died in prison
BREWER, William T., Lo-187-1; Mary A. Wallace formerly widow of; Cpl A Co 5th TN Inf; 25 Feb 62 to 4 Apr 65; Loudon PO
BREWINGTON, Joseph, Wh-187-3; Pvt D Co 8th TN Inf; 3-65 to 8-65; Key PO; contracted rheumatism
BRIANT, Nathanial, Ge-90-3; Sgt B Co 13th TN Cav; 63 to 66; Greenville PO
BRIANT, Robert, H-58-4; Pvt I Co 2nd TN Inf; 11-11-61 to 10-26-64; Sale Creek PO; loss of health
BRICE, John W., Hu-104-1(2); Pvt C Co 1st Reg Cav; Feb 19 64 to Mar 31 66; McEwen PO; wound in right hip
BRICE, Nelson, Hw-134-1; Sally widow of; Rogersville PO; disease unknown, no account of his service given
BRICE, Nelson, Hm-103-1; Pvt G Co 1st TN Hvy Art; 63 to 65; Morristown PO
BRICE, Richard, Hw-127-2; Pvt G Co 1st US Hvy Art; May 64 to 31 Mar 66; Rogersville PO; spinal disease, chron. diarrhea
BRICKELL, James, Mc-109-1; Pvt B Co 7th TN Inf; 10-27-64 to ___; Chuckaluck PO; prisoner at Andersonville 3 months
BRICKELL, Joshua, Mc-109-1; Pvt B Co 7th TN Inf; 10-20-64 to 7-27-65; Chuckaluck PO
BRICKEY, John B. J., Bo-14-4; Pvt D Co 2nd TN Cav; 9-1-62 to 7-6-65; Maryvill PO
BRICKEY, Merrity C., Ma-128-1; Pvt 21st KY; Apr 61 to 65; Jackson PO; internal injuries, hernia, pressure of cartridge box while on march
BRICKEY, William, Bo-23-1; Pvt D Co 2nd TN Cav; 9-1-62 to 7-6-65; Tang PO; discharged by reason Gen Or 88?, now suffering from liver disease
BRICKLE, James, Ru-241-4; Cpl A Co 12th TN Inf; 63 to 66; Murfreesboro PO; shot in leg, swelled so that can't work
BRIDGE, James, A-13-3; Pvt B Co 1st WV Lt Art; 10-1-61 to 6-28-65; Briceville PO
BRIDGEFORD, Thomas, F-42-2(4); Pvt H Co 11th USC Inf; Feb 24 64 to Jan 12 66; Rossville PO
BRIDGEFORTH, Benjamin H., Wi-276-1; Pvt B Co 9th TN Cav; Oct 62 to Jan 63; Beechville PO; CONF
BRIDGER, Richard C., Cr-4-5; Pvt; 4-64 to 8-64; Bells Depot PO; CONF
BRIDGES, David, S-216-1; Pvt F Co 7th TN Inf; 8 Nov 64 to 27 Jul 65; Gome Fork PO
BRIDGES, Edmond, Hd-44-1; Pvt H Co 144th IN Inf; 1-65 to 8-15-65; Clifton PO (Wayne Co.); cronic diarrhea & rumattic
BRIDGES, Elen C., K-154-2; widow; Col 10th TN Cav; Knoxville PO

BRIDGES, Isaac, Un-256-2; Pvt C Co 1st TN Inf; 9 Aug 61 to 17 Sep 64; Lost Creek PO; kidney trobble
BRIDGES, James R., Hd-54-1; Pvt US Tyler Gun Boat; 4 Mar 62 to 12 Apr 62; Saltillo PO; mumps & discharged on account of them
BRIDGES, John, A-1-1; Pvt S Co 9th TN Cav; 9-11-63 to 9-11-65; Andersonville PO
BRIDGES, W. A., Cr-16-3; Pvt G Co 2nd TN Cav; Aug 5 62 to Oct 25 63; Huntingdon PO; 2nd West TN Cav or 7th TN
BRIDGES, William, Un-256-2; Pvt I Co 7th TN Mtd Inf; 8 Nov 64 to 17 Jul 65; Lost Creek PO
BRIGES, Larkin W., Hd-52-1; Elza R. widow of; Pvt A Co 10th TN; Jun 4 62 to Jun 4 63; Adamsville PO; measles proved fatal
BRIGGS, Adolphus E., U-249-1; Cpl H Co 8th TN Cav; 28 Sep 63 to 11 Sep 65; Flag Pond PO; amarosis of eyes
BRIGGS, James L., We-231-1; Dist #13
BRIGGS, Jennie (see Boydan, John)
BRIGGS, John R., Ro-202-6; Elizabeth widow of; Cpl H Co 4th TN Inf; Oct 46 to 48; Kingston PO; dropsy, died in service, Mexican War
BRIGGS, Samuel F., Ro-202-6; Pvt H Co 3rd TN Inf; 20 Feb 62 to 25 Feb 65; Kingston PO; gun shot wound
BRIGGS, Stephen M., Cr-10-1; Pvt M Co 8th TN Cav; Mar 62 to 65; Friendship PO; right arm broke, 2 ribs right side, arm cramps from constant use
BRIGGS, Washington (C), Mt-140-1; Pvt D Co 12th Hvy Art; 64 to 5-65; Oak Wood PO
BRIGHAM, Henry Hart, St-164-1; Pvt D Co 8th KY Inf; 62 to 64; Stribling PO
BRIGHT, Alexander, K-178-2; Pvt E Co 1st TN Lt Art; 20 Oct 63 to 1 Jul 65; Virtue PO
BRIGHT, Andrew J., K-174-3(2); Pvt F Co 3rd TN Inf; 10 Feb 62 to 23 Feb 65; Church Grove PO; deseas of liver 25 yrs
BRIGHT, Armestrong, K-175-1; Pvt K Co 1st TN; 18 Aug 62 to 19 Aug 65; Pedigo PO
BRIGHT, Benjamin C., Lo-190-3; Pvt D Co 6th TN Inf; 1 Sep 62 to 12 Jun 65; Piney PO; neuratorphy
BRIGHT, David M., Wa-262-1; Elizabeth widow of; Pvt A Co 3rd TN Mtd Inf; 13 Jun 64 to Nov 13 64; Washington College PO
BRIGHT, David T., Lo-194-1; Pvt G Co 3rd TN Inf; 10 Feb 62 to 28 Feb 65; Muddy Creek PO
BRIGHT, Eli H., K-174-3(2); Pvt F Co 3rd TN Inf; 9 Aug 61 to __; Church Grove PO; deserted about Sep 62
BRIGHT, Fonze, Lo-187-3; Pvt D Co 3rd TN Mtd Inf; 64 to 64 (3 mos); Loudon PO
BRIGHT, Lemuel, We-223-5; Pvt G Co 5th KY Cav; Apr 64 to Jun 64; Palmersville PO; CONF
BRIGHT, Michael, K-174-3(2); Pvt C Co 9th TN Cav; 2 Jul 63 to 11 Sep 65; Church Grove PO; diseas of lungs & rheumatism 26 yrs, total disable from labor
BRIGHT, Robert H., K-165-2; Pvt I Co 3rd TN Inf; 4 Feb 62 to 29 Feb 65; Knoxville PO
BRIGHT, Sam R., Sh-153-1; Pvt; Bailey Sta. PO; did not know commisions
BRIGHT, William, K-175-1; Pvt F Co 1st TN Inf; 13 Sep 62 to 18 May 65; Bullrun PO
BRIGWATERS, Gilbert, Sm-174-2; Pvt G Co 4th TN Inf; Grant PO; discharge lost or misplaced
BRIGZWELL, William J., Ct-44-1; Cpl L Co 13th TN Cav; 9-5-63 to 6-21-65; Hampton PO
BRIME, Jackson, Dk-39-1; Pvt I Co 5th TN Cav; 2-8-64 to 8-14-65; Bozarth PO; crippled in right leg and hip by the falling of his horse
BRIMER, David, Se-226-3; Martha Henry formerly widow of; Pvt D Co 9th TN Cav; Sep 62 to 22 May 63; Sinking Springs PO; died at Galatin TN, measles
BRIMER, Jessee, V-178-1; Cpl D Co 4th KY Cav; 6-17-62 to 6-29-65; Spencer PO; cripled in right knee by horse falling
BRIMER, John, Je-139-2; Pvt F Co 9th TN Cav; 24 Jul 63 to 13 Sep 65; Oak Grove PO
BRIMER, Robert, Ro-209-4; Marsha J. widow of; Pvt F Co 4th TN Inf; Kingston PO
BRIMES, Andrew, Hm-107-2(1); Cpl G Co 4th TN Cav; 19 May 63 to 12 Jul 65; Witts Foundry PO; rheumatism & paralisis

BRIMLEY, Oren Benj., H-75-1; drummer B Co 14th MI Inf; 1-7-62 to __; Chattanooga PO; discharge papers lost
BRIN, James, A-6-6(4); Cpl J Co 11th TN Cav; 9-26-63 to __; Olivers PO
BRINK, Robert N., Sn-256-1; Pvt D Co 10th IN Inf; 8-14-62 to 8-14-65; Gallatin PO; rheumatism and neuralgia
BRINK, Samuel, Wi-279-1; Pvt A Co 64th OH Inf; Oct 61 to Oct 20 64; Franklin PO
BRINK, Samuel, H-59-1; Capt 15th MN Inf; 3-61 to 9-65; Chattanooga PO
BRINKLEY, Jerry, Mu-191-1; Pvt E Co 111th TN Vol; 2-10-64 to 4-30-66; Bigbyville PO
BRINKLEY, Robbert C., Cr-17-1; Pvt K Co 2nd TN Inf; 1-1-64 to 4-20-65; Buena Vista PO; general health impaired, not pention
BRINNAGER, Barbrey M. (see Posey, Hezikiah)
BRINT, Henry, Hr-96-2; on same line as Siler, W.; 4 yrs; Silers PO; Conf
BRISBO, Matt, D-44-2(1); Pvt I Co 2nd KY Cav; 62 to 65; Nashville PO; sun stroke & rhumatism
BRISENTINE, William A., Hi-84-1; 1st Civil Dist
BRISTOL, Jas., Dy-28-1; Pvt B Co 7th TN Cav; Feb 21 62 to Jul 10 65; Finley PO; chronic dirhea, pension of $14 per month
BRIT, Deby (see Britt, Henderson)
BRIT, William A., Cr-16-3; Pvt F Co 7th TN Cav; Aug 15 62 to Oct 25 63; Huntingdon PO; dislocation of knee
BRITON, Charley, Be-5-1; Nancey widow; Pvt F Co 7th TN Cav; 10 Jul 62 to Jun 63; PO omitted
BRITT, Andrew J., Wh-187-2; Pvt D Co 2nd TN Inf; 9-1-61 to 10-6-64; Sparta PO; contracted rheumatism
BRITT, Carter, St-162-1; Blacksmith; Cumberland City PO; enlisted at Clarksville, TN
BRITT, Franklin, Ct-38-2; Emily widow of; Pvt E Co NC Mtd Inf; Milligan PO
BRITT, Henderson, U-245-1; Deby Brit for. widoe of; Pvt K Co 13th TN Cav; 12 Sep 63 to 8 Sep 65; Marbleton PO
BRITT, John, Ge-97-4; Sol US; 16th Civil Dist
BRITT, John C., Ma-126-1; Sgt I Co 8th TN Cav; Sep 63 to Sep 65; Jackson PO; rheumatism & kidney affection; don't remember the exact days of months
BRITT, John D., Wa-263-5; Pvt H Co 8th TN Cav; 15 Sep 63 to 11 Sep 65; Conkling PO
BRITT, Wylie A., Cr-16-2; Pvt F Co 7th TN Cav; Huntingdon PO
BRITTIN, George E., Ge-97-2; Pvt C Co 4th TN Inf; 6 Jun? 63 to 2 Aug 65 (2 yrs 2 mos 28 days); Newmanville PO; weekness of the eyes
BRITTON, Benjamin F., Cr-4-3; Pvt F Co 9th TN Cav; 64 to 65; Bells Depot PO; CONF
BRITTON, Isaac, R-157-2; Sol; 12th Dist, Grandview PO
BRITTON, John A., Co-69-5; Sgt G Co 4th TN Cav; May 63 to Jul 65; Driskill PO; rheumatism in back for awhile, 2 weak
BRITTON, John M., A-5-6(2); Martha E. widow of; 1st Sgt B Co 3rd NC Mtd Inf; 6-18-64 to 8-8-65; Coal Creek PO
BRITTON, Joseph, Hw-125-3; Pvt K Co 19th TN Inf; 62 to 65; Surgoinsville PO; imprisoned at Cin. OH 7 mos; CONF
BRITTON, Theophilus P., Wa-274-2; 1st Sgt C Co 4th TN Inf; 6 Apr 63 to 10 Aug 65; Jonesboro PO
BRITTON, Thomas, Dk-32-1; Cpl A Co 5th TN Cav; 8-14-62 to 10-27-64; 2nd Lt D Co 4th TN Mtd Inf; 10-27-64 to 8-26-65; Liberty PO
BRITTON, Valentine S., Ge-93-1; Sgt G Co 4th TN Inf; 15 Mar 63 to 2 Aug 65; Greeneville PO
BRIXEY, Calvin L., W-193-1; Martha E. widow of; Capt; Vernilla PO; made up a company & was killed before organs in reg
BROADAWAY, Alexander, P-150-1; Pvt F Co 2nd TN Inf; Nov 15 63 to Jun 64; Dist 2
BROADWELL, William H., Wi-277-1; Pvt C Co 31st OH; Aug 20 61 to Sep 19 64; 8th Civil Dist
BROBECK, John G., Ge-91-4; Pvt H Co 8th TN Cav; Greeneville PO; scurvy, rheumatism
BROCK, Alexander, Ja-84-2; Pvt L Co 1st Strong Art TN; 65 to 66; Harrison PO; rheumatism, discharge in attorney's hands and cant give dates

BROCK, Andrew J., Br-6-3; Pvt E Co 7th TN Mtd Inf; 8-12-64 to 65; Chatala PO; disease of lungs & heart result injury
BROCK, Benjamin F., Mc-111-1; Cpl A Co 7th TN Mtd Inf; 9-18-64 to 7-27-65; Mortimer PO
BROCK, Elizabeth, Ro-205-2; widow US Sol; Demmond PO
BROCK, H. H., Cl-53-1; A. Manda widow of; Pvt C Co 1st TN Cav; Springdale PO
BROCK, Hezekiah, K-174-2(1); Pvt I Co 3rd TN Inf; 10 Feb 62 to 23 Feb 65; Snoderly PO; bronchitis; all most total disable from labor
BROCK, James, Ro-209-3; Pvt; Rockwood PO
BROCK, James M., K-174-1; US Sol; 5th Dist
BROCK, John, B-5-3; Pvt C Co 19th IN Inf; 63 to 6? (1 yr 6 mos); St. Elmo PO
BROCK, John L., Ro-204-1; Pvt H Co 4th TN Inf; Apr 63 to 12 May 65; Elverton PO; no discharge found
BROCK, Lawrence, Mc-117-1; Pvt A Co 7th TN Mtd Inf; 8-31-64 to 7-27-65; Mecca PO; piles and deafness
BROCK, Lewis, K-176-1; Pvt I Co 3rd TN Inf; 13 Feb 61 to 12 Jun 65; Mynott PO
BROCK, Martin V., H-58-1; Pvt B Co 10th TN Cav; Sale Creek PO; sick when regt. discharged
BROCK, Michael W., Bl-1-1; Pvt D Co 10th TN Cav; 12-15-63 to 5-20-64; Pikeville PO; crippled --thrown from horse
BROCK, Milton T., Mg-199-2; Pvt M Co 137th IN Inf; 65 to 66; Sunbright PO
BROCK, Moses, K-184-2; Cpl B Co 9th TN Cav; Sep 63 to Jun 65; Thorn Grove PO; defect of the eyes
BROCK, Nepthel I., Dk-35-2; Martha C. widow of; Sgt I Co 1st TN Mtd Inf; 1-1-64 to 7-22-65; Temperance Hall PO
BROCK, Obdiah, K-174-2(1); Pvt F Co 3rd TN Inf; 11 Feb 62 to __; Graveston PO; non as I can find out, deserted
BROCK, Raney W., A-9-6(4); Pvt C Co 2nd TN Inf; 8-6-61 to 2-4-63; Dutch Valley PO; catarrh of head & derangement of the nerves
BROCK, Richard W., H-53-3; 2 yrs 6 mos; Chattanooga PO; ruptured
BROCK, Robbert, K-184-2; Pvt B Co 9th TN Cav; Sep 63 to Jun 65; Thorn Grove PO
BROCK, William?, K-175-2; Pvt D Co 1st TN Inf; 28 Dec 62 to 28 Dec 65; Snoterly PO
BROCKER, Ernest, Gi-122-4; Quarter Gunner USS Kenwood, Missippi Sh. Road Inn?; 15 May 63 to 24 Jun 64; Prospect Sta. PO; discharged on account of being disabled
BROCKET, James H., M-107-5; Pvt B Co 5th TN Cav; 8-6-62 to 6-19-65; Gibbs Cross Roads PO; disease of chest, prisoner at LIbby Prison, VA 15 days
BROCKMAN, Lamuel, K-177-2; US Sol; PO omitted
BROCKUS, William K., U-247-1; Pvt B Co 13th TN Cav; 10 Sep 63 to 5 Sep 65; Erwin PO; disease lungs, injury to left shoulder
BROCKWAY, Chris T., K-160-2; Pvt 8? Co 67th OH; 61 to 7 Dec 65; Knoxville PO
BROCKWELL, Andrew, Wa-276-2; Elvira widow of; Pvt D Co 8th TN Cav; 63 to 5 Sep 65; Mosheim PO
BRODER?, William, Ro-210-7; Leanna widow of; Pvt; Rockwood PO; shot in the leg
BRODIE, John L., St-160-1; Alth A. widow of; Pvt 14th TN Inf; 61 to 64; Lafayette PO (Christian Co. KY); slightly wounded at Bat, Mation; CONF
BRODIE, Thomas, He-61-3; Lousann widow of; 1st Sgt C Co 7th TN Cav; 8 Aug 62 to died; 15th Civil Dist
BRODIGAN, Peter, G-63-1; Pvt F Co 1st AL Cav; Jun 29 63 to Jul 27 64; Milan PO
BROGDEN, Franklin, Mc-114-6; Pvt; Lamontville PO
BROGDON, Eleanor, Lo-188-1; Pvt C Co 3rd TN Cav; 5 Dec 62 to 3 Aug 65; Stockton PO
BROGDON, Henry M., Hm-104-3(1); Pvt F Co 1st TN Cav; 1 Mar 62 to 3 Mar 65; Alpha PO
BROGDON, James T., Hn-77-3(1); Pvt K Co 6th TN Cav; 15 Aug 62 to Aug 65; Henry PO
BROGDON, Matt W., K-183-1; Pvt F Co 1st TN Cav; 6 Mar 62 to 6 Mar 65; Riverdale PO
BROGDON, Thomas, K-184-1; Capt I Co 9th IN Inf; 1 Apr 61 to 11 Apr 65; Riverdale PO
BROIDEN?, Jerome, H-73-3; Pvt G Co 15th TN Inf; 1-20-64 to 4-7-66; Chattanooga PO
BROILS, Samuel N., D-57-4; Pvt A Co; 61 to 65; Nashville PO
BROMLEY, James, G-57-6; Pvt; 61 to 65; Yorkville PO; CONF
BROMLEY, Jason, Mt-140-1; Pvt A Co 83rd IL; 64 to 65 (1 yr 6 mos); Sailors Risk PO
BROMLY, Rily G., Hd-45-2; Pvt B Co 1st AL Cav; Sep 62 to Mar 64; Cerro Gordo PO; 3 ribs broken by horse jumping on right side of him
BROMWELL, William, D-71-1; US; Nashville PO
BRONARD, Edward, La-115-3; Cpl F Co 10th MS Inf; Aug 62 to Jul 65; Summertown PO
BRONAYER, Anthony, H-62-4; Bugler G Co 2nd MO Cav; 209 Market, Chattanooga PO
BRONER, Henry, Cy-27-5(3); Pvt; 63 to __; Spivey PO
BROOK, George W., Lo-193-1; Pvt E Co 10th TN Inf; 1 Mar 63 to 23 Jun 65; Unitia PO
BROOK, Henry, Ma-124-1; Indiana widow of; Pvt E Co MS Inf; Oct 62 to Mar 64; Jackson PO
BROOK, Henry D., Lo-192-2; Pvt E Co 1st TN; 20 Oct 63 to 4 Aug 65; Meadow PO; rheumatism
BROOK, John W., Cl-51-1; Pvt D Co 29th TN Inf; 9-10-62 to 8-20-65; Ritchie PO
BROOK, Willis, Sh-145-3; alias Brook, William; Marine? Conestoga Gunboat; Apr 63 to Jun 65; Millington PO; Capt Selvidge Conestoga transferred to Black Hawk Flag Ship then on the Tempest and discharged from the Tempest at Mound City, IL
BROOKER, Anus, D-50-2; Ellen widow of; Pvt; Nashville PO
BROOKS, Abner K., A-4-3; Pvt F Co 7th TN Mtd Inf; 11-25-64 to 7-27-65; Coal Creek PO
BROOKS, Albert, Hw-128-2; Sarah J. widow of; Sgt H Co 8th TN Inf; 25 Jul 63 to 30 Jun 65; Walnut Hill PO
BROOKS, Albert, Sh-159-8; US Sol; Memphis PO
BROOKS, Alexander, Je-144-2; Sarah E. widow of; Pvt D Co 9th TN Cav; 62 to 65; Talbotts PO; consumption, discharge lost
BROOKS, Alfred, Jo-150-5; Osborn PO; no record found
BROOKS, Alfred A., He-67-1; 2nd Ord Sgt C Co 6th TN Cav; Sep 18 62 to Mar 63; Sardis PO; no disability
BROOKS, Allen, Hy-83-1; Pvt B Co; May 3 63 to Jul 65; Brownsville PO; lost discharge
BROOKS, Amos, Lo-108-2; Pvt A Co 16th LA C Inf; PO omitted
BROOKS, Andrew K., K-184-2; Sgt L Co 2nd TN Cav; Sep 63 to 29 Jun 65; Thorn Grove PO
BROOKS, Anson M., A-5-3; Pvt F Co 7th TN Inf; 10-64 to 8-65; Clinton PO
BROOKS, Archibald T., Ha-112-2; Eliza Rogers formerly widow of; Pvt B Co 1st TN Cav; 11 Mar 62 to 5 Dec 63; Blackwater PO
BROOKS, Charley, Hw-130-2; Mary J. widow of; Pvt A Co TN; 62 to __; Lee Valley PO
BROOKS, Chidister?, Hw-118-2; Mary widow of; Pvt 4th TN Inf; St. Clair PO
BROOKS, Christfor, Ch-12-2; Pvt 21st TN Cav; 1-63 to 65; Custer Point PO; CONF
BROOKS, Daniel D., La-115-2; Pvt F Co 18th OH Inf; 23 Feb 64 to 16 May 65; Summertown PO
BROOKS, David, Ct-40-2; Pvt M Co 1st US Art; 10-14-64 to 3-31-66; Elizabethton PO; chronic diararrhea
BROOKS, David D., Co-61-5(2); Nancy widow of; recruiting officer K Co 9th TN Cav; __ to 1 Apr 65; Bridgeport PO; killed 9 Apr 1865
BROOKS, Edward, Sh-149-3; Pvt A Co 9th US Cav; 11 Nov 63 to Dec 66; Raleigh PO
BROOKS, Francis M., Je-125-1(3); Pvt B Co 9th TN Cav; 20 Sep 63 to 11 Sep 65; Fear Gap PO
BROOKS, G., Fe-44-2; Rhoada widow of; Pvt; Allardt PO
BROOKS, Hannah E. (see Moore, Doctor T.)
BROOKS, Henry, Hw-119-4(1); Pvt I Co 3rd TN Cav; 4 Mar 62 to Aug 65; Alum Well PO; erysipelus
BROOKS, Hiram, Hw-118-2; Pvt D Co 1st TN Cav; 15 Apr 62 to 15 Apr 65; St. Clair PO; cronic rheumatism
BROOKS, Isaac B., A-7-2; Robertsville PO
BROOKS, J. A., Je-135-2; Liza J. widow of; PVt B Co 13th IL Vol; 9 Aug 61 to 2 May 62; Flat Gap PO; diarhae
BROOKS, James, Hw-128-2; 2nd Lt H Co 8th TN Inf; 25 Jul 63 to 30 Jun 65; Walnut Hill PO

BROOKS, James F., Cl-50-1; Pvt J Co 8th TN Cav; 7-10-63 to 9-17-65; Tazewell PO; about 6-2-64
BROOKS, James L., A-4-1; Pvt 16th NC Inf; 61 to 65; Coal Creek PO
BROOKS, Joel, Co-61-6(2); Parthana widow of; Recruiting Officer K Co; Bridgeport PO
BROOKS, John, Gi-123-2; Pvt Col Troops; Bethel PO
BROOKS, John Jr., U-247-1; Pvt B Co 13th TN Cav; 3 Feb 64 to 5 Sep 65; Erwin PO; diarhoea, rheumatism & heart disease 25 yrs
BROOKS, John, Mn-125-1; Pvt D Co 49th US Col Inf; Oct 64 to Feb 66; Corinth, MS PO
BROOKS, John, St-164-1; Pvt A Co 39th OH Inf; Jul 61 to Oct 65; Stribling PO; re-enlisted veteran; CONF
BROOKS, John C., K-185-1; Pvt C Co 29th TN Inf; 63 to 65; Mascott PO; CONF
BROOKS, John L., We-221-4; Pvt A Co 9th TN Inf; Apr 61 to Apr 65; Martin PO; none but a flesh wound; CONF
BROOKS, John S., Li-144-1; Pvt E Battrie 1st KY Art; 11-63 to 8-4-65; Flintville PO
BROOKS, Joseph, Po-152-2; Pvt D Co 3rd TN Mtd Inf; 7-24-64 to 12-24-64; Ducktown PO; fever and jaundice
BROOKS, Joseph, Ha-112-1; 2nd Lt A Co 1st TN Cav; 9 Mar 62 to 4 Apr 65; Datura PO
BROOKS, Joseph A., A-2-1; Pvt C Co 2nd TN Inf; 8-7-61 to 10-6-64; Hynds Creek PO; crushed foot and sore legs
BROOKS, Louis, Sm-169-2; Pvt; Defeated PO; CONF
BROOKS, Luke S., Co-61-6(2); Pvt I Co 60th TN Inf; Bridgeport PO; CONF
BROOKS, Moses, Ro-204-4; Martha J. widow of; Pvt D Co 3rd TN Inf; 63 to 63; Kreis PO; no dis., died in army
BROOKS, Samuel, Mu-213-2; Pvt A Co US; May 61 to May 65; Rally Hill PO
BROOKS, Samuel, Li-155-1; Pvt A Co 42nd US Col Inf; __ to 66; Boon's Hill PO
BROOKS, Samuel, Je-145-2; Pvt D Co 8th TN Cav; 1 Dec 62 to 21 Jun 65; Dumplin PO
BROOKS, Spencer, Ge-69-2; Maria widow of; G Co 61st; 2 yrs 6 mos; Bartlett PO; spine disease
BROOKS, Stephen, Co-69-2; Sarah E. widow of; Pvt; Newport PO; dont know eny dates; CONF
BROOKS, Thomas, Sh-161-2; US Sol; 16th Dist
BROOKS, Thomas, Mc-112-5; Sgt A Co 17th PA Cav; 8-25-61 to 6-19-65; Athens PO; gunshot wound
BROOKS, Thomas, Gu-48-4(1); Pvt A Co 111th IL Inf; 6-6? to 64; Memphis PO
BROOKS, Thomas E., Cl-47-1; Pvt A Co TN Cav; Speedwell PO
BROOKS, Thomas N., K-182-1; Pvt E Co 10th MO Inf; Aug 62 to Sep 62; Shook PO; disabled 1861; rupture left side
BROOKS, Thomas P.?, Hm-106-2; Blacksmith L Co 9th TN Cav; 22 Dec 63 to 12 Oct 65; Morristown PO
BROOKS, W. W., M-108-3; Pvt I Co 9th KY Inf; 11-61 to 11-62; Godfrey KY PO; lung disease, dierhea, rheumatism
BROOKS, William, Hw-120-2; Wagonner G Co 1st TN Cav; 15 Sep 62 to 25 Apr 65; Eidson PO
BROOKS, William C., We-233-1(2); Pvt L Co 6th TN Cav; 2-1-64 to 7-26-65; Martin PO; bronchitis
BROOKS, William G., Sh-149-1; Betsy J. widow of; Pvt; Raleigh PO; papers lost by fire
BROOKS, Zachariah C., Cl-54-1; Pvt F Co 8th TN Cav; 8-6-63 to 9-11-65; Tazewell PO; chest affected
BROOKSHEER, Joel, Jo-153-2; P-t B Co 4th TN Inf; Pandora PO; rheumatism, deafness, heart trouble
BROOKSHIRE, Wyatt, Hn-73-1; Sgt Co B 131st? IL; Aug 12 62 to Sep 19 65; Como PO; bronchoines, draws pension
BROOMFIELD, William V., Br-7-3; Pvt I Co 4th TN Cav; 10-14-63 to 7-12-65; Cleveland PO
BROOMLY, Thomas, F-44-3; Pvt C Co 61st; Jun 63 to Jun 66; PO omitted
BROTHERTON, James M., Ge-92-3; Pvt K Co 1st TN Cav; 12 Jul 62 to 5 Jul 65; Laurel Gap PO; rheumatism & heart
BROTHERTON, Thomas, H-50-5; Rosannah formerly widow of; Pvt M Co 2nd R TN Cav; 11-8-62 to 7-6-65; Soddy PO; consumption
BROUN, John, Mn-121-2; Pvt A Co 6th TN Cav; Jul 62 to 26 Jul 65; Rose Creek PO
BROUN, William (see Mealpin, Calvin A.)
BROW, Andrew J., Ca-22-1; Pvt E Co 10th TN Inf; 3-1-63 to 6-23-65; Hollow Springs PO; wounded in ancle, now lame and blind
BROWDER, Anderson, Col, Lo-195-3(1); Eaton's X Roads PO
BROWDER, Benj. F., D-67-1; Pvt C Co 44th Col Inf; Apr 10 64 to Apr 30 66; Nashville PO
BROWDER, Isaac, Mc-112-1; Marjorie widow of; Pvt D Co 1st US Hvy Art; 3-1-64 to End 2-25-65; Athens PO
BROWDER, John D., Ro-203-7; Pvt TN Cav; 61 to 61; Wheat PO
BROWDER, Lafayette, H-67-2; Pvt C Co 14th US Col Inf; 11-1-63 to 3-25-66; Chattanooga PO; pierced in left shoulder & shot through left wrist, shoulder now ulcerated
BROWDER, Miller, H-69-6; widow US Sol; Chattanooga PO
BROWN, Abraham, Ms-174-1; Pvt D Co 17th US Inf; 18 Jan 63 to ___ (2 yrs); Chapel Hill PO
BROWN?, Acy A. A., Hy-84-1; Pvt A Co 9th TN; May 61 to Nov 63; Woodville PO; CONF
BROWN, Albert, Mu-198-2; 10th Dist
BROWN, Albert S., Sh-202-1; Pvt K B R Cav; 16 Apr 61 to 65; Memphis PO
BROWN, Aleck, H-63-2; Pvt C Co 1st Hvy Art; 62 to 64; 714 Poplar, Chattanooga PO
BROWN, Alexander, Wy-174-1; 9th Civil Dist
BROWN, Alexander, Su-233-1; Pvt D Co 13th TN Cav; 24 Sep 63 to 25 Sep 65; Vances Tank PO; injured in right foot, health impair from labor
BROWN, Alfred, Ro-210-4; Pvt 10th TN Cav; 1 yr 8 mos; Rockwood PO; rheumatism
BROWN, Anderson T., H-70-4(1); Pvt K Co 1st US Col Hvy Art; about 3 yrs; Chattanooga PO
BROWN, Andrew J., Ge-88-3; Pvt D Co 1st TN Cav; 18 Dec 62 to 20 Jun 65; Bulls Gap PO; spine aff., chronic diarrhea & lung trouble
BROWN, Andrew J., Ge-94-3; Ham PO
BROWN, Anim A., W-194-1; Pvt; 61 to 64; Morrison PO
BROWN, Ann, D-77-4; Bass St, Nashville PO
BROWN, Archale, Ge-93-2; Pvt I Co 1st TN Cav; 1 Aug 62 to 2 Jun 65; Cross Anchor PO
BROWN, Ashley A., Cf-40-1; Pvt A Co 5th MI Cav; 11 Aug 62 to 1 Jul 65; Tullahoma PO
BROWN, B. F., K-158-1; Pvt C Co 9th TN Cav; 62 to 65; Knoxville, 182 State St. PO; disabled from disease
BROWN, Ben, Mu-198-2; 10th Dist
BROWN, Benjamin H., Pu-146-2; Pvt I Co 1st TN Mtd Inf Vol; 8-12-64 to 7-22-65; H. I. PO; disease of lungs & stomach
BROWN, Bland, Gi-122-1; Pvt I Co 110th TN Inf; Dec 63 to 66; Prospect Sta. PO; run over by wagon
BROWN, Brittain, A-6-4(2); Sarah widow of; Pvt D Co; Fairview PO
BROWN, Cah?, O-140-1; Pvt H Co MI? Inf; Jan 62 to Apr 65; Union City PO; lost discharge, is able to work
BROWN, Campbell, Mu-210-2, Maj 3rd TN Inf; 61 to 5-61 (4 yrs-sic); Spring Hill PO
BROWN, Cato, Sh-188-1; Pvt; 6-63 to 4-65; Haynes Alley, Memphis PO
BROWN, Charles, Sh-179-1(2); Minerva widow of; Pvt E Co; Memphis PO; doesn't remember
BROWN, Charles, Sh-189-3; Pvt I Co 59th US Col Inf; 9-65 to 9-66; Memphis PO
BROWN, Charles, Sh-189-6; Sol US; Virginia Ave, Memphis PO
BROWN, Charles H., K-168-4; Sgt A Co 104th OH Inf; Knoxville PO
BROWN, Charles R., R-157-1; Mu(sician?) D Co 154th NY Vol Inf; 8-14-61 to ___; Lorraine PO; shot in both legs—lame in right
BROWN, Charley H., L-100-2; Pvt C Co 12th TN Cav; Dec 64 to 9 Oct 65; Ripley PO
BROWN, Churchill A., R-158-3; Pvt K Co 4th TN Cav; 2-64 to 7-65; Carp PO; effects of disease in service; discharge lost, exact dates not known
BROWN, Colman, We-231-1; Pvt; PO omitted
BROWN, Commodore C., Hw-130-1; Pvt E Co 1st TN Cav; 8 Feb 63 to 8 Feb 64; Lee Valley PO

BROWN, Crockett C., Je-143-3; Mary wife of; 1st TN Cav; Mossy Creek PO
BROWN, Dandy, Sh-200-1; Pvt I Co 9th US Lt Art; 4-26-64 to 1-10-66; 250 Trent St, Memphis PO
BROWN, Daniel W., O-138-3; Nellie V. widow of; 4th Cpl G Co 5th IN; 18 Apr 61 to 18 Jul 61; Minnick Box PO
BROWN, David, Wa-276-1; Pvt M Co 8th TN Cav; Jan 24 64 to Sep 11 65; Lees Burg PO; rheumatism & lung disease
BROWN, Deadrick S., Wa-261-1; Pvt E Co TN Cav; 61 to Jul 65; Canklin PO; diseas of eyes
BROWN, Easter, Sh-144-2; widow US Sol; First Dist
BROWN, Edward A., J-77-1; Pvt K Co 37th KY Cav; 63 to 1-20-65; Gainesboro PO; Andersonville GA & Florence SC 7 mos, disability caused by falling of mumps & rheumatism
BROWN, Edward P., D-103-1; Pvt H Co 134th NY Inf; Aug 9 62 to Jun 22 65; Joelton PO; chron. diarrhea, draws pension
BROWN, Elisha, H-53-6; T. E. widow of; Lt C Co 3rd WV Inf; 1 yr 9 mos; C Co WV Cav--no dates; Ridgedale PO; changed from inf to cavalry
BROWN, Eliza, Ru-241-1; widow; Murfreesboro PO
BROWN, Eliza D., Wa-261-2; Pvt I Co 1st TN Cav; 21 Sep 62 to 5 Jun 65; Nola Chuckey PO
BROWN, Felix W., Ge-93-1; Pvt E Co 4th TN Inf; 15 Mar 63 to Aug 65; Greeneville PO
BROWN, Franklin M., Ge-95-2; Catherine widow of; Pvt M Co 1st TN Cav; 25 Nov 62 to 19 Jun 65; Home PO
BROWN, Fredrick G., Hu-106-2; Pvt D Co 101st OH Inf; 31 Jul 62 to 2 Feb 64; Waverly PO
BROWN, George, Ge-91-3; Pvt H Co 16th US Col Inf; Mar 65 to Mar 66; Greenville? PO; piles & catarh
BROWN, George, C-24-2; Catherine widow; Pvt 49th KY Inf; Agee PO; lungs & piles (see Roach, William)
BROWN, George, F-42-2(4); Mary divorced widow of; Pvt P Co 59th USC Inf; May 17 63 to Jan 31 66; Rossville PO
BROWN, George, Di-34-2; Pvt; Dickson PO
BROWN, George, Gi-132-1; Hannah Reynolds formerly widow of; DeRay PO
BROWN?, George C., We-231-1; Pvt D Co 23rd KY Inf; Oct 65 to Oct 65; PO omitted
BROWN, George K., Wa-272-1; Pvt D Co 8th TN Cav; 6 Oct 64 to 11 Sep 65; Harmony PO; rheumatism heart and kidney disease
BROWN, George W., Pu-144-3; Pvt H Co 1stTN Mtd Inf; 2-15-64 to 5-28-65; Hudgins PO; kidney affections
BROWN, George W., D-103-1; Pvt K Co 4th TN Cav; Jul 65 to 65 (11 days); Whites Creek PO; unable to rejoin command
BROWN, Gotham, Ge-92-5; Nancy A. Weemes formerly widow of; Sgt D Co 8th TN Inf; Ottway PO
BROWN, Green B., He-67-2; Pvt C Co 6th TN Cav; Sep 18 62 to Jul 26 65; Sardis PO; chron. neuralgia head 26 yrs
BROWN, H., Sh-171-1; Pvt A Co 144th NY Vol; 8-15-62 to 7-65; Memphis
BROWN, Hardie R., K-177-4; Pvt & Lt, G Co 6th TN Inf; 18 Apr 62 to 17 May 65; Powells Station PO; gunshot wound in face
BROWN, Hawn', D-91-3; Pvt; Station C, Nashville PO
BROWN, Hector, D-60-2; Pvt 15 th Reg ___ Inf; 315 McNairy St, Nashville PO; colored
BROWN, Helen, Ro-210-6; Pvt E Co TN Inf; Rockwood PO
BROWN, Henry, Ro-205-2; Pvt A Co 1st Hvy Art; 8 Feb 64 to 31 Nov 66; Rockwood PO; pluerisy of side and reumatism for 24 yrs
BROWN, Henry, Col, Me-92-4(1); Pvt K Co 1st Col Hvy Art from TN; 6-63 to ___; Pin Hook PO; rheumatism, has no discharge, says that he was at home sick when discharged
BROWN, Henry M., Me-92-4(1); Ruhamey C. widow of; volunteered but captured before he reached army; Pin Hook PO; died in prison at Richmond
BROWN, Henson, Sh-179-1(2); Pvt; Memphis PO; doesn't remember
BROWN, Hiram, Sn-260-6; Pvt E Co 30th TN Inf; 6-61 to 9-16-62; Pondville PO; 8 mos in prison; CONF

BROWN, Houston, Lo-188-1; Sgt C Co 7th Mtd Inf; 20 Aug 64 to 27 Jun 65; Patties PO
BROWN, Isaac N., Dk-31-2; Cpl G Co 1st TN Mtd Inf; 3-2-64 to 4-21-65; Alexandria PO; suffering with rheumatism
BROWN, Jack, D-84-1; Drummer K Co 1st TN Inf; Mar 62 to May 65; LaVergne PO
BROWN, Jackson, Ro-205-1; 2 yrs 6 mos; Rockwood PO; rheumatism 25 yrs
BROWN, Jacob, Ge-89-1; Pvt A Co 12th TN Cav; 18 Ma__ 63 to 12 Jun 65; Mosheim PO
BROWN, James, Ca-23-1; Pvt K Co 52nd KY Inf; 12-63 to 3-11-65; Prater PO; injured by fall of horse
BROWN, James, Ca-24-2; Pvt K Co 52nd KY Mtd Inf; 12-14-63 to 3-11-65; Prater PO; injury in back, horse fell on him in the service
BROWN, James, C-24-3; Pvt K Co 47th KY Inf; 63 to 65 (15 mos); Girlton PO; chronic diarrhea & weak eyes
BROWN, James, Se-231-2; Pvt D Co 3rd TN Cav; 1 Jan 62 to 14 Jun 65; Boyds Creek PO; liver & dire 20 yrs, partial defness 25 yrs
BROWN, James, Gi-122-6; Pvt I Co 110th TN Inf; 1 Jan 63 to Mar 65; Veto, AL PO; 8 mos prison, Mobile AL
BROWN, James, Sh-190-2; Pvt; 159 Carolina St, Memphis PO; wounded on foot, could ascertain no further facts
BROWN, James, K-161-3; alias James Broyles; Cpl C Co 1st US Hvy Art; 26 Jan 64 to 31 Mar 66; Knoxville PO; reenlisted Mar 1, 1866
BROWN, James A., Fe-44-1; Pvt K Co 9th eN Cav; 6-6-62 to 7-5-65; Allardt PO; rupture abdomen
BROWN, James C., K-172-2; Pvt 3rd TN Cav; 62 to 65; Knoxville PO
BROWN, James D., Ge-97-2; Pvt A Co 4th TN Inf; 26 Jan 63 to 2 Aug 65; Locust Spring PO; lungs & heart disease
BROWN, James D., Ge-101-2; 2nd Sgt D Co 8th TN Inf; 15 Mar 63 to 30 Jun 65; Ottway PO; Atlanta, GA, result of mumps
BROWN, JAmes E., Col, Ca-23-3; Pvt K Co US Col Inf; 11-30-63 to 4-25-66; Morrison PO (Warren Co.); crushed by a horse
BROWN, James F., K-161-3; Pvt B Co 3rd TN Inf; 12 Feb 62 to 3 Feb 65; Knoxville PO
BROWN, James J., L-106-1; 4th Duty Sgt C Co 8th TN Cav; Oct 1 63 to Sep 11 65; Double Bridges PO
BROWN, James H., Br-12-6; McPherson PO; affected eyes
BROWN, James M., Ch-12-2; Pvt F Co 21st TN Cav; 10-63 to 5-65; Custer Point PO
BROWN, James M., H-53-5; Pvt K Co 9th TN Cav; 9-19-63 to 9-14-65; Ridgedale PO
BROWN, James M., S-213-3; Pvt E Co 1st TN Inf; 20 Aug 61 to 17 Sep 64; Capt D Co 191st OH Inf; 12 Feb 65 to 65; Robbins PO
BROWN, James N., Ca-22-1; Pvt E Co 10th TN Inf; 3-1-63 to 6-23-65; Hollow Springs PO
BROWN, James R., H-59-3; Pvt TN Inf; __ to 65 (3 yrs); Chattanooga PO
BROWN, James W., Cr-16-3; Pvt G Co 7th TN Cav; Aug 5 62 to Oct 25 63; Huntingdon PO; rheumatism
BROWN, Jane, Ca-23-3; widow of Sol; 5th Civil Dist
BROWN, Jasper, U-244-1; Pvt C Co 2nd NC Inf; Sep 63 to 16 Aug 65; Loganton PO; piles
BROWN, Jefferson, Gi-122-6; Pvt E Co 110th TN Inf; Nov 63 to Feb 65; Prospect Sta. PO; 8 mos in prison at Mobile AL
BROWN, Jeremiah, Pi-155-3; Pvt F Co 7th TN Mtd Inf; 11-8-64 to 7-27-65; Byrdstown PO
BROWN, Jesse M., H-50-2(1); Cpl I Co 13th R KY Vol Cav; 9-8-63 to 1-10-65; Bunch PO; kidney and liver disease incurred
BROWN, Jessey, S-218-3; Pvt E Co 1st TN Inf; 22 Aug 62 to Nov 64; Hughett PO; piles resulting disabilities of measels
BROWN, Jim, Ma-122-1; Pvt E Co 113th AR Inf; Jul 63 to Jan 64; Clay X Road? PO; leg broke while at Luvalls Bluff AR, has sent his discharge to Washington to the pension agt & dont remember the dates
BROWN, Mrs. John, Ro-205-3; Pvt D Co 7th TN Mtd Inf; 9 Feb 65 to 4 Jun 65; Hatch PO
BROWN, John, K-170-2; Pvt D Co 1st TN Art; 1 Sep 63 to 20 Jul 65; Knoxville PO

BROWN, John, Hw-125-1; A Co; Amis? PO
BROWN, John, Hw-127-3; alias William Fisher; Pvt C Co 16th US Inf; 20 Sep 62 to __; Amis PO; measles settled on lungs
BROWN, John, Hw-125-3; Mary widow of; 61 to 65; Stony Point PO
BROWN, John, Gr-70-1; Pvt L Co 8th TN Cav; 17 Sep 63 to 17 Sep 65; Rutledge PO; lungs & throat
BROWN, John, C-29-2; Pvt C Co 49th KY Inf; 7-13-63 to 12-26-64; Fincastle PO; lost bone out of finger
BROWN, John, W-189-1; Nancy A. widow of; Capt F Co 30th OH Inf; 4-61 to 63; McMinnville PO
BROWN, John, F-46-1; alias Brown May, F-46-1; Pvt D Co 49th KY Inf; 62 to __; LaGrange PO
BROWN, John, Mu-195-1; Sol; wife dont know; Columbia PO
BROWN, John, Sh-188-2; Saffaron St., Memphis PO
BROWN, John, Sh-189-6; Sol US; La. Ave, Memphis PO
BROWN, John, Sh-189-2; no record could be procured; Memphis PO; CONF?
BROWN, John A., K-171-6(5); Pvt A Co 3rd TN Inf; 62 to Apr 64; PO omitted; CONF
BROWN, John B., M-103-6; Pvt E Co 1st TN Inf; 10-21-62 to 1-22-65; Pvt D Co 8th TN Inf; 2-10-65 to 8-31-65; Union Camp PO
BROWN, John G., Ge-89-1; Pvt; Bulls Gap PO
BROWN, John H., Ge-101-1; Rachel E. widow of; Pvt D Co 8th TN Inf; Mar 63 to __; Locust Sp. PO; died in prison, Florence
BROWN, John I., H-56-3; Pvt E Co 36th OH Inf; 3-1-64 to 8-12-65; St. Elmo PO
BROWN, John M., F-44-1; Pvt B Co 15th TN; 63 to Jun 65; PO omitted; CONF
BROWN, John M., A-10-1; Pvt A Co 1st TN Lt Art; 3-4-64 to 8-5-65; Briceville PO; hearing
BROWN, John M., Ca-23-3; Pvt E Co 10th TN Inf; 3-1-63 to 6-23-65; Hollow Springs PO; health injured by cold
BROWN, John M., We-223-4; 5th Civil Dist
BROWN, John R., S-218-1; Pvt F Co 1st MO Inf; Nov 8 64 to 27 Jul 65; Huntsville PO; disease of head & hearing hard
BROWN, John S., Je-147-1; Pvt D Co 3rd TN Cav; 1 Dec 62 to 2 Aug 65; Shady Grove PO
BROWN, John T., Mo-118-2; Pvt M Co 1st US Hvy Art; 9-26-64 to 3-31-66; Longs Mills PO; chronic diarhea & pils & rupture 25 yrs
BROWN, John W., M-103-2; Cpl B Co 5th? TN Cav; 7-2-62 to 1-20-65; Lafayette PO
BROWN, John Z. A., Hm-107-3; Pvt H Co 32nd KY Inf; 1 Jan 63 to 12 Aug 63; Witts Foundry PO; partial blindness 25 yrs
BROWN, Jordan, Sh-190-1; Julia A. Williams former widow of; Gilfield Alley, Memphis PO; hearing
BROWN, Joseph, Ro-206-2; Pvt G Co 5th TN Inf; 64 to 65; Emory Gap PO
BROWN, Joseph, Bl-5-2; Pvt G Co 4th TN Cav; 7-22-63 to 7-12-65; Brayton PO; in prison
BROWN, Joseph, F-42-2(1); 1st Sgt, Sgt Major A Co 59th USC Inf; May 3 63 to Jan 31 66; Rossville PO
BROWN, Joseph, Sh-191-3; Emeline widow of; Sgt D Co 3rd Col Art; Memphis PO; records not seen
BROWN, Joseph A., A-5-5; Sgt B Co 3rd TN Inf; 2-62 to 2-65; Clinton PO; ruptured
BROWN, Joseph L., Dy-25-2; Capt E Co 6th TN Inf; Feb 61 to 65; Newbern PO; hip broken; CONF
BROWN, Joseph S., Cr-14-3; Pvt G Co 7th TN Cav; 5 Aug 62 to 15 Oct 63; Crider PO
BROWN, Joseph W., Sh-179-2; 423 Linden St, Memphis PO
BROWN, Killas, Co-67-1; Manerva widow of; PVt NC Cav; Bison PO; cannot give any dates
BROWN, Lafayette, H-69-3; Lt F Co 39th GA Inf; 62 to 64; Chattanooga PO; CONF
BROWN, Lewis, H-71-1; 62 to 65; Chattanooga PO
BROWN, Lewis, Ge-89-1; Pvt A Co 1st TN Cav; 28 Feb 64 to 1 Aug 65; Mosheim PO
BROWN, Lewis C., Sm-170-1; Pvt H Co 24th TN Inf; 12-10-61 to 6-16-65; Elmwood PO; shot in right foot; CONF
BROWN, Lissy, G-51-2; widow US Sol; Humboldt PO
BROWN, Louis, Sh-178-2; Cook I Co 14th IL; rear 96 Wellington, Memphis PO
BROWN, Lucus K., Hd-49-2; Sgt D Co 2nd TN Mtd Inf; Sep 1 63 to Feb 1 65; Lauryville PO; neuralga

BROWN, Lush, Bl-3-5; Pvt; Tanbark PO; CONF
BROWN, Lutrice, Sh-183-1; Pvt C Co 44th TN; 63 to 66 (2 yrs 6 mos); Memphis PO; CONF
BROWN, Marion C., Gi-123-1; Pvt F Co 110th TN Col Inf; 62 to Mar 65; Bethel PO
BROWN, Martha, Ge-93-4(1); widow US Sol; Greeneville PO
BROWN, Mrs. Martha A., Ro-205-2; Pvt D Co 7th TN Mtd Inf; 9 Feb 65 to 15 Jun 65; Hoods Landing PO
BROWN, Martha J., Ro-205-2; widow US Sol; Hatch PO
BROWN, Martin, K-180-4; Pvt; Ebenezer PO
BROWN, Martin S., H-60-3; Pvt I Co 4th MD Cav; 3-23-64 to 8-22-65; Chattanooga PO; wound on rt side
BROWN, Mrs. Mary, Hd-50-1; widow; Savannah PO
BROWN, Meaden, L-101-1; alias John Elam; Pvt H Co 55th C Inf; Henning PO; scalp wound, discharge in hand of atty.
BROWN, Milton, Col, Sh-171-1; Pvt E Co 2nd Col Art; Memphis PO
BROWN, Milton, Sh-193-2; Pvt; Memphis PO; papers in Washington
BROWN, Milton W., Sh-203-1; Pvt E Co Col Inf; Feb 63 to Apr 25 65; Memphis PO
BROWN, Moses, S-218-3; 2nd Cpl A Co; 13 Sep 63 to 13 Dec 63; Huntsville PO; diseas of stomach 7 yrs and back during ages
BROWN, Moses W., A-9-5(3); Mary widow of; Pvt H Co 1st TN Inf; 8-61 to __; Dutch Valley PO; died in service, date of death unknown
BROWN, Neal S., D-78-1; Pvt C Co 106th AL Inf; Jan 64 to Nov 17 65; Nashville PO
BROWN, Oates N., K-166-5; Cpl A Co 162nd OH Inf; May 64 to Sep 65; Knoxville PO
BROWN, Oscar F., G-51-1; Sgt B Co 117th IN Inf; 7-14-63 to 2-23-64; Humboldt PO; disabled
BROWN, Parthena, D-64-1; widow; Nashville PO
BROWN, Peter (see Boyd, Peter)
BROWN, Peter, Sq-164-5(1); 1st Lt E Co 6th TN Mtd Inf; 8-11-64 to 1-30-65; Brock PO
BROWN, Peter, Sh-175-1; Pvt I Co 103rd Inf; 63 to 65; Memphis PO
BROWN, Peter W., La-108-1; Pvt K Co 3rd M? Cav; 2-1-62 to 5-12-65; PO omitted
BROWN, Rachel (see Nickles, William)
BROWN, Return H., H-49-1; 2nd Sgt A Co 6th TN Mtd Inf; 8-2-64 to 6-30-65; Brown's Chapel PO
BROWN, Reuben H., Bl-2-2(1); Sgt G Co 6th TN Inf; 2-13-65 to 6-30-65; Orme's Store PO
BROWN, Reuben J., Co-67-5; Nancy Smith widow of; discharge lost; Naillon PO
BROWN, Richard, Col, Sh-145-1; Sgt B Co 1st? TN Lt Art; Mar 64 to Jan 10 66; Kerrville PO; cannot remember ex. day of enlistment or discharge
BROWN, Richard, Sh-189-2; Pvt F Co 3rd US Col Art Hvy; 7-15-63 to 4-30-66; Broadway, Memphis PO
BROWN, Richard H., Bo-23-2; Cpl B Co 2nd TN Cav; 8-15-62 to 7-6-65; PO omitted (Cades Cove?)
BROWN, Robbert, Mu-210-6; Pvt I Co OH Cav; 2 yrs; Spring Hill PO
BROWN, Robert, Ge-97-3; Pvt A Co 4th Inf; 5 Apr 63 to 2 Aug 65; Upchurch PO; hearing
BROWN, Robert C., Co-69-2; Capt D Co 12th TN Cav; 10 Sep 62 to 25 Apr 65; Rankin PO
BROWN, Ruffin, Gi-122-8; Pvt K Co 110th TN Inf; Mar 3 63 to Mar 3 65; Prospect Sta. PO
BROWN, Rufus B., Ro-207-3; Ord Sgt C Co 7th TN Mtd Inf; 20 Aug 64 to 27 Jun 65; Fossil PO; hemrage of lungs
BROWN, Sam, D-91-3; Waiter on Gen.; Davidson PO
BROWN, Samuel A., Cr-16-4; Pvt F Co 52nd __ Inf; Mar 24 62 to Mar 23 65; Huntington PO; chronic diarhea, affected 7 or 8 yrs
BROWN, Samuel C., Wi-281-1; Pvt H Co 5th TN; Apr 63 to Aug 65; Allisona PO
BROWN, Samuel H., Se-225-2; Sgt B Co 3rd TN Inf; 10 Feb 62 to 23 Feb 65; Millican PO; rheumatism, neuralgia and vericose vins 25 yrs, system debilitated and about blind
BROWN, Samuel T., Mu-198-2; 10th Dist
BROWN, Stephen, Sm-172-3(1); Cpl C Co US Inf; 8-20-63 to 1-16-66; Gordonsville PO; shot through the right leg
BROWN, Stephen C., Hm-109-4; Penelope C. widow of; Pvt C Co 8th TN Cav; 15 Apr 61 to 7 Jul 65; Whitesburg PO

BROWN, Sylvester S., Se-223-5(1); Blacksmith M Co 2nd TN Cav; 8 Nov 62 to 6 Jul 65; Sevierville PO; rheumatism and deafness
BROWN, Theadon F., H-60-4; Pvt IN Inf; Chattanooga PO; chronic diarrhoea
BROWN, Thomas, K-168-4; Adair's Creek PO
BROWN, Thomas, H-57-1; Pvt F Co 16th US Col; 63 to 65; Orchard Knob PO
BROWN, Thomas, Gu-48-4(1); Sgt A Co 14th KY Cav; 63 to 65; 118 Masy St, Knoxville PO; shot in right arm
BROWN, Thomas, Hm-108-3(2); Betsee Shipley widow of; Pvt; Russellville PO; loss of hearing
BROWN, Thos., Hy-75-2; PVt I Co 14th US Col Inf; 63 to __; Dancyville PO
BROWN, Thomas, Ms-171-1; Pvt TN Inf; Sep 64 to 64; Belfast PO
BROWN, Thomas, We-223-1; Ekuline? E. widow of; Set? L?; 35th TN Inf; Sep 61 to 7 Apr 62; Palmersville PO; died of brain trouble 1880; CONF
BROWN, Thomas, Cf-41-1; Pvt; Holly PO (care of Lawrence Sawmill); absent & wife did not know command
BROWN, Thomas B., Wl-292-1; Pvt B Co 5th TN Cav; May 62 to May 65; Buhler PO
BROWN, Thomas D., Mg-200-2; Pvt F Co 8th KY Inf; 62 to 65; Skene PO
BROWN, Thomas J., Ro-210-10; Pvt; Rockwood PO
BROWN, Thomas J., Gi-122-7; Pvt I Co 110th TN Inf; 1 Dec 63 to 10 Feb 66; Veto, AL PO; lost the sight of one eye
BROWN, Toliver N., Hm-107-3; Nancy A. widow of; Pvt H Co 32nd KY Inf; 1 Jan 63 to 12 May 63; Witts Foundry PO; ruptured
BROWN, Washington, T-209-1; Pvt C Co MS; 63 to 65; Randolph PO; can't find discharge
BROWN, Wilbren, C-33-2; Pvt; Jellico PO
BROWN, Wiley R., D-97-1; Pvt H Co 9th MS Inf; Nov 27 61 to Dec 20 64; Nashville PO; CONF
BROWN, William, Co-68-2; 16th NC Cav; 65 to 65; Sutton PO
BROWN, William A., Ge-101-1; Pvt M Co 1st TN Cav; 24 Nov 62 to 19 Apr 65; Ottway PO; diarrhoea resulting of rectun
BROWN, William A., Mc-114-6; Mary L. widow of; Pvt K Co 10th TN Cav; 11-3-63 to __; Folger PO
BROWN, William C., K-160-1; Martha J. widow of; Pvt K Co 32nd KY; 20 Jun 63 to 20 Sep 63; Knoxville PO
BROWN, William C., Sh-186-1; Pvt F Co 138th NY; 6-3-61 to 6-3-63; Memphis PO
BROWN, William C., Cy-27-4(2); Pvt C Co 39th KY Mtd Inf; 63 to 65; Spivey PO
BROWN, William H., Mc-112-1; Cpl A Co 7th TN Mtd Inf; 8-10-64 to 7-29-65; Athen PO; no discharge to get dates
BROWN, William H., Mu-210-7; Sgt Kellies Escort; 21 Oct 61 to 1 May 65; Spring Hill PO; CONF
BROWN, William R., Mu-210-4; Sgt A Co 48th TN Inf; 61 to 65; Carters Creek PO
BROWN, Willis, A-6-3(1); Pvt G Co 2nd TN Inf; 3-62 to 7-65; Olivers PO
BROWN, __, K-154-1; Nancy C. widow of; Knoxville PO
BROWNE, John, R-159-2; Sarah H. widow of; PVt; Spring City PO; died in the army; dont know what killed him
BROWNING, Abrahm, Un-257-3; Pvt; New Prospect PO; cant find out more
BROWNING, Elbert G., Wa-262-1; Pvt B Co 12th TN Cav; 22 Jul 63 to Oct 65; Telfords PO; cron. diareah, rheumatism
BROWNING, Robert S., Ge-85-2; Pvt G Co 4th TN Inf; 5 May 63 to 2 Aug 65; Cedar Creek PO; rheumatism & hemorrhoids 15 yrs
BROWNING, Thomas, Sh-158-2; Sgt Battery F Samberg's Col'd Lt Art; 62 to 65; Memphis PO; discharge papers at old house in _____ Co., AR; no doubt as to this case
BROWNING, Washington G., Un-257-2; Q Sgt D Co 1st TN Inf; Aug 9 61 to Sep 16 64; Little Baron PO; (died in army US, cant tell date in months and days--don't believe this info. belongs with this soldier, ed.); CONF
BROWNING, William A., Wa-262-1; Con S (sic) I Co 1st TN Cav; Telford PO; spine affection

BROWNLEE, Berry, Sh-153-3; Collierville PO; do not know company
BROWNLOW, Alexander, Wa-268-2; Mary A. widow of; Johnson City PO
BROWNLOWE, Joe, H-75-1; Pvt E Co 44th TN Inf; 5-63 to 65; Chattanooga PO; horses ran over him & turned his right foot around; never had discharge paper
BROYLE, Will A., Ge-83-3; Pvt E Co 4th TN Inf; 6 Apr 63 to 2 Aug 65; Painters PO; livir & kidney
BROYLES, Anderson, Ge-83-4; Pvt E Co 4th TN Inf; 25 Mar 63 to 2 Aug 65; Horse Creek PO; chronic diarrhear
BROYLES, Charles L., Ge-84-1; Sgt N Co 1st TN Cav; 18 Nov 61 to 11 Apr 65; Bird Bridge PO; chronic diarral, piles, hart diseas, rectum easy? from chronic diarrhea
BROYLES, George P., C-33-3; Pvt G Co 49th KY Inf; 10-1-63 to 12-26-64; Newcomb PO
BROYLES, James (see Brown, James)
BROYLES, King H., Ge-83-4; PVt E Co 4th TN Inf; 18 Mar 63 to 13 Aug 65; Horse Creek PO; chronic rheumatism
BROYLES, Riley, C-33-3; Pvt E Co 32nd KY Inf; 62 to 63; Newcomb PO
BROYLES, Thomas, Ge-84-2; Pvt A Co 4th TN Inf; 26 Ma_ 63 to 2 Aug 65; Greenville PO; chronic lung?, eyes
BROYLES, Thomas J., Ge-83-3; Pvt D Co 6th TN Inf; Nov 62 to 12 Jul 64; Painters PO
BRUCE, Airs M., Cl-48-1; PVt; Old Town PO; CONF
BRUCE, Daniel H., Gr-78-2; Capt A Co 51st VA Inf; 1 May 61 to 1 Jul 65; Spring House PO; (entry marked out, may be CONF)
BRUCE, James R., Gi-127-8; Pvt; Pulaski PO
BRUCE, John, D-54-3; Sadie widow of; PVt D Co; Nashville PO
BRUCE, John, Wl-308-3; Pvt 45th TN; Dec 61 to Sep 62; Mount Juliet PO; CONF
BRUCE, John N., C-34-2; Pvt H Co 2nd TN Inf; 3-9-62 to 3-9-65; Elk Valley PO; flesh wound head
BRUCE, Levy N., Co-62-1; Pvt E Co 7th Cal; 17 Apr 62 to Apr 65; Warrensburg PO; loss of springer?
BRUCE, Will, Gi-140-1; Pvt C Co 12th TN Inf; 6-10-63 to 6-20-6? (1 yr 11 mos 10 days); PO omitted
BRUCE, William, Sh-157-2; Pvt E Co 61st TN; 62 to 65; Dist 13; shot right side of the neck
BRUCE, William, Fe-40-1; Mary widow of; Pvt C Co 11th TN Cav; 63 to 64; Little Crabb PO
BRUER, Edward, Sh-147-1; Pvt K Co 7th ONG Inf; 9 Apr 64 to Jul 20 64; Ramsey PO
BRUKKER, Benjamin, Ru-13-2; Pvt I Co 172nd PA; Oct 62 to Aug 63; Murfreesboro PO
BRUMAGIM, Abraham, R-161-3; Pvt C Co 10th MO Inf--8-6-61 to 8-24-64; Pvt A Co Menill's Horse--9-28-64 to 6-15-65; Dayton PO; reenlisted veteran
BRUMAGIM, Nancy C. (see Nash, James M.)
BRUMBALOUGH, William J., Pu-141-2; Sgt K Co 1st TN Inf; 10-18-63 to 7-22-65; Goffton PO; discharged on account of fever
BRUME, Milton, We-223-2; Nancey C. widow of; have lost all papers and cant give dates; Palmersville PO; was killed in service; CONF
BRUMET, Thomas, U-245-1; Pvt B Co 12th TN Cav; 1 Jan 63 to 26 Aug 65; Marbleton PO
BRUMETT, Joseph H., Sm-166-3(1); Pvt D Co 1st TN Inf; 9-1-61 6o 4-1-63; Monoville PO
BRUMETT, William R., A-8-1; Pvt E Co 3rd TN Inf; 2-12-62 to 8-25-65; Scarborough PO; rheumatims, palpitation heart
BRUMEY, John, H-54-4; Pvt F Co 1st TN Cav; East Chattanooga PO
BRUMLEY, James, H-49-8; Pvt & Cpl __ Co 6th TN Mtd Inf; 9-5-64 to 6-30-65; Daisy PO; horse killed & fell upon him & crippled
BRUMLEY, William, Sq-165-2; Pvt E Co 5th TN Mtd Inf; 9-1-64 to 6-30-65; Delphi PO
BRUMMETT, James A., A-9-5(3); Hannah widow of; Pvt I Co 9th TN Cav; 6-20-63 to 6-12-65; Dutch Valley PO; gun shot wound in right side resulting in his death 3-26-72
BRUMMITT, Angelina, Wa-273-3; widow of; Pvt 4th MA; Bashors Mill PO; rheumatism, discharge in hands of a claim agent

BRUMNETT, Mason W., Tr-265-1; Pvt A Co 2nd KY Cav; 1 Jun 62 to 20 Jun 65; Dixons Springs PO
BRUNDIGE, Stephen C., We-220-1; Pvt A Co 7th TN Inf --Aug 18 62 to Aug 18 63; Pvt A Co 7th TN Cav --Aug 18 63 to Oct 21 63; Latham PO; confined to bed for 15 yrs
BRUNDIGE, William H., H-70-2(1); Drummer Boy C Co 3rd MD Inf; Chattanooga PO
BRUNER, Andrew J., Ge-92-3; Cpl K Co 1st TN Cav; 12 Jul 62 to 5 Jun 65; Laurel Gap PO; diseas of lungs
BRUNT, Jacob P., Mc-111-3; Pvt F Co (later 1st Lt & Capt F Co) 3rd TN Cav--11-1-62 to 5-18-64; Maj 3rd TN Cav--7-65 to 8-3-65; Mortimer PO; prisner Meridian MS 3 mos
BRUTON, J. B., Ov-134-1; Pvt J Co 1st KY Cav; 8-1-63 to 9-30-65; Hilham PO; wound of head by stroke with pistol & partial paralysis; also had fever which settled in leg
BRYAN, Alias (sic) W., Se-226-3; Oct 62 to 65; Henrys X Roads; sun strok & cripled side
BRYAN, Aljoumal, W1-300-1; Pvt G Co 5th TN Cav; 22 Sep 62 to Aug 65; Watertown PO
BRYAN, John N., W1-302-1; Pvt B Co 5th TN Cav; 28 Aug 62 to 14 Aug 64; PO omitted
BRYAN, Joseph A., Se-224-3; Sgt E Co 9th TN Cav; 1 Oct 63 to 11 Sep 65; Wears Valley PO; diarrhea 27 yrs
BRYAN, Joshua L., W1-300-2; Pvt G Co 5th TN Cav; 30 Sep 62 to 14 Aug 65; Watertown PO
BRYAN, Marcus M., G-51-1; Teamster K Co 4th TN Inf; Humboldt PO; wounded in privates
BRYAN, Peyton G., Se-224-2; Pvt H Co 9th TN Vol Cav; 1 Oct 63 to 11 Sep 65; Wears Valley PO; chronic diarrhea, came home on sick furlow
BRYANT, Allain M., Ge-90-3; Martha widow of; Sgt B Co 13th TN Cav; 23 Sep 63 to 5 Sep 65; Greeneville PO
BRYANT, Appollus, Co-67-4; Pvt G Co 60th NY Vt? Engineers; 12 Sep 61 to Mar 62; Naillon PO
BRYANT, Austin, Sh-197-1; Matilda widow of; Memphis PO; discharge lost or mislaid, Col Inf beginning of war, 3 yrs (no dates)
BRYANT, Brumest, Co-66-1; Pvt C Co 26th TN Inf; 13 Oct 62 to 5 May 63; English PO; wounded in arm; CONF
BRYANT, Charley O., Wy-175-2; Pvt B Co 10th TN Inf; 1-62 to 7-5 Jun 65; Cypress Inn PO
BRYANT, Ellis M., T-211-1; "found while examining work"; PO omitted
BRYANT, Fran Geo., Fr-112-1; Pvt I Co 44th Col Inf; Aug 62 to Aug 65; Tullahoma PO; shot through left arm & fracture of should., prisoner for 8 mos at Mobile AL
BRYANT, G. W., G-59-1; Pvt D Co 6th IL Cav; 15 Sep 64 to 15 Sep 65; Kenton PO
BRYANT, George, Sh-157-7; Insely Farm PO
BRYANT, George, D-64-6; 400 S. Sumner, Nashville PO
BRYANT, George W., He-67-1; Sgt C Co 6th TN Cav; Sep 18 62 to Aug 13 64; Sardis PO; hemorhoids & chronic rheumatism contracted in war
BRYANT, Gray, Wy-173-3; Nancy E. widow of; Pvt B Co 2nd TN Mtd Inf; 10-15-63 to 10-17-64; Sims PO
BRYANT, Henry A., Bo-14-5; Pvt L Co 2nd TN Cav; 9-8-63 to 7-6-65; Clover Hill PO
BRYANT, Hiram, Un-252-2; Pvt; Acuff PO; hearing
BRYANT, Jackson, Ar-95-2; Pvt I Co 70th TN Inf; 7-23-62 to 6-23-65; Ownes PO
BRYANT, Jake (see Ridley, Henry
BRYANT, James, Bo-12-3(1); Sol US; 17th Dist
BRYANT, James B., Br-11-2; Pvt A Co 3rd NC Mtd Inf; 7-62 to 8-65; Chatata PO; rheumatism 25 yrs
BRYANT, John C., Hr-92-1; Pvt F Co 6th TN Cav; 12-26-63 to 7-26-65; Saulsbury PO; had measles & settled on Lucy?
BRYANT, John T., Hu-103-1; Pvt C Co PA Inf; 14 Jan 61 to 64; PO omitted
BRYANT, Levi H., C2-40-1; Pvt L Co 2nd TN Cav; 8-15-63 to 7-16-65; Houk PO
BRYANT, Marrion, Cf-47-3; 1st Lt C Co 49th KY Inf; 8-8-63 to 12-26-64; Compensation PO; deafness & rheumatism, liver & kidneys, stomache & bowels 1864
BRYANT, Mary, Sh-145-4; Kerrville PO
BRYANT, McDonald, H-55-2; Pvt C Co 5th TN Cav; 2-27-62 to 7-31-65; Tyner PO; asthma
BRYANT, Nathen P., Br-11-1; Pvt F Co 53rd IL; 2-25-62 to 3-1-65; Chatala PO; wounded in shoulder near Miss county
BRYANT, Nedom J., Hd-53-3; Pvt C Co 7th TN Cav; Jun 6 63 to 23 Jun 65; Mellidyeville PO; hurt on head, Andersonville Prison 13 mos
BRYANT, Potter, B-18-1; 24th Dist
BRYANT, Saul, Sh-146-2; Pvt B Co 144th __; Lucy PO
BRYANT, Thomas, D-80-1; 2nd Civil Dist
BRYANT, William, Ca-22-3; Sol US; 13th Civil Dist
BRYANT, William (see Fitzpatrick, Alen)
BRYANT, William, Co-66-3(1); 1st Sgt F Co 5th TN Cav; 30 Nov 61 to 15 Apr 65; Newport PO; CONF
BRYANT, Wm. G., W1-308-1; Pvt I Co 20th TN; Jun 1 61 to Oct 10 63; Mount Juliet PO; shot through the arm and broken; CONF
BRYANT, William L., Sh-203-1; Pvt B Co 4th AR Bat; Aug 61 to 65; Memphis PO; CONF
BRYANT, Zacariah, O-142-1; Lucretia T. widow of; Pvt A Co 12th Col US Inf; 27 Jul 63 to 16 Jan 66; Obion PO
BRYMER, William, H-50-3(1); Jerusha widow of; Pvt H Co 9th R TN Cav; Igon's Ferry PO
BUCH, Robert, Wi-273-1; 4th Civil Dist
BUCHANAN, Abron, Sh-157-1; Ann widow of; Pvt A Co; 3 yrs; PO omitted
BUCHANAN, D. F., Gi-125-2; Pvt A Co 111th US Col Inf; 13 Jan 64 to 30 Apr 66; Weakly PO
BUCHANAN, F. W., G-57-7(4); 61 to 64; Yorkville PO; CONF
BUCHANAN, George, Po-148-2; Pvt K Co 1st Col Hvy Art; 8-5-64 to 3-31-66; Cog Hill PO
BUCHANAN, Katie, O-141-2; Union City PO; lost discharge papers
BUCHANAN, Moses R., D-99-5; Pvt; Sep 64 to Dec 64; Sante Fe PO (Grainger Co.); Central Hos. for Insane; CONF
BUCHANAN, Thomas, Mo-121-1; Sarah widow of; Pvt F Co 28th MI Inf; Eve Mills PO; chronic diarrhea; (may have died in service)
BUCHANAN, William P., Di-34-1; Pvt B Co 140th PA Inf; 9-6-62 to 6-26-65; Dickson PO; rheumatism & hemorhoids; transferred on account of disability to 9th Reg Co F URC
BUCHANAN, Widow US Sol, G-57-3; 8th Dist
BUCHELEW, George H., Je-141-2; Pvt K Co 3rd TN Inf; 10 Feb 62 to 24 Jun 63; Mossy Creek PO
BUCHER, Joshua, Dk-33-2; Pvt I Co 5th TN Cav; 11-2-62 to 8-14-65; 4th Civil Dist
BUCHETT, William, G-57-5(3); 63 to 64; Yorkville PO; CONF
BUCK, Alonzo, W-193-1; Mary J. widow of; Pvt M Co 2nd OH Art; 6-12-62 to 6-8-65; Vernilla PO
BUCK, Benjamin, R-162-3; Pvt E Co 7th US Vol; 1-30-64 to __-26-65; Dayton PO
BUCK, Dickens, Sh-158-1; Coal heaver Pvt Samson; Dec 10 62 to Jun 65; Memphis PO; chronic asthma or psthsis
BUCK, Nathaniel T., Wa-267-3; Pvt C Co 13th TN Cav; 5 Sep 63 to 5 Sep 65; Jonesboro PO; paralysis
BUCK, Osborn D., Ct-39-1; Pvt B Co 4th TN Cav; 62 to 65; Happy Valley PO; tumor in right hand
BUCK, Randolph B., Sm-171-1; Pvt K Co 1st TN Mtd Inf; Chestnut Mound PO
BUCK, Thomas Y., F-38-2; Capt C Co 13th TN Cav; Sep 63 to Sep 65; Stanton PO
BUCKALEW, Jasper, K-166-2; 1st Lt K Co 3rd TN Inf; 10 Feb 63 to 23 Feb 65; Knoxville PO; lung disease, rheumatism, drawing pension
BUCKELL, George W., H-49-11; Pvt D Co 22nd PA Cav; 6-27-63 to 2-5-64; Daisy PO
BUCKELS, Eli, Pi-155-1; Pvt G Co 14th KY Cav; 62 to 3-64; Otto PO; rheumatism & sore eyes
BUCKETS, Wm. Jr., Ct-43-3; PO omitted
BUCKHANEN, George W., Ge-92-2; Adaline widow of; 3rd NC Inf; Romeo PO
BUCKLEY, John, We-223-4; Pvt F Co 46th TN Inf; Oct 61 to 3 Nov 62; Palmersville PO; CONF
BUCKLEY, Joseph V., H-71-1; Pvt C Co 11th IN ___; 61 to 65; Chattanooga PO
BUCKNER, Alfred, Wa-268-1; alias Wyatt; Sgt D Co 3rd NC Mtd Inf; 12 Aug 64 to 8 Aug 65; Johnson City PO; heart disease
BUCKNER, James, D-64-2; Pvt K Co 15th TN Inf; Nashville PO
BUCKNER, Jasper, Co-69-6(12); Pvt F Co 4th TN Inf; 1 Jan 64 to 2 Aug 65; Bibee PO; not pensioner

BUCKNER, Jane, Di-34-4; widow of US Sol; Dickson PO
BUCKNER, Levy, Co-69-6(1); Pvt D Co 8th TN Inf; 24 May 63 to 1 Jul 64; Driskill PO; Mcleavill (McCavill?) KY, a pensioner
BUCKNER, Lige?, Co-62-2; Pvt D Co 8th tN Inf; 24 Mar 63 to ___ (9 mos); Rankins PO
BUCKNER, Thomas J., Un-252-1; Sarah widow of; Capt 11th TN Cav; Esco PO; discharge destroyed
BUCKNER, William, Mt-147-1; Pvt C Co 15?th US Col Cav TN; Feb 64 to May 66; McCalisters X Road PO; discharge sent to Washington
BUCKNER, William, H-74-1; Pvt D Co 42nd Pioneer Corps; 10-63 to 2-65; 36½ Slayton St., Chattanooga PO
BUCKNER, William, K-171-2; US Sol; 12th Civil Dist
BUDD, Jake, Gi-127-2; Sarah widow of; Pvt F Co 111th TN C Inf; Jan 6 76 to ___; Pulaski PO; died in prison, Mobile AL
BUDLONG, Loranzo D., Mn-121-2; Pvt B Co 1st R? Art; 13 Aug 61 to 13 Mar 63; Rose Creek PO
BUDRIANS, Nashua, H-50-5; Margaret D. widow of; Soddy PO
BUELL, George P., D-87-2; Rachie B. widow of; Colo? 15th US Inf; 28 Jul 66 to 31 May 83 (sic) (18 yrs); Nashville PO
BUFORD, George, Gi-132-1; Phoebe Hartford formerly widow of; Sgt D Co 111th USCV; DeRay PO; died in the service
BUFORD, Hardin, Mu-210-1; Pvt; Spring Hill PO
BUFORD, Landon, Gi-127-3; Pvt B Co 110th TN Col Inf; Pulaski PO; shot in foot and hand, but does not affect his use of them
BUFORD, Lorenzo, Gi-132-3; alias Buford, Don?; Cpl D Co 110th USCV; Dec 63 to Feb 8 66; Pulaski PO
BUFORD, Nicy (see Lewis, Frederick)
BUFORD, Peter, Gi-132-3; Mary Reynolds formerly widow of; Pvt B Co 110th USCV; ___ to Feb 66; DeRay PO
BUFORD, Ronnel, T-211-1; Pvt G Co 3rd Inf; 11 Oct 65 to 31 Oct 68; Munford PO
BUFORD, William, Mu-195-1; A Co 110th TN Vol; Columbia PO
BUG, Jesse N., D-75-2; Pvt A Co 15th TN Brit?; Jan 62 to 1 May 65; Stewarts Ferry PO; surrendered to Nashville; CONF
BUGG, James, D-79-2; Pvt A Co 14th US Col Inf; about Oct 63 to about Mar 66; Nashville, 315 Berry PO; sight poor, smallpox in army
BUGG, James, Sn-254-1; Pvt C Co 14th US Col Inf; 10-1-63 to ___; Hendersonville PO
BUHLER, Jos. M., Sh-189-1; Blacksmith D Co 16th KY Inf; 62 to 7-3-63; Iowa Ave, Memphis PO
BULINGTON, William K., Cr-13-1; Pvt B Co 1st W TN; 22 May 62 to sent home sick Nov 17 62; Atwood PO; Sept 30 or thereabout was discharge
BULL, James, Cl-48-2; Cav; Pleasant PO; CONF
BULL, Wesley, Gr-77-1; Pvt F Co 8th TN Cav; 13 Jul 63 to 11 Sep 65; Y. Z. PO
BULLARD, George A., Mu-195-3; Sol; Columbia PO
BULLARD, Isaac, K-186-3; Pvt; Knoxville PO
BULLARD, Silas, C-24-3; Mary widow of; Pvt C Co 1st TN Inf; 8-6-61 to ___; Girlton PO; rheumatism
BULLARD, William, Sh-159-5; PO omitted
BULLARD, William, Sn-169-3(5); Pvt D Co 4th TN Mtd Inf; 62 to 8-65; 2nd Dist
BULLINGER, James J., Ge-102-1; Pvt B Co 2nd NC Mtd Inf; Sep 63 to Aug 65; Camp Creek PO; rheumatism
BULLINGTON, Chesley, Dk-32-1; Pvt I Co 21st Col Inf; 10-14-64 to 5-15-65; Liberty PO
BULLINGTON, Frederick F., K-167-4; Lucinda widow of; Pvt; 62 to 65; Knoxville PO
BULLINGTON, John R., We-221-1(4); Pvt B Co 6th TN Cav; Jun 62 to May 63; Martin PO; constitution ruined
BULLINGTON, Mounce, J-81-3; Pvt I Co 1st TN; 9-1-64 to 4-1-65; Maryfield PO
BULLINGTON, Wesley R., J-82-1; Cpl I Co 1st TN Mtd Inf; 1-1-65 to 7-27-65; Irby PO; general debility
BULLNER, George, Ch-18-2; 31st TN; PO omitted; CONF
BULLOCK, Adam H., K-158-1; 1st Lt E Co 63rd TN Inf; May 61 to May 65; Knoxville, 182 State St.

PO; shot in leg & head; CONF
BULLOCK, Burton (Wm. B.), C-25-2; Pvt G Co 7th TN Inf; 11-20-64 to 7-27-65; Hatmaker PO; rheumatism
BULLOCK, Francis, A-4-5; Cpl C Co 2nd TN Inf; 8-61 to 7-65; Coal Creek PO; shot wound of right fore arm, date of enlistment & discharge lost
BULLOCK, John, C-27-2; Cpl G Co 17th TN Inf; 11-18-64 to 5-13-65; Caryville PO
BULLMAN, Eziekel, Ge-102-3; Mary J. Bowman, formerly widow of; Pvt 2nd NC; Henshaw PO
BULMASS, John W., Ge-84-1; Pvt A Co 2nd NC Mtd Inf; 15 Sep 63 to 15 Aug 65; Whig PO; chronic dis. measels and mumps
BUMBALOUGH, John F., Pu-142-1; PVt 5th TN Mtd Inf; Fourth Civil Dist
BUMGARDNER, David, Jo-150-3; Pvt I Co 13th TN Cav; 12 Jun 64 to 5 Sep 65; Trade PO
BUMGARNER, George W., Jo-150-5; Pvt CT; 10 Jun 64 to ___ (1 yr 2 mos 1 day); Osborn PO; rheumatism
BUMGARTNER, James A., Sq-164-3(1); Pvt; Dunlap PO
BUMPAS, Adam, Hd-55-1; Pvt IN Cav; 28 Dec 61 to 15 May 64; Cerro Gordo PO; Negro and can't remember
BUMTON, William, Sh-157-6; Cpl E Co 61st C; Aug 24 63 to Dec 30 65; Memphis, Calhoun St. PO
BUNCH, Francis, K-154-1; Pvt B Co 3rd TN Mtd Inf; 64 to Dec 65; Knoxville PO
BUNCH, George H., Sh-167-3; PO omitted; CONF
BUNCH, Isaac, A-9-2; Pvt G Co 7th TN Mtd Inf; 11-8-64 to 7-27-65; Podopholine PO; rupture
BUNCH, James, Gr-76-1; Sgt M Co 1st TN Cav; 20 Dec 62 to 19 Jun 65; PO ommited; hemorrhoids
BUNCH, James M., A-9-2; Sarah C. widow of; Pvt I Co 7th TN Mtd Inf; 11-8-64 to 7-27-65; Podopholine PO; died of lung disease
BUNCH, James W., Mu-210-5; Pvt A Co 48th TN Inf; 10-62 to 5-20-65; Carters Creek PO; CONF
BUNCH, John, A-9-2; Mary widow of; Pvt A Co 1st TN Inf; 8-2-61 to 9-17-64; PO ommited
BUNCH, Layford L., S-218-3; US Sol; 9th Civil Dist
BUNCH, Mathew, A-9-2; Pvt I Co 7th TN Mtd Inf; 11-8-64 to 7- 27-65; Podopholine PO
BUNCH, Robert C., Gr-78-2; Pvt D Co 2nd TN Cav; 21 Oct 62 to 21 Nov 64; Spring House PO; this entry was marked out, might be CONF
BUNCH, Sidney E., Me-91-1; 4th Civil Dist
BUNCH, William, C-33-2; Cpl F Co 16th KY Inf; 7-62 to 8-4-65; Jellico PO
BUNDON, Lightle (see Hilliard, Lightle)
BUNDRANT, William H., Hw-127-3; Pvt E Co 4th US Inf; 17 Oct 64 to 18 Jun 66; Amis PO; disease of eyes and stomach
BUNDY, David, H-51-4; PVt L Co 4th TN Cav; 3-1-64 to 7-12-65; Hill City PO
BUNER, Marler, C-32-2; Pvt C Co 9th TN Cav; 7-10-63 to 9-11-65; Clearfield PO; cripel right hip 25 yrs
BUNIRO, James R., B-11-1; Sgt F Co 5th TN Cav; 9-6-62 to 6-25-65; Shelbyville PO; piles
BUNN, George (see Washington, George L.)
BUNTING, Bland, D-77-1; Nancy widow of; PVt 14th US Col Inf; Nashville PO
BUNTING, Daniel, T-209-1; Sgt H Co 71st MO; Jun 1 62 to Jun 6 65; Randolph PO
BUNTING, Nancy (see Willhour, Joshua)
BUNTON, Eli, Black, Sn-264-1; Cpl A Co 14th Col Inf; Oct 1 63 to Mar 26 66; Mitchellsville PO; twice wounded in left leg & left arm; he has all his papers all right; mustered out at Nashville; C. W. Baker, Capt.
BUNTON, Joe, Sn-264-1; Pvt 112th TN Inf; Jul 63 to Jul 65; Mitchellsville PO; this man badly afflicted with rheumatism, his papers lost; mustered out in Nashville, Capt. Ayers, Gen. Gilliam
BUNTON, Samuel, Sh-157-2; Pvt E Co 61st US Col Inf; 63 to 66; Memphis PO
BUNTON, William, Sh-157-3; ___ to 65; Memphis PO
BUNTON, William, Jo-151-2; Jane widow of; Pvt I Co 13th TN Cav; 22 Sep 63 to ___; Casper PO; diarrhoea, died in service
BUNTON, William H., Jo-151-1; Pvt K Co 8th TN Cav; 13 May 63 to 11 Sep 65; Casper PO; rheumatic bronchitis

BURBANKS, Andy, Sn-264-1; Pvt H Co 8th Hvy Art; May 2 64 to Feb 10 66; Mitchellsville PO; this mans paper all right, suffering with hemorrhoids bad; discharged Victoria, TX, Cap. Norton, Col. H. C. Demming

BURCH, Thomas, Cl-56-2(1); Pvt C Co 47th KY Inf; 8-12-63 to 12-26-65; Big Barren PO; neuralgia of the heart & eyes

BURCHAM, Pleasant, P-151-1; Pvt G Co 6th Reg TN Cav; 18 Sep 62 to 26 Jul 65; Pope PO; hemorrhoids

BURCHARD, Henakiah E., R-106-2(3); Pvt M Co MS Art; 2 or 4-61 to 2-10-64; 7th Civil Dist

BURCHELL, Daniel, Hm-105-1; Pvt A Co 9th TN Cav; 10 Sep 64 to 11 Sep 65; Jarnagan PO

BURCHFIELD, Henry H., Se-225-1; Pvt F Co 9th TN Cav; 24 Jul 63 to 11 Sep 65; Allensville PO; chronic diarrhoea 25 yrs; now dead

BURCHFIELD, James, Hw-125-5; B Co 2nd KY Cav; Mar 62 to 65; Surgoinsville PO; CONF

BURCHFIELD, Jessey Y., S-218-2; L Co 2nd TN Cav; 8 Sep 63 to 6 Jul 65; Hughett PO; herrena (sic)

BURCHFIELD, Robert, S-216-1; Pvt F Co 12th KY Vol; 16 Sep 63 to 2 Jun 65; Windfild PO; cripeld in righ hand, kidny deseas 25 yrs

BURCHFIELD, Samuel S., Bo-23-2; Pvt B Co 1st TN Mtd Inf; 8-20-62 to 2-20-64; PO omitted (may be Cades Cove)

BURCHFIELD, ___, Hw-125-2; Maggie widow of; Cpl; 63 to 65; Yellow Stone PO

BURDETT, Thoma, Bl-3-5; Pvt A Co 25th TN Inf; 2-63 to __; Tanbark PO; CONF

BURDINE, L. P., Cl-53-1; Elisabeth Payne formerly widow of; Pvt M Co 8th TN Cav; 63 to 12-64; Springdale PO; died in hospital at Nashville, TN

BURDINE, William, D-68-3; 117 Lewis St, Nashville PO

BURDWELL, Jackson, Wa-272-1; Pvt C Co 3rd NC Inf; Aug 64 to 65; Locust Mount PO; rheumatism

BUREM, Henry S., Hw-133-2; Quartermaster Department K Co 13th TN Inf; 5 Apr 61 to 18 Aug 65; Burem's Store PO; wounded in battle; CONF

BURETT, John, H-56-7; Pvt; 61 to 65; St. Elmo PO

BURGAR, Joseph E., Po-152-2; Nancy widdow of; Pvt D Co 10th TN Cav; 1-4-64 to 8-1-65; Ducktown PO; relapse of measles and mumps

BURGE, James R., Wl-295-1; Pvt B Co 5th __ IN; 61 to __; Lebanon PO; cannot give dates, his papers in Washington DC

BURGEN, Sam, R-162-4; Dayton PO

BURGER, George E., Mc-111-1; Cpl F Co 4th TN Cav; 2-27-63 to 7-12-65; Nonaburg PO

BURGER, Joseph, Ge-95-1; Pvt B Co 8th TN Cav; 22 Jul 63 to 11 Sep 65; Home PO; shot in foot

BURGER, Michael D., Mc-111-1; Pvt E Co 9th TN Cav; 9-28-63 to 9-11-65; Nonaburg PO; left arm shot

BURGER, W. G., Hy-81-1; 7th Civil Dist

BURGES, Aden H., Ge-102-2; Pvt E Co 2nd NC Mtd Inf; 1 Sep 63 to 16 Aug 65; Woolsey College PO; ruptured by fall, now the piles

BURGESS, Andrew J., Hu-104-1(2); Pvt G Co 12th TN; Jan 6 64 to Oct 65; McEwen PO; by measles & constipation of bowels

BURGESS, Benjamin, H-72-2(1); Pvt G Co 5th US Col Inf; 2-64 to 8-65; Chattanooga PO

BURGESS, Charles L., Pu-144-3; Pvt B Co 1st TN Mtd Inf; 3-15-64 to 4-18-65; Ditty PO; leg injured in fall of horse

BURGESS, David, Hu-106-2; Pvt H Co 26th NY Col Inf; 1-64 to 8-65; Waverly PO

BURGESS, Edward, Br-9-2; Pvt H Co 10th TN Cav; 1-16-64 to 8-1-65; Cleveland PO

BURGESS, Isaac, H-59-1; Pvt TN Inf; Chattanooga PO

BURGESS, Jefferson T., J-83-1; Pvt B Co 8th TN; 1-8-65 to 8-17-65; Flynns Lick PO

BURGETT, Barton S., Wl-279-1; Pvt A Co OH; 62 to 65; Carl PO

BURGNER, Daniel, Wa-260-2; Hannah L. widow of; Sgt F Co 8th TN Cav; Apr 5 63 to Sep 11 65; Pilot Hill PO; by reason No. 49 Hd. Qrs. Dep. TN

BURGNER, Isaac M., Ge-96-4; PVt F Co 8th TN Cav; 5 Apr 63 to 11 Sep 65; Chucky City PO; deafness

BURK, James, K-161-2; Knoxville PO; ruptural hernia

BURK, John, H-62-1; 501 West Sixth, Chattanooga PO

BURKE, Thomas, Ma-128-1; Cpl K Co 118th MY (sic); Aug 13 62 to Jun 26 65; Jackson PO; wound in right leg, Drurys Bluff PO

BURKETT, Isaac F., We-225-2(1); Pvt A Co 7th TN Cav; Aug 4 62 to Aug 7 65; Sharon PO; axe cut, cut foot while chopping

BURKETT, William, Se-224-3; Pvt D Co 2nd TN Cav; 1 Sep 62 to 6 Jul 65; Wears Valley PO; rheumatism & heart

BURKHART, Morgan N., Un-254-1; Maj C Co 1st TN Cav; 1 Apr 62 to 6 Aug 63; Paulett PO; rheumatism, discharged from dissibility

BURKHEAD, Eli H., Ch-18-1; Pvt C Co 51st TN Cav; 25 Jul 63 to 14 May 65; PO omitted; CONF

BURKHEIMER, Wm. H., T-210-1; Dist No. 5

BURKHOLTS, Martin, D-54-2; Pvt A Co 2nd MI Inf; 21 Apr 61 to 21 Apr 64; Nashville PO

BURKLEY, Wri. N., Mg-197-4; Wartburg PO; command not known

BURKS, George P., Cf-33-1; 2nd Lt E Co 31st WI; Apr 63 to Nov 63; Gossburg PO

BURKS, Richard, Cs-62-3; Pvt B Co 7th PA Cav; 5-15-62 to __; Hollow Springs PO

BURL, Jiles, Co-62-3; Pvt A Co 9th TN Cav; 13 Jul 63 to 11 Sep 65; Bybee PO; ingered by horse

BURLESON, Greeberry, Wa-268-1; Pvt B Co 13th TN Cav; Sep 63 to Sep 65; Johnson City PO; dierrhea

BURLESON, Jefferson, Wa-167-1; Cpl F Co 8th TN Cav; 31 May 63 to 11 Sep 65;Jonesboro PO

BURLESON, Oliver, Wa-268-1; Pvt B Co 13th TN Cav; Sep 63 to Sep 65; Johnson City PO; rheumatism

BURLESON, Thomas, Wa-267-1; Susannah widow of; Pvt I Co 8th TN Cav; 5 Sep 63 to 11 Sep 65; Johnson City PO

BURLIN, Berry, S-218-3; US Sol; 9th Civil Dist

BURLIN, Ewel, S-218-3; US Sol; 9th Civil Dist

BURLISON, David C., Hy-84-1; Sgt K Co 48th TN; 1 Nov 62 to 1 Nov 64; Forked Deer PO; CONF

BURLISON, Van Buren, Lo-190-1; Pvt H Co 3rd TN Inf; Oct 63 to 65; Loudon PO; CONF

BURNELL, Charles A., Br-8-1; Pvt K Co 13th VT Inf; 9-11-62 to 1-31-63; Cleveland PO; general lung health

BURNES, George, T-214-1; Pvt G Co US Hvy Art; 63 to 65; Dist 9

BURNES, George W., Wi-276-1; Pvt B Co 10th TN Cav; 10 May 61 to Nov 62; Beechville PO; prisoner at Springfield 8 mos; CONF

BURNES, Green, La-117-2; Delila L. widow of; Pvt B Co 2nd TN Cav; May 63 to May 65; 15th Dist; CONF

BURNES, James B., Mu-200-1; Pvt B Co 31st OH Inf; 21 Feb 64 to 19 or 20 Jul 65; Rockdale PO

BURNES, James W., D-57-3; Nashville PO; CONF

BURNES, Joseph, Mg-198-3; Pvt C Co 3rd TN Inf; Dec 64 to __ (3 mos); Hunnicutt PO

BURNES, Martain V., He-64-2; Sgt A Co 2nd West TN Cav; 9 Aug 62 to 2 May 63; Middle Fork PO; disease of lungs; captured 20th Dec 1862

BURNET, Mit, Gr-71-2; Jarmine PO

BURNETT, Barbara, B-64-3; widow US Sol; 310 Earley St., Chattanooga PO

BURNETT, Caroline, G-51-2; widow US Sol; Humboldt PO

BURNETT, Edmond M., K-182-2; Mary J. widow of; Pvt E Co 3rd TN Cav; 62 to __; Shooks PO; was killed when the Str. Sultana blowed up

BURNETT, Edward, Sh-191-3; Pvt Gunboat Ratliff; 2 yrs; Memphis PO; records not seen

BURNETT, Hugh O., K-182-2; Pvt E Co 3rd TN Cav; 62 to 65; Shooks PO

BURNETT, Jackson C., K-184-1; Pvt B Co 6th TN Inf; 63 to Jul 65; Asbury PO

BURNETT, Jacob, D-87-1; Pvt A Co 12th TN Inf; 2 yrs 6 mos; Nashville PO

BURNETT, James, Un-257-2; Pvt L Co 1st TN Cav; 64 to 65; Little Barren PO; CONF

BURNETT, James M., Pu-142-2; 5th Civil Dist

BURNETT, James R., R-161-4; Pvt A Co 6th TN Inf; 3-8-62 to 4-27-65; Dayton PO; striffin of side tom

BURNETT, James W., K-154-3; Nancy E. widow of; Pvt B Co 6th TN Inf; 18 Jun 62 to 30 Jun 65; PO omitted

BURNETT, John, Se-228-2(3); Pvt K Co 3rd TN Cav; New Knob Creek PO; wounded in back; pensioner
BURNETT, John, Un-257-2; Pvt L Co 1st TN Cav; 64 to 65; New Prospect PO; disease of eyes; CONF
BURNETT, Jno. C., W1-291-1; Bugler K Co 15th TN; Feb 22 63 to Aug 14 65; Laynardo PO
BURNETT, Mart, Un-257-2; Pvt L Co 1st TN Cav; 64 to 65; Little Barren PO; CONF
BURNETT, Merideth, Mg-198-2; Jane widdow of; Pvt; Kismet PO
BURNETT, Morguis D. L., Lo-194-1; Lt C Co 5th TN Cav; 25 Feb 62 to Aug 62; Muddy Creek PO
BURNETT, Pleasant, Un-259-2; Pvt E Co 1st TN Inf; 2 May 62 to 18 Apr 64; Rhodelia PO; CONF
BURNETT, Samuel, Mr-96-1; Pvt 10th TN Inf; 8-62 to 1-13-64; Whitwell PO; foot mashed
BURNETT, William, K-182-4; Pvt F Co 9th TN Cav Vol; Sep 62 to __; Riverdale PO; scrofula
BURNETT, William A., G-66-1; Willam Davis alias; Pvt G Co 12th Cold. Inf; 12 Aug 63 to 16 Jan 66; Trenton PO; small pox, caused stiff ankle
BURNETT, William B., Hm-109-8; Pvt; PO not legible
BURNETT, William B., K-182-1; Pvt E Co 3rd TN Cav; Feb 63 to Jun 65; Shooks PO; disabled 1865, rheumatism, heart disease
BURNETT, William C., Lo-188-3; Capt C Co 7th TN Mtd Inf; 20 Aug 64 to 29 Jun 65; Stockton PO
BURNETTE, Alcana A., Ov-133-1; US Sol; 1st Civil Dist
BURNS, Columbus C., Wy-173-2; Pvt H Co 2nd TN Mtd Inf; 63 to 64; Houston PO
BURNS, Frank, H-49-10; Sgt; Daisy PO
BURNS, George, Hr-201?-1; Drummer by A. Reg. from Maine; Bolivar PO
BURNS, Gideon, Mc-118-5; Pvt H Co 5th TN Mtd Inf; 10-1-64 to 11-30-64; Calhoun PO; catarrh in head 26 yrs
BURNS, Hardy A., T-216-3; 14th Civil Dist
BURNS, Henry C., Ro-202-6; Pvt I Co 1st TN Inf; 11 Aug 61 to 30 Aug 64; Kingston PO; lung disease, also sun stroke
BURNS, Henry W., Mg-200-1; Pvt B Co 5th TN Inf; 25 Feb 62 to 7 Apr 65; Kismet PO; asthma, heart disease
BURNS, James H., Cr-8-1; Pvt F Co 7th TN Cav; 20 Sep 62 to 25 Oct 63; Lavinia PO
BURNS, Joseph H., S-214-3; Pvt I Co 11th TN Cav; 26 Sep 65 to __; Glenmary PO; was not discharged
BURNS, Paul, Sh-178-3; US Sol; rear 313 Union St, Memphis
BURNS, Robert J., Le-119-1; Mary Pope widow of; Pvt A Co 10th TN Inf; 16 Apr 62 to 25 May 65; Chief PO
BURNS, Sarah B., Ro-203-2; widow; Wheat PO
BURNS, Stephen, Mu-213-2; Pvt F Co 1st US TN Inf; 63 to 65; Rally Hill PO
BURNS, Tilmon, Br-7-3; Pvt A Co 10th TN Cav; 8-7-63 to 8-1-65; Old Fort PO (Polk Co.); disease of lungs
BURNS, William B., Hw-121-6(1); Pvt B Co 3rd TN Cav; 30 Jun 64 to 30 Nov 64; New Hope PO; rheumatism
BURNS, William C., Se-224-3; Pvt H Co 9th TN Cav; 1 Oct 63 to 63 (2 mos); Wears Valley PO; anneurism of the abdomen, Captain sent me home sick
BURNS, William P., Se-227-1; Sarah M. widow of; Pvt Detach 2nd TN Inf; 1 Jun 63 to 3 Aug 65; Trundles X Roads PO; hernia & heart disease
BURNS, ____, K-154-4; Jane widow of; Knoxville PO
BUROUGHS, B. F., We-230-4; Pvt E Co 22nd TN Reg; Sep 7 63 to Sep 8 64; McKinzie PO; CONF
BUROUS, Soloman F., Hd-50-2; Pvt E Co 1st TN Inf; Oct 12 63 to Jan 16 64; Walnut Grove PO; gun shot wound leg, head
BURRELL, Samuel, Hw-121-4(3); Pvt M Co 9th TN Cav; 30 Jun 63 to 20 Sep 65; Van Hill PO; broken rib, flash wound, hand
BURRESS, Alexander, A-9-5(3); Pvt C Co 2nd TN Inf; 11-1-61 to 11-5-64; Dutch Valley PO; rheumatism & neuralgia of bowels, prisoner 11 mos 17 days in B. Isle & Andersonville
BURRIS?, Elijah, Wa-267-2; Pvt E Co 3rdNC Inf; Dec 64 to 1 Apr 65; Febuary PO; chrc. rheumatism
BURRIS, Fernandes H., H-53-3; Lt A Co 10th KY Inf; 7-16-61 to 4-62; Chattanooga PO; left service on a/c of sickness, enlisted 4th then 10th reg. Lt A Co 4th KS Inf, no dates
BURRIS, James M., Sh-201-2; Pvt 2nd TN Cav; Memphis PO
BURRISS, Charles, Lo-191-2; Pvt H Co 1st TN Hvy Art; 7 Jun 63 to Mar 65; Morganton PO; ruptured while on force march
BURROUGHS, Jacob, Mr-99-2; Pvt I Co 10th TN Inf; 7-23-62 to 6-23-65; Jasper PO
BURROUGHS, Samuel S., S-214-1; Pvt E Co 9th IL Cav; 28 Feb 65 to 31 Oct 65; Robbins PO; disease of back
BURROUGHS, Thomas A., Mr-99-2; Pvt I Co 10th TN Inf; 6-23-62 to 7-3-65; Jasper PO; discharge lost
BURROW, George, M-106-3(2); Pvt D Co 40th US Col Inf; 8-63 to 4-65; Killsdale PO; applied for bounty money, discharge burned up
BURROW, George W., B-7-1; Sgt F Co 5th TN Cav; 9-10-63 to 6-25-65; Shelbyville PO
BURROW, Hiram W., Ms-172-1; Pvt M Co 5th TN Cav; Rich Creek PO
BURROW, Jarrell, B-7-1; Pvt C Co 4th TN Mtd Inf; 11-64 to 8-65; Shelbyville PO
BURROW, Martin, M-106-3(2); Martha widow of; Col Pvt I Co 14th US Col Inf; 12-15-63 to 3-26-66; Hillsdale PO; applied for pension
BURROW, Newt, Cr-8-2; B Co 22nd TN Inf; Jul 61 to 24 Dec 62; McBride PO; CONF
BURROW, Solomon, F-42-2(4); Pvt D Co 55th Col Inf; Canadaville PO; enlisted in Memphis
BURROWS, James M., Hd-53-2; Scout Cumberland Div; 12 Aug 64 to 27 Oct 64; Cravens Landing PO; rheumatism & bowel disease
BURROWS, John, D-71-1; Pvt H Co 12th Reg; 12 Feb 64 to Oct 12 65; Nashville PO
BURRTON?, Peter, Sh-145-2; Pvt A Co 11th US Col Inf; 1 May 64 to 12 Jan 66; Millington PO; rheumatism, Capt. Walter H. Fifull? US Col Inf, Co A
BURRUR, Jack, Tr-268-2; Pvt B Co; Hartsville PO; rheumatism, pensioned
BURSETT, William, Un-257-2; Pvt B Co 2nd TN Cav; Oct 61 to Apr 65; Sharps Chapel PO; CONF
BURT, Charles H., K-180-2; Pvt B Co 103rd OH Vol Inf; 2 Aug 62 to 12 Jun 65; Bearden PO; heart trouble
BURT, James, A-4-5; Pvt D Co 11th PA Vols; Coal Creek PO; shot wound of right fore arm, date of enlistment & discharge lost
BURT, John, Sh-189-5; Cpl 59th US Col Inf; 6-1-63 to 1-31-66; La. Ave, Memphis PO
BURT, Mason, H-51-4; Pvt G Co 16th US Inf; 8-12-61 to 3-31-65; Hill City PO
BURT, Mason, H-63-1; Rena widow of; Pvt 16th TN Inf; 707 Cypress, Chattanooga PO
BURT, Noah, Sh-153-3; Pvt G Co 61st; Jun 63 to Jan 66; Collierville PO
BURT, Thomas J., Ma-115-1; Pvt C Co 144th Inf; Jan 65 to Apr 65; PO omitted
BURT, Zephaniah, H-53-3; Julia A. widow of; Pvt A Co 122nd OH Inf; 5-1-64 to 9-64; Ridgedale PO; bowel trouble, discharge on account sickness
BURTIN, John C., La-117-3; Pvt F Co 1st AL Mtd Inf; Feb 11 62 to __ (1 yr 5 mos 17 days); 15th Dist; CONF
BURTON, Alford, Me-89-2; Pvt B Co 6th TN Inf; 8-15-64 to 6-20-65; Maloney PO; diarhea
BURTON, Andrew J., J-80-2; Pvt H Co 1st TN Inf; 4-18-64 to 5-23-65; Granville PO
BURTON, Charles C., Dk-39-1; Sarah E. widow of; Pvt D Co 1st TN Mtd Inf; Bozarth PO; death
BURTON, George M., Tr-269-2; Pvt G Co 6th TN Cav; 18 Mar 63 to 20 Apr 65; Knobton PO
BURTON, Hiram, Jo-151-1; Pvt E Co 13th TN Cav; 22 Sep 63 to 5 Sep 65; Stump Knob PO; measles-- results
BURTON, James, Pu-140-1; Pvt E Co 88th TN Inf; 11-14-64 to 1-66; Cookeville PO; discharged on disability
BURTON, James A., Cr-14-2; Pvt D Co 7th TN Cav; 5 Aug 62 to 25 Oct 63; Clarksburg PO; re-enlisted 8 Mar 65 - 9 Aug 65, Com. 7th TN Cav Discharge

BURTON, John, Dk-39-1; Margarett widow of; Pvt; Bozarth PO
BURTON, John, H-56-8; Sol US; St. Elmo PO
BURTON, Richard, We-220-1; Pvt C Co 40th IL State Troops; May 20 64 to Feb 28 65; PO omitted
BURTON, Simon, H-50-3(1); Emeline widow of; Soddy PO; killed
BURTON, William H., Su-232-1; Pvt I Co 50th VA Inf; 18 Jun 61 to ___ (3 yrs); Ruthton PO
BURTS, Isaiah, Wa-274-2; Pvt D Co 27th OH Inf (Col); 27 Jan 64 to 21 Sep 65; Jonesboro PO
BURUM, Absolom J., Ro-203-7; Sgt K Co 1st NC Inf; Oct 62 to ___; Wheat PO; CONF
BURUS, John, Mu-195-3; Mary widow of; Sol C Co 57th IL Vol; 62 to 66; Columbia PO
BURY, James E., Wy-171-3; Pvt H Co 6th TN Cav; 11-22-62 to 7-26-65; Sorby PO; shot through the foot
BURSY, Martin, H-76-1; Pvt I Co 4th US Vol Inf; 6-25-62 to 6-26-65; Chattanooga PO
BUSH, Asa A., H-73-2(1); Pvt K Co 149th NY Inf; 8-62 to 1-62 (sic); Chattanooga PO
BUSH, Cassius M., H-53-5; Lt WI Inf; ___ to 6-65 (3 yrs); Ridgedale PO
BUSH, Grantison Laton, Sm-169-3(5); Pvt C Co 8th TN Mtd Inf; 1-4-64 to 8-14-65; Donoho PO; neuralgia bursted out one eye and still afflicted; reenlisted veteran
BUSH, Henry, Sh-158-2; Rithey? widow of; Pvt H Co 55th Col'd. Inf; Memphis PO; partialy paralysed and partially supported by relatives
BUSH, Ivary, Ca-22-1; Pvt A Co 1st TN Inf; 2-17-64 to 4-18-65; Hollow Springs PO; sunstroke, reenlisted veteran
BUSH, John S., Cf-39-1; Pvt H Co 69th OH Inf--5 Aug 62 to 12 Nov 63; 168th OH Inf--2 May 64 to 8 Sep 64; Decherd PO (Franklin Co.)
BUSH, Leroy P., Ru-249-1; 1st TN; 12-10-63 to 8-17-65; Carlocksville PO; afflicted with rheumatism but able to work
BUSH, Mollie J., Ru-238-3; widow; Murfreesboro PO
BUSH, Phelix, Sm-171-1; Pvt H Co 1st TN Mtd Inf; 11-1-64 to 5-4-65; Chestnut Mound PO
BUSH, Timothy, Sm-171-1; Pvt L Co 5th TN Cav; 8-18-63 to 8-14-65; Chestnut Mound PO
BUSH, Timothy G., D-59-1; Pvt G Co 7th US Cav; whole service 61 (all the time to 65, to the end); 1707 Church St, Nashville PO
BUSH, William H., Pu-147-2; Pvt K Co 5th IL Inf; 4-8-65 to 11-13-66; Byrne PO
BUSH, Yocum C., Ro-201-5(3); Lt Col I Co 1st TN Inf; 9 Aug 61 to 28 Nov 64; Kingston PO
BUSH, Zachariah, Ca-22-2; Pvt F Co 1st TN Videt Cav; 6-63 to ___; Hollow Springs PO; measles
BUSHINGS, William, Be-5-1; Pvt A Co 7th TN Cav; 12 Jul 62 to Aug 65; Camden PO
BUSHNELL, Henry N., Cu-17-2; Sgt D Co 2nd CT Hvy Art; 7-62 to 7-23-65; Crossville PO; wounded
BUSHONG, Joseph, Mc-109-6; Pvt D Co 21st OH Inf; 8-26-61 to 7-25-65; Sweetwater PO (Monroe Co.) crippled in right hip & foot
BUSHYHEAD, George (Indian), Lo-190-1; Pvt G Co TN Inf; 62 to 65; Loudon PO; CONF
BUSIC, Calvin, Ha-115-1; Emeline widow of; Pvt A Co 1st TN Cav; Jun 62 to ___; Alanthers Hill PO; not disabled, died of malarial fever while on duty
BUSSELL, James W., Pu-145-1; Pvt L Co 5th Cav Vol; 8-5-63 to 08-4-65; Burton PO
BUSSELL, John L., Hw-133-4; Pvt B Co 60th TN Cav; Sep 62 to 10 Apr 65; Yellow Ston PO; rheumatism; CONF
BUSSELL, Mc D., Cl-51-1; Emeline widow of; Pvt L Co 8th TN Cav; 4-28-63 to 11-13-64; Cedar Fork PO; killed at Morristown 11-13-64
BUSSELL, William, Cl-51-2; Pvt I Co 3rd TN Inf; 9-10-63 to 9-15-65; Cedar Fork PO
BUTCHER, Layfaytt, Un-255-2; Pvt; Warwicks X Roads PO; rumatism
BUTLER, Dan J., Pi-154-2; Pvt H Co 12th KY Inf; 61 to 61; Hull PO
BUTLER, Daniel, Sh-178-1; Cook B Co 2nd IA; 64 to 65; rear 315 Union, Memphis PO
BUTLER, Frank, K-161-4; Pvt B Co 1st US Hvy Art; 24 Jan 64 to 4 Mar 66; Knoxville PO; kicked by horse--testicle mashed
BUTLER, Galston W., Cr-20-2; Pvt I Co 7th TN Cav; 9-15-63 to 6-27-65; Hollow Rock PO; diareah 26 yrs & scroffalo, not able to do hard labor
BUTLER, Gibson, Ru-241-3; Margaret widow of; Pvt; 63 to ___; PO omitted
BUTLER, Henry C., Cr-14-3; Nancy A. widow of; 2nd Lt D Co 7th TN Cav; 5 Aug 62 to 25 Oct 63; Crider PO
BUTLER, Henry H., Cr-17-1; Pvt B Co 7th TN Cav; 8-62 to 8-65; Buena Vista PO; general health impaired, not pentioned
BUTLER, James, Wa-270-1; Pvt H Co 9th TN Inf; 63 to 64; Austins Springs PO
BUTLER, John, De-22-2; Pvt OH Cav; 1 May 63 to 1 Jul 63; New Era PO
BUTLER, John M., Cl-56-2(1); Sarah widow of; Pvt B Co 11th TN Cav; 6-3-62 to ___ (1 yr 9 mos 23 days); Head of Barren PO; died of typhoid pneumonia 4-15-64
BUTLER, Keziah, Co-66-3(1); widow of US Sol; PO omitted
BUTLER, Lewis, Mu-190-1; Pvt F Co 110th Col Inf; 63 to ___; Culleoka PO
BUTLER, Markus D., W-193-1; Pvt; Vernilla PO; belong to a Missouri Reg, his discharge is in Washington
BUTLER, Mary, R-157-1; widow; Spring City PO; lung disease
BUTLER, Oliver, F-37-1; alias William Otes; Pvt I Co 11th US Inf; Stanton Depot PO; shot in right leg
BUTLER, Rillar (see White, Alex)
BUTLER, Samuel D., Sn-254-2; Sgt B Co 11th Vol Inf; 4-14-61 to 12-23-65; Hendersonville PO; heart disease, inflamatory rheumatism
BUTLER, W. W., Cr-17-2; Nancy widow of; Pvt B Co 7th TN Cav; 8-7-62 to died 1864; Buena Vista PO
BUTLER, William, Mo-130-1; Pvt G Co 1st NY Marine Art; 3-8-62 to 3-16-63; Ballplay PO; wound saber, reenlisted veteran--Pvt G Co 17th NY Inf; 9-14-63 to 8-8-65
BUTLER, William, D-70-1; widow of; Hospital Steward G Co 12th Inf; 63 to ___ (3 yrs); Nashville PO
BUTLER, William, Bo-12-2(1); Pvt B Co 13th TN Cav; 9-23-63 to 9-5-65; Rason PO; spinal disorder, can't see or hear well
BUTLER, William, Gr-81-1; Juley R. Hopson widow of; Pvt Bat 1st KY Mtd Cav; 62 to 63; Clear Spring PO; chron. in. of liver, totly disabled
BUTLER, William, A-6-4(2); Pvt E Co 3rd TN Inf; 2-12-62 to 6-22-65; Olivers PO; shoulder broke by wagon
BUTLER, William, Lo-195-1; Pvt K Co 5th TN Inf; 19 May 62 to 19 May 65; Eaton's X Roads PO
BUTLER, William J., Hd-50-6; Sol MS; 17th Civil Dist
BUTLER, Willis, T-206-1; Pvt G Co 61st TN Inf; Jun 1 63 to Dec 65; Dovington PO
BUTRAM, James, M-108-1; Margaret widow of; Pvt; Akersville, KY PO; discharge not at home
BUTRUM, Jacob B., M-108-4; Pvt A Co 9th KY Inf; 9-18-61 to 10-12-62; Lafayette PO; breast disease
BUTRUM, John J., M-108-3; Elizabeth E. widow of; Pvt D Co 8th TN Mtd Inf; 3-10-65 to 8-31-65; Lafayette PO
BUTTER, Adam, Sh-198-2; Pvt Teamster 11th, 12th & 20th Corps in VA; Capt. Lacey, QM during 1863 and 64; Memphis PO; was separated in battle (claimes a year's pay)
BUTTER, Calvin M., Hm-104-1; Pvt C Co 1st TN Cav; 1 Apr 62 to 1 Apr 65; Mossy Creek PO (Jefferson Co.); frost bite or chilblain, cancer on back, both legs ulcerated, helpless
BUTTER, Geo., T-212-1; found while examining work; no address on blank
BUTTER, Richard H., Jo-149-2; Pvt D Co 13th TN Cav; 24 Sep 63 to 1 Nov 64; Mountain City PO
BUTTER, Rodrick R., Jo-149-1; Lt Col 13th TN Cav; 8 Oct 63 to 11 Apr 64; Mountain City PO; piles
BUTTER, Sarah, D-100-1; widow of Battle, Andrew; Pvt D Co 7th TN Inf; Nashville PO; totally deaf and dumb by jar of canon, Battle died in Dec 1889 & his wife is weak minded & cannot obtain dates correctly

BUTTER, Willis, Gi-132-3; Pvt D Co 110th USCV; Nov 63 to Aug 15 65; Wales PO
BUTTERBOUGH, William M., Dk-33-4; Pvt F Co 74th PA Inf; 3-4-64 to 8-27-65; Cathage Home PO; lung trouble caused by meassels
BUTTERS, James, C-34-3; Pvt C Co 2nd WI Cav; fall 63 to fall 65; Pioneer PO
BUTTLER, Doctor C., C-8-2; Pvt H Co 9th TN Cav; 7-15-63 to 9-11-65; Well Spring PO; catarrh in head & bronchitis; receivs $72 per yr
BUTTLER, Jessie G., G-67-1; Pvt M Co 6th TN Cav; 11 Aug 62 to 26 Jul 65; Treynant? PO; rheumatism
BUTTLER, Oliver C., Jo-148-1; Eliza widow of; Saddler D Co 13th TN Cav; 5 Nov 63 to 5 Sep 65; Laurel Bloomery PO
BUTTN (sic), Alexander T., Cr-16-2; Cpl I Co 7th TN Cav; Aug 10 62 to Jun 26 65; Huntingdon PO; scurvy, piles & heart trouble, contracted Andersonville
BUTTRAM, Caroline, Lo-188-4; widow US Sol; 3rd Civil Dist
BUTTRAM, Daniel, Col, S-214-2; Manda widow of; Pvt; Glenmary PO
BUTTRAM, Joel, S-214-1; Arbama Willoby formerly widow of; G Co 2nd TN Inf; Robbins PO
BUTTRAM, Mary, S-213-3; widow US Sol; 2nd Civil Dist
BUTTRY, William, Ha-116-3(1); L Co 8th TN Cav; Aug __ to __; Clinch PO
BUTTS, Jothodara I., He-60-1; Pvt H Co 16th IL Cav; 8-28-63 to 8-19-65; Lexington PO; suffers with rheumatism in legs & arm
BUTTS, Sam., Hd-51-2; US Sol; Hamburg PO
BYARS, John R., We-223-1; Pvt I Co 6th TN Cav; 5 Jun 62 to 26 Jul 65; Palmersville PO; chronick cattarh
BYATT, Elisha, S-212-2; Pvt K Co 30th KY; 2 Feb 64 to 18 Apr 65; Onida PO; leg broak
BYERLY, Newton, Je-140-2; 15th Dist
BYERLY, Nuton, Je-140-2; Pvt E Co 5th TN Inf; 12 Feb 62 to 23 Feb 65; Strawberry Plains PO
BYERS, Andrew F., Pu-144-1; Pvt H Co 1st TN; 2-4-64 to 5-26-65; Double Springs PO; right leg shot off
BYERS, Henry T., Ct-38-2; Pvt K Co 8th IL Cav; 2-1-64 to 6-17-65; Carthage MO PO
BYFORD, George W., Dk-33-4; 4th Civil Dist
BYNUM, Henry, K-173-4; US Sol; 3rd Dist
BYNUM, Noah, Sh-145-4; Pvt A Co 55th US Co Inf; Apr 63 to 31 Dec 65; Millington PO; Capt. Henry Simmons,____ Kelley
BYONS, Doctor H., Se-228-3; Pvt M Co 9th TN Cav; 12 Jun 63 to 11 Sep 65; Henrys X Roads PO
BYONS, Elisha, Je-140-2; Pvt B Co 9th TN Cav; 21 Jun 63 to 9 Sep 65; PO omitted
BYRAMS, George W., D-59-1; Pvt B Co 111th NY Inf; 31 Aug 64 to 4 Jun 65; 1911 Patterson St, Nashville PO; rheumatism, fistula & piles; above diseases in service
BYRD, Chas. L., Sh-171-1; Pvt G Co OH Vol Inf; 65 to 66; Memphis PO
BYRD, David, Mo-120-3(1); Amanda J. widow of; Pvt TN Inf; Sweetwater PO; died in service
BYRD, Isaac, R-160-1; Pvt A Co 7th TN; 9-8-64 to 7-27-65; 6th Civil Dist
BYRD, James R., R-160-1; 7th Civil Dist; discharge not at hand
BYRD, James S., Br-11-1; Pvt I Co 1st TN Inf; 61 to 64 (3 yrs 6 mos 2 days); Chatala PO; chronic dyspepsia
BYRD, Jersiell, Sh-175-1; Sgt B Co 110th MS? Inf; 7-63 to 65; Memphis PO
BYRD, Jesse L., S-215-1; Pvt B Co 7th KY Inf; 7 Oct 61 to 11 Mar 66; Huntsville PO; rheumatism caused by exposure
BYRD, John H., Mg-198-4; Pvt F Co 1st TN Inf--9 Aug 61 to 15 Sep 62; Lt L Co 2nd TN Cav--15 Sep 62 to 4 Mar 64; Capt A Co 2nd TN Cav--3 Mar 64 to 6 Jul 65; Island Ford PO; affected spine
BYRD, Melton A., S-213-2; Pvt F Co 7th TN Inf; 63 to 15 Jul 65; Hellenwood PO; piles & left eye injured
BYRD, Robert K., Ro-201-4(2); Mary L. widow of; Col 1st TN Inf; 9 Aug 61 to 20 Sep 64; Kingston PO

BYRELEY, William J., K-180-1; Pvt E Co 3rd TN Cav; 29 Jan 63 to 14 Jun 65; Ebenezer PO
BYRGE, Calaway, A-9-1; Pvt I Co 7th TN Mtd Inf; 11-8-64 to 7-27-65; Ligias PO
BYRGE, William, A-9-2; Pvt A Co 1st TN Inf; 8-2-61 to 9-17-64; Podopholine PO
BYRLEY, James, Gr-77-1; Pvt E Co 3rd TN Inf; 12 Feb 62 to 25 Mar 65; Y.Z. PO; rupture
BYRLEY, James C., Lo-190-1; Pvt A Co 1st TN Inf; Jul 63 to ___; Loudon PO; chronic diarhoea
BYRLEY, Martin, Gr-77-1; Pvt E Co 3rd TN Inf; 12 Feb 62 to 13 Feb 65; Y.Z. PO; piles
BYRNES, James, L-100-2; Pvt C Co 4th US Col Hvy Art; Jan 63 to Feb 63; Ripley PO; wounded in right leg? and contracted hernia
BYRUM, Amos H., Mo-128-1; Pvt B Co 34th KY Inf; 11-15-62 to 7-15-65; Belltown PO
BYRUM, Joel, Mo-121-2; Pvt A Co 5th TN Inf; 2-25-62 to 4-4-65; Philadelphia PO; neuralgia results of smallpox, frost bitten feet
BYRUM, William M., Bo-13-2; Pvt F Co 2nd TN Inf; 1-63 to 7-6-65; Tutt PO; injured in back
CABBLE, James P., Co-69-5; Pvt B Co 9th TN Cav; 15 Aug 63 to Sep 65; Help PO; no as I remember dates not noun
CABE, Lucius H., Lo-191-2; Pvt C Co 3rd TN Mtd Inf; 26 Jul 64 to 30 Nov 64; Morganton PO
CABLE, Richard, Ct-35-4; Pvt G Co 13th TN Cav; Elk Mills PO; in the US Army; discharge mislayed, no date of enrollment or discharge
CADE, L. D., De-22-1; Alma E. widow of; Comisary? C Co 9th TN Cav; 1 Nov 62 to 1 May 65; Clifton PO; CONF
CADL (sic), Bengaman F., De-26-1; Millsers Hawkins; 6 mos; Bible Hill PO
CADY, George W., Wy-175-1; Pvt H Co 2nd TN Mtd Inf; 12-9-63 to 1-22-65; Cypress Inn PO; eyes affected from measles
CADY, J. H., H-66-1; Quartermaster Sgt 11th Cav; 8-22-63 to 9-22-65; Chattanooga PO
CAFFE, James R., Wi-278-1; Cornelia N. widow of; Pvt C Co 5th OH Cav--Apr 5 64 to Oct 5 65; 2nd Lt L Co 1st TN Cav--Nov 1 64 to Jul 14 65; Franklin PO
CAGLE, Burton?, Ch-18-3(5); Pvt F Co 3rd TN Inf; Dutch Valley PO; measles resulting in lung disease; discharge in hands of attorney
CAGLE, Henry, Dy-25-3; Pvt 27th TN Inf; Aug 61 to Sep 63; Newbern PO; CONF
CAGLE, Henry C., He-61-1; Pvt D Co 7th TN Cav; 6 Sep 62 to 25 Oct 63; Morgan PO
CAGLE, John, R-161-1; Pvt D Co 3rd TN Inf; 7-25-64 to 11-30-64; Dayton PO
CAGLE, Peter, H-49-3; Pvt 3rd TN Mtd Inf; 4 mos; PO omitted
CAGLE, William, Se-227-3; Pvt K Co 12th TN Cav; about Oct 63 to 65; Trundles X Roads PO
CAGLEY, Isaac, A-7-3; Pvt K Co 5th TN; 2-26-61 to 3-20-65; Robertsville PO
CAGLEY, Lewis F., Ro-203-5(1); Sarah G. widow of; Pvt I Co 7th TN Mtd Inf; 8 Nov 64 to 27 Jul 65; Burns Mills PO
CAHILL, Michael, Hr-2013-1; Sailor; Bolivar PO
CAHOON, Samuel, Hw-123-1; Eliza widow of; Pvt H Co 8th TN Cav; Rotherwood PO
CAILLONETT, Benj. F., D-76-1; Pvt D Co 150th IL Inf; Jan 1 65 to Jan 16 66; Nashville PO
CAIN, Almers A., G-71-1; Bugler L Co 6th TN Cav; 6 Jul 62 to 6 Jul 65; Bradford PO
CAIN, Benjamin F., K-168-1; Pvt L Co 10th TN Cav; 63 to 65; Knoxville PO
CAIN, Edward L., O-134-1; Pvt D Co Art; Sep 23 61 to Dec 23 62; Hornbeak PO; shot in face, afficted yet; CONF
CAIN, Franklin, Mc-113-2; Pvt A Co 5th TN Inf; 64 to __ (6 mos); Riceville PO; rheumatism, discharge sent off, couldn't give dates
CAIN, Homer C., K-166-4(2); Sgt B Co 123rd IN Inf; 26 Nov 63 to 25 Aug 65; Knoxville PO
CAIN, John G. (see Kean, John G.)
CAKES, Joseph, Sh-150-2; Pvt G Co 2nd TN Inf; Mar to 65 (3 mos); Bartlett PO
CALAWAY, Thomas, Mo-122-2; Mary J. wife of; Pvt G Co 3rd TN Inf; 11-61 to 8-20-63; Madisonville PO; further dates could not be gotten; CONF
CALDWELL, Charles Y., Lo-189-1; Pvt Art; 64 to 65; Philadelphia PO; CONF

CALDWELL, David M., Je-142-1; Capt B Co 9th TN Cav; 21 Mar 63 to 11 Sep 65; New Market PO; hemorrhoids & diarhea
CALDWELL, Elizabeth E., Dk-36-3; widow US Sol; 9th Dist
CALDWELL, Hugh D., Cr-16-1; Pvt I Co 7th TN Cav; Mar 7 64 to Aug 9 65; Huntingdon PO; chronic diarreha; taken in Andersonville
CALDWELL, James, Un-250-1; Pvt 1st TN Inf; Maynardville PO; herney from injury received while in service
CALDWELL, James, Gi-122-1; Pvt D Co 111th TN Inf; 61 to 63; Prospect Sta. PO
CALDWELL, James R., Hw-121-3(2); Pvt A Co 9th TN Cav; 1 Oct 63 to 12 Sep 65; New Hope PO; none in war
CALDWELL, John, K-176-3; PO omitted
CALDWELL, John, K-176-2; Pvt F Co 3rd TN Inf; 62 to 65; Halls X Roads PO
CALDWELL, John F., H-63-4; Pvt K Co 100th PA Inf; 10-8-61 to 10-7-65; Co. Chestnut & Broad, Chattanooga PO
CALDWELL, John M., Br-10-2; Pvt D Co 4th TN Cav; 12-16-62 to 7-12-65; Cleveland PO
CALDWELL, John W., Mu-209-5; Pvt C Co 3rd TN Inf; Jun 1 61 to May 1 65; Darks Mills PO; prisoner 7 mos Fort Warren, MA; CONF
CALDWELL, Joseph, H-72-1; Pvt 1st US Col Art; Chattanooga PO
CALDWELL, Mark, Un-254-2; Pvt G Co 2nd TN Inf; 16 Apr 62 to 18 Apr 65; Bartheney PO
CALDWELL, Patrice, Hw-125-2; Pvt TN Inf; 62 to 64; Stony Point PO; CONF
CALDWELL, William A., Mu-209-7; Pvt C Co 3rd TN Inf; 5-61 to 5-23-65; Columbia PO; CONF
CALES, James, Sh-173-1; Pvt M Co 3rd US Hvy Art; 12-22-63 to 4-30-66; Memphis PO
CALET, James M., Mu-203-1; 15th Civil Dist
CALES, John W., C-33-5; Sgt C Co 9th TN Cav; 7-4-63 to 9-11-65; Newcomb PO
CALFEE, Seth R., Co-69-6(1); Pvt I Co 62nd TN Inf; 28 Sep 61 to 64; Driskill PO; non, dont remember dates captured & paroled
CALHOUN, David, Sh-159-3; Sgt F Co 88th TN; 25 Jan 65 to 1 Jan 66; Memphis PO
CALHOUN, Geo. W., Ha-114-2; Pvt R Co 11th MO Inf; 1 Sep 64 to 29 Oct 65; Yellow Springs PO; CONF
CALHOUN, John C., H-60-5(2); Hattie widow of; Pvt 44th US Col Inf; Chattanooga PO
CALHOUN, Johnson, D-61-2; Mary widow of; Pvt; 61 to 65; Ament Cor. Jackson, Nashville PO; this party is dead
CALHOUN, William, Dh-34-3; Mary widow of; Pvt B Co 15th US Col Inf; Colesburg PO; discharge filed for pension
CALL, Frances L., Wa-266-1; Matilda C. formerly widow of; Lt; Haws X Roads PO; wounded Lookout Mt., died 14th Feb 64
CALL, George, F-43-2; Drum?; Colliervile PO; cannot get any information
CALL, Henry C., Mo-121-1; Cpl K Co 8th MI Inf; 9-12-61 to 9-23-62; Philadelphia PO; wound in right ankle, left foot, pensioner; Sgt I Co 1st MI Sharpshooters--8-26-63 to 12-20-64; asthma and rheumatism
CALL, William, We-224-1; Pvt A Co TN Inf; 61 to 64; Como PO (Henry Co.); contracted piles, discharged by reason of over age
CALLAHAN, Rufas K., R-161-6; Pvt G Co 6th TN Mtd Inf; 2-20-65 to 6-30-65; Dayton PO; shot in right leg
CALLAWAY, Andrew, Lo-191-2; Hilah widow of; Pvt; Morgantown PO
CALLAWAY, James M., K-186-4; Pvt G Co 8th TN Cav; 11 Aug 63 to 11 Sep 65; Balls Camp PO
CALLAWAY, John Q., K-186-3; Pvt H Co 1st TN Inf; 9 Aug 61 to 13 Nov 63; Beaver Ridge PO
CALLENDER, John Hill, D-99-5; Maj 11th TN Inf; Aug 20 61 to Feb 20 62; Nashville PO; Central Hos. for Insane; CONF
CALLEN, Samuel M., Dy-32-1; Pvt G Co 2nd KS Cav; 28 Mar 61 to 13 Jan 65; Trimble PO
CALLENS, J. C., Bo-11-3; Mary widow of; Pvt I Co 5th TN Inf; 6 mos svce; Brick Mill PO
CALLET, William N., Ge-96-4; Pvt M Co 1st TN Cav; 1 Aug 62 to 65 (2 yrs 10 mos 6 days);

Limestone PO; mashed testicle, gun shot wound in hip, diareah & fever
CALLETT, Charles U., K-156-2; 2nd Lt I Co 2nd E TN Mtd Inf; 28 Dec 61 to 28 Dec 64; 69 Church? St., Knoxville PO
CALLETT, James H., Gr-72-1; Pvt I Co 8th TN Inf; 1 Mar 63 to 28 May 65; Noelon PO; extreme marching
CALLETTS, Thomas, Je-144-2; Pvt I Co 8th TN Inf; 1 Mar 63 to Jun? 65; Talbotts PO; lung trouble by measles, discharge close ware
CALLISON, John L., We-227-1; Pvt I Co 6th TN Cav; 19 Jul 62 to 9 Aug 65; Greenfield PO
CALLMAN, Arthur W., Mo-119-2; Pvt H Co US Col Hvy Art; 65 to 66; Sweetwater PO; shot in left leg
CALLOWAY, Nancy, K-177-2; widow Sol US; PO omitted
CALLOWAY, Nelson, K-164-3; Cpl M Co 1st US Art; 15 Oct 64 to 31 Mar 66; PO omitted (Knoxville?)
CALLUM, George, Ov-138-1; 5th Civil Dist
CALOWAY, Robert, Hm-108-1; Pvt B Co; facts not known; Russellville PO; shot in leg, catarrh
CALTON, Robert, Ru-239-1; Pvt E Co TN? Inf; 63 to 63 (1 mo); Versailes PO; took measles, a conscripted soldier
CALVERT, James J., H-69-4; Pvt C Co 49th AL Inf; 61 to 64 (3 yrs 6 mos); Chattanooga PO; CONF
CALVIN, Lawson, Hw-127-4; Pvt; Amis PO
CALVIN, Newman, H-58-1; Pvt B Co 1st TN Inf; 8-3-62 to 6-21-65; Sale Creek PO; partial deafness & piles
CALVIN, Read, Mu-193-1; Pvt; Columbia PO
CALWELL, Hardy Sr., Sn-260-6; Pvt B Co 1st TN Cav; 9-27-61 to 7-4-62; Westmoreland PO; right arm shot off in battle; discharged on surgeons certificate; CONF
CALWELL, Petty, Dk-36-1; 1st Lt I Co 5th TN Cav; 63 to 64; Smithville PO
CAMADY, John H., D-87-1; Pvt G Co 84th IN Inf; 2 yrs mo; Nashville PO
CAMAL, Morna S., Cr-14-2; Quartermaster Sgt B Co 2nd TN Mtd Inf; 29 Dec 64 to __; Clarksburg PO; wounded; Maj. of batalion killed and batalion scattered, was not discharged
CAMAL, Moses D., Cr-14-1; Pvt G Co 2nd TN Mtd Inf; 29 Dec 63 to 1 Feb 65; Clarksburg PO; Mtd Inf
CAMBELL, Paris S., Wl-299-2; 15th Civil Dist
CAMEL, Neuton, Hd-48-1; Savannah PO; back injured
CAMELL, Jane, He-62-2; widow; 16th Dist
CAMERON, James, Me-89-1; Pvt E Co 5th TN Reg; 5-2-62 to 5-11-65; Big Spring PO
CAMERON, James M., Ct-40-6; Asst Surg 13th TN Cav; 11-7-63 to 7-19-65; Elizabethton PO
CAMERON, Samuel, Bo-21-2; Pvt I Co 3rd TN Cav; 10-1-63 to 9-11-65; Ellijay PO
CAMERON, Wm. B., Gr-70-1; Pvt F Co 1st TN Cav; 1 Apr 62 to 31 Mar 65; Rutledge PO; catarrh of head
CAMP, George L., Mc-112-3; Sgt G Co 92nd OH Inf; 8-15-62 to 6-20-65; Athens PO; rheumatism, deafness, kidney disease
CAMP, W. T., Mc-117-3; Pvt D Co 1st TN Art; 11-6-63 to 7-20-65; Carlock PO; kidney trouble
CAMPBEL, Adam C., Co-69-6(12); Susan C. widow of; Pvt G Co 4th TN Cav; __ to 65; Driskill PO; palpations of heart; discharge no at home, cant give dates
CAMPBEL, Ann, T-216-2; 14th Civil Dist
CAMPBELL, Abraham S., Gi-124-1; Pvt A Co 12th TN Cav; 29 Mar 63 to 15 Oct 65; Merritt PO
CAMPBELL, Al, Mu-191-1; Susan widow of; Pvt G Co 13th TN Vol; 63 to 66; Bigbyville PO
CAMPBELL, Alexander, Ct-35-1; Nancy J. widow of; Pvt 4th TN Inf; Hampton PO; discharge not at home
CAMPBELL, Alexander, Br-9-2; Pvt E Co 8th TN Cav; 4-20-63 to __; Cleveland PO
CAMPBELL, Alexander, Gu-45-1; Pvt E Co 1st TN Cav (Vidette); 63 to 64 (8 mos); Altamont PO
CAMPBELL, Alfred, Wl-295-1; Pvt F Co 13th Reg Inf; Sep 24 63 to May 25 65; Lebanon PO
CAMPBELL, Amy M. (see Russell, John
CAMPBELL, Andrew J., Wl-295-2; Lebanon PO
CAMPBELL, Andrew J., Wa-274-1; Lily S. widow of; Pvt I Co 8th TN Cav; 25 Sep 63 to 11 Sep 65; Jonesboro PO
CAMPBELL, Arch, W-193-2; Harriet widow of; Pvt; Viala PO

CAMPBELL, Benjamin D., Fr-112-3; Pvt H Co 7th AR Inf; 6-1-61 to 6-1-65; Tullahoma PO; wounded shoulder, back and leg; CONF
CAMPBELL, Canis C., Jo-152-3; widow US Sol; High Health PO
CAMPBELL, Carter, Ct-35-1; Cpl E Co 3rd MD Cav; 9-11-63 to 9-7-65; Hampton PO
CAMPBELL, Charles, Ru-241-2(1); Pvt K Co 14th TN Inf; 3 Apr 63 to 18 Jan 64; Murfreesboro PO; shot in the arm
CAMPBELL, Charles B., Co-62-2; Sgt M Co 1st TN Cav; 15 Jul 62 to 5 Jun 65; Help PO; rheumatism & local ingery
CAMPBELL, David F., Hn-69-1; PO omitted
CAMPBELL, Davis, Gr-80-2; Pvt C Co 4th TN Cav; 5 Dec 62 to 18 Jul 65; Red Hill PO; chronic diarhea
CAMPBELL, Duncan, Cf-35-1; Sgt B Co 1st TN Inf; 26 Apr 62 to 26 Sep 63; Tullahoma PO; CONF
CAMPBELL, E. N. (see Reynold, William H.)
CAMPBELL, E. R. (see Green, Thomas, D-94-1)
CAMPBELL, Ethelbert J., Hn-75-1; Pvt A Co 1st TN Cav; 8 Apr 64 to 10 Apr 65; Manlyville PO
CAMPBELL, Font G., D-57-1; Pvt A Co 11th TN Cav; 62 to 66; PO omitted; 8th Ward; CONF
CAMPBELL, George, L-103-1; Pvt D Co 13th TN Inf; 63 to Dec 24 64; Ashport PO
CAMPBELL, George F., Ct-35-1; Pvt G Co 13th TN Cav;    to 9-5-65; Hampton PO; in sevis of US Army, discharge not at home
CAMPBELL, George J., Sh-159-6; Pvt; Memphis PO; CONF
CAMPBELL, Geo. P., D-91-3; Ada B. Stier widow of; Pvt 19th IL Inf; 3 yrs; Market House, Nashville PO
CAMPBELL, George P., Sm-174-1; Pvt G Co 4th TN Inf; 11-1-64 to 8-25-65; New Middleton PO
CAMPBELL, Green, Bl-3-2; Pvt; Billingsly PO; CONF
CAMPBELL, Hardie H., Gu-45-1; Pvt E Co 1st TN Cav Vidette; 63 to 64 (8 mos); Altamont PO
CAMPBELL, Harrison, Gu-48-1; Sgt E Co 1st AL Vidette Cav; 10-7-63 to 6-6-64; 1st Lt M Co 10th TN Cav--10-11-64 to 8-1-65; Tracy City PO
CAMPBELL, Henderson, Ct-44-2; Pvt C Co 13th TN Cav; 9-5-63 to 9-5-65; Hampton PO
CAMPBELL, Hensree, Se-220-2; Pvt B Co 4th TN Cav; 15 May 60 to 11 Sep 65; Emerts Cave PO; prisner at Richman; died
CAMPBELL, Henry, U-245-2; Pvt B Co 13th TN Cav; 1 Oct 64 to May 65; Limestone Cove PO; nerviness of the heart, week trimbles
CAMPBELL, Henry C., Gi-127-3; alias Henry Clay; Cpl B Co 12th Reg Col Inf; 2 yrs 6 mos; Pulaski PO; discharge lost
CAMPBELL, Herv. L., Ja-84-2; Fifer Musitan C Co 5th TN Inf; Harrison PO; hemorge of lungs
CAMPBELL, Hiraim W., Cr-8-1; Pvt A Co 50th MO Inf; 21 Aug 64 to 7 Jul 65; Lavinia PO
CAMPBELL, Hiram, Hw-118-3; Sol; St. Clair PO
CAMPBELL, Howard, H-58-6; alias James; Mary C. widow of; Pvt; Retro PO; discharge lost, joined Shermans army in S. Carolina
CAMPBELL, Hugh, Gu-48-2; Pvt D Co 1st TN Idpt Vidette Cav; 8-4-63 to 6-16-64; Tracy City PO
CAMPBELL, Isaac, Pu-146-1; Michal widow of; Pekin PO; died in service
CAMPBELL, Isaac A., Cl-54-1; Pvt A Co 1st TN Cav; 9-1-62 to 6-8-63; Bacchus PO; typhoid fever
CAMPBELL, Ivie, Ca-19-1; Cpl H Co 4th TN Cav; 10-1-64 to 8-1-65; Woodbury PO; measels set back 45 days, fornest? batte at Murfreeboro
CAMPBELL, Jacob, K-161-6; Knoxville PO
CAMPBELL, James, Co-62-2; Pvt H Co 3rd NC Inf; Feb 65 to __ (5 mos); Givens PO; measles
CAMPBELL, James, Ca-22-2; Pvt IN Inf; 1-1-64 to 5-64; Burt PO; served in wagon train
CAMPBELL, James, Mr-96-3(2); Pvt 1st AL Cav; Tracy City PO; relaps measals
CAMPBELL, James A., Mr-99-3; Pvt I Co 10th TN Inf; 7-23-62 to 6-23-65; Jasper PO
CAMPBELL, James F., Br-12-1; 1st Lt G Co 11th TN Cav; 9-1-63 to 10-5-64; Charleston PO
CAMPBELL, James M., Ja-85-6; Lucy E. White widow of; Pvt E Co 5th TN Mtd Inf; 9-1-64 to 6-26-65; Georgetown PO

CAMPBELL, James P., Gi-122-1; Pvt A Co 53rd TN Reg; 1 Nov 61 to 18 May 65; Prospect Sta. PO; CONF
CAMPBELL, Jesse P., Br-7-1; Pvt E Co 5th TN Inf; 3-2-62 to 4-4-65; Felker PO; wound
CAMPBELL, James W., D-57-3; Lt A Co 1st TN; 61 to Apr 9 65; PO omitted, 8th Ward; CONF
CAMPBELL, Jesept, Gr-81-2; Martha widow of; Pvt C Co TN Inf; Jul 63 to Oct 65; Clear Spring PO; chronic dyrhie, now dead
CAMPBELL, John, Ct-44-1; Pvt G Co 13th TN Cav; 9-24-63 to 9-5-65; Hampton PO
CAMPBELL, John D., Mc-112-5; Pvt F Co Pioneer Inf; 9-64 to 11-64; Atens PO; chronic diarrhea; discharge lost, cannot get exact dates
CAMPBELL, John J., Ct-45-1; Sgt B Co 13th TN Cav; 9-23-63 to 6-20-65; Stony Creek PO; on march Kentucky to Nashville 1864
CAMPBELL, Joseph, Co-68-2; Pvt C Co 8th TN Cav; 3 Oct 63 to 11 Sep 65; Cashy PO; fevar settled in left knee
CAMPBELL, Joseph L., Jo-152-1; Pvt B Co 13th TN Cav; 22 Sep 63 to 6 Sep 65; Doeville PO; gun shot
CAMPBELL, Joseph P., Jo-151-1; Pvt E Co 13th TN Cav; 22 Sep 63 to 5 Sep 65; Stump Knob PO; diarrhoia, hip injured, thrown from horse
CAMPBELL, Lemuel J., Gu-47-1; PVt TN; 63 to 63 (6 mos); Pelham PO
CAMPBELL, M. C., Mu-210-3; Pvt & Capt G Co 1st TN Inf; 5-1-61 to 5-1-65; Spring Hill PO; shot in right leg; CONF
CAMPBELL, Mage, Hd-51-1; Capt E Co 55th US Inf; 14 Jun 63 to 24 Dec 66; Hamburg PO
CAMPBELL, Mandy, Hd-51-2; widow US Sol; 10th Civil Dist
CAMPBELL, Manuel H., Wa-268-4; discharge away from home; Johnson City PO
CAMPBELL, Martha J., Hw-131-4; PO omitted
CAMPBELL, Mary A. (see Pointer, R. W.)
CAMPBELL, Mary E., Dy-28-1; widow of US Sol; 10th Civ Dist
CAMPBELL, Mike O., Wh-180-1; Pvt B Co 9th IL Cav; 3-7-65 to 10-31-65; Methodist PO; lost right eye
CAMPBELL, Nathaniel T., Ct-44-1; Pvt G Co 13th TN Cav; 9-24-63 to 9-5-65; Hampton
CAMPBELL, R. N., Gi-139-3; Pvt K Co 53rd TN Inf; 11-15-62 to 4-65; Campbellsville PO; CONF
CAMPBELL, R. S., Ha-114-2; Pvt A Co 19th OH Cav; 19 Apr 62 to 1 May 64; New Cedalee PO; CONF
CAMPBELL, Richard, Hd-51-2; Mandy widow; Cpl E Co 50th US Inf; 14 Jun 63 to 66; Hamburg PO; killed in army, shot in body
CAMPBELL, Robert Calvin, Mn-121-1; Mary A. widow of; Pvt A Co 6th TN Cav; Sep 62 to __; Bethel Springs PO; died in Jun 1864 in army
CAMPBELL, Robert J., Hm-109-4; Pvt; Whitesburg PO
CAMPBELL, Robert M., Di-31-1; Quartermaster E Co 1st TN Cav; 9-5-64 to 65; 2nd Civil Dist; cant get to see his discharge
CAMPBELL, Robert V., Hw-134-1; Sgt G Co PA Inf; 62 to 65; Rogersville PO
CAMPBELL, Samuel, Jo-152-2; Emily J. widow of; B Co 13th TN Cav; Doeville PO; cause of loosing eyesight
CAMPBELL, Smith, Bo-20-2; Pvt E Co 4th TN Cav; 1-28-64 to 8-2-65; Maryville PO; diarhea, very poor, unable to work
CAMPBELL, Sparken M., Pu-144-3; Pvt C Co 1st TN Mtd Inf; 4-6-64 to 7-5-65; Hudgins PO; back hurt
CAMPBELL, Surreppta R., Po-150-1; widow of US Sol; 5th Civil Dist
CAMPBELL, Thomas, Ct-45-1; Levicey widow of; Pvt B Co 13th TN Inf; 9-21-63 to __; Stony Creek PO; died at Gallatin TN 1864
CAMPBELL, Thomas H., Sm-174-1; 1st Cpl G Co 4th TN Inf; 11-1-64 to 8-25-65; New Middleton PO; shot in right leg
CAMPBELL, Thomas J., A-3-2; Pvt A Co 6th TN Inf; 3-6-62 to 4-27-65; Wilson PO; dierea
CAMPBELL, W. A., Gi-122-2; Pvt A Co 3rd TN Inf; 61 to 65; Prospect Sta. PO; CONF
CAMPBELL, W. W., Cr-7-1; Pvt F Co 2nd TN Mtd Inf; 11-20-62 to 1-19-65; Eaton PO (Gibson Co.)
CAMPBELL, Washington C., Cu-16-2; Pvt F Co 7th TN Inf; 12-20-62 to 7-8-65; Wine Sap PO; relapse measles, lung disease

CAMPBELL, William A., H-61-5; Pvt G Co 3rd TN Cav; 8-63 to 10-63; 1st Lt H Co 3rd TN Cav--10-63 to 6-64; Capt G Co 3rd TN Cav--6-64 to 9-65; Chattanooga PO
CAMPBELL, Wm. H., Co-62-1; Cpl M Co 1st TN Cav; 15 Jul 62 to 5 Jun 65; Help PO; rheumatism
CAMPBELL, William R., Ct-35-2; Pvt G Co 13th TN Cav; 9-22-63 to 9-5-65; Lineback PO; in US Army
CAMPBELL, Wm. S., Je-141-1; Pvt C Co 1st TN Cav; 20 Dec 63 to 19 Jun 65; New Market PO
CAMPBELL, William W., Cf-41-1; Pvt H Co 13th TN Cav; 9-24-63 to 9-5-65; South Wattauga PO; chronnic dyrear and rhumatism
CAMPBELL, Wm. Y., Ha-113-2; Lizzie widow of; Sgt E Co 8th TN Cav; 13 Oct 63 to 11 Sep 65; Sneedville PO
CAMPBELL, Zachariah C., Ct-44-1; Pvt A Co 12th DE Hvy Art; 7-15-63 to 7-25-65; Hampton PO
CAMPBILL, Meredith G., Su-242-2; Lou A. widow of; Pvt B Co 4th TN Inf; 1 Oct 63 to 2 Aug 65; Bluff City PO; diarrhea and lung trouble; sol. died Jan 23 85, having troble, family in destitution who are now on pension
CAMPELL, George W., K-184-2; Pvt G Co 1st Hvy Art; Thorn Grove PO
CAMPELL, James H., K-184-2; Pvt G Co 1st Hvy Art; Thorn Grove PO
CANADA, David, Sh-189-3; no record could be had; Memphis PO; CONF
CANADA, David, Sh-189-6; Sol US; Prominade St, Memphis PO
CANADA, William, T-219-1; Elizabeth widow of; Cpl K Co 4th Hvy Art; 63 to 66; Phelan PO
CANADA, William C., M-107-1; Pvt D Co 9th KY Inf; 9-20-61 to 12-15-64; Red Boiling Springs PO; blind right eye & deaf right ear
CANADA, William C., M-107-1; Pvt D Co 9th KY Inf; 9-61 to ___; Red Boiling Springs PO
CANADAY, Robbert K., G-61-1; Pvt M Co 6th TN Cav; Aug 11 62 to Jun 10 65; 12th Civil Dist
CANADY, Adam, Lo-191-2; Sgt I Co 5th TN Inf; 1 Nov 62 to 30 Jan 65; Morganton PO; chronic diarrhoea
CANADY, Charles, B-11-2(1); Pvt C Co 5th Non? Cav; 8-30-62 to 6-5-65; Poplins X Roads PO; died in service
CANADY, Evner C., Ch-14-2; Eliza J. widow of; Pvt; PO omitted
CANADY, Thomas, Hd-55-1; Milber J. Hendricks late widow of; P Scout 9th & 10th IN Cav; May 63 to 65; Whitton PO; contracted lun disease, died from lung disease
CANAL, John C., Ro-208-3; Pvt A Co 2nd TN Inf; 10 Aug 61 to 6 Oct 64; Welker Mines PO
CANAN, William, Ge-83-2; Jane widow of; Pvt F Co 4th TN Inf; 5 Nov 62 to 26 May 65; Henshaw PO; fever & chills
CANBARY, John, Su-240-1; Pvt G Co 60th Con Inf; 61 to 63; Easley PO; crushed R R train; CONF
CANEY, Riley, Sn-261-1; Pvt B Co 60th MO Cav; 8-62 to 3-63; Rapids PO (Simpson Co., KY) discharged by officers (duplicate on Sn-261-3(2))
CANFIELD, William W., H-51-3; Pvt E Co 6th IA Cav; 4-25-64 to 10-17-65; Hill City PO
CANNADY, James H., Gr-78-1; Pvt C Co 17th VA Inf; Mar 62 to May 63 (70 days)?; Larkeyton PO
CANNEDY, Sterlin, Ct-37-3; Pvt I Co 7th ___; 11-8-64 to 7-27-65; Robertsville PO
CANNON, Benjamin B., Ja-86-2; Pvt C Co 60th Cav; 1-20-62 to 7-8-65; Ootewah PO; mups fell on me
CANNON, Benjamin F., Lk-113-1; High Pvt A Co 2nd AR Cav; 61 to 21 Sep 65; 4th Civil Dist
CANNON, Dennis, Ru-238-2; alias Dennis William; Pvt F Co 15th USC Inf; 15 Jan 64 to 7 Apr 66; Murfreesboro PO
CANNON, Elbert, Ct-42-2; Pvt L Co 13th TN Cav; 9-22-63 to 9-5-65; Watauga PO
CANNON, Eliga, Ro-207-3; Elizabeth widow of; Pvt; Paint Rock PO; straned in bowels
CANNON, Ezekiel M., Mc-112-8; Pvt I Co 5th Col Vol Inf; 11-1-61 to 9-15-66; Athens PO; varicose veins, enlisted in Co I & E
CANNON, George, Ge-90-3; Pvt K Co 8th TN Inf; 1 Jul 63 to 30 Jun 65; Greenville PO

CANNON, Horatio L., We-226-2; Pvt K Co 6th TN Cav; 13 Aug 62 to 26 Jul 65; Sharon PO
CANNON, J? Harrison, D-72-3; (Harrison Thompson); Pvt B Co 51st TN Inf; May 3 65 to Jun 16 66 (3 yrs 5 mos 3 days); Nashville PO
CANNON, James M., Ro-210-8; Pvt? D Co 1st? TN Cav; Aug 1 63 to 11 Sep 65; Rockwood PO
CANNON, Jessee, Se-223-4; Pvt I Co 1st TN Bat; 10 Jul 64 to 31 Mar 66; Sevierville PO
CANNON, John W., Se-223-4; Pvt L Co 1st TN Bat; Sevierville PO
CANNON, Joseph, Je-143-2; Ann D. wife of; Quartermaster Sgt D Co 9th TN Cav; 6 May 63 to 11 Sep 65; Mossy Creek PO; spinal affection
CANNON, Joseph M., Ge-94-2(1); Pvt E Co 4th TN Inf; 1 Sep 63 to Aug 65; Greeneville PO; rheumatism in 1863
CANNON, Lee, Ge-91-3; Cpl G Co 1st US Col Hvy Art; 64 to 29 Ma_ 66; Greeneville PO; kidney & liver
CANNON, Mariah (see McCulee, Wm. H.)
CANNON, Michael, B-3-2; 3rd Civil Dist
CANNON, Newton, Ge-91-3; Lizzie widow of; PO omitted
CANNON, Samuel C., Mc-118-3; Pvt A Co 5th TN Mtd Inf; 9-1-64 to 6-26-65; Joshua PO
CANNON, Solomon, Mo-124-1; 9th Civil Dist
CANNON, Zachariah, Mu-201-1; Pvt G Co 40th USC Inf; 23 Dec 63 to 6 Feb 66; Mt. Pleasant PO
CANNON, ___, Ja-85-2; Melinda J. widow of; Birchwood PO
CANON, Fredric, Sh-188-3; US Col; Haynes Alley, Memphis PO
CANON, Samuel B., S1-164-2(1); Sarah widow of; Pvt E Co 6th TN Mtd Inf; 8-11-64 to ___; Dunlap PO
CANSELL, Davis, Se-219-3; Elisabeth widow of; Pvt; Jones Cave PO
CANTELL, Andrew J., We-223-2; Pvt C Co 7th TN Cav; 28 Jun 62 to 30 Jun 65; Palmersville PO; 12 months in Andersonville Prison; is in feble condition
CANTER, Robert W., Wa-274-1; Pvt I Co 8th TN Cav; 1 Mar 65 to 21 Nov 65; Jonesboro PO
CANTER, William H., Jo-149-4; Pvt I Co 13th TN Cav; 24 Sep 63 to 5 Sep 65; Mountain City PO; injury hip thrown from horse
CANTEWELL, John, Ha-111-2; Pvt G Co 5th TN Cav; Jan 62 to Jan 65; Kyle's Ford PO
CANTRELL, James K., G-67-1; Pvt C Co 7th TN Cav; 1 Mar 65 to 9 Aug 65; Bradford PO
CANTRELL, Jesse R., Dk-38-2; Pvt F Co 4th TN Inf; 9-24-64 to 8-25-65; Smithville PO; injury to right knee
CANTRELL, John, R-161-5; Bugler G Co 3rd TN Cav; 7-6-63 to 6-10-65; Dayton PO; bayonett wound in left arm
CANTRELL, Stephen, W-189-2; Pvt M Co 5th TN Cav; 2-25-64 to 8-14-65; McMinnville PO; ruptured
CANTRELL, Starling W., Wh-185-1; Pvt H Co 37th KY Inf; 6-29-63 to 12-29-64; Peeled Chestnut PO; sight afcd., chronic rheumatism
CANTRELL, William M., G-67-3; Pvt M Co 6th TN Cav; 2 May 61 to Aug 64; Miland PO; rheumatism
CANTS, John A., Hw-122-1; Pvt K Co 8th TN Cav; 15 Aug 63 to 11 Sep 65; Clover Bottom PO; disease of spine & piles, almost totally disabled
CANTWELL, Abraham, Wa-268-1; Pvt C Co 17th IN Mtd Inf; 1st Lt G Co 120th IN Inf; 24 Apr 61 to 29 Jan 66; Johnson City PO
CANTWELL, O. F., G-63-1; 13th IN? Lt Art; Apr 63 6o Jul 65; Milan PO
CAPERTON, John H., Mu-210-7; Marget J. widow of; Pvt C Co Mis Inf; 62 to 63; Spring Hill PO; CONF
CAPHART, Hugh H., Ro-210-2; Margaret widow of; Pvt; 3 yrs; Rockwood PO
CAPILINGER, John, Dk-34-6(5); Pvt K Co 5th TN Cav; 7-26-63 to 8-14-65; Close PO; rheumatism & kidney disease
CAPLE, James L., He-58-1; Pvt C Co 12th TN Vol Cav; 2-10-63 to 6-29-65; PO omitted
CAPLEY, Freeling, B-14-1; Non Comm. Officer D Co 10th TN Inf; 4-10-62 to 6-10-65; Brandville PO

CAPLEY, Gabrel, Wi-270-1; Pvt E Co 10th TN Inf; 12 Mar 64 to 23 Jun 65; Union Valley PO

CAPLEY, Wilson A., B-11-3(2); Pvt E Co 10th TN Inf; 3-17-62 to 6-23-65; Poplins X Roads PO; reumatism, drawing pension $5

CAPLINGER, Samuel F., Sh-200-2; Pvt I Co 137th IN Inf; 5-9-64 to 9-21-64; 496 Orleans St, Memphis PO

CAPLINGER, Samuel G., Sh-200-2; Pvt A Co 52nd OH Inf; 6-5-62 to 5-5-64; 496 Orleans St., Memphis PO

CAPOLINGER, William R., Dk-34-6(5); Cpl K Co 5th TN Cav; 7-26-63 to 8-14-65; Close PO; rheumatism & frost bite

CAPP, Simon, D-57-2; widow; Pvt C Co 101st US Inf; Aug 12 63 to Aug 3 65; PO omitted, 8th Ward

CAPPER, Alford M., Ro-208-3; Pvt K Co 10th MI Cav; 23 Jul 64 to 11 Nov 65; Kingston PO

CAPPLES, Daniel, Ch-18-2; Pvt Independent Co Col F Hurst, 6th TN Cav; Spring of 62 to can't give date, his papers are away from home; Montezuma PO; rhumatism & chonic diarrahoea &c; Heavy Art Capt J. K. Cotton gave Col. Finley Hurst who lived at Purdy, TN, an independent co., did not belong as an army regular

CAPPS, Amis K., Hm-108-4(3); Cpl E Co 3rd US Inf; Oct 64 to 12 Jun 65; Russellville PO; piles

CAPPS, Persillor (see Owen, Anzil D.)

CAPPS, William, Cl-57-1; Lucinda widow of; Sgt E Co 6th TN Inf; 3-6-62 to 4-25-65; Cappsford PO

CAPPS, William F., Ja-84-2; Martha C. widow of; Pvt F Co 12th TN Cav; 12-23-63 to died 3-13-64; Harrison PO; died of mesels while in the service

CAPSHAW, Wayman C., Dk-36-1; Pvt B Co 4th TN Mtd Inf; 9-25-64 to 8-25-65; Smithville PO

CAR, Isaac, Ma-124-1; Loisanna formerly a widow of; Mis Inf; Jackson PO

CARATHERS, David, Wa-270-2; Pvt I Co 63rd TN Inf; 62 to 65; Jonesboro PO

CARAWAY, William R., Ct-36-2; Martha widow of; Pvt C Co 13th TN Cav; Shell Creek PO

CARD, Abraham R., R-163-1; Sarah J. widow of; Pvt F Co 5th TN Cav; 2-25-62 to 3-29-65; Graysville PO

CARD, Andrew C., Li-147-1; Capt C Co 4th TN Inf; 8-13-62 to 8-25-65; Norris Creek PO; chronic catarrh

CARD, Zimariah, Bl-4-2; Pvt F Co 5th TN Inf; 4-1-62 to 4-1-65; Morgan Springs PO (Rhea Co.)

CARDAR, John E., He-58-1; Pvt A Co 5th TN Vol Cav; 9-1-62 to 6-12-65; PO omitted

CARDEN, Alexander, K-161-1; Eliza widow of; Pvt I Co TN Inf; Knoxville PO; wounded in leg

CARDEN, Alphard, K-174-4(3); Pvt A Co 1st TN Inf; 28 Feb 63 to 9 Aug 65; Floyde PO; rheumatism no disability from apperance

CARDEN, Andrew C. Br-9-4; Pvt I Co 14th IL Cav; 64 to 65; Cleveland PO

CARDEN, Ansel C., Ct-42-2; Pvt A Co 13th TN Cav; 9-22-63 to 9-22-65; Watauga PO

CARDEN, Doctor D., H-49-7; Nancy widow of; H-49-7; Pvt D Co 1st TN Lt Art; 9-22-62 to 8-19-65; Igon's Ferry PO; lung troubles from pneumonia

CARDEN, Elihu P., A-2-2; Pvt C Co 52nd TN Inf; 3-7-62 to ___; Andersonville PO; this soldier was a union man; was conscripted & made his escape

CARDEN, Francis M., Po-149-3(2); Pvt F Co 5th TN Mtd Inf; 64 to 65; Fetzeton PO; date of enlistment & discharge unknown

CARDEN, Franklin A., H-49-5; Pvt D Co 4th TN Lt Art; 3-22-64 to 7-20-65; Daisy PO; diarhea

CARDEN, Giles, Gi-127-3; Mattie Gentry formerly widow of; Cpl F Co 110th TN Col Inf; Feb 64 to Mar 66; Pulaski PO; contracted galloping consumption

CARDEN, Jasper F., Po-151-1; Pvt E Co 10th TN Cav; 1-6-63 to 8-1-65; Servilla PO

CARDEN, Landon C., Ct-35-1; Emily C. widow of; Pvt G Co 13th TN Cav; 9-22-63 to 9-5-65; Hampton PO

CARDEN, Right R., Ja-86-1; Pvt A Co 4th TN Cav; 10-23-62 to 7-12-65; Oottewah PO

CARDER, John, Dk-35-1; Pvt A Co 5th TN Cav; Temperance Hall PO

CARDER, Thomas F., Ca-23-3; Pvt G Co 6th TN Inf; 2-64 to 7-64; Leoni PO; hip and thigh injured, fall horse

CARDIN, Andrew, Col, Mo-123-2; Pvt B Co 44th Col Inf; 3-25-64 to 10-13-64; Jalapa PO; captured at Dalton GA

CARDIN, James, Mo-123-2; Nancy widow of; Pvt K Co 12th TN Cav; 3-26-64 to ___; Mt. Vernon PO; deserted, time not known

CARDIN, Robert H., Mo-123-2; Pvt K Co 12th TN Cav; 3-26-64 to 10-7-65; Mt Vernon PO

CARDON, Nathan, Gi-127-2; Margaret Rivers formerly widow of; Pvt F Co 110th TN Col Inf; Pulaski PO

CARDWELL, Anthony, Ro-202-2; Sgt D Co 5th TN Inf; 7 Mar 62 to 14 Oct 63; Oral PO; frost bites wound in right arm

CARDWELL, Clisbey A., Se-229-1; Pvt C Co 1st TN Cav; 1 Jan 63 to 20 Jul 65; Galinburg PO; chronic rheumatism, diarea

CARDWELL, James A., Sm-169-2; Pvt; 61 to 62; no PO; CONF

CARDWELL, John, Se-220-2; Pvt D Co 2nd TN Cav; 16 Jul 63 to 6 Jul 65; Emerts Cave PO; piles & enlargement of liver, no confined to bed

CARDWELL, Richard, Un-252-1; Pvt H Co 8th TN Cav; Jun 3 63 to ___ (7 mos); New Flat Creek PO; heart disease

CARDWELL, Richard, Un-252-1; Pvt B Co 1st TN Inf; Aug 4 62 to ___ (3 mos 15 days); New Flat Creek PO

CARDWELL, W. S., Gi-122-8; 2nd Lt A Co 3rd TN Inf; 62 to 63 (1 mo); Prospect Sta. PO; CONF

CAREL, James, Un-255-2; Sarah widow of; PO omitted

CAREY, William, K-156-3; Pvt B Co 1st E TN Col Inf; 63 to 65; 98 Crozier St, Knoxville PO

CAREY, Wm. W., D-59-1; Pvt 4th PA Cav; 1620 Church St, Nashville PO

CARGILE, Jacob, Pi-155-1; Pvt H Co 4th TN Inf; 3-14-65 to 8-25-65; Neal PO; rheumatism

CARLIN, D. B., H-64-1; Lt C Co 18th OH V Inf; 8-20-61 to 65; Chattanooga PO; wounded 7 times

CARLISLE, Andrew J., Ge-99-2; Pvt L Co 8th TN Cav; 12 Sep 63 to 11 Sep 65; Limestone Springs PO; ribs broke by horse

CARLISLE, Eli, He-67-3; Martha J. widow of; Pvt B Co 15th IL Cav; Aug 7 61 to Aug 25 64; Scotts Hill PO; unknown more than heart disease

CARLISLE, James D., Co-61-1; Saddler L Co 8th TN Cav; 12 Sep 63 to 11 Sep 65; Parrottsville PO; rhumatism, not able for manuel labor

CARLISLE, Joseph G. W., Co-59-2; US Sol; 1st Dist

CARLISLE, Moses S., Wi-271-1; Seaman Beacon; 20 Nov 63 to 20 Nov 64; Boston PO

CARLOCK, Daniel, Mc-117-3; Clar widow of; Carlock PO

CARLOCK, William H., Sh-158-3; Mary Southall formerly widow of and now widow of Henry ___; Pvt A Co 55th Col Inf; (Capt Day); Jan 64 to killed (5 mos 10 days); Memphis PO; killed at Guntown, MI 1864; the deceased never got his bounty & his wife, now widow, wishes to get it

CARLSON, Christian, Sh-191-3; Sol & Sail; Memphis PO

CARLTON, Goodwin, Bl-5-2; Amanda A. Morell formerly widow of; Capt B Co 54th IN Inf--3 mos this service, is mustered?; Capt D Co 11th IN Cav--12-23-63 to 11-3-64; Brayton PO; discharged on account of wound, Carlton A. Goodwin lost right leg by gunshot wound--died

CARLTON, J. C., G-57-6; Pvt; 61 to 65; Yorkville PO; CONF

CARLTON, John C., We-233-1(2); Pvt L Co 6th TN Cav; 7-10-62 to 7-10-65; Ralston PO; chronic diarrhea

CARLTON, Joshua, Br-12-5; Pvt C Co 6th TN Inf; 9-2-64 to 6-30-65; Sydneyton PO

CARLTON, Lewis, Mr-68-1; Cpl D Co 10th TN Inf; 8-2-62 to 6-13-65; Kelly's Ferry PO; right fore finger shot off

CARLTON, Sarena, D-90-1; widow; 12th Dist

CARLTON, William R., Ms-173-1; Pvt F Co Independent TN Cav; 27 Aug 63 to 16 Jun 64; Rich Creek PO

CARMACK, Evan, Cl-48-3; Pvt; 1 mo; Pleasant PO; fell and broke left arm, not at home, wife dont know date of enlistment & discharge; CONF
CARMACK, Gilbert, Hw-134-1; Cpl M Co 1st US Art; Sep 64 to Sep 66; Rogersville PO; deafness
CARMACK, John, Hw-127-4; Rachel widow of; 1s TN Hvy Art; Rogersville PO
CARMACK, Richard, Hw-129-1; Sgt G Co 42nd US (Coler) Inf; 15 Feb 65 to 31 __ 66 (3 yrs); Dellmonell PO
CARMACK, Richard, Hw-125-3; Pvt? M Co 1st US; Oct 64 to Mar 65; Yellow Stone PO
CARMACK, _____, Hw-125-3; Ann L. widow of; A Co 19th TN Inf; May 61 to 63; Yellow Stone PO; shot 3 times in body; CONF
CARMAN, George F., H-65-1; Pvt E Co 12th OH Art; 8-13-61 to 7-11-65; Chattanooga PO
CARMAN, Jas. W., Dy-20-1; US Sol; Dist No 2
CARMICHAEL, George, Lo-187-2; Mandia widow of; Pvt 1st US Col Hvy Art; Loudon PO; lungs, from which died
CARMICHAEL, George W., Ro-203-1; Pvt; Ethel PO; CONF
CARMICHAEL, John, Je-135-2; Catherine widow of; Pvt; Fear Gap PO
CARMICHAEL, John M., Ro-210-8; Pvt D Co 9th TN Cav; 12 Sep 63 to 26 Mar 65; Rockwood PO
CARMICHAEL, P. J., Je-135-4; Cpl C Co 1st TN Cav; 1 Apr 61 to 1 Apr 64; Piedmont PO
CARMICHAEL, Proter L., Se-226-5; Pvt M Co 10th KY Cav; 17 Sep 62 to 17 Sep 63; Henrys X Roads PO
CARMICHAEL, W. W., Je-135-3; Pvt C Co 1st TN Cav; 1 Apr 62 to 1 Apr 65; Piedmont PO
CARMICHEAL, James, Hm-103-3; Cpl F Co 1st TN (Col) Hvy Art; __ to Mar 15 66 (2 yrs); Morristown PO; deafness
CARMICHIMA, Samuel W., Je-145-2; Pvt? K Co 9th TN Cav; 11 Aug 65 to 9 Jun 65; Dumplin PO
CARMON, William H., Un-252-1; Pvt C Co 1st TN Inf; 9 Aug 61 to 17 Sep 64; Haynes PO
CARMOR, Martha J., Cl-58-3; widow?; Tazewell PO
CARNAHAN, Bransford, J-78-1; Pvt I Co 59th OH Inf; 1-1-62 to 1-5-65; Rough Point PO; rumatism & eyes, crippled in hip & legs
CARNAHAN, Jacob, Sh-198-2; Pvt D Co 55th Col Inf; 5-21-63 to 12-31-65; Memphis PO; has his discharge
CARNAHAN, William, Cy-27-5(3); Pvt I Co 58th OH Inf; 1-62 to 1-65; Spivey PO
CARNEHAN, James M., J-79-2; Pvt K Co TN Mtd Inf; 64 to 65; Haydensburg PO; could not furnish dates
CARNEHAN, William, J-79-2; Pvt C Co 6th IL Cav; 10-1-63 to 11-5-65; Haydensburg PO; cronic rheumatism & piles
CARNER, William R., Mc-118-5; Pvt B Co 40th OH Cav; 10-1-63 to __; Calhoun PO
CARNES, J., K-167-2; Druller? widow; Pvt 3rd TN Inf; 1-62 to 65; Knoxville PO
CARNES, James G., Se-224-1; Sgt K Co 2nd TN Cav; 16 Oct 62 to 6 Jul 65; Waldens Creek PO; heart disease from exposure
CARNES, John B., K-154-1; Knoxville PO; CONF
CARNES, William C., A-2-2; Mary widow; Capt C Co 2nd TN Inf; 8-7-61 to __; Andersonville PO; severely wounded at Monticello, KY, captured Rogersville, TN 11-6-63
CARNEY, Elize (see Gaines, Wily)
CARNEY, George W., Mc-112-6; Pvt K Co 3rd TN Cav; 1-10-64 to 6-10-65; Athens PO; heart disease & rheumatism
CARNEY, Henry, Mt-137-1; Civ. in Gov. Employ, papers lost; St. Bethlehem PO
CARNEY, James W., Wl-307-1; Pvt H Co 4th TN Inf; 1 Dec 64 to 25 Aug 65; Beckwith PO
CARNEY, John, D-50-1; Pvt A Co 17th US Inf; Mar 7 62 to Jul 66; N. Cherry, Nashville PO; wounded in r. shoulder, papers lost
CARNEY, Lott, Po-149-1; Pvt D Co 1st GA Cav; 7-64 to 65; Helithrope PO; subsequently 4th TN Mtd Inf; no discharge
CARNEY, Martin, Mr-102-2; Pvt L Co 46th IN Cav; 3-1-63 to 7-25-65; South Pittsburg PO; gun shot wound in right knee
CARNEY, Nickolas, Fe-44-2; Emeline widow of; Pvt; Allardt PO
CARNIE, Mollie (see Motti, Clarance M.)
CARNS, Catharine (see Runnyan, John H.)
CARNS, Harve, Co-69-7(3); Mary widow of; Pvt TN; Rankin PO; died in the service, cant give dates, no papers here
CARNS, John H., Se-223-2; Pvt K Co 2nd TN Cav; 16 Oct 62 to 6 Jul 65; Hendersons Springs PO; diarrhea, disease of eyes & piles
CARNS, S. H., A-1-3; M. A. widow of; Pvt C Co 1st TN Cav; 7-14-62 to 4-28-65; Twinville PO (Knox Co. PO)
CARNYHAM, Franklin, Ov-139-2; Mary E. C. widow of; Pvt I Co; 61 to 65; Lovejoy PO
CAROLL, Edward, Sh-169-1; 1st Sgt I Co MO Inf; 61 to 64; Memphis PO
CAROLOS, Christophor, K-155-1; Pvt I Co 12th TN Cav; 20 Mar 64 to 16 Oct 65; Knoxville PO
CAROUTHERS, James M., M-103-3; Pvt F Co 32nd KY Inf; 8-26-63 to 1-19-65; Lafayette PO
CAROWTHER, Embery, Co-59-1; Sgt C A 2nd NC Mtd Inf; 9-15-63 to 8-18-65; Del Rio PO
CARPENTER, Alexander, K-174-2(1); Pvt B Co 8th TN Cav; 24 Apr 63 to 11 Sep 65; Church Grove PO; disease of lungs
CARPENTER, Charles C., Wa-268-1; discharge away from home; Johnson City PO; ruptured
CARPENTER, Charles H., Sq-164-3(1); Pvt E Co 3rd V I Inf; 5-28-61 to 6-27-64; Dunlap PO
CARPENTER, Daniel A., K-170-3; Maj 2nd TN Inf; 10 Aug 61 to 8 Oct 64; Knoxville PO
CARPENTER, David J., H-63-1; Sgt H Co 150th OH Inf; 5-3-64 to 8-23-65; 206 Prospect, Chattanooga PO; kidney disease
CARPENTER, Emanuel, Li-143-1; Pvt C Co 7th US Cav; 7-6-63 to 8-9-65; PO omitted
CARPENTER, Henry J., Sh-201-1; Pvt; Memphis PO; discharge lost; CONF
CARPENTER, John, Ms-171-1; Teamster I Co 4th TN Inf; 10 Jun 64 to Dec 65; Belfast PO
CARPENTER, John, Bo-14-3; Pvt L Co 2nd TN Cav; __ to 7-6-65; Huffstetlers Store PO
CARPENTER, John, Hw-128-2; Pvt H Co 8th TN Inf; 5 Feb 64 to 30 Jun 65; Walnut Hill PO; rheumatism, disease of heart, lost left eye
CARPENTER, John H., Cl-53-2; Elizabeth widow of; Pvt H Co 9th TN Cav; 9-21-63 to 9-11-65; Springdale PO
CARPENTER, John T., Lo-192-1; Sarrah A. widow of; 1st Lt K Co 5th TN; May 62 to 30 Jun 65; Coytee PO; chronic diarhoea, died Sep 27 1883
CARPENTER, Mary J. (see Wilkerson, Doctor)
CARPENTER, Richard, Gi-135-1; Pvt B Co 110th TN Inf; 63 to 65; Lynnville PO
CARPENTER, William, Gr-79-2; Pvt H Co 8th TN; 62 to 65; Ball Point PO; wounded in right shoulder
CARPENTER, William F., Mc-109-1; Cpl B Co 7th TN Inf; 9-12-64 to 7-27-65; Chuckaluck PO; measles and results
CARPENTER, Wilson, Hw-128-2; Cpl O Co 4th KY Inf; 27 Aug 61 to 27 Oct 64; Walnut Hill PO; loss of right eye
CARPER, Henry, K-154-6(3); Pvt I Co 27th OH Cav; Jul 64 to 65; Knoxville PO
CARR, Aaron, Sn-261-2(1); Sarah F. widow of; Pvt; New Roe PO (Allen Co. KY); priso(ner?); CONF
CARR, Allen, Cr-1-1; Lucetta widow of; Gadsden PO; killed Ball Point Pillow; forgotten Regt
CARR, Almon B., Mc-112-2; Pvt G Co 20th ME Inf; 8-20-62 to 7-65; Athens PO
CARR, Anderson, Sn-253-2; Sgt A Co 14th US Inf; 11-16-63 to 3-29-66; Gallatin PO
CARR, Andrew C., Wa-269-1; Pvt H Co 13th TN Cav; Sep 63 to Aug 65; Carters Depot PO (Carter Co.); leg & back injured
CARR, Andrew J., Ja-86-2; Pvt G Co 5th TN Inf; 3-1-62 to 5-16-65; Snowhill PO; chronic diarhea
CARR, B. S., Mn-120-1; Pvt G Co 6th TN Cav; Sep 25 62 to Jul 26 65; Ramer PO
CARR, Barton L., We-220-1; Seeman Gunboat No. 58 Huntress; May 21 64 to Oct 21 65; confined in Andersonville Prison 6 mos, dyspepsia, rheumatism, neuralgia, resulting heart disease
CARR, C. C., O-142-1; Pvt B Co 1st KY Capt. Guards; 3 Jul 64 to 13 Feb 65; Obion PO; C. V. fot Gulf?

CARR, David F., Cl-48-3; 3rd Civil Dist
CARR, David W., Cl-56-2(1); Pvt F Co 6th IN Cav; 8-18-63 to 9-14-65; Sandlick PO; spleen enlarged from ague
CARR, Hamilton, Gi-122-4; 1st Sgt D Co 111th TN Inf; 64 to 1 May 66; Aspen Hill PO; shot in thigh & knee
CARR, Henry C., Sn-260-6; Pvt A Co 4th MO Cav; 6-29-61 to 64; A.B.C. PO; CONF
CARR, Ira, Pu-145-3(4); Martha J. widow of; Pvt C Co 1st Mtd Inf; 10-21-63 to 12-13-64; Silver Point PO
CARR, John A., K-154-2; Knoxville PO
CARR, John H., Cl-56-2(1); Pvt E Co 2nd TN Inf; 6-1-63 to 8-8-65; Sandlick PO
CARR, Joseph C., Pu-140-1; Pvt L Co 5th TN Cav; 7-28-63 to 8-14-65; Cookeville PO; shot through rt. foot, had the smallpox
CARR, Simon, Pu-146-1; Pvt E Co 40th US Col Inf; 2-7-65 to 4-25-66; Pekin PO; now suffering with disease
CARR, Thomas J., Su-241-1; Pvt H Co 4th TN Cav; 8 Sep 62 to 12 Jul 65; Blairs Gap PO; shot in foot sige (sic) injured
CARR, W. B., H-60-1; Capt K Co 58th IN Inf--11-15-61 to __; Capt D Co 135thIN Inf--4-64 to 9-28-64; Chattanooga PO
CARR, William B., K-161-1; Pvt E Co 2nd TN Inf; 1 Jun 63 to 9 Aug 65; Knoxville PO
CARRAWAY, E. W., F-38-1; Pvt G Co 13th TN Inf; Apr 61 to Apr 63; Stanton PO; CONF
CARRELL, David, Bo-12-2(1); Pvt A Co 8th TN Cav; 9-12-63 to 1-5-64; Chilhowee PO
CARRELL, Dennis G., H-49-7; Pvt B Co 6th TN Inf; 3-8-62 to 3-15-65; Daisy PO; wounded by shell
CARRELL, Felen M., Co-69-6(1); Pvt C Co 2nd NC Inf; 26 Sep 63 to 17 Aug 65; Driskill PO; Campuelson KY, not a pensioner
CARREY, Elijah, Wa-272-2; Sgt I Co 8th TN Cav; 18 Sep 63 to 11 Sep 65; Morning Star PO; rheumatism and resulting disease of heart
CARREY, William M., Se-220-1; Pvt M Co 2nd TN Cav; 8 Mar 62 to 13 Jun 65; Emurts Cave PO
CARRIGAR, Aleon J., Ct-35-3; Pvt F Co 13th TN Cav; 9-24-63 to 9-5-65; Fish Spring PO; in the US Army
CARRIGER, Chrisley C., Ct-42-3; Rachel Bowers former widow of; Pvt A Co 13th TN Cav; PO omitted
CARRIGER, Isaac R., Su-242-2; Cpl F Co 13th TN Cav; 21 Sep 63 to 5 Sep 65; Bluff City PO; diarrhoea and pain in side; pension rate $6/month
CARRIGER, Joel N., Cf-44-2; Pvt A Co 13th TN Cav--9-22-63 to 12-31-63; 2nd Lt A Co 13th TN Cav--12-31-63 to 1-14-65; Hampton PO; chronic dysentery, now paralysis
CARRIGER, Nicholas T., Ct-40-5; Pvt B Co 4th TN Inf; 1-9-63 to __; Elizabethton PO
CARRIGER, Alxander, U-245-1; Pvt D Co 13th TN Cav; 24 Sep 63 to 5 Sep 65; Marbleton PO
CARROL, Edward, Br-10-2; Pvt K Co 5th TN Mtd Inf; 1-6-65 to 7-12-65; Cleveland PO
CARROL, Joel W., Wl-303-1; Nancy A. widow of; Pvt E Co 4th TN Mtd Inf; Nov 12 64 to 25 Aug 65; PO omitted
CARROL, William, Wh-180-1; Margrett widow of; Sparta PO
CARROL, William C., C-30-2; Mary S. widow of; Pvt C Co 1st TN Inf; 2-62 to __; Well Spring PO; died during service
CARROL, ____, Hu-106-1; Francis widow of; Waverly PO
CARROLL, Byrd, A-9-1; Pvt H Co 2nd TN Inf; 12-1-61 to 6-19-65; Ligias PO
CARROLL, Charles F.?, K-163-1; Chaplain 4th VA Reg; Mar 62 to 65; Knoxville PO; CONF
CARROLL, George W., Je-141-4; US Sol; 4th Dist
CARROLL, George W., K-170-3; US Sol; Dist 12
CARROLL, Henry, Cf-35-1; Pvt D Co 23rd TN Inf; 2 Nov 62 to 22 Dec 64; Normandy PO; CONF
CARROLL, Henry C., K-186-1; Pvt F Co 2nd TN Inf; 1 Jun 63 to 3 Aug 65; Beaver Ridge PO; diarrhea, at home, unable to work
CARROLL, Huston, S-215-2; Pvt I Co 7th TN Inf; 1 Jan 65 to 27 Jul 65; High House PO
CARROLL, Isaac H., Wa-263-4; Pvt D Co 13th TN Cav; Sep 24 63 to Sep 5 65; Garbers Mills PO
CARROLL, James A., Br-13-4; Pvt A Co 8th TN Inf; Pvt I Co 5th Roring? Corps; 5-3-62 to 7-13-65; Cleveland PO; chronic rheumatism
CARROLL, James H., Mc-109-1; Pvt B Co 7th TN Inf; 9-24-64 to 7-27-65; Chuckaluck PO; rheumatism
CARROLL, John L., Cr-7-2; Pvt B Co 6th TN Inf; 11-5-63 to 6-30-65; Felker PO; blind and wounded
CARROLL, Jordon, Hw-122-1; Pvt K Co 8th TN Cav; Aug __ to 3 Aug 64; Blairs Gap PO; disease of lungs & rupture, discharged on account of disability
CARROLL, Joseph S., Ch-12-2; Pvt B Co 10th TN Cav; 9-62 to 5-65; Custer Point PO; CONF
CARROLL, Samuel Q., Wh-187-3; Pvt K Co 1st TN Inf; 9-29-64 to 7-22-65; Newark PO
CARROLL, Thomas, H-51-4; Pvt A Co 2nd CA Cav; 11-13-62 to 10-2-65; Hill City PO
CARROLL, William C., Ct-38-2; Emma E. widow of; Pvt B Co 4th TN Inf; 12-26-62 to 8-2-65; Milligan PO
CARROLL, William R., Mg-199-3; Pvt 1st TN Inf; Emory PO
CARROLL, William S., H-58-2; PVt C Co 7th TN Mtd Inf; 8-20-64 to 6-5-65; Sale Creek PO; right side & arm affected by measles
CARRUTH, John T., H-56-7; Pvt E Co 1st TN Art; 9-22-64 to 8-1-65; St. Elmo PO
CARRY, Thomas, Cl-47-2; Cpl E Co 1st TN Cav; 7-1-62 to 6-9-65; Cappford PO; rheumatism & pneuralysis 1864
CARSON, Anderson, Je-136-3; Cpl B Co 42nd TN Inf; 2 yrs; PO omitted
CARSON, Andrew J., Hd-51-1; Pvt D Co 2nd TN Inf; Apr 64 to 65; Pickens PO
CARSON, Bob, Hy-85-1; Nut Bush PO
CARSON, David H., H-69-6; Blacksmith; 2 yrs (62 to 64); Chattanooga PO
CARSON, James, Hd-49-3; US Sol; 4th Civil Dist
CARSON, John, Hm-108-3(2); Pvt A Co 1st TN Art; 63 to 64 (1 yr 10 mos); Russellville PO; piles, rupture & rheumatism
CARSON, John A., C-28-2(1); Pvt C Co 7th TN Inf; 9-11-__ to __; Big Creek Gap PO
CARSON, John L., Cy-28-2; Pvt A Co 28th TN Inf; 10-7-61 to 7-18-62; Butlers Landing PO
CARSON, John M., H-61-1; Lt I Co 31st TN Mtd Inf; 3-62 to 4-65; Chattanooga PO; CONF
CARSON, Joseph S., Je-146-3; Pvt A Co 1st TN Art; 16 Sep 63 to 3 Aug 65; White Pine PO; rheumatism
CARSON, Rufus E., Je-143-1; Pvt A Co 1st TN Art; 1 Apr 62 to 1 Apr 65; Mount Horeb PO; catarrh of head & general debility
CARSON, Tipton, Hm-107-1; Pvt D Co 4th TN Inf; 18 Jan 63 to 23 Jun 65; Chestnut Bloom PO; diarrhea
CARSON, Wiley W., Col, Rb-222-1; Pvt F Co 2nd US Inf; 63 to __ (3 yrs); Cedar Hill PO
CARSON, William, Ca-22-2; Pvt G Co 5th TN Cav; 9-62 to 8-65; Burgen PO; rupture
CARSON, William L. R., Moo-215-1; Pvt C Co 6th USV; Mar 18 65 to Oct 14 66; Sevally PO; general disability, he is not to work
CARTER, Abner, Wi-275-1; Milly widow of; Bingham PO; left arm broken, gun shot wound; papers taken by Isaac Ivy, Esq., cant give information; called for alm, was drawing pension at death, widow was never drawing pension
CARTER, Abram, Ro-210-3; Pvt; Rockwood PO
CARTER, Alex A., D-67-1; Mary A. widow of; 1st Lt E Co 5th TN Cav; 61 to 65; Nashville PO
CARTER, Alexander W., Ge-92-4; Pvt D Co 1st TN Cav; 12 Jul 62 to 5 Jun 65; Laurel Gap PO; deefness of right ear & parial of left ear
CARTER, Alford, F-39-1; Cpl G Co 88th Inf; 16 Jan 63 to __; Galloway PO; has lost his discharge
CARTER, Allen (see Porter, Allen)
CARTER, Andrew M., A-4-5; Pvt I Co 11th TN Cav; Coal Creek PO; lost hearing left ear, back hurt; discharge not at home
CARTER, Barrons, F-37-2; 4th Civil Dist
CARTER, Camiel, Mc-114-7; Winnie widow of; Pvt; Calhoun PO
CARTER, Charlie L., Ms-174-1; Mamie M. widow of; Sgt H Co 3rd KY Inf; 4 Oct 61 to 30 Oct 64; Chapel Hill PO

CARTER, Chesley C., Mo-122-2; 2nd Sgt B Co 59th TN Inf; 12-61 to 65 (3 yrs 7 mos); Madisonville PO; CONF
CARTER, David, Sh-152-2; Fisherville PO
CARTER, D. H., Sh-145-2; Cpl E Co 59th US Col Inf; 15 Feb 64 to 31 Jan 66; Millington PO
CARTER, D. M., Mc-117-4-; Pvt A Co 5th TN Inf; 2-25-62 to 4-24-65; Carlock PO; rheumatism; aplication filed for increase of pension
CARTER, E. S., C-34-3; Capt A Co 48th VA Inf; 5-61 to 2-28-65; Abbott PO; CONF
CARTER, Elias J., Hd-53-1; Pvt C Co 6th TN Cav; 18 Sep 62 to 26 Jul 65; Sibley PO; deafness and piles; cause of deafness getting wet while under the influence of quinine
CARTER, Emberson, Ge-92-1; Hannah widow of; Pvt B Co 8th TN Inf; Romeo PO; hert of life?
CARTER, Enoch H., Su-236-1; Pvt G Co 14th KY Inf; 16 May 62 to 25 Oct 65; Arcadia PO
CARTER, Georg W., Cy-26-2; Pvt B Co 9th KY Inf; 10-25-61 to 12-15-65; Moss PO
CARTER, George, Rb-228-2; Malisa R. widow of; Pvt; ___ to Feb 1 62 (5 mos); Crunk PO; CONF
CARTER, George S., Sm-169-1; TN unit; Elmwood PO; bloody piles; CONF
CARTER, Geo. W., Se-227-1; Pvt E Co 9th TN Cav; 1 Oct 63 to 11 Sep 65; Trundles X Roads PO; general disability
CARTER, George W., K-166-2; Pvt A Co 72nd IN Inf; 21 Jul 62 to 11 Jan 63; Knoxville PO; asthma, heart disease; drawing pension
CARTER, Harrison B., D-101-1; 1st Lt H Co 3rd KY Inf; 8 Oct 61 to 15 Oct 64; 22nd Civil Dist
CARTER, Henry, Sn-260-5; Pvt A Co; 62 to ___; A.B.C. PO; thrown from horse & ruptured & dislocated hip
CARTER, Hue Y., Se-222-1; Pvt K Co 2nd TN Cav; 16 Oct 62 to 6 Jul 65; Harrisburg PO; gun shot wound, rumatism
CARTER, J. M., Gi-139-2; Pvt K Co 5th TN Inf; 12-1-62 to 5-65; Campbellsville PO; CONF
CARTER, James, Po-149-3(2); Pvt B Co 1st Col US Hvy Art; 63 to 65; Fetzelton PO; discharge lost or misplaced
CARTER, James C., K-165-3; 146 Tulip St, Knoxville PO
CARTER, James E., K-163-1; Sol 1st TN Reg; 8 Aug 61 to 21 May 65; Knoxville PO; CONF
CARTER, James H., Hw-123-2; Pvt F Co 2nd TN; 64 to 65; Rotherwood PO
CARTER, James M., Ge-87-2; Pvt D Co 8th TN Inf; 28 Mar 63 to 30 Jun 65; Little Chucky PO; diseased back
CARTER, Jessie, Bo-15-3; Martha L. Redwine widow of; Pvt I Co 2nd TN Inf; 11-61 to ___; Maryville PO
CARTER, John, Mc-112-4; Pvt I Co 32nd OH Inf; 8-9-62 to 2-66; Athens PO
CARTER, John, D-99-1; Poorhouse; Pvt F Co 14th TN Inf; 63 to 65; Nashville PO; wounded once clightly
CARTER, John, Col, Ct-39-2; Pvt M Co Reg US Hvy Art; Elizabethton PO; chronic diorhea
CARTER, John, Wl-300-1; Pvt 14th TN Inf; 64 to 66; Cherry Valley PO; foot frozen
CARTER, John A., K-173-2; Pvt E Co 52nd KY Inf; Sep 63 to 65; Troutman PO
CARTER, John H., Mc-114-1; Pvt; Folger PO
CARTER, John M., Cr-16-3; Pvt F Co 5th US Inf; Apr 1 65 to Oct 15 66; Huntingdon PO
CARTER, John P., K-163-1; Conf Sol 1st TN Reg; 8 Aug 61 to 21 May 65; Knoxville PO; CONF
CARTER, Jno. W., Je-135-1(3); Cpl B Co 9th TN Cav; 15 Sep 63 to 11 Sep 65; Piedmont PO; chronic diarbar
CARTER, Josephus F., Rb-228-2; Pvt A Co 30th TN Inf; Sep 61 to Feb 63; Coopertown PO; CONF
CARTER, Joshua, Hd-54-2; Susan M. widow of; Sgt H Co 6th TN Cav; 18 Sep 62 to 26 Jul 65; Saltillo PO; died Apr 23 1882
CARTER, Joshua C., Ro-210-10; Pvt H Co 1st TN Inf; Aug 61 to Sep 64; Rockwood PO
CARTER, Landen, Ct-41-2; Capt H Co 18th TN Cav; 9-63 to 9-8-65; Keensburgh PO; rhumatism, hearing
CARTER, Lawson, Sh-146-3; US Sol; 3rd Civ Dist
CARTER, Louis, H-49-2; Katharine F. Westbrooks formerly widow of; Pvt; Lake Side PO
CARTER, Mary, Ge-93-2; W. Sol (US); Greeneville PO
CARTER, Matison G., Se-224-1; Pvt E Co 9th TN Cav; 1 Oct 63 to 11 Sep 65; Waldens Creek PO; hearing
CARTER, Minor, Gi-127-5; Pulaski PO
CARTER, Monroe, K-185-1; Lucretia L. wife of; Pvt; 61 to 65; Scaggston PO; hemorroids
CARTER, Nathan, Su-236-1; Pvt K Co 9th TN Cav; 1 Oct 64 to 11 Sep 65; Arcadia PO
CARTER, Nelson V. S., Je-144-1; Pvt F Co 9th TN Cav; 1 Sep 63 to 11 Sep 65; Talbotts PO; frodbitten feet & heat disease
CARTER, Obediah C., Mc-109-1; D Co 12th TN Cav; 11-5-63 to 10-7-65; Chuckaluck PO; piles and rheumatism
CARTER, Parish, Gi-125-2; Pvt C Co 12th US Col Inf; 12 Jul 63 to 64; Wales PO
CARTER, Phillip P., Mc-109-5; Mary widow of; Pvt D Co 12th TN Cav; Erie PO (Loudon Co.); discharge misplaced
CARTER, Pinkney, We-227-1; Pvt I Co 6th TN Inf; 5 Jun 62 to 25 Aug 65; Greenfield PO
CARTER, Robert C., Ge-93-4(2); Capt C Co 4th TN Inf; 25 Aug 63 to (resined?) 64; Greeneville PO
CARTER, Robert S., B-7-1; Blacksmith M Co 5th TN Cav; 3-26-64 to 8-14-65; Shelbyville PO
CARTER, Stephen, Col, Li-144-1; Pvt A Co Inf; 11-63 to 4-65; Flintville PO; he has forgot the name of his regiment, his captain was Bowers
CARTER, Thos., T-210-1; Drum Maj 29th IL; Jul 61 to Jul 65; Richardson Ldg. PO
CARTER, Thomas F., Mo-122-2; Pvt; 11th Civil Dist
CARTER, W. R., K-166-1; Sgt C Co 1st TN Cav; 1 Apr 62 to 1 Apr 65; Knoxville PO; rheumatism and piles
CARTER, W. T., K-167-1; Susan widow of; 1st Hvy TN; 62 to 65; Knoxville PO
CARTER, Walker, Sh-157-1; Pvt A Co 12th Lt Art; 63 to 64; PO omitted
CARTER, Walter J., Dk-35-1; Pvt F Co 4th TN Cav; Temperance Hall PO
CARTER, Wesley, J-78-1; Pvt B Co 8th TN Inf; 1-15-65 to 8-17-65; Rough Point PO; lungs & rumatism; total confined to bed 11 yrs
CARTER, William, Col, Hn-73-1; Teamster Co G 71st OH; 63 to 65; Paris PO; shot in finger
CARTER, Wm., Di-37-1; Pvt G Co 12th TN Inf; 8-14-63 to 1-16-66; Cumberland Furnace PO
CARTER, William, Br-11-1; Pvt E Co 3rd MD Conf? Cav; 63 to 65; CONF?; 7th Civil Dist
CARTER, William, Hw-132-3(1); Pvt B Co 8th TN Inf; 20 Jan 63 to ___ (19 mos); Romeo PO (Greene Co.) did not get any discharge
CARTER, William, K-174-2(1); Pvt F Co 4th TN Inf; 12 Feb 62 to 2 Aug 65; Graveston PO; rheumatism
CARTER, William H., U-249-1; Jane Hardon formerly widow of; Pvt H Co 3rd NC Mtd Inf; Nov 64 to 65; Flag Pond PO; death May 10 65; died in hospitle at Knoxville
CARTER, William J., Wh-186-1; Pvt K Co 10th TN Cav; 2-1-64 to 3-20-65; Oconnor PO
CARTER, Wilson E., Lo-189-2; Pvt A Co 5th TN Inf; 16 Feb 62 to 5 Apr 65; Philadelphia PO
CARTER, Winfield, Ha-113-2; Emeline widow of; Pvt F Co 1st TN Cav; 7 Jan 64 to 19 Jun 65; Sneedville PO
CARTER, Young, Ge-92-1; Pvt A Co 4th TN Inf; 27 Jan 63 to 2 ___ 65; Romeo PO; hart trouble
CARTER, ___, Po-152-1; Anna widow of; Ducktown PO; Mrs. Carter so deaf she cant hear me
CARTHY, Alex, Hi-87-1; Sol US; Civil Dist 5
CARTRIGHT, Henry, Sh-144-1; alias James Pierce; Pvt I Co 68th US Col Inf; Apr 64 to 5 Feb 65; Brunswick PO
CARTRIGHT, Joseph, Ru-241-5; Pvt K Co 12th TN Inf; 63 to 66 (2 yrs 6 mos); Murfreesboro PO
CARTRIGHT, Tilman, Wl-300-1; Pvt E Co 40th TN Inf; 10 Nov 64 to 25 May 66; Watertown PO
CARTWRIGHT, Dixon C., M-106-3(2); Pvt D Co 8th TN Mtd Inf; 3-15-65 to 9-2-65; Hillsdale PO; heart disease, applied for pension
CARTWRIGHT, Henry, Bl-4-1; Wagoner G Co 49th KY Inf; 10-20-63 to 12-26-64; Pikeville PO
CARTWRIGHT, Isaac F., Br-7-4; Pvt; Cleveland PO

CARTWRIGHT, James H., Wl-294-1; Sgt A Co 1st KY Inf; Apr 63 to Sep 65; Jennings PO; no disability incurred, health good
CARTWRIGHT, Louis, D-99-1; Pvt G Co 13th TN Inf; Oct 10 63 to Jan 13 66; Chanerly PO
CARTWRIGHT, Samuel, Sl-165-1; Pvt; Delphi PO
CARTWRIGHT, Timothy M., F-40-1; Pvt B Co 13th TN Inf; 28 May 61 to 17 May 65; Oakland PO; CONF
CARUTHER, William, Tr-268-2; Pvt; Dist 7
CARUTHERS, Adam, Sh-158-3; Adam Davis alias; Pvt F Co 11th Col TN Inf; 15 Jan 64 to 12 Jan 66; Memphis PO; papers, discharge--in good order
CARUTHERS, Lee, Mu-193-1; Pvt D Co 111th OH Cav; 5-2-63 to 3-15-65; Columbia PO
CARVELL, Coleman, Cr-16-3; Pvt F Co 15th US Col Inf; Jan 3 64 to Apr 7 66; Huntingdon PO; present name Coleman Anderson
CARVER, A. J., Wl-308-3; Col Guard F Co 45th TN; Nov 1 61 to May 1 65; Mermatage PO; left arm shot off; CONF
CARVER, Benjamin, D-71-2; Nashville PO
CARVER, Camel A., Bo-14-1; Cpl D Co 5th TN Mtd Inf; 8-31-64 to 6-26-65; Clover Hill PO
CARVER, Cornelus C., Br-11-1; Pvt D Co 5th TN Mtd Inf; 9-10-64 to 6-26-65; Cleveland PO; rupture
CARVER, Geo., Ct-37-1; Pvt B Co 13th TN Cav; 9-24-63 to 9-8-64; Hopson PO; epsylepsy, caused small pox
CARVER, Jesse, Se-227-1; Pvt B Co 3rd TN Cav; 5 Nov 62 to 3 Aug 65; Trundles X Roads PO; theumatism & scurvey, was a prisoner
CARVER, John, Hw-128-1; Pvt B Co 13th TN Cav; 23 Sep 63 to 5 Sep 65; Choptack PO; thrown from horses
CARVER, John E., Mc-117-1; Pvt E Co 7th TX Mtd Inf; Kimbrough's Store PO
CARVER, Jonas, Wl-308-3; Sue widow of; Pvt 7th TN; May 20 61 to May 65; Mount Juliet PO; wounded at Shilo in back of neck on April 6, 1862; CONF
CARVER, Joseph, Sh-199-1; Lt; 61 to 65; 4213 Lauderdale, Memphis PO
CARVER, Louisa C., Je-138-2; widow of US Soldier; 4th Civil Dist
CARVER, Ruben, Po-149-2(1); Pvt C Co 2nd TN Cav; 8-6-63 to 7-6-65; Helithrope PO; Mt Inf one yr
CARVER, Samuel, Sm-168-1; Pvt B Co TN Inf; 64 to 65; Difficult PO
CARVER, Thomas, Br-11-1; Pvt D Co 5th TN Mtd Inf; 9-64 to 6-26-65; Cleveland PO; rupture 25 yrs
CARVER, William, Bo-12-1; Sarah W. widow; Pvt 1st TN Inf; 60 to __; Houk PO
CARVES, Sam, Sh-160-1; Pvt 43rd OH Inf; Apr 62 to Apr 65; Memphis, Poplar St (126 to 130) PO
CARY, Christopher C., Je-137-2; Capt F Co 9th TN Cav; 24 Jul 63 to __; Hickory Ridge PO
CARY, David, He-57-1; Sgt I Co 21st TN Cav; 7-1-61 to 4-1-62; Juno PO
CARY, David S., Je-142-2; Pvt E Co 6th TN Inf; 22 Mar 62 to 27 Apr 65; New Market PO; back and left ankle injured by a log falling from breast works
CARY, Lee, C-33-6; US Soldier; Standard PO
CARY, Mrs. (see Gallman, Andrew)
CARY, Thos., He-59-1; Sol US; PO omitted
CARY, William, Sh-185-1; Pvt K Co 48th US Col Inf; 8-8-63 to 1-4-66; 288 Ross, Memphis PO
CARYER, John, Ct-41-4; Pvt H Co 4th TN Cav; 1-1-64 to __; Keensburgh PO; rhumatism and heart trouble; CONF
CASADA, John A., Cl-55-1; Gems? A Co 2nd TN Cav; 8-1-62 to 6-20-65; Lone Mountain PO; hard of hearing
CASADY, Jeramise C., Hm-103-1; Pvt H Co 4th OH Cav; 63 to 15 May 65; Morristown PO; chronic bronkitis
CASAM, Henry, Sn-250-1; Pvt C Co 2nd __; 10-16-62 to 63; Castalian Springs PO; CONF
CASE, Efriam, We-225-2(·); Pvt L Co 1st NJ Cav; 13 Sep 61 to 23 Sep 64; Dresden PO; catarrh for 25 yrs
CASE, Halbert B., H-60-2; Pvt H Co 7th OH V Inf; 4-17-61 to 3-1-62; Chattanooga PO
CASE, John H., Gi-122-2; Pvt H Co 32nd TN Inf; Oct 19 62 to 65; Prospect Sta. PO; shot in left foot; CONF
CASE, John R., Je-135-3; Pvt 39th NC Inf; Piedmont PO; rheumatism; CONF
CASE, Joshua, Co-66-2(1); Pvt F Co 2nd NC Inf; 1 Oct 63 to 16 Aug 65; English PO
CASENBURY, John C., Bo-13-1; Cpl B Co 6th IL Inf; 2-15-62 to 3-15-65; Freindsville PO; injured in back and head
CASEY, Danial, Ge-83-3; Pvt K Co 65th TN Inf; Oct 62 to Sep 65; Painters PO; eye kaucked out
CASEY, I. N., Sh-161-2; US Sol; 16th Dist
CASEY, Isaac, Ja-85-3; Emeline widow of; Pvt E Co 5th TN Inf; 3-2-62 to __; Birchwood PO
CASEY, Jacob, Be-6-1; Pvt E Co 12th KY Cav; Big Sandy PO
CASEY, John, Ro-207-3; Sallie A. widow of; Fossil PO
CASEY, John, R-157-1; Pvt B Co 6th Mtd Inf E TN; 1-1-65 to 1-3-65; Spring City PO
CASEY, John, Mc-115-1; Pvt G Co 10th TN Cav; 4-18-63 to 8-1-65; Riceville PO; piles & heart trouble
CASEY, Thomas, Br-11-2; Pvt J Co 4th TN Cav; 63 to 65; Chatata PO
CASEY, Thomas J., Ja-86-2; Pvt C Co 10th TN Cav; Snowhill PO; shoot in left leg, hurts me now
CASH, James M., H-54-4; Pvt L Co 4th KY Cav; 12-25-63 to 8-21-65; Sherman Heights PO; rheumatism contracted in the army, not able to work half the time, chronic diarrhea
CASH, John, Br-12-3; Pvt G Co 14th IL Cav; Raht PO; wounded in leg
CASH, John, Cy-29-1; PVt I Co 1st KY Cav; 6-61 to 10-17-64; Fox Springs PO
CASH, John, Ms-176-1; Col; Pvt G Co 42nd TN; Apr 1 61 to Nov 65; Caney Springs PO; cannot tell when he was discharge
CASH, L. W., G-64-2; Sol; Bradford PO
CASH, Robert B., Br-14-3; Pvt E Co 1st TN Lt Art; 10-29-63 to 8-5-65; Black Fox PO; rheumatism 24 yrs
CASHAN, Dr. Pleasant A., We-221-5(2); Surgeon: Apr 65 to 26 Jul 65; Martin PO
CASHAN, Jhon F., We-221-3; Virginia widow of; Pvt 31st TN Inf; 62 to 63; Martin PO; CONF
CASLIN, Abner W., Dl-34-4; Sol US; 5th Civil Dist
CASON, Griffin, Po-149-3(2); Pvt B Co 22nd KY Mtd Inf; 9-62 to 12-23-64; Ocoee PO; discharge lost
CASON, Haver, Wl-301-1; 1st Capt, afterward Major L Co 5th TN Cav; Sep 4 63 to Aug 65; Cainesville PO
CASON, Joseph, Ch-18-1; Pvt K Co 27th TN Cav; 6 Apr 64 to 15 Apr 65; PO omitted; CONF
CASS, Daniel, Mc-114-2; Cela widow of; Pvt E Co 1st TN Inf; 3-64 to 4-66; Magellan PO
CASS, Geo. W., D-103-1; Pvt A Co 25th OH Inf; Jun 3 61 to Jan 23 63; Joelton PO; chron. diarrhea
CASSADAY, Alexander, Un-254-3; Pvt B Co 3rd TN Inf; 10 Feb 62 to 23 Feb 65; Gravestown PO
CASSADAY, George W., Un-254-3; Pvt D Co 1st TN Inf; 7 Aug 61 to 27 Sep 64; Gravestown PO
CASSADY, Andrew J., K-173-3; Pvt B Co 3rd TN Inf; 10 Feb 62 to 10 Feb 62 (sic) (3 yrs); Union Church PO; rheumatism & lung trouble
CASSADY, James M., Wa-267-1; Mary widow of; Pvt M Co 13th TN Cav; __ to 5 Sep 65; Jonesboro PO; paralysis
CASSEY, Frank, Sh-149-3; Pvt I Co 14th US Inf; 63 to 66; Frazer PO
CASSEY, Joseph P., Sh-183-1; No C S C Co 65th IL; 63 to 65 (1 yr 2 mos); Memphis PO
CASTEEL, C. F., K-167-5; Pvt G Co 11th TN Cav; 17 Nov 63 to 63; Knoxville PO; served 6 mos, got sick, cansole dated to 9th, I never got able to back &c
CASTEEL, George W., Mc-110-2(1); Pvt E Co 5th TN Inf; 8-26-64 to 6-26-65; Mouse Creek PO
CASTEEL, James H., Wy-173-5(1); Nancy J. Wright formerly widow of; Capt G Co 10th TN Inf; Houston PO
CASTEEL, Rearson B., Mc-114-6; Pvt A Co 1st TN Inf; 62 to 65; Raht PO; fever
CASTEEL, William, Ge-101-1; Pvt A Co 10th TN Cav--Nov 64 to 1 Aug 65; A Co 10th TN Inf--Jun 64 to 28 Nov 64 (1 yr 1 mo 1 day); Cross Anchor PO; linore Station Hospitle, measles & rheumatism
CASTLEBERRY, Elizebeth, Hd-50-1; widow; Pvt A Co 2nd TN Mtd Inf; Sep 63 to Sep 64; Savannah PO

CASTELOW, Charles W., Rb-226-1; Nancy A. widow of; Pvt A Co 10th TN Cav; 10 Aug 63 to 5 Aug 65; Greenbrier PO; died of consumption; she is drawing pension
CASTER, George E., Br-9-3; Cpl E Co 10th MD Inf; 7-6-63 to 6-29-64; Cleveland PO
CASTEX, Louis, Sh-158-3; PVt A Co 26th MO Inf; 61 to 65; Memphis PO; discharge papers lost
CASTILLO, ____, Dk-36-3; 9th Dist
CASTLE, Linnon, Sh-175-2; Pvt I Co 25th IN Inf; 7-9-61 to 8-18-64; Memphis PO
CASTLEMAN, Andrew, D-75-3; Pvt I Co 20th TN Inf; 1 Jun 61 to 1 Jun 63; Stewarts Ferry PO; CONF
CASTLEMAN, Benjamin, D-75-2; Pvt D Co 30th TN Inf; 1 Nov 61 to 1 Jul 62; Stewarts Ferry PO; shot through thigh; prisoner Louisville 4 mos; CONF
CASTLEMAN, Charles C., D-75-2; Sgt D Co 30th TN Inf; 15 Dec 61 to 15 Aug 62; Stewarts Ferry PO; prisoner at Boning, TN 8 mos; CONF
CASTLEMAN, John J., O-141-3; Pvt K Co 6th TN Vol Cav; Aug 7 62 to Jul 26 65; Union City PO
CASTLEMAN, Josiah, D-75-3; Pvt F Co 20th TN Inf; 1 May 61 to 1 Jun 61; Stewarts Ferry PO; discharged on certificate; CONF
CASTLEMAN, Lewis B., D-75-3; Pvt I Co 20th TN Inf; 1 Jun 61 to 1 Nov 63; Stewarts Ferry PO; CONF
CASTLEMAN, Parton, D-75-3; Pvt D Co 30th TN Cav; 1 May 61 to 1 Jun 62; Stewarts Ferry PO; CONF
CASTOLES, John T., Sh-202-1; Pvt B Co 13th Inf; 9 Aug 61 to 63; Memphis PO
CASTOLOW, Isaac, T-216-1; Harriet widow of; Pvt H Co 55th Col Inf; 3 yrs; Corona PO
CASTRET, Peter, Br-8-2; Pvt K Co OH Inf; 62 to 65; Cleveland PO
CASWELL, Edward R., Ro-211-3; Pvt C Co 4th VA Inf; Jun 61 to Sep 65; Harriman PO; iternal piles
CASWELL, Isaac, Hy-76-2; Pvt A Co 42nd Col Inf; 1 Mar 64 to 31 Jan 66; Stanton Depot PO
CASWELL, Seymore, Un-250-3(1); Pvt F Co 4th TN Inf; 12 Jan 64 to 2 Aug 64; Maynardville PO; piles
CASWELL, Solomon, K-161-2; Martha Thomas widow of; Knoxville PO
CATE, Abraham, Se-226-4; Cpl K Co 2nd TN Inf; 29 Dec 61 to 29 Dec 64; Sinking Springs PO; by exposure in service
CATE, Carr, Je-145-2; ____ A Co 8th TN Cav; Dumplin PO
CATE, Elijah, Se-226-1; Pvt F Co 9th TN Cav; 19 Oct 63 to 13 Sep 65; Cynthiana PO (Jefferson Co.); falling of horse on leg & wholly unable to work
CATE, George W., Me-92-2; Pvt G Co 5th TN Mtd Inf; 9-1-64 to 6-26-65; Decatur PO; lung disease, not able to work
CATE, Henry C., Se-226-3; Sgt F Co 9th TN Cav; 12 Jun 63 to 11 Sep 65; Henrys X Roads PO
CATE, Humphrey, Se-226-1; Pvt F Co 9th TN Cav; 1 Oct 63 to 11 Sep 65; Cynthiana PO (Jefferson Co.); dropsy of heart, rheumatism, spinal affection (fracture of spine); mustered in Co D Miss ____?
CATE, Isaac, K-183-2; Pvt B Co TN Inf; 8 Mar 62 to 22 Apr 65; High Point PO
CATE, James B., Je-145-1; Pvt A Co 9th TN Cav; 8 Sep 63 to 1 May 64; Cynthiana PO
CATE, Jefferson, K-184-3; Pvt D Co Hvy Cav; Thorn Grove PO
CATE, John, Ro-202-1; Pvt I Co 1st TN Inf; 9 Aug 61 to 17 Sep 64; Paw Paw Ford PO; lun, kindey & throat disease
CATE, John T., H-49-8; Talitha Gann formerly widow of; Pvt H Co 3rd TN Inf; 2-10-62 to 2-23-65; Igon's Ferry PO
CATE, Joshua, Br-6-2; Pvt I Co 1st US Col; 64 to 3-31-66; Chatala PO; partial paralysis hips & legs
CATE, Mary (see Thornburgh, Lowery)
CATE, Nelson, Mc-113-2; Pvt A Co 1st TN Hvy Art; 2-4-64 to 3-31-66; Athens PO; rheumatism
CATE, R. C., Mc-117-4; Pvt F Co 3rdTN Cav; 9-11-63 to 4-65; Williamsburg PO; Cohawba AL prisoner 6 mos
CATE, William, Je-145-1; Pvt F Co 9th TN Cav; 1 Apr 64 to 11 Sep 65; Cynthiana PO
CATE, William G., Ro-202-1; Caroline widow of; Pvt I Co 1st TN Inf; 9 Aug 61 to 17 Sep 64; Paw Paw Ford PO; fever caused cuott?
CATE, William T., H-61-1; Alice I. widow of; 63 to ____; Chattanooga PO
CATES, Dave, Mr-95-2; Pvt C Co 9th TN Cav; 7-28-63 to 9-11-65; Victoria PO
CATES, George W., Hw-129-1; Pvt L Co 13th TN Cav; 63 to 65; Dellmonell PO; rheumatism 26 yrs; horspill sick 7 weeks
CATES, Isaac, Co-67-4; Pvt K Co 8th TN Cav; 27 Sep 63 to 11 Sep 65; Naillon PO
CATES, Lafayette, Je-143-2; Com Sgt B Co 9th TN Cav; 12 Jun 63 to 11 Sep 65; Mossy Creek PO
CATES, Solomon, Mu-200-1; Pvt E Co 111th USC Inf; 10 Feb 64 to 30 Apr 66; Mt Pleasant PO
CATES, Tony, Mc-115-1; Pvt D Co 1st TN Hvy Art; 12-8-64 to 3-31-65; Riceville PO; yellow jaundice
CATHAM, John C., Co-65-2; Pvt; 8th Dist
CATHCART, Joseph G., Mo-121-1; Pvt E Co 2nd US Vol; 10-6-64 to 11-7-65; Philadelphia PO; dispepsia, prisoner Belle Isle & Andersonville 12 mos.
CATLE, John B., K-165-2; Pvt D Co 1st ____ Cav; 16 Feb 62 to Jan 64; Knoxville PO
CATLETT, John B., Se-225-4; Sol; Cotlettsburg PO; from a shell bursting over his head 25 yrs
CATON, John R., Se-222-1; Cpl B Co 2nd TN Cav; 15 Aug 62 to 6 Jul 65; PO omitted
CATON, Mathew, G-56-1; Pvt F Co 23rd OH Inf; 61 to 65 (4 yrs 6 mos); Trenton PO; prisoner 4½ mos at Danville, VA
CATON, W. B., O-137-1; Pvt D Co 89th IL Inf; 13 Aug 62 to Jun 65; Kenton PO; detail out of order on this sched. (ed)
CATRAN, John A., F-37-2; Pvt 48th US Col Inf; Yum Yum PO; somewhat feebleminded
CATRON, James, Hw-127-4; Pvt KY; Rogersville PO; chronic diarrhea
CATRON, Rachel, D-100-1; widow of George Pigram; US Sol; White Creek PO
CATS, Ephrim, Co-66-2(1); Pvt B Co 15th TN Art; 1 Mar 63 to 18 Jul 64; English PO; shot in left hip; CONF
CATTAN, Thos., Mn-126-3; Chap(lain?) in Gen. Hawes Brigade; C Co 129th IL Inf; 62 to 8-65; Purdy PO; saw wife & she could not tell dates etc.
CATTRILL, York, D-68-1; Cpl A Co Meggs Battery Lt Art; 102 Green, Nashville PO; received musket shot
CAUGHRON, James, K-182-4; Pvt A Co 10th TN Inf; Sep 62 to Jul 65; Gap Creek PO; CONF
CAUGHRON, William, Bo-23-2; Pvt D Co 2nd TN Cav; 8-1-63 to 7-6-65; Tuckaleechee Cove PO; pain in brist, now suffering with pain in brest
CAULER, Thomas D., Co-69-8(1); Pvt I Co 64th NC Inf; 61 to May 65; Rankin PO; dont no dates; CONF
CAURENTON, John, K-173-2; Pvt K Co 4th TN Inf; 1 Nov 64 to 25 Aug 65; Troutman PO; rheumatism
CAVE, Thomas H., H-70-3(1); Bugler B Co 44th IL Inf; 8-13-61 to 11-20-65; Chattanooga PO; hurt back in RR Transportation
CAVENDER, W., D-72-2; Pvt E Co 17th TN Inf; Jan 7 65 to Apr 25 66; Nashville PO; CONF
CAVENDER, William, Ge-84-2; Mrs. J. Girdner widow of; Assistant Sgt A Co 4th TN Inf; Greeneville PO; chronic diarrea
CAVNESS, M. C., He-57-1; Pvt C Co 7th TN Cav; 7-7-63 to 7-7-65; Claybrook PO; in Andersonville prison 13 mos
CAVNESS, W. H., He-57-1; Sgt C Co 7th TN Cav; 7-7-63 to 8-9-7? (2 yrs 1 mo 2 days); Claybrook PO; prison at Andersonville 9 mos, now blind in one eye
CAWAN, George W., Ro-201-3(1); Cpl F Co 1st TN Hvy Art; 28 Mar 64 to 31 Mar 66; Kingston PO
CAWEIN, John, Sh-158-1; Pvt E Co 22nd OH Vol--23 Apr 61 to 19 Aug 61; Pvt K Co 27th OH Vol--4 Sep 61 to 3 Sep 64; Pvt I Co 1st US ?--2 Feb 65 to 20 Feb 66; Memphis PO; rheumatism, knees & shoulders past? time 5 yrs; re-enlisted veteran, now much disabled by rheumatism
CAWHORN, Sarah, D-64-6; 118 S. Sumner, Nashville PO
CAWOOD, Thomas S., Br-13-1; Sgt L Co 1st TN Cav; 9-1-62 to 6-5-65; Georgetown PO
CAWTHON, David, Ca-22-2; Pvt E Co 10th TN Inf; 3-1-61 to 7-4-65; Hollow Springs PO
CAWTHON, John F?, Ru-13-1; A Co 2nd TN; May 61 to 65; Murfreesboro PO; faithful sol; CONF

CAWTHON, William, Ca-22-1; Pvt E Co 10th TN Inf; 6-1-62 to 63; Hollow Springs PO
CAYDELL, Joseph, Ge-90-2; Cpl D Co 10th? TN Cav; 9 Nov 63 to 1 Aug 65; Greeneville PO; piles
CAYLOR, Daniel, Bo-15-4; PVt B Co 6th TN Inf; 3-7-62 to 4-27-65; Maryville PO
CAYLOR, James, Bo-11-7; Pvt I Co 5th TN Inf; 10-62 to 6-65; Big Gulley PO
CEAKINS?, James E., Wa-260-1; Maj 8th Reg Cav; 1 Aug 63 to 10 Jun 65; Clarkson PO; concussion of brain
CEATHLY, William R., S-215-1; Pvt G Co 2nd TN Inf; 15 Jun 62 to 19 Jun 65; High House PO; rheumatism caused by exposure
CECIL, Batie, S-213-2; Pvt F Co 7th TN Inf; Nov 64 to 27 Jul 65; New River PO
CECIL, Charity, S-213-3; widow US Sol; 2nd Civil Dist
CECIL, Joseph, Mu-199-1; Pvt E Co 12th TN Inf; Mt. Pleasant PO; shot through right ankle
CECIL, Joseph, Mu-203-1; Pvt E Co 111th TN Inf; 20 Apr 64 to 30 Apr 66; Hampshire PO; wagon ran over him, was driving teams; is very much troubled with left hip and index finger of left hand is almost useless
CECIL, William, S-213-2; Lt G Co 7th TN Inf; 22 Jan 62 to __; Hellenwood PO; piles & rheumatism; not discharged, was captured & excaped and was takin sick and was away from the reg. sick when it was mustered out
CECIL, William H., Me-92-2; Sarah J. widow of; Pvt G Co 2nd TN Inf; 10-61 to 64; Sewee PO
CEICLE?, Ben, Mu-197-2; Adaline Frierson formerly widow of; Pvt; 63 to 65; Columbia PO
CENTER, Angeline (see Osburn, Aleck)
CENTER, John, H-61-3; Pvt 37th Cav; 61 to 65; Chattanooga, Burk's Alley PO; contracted diarrhea
CHADWELL, James, C-32-2; Pvt C Co 9th TN Cav; 7-4-62 to 9-11-64; Well Spring PO; relapesan measels & mumpes 26 yrs
CHADWICK, Henry H., R-161-1; Pvt B Co 11th TN Mtd Inf; 9-61 to __ (1 yr 10 mos); Dayton PO; no discharge
CHADWICK, Jacob, Di-34-4; Sol US; 5th Civil Dist
CHADWICK, Johnathan, R-161-1; Pvt C Co 6th TN Mtd Inf; 9-61 to __ (10 mos); Dayton PO; no discharge
CHAFFIN, William R., J-82-2; Sgt C Co 8th TN Inf; 2-10-65 to 8-17-65; Gainesboro PO; rupture on left side
CHAIN, Chas. H., Sh-189-2; widow of; Cpl G Co 6th MO Inf; Fall 61 to 64; Broadway, Memphis PO
CHAIRS, Isaac, Di-34-3; Pvt; Dickson PO
CHAIRS, Janis, Hi-85-1; Pvt F Co 100th KY Inf; 63 to 65; Lick Creek PO; shot right knee
CHAIRS, Nancy, Mu-211-1; mother & widow; Kedron PO
CHAIRS, Nathaniel F., Mu-210-7; M Y 3rd TN Inf; 61 to May 65; Spring Hill PO; CONF
CHALK, George W., Hy-84-3(5); Pvt F Co 31st TN; Sep 20 61 to Jul 15 64; Woodville PO; CONF
CHALK, John W., Hy-84-1; Gates PO; caused piles to be worse; CONF
CHALLIN, Luke, R-162-4; Pvt D Co 42nd US Inf; 8-12-64 to 6-31-66; Dayton PO; Lewis Cheddin--name on discharge
CHAMBER, M. L., F-44-2; Conf outlaw; 61 to 61 (2 mos); PO omitted; CONF
CHAMBERLAIN, Craven, Lk-113-2; Seaman, Fearnot; Mar 61 to Aug 65; Civil Dist 6
CHAMBERLAIN, Hiram S., H-67-2; Cpl B Co 2nd OH Vol Cav--8-61 to 8-62; 1st Lt B Co 2nd OH Vol--8-62 to 12-62; 2nd Lt B Co 2nd OH Vol--12-62 to 8-63; Quartermaster Sgt 1st Bat 2nd OH Vol--8-63 to 12-63; Capt B Co 2nd OH Vol --12-63 to 8-64; Quartermaster 1st Baty OH Vol--8-64 to 11-65; Chattanooga PO; also Capt & AOM
CHAMBERLAIN, Wesley, H-64-2; Henrietta widow of; Pvt C Co 1st MN Inf; 4-29-61 to 10-24-62; Chattanooga PO; congestion of lungs; died 9-25-1887
CHAMBERLIN, James, D-49-4; Col; he was away and his son could not find papers; Nashville PO
CHAMBERS, Arch, O-140-2; Pvt K Co 4th KY Hvy Art; __ to Apr 65; Union City PO; discharge is lost

CHAMBERS, Charles, Bo-14-1; Sarah widow of; Pvt L Co 2nd TN Cav; 63 to 7-6-65 (2 yrs 9 mos); Clover Hill PO
CHAMBERS, David, Mu-211-1; Com Sgt M Co 28th IN Cav; Oct 15 63 to Jul 12 64; Spring Hill PO; crippled in back, heart disease
CHAMBERS, David T., Ru-237-1; Pvt F Co 5th TN Cav; 20 Sep 62 to 2 Jul 64; Eagleville PO; ruptured
CHAMBERS, David T., Ct-40-4; Pvt A Co 13th TN Cav; 9-22-63 to 9-5-65; Elizabethton PO
CHAMBERS, David T., Ru-237-2(1); Pvt F Co 5th TN Cav; 20 Sep 62 to 2 Jul 65; Eagleville PO
CHAMBERS, Georg W., K-174-1; dont no ____; House Mountain PO
CHAMBERS, George W., K-167-3; Pvt G Co 8th TN Inf; Feb 63 to Jun 65; Knoxville PO
CHAMBERS, Joel, Cr-14-3; May J. Pruett formly widow of; 1st Lt G Co 7th TN Cav; 5 Aug 62 to 25 Oct 63; Crider PO; reenlisted Capt. Hardies Batalion
CHAMBERS, Mary, S-216-2; widow; Huntsville PO
CHAMBERS, Oliver P., Je-137-3; Pvt A Co 11th TN Cav; 1 Oct 62 to 12 Sep 65; Chestnut Hill PO
CHAMBERS, Richard, H-69-6; Pvt; Chattanooga PO; CONF
CHAMBERS, Richard J., H-69-4; Pvt D Co 5th TN Mtd Inf; 63 to 65; Chattanooga PO
CHAMBERS, Samuel R., Co-63-1; Sarah A. widow of; Cpl G Co 9th TN Cav; 8 Nov 63 to 11 Sep 65; Newport PO
CHAMBERS, Silas L., S-213-1; Pvt G Co 2nd TN Inf; 4 Nov 61 to Nov 64; Huntsville PO; chronic rheumatism, not able to work any
CHAMBERS, Simon P., Ge-91-3; Pvt E Co 8th TN Cav; 1 Oct 63 to 29 Jun 64; Greeneville PO; catarh, wounded & other things
CHAMBERS, Thomas, Lo-187-2; Pvt C Co 80th IN Inf; 15 Aug 62 to 22 Jun 65; Loudon PO; sunstroke & heart
CHAMBERS, Thomas, S-216-1; Pvt F Co 2nd TN Vol; 3 Aug 61 to 13 Sep 64; Huntsville PO; rheumatism 20 yrs
CHAMBERS, W. R., Pi-153-1; Elizabeth widow of; Chanute PO
CHAMBERS, Walker, La-112-2; Pvt K Co 16th IN Inf; 6-10-61 to 7-27-62; Lawrenceburg PO
CHAMBERS, William, Ct-37-1; Pvt L Co 14th NY Cav; 5-10-63 to 8-6-65; Plato PO; liver disease; suffering 27 yrs
CHAMBERS, William B., Ro-202-6; Rebecca L.; Pvt H Co 6th TN Inf; Feb 62 to 63; Kingston PO; smallpox; died in service
CHAMBERS, William B., S-215-2; Pvt F Co 7th TN Mtd Inf; Dec 64 to __; Huntsville PO; could not get rest of information
CHAMBERS, Wilson, W1-292-1; Pvt I Co 14th TN Cav; Dec 62 to Mar 65; Lebanon PO
CHAMBLIN, William, K-169-2; Lt 23rd OH Inf; Apr 61 to Apr 65; Knoxville PO
CHAMBLISS?, Henry, Ro-201-3(1); Ad'gt. F Co 1st TN Inf; 20 Aug 61 to 29 Nov 64; Kingston PO
CHAMP, Margaret C. (see Parker, Nimrod E.)
CHAMPION, James A., Ru-245-1; 19th Civil Dist
CHAMPION, Whit, Sh-146-3; under name of Bolton, Whit; Sgt F Co St. F Lt Art; Jan 63 to 65; Woodstock PO
CHAMSON?, William H., Ge-91-5; Pvt E Co 8th TN Cav; 17 May 62 to 10 Nov 64; Greeneville PO
CHANCE, Anderson, Se-222-2; Margarett P. widow of; Sgt M Co 2nd TN Cav; 8 Nov 62 to 14 Jul 63; Pigeon Forge PO; tiphoide fever
CHANCE, Caleb, Se-222-2; Nancy A. widow of; Pvt M Co 2nd TN Cav; 8 Nov 62 to 2 Feb 64; Sevierville PO; shot, died of wound
CHANCEY, Joseph, Po-152-2; Cpl B Co 10th TN Cav; 9-15-63 to 8-6-65; Ducktown PO; diarrhoea and liver disease
CHANCEY, Mathew, H-50-1; Cpl E Co 10th R TN Cav; 1-18-64 to 8-1-65; Soddy PO; wind galls
CHANDLER, Benjamin, H-57-3; Pvt G Co US Inf; 63 to 65; Orchard Knob PO
CHANDLER, Cynthia, K-155-2(1); widow Sol; Knoxville PO; rheumatism
CHANDLER, David C., M-103-3; Pvt C Co 9th KY Inf; 9-15-61 to 12-17-64; Lafayette PO
CHANDLER, Elisha, Hd-53-2; Pvt G Co 6th TN Cav; 15 Dec 62 to 26 Jul 65; Cravens Landing PO; gun shot wound

CHANDLER, Henry H., H-61-2; Pvt B Co 1st WI Inf--4-27-61 to 8-27-61; Ord Sgt B Co 1st WI Inf--10-8-61 to 7-3-63; Chattanooga PO; 2nd Lt B Co 1st WI Inf--7-3-62 to 9-63; 1st Lt B Co 1st WI Inf--9-63 to 7-2-64; Capt G Co 1st USAN Engineers--7-2-64 to 4-9-65
CHANDLER, James J., We-224-3(1); Pvt CW (sic); Dec 64 to 64 (4 days); Dresden PO; conscripted and ___ ran away; CONF
CHANDLER, Joseph, K-155-1; Pvt B Co 1st Col Hvy Art; Knoxville PO
CHANDLER, Richard P., Bo-20-2; Pvt B & F Co 3rd TN Cav; 9-22-62 to 6-21-65; Maryville PO; bronchittus
CHANDLER, William, Sh-147-2; Civil Dist
CHANDLER, William G., U-248-1; Pvt K Co 13th TN Cav; 20 Sep 63 to 5 Sep 65; Clear Branch PO
CHANDLER, Wm. Richard, P-156-1; Sallie widow?; Lt 48th TN Inf; 61 to __ (3 yrs); Lobelville PO; shot through the body; died in five weeks; CONF
CHANEY, E. J., Cr-8-1; Pvt C Co 10th TN Inf; 3-10-62 to 7-15-64; Maury City PO; CONF
CHANLEY, James, Sh-174-2; Pvt H Co 14th GA Inf, colored Aretemus; 63 to 7-29-65; 25 Turley St., Memphis PO
CHAPELL, Francis M., Jo-149-1; Sgt D Co 13th TN Cav; 24 Sep 63 to 5 Sep 65; Mountain City PO; chronic bronkitis and dirrhia
CHAPELL, Freeman, Li-149-1; Pvt H Co 136th US Col Inf; 5-1-65 to 12-65; Fayetteville PO
CHAPMAN, George W., C-27-3; Pvt C Co 9th TN Cav; 6-1-62 to 11-65; Jacksboro PO
CHAPMAN, James, Mo-119-1; Elizabeth C. Hall widow of; Pvt 79th IL Cav; Sweetwater PO
CHAPMAN, James, Su-240-2; Pvt C Co 29th TN Inf; Aug 62 to 1 Mar? 64; Ford Town PO; Droplep PO; CONF
CHAPMAN, John, Sh-163-1; Pvt H Co 109th IN Cav; Apr 64 to Nov 66; Buntyn PO; he lost his discharge
CHAPMAN, Lemuel, H-53-6; Sgt; __ to 65 (3 yrs); Ridgedale PO; chronic diarrhoea
CHAPMAN, Luke, Hy-79-2; Civil Dist No 6
CHAPMAN, Pleasant, Bo-13-2; Pvt A Co 3rd TN Inf; Freindsville PO
CHAPMAN, William, Jo-149-4; PO omitted
CHAPPELL, ___, D-77-2; Nashville PO; papers burned in Pulaski, TN
CHAPPLE, ___, Irris widow of; Sh-191-5(1); Memphis PO; records not seen
CHAPWELL, Morgan, Ma-176-1; Pvt I Co 12th TN; 8-15-61 to 1-20-65; Caney Springs PO
CHARLES, George W., Hw-132-3(1); Francis widow of; Pvt; Strahl PO
CHARLES, James, Gi-122-3; Rosa Powers widow of; Pvt; 62 to ___; Prospect Sta. PO; died in 1862 in the service; CONF
CHARLES, Wiley W., Hw-133-3; Pvt A Co 12th TN Bat; 17 Apr 62 to 1 Mar 65; Burem's Store PO; CONF
CHARLES, William A., Hw-131-4; Cpl H Co 1st TN Cav; 15 Jul __ to 5 Jun 65; White Horn PO; killed by service
CHARLTON, Isaac, H-57-1; Pvt H Co 16th US Col; Fall of 63 to 65 (2 yrs); Chattanooga PO
CHARLTON, John J., Sn-260-5; Pvt 1st TN Cav; 9-61 to 6-63; Pondville PO; 6 mos in prison; CONF
CHARLTON, LaFayett, Wl-358-3; Pvt Freemans Art; May 63 to 65; Mount Juliet PO; captured; CONF
CHARLTON, Moses, Ge-98-5; Pvt G Co 8th TN Inf; 15 Mar 63 to 65; Jeroldstown PO; disease of heart
CHARTON, William, Col, D-75-1; Pvt H Co 24th OH Inf; 4 Dec 62 to 19 Apr 65; Stewarts Ferry PO; captured at Murfreesboro
CHASE, Daniel H., H-61-5; 39th OH Inf; 61 to __; Cincinnati, OH, 18 E. 9th St. PO; inflam rheum. resulting in heart disease
CHASTAIN, Daniel ___, U-247-3; Pvt F Co 3rd NC Mtd Inf; 64 to __; Erwin PO; died, marked deserter
CHASTAIN, Edward P., Po-152-5(1); Pvt A Co 7th TN Mtd Inf; 9-16-64 to 7-27-65; Ducktown PO; chronic diarrhoea and rheumatism
CHASTAIN, Elisha, Ov-136-1; Capt F Co 10th TN Inf; 5-1-61 to 6-10-65; Livingston PO; hemorrhoids & locomotor ataxia
CHASTAIN, John W., Mc-114-5; Pvt A Co 1st GA Inf; 3-7-65 to 7-19-65; Santfordville PO; hemorrhoid
CHATMAN, Joe S., A-3-3; Sgt H Co 1st TN Inf; 8-9-61 to 9-17-64; Clinton PO; deafness
CHATMAN, Pombat, Mu-210-2; Cpl C Co 40th TN Inf; 2 yrs 6 mos; Spring Hill PO
CHATMAN, Primus, K-168-4; Adair's Creek PO
CHAVANES, Emma, K-154-6(3); widow Sol; Knoxville PO
CHAVENNESS?, Alexis, K-171-4(3); Sgt 1st TN Cav; Jun 61 to 2 Feb 65; PO omitted; CONF
CHAVES, Isaac L., A-7-1; Robertsville PO
CHAVIS, Archibald, H-70-3(1); Bettie widow of; Pvt I Co 111th US Col Inf; Chattanooga PO; contracted cancer or something
CHAVIS, Franklin, A-13-2; Pvt; Briceville PO
CHAVIS, Peter, A-7-3; Pvt K Co 9th __; 10-20-63 to 9-11-65; Robertsville PO
CHAVIS, Peter, A-7-3; Pvt H Co 32nd KY __; 1-6-63 to 8-12-63; Robertsville PO
CHEAK, Preston B., K-165-1; Pvt D Co 37th GA Inf; 10 Mar 62 to 14 May 65; Knoxville PO
CHEASTIANS, Jordan, D-50-4; 418 Jackson, Nashville PO; stone blind
CHEATHAM, A. H., Gi-139-1; 2nd Sgt F Co 48th TN Inf; 9-62 to 4-13-65; Barcheers PO
CHEATHAM, John W., K-161-1; Pvt B Co 1st TN Lt Art; 17 Oct 64 to 20 Jul 65; Knoxville PO
CHEATHAM, Jordan, D-50-2; Pvt; Nashville PO; lost record
CHEATHAM, William A., Mu-195-1; Sol, wife dont know; Columbia PO
CHEDDIN, Lewis (see Challin, Luke)
CHEEK, John W., Mg-196-1; Pvt B Co 5th TN Inf; 23 Aug 64 to Jul 65; Olivor Springs PO
CHEEK, Robert L., O-138-2; Pvt B Co 2nd TN; 1 May 61 to 10 May 65; Lanes PO; CONF
CHEEK, William B., Sm-174-1; Pvt G Co 4th TN Inf; 11-1-64 to 8-25-65; New Middleton PO
CHEEKS, David, Ct-35-4; 13th TN Cav; Shell Creek PO; gone from home, discharge could not be found
CHEEKS, James T., Mg-196-3; Pvt F Co 5th TN Inf; 1 Sep 64 to Jun 65; Hunnicutt PO
CHEERS, Jerry, Ru-13-3; Pvt F Co 111th Reg; Jan 64 to May 66; Murfreesboro PO; wounded
CHEESE, Dellia, Sh-167-3; widow US Sol; 34 Exchange St, Memphis PO
CHEETHAM, Benjamin T., K-156-2; Pvt B Co 1st TN Lt Art; 15 Sep 63 to 29 Oct? 65; Pine 103, Knoxville PO
CHENEY, Robert D., H-61-5; Sgt A Co 15th AR Inf; 4-61 to 4-26-65; Memphis PO; shot through knee and rec'd 5 other wounds; CONF
CHERRY, Caroline F., Cy-27-6(4); widow US Sol; 12th Civil Dist
CHERRY, Henry J., St-161-2; Marthy Jane widow of; Pvt I Co 17th KY Cav; Sep 1 64 to Sep 20 65; Blue Creek PO
CHERRY, Isaac, Hd-47-1; Cpl B Co 55th US Col Inf; May 63 to 65; Savannah PO; piles
CHERRY, John B., Ms-175-1; Pvt I Co 1st V C; 63 to 64; Holts Corner PO; diseased, masles set lungs
CHESER, Epharm, Hw-132-4; Pvt H Co 52nd NC Inf; 62 to 14 Jun 65; Otes PO; consumption; changed from CONF to US; CONF
CHESHER, James L., Gr-75-1; Sgt A Co 8th MO Cav--Nov 65 to 20 Jan 65; H Co 2nd MO Hvy Art --18 Dec 61 to 20 Nov 65; Tampico PO; rheumatism & heart trouble & neuralgia; this person was mustered twice
CHESHER, Samuel, Gr-75-1; Pvt B Co 8th TN Cav; 15 May 63 to 11 Sep 65; Tampico PO; catarrh & lungs
CHESHER, Thos. J. Mn-126-2; Cintha J. widow of; Cpl A Co 6th TN Cav; 7-62 to 8-5-65; Bethel Springs PO
CHESLEY, George, H-72-3(2); Pvt; Chattanooga PO
CHESNEY, Edward, K-184-3; Mary E. wife of; Pvt K Co 2nd TN Cav; Thorn Grove PO
CHESTER, Hanible, F-43-2; alias Hanible Long; Pvt C Co 55th US Inf; 63 to May 65; Piperton PO
CHESTER, Thomas, Hw-126-1; Pvt G Co 1st TN Cav; 3 yrs 6 mos; Fishers Creek PO; reenlisted vet

CHESTNEY, Oliver, Un-254-2; Pvt A Co; Oct 62 to 20 May 65; Meltebarger PO
CHESTNUT, Rahleigh, Hw-132-1; Sgt H Co 8th TN Inf; 25 Jul 63 to 30 Jun 65; Persia PO; bone scrofulus & rheumatism
CHETMAN, Henry, L-100-1; Pvt B Co 4th TN Hvy Art; 62 to Feb 28 65; Ripley PO; contracted rumotism, cannot give dates
CHEVIRS, Adam, Hr-87-1; Pvt D Co 55th MS Inf; 5-21-63 to 12-31-65; Hickory Valley PO; eyes powder burned
CHEVIRS, Handy, Hr-87-1; Pvt D Co 55th MS Inf; 5-21-63 to 12-31-65; Hickory Valley PO; discharge special order
CHILCUTT, Milton, Br-6-2; Pvt I Co 4th TN Cav; 1-18-64 to 7-12-65; Chatala PO; rheumatism & heart
CHILDER, John, Gi-128-2; Pvt; 63 to 65; Pulaski PO
CHILDERS, Berry, Di-34-3; Dickson PO
CHILDERS, James, Hd-51-1; Susan H. widow; Pvt E Co 7th TN Inf; Jun 63 to __; Hamburg PO; died at Mobile by exposure
CHILDERS, John D., Gi-128-2; Pvt L Co 10th TN Cav; 63 to Aug 1 65; Pulaski PO
CHILDES, Isaac L., Ms-167-1; Pvt B Co 111th AL Inf; Jan 15 62 to Jun 20 64; Ostello PO; leg mased by bbl. pork
CHILDREN, Thomas, D-72-2; Childris, Thomas; Pvt K Co 15th TN Inf; Mar 6 64 to Apr 17 65; Nashville PO
CHILDRES, Alen, D-47-1; Pvt K Co 111th Inf; 3-10-63 to 12-23-66; Jackson St, Nashville PO
CHILDRESS, A. B., G-57-1; Pvt D Co 12th TN Cav; 4-1-64 to 5-15-65; Yorkville PO; CONF
CHILDRESS, Alber, Ru-241-5; Margaret widow of; Pvt TN Inf; 61 to 65; Murfreesboro PO
CHILDRESS, Andrew, D-61-2; Ament Cor W Jackson, Nashville PO
CHILDRESS, Authar L., S-217-1; Pvt I Co 2nd TN Inf; 8 Aug 61 to 18 Apr 65; Isham PO; breast & piles
CHILDRESS, Carroll, D-49-3; Pvt D Co 13th __; Sep 10 63 to 8 Aug 65; 611 N. High St, Nashville PO; loss of right foot
CHILDRESS, George W., Su-239-1; Pvt K Co 8th TN Cav; 20 Sep 63 to 11 Sep 65; Horace PO
CHILDRESS, Gimeon (see Garris, Wiley)
CHILDRESS, John M., K-166-2; Sgt D Co 9th TN Cav; 20 Sep 63 to 11 Sep 65; Knoxville PO; kidney liver and spine trouble
CHILDRESS, Noah, Su-239-1; Pvt K Co 8th TN Cav; 20 Sep 63 to 11 Sep 65; Edens Ridge PO
CHILDRESS, Samuel L., Ro-201-4(2); Sgt F Co 5th TN Inf; 25 Feb 62 to 18 Feb 63; Kingston PO
CHILDRESS, William T., Ro-201-3(1); Mary S. widow of; Pvt F Co 1st TN Inf; 11 Aug 61 to 17 Sep 64; Kingston PO
CHILDRIS, Thomas (see Children, Thomas)
CHILDS, John, K-165-3; Capt H Co 1st TN Inf; 1 May 61 to 17 Sep 64; Knoxville PO
CHILDS, ___, Ro-208-3; Amanda widow of; she was from home and could not give information; Keyston PO
CHILDSIS, Rosetta, Cf-38-1; widow; 10th Civil Dist
CHILES, William, A-6-4(2); Pvt K Co "legion" Inf; 2-63 to 63 (9 mos); Olivers PO; CONF
CHIPLEY, James, Sh-162-1; Pvt D Co 4th KY Inf; Jul 4 61 to Aug 28 65; 2 Front St, Memphis PO c/o NA Bills; chronic rheumatism; enlisted at Camp Duck Robinson
CHISHON, Teale, Ru-241-1; Pvt C Co 113?th TN Inf; 5 Oct 63 to 10 Jan 66; PO omitted
CHITTUM, John W., Se-227-2; Pvt G Co 3rd TN Cav; 63 to 65; Trundles X Roads PO
CHITWOOD, Alvona, Dy-27-2; Pvt D Co 15th TN Cav; 9-10-63 to 5-64; Ro Ellen PO; CONF
CHITWOOD, Richard R., M-107-1; Cpl A Co 8th TN Mtd Inf; 11-22-64 to 8-1-65; Red Boiling Springs PO
CHITWOOD, Shadrach, M-107-1; Perndilla M. Bell former widow of; Pvt D Co 9th KY Inf; 9-61 to __; Red Boiling Springs PO; small pox
CHITWOOD, William W., Cy-26-1; Pvt B Co 9th KY Inf; 9-24-61 to 12-15-64; Moss PO; spinal disease
CHLUM, Charles C. D., H-76-3; Sgt G Co 1st NY Cav "Lincoln"; 5-20-61 to 6-28-65; Hamilton Co.

Hospital PO; shot through right breast and lung
CHOAT, James M., L-100-2; Pvt F Co 47th KY Inf; 4 Jul 63 to __ (1 yr 6 mos); Pvt L Co 17th KY Cav--Apr 65 to __ (6 mos); Ripley PO; wounded as scout in ankle, May 1865; cannot give date, reinlisted veteran
CHOAT, William E., Mc-116-3; Pvt I Co 7th TN Mtd Inf; 8-20-64 to 6-23-65; Williamsburg PO; rheumatism & kidney disease, contracted while in service
CHOATE, Austin, Fe-41-1; Pvt R Co 30th KY Cav; 61 to 64; Jamestown PO
CHOATE, Christopher C., Fe-42-3; Pvt K Co 9th TN Cav; 7-15-63 to 9-5-65; Boatland PO
CHOATE, John, Fe-40-2(1); Pvt B Co 2nd TN Mtd Inf; 8-10-61 to 12-20-65; Moodyville PO; injured lungs from measels in Andersonville prison
CHOTE, Shelby F., Pi-155-1; Pvt C Co 32nd KY Inf; 11-8-62 to 1-10-65; Byrdstown PO; rheumatism
CHRISMAN, Atlantic M., Cr-4-2; widow of Mr. F. Chrisman; Nurse; 47th TN Inf; Dec 61 to Dec 62; Bells Depot PO; health injured; CONF
CHRISMAN, Martha J., Cr-15-2; widow US Sol; Maple Creek PO
CHRISTAIN, Samuel M., Dk-32-3; Pvt E Co 4th TN Mtd Inf; 12-64 to 5-25-65; Temperance Hill PO
CHRISTENBERRY, Susan, G-51-2; widow US Sol; Humboldt PO
CHRISTIAN, Arkley F., Ov-134-1; Pvt C Co 39th IL Inf; 3-31-65 to 12-6-65; Hilham PO
CHRISTIAN, James, Mr-98-2(5); US Sol; 6th Civil Dist
CHRISTIAN, John, Ro-210-10; Pvt I Co 1st TN Inf; Rockwood PO
CHRISTIAN, John, Sh-195-2; US Sol; Memphis PO
CHRISTIAN, John Y., Ro-201-3(1); Pvt F Co 1st TN Inf; 9 Aug 61 to 22 Sep 64; Kingston PO
CHRISTIAN, Paul, Sh-191-4; alias Paul Christopher; Memphis PO; records not seen
CHRISTIAN, W. B., K-178-1; Pvt B Co 63rd TN Inf; 5 May 62 to 9 Apr 65; Vancouver PO
CHRISTIAN, Wiley M., Wa-268-1; 1st Lt F Co 1st TN Inf; 9 Aug 61 to 5 Aug 65; Johnson City PO
CHRISTIAN, William, Rb-224-1; Pvt K Co 11th OH Inf; 7- Mar 63 to Jul 65; Springfield PO
CHRISTMAN, Jeff, D-49-2; Lettie former widow of; Nashville PO; no papers to show
CHRISTMAN, Thomas, Sh-159-7; Cpl B Co 15th TN; 2 yrs 6 mos; Memphis PO
CHRISTMAS, William W., Mg-196-3; Pvt D Co 4th TN Inf; 63 to Aug 64; Webster PO
CHRISTOPHER, Austin C., Se-223-3; Pvt D Batt; Sevierville PO
CHRISTOPHER, Jefferson (see Green, Jefferson)
CHRISTOPHER, John W., He-64-1; Pvt A Co 7th TN Cav; 20 Sep 63 to 9 Aug 65; Lexington PO; discharged at Nash.
CHRISTOPHER, Paul (see Christian, Paul)
CHRISTY, Jasper, Wa-270-2; Pvt F Co 63rd TN Inf; 63 to 65; Johnson City PO
CHRISTY, Thomas J., Ce-27-1; South Side PO
CHUMLEY, George, Dk-33-2; Adaline widow of; Pvt I Co 5th TN Cav; 11-27-62 to 8-14-65; Gasaway PO
CHUMLEY, Jackson S., H-51-3; Pvt D Co 3rd TN Inf; 9-1-62 to 5-25-65; Hill City PO
CHUMNEY, Veverley R., He-63-1; Pvt C Co 7th TN; 12 Aug 62 to Jun 65; Long PO; in Andersonville Prison & ___ 8 mos
CHURCH, Allen B., Ro-210-4; Pvt E Co 9th TN Cav; 9-65 to 65 (3 mos); Carters Creek PO; CONF
CHURCH, George, Ha-111-3; Pvt; PO omitted; CONF
CHURCH, Hiram, Ha-111-1; Pvt C Co 2nd TN Cav; 62 to 65 (about 3 yrs); Upper Clinch PO; CONF
CHURCH, Jesse C., Jo-153-1; Sgt M Co 13th TN Cav; 2 Feb 64 to 5 Sep 65; Pandora PO; hernia, asthma
CHURCHILL, Comfort J., De-25-2; widow; Decaturville PO
CHURCHMAN?, Joseph E., Sh-159-1; Pvt IL Cav; 62 to __ (4 yrs); Memphis PO
CHURCHMAN, William A., Gr-75-2; Pvt H Co 1st TN Cav; 15 Apr 62 to 14 Apr 65; Tampico PO; injury to left side
CHURCHWELL, Henry T., Su-239-3; Pvt B Co 4th TN Cav; 27 Nov 62 to 12 Jul 65; Kingsport PO

CHURCHWELL, John W., Su-239-3; Pvt B Co 4th TN Cav; 27 Nov 62 to 12 Jul 65; Kingsport PO; chronic rumatism
CHURCHWELL, Marcus L., P-151-2; Pvt F Co 2nd TN Mtd Inf; 20 Nov 63 to 19 Jan 65; Mousetail PO; lightening struck him
CILLON, George C., R-158-2; Pvt F & A Cos 96th OH Inf; 7-26-62 to 7-29-65; Rhea Springs PO; gunshot wound
CIRTIN, Lisbeck, Dk-33-4; widow; 4th Civil Dist
CISCO, Frederick, H-62-5; Cor Chestnut & 4th, Chattanooga PO
CISCO, Wade, J-79-1; Pvt I Co 59th OH Inf; 1-1-62 to 62 (11 mos); Whitleyville PO; shot in left hip; retired on act of wound
CIVET, Hiram, Un-58-2(1); Pvt E Co 6th TN Inf; 10 Mar 62 to 27 Apr 65; Longhollow PO
CIVET, John Z., Un-258-2(1); Elizabeth E. widow of; Pvt 2nd TN Inf; Nov 61 to __; Longhollow PO
CLABAUGH, Archibald T., Se-223-1; Pvt K Co 2nd TN Cav; 1 Dec 62 to 6 Jul 65; Pigeon Forge PO; diarrhea & gun shot
CLABAUGH, John, Se-223-1; Pvt K Co 2nd TN Cav; 16 Oct 62 to 6 Jul 65; Pigeon Forge PO; heart disease, diarrhea
CLABE, James, Sh-175-1; Pvt M Co 6th US Inf; 63 to 65; Memphis PO
CLABORN, Robert L., Fe-41-2; Pvt D Co 1st TN Inf; 64 to 65; Fitz PO
CLABOUGH, James, Se-229-1; Pvt I Co 2nd TN Cav; 7 Aug 63 to 6 Jul 65; Banner PO; diarea & rheumatism
CLABOUGH, Nathaniel M., Se-229-1; Pvt E Co 9th Cav; 1 Oct 63 to 11 Sep 65; Pigeon Forge PO
CLABOUGH, William, Se-222-1; Pvt K Co 2nd TN Cav; 16 Oct 62 to 6 Jul 65; Harrisburg PO; defected site, rumatism
CLABURN, ____, Mo-130-1; Margaret Blanton widow of; Pvt B Co 3rd TN Mtd Inf; 63 to 63; Povo PO
CLAERRY, Wilson, Cy-27-5(3); Pvt D Co 8th TN Mtd Inf; 65 to 65; Spivey PO
CLAFFAIN, Hollis O., K-160-2; 1st Lt D Co 17th VA; Knoxville PO; chronic direah, invalid confined to bed
CLAGET, Joseph, Hi-84-1; Pvt D Co 8th IA Cav; 63 to 65; Centerville PO
CLAIBORNE, Arthur, Sh-158-1; Pvt (under cook, drummer) C Co 30th IL Inf; 3 Dec 63 to Jul 65; Memphis PO; discharge papers in good condition
CLAIBORNE, John H., C-30-1; 2nd Lt F Co 6th TN Inf; 3-10-62 to 3-24-65; Well Spring PO
CLAIBORNE, John W., B-12-1; Lt F Co 1st AL Vidette Cav; __ 6-16-64; Palmetto OP; discharge burnt up in house, could not give dates
CLAIBURN, Burl, Ma-181-1; Pvt B Co 11th TN Inf; 6-30-63 to 4-12-65; Cochran PO
CLAK, Christopher C., P-157-1; Pvt F Co 17th KY Cav; 9-22-64 to 9-20-65; Lark PO; wond on head by horse falling in a charge
CLAMONS, Jacob L., Hw-134-1; Pvt F Co 5th Mtd Inf; 64 to ___ (3 mos); Rogersville PO; wounded in left breast & left shoulder; furloughed & not able to get back
CLAPP, James A., K-173-1; Pvt F Co 1st TN Art; 23 Apr 64 to 31 Mar 65; Caswell PO; rheumatism
CLAPP, James M., Gr-82-1; Pvt F Co 3rd TN Inf; 12 Feb 62 to 23 Feb 65; Ambro PO
CLAPP, Thomas F., K-174-1; Pvt A Co 2nd TN Cav; 1 Aug 62 to 6 Jul 65; Graveston PO; catarr of head, sane, got leg brok
CLAPP, William A., K-174-4(3); Pvt G Co 7th TN Inf; 12 Nov 64 to 27 Jul 65; Hargus PO; no disability
CLAPTON?, Harry, Sh-200-1; Pvt H Co 11th US Col Inf; 3-12-64 to 1-12-66; Broadway St, Memphis PO
CLARK, Abner, Sh-157-1; Penny formerly widow of; Cap? B Co 25th NY Inf; Jan 63 to 65; Dist 13
CLARK, Abner J., H-76-1; Chattanooga PO
CLARK, Alexander, Co-69-3; Pvt I Co 1st TN Inf; 1 Jun 65 to 11 Sep 65; Rankin PO; no pension yet
CLARK, Alfred, Sh-155-1; Pvt Inf; Germantown PO
CLARK, Ben, D-72-1; Turner Mary J. (Bradford) widow of; Pvt TN Inf; 63 to 65; Nashville PO; nothing can be found out about him but supposed to bed dead
CLARK, Benjamin, Fr-118-1; Pvt I Co 41st TN Inf; 10-62 to 62 (2 yrs 2 mos); Winchester PO; CONF
CLARK, Beriah C., H-53-5; Pvt G Co 23rd NY Inf; 61 to 2-63; Ridgedale PO; rhumatism
CLARK, Burlin, Bl-3-3; Mary A. widow of; Pvt; Billingsly PO; weak lungs; CONF
CLARK, Dennis (army name Rutland), Sh-189-1; Pvt F Co 3rd US Hvy Art; 6-5-63 to 4-30-66; Iowa Ave, Memphis PO
CLARK, Ew;d. C., Sh-201-3; Amelia widow of; Memphis PO; CONF
CLARK, Edward P., Mo-122-3(1); Mary A. wife of; Pvt B Co 59th TN Inf; 61 to 5-15-65; Hiwassee College PO; CONF
CLARK, Ellis, Co-69-3; Pvt I Co 1st TN Inf; 1 Jan 65 to 1 May 66; Rankin PO; rheumates, Johnson City, TN, no pension
CLARK, Francis H., Sh-146-4; US Sol; 3rd Civ Dist
CLARK, G. W., A-1-2; Pvt F Co 6th TN Inf; 11-8-64 to 7-25-65; Andersonville PO
CLARK, George, Hl-24-1; Sgt G Co 17th TN Inf; 1-8-64 to 5-65; Lowe PO
CLARK, George M., Bo-14-2(1); Martha E. widow of; Cpl K Co 2nd TN Cav; 1-9-62 to 5-27-65; Yellow Sulphur PO; prisoner in Andersonville 16 mos
CLARK, George R., K-156-1; Sgt B Co 1st KY Cav; 15 Mar 61 to 10 Apr 65; 266 Main St, Knoxville PO
CLARK, George W., W-191-1; Pvt C Co 4th TN Mtd Inf; 63 to 8-65; Increase PO; right should hurt by falling horse, transferred from 4th MI Cav to 4th TN Inf
CLARK, Gholston, Mt-147-1; Pvt H Co 101st US Col; Jul 26 64 to Jan 24 66; McCalister X Roads PO; stout & healthy
CLARK, Hal, Col, Hr-92-1; 3rd Sgt G Co 59th TN; 5-15-63 to 1-66; Saulsbury PO; health was injured
CLARK, Henry, Mt-148-1; Cpl A Co 2nd US Art; 3-28-64 to 1-13-66; Orgains X Roads PO
CLARK, Henry A., Pi-154-1; Pvt D Co 2nd TN Inf; 8-12-61 to 10-3-63; Byrdstown PO; rheumatism, slightly paralized now
CLARK, Henry C. C., B-11-3(2); Pvt C Co 4th TN Mtd Inf; 9-1-64 to 8-19-65; Poplins Cross Roads PO; leg hurt, drawing pension $12
CLARK, Henry S., Wa-272-1; Pvt K Co 5th TN Cav; 9 Aug 62 to 12 Jun 65; Locust Mount PO; lung disease
CLARK, Ira N., K-166-2; Knoxville PO; absent from home, family could not tell reg't.
CLARK, Isiac, Su-241-1; Pvt B Co 4th TN Cav; 15 Nov 61 to 12 Jul 65; Blairs Gap PO; exposure
CLARK, James, Fe-41-2; Pvt D Co 1st TN Inf; 1-1-64 to 4-25-65; Fitz PO
CLARK, James, Bl-3-5; Sgt TN Cav; 62 to 63; Tanbark PO; CONF
CLARK, James?, D-57-2; Pvt I Co 121st OH; 63 to 65; PO omitted, 8th Ward
CLARK, James, L-108-1; Parthenia Fisher, widow?; Pvt G Co 52nd IN Inf; 62 to 64; Glimpville PO
CLARK, James, Mu-200-1; Pvt D Co 13th Inf; 1 May 65 to 6 Jan 66; Mt. Pleasant PO
CLARK, James B., H-73-1; Ellen widow of; Surgeon Asst K Co 19th AR; 61 to 5-10-65
CLARK, James K., K-170-1; Cpl K Co 8th TN Cav; 11 Sep 63 to 11 Sep 65; Knoxville PO
CLARK, James M., Lk-113-1; Pvt C Co 16th KY Cav; 62 to 65; 4th Civil Dist
CLARK, James M., M-107-6; Pvt B Co 9th KY Inf; 9-61 to 12-6-64; Willette PO; bronchitis
CLARK, Jason, Fe-41-1; Pvt G Co 10th MO Inf; 10-7-61 to 8-1-65; Jamestown PO
CLARK, John, S-213-3; Glenmary PO; loss of left arm, was in a prison; this man is dead since June th 1st 1890
CLARK, John A., Cl-58-1; Pvt C Co 1st TN Art; 4-1-63 to 7-20-65; Davo PO; kidneys & lungs; able to work on farm part time
CLARK, John B., Hy-79-1; Engineer 9th IL; 62 to 65; Brownsville PO; by explosion of shell, discharge papers lost
CLARK, John H., Co-69-3; Eliza widow of; Pvt K Co 8th TN Cav; 15 Apr 63 to 15 Apr 65; Rankin PO; discharge lost

CLARK, John M., Ro-209-2; Jane widow of; Pvt; 1812; Rockwood PO
CLARK, Lom M., H-66-1; 2nd Sgt 6th TN Inf; 2-25-62 to 4-14-65; Chattanooga PO
CLARK, Martin (see Manson, Martin C.)
CLARK, Martin V., G-69-1; Pvt E Co 10th IN Cav; 11 Dec 63 to 19 Jun 65; Rutherford PO
CLARK, Mitch, G-63-1; US Sol; Milan PO
CLARK, Patrick F., D-77-3; Pvt G Co 77th PA Vol Inf; Sep 64 to Jan 66; Nashville PO
CLARK, Peter, Gi-127-7; Pvt E Co 110th TN Inf Col; Nov 1 62 to A pr 30 66; Pulaski PO
CLARK, Peter, Ru-241-1; Sol; Murfreesboro PO
CLARK, Reuben, Pi-154-1; Emalin widow of; Pvt D Co 2nd TN Inf; 8-12-61 to __; Byrdstown PO; came home sick, no discharge
CLARK, Richard C., Sn-260-5; Pvt F Co 20th TN Inf; 3-61 to __ (1 yr 6 mos); Westmoreland PO; CONF
CLARK, Robert, R-161-3; Pvt I Co 5th TN Inf; 11-13-62 to 6-30-65; Dayton PO; gun shot in calf of leg
CLARK, Robert, Su-241-1; Pvt B Co 4th TN Cav; 11 Sep 62 to 4 Jul 65; Blairs Gap PO; dyrhear and piles
CLARK, Robert, Fr-118-1; Permelia Jane widow of; Pvt; 2 yrs; Winchester PO; CONF
CLARK, Samuel, Mo-119-1; Pvt D Co 1st US Col Hvy Art; Sweetwater PO
CLARK, T. L., Bo-21-3; Pvt D Co 3rd TN Inf; 2-28-62 to 3-11-65; Ellijay PO
CLARK, Thomas, Ov-138-1; Pvt G Co 4th TN Inf; 1-1-65 to 10-1-65; 5th Civil Dist
CLARK, Vachael M., J-80-1; Hospital Steward K Co 9th KY Inf; 61 to 65; Bagdad PO; discharge has been misplaced
CLARK, Virgil, K-171-4(3); Alice widow of; Pvt 1st US Hvy Art Col; 62 to 65; no PO
CLARK, Walter M., J-79-2; Pvt B Co 9th KY Inf; 9-11-61 to 12-25-64; North Springs PO
CLARK, Wiley, R-162-2; Lucretia widow of; Cpl A Co 1st US Col Hvy Art; 2-8-64 to 3-30-66; Dayton PO
CLARK, William, Br-9-2; alias Henry Smith; Pvt D Co 1st TN Hvy Art; 2-6-64 to 3-31-66; Cleveland PO
CLARK, William, Co-59-1; Pvt Co C 7th IN Cav; 8-22-63 to 2-18-86; Del Rio PO
CLARK, William, D-72-2; Pvt D Co 17th OH Inf; 63 to 65; Nashville PO; lost his discharge by fire
CLARK, William, B-11-2(1); Christena R. widow of; Pvt C Co 4th TN Mtd Inf; 11-2-64 8-25-65; Unionville PO
CLARK, William A., Jo-152-1; Cpl F Co 13th TN Cav; 20 Sep 63 to 5 Sep 65; High Health PO; chills & fever & lame back
CLARK, William A., Sh-159-2; Sgt B Co; 63 to 65; Memphis PO; horse fell down and mashed; CONF
CLARK, William L., Sh-202-1; 2nd Sgt C Co 4th IN Vol Cav; 8 Aug 62 to 20 Feb 63; Memphis PO; discharged on surgeons certificate--of disability
CLARK, William M., A-2-1; Sgt C Co 2nd TN Inf; 8-7-61 to 10-6-64; Twinville PO (Knox Co.); heart disease, piles, rheumatism
CLARKE, Amry, D-78-1; Pvt F Co 13th; Aug 63 to Jan 10 65; Nashville PO; was wounded in right side by a gun shot
CLARKE, Columbus, Je-135-3; Pvt A Co 9th TN Cav; 16 Aug 64 to 11 Sep 65; Flat Gap PO; bronchitis and rheumatism
CLARKE, William K., Dk-39-5(1); Cpl C Co 9th KY Inf; 9-15-61 to 12-16-64; Laurel Hill PO; hemorrhoids, front broken by gun shot
CLARKS, Charles, C-33-4; Jellico PO
CLARKSON, Samuel, Ha-115-1; Elizabeth T. widow of; Pvt F Co 8th TN Cav; 31 May 63 to 20 May 65; Alanthers Hill PO; bronchitis incurred, died since 65
CLARNY, Francis M., Ch-17-2; Pvt K Co 11th TN Cav; 4-12-61 to 5-5-65; Henderson PO; CONF
CLARY, James, Wl-293-1; H Co Inf; 62 to 64; Austin PO; CONF
CLARY, Patrick, Ma-125-1; Pvt B Co; 61 to 65; Jackson PO
CLATINGER, Margaret, D-78-2; widow US Sol; Nashville PO
CLATON, James H., K-181-5(2); Pvt C Co 6th TN Inf; Aug 63 to __; Knoxville PO
CLAXTON, Andrew J., Sm-170-2; Pvt I Co 1st TN Mtd Inf; 63 to 64; Maggart PO; inflamtory rheumatism; discharge is at Washington, cannon get dates
CLAXTON, Fernando, Ha-114-2; Pvt C Co 9th TN Cav; 11 Jun 62 to 17 Aug 64; Yellow Springs PO
CLAXTON, James L., Ce-23-1; Pvt TN; 61 to 65; Thomasville PO; CONF
CLAXTON, John W., Ru-249-1; Pvt C Co 2nd KY Cav; 8-20-63 to 8-25-65; Hoover PO; from saber; insane for the last 3 mos
CLAXTON, Nancy, Ha-114-2; Pvt; cannot get dates; Yellow Springs PO
CLAY, Albert, Gi-127-8; Pvt; 7th Dist
CLAY, David D., D-72-5; Pvt; 61 to 65; Nashville PO; loss of right arm; CONF
CLAY, Frank, Hy-81-1; 7th Civil Dist
CLAY, Henry, F-47-1; US Sol; 14th Civil Dist
CLAY, Henry (see Campbell, Henry C.)
CLAY, Henry, Ms-170-1; Pvt D Co 10th TN Inf; Mar 2 62 to Nov 3 65; 4th Dist
CLAY, Henry, Sh-174-3; Pvt F Co 3rd US Inf; 1-17-63 to 8-7-65; 143 Beale St, Memphis PO
CLAY, Henry, Sh-174-3; Mary widow of; Pvt Inf & Cav; 63 to 65; 22 Hadden Ave, Memphis PO; ruptured and hip dislocated by horse falling upon him; crippled for life; died from his injuries
CLAY, Hury, Sm-172-1; Pvt K Co 9th TN Inf; 9-4-62 to __ (2 yrs 8 mos); Lancaster PO
CLAY, Isaac C., Wy-177-1; Pvt H Co 2nd TN Mtd Inf; 11-63 to 11-65; Waynesboro PO; heart disease
CLAY, Mathew C., D-57-3; Pvt; Nashville PO; CONF
CLAY, Richard, H-57-2; Pvt I Co 1st TN; 62 to 65; Orchard Knob PO
CLAY, William C., La-117-3; nothing known; 15th Dist; CONF
CLAY, William R., Hd-45-1; Pvt A Co 10th TN Inf; 12 Apr 62 to 25 May 65; Cerro Gordo PO; piles
CLAYBROOK, Albert, Wi-281-2; Sol; 21st Dist
CLAYMAN, Levi, Sn-254-2; Pvt Battery B 6th WI; 10-1-61 to 10-10-64; Hendersonville PO
CLAYTON, Allen, Ms-183-1; Lucinda widow of; Pvt I Co 14th US Col Inf; 63 to 66; Roberson Fork PO; ought to have a pension
CLAYTON, Annie, Wl-291-1; Lagnordo PO
CLAYTON, Austin, Mc-114-3; Pvt; Folger PO
CLAYTON, Cornelius C., Mc-110-2(1); Pvt K Co 12th TN Cav; 3-14-64 to 8-5-89 (sic); Mt Vera PO
CLAYTON, Eligah, H-51-1; Pvt C Co 10th R TN Cav; 64 to 65; Soddy PO; camp cough
CLAYTON, George W., Ch-18-1; Pvt 31st TN Inf; 61 to Apr 62; PO omitted; CONF
CLAYTON, Hamilton M., Ma-126-1; Pvt I Co 60th IL Inf; Feb 1 62 to Aug 1 65; Jackson PO
CLAYTON, James, H-49-4; Pvt B Co 1st TN Lt Art; 11-15-62 to 7-20-65; Lake Side PO
CLAYTON, James M., La-112-2; Pvt 6th TN Cav; Venus PO; now blind in right eye
CLAYTON, Stephen H., Wy-177-2; Sgt F Co 6th TN Cav; 9-21-62 to 7-26-65; Moon PO; deafness
CLAYTON, Thomas, D-45-3; Mary D. widow of; Blacksmith K Co 16th IL Cav; 8-21-63 to 8-19-65; Nashville PO
CLAYTON, Thomas D., Br-8-3(1); Sarah A. widow of; Pvt F Co 8th IN Vol Cav; Red Clay, GA PO
CLEAG, Jefferson, R-158-2; Pvt A Co 14th TN Inf; 1-64 to 65; Carp PO
CLEAGE, Charles A., Mc-112-3; Pvt A Co 1st US Art Hvy Col; 4-63 to 4-65; Athens PO; heart disease
CLEAGE, Philip (alias Clegg); H-62-1; Katie widow of; Sgt A Co 1st US Col Hvy Art; 2-4-64 to 3-66; 521 Cedar, Chattanooga PO; died in hospital March 1866
CLEANSMAN, Albun, A-9-3(1); 1st Sgt B Co 2nd Reg Inf; 7-20-67 to 7-28-82; Briceville TN PO; exchanged May 1864 (must refer to previous service)
CLEANSMAN, Albun, A-9-3(1); Bugler C Co 2nd US Cav; 11-17-59 to 6-30-6_; Briceville PO; piles; 7 months in prison on Bells
CLEANSMAN, Albun, A-9-3(1); Pvt C Co 2nd US Cav; 6-32(sic) 62 to 6-30-67; Briceville PO; island? in castle thunder

CLEANSMAN, Nancy M. (see Johnson, Samuel H.)
CLEAVES, Lilborn, F-20-3; Sgt D Co 11th TN Inf; Jun 63 to Jun 64; Arlington PO
CLEEK, Henry J., Su-239-2; Pvt F Co 8th TN Cav; 12 Aug 63 to Sep __; Bloomingdale PO
CLEEK, John Riley, Fr-117-1; Cpl H Co 5th TN Cav; 9-10-62 to 8-13-6? (2 yrs 11 mos 3 days); PO omitted
CLEEK, Shad R., Cr-8-2; 10th Dist
CLEGG, Philip (see Cleage, Philip)
CLEGGETT, John, D-69-1; Ride? Cook K Co 8th TN; 30 Jan 64 to 30 Jul 64; Nashville PO
CLEGGETTE, John, Mu-197-1; Sgt K Co 12th __; 63 to 65; Columbia PO; shot in the right side
CLEGIT, John, Mu-210-7; Annis widow of; Pvt; Spring Hill PO
CLEM, John, Ge-97-3; Pvt A Co 4th TN Inf; 7 Mar 63 to Aug 65; Upchurch PO; weak eyes
CLEMDENEN, Robert A., Ca-23-3; Rebecca widow of; Pvt G Co 7th PA Cav; 4-62 to 6-24-62; Narla PO; husband killed in war, husband shot in head, ear and back, died from his wounds on the 24th day of June 1862
CLEMENS, Benjaman, Ct-40-2; Pvt A Co 13th TN Cav; 9-22-63 to 9-5-65; Elizabethton PO; neuralgia & rheumatism
CLEMENS, Elija N., Mn-129-1; Pvt B Co 6th TN Cav; 8-62 to 8-65; Adamsville PO; eyes affected
CLEMENS, Haywood, Hy-82-1; Cpl K Co 55th TN Inf; Jun 64 to 66; Brownsville PO
CLEMENS, Joseph, Dk-35-1; Pvt L Co 5th TN Cav; Temperance Hall PO; shot in right side
CLEMENT, Steven N., Be-7-1; Pvt G? Co 7th TN Cav; 13 Jan 64 to 26 Jun 65; Big Sandy PO; rumatism and kidney trubble while in Andersonville prison 13 mos 4 days
CLEMENTS, Ancel, Dk-39-6(2); Pvt L Co 5th TN Cav; 7-63 to 8-24-65; Laurel Hill PO
CLEMENTS, Francis M., D-75-1; Pvt F Co 20th TN Cav; 12 Aug 64 to 1 Feb 65; Stewarts Ferry PO; surrendered at Nashville; CONF
CLEMENTS, George W., Cy-27-2; 1st Lt I Co 1st TN Mtd Inf; 3-1-64 to 5-10-65; Clementsville PO
CLEMENTS, James, H-58-1; Pvt F Co 2nd TN Inf; 2-6-62 to 4-10-65; Sale Creek PO; side pleurisy, prisoner at Andersonville etc
CLEMENTS, John, H-50-5; Pvt I Co 59th R OH Inf; 12-24-61 to 10-1-62; Soddy PO; chronic diarhea
CLEMENTS, John C., Sh-157-6; Martha J. widow of; White Haven PO; CONF
CLEMENTS, Willie B., S-214-1; Capt I Co 7th NY Cav; 16 Jun 61 to 20 Oct 65; Robbins PO
CLEMMONS, Arrena M., La-112-2; former widow US Sol; 7th Civil Dist; Vengia PO
CLEMONS, J. J., Hu-103-1; E Co 10th TN Cav; 61 to 64; PO omitted
CLEMONS, John, Ge-84-3; Elizabeth C. widow of; Pvt A Co 2nd NC Inf; Bird Bridge PO
CLEMONS, Thomas, J-79-1; Pvt 9th KY Cav; 9-64 to 65 (1 yr); Whitleyville PO
CLEMONS, Washington, Di-34-2; Dickson PO; discharge lost
CLEMONS, William C., D-50-2; Pvt I Co 21st KY; Jan 2 62 to Dec 9 65; 519 Jefferson, Nashville PO
CLENDENING, James G., Sn-261-2(1); Pvt C Co 7th TN Inf; 4-1-61 to 4-4-65; Culfaria PO; surrendered by Bell Sep 6, 1865
CLENDENNING, Benjamine, Sn-254-2; PO omitted
CLERINGER, Elizander, Co-66-2(1); Sgt A Co 8th TN Cav; 11 Jun 63 to 11 Sep 65; Newport PO; disease stomach brest & bouls
CLESSER, J. E., Bo-11-1; Cpl D Co 8th TN Cav; 63 to 64; Cloids Creek PO
CLEVELAND, Benjamin F., Ro-205-3; Pvt D Co 51st TN Col Inf; 3 yrs; Hatch PO
CLEVELAND, Charles, H-57-1; Pvt K Co 44th US Inf; 63 to 65; Orchard Knob PO
CLEVELAND, Uriah, Sh-189-2; Pvt I Co 61st US Col Inf; 4-28-65 to 12-30-65; Penn Ave, Memphis PO
CLEVELAND, Wm. A., La-109-1; Musician H Co 57th OH Inf; 7-61 to parolled 63 (2 yrs 6 mos); St. Joseph PO
CLEVENGER, Elihu M., Ro-202-1; Pvt I Co 1st TN Inf; 9 Aug 61 to 17 Sep 64; Union X Roads PO; injury to left shoulder
CLEVENGER, Isaac, Co-63-4; Blacksmith A Co 8th TN Cav; 62 to 65; Newport PO; right leg injured
CLEVENGER, Jacob A., C-33-4; Pvt A Co 184th PA Inf; 8-64 to 7-65; Jellico PO
CLEVER, A. E., Cr-20-2; Charlotte widow of; Pvt 7th TN Cav; Aug 62 to __; Hollow Rock PO
CLEVINGER, Allen, Co-67-1; Mitilda widow of; 2nd Lt C Co 26th TN Inf; Jun 61 to 13 Mar 65; Bison PO; CONF
CLIBORNE, Henry S. R., Un-254-1; Cpl G Co 6th TN Inf; 20 Apr 62 to 14 May 65; Paulett PO; shot through right side, not able for manuel labor
CLIBOURN, Elijah, Lo-190-1; Pvt I Co 5th TN Inf; 1 Jan 63 to 30 Jun 65; Piney PO
CLICE, Henry, Sh-196-1; Laura Smithforme widow of; Sgt K Co 55th LA Inf; 2-16-64 to 12-31-65; 120 Dunlap St, Memphis PO
CLICK, Green, Ge-102-1; Lt E Co 4th TN Inf; __ 63 to Jul 64 (1 yr 4 mos); Henshaw PO; diarear & liver disease
CLICK, Isaac, Hw-125-1; Pvt B Co; 63 to 65; Surgoinsville PO; shot by minnie ball in the side
CLICK, James R., Ge-102-1; Pvt E Co 4th TN Inf; Nov 62 to Aug 65; Henshaw PO
CLICK, John L., Ge-83-3; Pvt E Co 4th TN Inf; 15 Nov 65 to 2 Jul 65; Henshaw PO; chronic piles & lungs?
CLICK, Marion F., Ge-102-2; Pvt E Co 4th TN Inf; 5 Sep 63 to 15 Aug 65; Henshaw PO; disease of stomache
CLICK, Michael, We-232-1; Susan widow of; Cpl D Co 13th TN Cav; 7-14-62 to killed 4-3-64; Mount Pelia PO; killed
CLICK, Wm. H., Co-65-1; Pvt K Co 8th TN Cav; 3 mos; Bridgeport PO; never discharged
CLIFFIN, Horice, K-182-3; Pvt D Co 6th TN Vol Inf; 2 Mar 61 to 4 Aug 64; Gap Creek PO
CLIFFIN, William P., K-184-2; Pvt B Co 1st TN Inf; 14 Mar 62 to 64; Thorn Grove PO
CLIFFORD, John D., Wl-293-2; Pvt; 61 to 63; Lockport PO; CONF
CLIFT, James, W-189-1; Capt M Co 5th TN Cav; 9-18-63 to 8-14-65; McMinnville PO; deafness
CLIFT, John, H-50-5; Mary formerly widow of; 4th TN Cav; Soddy PO
CLIFT, Joseph W., H-52-2; Cpl A Co 9th TN Cav; 8-62 to __; Lookout Mt. PO
CLIFT, William, H-58-1; Elizabeth H. widow of; Col 7th TN Inf; 62 to __; Sale Creek PO; regiment not organized but companies distributed among other regiments
CLIFT, William J., H-66-2; Pvt; Chattanooga PO
CLIFTON, James M., Gi-134-1; Pvt F Co 6th Mtd Inf; 1-13-65 to 6-30-65; Southport PO (Maury Co.)
CLIFTON, James W., Mn-121-2; Pvt B Co 6th TN Cav; 11 Aug 62 to 26 Jul 65; Rose Creek PO
CLIFTON, Nathaniel, La-112-1; Pvt F Co 6th TN Cav; 9-21-62 to 6-26-65; Venus PO
CLIMBER, James, Hm-109-1; Pvt G Co 2nd TN Cav; 1 Oct 62 to 6 Jul 65; Three Springs PO; hornea, his wife told me shot &c for which is drawing pension
CLIMER, Bengam F., D-66-2; Pvt H Co 4th TN Inf; 25 Sep 64 to 25 Aug 65; Nashville PO; blood folan near fillment?, shot through face and left leg; cant follow his busnes on account of his wound, which was farming
CLIMER, Wan W., Br-6-1; Pvt A Co 10th TN Cav; 8-12-63 to 1-65; Climer PO; disease of liver & bronchitis
CLINARD, Sam., Rb-228-1; Pvt F Co Cav; 61 to __ (1 yr); Crunk PO
CLINE, Alfred J., Hm-107-2(1); Pvt D Co 4th TN Inf; 6 Dec 62 to 2 Aug 65; Witts Foundry PO; chronic diarhea & disease of rectum
CLINE, Charly C., Hm-104-3(1); Pvt G Co 4th TN Inf; 9 Dec 62 to 18 Aug 63; Alpha PO; discharge acct rheumatism, deaf ____?
CLINE, David A., Mo-123-2; Edith C. Martin widow of; Pvt K Co 12th TN Cav; 3-26-64 to 1-28-65; Mecca PO (McMinn Co.); died in service
CLINE, George, Co-61-3(1); Pvt D Co 8th TN Inf; 1 Mar 63 to 1 Jun 65; Parrottsville PO; blind for 7 yrs

CLINE, George H., D-57-4; Pvt K Co NC; Jun 63 to Apr 65; Nashville PO; wounded at Clemment?; CONF
CLINE, Henry W., H-53-7; Pvt C Co 29th IN Inf--10-1-61 to 12-4-63; Pvt C Co 29th IN Inf--12-5-63 to 12-2-65; Churchville PO; thrown by mule, reenlisted veteran
CLINE, Isreal, Co-63-1; Pvt D Co 8th TN Inf; 1 Apr 63 to 30 Aug 64; Newport PO; rheumatism
CLINE, Jacob W., Ro-201-5(3); 1st Lt D Co 49th OH Inf; 14 Jun 61 to 14 Jun 65; Kingston PO
CLINE, John L., Gi-135-1; Olive J. widow of; Pvt & 2nd Lt L Co 8th MI Cav; 3-8-63 to 9-22-65; Lynnville PO
CLINE, John W., Mr-96-2; Pvt F Co 10th TN Inf; 2-16-64 to 6-20-65; Sunyside PO; lung trouble
CLINE, Joseph C., Mo-123-2; Pvt E Co 7th TN Mtd Inf; 9-15-64 to 7-27-65; Mecca PO (McMinn Co.)
CLINE, Peter H., Co-62-1; Pvt D Co 8th TN Inf; 1 Jun 63 to 11 Jun 65; Warrensburg PO; measles
CLINE, Samuel R., Hw-131-3; Pvt B Co 8th TN Inf; Mar 63 to 30 Jun 65; St. Clair PO
CLINE, William, K-176-1; Pvt I Co 3rd TN Inf; 30 Sep 61 to 30 Sep 61 (sic) (3 yrs); Preston PO
CLINGAN, James, H-58-3; Pvt B Co 6th TN Mtd Inf; 9-12-64 to 6-30-65; Sale Creek PO
CLINGAN, Washington, K-168-1; Pvt E Co 136th OH Mtd Inf?; 2 May 64 to 31 Aug 64; PO omitted; in very bad health
CLINGER, Henry, T-209-1; Capt; Giledge PO; he is away from home, his wife only knows that he was a ___ soldier
CLINGMAN, Andrew, F-47-1; Pvt I Co 40th TN Inf; Aug 65 to Aug 66; Williston PO
CLINON, Moses, Sh-147-1; Pvt E Co 42nd TN Inf; 15 Sep 62 to 10 Apr 65; Woodstock PO
CLINTON, Charles, R-159-1; Capt B Co 1st MO Cav; 7-1-61 to 11-63; Spring City PO; sick in army had measles
CLINTON, Charles P., Rb-226-1; Sgt B Co 4th KY Cav; 25 Sep 62 to 24 Jul 65; Chanury? PO
CLINTON, William C., Pu-140-1; Pvt K Co 8th TN Inf; 3-3-64 to 8-20-65; Cookeville PO; rheumatism, has rheumatism & cannot walk
CLIPPINGER, Daniel L., H-60-1; Musician Band 4th IA Inf; 10-27-61 to 6-63; Chattanooga PO; none except somewhat rheumatic
CLISAM, William G., W-195-1; Pvt G Co 5th TN Cav; 9-62 to 8-65; Goth PO; over heat
CLOAR, Henry, A-5-3; Pvt C Co 9th TN Cav; 10-20-63 to 9-11-65; Clinton PO; shot in left side
CLOER, Andrew J., Dy-20-1; Pvt I Co 1st AL Cav; 15 Sep 63 to 11 Dec 65; Dyersburg PO
CLOID, Asibee (see Phillips, Cap)
CLONCH, Wiley B., Ge-92-3; Pvt D Co 8th TN Inf; 15 Mar 63 to 30 Jun 65; Laurel Gap PO; diseas of heart & stomach
CLONTZ, William B., Br-8-3(1); Pvt F Co 2nd TN Cav; 8-1-62 to 7-6-65; Red Clay, GA PO; crippled in knee
CLOSE, Francis M., Dk-35-2; Sgt A Co 5th TN Cav; 8-9-62 to 6-25-65; Temperance Hall PO
CLOSE, John G., Dk-35-1; Pvt K Co 5th TN Cav; 6-8-63 to 8-14-65; Temperance Hall PO; thrown from horse and back hurt
CLOSE, Sperry B., D-79-2; Pvt K Co 2nd OH Cav; Feb 23 65 to Aug 25 66; Nashville, 304 Trentland PO
CLOSE, Thomas A., Dk-34-5(4); Cpl K Co 5th TN Cav; 6-8-63 to 8-14-65; Close PO; kidney affection
CLOSE, Thomas N., Dk-35-2; US Sol; 10th Civil Dist
CLOTNORTHY, William, K-170-3; US Sol; Dist 12
CLOUD, Gerge C., Su-239-2; Pvt B Co 4th TN Cav; 27 Nov 62 to 12 Jul 65; Kingsport PO
CLOUD, L.? B., Gi-122-8; Pvt TN Inf; 62 to 65; Lesters Sta. PO; CONF
CLOUD, Robert, Su-239-2; Pvt B Co 4th TN Cav; 27 Nov 62 to 12 Jul 65; Kingsport PO
CLOUD, Samuel N., Su-239-2; Pvt G Co 8th TN Cav; 12 Aug 63 to 5 Sep 65; Kingsport PO; Spring 65, rheumatism, neuralgia
CLOUD, William W., Ha-114-1; Pvt C Co 1st TN Inf; 8 Nov 62 to 1 Dec 64; Xenophon PO
CLOUDES, Joe (see Jones, Joe)
CLOUSE, Francis M., Pu-145-1; Pvt B Co 1st Mtd Inf; 12-25-63 to 4-14-65; Burton PO

CLOUSE, Jno. W., R-163-1; Pvt & Cpl E Co 5th TN Inf; 3-2-61 to 12-12-64; PO omitted
CLOUSE, Jno. W., R-163-2; 1st Lt E Co 5th TN Inf; 12-13-64 to 4-4-65; Graysville PO; acted in capacity as captain
CLOWARS, Andy, Ge-100-2; Pvt; Midway PO; gone from home
CLOWERS, Jasper N., Hm-104-1; Pvt B Co 9th TN Cav; 28 Jul 63 to 11 Sep 65; Talbotts PO (Jefferson Co.); maimed in right 3 finers off; Battlewild Cat KY
CLOWSON, Asher, Je-145-1; Mary A. widow of; Pvt B Co 9th TN Cav; Cynthiana PO
CLOYD, Andrew, D-91-1; Pvt A Co 14th TN Inf; 2 yrs 6 mos; Union Stock Yards, Nashville PO
COYD, David N., Wa-262-1; Sgt A Co 12th TN Cav; 27 Mar 63 to Oct 65; Telfords PO; rheumatism
CLOYD, Sallie, Col'd., Ru-234-1; widow; Pvt A Co 14th ___ ; 2 yrs; Jefferson PO
CLOYS, Marcus C., O-141-3; Pvt C Co 13th Reg US Vol Cav (or Col?); 63 to ___ ; this entry marked out and marked dead; Union City PO
CLOYS, Maria M., O-141-3; PO omitted
CLUSEMAN, Jack, H-49-10; Belle C. widow of; Pvt; Daisy PO; shot in shoulder & leg
CLYBORNE, John F., Ro-210-10; Pvt; Rockwood PO; CONF
CLYMER, Noah W., Hn-72-1; Pvt C Co 48th KY Cav; 7 Sep 64 to 8 Mar 65; Paris PO; neuralgia of stomach contracted by fever? cold in line of duty
CLYOFF, Anderson, Hy-79-1; Pvt C Co 59th TN Col Inf; Jun 1 63 to Jan 31 66; Brownsville PO
COAL, Oscar G., Ho-95-1; Pvt K Co 16th KY Cav; May 1 64 to Sep 6 65; McKinnon PO; re-enlisted veteran
COALSTONE, Solomon, He-64-3; Pvt A Co 32nd TN Inf; 1 Oct 61 to 15 Nov 63; Reagan PO; CONF
COAT, William A., Mc-109-1; Pvt D Co 3rd TN Inf; 2-10-62 to 2-23-65; Sewee PO (Meigs Co.); heart disease
COATER, Elixzander W., Ge-89-4; Romeo PO; cant give any dates
COATNEY, Reece R., Hd-45-2; Pvt 2nd IN? Mtd Inf; Nov 64 to May 65; Cerro Gordo PO; discharge lossed
COATNEY, Simeon F., Wh-187-1; Orderly Sgt K Co TN Cav; 2-64 to 8-65; Cherry Creek PO; contracted fever
COATS, Carol, Mr-98-1; Caraline widow of; Pvt; Kelley's Ferry PO
COATS, Henderson C., Su-239-1; Sarah widow of; Pvt B Co 4th TN Cav; Horace PO
COATS, James S., Su-239-1; Cpl K Co 4th TN Cav; Apr 64 to Jul 65; Peltier PO; Sep 64, back & vertigo
COATS, William, Su-240-1; Pvt K Co 8th US Cav; 15 Aug 63 to 11 Sep 65; Butterfly PO
COBB, Benjamin J., Mc-117-4; Pvt D Co 1st US Art; Carlock PO; rheumatism, heart disease
COBB, Cesar, Mc-117-4; Pvt D Co 1st US Art; Carlock PO; 1 leg? lost in army
COBB, Daniel, Br-9-3; Daniel Price alias; Cpl A Co 1st ___ ; Cleveland PO
COBB, David, H-63-3; Pvt F Co 1st Col Hvy Art; 12-65 to 3-66; 809 Pine, Chattanooga PO
COBB, Elie, L-103-2; Pvt G Co 6th Hvy Art; 63 to 65; Plum Point PO; very poor
COBB, George, Hy-76-1; Pvt A Co 55th US Col Inf; 15 Jan 65 to 3 Dec 65; Stanton Depot PO
COBB, Jackson, Mc-117-3; Carlock PO; CONF?
COBB, Jacob, K-185-1; Pvt G Co 1st TN Art; 63 to 65; Scaggston PO
COBB, John, T-213-1; Pvt E Co 3rd US Inf; Feb 63 to ___ (1 yr 6 mos); Braden PO
COBB, John L., Dy-25-4; Pvt; 3 yrs 6 mos; Newbern PO; CONF
COBB, Madison M., O-132-1; US Sol; Dist 3
COBB, Stephen, K-156-5; US Sol; 141 Pine St, Knoxville PO
COBB, Stephen, Rb-221-3; Pvt; Adams Station PO; CONF
COBB, Willis, D-72-5; Pvt G Co 12th TN Inf; Aug 12 63 to Jan 16 66; Nashville PO
COBBINS, Gilson O., Ct-40-4; Capt M Co 13th TN Cav; 3-22-65 to 9-5-65; Elizabethton PO; hernia

COBBLE, Bradford F., Hm-109-3; Sgt C Co 8th TN Cav; 17 Apr 63 to 22 May 65; Whitesburg PO
COBBS, Felix G., Rb-222-1; Pvt B Co 26th KY Inf; Oct 61 to 64; Cedar Hill PO
COBELL, Calvin, G-63-1; US Sol; Milan PO
COBLE, James A., D-44-1; Capt B Co 7th NH; 4-61 to 12-65; 1219 N. Vine, Nashville PO
COBLE, William R., P-156-1; Sgt F Co 48th TN Inf; 11-61 to 8-63; Lobelville PO; CONF
COBURN, Margaret, Hr-96-1; widow Pvt B Co 7th TN Cav; 62 to Sep 64; Bolivar PO; CONF
COBURN, William T., H-69-4; Cpl H Co 19th US Inf; 1-1-62 to 1-1-65; Chattanooga PO
COCHNUS, James A., Mc-110-1; Pvt H Co 1st KY Cav; 91-1-61 to 12-31-64; Athens PO
COCHRAM, John B., Mc-111-2; Pvt A Co 7th TN Mtd Inf; 8-13-64 to 7-27-65; Nonaburg PO
COCHRAM, Robert, Mc-111-2; Capt E Co 9th TN Cav; 9-18-63 to 3-10-65; Nonaburg PO
COCHRAM, William H., Mc-111-2; Sgt E Co 9th TN Cav; 3-16-63 to 9-11-65; Nonaburg PO
COCHRAN, James N., Mo-130-3; 16th Civil Dist
COCHRAN, J. M., Cr-7-1; Pvt D Co 12th TN Inf; 5-28-61 to 63; Friendship PO; CONF
COCHRAN, John A., Mg-197-4; Pvt H Co 3rd TN Inf; 10 Feb 62 to 23 Feb 65; Wartburg PO; rheumatism, tumor right rist
COCHRAN, John S., Wa-275-1; Sgt B Co 4th TN Cav; 1 D-c 62 to 20 __ 65 (2 yrs 6 mos 19 days); Pettibone PO; gunshot back, left side
COCHRAN, William A., Mc-116-3; Mary A. widow of; Capt A Co 7th TN Mtd Inf; 12-22-64 to 7-27-65; Athens PO
COCHREHAM, George W. (see Phillips, George W.)
COCHREN, John D., We-234-1; Pvt M Co 6th TN Cav; 10-16-62 to 5-65; Greenfield PO; croneck direey
COCK, William, Cl-53-1; Pvt A Co 12th TN ; 8-1-63 to 7-1-65; Springdale PO; heart diseast
COCKE, Thornton H., La-114-1; Pvt E Co 85th OH; 4 Jun 62 to 23 Sep 62; Lawrenceburg PO; chronic diarhea
COCKERELL, Jerry, Sh-159-6; Cpl SC; 63 to 65; Memphis PO; CONF
COCKRUM, William, Hi-87-1; Pvt G Co TN Vol; 12-15-63 to 5-14-65; Bonaqua PO
CODY, John, Ro-210-2; Pvt C Co 1st US Vol; Apr 64 to Oct 65; Rockwood PO; scurvy
CODY, Thomas, Ha-112-2; Pvt L Co 9th TN Cav; 4 Oct 64 to 18 Jul 65; Shortburg PO
CODY, William, Ha-112-1; Mahala widow of; Pvt; Datura PO
COE, Andrew (see Tate, Andrew)
COE, William, Po-148-1; Pvt A Co 5th TN Mtd Inf; 9-1-64 to 6-26-65; Chestewee Mills PO; shot in spine
COFER, George W., Me-88-2; Pvt E Co 5th TN Inf; 3-2-62 to 4-4-65; Georgetown PO
COFER, John H., Cr-4-4; Bugler B Co 13th TN Cav; 9-63 to 8-65; Bells Depot PO
COFER, Joseph, Me-88-4; Sol US; PO omitted
COFF, Areal L., Sh-157-6; Ardly L Co 154th TN; 1 yr; White Haven PO; shot left leg and left shoulder
COFFEE, Edwin, D-67-3; Com Sgt 12th Col Inf; Nashville PO
COFFEE, Elijah P., U-246-2; Pvt M Co 8th TN Cav; 15 Sep 63 to __ (2 yrs); Erwin PO
COFFEE, George, Hw-132-4; Pvt D Co 8th TN Inf; 15 Mar 63 to __; Otes PO; rheumatism, marked as a deserter
COFFEE, James, Mu-193-1; Jane widow of; Pvt D Co; 63 to 3-15-75; Columbia PO
COFFEE, Thomas, Co-69-2; Cpl M Co 1st TN Inf; 15 Aug 64 to 15 Mar 65; Rankin PO; rheumaties, Knoxvill TN, no pension yet
COFFEE, William, Ha-116-1; US Sol; 13th Dist
COFFEE, William B., Dk-34-3; Cpl D Co 4th TN Inf; 9-64 to 8-25-65; Dowelltown PO; general disability
COFFEE, William C., Ge-92-2; Pvt D Co 8th TN Inf; 15 Mar 63 to 30 Jun 65; Laurel Gap PO; chronic rheumatism, Tottireck?
COFFELT, Martin V., Mr-102-2; Cpl F Co 5th TN Cav; 9-8-62 to 6-25-65; South Pittsburg PO
COFFER, John A., K-171-1; Pvt 63rd VA Inf; 61 to Apr 65; Knoxville PO; CONF

COFFEE, Austin, Gr-79-1; Laura widow of; L Co Cav; to 65; Thorn Hill PO; not disabled; CONF
COFFEY, James, Mg-199-1; Pvt B Co 13th KY Cav; Nov 63 to 10 Jun 65; disease of lungs; PO omitted; wounded in face with wagon
COFFIN, Hector, K-171-1; Pvt I Co 2nd TN Cav; Sep 63 to Apr 65; Knoxville PO; CONF
COFFIN, James, Mo-126-2; Sol; 12th Civil Dist
COFFIN, Maria (see Smith, Edward)
COFFIN, York, Sh-196-2; Pvt I Co 11th US Inf; 3-1-64 to 11-22-65; Providence Chapel Memphis PO; permanently injured by cold contracted; served under Capt F. M. Marion
COFFINGER, Isaac, L-104-1; Pvt 75th NY Inf; Ripley PO
COFFMAN, D. M., Ro-210-1; Pvt 7th OH Cav; 17 Aug 61 to 3 Jul 65; Rockwood PO; in prison 14 mos
COFFMAN, George W., Hm-106-2; Pvt L Co 8th TN Cav; 63 to 65; Chestnut Bloom PO
COFFMAN, Michael, C-33-8; US Sol; PO omitted
COFFMAN, Moses, Hm-108-5(4); Pvt M Co 1st Col US Art; 14 Oct 64 to 31 Mar 66; Russellville PO; ruptured
COFFMAN, William, Gr-81-4(2); Pvt C Co 4th TN Cav; 18 Oct 62 to 12 Jul 65; Liberty Hill PO; rheumatism, partly disabled
COFFMAN, William, Lo-190-1; Pvt I Co 11th TN Cav; Sep 63 to Sep 65; Piney PO; lungs
COFFY, Ira, Gr-79-2; Pvt D Co 26th TN; 2 Jul 61 to __; Ball Point PO; rheumatism and heart disease; CONF
COFMAN, William, He-57-1; Pvt G Co 7th TN Inf; 7-1-61 to 4-1-62; Atkins PO; CONF
COGBURN, Hiram, Ge-86-1; Margret E. widow of; Pvt F Co 2nd TN Inf; Pates Hill PO
COGDILLE, Jonathan, Se-230-2; Pvt B Co 2nd TN Cav; 15 Aug 62 to 6 Jul 65; Pokeberry PO; chronic brochitis
COGDILLE, Lenard, Se-230-2; Pvt 9th TN Cav; Oct 63 to __ (3 mos); Ogles X Roads PO
COGGINS, Eli A., Dk-35-3(1); Frances M. widow of; Pvt I Co 5th TN Cav; Capling PO
COGGINS, John W., Hr-96-1; Pvt C Co 6th TN Inf; 61 to 63; Dorris PO; CONF
COGGINS, William, Pu-142-1; Martha widow of; Pvt; Calf Killer PO; insane
COGLE, Geo (see Harris, George)
COGSBELL, Benjamin, L-99-1; Pvt D Co 63rd US Col Inf; Nov 6 63 to Jan 9 66; Henning PO; wounded in breast and r arm
COGSHELL, Thomas, L-99-2; US Sol; Durhamville PO
COGSWELL, Minerva (see Mossell, Harrison)
COGUIR, John W., L-99-2; US Sol; Durhamville PO
COHEN, Isadore, Sh-182-1; 358 Washington St., Memphis PO
COIL, David N., Je-140-1; Pvt E Co 1st TN Art; 23 Nov 63 to 1 Aug 65; Hodges PO
COIL, Martin H., Br-74-4; Pvt E Co 1st TN Lt Art; 10-14-63 to 81-65; Ocoee PO; rupture, deaf & gravel
COIN, Amanda A., K-185-3; widow; River Dale PO
COKER, Charles, Ro-204-2; Nancy T.; Pvt C Co 6th TN Inf; Oliver Springs PO; died in army
COKER, Charles W., H-59-2; Capt E Co 3rd TN Cav; 62 to 65; Chattanooga PO
COKER, Francis N., K-180-1; Pvt C Co 6th TN Inf; 18 Apr 62 to 27 Apr 65; Ebenezer PO
COKER, Jonathan, K-180-1; Mary E. widow of; Pvt C Co 6th TN Inf; 18 Apr 62 to died in Jan? 65; Bearden PO; killed in rock of cav?
COKER, Jonathan, Ro-204-2; Pvt 1st TN Inf; Oliver Springs PO; no discharge found
COKER, M. P., K-180-1; Pvt C Co 6th TN Inf; 18 Apr 62 to 27 Apr 65; Ebenezer PO
COKER, Richard M., Sn-261-3(2); Pvt I Co 30th TN Inf; 11-3-61 to 9-7-62; Rapids PO; prison Camp Butler 7 mos 20 days, discharged 9-7-62 at Camp Butler; CONF
COKER, Thomas, C-26-1; Pvt D Co 5th TN Inf; 3-7-62 to 3-20-65; Jacksboro PO
COKER, ____, K-156-6; widow Sol USA; E Main St, 265, Knoxville PO
COKHER, John H., Cf-40-1; Cpl H Co 1st KY Inf; Jun 23 61 to 18 Jun 65; Tullahoma PO

COKHER, William H., Cf-40-1; Sgt K Co 26th IN Vol; 6 Aug 61 to 31 Jan 64; Tullahoma PO; served 2 yrs 5 mos & 25 days, reenlisted for 1 yr 11 mos & 6 days
COKINAUR, David, Je-142-1; Mary A. widow of; Pvt K Co 3rd TN Inf; 10 Feb 62 to 23 Feb 65; Alena PO
COLBOUGH, Teter N., Ct-43-1; Pvt A Co 3rd TN Mtd Inf; 6-30-64 to 2-22-65; Carter Furnace PO; prisoner Danville VA 4 mos
COLBY, Dalton, Gr-79-1; D Co 25th? TN Inf; 2 Jul 61 to 15 Mar 65; Ball Point PO; nose cut by bomb shell; CONF
COLBY, James L., H-54-4; Lt K Co 3rd WI Inf; East Chattanooga PO; right leg marred by a wagon, a cripple for life
COLDMAN, Thomas E., Gi-138-2; 18th Dist
COLDWELL, Archibald, Jo-152-1; Pvt H Co 13th TN Cav; 24 Sep 63 to 22 May 65; High Health PO; gun shot wound & h. disease
COLDWELL, Benn P., Hw-129-1; Pvt Reeling? I Co 8th TN Inf; 2 Jan 63 to ___ (3 yrs); Norisburg PO; diarrhea, rheumis, piles, hearing, sight; no discharge
COLDWELL, James, Mr-96-3(2); Pvt D Co 1st AL Cav; 6-63 to 6-16-64; Owen PO; injured breast
COLDWELL, John, Li-144-1; Pvt M Co 10th TN Cav; 10-28-64 to 8-1-65; Flintville PO; catah of breast 10 yrs
COLDWELL, Sammel S., Hw-129-1; Pvt B & G? Co 8th TN Inf; 2 Jan 63 to 1 Jan 64; Morisburg PO; cronic diare & hart & rheumts & kidney; no discharge, gave out on march
COLE, Anderson L., Ct-45-2; Amanda widow of; Pvt B Co 4th TN Inf; 6-63 to 8-2-65; Carter Furnace PO
COLE, Andrew, Wy-171-1; Pvt F Co 6th TN; Sep 21 62 to Jul 26 65; Waynesboro PO; rumatism, has to use crutches
COLE, Benjamin F., Ct-45-1; Pvt L Co 13th TN Cav; 2-19-65 to 5-23-65; Stony Creek PO; diarrhea Knoxville 1865
COLE, Ceasa, Sh-198-1; Pvt C Co US Col Inf; 6-10-63 to 12-30-65; Memphis PO; has his discharge
COLE, Charles H., Cf-40-2; Logan, Mary E. former widow of; Pvt B Co 83rd OH Inf; 62 to 65; discharge at pension offices
COLE, Claborn (Col?), Hm-105-2; Ambulance driver 6th Caney Fork?; 16 May 62 to ___ ; Jarnagon PO; chronic drarihia and injured
COLE, Clem, Sh-150-2; Pvt B Co 61st TN Inf; 15 May 63 to 30 Dec 65; Mullins Station PO
COLE, Daniel A., D-56-1; Pvt A Co 1st TN Inf; 64 to 65; Nashville PO
COLE, Ebenezer, H-54-6; Pvt 20th Batt IN Art; 2-10-62 to 1-28-65; Sherman Heights PO
COLE, Edmond, Sh-198-1; Pvt E Co 65th Col Inf; 12-30-63 to 6-8-65; Memphis PO; has his discharge
COLE, Fisher J., D-97-1; Mollie A. widow of; Lt C Co 21st ___ ; 61 to 65; Nashville PO; CONF
COLE, Franklin, Wy-171-1; Pvt F Co 6th TN Cav; 9-21-62 to 7-26-65; Waynesboro PO
COLE, Garner, Dy-27-2; Pvt H Co TN Cav; Nov 62 to May 65; Newbern PO; CONF
COLE, Isreal, K-167-6; Pvt F Co 55th KY Mtd Inf; Oct 64 to Oct 65; Knoxville PO; hip and ankle mased, no pension
COLE, Jackson, Su-235-1; Rebecca widow of; Pvt E Co 32nd NC Inf; 63 to 65; Blountville PO; exposure in war
COLE, James, Sh-152-1; non commissioned officer Pvt D Co 3rd Hvy Inf; Jul 63 to 65; Collierville PO
COLE, James, Dy-27-2; Pvt H Co 12th TN Inf; Oct 61 to Apr 63; Newbern PO; CONF
COLE, James F., Dy-27-3; Pvt C Co 17th TN Cav; Oct 64 to Apr 65; Yorkville PO; CONF
COLE, James Henry (see Nunly, Henry)
COLE, James L., K-179-2; Pvt G Co 6th TN Inf; 18 Apr 62 to 17 May 65; Virtue PO
COLE, James M., Se-229-2; Pvt B Co 2nd TN Cav; 15 Sep 62 to 6 Jul 65; Trentville PO; bronchitus
COLE, Jefferson, Sh-158-5(1); Cpl B Co 63rd US Col Inf; 27 Oct 63 to 9 Jan 66; Memphis PO; discharged at close of war with a discharge paper
COLE, John, Su-233-1; Pvt E Co 3rd NC: Bluff City PO; left leg hurt by collision of train, disabled considerable
COLE, John, Sh-145-2; alias John Washington; Pvt I Co 2nd Reg US Col Lt Art; 25 Apr 64 to 10 Jan 66; Millington PO; Capt Louis B. Smith, LA I Comp.
COLE, John, G-57-2; Yorkville PO; CONF
COLE, John, Cl-56-1; Pvt F Co 8th TN Cav; 4-13-63 to 9-11-65; Head of Barren PO; broken shoulder transfered to 1st TN Lt Art
COLE, John M., Po-152-5(1); Pvt C Co 5th TN Mtd Inf 9-4-64 to 7-16-65; Ducktown PO; lung and heart disease
COLE, John P., A-4-1; Cornellia divorced (and widowed 1876?); Pvt B Co 2nd TN Inf; 8-5-61 to 10-5-62; Coal Creek PO
COLE, John R., Wa-275-1; Rhoda E. Dunn late widow of; Pvt E Co 13th TN Cav; 24 Sep 63 to 5 Sep 65; Pettibone PO
COLE, Joseph, Hw-121-1; Pvt K Co 9th TN Cav; 20 Sep 63 to 11 Sep 65; Van Hill PO; lungs affected worse
COLE, Joseph E., Di-34-4; Sgt A Co 4th enrolled West TN Mill?; 1-1-65 to ___ ; Dickson PO
COLE, Joshua F., Br-12-3; Pvt C Co 5th TN Inf; 9-15-64 to 7-16-65; Raht PO
COLE, Josiah, Cl-56-1; Pvt C Co 1st TN Lt Art; 8-1-63 to 8-1-65; Big Barren PO
COLE, Marion R., Ge-99-2; 64 to Nov 65; Limestone Springs PO; thrown by horse, Mr. Cole was in NC & his wife didn't know anything about it
COLE, Newton, Hn-70-1; Mary S. Foust widow of; Pvt A Co 1st TN Mtd Inf; Paris PO
COLE, Newton D., Po-152-5(1); Pvt C Co 5th TN Mtd Inf; 9-15-64 to 7-16-65; Ducktown PO
COLE, Robert M., Po-152-5(1); Pvt C Co 5th TN Mtd Inf; 9-15-64 to 7-16-65; Ducktown PO
COLE, Sam A., Dy-29-3; Pvt G Co AR Inf & Cav; Aug 62 to May 65; Trimble PO; CONF
COLE, Solomon R., Pu-145-2; Sgt B Co 1st Mtd Inf; 12-3-63 to 4-14-65; Fancher's Mills PO
COLE, Thomas R., Mc-117-2; 13th Civil Dist
COLE, Tom, Sh-155-1; Teamster A Co 1st TN Inf; Jun 62 to 65; Germantown PO; CONF
COLE, William, We-221-6(2); Missouri? J. widow of; Pvt TN Inf; Aug 62 to 27 Jul 65; Martin PO; injured to death; CONF
COLE, William C., A-2-3; Cpl D Co 1st TN Lt Art; 10-20-63 to 7-20-65; Hinds Creek PO; rheumatism
COLE, William N., We-221-7; Pvt TN Inf; Martin PO
COLEBURN, Lewis, La-117-3; Pvt C Co 9th TN Cav; 62 to ___ ; 15th Dist
COLEMAN, Alvis, Cl-51-1; Louisa widow of; Pvt D Co 29th TN Cav; 8-10-63 to ___ ; Cedar Fork PO; CONF
COLEMAN, Ambrose B., Wh-180-2; Sparta PO; cant remember
COLEMAN, Anderson (see Carvell, Coleman)
COLEMAN, Benjamin C., Sq-164-5(1); Pvt H Co 9th TN Cav; 11-3-61 to 9-11-65; Soddy PO
COLEMAN, Benjamin F., H-58-5; Martha C. widow of; Pvt H Co 3rd TN Inf; 2-10-62 to 2-23-65; Retro PO
COLEMAN, Berry, Mu-210-5; Pvt H Co TN Cav; 63 to 64 (4 mos); Carters Creek PO; CONF
COLEMAN, Carden, Mc-112-1; Pvt A Co 42nd US Inf; 3-26-64 to 1-15-66; Athens PO
COLEMAN, Charles, Col, G-73-1; Pvt E Co 15th US Cav; Apr 1 63 to Apr 1 65; Trenton PO
COLEMAN, Dennis, Wa-276-2; Pvt Sailor Capt Smith; Oct 61 to Jun 65; Saginouw City, MI, PO; shot twice by minnie ball
COLEMAN, Evan E., H-51-5; Staff Sgt G Co 1st TN Cav; 7-1-62 to 6-5-65; Hill City PO
COLEMAN, George W., Br-9-1; Sgt A Co 63rd IL Inf; 12-1-61 to 7-18-62; Cleveland PO
COLEMAN, Harrison H., Sh-159-1; Pvt; Memphis PO; CONF
COLEMAN, Horace, Sh-158-6(4); Cpl K Co Col Hvy Art; 63 to 65; Memphis PO; shot in small of back causing partial paralysis of the leg; was captured in 64 by Forrest & got no discharge papers
COLEMAN, Jacob, Gi-122-2; Sgt? A Co 16th AL Inf; 62 to 2 Apr 65; Prospect Sta. PO; CONF

COLEMAN, James, Sh-144-2; Pvt A Co 3rd Col Hvy Art; Mar 63 to 30 Apr 66; Arlington PO
COLEMAN, James H., K-171-2; 1st Lt D Co 6th TN Inf; 18 Apr 62 to Jul 64; Knoxville PO
COLEMAN, James M., Mu-211-1; Cpl A Co 12th Rells? Inf Col; Jul 21 63 to Jan 16 66; Britton PO; rheumatism; this entry crossed out and written in below is McKissick, Augustus, Col.
COLEMAN, James S., Po-152-3(1); 1st Cpl E Co 7th TN Mtd Inf; 9-30-64 to 7-11-65; Ducktown PO
COLEMAN, John, Ru-239-1; Pvt Signal Service; 63 to 65; Murfreesboro PO
COLEMAN, John, Ch-17-1; Iby J. widow of; Pvt A Co 6th TN Cav; 62 to 65; Henderson PO; CONF
COLEMAN, Jos. (see Farney, Dennis)
COLEMAN, Lewis, Sh-157-6; Pvt H Co 65th C; 63 to 66; Dist 13
COLEMAN, Lewis W., H-51-1; Pvt H Co 3rd R TN Inf; 2-62 to 2-65; Soddy PO; rheumatism
COLEMAN, Louis L., Po-156-2; Pvt; no PO; CONF
COLEMAN, Mary J., K-170-3; widow of US Sol; Dist 12
COLEMAN, Myatt, Po-156-2; Sgt K Co 42nd TN Inf; 9-4-61 to 10-17-64; Lobelville PO; CONF
COLEMAN, Robert, Rb-221-1; Pvt 11th TN; Apr 1 62 to Apr 1 65; Barren Plains PO; CONF
COLEMAN, Samuel, De-26-1; C Co 32nd TN; Oct 61 to 63; Genett PO; CONF
COLEMAN, Thomas, Sh-189-1; could not get his record; Bomgrade? St., Memphis PO
COLEMAN, Thomas J., H-50-4; Pvt C Co 17th KY Vol; 9-17-64 to 10-4-65; Soddy PO
COLEMAN, William, K-172-2; Pvt A Co 6th TN Inf; 24 Apr 62 to 27 Apr 65; Knoxville PO
COLEMAN, William H., Hn-82-1; Pvt M Co 12th KY Cav?; 3-4-64 to 8-9-65; Buchanan PO
COLEMAN, William T., Ge-81-2; Sgt M Co 8th TN Cav; 15 Sep? 63 to 13 Sep 65; Greeneville PO; horse fell on me & broke my ankle
COLEMAN, Zachariah T., Dk-39-5(1); Pvt D Co 6th TN Mtd Inf; 9-63 to 6-6-65; Laurel Hill PO; lost arm by accident; through error mustered as John Coleman
COLEY, James M., Ro-210-4; Pvt H Co 1st TN Cav; yrs 6 mos; Rockwood PO; CONF
COLEY, John, M-103-2; Pvt H Co 1st KY Inf; 12-2-61 to 1-5-65; Lafayette PO
COLEY, Julius, M-103-3; Pvt I Co 9th KY Inf; 12-1-61 to 7-1-62; Lafayette PO
COLEY, William F., Ro-203-6; Pvt F Co 5th TN Cav; 6 Jan 62 to __; Burns Mills PO; sunstroke & rheumatism; CONF
COLIE?, William S., M-103-1; Pvt H Co 1st KY?; 12-2-61 to 1-8-65; Lafayette PO; shot in mouth
COLIER, Ben, Hd-54-2; Harrett Finger widow of; Pvt; Saltillo PO; died, no data (Colored sole)
COLINAN, James M., Mu-210-2; Pvt; 61 to 65; Spring Hill PO; CONF
COLINS, David J., Re-210-2; Pvt D Co 1st TN Inf; Aug 61 to 17 Sep 64; Webster PO; measles settled in eyes; dont know date of inlistment
COLL, Buch, Hr-86-2; Pvt; 63 to 66; Grand Junction PO
COLLER, James H., H-53-5; Phillipher C Bat OH Art; 61 to __; Ridgedale PO
COLLESTER, Charles, L-102-1; Pvt D Co 98th IL; Aug 9 62 to Jul 6 65; Fulton PO
COLLET, Joseph L., Mo-222-2; Pvt E Co 3rd TN Inf; 4-9-61 to 4-15-65; Dancing Branch PO; CONF
COLLETT, Charles, Wa-276-1; Pvt 12th TN Cav; 18 mos; Crokshanks PO; side pleuracy, no discharge, no dates
COLLETT, Elbert, Un-253-2; Cpl F Co 3rd TN Inf; 10 Feb 62 to 23 Feb 65; Meltabarger PO; chronic diarhea & piles
COLLETT, William H., K-159-2; 1st Lt F Co 11th W VA Inf; __ to Aug 25 65; Knoxville PO; gun shot wound ankle & leg; pentioned dischgd spl. order
COLLEY, William H., Wl-298-2; Pvt H Co 4th KY Cav; 61 to 62; Pvt G Co 4th KY Cav--61 to 62; Pvt G Co 4th TN Mtd Inf--64 to Aug 65; Cottage Home PO; disability of the left ankle, not able to work but very little
COLLIER, Augustus, Sh-193-1; Pvt; Memphis PO
COLLIER, Benj. B., Sh-159-3; Pvt; 2 yrs; Memphis PO; CONF
COLLIER, Dabney W., Sh-159-2; Lt Bluff City Grey; 154th? Mex Cav; Apr 61 to 26 Sep 63; Memphis PO; shot and leg amputated; CONF
COLLIER, Elija, Mt-149-1; Pvt F Co 15th US Inf; 3-27-64 to 4-12-66; Carbondale PO
COLLIER, Jeff (see Ross, William)
COLLIER, Joseph, Gi-132-4; Barbary Rodes formerly widow of; Wales PO
COLLIN, John K., Hw-119-2(1); Pvt E Co 8th TN Cav; 10 Oct 63 to 11 Sep 65; Lee Valley PO; rheumatism & heart disease
COLLING, Perrey, Cl-53-2; Pvt; Hipatia PO
COLLINS, Absalom G., Mo-120-3(1); Pvt C Co 7th OH Mtd Inf; 9-13-61 to 3-18-65; Sweetwater PO; chronic diarrhea etc.
COLLINS, Aliga, Cl-57-1; Pvt C Co 1st TN Vol; 11-16-61 to 12-10-64; Kecks Chappel PO; on crutches from rheumatism in legs & veins legs & shins cracked
COLLINS, Amanda A. (see Hall, George W.)
COLLINS, Armstrong, Ha-115-4; Pvt A Co 7th TN Inf; 20 Mar 63 to 20 Oct 63; Mulberry Gap PO; CONF
COLLINS, Baily, Ha-112-1; Pvt A Co 1st TN Cav; 1 Dec 62 to 15 Jun 65; Datura PO
COLLINS, Baty, Ha-117-3; Pvt E Co 8th TN Cav; 23 Sep 63 to 11 Sep 65; Sneedville PO; gunshot mumps? & piles
COLLINS, Benjamin, Hw-128-1; Pvt C Co 7th TN Cav; 22 Jul 62 to 22 Jul 65; Choptack PO; chills and fever
COLLINS, Calaway, Ha-113-1; Pvt A Co 1st TN Cav; 10 Jul 61 to 5 Jun 65; Sneedville PO; wounded in neck and head; fits at times
COLLINS, Caleb, Gr-79-4; 10th Dist
COLLINS, Charles (see Hughes, Charles)
COLLINS, Charlotte, R-106-2(3); 5th Civil Dist
COLLINS, Conoway, Ha-113-1; Cpl H Co 1st TN Cav; 10 Jul 62 to 5 Jun 65; Sneedville PO
COLLINS, Crocket, Cf-38-2; Pvt B Co 61st US Inf; 62 to 65; Somerville PO
COLLINS, David, K-176-2; Halls X Roads PO
COLLINS, David B., Ro-202-2; Pvt B Co 3rd TN Inf US; 14 Oct 64 to 9 Nov 65; Union X Roads PO; chronic rheumatism; CONF
COLLINS, Duncan, K-185-2; Pvt A Co 8th TN Cav; Mascott PO
COLLINS, Evan C., Ha-117-2; Pvt E Co 8th TN Cav; 23 Sep 63 to 11 Sep 65; Kyle's Ford PO; left arm, left lung?, left shoulder
COLLINS, Franklin, Ha-117-3; Pvt A Co 1st TN Cav; Dec 62 to Jan 15 65; Sneedville PO
COLLINS, George, Je-146-2; Pvt H Co 2nd NC Mtd Inf; 1 Oct 64 to 16 Aug 65; White Pine PO; spinel disease of hed & back, bad off
COLLINS, Henry W., Mc-112-10; Pvt C Co 1st TN Scout and Guide; Mount Verd PO; gunshot wound & deafness
COLLINS, Howard, Ha-117-3; Pvt E Co 8th TN Cav; 61 to 64; Sneedville PO; chronic diarrhea
COLLINS, Ira, Je-146-1; Martha E. widow of; Pvt H Co 2nd NC Mtd Inf; 1 Oct 63 to 14 Aug 64; Oak Grove PO
COLLINS, James Sen., Wa-270-1; Pvt G Co 7th TN Inf; 63 to 65; Austins Springs PO
COLLINS, James, Ha-117-1; Pvt E Co TN Inf; 61 to Oct 62 (13 mos); Kyle's Ford PO; CONF
COLLINS, James, S-214-4; Pvt A Co 44th TN Inf; Robbins PO; discharge lost, cat tell dates
COLLINS, James, Hw-130-1; Pvt E Co 8th TN Inf; 20 Oct 63 to 11 Sep 65; Lee Valley PO
COLLINS, James, Gr-75-2; Pvt K Co 3rd TN Inf; 10 Feb 62 to 14 Apr 65; Tampico PO; gun shot
COLLINS, James B., Hd-52-1; Pvt B Co 13th TN Cav; Mar 10 61 to 65; Pittsburg PO; wounded in head
COLLINS, James M., Hd-50-1; Pvt F Co 24th MI Inf; Apr 26 62 to Jun 24 65; Savannah PO
COLLINS, James P., Je-146-1; Pvt H Co 2nd NC Mtd Inf; 1 Oct 63 to 14 Aug 64; Oak Grove PO; piles & rheumatism, he looks very badly
COLLINS, James R., Br-10-1; Pvt F Co 3rd TN Cav; 11-11-62 to 6-10-65; Cleveland PO
COLLINS, Jerry, D-91-1; Pvt F Co 13th TN Inf; Sep to 10 Jan __ (2 yrs 3 mos); 808 Cedar St, Nashville PO; CONF
COLLINS, Jessee, Gr-79-3; Elizabeth widow of; Sgt C Co 2nd TN Cav; Aug 62 to Oct 65; Ball Point PO; killed

COLLINS, Jessee, Gi-122-7; Pvt H Co 43rd TN Inf; 1 Dec 62 to May 65; Veto, AL, PO; slight wound; CONF
COLLINS, John, D-98-1; Pvt K Co 2nd TN; Jan 25 64 to Apr 20 65; 19th Civil Dist
COLLINS, John C., D-46-2; Sophrona widow of; Pvt I Co 10th TN Inf; 7-23-62 to 6-23-65; Nashville PO
COLLINS, John C., Cl-57-1; Pvt E Co 6th TN Inf; 3-6-62 to 3-7-65; Kecks Chappel PO; sore legs & rheumatism for 27 yrs
COLLINS, John C., Cl-57-2; Pvt E Co 6th TN Inf; 3-6-62 to 3-7-65; Kecks Chappel PO
COLLINS, John H., Ha-115-4; Pvt H Co 50th VA Inf; 1 Aug 61 to 21 Jun 65; Mulberry Gap PO; prisoner at Ft. Deleware 13 mos; CONF
COLLINS, John L., Cl-57-1; Pvt D Co 1st TN Inf; 11-21-61 to 12-14-64; Goin PO; lung affected & rheumatism 27 yrs
COLLINS, Joseph, Mc-115-1; Pvt A Co 5th TN; 10-25-64 to 7-14-65; Riceville PO; chronic diorhea
COLLINS, Joseph, Cl-52-2; Lizebeth widow of; Pvt 8th TN Inf; 64 to 65; Hypratia PO; may have been killed in battle
COLLINS, Joshua, Gr-80-1; Pvt I Co 29th KY Inf; Sep 61 to 64; Thorn Hill PO; in prison at Richmond 4 mos, cannot recollect dates omitted
COLLINS, Lewis K., Ha-115-4; Pvt A Co 1st TN Cav; 1 May 62 to 1 May 65; Sneedville PO; shot through leg
COLLINS, Mathew C., Cl-57-1; Pvt E Co 6th TN Inf; 3-6-62 to 4-25-65; Kecks Chappel PO; gun shot in left arm & side, in prison at Libey & Belle Ile
COLLINS, McKinley, Ha-115-5; Pvt E Co 8th TN Cav; 23 Sep 63 to 29 Jun 65; Mulberry Gap PO; diarrhea, pensioner
COLLINS, Milam, Ha-115-4; Pvt A Co; Sneedville PO
COLLINS, Noble, Gr-79-4; Jelina E. widow of; Pvt 26th TN; 62 to 65; Thorn Hill PO; consumption; CONF
COLLINS, Perry L., Mo-126-1; Pvt I Co 5th TN Inf; Tevis PO
COLLINS, Richard K., Wa-268-4; Susan A. widow of; discharge away from home; Johnson City PO
COLLINS, Silas, Ha-113-3; Orpha wife of Simeon widow of; Pvt A Co 1st TN Cav; 14 Dec 62 to ___; Sneedville PO; died in the army Apr or May 63
COLLINS, Simeon, Ha-113-1; Pvt A Co 1st TN Cav; 9 Mar 62 to 5 Apr 65; Sneedville PO
COLLINS, Stokely, Gr-71-2; Tate Spring PO; discharged misplaced
COLLINS, Thomas L., K-165-1; Pvt F Co 10th TN Cav; 20 Oct 63 to 1 Aug 65; Knoxville PO
COLLINS, Vardymon, Ha-115-4; Pvt E Co 2nd TN Inf; 1 Feb 62 to 1 May 65; Mulberry Gap PO
COLLINS, Watson, Ct-42-1; Eveline widow of; Pvt H Co 2nd TN Inf; Watauga PO
COLLINS, William A., Un-252-1; Pvt E Co 49th KY Inf; 63 to 64; Nave Hill PO
COLLINS, William B., Mo-126-1; Mary L. widow of; Pvt A Co 2nd TN Cav; 8-62 to 7-9-65; Hopewell Springs PO; diarrhea; died 7-9-65 with command
COLLINS, William D., Su-241-2; Pvt F Co 8th TN Cav; 10 Aug 63 to 11 Sep 65; Clover Bottom PO; exposure
COLLINS, William J., B-11-3(2); Pvt F Co 1st IN Vidette Cav; 9-27-63 to 64 (11 mos 20 days); Unionville PO
COLLINS, William N., Mo-126-1; Pvt TN Cav; 10-15-63 to ___; Hopewell Springs PO; was in Col Brisons Reg, was shot and lay out in mountains, no discharge
COLLINS, William R., We-225-3(2); Sgt I Co 6th TN Reg; Jun 20 62 to Jul 26 65; Dresden PO; rheumatism & broken thumb in action at Nashville, ailing & not able to work
COLLINS, William T., Fr-116-1(2); Pvt I Co 10th Reg TN Inf; 7-23-63 to 6-23-65; Sherwood PO
COLLINS, Winfley, Gr-72-2; Pvt C Co 4th TN Cav; 1 Jan 63 to 13 Jun 65; Marshals Ferry PO; exposure in service
COLLYOR, Nathan, D-60-2; 130 Stonewall St, Nashville PO; colored
COLMAN, Peter, Hr-89-1; Pvt A Co 29th IL; 9-62 to 65; Whiteville PO

COLSON, Milton K., Cy-30-1; Ruth E. Ledbetter formerly widow of; Pvt KY Cav; 61 to 62 (10 mos); Mouth of Wolf PO; measles; no discharge given
COLTON, Criss, T-216-2; 11th Civil Dist
COLWELL, Amos, Gi-139-3; Pvt D Co 52nd IL Inf; 12-63 to 7-65; Bercheers PO; CONF
COLWELL, William B., Dk-36-2; Pvt B Co 4th TN Mtd Inf; 9-25-64 to 8-25-65; Smithville PO
COLYER, Geo., Ge-91-3; Wagon C Co 8th TN Cav; 5 May 63 to 11 Sep 65; Greeneville PO; kidney & rheumatism
COLYER, John, Ge-84-2; Rutha widow of; Pvt B Co 8th TN Cav; Jul 63 to ___; Greenville PO; not got discharge in hand
COLYER, John, Ro-205-3; Cpl B Co 1st TN Inf; 6 Mar 62 to 7 Mar 65; Dearmond PO; eyes sore
COLYER, John, Ck-185-2; Pvt F Co 8th TN Cav; Sep 63 to Sep 65; McMillans PO; ruptured
COLYER, Peter, Wa-274-2; Pvt F Co 1st US Hvy Art; 12 Apr 64 to 31 Mar 66; Jonesboro PO; rupture and frost bite
COMBS, Emanuel J., Wa-267-3; Pvt; Johnson City PO
COMBS, Fielding, Ha-115-2; Pvt E Co 5th NJ Art; 27 Nov 63 to 12 Jun 65; Alanthers Hill PO; shot in face, reenlisted veteran
COMBS, John F. M., D-60-2; 130 Morgan St, Nashville PO
COMBS, Marcus, D-73-2; Black ___ (either blacksmith or blackman, cant tell) A Co Capt John? IN Inf; Jun 1 62 to not discharged, transferred to Express 65; 314 Line St, Nashville PO; says never received one cent pay
COMBY, Samuel, Sh-178-4; US Sol; 323 Madison, Memphis PO
COMER, Frank M., C-27-4; Cpl G Co 65th IN Inf; 7-15-62 to 6-22-65; Jacksboro PO
COMER, Levi, C-24-1; Pvt in an IN Reg; Boy PO
COMIKLE, Jacob, T-216-3; 14th Civil Dist
COMMONS, Wiley, Li-149-2; Fayetteville PO
COMPTON, James, Wl-298-1; Pvt L Co 5th TN Cav; 5 Jun 63 to 14 Aug 65; Alexandria PO; chronic rheumatism--10 yrs, heart disease
COMPTON, James H., Ge-83-4; US Sol; Chickey City PO
COMPTON, Jeremiah, Se-223-2; Elizabeth B. widow of; Pvt K Co 2nd TN Cav; Hendersons Springs PO; diarrhea, discharge lost
COMPTON, Mills?, D-72-5; Lu? widow of; Pvt F Co 12th TN Inf; Aug 12 63 to Jan 16 66; Nashville PO
COMPTON, Richard H., Ru-244-1; Pvt B Co 5th TN Cav; 8-1-62 to 7-25-65; Milton PO; horse fall near Sporty, White Co.
COMPTON, William, Bo-11-1; Pvt I Co 2nd TN Cav; 62 to 63; Cloids Creek PO; ruptured, cannot give dates
COMPTON, William, O-135-1; Pvt K Co 2nd OH Inf; 5 Dec 62 to 2 Sep 65; Troy PO
COMPTON, William F., Cu-17-2; Pvt E Co 184th NY Inf; 9-15-64 to 7-12-65; Pomona PO
COMSTOCK, Silas G., D-56-1; 2nd Lt 11th MI Inf; 24 Aug 61 to ___; Nashville PO
CONAWAY, William, Ro-209-2; Pvt K Co 10th OH Inf; 11 Aug 61 to 15 Aug 65; Glen Alice PO
CONATSER, George W., Fe-41-2; Pvt D Co 1st TN Cav; 61 to 64; Fitz PO
CONATSER, John, Fe-40-1; Pvt Capt Beaty's Co. Independent Scouts TN Vol Inf; 62 to 65; Little Crabb PO; injury left leg
CONATSER, Johnathan, Se-225-3; Pvt 3rd TN Cav; Cotlettsburg PO; heart disease 25 yrs; enrolled but not mustered in, captured and put in prison at Andersonville 14 mos
CONATSER, Phillip, Fe-40-2(1); Abigil widow of; Pvt D Co 2nd TN Inf; Moodyville PO; Phillip Conatser died, died in prison at Charleston, SC
CONATSER, William, Fe-41-2; Pvt D Co 11th TN Inf; 61 to 65; Moodyville PO
CONCH, John E., Hd-50-5; Pvt E Co 8th TN Mtd Inf; 5-1-65 to 9-5-65; Nixon PO; mumps falling and rheumatism
CONELY, Wash, Sh-157-3; Pvt K Co 63rd ___; Nov 2 63 to Jan 9 66; Memphis, 88 7th St, PO
CONKIN, John W., Hm-107-5; Pvt B Co 4th TN Cav; 18 Aug 62 to 12 Jul 65; Chestnut Bloom PO; run over by horse, head injured

CONKIN, William J., Su-241-1; Pvt B Co 4th TN Cav; 15 Nov 61 to 12 Jul 65; Blairs Gap PO; by sunstroke trow off horse
CONKLIN, Alford, L-106-1; US Sol; 8th Dist
CONLEY, Dudley, Sol, Sh-190-2; 226 KY Ave, Memphis PO
CONLEY, John, Dk-32-2; Pvt I Co 1st TN Mtd Inf; 4-4-64 to 5-25-65; Liberty PO; ruptured
CONLEY, William, Ge-96-1; Pvt K Co 1st TN Cav; 3 Aug 62 to 4 Jun 65; Hascue PO
CONNANY, Martin, Ro-202-5; Elizabeth widow of; Cpl & Pvt I Co 1st TN Inf; 11 Aug 61 to died (1 yr 11 mos); died in service at Cumberland Gap
CONNATCHER, Margaret, Se-222-3; widow; 4th Dist
CONNELL, Frank, D-99-1; Pvt G Co 13th TN Inf; Oct 10 63 to Jan 10 66; Goodlettsville PO
CONNELL, John, Wi-281-1; Malinda A. widow of; Cpl H Co 5th TN; Aug 65; Allisona PO
CONNELL, Thomas, D-100-1; Pvt D Co 1st TN Inf; Sep 1 62 to __; Nashville PO; wounded twice, flesh wounds
CONNELLY, Owen, Mr-99-4; Sol US; Jasper PO
CONNER, Ellen F. (see Torrott, Nothlet)
CONNER, Frank, Mu-196-2; Sgt A Co 111th US Inf; Jan 1 64 to Apr 13 66; Columbia PO
CONNER, George, Se-226-2; Sarah widow of; Pvt Waters' Cates X Roads PO
CONNER, Jackson, Gi-132-2; Pvt D Co 110th USCV; Dec 15 63 to Feb 18 66; Pulaski PO
CONNER?, James, K-175-1; Pvt G Co 6th TN Inf; 18 Apr 62 to 18 May 65; Pedigo PO
CONNER, James, La-113-2; Pvt G Co 27th MI Inf; 10 Aug 63 to 26 Jul 65; Crowson PO; in prison, Richamon VA
CONNER, John, Hd-45-2; Pvt A Co 4th TN Cav; 4 Jul 62 to 63; Cerro Gordo PO
CONNER, Richard A., H-56-1; Pvt I Co 6th IN Inf; 3-1-62 to 4-27-65; St. Elm(o) PO
CONNER, Torrence O., Dk-33-2; Pvt I Co 5th TN Cav; 11-27-62 to 8-14-65; Dowelltown PO; piles & rheumatism
CONNER, Zerada, K-177-2; widow of US Sol; PO omitted
CONNOR, David, S-214-2; Pvt H Co 7th KY Cav; 20 Aug 62 to 5 Oct 64; Glenmary PO
CONNOR, Jeremiah L., Ma-126-1; Pvt E Co 46th NY Lt Art; 4 Sep 64 to Apr 65; Jackson PO
CONNOR, Lenard, Lo-191-2; Cpl I Co 5th? TN Vols; Morganton PO; gunshot right shoulder
CONNOR, Mabell (see McDowel, Charles E.)
CONNORISH, Wm., Sh-151-1; Pvt K Co Miss St. Oneida; 15 May 62 to 15 Jun 65; Arlington PO; shot in arm; discharge on surgeons certificate
CONNOWAY, Lucy, D-77-3; 21 Winter, Nashville PO
CONRY, George B., Wl-293-2; Cav G Co 6th GA; 62 to 64; Buhler PO; CONF
CONSTABLE, Jacob, Wa-263-3; Pvt; Garbers Mills PO; piles
CONSTOCK, Fredric, La-115-2; Pvt G Co 43rd WI Inf; Sep 64 to 3 Jul 65; Summertown PO
CONTRELL, Andrew J., Br-14-4; 11th Dist
CONUN?, Thomas J., Pi-154-2; Pvt D Co 2nd TN Inf; 62 to 65; Otto PO; rheumatism; 100 days troops
CONVERSE, Jerome D., Sh-144-1; Pvt G Co 81st NY; 15 Oct 61 to Jun 65; Brunswick PO; shot in leg
CONWAY, James C., Su-243-1; Ord Sgt D Co 13th PA Cav; 22 Jul 62 to 22 Jun 65; Bristol PO; shot in leg; re-enlisted
CONWAY, Jefferson, Hm-107-5; Pvt F Co 1st US Art; 5 May 64 to 31 Mar 66; Springvale PO; rheumatism
CONWAY, Joseph E., Je-139-1; Sgt M Co 9th TN Cav; 1 May 64 to 11 Sep 65; Trion PO
CONYERS, T. F., Cr-8-1; Pvt C Co 15th TN; 28 Jun 63 to 12 May 65; Maury City PO; CONF
CONYESS, Lewis, H-73-2(1); Sophia widow of; Pvt; Chattanooga PO
COODY, Ransom L., De-23-1; Pvt G Co 23rd TN Inf; Jul 9 61 to Jul 65; Bath Springs PO; wounded 6 times; prisner Pt. Lookout, MD; CONF
COOK, Alexander, O-141-3; Pvt I Co 70th Reg US Col Vol Inf; Nov 22 64 to Mar 7 66 (at vix?); Union City PO
COOK, Alford, Cr-4-3; Sophia A. widow of; Pvt; Bells Depot PO; wounded foot; CONF
COOK, Alfred, M-108-3; Pvt & Color bearer A Co 3rd KY Inf; 9-25-61 to 12-15-64; Lafayette PO; piles
COOK, Anson B., Sh-184-1; Pvt D Co 6th NY Cav; 10-1-61 to 10-21-63; 29 Alabama, Memphis PO
COOK, Chas. E., D-58-1; Sgt F Co 44th MA Inf--29 Aug 62 to 18 Jan 63; 5th MA Inf--12 Jul 64 to 17 Nov 64; Nashville PO
COOK, Charloty E., Gi-138-2; widow? 18th Dist
COOK, David C., K-156-3; Elizabeth J. widow of; 2nd Lt E Co 3rd NC Mtd Inf; 14 Mar 65 to 8 Aug 65; 20 Church St, Knoxville PO; feet and hands frost bitten, perfectly helpless at times
COOK, Frank (see Smith, Frank)
COOK, George, Co-67-6; Polly widow of; Pvt B Co 8th TN Cav; Mar 63 to __; PO omitted
COOK, George C., Ro-210-2; Pvt; Rockwood PO
COOK, George K., Hw-121-4(3); Pvt B Co 3rd TN Mtd Inf; 30 Jun 64 to 30 Nov 64; New Hope PO; rheumatism, piles
COOK, Goins H., Mg-198-3; Pvt I Co 7th TN Inf; 1 Jan 65 to 13 Jul 65; Rockwood PO
COOK, Harry J., K-160-2; Pvt J Co?, unknown to wife; Knoxville PO
COOK, Hugh, Bo-11-1; Pvt; Cloids Creek PO; canot give dates
COOK, James, H-69-5; Pvt; Chattanooga PO
COOK, James W., St-162-1; Pvt B Co 16th KY Inf; 24 Nov 64 to 3 Jul 65; Cumberland City PO
COOK, John E., D-75-1; Pvt I Co 20th TN Inf; 7 Jun 61 to 15 May 65; Stewarts Ferry PO; CONF
COOK, John F., Mo-122-3(1); Pvt TX Inf; 62 to 65; Hiwassee College PO; CONF
COOK, John H., O-138-1; Pvt D Co 14th TN; 15 Nov 62 to 15 Dec 63; Lanes PO; CONF
COOK, Johnithan, Cl-52-2; Pvt C Co 2nd TN Cav; 7-27-62 to 7-17-65; Hypratia PO
COOK, Joseph, M-108-3; Pvt A Co 9th KY Inf; 9-25-61 to 62; Lafayette PO; shot in right hip, discharge not at hand
COOK, Martin L., Ro-207-1; 1st Lt C Co 7th TN Mtd Inf; 22 Nov 64 to 27 Jun 65; Patties Gap PO
COOK, Pleasant, D-64-4; Nashville PO
COOK, Robert, Hm-109-3; Pvt G Co 8th TN Inf; 63 to 65; Whitesburg PO
COOK, Rwlim (sic) M., Cl-54-2; Pvt I Co 3rd TN Inf; 2-10-62 to 2-28-65; Tazewell PO; cist? affetd
COOK, Sol, Dy-29-4; Newbern PO; CONF
COOK, Thomas J., Co-65-2; Pvt F Co 4th TN Inf; __ 63 to 2 Aug 65; Bridgeport PO; ruptured, pensioned
COOK, W. T., Rb-220-1; Pvt H Co 2nd KY; Oct 15 62 to Apr 10 65; Adairsville, KY PO; CONF
COOK, Walter O., Mg-200-3; Pvt L Co 9th TN Cav; Jul 64 to 11 Sep 65; Stower PO
COOK, William, S-213-3; US Sol; 2nd Civil Dist
COOK, William G., Mo-125-1; Mary E. widow of; Pvt E Co 1st TN Cav; 7-15-62 to 4-10-65; Kinkaid PO
COOK, William G., Co-61-1; Annie widow of; Pvt H Co 1st TN Cav; Salem PO
COOK, William S., Cl-51-2; US Sol; 6th Civil Dist
COOKE, Emma, Sh-178-3; widow; 441 Union, Memphis PO
COOKE, John, D-91-2; Pvt Indp 4th OH Art; 13 Jun 61 to 21 Aug 65; Chris Eberhardt, Church & Market St, Nashville PO; flesh wound right leg
COOKERLY, John, H-56-2; 64 to 65; East End PO
COOKSON, Joseph, Ja-85-1; Pvt E Co 5th TN Inf; 3-2-62 to 4-4-65; Birchwood PO
COOLEY, Elisha, Ja-84-3; Pvt A Co 10th TN Cav; 7-22-63 to 8-8-65; Normans Store PO; wounded in shoulder
COOLEY, Robert S., Me-94-1; Pvt K Co 9th TN Cav; 4-2-63 to 9-11-65; Knott PO
COOLEY, William, Cf-41-1; Pvt; Hollow Springs PO; absent & family did not know co & reg
COOLLEY, Jehew J., Ro-207-1; Pvt C Co 7th TN Inf; 20 Aug 64 to 27 Jun 65; Erie PO (Loudon Co.); kidney & lungs
COOMB, Archibald C., Cf-40-3; Pvt G Co 9th KY Cav; Sep 63 to Sep 64; Tullahoma PO
COONRADT, Benjamin F., Ms-168-1; Pvt A Co 66th IL Inf; Oct 61 to 10 Jul 65; Second Dist
COOP, John H., K-179-4; Cpt C Co 3rd TN Inf; 10 Feb 62 to 23 Feb 65; PO omitted

COOPER, Aaron, Hw-127-4; Viney widow of; Sgt K Co 14th __ Inf; Rogersville PO; chronic diarrhoea & rheumatism, died of same
COOPER, Absalom, Ro-204-4; Pvt E Co 1st TN Inf; 9 Aug 61 to 17 Sep 64; Kreis PO; piles
COOPER, Alexander, K-178-2; Pvt F Co 1st TN Inf; 9 Aug 61 to 17 Sep 64; Ball Camp PO
COOPER, Anderson, H-55-2; Pvt D Co 4th TN Cav; 1-20-63 to 6-25-65; Tyner PO; sore eyes, discharged on surgeon's certificate
COOPER, Archie, H-69-3; Pvt; Chattanooga PO
COOPER, Benjamen M., Mc-116-3; Pvt E Co 7th TN Mtd Inf; 10-29-64 to 7-27-65; Athens PO
COOPER, Chas. N., Br-10-1; Pvt B Co 46th IA Cav; Cleveland PO
COOPER, Counsel, Pi-156-2; Nancy A. widow of; Pvt B Co 2nd TN Inf; 9-61 to __; Chanute PO; died in prison
COOPER, Daphne (see Dixon, Alfred)
COOPER, David G., Br-9-3; Pvt E Co 4th TN Cav; 2-13-63 to 7-12-65; Cleveland PO
COOPER, David Y., Mu-209-6; PVt 7th TX; 62 to 64; Columbia PO; CONF
COOPER, Epham, A-9-3(1); Pvt A Co 1st TN Inf; Briceville PO; captured and died in Andersonville prison
COOPER, George, Sh-174-2 (alias Cooper, George W.); Pvt H Co 26th US Col Inf; 1 yr 10 mos; 36 Turley St, Memphis PO; cataract in left eye, pneumonia, right lung permanently affected
COOPER, George W., A-3-3; Pvt H Co 1st TN Inf; 8-9-61 to 9-16-64; Bud PO; dierea, rheumatism
COOPER, Ira A. (see Gordon, Charles L.)
COOPER, Isaac, K-175-1; Pvt G Co 6th TN Inf; Bullrun PO; cant get eny information
COOPER, J. W. B., Gr-78-2; Pvt I Co 59th TN Cav; 26 Feb 63 to 26 Mar 65; Spring House PO; marked out, might be CONF
COOPER, James, C-34-1; Addie J. widow of; Pvt B Co 2nd TN Inf; 12-1-61 to __ (2 yrs 11 mos 25 days); Elk Valley PO; killed
COOPER, James, Br-7-1; Pvt A Co; 2-22-63 to 4-28-65; Felker PO; wounded in left leg
COOPER, James, Hw-127-1; Pvt I Co 38th MO Inf; 62 to 64; Rogersville PO
COOPER, James D., Gi-122-5; Pvt B Co 19th AL Inf; 10 Mar 61 to 18 Jun 65; Prospect Sta. PO; prison 6 mos; CONF
COOPER, James E., B-12-1; C Co 4th TN Mtd Inf; Wheel PO; was not at hime, wife could not give dates
COOPER, James K. P., Hd-53-2; McFerrin, James P. alias; Pvt C Co 6th TN Cav; 9 Nov 63 to 26 Jul 65; Morris Chapel PO
COOPER, James O., Gr-72-1; Pvt G Co 1st US Inf; __ to May 66; Noeton PO; exposure on plains and rivers
COOPER, Jerry, F-46-1; Pvt C Co 59th Col Inf; 6 Jun 63 to 6 Aug 65; LaGrance PO; rheumatism & deafness
COOPER, John, Di-20-1; Pvt A Co 4th TN Cav; 62 to 65; Dickson PO
COOPER, JOhn, R-69-3; Pvt; Rockwood PO
COOPER, John O., H-69-5; Pvt A Co 35th TN Inf; 62 to 65; Chattanooga PO; CONF
COOPER, Joseph, Gi-127-6; Pvt B Co 13th US Col Inf; Sep 63 to Jun 3 66; Pulaski PO
COOPER, Joseph D. (see Bowing, Isaac R.)
COOPER, Joseph W., Hw-128-2; Allice widow of; Pvt A Co 33rd MO Inf; Aug 62 to __; Choptack PO; shot through left wrist
COOPER, Levy, Mu-205-1; Pvt; 6 mos; Water Valley PO; engaged in building works at Columbia TN
COOPER, Lewis, Wa-274-3; Bernettie A. widow of; Ast Lt K Co 1st TN Cav; 22 Dec 62 to 10 Jun 65; Jonesboro PO
COOPER, Lindsay, Mg-196-2; 2nd Lt A Co 1st TN Inf; 2 Aug 61 to 25 Feb 65; PO omitted
COOPER, Mathew, C-26-1; Pvt A Co 1st TN Inf; 8-1-61 to 9-17-64; Jacksboro PO
COOPER, Minerva, T-219-1; Widow US Sol; Dist 15
COOPER, Naro, D-64-2; Pvt A Co 12th TN Inf; Aug 63 to Jan 66; Nashville PO
COOPER, Oberton M., Sm-170-1; Pvt C Co 28th TN Cav; 1-63 to 4-15-65; Maggart PO; CONF
COOPER, Stephen, Sh-144-2; US Sol; First Dist
COOPER, Stephen, H-57-3; Pvt IL Cav; 63 to 65; Orchard Knob PO
COOPER, Thomas B., Br-6-2; Pvt I Co 4th TN Cav; 10-4-63 to 7-12-6?; Chatala PO; disease of lungs
COOPER, Washington, D-61-2; Bell Childress widow of; Cpl A Co 12th Reg; Jul 21 63 to Jan 16 66; Ament Cor W. Jackson, Nashville PO; dead
COOPER, Wesley, Un-254-2; Pvt E Co 9th TN Cav; 1 Oct 63 to 11 Sep 65; Bartheney PO
COOPER, Wiley, Ge-95-2; Rebecca J. widow of; Pvt K Co 1st TN Cav; Home PO
COOPER, William, C-25-2; Sgt A Co 1st TN Inf; 8-2-61 to 9-17-64; Hatmaker PO; liver, heart, piles, bronchitis of lungs
COOPER, William, A-3-2; Mary widow of; Pvt H Co 1st TN Inf; 8-19-61 to about 2-62; Wilson PO; died in service
COOPER, William, H-57-2; Jeanie widow of; Pvt 15th TN Col; 63 to 64; Orchard Knob PO; died in camp near Murfreesboro, probably 15th US Col
COOPER, William, Col, K-162-1; Pvt 42nd TN Hvy Art; 63 to __; Knoxville PO
COOPER, William B., Dk-38-1; Pvt; Holmes Creek PO
COOPER, William M., Je-146-1; Pvt C Co 8th TN Cav; 15 Sep 63 to 11 Sep 65; White Pine PO; neuralga
COOPER, William W., Ja-87-1; Pvt I Co 4th TN Cav; 10-4-63 to 8-1-65; Apison PO; rheumatism
COOPER, Willis, H-50-4; Pvt K Co 72nd R IL Mtd Inf; 8-6-62 to 7-6-65; Soddy PO
COOPERWOOD, Henry, Sh-159-5; Henrietta widow of; Pvt B Co Inf; 11 Mar 64 to 1 Dec 65; PO omitted
COOPPER, Jerry, Un-255-2; Pvt I Co 7th TN Inf; 8 Nov 64 to 27 Ju_ 65; Gale? PO; rumatism & piles
COOTER, Phillip, Ge-90-4; Sgt F Co 4th TN Inf; 1 Jan 63 to 2 Aug 65; Greeneville PO; chronic rumatism, army exsposure the cause
COPE, Alfred, Ha-112-2; Pvt A Co 47th KY Inf; 3 Jul 63 to 27 Dec 64; Shortburg PO
COPE, Andrew J., Sn-261-5(4); Pvt K Co 16th TN Inf; 10-10-61 to 6-63; Perdue PO; rheumatism from exposure; CONF
COPE, Calaway, Hw-119-1; Sgt M Co 1st TN Cav--__ to 19 Jun 65; Pvt A Co 1st TN Cav--15 Apr 63 to __; Lee Valley PO; piles & rheumatism
COPE, James A., Pi-154-1; Pvt D Co 32nd KY Inf; 8-12-62 to 8-12-63; Hull PO; lung disease result of measles
COPE, John W., Hw-119-1; Lt E Co 8th TN Cav; 63 to 12 Sep 64 (1 yr 3 mos); Lee Valley PO; liver disease
COPE, John W., H-56-1; Mary C. widow of; Col OH; 61 to 65; St. Elm(o) PO
COPE, Mattison, Hw-119-1; Pvt E Co 8th TN Cav; 10 Oct 63 to 11 Sep 65; Lee Valley PO; diarrhea & jaundice
COPE, Richard, Hw-127-3; Pvt E Co 8th TN Cav; 20 Oct 63 to 11 Sep 65; Rogersville PO; liver kidney & diarrhea (ch)
COPE, Samuel J., H-63-2; Clerk Provost Marshal; 63 to 64; 407 W. 7th, Chattanooga PO
COPE, William A., Ha-110-3; 1st Lt E Co 8th TN Cav; 10 Sep 63 to __; Luther PO; served 6 mos, got separated from the Co before discharged
COPE, William A., Hw-119-1; Pvt A Co 1st TN Cav; 13 Apr __ to 19 Jun 65 (2 yrs 2 mos 4 days); Lee Valley PO
COPE, Woodson, Gr-80-1; Pvt E Co 8th TN Cav; 10 Oct 63 to 12 Sep 65; Red Hill PO; gun shot in head
COPELAND, Andrew, Br-6-1; Dorcus I. widow of; Pvt E Co 6th TN; 4-18-62 to __ (died) 2 yrs 3 mos 10 days; Chutala PO
COPELAND, Isaac, T-209-1; Pvt 15 and (sic) Inf TN; 61 to 64; Randolph PO
COPELAND, Jacob, Wy-171-1; Pvt A Co 10th TN Mtd Inf; 10-4-63 to 6-24-65; Waynesboro PO; erysipilias
COPELAND, James K., Ro-203-6; Cpl I Co 7th TN Mtd Inf; 8 Nov 64 to 27 Jul 65; Burns Mill PO; hernia
COPELAND, James W., Ov-137-1; Pvt I Co 11th TN Cav; 9-15-63 to (was never discharge); Nettle Carrier PO; pneumonia; was left sick in hospital during siege of Knoxville

COPELAND, John H., Ro-203-5(1); Pvt F Co 5th TN Inf; 25 Feb 62 to 29 Mar 65; Burns Mills PO; disease of lungs & shell wound
COPELAND, Jonathan B., Wy-173-2; Cpl 2nd TN Mtd Inf; 10-15-63 to 10-17-64; Lutts PO
COPELAND, John M., Mc-116-3; Pvt A Co 55th IL Inf; 2-64 to 12-65; Athens PO; discharge misplaced and exact dates of service cant be given
COPELAND, Joseph S., A-5-4; Pvt D Co 3rd TN Inf; 2-10-62 to 6-10-65; Clinton PO; wound caused blinens?
COPELAND, Samuel, Gi-127-8; Pvt; 9th Dist
COPELAND, Samuel, D-77-1; Cpl H Co; papers lost and can give no dates; Nashville PO
COPELAND, Solomon A., Cu-15-2; Pvt C Co 25th TN Inf; 62 to 63; PO omitted; CONF
COPELAND, Thomas, D-70-1; Pvt; 61 to 65; Nashville PO
COPELAND, Thomas, La-114-1; US Sol; PO omitted
COPELAND, Thomas S., Wy-174-1; Pvt G Co 10th TN; 6-14-64 to 5-20-65; Lutts PO
COPELAND, Van B., R-158-3; Mary C. widow of; Pvt; (no information procured); Breedenton PO (Meigs Co.); widow away from home--no information
COPELAND, William H., Wi-286-1; Pvt B Co 87th IN Inf; Nolinsville PO; gunshot wound in right groin, shell wound right knee, drawing 24 dollars per yr for pension
COPELAND, William L., K-177-6; Pvt B Co 3rd TN Inf; 10 Feb 62 to Mar 65; Powells Station PO; chronic rheumatism since 1864
COPLAND, James, K-173-1; Ellen S. widow of; Sgt B Co 8th TN Cav; 62 to 65; McMillen PO; insane
COPLEY, James, D-48-1; Capt E Co 101st Reg US Vols; 13 Aug 62 to 25 Jun 65; Nashville PO
COPPAGE, Phillip B., G-56-1; Bugler M Co 3rd KY Cav; 9-1-61 to 12-17-62; Trenton PO; ruptured
COPPINGER, Austin, Mr-95-2; Pvt C Co 6th TN Inf; 8-27-64 to 6-13-65; Ownes PO
COPPOCK, John, Un-255-2; Pvt; 63 to 65; PO omitted
COPPOCK, Thomas, A-1-1; Caroline widow of; Pvt D Co 1st TN Inf; 8-6-61 to 9-4-62; Bayless PO
COPPOCK?, William, Un-255-1; read CPPOCK; Pvt F Co 6th TN; 10 Nov 62 to 10 Jul 65; Warwicks X Roads PO
COPPS, Marcus, K-169-2; Susan widow of; Pvt B Co 11th TN Inf; 62 to 65; Knoxville PO
CORAM, John W., Un-254-4; Pvt F Co 3rd TN Inf; 12 Feb 62 to 11 Feb 65; Gravestown PO; rheumatism
CORAM, Henderson, K-167-1; Pvt 3rd TN Inf; Apr 62 to Mar 65; Knoxville PO; catarrh of head
CORAM, LeRoy, Un-253-2; Pvt F Co 3rd TN Inf; 12 Feb 62 to 23 Feb 65; Meltabarger PO; kidney disease
CORAM, Temple H., K-186-3; Pvt D Co 6th TN Cav; 18 Apr 62 to 27 Apr 65; Balls Camp PO
CORAM, Thomas J., K-186-2; Pvt D Co 6th TN Inf; 18 Apr 62 to 23 Apr 65; Balls Ridge PO
CORANN, Wilson A., K-174-4(3); Pvt G Co 7th TN Inf; 25 Oct 64 to 16 Apr 65; Floyde PO; no disability
CORBETT, Michael M., Je-136-1; 3 Sep 62 to Apr 65; Dandridge PO
CORBETT, Shederict J., Je-136-1; Pvt D Co 3rd TN Cav; 1 Dec 62 to 1 Mar 63; Dandridge PO
CORBIN, James M., Wy-173-3; Pvt F Co 10th TN Inf; 12-26-63 to 6-29-65; Houston PO; dates given from memory
CORBLY, Aaron S., H-56-5; A Co 34th OH Inf; 61 to 65; East End PO
CORBLY, Milton, H-53-7; Pvt A Co 34th OH Inf; 1-1-61 to 1-1-64; Chattanooga PO; deaf from report of cannon
CORCORAN, Allen (see Norman, Allen)
CORCORAN, David E., Mu-195-1; Emaline widow of; Sol, widow dont know; Columbia PO
CORD, Charles P., H-50-3(1); 1st Lt F Co 6th R TN Mtd Inf; 7-12-64 to ___; Daisy PO
CORD, William H., H-50-4; Pvt A Co 6th R TN Inf; 61 to 6? (1 yr); Soddy PO
CORDELL, Dorphus, Ct-35-3; Pvt C Co 3rd NC Inf; 1-65 to 8-65; Elks Mills PO; in US Army, discharge at Washington, exact dates of enrollment now known
CORDELL, William J., Sq-164-2(1); Pvt 1st TN Cav; 64 to 6-30-65; Dunlap PO
CORDEN, John, Gi-122-2; Pvt F Co 110th TN Inf; 63 to Jul 66; Prospect Sta. PO; prison 8 mos; CONF?
CORDER, John H., G-51-1; Pvt C Co 31st IL Inf; 1-7-62 to 1-7-63; Humboldt PO; wound in right leg; wounded in action at Ft. Donelson
CORDING, Lucy, O-141-2; Union City PO
CORE, Tom (see Douglass, Mariah)
CORIGAN, Patrick, D-69-1; Pvt K Co 9th R Cav?; 16 Sep 61 to 24 Dec 64; 15 Perkins St, Nashville PO
CORLEY, William B., Dk-36-1; Pvt B Co 4th TN Mtd Inf; 9-25-64 to 8-25-65; Smithville PO; back & hip hurt
CORMER, A. W., C-33-5; PVt E Co 6th WV Cav; 3-64 to 5-66; Newcomb PO
CORNELIUS, Richard, Ru-13-2; Pvt US; 61 to 61 (5 mos); Murfreesboro PO
CORNELL, Willis, Mt-135-1; Pvt K Co 16th TN Inf; 2-13-64 to 4-30-66; Jordon Springs PO
CORNETT, Cinley F., Mo-124-1; Pvt C Co 7th TN Inf; 4 yrs; Breakbill PO; enlisted 1st in 1861, afterwards--again
CORNETTE, Reubin, Jo-148-2; Pvt I Co 2nd WV Cav; 21 Apr 63 to 4 Jul 65; Head of Laurel PO; wounded in right shoulder by gun shot
CORNEY, James P., Br-13-3; Sgt G Co 30th IN Inf; 9-5-61 to 11-25-65; Cleveland PO
CORNISH, Harry B., G-58-1; Pvt 30th WI Inf; 10 Sep 63 to 10 Sep 64; Rutherford PO
CORNISH, Thomas J., Cf-40-2; Pvt D Co 13th IN Inf; 19 Jun 61 to 4 Jul 64; Tullahoma PO; chronic rheumatism
CORRAN, John R., K-174-1; US Sol; 4th Dist
CORREL, Elias S., Un-256-3; Lt 9th TN Cav; Loy X Roads PO; lung trobble
CORRELL, George, Su-242-1; Elizabeth F. Nickels formerly wid. He was captured by the rebels about Dec 62 and taken to Fort Hudson whence he deserted and went to "Yankees". He is believed to have been killed in the battle of Chickamanga 63. Widow remarried Sep 23 1868. Has never made any eff. to even get pay due to husband.
CORRELL, Geo. W., Wa-267-3; Pvt A Co E? TN Cav; 63 to 65; Johnson City PO; rheumatism, chrc.
CORRELL, Wm., Wa-267-2; Pvt H Co 3rd NC Inf; 15 Aug 64 to 8 Aug 65; Johnson City PO; lung & ht. dis.
CORREY, John H. H., Hd-50-3; Cpl E Co 2nd TN Mtd Inf; 64 to ___; Stout PO; foot mashed in war
CORRINGTON, W. H., Hd-47-1; Pvt H Co 6th OH Inf; Apr 61 to captured 62; Savannah PO; captured Sep 62
CORUTT, James S., Wl-293-1; G Co; 62 to 64; Austin PO; CONF
CORY, James, Se-222-2; Pvt C Co 9th MI Cav; Feb 62 to Apr 62; Harrisburg PO; defected stomech & bowels, cidney trubel
CORY, John D., Hm-109-1; Pvt A Co 1st TN Art; 63 to Aug 10 65; Three Springs PO; left year (sic) deaf
COSAM, Wm., Sn-250-1; Pvt C Co 2nd ___; 5-16-62 to 7-20-65; Castalian Springs PO; CONF
COSBY, David R., Lk-113-3; Bugular C Co 65th IN; Dec 26 62 to Feb 1 65; 6 Civil Dist
COSLEY, H. C., G-57-1; Pvt; 62 to 65; Yorkville PO; CONF
COSS, William, K-265-1; K Co 1st TN Inf; 9 Aug 61 to 23 Feb-Mar 65; Knoxville PO; deffness, bowl trobel; Cornel 1 yr and 8 mos
COSSE, Luke, Hd-49-2; Pvt B Co 8th TN Mtd Inf; Mar 17 65 to Sep 1 65; Stouts PO
COSTER, John, We-230-1; Lt E Co 22nd TN Reg; Apr 1 62 to Apr 1 63; Greenfield PO; CONF
COSTIGAN, Henry R., H-62-2; Hattie widow of; Lt; 524 Poplar, Chattanooga PO
COSTNER, David J., Bo-140-5; Pvt H Co 2nd TN Cav; 10-10-62 to 7-6-65; Clover Hill PO; shot in left leg
COSTOLOW, James, R-106-2(3); 5th Civil Dist
COTHRAN, Daniel R., Mn-121-1; Bugler E Co 1st AL Cav--Sep 63 to 4 Jan 63; reinlisted M Co 1st AL Cav--1 Jan 63 to 25 Sep 65; Rose Creek PO; served turm 12 mos & reinlisted for 3 yrs
COTHRAN, John B., Sm-173-1; Pvt B Co 5th TN Cav; 7-23-62 to 6-25-65; Brush Creek PO; left arm shot off, piles and rheumatism
COTHRON, Charles, Gi-127-1; Pvt G Co 13th TN C Inf; Pulaski PO; was discharged M101 Co B, TN C Inf

COTHRON, Joel F., K-181-6(3); Pvt A Co the Legion Vol; 13 Jan 62 to 65; Knoxville PO; CONF
COTLETT, James E., Se-225-3; Dollie A. widow of; Pvt A Co 3rd TN Cav; 10 Nov 62 to 27 Jun 65; Allensville PO
COTTEN, Jessee, We-225-2; Cpl M Co 3rd US Art; Dresden PO
COTTER, James H., Se-224-2; Pvt G Co 6th TN Mtd Inf; 20 Apr 64 to 30 Jun 65; Line Spring PO; kidney trouble
COTTON, George, Sh-158-5(1); Pvt A Co 63rd US Col Inf; 64 to 9 Jan 66; Memphis PO; discharged at close of war with a discharge
COTTON, Jas. H., K-15-62; Pvt E Co 3rd ___ Inf; 61 to 65; 19 Owen St, Knoxville PO; CONF
COTTON, Joseph S., Sh-212-1; Mate Empire State; 55 to 75 (sic--20 yrs); Memphis (Enumeration District is USM Hospital) PO
COTTON, Thomas M., Dy-25-1; Pvt G Co; ___ to 65; Newbern PO; CONF
COTTON, Willis D., D-49-3; Pvt K Co 55th MA; 15 Jun 63 to 20 Oct 65; Nashville PO
COTTORGIN, John R., Hr-97-1; Pvt A Co; Jun 63 to 65; PO omitted
COTTRAL, George, He-62-1; Elizia Anders widow of; Pvt Co C 7th TN Cav; Aug 62 to Dec 63; Darden PO; died in Andersonville Prison
COTTRELL, Adam F., K-154-2; Capt C Co 6th TN Inf; Knoxville PO
COTTRELL, John, K-181-6(3); C Co 6th TN Inf; Apr 62 to 24 Apr 65; Knoxville PO
COUCH, Alferd, Ge-92-2; Eliza widow of; Capt D Co 8th TN Inf; 62 to 64; Romeo PO
COUCH, John W., Ca-20-1; Pvt E Co 1st MO Inf; 8-1-62 to 9-1-64; Braxton PO
COUCH, Joseph, Hm-108-1; Pvt C Co 8th TN Cav; 17 Apr 63 to 11 Sep 65; Russellville PO; rheumatism, heart trouble
COUCH, Peter, Hw-132-4; Casander widow of; Pvt D Co 8th TN Inf; 15 Mar 63 to 30 Jun 65; Otes PO
COUCH, Reuben A., B-2-1; Lt F Co 23rd TN Vol; 6-25-61 to 6-25-62; Wartrace PO; CONF
COUCH, Reuben C., B-4-1; Capt F Co 5th Reg TN Cav; 9-62 to 8-65; Bell Buckle PO
COUCH, Robert W., B-2-2; Lt F Co 9th TN Cav; 11-62 to 64; Fairfield PO; CONF
COUCH, W. R., La-117-3; Pvt F Co 3rd TN Inf; May 61 to 63; 15th Dist; CONF
COUCH, William, Ge-92-2; Pvt F Co 1st TN Cav; 1 Mar 62 to 30 Mar 65; Romeo PO
COULTER, James J., H-60-5(2); Pvt I Co 2nd OH Art; 8-63 to 65; Chattanooga PO
COUNTISS, John M., De-24-1; alias John Martin; Pvt C Co 5th TN Cav; 1 Sep 62 to 25 Jun 65; Decaturville PO
COUNTZAR, Geo. M., Cr-3-1; Pvt K Co 6th US Inf; Mar 31 65 to Oct 11 66; Gadsden PO
COURTNEY, David, Hw-119-2(1); Pvt B Co 2nd NC Mtd Inf; 26 Mar 65 to 16 Aug 65; Alum Well PO; measles
COURTNEY, George, Cl-55-1; Pvt L Co 8th TN Cav; 9-17-63 to 9-11-65; Lone Mountain PO
COURTNEY, George J., Sm-174-1; Sgt Q Co 4th TN Mtd Inf?; 11-1-64 to 8-25-65; New Middleton PO
COURTNEY, James, Hm-108-5(4); Pvt D Co; Russellville PO
COURTS, Rodolphus, U-247-3; Pvt M Co 6th NY Cav; Dec 63 to 28 May 65; Erwin PO; lung disease, result of brain fever
COUSINS, Gilbert, Co-63-2; Pvt D Co 17th KY Inf; 1 yr; Newport PO; rheumatism, discharge lost
COUSINS, Robt. T., Cr-4-4; Pvt E Co 7th TN Cav; 5-63 to 4-65; Bells Depot PO
COVAN, Edward, K-160-1; Pvt B Co 4th TN; 8 Mar 63 to ___; Knoxville PO; kicked on leg by mule while on duty
COVEY, Charles B., Mn-122-1; Mary widow of; Pvt B Co 6th TN Cav; 8-25-62 to ___ (2 mos 27 days); PO omitted; died 11-22-62
COVIL, Andrew J., Br-9-3; Pvt; Cleveland PO
COVINGTON, Andrew, Se-231-2; Pvt K Co 2nd TN Inf; 13 Dec 61 to 15 Dec 64; Arther PO; gunshot in left side 17 yrs
COVINGTON, Anthony, D-68-2; Sgt K Co 17th US C Inf; 63 to 66; 118 Lewis, Nashville PO
COVINGTON, Arnol, Se-226-2; Martha widow of; Pvt K Co 2nd TN Cav; 2 Mar 62 to 6 Nov 63; Sinking Springs PO; died in Andersonville; was captured at Rogersville? TN
COVINGTON, Bengaman, Se-231-2; Pvt K Co 2nd TN Inf; Feb 63 to 3 Aug 65; Arther PO; chronic rheumatis 25 yrs
COVINGTON, James H., Se-231-1; Pvt K Co 2nd TN Inf; 13 Dec 61 to 15 Dec 64; Boyds Creek PO; chronic rheumatis 25 yrs
COVINGTON, Jefferson, Se-226-6; Pvt K Co 2nd TN Mtd Inf; 13 Dec 61 to 3 Aug 65; Sinking Springs PO; rhumatism & cattarrh
COVINGTON, Peter, Sh-200-3; Pvt; 433 Georgia St, Memphis PO
COVINGTON, Samuel (see Haly, Samuel)
COVINGTON, Susan, Wi-281-2; 20th Dist
COVINGTON, William H., Co-64-2; Pvt 3rd TN Cav; 13 Dec 61 to 15 Feb 65; Philips PO; fever fell in boath legs
COWAN, Abner, Hn-73-1; Pvt Co E 113th AR; Apr 63 to Feb 65; Paris PO; eye put out
COWAN, Benjamin, Mr-95-1; Orderly Sgt C Co 6th TN Inf; 9-2-64 to 7-1-65; Whitwell PO
COWAN, David M., Pi-155-2; Eliza A. widow of; Pvt C Co 11th TN Cav; 1-6-62 to 4-8-65; Byrdstown PO
COWAN, Henry T., B-12-1; Pvt I Co 13th TN Inf; 10-31-63 to 5-15-65; Wheel PO; attorney got his discharge and he could never get it returned
COWAN, James, K-161-4; Pvt; Knoxville PO; hurt in hip and leg
COWAN, Joseph G., J-80-2; Pvt A Co 1st TN Inf; 1-4-64 to 1-30-65; Granville PO; nervous disability & frost bite & also the sounding of artillery rendered him deaf
COWARD, Henry C., A-3-2; Pvt J Co 4th TN Cav; 3-9-64 to 6-10-65; Wilson PO
COWARD, John, A-3-2; Cpl C Co 2nd TN Cav; 11-7-62 to 7-6-65; Wilson PO; gunshot
COWARD, Lot, Mu-192-1; Pvt C Co 57th IL Inf; 1-1-63 to 7-1-64; Columbia PO; rheumatism in ankle
COWARD, Pery H., A-3-2; Pvt G Co 7th TN Inf; 11-8-64 to 6-9-65; Beveridg PO (Knox Co.); malera
COWDEN, Wm. S., Je-141-2; Cpl H Co 9th TN Cav; 3 Mar 63 to 14 Sep 65; New Market PO
COWDER, William, P-151-3; Pvt D Co 3rd TN Inf; 61 to 62; Linden PO; rhumatism
COWDERY, Asa A., H-63-2; 1st Lt D Co 124th IL Inf; 61 to 64; 517 W. 9th, Chattanooga PO; bronchial
COWELL, Robert, Wi-274-1; Pvt F Co 133rd IL Inf; 64 to 65; Franklin PO
COWENS, Milacan, K-174-5; Rachel M. widow of; cant finde out what regiment he belongs to; House Mountain PO
COWHERD, James H., Mt-135-1; Pvt D Co 63rd TN Inf; 2-15-63 to 65; PO omitted
COWLEY, Richard, Li-166-1; Pvt B Co 25th TN Cav; 65 to 65 (3 mos); Oregon PO; slight flesh wound in right leg
COWSEIT, W. S., G-57-2; Cpl; 64 to 64 (1 mo); Yorkville PO; CONF
COWSEY, John, R-159-2; Pvt G Co 3rd TN Cav; 8-11-63 to 7-3-65; Sheffield PO; rheumatism, measles, hurt by horse
COX, Abraham, Un-257-1; Pvt B Co 1st TN Inf; 9 Aug 61 to 17 Sep 64; Sharps Chapel PO; rheumatism, paralysis, rupture
COX, Abraham, Pu-147-2; Mary C. widow of; Pvt (Thomburgs); 62 to ___; Gabatha PO (Jackson Co.)
COX, Abraham, Ro-204-4; Anna M. widow of; Pvt K Co 9th TN Cav; 13 Jul 63 to 11 Sep 65; Elverton PO
COX, Albe, Ro-201-4(1); Sgt F Co 1st TN Inf; 9 Aug 61 to 17 Sep 64; Kingston PO
COX, Alexander B., S-217-1; Pvt K Co? 11th KY Inf; 1 Oct 61 to 16 Dec 64; Winfield PO
COX, Alfred M., A-4-5; Pvt H Co 1st TN Inf; 8-9-61 to 9-17-64; Coal Creek PO; chronic dia., rheumatism
COX, Andrew J., Bo-19-1; Pvt C Co 1st Col Hvy Art; 64 to 65; Rockford PO
COX, Andy (see Rogers, Pumas)

COX, Anthony, W-195-1; Pvt H Co 1st TN Inf; 6-63 to __; Pvt G Co 1st TN Mtd Inf--64 to 7-31-65 (1 yr 3 mos); Dibrell (or Evenston?) PO; bad health from exposure, now a poor farmer
COX, Bannis?, Sh-161-1; US Sol; 16th Dist
COX, Charles, Ma-273-2; Cpl I Co 8th TN Cav; 1 Jun 64 to 11 Sep 65; Keeblers X Roads PO; diarrhoea and disease of lungs
COX, Charles H., H-56-4; Pvt E Co 70th IN Inf; 8-4-62 to 6-8-65; East End PO
COX, Charley, Mg-198-1; Nancy A. widdow of; Pvt F Co 1st TN Inf; 19 Aug 61 to Sep 63; Deer Lodge PO; scroffulow
COX, Charley R., Cl-57-1; Cpl C Co 1st TN Lt Art; 6-1-63 to 8-1-65; Kecks Chappel PO
COX, Ching, K-154-2; Knoxville PO
COX, Cook, Mc-115-2; Eliza widow of; Pvt I Co; Riceville PO; dont know dates
COX, Edward, Hr-96-1; Pvt C Co 6th TN Cav; Ma_ 63 to Jul 65; Crainsville PO
COX, Elisiah, Ge-93-4(1); Pvt D Co 8th TN Inf; 15 Mar 63 to 3 Jul 65; Greeneville PO
COX, Finley, Wa-268-3; Johnson City PO
COX, Freeland H., A-4-2; Pvt B Co 3rd TN Inf; 12-16-62 to 2-23-65; Coal Creek? PO; hearing & sight effected
COX, Giles H., La-115-1; Pvt H Co 9th TN Cav; 24 Aug 62 to 6 Nov 63; Henryville PO; this entry marked through
COX, Hanna, K-176-1; widow US Sol; Pvt B Co 3rd TN Inf; 22 Apr 61 to 31 May 63; Preston PO
COX, Harvis N., Wl-299-1; Pvt E Co 4th TN Inf; 1 Nov 64 to 25 Aug 65; Statesville PO
COX, Henderson, Hw-127-1; Martha J. widow of; Pvt (papers lost in high water of 1867); Rogersville PO; cold settled on lungs, died from effects of same
COX, Henry, Gi-122-7; Annie widow of; Pvt H Co 110th TN Inf; 10 Dec 62 to __; Prospect Sta. PO; shot & killed at Mobile, AL
COX, Henry, Sh-150-3; Pvt A Co 2nd TN Inf; 3 yrs; Dexter PO
COX, Henry A., Hm-103-2; Pvt A Co 4th TN Cav; 15 Dec 62 to 12 Jul 65; Morristown PO; deaseased lungs
COX, Horten, Ge-89-3; Nancy widow of; Pvt D Co 1st TN Cav; 28 Mar 63 to __; Marvin PO; died 189(1?)
COX, Hugh, Se-228-2(3); Pvt A Co 16th TX Cav; Oct 61 to __; Cox PO; fought until disbanded; CONF
COX, Hugh L., Ov-137-1; Pvt K Co 4th TN Mtd Inf; 11-9-64 to 8-25-65; Nettle Carrier PO; rheumatism
COX, Isaac, A-3-1; Pvt K Co 1st TN Art; 7-20-64 to 3-31-66; Willson PO; rhumtism
COX, Jack, Hy-85-1; Pvt I Co 55th US Col Inf; 63 to 65; Nut Bush PO
COX, Jacob R., Su-240-2; Sgt G Co 29th TN Inf; 7 Aug 61 to 25 Feb 65; Ford Town PO; rupture; CONF
COX, James, A-8-2; Pvt K Co 5th TN Inf; 3-4-62 to 6-29-65; Ledom PO; absent from comand about 13 mos deduction from time marked above
COX, James, Je-144-2; Pvt C Co 1st TN Cav; 10 Apr 62 to 10 Apr 65; Kansas PO; cripple in left hip
COX, James F., Wa-272-3; Landman? Crew US Nafeant?; 20 May 64 to 20 Aug 65; Nellie PO; erysipelas lung disease
COX, James H., K-179-3; Sgt C Co 2nd TN Cav; 11 Nov 62 to 6 Jul 65; Ball Camp PO; now has bronchitis, rheumatism & piles
COX, James H., Su-239-3; 1st Lt K Co 13th TN Cav; Jul 63 to Sep 65; Kingsport PO
COX, James M., Cu-17-3; Pvt TN Cav; 1-65 to 5-65; Grassy Cove PO; perhaps deserted
COX, James R., A-3-3; Pvt L Co 4th TN Cav; 11-62 to 5-65; Bud PO; CONF
COX, Jane (see Taylor, Georg M.)
COX, Jasper, Me-90-2(1); I Co Str. Lookout; __ to 5-62; Rine Land PO
COX, Jessie B., Dy-27-3; Pvt 4th TN Cav; 1 Sep 61 to Apr 65; Tatemville PO; CONF
COX, Jim, Ms-175-1; 3rd Sgt D Co 17th TN; 63 to 65; Marshall Co. PO; catarrh in head
COX, Joe B., A-3-3; Pvt G Co 8th TN Cav; 7-3-63 to 9-8-65; Bud PO
COX, John, D-50-3; Pvt G Co 12th US Inf; Aug 63 to Jan 6 66; 945 N College, Nashville PO; eyesight fr. pox
COX, John A., Mg-200-2; Pvt F Co 1st TN Inf; 9 Aug 64 to 17 Sep 64; Glades PO; disease of stomach & bowels, result of fever
COX, John B., K-186-1; Beaver Ridge PO; chronic diareah
COX, John B., K-174-3(2); Pvt C Co 9th TN Cav; 10 Aug 63 to 11 Sep 65; Church Grove PO
COX, Joseph, K-159-1; Eliza widow of; Knoxville PO
COX, Joseph, Je-141-3; Pvt E Co 1st TN Lt Art; 28 Sep 63 to 1 Aug 65; Mill Springs PO
COX, Joseph, K-186-2; Margaret A. Oakes formerly widow; Pvt C Co 2nd TN Cav; 13 Sep 62 to __; Balls Camp PO
COX, Lafayett, K-171-6(5); Pvt 1st US Hvy Art Col; 64 to 65; PO omitted
COX, Leroy P., M-106-2(1); Pvt I Co 9th KY Vol Inf; 11-2-61 to 12-15-65; Lafayette PO; suffer from relapse of measles
COX, Louis C., A-8-2; Pvt D Co 6th TN Inf; 4-18-62 to 4-23-65; Scarborough PO; right leg shot off
COX, Maley, Hm-104-3(1); alias Joseph W. Cox; Pvt C Co 1st TN Cav; 7 Jan 63 to 19 Jun __ (3 yrs 6 mos); PO omitted; discharged act. rheumatism, ruptur cause
COX, Mary, Ms-181-1; wife; Cpl B Co 11th TN Inf; 6-30-63 to 4-12-65; Lewisburg PO
COX, Mary, K-176-1; widow US Sol; Pvt B Co 9th TN Cav; Preston PO
COX, Matha, K-176-2; Halls X Roads PO
COX, Matilda (see Rogers, Pumas
COX, Miheel?, D-69-2; US Sol; Nashville PO
COX, Nancy S. (see Foster, James, A-2-2)
COX, Phillip, Mc-115-1; Pvt C Co 3rd TN Cav; 12-16-62 to 9-10-63; Riceville PO; discharged on acct. disability
COX, Richard, Ro-204-1; Pvt K Co 5th TN Inf; Jul 61 to Jul 65; Elverton PO; no discharge found
COX, Robert, Sh-173-1; 206 Beale St, Memphis PO
COX, Thomas (see Smith, Thomas)
COX, Thomas, Cl-50-2(1); Pvt A Co 2nd TN Cav; 6-15-62 to 12-15-62; Bacchus PO; captured and paroled
COX, Thomas, F-48-1; Pvt K Co 7th TN nn?; 7-20-63 to 8-10-65; Somerville PO
COX, Thomas A., A-8-2; Sgt K Co 1st TN Inf; 8-9-61 to 9-14-64; Scarborough PO; contracted rheumatism 6-63
COX, Virginia (see Dyer, Andy)
COX, W. P., G-57-6; Pvt; 63 to 64; Yorkville PO; CONF
COX, Warren, M-105-1; Pvt I Co 9th TN Inf; 11-15-61 to 12-15-64; Echo PO
COX, William R., Cl-56-1; Pvt C Co 1st TN Inf; 7-1-62 to 6-21-65; Big Barren PO
COX, Eyley, Cl-54-1; Pvt I Co 3rd TN Inf; 2-10-62 to 2-28-65; Bacchus PO; expiration of time
COY, Alexandrew, Ho-95-1; Pvt K Co 147th IN; Ma_ 22 65 to Aug 22 65; McKinnon PO
COZART, John M., Ge-95-1; P-t E Co 4th TN Inf; 15 Apr 63 to 2 Aug 65; Home PO; rheumatism
COZART, Joseph, Dy-25-9(1); Pvt E Co 6th TN Cav; 64 to 65; Newbern PO; suffering from piles
CRABTREE, A. B., Ge-97-1; Pvt C Co 4th TN Inf 15 Jan 63 to 2 Aug 65; Maltsberger PO; mesel & some leg rheumatism
CRABTREE, B. F., Fr-118-2; Pvt E Co 2nd US; 6 Oct 64 to 6 Oct 65; PO omitted
CRABTREE, B. F., Sr., Fr-118-1; Pvt I Co 17th TN Inf; May 61 to Nov 63; Winchester PO; jeneral disability; CONF
CRABTREE, George W., Ro-205-3; Pvt M Co 8th TN Cav; 4 Mar 62 to 4 Dec 63; Hatch PO; piles
CRABTREE, J. M., Fr-118-1; Nancy widow of; PO omitted; CONF
CRABTREE, Jacob, Ge-97-4; Sol US; 20th Civil Dist
CRABTREE, James M., Cy-28-1; 4th Sgt B Co 9th KY Inf; 4-24-61 to 12-15-64; Celina PO
CRABTREE, John, Hw-118-2; Pvt K Co 13th TN Cav; St. Clair PO
CRABTREE, Susan, Ro-205-2; widow; Hatch PO
CRABTREE, Thomas, Mc-118-1; Pvt A Co 5th TN Mtd Inf; 9-1-64 to 6-26-65; Cogshill PO; piles, side pleurisy 24 yrs

CRABTREE, William, Pi-156-3; Pvt David Beaty Independent Scouts; Mt. Pisgah PO (Wayne Co. KY); heart disease, now totally disabled
CRADDOCK, N. L., G-64-2; Pvt; 61 to 65; Bradford PO; CONF
CRADDOCK, Nathanal H., Dk-33-3; Pvt A Co 5th TN Cav; 7-22-62 to 8-14-65; Halesville PO; small pocks
CRADINGTON, Robert, K-186-4; Pvt H Co 5th TN Inf; 10 Mar 62 to 16 May 65; Balls Camp PO
CRAFORD, Robert, Sh-148-1; Pvt D Co 59th; Dec 12 63 to Feb 3 66; Memphis PO
CRAFTON, G. G., Gi-125-2; Sgt I Co 2nd TN Mtd Inf; 7 Nov 63 to 21 Jun 65; Bodenham PO
CRAFTON, George W., Wi-287-1; Pvt B Co 12th TN Cav; 7 Sep 63 to 11 Oct 65; Civ Dist No 18
CRAFTON, James, H-59-4; Susie widow of; Pvt TN Inf; 62 to 65; Chattanooga PO
CRAFTON, William H., Wi-281-1; Pvt H Co 5th TN; 3 yrs; Reeds Store PO
CRAGHEAD, John H., M-103-2; Pvt B Co 8th TN Inf; Lafayette PO
CRAGHEAD, Shelton, Cy-27-2; Pvt G Co 5th KY Cav; 12-11-61 to 5-30-65; Boles PO (Monroe Co. KY)
CRAIG, Andrew D., P-161-4; Dist 6
CRAIG, Charley, Gi-131-1; Pvt H Co; Aug 63 to 65; Young PO; knee badly hurt
CRAIG, Danial, Sh-202-1; Pvt I Co Cav; 3 Mar 63 to 63 (3 yrs); Memphis PO
CRAIG, Henry, T-206-2; Covington PO
CRAIG, Henry C., B-12-1; Pvt K Co 6th TN Cav; 9-15-62 to 8-11-65; Wheel PO; liver & kidney trouble
CRAIG, Isaac S., A-13-3; Pvt F Co 7th TN Inf; 11-8-64 to 7-27-65; Briceville PO; heart disease
CRAIG, Isac, Hy-76-1; Pvt C Co 12th __ Inf; 2 yrs 11 mos; Stanton Depot PO
CRAIG, Jane M., Mu-191-3; widow; 7th Dist
CRAIG, John, G-51-2; US Sol; 3rd Civil Dist
CRAIG, John R., Un-257-2; Pvt M Co 9th TN Cav; 12 Oct 63 to 17 Sep 65; New Prospect PO; rheumatism
CRAIG, William, Gi-122-1; Kissiah widow of; Pvt 111th TN Inf; 61 to __ (2 yrs 6 mos); Prospect Sta, PO; CONF
CRAIG, William B., Lo-191-1; Pvt I Co 5th TN Inf; 1 Nov 62 to 30 Jun 65; Morganton PO; piles deafness
CRAIGHEAD, Murphy H., J-78-1; 2nd Sgt B Co 8th TN Inf; 12-31-64 to 8-17-65; Haydensburg PO; rumatism & cronic diarea
CRAIGHEAD, William H., J-78-2; Pvt F Co 3rd US Inf; 10-27-64 to 11-27-65; Haydonsburg PO; rumlus & bone skivey
CRAIGLOW, Daniel, Cr-4-1; Rebecca J. widow of; Pvt E Co 31st IL Inf; 61 to 65; Bells Depot PO
CRAIN, William A., S-213-3; Pvt K Co 10th TN Cav; 64 to Mar 65; Hellenwood PO; rheumatism, rupture, piles
CRAIN, Wilson, Sh-151-1; Cpl B Co 116th TX Inf; 28 Jun 64 to 18 Mar 66; Brunswick PO; disease of lung; discharged on surgeons certificate
CRALL, Samuel P., Cf-39-1; Pvt C Co 101st OH Inf; 11 Aug 62 to 12 May 65; Prairie Plains PO
CRAMER, Fred W., D-63-1; Johanna widow of; Pvt G Co 9th OH Inf; May 61 to 64; Nashville PO
CRANDALL, William H., La-115-1; Pvt A Co 1st MI Inf; 16 Apr 64 to 30 Jul 65; Blake Mills PO; gun shot left hand? and leg
CRANE, Nathanal, Cl-50-1; Pvt E Co 38th VA Inf; 3-9-62 to 4-17-65; Tazewell PO; about 5-24-63
CRANE?, Shappard, Hy-75-2; Dancyville PO
CRATTON, Stephen (see Nutson, Thomas)
CRAVETTE, Erastus M., D-99-6; Staff officer, Chaplain 101st OH VI; Jan 1 63 to Jun 1 65; Fisk University, Nashville PO
CRAVINS, Peter, Ov-138-1; Nansie widow of; Pvt 3rd KY R; 62 to 65; 10th Civil Dist
CRAWFORD, Americe, D-70-2; widow; Berrien St, Nashville PO
CRAWFORD, Charley Y., Gr-78-1; Pvt G Co 22nd VA Cav; 1 Apr 61 to 10 Apr 65; Larkeyton PO; CONF
CRAWFORD, David S., D-70-1; Color Sgt C Co 22nd IL; Nashville PO
CRAWFORD, Dawes, Hn-73-1; Pvt Co I 4th KY; 66 (sic) to 65 (1 yr 2 mos); Como PO
CRAWFORD, Frank, Sh-158-6(4); Pvt F Co 61st US Col Inf; 14 Jan 63 to 30 Dec 65; Memphis PO; discharged at close of war with discharge
CRAWFORD, George, Mu-205-1; Jane widow of; Water Valle PO; all papers lost
CRAWFORD, George G., Hw-133-3; Pvt B Co 4th TN Cav; 18 Jul 62 to 12 Jul 65; Fry PO; brinchitus, chronic diareah
CRAWFORD, Gilbert, H-49-3; Pvt G Co 15th TN Vol; 63 to 65; Lake Side PO
CRAWFORD, Hannah, Su-241-2; widow of US Sol; Dist No 15
CRAWFORD, Isaac C., Hm-103-2; Pvt F Co 3rd? TN Cav; 64 to 65; Morristown PO; nervis rheumatism
CRAWFORD, Isaac M., Cy-27-2; Pvt; Clementsville PO
CRAWFORD, Isabell W., Lo-194-2; widow; Lenoir PO
CRAWFORD, Jennie (see Sampler, Charles)
CRAWFORD, Joh, Su-240-1; Pvt K Co 29th Conf Inf; 25 Dec 61 to 25 Oct 64; Butterfly PO; shot in right hip; CONF
CRAWFORD, John H., G-67-1; Pvt M Co 6th TN Cav; 11 Aug 62 to 26 Jul 65; Bradford PO; epilepsy
CRAWFORD, Johnathan B., Cy-27-2; Pvt I Co 1st TN Mtd Inf; 3-64 to 5-26-65; Clementsville PO
CRAWFORD, Johnathan H., Bl-2-2(1); Pvt D Co 7th TN Mtd Inf; 10-9-64 to 8-11-65; Farmingdale PO; chronic sore eyes
CRAWFORD, Lucinda, Su-241-2; widow US Sol; Dist No 15
CRAWFORD, Lurman G., H-61-3; 2nd Lt G Co 3rd MI Inf; 7-64 to 5-65; Chattanooga PO
CRAWFORD, Martin, Ov-137-1; Cpl G Co 9th TN Cav; 6-27-63 to 9-11-65; Nettle Carrier PO; lung disease
CRAWFORD, Roller F. A., Hw-122-1; Cpl B Co 8th TN Cav; 23 Jul 63 to 11 Sep 65; Churchill PO; disease of lungs & rheumatism, partially disabled
CRAWFORD, Samuel, Su-239-3; Pvt 8th TN Cav; Kingsport PO
CRAWFORD, Shadric, Su-241-2; US Sol; Dist No 15
CRAWFORD, Thomas E., K-156-3; Pvt C Co 24th VA Inf; 24 May 61 to 24 Jun 65; 83 E. Cumberland St, Knoxville PO; CONF
CRAWFORD, William, K-175-2; 2nd Lt H Co 2nd TN Inf; 18 Mar 62 to 18 Mar 65; Twinville PO
CRAWFORD, William, Hw-122-1; Sgt B Co 8th TN Cav; 11 Jun 63 to 11 Sep 65; Blairs Gap PO; lumbago & piles, partially disabled
CRAWFORD, William C., D-45-4; Sgt D Co 1st TN Art; to 65 (3 yrs 5 days); Nashville PO
CRAWFORD, Winfield S., Dk-38-2; US Sol; 18th Civil Dist
CRAWFORD, ____, Wa-268-2; Carrie E. widow of; Johnson City PO
CRAWFORT, William, Sh-149-1; Pvt D Co 61st Col Inf; Mar 63 to Mar 66; Raleigh PO
CRAWLEY, Con, D-50-3; Sgt Navy USN; May 15 61 to Jan 30 65; 920 N. College, Nashville PO; injured back, suffering
CRAZE, Hack (see Wilson, Hack)
CREASEMAN, F. P., Hw-133-2; Mary widow of; recruiting Off E Co; Slide PO
CREASMAN, Joseph H., Mc-114-1; Pvt A Co 8th TN Inf; 6-18-63 to no discharge (1 yr 8 mos); Lamontville PO
CREECH, Cleave, Hm-108-5(4); Pvt I Co 8th TN Inf; 1 Jun 63 to 1 Jan 66; Russellville PO; crippled & lung disease
CREG, William H., O-138-1; Pvt A Co 1st TN Cav; May 61 to 1 May 65; Lanes PO; wound in hip caused by gun shot; CONF
CREGS, Robert, Sh-150-2; Pvt H Co 3rd US Hvy Art; 2 yrs 11 mos; Bartlett PO
CRENCHAW, Jordan, Tr-268-1; Pvt 40th TN Inf; Hartsville PO; shot in chest, disabled
CRENCHAW, Samuel (C), Tr-268-1; Pvt A Co 2nd TN Inf; 28 Jan 64 to 15 Nov 65; Hartsville PO; shot in knee joint
CRENSHAW, James C., D-72-4; Pvt C Co 44th TN Inf; Nov 12 62 to Apr 15 65; Nashville PO; CONF
CRENSHAW, Lamuel, Ro-201-4(1); Susan widow of; Pvt F Co 1st TN Inf; 9 Aug 61 to 22 Sep 65; Kingston PO
CRENSHAW, William B., Mg-197-4; Agness H. widow of; Pvt B Co 2nd TN Inf; 61 to __; Wartburg PO; time served not known

CRENSHAW, _____, G-57-6; Pvt C Co; 1 Nov 63 to 2? Apr 64; Dyer PO; CONF
CRESS, Daniel, Jo-151-3; Duty Sgt D Co 13th TN Cav; 22 Sep 63 to 5 Sep 65; Vaughtsville PO; injured by being thrown from horse, right testicle, left hip
CRESWELL, John E., Se-231-2; Pvt G Co 3rd TN Inf; Feb 1 64 to 2 Aug 65; Arther PO; piles & atrophy 26 yrs
CRESWELL, Joseph C., Wi-281-1; Pvt B Co 12th TN; Sep 9 63 to Oct 65; Reeds Store PO
CRESWELL, Laben C., Wi-281-1; Pvt H Co 5th TN; Jul 25 63 to Aug 25 65; Bathesda PO
CRESWELL, Samul A., Se-231-2; Pvt G Co 3rd TN Inf; 10 Feb 62 to 23 Feb 65; Boyds Creek PO; chronic rheumatis 20 yrs
CRESWELL, William C., Wi-281-1; Pvt H Co 5th TN; May 25 63 to Aug 14 65; Allisona PO; general debility
CREWS, Daniel B., La-113-1; Pvt; Jul 64 to 64; Lawrenceburg PO; discharge misslayed, cannot answer
CREWS, George, Ma-125-1; Paralee widow; Pvt H Co 55th AL Inf; Jun 63 to Dec 66; Jackson PO; information not reliable
CREWS, Gordon N., Cr-4-4; Pvt G Co 6th TN Inf; 5-61 to 11-61; Bells Depot PO; CONF
CREWS, Polk, Mu-190-1; Pvt A Co 14th Col Inf; 12-63 to 66; Culleoka PO; says his papers got destroyed and cant give dates accurately
CREWS, Robert T., La-112-1; Scout; 71-1-4 to 11-10-64; Knob Creek PO
CREWS, William R., La-112-1; Pvt G Co 29th IL Inf; 8-11-64 to 11-6-65; Knob Creek PO; kidney disease
CREWS, William S., G-58-1; Rutherford PO
CREWSBY?, Esquire, D-67-3; Pvt B Co 101st Col Inf; Feb 24 64 to Jan 21 66; Nashville PO
CRICK, Dallas, B-10-1; Pvt G Co 10th TN Inf; 5-1-63 to 6-6-65; PO omitted
CRICK, George W., B-10-1; Julia A. widow of; Cpl C Co 10th TN Inf; 5-1-63 to 6-20-65; PO omitted
CRICK, Polk, Fr-112-1; Pvt G Co 10th TN Inf; May 1 63 to Jun 24 65; Tullahoma PO; right shoulder broken & collar bone dislocated
CRIDENTON, Wiley, Sh-157-2; Cpl C Co 55th Col US Inf; 62 to 65; Memphis PO; middle finger of the left h. shot
CRIDER, Jane, De-25-2; widow; Decaturville PO
CRIDER, Labern, G-64-1; Stublefield, Nancie widow of; Pvt 12th TN; 61 to 65; Bradford PO
CRIDER, Robert A., We-226-2; Lt; Sharon PO
CRIGGER, George W., Hw-118-2; Pvt M Co 8th TN Cav; Feb ___ to ___; St. Clair PO; wound in kee (sic)
CRIGGER?, Robert, Ge-98-2; Pvt M Co 8th TN Cav; Aug 64 to Sep 65; Lovelace PO; spinal disease and meningitis
CRINER, Joe H., Ch-14-1; Jane widow of; Pvt C Co 52nd TN Inf; 3-1-61 to 10-1-61; Sweet Lips PO; shot in left leg; CONF
CRIPPEN, William F., K-180-2; 2nd Lt G Co 7th TN Mtd Inf; Mar 62 to Aug 65; Bearden PO
CRIPPING, Henry C., K-161-3; Ellen widow of; Knoxville PO
CRIPS, Yean, Dk-33-4; Pvt L Co 5th TN Cav; 9-8-63 to 8-14-65; Dowellltown PO; lungs & piles
CRISCILLIS, James, C-33-3; Pvt E Co 32nd KY Inf; 1-6-63 to 8-12-63; Capuchine PO
CRISE, William H. H., K-172-1; Pvt E Co 3rd TN Cav; 1 Mar 63 to 1 Aug 65; Knoxville PO
CRISP, A. J., Bo-11-2; Pvt A Co 3rd TN Inf; 2-10-62 to 2-23-65; Cliff PO; rhumatism
CRISP, H. C., Bo-11-1; Pvt K Co 5th TN Inf; 8-4-62 to 6-12-65; Meadow PO (Loudon Co.)
CRISP, John P., Hw-131-3; Pvt E Co 6th KY Cav; 16 Sep 63 to 6 Sep 65; St. Clair PO
CRISP, William, Bo-12-2(1); Pvt C Co 3rd TN Mtd Inf; 7-26-64 to 11-30-64; Montvale Springs PO; rupture
CRISP, William, Hw-118-1; Pvt A Co 3rd NC Cav; Feb 65 to Aug ___; St. Clair PO
CRISTENBERY, William A., Cr-20-2; Pvt K Co 2nd Mtd Inf; 2-4-64 to 5-30-65; Bilbry PO
CRISWELL, George W., Hm-33(103)-1; Pvt C Co 42nd IN; 61 to 62; Dyersburg PO
CRISWELL, John F., Wl-308-3; Pvt I Co 7th TN; May 20 61 to May 20 65; Mount Juliet PO; CONF
CRITCHFIELD, John, Hn-74-1; Nancey E. widdow of; Pvt K Co 6th TN Cav; Jul 62 to Aug 66; Henry Station PO; congestion, discharged special order
CRITENDON, Wash, F-43-1; Pvt I Co 55th TN; 62 to May 65; New Kent PO; party doesnt know date of enlistment, col & divis; colored and can neither read nor write
CRITER, Paul, Br-9-4; Cpl K Co 1st WI Inf; 9-6-61 to 12-20-64; Cleveland PO
CRITTENDEN, Columbus C., Mc-111-1; Pvt D Co 5th TN Mtd Inf; 8-31-64 to 6-26-65; Nonaburg PO
CRITTENDEN, Noel, K-166-1; Pvt K Co 11th MN Inf; 25 Aug 64 to 26 Jun 65; Knoxville PO; diarhea and piles
CRITZ, Joseph, Wi-281-2; Pvt H Co 13th US; ___ to Jan 65 (2 yrs); Colle e Grove PO; rheumatism, could not ascertain comp, regt, lenth of time &c
CROACH, James H., O-141-3; Pvt K Co 20th Reg MO Inf; Mar 15 65 to Aug 6 76; Union City PO
CROCKER, John Y?, Mn-120-1; Cpl G Co 1st AL Cav; 62 to Jan 4 64; Pocahontas PO
CROCKER, Alexander, Mc-116-2; Pvt D Co 1st US Art; 3-6-64 to 3-31-66; Williamsburg PO; rheumatism, contracted while in service
CROCKET, Anderson, D-49-3; Pvt K Co 12th ___; 13 Aug 63 to 16 Jan 66; Nashville PO
CROCKET, David, D-60-1; 1148 Brood St, Nashville PO; got no information
CROCKET, George, K-167-2; 1st Hvy TN; 62 to 65; Knoxville PO
CROCKET, Jacob, K-185-2; Pvt L Co 10th MS Cav; 64 to 65; Scaggston PO; ruptured
CROCKET, Milton G. M., H-57-1; Pvt I Co 16th US Col; 63 to 65; Orchard Knob PO
CROCKET, Richard, Sh-159-4; Margret widow of; Pvt K Co TN Inf; Memphis PO
CROCKET, Stanley, Gi-122-7; Pvt K Co 110th TN Inf; 10 Dec 62 to 64; Prospect Sta. PO
CROCKET, Thomas D., D-52-1; Pvt C Co 13th OH Cav; Fall 62 to 63; Nashville PO
CROCKETT, Charles, Sn-252-2; Pvt H Co 14th RJ Hvy Art; Gallatin PO
CROCKET, David R., Ro-208-1; Pvt A Co 5th TN Inf; 22 Feb 62 to 11 Jun 65; Morris Gap PO
CROCKETT, J. R., Pi-153-1; Cpl F Co 13th KY Cav; 9-63 to 6-10-65; Chanute PO
CROCKETT, Jonas, Sh-174-4; Mary D. widow of; US Hvy Art; 63 to 65; Memphis? PO
CROCKETT, Joseph, Pi-156-1; David Beaty's Independent Scouts; 63 to 65; Travisville PO; consumption, disabled from work
CROCKETT, Josiah H., Mc-111-1; Pvt F Co 4th TN Cav; 2-27-63 to 6-12-65; Mortimer PO
CROCKETT, Oliver P., Co-61-4(1); Sgt; 1 Nov 62 to 15 Apr 65; Parrottsville PO; CONF
CROCKETT, Robert P., D-97-1; Capt C Co 18th TN; 61 to 65; Nashville PO; CONF
CROCKETT, Thomas J., Mc-116-3; Pvt F Co 4th TN Cav; 10-20-62 to 7-12-65; Athens PO; wounded in right foot
CROCKETT, Wyatt, D-87-2; Eliza widow of; PVt; ___ yrs; Nashville PO; caught cold in armey, died from effects afterward
CROFFERD, George, La-115-3; Pvt G Co 18th MI Inf; 5 Aug 62 to 11 Jul 65; Summertown PO
CROFFORD, Francis A., A-8-3; Sgt E Co 3rd TN Inf; 2-12-62 to 2-22-65; Scarborough PO
CROFT, W. C., Hu-103-3; Pvt E Co 10th TN Inf; 1 Jan 62 to 25 Dec 64; PO omitted
CROMLEY, Frederick J., Ct-43-3; Pvt H Co 4th TN INfl; 4-23-64 to 8-2-65; Watauga PO
CROMWELL, John S., Wy-173-5(1); US Sol; 8th Civil Dist
CROMWELL, Oliver B., F-42-1(3); Pvt Forrests Brig Cav; 61 to 65; Collierville PO; CONF
CRONIN, Elijah N., Po-148-2; Pvt C Co 1st AL Vidette? Cav; 12-1-63 to 8-8-64; Benton PO
CRONY, Benjamin, Gi-122-1; Pvt I Co 27th AL Inf; 1 Feb 61 to 2 Apr 65; Prospect Sta. PO; CONF
CROOK, Henry W., Dk-33-3; Pvt G Co 1st TN Inf; 2-5-64 to 4-21-65; Halesville PO; two ribs broke in the service
CROOK, James M., D-104-1; Sgt B Co 4th TN Cav; 64 to 65; Whites Bend PO

CROOK, James W., Dk-33-4; Pvt A Co 5th TN Cav; 7-28-62 to 7-25-65; Liberty PO
CROOK, Jerry, Tr-268-1; Pvt E Co 2nd TN Cav; __ to 65; Harsville PO; poisoned, living and doing well
CROOK, Sciota, Ha-111-1; Pvt A Co 27th VA Cav; 62 to 65; about 3 yrs; Upper Clinch PO; CONF
CROOK, William R., Dk-32-3; Pvt L Co 5th TN Cav; 8-25-63 to 8-14-65; Doneltown PO
CROOK, Wyly J., We-221-6(2); Capt Quartermaster Guard Army Supply T; May 61 to 2 May 65; Martin PO; none but exposure; CONF
CROOM, George, F-37-1; Cpl G Co 3rd US Col Hvy Art; Jan 65 to Apr 13 65; Taylors Chapel PO
CROOMS, Henry, Sh-158-3; Cpl A Co 3rd US Col Hvy Art; 6 Jun 63 to 30 Apr 66; Memphis PO; no disability
CROP, James M., D-54-2; Pvt C Co 101st US Col Inf; Apr 64 to 24 Apr 66; Nashville PO; rheumatism & rupture
CROSBY, Joel S., R-159-2; Pvt C Co 17th IN Inf; 5-15-61 to 11-1-62; Spring City PO
CROSLIN, William, Sn-171-2; Sarrah A. Wyatt former widow of; Pvt K Co 5th TN Mtd Inf; 64 to 65; Chestnut Mound PO; killed
CROSNOR, John W., Ma-123-1; Pvt Co F 18th IL, re-inlisted--changed to Co C; Aug 1 61 to Jan 66; Jackson PO; lungs diseased & nervousness; has failed in getting pension because of being away from comrades
CROSS, Charles W., A-5-2; Capt F Co 7th TN Mtd Inf; 9-64 to 7-27-65; Clinton PO
CROSS, Danill, H-76-1; D Co 5th TN Cav; Chattanooga PO
CROSS, Elisha, J-79-2; Pvt F Co 1st TN Mtd Inf; 2-64 to 5-65; North Springs PO
CROSS, Isaac, Cy-27-3(1); Pvt B Co 37th KY Mtd Inf; 7-20-63 to 12-20-64; Miles Cross Roads PO
CROSS?, Isaac, F-47-1; Pvt C Co 59th TN Inf; Jun 1 63 to Jan 31 66; Williston PO
CROSS, James, Cy-27-3(1); Pvt B Co 9th KY Inf; 9-61 to 3-65; Miles Cross Roads PO
CROSS, James M., Mg-197-3; Jane widow of; Sgt; Crooked Fork PO; command not known
CROSS, Joel J., La-109-1; Pvt A Co 2nd TN Inf; 10-2-63 to 10-14-64; Loretto PO; husband killed in battle (this may apply to Mary Goolsby, widow); nothing definite
CROSS, John, K-154-3; Pvt 3rd TN Cav; __ to 65; Knoxville PO
CROSS, John C., H-58-2; Pvt F Co 1st TN Inf; 11-13-61 to 7-65; Sale Creek PO; right rist and hand stiff
CROSS, Joseph W., Ge-85-1; Pvt H Co 3rd NC Inf; Cavey Branch PO
CROSS, Nancy A., A-7-1; widow of __; Robertsville PO
CROSS, Sarah (see Smith, Nathanial)
CROSS, Wm., Sh-172-1; Cpl E Co 1st MO Inf; 7-20-61 to 8-2-64; 386 Main St, Memphis PO
CROSTON, Joseph C., Wi-281-1; Pvt H Co 5th TN; Jul 25 63 to Aug 25 65; Bathesda PO; piles during war
CROSSWAY, Louis (Henry), D-99-1; Pvt G Co 13th TN Inf; Oct 10 63 to Jan 10 65; Goodlettsville PO
CROSSWHITE, Abraham L., Jo-151-1; Asst Surgeon I Co 13th TN Cav; 22 Sep 63 to 5 Sep 65; Stump Knox PO; small pox--resulting diseases--hemorrhoids--disease of eyes
CROSSWHITE, John M., Jo-153-2; Pvt B Co 4th TN Inf; 22 Aug 62 to 17 Jul 85; Little Doe PO; bronchitis
CROSSWHITE, Thomas J., Jo-149-1; Cpl B Co 4th TN Inf; 22 Aug 62 to 7 Jul 65; Mountain City PO; nerves disease & general debility
CROSSWHITE, William C., Jo-153-1; Pvt B Co 4th TN Inf; 30 May 63 to 18 Jul 65; Little Doe PO; bronchitis, piles
CROTHERS, Mary, Hi-88-1; widow? 6th Dist
CROTTS, Joseph V., Hd-46-2; Pvt D Co 2nd TN Mtd Inf; Dec 1 64 to Feb 1 65; Savannah PO
CROUCH, James W., Hd-53-2; Pvt D Co 6th TN Cav; 24 Oct 62 to 26 Jul 65; Morris Chapel PO; consumption
CROUCH, Jessee P., Pi-154-1; Pvt H Co 3rd KY Inf; 12-62 to 9-64; Spurrier PO

CROUDER, Joe S., Hu-103-1; Pvt C Co PA Inf; 20 Feb 61 to Oct 10 65; PO omitted
CROW, James L., Mc-112-7; Sgt B Co 7th TN Mtd Inf; 9-24-64 to 7-27-65; Athens PO
CROW, Jessy, Ro-210-12; Pvt E Co; Cardiff PO
CROW, John, Ct-42-1; Pvt A Co 13th TN Cav; Watauga PO; chronic diarrhea
CROW, Walter H., He-60-1; Pvt C Co 6th TN Cav; 9-11-62 to 7-26-65; Lexington PO; wound in left leg
CROWDER, Alice W. (see Kindrick, Robert G.)
CROWDER, Charley B., Dk-39-3(1); Cpl B Co 42nd US Col Inf; 4-10-64 to 1-31-66; Dekalb PO
CROWDER, Edom, H-73-4(2); Chattanooga PO
CROWDER, James M., Ro-201-3(1); Pvt B Co 5th TN Inf; 25 Feb 62 to 7 Apr 65; Kingston PO
CROWDER, Mary (see Luttrell, Silas)
CROWDER, Richard F., K-180-3; Pvt K Co 11th TN Cav; 15 Sep 63 to 14 Sep 65; Ebenezer PO; chronic plueretus, heart disease
CROWDER, Robt., Mc-115-1; Martha widow of; Cpl B Co 1st IN Mtd Cav; 9-10-63 to 6-16-64; Riceville PO; lung disease
CROWDER, Robert P., Mo-125-1; Appointed Asst. Surgeon; Madisonville PO
CROWDER, Taylor C., M-103-4; Pvt B Co 37th KY Inf; 6-8-63 to 12-29-64; Lafayette PO
CROWDER, Thomas M., Mo-127-2; Notchy PO
CROWE, Giddian, W-196-2; Pvt C Co 44th WI Vol; 10-24-64 to 8-65; Goth PO; enlargement of splene
CROWE, Thompson P., W-189-1; Pvt D Co 37th WI Inf; 3-27-64 to 7-27-65; McMinnville PO
CROWEL, John, B-11-3(2); Sgt B Co 15th US Col; 6-1-64 to 4-7-66; Unionville PO
CROWELL, Hiram B., B-12-2; 10th TN Inf; __ to 6-23-65; Shelbyville PO; was not at home & wife could not give dates
CROWELL, John, Wi-270-1; Pvt L Co 5th TN Cav; 1 Jun 64 to 1 Nov 64; Union Valley PO
CROWELL, John W., Hu-103-2; Pvt 10th TN R Inf; 25 May 61 to 20 May 63; PO omitted
CROWNOVER, Daniel G., Ma-129-1; Pvt C Co 6th TN Cav; Nov 62 to Aug 5 65; Jackson PO
CROX, Charles, Lo-195-2(1); Pvt K Co 6th PA Cav; 4 Nov 61 to 30 Nov 64; Lenoirs PO; nervous prostration
CROX, Henry A., Po-148-3; Pvt K Co 6th PA Cav; 11-14-61 to 11-30-64; Benton PO
CROXVILLE, Granville, Ge-96-3; Pvt B Co 8th TN Cav; 23 Jul 63 to 11 Sep 65; Jockey PO
CROYON, Zion, H-51-6; Pvt A Co 6th TN Inf; Albion View PO
CROZIER, Samuel N., Ge-89-4; Pvt B Co 3rd TN Mtd Inf; 30 Jun 64 to 25 Oct 64; Pilot Knob PO
CRUDUP, Joseph, Ru-231-1; Teamster A Co 1st IN Inf; 25 Dec 63 to Mar 65; Rural? Hill PO
CRUM, Peter, La-115-1; Louisa widow of; Cpl B Co 32nd IN Vol; Henryville PO; discharge got lost at this pention office but he was granted a pention
CRUM, William A., Ja-87-1; Pvt L Co 1st TN Cav; 12-18-63 to 7-12-65; Howardville PO; relapse of measles
CRUMB, John, Co-67-2; Pvt I Co 69th TN Inf; 18 Oct 62 to Feb 65; Bison PO; CONF
CRUMB, Michael L., Ge-84-1; Pvt F Co 4th TN Inf; 11 Jul 62 to 7 Jul 65; Bird Bridge?; spasmodic colic, crying grate distress
CRUMBY, Carrol K., He-66-1; Pvt D Co 6th TN Cav; Sep 22 62 to Jul 4 65; Lexington PO; rheumatism
CRUMLEY, John H., Wa-270-1; Pvt D Co 60th TN Inf; 3 Dec 63 to 65; Austin's Springs PO; Point Lookout MD, 21 mos
CRUMLY, Elexander, Hw-118-3; Pvt A Co 4th TN Inf; St.Clair PO
CRUMLY, John, Ge-97-4; Pvt D Co 8th TN Inf; 15 Mar 63 to 30 Jun 65; 16th Civil Dist
CRUMP, Grundy, K-180-2; Sgt E Co 14th TN Col Inf; 1 Nov 63 to 26 Mar 66; Bearden PO; weak eyes result small pox
CRUMP, James L., Wa-272-3; Pvt H Co 9th TN Cav; 1 Jan 65 to 11 Sep 65; Free Hill PO; sunstroke, defective in sight and mind
CRUMRINE, Aaron A., H-56-6; Cpl 152nd OH Inf; 61 to 62; St. Elmo PO

CRUSE, Harvy L., K-181-2; Pvt E Co 3rd TN Cav; 1 Jan 62 to 12 Jun 65; Nast PO; rheumatism
CRUSE, William, K-181-2; Pvt A Co 5th tN Cav; Jan 62 to 62; Nast PO; CONF
CRUTCHER, Neal, Ru-238-2; Sgt B Co 111th USC Inf; 15 Jul 64 to 30 Apr 66; Murfreesboro PO
CRUTCHER, Samuel, Mu-213-1; Commissary & Pvt; Mar 63 to Oct 63; Glenns Store PO; was in Commisary service
CRUTCHERVILLE, Harrison, Mu-210-1; Cpl D Co 44th TN Inf--Col troops; 4-26-64 to 5-1-65; Spring Hill PO; captured by Hoods rade
CRUTCHERVILLE, Leah, Wl-288-1; Dist No. 2
CRUTCHFIELD, Amos, Cl-54-3(1); Pvt A Co 63rd TN; 9-1-61 to 7-65; Tazewell PO; never discharged from reg; CONF
CRUTCHFIELD, Henry M., Hu-106-1; 2nd Lt E Co 16th KY Cav; 1 Dec 63 to 65; Waverly; wound in head; pensioner
CRY, Hugh H., Bo-13-1; Pvt H Co 4th TN Inf; 7-4-64 to 8-12-65; Unitia PO (Loudon Co.)
CUFF, Benjamin, Sn-262-3(2); Fountain Head PO; have got all the information we can
CULBERSON, Caswell, Ge-85-2; Pvt G Co 1st TN Cav; 1 Jul 62 to 5 Jun 65; Cavey Branch PO; rheumatism, chronic diarhea, frost bitten feet
CULBERSON, Peter, Mc-111-2; Pvt F Co 3rd TN Cav; 4-6-63 to 6-10-65; Mortimer PO; prisner at Cahaba, AL 6 mos
CULBERSON, Peter, Mc-116-3; Pvt F Co 3rd TN Cav; 4-26-63 to 6-10-65; Mortimer PO
CULBERT, Robert, Wa-270-1; Pvt C Co 8th TN Inf; 65 to 65 (6 mos); Austins Springs PO
CULBERTSON, Benjamin F., Br-9-2; Bugler A Co 21st IN Inf; 7-23-61 to 1-10-66; Cleveland PO
CULIFER, Nabb, Gr-75-1; Pvt F Co 1st TN Cav; 30 Mar 62 to 30 Mar 65; Doyal PO; rupture
CULLEFER, Benjamin, Gr-76-1; Pvt M Co 1st TN Cav; 12 May 63 to Jun 19 65; Tampico PO; injury to right foot and leg
CULLOM, Daniel W., Cy-28-2; Pvt G Co 86th IL Inf; to 6-6-65; Celina PO
CULLUM, George, Sn-254-2; PO omitted
CUPLE, Houston, D-61-1; Pvt E Co 17th Army Cumber.; Oct 18 63 to Apr 25 66; Nashville PO
CULTON, George P., K-161-2; Cpl E Co 3rd TN Mtd Inf; Jul 64 to ___ 64; Knoxville PO
CULVAHOUSE, John M., H-58-1; Pvt A Co 5th TN Inf; 7-12-63 to 4-24-65; Sale Creek PO; scurvy, in very feeble health
CULVAHOUSE, Rutha (see Jackson, George W.)
CULVER, Dwight V., R-162-1; 1st Lt H Co 3rd TN Mtd Inf; 5-5-64 to 11-30-64; Dayton PO
CULVER, Lorenza D., Fe-42-2; Pvt Capt David Beaty's Co TN Ind Scouts; Jamestown PO
CULVERHOUSE, Edgar F., Ro-210-7; Pvt; Rockwood PO
CULVEYHOUSE, William, Ro-207-3; Pvt A Co 5th TN Inf; 25 Feb 62 to 3 Mar 65; Stockton PO (Loudon Co.) vronchitis
CULVYHOUSE, Elias W., Ro-208-1; Pvt A Co 5th TN Inf; 1 Mar 63 to 18 Sep 64; Morris Gap PO
CULY, Cubyhus, Ro-208-3; US Sol; 9th Civ Dist
CUMANOM, Joseph, Un-257-3; Pvt; 63 to 64; New Prospect PO; cant tell more about it; CONF
CUMBRY, Christopher, H-56-6; E Co ___ TN Inf; 64 to 65; St. Elmo PO; CONF
CUMBY, Wiliam T., Pu-141-1; Pvt K Co 4th TN Inf; 11-1-64 to 8-25-64 (sic); Cookville PO
CUMINS, A. Gustis, Co-59-1; Pvt Co B 3rd TN Cav; 11-62 to 1-16-64; Del Rio PO; rheumatism
CUMMING, Wm., Ca-20-2; Pvt C Co 5th TN Cav; 9-15-62 to 9-15-64; Talvine PO
CUMMINGS, Alfred, Sn-264-2; Pvt F Co 17th KY Cav--64 to Sep 64; G Co 8th KY Cav--Sep 63 to Sep 64; Mittchellsville PO; this man deaf in one ear from army service; Capt Alsup, Col Sam Johnson, Gen Judah, paper allright, can be produced when needed
CUMMINGS, Cicen, D-56-1; Cpl K Co 16th US Inf; 9 Feb 64 to 30 Apr 66; Nashville PO
CUMMINGS, Elizabeth, Gr-82-2; 14th Dist
CUMMINGS, Frank, Bo-21-3; Elizabeth widow of; Ellijay PO; died at close of war; no information
CUMMINGS, George, Sh-191-1; Pvt L Co 3rd Col Art; 2-65 to 4-66; Memphis PO
CUMMINGS, Jackson R., Se-255-3; Pvt I Co 5th TN Inf; Oct 62 to Jun 65; Cotlettsburg PO; hurtin in stomach caused by a cealing? 25 yrs ago
CUMMINGS, James K., Wl-299-1; Pvt H Co 4th TN Inf; 1 Nov 64 to 25 Aug 65; Statesville PO
CUMMINGS, Levi, D-104-1; Pvt R (sic) Co 80th IL; 61 to 64; Whites Bend PO; shot in the leg & finger shot off
CUMMINGS, Peter, D-72-1; Turner, Mary J. also widow of; Pvt B Co 44th TN Inf; Nov 18 63 to Nov 19 65; Nashville PO
CUMMINGS, Rosa (see Plumley, Anderson)
CUMMINS, Andrew, Sh-174-4; Martha Hanis formerly widow of; Pvt D Co 59th US Col Inf; 64 to ___; Memphis? PO; dysentery (chronic) enlisted at La Mange, TN
CUMMINS, Andrew N., Wl-302-1; Pvt H Co 4th TN Mtd Inf; 5 Dec 64 to 25 Aug 65; Greanvail PO
CUMMINS, John, Hy-81-1; Pvt; discharge with pension agt; Brownsville PO; frost bitten & toes off
CUMMINS, John, F-37-2; Josephine Hobson form. widow of (also widow of Charles Johnson); Pvt US Col; 2 yrs; Taylors Chapel PO; wounded in the thigh (both in same reg & comp as Charles Johnson)
CUMMINS, John C., Hm-103-3; Sgt G Co 102nd IL Inf; 6 Aug 62 to 6 Jun 65; Morristown PO; gun shot
CUMMIS, William C., K-172-2; Pvt B Co 3rd TN Cav; 5 Nov 62 to 10 Jun 65; Knoxville PO; in prison 7 mos
CUNDIFF, G. J., Ro-208-1; Pvt D Co 1st TN Inf; 64 to 65; Morris Gap PO
CUNINGHAM, George (see Washington, George)
CUNINGHAM, Lawrence, Sh-152-3; Eads PO
CUNINGHAM, Robt., D-49-2; Pvt; Nashville PO; cant remember
CUNINGHAM, Washington, Pu-141-2; Pvt B Co 42nd TN Inf; 62 to 65; Goffton PO; discharged close of war
CUNINGHAM, William, Cr-13-2; Pvt; Atwood PO; cannot find out when enlisted
CUNINGHAM, William (see Simmons, William)
CUNNINGHAM, Ab., L-99-2; Pvt B Co 44th US Col Inf; 63 to 66; Durhamville PO; frost bitten; date of enlistment uncertain
CUNNINGHAM, Calvin J., Cl-54-1; Pvt G Co 1st TN Cav; 7-1-62 to 5-20-65; Bacchus PO; smol pock & over head of blood
CUNNINGHAM, James H., Ja-86-4; Pvt K Co 2nd TN Inf; 2-61 to ___; Apison PO; chronic diarhea
CUNNINGHAM, John H., Wl-302-1; Pvt H Co 4th TN Mtd Inf; 7 Nov 64 to 25 Aug 65; no PO
CUNNINGHAM, John W., B-15-1; Pvt A Co 4th TN Inf; 8-13-64 to 8-26-65; Shelbyville PO; gun shot wounds
CUNNINGHAM, Massy J., H-54-3; Pvt I Co 11th KY Cav; 2-63 to 8-23-65; Sherman Heights PO; contracted sciatic rheumatism and neuralgia
CUNNINGHAM, William, Sh-196-2; Pvt I Co 90th IL Inf; 8-5-62 to 10-31-62; Duffy Hotel, Main St, Memphis PO; permanently injured at Mission Ridge; pensioner; Capt I Co 90th IL Inf; 10-31-62 to 7-24-64
CUNNINGHAM, William H., Cl-51-1; Pvt G Co 1st TN Cav; 7-1-62 to 6-5-65; Cedar Fork PO
CUPP, James, Sh-149-1; Cerenda widow of; Pvt; National Cemetery PO
CUPP, James E., Bo-15-4; Pvt H Co 2nd TN Cav; 10-10-62 to 7-6-65; Maryville PO; wound in back
CUPP, James F., Bo-15-4; Pvt A Co 3rd TN Cav; ___ to 8-3-65; Maryville PO
CUPP, James O., Ge-88-1; Pvt A Co 63rd TN Inf (R Co? C Co?); 62 to 65; Bulls Gap PO
CUPP, John, Bo-21-3; Pvt M Co 2nd TN Cav; 11-8-62 to 7-6-65; Veeba PO
CURBY, John, Bo-21-3; Pvt M Co 2nd TN Cav; 11-8-62 to 7-6-65; Veeba PO
CURD, Isiah, Ge-94-3; C Pvt 4th TN Inf; 65 to 65 (6 mos); Ham PO; dropsy 10 yrs, gun shot through left leg during war in 1865
CURD, James A., Ro-202-5; Cpl E Co 13th TN Cav; Sep 63 to 15 Oct 64; CaveCreek PO; heart disease cause by measles
CURETON, James E., Co-63-1; Pvt D Co TN Inf; 1 yr; Newport PO; phthisis, deserted
CURL, John M., Hm-106-1; Pvt D Co 3rd KY Cav; 25 May 61 to 15 Aug 65; Morristown PO
CURLIN, Charles, St-161-1 (Col); Pvt A Co 13th KY Art; Oct 64 to Nov 65; Tobacco Port PO; exact date of inlistment forgotten

CUROWN?, Joseph, Je-143-3; Pvt K Co 1st Hvy Art; 65 to Mar 66; Mossy Creek PO; wounded; discharge lost
CURREY, Jake, D-64-3; Nashville PO
CURRIER, Andrew L., Ro-203-6; Pvt K Co 1st TN Inf; 9 Aug 61 to 17 Sep 64; Ethel PO; diarrhea & lung & heart disease
CURRIER, Benjamin, Ro-203-2; US Sol; Wheat PO
CURRIER, James, Ro-203-8; Union Cross Roads PO
CURRIER, Richard, Ro-203-5(1); Colorbearer A Co 1st TN Mtd Inf; 8 Nov 64 to 27 Jul 65; Burns Mills PO
CURRIER, William, A-5-1; Pvt K Co 1st TN Inf; 8-61 to 4-65; Clinton PO
CURRY, Brice E., Hr-96-1; Lt F Co 13th TN Inf; 24 May 61 to 14 Apr 65; Carinsville PO; CONF
CURRY, Cornelious, Gi-128-2; Pvt G Co 10th IN Cav; 62 to 65; Pulaski PO
CURRY, Samuel, Col, W-189-2; Cpl E Co 17th TN Inf; 63 to 65; McMinnville PO; discharge lost
CURRY, W. M., Gi-122-6; Pvt E Co 7th TN Cav; Mar 61 to Apr 65; Lesters Sta. PO; CONF
CURSEY, John C., Po-149-1; Pvt G Co 11th TN Cav; 9-27-63 to 9-11-65; Conasauga PO; subsequently Co L 8th TN Cav
CURTICE, John, Mr-99-4; Sol US; Jasper PO
CURTICE, William, Mn-121-4; Pvt A Co 6th TN Cav; 9-1-62 to 7-26-65; Bethel Springs PO
CURTIS, Andrew, T-209-1; Hostler? 3rd IL Cav; 3 yrs; Randolph PO; lost discharge
CURTIS, Archabld, Ct-41-1; Pvt B Co 4th TN Inf; 11-24-62 to 8-3-65; South Wattauga PO; rhumatism and hearing
CURTIS, Bowling, Je-146-1; Pvt; Leadvale PO; deafness, bad fix
CURTIS, Burnett, Ru-232-1; Pvt A Co 10th TN Inf; Jun or Jul 63 to __ (1 yr 10 mos); LaVergne PO
CURTIS, Charley F., Cr-10-1; Pvt G Co 2nd TN V Cav; Stokes PO (Dyer Co.); heart disease winter of 62 to 63, able to perform duty on farm
CURTIS, Daniel W., L-103-1; Pvt H Co 31st IL Inf; Sep 17 61 to Oct 65; Island 25 PO; left shoulder broken, lost use of arm in past
CURTIS, Dearl H., La-109-1; did not know anything of his co, regt; Loretto PO; chronic diorhea, could not tell nothing
CURTIS, Henry, Wa-272-3; Rachel widow; Pvt E Co 8th TN Cav; 1 Feb 64 to 30 Jun 65; Clara PO
CURTIS, Henry, Mn-121-4; Pvt A Co 6th TN Cav; 9-1-62 to 7-26-65; Bethel Springs PO
CURTIS, J. W., K-158-1; Pvt 5th Pvt Art; Aug 62 to Sep 65; Knoxville, 7 W. Clinch PO
CURTIS, James M., Bo-13-2; Pvt A Co 3rd TN Cav; 12-11-63 to 6-10-65; Tutt PO
CURTIS, John W., Po-148-1; Pvt B Co 10th TN Cav; 1-21-64 to 8-1-65; Chestewee Mills PO
CURTIS, Pinkney A., Mo-126-2; Sol; 12th Civil Dist
CURTIS, S., D-54-3; 1405 Summer St, Nashville PO
CURTIS, Thomas J., Dk-34-2; 2nd Sgt F Co 4th TN Inf; 9-24-64 to 8-25-65; Dowelltown PO; liver & kidney disease
CURTIS, William, W-192-1; Pvt A Co; 6-17-63 to 65; 6th Civil Dist
CURTIS, William, Dy-25-2; Pvt A Co 10th TN Inf; 62 to 65; Newbern PO; wounded
CURTON, Isaac E., Mc-112-1; Pvt H Co 7th TN Inf; 2-65 to 4-30-65; Athens PO
CURTON, Pleasent S., K-165-1; Pvt D Co 43rd __; 61 to 15 Ju_ 63; Knoxville PO
CUTHBERT, B., Po-61-1; Eliza Ann Word widow of; Capt E Co Governer Staff; Jun 1 62 to Jun 1 65; Belmont Av, Nashville PO; Capt Co E; Governos Guard
CUTSHALL, David, Ge-99-2; Pvt A Co 7th IN Cav; 24 Aug 63 to 15 May 65; Woolsey College PO; ruptured
CUTSHAW, Andrew, Ge-99-2; Pvt M Co 1st TN Cav; Nov 62 to 64; Woolsey College PO; crippled in shin bone, could not get dates
CUTSHAW, Henry, Ge-89-2; Pvt K Co 13th TN Cav; 1 Sep 64 to 5 Sep 65; Mosheim PO
CUTTS, Lartan, W-189-3(2); Pvt D Co 9th TN Cav; 9-23-63 to 9-11-65; McMinnville PO
CUTTYMAN, Puckett, Dk-36-1; Mary F. widow of; Lt I Co 5th TN Cav; 63 to 64; Smithville PO
CYPERT, Thomas J., Wy-175-1; Capt A Co 2nd TN Mtd Inf; 9-2-63 to 10-14-64; Cypress Inn PO; in bad health
DABNEY, David, C-27-1; Sgt A Co 1st TN Inf; 8-2-61 to 9-15-64; Jacksboro PO
DABNEY, James D., Me-90-1; Matilda E. wife of; Pvt 8th TN Inf; 3-62 to __; Tabor PO; died of fever while in service
DABNEY, Payton, Me-90-1; Pvt A Co 8th TN Inf; 2-26-63 to 6-30-65; Tabor PO
DACKRY, Alford, Se-219-3; Pvt C Co 2nd NC Inf; 9-26-63 to 8-16-65; Jones Cave PO; rumatism & piles, yellow janders
DAGLEY, Feral H., A-9-4(2); Manerva V. widow of; Sgt E Co 3rd TN Inf; 2-12-62 to 2-25-64; Marlow PO; gun shot wound in boeth thighs; died 1-12-64
DAIL, James I., Ro-201-3(1); Lt Col 7th TN Inf; 2-10-62 to 7-27-65; Kingston PO; back & r. hip injured
DAIL, John, Ro-210-3; Laura widow of; Pvt; Rockwood PO
DAILEY, William B., Mo-129-3; Pvt C Co 6th TN Inf; 4-13-61 to 7-4-65; Lomotley PO
DAILLON, David, Mr-97-1; Mary J. widow of; Pvt C Co 6th TN Inf; 9-15-64 to 6-30-65; Inman PO; shoulder nocked out of place, horse fell down with him
DAILY, Ely, Col, Gr-70-1; Pvt K Co 1st TN Hvy; 12-19-64 to 3-31-66; Rutledge PO; rheumatism, side out of shape
DAILY, Henry, Col, Gr-70-1; Pvt K Co 1st TN Hea.; 7-18-64 to 3-31-65; Rutledge PO; daarhea
DAILY, Hiram P., Hm-103-1; Sarah E. widow of; Pvt 3rd TN Cav; 1-1-62 to __; Morristown PO
DAILY, James W., K-167-3; Pvt F Co 3rd TN Cav; 63 to 9-65; Knoxville PO
DAILY, William, Sh-159-2; Pvt C Co 61st Inf; 3-63 to 12-66; Memphis PO; feet frosted, fingers frosted
DAIMWOOD, George G., Mu-209-1; Pvt G Co 24th TN Cav; Columbia PO; CONF
DAKE, James W., Ro-205-4; Pvt B Co 5th TN Inf; 2-28-62 to 4-28-65; Kingston PO; spineal affecttion and lung trouble
DAKE, Samuel J., A-2-2; Cpl-Pvt J Co 5th TN Inf; 7-1-63 to 6-30-65; Bull Run PO (Knox Co.); gun shot left fore arm
DALE, Charles H., K-161-3; Knoxville PO
DALE, Duncan, Mu-210-6; Sgt C Co 15th TN Inf; 62 to 65; Mallard PO
DALE, James R., Dk-35-4(2); Pvt H Co 5th TN Cav; 8-15-62 to 8-14-65; Capling PO; ruptured
DALE, Wilbur P., H-70-1; Mary widow of; Cpl A Co 12th WI Inf; 61 to 64; Chattanooga PO; health ruined
DALE, William, R-106-1; Pvt C Co; 5th Civil Dist
DALEY, Andser, Sn-250-2; Dist 1 & 2
DALFORD, Green, Gi-137-6; Belle Milton formerly widow of; Pvt F Co 111th TN Col Inf; Pulaski PO; particulars not known
DALLAS, George, Gi-140-1; Pvt A Co 105th IL Inf; 6-10-63 to 6-20-65; PO omitted
DALLAS, William, A-4-6(2); Pvt C Co 44th USC Inf; 8-62 to 4-65; Coal Creek PO; has no discharge
DALTON, David, Gr-81-1; Pvt H Co 1st TN Cav; 10-1-62 to 6-28-65; Clear Spring PO; rheumatism, partly disabled
DALTON, Geo. W., Gr-79-2; D Co 26th TN Inf; 2-3-61 to 65; Ball Point PO; yellow janders, lost left lung; CONF
DALTON, Hiram, Gr-79-1; Pvt 7th TN Inf; shot through right hip; now has pulsey; CONF
DALTON, Isaac, Col, Wi-283-1; Pvt B Co 14th TN Inf; 11-10-62 to 6-1-65; Rock Hill PO
DALTON, Jeramire T., Dy-25-1; Pvt; Newbern PO; enlistment dates unknown
DALTON, John W., Gr-71-1; Pvt K Co 8th KY Inf; 9-22-61 to 1-3-65; Tate Spring PO; no discharge from service
DALTON, Lacy, Gr-79-1; Elizabeth widow of; Ball Point PO; killed; CONF
DALTON, Micheal, D-45-3; Pvt A Co 1st LA Cav; 62 to 7-65; Nashville PO
DALTON, Mirie (see Mallicot, Fayette)
DALTON, Nathan P., Gr-79-2; Pvt C Co 12 Batt; 8-63 to 64; Thorn Hill PO; not disabled; CONF

DALTON, Porter, Je-140-2; Pvt D Co 9th TN Cav; 1-1-64 to 9-11-65; Strawberry Plains PO
DALTON, Rebecca (see Wolfe, Adam)
DALTON, Rheuben, Gr-70-3; Pvt K Co 37th TN Inf; 61 to 64; Rutledge PO; spinal aff.
DALTON, William N., Gr-79-1; Cpl D Co 26th TN; 7-2-61 to 3-15-65; Ball Point PO; CONF
DALY, Patin R., Wy-174-1; Pvt A Co 2nd TN; 12-5-64 to 12-26-65; Lutts PO
DAMEWOOD, John H., K-174-5; Pvt A Co 4th Ioway Cav; 8-10-61 to 8-24-65; PO omitted
DAMIER, Peter F., Wa-268-1; Pvt F Co 3rd NC Mtd Inf; 9-64 to 8-65; Johnson City PO; heart disease
DAMPTON, Frank, Mt-137-1; Pvt K Co 16th KY Inf; 62 to 65; papers lost; St. Bethlehem PO
DAMRAN, Green B., B-6-1; Pvt A Co 4th TN Mtd Inf; __ to 65; Haven PO; gun shot wound
DAMRON, James W., We-225-2(1); Narsisa A. Hopps widow of; Pvt C Co 40th IL Inf; 12-8-61 to 5-65; Dresden PO; now dead 24 yrs
DAMRON, Mary C. (see Neal, Charles B.)
DAMS, George, Bo-20-2; Gunboat; 12-9-62 to 12-9-65; Maryville PO; lost two toes
DAMWOOD, Samuel M., Mu-209-1; Pvt G Co 24th TN Cav; 61 to 65; Columbia PO; CONF
DANALLS, William, Ca-25-2; Pvt L Co 5th TN Cav; 2-3-63 to __; Gassoway PO; stroke on head with a gun
DANBAR, Hamilton, Ge-83-3; Elizabeth widow of; Pvt I Co 1st TN Inf; 2-1-63 to 63?; Horse Creek PO; consumption from measels
DANCE, Jonathan A., Je-142-1; Pvt B Co 9th TN Cav; 5-30-64 to 9-11-65; Lucilla PO; hemorrhoids
DANCY, Andrew, Sh-191-6(2); Pvt A Co 3rd Hvy Art; 6-4-63 to 5-30-66; Memphis PO
DANCY, Jacob E., Cy-28-1; Pvt K Co 12th KY Inf; 3-12-63 to 7-11-65; Celina PO
DANDRIDGE, Edmond, Hy-81-2; Pvt K Co 59th US Inf; 7-64 to 1-66; 7th Civil Dist
DANELL, Levi N., Je-146-1; Pvt D Co 4th TN Inf; 1-63 to 9-65; White Pine PO; lung trouble
DANFORTH, Henry C., Ma-126-1; Pvt B Co 3rd VT Inf; 6-11-61 to 7-25-65; Jackson PO
DANGERFIELD, Thos., Gi-131-2; Pvt I Co 111th Col Inf; 62 to 65; Sumac PO
DANIALS, Henry, He-62-1; Martha Pettigrew widow of; Pvt; Darden PO; drowned on way home
DANIEL, Calvin, Mg-199-2; Catharine widow of; Pvt 2nd TN Inf; Sunbright PO
DANIEL, Fannie (see Irwin, Jo)
DANIEL, Franklin W., Dk-38-1; Pvt L Co 13th KY Cav; 10-63 to 1-65; Magness Mills PO; ruptured
DANIEL, George, Cl-58-2; Pvt Co E 2nd NC Inf; 8-64 to 8-65; Davo PO; can't give full account
DANIEL, Isaac, Hm-105-1; P-t D Co 4th TN Inf; 4-16-62 to 6-7-65; Turley Mill PO
DANIEL, Jeremiah, Lo-187-1; Pvt G Co 1st TN Inf; 8-9-61 to 9-17-64; Loudon PO; heart & lungs
DANIEL, John, Cl-58-2; Lewesana widow of; Pvt C Co 1st TN Inf; 8-8-61 to 62; Davo PO; died in service, Cumberland Ford KY, was not wounded, can't find out his desease
DANIEL, John T., Cl-58-1; Nancy M. widow of; Pvt 2nd TN; Davo PO
DANIEL, Johnathan S., Cl-58-2; Pvt C Co 1st TN Inf; 8-61 to 9-64; Davo PO; injured in back from lifting log, not at home, information from wife
DANIEL, Lewis W. sr., Cr-4-5; Major D Co 9th TN Cav; 62 to 62 (8 mos); Bells Depot PO; CONF
DANIEL, Marcus, Gr-70-1; Pvt D Co 4th TN Inf; 8-15-63 to 8-2-65; Rutledge PO; injured by vaccination
DANIEL, Thomas, Gr-80-1; Pvt B Co 1st TN Lt Art; 65 to 65; Thorn Hill PO; yellow janders & cannot recollect dates omitted
DANIEL, Thomas, Cf-35-3; Malinda widow of; Gould PO; CONF
DANIEL, Thomas L., Je-146-2; Pvt D Co 9th TN Cav; 10-1-63 to 9-11-65; White Pine PO; failed to get disease of any
DANIEL, William K., Gr-78-1; Pvt G Co 8th TN Cav; 7-18-64 to 8-12-65; Spring House PO; imflamatory rheumatism
DANIEL, Wootson T., Gr-73-2; Pvt F Co 1st TN Cav; 4-62 to 3-31-65; Turley's Mills PO
DANIELS, David, Wi-283-1; Lusinda widow of; Pvt A Co 38th OH Cav; 8-3-61 to 5-30-62; Rock Hill PO
DANIELS, Elias R., Sh-191-6(2); alias J. Daniel Reese; Pvt D Co 61st Col Inf; 63 to 65 (2 yrs 6 mos); Memphis PO
DANIELS, George W., A-2-3; Minerva E. Daniels widow of Albert Daniels formerly widow of George W. Daniels; 7th TN Mtd Inf; __ to __; Hinds Creek PO; discharge burned with his dwelling
DANIELS, alias Robinson, Joseph, A-4-5; Pvt L Co 4th OH Cav; 9-28-62 to 7-17-65; Coal Creek PO; gunshot left hand
DANIELS, Martha, La-117-4; widow; Pvt; 15th Dist
DANNELL, Joel, B-12-1; Amanda V. Haskins widow of; Pvt E Co 10th TN Inf; Palmetto PO; first husband Joel Dannell died in service; could not give dates
DANNELS, Willum, Un-255-2; Pvt G Co 7th TN Inf; 64 to Ju_ 65; Gale PO; parlitic
DANNIEL, Alexander H., Me-94-2; Sgt D Co 7th TM Mtd Inf; 10-9-64 to 7-27-65; Euchee PO
DARD, Christofer C., Sh-201-1; Pvt B Co 151st NY Inf; 8-15-62 to 2-7-65; Memphis PO
DARDEN, Andrew, Mt-136-1; Cpl.C Co 16th TN; 7-64 to 5-30-66; Port Royal PO; wound in ankle, sometimes painful now
DARDEN, Richard C., Rb-221-3; Pvt; Adams Station PO; CONF
DARDEN, Robert, Rb-221-3; Pvt E Co 14th US; Oct 1 63 to Mar 1 65; Adams Station PO
DARDIS?, Joseph (Black?); Fr-107-1; Pvt 33rd OH Inf 9-62 to 65; Winchester PO; lost discharge
DARDIS, Monroe; Fr-113-1(4); 8th Dist
DAREN, Bartlet M., Hd-49-1; Elizabeth widow of; Pvt D Co 2nd TN Inf; 11-1-63 to 64; Olive Hill PO
DARICOVE, W. M., G-57-1; Yorkville PO; CONF
DARLEY, Henry P., Co-69-3; Pvt D Co 22nd SC Inf; 1-1-61 to 4-15-65; Rankin OP; back effected at Pines MD; CONF
DARLING, Henry A., H-61-5; Pvt 27th MA Inf; Spring 62 to Spring 65; Chattanooga PO
DARMAN, John S., S-217-1; Pvt D Co 157th NY Inf; 8-15-62 to 2-14-65; Winfield PO
DARMOND, John H., Bo-15-4; Sgt H Co 2nd TN Cav; 10-10-62 to 7-6-65; Maryville PO
D'ARMOND, Samuel H., Br-9-2; Pvt E Co 5th TN Inf; 10-64 to 8-65; Cleveland PO
DARNELL, Allan, B-12-2; PO omitted
DARNELL, Isaac M., L-105-1; PVt; 7th Civil Dist
DARNELL, John F., Ms-172-1; Farmington PO
DARR, Fannie, D-77-3; No 6 Winter St, Nashville PO
DARROW, William J., St-16-22; Pvt G Co 10th TN Inf; 6-16-62 to 7-65; Cumberland City PO
DAUGHARTY, John, Mg-197-3; Pvt A Co 1st TN Inf; 8-2-61 to 9-17-64; 2nd Dist
DAUGHERTY, Albert, Dk-32-5; Sol; Liberty PO
DAUGHERTY, Charles K., Mc-117-1; Pvt E Co 7th TN Mtd Inf; 9-15-64 to 6-18-65; Mecca PO
DAUGHERTY, Edward, Wa-268-3; Johnson City PO; discharge away from home
DAUGHERTY, Elasha, A-9-2; Nancy widow of; Pvt I Co 7th TN Mtd Inf; 11-8-64 to 7-27-65; Podopholine PO; disease of head resulting in his death
DAUGHERTY, John, S-213-3; Pvt H Co 9th TN Cav; 62 to 7-5-65; Robbins PO; gunshot wound, piles & gravil
DAUGHERTY, John, A-9-2; Pvt G Co 7th TN Mtd Inf; 11-8-64 to 7-27-65; Podopholine PO
DAUGHERTY, John, Mc-117-2; Pvt E Co 7th.Mtd Inf; 9-2-64 to 7-27-65; Mecca PO
DAUGHERTY, John B., A-9-2; Pvt A Co 1st TN Inf; 8-2-61 to 9-17-64; Podopholine PO
DAUGHERTY, John H., Jo-149-2; Pvt E Co 13th TN Cav; 9-24-63 to 9-5-65; Mountain City PO; chronic rheumatism
DAUGHERTY, Josiah, Mo-123-1; P-t E Co 7th TN Mtd Inf; 1-23-64 to 7-27-65; Jalapa PO
DAUGHERTY, Moses, A-9-1; Pvt I Co 7th TN Mtd Inf; 11-8-64 to 7-27-65; Podopholine PO
DAUGHERTY, Noah, A-9-3; Mary widow of; Pvt A Co 1st TN Inf; 8-2-61 to 9-17-64; Podopholine PO
DAUGHERTY, Reason, A-9-2; Pvt F Co 7th TN Mtd Inf; 11-8-64 to 7-27-65; Podopholine PO; slight deafness

DAUGHERTY, Thomas F., D-66-1; Pvt K Co 32nd NY Inf; 6-15-61 to 5-5-63; 619 S Colleg, Nashville PO; gun shot wound in face, dimness of sight, deafness, catarrh & rheumatism & piles, ___ ___ bled from the wound
DAUGHERTY, Thomas O., Gi-124-1; Sgt I Co 2nd TN Cav; 11-4-63 to 1-19-65; Marbuts PO
DAUGHERTY, William, A-9-2; Pvt G Co 7th TN Mtd Inf; 11-8-64 to 7-27-65; Podopholine PO; measles resulting in lung disease
DAUGHTREY, Richard A., H-49-10; Sarah J. widow of; Pvt; Daisy PO
DAUGHTY, J. W., La-109-1; Pvt F Co 45th IL Inf; 9-25-64 to 12-8-65; Mockeson PO; diarhoes chronic; served in 7th Cav IL Vol
DAULTON, Isen, Hw-121-1; Pvt K Co 29th TN Inf; 6-1-61 to 5-1-65; Pullum PO; flash wound on the chin
DAVAULT, William, Un-253-3; US Sol; 4th Civil Dist
DAVENPORT, Elizabeth, Ct-39-2; widow?; Pvt; Gap Run PO
DAVENPORT, Gore D., Mg-200-3; 6th Dist
DAVENPORT?, Henry F., We-223-4; Pvt H Co 33rd TN Inf; 9-61 to 2-15-64; Palmersville PO; CONF
DAVENPORT, Isaac N., He-67-2; Pvt C Co 7th TN Cav; 8-28-62 to 6-29-65; Scotts Hill PO; chron. paralysis of right side contracted from effects of war
DAVENPORT, Jacob D., K-172-2; Pvt 6th TN Inf; 4-20-62 to 4-27-65; Knoxville PO
DAVENPORT, James, D-99-3; Cpl A Co 11th TN Inf; 5-63 to 1-65; State Penitentiary PO
DAVENPORT, John R., Ha-115-1; Alanthers Hill PO; CONF
DAVERSON, Jacob, Ru-241-3; Pvt B Co 107th TN Inf; 12-64 to 1-6-66; Murfreesboro PO; ruptured
DAVICE, Brownlow, Ct-41-3; Pvt H Co 13th TN Cav; 9-24-63 to 9-5-65; Turkey Town PO; rhumatism
DAVICE, Phillip, S-212-1; Pvt G Co 7th TN; 11-8-64 to 7-25-65; Hellenwood PO; shot threw left leg
DAVICE, Trave, S-212-1; Pvt H Co 7th TN; 11-1-64 to 8-15-65; Hellenwood PO; sprand leg
DAVID, Henry C., Ru-244-1; Milton PO
DAVID, Mary A., Hw-129-2; widow; Sol; no PO
DAVIDS, William H., Dy-23-1; Pvt F Co 3rd NY Cav; 4-16-61 to __ (4 yrs 6 mos); Dyersberg PO
DAVIDSON, Aaron G., Sh-167-1; H Pvt A Co 6th Ark; 6-17-61 to 63; PO omitted; CONF
DAVIDSON, Ezekiel, Wa-272-1; Cpl L Co 14th KY Cav; 12-20-62 to 3-24-64; Cpl M Co 4th? TN Cav; 3-30-64 to 7-12-65; Harmony PO; heart disease
DAVIDSON, Hugh A., B-2-1; Pvt F Co 41st TN Inf; __ to 4-16-65; Wartrace PO; CONF
DAVIDSON, James, Ha-117-3; Sgt F Co 8th TN Cav; 6-63 to 9-11-65; Sneedville PO
DAVIDSON, James, Mg-200-2; Hannah widow of; Pvt F Co 1st TN Inf; Skene PO
DAVIDSON, John, J-82-2; Mariah widow of; Pvt C Co 1st TN Mtd Inf; 64 to 65; Gainesboro PO; consumption
DAVIDSON, John C., K-179-4; Pvt D Co 6th TN Inf; 4-18-62 to 4-27-65; PO omitted
DAVIDSON, John C., G-64-2; Bradford PO
DAVIDSON, Leroy, Ms-171-1; Sarah wife of; Lt D Co 4th TN Inf; 8-64 to 11-65; Belfast PO
DAVIDSON, Melvina, Mu-191-1; widow; 7th Dist
DAVIDSON, Thomas B., G-70-1; Sgt G Co 15th KY Cav; 1-13-63 to 10-6-63; Dyer PO
DAVIDSON, Thomas W., G-71-1; Cpl L Co 12th TN Inf; 1-5-61 to 6-1-62; Greenfield PO; CONF
DAVIDSON, William A., Ch-17-2; Pvt G Co 51st TN Inf; 62 to 62 (6 mos); McNairy PO; CONF
DAVIDSON, William C., Ro-203-8; Cpl K Co 1st TN Inf; 8-9-61 to 9-17-64; Wheat PO; rheumatism
DAVIDSON, Wm. E., We-220-2; Pvt M Co 13th IL Cav; 12-1-63 to 9-1-65; 4th Civil Dist
DAVIDSON, William I., P-156-2; Pvt A Co 10th TN Cav; 66 (sic) to 63 (9 mos); Lobelville PO
DAVIE, Martin H., Hy-81-2; Brownsville PO; old & rheumatic; discharge with him
DAVIES, Doctor A., Dk-39-5(1); Amanda E. widow of; Pvt A Co 5th TN Cav; 8-4-62 to 2-15-63; Laurel Hill PO; died of disease 2-15-63
DAVIES, Eban, Cf-40-2; Ruth former widow of; Pvt D Co 1st MI Cav; 9-61 to 9-64; Tullahoma PO; Ruth Davies married Davies, ___
DAVIES, L. L., K-176-3; PO omitted

DAVIS, Adair, Me-88-1; Pvt I Co 5th TN Inf; 10-2-63 to 6-30-65; Birchwood PO
DAVIS, Adam (see Caruthers, Adam)
DAVIS, Alexander, D-63-3; Pvt C Co 15th OH Vol; Dec 63 to Apr 66; Nashville PO
DAVIS, Alexander A., Sm-173-2; Sgt B Co 5th TN Cav; 8-1-62 to 1-21-63; Brush Creek PO; discharged on surg. certificate
DAVIS, Allen, Cy-27-5(3); Pvt E Co 1st TN Mtd Inf; 1-12-63 to 1-12-64; Spivey PO
DAVIS, Amey, Ru-243-1; widow of US Sol; PO omitted
DAVIS, Andrew, K-170-2; Pvt L Co 8th TN Cav; 28 Jul 63 to 13 Sep 65; Knoxville PO; head disease for 24 yrs
DAVIS, Andrew, Cy-27-5(3); Pvt D Co 8th TN Mtd Inf; 4-65 to 8-65; Red Springs PO (Macon Co.)
DAVIS, Andrew J., Sh-200-1; Pvt L Co 11th US Cav; 6-11-61 to 8-1-62; rear of Polk St, Memphis PO; prisoner 2 mos & paroled
DAVIS, Anna, Sh-178-4; widow US Sol; 86 Marshall Ave, Memphis PO
DAVIS, Anten, K-167-2; Dora Nickles widow of; Sgt? 1st Hvy TN; 62 to 65; Knoxville PO
DAVIS, Archibald, Sm-173-2; Pvt B Co 5th TN Cav; 8-28-62 to 6-25-65; Brush Creek PO; left arm lame G.S. wound
DAVIS, Archie, T-206-1; alias Archer Langford; Pvt I Co 2nd IL Cav; Fall of 64 to Jun 66 (in prison); Covington PO
DAVIS, Arthur, Sh-195-1; Cpl K Co 61st Col Inf; Memphis PO
DAVIS, Ben Sr., Sh-158-2; Louisa widow of; 63 to died (2 yrs); Memphis PO; died in service, widow receives pension of $108 per year; old and feeble & not able to give details
DAVIS, Ben Jr., Sh-158-2; Pvt K Co 63rd Col Inf; Nov 63 to 9 Jun 66; Memphis PO; no disability, discharge burnt in 66 in riot, unable to give particulars, is feble
DAVIS, Ben J., H-53-4; Sgt F Co 10th or 11th KY Cav; __ to 6-65 (3 yrs); Ridgedale PO; cough & kidney disease
DAVIS, Benjamin, K-182-4; Pvt A Co 10th TN Cav; Sep 61 to 1 Jul 65; Riverdale PO; CONF
DAVIS, Benjamin, Sp-165-3; Pvt E Co 6th TN Mtd Inf; 9-11-64 to 6-12-65; Dunlap PO; received an honorable disc.
DAVIS, Benjamin F., Me-90-3(2); Pvt B Co 4th TN Cav; 3-2-62 to 8-16-65; Meigs PO
DAVIS, Benjamin H., Cr-14-1; Isabel L. widow of; Pvt K Co 2nd TN Mtd Inf; 1 Jan 64 to Apr 20 65; Clarksburg PO
DAVIS, Calvin M., Ch-14-2; Pvt K Co 43rd NC Inf; 5-10-61 to 6-19-65; Sweet Lips PO; in prison Point Lookout 2 mos
DAVIS, Caswell C., Ge-86-1; Pvt M Co 9th TN Cav; 1 Jun 63 to 11 Sep 65; Thula PO; deafness, rheumatism & serofula?
DAVIS, Charles, K-154-1; Pvt; Knoxville PO
DAVIS, Charley, Mu-197-2; Pvt D Co 110th; 63 to May 65; Columbia PO; shot in right leg & left flank and is and inturnel injured man (sic)
DAVIS, Charley, Lk-113-3; SM A Co 3rd US Inf; Dec 12 64 to Dec 12 69; Civil Dist No 5
DAVIS, Colvy, La-115-1; Pvt H Co 20th TN Inf; 1 Aug 62 to 15 Apr 64; Henryville PO; CONF
DAVIS, Daniel, W-291-1; Sol US; Labanon PO
DAVIS, Dave D., Dk-36-3; 9th Civil Dist
DAVIS, David, Gr-78-1; Pvt F Co TN Cav; Spring House PO; inflamatory rheumatism
DAVIS, David H., Sm-173-2; Pvt D Co 4th TN Mtd Inf; 9-20-64 to 8-25-65; Brush Creek PO
DAVIS, David W., Ov-135-1; 11th TN Mtd Inf; Ward PO; Mr Davis was not at home, his family could not give dates
DAVIS, Dennis, Sh-162-2(1); US Sol; Ramsey PO
DAVIS, Dock, D-45-2; 4th Sgt A Co 30th LA Inf; 8-8-62 to 64; Nashville PO
DAVIS, Dock H., Mu-209-5; Pvt A Co 9th TN Cav; Oct 62 to Aug 3 63; Columbia PO; prisoner 1 month New Orleans; CONF
DAVID, Edmond, W1-291-1; Pvt B Co 40th TN; 63 to 65; Laguards PO; wounded at Lebanon, TN, in the leg
DAVIS, Edmond, Gi-127-2; Rachal widow of; Cpl 111th TN Col Inf; Pulaski PO
DAVIS, Eli, Mu-209-3; Pvt; Columbia PO

DAVIS, Eli, Mu-209-6; Pvt; Columbia PO; CONF
DAVIS, Eligah, Sh-189-2; Pvt K Co 6th US Col Hvy Art; Spring 63 to Spring 65; La. Ave, Memphis PO
DAVIS, Ephraim A., Jo-153-2; Lt F Co 3rd NC Inf; 14 Feb 64 to 2 Aug 65; Pvt E Co 13th TN Cav; 21 Sep 63 to 13 Feb 64; Little Doe PO; bronchitis
DAVIS, Fletcher, D-57-2; Pvt Gunboat Mont City; 62 to 65; Nashville PO; wounded in back by shell
DAVIS, Francis, K-168-3; Pvt F Co 3rd TN Inf; 12 Mar 62 to 22 Feb 65; Smithwood PO
DAVIS, Francis M., Sn-261-2(1); Pvt F Co 20th TN Inf; 6-1-61 to 9-7-63; Perdue PO; prisoner at Camp Butler 6 mos; taken oath of allegiance
DAVIS, Francis M., Cl-56-2(1); Margaret widow of; Pvt E Co 2nd TN Inf; 3-22-63 to 8-8-65; Head of Barren PO; died with chronic diarhea
DAVIS, Frank, La-115-2; Pvt; Henryville PO; this entry marked through
DAVIS, Frank M., Dy-25-4; Pvt; 61 to 65; Newbern PO; CONF
DAVIS, Geor W., D-63-3; Pvt I Co 3 th IA Inf; Jul 62 to Aug 65; Nashville PO
DAVIS, George, Sh-169-2; US Sol; 216 Front St, Memphis PO
DAVIS, George, Sh-158-3; Amanda widow of; Pvt 61st Col Inf; Jun 63 to 64 (9 mos); Memphis PO; can learn very little about this case, he died early in Jun 1870
DAVIS, George, D-50-1; Pvt A Co 2nd TN Inf; Nov 64 to Jan 65; 190 Crawford, Nashville PO; wounded in r. leg; papers lost
DAVIS, George, Cy-27-4(2); Pvt E Co 1st TN Mtd Inf; 12-27-63 to 1-5-65; Spivey PO
DAVIS, George Jr., Bo-21-2; Sgt B Co 3rd TN Cav; 9-21-62 to 6-20-65; Ellijay PO
DAVIS, George C., Bo-21-3; Pvt B Co 3rd TN Cav; 9-21 62 to 7-6-65; Ellijay PO
DAVIS, George C., Po-148-1; Pvt A Co 5th TN Mtd Inf; 9-1-64 to 6-26-65; Chestewee Mills PO
DAVIS, George S., Hm-107-4; Pvt E Co 1st US Lt Art; 4 Apr 64 to 31 Mar 66; Springvale PO; blind left eye
DAVIS, George W., Ha-112-1; Lt E Co 8th TN Cav; 23 Sep 63 to 8 Jan 64; Blackwater PO
DAVIS, George W., Wy-171-3; Cpl H Co 6th TN Cav; 9-21-62 to 7-26-65; Sorby PO
DAVIS, George W., Su-243-1; Pvt B Co 4th US Inf; Bristol PO; shot in hip
DAVIS, Gilbert, Sh-174-2; Elizabeth widow of; Pvt E Co 59th US Inf; 154 De Soto St, Memphis PO; lay in hospital several months, died in hospital in early part of 1866
DAVIS, Hamilton, Me-92-1; Pvt G Co 1st TN Hvy Art (Col); Cate PO
DAVIS, Henry, Hw-119-1; Orderly Sgt L Co 8th TN Cav; Sep 63 to Sep 65; Lee Valley PO; rheumatism & short breath
DAVIS, Henry, Sh-150-1; PVt I Co 61st TN Inf; 2 yrs; Bonds PO
DAVIS, Humes I., A-9-5(3); Pvt C Co 3rd TN Mtd Inf; 8-8-64 to 11-30-64; Bull Run PO (Knox Co.); chronic liver disease
DAVIS, Isaac, Sh-200-3; Ella widow of; Pvt D Co 113th US Col Inf; 740 Georgia St, Memphis PO; died in service
DAVIS, Isaac, H-73-5(3); 217 Foster St, Chattanooga PO
DAVIS, Isaac B., O-139-1; PVt; 63 to 64; Protemus PO
DAVIS, J. C., W-194-1; Pvt M Co 5th TN Cav; 10-63 to 8-65; Davenport PO
DAVIS, Jack, D-64-2; 61 to 64; Nashville PO
DAVIS, Jack, Dk-37-1; 5th Civ Dist
DAVIS, Jack, Dk-36-3; 5th Civ Dist
DAVIS, Jackson, Se-227-1; PVt H Co 1st USC Hvy Art; 9 Jun 64 to 31 Nov 66; Trundle's X Roads PO; diarrhea & rheumatism
DAVIS, Jackson, Po-149-1; Pvt A Co 7th AL Cav; 8-28-63 to 6-16-64; Old Fort PO
DAVIS, Jacob, D-64-1; Mattie widow of; Pvt; Nashville PO; killed in war
DAVIS, Jacob A., H-70-2(1); Pvt A Co 1st NY Mtd Rifles; 9-13-64 to 5-8-65; Chattanooga PO; legal residence America, NY
DAVIS, Jacob C., Be-6-1; Cpl C Co 6th TN Inf; 11 Aug 64 to 30 Jun 65; Big Sandy PO
DAVIS, Jacob D., La-111-3; Pvt O Co 1st MS Inf; 1 yr 6 mos; PO omitted
DAVIS, James, Ja-85-5; Pvt L? Co 5th TN Inf; 2-22-62 to 5-15-65; Long Savannah PO; shot through right foot
DAVIS, James, Hw-120-2; Sgt G Co 1st TN Cav; 1 Jun 62 to 5 Jun 65; Eidson PO
DAVIS, James, K-165-2; Pvt I Co 3rd E TN Cav; Sep 63 to 12 Jun 65; Knoxville PO; back an limbs
DAVIS, James, Ro-204-1; Pvt C Co 7th TN Inf; Mar 62 to 63 (1 yr 2 mos); Elverton PO
DAVIS, James, B-4-1; Pvt A Co 40th Col US Reg; 11-63 to 4-66; Bell Buckle PO; sound
DAVIS, James, Gi-127-3; Pvt H Co 1st Reg OHB MD Vol; Sep 16 61 to Oct 25 64; Pulaski PO; contracted epilepsy, prisoner
DAVIS, James, Wl-291-1; Pvt F Co 13th KY; 63 to 65; Lebanon; rheumatism & jaundice, eyes damaged by jaundice
DAVIS, James, Br-12-5; Rachel widow of; McPheron PO; CONF
DAVIS, James A., Mc-109-6; Quartermaster Sgt B Co 3rd TN Cav; 11-16-62 to 6-14-65; Mouse Creek PO; injury of back and resulting atrophy of mussels of same
DAVIS, James A., M-107-3; Pvt E Co 1st TN Mtd Inf; 10-21-63 to 1-22-65; Red Boiling Springs PO; disease of eyes
DAVIS, James B., Je-136-2; PVt B Co 9th TN Cav; 11 Sep 63 to 28 Sep 65; PO omitted
DAVIS, Jas. F., Wa-268-4; Johnson City PO
DAVIS, James H., K-170-2; Pvt A Co 9th TN Cav; Knoxville PO; gun shot in shoulder; rheumatism 20 yrs
DAVIS, James J., Wy-173-2; Sgt H Co 6th TN Cav; 9-18-62 to 7-25-65; Houston PO
DAVIS, James M., H-59-2; Rachael widow of; Sgt 1st TN Bat; 62 to 9-65; Chattanooga PO
DAVIS, James M., Ms-171-1; SgtF Co 3rd R Inf; 17 Oct 64 to 29 Nov 65; Belfast PO
DAVIS, James P., Bo-13-3(1); Pvt I Co 5th TN Inf; 4-1-62 to 7-6-65; Louisville PO; 2 fingers torn off by shell
DAVIS, James R., Ro-204-1; Pvt B Co 2nd TN Inf; 63 to 13 Aug 65; Oliver Springs PO; no discharge produced
DAVIS?, Jasper, Cl-56-2(1); Pvt E Co 2nd TN Inf; 8-9-61 to 10-64; Head of Barren PO; injured testes from mumps, loss of teeth from scurvy
DAVIS, Jim (see Murry, Alferd)
DAVIS, Joe, Sh-200-2; or Joseph Green; Pvt I Co 61st US Col Inf; 7-31-63 to 12-30-65; 6 Polk St, Memphis PO
DAVIS, John, Hu-104-1(2); Pvt 1st Kain.; Aug 62 to Jul 65; McEwen PO; cronic diarhea & rumatis
DAVIS, John, H-69-3; Pvt I Co 1st US Col Hvy Art; 64 to 66; Chattanooga PO
DAVIS, John, H-50-1; Pvt E Co 6th R TN Mtd Inf; 8-16-64 to 6-20-65; Soddy PO
DAVIS, John, We-222-1; Pvt F Co 45th TN Reg; 9 Jul 61 to 16 Jan 63; Gardner PO; CONF
DAVIS, John, Bo-15-3; Pvt L Co 8th TN Cav; 10-10-63 to 12-1-63; Maryville PO
DAVIS, John A., Ro159-2; Pvt G Co 8th TN Cav; Sheffield PO
DAVIS, John B., K-176-1; Pvt K Co 8th MI Cav; 15 Jun 61 to 19 Jul 66; Halls X Roads PO; CONF
DAVIS, Jno. C., Dy-21-1; Pvt B Co 42nd MS Cav; 5 Mar 62 to 64; Chestnut Bluff PO; CONF
DAVIS, John C., Pu-140-1; Pvt TN Inf; 64 to 65; Cookeville PO
DAVIS, John C., Cy-27-1; Pvt A Co 8th KY Mtd Inf; 1-2-65 to 8-17-65; Clementsville PO
DAVIS, John H., Sh-188-1; Pvt US Art; 63 to 65; 60 Mannassas St, Memphis PO
DAVIS, John L., Mg-196-1; Pvt 11th TN Cav; 63 to 64; First Dist
DAVIS, John M., Hd-53-3; Pvt E Co 10th TN Inf; 12 Sep 62 to 3 Jul 65; Coffee Landing PO
DAVIS, John M., Ge-98-4; Sarah J. widow of; Pvt C Co 4th TN Inf; PO omitted; dyspepsia and heart disease
DAVIS, John P., Co-61-4(1); Pvt; Parrottsville PO; Mary A. Stokely widow; CONF

DAVIS, John S., Ge-86-1; Pvt C Co 7th IN Cal; 18 May 64 to 18 Feb 66; Thula PO; right eye out & rheumatism
DAVIS, John T., Ge-90-1; Sgt A Co 3rd MO Inf; 30 Jun 64 to 30 Nov 64; Greeneville PO
DAVIS, John W. P., Sm-173-3; Pvt B Co 5th TN Cav; 8-1-62 to 6-25-65; Brush Creek PO
DAVIS, John W., K-161-6; Sgt B Co 3rd TN Lt Art; 1 Jul 62 to 20 Jul 65; Knoxville PO
DAVIS, John W., Ro-203-8; Pvt G Co 1st TN Inf; 9 Aug 61 to 17 Sep 64; Wheat PO; chronic diarrhea
DAVIS, Jonathan B., Mc-112-4; (the name Moore appears here with no explanation); Pvt A Co 1st TN Cav; 1-24-65 to 9-11-65; Athens PO; shot in the neck
DAVIS, Joseph, D-71-2; Nashville, Market St. PO
DAVIS, Joseph, Hm-109-2; Pvt H Co 7th KY Inf; 22 Sep 61 to 11 Aug 64; Whitesburg PO
DAVIS, Joseph, Ro-206-2; Pvt K Co 9th TN Cav; 1 Jan 65 to 11 Sep 65; Emory Gap PO
DAVIS, Joseph F., Wa-268-2; Johnson City PO; asthma
DAVIS, Joseph N., Wy-173-3; Pvt B Co 2nd TN Mtd Inf--10-15-63 to 10-17-64; Sgt E Co 8th TN Mtd Inf--3-1-65 to 9-1-65; Houston PO
DAVIS, Joseph P., Dk-34-5(4); Pvt A Co 5th TN Cav; 8-9-62 to 6-5-65; Temperance Hall PO; spinal affection & piles
*DAVIS, James K. P., Mu-209-5; Pvt A Co 9th TN Cav; Oct 1 62 to Apr 16 63; Columbia PO; wounded in neck; CONF
DAVIS, Leml., Sh-157-2; Pvt B Co; 63 to ___ (3 mos); Dist 13
DAVIS, Littleton, H-67-2; Pvt A Co 42nd US Col Inf; 65 to 66 (1 yr 2 mos); Chattanooga PO
DAVIS, Littleton, Br-9-4; Pvt A Co 43rd TN Inf; 64 to 66; Cleveland PO
DAVIS, Lizzie (see Anderson, Amos J.)
DAVIS, Louis J., Hw-127-2; Pvt A Co 1st TN Lt Art; 10 Oct 63 to 3 Aug 65; Rogersville PO; small pox & disease of lungs
DAVIS, Manuel, Sh-157-5; Pvt H Co 88th IL; 63 to 65; White Have PO; stomache; I claim that this trouble has made me somwhat disable to som extent in regards to health and labor and I am a man of a large family and growing considerable in age
DAVIS, Manuel, Hy-83-1; Pvt 11th IL; 62 to 65; Brownsville PO; lost discharge
DAVIS, Margaret H. (see Mull, Samuel)
DAVIS, Marion, Mc-114-4; Sarah M. widow of; Pvt A Co 9th TN Cav; 7-15-63 to 9-11-65; Calhoun PO
DAVIS, Martha E. (see Montgomery, James)
DAVIS, Mart., B-22-2; Pvt H Co 3rd TN Cav; 9-63 to 8-3-65; Hebronville PO
DAVIS, Mary (see Duggay, W. H.)
DAVIS, Mary J., D-43-2; Sol widow; Nashville PO
DAVIS, Mathew P., S-214-2; Sarah widow of; Pvt; Glenmary PO; is not a pensioner
DAVIS, Mathew W., Sh-201-2; Pvt A Co 36th AL Inf; 15 Aug 61 to 15 Aug 65; Memphis PO; CONF
DAVIS, Mattie, Fr-120-1; 18th Civil Dist
DAVIS, Milton, T-216-1; Pvt L Co 44th US Inf; 64 to 30 Apr 66; Corona PO
DAVIS, Moses, A-6-4(2); Addaline widow of; Sgt J Co 7th TN Inf; 11-4-64 to 7-23-65; Olivers PO
DAVIS, N. C., De-22-1; Pvt F Co 9th TN Cav; 1 Aug 62 to 5 May 65; Bath Springs PO; CONF
DAVIS, Nathan, Co-67-5; Pvt K Co 8th TN Cav; 10 Sep 63 to 11 Sep 65; Naillon PO
DAVIS, Noel, Mg-197-5; K Co 9th & 11th TN Cav; 63 to 65; Nemo PO
DAVIS, Owen E., Ct-41-4; Pvt TN Cav; 62 to 65; Keensburgh PO; CONF
DAVIS, Peter, D-99-1; PVt G Co 13th TN Inf; Oct 10 63 to Jan 10 66; Bakers PO
DAVIS, Phillip, Ge-96-1; Cpl C Co 4th TN Inf; 63 to 65 (2 yrs 4 mos 25 days); Limestone PO; nerves shattered
DAVIS, Presley J., Sh-174-2; Pvt K Co 11th MO Cav; about 75 to 8-65; 102 Hernando St, Memphis PO; shot in right arm--crippled rheumatism
DAVIS, R. N., Mr-97-2; Pvt G Co 5th TN Cav; 8-29-61 to 9-25-65; Jarman? PO; shot in the head--eye out, shot in the side & arm
DAVIS, Ransom J., A-9-1; Pvt C Co 2nd TN Inf; 8-61 to 10-64; Ligias PO; rheumatism, discharge in hands of pension attorney
DAVIS, Rector, Po-148-1; Pvt A Co 5th TN Mtd Inf; 9-1-64 to 6-26-65; Chestewee Mills PO; cronic diarrhea
DAVIS, Rhubin P., Dk-37-1; 31st Civ Dist
DAVIS, Robbert, Mu-210-2; Eliza widow of; Pvt; 2 yrs; Spring Hill PO
DAVIS, Robbert, Ms-183-1; Pvt I Co 111th US Col Inf; 3-1-64 to 10-65; Comenville PO; old, feeble & poor, no pension, ought to have a pension
DAVIS, Robert, Po-148-1; Pvt A Co 5th TN Mtd Inf; 9-1-64 to 6-26-65; Chestewee Mills PO
DAVIS, Robert N., M-107-2; Eliza M. widow of; PVt E Co 1st TN Mtd Inf; 10-28-63 to 1-27-65; Walnut Shade PO; disease of lungs
DAVIS, Robt. P., Sh-201-2; Pvt F Co 12th KY Cav; 13 Aug 62 to 16 Nov 63; Memphis PO
DAVIS, Rubin A., Mg-197-2; Lt Col 11th TN Cav; 10 Mar 63 to Oct 64; Wartburg PO; wounds in war, 3 in number
DAVIS, Samuel, Ja-85-3; Pvt I Co 5th TN Inf; 10-2-63 to 6-30-65; Thatcher PO
DAVIS, Samuel, Hn-73-1; Pvt Co E 110th IL; 63 to 64; Como PO; no disabilaty incured at Fort Pillow
DAVIS, Saml. B., Ge-97-1; Pvt C Co 4th TN Inf; Apr to May 2 65 (1 yr 2 mos 27 days); Locust Spring PO; consumptive
DAVIS, Sandy, D-67-2; Pvt A Co 113th Col Inf; Nov 63 to Nov 66; Nashville PO
DAVIS, Sarah J., Dy-29-1; widow US Sol; 9th Civil Dist
DAVIS, Seth B., Dy-27-3; Pvt I Co 15th TN Cav; Sep 62 to 20 Mar 65; Ro Ellen PO; prisoner at Camp Douglas; CONF
DAVIS, Simon P., G-63-1; Mary widow of; Pvt C Co 1? IL Cav; Oct 62 to 64; Milan PO; fistula, died from disease contracted
DAVIS, Solamon, Ms-183-1; 17th Civil Dist; dropsy 3 yrs
DAVIS, Squire, Sh-189-2; Memphis PO; CONF?
DAVIS, Stephen (see Mays, Stephen)
DAVIS, Stephen E., S-214-3; Pvt C Co 11th TN Cav; 62 to 14 Sep 65; Robbins PO
DAVIS, Sullivan W., Ja-86-3; Pvt B Co 1st TN Art; 10-18-62 to 7-65; Long Savannah PO; shoulder broken by horse while in service near Rogersville, TN
DAVIS, Swillivan, Ja-84-3; Pvt B Co 7th TN Lt Art; 4-7-63 to 7-10-65; Normans Store PO; cronic diarrhea
DAVIS, Syntha, P-150-2; widow US Sol; 1st Dist
DAVIS, T. D., Hy-82-1; Pvt C Co 8th TN Cav; Sep 61 to Sep 65; Rudolph PO
DAVIS, Theodore, Ma-128-2; 15th Civil Dist
DAVIS, Thomas, Ca-25-2; Pvt E Co 4th TN Mtd Inf; 8-64 to 8-65; Gassoway PO
DAVIS, Thomas, Sh-155-1; Pvt B Co 63rd TN Inf; 27 Jul 64 to Feb 65; Germantown PO
DAVIS, Thomas, W-196-1; Sgt A Co 4th MI Cav; 8-5-62 to 7-5-65; Dibril PO; deafness, CONF
DAVIS, Thomas, Mc-118-2; Pvt F Co 4th eN Cav; 12-22-62 to 6-10-65; Joshua PO; chronic diarrhea 25 yrs
DAVIS, Thomas D., U-247-1; Cpl E Co 1st TN Lt Art; 28 Sep 63 to 1 Aug 65; Erwin PO; deafness, rheumatism into back
DAVIS, Thomas D., Ja-86-3; Sgt E Co 5th TN Mtd Inf; 64 to 6-65; Snowhill PO; chronic diarhea
DAVIS, Thomas H. A., K-181-4(1); H Co 4th TN Cav; 24 May 63 to 19 Jul 65; Knoxville PO
DAVIS, Thomas J., Dk-34-5(4); Pvt K Co 5th TN Cav; 5-18-63 to 8-14-65; Dowelltown PO
DAVIS, Thomas J., Ch-17-2; Annie E. Allen widow of; Pvt B Co 49th IL Inf; 11-4-62 to 9-9-65; Masseyville PO; liver complaint, died 4-5-1878
DAVIS, W. N., Bo-22-3; Pvt A Co 6th TN Inf; 3-1-62 to 4-8-65; Gamble's Store PO
DAVIS, W. S., Gi-139-2; Ofe (officer?) I Co 2nd TN Cav; 64 to 65; Bercheers PO; CONF
DAVIS, Welcome H., Mg-199-3; Pvt K Co 30th KY Inf; 64 to 65; Glen Mary PO (Scott Co.)
DAVIS, Wiley M., Hw-119-3(1); Pvt 3rd TN Cav; Sep 63 to ___; Fisher's Creek PO

DAVIS, William, W1-291-1; Pvt F Co 13th KY; 63 to 65; Lebanon PO; horse fall during war, eyes damaged by Wood in 1882
DAVIS, William (see Burnett, William A.)
DAVIS, William, K-179-3; Pvt F Co 1st TN Hvy Art; 12 May __ to 12 May __ (2 yrs); Concord PO
DAVIS, William, K-182-1; Pvt D Co 4th NC Cav; 19 May 63 to 28 Jun 65; Shooks PO; disabled 1864, shot in left leg
DAVIS, William, Ha-116-3(1); 1st Sgt G Co 8th TN Inf; 1 Mar 63 to 30 Jun 66; Lee Valley PO; cronic rumatism
DAVIS, Wm., D-64-5; Katie Jackson widow of; Nashville PO
DAVIS, William, R-161-6; Louisa widow of; Pvt G Co 5th TN; Dayton PO; discharge lost
DAVIS, William A., Co-62-2; Pvt K Co 2nd TN Inf; 8 Aug 62 to Mar 65; Hartsville PO
DAVIS, William A., H-51-5; Pvt E Co 6th TN Inf; 9-12-64 to 9-22-65; Hill City PO
DAVIS, William B., Hd-50-5; Pvt F Co 6th TN Cav; 12-2-62 to 7-26-65; Nixon PO
DAVIS, William B., Ha-112-1; Maj E Co 8th TN Cav; 23 Sep 63 to 25 Jan 65; Blackwater PO
DAVIS, William C., Dk-34-3; Cpl C Co 5th TN Cav; 12-1-63 to 8-24-65; Dowelltown PO; back, hips & ankle, heart
DAVIS, William A., Mg-196-1; Rebecca widow of; Pvt; First Dist
DAVIS, William F., K-168-1; Pvt C Co 6th TN Inf; 18 Apr 62 to 27 Apr 65; Knoxville PO
DAVIS, William G., Pu-145-2; Capt A Co 5th Cav Vol; Fancher's Mills PO; discharge lost
DAVIS, William G., W-298-1; Pvt B Co 5th TN Cav; 2 Aug 62 to 13 Dec 62; Alexandria PO; lung disease or affectious, suffering for 25 yrs
DAVIS, William H., Wy-175-1; Pvt F Co 6th TN Cav; 12-2-62 to 7-26-65; Cypress Inn PO; eyes affected from liver, wears glasses
DAVIS, William J., Fr-107-1; Capt A Co 5th TN Cav; Jul 21 62 to Aug 22 65; Winchester PO; ruptured and broken leg
DAVIS, William K., Cr-19-1; Pvt M Co 6th TN Cav; 7-31-62 to 7-26-65; Buxter PO
DAVIS, William M., C-33-3; Pvt G Co 49th KY Inf; 10-1-63 to 12-26-64; Newcomb PO
DAVIS, William M., Bo-21-3; Pvt A Co 3rd TN Cav; 8-10-62 to 8-3-65; Cox PO
DAVIS, Wm. M., O-139-1; Nancy E. widow of; Pvt; 63 to 64; Protemus PO
DAVIS, William R., Mc-112-7; 1st Lt 5th TN Mtd Inf; 9-23-64 to __; Athens PO
DAVIS, William R., Fe-41-2; Pvt B Co 2nd TN Inf; 62 to 65; Travisville PO
DAVIS, William T., Dy-25-4; Pvt E Co 6th TN Cav; 61 to 65; Newbern PO; CONF
DAVIS, Woodson R., Br-11-2; 7th Civil Dist
DAVIS, Zebulan, Bo-12-3(1); Pvt C Co 8th TN Cav; 10-4-63 to 9-11-65; Millers Cove PO
DAVIS, __, Hw-134-2; Sally widow of; 20th Civil Dist
DAVISH, Luthur, H-56-2; Pvt E Co 79th PA Inf; 2-9-64 to 7-12-65; East End PO
DAVY, Frank, Hd-54-1; Sgt C Co 8th KY Col Hvy Art; 24 Mar 64 to Feb 15 66; Saltillo PO; kidney
DAVY, William, Mt-135-1; Pvt 14th TN Inf; 63 to 65; Jordan Springs PO; prisoner
DAWKINS, Kearney, Sh-174-1; Sgt B Co 11th US Col Inf; 3-1-64 to 1-12-66; 155 Linden St, Memphis PO
DAWLEY, Jesse, H-49-2; Harriett C. widow of; Pvt E Co 90th NY Vol; 9-20-64 to 6-30-65; Red Bank PO
DAWN, Henry C., S-213-3; Pvt F Co 1st TN Inf; 9 Aug 61 to 17 Sep 64; Glenmary PO
DAWSEN, Drury, Co-62-2; Elizabeth widow of; Pvt D Co 1st TN Cav; 26 Jan 63 to 19 Jun 65; Help PO; ingenial hernia
DAWSEY, Daniel, Sh-162-2(1); US Sol; Ramsey PO
DAWSON, Abraham, Co-61-2(1); Pvt D Co 1st TN Cav; 25 Jan 63 to 19 Jun 65; Parrottsville PO
DAWSON, Alexander, Co-69-6(1); Pvt C Co 8th TN Inf; 1 Jan 63 to 3 Jun 65; Driskill PO; non as remark

DAWSON, Alferd, Co-62-2; Pvt D Co 1st TN Cav; 1 Jan 63 to Jun 64 (2 yrs 6 mos); Help PO; ingered by a horse
DAWSON, Cato, Mu-200-2; Cpl E Co 111th TN Inf; 63 to 65; Terry PO
DAWSON, Charles, La-115-2; Pvt D Co 111th IN Vol; 6 Sep 61 to 19 Sep 64; Summertown PO; back wond by bayonet
DAWSON, David, Co-61-2(1); Pvt D Co 1st TN Cav; 25 Jun 63 to 9 Jun 65; Parrottsville PO; leg broke
DAWSON, David H., H-56-6; Pvt K Co 1st WV Cav; 63 to 65; St. Elmo PO
DAWSON, Edward, K-170-2; Pvt D Co 127th OH Inf; 62 to 65; Knoxville PO
DAWSON, Elijah L., Lo-191-3; Pvt K Co 2nd TN Cav; Morganton PO
DAWSON, Eugene, Ma-127-1; Pvt D Co 45th IL Inf; Feb 19 64 to Jul 20 65; Jackson PO; contracted rhumatism which caused amputation of right leg
DAWSON, Henry, Br-10-2; Pvt P Co 16th OH Hp? Bat; 9-8-64 to 6-8-65; Cleveland PO
DAWSON, Isaac, Co-61-2(1); Pvt C Co 8th TN Cav; 1 Jan 63 to __; Parrottsville PO
DAWSON, John, Lo-191-2; Morganton PO; CONF
DAWSON, John W., Mt-145-1; Pvt E Co 43rd OH Inf; 10-15-64 to 7-18-65; Palmyra PO
DAWSON, Lewis N., T-218-1; Cpl G Co 1st AL Cav; 5 Mar 63 to 1 Jan 64; Covington PO
DAWSON, Robert A., K-172-2; 1st Lt; Knoxville PO; CONF
DAWSON, Warren, Mu-201-1; Pvt E Co 111th TN Inf; 10 Feb 64 to 30 Apr 66; Mt. Pleasant PO; pistol shot in left arm, suffers from ___ wounds all the time
DAWSON, William, Sh-195-1; Fort Kenan; Memphis PO
DAWSON, William D., H-69-3; Pvt; Chattanooga PO; CONF
DAY, Alfred A., Mg-199-1; Sgt F Co 8th MN Inf; 15 Aug 62 to 27 Jul 65; Sunbright PO; chronic diarrhoea & piles
DAY, Benjamin, Br-11-2; Pvt K Co 1st US Hvy Art; 8-64 to 3-66; 7th Civil Dist
DAY, Charles D., Cf-42-1; Sgt F Co 15th IL Inf; 8-61 to 6-65; Hickerson PO
DAY, David A., Br-9-1; Mary J. widow of; Sgt C Co 3rd IA Cav; 8-29-61 to 9-20-62; Cleveland PO
DAY, Felix G., Hm-106-2; Pvt A Co 12th TN Cav; 5 Feb 63 to 7 Oct 65; Chestnut Bloom PO
DAY, James, Je-140-1; Pvt B Co 1st TN Cav; 62 to Aug 64; Lucilla PO; rumatism, discharge lost
DAY, James R., Gage-86-1; 1st Sgt C Co 8th TN Inf; 1 Jan 63 to 30 Jun 65; Thula PO; desease of stomach
DAY, James T., K-186-4; Pvt E Co 1st TN Cav; Balls Camp PO
DAY, Marion, H-54-2(3); Sgt F Co 81st OH Inf; 1-1-64 to 7-13-65; 1710 Market St, Chattanooga PO; rheumatism, loss in part of hearing in both ears
DAY, Mary E., Ct-39-3; widow; Johnson City PO
DAY, Mikial, Ge-89-3; Nancy A. widow of; Pvt A Co 12th TN Cav; 9 Feb 63 to 7 Oct 65; Marvin PO
DAY, Samuel, Jo-151-1; Pvt H Co 2nd NC Inf; 15 Apr 65 to 16 Aug 65; Stump Knob PO; piles -diarrhora-rheumatism
DAY, William, Cy-28-2; Pvt B Co 8th TN Inf; 3-63 to 4-64; Butlers Landing PO; could not give dates
DAYBERRY, Thomas, K-154-4; Knoxville PO
DAYTON, J. H., L-105-1; Pvt; 7th Civil Dist
DEADERICK, Enslee, K-182-1; Pvt I Co 2nd TN Cav; Jun 61 to Apr 65; Shooks PO; disabled 1864; rheumatism, heart disease; CONF
DEADERICK, Oakley, K-182-2; Pvt I Co 2nd TN Cav; 61 to 64; Shook PO; CONF
DEAKENS, David R., Mr-96-3(2); Sol US; 3rd Dist
DEAKINS, Richard M. K., Wa-273-1; Pvt M Co 8th TN Cav; 27 Jun 64 to 19 May 65; Morning Star PO; gunshot
DEAL, Henry E., O-138-4; P t; 14th Civil Dist
DEAL, Jordon, Mo-129-2; Pvt F Co 2nd OH Inf; 61 to 65; Lomotley PO
DEAN, David, Mu-196-2; Nancy Johnson formerly widow of; Columbia PO
DEAN, George W., Cr-8-1; PVt B Co 14th TN; Jun 28 61 to Jun 28 65; Maury City PO; CONF

DEAN, Hiram, Hw-132-4; Pvt D Co 1st TN Cav; 15 Apr 62 to 15 Apr 65; Otes PO; nasal catarrh & bronchitis
DEAN, James, P-156-3; Pvt 20th TN Inf; 7-20-61 to 10-62; Lobelville PO; wounded in foot, leg and shoulder; CONF
DEAN, John H., Ha-111-2; Pvt E Co Brittalian (sic) VA Cav; Sep 62 to Jan 64; Upper Clinch PO; CONF
DEAN, LeGrand B., D-79-2; 2nd Ast Engineer, Seaman; 2 or 3 yrs; Nashville PO; unable to get exact facts
DEAN, Peter, F-43-2; Pvt F Co 59th TN; Jun 1 63 to Jan 66; Collierville PO
DEAN, Robert T., Ge-88-2; Sarah H. widow; Pvt G Co 8th TN Inf; 62 to 64; Bulls Gap PO; family dont know what decease
DEAN, Rufus, B-4-1; Bell Buckle PO
DEAN, William A., Hm-109-2; Pvt A Co 8th TN Cav; 11 Jun 63 to 11 Sep 65; Whitesburg PO
DEAN, William R., Mo-125-1; Pvt H Co 29th TN Mtd Inf; 9-64 to 12-24-64; Gudger PO
DEANE, James M., Hs-129-2; Pvt A Co 1st TN Art; 4 Sep 63 to 3 Aug 65; Mooresville PO; rhumitism, hart trouble, sight
DEARING, John H., Cy-26-2; Pvt L Co 8th TN Cav; 3-62 to 9-16-65; Rocktown PO
DEARING, Noah, Pu-141-1; Cpl K Co 1st TN Inf; 10-8-64 to 7-22-65; Cookville PO; chronic rheumatism, discharged at expiration of time
DEARING, Theodore C., Mr-99-4; Sol US; Jasper PO
DEARING, William J., Me-107-1; Pvt G Co 9th KY Inf; 9-61 to 8-62; Pvt A Co 8th TN Mtd Inf; 2-10-65 to 8-17-65; Riddleton PO; rheumatism & heart disease, now drawing pension
DEARMAN, John P., W-192-2; Pvt B Co 1st WV Art; 11-1-61 to 1-18-64; Viala PO
DEARMOND, John T., Br-9-3; Capt E Co 5th TN Mtd Inf; 9-64 to 8-65; Cleveland PO
DEARSTONE, C. C., Ge-91-5; Cpl F Co 4th TN Inf; 6 Apr 63 to 16 May 65; Greeneville PO; piles & liver & kidney trouble
DEARSTONE, Jacob, Ge-90-3; Pvt F Co 4th TN Inf; 6 Apr 63 to Oct 63; Greenville PO; indigistion & piles; exposure in servis
DEATHRAGE, Alexander, Ge-98-1; Pvt G Co 8th TN Inf; 5 Jun 63 to __ (2 yrs); PO omitted; general debility
DEATOR, William H., Sh-189-4; Pvt F Co 3rd IL Cav; 5-20-64 to 10-65; Memphis PO
DEAVER, Levi L., H-61-4; Pvt D Co 97th OH Inf; 9-62 to 4-9-65; Chattanooga PO; shot in right side
DEBAUSK, Elisha, Ge-87-1; Pvt G Co 4th TN Inf; 6 mos; Timberridge PO
DEBERRY, Henry E., Ca-24-2; Sgt K Co 52nd KY Mtd Inf; 12-14-63 to 3-11-65; Gassaway PO; stiffness, pain left hipp & side, relapse from measles in the service
DEBERRY, James, Ca-24-1; Pvt K Co 52nd KY Cav; 3-62 to 3-64; Talvine PO; right arm flesh wound, phthisic, disabled for work
DEBERRY, Lafayette, Ch-18-2; TN Cav; PO omitted; CONF
DEBERRY, Mail J., Ch-18-2; Pvt; PO omitted; CONF
DEBO, Bob, Wl-290-1; PVtt K Co 27th OH; May 1 64 to Aug 1 65; Lebanon PO; discharged
DEBO, Peter, Sn-259-1; Mary A. widow of; Pvt C Co 40th __; 10-8-63 to 5-2-65; Bethpage PO
DEBORD, William H., Gr-71-2; Cpt C Co 8th TN Cav; 18 May 63 to 11 Sep 65; Jarmine PO
DEBRO, Sam, Mu-189-1; alias William Vaner; Pvt B Co 15th Inf; 7-64 to 4-10-66; Hurricane Switch PO
DeBUCK, Andrew J., Co-60-1; Mary E. widow of; Co K 8th TN; 4 mos; Peanut PO; ruptured, cannot ascertain in full
DECK, Joseph F., Ov-135-1; Sgt K Co 4th TN Cav; 3-15-65 to 8-25-65; Eagle Creek PO
DECK, Nin H., Ov-138-1; Pvt I Co 1st TN Inf; 12-1-64 to 7-22-65; 10th Civil Dist
DECKARD, Robert J., M-106-2(1); Pvt A Co 8th TN Inf; 10-9-64 to 8-15-65; Lafayette PO; lung disease, pension appl. for
DECKER, Daniel S., Je-142-2; Pvt I Co 45th OH Inf; 13 Dec 63 to 23 Aug 65; New Market PO; gun shot--right heel and ankle, transferred to 2nd Bat N.R.C. 93 Co
DECKER, Frederick, D-44-2(1); Wagoner B Co 1st OH; 8-15-62 to 6-9-65; Nashville PO; rhumatism
DECKER, William B., Cy-27-1; Pvt I Co 52nd KY Mtd Inf; 12-63 to 3-65; Clementsville PO
DEDMON, Thos. H., Dy-27-2; Pvt F Co 42nd NC Inf; 12 Aug 63 to 12 Jun 65; Tatemville PO; imprisoned 3 mos; CONF
DEDRICK, George, Mc-112-6; Pvt I Co 1st US Art TN; 7-12-64 to 3-21-66; Athens PO; relaps of measles
DEEM, Quindom A., Hi-86-1; Duck River, Main PO
DEES, Eli, Un-257-3; Pvt F Co 3rd TN Inf; Feb 12 62 to Mar 2 65; New Prospect PO; shot in shoulder, broke his foot?
DEES, Isaac, Sh-159-4; Cathern widow of; Cpl; Memphis PO
DEESON, Sidney F., Sh-159-4; Pvt MS Inf; 63 to 65; Memphis PO; CONF
DEFORD, George W., Lo-193-1; Pvt E Co 3rd TN Mtd Inf; 15 Jul 64 to 30 Nov 64; Unitia PO; disease of left leg and thigh
DEFORD, James P., Hd-49-1; Pvt A Co 2nd TN Inf; Oct 63 to Oct 14 64; Olive Hill PO; rheumatism & piles
DeFORD, Risden D., Hd-49-2; Capt H Co 6th TN Cav; 4 Jul 62 to 26 Jul 65; Olive Hill PO; gun shot wound in left thigh
DeFOREST, Sylvester, Fr-120-1; Pvt E Co 1st MI Cav; Mar 6 65 to Aug 65; Sewanee PO
DEGEER, William, Cl-48-2; Sarah widow of; Pvt B Co 34th KY; 3 yrs 20 days; Pleasant PO; stabed in r nee with bayonet, the widow dont know date of E & D
DEGERN?, Hezekiah, Ge-98-5; Pvt A Co 1st TN Cav; 26 Mar 62 to 9 Apr 65; Jeroldstown PO; chronic diarhea
DEGRAFFREAD, James, Col, D-45-1; Pvt I Co 12th US Col Inf; 8-12-63 to 1-16-66; Nashville PO
DeHART, Isaac N., D-60-2; 1317 Grundy St, Nashville PO; white
DUHUFF, Ames, K-184-1; Pvt I Co 9th IN Inf; 1 Apr 61 to 11 Apr 64; Riverdales PO
DeJARNETT, John (see West, John)
DELAMITES, William·H., R-161-4; Pvt C Co 1st MI Art; 6-13-64 to 5-10-65; Dayton PO
DELANEY, Edward M., H-71-1; sailor; 62 to 65; Chattanooga PO
DELANEY, John, Mc-114-4; Pvt B Co 14th TN Inf; Santford PO
DELANEY, Sherwood, Ro-205-2; Pvt; Rockwood PO
DELANEY, Thomas, Ro-205-2; Pvt; Kingston PO
DELANEY, Toursaint L. O., D-60-3; Pvt D Co 54th MA Vol; 63 to 65; 1309 Hardee St, Nashville PO; white
DELANIE, George, K-167-5; Pvt E Co; 65 to May 65; Knoxville PO
DELANY, John J., Ro-208-3; Pvt A Co 2nd TN Inf; 11 Aug 61 to 14 Jun 65; Kingston PO; rheumatism
DELANY, Robt. H., Ro-208-3; Pvt A Co 5th TN Inf; 25 Feb 62 to 12 Jun 65; Keyston PO
DELASS?, George W., Ro-202-5; Pvt F Co 1st TN Cav; 11 Sep 63 to 4 Aug 64; Cave Creek PO; no disability; CONF
DELBRIDGE, George, D-70-3; Pvt 100th __; Oct 14 65 to Dec 28 66; 917 S. High St, Nashville PO; rheumatism
DELFFS, Arnold, B-20-1; Hospital Steward 5th TN Cav; 8-22-62 to 8-14-65; Bedford PO
DELINS, Charles H., Mg-197-4; Margaret T. widow of; Hospital Steward 3rd NC; Wartburg PO
DELK, Wilkin, Col, Hi-86-1; Pvt A Co 10th TN; 63 to 64; 3rd Dist; Wilkin Delk Col. free from wond and disease
DELOCH, James, Ct-40-3; Pvt A Co 13th TN Cav; 9-22-63 to 9-5-65; Elizabethton PO; liver & kidney disease
DE LONG, Thomas J., Ce-20-2; 2nd Lt E Co 24th OH Inf; 1-61 to __ (3 yrs 8 mos 16 days); PO omitted
DELORAS, James, Bo-21-1; Pvt A Co 6th TN Inf; 3-8-62 to 4-27-65; Veeba PO
DELOZIER, Campbell, Mg-196-4; US Sol; 10th Dist
DELOZIER, George H., Ro-206-3; Pvt B Co 5th TN Inf; 27 Feb 62 to 28 Mar 65; Emory Gap PO
DELOZIER, George L., Se-228-2(3); Pvt H Co 3rd TN Cav; 4 Jan 64 to 12 Jun 65; New Knob Creek PO

DELP, James, Ha-117-3; Pvt E Co 8th TN Cav; 23 Sep 63 to 11 Sep 65; Sneedville PO; disease of breast
DEMAR?, Thomas, Wl-302-2; Permelia V. Leeman widow of; Sgt H Co 4th TN Mtd Inf; Nov 1 64 to Aug 25 65; PO omitted
DEMARCUS, Amos, K-177-2; Sol US; PO omitted
DEMEES, Samuel T., H-62-2; Pvt I Co 64th OH Vol Inf; 11-61 to 4-65; 309 West Sixth, Chattanooga PO
DEMONBREUN, John R., Rb-228-2; 1st Lt H Co 30th TN Inf; Crunk PO; CONF
DEMONBREUN, Timothy, Rb-228-2; Pvt; 61 (6 mos); Springfield PO; CONF
DEMORRIS, Flaven, H-72-3(2); Ammunition Corps; Chattanooga PO
DEMOSS, Henry H., Ro-208-2; Pvt A Co 6th TN Inf; 25 Feb 62 to 4 Apr 65; Moris Gap PO; lung disease
DENISON, Jas. H., Je-135-2; Pvt; Dumplin PO; rheumatism; CONF
DENISON, Martha E., Mr-102-1; widow; Pvt B Co 6th TN Cav; 6-4-63 to 7-26-65; South Pittsburg PO (see Kelly, Jordon)
DENISON, Robert, Je-135-2; Pvt; Dumplin PO; shot in elbow; CONF
DENN, John M., Ch-13-2; Civ. Dist #2
DENNEY, Thomas W., Ja-84-2; Madra M. widow of; 1st Lt G Co 5th TN Inf; 3-1-62 to 5-15-65; Harrison PO
DENNEY, Wm. H. H., Su-238-1; Cpl H Co 13th TN Cav; 24 Sep 63 to 5 Sep 65; Piney Flats PO; chronic diarrhea and resulting piles and desease of chest, results of measles
DENNIS, Allen, Co-67-3; Nancy widow of; Pvt C Co 3rd TN Cav; 1 May 63 to ___; Cosby PO; died Apr 4, 1865
DENNIS, Cary, Co-67-3; Cpl I Co 62nd TN Inf; 25 Oct 62 to Jul 63; Cosby PO; captured & parolled Vicksburgh; CONF
DENNIS, Samuel B., H-54-3; Sgt D Co 148th PA; 8-19-62 to 1-31-65; Sgt H Co 148th OH Inf; 4-18-61 to 7-26-65; Sherman Heights PO; contracted rheumatism
DENSIN, Richard, Fr-115-1; this man has lost his discharge and has no information; 1 yr 4 mos; Cowan PO
DENSON, James B., H-58-3; Minda widow of; Pvt H Co 12th TN Cav; Sale Creek PO; died in hospital
DENSON, Thiela (see Jehles, John B.)
DENT, Benjamin C., We-226-1; Pvt L Co 6th TN Cav; 1 Jun 62 to 26 Jul 65; Sharon PO
DENT, George W., We-226-1; Pvt L Co 6th TN Cav; 20 Aug 62 to 25 Jul 65; Sharon PO
DENTON, Gideon F., Br-14-3; Pvt H Co 2nd TN Vol; 12-7-62 to 6-18-63; Black Fox PO; pheiser palmononia
DENTON, James C., Br-14-3; Pvt H Co 7th TN Inf; 12-7-62 to 5-65; Cleveland PO; piles & general disability, discharged for general disability
DENTON, Jero P., Me-90-2(2); Sgt Major H Co 5th TN Inf; 3-27-62 to 5-20-65; Goodfield PO
DENTON, John, Mo-129-2; Pvt B Co 11th TN Inf; 63 to 65; Loco PO
DENTON, John, Je-147-2; Pvt M Co 2nd TN Cav; Nov 62 to 6 Jul 65;; Shady Grove PO; paralyzed
DENTON, John H., A-6-3(1); Pvt Co B 16th TN Inf; 4-21-61 to 1-65; Olivers PO; CONF
DENTON, Jno T., D-50-2; Cpl & 1st Sgt F, D & H Cos. 25th KY, 17th KY & 48? I Inf; Nov 17 61, Nov 20 62 to Apr 26 65, Sep 63 to Dec 19 64; 519 Jefferson, Nashville (at present); wounded in r leg
DENTON, Thos., P-151-3; Pvt E Co 2nd TN Mtd Inf; 64 to 65; Linden PO
DENTON, Thomas, Co-66-1; Pvt K Co 2nd TN Cav; 1 Nov 62 to 6 Jul 65; Birdsville PO; measels in left brest & lungs
DENTON, William, Hm-208-4(3); Pvt A Co VA Inf; 62 to 65; Russellville PO; CONF
DENTON, William, Je-147-1; Pvt M Co 2nd TN Cav; 8 Nov 62 to 6 Jul 65; Shady Grove PO
DENTON, William H., Wa-274-2; Pvt H Co 8th TN Cav; Jonesboro PO
DEPEW, Elbert E., Su-241-2; he wasent at home; Pvt I Co 8th TN Cav; Slaughter PO
DEPEW, Lilburn W., Wa-264-1; Pvt I Co 8th TN Cav; 18 Sep 63 to 11 Sep 65; Jonesboro PO; shot through right thigh, discharged on sur. cert.

DEPEW, Robt. E., Wa-271-2; Pvt E Co 1st KY Lt Art; 28 Sep 63 to 5 Oct 64; Jonesboro PO; injured back, diarhea & lungs
DEPEW, William D., Su-240-1; Pvt K Co 8th US Cav; 2 Sep 63 to 11 Sep 65; Butterfly PO; catar of the head
DEPEW, William W., Wa-272-3; Pvt, Mariner; Free Hill PO; spinal disease for 24 yrs
DERBY, George W. (see Wason, Clyde)
DERETT, Preston, H-56-7; Arvilla widow of; Pvt K Co 97th NY Inf; ___ to 5-6-65 (2 yrs); St. Elmo PO
DERRICK, Erastus L., Mc-117-2; Pvt A Co 7th TN Mtd Inf; 9-6-64 to 7-27-65; Mortimer PO
DERRICK, Maranda J., Mc-111-1; Pvt A Co 7th TN Mtd Inf; 9-18-64 to 7-27-___ (1 yr 10 mos 27 days); Nonaburg PO
DERRICK, William F., Me-92-4(1); Sarah J. widow of; Pin Hook PO; could not answer correct
DERRYBERRY, Wesly M., Hd-62-3; Sousan C. widow of; Capt Co ___ 7th TN Cav; Spring 62 to died in Andersonville Prison; Chesterfield PO
DERRYBURY, Cyntha, He-59-1; widow US Sol; PO omitted
DERSTINE, Joseph K., Di-34-2; 1st Sgt H Co 4th Col Inf; 12-13-61 to 11-30-65; Dickson PO; re-enlisted veteran
DESARN?, Elisha, L-166-2; Pvt C Co 2nd TN Cav; 27 Jul 62 to 6 Jul 65; Knoxville PO; indigestion, chronic diarrhea
DeSHIELDS, William, Rb-221-2; Pvt G Co 8th TN; 17 May 61 to Jan 1 63; Adams Station PO; CONF
DEUNEY, Samuel, Sm-174-1; Pvt G Co 4th TN Inf; 11-1-64 to 8-25-65; New Middleton PO
DEVANEY, Thomas W., Ro-201-1; Pvt K Co 79th IL Inf; 5 Aug 62 to 29 Oct 65; Kingston PO
DEVASIER, Alexander L., Rb-219-1; Pvt L Co KY Reg; 62 to 63; Black Jack PO; Morgan's Brigade, KY; CONF
DEVASIER, Alexander L., Rb-219-1; PVt I Co MO Reg; Jun 61 to Sep 61; Black Jack PO; CONF
DEVAULT, H. C., R-160-1; Pvt A Co 9th TN; 6-11-63 to 9-11-65; 7th Civil Dist
DEVENAUGH, Daniel D., Sh-151-1; Cpl E Co 2nd MN Inf; 21 Jan 61 to 25 Aug 62; Arlington PO; defective eyesight & lung? disease, discharged on surgeons certificate
DEVER, William B., Di-42-1; Pvt 32nd TN Inf; 7-12-61 to 63; Tenn City PO; CONF
DEVINE, Harrison, Mu-193-1; 1st Lt E Co 33rd IL Inf; 8-19-61 to 11-26-65; PO omitted
DEVINPORT, Marlin S., J-78-2; Pvt B Co 8th TN Inf; 1-15-65 to 8-17-65; Highland PO; rumatism
DEVLIN, John, H-59-3; Pvt IN Cav; Chattanooga PO; wounded right side
DEVREESE, William B., M-106-2(1); Pvt K Co 4th TN Mtd Inf; Hillsdale PO; hearing and a lung dis, lost his discharge
DEW, Robbert C., A-5-4; Pvt I Co 7th TN Inf; 10-8-64 to 7-28-65; Clinton PO
DEWALD, James M., Wa-261-2; Pvt H Co 5th TN Cav; 21 Oct 61 to 19 Apr 65; Conkling PO; CONF
DEWBERRY, John H., Ch-14-3; Pvt A Co 27th TN Inf; 4-1-61 to 5-1-62; PO omitted; CONF
DEWCISE, Meredith, Pu-145-2; Sgt C Co 1st Mtd Inf; 10-21-63 to 12-13-64; Burton PO
DEWEASE, Elias W., Dk-39-3(1); Pvt K Co 1st TN Mtd Inf; Dekalb PO; whie swelling PO
DEWEASE, Isaac, Dk-39-3(1); Pvt B Co 1st TN Mtd Inf; Dekalb PO
DEWEY, Orange S., Mg-198-2; Pvt B Co 30th MS Inf; 13 Dec 64 to 30 Jun 65; Deer Lodge PO
DEWIT, Jack A., F-43-1; Drumer B Co 59th Col US Inf; Jan? 64 to Mar 66; Rossville PO
DeWOLF, St. George, Sh-171-1; Pvt 23rd MA unattached; 8-63 to 11-63; Memphis PO
DEWS, Alfred, D-64-6; Nashville PO
DEXTER, John C., Mu-195-1; Ella C. widow of; Sol wife dont know; Columbia PO
DIAL, William, Un-258-3; Pvt F Co 2nd TN Inf; Dec 61 to Jan 65; Longhollow PO
DIBBLE, Chas. E., Sh-204-1; Pvt E Co 3rd OH; 62 to 64; McLemore Ave, Memphis PO
DICARSON, Side (see Stephens, Joseph C.)
DICE, George, Sm-176-1; Pvt; 1-25-65 to 4-25-65; Rome PO

DICE, John H., Tr-269-1; Lt C Co 4th TN Cav; 3 Nov 61 to 5 Jun 65; Knobton PO
DICE, John S., Tr-269-2; Pvt A Co 8th TN Inf; 1 Sep 62 to 5 Dec 62; John PO
DICK, John (see Brazzleton, John)
DICKENS, Allen, Sh-152-3; Fisherville PO
DICKENS, Briant, Sm-170-3; 1st Cpl A Co 1st TN Mtd Inf; 1-21-64 to 1-30-65; Maggart PO; hidrowseal
DICKENS, Dickson, Sn-264-2; Martha F.; Pvt A Co; Mittchellsville PO; this woman draws a pension, she is certain OK; she has paper but I have not seen them
DICKENS, Dred, T-213-2; Pvt; 8th Civil Dist
DICKENS, Felix G., Sm-170-3; Pvt G Co 28th TN Inf; 9-7-61 to 65; Maggart PO; CONF
DICKENS, James M., Sm-170-3; 2nd Sgt L Co 1st TN Cav; 6-63 to 65; Maggart PO; rheumatism & hemerage of bowels
DICKENS, Jasper, B-11-3(2); Pvt E Co 10th TN Inf; 3-1-63 to 6-23-65; Unionville PO
DICKENS, Joshua, Sm-170-3; Pvt A Co 1st TN Mtd Inf; 12-30-63 to 1-30-65; Maggart PO; typhoid fever
DICKENS, Joshua, Sm-170-2; Pvt A Co 1st TN Mtd Inf; 64 to 65; Chestnut Mound PO; shot in right shoulder
DICKENS, Lewis B., Sm-169-1; Cpl L Co 5th TN Cav; 8-14-63 to 8-14-65; Maggart PO; bronchitis
DICKENS, Mat, Mt-138-1; (blk) US Sol; Dist 7, New Providence PO
DICKENS, Michel A., Sm-170-3; 2nd Lt A Co 1st TN Mtd Inf; 12-30-63 to 1-20-65; Maggart PO
DICKENS, William C., Ms-173-1; Cpl A Co 4th TN Mtd Inf; 4 Aug 64 to 25 Aug 65; Rich Creek PO
DICKERSON, Franklin, Li-144-1; 3rd Civil Dist
DICKERSON, Albert, Sh-144-2; US Sol; First Dist
DICKERSON, Ben, T-214-2; US Sol; 9th Dist
DICKERSON, Charles H., Ce-20-2; Mary J. widow of; Pvt F Co 35th KY Reg; PO omitted
DICKERSON, David J., Hd-47-1; Capt F Co 6th TN Cav; Sep 21 62 to 65; Savannah PO
DICKERSON, Frank, Col, Li-144-1; Pvt A Co 24th IL Inf; 1-62 to 5; Flintville PO; he was taken prisoner at the Battle of Stones River & was exchanged & never reentered the army
DICKERSON, Isaiah, Ro-203-8; Pvt F Co 26th TN Inf; 20 Jul 62 to 20 Aug 62; Burns' Mills PO; piles; CONF
DICKERSON, James M., Wy-171-3; Sarah A. widow of; Major A Co 2nd TN Mtd Inf; __ to 5-15-66 (1 yr 6 mos); Sorby PO
DICKERSON, Jno., Sh-187-1(5); Sol; Memphis PO
DICKERSON, Joshaway, D-99-2; US Sol; Davidson Co. Poor House PO
DICKERSON, Solomon, Gu-47-1; Pvt TN; 62 to 63; Pelham PO
DICKERSON, Wiliam, Sh-155-1; Pvt B Co 59th TN Inf; 63 to 65; Germantown PO
DICKEY, J. C., Gi-139-1; Pvt K Co 53rd TN Inf; 12-15-61 to 12-15-64; Campbellsville PO; CONF
DICKEY, John M., Br-9-2; Alice C. widow of; Pvt G Co 25th OH Inf; 7-12-61 to 7-26-64; Cleveland PO
DICKEY, Phillip R., Ro-204-3; Pvt I Co 7th TN Cav; Elverton PO
DICKINS, Thomas T., Cy-26-2; Pvt C Co 32nd KY Inf; 4-13-62 to 62 (1 mo r days); Rocktown PO
DICKINSON, Henry, D-79-3; Pvt B Co 14th US Col Inf; about Oct 63 to about Mar 66; Nashville, 33 Liscke PO
DICKINSON, Mathew, Sh-191-3; Memphis PO; records no seen
DICKINSON, Nancy (see Williams, Archie)
DICKISON, Charles C., Hm-107-5; Mary J. widow of; Pvt C Co 2nd IL Lt Art; 62 to 65; Chestnut Bloom PO; cronic diarrhia, discharge lost
DICKISON, Will W., T-216-3; 14th Civil Dist
DICKMAN, Henry, Sh-184-1; Pvt 8th OH Art; 3-1-62 to 4-25-65; 183 High, Memphis PO
DICKSON, Henry, Sh-184-1; Pvt 8th OH Art; 3-1-62 to 4-25-65; 183 High, Memphis PO
DICKSON, Alexander R., Hd-54-3; US Sol; PO omitted
DICKSON, Augustus F., Dy-25-5(1); Pvt D Co 12th TN Inf; May 61 to 6 Apr 62 Newbern PO; crippled balance of life; CONF
DICKSON, Ed., T-210-1; 3rd US Colort; Jun 62 to 64; Richardson Ldg. PO

DICKSON, Eliza, Mu-200-2; widow; Mt Pleasant PO
DICKSON, George W., W-189-3(2); Mary J. widow of; Pvt D Co 8th TN Inf; 3-17-62 to 7-65; McMinnville PO
DICKSON, Henry (see Foster, Henry)
DICKSON, Isaac W., Dy-25-1; Pvt G Co 20th TN Inf; 12 May 61 to end war (4 yrs 6 mos); Newbern PO; wounded three times, enlistment dates unknown; CONF
DICKSON, James H., Hd-54-2; Pvt C Co 6th TN Cav; 18 Sep 62 to 26 Jul 65; Sardis PO; piles & fistilla in arm
DICKSON, James M., Ov-139-1; PVt K Co 4th TN Cav; 2-14-64 to 8-25-65; France PO
DICKSON, Joe, Gi-128-1; Pvt G Co 111th TN Inf; 63 to 65; 8th Civil Dist
DICKSON, John, Su-239-1; Pvt G Co 8th TN Cav; 18 Aug 63 to 17 Sep 65; Edens Ridge PO; diseased of piles
DICKSON, Jno T., T-210-1; Pvt Gralet Growlet; Sep 62 to Jan 63; Quito PO; shot in the head
DICKSON, Milton, Gi-128-1; Pvt F Co 110th TN Inf; 63 to 65; 8th Civil Dist
DICKSON, Walter, Cu-17-1; 2nd Lt G Co 144th NY Inf; 8-26-62 to 7-65; Crossville PO; asthma & kidney trouble, unable for work
DICKSON, William H., Dy-32-1; Pvt I Co 58th OH Inf; Apr 62 to Dec 62; Trimble PO
DICUS, Stewart (see Hutchinson, James)
DIES, John, Tr-269-1; Staff; 62 to 63; John PO
DIGGS, Dudley, Mu-197-1; Cook I Co 12th IL Reg; Apr 17 65 to Jul 10 65; Columbia PO
DIGGS, Edward, Sh-189-5; Sgt I Co 88th US Col Inf; about 7-63 to about 12-63; Ark. Ave, Memphis PO
DIGGS, George W., Ro-203-8; Pvt K Co 1st TN Inf; 9 Aug 61 to 17 Sep 64; Burns' Mills PO; injury of side and ankle
DIGGS, Henry C., A-2-3; Andersonville PO; hernia; not at home & discharge in Washington
DIGGS, James E., A-8-1; Pvt K Co 1st TN Inf; 8-9-61 to 9-17-64; Ledom PO; contracted sore eyes 6-62
DIGGS, John, A-5-3; Rhal? widow of; Pvt 2nd TN Mtd Inf; 10-61 to ___; Clinton PO
DIGGS, Presley K., T-7-3; Pvt K Co 1st TN __; 8-9-61 to 9-17-64; Robertsville PO
DIGGS, William, A-8-1; Wagoner Co K 1st TN Inf; 8-9-61 to 9-17-64; Ledom PO; now entirely helpless
DIGGS, William J., A-8-2; Pvt F Co 32nd KY Inf; 12-14-62 to 9-12-63; Ledom PO; chronic dispepsia & diarhea, reenlisted
DIGGS, William J., A-8-2; Pvt M Co 9th TN Cav; 3-29-64 to 9-11-65; Scarborough PO
DIGGS, Wilson (black), Hm-104-4(2); Pvt H Co 1st US Inf; 63 to 65; Morristown PO; from shell wound Fort Fisher, NC, lost discharge
DIGHT, William J., Cy-27-3(1); Pvt B Co 5th IN Cav; 3-63 to 64; Miles PO
DIKE, William, C-8-1; Pvt E Co 2nd TN Inf; 6-10-63 to 8-3-65; Well Spring PO; c(hronic) dorhea, deafness, pain in side & rheumatism
DIKIMAN, Joel, Di-34-3; Catharine E. widow of; Pvt I Co 83rd PA Inf; 7-25-61 to 7-25-64; Dickson PO
DILDINE, James D., W-222-2; Pvt B Co 41st TN; Nov 62 to Mar 64; Gardner PO; CONF
DILL, A., Ca-20-1; Major A Co 4th TN Cav; 1-15-62 to 2-1-63; Woodbury PO; CONF
DILL, Overton, Sq-16-5; Sarah widow of; Pvt E Co 6th TN Inf; 4-1-62 to 5-1-65; Sunnyside PO; received an honorable disc.
DILL, Thomas H., H-69-2; Pvt G Co 3rd TN Inf; 11-20-61 to 12-25-65; Chattanooga PO; CONF
DILL, William, Po-149-1; Pvt F Co 5th TN Inf; 10-4-64 to 7-18-65; Conasauga PO; Mont. Inf
DILL, William, C-33-1; Pvt A Co 10th MI; 4-63 to 65; Newcomb PO
DILL, _____, Mc-112-10; Margaret widow of; Athens PO
DILLAR, Lewis, Ge-100-2; Pvt D Co 14th US Cav Ord Troop; 63 to 25 Dec 65; PO omitted
DILLARD, Chales, Col, Tr-268-1; Harriett widow of; Pvt A Co; 63 to 65; Hartsville PO; killed at Chattanooga

DILLARD, Ephram, W1-293-1; E Co 4th TN Inf; 18 Dec? 61 to Apr 2 65; Austin PO; CONF
DILLARD, F. P., M-208-4; Pvt B Co 52nd KY Mtd Inf; 9-24-63 to 1-17-65; Lafayette PO; rist thrown out of place by ball
DILLARD, Frank, K-156-3; Cpl L Co 1st US Hvy Art; Dec 6 64 to 1 Mar 66; 130 E Clinch St, Knoxville PO; injured internally, caused by excessive drilling and marching
DILLARD, Henry, Sh-196-1; Pvt C Co 61st TN Inf; 2-27-64 to 12-30-65; 120 Dunlap St, Memphis PO; frost bitten from exposure, still suffers
DILLARD, Henry, Sh-196-2; Loader Ouachita; 63 to 65; Providence Chapel, Memphis PO; injured by cannon jars, served under Capts. Wilson and Fitzhugh
DILLEHAY, B. T., Sm-169-2; Pvt A Co 1st TN Mtd Inf; 1-28-64 to 11-28-65; Elmwood PO; back affected
DILLERHOY?, Joel L., M-103-5; Pvt A Co 8th TN Inf; 11-27-64 to 8-17-65; Lafayette PO
DILLON, David H., Cu-15-3; Pvt E Co 16th TN Cav; 11-61 to 9-62; Woody PO; CONF
DILLON, Thomas J., Su-239-1; Pvt K Co 8th TN Cav; 15 Aug 63 to 11 Sep 65; Edens Ridge PO; Dec 20 1864, lungs & frost bite
DILLS, Jerry, Fe-41-1; Pvt E Co 7th TN Inf; 7-24-62 to 12-20-62; Pall Mall PO
DILTHNTY (sic), Abraham, Sol MS, Hd-50-6; 8th Civil Dist
DIMSON, Joseph, Je-146-3; Pvt B Co 2nd TN Cav; 15 Aug 63 to 15 Aug 65; White Pine PO; mashed up in hip, horse fall, looks slim
DINE, George W., L-101-1; alias George W. Haden, Pvt H Co 3rd Reg Cav; Mar 80 to Mar 1 81; Ripley PO; left leg broken above ankle, rec. injury in game baseball
DINES, William M., K-179-1; Pvt G Co 1st TN Inf; 9 Aug 61 to 17 Sep 64; Virtue PO
DINGS, James, Sh-158-3; Seaman, Lehigh, Flagship Massachusetts; Jul 64 to 24 Feb 66; Memphis PO
DINKINS, James B., Hn-74-1; Luisa J. widow of; Pvt A Co 2nd MO Cav; 61 to 65; PO omitted; cronic direar, discharged on disability
DINKINS, Thomas, A-5-1; Bethena widow of; Pvt C Co 11th TN Cav; 1-1-63 to 9-65; Clinton PO
DINSMORE, John W., Hw-126-1; Pvt A Co 1st TN Art; 20 Sep 63 to 3 Aug 65; Starns PO; eyes affected
DINSMORE, Samuel, Cf-45-3; Nancy J. widow of; Pvt L Co 13th TN Cav; 6-4-64 to 9-5-65; Carter Furnace PO
DINWIDDIE, Henry, Hn-77-3(1); Ann widow of; Henry PO; dead & discharge mislaid
DINWIDDIE, James H., Je-141-4; US Sol; 4th Dist
DINWIDDIE, John R., Je-141-2; Pvt B Co 9th TN Cav; 15 Sep 63 to 11 Sep 65; New Market PO
DINWIDDIE, Joseph F., Je-142-2; Nancy J. widow of; Pvt B Co 9th TN Cav; 15 Sep 62 to 11 Sep 65; Lucilla PO
DINWIDDIE, Rufus, Hn-77-1; Pvt D Co 4th Hvy Art; 63 to 66; PO omitted
DIO, Absalen, B-11-1; Pvt C Co 6th TN Inf; 9-12-64 to 6-30-65; Normandy PO
DIRK, Archie, Ms-174-1; Pvt H Co 17th US Inf; 30 Nov 63 to 25 Apr 66; Chapel Hill PO
DISMUKES, Robert, D-87-2; Pvt A Co 111th TN Inf; Jan 64 to 66; Nashville PO; prisoner 9 mos
DIVINE, Frederic, H-76-1; Chattanooga PO
DIX, Henry F., Sh-192-1; Capt F Co 16th US VT Vol; 10-23-62 to 11-16-63; Memphis PO
DIXON, Alfred, Sh-200-1; Daphne Cooper formerly widow of; Pvt TN Cav; corner McKinley & Dixon Sts, Memphis PO; right arm shot off; died with lockjaw after his discharge
DIXON, Alfred, St-162-1; Pvt K Co 8th KY Cav; May 64 to Mar 65; Cumberland City PO; eyes affected
DIXON, Dalis, Mr-95-2; Pvt E Co 6th TN Inf; 9-9-64 to 7-1-65; Ownes PO
DIXON, Dudley, Gi-127-2; Artelia widow of; Sgt F Co 110th TN Col Inf; Dec 9 63 to Feb 3 66; Pulaski PO
DIXON, Giles, Gi-127-3; Pvt F Co 110th TN Col Inf; ___ to Feb 66; Pulaski PO; foot mashed
DIXON, James H., Mc-111-3; Sgt E Co 9th TN Cav; 9-18-63 to 65; Mortimer PO
DIXON, John, De-24-1; Pvt I Co 3rd TN Inf; 18 Aug 63 to 30 Apr 66; Decaturville PO
DIXON, John, J-79-1; Martha A. widow of; Pvt F Co 13th KY Cav; 63 to 10-2-65; Whitleyville PO; reenlisted vet, date of discharge
DIXON, Jonathan M., Wy-172-1; Bugler A Co 2nd TN Inf (Mtd); 10-2-63 to 10-14-64; Waynesboro PO; diarrhea
DIXON, Joseph F., Mg-200-2; Pvt K Co 60th IL Inf; 28 Oct 61 to 20 Mar 65; Glades PO; varicose veins (neuratrophy)
DIXON, Mariah (see Gallaher, Thomas M.)
DIXON, Nicholas, D-89-2; 11th Civil Dist
DIXON, Onslo M., Mo-122-3(1); Margaret widow of; Pvt; 4-22-63 to 7-15-63; Hiwassee College PO; CONF
DIXON, Robert A., D-86-1; Brentwood PO
DIXON, Samul, Gi-127-1; Pvt F Co 110th TN C Inf; Pulaski PO
DIXON, Thomas J., M-106-2(1); Pvt I Co 9th KY Vol Inf; 11-21-61 to 12-15-64; Lafayette PO; chronic diarrhea and piles; pensioner
DIXON, Thos. L., Mc-115-1; Cpl A Co 10th TN Cav; 8-12-63 to 8-1-65; Riceville PO; dont know anything about it
DIXON, Wm., Je-141-3; Susan widow of; Pvt F Co 1st TN Cav; Mill Springs PO; papers at Washington, no way to get dates
DIXON, William M., H-70-4(1); Sol (Fed); 313 Gilmer St, Chattanooga PO
DIXON, William R., B-20-1; Sgt C Co 5th TN Cav; 9-4-62 to 6-25-65; Shelbyville PO
DIXSON, William, Ge-99-2; Pvt I Co 1st TN Cav; 1 Aug 62 to 5 Jun 65; Woolsey College PO; gunshot wound
DIZARX, John, D-91-1; Sgt F Co 15th; Jerry Sullivan's Nashville PO; CONF
DIZERNE, William, Gr-80-1; Pvt H Co 8th TN Cav; Oct 63 to Aug 65; Meltabarger PO
DOAK, Henry M., D-61-1; Lt E Co Marine Corps; Apr 1 61 to Apr 10 65; Nashville PO; shot in hand; CONF
DOAK, Wyley, Hm-108-5(4); CONF; Pvt A Co 2nd KY Cav; 12 Aug 61 to 12 Feb 65; Russellville PO; wounded in hand
DOAKE, Willis, Ru-241-4; Murfreesboro PO
DOBBINS, Minerva, D-70-1; widow Sol; No 1 Maple St, Nashville PO
DOBBINS, Nelson, Mu-210-5; Pvt F Co 110th TN Inf; 1-63 to 12-64; Carters Creek PO; weak lungs from measles
DOBBINS, William A., Mu-209-4; Pvt E Co 9th TN Cav; 63 to 65; Columbia PO; CONF
DOBBS, James T., Pi-156-3; Pvt I Co 12th KY Inf; 11-1-61 to 8-1-65; Travisville PO
DOBBS, John P., Ca-19-1; Woodbey PO
DOBBS, Johnson S., Hw-122-1; Catherine widow of; Pvt; Blossom PO; family has no record of service
DOBBS, Sith, We-221-1(4); Rebecca widow of; Pvt 1st TN Cav; 61 to 64; Martin PO; CONF
DOBSON, John N., Ge-94-1; Pvt H Co 24th MI Inf; 8 May 65 to 30 Jul 65; Tusculum PO
DOBSON, William J., D-73-1; Cpl H Co 38th TN Conf Inf; 20 Nov 61 to Jul 11 63; Nashville PO; CONF
DOCKERY, William P., Lo-192-1; Pvt L Co 2nd TN; 16 Nov 63 to 24 May 65; Griffitts PO; rheumatism & heart disease
DOCKEY, Chares, Sh-158-6(4); Pvt I? Co 63rd Col Inf; Mar 64 to 9 Jan 66; Memphis PO; cant read remarks
DOCKEY, Green, J-83-1; Pvt KY; Flynns Lick PO
DOCKINS, John, W1-293-1; H Co Cav; 63 to 64; Lockport PO; CONF
DOCY, Moses, B-10-1; Lucy A. widow of; Pvt A Co 4th TN Cav; 64 to 65; PO omitted
DODD, Benjamin F., De-26-1; E Co 7th ___; 28 Jun 62 to ___ (8 mos); Bible Hill PO
DODD, Eli, Hn-77-3(1); Pvt I Co 6th TN Cav; 7-62 to 8-65; Henry PO
DODD, John B., D-72-3; Pvt C Co 10th TN Inf; Aug 12 61 to Feb 15 65; Nashville PO; CONF
DODD, Joseph B., R-162-3; Sgt D Co 12th TN Cav; 11-24-63 to 10-7-65; Dayton PO; health injured from exposure

DODD, Samuel F., Cr-14-2; Pvt C Co 7th TN Cav; 4 Jul 62 to 27 Jun 65; Clarksburg PO
DODD, William, Br-7-2; Elisabeth widow of; Pvt L Co 1st TN Cav; 9-1-62 to __ (11 mos); Falker PO
DODD, William, H-72-1; Mary A. widow of; Chattanooga PO
DODDS, Andrew C., Hd-49-2; Pvt H Co 2nd TN Mtd Inf; Sep 1 63 to Apr 17 65; Gillis Mills PO; neuralgia & rheumatism
DODDS, Joseph, Sh-145-2; Pvt K Co 4th TN Col US Hvy Art; Dec 63 to Mar 65; Millington PO; Capt A Brewer, 1st Lt Gaughf; 2nd Lt Rice
DIDDS, Robert, D-50-4; 316 Line, Nashville PO
DODGE, Alvin, H-68-1; Pvt H Co 4th MI Vol; 3-61 to 12-63; Chattanooga PO
DODGE, George C., R-159-1; Maj D Co 41st OH Inf; 8-3-61 to 12-3-64; Spring City PO
DODGE, John W., Tr-269-1; Pvt 2nd KY Inf; May 61 to Apr 65; Hartsville PO
DODGE, Talbert C., Sh-201-3; Pvt A Co 27th OH Inf; 10 Mar 63 to 10 Mar 65; Memphis PO
DODSON, Charles G., Wh-181-1; Pvt G Co 21st IL Inf; 3-6-65 to 6-26-65; Dodson PO; diarrhoea, injured hearing, applied for pension
DODSON, Edward A., Mc-115-1; Pvt D Co 5th TN Mtd Inf; 8-31-64 to 6-26-65; Riceville PO; shoulder dislocated
DODSON, Elias, P-151-3; Pvt E Co 6th TN Cav; Linden PO; no discharge
DODSON, Isum, L-102-1; soldier was not at home, couldn't get his record; Mack PO
DODSON, J. M., Mc-114-2; Pvt G Co 3rd TN Cav; 10-63 to 5-10-65; Santfordville PO; CONF
DODSON, James, Col, S-214-2; Pvt I Co 1st US Hvy Art; Jul 64 to 31 Mar 66; Glenmary PO; broncitos, scraflo, disease lung, rheumatism
DODSON, James, Ro-210-4; Pvt H Co; Rockwood PO
DODSON, James M., P-151-3; Linden PO
DODSON, Jessee, Mc-111-3; Pvt F Co 3rd TN Cav; 5-25-63 to 6-27-65; Nonaburg PO; prisner Cahaba AL 6 mos
DODSON, Joel, Ro-210-7; Pvt H Co TN Mtd Inf; Cardiff PO; consumption
DODSON, John M., Ro-209-1; Eliza widow of; Rockwood PO; CONF
DODSON, Lewis, Mu-198-1; Pvt A Co 13th US Reg; 63 to 64; Saw Dust PO; right leg wounded
DODSON, Noah see McQueen, Noah)
DODSON, Robert S., Wh-181-1; Pvt D Co 60th IL Inf; 2-22-65 to 7-31-65; Solon PO; suffers from relapse of measles
DODSON, Samuel. (see Mevon, Samuel)
DODSON, Thomas, Mc-118-2; Pvt A Co 4th TN Cav; 10-24-62 to 7-24-65; Joshua PO; measles settled in breast 25 yrs
DODSON, W. H., G-57-1; Pvt K Co 47th TN Inf; 12-7-61 to 12-5-62; Yorkville PO; CONF
DODSON, William, Hy-74-1; 1st Civil Dist
DODSON, William, Ro-210-1; Pvt G Co 6th KY Mtd Inf; 8 Jul 62 to 8 Apr 65; Rockwood PO
DOGER, William, Sh-152-3; Dexter PO
DOGGED, William A., Hm-108-3(2); Mary widow of; Pvt F Co 4th TN Inf; 17 Jan 62 to 17 Mar 63; Russellville PO; death
DOLE, Josiah, H-51-3; Minerva widow of; Pvt I Co 4th TN Cav; 63 to 65; Hill City PO
DOLEN, John N., Su-241-1; Quartermaster B Co 4th TN Cav; 15 Nov 62 to 12 Jul 65; Butterfly PO; injure to right side, dyreah
DOLES, John, Mn-120-1; Pvt A Co 6th TN Cav; Falcon PO; dropsey; captured & never got any discharge
DOLLEY, Roberta (see Liggin, Alfred)
DONAHOE, James, Hm-108-5(4); Pvt A Co 149th TN Inf; Feb 65 to Nov 65; Russellville PO; ruptured
DONAHOE, John, Je-143-2; Sgt C Co 4th TN Cav; 26 Nov 62 to 6 Jul 65; Mossy Creek PO; catarrh & throat trouble
DONAHOE, Robert F., K-156-2; Trival? 1st E TN Vol; 61 to 65; Kennady 120, Knoxville PO
DONALDSON, Henry C., H-56-5; Cpl B Co 12th Inf; 12-15-64 to 65; East End PO
DONALDSON, Robert, A-9-4(2); NCO Capt Carns Lt Art; 5-27-61 to 6-1-62; Marlow PO: CONF
DONALLY, James C., C-33-2; Pvt L Co 3rd Col Cav; 8-19-64 to 12-31-64; Jellico PO
DONEHOE, William, H-51-3; Pvt A Co 1st TN Art; 1-18-64 to 3-31-65; Hill City PO

DONELEY, Frederic W., H-51-3; Drummer I Co 2nd TN Inf; 61 to 63; Hill City PO
DONIELS, Elijah, D-49-1; Martha former widow of; Pvt F Co 12th US Inf; 12 Aug 63 to 16 Jan 66; Nashville PO
DONNELL, Allen, St-162-2; Pvt K Co 6th IL Cav; 63 to 65; Erin PO
DONNELLS, Siles, L-100-1; Pvt F Co 138th US Col Inf; 1 yr 6 mos; Ripley PO; wounded by lightning, cannot give date of discharge or enlistment
DONNELLY, Alfred T., Jo-149-2; Capt D Co 13th TN Cav; 15 Oct 63 to 8 Sep 65; Mountain City PO
DONNELLY, James C., Jo-149-1; Cpl B Co 4th TN Inf; 1 Oct 62 to 7 Jul 65; Mountain City PO; liver and kidneys & spine, rheumatism
DONNELLY, John, D-103-2; 24th Dist
DONNELLY, John M., Ct-35-2; Pvt B Co 4th TN Inf; 7-7-62 to 7-7-65; Butler PO (Johnson Co.); in the US Army
DONNELLY, Margaret, Sh-176-1; widow of US Sol; 67 Beale St, Memphis PO
DONNELLY, Robert H. M., Ge-96-4; Maj 13th TN Cav; 25 Apr 63 to 5 Sep 65; Chuckey City PO; rheumatism & eye disease
DONNELLY, William, Sh-199-2; Wagon Master; 47 Frasur St, Memphis PO
DONNER, George, Dk-34-1; Elizabeth widow of; Sgt E Co TN Inf; 11-23-64 to 8-25-65; Dowelltown PO; consumption
DONOHO, John H., M-107-5; Sgt G Co 23rd KY Inf; 12-7-61 to 1-24-65; Willette PO; disease of lungs
DONOHO, Leroy, M-107-5; Pvt E Co 9th KY Cav; 12-7-61 to 9-17-64; Willette PO; gunshot wound right arm
DONOHUE, James, Sh-158-4; US Sol; 14th Civil Dist
DONOHUE, T. R., D-78-1; 1st Sgt I Co 27th OH Inf; Aug 16 61 to Aug 17 64; Nashville PO
DONOHUE, Thade, Sh-167-3; Sgt in Hospital; 8 Oct 62 to 5 Feb 65; PO omitted; Dr. in the army
DONOVAN, Daniel, G-51-1; Storekeeper USN Iroquois; 61 to 65; Humboldt PO
DONOVAN, Patrick H., Mt-149-1; Sgt G Co 6th KY Cav; 7-28-62 to 7-14-65; Carbondale PO
DONTHCON, A. J., Hy-85-1; Pvt D Co 1st AL Cav; 62 to 64; Nut Bush PO; kicked by horse on boat going from Memphis to Nashville & head injured
DOOGAN, ___, H-54-2(3); Sherman Heights PO
DOOLEE, John, Hy-76-1; Teamster D Co Col Inf; 2 yrs; PO omitted
DOOLEY, Francis M., Mu-194-1; Scout 14th MI Mtd Inf; 11-1-63 to 1-20-65; Columbia PO
DOOLEY, John L., Mu-209-6; Mary widow of; Pvt G Co 9th TN Inf; 3-62 to 63; Columbia PO; CONF
DOOLEY, Mack H., K-166-5; Col Orderly; 102nd OH Inf; Oct 63 to Oct 65; Knoxville PO
DOOLEY, Peter J., Mu-209-1; Columbia PO; CONF
DOOLING, Joe (see Garner, Joe)
DOOLITTLE, L. S., D-98-1; Pvt C Co 9th? IL; Aug 7 62 to Jun 21 65; 19th Civ Dist
DORCH, Edmond, Gi-135-1; Pvt D Co 15th TN Inf; 10-2-63 to 3-66; Lynnville PO
DOREMUS, Charles, D-79-1; 1st Sgt 13th MY Inf; Apr 61 to Jul 61; Nashville PO, N. 1st 93
DORITY, B. T., Rb-224-1; Sarah J. widow of; Pvt MI Inf; 61 to 65; Springfield PO
DORON, Thomas J., We-223-5; Pvt H Co 33rd TN Inf; Oct 61 to Jan 65; Palmersville PO; well and harty; CONF
DORRET, Robert, Un-258-2(1); Pvt A Co 9th TN Cav; 61 to 64; Rhodelia PO
DORRETT, Andrew, Un-258-2(1); US Sol; 1st Dist
DORRIS, Henry H., D-82-1; Pvt Home Guard; May 1 62 to Jan 5 63; Hermitage PO
DORRIS, Wm. D., D-71-1; Nashville PO
DORTCH, Richard W., We-226-1; Pvt K Co 6th TN Cav; Sharon PO
DORTON, Azariah, Cu-17-3; Sgt D Co 2nd TN Inf; 9-1-61 to 10-6-64; Grassy Cove PO; spinal affection, enlargement of testicle glands
DOSS, Alfred H., M-108-4; Clara A. widow of; Pvt 57th KY Cav; Lafayette PO; discharge lost
DOSS, Charles W., Cr-8-1; Pvt I Co 7th TN Cav; 63 to 65; Lavinia PO; thrown from horse, his discharge is at Washington
DOSS, J. C., M-108-4; Pvt C Co 9th KY Inf; 61 to 63; Lafayette PO; lung disease, discharge not at hand

DOSS, William J., Hd-53-3; Pvt M Co 7th TN Cav; 6 Jul 63 to 23 Jun 65; Adamsville PO; Andersonville Prison 18 mos
DOSSETT, Jacob, A-9-4(2); Pvt I Co 7th TN Cav; 5-28-63 to 9-11-65; Dossett PO; heart disease; prisoner 1 mo. Belle Island
DOSSETT, John, C-24-3; Elisabeth widow of; Pvt B Co 1st TN Inf; 61 to 63 (1 yr 10 mos); Fork Vale PO ingery of left side
DOSSETT, John W., C-30-1; Pvt C Co 3rd TN Inf; 2-13-62 to 2-13-65; Stockville PO; shot through right arm
DOSSETT, William, C-29-2; Fincastel PO; rheumatism
DOTSON, Charles, Gr-79-4; Mary widow of; Pvt; Thorn Hill PO; killed; CONF
DOTSON, Charles L., R-161-2; Pvt I Co 1st Hvy Art Cav; 7-13-64 to 3-31-66; Dayton PO
DOTSON, David M., Gr-79-3; Pvt K Co 37th TN; Thorn Hill PO; right foot shot off; CONF
DOTSON, Isaac, Hw-132-5; Pvt H Co 8th TN Inf; Mar 63 to 15 Jun 65; Strahl PO; wounded in the head
DOTSON, Joel, Gr-70-3; Capt D Co 2nd TN Inf; 14 Jul 61 to 20 Jan 62; Rutledge PO; diarhea
DOTSON, John H., We-230-2; Pvt I Co 19th TN Cav; Apr 1 64 to May 1 65; PO omitted; CONF
DOTSON, Squire, Sh-174-1; Pvt F Co 57th US Col Vol; 4-20-63 to 2-66; 234 Pontotoc St, Memphis PO; left arm broken, mustered out at Memphis
DOTSON, Thomas, Ro-210-4; Manerva J. widow of; Pvt; Rockwood PO; CONF
DOTSON, William S., M-108-2(1); Cpl D Co 8th TN Mtd Inf; 3-1-65 to 8-31-65; Pvt A Co 9th Reg Inf; 9-15-61 to 12-15-65; Salt Lick PO; ruptured, nervous debility
DOTY, Lucinda C., Ge-97-4; widow US Sol; 16th Civil Dist
DOUD, James, Ge-89-1; Pvt B Co 3rd TN Inf; 30 Feb 64 to 30 Oct 64; Pilot Knob PO
DOUDY, Perry C., Pi-153-2; Sgt D Co 1st TN Inf; 10-62 to 8-13-63; Chanute PO; CONF
DOUDY, Rufus, Pi-153-2; Capt D Co 1st TN Inf; 61 to 65; Chanute PO
DOUGHERTY, Mitchell (see Maxwell, Mitchell)
DOUGHERTY, Samuel, Gi-127-6; Pvt; Pulaski PO
DOUGHERTY, Wm. Ransom, C-34-2; Pvt C Co 4th TN Inf; ___ to 65 (2 yrs 11 mos); Elk Valley PO
DOUGHTY, B. F., K-180-3; Pvt D Co 6th TN Cav; 18 Apr 62 to 27 Apr 65; PO omitted
DOUGHTY, James A., K-169-1; Col K Co 2nd TN Cav; 1 Jul 63 to Feb 64; Knoxville PO; totally disabled
DOUGHTY, James S., Be-7-1; Bugler A Co 7th TN Cav; 13 Jan 64 to 9 Aug 65; PO omitted
DOUGHTY, William N., Ru-241-5; Sarah widow of; Capt I Co 37th TN Inf; 61 to 66; Murfreesboro PO
DOUGLAS, Attison, F-37-1; Carroll Douglas alias; Cpl K Co 5th US Col Inf; May 62 to Oct 65; Taylors Chapel PO; shot through the thumb, very old
DOUGLAS, G. W., Ro-203-8; Burns' Mills PO
DOUGLAS, Harrison, Sm-175-2(1); Pvt I Co 1st TN Inf; 5-64 to 8-6? (1 yr 3 mos); Enoch PO; lung trouble
DOUGLAS, James, Ms-176-1; Pvt E Co 44th TN; Caney Springs PO; stiffness from rheumatism, does not know what month or year he was enlisted—was discharge in April but does not know the year
DOUGLAS, James T., Ro-203-8; Sarah C. widow of; Pvt; Wheat PO; strain of hip
DOUGLAS, Matthew, C-34-2; Nancy widow of; Pvt G Co 7th TN Cav; 11-8-64 to 7-28-65; Elk Valley PO; (believe died after war from disease contracted in army)
DOUGLAS, Nancy E. (see Lowery, David L.)
DOUGLAS, Stephen, Gi-125-1; Pvt E Co 101st US Col Inf; 63 to 65; Bodenham PO
DOUGLAS, William, Ce-30-1; Pvt A Co 12th TN Inf; 63 to 65; Kingston Springs PO
DOUGLASS, Adem A., Je-140-2; Ord Sgt G Co 9th TN Cav; 1 Oct 63 to 4 Mar 65; PO omitted
DOUGLASS, Alexander, Ct-39-3; Pvt A Co 13th TN Cav; 63 to 65; Gap Run PO; sore leg from fever
DOUGLASS, Edmond, Sn-257-1; Pvt D Co 14th TN Inf; 11-63 to 3-65; Gallatin PO

DOUGLASS, Edward M., Je-135-3; Sarah widow of; Cpl D Co 3rd TN Cav; Dec 62 to death 65; Piedmont PO; death
DOUGLASS, Frank, Sh-193-1; Pvt; Memphis PO
DOUGLASS, Guy, Dy-25-3; Pvt; Newbern PO; CONF
DOUGLASS, Henry, Wl-295-2; Lebanon PO
DOUGLASS, Henry, He-61-1; Pvt D Co 7th TN Cav; Sep 62 to 25 Oct 63 (papers lost); Pvt K Co 2nd TN Mtd Inf; 28 Mar 64 to 20 Apr 65; Poplar Springs PO; dyspepsia, this soldier was considered one of the best sol. in reg.
DOUGLASS, James, Ct-39-3; Pvt A Co 13th TN Cav; 63 to 65; Gap Run PO; rheumatism
DOUGLASS, James E., Se-226-5; Cpl D Co 3rd TN Cav; 1 Dec 62 to 10 Jun 65; Trotters Store PO; in Andersonville prison
DOUGLASS, James W., Je-149-2; Coms Sgt 9th TN Cav; 1 Oct 63 to 11 Sep 65; PO omitted
DOUGLASS, John W., Se-226-5; Pvt C Co 9th TN Cav; 12 Jun 63 to 11 Sep 65; Henrys X Roads PO
DOUGLASS, Joseph N., Je-142-1; Atha M. widow of; Cpl B Co 9th TN Cav; 5 Aug 63 to 24 Mar 65; Alena PO
DOUGLASS, Madison, Hy-75-1; Pvt B Co 12th MI; fall 62 to summer 63; Dancyville PO; cooked for Lt. King
DOUGLASS, Mariah, Hy-76-1; widow of Tom Core; Stanton Depot PO
DOUGLASS, Mathew A., Dy-25-7(3); Lucy A. widow of; 4 yrs; Newbern PO; CONF
DOUGLASS, Michael, H-62-1; Pvt B Co 10th WI Inf; ___ to 65 (3 yrs 4 mos); 138 Chestnut, Chattanooga PO; cook, driver of ambulance & private
DOUGLASS, Simon B., Se-226-5; Pvt D Co 3rd TN Cav; 1 Dec 62 to 17 Jun 65; Henrys X Roads PO; shot in left shoulder
DOUGLASS, William, Ct-39-2; Pvt A Co 9th TN Cav; Gap Run PO; rheumatism, piles & chronic diorhoea
DOUGLASS, William A., He-58-2; Sol; 8th Civil Dist
DOUGLASS, William C., Se-226-*; Pvt D Co 3rd TN Cav; 1 Dec 62 to 8 Aug 65; Henrys X Roads; shot in left knee
DOUGLASS, William H., He-58-2; Sol; 7th Civil Dist
DOUGLESS, Henry, D-72-2; Pvt G Co 17th TN Inf; May 21 61 to Sep 28 63; Nashville PO; wounded in leg, now paralyzed
DOUTHAT, William B., Li-149-2; 1st Lt A Co 12th TN Cav; 9-7-63 to 10-27-65; Fayetteville PO; gun shot wounds in thigh & arm
DOVE, Josiah P., Wa-263-3; Pvt B Co 8th TN Cav; Jul 23 63 to Sep 11 65; Alfred PO
DOVENS, David A., Bo-12-1; Pvt H Co 10th TN Cav; 2-8-64 to 8-4-65; Houk PO
DOW, William, Gi-127-7; Pvt B Co 13th US Inf (Col); Sep 5 62 to Jun 3 66; Pulaski PO
DOWDY, Wesley, St-162-2; Sarah widow of; Cumberland City PO
DOWEL, Curtis C., Cy-29-1; Pvt C Co 8th TN Inf; 3-10-65 to 8-17-65; Fox Springs PO
DOWEL, Mollie, Dy-25-9(1); widow; PO omitted
DOWEL, Mollie (see Howard, Jack)
DOWEL, Pink, C-34-2; Pvt; Elk Valley PO; could not get any information, Dowell gone from home
DOWELL, James E., Jo-150-5; Pvt D Co 13th TN Cav; 22 Sep 63 to 5 Sep 65; Osborn PO
DOWELL, John L., Su-233-1; Pvt G Co 13th TN Cav; Sep 63 to Sep 65; Kings Mills PO; rupture & crippled shoulder, almost entirely disabled
DOWELL, Major C., We-222-1; Pvt B Co 24th TN Inf; Jun 24 61 to 65; Terrill PO; CONF
DOWELL, Watson G., J-83-1; Sgt C Co 8th TN; 4-4-65 to 8-17-65; Flynns Lick PO
DOWELL (Dannell?), William, Hm-103-2; 2nd Lt G Co 4th TN Cav; 4 Mar 62 to 12 Jul 65; Morristown PO; gun shot left shoulder
DOWLAND, Robt. I., G-67-1; Pvt M Co 5th TN Cav; 11 Feb 64 to 1 Jul 65; Bradford PO
DOWLER, James W., Sh-157-6; Insely's Farm PO
DOWNER, A. W., D-60-1; Musician Co F 179th OH Inf; Sep 23 64 to Jun 18 65; 1154 Brood St, Nashville PO
DOWNEY, J. A., Bo-11-3; Pvt L Co 2nd TN Cav; 9-8-63 to 7-6-65; Brick Mill PO
DOWNEY, William G., Lo-191-2; Pvt A Co 3rd TN Inf; 4 Mar 62 to 4 Mar 65; Morganton PO; leg broken, varicose veins

DOWNING, George E., Mr-102-3; 1st Lt & Adjutant? B Co 2nd WV Cav; 10-13-61 to 5-19-63; South Pittsburg PO
DOWNING, Jessee, Wy-173-3; Lida widow of; Pvt G Co 10th TN Inf; 6-14-62 to 6-24-65; Sims PO
DOWNING, John A., Hd-45-2; Sarah C. Smith widow of; Pvt E Co 8th TN Mtd Inf; 1 M 65 to 1 Sep 65; Cerro Gordo PO
DOWNING, John G., La-117-3; Pvt K Co 42nd TN Cav; Oct 62 to 65; 15th Dist; CONF
DOWNING, Peter P., Hd-49-1; Pvt D Co 2nd TN Inf; Sep 1 63 to Feb 1 65; Olive Hill PO
DOWNING, Washington, T-206-1; Pvt I Co 88th TN Vol Inf; 20 Apr 65 to Apr 30 66; Covington PO
DOWNS, Jessee, Fe-42-1; Elisabeth widow of; Pvt Capt David Beaty's Co of TN Indpt Scouts; Jamestown PO
DOWNS, John J., Ro-211-4; US Sol; 16th Civil Dist
DOWNS, William H., Sm-166-3(1); Pvt A Co 23rd TN Inf; 1-62 to 7-63; Monoville PO
DOWTHAT, Jonithan, Hw-118-3; Eliza widow of; Pvt; St. Clair PO
DOYAL, Joseph S., Gr-75-1; Amanda widow of; Sgt B Co 1st TN Lt Art; 18 Apr 63 to 20 Jul 65; Doyal PO; chronic diarrhea
DOYLE, Andrew J., Wa-263-5; Nancy J. widow of; Pvt F Co 60th TN Inf; Conkling PO; CONF
DOYLE, Archi, C-33-1; Pvt J Co 7th TN Cav; 11-8-64 to 7-27-65; Newcomb PO
DOYLE, Daniel, Sh-151-1; Sgt F Co 59th; 2 yrs 9 mos; Arlington PO
DOYLE, Edward S., K-172-1; Pvt A Co 6th TN Inf; 1 Dec 64 to 30 Jun 65; Knoxville PO; service pension bil
DOYLE, Jackson, T-214-1; Pvt I Co 55th US Inf; Oct 62 to 65; Mason Depot PO
DOYLE, Jacob H., K-156-1; Melissa C. widow of; Pvt TN; Patton St 54, Knoxville PO
DOYLE, James A., K-172-3; Pvt A Co 6th TN Inf; 62 to 65; 14th Dist, South Knoxville PO
DOYLE, Joseph W., P-151-4; Linden Hotel de Linden PO
DOYLE, William, A-6-6(4); Sarah widow of; Pvt; 62 to 65; Olivers PO; CONF
DOYLE, Woodran, K-176-2; Pvt F Co 2nd TN Inf; 62 to 65; Halls X Roads PO
DOZIER, Benjamin, D-102-1; Pvt E Co 30th GA Inf; Drake PO
DOZIER, Edward, D-49-2; Ellen former widow of; Pvt D Co 106th US Inf; Nashville PO; just knows this
DOZIER, Henry E., Dy-29-5; Pvt B Co 12th TN Inf; Jul 61 to Feb 65; Newbern PO; CONF
DOZIER, J. J., G-57-5(3); Pvt; Yorkville PO; CONF
DOZIER, James, Mu-209-3; Pvt F Co 138th GA; May 1 65 to Dec 23 65; Columbia PO
DOZIER, James, Mu-209-6; Pvt F Co 138th GA; May 1 65 to Dec 23 65; Columbia PO
DOZIER, Lizzie (see Stanley, John)
DOZIER, W. A., G-57-4(1); Pvt; 6-1-61 to 6-1-64; Yorkville PO; CONF
DRAKE, Albert, D-50-3; Louise widow of; Nashville PO
DRAKE, Burgess, Ce-30-1; Pvt H Co 12th TN Inf; 63 to 65; Craggie Hope PO
DRAKE, Charles M., H-56-7; Pvt E Co 4th MI Inf; 4-61 to 6-62; St. Elmo PO
DRAKE, David J., Dy-25-1; Pvt B Co 12th KY Cav; 62 to 65; Newbern PO
DRAKE, George, D-78-2; Nashville PO
DRAKE, Granvill Col, Li-152-1; Pvt H Co 12th TN; 62 to 65; PO omitted; shot 5 times
DRAKE, James, Cf-35-3; Pvt I Co 4th TN Inf; 6 Nov 61 to 1 Apr 63; Gould PO; CONF
DRAKE, Mulford F., H-53-8; enlisted as Foster Drake; Sgt G Co 11th MI Inf; 8-24-61 to 9-30-64; Chattanooga PO
DRAKE, Thomas J., Bo-15-1; Pvt B Co 1st TN Inf; Blockhouse PO
DRAM, Val, D-99-2; Elizabeth widow of; Pvt 14th TN Inf; Edgefield Junction PO
, J. M., G-57-4(1); Pvt C Co 12th TN Inf; 7-1-61 to 5-1-65; Yorkville PO; CONF
DRAPER, John R., Un-256-2; Pvt C Co 16th IA Inf; 1 Nov 61 to 4 Jan 65; Lost Creek PO; constapatien, piles & heart diseas
DRAPER, Prier L., K-175-1; Pvt A Co 1st TN Cav; 13 Apr 62 to 1 Aug 65; Pedigo PO
DRATON, Edward, Sh-159-1; Sylvia widow of; Memphis PO; CONF
DRATON, Rosier, C-28-1; Fincastle PO
DRAUGHN, Albert, D-77-3; Foster St, Nashville PO
DRAUGHON, J. S., Rb-221-3; Pvt; Sep 1 64 to Oct 1 65; Adams Station PO; CONF
DRESKILL, Benjamin F., Co-61-2(1); C Sgt 8th TN Inf; 1 Jul 63 to 30 May 65; Parrottsville PO; neuralgia from fever
DRESSER?, Nicholas, D-50-4; Pvt; 1045 N. Cherry, Nashville PO; lost records
DREW?, Leander E., Sh-148-1; Assistant PM at Memphis; Memphis PO
DREWRY, Harvy, We-227-1; Pvt A Co 7th TN Cav; 27 Dec 64 to 11 Aug 65; Greenfield PO
DRIGGS, Nelson C., Sn-201-1; Pvt G Co 50th IL Inf; 10-12-61 to 10-12-64; Memphis PO
DRINEN, William B., Hm-107-5; Pvt D Co 9th TN Cav; 26 Oct 63 to 11 Sep 65; Springvale PO; heart
DRISKELL, Moses, Je-146-5; Pvt D Co 8th TN Inf; 28 Mar 63 to 25 Jan 65; White Pine PO; disease of lungs & throat
DRISKILL, Richard, Ro-202-4; Pvt I Co 1st TN Inf; 9 Aug 61 to 30 Sep 64; Paw Paw Ford PO; lungs & left eye
DRISKILL, Robert A., Sol, Gr-82-2; 13th Dist
DRIVER, Alvin, M-108-3; Pvt H Co 5th KY Cav; 12-31-61 to 5-3-65; Akersville, KY PO; deafness & injure in back & hips from fall of horse
DRIVER, Asa D., Dk-34-5(4); Pvt F Co 4th TN Inf; 9-2-64 to 8-24-67; Dowelltown PO
DRIVER, Dempsy D., Dk-34-6(5); Pvt A Co 5th TN Cav; 7-25-62 to 6-25-65; Copling PO; thrown from horse and hurt
DRIVER, James A., M-108-5; Pvt; Lafayette PO; discharge lost
DRIVER, John H., M-108-2(1); Pvt K Co 5th KY Cav; 12-61 to 65 (3 yrs); Salt Lick PO; chronic diarhea
DRIVER, Joseph Y., M-108-3; Pvt & Cpl H Co 5th KY Vol Cav; 11-5-61 to 5-6-65; Akersville KY; rheumatism, discharge not at home
DRIVER, Thomas, Di-36-1; Pvt D Co 16th TN Inf; 62 to 65; Bellsburgh PO
DRIVER, Thomas, M-108-4; Jane widow of; Pvt I Co 9th KY Inf; 62 to __; Lafayette PO; discharge lost
DRIVER, William R., M-108-3; Pvt H Co 5th KY Cav; 61 to 5-3-65; Akersville PO; rheumatism, discharge not at home
DROKE, Jobe K., Su-235-1; Pvt G Co 23rd IN Inf; 1 Aug 62 to 1 Jul 65; Blountville PO; exposure in war
DRONDIARD, James P., D-56-1; Capt ADC on Rosencranzs staff & with regular troops at first battle of Bull Run; Spring 66 (7 yrs 6 mos); this includes time at West Point; graduated there after 1st battle of Bull Run, served as Major, _____ Irwin Mc Donell staff till ___ 63 then on the staff of Genl. Rosencrans till close of war; Nashville PO
DROSSETT, Andrew L., A-5-2; Pvt H Co 19th TN Inf; 4-62 to 4-65; Dossett PO; rheumatism
DROUNE, Charles H., Ro-211-4; US Sol; Harriman PO
DROWN, John, Ge-89-3; PVt K Co 1st TN Cav; 12 Jul 62 to 5 Jun 65; Albany PO; hernia
DRUHAM, Urls?, H-114-2; Pvt I Co 4th IL Cav; 9 May 62 to 1 Aug 64; Xenophon PO; died since war
DRUHOT, JOhn, H-76-2; Pvt C Co 184th OH Vol; 5-3-64 to 7-25-65; Chattanooga PO
DRUMBAR, Geo. E., H-68-1; Pvt B Co 3rd OH Inf; 7-61 to 8-64; Chattanooga PO
DRUMING, William R., Se-223-1; Pvt B Co 2nd TN Cav; 15 Sep 62 to 6 Jul 65; Pigeon Forge PO
DUMMEN, John, Ha-110-3; Cpl L Co 8th TN Cav; 17 Sep 63 to 11 Sep 65; Treadway PO; nasal catarrh & rheumatism
DRURY?, Harland P., Cf-40-1; Sgt H Co 18th MI Inf; 15 Aug 62 to 26 Jun 65; Tullahoma PO
DRUVAULT, Martan V., Cl-53-2; Pvt A Co 9th TN Cav; 8-9-63 to 9-11-65; Springdale PO
DRYDEN, Mary A., B-12-2; widow?; PO omitted
DUBERRY, Bragg, H-57-4; US Sol; 10th Civil Dist
DUBERRY, Thomas, Ch-17-1; Pvt A Co 27th TN Inf; Henderson PO; CONF

DUBOSE, Frank, H-57-1; Bugler 6th US Col; 63 to 65; Orchard Knob PO
DUCHMAN, John W., H-61-1; Capt G Co 60th TN Inf -- 5-61 to 10-64; Capt G Co 60th TN Inf--10-64 to 4-65; Chattanooga PO; in siege of Vicksburg
DUCKET, Enoch C., Br-8-4(2); Sgt H Co 12th TN Cav; 2-61 to __; Cleo PO
DUCKET, James, D-47-1; Rebecker widow of; Pvt A Co 44th US Inf; Jackson St, Nashville PO
DUCKETT, Robert C., Po-151-1; Pvt; Serville PO
DUCKWORTH, John B., O-138-4; Pvt; 9th Civil Dist
DUCKWORTH, John B., O-138-3; Pvt H Co 6th KY; spring 63 to May 65; Elbridge PO; shot in knee and head; CONF
DUCKWORTH, John H., Ms-169-1; Louisa A. widow of; Pvt E Co 10th TN Inf; 22 Jun 62 to 23 Jun 65; Petersburg PO; dislocation of right hip, discharged on surgeons certificate
DUCKWORTH, Morgan D., Ms-169-1; Pvt G Co 31st IN Inf; 8 Feb 64 to 8 Dec 65; Petersburg PO; lungs injured by exposure, discharged on surg. certificate
DUCKWORTH, William S., D-67-2; Nashville PO
DUDLEY, Bartlett T., Bo-21-2; Cpl C Co 1st TN Art; 7-20-63 to 5-1-65; Ellijay PO
DUDLEY, Isaac N., Cf-39-1; Pvt B Co 2nd KY Art; Sep 61 to 8 Nov 64; Prairie Plains PO; fractured tibia left leg, piles, resulting from chronic diarrhoea
DUDLEY, Joseph, Mt-135-1; Pvt A Co 16th TN Inf; 63 to 3-1-65; Jordan Springs PO
DUDLEY, Perry, Mu-205-1; Pvt F Co 138th GA US Inf; Aug 64 to May 65; Water Valley PO; all papers lost
DUDLEY, Ransona, Wi-276-2; widow of; Pvt D Co 10th TN Cav; Oct 62 to Oct 63; Beechville PO; CONF
DUDLEY, Reubin, Mt-137-2; in USA employ; papers lost; St. Bethlehem PO
DUDLEY, Solomon, Ge-99-2; Pvt C Co 1st TN Lt Art; 20 Jul 63 to 1 Aug 65; Limestone Springs PO; gunshot wound in right arm
DUFF, Donnis, P-156-3; Pvt H Co 10th TN Cav; 2-63 to 7-63; Lobelville PO
DUFF, Gilbert R., Mc-117-2; Nonaburgh PO
DUFF, Harris, Wa-274-1; Jane widow of; Pvt F Co 121st US Col Vol; Jonesboro PO
DUFF, James P., Gr-78-2; Pvt B Co 8th TN Cav; 11 Jun 63 to 11 Sep 65; Spring House PO; rheumatism
DUFF, John J., Lo-187-1; Pvt D Co 5th TN Inf; 25 Mar 62 to 30 Apr 65; Loudon PO; injury left ankle
DUFF, Peter, H-64-3; Pvt; Chattanooga PO; shocked by cannon; deaf in 1 ear
DUFF, Thos., We-220-3; Pvt I Co 6th TN Cav; Jan 16 62 to Jan 16 65; PO omitted
DUFF, Wiliam H. H., Gr-75-1; Pvt F Co 1st TN Cav; 1 Mar 62 to 30 Mar 65; Tampico PO; eye and hearing and rhumatics
DUFFEY, James, Sh-188-2; US white; 129 Jackson St, Memphis PO
DUFFINE, I., Col, Sh-146-2; Pvt E Co 53rd __; Woodstock PO
DUFFLE, George W., We-233-2; Pvt M Co 2nd IA Cav; 3-16-62 to 3-16-65; Latham PO
DUFFY, Daniel J., H-62-1; Lt D Co 9th MO Cav; 9-61 to 4-65; 517 Poplar St, Chattanooga PO; wounded in left arm, 3rd knuckle broken
DUGAN, John, Ro-209-1; Eliza widow of; Pvt D Co; Rockwood PO
DUGAN, John N., Ja-85-5; Pvt E Co 5th TN Mtd Inf; 9-17-64 to 6-26-65; Long Savannah PO
DUGDALE, W. H., Hd-47-1; Sgt D Co 16th OH Inf; Apr 61 to __ (4 yrs); Savannah PO; enlisted 1861? 44th OH Inf
DUGGAN, Archibal M., Se-226-1; Pvt A Co 2nd TN Cav; 16 Sep 62 to 5 Jul 65; Straw Plains PO; rupture in battle
DUGGAN, Daniel, Se-221-3; Sarah Feezel former widow of; Pvt M Co 2nd TN Cav; 8 Nov 62 to __; Harrisburg PO
DUGGAN, James M., Je-140-1; 2nd Lt B Co 7th TN Cav; 15 Aug 62 to 6 Jul 65; Lucilla PO; rumatism & piles
DUGGAN, John F. M., Mc-117-1; Pvt; Mecca PO
DUGGAN, Thos. C., Mc-117-4; Capt E Co 7th __ Mtd Inf; 8-16-64 to 7-27-65; Carlock PO; rheumatism & neuralgia
DUGGAN, Wilson M., Lo-195-1; Pvt E Co 5th TN Inf; 5 Sep 64 to __; Eatons X Roads PO
DUGGAY, W.? H., Se-228-3; Mary David formerly widow of; Pvt G Co 6th TN Inf; 10 May 62 to __; Cox PO
DUGGER, George M., Ct-35-1; 2nd Lt & M Sgt A Co 13th TN Cav; 9-22-63 to 10-14-64; Hampton PO
DUGGER, John F., Ct-35-3; Sarah widow of; Pvt G Co 13th TN Cav; 9-24-63 to 9-5-65; Elk Mills PO; in US Army
DUGGER, John S., Ge-97-2; Pvt D Co 8th TN Inf; 4 Mar 64 to 30 Jan 65; Locust Spring PO; rheumatism
DUGGER, William L., H-62-2; 415 Poplar, Chattanooga PO
DUGGAR, Hardin G., Cu-16-2; Pvt K Co 1st TN Inf; 8-12-61 to 9-17-64; Mt. Gilean PO; shot in left hand
DUGLAS, William H., H-69-6; Ann widow of; Pvt; Chattanooga PO; killed in war; CONF
DUGLASS, Samuel L., Je-145-2; Elizabeth widow of; Cpl C Co 9th TN Cav; 12 Jun 63 to 4 Mar? 65; Dumplin PO
DUGLIS, Eebb, Gi-138-2; Sgt D Co 110th Cav; 63 to 66; Valesville PO
DUGLISS, Julins, T-216-1; Pvt L Co 3rd TN Inf; __ tured May 65; Corona PO
DUKE, Ben, D-91-2; Pvt; Nashville PO
DUKE, Benjamin R., Bl-1-1; Pvt E Co 10th TN Inf; 3-1-63 to 6-23-65; Pikeville PO rheumatism & deafness
DUKE, Dolphin, Sh-161-2; US Sol; 16th Dist
DUKE, Elvin, A-1-3; Pvt G Co 7th TN Cav; 11-8-64 to 7-28-65; Andersonville PO; hurt in the back
DUKE, Gideon F., Ca-23-3; Pvt E Co 10th TN Inf; 3-1-63 to 6-23-65; Narla PO; health injured by cold
DUKE, James J., D-45-4; Pvt E Co 10th TN Inf; 3-1-63 to 6-2-65; Nashville PO
DUKE, Napoleon C., J-80-2; Pvt A Co 7th? TN Inf; 1-10-65 to 8-7-65; Donahoe, Smith Co. PO; measles followed by diarhea & disease of kidneys & bladder; Mr. Duke was enlisted as Clay Duke
DUKE, Samuel J., Sm-170-1; Pvt B Co 7th TN Inf; 5-20-61 to 8-20-63; Maggart PO; CONF
DUKE, William, Sh-145-1; alias Seniggo, William; Cpl I Co 59th US Col Inf; 1 Jun 63 to 31 Jan 66; Millington PO; Cap. A. J. Henderson, Co I
DUKE, William L., Sm-170-3; Orderly Sgt G Co 28th TN Inf; 10-10-61 to 1-25-65; Chestnut Mound PO
DUKES, Amis, Sh-157-5; Pvt A Co; 2 yrs 6 mos; White Haven PO
DUKES, Arnold, Sh-162-2(1); Pvt I Co 44th TN Inf; 62 to 65; Ramsey PO; discharged at Nashville
DULAN, Jackson, K-166-5; US Sol; North Knoxville PO
DULEY, Eli, D-78-1; Pvt H Co 1st MI Inf; Sep 63 to Sep 65; Nashville PO
DULWORTH, Mathias T., Cy-30-1; Pvt G Co 5th KY Cav; 10 mos; Willow Grove PO; lung disease, discharged from disabilities
DUMACK, Washington, Hu-99-1; Cpl H Co 13th Col US Inf; 2 Oct 63 to 13 Jun 66; Johnsonville PO; shot in left hand, frequent pain
DUMAGER, Andy C., Hu-103-2; Pvt E Co 10th TN Inf; 10 Aug 61 to 28 Dec 64; PO omitted
DUMAS, Livina P., Cr-16-4; widow of Sol; 11th Civil Dist
DUN, James, Sh-161-1; on same line as Hicks, Petter; perished in Mexico; PO omitted
DUN, John, Ch-17-2; Lucinda widow of; Pvt A Co 6th TN Cav; Sep 62 to Mar 65; McNairy PO
DUN, John W., Dk-36-2; Pvt B Co 4th TN Mtd Inf; 9-25-64 to 65; Smithville PO
DUN, Thomas, D-69-3; Mygie widow of; US Sol; no record; Nashville PO
DUN, Willia, Hu-103-4; Pvt A Co 6th GA Inf; 62 to 64; PO omitted; marked through, probably CONF
DUNAGAN, Goerge, Col, Dy-20-1; Pvt D Co 4th TN Art; May 63 to Aug 64; Friendship PO
DUNAWAY, George, H-59-3; Lt MS Inf; 7-62 to 12-62; Chattanooga PO
DUNBAR, Charles, Lo-188-3; Sweetwater PO; CONF

DUNBAR, Charles D., Lo-188-3; Sweetwater PO
DUNBAR, George E., Sh-174-1; Quartermaster Sgt 74th IL Inf; 8-62 to 65; 185 Willington St, Memphis PO
DUNBAR, George W., Wa-260-1; Pvt G Co 4th Reg Inf; Nov 12 62 to Aug 2 65; Pilot Hill PO; chronic diarear & piles
DUNBAR, Johnson, F-39-1; Pvt D Co 57th US Col Inf; 63 to 65; Braden PO; discharge in Washington
DUNBAR, Miles, Hn-81-1; Teamster G Co IN; 62 to 64; Elkhorn PO; colored, & is not able to give regt., no month enlisted
DUNBAR, Wm., T-212-1; "found while examing work', no address on blank
DUNBAR, William, Wa-260-1; Pvt K (or H?) Co 3rd NC Cav; Nov 26 64 to Aug 8 65; Cassi PO; catar of head & scarfulus
DUNBAR, William, Ge-83-3; Pvt G Co 4th TN Inf; 25 Nov 62 to 2 Aug 65; Painters PO; reaps of measels & cronic diar.
DUNCAN, Alfred, W-189-1; Pvt D Co 4th TN Cav; 4-18-63 to 7-18-65; McMinnville PO
DUNCAN, Calloway H., A-2-3; Cpl-Pvt C Co 2nd TN Inf; 12-14-61 to 12-15-64; Hinds Creek PO; gun shot wound right side & leg
DUNCAN, Coleman, H-61-5; 2nd Lt B Co 18th IN Inf; 7-8-61 to 11-22-64; Chattanooga PO; gunshot wound in right hip
DUNCAN, Craven, S-213-3; Cpl F Co 9th TN Inf; 9 Aug 61 to 17 Sep 64; Glenmary PO
DUNCAN, Elijah, A-13-3; Nancy Turp widow of; Briceville PO; his discharge not at home
DUNCAN, George, Hr-87-1; Hickory Valley PO
DUNCAN, George S., H-73-4(2); Pvt A Co 62nd PA Inf; 9-20-61 to 1-23-65; Chattanooga PO
DUNCAN, George W., Hd-53-1; Pvt F Co 6th TN Cav--21 Sep 62 to 25 Jun 63; Pvt B Co 2nd TN Mtd Inf--15 Oct 63 to 17 Oct 64; O Sgt I Co 4th TN Mtd Inf--15 Nov 64 to 15 Aug 65; Sibley PO; disabled in head, thrown from horse & hearing injured
DUNCAN, Granderson, Pu-145-2; Pvt B Co 1st Mtd Inf; 2-4-64 to 7-20-65; Burton PO
DUNCAN, Henry, D-68-1; alias Harding, Henry; Pvt A Co 100th USC Inf; __ to 65 (2 yrs 8 mos); 156 Fillmore, Nashville PO; this man has not his discharge papers with him
DUNCAN, Henry, Lo-187-3; Pvt; Loudon PO; deafness
DUNCAN, Henry C., Cu-17-1; Pvt C Co 1st TN Inf; 1-61 to 5-27-65; Crossville PO
DUNCAN, Henry H., Cf-35-3; Pvt I Co 4th TN Inf; 6 Nov 61 to 1 Apr 63; Normandy PO; CONF
DUNCAN, Isaac A., Je-147-2; Capt F Co 9th TN Cav; 16 Dec 63 to 10 Jun 64; Shady Grove PO
DUNCAN, Isaac A. (William I. alias); A-9-1; Pvt I Co 9th TN Cav; 10-20-64 to 9-11-65; Ligias PO; measles resulting in disease of lungs
DUNCAN, James M., A-6-3(1); Annie widow of; Pvt G Co 2nd TN Inf; 1-62 to 4-65; Wind Rock PO
DUNCAN, James F., A-5-1; Cpl F Co 7th TN Inf; 11-8-64 to 7-27-65; Clinton PO; rheumatism
DUNCAN, James M., Wa-26-1; Pvt K Co TN Inf; 10 May 62 to Jul 20 63; Cankling PO; lung disease
DUNCAN, James H., H-56-6; K Co 3rd PA; 4-20-61 to 5-26-63; St. Elmo PO; reenlisted
DUNCAN, James W., R-159-2; Pvt B Co 7th TN Mtd Inf; 10-14-64 to 7-26-65; Spring City PO
DUNCAN, John, A-6-3(1); Pvt C Co 11th TN Inf; 5-1-64 to 8-2-65; Wind Rock PO; relaps of measles
DUNCAN, John, A-2-3; Susan J. widow of; Pvt C wnd TN Inf; Hinds Creek PO; house burned & discharge lost
DUNCAN, John H., Hw-133-2; Catharine widow of; Pvt K Co 1st TN Cav; Burem's Store PO
DUNCAN, John M., Hw-121-1; US Sol; PO omitted
DUNCAN, Joseph G., Wa-261-1; Pvt G Co TN Inf; 20 Oct 63 to 14 Apr 64?; Brownsboro PO; CONF
DUNCAN, Lode, P-151-4; Dist 6
DUNCAN, Robert, H-73-2(1); Susan widow of; Pvt; Chattanooga PO
DUNCAN, Robert, Lo-187-3; Pvt H Co 5th TN Inf; 62 to 65; Loudon PO
DUNCAN, Sam D., H-73-4(2); Pvt; Chattanooga PO
DUNCAN, Solomon, Hm-107-1; Pvt D Co 4th TN Cav; Chestnut Bloom PO; bronchitis
DUNCAN, Tampa, K-162-1; widow, sol; #83 Common Alley, Knoxville PO

DUNCAN, Thomas, A-9-3(1); Pvt G Co 2nd TN Inf; 3-12-62 to 8-9-65; Wind Rock PO; rheumatism & kidney disease
DUNCAN, Thomas L., A-6-3(1); Pvt I Co 7th TN Inf; 11-64 to 7-65; Wind Rock PO; shot in the neck
DUNCAN, Thomas N., Cr-20-2; Pvt I Co 7th TN Cav; Aug 15 63 to __; Hollow Rock PO
DUNCAN, Wm. C., C-34-3; Pvt G Co 2nd TN Inf; 12-23-61 to 12-63; Caryville PO; sickened & furloughed
DUNCAN, Wm. F., Br-6-2; Sgt H Co 4th TN Cav; 5-6-64 to 7-12-6? (1 yr 2 mos 6 days); Chatala PO; disease lungs, diarrhoea & nephritis, injured in RR act Aug 19, 1864
DUNCAN, William R., A-6-3(1); Pvt G Co 3rd TN Inf; 2-10-62 to 2-13-65; Olivers PO
DUNCUM, Gannin?, K-174-5; Pvt E Co 3rd TN Inf; 22 Feb 62 to 23 Feb 65; Floyd PO
DUNCUM, Thorough, K-173-3; Luisa widow of; Pvt K Co 3rd TN Inf; 62 to 2 Jun 65; Troutman PO
DUNDERMAN, Jacob, Sh-151-1; Pvt D Co 1st OH Art; 10 Sep 61 to 18 Jul 63; Arlington PO; thrown from horse in baggle & disabled in arm, discharged on surgeons certificate
DUNGAN, James L., Ja-85-3; Capt H Co 5th TN Inf; 5-21-62 to 5-16-65; Birchwood PO
DUNHAM, Aaron, Mr-102-2; Cpl A Co 68th IN Inf; 8-5-62 to 6-20-65; South Pittsburg PO; chronic diarhea
DUNKIN, Charley, C-26-1; Lt A Co 1st TN Inf; 8-2-61 to 9-17-64; Jacksboro PO
DUNKIN, John H., Ja-84-1; Rebecca widow of; Pvt H Co 12th TN Cav; __ to 63; Harrison PO; died in survis
DUNKIN, Taylor, Mt-132-1; Pvt B Co 16th TN Inf; 7-4-62 to 10-1-65; Guthrie, KY PO; blind
DUNKIN, William A., Dy-25-2; Ellen E. widow of; Pvt; Mar 62 to __; Newbern PO; died Apr 19 62, pneumonia cause of death; CONF
DUNKINS, John M., Hw-121-1; Pvt K Co 9th TN Cav; 4 Aug 63 to 15 May 65; Chimny Gap PO; rhumatism spinal affection
DUNLAP, Charles, Hn-77-2; Tennessee widow of; Pvt; Sep 63 to __; PO omitted
DUNLAP, F. A., Bo-11-2; Pvt E Co 3rd TN Inf; 7-15-64 to 11-30-64; Cloids Creek PO
DUNLAP, James J., Bo-22-2; Pvt H Co 3rd TN Cav; 9-63 to 8-8-65; Hebronville PO
DUNLAP, Jasper F., Ct-44-2; Pvt E Co 6th IN Inf; 4-20-61 to 8-2-61; Cpl D Co 6th IN Inf--9-20-61 to 11-13-62; Pvt E Co 10th IN Cav--11-13-63 to 11-24-63; 1st Lt E Co 10th IN Cav--11-24-63 to 7-10-64; Hampton PO; reumittant fever, now consumption, rheumatism
DUNLAP, John, Sh-184-1; US Sol; 179 Carroll Ave, Memphis PO
DUNLAP, John, Mo-119-3; Pvt B Co 169th OH NG Inf; 64 to 9-4-64; Sweetwater PO
DUNLAP, John, Bo-21-1; Cpl A Co 6th TN Inf; 3-8-62 to 4-27-65; Veeba PO
DUNLAP, John M., H-70-2(1); Lt K Co 4th OH Inf; 7-61 to 64 (4 yrs); Chattanooga PO; wounded in left foot by shell
DUNLAP, Polly A., R-157-1; widow; Lorraine PO; hard hearing
DUNLAP, Presley E., We-230-4; Pvt K Co 10th TN Reg; May 1 61 to May 1 62; Greenfield PO; CONF
DUNLP, Benjamine, Mt-137-1; Cpl A Co 16th TN Col Inf; in service over two years, papers lost; St. Bethlehem PO
DUNMEYER, Louis L., H-60-2; alias Louis Meyers; Capt C Co 84th OH Inf--5-1-62 to 9-30-62; Eng asst L and Harvest Moon, New Hampshire & Phila --fall 63 to 9-65; Chattanooga PO; enlisted in Navy, assumed name
DUNN, Caleb W., Jo-149-3; Pvt M Co 10th Genl? Cav; 1 Feb 64 to 1 Aug 65; Mountain City PO; failed to see the soldier in person
DUNN, Elijah, K-182-2; Wagon master; 63 to 64; Nast PO
DUNN, Emanuel, Jo-150-4; Pvt E Co 13th TN Cav; 24 Sep 63 to 5 Sep 65; Osborn PO
DUNN, George, C-33-3; Pvt Navy Carondelette; 63 to 65; Newcomb PO
DUNN, George H., We-228-1(9); Pvt E Co 6th TN Cav; 20 Nov 63 to 26 Jul 65; Gleason PO; loss of right ear, now deaf in right ear

DUNN, Godfrey B., Jo-150-1; Pvt F Co 13th TN Cav; 22 Sep 63 to 5 Sep 65; Osborn PO
DUNN, Harry, D-49-4; Helen widow of; 1st Lt B Co 100th USC Inf; 9 Dec 65 to 21 Jan 66; Nashville PO
DUNN, Harvey T., O-140-1; Pvt F Co 61st IL Ver?; 21 Nov 63 to 8 Sep 65; Union City PO; feet frozen
DUNN, Henry, Jo-151-3; Pauline widow of; Pvt F Co 13th TN Cav; 22 Sep 63 to 5 Sep 65; Vaughtsville PO; dyspepsia, liver disease
DUNN, Henry W., Hu-104-1(2); Buglar G Co 12th TN Cav; Feb 10 64 to Ju_ 17 65; McEwen PO; fall inguring left hip & cankered sore throat
DUNN, Jackson, Gi-122-2; Pvt AL Inf; Apr? 15 64 to _ (3 yrs); Prospect Sta. PO; CONF
DUNN, Jacob N., Jo-150-1; Pvt F Co 13th TN Cav; 22 Sep 63 to 5 Sep 65; Rheas Forge PO; hearing
DUNN, James D., Po-148-2; Pvt A Co 44th Col Inf; 12-15-63 to 3-26-66; Benton PO; cold settle in eyes
DUNN, John, Col, Rb-222-1; Pvt D Co 101st US Inf; 1 Jul 64 to 31 Jan 66; Turnersvill PO
DUNN, John, C-30-1; Catherine Spangler formerly widow of; Pvt F Co 6th TN Inf; 3-10-62 to _; Well Springs PO; died during service
DUNN, John L., Dy-27-3; Pvt I Co 45th TN Inf; Oct 62 to Apr 65; Tatemville PO; CONF
DUNN, John L., Pu-145-2; Pvt E Co 1st Mtd Inf; 11-5-63 to 1-22-65; Burton PO
DUNN, John L., Jo-151-3; Pvt F Co 13th TN Cav; 22 Sep 63 to 5 Sep 65; Shown's & Roads PO; liver disease, died in January 1889
DUNN, John M., Be-6-1; Pvt L Co 12th KY Cav; 63 to 65; Big Sandy PO
DUNN, John M., Ch-13-2; Pvt B Co 6th TN Vol; 7-20-63 to 7-26-65; Henderson PO
DUNN, John R., Dk-39-2; 8th Civil Dist
DUNN, John T., We-220-3; 1st Civil Dist
DUNN, Josep, Jo-150-5; Pvt Pontiac, 3 Jun 64 to 27 Jun 65; Osborn PO
DUNN, Lucinda, Bl-3-6; widow of US Sol; 5th Civil Dist
DUNN, Martin, K-164-2; Pvt D Co 2nd IN Cav; 22 Oct 62 to 22 Jul 65; PO omitted (Knoxville?)
DUNN, Nathaniel, Gr-82-1; Malinda widow of; Pvt 9th TN Cav; Ambro PO
DUNN, Phillip, Ge-97-3; Pvt F Co 3rd TN Cav; 1 Jun 62 to 5 Jun 65; Upchurch PO; lungs
DUNN, Rhoda E. (see Cole, John R.)
DUNN, Samuel, Ct-39-2; Pvt E Co 7th TN Mtd Inf; 61 to 65; Happy Valley PO; shot through left breast
DUNN, Samuel, Su-236-1; Cpl B Co 45th KY Inf; 24 Aug 63 to 4 Dec 64; Arcadia PO
DUNN, Thomas, La-113-1; Pvt A Co 5th KY Inf; 1 Nov 61 to 4 Nov 64; Lawrenceburg PO
DUNN, W. W., K-155-1; 2nd Sgt A Co 6th TN Inf; 8 Mar 62 to 27 Mar 63; Knoxville PO; disease of spine & kidneys
DUNN, William, Jo-150-1; Pvt D Co 13th TN Cav; 24 Sep 63 to 5 Sep 65; Rheas Forge PO; sight
DUNN, Wilson B., Sn-259-1; Pvt C Co 5th _; 10-12-62 to 6-20-64; Bransford PO; wounded with horse
DUNN, Zephering, Gr-78-2; Pvt B Co 9th TN Cav; Sep 63 to Mar 65; Spring House PO
DUNNE, Burl H., Br-7-3; Artificer L Co 3rd TN Cav; Cleveland PO; rheumatism
DUNNIGAN, Dorcey, K-174-1; Pvt F Co 1st TN Cav; 1 Nov 62 to 25 May 65; Church Grove PO
DUNNING, Andrew, Hn-74-1; Cpl I Co 6th TN Cav; 26 Jun 62 to 28 Jul 65; Como PO; discharged special order
DUNSMORE, Frank, K-174-4(3); Pvt G Co 8th TN Cav; 6 Aug 63 to 11 Sep 65; Church Grove PO; deseas of eyes and wound
DUNSMORE, John, Gr-81-1; Pvt H Co 1st TN Cav; 15 Jul 62 to 8 Jun 65; Clear Spring PO; spinal affection; totly disabled
DUNSMORE, Joseph J., K-156-4; Pvt H Co 8th TN Inf; 15 Aug 63 to 8 Apr 65; 119 Kennedy St, Knoxville PO; received wounds which destroyed health, had skull cracked gun barel
DUPES, Andrew J., Mo-124-1; 9th Civil Dist
DUPREE, James, Sh-191-7(3); Memphis PO; records not seen

DURANT, Jerry, Sh-197-1; Col unit; Memphis PO; not at home
DURANT, Robert R., Sh-159-6; Pvt A Co 113th IL; Oct 61 to Dec 64; Memphis PO; shot three times twice in legs and once in body, sunstroke at Wellsbury, not able to work, this entry marked out
DURHAM, James A., St-162-2; Pvt H? Co 3rd IL Inf; Nov 63 to _; Erin PO; lost one eye & the other damaged & now drawing pension; Pvt G Co 61st IL Inf--Jul 64 to 65
DURHAM, Oliver P., Dk-32-3; Sariah widow of; Pvt G Co 1st TN Mtd Inf; 3-5-64 to _; Temperance Hall PO
DURHAM, Samuel D., Ms-173-1; Pvt L Co 8th E TN Cav; 28 Mar 64 to 11 Sep 65; Rich Creek PO
DURHAM, Thomas, Sn-260-6; Pvt B Co 1st KY Mtd Inf; 64 to 65; A.B.C. PO
DURHAM, William C., Sn-261-3(2); Pvt E Co TN Cav; 62 to 6-19-65; Reddick PO; imprisoned at Camp Morton, IN, Chicago IL, Point Lookout 23 months; come home at the close of the war; CONF
DURHAM, William J. B., Sn-261-3(2); Pvt E Co TN Cav; 62 to 5-10-65; Sulphuria PO; imprisoned Camp Chase OH about 6 mos, came home on discharge 5-10-65; CONF
DURWIN, Houston, L-108-1; Pvt F Co 101st US Inf; Aug 18 64 to Jan 1 66; Henning PO
DUSTAN, Samuel, Sh-191-5(1); 1st Lt E Co 9th IN Inf; Memphis PO; wounded in leg, records not seen
DUSTER, J. John, Co-69-1; Juley A. widow of; Pvt; 63 to 64; Driskill PO; no reported, dont no date of inlistment
DUYER, Michael, Sn-262-2(1); Pvt A Co 1st OH Lt Art; South Tunnell PO; deafness, dont know the day in April
DWANEY, Ellis M., Ro-210-2; Pvt F Co 1st TN Inf; Rockwood PO
DWIGINS, Alexander (see Peacock, Alexander)
DWIGINS, Peter, Ru-241-2(1); Jane widow of; Pvt B Co 98th OH Inf; Jul 63 to Jun 66; Murfreesboro PO
DWYER, William, Gi-134-1; Pvt K Co 1st AL Cav; 11-13-62 to 6-20-65; Yokley PO; frostbitten feet, by escaping prison at Coherty
DYAR, Chalton, Un-255-1; Pvt D Co 8th TN Cav; Aug 63 to 66; Warwicks X Roads PO; rumatism
DYAR, Samuel L., Be-7-1; Pvt F Co 97th IN Inf; Aug 62 to Jun 65; Big Sandy PO
DYCHE, William H., Lo-188-2; Pvt G Co 9th TN Cav; 23 Aug 63 to 11 Sep 65; Philadelphia PO
DYE, Billy, T-215-2; US Sol; Mason PO
DYE, Isaac, Mc-117-2; Pvt B Co 7th TN Mtd Inf; 10-8-64 to 7-27-65; Mortimer PO
DYE, James, H-55-2; Pvt D Co 6th TN Mtd Inf; 8-16-64 to 6-30-65; Chickamauga PO
DYE, Jennings, Mo-123-2; Pvt E Co 7th TN Mtd Inf; 9-15-64 to 7-27-65; Jalapa PO
DYE, Orland W., K-160-1; Sailor, all wife knows; Knoxville PO
DYE, William H., Bl-1-2; Pvt D Co 6th TN Inf; 9-5-64 to 6-30-65; Fillmore (Sequatchie Co.); scrofula and crippled in left leg
DYE, William M., Mo-128-1; Cpl K Co 11th TN Cav; 10-10-63 to 3-25-65; Belltown PO
DYENS, Thomas E., Dy-25-3; Pvt I Co 154th TN Inf; May 61 to _ (4 yrs); Newbern PO; CONF
DYER, Andy, Sm-166-1; Virginia Cox formerly widow of; Pvt A Co 1st TN Inf; 12-18-63 to 1-30-65; Carthage PO
DYER, Augustus, Hw-121-6(1); Pvt B Co 7th Oct 62 to 1 Mar 63; New Bope PO; non in war; CONF
DYER, Charles H., H-66-1; 1st Lt 2nd Batt 2nd OH Vol; 4-19-61 to 1-31-65; Chattanooga PO
DYER, Elijah, Mc-113-1; Pvt D Co 3rd TN Inf; 2-10-62 to 2-23-65; Fiketon PO; rheumatism
DYER, Gandy, Mo-128-1; Mariah widow of; Sink PO
DYER, James A., Un-254-2; Pvt A Co 1st TN Inf; 4 Apr 63 to 3 Aug 65; Meltebarger PO; neuralgia
DYER, John F., Bo-19-3; Pvt D Co 19th TN Inf; 61 to _; Rockford PO; CONF
DYER, Joseph, Gr-81-4(2); Pvt A Co 12th TN Cav; 10 Jul 63 to 5 Sep 65; Liberty Hill PO; dyerhie, disabled some
DYER, Lawson, Hw-119-1; Lucinda Manis formerly widow of; Lee Valley PO; spinal affection

DYER, Leroy, Wa-270-1; Pvt H Co 13th TN Cav; 4 Nov 63 to 8 Sep 65; Austins Springs PO; rheumatism
DYER, Marion, Un-253-2; Pvt B Co 7th TN Inf; 7 Aug 61 to 17 Oct 64; Meltbarger PO
DYER, Richard F., Hw-121-6(1); Pvt K Co 1st TN Cav; 4 Sep 62 to 4 Oct 65; New Hope PO; defective in hearing
DYER, Thomas L., Pu-142-2; Teamster D Co 4th TN Mtd Inf; 4-15-62 to __ (2 yrs 4 mos); Standing Stone PO
DYER, William B., Mo-120-1; Pvt E Co 80th IN Inf; __ to 65 (2 yrs 6 mos); Glenloch PO; eye put out at Battle of Virginia
DYER, William C., Dk-39-1; Cpl C Co 1st TN Mtd Inf; 10-21-63 to 12-13-64; Bozarth PO; eyes affected result of having the small pox
DYER, William S., Hm-109-1; Pvt D Co 4th TN Cav; 12 May 62 to 12 May 65; Three Springs PO; rheumatism fr. which is having pension
DYER, Winship, He-63-1; Matilda J. widow of; Pvt K Co 7th TN; Long PO
DYKE, Robt. J., Sh-204-1; Elizabeth M. (formerly Whitt); widow of Pvt; Bethel Avenue, Memphis PO; could not tell a thing
DYKE, William, Ro-209-3; Elizebeth widow of; Pvt A Co 43rd TN; Glen Alice PO; CONF
DYKE, William R., H-50-1; Pvt I Co 14th R IL Cav; Soddy PO; bone scurvey
DYKES, Abraham J., Ge-98-1; Pvt D Co 4th TN Inf; 62 to 14 Jul 63 (9 mos); PO omitted; rheumatism and disease heart
DYKES, Isem B., Hw-121-1; Lt D Co 31st TN Inf; 5 Feb 62 to 13 Sep 64; New Hope PO; loss of right leg; CONF
DYKES, Jasper, Ge-98-2; Mary A. widow of; Pvt D Co 4th TN Inf; 1 Dec 62 to 2 Aug 65; Lovelace PO
DYKES, Jessey, Hw-121-5(4); Pvt; Blairs Gap PO; CONF
DYKES, John N., Ge-98-1; Pvt H Co 4th TN Cav; 15 Nov 61 to 13 Jul 65; PO omitted; rheumatism resulting in disease of heart
DYKES, Joseph, Hw-121-5(4); Pvt D Co 4th TN Inf; 12 Nov 62 to 2 Aug 65; Blairs Gapp PO; sight of right eye from artillery, rheumatism
DYKES, Levy, Se-226-3; Viny Smith formerly widow of; Henrys X Roads PO; rhumatism; cannot obtain any more information of him
DYKES, Samual, Hw-121-1; Pvt I Co 8th TN Cav; 11 Sep 63 to 11 Sep 65; Van Hill PO; throw of horse, captured and wounded in testicles, __ imprisined 6 mos
DYKES, Thomas, Hw-121-5(4); Pvt; Blairs Gapp PO; CONF
DYRE, Joseph, Ge-88-2; Mattie widow of; Pvt C Co 1st TN Cav; 62 to 63; Mohawk PO; fall of mumps
DYZON, Paul, T-206-1; Pvt G Co 4th TN Col Hvy Art; Oct 13 63 to Feb 25 66; Covington PO
EADES, Benjamin, Mc-114-6; Pvt; Santfordville PO; CONF?
EADES, Robert M., Su-241-2; Pvt P Co 8th TN Cav; Sep 62 to Apr 65; Meadow Brook PO
EADS, Andrew, Cl-47-2; Pvt E Co 2nd TN Inf; 8-9-61 to 2-9-65; Cappford PO; rheumatism, scurvey & heart 1864
EADS, Isiac, Su-241-2; he was not at home; Pvt 8th TN Cav; 62 to Apr 65; Clover Bottom PO
EADS, Samuel, Ge-91-1; Pvt 8th TN Inf; Greeneville PO; dont know any dates
EAKIN, Hugh M., Li-149-1; Cpl B Co 4th TN Inf; 4-63 to 8-65; Fayetteville PO
EAKIN, William L., H-61-1; Col 39th TN Inf; 12-61 to 6-65; Chattanooga PO; CONF
EAKLE, Henry, Cy-27-2; Pvt C Co 31st KY Inf; 5-25-63 to 12-23-64; Clementsville PO
EAKS, Frank, Wl-308-2; Pvt TN; 61 to 63; Rural Hill PO; captured; CONF
EALY, Frank M., Ms-167-1; Pvt I Co 3rd NC Inf; 1 Jan 65 to 8 Aug 65; Second Dist
EALY, John, Co-63-2; Pvt A Co 8th TN Cav; 11 Jun 63 to 11 Sep 65; Newport PO; broken ankle & dispepsia
EARHART, Jacob J., D-78-2; Nashville PO
EARHERT, J. L., Wl-308-3; Pvt I Co 20th TN; Jun 1 61 to Sep 1 62; Green Hill PO; CONF
EARLES, Thomas, W-195-1; Pvt M Co 5th TN Cav; 10-17-62 to 8-14-65; 12th Dist; fracture of right leg?

EARLIE, William H., Lo-187-1; 2nd M Sgt I Co 95th IL Inf; 4 Sep 62 to 4 Sep 65; Loudon PO
EARLS, Alexander W., Ca-23-2; Pvt M Co 5th TN Cav; 11-18-62 to 8-24-65; Leoni PO; rheumatis caused by exposure
EARLY, Abraham, Mo-119-1; Pvt; Sweetwater PO; chronic diarrhoea, drawing a pension
EARLY, Fielder O., Mc-113-1; Pvt D Co 3rd TN Inf; 2-10-62 to 2-23-65; Rock Creek PO; rheumatism
EARLY, J. V., Hu-103-1; Pvt F Co 10th TN; 10 Mar 61 to 12 May 64; PO omitted
EARLY, James, Wa-272-2; Pvt 1st TN Inf; Feb 62 to __; Harmony PO; chronic diarrhoea, disease of heart
EARLY, John G., H-51-6; 1st Sgt H Co 12th TN Cav; 1-17-64 to 10-23-66; Red Bank PO
EARLY, Thomas J., K-179-1; Pvt D Co 3rd TN Inf; 10 Feb 62 to 23 Feb 65; Rodelin PO
EARLY, William K., K-179-3; Pvt D Co 3rd TN Inf; 10 Feb 62 to 23 Feb 65; Rodelin PO
EARMIKLE, Jesse, Co-69-2; Pvt F Co 1st TN Art; 4 May 64 to 31 Mar 66; Rankin PO; rheumaties at Knoxvill TN, no pension yet
EARVIN, Driver, Dk-32-4; Luisie widow of; Pvt D Co 4th TN Mtd Inf; 9-23-64 to 5-10-65; Liberty PO; died in hospital since 1865
EASARY, William P., He-62-1; Pvt C A 110th IL; Aug 20 62 to Jul 13 65; Chesterfield PO; wounded in hip
EASELEY, Benj., D-50-2; 1st Lt Co 111th US Inf; Nov 63 to Apr 66; 318 Line, Nashville PO; wounded in 1 arm
EASLEP, Alfred, Wa-263-2; US Pvt A Co 8th TN Cav; 11 Jun 63 to Sep 11 65; also in CONF; Garbers Mills PO; gun shot wound & rheumatism
EASLEY, George, Mt-149-1; Cpl D Co 8th KY Hvy Art; 3 Mar 64 to 11 Mar 66; Palmyra PO
EASLEY, Henry, K-161-2; Knoxville PO
EASLEY, Thomas, Su-241-1; Capt B Co 4th TN Cav; 22 Dec 62 to 12 Jul 65; Clover Bottom PO; exposure, bad dyet
EASLY, Harrison, D-72-2; McLaron, __ formerly widow of; Cpl D Co 17th TN Inf; 63 to 65; Nashville PO
EASON, Francis M., Ch-14-1; Pvt D Co 48th TN Inf; 12-10-62 to 2-20-63; Sweet Lips PO
EASON, George (see Wilson, George)
EASON, Robert W., De-22-2; Pvt E Co 55th TN Inf; 1 Dec 61 to 1 Jun 62; Dunbar PO; CONF
EASON, __, Gi-127-4; Mary Kimble formerly widow of; Pulaski PO
EAST, Abner, Sh-191-2; Memphis PO; records sent to Washington
EAST, Elonzo, Ro-209-3; Pvt G Co 5th US Inf; 4 Apr 65 to 26 Sep 65; Glen Alice PO
EAST, Joseph R., C-29-2; Pvt F Co 22nd VA Cav; 9-63 to 4-9-65; Fincastle PO
EAST, Washington, Sh-191-6(2); Memphis PO; records not seen
EASTEP, Beral H., Cl-50-2(1); Pvt B Co 9th TN Cav; 8-14-63 to 9-11-65; Sprowles PO
EASTEP, William, Ge-95-1; Pvt M Co 8th TN Cav; 3 Dec 63 to 11 Sep 65; Home PO
EASTER, John, Ro-207-4; Pvt B Co 11th IN foot; 24 Jun 63 to 23 Feb 64; Fossil PO
EASTER?, Wm. T., Ro-207-3; Mady J. widow of; Pvt A Co 5th TN Inf; 61 to __; Stockton PO (Loudon Co.); chron. diarrhea
EASTERLY, Abraham H., Ge-85-1; Pvt A Co 4th TN Inf; 13 Dec 62 to 2 Aug 65; Cavey Branch PO; rheumatism
EASTERLY, George, D-61-2; Pvt K Co 8th Inf; 3 yrs; Catron Ave, Nashville PO
EASTERLY, Philip A. C., Ge-86-2; Sgt A Co 8th TN Cav; 11 Jul 63 to 11 Sep 64; Warrensburgh PO; rheumatism & catarrh
EASTERLY, R. H., Ge-85-1; Sgt A Co 4th TN Inf; Dec 13 62 to 2 Aug 65; Cavey Branch PO; nervous dibility
EASTERWOOD, William, O-134-2; Hornbeak PO; CONF
EASTES, Thomas F., Wl-294-1; Pvt G Co 4th TN Inf; 64 to Nov 65; Jennings PO; measles, settled on kidneys but able to do work
EASTHAM, James, Wl-301-1; Pvt A Co 8th TN Mtd Inf; Jan 1 65 to Aug 65; Cainesville PO; shot through left foot, accidental; belonged to Capt. B. J. Terry Co.

EASTMAN, Adonirum?, La-113-1; Sgt F Co 3rd MN Inf; 5 Oct 61 to 3 Sep 65; Lawrenceburg PO; shot in right thigh
EASTMAN, Thomas A. H-49-7; Pvt K Co 58th IN Vol; 12-22-61 to 4-16-62; Daisy PO
EASTRIDGE, Barnibas, Jo-150-1; Pvt G Co 6th IN Inf; 4 Mar 64 to 28 Aug 65; Osborn PO
EASTRIDGE, Isham, Cl-48-1; Pvt C Co 49th KY Inf; 5-15-63 to 12-64; Old Town PO
EASTRIDGE, Joel, Jo-150-5; Pvt G Co 4th TN Inf; 11 Jan 63 to 7 Aug 65; Osborn PO; diarrhea
EASTRIDGE, John R., Cl-56-2(1); Pvt I Co 3rd TN Inf; 2-10-62 to 5-15-63; Big Barren PO; injured by a fall & resulting disease of heart
EASTWOOD, Benjamin, James W., W-189-1; Lean widow of; Coin Sgt M Co 13th OH Cav; 3-17-65 to 7-4-65; McMinnville PO
EATHERLY, George W., Ca-22-2; Pvt K Co 10th TN Inf; 4-1-63 to 6-24-65; Burgen PO
EATHERLY, William A., Dy-25-8(4); Georgia widow of; Pvt 18th TN; 61 to 65; Nashville PO (Davidson Co.); measels & consumption; enlistment dates unknown
EATON, Allen C., Mr-98-2(5); Pvt K Co 50th MA Inf; 9-63 to 10-64; Whiteside PO
EATON, Benjamin, Li-147-1; Pvt 1st TN Cav; Norris Creek PO; none except lame at times from a wound; this is an ignorant negro who has lost his papers
EATON, Charles, H-72-2(1); Pvt 1st US Inf; Chattanooga PO
EATON, Clement H., R-162-5; Sarah widow of; Pvt; Dayton PO
EATON, Eli A., Mc-116-1; Pvt L Co 10th TN Cav; 7-17-64 to 8-1-65; Longs Mills PO; eye sight injured, contracted while in service
EATON, George W., Br-12-5; McPherson PO
EATON, Joshua, L-109-1; Pvt I Co 10th TN Cav; 1 Dec 62 to 1 Jun 65; Lightfoot PO
EATON, Lucien B., Sh-172-1; Col; 352 Second St, Memphis PO; not at home, in Washington, can't give better information
EATON, Pleasant, Wy-174-1; US Sol; 9th Civil Dist
EAVANS, D. V., Bo-19-2; Pvt C Co 6th TN Inf; 4-62 to 4-65; Rockford PO; shot in right hand
EAVANS, Thomas A., H-54-1; Pvt H Co; 1-6-62 to __ (1 yr 10 mos); Chattanooga PO
EAVENS, John, Sh-144-1; Pvt K Co 61st US Col Inf; 19 Mar 64 to 13 Dec 65; Brunswick PO
EAVES, Elizabeth, Be-2-1; Pvt B Co 2nd TN Mtd Inf; 62 to 65; Holladay PO
EAVES, John H., We-220-1; Pvt I Co 6th TN Cav; Feb 1 64 to May 13 65; Dresden PO
EAVES, William B., Hn-82-1; Pvt E Co 145th IN Inf; 1-26-65 to 1-26-66; Buchanan PO
EAVINS, Richard G., Br-12-3; Pvt G Co 24th MI Inf; 3-21-65 to 3-30-65; Raht PO
EBERHARDT, Chris (see Cooke, John)
EBERSTEEN, Henry, W-193-1; Cpl C Co 1st MI Cav; 2-12-64 to 3-10-66; Vernilla PO
EBLIN, Thomas A., Ro-201-5(3); Pvt C Co 7th TN Inf; 20 Aug 64 to 27 Jun 65; Kingston PO
EBLING, Addis, M-64-3; Pvt E Co 50th OH; Chattanooga PO
ECHHOM, Philip, H-70-3(1); Pvt F Co 73rd IL Inf; 7-20-62 to 9-29-65; Chattanooga PO; 7-2-64 promoted to 1st Lt Co E 1st US Vet Vols Engineers
ECHOLS, Cyrus, Sh-152-2; Pvt H Co 55th US Inf; Feb to Jan 65 (1 yr 11 mos); Leno PO
ECKEL, Alexander, Hm-103-3; Cpl C Co 4th TN Cav; 10 Dec 62 to 20 Jul 65; Morristown PO; chronic diarrhea
ECKEL, Allen, Hm-109-8; Pvt; Three Springs PO
ECKHARDT, Gustavus, D-44-1; messenger?; 62 to 65; 718 Jefferson, Nashville PO
ECKLES, John G., H-61-2; Pvt 11th GA Reg; 6-61 to 62; Pvt 2nd GA Cav; 62 to fall 63; Chattanooga PO; CONF
EDDE, James, Cf-37-1; Pvt C Co 5th TN Cav; Sep 29 63 to Aug 14 65; Stick PO
EDDINGS, Eliza, Sh-149-3; widow US Sol; 6th Civil Dist
EDDINGTON, Thomas B., Sh-185-1; US Sol; 120 Jones Ave, Memphis PO
EDDS, James (see Price, Gustavus)
EDDY, Marvin L., Mu-195-2; Sol D Co 1st OH Vol; Apr 6 61 to Feb 65; Columbia PO; exposure, pneumonia
EDEN, Samuel, D-61-1; Pvt; Nashville PO
EDENS, Andrew, Hw-120-1; Pvt E Co 1st TN Cav; 17 Mar 62 to 64; Upper Clinch PO; gun shot
EDENS, George, Ha-111-4(1); Pr. Cpl E Co 1st TN Cav; 17 Mar 62 to 21 Apr 63; Upper Clinch PO
EDENS, Isom, Ha-111-1; Pvt G Co 1st TN Cav; 10 Jul 62 to 5 Jun 65; Upper Clinch PO
EDGAR, James, Mu-200-1; Sgt G Co 9th IN Inf; 16 Apr 61 to Sep 65; New Lothel PO (Discarrer? Co., MI); reenlisted in 87th & 1st US Vet Vol Engineers
EDGE, Elam, Dk-33-2; Pvt K Co 5th TN Cav; 12-1-63 to 8-14-65; Dowelltown PO; piles & liver
EDGE, Smith M., He-64-2; Pvt C Co 1st AL Cav; 1 Feb 65 to 1 May 65; Center Point PO; CONF
EDGEMAN, Thomas K., Mc-112-10; Pvt; Athens PO
EDINGTON, Harrison, Co-62-3; Pvt L Co 8th TN Cav; 6 mos; Rankins PO
EDINGTON, James A., K-172-3; Pvt A Co 6th TN Inf; Mar 8 62 to 15 Ma_ 65; 14th Dist, South Knoxville PO
EDINGTON, Robert H., K-171-5(4); Pvt 6th TN Inf; 62 to 65; Bearden PO
EDINGTON, Thomas D., K-181-6(3); D Co 6th TN Inf; 8 Mar 62 to 27 Apr 65; Knoxville PO
EDINGTON, William, Je-146-2; Pvt D Co 4th TN Inf; 63 to 65; White Pine PO; soldier cant give dates
EDINGTON, William H., K-172-2; PVt A Co 6th TN Inf; 8 Mar 62 to 27 Apr 65; 14th Dist
EDINTON, W. H., F-44-2; Pvt B Co Forest; Aug 66 to May 11 65; PO omitted; CONF
EDMISTON, Charles (see Smith, Charles)
EDMON, Henry, Mg-196-2; Pvt H Co 17th Col TN Inf; Oct 63 to 29 Apr 66; Oliver Springs PO
EDMONDS, George P., D-64-2; Nashville PO
EDMONDS, John, Pu-146-1; Byrna PO; shot -in hip
EDMONDS, William, Lo-194-1; Pvt B Co 24th WI Inf; 1 Feb 63 to 65; Muddy Creek PO
EDMONDSON, Alexander, Gi-126-1; Cpl F Co 110th Col Inf; Pulaski PO
EDMONDSON, Ambrose (see Beavers, Sarah J.)
EDMONDSON, John, Sh-157-3; __ to 65; Ensly PO
EDMONDSON, John, Sh-157-4; Pvt D Co 5th Corp hill?; 63 to 65; Ensely PO; I am due 60, get from pension?
EDMONDSON, John C., Bo-13-2; 1st Lt E Co 3rd TN Lt Inf?; 8-12-64 to 11-30-64; Tutt PO
EDMONDSON, Marthey, Li-148-1; widow; PO omitted
EDMONDSON, Robt. H., Di-36-2; Pvt C Co 14th TN Inf; 5-13-61 to 62; Bellsburgh PO; CONF
EDMONDSON, William H., Bo-13-2; Pvt E Co 98th IL Inf; 8-12-62 to 12-28-63; Tutt PO
EDMUNDS, Calloway, Pc-151-1; Francis widow of; Pvt E Co 2nd TN Mtd Inf; 62 to Jul 65; Pope PO; poisened
EDMUNDS, Theodore, Je-137-1; Pvt B Co 9th TN Cav; 12 Sep 65 to 22 Aug 66; Hickory Ridge PO
EDMUNDS, Tillman W., Ge-91-3; Pvt B Co 2nd NC Inf; 25 Sep 63 to 16 Aug 65; Greeneville PO; rheumatism &c
EDMUNDSON, Austin (see Fitzpatrick, Austin)
EDMUNDSON, John L., G-69-1; Pvt E Co 6th IL Cav; 12 Jun 63 to 5 Jul 65; Rutherford PO
EDMUNDSON, Thomas M., Bl-4-2; Musician F Co 7th TN Mtd Inf; 11-8-64 to 7-31-65; Pikeville PO
EDMUNDSON, William L., A-2-1; Cpl F Co 7th TN Inf; 11-8-64 to 7-27-65; Hynds Creek PO; lung, liver & kidney disease
EDMUNSON, James, Cr-13-1; Pvt A Co 15th IA Cav; Jul 10 62 to Aug 65; PO omitted
EDNEY, John B., Di-31-1; Pvt F Co 4th TN Mtd Inf; 10-5-64 to 5-10-65; Hazel Ridge PO; piles
EDNEY, William H., Di-31-1; Sgt H Co 10th TN Inf; 11-10-63 to 4-7-65; Hazel Ridge PO; diarrhoea & rheumatism
EDSALL, James S., H-54-3; Pvt C Co 24th OH Inf; 4-61 to __; Sherman Heights PO
EDWARDS, Allen, Rb-221-1; Winnie A. widow of; Pvt; May 1 61 to May 1 65; Barren Plains PO; CONF
EDWARDS, Andrew R., K-154-5(2); Knoxville PO; hernia 34 yrs
EDWARDS, Burgess A., Br-12-2; Pvt L Co 9th TN Cav; 9-30-63 to 9-11-65; Charleston PO

EDWARDS, Carrick S., Ro-204-1; Mary E. widow of; Pvt B Co 5th TN Inf; 27 Feb 62 to __; Elverton PO; died in Andersonville, GA prison

EDWARDS, Charles A., La-112-1; Pvt A Co 2nd MO? Inf; 6-22-61 to 2-11-64; Abner PO; gun shot wound in right hand

EDWARDS, Cyrus, S-214-3; Pvt B Co 13th KY Cav; Robbins PO; and was over look first week (sic); cannot remember dates

EDWARDS, Edmon, U-248-1; Ruth widow of; Pvt M Co 8th TN Cav; 16 Sep 63 to 11 Aug 65; Clear Branch PO

EDWARDS, Edward Jef, Cr-17-1; Rebecca J. widow of; Buena Vista PO

EDWARDS, Elijah, H-51-6; Pvt H Co 7th TN Inf; 10-8-62 to 10-8-64; Albion View PO

EDWARDS, G. W., Je-135-2; Pvt C Co 3rd NC Art; May 63 to __; Flat Gap PO; catarrh; CONF

EDWARDS, Henry, Sh-172-1; Pvt does not remember detail, papers lost; 67 Hernando St, Memphis PO; papers claim to be burned

EDWARDS, J. C., W-194-1; Pvt G Co 5th TN Cav; 9-11-62 to 8-14-65; Morrison PO; discharge lost

EDWARDS, J. W., Gi-122-7; Pvt H Co 53rd TN Inf; 61 to 65; Lesters Sta. PO; CONF

EDWARDS, Jackson E., U-244-1; Pvt M Co 8th TN Cav; not discharged; Loganton PO; diarrhear & piles

EDWARDS, Jacob, Wl-296-1; Sallie McBrient divorced from; Pvt; Shop Spring PO; disease of lungs; cannot hear well

EDWARDS, James, Sn-255-1; Pvt G Co 49th IL Inf; 1-2-61 to 3-25-64; Goodlettsville PO (Davidson Co.); went through unhurt

EDWARDS, James, Cr-16-3; Pvt B Co 21st US Inf; Jan 63 to Apr 30 65; Huntingdon PO; bronchitis & rheumatism, fails to remember day of enlistment

EDWARDS, James, Cl-47-2; Speedwell PO; rheumatism 1863

EDWARDS, Jas. P., W-194-1; Pvt L Co 126th IN Cav; 8-63 to 9-64; Morrison PO

EDWARDS, James R., H-63-3; 1st Lt A Co 6th TN Inf; 61 to 65 (3 yrs 10 mos); 308 W 8th St, Chattanooga PO; shot in hip & groin, kidney disease dangerous

EDWARDS, James W., Gr-71-2; Pvt 10th TN Inf; Jarmine PO; discharge destroyed

EDWARDS, Jeremiah, Wa-274-1; Artificer F Co 1st US Col Art; Jonesboro PO

EDWARDS, John (Jack) (Col), Ru-247-1; PVt K Co 14th Reg; 1-1-62 to 3-26-66; Sharperville PO

EDWARDS, John, Wa-263-6; Lue J. Enser widow of; Pvt C Co 63rd NC Inf; Conkling PO; CONF

EDWARDS, John E., Rb-221-2; Pvt E Co 50th TN; May 1 61 to Feb 1 65; Adams Station PO; slightly wounded; CONF

EDWARDS, John H., We-226-2; Capt L Co 6th TN Cav; 8 Jul 62 to 26 Jul 65; Sharon PO

EDWARDS, Joseph, G-63-1; 4th Cpl A Co 15th TN Vol; Mar 63 to Sep 65; Milan PO

EDWARDS, Joseph J., Cr-4-5; Pvt TN Cav; 4-1-64 to 9-64; Bells Depot PO

EDWARDS, Lewis T., St-160-1; Pvt 1st KY Cav; May 15 61 to Aug 1 __ (2 yrs); Lafayette PO (Christian Co. KY); CONF

EDWARDS, Martin, Cl-57-2; Kecks Chappel PO

EDWARDS, N. B., Mc-114-3; Pvt D Co 3rd NC Inf; 8-6-64 to 8-8-65; Raht PO

EDWARDS, Nathan J., Cr-20-2; Pvt 7th TN Cav; Aug 15 62 to Aug 9 65; Hollow Rock PO; bronchitis 25 yrs, con. in the service

EDWARDS, Polk, Mu-200-2; Pvt F Co 55th US Inf; 20 May 63 to 31 Dec 65; Terry PO

EDWARDS, Richard M., Br-9-3; Col 4th TN Cav; 8-62 to 65; Cleveland PO

EDWARDS, Robert, F-43-2; PVt A Co 1st TN; 62 to __ (1 yr); Collierville PO; does not know about discharge

EDWARDS, Samuel, Wa-265-1; US Sol; Emberville PO; rheumatism

EDWARDS, Samuel T. Sr., Dy-25-4; PVt D Co 20th TN Inf; 28 Aug 61 to 65; Newbern PO; wounded; CONF

EDWARDS, Sterling H., We-225-1; Cpl C Co 7th TN Inf; Aug 62 to __ (11 mos); Dresden PO; rheumatism

EDWARDS, Thomas, Co-60-1; I Co 3rd NC Inf; Syrensburg PO; lung trouble

EDWARDS, Thomas J., Pu-145-1; Pvt B Co 1st Mtd Inf; 12-3-63 to 4-20-65; Burton PO

EDWARDS, Wiley, Rb-221-5; Pvt F Co 11th TN; May 1 62 to Oct 1 64; Adams Station PO; CONF

EDWARDS, William, Sh-195-2; Pvt D Co 1st Col Hvy Art; 63 to 66; Memphis PO

EDWARDS, William (see Allen, William, Hy-84-3(5))

EDWARDS, William A., Fe-42-2; Sarah A. widow of; Pvt 7th TN; 5-62 to __; Jamestown PO

EDWARDS, William H., Sh-202-1; Lt B Co 4th Inf; 8 Aug 61 to 65; Memphis PO; wounded in right lung

EDWARDS, Wm. H., A-4-3; Nancy L. widow of; Sgt L Co 4th TN Cav; 4-12-62 to 4-14-65; Coal Creek PO; discharge not at home

EDWARDS, Wyatt, Sh-191-7(3); Pvt A Co 1st Col Inf; Memphis PO

EDYNS, Miles, Mg-198-4; Sarah G. widow of; Pvt 5th OH Inf; Rockwood PO; lost left eye

EGGEN, Clevelin H., Jo-153-1; Pvt D Co 13th TN Cav; 24 Sep 63 to 5 Sep 65; Little Doe PO; hearing, frost bite

EGGERS, Landrine, Jo-148-1; Cpl D Co 13th TN Cav; 24 Sep 63 to 8 Sep 65; Laurel Bloomery PO; rheumatism & disease of the lungs

EGGLESTON, Joseph, W-194-1; Pvt; 9-64 to 5-65; Morrison PO; discharge lost

EGGRT, Louis, Mr-95-1; PVt D Co 1st IN? Cav; 7-15-61 to __-24-65 (3 yrs 9 mos); Whitwell PO

EHRLICA, Adolph, Sh-178-2; Pvt G Co 107th OH; 62 to 64; 378 Madison St, Memphis PO

EICHHORN, Phillip J., H-50-2(1); Lt E Co 1st R US Vol E; 7-20-62 to 9-29-65; Daisy PO; piles

EKINS, Stokely M., Hw-128-1; Pvt E Co 8th TN Cav; 10 Oct 63 to 11 Sep 65; Walnut Hill PO; piles

ELAM, John (see Brown, Meaden)

ELBRICK, Fredrick, D-54-2; Pvt A Co 39th NY Inf; May 61 to Jun 64; Nashville PO

ELDER, Casper W., H-50-3(1); Pvt F Co 4th R TN Inf; 11-16-61 to 7-7-65; Soddy PO

ELDER, James H., Gi-122-6; Pvt A Co 3rd TN Inf; 61 to 65; Prospect Sta. PO; 7 months in prison; CONF

ELDER, Jerrs. M., F-42-2(4); Pvt Phillips Battery; May 62 to May 65; Rossville PO; CONF

ELDER, Peter, Ge-102-2; Catharine M. Burges formly widow of; Pvt F Co 2nd TN Inf; 24 Nov 62 to __; Woolsey College PO; died in prison

ELDER, Philip, G-55-1; Pvt A Co 63rd Col Inf; 2-22-65 to 1-9-66; Trenton PO

ELDER, William L., Cu-18-1; Pvt H Co 7th TN Inf; 2-10-65 to 7-27-65; Manning PO

ELDREDY, Andre, Gi-138-1; Pvt A Co 110th TN; 64 to 66; Valesville PO

ELDRIDGE, James C., K-182-3; Pvt D Co 9th TN Cav; Aug 62 to Oct 65; Riverdale PO; right leg broke

ELDRIDGE, James W., Ge-86-1; Pvt D Co 9th TN Cav; 31 Aug 63 to 11 Sep 65; Warrensburgh PO; lung injured

ELDRIDGE, Jessie C., Ja-84-3; Pvt B Co 1st TN Lt Art; 1-2-62 to 1-23-65; Normans Store PO; loss of left arm

ELECANDER, ____, K-177-3; Pvt K Co 20th NC Inf; 18 Mar 63 to 17 Apr 65; PO omitted; CONF

ELESON, George R., Un-258-2(1); Pvt 2nd TN Inf; Sep 61 to Sep 64; Longhollow PO; shot threw wright leg

ELEXANDER, Bengman F., He-62-2; Pvt Co C 10th Ridgment Inf; Jul 1 62 to 62 (4 mos); Alexander's Mill PO

ELI, Henry, K-179-1; Sarah C. widow of; Pvt I Co 1st TN Inf; 9 Aug 61 to __; Campbell PO

ELISON, Berry, Un-258-1; Pvt C Co 1st TN Inf; 9 Aug 61 to 17 Sep 64; Phebe PO

ELISON, Henry, Un-258-1; PVt C Co 1st TN Inf; 9 Aug 61 to 17 Sep 64; Phebe PO; shot through left leg

ELKINGS, J. N. (see Alkings, J. N.)

ELKINS, Ralph E., Hw-128-2; Pvt F Co 5th TN Cav; Jun 63 to 30 Jun 65; St. Clair PO; shot in left knee

ELKINS, Spencer, K-177-4; Pvt C Co 1st TN Cav; 62 to Jul 65; Powells Station PO; measles

ELLARD, Silas, D-63-1; Pvt I Co 101st OH; Nashville PO

ELLENBURGE, Thomas, Ge-88-3; Marvin PO; none of family at home & dont get nothing
ELLER, John, Jo-148-2; Pvt B Co 3rd NC Inf; Sep 64 to Nov 65; Head of Laurel PO; wounded
ELLER, Joseph A., M-106-2(1); Pvt Ethan Allen; 5-20-64 to 7-65; Hillsdale PO; never received any bounty
ELLIGIT, Michael, Hw-125-2; Cpl A Co 12th TN Cav; 61 to Dec 64; Yellow Stone PO; shot in the breast; CONF
ELLIOT, Alfred, D-64-5; Pvt G Co 10th TN Inf; Jan 64 to Nov 64; Nashville PO; sick in war--blind
ELLIOT, Wesley, Sh-186-1; Pvt B Co 55th Col; 3 yrs; Memphis PO; buried 1890, has wife Mary Morris
ELLIOT, William N., Ru-239-1; Pvt A Co; 63 to 65; Rockvale PO; conscripted sol.
ELLIOTT, David M., D-78-1; Pvt F Co 24th WI Inf; Aug 11 62 to Jun 22 65; Nashville PO
ELLIOTT, Grandville, We-221-5(2); Pvt; 61 to 65; PO omitted
ELLIOTT, Hesikiah T., U-247-1; Pvt I Co 13th TN Cav; 15 Jan 64 to 5 Sep 65; Erwin PO; partial deafness & lung disease 26 yrs
ELLIOTT, James M., A-4-4; Pvt C Co 3rd TN Inf; 2-12-62 to 2-23-65; Coal Creek PO
ELLIOTT, John, Mc-117-1; Sgt E Co 7th TN Mtd Inf; 9-15-64 to 7-27-65; Mecca PO
ELLIOTT, John C., A-13-4; Pvt H Co 2nd TN Inf; 3-24-62 to __; Thomas Mill PO; piles, has no discharge, only in 6 mos
ELLIOTT, John F., A-5-2; Pvt 2nd TN Inf; Clinton PO
ELLIOTT, John G., Jo-150-3; Pvt I Co 13th TN Cav; 22 Sep 63 to 5 Sep 65; Trade PO
ELLIOTT, John T., Sh-179-3(1); Sgt B Co 100th TN Inf; 8-20-61 to __; Memphis PO; lost a hand in battle
ELLIOTT, Levi P., H-62-4; Capt 8th KY; West Sixth, cor. Cedar, Chattanooga PO
ELLIOTT, Michael P., Ct-43-1; Pvt B Co 13th TN Cav; 9-22-63 to 9-5-65; Carter Furnace PO; testicles & rheumatism
ELLIOTT, Stokly J., Di-31-1; Pvt 10th TN Cav; Hazel Ridge PO; piles, not discharged--deserted
ELLIOTT, William H., Ct-45-3; Pvt F Co 13th TN Cav; 9-12-64 to 9-5-65; Carter Furnace PO; wounded Marion VA 1864
ELLIOTTE, Thomas R., H-55-1; Pvt G Co 5th TN Inf; 3-1-62 to 5-15-65; Tyner PO; partially deaf
ELLIS, Albert, G-55-1; Pvt F Co 111th Col Inf; 64 to 66; Trenton PO; lost discharge
ELLIS, Andrew Harris, Je-137-3; Pvt B Co 9th TN Cav; 24 Sep 63 to 11 Sep 65; Chestnut Hill PO
ELLIS, Asberry, Br-11-2; Pvt C Co 9th TN Cav; 4-63 to 9-64; Chatata PO
ELLIS, Benj. J., D-75-1; Sgt F Co 30th TN Inf; 15 Jul 61 to 1 Apr 64; Stewarts Ferry PO; prisoner 18 mos. Rock I. IL; CONF
ELLIS, Clark, Mr-98-1; Pvt F Co 5th TN Cav; 6-1-65 to 7-65; Oat's Island PO
ELLIS, Daniel, Ct-40-3; Capt A Co 13th TN Cav; 1-13-65 to 9-5-65; Elizabethton PO; served in Mexican War and was engaged piloting Union men through lines in East Tenn. early part of war, famous Union scout
ELLIS, Ezira W., Rb-218-1; Pvt D Co 16th WI Inf; 15 Oct 61 to 3 Sep 62; Handleyton PO; shot in left instept; draing pension
ELLIS, Francis M., Ch-12-1; Pvt B Co 21st TN Cav; 63 to 65; Wild Goose PO; CONF
ELLIS, George L., D-68-2; Sgt C Co 13th TN Cav & E Co 6th TN Cav; 28 Nov 63 to 28 Jul 65; 137 Whart Ave, Nashville PO
ELLIS, Louiza J. widow of; Pvt I Co 9th KY Vol Inf; 10-25-61 to 12-15-64; Lafayette PO; discharged sick, died on 12-23-64; pensioner
ELLIS, James, Cu-17-2; Pvt D Co 50th NY Inf; 3-14-64 to 4-64; Pomona PO; discharged fro previous disability
ELLIS, James C., Bo-13-3(1); Pvt I Co 78th IL Inf; Freindsville PO; injured in right leg and head by shell
ELLIS, James H., G-55-1; Cpl D Co 16th IA Inf; 1-18-62 to 1-25-64; Trenton PO; resulated rectum; Cpl D Co 16th IA Inf; 1-25-64 to 7-19-65
ELLIS, James J., D-75-1; Musician I Co 20th TN Inf; 28 May 61 to 31 Mar 64; Stewarts Ferry PO; shot through the arm; CONF
ELLIS, John, Jo-150-1; Grayson PO
ELLIS, John, Ro-211-1; Lt Col 1st TN Inf; 20 Aug 61 to 15 Nov 64; Webster PO
ELLIS, John, D-46-2; 1st Class Fireman, Hydrangea; 2-24-64 to 3-29-65; Nashville PO
ELLIS, John H., Sh-201-1; Gertrude V. widow of; Memphis PO; discharge papers misplaced; CONF
ELLIS, Joseph, Sh-191-6(2); Cpl E Co 11th Col Inf; 1-1-64 to 1-1-66; Memphis PO
ELLIS, Katie, Sh-178-4; widow US Sol; 227 Monroe, Memphis PO
ELLIS, Martin, S-214-2; Pvt F Co 7th TN Inf; 64 to 65; Glenmary PO
ELLIS, Samuel (see Hunt, Samuel)
ELLIS, Sandon E., Cl-47-3; Mary Jane widow of; 6-3-64 to 8-23-65; Cappford PO; dropsey 1865; naval servis
ELLIS, Sidney, T-215-2; US Sol; Mason PO
ELLIS, Taylor, Col, Mt-139-1; Cpl E Co 16th US; 63 to __ (2 yrs 6 mos); New Providence PO
ELLIS, Wesley, H-73-2(1); Pvt 44th TN Inf; Chattanooga PO
ELLIS, West W., Ro-211-4; US Sol; 16th Civil Dist
ELLIS, William C., Sh-189-6; Sol US; Ark. Ave, Memphis PO
ELLIS, William L., K-164-1; Mary A. widow of; Pvt C Co 6th TN Vol; 62 to May 14 64; PO omitted (Knoxville?); killed at Resacca, GA
ELLIS, William W., Pu-146-2; Pvt D Co 8th TN Mtd Inf Vol; 1-1-65 to 9-2-65; Bloomington PO; rupture
ELLISIN, Benjamin, Je-137-1; Pvt K Co 3rd TN Inf; 63 to 5 Aug 65; Hickory Ridge PO
ELLISON, Charles, D-57-1; Liza widow of; Pvt I Co 12th US Inf; Aug 12 63 to Jan 16 66; PO omitted, 8th Ward
ELLISON, John, Ct-36-2; Pvt A Co 12th NY Cav; 63 to 9-65; Roan Mt. PO
ELLISON, John F., K-154-4; Knoxville PO; CONF
ELLISON, John F., Co-61-4(1); Pvt D Co 8th TN Inf; 12 Jan 63 to 30 Jun 65; Parrottsville PO; in prison 125 days
ELLISON, Jonithan, Co-62-3; Pvt C Co 8th TN Vol; 1 Jan 63 to 30 Jun 65; Bybee PO; loss of finger
ELLISON, Joseph H., Ge-92-2; Pvt K Co 8th TN Inf; 20 Jul 63 to 30 Nov 65; Romeo PO
ELLISON, Robert, Un-251-2; Pvt F Co 2nd TN Inf; 61 to Aug 65; Hurricane Branch PO; scrofula
ELLISON, Thomas, Cl-54-1; Pvt I Co 3rd TN Inf; 2-10-62 to 5-26-65; Tazewell PO; expiration of time
ELLISON, William, H-51-1; Pvt G Co 5th R TN Cav; Soddy PO
ELLSWICK, John, St-163-1; Pvt G Co 1st VA Vets; Dec 63 to Jul 65; Dover PO; shot in left hand & rist
ELLSWICK, William T., St-163-1; US Sol; Dover PO
ELMORE, Edmond, Je-143-1; Pvt K Co 3rd TN Inf; 2 Dec 62 to 2 Aug 65; Kansas PO; shell bone left shoulder and glage? ball on chin
ELMORE, Francis M., Cu-15-2; Pvt I Co 13th KY Cav; 10-63 to __ (6 mos); Genesis PO; bronchitis, discharged on account disability
ELMORE, John A., Pu-144-3; Pvt I Co 5th TN Cav; 11-15-62 to __; Pine Fork PO
ELMORE, Matthew, Se-221-1; Seaman Ioscoe; 19 Jan 64 to 25 Aug 65; Fair Garden PO; now blind in one eye
ELMORE, Mitchel, Je-142-2; Pvt F Co 6th IN Cav; 63 to 65; Lucilla PO; crippled back--thrown from horse, discharge misplaced
ELROD, Anthony D., Pu-145-2; Pvt; Fancher's Mills PO; discharge lost
ELROD, James M., Br-6-3; Pvt G Co 10th TN Cav; 2-20-64 to 8-1-65; Charleston PO; nervous prostration result of fever
ELROD, Joseph E., Jo-149-4; Pvt B Co 4th TN Inf; 1 Mar 65 to 2 Aug 65; Mountain City PO
ELSEA, George N., H-58-2; PvtM Co 7th PA Cav; 8-23-63 to __; Sgt I Co 4th TN Cav; __ to 7-12-65 (1 yr 10 mos 19 days); Coulterville PO; lung trouble

ELSEA, James C., H-58-3; Pvt A Co 6th TN Mtd Inf; 8-9-64 to 4-5-65; Sale Creek PO
ELSEA, William C., H-58-3; Pvt I Co 9th TN Mtd Inf; 11-11-61 to 8-3-65; Sale Creek PO
ELZIE, Robert M., K-168-4; Cpl E Co 3rd TN Cav; 19 Feb 63 to 18 Jun 65; Knoxville PO; back hurt
EMANEUL, William L., Hw-133-3; Pvt E Co 64th VA Inf; 15 Nov 62 to 15 May 64; Burem's Store PO; CONF
EMANUEL, Tobias, Sh-148-1; Pvt K Co 16th ___; Memphis PO
EMBELINE?, William A., H-50-1; Sarah widow of; Cpl B Co 14th R OH Inf; 9-9-61 to 9-12-64; Daisy PO
EMBY, Joseph, Fr-115-1; Margrett widow of; Capt KY; 62 to 62 (2 yrs 6 mos--sic); Cowan PO; Mrs. E. does not have or can anser ony question from 4 ___
EMERSON, Alison, Mc-112-8; Hannah B. widow of; Pilot; ___ to 9-66; Athens PO; no papers to get dates
EMERSON, John, Hr-97-2(1); Susan F. widow of; Pvt; 63 to 65; PO omitted
EMERSON, Samuel, Gi-133-1; Sgt I Co 53rd TN; 1 Jan 62 to Dec 25 64; Bufords PO; CONF
EMERT, Alexander C., Se-224-1; Pvt G Co 2nd TN Cav; 8 Sep 63 to 6 Jul 65; Waldens Creek PO; piles & diarea
EMERT, Daniel G., Se-221-2; Pvt K Co 2nd TN Cav; 30 Nov 62 to 6 Jul 65; Fair Garden PO
EMERT, Daniel M. J., Gr-74-2; Clearsy widow of; Cpl 9th TN Cav; Dyers Ferry PO
EMERT, F. S., Se-222-1; Pvt B Co 2nd TN Cav; 15 Sep 62 to 23 Jan 65; Sevierville PO; vericose veins, rumatism, heering & site
EMERT, James S., Se-230-1; Asa widow of; Pvt M Co 2nd TN Cav; Nov 62 to ___; Richison's Cove PO; consumption
EMERT, John B., Se-223-5(1); Martha J. widow of; Lt K Co 2nd TN Cav; 8 Nov 62 to ___; Sevierville PO; gun shot right thigh
EMERT, Phillip J. M., Se-221-2; Louisa J. widow of; Pvt B Co 2nd TN Cav; Harrisburgh PO; could not get any dates
EMERY, Benjamin, H-58-5; Pvt I Co 2nd TN Inf; 11-11-61 to 2-5-63; Soddy PO; chronic diarrhea, discharged on surgeon's certificate
EMERY, Georg, Sh-157-3; Pvt I Co 3rd US L; 63 to 65; Memphis PO
EMERY, William, H-58-6; Pvt E Co 1st TN Inf; Retro PO; chronic ophthalmia, discharge in Washington DC
EMMENT, L. J., Bo-23-1; Louiza Jane (widow?); Pvt B Co 2nd TN Cav; 9-15-62 to 1-2-63; Tuckaleechee Cove PO; died with measels, his widow is in health
EMMERT, Caleb M., Ct-40-6; 2nd Lt H Co 13th TN Cav; 9-24-63 to 9-5-65; Elizabethton PO
EMMERT, Gorge W., Ct-41-2; Lt C Co 13th TN Cav; 9-24-63 to 9-5-65; Keensburg PO; gunshot through the bowels
EMMERT, John R., K-179-3; Pvt A Co 9th OH Cav; Virtue PO
EMMERT, Philip H., Cy-26-1; Pvt B Co 9th KY Inf; 11-27-61 to 12-27-65; Moss PO
EMMIAN, Lowry W., Sq-164-2(1); Cpl D Co 6th TN Inf; 10-12-64 to 4-63 to 65; Dunlap PO
EMMONS, Eugene, Mt-140-1; Cpl B Co 197th OH Vol Inf; 3-2-65 to 8-66; Thomason PO
EMMONS, Pink (see Myers, Pink)
EMSEY, Caser (colored), Ch-18-3(5); Cpl D Co 14th USA; Oct 63 to Spring 66; Montezuma PO; broken veins in leg, sun stroke, has made application for pension
ENAM?, Thomas J., Cl-56-1; Pvt A Co 49th KY Inf; 1-27-63 to 12-26-64; Halpnes? PO; shot through left leg
ENCHENBURGER, John, Fr-110-1; Music. 4th OH; Jun 13 61 to Aug 15 62; Belvidere PO
ENDSLEY, Henry W., Ms-171-1; Teamster I Co 4th TN Inf; 10 Jun 64 to Dec 65; Belfast PO
ENGLAND, Alexander, Cl-58-2; Pvt B Co 1st TN Lt Art; 4-1-63 to 7-20-65; Minkton PO; debilaty from small pox, rheumatism & hart trouble, now partli able to work but little
ENGLAND, James, A-6-4(2); Pvt E Co 3rd TN Inf; 2-12-64 to 2-23-65; Olivers PO

ENGLAND, James A., Cl-54-1; Cpl I Co 3rd TN Inf; 2-10-62 to 2-28-65; Bacchus PO; expiration of time
ENGLAND, John, Mg-198-1; Pvt K Co 5th TN Inf; 17 Apr 62 to 30 Jan 65; Lavender PO; rheumatism, broke right leg and two ribs
ENGLAND, John, Cl-57-1; Pvt B Co 1st TN Bat; 4-1-63 to 7-20-65; Goin PO; deefness & kidney 27 yrs
ENGLAND, John, B-14-1; Pvt B Co 13th IN Cav; 10-10-63 to 11-2-65; Brandville PO; lost his discharge
ENGLAND, Layne, K-173-1; Pvt D Co 2nd TN Cav; 64 to ___; McMillen PO; rheumatism; CONF
ENGLAND, Thos., Cl-47-3; Pvt B Co 1st TN Hvy Art?; 4-1-63 to 6-13-65; Cappford PO
ENGLAND, Valentine, Cl-55-1; Pvt C Co 1st TN Bat; 63 to ___; Lone Mountain PO
ENGLAND, Wibbey F., Di-30-2; Pvt E Co 10th TN Art?; 2-12-63 to 5-8-65; Dickson PO
ENGLAND, William, Se-223-2; Pvt D Co 2nd TN Cav; 1 Sep 62 to 9 Jul 65; Pigeon Forge PO; diarrhea & hurt by horse falling
ENGLEHARD, John, H-69-4; Cpl F Co 32nd IN Inf; 62 to 65; Chattanooga PO; shot through the ankle
ENGLETT, John, Gi-127-3; Pvt F Co 12th TN Cav; Pulaski PO; shot between temple & forehead and in thigh, hostilities ceased before he resigned army
ENGLISH, Alexander, A-6-5(3); Pvt K Co; 11-63 to 5-65; PO omitted
ENGLISH, Allen, Ge-98-1; Pvt G Co 8th TN Inf; 15 Mar 63 to 26 Jul 65; chronic diarhea; PO omitted
ENGLISH, Henry J., Le-118-1; Pvt D Co 110th TN Inf; 8 Dec 63 to 6 Feb 66; Palistine PO
ENGLISH, J. T., Gi-139-2; Pvt K Co 53rd TN Inf; 11-61 to 5-65; Campbellsville PO; S. B. English wife of J. T. English; CONF
ENGLISH, John, Mn-123-2; Sol US; 4th Dist
ENGLISH, John W. (see Henderson, John)
ENIS, Jessie C., R-161-1; Mary E. widow of; Lt Col; 61 to ___; Dayton PO; very old, has no papers, has forgotten
ENLOE, John T., A-9-4(2); Pvt A Co ___ NC Inf; 8-63 to 4-65; Lowe Sulphur Springs PO; CONF
ENNIS, David, Sh-191-7(3); Pvt; Memphis PO; records not seen
ENOCH, David R., W1-302-2; PO omitted
ENOCH, John M., Sm-174-2; 3rd Sgt G Co 4th TN Inf; 11-1-64 to 8-25-65; Grant PO
ENOCH, William, Ro-201-5(3); Pvt H Co 1st TN Inf; 20 Aug 61 to ___; deserted; Kingston PO
ENOCHS, Robert, Dy-25-4; Sarah F. McKnight widow of; Pvt; 61 to ___ (3 yrs); Newbern PO; died from fever; CONF
ENSER, Lue J. (see Edwards, John)
ENSER, William T., Wa-263-6; Pvt H Co 26th TN Inf; Conkling PO; deserted and joined US; Cpl H Co 8th TN Cav; 15 Sep 63 to 15 Sep 65; CONF
ENSLEY, Carriel S., Ch-18-1; Pvt G Co 1st TN Cav; 62 to ___ (2 yrs); PO omitted; CONF
ENSLEY, John C., R-158-2; Pvt E Co 7th TN Mtd Inf; 63 to ___ (10 mos); Rhea Springs PO
ENSLY, Henry, D-64-6; High & Broad, Nashville PO
ENYSTFIELD, Frederick, Sh-175-1; Cpl C Co 32nd IN Inf; 65 to 65; Memphis PO
EONIX, Harrison, Dy-25-1; Harriett Haskin widow of; Pvt; Newbern PO; enlistment dates unknown
EPISON, Mary, Ma-124-1; Pvt; Jackson PO
EPISON, Wiley, Cl-52-2; Eliza widow of; Wag(oner); Hypratia PO
EPLEY, William, H-55-1; Pvt K Co 1st TN Cav; 7-12-62 to 6-5-65; Harrison PO
EPPELMAN, Theophilus, H-63-4; Pvt PA Inf; 65 to 65 (3 mos); Chattanooga PO
EPPERSON, James T., Dy-25-5(1); Pvt C Co 11th TN Cav; Dec 62 to 12 May 64; Newbern PO; CONF
EPPERSON, Jesse N., Br-7-1; Pvt L Co 1st TN Cav; 9-1-62 to 6-5-65; Felker PO; disease of the eyes
EPPERSON, Joseph, Br-7-1; Pvt L Co 1st TN Cav; 9-1-62 to 6-5-65; Felker PO; displaced shoulder
EPPERSON, Nathaniel W., Po-149-1; Pvt A Co 8th TN Inf; 2-20-63 to 6-30-65; Heliothrope PO; nerves, rheumatism--heart disease

EPPERSON, Thomas, Ja-86-4; Pvt E Co 6th TN Inf; 4-10-62 to 4-27-63; Apison PO; skivoy (scurvy?)
EPPISON, John, S-214-3; Pvt H Co 2nd TN Inf; New River PO
EPPS, Alexander, Hw-119-2(1); Pvt C Co 63rd TN Inf; 62 to 64; Choptack PO; back affected; CONF
EPPS, Elbert, Cs-63-2; Pvt B Co 1st TN Cav; ___ 62 to Apr 65 (2 yrs 9 mos); Newport PO
EPPS, Harrison, Mu-210-1; Pvt; Spring Hill PO; CONF
EPPS, William, Sh-191-1; Pvt; 8-63 to 11-63; Memphis PO; records lost
ERLY, James, Co-67-3; Pvt E Co 1st TN Art; 19 Sep 63 to 1 Aug 65; Cosby PO
ERVAN, Isaac V., Je-144-2; Lt G Co 4th TN Inf; Nov 63 to 65; Talbotts PO; no discharge
ERVAN, Wm., Ro-202-4; Sarah J. widow of; Pvt A Co 2nd TN Inf; Aug 61 to Jul 62; Cave Creek PO; head ache, blind in one eye, lungs
ERVIN, David Jr., U-247-2; Quartermaster M Co 8th TN Cav; 27 Sep 63 to 11 Sep 65; Erwin PO; rheumatism & heart disease
ERVIN, John, Lo-189-3(1); Pvt I Co 7th TN Mtd Inf; 1 Aug 63 to furloughed 5 May 65; Philadelphia PO; not discharged, he home on furlough with fever when co. dis.
ERVIN, Thomas J., Ro-210-5; Pvt; Rockwood PO
ERVIN, William, Co-66-3(1); Pvt A Co 15th TN Inf; 1 Feb 63 to 11 Sep 65; Newport PO; CONF
ERVINE, Frank M., H-63-2; Pvt A Co 3rd Col Cav; 64 to 65 (10 mos); 501½ W. 7th, Chattanooga PO
ERWIN, Brownlow, Mc-114-1; Pvt; Lamontville PO
ERWIN, Charles (see Irwin, Charley)
ERWIN, Isaac, K-182-2; Pvt A Co 2nd TN Inf; Mar 62 to Mar 65; Gapcreek PO; jaundice, rheumatism
ERWIN, James A., Mg-198-3; Pvt F Co 1st TN Inf; 19 Aug 61 to 17 Aug 64; Kismet PO; mashed leg, by now amputated
ERWIN, James M., Wa-268-3; Johnson City PO
ERWIN, John A., Ro-210-4; Pvt; Rockwood PO; CONF
ERWIN, Joseph, Ge-101-2; Martha A. widow of; Pvt C Co 4th TN Inf; 63 to 65; Locust Sp. PO; died Apr 3, 1864
ERWIN, P. P., U-248-2; Pvt G Co 8th TN Cav; 17 Jul 63 to 11 Sep 65; Indian Creek PO
ERWIN, Preston, Hm-109-4; Pvt B Co 1st TN Art; Whitesburg PO
ERWIN, Samuel, Wa-263-6; Minerva D. T. Kyker widow of; Capt TN Cav; 64 to ___; May Day PO
ERWIN, William, H-72-2(1); Disie widow of; Chattanooga PO
ESCUE, Lenard J., Sn-261-2(1); Pvt Burton's Cav; 2-63 to 64 (1 yr 9 mos); Brackentown PO; cast of from regular army; CONF
ESCUE, William, Hy-84-1; Pvt A Co; Jun 62 to ___ (2 yrs 6 mos); Forked Deer PO; rhumatism caused by war; CONF
ESERY, George W., He-63-2; Cpl H Co 7th TN Cav; 62 to 65; Long PO; died Bell Isle
ESKERIDGE, Wiley, R-162-1; Pvt F Co 13th KY Inf; 3-13-65 to 11-16-65; Dayton PO; sunstroke
ESKRIDGE, Hiram, Ro-210-3; Pvt; Rockwood PO
ESKRIDGE, John H., D-75-3; Pvt A Co 22nd TN Inf; 15 Oct 64 to 30 Jun 65; Stewarts Ferry PO; company disbanded; CONF
ESKRIDGE, Richard W., We-225-2(1); 1st Lt 13th TN Cav; 4 Jul 62 to 25 Aug 65; Dresden PO; bronchitis for 6 yrs
ESKRIDGE, Samuel B., Ro-210-3; Pvt; Rockwood PO; CONF
ESLINGER, Thomas, Je-137-1; Mary widow of; Hickory Ridge PO
ESLINGER, William, Je-137-1; Pvt F Co 6th IN Cav; Aug 8 63 to 15 Sep 65; Hickory Ridge PO
ESMON, Hiliare, Wi-281-2; Milly widow of; College Grove PO
ESPY, Mary E., Ca-22-3; widow US Sol; 4th Civil Dist
ESPY, Moses, Col'd, Ru-234-1; Pvt D Co 45th OH Inf; Mar 62 to Jun 30 64; Jefferson PO; rheumatism by exposure
ESSARY, Mary, Ma-129-1; widow US Sol; PO omitted
ESSELMAN, David, D-90-1; Pvt G Co 4th OH Inf; 63 to 65; Vaughns Gap PO; not hurt; had papers but they are lost, doesn't recollect dates

ESSERY, John M., He-63-2; Pvt A Co 48th IL Inf; 62 to ___; Catharine J. widow of; Shady Hill PO; 14 months in Mobeil Ala
ESSLINGER, James, D-57-1; Pvt A Co 2nd LA CONF Inf; Sep 4 63 to Sep 4 65; PO omitted, 8th Ward
ESTEP, Andrew J., Ct-40-2; Pvt A Co 64th VA inf; 5-1-61 to ___ (4 yrs); Elizabethton PO; CONF
ESTEP, Henry C., Ct-45-1; Pvt H Co 4th TN Inf; 4-64 to 6-6-65; Stony Creek PO; Knoxville 1865, fever and mind, discharged surgeon's certificate
ESTEP, Rebecca (see POWEL, Arnold)
ESTEP, Samuel M., Ct-42-1; Pvt A Co 13th TN Cav; Watauga PO
ESTEP, William, Ct-45-3; Pvt H Co 4th TN Inf; 6-1-64 to 8-2-65; Carter Furnace PO
ESTES, Brazel, Gr-71-1; Pvt K Co 8th KY Inf; 22 Sep 61 to 3 Jan 65; Jarmine PO; trans. from Co K to Co I & Reg KY Inf
ESTES, George, Mu-199-1; Sgt E Co 111th TN Inf; Ashwood PO
ESTES, James, Hm-108-4(3); Pvt B Co 12th TN Cav; 20 Nov 63 to 12 Oct 65; Russellville PO; catarrh head
ESTES, James A., Wa-268-1; Pvt D Co 8th TN Cav; 14 Jan 63 to 19 Feb 65; Johnson City PO; rheumatism
ESTES, John Dk-33-1; Pvt A Co 5th TN Cav; 12-1-63 to 8-14-65; Dowellton PO
ESTES, John H., Lo-195-2(1); Pvt B Co 11th TN Cav; 5 Oct 63 to 13 Sep 65; Cave Creek, Roane Co PO; heart disease & epilepsy fits
ESTES, Joseph, Wa-268-4; Johnson City PO
ESTES, Paralee (see VANCE, James Sr)
ESTES, Peter, Mg-196-1; Jennie widow of; Pvt B Co 11th TN Cav; 19 Jul 63 to ___; Coalfield PO; died in the service
ESTES, Richard, K-186-1; US Sol; Beaver Ridge PO
ESTES, Robert, Hm-109-8; Pvt B Co 12th TN Cav; 12 Dec 63 to 25 Oct 65; Whitesburg PO; weak lungs from pneumonie
ESTES, Thomas, Dk-33-3; Pvt A Co 5th TN Cav; 12-1-63 to 8-14-65; Dowelltown PO; rheumatism
ESTES, William, Hm-107-3; Pvt B Co 8th TN Cav; 30 Nov 63 to 26 Oct 65; Witts Foundry PO; diarrhea & piles
ESTRIDGE, Hiram, K-170-1; Pvt K Co 13th TN Cav; 13 Oct 63 to 5 Sep 65; Knoxville PO
ESTRIDGE, Moses, H-73-1; Pvt; Chattanooga PO
ESTUS, Newton W., Lo-187-4; Pvt I Co 5th TN Inf; 62 to 65; Loudon PO
ETHERLY, Alferd, R-162-4; Pvt D Co 16th US Inf; 11-10-63 to 4-30-66; Dayton PO
ETHRIDGE, Henry, O-138-3; Pvt E Co 6th TN; 17 Oct 64 to 21 Jul 65; Hornbeak PO; brken ankle cause by gun shot
ETHRIDGE, William A., He-64-3; Quartermaster US Navy Gunboat Tyler and Rob; 9 Feb 62 to 9 Feb 65; Reagan PO; wounded in buttics, ruptured double
ETHRIDGE, William T., Hu-103-1; Pvt E Co TN Inf; Mar 63 to ___ (2 yrs 10 Mos); PO omitted
ETRASOV, Elias, Di-30-1; Pvt H Co 12th TN Inf; 11-16-63 to 1-16-66; Dickson PO
ETTER, Lemuel, Mc-118-2; Pvt D Co 4th TN Cav; 3-1-63 to 7-12-65; Joshua PO; hemorag of lungs & catarack in both eyes, rheumatism in right leg 25 yrs
EUBANK, Edward, He-57-1; Pvt G Co 7th TN Cav; 8-10-61 to 8-1-62; Law PO; back & hip dislocated
EUBANKS, Isaac, D-87-1; Pvt TN Inf Nashville PO
EUDALEY, Robert, D-103-1; Sgt F Co 2nd TN Cav; 62 to 65; Ridge Post PO; gun shot left breast, draws pension
EUSTICE, John, H-50-4; Soddy PO
EVANS, Augustus, Hw-132-3(1); Pvt A Co 8th TN Inf; 28 Oct 63 to 64; PO omitted
EVANS, Blenty, Se-226-5; Cpl D Co 42nd US Col Inf; 5 Aug 64 to 31 Jan 66; Sinking Springs PO
EVANS, Charles, Hm-108-1; 1st Lt K Co 76th PV Inf; 18 Apr 61 to 18 Jul 65; Russellville PO; ruptured
EVANS, Cristopher C., Hm-109-2; Pvt D Co 1st TN Cav; 15 Apr 62 to 15 Apr 65; Whitesburg PO
EVANS, Conrad, Po-149-3(2); Pvt; Oconee PO; regiment & co unknown

EVANS, E. Nicholas, De-26-1; I Co 9th ___ ; 62 to (1 yr 6 mos); Bible Hill PO; CONF
EVANS, Eli J., Dk-36-1; Pvt I Co 4th TN Mtd Inf; 9-25-64 to 8-25-65; Smithville PO
EVANS, Evan E., A-8-1; Pvt F Co 5th TN Inf; 2-25-62 to 4-7-65; Wheat, Roan Co PO
EVANS, George, Sm-176-1; Pvt A Co; 12-6-63 to 5-28-65; Rome PO; shot in the breast
EVANS, George W., Se-225-2; Cpl B Co 18th Jun 64 to Mar ___ (1 yr 6 mos 13 days); Trotters Store PO; rheumatism resulting in heart disease 25 yrs
EVANS, Henry, K-168-2; Pvt A Co 16th TN Inf; Knoxville PO
EVANS, Henry Clay, H-67-2; Quartermaster Sgt A Co 41st WI Inf; 5-2-64 to 11-2-64; Chattanooga PO
EVANS, Holden G., Lo-190-2; Pvt A Co 5th NC Cav; Aug 62 to ___ ; Loudon PO; prisoner 2 yrs and 6 mos; CONF
EVANS, Hugh, Ro-203-6; Drummer A Co 49th KY Inf; 27 Jun 63 to 26 Dec 64; Wheat PO; chronic rheumatism
EVANS, Jack, Ro-209-2; Pvt E Co 1st TN Inf; Nov 62 to Aug 65; Kings Creek PO
EVANS, James, Hy-85-1; Pvt K Co 55th Col US Inf; 62 to 65; Tibbs PO; this entry marked through
EVANS, James, Gr-78-1; Pvt F Co 8th TN Cav; 13 Jul 63 to 11 Sep 65; Larkeyton PO; pharaerceal? taken whiel in army
EVANS, James, K-167-2; Cyrena M. widow of; Pvt 3rd TN Cav; Sep 62 to died 65; Knoxville PO
EVANS, James F., Mu-209-1; Columbia PO; CONF
EVANS, James J., Dk-34-1; 2nd Lt A Co 5th TN Cav; 8-28-62 to 1-24-63; Pvt D Co 14th IL Inf; 64 to 6-65; Dowelltown PO; piles & rheumatism
EVANS, Jesse, H-49-3; Lake Side PO
EVANS, Jesse M., Gr-78-1; Pvt K Co 8th TN Cav; 6 Aug 63 to 11 Sep 65; Larkeyton PO
EVANS, John, Cr-14-4; Pvt K Co 2nd TN Mtd Inf; 1 Jan 64 to 15 Mar 65; Cawthon PO
EVANS, John C., Ca-20-1; Pvt A Co 4th TN Cav; 8-1-63 to 9-1-64; Woodbury PO
EVANS, John H., F-44-1; Pvt H Co 19th MS; May 1 61 to May 26 65; PO omitted; CONF
EVANS, John O., Cl-48-1; Pvt K Co 14th KY Cav; 12-22-62 to 2-25-64; Old Town PO
EVANS, Joseph, Un-259-1; Pvt E Co 6th TN Inf; 6 Mar 62 to 27 Apr 65; Rhodelia PO (this post office crossed out on schedule)
EVANS, Julien L., D-70-1; Sol; 1016 Market St., Nashville PO
EVANS, Laura, Gr-71-2; widow; 2nd Dist.
EVANS, Noi (see HODGES, James)
EVANS, Otaria, Sh-178-2; 58 Wellington St., Memphis PO
EVANS, P. W., Ro-205-1; 1st Sgt A Co 5th TN Inf; 25 Feb 62 to 4 May 65; Post Oak Springs PO
EVANS, Pleasant, Ma-128-1; Pernella P. widow of; PO omitted
EVANS, Samuel, Hn-80-1; Pvt K Co 3rd IL Cav; 3-17-65 to 10-14-65; Paris Landing PO
EVANS, Samuel P., K-159-1; Capt A Co 5th TN Inf; Feb 62 to 65; Knoxville PO; lost left leg below knee, pentioned-discharged exp. term served
EVANS, Sarah, He-61-2; widow Sol; 15th Civil Dist.
EVANS, T. T., Cr-4-2; Musician C Co 12th TN Cav; 4 Dec 61 to 12 May 63; Bells Depot PO; CONF
EVANS, Thomas, K-170-1; Pvt E Co 123rd PA Inf; 21 Feb 65 to 18 Nov 65; Knoxville PO; lame from gun shot
EVANS, Thomas J., Hm-108-2(1); Pvt A Co 3rd TN Bat; 1 Jun 61 to 9 Apr 65; Chestnut Bloom PO; CONF
EVANS, Will M., Ge-85-1; Pvt M Co 9th TN Cav; 1 Jun 63 to 16 Sep 65; Cavey Branch PO; kidneys affected 2 yrs
EVANS, William, H-69-2; Pvt; Chattanooga PO
EVANS, ___ , K-167-2; Cyrena Widow of; Pvt 3rd TN Inf; 61 to 65; Knoxville PO
EVEHART, Daniel, Ge-92-2; 3rd Sgt K Co 1st TN Cav; 12 Jul 62 to 5 Jun 65; Romeo PO
EVENS, Planus, Sh-183-1; Pvt A Co; Memphis PO; blind, papers lost
EVENS, Simpson, F-40-1; Pvt G Co 5th AR Inf; 13 Jun 62 to 5 May 65; Eads, Shelby Co. PO; CONF
EVENTRON, Alexander, Mc-117-2; Caroline widow of; Mecca PO

EVERET, Isiah, Cf-40-2; Tullahoma PO
EVERET, Richard, K-172-1; Pvt A Co 6th TN Inf; 16 Apr 62 to 8 May 65; Knoxville PO
EVERETT, Aaron, Bo-15-4; Pvt H Co 2nd TN Cav; 10-10-62 to 7-6-65; Maryville PO
EVERETT, Brayton O., Mc-112-4; Pvt; Athens PO; this man not at home, cannot get dates
EVERETT, Chas., D-58-2; Cpl C Co 40th US Inf; Jan 63 to 65; Nashville PO
EVERETT, Chas. H., D-58-1; Pvt C Co 143rd NY Inf; Aug 62 to 65; Nashville
EVERETT, George W., R-161-4; Sgt B Co 1st TN Lt Art; 1-24-62 to 1-24-65; Dayton PO
EVERETT, John, Bo-15-2; Pvt L Co 2nd TN Cav; ___ to 7-6-65; Blockhouse PO
EVERETT, Lorenza, Bo-15-4; Pvt E Co 3rd TN Mtd Inf; 7-15-64 to 11-30-64; Maryville PO
EVERETT, Orville R., Ro-201-4(2); Pvt F Co 1st TN Inf; 9 Aug 61 to 17 Sep 64; Kingston PO
EVERETT, Robert, Lo-191-3; Pvt H Co 2nd TN Cav; 10 Oct 62 to 1 Jul 63; Pvt H Co 15th V R C; 1 Jul 63 to 7 Aug 65; Morganton PO
EVERETT, Wm. L., Bo-22-2; Mary widow of; Pvt K Co 3rd TN Cav; Gamble's Store PO
EVERHART, Daniel, Hw-132-4; Cpl A Co 1st TN Inf; 24 Jan 64 to 10 May 66; Persia PO; heart disease
EVERHART, James, Ge-92-2; Pvt K Co 1st TN Cav; 12 Jul 62 to 5 Jun 65; Romeo PO; feber seteled right sholder
EVERHART, James, Hw-132-4; Pvt A Co 8th TN Inf; Dec 62 to 65; Otes PO; supposed to be rheumatism, could not get further information
EVERHART, James H., Hw-133-3; Sgt D Co 31st TN Inf; 18 Feb 62 to 11 Jun 63; Burem's Store PO; hand off; CONF
EVERIT, Blunt, St-164-2; Pvt D Co 13th TN Inf; Oct 63 to Jan 66; Stribling PO
EVERLY, Abriham, D-67-1; Pvt C Co Col Inf; Nashville PO
EVERLY, Thomas, De-46-2; Sarah Johnson formerly widow of; Cpl I Co 12th US Col; Nashville PO
EVES, W. R., O-136-1; Pvt K Co 6th TN Cav; Jul 10 62 to Jul 26 65; Mt. Pelia PO; contracted lung trouble
EVESINE, Philip I. (see METZGER, Philip)
EVINS, Jack, Mu-198-2; 10th Dist.
EVINS, William, Sh-160-2; Pvt; 15th Dist.
EVITT, William, B1-3-5; Pvt 1 Co 10th IN Cav; 12-63 to 9-65; Letton PO
EWELL, Gilbert, F-46-2; Pvt F Co 59th TN; 63 to 65; LaGrange PO
EWERS, Jus. E., R-163-4; Pvt I Co 116th OH Inf; 8-19-62 to 6-24-65; Dayton PO; recieved sunstroke in service
EWIN, Callie (see SMITH, George, D-50-3)
EWIN, Henry (see HAMLETT, Thomas)
EWIN, Simon, Hu-100-1; 3rd Civil Dist.
EWING, Andrew, D-80-1; 1st Sgt B Co 2nd USC Inf; Aug 12 63 to ___ (2 yrs 2 mos); Donelson PO; ankle broken
EWING, Celia, Mt-138-2; widow US Sol; Dist. no. 7, N. Providence PO
EWING, George, Sh-152-3; Dexter PO
EWING, Jackson, Ms-181-1; Pvt A Co 10th TN Inf; 6-10-63 to 4-12-65; Lewisburg PO; bone scurvey
EWING, James, Sh-152-3; Pvt K Co 11th US Inf; 1 Mar 63 to 1 Mar 66; Dexter PO
EWING, Mary, D-91-3; widow of Hands; Davidson PO
EWING, Sallie, D-58-2; widow US Sol; Cedar St., Nashville PO
EWING, Zacariah, D-49-1; Francis widow of; Drum Maj. D Co 12th TN Inf; 3 yrs; Nashville PO; widow dont know dates
EWLLIS, Thomas, Sm-171-1; Pvt A Co 1st TN Mtd Inf; 9-9-64 to 8-8-65; Chestnut Mound PO
EXUM, Henry G., We-226-1; Lucy A. widow of; Pvt L Co 6th TN Cav; 1 Feb 64 to 8 May 64; Sharon PO
EXUM, James T., Dk-39-5(1); Capt I Co 5th TN Cav; 8-24-62 to 3-22-65; Laurel Hill PO; chronic rheumatism
EXUM, Matthew, We-226-2; Candace Shaw formerly widow of; Cpl L Co 6th TN Cav; 5 Jun 62 to 26 Jul 65; Sharon PO
EZELL, Caye, Gi-127-1; Patsy Walker widow of; Pvt F Co 110th USC Inf; Pulaski PO; died while in service

EZELL, George, We-222-1; Kitten widow of; Pvt F Co 17th TN Inf; 11 May 61 to 11 May 65; Gardner PO; CONF
EZELL, Isaac B., We-221-6(2); Pvt A Co 4th TN Cav; Sep 61 to 5 May 65; Martin PO; CONF
EZELL, James M., O-134-2; Pvt H Co 12th TN Cav; Jul 18 61 to May 10 65; Hornbeak PO; CONF
EZELL, Joseph B., We-223-1; Pvt K Co 10th TN Cav; Palmersville PO; CONF
EZELL, Lemuel, Gi-131-1; Pvt K Co 110th Col Inf; Dec 63 to Feb 65; Young PO; diarrhea, prisoner 6 months, Mobile AL
FACING, Robert, Sh-188-1; Pvt I Co 88th US Col; 63 to 65; Memphis, 62 Mannassas St., PO
FAGAN, Robert, La-117-3; Pvt B Co 90th OH Inf; Sep 62 to Jun 28 65; 15th Dist.
FAGG, Dr. Johnathan W., He-67-1; Pvt H Co 101st IL Inf; 62 to 65; Sardsi PO; paralysis & deafness
FAGUE, Calvin, S-215-1; Pvt E Co 44th IA? Inf; 7 Apr 64 to 28 Sep 64; Pioneer PO
FAHEY, Patrick, D-59-1; Pvt 4th MS Inf; 213 Williams Ave, Nashville PO
FAIDLEY, Charles, H-59-3; Susie widow of; Pvt TN Cav; 10-61 to 12-18-64; Chattanooga PO
FAILMY?, John W., K-186-5; 1st Sgt K Co 1st Cal? Cav; May 63 to Jul 66; Beaver Ridge PO
FAIN, Alexander, Je-136-3; Pvt 44th GA Inf; 2 yrs; PO omitted
FAIN, George, Hy-76-2; US Sol; Stanton Depot PO
FAIR, Samuel H., Ct-40-6; Elizabethton PO; CONF
FAIR, William, Ct-41-1; Cpl H Co 15th TN Cav; 9-24-63 to 9-5-65; South Wattauga PO; left foot broken ankle mashted
FAIRCLOTH, James, Dy-25-7(3); Pvt C Co 4th MS Cav; 10 Mar 62 to 20 Apr 65; Newbern PO; in prison, wounded knee; CONF
FAIRFIELD, Cyrus E., Mg-200-1; Pvt H Co 86th OH Inf; 6 Jun 62 to Jun 65; PO omitted
FALCONNIER, Louis, K-154-1; Sgt L Co 9th TN Cav; 11 Sep 63 to 11 Sep 65; Knoxville PO; bronchitis, rheumatism
FALK, Charles W., H-62-2; Pvt A Co 165th OH Inf; 410 Cedar, Chattanooga
FALKNER, Isaac, Cl-57-1; Cpl G Co 2nd TN Cav; 10-62 to 7-65; Kecks Chappel PO; rheumatism & lungs
FALKNER, Mary, Mt-139-2; Dist. 21
FALKNER, William (see HOLLOWAY, William B.)
FALLENS, Patrick, D-60-2; 133 Morgan St., Nashville PO
FALLON, Terrence, Ma-127-1; Pvt US Ship Lancaster; Aug 6 61 to Mar 65; Jackson PO; broken skull went home on leave of absence, war over, he did not report back & got no discharge. Skull broke in suffering riot on board his vessel (Lancaster); cannot stand heat
FALLS, John, H-59-4; Lucetta C. widow of; PA Cav; 61 to 65; Chattanooga PO
FALLS, Jno. N., Hd-47-1; Seaman Gunboat "Robb"; Feb 22 62 to Feb 23 65; Savannah PO; rheumatism, has been suffering from rheumatism for 19 yrs
FALLS, Wm. A., Hd-1; Pvt D Co 2nd TN Mtd Inf; 63 to 64; Paulks PO
FALLS, William F., Hd-46-2; Third Civil Dist.
FALMOR, Thomas, K-173-3; US Sol; 3rd Dist.
FALWELL, James F., We-222-2; Pvt A Co 4th TN; Sep 64 to Apr 65; Gardner PO; CONF
FAMIN, James, Li-166-1; Pvt A Co 4th KY Inf; 64 to 65; Smithland PO
FAN, Alfred, Ge-99-1; Mary J. widow of; Pvt E Co 2nd NC Inf; Limestone Springs PO; rheumatism, impossible to get dates
FANCE, Joseph M., D-79-4; #7 Lerchey, Nashville PO
FANCHER, H. T., Co-61-4(1); Pvt; Parrottsville PO
FANCHER, James A. P., Wh-185-1; Pvt F Co 3rd US Inf; 10-18-64 to 12-10-65; Fanchers Mills PO; chronic indigestion, loss hearing
FANCHER, John, Col, Wh-185-1; Cpl B Co 42nd US Col Inf; 3-31-64 to 2-4-66; Fanchers Mills PO
FANCHER, Levi L., Co-67-2; Pvt D Co 2nd TN Cav; 1 Sep 62 to 6 Jul 65; Cosby PO
FANCHER, William C., Co-61-1; Pvt M Co 9th TN Cav; Parrottsville PO
FANN, Robert, Br-14-4; Pvt A Co 4th TN Cav; 10-20-62 to 7-12-65; McDonald PO; lung disease from pneumonia, general disability
FANN, Wm. H., Ca-20-1; Pvt A Co 4th TN Cav; 63 to 5-64; Woodbury PO
FANNER, William, Br-12-4; Pvt A Co 8th TN Inf; Sydneyton PO; neuralgia
FANNIN, Joseph, Sh-189-2; Pvt Capt Stevenson Lt Art 6th Corps MA; 64 to 65; Penn. & Va. Ave. Memphis PO
FANNING, William, Ge-102-3; Pvt G Co 4th TN Inf; 5 May 62 to 16 Jul 65; Whig PO; gun shot, now crippled in hipp
FANNON, John, Ge-99-3; Pvt B Co 12th TN Cav; 29 Sep 63 to 7 Oct 65; Cedar Creek PO; rheumatism & neuralgia
FANON, Nathaniel, Ge-102-3; Pvt B Co 12th TN Cav; 29 Sep 63 to Oct 65; Whig PO; disease of stomach, no rheumatism
FANZ, Ignaz, K-159-2; 1st Sgt G Co 6th TN Inf; 14 Apr 62 to 17 May 65; Knoxville PO
FARABY, Henry, H-62-1; Henry Wilson alias; Pvt & Cpl I Co 1st US Hvy Art; 7-6-64 to 3-31-66; Rear 513 Cedar, Chattanooga PO
FARAR, William K., Se-220-2; Pvt H Co 1st TN Cav; 22 Dec 62 to 17 Jun 65; Emerts Cave PO; disease of the lungs
FARBY, David, S-217-2; Pvt E Co 1st TN Cav; 62 to 64 Oneida PO
FARCE, Charles, Mr-98-2(5); Drummer Cav; Pvt Inf; Whiteside PO
FARELL, John W., Ch-18-2; Pvt B Co 31st TN Inf; Sep 15 61 to Jul 15 62; PO omitted; CONF
FARER, George W., F-44-2; Lt F Co 12th TX; May 7 61 to May 65; PO omitted; CONF
FARGESON, Francis M., W-189-2; Pvt K Co 4th TN Mtd Inf; 2-20-64 to 8-65; McMinnville PO; discharge lost
FARGO?, Jessey B., We-230-4; Lue S. widow of; Pvt KY; Greenfield PO; CONF
FARINGTON, Preston, K-154-6(3); Knoxville PO
FARIS, Caleb, Un-259-2; Cpl E Co 2nd US Inf; 2 Sep 64 to 2 Oct 65; Lost Creek PO
FARLER, Jesse B., Dk-34-3; Pvt F Co 4th TN Inf; 9-24-65 to 8-25-65; Dowelltown PO
FARLEY, William, Sm-169-1; Pvt 44th TN Inf; 11-15-61 to 12-30-62; Carthage PO; CONF
FARLEY, Wm., F-42-2(4); Julia widow of; Pvt Richardsons Cav; Spring 62 to 63; Rossville PO; disabled from prison life to the extent that he was unable to serve longer after being discharged; CONF
FARLING, John W., K-186-2; Balls Camp PO; CONF
FARLY, Dick, Ce-26-1; Col; Pvt I Co 12th KY; 61 to 65; Neptune PO
FARLY, James, Pu-142-1; Pvt; Calf Killer PO
FARMER, Alexander L., Cf-39-1; Pvt H Co 4th TN Cav; 1 Nov 64 to 25 Aug 65; Hillsboro PO
FARMER, Benjamin, Fr-105-1; Pvt E Co 1st TN Vol Inf; 20 Aug 61 to Oct 64; Winchester PO
FARMER, Berry, C-29-1; Sgt A Bat Art; 7-61 to 4-65; Fincastle PO; shot through left knee
FARMER, Cynthia (see ROYSDEN, George W.)
FARMER, David, Mg-196-1; Blacksmith H Co 4th TN Cav; 27 Jul 63 to 12 Jul 65; Oliver Springs PO; wounded in side
FARMER, Dillon? C., Be-6-1; Pvt T? Co 21st KY Inf; 27 Feb 65 to 9 Dec 65; Big Sandy PO
FARMER, Edward, Se-226-3; Pvt K Co 2nd TN Cav; Jun 63 to 11 Aug 65; Sinking Springs PO; injured 1 hip, ruptured r side
FARMER, Eli, Bo-22-3; Pvt A Co 3rd TN Cav; 9-18-62 to 8-3-65; Gamble's Store PO
FARMER, George, Hw-133-4; Pvt A Co 1st TN Lt Art; Sep 63 to Apr 65; Sigornsvill PO; chronic bronchitus & rheumatism
FARMER, Henry J., O-140-1; Pvt C Co 1st KY Cav; Jul 65 to Apr 65; Union City PO; was first CONF sol, discharge lost
FARMER, Henry P., A-9-6(4); 1st Sgt & Ast Lt I Co 9th TN Cav; 5-28-63 to 9-11-65; Dutch Valley PO; rheumatism & lung disease, prisnor 1 mo on Belle Island
FARMER, Horace L., Dk-34-1; Pvt G Co 1st TN Inf; 3-4-64 to 4-21-65; Dowelltown PO; rheumatism & heart disease
FARMER, Isaac, A-3-4; Lt H Co 1st TN Inf; 8-9-61 to 2-4-65; Clinton PO; catarrh, liver & rheumatism

FARMER, James, Cl-55-2; Cpl C Co 4th TN Cav; 11-18-62 to 7-12-65; Lone Mountain PO
FARMER, James, K-176-3; Sgt H Co 2nd TN Inf; 1 Dec 61 to 18 Apr 65; Halls X Roads PO
FARMER, James A., Se-226-5; Pvt 9th TN Cav; Straw. Plains PO
FARMER, Joe H., B-18-1; Pvt C Co 5th TN Cav; 4-9-63 to 8-20-65; Flat Creek PO
FARMER, John, Br-12-3; Sgt B Co 1st TN Inf; 61 to 65; Raht PO
FARMER, John, K-168-3; Adair's Creek PO
FARMER, John, Ro-202-2; 1st H Co McClurg PO; 12 Nov 61 to 20 Feb 63; Union X Roads PO; injury result of measles & fever
FARMER, John L., We-222-2; Pvt A Co Forrest TN Cav; Oct 63 to Oct 64; Gardner PO; leg broken; CONF
FARMER, Joseph, Je-135-1(3); Cpl B Co 9th TN Cav; 10 Aug 63 to 10 Apr 65; Piedmont PO; paralysis
FARMER, Nelson, Je-135-1(3); Pvt B Co 9th TN Cav; 10 Aug 63 to 11 Sep 65; Piedmont PO; affected lungs
FARMER, Samuel T., A-3-3; Pvt D Co 1st TN Art; 11-20-63 to 7-20-65; Clinton PO; eplepsy
FARMER, Steven, We-221-4; Pvt A Co 3rd KY Cav; Feb 64 to 64 (8 mos); Martin PO
FARMER, Thomas, Wh-186-1; Landsman Navy; 2-6? to 3-6?; Oconor PO; could tell nothing definite
FARMER, William, Ja-85-1; Pvt E Co 5th TN Inf; 3-2-62 to 4-4-75; Georgetown PO; chronic diarrhoea
FARMER, William, Bo-22-2; Capt H Co 3rd TN Cav; 11-12-63 to 7-11-64; PO omitted
FARMER, William B., Dk-34-2; Pvt G Co 1st TN Mtd Inf; 2-10-64 to 4-21-65; Dowelltown PO; rheumatism hernia, hand shot
FARMLEY, Genetie Gildon (See ONESBY, Sick)
FARNEY, Dennis, Sh-189-3; enlisted in name of Jos. Coleman, Pvt G Co 5th NJ Inf; 3-8-65 to 7-20-65; Broadway, Memphis PO
FARNHAM, George M., Wa-274-3; Cpl H Co 4th US Inf; 15 Nov 62 to 15 Nov 65; Jonesboro PO
FARR, David G., Bo-12-4; Sol US; 18th Dist.
FARR, John H., Mc-111-3; Pvt E Co 3rd TN Mtd Inf; 7-16-64 to ___; Mortimer PO
FARRAR, Hartwell P., Ma-127-1; 1st Lt D Co 48th IL Inf; Sep 10 61 to late in that year, don't know dates (64); Jackson PO; bodily wounded, wounded at Shiloh & Cornith, mustered out as Captain. Sent his papers all to claim agt soon after war & is unable to give exact dates
FARRELL, Michael, Sh-174-2; Pvt OH Vol Inf; 64 to 65; 163 De Soto St, Memphis PO; struck by piece of shell--shot in collar bone by rifle ball--injuries permanent, mustered out at Columbia, OH, in 1865
FARRELL, Theopilus L., Mc-109-2; Pvt D Co 7th TN Inf; 12-1-64 to 7-27-65; Regret PO
FARRENTINE, Robt., Mu-205-1; Pvt C Co 13th US TN Inf; 15 Jan 63 to 15 Feb 65; Jones Valley PO; all papers lost
FARRER, James A., Mu-200-2; Mt. Pleasant PO; wounded in knee
FARRER, Polean, St-162-2; Pvt G Co 13th TN Inf; Feb __ to __ (2 yrs); 6th Civil Dist
FARRIS, Becca, Hd-47-2; Savannah PO
FARRIS, Jack, G-71-2; Pvt 20th TN Inf; 15 Jan 61 to 15 Jul 63; Rutherford PO
FARRIS, Jasper, Me-89-1; Pvt D Co 5th TN Inf; 9-1-64 to 6-26-65; Tabor PO
FARRIS, John, Ha-115-2; Pvt H Co 4th TN Inf; 6 Apr 65 to 2 Aug 65; Fenton PO
FARRIS, John D., Mu-209-1; Mollie A. widow of; Columbia PO; CONF
FARRIS, Muggy, Mr-97-2; Jarman? PO
FARROW, Edward, Gr-74-2; Nancy widow of; Pvt; Dyers Ferry PO; CONF
FARROW, Thomas G., Gr-74-2; Caroline widow of; Pvt C Co 1st TN Cav; 1 Apr 62 to 1 Apr 65; Dayal PO
FARTHING, John S., Jo-151-2; Pvt G Co 1st US Inf; 26 Feb 64 to 21 May 66; Bakers Gap PO; bronchitis-sore eyes, heart disease resulting
FASIP, David, Je-146-5; Pvt; White Pine PO; he is gone & wife dont know anything
FASTER, Joseph M., Mu-210-4; Pvt G Co 1st TN Inf; 3-1-61 to 6-18-65; Carters Creek PO; CONF
FATIS, James, Br-6-2; Judith Stevenson widow of; this man belonged to a Michigan regt. and his widow dusnt know when in W he died; Chatala PO; died of injuries receaved in sirvice
FAUBION, Robert P., Ge-87-1; Pvt K Co 8th TN Inf; 4 Feb 62 to ___; Mosheim PO; chronic diarrhea
FAUKNER, George, K-157-1; Pvt; Knoxville PO
FAULKNER, Clay, W-189-4; Pvt G Co 5th TN Cav; 10-62 to 6-65; McMinnville PO; discharge lost
FAULKNER, Thomas, K-174-4(3); Pvt F Co 3rd TN Inf; 10 Feb 62 to 23 Feb 65; House Mountain PO
FAULKNER, Thomas K., Su-240-3; Margaret widow of; Pvt C Co 79th TN Inf; 1 Oct 62 to 63; Kindricks Creek PO; no discharge; CONF
FAUVER, Isaac, Hm-108-4(3); Pvt D Co 4th TN Inf; 4 Jul 63 to 4 Aug 65; Russellville PO; ruptured
FAYSE, Logan M., Ov-136-1; Pvt K Co 9th TN Cav; 7-13-63 to 9-11-65; Livingston PO; rheumatism
FEATHERS, Geo. W., Hw-125-5; K Co 26th TN Inf; 61 to Apr 65; Surgoinsville PO; shot in the left leg; CONF
FEATHERS, John, Su-238-1; Sgt L Co 1st TN Cav; 1 Nov 62 to 19 Jun 65; Piney Flats PO; rheumatism
FEATHERS, Martha (see Williams, James)
FEATHERS, William, Wa-269-1; Hannah widow; Carters Depot PO (Carter Co.); discharge away from home
FEATHERSTON, William J., Dy-27-3; Pvt F Co 47th TN Inf; Feb 62 to Feb 63; Tatemville PO; CONF
FEBUARY, Joseph A., Wa-274-1; 1st Lt G Co 4th TN Inf; 1 Jun 63 to 2 Aug 65; Jonesboro PO
FECKLER, Joseph, R-157-1; Pvt E Co 8th TN Inf; 4-19-61 to 8-61; Spring City PO
FEDDER, Spencer J., Ro-205-1; Capt E Co 1st TN Inf; 18 Aug 61 to 63; Post Oak Springs PO; piles since 1863
FEEDS, James, Fr-110-1; alias James Anderson; Cook; May 11 65 to Nov 10 65; Belvidere PO; imperfect dates
FEEZEL, John, Se-221-3; Pvt G Co 6th TN Inf; 10 May 62 to 18 May 65; Harrisburgh PO; could not get date of death (sic)
FEEZEL, Sarah (see Duggan, Daniel)
FEHR, John C., D-63-1; Pvt A Co 2nd TN; Nashville PO
FELKER, Joseph, Br-6-4; Pvt E Co 6th TN Inf; 4-10-62 to 65; Charleston PO; diarhoea, rheumatism and deafness
FELKNER, Alexander, Je-146-2; Pvt C Co 9th TN Cav; 7 Aug 63 to 11 Sep 65; White Pine PO; deafness
FELKNER, William, Je-146-2; Pvt C Co 9th TN Cav; 7 Aug 63 to 11 Sep 65; White Pine PO
FELKNOR, John L., Je-138-1; Pvt C Co 9th TN Cav; 1 Aug 63 to 11 Sep 65; Oak Grove PO; colemn spine dislocated
FELKNOR, Shadrach J., Je-138-1; Pvt M Co 1st TN Cav; 2 Dec 62 to 19 Jun 65; Oak Grove PO; leg hurt
FELLENS, Thomas, Ge-83-3; Sarah widow of; Pvt E Co 4th TN Inf; Painters PO; chronic sore eyes
FELLERS, Samuel, H-53-6; Margaret widow of; Lt G Co 73rd OH Inf; __ to 9-62 (1 yr 6 mos); Ridgedale PO; shot through right lung
FELLERS, Washington G., Wa-260-2; Pvt E Co 4th TN Inf; Apr 6 63 to Aug 2 65; Pilot Hill PO; eyes and liver
FELLERTIN?, Andrew J. G., Ge-94-2(1); Pvt 103rd 2nd Bat URC; 6 Apr 63 to 26 Jul 64; Ham PO; during the late war
FELLINGTON, Alexander, Cl-56-1; Abbigail widow of; Pvt D Co 1st TN Inf; 8-26-61 to 9-26-64; Big Barren PO
FELTON, Floyd, Col, H-56-2; Pvt F Co Inf; East End PO
FELTS, Calaway, Ro-210-6; Pvt G Co; Rockwood PO
FELTS, John C., Ro-210-6; Pvt; Rockwood PO
FELTS, Julies C., Rb-228-1; Pvt C Co 20th TN Inf; 20 May 62 to Apr 65; Crunk PO; prisoner at Rock Isl. IL 17 mos; CONF
FELTS, Mary M. (see Kirkland, George W.)
FELTY, Granville, Mo-130-2; Pvt; Ballplay PO

FELURE, Lewis, Wl-302-3(5); Pvt G Co 22nd OH Inf--May 61 to Jul 61; Pvt C Co WV Lt Art--Sep 61 to Sep 64; Pvt E Co 1st VA Lt Art--Jan 65 to 29 Jun 65; Lebanon PO
FENDREN, Andrew J., Wa-263-1; Pvt B Co 4th TN Inf --Aug 62 to Apr 29 64; Lt M Co 13th TN Cav-- Apr 29 64 to Sep 5 65; Garbers Mills PO; chronic rheumatism & diarrhea (blind 1 eye 25 yrs)
FENING, Peter, D-91-2; Pvt C Co 32nd IN Inf; 60 to 61; Market House, Nashville PO; rec'd a sun stroke
FENNEL, Larkin (see Anderson, Larkin)
FENNELL, J. T., Gr-76-1; Martha J. widow of; Sgt B Co 8th TN Cav; 7 Jun 63 to Sep 11 65; Indian Ridge PO; chronic diarrhea; died Aug 4 1888
FENTON, Clark (see Smith, Fenton)
FENTRES, Costilla, Ho-97-1; Pvt A Co 16th TN Inf; 10 Sep 63 to 26 Feb 65; Medcalf PO; discharged on accoun of close of war
FENTRESS, Caleb, Ho-97-1; Pvt B Co 12th TN Inf; 5 Mar 64 to 16 Jan 66; Yellow Creek PO
FENTRESS, Durke, Ho-97-1; Pvt B Co 12th TN Inf; 5 Mar 64 to 16 Jan 66; PO omitted
FERGERSON, Charles A., D-79-2; Clara widow of; Pvt E Co 123rd IN Inf; Nashville, 3rd & Foster PO
FERGERSON, Frank, K-170-2; Pvt D Co 6th TN Cav; 18 Jun? 62 to 27 Apr 65; Knoxville PO
FERGERSON, Gerry, Ha-114-1; Pvt D Co 5th TN Cav; 1 Jul 63 to 13 Aug 64; Xerxes PO
FERGERSON, Isaac H., K-172-2; Mary E. Anderson widow; Pvt A Co 6th TN Inf; 62 to ___; CONF
FERGERSON, James F., He-63-1; Pvt C Co 7th TN; 63 to 65; Shady Hill PO; lungs; in Andersonville 7 mos
FERGUSON, John H., H-59-1; Pvt TN Inf; 1 yr; Chattanooga PO
FERGUSON, Charles, Bl-1-1; Pvt G Co 6th TN Inf; 2-20-65 to 6-30-65; Pikeville PO; chronic rheumatism, chron. rheum and deafness
FERGUSON, Charles A., Ro-201-2; Pvt D Co 6th TN Inf; 11 Dec 62 to 30 Jun 65; Kingston PO
FERGUSON, Elihu E., Su-241-2; 62 to 65; he was not at home; Clover Bottom PO
FERGUSON, Elisha, Un-253-2; Pvt F Co 3rd TN Inf; 10 Feb 62 to 10 Feb 65; Meltabarger PO; bronchitis, lung, defness
FERGUSON, George, Sh-146-1; Pvt E Co 184th Inf; 62 to 65; Lucy PO
FERGUSON, Henry, Wa-275-1; Drucilla widow of; Pvt D Co 3rd TN Cav; Pettibone PO
FERGUSON, James P., O-138-1; Pvt H Co 11th AL; 11 May 61 to 11 May 65; Lanes PO; CONF
FERGUSON, Joel M., St-163-1; US Sol; Dover PO
FERGUSON, John, Sh-169-2 US Sol; 32 Adams St, Memphis PO
FERGUSON, John, H-74-1; Chattanooga PO
FERGUSON, John, Gr-76-1; Hannah formerly widow of; Pvt E Co 8th TN Cav; 10 Oct 63 to 11 Sep 65; PO omitted
FERGUSON, John W., Sh-169-2; US Sol; 9 Jefferson St, Memphis PO
FERGUSON, Julia A. (see White, James L.)
FERGUSON, Robert, Se-221-2; Sidney H. Shrader former widow of; Pvt M Co 2nd TN Cav; 8 Nov 62 to 12 Mar 63; Fair Garden PO; died Mar 12, 8165 (sic)
FERGUSON, Silas B., M-107-3; 4th Sgt F Co 1st TN Mtd Inf; 2-13-64 to 5-3-65; Gamaliel PO (Monroe Co.)
FERGUSON, Thomas, Se-2 6-5; Sgt L Co 9th TN Cav; 12 Jun 63 to 24 Mar 65; Henrys X Roads PO
FERGUSON, Thomas B., H-65-1; Musician 3rd J. E. Brown Inf; 7-18-61 to 64; Chattanooga PO; CONF
FERGUSON, Wesley, Ha-113-2; Pvt E Co 8th TN Cav; 10 Oct 63 to 11 Sep 65; Sneedville PO
FERGUSON, William R., Mn-126-2; Pvt K Co 12th TN Cav; 4-63-to ___; Puryd PO; did not get any discharge
FERGUSON, Zene, Sh-174-3; Pvt E Co 3rd US Hvy Art; about 6-63 to 4-66; rear 150 De Soto St, Memphis PO; discharge lost through claim agt.
FERGUSSON, Hugh L., A-3-2; Pvt G Co 7th TN Inf; 11-18-64 to 7-29-65; Wilson PO; measles
FERNANDEZ, Gideon, Sh-174-1; Sgt K Co 46th Col US Inf; 4-63 to 66; 78 Hadden Ave, Memphis PO
FERREE, Daniel L., R-157-2; Sol; 12th Dist; Grand View PO
FERRELL, David T., Dy-25-5(1); Pvt C Co 15th TN Cav; Aug 62 to Apr 65; Newbern PO; enlistment & discharge dates forgotten; CONF
FERRELL, Elija P., Ge-85-2; Sgt A Co 3rd TN Inf; 29 Jul 64 to 29 Dec 64; Cavey Branch PO
FERRELL, Evaline, Ov-136-1; widow of US Sol; Livingston PO
FERRILL, James A., Cf-35-2; Pvt A Co 37th TN Inf; 61 to 64; Tullahoma PO; right arm shot off; CONF
FERULL, Frank, G-61-1; Pvt G Co 4th NY; May 6 61 to May 5 63; 12th Civil Dist
FETTERMAN?, John, S-216-1; Pvt A Co 2nd Milw. Inf; 26 Mar 61 to 27 Jun 64; Oneida PO; chronick diree since 1862 & 3
FEW, James, Di-30-1; Pvt A Co 4th TN Inf; 11-62 to 65; Dickson PO; CONF
FEW, Peter B., H-67-1; Anna M. widow of; Pvt 73rd IL Inf; 61 to 6-65; Chattanooga PO
FEW, William, Di-30-1; Cintha F. widow of; Pvt A Co 4th TN Inf; 62 to 64; Dickson PO; CONF
FEWLER, Joseph N., H-68-2; Pvt; 609 Boyd St, Chattanooga PO
FIBBS, Wayne, K-164-1; Pvt G Co 8th TN Vol; 26 Jul 63 to 11 Sep 65; no PO (Knoxville?)
FICKLE, Danial H., Sh-153-3; Pvt 3rd KY Cav; Oct 61 to May 25 65; Collierville PO; shot through hand
FIELD, Johnson, Sh-157-4; Pvt G Co 11th US; 62 to 65; Enesly PO
FIELDEN, Arwine, Cl-55-2; Mary widow of; Pvt A Co 12th TN Cav; 7-8-63 to 6-12-65; Lone Mountain PO
FIELDEN, Mary (see Haworth, Calvin)
FIELDER, William, Cr-8-2; Pvt H Co 4th AL; Jul 1 61 to 1 Jul 61 (3 yrs 8 mos); Maury City PO; CONF
FIELDON, Calvin M., K-158-2; Scout B Co 1st TN Cav; 63 to 64; Knoxville PO, 190 Mabry
FIELDS, Abner, Cl-48-2; Pvt C Co 29th TN Inf; 6-62 to 63; Pleasant PO; CONF
FIELDS, Absolom, Sh-152-2; Pvt G Co 11th US Inf; Jan 63 to Jan 66; Dexter PO; wounded in hip
FIELDS, Alfred, D-54-1; Pvt; Nashville PO
FIELDS, Asberry, Ha-114-3; Pvt G Co 2nd TN Cav; 1 Oct 62 to 20 Aug 65; Sneedville PO
FIELDS, Cyrus, Sh-144-3; US Sol; 6th Civil Dist
FIELDS, Darwin S., H-60-3; Pvt C Co 4th OH Cav; 4-7-63 to 7-15-65; Chattanooga PO
FIELDS, David, Un-251-1; Pvt M Co 9th TN Cav; 2 Sep 63 to 11 Sep 65; Effie PO; heart disease
FIELDS, George W., Mo-129-2; Pvt I Co 5th TN Inf; 11-1-62 to 6-30-65; Lomotley PO
FIELDS, James, Sh-153-1; Pvt B Co 17th USC Inf; 62 to 65; Collierville PO
FIELDS, James R., Pu-145-3(4); Sgt I Co 12th KY Inf; 11-10-61 to 12-31-64; Silver Point PO
FIELDS, James S., Sh-195-2; US Sol; Memphis PO
FIELDS, Jefferson L., Gr-79-2; Pvt D Co 3rd KY Inf?; Jun 61 to 23 Jul 65; Thorn Hill PO; shot in right arm and now suffering with rheumatism
FIELDS, Jesse, O-135-1; Pvt H Co 31st IL Inf; 17 Sep 61 to 1 Aug 65; Troy PO
FIELDS, Johnson, Sh-157-3; ___ to 65; Ensley PO
FIELDS, Joseph P., Hw-119-3(1); Pvt F Co 16th TN Cav; 62 to ___ (2 yrs); Alum Well PO; CONF
FIELDS, Linsey, A-6-4(2); Cpl B Co 1st TN Inf; 8-14-62 to 8-3-65; Robertsville PO
FIELDS, M. L., Bo-11-7; Pvt I Co 5th TN Cav; 11-1-62 to 6-30-65; Houk PO
FIELDS, Oshy, Hy-76-2; Pvt Inf; 6 mos; Stanton Depot PO
FIELDS, Richard, Ha-111-1; Pvt 49th KY Inf; 8 May 63 (about) to 26 Dec 64; Upper Clinch PO
FIELDS, Shadrack, Ha-111-2; Pvt E Co 1st TN Cav; 1 Apr 62 to 11 Apr 65; Upper Clinch PO
FIELDS, Thomas F., Sh-152-1; alias Fields, Frank; Pvt D Co 61st US Inf; Jun 63 to 8 Jan 65; Collierville PO; rhematism
FIELDS, Thomas J., We-223-3; Martha A. widow of; Pvt F Co 20th TN Inf; Aug 62 to May 65; Palmersville PO; died 12 January 1865, consumption; CONF
FIELDS, Thomas W., Dy-25-2; Pvt A Co 12th TN Inf; 26 May 61 to 20 May 65; Newbern PO; CONF

FIELDS?, ____, Ha-111-4(1); Juda Wallen formerly widow; Upper Clinch PO
FIGGINS, Gilbert, Sm-174-1; Pvt A Co 14th TN Inf; 12-22-63 to 65; Grant PO
FILTON?, George, D-69-3; US Sol; has no record; Nashville PO
FINCH, Caleb, Mt-135-1; Pvt A Co 16th TN Inf; 2-15-64 to 4-30-66; Jordan Springs PO; shot in the rt leg, he is very badly injured
FINCH, Julius, D-54-3; Carolin widow of; 1st Lt M Co 1st OH Art; Nashville PO; papers lost & cant give dates
FINCH, Paul, Fr-119-1; Mtd Inf; 64 to 65; Civil Dist 17
FINCH, William M., Li-161-1; Pvt C Co 88th Inf; Sep 64 to Sep 65; Fayettville PO; piles & weak eyes, from what I learn this is an Able Bodie Man
FINCHER, Andrew J., Mt-132-1; Cpl M Co 1st TN Cav; 11-25-62 to 6-19-65; 1st Civil Dist
FINCHER, David B., Ge-98-2; Pvt G Co 8th TN Inf; 10 Mar 63 to 30 Jun 65; Lovelace PO; testicle result of mumps
FINCHUM, Anderson, Co-66-3(1); Pvt D Co 8th TN Cav; 15 Oct 63 to 11 Sep 65; English PO
FINCHUM, William, Se-225-2; Trotters Store PO; chronic diarrhoea 25 yrs
FINDLO?, William, Ro-209-4; Pvt B Co 1st TN Inf; Aug 63 to 64; Kings Creek PO
FINE, William R., Co-69-2; Pvt I Co 60th TN Inf; 15 Oct 62 to 29 Feb 65; Rankin PO; CONF
FINGER, Harrett (see Colier, Ben)
FINGER, Henry, Bo-14-5; Pvt H Co 5th TN Inf; 62 to 65; Clover Hill PO
FINLEY, Albert, G-57-4(1); Sgt D Co 5th AR Inf; 6-1-61 to 10-8-62; Nebo PO; left leg shot off; CONF
FINLEY, Book, Br-12-5; McPherson PO
FINLEY, Charles, Jo-149-3; Pvt I Co 119th US Col Inf; 14 Apr 65 to 27 Apr 66; Mountain City PO; wound or injury by cannon, leg or knee
FINLEY, David G., Hu-105-1; Pvt G Co 10th TN Inf; 1 Mar 63 to 24 Jun 65; McEwen PO; piles, rheumatism, chronic diarrhea
FINLEY, George A., K-179-2; Pvt I Co 1st TN Inf; 11 Jul 63 to 3 Aug 65; Virtue PO
FINLEY, Guthrie Sr., Mu-200-2; Mt. Pleasant PO
FINLEY, Jackson, Gi-135-2; Pvt L Co; 62 to 65; Lynnville PO
FINLEY, James H., Je-141-2; Pvt I Co 7th TN Inf; 8 Nov 64 to 27 Jul 65; New Market PO
FINLEY, John, H-59-2; Pvt OH Cav; 62 to 65; Chattanooga PO; wounded leg
FINLEY, John, Se-228-1(2); Mary widow of; Pvt A Co 3rd TN Cav; 15 Oct 62 to __; Cusicks X Roads PO; pensioner
FINLEY, Julia, Sh-163-1; widow US Sol; PO omitted
FINLEY, Lewis, H-67-1; Pvt C Co 1st US Col Hvy Art; 12-18-64 to 3-31-66; Chattanooga PO; now suffers from side pleurisy
FINN, Frank, K-155-1; Pvt E Co 1st Col Inf; 14 Apr 64 to 31 Mar 65; Knoxville PO
FINNELL, James W., Br-7-2; Pvt L Co 1st TN Inf; 4-1-64 to 9-11-65; Coahulla PO; deafness in left ear
FINNEY, James W., La-112-1; Arrence M. Gurmely widow of; Pvt; Ulnus PO; died in prison
FINNEY, Richard W., Dy-25-7(3); Pvt C Co 45th TN Inf; Nov 61 to Apr 62; Newbern PO; contracted rhumatism, afterward reinlisted; CONF
FINNY, Matthew M., La-113-2; Pvt I Co 85th OH Inf; 9 Jun 62 to 23 Sep 62; Lawrenceburgh PO
FIPPS, John H., Un-254-3; Pvt D Co 1st TN Inf; 23 May 62 to 17 Sep 64; Gravestown PO; CONF army
FIPPS, Peter, Ct-45-3; Pvt M Co 13th TN Cav; 8-1-64 to 9-5-65; Carter Furnace PO
FIRESTONE, Fed?, H-69-1; Pvt E Co 1st US Col Hvy Art; 3-64 to 3-66; Chattanooga PO
FISCHER, Fredrick A., Sh-189-1; Pvt A Co 58th NY Inf; 64 to Fall 65; Ark. Ave, Memphis PO
FISCHER, William, D-63-2; Nashville PO
FISCHER, William M., K-161-6; Knoxville PO
FISH, Edwin, Dk-31-3; Pvt L Co 5th TN Cav; 2-63 to 8-14-65; Alexandria PO; hard of hearing in left ear
FISH, Ethel D., Dk-35-1; Anna E. widow of; Pvt F Co 4th TN Mtd Inf; 9-24-64 to 8-25-65; Temperance Hall PO; collar bone & two ribs broken
FISH, Frank P., Cf-40-3; Pvt 7th MA Bat; 13 Dec 64 to 10 Nov 65; Tullahoma PO
FISH, Stephen W., Ch-16-1; Pvt A Co 6th TN Cav; 1-6-64 to 7-65; Henderson PO
FISHBUNIC, Jacob, M-103-1; Rhacal widow of; Pvt B Co 9th KY Inf; discharge lost; Lafayette PO; killed at Shilo after discharged
FISHBURNE, Bluford M., M-103-3; Betsie widow of; Pvt C Co 9th KY Inf; 9-15-61 to 12-15-64; Lafayette PO
FISHER, Albert A., Sh-186-1; Quartermaster Sgt 2nd OH; 7-27-61 to 10-10-64; Memphis PO
FISHER, Amy, Sh-189-6; widow US Sol; La. Ave, Memphis PO
FISHER, Daniel, K-183-1; Jane widow of; Pvt B Co 6th TN Cav; 15 Oct 62 to __; Riverdale PO
FISHER, F. M., Ro-202-3(1); Pvt A Co 5th TN Inf Vols; Jan 63 to Jul 65; Paw Paw Ford PO; rheumatism
FISHER, Francis H., R-162-3; Cpl M Co 9th TN Cav; 9-5-63 to 9-11-65; Dayton PO; lungs & sight injured from exposure, draws pension of $4 per month
FISHER, Freeman I., La-114-1; Pvt C Co 21st OH Inf; 5 Jun 62 to 15 Oct 65; Lawrenceburg PO
FISHER, Garret, Sh-146-3; Pvt K Co 3rd US Hvy Art; 62 to 65; Lucy PO
FISHER, Garret, Sh-146-1; Pvt K Co 3rd US Hvy Art; Lucy PO
FISHER, George W., Me-88-3; Nancy J. widow of; Pvt E Co 5th TN Inf; Georgetown PO
FISHER, Henry, Je-146-4; 1st Sgt B Co 170th OH NA Guards; 13 May 64 to 10 Nov 64; White Pine PO; dont know disease, soldier was not at home
FISHER, Isaac, Sh-160-1; Driver TN; Apr 61 to Apr 65; Memphis, Poplar St (126 to 130) PO
FISHER, James B., Dk-36-2; Pvt B Co 4th TN Mtd Inf; 9-25-64 to 8-25-65; Smithville PO
FISHER, John I., H-64-2; 53rd KY; Chattanooga PO
FISHER, Joseph, Ha-111-4(1); Pvt B Co? 2nd TN Inf; Jan or Feb 65 to left in Apr 65; Upper Clinch PO; CONF
FISHER, Joseph, Ge-92-4; PVt B Co 8th TN Cav; 62 to __; Romeo PO; deafness and heart trouble
FISHER, Joseph D., H-61-1; 2nd Lt C Co 58th IN Inf; 8-61 to 4-19-62; Chattanooga PO; hernia, has suffered from rheumatism caused by war
FISHER, Parthenia (see Clark, James, L-108-1)
FISHER, Samuel, Wi-278-1; Pvt E Co 2nd OH Hvy Art; Jan? 22 63 to Aug 28 65; Franklin PO; suffering from lung pneumonia
FISHER, Samuel, Gi-122-8; Pvt K Co 110th TN Inf; Mar 3 63 to Mar 3 65; Prospect Sta. PO
FISHER, Shadrach, Ha-111-3; Mary widow of; PO omitted
FISHER, Thomas E., Dy-27-3; Mary E. wife of; Pvt C Co TN Inf; Dec 61 to Apr 65; Tatemville PO; CONF
FISHER, Thomas F., J-79-2; 4th Sgt I Co IL Inf; 61 to 9-25-65; Haydensburg PO; could not furnish dates
FISHER, Thomas C., B-8-1; Pvt A Co 4th TN Mtd Inf; 7-23-64 to 8-1-65; Fall Creek PO
FISHER, W. H., Hd-53-1; Pvt G Co 10th TN Inf; 10 Jun 62 to 24 Jun 65; Saltillo PO
FISHER, William, Ha-111-2; Pvt E Co 1st TN Cav; 1 Apr 62 to 11 Apr 65; Upper Clinch PO
FISHER, William (see Brown, John, Hw-127-3)
FISHER, William T., Dk-39-5(1); Pvt F Co 4th TN Mtd Inf; 3-4-64 to 5-5-65; Laurel Hill PO; loss of eyesight so claimed
FISK, Elear, Sh-169-1; (P. Etcar)?; Pvt D Co NY; Memphis PO; enlisted in 100 days men
FITCH, William H., Hn-75-1; Pvt I Co 136th IL Inf; 22 May 64 to 22 Oct 64; Springville PO; wounded in left leg
FITCH, William S., Ro-211-3; Musician A Co 60th OH Inf--1 Jul 62 to 20 Nov 62; Musician K Co 9th OH Cav--28 Oct 63 to 20 Jul 65; Harriman PO
FITE, Nathaniel M., Mc-114-5; Pvt; Santfordville PO
FITSPATRICK, James E., Hn-81-1; Pvt D Co 56th IL; 2-4-64 to 8-12-65; Gillie PO; rheumatism, result of exposure, rheumatism
FITTS, Jasper N., Dk-35-4(2); Pvt A Co 5th TN Cav; 11-14-63 to 8-14-65; Temperance Hall PO

FITTSGERALD, William C., K-174-3(2); Pvt B Co 1st TN Lt Art; 1 Oct 63 to 29 Jul 65; Graveston PO; wound in left side
FITZGERALD, Arch, Ja-87-1; 3rd Sgt H Co 8th TN Inf; 8-8-62 to 5-27-65; Howardville PO; gun shot varicose veins & rheumatism
FITZGERALD, Beverly A., Di-34-3; Elisabeth widow of; Dickson PO
FITZGERALD, C., Cf-41-1; Clara widow of; Pvt F Co 1st ME Inf; 61 to 65; Holly PO
FITZGERALD, Edward M., O-137-1; 1st Sgt H Co 31st NY Vol; 3 May 61 to Jun 63; detail out of order on this sched.
FITZGERALD, Francis M., Mu-210-5; Lt A Co 48th TN Inf; 11-61 to 5-65; Carters Creek PO; CONF
FITZGERALD, James, Su-242-2; US Sol; 16th Civil Dist
FITZGERALD, John F., Ja-86-3; Cpl B Co 1st TN Lt Art; 6-1-63 to 7-1-65; Oottewah PO; head jarred by cannon
FITZGERALD, Margaret A., Wi-280-1; Dist #11
FITZGERALD, N. A., Ja-86-4; Lt 4th TN Cav; Apison PO
FITZGERALD, Patrick, Mu-189-1; Carrie E. widow of; Pvt; Hurricane Switch PO
FITZGEURLS, Nathan, Sh-191-1; Cpl K Co 7th Col Art; 3-1-64 to 7-18-65; Memphis PO; an affected arm
FITZGIBBONS, Thomas J., H-49-8; Pvt H Co 24th MI Inf Vol; 5-19-61 to 11-63; Daisy PO; deafness & double rupture; in Andersonville prison 2 mos
FITZPATRICK, Alen, Mu-189-1; Emeline widow of; Wm. Bryant alias; Pvt TN Inf; Hurrican Switch PO
FITZPATRICK, Austin, Gi-132-3; alias Edmundson, Austin; Cpl K Co 12th USCV; 63 to 65; Pulaski PO
FITZPATRICK, Ephram, L-101-2; Pvt; Henning PO; belong to gun boat fleet, cant give boat
FITZPATRICK, Milem, Gi-135-1; Myra widow of; Pvt E Co 111th TN Inf; 62 to 66; Lynnville PO
FITZPATRICK, Rolly, Ms-180-1; alias Rowel Patrick; Pvt C Co 110th TN Inf; 63 to 65 (2 yrs 9 mos); Mooresville PO; heart disease; large family & homeless
FITZPATRICK, Thomas 2nd, Mu-190-2; Pvt G Co 110th Col Inf; 63 to 3-65; Culleoka PO; this man does not recollect date of enlistment or discharge
FITZPATRICK, William J., We-220-3; 1st Civil Dist
FITZWATER, James S., K-185-2; Pvt; McMillan PO; CONF
FLACK, John Y., Dy-25-4; Margret widow of; Pvt; Newbern OP; wounded twice; CONF
FLAGG, Henry G., Hm-109-3; Maj E Co 5th? TN Cav; 15 Apr 61 to 3 Apr 65; Whitesburg PO; hearnea
FLAKE, Alexander, Col, He-66-1; does not know anything at his rank; prisner 6 mos in Andersonville, said that he worked on breastworks; Lexington PO
FLANAGAN, Felix, Ru-231-1; Pvt; Couchville PO
FLANAGIN, Patrick, Sh-167-2; Pvt E Co 2nd TN; 18 Apr 61 to 65; PO omitted; one arm
FLANAGIN, Robert A., Bo-21-1; Pvt I Co 3rd TN Cav; 1-15-64 to 5-15-65; Bank PO
FLANEGHAN, Thomas, Sh-167-1; 2nd Lt A Co 1st Bat Ark; 61 to 62; PO omitted; dont know dates; CONF
FLANIGAN, James, D-99-1; poorhouse; Pvt I Co 23rd IL Inf; 62 to Jul 65; Nashville PO; feeble minded and right leg off
FLANIGAN, John, Gu-48-1; Pvt G Co 2nd OH Cav; 8-22-61 to 2-19-63; Tracy City PO; shot through right instep, right leg now useless
FLANNAGIN, Isaac, Hw-125-4; Pvt; 61 to 65; Stony Point PO; shot in the back & chin by minnie ball; CONF
FLASHER, John, K-168-2; Nancy widow of; Pvt 19th TN Lt Art; Knoxville PO
FLATT, Henry M., Dy-29-3; Ord Sgt A Co; Dec 61 to May 65; Newbern PO; CONF
FLEENER, John, Ha-111-3; Pvt E Co 1st TN Cav; 11 Apr 62 to 11 Apr 65; PO omitted
FLEENOR, Abraham, Hw-124-1; Pvt H Co 8th TN Cav; 6 Oct 63 to 20 Oct 65; Church Hill PO
FLEENOR, Eleana, Hw-124-1; Pvt H Co 8th TN Cav; 6 Oct 63 to 20 Oct 65; Church Hill PO

FLEIT, Gorge W., Di-40-1; Elizy J. Reynolds formerly widow of; Pvt H Co 18th TN Inf; 10-10-63 to deserted 1864; Adinburg PO; deserted
FLEMAN, David C., Gi-132-4; Pvt I Co 4th TN Mtd Inf; Sep 25 64 to Aug 25 65; Wales PO
FLEMING, Battey, Cl-56-2(1); Lt? D Co 100th OH Inf; 8-10-62 to 6-25-65; Head of Barren PO; injury of eyes by heat, reinlisted
FLEMING, Elizabeth A., Wi-280-1; Dist #11
FLEMING, J. H., Fr-112-1; Pvt K Co 150th US Inf; 8-15-62 to 6-15-65; Tullahoma PO
FLEMING, Jackson, F-42-1(3); Pvt D Co 59th US Inf; Dec 12 63 to Jan 31 66; Candaville PO; hernia left side in ditches
FLEMING, Jacob, Mu-198-2; 10th Dist
FLEMING, Matheu, W1-301-1; Pvt I Co 13th Col Inf; 63 to 65; Cainesville PO
FLEMING, William, Wi-274-1; Pvt F Co 17th TN Inf; 62 to 65; Franklin PO; dont know dates
FLEMINGS, John, Se-223-3; Pvt K Co 2nd TN Cav; __ to 6 Jul 65; Middle Creek PO
FLEMMING, Joseph, Ru-238-1; Cpl E Co 111th USC Inf; 20 Feb 64 to 66; Murfreesboro PO
FLEMMING, Robert, F-44-1; Pvt B Co 14th TN; 64 to 65; PO omitted; CONF
FLEMMING, Thomas, Sh-191-7(3); Pvt A Co 1st MS Rg; Memphis PO
FLEMMING, William, H-73-3; Pvt 14th TN; Chattanooga PO
FLENEKIN, Burrell P., K-172-3; Pvt 63rd TN Inf; PO omitted; CONF
FLENNIKEN, Robert G., K-181-5(2); Pvt C Co 6th TN Inf; 25 Aug 63 to 13 Jun 65; Knoxville PO
FLETCHER, Alexander, Wh-182-1; Pvt E Co 13th KY Cav; 8-25-63 to 6-10-65; Doyle's Sta. PO
FLETCHER, Benjamin, Mt-148-1; Sgt A Co 16th US Col Mtd Inf; 11-5-63 to 4-13-66; Orgains X Roads PO
FLETCHER, Elijah, Hw-124-1; PVt H Co 8th TN Cav; 6 Oct 63 to 20 Oct 65; New Canton PO; rhumatism in hands and feet, unable to do manual labor
FLETCHER, Giles, H-68-2; Pvt; 2 yrs 6 mos; Chattanooga PO; left side partly paralyzed, not able to work 1/3 of the time
FLETCHER, John, Jo-152-2; Pvt G Co 4th TN Inf; 25 Aug 63 to 7 Jul 65; Butler PO; pain in left breast, nervous, heart disease, unary organ, chronic dirhea
FLETCHER, John, Ha-115-3; Pvt C Co 29th TN Inf; 5 Aug 61 to 18 Apr 65; Jap? PO (Lee Co., VA); CONF
FLETCHER, John W., H-63-1; Mary P. widow of; Capt Art; 61 to 65; 13 Magazine, Chattanooga PO; dead
FLETCHER, Leonadus, Hm-108-1; Eliza widow of; Pvt; facts not known; Russellville PO; CONF
FLETCHER, Sara (see Thompson, Ezra)
FLETCHER, William, Ct-45-2; Manerva Garland formerly widow of; Pvt A Co 13th TN Inf; 6-1-64 to ___; Stony Creek PO; died Danville VA, 29th Dec 1864, prisoner
FLIER, Henry A., D-96-1; Pvt Inf IN Reg; 65 to 65 (3 mos vol); Nashville PO; husband not at home, information from wife
FLINN, George W., H-55-1; Pvt D Co 1st TN Hvy Art; 6-15-62 to 7-20-65; Harrison PO; weak eyes
FLINN, Mike, K-173-2; Pvt F Co 29th TN Inf; 61 to 63; Troutman PO; CONF
FLINN, William W., Se-225-1; Sarah A. widow of; Cpl TN Cav; Allensville PO; typhoid fever, died at Nashville, TN
FLINT, Charlie, Sh-162-2(1); Cpl E Co 59th TN Inf; May 20 62 to Jan 15 66; Ramsey PO
FLINT, Harrison T. (see Harrison, Benjaman)
FLIPPIN, James, Col, M-103-2; Pvt I Co 14th TN Vol Inf; 2-1-64 to 3-26-66; Lafayette PO; shot in knee
FLIPPS, Houston, H-49-6; Martha E. widow of; Pvt; PO omitted
FLONNOY, Bateman, Gi-127-7; Pvt D Co 112th TN Col Inf; Nov 1 62 to Apr 30 66; Pulaski PO
FLORA, Joseph D., H--107-2(1); Pvt L Co 19th TN Cav; 11 Apr 63 to 11 Sep 65; Witts Foundry PO; partial deafness 26 yrs
FLORA, Nat A., Hw-133-1; Pvt C Co 60th TN Cav; 12 Jul 64 to 12 Apr 65; Slide PO; CONF
FLORA, William M., H-51-7; 3rd Dist

FLOWERS, Allen, G-69-1; Sgt B Co 13th TN Cav; 20 Dec 62 to 20 Apr 63; Rutherford PO
FLOWERS, B. L., G-57-2; Yorkville PO; CONF
FLOWERS, James, G-69-1; Elizabeth A. widow of; Pvt E Co 6th IL Cav; 12 Jun 63 to 18 Jul 65; Kinton PO (Obine Co.)
FLOWERS, James R., Pi-154-1; Pvt A Co 26th KY Inf; 10-5-64 to 6-23-65; Otta PO; bronchial troubles
FLOWERS, Thos. J., G-71-1; Pvt F Co 12th TN Inf; 27 May 61 to 2 Mar 62; Rutherford PO; CONF
FLOWERS, William H., Pi-155-2; Susan widow of; Pvt H Co 3rd KY Inf; 12-13-61 to 9-8-62; Byrdstown PO; fever & jaundice
FLOYD, Abraham, K-180-1; Pvt H Co 2nd TN Inf; 21 Dec 62 to 17 May 65; Ebenezer PO; diarrhoea nad rheumatism
FLOYD, Andrew, Hw-127-2; Pvt G Co 12th NH Inf; 8 Dec 63 to 19 Sep 65; Rogersville PO; bronchitis or lung trouble
FLOYD, Fredrick J., Mn-122-2; Pvt B Co 6th TN Cav; 8-25-62 to 7-26-65; McNairy PO; chronic diarhea, discharge GO No 12
FLOYD, Isaac B., Se-223-1; Flag Bearer K Co 2nd TN Cav; 1 Dec 62 to 6 Jul 65; Pigeon Forge PO; chronic diarrhea & piles
FLOYD, James J., Me-92-3; Louisa J. widow of; Pvt D Co 7th TN Mtd Inf; 10-9-64 to 7-27-65; Hester Mills PO
FLOYD, James W., B-18-1; 1st Sgt F Co 5th TN Cav; 10-20-63 to 8-20-65; Flat Creek PO
FLOYD, Joseph, D-68-2; Mandy widow of; Pvt 14th USC Inf; 194 Fillmore St, Nashville PO; received a shock from a shell that injured his health
FLOYD, Preston, Gu-48-1; Nancy A. widow of; Pvt C Co 6th TN Inf; 9-7-64 to 6-13-65; Tracy City PO
FLOYD, Robert, Se-222-1; Pvt E Co 9th TN Cav; 1 Oct 63 to 12 Sep 65; Midel Creeke PO; rumatism, dierea, cidney diseas
FLOYD, Thomas H., Se-229-1; Pvt G Co 6th TN Cav; 10 May 62 to 16 May 65; Gatlinburg PO; rheumatism, eyesight, hearing
FLOYD, Wm., Gr-70-2; Pvt D Co 10 Sep 61 to 10 Dec 64; Bowen PO; regiment unknown
FLUAMAN, William B., Hd-45-2; Pvt I Co 4th TN? Mtd Inf; 21 Sep 64 to 25 Aug 65; Cerro Gordo PO
FLUMAN, James W., La-114-1; Pvt I Co 4th TN Mtd Inf; Sep 21 64 to 25 Aug 65; Lawrenceburg PO
FLYNN, Andrew M., J-81-3; 8th Civil Dist
FLYNN, Ruben, Su-241-2; Pvt A Co 1st TN Art; 6 Mar 64 to 3 Aug 65; Clover Bottom PO; exposure
FOCKNER, John, Mo-120-1; Minerva J. Snapp formerly widow of; Pvt 3rd TN Cav; 62 to 8-19-64; Sweetwater PO; died in service in 1864
FOEHANT, Edmond B., Cr-16-4; US Sol; Huntingdon PO
FOGARTY, John J., D-60-3; Pvt 4th KY Cav; 1307 Hynes St, Nashville PO; white
FOGG, N. U., Gi-122-6; Pvt A Co 53rd TN Inf; Mar 62 to May 65; Prospect Sta. PO; shot in left shoulder, in prison 6 mos, Fort Donalson, IN; CONF
FOITZ, William W., A-4-1; Pvt G Co 1st TN Inf; 6-24-63 to 8-3-65; Coal Creek PO; chronic dia. & rheumatic pains, enlisted in Co G, discharged or mustered out in Co B
FOLAN, William, Je-147-1; Emily J. widow of; Pvt E Co 9th TN Cav; 10 Oct 63 to 11 Sep 65; Shady Grove PO
FOLEY, Harden C., Ha-114-1; Sgt E Co 1st TN Cav; 1 Jun 62 to 3 Jun 64; Xenophon PO
FOLEY, Jordon B., Tr-269-2; Pvt I Co 8th TN Inf; 4 Jul 61 to 14 Apr 63; Knobton PO
FOLLEY, Charles P., Co-61-3(1); Susan A. widow of; Pvt D Co 8th TN Inf; 28 Mar 63 to 30 Jun 65; Parrottsville PO; died in war
FOLSON, George W., Hm-106-2; Cpl; Morristown PO; in Genl. Jacksons Brigade; CONF
FOLSOM, Henderson M., Ct-40-5; Maj. on staff of Genl. A. E. Jackson; Elizabethton PO; CONF
FOLWELL, Frank, Sh-197-1; Jennie Williams formerly widow of; Pvt G Co 61st Col Inf; 6-13-63 to 12-30-65; Memphis PO
FONE, Lorenzo Dow, Mc-112-8; Jemima widow of; Athens PO
FONSHEE, George A., Mo-122-3(1); Pvt A Co 3rd TN Inf; 62 to 7-13-63; Hiwassee College PO; CONF
FONTLEROY, William, Mt-147-1; Pvt C Co 16th TN Cav; 7-64 to 66; Collinsvill PO; discharge lost, can't tell date
FONTNER, William, Ge-93-1; Pvt E Co 4th TN Inf; 15 Mar 63 to 2 Aug 65; Greeneville PO
FONVILLE, W. A., G-57-6; Pvt; 62 to 64; Yorkville PO; shot through neck; CONF
FOOKES, Daniel R., Ct-43-1; Sgt B Co 13th TN Cav; 9-22-63 to 9-5-65; Carter Furnace PO; neuralgia and piles
FOOTE, David, Ma-116-1; US Sol; 4th Civil Dist
FOOTE, Peter, D-91-1; Bettie widow of; Sgt B Co 111th TN Inf; 3 yrs; Nashville PO
FORBES, Alexander, Mu-210-6; Pvt M Co 8th MI Cav; 25 Aug 64 to 30 May 65; Mallard PO; lost sight of left eye
FORBS, William, U-245-1; Pvt E Co 3rd NC Inf; 24 Jun 63 to 16 Aug 65; Okolona PO (Carter Co.); in US Service
FORBY, Greene, Col, Ge-87-2; Pvt M Co Art; Almeda PO; rheumatism
FORD, Benjamin, Su-233-2; Dist 3
FORD, Boaz B., K-172-3; Pvt A Co 6th TN Inf; 62 to 65; 14th Dist, South Knoxville PO; gun shot wound right hand at the Big Black River
FORD, Carley, Su-240-2; Pvt G Co 29th TN Inf; Aug 62 to Apr 65; Ford Town PO; bronchitis; CONF
FORD, Daniel M., C-8-2; Pvt C Co 1st TN Inf; 7-18-63 to 8-3-65; Powells River PO; relapse on measels & lame hip, receives $24 per year
FORD, Edmon, Mc-109-6; US Sol; 2nd Civil Dist
FORD, George, Sh-157-8; 62 to 65; Dist 13
FORD, George, Hw-132-5; Pvt E Co 29th TN Inf; May 61 to Apr 65; Persia PO; CONF
FORD, Gilbert, K-171-4(3); Pvt E Co 3rd TN Cav; 17 Dec 62 to 10 Jun 65; Craigville PO; courier thrown from horse, chronic rhumatism contracted in Cahaka prison 6 mos
FORD, Harry, D-64-3; Mary widow of; Nashville PO
FORD, Isaac, Wa-273-1; Mary widow of; Pvt 9th KY Inf; May 63 to __; Morning Star PO; a difficult case to obtain any information on
FORD, James, Wa-272-3; Sarah widow; Pvt I Co 8th TN Cav; Nellie PO
FORD, James W., Hd-44-1; Pvt A Co 6th TN Inf; 11-62 to 3-1-64; Clifton PO (Wayne Co.)
FORD, John, Wa-270-1; Pvt I Co 8th TN Cav; 22 Sep 63 to 15 Sep 65; Austins Springs PO; rheumatism
FORD, John, Wa-267-1; Pvt H? Co 27th OH Inf; 6 Aug 64 to 7 Sep 65; Johnson City PO; hemorage lungs
FORD, John, K-175-2; Pvt D Co 5th TN Cav; 12 Apr 62 to 12 Aug 65; Pedigo PO
FORD, John C., Un-256-1; Pvt C Co 1st TN Inf; 18 Jul 63 to Aug 3 65; Starkvale PO; scurvy, vericois veins, liver & heart disease
FORD, John L., K-172-1; Cpl, Sgt, A Co 6th TN Inf; 2 Apr 62 to 3 Apr 65; Knoxville PO
FORD, John S., Wa-261-1; Pvt G Co TN Inf; 12 May 63 to 30 Jul 65; Washington Colleg PO; rheumatism
FORD, Joseph M., K-172-5(1); Margaret widow of; Pvt A Co 6th TN Inf; 62 to __; 14th Dist, South Knoxville PO
FORD, Joseph S., Se-223-5(1); Ord Sgt K Co 9th TN Cav; 30 Sep 63 to 11 Sep 65; Sevierville PO
FORD, Josiah H., We-225-3(2); Pvt L Co 6th TN Inf; Jun 22 62 to Jul 26 65; Dresden PO; rheumatism been ailing ever since
FORD, Loranso Doro, Mc-112-4; Jemima widow of; Pvt I Co 1st TN Col Hvy Art; 61 to 65; Athens PO; no papers to get dates
FORD, M., K-155-2(1); Pvt E Co 3rd TN Cav; Dec 62 to Jun 65; Knoxville PO
FORD, Marlin A., H-64-3; US Sol; 403 Gillisfrie St, Chattanooga PO
FORD, Patrick, Sh-178-1; Pvt C Co TN; 2 yrs; 239 Union, Memphis PO
FORD, Peter, F-38-2; Pvt B Co 14th US Inf; 2 Jun 64 May 65; Lambert PO
FORD, Scott, D-43-1; Nashville PO
FORD, Stephen A., C-24-1; Pvt F Co 6th Inf; 3-62 to 4-65; Boy PO; hernia
FORD, Stephen D., C-24-1; Pvt C Co 1st Inf; 7-18-63 to 8-10-65; Boy PO; piles & rheumatism

FORD, Susan (see Albright, Susan)
FORD, William H., H-63-2; Pvt B Co 2nd MD Cav; 62 to 62 (3 mos); 608 Cedar, Chattanooga PO; rheumatism
FORD, William R., Ja-84-3; Pvt G Co 5th TN Cav; 10-2-63 to 8-14-65; Normans Store PO; loss of sight
FORD, William R., Un-259-2; Pvt A Co 12th TN Cav; 2 Jul 63 to Sep 65; Sharps Chapel PO
FORDE, Peter (see Taylor, Peter)
FORDHAM, James W., Hn-75-1; Pvt B Co 109th KY Inf; 12 Jun 63 to 15 Mar 65; Springvale PO
FOREBUSH, Louis, K-166-2; Pvt D Co 1st US Hvy Art; 4 Mar 64 to 6 Mar 66; Knoxville PO; right eye injured, rheumatism
FOREST, Henry M., Wi-270-1; Pvt K Co 5th TN Mtd Inf; 1 Dec 64 to 12 Jul 65; Naomi PO; jury of right arm; pensioned
FOREST, Minnie, Sh-167-3; widow US Sol; rear 40 Exchange St, Memphis PO
FORESTER, John C., Bo-14-4; Sarah Petty widow of; Pvt A Co 3rd TN Cav; Mint PO; died at Nashville TN in 1863
FORESTER, Matilda, Li-149-2; widow?; 8th Civil Dist
FORESTER, Richard, K-167-5; Pvt B Co 8th TN Cav; 11 Jun 63 to Sep 65; Knoxville PO
FORESYTH, Daniel, Mu-197-2; Lizzie widow of; Pvt C Co 9th TN; 62 to 65; Columbia PO
FORFLEET, Henry, Sh-196-2; Gunnel W. Norfleet alias; Pvt E Co 3rd TN Hvy Art; 7-63 to 65; Providence Chapel, Memphis PO; served under Cats. Reed and Seers
FORGESON, Linyer, Mn-121-2; Pollie widow of; Pvt 6th TN Cav; 62 to 26 Jul 65; Cramsville PO; intirrely insane
FORISTER, Hiram K., Lo-191-4; Pvt; Greenback PO
FORISTER, William T., K-181-1; Pvt F Co 8th TN Cav; 12 Jun 63 to 15 Sep 65; French PO
FORKUM, Thomas J., J-78-1; Pvt K Co 14th TN Inf; 3-30-64 to 7-22-65; Highland PO; stomach & bowels & crippled and hasn't worked in near 2 yrs
FORLER, William B., Dk-34-3; Pvt A Co 5th TN Cav; 8-2-62 to 6-25-65; Dowelltown PO
FORNSHELL, Frank L., Mo-125-1; Pvt F Co 12th OH Inf; 4-19-61 to 7-13-64; Madisonville PO; gunshot wond
FORREST, William, Col, Ce-29-1; Mary Harris widow of; Mary Harris, former widow of William Forrest, decd, says he belonged to one of the Tennessee Col regiments but she does not know which, she married him after the close of the war
FORRESTER, Chas, Li-147-1; 6th Civil Dist
FORRESTER, Samuel, Jo-151-3; Pvt M Co 13th TN Cav; 2 Feb 64 to 5 Sep 65; Shown's X Roads PO; rheumatism, disease eyes, head
FORRESTER, Thomas, Jo-151-3; Pvt M Co 13th TN Cav; 2 Feb 64 to 5 Sep 65; Vaughtsville PO; chronic diarrhoea
FORRESTON, Edward, Br-9-5; Pvt A Co 7th TN Mtd Inf; 9-27-64 to 5-20-65; Cleveland PO
FORRISTER, Andrew, Jo-149-2; Pvt M Co 13th TN Cav; 2 Feb 64 to Jul__ (1 yr 7 mos 3 days); Mountain City PO; chronic dirrhea, rheumatism, hart
FORRISTER, John F., Jo-148-2; Pvt F Co 13th TN Cav; 22 Sep 63 to 8 Sep 65; M't. City PO; lung disease
FORRISTER, Marshal H., Ro-201-6; Pvt F Co 1st TN Inf; 9 Aug 61 to 17 Sep 64; Kingston PO
FORRISTER, William, Fr-118-1; Pvt D Co 22nd AL Inf; Feb 62 to Sep 64; Winchester PO; CONF
FORSTER, John, Jo-150-2; Pvt I Co 13th TN Cav; 22 Sep 63 to 5 Sep 65; Key Station PO
FORT, Benjamin, Hu-105-1 (Black); Pvt F Co 16th Col Inf; 26 Dec 62 to 64; McEwen PO; discharge lost, cannot get dates of enlistment and discharge
FORT, David, C-33-6; US Soldier; PO omitted
FORTNER, Adam (see Green, Adam)
FORTNER, Joab Jr., Cl-48-3; Nancy M. Alford formerly widow of; Pvt H Co 2nd TN Inf; 3-1-62 to __; Pleasant PO; served 1 mo 11 days & died
FORTNER, John, Ge-94-3; Pvt E Co 4th TN Inf; 5 Apr 63 to 2 Aug 65; Greeneville PO; hearing impaired during war in 1865

FORTNER, John L., K-185-1; Pvt H Co 9th TN Cav; 63 to 65; Scaggston PO; ruptured
FORTNER, Joseph F., Ja-86-1; Bugler M Co 8th TN Cav; Oottewah PO
FORTNER, Josiah, Lo-193-1; Sgt I Co 5th TN Inf; 1 Nov 62 to 12 Jul 65; Unitia PO; wounded in right leg
FORTNER, Josua, Ru-241-3; Celia widow of; Pvt; 63 to 66; PO omitted
FORTNEY, James H. Br-14-3; Chief Bugler B Co 5th TN Mtd Inf; 64 to 7-4-65; Cleveland PO
FORYSTER, John, Ro-210-3; Pvt; 3 yrs; Rockwood PO
FOSHE, John H., Ge-93-2; Pvt B Co 8th Inf; Greeneville PO
FOSHER, Louis, Dy-29-3; Trimble PO; shot in leg & shoulder; CONF
FOSTER, Albert F-44-4; no PO
FOSTER, Ambers, Ro-211-2; Pvt G Co 1st TN Inf ; 9 Aug 61 to 17 Sep 64; Oliver Springs PO; broken ribs also, breard, measels
FOSTER, Ambrose, Ro-204-2; Pvt 1st TN Inf; 61 to__; Oliver Springs PO; no discharge found
FOSTER, Asa, Gi-127-8; Pvt; Pulaski PO
FOSTER, Asa C., Wa-264-1; Levinia widow of; Pvt 13th TN Cav; Tilford PO; could not get facts, want of record
FOSTER, Benjaman N., Br-14-3; Pvt C Co 5th TN Mtd Inf; 62 to 7-4-65; Daisy PO (Hamilton Co.); crippled in joint, regiment on leave of absence, discharged
FOSTER, Benjamin H., Ro-203-1; Mary A. widow of; Pvt; Oct 62 to __; Guenther PO; CONF
FOSTER, Enoch, D-86-1; Brentwood PO
FOSTER, Ephraim H., Bl-2-3; Pvt L Co 4th TN Cav; 2-4-64 to 7-2-65; Orme's Store PO; measles settled in left leg causing lameness, can do moderate work
FOSTER, Francis M., Wy-173-2; Pvt B Co 2nd TN Mtd Inf; 10-15-63 to 10-17-64; Lutts PO
FOSTER, George W., Wy-173-5(1); Pvt A Co 10th TN Inf; 4-12-62 to 6-26-65; Victory PO
FOSTER, George W., Mc-112-4; Sgt A Co 10th TN Mtd Inf; 64 to 7-65; Athens PO
FOSTER, Henry, Sh-195-1; soldier name, his father's name Henry Dickson; Pvt A Co 54th US Col Inf; 7-20-63 to 8-8-66; Memphis PO
FOSTER, Henry, H-52-1; Pvt F Co 9th IN Cav; 8-64 to 65; Wauhatchie PO
FOSTER, Isaac B., Ge-101-2; Rebecca Malone form. widow of; Pvt I Co 1st TN Cav; Locust Sp. PO
FOSTER, James, A-2-2; Nancy S. Cox formerly widow; Pvt J Co 7th TN Inf; 11-8-64 to 7-27-65; Twinville PO
FOSTER, James A., R-161-3; Sgt B Co 6th TN Mtd Inf; 9-12-64 to 6-30-65; Dayton PO
FOSTER, James F., Je-141-3; Pvt F Co 9th TN Cav; 28 Sep 63 to Sep 65; Mill Springs PO
FOSTER, John, Sh-157-2; Julia widow of; PVt D Co 14th __; 63 to 66; Memphis PO
FOSTER, John, D-93-1; Pvt I Co 30th KY Inf; 8 Feb 64 to 18 Apr 65; Newsom Sta. PO
FOSTER, John W., Sh-191-2; Memphis PO; records not here
FOSTER, Joseph, Hn-74-1; PO omitted
FOSTER, Julia, Sh-184-1; widow US Sol; 125 rear of Alabama, Memphis PO
FOSTER, Lucy, O-133-1; widow US Sol; Rives PO
FOSTER, Maniah, Ge-93-1; wid. of US So; PO omitted
FOSTER, Marget, D-99-2; widow of Sol; Davidson Co. Poor House & Asylum PO
FOSTER, Marth E., D-56-1; 205 Gondy St, Nashville PO
FOSTER, Martin, Po-149-1; Pvt D Co 4th TN Cav; 7-25-64 to 12-24-64; Conasauga PO; hundred days regiment
FOSTER, Mary A., Dk-38-2; widow? US Sol; 18th Civil Dist
FOSTER, Mary J., He-61-2; widow Sol; 15th Civil Dist
FOSTER, Pat, S-212-2; Pvt F Co 12th KY; 30 Nov 61 to 64; Porch Corn PO
FOSTER, Peter, Mc-112-3; Pvt D Co 32nd IN Inf; 63 to 65; Athens PO; rheumatism, no papers to get dates
FOSTER, Sarah T., Wy-173-5(1); widow US Sol; 7th Civil Dist

FOSTER, Thomas, Rb-226-1; Capt US Comisary; Greenbrier PO; in government employ
FOSTER, Thos., U-248-2; Pvt H Co 10th TN Cav; 1 Mar 64 to 1 Aug 65; Kittyton PO
FOSTER, William, Sh-159-8; US Sol; Memphis PO
FOSTER, William, Sq-165-3; Pvt K Co 4th TN Cav; 6-64 to 1-11-65; Dunlap PO
FOSTER, William, Gu-48-2; Pvt F Co 10th TN Cav; 62 to 65; Tracy City PO; lost record of discharge
FOSTER, William B., Dk-36-2; Pvt B Co 4th TN Mtd Inf; 9-25-64 to 8-25-65; Smithville PO
FOUCHEA, Andrew (see Jackson, Andrew J.)
FOULER, Asbery, Co-68-1; Capt K Co 8th TN Cav; 63 to 64; heart disease, lungs efected, piles
FOULER, Lorenzo T., Wy-178-1; Pvt B Co 2nd TN Mtd Inf--10-15-65 to 10-15-64; Pvt E Co 8th TN Mtd Inf--3-1-65 to 9-1-65; Pleasant Valley PO
FOUST, Dannell, Ct-41-2; Pvt B Co 40th TN Inf; 12-25-62 to __; South Wattauga PO; ruptured and jandles (jaundice?)
FOUST, David, A-13-4; Pvt F Co 7th TN Inf; 9-63 to 7-65; Prosise PO; nuraliga & piles & rheumatism
FOUST, George W., C-24-3; Pvt 9th TN Cav; 63 to __; Fork Vale PO; rheumatism
FOUST, Jacob, Dy-27-1; Pvt K Co 47th NC Reg; 11-61 to 6-20-65; Ro Ellen PO; shot 3 times, prisoner at Ft. Delaware; CONF
FOUST, John, C-24-3; Pvt G Co 9th TN Cav; 63 to 9-11-65; 1st Dist
FOUST, Mary S. (see Cole, Newton)
FOUTCH, Jason A., Sm-173-1; Pvt G Co 1st TN Mtd Inf; 3-9-64 to 4-25-65; Sykes PO
FOUTCH, John H., Dk-31-2; Pvt A Co 1st TN Mtd Inf; 7-14-64 to 7-22-65; Alexandria PO; blind in one eye
FOUTCH, William J., Sm-173-1; Pvt G Co 1st TN Mtd Inf; 3-5-64 to 4-21-65; Sykes PO; blind in one eye
FOWLER, Alexander, Co-62-2; Pvt C Co 8th TN Inf; 1 Jan 63 to 16 Sep 63; Help PO; cataarh of head & lungs
FOWLER, Berry M., Dk-35-2; Pvt I Co 1st TN Mtd Inf; 9-25-64 to 7-22-65; Temperance Hall PO; lung trouble
FOWLER, Catrin J. (see Solomon, Baulden)
FOWLER, Eliga W., Me-88-3; Pvt E Co 5th TN Inf; 3-2-62 to 9-4-65; Brittsville PO
FOWLER, Green L., De-26-3; Martha C. widow of; Bible Hill PO
FOWLER, Henry W., Ho-96-1; Pvt A Co 8th KY Inf; Apr 63 to Mar 5 65; Erin PO
FOWLER, Isaac, Co-69-5; Pvt C Co 8th TN Inf; May 63 to Sep 63; Driskill PO
FOWLER, James O., Ge-91-5; US Sol; Greeneville PO
FOWLER, John, Pi-153-2; Pvt I Co 13th KY Cav; 10-63 to 1-65; Byrdstown PO
FOWLER, John, D-58-1; Pvt; Nashville PO
FOWLER, John M., Gi-136-1; Pvt I Co 3rd IL Inf; 11-14-64 to 11-14-65; Odd Fellow Hall PO
FOWLER, Martin V., Ov-137-2; Pvt H Co 3rd KY Inf; 8-26-61 to 1-24-63; West Fork PO; lung disease and rupture, was discharged for disabilities
FOWLER, Nancy L., Wy-175-2; widow; Pvt; 10th Civil Dist
FOWLER, Orin P., Mg-199-2; Pvt A Co 5th US Art; 25 Oct 62 to 2 Oct 64; Sunbright PO; enlargement of the liver
FOWLER, Prior, Mo-120-2; Pvt H Co 1st TN Hvy Art; 7-__ to 3-__ (1 yr 10 mos); Glenloch PO; rheumatism
FOWLER, Whig H., Co-61-4(1); Pvt; Parrottsville PO
FOWLER, William F., Ge-91-1; Lt A Co 1st TN Cav; 1 Aug 62 to 62; Greeneville PO; cant tell as to dates
FOX, Alx., Co-69-1; Mary A. widow of; Pvt E Co 4th TN Cav; 1 Mar 61 to 18 May 65; Driskill PO; leg affected, don no cause not a pensioner
FOX, Carroll, Se-221-1; Pvt I Co 2nd TN Cav; 1 Jan 64 to 6 Jul 65; Fox PO
FOX, Carter B., Co-61-2(1); Pvt; Givens PO
FOX, Caswell, Se-221-2; Pvt A Co 9th TN Cav; 21 Sep 63 to 11 Sep 65; Fair Garden PO
FOX, Christopher, Je-137-3; Eliza widow of; Sgt F Co 9th TN Cav; 13 Sep 63 to 24 Mar 65; Fox PO
FOX, Daniel S., Un-254-3; Lt B Co 1st TN Cav;

1 Mar 62 to 11 Apr 65; Gravestown PO; gun shot through right arm
FOX, David, Pu-147-2; Pvt I Co 1st TN Mtd Inf; 6-2-64 to 7-22-65; Byrne PO; rupture
FOX, Elbert S., Ge-98-2; Co Sgt K Co 1st TN Cav; 11 Aug 62 to 6 Jun 65; Lovelace PO; rheumatism resulting disease of heart
FOX, Elijah, Co-61-3(1); Caroline widow of; Pvt C Co 8th TN Inf; Givens PO; shot in shoulder
FOX, Frank, C-33-1; Pvt B Co 8th TN Cav; 5-14-63 to 9-11-65; Newcomb PO
FOX, Furgeso, Un-256-2; Pvt F Co 6th TN Inf; 10 Ma_ 62 to Apr 65; Duke PO; lung trobble & rheumatism
FOX, George, D-99-1; Pvt A Co 2nd MO Art; Jan 62 to Dec 22 64; Bakers PO; wounded in thigh
FOX, George W., Mc-116-2; Pvt F Co 12th KY Inf; 10-22-61 to 12-31-65; Williamsburg PO; rheumatism, contracted while in service
FOX, Gilbert, Se-221-1; Pvt A Co 9th TN Cav; 21 Sep 63 to 11 Sep 65; Fair Garden PO
FOX, James R., A-5-5; Pvt G Co 47th IL Inf; 3-6-65 to 2-6-66; Clinton PO
FOX, John E., Gi-125-1; Pvt C Co 4th TN Mtd Inf; 13 Sep 64 to 25 Sep 65; Bodenham PO
FOX, John M., Co-69-1; Pvt C Co 8th TN Inf; 1 Mar 65 to 15 Apr 65; Driskill PO; no pension
FOX, John M., Co-69-1; Pvt C Co 8th TN Inf; 1 Apr 63 to 1 Jul 64; Driskill PO; CONF
FOX, John W., Co-69-5; Sallie A. widow of; Pvt 4th TN Inf; 62 to Jul 65; Help PO; fever & side plursey, correct date can be given
FOX, Joseph W., Wa-276-1; Pvt M Co 8th MO Inf; Jul 63 to 65; Limestone PO; discharge missplaced
FOX, Robert M., Co-69-6(1); Pvt C Co 8th TN Inf; 1 Jan 63 to 1 Aug 65; Driskill PO; dirhea & dispepa; dates at best recollection
FOX, Robert M., Co-69-1; Juley M. widow of; Driskill PO
FOX, Samuel D., Su-238-1; Sgt H Co 4th TN Cav; 4 Aug 63 to 24 Jul 65; Piney Flats PO; rheumatism, diarhea
FOX, Thomas, Co-69-5; Pvt A Co 7th IN? Cav; 10 Aug 63 to 18 Feb 66; Driskill PO; chronic side purrisy 26 yrs, no pension yet
FOX, William, Hw-126-1; Pvt G Co 13th TN Cav; 6 Apr 64 to __ (1 yr 6 mos); Vogel PO; scurvy, no discharge given
FOX, William D., R-106-1; Pvt C Co 36th OH Inf; 6-10-61 to 9-19-64; 6th Civil Dist
FOX, Wm. R., Br-7-3; Sgt H Co 4th TN Cav; 2-13-63 to 7-12-65; Cleveland PO
FOX, Wilson D., Hd-50-3; Pvt I Co 2nd TN Vol; Sep 1 62 to Jan 1 65; Walnut Grove PO; rheumatism incurred in war, half the time confined to his bed
FOXHALL, John J., Mu-209-5; Pvt 48th TN; Sep 62 to Aug 65; Columbia PO; rheumatism
FOY, Francis M., H-52-1; 19th Dist
FRANK, Salley (see Roberson, Garner)
FRANKLIN, Andrew, K-161-4; Pvt G Co 1st US Hvy Art; _-64 to 30 Mar 66; Knoxville PO; shot in right hand
FRANKLIN, Andrew J., Ov-137-1; Matilda widow of; Pvt D Co 1st TN Mtd Inf; Nettle Carrier PO; widow could give no further information
FRANKLIN, Benjamin, F-45-1 (also 45-3); Cpl I Co 59th USCA; 62 to 65; Moscow PO; Benjamin Franklin does not recollect the date of enlistment. Says he was with Genl. Sturgis in the battle with Genl. Forrest at Guntown. Says Col. Bowdwin was his Col. Discharged at the close of the war, 1865; I believe his statement to be truthful
FRANKLIN, Benjamin, Hr-89-1; Pvt K Co 17th TN; __ to 65 (1 yr 6 mos); Vilar PO
FRANKLIN, Benjamin, Je-136-2; Cpl B Co 9th TN Cav; 11 Aug 63 to 11 Sep 65; PO omitted
FRANKLIN, Benjamin, H-64-3; US Sol; 3 Locust Alley, Chattanooga PO
FRANKLIN, C. F., Je-135-1(3); Pvt F Co 9th TN Cav; 24 Sep 63 to 11 Sep 65; Piedmont PO
FRANKLIN, Clabe, H-61-3; Pvt A Co 1st TN Hvy Art; 12-62 to 4-9-65; Chattanooga PO; contracted rheumatism
FRANKLIN, George W., S-214-1; Sgt D Co 1st TN Inf; 1 Sep 63 to 25 Apr 65; Robbins PO; disease of heart & rheumatism

FRANKLIN, Heanley, Fe-41-3(1); Pvt A Co 11th TN Cav; 4-11-63 to 6-25-65; Boat Land PO; rheumatism & weak lungs; measels & yellow jaundice when in service of U.S.
FRANKLIN, James, D-64-4; Nashville PO
FRANKLIN, James, H-73-3; Pvt G Co or B Co 1st Hvy Art; Chattanooga PO
FRANKLIN, James H., Co-65-1 (alias Franklin, James); Pvt C Co 3rd TN Cav; 19 Dec 62 to 3 Aug 65; Wilton Springs PO; piles, not pensioned
FRANKLIN, James H., K-181-5(2); Nancy J. widow of; 3rd TN Cav; May 62 to __; Knoxville PO
FRANKLIN, James K., Se-226-1; Margaret widow of; Pvt K Co 2nd TN Cav; __ to 14 May 62; Straw Plains PO
FRANKLIN, James M., Je-142-1; Pvt G Co 1st TN Cav; 1 Jul 62 to 5 Jun 65; Alena PO; injured lungs
FRANKLIN, John, Bo-12-2(1); Pvt D Co 9th TN Cav; 63 to 65; Rasor PO
FRANKLIN, John K-167-4; Pvt B Co 1st Cav Hvy; 64 to Mar 66; Knoxville PO
FRANKLIN, L. M., Hu-103-1; L. A. Col B Co US Cav; 14 Jan 62 to     (3 yrs); Knoxville PO
FRANKLIN, Lossen, Sn-255-1; Pvt D Co 9th IN Inf; 9-1-61 to 5-1-64; Saundersville PO
FRANKLIN, M., Po-150-1; Merry E. widow of; Pvt B Co 5th __; 2-20-65 to 7-13-65; Sylco PO; cancer of eyesyplis
FRANKLIN, Sylvester, Fe-41-4(2); Pvt A Co 1st NC Mtd Inf; 11-63 to 65; Boat Land PO; cr. dis. of lungs; in prison in Atlanta GA 2 mos
FRANKLIN, Thomas P., Je-136-2; Sgt B Co 9th TN Cav; 11 Aug 63 to 11 Sep 65; PO omitted
FRANKLIN, William D., Je-136-2; Mary A. widow of; Pvt D Co 9th TN Cav; 4 Jul 63 to 11 Nov 63; PO omitted
FRANKLIN, William P., Bo-20-1; Sgt C Co 6th TN Cav; 4-18-62 to 4-27-65; Bank PO
FRANKLIN, William T., J-80-1; Pvt I Co 1st TN Mtd Inf; 64 to 65; Kempville PO; rupture incurred in last of yr 1864 to 1st of yr 1865; discharge has been destroyed by fire
FRANKLIN, ___, Wa-274-4; Ruth widow of; Jonesboro PO
FRABA, William M., Sn-252-4; Pvt F Co 15th KY Cav; 11-6-62 to 10-20-63; Pvt D Co 17th KY Cav-- 8-10-64 to 9-20-65; Sycamore PO; this man served in to reg.
FRABEK, James, Me-99-2; Pvt K Co 10th TN Cav; 64 to 8-1-65; Sewee PO
FRAE, T. K., La-117-3; Pvt A Co 48th TN Inf; Jan 2 62 to May 65; 15th Dist; CONF
FRAIZIER, William, Dy-28-1; Sarrah widow of; Pvt A Co 13th TN Cav; Aug __ to __; Finley PO; for man being killed army drawing pension $8 per m
FRALEY, W. J., Hd-51-1; Pvt D Co 5th? US Inf; 65 to Oct 66; Hamburgh PO
FRAME, Thomas, Ru-238-2; Pvt M Co 2nd US Art--53 to 58; Pvt F Co 4th US Cav--60 to 65; Murfreesboro PO; wounded in left arm & leg
FRANCIOLA, Samuel, Sh-173-1; Cpl A Co Hvy Art; __ to 4-66 (1 yr 2 mos); Memphis PO; eruption
FRANCIOLA, Wm. Samuel, Sh-173-1 (this was a separate entry in remarks section); first enlisted in company A and was transferred to 3rd Hvy Art bn.
FRANCIS, John H., St-160-1; Pvt F Co 48th KY Mtd Inf; Jun 1 63 to Dec 65; Weavers Store PO; piles contracted
FRANCIS, John W., Bl-5-1; 2nd Lt 14th OH Independent Battery Lt Art; 8-20-61 to 8-9-65; Brayton PO; hearing injured, reenlisted veteran
FRANCIS, Louisa, D-43-2; sol widow; Vine St, Nashville PO
FRANCIS, Robert A., Ct-39-2; Pvt D Co 13th TN Cav; Happy Valley PO; kidney disease, paroehora
FRANCIS, William B., Mg-197-5; Pvt G Co 2nd TN Inf; Sep 61 to 12 Oct 64; Wartburg PO; wounded left ancle
FRANCISCO, Henry C., H-58-3; Pvt A Co 8th TN Inf; 11-11-61 to 3-3-65; Sale Creek PO; gunshot wound in left shoulder
FRANCISCO, James T., Cl-57-2; 9th TN Reg; Goin PO
FRANK, Augustus, D-46-1; Mena Braun formerly widow of; Pvt C Co 32nd IN Foot V; 9-1-62 to 6-14-65; Nashville PO
FRANK, E. A., Je-135-2; Pvt B Co 8th TN Cav; 11 Jun 66 to 15 Sep 65; Piedmont PO; diarhea, dyspepsia
FRANK, Geo. H., Je-135-4; PVt B Co 6th TN Inf; 14 Apr 62 to 7 Apr 65; Piedmont PO
FRANK, Peter, Mg-199-1; Pvt C Co 57th OH Inf; Feb 64 to Jul 64; Sunbright PO; 2 fingers cut off (by his self)
FRANK, Samuel B., D-45-2; Pvt L Co 12th MO Cav; 2-4-64 to 4-9-66; Nashville PO; contracted rheumatism while in army and has never recovered
FRANK, William H., Ro-210-6; Pvt; Rockwood PO
FRANKLIN, Jery, Hm-108-3(2); Rebeckah Robertson widow of; Pvt B Co 8th TN Inf; Russellville PO; rheumatism
FRANKLIN, John H., Hm-108-4(3); Pvt D Co 1st TN Cav; 12 Aug 62 to 5 Jun 65; Russellville PO; heart disease
FRANKLING, John, K-167-2; 1st Hvy __; 62 to 65; Knoxville PO
FRANKS, Green, La-111-3; Pvt I Co 2nd TN Inf; 3-63 to 7-65; PO omitted
FRANKS, Jefferson, Hd-49-2; Pvt D Co 2nd TN Mtd Inf; Sep 1 63 to __; Gillis Mills PO
FRANKS, John M., La-111-3; Pvt I Co 10th MI Inf; 6-3-62 to 7-65; PO omitted
FRANKS, William, Wy-173-2; Pvt G Co 10th TN Inf; 1-20-62 to 6-24-65; Marins Mills PO
FRANSELIN, Thomas, Fe-42-3; Pvt D Co 1st TN; 62 to __ (11 mos); Boatland PO
FRANSIOLI, Phillip, Sh-172-2; Pvt B Co 1st HG Inf; 63 to 65; Co. Union & 2nd Sts, Memphis PO; served as home guard
FRASIER, Alexander D., Ct-42-2; Lt U Co 13th TN Cav; 9-22-63 to 9-5-65; Watauga PO; neuralgia
FRASIER, Jacob L., Ct-43-2; Cpl B Co 13th TN Cav; 9-22-63 to 9-5-65; Carter Furnace PO
FRASIER, James, Col, Me-94-1; Pvt K Co 40th US; Knott PO
FRASIER, John W., Ct-42-3; Annie widow of; Pvt B Co 13th TN Cav; Watauga PO
FRASURE, Carrel, O-136-1; alias Charles Savage; Pvt E Co 14th TN Inf; Apr 16 64 to Mar 26 66; Crocket Sta? PO
FRAYSER, John Albert, Sh-152-1; alias Frayser, Albert; Pvt D Co 23rd PA Inf; 63 to Jan 65; Collierville PO; wounded in head
FRAYSER, Robert, Sh-160-2; Pvt 59th TN Inf; 61 to 65; Memphis PO
FRAYSER, Sabey, Sh-163-1; Pvt 104th SC Inf; Apr 24 65 to Apr 66; Memphis PO
FRAZEE, John, K-169-2; Chap; gone from home; Knoxville PO
FRAZER, Henry H., Br-12-1; Pvt F Co 14th OH Inf; 8-12-61 to 10-24-64; Charleston PO; sciatic rheumatism
FRAZER, John, Sh-191-5(1); Memphis PO; records not seen
FRAZIER, Abner J., Ge-91-3; Lt E Co 4th TN Inf; Dec 62 to Aug 2 65; Greeneville PO; lung trouble & diarhea & ankle
FRAZIER, Adison N., Ge-98-2; Pvt K Co 12th TN Cav; 12 Jan 62 to 5 Jun 65; Lovelace PO; spinal disease of back
FRAZIER, Alex, D-103-1; Pvt C Co 1st TN Cav; Jul 12 62 to 5 Jun 65; Ridge Post PO
FRAZIER, Andrew J., Ho-96-2; Pvt I Co 2nd IL Cav; Aug 6 61 to __; Erin PO; received captains comm.
FRAZIER, Gilbert R., Br-7-1; Pvt A Co 7th TN Inf; 2-27-62 to 7-12-65; Cleveland PO; diarhea
FRAZIER, Harrison, H-55-3; Cathrine widow of; Pvt A Co 1st TN Cav; 62 to 65; Harrison PO; rheumatish
FRAZIER, Jane (see Perkins, Samuel)
FRAZIER, John B., Cf-35-3; Pvt I Co 4th TN Inf; 6 Nov 61 to 1 Feb 62; Normandy PO; CONF
FRAZIER, John M., Br-7-2; Cpl H Co 4th TN Cav; 9-12-63 to 7-12-65; Earnest PO; chronic diarhea
FRAZIER, Nathan, B-3-2; 3rd Civil Dist
FRAZIER, Onslow G., Br-7-1; Pvt A Co 4th TN Inf; 2-27-62 to 7-12-65; Felker PO; sunstroke & catarrh

FRAZIER, Russell D., Cy-26-2; Pvt H Co 9th KY Inf; 10-25-61 to 12-15-64; Boles PO (Monroe Co. KY); gun shot in right foot
FRAZIER, Williamson, H-55-3; Pvt F Co 6th TN Mtd Inf; 10-20-64 to 6-30-65; Harrison PO; rheumatism, now helpless
FRAZIER, _____, K-168-3; Pvt; Knoxville PO
FRAZUR, Henry alias Jones, Sh-158-51; Pvt E Co 3rd US Col Cav; 1 Nov 63 to __; not discharged but captured by the Conf army
FREDRICK, Jassee, Mr-96-2; Pvt C Co 6th TN Inf; 10-30-64 to 6-20-65; Cedar Spring PO; vricosela
FREEBERGER, George, Sh-159-1; Memphis PO; CONF
FREEBURGER, J. F. A., W-193-1; Pvt A Co 57th OH Inf; 9-2-61 to 6-23-65; Vernilla PO
FREED, Richard K., Ho-97-1; Cpl Co B 5th PA __; Aug 64 to 30 Jun 65; Erin PO; discharged on account of expiration of ware
FREELS, Isaac, Ro-203-5(1); Pvt A Co 4th TN Cav; 1 Dec 63 to 12 Jul 65; Burns Mills PO; disabled back resulting from chills & fever
FREELS, Jackson, We-220-2; Pvt C Co TN; at about 64 to Feb 10 65; PO omitted; discharge lost and dates forgotten; CONF
FREELS, James A., A-8-4; 1st Lt H Co 13th TN Cav; 10-1-63 to 9-9-65; Scarborough PO; contracted rheumatism, catarrh & asthma, Dec 1864
FREELS, John T., A-8-3; Pvt I Co 9th TN Cav; 5-8-63 to 9-14-65; Scarborough PO; crippled in foot 10-65
FREELS, Judge A., A-9-4(2); Pvt C Co 7th TN Mtd Inf; 11-8-64 to 7-27-65; Marlow PO; measles resulting in lung disease
FREELS, Pleasant N., A-8-1; Nancy J. widow of; Pvt E Co 3rd TN Inf; 62 to 12-25-63; Ledom PO
FREELS, Samuel, Ro-203-3; Pvt G Co 7th TN Inf; 8 Nov 64 to 27 Jul 65; Ethel PO; injury from relapse of measles
FREELS, William M., Ro-203-5(1); Pvt H Co 7th TN Inf; 15 Feb 65 to 27 Jul 65; Burns Mills PO; piles, rheumatism
FREEMAN, Andrew, A-7-1; Robertsville PO
FREEMAN, Bird, Bl-4-3; Cpl B Co 16th Reg MO Cav; 8-15-64 to 6-30-65; Pikeville PO
FREEMAN, Danel, F-36-1; Pvt F Co; Aug 62 to Jul __ (3 yrs 6 mos); Taylors Chappel PO
FREEMAN, Ewerd S., We-221-6(2); Pvt TN Cav; Oct 61 to Feb 63; Martin PO; CONF
FREEMAN, George, D-50-3; Emma widow of; Mus D Co 13th US Inf; 903 N College, Nashville PO; wid. has no more recollect
FREEMAN, James M., Bl-4-3; Pvt C Co 43rd TN Inf; 10-1-61 to 8-1-63; Pikeville PO; CONF
FREEMAN, James M., Cf-35-2; Pvt D Co 23rd TN; Jul 61 to Jul 62; Normandy PO; discharged on surgeon certificate; CONF
FREEMAN, James P., Lo-187-3; Sgt I Co 1st TN Inf; 9 Aug 61 to 17 Sep 64; Loudon PO
FREEMAN, John, H-49-8; Elisabeth widow of; Pvt; Igon's Ferry PO
FREEMAN, John A., Mo-131-1; Pvt E Co 71st TN Cav; 7-15-62 to 6-65; Joe PO
FREEMAN, John L., Pu-143-1; Elizabeth A. widow of; C Co 8th TN Inf; 3-13-65 to 8-17-65; Cookville PO
FREEMAN, John T., Ha-115-4; Pvt 44th SC Cav; Mulberry Gap PO; CONF
FREEMAN, Lewis R., Jo-150-3; Anne widow of; Pvt E Co 13th TN Cav; 24 Sep 63 to 5 Sep 65; Osborn PO
FREEMAN, M. B., M-108-3; Pvt E Co 1st TN Mtd Inf; 1-11-63 to 64; Lt B Co 8th TN; 4-7-65 to 8-31-65; Lafayette PO; discharge not at home
FREEMAN, Molly, Cr-16-4; widow of Sol; Huntington PO
FREEMAN, Rily D., Bo-12-2(1); Pvt; Chilhowee PO
FREEMAN, Ryman, Lo-189-2; Mary A. widow of; Pvt VA Hvy Art; Philadelphia PO
FREEMAN, Sandy, D-49-1; Silvester widow of; Nashville PO
FREEMAN, W. H., He-57-2; Pvt I Co 13th TN Inf; 5-10-61 to 9-10-62; Law PO; prisoner Jackson 2 mos; CONF?
FREEMAN, William, Sh-200-2; Millie S. widow of; Cpl E Co 59th US Col Inf; 27 Wilkerson St, Memphis PO
FREEMAN, William A., St-160-1; Cpl G Co 1st Mtd Inf; 6-1-62 to 6-1-63; Legate PO
FREEMAN, Wm. L., Li-154-1; Mrs. Jane widow of; Pvt I Co 17th KY Cav; 11-12-64 to died 8-25-65; Clardy Ville PO; her husband died in army, she draws a pension of $6 a mo
FREEMON, James, Wa-260-2; Pvt I Co 1st TN Cav; Sep 22 62 to Jun 14 65; Pilot Hill PO; rheumatism
FREEMONT, Ross, Sh-155-2; Pvt; 63 to 66; White Station PO
FREIZE, Lottie, C-38-1; widow; 10th Civil Dist
FRELAND, William, Gi-140-1; Dist 20
FREMAN, James, C-8-1; Pvt G Co 49th KY Inf; 11-5-63 to 12-25-64; Well Spring PO
FRENCH, Charles M., Je-135-2; Pvt E Co 50th IL Inf; 24 Feb 64 to 10 Jul 65; Leonidas PO; rheumatism, diarhea
FRENCH, George H., Ho-96-2; Pvt K Co 111th USC Inf; Mar 15 64 to Apr 9 66; Erin PO
FRENCH, George W., Wa-268-3; Johnson City PO
FRENCH, Gordon, S-215-2; Pvt K Co 7th KY Cav; Aug 61 to Nov 64; Pioneer PO; fever fell in arm, partly useless
FRENCH, James W., Bo-20-1; Pvt E Co 3rd TN Inf; 7-15-64 to 11-30-64; Bank PO; deafness, defective eye site, was thrown from a horse
FRENCH, Jas. R., Je-135-2; 1st Sgt A Co 8th TN Cav; 11 Jun 63 to 11 Sep 65; Dumplin PO; diarhea & piles
FRENCH, John, Ge-88-1; Pvt E Co 1st TN Lt Art; 63 to 65 (2 yrs 10 mos); Marvin PO; rheumatism
FRENCH, Joseph P., Lo-195-3(1); Sarah A. widow of; Pvt D Co 3rd TN Inf; 10 Feb 62 to 23 Feb 65; Loudon PO
FRENCH, Michael, K-181-3; Pvt E Co 44th PA Inf; 2 Sep 63 to 20 Feb 64; French PO
FRENCH, Oliver T., Ge-91-2; Pvt E Co 4th TN Inf; 15 Oct 62 to 2 Aug 65; Greeneville PO; neuralgia
FRENCH, Richar E., Cr-20-1; Mary F. widow of; Pvt B Co 7th TN Cav; 8-62 to __ (2 yrs 6 mos); Proffitt PO
FRENCH, Rufus A., Se-224-1; Pvt F Co 2nd TN Cav; 1 Aug 62 to 6 Jul 65; Waldens Creek PO; spinal affection of back
FRENCH, William B., K-168-4; Pvt G Co 4th TN Inf; Smithwood PO
FRENCH, Wm. J., Je-135-1(3); Pvt B Co 9th TN Cav; 16 Sep 63 to 11 Sep 65; Leonidas PO; discharged--war ended
FRENCH, Wright R., Bo-13-3(1); Pvt H Co 13th TN Cav; 9-1-64 to 9-5-65; Miser PO
FRESHAM, George, Co-60-2; Susan widow of; Sgt K Co 8th TN Inf; Parrottsville PO; bronchitis & diarhea
FRESHENOR, Oliver, Co-62-2; Marget widow of; Pvt M Co 9th TN Cav; Jun 63 to 65 (2 yrs); Rankins PO; rheumatism
FREUDINBERG, John N., H-51-6; Pvt I Co 7th OH Inf; 6-10-61 to 4-18-63; Albion View PO
FRIARSON, Polk, G-52-1; Pvt A Co 14th TN Col; Fruitland PO
FRIARSON, Porter, G-52-1; Drum Major A Co 43rd TN Col; 3-63 to __; Fruitland PO
FRIDDLES, Moses S., Jo-151-3; Martha C. widow of; Pvt M Co 13th TN Cav; 2 Feb 64 to 5 Sep 65; Vaughtsville PO; chronic diarrhoea, piles, rheumatism
FRIDELL, Joseph, H-59-1; Elizabeth widow of; Sgt IN Cav; 6-61 to 9-65; Chattanooga PO
FRIEL, Peter, O-139-1; Margaret D. widow of; Crystal PO
FRIER, Nancy, Rb-226-2; widow; Dist 12
FRIERSON, Adaline (see Ceicle?, Ben)
FRIERSON, Arthur, Mu-198-2; 10th Dist
FRIERSON, Bill, Mu-197-1; Sallie widow of; Pvt; 63 to 65; Columbia PO; now dead
FRIERSON, Billy, Mu-198-1; Pvt 13th US Reg; 63 to 65; Frierson PO; sickness caused by exposure, a pensioner wounded in foot; pensioner, wounded at Nashville
FRIERSON, Chafin, Mu-194-1; Pvt E Co 15th US Col Inf; 2-10-64 to 4-30-66; Columbia PO
FRIERSON, Charley H., Hi-92-1; Pvt; Hamshire PO
FRIERSON, James D., Mu-64-5; Pvt I Co 111th US C Inf; 1 Feb 64 to 30 Apr 66; Nashville PO; plurisey & diarhorea contracted in service
FRIERSON, John, Mu-197-1; Pvt; 62 to 65; Columbia PO

FRIERSON, Peter, Mu-197-2; Pvt; 62 to Mar 65; Columbia PO; feet frosted and all his toes came off
FRIERSON, Shaw, Mu-199-1; Pvt E Co 11th TN Inf; Ashwood PO
FRIERSON, W. W. S., K-167-6; Capt (L Col) 1st TN Cav; May 61 to May 65; Knoxville PO; CONF
FRILTY, Fransis, Cl-58-2; Pvt Co C 1st TN Inf; Aug 61 to Oct 64; Davo PO; injured in back of neck?, miniball
FRINK, George W., Ro-208-3; US Sol; 9th Civ Dist; nervous
FRISBEY, John V., Cu-18-1; Pvt G Co 30th IN Inf; 8-31-61 to 9-29-64; Manning PO
FRITH, Joseph A., D-59-1; Pvt 71st NY State Militia; 3 mos; 1802 Hays St, Nashville PO
FRITTS, David M., Jo-149-2; Pvt D Co 13th TN Cav; 24 Sep 63 to 5 Sep 65; Mountain City PO; rheumatism and hart
FRITTS, George (see Stufflestreet, George)
FRITTS, Jeremiah, Ro-203-7; Pvt D Co 5th TN Inf; 26 Feb 62 to __; Vancouver PO; injury from mumps & measles
FRITTS, John, Ro-203-7; Pvt K Co 5th TN Inf; 18 Oct 62 to 30 Jun 65; Union X Roads PO; loss of left eye
FRITTS, Ransom, S-218-1; Pvt D Co 5th TN Inf; M 62 to __ (7 mos); PO omitted
FRITTS, Wiley H., Ro-206-2; Cpl B Co 5th TN Inf; 25 Feb 62 to 30 Mar 65; Emory Gap PO
FRITTS, William, Mc-109-5; Sarah J. widow of; Prigmore PO; died in hospital at Chattanooga
FRITZ, George, K-169-1; Pvt G Co 1st KY Inf; 62 to 65; Knoxville PO
FRITZ, John, Su-233-1; Pvt M Co 13th TN Cav; 64 to Sep 65; Holston Vally PO; week brest, partly disabled
FRITZ, Phillip, D-51-1; Pvt C Co 10th TN Inf; Oct 62 to 65; 333 Deadrick St, Nashville PO; dont know date of enlistment
FRIZZELL, Jane, De-26-3; widow of Sol US; Poplar Springs PO
FROMAN, Alfred, Sh-172-2; US Sol; 17 Hernando St, Memphis PO
FRONEYBERGER, Joseph, K-173-3; US Sol; 3rd Dist
FROST, Benjamin F., H-54-3; Pvt E Co 5th ME? Vol; 5-2-61 to 3-8-62; Sherman Heights PO; sprain of the back, reenlisted but was rejected on medical examination
FROST, Calvin, Un-253-1; Sgt F Co 11th OH Cav; 10 Ju 63 to 10 Ju 66; Lorenaton PO
FROST, Constan, Gr-77-1; Leesean J. widow of; Y.Z. PO; husband died of measels
FROST, John F., Un-253-1; Pvt F Co 11th OH Cav; 10 Ju 6e to 10 Ju 66; Lorenaton PO
FROST, Wm C., H-60-5(2); Pvt B Co 10th TN Cav; 10-21-63 to 8-1-65; Chattanooga PO
FROTHINGHAM, Samuel H., Cf-41-1; 15th Civil Dist
FRUMAN, William J., Ch-17-1; Pvt H Co 21st TN Cav; 63 to 65; Henderson PO; CONF
FRY, Abraham, Sn-251-1; Cpl D Co 79th PA Vol; 9-12-61 to 9-12-64; Gallatin PO; spinal disease
FRY, Daniel, Je-138-1; Kate Tillett formerly widow of; Capt F Co 2nd TN Inf; 22 Oct 61 to 65; White Pines PO
FRY, Henry, L-104-1; Pvt E Co 9th NY Hvy Art; Aug 64 to Jun 65; Ripley PO
FRY, Henry, Sn-253-1; Pvt H Co PA; 10 days; Saunders Mills PO; ankle broken
FRY, James B., D-72-3; Margret B. widow of; Musician; Jun 16 61 to May 18 65; Nashville PO; CONF
FRY, James S., Ge-89-3; Pvt D Co 1st TN Cav; Aug 12 62 to 5 Jun 65; Marvin PO
FRY, John A., Ch-17-2; Pvt F Co 49th IL Inf; 1-15-62 to 9-9-65; Menary PO
FRY, John B., Je-146-1; Pvt A Co 124th IN Inf; 12 Nov 63 to 31 Aug 65; White Pine PO; diarrhea & piles; badly affected
FRY, John W., Ma-126-1; Sgt K Co 3rd TN Inf; 10 Feb 62 to 23 Feb 65; Jackson PO
FRY, Joseph W., Ch-18-2; Pvt TN Reg; PO omitted; CONF
FRY, M., D-43-1; Pvt F Co 21st KY; 61 to 64; Nashville PO
FRY, Parker, D-87-1; Cpl A Co 2nd MS Hvy Art; Nashville PO

FRY, Thomas, Je-146-4; Pvt C Co 8th TN Inf; 1 Dec 62 to 30 Jun 65; White Pine PO; he's a good one
FRYAR, Joseph, H-55-1; Elizabeth widow of; Pvt Inf; 62 to 65; Tyner PO; shot through left arm
FRYAR, Pleas, D-99-3; Pvt F Co 6th TN Mtd Inf; Aug 64 to 65; State Penitentiary PO
FRYBERBER, William, D-57-3; OH; PO omitted; 8th Ward; CONF
FRYER, William M., Rb-228-1; Pvt; 63 to __ (1 yr 6 mos); Greenbrier PO
FUGATE, Elvenia (see Smith, John H.)
FUGATE, James H., Cl-52-2; Pvt A Co 8th TN Cav; 6-2-63 to 9-11-65; Hypratia PO
FUGATE, Joseph H., Ha-116-2; US Sol; Dist No 10
FUGATE, Mary, Ha-116-2; widow US Sol; Dist No 10
FUGELBERGER, William C., Fr-119-1; Pvt C Co 1st US TN; Debret? 1863; 1 yr 8 mos; Winchester PO; wounded in the right leg, struck by shell
FUGERSON, Thomas, Hi-85-1; Pvt C Co 12th TN Cav; 2-15-64 to 10-10-65; Spinars Mill PO; & is now broke down
FUGET, Lewis F., R-158-2; Pvt B Co 6th TN Mtd Inf; 9-12-64 to 6-30-65; Rhea Springs PO; lung disease and paralasis
FUGUE, James, Cl-46-2; PO omitted
FUKEWAY, William E., J-83-2; Pvt I Co 1st TN; 7-7-64 to 7-22-65; Nameless PO
FULFER, Nicholas, Mr-99-2; Pvt K Co; Owen PO
FULKERSON, Jesse C., Wa-266-1; Pvt F Co 8th TN Cav; 31 May 63 to 11 Sep 65; Meadow Brook PO
FULKS, William B., Ge-91-2; Cpl A Co 3rd TN Inf; Nov 64 to Ma 65; Greeneville PO; lungs & eyes
FULLBRIGHT, Miles W., Po-148-3; Pvt I Co 3rd US Inf; 10-31-64 to 11-29-65; Benton PO
FULLER, Arch B., W1-300-1; Pvt G Co 4th TN Inf; 14 Dec 64 to 30 Aug 65; Watertown PO
FULLER, Buck, Sh-189-2; Sgt 3rd US Col Cav; alley off Broadway, Memphis PO
FULLER, George C., O-134-2; Pvt B Co 48th TN Inf; Sep 15 61 to Dec 15 63; Hornbeak PO; CONF
FULLER, Henry R., Ro-210-11; Pvt C Co 16th TN Bat; 11 May 62 to Dec 64; Post Oak Springs PO; CONF
FULLER, John, H-58-4; Alice widow of; Pvt E Co 3rd TN Inf; 7-15-64 to 11-30-64; Sale Creek PO
FULLER, Levi, Dk-32-1; Pvt H Co 10th TN Inf; 3-3-65 to 6-23-65; Liberty PO
FULLER, Luman, K-172-2; alias Luman Adams, K-172-2; Pvt C Co 124th OH Inf; 21 Dec 63 to 10 Jul 65; 14th Dist; gun shot wound right shoulder, contusion right hip
FULLER, William J., Sm-174-1; Pvt G Co 4th TN Inf; 11-1-64 to 8-25-65; New Middleton PO
FULLINGTON, Armintie, He-59-1; widow; PO omitted
FULLINLOVE, Thomas, K-158-2; Pvt IN Inf; 61 to 65; Knoxville PO; 222 Mabry; suffering from effects of measles
FULNOR, Chas. L., R-163-2; Pvt F Co 75th Inf; 8-12-62 to 8-20-65; Graysville PO
FULQUM, Matilda (see Pickering, Ephriham)
FULTON, John, Je-140-2; Pvt D Co 2nd TN Cav; PO omitted
FULTS, Daniel, Gu-45-1; Pvt E Co 1st TN Cav Vidette; 63 to 64 (8 mos); Altamont PO
FULTS, David Sr., Gu-45-1; Pvt E Co 1st TN Cav Vidette; 63 to 64 (8 mos); Altamont PO
FULTS, Marsh, W-198-2; Nancy widow of; Lt--dont know the co. or regiment; Viala PO; discharge is at Washington, she drew 1500 H sane 2 yrs ago & is now trying for a pension
FULTS, W. C., Cf-40-4; Caroilen widow of; E Co 1st IN Cav; 7 Oct 63 to 65; Tullahoma PO; discharge at pension office
FULWILER, Samuel, Su-241-2; Pvt D Co 47th KY Inf; 11 Aug 63 to 26 Dec 64; Butter Fly PO; exposure
FUNDERBURK, David A., De-22-3; Pvt F? Co 26th SC Inf; 30 Apr 62 to 12 Apr 65; Dunbar PO; CONF
FUQUA, Gabriel, Rb-228-1; Mineva widow of; Pvt; Oct 61 to __; Crunk PO; CONF
FUQUA, Hamson, H-76-2; Pvt H Co 111th TN Col Inf; Chattanooga PO
FUQUA, Jessie, Hu-103-2; Pvt 10th TN R; 25 May 61 to 20 May 63; PO omitted

FUQUA, John, Gi-127-1; Pulaski PO
FUQUA, Levi W., Rb-228-1; Catherine M. widow of; Pvt; Springfield PO
FUQUA, Sam., D-49-3; Cpl H Co 111th __; 1 Feb 64 to 30 Apr 66; Nashville PO
FUQUA, Thomas, D-75-1; Sallie A. widow; Pvt F Co 30th TN Inf; 1 Oct 61 to 1 Sep 62; Stewarts Ferry PO; CONF
FURGERSON, James R., Mc-116-3; Pvt A Co 7th TN Mtd Inf; 8-13-64 to 7-27-65; Mortimer PO
FURGESEN, Andrew, Br-12-4; Lucinda widow of; Pvt E Co 5th TN Inf; Etola PO
FURGUSON, James, Gi-127-3; Rachel Williams formerly widow of; Pulaski PO; said to have been killed in battle, Rachel does not know the particulars
FURGUSON, John, Cl-51-2; US Soldier; 6th Civil Dist
FURGUSON, Thomas, Ro-209-3; Pvt D Co 47th MO Inf; 63 to 65; Rockwood PO
FURGUSSON, Bengamin W., Mr-99-2; Pvt E Co 10th TN Inf; 5-23-62 to 7-6-65; Jasper PO
FURMAN, Elijah V., D-99-5; Pvt; Central Hos. for Insane PO
FURMAN, Thomas B., Gu-47-1; Pvt NY; 61 to 62; Mont Eagle PO
FURRINGTON, Daniel, Mg-198-2; Pvt I Co 150th PA Inf; 21 Aug 62 to 19 Jan 65; Deer Lodge PO; shot left hip
FURROW, Marion, Gr-70-3; Pvt A Co 9th TN Cav; 24 Sep 63 to 11 Sep 65; Lulaville PO; heart disease
FUTRAR, Ruben, Ru-241-4; Pvt; 63 to 66; Murfreesboro PO
FUTRELL, John, Mg-196-3; Pvt H Co 3rd TN Inf; 23 Feb 62 to Feb 65; Elverton PO
FUTTS, Jessee, Gu-47-1; Pvt TN; 63 to __ ( yr); Pelham PO; feet frozen; trouble him in winter
GABBERT, James T., Rb-226-1; Pvt E Co 145th Inf; 27 Jun 65 to 26 Jun 66; Greenbrier PO; diarrhea resulting in piles, drawing pension
GABBERT, Joel C., Pu-140-1; Pvt C Co 8th TN Cav Inf; 65 to 65; Cookeville PO; chronic inflamation of kidneys
GABLE, James, Hr-92-1; Pvt F Co 27th Reg; 9-7-64 to 9-7-67; Bolivar PO; think exposure caused piles
GABRIEL, Casper, D-46-2; Pvt C Co 10th TN Inf; 4-19-62 to 5-25-65; Nashville PO
GABY, George W., Ge-92-1; Pvt B Co 3rd TN Mtd Inf; 13 Aug 64 to 15 Oct 64; Romeo PO
GABY, Henry H., Ge-92-4; Pvt 4th TN Inf; Ottway PO; deafness
GABY, John N., Ge-92-1; Pvt B Co 3rd TN Mtd Inf; 30 Jun 64 to 30 Nov 64; Romeo PO
GAD, Jno. D., Br-10-2; Pvt G Co 37th TN Inf; 10-15-61 to 11-4-62; Cleveland PO
GADDIS, James, Je-137-1; Mary widow of; Pvt B Co 3rd TN Cav; Hickory Ridge PO
GADSON, Eliga, A-3-1; Sgt F Co 42nd TN Inf; 10-10-64 to 1-8-66; Bull Run PO (Knox Co.)
GAFFORD, John D., H-56-7; Pvt NY; St. Elmo PO
GAGE, Francis M., Ro-208-1; Pvt C Co 7th TN Inf; 20 Aug 64 to 10 Jun 65; Morris Gap PO
GAGE, Mrs. George W., Ro-205-3; Pvt F Co 5th TN Inf; 14 Feb 61 to __; Halfmoon Island PO
GAGE, John T., Mn-126-2; Pvt B Co 6th TN Cav; 8-25-62 to 6-29-65; Bethel Springs PO
GAGE, William A., K-158-1; Col 12th OH Cav; Aug 61 to May 65; Knoxville PO; 32 Mabry St, wounded in cheeck by sword
GAIN, Moses, D-57-2; Pvt A Co 12th US? Inf; 62 to 65; Nashville PO; lossed eye
GAHAGAN, Andrew J., H-59-1; 1st Lt D Co 1st TN Cav; 1-20-62 to 4-15-65; Chattanooga PO
GAINES, Charlie, D-64-1; Nashville PO
GAINES, Edward, H-51-1; Pvt H Co 16th R PA Cav; 11-6-62 to 8-11-65; Soddy PO; rupture and wounded
GAINES, Jerry, Mt-136-1; Pvt F Co 16th TN; Jan 63 to Apr 66; Omar PO
GAINES, T. L., Bo-19-3; Pvt C Co 13th TN Cav; 6 mos; Rockford PO
GAINES, Wily, Mt-136-1; Eliza Carney widow of; Pvt K Co 16th TN; Mar __ to __; Port Royal PO
GAINLERS, Thomas, Bo-12-2(1); Pvt C Co 13th TN Cav; 65 to 11-11-66; Montvale Springs PO
GAINS, Thomas E., Gr-78-2; Pvt C Co 12th TN Cav; 4 Aug 62 to 4 Apr 65; Maples PO; this was marked out, might be CONF
GAINS, Uriah, Cl-56-2(1); Rebecca widow of; Pvt C Co 1st TN Lt Art; Head of Barren PO; died of small pox
GAINT, Jeff, L-108-1; Pvt I Co 3rd US Art; 63 to 64; Glimpville PO
GAITHER, Silas, Ca-19-1; Cpl F Co 1st TN Mtd Inf; 8-27-63 to 6-27-64; Auburn PO
GALAWAY, George W., Hw-123-1; Pvt K Co 8th TN Cav; Oct 62 to 64; New Canton PO
GALAWAY, Noah, Su-241-2; Pvt K Co 8th TN Cav; 10 Oct 63 to 11 Sep 65; Fall Branch PO; gun shot in left arm, chronic diarrhoea
GALBRAITH, Henry, A-7-2; Robertsville PO
GALBRAITH, James H., R-158-2; Capt; Rhea Springs PO; family away from home--no information, pensioner
GALBRAITH, James N., He-64-2; Pvt 13th TN Reg; Aug 61 to 63; Center Point PO; CONF
GALBRAITH, John T., A-7-1; Robertsville PO
GALBRAITH, Mary J., A-7-1; widow of; Robertsville PO
GALBRAITH, Robert F., B-2-1; Fannie widow of; Lt Col 5th TN; Wartrace PO
GALBRAITH, Thomas E., K-179-4; Pvt D Co 3rd TN Inf; 10 Feb 62 to 23 Feb 65; PO omitted
GALBRAITH, Willis, Hw-124-2(1); Pvt A Co 1st US Art; 26 Jan 64 to 31 Nov 66; New Canton PO
GALBRETH, John B., Mu-209-4; Pvt G Co 48th TN Inf; Nov 62 to Aug 1 65; Darks Mills PO; sunstroke; CONF
GALE, James, Sh-146-1; Pvt; 64 to 65; Lucy PO; this man was evidently a soldier but is unable to tell anything about it except that he enlisted in Memphis
GALES, Columbus C., We-225-2(1); Nancy E. widow of; Pvt L Co 6th TN Cav; Jul 14 62 to Jul 26 65; Dresden PO; piles & bad health, now dead
GALIAN, Joshua, K-167-3; Nancy C. Morris widow of; Pvt 2nd TN Mtd Inf; 61 to died, Knoxville PO
GALIMORE, Dave, Ro-210-2; Pvt; 3 yrs; Rockwood PO
GALLAGHER, John, D-49-2; Cpl D Co 74th OH Inf; 5 Feb 62 to 16 Jul 65; Nashville PO
GALLAHER, David H., Ro-203-7; Lt K Co 1st TN Legion Inf; Mar 62 to May 65; Wheat PO
GALLAHER, Hiram J., K-178-2; Cpl G Co 8th TN Cav; 21 May 64 to 31 Mar 66; Hardin Valley PO
GALLAHER, Thomas M., Wy-177-1; Mariah Dixon formerly widow of; Pvt; Moon PO; got wounded in Shilo battle and died from effects thereof in hospital
GALLAHER, William M., Wy-177-2; Pvt A Co 10th TN Inf; 4-26-62 to 6-25-65; Moon PO
GALLAWAY, Allbert, Hr-94-1; Lottie widow of; Saulsbury PO
GALLAWAY, Charlie, D-64-5; Pvt; Nashville PO
GALLAWAY, Frank, K-183-1; Pvt K Co 5th TN Inf; 9 Aug 66 (sic) to 12 Jun 65; Riverdale PO
GALLEHEN, John, F-46-2; LaGrange PO; John Gallehen said he belon to Vicburgh malisha
GALLESPIE, Alexander, Hm-103-3; Morristown PO
GALLIAN, Albert (see Pearcely, Albert)
GALLIEN, Dicemous G., Wy-178-1; Pvt E Co 2nd Mtd TN Inf; 12-10-63 to 5-10-65; Light PO
GALLIMORE, James, Mg-196-3; Pvt F Co 1st TN Inf; 9 Aug 61 to 17 Sep 64; Hunnicutt PO
GALLIMORE, John R., We-225-2(1); Pvt; Dresden PO
GALLMAN, Andrew, Mo-119-1; Mrs. Cary widow of; Pvt 32nd IN Inf; Sweetwater PO
GALLOWAY, Jennie (see Lee, Sam)
GALLOWAY, Jesse B., Wa-273-1; Pvt K Co 13th TN Cav; 21 Aug 63 to 5 Sep 65; Morning Star PO; chronic diarrhoea
GALLOWAY, Lucintha W., We-234-1; US Sol; PO omitted
GALLOWAY, Miles L., Br-14-3; Quartermaster Sgt C Co 6th IL? Cav; 1-11-63 to 9-15-65; Cleveland PO; bad hearing and general disability
GALYAN, Calvin, Ro-210-5; Pvt D Co 5th TN Inf; 61 to __; Rockwood PO
GALYAN, Franklin, Ro-205-3; Pvt A Co 2nd TN Inf; 10 Aug 62 to 6 Oct 64; Hatch PO
GALYON, John, Ro-207-2; Pvt H Co 5th E TN Inf; 25 Feb 62 to 10 Dec 63; Morris Gap PO; kidney affection
GALYON, John W., Ro-210-8; Pvt L Co 1st TN Cav; 1 Nov 62 to 19 Jun 65; Rockwood PO

GALYON, Wesley H., Gr-74-1; Pvt D Co 2nd TN Cav; Rutledge PO; lameness in hip on acct of horse running
GAMBER, Theodore W., H-57-3; Pvt 104th OH Inf; 62 to 65; Orchard Knob PO
GAMBILL, Jesse, D-84-1; Celia F. widow of; Pvt 24th IL Inf; Sep 64 to Jan 65; LaVergne PO
GAMBILL, Jesse W., Jo-151-2; Pvt M Co 13th TN Cav; 2 Feb 64 to 5 Sep 65; Bakers Gap PO; chronic diarrhoia, spinal affection, enlargement left testicle
GAMBLE, A. Marion, Bo-22-2; Major 6th TN Inf; 3-8-62 to 4-17-65; Gamble's Store PO; hurt back aggravated by small pox
GAMBLE, Aron, Mc-117-4; Pvt A Co 44th TN Inf; 3-7-64 to 4-30-66; Carlock PO; wounded in back
GAMBLE, Charles, Me-89-1; Pvt E Co 5th TN Reg; 7-7-64 to 6-26-65; Big Spring PO
GAMBLE, Charles P., Ja-85-5; Sarah A. widow of; Pvt E Co 5th TN Inf; 3-2-62 to 4-4-65; Georgetown PO
GAMBLE, Mariah, Po-148-3; widow of US Sol; 2nd Dist
GAMBLE, Moses, Bo-22-1; Angeline F. widow of; Pvt A Co 3rd TN Cav; 9-3-62 to 4-27-65; killed; PO omitted
GAMBLE, Moses, Mo-123-1; Pvt K Co 3rd TN Cav; 3-10-64 to 6-10-65; Jalapa PO
GAMBLE, Robert L., Me-88-3; Capt G Co 4th TN Cav; 12-2-62 to 7-12-65; Georgetown PO; gun shot right thigh; prisner 61 days, Charleston SC
GAMBLE, Samuel H., Me-88-2; Pvt E Co 5th TN Inf; 6-11-62 to 6-11-65; Georgetown PO
GAMBLE, Vince, Br-12-1; Pvt M Co 1st TN Hvy Art; Charleston PO; hemorrhoids
GAMBOL, John, Rb-223-3(5); Nancy widow of; 9th Dist
GAMBREL, James, Wy-177-1; Pvt B Co 2nd TN Mtd Inf; 10-15-63 to 10-17-64; Wayland Springs PO
GAMBRELL, Bradford C., Wy-177-2; Sol US; 12th Dist
GAMBULL, John R., Jo-149-3; Blacksmith M Co 13th TN Cav; 2 Feb 64 to 65; Mountain City PO
GAMIS, James H., Cy-27-5(3); Pvt I Co 55th OH Inf; 1-6-62 to 3-22-63; Spivey PO; discharged by reason of disability
GAMMON, Harrison, Ro-203-4; Pvt; Ethel PO
GAMMON?, William M., M-106-2(1); Sgt I Co 9th KY Vol Inf; 11-2-61 to 12-15-64; Lafayette PO; ruptured, pensioner
GAMMON, William T., Br-13-2; Cpl G Co 5th TN Inf; 4-1-62 to 4-19-65; Ora PO
GAN, Wesley, Je-145-1; Pvt B Co 9th TN Cav; Cynthiana PO
GANDY, William F., Dk-39-4(2); Mary A. widow of; Sgt E Co 1st TN Mtd Inf; Dekalb PO
GANILIN, James G., P-151-1; Pvt F Co 2nd TN Mtd Inf; 20 Nov 63 to 19 Jan 65; Lindon PO; injured by lightening
GANN, Alexander, Se-225-2; Pvt F Co 9th TN Cav; Jul 63 to 11 Sep 65; Trotters Store PO; crippled in left shoulder and left arm fractured 25 yrs, thrown from horse in action at Russellville, TN and run over
GANN, Amanda (see Bean, James Wm.)
GANN, Andy, H-49-9; Pvt F Co 6th TN Mtd Inf; 8-2-64 to 6-30-65; Igon's Ferry PO; hurt hip in jumping off a train
GANN, Campbell A., H-49-8; Pvt C Co 5th TN Inf; 2-25-62 to 4-4-65; Igon's Ferry PO
GANN, Christopher, M-106-2(1); Pvt C Co 5th TN Cav; 62 to 65; Lafayette PO; thrown from a horse & bruised, his discharge is at Washington
GANN, Daniel, M-106-2(1); Pvt I Co 5th TN Inf; 11-1-62 to 7-65; Hillsdale PO; enlargement of testicles, wounded in right thigh, pensioner --discharge at Washington
GANN, Elisha, H-49-8; Pvt C Co 5th TN Inf; 2-25-62 to 4-4-65; Igon's Ferry PO; dyspepsia
GANN, James M., H-49-9; Mary Jones formerly widow of; Pvt C Co 5th TN Inf; 2-25-62 to ___; Igon's Ferry PO; died in the service
GANN, Jarett, H-49-9; Pvt A Co 6th TN Mtd Inf; 8-2-64 to 6-30-65; Igon's Ferry PO
GANN, John, H-49-9; Pvt F Co 6th TN Mtd Inf; 9-12-64 to 6-30-65; Igon's Ferry PO; rheumatism
GANN, John R., Dk-33-3; Frances widow of; Pvt L Co 5th TN Cav; 5-13-63 to 8-14-65; Halesville PO; injury to left hip by horse in service
GANN, Preston, H-49-2; Susan wife of; Pvt; Falling Water PO
GANN, Russell, Dk-33-3; Pvt I Co 5th TN Cav; 11-27-62 to 8-14-65; Halesville PO
GANN, Talitha (see Cate, John T.)
GANNILL, Mires, Hd-50-6; Sarah widow of; Pvt M Co 7th TN Cav; 63 to 65; Nixon PO; one arm most? useless
GANNON, William D., Hm-106-3; Lt C Co 19th TN Inf; 15 Nov 61 to 10 to 10 Nov 65; Morristown PO; CONF
GANNUM, W. H., Ge-87-3; Pvt E Co 8th TN Inf; 20 Jun 63 to 30 Jun 65; Timerridge PO; spinal & kidney trouble
GANON, Harvey A., Ru-13-2; Pvt Nichols; 62 to 63; Murfreesboro PO; wounded; CONF
GANT, Cranford, Ms-181-1; Pvt A Co 10th TN Inf; 6-10-63 to 4-12-65; Lewisburg PO
GANT, Dareld, Hd-50-4; Elizebeth widow of; Pvt F Co 1st TN Mtd Inf; Apr 22 62 to Apr 22 65; Nixon PO
GANT, William J., Ch-18-3(5); Pvt A Co 9th MS; Mar 62 to 65; PO omitted; CONF
GARDENER, Overton, Sh-150-3; Cpl D Co 88th US Inf; 63 to Apr 66; Bartlett PO
GARDNER, Adam, Se-228-1(2); Pvt H Co 3rd TN Cav; 3 Sep 63 to Aug 65; Cusicks X Roads PO
GARDNER, Algernon C., We-222-1; Capt G Co 9th TN Reg; 15 May 61 to 15 May 65; Gardner PO; CONF
GARDNER, Amos, Se-228-3; Pvt H Co 3rd TN Cav; 27 Sep 63 to 5 Aug 65; Cox PO
GARDNER, Charly, F-43-1; Carsie? widow of; Pvt; 61 to 65; New Kent PO; cannot give much information
GARDNER, George W., Sh-158-2; Pvt D Co 11th IN Vol; 6 Jul 61 to 16 Jun 62; 2nd enlistment Pvt Bat F 2nd IL Lt Art; 4 Jan 64 to Sep 65; Memphis PO; re-enlisted veteran
GARDNER, Henry, Hw-121-4(3); Pvt I Co 8th TN Cav; 25 Oct 63 to 25 Oct 65; Van Hill PO; contracted rheumatism
GARDNER, Jackson, Se-228-1(2); Pvt B Co 46th NC Inf; Mar 61 to 62; Cusicks X Roads PO
GARDNER, James, Gi-129-1; Pvt B Co 106th TN Inf; 15 Jan 64 to 29 May 65; Elkton PO
GARDNER, James A., Ro-210-4; Pvt C Co 2nd TN Cav; 5 Nov 62 to 6 Jul 65; Rockwood PO; shot through the foot
GARDNER, James V., We-230-3; Pvt F Co 18th KY Inf; Jan 15 63 to Feb 15 65; McKinzie PO; CONF
GARDNER, Jefferson, D-68-2; Pvt C Co 2nd TN Cav; 272 Fillmore St, Nashville PO
GARDNER, John, Gi-127-6; Pvt; 9th Dist
GARDNER, John, Gi-127-6; Pvt C Co 13th US Col Inf; Sep 5 62 to Jun 3 66; Pulaski PO
GARDNER, Lee, D-72-5; Pvt G Co 4th TN Cav; Sep 15 64 to May 17 65; Nashville PO; CONF
GARDNER, M. A., Bo-11-1; Pvt B Co 5th US Vol; 3-15-65 to 3-15-65; Cloids Creek PO
GARDNER, M. A., Bo-11-1; Pvt A Co 3rd TN Inf; 2-10-62 to 5-16-64; Cloids Creek PO; renlisted in US Volunteer
GARDNER, Mack, Hi-91-1; US Sol; Pleasantville PO
GARDNER, N. A., He-57-1; Sgt G Co 6th TN Inf; 3-25-62 to 2-25-65; Juno PO; CONF?
GARDNER, Samuel, Sh-174-2; Hagar A. widow of; Pvt; 164 De Soto St, Memphis PO; shot in head and side, died from wounds
GARDNER, Solomon, Gi-129-1; Pvt B Co 12th TN Inf; 31 Jul 63 to 16 Jan 66; Elkton PO
GARDNER, Thos. M., Bo-14-2(1); Pvt H Co 2nd TN Cav; 9-22-62 to 2-18-63; Yellow Sulphur PO
GARDNER, William, Ge-92-3; Pvt 3rd TN Mtd Inf; Laurel Gap PO
GARETT, James, D-68-2; 227 Fillmore St, Nashville PO; discharge papers lost
GAREY, Bartley, Hd-53-2; Pvt H Co 6th TN Cav; 18 Sep 62 to 26 Jul 65; Cravins Landing PO
GARISON, James L., F-40-2; Lucy A. widow of; Capt B Co 15th TN Cav; Feb 62 to Sep 64; Hickory Withe PO; Camp Douglass, 11 mos 16 days; CONF
GARISON, John C., R-161-3; Pvt C Co 5th TN Mtd Inf; 8-5-64 to 7-16-65; Dayton PO
GARLAND, Ambros, Jo-153-2; Pvt A Co 47th KY Inf; 3 Jul 63 to ___; Shady PO; bronchitis, rheumatism, hearing

GARLAND, Benjamin I., Ct-45-1; Nancy A. widow of; Pvt L Co 13th TN Cav; 4-8-64 to 8-23-65; Stony Creek PO
GARLAND, Dicey (see Anderson, William A.)
GARLAND, James D., Ct-45-1; Sarah widow of; Pvt H Co 4th TN Inf; Stony Creek PO; no record of enlistment or discharge
GARLAND, Jessee H., Jo-153-2; Pvt E Co 13th TN Cav; 21 Sep 63 to 5 Sep 65; Shady PO; gun shot, rheumatism
GARLAND, John R., Ct-45-3; Cpl L Co 13th TN Cav; 4-8-64 to 9-5-65; Stony Creek PO; Boyeds Ferrn TN 1865; paralysis
GARLAND, Lewis, Jo-152-1; 8th? Sgt E Co 13th TN Cav; 20 Sep 63 to 5 Sep 65; Doeville PO; gun shot & mumps
GARLAND, Manerva (see Fletcher, William)
GARLAND, Mordecai, Ct-45-1; Pvt H Co 4th TN Inf; Stony Creek PO; no record of enlistment or discharge
GARLAND, Ples, T-215-2; US Sol; Mason PO
GARLAND, Prior L., Su-232-1; Pvt H Co 4th TN Inf; 63 to 65; Holston Valley PO; hearing and rheumatism 27 yrs
GARLAND, Russell, Lo-188-1; Pvt A Co 2nd TN Inf; 10 Aug 61 to 15 Mar 66; Stockton PO; loss of eyes
GARLAND, Samuel, Jo-152-2; Pvt E Co 13th TN Cav; 24 Sep 63 to 5 Sep 65; Pandora PO; rheumatism & eyes
GARLAND, William W., U-245-2; Sgt B Co 12th TN Cav; 30 Nov 63 to 25 Oct 65; Limestone Cove PO; Pulaskey TN 1864
GARMEN, Thendonius M., H-56-5; Orderly Sgt G Co 15th WI Inf; 2-4-62 to 65 (3 yrs 5 mos); St. Elmo PO
GARNER, Abraham B., Gi-126-1; Pvt I Co 2nd TN Inf; 16 Nov 63 to 21 Jan 65; Pulaski PO
GARNER, Andrew J., Mn-126-2; Purdy PO; lost right eye in service; could not give dates of en. & dis.
GARNER, Isaac J., Fr-112-3; Pvt H Co 7th MI Inf; 8-10-61 to 8-21-64; Tullahoma PO (Coffee Co.)
GARNER, Isaiah, Le-118-1; Manerva widow of; Pvt TN Inf; 61 to 62; Newburg PO; cannot get the dates
GARNER, James C., A-3-3; Pvt G Co 4th TN Inf; 8-15-63 to 6-7-65; Beverid? PO
GARNER, John, Se-228-3; Elisabeth A. widow of; Pvt K Co 2nd TN Inf; 9 Jan 62 to __; Shiloh Church PO; was captured at Rogersville, Nov 6, 63
GARNER, John, A-4-1; Pvt G Co 4th TN Inf; 8-15-63 to 8-2-65; Coal Creek PO; chronic diarrhea
GARNER, John A., He-62-3; Pvt Co A 7th TN Cav; Mar 64 to 64 (2 mos); Lexington PO; mesles
GARNER, John D., G-57-5(3); Pvt; Yorkville PO; CONF
GARNER, Joe (or Dolling, as alias?); Sarah widow of, A-3-2; Pvt J Co 1st TN Inf; Wilson PO
GARNER, Joseph B., K-186-3; Pvt H Co 1st TN Inf; 9 Aug 61 to 17 Sep 64; Chumlea PO
GARNER, Plesant H., A-3-3; Pvt C Co 2nd TN Cav; 62 to 65; Beveridg PO (Knox Co.); lung disease
GARNER, Robt., Sol, Sh-187-1(5); Memphis PO
GARNER, Thomas, G-57-3; Yorkville PO; deafness, deafness occured from cannon; CONF
GARNER, Vincent, Br-13-3; Sgt A Co 10th TN Cav; 8-12-63 to 8-1-65; Cleveland PO
GARRARD, F. B., De-23-1; Julia M. widow of; Sgt; 61 to 65; Swallow Bluff PO; CONF
GARRELL, William, Co-66-1; Pvt F Co 8th TN Inf; 10 Dec 62 to 6 Mar 65; English PO; CONF
GARRET, Noah, Gr-71-1; Cpl F Co 1st TN Inf; Jarmine PO; fracture of ankle bone; discharge in pension office
GARRETT, Abraham E., Sm-166-1; recruiting service; 61 to 1-1-62; Carthage PO; shot through the stomache & right hip; 1st Lt TN Mtd Inf; 7-1-63 to 11-20-65; Carthage PO
GARRETT, B. J., Fe-44-1; Pvt F Co 1st E TN Inf; 8-61 to __ (8 mos); Allardt PO; rupture
GARRETT, Calvin, B-6-1; Pvt A Co 17th US Col Inf; 9-64 to 66; Shelbyville PO
GARRETT, Charles, Mt-148-1; Pvt A Co 2nd US Art; 3-28-64 to 1-13-66; Orgains X Roads PO
GARRETT, Charley, D-77-3; Spring St, Nashville PO
GARRETT, Daniel, Mg-197-1; Margaret Jones formerly widow of; Pvt B Co 2nd TN Inf; Wartburg PO
GARRETT, Elijah, Pi-155-2; Pvt D Co 1st TN Mtd Inf; 1-25-64 to 4-25-65; Byrdstown PO; rheumatism in back
GARRETT, George W., Cy-28-2; 1st Sgt C Co 10th TN Cav; 12-12-63 to 8-1-65; Butlers Landing PO
GARRETT, George W., D-51-2; Pvt I Co 15th TN C Inf; 456 N Market, Nashville PO
GARRETT, J., K-156-5; Rachael widow US Sol; 11 Patterson St, Knoxville PO
GARRETT, Jerry M., Cr-17-2; Pvt; 11-13-64 to 5-6-65; Buena Vista PO
GARRETT, John, M-106-1; Nancy J. widow of; Pvt I Co 42nd IN Inf; 9-26-60 to 1-18-65; Lafayette PO
GARRETT, John H., K-174-3(2); Pvt K Co 8th TN Cav; 17 May 63 to 19 May 65; Graveston PO; deseas of spine of back
GARRETT, Major, Col, Mt-139-1; Pvt E Co 15th US; 64 to 66 (1 yr 6 mos); Woodlawn PO
GARRETT, Sam, Mt-139-1; Pvt I Co 101st US; 64 to 66 (1 yr 6 mos); Woodlawn PO
GARRETT, Shaderick H., Fe-44-1; Pvt F Co 1st TN Inf; 8-61 to __ (7 mos); Allardt PO; congestion of lungs
GARRETT, Sige, Ov-138-1; Pvt; 1-1-61 to 1-1-63; 5th Civil Dist
GARRETT, Silas S., Sh-158-1; Sarah widow of; Pvt A Co 3rd US Hvy Art & 55th IL Inf; 1 Sep 61 to 30 Apr 66; Memphis PO; diabetes or Brights disease when discharged he was 1st Lt 3rd Hvy Art; discharged for physical disability at Helena, AR, 1 Oct 63 by Edward Langer, Capt. Comp 5th MO Cav
GARRETT, Stephan, K-174-3(2); Pvt F Co 3rd TN Inf; 10 Feb 62 to 23 Feb 65; Graveston? PO; gun shot in left leg
GARRETT, Stephen, Po-148-2; Pvt H Co 10th TN Cav; 12-25-63 to 8-1-65; Benton PO
GARRETT, Timothy W., Rb-219-2; Pvt H Co 2nd TN Reg; May 61 to Apr 2 65; Duerville PO; two fingers of left hand shot off; furloughed in May 1862; CONF
GARRETT, Volney F., K-172-3; Lt A Co 6th TN Inf; 62 to 65; 14th Dist; South Knoxville PO
GARRETT, Woodson, K-173-3; Pvt; McMillen PO
GARRETTE, Lizzie (see Maddock, John)
GARRIS, Wiley, Ro-210-5; Gimenon Childress formerly widow of; Pvt; Rockwood PO
GARRISON, Henry, Ro-210-7; Pvt; Cardiff PO; CONF
GARRISON, Jacob, G-54-1; Pvt E Co; 61 to 64; Eaton PO; wound in shoulder
GARRISON, James, Cu-18-1; Pvt B Co 28th TN Inf; 1 yr 2 mos; Jewett PO; no discharge; CONF
GARRISON, John, Dk-31-2; Jane widow of; Pvt A Co 5th TN Cav; 8-9-62 to 6-25-65; Alexandria PO
GARRISON, John E., Dk-31-1; Pvt I Co 5th TN Cav; 2-11-63 to 8-14-65; Alexandria PO; suffering with rheumatism
GARRISON, John R., Rb-221-1; Pvt I Co 56th VA; May 8 61 to Jun 13 65; Barren Plains PO; prisoner at Point Lookout, MD?; CONF
GARRISON, Robert M., We-225-1; Pvt A Co 23rd KY Inf; 64 to 65; Dresden PO
GARRISON, Susan (see Keeton, William)
GARROTT, George W., Ov-137-3; Pvt H Co 5th KY Cav; 12-4-61 to 11-10-62; Monroe PO
GARROTT, William Jorden, Ov-137-3; Pvt C Co 13th KY Cav; 11-63 to __; Monroe PO; piles and left leg injured
GARTNER, Howell, Mu-195-1; was not at home and wife dont know; Columbia PO
GARTNER, Micheal W., Mu-195-1; Sol, wife dont know; Columbia PO
GARVEY, Thomas, Sh-167-2; PO omitted; CONF
GARVIN, Franklin, H-49-4; Cpl F Co 6th TN Mtd Inf; 8-2-64 to 6-30-65; Lake Side PO
GARVIN, Henry, K-158-2; Pvt KY Cav; 61 to 64; Knoxville PO, 156 Mabry; rheumatism from exposure
GARVIN, James T., Wa-263-5; Nettie E. widow of; Telford PO; CONF
GARY, John W., Mu-210-3; Eliza J. widow of; Pvt; 63 to 63 (1 mo); Spring Hill PO; CONF
GASAGNON, H., Sol, Sh-187-1(5); Memphis PO
GASKEL, Hayes, Dy-22-1; Sgt A Co 4th US Art; Nov 61 to Jun 17 65; Dyersburg PO; rheumatism
GASS, Charles, Ge-93-1; Sgt B Co 8th TN Cav; 23 Jul 63 to Sep 65; Greeneville PO

GASS, David A., Ge-101-2; Pvt A Co 4th TN Inf; 1 Sep 63 to 2 Aug 65; Cross Anchor PO; between Knoxville & Paint Rock
GASS, Joseph W., Br-14-1; Pvt G Co 4th TN Cav; 9-21-63 to 6-26-65; Cleveland PO; right leg off below knee
GASSOWAY, George W., Cf-40-2; Cpl D Co 58th IN Inf; 5 Dec 61 to 24 Jan 64; Tullahoma PO; one finger gone, hearing in one ear gone
GASSOWAY, Logan, Cf-40-2; Cpl B Co 65th IN Inf; 5 Aug 62 to 8 Feb 63; Tullahoma PO; discharged on account of disability
GASSOWAY, Robert L., Cf-40-2; Pvt C Co 136th IN Vol; 11 May 61 to 2 Sep 64; Tullahoma PO; gun shot in arm
GASTON, Ephraim, Mc-112-7; Pvt I Co 143rd OH; 5-2-64 to 12-64; Athens PO; lung trouble
GATES, Moses, Sh-197-1; Lydia Jackson formerly widow of; Pvt C Co 3rd Col Cav; 2-15-64 to 1-26-66; Memphis PO; not at home
GATEWOOD, Calvin O., We-222-2; Pvt A Co 18th __; 62 to 65; Martin PO
GATEWOOD, Harvey, We-220-2; Pvt I Co 6th TN Cav; Jun 62 to Aug 5 65; PO omitted
GATEWOOD, Lawrence D., We-223-1; Marthy J. Burton former widow of; Pvt I Co 6th TN Cav; 5 Jun 62 to 26 Jul 65; Palmersville PO; dead 14 yrs, killed by City
GATEWOOD, Pinkney, We-224-1; Pvt C Co 7th TN Inf; 62 to 20 Dec 62 (6 mos); Dresden PO; captured, parolled and never returned
GATLEY, William, Ch-14-2; Pvt K Co 7th TN Cav; 8-6-63 to 1-31-64; PO omitted
GATLIN, Jas. T., Gi-123-2; Pvt I Co 2nd TN Mtd Inf; Jan 64 to Jan 65; Stella PO
GAUDEN, Daniel, G-64-1; 1 yr; Bradford PO; CONF
GAUL, William H., Sn-260-6; Sgt B Co 1st TN Cav; 9-61 to 4-6-65; Pondville PO; contracted rheumatism; CONF
GAULDEN, Mikel D., Dy-25-2; Pvt A Co 1st TN Inf; 26 May 61 to 20 Apr 65; Newbern PO; wounded twice, in arm & hip; CONF
GAULLEY, Elexander, Hw-118-1; Pvt D Co 8th TN Inf; St. Clair PO
GAULLEY, John, Hw-118-2; Pvt D Co 8th TN Inf; St. Clair PO
GAULT, John C., K-177-5; Pvt C Co 1st TN Cav; 1 Nov 62 to 24 Aug 65; Powells Station PO
GAULT, Peter, K-177-5; Pvt K Co 1st US Hvy Art; 62 to 64; Powells Station PO
GAULT, Samuel H., Hw-127-1; 2nd Lt A Co 3rd TN Inf; 10 Feb 62 to 23 Feb 65; Rogersville PO
GAULT, Thomas, K-176-2; Pvt F Co 3rd TN Cav; 1 Apr 62 to Apr 65; Halls X Roads PO; one leg off
GAUNT, Henry C., G-71-1; Cpl Carethers Artillery; 10 Jan 62 to 10 Jul 63; Bradford PO; reinlisted in cavilry; CONF
GAUNTT, John F., Ge-97-3; Pvt F Co 3rd TN Mtd Inf; 1 Jul 64 to 30 Nov 64; Upchurch PO; lung disease
GAUST, Thomas, K-176-2; Halls X Roads PO
GAVEN, Samuel, Sh-159-3; 2nd? (V?) Pvt K Co 17th OH Inf; Memphis PO
GAY, Sam, Dk-36-3; Pvt B Co 4th TN Mtd Inf; 9-25-64 to 8-25-65; Smithville PO
GAYLOR, Thornton (see Graves, Thornton)
GEARN, Joal K., Br-9-5; Cleveland PO
GEARY, Thomas, Gu-48-2; Pvt A Co 31st MA Inf; 63 to 65; Tracy City PO; no discharge record
GEASLAND, Stephen, Ro-211-4; US Sol; 16th Civil Dist
GEASLAND, Steven A., Ro-210-8; Pvt B Co 2nd TN Inf; 19 Oct 63 to __; Rockwood PO; prisoner at Sawton? Prison
GEE, John J., Mc-114-2; Pvt D Co 5th TN Inf; 5-3-63 to 6-26-65; Folger PO
GEE, Thos., T-210-1; Cpl C Co 4th TN; Jul 63 to Aug 64; Quito PO
GEE, Wily J., Hr-96-2; PO omitted
GEER, Samuel, A-8-1; Chaplain 11th TN Cav; 12-1-63 to 9-11-65; Scarborough PO
GEERS, William, A-6-1; Lt 2 RM 11th TN Cav; 8-20-63 to 10-7-63; Olivers PO
GEETERS, Esic, Sh-157-7; Uncomis. F Co 11th; Jan 64 to 66; White Haven PO
GEETERS, Henry, Sh-157-7; Memphis PO
GEETERS?, Henry, Sh-157-6; Sgt B Co 64th Inf; 63 to __; Memphis, Trent? St, 300, PO
GEETERS, Jack, Sh-157-7; Pvt F Co 11th; Jan 64 to 66; White Haven PO
GEFELLERS, James M., Ge-83-1; Pvt E Co 4th? TN Inf; 6 Apr 63 to 6 Aug 65; Chucky City PO; hypertraphy liver & sore eyes; CONF
GEFELLERS, Joe, Ge-83-1; Pvt E Co 4th TN Inf; 22 Jul 63 to 6 Aug 65; Chucky City PO; back & mumps
GEHRETT, Jacob, B-7-2; Pvt A Co 68th OH Inf; 10-28-61 to 10-22-64; PO omitted
GEILER, John, H-60-2; Pvt A Co 106th OH Inf; 8-7-62 to 8-26-65; Chattanooga PO; rheumatism & shot left leg, says injured mentally also
GEISER, Phillip, A-9-5(3); Rosey widow of; Pvt; Dutch Valley PO
GEISSLER, Henry, Gu-46-3(1); Pvt A Co 10th NY Inf; 7-63 to 11-15-65; Tracy City PO
GELSTON, William A., A-7-2; Robertsville PO
GENETTE, Henry, Ru-231-1; Pvt I Co 74th LA Inf; 12 Oct 62 to Nov 65; Lamar PO
GENSLEY, Samule G., Cy-26-2; Pvt H Co 13th MO Cav; 3-7-62 to 5-66; Moss PO
GENTER, Dominic, H-66-2; Pvt D Co 13th US Inf; 1-2-62 to 1-2-65; Chattanooga PO
GENTLE, John S., Gr-72-2; Pengum (name of boat?); 22 Jan 64 to 22 Aug 65; Marshals Ferry PO; diarhea--in service
GENTRY, Albert A., K-177-5; non com. off. L Co 9th TN Cav; 15 Oct 63 to 15 Aug 65; Powells Station
GENTRY, Andrew M., Jo-148-2; Sgt I Co 13th TN Cav; 2 Sep 63 to 22 Sep 65; Head of Laurel PO; contracted rheumatism
GENTRY, Charles W., Mc-117-1; Pvt E Co 7th TN Mtd Inf; 9-15-64 to 7-27-65; Mecca PO
GENTRY, Hartsell, Wa-274-1; Pvt F Co 1st TN Col Hvy Art; 15 May 63 to Aug 65; Jonesboro PO; lost his discharge
GENTRY, James, Bl-3-3; Pvt C Co 43rd TN Inf; 10-61 to 7-12-63; Billingsly PO; CONF
GENTRY, James P., Je-146-2; Pvt B Co 11th TN Cav; 63 to 9 Mar 65; White Pine PO
GENTRY, James R., Jo-152-1; Cpl A Co 13th TN Cav; 22 Sep 63 to 5 Sep 65; Doeville PO; measles & resultant chronic disease
GENTRY, John, Fe-44-1; recruting Lt E Co 7th TN Inf; 7-15-62 to __; Allardt PO
GENTRY, John W., Cy-27-2; Pvt E Co 9th KY Inf; 9-61 to 3-62; Spivey PO
GENTRY, Joseph A., Mc-117-1; 5th Sgt C Co 9th TN Cav; 4-23-63 to 9-11-65; Mecca PO; piles & rupture
GENTRY, Mallin, Jo-153-2; Sgt D Co 10th TN Cav; 24 Sep 63 to 5 Sep 65; Shady PO; hurt by a horse
GENTRY, Mattie (see Carden, Giles)
GENTRY, Meridith J., Pu-144-2; Pvt B Co 1st TN Inf; 1-13-64 to 4-14-65; Bloomington PO
GENTRY, Ned, G-54-1; Jane widow of; Pvt E Co 18th US Col Inf; Eaton PO
GENTRY, Prior, K-177-6; Pvt F Co 3rd TN Inf; 11 Feb 62 to 23 Feb 65; Powells Station PO
GENTRY, Robert, Pu-14-2; Pvt B Co 1st TN Inf; 1-64 to 4-65; Double Springs PO
GENTRY, Robert P., Wa-263-2; Pvt A Co 2nd NC Mtd Inf; Nov 13 63 to Aug 65; Garbers Mills PO; gun shot wound & cause of nerveness & deafness
GENTRY, Samuel A., Mc-116-3; Charlotte widow of; Sgt E Co 9th TN Cav; Mortimer PO; died while in service, exact dates not known as when was wounded
GENTRY, Thomas, J-78-1; Pvt B Co 8th TN Inf; 1-28-64 to 8-16-65; Gainesboro PO; sickle & so on which trobles a great deal
GENTRY, Thomas M., J-83-2; Pvt B Co 8th TN; 11th Civil Dist
GENTRY, William, J-79-1; Pvt B Co 8th TN Mtd Inf; 1-15-65 to 8-17-65; Whitleyville PO; wounded in left hip
GEORGE, B. F., Cr-7-1; Pvt F Co 47th TN Inf; 61 to 63; Friendship PO; CONF
GEORGE, Cornelius W., Ge-84-3; Pvt G? Co 1st TN Cav; 13 Sep 62 to 16 Jun 65; Bird Bridge PO; chronic of liver
GEORGE, Edward, H-66-2; Pvt B Co 7th OH Inf; 4-22-61 to 4-22-61 (4 mos); Chattanooga PO

GEORGE, Henry, Un-154-1; Elizabeth widow of; Pvt; Paulett PO
GEORGE, Huston F., K-154-3; Cpl 7th TN Mtd Inf; __ to 8 Nov 64; Knoxville PO
GEORGE, James, S-214-3; Cpl H Co 1st WI Inf; 26 Oct 61 to 20 Jan 63; New River PO
GEORGE, John, Rb-221-3; Pvt; Adams Station PO; CONF
GEORGE, Malory, Ce-23-1; Pvt; 61 to 65; Thomasville PO
GEORGE, Samuel D., K-161-1; Mattie widow of; Pvt G Co; Knoxville PO
GEORGE, Samuel L., Ca-25-2; Pvt B Co 5th TN Cav; 8-5-62 to 6-30-65; Gassoway PO; shot in right leg
GEORGE, Susan, Wl-297-2; widow; Dist No 12
GEORGE, William, Ct-35-2; Pvt B Co 12th TN Inf; 12-22-63 to 11-25-65; Butler PO (Johnson Co.); in US Army
GEORGE, William, Rb-219-2; Pvt D Co 32nd KY Reg; 64 to 65; Duersville PO; spell of typhoid fever, by which his mind was affected
GEORGE, William H., Tr-265-1; Pvt L Co 5th TN Cav; 1 May 63 to 14 Aug 65; Dixon's Springs PO; rhumatish-jaundice
GOERGE, William W., Ge-102-2; Pvt G Co 4th TN Inf; 15 Nov 61 to 7 Jul 65; Whig PO
GEORGE, Willis, Sh-195-1; Pvt I Co Spen.; Memphis PO
GEORGESON, John, H-54-2(3); Wagoner F Co 1st WI Cav; 12-25-61 to 9-3-63; Sherman Heights PO
GERARD, Ambros, Mc-114-6; Ord Sgt B Co 83rd IN Inf; 8-61 to 12-10-64; Santfordville PO
GERATY, Pat, Dk-34-1; Pvt G Co 4th US Cav; 3-12-57 to 3-13-65; Dowelltown PO; bowel trouble hernia & deafness
GERDNER, David, Ge-88-3; Pvt F Co 4th TN Inf; Mohawk PO; chronic diarrhe
GERDON, Lemual, Sh-188-2; Pvt US Col Inf; 58 Mannassas, Memphis PO
GERKINS, Benj. J., H-68-2; Pvt D Co 10th TN Cav; Chattanooga PO; has fits frequently, not able to do much
GERLY, Thomas, D-71-1; Nashville PO
GERMAN, Anderson, Gr-72-1; Sgt B Co 8th TN Inf; 5 Jan 63 to 30 Jun 65; Noelon PO; result of measles
GERMAN, Christian, Fr-110-1; Pvt H Co 18th MI; Jul 26 62 to Jun 26 65; Belvidere PO
GERMAN, Isaac, C-25-2; chief of scouts; Hatmaker PO; belong to Capt Wm. Runnels chief of scouts secret service
GERMMIE, Hester (see Kennedy, Westly)
GERON, John A., K-160-3; Pvt 3? Co 23rd MI; Aug 62 to Jul 65; Knoxville PO
GERRELL, Hiram, Mt-139-1; Pvt H Co 17th US; 4 yrs; Woodlawn PO
GERRON, William, Sh-153-2; Pvt E Co 61st USC Inf; Collierville PO
GEST, Jeremiah H., Br-13-2; Cpl G Co 154th OH Inf; 5-2-64 to 9-1-64; Ora PO; muscular rheumatism
GESTES, Abe, Mu-198-1; 10th Dist
GETTYS, James R., Mc-112-7; Adjudant B Co 7th TN Mtd Inf; 9-10-64 to 7-27-65; Athens PO
GETTYS, John B., Br-12-1; Charleston PO
GETTYS, Samuel A., R-161-4; Pvt I Co 3rd PA Inf; 4-16-61 to 7-9-65; Dayton PO; gunshot in right leg & left ear; reenlisted veteran
GIBBEN, John A., Je-144-1; Pvt B Co SCB KY Art; Mar 65 to 65 (10 mos); Valleyhome PO; diarrhea from exposure
GIBBINS, Bushrod T., K-181-5(2); Knoxville PO
GIBBINS, Georgia, Mc-115-1; Pvt; Riceville PO; shot in leg
GIBBINS, William E., K-162-1; Sgt D Co 14th KY Inf; Sep 61 to Jan 65; Knoxville PO; right foot with gun shot
GIBBONS, Asbury, Sh-158-1; Pvt F Co 61st C Inf; 23 Aug 63 to 30 Dec 65; Memphis PO; rheumatism in shoulders, able to drive his express wagon
GIBBONS, Jacob L., Je-144-2; Jane widow of; Pvt; Talbotts PO; died since ware
GIBBS, Franklin, K-164-1; Pvt C Co 13th TN Vol; 20 Jan 64 to 5 Sep 65; PO omitted (Knoxville?)
GIBBS, French, Ct-40-3; Pvt Co 40th TN Col Inf; 1 yr 6 mos; Elizabethton PO; rheumatism
GIBBS, James B., Cl-57-1; Louisa P. widow of; died 4-16-1890; Pvt E Co 6th TN Inf; 3-6-62 to 65; Kecks Chappel PO
GIBBS, James J., K-161-3; Knoxville PO; shot in breast
GIBBS, Jessee D., We-231-1; Pvt L Co 6th TN Cav; 15 Aug 62 to 26 Aug 65; Fulton KY PO
GIBBS, John F., D-74-1; Pvt H Co 313 Fatherland, Nashville PO
GIBBS, John P., We-225-2(1); Pvt D Co 5th TN Cav; 15 Jun 62 to 26 Jul 65; Dresden PO; rheumatism 27 yrs
GIBBS, Levi, K-167-1; Pvt 3rd TN Inf; 62 to 65; Knoxville PO
GIBBS, Martin (see Sikes, Martin)
GIBBS, Mary (see Baker, John, K-167-4)
GIBBS, Nicholas, A-9-4(2); Sgt C Co 2nd TN Inf; 8-7-61 to 10-6-64; Marlow PO; gun shot wound resulting in lung disease
GIBBS, Robert W., Bo-13-1; Pvt B Co 3rd TN Inf; 6-13-62 to __; Disco PO
GIBBS, William A., St-159-1; Pvt K Co 83rd IL Inf; 8-19-64 to 9-8-65; Oakwood PO (Montgomery Co.)
GIBSON, Ace Y., Pu-144-2; Bloomington PO
GIBSON, Benjamin, We-229-1; Pvt D Co 5th TN Inf; 20 May 61 to 25 Jul 63; Gleason PO; wonded in hip and thy, still gives me pain
GIBSON, David, Se-223-3; Pvt I Co 3rd TN Cav; Sevierville PO
GIBSON, David, H-56-2; Pvt; 65 to 65; East End PO
GIBSON, David H., Lo-195-2(1); Bugler C Co 4th TN Cav; 8 Aug 62 to 12 Jul 65; Union X Roads PO
GIBSON, Elisha S., R-161-5; Pvt A Co 4th TN Cav; 7-30-63 to 5-18-65; Dayton PO; scrofula in camp
GIBSON, Green B., He-61-2; Sol; 15th Civil Dist
GIBSON, Henry, Cl-48-2; Pvt; 63 to 65; Old Town PO; gun shot across forehead, he does not remember the name of his company & reg; CONF
GIBSON, Henry R., K-159-1; Bravett Capt Comissary Staff Off; 17 Mar 63 to 4 Aug 65; Knoxville PO
GIBSON, James C., Mu-201-1; Pvt H Co 5th TN Cav; 20 Dec 61 to 1 Jan 65; Mt. Pleasant PO
GIBSON, James E., Ro-205-3; Pvt I Co 26th TN Cav; 2 yrs 9 mos; Hatch PO
GIBSON, Jerimiah, Su-239-1; Margrate E. widow of; Cpl M Co 8th __; Horace PO
GIBSON, John, D-82-1; Pvt; 61 to 65; Edgefield Junction PO
GIBSON, John, H-50-2(1); Pvt E Co 6th R TN Mtd Inf; 9-12-64 to 6-30-65; Bunch PO; pneumonia fever
GIBSON, John, Bo-21-4; Cpl H Co 2nd TN Cav; 10-10-62 to 7-15-65; Ellijay PO
GIBSON, John P., Ct-41-1; Bosan J. widow of; Pvt B Co 4th TN Inf; 11-24-62 to 8-2-65; South Wattauga PO
GIBSON, John W., Cl-47-2; Pvt G Co 8th TN Cav; 5-26-63 to 9-11-65; Pleasant PO
GIBSON, Joseph, Ha-117-3; Pvt B Co 50th VA Inf; Sneedville PO; gunshot r. shoulder, hand crippled; CONF
GIBSON, Lanney, Sh-197-1; Frances Smith formerly widow of; Sh-197-1; Pvt Col Art; Memphis PO; killed at Shilogh
GIBSON, Mason L., Se-225-2(1); Pvt G Co 1st TN Inf; 26 Nov 62 to 25 May 65; Easton's X Roads PO; head, heart & lung trouble
GIBSON, Reuben, H-58-2; Quartermaster Sgt A Co 1st TN Cav; 2-17-62 to 4-4-65; Sale Creek PO; partial deafness & hernia
GIBSON, Samuel, Se-224-1; Pvt E Co 3rd NC Mtd Inf; 8 Nov 64 to 8 Aug 65; Hornett PO; rupture
GIBSON, Stephen, Se-224-1; Pvt E Co 3rd NC Mtd Inf; 8 Nov 64 to 8 Agu 65; Grapeton PO
GIBSON, Thomas, F-46-1; Pvt H Co 59th TN; 63 to 66; LaGrange PO; lost left eye & deafness
GIBSON, Thomas, Ge-96-1; Patience widow of; Pvt B Co 4th TN Cav; 1 Feb 63 to died Mar 30 65; Jockey PO; husband dead
GIBSON, Thomas F., Cr-9-1; Pvt L Co 7th KY Cav; Aug 11 62 to Apr 23 63; Crockett Mills PO; surgs. cert. disch.
GIBSON, William, Wa-269-1; Pvt B Co 4th TN Inf; 24 Nov 62 to 2 Aug 65; Carters Depot PO (Carter Co.); neuralgia, heart & stomach
GIBSON, William, Wy-172-1; Laura S. Poag formerly widow of; Waynesboro PO; it is thought that he caught his death

GIBSON, William, Se-224-2; Pvt E Co 3rd NC Mtd Inf; 8 Nov 64 to 8 Aug 65; Hornett PO
GIBSON, William H., Co-69-6(1); Pvt NC Cal; Mar 64 to May 65; Driskill PO; CONF
GIBSON, Zacarah S., Cl-48-1; Sgt E Co 1st TN Cav; 63 to 65; Old Town PO; CONF
GIDEON, Abigia, K-160-1; Harret E. widow of; Pvt D Co 6th TN; 18 Apr 61 to 18 Mar 64; Knoxville PO
GIDEON, Scarlott, K-157-1; Pvt C Co 9th TN Cav; 12 Jun 63 to 11 Sep 65; Knoxville PO
GIDEON, William, Bo-14-1; Pvt D Co 6th TN Inf; 11-11-62 to 6-30-65; Clover Hill PO; rheumatism & diarrhea
GIDER, Joseph, Lo-192-2; Harret widow of; Recruiting Officer; Griffitts PO; lost health, discharge lost
GIEBER, James A., A-7-3; Pvt G Co 7th __; 11-64 to 6-12-65; Robertsville PO
GIFFE, Ths., H-60-5(2); Capt H Co 16th US Col Inf; 4-29-64 to 4-30-66; Chattanooga PO; gunshot wound in shoulder & leg (listed as duplication by enumerator)
GIFFE, Thos. M., H-60-4; Pvt B Co 74th OH Inf; 10-10-61 to 4-28-64; Chattanooga PO
GIFFIN, Gerge W. L., K-172-4; 78 Cpl A Co 6th TN Inf; 21 Sep 62 to 13 Jun 65; PO omitted
GIFFIN, John C., K-172-4; 2nd Lt E Co 3rd TN Cav; 29 Jan 63 to 7 Jan 65; PO omitted
GIFFIN, John H. (alias), K-172-1; Pvt A Co 6th TN Inf; 8 Nov 62 to 27 Feb? 65; Knoxville PO; rupture
GIFFIN, Volney, K-172-2; Pvt A Co 6th TN Inf; 21 Sep 62 to 29 Jun 65; Knoxville PO; gun shot wound in knee
GIFFORD, Charles F., D-77-1; Mary Hill widow of; Pvt; 3 yrs; Nasvhille PO; papers destroyed by rats, but was honorably from a Michigan Regt.
GIFFORD, Samuel M., H-51-7; Hill City PO
GIHOS, Henry C., Gi-138-1; Pvt F Co 6th TN; 2-3-63 to 7-26-65; Bodinham PO
GILAFRO, W. S., Mt-145-1; Pvt F Co 103rd PA Vol; 10-1-61 to 7-1-65; Palmyra PO; gunshot wound in left arm; shot at battle Kingston NC
GILB, Joseph, Hw-129-1; Pvt H Co 8th TN Inf; 15 Apr 62 to 9 Jun 65; Galbrath Springs PO; rheumatism, hearting
GILBER, Alford, K-172-4; Pvt E Co 3rd TN Cav; PO omitted
GILBER, Rhebert, Mt-132-1; Sgt K Co 13th TN Inf; 7-4-62 to 4-1-64; 1st Civil Dist
GILBERT, Alex, Gi-123-2; Pvt F Co 110th TN Col Inf; 63 to Feb 66; Stella PO
GILBERT, Andreson, Gr-79-2; Ailsie widow of; Pvt 1st TN; 62 to 65; Ball Point PO; wounded in arm
GILBERT, Andrew J., Wl-305-1; Pvt L Co 5th Stokes; Aug 14 62 to 6 Mar 64; Partlow PO; shot through right foot
GILBERT, Bernhart, Me-93-1; Pvt C Co 124th IL Vol Inf; 1-62 to 9-65; Ten Mile Stand PO; loss of one eye &c
GILBERT, Charly, Gi-123-1; Cpl G Co 110th TN Col Inf; Jan 63 to 65; Bethel PO
GILBERT, Chritopher C., St-160-1; Pvt D Co 17th KY Cav; Jul 3 63 to Sep 6 65; Lafayette PO (Christian Co. KY); wounded hip & back; not able to work at trade
GILBERT, Daniel, Ha-113-1; Cpl E Co 8th TN Cav; 10 Oct 63 to 11 Dec 64; Sneedville PO
GILBERT, David, Gi-122-4; Pvt D Co 1st TN Inf; 1 Jan 64 to 1 May 66; Lesters Sta. PO; 2 mos in prison
GILBERT, George G., Mc-112-7; Pvt I Co 24th & 33rd IL Inf; 1-64 to 11-65; Athens PO
GILBERT, Harrison, Gi-123-2; Pvt Co F 110th TN Inf (Col); 63 to 66; Stella PO
GILBERT, Hezekiah, Ma-128-1; Pvt 20th KS; Jackson PO; wound in leg; could get no information
GILBERT, James A., Ge-84-1; Pvt C Co 3rd NC Mtd Inf; 11 Jun 64 to 8 Aug 65; Wolsey College PO; chronic diarrea
GILBERT, James F., De-24-1; Pvt C Co 7th TN Cav; Feb 64 to Aug 65; Decaturville PO; prisoner at Andersonville 10 mos, cant give dates of month
GILBERT, John, Lo-191-4; Trigonia PO; CONF

GILBERT, John E., Gi-122-3; Capt B Co 50th AL Inf; 1 Sep 61 to 5 May 65; Prospect Sta. PO; shot in wrist & in thigh; CONF
GILBERT, John M., Dk-36-1; Pvt F Co 4th TN Mtd Inf; 9-25-64 to 8-25-65; Smithville PO; curvature
GILBERT, John N., Gi-123-1; Pvt G Co 110th TN Col Inf; Jan 63 to 65; Bethel PO
GILBERT, Randal, Gi-123-1; Margaret widow of; Pvt K Co 110th TN Col Inf; 62 to 65; Bethel PO
GILBERT, Reece B., Gr-70-3; Pvt F Co 8th TN Cav; 10 Oct 62 to 11 Sep 65; Spring House PO; rheumatics
GILBERT, Ruben, Cl-49-2; Cpl C Co 2nd TN Cav; 62 to 6-65; Zeb PO; brest comprint
GILBERT, Sam, Gi-123-2; Pvt I Co 110th TN Col Inf; 62 to 65; Heron PO
GILBERT, Thomas Henry, Gi-122-1; Amy widow of; Capt AL Inf; 15 Oct 61 to 15 Oct 64; Prospect Sta. PO; CONF
GILBERT, Thomas W., Bl-2-1; Pvt KY Cav; 2 yrs; Glade Creek PO
GILBERT, William, He-60-2; Fanny A. widow of; Cpl C Co 7th TN Cav; 62 to died Jan 12 65; Alberton PO; died in Andersonville Prison
GILBERT, William, Gi-123-2; Pvt F Co 110th TN Col Inf; 63 to Feb 66; Stella PO
GILBERT, Witt W., Me-88-2; Pvt D Co 1st TN Art; 9-2-63 to 7-20-65; Brittsville PO
GILBREATH, Franklin, Ro-210-9; Pvt D Co 1st TN Art; Rockwood PO
GILBREATH, James, Mg-198-2; Pvt B Co 98th OH Inf; 15 Aug 62 to 15 May 65; Deer Lodge PO; rupture rheumatism, discharged on surgents certificate
GILBREATH, William, R-162-2; Cpl C Co 88th OH Vol Inf; 8-7-62 to 7-3-65; Dayton PO
GILCHRIST, John, Hd-53-1; Pvt E Co 8th US Col TN Inf; 20 Mar 64 to 20 Mar 66; Saltillo PO; deafness caused by firing of artilery
GILCHRIST, John D.?, Hr-96-1; Sgt H Co 3rd AR Cav; Feb 13 64 to 21 Jul 65; Crainsville PO
GILCHRIST, Malcomb, Wy-175-1; Pvt A Co 2nd TN Mtd Inf; 10-2-63 to 10-14-64; Whitting Stand PO; lung disease from measles
GILDERLAND, Majr. (see Bates, Major)
GILENTINE, Robert G., Pi-156-1; Pvt A Co 11th TN Cav; 4-23-64 to 64; Permalia PO; lumbago, deafness
GILES, Absalom, Br-7-2; Pvt G Co 10th TN Cav; 2-15-64 to 8-31-65; Felker PO; wounded
GILES, Albert, Br-9-3; Cleveland PO
GILES, Gilman, Mo-128-1 (Robert Powal listed on same line); Pvt D Co 3rd TN Mtd Inf; 7-25-64 to 11-30-64; Bell Town PO
GILES, James M., Mo-130-3; Lt D Co 3rd TN Mtd Inf; 7-26-64 to __; Ballplay PO
GILES, John, Sm-175-2(1); Lucy J. Pope formerly widow of; Pvt 4th TN Inf; Enoch PO
GILES, Larkin, Br-7-2; Cpl G Co 10th TN Cav; 2-15-64 to 8-31-65; Felker PO; wounded
GILES, Solomon H., S-214-3; Pvt B Co 21st NY Cav; Jan 64 to Jun 65; New River PO
GILES, Thomas J. R., Mo-128-2; Pvt D Co 3rd TN Mtd Inf; 7-25-64 to 11-30-64; Belltown PO
GILESPIE, Thomas H., F-44-1; Pvt E Co 7th TN; Aug 25 62 to May 8 65; PO omitted; CONF
GILIAN, Verge, Sh-157-2; Louisia Gillian widow of; Cpl F Co or L Co 61st US Col Inf; Aug 20 63 to Dec 31 65; Memphis PO; consumption contracted in war
GILILLAND, Hiram H., Je-138-1; Pvt F Co 8th TN Cav; 1 Jun 63 to 13 Sep 65; Oak Grove PO
GILISPIE, Robert A., Ms-175-1; 1st Sgt H Co 5th TN; 62 to __ (3 yrs); Holts Corner PO
GILL, John K., Cr-13-1; Pvt M Co 6th TN Cav; Feb 62 to Jul 26 65; Atwood PO; none incured; dont kno exact date enlistment
GILL, Robert M., Cr-13-1; Rebecca widow of; Pvt M Co 6th TN Cav; Feb 62 to 62; Atwood PO; none incured; dont know when discharged
GILL, Steven, Gr-71-2; Fannie widow of; Tate Springs PO
GILL, William B., Hd-44-2; Rebecca widow of; Pvt 27th KY Inf; PO omitted
GILL, William H., Wl-302-3(5); Pvt H Co 4th TN Inf; 1 Jan 65 to 25 Aug 65; Baird's Mill PO

GILLAM, John W., D-92-1; Pvt D Co 81st OH Inf; 1 Sep 61 to 9 Mar 65; West Nashville PO; deaf, partly from scurvey; prisoner at Andersonville

GILLAN, Willis N., We-230-2; Pvt C Co 21st TN Reg; May 1 63 to May 10 65; Greenfield PO; left arm shot off; CONF

GILLAND, Benjamin F., L-106-1; Pvt I Co 12th TN Cav; Sep 11 62 to Sep 11 65; Naukapoo PO

GILLBERT, Jessie, Me-88-2; Pvt C Co 7th TN Cav; 5-28-63 to 8-14-65; Athens PO

GILLE, John, H-61-1; Pvt D Co 42nd TN Inf; 62 to 4-9-65; Chattanooga PO; 3rd of 3rd finger of R.H. shot off

GILLEM, Joseph, Je-144-1; Pvt G Co 4th TN Cav; Jan 62 to 65; Valleyhome PO; rheumatism, direah, shot in side, discharge at close ware

GILLEM, Luke P., D-94-1; Lt G Co 1st TN Cav; Jan 10 64 to May 10 65; Donelson PO; good sircumstances

GILLEM, William S., Pu-140-1; Sgt K Co 13th E TN Cav; 8-11-63 to 5-23-65; Cookeville PO; lung and kidney diseases, now blind in one eye

GILLENWATER, James, Hw-119-2(1); Emily J. widow of; Pvt; 62 to __; Hales Spring PO; dead, cause fever & meningitis; CONF

GILLES, Thomas J., Hd-49-1; Pvt A Co 2nd TN Inf; Oct 11 63 to Oct 17 64; Olive Hill PO

GILLESPIE, J. J., Wi-282-1; Pvt H Co 5th TN Reg; Mar 63 to Aug 14 65; Peytonsville PO; dislocated knee

GILLESPIE, Matthew, K-177-4; Pvt K Co 2nd TN Cav; Nov 62 to 5 Apr 63; Powells Station PO; rheumatism; CONF

GILLESPIE, William, La-111-2; Carolina widow of; Pvt 9th TN Cav; 2-62 to 4-63; PO omitted; CONF

GILLESPIE, William A., Wi-286-1; Pvt K Co 9th MS?; 1 Jul 63 to 7 Aug 64 to Jan 66; Nolinsville PO

GILLETT, Edwin R., R-163-2; Pvt A Co 46th IL Inf; 9-10-61 to 12-26-62; 1st Lt 46th IL Inf; 12-26-62 to 10-5-64; Graysville PO

GILLETT, James A., Ja-85-3; Pvt E Co 5th TN Inf; 3-2-62 to 11-16-64; Birchwood PO; paralysis

GILLIAM, Clem S., D-73-1; Pvt TN Conf Inf; Feb 62 to 65; Grand? Ave, Nashville PO; CONF

GILLIAM, Jacob, Ha-111-1; Pvt 26th VA Cav; 65 to Apr 65 (about 3 mos); Upper Clinch PO; CONF

GILLIESPY, Gilbert, Sh-157-8; Pvt D Co US Lt Art; Ma 64 to 66; Memphis PO

GILLILAND, Adelbert B., H-55-2; Musician E Co 23rd MO Inf; 10-6-62 to 7-18-65; Chickamauga PO; paralysis agitans

GILLILAND, James, K-159-1; Pvt D Co 17th MO Vols; 4 Jul 61 to 27 Jan 62; Knoxville PO; contracted lung trouble, wound right hip, re-inlisted M.S.M. Lt Art

GILLILAND, James, Co-68-3; Cpl E Co 1st TN Bat; 63 to 65; Sutton PO; liver & lungs & piles

GILLILAND, William, Co-68-2; Sutton PO

GILLINWATERS, Geo., Hw-125-5; Surgoinsville PO; right eye knocked out by ramrod

GILLIS, John, Ru-249-1; Mariah widow of; 2nd Lt 33rd IN Regt; 4-1-65 to __; Hoover PO; dead, drawing a pension

GILLIS, Levi, Co-61-5(2); Clarrissia, divorced wife of; Pvt 64th NC Inf; Bridgeport PO; CONF

GILLISPIE, Hardin, Ge-96-3; Pvt F Co 1st TN Art; 29 Apr 64 to 31 Mar 66; Rheatown PO; cataarh

GILLMORE?, John S., Mu-195-2; Sol H Co IL Fau? Vol; Fall of __ to 4 May 66 (1 yr 6 mos); Columbia PO

GILLMORE, William C., Wl-293-2; 61 to 64; Lockport PO

GILLS, Williamson P., We-222-1; Pvt I Co Falkners TN Reg; Nov 63 to 65; Martin PO: CONF

GILLUS, Quillen, Mg-198-3; Cpl K Co 13th TN Cav; 1 Oct 63 to 5 Sep 65; Rockwood PO; injured spine

GILLY, James M., Hw-119-4(1); Lt A Co 51st VA Inf; Nov 61 to 19 Jun 65; Gillenwater PO; shot through left hip; CONF

GILMAN, James, Gu-48-1; Seaman Galena; 12-1-63 to 5-22-64; Tracy City PO; fell and hurt left elbow; left forearm now paralyzed

GILMORE, Charles, alias Washington, Charles, Sh-153-2; Pvt Pioneer Corp 1st Div 16th Army Corp; Jul 63 to Dec 65; Bailey Sta. PO

GILMORE, Homer, K-154-2; Capt B Co 8th TN Cav; 12 May 63 to 11 Sep 65; Knoxville PO; wound from gun shot

GILMORE, Irvin, C-33-1; Pvt L Co 6th US Col Cav; 64 to 4-66; Newcomb PO

GILMORE, John J., K-156-3; Pvt G Co 7th OH Inf; 10 Mar 63 to 10 Jun 65; 28 Clinch St, Knoxville PO

GILMORE, Robert, D-72-3; Pvt D Co 17th TN Inf; Oct 7 64 to Apr 25 65; Nashville PO

GILMORE, Sidney, C-33-1; Sgt L Co 6th US Col Cav; 64 to 4-66; Newcomb PO

GILMORE, William, Le-119-1; Charity A. widow of; Pvt; Strathmore PO; her son has husbands discharge & papers, Riley Gilmore, Dallas, TX

GILREATH, Barnabas, A-9-4(2); Mary J. widow of; Pvt Capt Cain's Lt Art; 1-4-62 to 1-4-63; Marlow PO; CONF

GILSON, Samuel L., K-180-3; 1st Lt 6th TN Inf; 18 Apr 62 to 6 Apr 63; Bearden PO; lung disease and disease of testicles

GILTNER, Henry L., Rb-13-2; Col 4th KY Cav; Aug 61 to Apr 30 65; Murfreesboro PO; arm shot off; CONF

GIM, Francis B., K-181-6(3); Pvt L Co 9th TN Cav; 1 Oct 63 to Sep 65; Knoxville PO

GIMERSON, Charley, Sh-149-4; US Sol; 6th Civil Dist

GINN, James B., K-179-2; Pvt C Co 6th TN Inf; 18 Apr 62 to 27 Apr 65; Muddy Creek PO; right ankle broken

GINUM?, David, Ct-36-2; Pvt C Co 13th TN Cav; 9-63 to 9-65; Roan Mt. PO

GIPSON, Ed (see Lemmons, Ed)

GIPSON, Elie, Cl-52-3; Nancy widow of; Pvt A Co 1st TN Cav; 62 to __ (1 yr); Hypatia PO; killed at Louisville

GIPSON, Isaac, J-83-1; Pvt B Co 8th TN; Flynns Lick PO

GIPSON, James, Ro-208-3; US Sol; 9th Civil Dist

GIPSON, Perry F., Hw-132-5; Pvt VA Cav; Feb 62 to 65; Strahl PO; CONF

GIPSON, Thomas, Ct-39-3; Johnson City PO; piles, breast disease, heart trouble

GIPSON, Thomas, Pi-156-2; Pvt; Byrdtown PO

GIPSON, Willis, Cl-52-2; Eva R. widow of; Pvt E Co 8th TN Cav; Hypratia PO

GIRARD, Joseph H., D-46-1; Cpl E Co 113th OH Vol Inf; 9-62 to 7-65; Nashville PO

GIRDNER, Mrs. J. (see Cavender, William)

GIRDNOR, Michael L., Ge-84-1; Pvt K Co 8th TN Inf; 1 Jul 63 to 5 Jun 65; Bird Bridge PO; chronic diseas of stomach and liver

GIST, Hiram L., Cy-27-2; Pvt D Co 9th KY Cav; 10-13-62 to 10-13-65; Clementsville PO

GIVAN, Henry, Dk-38-1; Sarah J. Hayes former widow of; Pvt; Crawfordton PO

GIVAN, William J., Sm-172-4; Pvt A Co 5th TN Cav; 9-6-63 to 8-14-65; Hickman PO

GIVENS, Jessee M., Gu-45-2; Cpl M Co 10th TN Cav; 64 to 65 (11 mos); Altamont PO; ruptured

GIVENS, John M., Hi-84-1; Pvt F Co 3rd TN Cav; 11-1-62 to 6-1-65; Goodrich PO

GIVENS, Joshua, Ha-113-2; 6th Civil Dist

GIVENS, Thomas B., Ha-113-2; Sgt E Co 8th TN Cav; 10 Jul 63 to 11 Aug 65; Sneedville PO

GIVENS, William, Bo-21-3; Pvt E Co 8th IN Cav; 7-25-62 to 4-1-65; Cox PO

GIVINGS, Ephrom, Mn-125-1; Pvt B Co 110th US Hvy? Col Inf; Caffey PO; 3 Jan 64 to 3 Feb 65

GIVINS, John, K-167-6; Pvt H Co 1st TN Cav; 62 to Jun 65; Knoxville PO; discharge lost

GIVINS, L. R., Cu-18-2; Mary R. widow of; Pvt I Co 5th TN Inf; 5-8-62 to 7-9-65; Rockwood PO

GIVINS, Peter H., Je-146-1; Martha A. widow of; Pvt K Co 9th TN Cav; Leadvale PO; can't give dates

GIVONS, Cebastin, Gr-82-1; Pvt E Co 2nd TN Inf; 25 Apr 62 to May 65; Liberty Hill PO

GLADDING, James W., Je-138-1; Capt B Co 2nd MI Cav; 9 Aug 61 to 26 Jul 65; White Pines PO; shot through right leg

GLADIS, J. M., Mn-129-1; Pvt 49th IL Inf; 63 to 65; Adamsville PO; this is as right as I can ___ ___

GLASE, Thomas M., Mc-118-1; Pvt D Co 10th TN Cav; 6-18-64 to 8-1-66; Longs Mills PO; disease of heart 25 yrs
GLASGOW, Jessee, St-162-3(1); Pvt K Co 83rd IL Inf; 25 Nov 62 to 20 Sep 65; Cumberland City PO; left hand crippled, eyes also affected & partially deaf
GLASGOW, William D., We-224-3(1); Pvt C Co 7th TN Inf; 62 to 65; Dresden PO; he does not remember the dates
GLASNER, John, Hu-105-1; Pvt H Co 1st WI Cav; McEwen PO; partial loss of hearing, leg broken, discharged from hospital
GLASS, Chaney, Sh-196-3; Memphis PO
GLASS, George, Sh-191-7(3); rear of DeSoto St, Memphis PO
GLASS, Job?, Sh-157-1; Emly widow of; Pvt M Co 3rd Art; 63 to __ (2 yrs 6 mos); PO omitted
GLASS, John, Lo-187-1; Pvt F Co 10th TN Cav; 18 Dec 63 to 1 Aug 65; Loudon PO; rheumatism
GLASS, Samuel B., We-223-4; 2nd Sgt E Co 7th KY Inf; 21 Aug 61 to 27 Nov 64; Elm Tree PO; shot in ankle; CONF
GLASSCOCK, George, Ms-171-2; Pvt C Co 4th TN Cav; Sep 64 to 30 Aug 65; Belfast PO
GLAYE, Mary (see Holt, John)
GLAYS, Jacson, Je-138-1; Jacson Bragg alias; Pvt F Co 1st US Col Inf; __ to 6 Mar 65 (2 yrs 6 mos); Oak Grove PO
GLEAVER, Isaac L., H-59-1; 2nd Lt D Co 86th IL Inf; 8-14-62 to 6-6-65; Chattanooga PO
GLEAVES, Alexander, D-66-1; lost his papers; Pvt Col; Nashville, 518 S Chery PO
GLEAVES, J. Monroe, D-78-2; Nashville PO
GLEDHILL, Charles H., H-56-2; Maggie widow of; 61 to 65; East End PO
GLEESON, John, Dk-32-1; Drummer F Co 3rd TN Inf; 10-1-63 to 9-1-65; Liberty PO
GLEIM, Jake, Ms-181-1; Pvt B Co 11th TN Inf; 6-30-63 to 4-12-65; Lewisburg PO
GLENN, John W., Mo-120-3(1); Pvt A Co 89th OH Inf; 8-22-62 to 6-7-65; Sweetwater PO; wounded at Chickamauga
GLENN, Osborne, Mu-213-1; Cook; Sep 61 to Nov 61; Glenns Store PO; no discharge
GLENN, Pascall, Se-226-2; Pvt B Co 6th TN Inf; 13 Apr 64 to 5 Jun 65; Sinking Springs PO
GLENN, Samuel O., Sh-201-1; Mary A. widow of; Pvt A Co 36th AL Inf; 10 Nov 63 to 1 Dec 65; Memphis PO; CONF
GLENN, Thomas, Sn-250-2; Pvt K Co 2nd __; 5-3-61 to __ (4 yrs); Castalian Springs PO; CONF
GLIDEWELL, James T., Dy-29-2; Pvt A Co Cav; Apr 63 to Jul 63; Newbern? PO; CONF
GLIDEWELL, William L., Dy-29-2; Pvt D Co 26th MN Inf; 62 to __ (4 yrs); Newbern PO; taken prisoner; CONF
GLISSON, Dennis J. M., We-224-1; Pvt D & K Cos 6th TN Cav; Aug 63 to Oct 64; Dresden PO; contracted piles, also breastbone broken, discharged by reason of disability
GLISSON, Huston, Hn-74-1; Sarah C. widow of; McKenzie PO; discharged special order
GLISSON, Isaac D., We-229-1; Pvt G Co 7th TN Inf; 27 Aug 61 to 1 Aug 65; McKinzie PO (Carrol Co.)
GLOSSIP, John F., Je-146-3; Nancy widow of; Pvt M Co 9th TN Cav; 1 Jun 63 to 11 Sep 65; White Pine PO
GLOSSON, Alex, Cr-20-1; Ann F. widow of; Pvt B Co 7th TN Cav; 8-63 to __ (5 mos); Hollow Rock PO; diorh
GLOTHEN, John, Ro-206-2; Catharine widow of; Pvt H Co 5th TN Inf; 27 Feb 62 to 16 May 65; Emory Gap PO
GLOVER, George G., Cf-40-2; alias Glover, Zacharis; Pvt E Co 1st TN Inf; Sep 63 to Mar 65; Tullahoma PO; discharged at expiration of service, discharge at pension office
GLOVER, George L., M-103-1; Sinthy widow of; Pvt B Co 37th KY Inf; Lafayette PO; killed in 1863
GLOVER, James, Ro-209-2; Pvt A Co 1st TN Inf; Aug 64 to Aug 65; Glen Alice PO
GLOVER, John, Ct-39-2; Pvt B Co 4th TN Inf; 8-62 to 8-65; Elizabethton PO; diorhoea
GLOVER, Richard, Ct-39-2; Pvt A Co 13th TN Cav; 9-62 to __; Gap Run PO; frost bitten & rheumatism

GLOVER, Thomas, Gi-138-2; Pvt D Co 24th Art; 64 to 65 (1 yr 6 mos); Valesville PO
GLOVER?, William C., D-75-1; Sgt F Co 30th TN Inf; 1 Oct 61 to 15 Dec 63; Stewarts Ferry PO; prisoner 4 mos Nashville; CONF
GOAD, Benjamin, D-64-3; Pilot & Master Newsboy & M. B. Beard; 63 to 65; Nashville PO
GOAD, James O., D-47-1; Pvt H Co 10th TN Cav; 10-63 to 8-2-65; Station B Jackson St, Nashville PO; shot in thigh and neck; paralised from shot in thigh
GOAD, Joshua, Sm-168-1; Pvt H Co TN Inf; 10-61 to 62; Difficult PO; sick a good deal
GOAD, Peter, Wa-266-1; Pvt F Co 3rd TN Mtd Inf; Meadow Brook PO
GOAD, Richard H., M-106-3(2); Cpl K Co 9th KY Vol Inf; 11-30-61 to 1-11-65; Hillsdale PO; wounded in left shoulder; pensioner
GOAN, Ezekel, Hw-131-2; Pvt B Co 8th TN Inf; 4 Mar 63 to 18 Jul 65; White Horn PO
GOAN, Rufis J., Ge-89-3; M Co 1st TN Cav; Albany PO; dont remember dates
GOAN, William M., Hm-108-2(1); Pvt G Co 4th TN Inf; 1 Jan 63 to 2 Aug 65; Chestnut Bloom PO; c. rheumatism
GOANS, Steven A., Mo-122-3(1); Pvt C Co 31st TN Inf; 62 to 65; Madisonville PO; CONF
GOANS, William P., Gr-71-1; Cpl F Co 8th TN Cav; 31 Aug 63 to 11 Sep 65; Bean Station PO
GOBBEL, William A., La-112-1; Pvt A Co 2nd TN Mtd Inf; 10-2-63 to 10-14-64; Knob Creek PO; typhoid fever damaged left arm
GOBBELL, Edward W., Wy-172-1; Pvt A Co 2nd TN Mtd Inf; 10-63 to 64 (9 mos); Waynesboro PO; captured 7-64, Centerville, TN
GOBBELL, Isaac H. (now Sr.), Wy-172-1; Pvt A Co 10th TN; 4-13-62 to 7-5-65; Waynesboro PO; captured 12-4-62, parolled
GOBBELL, James T., Wy-177-2; Pvt A Co 10th TN Inf; 10-3-63 to 7-25-65; Moon PO
GOBBLE, Amos, Se-228-1(2); Pvt B Co 2nd TN Cav; 15 Sep 62 to 6 Jul 65; New Knob Creek PO; wounded right knee
GOBBLE, Chas., Ct-39-4; US Soldier; 6th Dist
GOBBLE, Henry, Se-223-2; Blacksmith E Co 9th TN Cav; 1 Oct 63 to 11 Sep 65; Pigeon Forge PO; chronic diarrhea
GOBLE, Lewis, Gr-74-2; Cpl M Co 2nd TN Cav; 7 Nov 62 to 14 Jul 65; May Spring PO
GODARD?, James A., Hm-106-3; Capt H Co 3rd TN Cav; 6 Nov 62 to 3 Aug 65; Morristown PO
GODARD, Wesley, Mg-196-1; Pvt 2nd TN Art; First Dist
GODDARD, Francis M., Mg-196-3; Cpl F Co 5th TN Inf; 25 Feb 62 to 29 Mar 65; Hunnicutt PO
GODDARD, James, Ro-206-3; Martha H. widow of; Pvt; 62 to 64; Kingston PO; CONF
GODDARD, Joseph, Bo-15-4; Pvt A Co 2nd TN Cav; 10-10-62 to 7-6-65; Maryville PO
GODDARD, Nathaniel, Bo-15-4; Pvt H Co 2nd TN Cav; 10-10-62 to 7-6-65; Maryville PO
GODDARD, Thomas L., Ro-206-2; Pvt B Co 11th TN Inf; 15 Jul 63 to 24 Oct 63; Emory Gap PO
GODDARD, Wiley G., Ro-206-1; Cpl B Co 11th TN Cav; 21 Jul 63 to 11 Sep 65; Kingston PO
GODDARD, William, Bo-20-2; Pvt A Co 3rd TN Cav; 9-18-62 to 6-10-65; Bank PO
GODENER, Mose, F-44-1; Pvt; 62 to 65; PO omitted
GODFREY, Edwin J., Cu-17-2; Pvt Rhode Island; 61 to 5-64; Pomona PO
GODFREY, Robert G., K-177-5; Pvt C Co 6th TN Inf; Feb 62 to 65; Powells Station PO; fever, rheumatism & chills & fever
GODLOE, Martain B., Co-68-1; Cap E Co 11th GA; 61 to 65; Cosby PO; spinal effected; CONF
GODSEY, John, Wa-268-3; Johnson City PO
GODSEY, Mary, H-51-7; 3rd Dist
GODSEY, Samuel, Ja-85-5; Pvt H Co 10th TN Cav; Long Savannah PO
GODWIN, Charles M. (see Mallory, Charles H.)
GODWIN, Samuel C., Hd-55-1; Pvt E Co 3rd KY Batt; 1 Oct 64 to 18 Feb 65; Clifton PO (Wayne Co.); now breasted and lung disease
GOEBEL, Fredrick, Ma-127-1; Band Leader M Co 4th PA Cav; 61 to Jul 20 65; Jackson PO; astma
GOFF, DeWitt C., Br-9-3; Pvt E Co 9th MI Cav; 1-12-63 to 7-21-65; Cleveland PO

GOFF, Elias P., He-64-2; Martha widow of; Pvt K Co 7th TN Cav; 20 Jun 62 to __ (3 yrs); Center Point PO; died in Camp Cotten
GOFF, Frank, H-63-1; Eliza widow of; Sgt E Co 1st Col Hvy Art; 63 to 65; 629 W. 7th, Chattanooga PO
GOFF, Henry C., Sh-148-1; E Co; Mann the rifles; Memphis PO
GOFF, Henry G., Bo-20-2; Cpl I Co 9th TN Cav; 3-28-63 to 9-11-65; GOFF, Jas. M., Wa-267-1; Pvt 23rd Army Corp; Gen. Scofield Inf; Blacksmith; 21 May 64 to 4 Mar 65; Jonesboro PO; chc. diarhea, rheumatism & bone scrofula, brain fever in Anapolis, MD, hospital
GOFF, Joel, Ch-14-2; Pvt 65th IN Art; 12-1-61 to 10-21-63; Sweet Lips PO; finger shot off
GOFF, Josep W., Hd-54-1; Pvt F Co 145th IL Inf; 20 May 64 to 23 Sep 64; Saltillo PO; mumps
GOFF, Walrus E., D-72-1; Pvt A Co 21st TN Inf; Aug 23 __ to Jul 27 64 (1 yr 1 mo 4 days); Nashville PO
GOFORTH, Alfred, Su-239-2; Pvt I Co 3rd NC Inf; 64 to 65; Kingsport PO
GOFORTH, Drury, H-63-3; Pvt L Co 10th TN Inf; 63 to 65; 714 Pine, Chattanooga PO; inflammatory rheumatism
GOFORTH, James P., Cl-57-2; Pvt H Co 8th Reg Cav; 7-24-63 to __; Goin PO; rheumatism & pasied in legs; not able to walk without 2 sticks, not discharged, left near Knoxville
GOFORTH, John F., Wh-183-1; Sgt A Co 11th TN Cav; 7-13-63 to 9-11-65; Quebeck PO; wounded in right leg
GOFORTH, Miles, Mc-114-2; Pvt F Co 1st TN Inf; 62 to no discharge (2 yrs); Magellan PO; hemorrhoids
GOFORTH, Sebran, Je-139-2; Pvt I Co 2nd TN Cav; 22 Sep 62 to __ (2 yrs 6 mos); Trion PO
GOFORTH, Thomas J., Hy-78-1; Pvt B Co 12th TN Cav; 22 Jul 63 to 25 Oct 65; Brownsville PO
GOIN, Francis M., Ca-23-3; Pvt B Co 1st TN Art; 9 62 to 7-25-65; Burt PO; mash from fall of a log
GOIN, Harvel R., Je-146-4; White Pine PO; dont know disease, soldier was not home
GOIN, Henry, H-58-2; Pvt K Co 4th TN Cav; __ to 7-12-65; Coulterville PO
GOIN, John, Cl-58-2; Pvt Co C 1st TN Art; 5-12-63 to 8-1-65; Davo PO; helth impared from small pox, able to work part of his time
GOIN, Joshua G., Cl-57-2; Pvt C Co 1st TN Reg Art; 7-1-63 to 8-1-65; Goin PO; gone from home
GOIN, Miller, R-163-3; Pvt C Co 5th TN Inf; 61 to 65; Graysville PO; shot in left thigh
GOIN, Robbert, Je-146-3; Cpl A Co 12th TN Cav; 1 Sep 63 to 7 Oct 65; White Pine PO; jaundice, old feller is thin
GOINS, Alfred, Ja-84-3; Pvt B Co 1st TN Lt Art; 1-2-62 to 1-23-65; Normans Store PO; cronic diarhea
GOINS, Alfred, Ha-117-3; Pvt A Co 1st TN Cav; 62 to 65; Sneedville PO; chronic diarrhea, lungs
GOINS, Elijah J., Ro-204-3; Pvt A Co 12th __; 64 to 65; Elverton PO
GOINS, Elisabeth A. (see Morgan, Wm. B.)
GOINS, Felix W., K-185-2; Pvt; 63 to 65; Mascott PO; CONF
GOINS, Henry B., Gr-80-1; Pvt G Co 14th KY Inf; 15 Jun 63 to 2 Apr 64; Thorn Hill PO
GOINS, Isaac, Hw-130-2; Oma widow of; Pvt F Co 2nd TN Cav; 62 to __; PO omitted
GOINS, James (Indian), Lo-190-1; Pvt Cav; 62 to 65; Loudon PO
GOINS, John, Ca-25-3; Pvt K Co 4th TN Cav; 5-3-64 to 7-12-65; Gassoway PO; shot on top of left foot with __ shell
GOINS, John, Ha-115-4; Pvt H Co 24th KY Inf; 1 Nov (Oct) 61 to 19 Sep 65; Mulberry Gap PO; re-enlisted veteran
GOINS, John, Ha-113-1; Pvt A Co 1st TN Cav; 14 Dec 62 to 19 Jun 65; Sneedville PO
GOINS, John G., Gr-80-1; Pvt 8th TN Cav; 63 to 63 (3? yrs); Thorn Hill PO chronic diarhea, cannot recollect dates omitted
GOLDEN, Charles, Col, D-63-1; Nashville PO
GOLDEN, Henry C., We-221-4; Pvt I Co 6th TN Cav; 9 Aug 62 to 26 Jul 65; Martin PO; hernia, thrown from horse

GOLDEN, Henry H., Hi-87-1; Mariah widow of; Pvt G Co TN Cav; 12-15-63 to died in 2 mos; Civil Dist 5
GOLDEN, Herman G., H-62-3; 438 Pine, Chattanooga PO
GOLDEN, James P., Hw-125-4; Cpl K Co 8th TN Cav; Aug 63 to 19 Sep 65; Surgoinsville PO
GOLDEN, Joshua, Wh-187-1; Caroline widow of; Orderly Sgt KY Inf; 62 to 65; Cherry Creek PO; contracted rheumatism
GOLDEN, Richard, Cl-55-1; Pvt C Co 3rd TN Inf; 8-64 to 65; Lone Mountain PO
GOLDEN, William F., A-2-4; Pvt 2nd Pioneer Corps (commanded last by Capt Rogers); Andersonville PO; measles and sequences; gun shot wound in leg; papers in Green Co., cant make record complete
GOLDEN, William T., Cl-55-1; Sgt C Co 3rd TN Inf; 8-64 to 65; Lone Mountain PO
GOLDMAN, John M., Gi-122-3; Pvt F Co 55th VA Inf; 1 Jan 62 to 1 Jun 64; Prospect Sta. PO; shot in head; prison 12 mos; CONF
GOLDMON, John, Gi-138-2; Pvt; 63 to 64; Valesville PO
GOLDSBERRY, John C., H-54-6; Pvt K Co 46th OH Inf; 61 to 62; East Chattanooga PO
GOLDSMITH, John, H-54-2(3); John G. Smith; Pvt D Co 35th IN Inf; 61 to __; Sherman Heights PO; wounded in the right thigh by gunshot, fell out on the Atlanta on account exhaustion, served three years and ____ and could never reach his command
GOLDSTONE, Louis E., H-64-2; Chattanooga PO
GOLLAHORD, William A., Mc-114-7; US Sol; 9th Civil Dist
GOLLIHOR, P. B., Mc-114-4; Ruth widow of; Pvt M Co; 3-14-63 to no discharge; Sandford PO
GOLMAN, James N., Cy-26-2; Pvt D Co 9th KY Inf; 9-16-61 to 5-15-63; Moss PO; wounded from shot
GOLOWAY, Johnson, Mc-114-7; US Sol; Calhoun PO
GOOCH, Ellis, Hr-96-1; alias Ellis Beany; Pvt H Co 3rd AR Cav; 61 to 65; Dorris PO
GOOCH, Hariette, Ru-231-1; 1st Dist
GOOCH, Littleton O., Cr-14-3; Pvt K Co 2nd TN Mtd Inf; 10 May 64 to 27 Jun 65; Crider PO
GOOCH, Willice C., Cr-6-1; Pvt G Co 7th TN Cav; 8-1-62 to 10-15-65; Cairo PO
GOOD, Abraham H., Ja-87-1; Pvt H Co 4th TN Cav; 10-25-62 to 7-12-65; Howardville PO; rheumatism & indigestion
GOOD, Edward J., Ja-85-4; 1st Lt E Co 6th TN Inf; 4-1-62 to 1-15-64; Georgetown PO
GOOD, Jacob M., Wa-272-2; Sgt D Co 8th TN Cav; 18 Sep 63 to 11 Sep 65; Cedar Lane PO; chronic rheumatism
GOOD, James, M-103-4; Susan V. widow of; Pvt I Co 9th KY; Alton Hill PO
GOOD, James M., Wa-272-1; Sgt F Co 8th TN Cav; 4 Mar 63 to 11 Sep 65; Locust Mount PO; varicose veins both legs
GOOD, Joshua, S-218-3; US Sol; 9th Civil Dist
GOOD, LaFayette, Ha-115-2; Pvt C Co 64th VA Cav; 9 Apr 63 to 9 Apr 65; Fenton PO
GOOD, Little B., S-214-3; Pvt E Co 11th TN Cav; 26 Jul 62 to 5 Jul 65; Robbins PO; shot in right shoulder
GOOD, Nattan M., Ge-94-1; Home PO
GOODALL, Albert, Tr-268-1; Pvt H Co 14th TN Inf; Sep 62 to 66; Albert Goodall shot in hip, pensioned; PO omitted
GOODALL, Edward, H-67-1; Pvt G Co 14th US Col Inf; 11-63 to 3-66; Chattanooga PO
GOODE?, Bettis? (see Tomlinson, David M.)
GOODE, Edward, Cu-17-4; Pvt B Co 5th TN Inf; 2-25-62 to 3-30-65; Northville PO; chronic diarrhea
GOODE, Marion, Br-6-3; Pvt E Co 6th TN Inf; 4-10-62 to 65; Chatala PO; diarhoea, nervous prostration & rheumatism
GOODE, Richard, Br-12-2; Pvt 42nd TN Inf; Charleston PO
GOODE, Thomas, D-54-1; Pvt A Co 10th IL Inf--18 Apr 61 to 18 Jul 61; Pvt A Co 10th IL Inf--Jan 66 to 4 Jul 66; Nashville PO; got piles and suffered with them since
GOODELL, Charles, Fe-43-1; Clark Range PO
GOODELL, George B., Br-7-4; Pvt A Co 55th OH Inf; 9-30-61 to 7-22-65; Cleveland PO; rupture
GOODEN, Ellitt S., Ge-89-2; Pvt 1st TN Cav; Mosheim PO

GOODEN, Hugh, Mo-121-1; Pvt H Co 1st OH Hvy Art; 8-6-64 to 6-20-65; Eve Mills PO; dis. right leg--res. varicose veins, pensioner
GOODEN, John C., Ge-100-1; Pvt E Co 1st TN Cav; Sep 63 to May? 65; Mosheim PO
GOODEN, Needham, Su-239-2; Ann widow of; Pvt 4th TN Cav; Horace PO
GOODHEART, Briscoe, K-163-1; Pvt A Co LCR?; Aug 62 to 65; Knoxville PO; crippled; CONF?
GOODING, Richard, Cf-38-1; Sgt G Co 5th TN Cav; 6 Sep 62 to 14 Aug 65; 10th Civil Dist
GOODLOE, Abriham, Hu-99-1; Pvt A Co 110th Col US Inf; Johnsonville PO
GOODLOE, Frank, Hu-99-1; Cpl A Co 110th Col US Inf; 5 Jul 64 to 10 Dec 65; Johnsonville PO
GOODLOE, Gilbreath, Mu-195-1; E Co 111th TN Vol; 3-1-62 to 5-3-65; Columbia PO
GOODLOE, William, Hu-99-1; Sgt A Co 110th Col US Inf; Johnsonville PO
GOODMAN, Arch. W., Be-6-1; Pvt E Co 2nd TN Inf; Mar 64 to 10 May 65; Camden PO; right shoulder dislocated
GOODMAN, George, Wa-270-2; Pvt D Co 60th TN Inf; 63 to 65; Jonesboro PO; shot through left wrist
GOODMAN?, George W., Ms-177-1; Pvt B Co 111th TN Inf; 4-15-64 to 5-1-65; Berlin PO
GOODMAN, Green B., Wl-298-1; Pvt I Co 4th TN Mtd Inf; 1 Jan 65 to 25 Aug 65; Statesville PO; ruptured on left side, 25 yrs, right leg broken in a
GOODMAN, Henry, S-216-1; Pvt G Co 2nd TN Inf; fall of 61 to 62; Huntsville PO; brest broak
GOODMAN, John, S-215-2; Jennie widow of; Pvt; High House PO
GOODMAN, John, A-6-1; Pvt A Co 11th TN Cav; 5-28-63 to 9-11-65; Olivers PO
GOODMAN, Kemp., La-109-1; Pvt A Co 10th KY Inf; 9-22-62 to 3-2-64; Pleasant Pt. PO; exact dates uncertain
GOODMAN, Lewis (see Adkins, Arthur)
GOODMAN, Madison, Ha-113-1; Pvt A Co 1st TN Cav; 9 Mar 62 to 5 Apr 65; Sneedville PO
GOODMAN, Milton J., La-112-1; Pvt I Co 2nd TN Mtd Inf; 12-15-63 to 1-21-65; Venus PO
GOODMAN, William, H-53-8; Pvt; 1 yr 6 mos; Fifth Civil Dist
GOODALL, Jerry, Col, Tr-268-1; Rachel widow of; Pvt F Co; Hartsville PO; mustered out
GOODNER, Gennie?, Wl-299-1; Emma J. widow of; Pvt K Co 5th TN Inf; 22 Aug 62 to 25 Aug 65; Statesville PO
GOODNER, Thomas, Br-10-2; Pvt E Co 4th US Col Inf; 10-1-64 to 1-31-66; Cleveland PO
GOODNOW, Chas. E., Ke-169-2; Pvt I Co 3rd MS Inf; 9 Nov 61 to 14 Apr 63; Knoxville PO; left arm off, chronic dysentery
GOODPASTURE, Martha A., Cy-29-2; widow of US Sol; 8th Civil Dist
GOODRICH, Bryant, D-69-3; 31 Murry St, Nashville PO
GOODRING, Andrew A., Fe-42-1; Sgt D Co 2nd TN; 9-1-61 to 10-6-64; Jamestown PO
GOODSON, Cyrus, Hw-121-3(2); Pvt A Co 37th VA Inf; 12 Feb 64 to 11 Oct 65; New Hope PO; catarrh in head
GOODSON, William, Hm-106-3; Pvt; Morristown PO
GOODSON, William S., H-58-5; Pvt B Co 120th IL Inf; Retro PO; discharge misplaced
GOODWIN, Andrew J., Ro-202-2; Pvt B Co 63rd TN Inf; Sep 62 to 9 Apr 65; Union X Roads PO; horse thrown him; CONF
GOODWIN, Carlton A. (see Carlton, Goodwin)
GOODWIN, Chesley H., We-221-4; Pvt KY Cav; 61 to 64; Martin PO; CONF
GOODWIN, James M., Ct-35-3; Pvt G Co 13th TN Cav; 9-24-63 to 9-5-65; Elk Mills PO; in US Army
GOODWIN, James W., Ja-85-3; Pvt E Co 4th TN Cav; 12-5-62 to 7-12-65; Thatcher PO
GOODWIN, John D., Ro-203-7; Pvt B Co 63rd TN Inf; Oct __ to __; Vancouver PO; gunshot wound in both legs, never discharged, parolled prisoner; CONF
GOODWIN, John S., H-53-3; Pvt F Co 10th TN Inf; 12-27-63 to 6-21-65; Chattanooga PO; rhumatism & paralysis
GOODWIN, John W., Wh-186-2; Pvt K Co 1st TN Mtd Inf; 9-29-64 to 7-22-65; Bakers Cross Roads PO; general break down
GOODWIN, Joseph, Ca-22-1; Pvt G Co 5th TN Cav; 8-11-63 to 8-14-65; Hollow Springs PO; cataarh in head
GOODWIN, Joseph A., K-162-1; O Sgt H Co 8th TN Inf; 1 Aug 63 to 65; Knoxville PO; rheumatism, ruptured
GOODWIN, Lymen, H-56-3; Pvt H Co 6th MN Inf; 7-28-62 to 7-31-64; St. Elmo PO; dropsy of chest, hospital 2 mos
GOODWIN, Munroe M. (see Harvey, Munroe)
GOODWIN, Peter, Ro-202-3(1); Pvt E Co 19th TN Inf; 8 Nov 62 to 19 May 65; Union X Roads PO; CONF
GOODWIN, William A., Ca-23-3; Pvt G Co 5th TN Cav; 2-17-63 to 65 (not discharged); Narla PO; health injured by cold
GOODWINE, Eli, Me-88-2; Pvt A Co 9th TN Cav; 12-63 to 9-13-65; Georgetown PO; prisoner at Danville VA, now deaf & cripple
GOOL, Archie, H-63-1; Celia widow of; Cpl A Co 1st Col Hvy Art; 63 to 65 (1 yr 9 mos); 613 W 7th, Chattanooga PO
GOOLSBY, James L., Cy-26-1; Mary L. widow of; Pvt I Co 1st TN Inf; 6-63 to 64; Moss PO
GOOLSBY, Mary (see Cross, Joel J.)
GOOLSBY, Mary, La-109-1; soldiers widow; Pvt; husband killed in US Army; St. Joseph PO
GOOLSBY, Nancy, Mr-102-1; widow? Pvt 6th TN Inf; South Pittsburg PO
GOOLWIN, Willia- D., D-57-3; (Susie); Pvt 18th TN Inf; Mar 61 to Nov 65; Nashville PO; CONF
GORDAN, Silas, Ru-237-1; Pvt F Co 14th TN Inf; 63 to 65; Eagleville PO
GORDAN, William B., Mu-210-6; Pvt E Co 1st TN Cav; 61 to caputred 63; Columbia PO; shot trhough both feet; CONF
GORDEN, David, Gi-122-1; Pvt F Co 110th TN Inf; Dec 61 to __ (2 yrs 6 mos); Prospect Sta. PO
GORDEN, Samuel, Gi-129-1; Cpl I Co 17th TN Inf; __ to Apr 66; Conway PO
GORDON, Carol, Gi-136-1; Pvt K Co 38th TN Inf; 1-15-63 to 2-15-65; Odd Fellow Hall PO; shot in foot, suffers good __ with wound
GORDON, Charles L., Wh-181-1; alias Ira A. Cooper; Frankey A. widow of; Pvt A Co 3rd KY Cav; River Hill PO; applied for pension, needs it
GORDON, Edwin R., Sh-177-1; 120 Mulberry, Memphis PO
GORDON, Harrison, Gi-135-2; Pvt; Lynnville PO
GORDON, Henry, Hn-77-1; Eliza widow of; Pvt; PO omitted
GORDON, Jasper, Gi-135-3; Pvt E Co 110th TN Inf; Lynnville PO
GORDON, Jeff, D-73-1; Pvt; Nashville PO; care Willis Bateman
GORDON, Jefferson, Gi-132-3; Maria Buford formerly widow of; D Co; Pulaski PO
GORDON, Jessie, Sh-191-1; Cpl F Co 46th IN; 5-1-63 to 12-1-65; Memphis PO
GORDON, John, Mu-195-1; Lou widow of; A Co 13th TN Vol; 8-12-63 to 1-10-66; Columbia PO
GORDON, John, Lo-189-3(1); Pvt K Co 10th OH Cav; 11 Nov 62 to 24 Jul 65; Philadelphia PO; enlarged veins caused by over heat, suffering from enlarged veins
GORDON, Milton, Gi-132-3; Pvt H Co 110th USCV; Dec 63 to Feb 9 66; Pulaski PO; injury to eye
GORDON, Milton, Ms-183-1; Pvt C Co 110th US Col Inf; 1-25-64 to 2-6-66; Comenville PO; not drawing a pension
GORDON, Neel, Gi-135-3; Pvt A Co 110th TN Inf; Lynnville PO
GORDON, Noah K., Sh-195-1; Pvt A Co 73rd IN Inf; 63 to 2-18-66; Memphis PO; this man enlisted twice; C Co 7th IN Cav; 8-2-62 to
GORDON, Pleas W., Cr-14-4; Pvt G Co 7th TN Cav; 5 Aug __ to 25 Oct 63 (1 yr 1 mo 20 days); Cawthon PO
GORDON, Prinze, Ho-97-1; Pvt A Co 2nd US Inf; 10 Sep 63 to 24 Feb 65; Yellow Creek PO; discharged on account of close of war
GORE, Alfred, Col, D-101-1; Cpl F Co 15th US Inf; Dec 62 to May 65; 22nd Civil Dist
GORE, Overton, Ov-134-1; Hilham PO; has forgotten dates & names
GOREN, Francis M., Br-14-2; Pvt D Co 10th TN Cav; 1-1-64 to 65; McDonald PO

GOREN, Scobard J., Br-14-2; Pvt D Co 10th TN Cav; 1-1-64 to 65; McDonald PO
GOREN, Washington L., Mr-99-3; Pvt Vancleve Div, Capt Drewry; Jasper PO
GORHAM, Hiram I., La-113-1; Sgt I Co 4th VT Inf; Feb 62 to Jun 65; Lawrenceburg PO
GORLEY, Nathanill T., Hm-102-1; Pvt F Co 8th TN Cav; 8 Jun 63 to 11 Sep 65; Morristown PO; chronic diarrhea
GORMAN, Thomas, A-6-6(4); Pvt B Co 19th OH Inf; 62 to 1-65; Olivers PO; shot in the left arm
GOSNELL, Isaac, H-68-1; Pvt K Co 8th TN Inf; 5-62 to 5-65; Chattanooga PO
GOSSAGE, Thomas J., Fr-112-3; Pvt D Co 17th TN Inf; 8-9-61 to 8-65; Decherd PO; CONF
GOSSET, Henry J., Se-231-1; Pvt A Co 6th IN Cav; 18 Aug 63 to 15 Sep 65; Boyds Creek PO; malary poisen 27 yrs
GOSSETT, Calaway B., K-181-4(1); Sgt A Co 6th TN Inf; 1 Mar 62 to May 65; Knoxville PO
GOSSETT, Jason R., K-181-4(1); Recruiting Officer 3rd TN Cav; French PO
GOSSETT, Will. T., Hd-51-1; Pvt B Co 4th AL Inf; 1 Aug 63 to 65; Pickens PO; CONF
GOSSETT, William H., We-222-2; Pvt F Co 11th TN Inf; 18 May 61 to 18 May 65; Gardner PO; CONF
GOTHARD, Elizabeth (see Jasper Lea)
GOTHERD, William B., R-161-1; Arvazena widow of; Lt Col B Co 6th TN Mtd Inf; 10-26-64 to 6-30-65; Dayton PO; discharge is at W., appointed 10-26-64
GOTT, David, Su-240-2; Cpl E Co 64th VA Cav; 20 Sep 63 to Apr 65; Ford Town PO; CONF
GOTT, Georgia A., Mr-97-1; widow of; 2nd Briga ? H Co TN Cav; 10-24-63 to 6-16-64; PO omitted
GOTT, William H., Mr-97-1; Pvt D Co TN Cav--9-7-63 to 6-16-64; Sgt C Co 6th TN Cav--9-10-64 to 6-30-65; PO omitted; calara in the head
GOUCH, Sam'l J., Sh-207-3; Soldier; Memphis PO
GOUGH, Anderson, Gi-127-4; Cpl C Co 12th TN Col Inf; 8-1-63 to 1-16-66; Pulaski PO
GOUL, Frank, Sh-191-4; Memphis PO; records not seen
GOULD, Heiser D., Fe-42-4; 3rd Civil Dist
GOUND, Robert J., Lo-194-1; Muddy Creek PO
GOURLEY, Charles, Ge-96-1; Pvt C Co 2nd TN Cav; 27 Jul 62 to 11 Aug 65; Jockey PO
GOURLEY, George W., Ct-39-1; H Co 8th TN Cav; Carters Depot PO
GOURLY, J. W. (Colored), K-179-1; Pvt D Co 1st TN Col Hvy Art; Mar 64 to 66; Rodelin PO
GOURLY, Lorind L. (see Awood, James)
GOVERS, Joshway C., Fr-107-1; Pvt B Co 12th TN Cav; 63 to 65; Winchester PO; discharge on surgeon certificate and claiming pension for ____ that wound; and 6th Mtd Inf, 64 to ____
GOWAN, James M., Ru-240-1; Pvt 5-33rd IN Inf; 4 Sep 64 to 19 Sep 64; 11th Civ Dist
GOWEN, Zechariah, Ha-111-3; Pvt G Co 1st TN Cav; 1 Jul 62 to 5 Jun 65; PO omitted
GOWER, Thos? J., Hd-50-4; Sarah M. widow of; Seaman; Nixon PO; kidney disease of which he died some years ago leaving widow
GOWERS, Fuston, Dk-31-2; Pvt H Co 8th IN Cav; 5-62 to 8-11-65; Alexandria PO; transferred to 9th TN Inf
GOWERS, George W., He-64-1; Pvt C Co 7th TN Cav; 19 Oct 63 to 9 Aug 65; Lexington PO; discharged at Nash.
GOWLACE, Ben, Mu-198-1; 10th Dist
GRACE, Jacob M. (James), D-103-1; Sgt F Co 1st PA Inf; Aug 7 62 to Jun 16 63; Joeton PO; chron. diarrhea, draws pension
GRACE, Walker, Cy-26-2; Pvt B Co 5th KY Cav; 10-10-61 to 5-3-65; Celina PO; cripled from fever
GRACE, Wiliam C., K-172-4; Pvt H Co Callent? NC Reg; 11 Nov 63 to 10 May 65; PO omitted; CONF
GRACEN, Lemiel F., Dy-25-7(3); Pvt; Newbern PO; CONF
GRACY, John, Dk-39-3(1); Elisabeth widow of; Pvt K Co 1st TN Mtd Inf; Dekalb PO
GRADFORD, Mary F., Cr-15-2; widow US Sol; Maple Creek PO
GRADY, George W., D-43-1; Pvt; Nashville PO
GRADY, James, Lo-190-2; Mary widow of; Pvt TN Inf; Jan 61 to ____; Loudon PO; CONF
GRADY, Joseph, Di-34-1; Pvt E Co 12th TN Inf; 10-26-61 to 1-66; Dickson PO; reenlisted veteran
GRAGG, Benjamin F., Co-63-2; Pvt C Co 4th TN Inf; Apr 63 to ____ (8 mos); Newport PO; no discharge in prison
GRAGG, Henry, Co-63-2; Pvt 8th TN Inf; Newport PO; measles caused deafness
GRAGG, John, Po-148-3; Pvt E Co 4th TN Cav; 5-1-63 to 7-25-65; Benton PO; discharge lost or misplaced
GRAGG, Samuel, Co-63-2; Mahala widow of; Pvt C Co 4th TN Inf; Apr 63 to ____; Newport PO; no discharge, in prison
GRAGGS, Marshal, Po-148-3; Pvt E Co 4th TN Cav; 5-1-63 to 7-65; Benton PO
GRAHAM, Alexander, Ge-93-2; Pvt C Co 4th TN Inf; 1 Apr 64 to 1 Aug 65; Greeneville PO
GRAHAM, Andrew, Dk-36-1; Pvt E Co 1st TN Mtd Inf; 11-2-63 to 1-22-65; Smithville PO
GRAHAM, Andrew J., Ge-101-1; Pvt A Co 100 Day Cav; 1 Feb 64; Cross Anchor PO; never discharged
GRAHAM, Andrew J., Ge-92-5; Margaret Tucker formerly widow of; Pvt A Co 4th TN Inf; Romeo PO
GRAHAM, Benjamin, Sh-191-5(1); Memphis PO; records not seen
GRAHAM, Charley, Sh-157-7; Pvt K Co 23rd Dist; 63 to 65; Memphis, Beal St. 107; deaf and pnumonia
GRAHAM, Daniel J., Sq-164-1; Pvt K Co 5th TN Inf; 8-63 to 6-30-65; Fillmore PO; rheumatism & diarhoea
GRAHAM, G. W., C-28-2(1); Capt J Co 8th TN Inf; 8-1-61 to 9-17-64; Big Creek Gap; diarrhea and piles
GRAHAM, James, Ge-93-2; Pvt F Co 1st TN Cav; 1 Aug 62 to 10 Jun 65; Greeneville PO
GRAHAM, Jane (see Andrews, Peter)
GRAHAM, Jasper, C-34-1; Pvt M Co 9th TN Cav; 11-62 to 5-65; Elk Valley PO; shot in jaw
GRAHAM, John B., Bl-1-2; Pvt C Co 5th TN Inf; 8-15-63 to 7-15-65; Stevens Chapel PO; chronic rheumatism
GRAHAM, John W., Cl-54-3(1); Capt G Co 3rd TN; 4-62 to 11-65; Tazewell PO; US Soldier, Mexican War; CONF
GRAHAM, Martin V., Po-149-3(2); Pvt H Co 4th TN Cav; 8-14-63 to 7-12-65; Conasauga PO; spinel --back since 1866
GRAHAM, Mitchell, D-62-1; Mis? F Co 77th IL; Sep 8 62 to Jul 1 64; Nashville PO, 1305 McGavock; injury to left ankle
GRAHAM, Robt., Sh-195-2; US Sol; Memphis PO
GRAHAM, Wash., Sh-161-1; US Sol; 16th Dist
GRAHAM, William, Bl-1-2; Cpl D Co 99th NY Inf; 7-23-61 to 8-5-64; E. Nashville PO; moon blindness, RR contractor
GRAHAM, Wm. A., Ge-93-1; USS; PO omitted
GRAHAM, William M., Bl-2-2(1); Pvt K Co 1st TN Mtd Inf; 7-22-64 to 7-22-65; Schoolfield PO; cough from exposure, occasional cough
GRAINGER, John P., Su-240-2; Pvt E Co 63rd Hvy Art; Aug 62 to 1 May 65; Slaughter PO; CONF
GRAMMAR, William L., Lo-195-2(1); Cpl G Co 1st TN Inf; 9 Aug 61 to 17 Sep 64; Oral PO (Roane Co)
GRANBERRY, James, Sh-146-1; Pvt B Co 6th Inf; 63 to 65; Lucy PO; this man is a negro who says that he was mustered in at Columbus, KY. He things about the 3rd year of the war captured in Graves County by Forrests Cavalry and retaned a prisoner that he never was discharged because he never reached his command in time, that his captains name was Johnston
GRANBERRY, John, Sh-146-2; Ann widow of; Inf; 63 to 65; Lucy PO
GRANBERRY, John, Sh-153-2; Com Sgt D Co 59th USC Inf; 9 May 63 to 31 Jan 66; Collierville PO
GRANBERY, Alferd, F-44-3; Rose widow of; Pvt B Co 59th ____; May 63 to Feb 66; PO omitted
GRANBERY, John, F-42-1(3); Pvt A Co 59th US Col Inf; May 8 63 to Jan 31 66; Collierville PO (Shelby Co.); right leg partially disabled on train
GRANBERY, Rhoden, F-44-3; Pvt B Co 59th ____; May 63 to Feb 66; PO omitted; CONF
GRANDSTAFF, William B., Sm-173-1; Pvt L Co 5th TN Cav; 5-8-63 to 8-14-65; Sykes PO
GRANDY, Ashman G., Di-34-1; Pvt H Co 87th PA Inf; 2-25-65 to 6-29-65; Dickson PO; chronic diarrhea

GRANGER, Charles, H-52-2; Pvt E Co 2nd TN Inf; 9-28-61 to 11-28-64; Lookout Mt. PO
GRANGER, Morris C., H-56-3; St. Elmo PO
GRANLEES, John W., Hw-133-1; Pvt I Co 1st PA Inf; 18 Apr 61 to 21 Oct 65; Slide PO; ribs fractured in left sidGRANT, Heman W., H-52-2; 1st Lt J Co 4th MS Cav; 5-61 to 65; Lookout Mt. PO
GRANT, Henry R. (Blk), Mt-138-2; US Sol; Dist 7, New Providence PO
GRANT, Isaac, Je-136-3; Cpl B Co 9th TN Cav; Sep 63 to Nov 65; PO omitted
GRANT, John F., Mu-209-1; Margaret widow of; Pvt; Columbia PO; CONF
GRANT, John Jackson, Wa-270-1; Pvt H Co 13th TN Cav; 63 to 65; Austin's Springs PO; rheumatism
GRANT, Marcus, H-62-3; Senior Major H Co 1st MI Mech Engr; __ to 10-65; 413 West Fifth, Chattanooga PO
GRANT, Robert, C-24-1; Pvt F Co 6th Inf; 3-62 to 4-63; Boy PO
GRANT, Theodore B., Me-93-1; Pvt M Co 8th TN Cav; 3-64 to 9-16-65; Regret PO (McMinn Co.); lungs injured, measles
GRANT, Thomas B., Sq-164-5(1); Cpl A Co 9th TN Cav; 9-1-63 to 8-2-65; Brock PO
GRANT, Tom, F-46-2; alias Thomas Jones; Pvt H Co 59th TN; 63 to 66; LaGrange PO
GRANT, William, Ge-91-4; Pvt __ 3rd NC Inf; Greeneville PO; went by name of Billington
GRANT, Wm., Mo-119-2; Jane widow of; Pvt; Sweetwater PO
GRANT, William H., Lo-189-2; Elizabeth J. widow of; Pvt 9th TN Inf; 4 Oct 63 to 65; Philadelphia PO; furloughed at time of surrender; CONF
GRANT, William T., T-213-1; Pvt E Co 5th SC Inf; 11 Apr 62 to 9 Apr 65; Brighton PO; CONF
GRANTHAM, Pleasant A., Gu-48-2; Cpl M Co 10th TN Cav; 11-2-64 to 8-1-65; Tracy City PO
GRANTT, Francis M., K-180-2; Pvt D Co 6th TN Inf; 18 Apr 62 to 27 Apr 65; Ebenezer PO; scurvy, rheumatism, bronchitis
GRASSHAM, Anderson, Cu-15-1; Pvt E Co 1st TN Inf; 8-31-62 to 6-9-65; Hebbertsburg PO; spine effected and sore eyes
GRATTAN, John, O-135-1; 6th Civil Dist, Polk, Obion Co. PO
GRATY, Louis A., K-166-1; Maj 6th KY Cav; Apr 61 to Jul 65; Knoxville PO
GRAVES, A. K., K-167-5; Pvt TN Cav; 61 to 65; Knoxville PO; drawes pension
GRAVES, Benjamin, Mg-198-3; Hunnicutt PO
GRAVES, Harrison, Se-228-1(2); Pvt A Co 6th TN Inf; 8 Mar 62 to 27 Apr 65; New Knob Creek PO; was a good soldier
GRAVES, James, K-174-4(3); Pvt F Co 3rd TN Inf; 10 Feb 62 to 23 Feb 65; Graveston PO; dropsey, very feable
GRAVES, James R., Sh-159-6; Lt; Memphis PO; CONF
GRAVES, James Richard, Ru-235-1; Pvt KY; Smyrna PO; feet frost bitten
GRAVES, Jessee, Un-257-1; Pvt; New Prospect PO
GRAVES, John, Un-257-1; Isabel widow of; Pvt I Co 1st TN Vol; Aug 61 to 3 Oct 61; Sharps Chapel PO
GRAVES, John W., Bo-19-2; Pvt B Co 6th NC Cav; 10-1-62 to __ (3 yrs); South Rockford PO; stabed with bayonet
GRAVES, Thornton, Sh-191-7(3); alias Thornton Gaylor; Pvt F Co 61st IN; 63 to 65; Memphis PO
GRAVES, William, Un-259-2; Cpl E Co 2nd TN Inf; 10 Feb 62 to 9 Feb 65; Lost Creek PO; rheumatism & bronchitis, exposure in war
GRAVES, Willis, D-50-1; Emily widow of; Pvt H Co 13th US Inf; 63 to 65; 186 Crawford, Nashville PO; shot in face, died, papers lost
GRAVET, Frank, D-73-1; Pvt H Co 71st OH; 62 to 65; 705 Kascis? Av, Nashville PO; Dec 1864, portions of feet frozen off
GRAVINOR?, Benjamin F., Ro-206-2; Pvt D Co 3rd TX Cav; 13 May 61 to 28 Jun 65; Emory Gap PO; CONF
GRAY, Andrew C., Ge-83-2; Pvt E Co 4th TN Inf; 12 Nov 62 to 27 May 65; Horse Creek PO; hart disease
GRAY, Benjamin, Me-89-2; Dinah Baggert formerly widow of; Pvt B Co 44th IA Reg; Big Spring PO
GRAY, Charlie, Hr-94-1; Pvt I Co 59th TN Inf; __ to 1-31-66; Saulsbury PO
GRAY, Deasant J., Gr-74-1; Pvt I Co 59th TN Cav; 18 Apr 62 to 8 May 65; May Spring PO; CONF
GRAY, Dock, Sh-193-2; Dunlap Ave, Memphis PO
GRAY, Edward, C-33-6; US Soldier; Jellico PO
GRAY, Elizebeth, H-56-8; widow Sol US; 17th Civil Dist
GRAY, Frank F., D-72-5; Pvt G Co 4th TN Cav; Sep 15 64 to May 17 65; Nashville PO; CONF
GRAY, Henry, Gi-132-4; Sgt D Co 13th USCV; 63 to Jan 5 66; Wales PO
GRAY, Isaac B., Ge-97-3; Cpl? C Co 4th TN Inf; 6 Aug 63 to 2 __ 65 (2 yrs 3 mos 26 days); Upchurch PO; heart
GRAY, Ivie, Co-66-3(1); Elizabeth widow of; Pvt B Co 26th TN Cav; 24 Nov 62 to 15 Sep 63; Newport PO
GRAY, James H., Gi-135-2; Annie E. widow of; Pvt; Lynnville PO
GRAY, James H., O-138-3; Pvt H Co 9th? TN; 25 Mar 61 to 25 Jan 65; Elbridge PO
GRAY, Jayhew A., Sq-165-2; Pvt E Co 6th TN Mtd Inf; 9-64 to 6-65; Sunnyside PO; received an honorable disc.
GRAY, Jessee V., Hw-122-1; Pvt D Co 4th KY Mtd Inf; 31 Mar 64 to 17 Aug 65; New Canton PO
GRAY, John, Hm-108-5(4); Pvt M Co 8th TN Cav; 4 Mar 64 to 11 Sep 65; Russellville PO; heart disease & liver
GRAY, John, Ge-84-4; Pvt H Co 13th TN Cav; 9 Oct 64 to 5 Sep 65; Greenville PO; spinal infecttion, ructum
GRAY, John N., Cf-35-1; Pvt D Co 23rd TN Inf; 2 Nov 62 to 22 Dec 64; Tullahoma PO; CONF
GRAY, Joseph (Col), H-56-1; Pvt; 64 to 65; St. Elm(o) PO
GRAY, Lowry M., Gi-125-1; Pvt; Bodenham PO; could not get command; CONF
GRAY, M. L., P-151-3; E Co 6th TN Cav; 2 yrs 10 mos; Linden PO
GRAY, Marshal M., K-180-3; Pvt D Co 6th TN Inf; 18 Dec 62 to 13 Jun 65; Bearden PO; chronic rheumatism
GRAY, Mary Ann (see Mosby, James)
GRAY, Newton, Co-64-1; Pvt A Co 8th TN Cav; 10 Sep 63 to __ (9 mos 15 days); Newport PO; shot in the left leg
GRAY, Robert H., K-180-2; Pvt D Co 6th TN Inf; 14 Dec 62 to 15 Aug 65; Bearden PO
GRAY, S. S., M-108-4; Pvt F Co 52nd KY Mtd Inf; 8-24-63 to 1-18-65; Lafayette PO
GRAY, Samuel, Su-235-1; Pvt A Co 26th KY Cav; 62 to Aug 65; Bluff City PO; by horse falling down
GRAY, Thomas J., T-212-1; Pvt G Co 52nd IN Inf; 12 Dec 62 to 16 Sep 64; Brighton PO; rhumatism
GRAY, Thomas W., Mo-122-3(1); Pvt F Co 2nd TN Cav; 8-1-62 to 6-6-65; Hiwassee College PO; CONF
GRAY, Tilman, Co-66-2(1); Sgt A Co 5th TN Cav; 15 Oct 61 to 1 Mar 65; English PO; shot in right leg; CONF
GRAY, Tilman Y., Hu-103-1; Pvt E Co 10th TN Inf; 10 Jul 62 to 10 Dec 65; PO omitted
GRAY, William, Hw-142-1; Pvt B Co 3rd TN Mtd Inf; 30 Jun 64 to 25 Oct 64; Mole? PO
GRAY, William A., Ge-83-4; Pvt E Co 4th TN Inf; 12 Nov 63 to 5 Aug 65; Painters PO; liver & kidney disease
GRAY, William J., M-103-2; Pvt 9th KY Inf; 12-1-61 to 1-5-65; Lafayette PO
GRAY, Wm. K., R-163-2; Pvt B Co 6th TN Mtd Inf; 8-15-64 to 6-30-65; Graysville PO
GRAY, Yancy W., Ma-116-1; Pvt C Co 6th TN Cav; 1 Jul 62 to 10 Jul 64; Uptonville PO
GRAY, Yancy W., Ma-116-1; US Sol; 4th Civil Dist
GRAY, _____, K-154-1; Mary J. widow of; Knoxville PO
GRAYHAM, Cornelias, Mn-121-4; Sgt G Co 6th TN Cav; 9-15-62 to 7-26-65; Bethel Springs PO; cant tell when he went in & when he was mustered out
GRAYHAM, George W., Sq-164-5(1); Pvt D Co 6th TN Mtd Inf; 9-8-64 to 7-16-65; Brock PO

GRAYHAM, Robert, Hu-106-1; Pvt K Co 1st USC Art; May 63 to May 65; Waverly PO; cannot get furtherinformation now
GRAYHAM, William A., Ge-93-1; Pvt E Co 4th TN Inf; 15 Mar 63 to 2 Aug 65; Greeneville PO
GRAYHAM, William P., Hm-105-1; Pvt C Co 1st KY; 63 to 65; Morristown PO; poils (sic)
GRAYHEAL, Alex, K-176-1; Pvt B Co 9th TN Cav; 15 Aug 63 to 5 Sep 65; Hall X Roads PO
GRAYHEAL, William, K-176-1; Pvt B Co 9th TN Cav; 15 Aug 63 to 5 Sep 65; Hall X Roads PO
GRAYSON, Ben C., Jo-148-1; Pvt G Co 4th TN Inf; 25 Aug 62 to 23 May 65; Laurel Bloomery PO; rheumatis caused paralysis
GRAYSON, John R., O-142-1; Obion PO; I went twice but failed to see him, discharge is in Washington DC
GRAYSON, Joseph F., Mo-119-1; Pvt F Co 10th TN Cav; 10-20-63 to 8-4-65; Sweetwater PO; measles settled on lungs, drawing a pension
GRAYSON, Please C., Mr-96-2; Sgt I Co 10th TN Inf; 7-23-62 to 6-23-65; Sherleyton PO; deftness
GRAYSON, William, Mr-95-1; Pvt C Co 6th TN Inf; 9-2-64 to 7-11-64; Whitwell PO
GREAN, Edward, Mg-197-5; Rebecky widow of; Pvt F Co 1st TN Inf; 9 Aug 61 to ___; Crooked Fork PO; dates of discharge not known
GREAR, Joe W., G-61-1; Pvt M Co 5th TN; 63 to May 15 65; 12th Civil Dist
GREAR, Jourdon, L-100-1; Pvt C Co 55th US Col Inf; Ripley PO; contracted chronic diorea, cannot give dates
GREASLEE, Andrew, D-44-2(1); Pvt (148 2nd Bat)? Res Corps; Nashville PO
GREDIG, Abraham, K-154-1; Knoxville PO; CONF
GREEAR, Benjamin F., Fe-41-1; Pvt K Co 9th TN Cav; 7-14-63 to 9-10-65; Jamestown PO
GREEAR, John A., Hi-85-1; Pvt K Co 7th IL Inf; 3-15-63 to 4-65; Little Rock Mill PO
GREEAR, John C., Fe-41-1; Pvt K Co 9th TN Cav; 7-14-63 to 9-10-65; Jamestown PO
GREEN, Abner J., Po-149-1; Pvt I Co 5th TN Inf; 9-5-64 to 6-26-65; Hellithrope PO; Mtd Inf one yr
GREEN, Adam, L-99-1; Cpl K Co 4th US Hvy Art; 63 to 66; Durhamville PO; small pox caused from exposure
GREEN, Adam, Wa-267-2; alias Adam Fortner; Pvt B Co 12th TN Cav; 30 Nov 62 to 11 Sep 65; Jonesboro PO; chrc. rheumatism & diarhea
GREEN, Alexander, Sq-164-5(1); Sailor US and Escot SC US Navy; 1-8-62 to 1-26-64; Brock PO; vice cap pishcated (sic)
GREEN, Dan, D-77-1; Pvt B Co 17th TN Inf; __ to 65 (3 yrs); Nashville PO
GREEN, Dempsey, Hu-99-1; Pvt A Co 13th Col US Inf; Johnsonville PO
GREEN, Dury D., H-76-2; Pvt A Co 2nd TN Vol; 8-3-61 to 10-4-64; Chattanooga PO
GREEN, Ebbert, Cr-20-2; Pvt A Co 13th TN Col Inf; Aug 63 to Aug 15 65; Hollow Rock PO
GREEN, Elizabeth (see Greenfield, Green)
GREEN, Ellen (see Yokely, Scott)
GREEN, Enoch, Ge-84-2; Pvt F? Co 4th TN Inf; 15 Feb 62 to 2 Aug 65; Greeneville PO; chronic diarrea
GREEN, Fuscius C., Ho-96-1; Pvt D Co 2nd Col Cav; Nov 2 63 to May 2 65; Erin PO
GREEN, George, G-69-1; Leeann A. widow of; Rutherford PO
GREEN, George, L-108-2; Pvt; McIntyre PO; ignorant
GREEN, George, Gu-48-4(1); Cpl D Co 56th IN Inf; 62 to 65; Stouts PO (Wayne Co.); shot in left leg
GREEN, George H., H-63-3; Pvt A Co 1st MI Eng; 62 to 62 (3 mos); 606 Pine, Chattanooga PO
GREEN, George H. W., Po-149-3(2); Pvt I Co 5th TN Mtd Inf; 9-5-64 to 8-7-65; Fetzeton PO; asma from discharge
GREEN, George W., Ge-84-3; Susan widowed of; Pvt K Co 8th TN Inf; Bird Bridge PO; dates not given
GREEN, Gilbert, R-161-5; Pvt H Co 136th Inf; 5-29-65 to 6-26-66; Dayton PO
GREEN, Henry C., Wy-173-1; Cpl D Co 2nd TN Mtd Inf; 12-1-63 to 2-1-65; Lutts PO
GREEN, Henry C., Mc-113-1; Pvt K Co 10th TN Cav; 63 to 65; Riceville PO; hemorhage of lungs from measles during war; cant give exact dates
GREEN, Ike, Cr-8-2; Pvt A Co 12th AL; 1 Jun 63 to May 64; Maury City PO; CONF
GREEN, Isaac, D-45-1; alias Isaac Holms; Pvt A Co 15th US Col Inf; 11-28-63 to 4-7-66; Nashville PO
GREEN, Isaiah, T-214-1; Pvt E Co 5th US Inf; Mar 62 to 65; Dist 9
GREEN, Jack A., Hm-108-2(1); Pvt A Co 1st TN Lt Art; 8 Sep 63 to 3 Aug 65; Springvale PO; sight injured
GREEN, Jackson, Mc-118-2; Tidice widow of; Pvt B Co 10th TN Cav; 64 to ___; Joshua PO
GREEN, James, Sh-152-2; Dexter PO
GREEN?, James G., Cf-35-1; Sgt A Co 37th TN Inf; 4 Oct 61 to 19 May 65; Rhodelia PO; head disease, typhoid fever 27 yrs
GREEN, James R., Su-236-1; Pvt B Co 45th KY Cav; 28 Oct 63 to 14 Feb 65; Arcadia PO
GREEN, Jans D., Cr-20-1; Luiss E. widdow of; Pvt O Co 7th TN Cav; 9-13-63 to ___; Proffit PO; death, killed in hospitl
GREEN, Jans H., Cr-20-1; P-t B Co 7th TN Cav; 8-16-62 to 6-16-65; Proffit PO; scurvey in ___
GREEN, Jefferson, T-206-2; alias Jefferson Christopher; Pvt F Co 57th TN Inf; Sep 62 to 65; Rialto PO; discharge burned when home was burned
GREEN, Jesse P., K-182-4; 2nd TN Cav; 1 Sep 62 to 6 Jul 65; Gap Creek PO; rheumatism, lost hearing
GREEN, John, D-44-2(1); Pvt D Co 10th TN Inf; ___ to 65; Nashville PO
GREEN, John, Un-259-1; Pvt A Co 1st TN Inf; 2 Aug 61 to 17 Sep 64; Rhodelia PO; head disease, typhoid fever 27 yrs
GREEN, John, Ge-84-3; Pvt L Co 8th TN Cav; 12 Sep 63 to 11 Sep 65; Wolsey College PO; chronic dyspeptic
GREEN, John, H-60-5(2); Pvt US Col Inf; Chattanooga PO; gunshot wound in head
GREEN, John, Hm-105-1; Pvt G Co 9th TN Cav; 24 Oct 64 to Sep 65; Russellvill PO; deafness & rheumatism
GREEN, John, K-161-1; Mima Petty widow of; Knoxville PO
GREEN, John, H-70-2(1); Margaret Hergan formerly widow of; Pvt 9th TN Cav; 8-63 to 7-65; Chattanooga PO
GREEN, John C., Cr-20-2; Mary P. widow of; Pvt I Co 7th TN Cav; Oct 63 to ___; Profit PO; scurvy & exemer
GREEN, John E., Hw-118-1; Pvt D.Co. 6th IN Cav; 11 Jun 63 to 9 Jul 65; St. Clair PO; rupture
GREEN, Joseph (see David, Joe)
GREEN, Joseph, Br-9-3; Pvt E Co 1st US Hvy Art; 3-3-64 to 3-31-66; Cleveland PO
GREEN, Joseph M., O-132-1; Pvt E Co 6th TN; Oct 63 to Jul 65; Clayton PO; wounded at Ft. Pillow
GREEN, Joseph R., K-179-5; Pvt A Co 35th KY Cav; 27 Jun 63 to Jul 65; Concord PO
GREEN, Joseph S., Co-67-6; Cpl L Co 9th TN Cav; 1 Jun 63 to 11 Sep 65; PO omitted
GREEN, Joseph W., Ct-35-3; Pvt G Co 13th TN Cav; 9-24-63 to 9-5-65; Lineback PO; in US Army
GREEN, Key, J-81-1; Pvt D Co 9th KY; 9-13-61 to 2-13-63; 8th Civil Dist
GREEN, Kutildey, K-184-2; Rutildal widow of; Pvt B Co 5th TN Inf; 23 Oct 63 to Apr 65; Thorn Grove PO
GREEN, Leander N., Co-67-6; Pvt C Co 2nd NC Mtd Inf; Jan 64 to 13 Jun 65; PO omitted
GREEN, Levi, R-106-1; Pvt C Co 7th TN Mtd; 6-64 to 6-26-65; 6th Civil Dist
GREEN, Levi, Di-31-1; 2nd Civil Dist
GREEN, Lugana E., He-58-2; Sol; 7th Civil Dist
GREEN, Lunia, Su-243-1; Sgt G Co 5th OH Inf; 28 Sep 63 to 25 Mar 65; Bristol PO; shot through 2 legs, reenlisted
GREEN, Mark, D-49-1; Pvt I Co 12th TN; 1 yr 8 mos; Nashville PO; soldier dont remember dates
GREEN, Mark (Col), H-56-4; Pvt C Co 1st Art; 2-7-64 to 3-31-66; St. Elmo PO
GREEN, Marion, La-111-2; Pvt 3rd ___ Cav; 62 to 65; PO omitted; wounded in the thigh; CONF
GREEN, Martha A. (see Greer, James)
GREEN, Mary, Hy-82-3(5); widow; Pvt; 8th Dist

GREEN, Michael D., C-8-1; Pvt H Co 9th TN Cav; 7-19-63 to 8-23-65; Well Spring PO; rheumatism; pension $14 per month
GREEN, Miles, Sh-161-1; US Sol; 16th Dist
GREEN, Mordica, Gu-46-3(1); Pvt E Co 1st TN (AL) Cav; 10-10-63 to 6-16-64; Tracy City PO
GREEN, Nelson (see Nelson, Green)
GREEN, Richard, Un-257-1; Pvt E Co 3rd TN Inf; 63 to 65; New Prospect PO; gun shot
GREEN, Richard, D-99-3; Pvt B Co 1st TN Cav; 10 Apr 62 to 10 Apr 65; State Penitentiary PO
GREEN, Robert, Sh-204-1; Pvt; Franklin Ave, Memphis PO
GREEN, Robert, Se-229-1; Pvt H Co 9th TN Cav; Pigeon Forge PO; rheumatism
GREEN, Robert S., Wa-262-1; Jeraldine widow of; Pvt I Co 1st TN Cav; Washington College PO
GREEN, Rosa (see Pitts, Larkin)
GREEN, Roten, Me-94-2; Pvt G Co 1st TN Inf; 12-13-62 to 12-18-63; Euchee PO
GREEN, Ruben P., K-172-3; Cpl C Co 2nd NC Inf; 26 Sep 63 to 6-26-65; 14th Dist, South Knoxville PO
GREEN, Thomas, Un-257-1; Pvt E Co 3rd TN Inf; Feb 62 to Feb 65; New Prospect PO; mumps & measles settled on lungs
GREEN, Thomas, D-94-1; Pvt A Co 101st OH Inf; Aug 4 62 to Aug 26 63; c/o E. R. Campbell, Nashville PO; contracted dysentery; helpless & in need/small pension
GREEN, Thomas H., J-81-3; Pvt K Co 1st TN; 1-1-62 to 5-1-62; Quiz PO (Putnam Co.)
GREEN, Wade, Co-62-3; Pvt C Co 8th TN Vol; 1 Jan 63 to 30 Jun 65; Bybee PO; piles & direah, ingery on head
GREEN, Wash, L-108-1; Pvt L Co 4th US C Art; 25 Feb 64 to 25 Feb 66; Glimpville PO
GREEN, Watson, Sh-173-1; 151 Union St, Memphis PO
GREEN, William, Sh-169-1; Pvt D Co Freemans, Baily Guard?; Sep 61 to Jan 62; Memphis PO
GREEN, William, C-27-4; Pvt I Co 1st TN Inf; 7 mos; Jacksboro PO
GREEN, William C., H-59-2; 2nd Lt NY Inf; 61 to 62 (8 mos); Chattanooga PO; wounded left leg
GREEN, William F., G-71-3; Pvt L Co 27th TN Inf; 12 May 61 to 20 Jul 64; PO omitted; CONF
GREEN, William L., Me-90-2(1); Sgt Major 1st Regt US Vol Eng; 6-62 to 65; Goodfield PO
GREEN, William N., Po-148-2; Cpl I Co 5th TN Mtd Inf; 9-10-64 to 6-26-65; Benton PO
GREEN, William R., Ja-86-1; Elizabeth J. widow of; Pvt C Co 5th TN Inf; 3 yrs; Oottewah PO; side pleurisy & heart disease
GREEN, Willice Mlnc-121-2; Lizey Jane widow of; Pvt A Co 6th TN Cav; 62 to 26 Jul 65; Bethel Springs PO
GREENE, A. J., Ha-110-2; Pvt B Co 8th TN Cav; 11 Mar 62 to 10 Apr 65; Luther PO; diarhea
GREENE, Andrew J., Wh-182-1; Pvt I Co 3rd KY Cav; 3-28-64 to 7-15-65; Doyle's Sta. PO
GREENE, Harris S., S-217-2; Maj 4th AR Cav; 24 Aug 61 to 5 Jul 65; Oneida PO; wounded in both hands
GREENE, Joseph, Ge-87-3; Pvt C Co 8th TN Inf; 1 Jan 63 to 30 Jun 65; Pates Hill PO
GREENE, Joseph, Ha-113-2; Pvt B Co 1st TN Cav; 1 Jun 62 to 5 Jun 65; Sneedville PO
GREENE, Joseph, Mo-129-1; Sarah widow of; Pvt; Loco PO
GREENE, Perry, Ha-116-1; Pvt E Co 9th TN Cav; Sep 63 to Sep 15 65; Luther PO
GREENE, Samuel T., K-182-4; Pvt D Co 2nd TN Vol Cav; Sep 62 to 6 Jul 65; Gap Creek PO
GREENE, Sebert, Ha-113-2; Pvt G Co 8th TN Inf; 27 Jul 63 to 30 Jun 65; Sneedville PO
GREENE, Sol D., Rb-227-1; Pvt C Co 16th KY Cav; 12 Feb 64 to 25 May 65; Turnersville PO; lung disease
GREENE, Thomas, Ro-210-4; Pvt; Rockwood PO; CONF
GREENE, Washington, Ru-248-1; 9th MI Inf; 61 to 63; Murfreesboro PO; Wash was a teamster
GREENE, William H., H-69-1; Cpl H Co 136th GA Inf; 2-65 to 1-4-66; Chattanooga PO
GREENFIELD, Green, Mu-205-2; Elizabeth Green widow of; Pvt 39th OH Inf; 63 to 65; Williamsport PO; papers lost
GREENLEE, Alaxander H., Gr-75-2; Pvt G Co 2nd TN Cav; 12 Oct 62 to 6 Jul 65; Tampico PO; hearnia and varico vains
GREENLEE, James L., Jr., K-167-6; Lt? D Co 4th GA? Inf; Apr 62 to 65; Knoxville PO
GREENLEE, James L., Ge-90-2; Mary J. widow of; Pvt D Co 4th TN Inf; 30 Jan 63 to 15 Aug 65; Greenville PO; eye weakness, widow dont remember
GREENLEE, John, Mc-112-1; Margaret widow of; Pvt Inf; 64 to 65; Athens PO; no papers to get exact dates
GREENLEE, Saml. J., Gr-70-1; Pvt B Co 8th TN Cav; 15 May 63 to 11 Sep 65; Rutledge PO; piles & lungs aff.
GREENLEE, Saml. P., Gr-70-1- Malissia widow of; Sgt 8th TN Cav; Rutledge PO; co & dates unknown
GREENLOW, William E., Mu-210-7; Pvt A Co 1st TN Cav; 1 Jul 62 to May 65; Spring Hill PO; CONF
GREENWAY, Edward M., Lo-192-1; Cpl I Co 2nd TN; Jun 22 62 to 21 Jun 65; Coytee PO; chronic rheumatism & lung trouble
GREENWAY, James K., Ct-41-2; Pvt H Co 13th TN Cav; 9-24-63 to 9-5-65; South Wattauga PO; gunshot through left thy
GREENWAY, John H., Ge-91-5; Pvt G Co 4th TN Inf; 8 May 62 to 8 Jul 65; Greeneville PO; scurvey hemroids & others
GREENWOOD, Bartley G., H-56-7; Pvt C Co 129th IN Inf; 1-30-64 to 9-13-65; St. Elmo PO
GREER, Andrew, Hw-133-4; Pvt J Co 18th TN Cav; Sep 63 to Sep 65; Fry PO
GREER, Benjamin F., Cl-58-1; Pvt I Co 3rd TN Inf; 2-7-62 to 6-8-62; Davo PO; lungs affected; discharged on surgeons certif.
GREER, George, D-75-3; Lt D Co 1st TN Inf; Apr 61 to 1 Sep 64; Stewarts Ferry PO; CONF
GREER, Henry C., Bl-4-3; Sgt C Co 43rd TN Inf; 7-1-62 to 5-1-65; Pikeville PO; CONF
GREER, James, Hn-70-1; Mary A. widow of; Pvt B Co 7th TN Cav; Paris PO; died in prison
GREER, James, Cy-27-5(3); Martha A. Green widow of; Clementsville PO; died in service
GREER, James E., Gr-75-2; Cpl B Co 8th TN Cav; 11 Jun 63 to 11 Sep 65; Tampico PO; varicocele, rheumatism & heart trouble 27 yrs
GREER, Jessie, Cl-49-2; Pvt A Co 2nd TN Cav; 8-1-62 to 7-6-65; Zeb PO; general disability
GREER, John A., P-151-2; Susan widow of; Pvt A Co 2nd TN Mtd Inf; Mar 64 to May 65; Aldon PO
GREER, John P., Wi-276-1; Pvt D Co 10th TN Cav; Oct 62 to 22 May 65; Beechville PO; CONF
GREER, Joseph, K-158-2; Pvt E Co 3rd TN Inf; Jul 64 to May 65; Knoxville PO; chronic rheumatism
GREER, Joseph A., P-156-1; Lt G Co 20th TN Inf; 6-61 to 63; Lobelville PO; shot in left arm
GREER, Lawson, Gr-77-2; Maud E. widow of; Pvt A Co 1st TN Cav; 62 to 65; Y.Z. PO; husband died of smallpox
GREER, Noah N., Gr-76-1; Pvt F Co 1st TN Cav; 1 Mar 62 to 30 Mar 65; Tampico PO
GREER, William, P-156-2; Huldy widow of; Lobelville PO; CONF
GREER, William H., Ge-84-2; Pvt L Co 8th TN Cav; 12 Sep 63 to 11 Sep 65; Greenville PO; dis. back an hips
GREER, Williburn R., K-165-3; Wagonner C Co 1st TN Cav; 6 Aug 62 to 6 Jul 65; 72 Hauer Ave, Knoxville PO
GREGG, James, Br-7-4; Artificer E Co 4th TN Cav; 3-15-63 to 7-12-65; Cleveland PO; chronic diarhea
GREGG, John, Co-60-1; Pvt Co B 58th IL; 7-20-63 to 4-1-66; Peanut PO; broken finger & rheumatism
GREGG, John R., U-246-2; Pvt F Co 3rd NC Mtd Inf; 30 Jul 64 to Aug 65; Limonite PO
GREGG, Joseph, Ms-171-1; Pvt F Co 4th TN Cav; 1 May 63 to 12 Jul 63; Belfast PO
GREGG, Joseph U., K-156-3; Pvt A Co 1st VA Hvy Art; 4 Mar 62 to 2 Apr 65; 89 E. Cumberland St, Knoxville PO; CONF
GREGG, William, Co-60-1; K Co 8th TN Inf; 2-14-63 to 6-20-64; Syrensburg PO; diarhea
GREGORY, David, Ja-85-1; Pvt E Co 8th TN Inf; 6-7-63 to 6-30-65; Birchwood PO
GREGORY, David S., Mu-209-5; Pvt A Co Gants Bat; Nov 62 to 65; Columbia PO; shot in leg at Nashville; CONF

GREGORY, Frank, Sh-149-3; Pvt H Co 55th AL Inf; 3 Feb 63 to 66; Frazer PO
GREGORY, George W., Dy-25-5(1); Pvt 15th TN Cav; Apr 64 to M 65; Newbern PO; CONF
GREGORY, George W., Sh-175-2; 101 Vance St, Memphis PO
GREGORY, Green A., C-8-2; Pvt C Co 4th TN Cav; 8-15-62 to 8-15-65; Powells River PO; relapsion measels etc., also rheumatism
GREGORY, Jesse A., Sm-168-2; Pvt B Co 8th TN Inf; 3-27-65 to 8-27-65; Pleasant Shade PO; weak back and breast
GREGORY, John, C-28-1; Cpl C Co 9th TN Cav; 2 yrs 6 mos; Fincastle PO
GREGORY, John K., white, Li-154-1; Sgt N Co 73rd MO Cav; 1-3-64 to 3-20-65; Clardy Ville PO; he enlisted in MO
GREGORY, John M., Dy-25-8(4); Pvt D Co 13th TN Inf; 5-61 to close of war; Newbern PO; wounded at Shilow; CONF
GREGORY, Samuel, Bo-22-2; Pvt C Co 1st US Art; 2-12-64 to 3-31-66; Bank PO
GREGORY, Simpson L., M-106-1; Pvt E Co 1st TN Mtd Inf; 1-12-64 to 1-22-65; Union Camp PO; shot in left ankle, liver & kidney dis., measles resulting in; applied for pension
GREGORY, Thomas, H-49-10; Pvt G Co 3rd TN Cav; __ to 6-65; Daisy PO
GRENADE, James, M-107-4; Pvt F Co 38th IN Inf; 11-10-64 to 7-15-65; Red Boiling Spring PO
GRENADE, Semma A., M-107-6; widow of US Sol; 6th Civil Dist
GRESHAM, George W., Dy-25-7(3); Pvt; Newbern PO; CONF
GRESHAM, Thomas M., Dy-29-4; Pvt F Co 9th MS Inf; 8 Jun 62 to 15 May 65; Trimble PO; CONF
GRESS, Payton (see Randle, John)
GREVE, Chas. M., H-60-4; Pvt B Co 2nd KS Cav--10-1-61 to 10-3-62; Sgt 3rd KS Battery--fall 62 to 11-22-64; Chattanooga PO
GREY, Anthony, Sh-192-1; US unit; Henetta St, Memphis PO
GREY, Green, G-57-6; Pvt; 1 yr 6 mos; Yorkville PO; CONF
GREY, Henry (See Horton, Henry)
GREY, Joseph, Sh-146-1; Pvt A Co 55th I?; autumn 63 to autumn 65; Woodstock PO; wounded at Guntown, MS, about May 1864 in the left foot by shell and hurt in back by caison
GREY, Mat (see Horton, Madice)
GREY, Richard F., Wy-175-1; Pvt A Co 2nd TN Mtd Inf; 3-10-64 to 5-13-65; Whittens Stand PO
GREY, Whitney, Sn-254-1; Pvt F Co 101st US Col Inf; 10-1-64 to 1-12-66; Hendersonville PO
GRICE, William R., He-63-2; Pvt H Co 7th? TN Cav; 62 to 65; Long PO; 13 mos Andersonville
GRIDER, Henry S., M-108-2(1); Mary H. widow of; Pvt Co 9th KY Inf; 61 to 65; Salt Lick PO; shot through arm (right)
GRIDER, John, Cy-27-2; Pvt E Co 1st TN Mtd Inf; 10-23-63 to 1-65; Clementsville PO
GRIDER, William H., Cy-27-3(1); Margret I. widow of; Pvt A Co 8th TN Mtd Inf; 3-18-65 to 8-17-65; Miles Cross Roads PO
GRIER, Harden, H-67-2; Sgt F Co 40th US Col Inf; 4-7-65 to 4-25-66; Chattanooga PO; now suffers withchronic diarrhoea
GRIFFEN, John E., Co-62-3; Pvt A Co 2nd NC Inf; Oct 63 to 29 Feb 65; Rankins PO; wounds & neales
GRIFFIN, Martha J., Wa-268-4; widow of US Soldier; Johnson City PO
GRIFFETH, Harris L., Mr-96-3(2); Pvt T Co 12th TN Cav; 1-64 to 1-65; Whitwell PO
GRIFFETH, John R., Mr-96-2; Pvt C Co 6th TN Inf; 10-30-64 to 1-30-65; Shirleton PO
GRIFFETH, Josiah, Dk-32-5; PVt K Co 5th TN Cav; 6-8-63 to __ (6 mos); Liberty PO; liver and lung trouble, taken sick & never mustered
GRIFFETH, Martha H. (see White, William R.)
GRIFFETH, Thomas C., D-58-2; Celia widow of; 4th Sgt H Co 3rd US KY; Nashville PO
GRIFFETH, William E., Mr-96-2; Pvt G Co 6th US Vol; 3-24-65 to 10-12-66; Whitwell PO
GRIFFIN, Acy J., Hy-84-1; Pvt D Co 35th MS; 2 May 62 to 28 Apr 65; Forked Deer PO; CONF
GRIFFIN, Andrew, Hd-55-1; Lucinda B. widow of; Pvt D Co 6th TN Cav; 19 Mar 62 to 64; Clifton PO; killed in war
GRIFFIN, Calab, Pu-141-2; Pvt K Co 27th IL Inf; 61 to 64; Dry Valley PO; discharge at expiration time
GRIFFIN, George, Sh-144-1; Pvt D Co 1st LA; 62 to 65; Brunswick PO
GRIFFIN, Isaac, Hr-86-2; Grand Junction PO
GRIFFIN, Jacob M., K-183-2; Pvt L Co 1st TN Cav; 1 Apr 63 to 19 Jun 65; Riverdale PO
GRIFFIN, James, P-150-1; 2nd Lt C Co 3rd KY Cav; to 64; Dist 2
GRIFFIN, James H., B-14-1; Pvt F Co 1st TN Vidette Cav, M TN; 8-27-63 to 6-16-65; Bedford PO
GRIFFIN, James H., K-168-1; Pvt C Co 6th TN Inf; 18 Dec 62 to 20 Jun 65; Hercules PO
GRIFFIN, James K., K-155-1; Pvt F Co 3rd TN Cav; 4 Aug 63 to 20 Jun 65; Knoxville PO
GRIFFIN, James M., Sn-261-5(4); Pvt C Co 30th TN Inf; 10-61 to 2-62; New Roe, Allen Co. KY, PO; came home on furlow; CONF
GRIFFIN, James P., Gr-77-1; Pvt K Co 3rd TN Inf; 5 Feb 64 to 2 Aug 65; Y. Z. PO; piles
GRIFFIN, James P., Tr-269-1; Pvt G Co 2nd TN Cav; Dec 61 to 65; John PO
GRIFFIN, Jessie E., Su-238-1; Pvt B Co 3rd US Vol; 14 Oct 64 to 29 Nov 65; Piney Flats PO; rheumatism, hart trouble
GRIFFIN, Jobe, Co-69-2; Pvt I Co 2nd TN Cav; 18 Sep 63 to 18 Feb 65; Newport PO; no pension
GRIFFIN, Joel J., Hd-53-1; Cpl D Co 6th TN Cav; 24 Oct 62 to 26 Jul 65; Coffee Landing PO; rheumatism
GRIFFIN, Joel R., D-51-1; Col 82nd GA Cav; Apr 26 61 to Apr 1 65; 500 North College, Nashville PO; suffering from wounds; CONF
GRIFFIN, John, K-184-3; Sarah wife of; Pvt; Thorn Grove PO
GRIFFIN, Jos. B., Wl-291-1; Labanon PO; Sol US Inf; 18 Apr 62 to __; PO omitted; Knoxville?
GRIFFIN, Pateric J., K-171-3(2); Pvt D Co 6th TN Inf; 18 Apr 62 to __; PO omitted; Knoxville?
GRIFFIN, Richard, K-182-4; Fanny widow of; Pvt G Co 9th TN Vol Inf; Sep 62 to __; Knoxville PO; died of diarrhoea in US Service
GRIFFIN, Rufus H., Un-254-1; Sgt A Co 3rd TN Inf; 18 Sep 64 to __; Paulett PO; piles & diarhea
GRIFFIN, Wm. B., Dy-21-1; 1st Lt B Co 55th TN Inf; 20 May 62 to 65; Chestnut Bluff PO; CONF
GRIFFIN, William T., B-14-1; Pvt F Co 1st TN Vidette Cav, M TN; 8-27-63 to 6-16-65; Bedford PO; lost leg by saw mill, goes on a crutch
GRIFFIS, James R., H-49-10; Pvt E Co 1st TN Inf; Daisy PO
GRIFFIS, William L., Mg-198-4; Nancy L. widdow of; Pvt E Co 1st TN Inf; 20 Aug 61 to 9 Apr 63; Emory Gap PO; Pvt C Co 2nd KY Cav; 26 Mar 64 to 17 Jun 65
GRIFFITH, A. S., D-99-3; Capt D Co 1st TN Inf; 9 Aug 61 to 17 Sep 64; State Penitentiary PO; thrown from horse & shoulder mashed
GRIFFITH, Andrew J., We-221-3; Martha L. widow of; Pvt; 61 to 65; Martin PO; Bud died from sickness in war; CONF
GRIFFITH, Hamilton, S-218-1; Pvt A Co 4th __ Cav; 1 May 64 to __; Huntsville PO; Co E 7th TN Cav; Co H 9th TN
GRIFFITH, Henry, H-59-3; Hester widow of; Pvt IN Inf; 62 to __; Chattanooga PO
GRIFFITH, Isaac D., Dk-31-2; Pvt K Co 5th TN Cav; 1-1-63 to 8-14-65; Alexandria PO
GRIFFITH, Jacob, Mr-97-1; Pvt C Co TN Inf; 8-20-64 to 6-30-65; PO omitted
GRIFFITH, James, Dk-31-2; Sgt I Co 5th TN Cav; 2-10-63 to 8-14-65; Alexandria PO
GRIFFITH, Jasper B., La-113-1; Pvt E Co 3rd WI Inf; 18 Apr 61 to 6 Jul 65; Lawrenceburg PO; right lun affected
GRIFFITH, Joel, Mg-199-2; Cloa widow of; 1st TN Inf; PO omitted
GRIFFITH, Joseph, S-218-2; Pvt C Co 9th TN Cav; 7 Jun 62 to 7 Jul 65; PO omitted
GRIFFITH, Prince, Gi-127-6; Pvt H Co 111th US Col Inf; Pulaski PO; dates lost
GRIFFITH, William, S-218-3; Pvt F Co 7th TN Inf; 7 Jun 62 to 63; Hughett PO
GRIFFITH, William L., Ro-201-4(2); Hattie widow of; Kingston PO

GRIFFITS, Simeon, Bo-14-2(1); Cpl C Co 89th IN Inf; 8-25-62 to 7-19-65; Mint PO
GRIFFITTS, Elijah, Lo-193-1; Pvt C Co 1st Hvy Art; 3 Feb 64 to 31 Mar 66; Unitia PO; defect in both eyes
GRIFFITTS, Lewis, K-164-3; Pvt C Co; __ to 66; PO omitted (Knoxville)
GRIFFY, John, H-73-2(1); Pvt; Chattanooga PO
GRIGBY, Alfred, T-215-2; Pvt G Co 61st TN Inf; Mason PO
GRIGG, James T., Jo-151-1; Harriet L. widow of; Pvt D Co 3rd NC Inf; 8 Nov 64 to 8 Aug 65; Stump Knob PO; lung disease, killed after discharge
GRIGGS, James D., Wy-177-2; Cpl A Co 10th TN Inf; 4-16-62 to 5-25-65; Waynesboro PO; frozent
GRIGORY, Benard, H-106-3(2); Pvt I Co 1st TN Inf; Hillsdale PO; applied for invalid pension
GRIGSBIE, Jesse, Hw-132-5; Pvt D Co 31st TN Cav; Fall 61 to Apr 65; Strahl PO; lung trobles; CONF
GRIGSBY, Alexander, Sh-144-1; Pvt G Co 15th US Col Inf; Feb 1 64 to Apr 7 66; Brunswick PO
GRIGSBY, Benjamin F., Me-91-1; Decatur PO
GRIGSBY, Candas, Gi-129-3; Dist No 9
GRIGSBY, Henry H., K-167-4; Pvt B Co 1st US Hvy; 22 May 64 to 1 Mar 66; Knoxville PO; liver complaint
GRIGSBY, Jacobe, Gi-129-1; Pvt B Co 12th TN Inf; 31 Jul 63 to 18 Jan 66; Elkton PO
GRIGSBY, Joseph, Hm-103-2; Capt C Co 1st TN Lt Art; 16 Sep 63 to 1 Aug 65; Morristown PO; chronic diarrhea
GRIGSBY, Perlina, Gi-129-1; widow; Elkton PO
GRIGSBY, Samuel, Hw-132-1; Pvt B Co 60th TN Inf; 62 to Apr 65; Strahl PO; was not discharged until close war; CONF
GRIGSBY, Thomas, Po-149-3(2); Eliza widow of; Ocoee PO; regment & co. not known
GRIGSBY, William E., Ja-85-3; Pvt G Co 3rd TN Cav; 8-31-63 to 8-3-65; Georgtown PO
GRIGSTON, James M., Jo-149-1; Pvt D Co 13th TN Cav; 24 Sep 63 to 5 Sep 65; Mountain City PO; frost afect lungs and rheumatism
GRILES, Rufus S., K-177-1; Pvt D Co 8th TN Cav; 1 Jan 63 to 10 May 65; Dante PO; measles and rheumatism; CONF
GRILLS, James, A-8-2; Pvt K Co 5th TN Inf; 8-9-62 to 6-12-65; Scarborough PO; crippled in ryte hand by explosion shell
GRIM?, Phillip, D-44-3; Nashville PO
GRIME, William H., Pu-144-3; Pvt C Co 8th TN Mtd Inf; 2-21-65 to 8-17-65; Hudgins PO; rheumatism & piles
GRIMES, Bengiman F., Ch-12-1; Pvt MS Cav; 8-1-62 to 5-1-65; Custer Point PO; CONF
GRIMES, Dusom (see Harmar, Moses)
GRIMES, Henry, Sol, Sq-165-3; 6th Civil Dist
GRIMES?, James M., We-221-6(2); Pvt E Co 15th KY Cav; Apr 63 to Oct 63; Martin PO; none but constitution weakened
GRIMES, Jas. M., C-34-2; Pvt 2nd TN Inf; 61 to (deserted about 4 mos); Elk Valley PO; conscripted CONF
GRIMES, John S., Hu-103-4; Pvt; 10 Jul 61 to 12 Feb 64; PO omitted
GRIMES, Peter, Hw-131-1; Pvt A Co 33rd NY Inf; May 63 to 16 May 65; PO omitted
GRIMES, Robert W., Wy-171-3; Pvt A Co 10th TN Inf; 5-5-62 to 5-25-65; Sorby PO; pain in the head
GRIMES, Samuel, O-135-1; Pvt E Co 2nd PA Inf; 6 Oct 64 to 7 Nov 65; PO omitted
GRIMES, William, La-117-4; Martha C. widow of; 48th TN Inf; May __ to __; 15th Dist; CONF
GRIMES, William, Lo-189-1; Mary widow of; Pvt A Co 2nd TN Inf; 63 to died 23 Aug 64; Philadelphia PO; died in prison at Andersonville; taken prisoner at Carter Station TN, taken to Libby & then to Andersonville
GRIMSLEY, Jas. M., R-163-2; Cpl F & K Cos 5th TN Inf; 11-26-62 to 6-30-65; Graysville PO; shell wound left hand, transfered to 110 Wm. 2 Batt VA
GRIMSLEY, Meridieth M., He-63-2; Pvt A Co 7th TN Cav; Mar 24 62 to Jul 22 62; Long PO
GRINDSTAFF, Isaac, Co-65-1; Pvt; Sep 21 63 to 5 Sep 65; Big Creek PO; back & kidney diseas, result of mumps, pensioned
GRINDSTAFF, Isaac, Ct-44-2; Pvt G Co 13th TN Cav; 9-15-63 to 9-5-65; Hampton PO; hips and breast mashed, now rheumatism
GRINDSTAFF, Jacob F., Jo-152-2; Pvt M Co 13th TN Cav; 2 Feb 64 to 21 May 64; Mouth of Doe PO
GRINDSTAFF, James D., Dk-31-3; Pvt K Co 5th TN Cav; 7-8-63 to 8-14-65; Alexandria PO; piles 25 yrs & fistula PO; orchitis 5 yrs
GRINDSTAFF, John, Bo-13-3(1); Pvt L Co 2nd TN Cav; 11-20-63 to 7-6-65; Miser PO; injured in left side and back
GRINDSTAFF, Maraly (see Roberts, John)
GRINDSTAFF, William C., Bo-15-2; Quartermaster Sgt L Co 2nd TN Cav; 9-8-63 to 7-6-65; Blockhouse PO
GRINNEY?, Joshua C., Ha-115-1; Pvt I Co 54th VA Cav; 12 Oct 62 to 7 Aug 63; Alanthers Hill PO; not disabled, yet living; CONF
GRISHAM, Edmund I., Br-14-2; Mary J. widow of; Pvt E Co 5th TN Mtd Inf; __ to 65; McDonald PO; died of bronchitis
GRISHAM, George E., Wa-274-3; Margaret J. widow of; Capt I Co 8th TN Cav; Jonesboro PO
GRISHAM, J. H., Mc-117-4; Pvt A Co 10th TN Cav; 8-1-63 to 8-12-65; Cog Hill PO; loss of left leg and rheumatism
GRISHAM, James M., K-154-6(3); Pvt I Co 8th TN Cav; 11 Sep 66; Knoxville PO
GRISHAM, James M., Wa-272-3; Pvt I Co 8th TN Cav; 63 to __; Clara PO; bronchitis
GRISHAM, Samuel, Cy-26-2; Ellza A. widow of; Sgt E Co 5th KY Cav; 62 to 64; Ascot PO; disabled from poisoning
GRISHAM, Thomas Y., Wi-276-1; Pvt C Co 11th TN Cav; Oct 62 to Nov 63; Beechville PO; CONF
GRISSOM, Americus, Sm-168-2; Pvt F Co 1st TN Inf; 1-64 to 5-15-65; Pleasant Shade PO; mump and throwed by horse, one side partially useless
GRISSOM, William W., B-3-1; Cpl C Co 5th TN Cav; 8-14-62 to 6-25-65; Shelbyville PO; deafness 11-64
GRISWOLD, Osmund C., Cu-17-1; 2nd Lt G Co 56th IL Inf; 11-23-61 to 3-4-64; Crossville PO; chronic diarrhea; reenlisted, served 1 yr
GRIUR?, George W., A-7-3; Pvt K Co 5th __; 2-5-64 to 6-30-65; Robertsville PO
GROGG, Louis G., Su-239-2; Horace PO
GROLBY?, Lewis, J-78-2; Pvt I Co 57th IN Inf; 12-27-61 to 1-19-65; Highland PO; hearing, sight, not able to do anything
GRONVILLE, Cecil, Me-91-1; Pvt C Co 3rd TN Cav; 11-1-62 to 8-3-65; Decatur PO; disease of lungs from effects of measles
GROOM, William H., Cr-20-2; Pvt B Co 7th TN Cav; 8-15-62 to 8-9-65; Profit PO; scurvey 25 yrs, can--in the service
GROOMS, Frank, D-102-1; Pvt G Co 12th TN Inf; Jordonia PO
GROOMS, Wash. W., We-230-2; Pvt C Co 16th KY Inf; Jan 15 61 to Jan 15 64; PO omitted
GROONS, Isaac R., Cr-20-1; Sarah J. widow of; Pvt I Co 7th TN Cav; 11-63 to __; Proffit PO; death, dide with scurvy
GROSLUR, Samuel S., De-23-2; Pvt G Co 27th TN Inf; 61 to 65; Bath Springs PO; CONF
GROSS, Abe, C-27-1; Pvt F Co 6th TN Inf; 3-10-62 to 3-30-65; Jacksboro PO
GROSS, Charles, Bl-3-5; Pvt B Co 10th MS? Inf; 10-22-61 to 10-5-65; Tankark PO; cron. rheumatism
GROSS, George W., C-28-2(1); Pvt D Co 58th KY Mtd Inf; 8-29-64 to 9-15-65; Big Creek Gap PO; liver & kidney disease
GROSS, James, D-49-2; Nashville PO; only knows he was a soldier
GROSS, Jeremiah, D-49-2; Sarah widow of; Cpl H Co 14th US Cav; 61 to 28 Mar 65; all she knows; PO omitted
GROSS, John, Sm-171-1; Sarah C. widow of; Pvt D Co 5th KY Mtd Inf; 9-1-61 to 10-14-65; Chestnut Mound PO
GROSS, John, Ja-85-2; Cpl E Co 5th TN Inf; 3-2-62 to 4-4-65; Birchwood PO
GROSS, Lewis, H-58-5; Pvt C Co 5th TN Inf; Retro PO; hernia, discharged on surgeon's certificate

GROSS, Loranzo, Sn-262-3(2); Sgt E Co 58th MO? Inf; 17 Jun 63 to 17 Apr 65; Fountain Head PO; shot in right side
GROSS, Thomas, Hw-126-1; Pvt K Co 13th? TN Cav; 1 Jan 65 to Jul 65; Fishers Creek PO; dates given from memory
GROVE, Perry, Sh-191-7(3); 343 South St, Memphis PO
GROVER, George P., Le-118-1; Pvt; Hakenwald PO; gone from home, could not get dates
GROVER?, John W., P-150-2; US Sol; 1st Dist
GROVES, Abraham, Mo-127-1; Pvt; Notchy PO
GROVES, Jacob A., T-216-2; 11th Civil Dist
GROVES, Patison, Hr-97-2(1); Sgt M Co 1st AL Cav; 6 Feb 63 to 12 May 66; PO omitted
GROVES, Press (Black), Sn-264-1; Pvt A Co; 63 to 65; Portland PO; this man joined at Gallatin, TN, his papers lost, mustered out at Huntsville, AL
GRUBB, Alford C.?, We-223-2; Pvt A Co 25th VA Pat?; 1 Jul 61 to 2 Jul 65; Palmersville PO; CONF
GRUBB, Franklin B., Ro-203-8; Pvt G Co 1st TN Inf; 9 Aug 61 to 17 Sep 64; Burns Mills PO
GRUBB, Isaac J., K-178-1; Pvt F Co 5th TN Inf; 25 Feb 62 to 29 Mar 65; Hardin Valley PO
GRUBB, James M., Me-90-1; Pvt L Co 4th TN Cav; Tabor PO
GRUBB, James M., Lo-194-2; Pvt D Co 5th TN Inf; 28 Mar 62 to 23 Sep 64; Muddy Creek PO
GRUBB, King W., Lo-195-1; Pvt F Co 5th TN Inf; 25 Feb 62 to 29 Mar 65; Eaton's X Roads PO
GRUBB, Marshall J., Gr-76-2(1); Indian Ridge PO; bill now pending for muster roll
GRUBB, Peter J., Mc-116-1; Pvt D Co 5th TN Art; 8-31-61 to 1-27-65; Riceville PO; vara course veins in left leg
GRUBB, Ruben L., Me-89-1; Pvt D Co 7th TN Reg; 65 to 2-65; Big Spring PO
GRUBB, Samuel, Hw-125-4; Pvt C Co 63rd TN Inf; 12 Aug 62 to 27 J 65; Surgoinsville PO; shot under left shoulder blade
GRUBBS, David N., Ge-88-2; Eliza C. widow of; Pvt D Co 8th TN Inf; 63 to 7 Aug 64; Marvin PO; wounded in leg below knee
GRUM, Sam., Sh-175-1; Pvt A Co 55th Inf; 62 to 65; Memphis PO
GRUMWELL, Frank M., Sh-188-2; US white; 258 Looney St, Memphis PO
GRUNDY, Dennis, Ho-96-2; Pvt C Co 24th TN Inf; Sep 3 70 to Sep 3 75; Erin PO; United States Regular, lost discharge (this entry crossed through)
GRUNDY, Owen, Mu-194-1; Sgt B Co 15th US Col Inf; 12-4-63 to 4-7-66; Columbia PO
GUBER, Samuel, Ru-13-3; Pvt K Co 12th Reg; Aug 63 to Feb 65; Murfreesboro PO
GUDGER, Robert, Mc-112-7; Pvt E Co 2nd US Inf; Athens PO
GUESS?, Collins, Wa-270-1; Pvt A Co 63rd VA Inf; 61 to 65; Austins Springs PO
GUESS, John W., Mu-205-2; Eliza widow of; Pvt B Co 1st MS Rifle; Williamsport PO; deranged, died in asylum, papers sent to Washington DC
GUESS, Lafayette, Sq-165-2; Rustie A. widow of; Pvt C Co 6th TN Mtd Inf; 9-12-64 to 6-31-65; Sunnyside PO; received an honorable disc.
GUESS, William M., Hd-53-3; Pvt C Co 1st AL Cav; 20 Feb 63 to 1 Aug 65; Cravens Landing PO
GUEST, Elvira H., Wl-295-2; E Main St, Lebanon PO
GUFFEE, John H., We-230-1; Cav K Co 21st TN R; May 5 63 to May 5 64; Greenfield PO; CONF
GUFFEY, George W., Mc-113-1; Pvt F Co 32nd KY Mtd Inf; 12-62 to 8-63; Athens PO
GUFFEY, Isaac, Fe-42-2; Luverna widow of; Pvt I Co 13th KY; Jamestown PO
GUFFEY, Thomas F., Mc-113-2; Pvt D Co 32nd KY Inf; 10-28-62 to 8-12-63; Riceville PO
GUFFY, Harrison, Pi-155-2; Pvt Baty's Scout Reg TN Cav; 1-64 to 65; Byrdstown PO; right testicle hurt by horse
GUICE, William J., H-53-4; Pvt F Co 10th TN Inf; 2-14-64 to 6-20-65; Chattanooga PO; crippled feet from marching
GUILLE, Andras, Ja-86-4; Pvt K Co 97th OH Inf; 8-11-62 to 4-24-64; Ooltewah PO; shot left hand right shoulder & face
GUIN, Isaac T., Je-142-2; Pvt K Co 8th TN Cav;
New Market PO; crippled--left hip, discharge carried off by pension agt.
GUINAN, Michael, G-51-1; Pvt 5th KY Inf; Humboldt PO
GUINE, William, Sh-178-2; Pvt C Co 3rd LA; 263 Monroe, Memphis PO; shot in head
GUINN, Griffin, Fr-116-1(2); Pvt I Co 10th TN Inf; 7-23-62 to 7-3-65; Sherwood PO
GUINN, James, De-26-1; C Co 2nd TN; 4 mos; Bible Hill PO
GUINN, James H., K-178-2; Mary widow of; Sgt H Co 1st TN Cav; 21 Sep 63 to 11 Sep 65; Hardin Valley PO
GUINN, John, Fr-116-1(2); Pvt I Co 10th TN Inf; 7-23-62 to 7-3-65; Sherwood PO; rheumatism from service
GUINN, McD., Ge-85-1; W. Susan widow of; Pvt F Co 4th TN Inf; 14 May 63 to __ (1 mo 9 days); Cavey Branch PO
GUINN, Pierce, Be-2-2; Pvt B Co 3rd TN Mtd Inf; 63 to deserted; Holladay PO
GUINN, Pleasant M., Ge-86-1; Pvt E Co 1st KY Lt Art; 22 Sep 63 to 5 Aug 65; Warrensburgh PO
GUINN, Zuda L., K-177-2; widow; PO omitted
GULLEY, Joseph, Cy-27-2; Pvt I Co 1st TN Mtd Inf; 3-8-64 to 5-16-65; Clementsville PO
GULLIDAY, Adams, F-39-1; Pvt H Co 61st US Col Inf; 2 yrs; Galloway PO; discharge in Washington
GUNDO, William A., Sm-168-1; Pvt A Co TN Inf; 62 to 6-62 (6 mos); Pleasant Shade PO
GUNIES, Dock G., La-115-2; Pvt H Co 14th AR Inf; 1 Jun 63 to 1 Apr 65; Summertown PO; CONF
GUNKLE, John F., Di-34-3; Major B Co 4th KY Cav; 12-13-61 to 2-3-63; Colesburg PO
GUNN, Andrew J., Di-42-1; Pvt G Co 11th TN Inf; 2-63 to 63 (6 mos 8 days); Tenn City PO; CONF
GUNN, Edmond W., Rb-221-1; Pvt F Co 11th TN Inf; May 24 61 to May 24 65; Cedar Hill PO; flesh wound through body; CONF
GUNN, Simpson, B-18-1; 24th Dist
GUNNELS, James P., Ov-135-2; Sarah A. widow of; Sgt D Co 1st TN Mtd Inf; Livingston PO; discharge with pention, forgot date
GUNTER, James, H-72-3(2); Pvt F Co 15th TN Inf; 63 to 65; Chattanooga PO
GUNTER, John, Co-68-2; Pvt E Co 2nd TN; 62 to 65; Cashy PO; chills
GUNTER, John W., He-58-2; Sol; 8th Civil Dist
GUNTER, Radolphus H.?, We-229-1; Cpl B Co 7th TN Cav; 4 Oct 64 to 7 Aug 65; Gleason PO; rheumatism
GUNTER, Robert, Cl-49-1; Pvt F Co 8th TN Cav; 6-3-62 to 65 (2 yrs 8 mos); Zib? PO; side plurecey
GUNTHER, Andrew, Sh-158-2; Pvt K Co 51st NY Inf; 18 Mar 64 to 7 Jul 65; Memphis PO; spine injured & left leg paralysed
GUNTNER, John H., Su-243-1; Sgt H Co 5th NH Inf; 24 Aug 64 to 8 Jul 65; Bristol PO; slight wound, reenlisted
GUONIAN, Budas, D-60-1; Bridget S. widow of; 304 McCrairy, Nashville PO; white
GUPTON, Steven M., Rb-223-1; Capt F Co 28th KY Inf; 14 Oct 61 to Jan 66; Springfield PO; varicose vains left leg
GURLEY, Clement, D-77-1; claims to have served three years but can give no facts; Nashville PO
GURLEY, John A., He-64-1; Pvt A Co 16th TN Cav; 15 Nov 63 to Apr 65; Reagan PO; flesh wound in left hand; CONF
GURNEY, Thoms., Sh-189-2; Eliza widow of; Pvt I Co 55th US Col Inf; 2-1-63 to 12-31-65; Penn Ave, Memphis PO
GURVIN, Jame C., K-165-1; Cpl D? Co 8th TN Cav; 28 Sep 63 to 26 Jun 65; Knoxville PO
GUSAWAY, George W., Fr-105-1; 1st Sgt D Co 58th IN Inf; 22 Oct 61 to 3 Aug 65; Winchester PO
GUSBEE, John, K-181-5(2); Elizabeth Wright widow of; Pvt A Co 6th TN Inf; Mar 62 to May 65; Knoxville PO
GUSHER, Henry H., Cu-17-4; Pvt B Co 33rd MO? Inf; 6-6-62 to 6-11-65; Northville PO; chronic diarrhea
GUSTAVUS, Gaspaino?, Sh-173-1; Memphis, 91 De Soto St, PO
GUTERWOOD, William, T-206-2; Pvt; Rialto PO; lost his discharge, can't give company or regiment

GUTHREY, John, Hi-92-1; Aetna PO; catarh of the head 25 yrs, coulden find out anything about enlistment
GUTHRIE, Antony, Mu-195-2; Sol wife dont know; Columbia PO
GUTHRIE, James G., P-151-2; Pvt F Co 2nd TN Mtd Inf; 64 to 65; Linden PO
GUTHRIE, John, Mu-200-2; Mt. Pleasant PO
GUTHRIE, John, Ge-88-1; Pvt B Co 3rd TN; PO omitted; rheumatism, not at home & cant get facts
GUTHRIE, Joseph, Me-93-1; Pvt C Co 10th OH Inf; 6-17-61 to 6-17-64; Ten Mile Stand PO; shot in right hip, suffering from rheumatism and varicose veins
GUTHRIE, Seborn, La-113-1; Pvt B Co 1st AL Cav; 64 to __; Lawrenceburg PO; discharge lost, cannot answer
GUTHRIE, Shaderick A., Mc-113-1; Arabella F. Hutsell formerly widow of; Pvt 2nd TN Inf; Athens PO
GUTHRIE, William E., Wy-178-1; Pvt L Co 1st AL Cav; 10-62 to 10-63; Pleasant Valley PO
GUTHRIE, William S., Ov-135-1; Cpl C Co 12th KY Inf; 10-3-61 to 7-11-64; Oakley PO; concussion of head
GUY, Daniel M., A-5-4; Pvt E Co 13th TN Cav; 9-1-64 to 9-7-65; Clinton PO; rheumatism
GUY, Isham W., A-5-4; Pvt B Co 3rd TN Inf; 2-10-62 to 2-20-65; Clinton PO; piles
GUY, William, Cl-49-2; Cpl A Co 2nd TN Cav; 8-1-62 to 7-6-65; Zeb PO; broncitis & nervous debility
GWALTNEY, Archibal, Sm-172-4; Sgt G Co 4th TN Inf; 11-1-64 to 8-15-65; Hickman PO
GWATTNEY, Dawson B., Sm-173-1; Cpl G Co 4th TN Mtd Inf; 11-1-64 to 8-25-65; Hickman PO
GWATTNEY, John T., La-115-2; Cpl D Co 17th WI Inf; 3 Feb 64 to 14 Jul 65; Henryville PO
GWINN, Elijah F., R-163-4; Pvt A Co 46th IN Vet Inf; 2-19-64 to 6-26-65; Dayton PO; camp diarhea contracted
GWINN, Shadrach, D-77-1; Laborer 19th MI Inf; 61 to 63; Nashville PO; Pvt 17th TN Inf--63 to 65
GWINN, William, Mc-110-1; Pvt G Co 7th TN Inf; 10 Nov 64 to 5 Aug 65; Bray's PO; neuralgia, re-enlisted, first dates last
GYE, Narcissas (see Ricketts, Robert)
HACKER, Alfred M., Mc-114-4; Pvt H Co 5th TN Inf; 3-21-62 to 5-16-65; Calhoun PO; wounded in neck with gunshot at Resackey GA
HACKER, George W., Me-94-2; Pvt D Co 7th TN Mtd Inf; 11-29-64 to 7-25-65; Pin Hook PO
HACKER, Isaac H., K-156-5; 2nd Sgt H Co 5th TN Cav; 3 Oct 61 to 4 Nov 64; 84 Church St, Knoxville PO; CONF
HACKER, Joel, Ro-204-4; Sarah widow of; Pvt B Co 5th TN Inf; Kreis PO; no dos., died in army
HACKER, Newton, Wa-274-2; Capt C Co 4th TN Inf Vol; 27 Feb 63 to 2 Aug 65; Jonesboro PO
HACKET, Henry, H-73-2(1); Pvt H Co 13th US Inf; 12-1-65 to __; Chattanooga PO
HACKLER, George, Mc-109-2; Cpl B Co 7th TN Inf; 10-12-64 to 7-27-65; Sewee PO (Meigs Co.)
HACKLER, John, Mc-109-3; Pvt B Co 7th TN Inf; 12-1-64 to 7-27-65; Sewee PO (Meigs Co.); rheumatism, totally disabled
HACKNEY, Calvin, Sn-252-2; Sgt E Co 14th US Inf; 11-16-63 to 3-29-66; Gallatin PO
HACKNEY, James, Hr-96-2; 2 yrs; Crainville PO; CONF
HACKNEY, John, Mt-137-2; in government employ; no papers; 62 to 65; St. Bethlehem PO
HACKNEY, Lafayett, Lo-193-1; Pvt M Co 1st US Art; 18 Oct 64 to 31 Mar 66; Unitia PO
HACKNEY, William H., H-56-3; Pvt C Co 129th IN Inf; 10-3-63 to 8-29-65; St. Elmo PO; wounded
HACKWORTH, Gabriel S., A-8-3; Wagoner H Co 1st TN Inf; 8-9-61 to 9-17-64; Scarborough PO; contracted measel Oct 1861
HACKWORTH, Larkin, A-6-3(1); Pvt E Co 3rd TN Inf; 2-12-62 to 2-23-65; Olivers PO; afflicted by small pox
HACKWORTH, Louis, A-8-3; Pvt H Co 1st TN Inf; 8-9-61 to 9-17-65; Scarborough PO; contracted diarhea & rheumatism in 1862
HACKWORTH, Martha, A-7-1; widow; Robertsville PO

HACKWORTH, Morgan C., A-8-3; Sgt H Co 1st TN Inf; 8-9-61 to 9-17-64; Scarborough PO
HACKWORTH, William C., K-186-3; Pvt A Co 1st TN Inf; 14 Aug 63 to 3 Aug 65; Beaver Ridge PO
HADDOX, Andrew, K-181-2; Pvt G Co 6th TN Inf; 18 Apr 62 to 17 May 65; French PO
HADDOX, Henry, Mu-196-1; Pvt G Co 101st Reg; 3 or 4 yrs; Columbia PO; rheumatism
HADEN, Alex, K-168-1; Pvt C Co 42nd TN Inf; 13 Jul 64 to 6 Feb 66; Hercules PO
HADEN, George W. (see Dine, George W.)
HADEN, Jordan, C-33-6; US Soldier; Standard PO
HADOX, Sam, D-51-1(Col); Pvt 21st Col TN Inf; 64 to 65; Nashville PO
HADSPETH, Samuel, Col, Li-154-1; Pvt A Co 1st US Inf; 12-62 to __ (3 yrs); Clardy Ville PO; crippled by falling from breas works so he says
HAEGER, John F., H-51-3; Pvt I Co 7th NY Inf; 9-11-64 to 6-25-65; Hill City PO
HAESLETT, James, F-44-3; Pvt C Co 59th __; May 63 to May 65; PO omitted
HAFLEY, Andrew, Bo-20-1; 1st Sgt A Co 3rd TN Cav; 11-10-62 to 7-19-65; Bank PO
HAFLEY, Charls A., Bo-20-2; Pvt A Co 3rd TN Cav; 9-18-62 to 6-12-65; Bank PO
HAGANS, James, Sh-171-2; Pvt F Co 11th Col Inf; 1-12-64 to 1-12-66; 147 Madison St. in R., Memphis PO
HAGART, T. R., A-1-3; C Sgt 2nd TN Cav; 7-27-62 to 6-13-65; Andersonville PO; pils (sic)
HAGER, Joseph, Sn-255-1; Orderly Sgt K Co 2nd WI Cav; 10-1-61 to 6-1-65; Goodlettsville PO (Davidson Co.)
HAGEY, William J., Di-34-2; Jane G. widow of; Pvt E Co 57th PA Inf; 2-9-64 to 4-19-65; Dickson PO; lost left arm
HAGGARD, Henry, Ro-202-5; Pvt K Co 3rd KY Inf; 24 Jul 61 to 15 Oct 65; Cave Creek PO; lung disease
HAGGARD, John A., Ch-12-2; Sgt I Co 55th TN Inf; 5-61 to 4-65; Custer Point PO; CONF
HAGGARD, John S., Hd-44-1; Sgt C Co 2nd TN Mtd Inf; 12-25-63 to 5-13-65; Clifton PO (Wayne Co.)
HAGGARD, Squire, Hd-47-1; Cynthia A. widow of; Pvt H Co 6th TN Cav; 62 to 65; Savannah PO; death from small pox
HAGINS, John, Hy-81-1; Pvt, discharge with pension agt.; Brownsville PO; lung disease; this entry crossed through
HAGLER, Jacob S., Ro-203-5(1); Capt F Co 5th TN Inf; 9 Aug 61 to 3 Aug 62; Burns Mills PO; hand disabled
HAGLOR, Manul L., Be-5-1; Pvt C Co 4th KY Hvy Art; 31 May 65 to 7 Feb 66; Eggville PO; deseased from measles
HAGOOD, Wiley B., Hw-125-2; Pvt C Co 1st TN Art; 17 Sep 63 to 1 Aug 65; Surgoinsville PO; diseased
HAGUE, John A., Br-8-1; Pvt F Co 4th TN Cav; 9-17-63 to 7-12-65; Cleveland PO
HAGY, Frank, Hy-84-3(5); Woodville PO
HAHN, John G., Co-59-1; he cannot give any further instruction; Del Rio PO
HAIL, Gails, Ru-241-3; Anna widow of; Pvt B Co 14th TN Inf; 7-63 to 3-66; Murfreesboro PO; shot in leg
HAILEY, George W., Sm-169-3(5); Pvt A Co 1st TN Mtd Inf; 1-21-64 to 1-13-65; 2nd Dist, nasal catarrh and bronchitis, atrophy left testicle
HAILEY, John A., O-138-1; Pvt B Co 27th TN; 17 Oct 61 to 30 Jan 64; Elbridge PO; left ancl? broken by gunshot; CONF
HAIN (Hann?), Andrew, Hm-108-4(3); Pvt G Co 2nd TN Cav; 1 Oct 62 to 6 Jul 65; Russellville PO; chronic diarea
HAIN, Francis A., Ru-245-1; Pvt A Co 6th KY Cav; 12-15-63 to 9-6-65; Hall Hill PO
HAIN (Haus?), Jacob A., Ge-88-3; Pvt L Co 12th KY Cav; 63 to 65; Mohawk PO; spinal & kidney affections
HAINES, Burrell, H-57-3; Pvt D Co 16th US Col; 63 to 65; Orchard Knob PO
HAINES, Robert, Sh-145-2; Pvt K Co 17th US Col Inf; 30 Nob 63 to 14 Jul 65; Kerrville PO; feet & hands frostbitten, fingers & toes off, each hand and foot

HAINS, Jackson, H-54-5; Ruth widow of; Pvt G Co 5th TN Inf; 6th Dist
HAIR, James M., Ge-99-2; Emeline Ricker formerly widow of; Recruit. Officer E Co 8th TN Inf; Apr 63 to killed Mar 65; Cedar Creek PO; killed, couldnt get date of death
HAIR, Mary (see Ivry, Garland)
HAIRE, John, T-212-1; found while examining work, no address on blank
HAIRSON, William J., Ge-89-2; Pvt G Co 1st TN Cav; 61 to 65; Mosheim PO
HALBROOKS, Ethelbert A., P-151-1; Ord Sgt F Co 2nd TN Mtd Inf; 20 Nov 63 to 19 Jan 65; Pope PO; injured by lightening being struck
HALE, Alexander E., Hm-108-3(2); Pvt L Co 1st TN Cav; 63 to Jun 65 (1 yr 8 mos); Russellville PO
HALE, Armsted B., Fe-43-1; Pvt D Co 1st TN Art; 9-63 to 7-25-65; Clark Range PO
HALE, Elijah B., Hm-104-1; Sgt 4th TN Cav; 28 Jul 63 to 12 Jul 65; Mornston PO
HALE, Enos N., Mo-120-3(1); Serena C. widow of; D Co 4th TN Cav; Sweetwater PO; wounded, deserted his wife
HALE, Henry, Hm-107-4; Pvt D Co 1st TN Cav; 1 Jul 62 to 5 Jun 65; Chestnut Bloom PO; diarrhea & heart & hips
HALE, Henry, Hw-127-1; Cpl L Co 4th TN Cav; 12 May 64 to 19 Jul 65; Rogersville PO; contracted spine & kidney trouble
HALE, Isac, Bl-3-2; Pvt H Co 1st KY Cav; 6-1-63 to 9-25-65; Billingsly PO
HALE, J. C., Bo-11-4; 1st Lt; Brick Mill PO
HALE, J. P., G-57-4(1); Pvt D Co 13th TN Inf; 6-1-62 to 6-1-62 (sic); Yorkville PO
HALE, James, Wa-263-3; Pvt H Co 8th TN Cav; Sep 28 63 to Sep 11 65; Alfred PO; shot through right breast & left hip
HALE, James, Dk-33-1; Mary A. widow of; Pvt K Co 5th TN Cav; 5-13-63 to unknown; 4th Civil Dist
HALE, James, Bl-3-1; Sgt G Co 6th Mtd Inf; 2-20-63 to 6-30-63; Patten PO
HALE, James C., Je-142-1; Pvt B Co 9th TN Cav; 1 Oct 63 to 11 Sep 65; Alena PO; gunshot wound
HALE, James H., Ge-87-3; Sgt L Co 11th TN Cav; 1 Jun 63 to 17 Jun 65; Pates Hill PO; lung & heart deseas
HALE, Jeremiah B., Wa-272-3; Sgt 1st AR Cav; 8 Nov 62 to 3 Aug 65; Free Hill PO; rheumatism and disease of mouth, results scurvy
HALE, John H., A-8-2; Cpl K Co 1st TN Inf 8-9-61 to 9-17-64; Leadom PO; prisoner at Beel Island 6 mos
HALE, John P., R-162-1; Pvt G Co 6th TN Inf Vols; 2-64 to 7-65; Dayton PO
HALE, John W., Co-60-2; Pvt B Co 8th TN Inf; 1-5-63 to 6-13-65; Bridgeport PO; heart disease & gravel
HALE, Johnathan, K-186-2; Pvt; Balls Camp PO
HALE, Lamar, Wa-274-2; Pvt F Co 1st US Col Art; Jonesboro PO
HALE, Nepolian, Hm-108-3(2); Pvt I Co 1st TN Cav; 5 Jun 62 to 5 Jun 65; Russellville PO; diarea
HALE, Patric H. C., Hm-107-5; Pvt D Co 1st TN Cav; 17 Aug 62 to 5 Jun 65; Chestnut Bloom PO; diarrhea & rheumatism
HALE, Reubin B., Dk-33-2; Pvt K Co 5th TN Cav; 6-6-63 to 8-14-65; Dowelltown PO; rheumatism
HALE, Rubin B., Dk-36-2; Pvt B Co 4th TN Mtd Inf; 64 to 64?; Smithville PO
HALE, Sallie A. (W), Be-2-1; Pvt I Co 7th TN; Sep 15 63 to Aug 9 65; Holladay PO
HALE, Silas, C-33-4; Pvt G Co 1st Reg Col Hvy Art; 5-64 to 3-66; Jellico PO
HALE, Thomas, Dk-33-4; 4th Civil Dist
HALE, William C., Wa-272-2; Bugler H Co 4th TN Cav; Aug 63 to Jun __; Pettibone PO; rheumatism and resulting disease of heart
HALE, William C., H-49-2; P-t A Co 6th TN Mtd Inf; 8-2-64 to 30-60-65; Falling Water PO
HALE, William L., Dk-32-3; Pvt K Co 5th TN Cav; 5-13-63 to 8-14-65; Alexandria PO
HALEY, Albert A., R-159-2; Sgt H Co 2nd MS Art; 11-1-63 to 11-20-65; Spring City PO
HALEY, Alexander, Mc-118-1; Harriet widow of; Pvt I Co 1st Col US Hvy Art; 7-13-64 to dide 12-13-64; Coghill PO
HALEY, Charles, Mc-114-5; Pvt A Co 42nd TN Inf; 3-1-64 to 1-31-66; Santfordville PO
HALEY, Frank (Col), Me-92-5(2); Pvt; Pin Hook PO; crippled leg
HALEY, Harvey V., Mu-209-5; Pvt G Co TN; Feb 63 to Oct 63; Columbia PO; CONF
HALEY, Isaac, Wi-279-1; Pvt 1st TN Art; Nov 64 to Apr 26 66; Franklin PO
HALEY, Jesse, Ru-237-1; Pvt TN Inf; Feb 63 to 64; Eagleville PO
HALEY, John, D-60-2; 1109 Cedor St, Nashville PO; white
HALEY, John B., Bl-2-3; H Co 2nd MO Art; 11-1-63 to 11-20-65; Litton PO; chronic diarhea
HALEY, Nan, Tr-267-1; widow US; PO omitted
HALEY, Samuel, Mc-114-6; Pvt A Co 42nd TN Inf; 3-61 to 1-31-64; Santfordville PO
HALEY, Wellington M., K-154-3; Knoxville PO
HALEY, Zacariah, Ru-237-1; Pvt G Co 13th IL Cav; 26 Dec 62 to 26 Dec 64; Eaglesville PO; right lung
HALFACKER, George, L-100-1; Pvt L Co 4th US Col Inf; Mar 62 to 19 Oct 65; Ripley PO; cannot give dates of enlistment
HALFORD, William J., G-70-1; Pvt C Co 2nd TN; 17 Dec 63 to May 6 65; Dyer PO
HALL, Abner, Ms-183-1; Landsman (navy) Koon; 8-14-62 to 8-14-65; Comenville PO; dropsy & other disease, is certainly entitled to pension
HALL, Alexander H., Su-240-2; Pvt G Co 60th TN Inf; 1 Sep 62 to 1 Mar __ (2 yrs 20 mos); Ford Town PO; CONF
HALL, Allen, Fe-43-1; Pvt F Co 1st TN Cav; 8-9-61 to 9-17-64; Boiling PO; chronic disease of right lung
HALL, Arafiolan, Mc-118-5; Pvt E Co 4th TN Cav; 1-1-63 to 7-2-65; Calhoun PO; cripled in left arm, hip & leg 29 yrs
HALL, Baily B., Ro-202-5; Pvt I Co 1st TN Inf; 9 Aug 61 to __ (17 mos); Cave Creek PO; kidney affection & piles
HALL, Benjaman F., Dk-33-3; 1st SgtF Co 4th TN Inf; 9-5-64 to 8-25-65; Gasaway PO; disease of kidneys
HALL, Benjamin F., We-221-5(2); Pvt A Co 31st TN Inf; Oct 61 to Nov 62; Martin PO; CONF
HALL, Chester B., Cl-52-1; Pvt E Co 8th TN Cav; 6-1-63 to 3-13-64; Springdale PO; prisoner Knoxville 4 mos
HALL, Church T., K-174-3(2); Cpl G Co 8th TN Cav; 6 Jul 63 to 11 Sep 65; Mynott PO; disability non
HALL, Daniel B., K-168-4; Pvt B Co 10th KY Cav; Adair's Creek PO; Pvt M Co 18th KY Inf
HALL, Dannel? J., Co-64-2; Pvt C Co 26th TN Inf; Nov 62 to Nov 63; Newport PO
HALL, David E., Dk-39-5(1); Pvt H Co 1st TN Mtd Inf; 3-24-64 to 5-25-65; Laurel Hill PO
HALL, Edward E., Be-2-1; Pvt I Co 7th TN; Mar 8 65 to Aug 9 65; Holladay PO
HALL, Edwin R., K-160-1; 1st L K Co 1st US Art; 12 Aug 62 to 31 Mar 66; Knoxville PO
HALL, Elija, Mg-198-1; Pvt I Co 39th KY; 62 to 64; Lavender PO
HALL, Elisha, Mg-199-3; Pvt F Co 4th TN Cav; Apr 64 to Jul 65; Sunbright PO; left arm broken by horse falling
HALL, Elizabeth C. (see Chapman, James)
HALL, Elsie B., Cr-15-2; widow US Sol; Maple Creek PO
HALL, Fairfax, D-99-1; Pvt G Co 13th TN Inf; Oct 10 63 to Jan 10 66; Goodlettsville PO
HALL, Felix H., Ro-201-6; Pvt I Co 1st TN Inf; 9 Aug 61 to 17 Sep 64; Kingston PO
HALL, Fleman, Ru-13-3; 1st Lt H Co 99th OH Vol Inf; Aug 11 62 to Jan 31 63; Murfreesboro PO; chronic disease
HALL, Geary, Sh-200-1; Pvt F Co 55th US Col Inf; 5-20-63 to 12-31-65; Broadway St., Memphis PO
HALL, George U., Mo-12-4; Sol US; 17th Dist
HALL, George W., Mo-126-1; Amanda A. Collins former widow of; Lt K Co 12th TN Cav; 4-12-63 to 65; Hopewell Springs PO; left four finger shot off, this applies to deceased

HALL, George W., K-174-5; Pvt G Co 2nd TN Cav; 1 Oct 62 to 25 Mar 64; House Mountain PO; rheumatism, in bad health
HALL, George W., Co-64-2; Pvt I Co 26th NC Inf; Jun 61 to 8 May 65; Philips PO; CONF
HALL, Green, Li-161-1; Pvt; Fayetteville PO; I hear that he was honorably discharged, I don't know how long he served
HALL, Henderson, Ru-241-2(1); Pvt H Co 14th TN Inf; 15 Nov 63 to 20 Mar 66; Murfreesboro PO
HALL, Henry, Sh-173-2; Gayose St, Memphis PO
HALL, Henry, Se-223-3; Pvt 3rd TN Cav; Sevierville PO
HALL, Henry, D-61-2; Ament St, Nashville PO; impossible to get information, party not at home
HALL, Henry, Cu-16-2; Pvt G Co 6th TN Mtd Inf; 3-25-65 to 6-30-65; Litton PO; fever settled in back
HALL, Henry B., We-221-3; Pvt E Co 4th TN Cav; Jun 62 to Jul 63; Martin PO; struck by a spent ball with? thigh; CONF
HALL, J. R., G-57-7(4); Pvt D Co 13th TN Inf; Apr 61 to May 65; Yorkville PO; CONF
HALL, J. S., T-213-1; Capt C Co 9th TN Inf; May 61 to May 65; Covington PO; shot through body, thigh & head; CONF
HALL, James, Di-37-1; Pvt F Co 16th TN Inf; 12-24-63 to 4-30-66; Cumberland Furnace PO
HALL, James A-3-4; Sgt H Co 9th TN Cav; 63 to __; Bud PO; rhumatism
HALL, James A., Sh-25-6(2); Pvt 18th TN Inf; Apr 61 to Apr 65; Newbern PO; CONF
HALL, James A., Hm-106-1; Pvt C Co 8th TN Inf; 20 Dec 62 to __; Chestnut Bloom PO; deserted, dates not known
HALL, James K. P., Ge-91-2; Lt B Co 4th TN Cav; 11 Aug 61 to 12 Jul 65; Greeneville PO; derangement ner. system
HALL, James M., Dy-29-5; PVt G Co TN Cav; 4 Dec 64 to Jun 65; Newbern PO; CONF
HALL, James M., H-58-6; Artificer B Co 1st Regt Eng; 1-4-64 to 9-26-65; Retro PO; transferred from Co D 8th KY Vol; reenlisted
HALL, James R., Sol US, He-59-1; PO omitted
HALL, James T., D-46-1; Pvt G Co Berdans 1st S.S.S.; 9-10-61 to 7-9-62; Nashville PO
HALL, James W., Bo-15-2; Pvt L Co 2nd TN Cav; 9-8-63 to 7-6-65; Blockhouse PO
HALL, John, Mu-193-1; Martha widow of; Pvt; 1-1-64 to 6-1-64; Columbia PO
HALL, John, Ge-98-2; Catharine widow of; Pvt B Co 9th TN Cav; Lovelace PO
HALL, John, Lo-190-2; Capt G Co 59th TN Cav; 62 to 65; Loudon PO; CONF
HALL, John, Hw-127-3; Pvt H Co 8th TN Inf; Rogersville PO; rupture, rheumatism, kidney & liver
HALL, John, Mg-197-4; Pvt B Co 2nd TN Inf; Aug 61 to Oct 64; Wartburg PO; rheumatism
HALL, John, Co-66-3(1); Pvt A Co 5th TN Cav; 1 Feb 63 to 1 Aug 65; English PO; CONF
HALL, John, Lo-194-1; Elarry L. widow of; Sgt D Co; 3 yrs; Muddy Creek PO
HALL, John A., Co-62-1; Pvt H Co 1st TN Cav; 1 Sep 62 to 65 (3 yrs); Warrensburg PO; catarrh of head
HALL, John M., R-161-5; Cpl I Co 38th OH Inf; 9-4-61 to 9-13-64; Dayton PO
HALL, John T., K-160-1; Sgt G Co 2nd MI; Oct 61 to Oct 65; Knoxville PO
HALL, Johnathan H., Po-152-3 (1); Capt H Co 10th TN Cav; 63 to 12-28-64; Ducktown PO; lung disease
HALL, Joseph, Bo-15-1; Amanda widow of; Pvt J Co 3rd TN Cav; 9-6-63 to 12-14-63; Blockhouse PO
HALL, Joseph R., T-213-1; Pvt G Co 51st TN Inf; Nov 61 to Apr 65; Covington PO; shot through right leg; CONF
HALL, Josiah, Co-62-2; Pvt F Co 3rd TN Inf; 18 Feb 62 to 23 Feb 65; Givens PO; piles
HALL, Levi H., La-109-1; Pvt C Co 125th OH Vol Inf; 9-21-62 to 2-28-65; Lexington, AL, PO; physical disability
HALL, Lilborn H., S-214-2; Pvt E Co 29th OH Inf; does not know dates &c; Glenmary PO
HALL, Nathan E., T-213-1; Pvt C Co 12th TN Cav; Aug 62 to Apr 65; Covington PO; CONF
HALL, Oliver, Ct-44-2; Elizath widow of; Pvt E Co 2nd TN Inf; 8-26-62 to 7-26-65; Hampton PO
HALL, Perry, A-9-4(2); Pvt; Marlow PO
HALL, Perry, Co-64-2; Pvt F Co 9th TN Cav; 24 Jul 63 to 11 Sep 65; Philips PO; feet frost bite
HALL, Pinkney D., Wy-173-2; Pvt B Co 1st AL Cav; 1-20-63 to 1-22-64; Victory PO
HALL, Pleasant H., Hw-123-1; Pvt I Co 13th TN Cav; 63 to 65; Rotherwood PO
HALL, Polly (see Hyde, Boyd)
HALL, Richard B., A-3-1; Pvt D Co 20th __ Art; 9-10-63 to 7-20-65; Bud PO; lung disease
HALL, Robert, Sh-159-7; Eliza widow of; Pvt 61st US; PO omitted
HALL, Robert H., Cl-46-1; Capt B Co 8th TN; 6-1-63 to 9-65; Clairfield PO; hart & liver
HALL, Samuel (see Jenkins, Samuel)
HALL, Samuel D., Su-240-2; Pvt G Co 60th TN Inf; 1 Sep 62 to 1 May 65; Ford Town PO
HALL, Samuel H., Cu-16-1; Pvt C Co 32nd KY Inf; 4-13-63 to 8-12-63; Crossville PO
HALL, T. W., G-57-2; Pvt; Yorkville PO; CONF
HALL, Washington, K-176-2; Pvt 2nd TN Inf; 6-29-63 to 8-3-65; Andersonville PO
HALL, Wm., Sh-204-1; Pvt A Co 3rd US Inf; 63 to 65; Orleans Extd., Memphis PO.
HALL, William, Wa-272-3; Pvt F Co 4th TN Cav; 1 Jul 63 to 2 Aug 65; Fordtown PO; heart disease, general debility, lung disease, rheumatism, varicose veins of left leg
HALL, William, K-168-3; Smithwood PO
HALL, William, H-57-3; Pvt B Co 34th KY Inf; 62 to 65; Orchard Knob PO
HALL, William, Je-142-1; Pvt H Co 7th KY Inf; 20 Aug 61 to 5 Oct 64; Lucilla PO; paralysis & heart disease
HALL, William, Co-62-2; Pvt K Co 8th TN Inf; 29 Jul 62 to 64 (2 yrs); Bybee PO; measles
HALL, William A., Wy-173-5(1); Sgt B Co 1st AL Cav; 1-20-63 to 1-22-64; Victory PO
HALL, William C., Wa-270-1; Pvt H Co 4th TN Cav; 6 Nov 62 to 17 Jul 65; Austin's Springs PO; injury to left ankle
HALL, William M., Dy-29-5; Pvt G Co TN Cav; 4 Dec 64 to Mar 65; Newbern PO; CONF
HALL, William M., Ro-202-4; Pvt I Co 1st TN Inf; 9 Aug 61 to Sep 62; Cave Creek PO; lost use of leg & l. eye, caused by fever
HALL, William M., K-178-1; Pvt M Co 5th TN Cav; 15 Nov 61 to 11 Apr 65; PO omitted
HALL, William R., Cr-13-1; Pvt H Co 7th KY Inf; Aug 61 to Oct 64; Whitthorne PO; dont know date of enlistment or discharge
HALLIBURTON, John, G-58-1; Pvt B Co 7th IL Inf; 10 Jan 63 to 10 Jun 65; Rutherford PO
HALLIDAY, Edward O., Sh-178-3; US Sol; Cor. Dunlap & Union Ave, Memphis PO
HALLOCK, William S., Ro-211-2; Capt D Co 1st MO Cav; 1 Aug 61 to 1 Aug 65; Harriman PO; broken ankle
HALLOWAY, Andrew J., Mr-96-1; Pvt C Co 6th TN Mtd Inf; 8-27-64 to 13-30-65; Whitwell PO
HALLOWAY, Green P., Mr-96-2; Pvt; Whitwell PO
HALLOWAY, Jerry, Mr-96-2; Pvt C Co 6th TN Mtd Inf; 9-12-64 to 1-64; Whitwell PO
HALLOWAY, John R., Mr-96-1; Sgt I Co 2nd E TN Vol; 3-62 to 3-65; Whitwell PO; dislocated ancle
HALLSON, D. A., Fr-120-1; Pvt I Co 1st MN Vol; Apr 10 65 to Aug 7 65; Sewanee PO
HALLUM, Lanerania, Dy-29-3; widow Conf Sol; Trimble PO; CONF
HALLUM, Robert P., We-222-2; 1st Cpl E Co 21st TN Cav; Sep 64 to Sep 67; Gardner PO; CONF
HALLUM, William, Wa-268-3; Johnson City PO
HALT, Thomas H., K-156-6; Wol USA; 132 Kennedy St, Knoxville PO
HALTON, Elisha S., Ma-114-1; Lt G Co 41st TN Cav; Oct 62 to Apr 65; Pinson PO; CONF
HALY, Samuel, Ms-175-1; alias Covington; Pvt A Co 2nd USC; Holts Corner PO; "I get this information from a letter"
HAM, Anderson, Sh-201-4; Pvt I Co 61st US Col Inf; 23 Aug 63 to 20 Dec 65; Memphis PO
HAM, Charles C., H-73-5(3); Chattanooga PO

HAM, Monroe, He-67-2; Jolina A. widow of; Pvt Co C 6th TN Cav; Sep 18 62 to Jul 26 65; Sardis PO; gun shot in left shoulder & right thigh in war
HAMBLETON, James, J-83-2; Pvt G Co 3rd TN; 62 to 65; Nameless PO
HAMBLIN, Dant, Cl-46-4(2); Pvt C Co 9th TN Inf; 63 to 66; Ibex PO; health injured; draws pension
HAMBLIN, Lenard, Hw-118-2; Pvt C Co 1st US Inf; 2 Feb 64 to 27 Nov 65; St. Clair PO
HAMBLIN, William, Hw-128-1; Pvt B Co 3rd US Vol; 14 Oct 64 to 29 Nov 65; Rogersville PO; rheumatism & disease of eyes
HAMBRICK, John W., Je-135-1(3); Pvt F Co 50th TN Inf; 15 Sep 62 to 11 Sep 65; Piedmont PO; mashed by artillery
HAMBRIGHT, Aron, Lo-190-2; Pvt E Co 1st GA Inf; Jan 62 to 65; Loudon PO; shot in hips; CONF
HAMBRIGHT, Benjamin T., Br-8-1; Pvt L Co 1st TN Vol Cav; 9-1-62 to 6-5-65; Blue Springs Stn PO
HAMBRIGHT, Frederick, Br-12-1; Charleston PO
HAMBRIGHT, Jacob, Po-148-1; Pvt A Co 5th TN Mtd Inf; 9-1-64 to 6-26-65; Chestewee Mills PO
HAMBRIGHT, James R., H-68-1; Pvt L Co 1st TN Cav; 9-62 to 6-65; Chattanooga PO
HAMBY, James N., Ro-209-3; Pvt E Co 1st TN Inf; 20 Aug 61 to 17 Sep 64; Rockwood PO
HAMBY, Hebbert, Cu-15-1; Mary widow of; Cpl E Co 1st TN Inf; 8-17-64; Hebbertsburg PO; ulceration of the head
HAMBY, James H., Cu-15-1; Elisabeth A. Ayles widow of; Pvt E Co 1st TN Inf; 8-20-61 to 18-9-64; Hebbertsburg PO; cause of death, measeles, died after his return home
HAMBY, Reuben S., Cu-15-1; Pvt E Co 1st TN Inf; 8-20-61 to 11-22-62; Hebbertsburg PO
HAMBY, Thomas, K-171-5(4); Pvt; Bearden PO
HAMBY, William, Gi-122-2; Pvt C Co 14th AL Cav; Sep 62 to Jul 65; Elkton PO; prison 9 mos; CONF
HAMELTON, David B., Mc-116-2; Elisabeth widow of; Pvt B Co 7th TN Mtd Inf; 11-21-64 to 7-27-65; Athens PO; diseased since the war
HAMELTON, Jasper N., Mo-123-1; Pvt A Co 11th TN Cav; Mt. Vernon PO; claims he was cut off from command & got no discharge
HAMELTON, Jefferson Albert, D-59-1; Pvt I Co 1st US Cav; 14 Jul 64 to 31 Mar 66; 133 Belmont Ave, Nashville PO; shot in right knee; never drawn any pension
HAMER, Harry, Br-8-2; Catherine widow of; Capt E Co 3rd VT Cav; __ to 6-5-65 (4 yrs 2 mos); Cleveland & Blue Springs Station PO
HAMER, William, Cl-46-1; Pvt C Co 1st TN; 8-9-61 to 9-17-64; Clairfield PO; pawler? dirie
HAMERS, John H., Rb-228-1; Pvt A Co 1st TN Inf; 10 Apr 61 to 22 Aug 63; Crunk PO; CONF
HAMES, Reuben L., H-52-2; Lookout Mt. PO
HAMIEL, John W., Bo-13-1; 11-27-64 to 12-24-64; Freindsville PO
HAMILTON, Daniel, Dy-20-1; US Sol; Dist No 1
HAMILTON, David, Mc-112-4; Pvt I Co 1st US Col Art TN; 7-7-64 to 3-31-66; Athens PO
HAMILTON, David, O-134-1; Pvt K Co 15th TN Inf; Apr 1 61 to 64; discharged from US Service; Hornbeak PO; shot in the foot 1 time; CONF
HAMILTON, David B., Li-153-1; Pvt E Co 196th IL Inf; 5-12-64 to 10-22-64; Fayetteville PO
HAMILTON, F. M., D-78-2; Pvt 30th IN Inf; Sep 61 to Apr 17 63; Nashville PO
HAMILTON, George, Ru-241-4; Rachel widow of; Cpl TN Inf; 63 to 63 (3 mos); Murfreesboro PO; died with pneumonia
HAMILTON, George, K-177-5; Cook B Co Johnson & McClure VA Inf; Nov 61 to Jun 65; Powells Station PO
HAMILTON, George, H-75-1; Musician M Co USC VA Art; 11-3-64 to 3-31-66; Chattanooga PO
HAMILTON, Henry H., H-49-3; 2nd Lt G Co 81st NY Inf; 9-18-61 to 63 (2 yrs); Pvt G Co 1st MN Hvy Art; 2-63 to 65; Chattanooga & Kings Point PO
HAMILTON, Isaac, H-63-2; Virginia widow of; Sgt Cav; 61 to 65; 706 Cedar, Chattanooga PO
HAMILTON, Isaac N., Mr-97-2; Pvt E Co 6th TN Inf; 10-14-64 to 6-30-65; Victoria PO
HAMILTON, J. G., G-57-2; Sgt 9th TN Mtd Inf?; 61 to 65; Yorkville PO; CONF
HAMILTON, James H., Li-153-1; Pvt A Co 111th IL Inf; 8-12-62 to 6-6-65; Fayetteville PO; shot through left hand
HAMILTON, John, Ru-241-2(1); Minnie widow of; Cpl I Co 17th TN Inf; 21 Nov 63 to 25 Apr 66; Murfreesboro PO
HAMILTON, John, R-162-3; Pvt A Co 1st TN Col Hvy Art; Dayton PO
HAMILTON, John, Bo-15-1; Pvt D Co 2nd TN Cav; 9-62 to 7-6-65; Mountvale PO; wound in shoulder & breast
HAMILTON, John B., Mc-111-1; Pvt F Co 3rd TN Cav; 7-12-62 to 6-10-65; Nonaburg PO; prisner at Cahaba AL 6 mos
HAMILTON, John L., Sn-250-2; Pvt K Co 2nd __; 5-3-61 to 5-7-65; Castalian Springs PO; CONF
HAMILTON, Joseph, D-71-1; Nashville PO
HAMILTON, Lewis M., Ma-126-2; Cpl K Co 150th PA Inf; Aug 62 to Jul 65; Jackson (resident) PO; forgot day of enlistment, also discharge
HAMILTON, R. W., Ce-31-1; Cpl C Co 30th IL Inf; 3 Dec 61 to 15 Oct 62; Petway PO; shot in thigh, re-enlisted veteran; Sgt G Co 8th IO? Cav; May 63 to 64
HAMILTON, S. B., G-57-6; Cpl; 62 to 63; Yorkville PO; CONF
HAMILTON, Samuel, Ro-202-6; Pvt I Co 5th TN Inf; 11 Oct 62 to 1 Jul 65; Kingston PO; right scrotal, left foot and side
HAMILTON, Samuel, K-167-6; Pvt TN; 3 yrs; Knoxville PO; wife dont know anything
HAMILTON, Stephen J., Po-148-1; Sgt F Co 101st IN Inf; 8-15-62 to 6-24-65; Benton PO
HAMILTON, Thomas, Wh-185-1; Pvt K Co 13th TN Cav; 9-22-63 to 6-2-65; Cassville PO; chronic rheumatism & shot in right leg
HAMILTON, Thomas J. (Col), Ru-247-1; Pvt B Co 1st TN Reg; 12-20-64 to 4-66; Murfreesboro PO; left ankle, now lame
HAMILTON, Warren, H-56-8; Sol US; St. Elmo PO
HAMILTON, William, Bo-12-2(1); Pvt B Co 8th TN Cav; Rasor PO
HAMILTON, William R., Mc-118-2; Pvt G Co 5th TN Mtd Inf; 10-18-64 to 7-13-65; Joshua PO; chronic diarrhea, measles settled in eyes 25 yrs
HAMILTON, Wm. S., G-57-5(3); Pvt; 61 to 65; Yorkville PO; CONF
HAMLET, Lucius (see Irvin, Lucus)
HAMLET, Thomas, Col, D-85-1(2); Pvt B Co 17th TN Inf; Nov 30 63 to Apr 25 66; Wrencoe PO
HAMLETT, Thomas, D-50-3; Henry Ewin alias; Pvt I Co US Inf; 3 yrs 6 mos; 901 N College, Nashville PO; shot in head, hand & back in battle of Murfreesboro
HAMLIN, Dyer, V-178-1; Nancy A. widow of; Pvt; River Hill PO; died in hospital Lexington, KY
HAMLIN, Paul, Di-37-1; Pvt K Co 12th TN Inf; 8-12-63 to 1-16-66; Cumberland Furnace PO; in both CONF & US Service
HAMLIN, Vina, D-45-5; Fillmore Ave, Nashville PO
HAMM, George W., K-167-5; Pvt 7th OH Bat; 62 to 65; Knoxville PO
HAMMAN, Albian O., We-227-1; Pvt 2nd ME Battery, 1st ME Inf; 8 Nov 63 to 16 Jun 65; Greenfield PO; injured in back by stirup being shot and striping me
HAMMER, Robert, Gr-74-1; Pvt G Co 2nd TN Cav; 1 Oct 62 to 6 Jul 65; May Springs PO
HAMMER, Samuel M., Se-231-1; Cpl E Co 1st TN Art; 1 Sep 63 to 1 Aug 65; Boyds Creek PO; hearing 25 yrs
HAMMETT, David, Wa-273-2; Elizabeth widow of; Cpl A Co 8th TN Cav; 11 Jun 63 to 11 Sep 65; Keeblers X Roads PO
HAMMIT, Rollin, Su-237-1; Pvt H Co 13th TN Cav; Oct 62 to Oct 64; Wahoo PO; his discharge has been misplaced
HAMMIT, Samuel, Wa-267-2; Pvt H Co 13th TN Cav; 63 to Nov 65; Febuary PO; bronchitis &c
HAMMOCK, Alexander, M-103-3; Pvt A Co 1st TN Col Inf; Lafayette PO
HAMMOCK, Levi, Un-252-1; Pvt D Co 8th TN Cav; 5 Dec 63 to 16 Jun 65; Simcoe PO; eyes injured

HAMMOCK, Thos., K-167-1; Pvt F Co 6th TN Inf; Mar 62 to 65; Knoxville PO; side and eyes, rheumatism
HAMMON, Goulder, Bo-12-4; Sol US; 3rd Dist
HAMMON, Russell M., Pi-155-1; Pvt G Co 8th TN Inf; 62 to 7-1-65; Byrdstown PO; lung disease
HAMMOND, Charles N., Ma-119-1; Pvt F Co 96th IL Inf; Artificer G Co 1st US Vol; 64 to Jun 30 65; Jackson PO; transferred in Jun 64 at Chattanooga
HAMMOND, Gilbert E., La-115-3; Pvt A Co 31st WI Inf; 14 Aug 62 to 20 Jun 65; Summertown PO
HAMMOND, James, K-166-3; Seaman Ship Kearsarge; 64 to __; Knoxville PO; nearly blind, rheumatism
HAMMOND, Presly, Mu-190-1; alias Presly Owen; this man was only servant not a soldier; Stiversville PO; contracted hoemorhoids & suffers badly from them; by failure to get back to command, says he was cut off & never discharged
HAMMONS, Gilbert, Br-9-3; Cleveland PO
HAMMONS, James, Co-63-1; Pvt H Co 2nd NC Mtd Inf; 1 Oct 63 to 16 Aug 65; Newport PO; measels settled in eyes & r. lung
HAMMONS, Jesse G., Ro-211-2; Pvt H Co 13th KY Cav; 1 Dec 63 to 20 Jan 65; Webster PO; blindness right eye and gravel
HAMMONS, John C., Ro-204-2; Pvt H Co 3rd TN Inf; 10 Feb 62 to 25 Jul 62; Oliver Springs PO; rheumatism &c
HAMMONS, Madison J., Mc-112-3; Cpl E Co 42nd US Col TN Inf; 9-23-64 to 1-21-66; Athens PO
HAMMONS, Willis M., K-162-1; Pvt D Co 3rd TN Inf; 10 Feb 61 to Feb 64; Knoxville PO; paralaryse in left side
HAMMONTREE, Alexander, Lo-192-1; Cpl H Co 5th TN; 27 Feb 62 to 16 May 65; Griffitts PO; rheumatism
HAMMONTREE, Harvey A., Lo-191-1; Pvt; Morganton PO
HAMMONTREE, Hyram, Mo-129-2; Pvt H Co 5th TN Inf; 7-1-62 to 6-5-65; Lomotley PO
HAMMONTREE, James E., Lo-191-1; 1st Sgt H Co 5th TN Inf; 25 Feb 62 to 15 May 65; Greenback PO; gunshot right arm & shoulder, wounded at New Hope Church, GA
HAMON, Jacob, S-215-1; Pvt GCo 8th TN Inf; 3 Jun 62 to 7 Jun 65; Norma PO; hurt in stomach, caused by falling
HAMON, John B., Ge-93-2; Pvt A Co 4th TN Cav; 27 Jun 63 to 5 Aug 65; Greeneville PO
HAMPTON, Aaron A., Cf-40-3; Melissa widow of; Pvt C Co 13th US Inf; 63? to 65; Tullahoma PO; wounded in chest; Col? received pension till he died
HAMPTON, Abraham, T-215-2; Pvt K Co 3rd USC Cav; Mason PO
HAMPTON, Alfred, Ro-210-9; Pvt I Co 4th TN Cav; 20 Feb 64 to 12 Jul 65; Rockwood PO
HAMPTON, Daniel H., Ct-36-1; Cpl F Co 6th IN Cav; 12-7-63 to 9-15-65; Roan Mt. PO; prisoner at Tilina GA
HAMPTON, David H., K-157-1; Pvt H Co 1st US Art; Knoxville PO
HAMPTON, Eb, Be-2-1; Pvt D Co 7th TN Cav; 62 to 65; Holladay PO
HAMPTON, Ezekiel G., L-106-1; July widow of; Pvt C Co 8th TN Cav; Oct 6 63 to Sep 11 65; Double Bridges PO; crippled in knee
HAMPTON, George W., C-29-2; Pvt F Co 6th TN Inf; 3-10-62 to 3-28-65; Fincastle PO; heart disease
HAMPTON, James F., G-67-1; Pvt M Co 6th TN Cav; 11 Aug 62 to 1 Jul 65; Bradford PO; diarrhea
HAMPTON, John A., Di-37-1; Pvt G Co 10th TN Inf; 12-20-64 to 6-24-65; Cumberland Furnace PO
HAMPTON, John P., Dy-25-3; Pvt G Co TN Cav; May 64 to __ (3 mos); Newbern PO; CONF
HAMPTON, Joseph, Me-92-2; Pvt A Co 2nd IL? Cav--  to 2-64; Pvt B Co 7th TN Mtd Inf--6-10-64 to 7-27-65; Chuckaluck PO; rheumatism & disease of eyes, regiment disbanded
HAMPTON, Martha A. (see Johnson, Joseph)
HAMPTON, Mose, Sh-153-2; Pvt 16th IL Cav; Bailey Sta. PO
HAMPTON, Orwin, Cr-14-2; Pvt G Co 2nd TN Mtd Inf; 5 Aug 62 to Oct 25 63; Crider PO

HAMPTON, Richard, Hm-106-3; Mary L. widow of; Pvt F Co; 63 to __; Morristown PO
HAMPTON, Thomas, Mc-110-2(1); Pvt B Co 7th TN Inf; 9-7-64 to 7-27-65; Fiketon PO
HAMPTON, Tom, L-99-1; Pvt; 61 to 66; Orysa PO; as much information as could be had
HAMPTON, Wesley A., Ct-38-1; Cpl K Co 4th TN Cav; 4-12-64 to 7-12-65; Happy Valley PO; supposed to be consumption
HAMPTON, William, U-247-4; US Sol; 5th Civil Dist
HAMPTON, Wm. F., Wa-267-2; Pvt G Co 4th TN Inf; 27 Nov 62 to Aug 64 65; Febuary PO; chrc. diarhea
HAMPTON, William H., Gu-48-2; Capt M Co 10th TN Cav; 11-10-64 to 8-16-65; Tracy City PO
HAMSTEAD, Henry C., Se-226-4; Col 4th MO Cav; 2 yrs; Sinking Springs PO; left eye knocked out by shell
HANAHAN, Thomas, R-162-4; Pvt B Co 32nd OH Inf; 12-63 to 4-12-65; Dayton PO; gunshot in left arm
HANBY, William Henry, H-73-1; Pvt M Co 1st US Inf; 63 to 65; Chattanooga PO
HANCE, Calvin, Je-139-2; Trion PO
HANCE, Mordica, J-79-2; Millie widow of; Pvt B Co 5th KY Cav; 9-10-61 to 7-16-65; North Springs PO; reenlisted veteran
HANCE, Samuel, Co-63-3; Sarah widow of; Pvt D Co 9th TN Cav; Newport PO; died at Knoxville during service
HANCHER, James, Bo-23-1; Pvt B Co 2nd TN Cav; 9-18-62 to 6-14-65; PO omitted
HANCLE, Carlos, Co-63-1; Pvt 10th TN Inf; 3 yrs; Bibee PO; rheumatism, kidneys & eyes affected
HANCOCK, Adam, Se-228-2(3); Pvt A Co; Mar 63 to __; Cusick's X Roads PO; was paroled; CONF
HANCOCK, Bethuel, We-221-6(2); Pvt 8th NC Cav; 64 to 65; Martin PO; none but exposure; CONF
HANCOCK, Charles, Mr-99-2; Pvt G Co 1st WI Inf; 11-15-63 to 12-25-65; Jasper PO
HANCOCK, Dan (see Jordon, Dan)
HANCOCK, Henry C., H-69-4; Pvt B Co 11th GA Cav; 4-11-63 to 65; Chattanooga PO; CONF
HANCOCK, Margret, Hm-33(103)-1; widow of; Civil 17
HANCOCK, Ortan, K-176-3; PO omitted
HANCOCK, Wm., Gr-70-1; Orlenia widow of; Pvt; Spring House PO; co & dates unknown
HANCOCK, William D., K-168-1; Nancy A. widow of; Pvt D Co 3rd TN Cav; 30 Nov 62 to killed in service; Knoxville PO
HANCOCK, Zinnis?, We-221-7; Pvt K Co 10th NC __?; Dec 62 to 18 Jul 65; Martin PO; imprisoned 7 mos in Elmiry, New York; CONF
HANCOCK, _____, Sn-252-2; Isabella E. widow of; Pvt A Co 8th KY Cav; Gallatin PO
HAND, George R., K-179-2; Pvt B Co 9th TN Inf; Virtue PO
HANDCOCK, Jseoph E., D-72-2; Sgt E Co 12th TN Inf; Aug 12 64 to Jan 16 66; Nashville PO
HANDCOCK, Randall, Gi-122-1; Pvt AL Inf; 61 to __ (1 yr); Prospect Sta. PO; CONF
HANDLEY, William P., Hd-55-1; Pvt C Co 1st AL Cav; 15 Nov 63 to 3 Mar 64; Olive Hill PO; wounded in sholder, ammunition wagon run over and crushed ankle, now suffering from hemorrage of the lungs
HANDS, William, Gu-47-1; Mont Eagle? PO
HANDS, _____ (see Ewing, Mary)
HANEL, Moses, Gi-138-2; 18th Dist
HANES, Ezekial S., Mr-99-2; Pvt C Co 6th R Mtd Inf; 9-12-64 to 1-30-65; Jasper PO
HANES, J. R., A-1-1; Sgt F Co 3rd TN Inf; 10-9-62 to 66; Turnville PO; rheumatism
HANEY, Cash, Br-6-1; Malicen widow of; Pvt; Stamper PO; soldirs names, co & regt I did not get, she dus pension?
HANEY, Colonel W., A-13-3; Cpl H Co 22nd KY Inf; 10-10-61 to 3-11-66; Briceville PO; first belonged 22nd KY reenlisted 7th KY
HANEY, Frank M., Br-12-3; Pvt G Co 10th TN Cav; McPherren PO; injured in side
HANEY, James H., Ro-210-5; Rachel widow of; Pvt H Co 3rd NC Inf; 64 to 65; Rockwood PO
HANEY, John, Jn-82-2; Pvt H Co 1st TN Mtd Inf; 64 to 65; Bloomington PO; rupture on right side
HANEY, John L., H-49-3; Pvt H Co 2nd US Inf Vol; 10-13-64 to 11-13-65; Lake Side PO
HANEY, Samuel C., Ge-102-2; Polly A. widow of; Camp Creek PO

HANEY, William R., Ja-85-1; Cpl E Co 5th TN Inf; 3-2-62 to 4-4-65; Birchwood PO; chronic diarrhoea
HANIS, Martha (see Cummins, Andrew)
HANKER, William H., Dk-32-4; Pvt K Co 5th TN Cav; 2-8-63 to 8-14-65; Liberty PO; liver & kidney disease
HANKINS, Dannel, Me-93-1; Pvt H Co 5th TN Inf; 3-18-62 to 5-16-65; Ten Mile Stand PO; varicose veins, injury to eyes
HANKINS, Jeremiah, Cf-42-2; Pvt KY Cav; 62 to 65; Manchester PO; war papers lost
HANKINS, John E., Ge-93-1; Pvt A Co 4th TN Inf; 15 Mar 63 to 2 Aug 65; Greeneville PO
HANKINS, Marcus Z., We-222-1; Pvt G Co 15th MI Inf; 11 Mar 61 to 11 May 65; Gardner PO; CONF
HANKINS, William, L-105-1; Pvt G Co 59th IL Inf; Jul 4 61 to 65; Edeth PO; forgotten date of discharge
HANKLE, Michael R., Ct-39-1; Pvt G Co 29th TN Inf; 8-61 to 65; Johnson City PO
HANKS, William R., Hm-103-1; Pvt H Co 8th TN Inf; 1 Mar 63 to ___; Morristown PO
HANLEY, Thomas J., Ce-23-1; Pvt G Co 30th TN; Aug 61 to Sep 62; Thomasville PO; measels 3 mos
HANN, Andrew C., Hm-108-3(2); Pvt D Co 1st TN Cav; 2 Jan 63 to 25 May 65; Russellville PO; eyes, kidneys & back
HANN, Daniel, U-247-2; Pvt B Co 3rd NC Mtd Inf; 19 Jul 64 to 8 Aug 65; Erwin PO; rheumatism, piles & heart disease
HANN, George E., Hm-108-3(2); Pvt G Co 2nd TN Cav; 1 Oct 62 to 7 Jul 65; Russellville PO; liver complaint
HANN, George W., Je-141-1; Pvt D Co 4th TN Inf; 1 Mar 63 to 2 Aug 65; New Market PO
HANN, Lewis, Hm-109-2; S. M. C Co 3rd TN Cav; 3 Dec 62 to 3 Aug 65; Whitesburg PO
HANN, William H., Hm-109-4; Pvt D Co 8th TN Inf; May 62 to 30 Jun 65; Whitesburg PO
HANN, Zachariah, Hm-108-2(1); Pvt G Co 8th TN Inf; 18 Nov 62 to 30 Jun 65; Russellville PO; chronic diariah
HANNA, Calvin, Hd-54-3; Sgt H Co 6th TN Cav; 11 Oct 62 to 26 Jul 65; Saltillo PO; chronic rheumatism; promoted to 1st Lt Oct 7 64
HANNA, John W., Hd-54-3; US Sol; PO omitted
HANNAH, Andrew B., Bo-14-2(1); Pvt L Co 2nd TN Cav; 9-8-63 to 7-6-65; Huffstetlers Store PO
HANNAH, Harvey, Se-230-4; Sarah E. Hill formerly widow of (see Messer, Samuel); Richison's Cove PO; her husband, sol (CONF) is still living but not with her
HANNAH, Isaac A., Bo-14-3; Pvt H Co 2nd TN Cav; 10-10-62 to 7-5-65; Huffstetlers Store PO
HANNAH, John H., Bo-14-5; Pvt A Co 3rd TN Inf; 2-10-62 to 2-23-65; Clover Hill PO
HANNAH, William A., Bo-14-5; Pvt A Co 3rd TN Inf; 11-2-63 to 8-2-65; Clover Hill PO
HANNAN, Fred, Mu-210-6; Pvt A Co 9th TN Cav; Oct 62 to 64; Mallard PO; CONF
HANNER, Disney, M-137-1; Pvt K Co 16th TN Col Inf; Ma 62 to 21 Jan 66; papers lost; St. Bethlehem PO
HANSFORD, Benjamin F., Wa-274-1; Mary M. widow?; Pvt I Co 1st TN Cav; 21 Sep 62 to 24 Jan 64; Jonesboro PO
HANSLEY, Andrew, D-72-2; Pvt D Co 1st TN Art; Sep 30 63 to Jul 28 65; Nashville PO
HANSON, Frank, H-53-3; Sgt E Co 52nd IL Inf; 61 to 64; Chattanooga PO
HANSON, Jno. D., B-7-2; Pvt C Co 5th TN Cav; 8-21-62 to 1-25-65; PO omitted
HANWILL, Robert, Gi-138-1; Pvt D Co; 61 to 12-24-62; Bodinham PO
HANY, George W., Br-12-1; Pvt D Co 5th TN Inf; 8-20-64 to 7-2-65; Charleston PO; piles
HANY, Henry, Br-12-3; Pvt D Co 5th TN Inf; 10-64 to 7-2-65; Raht PO; hart pluersy
HANY, Peter, We-232-1; Pvt E Co 13th TN Cav; 63 to 65; Mount Pulie PO
HAPPER, George W., Cl-57-1; Cpl C Co 1st TN Inf; 2-1-62 to 2-1-65; Kecks Chappel PO; hart trouble, rheumatism & mumps, Feb 1862
HARACE, Haran, K-175-2; Pvt D Co 17th KY Cav; 3 Dec 64 to 3 Dec 65; Bayless PO
HARALD, Arnist, La-111-4; US Sol; 5th Civil Dist

HARALSON, Ephram F., D-75-3; Pvt H? Co 38th TN Inf; Nov 62 to 15 Jun 64; Stewarts Ferry PO; CONF
HARALSON, William L., D-75-1; Pvt H Co 38th TN Inf; 12 Apr 61 to 1 Sep 63; Stewarts Ferry PO; CONF
HARBER, J. W., Cr-7-1; Pvt D Co 12th TN Inf; 5-28-61 to 65; Eaton PO (Gibson Co.)
HARBERT, Benjamin F., Sh-167-1; Annie M. widow of; PO omitted; CONF
HARBERT, Harrison L., Hd-53-2; 1st Sgt C Co 6th TN Cav; 11 Sep 62 to 26 Jul 65; Morris Chapel PO
HARBERT, Terriel P., Hd-53-2; Sgt C Co 6th TN Cav; 11 Sep 62 to 26 Jul 65; Morris Chapel PO
HARBIN, Jacob, Gr-73-2; Pvt F Co 1st TN Cav; 1 Apr 62 to Apr 65; Turley's Mills PO
HARBIN, James D., Hi-86-1; Pvt G Co 12th TN; 63 to ___; goon shot in sholder (James D. Harbin was gun shot at Nashville)
HARBIN, Joseph, Gr-73-1; Pvt C Co 4th TN Cav; Jan 1 63 to 65; Westerville PO
HARBISON, John, D-87-1; Elizabeth B. widow of; IL; Nashville PO
HARBOUR, Elisha, Su-241-1; 2nd Lt F Co 2nd TN Inf; 4 Nov 61 to 3 Aug 65; Harbours PO; Mexican Soldier
HARBOUR, Martha, Hd-47-2; 4th Civil Dist
HARDAN, George W., Lo-249-1; Pvt 1st Indep. DE Bat; Jul 63 to 1 Jul 65; Flag Pond PO
HARDAN, John L., Mn-121-2; Pvt G Co 1st AL Cav; 5-63 to 1-66; Bethel Springs PO; woonded at Cross Rods AL; lost discharge, can't tell exact dates
HARDAWAY, Cyrus, Sh-198-1; Cyrus Harwell alias; Pvt K Co 63rd Col Inf; 11-2-63 to 1-9-66; Memphis PO; has his discharge
HARDBARGER, Rufus, R-160-1; Pvt H Co 13th TN; 10-1-63 to 2-21-64; 6th Civil Dist
HARDCASTLE, William L., Dk-39-6(2); Pvt; Laurel Hill PO
HARDDIN, Ben, Sn-264-1; Pvt K Co 6th KY Cav; Jul 14 62 to Jul 15 65; Portland PO; wounded in rt. hand, papers all right, muster out in Nashville, Col Roper, Cap Jim McCowan
HARDEN, Alfred, Sh-162-1; Pvt 78th IN Inf; Jun 16 62 to Dec 63; Ramsey PO; shot in thigh and breast
HARDEN, Alvin P., Ct-43-2; Pvt C Co 47th KY Inf; 7-9-63 to 12-28-64; Carter Furnace PO; injury to spine falling bridge
HARDEN, Charley O., T-211-1; Pvt C Co 30th KY Inf; 1 Jan 63 to 21 Apr 65; Brighton PO; rheumatism, eyes effected
HARDEN, Eli, Ct-42-2; Pvt A Co 13th TN Cav; 9-22-63 to 9-22-65; Watauga PO; in prison 3 mos
HARDEN, Elijah D., Ct-42-3; Pvt L Co 13th TN Cav; 3-19-63 to 9-8-65; Elizabethton PO; rheumatism
HARDEN, Georg W., Lo-194-1; Pvt F Co 26th TN Inf; 1 Oct 62 to 18 Aug 64; Muddy Creek PO; right arm shot off
HARDEN, Harvy A., Se-224-2; Pvt B Co 2nd TN Cav; 15 Aug 62 to 6 Jul 65; Line Spring PO; diarea & piles, horse fell on me & held me
HARDEN, Hoe?, Co-69-2; Pvt I Co 62nd TN Inf; 17 Oct 62 to 8 Jul 63; Rankin PO; CONF
HARDEN, Isaac P., K-186-4; Pvt H Co 1st CA Art; 9th Jun 64 to 31 Mar 66; Beaver Ridge PO
HARDEN, James M., Se-223-3; Pvt G Co 6th TN Inf; 1 May 62 to 17 May 65; Sevierville PO
HARDEN, Jasper, Wh-185-2; Pvt E Co 4th TN Inf; 11-1-64 to 8-25-65; Cassville PO; sight affected
HARDEN, John, Mc-114-6; Pvt K Co 1st TN Cav; 2-10-61 to 4-1-61; Santfordville PO
HARDEN, John H., Ct-42-3; Pvt F Co 13th TN Cav; 9-21-63 to 9-5-65; Watauga PO; rheumatism
HARDEN, Joshuwa, Mu-210-6; Margett widow of; Pvt; 62 to 65; Mallard PO
HARDEN, Solomen, Ja-84-3; Thatchers Landing PO
HARDEN, William E., Mo-131-2; Recruit Officer; 20th Civil Dist
HARDERSON, Isaac, Mu-279-1; Pvt B Co 4th TN Inf; May 63 to May 65; Franklin PO
HARDESON, Joshua, Sh-193-1; Pvt; Memphis PO
HARDESTY, Jno. C., Br-10-1; Pvt F Co 122nd OH Inf; 1-2-64 to 7-2-65; Cleveland PO
HARDIE, Dudley, D-49-2; Pvt B Co; 61 to 64; Nashville PO; only remembers what is given

HARDIN, Andrew, Fe-41-1; Pvt H Co 1st KY Cav; 10-14-61 to 12-31-64; Pall Mall PO
HARDIN, Enoch, H-49-6; Pvt F Co 6th TN Mtd Inf; 8-2-64 to 6-30-65; Trewhitt PO
HARDIN, James O., Mu-210-1; Pvt Independent Orleans Lighthouse; 3-62 to 5-20-65; Spring Hill PO; CONF
HARDIN, John, Hd-46-1; Harriet widow of; Pvt A Co 11th US Col Inf; __ to Apr 13 64; Cerro Gordo PO
HARDIN, John, Ge-91-5; Pvt A Co 4th TN Inf; 6 Apr 63 to 18 Aug 65; Greeneville PO; chronic diarhea & others
HARDIN, John W., Ct-40-1; Pvt A Co 13th TN Cav; 9-22-63 to 9-5-65; Elizabethton PO; diarrhea
HARDIN, Louis R., Wy-177-1; Pvt A Co 10th TN Inf; 9-10-62 to 4-9-63; Waynesboro PO
HARDIN, Martin J., La-117-2; Cpl B Co 23rd TN Inf; Jul 9 61 to Aug 62; Pinkery PO; CONF
HARDIN, Oliver, Ge-93-2; Pvt A Co 4th TN Inf; Mar 62 to Aug 65; Greeneville PO
HARDIN, Samuel W., Wa-260-2; Quartermaster Sgt 3rd NC Inf; Jul 24 64 to Aug 8 65; Pilot Hill PO; had his discharge with him at Greenvill, TN
HARDIN, Samuel W., Ge-83-1; Sgt C Co 8th? NC Mtd Inf; 2 Jul 64 to 8 Aug 65; Horse Creek PO; disease of stomic
HARDIN, Thomas G., De-22-2; Pvt H Co 16th TN Cav; 10 Jun 62 to 9 May 65; Clifton PO; shot in left leg & hand?; CONF
HARDIN, Wm. A., Ch-15-1; Henderson PO
HARDINBROOK, Theophilus, Sn-262-3(2); Pvt L Co 3rd MI Cav; 20 Sep 61 to 12 Sep 65; Fountain Head PO; rheumatism & shot in the ankle
HARDING, Benjamin F., K-179-4; Cpl A Co 40th US Inf; 17 Mar 63? to 30 Apr 65; PO omitted
HARDING, Henry (see Duncan, Henry)
HARDING, Hezikiah, D-77-2; Sgt B Co 40th US Inf; Nashville PO
HARDING, John H., Rb-221-1; Pvt 13th IN; Jan 16 62 to Apr 1 65; Barren Plains PO
HARDING, Narcissus, Ca-25-1; widow US Sol; 9th Civil Dist
HARDING, Rebecca, D-80-1; 2nd Civil Dist
HARDING, William B., Un-252-2; Cpl B Co 8th TN Cav; 27 Apr 63 to 11 Sep 65; Acuff PO
HARDISON, Ben, Gi-128-2; Pvt K Co 123rd IN Inf; 63 to 65; Pulaski PO
HARDON, William A., Mo-129-2; Pvt; Povo PO
HARDWICK, James A., Pi-154-2; Pvt F Co 12th KY Inf; 8-20-63 to 7-3-65; Otto PO
HARDY, Lewis, Gi-123-3; Caroline widow of; Pvt F Co 110th TN Inf; Nov 62 to Apr 65; Bethel PO; wounded with bomb shell which caused his death, she says
HARDY, Thomas, D-68-3; Pvt A Co 14th USC Inf; 17 Sep 63 to 26 Mar 66; River St, Nashville PO; shot in right side and two toes shot off right foot, Dec 18 64, had measles Mar 1864 and they settled in the eyes and right eye went out Mar 1867
HARE, Charley H., T-215-2; 1st Lt 27th IN Cav; 119th Reg; 61 to 65; Mason PO; shot twice, ba-1 still in left thigh
HARE, Richard B., H-61-2; Capt B Co 45th TN Inf; 1-62 to 2-63; Chattanooga PO
HARELSON, Henry, Mt-138-2; US Sol; Dist. No. 7, N. Providence PO
HAREN, James N., K-178-1; Pvt C Co 6th TN Cav; 18 Apr 62 to 27 Apr 65; Campbell PO
HARGES, Charles F., M-103-1; Cpl I Co 9th KY Inf; 10-25-61 to 12-13-64; Lafayette PO; diseased lungs
HARGES, Shadrack B., M-103-1; Pvt K Co 9th KY Inf; 11-28-61 to 1-8-65; Lafayette PO; gun shot in hand
HARGIN, Henry J., Dk-32-3; Rachel widow of; Saddler K Co 5th KY Cav; 3-8-63 to 8-14-65; Liberty PO
HARGRAVE, Spencer, Ms-175-1; Eanesa White widow of; Dist 9; gun shot wound
HARGRAVES, Ben, Ch-12-2; Pvt 48th TN Inf; 10-61 to 64; Custer Point PO; CONF
HARGROVE, John R., Gi-122-2; Pvt 3rd TN Inf; 63 to 64; Prospect Sta. PO; prison 6 days; CONF
HARGROVE, Thomas W., Gi-133-1; Ord Sgt K Co 3rd TN; Aug 62 to 65; Bufords PO; CONF

HARGUS, Adam D., Ca-24-1; Pvt I Co 5th TN Cav; 63 to 8-14-65; Talvine PO; shot in leg, arm displaced when in the service
HARGUS, David, Bo-11-3; Sarah A. widow of; Pvt A Co 3rd TN Inf; 2-10-62 to __ (2 yrs); Hout PO; died in svce.
HARGUS, S. T., Bo-11-2; Pvt A Co 3rd TN Inf; 2-10-62 to 2-23-65; Houk PO
HARIL, Ruffin, Be-5-2; Patcey widow of; Pvt B Co 64th __ Inf; Feb 64 to Mar 66; Eggville PO; cronick diarrhea
HARIS, Paton, Ru-248-1; H Co 14th TN Inf; 11-63 to 4-9-66; Floraton PO
HARISON, Gran, Ru-239-2; Sol; 12th Civil Dist
HARISON, Henry, Bo-20-1; Bank PO
HARISON, James, G-64-1; Pvt G Co 7th __; May 62 to 63; Bradford PO; CONF
HARKEN, Aaron, K-175-2; Pvt A Co 4th TN Cav; 18 Aug 62 to 18 Mar? 65; Bullrun PO
HARLAN, Elihu B., K-159-3; Pvt B Co 3rd IA Cav; 29 Feb 64 to 9 Aug 65; Knoxville PO; 1st enlisted 4th Iowa Baty and then in Cav
HARLAN, Thomas, Mu-209-4; Pvt A Co 14th TN Inf; Oct 63 to Mar 13 65; Darks Mills PO; shot in left thigh; CONF
HARLAND, Randal, Mu-200-2; Pvt D Co 13th TN Inf; 12 Aug 63 to 10 Jan 66; Mt. Pleasant PO; back crippled in service
HARLAND, William, Ru-238-2; Sgt F Co 111th USC Inf; 64 to 65; Murfreesboro PO; prisoner 3 months
HARLEN, William H., Un-254-2; Pvt F Co 6th TN Inf; 10 Mar 62 to 27 Mar 65; Bartheney PO
HARLESS, William, C-24-2; Kisabert? widow of; Pvt C Co 9th TN Inf; 7-11-63 to 9-11-65; Girlton PO; died of consumption
HARLESS, William, Hw-127-4; Pvt; Amis PO
HARLEY, Alexander, D-71-2; Nashville PO
HARLIN, Margarett (see Lawson, William)
HARLOW, John, Le-119-1; Pvt G Co 10th TN Inf; 9 May 62 to 9 Jun 64; Chief PO; chronic rheumatism and diarrheah
HARLOW, Mary, Le-119-1; widow US Sol; Dist No. 8, Rapier Furnace? PO
HARMAN, D. P., Cl-54-2; Soldier US; PO omitted
HARMAN, James W., B-5-1; Pvt E Co 10th TN Inf; 6-17-62 to 7-3-65; Shelbyville PO; crippled left arm & back
HARMAR, Moses, Br-6-1; Dusom Grimes widow of; Pvt A Co 8th TN Inf; 2-20-63 to 64 (1 yr 1 mo 2 days); Climer PO
HARMING, Garrett, Cf-40-1; Lt Col MI Cav; Sep 22 61 to 22 Dec 65; Tullahoma PO
HARMON, Benton, Mt-139-2; Pvt C Co 1st MN (Artificer?); 11-10-63 to 7-22-65; Dist 21
HARMON, Ephraim, C-27-1; Pvt A Co 1st TN Inf; 8-8-61 to 9-17-64; Jacksboro PO
HARMON, Franklin H., A-13-2; Pvt B Co 1st TN Inf; 8-9-61 to 3-23-65; Briceville PO
HARMON, Isaac B., Ge-100-3; Pvt A Co 4th TN Inf; 27 Jan 63 to 2 Aug 65; Midway PO
HARMON, Jacob, K-170-3; US Sol; Dist 12
HARMON, Jacob H., Bo-21-3; Pvt C Co 6th TN Inf; 8-25-63 to 6-13-65; Ellijay PO
HARMON, Jacop F.?, Ge-100-2; Pvt E Co 8th TN Inf; 4 Jun 63 to Nov 63; Mohawk PO
HARMON, James T., Ge-100-3; Cpl A Co 8th TN Inf; 14 Sep 63 to 14 Sep 65; Midway PO
HARMON, John, Po-149-3(2); Louisa widow of; Pvt G Co 3rd TN Cav; 7-1-63 to 65; Ocoee PO
HARMON, John A., K-180-1; Pvt C Co 6th TN Cav; 18 Apr 62 to 27 Apr 65; Bearden PO
HARMON, John B., T-208-1; Nancy J. Walker widow of; Pvt B Co 1st TN; 62 to 64; Garland PO
HARMON, John W., Lo-190-1; Pvt A Co 3rd TN Inf; 10 Feb 62 to 65; Piney PO; rheumatism; CONF
HARMON, Kawly? B., Ge-100-1; Margret widow of; Pvt A Co 4th TN Inf; 30 Jan 64 to 4 Jun 64; Mosheim PO
HARMON, Robert L., Ge-93-4(1); Pvt A Co 4th TN Inf; 6 Apr 63 to 15 Aug 65; Greeneville PO
HARMON, Sperling B., Ge-93-4(1); Pvt A Co 4th TN Inf; 27 Jan 63 to 15 Aug 65; Greeneville PO
HARMON, Thomas, Ge-93-4(1); Pvt A Co 4th TN Inf; 6 Apr 63 to 15 Aug 65; Greeneville PO
HARMON, William R., Bo-21-4; Pvt H Co 4th TN Inf; 7-30-63 to 8-2-65; Ellijay PO

HARMUN, J. C., C-33-4; Capt C Co 22nd PA Cav; 62 to 65; Jellico PO
HARNED, William, Co-61-1; 2nd Lt K Co 8th TN Inf; 4 Jul 63 to 30 Jun 65; Ottinger PO
HARNESS, John, A-9-3(1); Pvt I Co 9th TN Cav; 9-16-63 to 9-11-65; Dutch Valley PO; rheumatism
HARNESS, Thomas, S-215-2; Pvt; Pioneer PO
HAROESTON, William, Bo-19-4; PO omitted
HAROLD, Elbert L., Ge-93-1; Pvt C Co 4th TN Inf; Mar 15 63 to 2 Aug 65; Greenville PO
HAROLL, James M., Hd-50-1; Pvt D Co 2nd TN Mtd Inf; Dec 29 63 to Feb 1 65; Savannah PO
HARP, William D., Bo-13-1; Pvt M Co 13th TN Cav; 2-2-64 to 9-5-65; Unitia PO (Loudon Co.)
HARPER, Alferd M., Dy-25-2; Lt; 61 to 65; Newbern PO; CONF
HARPER, Alfred, M-108-5; Pvt A Co 8th TN Mtd Inf; 3-20-65 to 8-7-65; Lafayette PO
HARPER, Allen, Sh-157-3; Pvt I Co 3rd US; 63 to 65; Lake View, MS PO; rib broken
HARPER, Edward, Sh-159-6; Memphis PO
HARPER, George, Sh-191-2; Elmira widow of; Memphis PO; records not seen
HARPER, Henry, Sh-152-2; Pvt H Co 68th MI Inf; 30 Jan 64 to 5 Feb 65; Leno PO
HARPER, Jasper N., Dk-38-1; Pvt A Co 5th TN Cav; 8-9-62 to 6-25-65; Crawfordton PO
HARPER, John P., Br-12-5; Sarah widow of; Lt E Co 4th TN Cav; Georgetown PO; died in hospital
HARPER, John W., J-83-1; Pvt TN; 64 to 65; Flynns Lick PO
HARPER, Joseph, Sh-145-2; Pvt F Co 14th USC Hvy Art; Aug 64 to 23 Dec 66; Millington PO; enlisted under Maj. Jinester at Newbern, NC; Capt Mills, Col Pre, Maj Moore
HARPER, Robt. L., Dy-27-2; Mary F. wife of; Pvt TN Cav; May 61 to May 65; Newbern PO; CONF
HARPER, Sterling, D-45-2; Pvt F Co 12th TN Cav; 9-7-64 to 10-7-65; Nashville PO
HARPER, Thomas D. A., Co-61-5(2); Pvt F Co 5th TN Cav; 21 Jun 61 to __; Bridgeport PO; CONF
HARPER, William, Sh-159-6; Pvt; Memphis PO
HARPER, William A., K-158-2; 1st Lt H Co 128th IN Inf; 6 NOv 63 to 10 Apr 66; Knoxville, 39 Payne St., PO; rheumatism and resulting in disease of heart
HARRASS, William, F-43-2; alias William Barton; Pvt K Co 55th TN Cav; 63 to Jan 66; Rossville PO
HARREL, Samuel, K-172-5(1); Pvt A Co 1st TN Inf; 2 yrs 10 mos; Knoxville PO
HARRELL, Columbus, Cr-16-2; Pvt B Co 64th US Col Inf; Feb 15 64 to Mar 13 66; Huntingdon PO; had typhoid fever whiel in service which produced bed sores on hips
HARRELL, Henry J., Gr-72-1; Pvt F Co 1st TN Cav; 1 Mar 62 to 1 Mar 65; Noelon PO; long contrived riding
HARRELL, Isaac O., Ge-91-2; Pvt 26th IN Bat; 14 Aug 62 to 19 Jul 65; Greeneville PO; catarh & several other disabilities
HARRELL, Joseph B., Mc-112-5; Cpl I Co 32nd MO Cav; 7-65 to __; Athens PO; this man took sick & went home, no discharge
HARRELL, Maxfield, A-3-1; Pvt H Co 1st TN Inf; 8-9-61 to 9-17-64; Bull Run PO (Knox Co.); fever
HARRELL, Milton, Hw-124-2(1); Sgt H Co 8th TN Cav; 19 Nov 63 to 11 Sep 65; New Canton PO
HARRELL, William, Sh-148-1; papers lost; Memphis PO
HARRELL, William A., A-3-3; Pvt C Co 3rd TN Inf; 2-12-62 to 2-23-65; Clinton PO; catarrh and piles
HARRELL, William C., A-4-4; Pvt A Co 1st TN Inf; 8-2-61 to 9-17-64; Coal Creek PO; leg injured
HARRELL, William P., Gr-72-1; Pvt A Co 9th TN Cav; 24 Oct 64 to 11 Sep 65; Noeton PO; discharges are at Washington
HARRIES, Mack, Mu-197-2; Chancy widow of; Pvt; 62 to 65; Columbia PO
HARRIGHAN, Dave, Sh-167-1; Pvt M Co 1st TN Cav; 5 Aug 61 to 9 Sep 64; 9 Washington, Memphis PO
HARRIMAN, George, Wi-277-1; 2nd Lt B Co 31st OH, 174th OH; Aug 61 to Jul 5 65; 8th Civil Dist
HARRIMAN, John, Ca-20-2; Pvt C Co 5th TN Cav; 3-1-62 to 5-64; Talvine PO

HARRINGTON, George W., Ce-21-1; Pvt G Co 10th TN Inf; 7-10-62 to 65; Hoffas Wells PO
HARRINGTON, John, D-44-2(1); __ Gunner Bat 1 US Navy; 12-2-62 to 12-24-64; Nashville PO; deaf in one ear
HARRINGTON, John C., A-3-1; Pvt C Co 3rd TN Inf; 2-12-62 to 2-28-65; Bud PO; rhumatism and catarrh
HARRINGTON, Osborn R., K-180-4; US Sol; 11th Dist
HARRINGTON, Osborne, K-180-4; Pvt; Ebenezer PO
HARMS, John W., Dk-32-3; Cpl H Co 1st TN Mtd Inf; 1-26-64 to 5-23-65; Gordensville PO; shot in head, shouler & neck
HARRIS, Abrim, F-46-1; alias Thomas Parham; Pvt I Co 59th TN; LaGrange PO; dislocated sholder
HARRIS, Ambrose, L-104-1; US Sol; 6th Civil Dist
HARRIS, Andrew, Sm-176-1; Pvt; 5-64 to 65; Knolton PO
HARRIS, Andrew, Mr-95-2; Pvt I Co 10th TN Inf; 3-1-63 to 6-23-65; Victoria PO
HARRIS, Andrew A., Hd-53-3; Pvt C Co 111th US Col Inf; 8 Oct 63 to 23 May 66; Coffee Landing PO; discharged lost
HARRIS, Armstrong, U-249-1; Pvt E Co 2nd NC Inf; 14 May 64 to 16 Aug 65; Flag Pond PO
HARRIS, Aron V. B., Hu-106-2; Pvt E Co 8th KY Art; Apr 63 to Mar 64; Waverly PO
HARRIS, Axy C. (W), Be-2-1; Pvt E Co 7th TN Cav; 61 to died 64; Holladay PO
HARRIS, Bartlet Y., Gr-71-2; Pvt I Co 8th TN Inf; 1 Mar 63 to 30 Jun 65; Jarmine PO; wounded by gunshots
HARRIS, Burges, Ce-23-2; Cpl G Co 42nd TN; May 61 to May 65; Thomasville PO; chronic diarhoea 2 yrs, flux
HARRIS, Buryl, Hw-130-1; Pvt L Co 4th KY Cav; 10 Jan 64 to 2 Aug 65; Lee Valley PO
HARRIS, Carter, J-80-2; Pvt E Co 10th IN Cav; 63 to 6-30-65; Granville PO; blind caused by neuralgia & exposure, discharge not in Harris possession
HARRIS, Dewitt E., Mo-122-1; Sgt F Co 3rd TN Cav; 4-26-63 to 6-10-65; Dancing Branch PO
HARRIS, Emily (see Rankin, William T.)
HARRIS, Emmaline (see Booker, Green)
HARRIS, Ezekiel, Co-61-1; Pvt L Co 8th TN Cav; 1 Oct 63 to 11 Sep 65; Parrottsville PO; bloody piles, badly crippled in back
HARRIS, Frank, Sh-148-1; papers lost; Memphis PO
HARRIS, Frank M., W1-295-2; Lebanon PO
HARRIS, George, G-68-1; alias Geo. Cogle; Pvt K Co 4th KY; 61 to 65; Gibson PO; loss one eye
HARRIS, George, Di-37-2; Pvt D Co 16th IN Inf; 12-24-63 to 4-30-66; Cumberland Furnace PO
HARRIS, George, Mu-189-1; Pvt 128th IL Cav; Hurrican Switch PO
HARRIS, George T., Ge-96-1; Lt M Co 1st TN Cav; 13 Aug 62 to 1 Jun 65; Limestone PO; neuralgia &c
HARRIS, H. C., Mn-123-2; Pvt B Co 6th TN Cav; Falcon PO; was goone from home and discharge locked up
HARRIS, Henry H., T-210-1; Orderly T (sic) Co 1st US Hvy Art; Apr 63 to Apr 65; Uril PO
HARRIS, Hooper, D-72-4; Maj. Nashville PO; CONF
HARRIS, Isaac, Sh-159-3; Ora widow of; Memphis PO; husband lost one arm; CONF
HARRIS, James, H-54-5; Pvt E Co 10th IN Cav; 11-3-63 to 8-1-65; PO omitted (Chattanooga?)
HARRIS, James, Ha-113-2; Pvt A Co 1st TN Cav; 1 Jun 62 to 12 Apr 65; Sneedville PO
HARRIS, James H., F-38-1; Sgt C Co 3rd TN Cav; May 62 to May 65; Mason PO
HARRIS, James M., Mo-130-2; Pvt; Ballplay PO
HARRIS, James P., Dy-25-3; Pvt K Co 12th TN Cav; 64 to 12 Apr 65; Newbern PO; CONF
HARRIS, Jock, Gi-123-3; PO omitted
HARRIS, John, Ct-40-2; Pvt J Co 13th TN Cav; Elizabethton PO
HARRIS, John, Hm-106-3; Morristown PO; refuse to answer; CONF
HARRIS, John, D-79-1; Mary E. widow; Pvt E Co 100th OH Inf; Aug 7 62 to Jun 20 65; Nashville, Joseph Ave, PO
HARRIS, John, Mo-123-2; 8th Civil Dist
HARRIS, John A., A-1-12; Pvt C Co 1st TN Inf; 8-7-61 to 10-6-64; Andersonville PO; piles

HARRIS, John H., Hd-52-1; Pvt E Co 8th TN; Oct 15 63 to __ (11 mos); Adamsville PO
HARRIS, John L., Hw-121-5(4); Pvt D Co 10th VA Reg; 25 May 62 to 30 Apr 63; Lucas PO; CONF
HARRIS, John S., Sh-159-6; Agt Lt I Co 17th MS; 29 Apr 61 to __ (2 yrs); Memphis PO; CONF
HARRIS, John T., Sh-149-1; Pvt F Co 12th TN Cav; 20 Jul 61 to 30 Jul 65; National Cemetery PO; CONF
HARRIS, John W., A-4-5; Pvt G Co 11th GA? Inf; 6-61 to 12-64; Coal Creek PO; CONF
HARRIS, Judee (see Surratt, Abe)
HARRIS, L. H., Gi-139-2; Pvt G Co 44th TN Inf; 12-61 to 5-65; Campbellsville PO; CONF
HARRIS, Little A., We-220-3; 1st Civil Dist
HARRIS, Louisa (see Herrington, John K.)
HARRIS, Madison M., K-162-1; Pvt C Co 9th TN Cav; 11 Jul 63 to 11 Sep 65; Knoxville PO
HARRIS, Mary (see Forrest, William)
HARRIS, Nancy M., Br-14-2; widow of US Sol; 12th Dist
HARRIS?, Nat, Wi-278-1; Drummer C Co 25th MO Inf--Mar 5 62 to Apr 64; Drummer H Co 43rd MO Inf --Sep 1 64 to Jul 65; Franklin PO
HARRIS, Nathan, Ha-111-2; Elisabeth widow of; Kyles Ford PO
HARRIS, Nathan, Li-155-1; Pvt F Co 111th US Regt Col Inf; 1-6-64 to 4-30-66; Boon's Hill PO; measles fell in eyes; spine affected while in CS prison
HARRIS, Nathan M., Lo-189-3(1); Pvt & Sgt A Co 11th KY Cav; Aug 62 to Apr 65; Philadelphia PO; not mustered out with company
HARRIS, Newson, Ce-23-1; Sarah widow of; Pvt 1812 to 1812; Thomasville PO
HARRIS, Notley, Mt-149-1; Pvt C Co 2nd IL Lt Art; Dec 64 to Aug 65; Riggins PO
HARRIS, Orren, F-39-2(1); Cpl C Co 66th US Col Inf; 29 Feb 64 to 20 Dec 65; PO omitted
HARRIS, Payton, Sh-149-1; Pvt US Nav Mail Line; 64 to 65; Raleigh PO
HARRIS, Perminius L. (77--sic), Hm-104-1; Pvt A Co 4th TN Inf; 5 Jan 63 to 2 Aug 65; Talbotts PO (Jefferson Co.); Black tounge fever setted on brain, feble minded, head sore
HARRIS, Pink, Gi-131-2; Mary widow of; Pvt; Sumac PO; widow now gets a pension
HARRIS, R. M., Je-141-2; Emily M. widow of; Sgt; New Market PO
HARRIS, Robert P., Ge-85-2; Cpl A Co 3rd TN Inf; 30 Jun 64 to 5 Nov 64; Cavey Branch PO; hors falling on me and mashed right side & back--captured and in Wittville VA prison
HARRIS, Samuel, H-68-1; Pvt A Co 3rd VA Vol; 1-62 to 2-13-65; Chattanooga PO
HARRIS, Samuel, Pu-145-3(4); Nancy D. widow of; Pvt L Co 5th Cav Vol; 4-24-63 to 8-14-65; Silver Point PO
HARRIS, Samuel, Mr-95-2; Pvt I Co 10th TN Inf; 5-14-63 to 5-25-65; Victoria PO
HARRIS, Samuel, Ru-241-3; Pvt 111th __; 63 to 66; PO omitted
HARRIS, Shadrack, K-162-1; Capt D Co 3rd TN Cav; Dec 62 to Apr 65; Knoxville PO; eyes, throat & lungs; Capt also contracted cronic dyreah
HARRIS, Thomas, D-54-1; Hattie widow of; Pvt US Col Art; Nashville PO
HARRIS, Thomas, Cf-41-1; 15th Civil Dist
HARRIS, Thomas G., Sn-260-5; Pvt K Co 20th KY Inf; 5-9-61 to 5-25-65; Westmoreland PO; shot through leg & broken; CONF
HARRIS, Thomas L., Hm-107-4; Lellie J. widow of; Pvt I Co 8th TN Inf; Jun 62 to 65 (3 yrs 8 mos); Chestnut Bloom PO; dropsy
HARRIS, Thomas R., H-56-1; Massachusetts; 6-22-64 to 8-12-65; St. Elm(o) PO
HARRIS, Vinnie, Wl-291-1; Sol US; Lebanon PO
HARRIS, William, Br-14-2; Pvt 4th TN Cav; __ to 7-12-65; McDonald PO
HARRIS, William, Je-146-5; Pvt C Co 1st US Col Art; 31 Jul 64 to 31 Mar 66; White Pine PO; lung disease, he's a poor old man
HARRIS, William, Wa-261-2; Pvt L Co 4th KY Cav; 19 Jan 64 to 21 Aug 65; Conkling PO
HARRIS, William, Mr-97-1; I Co KY Cav; 7-18-63 to 7-17-65; PO omitted
HARRIS, William D., Ge-92-5; US Sol; 11th Dist

HARRIS, William H., Ja-86-1; Pvt G Co 4th TN Cav; 5-61 to 65 (3 yrs 8 mos); Oottewah PO
HARRIS, William M., K-174-4(3); Pvt F Co 3rd TN Inf; 18 Feb 62 to 23 Feb 65; Graveston PO; gun shot in left side
HARRIS, William R., De-26-3; D Co 7th TN; 15 Sep 62 to 25 Oct 63; Poplar Springs PO
HARRIS, William R., J-81-3; Pvt K Co 1st TN; 9-64 to 65 (9 mos); Meringo PO; pneumonia from 3 month; CONF
HARRIS, William R., J-81-3; 9th Civil Dist
HARRIS, William S., K-159-2; Pvt C Co 1st TN Cav; 1 Nov 62 to 25 Jul 65; Knoxville PO; discharged Co "L" Consolidated
HARRIS, William T., Sn-260-5; Capt K Co 20th TN Inf; 5-9-61 to 1-16-65; Westmoreland PO; shot through arm & hands
HARRIS, William W. (see Harrison, William H.)
HARRIS, Wishinghan, Mc-114-4; Pvt I Co 10th TN Cav; Santfordville PO; brain fever during war
HARRIS, ___, Sh-159-1; Jane widow of; Memphis PO
HARRISON, Add, Co-67-2; Mary J. Layman widow of; Pvt F Co 2nd TN Cav; 22 Sep 62 to 31 May 65; Cosby PO
HARRISON, Alexander, Ro-208-1; Pvt I Co 12th TN Cav; 21 Mar 64 to 28 Jun 65; Welker Mines PO
HARRISON, Amos I., Ge-92-4; Sgt I Co 1st TN Cav; 1 Aug 62 to 5 Jun 65; Ottway PO; disease of lungs
HARRISON, Andrew J., K-174-1; Pvt G Co 7th TN Inf; 12 Nov 64 to 27 Jul 65; Graveston PO; shake by lighing (lightning?)
HARRISON, Baxter, Co-68-3; Sgt I Co 2nd TN Cav; 62 to 65; Sutton PO; diarrhea
HARRISON, Benjaman, Li-148-1 (Harrison T. Flint on same line without explanation--an alias?); Pvt E Co 101st Col Inf; 4-25-61 to 1-21-62; Renegar PO; honorable discharge
HARRISON, Carter B., Ru-13-3; Capt 61st OH Vol Inf; Apr 61 to 64; Murfreesboro PO
HARRISON, David F., Lo-187-2; Sarah A. widow of; 2nd Class Fireman Gunboat Louisville; Loudon PO; chronic diarhea
HARRISON, David N., Wa-275-1; Pvt C Co 4th TN Inf; 10 Sep 62 to 7 Jul 65; Pettibone PO; helpless, equivalent to both arms and legs off
HARRISON, Elija P., B-12-2; Pvt C Co 5th TN Cav; Wheel PO; attorney has discharge and could not give dates
HARRISON, Emaline, Mo-131-1; widow; 17th Civil Dist
HARRISON, George, H-69-2; Pvt E Co 138th GA Inf; 7-65 to 1-1-66; Chattanooga PO
HARRISON, George (alias), Me-89-2; Lancy A. widow of; Big Springs PO
HARRISON, George D., Ge-102-2; Pvt E Co 4th TN Inf; 22 Jul 63 to 7 Aug 65; Whig PO
HARRISON, Henry M., Ge-84-1; Pvt G Co 4th TN Inf; 5 Nov 62 to 2 Aug 65; Bird Bridg PO; dis. of lungs, bowels
HARRISON, James, D-54-3; Fannie widow of; Pvt H Co 13th US Col Inf; Nashville PO
HARRISON, Jessie Y., Hm-109-4; Pvt D Co 8th TN Cav?; 20 Apr 63 to 11 Sep 65; Whitesburg PO
HARRISON, John, Mc-112-4; Pvt F Co 4th IN Cav; 8-4-62 to 7-65; Athens PO; rheumatism
HARRISON, John, Je-147-2; Sgt C Co 9th TN Cav; 12 Jun 63 to 24 Mar 65; Shady Grove PO
HARRISON, John, Je-146-3; Pvt G Co 1st TN Cav; 62 to 15 Apr 65; Leadvale PO; wounded 7 times with bulletts, he is old and a ball in his hip
HARRISON, Dr. John B., O-141-2; Union City PO; in the Mexican War
HARRISON, John C., Mc-117-3; Pvt K Co 10th TN Cav; 8-4-64 to 8-1-65; Cog Hill PO; phthisic
HARRISON, John G., Hd-53-1; Cpl B Co 2nd TN Mtd Inf--15 Oct 63 to 17 Oct 64; Pvt E Co 8th TN Mtd Inf--11 Mar 65 to 1 Sep 66; Saltillo PO; rheumatism & chronic diarhea
HARRISON, Joseph, Je-136-2; Pvt K Co 3rd TN Inf; PO omitted
HARRISON, Lewis, Sh-149-3; Pvt Gun Boat Oszark US; 63 to 66; Raleigh PO
HARRISON, M. F., Mc-117-3; Cpl D Co 5th TN Mtd Inf; 11-64 to 7-65; Cog Hill PO
HARRISON, Merrey, Sh-157-5; Pvt A Co 61st Hvy Art; White Haven PO; weakness in the back

HARRISON, Moses, Sh-148-1; Pvt H Co 55th Cav; Memphis PO
HARRISON, Phillip, L-103-1; Pvt H Co 15th NC; cant read dates; Ashport PO; badly wound in spine, gets no pension or help
HARRISON, Rachel (see Payne, Thomas)
HARRISON, Ruffin, Sh-174-1; Pvt I Co 10th OH Inf; 219 Linden St., Memphis PO; run over by horse in skirmish and crippled in abdomen; discharged on acct of disabilities
HARRISON, Russel, Br-14-3; Elisabeth widow of; Pvt I Co 2nd TN Cav; 9-22-62 to 7-6-65; Black Fox PO; cancer in right arm
HARRISON, Samuel, Sm-166-3(1); Pvt A Co 8th TN Inf; 1-10-65 to 4-27-65; Monoville PO
HARRISON, Salts, Wa-263-5; Pvt B Co 12th TN Cav; 9 Jul 63 to 6 Jul 65; Telford PO; discharged on surgeon's certificate
HARRISON, Wesley, Cl-47-3; Pvt E Co 6th TN Inf; 3-14-62 to 4-27-65; Compensation PO; catarrh in the head 64
HARRISON, William, Mo-131-1; Cpl H Co 3rd TN Inf; 9-20-64 to 11-30-64; Ipe PO
HARRISON, William H. (William W. Harris on sched. 1); C-28-2(1); Cpl G Co 9th TN Cav; 7-8-63 to 9-11-65; Big Creek Gap PO; hernia
HARRISON, William L., H-57-4; US Sol; 10th Civil Dist
HARRISSON, Landon C., Wa-272-3; Pvt D Co 1st US Inf; 24 Jun 64 to 27 Nov 65; Free Hill PO; rheumatism
HARRISTON, Giles B., D-66-1; Musician 97th IN; 22 Aug 62 to 9 Jun 65; Nashville, 718 S. Cherry PO
HARRITAGE, John L., Co-62-3; Pvt A Co 3rd TN Mtd Inf; 20 Jun 63 to May 65; Bybee PO; shot in ankle & scurvey
HARROLD, William C., Ge-90-2; Cpl E Co 4th TN Inf; 6 Apr 63 to 3 Aug 65; Greeneville PO; side & kidney truble
HARROWAY, Lewis, D-66-2; Pvt H Co 3rd US Col Inf; Jun 64 to 30 Apr 66; Nashville, 19 Liberty St PO; chronic diases from piels
HARSHA, ___, Hy-81-1; Mrs. Emily C. widow of; Pvt A Co 6th WI; 17 Dec 63 to May 24 65; Brownsville PO; husband dead & her daught. epilepsy, last year in alm house
HART, Absalem, He-67-1; PvtK Co 7th TN Cav; May 63 to Aug 65; Sardis PO; hemorhoids 26 yrs; contracted in Andersonville Prison
HART, Amos, Ro-202-5; Mary A. widow of; Sgt I Co 1st TN Inf; 9 Aug 61 to 17 Sep 64; Cave Creek PO; crippled by fall from horse
HART, Christtzele, Ct-41-1; Pvt H Co 13th TN Cav; 9-24-63 to 9-5-65; Elizabethton PO; piles and rheumatism, hearing
HART, Easley, Hy-82-1; B Co 2nd IL Inf; May 1 ___ to ___ (9 mos); Brownsville PO; now almost blind
HART, Edd, Sh-189-3; Pvt A Co 61st Reg US Col Inf; 5-16-63 to 12-30-65; Dee Ave, Memphis PO
HART, Franklin, Hw-120-2; Amanda widow of; Pvt M Co 13th TN Cav; 64 to 65; Eidson PO
HART, George, Sh-178-4; US Sol; 284 Union, Memphis PO
HART, Green, Sh-191-3; Pvt F Co 3rd Hvy Art; 8-10-63 to 10-65; Memphis PO
HART, Harvey, La-113-2; Pvt F Co 58th OH Inf; 3 Nov 61 to 17 Jul 62; Crowson PO
HART, Henry, Sh-200-2; 21 Polk St, Memphis PO
HART, Henry K., Cr-4-3; Pvt 157th TN Inf; 9-61 to 4-65; Bells Depot PO; wounded in right leg; CONF
HART, James W., Rb-219-1; Pvt C Co 49th TN Reg; Sep 9 61 to Jun 27 65; Black Jack PO; Quarles Brigade
HART, John, Hy-82-3(5); Cornelia widow of; 61 to 65; Johnsons Grove PO
HART, John A., H-66-1; Pvt Ind. Battery 8th OH; 1-3-63 to 8-7-65; Chattanooga PO
HART, Mariah, Hy-82-3(5); widow Pvt; 8th Dist
HART, Moses, Ca-25-1; Pvt E Co 4th MN Inf--3-30-62 to 8-10-62; Mechanicsville PO; farier? C Co 2nd MN Cav--12-1-63 to 11-17-65
HART, Peter E., Ct-38-1; Pvt H Co 13th TN Cav; 9-24-63 to 9-5-65; Milligan PO; chronic diarrhea

HART, Stephen, Sh-157-8; Dist 13
HART, Thomas C., Ct-41-1; Eliza M. widow of; Pvt B Co 4th TN Inf; 11-24-62 to 8-3-65; Elizabethton PO
HART, William A., K-180-4; Pvt E Co 3rd TN Cav; 14 Dec 62 to 14 Jun 65; Ebenezer PO; chronic diarrhoea, defect. sight
HARTDGEN, William, Br-9-2; Anna C. widow of; Cleveland PO; discharge in hands of agent
HARTFORD, Hosee, C-33-2; Lucinda widow of; Pvt B Co 6th NH Inf; 63 to 64; Jellico PO
HARTFORD, Phoebe (see Buford, George)
HARTFORD, Richard F., H-62-1; Acting Ensign, Stepping Stone, Haunch Back; 1-23-62 to 8-23-65; West Fifth, Chattanooga PO
HARTLEY, James M., Lo-194-1; Pvt G Co 1st TN Inf; Aug 61 to Aug 63; Muddy Creek PO
HARTLEY, Laben, Wi-281-1; Pvt H Co 5th TN; Feb 63 to Aug 65; Reeds Store PO; suffering from liver disease since war
HARTLEY, William G., H-61-2; Lt A Co 1st TN Inf; 8-9-61 to 8-65; Chattanooga PO
HARTMAN, Andrew J., Ge-90-2; Pvt; Greeneville PO
HARTMAN, Charety, D-45-6; Buva Vonta Pike, Nashville PO
HARTMAN, Enoch, Ge-87-1; 1st Sgt E Co 4th TN Inf; Apr 63 to 12 Aug 65; Midway PO
HARTMAN, Fred B., Ja-86-3; Pvt C Co 2nd MO Inf; Snowhill PO
HARTMAN, George, Ge-90-2; Eliza J. More, formerly widow of; Myers Port PO; dates not remembered
HARTMAN, George S., H-51-6; Pvt A Co 6th TN Inf; 8-6-62 to 6-30-65; Red Bank PO
HARTMAN, John B., Wa-273-1; Sgt I Co 8th TN Cav; 25 Sep 63 to 11 Sep 65; Morning Star PO; fever in leg
HARTMAN, Madison, H-51-5; Pvt C Co 5th TN Inf; 8-18-63 to 6-30-65; Red Bank PO
HARTMAN, Margaret C., K-177-2; widow Sol US; PO omitted
HARTMAN, Newton C., Ge-100-2; ___ 12 Aug 62 to ___; Midway PO; emprisoned before to Co. (sic)
HARTMAN, Thomas J., H-49-2; Pvt C Co 5th TN Inf; 7-63 to 6-3-65; Red Bank PO
HARTMAN, William R., K-174-3(2); Pvt C Co 8th TN Cav; 6 Oct 63 to 11 Sep 65; Church Grove PO; rheumatism and piles, 25 yrs
HARTS, Stephen, Sh-157-8; Pvt K Co 55th Col?; 2 yrs 8 mos; PO omitted
HARTSEL, Charles C., Ge-84-3; Lt C Co 2nd NC Inf; 26 Sep 63 to Aug 65; Bird Bridge PO; spinal afecttion
HARTSELL, Abraham, Ge-96-2; Pvt L (F?, T?) Co 56th PA Inf; 19 Sep 64 to 3 Mar 65; Rheatown PO; chronic diareah, loss sight
HARTSFIELD, Durham, D-79-2; Lucy widow of; Pvt I Co 14th US Col Inf; about Oct 63 to about Mar 66; Nashville, 315 Berry PO
HARTSFIELD, Elias, H-67-3; Teamster 20th MO; 5-63 to 65; Chattanooga PO; shot through right & left hips
HARTWELL, James, Pu-144-2; Sarah T. widow of; Bloomington PO
HARTWELL, Warrel, Ru-241-3; Millie widow of; Pvt G Co 58th MS Inf; ___ to 66; Murfreesboro PO
HARVEY, Francis M., Bl-5-1; Pvt I Co 2nd TN Mtd Inf; 9-17-61 to 5-27-65; Soddy, Hamilton Co. PO; chronic diarrhea, captured 6 Nov 1863, paroled 27 Feb 65
HARVEY, Franklin S., Dy-25-6; Pvt; Newbern PO; CONF
HARVEY, Henry M., K-179-2; Sgt D Co 3rd TN Inf; 10 Feb 62 to 23 Feb 65; Rodelin PO; gun shot wound left thigh and leg
HARVEY, Joe, D-91-2; Sgt D Co 12th Inf; 1 Aug 63 to 17 Jan 66; Johny Winns Grocery, Cedar St, Nashville PO
HARVEY, John F., Ro-201-6; Pvt C Co 7th TN Inf; 20 Aug 64 to 16 Jun 65; Kingston PO
HARVEY, Muroe, F-38-2; alias Munroe M. Goodwin; Sgt F Co 3rd US Inf; Nov 63 to 30 Apr 65; Mason PO
HARVEY, Simon, D-91-2; Silvia widow of; Pvt D Co 12th TN Inf; 1 Aug 63 to 17 Jan 66; John? Winns Grocery, Cedar St, Nashville PO
HARVEY, Thomas, Gr-78-2; Pvt G Co ___ TN Cav; 4 May 63 to 4 May 65; Spring House PO
HARVEY, William, Sh-168-1; Pvt A Co 40th TN Inf; Feb 15 63 to Mar 20 65; 87 Poplar St, Memphis (rear) PO

HARVEY, William H., Sq-164-5(1); Pvt; Brock PO
HARVEY, William J., K-179-3; Pvt D Co 3rd TN Inf; 10 Feb 62 to 23 Feb 65; Rodelin PO; shot in ankle
HARVEY, Zore B., Cl-52-2; Pvt A Co 9th TN Cav; 6-1-63 to 9-11-65; Hypratia PO
HARVILLE, Birket F., Sm-170-2; Pvt C Co 8th TN Mtd Inf; 3-15-65 to 8-15-65; Maggart PO; rheumatism & loss of 1 eye from small pox
HARVILLE, David B., Sm-170-2; Pvt A Co 1st TN Mtd Inf; 1-7-64 to 1-30-65; Maggart PO
HARVY, Akhel N., Ja-85-2; Mary E. widow of; Pvt E Co 5th TN Inf; 3-2-62 to __; Birchwood PO
HARVY, James (see Alexander, James)
HARVY, James C., Bl-1-1; 1st Sgt D Co 6th TN Mtd Inf; 9-12-64 to 6-29-65; Pikeville PO; chronic rheumatism
HARVY, John, Cy-30-1; Pvt K Co 4th E TN Cav; 2-62 to __ (8 mos 12 days); Speck PO; no discharge given
HARWELL, Allen C., Sh-159-4; Pvt MS Inf; Memphis PO; CONF
HARWELL, Carsen, Gi-131-1; Pvt (Cook) H Co 7th IA Inf; 11 Dec 63 to 18 Jan 66; Pulaski PO
HARWELL, Cyrus (see Hardaway, Cyrus)
HARWELL, David, Gi-131-1; Pvt H Co 111th Col Inf; Feb 64 to 65; Pulaski PO; smallpox injured left eye
HARWELL, Grant W., Hd-54-3; US Sol; PO omitted
HARWELL, William M. R., Lo-189-3(1); Sgt B Co 1st TN Inf; 14 Nov 62 to 3 Aug 65; Philadelphia PO; consumption, unable for any duty
HARWICK, Ansel P., Un-250-2; Nancy widow of; _ck Pvt D Co 1st TN Inf; 9 Aug 61 to 17 Sep 64; Have Hill PO
HARWICK, Briton, A-1-1; Pvt I Co 5th TN Inf; 11-1-64 to 8-5-65; Andersonville PO; deafness
HARWICK, F. P., A-1-1; Pvt B Co 3rd TN Inf; 1-1-64 to 12-1-65; Andersonville PO
HARWOOD, Benjamine, Bl-4-2; Sgt A Co 1st TN Cav; 7-25-61 to 4-16-65; Morgan Springs PO (Rhea Co.); CONF
HARWOOD, Francis M., M-108-2(1); Elizabeth C. widow of; Pvt A Co 9th KY Inf; 3-61 to 65 (3 yrs 8 mos); Salt Lick PO
HARWOOD, John, Me-92-1; Jane? widow of; Pvt D Co 12th TN Cav; 11-5-63 to __; Cate PO
HARWOOD, John W., Cr-13-2; Ass Surgeon B Co 1st TN Inf; May 24 66 to Mar 3 63; Atwood PO; bowel disease
HARWOOD, Peter, Gi-132-4; Pvt Co D 110th USCV; __ to Feb 66; Wales PO
HARWOOD, W. R., M-108-2(1); Pvt I Co 9th KY Inf-- 12-1-61 to 1-24-63; Cpl E Co 1st TN Mtd Inf-- 10-28-63 to 1-22-65; Salt Lick PO; general prostation consumption
HARWOOD, William, Gi-125-1; Cpl F Co 111th US Col Inf; 15 Jan 64 to 30 Apr 66; Bodenham PO
HARWOOD, William, R-160-1; Pvt TN; 6th Civil Dist
HASBARG, Nancy P. (see Andrews, Orville T.)
HASHBARGER, David A., Ge-96-3; Pvt D Co 8th TN Cav; 28 Sep 63 to 11 Sep 65; Jockey PO
HASHBARGER, Zachariah S., Ge-97-3; Pvt K Co 1st TN Cav; 10 Aug 62 to 5 Jun 65; Newmanville PO; piles, rheumatism & diarrhea
HASKELL, Ferdinand, K-180-3; Pvt B Co 2nd KY Inf; 21 Apr 61 to Jun 65; Ebenezer PO; injury to eyes and loss of toes by freezing
HASKELL, Isaac, H-67-3; Sol US; Chattanooga PO
HASKIN, Creed, Dy-25-2; Pvt 13th TN Cav; 3 yrs; Newbern PO; CONF
HASKIN, Harriett (see Harrison, Eonix)
HASKIN, John C., Dy-25-2; Pvt; 8 mos; Newbern PO; CONF
HASKINS, James R., B-12-2; F Co 1st TN Ind Cav; Wheel PO; claims chronic diarhea, discharge faded out, could not give dates
HASKINS, John B., Sh-203-1; Pvt ME? (Marne?) Comp; 61 to 65; Memphis PO; CONF
HASKINS, John P., B-12-1; Pvt C Co 4th TN Mtd Inf; 64 to 8-25-65; Palmetto PO; claims he incurred liver & kidney trouble, discharge in hands of attorney, could not give date of enlistment
HASLE, Jacob, G-56-1; Pvt; Trenton PO
HASLEY, William C., Di-40-1; Elisabeth widow of; Pvt H Co 10th TN; 10-63 to died 1864; Adinburgh PO; died with small pox, died without discharge
HASLING, William J., D-70-1; Rosana R. widow of; Pvt B Co 22nd Reserve Core?; 4 Feb 64 to 66; Nashville PO
HASS, John, Dk-35-3(1); Annie widow of; Pvt; Capling PO; consumption
HASS, Thomas, Dk-33-1; Pvt E Co 4th TN Inf; 9-24-64 to 8-25-65; 4th Civil Dist; rheumatism & ruptured
HASSELL, Henry L., De-22-1; Pvt A Co 9th TN Cav; 1 Apr 62 to 1 Apr 62; Clifton PO; CONF
HASSELL, Hordee, De-23-1; Cpl A Co 40th TN; Jan 21 64 to Apr 25 65; Thurman PO
HASSETT, Charles, H-63-4; Pvt D Co 5th OH Inf; 61 to 63; 827 Broad St, Chattanooga PO; lost sight, wound right eye
HASSH, George, Sn-250-1; 2nd Lt I Co 3rd __; 5-6-61 to __ (1 yr 6 mos); Castalian Springs PO; CONF
HASSLE, William, D-76-1; Pvt D Co 129th US Inf; Sep 62 to Mar 64; Nashville PO
HASSON, James, Se-219-2; Nancy widow of; Pvt E Co Jones Cav; piles & rematism
HASTINGS, George, Gi-127-3; Maggie widow of; Pvt 12th TN Col Inf; Pulaski PO; supposed to have been killed, widow does not know particulars
HASTY, Benjamin F. (dec), Hd-54-2; Mary Alexander wife of; Pvt F Co 6th TN Cav; Aug 62 to May 64; Saltillo PO; died in a hospital at Memphis TN
HATCH, Winnie C., Cr-16-2; widow US Sol; Maple Creek PO
HATCHER, E. L., Bo-11-2; Pvt D Co 2nd TN Cav; 9-1-62 to 7-7-65; Brick Hill PO
HATCHER, Elijah, Bo-22-3; 14th Dist
HATCHER, James, K-165-1; Pvt D Co 2nd TN; 1 Sep 62 to 26 Jun 64; Knoxville PO; epletic fites cose by hors faling
HATCHER, James, Se-224-2; Pvt E Co 9th TN Cav; 1 Oct 63 to 11 Sep 65; Wears Valley PO; loss of sight, came home on sick furlow
HATCHER, Joseph W., Bo-12-3(1); Cpl D Co 2nd TN Cav; 9-1-62 to 7-6-65; Millers Cove PO
HATCHER, Richard, Bo-22-2; Pvt D Co 1st TN Art; 9-1-63 to 7-20-65; Seaton PO
HATCHER, Rubin, Se-224-2; Pvt E Co 1st TN Lt Art; 1 Sep 63 to 1 Aug 65; Wears Valley PO; diarrhea & jandice
HATCHER, Samuel, D-58-1; Sgt K Co 40th US Col Inf; Nashville PO
HATCHER, William, K-156-4; Pvt B Co 9th OH Inf; 9 Apr 62 to 11 Apr 65; 23 W. Cumberland St, Knoxville PO
HATCHER, William, Hu-106-2; Waverly PO
HATCHETT, Lucinda (see Vance, Clinton)
HATELY, John F., Ct-35-2; Pvt E Co 13th TN Cav; 9-24-63 to 9-5-65; Lineback PO; in US Army
HATELY, Wiley S., Ct-35-3; Sgt E Co 13th TN Cav; 9-24-63 to 9-5-65; Lineback PO; in US Army
HATFIELD, Andrew D., H-50-2(1); Pvt E Co 6th R TN Mtd Inf; 8-16-64 to 6-30-65; Bunch PO; measles
HATFIELD, David, S-213-2; Pvt I Co 12th KY Inf; Nov 61 to 5 Sep 65; Hellenwood PO; chronic diar. measels & cold, condition absolutely helpless
HATFIELD, Emanuel, Fe-41-2; Pvt H Co 30th KY Cav; 1-1-64 to 7-1-64; Travisville PO
HATFIELD, Francis M., Pi-156-2; Pvt H Co 30th KY Cav; 1-1-63 to 7-21-63; Travisville PO; fell from a horse, paroled 7-21-83?, sickness
HATFIELD, Georg W., C-34-3; Pvt G Co 7th TN Inf; 1-65 to 7-65; Pioneer PO
HATFIELD, Henry, Cl-46-1; Pvt A Co; Speedwell PO; wound
HATFIELD, James, Cl-54-3(1); Pvt G Co 2nd TN Cav; 4-7-61 to __; Tazewell PO
HATFIELD, Jasper, Cl-53-1; Pvt K Co 9th TN Cav; 12-1-64 to 9-11-65; Springdale PO; chronic rheumatism
HATFIELD, John, Sq-165-2; Pvt F Co 5th TN Cav; 9-1-62 to 6-25-65; Delphi PO; received an honorable disc.
HATFIELD, John B., Sq-164-3(1); Pvt E Co 6th TN Mtd Inf; 8-11-64 to 6-30-65; Dunlap PO

HATFIELD, Joseph F., S-218-2; Pvt C Co; Sep 64 to Dec 64; Norma PO
HATFIELD, Linch, Ja-85-3; Flag barer A Co 2nd NC Mtd Inf; 7-62 to 8-19-65; Thatcher PO
HATFIELD, Nadisen? H., H-73-4(2); Chattanooga PO
HATFIELD, Robert, Pi-156-3; Pvt H Co 30th KY Cav; 1-1-63 to 7-21-63; Travisville PO
HATFIELD, William, Fe-41-1; Pvt C Co 2nd KY Inf; 62 to 64; Pall Mall PO
HATFIELD, William, H-69-1; Martha widow of; Pvt; 61 to 65; Chattanooga PO
HATFIELD, William C., Gi-130-1; Pvt A Co 6th TN Inf; 2 Aug 64 to 30 Jun 65; Bradshaw PO
HATFIELD, William M., Sq-165-3; Sol; 8th Civil Dist
HATHAWAY, Albert, Dk-34-3; Pvt I Co 1st TN Inf; 10-9-64 to 7-22-65; Dowelltown PO; left arm hurt
HATHAWAY, James C., Dk-33-2; Pvt H Co 5th TN Cav; 10-13-62 to 8-14-65; Dowelltown PO; rheumatism
HATHWAY, James, Dy-27-2; Pvt A Co 12th TN Inf; Apr 61 to Apr 62; Tatemville PO; CONF
HATLEY, A. J., Di-41-1; alias Man Hatley; Pvt E Co 41st IL Inf; 8-61 to 7-65; White Bluff PO; gravels, reenlisted veteran
HATLEY, John, Ge-92-1; Rachel widow of; Pvt C Co 56th IL Inf; 12 Nov 61 to 12 Jul 62; Romeo PO
HATMAKER, Duncan, C-25-1; Pvt A Co 1st TN Inf; 8-2-61 to 9-17-64; Agee PO
HATMAKER, Jacob Sr., C-25-2; Pvt A Co 1st TN Inf; 8-2-61 to was not discharged; Hatmaker PO; liver affection, rheumatism; reinlisted G Co 7th TN on 11-8-64, discharged 7-27-65
HATMAKER, Jacob Jr., C-25-2; Pvt G Co 7th TN Inf; 11-8-64 to 7-27-65; Hatmaker PO; lung affection
HATMAKER, James, C-25-2; Sarah widow of; Pvt A Co 1st TN Inf; 9-2-61 to __; Coal Creek PO (Anderson Co.); died 2-62
HATMAKER, Milley A. (see Walace, Johnson)
HATMAKER, Thomas, A-4-1; Jane M. widow; Pvt A Co 1st TN Inf; 62 to 65; Coal Creek PO
HATMAKER, Thomas, C-25-2; Pvt A Co 1st TN Inf; 8-2-61 to 9-17-64; Hatmaker PO; rheumatism
HATMAKER, Wm. H., Sr., A-4-2; Cpl H Co 1st TN Inf; 8-9-61 to 9-17-64; Coal Creek PO; rheumatism
HATON, Richard C., L-105-1; Pvt F Co 6th IN Cav; Jul 62 to Jun 65; Curve PO; injure to breast, draws a pension
HATTENDORF, Charles, Sh-180-1; Pvt H Co 3rd MI Cav; 8-16-61 to 11-20-64; 352 Vance St, Memphis PO
HATTLEY, John H., Mg-198-3; Pvt F Co 5th TN Inf; 10 Feb 65 to 12 Jul 65; Rockwood PO; mashed blaksmithing
HATTLON, Philip, Mu-213-1; Margaret widow of; Blacksmith; Mar 62 to Mar 63; Glenns Store PO
HAUGHER, Jackson L., Se-220-2; Pvt E Co 1st TN LT; 6 Oct 63 to 1 Aug 65; Emerts Cave PO
HAUL, Alfred, Sh-155-1; Pvt K Co 61st TN Inf; 15 Aug 63 to Feb 15 65; Germantown PO
HAUL, Arch, Sh-155-1; Musiton (Musician?) F Co 55th AL Inf; 63 to 66; Germantown PO
HAUN, Gilbert L., Mc-111-2; Pvt; 8-65 to __; Athens PO
HAUN, John R., Ge-88-3; Cathern M. widow of; Cpl D Co 1st TN Cav; 12 Aug 62 to 5 Jun 65; Mohawk PO
HAUN, Peter L., U-246-1; Pvt B Co 3rd NC Mtd Inf; 26 Mar 64 to 6 Aug 65; Erwin PO
HAUN?, Pleasant, Hw-132-2; Pvt; Persia PO; could not get any information
HAUN, William, Un-253-1; Sgt G Co 2nd TN Cav; 7 Oct 62 to 24 May 65; Ambro PO (Grainger Co.); rheumatism, fistula &c
HAVERKAMP, Henry, H-62-2; 212 West Fifth, Chattanooga PO
HAW, Jacob W., We-221-2; Pvt H Co 20th TN Inf; 18 May 61 to 19 May 65; Martin PO; three flesh wounds and left thigh bone busted; CONF
HAWK, James, Br-12-6; Pvt A Co 8th TN Inf; 11-11-61 to 12-24-64; McPherson PO; granulated sore eyes
HAWKIN, Joseph, Sh-144-2; Pvt C Co 3rd Col Art; Apr 63 to 30 Apr 66; Brunswick PO; shot in face
HAWKINS, Alfred, Jo-148-1; Pvt D Co 13th TN Cav; 24 Sep 63 to 5 Sep 65; Laurel Bloomery PO
HAWKINS, Andrew, R-162-4; Matilda widow of; Pvt H Co 7th TN Inf; 2-15-65 to 7-7-65; Dayton PO; health injured from exposure in the service
HAWKINS, Charles (see Patterson, Charles)
HAWKINS, Charles, Ge-92-2; Elizabeth widow of; Pvt G Co 8th TN Inf; 10 Mar 63 to __; Laurel Gap PO
HAWKINS, Creed A., Sh-191-4; Memphis PO; records not seen
HAWKINS, Curry N., J-77-1; Pvt B Co 8th TN Cav; 2-10-65 to 8-17-65; Gainesboro PO; lung disease
HAWKINS, Danel, Sh-145-3; Pvt A Co 48th US Col Inf; Jul 64 to Jan 66; Kerrville PO; Cap Bradford, 1st Lt Badie, enlisted Gorrich Ldg., LA, 1st Lt Mayhu
HAWKINS, George, Sh-152-1; alias Webber, Jacob; Pvt C Co 61st 1st TN Inf; 17 Aug 63 to Jan 64; Collierville PO
HAWKINS, Henry, Sh-178-1; Pvt H Co 3rd TN; 3 yrs; 304 Union St, Memphis PO
HAWKINS, Henry, Sh-191-6(2); Memphis PO; records not seen
HAWKINS, James, Sh-190-1; Pvt M Co 3rd Col Cav; 63 to 1-26-66; Alley bt. Broadway & 7th, Memphis PO; foot mashed by mule
HAWKINS, John, Gu-48-5(2); Tracy City Branch Prison PO
HAWKINS, John B., Ge-101-2; Sally widow of; Pvt H Co 8th TN Inf; 5 Aug 63 to 16 Jun 64; Locust Sp. PO
HAWKINS, John E., Ro-210-12; Pvt; Rockwood PO
HAWKINS, John R., Li-166-1; Cpl D Co 27th KY Inf; 61 to 65; Smithland PO; wounded in left foot
HAWKINS, Joseph E. J., We-224-3(1); ___, Serena formerly widow of; Pvt 15th TN Cav; 61 to __; PO omitted; CONF
HAWKINS, Joshua, M-107-2; Pvt F Co 26th KY Inf; 2-26-63 to 7-10-65; Red Boiling Springs PO; gunshot wound right thigh
HAWKINS, Landon H., Jo-148-2; Sgt D Co 13th TN Cav; 24 Sep 63 to 8 Sep 65; Laurel Bloomery PO; wounded in right arm & breast by gun shot
HAWKINS, Mack, Hw-118-2; Pvt 1st TN Cav; St. Clair PO
HAWKINS, Marion J., H-50-2(1); Pvt H Co 7th R TN Mtd Inf; 2-14-62 to 6-13-65; Sardy (Soddy?) PO
HAWKINS, Patrick, H-57-3; Pvt E Co 16th US Col; 63 to 65; Orchard Knob PO
HAWKINS, Rhoda A. (see Borden, Nathaniel)
HAWKINS, Samuel W., Cr-16-2; 7th TN Cav; Huntingdon PO; maimed back, horse was shot and fell on him
HAWKINS, Thos. Jefferson, Sh-179-3(1); Pvt C Co 66th IN Inf; 63 to 63 (8 mos); Memphis PO
HAWKINS, William, Ge-97-2; Pvt G Co 8th TN Inf; 1 Mar 63 to 21 May 64; PO omitted
HAWKINS, William H., A-4-1; Pvt D Co 1st TN Lt Art; 12-24-63 to 7-20-65; Coal Creek PO; rheumatism
HAWKS, Linda W., Mr-102-2; widow? Orderly Sgt F Co 6th US Inf; 3-5-62 to 10-12-66; South Pittsburg PO
HAWLEY, Romain M., Fr-112-1; Pvt H Co 59th IL Col Inf; Oct 7 64 to Nov 15 65; Tullahoma PO; contr. hemorrhage of bowels & piles
HAWN, James K., Ge-89-3; Pvt F Co 2nd TN Inf; 8 Nov 61 to __ (4 mos); (and firded? to reach the command); Mosheim PO
HAWN, Thomas, Co-62-2; Pvt H Co 3rd NC Inf; Feb 65 to __ (5 mos); Givens PO
HAWORTH, Calvin, Je-141-3; Mary Fielden widow of; Pvt K Co 3rd TN Inf; 62 to __; Mill Springs PO; killed in battle
HAWORTH, Jonathan, Je-141-1; Lt F Co 1st TN Cav; 1 Mar 62 to 31 Mar 65; New Market PO
HAWORTH, Richard, Je-141-1; Sgt F Co 1st TN Cav; 1 Mar 62 to 30 Mar 65; New Market PO
HAWS, Albert, K-168-1; Pvt H Co 3rd TN Inf; 11 Apr 62 to 1 Aug 62; Knoxville PO; chronic flux
HAWS, John S., Wa-273-2; Nancy E. Beals formerly widow of; Pvt B Co 4th TN Inf; Nov 62 to Jan 63; Jonesboro PO; killed in battle
HAWS, Wyatte C., Hn-82-1; Pvt K Co 2nd TN Mtd Inf; 1-61 to 4-20-65; Buchanan PO

HAWSHAW, William, Br-9-4; Pvt I Co 15th Col US Inf; 1-24-64 to 8-21-65; Cleveland PO
HAYDEN, Henry, K-166-3; Pvt B Co 4th MN Cav; 2 Dec 62 to 2 Dec 65; Knoxville PO; dead 16 yrs
HAYES, Abner, Sh-159-5; Lettie widow of; Pvt 11th US; Memphis PO; husband in May 1865 in service
HAYES, Benjamin, Wy-175-1; Pvt E Co 8th TN Mtd Inf; 3-1-65 to 9-5-65; Cypress Inn PO
HAYES, Charles (see Williams, Charles)
HAYES, David D., Me-88-1; Octavia A. widow of; Pvt F Co 3rd TN Cav; 3-16-63 to 7-12-65; Birchwood PO
HAYES, Harman M., Ha-116-2; US Sol; Dist No 10
HAYES, Jackson, He-60-2; Mary M. widow of; Pvt C Co 7th TN Cav; Aug 62 to died Apr 65; Chesterfield PO; died in Andersonville Prison
HAYES, James H., H-63-2; Pvt C Co 36th IL Inf; 8-31-62 to 6-14-65; 713 Poplar, Chattanooga PO; hearing
HAYES, James M., Dk-39-3(1); Pvt A Co 5th TN Cav; 8-4-62 to 8-24-65; Dekalb PO
HAYES, John, Wy-175-1; Pvt E Co 8th TN Mtd Inf; 3-1-65 to 9-5-65; Whittens Stand PO
HAYES, John C., Me-90-1; Pvt D Co 5th TN Mtd Inf; 8-31-64 to 6-26-65; Goodfield PO
HAYES, John S., K-154-2; Knoxville PO; CONF
HAYES, King S., Sn-264-1; alias King S. Allen; Pvt B Co 9th Hvy Art; Sep 2 64 to Sep 3 65; Portland PO; wounded twice, small pox, rheumatism, discharged at Nashville, Cap. P. Comodore
HAYES, Lewis Black, Mo-124-1; 9th Civil Dist
HAYES, Robert, Ct-38-1; Rebecca L. widow of; Sgt E Co 13th TN Cav; Milligan PO; died of blood poisoning
HAYES, Sarah J. (see Givan, Henry)
HAYES, Sarah J. (see Reeves, James)
HAYES, William, Sh-174-3; Pvt 58th LA Cav; 1-15-63 to 5-6-65; 226 Pontotoc St, Memphis PO
HAYES, William H., Dk-39-3(1); Pvt K Co 5th TN Cav; 4-8-63 to 8-14-65; Dekalb PO
HAYFIELD, John T., Rb-221-2; Capt B Co 39th IN; May 9 62 to Aug 20 65; Adams Station PO; wounded in arm and shot in ____; taken prisoner
HAYMES, James P., Mc-114-2; Pvt C Co 3rd TN Cav; 12-16-62 to 8-3-65; Leamontville PO
HAYMOND, John W., R-161-1; Pvt D Co 91st IL Inf; 8-11-62 to 7-12-65; Dayton PO
HAYNES, Alferd, Hn-77-2; Pvt H Co 61st TN Inf; Jul 63 to 65; PO omitted
HAYNES, Alfred, Hd-44-1; Pvt B Co 8th TN Inf; 5-1-65 to 9-1-65; Clifton PO (Wayne Co.)
HAYNES, Daniel, Un-252-1; Sgt G Co 8th TN Cav; 24 Jul 63 to 11 Sep 65; Acuff PO
HAYNES, Dennis, Hn-77-1; Pvt F Co 3rd Hvy Art; Jul 63 to Feb 66; PO omitted
HAYNES, George A., Se-226-4; Pvt H Co 18th IL Inf; 1 Mar 65 to 9 Jul 66; Henrys X Roads PO; malarial, typhoid fever & rheumatism
HAYNES, Henry, Hn-77-2; Pvt K Co 13th KY Inf; May 64 to Feb 66; PO omitted
HAYNES, Henry J., Hd-50-3; Pvt D Co 2nd TN Inf; Mar 1 64 to May 13 65; Loweryville PO
HAYNES, Isaac C., Un-252-2; Pvt H Co 8th TN Cav; Jun 63 to 65; Acuff PO; no discharge
HAYNES, Joe A., Cr-4-3; Sgt B Co 51st TN Inf; 9-62 to 4-65; Bells Depot PO; wounded right leg; CONF
HAYNES, John M., Hw-134-1; Pvt E Co 8th TN Cav; Oct 63 to Apr 65; Rogersville PO; disease of eyes
HAYNES, John T., Hd-55-1; Pvt; Cerro Gordo PO
HAYNES, John T., Hd-46-1; Pvt D Co 2nd TN Mtd Inf; Nov 12 63 to Dec 12 64; Lowryville PO
HAYNES, Napoleon B., Br-13-3; Manerva Rucker formerly widow of; 4th TN Cav; Cleveland PO
HAYNES, P. Z., B-10-1; Pvt G Co 4th TN Cav; 5-23-63 to 7-12-65; PO omitted
HAYNES, Row D., Hn-77-1; Pvt F Co 3rd Hvy Art; 16 Jul 63 to Apr 66; PO omitted
HAYNES, Samuel H., Sh-188-2; Pvt A Co 27th KY Inf; 9-61 to 5-64; 308 Johnson Ave, Memphis PO
HAYNES, William A., K-170-2; Pvt D Co 6th TN Inf; 18 Apr 62 to 30 Jun 65; Knoxville PO
HAYNES, William J., Hn-68-1; 1st Sgt A Co 4th Hvy Art; 4 Jun 63 to 25 Feb 66; Paris PO
HAYNIE, James M., Sh-201-2; Elizabeth widow of; Memphis PO; papers all lost; CONF
HAYON, Solomon, Sh-157-8; Pvt G Co 11th __; 62 to 65; Dist 13
HAYS, Balinda P., He-62-1; Sgt C Co 7th TN Cav; Aug 62 to Aug 65; Darden PO; crippled in breast
HAYS, Capting Asa N., De-26-2; Martha A. widow of; Capt; Bible Hill PO
HAYS, Eli M., A-4-2; Pvt B Co 1st TN Inf; 8-1-64 to 9-17-64; Coal Creek? (no place of res. given)
HAYS, George, D-50-2; Alice Braughman formerly widow of; Pvt; Nashville PO
HAYS, Isaac, Ge-89-3; Pvt M Co 1st TN Cav; 25 Nov 62 to 30 Jun 63; Mosheim PO; gun shot
HAYS, Jacob, Ge-98-3; Susanah G. widow of; Pvt C Co 4th TN Inf; Cedar Lane PO; relapse of measels
HAYS, James H., Po-149-2(1); Pvt E Co 5th TN Mtd Inf; 10-10-64 to 7-12-65; Conasauga PO; Mtd Inf one year
HAYS, James L., Ct-41-2; Pvt H Co 13th TN Cav; 8-12-64 to 9-8-65; Elizabethton PO; hart trouble
HAYS, John, Ct-41-3; Pvt; South Wattauga PO; liver trouble, hearing and speach
HAYS, John B., He-62-3; Sgt C Co 7th TN Cav; Aug 62 to Jun 65; Lexington PO; scurvey
HAYS, John M., C-25-2; Sgt B Co 1st TN Inf; 8-2-61 to 9-17-65; Hatmaker PO; chronic diareah & rheumatism & scurvy
HAYS, N. S., Wl-308-3; Pvt I Co 20th TN; Jul 1 61 to Jul 1 64; Green Hill PO; CONF
HAYS, Robert, Ge-98-2; Pvt G Co 4th TN Inf; 5 Apr 63 to 2 ___ 65 (2 yrs 3 mos 27 days); Cedarlane PO; diarhea & rheumatism
HAYS, Virginus H., Sh-178-2; Sgt A Co 1st Caps Afrie; 63 to ___; 231 Monroe, Memphis PO
HAYS, William, Ct-35-4; Pvt 1st US Inf; 2-64 to 11-27-65; Elk Mills PO; in the 22 S Army (disability); no discharge to get the exact dates
HAYS, William H., He-62-3; Pvt Co A 7th TN Cav; Aug 17 62 to Aug 17 65; Darden PO; catarh in head and disease of throat
HAYS, Zachary T., Gi-131-1; Pvt A Co 111th Col Inf; 63 to 65; Bradshaw PO
HAYSE, Thomas H., H-58-2; Pvt C Co 7th OH Inf; 8-64 to ___; Coulterville PO
HAYWOOD, Paul, H-67-3; Pvt E Co 33rd US Col Inf; 62 to 66; Chattanooga PO
HAYWOOD, Robt. W., Hy-85-1; Nut Bush PO; US Soul
HAYWOOD, W. T., Cr-15-1; Pvt D Co 7th TN Cav; 25 Oct 63 to Aug 25 65; Maple Creek PO
HAYWOOD, William, Pe-88-2; alias Phillips, William; Ord Sgt G Co 53rd USC Inf; ___ to 65; 186 Fillmore St, Nashville PO; gunshot in hand and knee
HAYWORTH, Z. K., Hm-105-2; Sgt I? Co 11th IN Cav; 27 Jul 63 to 29 Sep 65; Morristown PO; gunshot & rheumatism
HAZELWOOD, Restin? A., We-221-6(2); Pvt TN Inf; 62 to 65; Martin PO; CONF
HAZELY, John W., Hd-53-2; Scout Cumberland Div.; 27 Jul 64 to 27 Oct 64; Cero Gordo PO
HAZLETT, James H., Mn-129-2; Sol US; PO omitted
HAZLEWOOD, Daniel, Gi-122-6; Pvt K Co 110th TN Inf; Jan 63 to Feb 65; Prospect Sta. PO; CONF
HAZLEWOOD, Dannel, Gi-122-8; Pvt K Co 110th TN Inf; Mar 3 63 to Mar 3 65; Prospect Sta. PO
HAZLEWOOD, Henry, O-136-2; Pvt E Co 4th TN Cav; Jun 2 63 to Apr 14 66; PO omitted
HAZLEWOOD, Robert H., Gi-122-4; Pvt A Co 53rd TN Inf; 1 Dec 61 to Mar 63; Prospect Sta. PO; 6 mos in prison; CONF
HEABLER, David, Mo-119-1; Pvt C Co 164th OH V Inf; 5-64 to 8-64; Sweetwater PO
HEAD, Caleb, Cy-26-1; Pvt B Co 37th KY Inf; 7-17-63 to 12-29-64; Moss PO
HEAD, Charles G., Mu-191-1; 7th Dist
HEAD, Daniel S., Jo-150-5; Mary J. widow of; Pvt D Co 13th TN Cav; 24 Sep 63 to ___; Osborn PO
HEAD, Elias, Sn-252-1; Pvt A Co 11th KY Cav; 1-13-63 to 5-15-63; Gallatin PO; shot in left leg
HEAD, James A., C-25-3; Pvt H Co 24th MO Inf; Aug 63 to Jul 65; Union City PO; rheumatism
HEAD, John, D-49-4; made 3 trips but could not find him to get rank &c; Nashville PO

HEAD, Kaney, Sn-250-2; Pvt K Co 2nd __; 4-25-61 to 5-7-65; Castalian Springs PO; CONF
HEADDEN, John T., D-75-3; Pvt 18th GA; Stewarts Ferry PO; shot in leg; CONF
HEADERICK, William A., Wa-260-1; 2nd Sgt K Co 1st Reg Cav; 15 Nov 62 to 1 Dec 65; Pilot Hill PO; failed to make any out of it
HEADRICK, Absilom B., Co-61-6(2); Pvt E Co 16th TN Cav; 1 Jan? 64 to __; Bridgeport PO; CONF
HEADRICK, Alexander, Ro-202-3(1); Pvt I Co 1st TN Inf; Aug 61 to Sep 64; Union Cross Roads PO; rheumatism & deafness
HEADRICK, Charles, Ct-40-4; Jane widow of; Sgt A Co 13th TN Cav; 9-22-63 to 9-5-65; Elizabethton PO
HEADRICK, Daniel A., K-181-1; Pvt A Co 3rd TN Cav; 18 Sep 62 to 2 Jun 65; French PO
HEADRICK, Ezekel, Je-140-2; Pvt C Co 9th TN Cav; 1 Jun 63 to 11 Sep 65; Strawberry Plains PO
HEADRICK, John B., Po-149-3(2); Blacksmith B Co 2nd TN Cav; 8-15-62 to 6-6-65; Ocoee PO
HEADRICK, John W., Ct-40-4; Cpl A Co 13th TN Cav; 9-22-63 to 9-5-65; Elizabethton PO; chronic diarrhea
HEADRICK, Orvill B., Ge-91-2; Sgt M Co 1st TN Cav; 8 Sep 62 to 5 Jun 65; Greeneville PO; side plurasy
HEADRICK, Peter Sr., Se-224-2; Pvt B Co 2nd TN Cav; 15 Sep 62 to 6 Jul 65; Line Spring PO; rheumatism, sight, hearing
HEADRICK, Peter, Bo-11-7; Mary widow of; Pvt 1 Co 5th TN Cav; 11-1-62 to killed; Big Gulley PO; died in service
HEADRICK, Peter Jr., Se-224-2; Pvt B Co 2nd TN Cav; 15 Sep 62 to 6 Jul 65; Line Spring PO; fever settled in back, in hospital 2 months
HEADRICK, William H., Co-61-6(2); Bridgeport PO; CONF
HEADRIX, John, Mg-197-4; Sousan widow of; Pvt B Co 2nd TN Inf; Wartburg PO
HEAGAN, Harry, Sh-199-2; Pvt B Co 19th KY Reg; 62 to 63; 55 St. Paul St., Memphis PO
HEAGENS, Wilson N., Ct-40-2; Pvt H Co 13th TN Cav; 11-1-63 to 9-5-65; Elizabethton PO; gunshot wounds one through lungs
HEALD, Thomas H., K-160-2; Sgt 15th MD Vol; 22 Aug 61 to 3 Sep 63; Knoxville PO
HEALINGTON, John W., He-61-1; Pvt C Co 7th TN Cav; 7 Aug 62 to 7 Aug 65; Shermans Mill PO
HEARD, Berry (Col), H-56-3; Pvt AL; St. Elmo PO
HEARD, George W., Sq-165-3; Pvt E Co 6th TN Mtd Inf; 61 to 65; Sunnyside PO; received an honorable disc.
HEARD, James C., B1-5-3; Pvt E Co 6th TN Mtd Inf; 9-11-64 to 6-30-65; Stephens Chapel PO; sick with fever in 1865 and lung diseased ever since
HEARD, Levander, H-49-6; 1st Sgt E Co 6th TN Mtd Inf; Daisy PO
HEARN, Eli M., W1-295-2; Pvt B Co 5th Reg Cav; 6 Aug 63 to 1 Jul 65; Lebanon PO
HEARN, Granville, St-164-1; Pvt C Co 2nd VA Cav; 7 Sep 61 to 4 Jul 65; Stribling PO; reinlisted veteran
HEARN, James W., W1-300-2; Pvt H Co 4th TN Cav; 25 Oct 64 to 25 Aug 65; Cherry Valley PO
HEATH, Ai T., Sn-261-3(2); Pvt E Co 7th TN Cav; 9-15-62 to 12-25-63; Pondville PO; prison Bowlingreen KY 2 mos; come home on furlough; CONF
HEATH, Chapal, Ch-12-2; Pvt B Co 6th TN Cav; 8-25-62 to 7-26-65; Custer Point PO
HEATH, Green, Ge-88-2; Sarah widow of; Pvt A Co 8th TN Cav; Bulls Gap PO; died with fever in the war
HEATH, James L., K-186-2; Cpl L Co 1st MN Inf; 13 Feb 62 to 31 Aug 66; Powels Station PO
HEATH, James M., Cl-56-1; Pvt L Co 1st TN Inf; 8-6-61 to 10-17-64; Big Barren PO; fistula set issue from exposure
HEATH, John J., D-102-1; Mary A. widow of; Pvt I Co 4th TN Inf; 7 Nov 64 to 25 Aug 65; Jordania PO
HEATH, L. R., K-158-1; Pvt; 3 yrs; Knoxville, Gay St. PO
HEATH, Oscar F., Gr-72-1 Pvt C Co 7th KY Cav; 6 Aug 61 to 18 Apr 62; Noeton PO; general exposure; discharges are at Washington

HEATH, Samuel, La-116-1; Cono? B Co 1st AL Cav; 10 Jan 62 to 25 Mar 65; PO omitted
HEATH, Sarah A., Dy-29-3; widow of Conf Sol; Newbern PO
HEATH, William W., 0-138-4; 9th Civil Dist.
HEATH, William W., 0-138-1; Pvt 1 Co 4th TN; 9 Nov 64 to 25 Aug 65; Lanes PO; CONF
HEATHCOCK, George W., Ru-235-1; Maria widow of; Pvt A Co 10th TN Inf; __ to 24 June 65; Smyrna PO
HEATHCOTT, George W., We-221-2; Pvt B Co 16th KY Cav; Nov 63 to Apr 65; Martin PO
HEATHERLY, Godfrey N., Ct-45-2; Cpl H Co 13th TN Cav; 9-24-63 to 9-5-65; Stony Creek PO; measles Nashville TN 1864
HEATON, Murphey, Bo-15-1; Pvt M Co 13th TN Cav; 2-2-64 to 9-5-65; Mountvale PO; diarrhea
HEATON, Robert, R-161-2; Pvt G Co 5th TN Inf; 4-1-62 to 5-15-65; Dayton PO; shot through left ankle & right great toe
HEATON, William, Bo-12-1; Pvt M Co 13th TN Cav; 2-2-64 to 9-5-65; Houk PO (this crossed out)
HEATON, William, Ja-86-2; Pvt G Co 5th TN Inf; 2-62 to 5-15-65; Long Savannah PO; throwed off train & back burt while in service
HEATON, William J., Jo-152-2; Rebecca K. widow of; Pvt B Co 13th TN Cav; 23 Sep 63 to 5 Sep 65; Doeville PO; thrown off horse & back injured
HEBBERD, Erskine, Sh-204-2; Pvt B Co 3rd NC Vol Inf; 5 Aug 61 to 28 Jul 62; McLeMore Ave, Memphis PO
HEBBERTS, John, K-180-2; Sgt D Co 3rd TN Mtd Inf; 25 Jul 64 to 13 Nov 64; Bearden PO; vericose veins
HEBERT, Louis, Sn-262-2(1); Pvt H Co 46th MI Inf; 8 Feb 65 to 27 Sep 65; Fountain Head PO; rheumatism & diarrhea
HECK, Adam S., Hw-132-3(1); Pvt D Co 31st TN Inf; Nov 62 to 65; Strahl PO; rheumatism, was not discharged; CONF
HECK, Charles, Sh-191-4; Memphis PO; crippled; records not seen
HECK, Layfayette F., Hw-127-3; Pvt G Co 1st TN Cav; Dec 62 to 5 Jun 65; Rogersville PO; rupture & frost bitten feet
HECTER, James, Sh-202-1; Pvt Stanford Battery Cav; 8 Sep 61 to 65; Memphis PO; served till the close of war
HECTOR, Jim, Sh-158-4; Pvt D Co 10th OH Vol Inf; 16 Apr 61 to 3 Jun 65; Memphis PO
HEDGE?, Hiram, Mc-112-4; Bertie McGee former widow of; Cpl A Co 1st US Col Art; 2-11-64 to 3-21-66; Athens PO
HEDGECATH, John G., Cu-17-4; Pvt I Co 3rd E TN Inf; 2-10-62 to 2-23-65; Crab Orchard PO; chronic diarrhea
HEDGECOCK, James M., We-224-1; Pvt E Co TN Cav; 62 to 65; Como, Henry Ctr. PO; discharged by reason of disabilities; CONF
HEDGECOCK, Thomas, Ro-201-1; 2nd Lt G Co 1st TN Inf; 9 Aug 61 to 17 Sep 64; Kingston PO
HEDGECOCK, Willis E., K-178-1; Capt H Co 5th TN Inf; 61 to 2 May 63; Vancouver PO; chronic diarrhea
HEDGECOTH, Doctor G., R-160-1; Pvt I Co 3rd TN; 2-5-62 to 2-23-65; 6th Civil Dist.
HEDGPATH, Betsey (see Watts, Horton)
HEDRIC, William W., Bo-52-3(1); Pvt L Co 2nd TN Cav; 9-8-63 to 7-6-65; Millers Cove PO
HEDRICK, Phillip L., D-61-1; Cpl A Co 4th OVC; 23 Apr 61 to 31 Oct 64; Nashville PO
HEFLIN, Joseph, Sm-174-1; 1st Sgt A Co 7th TN Cav; 6-22-62 to 65; Grant PO
HEINBREE, Joel D., Bl-4-1; Pvt A Co 16th TN Cav; 3-1-62 to 2-1-64; Pikeville PO; wounded in leg at Fort Donaldson, badly crippled; CONF
HEISKEL, Luke M., R-157-1; Pvt; Lorraine PO; lost all papers etc. on discharge
HEISKELL, Isaac, Mo-119-2; Pvt A Co US Col Hvy Art; Sweetwater PO; contracted rheumatism
HEISKELL, John, R-162-2; Harriet widow of, Pvt A Co 1st TN Hvy Art; Dayton PO
HELEMAN, Henry H., Ho-95-1; Cpl D Co 2nd W VA Cav; 1 Sep 61 to 30 Jun 65; McKinnon PO
HELLAN, Warner S., K-165-2; Sgt E Co 1st TN Art; 3 Oct 63 to Aug 65; Knoxville PO
HELLINGHEART, Thomas, Sh-169-2; Lt K Co 4th MO Inf; 61 to 65; Memphis PO

HELLSTRON, John, Sh-183-1; Memphis PO
HELLUMES, James, M-107-2; Sgt H Co 14th TN Vol Inf; 12-63 to 3-29-66; Red Boiling Springs PO
HELLUMS, Marcus, Pu-145-4(5); Pvt H Co 1st Mtd Inf; Silver Point PO; discharge not at hand
HELM, Alexander, Mu-189-2; Jane widow of; Pvt A Co 13th TN Inf; 3 yrs 4 mos; Hurricane Switch PO
HELM, James, Mt-146-1; Cpl F Co 6th KY Cav; Sixth US Cav; Sep 64? to Apr 64; Clarksville PO; frost bit & ruptured
HELMANTALLER, Archabol D., B-6-1; Pvt G Co 4th TN Mtd Inf; 2-1-65 to 8-25-65; Shelbyville PO
HELMES, Miles F., Ch-13-2; Pvt A Co 7th TN Vol; 11-28-62 to 8-9-65; Jacks Creek PO; left eye nearly out
HELMS, George W., Hy-82-1; Pvt F Co 12th TN Inf; Aug 64 to Feb 66; Brownsville PO
HELSLEY, Henderson, K-186-3; Pvt D Co 6th TN Inf; 17 Apr 62 to 20 Jun 65; Balls Camp PO
HELTON, Bazil, Se-222-2; Pvt K Co 2nd TN Cav; 15 Aug 62 to 6 Jul 65; Sevierville PO; disabeled in hips by horse falling on me
HELTON, Daniel, R-162-2; Sarah J. widow of; Pvt G Co 9th TN Cav; 9-15-63 to 9-11-65; Dayton PO
HELTON, Eli, Se-224-1; Martha widow of; Pvt K Co 2nd TN Cav; 62 to __; Waldens Creek PO; died
HELTON, H. C. (see Heton, K. T.)
HELTON, James H., Ro-210-6; Pvt H Co 9th TN Cav; 18 Sep 63 to 11 Sep 65; Rockwood PO
HELTON, James H., Po-152-2; Pvt B Co 5th TN Mtd Inf; 2-64 to 4-65; Ducktown PO; sore eyes and mumps
HELTON, John, Po-149-3(2); Sallie widow of; Fetzerton PO; regment & co not known
HELTON, Jno., Wa-268-4; Sallie widow of; discharge away from home; Johnson City PO
HELTON, K. T., Wa-263-2; alias H. C. Helton, alias Robert Helton; Sarah A. divorced widow of; Pvt; Garbers Mills PO
HELTON, Miles W., Po-148-3; Pvt G Co 10th TN Cav; 9-64 to 8-65; Benton PO
HELTON, Milton E., Hn-71-1; Pvt C Co 54th IL Inf; Sep 61 to Nov 65; Spring Hill Academy PO; heart disease from exposure, Mr. Helton lost discharge but thinks about dates nearly correct
HELTON, Pleasant, Hw-134-2; US Sol; 20th Civil Dist.
HELTON, Sallos M., Ro-210-11; Pvt; Post Oak Springs PO
HELTON, Silas M., Ro-205-4; Pvt I Co 1st TN Inf; 12 Aug 61 to 12 Oct 64; Rockwood PO; piles for 25 years
HELTON, Vanice, Ha-114-3; widow; 7th Civil Dist.
HELTON, Willey B., Hw-130-1; Pvt A Co 8th TN Inf; Jul 64 to May 65; Lee Valley PO; gantgreene
HELTON, William J., Ha-110-3; Manerva widow of; Pvt L Co 8th TN Cav; Treadway PO
HEMBREE, David A., Dk-35-2; US Sol; 10th Civil Dist.
HEMBREE, Hamilton, S-215-2; Pvt K Co 49th KY Inf; 1 Sep 62 to 26 Dec 64; High House PO; chronic diarhea contracted in 1863
HEMBREE, Joseph, Ro-203-3; Cpl G Co 1st TN Inf; 9 Aug 61 to __ (1 yr 2 mos); Ethel PO; broken rib & crippled leg
HEMBREE, William, Ro-203-1; Pvt G Co 1st TN Inf; 10 Mar 62 to 11 Mar 65; Wheat PO; chronic rheumatism
HEMBRY, William, Se-231-1; Pvt K Co 1st TN Inf; Boyds Creek; clame agent got his discharge
HEMHILL, Jasper, K-176-2; Halls Roads PO
HEMPHILL, John J., Ms-169-1; Pvt E Co 9th TN Cav; Aug 63 to Feb 64; Petersburg PO; no disability incured, not regularly discharged
HEMPHILL, Samuel C., Bl-2-1, Mary C. widow of; Pvt A Co 3rd OH Inf; 61 to 64; Sampson PO; shot in left leg
HEMPLE, Henry, Sh-172-1; Sgt F Co 2nd MO Art; 9-19-61 to 10-13-64; 11 McCall St., Memphis PO; deaf from war; lost his hearing
HEMPPAIL, John W., Sh-150-1; John H. Smigh; Pvt D Co US Hvy Art; Bartlett PO; shot in left shoulder
HENARD, Benjamin, F-37-2; Pvt M Co 41st or 14th NC Col Art; 64 to 65; Yum Yum PO; wounded at Ft. Macon under Col Poe and Capt Mills
HENARD, Elijah A., Hw-119-2(1); Pvt H Co 8th TN Inf; 23 Jul 63 to 16 Jun 65; Alum Well PO; rheumatism & dis eyes

HENARD, James M., Hw-121-3(2); Pvt; 1 Sep 63 to 15 Jul 65; New Home PO; CONF
HENARD, William, Hw-133-3; Pvt OH Pat?; 64 to 65; Fry PO; rhumatism with other
HENCHEY, Albert L., Je-135-3; Mary F. widow of; Pvt D Co 3rd TN Cav; 19 Jan 64 to 3 Aug 65; Flat Gap PO; catarrh & lung trouble
HENCKLE, William C., D-45-2; Pvt E Co 41st NY Vol; 9-1-62 to 9-20-63; Nashville PO
HENDEN, James W., Bl-5-1; Pvt I Co 2nd TN Mtd Inf; 11-11-61 to __ (no discharge); Brayton PO; pleurisy--measles and relapse, absent without leave in 62, returned to duty in 64 but not recorded
HENDERSON, Charles A., Ma-119-1; Sgt C Co 92nd IL Inf; Aug 62 to Jun 65; Jackson PO; kidney trouble, draws a pension
HENDERSON, David, Sh-195-2; US Sol; Memphis PO
HENDERSON, Edward, Ge-94-2(1); Pvt G Co 1st TN Art; May 64 to 31 Mar 66; Tusculum PO; during Civil War
HENDERSON, Elizabeth, K-181-6(3); widow of Sol (CONF) Pvt; Jan 62 to __; Knoxville PO; CONF
HENDERSON, Emma C., Lo-194-2; widow; Muddy Creek PO
HENDERSON, Finley H., K-158-1; Maj Ashby's Bat; May 61 to 13 May 65; Knoxville, c/o Hattie House PO; CONF
HENDERSON, G. L., Hw-125-2; Pvt A Co 12th TN Cav; 62 to 65; Surgoinsville PO; shot in the left leg
HENDERSON, George, Col, Li-154-1; Pvt A Co 1st US Inf; 12-62 to __ (3 yrs 8 mos); Clardy Ville PO, ran away and joined the army in 1862, no discharge
HENDERSON, George J., B-7-2; Sgt 2nd KY Battery; 7-20-61 to 4-24-64; PO omitted
HENDERSON, George W., Se-231-2; Pvt H Co 9th TN Cav; 1 Oct 63 to 11 Sep 65; Boyds Creek PO; lung diseas 26 years, partial defness, 15 years
HENDERSON, George W., Mc-112-2; Pvt H Co 1st US Col Art; 10-64 to 3-21-66; Athens PO
HENDERSON, Hattie, (see Robinson, Robert)
HENDERSON, Henry, Sh-158-4; Pvt; 2 yrs; Memphis PO; Henderson absent & wife too sick to get his papers, but __ is clear that he was soldier
HENDERSON, Isic, D-47-1; Pvt K Co 111th TN Inf; 64 to 65; Jefferson St., Nashville PO
HENDERSON, J. W., A-1-3; M. J. widow of; Pvt F Co 6th TN Inf; 3-10-62 to 3-15-65; Andersonville PO; husband died in prison
HENDERSON, James, D-56-1; 418 Spruce, Nashville PO
HENDERSON, James C., K-160-1; Sgt H Co 9th TN Vol; 28 Oct 63 to 7 Apr 65; Knoxville PO; chronic bronchitis
HENDERSON, James H., A-3-3; Pvt G Co 8th TN Cav; 7-1-63 to 9-11-65; Clinton PO; lungs and eyes
HENDERSON, James P., Mc-114-7; 16th Civil Dist; CONF
HENDERSON, James R., Hw-118-3; Pvt D Co 1st TN Cav; 15 Apr 62 to 15 Apr 65; St. Clair PO; rheumatism & piles
HENDERSON, Jasper, Bl-3-6; Pvt; 62 to 62; Tanbark PO; CONF
HENDERSON, John, Mu-190-1; alias John H. English; Pvt D Co 110th Col Inf; 10-64 to 2-66; Culleoka PO
HENDERSON, John, Ge-94-2(1); Pvt G Co 1st TN Art; Apr 64 to Mar 66; Tusculum PO; during the Civil War
HENDERSON, John C., Mo-152-1; Cpl K Co 9th TN Cav; 9-16-63 to 9-11-65; Dancing Branch PO; camp diarrhea & rupture
HENDERSON, Joseph, Dk-37-1; 5th Civ District
HENDERSON, Joseph, Dk-36-3; 5th Civl Dist.
HENDERSON, Josiah S., Dk-35-1; Nancy A. widow of; Pvt F Co 4th TN Mtd Inf; 9-25-64 to 8-25-65; Temperance Hall PO
HENDERSON, Mark, Lo-193-1; Cpl D Co 1st US Art; 7 Mar 64 to 31 Mar 66; Unitia PO
HENDERSON, Milton H., Gi-139-1; Pvt E Co 18th TN Cav; 11-64 to 65 (6 mos); Barcheers PO; CONF
HENDERSON, Orter, D-57-3; Pvt; PO omitted, 8th Ward
HENDERSON, Perry, Gi-129-2; Clycey widow of; Pvt 110th TN Inf; Elkton PO
HENDERSON, Robert, Bl-3-6; Pvt; 62 to 62; Tanbark PO; CONF
HENDERSON, Robert, Sh-15-9-1; Pvt 16th IL Inf; 6 mos; Bartlett PO

141

HENDERSON, Robert F., H-54-5; Cpl M Co 1st TN Cav; 12-20-62 to 5-65; Sherman Heights PO; broken in health, heart & lungs, diseased
HENDERSON, T. J., Mc-117-5; Pvt E Co 7th TN Mtd Inf; 3-25-64 to 7-27-65; Carlock PO; throat skin & impore vaccination
HENDERSON, Thomas, (see Voorhies, Thomas)
HENDERSON, William, D-45-2; Pvt E Co PA Art; 10-31-64 to 6-14-65; Nashville PO
HENDERSON, William, Ms-181-1; Cpl C Co 10th TN Inf; 1-7-63 to 4-12-65; Lewisburg PO
HENDERSON, William, D-50-1; Pvt; 522 Line, Nashville PO
HENDERSON, William, Co-67-5; Cpl I Co 6th NC Inf; 9 Mar 65 to 9 Oct 66; Naillon PO; loss of two toes
HENDERSON, William, K-161-2; Knoxville PO
HENDERSON, William C., Mn-120-1; Pvt G Co 6th TN Cav; 25 Sep 62 to 26 Jul 65; Ramer PO
HENDERSON, William H., Mo-129-2; Pvt B Co 7th TN Cav; 5-62 to 65; Lomotley PO; shot in the head and arm
HENDERSON, Wm. W., Hw-125-1; Pvt E Co 2nd TN; 7 Jul 61 to 10 May 65; Stony Point PO; CONF
HENDERSON, _____, Hw-125-2; Sarah widow of; E Co 2nd TN Cav; 61 to 65; Surgoinsville PO; eyes afflicted
HENDERSON, _____, H-73-3; Minnie widow of; Pvt; Chattanooga PO
HENDESON, Joseph, Mr-102-3; Pvt E Co 6th TN Mtd Inf; 64 to 7-65; South Pittsburg PO; piles contracted in war, discharge ___ burned in house
HENDLEY, Benjamin F., Rb-219-3; Elizabeth widow of; Pvt C Co 14th TN Reg; May 61 to ___; Black Jack PO
HENDLEY, Charles F., Rb-219-1; Pvt B Co 6th US Inf; Apr 65 to Sep 65; Orlinda PO
HENDLEY, Charles F., Rb-219-1; Sgt B Co 14th KY Cav; Aug 64 to Dec 64; Orlinda PO
HENDLIN, Joseph B., H-53-6; Ridgedale PO
HENDON, William, H-50-1; Pvt A Co 9th R TN Cav; 8-12-63 to 9-11-65; Daisy PO; chronic diorreah and piles
HENDREW, Eli, A-9-5(3); Pvt I Co 9th TN Cav; 9-63 to 9-11-65; Clinton PO; rheumatism
HENDRICKS, Charles, Gu-48-4(1); Pvt L Co 53rd LA Inf; 6-10-62 to 3-20-65; Jackson PO (Madison Co)
HENDRICKS, John, Ma-188-1; Cpl D Co 17th OH Inf; 3-13-63 to 7-16-65; Parks Station PO
HENDRICKS, Joseph B., K-180-4; US Sol; 11th Dist
HENDRICKS, Milber J., (see Canady, Thomas)
HENDRICKS, Nathan G., Me-88-1; Pvt G Co 5th TN Inf; 4-1-62 to 4-11-65; Birchwood PO; discharged surgeons ctf
HENDRICKS, William, H-64-3; US Sol; 407 Lenore St., Chattanooga PO
HENDRICKS, Benj. L., Ro-204-3; Pvt B Co 5th TN Inf; 25 Feb 62 to 30 Mar 65; Elverton PO
HENDRICKSON, Jacob M., Su-234-1; Capt K Co 8th TN Cav; 22 Jul 62 to 2 Feb 64; Lella PO; Morristown 28 Oct 1864, injury of the hips by horse falling
HENDRICKSON, Joseph, D-45-4; Pvt A Co 5th TN Cav; 6-62 to 64 (2 yrs 9 mos); Nashville PO
HENDRIX, Daniel M., Sn-262-2(1); Cpl I Co 66th OH Inf; 10-8-61 to 7-15-65; Fountain Head PO; diabetes
HENDRIX, Farlington, K-186-1; Musician E Co 3rd TN Inf; 12 Feb 62 to 23 Feb 65; Beaver Ridge PO; piles, fever in left hip, at home unable to work
HENDRIX, Hand A. C., De-26-2; D Co; 2 Dec 61 to ___ (1 yr); Pakers Ld? PO; CONF
HENDRIX, Harvy, Sq-165-1; Pvt I Co 6th TN Cav; 10-1-64 to 65; Delphi PO
HENDRIX, Henry C., We-223-5; Pvt C Co 3rd KY Inf; 1 Jan 63 to 14 Feb 64; Elm Tree PO; shot in head
HENDRIX, Isaac, Ru-237-1; Pvt K Co 17th TN Inf; 64 to Apr 65; Eagleville PO
HENDRIX, James H., A-8-4; Lirzer widow of; Pvt E Co 3rd TN Inf; Scarborough PO; killed 1-27-63
HENDRIX, Jarome B., K-181-5(2); Pvt A Co 6th TN Inf; Knoxville PO
HENDRIX, Joseph, Mc-109-5; Pvt K Co 10th TN Cav; Sweetwater PO (Monroe Co)
HENDRIX, Newton, A-7-3; Pvt C Co 11th ___; 5-22-63 to 4-28-65; Robertsville PO

HENDRIX, Robert W., Wl-293-1; Pvt B Co 1st TN; 60 to 62; Austin PO; CONF
HENDRIX, Soloman M., Ct-41-3; Hospital steward 1st TN Cav; 10-6-62 to 9-29-65; South Wattauga PO; Rhumatism, hearing
HENDRIX, William H., He-61-1; Pvt G Co 7th TN Cav; 5 Aug 62 to 14 Oct 63; Sgt G Co 2nd TN Mtd Inf; 30 Nov 63 to 28 Dec 64; Sherman Mill PO
HENDRIX, William L., Dy-29-2; Pvt I Co 12th TN Cav; 3 Dec 64 to 18 Mar 65; Newbern PO: CONF
HENDRIXON, Jeremiah, Dk-35-4(2); Pvt A Co 5th TN Cav; 11-14-63 to 8-14-65; Temperance Hall PO; shot in mouth
HENDRIXON, Wilson, Dk-35-3(1); Pvt A Co 5th TN Cav; 1-20-64 to 8-14-65; Hicks PO; arm broken
HENDRIXSON, Jacob, Wa-268-3; Capt K Co 8th TN Cav; 22 Jul 62 to 22 Feb 65; Johnson City PO; spinal disease
HENDRIXSON, John F., Martha A widow of; D-34-3; Pvt F Co 4th TN Inf; 10-30-64 to 8-25-65; Dowellton PO; lungs
HENDRON, Daniel R., A-5-1; Pvt C Co 2nd TN Inf; 8-7-61 to 2-14-65; Clinton PO; piles & constipation
HENDRY, William B., Ge-101-2; Recr. Off 2nd NC Cav; Nov 63 to ___ (2 yrs); Locust Sp PO
HENDRY, William B., Ge-101-2; Pvt H Co 8th TN Inf; 25 Jul 63 to 17 Aug 65; Locust Sp PO; rectum near Nashville
HENDSON, Elijah, A-6-6(4); Pvt CS Co 3rd TN Inf; 2-12-62 to 2-29-65; Olivers PO
HENDSON, John, A-6-6(4); Pvt K Co 1st TN Inf; 4-23-63 to 5-25-65; Olivers PO
HENDSON, John, A-6-1; Pvt K Co 1st TN Inf; 8-9-61 to 9-17-64; Olivers PO
HENELY, William, Ge-83-3; Pvt E Co 2nd NC? Inf; 63 to Aug 65; Painters PO; wound in anus, chronic diarrhea
HENERY, John E., (W.S.), Ge-89-3; Pvt D Co 8th TN Inf; 20 Jan 63 to 30 Jun 65; Marvin PO; lungs
HENGLEY, T. M., Ru-231-1; Pvt C 73rd IN Inf; May 63 to 65; May Ella PO
HENIGER, Andrew J., Un-258-3; Pvt E Co 6th TN Inf; Mar 62 to Apr 65; Longhollow PO; shot throu wright leg
HENKLE, Joseph, Ge-87-1; Pvt G Co 4th TN Inf; 15 Jan to Aug 65; Midway PO
HENLEY, Charles B., Mo-124-1; Pvt; 4 mos 15 days; 4 Mile Branch PO; spasms, other afflictions, discharge lost, but proof can be made
HENLEY, George E., Dk-31-2; Pvt K Co 5th TN Cav; 2-22-63 to 8-14-65; Alexandria PO
HENLEY, Samuel, Dk-31-3; Pvt I Co 5th TN Cav; 2-11-63 to 8-14-65; Alexandria PO; now suffering with general debility, nervousness & weakness
HENLEY, William, Dk-31-1; Cpl C Co 5th TN Cav; 2-11-63 to 8-14-65; Alexandria PO; blind in one eye
HENLEY, William, Sh-144-2; US Sol; First Dist
HENLY, Joel J., Ov-133-1; Pvt K Co 28th TN Cav; 1-6-65 to 7-1-65; Jeremiah PO
HENLY, Robert, K-168-2; Pvt L Co 3rd TN Col Inf; Knoxville PO
HENLY, Robert, K-168-2; Pvt I Co 1st TN Hvy Art; 1 Jul 62 to ___; Knoxville PO
HENNESSEE, Wm. F., W-194-2; US Sol; 11th Dist
HENNICK, Cornelius, Sh-158-4; Sgt B Co 46th IL Inf; 10 Sep 61 to 2 Feb 66; Memphis PO; in 10 Genl Eng regiments? & never wounded
HENNINGHAM, Thomas, Fe-40-1; Pvt D Co 2nd TN Cav; Little Crabb PO; piles & hurt by horse
HENREY, John, O-138-1; Pvt F Co 54th & 48th TN; 1 Mar 62 to 1 Nov 64; Lanes PO; wounded in right arm? caused by gun shot; CONF
HENRICK, Jefferson, K-175-1; Pvt; Bullrun PO
HENRICKS, John, D-64-2; Nashville PO
HENRY, Anderson, Je-140-2; Mollie widow of; Pvt B Co 9th TN Cav; PO omitted
HENRY, Anderson, Hw-120-1; Pvt B Co 9th TN Cav; Jul 63 to 17 Sep 65; War Gap PO; heart trouble
HENRY, Charles, D-44-2(1); Wilhelmina widow of; Pvt K Co 9th OH; 3-18-63 to 7-25-65; Nashville PO
HENRY, Charles, G-58-1; Rutherford PO
HENRY, George, Sh-199-1; Pvt; 574 Georgia St., Memphis PO
HENRY, George W., Se-227-2; Pvt 2nd TN Cav; PO omitted

HENRY, James, Sh-189-4; Coal Heaver Steamer Stockaver?; 2-64 to 2-7-67; Carolina, Memphis PO
HENRY, James F., Bl-4-1; Sgt E Co 22nd PA Cav; 10-13-62 to 7-10-65; Pikeville PO; chronic bronchitis, not able to labor
HENRY, James M., Gr-70-4; Cpl B Co 1st TN Cav; 9 Apr 61 to 1 Apr 64; Rutledge PO
HENRY, John, Se-219-3; Capt E Co 2nd TN Cav; 16 Sep 62 to 11 Apr 65; Richardsons Cave; chronic diarhoe, rumatism
HENRY, John, Je-136-1; Dandridge PO
HENRY, John, Gr-80-1; Sgt B Co 1st TN Cav; 9 Apr 62 to 9 Apr 65; Thorn Hill PO; rumatism
HENRY, John C., S-219-2; Pvt G Co 8th Inf; 14 Jul 62 to __; Hughett PO; absent without leave
HENRY, John F., Bo-14-1; Cpl L Co 2nd TN Cav; 9-5-63 to 7-6-65; Clover Hill PO; chronic diarrhea, rheumatism and
HENRY, Jos. A., Ge-87-2; Pvt M Co 9th TN Cav; Mar 65 to Sep 65; Timberridge PO; chronic diarrhea
HENRY, Martha, (see Brimer, David)
HENRY, Samuel, Bo-22-2; Pvt A Co 3rd TN Cav; 9-18-62 to 8-3-65; Gamble's Store PO; chronic diarea & piles
HENRY, Samuel, Bo-14-4; Mary S. widow of; Sgt L Co 2nd TN Cav; 9-8-63 to 9-15-65; Clover Hill PO; chronic rheumatism
HENRY, Samuel A., Se-225-2; Pvt B Co 2nd TN Cav; Aug 62 to Jul 65; Allensville PO; wounded in right thigh
HENRY, Samuel P., Se-226-3; Malinda widow of; Pvt; Henrys X Roads PO
HENRY, Samuel W., Bo-22-3; Pvt D Co 1st TN Art; 9-63 to 7-65; Gamble's Store PO
HENRY, Spencer H., Bo-15-3; Pvt L Co 2nd TN Cav; 9-8-63 to 3-5-65; Corn PO
HENRY, Spruce W., Sq-164-3(1); Pvt; Dunlap PO
HENRY, Thomas, Ru-246-1; Cook A Co 23rd MI Inf; 2-64 to 65; Murfreesboro PO
HENRY, Thomas, Sh-195-1; Pvt C Co 11th Col Inf; __ to 11-66; Memphis PO
HENRY, Thomas C., Mc-110-1; Nancy E. widow of; Pvt 8th TN Inf; Rock Creek PO; came home on sick furlow
HENRY, Ulrich, Gr-74-2; Cpl H Co 2nd TN Mtd Inf; Mar 63 to __; Dyers Ferry PO; prisoner 16 months, Bell Island, Andersonville, Florence; CONF
HENRY, William, D-75-1; Mary A. widow of; Pvt; 1 May 61 to 1 Oct 64; Stewarts Ferry PO; discharged from age; CONF
HENRY, William, S-218-21 Pvt D Co 62nd KY Inf; Aug 63 to Jul 65; PO omitted
HENRY, William, Se-219-3; Pvt E Co 2nd TN Cav; 16 Sep 62 to 5 Jul 65; Jones Cave PO; broken collar bone
HENRY, William, Bo-11-3; Pvt L Co US Hvy Art; 64 to __ (7 mos); Largonia? PO
HENRY, William M., We-232-1; Pvt E Co 13th TN Cav; 63 to 65; Mount Pulon PO
HENRY, William M. (US), Hw-119-2(1); Sgt E Co 1st TN Cav; 2 Mar 62 to 11 Apr 65; Hales Spring PO; heart dis. & nerv. debility
HENSELY, Benj. F., Ro-208-2; Pvt C Co 7th TN Inf; 20 Aug 64 to 27 Jun 65; Welker Mines PO; lung trouble
HENSER, James, Sol, D-43-2; Cheny St., Nashville PO
HENSLEY, Calam L., Po-152-4(2); Pvt G Co 8th TN Cav; 3-1-64 to 9-11-65; Ducktown PO; deafness and gun shot wound of head
HENSLEY, Clingman, U-249-1; Pvt C Co 3rd NC Mtd Inf; 5 Nov 64 to 8 Aug 65; Flag Pond PO; rheumaties and chronic diarea
HENSLEY, Cornelies, Ge-102-2; Pvt M Co 1st TN Cav; 25 Nov 62 to 19 Jun 65; Whig PO
HENSLEY, Daniel, Le-119-1; Mary E. Beckurn, formerly widow of; Simmestown PO; chronic diarrhoes from which he died; it is supposed discharged on surgeons certificate, all discharges ar lost
HENSLEY, Daniel P., A-2-2; Bull Run PO (Knox Co); not at home, discharge in Sullivan Co
HENSLEY, Ezekiel S., Co-67-6; Sgt D Co 3rd NC Mtd Inf; 12 Aug 64 to 16 Aug 65; PO omitted
HENSLEY, Francis E., Co-60-2; M Co 1st TN Cav; 11-25-62 to 6-19-65; Syrusburg PO; wounded legs
HENSLEY, George, Su-239-1; Pvt H Co 8th TN Cav; 28 Sep 63 to 11 Sep 65; Peltier PO

HENSLEY, Geo. W., Hi-91-1; Pvt F Co 48th MO Inf; 64 to 8-5-65; Pleasantville PO
HENSLEY, Harrison H., Jo-153-1; Pvt F Co 13th TN Cav; 21 Sep 63 to 5 Sep 65; Pondora PO; hernia, frost bite
HENSLEY, Isaac, Sm-169-2; Pvt; Elmwood PO; CONF
HENSLEY, Isaac, Wa-266-1; Pvt A Co 1st TN Cav; 19 Mar 62 to 4 Apr 65; Fall Branch PO
HENSLEY, Joel, Le-118-1; Pvt B Co 5th US Cav; 13 Jun 66 to 24 Sep 66; Hakenwalk PO; chronic diarrhea
HENSLEY, John, Wa-266-2; Pvt E Co 1st TN Lt Art; 1 Sep 63 to 1 Aug 65; Fall Branch PO
HENSLEY, John, Ge-98-1; Pvt H Co 1st TN Cav; 1 Jul 62 to 5 Jun 65; disease of left eye, PO omitted
HENSLEY, John C., Ru-239-1; Pvt D Co 17th KY Cav; 18 Nov 64 to 20 Sep 65; Overall PO; served till the end
HENSLEY, John W., Je-146-1; PO omitted
HENSLEY, Lue S. (see McCay, P.)
HENSLEY, Michael Jr., Ge-98-5; Pvt A Co 1st TN Cav; 19 Mar 62 to 4 Apr 65; Jeroldstown PO; chronic diarhea
HENSLEY, Michael, Ge-98-1; Pvt 1st TN Cav; PO omitted; chronic diarhea
HENSLEY, Wesley, Ge-99-2; Pvt, didn't belong to any co., 1st TN Cav; Limestone Springs PO; gunshot wound in hip, couldn't get dates
HENSLEY, William, Hw-49-5; Cpl C Co 5th TN Inf; 2-25-62 to 4-4-65; Daisy PO; piles & rheumatism
HENSLEY, William, Ro-210-9; Pvt; Rockwood PO; CONF
HENSLEY, William H., U-248-1; Cpl M Co 8th TN Cav; 16 Sep 63 to 15 Sep 65; Clear Branch PO
HENSLEY, William K., U-248-1; Elvira widow of; Cpl M Co 8th TN Cav; 15 Sep 63 to 11 Sep 65; Clear Branch PO
HENSLY, Amos, Ge-84-3; Elizabeth widow of; Pvt M Co 1st TN Cav; Wolsey College PO; discharge not found
HENSON, Christopher C., D-57-2; Pvt A Co 10th MO Inf; 1 Nov 63 to 15 Apr 65; PO omitted, 8th Ward; CONF
HENSON, Daniel, Hr-96-2; Pinetop PO
HENSON, Edmund D., Ro-210-8; Pvt G Co 3rd TN Mtd Inf; 8 Aug 64 to 13 Nov 64; Rockwood PO
HENSON, J. E., Bo-11-1; Pvt M Co 8th TN Cav; 1-63 to 9-65; Grice Buck PO; weak eyes
HENSON, James, C-34-1; Nancy J. widow of; Cpl 12th KY Inf; 61 to 65 (3 yrs 4 mos); Stanfill PO; contracted consumption
HENSON, Jessee, St-160-2; Pvt 50th TN Inf; Oct 62 to Apr 65; Big Rock PO; CONF
HENSON, Robert, U-245-2; Marbleton PO
HENSON, Thomas, Hr-97-1; Pvt; Aug 64 to __ (2 yrs); Toone PO
HENSON, Thos. Iben, La-117-3; Pvt A Co 2nd TN; 14 Oct 64 to 14 Oct 65; 15th Dist
HENSON, William, R-161-2; Mary Thompson formerly widow of; Pvt A Co 5th TN Inf; 2-62 to 65; Dayton PO; died in hospitle at Nashville, TN
HENSON, William A., Dy-25-5(1); Pvt A Co 38th GA Inf; 9 Sep 61 to 12 May 65; Newbern PO; CONF
HENTY, Charles, L-106-1; US Sol; 8th Dist
HEPLEY, Delas, Hm-33(103)-1; Pvt I Co 1st MI Cav; Dec 63 to 66 (3 yrs); Dyersburg PO; palsey & piles
HERAL, Jacob, Hw-128-2; Pvt H Co 8th TN Inf; 25 Jul 63 to 30 Jun 65; Walnut Hill PO; rheumatism & resulting in disease of heart
HERALD, James, Sh-38-1; Pvt E Co 10th IN Cav; 63 to 65 (2 yrs 6 mos); Silver Point PO
HERALD, Thomas, Ja-84-2; Pvt C Co 5th TN Inf; 2-25-62 to 4-4-65; Harrison PO; inflamatory rheumatism
HERALD, William V., Sm-175-2(1); Pvt H Co 11th KY Cav; __ to 1-65; Bluff Creek PO
HERBERT, R. N., Gi-139-2; Pvt A Co 1st TN Inf; 5-10-61 to 5-6-6? (4 yrs 1 mo 10 days); Campbellsville PO
HERD, Carter D., Ha-111-1; 1st Sgt L Co 8th TN Cav; 17 Sep 63 to Sep 65; Upper Clinch PO
HERD, James, Ha-111-3; Pvt E Co 1st TN Cav; 17 Mar 62 to 15 Nov 63; PO omitted
HERD, Wiley, Ha-111-2; Pvt L Co 8th TN Cav; 17 Sep 63 to 11 Sep 65; Kyle's Ford PO
HERGAN, Margaret, (see Green, John, H-70-2(1))

HERILL, David M., Ge-90-2; Pvt F Co 4th TN Inf; 15 Apr 63 to 2 Aug 65; Myers PO; smothering of the heart
HERMAN, Isaac, T-216-2; 11th Civil Dist
HERMAN, John, H-53-7; Pvt I Co 44th PA Inf; 10-62 to 7-63; Chattanooga PO
HERMAN, John H., Ca-23-1; Pvt L Co 5th TN Cav; 2-63 to 8-14-65; Leoni PO; health injured by exposure
HERMAN, Joseph, Dk-33-4; 3rd Civil Dist
HERN, Alen, Wl-302-2; Shopsprings PO
HERN, Russ, Hd-52-2; Lucrecia widow of; Pvt 6th TN Cav; 62 to 65; Shelohville PO
HERNDON, Thomas D., G-67-3; Sarah L. widow of; Sgt K Co 7th TN Cav; Apr 63 to __; Idlewild PO; killed in battle
HERNYCUT, Andrew J., Ov-139-1; Marah H. widow of; Pvt; 61 to __; France PO
HERRELL, Drew P., Cl-53-1; Milley Reanson former widow of; Capt H Co 1st TN Cav; 6-13-62 to 8-24-63; Springdale PO
HERRELL, William M., K-177-6; Pvt C Co 3rd TN Inf; Feb 62 to Feb 65; Powells Station PO; piles, rheumatism & spinal disease since 1862
HERREN, John W., Se-231-1; Pvt H Co 2nd TN Cav; 10 Oct 62 to 14 Jul 65; Boyds Creek PO
HERRIMAN, Stephen, Ca-24-2; Pvt D Co 4th TN Mtd Inf; 9-22-64 to 8-25-65; Woodbury PO; none whatever thank God
HERRIN, Charles F., La-117-3; Pvt I Co 3rd TN Inf; May 61 to 64; 15th Dist; CONF
HERRIN, Jas. L., La-117-3; Pvt I Co 3rd TN Inf; May 61 to __ (4 yrs); 15th Dist; CONF
HERRIN, Robert, Pu-145-1; Pvt C Co 1st Mtd Inf; 10-21-63 to 12-13-64; Burton PO
HERRIN, Wiseman, Pu-145-1; Pvt C Co 1st Mtd Inf; 10-21-63 to 12-13-64; Burton PO
HERRING, Benjamin, Mt-138-1; (Mulatto) US Sol; Dist 7, New Providence PO
HERRINGTON, John K., Dk-39-1; Louisa Harris formerly widow of; Pvt; Bozarth PO
HERRITAL, Jacob, Mc-117-4; Pvt A Co 48th IN Inf; 6-3-65 to 8-26-65; Williamsburg PO; liver trouble
HERRON, Hiram, Ha-111-1; Pvt E Co 13th TN Cav; Sep 62 to Apr 65; Upper Clinch PO; CONF
HERRON, Jackson, Dk-39-2; Pvt C Co 1st TN Mtd Inf; 10-24-63 to 12-20-64; Bozarth PO; right thigh smashed severely ___ and many other complaints the result of his service
HERRON, John, Hy-76-2; US Sol; Stanton Depot PO
HERRON, Richard B., Dk-39-2; Abby widow of; Pvt 1st TN Mtd Inf; BozarthPO
HERRON, Richmond, Dy-29-2; Cpl I Co 22nd TN Inf; Dec 61 to Mar 62; Newbern PO; CONF
HERRON, William, Sh-196-1; Pvt E Co 3rd US Hvy Art; 64 to 65; 120 Dunlap St., Memphis PO; papers lost
HERSEY, N(op?), Hr-94-1; Emily widow of; Pvt; Saulsburg PO
HERSEY, Sylvanus, K-171-3(2); Sgt KY Inf; Knoxville PO
HERSHAW, Alfred, H-68-2; 1st Sgt G Co 15th US Col Inf; 2 yrs 9 mos 17 days; Chattanooga PO
HERWIG, E., D-54-3; Dusie widow of; Surgeon; 3 yrs; Nashville PO; in charge of hospitals at Nashville & Memphis
HESIR, James, Ro-209-3; Pvt B Co; Rockwood PO
HESS, Nelson P., Cr-4-2; Asst Sgt H Co 12th TN Inf; 1 Apr 61 to 1 Apr 65; Bells Depot PO; wounded --shouls, also ankle; CONF
HESSE, Fred, D-86-1; Pvt E Co 2nd KY Inf; 6 Jun 61 to 19 Jun 64; PO omitted
HESSEY, Flavin? F., D-75-2; Pvt D Co 30th TN Inf; 1 Oct 61 to 15 Jun 64; Stewarts Ferry PO; shot in hip, Franklin Pris. 9 mos, Springfield IL; CONF
HESSEY, James M., D-75-2; Teamster I Co 20th TN Inf; 15 Apr 61 to 1 Jun 65; Stewarts Ferry PO; surrendered under Gen. Paine, Gallatin; CONF
HESTER, Chruchwell, Ro-204-4; Mary A. widow of; Pvt I Co 1st TN Inf; 2 Nov 61 to 5 Nov 64; Kreis PO
HESTER, Daniel W., Mn-126-2; Sgt A Co 6th TN Cav; 8-11-62 to 6-26-65; Bethel Springs PO
HESTER, Enoch M., Mn-126-2; Pvt A Co 6th TN Cav; 8-11-62 to 6-26-65; Bethel Springs PO

HESTER, Hardy A., Sol US, He-59-1; PO omitted
HESTER, James I., Sol US, He-59-1; PO omitted
HESTER, John W., Mn-126-2; Pvt A Co 6th TN Cav; 8-11-63 to 1-63; Bethel Springs PO; was paroled, got no discharge
HESTER, Lewis, Ro-204-4; Pvt I Co 9th TN Cav; 12 Oct 63 to 11 Sep 65; Kreis PO; broken arm & c
HESY, William M., Cr-14-4; Mary J. widow of; Pvt G Co 2nd TN Cav; 5 Aug 62 to 25 Oct 63; Cawthorn PO
HETON, K. T., Wa-263-2; alias Helton, H. C.; Pvt; Garbers Mills PO; he says he was a soldier but I think he lies
HEUBLER?, O. H., P-156-2; Pvt G Co 20th TN Inf; 6-7-61 to 11-62; Lobelville PO; wounded in the head; discharged on account of wound; CONF
HEUGLEY, Brethet, Wl-308-2; Pvt H Co 7th TN; 1 May 61 to Apr 65; Mount Juliet PO; captured; CONF
HEULSE, Alford F., H-70-3(1); Pvt H Co 97th OH Inf; 8-5-62 to 9-64; Chattanooga PO; enlisted again K Co 1st US Engineers, discharged 9-28-65
HEUST, Vincent, Me-90-1; Pvt E Co 2nd TN Cav; 9-62 to 7-65; Decatur PO
HEWETT, Febery, T-213-2; widow Pvt; 8th Civil Dist
HEWETT, John M., O-134-2; Pvt 12th 10SC Cav; 15 Jun 62 to 12 Apr 65; Hornbeak PO; CONF
HEWETT, Lewis T., St-160-1; Pvt C Co 50th TN Inf; Nov 61 to Jan 62; Layfayette PO (Christian Co); CONF
HEWGHS, John R. Ge-89-2; Susie P. widow of; Pvt G Co 8th TN Inf; Nov 61 to Jul 65; Mosheim PO
HEWITT, Harry J., Dy-29-4; Sailor, Trimble PO
HEWITT, William, G-70-1; Pvt H Co 81st PA Inf; 1 Oct 61 to 1 Oct 64; Dyer PO
HEWEITT, William, Ce-23-1; Pvt Lockhards 14th Reg; 61 to 61 (4 mos); Thomasville PO; chronic sore eyes
HEWSON, James D., Mg-196-4; US Sol; 10th Dist
HEYERS, Mary A., widow of Stephan; D-66-1; sayes her papers at Col Gippers off; O Sgt 10th TN Cav; Oct 63 to 66; Nashville, 406 S Front PO; draws a pension; wounded in left arm from effects of which produced paralasis of heart, killed him
HEYGOOD, George, D-69-3; 20 E. Hill St. Nashville PO
HEYSMITH, E. J., Hd-56-1; Pvt B Co 6th TN Cav; 9-1-62 to 7-26-64; Adamsville PO; ruptured in US army
HIBDON, Champion, D-58-2; Pvt M Co 5th US Inf; Jan 64 to Aug 65; Nashville PO; small pox in service
HIBDON, John C., Ce-20-2; Pvt D Co 4th TN Inf; 9-22-64 to 8-25-65; Ashland City PO; chronic diarear and fistula
HIBLER, Bettie Little widow of; Sh-198-2; Pvt C Co 1st TN Hvy Art; 12-22-63 to died 4-21-64; Memphis PO; was on Garrison duty 3-11-64, died 4-21-64; in small pox hospital on Union Ave nr. Memphis (J. T. Whitten hospital steward)
HICE, Henry, Ge-96-3; Pvt C Co 1st TN Art; 16 Sep 63 to 1 Aug 65; Rheatown PO; injured by horse fall, back
HICK, Charles C., Jo-149-4; Emaline widow of; Pvt F Co 13th TN Cav; 2-2-64 to 9-5-65; Mountain City PO; epileptic fits
HICK, Nathaniel H., Ha-110-1; Pvt G Co 1st TN Cav; 1 Jul 62 to 5 Jun 65; Treadway PO
HICK, William R., A-5-2; Pvt C Co 2nd TN Inf; 8-7-61 to 2-8-65; Clinton PO
HICKASON, James J., P-150-1; Pvt E Co 2nd TN Inf; Apr 63 to Jul 64; Dist 1
HICKERSON, William J., P-150-2; US Sol; 1st Dist
HICKES, John, K-175-2; Pvt E Co 1st KY? Cav? Apr 62 to Aug 65; Bayless PO
HICKEY, Benjamin F., Hm-104-3(1); Pvt C Co 1st TN Cav; 1 Jan 63 to 24 Apr 65; Valley Home PO: spinal back caused by fall from horse in the service.
HICKEY, Cornelious, K-169-1; Cpl C Co 2nd TN Cav; Nov 62 to Jul 65; Knoxville PO
HICKEY, David A., Pu-145-2; Pvt D Co 1st Mtd Inf; 12-23-63 to 4-25-65; Burton PO
HICKEY, Thomas C., Br-7-3; Pvt L Co 9th TN Cav; 9-1-63 to 9-11-65; Felker PO; ulceration of left leg

HICKEY, W. J., K-182-1; Pvt E Co 3rd TN Cav; Nov 62 to May 65; Knoxville PO; disabled 1865; rupture left side; Andersonville 2 mos
HICKEY, William B., K-171-3(2); Pvt C Co 6th TN Inf; 17 Apr 62 to Apr 65; Knoxville PO
HICKLE, Ezra, Un-253-3; Pvt F Co 4th TN Inf; 10 Jan 64 to 2 Aug 65; Lorenaton PO
HICKLE, George, Un-253-2; Cpl F Co 3rd TN Inf; 10 Feb 62 to 2 Mar 65; Lutterell PO; shot through right thigh
HICKLE, James K., Un-253-1; Pvt G Co 2nd TN Cav; 7 Feb 63 to 6 Jul 65; Lorenaton PO; rheumatics, diarhea
HICKLE, John W., Un-253-1; Pvt D Co 1st TN Inf; 15 Jul 62 to 30 Jul 65; Lorenaton PO; loss of 1 eye, rheumatism
HICKMAN, Elias, H-49-6; Pvt K Co 5th TN Inf; 6-17-62 to 6-12-65; Daisy PO
HICKMAN, Frank A., H-52-1; Sgt C Co 16th IN Cav; Lookout Mt. PO
HICKMAN, Fred, A-13-2; Martha (widow?); 61 to 64; Briceville PO; no discharge can be found
HICKMAN, Frederic P., Se-226-2; Mary M. widow of; Pvt K Co 2nd TN Mtd Inf; 2 Mar 62 to 24 Mar 64; Cynthiana PO (Jefferson Co); died Bell's Island prison
HICKMAN, George W., Su-241-2; Pvt S Co 13th MO Cav; 7 Sep 64 to 15 Jul 65; Clover Bottom PO; throw off horse off a bridge
HICKMAN, Henry M., Di-30-2; Pvt 312th TN Inf; 11-62 to 62 (4 mos); Dickson PO; CONF
HICKMAN, Humphrey, Se-226-2; Pvt F Co 9th TN Cav; 1 Oct 63 to 11 Sep 65; Cynthiana PO (Jefferson Co); right testacle hurt
HICKMAN, Isaiah, Ro-203-8; Cpl G Co 3rd TN Inf; 10 Feb 62 to 23 Feb 65; Burns' Mills PO
HICKMAN, James A., H-50-4; Pvt A Co 6th R TN Mtd Inf; 8-2-64 to 6-30-65; Soddy PO
HICKMAN, James A., Je-145-2; Pvt H Co 12th KY Inf; 9 Sep 63 to 11 Jul 65; Dumplin PO
HICKMAN, James H., Dk-31-2; Pvt E Co 4th TN Mtd Inf; 10-20-64 to 8-25-65; Alexandria PO
HICKMAN, Nancy, (see Saunders, David)
HICKMAN, Pleasant P., Je-141-3; Rebecca widow of; Pvt B Co 11th TN Cav; Mill Springs PO
HICKMAN, Samuel, Je-145-2; Mary widow of; Pvt K Co 2nd TN Inf; 1 Sep 62 to 28 Jul 65; Dumplin PO
HICKMAN, Thomas, Pu-144-4; Pvt I Co 5th TN Cav; 11-27-62 to __; PO omitted, side hurt
HICKMAN, Thomas, Se-226-6; Elizabeth widow of; Sinking Springs PO
HICKMAN, Thomas, Se-226-2; Cpl F Co 9th TN Cav; Cynthiana PO (Jefferson Co)
HICKMAN, Thomas A., Se-226-2; Pvt D Co 14th IL Cav; 18 Sep 62 to 18 Jul 65; Sinking Springs PO; liver, heart & catarrh diseases
HICKMAN, Thommas, Se-231-2; Pvt K Co 2nd TN Inf; 29 Dec 61 to 29 Dec 64; Arther PO; cattarh of head 25 hears, nearly blind in both eyes 29 years
HICKMAN, William, K-164-2; Mary C. widow of; Pvt G Co 3rd TN Vol; 1 Jul 63 to 20 Jul 64; PO omitted (Knoxville?); died in Andersonville Prison
HICKMAN, William M., Me-92-1; Pvt G Co 4th TN Cav; 6-27-63 to 7-12-65; Hester Mills PO; chronic diarrheoa
HICKOK, Frank, Co-133-1; Pvt I Co 60th Ohio Inf; 5-64 to 1-65; Rives PO
HICKOK, William W., Sh-178-1; Pvt C Co 5th ME; 61 to 11-62; 174 Lauderdale, Memphis; sight effected & hearing
HICKS, Adam, Se-227-1; Mary J. widow of; Pvt B Co 6th TN Inf; 3-8-62 to 4-27-65; Arthur PO; gun shot of left arm
HICKS, Alexander H., Ge-98-4; 1st Lt F Co 3rd TN Mtd Inf; 9-8-62 to 5-13-64; PO omitted; loss of left testicle & rheumatism
HICKS, Allen, cold., Ru-234-1; Pvt F Co 39th Ind Cav; 3-62 to 3-65; Jefferson PO; mashed by horse
HICKS, Anderson, C-34-63; Pvt E Co 32nd KY Vol; 12-26-62 to 8-12-63; Elk Valley PO
HICKS, Andrew J., R-159-1; Pvt F Co 1st TN Cav; 3-1-62 to 3-31-63; Spring City PO; lung trouble brought on by exposure

HICKS, Aquin Saml., Sh-189-3; Pvt E Co 9th KY Cav; 8-8-62 to 9-10-63; Va. Ave., Memphis
HICKS, Berry, Mo-125-1; Pvt E Co 3rd TN Cav; 63 to 64; Mt. Vernon PO
HICKS, Daniel, Bo-14-3; Pvt D Co 8th TN Cav; 5-63 to ?; Mint PO; taken prisoner, never discharged
HICKS, Daniel R., K-154-5(2); Pvt L Co 9th TN Cav; 9-6-63 to 9-14-65; Knoxville PO; rheumatism since war
HICKS, David, Co-66-3(1); US Sol; 1st Dist
HICKS, Erasmus F., Cr-4-3; Alice J. widow of; Pvt C Co TN Cav; Bells Depot PO; CONF
HICKS, Fenton, J-78-2; Pvt K Co 1st TN Inf; 11-30-64 to 12-22-65; Haydensburg PO; kidneys & dyrear
HICKS, George D., D-45-4; Pvt F Co 6th Ky Cav; 12-3-63 to 9-6-65; Nashville PO; contracted heart deasease from exposure not able to do anything
HICKS, J. D., Bo-19-2; Stg E Co 63rd TN Inf; 1-5-61 to __ (2 yrs); Louisville PO; CONF
HICKS, Jacob R., Mo-124-2; Pvt E Co 1st MO Cav; 4-60 to 8-20-61; 4 Mile Branch PO; breast and rheumatism
HICKS, James, Col., Ms-176-1; Pvt G Co 1st TN; __ to 11-26-__; Caney Springs PO; cannot tell when enlisted
HICKS, James, Se-222-2; Harrisburg PO; gunshot wounds, defect of meazels & speach
HICKS, James, Mo-119-2; Pvt D Co 3rd TN Inf; 7-25-64 to 11-30-64; Sweetwater PO
HICKS, James, Dk-38-1; Pvt A Co TN Cav; 61 to 62 (9 mos); Capling PO
HICKS, James, Fe-44-1; Pvt E Co 7th TN Inf; 8-2-64 to __ (2 yrs); Allart PO
HICKS, James F., A; Pvt C Co 2nd TN Inf; 8-7-61 to 2-8-65; Bull Run PO (Knox Co); disease of stomach, kidney & liver, captured Rogersville TN 11-6-63
HICKS, James K., Mc-112-1; Pvt A Co 7th TN Mtd Inf; 10-6-64 to 7-27-65; Athens PO; hips injured by falling horse
HICKS, James K., Hu-100-1; Pvt E Co 6th US Inf; 3-24-65 to 10-10-66; Hustburg PO; CONF
HICKS, James N., Cr-4-3; Pvt E Co TN Cav; 3-1-62 to 4-15-65; Bells Depot PO; CONF
HICKS, Joel W., Mu-205-1; Sgt E Co 2nd TN Cav; 9-16-62 to 7-7-65; Williamsport PO
HICKS, John, C-24-3; Pvt B Co 1st TN Inf; 8-10-61 to 9-17-64; Agee PO; rheumatism disease of heart
HICKS, John, J-78-2; Pvt C Co 5th IN Inf; 2-2-64 to 7-31-65; Rough Point PO; lungs & kidney & broke arm
HICKS, John, Cl-47-1; Cpl C Co 1st TN Inf; 8-6-61 to 64; Speedwell PO
HICKS, John, Co-66-2(1); Sarah C., widow of; Pvt E Co 2nd TN Cav; 9-15-62 to 7-5-65; Birdsville PO
HICKS, John, H-64-3; Sgt; Chattanooga PO; shot in arm
HICKS, John S., Mo-120-3(1); Elizabeth V. widow of; Cpl G Co 1st TN Cav; 4-10-62 to 4-14-65; Sweetwater PO
HICKS, John W., Fe-43-1; Pvt B Co 11th TN Cav; 7-23-63 to __ (1 yr 4 mos); Beauty PO; typhoid fever affecting left side
HICKS, John W., Cr-4-1; Pvt E Co TN Cav; 3-62 to 4-65; Bells Depot PO; CONF
HICKS, Joseph, J-79-1; Pvt B Co 8th TN Mtd Inf; 1-15-65 to 8-17-65; Whitleyville PO
HICKS, Josiah, Dk-31-2; Pvt G Co 1st TN Mtd Inf; __ to 65; Alexandria PO
HICKS, Martha C., (see Wrigh(t), John E.)
HICKS, Mary A., (see Keener, John)
HICKS, Mathew J., Mr-99-4; Sol US; Jasper PO
HICKS, Moses, Co-67-3, Pvt L Co 8th TN Cav; 7-17-63 to __; Cosby PO
HICKS, Napoleon B., Br-13-3; Pvt F Co 1st TN Cav; 4-1-62 to 4-15-65; Cleveland PO; ventral hernia
HICKS, Petter, (see DUN, James)
HICKS, Rhodes, C-34-1; 2nd Sgt G Co 7th TN Mtd Inf; 11-8-64 to 7-27-65; Elk Valley PO

HICKS, Richard M., K-166-1; Pvt D Co 1st TN Art; 10-20-63 to 7-20-65; Knoxville PO; erysilos, 1 eye nearly gone
HICKS, Richard S., We-221-2; Pvt 5th TN Inf; 10-62 to 10-63; Martin PO; contracted bad health; CONF
HICKS, Robert W., Mr-98-1; Pvt K Co 9th TN Cav; 9-18-63 to 9-11-65; Whiteside PO
HICKS, Thomas, Lo-191-1; Pvt B Co 9th PA Cav; 2-23-64 to 7-18-65; Morganton PO; Andersonville Prison 9 mos
HICKS, Thomas J., Mo-125-1; Pvt 7th TN Cav; 4-63 to 64; Gudger PO
HICKS, William, Sh-159-2; Pvt & Sgt G Co 18th MO Inf; S ep __ to 3-9-66 (1 yr 6 mos); Memphis PO
HICKS, William, Mr-97-1; US Sol; Jarman PO
HICKS, William, Hw-134-1; US Sol; 20th Civil Dist
HICKS, William, C-24-3; Pvt 1st TN Inf; 8-10-61 to 9-17-64; Agee PO
HICKS, William L., Br-13-3; Sgt H Co 1st KY Cav; 9-1-61 to 12-31-64; Cleveland PO
HICKS, William N., Je-136-2; Pvt F Co 9th TN Cav; 9-15-63 to 5-1-64; PO omitted
HICKS, Windfield S., We-221-1(4); Pvt D Co TN Inf; 2-61 to 12-1-61; Martin PO; CONF
HICKSON, Samuel P., Hm-104-4(2); Julia A. widow of; Sgt F Co 9th TN Cav; 9-63 to 9-65; Alpha PO; rheumatism while in the service, discharged as Regimental Black Smith
HIDWELL, Benjamin F., Wh-183-1; Pvt G Co 4th TN Mtd Inf; 64 to 65; Quebeck PO; no disability inucrred; lost discharge
HIGBY, George D., Mu-195-3; Sol; Columbia PO
HIGDON, Robert S., Mr-96-1; Pvt D Co 10th TN Cav; 6-7-64 to 8-1-65; Whitwell PO
HIGDON, Vecey, Mu-190-1; widow; Fountain Creek PO; does not know command of husband
HIGGIN, Isaac, Ca-20-2; Pvt C Co 5th TN Cav; 8-3-63 to 9-1-64; Woodbury PO
HIGGINS, Charles W., H-63-3; Surgeon 5th IL Cav; 9-27-61 to 7-63; Room 34, 1st Nat'l Bank Bldg, Chattanooga PO
HIGGINS, David A., Wa-260-2; Olivia C. widow of; Pvt D Co 8th TN Cav; 9-15-63 to __; Pilot Hill PO; killed in action at Marien VA, 12-16-64
HIGGINS, Ephraim B., Hm-104-1; Pvt B Co 5th TN Cav; 5-20-62 to __ (1 yr 2 mos); Alpha PO; neuragia & rheumatism
HIGGINS, James H., Mr-96-3(2); Pvt D Co 1st AL Cav; 1-63 to 6-64; Owen PO
HIGGINS, Jas. P., Hi-91-1; Pvt I Co 23rd MI Inf; 63 to Jul 63 (1 mo 10 days); Pleasantville PO
HIGGINS, John J., Hi-91-1; Sarah C. widow of; Pvt K Co 4th KY? Col; 5-15-62 to 5-25-65; Pinewood PO
HIGGINS, Thomas, Mc-114-3; Millie widow of; Pvt; Calhoun PO
HIGGINS, William T., U-249-1; Sgt M Co 8th TN Cav; 9-15-63 to 9-11-65; Flag Pond PO; surgery to left testicle
HIGGS, James, Gr-75-2; Sgt F Co 1st TN Cav; 3-1-62 to 3-1-65; Tampico PO; sight & crippled
HIGGS, Thomas J., We-221-7; Cpl A Co 31st TN Inf; 8-14-61 to 5-2-62; Martin PO; CONF
HIGHAND, William, Hd-50-2; Pvt E Co 21st IL Vol; 8-1-61 to 10-31-64; Walnut Grove PO
HIGHERS, Josiah T., Sm-175-2(1); Cpl G Co 4th TN Inf; 11-1-64 to 8-25-65; Carthage PO
HIGHERS, Simon, Sm-174-2; Pvt G Co 4th TN Inf; 11-1-64 to 8-25-65; Grant PO
HIGHTOWER, Henry, H-62-1; Pvt; 519 Cedar, Chattanooga PO
HIGHTOWER, Leander, A-13-3; Pvt G Co 63rd TN Inf; 8-62 to 12-64; Briceville PO; CONF
HIGHTOWER, Pleasant, Mo-122-1; Alsey widow of; Pvt D Co 62nd TN Mtd Inf; Dancing Branch PO; CONF
HIGHTOWER, William H., H-61-1; Mary A. widow of; 1st Lt; 62 to 65; Chattanooga PO; CONF
HIGS, George W., We-220-1; Pvt I Co 6th TN Cav; Feb 1 64 to May 13 65; Catham PO; discharged on account of disability
HILAND, A. P., Ce-31-1; Pvt G Co 50th TN Inf; 26 Nov 61 to 17 Jul 63; Petway PO; CONF

HILBEE, William, C-25-3; Pvt M Co 13th TN Cav; 2-15-63 to 9-3-64; Whitman PO; deafness & nearvis debility
HILDERBRAND, Jacob, D-44-2(1); Cpl C Co 23rd IN Inf; 9-8-62 to 6-12-65; Nashville PO; wounded in leg
HILDERBRAND, John, Br-7-3; Pvt D Co 10th TN Inf; 1-2-61 to 8-1-65; Cleveland PO; rupture
HILFER, Daniel E., Co-61-5(2); Pvt H Co 13th TN Cav; 24 Sep 63 to 5 Sep 65; Bridgeport PO
HILL, A. C. P., Je-139-1; Pvt A Co 9th TN Cav; 12 Dec 62 to 17 Sep 63; Trion PO; dispeptic
HILL, Abe, Mu-198-1; 10th Dist
HILL, Alfred H., Un-253-2; Cpl B Co 11th IL Inf; 15 Aug 62 to 14 Jul 65; New Flat Creek PO
HILL, Allen, Ct-37-2; Pvt C Co 13th TN Cav; 9-23-63 to 4-8-65; Ripshin PO; liver complaint
HILL, Amand (see Robertson, George)
HILL, Amon J., T-218-1; Pvt G Co 4th Hvy Art; 13 Oct 63 to 25 Feb 66; Covington PO
HILL, Andrew, Hm-107-4; Pvt D Co 1st TN Cav; 15 Apr 62 to 16 Apr 65; Chestnut Bloom PO; throat & lung trouble
HILL, Ben, Hy-75-2; Pvt H Co 2nd W TN Col Inf; Aug 63 to __; Koko PO
HILL, Booker (see Bets, Booker)
HILL, Chorly, De-23-2; Pvt K Co 2nd TN Inf; Jul 29 63 to Aug 65; Swallow Bluff PO; received injuri in ankle, sun stroke, head affected
HILL, David, G-54-1; Pvt B Co 7th US Col Inf; 11-5-62 to 11-25-65; Eaton PO
HILL, David, R-158-1; 2nd Lt C Co 8th TN Vol; 9-1-62 to 10-26-63; resigned; Lucknow PO
HILL, David, Ha-115-1; Llarisa widow of; Pvt I Co 9th TN Cav; 13 Aug 63 to 1 Sep 65; Alanthers Hill PO; not disabled, died of dropsy after leaving army
HILL, Elijah F., H-76-1; Chattanooga PO
HILL, Emanuel, Cl-47-4; Compensation PO; not at home; CONF
HILL, Emanuel, Sh-147-1; Pvt M Co 3rd TN Art; 26 Dec 63 to Apr 30 66; Cuba PO
HILL, Fred A., Su-243-1; Maj E Co 6th ME? Inf; 15 Aug 61 to 15 Aug 64; Bristol PO
HILL, Frederick J., Hd-46-1; Pvt I Co 5th TN Cav; Sep 5 62 to Aug 5 65; Cerro Gordo PO
HILL, G. W., De-26-1; F Co 51st TN Inf; 62 to __ (2 yrs 3 mos); Bible Hill PO; CONF
HILL, George W. T., Se-225-2; Nancy F. widow of; Pvt 2nd AR Cav; Millican PO
HILL, Gooden M., A-44-5; Sarah A. widow of; Pvt F Co KY Cav; Coal Creek PO; discharge at Washington DC
HILL, Hazel, C-32-2; Pvt J Co 7th TN Inf; 10-8-64 to 6-27-65; Big Creek Gap PO; hepthes bronkitis & hart disease 25 yrs
HILL, Henary, Un-256-2; Sgt G Co 2nd TN Cav; 1 Feb 63 to 14 Jul 65; Lost Creek PO; general disability & deafness
HILL, Henry, Sh-191-6(2); Memphis PO; records not seen
HILL, Henry, Mu-198-1; 10th Dist
HILL, Henry F., Sh-167-1; Lt F Co 9th IL Cav; Jan 62 to 13 Oct 65; PO omitted
HILL, Hinton A., Dk-33-1; Pvt K Co 5th TN Cav; 5-2-63 to 4-22-65; Dowellton PO; hemerage of lungs, heart & sight
HILL, Hugh A., Dy-25-1; Jane J. widow of; Newbern PO; wounded & died; CONF
HILL, Isaac A., Ro-205-1; Cpl E Co 1st TN Inf; 20 Aug 61 to 17 Sep 64; Kings Creek PO; chronic diarrhoea
HILL, Isaac A., Pu-142-1; Pvt; Calf Killer PO
HILL, Jame H., C-30-2; Pvt B Co 2nd TN Inf; 6-62 to __; Well Spring PO; no discharge
HILL, James A., Hy-84-1; Pvt B Co 24th TN; Jun 61 to Dec 61; Forked Deer PO; wounded; CONF
HILL, James F., R-106-1; Pvt A Co 86th __; 5th Civil Dist
HILL, Jas. H., La-109-1; Pvt C Co 2nd TN Mtd Inf; 12-10-63 to 5-10-65; Lexington PO
HILL, James H., Mc-118-2; Pvt E Co 3rd TN Mtd Inf; 7-15-64 to 11-30-64; Joshua PO
HILL, James J., Hd-49-3; US Sol; 4th Civil Dist
HILL, James M., Wy-173-2; Pvt A Co 10th TN Inf; 4-11-62 to __; Lutts PO; discharge lost, dates not given

HILL, James O., He-61-1; Pvt K Co 2nd TN Mtd Inf; 28 Mar 64 to 20 Apr 65; Shermans Mill PO; reumatism, torpor, liver, eresyplus
HILL, James P., Je-147-1; Sgt F Co 9th TN Cav; 18 Sep 63 to 11 Sep 65; Shady Grove PO; shot in the head? (heart?)
HILL, James R., Co-67-5; Cpl C Co 62nd NC Inf; Aug 61 to 14 Jun 65; Naillon PO; gunshot wound through right lung; CONF
HILL, James T., H-67-3; Sgt H Co 2nd MD Pot Home Brig; 8-24-61 to 9-29-64; Chattanooga PO; rheumatism in both legs & chronic diarrhoea
HILL, James T., Wi-276-1; Pvt F Co 4th TN Cav; Oct 61 to May 65; Beechville PO; shot in the left arm, crippled; CONF
HILL, Jefferson L., Pi-156-1; Pvt K Co 4th TN Inf; 3-10-65 to 6-18-65; Permelia PO; from measles, now deaf in one ear (right)
HILL, John, Gr-82-1; Pvt B Co 48th MD Inf; Aug 63 to Apr 65; Powder Spring PO
HILL, John, Ro-210-5; Mary E. widow of; Pvt; Rockwood PO
HILL, John A., Pi-154-1; Pvt K Co 4th TN Inf; 6-64 to 7-65; Byrdstown PO
HILL, John C., Ms-182-1; 16th Dist
HILL, John E., O-136-1; Pvt L Co 6th TN Cav; Aug 1 62 to Aug 22 64; Limbs PO; discharged on account of bad health
HILL, John H., D-72-1; Alton, Maggie M. formerly widow of; Pvt TN Inf; Ju 63 to 65; Nashville PO; wounded in left leg; discharged on surgeon certificate
HILL, John H., Sh-175-1; Pvt A Co 97th LA Inf; 5-65 to 3-66; Memphis PO
HILL, John M., Ro-210-11; Pvt E Co 1st TN Inf; Post Oak Springs PO
HILL, John N., Ca-22-3; Pvt E Co 5th TN Cav; Burgen PO
HILL, John W., G-53-4; Pvt M Co 6th TN Cav; 5-62 to 8-65; Brazil PO
HILL, Joseph, K-173-3; Pvt D Co 9th TN Cav; 13 Sep 63 to 25 Sep 65; Union Church PO; left arm off
HILL, Joseph H., Je-136-2; Pvt F Co 9th TN Cav; 25 Sep 63 to 25 Apr 65; PO omitted
HILL, Lamont B., Pu-144-2; Pvt B Co 14th PA Cav; 9-62 to 65; Double Springs PO
HILL, Leonard B., H-53-5; Pvt D Co 58th MA Inf; 63 to 7-65; Ridgedale PO; lame in right foot and chronic diarrhoea
HILL, Lewis, Sh-190-2; Jeane House widow of; Pvt E Co 59th Col Inf; 6-27-63 to 65; 168 Kansas Ave, Memphis PO
HILL, Livel, C-26-1; Pvt F Co 6th TN Inf; 3-10-62 to 3-10-65; Coal Creek PO
HILL, Marcus, Un-256-1; Pvt D Co 1st TN Inf; 9 Aug 61 to 17 Sep 64; Rule PO
HILL, Mary (see Gidger, Charles F.)
HILL, Moses, Sh-178-4; 281 Monroe, Memphis PO
HILL, Narvel, C-24-3; Pvt F Co 6th TN Inf; 3-10-62 to 3-24-64; Fork Vale PO; piles, nasel cattarr
HILL, Ned, Hr-92-1; (found while examining work); Hardeman Co.
HILL, R. C., Cr-15-1; Pvt E Co 7th TN Cav; 4 Aug 62 to 16 Jun 65; Bueno Vista PO; pneumoniz, scurvy
HILL, Randall, Dk-35-4(2); Pvt F Co 4th TN Mtd Inf; 9-29-64 to 8-25-65; Hicks PO; consumption
HILL, Rheuben, H-51-1; Pvt A Co 8th R MI Cav; 9-22-63 to 11-6-65; Soddy PO
HILL, Richard, Ms-178-1; Cpl I Co 111th Col; 64 to 66; Silver Creek PO; leg mashed by loading siege gun
HILL, Richard, Sh-147-2; Buglar C Co 2nd MO Cav; 10 Sep 64 to 15 Oct 65; Cuba PO; wounded in leg and arm
HILL, Robert, Wy-173-2; Pvt A Co 10th TN Inf; 4-11-62 to 5-25-65; Lutts PO
HILL, Robert G., Ms-182-1; Pvt C Co 4th TN Cav; 12-5-64 to ___ (6 mos); Venna PO; able to perform a day's labor
HILL, Russell B., Mc-114-1; Pvt; 1 yr; Folger PO
HILL, Salina, We-224-1; Pvt K Co 4th KY Inf; 62 to 65; PO omitted
HILL, Sarah E. (see Messer, Samuel)
HILL, Seymour E., Se-226-1; Pvt B Co 17th MI Inf; 26 Aug 62 to 10 Jun 65; Straw Plains PO; in Andersonville Prison 1121?; totally disabled from labor
HILL, Stephen, Mc-114-1; Cpl L Co 9th TN Cav; 9-28-63 to 9-11-65; Folger PO
HILL, Stephen, Ma-124-1; Jackson PO
HILL, Tate, Ms-181-1; Pvt A Co 10th TN Inf; 6-10-63 to 4-12-65; Lewisburg PO
HILL, Thomas, Co-64-1; Pvt M Co 10th KY Cav; 5 Dec 62 to Jan 63; Philips PO
HILL, Thomas J., Mu-197-2; Pvt 14th Col TN; 62 to 65; Columbia PO
HILL, Union, Un-256-2; Pvt I Co 7th TN Mtd Inf; 8 Nov 64 to 30 May 65; Lost Creek PO; contracted momp
HILL, W. H., O-136-1; Pvt L Co 6th TN Cav; Aug 1 62 to Jul 26 65; Limbs PO
HILL, W. S., Bo-22-3; Pvt L Co 3rd TN Cav; 9-62 to 6-10-65; Gamble's Store PO
HILL, William, We-233-1(2); Pvt I Co 1st TN Inf; 8-62 to 4-6; Ralston PO; paroled by Forrest at Trenton
HILL, William, Sh-195-1; Landsman on a vessel; Memphis PO
HILL, William (see Minx, William)
HILL, William, F-37-1; Cpl C Co 61st US Col Inf; Jun 10 61 to Dec 13 65; Dayleyville? PO (Haywood Co.)
HILL, William, C-28-1; Pvt H Co 2nd TN Inf; 63 to ___; Fincastle PO; hemorage of the lungs
HILL, William, Cl-47-4; Compensation PO; not at home; CONF
HILL, William A., Dy-29-3; Pvt D Co 47th TN Inf; 62 to 62 (6 mos); Newbern PO; CONF
HILL, William B., Pi-154-1; Emily B. widow of; Pvt K Co 4th TN Inf; 6-64 to 7-65; Olympus PO
HILL, William C., Ro-205-2; Pvt E Co 1st TN Inf; 10 Sep 62 to 5 Aug 65; Kingscreek PO; eyes sight not good, also a kidney affection for 25 yrs
HILL, William D., Ms-173-1; Mary J. widow of; Pvt C Co 4th TN Mtd Inf; Rich Creek PO
HILL, William L. D., We-224-3(1); Pvt D Co 31st NC Inf; Sep 61 to 13 Apr 65; Como PO (Henry Co.); CONF
HILL, William R., Dk-35-3(1); Elizabeth widow of; Pvt E Co 4th TN Mtd Inf; 11-26-64 to 8-25-65; Capling PO; rheumatism
HILL, ___, H-62-4; Susan E. widow of; 232 Chestnut, Chattanooga PO
HILLARD, John A., F-40-2; Cpl B Co 7th TN Cav; 7 Apr 61 to 5 Feb 65; Hickory Withe PO; CONF
HILLHOUSE, David L. D., Sh-201-2; Pvt G Co 50th IL Inf; Oct 5 62 to Jul 10 65; Memphis PO
HILLIARD, Lightle, Sh-150-3; Bundon, Lightle; Pvt I Co 61st TN Inf; 3 yrs 3 mos; Bartlett PO
HILLIARD, Sikes, Su-233-1; Pvt 10th MI Cav; Island Mills PO; week brest, hearing impaired, cripple gunshot, disabled considerable
HILLIARD, Spencer, F-38-1; Sgt A Co 59th US Inf; May 61 to May 65; Mason PO
HILLIARD, William B., Mr-95-1; Pvt C Co 6th TN Cav; 9-2-64 to 7-11-65; Victoria PO
HILLIMAN, E. N., H-74-1; Cpl C Co 68th IN; 8-8-62 to 6-20-65; 115 Montgomery Ave, Chattanooga PO
HILLIS, Francis M., V-177-1(2); Pvt L Co 1st AR Cav; 62 to 8-1-65; Paineville PO; rupture; date of enlistment unknown
HILLMAN, Thomas, Mt-146-1; Pvt G Co TN Inf; 3 yrs; Henrietta PO
HILTON, Isaac M., Wa-274-4; Mack Hilton alias; Pvt; Jonesboro PO
HILTON, James, K-181-5(2); Pvt G Co 19th TN Inf; 62 to Feb 64; Knoxville PO; CONF
HILTON, Martin L., Su-239-3; Pvt K Co 13th TN Cav; 10 Sep 63 to 5 Sep 65; Rotherwood PO
HILTON, William G., Ge-84-1; Pvt B Co 49th IN Inf; 15 Oct 61 to ___; chronic diarrea; captured and was not discharged
HIMES?, James H., Cf-35-2; Pvt; Tullahoma PO; CONF
HIMES, Lem, Gi-135-2; Pvt A Co 1st TN Art; 1-63 to 4-66; Lynnville PO
HINCKEY, James G., Je-143-2; Pvt A Co Home Guard; Oct 63 to 65; Mossy Creek PO; catarrh
HINCKLEY, James H., A-5-2; Pvt C Co 7th TN Cav; 6-11-61 to 65; Clinton PO; rheumatism
HINCKLEY, Theodore D., H-69-6; Chattanooga PO

HINDERSON, Robert, D-103-2; Pvt G Co 10th TN Inf; Jun 20 62 to Jun 22 65; Marry PO; chronic diarhea; draws pension
HINDES, George W., A-4-6(2); Pvt; Coal Creek PO; couldn't get data
HINDEX, G. W., We-223-4; Sarah J. widow of; Pvt C Co 13th TN Inf; 1 Jan 63 to Apr 63; Elm Tree PO; died of malarial fever in 1886, Oct 27th
HINDMAN, Bird, B1-3-5; Pvt; 7-9-6_ to __; Tanbark PO; CONF
HINDMAN, John, D-72-5; Amanda widow of; Pvt 53rd TN Inf; Oct 61 to Mar 65; Nashville PO
HINDMON, E. L., Gi-133-2; D Co 3rd TN; 63 to 63 (7 days); Bufords PO; CONF
HINDS, Austin, Ma-119-1; Pvt E Co 105th IL Inf; Sep 62 to Jun 65; Malesus PO
HINDS, Francis M., Un-254-1; Sgt B Co 1st TN Inf; 4 Aug 61 to 17 Sep 64; Paulett PO; shot in the head
HINDS, George, Ro-209-2; Eliza widow of; Pvt E Co 1st TN Inf; 12 Aug 61 to 65; Glen Alice PO
HINDS, James K., Ro-202-5; Cpl H Co 9th TN Cav; 4 Apr 63 to 14 Sep 65; Cave Creek PO; injury to left side by horse running away
HINDS, John I. D., W1-295-1; Pvt I Co 18th IA Inf; Lebanon PO; lost his papers
HINDS, Joseph, Ro-209-2; Pvt E Co 1st TN Inf; Aug 63 to Aug 65; Glen Alice PO
HINDS, Simeon, Pi-153-2; Pvt D Co 11th TN Cav; 7-63 to 11-64; Spurnier PO; CONF
HINDS, Susan E. (see Breazeal, James)
HINEMAN, Thos. J., Ja-84-3; 2nd Dist, Harrison PO
HINES, Henry, D-73-2; Pvt; Granry White Pike, Nashville PO; he's not at home, can't get information
HINES, Henry, Gi-127-2; Patsey widow of; Pvt H Co 110th TN Col Inf; Pulaski PO
HINES, Isaac, Sm-169-3(5); Pvt; Defeated PO; gun shot; CONF
HINES, Joseph, K-182-1; Pvt I Co 3rd TN Cav; Oct 63 to Jun 65; Shooks PO; disabled 1864; diarrhoea
HINES, Joshua, Bo-21-1; Sgt B Co 3rd TN Cav; 11-5-62 to 8-3-65; Veeba PO
HINES, Sebron, F-43-2; Pvt C Co 55th TN Col Hvy Art; May 63 to May 65; Piperton PO
HINES, Thomas, Hi-85-1; Pvt G Co TN Inf; 3-15-63 to __; Tatty's Bend PO; served 3 mos and deserted
HINES, William, Bo-21-1; Pvt A Co 6th TN Inf; 3-11-62 to 3-11-65; Bank PO
HINES, William, Hi-85-1; Pvt E Co 13th TN Inf; 10-1-62 to 4-1-65; Tatty's Bend PO
HINES, William, Sn-254-1; Sgt D Co 70th OH Vol Inf; 9-10-61 to 8-15-65; Hendersonville PO
HINESLY, Robert, Dk-58-1; Pvt K Co 5th TN Cav; 4-24-63 to 8-14-65; Temperance Hall PO
HINGS, William, Ro-209-2; Pvt E Co 1st TN Inf; Jul 61 to 64; Glen Alice PO
HINKLE, George W., Ja-85-5; Pvt B Co 5th TN Mtd Inf; 8-13-64 to 7-13-65; Georgetown PO
HINKLE, Henry R., Hd-50-1; Sgt C Co 152nd IL Inf; Feb 10 65 to Sep 22 65; Savannah PO; rheumatism; also Seaman, Robb; Aug 10 63 to Aug 10 64
HINKLE, John, Ge-87-1; Cpl G Co 4th TN Inf; Jan 63 to Aug 65 (1 yr 1 mo); Midway PO; catarrh, rheumatism
HINKLE, William F., Hd-54-1; Pvt K Co 44th IN Inf; 25 Sep 61; 1st Lt A Co 26th PA Mal--16 Sep 63 to 30 Jul 63; Saltillo PO; chron. rheumatism & piles
HINKLEY, James P., K-159-3; Cpl E Co 34th Vet Vols Inf; 20 Aug 61 to 13 Sep 64; Knoxville PO; kidney and liver trouble, enlisted 3 mos, serve and then vet vols
HINMAN, George W., Sh-191-8(4); 41 Wrights Ave, Memphis PO
HINMAN, Hurbert, O-137-1; Pvt I Co 10th MI Cav; 30 Sep 63 to 6 Sep 65; Kenton PO; detail out of order on this schedule
HINSHAW, William, Ge-89-3; Nancy widow of; Pvt 1st IL Baty; Marvin PO
HINSON, Cary, Sh-203-1; Sgt Young Co 2nd AR Bat; Apr 1 61 to Apr 6 62; Memphis PO; shot in shoulder; CONF
HINSON, James P., P-156-1; Cpl G Co 5th US Inf; 4-24-65 to 10-13-66; Lobelville PO; ruptured; also 11-61 to 8-11-64
HIPSHER, Henry, Gr-79-2; Pvt F Co 1st TN Inf; 62 to 65; Thorn Hill PO; not disabled; CONF
HIPSHER, William L., Gr-79-2; Pvt K Co 19th TN; 21 May 61 to 26 Apr 64; Thorn Hill PO; CONF
HIPSHIRE, William, Gr-72-1; Com Sgt E Co 9th TN Cav; 28 Sep 63 to 5 Apr 65; Noeton PO; result of mumps & fever
HISE, Robt. E., Wa-267-1; Martha A. Onkst formerly widow of; Pvt M Co 13th TN Cav; Apr 63 to 5 Sep 65; Jonesboro PO; gunshot wound of heel & lung dis.
HISTON, Calvin, Mo-129-3; Pvt; Huling PO
HITCHCOCK, George, Fr-116-1(2); 2nd Bat MN Lt Art; 2-20-62 to 8-28-65; Sherwood PO
HITCHCOCK, Harry H., O-142-1; Lt & Capt 60th IN Vol Inf; 11 May 62 to __ (3 yrs); PO omitted
HITE, James E., Hu-103-4; Pvt 11th TN Inf; 10 Jan 64 to Apr 66; PO omitted; marked through, probably CONF
HITE-SMITH, Charles, H-53-2; Capt; Chattanooga PO
HITER, William Y., Cr-4-4; Pvt D Co 23rd VA Inf; 4-61 to 4-65; Bells Depot PO; wounded--left shoulder
HITTON, Joseph, Gr-70-2; Pvt A Co 9th TN Cav; 24 Oct 64 to 11 Sep 65; Rutledge PO; lungs & throat
HIX, Anderson, S-218-3; US Sol; 9th Civil Dist
HIX, Jackson, Ro-207-4; Malinda widow of; Pvt; Paint Rock PO
HIX, James, Wa-273-2; Cpl I Co 8th TN Cav; 25 Sep 63 to 25 May 65; Locust Mt. PO; disease of lungs
HIX, John, Fe-42-1; Pvt Capt David Beaty's Co TN Ind Scouts; Jamestown PO
HIX, Thomas, S-216-2; Pvt B Co 1st TN Inf; 1 Aug 61 to 5 Aug 66; Huntsville PO; hart deseas 10 yrs, ring finger off in war
HIXON, David, H-49-1; Lucy A. widow of; Pvt A Co 6th TN Mtd Inf; 8-2-64 to 6-30-65; Falling Water PO
HIXON, Jno. H., B1-1-2; 9th Civil Dist; chronic rheumatism 25 yrs
HIXON, John M., H-50-2(1); Pvt G Co 1st US Cav; 10-14-57 to 10-14-62; Pvt E Co 1st R OH Lt Art--7-3-63 to 7-18-65; Sardy (Soddy?) PO; chronic rheumatism
HIXON, Marion, Sq-164-1; Pvt E Co 10th TN Inf; 8-61 to __ (1 yr); Fillmore PO
HIXON, Newton J., Sq-164-1; Nancy A. widow of; Pvt; Fillmore PO
HIXON, Samuel, H-49-3; Sarah Johnson formerly widow of; Pvt H-49-3; Pvt I Co 1st TN Inf; 2-62 to __; Lake Side PO; capt & died in Andersonville Prison
HIXSON, Andrew J., Co-59-2; US Sol; 1st Dist
HIXSON, Ephraim F., Sr., H-49-6; Pvt F Co 6th TN Mtd Inf; 9-12-64 to 6-30-65; Trewhitt PO
HIXSON, George W., B1-1-2; Pvt D Co 6th TN Inf; 8-16-64 to 6-30-65; Stevens Chapel PO; chronic rheumatism and hearing
HIXSON, George W., H-49-5; Pvt & 1st Lt F Co 6th TN Mtd Inf; 9-13-64 to 6-30-65; Daisy PO
HIXSON, Houston, H-49-3; Ord Sgt F Co 6th TN Mtd Inf; 9-64 to 6-30-65; Lake Side PO
HIXSON, James F., H-49-5; 4th Cpl A Co 6th TN Mtd Inf; 8-2-64 to 6-30-65; Lake Side PO
HIXSON, James M., B1-1-2; Sgt D Co 6th TN Inf; 8-16-64 to 6-30-65; Stevens Chapel PO; chronic rheumatism
HIXSON, John, H-49-4; Mary widow of; Sgt F Co 6th TN Mtd Inf; Lake Side PO
HIXSON, John B., B1-1-2; Pvt I Co 2nd TN Inf; 11-62 to Spring 65; Stevens Chapel PO; chronic rheumatism
HIXSON, John M., B1-5-2; Pvt D Co 6th TN Mtd Inf; 8-15-64 to 6-30-65; Stevens Chapel PO; chronic diarhoea and dyspepsia
HIXSON, Josiah, B1-1-2; Sarah E. widow of; Pvt H Co 9th TN Cav; 5-10-63 to 9-18-65; Fillmore PO (Sequatchie Co.)
HIXSON, Reuben, H-58-6; Pvt I Co 14th TN Inf; Retro PO; discharge burned
HIXSON, Timothy, H-49-4; 1st Lt A Co 6th TN Mtd Inf; Lake Side PO

HIXSON, William A., Bl-5-3; Artificer D Co 6th TN Mtd Inf; 10-1-64 to 6-30-65; Sequachee College PO; discharge states comissary blacksmith
HIXSON, William Carol, Bl-1-2; Sgt D Co 6th TN Inf; 8-16-64 to 6-30-65; Mt. Airy PO; chronic rheumatism
HIXSON, William M., H-55-1; Pvt Co 4th TN Cav; 1-20-63 to 7-12-65; Tyner PO
HOBACK, John G., Me-93-2; Pvt I Co 3rd TN Cav; 10-7-63 to 8-3-65; Ten Mile Stand PO
HOBACK, William, Mc-109-1; Pvt B Co 7th TN Inf; 9-13-64 to 7-27-65; Chuckaluck PO
HOBBERT, Joseph, Je-137-2; Nancy widow of; Pvt F Co 9th TN Cav; Sep 63 to __; Hickory Ridge PO; shot & killed
HOBBS, Alexander, Gu-45-2; Pvt E Co 1st TN Cav Vidette; 63 to 64 (8 mos); Altamont PO
HOBBS, Christopher, Gu-45-1; Pvt E Co 1st TN Cav Vidette; 63 to 64 (8 mos); Altamont PO
HOBBS, Cristopher C., G-70-1; Pvt E Co 1st TN; 1 Feb 63 to Jul 10 64; Dyer PO
HOBBS, James W-193-2; Pvt; Viala PO; discharge at Washington
HOBBS, James N., Wl-298-1; Cpl E Co 1st TN Vid Indt Cav; 10 Oct 63 to 16 Jun 64; Round Top PO
HOBBS, Webster, R-161-6; Pvt C Co 10th OH Cav; 2-10-63 to 7-24-65; Dayton PO
HOBBS, Wesley, Gu-45-1; Pvt E Co 1st TN Cav Vidette; 63 to 64 (8 mos); Altamont PO
HOBBS, William, Sq-164-2(1); Sol; 3rd Civil Dist, Dunlap PO
HOBGOOD, Benjamin F., Sh-176-1; Main-Waldran Block, Memphis PO
HOBSON, Ezekiel, Gi-139-2; Sgt A Co 110th TN Inf; 61 to 65; Campbellsville PO
HOBSON, Josephine (see Cummins, John)
HOBSON, Mandy, D-64-1; widow; Nashville PO
HOCKADY, Larkin L., Jo-153-1; Pvt G Co 4th TN Inf; 15 Aug 62 to 17 Jul 65; Little Doe PO; lung and liver affection
HOCKETT, Wesley, D-80-1; 2nd Civil Dist
HODG, Thomas, L-103-2; Cpl D Co 13th Inf; __ to 65 (2 yrs 8 mos); Plum Point PO
HODGE, Charley H., Cr-11-1; Pvt I Co 60th NY Inf; 4 Jan 64 to 17 Jul 65; Johnson Grove PO
HODGE, David N., Cu-16-3; Orderly Sgt B Co 2nd TN Cav; 8-62 to 12-65; Pleasant Hill PO; rheumatism
HODGE, Frank, Ct-40-1; Nancy widow of; Pvt; Elizabethton PO
HODGE, Horry, Mn-126-2; Mary E. widow of; Capt B Co 6th TN Cav; __ to 5-5-64; Bethel Springs PO; died with small pox 5-5-64
HODGE, Isaac, Ct-45-1; Pvt G Co 4th TN Inf; 2-15-64 to 8-2-65; Stony Creek PO
HODGE, James, Wa-271-2; Pvt B Co 4th TN Inf; 25 Nov 62 to Apr 65; Jonesboro PO; rumatism, hearing, sight, peralisis, ruptured
HODGE, James I., Mg-198-2; Pvt K Co 63rd TN Inf; 1 Aug 61 to 1 Aug 64; Deer Lodge PO
HODGE, James M., Cr-20-2; Pvt I Co 7th TN Cav; 10-63 to 5-28-65; Profit PO; scurvey 25 yrs; can --in the service
HODGE, Jesse, Gr-75-2; Sgt C Co 4th TN Cav; 29 Nov 63 to 12 Jul 65; Doyal PO; rheumatism & gun shot
HODGE, Jerry, F-258-2; US Sol; PO omitted
HODGE, John, La-113-1; Sarah widow of; Pvt; 63 to 65; Lawrenceburg PO; discharge lost, widow cannot ans.
HODGE, John, Cu-18-2; Pvt E Co 1st TN Inf; 8-22-61 to 9-17-64; Manning PO
HODGE, Josiah, Wa-270-2; Pvt I Co 60th TN Inf; 1 Apr 63 to 1 Apr 65; Piney Flats PO (Sullivan Co.)
HODGE, Levi, Ct-45-2; Pvt C Co 8th TN Inf; 12-29-62 to 7-7-65; Stony Creek PO; discharge surgeon's certificate
HODGE, Mack, Je-140-1; Cpl I Co 1st US Art; 14 Jul 64 to 31 Mar 66; PO omitted
HODGE, Marcus D., K-177-1; Pvt H Co 1st TN Inf; 9 Aug 61 to 20 Sep 64; Chumlea PO
HODGE, Newton, M-103-5; Pvt E Co 4th TN Cav; 8-23-65 to 9-25-65; Union Camp PO
HODGE, Peter, Hw-131-2; Pvt L Co 1st US Reg Hvy Art; 11 Aug 64 to 31 Mar 64; Bulls Gap PO
HODGE, Reverby M., Bo-23-3; (no detail--evidently deceased); 15th Dist
HODGE, Sam, Ru-13-3; Pvt; 3 yrs 2 mos 11 days; Murfreesboro PO
HODGE, Samuel, H-57-2; Pvt D Co 15th US Col; 63 to 65; Orchard Knob PO
HODGE, Samuel, Ct-36-2; Pvt F Co 8th TN Cav; 5-18-63 to 9-9-65; Roan Mt. PO
HODGE, Thomas, Se-226-1; Pvt D Co 12th US Hvy Art; 25 Jan 64 to 25 Jan 65; Straw Plains PO; hearing injured in serviced, mustered in 72nd US Inf & transf (12th US Hvy Art)
HODGE, Watsie A., Ct-39-4; Pvt 13th TN Cav; Dry Creek PO; liver trouble, breast disease & left hip
HODGE, William, Sh-158-1; Pvt B Co 13th IN Inf; Dec 64 to Jan 65; Memphis PO; ruptured; discharged at Goldsband NC and rec'd. at Indianapolis, discharge sent to Gilma _____ & Co., attys., Washington DC
HODGE, William, K-159-3; Pvt C Co 1st US Hvy Art; 64 to May 66; Knoxville PO
HODGE, William, K-161-6; Pvt B Co 1st US Hvy Art; Knoxville PO; ruptural hernia
HODGE, William R., Ct-36-3; Pvt A Co 13th TN Cav; 4-63 to 9-25-65; PO omitted
HODGES, Andrew, D-80-1; 2nd Civil Dist
HODGES, Edmond S., Se-231-2; Cpl G Co 3rd TN Inf; 10 Feb 62 to 17 Apr 65; Boyds Creek PO; scurvy 25 yrs
HODGES, Edward P., We-223-3; 1st Sgt B Co 38th VA? Inf; 5 Jun 61 to 20 Jun 65; Palmersville PO; prisnor for 6 mos, was paroled from Hacots? Island Prison 20 Jun 1865; CONF
HODGES, Ephraim L., Se-231-2; Pvt C Co 4th TN Inf; 14 Feb 63 to 2 Aug 65; Boyds Creek PO; chronic rheumatis 16 yrs
HODGES, Granville, Cl-55-1; Sgt A Co 2nd TN Cav; 8-1-62 to 7-6-65; Lone Mountain PO
HODGES, Henry, Hm-103-2; Capt G Co 3rd TN Inf; 61 to 65 (3 yrs); Morristown PO
HODGES, Henry W., Gr-71-1; Pvt K Co 8th TN Cav; 17 Feb 65 to 11 Sep 65; Bean Station PO
HODGES, Hesiciah, We-223-3; cant say anything about record; Palmersville PO; CONF
HODGES, Howell, Ja-84-2; Amand J. widow of; Cpl B Co 1st TN Inf; 12-62 to 8-65; Harrison PO
HODGES, James, W-189-3(2); Meeky J. widow of; Pvt E Co 4th TN Mtd Inf; Leeds PO; gunshot wound in leg; discharge placed in hands of Noi Evens claim agent at Alexandria TN who ran away with it
HODGES, James W., Se-231-3; Martha J. widdow of; Pvt F Co 3rd TN Cav; 15 Jun 63 to 10 Jun 65; 14th Civil Dist
HODGES, Jordun, Je-140-1; Pvt G Co 1st US Art; Hodges PO
HODGES, Marion R., Sn-261-3(2); Pvt 1st TN Cav; 11-61 to 11-63; Brackentown PO; prison Springfield 7 mos, come home on furlow 11-63; CONF
HODGES, Martha H., Mn-122-2; 3rd Civil Dist
HODGES, Roland, Wa-271-1; Sgt K Co 13th TN Cav; 22 Aug 63 to 8 Sep __ (2 yrs 2 mos 16 days); Flourville PO; rumatism & piles
HODGES, Wilburn, Wa-268-3; discharge away from home; Johnson City PO; scurvy
HODGES, William B., Cl-53-1; Pvt G Co 9th TN Cav; 1-18-65 to 9-11-65; Lone Mountain PO
HODGES, William P., H-49-6; 2nd Lt I Co 2nd E TN Inf; 8-23-61 to 11-26-64; Trewhitt PO; diahrrea & infu? for measles
HODGES, William R., K-164-1; Pvt; PO omitted (Knoxville?)
HODGES, Willis, Sh-155-1; alias Pond, Kit; Cpl A Co 11th US Inf; 64 to 66; Germantown PO
HODSDEN, Matilda, Se-227-2; widow of US Sol; 9th Dist
HOFFMAN, John, Sn-257-1; Pvt; 9th Civil Dist
HOGAN, Dave, Sh-197-2; Col unit; Memphis PO; not at home
HOGAN, Granvil M., Cy-30-1; Sgt A Co 1st SC Batt; 2-7-64 to 10-23-65; Willow Grove PO; paralysis
HOGAN, James L., Cy-30-1; Cpl A Co Bristoe's Battalion; 2-7-64 to 10-20-65; Willow Grove PO
HOGAN, John H., H-56-5; Sgt H Co 33rd PA Inf; 6-17-6? to 8-5-65; East End PO

HOGAN, Nathaniel, Mt-145-1; Pvt K Co 4th TN Cav; 1 Feb 63 to 18 Jul 65; Clarksville PO
HOGAN, Reuban, Sh-146-3; Pvt B Co 55th Reg Inf; 62 to 65; Lucy PO; wounded in the left hand at Guntown, MS, partially disabled
HOGAN, Timothy, D-43-2; Sol; Cheny St, Nashville PO
HOGE, James L., Bl-4-1; Pvt F Co 9th TN Cav; 1-7-62 to 5-1-62; Pikeville PO; CONF
HOGE, Joel W., R-163-3; Margaret I. Martin formerly widow of; Pvt C Co 11th CI Cav; 61 to 65; Graysville PO; contracted breast complaint, reenlisted veteran
HOGE, Lemuel, Bl-4-3; Pvt D Co 6th TN Inf; 8-16-64 to 6-30-65; Pikeville PO
HOGE, Preston, Bl-3-1; Pvt B Co 1st TN Art; 10-18-62 to 7-20-65; Patten PO; CONF
HOGE, Walace N., Mc-112-3; 1st Lt K Co 26th OH Vol Inf; 6-17-61 to 7-24-64; Athens PO; gun shot, rheumatism, neuralgia
HOGG, Frank, D-68-2; Emily widow of; Sgt F Co 13th USC Inf; __ to 28 Dec 65; 105 Claiborn St, Nashville PO
HOGLE, James B., D-49-4; Pvt G Co 15th IN; 6 Jun 61 to 27 Jun 64; Nashville PO
HOGLE, Lorenza D., D-49-4; 2nd Ast Sgt 2nd TN Vol; 1 Mar 64 to 15 May 65; Nashville PO
HOGUE, Milborn, Fe-42-3; Rachel widow of; Pvt Capt David Beaty's Co TN Ind Scouts; Boatland PO
HOKE, Jacob B., Fr-105-1; Cpl G Co 23rd OH V Inf; 6 Jun 61 to 29 Jul 64; Winchester PO; pensioned
HOLAMAN, Joe, F-44-2; Pvt; May 62 to May 65; PO omitted
HOLAND, John H., Hr-97-1; Sgt M Co 1st AL Cav; 1 Nov 63 to 12 May 66; PO omitted
HOLBERT, Irvin, Je-139-1; Pvt F Co 9th TN Cav; Sep 62 to Sep 65; Trion PO
HOLBERT, Jake C., Gi-130-1; Pvt I Co 16th MO Col Inf; 63 to 65; Bradshaw PO
HOLBERT, James, Co-69-2; Linda widow of; Pvt; Rankin PO; no disability, discharge not here
HOLBERT, Nathaniel, Pi-153-2; Pvt D Co 2nd TN Inf; 12-15-61 to 12-15-64; West Fork PO; CONF
HOLBROOKS, John H., He-61-3; Rebecky L. widow of; Pvt G Co 7th TN Cav; 5 Aug 62 to 25 Oct 63; 18th Civil Dist
HOLCOMB, Benjamin S., M-107-3; Pvt F Co 52nd KY Mtd Inf; 8-3-63 to 1-18-65; Gamaliel, Monroe Co. KY PO; lameness in back & hip
HOLCOMB, C., La-109-1; Pvt B Co 1st OH Lt Art; 2-27-64 to 7-22-65; Lexington AL PO; hert & breast affected
HOLCOMB, Pleasant M., Mu-209-4; Cap G Co 1st AR Cav; May 3 62 to May 25 65; Columbia PO; prisoner, Jacksonport 6 wks; CONF
HOLCOMB, William, U-244-1; Pvt H Co 10th TN Cav; 1 Mar 64 to 1 Aug 65; Ernestville PO; disease of lungs & eyes, nearly blind in right eye
HOLDAM, Samuel J., Br-9-1; Pvt H Co 10th TN Cav; 1-16-64 to 9-15-64; Cleveland PO
HOLDEN, Green J., Pi-156-2; Sarah widow of; Pvt; Byrdtown PO; CONF
HOLDEN, James, Ru-235-1; Sallie widow of; Cpl G Co 17th TN Inf; Smyrna PO; jard by cannon ball, right shoulder disabled
HOLDEN, James J., Jo-152-2; Pvt M Co 13th TN Cav; 2 Feb 64 to 5 Sep 65; Butler PO; testical disease
HOLDEN, John, Co-65-1; Pvt K Co 8th TN Cav; 11 Jun 61 to 11 Sep 65; Wilton Springs PO; pensioned
HOLDEN, Lavis, Je-138-1; Oral Rankin formerly widow of; Capt E Co 20th MI Inf; Jul 62 to Jul 64; Dandridge PO; shot through body
HOLDEN, Richard, Ct-44-2; Pvt G Co 13th TN Cav; 9-15-63 to __; Hampton PO; chronic dysentery, discharge lost
HOLDER, Columbus, W-195-2; Pvt M Co 5th TN Cav; 10-63 to __; Mangrum PO; dislocation of shoulder
HOLDER, Dillard, Co-67-2; Pvt I Co 69th TN Inf; 18 Oct 62 to 65 (2 yrs 6 mos); Bison PO
HOLDER, Gabrel W., K-179-3; Pvt D Co 3rd TN Cav; 10 Feb 62 to 22 Feb 65; Rodelin PO
HOLDER, Harrison, Co-67-1; Pvt F Co 5th TN Cav; Oct 62 to May 65; Bison PO; CONF
HOLDER, James, Mg-197-2; Pvt A Co 11th TN Cav; Feb 62 to __; Crooked Fork PO; kidney disease, not discharged
HOLDER, James A., Gr-78-2; Pvt 1st TN Art; 4 Jul 62 to 4 Jul 63; Maples PO; lung, taken son after war (this was marked out, might be CONF)
HOLDER, Jesse M., H-54-1; Pvt E Co 4th TN Cav; 3-19-6? to 7-12-65; Chattanooga PO; contracted erysipilus, rheumatism and kidney disease in the army
HOLDER, JOhn W., K-179-1; Pvt G Co 1st TN Inf; 9 Aug 61 to 17 Sep 64; Rodelin PO; eyes and heart affected since 1862
HOLDER, Louis, W-195-1; Pvt L Co 5th TN Cav; 4-63 to 8-65; Evenston PO
HOLDER, Mary, B-11-1; widow?; 25th Civil Dist
HOLEMAN, Andrew, Je-143-2; Rhoda wife of; Pvt TN Cav; Mossy Creek PO
HOLIFIELD, Joel A., C-27-3; Pvt A Co 3rd NC Inf; 6-6-63 to 8-18-65; Caryville PO
HOLIWAY, Jerry M., Pu-143-1; Pvt K Co 8th TN Cav; 9-62 to 9-12-65; Jeremia PO; eyes injured, now paralyzed
HOLLAND, A. C., De-22-3; Pvt G Co 51st TN Inf; 1 Sep 61 to 1 Dec 62; Thurman PO; CONF
HOLLAND, Charley, M-108-3; Nancy M. widow of; Pvt H Co 5th KY Cav; 12-31-61 to 5-5-65; Lafayette PO
HOLLAND, Dave, T-206-2; Covington PO
HOLLAND, Frank A., Cf-35-4; Pvt B Co 16th TN Inf; 15 Oct 61 to 20 Nov 63; Normandy PO; CONF
HOLLAND, George W., Hu-104-1(2); Pvt G Co 12th TN; Feb 6 64 to Oct 65; Tennessee City PO; rumatism, dropsy & sore eyes
HOLLAND, George W., Mr-96-2; Pvt I Co 3rd TN Inf; Whitwell PO; sore eyes
HOLLAND, Leonidas T., J-80-1; Pvt H Co 4th TN Cav; 64 to 65; Bagdad PO
HOLLAND, Newton J., Hu-104-1(2); Buglar G Co 12th TN; Feb 4 64 to Ju 17 65; Tennessee City PO; sun stroke, piles & lung disease
HOLLAND, Peter, H-66-1; Pvt A Co 16th Col Inf; 1-25-62 to 65; Chattanooga PO
HOLLAND, Phillip H., Dy-27-1; Pvt 47th TN Inf; 62 to 65; Newbern PO; CONF
HOLLAND, Robert, J-80-2; Pvt I Co 1st TN Mtd Inf; Granville PO; wounded by horse falling down with him in line of duty, discharge not in Holland's possession
HOLLAND, William H., Bl-1-1; Sgt I Co 1st Mtd Inf; 7-7-64 to 7-29-65; Sequatchie College PO; diseased from measles in US service
HOLLANDWORTH, Francis, Ca-25-1; US Sol; 10th Dist
HOLLAR, Noah, Co-61-5(2); Pvt; Bridgeport PO; CONF
HOLLAWAY, Alaxander, K-186-4; Pvt D Co 6th TN Inf; 18 Apr 62 to 27 Apr 65; Balls Camp PO
HOLLAWAY, John, Co-66-3(1); Susie Blackwell family widow of; Pvt D Co 8th TN Cav; 15 Oct 62 to 11 Sep 63; Newport PO
HOLLAWAY, M. Seals, Di-40-1; Cpl G Co 38th KY; 7-1-62 to 65; Charlotte PO; family burned out and went to them before time out
HOLLAWAY, Picking, Ho-95-1; Pvt B Co 7th TN Inf; Jun 6 64 to Sep 1 65; McKinnon PO
HOLLEMAN, Henry, Sm-169-3(5); Pvt; Defeated PO; CONF
HOLLEN, Jane, Ge-97-4; widow US Sol; 20th Civil Dist
HOLLEWAY, John, Cl-47-2; Margaret Leach Jones widow of; Speedwell PO; rheumatism 30 yrs
HOLLEY, Calvin A., Hd-53-2; Charllottie T. widow of; Pvt D Co 6th TN Cav; 24 Oct 62 to 26 Jul 65; Morris Chapel PO
HOLLEY, Isaac D., Gi-122-3; Pvt B Co 32nd TN Inf; 61 to 65; Prospect Sta. PO; CONF
HOLLEY, Jacop, Ge-100-1; Cpl F Co 4th TN Inf; 30 Jan 63 to 2 Aug 65; Midway PO
HOLLEY, James M., De-25-1; Gunner PO; 19 M 62 to 19 Apr 63; Decaturville PO
HOLLEY, John S., Dk-35-2; Pvt; Temperance Hall PO
HOLLEY, Moses, Je-135-3; Pvt D Co 1st Cherokee NC Inf; 61 to 11 Sep 65; Flat Gap PO; Indian from Cherokee NC
HOLLEY, William H., Hu-103-2; C Co 22nd TN Inf; 20 Jun 61 to Dec 64; PO omitted; crossed through, probably CONF

HOLLIER, John H., We-223-2; Pvt, has lost all papers and cant remember anything about comp or regiment; Palmersville PO; is cripled in leg or foot
HOLLIMAN, Benjamin G., M-107-1; Cpl K Co 5th TN Cav; 4-23-63 to 8-14-65; Red Boiling Springs PO; lumbago & disease of eyes
HOLLIMAN, Lucinda J. (see Hudson, William)
HOLLINGER, Wm. H., Hu-106-2; 2nd Sgt I Co 92nd IL Inf; 7-62 to 9-63; 1st Sgt & AR2 M Co 13th US Col Inf; 9-63 to 1-16-66; Waverly PO
HOLLINGSHEAD, James W., Mo-131-1; Pvt E Co 3rd TN Inf; 7-26-64 to 11-3-65; Joe PO
HOLLINGSHEAD, John W., He-64-1; Pvt C Co 6th AL Cav; 15 Oct 64 to May 13 65; PO omitted
HOLLINGSWORTH, Ericus E., C-27-4; Capt I Co 9th TN Cav; 63 to 65 (2 yrs 6 mos); Jacksboro PO
HOLLINGSWORTH, James P., C-33-6; US Soldier; Jellico PO
HOLLINGSWORTH, John C., C-27-4; Pvt B Co 1st TN Inf; 8-1-61 to 9-64; Jacksboro PO; shot left arm
HOLLINGSWORTH, Wm. M., Cl-48-3; Orderly Sgt H Co 2nd TN Inf; 7-62 to 63 (1 yr 6 mos); Pleasant PO; dont know exact date of enlistment & dis.
HOLLINGWORTH, Harry, A-5-2; Colliervile PO; did not know commision
HOLLINGWORTH, Harry M., A-5-2; Alice A. widow of; Clinton PO; varioloid?; Sgt C Co 9th TN Cav; 7-14-63 to 9-11-65
HOLLINS, Shed, D-64-2; 12th TN Inf; Nashville PO
HOLLINS, Speaker, Hy-81-2; Brownsville PO
HOLLINS, Speaker, Hy-81-1; PO omitted; this entry crossed through
HOLLIS, David C., Dy-29-4; Pvt A Co 29th Mis Inf; Apr 62 to May 65; Trimble PO; CONF
HOLLIS, John B., Wy-177-1; Sgt B Co 2nd TN Mtd Inf; 10-15-63 to 10-17-64; Moon PO
HOLLIS, John W., Dy-29-4; Pvt A Co 6th TN Cav; 63 to 64; Newbern PO; CONF
HOLLIS, Newton M., La-117-4; 15th Inf Dist
HOLLIS, William J., Wy-177-2; Sol US; 12th Dist
HOLLISTER, Edwin J., K-160-1; Pvt A Co 2nd MI; Knoxville PO
HOLLOWAY, Dan, We-225-1; Sgt L Co 4th US Art; Feb 63 to 26 Feb 66; rheumatism
HOLLOWAY, Harry, Gi-129-2; Pvt 110th TN Inf; 6 Feb 64 to 6 Feb 66; Conway PO
HOLLOWAY, Preston O., Mg-200-1; P-t B Co 2nd TN Inf; 3 May 63 to Jul 65; Kismet PO; rupture
HOLLOWAY, Thomas, Sh-150-2; Pvt H Co Inf; 3 yrs; Bartlett PO
HOLLOWAY, Thomas C., K-159-3; C Sgt G Co 4th TN Cav; 2 May 63 to 12 Jul 65; Knoxville PO
HOLLOWAY, William B., Mr-96-2; (William Falkner); Pvt I Co 2nd E TN Inf; 2-20-62 to 2-20-65; Whitwell PO; dirhea
HOLLOWELL, Joseph, Sh-169-1; Pvt I Co Merchen?; Memphis PO
HOLLOWELL, Stephen, He-61-1; Sgt D Co 7th TN Cav; 62 to 25 Oct 63; Shermans Mill PO; has dispepsia
HOLLUM, Violet, D-64-6; 112 S High St, Nashville PO
HOLLY, Danill, Ho-96-1; Pvt D Co 1st MI Inf; Dec 19 61 to Jan 9 64; Tennessee Ridge PO
HOLLY, George, H-60-1; Betty widow of; TN Col; Chattanooga PO
HOLLY, John, Ct-40-1; Pvt C Co 13th TN Cav; 9-24-63 to 9-5-65; Elizabethton PO; rheumatism & frostbitten feet
HOLLY, John P., Gi-133-3; Pvt H Co 3rd TN; 5-61 to 8-65; Bufords PO
HOLLY, Joseph, K-167-5; Pvt 1st Hvy; Knoxville PO
HOLLY, Thomas R., Ch-12-1; Sophia widow of; Pvt 7th TN Cav; 2-62 to 64; Custer Point PO
HOLM, John, H-55-2; ABS (able seaman) (name of boat illegible) Mass; 61 to 64; Chickamauga PO
HOLMAN, Daniel, Mu-210-6; Mollie widow of; Pvt Inf; Mallard PO
HOLMAN, William, Mu-209-4; Pvt G Co 9th TN Cav; Oct 61 to May 65; Columbia PO; CONF
HOLMAN, William P., Sh-159-6; Pvt C Co 7th TN; Jun 61 to Jun 65; Memphis PO; CONF
HOLMES, B. E., G-57-7(4); Lt Col 47th TN Inf; 1 Nov 61 to 1 Jul 62; Yorkville PO; CONF
HOLMES, Daniel, Wl-294-1; Pvt I Co 72nd PA Reg Cav; Apr 62 to Jul 65; Bellwood PO; shot in hip at Chicamanga, able to work
HOLMES, Henry, Sh-149-2; Pvt D Co 66th US Inf; 65 to 66; Raleigh PO
HOLMES, Jas., T-209-1; Pvt; 62 to 64; Randolph PO
HOLMES, John, Sh-204-1; Pvt; Bethel Ave, Memphis PO
HOLMES, Wiliam, Wi-271-1; Pvt A Co 5th MA Cav; 3 yrs 6 mos; Boston PO; discharge lost, time of enlistment unk
HOLMON, John, Mu-190-2; alias Jack Holmon; Pvt D Co 15th Col Inf; 9-12-64 to 4-7-66; Culleoka PO
HOLMON, William B., Me-88-1; Sgt F Co 4th TN Cav; 2-15-63 to 7-11-65; Birchwood PO
HOLMS, Isaac (see Green, Isaac, D-45-1)
HOLOWAY, William, Ro-209-3; Pvt C Co; 61 to 65; Kings Creek PO; CONF
HOLSTON, Virginia, Ja-86-4; widow of US and CONF sol; 5th Dist
HOLT, Augustus, Wa-260-1; Pvt C Co 1st Reg Cav; Jul 5 62 to Jun 5 65; Nola Chucky PO; rheumatism
HOLT, Austin M., Wy-175-1; Pvt H Co 2nd TN Mtd Inf; 12-20-63 to 1-21-65; Cypress Inn PO
HOLT, Benjamin, Mu-209-5; Pvt A Co 1st TN Inf; Oct 1 61 to Aug 1 63; Columbia PO
HOLT, Bradley, Ge-102-3; Nancy widow of; Pvt F Co 4th TN Inf; 21 Jan 63 to 65; Whig PO
HOLT, Catharine, Wi-277-1; 8th Civil Dist
HOLT, Christopher, Je-138-2; Mary widow of; Pvt; Mount Hareb PO; died of measles; his discharge is at Washington DC
HOLT, Daniel, Ru-13-2; Pvt; Murfreesboro PO
HOLT, David S., Cf-39-1; Pvt H Co 4th TN Cav; 1 Nov 64 to 25 Aug 65; Prairie Plains PO
HOLT, Emily (see Whiteside, Thos.)
HOLT, Frank A., Br-9-3; Malissee D. widow of; Pvt 5th TN Inf; 1-1-62 to 9-6-65; Cleveland PO
HOLT, Gastevus, Sh-167-2; Col 3rd KY Inf; May 61 to Jun 65; PO omitted; CONF
HOLT, George, Co-69-6(12); Darcus E. widow of; Pvt C Co 8th TN Inf; 1 Jan 63 to 1 Apr 64; Bibee PO; fever in TN, drawing no pension
HOLT, George D., Co-61-3(1); Mary widow of; Pvt D Co 8th TN Inf; Givens PO
HOLT, Giles, Hd-50-1; Cpl A Co 2nd TN Mtd Inf; Sep 63 to Sep 64; Savannah PO
HOLT, Howard, Co-69-6(12); Pvt C Co 8th TN Inf; 1 Jan 63 to 1 Apr 64; Help PO; rheumaties KY; no pension yet
HOLT, Isaac, Ov-137-2; Pvt O Co 32nd KY Inf; 10-28-62 to 8-12-63; Monroe PO; lung disease
HOLT, Isaac, Co-62-1; Pvt C Co 8th TN Inf; 62 to 65; Help PO; kidney & rheumatism
HOLT, Jacob, Cr-3-1; USN, Jan 18 64 to Apr 8 65; Gadsden PO; wounded in hipo
HOLT, Jacob H., Ov-137-2; Pvt A Co So KY Inf; 1-25-65 to 10-23-65; Monroe PO; rheumatism, this soldier served in KY state troops but aided in putting down the rebellion
HOLT, James, Col, D-74-1; Pvt B Co; 62 to 65; 108 St. Inst? Nashville PO
HOLT, James, Co-69-7(12); Pvt C Co 8th TN Inf; 1 Jan 63 to 64 (1 yr); Help PO; no pension
HOLT, James, Ge-85-2; Pvt F Co 4th TN Inf; 25 Apr 63 to 3 Aug 65; Cedar Creek PO; enlargement kidneys & liver
HOLT, James W., Bo-21-2; Pvt A Co 5th TN Cav; 9-4-64 to 6-26-65; Ellijay PO
HOLT, John, Gi-132-3; Mary Glaye formerly widow of; Pvt H Co 111th USCV; Jan 10 64 to Apr 13 66; DeRay PO
HOLT, John, Wy-175-1; Pvt A Co 10th TN Inf; 5-1-62 to ___ (1 yr 6 mos); Cypress Inn PO
HOLT, John, Co-61-4; Pvt C Co 8th TN Cav; 1 Oct 63 to ___; Little Chucky PO
HOLT, Jonah, Ge-99-2; Pvt B Co 8th TN Cav; 23 Jul 63 to ___; Cedar Creek PO; horse fell & hurt back, didn't get any discharge
HOLT, Jonas, Ge-85-3; Mary A. widow of; Pvt B Co 8th TN Inf; Syren Burg PO; dont remember dates
HOLT, JOseph, Wy-175-1; Sgt A Co 10th TN Inf; 9-20-63 to 1-1-65; Whittens Stand PO
HOLT, Joseph, Co-61-6(2); C Sgt K Co 8th TN Cav; 1 Sep 62 to 17 Sep 65; Bridgeport PO

HOLT, Joseph C., Dy-25-5(1); Pvt D Co 13th TN Inf; 4 Apr 61 to 65; Newbern PO; shot nine times; CONF

HOLT, Louisa, D-70-2; widow; 21 Lafayette St, Nashville PO

HOLT, Moses, Ch-16-1; Pvt Battery 1 attached 6th IL Cav; 62 to 64; Henderson PO

HOLT, Nicholas P., Wi-276-1; Pvt F Co 17th TN Inf; 10 Apr 61 to 3 Jul 65; Beechville PO; shot in legs, crippled; CONF

HOLT, Obediah, Co-69-7(12); Pvt C Co 8th TN Inf; 1 Jan 63 to 64 (1 yr); Bibee PO; KY; no pension

HOLT, Philip, Ma-124-1; Jackson PO

HOLT, Pleasant, Ov-136-1; Pvt A Co South Cumberland Battalion; 1-25-65 to 10-23-65; Livingston PO; rheumatism & heart disease; belonged to South Cumberland Battalion KY state volunteers

HOLT, Pryor, Ha-110-1; Manerva widow of; Pvt G Co 8th TN Inf; 63 to ___; Luther PO; killed on Indian Creek, Gr. Co., TN, Oct 9, 1863

HOLT, Raph, Gi-128-1; SgtC Co 12th TN Inf; 62 to 65; 8th Civil Dist

HOLT, Robert R., Hd-55-1; Pvt A Co 2nd TN Cav; 15 Oct 63 to 15 Nov 64; Whitton PO

HOLT, Rock H., Ov-136-1; Livingston PO

HOLT, Samuel M., D-63-3; Pvt F Co 5th TN Cav; Sep 62 to Jan 65; Nashville PO

HOLT, Tobe?, Mu-195-2; Sol G Co 111th TN Vol; Jun 63 to May 66; Columbia PO

HOLT, William, Ce-30-1; Lt A Co 10th TN Inf; Apr 62 to May 65; Craggie Hope PO

HOLT, William, Mu-202-1; Pvt B Co 8th TN Cav; Mar 26 63 to Jul 27 65; 14th Civ Dist

HOLT, William (dee), Mu-189-1; Pvt G Co 110th TN Inf; Hurricane Switch PO

HOLT, William, Se-221-3; Pvt A Co 9th TN Cav; 13 Sep 63 to 11 Sep 65; East Fork PO

HOLT, William C., We-225-2; Capt M Co 6th TN Cav; 14 Mar 62 to Jun 65; Dresden PO; rheumatism & hearing

HOLTE, William C., We-234-1; Pvt F Co 1st KY Cav; 9-64 to 5-65; Greenfield PO

HOLTSINGER, George W., Je-136-2; Capt F Co 4th TN Inf; 26 Jun 63 to 2 Aug 65; PO omitted

HOLTZKNECHT, Jacob, Mr-102-2; Pvt B Co 26th MO Inf; South Pittsburg PO; cripled by musket ball in war, was captured and got no discharge papers

HOMAN, William, Sh-174-1; Eliza J. widow of; Pvt D Co 8th IA Inf; 1-1-64 to 4-24-66; 195 Linden St, Memphis PO; right arm partially disabled by rifle ball, reenlisted veteran--mustered out at Selma, AL

HOMER, Pleasant, Hw-131-1; Pvt A Battery 1st TN Lt Art; 20 Sep 63 to 3 Aug 65; Whites Burge PO; chronic diarhea, discharged pension $10

HOMER, William, H-76-1; Chattanooga PO

HOMES, John, Col, Mt-139-1; Pvt H Co 10th US Col Inf; 63? to 66 (2 yrs 3 mos 11 days); New Providence PO

HOMES, Riley, Mn-126-1; Pvt G Co 6th TN Cav; 64 to 8-65; Purdy PO

HOMES, Thomas, R-161-2; Pvt K Co 4th TN Cav; 4-9-64 to 7-12-65; Dayton PO

HOMES, Thomas A., Je-144-2; Caralin M. widow of; Pvt C Co 4th TN Cav; Feb 63 to ___ (2 yrs); Talbotts PO; died in army before war closed

HONEY, John, Pi-156-3; Pvt C Co 13th KY Cav; 7-3-63 to 1-10-65; Travisville PO; piles

HONEYCUTT, James M., Ro-209-3; Pvt 1st TN Cav; 18 Nov 46 to 47; Mexican War; Rockwood PO

HONEYCOTT, Lucinda, Ct-39-2; widow; Pvt 15th TN Reg; Elizabethton PO

HONEYCUT, William, S-213-3; Pvt E Co 2nd KY Inf; Mar 61 to 12 Aug 64; Hellenwood PO; rheumatism in right shoulder

HONEYCUTT, James, Sn-262-1; Pvt; PO omitted

HONEYCUTT, James A., Sn-264-1; reenlisted veteran; Cpl A Co 22nd ___; 11 May 61 to Jun 1 64; Pvt A Co 42nd ___; 1 Jun 64 to 3 Jun 65; Fountain Head PO; shot in head, shot in shoulder, eye & ear injured by wounds; this man badly wounded many times in shoulder, has come out

HONEYCUTT, Jas. A., Sn-262-1; Pvt TN Cav; 63 to 64; Fountain Head PO; CONF

HONEYCUTT, John M., U-247-1; 1st Lt B Co 13th TN Cav; 23 Sep 63 to 27 Aug 65; Erwin PO; rheumatism & heart disease 25 yrs

HONEYCUTT, Peter L., U-247-2; Erwin PO; kidney & lungs

HONEYCUTT, Sterling, Cl-57-2; Pvt B Co 8th TN Cav; 6-63 to 64; Goin PO; heptetides 1863; US Sol not discharged

HONEYCUTT, Thomas, S-217-1; Pvt G Co 8th TN Inf; 8 Dec 62 to ___ (13 mos); Winfield PO; rheumatism

HOOD, Alfred R., Su-239-2; Cpl G Co 8th TN Cav; 26 Aug 63 to Sep 65; Bloomingdale PO

HOOD, Benjamin F., Su-240-1; Pvt G Co 8th US Cav; 20 Oct 63 to 11 Sep 65; Butterfly PO; chronic (sic)

HOOD, Edwin T., Un-251-1; Pvt E Co 55th OH Inf; 25 Nov 61 to Feb 64; Effie PO; chronic diareah, discharged from disability

HOOD, Henry, Su-240-2; Blacksmith M Co 4th TN Cav; 8 May 64 to 12 Jul 65; Easley PO; lost 1 eye, discharge lost

HOOD, John, Sh-162-2(1); US Sol; Ramsey PO

HOOD, John, C-27-3; Susen widow of; Jacksboro PO

HOOD, John H., K-179-4; Pvt C Co 2nd TN Cav; 5 Nov 62 to 6 Jul 65; Ball Camp PO; ruptured--fall from horse

HOOD, John N., Di-31-1; Pvt G Co 6th TN Inf; 7-8-63 to ___ (1 yr 4 mos 16 days); 2nd Civil Dist

HOOD, William, K-181-2; Bugler 3rd TN Cav; 7 Dec 62 to 18 Jun 65; Nast PO; cattarh in head 18 yrs.

HOOD, William A., Hy-84-2; Hood, Neuton T. on same line; Pvt G Co 1st TN; Apr 64 to Jan 65; Forkeddeer PO; CONF

HOOD, William J., Di-31-1; Pvt G Co 6th TN Inf; 7-8-63 to 8-9-65; 2nd Civil Dist; piles; no information to be obtained

HOOD, William T., Ro-210-5(3); Pvt D Co 7th TN Cav; 1 Nov 64 to 16 Jun 65; Kingston PO

HOOD, Wyly A., Cr-19-1; Pvt F Co 7th TN Cav; 8-5-62 to 10-25-63; Clarksburg PO

HOODENPYLE, Robert, Sq-165-1; Pvt C Co 6th TN Cav; 10-1-64 to 9-20-65; Delphi PO; sick stuck in ear 3 inches, received an honorable disc.

HOOK, George, Sh-191-5(1); Memphis PO; records not seen

HOOK, Peter, Mu-205-2; Williams, Catherine formerly wid; Pvt; Williamsport PO; papers in Washington DC

HOOKER, Charles (see Barnes, Charles)

HOOKER, Cornelious S., Po-149-2(1); Pvt E Co 5th TN Mtd Inf; 9-23-64 to 6-26-65; Conasauga PO; Mtd Inf one yr

HOOKER, Foster L., B-11-3(2); Louviny widow of; Pvt A Co 10th TN Inf; 1-63 to 7-65; Unionville PO; discharge not found

HOOKER, Ruben, Dy-22-1; drawing a pension now; Dyersburg PO

HOOKER, Solomon N., R-157-1; 1st Lt F Co 89th OH; 8-7-62 to 6-7-65; Lorraine PO; chronic diarrhea

HOOKS, Ammon H., Le-119-1; Pvt E Co 9th MI Inf; 20 Feb 65 to 15 Sep 65; Strathmore PO; chronic diarrhoea and piles; discharged by S.O. No. 66 dated Sep 9/65

HOOKS, George H., A-7-2; Robertsville PO

HOOKS, Stephen, A-7-2; Robertsville PO

HOOKS, Thomas, A-6-4(2); Pvt "captains battery"; Spring 1862 to 6-27-65; Fairview PO

HOOPER, Elias, H-57-1; Pvt B Co 15th US Col; 63 to 65; Orchard Knob PO

HOOPER, Jehue, Br-12-5; Pvt A Co 8th TN Inf; 12-15-62 to 6-30-65; Raht PO

HOOPER, Kinsey C., Br-12-5; Pvt A Co 8th TN Inf; 12-25-62 to 7-30-65; Raht PO

HOOPER, Lemuel W., Co-63-3; Lt D Co 9th TN Cav; 22 Apr 63 to 11 Sep 65; Newport PO; rheumatism & heart disease

HOOPER, Thomas, Sh-178-2; Rosa widow of; Cpl C Co 4th US; 263 Monroe, Memphis PO; killed at Ft. Pillow

HOOPER, Wesley W., H-53-3; Pvt; 3 yrs; Chattanooga PO; loss of sight--left eye

HOORD, Pleasant, K-170-1; Pvt M Co 1st US Art; 5 Sep 63 to 20 Mar 65; Knoxville PO

HOOVER, Amelia A., Cf-38-1; widow; 10th Civil Dist

HOOVER, Henry, Fe-41-3(1); Mary Ann widow of; Pvt B Co 2nd E TN Inf; 61 to 65; Boat Land PO; died from starvation; in prison on Bells Island and died before he got home

HOOVER, James M., Fe-41-4(2); Pvt Capt Beaty's Co. Indpt TN Scouts; 62 to 65; Boat Land PO; chr. rheumatism & kidney dis.
HOOVER, James N., Pu-142-1; Pvt F Co 14th WI Inf; 9-22-61 to 9-31-62; PO illegible; shot in left eye
HOOVER, John M., Mg-197-5; Pvt E Co 10th MN Inf; Aug 62 to 65; Neom PO; rheumatism
HOOVER, John T., Wh-182-1; Cpl A Co Unat. PA Inf; 10-16-62 to 7-23-63; Doyle's Sta. PO
HOOVER, Lewis, Ov-139-2; Pvt I Co 25th TN Inf; 5-63 to 6-65; Lovejoy PO
HOOVER, Miles, Co-64-1; Conf Pvt 58th NC Inf; 63 to 65 (1 yr 7 mos); Newport PO
HOOVER, Robert, D-50-4; Robert Black alias; Pvt B Co 5th US Cav; 2 yrs; 1010 N Market, Nashville PO; pension at disch. 20 yrs ago
HOPE, Andrew N., Mc-114-3; Pvt; Riceville PO
HOPE, Cyrildan (see Boaz, Benjamin)
HOPE, David, Ge-97-2; Pvt 8th TN Inf?; 1 Mar 64 to 26 Jun 65; PO omitted
HOPE, Hardin, Me-94-1; Pvt K Co 10th TN Cav; 2-15-64 to 8-1-65; Knott PO
HOPKINS, Alex, Mt-139-1; Pvt I Co 15th US; 64 to 66 (1 yr 6 mos); New Providence PO
HOPKINS, Alexander D., Ms-171-1; Cpl A Co 4th TN Inf; Jun 64 to Jul 65; Belfast PO
HOPKINS, Arthur, Ha-114-2; Pvt D Co 3rd TN Inf; 14 May 62 to 1 Sep 64; New Cedalee PO
HOPKINS, Hillery, H-57-4; Pvt A Co 15th TN Inf; 63 to 65; Orchard Knob PO
HOPKINS, James C., Ro-207-3; Pvt I Co 11th TN Cav; 61 to __; Paint Rock PO; rheumatism
HOPKINS, James E., Su-233-1; Cpl H Co 4th TN Inf; Apr 63 to 65; Bristol PO; bronchitis, chronic, disabled entire year
HOPKINS, John S., J-83-1; 1st L t B Co 8th TN; 1-15-65 to 8-17-65; Flynns Lick PO
HOPKINS, Layfate, Fr-114-1; Pvt F Co 71st OH Inf; 63 to 64; Alto PO
HOPKINS, Moses, Sh-191-6(2); Memphis PO; records not seen
HOPKINS, Samuel J., Cr-4-3; Pvt L Co 7th TN Cav; 1 Jan 63 to 1 May 65; Bells Depot PO
HOPKINS, Samuel J., Cr-4-3; Pvt B Co 9th TN Cav; 5 Aug 61 to 5 Nov 62; Bells Depot PO; CONF
HOPPER, Daniel, Cl-47-2; Rachel widow of; Pvt E Co 6th TN Inf; Speedwell PO
HOPPER, James, Un-256-3; Linda Nelsor formerly widow of; Pvt D Co 1st TN Inf; 9 Aug 62 to __; Forkvale PO; died in army
HOPPER, James H., Ms-173-1; Pvt F Co 5th TN Cav; 20 Oct 62 to 20 Jun 65; Rich Creek PO
HOPPER, John, O-134-1; Pvt 23rd TN Inf; Aug 15 61 to Jun 20 62; Hornbeak PO; CONF
HOPPER, John, Cl-47-2; Pvt C Co 1st TN Art; 6-1-63 to 8-1-65; Speedwell PO
HOPPER, Solomon, Cl-47-2; Louisa T. widow of; Pvt C Co 1st TN Art; 6-8-63 to __; Speedwell? PO; small pox, died in service
HOPPER, William H., Je-142-2; Anna widow of; Cpl C Co 1st TN Vol; New Market PO; died in service
HOPPES, James, Ho-96-1; Pvt B Co 22nd OH Inf; Apr 15 61 to Dec 8 Oct 65; Erin PO
HOPSON, Albert, Sh-174-3; Sgt D Co 7th OH Col Inf; 5-25-62 to 11-11-63; 146 Liden St, Memphis PO
HOPSON, Dannel, Cl-53-2; Cathrine widow of; Cpl A Co 12th TN Cav; 7-28-63 to 10-7-65; Lone Mountain PO
HOPSON, David R., Gr-81-5(3); Sol US; PO omitted
HOPSON, Jessie, D-45-2; Pvt F Co 12th __; 8-63 to 11-3-63; Nashville PO
HOPSON, Juley R. (see Butler, William)
HOPSON, Thomas B., Un-252-2; Pvt A Co 12th TN Cav; 22 Dec 63 to 8 Oct 65; Simcoe PO
HOPSON, William, Gr-81-4(2); Pvt H Co 1st TN Cav; 1 Sep 62 to 7 Jun 65; Shelton's Ford PO; spinal affection, disabled
HOPSON, Young, Gr-81-1; Cpl L Co 1st TN Cav; 15 Jun 62 to 7 Jun 65; Clear Spring PO
HOPWOOD, Josephus, Ct-38-1; Pvt L Co 7th IL Cav; 9-61 to 10-64; Milligan PO; in Belle Isle prison 4 mos
HORD, James, K-167-6; Pvt; Knoxville PO; cant find out what redgement he was in
HORD, James K.?, K-179-3; Cpl F Co 2nd TN Cav;

1 Aug 62 to 6 Jul 65; Campbell PO
HORD, John Sol., Hw-132-3(1); Pvt TN Inf; Strahl PO; CONF
HORD, John A., Mn-121-3; Pvt C Co 1st AL Cav; 7-1-63 to 7-26-64; Falcon PO; reenlisted in Co E 20th __
HORD, William W., B-2-1; Pvt D Co 23rd TN Inf; 7-16-61 to 6-16-65; Wartrace PO; CONF
HORGAN, Catherine, Sh-189-6; widow US Sol; Broadway, Memphis PO
HORN, Albert, D-46-1; Pvt 4th IN Battery; 9-15-61 to 10-6-65; Nashville PO
HORN, Albert D., We-229-1; Pvt B Co 134th OH Inf; 6 May 64 to 31 Aug 64; McKinzie PO (Carroll Co.)
HORN, Calvin P., La-117-4; Pvt 48th TN Inf; 15th Dist; CONF
HORN, Green Berry, D-78-2; Pvt G Co 10th TN Inf; Dec 8 63 to 24 Jun 65; Nashville PO
HORN, John R., Pu-142-1; Pvt C Co 2nd IL Inf; 63 to 65; Calf Killer PO; nerveous complaint
HORN, John W., Mc-120-3(1); Lucy A. widow of; Pvt 3rd TN Inf; Sweetwater PO; drowned during service
HORN, Sidney H., Cr-14-4; Pvt K Co 2nd TN Mtd Inf; 1 Jan 64 to 15 Mar 65; Clarksburg PO; discharge lost, deserves a pension
HORN, W. R., Gi-139-3; Pvt TN Cav; 5-63 to 64; Campbellsville PO; M. C. Horn wife of W. R. Horn; CONF
HORNBACK, Sarah, Ch-13-4(1); widow of; Pvt K Co 7th TN; 62 to __ (nearly 3 yrs); Brinley PO; she living in household of Miles Presslar; soldier died Andersonville
HORNBERGER, Curtis E., Rb-221-2; Pvt E Co 50th TN; Sep 1 62 to May 1 65; Adams Station PO; CONF
HORNBERGER, George I., Rb-221-1; Pvt E Co 50th TN; Sep 62 to Mar 1 65; Adams Sta. PO; flesh wound through abdomen; prisoner at Camp Douglas; CONF
HORNBY, Julius E., Ro-210-10; Pvt E Co 1st TN Inf; 20 Aug 61 to 17 Sep 64; Rockwood PO; died
HORNE, Howel, M-108-4; Matilda widow of; Pvt 9th KY Inf; 61 to 65; Lafayette PO; discharge not at hand
HORNE, James, Gi-134-1; Dist 14
HORNE, John W., Su-241-2; Pvt I Co 1st TN Cav; Apr 62 to 65; Clover Bottom PO; sine-nerve affection-piles, rheumatism
HORNED, Samuel D., Co-61-4(1); Sgt M Co 1st TN Cav; 2 Jun 62 to 5 Apr 65; Parrottsville PO
HORNEDAY, Lish, Ru-239-1; Pvt; 63 to 63; Rockvale PO; conscripted soldier
HORNER, Andrew J., Rv-11-2; 7th Civil Dist
HORNER, Daniel, Hm-109-4; Pvt A Co 1st TN Art; 25 Mar 63 to 3 Aug 65; Whitesburg PO
HORNER, Elbert, Hm-109-5; USS; PO omitted
HORNER, George, P-156-2; Nancy J. widow of; Lobelville PO; CONF
HORNER, Thom., Ho-95-1; Pvt A Co 1st TN; Dec 1 63 to Aug 3 65; Stuart PO
HORNER, William R., Hm-109-8; Pvt A Co 1st TN Art; 62 to 65; Whitesburg PO
HORNERS, James, S-218-1; 64 to __; PO omitted; 7th regt captured & went to other companies
HORNERS, John, S-218-1; 64 to 65; Cavalry; PO omitted
HORNSBY, Frank, Me-94-2; Pvt I Co 5th TN Inf; 11-14-62 to 6-30-65; Euchee PO
HORNSBY, James H., Mc-112-3; Major 9th TN Cav; 6-22-63 to 9-24-65; Athens PO
HORNSBY, John, We-220-2; Pvt K Co 6th TN Cav; Aug 10 62 to Jul 26 65; PO omitted
HORNSBY, K. E., Hr-96-1; Texas CONF; 61 to 62; Crainsville PO; ranger forgot wo 7 reg
HORNSON?, Howisere? C., Ge-88-3; Pvt E Co 8th TN Inf; 1 Jun 63 to 30 Jun 65; Mohawk PO; rheumatism & heart trouble
HORRICE, John, Un-258-3; Pvt B Co 6th TN Inf; 14 Apr 62 to 13 Jul 65; Longhollow PO
HORSHAW, Calvin, Br-12-2; Pvt G Co;. 1-1-64 to 3-15-65; Charleston PO; catarrh
HORTON, Alexander, Ch-17-1; 63 to 65; Henderson PO; CONF
HORTON, Frank, H-67-2; Pvt F Co 13th US Col Inf; 9-16-63 to 1-15-66; Chattanooga PO; dropsy of chest, now suffers from shortness of breath

HORTON, George W., Wy-173-1; Pvt E Co 8th TN Mtd
    Inf--3-1-65 to 9-1-65; Pvt B Co 2nd TN Mtd
    Inf--10-15-63 to 10-17-64; Victory PO
HORTON, Henry, Wy-173-5(1); US Sol; 7th Civil Dist
HORTON, Henry (while in army), Sh-192-1; now Henry
    Grey; Pvt B Co 61st US Col Inf; 63 to 65
    (2 yrs 6 mos); Memphis PO
HORTON, James, Wy-173-1; Elizabeth widow of; Pvt F
    Co 6th TN Cav; 9-21-62 to 7-26-65; Houston PO
HORTON, James M., Ge-96-2; Pvt C Co 4th TN Inf; 7
    Apr 64 to Aug 65; Rheatown PO; enlarged liver
    &c; discharge gone, cant get dates
HORTON, Jesse D., He-64-1; Pvt A Co 10th TN Inf;
    4-12-62 to 5-25-65; Sims PO
HORTON, James W., Wy-173-4; Pvt I Co 13th __; 28
    May 61 to 28 Apr 66; Shady Hill PO; CONF
HORTON, John E., Wy-177-1; Pvt F Co 6th TN Cav; 10-
    62 to 8-65; Waynesboro PO
HORTON, Loney, Ge-84-3; Pvt H Co 4th US Inf; 5 Jun
    64 to 30 Jun 65 (1 yr 2 mos 1 day); Bird
    Bridge PO; dis of lung?
HORTON, Louis D., He-64-1; Pvt I Co 13th __; 29
    May 61 to __ (3 yrs 3 mos); Reagan PO; wound
    in left shoulder, from prison to US Army;
    CONF
HORTON, Madios (while in army--now Mat Grey),
    Sh-192-1; Pvt B Co 61st US Col Inf; 2-64 to
    12-65; Memphis PO
HORTON, Nathaniel, Wy-173-3; Margret widow of; Pvt
    B Co 2nd TN Mtd Inf; 10-15-63 to 10-17-64;
    Houston PO
HORTON, Robert, D-66-2; Cpl C Co 10th US C Inf;
    Jul 64 to Jan 66; Nashville PO; rolling
    mill
HORTON, Samuel, Sh-146-3; Pearly PO
HORTON, Wm. B., Wa-267-3; Pvt A Co NC Inf; 1 Jan
    65 to Aug 65; Johnson City PO; chrc. rheuma-
    tism
HORTON, William T., Sh-152-1; Dexter PO
HORTON, William H., Sh-159-2; Hollie E. widow of;
    Lt; 62 to 63; Memphis PO; leg shot and became
    useless; CONF
HOSKINS, Brittain, A-6-3(1); Pvt E Co 3rd TN Inf;
    2-12-62 to 2-23-65; Olivers PO
HOSKINS, Crineral, A-6-4(2); Cpl E Co 3rd TN Inf;
    2-12-62 to 63; Robertsville PO
HOSKINS, George, M-103-4; discharge lost; Alton
    Hall PO
HOSKINS, Marthey (see Towns, Shon)
HOSKINS, Wm. A., Mo-119-2; Col 12th KY Inf; 61 to
    64; Sweetwater PO
HOSNESS, Thomas, S-218-3; US Sol; 9th Civil Dist
HOSS, Henry, Wa-263-1; 1st Lt H Co 8th TN Cav;
    Garbers Mills PO
HOSS, James H., Ct-36-2; Pvt C Co 13th TN Cav; 2-
    14-64 to 9-5-65; Shell Creek PO
HOSS, Spencer, Gi-129-1; Pvt B Co 111th TN Inf;
    24 Mar 64 to 30 Apr 66; Elkton PO
HOSTINGS, Charley, C-34-3; Pvt US Col; Elk Valley
    PO; 2nd visit, absent from home
HOTCHKISS, Peter, Lo-187-4; Sallie J. widow of;
    Pvt 1st US Col Hvy Art; 64 to 66; Loudon PO
HOTES, William (see Ivey, Willis)
HOUK, John W., Se-227-1; Pvt F Co 3rd TN Cav; 15
    Jun 63 to 29 Jun 65; Trundles Cross Roads
    PO; dislocation of left shoulder
HOUK, Tilman A., Se-221-3; Pvt M Co 2nd TN Cav; 8
    Nov 62 to 6 Jul 65; East Fork PO
HOULDER, William, Br-13-1; Pvt D Co 14th TN Cav; 11-
    8-61 to 4-15-65; Cleveland PO; loss of eye
    sight
HOUSE, Alexander, F-39-2(1); Cpl B Co 61st US Col
    Inf; 29 May 63 to Jan 66; PO omitted
HOUSE, George, G-51-2; US Sol; Humboldt PO
HOUSE, George, Hy-74-1; Pvt B Co 61st Col Reg;
    May 63 to 65; Vildo, Midland R R PO; partial
    paralisis cause by bursting bomb shell
    during war close to him; he is partially
    able to work in the field
HOUSE, George, Ge-85-3; Chief Bugler E Co 2nd
    TN Cav; 16 Sep 62 to 6 Jul 65; Cavey Branch
    PO; I am now suffering from loss of voice
HOUSE, George W., H-55-1; Nancy P. widow of; Pvt
    G Co 4th TN Inf; 2-61 to 11-61; Chickamauga
    PO
HOUSE, Harvy J., Je-146-3; Pvt; White Plains PO
HOUSE, Hattie (see Henderson, Finley H.)

HOUSE, Henry, Sh-203-1; Pvt A Co TN Reg; Memphis
    PO; CONF
HOUSE, Jeane (see Hill, Lewis)
HOUSE, Symon, Hn-74-1; Pvt C Co 6th TN Cav; Jun 62
    to Feb 63; Como PO; cronic diariar, discharged
    on disability
HOUSEHOLDER, Wm. M., Se-227-1; Cpl A Co 6th TN Inf;
    8 Mar 62 to 27 Apr 65; Trundles X Roads PO;
    rheumatism & heart trouble
HOUSELEY, John, H-75-1; Emily widow of; Chattanooga
    PO; no record
HOUSEN, Lewis, Mu-198-1; 10th Dist
HOUSER, Ely, Ro-211-3; Pvt B Co 18th US Inf; 25
    Oct 62 to 25 Oct 65; Harriman PO; shot in left
    hip
HOUSER, Joseph A., K-182-1; Pvt A Co 6th TN Inf;
    62 to 64; Shook PO; disabled 1862; two
    fingers shot off right hand
HOUSER, Louis, Bo-20-1; Pvt E Co 3rd TN Cav; 9-18-
    62 to 5-1-65; Bank PO; heart trouble
HOUSER, Lucinda, K-181-2; widow US Sol; Knoxville
    PO
HOUSEWRIGHT, ____, Hw-125-3; Rebecca widow of;
    (see Kersey, Elijah--same Rebecca); Art E Co
    2nd TN; 63 to 65; Surgoinsville PO
HOUSHOLDER, James, K-167-4; Pvt H Co 9th TN Cav;
    Sep 63 to Nov 63; Knoxville PO; discharged--
    health bad
HOUSLEY, Benjamin F., Hw-124-2(1); Pvt M Co 1st TN
    Cav; 19 Jan 63 to 19 Jun 65; Stony Point PO
HOUSLEY, Harrison H., Ct-43-2; Lt L Co 13th TN Cav;
    9-22-63 to 9-5-65; Carter Furnace PO
HOUSLEY, James, C-28-2(1); Sgt F Co 6th TN Inf;
    3-10-62 to 3-24-65; Big Creek Gap PO
HOUSLEY, Pleasant, C-29-1; Sgt C Co 1st TN Art; 8-
    1-63 to 8-1-65; Fincastle PO; deafness, weak
    eyes & catarrh
HOUSTIN, Mathew, Sh-159-2; Cook I Co 7th IL; 62 to
    65; Memphis PO
HOUSTON, Benjamin F., Un-259-2; PVt C Co 8th TN
    Inf; 1 Feb 63 to 30 Jun 65; New Prospect PO;
    lungs, fever & measles
HOUSTON, Elbert S., Hr-86-2; Elizabeth wife of;
    Pvt B Co 4th TN Inf; 62 to 66; Grand Junction
    PO; powder burnt & lost health, & died since
    the war
HOUSTON, George, Sh-189-3; Pvt B Co 7th Regt US
    Col Hvy Art; 8-5-6? to 9-28-64; River Bank,
    Memphis PO
HOUSTON, James M., Wa-269-1; Pvt B Co 4th TN Inf;
    24 Nov 62 to 2 Aug 65; Carters Depot PO
    (Carter PO); rheumatism, piles, heart disease
HOUSTON, James N., De-26-3; A Co 52nd TN; 1 yr;
    Genette PO; CONF
HOUSTON, John P., Po-152-1; Pvt M Co 12th KY Cav;
    12-27-63 to 8-23-65; Ducktown PO
HOUSTON, Joseph, Un-258-1; Sgt E Co 6th TN Inf; 6
    Mar 62 to 27 Apr 65; Newprospect PO
HOUSTON, Robert L., Bo-21-2; Pvt D Co 2nd TN Cav;
    9-1-62 to 7-16-65; Bank PO
HOUSTON, Samuel D., R-162-3; Pvt B Co 6th TN Mtd
    Inf; 64 to 6-30-65; Dayton PO; had measles
    which settled in back and hips
HOUSTON, Wiliam W., Ma-114-1; Cpl I Co 13th TN;
    Aug 61 to Mar 65; Pinson PO; CONF
HOUSTON, William L., Bl-2-2(1); Sgt I Co 4th TN
    Cav; 12-8-63 to 6-20-65; Grape Vine PO;
    chronic diarhea, occasional diarhea
HOUTSON, Tilmon, Gr-81-1; Pvt C Co 4th TN Cav; 1
    Nov 62 to 13 Jul 65; Clear Spring PO; piles,
    partly disabled
HOWARD, Anthony, Col, Lo-191-1; Mary J. widow of;
    Pvt; Morganton PO
HOWARD, Anthony, Sh-174-3; Pvt G Co 78th TN Inf;
    10-64 to 10-65; 35 Turley St, Memphis PO
HOWARD, Charles, Sh-174-2; Lucy widow of; Pvt A Co
    11th US Hvy Art; rear 194 Linden St, Memphis
    PO; killed at Fort Pillow
HOWARD, Charles L., K-178-1; Catharine widow of;
    Pvt D Co 3rd TN Inf; 10 Feb 62 to 20 Feb 65;
    Campbell PO
HOWARD, Charles T., Lk-113-3; Sgt H Co 39th MO?;
    Sep 1 64 to Jun 5 65; 6 Civil Dist
HOWARD, Clark, Ho-95-1; Pvt H Co 1st W VA; Apr 1
    62 to May 30 65; McKinnon PO
HOWARD, Clark, St-164-1; Pvt H Co 9th W VA Inf;
    Apr 1 62 to Nov 30 65; Stribling PO; wounded
    in hip

HOWARD, David S., Hm-105-2; Pvt D Co 8th TN Cav;
63 to 64; Morristown PO; chronic dyare & other
disability
HOWARD, Edward, D-47-1; Phillips St, Nashville PO;
cant tell anything about reg. or length of
service
HOWARD, Elizabeth (see Woolart, John)
HOWARD, George, T-213-1; Pvt F Co; 2 yrs 6 mos;
Covington PO
HOWARD, George, A-5-1; Pvt M Co 13th TN Cav; 2-15-
63 to 9-17-65; Clinton PO
HOWARD, George W., Fe-41-2; Pvt D Co 5th TN Inf;
63 to 65; Fitz PO
HOWARD, George W., Col, Lo-192-3; Cpl L Co 1st TN;
Mar 64 to 65; Morganton PO
HOWARD, Hamilton, Ge-96-1; Pvt B Co 4th TN Inf; 8
Dec 62 to 2 Aug 65; Limestone PO; rheumatism
HOWARD, Harrison, D-64-2; Nashville PO
HOWARD, J. S., Bo-11-2; PVt L Co 7th TN Hvy Istel?;
9-64 to 3-30-66; Big Gulley PO; very corse
vains
HOWARD, Jack, Dy-25-5(1); Mollie Dowel widow of;
Newbern PO; killed at Island N. 10, TN, date
of enlistment & discharge forgotten; CONF
HOWARD, Jackson, K-173-3; Pvt; Troutman PO
HOWARD, James I., Mc-112-9; Pvt; Athens PO
HOWARD, James L., Lo-187-2; Pvt C Co 4th KY Inf;
61 to 65; Loudon PO
HOWARD, James R., We-223-5; Ernnar? widow of; Pvt;
lady cant say what co or regment belong to as
she has forgotten; Palmersville PO; CONF
HOWARD, James M., Gr-79-2; Atlanta widow of; Cpl;
Thorn Hill PO; not disabled; CONF
HOWARD, Joe, Gi-127-1; Pvt F Co 110th TN USC Inf;
Pulaski PO
HOWARD, John, Sh-191-6(2); Memphis PO; records not
seen
HOWARD, John, Se-219-2; Pvt B Co 9th TN Cav; Jones
Cave PO
HOWARD, John, Mg-200-1; Pvt K Co 11th TN Cav; 20
Aug 63 to 12 Sep 65; Kismet PO; diseas of
head & lungs, deafness, failing sight
HOWARD, John B., St-160-1; Pvt F Co 48th KY Mtd
Inf; Jun 1 63 to Dec 65; Weavers Store PO
HOWARD, John G., K-156-4; Colette E. widow of; Pvt
B Co 2nd TN Reg; 1 May 63 to 6 May 65; 19
Mill St, Knoxville PO
HOWARD, John H. B., D-92-2; US Sol; W. Nashville PO
HOWARD, John R., K-154-1; Knoxville PO
HOWARD, John W., D-62-1; Sol; 1220 McGavock St,
Nashville PO
HOWARD, John W., Sh-189-6; Wol US; Ark Ave, Memphis
PO
HOWARD, Joseph, K-179-1; Melvina M. widow of; Pvt
D Co 3rd TN Inf; 20 Feb 62 to 23 Feb 65;
Virtue PO
HOWARD, Joseph, Ro-202-5; Mary A. E. widow of; Pvt
M Co 13th TN Cav; 2 Feb 62 to 2 Aug 65; Cave
Creek PO; dropsy
HOWARD, Joseph B., Lo-190-2; Pvt H Co TN Cav; 64
to 65; Loudon PO
HOWARD, Joseph H., T-213-1; Pvt E Co 32nd MS Inf;
2 Mar 62 to 2 May 65; Covington PO; CONF
HOWARD, Joshua B., Mo-129-1; Sgt D Co 11th TN Cav;
3-28-63 to 2-24-65; Huling PO
HOWARD, Leroy, H-55-1; Pvt G Co 5th TN Inf; 10-5-
62 to 6-30-65; Tyner PO
HOWARD, Lirona?, Gi-138-1; Bodinham PO
HOWARD, Phillip, Hd-50-5; 1st Lt D Co 2nd TN Mtd
Inf; 12-18-63 to 2-1-65; Nixon PO; gimuhtur
of bowels
HOWARD, Reece, K-168-3; Smithwood PO
HOWARD, Rhoda, Jo-150-3; widow; Osborn PO
HOWARD, Robert, H-72-3(2); Cpl H Co 14th US Inf;
9-62 to 3-65; Chattanooga PO
HOWARD, Sallie (see Stultz, Chas.)
HOWARD, Samuel, Bo-11-4; Pvt canot give dates;
Brick Mill PO
HOWARD, Tillman A., Se-223-5(1); Mary L. widow of;
Pvt I Co 3rd TN Cav; 23 Sep 62 to 27 Apr 64;
Sevierville PO; lost on Sultanna
HOWARD, W. B., Bo-11-4; Pvt H Co 3rd TN Mtd Inf; 9-
15-64 to 12-30-64; Big Gulley PO
HOWARD, William, Mc-114-1; Pvt L Co 10th TN Cav;
3-42-64 to 6-8-65; Magellan PO
HOWARD, William, St-160-1; Teamster I Co WI Inf;
Sep 62 to May 65; Weavers Store PO; foot
broke, lame in walking
HOWARD, William, Ro-211-1; Milly A. Long formerly
widow of; PVt K Co 1st TN Inf; 9 Aug 61 to 17
Sep 64; Webster PO
HOWARD, William, Mg-198-1; Lt F Co 2nd TN Inf; 15
Aug 61 to 65; Lavender PO; measles affected
lungs, now deaf in right ear
HOWARD, _____, K-168-2; Jame widow of; Knoxville PO
HOWE, Henry, K-185-1; Mary A. wife of; Pvt;
Hargus PO (Granger Co.)
HOWE, James, R-158-1; Capt B Co 7th TN Mtd Inf; 7-
64 to 7-24-65; Rhea Springs PO
HOWE, Joseph M., Hw-119-3(1); Pvt D Co 16th IN
Mtd Inf; 19 Nov 64 to 30 Nov 65; Alum Hill PO;
disease of hd. & heart result sun stroke
HOWE, Leonadius C., K-160-3; Col 3rd TN Inf;
Knoxville PO
HOWEL, Alfonzo, Je-140-2; Pvt A Co US Art; 23 Jun
64 to 31 Mar 66; PO omitted
HOWEL, John G., J-78-2; Pvt K Co 1st TN Inf; 9-23-
64 to 7-22-65; Highland PO; arm broke
HOWEL, William A., Mg-197-3; Pvt H Co 4th TN Inf;
Feb 63 to 22 Aug 65; Crooked Fork PO; rheuma-
tism for 12 yrs
HOWELL, Charles, D-54-2; Nashville PO; gun shot
wound in mouth, could find nothing of record
HOWELL, Daniel, Ge-99-2; Pvt B Co 12th TN Cav; 29
Sep 63 to 7 Oct 65; Limestone Springs PO;
diarrhea & hemorrhoids
HOWELL, David C., H-70-3(1); Smina? widow of;
Scout Pvt C Co 65th OH Inf; 61 to 65; Chatta-
nooga PO
HOWELL, Harrison, K-160-2; Pvt T Co 149th TN Inf; 24
Jan 65 to 21 Jan 66; Knoxville PO; partial
lost of teeth?
HOWELL, Howell Stephen, D-59-1; Pvt; 1615 Church
St, Nashville PO
HOWELL, James F., Fr-112-3; Pvt A Co 37th TN Inf;
8-12-61 to 8-12-62; Tullahoma PO (Coffee Co);
CONF
HOWELL, John S., Wi-270-1; Pvt K Co 5th TN Mtd
Inf; 1 Dec 64 to 12 Jul 65; Naomi PO; silicia
right hip, pensioned
HOWELL, Joseph, Br-7-1; Pvt E Co 5th TN Inf; ___
to 5-65 (9 mos); Cleveland PO
HOWELL, Joseph, Gi-123-3; PO omitted
HOWELL, Manuel, Col, Li-144-1; Pvt G Co 40th TN
Inf; 3-1-63 to 4-25-65; Flintville PO; famur
in right side & blindness, now blind &
helpless
HOWELL, Mary (see Swofford, Aaron P.)
HOWELL, Reuben, Sh-196-2; Pvt 1st Div 15th A Corps
Rio; 8-11-63 to 6-30-65; Equitable Gas Co,
Memphis PO; served under Genl Woods, Capt
Phillips
HOWELL, Wm., G-57-5(3); Pvt; 6-1-61 to 6-1-64;
Yorkville PO; CONF
HOWELL, William P., Wh-186-2; Cpl B Co 1st TN Mtd
Inf; 12-3-63 to 4-14-65; Bakers Cross Roads
PO
HOWINGTON, Alford, H-55-3; Pvt D Co 10th TN Cav;
2-63 to 64 (6 mos); Chickamauga PO
HOWINGTON, Francis M., We-226-2; Pvt B Co 50th MO
Inf; Sharon PO; his discharge is in hands of
Talmadge, a pension attorney in Washington
DC
HOWINGTON, William P., Hm-163(2); Cpl A Co 187th
PA Inf; 6 Apr 64 to 24 Jul 65; Russellville
PO; lung disease
HOWLAND, Mary A. (see Todd, Granvill)
HOWLETT, S. B. (see Tuley, John M.)
HOWS, Henry, D-93-1; Pvt C Co 12th TN Inf; 16 Jan
64 to 16 Jan 66; Belleview PO
HOWSEN, Henry M., Me-90-2(1); Pvt G Co 5th TN Inf;
11-11-62 to 5-15-64; Goodfield PO; shot in
left hip & hand
HOYLE, Calvin, Hr-98-1; Pvt I Co 23rd MO Inf; 10
Jun 62 to 10 May 65; U-Bet PO
HOYLE, George, K-160-3; Knoxville PO
HOYNE, Andrew, D-63-1; Nashville PO
HUBB, William, Un-253-3; Pvt G Co 7th TN Inf; 7
Jun 65; Lorenaton PO; lungs & disease of eyes
HUBBARD, Creed M., Hd-50-1; Pvt K Co 50th TN Mtd
Inf; Feb 25 65 to Aug 1 65; Savannah PO
HUBBARD, J., K-166-5; Navy-ship Monondehala; Jul
64 to Aug 65; Knoxville PO

HUBBARD, Jacob P., Ge-95-1; Cpl L Co 8th IN Cav; 4 Sep 62 to 2 Sep 65; Rheatown PO; prisoner Salisberry
HUBBARD, John H., W-194-2; US Sol; 11th Dist
HUBBARD, Liddia (see Long, George)
HUBBARD, Mary A., C-30-2; widow of serviceman; Civil Dist #7
HUBBARD, William, D-50-1; 1st Sgt A Co 40th US Inf; __ to Jul 65; 318 Line, Nashville PO; wounded in 1. arm
HUBBARD, William C., K-166-2; Pvt H Co 1st MI Inf; 8 Dec 63 to 22 Sep 65; Knoxville PO; chronic diarrhea
HUBBARD, Willis, C-29-2; Pvt B Co 3rd TN Inf; 3-61 to 2-64; Fincastle PO; foot mashed
HUBERT, Peter, R-157-2; Sol; 12th Dist
HUBERT, William S., Sh-167-3; PO omitted; CONF
HUCABY, William, A-3-3; Nancy J. widow of; Pvt J Co 11th TN Inf; 8-62 to 6-14-65; Wilson PO; Risiny?
HUCKABA, George E., Wy-171-1; Capt H Co 2nd TN Mtd Inf; 6-19-64 to 4-17-65; Sorby PO
HUCKABEE, John, K-164-2; Pvt I Co 9th TN Cav; 1 Aug 63 to 11 Sep 65; PO omitted (Knoxville?)
HUCKABEY, James, Hw-125-4; Sarah A. widow of; Cpl; 62 to 65; Stony Point PO; CONF
HUCKABY, William, K-154-2; Knoxville PO; CONF
HUCKEBY, A. J., Pi-153-1; Pvt TN Cav; 4-63 to 4-65; Chanute PO
HUDDLESTON, David, A-1-2; Pvt C Co 9th KY Cav; 11-4-64 to 9-5-65; Andersonville PO
HUDDLESTON, J. M., Hr-96-2; 2 yrs; PO omitted; CONF
HUDDLESTON, John B., Pi-155-2; Pvt D Co 1st TN Mtd Inf; Byrdstown PO
HUDDLESTON, Joseph, Pu-140-2; Pvt I Co 1st TN Mtd Inf; 11-27-64 to 8-22-65; Cookeville PO
HUDDLESTON, Levey H., Hr-97-1; Pvt C Co 1st AL Cav; Mar 64 to Oct 65; Toone PO
HUDDLESTON, R. H., Hr-796-2; 2 yrs; Pinetop PO; CONF
HUDDLESTON, William, V-178-1; Pvt C Co 44th US Vol Inf; 3-20-64 to 5-66; Sparkman PO
HUDGENS, William D., K-180-4; Pvt E Co 9th TN Cav; 25 Oct 63 to 11 Sep 65; Ebenezer PO; disease of lungs, result of measles
HUDLESTON, David F., C-32-2; Elisebeth widow of; Pvt C Co 9th TN Cav; 7-4-62 to 9-11-65; Pine Mountain? PO
HUDSON, Andrew, A-7-1; Robertsville PO
HUDSON, Benjamin F., H-57-1; Pvt C Co 1st TN Inf; 63 to 65; Orchard Knob PO
HUDSON, Calup, Mg-196-1; Eliza widow of; Pvt B Co 11th TN Cav; 63 to __; First Dist
HUDSON, Charles, Di-34-1; Pvt B Co 14th Col US; 10-1-64 to 3-26-66; Dickson PO
HUDSON, George, Hw-123-2; Susan widow of; Pvt; Rotherwood PO
HUDSON, Jerome H., Be-6-1; Pvt E Co 6th IA Cav; 2 Dec 62 to 27 Oct 65; Big Sandy PO
HUDSON, Joseph, Sh-149-3; Pvt E Co 54th US Inf; Nov 63 to Dec 66; Raleigh PO
HUDSON, Kesley M., L-194-2; K Co 1st TN Inf; 25 May 63 to 25 May 65; Lenoir PO
HUDSON, Lee, La-114-1; US Sol; PO omitted
HUDSON, Richard, Sq-165-3; Pvt C Co 6th TN Mtd Inf; 9-18-64 to 6-30-65; Sunnyside PO; received an honorable disc
HUDSON, Riley W., J-79-2; 2nd Sgt B Co 9th KY Inf; 9-24-61 to 12-15-64; North Springs PO; gun shot in left thigh
HUDSON, Robert, Cy-27-4(2); Pvt F Co 1st TN Mtd Inf; 1-18-64 to 5-5-65; Spivey PO
HUDSON, Thomas, D-58-2; Pvt H Co 13th USC; 12 Aug 63 to 16 Jan 66; Nashville PO
HUDSON, Thomas D., Ch-18-2; 1st Sgt E Co 16th TN Cav; May 1 64 to Apr 65; Montezuma PO; CONF
HUDSON, Thomas Y., Ro-203-7; Cpl K Co 1st TN Inf; 9 Aug 61 to 17 Sep 64; Union Cross Roads PO; injury from measles, fever & mumps
HUDSON, William, M-107-1; Lucinda W. Holliman former widow of; Cpl D Co 9th KY Inf; 9-20-61 to __; Red Boiling Springs PO; gunshot wound of knee, died at Sherman's hospital at Nashville
HUDSON, William N., De-22-1; Pvt G Co 1st AL Cav; 1 Apr 63 to 1 Jan 64; Clifton PO

HUES, Martin, W1-299-1; Tilitha widow of; Pvt M Co 4th TN; Statesville PO
HUEY, Albert, Rb-223-3(5); Sallie widow fo; 9th Dist
HUFF, Andrew C., Hm-104-2; 1st Lt B Co 2nd NC Malitia; 3 Oct 63 to 1 Mar 65; Talbotts PO (Jefferson Co.)
HUFF, Daniel, Gi-127-7; Pvt C Co 110th TN Col Inf; Nov 1 62 to Apr 30 66; Pulaski PO
HUFF, George W., J-80-2; Pvt A Co 1st TN Inf; 1-64 to 1-65; Granville PO; discharged misplaced
HUFF, Henry, K-173-2; Pvt C Co 10th MS Inf; Aug 62 to Dec 65; McMillen PO
HUFF, James T., Co-61-6(2); Major 60th NC Inf; Bridgeport PO; CONF
HUFF, Jonas, Ge-88-3; Cpl F Co 4th TN Inf; 15 Apr 63 to 1 Aug 65; Mohawk PO
HUFF, Joshua, Sh-189-5; Malinda mother of; enlisted at Augusta, AR, no other record; Memphis PO
HUFF, Nathan, Sm-170-1; Liza C. widow of; Pvt; Maggart PO; Liza is widow of 2 US soldiers
HUFF, Samuel, Pu-147-2; Loucindia widow of; Pvt; 12-64 to 4-65; Gabatha PO (Jackson Co.)
HUFF, Stephen, Se-219-4; Pvt K Co 2nd TN Cav; 10 Oct 62 to 14 Apr 64; Jones Cave PO; general disability
HUFF, Swan B., Co-59-2; US Sol; 1st Dist
HUFF, William, Co-66-1; Pvt D Co 9th TN Cav; 12 Oct 63 to 13 Sep 65; English PO; piles and heart disese
HUFFAKER, Jessie, K-184-3; Pvt D Co 3rd TN Cav; 63 to 65; Thorn Grove PO
HUFFAKER, Jessie I., Ja-87-1; Sgt I Co 9th TN Cav; 9-29-63 to 9-11-65; Apison PO; piles, enlisted in 11th, discharged as 9th
HUFFAKER, Margarett E. (see Linville, ___)
HUFFAKER, Samuel, Se-225-3; Pvt D Co 3rd TN Cav; 1 Apr 63 to 3 Aug 65; Cotlettsburg PO; catarrh of head and throat 25 yrs
HUFFAKER, Wiley, H-73-4(2); Elizabeth A. widow of; Chattanooga PO
HUFFHINES, Drury S., J-80-1; 2nd Cpl D Co 8th TN Inf; 1-15-65 to 8-1-65; Bagdad PO; rupture, dyspepsia
HUFFHINES, Logan, Cy-27-1; Pvt B Co 37th KY Mtd Inf; 6-10-62 to 63 (1 yr 6 mos); Clementsville PO
HUFFINE, Abner, Wa-267-1; PVt B Co 8th TN Cav; Jul 63 to 11 Sep 65; Johnson City PO; varicose veins
HUFFINE, David B., Wa-267-3; Pvt B Co 8th TN Cav; 23 Jul 63 to 11 Sep 65; Jonesboro PO; chrc. diarhear & piles
HUFFINE, Jacob, Wa-267-3; Pvt B Co 8th TN Cav; 21 Jul 63 to 11 Sep 65; Johnson City PO; rheumatism & diarhea, blacksmith part time
HUFFINE, John, Ro-201-1; Pvt L Co 1st TN Hvy Art; Kingston PO
HUFFMAN, James F., Cr-20-3; Pvt I Co 7th TN Cav; Jan 64 to Aug 15 65; Huntingdon PO
HUFFMAN, Luch A., Tr-267-1; widow; Pvt; 6th Dist
HUFFMAN, William A., Ge-96-4; Pvt M Co 1st TN Cav; 2 Nov 62 to 19 Jun 65; Rheatown PO; one eye gone, the other almost, piles, catarrh
HUFFSTETLER, Eli, Bo-14-3; Pvt H Co 2nd TN Cav; 11-4-62 to 7-5-65; Huffstetler Store PO
HUFFSTETLER, George W., K-167-5; Cpl G Co 3rd TN Inf; Feb 62 to Mar 65; Knoxville PO; rheumatism & lunp on shoulder from
HUFFSTETLER, M. A., Bo-11-2; Pvt H Co 2nd TN Cav; 62 to 63; Brick Mill PO; cronic direah, cant give dates
HUFMAN, William, Mt-136-1; Pvt C Co 1st TN; 61 to 62; Woodford PO
HUGERELEY, Lucy E., Dy-29-3; widow US Sol; Newbern PO
HUGES, Almoda J. (see Richardson, Henry)
HUGGANS, John C., We-223-4; Nicy G. widow of; cant give record; PO omitted; died of abcess of lungs (laigs?) 1881, Jun 20; CONF
HUGGINS, Abraham, Sh-174-3; Abraham Johnson alias; Sgt A Co 11th US Col Inf; 7-63 to 66 (2 yrs 9 mos); rear 152 De Soto St, Memphis PO; partial paralysis of left arm, sometimes disabling from work; at Fort Pillow, rec'd sabre cut on head, bayonet thrust in right breast, and rifle butt in left breast

HUGGINS, Andrew J., Hm-108-2(1); Pvt M Co 1st TN Cav; 11 Jul 62 to 11 May 65; Sprigvale PO; rheumatism
HUGGINS, Benjamin, Mc-116-3; Pvt I Co 15th IN Cav; 3-20-63 to 7-1-66; Williamsburg PO; discharge papers lost, no true record
HUGGINS, Hamilton, Ge-86-2; Nancy A. widow of; Sgt M Co 1st TN Cav; 15 Jul 62 to 5 Jun 65; Beulah PO; lungs injured
HUGGINS, John T., Ms-178-1; 12th Dist
HUGGINS, Rhoda A., Mt-145-1; widow; 4 yrs 1 mo 15 days; PO omitted
HUGHES, Anderson W., R-162-2; Dayton PO
HUGHES, Andrew T., Br-8-2; Louisa widow of; Pvt E Co 7th TN Inf; 64 to 65; Cleveland PO; lung trouble
HUGHES, Archibald F., Ge-98-5; Pvt K Co 1st TN Cav; 12 Jul 62 to 5 Jun 65; Jeroldstown PO; hernia
HUGHES, Charles, Wi-275-1; alias Charles Collins; Pvt C Co 121st MA Inf; __ to 65; Franklin PO; papers lost
HUGHES, Edmond, Ho-96-1; Pvt I Co 16th TN Inf; Erin PO; this entry is marked through
HUGHES, Ewin W., Ma-127-1; Pvt B Co 3rd IL Cav; Jan 63 to 65; Jackson PO
HUGHES, Frances, H-58-4; Pvt D Co 6th TN Mtd Inf; 9-12-64 to 6-30-65; Retro PO; hemorrhage of lungs
HUGHES, George, F-47-3; Pvt K Co 26th IL Inf; 10-1-61 to 8-5-65; Medina PO
HUGHES, George W., Br-9-3; Elizabeth widow of; Pvt E Co 14th IL Cav; Cleveland PO
HUGHES, Harison, D-73-2; Blacksmith; 63 to 65; Granery White Pile, Nashville PO
HUGHES, Hezekiah, H-58-5; Pvt D Co 6th TN Mtd Inf; 9-12-64 to 6-30-65; Retro PO; rheumatism and ruptured from effect of mumps
HUGHES, Horace C., Ro-210-6; Pvt D Co 7th TN Inf; 21 May 61 to 9 Apr 65; Rockwood PO; shot five times; CONF
HUGHES, James, Mn-126-1; Pvt; 2-9-62 to 1-26-63; Adamsville PO
HUGHES, James B., Sm-176-1; 12th Civil Dist
HUGHES, James P., Rb-221-1; Pvt B Co 2nd KY; Nov 1 62 to May 1 65; Cedar Hill PO; prisoner Camp Douglas; CONF
HUGHES, James V., F-42-2; Pvt B Co 13th TN Cav; 62 to 65; Rossville PO; CONF
HUGHES, Jessee A., G-501-; Cpl K Co 49th IL; 61 to 64; Humboldt PO
HUGHES, John, Sh-172-1; Capt A Co 22nd KY Inf; 1-10-62 to 10-15-63; Maj 22nd KY Inf; 10-31-63 to 1-25-65; 20 Hernando St, Memphis PO
HUGHES, John B., Hd-56-1; Pvt F Co 64th IL Inf; 12 Aug 62 to 10 Jun 65; Coffee Ledg PO; in Andersonvill prison 8 mos
HUGHES, John M., Bl-5-1; Pvt A Co 6th TN Mtd Inf; 8-2-64 to 6-30-65; Soddy PO (Hamilton Co.)
HUGHES, John W., D-45-5; Madison St, Nashville PO
HUGHES, John W., Col, Rb-222-1; Pvt Steam Boat Fare Play; 64 to 65; Kinnie Station PO; shot through the right thigh
HUGHES, Joseph, Ct-22-1; Pvt C Co 13th TN Cav; 64 to 8-5-65; Johnson City PO; urinary disease
HUGHES, Lic----s, D-97-1; Pvt H Co 44th TN Inf; Dec 12 61 to May 12 64; Nashville PO; CONF
HUGHES, Peter L., D-91-2; Pvt C Co 15th TN Inf; 6 Jul 64 to 7 Apr 66; W. J. Phipps Grocery, Jefferson St, Nashville PO
HUGHES, Samuel, Mw-187-1; Elizabeth C. widow of; Pvt E Co 14th TN Cav; 11-10-64 to 8-25-65; Yankeetown PO; measles settled on lungs; died from sickness contracted there
HUGHES, Samuel P., Mc-115-1; Pvt E Co 7th TN Mtd Inf; 10-1-64 to 7-27-65; Riceville PO; measels settled on lungs
HUGHES, Thomas, Pu-145-3(4); Pvt G Co 4th Mtd Inf; 11-1-64 to 8-25-65; Silver Point PO
HUGHES, Thomas J., Pu-149-4(2); Mary E. widow of; Pvt E Co 5th TN Mtd Inf; 8-17-64 to 6-26-65; Fetzerton PO
HUGHES, William, Ru-105-1; Able Seaman, Michigan; May 64 to Jun 65; McEwen PO; discharge lost, cannot get dates of enlistment &c
HUGHES, William, Hd-53-3; Pvt F Co 64th IL Inf; 1 Sep 62 to 8 Jun 65; Coffee Landing PO; gun shot wound, drawing pension

HUGHETT, Allen, S-218-2; Pvt C Co; Sep 64 to Dec 64; PO omitted
HUGHETT, John, S-218-2; Pvt C Co; Sep 64 to Dec 64; PO omitted
HUGHETT, Robt. M., T-213-1; 1st Lt H Co 12th TN Cav; Jan 61 to May 65; Covington PO; broken arms & legs; CONF
HUGHLIN, Carry F., Hd-45-1; Nancy widow of; Pvt H Co 6th TN Cav; Dec 62 to 64; Cerro Gordo PO
HUGHLTT, Rubin T., Cl-53-2; Pvt D Co 8th TN Cav; 9-28-63 to 6-5-65; Springdale PO
HUGHS, George W., Sm-166-1; Pvt K Co TN Inf; 6-64 to 9-64; Carthage PO
HUGHS, Hugh H., La-117-4; Pvt F Co 12th US Col Inf; 8-12-63 to 1-66; Dickson PO
HUGHS, Rufus C., R-160-1; Pvt I Co 184th OH Inf; 2-8-65 to 9-65; 6th Civil Dist; Pvt B Co 1st TN Inf--12-28-62 to 8-3-65
HUGHS, Samuel B., Mc-110-2(1); Martha widow of; Pvt IN Hvy Art; Mt. Vera PO; discharge lost
HUGHS, W. E., Hd-48-1; Pvt H Co 11th KY Reg; Nov 4 61 to Dec 14 64; Savannah PO; ruptured
HUGHS, William, G-51-2; US Sol; Humboldt PO
HUGHS, William, Ro-209-1; Pvt; Rockwood PO; CONF
HUGHT, William, Rb-223-3(5); Denie Washington widow of; 9th Dist
HUGINESX?, Joseph, Hw-133-1; Pvt A Co 63rd TN Inf; 1 Sep 63 to 25 Mar 65; PO omitted; CONF
HUGLEY, James, H-72-3(2); Pvt G Co 20th KY Inf; 10-15-61 to 11-65; Chattanooga PO
HUKSTON, William, C-24-2; Pvt C Co 9th TN Cav; 9-63 to 9-11-65; Girlton PO; scrofferls etc
HULBURT, Frank, Sh-189-5; Pvt A Co 55th US Col Inf; Penn Ave, Memphis PO
HULETRON?, James, Bl-3-2; Sgt C Co 63rd TN Inf; 10-14-61 to 62; Orones Store PO; CONF
HULETRON, William, Bl-3-2; Lt F Co 2nd TN Cav; 6-61 to 7-11-65; Orones Store PO; CONF
HULETT, Jacob G., Ja-87-2; B Co 9th RI Cav; Tyner Station PO; discharge lost or mislaid, cant give dates
HULETT, John C., F-44-4; S. L. widow of; Pvt B Co 13th TN; May 61 to May 65; 11th Civil Dist; CONF
HULL, Andrew B., Ov-137-2; Caroline widow of; Pvt B Co 2nd TN Inf; 7-61 to 62; Monroe PO; soldier died 2-21-62
HULL, Benjamin C., Sh-191-5(1); Memphis PO; records not seen
HULL, Daniel, Mg-198-1; Pvt K Co 4th TN Inf; Sep 62 to Aug 64; Lavender PO
HULL, Henry, Co-65-2; Pvt B Co 8th TN Cav; 11 Jan 63 to 14 Sep __ (never discharged); Edwiney PO; week eyes
HULL, Isaac B., Ge-89-1; Cpl A Co 4th TN Inf; 8 Oct 63 to 2nd Aug 65; Mosheim PO
HULL, James, Co-65-1; Pvt K Co 8th TN Vol; Oct 63 to never discharged, 4 yrs; Wilton Springs PO
HULL, Peter, T-206-1; alias Peter Small; Pvt C Co 38th IL; 15 Jun 64 to 30 Aug 65; Covington PO; wounded at Aberdeen, MS; the party cant tell the exact time of enlistment
HULL, Rowland, B-6-1; Pvt H Co 10th MI Cav; 2-10-65 to 11-11-65; Shelbyville PO
HULLER, Samuel, Cf-40-1; Elizabeth widow of; Pvt F Co 27th IN Vol; 3 yrs; Tullahoma PO; both arms broken
HULLETT, Andrew, Sq-165-1; Pvt I Co 6th TN Inf; 63 to 6-30-65; Cedar Spring PO; received an honorable disc.
HULLIBARGER, William C., Rb-226-1; Pvt B Co 45th OH Inf; 22 Jan 64 to 3 Oct 65; Greenbrier PO; rheumatism, chronic diarhea resulting in piles, contracted in servis
HULLUM, Martin, Hr-87-1; Pvt B Co 3rd TN Hvy Art; 6-5-63 to 4-30-66; Hickory Valley PO
HULM, James W., Mg-198-3; Pvt F Co 1st TN Inf; 10 Aug 61 to 17 Sep 64; Heburtsburgh PO; measles 3 mos
HULME, Robt. C., Dy-27-2; Capt K Co 42nd TN Inf; Oct 61 to Apr 64; Newbern PO; shot, detained 2 mos; CONF
HULSE, Eldrige P., Ge-101-2; Lt A Co 48th PA Cav; Jan 62 to Feb 64; Locust Sp. PO; shot in right thigh

HULSE, John H., Ge-96-1; Ann J. widow of; Pvt K Co 8th TN Cav; 63 to May 65; Mill Brook PO; cant get dates
HULSE, Thomas, Wa-272-2; Pvt L Co 13th TN Cav; 1 Jan 64 to 1 Sep 63; Pettibone PO; chronic diarrhoea and hemorrhoids
HUMAN, Basil M., Mg-199-1; Cpl A Co 4th TN Cav; 15 Oct 62 to 12 Jul 65; Sunbright PO; liver disease
HUMAN, Edward F., Mg-199-3; Pvt A Co 4th TN Cav; 15 Oct 62 to 12 Jul 65; Mill Creek PO
HUMAN, Geo. A., Sh-203-1; Pvt A Co GA Regt; Jun 63 to May 65; Memphis PO; CONF
HUMAN, Jefferson M., Mg-199-3; Pvt F Co 4th TN Cav; Sep 62 to 12 Jul 65; Mill Creek PO
HUMBERD, Aden P., Ge-94-2(1); Pvt E Co 4th TN Inf; 15 Mar 63 to 2 Aug 65; Greeneville PO; during June 1865
HUMBERD, Samuel H., Br-7-3; Pvt F Co 1st TN Cav; 3-1-62 to 3-30-65; Cleveland PO; crippled, prostate glands & sight
HUMMEL, Frederick, Mu-193-2; High Pvt 79th OH; 7-62 to 6-65; PO omitted
HUMPHREY, Abraham J., Ro-207-2; Pvt; Fossil PO; son stroke
HUMPHREY, J. William, Ct-39-1; Cpl G Co 13th TN Cav; 9-63 to 9-65; Johnson City PO; rheumatism of heart, inflamatory rheumatism
HUMPHREY, James W., We-224-4; 6th Dist
HUMPHREY, Lewis, Be-8-1; Pvt B Co 2nd US Vol; 6 Oct 64 to 7 Nov 65; Spring Creek PO
HUMPHREY, Morris, R-163-4; Pvt I Co 116th OH V Inf; 8-19-62 to 5-65; Dayton PO; ruptured--hernia, asthma contracted
HUMPHREY, Young, Ct-40-3; Eliza widow of; Pvt A Co 13th TN Cav; 9-22-63 to 9-5-65; Elizabethton PO
HUMPHREYS, James, Br-13-1; Pvt E Co 11th OH Inf; 8-8-62 to 6-11-65; Cleveland PO; chronic diarhoea
HUMPHREYS, John, Mo-130-2; Pvt K Co 9th TN Cav; 5-7-63 to 9-11-65; Ballplay PO
HUMPHREYS, John, Wa-261-2; Pvt C Co MO Cav; Feb 62 to Apr 65; Conkling PO
HUMPHREYS, John S., Wa-267-3; Sgt G Co 13th TN Cav; 8 Sep 63 to 5 Sep 65; Johnson City PO; rheumatism, chrc.
HUMPHREYS, Lee H., Lo-192-2; Pvt E Co 3rd TN; 15 Jul 64 to 30 Nov 64; rheumatism; Cloyds Creek PO
HUMPHREYS, Washington, Mo-130-1; Pvt D Co 3rd TN Mtd Inf; 7-12-64 to 9-30-64; Acorn PO; rench in hip
HUMPHREYS, William J., Mo-128-1; Nancy E. widow of; Pvt D Co 11th TN Cav; Belltown PO
HUMPHREYS, William L., Co-61-6(2); Margrett widow of; Pvt; Bridgeport PO
HUMPHRYS, William, Ct-41-1; Pvt F Co 6th IN Cav; 8-8-63 to 9-15-65; South Wattauga PO; rhumatism crippled left leg
HUMPHRES?, James H., K-164-1; Pvt F Co 3rd TN Vol; 64 to 64; PO omitted (Knoxville?); was in prison at Vicksburg, MS
HUNDLEY, Jorden, Mr-96-1; Pvt C Co 6th TN Mtd Inf; 9-9-64 to 6-65; Whitwell PO; indigestion
HUNDLEY, Pryer, Un-251-1; Pvt D Co 1st TN Inf; 6 Aug 61 to Sep 64; Effie PO; ankle put out of place
HUNDLEY, Thomas, Un-252-1; Lucrecia widow of; Pvt E Co 2nd TN Inf; Esco PO
HUNEYCUTT, Samuel C., Ro-206-2; Martha A. widow of; Capt D Co 5th TN Inf; 1 Apr 62 to 24 Dec 64; Emory Gap PO
HUNGATE, Edger W., Je-146-4; Pvt K Co 86th IN Inf; 12 Jul 62 to 23 Mar 63; White Pine PO; diarrhea & deafness
HUNLEY, James, C-27-2; Pvt A Co 1st TN Inf; 61 to 9-17-64 (3 yrs 1 mo); Jacksboro PO
HUNLEY, John, C-27-3; Sgt A Co 1st TN Inf; 8-2-61 to 64 (3 yrs 2 mos); Jacksboro PO
HUNLY, John W., Rb-221-1; Pvt; Jan 22 65 to Apr 1 65; Keysburgh, KY PO
HUNNICUTT, Lewis, Gi-123-2; Mariah widow of; Pvt A Co 10th TN Col Inf; Heron PO
HUNT, Adam, F-47-1; Pvt H Co 59th TN Inf; Jun 63 to Jan 31 66; Somervile PO
HUNT, Calvin, Mo-130-1; Pvt D Co 3rd TN Mtd Inf; 7-25-64 to 11-30-66; Ballplay PO

HUNT, Charles, Mc-112-9; Pvt A Co 1st US Hvy Art TN; Athens PO
HUNT, Christopher (see Boyd, Christopher A.)
HUNT, Danl. A., Hd-47-1; Seaman US Navy "Robb"; Aug 10 63 to Aug 10 64; Pvt B Co 6th IL Cav--Mar 65 to 65 (8 mos 5 days); Savannah PO; rheumatism
HUNT, David, Sh-191-5(1); Memphis PO; records not seen
HUNT, Dennis, Sh-199-1; Pvt; Memphis PO
HUNT, Elisha, Hd-48-2; Pvt A Co transferd 2nd TN Mtd Inf; Dec 25 63 to Feb 1 65; Savannah PO; back injured; Pvt A Co 14th Mish? dates not known
HUNT, G. O., Hd-48-1; Savannah PO; rheumatism
HUNT, George E., Sh-201-4; Pvt; Memphis PO; piles
HUNT, Jackson P., Sm-170-1; Pvt E Co TN Inf; 4-15-62 to 11-15-62; Maggart PO; CONF
HUNT, Jacob, Mt-137-1; Pvt; 62 to 65; papers lost; St. Bethlehem PO
HUNT, Jasper, Hr-86-2; Pvt C Co 54th AR Inf; 8-8-63 to 8-27-66; Grand Junction PO; frost bitten
HUNT, Jessie, Hw-122-1; Mary widow of; Pvt I Co 8th TN Cav; Moer? PO; chr. diarhea, died of chr. diarhea
HUNT, John A., Sm-172-3(1); Lucy J. widow of; Pvt G Co 4th TN Inf; 11-1-64 to 8-28-65; Hickman PO
HUNT, John M., Sh-198-1; Pvt K Co 13th KY Inf; 10-7-61 to 1-19-63; Memphis PO; only injured by fall from a wagon, has a duplicate discharge
HUNT, John R., Lo-190-2; Pvt C Co 6th TN Inf; Loudon PO
HUNT, Johnson, Cl-46-1; Pvt A Co 8th KY; 9-8-61 to 7-20-65; Speedwell PO; schronic dir.
HUNT, Joseph D., We-226-2; Pvt L Co 6th TN Cav; 5 Jun 62 to 26 Jul 65; Sharon PO
HUNT, Moses F., S-213-2; Pvt I Co 30th KY Inf; 64 to Feb 65; New River PO
HUNT, Patrick, U-247-3; US Sol; 5th Civil Dist
HUNT, Robert (Newton), Mo-129-2; Pvt D Co 3rd TN Inf; 7-25-64 to 11-30-64; Povo PO
HUNT, Samuel, K-161-4; alias Samuel Ellis; Pvt F Co 1st US Hvy Art; Knoxville PO
HUNT, Syrus O., H-56-3; Cpl A Co 101st IN Inf; 8-62 to 1-63; St. Elmo PO; left engraveral hernia, discharged surgeon certificate
HUNT, William, Hr-86-2; Pvt C Co 54th AR Inf; 63 to 66; Grand Junction PO; was captured & put to work 1½ yrs
HUNT, William J., Sm-172-1; Pvt G Co 4th TN Inf; 1-64 to 8-15-65; Lancaster PO
HUNT, William W., Mo-131-1; Pvt E Co 56th IL Inf; 11-61 to 11-64; Joe PO; bronchitis, shot through left hand
HUNT, Zachary T., Mo-122-2; Pvt B Co 59th TN Inf; 1-13-63 to 4-20-65; Madisonville PO
HUNTER, Benjamin F., Ge-95-2; Pvt F Co 8th TN Cav; 31 May 63 to 11 Sep 65; Home PO
HUNTER, Daniel, Sh-146-1; Pvt G Co 137th Inf; 64 to 65; Lucy PO
HUNTER, Elias, St-163-1; Pvt 83rd IL Inf; 10 mos; Dover PO
HUNTER, Emily (see Waller, Wallis)
HUNTER, George, Hy-79-2; Pvt; Civil Dist No. 6
HUNTER, Green, Wl-293-3; Pvt F Co 7th TN Inf; Jan 61 to 61 (6 mos); Buhler PO; CONF
HUNTER, Harrison, Sh-204-2; Pvt E Co 11th US Inf; 62 to 65; Alley (1st) west of College Ave, Memphis PO
HUNTER, Henderson, Sh-150-1; Pvt A Co 57th Inf; 3 yrs; Bartlett PO
HUNTER, Henry, Br-12-3; Pvt B Co 44th TN Inf; Raht PO; wounded in hip; probably a CONF
HUNTER, Jack, Sh-150-2; Pvt 61st; 6 mos; Bartlett PO; disabled by sickness
HUNTER, Jacob, H-57-2; Pvt 16th US Col; 63 to 65; Orchard Knob PO
HUNTER, John, Gr-77-1; Pvt D Co 24 Feb 64 to 1 Aug 65; Lea Spring PO; rupture
HUNTER, John C., Wa-264-1; Pvt D Co 8th IA Cav; Jul 9 63 to Jul 25 65; Jonesboro PO; chronic rheumatism
HUNTER, Madison, Sh-175-1; Pvt C Co 48th US Inf; 5-63 to 4-65; Memphis PO
HUNTER, Mike, Sh-150-1; Mike Becton; Sgt A Co 11th US Inf; 3 yrs 1 mo; Bonds PO

HUNTER, Mike L., Bo-13-1; Sgt H Co 1st US __ Art; 6-14-64 to 3-31-66; Freindsville PO
HUNTER, Ralph E., H-56-5; 61 to 65; East End PO
HUNTER, Robert, H-50-5; Sarah J. formerly widow of; 1st Lt I Co 4th R TN Cav; 11-11-61 to 7-12-65; Soddy PO
HUNTER, Robt. B., Br-10-1; Rachel widow of; 2nd Lt I Co 2nd E TN Cav; 3-2-62 to __; Cleveland PO; died in hospital at Nashville Dec 23, 1864
HUNTER, Warren, Sh-174-2; Millie widow of; Pvt entered army 1863; 209 Linden St, Memphis PO; enlisted for 3 yrs or during the war at Ripley, Turnessie
HUNTER, Wayman, Pu-140-2; 1st Civil Dist
HUNTER, William, D-100-1; 21st Dist
HUNTER, William, C-34-3; Louisa widow of; Pvt G Co 2nd TN Inf; Fall 61 to Fall 64; Pioneer PO; conscripted think
HUNTER, William H., Ge-94-3; 2nd Lt D Co 8th TN Cav; Jun 62 to 63; Ham PO; during war in 1863
HUNTER, William H., H-54-3; Catharine E. widow of; Sherman Heights PO; husband was killed by the Rebels after he was discharged; he was a good soldier--was honorably discharged and was at home sick and the rebels came to his house and murdered him
HUNTER, William S., Me-88-2; 1st Lt E Co 5th TN Mtd Inf; 10-11-64 to __; Georgetown PO
HUNTES, Edman, Wl-293-3; Inf; 62 to 64; Lockport PO; CONF
HUNTLY, Isaac A., Ct-36-2; Martha A. widow of; Cpl 13th TN Cav; Shell Creek PO
HUNTSMAN, Joseph R., Ge-88-7; PO omitted
HURBERT, Samuel, Sh-149-1; Pvt I Co 8th TN Inf; Nov 63 to Nov 65; Frazer Station PO; papers lost
HURD, George M., H-62-3; Pvt E Co 84th OH Vol Inf; 4-36 (sic)-62 to 9-20-62; 413 Pine, Chattanooga PO
HURELT, Jesse, Wa-263-3; Cyntha A. widow of; Pvt A Co 3rd NC Mtd Inf; Garbers Mills PO; diarrhea & rheumatism
HURLBURSH, Pierre, H-56-5; Mass; 62 to 65; East End PO
HURLEY, William S., Hw-129-1; Eliza widow of; Pvt F Co 8th KY Cav; 5 Aug 62 to 20 Jun 63; Morrisburg PO
HURNEY, Albert, Gi-126-1; Cpl K Co 110th Col Inf; 15 Dec 63 to 6 Feb 66; Pulaski PO
HURRY, William, St-160-1; Pvt 5th TN Inf; Oct 62 to Nov 64; Lafayette KY PO (Christian Co.); CONF
HURSH, Andrew J., Ch-17-2; Pvt B Co 3rd Ing Trop?; 65 to 4-26-65 (4 mos); Massyeville PO
HURST, Daniel, Ro-201-2; Pvt K Co 5th IN Cav; Oct 62 to 65; Kingston PO
HURST, Emanuell, Se-219-1; Pvt C Co 8th TN Cav; 6 Oct 63 to 17 Sep 65; East York PO; chronic diarhoe
HURST, George, Se-219-3; Pvt C Co 9th TN Cav; 25 Sep 63 to 14 Apr 64; Richardson Cave PO; rumatism
HURST, Green M., Sn-252-4; Pvt C Co 18th TN Inf; 5-4-61 to 10-1-62; Pleasant View PO; CONF
HURST, Hiram, Un-252-1; Pvt K Co 8th TN Cav; 11 Aug 63 to 11 Sep 65; Esco PO
HURST, James, Mc-112-6; Pvt C Co US Col Art TN; 2-27-64 to 3-1-66; Athens PO; piles
HURST, James P., Cl-53-1; Pvt I Co 23rd TN Inf; 1-5-62 to 10-5-65; Lone Mountain PO
HURST, John, R-158-2; Pvt I Co 3rdTN Cav; 8-63 to __; Breedenton PO (Meigs Co.); weak lunged--from measles in army
HURST, John C., Cl-53-2; Pvt A Co 12th TN Cav; 12-27-64 to 11-7-65; Lone Mountain PO
HURST, John D., D-51-1; Pvt A Co 25th IN Inf; Jul 2 62 to Aug 64; 309 Cedar St, Nashville PO
HURST, Plesant, Se-219-2; Pvt I Co 2nd TN Cav; 22 Sep 62 to 6 Jul 65; East Fork PO
HURST, Samuell, Se-219-1; Pvt I Co 3rd TN Cav; 8 Sep 63 to 20 Jun 65; Jones Cave PO
HURST, Simon, Se-219-1; Pvt C Co 8th TN Cav; 15 Mar 65 to 11 Sep 65; East York PO
HURST, Telino, Mn-121-4; Melocky widow of; Col 6th TN Cav; 62 to 5-65; Hurst PO; old and cant give date of enlistment & discharge

HURST, William, Co-64-1; Pvt F Co 13th KY Cav; 28 Sep 63 to 20 Jan 65; Newport PO; rheumatism
HURST, William M., Se-219-1; Elisabeth widow of; Pvt I Co 2nd TN Cav; 62 to 65; heart trouble
HURT, Christmas, F-46-1; Susan widow of; A Co 61st TN; 3 yrs; LaGrange PO
HURT, Claiborne, Mu-213-1; Pvt K Co 12th TN Inf; 7 Aug 63 to Apr 65; Glenns Store PO
HURT, John, Mu-213-1; Susan J. widow of; Pvt 15th MI Cav; 12 Jul 61 to 1 Apr 64; Rally Hill PO
HURT, John, D-75-1; Lt F Co 30th TN Inf; 1 Oct 61 to 1 Jun 62; Stewarts Ferry PO; CONF
HURT, John Jr., Mu-213-1; Pvt K Co 12th TN Inf; 7 Aug 63 to Jan 65; Rally Hill PO; feet frost bit, now suffering from rheumatism
HURT, Robert R., We-223-2; Judith F. widow of; Pvt I Co 6th TN Cav; 5 Jun 62 to 26 Jul 65; Palmersville PO; died in Oct 1872
HURT, Thomas L., B-3-1; Pvt F Co 5th TN Cav; 9-1-62 to 6-25-65; Coldwell PO
HURT, Warner, D-91-3; Mary widow of; Pvt; 500 N. College St., Nashville PO
HURTT, Isham, S-213-3; Pvt B Co 2nd TN Inf; Aug 61 to Nov 64; New River PO; chronic direah, rheumatism & piles
HURTT, Ruben, S-213-1; Pvt K Co 30th KY Mtd Inf; 63 to 10 Apr 65; Huntsville PO
HUSE, M. F., Pi-153-1; Sgt D Co 12th KY Inf; 10-10-61 to 8-3-65; Chanute PO; rheumatism
HUSELBACHER, John Valentine, Gi-127-2; Pvt A Co 1st MI Engineers; Dec 24 63 to Sep 28 65; Pulaski PO; rheumatism in shoulder and fever in bowels
HUSKEY, Fredrick, Se-220-1; Pvt E Co 2nd TN Cav; Sep 62 to 63; Emurts Cave PO; disease of the liver
HUSKEY, Louis, Se-224-3; Pvt E Co 9th TN Cav; 1 Oct 63 to 11 Sep 65; Line Spring PO; rupture & rheumatism
HUSKY, Anna (see Webb, Riley)
HUSKINS, John, U-247-1; Pvt M Co 8th TN Cav; 15 Sep 63 to 11 Apr 65; Erwin PO; lung & heart disease
HUSKINS, Juble H., Wa-265-1; Pvt A Co 3rd NC Inf; Dec 65 to __; Trump PO; rheumatism
HUSKINS, William, U-244-1; Pvt N Co 8th KS? Cav; 15 Sep 63 to 11 Sep 65; Trump PO; gun shot wound right eye?
HUSKINS, William H., U-246-2; Cpl M Co 8th TN Cav; 15 Sep 63 to 11 Sep 65; Erwin PO
HUSKISSON, George M., Gr-74-2; Pvt B Co 8th TN Cav; 4 Jul 64 to 11 Sep 65; May Spring PO
HUSKITH?, James L., We-221-4; Pvt M Co TN Cav; 16 Dec 61 to 5 May 63; Martin PO; CONF
HUSKY, John, Se-220-1; Pvt E Co 2nd TN Cav; 3 Jun 63 to 3 Dec 63; Emurts Cave PO
HUSKY, Welcome (or William), Co-67-3; Rhoda Murr widow of; Pvt 2nd TN Cav; Sep 62 to __; Cosby PO; died in service
HUSTAND, Thos. J., Sh-203-1; Pvt 154th TN Reg; Memphis PO; US
HUSTON, Clark, Pu-142-1; Pvt K Co 4th TN Mtd Inf; 64 to 8-65; Shuyle PO; rheumatism
HUSTON, Henry, Col, Mg-196-4; Pvt D Co 29th IL Inf; Memphis PO
HUSTON, Nelson, Me-93-1; Pvt D Co 12th TN Inf; 11-63 to 10-65; Ten Mile PO; shot in left hip &c
HUTCHERSON, George, Ch-14-1; Sarah J. widow of; Pvt C Co 52nd TN Inf; 12-19-61 to __; Sweet Lips PO; CONF
HUTCHERSON, Jackson, Sh-149-2; Pvt M Co 3rd Hvy Art; 22 Dec 63 to 3 Apr 66; Frazer PO
HUTCHERSON, William T., We-221-2; Pvt I Co 10th NC Art; Mar 62 to Apr 65; Martin PO; CONF
HUTCHESON, John A., M-107-5; Francis widow of; Pvt; Willette PO
HUTCHINS, Rollin, W-189-4; 1st Sgt K Co 153rd NY Vol Inf; 5-30-62 to 10-2-65; McMinnville PO
HUTCHINS, Stiles L., H-57-1; Pvt A Co 15th US Col; 64 to 65; Chattanooga PO; all papers lost in flood, 1867
HUTCHINS, Thomas P., We-233-1(2); Pvt L Co 6th TN Cav; 63 to 65; Ralston PO; kidney disease, paroled by Forrest at Dresden
HUTCHINS, William K., H-51-3; Pvt; Hill City PO
HUTCHINSON, George, Un-255-1; Pvt F Co 6th TN; 10 Ma 62 to 24 Ma 65; Warwicks X Roads PO

HUTCHINSON, James, T-219-1; alias Stewart Dicus; Pvt I Co 4th PA Inf; Nov 62 to 4 Jul 65; Phelan PO
HUTCHINSON, John, A-2-3; Edith Pike formerly widow of; Co D 1st TN Inf; Andersonville PO
HUTCHISON, Andy, St-160-2; Pvt 50th TN Inf; 61 to Feb 14 62; Big Rock PO; CONF
HUTCHISON, Charles, Mu-195-2; Sol; Columbia PO
HUTCHISON, Mary A. (see Rodgers, Alexander)
HUTCHISON, Ruben, Bl-3-2; Sgt F Co 2nd TN Cav; 6-4-62 to 5-30-65; Billingsly PO; CONF
HUTCHISON, Sarah E., D-78-1; widow; Pvt Marine; 63 to 65; Nashville PO
HUTCHISON, William, Un-251-1; Effie PO
HUTCHISON, William, Un-254-2; Pvt D Co 6th TN Inf; 18 Apr 62 to 27 Apr 65; Paulett PO
HUTCHISON, William, A-1-1; Pvt S Co 9th TN Cav; 7-4-63 to 9-15-65; Andersonville PO
HUTCHSON, Maston, Un-255-1; Pvt H Co 9th TN Cav?; 4 Ju 63 to 11 Sep 65; Lay's X Roads PO; blind
HUTSELL, Arabella F. (see Guthrie, Shaderick A.)
HUTSELL, William H., Mc-112-10; Sgt A Co 7th TN Mtd Inf; 9-12-64 to __; Athens PO
HUTSON, George W., Po-148-3; 2nd Dist
HUTSON, Hugh L. W., Lo-193-1; Pvt M Co 1st Col Hvy Art; 25 Oct 64 to 31 Mar 66; Unitia PO
HUTSON, John E., S-215-1; 1st Lt A Co 1st TN Inf; 3 Aug 61 to 3 Jul 62; Jeffers PO; rheumatism caused by cold & exposure
HUTSON, Reuben, Gr-73-1; Pvt G Co 11th TN Cav; Oct 62 to Aug 65; Westerville PO; rupture of mumps while in US Service
HUTSON, Reuben, C-25-1; Pvt A Co 1st TN Inf; 8-2-61 to 9-17-64; Agee PO; diareah & piles
HUTSON, Richard, Un-251-2; Pvt H Co 7th TN Inf; Oct 63 to Jul 65; Esco PO
HUTSON, William R., C-24-3; Pvt I Co 173rd IN Inf; 12-8-63 to 8-25-75; 1st Dist
HUTTON, John C., K-171-6(5); Pvt C Co 29th TN Inf; 62 to 65; PO omitted; CONF
HUTTON, John N., Mo-129-1; Pvt 4th TN Inf; Four Mile Branch PO
HUTTON, William, K-175-2; Pvt D Co 6th TN Inf; 6 Mar 62 to 7 Mar 65; Bullrun PO
HUY, Zeachariah T., K-181-5(2); Pvt; 64 to 65; PO omitted; CONF
HUYES, Susan (see Barnnett, Jobe)
HYATT, Ephraim J., Hm-109-4; Elizabeth widow of; Lt L Co 9th TN Cav; 20 Sep 63 to __; Whitesburg PO
HYATT, John A., Cl-58-1; Pvt I Co 2nd TN Inf; 3 mos; Minkton PO; no discharge, can't tell much about it
HYATT, Nathan, Ja-87-1; Rachel widow of; Pvt C Co 8th TN Cav; 5-5-63 to 9-11-65; Apison PO; diarrhea
HYBARGAR, Isaac, Ge-100-2; Pvt B Co 8th TN Inf; 15 Dec 62 to 16 May 65; Midway PO
HYBARGER, Jacob H., Ge-91-5; Pvt K Co 1st TN Cav; 17 Mar 63 to 19 Jan 65; Greeneville PO; piles & rheumatism
HYBURGER, Jacob, Ge-90-2; Pvt B Co 8th TN Inf; 15 Dec 62 to 30 Jun 65; Greenvill PO; hear disease & piles, tifoid fevor the cause
HYDE, Absalom, St-163-1; US Sol; Dover PO
HYDE, Andrew J., Mc-110-2(1); Pvt I Co 7th TN Inf; 1-1-65 to 6-27-65; Zengles PO
HYDE, Boyd, D-91-3; Hall, Polly widow of; Pvt L? Co TN Inf; 3 yrs; Station C, Nashville PO
HYDE, Cornelius M., Po-152-5(1); Cpl D Co 7th TN Mtd Inf--9-16-64 to 7-28-65; Pvt G Co 11th TN Cav--9-16-63 to 65; Ducktown PO; gun shot wound of thigh, left the 11th and enlisted in the 7th
HYDE, George W., Mc-110-3(1); Pvt F Co 2nd TN Cav; Mouse Creek PO; discharge lost
HYDE, Gustavus A., Cr-13-1; Pvt G Co 3rd KY Cav; Sep 61 to Jun 1 65; Atwood PO; dont know exact date of enlistment or discharge
HYDE, Levy, Ce-23-1; Sol; 61 to 65; Thomasville PO
HYDE, Phineas, La-115-2; Pvt I Co 8th Con Inf; 1 Jan 64 to 1 Sep 65; Summertown PO
HYDE, Wesly, D-91-2; Pvt; Phipps Grocery, Jefferson St, Nashville PO
HYDE, William B., Po-149-2(1); Pvt E Co 5th TN Mtd Inf; 9-25-64 to 6-26-65; Conasauga PO; Mtd Inf one year

HYDER, Andrew J. F., Ct-38-1; Pvt B Co 4th TN Inf; 2-1-64 to 8-2-65; Happy Valley PO; injurie eyesight & lame shoulder
HYDER, Denson, Ct-40-4; 1st Sgt B Co 4th TN Inf; 4-13-63 to 65; Elizabethton PO; heart disease result of rheumatism
HYDER, Jacob, Ct-39-3; Pvt F Co 8th TN Cav; Gap Run PO; diorhoea & piles
HYDER, John L., Ct-44-1; Catherine widow of; 2nd Lt C Co 13th TN Cav; 63 to __: Hampton PO; heart disease from small pox, discharge lost
HYDER, Sampson, Cu-15-3; Cpl H Co 20th KY Inf; 1-9-64 to 4-18-65; Woody PO; I never received bounty
HYDER, Susanne, Ct-39-3; widow?; Gap Run PO
HYDER, William F. M., Ct-39-3; Lt R Co 13th TN Cav; 63 to __; Gap Run PO; thrown from horse, roar of cannon
HYDER, William P., Ge-95-1; Pvt A Co 13th TN Cav; 22 Sep 63 to 5 Sep 65; Home PO
HYDER, William R., Cu-16-1; Pvt G Co 6th TN Mtd Inf; 2-20-65 to 6-30-65; Crossville PO
HYMAN, David, Sh-179-3(1); Pvt E Co 137th US Inf; 4-8-65 to 1-15-66; Memphis PO
HYNDS, Constant H., We-233-2; Master Sgt K Co 6th TN Cav; 7-20-62 to 7-26-65; Ralston PO; imprisoned at Camp Butler IL 9 mos
HYNDS, David, We-233-2; 18th Dist
HYSAW, Henry, Sm-176-1; Pvt K Co KY; 11-7-63 to 4-18-65; Rome PO; unable to work
HYSINGER, Benjamin F., Br-13-1; Pvt E Co 4th TN Cav; 63 to 65; Cleveland PO; chronic bronchitis
HYSMITH, C. C., Rb-220-1; Pvt B Co 30th TN; Mar? 11 61 to May 20 65; Barrenplains PO; CONF
HYSOE, Fred, Pi-153-1; Anna widow of; Chanute PO
IDEMAN, Mason (see William, Henry)
IGO, James L., H-68-2; Batery Officer B Co 1st TN Vol Lt Art; 11-1-62 to 7-20-65; Chattanooga PO; now dead, widow living
IKARD, James M., Fr-114-1; Pvt I Co 53rd IN Inf; 3-6-64 to 1-20-65; Alto PO; heart disease
ILES, John, H-58-4; Pvt I Co 2nd TN Inf; Sale Creek PO; loss of jaw bone, has no discharge for some cause
INCH, Danial W., Ge-83-2; Horse Creek PO; suposed to hav be killed
ING, Fannie, Sh-178-3; widow US; 180 Lauderdale, Memphis PO
INGERS, Mary M. B., K-156-5; widow US Sol; 44 E Church St, Knoxville PO
INGERSOLL, Samuel, H-74-1; Pvt; 820 10th St, Chattanooga PO
INGG, __, D-57-3; Comisary; 61 to 65; Nashville PO; Co I 44th TN; CONF
INGHRAM, John H., Ch-14-2; Pvt C Co 33 1st TN Inf; 7-10-61 to 4-10-65; PO omitted; CONF
INGHRAM, Kim P., Ch-14-2; Pvt C Co 52nd TN Cav; 63 to 64; PO omitted; CONF
INGLE, Elbert C., Ja-85-3; Pvt A Co 8th TN Inf; __ to 6-30-65; Georgetown PO; chronic diarrhoea
INGLE, George H., Br-13-3; Pvt A Co 8th TN Inf; 5-6-63 to 6-30-65; Ora PO; chronic bronchitis
INGLE, Henry, Ge-86-1; Melvina widow of; died in service, enlistment and regiment not known; Thula PO
INGRAHAM, George, Sh-193-2; Pvt; Memphis PO
INGRAHAM, John, Ch-17-1; Jane widow of; Pvt B Co 55th Col Inf; Henderson PO
INGRAHAM, Marcena, H-49-7; Pvt E Co 104th NY? Inf; 11-20-61 to 11-24-64; Daisy PO; wounded in breast
INGRAIN, Dodson T., Dy-25-9(1); Pvt A Co; 8-62 to __ (6 mos); Newbern PO; dates of enlistment unknown
INGRAM, David, Ro-202-5; Sgt C Co 7th TN Inf; 2 Aug 64 to 6 Jul 65; Cave Creek PO; chronic diarrhea, lungs & indigestion
INGRAM, Henry P., He-62-2; Pvt Co A 7th TN Cav; Aug 62 to Aug 65; Lone Elm PO; chronic dirhea and scurvy
INGRAM, James, Dk-34-3; Sarah widow of; Pvt A Co 5th TN Cav; 7-28-62 to __; Dowelltown PO
INGRAM, Jas. E., Dk-36-2; Pvt F Co 4th TN Mtd Inf; 64 to 64; Smithville PO
INGRAM, Jessee, La-117-3; Pvt A Co 48th TN Inf; Jan 2 62 to 65; 15th Dist; CONF

INGRAM, Jim R., Gi-134-1; Dist 14
INGRAM, K., Je-137-1; Elizabeth widow of; Pvt C Co 6th IN Cav; Hickory Ridge PO
INGRAM, Lucinda (see Smith, Daniel)
INGRAM, Moses S., Lo-195-2(1); Pvt I Co 1st TN Inf; 8 Oct 62 to Aug 65; Oral PO (Roane Co.); lung & bowel trouble, measels settled on them
INGRAM, Nancy N., He-58-2; widow of soldier; 7th Civil Dist
INGRAM, Wash, F-39-1; Pvt E Co 59th US Col Inf; May 63 to 27 Jan 66; Galloway PO
INGRAM, Wesley, Col, Ma-119-1; Pvt G Co 107th or 111th AL Inf; 7 mos 13 days; Jackson PO; Hood chased him out of Block house at Tullahoma & he went home
INGRAM, William, Ct-38-2; Pvt F Co 8th TN Cav; 5-31-63 to 9-11-65; Dry Creek PO; diarrhea & jaundice
INGRHAM, Jordan, Hy-79-1; Pvt; Civil Dist No 6
INGRUM, John, K-173-1; Pvt C Co 1st TN Cav; 1 Apr 62 to 1 Apr 65; McMillen PO; measles settled in lungs
INMAN, Charles, Se-221-2; 2nd Maj 2nd TN Cav; 1 Dec 62 to 12 Mar 63; Fair Garden PO
INMAN, Green, Co-61-5(2); Pvt K Co 8th TN Cav; 10 Sep 63 to 11 Sep 65; Bridgeport PO; hurt shoeing horse
INMAN, James C., Dy-25-6(2); Francis widow of; Capt; Newbern PO; CONF
INMAN, James C., Hm-207-5; Pvt D Co 8th TN Inf; 28 Mar 63 to 17 Aug 65; Springvale PO; bronchitis lung trouble
INMAN, James T., D-90-1; Cpl G Co 10th TN Inf; Jun 62 to Jun 65; PO omitted
INMAN, Joseph, Co-67-1; Susannah Whitehead widow of; Pvt E Co 2nd TN Cav; 28 Dec 62 to ___; Cosby PO; died while on parole at Anapolis
INMAN, John M., Me-93-1; Sarah widow of; Pvt K Co 7th TN Mtd Inf; 64 to 65; Sewee PO; now disabled and homeless
INMAN, William, Hm-105-1; Pvt D Co 4th TN Inf; 20 Nov 62 to 10 Aug 65; Morristown PO; health injured
INNMAN, George W., Pu-144-2; Cpl C Co 10th TN Cav; 11-4-63 to 8-7-65; Bloomington PO
INNMAN, William, Co-63-3; Martha widow of; Pvt A Co 2nd TN Inf; Newport PO
INUSLEY?, Aron, Ro-210-9; Pvt; Rockwood PO; CONF
IRICH, Marcus, A-1-1; Pvt F Co 6th TN Inf; 3-10-62 to 3-10-65; Andersonville PO
IRICK, Robert, Un-251-1; Sarah M. widow of; Cpl G Co 2nd TN Cav; 1 Oct 62 to 63; Effie PO; gun shot in right wrist
IRON, George, T-218-1; Pvt C Co 13th TN Inf; 13 Jun 61 to 12 Aug 66; Tabernacle PO; shot in the arm
IRONS, Alvin J., Mo-122-2; Lt 7th TN Mtd Inf; Madisonville PO; dates could not be gotten
IRONS, Lafayett, Po-152-3(1); Pvt E Co 14th IL Cav; Ducktown PO
IRVIN, Albert, L-105-1; Pvt C Co 2nd IL Cav; Oct 62 to Dec 23 63; Curve PO; taken prisner Dec 21 1863
IRVIN, George, Hy-76-2; US Sol; Stanton Depot PO
IRVIN, Jennie (see Ventrici, Robert)
IRVIN, Jesse D., Wi-281-1; Pvt 77th OH; Jul 64 to Sep 65; Allisona PO
IRVIN, Lucas, Mu-210-5; alias Lucius Hamlet; Pvt I Co 111th US Col TN Inf; 2-1-64 to 64 (7 mos 25 days); Spring Hill PO; taken prisoner 9-25-64 at Sulphur Branch, TN
IRVIN, Richard, Co-69-2; Pvt E Co TN Cav; 62 to 64; Rankin PO; legions dont no dats
IRVINE, Nicholas, Mu-196-1; Sgt C Co 40th Reg; May 64 to 66; Columbia PO
IRVINE, Samuel, We-224-1; Savanna widow of; Pvt TN Cav; 62 to Dec 63; Como PO (Henry Co.); CONF
IRVING, Andrew J., H-69-3; Pvt A Co TN Cav; 6-5-63 to 9-5-65; Chattanooga PO
IRVING, John D., Lo-187-3; Capt B Co 26th IN Inf; 25 Jun 61 to Aug 63; Loudon PO
IRVING, Lindsay, H-57-2; Pvt C Co 15th TN Col; 63 to 65; Orchard Knob PO
IRWIN, Alexander, Bo-13-3(1); Pvt C Co 9th TN Cav; 6-9-63 to 12-9-63; Moser PO
IRWIN, Cal, Mu-197-1; Pvt B Co 15th Col Inf; 64 to Apr 12 65; Columbia PO; shot in both legs
IRWIN, Charley, Wa-263-3; alias Erwin, Charles; Pvt G Co 40th US Col; Apr 20 65 to Apr 20 66; Garbers Mills PO; powder burnt in eyes
IRWIN, George W., C-25-1; Pvt I Co 7th TN Mtd Inf; 11-10-64 to 7-27-65; Agee PO; consumption
IRWIN, Jo, B-5-1; Fannie Daniel formerly widow of; Pvt I Co 17th US Col Inf; 11-30-63 to 4-25-66; Bell Buckle PO; was afflected with small pox while in the service, died in 1881
IRWIN, Martha, Hd-48-1; Savannah PO
IRWIN, Miller F., C-24-4(3); Pvt I Co 7th TN Mtd Inf; 11-8-64 to 7-27-65; Forkvale PO; catarr of head, bronchitus & chronic diarhea
IRWIN, Robert, D-67-2; Pvt Col Inf; Nashville PO
IRWIN, Robert M., Se-227-3; Pvt A Co 2nd TN Inf; Aug 63 to 65; Trundles X Roads PO
IRWIN, William, D-64-1; Pvt; Nashville PO
IRWIN, William H., K-159-2; Martha C. widow of; Pvt H Co 9th MI Inf; 18 Mar 61 to 25 Sep 65; served 3 yrs and re-enlisted vetren; Knoxville PO
ISAAC, Edward (see Bradshaw, George)
ISAAC, Russell, Bo-15-2; Pvt H Co 2nd TN Cav; 10-10-62 to 7-6-65; Maryville PO
ISAACS, Solomon, Wa-274-3; Lts? Fort Henry; 10 Jun 64 to 15 Aug 65; Jonesboro PO
ISABLE, John W., H-52-1; Pvt A Co 31st MS Inf; 61 to 65; Wauhatchie PO
ISBELL, Anthony, Sh-204-1; Pvt G Co 11th TN Inf; Walker Ave, Memphis PO
ISBELL, George, Sh-150-3; George Smiff; Pvt D Co 59th TN Inf; Jan 64 to May 65; Bartlett PO
ISBELL, Henry, Sn-250-2; Dist 1 and 2
ISBELL, James R., Mu-199-1; Pvt B Co Cav; Mt. Pleasant PO
ISBELL, Marian, Mo-126-1; Pvt D Co 3rd TN Mtd Inf; 7-25-64 to 11-30-64; Hopewell Springs PO
ISBELL, Nelson, Mo-129-1; Pvt H Co 20th KY Inf; 12-25-63 to 8-64; Huling PO
ISBELL, Sarah A., Mo-122-2; widow of _____; 6th Civil Dist
ISBILL, Marques, Lo-190-1; Ord Sgt K Co 3rd TN Inf; May 63 to __; Loudon PO; CONF
ISBILL, Theodric L., Lo-190-2; Quartermaster 3rd TN Inf; 64 to 65; Loudon PO
ISENBERG, Jacob A., K-168-3; Knoxville PO
ISHAM, William F., Ro-208-1; Pvt B Co 5th TN Inf; 25 Feb 62 to 30 Mar 65; Barnardsville PO; chronic direa
ISIMINGER, Joseph, R-163-2; Pvt B Co 31st WI Inf; 8-15-62 to 6-20-65; Graysville PO; injured in back
ISOM, Charles, Ha-111-1; Pvt E Co 13th TN Cav; Sep 63 to Apr 65; Upper Clinch PO; CONF
ISRAEL, Andrew M., A-2-2; Pvt D Co 1st KY Cav; Bull Run PO (Knox Co.); wounds head, side & left knee (I have some doubts about this record--note by marshall)
ISREAL, John W., Mr-102-2; Cpl I Co 79th IN Inf; 8-14-62 to 6-7-65; South Pittsburg PO
ISS, John, Sn-252-1; Pvt I Co 1st KY Inf; 5-61 to 5-64; Gallatin PO
IVANES, Richerd Mc., Se-220-1; Pvt E Co 2nd TN Cav; 15 Sep 63 to Oct 64; Emurts Cave PO
IVANS, Andrew, K-181-1; Pvt C Co 6th TN Inf; 18 Apr 62 to 27 Apr 65; Flenekin PO
IVANS, Polk, Sn-252-1; Pvt K Co 14th tN Inf; 1-1-64 to 3-26-66; Gallatin PO
IVANS, S. C., Ge-96-2; Pvt D Co 8th TN Cav; 29 Sep 63 to 11 Sep 65; Jockey PO; catarrh, mashed testicle
IVANS, William N., K-181-1; Pvt D Co 4th TN; 12 Sep 62 to 12 Jul 65; Knoxville PO
IVES, William (white), Fr-115-1; Pvt C Co 12th IN? Cav; 9-21-61 to 7-15-62; Cowan PO; wounded by fall from horse
IVEY, Caloway B., Ch-18-1; Pvt H Co 52nd TN Inf; 19 Dec 62 to 6 May 63; PO omitted; CONF
IVEY, James, Je-137-3; Manerva widow of; Pvt; Chestnut Hill PO
IVEY, James B., Mo-129-2; Pvt TN; Povo PO
IVEY, Thomas W., Co-69-5; Pvt A Co 5th SC Inf; 22 Aug 62 to 9 Apr 65; Driskill PO; dont remember dates well; CONF

IVEY, Willis, Sh-148-1; William Hotes?; Pvt G Co; Memphis PO
IVIE, Mitchell, G-56-1; Pvt; Trenton PO
IVINS, Alexander, Bl-2-1; Pvt A Co; 2-62 to 65; Glade Creek PO; discharge lost
IVORY, John S., Sh-201-3; Memphis PO
IVRY, Garland, T-216-1; Mary Hair widow of; Corona PO
IVUNS, Alfred, Br-12-5; Pvt H Co 8th IL Inf; 6-14-63 to 8-29-65; Sydneyton PO; shot in jaw
IVY, Claborn, F-20-3; Pvt C Co Hvy Art Inf; May 62 to May 65; Hickory Withe PO
IVY, George, C-28-1; Nancy widow of; Pvt 6th TN; Fincastle PO
IVY, Jack, Sh-178-1; Fannie widow of; Rear 180 Wellington, Memphis PO; died from effects of wound; CONF
IVY, James, C-28-1; Pvt F Co 6th TN Inf; 3-10-62 to 3-15-65; Fincastle PO; pleurisy
IVY, James H., F-40-2; SgtB Co 15th TN Cav; Feb 64 to May 65; Hickory Withe PO; CONF
IVY, Joseph, C-29-1; Pvt C Co 4th TN Cav; 8-61 to 2-62; Fincastle PO
IVY, Robert L., F-40-2; Lt B Co TN Cav; May 61 to May 65; Hickory Withe PO; prisoner at Caro 10 days; CONF
JABES, William H., Dy-22-1; Clerk, MI Civil Engineers; Jul 18 62 to Apr 65; Quartermaster; Dyersburg PO; CONF
JACK, D. B., F-44-2; Pvt B Co 7th TN; Feb 62 to Apr 65; PO omitted; CONF
JACK, John, Co-63-3; Pvt H Co 1st TN Art; ___ 63 to Apr 65 (2 yrs); Newport PO
JACK, Samuel E. G., Mu-210-5; Pvt Mury Art Indp. Co; 10-61 to paroled 7-63; Carters Creek PO; CONF
JACK, Samuel H., Mc-117-2; Mecca PO
JACKS, Frances M., Mc-117-2; Pvt? K Co 3rd TN Cav; 2-1-64 to 6-10-65; Mortimer PO
JACKSON, Addison (see Stephens, Jerry)
JACKSON, Albert, Sh-196-3; Memphis PO
JACKSON, Alfred, Sh-149-4; US Sol; 6th Civil Dist
JACKSON, Alick, Mt-147-1; Pvt C Co 16th US Col Cav TN; 7-64 to 66; Collinsvill PO; discharge in Washington
JACKSON, Allison, Ms-182-1; Pvt A Co 38th IL; 63 to ___; Venna PO; defective right wrist, labors in Tarm
JACKSON, Amos L., Mc-112-3; Cpl L Co 1st TN Col Hvy Art; ___ to 3-64; Athens PO; discharge at Washington DC
JACKSON, Amos G., J-82-2; Pvt C Co 8th TN Mtd Inf; 2-10-65 to 8-17-65; Bloomington PO; rheumatism
JACKSON, Anderson (see Bradshaw, Anderson)
JACKSON, Andrew, Hw-130-1; Pvt B Co 48th VA Inf; 4 Jun 61 to Sep 64; Lee Valley PO; piles; CONF
JACKSON, Andrew, H-49-6; Nancy Minyard formerly widow of; Pvt A Co 6th TN Mtd Inf; 8-2-64 to 6-30-65; Lakeside PO
JACKSON, Andrew, H-67-3; Seaman Numkeap? #37; 63 to 65 (1 yr 6 mos); Chattanooga PO
JACKSON, Andrew, Sh-191-6(2); Memphis PO; records not seen
JACKSON, Andrew (see Partlow, Jack)
JACKSON, Andrew J., H-67-3; Andrew Fouchea alias; Pvt K Co 44th US Col Inf; 8-23-64 to 5-1-65; Chattanooga PO; shot in left shoulder, now ruptured, wears truss
JACKSON, Andy, Hw-125-5; Stony Point PO
JACKSON, Arthur B., Cy-27-3(1); Pvt E Co 5th KY Cav; 12-15-61 to 5-65; Exeda PO; fracture of right fore arm
JACKSON, Benjamin, Gr-79-3; Pvt B Co 1st TN; 9 Apr 62 to 10 Apr 65; Ball Point PO; shoulder mashed
JACKSON, Bill, J-81-1; Pvt G Co 37th KY; 8-1-63 to 2-21-65; 8th Civil Dist
JACKSON, Charles, K-158-2; Pvt A Co 9th TN Inf; 63 to 65; Knoxville PO, 117 Payne St; chronic rheumatism
JACKSON, Charles, Sh-158-3; 2nd Sgt F Co 61st Col Inf; 30 Jun 63 to Dec 66; Memphis PO; Jackson has a printed copy of his company record in which his name and rank appears, has $24 pension money, his discharge lost by A. D. Smith

JACKSON, Charles R., Ov-136-1; Livingston PO
JACKSON, David, Wl-293-1; F Co Inf; 61 to 63; Austin PO; CONF
JACKSON, David C., Mg-196-2; Sgt A Co 4th TN Cav; 15 Oct 62 to 12 Jul 65; Coalfield PO
JACKSON, Elijah J., Mu-213-2; 2nd Sgt G Co 47th NC Inf; May 61 to Jul 65; Hardisons Mills PO; CONF
JACKSON, Elisha S., Me-92-4(1); Pvt M Co 8th TN Cav; 1-15-64 to 9-11-65; Pin Hook PO; hurting in back & hip caused by being thrown from horse
JACKSON, Flemming, K-154-6(3); Knoxville PO; defective in sight 25 yrs; dont acertain rank
JACKSON, Frank, Sh-158-6(4); Pvt H Co 11th US Inf; 63 to 65; Memphis PO; discharged at close of war with discharge papers
JACKSON, Frank, Sh-191-4; Memphis PO; records not seen
JACKSON, George, L-108-1; Pvt H Co 17th TN Col US; Oct 63 to Apr 65; Glimpville PO
JACKSON, George A., Sh-196-2; Sgt A Co 75th US Inf; 7-10-63 to 8-65; 20 Madison St, Memphis PO; wounded at Ft. Fisher
JACKSON, George W., Dy-28-1; Pvt F Co 2nd TN Mtd Inf; Dec 25 63 to Dec 20 65; Finley PO; shocked by thunder & throwed by horse 4 times, no pension
JACKSON, George W., Gr-79-3; Pvt E Co 9th TN Cav; Mar 64 to 65; Thorn Hill PO
JACKSON, George W., H-58-1; Rutha Culvahouse formerly widow of; Sale Creek PO; discharge misplaced
JACKSON, Harris, Ha-110-3; Jemima widow of; Pvt L Co 8th TN Cav; Treadway PO
JACKSON, Henderson, Sh-147-1; Pvt G Co 63rd AR Inf; 10 Apr 63 to 4 Mar 65; Ramsey PO
JACKSON, Henry E., Gr-79-4; Lt E Co 9th TN Cav; 9 Apr 62 to 27 Jul 65; Thorn Hill PO; eyes & stomach
JACKSON, Huston, Je-139-1; Cpl; Trion PO
JACKSON, Isac, Wl-293-3; Pvt G Co TN; 63 to 63 (6 mos); Buhler PO; CONF
JACKSON, Isah G., Tr-269-1; Pvt A Co 7th TN Cav; 5 Sep 62 to 15 Jul 64; John PO
JACKSON, Jacob, L-103-1; J. F. Bratten (same line); Pvt E Co 1st Conf Cav; Nov 11 61 to 65; Ashport PO; leg broken; surrendered with army; CONF
JACKSON, James, Dy-25-3; Pvt 2nd TN Cav; 4 yrs; Newbern PO; CONF
JACKSON, James, Ha-110-1; Sgt L Co 9th TN Cav; Oct 63 to Mar 65; Bray's PO; rheumatism
JACKSON, James C., Ct-44-1; Pvt G Co 13th TN Cav; 9-24-63 to 9-5-65; Hampton PO
JACKSON, JAmes E., Mo-124-1; Pvt D Co 1st TN Art; 1 yr 10 mos; 4 Mile Branch PO; bone fever; discharge lost--can make proof
JACKSON, James H., Ge-87-3; 2nd Sgt M Co 9th TN Cav; Jun 63 to 11 Sep 65; Pates Hill PO; rheumatism
JACKSON, James K. P., Ge-98-1; Pvt F Co 3rd TN Mtd Inf; PO omitted; chronic diarhea
JACKSON, John, F-42-1(3); Pvt 1st US Cal; Spring 62 to ___; Elba PO; Horn? ran against tree in war, cant find particulars, lost papers
JACKSON, John (see Lyhugh, John)
JACKSON, John, Hy-82-1; Pvt A Co 4th KY Hvy Art; May 63 to Feb 66; Brownsville PO
JACKSON, John, Sh-146-4; 3rd Civil Dist
JACKSON, John, Fr-109-1; Sgt H Co 104th IL Inf; Jul 62 to 62 (5 mos); Huntland PO
JACKSON, John, Sm-166-2; Pvt K Co 17th TN Inf; 11-62 to 65; Carthage PO; shot 3 times, once arm & hand--leg
JACKSON, John, D-68-2; Pvt E Co 12th USC Inf; 123 Fairfield Ave, Nashville PO
JACKSON, John, Gr-79-2; Catharine widow of; Lt 9th TN; Ball Point PO; wounded in right hip
JACKSON, John, D-50-1; Addie widow of; Pvt; 63 to 66; 611 N. Summer, Nashville PO; no rec. or papers
JACKSON, John, Sh-173-1; Pvt C Co 13th OH Inf; 4-20-63 to 12-25-64; Memphis PO
JACKSON, John A., O-138-2; 2nd Sgt I Co 33rd TN; 15 Nov 61 to 15 May 65; Elbridge PO; CONF

163

JACKSON, John E., Dy-25-4; Pvt G Co 42nd AL Inf; 62 to 65; Newbern PO; CONF
JACKSON, John J., Mc-112-2; Pvt K Co 10th TN Cav; 2-10-64 to 7-15-64; Athens PO
JACKSON, Joseph, F-39-1; Pvt K Co 3rd US Cav; Feb 63 to Jan 66; Braden PO
JACKSON, Joshua S. P., J-82-2; Almira widow of; Pvt TN Mtd Inf; Bloomington PO; disease lungs & throat
JACKSON, Katie (see Davis, Wm., D-64-5)
JACKSON, Lemuel, Sh-197-1; Memphis PO
JACKSON, Levi, Pu-141-2; Pvt K Co 4th TN Inf; 11-1-64 to 8-25-65; Dry Valley PO; discharged at close of war
JACKSON, Liemoler?, Dk-32-2; Milly C. widow of; Pvt G Co 1st TN Mtd Inf; Alexandria PO
JACKSON, Logan, Pu-147-2; Pvt G Co 8th TN Mtd Inf; 1-1-65 to 8-24-65; Byrne PO; rupture
JACKSON, Lydia (see Gates, Moses)
JACKSON, Nancy, H-76-3; widow Sol US; Chattanooga PO
JACKSON, Nick, Sh-153-1; Pvt G Co 55th USC Inf; 1 Jun 63 to 31 Dec 65; Collierville PO
JACKSON, Peter, K-167-1; 1st Hvy TN; 62 to 65; Knoxville PO
JACKSON, Peter, Ha-116-2; widow US Sol; Dist No 13
JACKSON, Richard C., Ge-98-1; Pvt H Co 4th TN Cav; 4 Aug 63 to 12 Jul 65; PO omitted; rheumatism & disease of heart
JACKSON, Robert, Mt-148-1; Pvt I Co 16th OH; 11-63 to 2-65; Orgains X Roads PO; shot in right arm & left leg, the veteran does not remember date of discharge
JACKSON, Robert, Ge-94-3; Pvt L Co 1st US Cav Hvy Art; 14 Aug 62 to 9 Apr 66; Ham PO; rheumatism during war in 1865
JACKSON, Robert, D-51-1; Pvt F Co 14th US Col Inf; 63 to 65; 122 Gay St, Nashville PO
JACKSON, Simon, Sh-158-6(4); Cpl F Co 61st US Col Inf; Jun 63 to 14 Dec 65; Memphis PO; discharged at close of war with discharge papers
JACKSON, Stafford (see Townsend, Stafford)
JACKSON, Steven (see Turner, Steven)
JACKSON, Thomas J., Mc-115-1; Pvt I Co 1st US Hvy Art; 7-7-64 to 3-31-66; Riceville PO; dont know dates
JACKSON, Wesly, K-157-1; Knoxville PO
JACKSON, William, Cr-8-2; Pvt B Co 19th TN; 1 Sep 62 to 1 Sep 65; Maury City PO; shot thru r leg & l arm; CONF
JACKSON, William, D-101-1; Col; Frances widow of; Pvt F Co 15th US Inf; Dec 62 to May 65; 22nd Civil Dist
JACKSON, William, Gr-79-3; Pvt I Co 8th TN Inf; 9 Apr 62 to 10 Apr 65; Ball Point PO; fever, diarrhea and side pleurisy
JACKSON, William, Ge-91-4; Eliza J. widow of; Sgt B Co 14th US Inf; Greeneville PO
JACKSON, William, Rb-229-1; Pvt F Co 42nd TN Inf; Oct 62 to Apr 65; Keesburg, Logan Co., KY, PO; shot in left leg
JACKSON, William, Ce-31-2; Pvt 18th TN Inf; Mar 61 to 1 Mar 65; Ashland City PO
JACKSON, William A., H-49-5; Pvt A Co 6th TN Mtd Inf; 8-2-64 to 6-30-65; Lakeside PO
JACKSON, William H., Sh-159-5; Memphis PO; CONF
JACKSON, William J., Sm-172-1; Pvt K Co 1st TN Inf; 2-14-64 to 4-21-65; Temperance Hall PO (Dekalb Co); rheumatism of the chest
JACKSON, Wm. M., Rb-220-1; Pvt 80th TN; Oct 15 64 to Aug 20 65; Barrenplains PO; CONF
JACKSON, William T., H-53-1; 2 yrs; Chattanooga PO
JACO, Albert R., D-78-1; Pvt K Co 15th W VA Inf; Feb 15 65 to Jun 30 65; Nashville PO
JACO, Ellik J., Wl-299-1; Pvt M Co 5th TN Inf; 1 Oct 63 to Nov 65; Statesville PO
JACO, William, Wl-299-1; Pvt M Co 5th TN Inf; 1 Jan 64 to __ (9 mos); Statesville PO
JACOB, Sallie (see Allen, Charles, Sh-157-2)
JACOB, Wm., D-43-1; Pvt M Co 4th OH; 62 to 65; Nashville PO
JACOBS, George, H-60-1; Cora widow of; PA; Chattanooga PO; (prob. dead)
JACOBS, James, Sh-196-2; Pvt E Co 3rd US Hvy Art; 9-25-64 to 9-65; 120 Dunlap St, Memphis PO
JACOBS, John W., T-207-1; Covington PO
JACOBS, Wesley J., Je-137-3; Pvt G Co 4th TN Cav; 13 Nov 63 to 12 Jul 65; Chestnut Hill PO

JACOPS, Waren, Sh-188-2; Parine Service--Black Night? Squadron; 242 Looney St, Memphis PO
JACOX, Augustus, Cr-4-1; Cyrena F. widow of; Pvt; Bells Depot PO; wounded shoulder; CONF
JACSON, Ephraim (see Bowling, Ephraim)
JAMERSON, Abraham, Sh-152-2; Pvt C Co 88th TN Inf; Jan 63 to Jun 65; Dexter PO; trans'd to 59th Reg in 1863
JAMES, Alvin, Pu-145-3(4); Pvt C Co 37th KY Inf; 1-28-63 to 12-13-64; Silver Point PO
JAMES, Austin, Moo-215-1; Pvt B Co V Cav; 2 Aug 61 to 15 May 65; Tulahoma PO; gunshot in left knee
JAMES, Bartlett A., Sm-172-4; Pvt G Co 4th TN Inf; 11-1-64 to 8-15-65; Gordonsville PO
JAMES, Bryant, Co-66-2(1); Orpha B. widow of; Pvt E Co 2nd TN Cav; 16 Sep 62 to 5 Jul 65; Birdville PO
JAMES, Calvin, Je-140-1; Pvt 9th TN Cav; __ to 11 Sep 65; Lucilla PO; piles
JAMES, Davie, We-221-7; Cook E Co 54th IL Inf; 62 to 63; Martin PO
JAMES, David, Gi-122-6; Pvt G Co 110th TN Inf; Mar 62 to Apr 65; Prospect Sta. PO; military wagon run over leg
JAMES, Eule C., Ru-241-5; Cpl G Co 13th TN Inf; Murfreesboro PO
JAMES, Francis R., Co-64-2; Asener (sic) L. widow of; Pvt 2nd TN Cav; 61 to 64; Philips PO
JAMES, George W., H-57-3; Cpl I Co 104th OH Inf; 62 to 65; Orchard Knob PO
JAMES, Henry, Gr-81-5(3); Sol US; PO omitted
JAMES, Henry H., Br-8-3(1); Capt L Co 1st TN Cav; 9-1-62 to 7-26-65; Cleo PO; lame, caused by fever
JAMES, Henry W., Ro-210-3(1); Maria L. widow of; Pvt G Co 1st TN Inf; 9 Aug 61 to __; Kingston PO
JAMES, Hezekiah, Bl-5-2; Margaret widow of; Pvt E Co 5th TN Mtd Inf; 8-24-64 to 6-26-65; Pitts X Roads PO; died April 1889
JAMES, James, Wi-270-1; Pvt K Co 8th TN Inf; 5 Jul 62 to 25 Apr 65; Naomi PO; diseas of lungs; pensioned
JAMES, James, He-57-2; Sgt F Co 7th TN Cav; 10-1-63 to 12-1-63; Speim PO
JAMES, Joel H., Mn-122-1; Pvt B Co 6th TN Cav; 8-25-62 to 7-9-65; McNairy PO; discharge sergeons certif. disability
JAMES?, John N., We-221-7; Sgt F Co 5th TN Inf; 17 Jul 61 to Dec 64; Martin PO; CONF
JAMES, John W., Dk-39-2; Pvt D Co 2nd IN Cav; 8-5-62 to 6-27-65; Bozarth PO; liver disease and mind at times affected
JAMES, Lee, A-3-1; Mary A. widow of; Pvt B Co 14th TN Inf; Bud PO; died in service
JAMES, Monrow, Gi-139-1; Pvt F Co 9th AL Inf; 61 to 6-9-65; Barcheers PO; shot in thigh & shoulder; CONF
JAMES, Ray, Hr-98-1; Matild widow of; Pvt 6th TN Cav; Middleton PO; died from typhoid fever
JAMES, Saml., Co-66-4(1); Pvt B Co 2nd NC Inf; 15 Mar 64 to 1 Aug 64; Birdsville PO; palpitation of heart
JAMES, Smith J., Li-146-1; PVt A Co 5th TN Cav; 9-4-62 to 6-25-65; Mulberry PO; wounded right leg & skull fractured while in service
JAMES, Thos. E., Lk-112-2; Mary A. widow of; on a second visit to Mrs. James she says she is not certain whether her husband was in US service or not
JAMES, Thomson, K-170-3; Maj 4th OH Cav; 9 Sep 61 to 15 Jul 65; Knoxville PO
JAMES, Walter K., Lo-187-2; Sgt L Co 1st TN Inf; 1 Sep 62 to 5 Jun 65; Loudon PO
JAMES, William, H-62-3; 316 Chestnut, Chattanooga PO
JAMES, William, Gr-77-1; Elizabeth widow of; Y. Z. PO
JAMES, William, Co-67-6; Pvt F Co .8th TN Cav; 11 Aug 63 to __; PO omitted
JAMES, William A., Mo-120-3(1); Pvt H Co 31st IL Inf; 10-12-64 to 9-2-65; Sweetwater PO; chronic diarrhea
JAMES, William M., Dk-39-2; Pvt I Co 1st TN Mtd Inf; 11-10-64 to 7-22-65; Bozarth PO; heart & kidney trouble

JAMESON, Thomas E., Mu-210-4; Maj A Co 48th TN Inf; 11-27-61 to 7-27-65; Carters Creek PO; shot through left thigh; CONF
JAMESON, William A., Mu-210-4; Pvt C Co 9th TN Cav; 62 to 64; Carters Creek PO; CONF
JAMISON, Doc, Hy-75-1; Pvt; Dancyville PO
JAMISON, George P., G-67-3; Pvt G Co 2nd TN Mtd Inf; 30 Nov 63 to 19 Jan 65; Idlewild PO; ankle broken
JANES, Mat, F-44-1; Pvt; May 6 63 to Jun 2 65; PO omitted
JANKINS, Kelley H., We-230-3; Pvt A Co 7th TN Cav; Sep 1 62 to Nov 1 63; Greenfield PO
JANROIC, William R., Me-92-2; Pvt D Co 7th TN Mtd Inf; 11-16-64 to 7-27-65; Cate PO
JANUARY, John, Gi-129-2; Cpl E Co 12th TN Inf; Elkton PO
JARLS?, Palina E. (see Pulliam, Joseph M.)
JARNAGAN, Anderson, A-5-4; Pvt I Co 1st USC Hvy Art; 4-64 to 7-66; Clinton PO; chronic diarrhea
JARNAGAN, Henry, A-5-1; Pvt L Co 1st TN A (art?); 9-23-64 to 3-1-66; Clinton PO
JARNAGAN, Ruben, Ru-241-2(1); Kittie widow of; Pvt K Co 111th TN Inf; __ to Aug 66 (2 yrs); Murfreesboro PO
JARNAGIN, Gus H., H-61-2; Pvt TN Lt Art Battery; 9-62 to 5-15-65; Chattanooga PO; CONF
JARNAGIN, James, Co-63-1; Pvt K Co 13th TN Cav; 6 Oct 63 to 9 Sep 65; Newport PO; rheumatism & heart trouble
JARNAGIN, Robert E., Hw-129-1; Pvt A Co 9th TN Cav; Feb 64 to __ (1 yr); Morisburg PO; rheumatism & kidney & catar, no undischarged, not mustered in
JARNAGIN, Shadric, Hm-108-4(3); Pvt M Co 13th TN Cav; 7 Feb 62 to 9 Aug 65; Russellville PO
JARNIGAN, William G., De-26-2; C Co 2nd TN; 11 mos; Genette PO; CONF
JARNIKN, Elixander, Ha-116-1; US Sol; 13th Dist
JARRATT, Cy, Mu-210-5; Pvt A Co 12th TN Inf; 8-63 to 1-16-65; Carters Creek PO; weak eyes from smallpox
JARRELL, Andrew J., B-7-1; Pvt 4th TN Mtd Inf; 64 to 8-25-65; Shelbyville PO
JARRELL, Joseph, Hm-108-5(4); Mary widow of; Pvt; 4 yrs; Langdonic PO; CONF
JARRELL, Leaty, Cf-38-2; widow; 10th Civil Dist
JARRELL, William, B-7-2; Pvt C Co 5th Reg TN Cav; 8-63 to 65 (2 yrs 9 days); PO omitted
JARRETT, Thomas G., Di-36-2; Pvt M Co 45th TN Inf; 62 to 64; Bellsburgh PO; CONF
JARVIS, George W., Ha-113-3; Pvt 8th TN Cav; Nov 63 to Sep 65; Sneedville PO
JARVIS, Lewis M., Ha-113-2; Capt E Co 8th TN Cav; Sep 63 to Mar 65; Sneedville PO
JASPER, Jeffers, S-218-1; Cpl? E Co 11th TN Cav; 19-25 Ju 62 to __ (19 mos); Co H 9th TN Cav; Huntsville PO; chronick liver compt
JAYNES, James M., Cr-17-2; Mary E. King formerly widow of; Pvt B Co 7th TN Cav; 8-7-62 to died 8-64; Buena Vista PO
JEARS?, Richard F., D-57-3; Pvt G Co 8th LA Inf; Mar 8 61 to Sep 17 62; Nashville PO; shot in thigh at Sharpsburg PO; CONF
JEFF, Richard, Sh-189-6; Sgt K Co 48th US Col Inf; 5-63 to 1-9-66; Carolina Ave, Memphis PO
JEFFERS, Charles, A-13-3; Mariah widow of; Pvt 2nd TN; 62 to __; Briceville PO
JEFFERS, John, A-10-1; Pvt C Co 2nd TN; Briceville PO; chronic diarrhea 24 yrs
JEFFERS, Marien, S-218-1; Pvt; PO omitted
JEFFERS, Stephen, S-218-2; Pvt A Co; Sep 64 to Dec 64; Norma PO
JEFFERS, William, Je-147-2; Pvt K Co 9th TN Cav; 20 Sep 63 to 11 Sep 65; Shady Grove PO
JEFFERS, William, Ge-92-3; Pvt 8th TN Inf; Laurel Gap PO
JEFFERSON, Dean, Sm-168-1; Sophia widow of; Lt TN Inf; 10-61 to 7-62; Bagdad PO; died
JEFFERSON, Jenkins, Sm-168-2; Martha widow of; Pvt 9th KY Inf; 11-61 to 62; Pleasant Shade PO; died in Nashville, TN
JEFFERSON, Lucinda (sic), Ha-114-1; Pvt A Co 10th VA Inf; 15 May 64 to 20 Jun 65; Xenophon PO; CONF
JEFFERSON, Noah, Sh-152-1; Pvt C Co 3rd TN Inf; 63 to Jan 66; Collierville PO; cold & rheumatism

JEFFERSON, Norman G., A-8-1; Pvt D Co 1st TN Art; 9-25-64 to __; Scarborough PO
JEFFERSON, Norman G., A-8-1; Pvt H Co 1st TN Inf; 8-9-61 to 9-17-64; Scarborough PO; rheumatism, rupture & piles
JEFFERSON, Pateric, K-168-1; Pvt; Knoxville PO
JEFFERSON, Thomas (see Taylor, Steven)
JEFFERSON, Thomas (Lowe), R-162-3; Cpl D Co 137th Col US Vol; 4-8-65 to 6-15-66; Dayton PO
JEFFRE, James, Bo-13-3(1); Pvt C Co 6th TN Inf; 4-62 to 65 (3 yrs); Louisville PO; shocked by shell
JEFFRES, William, A-9-3(1); Pvt I Co 9th TN Cav; 6-30-64 to 9-11-65; Dutch Valley PO; measles resulting in lung disease
JEFFREWS, Theophilas D., We-222-2; Cpl A Co 31st __; Aug 61 to Apr 65; Gardner PO; CONF
JEFFRIES, Hugh, Bo-21-3; Pvt A Co 3rd TN Cav; 8-10-62 to 8-3-65; Veeba PO
JEFREY, J. F., Mn-129-1; Pvt C Co 6th TN Inf; 6-64 to __; Purdy PO
JEHLES?, John B., Pu-146-1; Thiela Denson widow of; Pvt C Co 8th TN Mtd Inf Vol W(hite?); __ to 8-11-65; Buffalo Valley PO
JELF, John T., H-69-2; Sgt B Co 5th US Art; 8-25-63 to 8-25-68; Chattanooga PO
JEMMERSON, Ed, D-64-2; Maggie widow of; Nashville PO
JENIT, Henry, Bo-12-3(1); Sol US; 17th Dist
JENKINS, Abraham, H-57-4; US Sol; 10th Civil Dist
JENKINS, Abraham, A-3-2; Pvt G Co 29th IA? Inf; 1-4-64 to 8-4-65; Wilson PO; measles
JENKINS, Abriham, Co-66-1; Pvt I Co 2nd TN Cav; 22 Sep 62 to 1 Jul 65; Bison PO
JENKINS, Andrew W., Jo-150-3; Trade PO
JENKINS, Cal (Col), Ma-119-1; Cook I Co 54th IL Inf; Jun 63 to Oct 65; Jackson PO; burned leg with hot water, is trying to get pension
JENKINS, D. M., B-11-1; Pvt F Co 5th TN Cav; 9-20-62 to 6-25-65; Healey PO; fistula
JENKINS, David, Ro-208-3; Fannie widow of; Pvt B Co 1st TN Inf; 6 Oct 62 to 3 Aug 65; Kingston PO; sore eyes & kidny disease
JENKINS, David B., Ct-40-1; Eveline widow of; Pvt F Co 2nd TN Cav; 10-26-61 to __; Elizabethton PO; also Capt & Lt C Co 13th TN Cav--10-28-63 to 9-5-65
JENKINS, Dixon A., M-107-5; Pvt K Co 9th KY Inf; 11-30-61 to 12-7-64; Gibb's Cross Roads PO; gun shot wound left knee & disease of eyes, etc
JENKINS, Dr. W., D-80-1; Pvt C Co 5th TN; Aug 14 63 to Aug 14 65; Donelson PO
JENKINS, Dugan, Co-68-3; Pvt; 62 to __; measles settled in back; PO omitted
JENKINS, Emely (see Salts, William)
JENKINS, Henry, Sh-146-3; US Sol; 3rd Civil Dist
JENKINS, Henry C., Wl-297-1; Cpl D Co 4th TN Mtd Inf; 12 Oct 64 to 25 Aug 65; Hennig PO
JENKINS, Houston, Co-68-1; Pvt E Co 1st TN Cav; 63 to 65; Costner PO
JENKINS, Hugh, Ct-40-1; Pvt A Co 13th TN Cav; 9-22-63 to 9-5-65; Elizabethton PO; rheumatism
JENKINS, Hugh A., Ro-202-4; Pvt I Co 7th TN Cav; 62 to 64; Cave Creek PO; sound
JENKINS, Jas. W., Cr-4-4; Pvt E Co 7th TN Cav; 5-63 to 10-63; Bells Depot PO
JENKINS, Jerry, Gi-122-5; Cpl K Co 110th TN Inf; 8 Jan 64 to 10 Feb 66; Prospect Sta. PO; 8 mos in prison
JENKINS, Jesse C., Jo-150-2; Pvt D Co 13th TN Cav; 22 Sep 63 to 5 Sep 65; Trade PO; sight
JENKINS, Joseph N., Jo-149-2; Pvt D Co 13th TN Cav; 2 Feb 64 to 5 Sep 65; Mountain City PO; liver __, chronic dirrhea & results
JENKINS, Josiah S., D-45-2; Pvt D Co 4th TN Mtd Inf; 2-24-65 to 8-25-66; Nashville PO
JENKINS, Leonidas?, Sm-168-1; Pvt B Co 8th TN Inf; 3-6-65 to 8-65; Pleasant Shade PO; deafness
JENKINS, Martin, Me-89-2; Pvt; Big Spring PO; rheumatism
JENKINS, Nat, Gi-129-1; Pvt B Co 12th TN Inf; 31 Jul 63 to 16 Jan 66; Conway PO
JENKINS, Neuton, Wl-308-1; Pvt 38th TN; Sep 1 61 to 64; PO omitted; CONF
JENKINS, Nicholas, M-107-5; Susan widow of; Pvt K Co 9th KY Inf; 11-30-61 to 62; Gibb's Cross Roads PO; chronic diareah

JENKINS, Patrick, Sh-203-1; Pvt B Co IL Regt; Jan 3 64 to Nov 18 65; Memphis PO
JENKINS, Phillip, Co-68-3; Pvt E Co 1st TN Bat; __ to 65; Sutton PO; diarehea, left ear effected
JENKINS, Reubin, M-106-3(2); Pvt K Co 9th KY Vol Inf; 10-25-61 to 12-26-63; Killsdale PO; physical disability, heart & lung disease, pensioner
JENKINS, Samuel, Sm-168-2; Pvt TN Cav; 64 to 65; Pleasant Shade PO; cold, lost sense of smell
JENKINS, Samuel, D-67-3; alias Hall, Samuel; Pvt A Co 2nd Col Art; Mar 20 64 to Jan 13 66; Nashville PO
JENKINS, Samuel W., H-50-5; Cpl L Co 3rd R TN Cav; 4-20-64 to 6-10-65; Soddy PO; rupture
JENKINS, Talever, Co-68-2; Pvt I Co 2nd TN Cav; 63 to 65; Sutton PO; fever & chills
JENKINS, Thomas E., K-173-1; Nancy E. widow of; Pvt B Co 6th TN Inf; Caswell PO; lung trouble
JENKINS, William, Gi-122-2; Rachell widow of; Pvt I Co 110th TN Inf; 62 to 64; Prospect Sta. PO; died while in service; CONF
JENKINS, William, Ct-40-3; Pvt A Co 13th TN Cav; 9-22-63 to 9-5-65; PO omitted; CONF
JENKINS, William A., K-156-1; Pvt; 32 Pine St, Knoxville PO
JENKINS, William B., M-103-5; Pvt D Co 9th KY Inf; 9-11-61 to 1-1-63; Alton Hill PO; gun shot in shoulder
JENKINS, William B., Hw-118-1; Pvt D Co 8th TN Inf; St. Clair PO
JENKINS, William D., Ct-36-3; Elizebeth J. widow of; Capt C Co ___; PO omitted
JENKINS, ____, K-166-3; Catherine widow of; Smithwood PO
JENNETT, Henry P., Wi-276-2; Pvt D Co 10th TN Cav; 4 May 62 to 1 May 65; Beechville PO; CONF
JENING, George, Ge-102-1; Pvt E Co 4th TN Inf; 15 Nov 61 to 2 Aug 65; Camp Creek PO; disease of stomach
JENNING, Rial, Cl-71-54-1; Pvt A Co 2nd TN Cav; 8-1-62 to 7-6-65; Lone Mountain PO
JENNING, William L., D-58-1; Pvt F Co 1st VA; Sep or Oct 63 to 14 Feb 64; Nashville PO; wounded right leg
JENNINGS, David F., Cl-55-1; Cpl G Co 8th TN Cav; 7-63 to __ (2 yrs); Lone Mountain PO
JENNINGS, Edward, H-71-1; Mattie widow?; 62 to 65; Chattanooga PO
JENNINGS, Elizah, Ge-102-2; Cpl E Co 4th TN Inf; 15 Nov 61 to 7 Jul 65; Camp Creek PO; rheumatism, now heart trouble
JENNINGS, Henry F., O-138-3; Pvt L Co 8th KY Cav; 14 Aug 62 to 20 Sep 63; Minnick Box PO
JENNINGS, James W., De-26-1; 3rd Sgt C Co 2nd TN Mtd Inf; 6 Jan 64 to 21 Jan 65; Bible Hill PO
JENNINGS, Jesse D., Sq-164-1; Pvt 5th TN Cav; Fillmore PO
JENNINGS, John, D-64-3; 2nd Lt A Co 3rd W VA Cav; 20 Feb 65 to 30 Jun 65; Nashville PO
JENNINGS, John, D-82-1; Catharine widow of; Pvt; Hermitage PO
JENNINGS, John, Jo-148-2; Pvt; PO omitted
JENNINGS, John H., H-69-6; Sgt H Co 19th AL Inf; 5-62 to 4-65; Chattanooga PO
JENNINGS, Leann? J., Cy-29-2; 9th Civil Dist; crippled by fall from horse
JENNINGS, Mikel R., Se-224-3; Pvt 10th TN Inf; Sep 64 to 65; Wears Valley PO
JENNINGS, Robert L., Ru-245-1; Pvt G Co 132nd IN Inf; 5-3-63 to 9-7-63; Readyville PO; kidney disease
JENNINGS, Samuel, D-75-1; Emily widow of; Pvt TN Cav; 1 Jun 61 to 15 Feb 63; Stewarts Ferry PO; shot through arm; taken at Ft. Donelson; CONF
JENNINGS, Stephen C., Ge-99-2; Pvt E Co 4th TN Inf; __ to 9 Jul 65; Limestone Springs PO; deafness & rheumatism, couldnt get dates
JENNINGS, S____, Cl-54-3(1); Pvt A Co 1st TN Bat; 4-61 to 4-65; Tazewell PO; CONF
JENNINGS, Thomas, Ms-174-1; Jane widow of; Chapel Hill PO; killed in service, nothing known
JENNINGS, Wesley, Wl-298-1; Pvt K Co 5th TN Cav; 25 Feb 63 to 14 Aug 65; PO omitted
JENSON, Robert, Dk-37-1; Pvt F Co 5th TN Cav; 10-11-62 to 9-11-65; Mechanicsville PO

JENT, T. H., M-108-5; Pvt A Co 1st TN Mtd Inf; 10-24-63 to 1-22-65; Haysville PO; breast disease, crippled by horse falling
JENTRY, Lewis L., Ge-89-1; Pvt 13th TN Cav; Mosheim PO
JERDEN, Thomas, H-72-2(1); Sgt K Co 14th US Col Inf; __ -15-63 to 3-26-66; Chattanooga PO
JERMUN, Granderson, C-24-1; Pvt F Co 12th KY Inf & D Co 32nd OH Inf; 6-1-63 to never mustered out; Whitman PO; sechurvia (scurvy?)
JERNIGAN, William, Cf-35-4; Martha E. widow of; Pvt K Co 24th TN Inf; 20 Jun 63 to __; Normandy PO; CONF
JEROLDS, Marcus F., Ge-98-4; Asst Sgt 2nd TN Cav; 12 Aug 62 to 5 Jul 65; PO omitted; phthisis pulmonalis
JERRILS, Devault, H-73-1; Adatme widow of; Pvt; Chattanooga PO
JERVIS, James, Hw-129-1; Pvt G Co 1st TN Cav; 5 Jun 62 to Jun 65; Morisburg PO; rheumatis, hearring & sight
JESTA, Andrew J., Ch-18-2; Pvt C Co 19th TN Cav (Col Ripple?); 62 to 65; PO omitted; CONF
JESTIS, Minerva (see Young, Lewis)
JESTLES, James N., K-167-5; PVtS B Co 2nd NC Cav; Sep 61 to Aug 65; Knoxville PO; frost bite and horse fell on him, draws 2 per month
JETER, James E., Ch-13-2; Pvt B Co 6th TN Vol; 8-25-62 to 10-23-65; Jack Creek PO; piles
JETT, Robert W., Rb-221-2; Ord Sgt K Co 14th TN; May 20 61 to Jul 12 64; Adams Station PO; wounded twice at Malvern Hill; CONF
JETTON, George, Ru-241-4; Sgt K Co 17th TN Inf; 1-5-64 to 4-25-66; Murfreesboro PO
JETTON, Robert, Cr-8-2; Sgt? I Co 12th TN; __ 62 to Apr 65; Maury City PO; CONF
JETTS, Franklin (see Taylor, Franklin)
JEWELL, George, U-247-3; US Sol; 5th Civil Dist
JEWETT, Mary A., R-157-2; Sol; 12th Dist
JHONSON, James, Cl-46-1; Pvt C Co 1st TN; 8-16-61 to 9-17-64; Clairfield PO; lungs, dirie
JILES, John M., Co-68-2; Pvt E Co 2nd TN Cav; Sep 62 to Jul 65; Cashy PO
JILES, William, Co-67-3; Pvt A Co 4th TN Cav; 1 Dec 62 to 19 Jun 65; Coxby PO
JIMISON, Joseah, Sh-145-3; alias Joseph Levar; Pvt B Co 3rd US Col Hvy Art; Oct 63 to Jan 66; Kerrville PO; very feeble sight caused by hard drilling in hot wether, 1st Capt Ball, 2nd Cap Johnson, enlisted at Memphis, TN
JINKENS, Josh, Sh-160-1; Nurse TN Inf; 62 to 65; Poplar St (126-130); Memphis PO
JINKINS, J. F., Mn-129-1; Cpl A Co 11th MO Cav; 62 to 8-65; Adamsville PO; shot through sholder
JINKINS, Lock, Hr-86-1; Pvt H Co 59th TN; 63 to Jun 17 65; Grand Junction PO; small pox, was in hospital at Memphis
JINKINS, Margaret, Lo-194-2; widow; Muddy Creek PO
JOBE, Presly D., Hr-89-1; Sgt C Co 11th IL; 9-62 to 6-6-65; Whiteville PO
JOHBILL, Penalton, Mo-126-2; Sol; 12th Civil Dist
JOHLING, William M., Mc-112-5; Pvt I Co 34th NJ Inf; 8-62 to 4-65; Athens PO; gunshot wound
JOHN, Willam, D-44-2(1); Sgt A Co 1st US Inf; 2-25-59 to 2-26-64; Nashville PO
JOHNS, Charles, Ru-241-4; Pvt I Co 102th MI Inf; 63 to 66; PO omitted
JOHNS, I. W., G-67-1; Lucil W. widow of; Pvt M Co 6th TN Cav; 11 Aug 62 to 26 Jul 65; Bradford PO; ruptured
JOHNS, Wm H., M-106-2(1); Pvt A Co 8th TN Inf; 12-64 to 9-65; Hillsdale PO; broken arm, discharge burned up
JOHNS, Joseph, Ha-110-1; Pvt L Co 8th TN Cav; 1 Dec 64 to 11 Sep 65; Treadway PO
JOHNS, Steven (see Stephens, John)
JOHNS, Thomas L., Sn-261-1; Pvt E Co 1st TN Cav; 12-26-63 to 1-20-65; Rapids, Simpson Co., KY PO
JOHNS, Thomas L., Sn-261-4(3); Pvt E Co 1st TN Cav; 12-26-63 to 1-20-65; Rapids, Simpson Co. KY PO; ruptured near carlhernze & wounded in left arm, came home on sesonal discharge 8-17-65
JOHNS, Wade M., R-161-3; Dayton PO; hart & lung trouble from fever; Cpl I Co 10th TN Inf; 4-13-63 to 6-20-65

JOHNS, Wyatt, D-103-1; Pvt D Co 18th OH Inf; Mar 9 64 to Oct 9 65; Whites Creek PO
JOHNSON, A. G., Cl-54-3(1); Pvt; Tazewell PO; CONF
JOHNSON, Alaxander, Cr-16-2; Cpl F Co 7th TN Cav; Aug 20 62 to Oct 25 63; Huntingdon PO
JOHNSON, Albert, D-91-3; alias Tilton; Pvt A Co 42nd Inf; 24 May 64 to 31 Jan 66; Station C, Nashville PO
JOHNSON, Albert M., Ct-36-1; Cpl C Co 13th TN Cav; 9-23-63 to 9-8-65; Roan Mt. PO; contracted rheumatism
JOHNSON, Alex, Gi-136-1; Cpl D Co 110th TN Inf; 11-1-63 to 1-1-66; Lynnville PO; shot in left leg, from which he suffers
JOHNSON, Alexander, Mt-138-1; Pvt E Co 16th US C Inf; 16 Feb 64 to 2 Aug 65; New Providence PO; sergeants surtificate
JOHNSON, Alford W., Hw-121-6(1); Pvt C Co 2nd NC Mtd Inf; 16 Sep 63 to 19 Aug 65; New Hope PO; liver deseas 27 yrs
JOHNSON, Alvin J., K-177-1; Pvt E Co 16th Inf; 14 Apr 61 to 20 May 62; Chumlea PO
JOHNSON, Ambors O., C-32-1; Pvt E Co 3rd TN Inf; 62 to __; Pine Mountain PO; one eye out 26 yrs
JOHNSON, Ambrose, Cl-58-3; Pvt Co I 9th TN Inf; Jun 62 to Mar 65; Bachus PO; slight debilitation, wooden left hand
JOHNSON, Ambrose L., H-55-3; Pvt I Co 4th TN Cav; 10-1-65 to 7-12-65; Harrison PO
JOHNSON, Anderson, Hu-106-1; Pvt D Co 13th US C T; Sep 63 to 65; Waverly PO
JOHNSON, Andrew, H-60-2; Pvt D Co 7th IL Cav; 7-19-61 to 11-13-65; Chattanooga PO
JOHNSON, Andrew, Jo-150-4; Pvt A Co 9th TN Cav; 4 Jun 64 to 5 Sep 65; Osborn PO
JOHNSON, Andrew, F-37-1; Pvt K Co 1st US Col Art; to Jul 65; Somerville PO
JOHNSON, Andy, Ro-210-7; Pvt; Cardiff PO; CONF
JOHNSON, Anthony, Sh-179-2; 10 Spring St, Memphis PO
JOHNSON, Asa, Mu-196-2; Sgt C Co 15th Reg; Fall 63 till mustered out; 2 yrs 4 mos; Columbia PO
JOHNSON, Bengeman F., Sh-188-1; Pvt B Co 77th OH Inf; 12-62 to 2-65; 230 Greenlaw St, Memphis PO
JOHNSON, Benjamin A., A-13-2; Pvt 11th TN Lt Art; 61 to 64; Briceville PO; no disability incurred
JOHNSON, Beverley, T-214-1; Pvt C Co 3rd US Inf; Aug 62 to 65; Mason Depot PO
JOHNSON, Bird, Wi-273-1; Pvt F Co 12th TN Inf; Aug 12 63 to Feb 66; Thompson Sta. PO; in good health & condition
JOHNSON, C. L., Br-12-3; Mary K. widow of; Lt A Co 8th TN Inf; 10-20-62 to 6-65; McPherren PO; killed in battle
JOHNSON, Carter, Ct-38-2; Pvt B Co 13th TN Cav; 9-23-63 to 9-5-65; Johnson City PO; rheumatism & heart disease
JOHNSON, Carter, Sh-160-1; Pvt H Co 3rd TN Inf; Feb 64 to Jan 66; Memphis, Poplar St (126-130); wounded __, r. hand and head
JOHNSON, Chancell, De-22-1; Pvt K Co 56th AL Reg; 26 Aug 63 to 15 Dec 64; Bath Springs PO; CONF
JOHNSON, Charles, Sh-37-2; Josephine Hobson form. widow of;Pvt US Col; 4 yrs; Taylors Chapel PO; wounded in the leg; (Josephine Hobson then widow of John Cummins--both in the same reg & comp)
JOHNSON, Chas. R., Cr-4-2; Bettie M. widow of; Lt 12th TN Cav; 63 to 65; Bells Depot PO; CONF
JOHNSON, Charlotte, Dy-32-1; widow US Sol; 15th Civil Dist
JOHNSON, Christopher, Un-254-2; Lucy formerly widow of; Pvt B Co; Paulett PO
JOHNSON, Claborne W., Wh-181-1; Drummer A Co 1st TN Inf; Green Tree PO
JOHNSON, Claiborne, Ha-115-2; Pvt E Co 61st TN Inf; 25 Oct 63 to 1 Jul 65; Jap? VA PO; CONF
JOHNSON, Clara, Sh-149-4; widow US Sol; 6th Civil Dist
JOHNSON, Daniel, Bl-5-1; Sgt D Co 6th TN Mtd Inf; 8-16-64 to 6-30-65; Stevens Chapel PO
JOHNSON, Daniel, Sh-160-2; Mary Wallace widow of; Pvt 59th TN Inf; 61 to __ (1 yr); Memphis PO; died small pox 1862, Dec.
JOHNSON, David, Hr-97-1; Pvt B Co 106th OH Cav; 2 yrs 6 mos; PO omitted
JOHNSON, David N., We-225-1; Pvt I Co 6th TN Cav; 1 Jan 64 to 26 Jul 65; Dresden PO; wounded in hands?
JOHNSON, David R. C., K-156-1; Pvt; Mar 61 to A pr 65; Pine 127, Knoxville PO; CONF
JOHNSON, Dobson, Dk-32-2; Pvt E Co 4th TN Mtd Inf; 11-64 to 8-25-65; Alexandria PO; liver and kidney disease, captured June 1863
JOHNSON, Drewry, Jo-149-2; Emily widow of; Blacksmith D Co 13th TN Cav; 24 Sep 63 to Jul 65; Mountain City PO; back or spinal disease, dirrhea
JOHNSON, Edd, Cr-8-1; Mira Lee widow of; Sgt B Co 9th TN; 3-25-61 to 8-2-63; Maury City PO; exposure caused rheumatism; CONF
JOHNSON, Edmund, Sh-163-1; Pvt G Co 52nd IN Inf; Sep 9 62 to Jan 3 65; Memphis PO; kidney disease & almost blind
JOHNSON, Edwin, H-63-1; Mariah widow of; Pvt Inf; 709 Cypress, Chattanooga PO; dead
JOHNSON, Eli H., A-9-4(2); Pvt C Co 1st TN Cav; 11-1-62 to 6-19-65; Lowe Sulphur Springs PO; mumps resulting in injury to testicles
JOHNSON, Elizabeth, Ge-97-4; widow US Soldier; 20th Civil Dist
JOHNSON, Elisabeth J. (see Boshel?, James W.)
JOHNSON, Elkany, Bo-14-5; Mary C. widow of; Pvt E Co 1st TN Lt Art; 10-10-62 to 8-1-65; Tut PO
JOHNSON, Felicks, We-230-3; Pvt A Co 7th TN Cav; Sep 1 62 to Nov 1 63; McKinzie PO; CONF
JOHNSON, Francis M., Je-147-1; Pvt B Co 9th TN Cav; 16 Sep 63 to 11 Sep 65; Shady Grove PO
JOHNSON, Frank J., F-45-1; US Sol; 12th Civil Dist
JOHNSON, George, H-70-4(1); Pvt; Chattanooga PO; didn't serve, was discharged because of bad cough
JOHNSON, George, Sh-152-3; Amanda widow; Dexter PO
JOHNSON, George, Sh-158-1; Pvt C Co 3rd C Hvy Art; Memphis PO; shot in skull and shoulder, almost helpless & wife earns meager support
JOHNSON, George, Sh-145-4; Pvt Bat 6 2nd US Lt Art; Oct 63 to Dec 66; Millington PO; Capt Rainey, 1st Lt while ? Border
JOHNSON, George, Sh-149-2; Pvt D Co 59th US Inf; 23 Nov 63 to 31 Feb 66; National Cemetery PO
JOHNSON, Geo., Hd-54-2; Pvt C Co 6th TN Cav; 20 Jul 63 to 26 Jul 65; Sardis PO; neuralgia in eyes
JOHNSON, George, Sn-254-2; Pvt K Co 17th Col Inf; 12-31-63 to 3-65; Hendersonville PO
JOHNSON, George L., H-51-2(1); Pvt B Co; 6-1-63 to 64; Hill City PO
JOHNSON, George L., H-51-3; Cpl B Co 9th IA Inf; 6-1-64 to 7-18-65; Hill City PO
JOHNSON, George W., Jo-150-2; Pvt I Co; Key Station PO
JOHNSON, George W., C-25-2; Coal Creek PO (Anderson Co.); CONF
JOHNSON, George W., O-138-2; Pvt K Co 4th TN; 15 Sep 61 to 20 Apr 65; Elbridge PO; CONF
JOHNSON, George W., Cr-14-3; Pvt M Co 6th TN Cav; 9 Aug 62 to 26 Jul 65; Crider PO
JOHNSON, George W., Sh-195-1; Pvt B Co 40th MO Inf; Memphis PO
JOHNSON, George W., A-3-4; Pvt B Co 63rd TN Inf; 8-63 to 5-12-65; Clinch River PO; CONF
JOHNSON, Hamer, Gu-48-5(2); Tracy City Branch Prison PO
JOHNSON, Hamsigh, Fr-114-1; Synthee widow of; Alto PO; I failed to find rank & she drawing pension
JOHNSON, Harry, Fr-110-1; Teamster; PO omitted
JOHNSON, Harvey, Sh-198-1; Pvt H Co 3rd US Col Inf; Fall 64 to about Jan 65; Memphis PO; gave his discharge to a claim agent
JOHNSON, Henrietta, Sh-178-3; 28 Marshall, Memphis PO
JOHNSON, Henry (Col), Gr-76-2(1); Pvt F Co 1st TN Cav; 29 Apr 64 to 31 Mar 66; Tampico PO
JOHNSON, Henry, Dk-38-2; Pvt F Co 5th TN Cav; 64 to 65 (10 mos); Smithville PO
JOHNSON, Henry, Hr-94-1; Pvt A Co 57th MO Inf; Oct 63 to __ (3 yrs); Saulsbury PO
JOHNSON, Henry, Sh-149-4; US Sol; 6th Civil Dist
JOHNSON, Henry, Gi-135-3; Pvt; Lynnville PO

JOHNSON, Henry, Sn-254-2; 14th US Col Inf; 3-7-63 to 3-12-65; Hendersonville? PO
JOHNSON, Henry, Sh-192-1; Pvt F Co 3rd US Hvy Art; 8-5-63 to 5-66; Memphis PO
JOHNSON, Henry, Sh-160-2; Pvt D Co 56th GA Inf; Jul 64 to 65; Memphis PO; shot through right hand
JOHNSON, Henry M., Hd-54-2; Pvt C Co 6th TN Cav; 11 Sep 62 to 26 Jul 65; Sardis PO; chron. diariah
JOHNSON, Hiram, Wa-271-1; Seaman Fort Henderson?; 3 Dec 64 to 5 Aug 65; Blizard PO
JOHNSON, Hugh, Se-226-3; Pvt F Co 9th TN Cav; 11 Oct 63 to 13 Sep 65; Sinking Springs PO; injured r. lung, r. knee, l. hip
JOHNSON, Ike, Mt-137-1; Civilian, in government employ; St. Bethlehem PO
JOHNSON, Isaac, K-161-4; Pvt K Co 3rd TN Inf; Knoxville PO
JOHNSON, Isaac, R-162-4; Pvt A Co 51st OH Inf; 9-7-61 to 11-5-64; Dayton PO; disabled from chronic diarrhea & typhoid fever
JOHNSON, Isaac A., Hd-46-2; Pvt B Co 2nd TN Mtd Inf; Oct 15 63 to Apr 12 65; Savannah PO
JOHNSON, Isaac C., Dk-33-2; Pvt F Co 4th TN Inf; 9-28-64 to 8-25-65; Halesville PO; lungs & heart
JOHNSON, Isaac G., H-69-4; Cpl; 62 to 65; Chattanooga PO; CONF
JOHNSON, Isac K., Sh-187-1(5); E Co 23rd MD? Inf; 8-64 to 12-65; 86 N. Front St, Memphis PO; my age do not alow me to make a liven
JOHNSON, Isah, Je-146-4; Pvt B Co 9th TN Cav; 13 Sep 63 to 11 Sep 65; White Pine PO; everything looks like very thin care
JOHNSON, J. S., La-117-3; TN Cav; 62 to 65; 15th Dist; CONF
JOHNSON, Jack, US Sol, Mt-138-2; Dist No 7, N. Providence PO
JOHNSON, Jacob G., Mt-135-1; Pvt C Co 3rd TN Art; 8-17-62 to 5-1-65; New Providence PO; prisoner at Clarksville 6 wks
JOHNSON, Jake, H-72-2(1); Pvt B Co 29th US Col Inf; 65 to 4-66; Chattanooga PO
JOHNSON, James, Ha-117-2; Pvt B Co 50th VA Inf; 62 to 65; Kyle's Ford PO; CONF
JOHNSON, James, Je-137-3; Pvt E Co 9th TN Cav; 1 Oct 63 to 11 Sep 65; Chestnut Hill PO; leg mashed
JOHNSON, James, Ro-210-11; Polly A. widow of; Pvt; Rockwood PO
JOHNSON, James, Br-12-2; Charleston PO; CONF
JOHNSON, James, R-162-2; Pvt I Co 1st US Col Hvy Art; 7-8-64 to 3-31-66; Dayton PO
JOHNSON, James, Sq-165-2; Pvt; Delphi PO; received an honorable disc.
JOHNSON, James, F-42-1(3); Pvt I Co 42nd US Col Inf; Apr 65 to Feb 6 66; Elba PO; arm partially disabled in service, runaway team ran over arm
JOHNSON, James, Mc-117-2; 13th Civil Dist
JOHNSON, James, Sh-190-2; Pvt C Co 59th US Inf; 63 to 66; 102 - 6th St, Memphis PO; broken finger, reenlisted
JOHNSON, James A., Sn-261-4(3); Pvt H Co 2nd TN Inf; 62 to 5-64; Rapids, Simpson Co., KY PO; came home on discharge
JOHNSON, James B., Fr-109-1; Pvt C Co 148th OH Inf; 17 May 64 to Sep 10 64; Huntland PO
JOHNSON?, James C., Un-255-1; (reads Johson); Pvt F Co 3rd TN Inf; 18 Feb 62 to 10 Aug 63; Warwicks X Roads PO; liver & bou & stum
JOHNSON, James C., Se-219-3; Pvt E Co 2nd TN Cav; 16 Sep 62 to 5 Jul 65; Jones Cave PO; general disability
JOHNSON, James E., Ja-85-2; Pvt E Co 5th TN Inf; 3-2-62 to 4-4-65; Birchwood PO
JOHNSON, James M., We-227-1; Cpl E & C Cos 7th TN Cav; 12 Aug 62 to 5 Aug 65; Greenfield PO
JOHNSON, James M., G-60-1; Sgt E Co 4th TN Mtd Inf; 26 Sep 64 to 25 Aug 65; Trenton PO
JOHNSON, James M., K-172-4; Pvt E Co 3rd TN Cav; 17 Dec 62 to 12 Jun 65; PO omitted
JOHNSON, James R. (see Miller, R. J.)
JOHNSON, Jerome, K-168-4; Adair's Creek PO
JOHNSON, Jerre, D-64-2; Sarah widow of; Pvt I Co 9th MI Inf; Nashville PO
JOHNSON, Joel, Bo-23-1; Pvt H Co 3rd TN Inf; 2-9-62 to 2-10-65; Tuckaleechee Cove PO; cut on sholder with sabre, shot rite side, discharged by time out
JOHNSON, John, Dk-38-1; Pvt I Co 35th TN Inf; 9-5-61 to 4-26-65; Smithville PO; CONF
JOHNSON, John, K-158-2; Betty widow of; Pvt K Co 3rd TN Inf; 61 to May 65; Knoxville, 94 Payne St PO
JOHNSON, John, Sq-164-4(1); Pvt G Co 3rd TN Cav; 8-12-63 to 8-3-65; Brock PO
JOHNSON, John, Gi-135-1; Pvt E Co 110th US Cav; Lynnville PO
JOHNSON, John, Mu-190-1; Pvt D Co 8th MI Cav; 4-14-63 to 6-10-65; Fountain Creek PO
JOHNSON, John, Mu-197-1; Pvt E Co 9th TN; 62 to 64; Columbia PO; cripled in right leg; CONF
JOHNSON, John, Ms-178-1; 12th Dist
JOHNSON, John A., La-117-4; 15th Dist; CONF
JOHNSON, John B., Di-36-2; Pvt G Co 50th TN Inf; 61 to 64; Bellsburgh PO; CONF
JOHNSON, John C., Su-243-2; Pvt A Co 9th TN Cav; 5 Jan 65 to __ (3 mos); Bristul PO
JOHNSON, John F., Br-6-2; Sarah B. widow of; Pvt I Co 10th TN Cav; 2-4-64 to 8-1-65; Chatala PO
JOHNSON, John H., Ms-181-1 (reads Johson); Pvt B Co 11th TN Inf; 6-30-63 to 4-12-65; Lewisburg PO
JOHNSON, John J., La-111-4; US Sol; 4th Civil Dist
JOHNSON, John J., Dk-39-5(1); Pvt H Co 1st TN Mtd Inf; 3-64 to 5-17-65; Laurel Hill PO; feet frost bitten and neuralgic affections
JOHNSON, John P., Sq-164-5(1); Pvt E Co 6th TN Mtd Inf; 8-11-64 to 1-30-65; Brock PO
JOHNSON, John S., M-103-1; Pvt F Co 7th TN Inf; 3-1-64 to 5-9-65; Lafayette PO
JOHNSON, John S., K-171-4(3); Pvt D Co 9th TN Cav; Sep 63 to Sep 65; PO omitted
JOHNSON, John S., Ge-102-1; Pvt K Co 1st TN Cav; Sep 61 to Jun 65; Camp Creek PO; shot in hand, now diarear
JOHNSON, John T., P-151-3; Cpl F Co 2nd Mtd Inf; 64 to 65; Linden PO; electric shock
JOHNSON, John T., Ca-19-1; Pvt D Co 2nd IL Art; 10-4-62 to 7-6-65; Auburn PO; paralyzed in August? 65 & Jun 67
JOHNSON, John W., Un-251-; Cpl F Co 3rd TN Inf; 14 Feb 62 to 17 May 65; Effie PO; pneumonia fever & gunshot
JOHNSON, John W., Bo-13-2; Pvt L Co 2nd TN Cav; 7-64 to 7-6-65; Miser PO
JOHNSON, John W., Cy-26-1; Mary E. widow of; Pvt B Co 5th KY Cav; 61 to 5-65; Moss PO
JOHNSON, John W., Ge-95-1; Pvt D Co 3rd NC Inf; 10 Jan 63 to 20 Oct 64; Home PO; shot through left arm; discharged sergon certificate
JOHNSON, Jonathan T., Se-226-3; Pvt K Co 2nd TN Mtd Inf; 14 Feb 62 to 8 Aug 65; Cates X Roads PO; measles contracting heart trouble
JOHNSON, Jordan, Sh-198-2; US Sol; Main St, Memphis PO
JOHNSON, Joseph, Un-254-2; Hannah widow of; Pvt B Co 20th TN Cav; Sep 62 to 65; Bartheney PO
JOHNSON, Joseph, Mc-110-2(1); Martha A. Hampton widow of; Pvt D Co 5th TN Inf; Mouse Creek PO; died in camp
JOHNSON, Joshua, Bo-21-1; Annie widow of; Pvt B Co 6th TN Inf; 4-22-61 to 10-22-61; Bank PO
JOHNSON, Joshua C., Cy-29-2; Pvt D Co 17 TN Cav; 9th Civil Dist
JOHNSON, Julius, Sh-179-2; 424 Pontotoc St, Memphis PO
JOHNSON, L. A., K-172-1; Pvt A Co 6th TN Inf; 62 to 65; Knoxville PO; shot through left thiy
JOHNSON, Lauranso D., K-181-1; Pvt A Co 6th TN Inf; 24 Apr 62 to 27 Apr 65; French PO
JOHNSON, Levi, Ha-117-3; Pvt B Co 50th VA Inf; 63 to __; Sneedville PO; was captured by Federals 5/12/64; CONF
JOHNSON, Louis F., Ge-84-3; Pvt G Co 1st TN Cav; 31 Sep 62 to 12 Jun 65; Bird Bridge PO; dis. wound & general disability
JOHNSON, Luke, Mo-119-2; Pvt C Co US Col Hvy Art; 3-25-62 to 3-30-65; Sweetwater PO
JOHNSON, Lucy, W1-297-2; widow; Dist No 12
JOHNSON, Mack, Sh-197-2; Pvt E Co 42nd Col Inf; 9-11-64 to 1-31-66; Memphis PO; both legs frost bitten
JOHNSON, Major, D-69-3; 108 Lowes St, Nashville PO

JOHNSON, Major, B-11-2(1); Pvt I Co 13th US Col; Ellen widow of; Unionville PO; died in service
JOHNSON, Malcom, Sq-164-2(1); Pvt E Co 6th TN Mtd Inf; 8-11-64 to 6-30-65; Dunlap PO; by measles
JOHNSON, Maniel, Sh-144-1; Pvt G Co 15th US Col Inf; Jan 64 to 66; Brunswick PO; shot in foot
JOHNSON, Margaret S., D-87-2; 9th Dist
JOHNSON, Marquis D. L., Ro-203-7; Pvt TB 1st TN Inf; Jul 62 to 21 Jun 65; Union Cross Roads PO; injury from mumps & measles
JOHNSON, Marry J. & A. C. Andies, K-181-4(1); widow of; Pvt A Co 2nd TN Cav; 5 Nov 62 to ___; Fleniken PO
JOHNSON, Martin, C-27-3; Sgt L Co 4th TN Cav; 63 to 7-65 (2 yrs); Caryville PO
JOHNSON, Mershon, H-69-1; Violet widow of; Pvt; 62 to 65; Chattanooga PO; CONF
JOHNSON, Millo, R-162-2; Susan Majors widow of; Pvt H Co 2nd TN Inf; 63 to ___; Dayton PO; died in the service
JOHNSON, Mitchell, W1-295-1; Pvt I Co 4th Hvy Art; Jy 63 to Mar 5 65; Lebanon PO
JOHNSON, Moses, Mo-121-1; Pvt L Co 1st US Co 1 Hvy Art; 9-17-64 to 5-20-65; Philadelphia PO; piles
JOHNSON, Moses (see Miles, Milo)
JOHNSON, Nancy (see Dean, David)
JOHNSON, Nancy (see Paschal, Richard)
JOHNSON, Nancy W., K-181-5(2); widow US Sol, Pvt C Co 6th TN Inf; 18 Apr 62 to 24 Apr 65; Knoxville PO
JOHNSON, Napolian B., G-71-2; Pvt G Co 47th TN Inf; 12 Jun 61 to 24 Jun 63; Edmonds PO; CONF
JOHNSON, Newton M., Fr-109-1; Pvt G Co 64th OH Inf; 15 Oct 61 to 25 Aug 63; Huntland PO; attracted rumatisms
JOHNSON, Noble, K-186-1; Pvt B Co 107th IL Inf; 13 Aug 62 to 20 Jun 65; Chumlea PO; rheumatism
JOHNSON, Noble, A-9-5(3); Cpl K Co Thomases Legion; 4-62 to ___; Dutch Valley PO; furlowed about July or Aug 64; never returned to his command; CONF
JOHNSON, Orange, Hw-127-4; Pvt; Rogersville PO; right eye kicked out by mule
JOHNSON, Oscar G., K-156-3; Pvt M Co 1st Col E TN Inf; 1 May 63 to 6 May 65; 54 Patton, Knoxville PO
JOHNSON, Patrick H., Wa-265-1; Pvt F Co 10th TN Cav; 6 Nov 63 to 1 Aug 62; Chuckey Valley PO; rhumatism
JOHNSON, Paul, Sh-189-4; Pvt H Co 55th US Col Inf; 2-10-63 to 1-65; Pewitt? Ave, Memphis PO
JOHNSON, Permelia J. (see Williams, Henry F.)
JOHNSON, Peter, K-185-2; Pvt; Scaggston PO
JOHNSON, Peter, K-167-4; Pvt D Co 10th TN Cav; Knoxville PO
JOHNSON, Peter, Ge-89-1; Pvt E Co 1st TN Lt Art; 14 Sep 63 to 1 Aug 65; Mosheim PO
JOHNSON, Peter, Sh-147-2; Pvt G Co 10th MS Inf; 10 May 62 to 20 Apr 65; Cuba PO
JOHNSON, Peter, Sh-158-3; Pvt I Co 3rd Col Cav; Oct 63 to Feb 66; Memphis PO; fistula in arm 25 yrs
JOHNSON, Pleasant, Cl-52-2; Pvt A Co 11th TN Cav; 1-1-64 to 9-11-65; Hypratia PO; prisoner at Richmond 9 mos
JOHNSON, Pleasant, Ha-110-2; Pvt L Co 8th TN Cav; 1 Jan 65 to 11 Sep 65; Luther PO; asthma
JOHNSON, Presley E., Fe-40-1; Pvt E Co 36th IN Inf; 8-23-61 to 9-21-64; Little Crabb PO; sciatica & rheumatism, wounded in left hip
JOHNSON, Reason P., H-53-7; Asst Surg 104th OH Inf; 3 yrs; Chattanooga PO
JOHNSON, Reuben E., A-4-2; Cpl A Co 1st US Hvy Art; 8-19-65 to 3-24-66; Coal Creek PO; erysipelas, cause of dis.
JOHNSON, Richard, Sh-149-1; Sgt M Co 3rd US MS Cav; Feb 63 to Nov 65; Memphis PO; paper in hand of claim agent
JOHNSON, Richard B., H-68-2; Pvt D Co 2nd NJ Cav; 8-10-63 to 8-4-65; Chattanooga PO; kindney disease, not able to be on duty at times
JOHNSON, Richard H., Sh-193-1; Pvt; Memphis PO
JOHNSON, Richard H., W1-298-1; Sgt K Co 5th TN Cav; 3 Mar 63 to 14 Aug 65; Round Top PO; catarrh of the head, able to do half work
JOHNSON, Richard H., O-141-2; Union City PO; no information

JOHNSON, Richard M., Cl-46-1; Pvt A Co 24th KY; 12-14-61 to 9-14-64; Clairfield PO; lung disis
JOHNSON, Rilie, R-162-1; Pvt E Co 1st AL Cav; 64 to 64 (6 mos); Dayton PO; rheumatic trouble from exposure in service
JOHNSON, Robert, H-55-2; Pvt C Co 110th TN Inf; 62 to 65; Jersey PO; shot through right hip
JOHNSON, Robert, L-101-1; 5th Sgt F Co 47th LA Cav; Henning PO; lost discharge (deserves pension)
JOHNSON, Robert, D-93-1; Pvt I Co 12th TN Inf; 12 Aug 63 to 16 Jan 66; Belleview PO
JOHNSON, Robert, D-64-4; Nashville PO
JOHNSON, Robt., La-117-4; Harriet E. widow of; nothing known; 15th Dist; CONF
JOHNSON, Robert A., Ge-87-2; Pvt C Co 2nd NC Inf; Oct 63 to 16 Aug 65; Timberridge PO; bronchitis
JOHNSON, Robert B., K-172-1; Pvt A Co 6th TN Inf; 20 Apr 62 to 27 Apr 65; Knoxville PO
JOHNSON, Ruffus P., K-184-4; Pvt C Co 1st TN Inf; Dec 62 to Jun 65; Riverdale PO; shot in the shoulder
JOHNSON, Rufus, Un-255-1; Pvt G Co 7th TN Inf; 8 Nov 64 to 10 Ju 65; Warwicks X Roads PO
JOHNSON, Russel R., Br-14-1; Pvt; McDonald PO
JOHNSON, Russel R., Mc-115-2; Pvt I Co 5th US Col; 7-15-64 to 5-22-65; Riceville PO; hurt in shoulder & head
JOHNSON, Sam, Sh-159-3; Jane widow of; Pvt; Memphis PO
JOHNSON, Samuel, K-161-2; O. S. L Co 1st TN Hvy Art; 14 Aug 64 to 31 Mar 65; Knoxville PO
JOHNSON, Samuel, Ha-115-2; Pvt E Co 61st TN Inf; 25 Oct 63 to 1 Jul 65; Jap? VA PO; shot through thigh; CONF
JOHNSON, Samuel, Fr-110-1; Pvt; Belvidere PO; right eye injured, no exactness as to dates
JOHNSON, Samuel, W1-297-2; Dist No 12
JOHNSON, Samuel A., Lo-190-2; Sgt L Co 1st TN Inf; 14 Aug 64 to 31 Mar 66; Loudon PO
JOHNSON, Samuel B., H-51-3; Sgt D Co 2nd IN Cav; 7-16-62 to 7-21-65; Hill City PO
JOHNSON, Samuel H., A-9-3(1); Nancy M. Cleansman formerly widow of; Pvt E Co 3rd TN Mtd Inf; 7-15-64 to 11-13-64; Briceville PO; catarrh of head resulting in his death, 12-10-88
JOHNSON, Samuel M., Su-239-2; Cpl 8th TN Cav; Bloomingdale PO
JOHNSON, Sarah (see Hixon, Samuel)
JOHNSON, Sarah (see Everly, Thomas)
JOHNSON, Sarah A. (see Teague, John W.)
JOHNSON, Sherade, He-63-2; Pvt A Co 7th TN Cav; Jul 20 64 to Jun 13 65; Long PO; Pvt A Co 48th IL Inf (Mar 24 62 to Jul 22 62)?
JOHNSON, Stephen, K-169-1; Cpl A Co 6th TN Inf; 24 Apr 62 to Jan 64; Knoxville PO
JOHNSON, Stephen, Br-13-1; Pvt I Co 4th TN Cav; 1-17-64 to 7-12-65; Georgetown PO
JOHNSON, Sylvester, H-63-2; Pvt 70th TN Inf; 61 to 63; 408 W 7th; Chattanooga PO; hearing
JOHNSON, Thomas, H-49-2; Pvt A Co 6th TN Mtd Inf; 8-2-64 to 6-30-65; Lakeside PO
JOHNSON, Thomas, K-157-1; Alice widow of; Pvt; Knoxville PO
JOHNSON, Thomas, D-79-3; Addie widow of; Pvt F Co 49th US Col T; Nashville, 323 Foster PO; hemorrhages, caused by cold and exposure
JOHNSON, Thos., De-25-1; Decaturville PO
JOHNSON, Thomas, Mu-200-1; Sofronia P. widow of; Pvt; Terry PO; has never recd. pension
JOHNSON, Thomas F., Ge-102-3; Pvt C Co 2nd NC Mtd Inf; 1 Oct 64 to 16 Aug 65; Whig PO; pain in back, now rheumatism
JOHNSON, Thomas J., He-61-3; Pvt H Co 3rd US Hvy Art; Aug 63 to Apr 65; 15th Civil Dist
JOHNSON, Thomas L., Hw-126-1; Pvt A Co 1st TN Inf; 10 Oct 63 to ___; Fishers Creek PO; prisoner at Rogersville 6 days, captured, no discharge
JOHNSON, Thomas R., H-55-1; Pvt G Co 5th TN Cav; 63 to 5-65; Tyner PO
JOHNSON, Thomas W., Gi-138-1; Cpl I Co 4th TN; 8-15-64 to 8-30-65; Bodinham PO
JOHNSON, Timothy A., Tr-269-1; Caroline widow of; Pvt 44th TN Inf; 19 Sep 61 to 20 Sep 66; Hartsville PO
JOHNSON, Tobe, Sh-153-1; alias Johnson, William; Pvt A Co 1st USC Cav; 20 Jan 64 to 31 Mar 66; Collierville PO

JOHNSON, Trannel, Dk-34-6(5); Lurah E. widow of; E Co 2nd TN Inf; 11-25-64 to __; Copling PO; consumption
JOHNSON, Valentine G., Ge-93-2; Pvt Co I 1st TN Cav; 1 Aug 62 to 5 Jul 65; Greeneville PO
JOHNSON, W. B., Sh-189-1; Wagonmaster with Capt Nye AQM Dept; 10-61 to 2-20-64; Iowa Ave, Memphis PO
JOHNSON, Walter, Sn-254-1; Pvt B Co 70th OH Inf; 9-16-61 to 8-15-65; Hendersonville PO
JOHNSON, Wash., Sn-161-1; US Sol; 16th Dist
JOHNSON, Wash., Ru-239-1; Cpl E Co 16th TN Inf; 6 yrs; Overall PO
JOHNSON, West, Wi-282-1; Pvt K Co 44th IL Reg; May 61 to Aug 65; Peytonsville PO; wounded in left arm & shoulder
JOHNSON, Wiley W., Mu-199-1; Pvt H Co 5th TN Cav; 16 Aug 63 to 14 Aug 65; Ashwood PO
JOHNSON, William, Co-68-3; Pvt 2nd TN Cav; 62 to 65; Sutton PO; fever & ague
JOHNSON, William, Bl-1-1; Pvt G Co M. Wrays Regiment, Capt Uriah Brown; 10-5-? to __ (dates lost and forgotten); Sequatchie College PO; paralys and loss of speech
JOHNSON, William, Ct-44-1; Hannah widow of; Pvt I Co 8th TN Inf; 7-64 to __; Hampton PO; killed by bushwhackers, never received a discharge
JOHNSON, William, Br-12-4; Sydneyton PO
JOHNSON, William, Ch-18-1; Pvt I Co; PO omitted
JOHNSON, William (see Johnson, Tobe)
JOHNSON, William, Mt-135-2; Sol US; PO omitted
JOHNSON, William, Ch-18-3(5); Pvt I Co Cav; Hawkins TN; Montezuma PO; had forgotten dates & time of service
JOHNSON, William, Hy-83-1; Pvt A Co; 63 to 65; Brownsville PO; lost discharge
JOHNSON, William, F-46-2; Capt E Co 17th IL; 62 to 65; LaGrange PO; rheumatism
JOHNSON, William, Sh-160-1; alias Johnson, Henry, Pvt B Co Hvy Art; 61 to 65; Memphis, Poplar St (126 to 130); right arm broken, now almost useless
JOHNSON, William, Gi-127-5; Sgt E Co 110th TN Inf; 5-64 to 1-66; Pulaski PO
JOHNSON, William, Mu-195-2; Mollie widow of; Sol; Columbia PO
JOHNSON, William, Sh-201-4; Pcr V Co 3rd US Col Reg Hvy Art; 10 Mar 63 to 10 Apr 66; Memphis PO
JOHNSON, William, We-222-2; 1st Cpl A Co 8th KY. Reg; 61 to 65; Gardner PO; piles, alias Samuel Johnson
JOHNSON, William A., W-189-3(2); Capt F Co 81st OH Inf; 9-10-61 to 7-20-65; McMinnville PO; served 4 mos previous to above enlistment from 4-22-__ to 8-19-61
JOHNSON, William B., O-138-1; Pvt 15th TN Cav; 15 Aug 62 to 20 Apr 65; Lanes PO; CONF
JOHNSON, William C., Ch-12-1; Cpl B Co 6th TN Cav; 8-15-62 to 7-26-65; Wild Goose PO
JOHNSON, William D., Ja-86-1; Pvt D Co 4th TN Cav; 4-63 to 8-65; Oottewah PO; chronic diarhea
JOHNSON, William H., Jo-149-3; Elizabeth widow of; Blacksmith D Co 13th TN Cav; 24 Sep 63 to 5 Sep 65; Mountain City PO; phthisic result measles
JOHNSON, William H., Me-88-2; Pvt F Co 5th TN Inf; 3-2-62 to 4-14-65; Birchwood PO
JOHNSON, William H., Mu-209-6; Pvt 1st TN Cav; 3-64 to 12-64; Columbia PO
JOHNSON, William P., Un-254-1; Sgt E Co 6th TN Cav; 15 Apr 62 to 27 Apr 65; Paulett PO; lost one eye from smallpox
JOHNSON, William R., Mg-196-3; Pvt A Co 1st TN Inf; 61 to 65; Hunnicutt PO
JOHNSON, William R., Lo-189-1; Mary widow of; Pvt C Co 3rd TN Cav; Nov 62 to kiled 25 Apr 65; Philadelphia PO; killed by blow up of Sultana
JOHNSON, Wilson L., K-182-3; Ord Sgt K Co 2nd TN Vol Inf; 62 to 65; Gap Creek PO
JOHNSON, Wilson N., Hw-119-4(2); Pvt C Co 63rd TN Inf; oct 63 to __; Alum Well PO; yellow jaundice; unsound
JOHNSON, Yancy, M-103-4; Pvt I Co 7th KY Vol Inf; 10-15-61 to 11-14-63; Sullivan PO. discharged on account of disability

JOHNSON, Zack, M-105-1; Pvt D Co 4th TN R; 6-63 to 8-6_ (1 yr 2 mos); Echo PO
JOHNSTON, Alen, Ro-201-4(2); alias Kimbrough, Alen; Teurice widow of; Pvt A Co 1st TN Hvy Art; 8 Feb 64 to 31 Mar 66; Kingston PO
JOHNSTON, Andrew F., Br-14-3; Mahala widow of; 5th TN Cav; 62 to 65; Black Fox PO; served in Stoke's Cavalry
JOHNSTON, Andrew W. Br-9-4; Pvt A Co 1st TN Inf; 12-16-62 to 8-3-65; Cleveland PO
JOHNSTON, Benjamin (Col); Ma-128-1; Margarette A. widow of; Pvt 3rd TN Hvy Art; Jackson PO; could get not information
JOHNSTON, Cary, Dy-25-9(1); Poll- A. widow of; Pvt A Co; Newbern PO; sicken & died 1863, now drawing pension
JOHNSTON, George M., Un-256-3; US Sol; PO omitted
JOHNSTON, Henry, Sh-203-2; US Sol; Memphis PO
JOHNSTON, James, Hd-45-2; Pvt F Co 9th IN Mtd Inf; 63 to Dec 64; Cerro Gordo PO; discharge not present, hence arregulars
JOHNSTON, James J., H-69-1; Pvt I Co 10th TN Vol Cav; 2-3-64 to 8-1-65; Chattanooga PO
JOHNSTON, John L., Ma-114-2; Pvt C Co 6th TN Inf; Jan 61 to Jul 16 62; Pinson PO; CONF
JOHNSTON, John N., K-174-5; Pvt A Co 4th TN Inf; 1 Aug 63 to 2 Aug 65; House Mountain PO
JOHNSTON, John W., Di-34-3; Pvt G Co 120th PA Inf; 2-24-64 to 3-24-65; Dickson PO; physical disability
JOHNSTON, John W., D-54-2; Pvt D Co 2nd OH Inf--Apr 61 to Aug or Jul 61; Sgt H Co 37th KY Inf--6 Jul 63 to 29 Dec 64; Nashville PO
JOHNSTON, Jno. W. A., La-117-4; Pvt; 15th Dist; CONF
JOHNSTON, Joseph W., H-69-6; Pvt K Co 2nd TX Cav; 75 yo 76; Chattanooga PO; CONF
JOHNSTON, Lewis, Br-13-2; Pvt F Co 42nd TN Col Inf; Ora PO
JOHNSTON, Manuel, Dy-25-3; Pvt A Co 7th TN Cav; Aug 62 to Aug 65; Newbern PO
JOHNSTON, Mariah (see Miller, Alfred)
JOHNSTON, Robert N., Ro-201-6; Pvt I Co 1st TN Inf; 9 Aug 61 to 17 Sep 64; Kingston PO
JOHNSTON, Rose (see Mitchell, Young)
JOHNSTON, Thomas J., La-116-1; Pvt H Co 2nd TN Cav; Dec 9 63 to Jan 21 65; Strathmore PO
JOHNSTON, Thomas M., Me-88-3; Pvt E Co 5th TN Mtd Cav; 1-1-64 to 12-1-64; Brittsville PO
JOHNSTON, Wm., Mo-109-2; Sgt E Co 5th TN Mtd Inf; 64 to 7-65 (9 mos); Sweetwater PO; exposure caused rheumatism
JOHNSTON, William J., Mr-99-3; Pvt C Co 6th TN Inf; 11-8-62 to 1-20-65; Jasper PO
JOHNSTON, William T., Mr-96-2; Pvt Ast AL Cav; 63 to 64; Sunyside PO
JOHSON, Lewis J., K-165-3; Ardely B Co 2nd CT __; 62 to 65; 35 Hauer Ave, Knoxville PO
JOHSON, William A., Sm-175-1; Pvt I Co 9th KY Inf; 12-1-61 to 1-25-65; Rome PO; oung trouble
JOHSTON, Robert M., Mr-99-2; Pvt C Co 6th TN Inf; 9-2-64 to 6-30-65; Jasper PO
JOICE, ____, Je-136-1; Sarah A. widow of; Pvt F Co 6th TN Cav; 20 Apr 62 to 20 Apr 65; Dandridge PO
JOINER, Abner, M-107-3; Sgt A Co 11th TN Cav; 62 to 64; Walnut Shade PO
JOINER, Daniel, Fr-112-1; Cook M Co 1st OH Cav; 61 to 65; Tullahoma PO
JOINER, Nickademus, K-186-4; Pvt C Co 2nd TN Cav; 20 Jan 62 to 14 Jul 65; Balls Camp PO
JOINES, Tilmon, Dk-33-2; Pvt F Co 4th TN Inf; 7-30-61 to 8-25-65; Dowelltown PO; disease of eyes
JOLLEY, Henry C., D-68-2; Cpl B Co 14th USC Inf; 63 to 65; 99 Claiborn St, Nashville PO
JOLLEY, Isaac B., We-225-1; Pvt E Co 15th KY Cav; 13 Oct 62 to 6 Oct 63; Dresden PO
JOLLEY, John, Cu-15-2; Pvt B Co 5th TN Cav; Genesis PO; left on furlough never returned; CONF
JOLLY, William T., H-69-3; Pvt; Chattanooga PO; CONF
JOMS, Henry H., Dk-35-3(1); Pvt G Co 6th TN Cav; 8-30-64 to 5-20-65; Hicks PO
JONES, Aaron, Sh-157-4; Pvt K Co 63rd __; Nov 2 63 to Jan 9 66; Lake View, MS PO
JONES, Acy, Hw-130-2; Pvt L Co 8th TN Cav; Lee Valley PO

169

JONES, Adolphus D., We-221-1(4); Pvt L Co 6th TN Cav; 62 to 65; Martin PO; shot in right ankle
JONES, Alex, Mu-209-5; Pvt D Co 1st TN Inf; 62 to 65; Columbia PO; prisoner 2 yrs Camp Morton, IN; CONF
JONES, Alexander, Ge-94-1; Paulina widow of; Pvt E Co 2nd NC Inf; Greeneville PO
JONES, Allen, Bo-21-4; Pvt H Co 1st TN Cav; 8-11-63 to 5-12-65; Ellijay PO
JONES, Allen, Sh-152-2; Dexter PO
JONES, Ammon D., Pu-145-2; Pvt G Co 5th Cav Vol; 9-27-62 to 8-14-65; Burton PO
JONES, Andrew, Co-63-3; Elenora widow of; Pvt; 61 to 65; Newport PO
JONES, Andrew, D-71-1; US; Nashville PO
JONES, Andrew C., H-58-2; Martha J. widow of; Sgt E Co 6th TN Mtd Inf; 9-12-64 to 6-30-65; Coulterville PO
JONES, Anthony, T-216-2; 11th Civil Dist
JONES, Asa, Hw-127-3; Pvt L Co 8th TN Cav; 18 Sep 63 to 18 Sep 65; Lee Valley PO; right thigh broken, deafness &c &c
JONES, Bartley R., Pi-156-1; Pvt F Co 2nd TN Cav; 8-1-62 to 7-6-65; Permelia PO
JONES, Bealey, O-136-1; Pvt E Co 4th TN Inf; Jun 3 64 to Apr 15 65; Terrell PO
JONES, Benjamin, Gr-81-4(2); Pvt A Co 12th TN Cav; 64 to 28 Oct 65 (1 yr 6 mos); Shelton's Ford PO; spinal, partley disabled
JONES, Benjamin, Col, H-56-6; TN Inf; 64 to 65; St. Elmo PO
JONES, Betsy, D-60-3; widow; 1116 Church St, Nashville PO
JONES, Bucker, Sh-147-1; Sgt C Co 3rd TN Art; 27 Dec 63 to 30 Apr 66; Cuba PO
JONES, Calvin, P-151-1; Nancy widow of; Pvt E Co 2nd TN Mtd Inf; 18 Sep 62 to 63; Pope PO; died in the service
JONES, Calvin J., Ha-115-3; Pvt A Co 63rd TN Inf; 15 May 62 to 20 Oct 62; Mulberry Gap PO; one hand cut off--left; CONF
JONES, Calvin R., Wa-263-3; Pvt H Co 8th TN Cav; Sep 63 to Aug 64; Garbers Mills PO
JONES, Carrol, Ca-23-3; Pvt I Co 4th TN Inf; 2-15-65 to 8-25-65; Morrison PO (Warren Co.); no injuries
JONES, Charity (see Williams, _____)
JONES, Charles, Sh-159-1; Ord 53rd IN; 3 yrs 5 mos; Memphis PO; shot twice in head and lip, affects head in warm weather
JONES, Charles, Sh-202-1; Pvt A Co Inf; 12 Apr 61 to 65; Memphis PO
JONES, Charles, Su-240-3; Pvt 1st Bat TN; Sep 64 to Apr 65; Slawghter PO; CONF
JONES, Charles, D-77-3; Pvt 14th US Col Inf; Nashville PO
JONES, Charley, Lo-187-1; Pvt K Co 1st US Col Hvy Art; 2 Aug 64 to 31 Mar 66; Loudon PO
JONES, Coulson C., Wl-308-1; A. D. widow of; Pvt TN; Jan 1 62 to Jan 1 66; Rural Hill PO; CONF
JONES, Creed H., Pu-145-3(4); Pvt L Co 5th Cav Vol; 7-17-63 to 8-14-65; Silver Point PO
JONES, Crude, Pu-146-1; Capt C Co 1st TN Mtd Inf W(hite?); 9-21-63 to 12-13-64; Buffalo Valley PO
JONES, Cyris, Jo-152-2; Pvt F Co 40th TN Inf; Mar 65 to May 66; Butler PO; chills & wound
JONES, Daniel, D-49-1; Pvt E Co US Hvy Art; Jul 64 to ___ (1 yr 6 mos); Nashville PO
JONES, Dave, D-99-1; Pvt G Co 13th TN Inf; Oct 10 63 to Jan 10 66; Chanerly PO
JONES, David, Je-147-2; Sgt F Co 9th TN Cav; 24 Jul 63 to 2 Aug 65; Shady Grove PO
JONES, David, Sh-144-2; US Sol; First Dist
JONES, David M., G-71-3; Pvt D Co 23rd TN Inf; 15 Jul 62 to 18 Sep 63; PO omitted; CONF
JONES, David W., He-63-1; Pvt C Co 6th TN; Sarah A. widow; Sep 18 62 to ___; Shady Hill PO; in Andersonville; death not known
JONES, Dice, Gi-123-1; Pvt TN Col Inf; 62 to ___; Bethel PO
JONES, Dirson, Ge-89-3; Pvt A Co 12th TN Cav; no dates (insane and dont know); Marvin PO; mind
JONES, Dollie, Sh-190-2; widow of Sol; 170 Kansas Ave, Memphis PO
JONES, Druerry, K-155-1; Susan widdow of; US Sol, War 1812, Pvt; Knoxville PO; draws pension, cannot recolect

JONES, E. G., Bo-11-1; Pvt A Co 3rd TN Inf; 2-10-62 to 2-10-65; Meadow PO (Loudon Co.); rhumatism
JONES, Edward, Sh-146-2; Pvt A Co 86th; Woodstock PO
JONES, Eli, Mu-192-1; Pvt D Co 44th TN Inf; 4-16-64 to 5-26-66; Columbia PO; not wounded
JONES, Elihu, C-33-5; Elizabeth J. widow of; Capt E Co 2nd TN Inf; 8-61 to 5-21-62; Newcomb PO
JONES, Elisha, H-58-5; Elizabeth A. widow of; Pvt D Co 1st TN Lt Art; Retro PO; died in hospital Nashville
JONES, Eliza (see Morris, William)
JONES, Erwin, Sh-153-3; Pvt B Co 61st ___; Jun 63 to ___ (2 yrs 6 mos); Collierville PO; struck by bullet at Guntown, I don't know anything about how long he served, he died in Sep 1866
JONES, Evan, K-165-3; 76 Adkin St, Knoxville PO
JONES, Fayette, G-57-3; Yorkville PO; CONF
JONES, Francis M., Bo-12-1; Pvt I Co 5th TN Inf; 7-1-62 to 6-14-65; Houk PO
JONES, Frank, Gi-131-1; Cpl I Co 111th Col Inf; 63 to 65; Pulaski PO; small pox injured sight
JONES, Frank, F-46-2; Lila widow of; Pvt H Co 59th TN; 63 to 64; killed in Gun Town fight, widow quite needy
JONES, Fredrick J., H-50-4; Sgt E Co 6th R TN Mtd Inf; 8-16-64 to 6-30-65; Soddy PO; rupture and piles
JONES, Garret, Ge-92-5; 1st Sgt K Co 1st TN Cav; 12 Jul 62 to 5 Jun 65; Romeo PO; rhumatism disease of heart
JONES, George, Gi-135-4; Pvt B Co 110th TN Inf; 11-1-63 to 2-13-66; Bufords Station PO; wounded in head, which greatly affects his eyes
JONES, George, Ro-210-4; Adlate Lewis formerly widow of; Pvt H Co 1st TN Inf; Rockwood PO
JONES, George, Ro-203-3; 2nd Lt I Co 11th TN Cav; 63 to 65; PO omitted
JONES, George, Ge-90-4; Lt E Co 8th TN Cav; 23 Jul 63 to 13 May 64; Greeneville PO; general disabilities
JONES, George, Gr-78-2; Pvt E Co ___ Cav; 9 Oct 64 to 28 Oct 64; Larkeyton PO
JONES, George, Hw-134-1; Pvt D Co 4th TN Inf; 62 to 65; Rogersville PO; disease of lungs
JONES, George, Mc-111-3; Sgt A Co 12th TN Cav; 5-29-63 to 10-7-65; Mouse Creek PO
JONES, George A., Ge-83-2; Pvt G Co 4th TN Inf; 12 Oct 63 to 2 Aug 65; Henshaw PO; chronic diarrhea
JONES, George H., Je-145-2; Hexter (sic) K Co 3rd TN Inf; 10 Feb 62 to 23 Feb 65; Dumplin PO
JONES, George W., Mc-113-2; Pvt D Co 2nd TN Inf; 5-16-63 to 5-22-65; Riceville PO
JONES, George W., Hm-33(103)-1; Pvt B Co 11th IL? Cav; 63 to Aug 64 (1 yr 11 mos); Dyersburg PO
JONES, George W., Ha-115-3; Pvt B Co 69th TN Cav; 1 Sep 63 to 1 Mar 65; Mulberry Gap PO; CONF
JONES, Grant, K-155-1; Pvt C Co 7th Col Inf; 18 Oct 64 to 31 Mar 66; Knoxville PO; eye hurt
JONES, Hamilton, Lo-189-2; Betsey widow of; Pvt L Co 1st TN Hvy Art; Philadelphia PO; pressed into service
JONES, Hardin, Ct-36-3; Roar Mountain PO
JONES, Harlin C., Lo-192-2; Cpl F Co 3rd TN; Jan 63 to Jun 65; Coytee PO
JONES, Henry, D-64-2; Tabitha widow of; Pvt 112th ___; Nashville PO
JONES, Henry, Col, Sh-145-1; Pvt I Bat 3rd TN USC Hvy Art; 25 Apr 64 to 13 Apr 66; Millington PO; hard of hearing, lost by firing cannon, Capt S. D. Thompson enlisted at Memphis TN and discharged at Memphis TN
JONES, Henry, Col, Sh-145-1; Musician G Co 1st US Col TN; Apr 64 to 65; Millington PO; I was cut off from my company in a skirmish near Greenville TN
JONES, Henry (see Frazur, Henry)
JONES, Henry, Sh-146-1; Pvt G Co 44th Inf; May 62 to 65; Lucy PO; wounded at Nashville by minnie ball
JONES, Henry, Cr-1-1; Mariah widow of; Sgt A Co 3rd US Hvy Art; ___ to 64; Gadsden PO; killed Memphis, TN 1864
JONES, Henry, Hw-134-2; US Sol; 20th Civil Dist
JONES, Henry, Hm-106-1; Caroline widow of; Pvt F Co 13th TN Cav; Morristown PO

JONES, Henry B., Ro-204-1; 2nd Lt A Co 17th TN Cav; 5 Mar 62 to __ (9 mos); Elverton PO; yellow jaundice, piles
JONES, Henry H., Dk-31-2; Cpl G Co 4th TN Mtd Inf; 11-1-64 to 8-25-65; Alexandria PO
JONES, Immanuel, H-59-3; Nancy widow of; Pvt K Co 5th US Art; 10-61 to 5-65; Chattanooga PO
JONES, Ira H., Je-147-1; Pvt M Co 2nd TN Cav; 8 Nov 62 to 23 Jun 65; Shady Grove PO
JONES, Isaac N., C-24-1; Sgt H & B Co 11th & 9th Cav; 7-1-63 to 9-11-65; Boy PO; heart & piles & rheumatism
JONES, Israel, Sh-174-4; alias "Doc" Jones; Pvt A Co 61st US Col Inf; 63 to 5-65; 10 Hadden Ave, Memphis PO; shot through abdomen, bowels permanently injured
JONES, J. D., Hu-103-3; Pvt E Co 11th TN Inf; 62 to 65; PO omitted; entry marked through, probably CONF
JONES, J. H., Ma-126-2; Jackson (at present) PO; given in by wife, could never catch him at home to get co, regt or enlistment &c
JONES, J. Ira, Dy-25-7(3); Pvt K Co 154th TN Inf; 7 May 61 to __; Newbern PO; wounded three times cutting tends Achilles; CONF
JONES, Jackson, Gi-127-7; Pulaski PO; papers misplaced
JONES, Jacob, Pi-156-1; Pvt H Co 1st KY Cav; 9-14-61 to 12-30-64; Permelia PO
JONES, James, D-80-1; 2nd Civil Dist
JONES, James A., Ge-92-5; Malinda widow of; Pvt H Co 8th TN Inf; Romeo PO; died in Andersonville Prison GA
JONES, James A., Hw-121-3(2); Pvt B Co 8th TN Inf; 18 Dec 62 to 30 Jun 65; New Hope PO; none in war
JONES, James B., B-11-3(2); Sgt A Co 10th TN Inf; 1-25-63 to 4-25-65; Poplins X Roads PO
JONES, James C., Su-240-3; Pvt; 63 to 65; Kindricks Creek PO; never discharged; CONF
JONES, James C., A-13-2; Pvt E Co 6th TN Cav; 8-6-63 to __ 64; Briceville PO; has no discharge
JONES, James C., Hw-118-3; Sgt D Co 4th TN Inf; 13 Apr 62 to 7 Jan 65; St. Clair PO; disabled back
JONES, James F., Hw-133-1; Pvt B Co 3rd TN Mtd Inf; 30 Jun 64 to 30 Nov 64; Beurams Store PO; chronic diareah
JONES, James L., Gi-133-1; Pvt B Co 3rd TN; May 18 61 to Jul 5 65; Bufords PO; CONF
JONES, Jas. M., Bo-14-2(1); Pvt H Co 5th TN Inf; Yellow Sulphur PO; discharged for disability, discharge lost, cannot give dates
JONES, James M., K-184-3; Pvt H Co 8th TN Cav; 18 Sep 62 to 15 Sep 65; Thorn Grove PO
JONES, James M., Mg-200-2; Sgt K Co 11th KY Inf; 20 Oct 61 to 1 Aug 65; Skene PO; heart disease
JONES, Jarrett, Sh-150-2; Pvt C Co 17th MO Inf; Jul 62 to Oct 66; Mullins Station PO
JONES, Jason, Mu-198-2; 10th Dist
JONES, Jasper A., Mg-198-1; Sgt B Co 137th PA; 3 May 62 to 5 May 63; Deer Lodge PO; shot in right ear
JONES, Jesse, Gi-127-7; Pulaski PO; papers & dates lost
JONES, Jehu, K-181-5(2); Pvt A Co 50th TN Cav; Mar 63 to 65; Knoxville PO; CONF
JONES, Jeramire M., Dy-25-6(2); Pvt E Co TN Cav; Mar 62 to Apr 65; Newbern PO; wounded & prisener & exchanged; CONF
JONES, Joe, Sh-153-2; alias Cloudes, Joe; Pvt I Co 44th US C Inf; May 64 to Dec 64; Collierville PO; captured and wounded
JONES, John, Sh-174-4; Rebecca widow of; 63 to __; 40 Hadden Ave, Memphis PO
JONES, John, Ha-115-3; Nancy widow of; Pvt; Mulberry Gap PO; CONF
JONES, John, Mg-196-1; Pvt I Co 1st TN Cav; Mar 63 to Sep 65; Oliver Springs PO
JONES, John, Lo-187-3; Pvt L Co 1st US Col Hvy Art; 64 to 66; Adolphus PO
JONES, John, Co-67-5; Pvt H Co 1st TN Cav; 11 Aug 62 to 12 May 65; Naillon PO
JONES, John, Ha-110-3; Pvt H Co 14th KY Inf; 25 Jan 63 to 25 May 65; Michburgh PO; collar bone, broken arm and shoulder joint dislocated, fell off "Wildcat Cliff" in a night march

JONES, John, Mr-96-2; Pvt D Co 9th TN Cav; 9-13-62 to 9-65; Shirleton PO; deftness
JONES, John, F-37-1; alias John Pulliam; Pvt D Co 61st US Col Inf; __ to Dec 30 65; Yum Yum PO
JONES, John C., Ro-202-3(1); Pvt B Co 63rd TN Inf; 26 Apr 62 to retired May 64; Union X Roads PO; gun shot wound; CONF
JONES, John J., Bo-13-2; Pvt I Co Del HA; 6-1-63 to 7-1-63; Freindsville PO
JONES, John J., Hw-125-1; Pvt K Co; 63 to 65; Blevins PO; prisoner at Chicago 18? mos; CONF
JONES, John J., Lo-187-4; Pvt L Co 1st US Col Hvy Art; 64 to 66; Adolphus PO
JONES, John L., D-102-1; Pvt B Co 161st OH Inf; 10 May 64 to __; Jordonia PO
JONES, John M., Mo-122-1; Pvt C Co 14th NY Inf; 63 to 65 (1 yr 3 mos); Madisonville PO
JONES, John M., Rb-219-2; Pvt C Co 14th TN Reg; May 61 to Apr 64; Orlinda PO
JONES, John M., Wl-299-1; Pvt K Co 5th TN Inf; 1 Feb 63 to 14 Aug 65; Statesville PO
JONES, John R., C-8-2; Pvt D Co 9th TN Cav; 7-17-63 to 9-12-65; Stockville PO; bashed left hip deased, receives $120 per yr
JONES, John W., Wl-308-2; Nancy A. widow of; Pvt H Co 45th TN; Dec 11 61 to Dec 11 63; Dodoburgh PO; CONF
JONES, John W., Pu-145-1; Pvt A Co 5th Cav Vol; 8-4-62 to 6-25-65; Burton PO
JONES, John W., Lo-190-3; Recruiting Off 11th TN Cav; Jan 63 to __; Piney PO
JONES, John W., Sn-250-2; Pvt K Co 2nd __; 5-3-61 to __-2-63; Castalian Springs PO; CONF
JONES, Johnson N., Mr-102-2; Eliza widow of; Pvt B Co 1st TN Cav; South Pittsburg PO; drawing pension, discharge lost
JONES, Josep, Ha-111-2; Pvt K Co 13th TN Cav; 15 Sep 63 to Aug 65; Upper Clinch PO
JONES, Joseph, Lo-189-1; Pvt L Co 1st TN Hvy Art; 19 Sep 64 to 31 Mar 66; Philadelphia PO; rheumatism
JONES, Joseph, Bo-14-4; Pvt C Co 1st TN Cav; 2-1-63 to 5-25-65; Clover Hill PO
JONES, Joseph, K-161-6; Knoxville PO; died in service
JONES, Joseph, Pu-144-1; Bloomington PO
JONES, Joshua L., Se-225-1; Pvt 15th TN Cav; Allensville PO; 1 rib broke
JONES, Juanias A., K-160-4; 38 N 3rd Ave, Knoxville PO
JONES, King E., Rb-219-1; on same line as Rippy, Jesse; Pvt 20th TN Reg; Nov 64 to May 65; Orlinda PO; CONF
JONES, Landon C., Hw-121-2; US Sol; PO omitted
JONES, Leander D., Ha-115-3; Pvt B Co 69th TN Cav; 1 Sep 63 to 1 Mar 65; Mulberry Gap PO; CONF
JONES, Lee, Sh-191-3; Memphis PO; records not seen
JONES, Lewis, K-182-3; Pvt B Co 3rd TN Vol Inf; 61 to 64; Gapcreek PO; mashed by falling
JONES, Lewis, Wa-267-3; Cpl F Co 8th TN Cav; 31 May 63 to 11 Sep 65; Jonesboro PO; indigestion & rheum, mustd. out in 8th TN Cav
JONES, Lewis J., Mg-200-1; Pvt F Co 1st TN Inf; 9 Aug 61 to 12 Sep 64; Kismet PO; rheumatism
JONES, Lilborn, Lo-189-1; Philadelphia PO
JONES, Lincon S., Hw-133-2; Pvt H Co 8th TN Inf; Jul 63 to 27 Jun 64; Burem's Store PO; ruptured
JONES, Lincy (see Smith, Z.)
JONES, Lon, F-37-1; alias Lon Tucker; Pvt D Co 59th US Col Inf; Somerville PO
JONES, Malinda Sinth (see Berry, P. L.)
JONES, Manuel, Mt-135-1; Pvt A Co 9th TN Art; 5-64 to 8-65; Jordan Springs PO
JONES, Manuel (see Scurlock, Jim)
JONES, Margaret (see Garrett, Daniel)
JONES, Margaret Leach (see Holleway, John)
JONES, Mark F., Ge-92-5; Pvt B Co 3rd TN Mtd Inf; Romeo PO
JONES, Martin, Mo-119-2; Pvt D Co 1st TN Cav; 1 yr; Sweetwater PO
JONES, Marvel, Je-139-1; Pvt C Co 8th TN Inf; 10 Aug 63 to __; Trion PO
JONES, Mary (see Gann, James M.)
JONES, Mary, H-49-11; widow Sol US; 2nd Civil Dist
JONES, Mathew, F-39-1; Pvt A Co 63rd US Col Inf; 20 Oct 63 to 28 Jun 65; Galloway PO

JONES, Matthew, Sm-176-1; Pvt; 63 to 65; Rome PO
JONES, Matthew F., Pu-145-1; Pvt A Co 5th Cav Vol; 7-21-62 to 6-25-65; Burton PO
JONES, Miles, T-210-1; Pvt M Co Hvy Art; Jun 63 to Jun 66; Quito PO
JONES, Miles, Je-135-3; Pvt K Co 3rd TN Inf; 10 Feb 62 to 23 Feb 65; Piedmont PO; shot in abdomen
JONES, Nicholas, S-212-1; Pvt D Co 27th NY; 10 Sep 62 to 10 Oct 64; Porch Corn PO
JONES, Nicholas T., Hw-133-1; Elizabeth J. widow of; Pvt B Co 3rd TN Mtd Inf; 30 Jun 64 to 25 Oct 64; Beurams Store PO; palpitation of the heart
JONES, Oadam A., Dy-24-1; Pvt E Co 6th TN Cav; Sep 8 64 to Aug 26 65; Dyersburgh PO; left hand broken, discharged at surrender
JONES, Otisway, Hu-106-1; Pvt 10th TN Cav; Waverly PO
JONES, Phenis S., Ge-84-2; Pvt B Co 8th TN Cav; 23 Jul 63 to 11 Sep 65; Greenville PO; cronic rhumatism
JONES, Pleas C., Hw-133-2; Pvt H Co 8th TN Inf; Slide PO
JONES, Pleasant F., Ro-204-1; Pvt H Co 3rd TN Inf; 27 Feb 62 to __ (5 mos); Elverton PO
JONES, Preller, T-216-2; 11th Civil Dist
JONES, Prettyman, Pu-145-5(6); 2nd Lt C Co 1st Mtd Inf; 8-63 to 5-16-64; Buffalo Valley PO, discharge not at hand
JONES, Ramon, Sn-250-2; Pvt K Co 2nd __; 5-3-61 to -3-62; Castalian Springs PO; CONF
JONES, Ransom T., He-62-3; Pvt Co H 55th TN; Feb 14 62 to Apr 14 62; Chesterfield PO; mumps & yellow janders; CONF
JONES, Rebecca (see McFarland, John)
JONES, Redding, Ms-173-1; 7th Civil Dist
JONES, Richard D., Ha-115-3; Pvt A Co 1st TN Cav; 18 Oct 61 to 3 Jul 65; Mulberry Gap PO; prisoner at Camp Chase 7 mos & Rock Island 18 mos; CONF
JONES, Richard J., Mg-199-3; Mary widow of; Pvt G Co 2nd TN Inf; 5 Oct 62 to __; Mill Creek PO
JONES, Richmond, Gi-132-1; Cpl K Co 110th US CV; Nov 19 63 to Feb 6 66; DeRay PO
JONES, Rievins?, Ge-88-2; Carthin widow of; Pvt E Co 1st KY Lt Art; 29 Feb 64 to 1 Aug 65; Mohawk PO; rheumatism & blind in left eye
JONES, Robert, Hw-133-3; Pvt C Co 1st TN Lt Art; 1 Apr 64 to 1 Aug 65; Burem's Store PO; disease of eyes
JONES, Robert S., Mo-120-1; Pvt E Co 7th TN Mtd Inf; Sweetwater PO; chronic diarhea
JONES, Rogert, Sh-162-1; Letha Winston widow of; Bings Town PO; rupture
JONES, Rufus, Mg-199-1; Pvt F Co 1st TN Inf; 27 Feb 62 to 27 Feb 65; Sunbright PO; general debility
JONES, Rufus F., Sh-178-2; Wardmaster B Co 38th KS; 5-13-67 to 5-17-69; rear 173 Orleans St, Memphis PO
JONES, Rufus J., Sh-201-2; Cpl B Co 12th TN Cav; 20 Sep 63 to 20 Oct 65; Memphis PO
JONES, Russel, Co-59-2; US Sol; 1st Dist
JONES, S. N., M-108-5; Evaline widow of; Pvt 9th KY Inf; Lafayette PO; discharge not at home
JONES, Saml., Or-70-1; Sgt D Co 4th TN Inf; 22 Dec 62 to 10 Aug 65; Rutledge PO
JONES, Samuel, Cl-48-2; Amanda widow of; Old Town PO
JONES, Samuel, Gr-81-4(2); Pvt H Co 1st TN Cav; 15 Jul 62 to 5 Jun 65; Clear Spring PO; rheumatism, partly disabled
JONES, Samuel, Pi-154-2; 4th Civil Dist; rheumatism 25 yrs
JONES, Samuel, U-246-2; Pvt M Co 8th TN Cav; 5 Feb 64 to 11 Sep 65; Limonite PO
JONES, Samuel B., Br-8-2; Pvt D Co 63rd IN Inf; 8-10-62 to 7-25-65; Cleveland PO; lost right arm—left hand
JONES, Seiben, H-69-1; Pvt; Chattanooga PO
JONES, Seyrus N., H-58-2; Lucy A. Leggett formerly widow of; Pvt G Co 6th TN Mtd Inf; 2-20-65 to 6-30-65; Sale Creek PO
JONES, Silas B., H-72-3(2); Evaline formerly widow of; Chattanooga PO
JONES, Silas M., Mc-114-3; Pvt 2nd TN Inf; 5-17-63 to 8-3-65; Folger PO; middle of one hand crippled by gunshot
JONES, Silas M., Mu-209-6; Pvt G Co 9th TN Cav; 3-64 to 9-65; Columbia PO; CONF
JONES, Silus M., Mu-209-1; Pvt G Co 9th TN Cav; Sep 64 to Mar 65; Columbia PO; CONF
JONES, Solomon, Hy-75-1; Pvt C Co Memphis Hvy Art; 62 to 65; Dancyville PO; diseased, ruptured, has recd. a bounty
JONES, Solomon H., K-179-2; Nancy C. Williams widow of; Pvt G Co 1st TN Inf; 9 Aug 61 to 11 Sep 64; Virtue PO
JONES, Solomon T., Lo-192-2; Pvt K Co 9th TN; 10 Oct 63 to 10 Sep 65; Coytee PO; lung disease
JONES, Spencer, Sh-147-1; Pvt A Co 55th TN Inf; 15 Aug 62 to 6 Apr 65; Cuba PO
JONES, Stephen, Mu-191-1; Bigbyville PO
JONES, Thomas, F-46-2 (see Grant, Tom)
JONES, Thomas, Ha-110-3; Allie E. widow of; Pvt G Co 1st TN Cav; 1 Jul 62 to 6 Jun 65; Luther PO
JONES, Thomas, St-162-2; Cumberland City PO
JONES, Thomas A., C-29-1; Capt B Co 2nd TN Cav; 8-15-62 to 7-6-65; Fincastle PO; bronchitis
JONES, Thos. J., Bo-14-2(1); Elizebeth J. widow of; Pvt F Co 2nd TN Inf; Yellow Sulphur PO; date of enlistment & discharge not known
JONES, Thomas P., Sn-256-1; Pvt E Co 4th TN Mtd Inf; 9-12-64 to 8-65; Cotton Town PO; discharge lost and cant say posative as to date of discharge
JONES, Thos. W., D-99-5; 4th Sgt C Co 1st TN Cav; Apr 21 61 to May 26 65; Nashville PO; Central Hos. for Insane; CONF
JONES, Thomas W., Ge-99-2; Bethia S. widow of; Sgt E Co 4th TN Inf; Limestone Springs PO; consumption, discharge at Washington & could not get dates
JONES, Tilman, Dk-32-4; Pvt L Co 5th TN Cav; 7-10-63 to 8-14-65; Doneltown PO; lost right eye
JONES, Tom, O-140-1; Pvt I Co 4th TN Inf; 63 to Apr 65; Union City PO; has discharge but not at home
JONES, Tom, Sh-144-2; Pvt S? Co Col Inf; Dec 22 63 to 20 Apr 66; Brunswick PO
JONES, Tom, Sh-144-2; US Sol; First Dist
JONES, Tommas, Ce-27-1; Pvt H Co 12th US Col; 12 Aug 63 to 1 Jan 65; Collensville PO; right injured slightly
JONES, Tony, Wl-302-2; Shopsprings PO; discharge absent
JONES, Tyler, Je-143-3; US Sol; Mossy Creek PO
JONES, W. H., Gi-122-3; 1st Lt A Co 3rd TN Inf; 14 May 61 to May 65; Prospect Sta. PO; shot in thigh, prisoner 7 mos; CONF
JONES, Wallace, K-167-6; Pvt H Co 1st Hvy TN; 62 to 65; Knoxville PO
JONES, Werly, Ge-96-2; Eliza J. widow of; Pvt B Co 4th TN Cav; 16 Oct 62 to 12 Jul 65; Theatown PO; cant get dates
JONES, Wesley J., Hu-106-1; Pvt 10th TN Cav; Waverly PO
JONES, Wiley C., Cl-52-1; Pvt A Co 9th TN Cav; 10-1-63 to 9-10-65; Quarter PO
JONES, Wiley W., Co-61-5(2); Pvt D Co 8th TN Cav; May 63 to __; Bridgeport PO
JONES, William, Sh-160-2; Pvt D Co TN; 63 to 65; Memphis PO
JONES, William, Ro-202-4; Pvt C Co 7th TN Inf; 6 Oct 62 to 3 Aug 65; Cave Creek PO; rheumatism & bowels, also heart? disease
JONES, William, K-178-2; Lucinda C. widow of; Pvt C Co 6th TN Inf; 18 Apr 62 to 24 Apr 65; Ball Camp PO
JONES, William, H-73-2(1); Lucinda widow of; Pvt; Chattanooga PO; shot in left side, ball still remains in side
JONES, William, Ha-110-1; Lidia widow of; 7th KY Inf; Mar 62 to 65; Treadway PO; died in the service
JONES, William, H-49-9; Mary widow of; Pvt C Co 5th TN Inf; 2-25-6 to 3-17-63; Igon's Ferry PO; widow of two soldiers
JONES, William, O-142-2; US Sol; Obion PO
JONES, William, U-244-1; Pvt H Co 10th TN Cav; 1 Mar 64 to Aug 65; Ernestville PO; small pox, rupture, captured

JONES, William A., M-103-4; 3rd Sgt B Co 8th TN Inf; 1-1-65 to 9-1-65; Lafayette PO; lost hearing
JONES, William A., Mg-196-2; Pvt C Co 2nd TN Cav; Nov 4 62 to 6 Jul 65; Coalfield PO; rheumatism, totally disabled
JONES, William B., O-141-3; Union City PO; no information
JONES, William C., Ca-24-1; Pvt G Co 1st TN Mtd Inf; 4-4-64 to 7-22-65; Gassaway PO; pain in head settled from effect fever when in the army
JONES, William C., Se-225-1; Pvt E Co 1st TN Cav; 2 Jul 62 to 5 Jun 65; Allensville PO; rheumatism and sore eyes 25 yrs caused by cold in the army, mustered out from Co E and trasnfered to Com G after returning from prison
JONES, William C., M-107-6; Sgt D Co 8th TN Mtd Inf; 12-64 to 9-1-65; Willette PO
JONES, William D., Mg-197-2; Pvt F Co 1st TN Inf; 9 Aug 61 to 11 Sep 64; Wartburg PO; measles resulting in fever of left side and leg
JONES, William E., Su-239-3; Cpl? GA malitia; 5 Jun 64 to 16 Aug 65; Kingsport PO
JONES, William G., Ja-86-1; Lt E Co 5th TN Cav; 1-62 to 5-22-65; Oottewah PO; diseased generally
JONES, William G. B., Pi-154-1; Pvt K Co 1st TN Mtd Inf; 6-64 to 7-65; Byrdstown PO
JONES, Wm. H., Wa-267-3; Cpl B Co 4th KY Inf; 4 Sep 61 to 3 Jan 64; Jonesboro PO; lung dis., catarrh & chc. rheum., reenlisted veteran, Andersonville Prison 8 mos
JONES, William H., Dk-34-6(5); Pvt K Co 5th TN Cav; 4-8-62 to 8-25-65; Copling PO; rheumatism & lung disease
JONES, William H., Ms-182-1; Pvt E Co 10th TN; 10-18-63 to 6-22-65; Venna PO; hydrocele, labors 1/3 of time of the farm
JONES, Wm. H., Wa-267-2; Sgt C Co 13th TN Cav; 22 Sep 63 to 8 Sep 65; Febuary PO; lung dis
JONES, William J., Dk-31-2; Pvt K Co 5th TN Cav; 7-4-63 to 8-14-65; Alexandria PO
JONES, William J., Bo-12-3(1); Sol US; 17th Dist
JONES, William K., Hw-121-3(2); Pvt I Co 8th TN Cav; 25 Sep 63 to 17 Sep 65; New Hope PO; crippled and deafness
JONES, William M., Mg-200-1; Cpl H Co 3rd TN Inf; 10 Feb 62 to 25 Mar 65; Kismet PO; back & shoulders by wagon upsetting
JONES, William O., K-180-2; Pvt B Co 8th TN Inf; 1 May 63 to ___; Ebenezer PO; disease of kidneys
JONES, William R., Co-62-4; USS; 4th Dist; heart trouble 1 month
JONES, Wm. S., D-57-4; PVt E Co 10th TN Inf; Jul 7 62 to Jul 3 64; Nashville PO
JONES, William T., Dy-25-4; Pvt; 4 yrs; Newbern PO
JONES, Willis, Hm-104-1; Landsman, Vessel Minnesota; 24 Jan 64 to 14 Apr 66; Alpha PO; spinal or kidny with rheumatism, discharged from Vessel Tirage
JONES, Wyatt, H-73-4(2); Pvt E Co 18th IN Inf; 8-63 to 9-65; Chattanooga PO
JONES, ___, Sh-179-1(2); Carrie widow of; Pvt; Memphis PO
JONES, ___, Sh-191-2; Pricilla widow of; Memphis PO; records not seen
JONSEN, William H., D-44-2(1); Pvt 18th IN Battery; 10-15-62 to 7-5-65; Nashville PO; defective in sight & mind, reenlisted 7-5-64
JONSON, John W., Cl-49-2; Pvt 30th MA Mtd Inf; 8-29-64 to 6-16-65; Zeb PO; kidney
JONSON, Robert, Dk-36-3; Pvt F Co 5th TN Cav; 10-11-62 to 9-11-65; Mechanicsville PO
JORDAN, Alfred, D-73-1; Caroline widow of; Pvt; Nashville PO
JORDAN, Edward (see Neal, Edward)
JORDAN, Harbert M., De-26-2; C Co 2nd TN; 13 Jan 64 to 1 Jan 65; Genette PO
JORDAN, Henry C., G-73-1; (Col) Bugler K Co 44th US Inf; Jun 1 64 to Apr 1 65; Trenton PO; captured at Dalton
JORDAN, James R., G-71-1; Pvt H Co 7th TN Cav; 16 Oct 61 to 25 Aug 63; Rutherford PO; chronic rheumatism of liver; CONF
JORDAN, James T., Ge-95-2; Cpl B Co 12th TN Cav; 1 Jul 63 to 3 Oct 65; Home PO; diarrhea, piles & sight, rheumatism and heart
JORDAN, Jim, Ru-237-1; Pvt G Co 5th TN Inf; 20 Aug 61 to 20 Aug 63; Alisona PO; thigh fractured
JORDAN, John M., T-219-1; US Sol; Dist 15
JORDAN, John R., L-101-2; 1st Lt A Co 1 Dak? C; Henning PO; flesh wound left breast, lost discharge
JORDAN, N. C., He-57-1; Pvt I Co 19th TN Cav; 4-1-64 to 7-1-65; Juno PO; CONF
JORDAN, Ozias, R-163-2; Pvt F Co 5th TN Inf; 2-25-62 to 3-29-65; Graysville PO
JORDAN, Peter, Ru-239-1; Mary A. widow of; Pvt; Patterson PO; smallpox
JORDAN, Pinckney C., Cu-15-2; Pvt 47th NC Inf; Genesis PO; Baitties Batt. recog. as US & paid; CONF
JORDAN, Teter, H-69-2; Sarah widow of; Pvt L Co 1st US Col Art; 7-18-65 to 3-31-66; Chattanooga PO
JORDAN, William A., Bl-4-2; Pvt A Co 1st KY Cav; 4-15-63 to 9-22-65; Morgan Springs PO (Rhea Co.)
JORDAN, William S., Sq-164-3(1); Pvt G Co 10th TN Cav; 62 to ___ (3 yrs); Dunlap PO; shot in right hip
JORDON, Dan, D-49-3; alias Hancock, Dan; Pvt F Co 44th US Cav; 29 Jul 64 to 30 Apr 66; 502 McLemore St, Nashville PO
JORDON, Henry, Ro-210-3; Pvt C Co 1st TN Inf; 62 to 8 Sep 66; Rockwood PO; rheumatism
JORDON, Orlando, D-57-1; Pvt I Co 4th TN Inf; Mar 1 65 to Aug 25 65; PO omitted, 8th Ward
JORDON, William, Sh-160-2; Pvt D Co 88th TN Inf; ___ to Jan 62; Memphis PO
JOSEPH, Henry C., D-77-2; Pvt A Co 27th OH Inf; 12 Sep 62 to 11 Jul 65; Nashville PO; chronic diarrhea, rheumatism
JOSEPHUS, ___, Li-160-1; 19th Civil Dist
JOSLIN, Joseph, Lo-187-2; Cpl A Co 46th MA Inf; Aug 62 to ___; Loudon PO
JOURDAN, Robert H., Wy-171-1; Pvt H Co 6th TN; Sep 18 62 to Jul 2 65; Waynesboro PO; rumatism
JOY, Elias W., Hi-92-1; Pvt K Co 6th MI Inf; Aug 25 61 to Sep 20 65; Aetna PO
JOYNER, Calvin G., Mg-197-3; Pvt B Co 1st TN Inf; Crooked Fork PO; rupture 1862
JOYNER, Nathan G., Cr-14-2; Martha E. widow of; Pvt A 7th TN Cav; 15 Aug 62 to 9 Aug 65; Clarksburg PO
JOYNES, Edgon, Fe-42-3; Pvt A Co 22nd IN; 61 to 63; Boatland PO
JUCKETT, James, Mt-139-2; Pvt I Co 4th MD Cav; 62 to 66; Palyra PO
JUDD, Mathias, Pu-140-2; Cpl I Co 1st TN Inf; 8-20-64 to 8-22-65; Cookeville PO; rheumatism & heart disease
JUDSON, Silas H., Gu-45-2; Lt B Co 1st OH ovelea?; 61 to 65 (3 yrs 10 mos 17 days); Beersheba Springs PO
JULES, Jessy A., Co-68-2; Cpl E Co 2nd TN Cav; 16 Sep 62 to 14 Jul 64; Cashy PO; deafness in one ear & partialy in the other
JULIAN, Drury C., K-182-1; Pvt A Co 6th TN Inf; 8 Mar 62 to 27 Apr 65; PO omitted
JULIAN, James J., Ct-36-2; Pvt E Co 2nd TN Inf; 8-2-62 to 6-19-65; Roan Mt. PO; 13 mos in Andersonville Prison
JULIAN, James N., O-141-1; Lt L Co 6th TN Vol CAv; 7 Aug 62 to Aug 16 64; Union City PO
JULIAN, John M., Br-11-1; Cpl A Co 4th TN Cav; 5-24-63 to 7-65; Chatala PO
JUNO, Lewis, Cf-40-1; Musician Pvt G Co 26th WI Vol; 16 Aug 62 to 21 Aug 65; Tullahoma PO; gun shot in left side
JURRICK, James, Sn-253-1; Pvt B Co MA Cav; 12-64 to 65; No. One PO; poor as Lazarus
JUSTICE, Danial K., Ge-89-4; Cpl D Co 8th TN Inf; 15 Mar 63 to Jun 6 65; Romeo PO; spinal afection, back and diarhea
JUSTICE, Henry D., Ge-97-1; Pvt C Co 4th TN Inf; 17 Mar 63 to 2 Aug 65; Newmanville PO; kidny disease
JUSTICE, Henry H., Hr-97-1; Pvt B Co 1st AL Cav; Mar 65 to Jun 65; Toone PO
JUSTICE, Nicholas, M-106-2(1); Pvt B Co 3rd NC & TN Mtd Inf; 64 to ___; Hillsdale PO; taken prisoner and held

JUSTIS, William A., Ge-101-1; Pvt K Co 1st TN Cav; 7 Jun 63 to none; Locust Sp. PO; shot in the back
JUSTUS, Alexander, Se-230-1; Pvt B Co 38th GA Inf; 62 to __ (3 yrs); Richison's Cove PO; hearing; CONF
JUSTUS, Julius A., Se-230-3; Cpl F Co 9th TN Cav; 25 Sep 63 to 11 Sep 65; Richison's Cove PO; back trouble, he had mumps, measles &c, thinks dregs of measles the cause of present trouble
JUSTUS, Martin, Se-230-3; PO omitted; CONF
KAGAR, George W. L., Ov-137-1; this soldier refused to give any information as to his service; Nettle Carrier PO
KAGLEY, Absalom F., Bo-14-2(1); Pvt H Co 2nd TN Cav; 10-10-62 to 7-6-65; Yellow Sulphur PO; kicked on head by horse
KAGLEY, William L., Bo-14-2(1); Cpl H Co 2nd TN Cav; 10-10-62 to 7-6-65; Yellow Sulphur PO; grovel?
KAIN, John G., H-59-3; Gunboat Miss. River; Chattanooga PO
KAIRE, Thomas, Sh-169-1; Pvt B Co 4th IN Inf; 61 to 64; Memphis PO
KAISER, Mathias, Cf-40-3; Sarah widow of; Pvt B Co 18th Reg Inf; Tullahoma PO; discharge at pension office
KANCE, Erastus S., Sm-169-3(5); Capt; Defeated PO; CONF
KANE, Alex, Ge-102-1; Cpl G Co 4th TN Inf; 5 May 63 to 2 Aug 65; Henshaw PO; hurt by gilling (getting?) smash up
KANE, Jacob, A-10-1; Pvt 1st TN HA; 6-22-64 to 3-31-66; Briceville PO; testicles injured from mumps
KANE, Joseph F., Ge-102-3; Pvt G Co 4th TN Inf; Oct 61 to 65; Henshaw PO; liver disease; now deaf in left ear
KANE, Mike, Wl-295-2; Pvt A Co 30th NY Reg Inf; 64 to Sep 65; Lebanon PO
KANIFE, Daniel, Hm-108-3(2); Pvt C Co 16th NC Inf; 2 yrs; Russellville PO
KAPLINGER, Frederick, W-194-1; Pvt G Co 52nd MA? Inf; 3-16-63 to 12-16-63; Morrison PO
KAPPER, Benjamin, Hw-119-3(1); Pvt C Co 63rd TN Inf; Alum Well PO; CONF
KARMAN, James, Mu-191-1; Pvt E Co 111th TN Vol; 2-10-64 to 4-30-66; Bigbyville PO
KARNS, John M., K-168-3; Pvt G Co 6th TN Inf; 18 Apr 62 to 17 May 65; Smithwood PO
KARR, George P., H-61-4; Pvt D Co 1st MO Inf; 4-1-61 to 7-15-61; Chattanooga PO; CONF
KARZ, William J. M. C., Mu-210-4; Pvt E Co 2nd TN Cav; 61 to 5-65; Carters Creek PO; CONF
KASSEFANG, Will Federick, C-34-2; Pvt & 1st Lt Co H 58th NY & 22nd Inf; 9-62 to 10-17-65; Buckeye PO
KATE, George W., Mo-122-1; Pvt B Co TN Inf; 12-63 to 3-3-64; Dancing Branch PO; further dates could not be given; CONF
KAUFMAN, S., Sh-201-1; Bertha widow of; Pvt; Memphis PO; discharge papers lost; CONF
KEAN, John G., D-49-2; enrolled as Cain by error; Pvt B Co 21st IL Inf; 27 Jun 61 to 4 Jul 64; Nashville PO; comp. fract. in both wrists, RR accident
KEANE, Stephen, Ch-18-2; Pvt 21st TN Cav; 63 to __ (12 mos 8 days); his wife did not know his war history; Montezuma PO; loss of left eye (minie ball)
KEAR, Joel, Se-223-3; Pvt B Co 2nd TN Cav; 15 Aug 62 to 6 Jul 65; Henderson Springs PO
KEAR, John, Se-222-3; Pvt M Co 2nd TN Cav; 8 Nov 62 to 2 Jun 65; Harrisburg PO; rumatism, mind, site & heering, head trubel
KEARLEY, Benjamin F., Cu-16-2; Pvt G Co 6th TN Mtd Inf; 2-20-65 to 6-30-65; Litton PO; diarrhea
KEARLEY, Calvin, Cu-16-2; Cpl G Co 6th TN Mtd Inf; 2-20-65 to 6-30-65; Litton PO
KEARNEY, Samuel, Sh-201-4; Julia M. widow of; Memphis PO
KEASEY, Louis, St-159-1; Meesy widow of; Pvt KY Cav; Indian Mound PO
KEATON, J. P., Lk-112-1; Sgt I Co 3rd KY Inf; 30 Jul 61 to Oct 13 64; Tiptonville PO; a little deaf
KEATON, James, Wl-298-2; Pvt D Co 4th TN Mtd Inf; 20 Oct 64 to 25 Aug 65; Cottage Home PO
KEATON, James, Ca-25-3; Pvt; Gassoway PO
KEATOR, Matthew S., H-63-1; Cpl I Co 89th NY Inf; 9-61 to 12-25-62; 21 Magazine, Chattanooga PO
KECK, John, Cl-57-2; PO omitted; CONF
KECK, Joseph W., K-160-4; 6 Luttrell St, Knoxville PO
KEE, Jerry, Mt-147-1; Dist 16
KEE, Martin L., Cr-14-2; Pvt K Co 2nd TN Mtd Inf; 22 Dec 63 to May 65; Clarksburg PO; discharge lost
KEEBLE, John, Wa-274-3; Pvt A Co 3rd TN Cav; Oct 62 to Jun 65; Jonesboro PO; diarrhoea, lung disease & heart disease
KEEBLE, P. M., Bo-22-3; Pvt 3rd TN Cav; Hebronville PO
KEEBLE, Samuel, K-179-2; Pvt G Co 3rd TN Inf; Feb 10 62 to 23 Feb 65; PO omitted
KEEBLE, Samuel, Bo-22-3; Pvt H Co 3rd TN Cav; 9-25-63 to 8-3-65; Ellijay PO; loss of health
KEEF, John, D-45-3; Nancy widow of; Pvt A Co 5th TN Cav; 3-5-63 to 8-4-65; Nashville PO
KEEL, John W., Ho-96-1; Pvt B Co 29th IL Inf; Aug 12 62 to Sep 15 65; Erin PO
KEELE, Michael, K-181-1; Pvt C Co 6th TN Inf; 18 Apr 62 to 24 May 65; Michael French (sic) PO
KEELER, E. J., St-162-1; Louisa widow of; Pvt; Cumberland City PO; wounded behind ear, lost eye from wound, papers all burned
KEELER, James M., Se-221-2; Pvt B Co 2nd TN Cav; 15 Aug 62 to 31 May 65; Fair Garden PO; discharged from hospital
KEELER, Smith, K-154-6(3); Cpl D Co 57th NY; Sep 61 to Sep 64; Knoxville PO
KEELIN, John J., Ro-210-9; Pvt B Co 2nd TN Inf; 10 Aug 61 to 12 Nov 64; Rockwood PO; relapse of measles
KEELING, Firdinand, K-185-1; Pvt G Co 8th TN Cav; 63 to 65; Scaggston PO; eyes afficted
KEEN, Abram, Cy-27-6(4); US Sol; 4th Civil Dist
KEEN, Abram, Cy-27-1; Pvt I Co 1st TN Mtd Inf; 2-8-64 to 5-3-65; Clementsville PO
KEEN, Alderson T., S-213-2; Maj I Co 1st KY Cav; 25 Jul 61 to 31 Dec 64; Hellenwood PO; hernia & tumor right arm
KEEN, David, Un-252-3; US Con; 15th Dist
KEEN, G. W., Lk-112-1; Pvt C Co 7th TN Cav; 19 Aug 62 to Jun 24 64; Tiptonville PO; scurvy--not serious; farm labor
KEEN, Pinkney M., Ch-14-2; Pvt; PO omitted; CONF
KEENER, Abraham, Co-63-3; Pvt I Co 2nd TN Cav; 22 Sep 62 to 5 Jul 65; Newport PO; piles, chronic diareah, paralysis
KEENER, Chas. L., Wa-271-1; Jonesboro PO
KEENER, Isaac H., Se-226-2; Cpl C Co 9th TN Cav; 22 Jul 63 to 24 Mar 65; Sinking Springs PO chronic diarrhoe & rheumatism
KEENER, James D., H-54-2(3); Pvt E Co 11th TN Cav; 11-13-61 to 2-65; Chattanooga PO; scurvy, chronic diarrhoea
KEENER, John, Co-67-2; Mary A. Hicks widow of; Pvt E Co 2nd TN Cav; Oct 62 to __; Cosby PO; killed accidentally
KEENER, Tillman, H-58-4; Margaret widow of; Pvt B Co 5th TN Mtd Inf; Sale Creek PO; failed to see discharge
KEENEY, Wiley, T-208-1; Susanah Terry widow of; Sgt A Co TN; 61 to 63; Covington PO; kild July 2 near Dalton, GA
KEENY, Robert, H-66-1; Pvt A Co 4th TN Cav; 10-15-62 to 7-12-65; Chattanooga PO
KEER, W. A., Hd-48-1; 2nd Class Fireman, Exchange; Jun 17 63 to Jun 17 64; Savannah PO
KEETAN, Burg, S-212-1; Pvt G Co 7th TN; 15 Sep 62 to __ (3 yrs); Hellonwood PO; rheumatism
KEETEN, Jacob, Me-92-2; Pvt C Co 3rd TN Cav; 12-10-62 to 8-3-65; Fiketon PO; lung disease
KEETHLEY, Jane (see York, James)
KEETON, John E., D-73-2; Pvt G Co E TN Inf; Oct 62 to Nov 65; Granry White Pike PO; Nashville PO
KEETON, Jonathan J., Wy-175-1; Pvt A Co 6th TN Cav; 9-9-63 to 7-20-65; Victory PO
KEETON, Samuel M., Ca-25-2; Pvt I Co 5th TN Cav; 11-62 to 8-4-65; Gassoway PO
KEETON, William, Dk-31-3; Susan Garrison formerly widow of; Cpl I Co 5th TN Cav; 12-62 to 4-63; Forks of Pike PO; killed in line of duty

KEEZEL, W. C., Wa-276-1; Sgt M Co 1st TN Cav; Sep 28 62 to Jun 5 65; Limestone PO; liver disease
KEFFER, Peter, O-133-1; Pvt G Co 21st OH Inf; 20 Apr 61 to 15 Aug 61; Rives PO; Cpl G Co 178th OH Inf; 28 Aug 64 to 30 Jun 65
KEGLEY, James, Hw-127-4; Jane McVey former widow of; Pvt; Austins Mills PO
KEICHER, Reuben A., Ge-100-2; Pvt G Co 4th TN Cav; 13 Apr 63 to 22 Jun 65; Midway PO
KEIFER, James M., Ge-100-1; Pvt K Co 8th TN Inf; 1 Dec 62 to 27 Jan 65; Midway PO; not curable
KEISER, Joseph, H-65-1; US Sol; 502 Carter St, Chattanooga PO
KEITH, Gabriel P., H-58-3; Pvt I Co 71st IN Inf; 6-11-63 to ___; Sale Creek PO
KEITH, Henry, Cy-27-1; Rebeca widow of; Pvt I Co 1st TN Mtd Inf; 64 to 5-65 (1 yr 3 mos); Clementsville PO
KEITH, Mack, H-70-3(1); Josephine widow of; Pvt A Co 44th TN Inf; 61 to 65; Chattanooga PO; chronic dysentery, recovered from it afterwards
KEITH, Mark, Dy-25-3; Pvt 13th TN Cav; 61 to ___ (3 yrs); Newbern PO; CONF
KEITH, William A., K-177-1; Pvt C Co 3rd E TN Inf; 1 Feb 62 to 10 Jun 65; Chumlea PO; prisoner at Andersonville 13 mos
KEITH, William J., A-8-3; Pvt E Co 8th TN Inf; 3-1-63 to 6-30-65; Scarborough PO
KELLAM, Orrin A., Sh-145-1; Pvt D Co 127th IL Inf; 12 Aug 62 to 5 Jun 65; Millington PO; Cap Robert Chandler, Com D, 60 yrs old, 19 May 1890
KELLAS, Robert B., H-70-1; Capt A Co 19th IL Inf; 6-17-61 to 5-8-65; Chattanooga PO
KELLEN, Nancy, Dy-20-1; widow; Dist 2
KELLER, David, Un-257-1; Pvt M Co 9th TN Cav; New Prospect PO
KELLER, Isaac M. H., Cl-47-3; Pvt M Co 9th TN Cav; 9-1-63 to 9-11-65; Compensation PO; back & kidneys 1863
KELLER, James N. J., Ge-99-1; Pvt B Co 8th TN Cav; 23 Jul 63 to 11 Sep 65; Limestone Springs PO; rheumatism, deafness & nasal catarrh
KELLER, Oscar, Hw-123-1; Pvt G Co 10th TN Cav; 9 Nov 63 to 1 Aug 65; Rotherwood PO
KELLER, Peter, Un-255-1; Pvt M Co 9th TN Cav; 8 Sep 63 to 11 Sep 65; Warwicks X Roads PO; rumatism
KELLER, Samuel D., Co-60-1; B Co 8th TN Inf; 1-5-63 to 6-13-65; Syrensburg PO; injured eyes
KELLER, William H., Bo-20-1; Pvt E Co 8th TN Inf; 2-10-62 to 12-13-65; Bank PO; heart disease, defective in hearing
KELLEY, Albert, H-58-6; Pvt I Co 4th MI Cav; 8-63 to 8-65; Retro PO; discharge in Washington DC
KELLEY, Daniel, Hw-132-2; Polly widow of; Pvt 8th TN Inf; Jun 63 to 64; Strahl PO; died in prison, could not get full particulars
KELLEY, Daniel H., Ge-99-1; Delilah widow of; Pvt F Co 2nd TN Vol; Limestone Springs PO; pleurisy, cant get dates
KELLEY, Donald H., Br-14-4; Pvt A Co 7th TN Inf--7-2-62 to 2-63; Lt D Co 1st TN Lt Art--2-63 to 7-26-65; McDonald PO; habitual constipation & piles, general disability
KELLEY, Eli, Mc-112-1; Pvt F Co 8th TN Cav; 10-10-62 to 9-11-65; Athens PO; ruptured veins
KELLEY, Elishu, De-22-3; Pvt C Co 51st TN Inf; 1 Dec 61 to 1 Oct 62; Point Pleasant PO; CONF
KELLEY, George, H-75-1; Sgt A Co 115th IL Inf; 8-11-62 to 1-11-65; Chattanooga PO
KELLEY, George, Mc-114-6; Pvt; Santfordville PO
KELLEY, George M., H-64-1; Pvt G Co 42nd OH V Inf; 9-19-61 to 12-20-64; Chattanooga PO
KELLEY, James, Br-12-6; Charleston PO
KELLEY, Jas. A., R-163-2; Pvt B Co 6th TN Mtd Vol Inf; 8-15-64 to 6-30-65; Graysville PO; bronchitis contracted
KELLEY, James B., Ge-84-1; Pvt A Co 9th TN Mtd Inf; 64 to ___; Wolsey College PO; rheumatism, was taken sick and left, got no discharge
KELLEY, James H., Re-210-1; Pvt H Co 43rd TN Vol; Sep 62 to May 65; Rockwood PO; CONF
KELLEY, James J., Mc-116-3; Cyntha widow of; Pvt H Co 9th TN Cav; 11-20-62 to 9-11-65; Mortimer PO

KELLEY, James J., Br-9-1; 2nd Lt C Co 5th TN Inf; 2-29(sic)-62 to 2-14-64; Cleveland PO
KELLEY, John M., H-64-2; Pvt D Co 7th Del; 64 to 64 (30 days); Chattanooga PO
KELLEY, Joseph, Lo-189-3(1); Polly widow of; Pvt TN Inf; 62 to 64; Philadelphia PO; gunshot wound through left leg, leg off, dis. on sur. cert; CONF
KELLEY, Joseph B., Hw-121-3(2); Pvt B Co 3rd TN Mtd Inf; 30 Jun 64 to 1 Nov? 64; New Hope PO; none in war
KELLEY, Lewis, La-111-1; Pvt H Co 1st AL Cav; 10-10-63 to 5-11-65; PO omitted
KELLEY, Mathew K., Ma-124-1; Pvt H Co 213th TN; Dec 64 to Oct 65; Jackson PO
KELLEY, Robert, Co-60-1; K Co 8th TN Inf; 7-25-63 to 6-30-65; Salem PO; chronic diarhea 26 yrs
KELLEY, Sam, Br-10-2; Pvt D Co 29th IN Inf; 9-13-61 to 12-2-65; Cleveland PO
KELLEY, Samuel N., Un-254-3; Pvt G Co; Meltibarger PO; CONF
KELLEY, Samuel S., Wy-178-1; Pvt B Co 2nd TN Mtd Inf; 10-15-63 to 10-17-64; Light PO; general debility & piles, has been in bad health since fall of 63
KELLEY, Thomas, Cl-52-3; Pvt A Co 9th TN Cav; 62 to 65; Hypatia PO; lost a finger
KELLEY, William, Hd-46-2; Pvt A Co 2nd TN Mtd Inf; Oct 2 63 to Oct 14 64; Lowryville PO
KELLEY, William B., Mc-112-2; 2nd Lt F Co 1st KY Vol Cav; 8-21-61 to 6-63; Athens PO; rheumatism
KELLEY, William H., K-165-1; Pvt C Co 42nd TN; Dec 62 to May 65; Knoxville PO
KELLEY, William M., Mc-116-2; Sgt A Co 7th TN Mtd Inf; 10-6-64 to 7-27-65; Williamsburg PO; injure in left ancle
KELLIS, James H., H-54-1; Pvt H Co 13th TN Cav; 2-1-65 to 9-5-65; Chattanooga PO; fever in the hospital at Knoxville 3 mos, suffering from rheumatism defective eyes
KELLMAR, Conrad, H-72-3(2); Pvt K Co 65th OH Inf; 9-26-61 to 1-1-64; Chattanooga PO; Pvt K Co 1st US Vol Eng; 1-1-64 to 12-26-65; transferred to engineer corps
KELLOGG, Joseph, D-60-1; 1047 Church St, Nashville PO; failed to find him
KELLY, Alex W., Ge-91-5; Pvt A Co 4th TN Inf; 15 Nov 61 to 25 Nov 64; Greeneville PO; piles & rheumatism & bronchitis
KELLY, Anna (see Roberts, John)
KELLY, Benjamin S., Sn-172-1; Pvt G Co 8th MO Inf; 6-22-61 to 7-4-64; PO omitted (Memphis)
KELLY, George W., Mc-112-2; Cpl C Co 5th TN Inf; 2-25-62 to 4-10-65; Athens PO; piles & heart disease
KELLY, James, Cr-4-1; Pvt I Co 13th IL Cav; 63 to 65; Bells Depot PO; eyes damaged
KELLY, James, M-106-2(1); Pvt I Co 9th KY Vol Inf; 11-2-61 to ___ (3 mos); Hillsdale PO; came home sick and taken prisoner and paroled
KELLY, James, H-57-2; Pvt H Co 16th US Col; 63 to 65; Orchard Knob PO
KELLY, James J., B1-4-3; Pvt C Co 6th TN Mtd Inf; 9-7-64 to 30-65; Pikeville PO
KELLY, John, D-44-3; Margaret widow of; Nashville PO
KELLY, John, Sh-179-3(1); Pvt H Co 1st MO Inf; 61 to 61; Memphis PO
KELLY, Jordon, Mr-102-1; Martha E. Denison widow of; Pvt A Co 42nd US Col Inf; South Pittsburg PO
KELLY, Joseph P., Gi-122-2; Elzira widow of; Pvt C Co 53rd TN Inf; Nov 62 to 64; Prospect Sta. PO; CONF
KELLY, Kenchen, Ge-23-1; Pvt; 64 to 65; Swallow Bluff PO; CONF
KELLY, Mathew, H-72-1; 1st Lt F Co 28th PA Inf; 7-6-61 to 4-9-65; Chattanooga PO
KELLY, Robert, H-69-5; Pvt B Co 44th AL Inf; 62 to 65; Chattanooga PO; shot in left shoulder
KELLY, Samuel, D-99-4; State Penitentiary PO
KELLY, Sheppar, D-58-1; Addie widow of; Pvt D Co 3rd US Col Inf; Nashville PO
KELLY, Timethy, D-60-3; Margaret Wilson former widow of; 1303 Hynes St, Nashville PO; Black
KELLY, William, Be-2-1; Pvt F? Co 2nd TN Mtd Inf; 64 to 65; Holladay PO

KELLY, William H., Mr-99-3; Pvt C Co 6th TN Inf; 9-7-64 to 6-30-65; Jasper PO; rheumatism
KELSEY, David C., Ro-208-1; 2nd Lt D Co 5th US Inf; 26 Feb 62 to 28 Mar 65; Morris Gap PO
KELSEY, Joseph M., Ro-205-3; Pvt A Co 2nd TN Inf; 10 Aug 61 to 6 Oct 64; Hatch PO; rheumatism
KELSIN?, Sarah, G-53-4; widow?; Brazil PO; this woman dont know anything
KELSIO, Drury, Ct-39-1; Johnson City PO; CONF
KELSO, Fredrick B., Dy-29-3; Conn? C Co 13th TN Cav; Dec 63 to 26 Jul 65; Trimble PO
KELSOE, William, H-53-3; 1st Lt; 62 to 65; Chattanooga PO
KELTON (Ketton?), James R., Ge-90-2; Sgt A Co 3rd TN Mtd Inf; 30 Jun 64 to 30 Nov 64; Myers PO; rumatism & heart truble
KELTON, W. D., La-110-1(2); Pvt A Co 3rd TN Inf; 10-17-64 to 11-65; Mockerson PO
KELTON, Wm., C-34-3; Pvt E Co 16th TN Cav; 1st SC Art; 6-61 to 5-65, went to TX about 5-62?; Buckeye PO; scouted to TX, rem'd till peace
KELTY, Samuel Dallas, La-117-2; Pvt B Co 23rd TN Inf; Jul 9 61 to Jun 2 65; West Point PO; CONF
KEMELL, J. N. J., Cr-4-4; Pvt B Co 9th TN Cav; 9-62 to 4-65; Bells Depot PO; wounded right leg; CONF
KEMP, Alfred, H-51-3; Pvt I Co 35th US Inf; 8-3-63 to 8-20-65; Hill City PO
KEMP, Alsa R., M-107-5; 5th Cpl D Co 87th TN Mtd Inf; 12-64 to 9-1-65; Willette PO
KEMP, Bailey R., M-107-6; Pvt D Co 8th TN Mtd Inf; 3-65 to 8-31-65; Gibbs Cross Roads PO; heart disease
KEMP, Crosby, Mu-193-1; Pvt; Columbia PO
KEMP, Henry, Sm-193-3(5); Pvt A Co 1st TN Mtd Inf; 1-2-64 to 1-13-65; 2nd Dist; fever settled in right shoulder, mumps fell
KEMP, J. J., Sh-157-7; 1st Sgt A Co 11th NY Sharp Shooters; 62 to 65; Memphis, 47 Ala. St PO; shot in the left arm
KEMP, J. J., Sh-189-1; could not get his record; Ark. Ave & Va. Ave, Memphis PO
KEMP, John B., Sh-172-2; US Sol; 386 Front St, Memphis PO
KEMP, Jno. B., Sh-172-1; Adjgt MD Inf; care Gayoso Hotel PO; will not give any further information
KEMP, Joseph W., Mn-126-2; Sgt C Co 6th TN Cav; 9-25-62 to 8-4-65; Bethel Springs PO
KEMP, Marl, Sm-169-2; Pvt; Defeated PO; also listed on p. Sm-169-4(6) as Federal—no detail
KEMP, Webster, Mu-203-1; Pvt F Co 13th TN Inf; 20 Feb 65 to 10 Jan 66; Hampshire PO
KEMP, Wiley, M-106-1; Pvt B Co 8th TN Inf; 4-65 to 8-65; Union Camp PO
KENADY, Samuel, Hw-127-3; Elizabeth Smith formerly widow of; Pvt; Rogersville PO; measles settled on lungs, died from effects of same
KENDALL, Alpheus, Cy-26-1; Pvt B Co 5th KY Cav; 10-10-61 to 5-3-65; Moss PO
KENDRICK, John D., Cu-18-2; Pvt E Co 1st TN Inf; 8-22-64 to 9-17-64; Manning PO; shot in left hand
KENEDY, Calvin, We-223-3; Pvt K Co 10th TN Cav; Dec 63 to Aug 64; Palmersville PO; wounded; CONF
KENEDY, Farris, K-167-1; Pvt 1st Hvy TN; May 62 to May 65; Knoxville PO
KENEDY, Francis M., S-213-3; Pvt F Co 32nd KY Inf; 1 Jan 63 to 12 Aug 63; Pvt A Co 13th KY Cav—1 Jan 64 to 10 Jan 65; Robbins PO; lung disease
KENEDY, Loranzy, A-9-1; Pvt I Co 7th TN Mtd Inf; 11-8-64 to 7-27-65; Ligias PO
KENEDY, Matterson, C-26-2; Pvt G Co 2nd TN Inf; 11-27-63 to 1-9-65; Hy House PO; heart trouble apoplexy, twenty sic yrs disable
KENHAM, James (see Bartee, James)
KENNEDY, A. H., K-158-1; Jane widow of; Pvt; 61 to 64; Knoxville, 19 W Clinch PO; CONF
KENNEDY, Charles J., Ge-94-2(1); Pvt M Co 1st US Cav, Hvy Art; 8 Oct 64 to 31 Mar 66; Tusculum PO; during Civil War
KENNEDY, David, He-67-1; Pvt C Co 6th TN Cav; Sep 18 62 to Jul 26 63; Sardis PO; hemorhoids & consumption, caused by measles in camp
KENNEDY, Dennis E., St-164-2; Cpl E Co 13th NY Inf; Jun 13 65 to 68; Stribling PO; reenlisted vetteren

KENNEDY, Edward, D-68-1; Sgt B Co 44th USC Inf; Mar 64 to 30 Apr 66; 56 Green St, Nashville PO feet frost biten and back injured by guard in Conf prison at Covint. MS 1864
KENNEDY, Isaac, He-67-2; Millie A. widow of; Pvt C Co 6th TN Cav; Sep 18 62 to fall of 63; Scotts Hill PO; discharged for disability, could not get the exact time
KENNEDY, J. W., K-158-1; Annie B. widow of; Pvt; 62 to 65; Knoxville, 19 W Clinch St, PO; CONF
KENNEDY, James, Gi-126-1; Pvt G Co 110th Col Inf; 23 Dec 63 to 6 Feb 66; Pulaski PO
KENNEDY, James, Se-227-3; Pvt A Co 3rd TN Inf; Mar 62 to 65; Trundles X Roads PO; two gun shot in leg, reenlisted 57th OH
KENNEDY, James M., K-154-6(3); Knoxville PO; diseased—badly, he cant or dont know
KENNEDY, John B., Mc-109-2; Pvt C Co 3rd TN Cav; 11-25-62 to 8-3-65; Ziegler PO; symptoms of apoplexy & rheumatism
KENNEDY, John M., K-156-2; Pvt I Co 2nd E TN Cav; 7 Mar 65 to Apr 65; 30 Kennedy St, Knoxville PO; CONF
KENNEDY, John W., Ov-137-3; Pvt F Co 37th KY Mtd Inf; 9-25-63 to 12-29-64; Monroe PO; diarhea & piles; left wrist dislocated at Glasgo, KY
KENNEDY, Thomas L., H-70-3(1); Pvt 30th OH Inf; about 3 yrs; Chattanooga PO
KENNEDY, Virtenvins J., H-58-1; Pvt D Co 1st TN Lt Art; 2-15-64 to 5-12-65; Sale Creek PO; chronic diarrhoea
KENNEDY, Westly, A-6-1; Hester Germmie formerly widow of; Pvt 2nd TN __; 62 to 63; Olivers PO
KENNEDY, William M., Mo-129-2; Pvt C Co 11th TN Cav; 3-28-63 to 9-11-65; Loco PO
KENNER, Benjamin F., K-173-3; Millie? E. widow of; Pvt G Co 8th TN Cav; 15 Jun 63 to 11 Sep 65; Troutman PO
KENNER, Hquston, Hw-128-1; Mary M. widow of; Pvt H Co 8th TN Inf; 25 Jul 63 to 13 Jun 65; Choptack PO; back lumbago
KENNER, Mark H., Hw-128-1; Sgt B Co 8th TN Inf; 25 Jul 63 to 13 Jun 65 (sic) (1 yr 10 mos 18 days); Choptack PO; eyes trouble
KENNER, Thomas H., Cr-3-1; Sarah E. widow of; Lt; to Jun 65; Gadsden PO
KENNER, William, Hw-128-1; Pvt D Co 1st TN Cav; 15 Apr 62 to 15 Apr 65; Choptack PO; chronic disease
KENNEY, Daniel, Ge-92-3; Pvt D Co 8th TN Inf; Romeo PO; varicose veins
KENNEY, Lorenzo D., Ge-92-2; Pvt B Co 3rd TN Mtd Inf; 30 Aug 64 to 30 Nov 64; Romeo PO
KENNEY, William J., Ge-89-1; Pvt B Co 2nd TN Mtd? Inf; 30 Jun 64 to 30 Oct 64; Romeo PO
KENSEER?, John Cf-40-3 (Col); Drum Major 14th US Inf; 63 to 65; Tullahoma PO
KENSER, William, Hw-134-2; US Sol; 20th Civil Dist
KENSINGER, Thomas, H-60-3; Pvt I Co 2nd TN Mtd Inf; 11-11-61 to 11-26-64; Chattanooga PO
KENT?, James, Gi-122-7; Pvt F Co 13th TN Inf; Dec 63 to Oct 65; Veto, AL, PO
KENT, John J., J-80-2; Pvt B Co 5th TN Cav; 7-29-62 to 9-9-62; Waggart PO (Smith Co.); cold settled on right lung; Mr. Kent's discharge is destroyed
KENT, William C., Wh-180-1; Poline widow of; Sparta PO; discharge misplaced, no information
KENYBOW?, Robert, Hr-97-1; Pvt D Co 40th __; 31 May 64 to 25 Apr 66; PO omitted
KERBOUGH, Samuel, Ge-90-2; Pvt D Co 4th TN Inf; 30 Jan 63 to 15 Aug 65; Greeneville PO; chronic lungs defect, caus—camp life
KERBOUGH, Thomas F., Ge-90-2; Pvt D Co 4th TN Inf; 30 Jan 63 to 15 Aug 65; Greeneville PO; eye weakness, caus—camp life
KERBY, John, Dk-38-1; Pvt I Co 4th TN Inf; 1-2-65 to 7-20-65; Drop PO
KERBY, Thomas, Pu-140-2; Pvt I Co 3rd TN Mtd Cav; 11-27-64 to 8-22-65; Cookeville PO; Capt Pearson's Co
KERBY, Wood, Wh-187-3; Elizabeth Lowe widow of; Pvt TN Cav; Newark PO
KERKLEN, Jessee, Mo-130-3; Pvt C Co 3rd TN Mtd Inf; 7-25-64 to 11-30-64; Ballplay PO
KERNAN, Mark D., Sh-201-1; Musician B Co 141st IL Inf; 5-10-62 to 9-15-65; Memphis PO

KERNEL, Larken, J-78-1; Pvt B Co 8th TN Inf; 1-15-65 to 8-17-65; Rough Point PO; trouble with head, spels with head & so on
KERNELL, Jessee, Pi-153-1; Pvt F Co 5th TN Inf; 5-62 to 7-14-65; Byrdstown PO; shot left foot
KERR, Daniel W., Se-225-2; Pvt B Co 9th TN Cav; 21 Aug 63 to 11 Sep 65; Allensville PO; chronic diarrhoea 25 yrs; disabilities originated in the service
KERR, Green, Ru-240-1; Viola A. widow of; Pvt F Co 42nd US Col Trops; Murfreesboro PO; died before mustered out
KERR, Henry C., Je-142-1; Pvt M Co 2nd TN Cav; 8 Oct 62 to 6 Jul 65; New Market PO; diarhea & rheumatism
KERR, James C., Lo-191-4; Greenback PO
KERR, James P., K-159-2; Pvt 3rd IN Batry, Lt Art; 24 Aug 61 to 24 Aug 64; Knoxville PO; skull fractured right side wounded near Mt Vernon, MO
KERR, James P., Mu-210-7; Pvt H Co 48th TN Inf; 12 Dec 61 to 1 Mar 63; Spring Hill PO; CONF
KERR, John W., Cy-29-1; Pvt C Co 10th TN Cav; 12-12-63 to 8-1-65; Batesville PO; speresipolus
KERR, Robbert M., Mu-210-6; Pvt H Co 48th TN Inf; 12-12-61 to 12-14-64; Mallard PO; incurred rheumatism; CONF
KERR, William H., Lo-191-2; Pvt K Co 3rd TN Cav; Sep 61 to Jan 64; Morganton PO; CONF
KERR, William M., H-68-1; Sarah widow of; Pvt; 6-27-62 to 4-15-65; Chattanooga PO; this woman has large family
KERR, William M., K-181-2; Pvt F Co 9th TN Cav; 29 Sep 63 to 11 Sep 65; Bank PO (Blunt Co.)
KERR, William P., Se-225-2; Perlina widow of; Pvt 3rd TN Cav; Allensville PO; died in prison with diarrhoea at Richmond VA
KERRAD?, William M., Mc-110-1; Pvt B Co 7th TN Inf; 10-29-64 to 7-27-65; Fiketon PO
KERSEY, Elijah (see Housewright, ____)
KERSEY, Elijah, Hw-125-3; Rebecca widow of; Inf E Co 2nd TN; 19 Mar 62 to 15 Aug 62; Surgoinsville PO; (see Housewright, ____)
KERSEY, Robert, Hw-120-1; Pvt E Do 1st TN Cav; 17 Mar 62 to 17 Apr 64; War Gap PO; rheumatism & paralysis of right side
KERTIS, Kyziah, Bl-3-6; widow of US Soldier; 10th Civil Dist
KESLING, Ruben, Co-69-6(1); Pvt D Co 8th TN Inf; 10 May 63 to 30 Jun 65; Driskill PO; rheumties at Knoxvill, TN, not drawin a pension
KESSER, Jim, D-72-2; Seaman; Jul 63 to Aug 64; Nashville PO
KESTERSON, James R., Mg-199-2; Pvt A Co 11th TN Cav; Sunbright PO
KESTERSON, William, A-4-3; Pvt C Co 2nd TN Inf; Coal Creek PO; discharge misplaced
KESTOR?, John A., D-75-2; Pvt C Co 30th TN Inf; 1 Oct 61 to 1 Aug 63; Stewarts Ferry PO; CONF
KETCHAN, David M., Mr-99-3; Frances widow of; Pvt C Co 6th TN; 9-7-64 to 6-30-65; Jasper PO
KETNER, Henry, Je-137-3; Pvt F Co 9th TN Cav; 28 Sep 63 to 11 Sep 65; Chestnut Hill PO
KEY, Franklin A., O-130-1; Francis widow of; Pvt D Co 13th TN Cav; Dec 63 to 64; Jordan, Fulton Co. KY, PO; killed at Fort Pillow
KEY, Hugh, Ge-101-1; Pvt I Co 1st TN Cav; Aug 62 to Jun 65; Locust Sp. PO
KEY, James T., Mc-110-2(1); Pvt B Co SCB KY Vet; 1-16-65 to 10-23-65; Chuckaluck PO
KEY, Jiles W., Lo-192-2; Pvt E Co 3rd TN; 1 Aug 64 to 23 Dec 64; Coytee PO; eyes effected
KEY, John, Mc-110-1; Pvt B Co 7th TN Inf; 9-21-64 to 7-27-65; Fiketon PO; heart trouble
KEYLON, William J., Me-94-1; Margaret A. White formerly widow of; Cpl; 10-18-64 to 7-13-65; Knott PO; disease of lungs from measles
KEYS, Aaron, Ge-96-1; Pvt A Co 8th TN Cav; 5 Jun 63 to May 65; Mill Brook PO; ruptured, crippled arms
KEYS, Elbert W., Wa-275-1; Pvt C Co 4th TN Inf; 25 Dec 62 to 2 Aug 65; Pettibone PO
KEYS, James, Je-137-1; Elizabeth widow of; Pvt B Co 3rd TN Cav; Hickory Ridge PO
KEYS, John, Wl-295-2; Pvt C Co 3rd TN Cav; Nov 18 61 to Mar 65; Lebanon PO

KEYS, John S., Wa-274-4; Pvt D Co 8th TN Cav; 26 Sep 63 to 14 Nov 65; Jonesboro PO; lung trouble with resulting heart disease; private for enrollment to Jan 12 64, then Cpl
KEYS, Mark, Wa-273-1; Lydia A. widow of; Pvt H Co 4th TN Cav; Aug 63 to 8 Oct 64; Morning Star PO; chronic diarrhoea
KEYS, William H., Wa-273-2; Nancy A. widow of; Pvt K Co 65th IN Inf; 5 Sep 63 to 6 Jul 65; Keeblers X Roads PO; lung disease
KIBBLE, William A., Mc-114-3; Pvt H Co 8th TN Inf; Folger PO
KIBBY, Hiram A., K-154-3; Knoxville PO
KIBLER, Sam, Br-11-2; Pvt D Co 12th TN Cav; 63 to 65; Chatata PO
KICKLE, Kannon, Un-253-3; US Sol; 4th Civil Dist
KID, William T., T-208-1; Pvt D Co 52nd IN; 62 to 65; Burleson PO
KIDD, Allen H., La-115-2; Pvt B Co 29th TN Inf; Sep 15 63 to 15 Mar 63; Summertown PO; shot left thigh; CONF
KIDD, Joe P., La-115-2; Pvt E Co 9th TN Cav; 15 Feb 63 to 10 May 65; Summertown PO; shot left leg; CONF
KIDD, Joseph O., K-171-5(4); Pvt C Co 7th TN Mtd Inf; 1 Nov 64 to 12 Jul 65; Bearden PO
KIDD, Mary A., K-154-6(3); widow US Sol; Knoxville PO; hernia
KIDD, William H., Bo-20-2; Pvt L Co 3rd TN Cav; 11-1-63 to 8-3-65; Maryville PO
KIDDY, James H., Wy-178-1; Pvt H Co 6th TN Cav; 4-5-63 to 7-26-65; Light PO
KIDDY, Paul W., Hd-52-1; Pvt B Co 2nd TN Cav; Oct 10 63 to 64; Adamsville PO
KIDDY, Thomas, Hd-52-2; Pvt C Co 7th TN Inf; 63 to 65; Hurley PO
KIDWELL, Benjamin F., Wh-183-1; Pvt G Co 4th TN Mtd Inf; 64 to 65; Quebeck PO; no disability incurred, lost discharge
KIELLAN, Edward D., H-69-5; Pvt Chattanooga PO
KIES, S. W., D-60-2; Mary widow of; Pvt C K 157th Reg Engineers; Oct 16 64 to Sep 26 65; 209 Hardie, Nashville PO
KIET, Edward, K-169-2; away from home; Knoxville PO
KIGLER, Henry, Sh-157-3; __ to 65; Memphis PO
KIKER, Jacob, Ge-85-1; 1st Sgt K Co 13th TN Cav; 1 Oct 63 to 5 Sep 65; Cavey Branch PO; chronic diarhaia and resulting disease of rectum
KIKER, Martain L., Ge-85-1; Cpl K Co 13th TN Cav; 1 Oct 63 to 5 Sep 65; Cavey Branch PO; now suffering from rheumatism & indigestion
KILBURN, Josiah, Wy-177-1; Pvt A Co 2nd TN Mtd Inf; 10-3-63 to 10-3-64; Waynesboro PO; chronic rheumatism
KILBURN, Roberson P. (Robertson), Wy-172-1; Pvt A Co 2nd TN Mtd Inf; Waynesboro PO; snagged at or near Clifton, TN
KILBURN, William A., Wy-177-1; Cpl A Co 2nd TN Mtd Inf; 10-15-63 to 10-17-64; PO omitted; throwed from mule, shoulder enlarged from fall
KILBY, William E., Wa-263-5; Mary A. widow of; Drummer I Co 13th TN Cav; Sep 63 to __; May Day PO
KILDAY, Carter L., Ge-98-3; Pvt C Co 7th KY Inf; 21 Nov 62 to 21 Nov 65; New Lebanon PO; ____ diarhea and general debility 25 yrs
KILDAY, Elijah, Ge-98-6; Sol US; 11th Dist
KILE, Amos H., Lo-188-1; Pvt D Co 5th TN Inf; 23 Nov 62 to 30 Jun 65; Stockton PO
KILE, Polly, Dk-32-5; widow of Soldier; Temperance Hall PO
KILE, Silvester, Sh-172-2; Pvt A Co 104th PA Inf--9-9-61 to 7-14-64; Cpl A Co 104th PA Inf--2-14-64 to 8-25-65; 55 Union St, Memphis PO
KILGORE, James, Gu-48-3; Mary A. widow of; Pvt D Co 1st TN Vidette Cav; 10-1-63 to 6-16-64; Tracy City PO
KILGORE, James, Ha-11-2; Pvt F Co 1st TN Cav; 62 63; Upper Clinch PO
KILGORE, Oliver, Gu-48-2; Pvt D Co 1st TN Indpt Vidette Cav--63 to 6-64; Pvt C Co 6th TN Mtd Inf--64 to 8-65; Tracy City PO; knife cut in left shoulder
KILGORE, William H., Hm-109-2; Pvt B Co 23rd OH Inf; Whitesburg PO

177

KILGROW, John W., Dk-39-1; Pvt D Co 8th TN Mtd Inf; 2-1-65 to 8-31-65; Bozarth PO; kicked by a mules and damaged internally
KILLDAY, John, Ge-97-2; Pvt B Co 3rd TN Inf; 3 Jun 64 to 30 Dec 64; PO omitted
KILLEBREW, Andrew J., We-223-3; 2nd Lt F Co 20th TN Cav; Aug 62 to May 65; Palmersville PO; CONF
KILLEBREW, John, We-223-3; Mary E. widow of; Pvt F Co 20th TN Cav; Aug 62 to May 65; Palmersville PO; died 12th Dec 1878 of typhoid pneumonia
KILLEBREW, Okser, St-160-2; Pvt G Co 100th KY Inf; May 63 to Dec 65; Weavers Store PO
KILLEBREW, Thomas L., We-223-3; Capt H Co 33rd TN Inf; May 61 to May 65; Palmersville PO; CONF
KILLEY, James T., Wa-273-2; Pvt I Co 9th TN Cav; Jan 65 to 11 Sep 65; Keeblers X Roads PO; rupture and liver disease, now blind
KILLFOILE, ___, Sh-191-3; Delila widow of; Memphis PO; records not seen
KILLGORE, Abraham, Mr-95-1; Pvt C Co 6th TN Cav; 9-2-64 to 7-11-65; Victoria PO
KILLGORE, Alexander, Mr-97-2; Pvt D Co 1st AL Cav; 7-31-63 to 6-16-64; Victoria PO
KILLGORE, Craven, Mr-95-1; Pvt L Co 1st TN Cav; 7-31-63 to __-16-64 (11 mos 15 days); Whitwell PO
KILLGORE, George W., We-223-3; Pvt H Co 33rd TN Inf; 13 Oct 61 to 20 Nov 65; Palmersville PO; CONF
KILLGORE, Isaac, Mr-96-3(2); Pvt D Co 1st AL Cav; 7-31-63 to 6-16-64; Victoria PO
KILLGORE, John, Mr-95-1; Pvt C Co 6th TN Cav; 9-2-64 to 7-11-65; Victoria PO
KILLGORE, Matterson, Mr-95-2; Pvt D Co 1st TN Cav; 7-31-63 to 7-16-64; Whitwell PO
KILLGORE, William, Mr-95-2; Pvt C Co 6th TN Inf; 8-27-64 to 6-13-65; Victoria PO
KILMER, Adam, Adam, G-68-1; Pvt 22nd NY Volunteers; Jun 61 to Nov 65; Gibson PO
KILPATRICK, John W., T-213-1; Pvt C Co 12th TN Cav; Aug 62 to May 65; Brighton PO; CONF
KILPATRICK, William W., De-22-2; Pvt E Co 6th TN Cav; 1 Sep 62 to 5 Aug 65; Bath Springs PO
KIMBALL, Levelle, H-61-1; Pvt A Co AL State Lt Art --3-61 to Fall 64; Sgt A Co AL State Lt Art--Fall 64 to 4-65; Chattanooga PO
KIMBER, Richard, H-56-4; Sgt C Co 51st NY Inf; 8-61 to 64 (3 yrs); St. Elmo PO
KIMBER, William H., Bl-4-3; US Sol; 6th Civil Dist
KIMBLE, James (see Shilcut, James)
KIMBLE, Mary (see Eason ___)
KIMBLE, Peter, Gi-127-5; Pvt F Co Col Inf; Pulaski PO; papers burnd
KIMBLE, Rile, We-220-3; Pvt I Co 6th TN Cav; Jan 16 62 to Jan 16 65; PO omitted
KIMBLE, Shead, Sh-158-6(4); Pvt G Co 11th US Col Inf; Jan 64 to 7 Jan 66; Memphis PO; discharged at close of the war with discharge papers
KIMBREL, Alec M., La-117-1; Pvt TN Cav; Mar 3 63 to __ (1 yr 8 mos); West Point PO; fingers of left hand shot off; CONF
KIMBREL, Francis, We-229-1; Teresa widow of; Pvt 6th TN Cav; Gleason PO
KIMBRO, Nat., D-72-1; Harret widow of; Pvt TN Inf; Sep 63 to Jun 65; Nashville PO; died in prison
KIMBRO, Stephen, Ca-20-1; Cook A Co 4th TN Cav; 62 to 12-25-63; Woodbury PO (this name lined out on schedule--no reason given)
KIMBRO, Thomas, Sh-188-2; Pvt F Co 55th US Col; 2-22-64 to 12-30-66; 258 Saffron St, Memphis PO
KIMBRO, ___, Sh-191-6(2); Sarah King alias Kimbro, widow of; Memphis PO; records not seen
KIMBROUGH, Alen (see Johnston, Alen)
KIMBROUGH, Butler, Gi-126-1; Cpl G Co 110th Col Inf; Pulaski PO
KIMBROUGH, Enoch N., Je-144-1; Pvt G Co 4th TN Cav; 63 to 65; Valleyhom PO; wond in right by waggen
KIMBROUGH, Rufus M., Ro-210-12; Pvt A Co; 61 to __; Post Oak Spring PO
KIMBROUGH, Suly, Ro-210-3; Pvt; Rockwood PO
KIMBROUGH, William, Br-8-4(2); Pvt D Co 4th TN Cav; Cleo PO; rheumatism
KIMBROUGH, William B., H-65-1; Capt A Co 21st GA Inf; 6-6-61 to 4-9-65; 1067 Market St, Chattanooga PO; CONF

KIMBY, Henry S., Bo-19-1; Pvt A Co 6th TN Art; 3-20-64 to 65; Rockford PO
KIMER, John V., Ov-139-1; Mary C. K. widow of; Pvt; Beaver Hill PO; killed before entering into the regular service
KIMEY?, Soan W., Ge-83-1; Pvt K Co 8th TN Inf; 2 Jul 63 to 8 Jun 65; Horse Creek PO; rheumatism
KIMSEY, William A., Po-152-3(1); Pvt C Co 5th TN Mtd Inf; 1-64 to 7-17-65; Ducktown PO; injury to back and side
KINCADE, James N., C-27-4; Pvt I Co NSCa Hy?; 7-19-63 to 3-31-66; Jacksboro PO
KINCAID, Hanson H., K-167-1; TN; 63 to 65; Knoxville PO; enlisted in 1st TN in Aug 8 61
KINCAID, John L., Mu-109-4; Pvt B Co 3rd TN Inf; Oct 10 61 to May 5 65; Columbia PO; prisoner, Camp Morton 7 mos; CONF
KINCAID, Timothy S., A-5-3; Pvt F Co 7th TN Mtd Inf; 11-64 to 8-65; Clinton PO
KINCAID, William, A-5-4; Pvt D Co 1st USC HA (hvy art); 12-6-64 to 3-31-65; Clinton PO
KINCAIDE, Henry H., K-167-1; Pvt 3rd TN Inf; 62 to Mar 65; Knoxville PO
KINCHELOE, James H., Wa-272-2; Pvt A Co 29th MO Militia; Mar 64 to Nov 64; Meadow Brook PO; rheumatism, deafness
KINCHEN?, Isaac, Ha-117-2; lost discharge, can't remember dates; Kyles Ford PO; no disability; CONF
KINDELL, Richard, Hd-47-1; Cpl H Co 55th US Col? Inf; Jun 63 to 65; Savannah PO
KINDER, George W., Je-143-2; 1st Lt H Co 1st TN Cav; 1 Apr 62 to 5 Jun 65; Mossy Creek PO
KINDLEY, John D., Hw-133-3; Pvt A Co 42nd NC Inf; 15 Oct 64 to 15 Apr 65; Fry PO; CONF
KINDRED, Thornton, Cu-18-2; Pvt E Co 1st TN Inf; 8-22-61 to 9-17-64; Rockwood PO
KINDRICK, Anderson, Co-63-1; Cook C Co 10th IN Cav; __ to Jul 65 (1 yr 7 mos); Newport PO; shot in right leg, discharge was stolen
KINDRICK, James P., H-59-1; Capt I Co 8th TN Cav; 8-20-61 to 9-11-65; Chattanooga PO
KINDRICK, Robert G., Ro-210-2; Alice W. Crowder formerly widow of; Pvt E Co 1st TN Inf; 11 Aug 61 to 1 Oct 64; Rockwood PO
KINDRICK, Rufus, Ro-209-2; Pvt; Rockwood PO
KINEY, David, C-32-2; Pvt A Co 1st TN Inf; 8-10-61 to 9-10-64; Clearfield PO
KING, Abram T., Bl-4-3; Pvt F Co 3rd Conf Cav; 10-1-61 to 5-16-65; Pikeville PO; CONF
KING, Albert, Ct-39-1; Johnson City PO
KING, Alex, Sh-157-5; Pvt K Co 1st TN; 62 to 66; Memphis PO
KING, Alfred, H-49-5; Pvt A Co 6th TN Mtd Inf; 8-2-64 to 6-30-65; Daisy PO
KING, Amos A., Di-32-1; Jennie R. Martin formerly widow of; Pvt F Co 121st PA Inf; 9-2-62 to 9-2-64; Spencers Mill PO
KING, Amos G., Cr-17-2; Pvt H Co 18th IA Inf; 7-7-63 to 5-23-65; Buena Vista PO
KING, Andrew J., K-166-4(2); Pvt C Co 3rd TN Inf; 2 Mar 62 to 12 Aug 65; Knoxville PO
KING, Austin, Sh-157-6; Pvt G Co 55th Inf; May 63 to 66; Dist 13
KING, Benjamin W., O-130-1; Mary C. widow of; Pvt D Co 13th TN Cav; 63 to 64; Union City PO; captured at Fort Pillow, died in prison
KING, Charles A., Mr-102-1; Pvt F Co 2nd OH Hvy Art; 7-16-63 to 8-23-65; South Pittsburg PO
KING, Charles B., B-3-1; Pvt F Co 5th TN Cav; 9-7-62 to 6-25-65; Wartrace PO; rheumatism June 1864, pulmonary Jan 1864
KING, Curby, S-212-2; Pvt I Co 30th KY; 15 Nov 63 to 18 Apr 65; Porch Corn PO; rheumatism
KING, David A., Cl-56-2(1); Susan widow of; Pvt E Co 6th TN Inf; 5-20-62 to 6-30-65; Head of Barren PO
KING, E. C., Bo-11-2; Pvt I Co 5th TN Inf; 10-31-62 to 6-28-64; Big Gulley PO
KING, Francis M., Mo-128-1; Pvt; Belltown PO
KING, Frank, D-50-1; Pvt F Co 17th US Inf; Nov 30 63 to Apr 25 66; 245 Crawford, Nashville PO
KING, Frank, La-108-1; Pvt P Co 16th KS Cav; 63 to 65; PO omitted
KING, George A., Bo-23-1; Pvt D & B Co, 2nd TN Cav; 9-1-62 to 6-14-65; Tuckaleechee Cove PO; prisoner at Whiliky? AL, now suffering from chr. diareah

KING, George, Wi-273-1; Pvt K Co 12th TN Inf; Aug 12 63 to Feb 66; Thompson Sta. PO; belly & hand injured by shell, pensioner
KING, George, He-62-3; Ann wid. of; Pvt Co I; 62 to 64; Lexington PO; wounded in left leg and head
KING, George, K-161-4; alias George Richardson; Mary Richardson widow of; Pvt C Co 1st US Hvy Art; 15 Feb 64 to 31 Mar 66; Knoxville PO
KING, Geo. W., Wl-291-1; Sol US; Labanon PO
KING, George W., Col, Cf-40-3; Pvt A Co 16th US Inf; Sep 64 to Sep 65; Tullahoma PO
KING, George W., O-138-2; Pvt H Co 9th TN; 1 Sep 61 to 1 Dec 63; Lane PO; CONF
KING, George W., Cu-18-1; Pvt E Co 1st TN Inf; 12-4-61 to 12-24-64; Manning PO
KING, George W., Cy-27-1; Pvt F Co 1st TN Mtd Inf; 3-13-64 to 5-16-65; Clementsville PO
KING, Herrod, Hy-76-2; US Sol; Stanton Depot PO
KING, Hiram, Hw-132-2; Van Hill PO
KING, Isaac, Se-223-2; Pvt I Co 2nd TN Cav; 22 Sep 62 to 6 Jul 65; Hendersons Springs PO; diarrhea, catarrh of head
KING, J. W., M-108-1; Pvt C Co 91st KY Inf--9-15-61 to 1-10-62; Sgt B Co 37th KY Mtd Inf--7-7-63 to 12-29-64; Lafayette PO; piles, gunshot wound left leg
KING, J. W., Mc-117-4; Pvt F Co 5th TN Inf; 9-9-64 to 3-15-65; Carlock PO
KING, Jackson J., Mn-121-2; Mary J. widow of; Falcon PO
KING, James, Ru-241-3; Millie widow of; Pvt; 63 to killed (1 yr); PO omitted
KING, James E., Se-225-3; Pvt A Co 8th TN Inf; 4 Mar 62 to 27 Apr 65; Sevierville PO; ruptured 25 yrs
KING, James H., Mn-121-1; Pvt G Co 6th TN Cav; Nov 63 to 26 Jul 65; Bethal Springs PO; disease of chest, result of pneumonia and rheumatism
KING, James M., Hw-132-1; Pvt B Co 3rd TN Inf; 30 Jun 64 to 30 Nov 64; Persia PO; disabled by frost bite & yellow janders
KING, James M., La-113-3; Pvt I Co 31st OH Inf; 19 Sep 61 to 1 Oct 64; Ethridge PO; blindness
KING, James P., Hw-133-2; Pvt C Co 31st TN Inf; 9 Apr 62 to 9 Apr 65; Slide PO; CONF
KING, James P. (Clayborne), D-57-2; Pvt I Co 12th US Inf; Aug 12 63 to Jan 16 66; PO omitted, 8th Ward
KING, James R., K-172-1; Pvt A Co 6th TN Inf; 20 Apr 62 to 28 Apr 65; Knoxville PO
KING, Jasper, Co-55-1; Pvt C Co 3rd NC Inf; 20 Nov 64 to 10 May 65; Wilton Springs PO; not pensioned
KING, Jehu, K-179-1; Pvt D Co 3rd TN Inf; 10 Feb 62 to 23 Feb 65; Rodelin PO
KING, Jeremiah, Fe-41-4(2); Ruth widow of; Pvt B Co 2nd TN Mtd Inf; 62 to 63; Boat Land PO
KING, John, K-184-2; Oma wife of; Thorn Grove PO
KING, John, S-217-1; Pvt D Co 8th TN Cav; 62 to 65; Isham PO
KING, John H., K-172-1; Cpl A Co 6th TN Inf; 8 Mar 62 to 3 Apr 65; Knoxville PO
KING, John L., Sh-145-2; Pvt B Co 10th TN Cav Vol; 15 Sep 63 to 1 Aug 65; Kerrvill PO; crippled by kick of a horse, 1864; Capt Story, lost Cap?, held offic of farrier when mustered out
KING, John T., Wa-269-1; Pvt B Co 4th TN Inf; 12 Aug 62 to 9 Jul 65; Johnson City PO; broken leg and ankle, rheumatism
KING, John W., K-177-6; Pvt G Co 8th TN Cav; 18 Aug 63 to 11 Sep 63; Pedigo PO; measles & chronic diarrhoe
KING, John W., Cr-17-2; Pvt K Co 2nd TN Inf; 63 to 65 (1 yr 2 mos); Buena Vista PO
KING, Joseph B., Hr-97-2(1); Pvt A Co; Jun 63 to 65; PO omitted
KING, Joseph L., K-172-5(1); Pvt A Co 6th TN Inf; 2 Apr 62 to Apr 66?; Knoxville PO; rheumatism, scurvy?
KING, Leander W., Ge-93-2; Pvt A Co 3rd Mtd Inf TN; 30 Jun 64 to 64 (3 mos 20 days); PO omitted
KING, Levi, Mc-114-3; Sallie widow of; Pvt; Calhoun PO
KING, Linoy, A-5-2; Pvt F Co 7th TN Inf; 64 to 7-27-65; Dossett PO

KING, Marion, Lo-101-3; Susan widow of; Cpl C Co qst TN Cav; Morganton PO
KING, Martin, Ca-22-2; Pvt F Co 1st TN Videt? Cav; 2-28-63 to 6-15-64; Hollow Springs PO; measles
KING, Martin V., K-172-4; Sgt E Co 3rd TN Cav; 29 Jan 62 to 7 Mar 65; PO omitted; scurvia, Cohoka AL, Cohoka Prison 6 mos
KING, Mary (see Whaley, West O.)
KING, Mary E. (see Jaynes, James M.)
KING, Mathew Sr., D-73-1; Pvt Steadman; Sep 62 to (7 mos); Verron? Av, Nashville PO, May 1863; hurt with ___; papers lost
KING, Maxel, Ge-90-1; Pvt 8th TN Inf; Greeneville PO
KING, Moses, Sh-192-1; US Unit; Memphis PO
KING, Noah, D-54-3; Malinda widow of; Pvt; Nashville PO; died in hospital at Nashville 186?
KING, Oliver, Hm-106-3; Pvt E Co 1st TN Cav; 25 Jan 61 to 65; Morristown PO; CONF
KING, Paljars (Dack King on same line without explanation); Li-148-1; Pvt M Co 5th TN Col; Fayetteville PO
KING, Porter, H-57-2; Pvt 15th US Col; 63 to 65; Orchard Knob PO
KING, Quinton C., We-222-1; Pvt Col Basts TN Reg; Apr 64 to 64 (3 mos); Gardner PO; CONF
KING, Richard, Wi-286-2(1); Pvt 36th IN Inf; 61 to 64; Rock Hill PO; details forgotten
KING, Robert, Mo-129-2; Pvt H Co TN; Loco PO
KING, Rufus, Gi-132-3; Pvt H Co 42nd USVC; 63 to 65; Pulaski PO
KING, S. B., K-172-3; Cathern E. widow of; Sgt E Co 3rd TN Cav; 14 Dec 62 to 12 Jun 65; PO omitted
KING, Saint Leger, Bo-13-4; Pvt G Co 1st TN Inf; 8-1-61 to 2-10-62; Freindsville PO; over heat (sun stroke); don't know exact dates
KING, Samuel T., Mr-96-2; Pvt A Co 8th TN Inf; 8-8-62 to 1-30-65; Cedar Spring PO; eryssipelas
KING, Sarah (see Kimbro, ___)
KING, Solomon, Dy-31-1; Pvt H Co 18th MO Inf; Aug 64 to 13 Mar 66; PO omitted
KING, Thomas, Di-30-2; Pvt E Co 42nd IN Inf; 63 to 65; Dickson PO
KING, Thomas, Lo-187-2; Mary A. widow of; Pvt G Co 1st TN Inf; 9 Aug 61 to 17 Sep 64; Loudon PO; lungs from which he died
KING, Thomas J., Po-149-1; Pvt B Co 5th TN Cav; 64 to ___; Conasauga PO; not discharged--at home sick
KING, Thos. S., H-74-1; Pvt G Co 158th IL; 2-7-65 to 2-8-66; 713 Montgomery Av, Chattanooga PO
KING, W. P., Cr-15-1; Pvt I Co 7th TN Cav; M 1 65 to Aug 25 65; Maple Creek PO; piles
KING, Washington, Gi-135-1; Sgt G Co. 1st US Art; 62 to 65; Lynnville PO
KING, William, Sh-161-1; Pvt B Co 59th TN Inf; PO omitted
KING, William, Se-220-1; Pvt E Co 9th TN Cav; 1 Oct 63 to 11 Sep 65; Emurts Cave PO
KING, William, Mc-112-10; Pvt H Co 34th IN Inf; Athens PO
KING, William, Mc-114-2; Pvt; Magellan PO
KING, William, S-216-1; Pvt D Co 30th KY; 1 Nov 63 to 18 Apr 65; Gome Fort PO; rhumatism, contracted in war
KING, William C., Ro-210-11; Pvt E Co 1st TN Inf; Dec 61 to Dec 64; Post Oak Springs PO
KING, William C., Cf-42-1; Pvt C Co 5th TN Cav; 8-24-62 to 6-28-65; Hickerson PO; chronic doreah
KING, William H., Se-224-2; Cpl B Co 2nd TN Cav; 15 Sep 62 to 6 Jul 65; Line Spring PO; neuralgia & dispepsy, sick & had throat burnt
KING, William H., Me-92-3; Sgt I Co 1st TN Inf; 8-9-61 to 9-17-64; Hester Mills PO; chronic diarrhea & disease of rectum
KING, William N., Ca-25-2; Pvt L Co 5th TN Cav; 7-7-63 to 8-5-65; Gassoway PO
KING, William R., La-117-2; Pvt 33rd OH Cav; 63 to 65; 15th Dist
KING, William W., Mr-96-2; Pvt H Co 11th TN Cav; 9-1-63 to 3-24-65; Cedar Spring PO; dirhea
KING, Willy V., K-172-3; Caroline B. widow of; Pvt B Co 2nd TN Cav; 16 Oct 62 to ___; 14th Dist, South Knoxville PO

KING, _____, Be-1-1; Lucinda widow of; Sol; 1st Dist
KINKEAD, Wm., Hw-125-1; Pvt B Co 5th Oct 62 to 15 Apr 65; Blevins PO; 21 mos in prison, Point Lookout PO
KINKLIN, Samuel, Mc-114-3; Pvt; Calhoun PO
KINLEY, Pat, St-164-1; Pvt C Co 10th tN Inf; Apr 15 62 to May 65; Stribling PO
KINMAN, Elijah W., H-61-3; Pvt A Co 19th TN Reg; 8-1-63 to 4-9-65; Chattanooga, Burk's Alley PO; CONF
KINMAN, Mary K. (see Moss, Wiliam)
KINNAIRD, John L., Sm-173-1; Pvt E Co 4th TN Mtd Inf; 11-25-64 to 8-25-65; Sykes PO
KINNARD, David M., Mu-210-5; Ophelia E. widow of; Pvt B Co 2nd KY Cav; 4-62 to 5-65; Carters Creek PO; dropsey; CONF
KINNEY, Andrew J., Wa-261-1; Pvt K Co TN Inf; 12 Feb 62 to 15 Feb 65; Cankling PO
KINNEY, Asa C., Li-149-2; Orderly Sgt C Co 100th US Col Inf; 5-24-64 to 12-25-65; Fayetteville PO
KINNEY, Sunon, Sol, Sh-187-1(5); Memphis PO
KINNY, John S., T-207-1; Pvt F Co M Reg Vol Inf; Aug 8 61 to Aug 8 64; Covington PO; bayonet wound, RR Employee away from home
KINSEL, Henry, K-168-2; Pvt G Co 6th TN Inf; 17 Apr 61 to _____ (3 yrs 3 mos); Beverly PO
KINSER, Henry C., Bo-13-2; Sgt I Co 10th TN Cav; 1-30-64 to 8-1-65; Freindsville PO
KINSER, Jacob, Mo-122-1; Sgt E Co 61st TN Inf; 10-62 to 7-9-63; Dancing Branch PO
KINSER, James H., Co-60-1; K Co 8th TN Inf; 1-5-63 to 12-9-63; Syrensburg PO; ruptured 27 yrs
KINSEY, Joel H., Gr-75-2; Pvt D Co 1st TN Lt Art; 24 Sep 63 to 20 Jul 65; Tampico PO; hearing
KINSEY, Samuel B., We-223-5; Pvt E Co 61st VA Inf; 1 Nov 62 to 1 May 65; Palmersville PO; CONF
KINZEL, John C., K-159-2; Pvt G Co 6th TN Inf; 21 Apr 62 to 31 May 65; Knoxville PO
KINZER, John H., Mu-197-2; Sgt D Co 44th Co ___; Mar 64 to 64; Columbia PO; frosted feet
KIPLINGER, Jno. H., Br-10-1; Pvt 48th IN Inf; 12-4-61 to 10-15-63; Cleveland PO
KIPPAS, Mathew, Mu-194-1; Drummer A Co 17th US Inf; 4-7-62 to 2-7-65; Columbia PO
KIRBY, Archibald, Se-223-5(1); Pvt H Co 17th KY Cav; 20 Oct 64 to 20 Sep 65; Sevierville PO
KIRBY, Calvin, Mc-116-4; Betsey widow of; Pvt F Co 4th TN Cav; 64 to 65; Mortimer PO; discharge papers lost and no exact date of service given
KIRBY, Claborn, Cy-27-5(3); Lt? D Co 9th KY Inf; 9-30-61 to 64 (2 yrs 8 mos); Red Springs PO (Macon Co.); captured
KIRBY, Haley S., M-103-6; Pvt A Co 8th TN Inf; 11-22-64 to 8-17-65; Lafayette PO
KIRBY, James V., M-103-6; Pvt A Co 8th TN Inf; 11-22-64 to 8-17-65; Red Boiling Spring PO
KIRBY, Layfaette, Bl-5-3; Pvt D Co 6th TN Mtd Inf; 9-16-64 to 6-30-65; Sequachee College PO; had malarial fever in 1885 and claims to be disabled since
KIRBY, Leonadas D., M-107-4; Montavilla H. widow of; Pvt K Co 9th KY Inf; 61 to ___; Gibbs Cross Roads PO
KIRBY, Melvin B., M-103-2; Cpl A Co 8th TN Inf; 11-1-64 to 8-17-65; Lafayette PO
KIRBY, Robert C., W-195-1; Sarah L. widow of; Cpl K Co 13th TN; 62 to 65; 13th Dist
KIRBY, Thomas, Ca-25-2; Pvt A Co 5th TN Cav; 7-28-62 to 6-25-65; Gassoway PO
KIRBY, William M., M-103-6; Pvt H Co 52nd KY Inf; 9-15-63 to 1-18-65; Red Boiling Spring PO
KIRBY, William W., Mn-126-1; 2nd Lt; 8-22-62 to 7-25-64; Purdy PO
KIRK, Alonzo C., Mn-120-1; Pvt L Co 6th TN Cav; 63 to Jul 26 65; Pochontas PO
KIRK, Daniel, U-247-2; Pvt C Co 2nd NC Mtd Inf; ___ to 16 Aug 65; Erwin PO; heart & lungs 25 yrs
KIRK, Ephriham L., K-164-2; Pvt C Co 1st TN Cav; 1 Mar 62 to 1 Apr 65; PO omitted (Knoxville?)
KIRK, Felix, F-42-1(3); Lt? D Co 38th TN Inf; Oct 61 to May 65; Colliervlle PO; CONF
KIRK, Henry, Dy-24-1; Pvt 13th TN; May 62 to 61 (sic)(3 yrs); Dyersburg PO; unhurt
KIRK, James A., Mn-120-1; Pvt L Co 6th TN Cav; ___ to Jul 26 65 (2 yrs); Pocahontas PO

KIRK, James F., Ge-91-5; Lt D Co 8th TN Cav; 30 Jun 63 to 30 Dec 63; Greenville PO; liver disease
KIRK, James R., K-168-2; Pvt C Co 1st TN Cav; 12 Mar 62 to 29 Apr 63; Knoxville PO; back hurt
KIRK, John M., Gr-81-1; Pvt K Co 8th TN Cav; Jul 63 to 29 May 65; Clear Spring PO; chron. diarhea & kidney loss, partly disabled
KIRK, Joseph W., Ge-86-1; Cpl C Co 8th TN Inf; 1 Dec 62 to 30 Jun 65; Warrensburgh PO; eyes injured, torpid liver and rheumatism
KIRK, Orvil R., Ge-100-1; Cpl I Co 3rd NC Inf; Nov 63 to Jun 65; Midway PO
KIRK, Sidney E., O-135-1; Pvt D Co 13th TN Inf; 14 Dec 63 to 3 Aug 65; Troy PO; ruptured
KIRK, William C., Wl-293-2; Pvt M Co 3rd KY Cav; Sep 63 to Dec 27 62; Lockport PO
KIRKHAM, Thomas, Sn-261-2(1); Pvt Bells; PO omitted; CONF
KIRKLAND, Elijah L., Lo-190-3; Pvt L Co 2nd TN Cav; 1 Aug 62 to 6 Jul 65; Piney PO
KIRKLAND, George W., Dk-39-3(1); Mary M. Felts formerly widow of; Pvt E Co 4th TN Lt Art; Dekalb PO
KIRKLAND, James A., Mo-129-2; Pvt K Co 12th TN Cav; Loco PO
KIRKLAND, Jefferson W., Ro-207-3; Pvt G Co 1st AL Cav; 10 Mar 64 to 20 Oct 65; Paint Rock PO; deafness
KIRKLAND, Rufus M., Mo-131-1; Pvt C Co 3rd TN Inf; 7-26-64 to 11-3-65; Joe PO
KIRKLAND, W. T., Bo-11-3; Pvt H Co 3rd TN Inf; 9-1-64 to 7-27-65; Rockwood PO; badly diseased
KIRKLIN, William, H-55-1; Martha A. Nowlen formerly widow of; 1st Lt 10th TN Cav; 63 to 65; Tyner PO
KIRKMAN, Shedrick, Sh-153-2; Pvt E Co 61st USC Inf; 62 to 65; Collierville PO; ruptured in army
KIRKMAN, William T., Ch-15-1; Henderson PO
KIRKPATRICK, Andrew J., Mu-209-1; Columbia PO; CONF
KIRKPATRICK, Humphry, Bo-21-3; Pvt K Co 8th TN Cav; 10-6-63 to 6-1-65; Ellijay PO
KIRKPATRICK, Jackson, Sn-254-2; Pvt 14th US Col Inf; Hendersonville PO
KIRKPATRICK, James, D-68-2; Pvt K Co 101st USC Inf; ___ to 65; Hamler St, Nashville PO; hip injured by gun shot
KIRKPATRICK, John R., K-174-3(2); Pvt I Co 3rd TN Inf; 10 Feb 62 to 21 Feb 65; Church Grove PO; deseas of hip, right hip 25 yrs, got don on the Sultanor, Mississippi River
KIRKPATRICK, Josiah M., Hm-109-4; Pvt D Co 1st TN Cav; 15 Apr 62 to 15 Apr 65; Whitesburg PO
KIRKPATRICK, Martha A., K-154-2; Knoxville PO
KIRKPATRICK, N.? B., Mo-124-5; Pvt L Co 7th TN Cav; 11-1-62 to 6-19-65; Santordville PO; scurvy of mouth & spained wrist
KIRKPATRICK, Robert, Gi-127-5; Pvt D Co 110th US Col Inf; Jan 2 64 to Apr 3 66; Pulaski PO
KIRKPATRICK, Thos. C., Cr-4-2; Pvt K Co 18th TN Inf; Dec 61 to 65; Bells Depot PO; CONF
KIRKPATRICK, Wm. C., K-173-3; US Sol; 3rd Dist
KIRTIS, Nurd?, Hd-45-1; 2nd Sgt E Co 2nd TN Mtd Inf; 4 Feb 64 to 10 May 65; Cerro Gordo PO
KIRTMAN, Hiram, Su-240-3; Pvt A Co 16th VA Cav; 62 to 65; Kindricks Creek PO; chronic rheumatism, no discharge; CONF
KISER, Asa, Wl-292-1; alias Asa C. Kiser; Pvt D Co 71st OH Inf; 16 Oct 61 to 15 Dec 64; Buhler PO; lungs diseased & feet frost bitten
KITCHELL, J. R., O-133-1; Amelia widow of; Sgt B Co 15th IL Cav; Rives PO; discharge lost
KITCHEN, John C., Mo-130-3; Pvt C Co; Ballplay PO
KITCHING, James H., Dk-31-1; Lt G Co 4th TN Mtd Inf; 2-2-65 to 8-25-65; Alexandria PO; re-enlisted, suffering with disabilities
KITE, A. N. D., Ct-39-2; Pvt A Co 13th TN Cav; 9-63 to 9-65; Elizabethton PO; heart disease, diorhoea, rheumatism, lung trouble
KITE, Alfred C., Ct-36-1; Pvt C Co 13th TN Cav; 9-63 to 9-65; Shell Creek PO
KITE, Daniel, Hw-132-1; Pvt D Co 31st TN Inf; 61 to May 65; Persia PO; CONF
KITE, Grandvill, Je-147-2; Pvt E Co 9th TN Cav; 8 Sep 63 to 8 Sep 65; Shady Grove PO

KITE, Hamelton, Ct-35-4; Cpl I Co 13th TN Cav; 9-22-63 to 9-5-65; Shell Creek PO; in the US Army
KITES, Lazarus, Ge-92-3; Pvt D Co 8th TN Inf; Romeo PO; rheumatism and heart trouble
KITE, Martin V., Hw-132-5; Pvt E Co 29th TN Inf; 61 to 64; Strahl PO; CONF
KITE, William H., Ge-94-2(1); Pvt B Co 4th TN Inf; 8 Dec 62 to 2 Aug 65; Greeneville PO
KITRELL, ____, Lo-187-3; 2nd Lt A Co 2nd TN Inf; 9 Aug 61 to __; Loudon PO; ruptured
KITTERELL, Charles, D-92-1; Pvt E Co 15th US Col Inf; Jan 64 to Apr 66; Nashville PO
KITTERLIE, John, Sh-196-3; Pvt 5th KY B; 62 to 65; Mullin's Store, Main St, Memphis PO
KITTINGER, Jacob, D-63-2; Pvt C Co 30th IL Inf; Oct 4 64 to Jul 65; Nashville PO
KITTINGER, John, Be-2-2; Pvt A Co; 14th Dist
KITTRELL, Allen, Mu-200-1; Pvt A Co 111th TN Inf; Feb 62 to May 65; Terry PO
KITTRELL, Hardy, Mu-198-1; Pvt A Co 111th US Reg; Jan 10 64 to Sep 12 64; Canaan PO; gunshot wound in leg, in the army of US
KITTRELL, Robert, R-158-2; Lt M Co 4th TN Cav; 10-18-64 to 7-12-65; Pin Hook PO (Meigs Co.)
KITTS, Andrew G., Un-250-1; Pvt A Co 1st TN Inf; Feb 63 to Aug 65; Maynardville PO; piles & gun shot wound incured & received while in service
KITTS, Calvin, Un-253-2; Pvt F Co 3rd TN Inf; 18 Feb 62 to 23 Feb 65; Luttrell PO; spinal effection
KITTS, David, Gr-82-1; Anice widow of; Pvt D Co 1st TN Inf; 26 Jul 63 to 17 Sep 64; Powder Spring Gap PO; piles, exposure
KITTS, Elizabeth, Gr-82-2; 14th Dist
KITTS, Henery, K-174-4(3); Pvt D Co 1st TN Inf; 26 Jul 62 to 25 Jun 65; Church Grove PO; no disability incurred
KITTS, Isaac, Gr-81-4(2); Pvt A Co 2nd TN Cav; 1 Aug 52 to 7 Jul 65; Shelton's Ford PO; liver, heart & sommac, partly disabled
KITTS, John, Gr-70-1; Pvt D Co 26th TN Inf; 10 Aug 61 to 10 May 64; Rutledge PO
KITTS, Mark, Un-250-2; Margrett A. widow of; Pvt C Co 4th TN Inf; 1 Feb 63 to died 16 Jun 63; Maynardville PO
KITTS, William M., Gr-82-1; Pvt D Co 1st TN Inf; 4 Jul 62 to Jun 20 65; Powder Spring Gap PO; piles, exposure
KIZER, Eugene, Hr-92-1; Pvt I Co 1st PHB MD; 10-61 to 10-64; Hickory Valley PO
KIZER, Jacob, K-173-1; Pvt C Co 1st TN Art; 11 Sep 63 to 1 Aug 65; Caswell PO; direah
KIZER, Philip, K-186-3; Pvt C Co TN Art; Beaver Ridge PO
KLAUSER, Benedict, D-103-2; Pvt D Co 165th PA Inf; Oct 1 64 to Jul 1 65; Marry PO; hearing injured, drafted 9 mos
KLAROON, Samuel W., H-74-1; 2nd Lt B Co 1st TN; 11-14-62 to 7-25-65; 342 East End Ave, Chattanooga PO
KLASSEN, John, H-73-5(3); Pvt IN; Chattanooga PO
KLEIN, Charles W., D-44-3; Nashville PO; could get not better information
KLEIN, Henry T. S., Ho-96-2; Pvt; Jane S. widow of; Pvt H Co 49th WI Inf; Feb 18 65 to Nov 18 65; Erin PO
KLEIN, Peter O., D-67-2; Pvt H Co 149th IL Vol; 64 to 65; Nashville PO
KLEPPE, Andrew J., Wa-271-1; Pvt; Blizard PO
KLINCK, Monroe, Sh-160-2; Pvt; 15th Dist
KLINE, Edward, Lo-187-1; Sgt E Co 1st US Col Hvy Art; 4 Apr 64 to 31 Mar 66; Loudon PO; lungs, affected from measles
KLINTWORTH, Charles, H-63-3; Pvt A Co 9th OH Inf; 4-25-61 to 5-65; 219 W. 7th, Chattanooga PO
KLOCK, Wm. D., D-71-2; Nashville PO
KLOENER, John C., H-51-2(1); Lt Col I Co 58th IN Inf; 4-17-61 to 2-18-62; Hill City PO
KMY (Sic), Thomas M., Cl-46-1; Pvt C Co 1st TN; 8-9-61 to 9-17-64; Clairfield PO; rumatism
KNEPPE, Joel, Un-251-1; Pvt C Co 27th IL Inf; 3 Aug 61 to 19 Jul 65; Effie PO; heart disease
KNESNER, Henry, D-66-1; Pvt 9th TN Cav; is a pensioner; Nashville, 711 S Market PO; pension applied for & got one, his papers are in Washington

KNIFE, Henry, Hm-108-3(2); Pvt K Co 49th NC Inf; 61 to 65; Russellville PO; CONF
KNIGHT, Andrew J., Fr-112-3; Pvt D Co 17th TN Inf; 61 to 65; Decherd PO; CONF
KNIGHT, Benjaman, Se-231-1; Pvt F Co 8th TN Cav; 25 Jul 63 to 23 May 65; Boyds Creek PO
KNIGHT, Catherine, Gr-71-2; Sol Widow; 2nd Dist
KNIGHT, Cornelius, Sh-198-2; Pvt C Co US Col Inf; 7-64 to 4-65; Memphis PO; discharge burned in his house
KNIGHT, Cornelius H., R-158-3; Pvt H Co 73rd IN Vol; 7-1-62 to 7-1-65; Sheffield PO; wounded left hip at bat. Murfreesborough, pensioner
KNIGHT, David, Co-67-5; Pvt F Co 8th TN Cav; 24 Jul 63 to 11 Sep 65; Naillon PO; malarial poison
KNIGHT, Frank M., Bl-4-1; Cpl I Co 4th TN Cav; 1-1-63 to 6-12-65; Pikeville PO
KNIGHT, Greeneville, Ge-97-3; Pvt K Co 1st TN Cav; Aug 62 to 5 Jun 65; Upchurch PO
KNIGHT, Henry, Hu-106-1; Pvt D Co 13th US C T; 64 to 65; Waverly PO
KNIGHT, James, Mn-121-4; Pvt E Co 1st AL Inf; 62 to 65; Bethel Springs PO
KNIGHT, James, R-159-2; Pvt H Co 3rd KY Inf; 10-61 to 7-65; Spring City PO; wounded, never applied for pension
KNIGHT, James H., Mc-118-5; Mary E. widow of; Pvt C Co 2nd TN Cav; 7-1-61 to 7-18-65; Calhoun PO
KNIGHT, Joel A., W-195-1; Pvt F Co 1st TN Inf; 3-64 to 5-66; Goth PO; ill health from measles
KNIGHT, John W., Mr-95-2; Pvt G Co 10th TN Inf; 11-10-64 to 7-27-65; Victoria PO
KNIGHT, Samuel, H-62-4; Silvia widow of; Pvt B Co 16th US Inf; cor West Fifth and Broad Sts, Chattanooga PO
KNIGHT, Thomas J., R-161-3; Pvt D Co 2nd TN Inf; 5-27-62 to 5-27-65; Dayton PO
KNIGHT, William, Sm-169-2; Pvt; Defeated PO; CONF
KNIGHT, William C., Rb-228-2; Pvt TN Inf; 62 to __ (8 mos); Crunk PO; CONF
KNOBLE, William R., We-233-2; Pvt I Co 6th TN Cav; 7-4-62 to 8-26-65; Ratham PO; blind left eye & cronic diarhea
KNOTT, James H., K-171-1; Sgt D Co 6th TN Inf; Apr 62 to May 63; Knoxville PO
KNOTT, John J., G-67-3; Pvt N Co 7th TN Inf; Aug 62 to __; Idlewild PO
KNOTT, Simon, Fr-109-1; Pvt B Co 14th TN Inf; Ma 64 to Ma 66; Huntland PO; shot through hip, not able to work
KNOTT, William G., G-67-2; Pvt M Co 6th TN Cav; 1 Aug 65 to 26 Jul 65; Bradford PO; disease of respiratory organs
KNOWLES, Jasper, Wh-183-1; Conf & Union Soldier; Fourth Civil Dist
KNOWLES, John F., Wh-184-1; Pvt F Co 3rd Regt US Vol; 64 to 65; Darkey Springs PO; his discharge not at home & cant give dates; voluntered out of prison, first a rebel
KNOX, Augustus, L-103-2; Cpl K Co 41st PA Inf; I Co 63rd Inf; 62 to 65; Plum Point PO; very poor, has had no help
KNOX, George W., H-72-2(1); Pvt D Co US Col Art; __ to 3-31-66; Chattanooga PO
KNOX, Henry, Hw-125-1; Pvt; 63 to May 65; Surgoinsville PO; CONF
KNOX, James, Ro-210-6; Seaman, Bienville; Rockwood PO
KNOX, Jeremiah, Me-92-2; Martha Ball formerly widow of; Pvt H Co 5th TN Mtd Inf; Hester Mills PO
KNOX, Jessie, Me-90-1; Pvt B Co 6th TN Mtd Inf; 8-15-64 to 6-30-65; Decatur PO
KNOX, Joseph P., Mr-97-1; Pvt I Co TN Cav; 11-22-62 to 8-24-65; PO omitted; hearing from measles
KNOX, Samuel D., Ro-210-4; Pvt H Co 3rd TN Cav; 62 to __; Rockwood PO; prisoner at Fort Delaware
KNUCKLES, Jerry, Mu-210-4; Pvt F Co 138th GA Inf; 4-65 to 12-65; Carters Creek PO; CONF
KOHLBEY, August, Sh-187-1(5); Pvt G Co 1st IA; 8-61 to 7-17-66; Volunteer who was enrolled on 4-20-61 to serve 3 mos; Memphis PO

KOLLOCK, Joseph, Lo-195-1; Martha E. widow of; 1st Lt D Co 5th TN Inf; Feb 62 to __; Eatons X Roads; chronic liver disease
KOME, James N., Pu-142-1; Pvt I Co 5th TN Vol Cav; Calf Killer PO
KOONCE, William W., B-3-2; Pvt F Co 5th TN Cav; 9-6-62 to 7-1-65; Shelbyville PO; chrnoic diarrhea 2-65; suffering from same disability
KOONTZ, James E., Un-254-3; Sgt F Co 3rd TN Inf; 10 Feb 62 to 23 Feb 63; Bartheney PO; pain in right side
KORNODLE, George W., G-55-1; Pvt B Co 6th TN Cav; 8-62 to 7-26-65; Trenton PO; hurt in the privates, discharge mislaid
KOSIRE, John, K-186-3; Ann widow of; Pvt; Chumlea PO
KOUNS, Abraham, St-164-1; Pvt K Co 4th KY Cav; Oct 23 63 to Feb 65; Stribling PO
KRANTZ, Michal, M-103-1; Pvt D Co 8th TN Inf; 3-1-65 to 8-1-65; Lafayette PO
KREIDER, Uriah, K-165-2; Pvt C Co 127th __; Knoxville PO
KREIN, Conrad, Sh-152-3; Fisherville PO
KREIS, Harmon, Mo-124-2; Pvt L Co 9th TN Cav; 10-4-63 to 9-11-6? (2 yrs); Hurklee PO (Knox Co.); indigestion, head trouble, first enlisted in 11th Co H, afterwards consolidated in Co L in 9th
KRIEGAR, Henry, Mr-98-2(5); Sarah E. widow of; Sgt B? Co 68th NY Inf; 8-26-64 to 11-13-65; Whiteside PO
KRIGER, Pearly S., Br-10-2; Pvt F Co 9th MI Inf; 1-24-65 to 9-16-65; Cleveland PO
KRISLY, John W., Mu-207-1; Pvt H Co 12th TN Inf; Jan 63 to Dec 65; Loco PO; misplaced discharge
KRMNE (sic), William G., Cf-39-1; Hospital Steward 13th OH Inf; 17 Apr 61 to Dec 5 65; Prairie Plains PO
KROCKET, Hanibal, D-72-6; Sol; Nashville PO
KROTZER, Henry J., Fr-105-1; Pvt F Co 67th TN Vol; 14 Oct 62 to 14 Jul 65; Winchester PO
KROUSS, Chas. P., Sh-172-1; Pvt A Co 17th OH Inf--4-22-61 to 8-15-61; Pvt A Co 17th OH Inf--8-22-61 to 10-2-64; 416 Main St, Memphis PO
KRUMM, Jacob, D-99-1; Bugler I Co 8th OH Cav; 4 Mar 62 to Aug 5 65; Nashville PO; poorhouse
KRYSHER, Wesley, Br-9-2; Wagoner C Co 39th TN Inf; 8-9-62 to 6-5-65; Cleveland PO; wounded in back (a CONF?)
KUBANKS, James L., Mn-122-1; Pvt F Co 10th TN Inf; 5-6-62 to 6-20-65; McNairy PO; sight impaired pension since 1883
KUDDER, Robert A. L., K-181-5(2); Pvt C? Co 7th TN Inf; Knoxville PO
KUHN, Joseph R., Ct-41-4; Lt C Co 53rd TN Inf; 12-20-61 to __; Keensburgh PO
KUMIG, Hamilton H., Ct-36-2; Sgt G Co 13th TN Cav; 9-24-63 to 9-8-65; Shell Creek PO
KUYKENDALL, Alfred, Ge-99-2; Pvt H Co 2nd NC Mtd Inf; 1 Oct 63 to 16 Aug 65; Woolsey College PO; rheumatism
KUYKENDALL, George W., Ge-99-1; Or S D Co 11th MI Cav; __ Mar 62 to 29 Apr 65; Limestone Springs PO; could not get day of month, enlistment
KYKER, Andrew J., Wa-263-2; Conf (worked in US) Pvt A Co 1st TN Hvy Art; 62 to Jul 4 __; May Day PO; CONF
KYKER, Benjamin E., Mc-109-3; B. E. Riker alias; Cpl B Co 7th TN Inf; 9-24-64 to 7-27-65; Regret PO; chronic diarhea & piles 26 yrs
KYKER, Marcus L., Mc-112-7; Pvt B Co 7th TN Mtd Inf; 9-17-62 to 7-27-65; Athens PO
KYKER, Minerva D. T. (see Erwin, Samuel)
KYLE, Erastus R., Cr-17-2; Pvt B Co 7th TN Cav; 8-20-62 to 6-16-65; Buena Vista PO; disease of gums, heart and kidneys, result of scurvy and disease of bowels
KYLE, James B., Sm-173-1; Pvt D Co 4th TN Mtd Inf; 9-20-64 to 8-25-65; Sykes PO
KYLE, Jesse, K-161-3; Hulda widow of; Knoxville PO; died in service
LABAR, Alexander, H-68-1; Pvt A Co 50th NY Vol Inf; 2-23-64 to 6-23-65; Chattanooga PO
LABBE, Frank, Sh-167-1; Elizabeth widow of; Pvt F Co 4th MO Cav; Sep 61 to __; PO omitted, died in war, dont know dates; CONF

LACEWELL, William, Mo-123-2; Pvt A Co 7th TN Mtd Inf; 11-18-64 to 7-27-65; Mt. Vernon PO
LACEWELL, William L., Br-12-2; Cpl A Co 7th TN Inf; 9-23-64 to 7-29-65; Charleston PO; deafness in right ear
LACEY, William J., B-14-1; Musician E Co 10th TN Inf; 6-5-62 to 6-16-64; Wisener PO; injured by falling off bridge
LACHRY, J. W., Pi-153-1; Pvt C Co 1st TN Inf; 5-62 to 12-64; Chanute PO
LACK, James, Pu-140-1; Pvt Ft. Donelson Ship; 64 to 8-17-65; Cookeville PO; hand injured
LACKEY, Emaline, Cy-28-2; widow of US Sol; 6th Dist
LACKEY, Emily (see Massingale, Louis)
LACKEY, Joel, S-214-1; Pvt I Co 30th KY Inf; Robbins PO; piles and chronic diarrhoea
LACKEY, John H., Ha-117-2; Pvt K Co 5th KY Cav; Oct 62 to Nov 65; Kyle's Ford PO; no disability
LACY, Andy, K-169-1; Pvt I Co 3rd MS Inf and Col Hvy Art; 14 May 63 to 31 Mar 65; Knoxville PO; partly disabled
LACY, Ezekiel M., B-7-1; Pvt F Co 5th TN Cav; 9-25-62 to __; Shelbyville PO; gun shot wound in neck, wound received in battle 6-27-63
LACY, James L., Pi-153-3; 2nd Lt G Co 9th TN Cav; 5-15-62 to 9-11-65; Spurnier PO; shot right foot
LACY, Reuben, Ro-208-1; Pvt D Co 5th TN Inf; 26 Feb 63 to 30 Mar 65; Morris Gap PO; chronic sore leg
LACY, Sam, Cr-1-1; alias Allen, Sam; Pvt C Co 4th Hvy Art; 62 to 65; Gadsden PO
LACY, Walter S., B-20-1; Marthey E. widow of; Pvt A Co Mtd Inf; 8-11-64 to 8-21-65; Shelbyville PO
LACY, William H., Sh-158-4; Orderly Sgt K Co 63rd Col Inf; 2 Nov 63 to 9 Jan 66; Memphis PO; asthma 20 yrs, nothing special, discharge papers all right
LADD?, Daniel, Sm-170-1; Pvt D Co 1st TN Cav; 6-2-64 to 1-15-65; Maggart PO; CONF
LADD, Jesse, Su-236-1; Petcy widow of; Pvt L Co 9th TN Cav; 20 Oct 63 to 11 Sep 65; Bloomingdale PO
LADD, John (see Payne, John)
LADD, John W., Ro-201-1; Salena A. widow of; Pvt H Co 60th IL Inf; 1 Sep 63 to 1 Sep 64; Kinston PO
LADD, Samuel N., Ro-201-1; Pvt F Co 1st TN Inf; Jul 63 to Aug 65; Kingston PO
LA DILLE, Charles, R-162-3; Rilla F. widow of; Dayton PO
LADY, Henderson, Ge-91-3; Pvt D Co 1st TN Cav; 8 Nov 61 to 15 Apr 65; Greeneville PO; blindness, total
LADY, Samuel A., Ge-100-2; Pvt D Co 1st TN Cav; 12 Aug 62 to 5 Jun 65; Mohawk PO
LAFATE, Bropher, Pi-156-1; Pvt C Co; 3-1-65 to 10-23-65; Permelia PO
LAFEVER, Andrew, Dk-39-3(1); Pvt H Co 1st TN Mtd Inf; 12-12-63 to 5-23-65; Dekalb PO; hemorrhoids and chronic diarrhea
LAFEVER, Jessee P., Dk-39-1; Pvt D Co 4th TN Mtd Inf; 10-15-64 to 8-25-65; Bozarth PO; chronic rheumatism & general debility
LAFEVOR, Lee, Ca-25-2; Pvt A Co 5th TN Cav; 8-7-62 to 6-25-67; Gassoway PO
LAFOLLETT, George, Se-221-1; Seaman, Ioscoe; 13 Jan 64 to 25 Aug 65; Fair Garden PO
LAFRADE, Henry, Rb-229-1; Pvt H Co 16th TN Inf; Apr 63 to Apr 65; Sadlersville PO
LAGLER, Russell, S-212-2; 12th Dist
LAHIFF, John, St-159-1; Pvt D Co 28th KY Inf; 5-8-63 to 7-65; Indian Mound PO; shot in left ankle
LAHR, James M., Rb-223-3(5); Pvt H Co 1st Mish Meck En (sic); 31 Oct 61 to 31 Oct 64; 9th Dist
LAIN, Few, Co-64-2; Jane widow of; Pvt C Co 8th TN Cav; 1 Oct 63 to __; philips PO
LAIN, John M., G-60-1; Adaline T. widow of; Pvt A Co 6th TN Cav; 11 Aug 62 to Jul 65; Trenton PO; chronic diarrhea
LAIN, William H., W1-305-1; Pvt I Co 43rd MO Inf; Aug 29 64 to Mar 6 65; Lebanon PO; diseased
LAINE, J. H., Fr-115-1; Pvt G Co 31st IN Inf; 10-8-61 to 12-10-63; Cowan PO

LAINE, John R., Ge-94-2(1); Pvt D Co 8th TN Cav; 28 Sep 63 to 11 Sep 65; Greeneville PO
LAINE, William, Cl-52-3; Pvt A Co 9th TN Cav; 9-1-62 to 9-18-65; Hypatia PO; shot in arm
LAIRD, Robert, Gi-127-7; Pvt F Co 110th TN Col Inf; Nov 1 62 to Apr 3 66; Pulaski PO
LAKE?, John, Hy-79-1; Pvt H Co 4th Col Hvy Inf; Oct 20 63 to Feb 25 66; Brownsville PO
LAKEY, Harmon, Wy-173-3; Pvt B Co 2nd TN Mtd Inf; 10-15-63 to 10-17-64; Sims PO
LAKEY, James H., Hd-50-2; Pvt C Co 10th TN Inf; May 16 62 to Jun 20 65; Walnut Grove PO; shot in back
LAKEY, Nancey J., Hd-49-2; Pvt D Co 1st R Ing; Aug 12 63 to Nov? 1 64; Martins Mills PO; kidney deseas
LAKEY, William M., Wy-173-3; Pvt B Co 2nd TN Mtd Inf; 10-15-63 to 10-17-64; Sims PO
LAKIN, John, Ha-110-1; Pvt L Co 9th TN Cav; Oct 63 to Mar 65; Bray's PO; dislocation of arm and shoulder joints
LAKINS, Alex, K-183-2; Pvt E Co 8th TN Cav; 10 Oct 63 to 11 Sep 65; Thorn Grove PO
LAKINS, Robert, Gr-79-4; Pvt K Co 9th TN; Thorn Hill PO; injury of head
LALLER, George W., Di-37-2; Pvt D Co 3rd US Inf; 10-15-64 to 11-29-65; Dull PO; in both US & CONF service
LAMARR, Joseph C., Ha-115-1; Pvt H Co 8th TN Cav; 63 to 65; Alanthers Hill PO; not disabled, yet living
LAMB, Albert, U-246-2; Capt K Co 129th IL Inf; 1 Sep 62 to 27 Dec 64; Limonite PO
LAMB, Buford, Hy-76-2; US Sol; Stanton Depot PO
LAMB, Eli, K-173-3; Pvt A Co 9th TN Cav; 8 Aug 63 to 11 Sep 65; Troutman PO; rheumatism
LAMB, Epharim, K-154-5(2); Pvt F Co 6th TN Inf; 10 Jun 62 to 6 Jun 65; Knoxville PO
LAMB, Henrietta, B-4-1; widow; Bell Buckle PO
LAMB, Henry, Hd-50-4; Pvt A Co 2nd TN Mtd Inf; 10-2-63 to 10-14-64; Nixon PO; defective in hearing
LAMB, Josiah H., Sq-165-3; Louisa D. widow of; Lt E Co 6th TN Inf; 9-11-64 to 6-13-65; Dunlap PO; received an honorable disc.
LAMB, Lucy J., Ru-237-1; Pvt 4th TN Inf; 62 to 65; Eagleville PO; skull fractured
LAMB, Noah, Un-257-1; Sarah widow of; Pvt B Co 8th TN Cav; Sharps Chapel PO
LAMB, Orris F., Fr-116-1(2); Pvt 177th OH Inf; 9-64 to 7-65; Sherwood PO
LAMB, W. H., B-10-1; Pvt A Co 10th TN Inf; 2-22-63 to 20 Jun 65; PO omitted
LAMB, William H., We-224-4; 6th Dist
LAMBDIN, John B., Br-8-3(1); Emily widow of; Sgt E Co 5th TN Mtd Inf; 10-3-64 to 7-12-65; Cleo PO
LAMBERT, Betsey J. (see Belt, Robert)
LAMBERT, Howard, Bo-14-4; Pvt A Co 3rd TN Inf; 2-10-62 to 2-23-65; Clover Hill PO; chronic diarrhea
LAMBERT, James L., Cl-54-1; Mary widow of; Pvt I Co 3rd TN Inf; 2-10-62 to __; Bacchus PO; typhoid fever; cannot get the date of his death, some time in 1865
LAMBERT, John C., Dy-29-3; Pvt D Co 2nd MS Cav; Feb 62 to Jun 65; Newbern PO; CONF
LAMBERT, Joseph, Cl-54-1; Pvt F Co 8th TN Cav; 7-10-63 to 9-11-65; Bacchus PO; expiration of time
LAMBERT, Robert, Sh-196-1; Rhoda widow of; Pvt C Co 59th US Lt Art; 63 to 66; 120 Dunlap St, Memphis PO; pensioner
LAMBETH, John, Mn-125-1; Pvt E Co 1st US __ Cav (AL?); 10 Jun 63 to 27 Jul 64; Caffey PO
LAMBKINS, Samuel, Su-239-2; Pvt F Co 8th TN Cav; 10 Aug 63 to 11 Sep 65; Horace PO; spring 65
LAMONS, Wasington A., Ge-91-4; Sgt C Co 2nd NC Inf; 23 Sep 63 to 16 Aug 65; Greeneville PO; deafness &c
LAMPKIN, Alfred, H-67-2; Cpl D Co 10th US Col Inf --5-25-64 to 5-65; Cpl D Co 40th US Col Inf-- 5-65 to 4-25-66; Chattanooga PO; left foot split by an ax, now crippled
LAMPKINS, Joseph, Gr-76-2(1); Angeline widow of; Pvt D Co 9th TN Vols; 13 Nov 63 to 11 Sep 65; Tampico PO; died, Aug 1, 1883

LAMSON, Isaac, Cl-55-2; Pvt B Co 1st TN Cav; 63 to 65; Lone Mountain PO
LAMY, James Mooney, C-8-1; Pvt C Co 9th TN Cav; Well Spring PO; piles; was in service only few months, got sick and was released without discharge
LAN, Alfred, M-108-1; Mary J. widow of; Pvt; Lafayette PO
LANARD, Howell, Su-235-1; Pvt A Co 13th TN Cav; 24 Sep 63 to 22 Jul 65; Blountville PO; small pox
LANCASTER, Benjamin M., De-22-3; Pvt B Co 52nd TN Inf; 1 Sep 62 to 1 Nov 64; Dunbar PO; CONF
LANCASTER, Jerre, K-161-1; Knoxville PO
LANCASTER, Jesse J., De-22-1; 1st Lt G Co 6th TN Cav; 18 Sep 62 to 1 Mar 63; Dunbar PO
LANCASTER, John A., Dy-29-4; Sgt F Co 55th TN Inf; Oct 61 to __; Newbern PO; taken prisoner & sworn allegiance; CONF
LANCASTER, John C., Mu-197-1; Pvt A Co; 63 to 65; Columbia PO; CONF
LANCASTER, Larkin, Gi-127-6; Pvt C Co 12th TN Col Inf; 2 yrs 6 mos; Pulaski PO; in jail and discharge not at han
LANCASTER, William H., P-156-2; Sgt F Co 53rd TN Inf; 61 to 64; Lobelville PO; CONF
LANCE, James K. P., Ca-24-1; Pvt B Co 5th TN Cav; 8-27-62 to 6-25-65; Prater PO; deafness, contraction of measles, left side face & ear
LAND, Newton, Bo-15-1; Matilda Blevins widow of; Pvt H Co 2nd TN Cav; 10-10-62 to 2-12-63; Corn PO
LAND, William L., Sq-164-4(1); Pvt; Brock PO
LANDAU, Robert, Mo-126-2; Pvt B Co 1st US Vol Inf; 1-26-64 to 11-4-66; Madisonville PO
LANDER, George, Mt-132-1; Pvt G Co 15th TN Inf; 10-10-64 to 4-7-66; Guthrie KY PO; now partly blind and paralyzed
LANDERS, Beuley, Wa-260-1; Pvt E Co 2nd NC; 1 Sep 63 to 15 Aug 65; Nola Chucky PO
LANDERS, George C., Sh-171-1; Pvt E Co 2nd OH Cav; 61 to 65; Memphis PO
LANDMAN, Johnson, Un-259-2; Pvt G Co 4th TN Cav; 10 Mar 61 to 10 Mar 65; Herricane Branch PO; catar of the head, exposure
LANDRETH, Wilkerson M., Wa-268-2; Johnson City PO; dyspepsia
LANDRUM, James W., G-71-2; Pvt D Co 13th TN Cav; 15 Dec 63 to 15 Apr 64; Rutherford PO
LANDRUM, Thomas D., G-60-1; Pvt B Co 13th TN Cav; Oct 63 to __; Dyer PO; certificate of discharge is at Washington and he can not give the dates for enlistment
LANDYMITE, George, Hw-118-2; Pvt; St. Clair PO
LANE, A. H., Bo-22-1; Pvt D Co 2nd TN Cav; 12-24-63 to 7-6-65; Seaton PO
LANE, Abraham B., Ge-101-2; Pvt C Co 4th TN Inf; 6 Apr 63 to 2 Aug 65; Locust Sp. PO; died Dec 7 1887
LANE, Benjamin, Su-232-1; Saddler H Co 13th TN Cav; 24 Sep 63 to 24 Sep 65; Bristol PO; epilepsey and stricture of bowels
LANE, Ferniand, Sh-149-3; US Sol; 6th Civil Dist
LANE, Gabriel (see McClelland, Calvin)
LANE, Garrot, Hm-109-8; Pvt C Co 8th TN Cav; Whitesburg PO
LANE, George W. (Col), Ja-86-3; Pvt I Co 44th Col Inf; 8-17-64 to 4-30-66; Oottewah PO
LANE, Isom, Col, Gi-133-1; Pvt B Co 110th __; 61 to 65; Bufords PO
LANE, James, Mc-114-5; Mollie widow of; Pvt; Santfordville PO
LANE, James, Mr-97-2; Pvt D Co 1st AL Cav; 8-3-63 to 6-16-64; Jarman? PO
LANE, James M., Hw-124-1; Pvt H Co 8th TN Cav; 19 Nov 63 to 17 Sep 65; Opossum PO
LANE, James T., H-75-1; Pvt C Co 3rd OH Inf; 1-15-61 to 12-29-65; Chattanooga PO
LANE, John, Co-69-3; Pvt K Co 8th TN Cav; 20 Sep 63 to 11 Sep 65; Rankin PO; health los in Reble Prim a Wythvill, GA, no pension
LANE, John C., Ja-85-2; Pvt E Co 5th TN Inf; 3-2-62 to 4-4-65; Birchwood PO
LANE, John W., Wa-263-3; Sarah J. widow of; Garbers Mills PO
LANE, Joseph, Mu-193-2; Pvt 53rd IL Cav; 3-15-62 to 3-15-65; PO omitted
LANE, M. E., Se-222-2; Pvt K Co 3rd TN Inf; 62 to 65; Harrisburg PO; site & hearing

LANE, Maggie A., K-154-2; Knoxville PO
LANE, Marshal, Sh-148-2; Memphis PO
LANE, R. R., Wl-308-1; Pvt F Co 43rd TN; Dec 2 61 to Jan 28 63; Dodoburgh PO; CONF
LANE, Richard S., Hm-108-3(2); Capt D Co 4th TN Inf; 4 Nov 62 to 2 Aug 65; Russellville PO; rheumatism
LANE, Samuel, K-180-3; Sarah widow of; Pvt 8th TN Inf; Ebenezer PO; died in army
LANE, Thomas, Br-12-3; Pvt G Co 5th TN Inf; 3-1-62 to 5-15-65; McPherren PO; rhumatism
LANE, W. C., Bo-22-1; Pvt D Co 2nd TN Cav; 9-1-62 to 7-6-65; Seaton PO
LANE, Washington, Sh-191-2; Memphis PO; records not seen
LANE, William, Ge-97-2; Pvt C Co 4th TN Inf; 15 Mar 63 to 2 Aug 65; Lost Mountain PO; rheumatism
LANE, William A., Je-146-3; Pvt C Co 8th TN Cav; 64 to 11 Sep 65; Leadvale PO; neuralga since the war, soldier is now suffering badly
LANE, William E., Ge-84-2; Sadler B Co 8th TN Cav; 23 Jul 63 to 11 Sep 65; Greenville PO; chronic diarria
LANE, William M., Mu-210-2; Pvt 2nd TN Inf; 5-1-63 to 8-3-65; Spring Hill PO
LANER, Christopher Sr., A-6-6(4); Sgt H Co 26th NY Inf; 61 to 63; Olivers PO
LANG, Isaac, Hw-131-3; Otes PO; CONF
LANG, Isoral, Dk-37-1; Pvt D Co 8th TN Cav; 64 to 65; Jonesville PO
LANG, Nicholous B., Hw-131-2; Pvt B Co 8th TN Inf; 15 Dec 62 to 30 Jun 65; White Horn PO
LANG, William M., Hw-131-4; Pvt D? Co 8th TN Inf; 15 Mar 63 to 8 Aug 65; Otes PO; gunshot hand, discharged on cirttificate
LANGFORD, Archer (see Davis, Archie)
LANGFORD, Richard A., Je-145-2; Sgt A Co 6th TN Inf; 8 Mar 62 to 27 Apr 65; Dumplin PO
LANGFORD, Vinson M., H-54-2; Pvt 1st TN Art; 9-63 to 65; Sherman Heights PO; hearing injured in left ear
LANGFORD, Walker, Hw-132-4; Pvt B Co 6th TN Inf; 62 to 65; Otes PO; rheumatism, was not discharged at close of war
LANGFORD, William M., Ov-134-1; Pvt E Co 14th MO Vol Mtd Cav; 4-1-65 to 10-26-65; Hilham PO; chronic diarhea & bronchitis, does not remember exact dates
LANGLEY, Eli, Un-256-3; Rachel widow of; Pvt 11th TN Cav; Loys X Roads PO; died in army
LANGLEY, Ephraim, Ro-203-3; Sarah widow of; Capt F Co 1st TN Inf; 61 to __; Ethel PO; injury from fever
LANGLEY, Henry, Sh-189-2; no record could be procured; La. Ave, Memphis PO
LANGLEY, James, Mg-197-6; Sgt F Co 1st TN Inf; 9 Aug 61 to 17 Sep 64; Crooked Ford PO; spinal & kidney disease from measles, chronic rheumatism 27 yrs, totally disabled from labor
LANGLEY, James M., K-182-2; Pvt K Co 3rd TN Cav; 63 to 65; Shook PO; Cahoba P. 6 mos
LANGLEY, James O., Mg-200-2; Pvt F Co 1st TN Inf; 9 Aug 61 to 27 Sep 64; Kismet PO
LANGLEY, Tomas H., O-134-2; Pvt C Co 9th TN Cav; Jan 1 63 to Mar 1 65; Hornbeak PO; CONF
LANGLEY, William B., Mg-196-3; Pvt F Co 2nd TN Inf; 9 Mar 62 to 11 Mar 65; Wartburg PO; shot
LANGLY, Sarah (see Robinson, Alvin J.)
LANGLY, Thomas L., P-156-2; Pvt C Co 42nd TN Inf; 62 to 7-12-65 (3 yrs 6 mos); Lobelville PO; shot in right leg and back; CONF
LANGSTON, Albert L., K-156-2; Mary E. widow of; Pvt TN Inf; E Main 259, Knoxville PO; CONF
LANGSTON, Benjamin, Se-228-2(3); Pvt D Co 9th TN Cav; 7 Sep 63 to 12 Sep 65; Cox PO; general disability, pensioner
LANGSTON, William, Br-9-4; Cleveland PO
LANHAM, Thoma H., Wl-297-2; Sgt H Co 4th TN Mtd Inf; 20 Oct 64 to 25 Aug 65; Commerce PO
LANIER, Thos. H., Dy-20-1; Mary S. widow of; Pvt E Co 13th TN Cav; Apr 63 to Apr 64; Dyersburg PO
LENIRE, Andrew, Mu-191-1; Cpl A Co 15th TN Vol; 11-63 to 2-16-66; Bigbyville PO
LANKASTER, Joseph G., Mr-99-2; Pvt B Co 1st OH Lt Art; 9-6-61 to 7-23-65; Jasper PO
LANKASTON, John M., P-157-1; PO omitted; never belonged to the service--has no discharge
LANKFORD, James M., H-56-8; Sol US; St. Elmo PO
LANKFORD, Silas J., Di-36-1; Pvt H Co 24th TN Inf; 6-24-61 to 1-14-65; Bellsburgh PO; CONF
LANKFORT, John W., Mg-200-3; Eliza E. widow of; Pvt G Co 2nd TN Cav; Jun 63 to died in prison
LANKIST, Lee W., Hi-91-1; Pvt E Co 2nd TN Inf; 63 to 64; Pleasantville PO
LANORE, Nancy, K-167-1; Pvt 1st Hvy TN; 63 to May 65; Knoxville PO
LANSFORD, Thomas A., Hw-127-2; Pvt F Co 7th IN Cav; 22 Aug 63 to 17 Nov 65; Rogersville PO; rheumatism resulting in heart disease
LANTHER, McLane, Ge-83-2; Bathia E. widow of; Cpl G Co 4th TN Inf; 62 to 65; Henshaw PO; chronic diorrhial
LANY, John L., K-179-2; Pvt E Co 3rd TN Mtd Inf; 15 Jul 64 to 13 Nov 64; Virtue PO
LAPHORN, Cement H., Mr-102-1; Pvt D Co 9th KY Cav; 8-22-62 to 8-21-63; South Pittsburg PO
LAPIER, Phelix, Fe-41-3(1); Zilphia widow of; Pvt, Little Crabb PO; wound in right hand
LAPPIN, Burton, D-60-2; Messenger Boy Col Cram Paymaster; 313 McNairy St, Nashville PO; mulatto
LaPROFIT, Danil, L-108-1; Pvt K Co 5th AL C Inf; 63 to 64; Glimpville PO
LARGE, Auston, Co-66-3(1); Levina widow of; Pvt B Co 26th TN Inf; 28 Jun 61 to 15 Feb 63; English PO; tunge shot off; CONF
LARGE, Emily, Gr-77-2; widow (USS); Strawberry Plains PO
LARGE, Isaac, Me-90-1; Pvt D Co 3rd TN Inf; 2-10-62 to 2-23-65; Goodfield PO
LARGE, John, Se-219-3; Pvt E Co 2nd TN Cav; 16 Sep 62 to 5 Jul 65; Richardsons Cave PO; chills, fever & rumatism
LARGE, Samuell, Se-219-2; Pvt E Co 2nd TN Cav; 1 Feb 64 to 5 Jul 65; Jones Cave PO; chronic diarhea
LARGE, Talitha (see Tallent, John)
LARGE, William, Ct-42-3; Pvt H Co 8th TN Cav; 11-19-63 to 9-1-65; Elizabethton PO; shot through foot
LARGE, William H., Co-67-3; Ritty widow of; Pvt B Co 1st KY Cav; 10 Nov 62 to 13 Sep 65; Cosby PO
LARHARITY, George W., K-182-4; Pvt D Co 2nd TN Cav; 1 Sep 62 to 6 Jul 65; Gap Creek PO; left leg mashed
LARKIN, G. T., Hm-104-2; Pvt; PO omitted
LARKIN, Joseph, Mu-197-2; Pvt E Co 49th __; __ to 64; Columbia PO
LARKIN, Onie, Fr-109-1; Huntland PO
LARKINS, Henry, Hw-125-6; Pvt B Co KY Bat; 63 to Jun 63 (6 mos); Blevins PO; CONF
LARNE, Abe, Ms-171-2; Teamster D Co 127th TN Inf; Mar 63 to Apr 65; Belfast PO
LARNE, John F., Ms-180-1; Pvt E Co 10th TN Inf; 3-12-64 to 7-2-65; Lewisburg PO; tumer on jaw, homeless
LARNER, Thomas, Fe-41-4(2); Eliza A. widow of; Pvt D Co 2nd TN Inf; 8-61 to 63; Sand Land PO; sickened & died in service with cholera morbus
LARREN, Rachael W., G-64-2; Bradford PO
LARRISON, Emiline, Rb-223-2; widow Sol US; PO omitted
LARSON, Valentine L., K-180-3; Pvt I Co 1st TN Cav; 22 Sep 62 to 5 Jun 65; Ebenezer PO; injury to eyes
LARUE, Joseph, K-176-1; Pvt G Co 6th TN Inf; 14 Apr 62 to 17 May 65; Halls X Roads PO
LARUE, Josiah, P-151-1; Pvt A Co 10th TN Cav; 63 to 64; Pope PO
LASATER, William, Mc-112-6; 1st Lt A Co 7th TN Mtd Inf; 6-63 to 5-65; Athens PO; gunshot wound
LASH, Julian, Br-9-5; Jane widow of; Cleveland PO; draws a pension, no discharge
LASLEY, Ahas B., Fe-58-6; Pvt I Co 2nd TN Mtd Inf; 10-25-61 to 2-18-63; Sale Creek PO; loss of health, discharged on surgeon's certificate
LASLEY, Lewis H., H-50-3(1); Sarah widow of; Pvt C Co 5th R TN Vol; Igon's Ferry PO; died of measles

LASSLY, William H., H-7-31; Pvt I Co 38th US Inf; 11-15-6? to ___ (3 yrs); Chattanooga PO
LASURE, Abram, De-25-1; Pvt; 15 May 61 to 15 May 65; Decaturville PO
LATHAM, Charles H., white, Li-154-1; Pvt D Co 11th US Cav; 1-62 to 10-8-65; Clardy Ville PO; he enlisted in Decatur, AL
LATHAM, Ely, We-225-4(3); Sol; Dresden PO
LATHROP, Alfred W., Sq-164-3(1); Pvt; Dunlap PO
LATHROP, Stanley E., Fr-116-1(2); Sgt M Co 1st WI Cav; 4-61 to 7-19-65; Sherwood PO
LATHUM, William, Br-9-3; Pvt H Co 3rd TN Cav; 63 to 6-65; Cleveland PO
LATIMORE, Loss, Mc-115-1; Riceville PO
LAUCHNER, John A., Ge-88-1; Pvt C Co 61st TN Inf; 62 to 63; PO omitted; spinal; CONF
LAUDERDALE, Daniel, Ma-128-1; Cook; 3 yrs; Jackson PO; could give no name of co.
LAUGHERTY, Thomas, K-184-4; Susana wife of; Pvt B Co 6th TN Inf; Thorn Grove PO
LAUGHLIN, W. W., Mn-121-1; Sarah J. widow of; Pvt A Co 6th TN Cav; 28 Jul 63 to 26 Jul 65; Rosecreek PO
LAUGHLIN, William, Mn-121-2; Pvt A Co 6th TN Cav; 11 Aug 62 to 26 Jul 65; Bethel Springs PO
LAUGHMILLER, John, Bo-21-2; Pvt D Co 4th TN Cav; 3-1-63 to 7-12-65; Ellijay PO
LAUGHTER, Samuel, Mo-130-2; Mary widow of; Pvt I Co 7th TN Mtd Inf; 1-1-65 to 7-27-65; Ballplay PO
LAURENCE, John, Tr-268-2; Pvt A Co 52nd KY Mtd Inf; Oct 63 to Jan 65; Hartsville PO; able bodied
LAURENCE, Joseph B., Di-36-1; Pvt B Co 11th TN Inf; 5-1-61 to 5-20-64; Bellsburg PO; CONF
LAURENT, Moses, Cf-40-2; Pvt I Co 6th MI Cav; 29 Aug 62 to 29 Jun 65; Tullahoma PO; ruptured in abdomen
LAUREY, John T., Wl-293-1; G Co 6th Gov Inf; 61 to 65; Lockport PO; CONF
LAUSON, Harry, H-64-1; Pvt; Chattanooga PO; asthma
LAUSON, James, Bl-3-3; Pvt K Co 5th TN Inf; 11-9-62 to 6-20-65; Billingaly PO; weak lungs
LAUSON, Lazerac, Bo-12-3(1); Sol US; 3rd Dist
LAUTER, Albert W., H-60-5(2); Pvt E Co 5th NY Inf; 4-18-61 to 7-61; Chattanooga PO; gunshot wound left arm
LAUTER, Amandus J., H-53-5; Pvt E Co 5th NY Inf; 4-61 to 8-61; Ridgedale PO
LAVALLEY, Jos. (see Walker, Jos.)
LAVENDER, John, Mg-200-1; Pvt F Co 1st TN Inf; 20 Aug 61 to 12 Sep 64; Kismet PO; disease of lungs
LAVENY, Evin J., We-221-2; Lt TN Cav; Nov 61 to Dec 62; Martin PO; CONF
LAW, A. H., Bo-22-2; Pvt D Co 2nd TN Cav; 9-1-62 to 7-6-65; Seaton PO
LAW, Addison A., Sm-169-3(5); Pvt; Defeated PO; CONF
LAW, Amos, H-75-1; SgtG Co 44th TN Inf; 63 to 66 (2 yrs 6 mos); Chattanooga PO; papers lost
LAW, Charley, Ca-22-3; Pvt F Co 5th TN Cav; 3-14-62 to 1-5-63; Burt PO
LAW, Joseph, S-218-3; Pvt G Co 2nd Inf; 61 to Sep 62; Hughett PO; in 1861, piles
LAW, Mathew A., Mr-99-2; Pvt G Co 5th TN Inf; 3-1-62 to 12-12-64; Jasper PO; chronic diorhoer ever since the war
LAW, William, Bo-13-1; Pvt C Co 3rd TN Lt Inf; 9-17-63 to 8-1-65; Freindsville PO
LAWBRUGH, Alford P., Ov-133-2(1); Hattie widow of; Pvt G Co 1st Bat US Inf; 4-15-61 to 2-12-61 (sic) (5 yrs); Oak Hill PO
LAWHORN, David A., Be-9-1; Pvt D Co 1st TN Inf; 4-23-63 to 8-25-65; Rockford PO
LAWHORN, Joel A., H-53-1; Pvt D Co 5th TN Inf; 2-26-62 to 5-15-65; Chattanooga PO; piles, deafness left ear
LAWLER, John A., Cr-13-1; Pvt A Co 7th TN Cav; May 63 to not discharged (9 mos); Atwood PO; none incured, regiment captured & scattered
LAWLER, Thomas, Hy-74-1; 1st Civil Dist
LAWLER, William T., We-221-4; 2nd Lt I Co 22nd TN Cav; May 61 to Sep 64; Martin PO; loss of right arm; CONF
LAWRENCE, Calaway, Se-226-1; Lt Art H Co 2nd TN; Straw Plains PO; both eyes diseased with powder

LAWRENCE, David, Je-140-2; Pvt D Co 1st TN Art; 15 Sep 63 to 20 Jul 65; PO omitted
LAWRENCE, Ellis, Sn-252-2; Pvt H Co 14th TN Inf; 11-63 to 2-65; Gallatin PO
LAWRENCE, Henry M., We-229-2; "found while examing work"; 11th Civil Dist
LAWRENCE, John, D-54-2; Emma E. widow of; Chap 15th US Col Inf; 3 Mar 64 to 17 May 66; Nashville PO
LAWRENCE, Joshua, D-61-2; Ord Sgt B Co 15th TN Inf; Nov 61 to Apr 65; Ament St, Nashville PO
LAWRENCE, Leonard B., G-64-2; Bradford PO
LAWRENCE, Richard, D-50-1; Julia widow of; Pvt; ___ to 66; 420 Line, Nashville PO
LAWRENCE, Rufus M., D-72-6; Pvt 13th TN Inf; 63 to 66; Nashville PO
LAWRENCE, Wm., Hw-129-1; Pvt A Co 5th IA Cav; 14 Sep 61 to 16 Sep 64; Morrisburg PO; disease of eyes & liver, deafness contracted from exposure while prisoner
LAWRENCE, William H., Ro-207-2; Pvt G Co 1st NC Inf; 25 Apr 63 to 27 Jun 65; Paint Rock PO; rheumatism & piles
LAWS, Gaston P., Wa-260-1; Pvt A Co 1st Reg East VA Vols; Jun 4 63 to Dec 1 65; Pilot Hill PO; failed to see discharge
LAWS, Isaac, Jo-152-3; Pvt F Co 13th TN Cav; 22 Sep 63 to 5 Sep 65; Butler PO; frost bitten feet & rheumatism
LAWS, John M., Co-65-2; Pvt I Co 3rd NC Inf; papers all lost in burning of his house; Nailon PO; rheumatism
LAWS, Joseph, Wa-267-2; Pvt F Co 13th TN Cav; 20 Aug 63 to 21 Jun 65; Febuary PO; wound w. foot
LAWSON, Calaway H., Hw-121-6(1); Pvt C Co 61st TN Inf; 6 Oct 63 to 12 Jul 64; Strahl PO; rheumatism, piles
LAWSON, Centre, Hm-107-3; Pvt I Co 8th TN Cav; 24 Nov 63 to 11 Sep 65; Witts Foundry PO; gun shot wound
LAWSON, Chisel, Mc-103-2; Pvt I Co 4th TN Cav; 9-25-64 to 8-25-65; Lafayette PO
LAWSON, Crocket, V-178-1; Cpl B Co 6th US Vol Inf; 3-14-65 to 11-66; Cummingsville PO; diarhea
LAWSON, Curren, Hw-130-2; Pvt L Co 8th TN Cav; 11 Sep 63 to 8 Sep 65; Lee Valley PO
LAWSON, Edward, Je-136-1; Caroline widow of; Pvt F Co 2nd TN Cav; 1 Feb 64 to 6 Jul 65; Dandridge PO
LAWSON, Fletcher, K-172-4; Pvt G Co 24th KY Inf; 9 Oct 61 to 31 Jan 65; PO omitted
LAWSON, Frank D., La-116-1; Pvt I Co 4th TN Inf; Jan 10 63 to Aug 25 63; Henryville PO
LAWSON, Frank M., Wa-270-2; Pvt I Co 8th TN Cav; 1 Apr 62 to Apr 65; Austin's Springs PO; diarhea, lung trouble
LAWSON, George, K-181-7(4); Knoxville PO
LAWSON, George, Hm-109-2; Pvt B Co 9th TN Cav; Sep 63 to 15 Sep 65; Russellville PO
LAWSON, George W., Br-7-2; Pvt A Co 2nd? TN Cav; 10-62 to 7-12-65; Coahulla PO
LAWSON, George W., Hw-120-1; Pvt F Co 8th TN Cav; Sep 63 to Nov 63; War Gap PO
LAWSON, George W., Bo-14-5; Pvt J Co 1st TN Inf; ___ to 65; Mint PO
LAWSON, Henry G., Hw-132-5; Pvt H Co 8th TN Cav; 63 to Jun 65; Strahl PO; could not obtain full details
LAWSON, Hudson, Gr-70-1; Pvt C Co 12th TN Cav; 1 Oct 62 to 1 Sep 63; Rutledge PO
LAWSON, Isariah, Ro-204-2; Mary A. widow of; Pvt 1st TN Inf; Aug 61 to ___; Oliver Springs PO; no discharge found
LAWSON, Isham, Br-6-3; Pvt A Co 8th TN Inf; 2-20-63 to 65; Charleston PO; disease eyes, diarhoea and rheumatism
LAWSON, James, O-134-2; Sgt I Co 36th IN Inf; Sep 16 61 to Sep 21 64; Hornbeak PO
LAWSON, James, Hw-130-1; Pvt L Co 10th TN Cav; 62 to 65; Lee Valley PO; rheumatis, no discharge
LAWSON, James, Ct-39-1; Pvt H Co 13th TN Cav; 9-63 to 9-65; Johnson City PO; frost bite & rheumatism
LAWSON, James, Mc-118-2; Betty J. widow of; Pvt 7th TN Mtd Inf; 64 to 65; Joshua PO
LAWSON, James M., M-103-3; Pvt E Co 4th TN Cav; 10-1-64 to 8-1-65; Lafayette PO

LAWSON, James N., Bo-14-5; Pvt 4th TN; Clover Hill PO
LAWSON, Jesse, Bl-2-1; Pvt C Co 1st AL Cav; 12-62 to 10-65; Clade Creek PO; palpitation of heart
LAWSON, John, Pi-156-2; Nancy E. widow of; Pvt; Byrdtown PO
LAWSON, John, Hw-130-1; Pvt G Co 8th TN Inf; 62 to 64; Lee Valley PO
LAWSON, John M. P., Ha-112-1; Nancy widow of; Pvt B Co 1st TN Cav; Datura PO
LAWSON, John W., Bl-2-1; Pvt D Co 4th TN Mtd Inf; 9-6-64 to 8-26-65; Pikeville PO; deafness, partialy deat, old, infirm
LAWSON, Lewis, Br-12-2; Orlena widow of; Cleveland PO; CONF
LAWSON, Marshal, Br-6-2; Pvt I Co 10th TN Cav; 2-10-64 to 4-15-65; Climer PO; appoplexy, result explosion shell
LAWSON, Martha, H-64-3; former widow US Sol; 105 Vaughn St, Chattanooga PO
LAWSON, Momen, Cl-52-3; Pvt A Co 11th TN Inf; 3-8-62 to 65; Hypatia PO; health injured
LAWSON, Nathan, Ca-22-1; Pvt E Co 155th IL Inf; 61 to 9-64; Hollow Springs PO
LAWSON, P. A., Mc-113-1; Cpl L Co 9th TN Cav; 9-1-63 to 9-11-65; Athens PO
LAWSON, Palistine, Hw-120-2; Sarah widow of; Pvt G Co 8th TN; Eidson PO
LAWSON, Preston, Hw-119-3(1); Pvt; Alum Well PO; taken sick from cold; CONF
LAWSON, Stephen, Ge-99-2; Pvt L Co 8th TN Cav; 12 Sep 63 to 11 Sep 65; Limestone Springs PO; throwed by horse, crippled in right hip and ruptured
LAWSON, Thomas, Br-6-2; this man was a substitute in Fed Regt; Chatala PO; rheumatism & hernie, never assigned to regt
LAWSON, Tyre, Mg-196-2; Smith (blacksmith?) L Co 10th TN Cav; 7-9-64 to 8-1-65; Pikeville PO; also veteran of Mexican War, pensioner
LAWSON, Wash, H-67-1; Pvt G Co 13th US Col Inf; 63 to 6-10-66; Chattanooga PO
LAWSON, William, F-46-2; Margarett Harlin widow of; Pvt B Co 7th IL; 3 yrs; LaGrange PO; shot in sholder & hip, widow quite needy
LAWSON, William, Mg-196-2; Mahala widow of; G Co 1st TN Inf; 61 to 62; Coalfield PO; died in service
LAWSON, William, Hw-130-2; Pvt L Co 8th TN Cav; 17 Sep 63 to 11 Sep 65; Lee Valley PO
LAWSON, William A., Ha-116-3(1); Pvt G Co 4th TN Cav; 19 May 63 to 10 Jul 65; Clinch PO; shot in right thie
LAWSON, William M., Br-11-2; Pvt M Co 9th TN Cav; 9-63 to 9-65; Chatala PO; total blindness
LAWSON, William P., Cr-4-1; Lt H Co 50th TN Inf; 62 to 65; Bells Depot PO; CONF
LAXAM, Jessie P., Wy-174-1; 9th Civil Dist
LAY, David, C-8-2; Pvt F Co 6th TN Inf; 3-10-62 to 3-25-65; Powells River PO; both lungs affected, has never applied for pension
LAY, Elizabeth, Gi-138-2; 18th Dist
LAY, Freelin H., Un-251-1; Pvt G Co 7th TN Mtd Inf; 64 to 27 Jul 65; Effie PO
LAY, Jack A., Dy-25-9(1); Dosia E. widow of; 61 to 63; Newbern PO; contracted consumption, enlistment dates unknown; CONF
LAY, James, C-34-2; Pvt A Co 1st TN Inf; 8-8-61 to 10-1-64; Elk Valley PO; died after war from disease contracted in army (believe this comment refers to another veteran)
LAY, Jessie, Un-257-3; Pvt B Co 1st TN Art; 1 Jul 64 to 12 Jul 65; New Prospect PO; measles & deafness, deafness by artillery shock
LAY, John, S-216-2; Pvt; Capushiene PO; away from home, no information
LAY, John R., H-69-5; Sgt; Chattanooga PO; CONF
LAY, Lewis, S-216-1; Pvt A Co 1st TN Inf; 2 Sep 63 to 3 Aug 65; PO omitted
LAY, Louis C., Un-259-2; Pvt D Co 2nd TN Cav; 12 Aug 61 to 12 Apr 64; Herricane Branch PO; CONF
LAY, Martha E., C-34-4; widow US Soldier; 11th Civil Dist
LAY, Martha J. (see Baird, Andrew)
LAY, William P., S-216-2; Sol; 6th & 7th Dist

LAYMAN, Asa, Se-221-2; Pvt M Co 2nd TN Cav; 8 Nov 62 to 6 Jul 65; Fox PO
LAYMAN, John T., Je-142-1; Pvt F Co 9th TN Cav; 29 Jan 64 to ___; Lucilla PO; shot three times
LAYMAN, William, Je-139-1; Cpl F Co 7th TN Cav; May 63 to 25 Mar ___; Trion PO; heart disease
LAYN, David E., H-70-1; Pvt D Co 38th OH Inf; 10-7-64 to 7-12-65; Chattanooga PO
LAYNE, Abraham, Sq-165-2; Pvt; Delphi PO; received an honorable disc.
LAYNE, Alexander, Sq-165-1; Delphi PO; received an honorable disc.
LAYNE, Charles, Mr-96-3(2); Pvt D Co 1st AL Cav; 7-3-63 to 6-16-64; Whitwell PO
LAYNE, Henry, Sq-165-2; Pvt C Co 6th TN Mtd Inf; 9-12-64 to 6-65; Sunnyside PO; died in service in 1865
LAYNE, Jackson, Mr-96-3(2); Pvt D Co 1st AL Cav; 7-31-63 to 6-16-64; Whitwell PO; deftness
LAYNE, James H., C-33-1; Pvt G Co 7th OH Cav; 9-8-62 to 6-22-65; Newcomb PO
LAYNE, John A., Mr-95-1; Pvt C Co 6th TN Cav; 9-2-64 to 7-11-65; Victoria PO
LAYNE, John B., Sq-165-2; Amanda L. widow of; Lt D Co 1st TN Cav; 8-1-63 to 6-16-64; Delphi PO
LAYNE, Morison, Sq-165-1; Pvt C Co 6th TN Mtd Inf; 9-12-64 to 6-30-65; Cedar Spring PO; received an honorable disc.
LAYNE, Richard H., Dy-27-1; Pvt G Co 15th TN Cav; 9-20-63 to 1-5-65; Taytonville PO; CONF
LAYTHEM, John, Pi-156-2; Pvt B Co; Travisville PO
LEA, Alfred, H-58-4; Pvt A Co 6th TN Mtd Inf; 8-2-64 to 6-30-65; Sale Creek PO
LEA, Jasper, H-58-4; Elizabeth Gothard formerly widow of; Cpl G Co 5th TN Cav; 9-11-62 to 8-14-65; Sale Creek PO; rheumatism, badly crippled
LEA, John, A-8-3; Pvt H Co 9th TN Cav; 9-1-63 to 9-11-65; Scarborough PO
LEA, Robet, L-101-2; Pvt D Co 106th C Inf; Jan 3 64 to Apr 25 66; Henning PO; discharge from Co H 40th US C T
LEAB, Jacob, Wa-273-1; Adjutant 8th TN Cav; 15 Sep 63 to 11 Sep 65; Locust Mt. PO; lung disease
LEAB, John, K-161-1; Anne widow of; Knoxville PO
LEACH, Charles, Sh-145-2; Cpl B Co 3rd TN Col Hvy Art; Jun 63 to Apr 66; Kerrville PO
LEACH, Madison, Wa-263-6; Sarah E. widow of; Pvt L Co 13th TN Cav; 16 Oct 64 to 5 Sep 65; Garbers Mills PO
LEACH, Preston, C-30-1; Pvt C Co 1st TN Inf; 6-63 to 8-65; Well Spring PO
LEACH, William, A-4-2; Mary J. widow of; Sgt C Co 11th TN Cav; 8-62 to 9-65; Coal Creek PO
LEADGERWOOD, Layfette, K-167-1; Capt I Co 3rd TN Inf; 8 Apr 62 to 25 Nov 65; Knoxville PO
LEADOM, Dan, T-216-3; 14th Civil Dist
LEAGUE, James R., Dk-39-2; Pvt K Co 5th TN Cav; 5-22-63 to 8-14-65; Bozarth PO; head the measles result health bad
LEAHY, Michael, K-162-1; Pvt I Co 2nd IL Inf; 15 May 60 to 15 Mar 64; Knoxville PO
LEAK, Adam, K-183-1; Cpl B Co 3rd TN Cav; 15 Nov 62 to 10 Jun 65; Riverdale PO
LEAMER, Fred A., D-57-4; Master at _____ Navy under Porter; Sep 12 62 to Sep 12 63; Nashville PO; contract kidney disease
LEANERA, Peter S., Mn-121-2; Pvt A Co 6th TN Cav; 1 Mar 64 to 26 Jul 65; Falcon PO
LEAPER, Tobias, K-164-2; Sarah E. widow of; Pvt A Co 1st US Art; 18 Jan 64 to 31 Mar 65; PO omitted (Knoxville?)
LEATERWOOD, Sallie, Ru-238-2; widow; Murfreesboro PO
LEATHERWOOD, Miles N., H-54-2(3); Jane widow of; Pvt E Co 9th TN Cav; 9-29-63 to 9-11-65; 213 Cherry St., Chattanooga PO; horse fell on him, mashed his shoulder
LEATHERWOOD, Nicholas C., H-54-3; Pvt G Co 5th TN Mtd Vol; 1-1-65 to 7-13-65; Sherman Heights PO
LEAUGHNER, John A., Gr-79-4; Musi. C Co 1st TN; Sep 63 to May 65; Ball Point PO; piles
LEAVE, Samuel, K-170-2; Pvt D Co 6th TN Inf; 18 Apr 62 to 27 Apr 65; Knoxville PO; consumption 25 yrs, hearing badly injured

LEAVENGOOD, John, Br-12-2; Sgt H Co 51st OH Inf; 9-10-61 to 11-5-65; Charleston PO; wounded in leg
LEBOW, Grinsfield T., Bo-19-2; Pvt G Co 3rd TN Cav; 7-62 to ___ (7 mos); South Rockford PO; CONF
LECK, Joh, Br-12-6; 9th Dist
LEDBETTER, Elmira, Ha-114-3; Pvt K Co 12th KY Cav; 1 Jun 64 to 27 Sep 65; Sneedville PO
LEDBETTER, Ham, Pi-153-3; Pvt G Co 9th TN Cav; 8-2-63 to 9-11-65; Spurnier PO
LEDBETTER, Thomas, Ca-25-3; Pvt; Gassoway PO; feet frost bitten
LEDFORD, Green, Wa-273-2; Pvt D Co 13th TN Cav; Jan 63 to Oct 65; Jonesboro PO; lung disease and diarrhoea, discharge misplaced
LEDFORD, James M., Cu-18-1; Forage Master 100th OH Inf; 64 to 65; Verdic PO; imprisoned at Point Lookout
LEDFORD, Lucius J., Fr-112-3; 3rd Sgt B Co 62nd NC Inf; 8-22-62 to 1-20-63; Decherd PO
LEDFORD, Plesant B., Hd-45-2; Mary A. widow of; 3rd Sgt F Co 10th TN Inf; 28 May 62 to 20 Jun 65; Cerro Gordo PO
LEDFORD, Samuel, A-6-6(4); Pvt A Co 43rd TN ___; 63 to 8-63 (9 mos); Olivers PO; CONF
LEDFORD, Thomas L., Ro-210-9; Pvt; Rockwood PO
LEDFORD, ___, Nancy T. widow of; H-50-5; Soddy PO
LEDGEWOOD, James L., K-161-1; Capt F Co 3rd TN Inf; 61 to Mar 65; Knoxville PO
LEDGEWOOD, John, Mr-98-2(5); Pvt C Co 7th IL Inf; 12-3-62 to 7-9-65; Whiteside PO
LEDSINGER, Andrew, Dy-25-6(2); Carline widow of; 1 yr; Newbern PO; want out with his Master; CONF
LEE, Albert T., Ro-211-4; Jennie A. widow of; Maj Surgeon 5th TN Inf; 12 Aug 62 to 15 May 65; Kingston PO
LEE, Aleck, Mu-213-2; Pvt A Co 12th US TN Inf; 62 to 65; Rally Hill PO
LEE, Alexander, Sh-179-3(1); Pvt E Co 59th TN Inf; 1-6-63 to 65; Memphis PO
LEE, Alexander F., Ct-40-1; Pvt D Co 30th VA Bat; 61 to 8-14-65; Elizabethton PO; rheumatism; CONF
LEE, Alsa, Mu-210-2; Pvt G Co 11th TN Cav; 3-61 to 4-65; Spring Hill PO; CONF
LEE, Ben, We-224-1; Pvt KY? Cav; 61 to ___ (1 yr); Como PO (Henry Co.); discharge by reason of over age
LEE, Benjamin F., Bl-2-3; Pvt G Co 6th TN Mtd Inf; 2-20-65 to 6-30-65; Orme's Store PO; health injured by small pox & measles, moderate health now
LEE, Berrey B., Cl-51-1; Pvt C Co 29th TN Inf; 8-15-61 to 8-15-63; Hoop PO; wounded at Kingsport 9-63
LEE, Berry D., Hd-53-2; Lucinda F. widow of; Seaman Tyler; Sibley PO; discharge papers on file at pension office, Washington City, hence no dates
LEE, Charley, Ma-124-1; Sgt; May 61 to 65; Jackson PO
LEE, Charlie, F-46-1; LaGrange PO; Lee is not at home, wife dont know reg.
LEE, Columbus W., We-221-7; Rebecca E. widow of; Pvt C Co TN Cav; 62 to 65; Martin PO; none, but constitution broken, thought to be cause of death
LEE, Elizabeth, L-99-2; widow US Sol; Durhamville PO
LEE, Emma O., D-46-2; widow of US Sol; Nashville PO
LEE, George, Hw-129-2; Pvt A Co 2nd NC Inf; 1 Apr 64 to 16 Aug 65; Dellmonell PO
LEE, George H., Ro-203-7; Pvt F Co 1st TN Inf; 9 Aug 61 to 17 Sep 64; Burns' Mills PO; defective in sight
LEE, George W., O-139-1; Pvt A Co 50th MO; 8 Oct 64 to 5 Aug 65; Protemus PO
LEE, Harman, Hm-107-4; Pvt 9th TN Cav; 62 to Aug 65; Springvale PO; discharged burned, dates forgotten
LEE, Harry, H-56-6; 64 to 65; St. Elmo PO
LEE, Henry, Ro-206-1; Pvt D Co 11th TN Cav; Mar 62 to Jul 64; Emory Gap PO
LEE, Henry N., Le-119-1; Pvt A Co 2nd TN Mtd Inf; 13 Oct 63 to 13 Oct 64; Strathmore PO; left leg fractured, drawing pension since Feb 86
LEE, Henry N., Wy-177-2; Capt A Co 10th TN Inf; 4-6-62 to 5-25-65; Waynesboro PO; heart disease, cattarrh, receiving pension
LEE, Isaac C., Sh-191-6(2); Memphis PO; records not seen
LEE, Jackson, Mr-99-2; Owen PO
LEE, Jas., Gr-71-1; Mary widow of; Cpl D Co; Bean Station PO; discharge pension office
LEE, James, Dk-34-5(4); Pvt K Co 5th TN Cav; 4-3-63 to 8-14-65; Copling PO; hernia
LEE, James H., Hw-127-3; Sgt D Co 1st TN Cav; 15 Apr 62 to 15 Apr 65; Amis PO; rheumatism
LEE, James R., Cl-51-1; Pvt L Co 9th TN Cav; 9-1-63 to 9-11-65; Hoop PO
LEE, John, Mo-127-1; Rachiel M. widow of; Pvt; 11-9-64 to 3-9-65; Notchy PO
LEE, John, Hw-123-1; Pvt G Co 1st TN Cav; 1 Sep 62 to 65; New Canton PO
LEE, John, J-82-1; Nancy H. widow of; Cpl B Co 8th TN Mtd Inf; Irby PO
LEE, John E., H-76-2; Pvt F Co 1st OH US Cav; 9-5-61 to 10-6-64; Chattanooga PO
LEE, John M., D-97-2; US Sol; 18th Dist
LEE, John W., Mg-198-2; Pvt F Co 1st TN Inf; 19 Aug 61 to 17 Sep 64; Kismet PO; fever 1 mo.
LEE, John T., M-108-3; Cpl & Pvt A Co 9th KY Inf; 9-25-61 to 12-15-64; Lafayette PO; right lung damaged & mumps, also right side, discharge not at home
LEE, John W., Pu-145-3(4); Violet widow of; Pvt D Co 8th Mtd Inf; 2-1-65 to 8-31-65; Silver Point PO
LEE, Jorden P., Ge-94-1; Pvt E Co 4th TN Inf; 17 Sep 62 to 20 Jul 65; Home PO; rheumatism
LEE, Joseph R., Pu-146-2; Pvt C Co 1st TN Mtd Inf Vol; 3-13-64 to 8-1-65; Buffalo Valley PO
LEE, Joseph W., Cr-19-1; Sgt M Co 6th TN Cav; 7-31-62 to 7-26-65; Buxter PO
LEE, Lewis H., Hw-125-5; 1st TN Inf; 7 Aug 63 to 65; Surgoinsville PO; imprisoned at Camp Douglas, IL, 9 mos; CONF
LEE, Louisa J., B-3-2; widow; 3rd Civil Dist
LEE, Major, D-64-4; Nashville PO
LEE, Marshall, Hd-46-1; Sgt H Co 55th Col Inf; ___ to Jun 3 65; Cerro Gordo PO
LEE, Mira (see Johnson, Edd)
LEE, Pinkney W., We-221-5(2); Sgt I Co 6th TN Cav; 5 Jun 62 to 23 Jul 65; Martin PO; none but exposure
LEE, Robert, Sh-150-1; Pvt A Co Inf; 2 yrs 6 mos; Bartlett PO
LEE, Sam, D-54-3; Jennie Galloway widow of; Pvt A Co 15th US Col Inf; Nashville PO
LEE, Samuel, D-91-4; Davidson PO
LEE, Samuel J., K-180-4; Ebenezer PO
LEE, Samuel W., Br-7-2; Paulina widow of; Artificer B Co 1st US VVE; 8-27-62 to 6-30-65; Felker PO; chronic diarhea
LEE, Shaderick, Ro-202-2; Pvt E Co 3rd TN Inf; Feb 62 to 17 Apr 65; Union X Roads PO; bone scurvy & kindey
LEE, Thomas, Hw-132-5; Lt D Co 31st TN Inf; 62 to 65; Strahl PO; hernia
LEE, Thomas A., Je-144-1; Easter J. widow of; Pvt E Co 4th TN Cav; 63 to ___; Talbotts PO; died in ware be if closed
LEE, Thomas F., We-221-5(2); Adjutant TN Inf; 5 Jan 62 to Feb 63; Martin PO
LEE, Thomas J., W-193-1; Pvt D Co 111th OH Inf; 8-18-62 to 7-27-65; Smartt PO
LEE, Turner, Rb-218-1; Pvt; Cross Plains PO
LEE, Uriah, J-78-1; Pvt B Co 8th TN Inf; 1-28-64 to 8-18-64; Rough Point PO; ancle and other troubles, and not able to walk much
LEE, William, Mu-211-1; Pvt; 62 to 65; Britton PO; rheumatism by exposure, lost his papers
LEE, William, R-162-2; Sarah widow of; Pvt D Co 12th TN Cav; 63 to ___; Dayton PO; died during the service
LEE, Wm., Hw-134-1; Rogersville PO
LEE, William A., H-73-4(2); Chattanooga PO
LEE, William A., Hw-118-2; Pvt C Co 8th TN Inf; St. Clair PO; bronchitis
LEE, William D., Sh-178-1; Mary A. widow of; Surgeon Baton Rouge Post Port Delaware; 239 Union, Memphis PO

LEE, William J., K-178-2; Pvt I Co 6th TN Inf; Ball Camp PO
LEE, William J., Mu-210-2; 2nd Lt A Co 48th TN Inf; 11-20-61 to 4-65; Spring Hill PO; CONF
LEE, William J., Mu-195-3; Columbia TN
LEE, William L., Gr-78-1; Pvt B Co 8th TN Cav; 10 Mar 62 to 10 Mar 65; Spring House PO
LEE, William W., H-69-3; Pvt F Co 39th GA Inf; 62 to __; Chattanooga PO; CONF
LEEDY, Joe, Ha-114-1; Pvt D Co 1st NC Inf; 3 Dec 62 to 1 Jan __; Xenophon PO
LEEHMAN, Charles F., K-156-1; Pvt A Co 3rd MO Inf; 10 Apr 61 to 14 Jul 61; Pine 167, Knoxville PO
LEEMAN, Henry, Wl-302-1; Pvt H Co 4th TN Mtd Inf; 1 Nov 64 to 25 Aug 65; PO omitted
LEEMAN, George W., Wl-302-1; Elisabeth E. widow of; Pvt H Co 4th TN Mtd Inf; 1 Nov 64 to 25 Aug 65; Henderson X Roads PO
LEEMAN, Permelia V. (see Demar?, Thomas)
LEEPER, John H., P-156-1; Pvt H Co 11th TN Inf; 5-1-61 to 65; Lobelville PO; CONF
LEEPER, John M., Je-147-1; Cpl K Co 3rd TN Inf; 10 Feb 62 to 23 Feb 65; Shady Grove PO
LEETHE, John U., Sh-145-3; Pvt B Co 34th IN Vol Inf; 21 Sep 61 to 3 Feb 66; Kerrville PO; struck with bombshill in left leg at Island No 10, reenlisted veteran, 14 day Dec 63
LE FAVEMIER, Frederick, H-70-3(1); Capt F Co 7th NY Inf; 9-62 to 5-8-63; Chattanooga PO; Capt 16th IL Cav; 9-63 to 5-65; became Major in 5th US Cav 11-7-65
LEFEN, Frank, Hw-125-1; 29th TN Inf; 61 to 64; Surgoinsville PO; shot in the head by bombshell; CONF
LEFEURE, Peter A., Sh-150-2; Mrs. A. M. widow of; Capt A Co 156th W TN Vol Inf; 31 Aug 62 to 11 Jan 64; Bartlett PO
LEFFERING, Herman, D-45-5; Annie E. Wessel widow of; Pvt F Co 10th OH; Nashville PO; husband shot through the body, married now to Geo. Wessel
LEFFEW, Jo, R-161-1; Pvt A Co 2nd TN Inf--8-61 to 11-22-62; Pvt H Co 5th US Cav--11-22-62 to 3-31-65; Dayton PO; scurvy from prison
LEFFEW, John H., Ro-205-1; Pvt G Co 5th TN Inf; 24 Oct 64 to 16 May 65; Kingston PO
LEFLAR, James W., Sh-196-2; Pvt F Co 196th OH Inf; 3-7-65 to 9-11-65; Bluff City Brick Co., Memphis PO
LEFLER, Charles, Jo-149-3; Esther widow of; 2nd Lt D Co 13th TN Cav; 24 Sep 63 to 8 Sep 65; Mountain City PO; rheumatism resulting paralysis
LEFTWICK, James, Wh-187-1; Cpl A Co 42nd TN Inf; 63 to 65; Bon Air PO
LEFTWICK, James, Rb-228-1; Pvt D Co TN Cav; 64 to 65; Crunk PO
LEGG, Jackson, Wi-273-1; Pvt F Co 110th TN Inf; Jan 6 63 to Feb 11 66; Shaw PO; claimed left leg, shoulder & side injured; applicant for pension
LEGG, John W., Hm-109-2; Francis N. widow of; Pvt D Co 1st TN Cav; Whitesburg PO; gunshot wound
LEGGETT, George A., H-58-2; Sale Creek PO; he was not at home & wife could not find papers
LEGGETT, Lucy A. (see Jones, Seyrus T.)
LEHMAN, William, Mg-197-4; Pvt Benton Battery IL 12 Nov 61 to 20 Nov 65; Wartburg PO; rheumatism, piles and kidney disease, Illinois Benton Battery
LEHN, Sylvester, Dy-32-1; US Sol; Trimble PO
LEINART, Charles H., C-28-2(1); Lt M Co 9th TN Cav; 5-1-63 to 9-15-65; Fincastle PO; piles
LEINART, Daniel, A-10-1; Pvt C Co 11th TN Cav; 7-63 to 9-65; Procise PO
LEINART, Jacob, A-5-3; Sarah A. widow of; Pvt C Co 9th TN Cav; 7-27-63 to 9-11-65; Clinton PO
LEINART, James H., A-9-4(2); Cpl E Co 3rd TN Inf; 2-22-62 to 2-22-65; Dutch Valley PO; hemorage of lungs & chrn. diarrhea
LEINART, Samuel D., K-186-1; Elizabeth widow of; Capt D Co 1st TN Art; 1 Nov 63 to 16 Aug 64; Beaver Ridge PO
LEINART, William M., A-9-6(4); Pvt C Co 11th TN Cav; 5-28-63 to 12-24-65; Dutch Valley PO; rheumatism resulting in heart disease
LEISURE, Abraham, P-150-2; US Sol; 1st Dist

LEMBURG, Christopher, Sh-188-1; Pvt B Co 8th IA Inf; 8-15-61 to 4-20-66; 26 Peyton St, Memphis PO
LEMING, Georg W., Bo-23-1; Mariah widow of; Pvt C Co 3rd TN Mtd Inf; 7-26-64 to 11-30-64; Lyon Springs PO; discharged by reason close of war, now dead
LEMING, Samuel W., Ge-94-1; Pvt L Co 4th TN Cav; 20 Sep 62 to 4 May 65; Tusculum PO; CONF
LEMLY, Lewis C., Rb-228-2; Pvt 26th AL; 1 mo; Springfield PO; CONF
LEMMINGS, William, Mo-130-1; Pvt A Co 7th TN Mtd Inf; 2-2-65 to 8-3-65; Povo PO
LEMMONS, Ed, F-39-1; alias Ed Gipson; Sgt K Co 3rd US Lt Art; 2 yrs; Galloway PO; dischage in Washington
LEMMONS, George W., Wa-263-2; Pvt 4th KY Inf; Conf & US; Garbers Mills PO
LEMONS, Ebenezer M., Ge-91-2; Cpl C Co 2nd NC Mtd Inf; 16 Sep 63 to 17 Aug 65; Greeneville PO; cronic diahhrea, piles, blader, liver
LEMONS, George W., Br-6-3; Arie Ann widow of; Pvt A Co 5th TN Mtd Inf; 9-4-64 to 65; Chatala PO
LEMONS, James B., Po-148-1; Elizabeth J. widow of; Cpl A Co 14th IL Cav; 6-7-64 to 7-31-65; Chestewee Mills PO
LEMONS, John, Gr-78-2; Caroline widow of; Pvt; Spring House PO; marked out, might be CONF
LEMONS, John, H-49-9; Pvt F Co 6th TN Mtd Inf; Daisy PO; hurt by fall of horse
LEMONS, Joseph B., Ca-23-3; Pvt K Co 5th TN Cav; 4-3-63 to 9-65; Narla PO; no injuries
LEMONS, Thomas J., Ge-88-3; Pvt G Co 8th TN Cav; Bulls Gap PO; rheumatism, not at home
LEMONS, Wesly, Ge-99-2; Sol; 18th Dist
LEMONS, William O., Ge-90-3; Pvt E Co 4th TN Inf; 63 to 65; Timberridge PO; chronic rumatism
LEMONS, Zagy, Mn-121-3; Pvt G Co 6th TN Cav; 11-9-63 to 7-26-65; Falcon PO
LEMONS, Reuben, Me-93-2; Pvt H Co 5th TN Inf; 3-18-62 to 5-16-65; Ten Mile Stand PO; rheumatism --piles
LENIX, Henry S., Ro-202-5; Martha widow of; Pvt PA Inf; 61 to 4 Aug 64; Cave Creek PO; no disability
LENNING, John F., G-71-3; Martha J. widow of; Pvt F Co 18th TN Inf; 5 Apr 61 to 25 Jun 63; PO omitted; CONF
LENNON, John, Mc-116-2; Margret A. widow of; Sgt C Co 4th TN Cav; 12-1-62 to 7-12-65; Longs Mills PO
LENNON, Louis, D-54-2; Rebecca widow of; Pvt L Co 4th OH Cav; 3 Sep 62 to 2 Jun 65; Nashville PO
LENOARD, William, Wa-263-1; Pvt A Co 66th TN Inf; May 4 62 to May 1 65; Garbers Mills PO; CONF
LENOIR, George W., Lo-195-1; Sgt E Co 1st TN Hvy Art; 4 Apr 64 to 30 Mar 66; Muddy Creek PO
LENOIR, Milos, Mc-111-3; Pvt E Co 1st CAH; 3-31-64 to 3-31-66; Mouse Creek PO
LENOIR, William, Lo-189-1; Sgt C Co 1st TN Hvy Art; 4 Apr 64 to 31 Mar 66; Philadelphia PO; rheumatism
LENORE, Ricard, K-177-2; Sol Vol; PO omitted
LENT, James M., Mu-193-1; 2nd Lt F Co 10th OH Cav; 9-14-62 to 1-14-65; Columbia PO
LENTS, George, B-11-2(1); Cpl G Co 14th US Col; 7-20-64 to 3-1-66; Fall Creek PO; rumatism
LENTZ, Solomon, Sh-153-2; Pvt I Co 109th IL Inf; 14 Aug 62 to 12 Jun 65; Bailey Sta. PO
LENVICK, Thomas J., Me-88-1; Pvt F Co 3rd TN Cav; 3-16-63 to 1-10-65; Birchwood PO; prisner 6 mos.
LEOB, John W., Wa-272-3; Sgt I Co 8th TN Cav; Clara PO; rheumatism, injury to the eyes
LEONARD, Elizabeth, Cy-27-6(4); widow US Sol; 5th Civil Dist
LEONARD, George W., Wa-269-1; Pvt G Co 7th IL Inf; about 10 Nov 63 to about 10 Jul 65; Johnson City PO; rheumatism
LEONARD, Joeanna, Sh-193-1; widow of LUSt? (S US t) (Sol US troops)?; Pvt; Memphis PO
LEONARD, John, Ct-40-1; Pvt G Co 6th TN Inf; 1 yr; Elizabethton PO; rheumatism; CONF
LEONARD, John R., Mo-123-1; Asst Surgeon 10th TN Cav; 2-11-64 to 4-21-65; Jalapa PO
LEONARD, Nancy E., Ms-170-1; 4th Dist
LEONARD, Sarah, Cy-27-6(4); widow US Sol; 5th Civ Dist

LEONARD, Thomas P. A., Mo-120-3(1); Pvt; Sweetwater PO; wounded on arm
LEONARD, William A., Hw-132-1; Pvt C Co 1st TN Inf; Jan 64 to 11 Nov 65; Persia PO; heart disease, rheumatism & c
LEONARD, William G., Dy-25-5(1); Pvt K Co 19th Mis Inf; May 61 to 65; Newbern PO; CONF
LEPHEM, Henry, Fe-41-1; Pvt E Co 4th TN Inf; 1-20-62 to 6-13-64; Pall Mall PO
LEPHFINE, Robert, Gr-81-4(2); Lucinda widow of; Pvt H Co 24th TN Inf; 62 to 65; Clear Spring PO; ded with consumption
LEPHINE, William J., Mg-198-3; Pvt D Co; Herburtsburgh PO
LEQUIN, Isaac, Bo-23-2; Pvt B Co 1st TN Inf; 5-20-62 to 9-20-64; Cades Cove PO; contracted rheumatism, was not discharged from service
LERCH, Michael, H-53-7; Pvt E Co 9th OH Inf; 11-62 to 6-65; Chattanooga PO
LERD, Gilbert, H-52-1; Pvt A Co 6th TN Inf; 8-2-64 to 6-30-65; Wauhatchie PO
LERNED, George F., Mo-122-2; Pvt C Co LA Cav; 62 to 65; Dancing Branch PO, further dates unknown; CONF
LESLEY, John, Mc-117-3; Pvt K Co 3rd TN Cav; 10-4-63 to 6-10-65; Cog Hill PO; kidney trouble
LESLIE, John A. H-69-2; Pvt E Co 101st US Col; 4-24-65 to 1-66; Chattanooga PO
LESTER, Henry, Gi-132-1; on same line as William H. Oliver; Pvt H Co 734d IL Inf; Nov 10 63 to Jun 1 65; DeRay PO
LESTER, William, Gi-13202; alias Shadden, William; Pvt D Co 110th USCV; Dec 6 63 to Feb 6 66; Pulaski PO; shot in hip
LESTER, William, Sm-172-1; Sgt L Co 5th TN Cav; 4-22-63 to 8-14-65; Lancaster PO, chronic sore eyes
LESTER, William W., R-161-4; Beckie widow of; 1st Lt C Co 23rd MO Inf; 7-13-61 to __; Dayton PO; died 3-28-62
LETHCO, Henry E. Se-221-1; Pvt I Co 13th TN Cav; 22 Sep 63 to 5 Sep 65; Fair Garden PO; now blind in one eye
LETHERS, Levy G., Sh-169-2; Pvt D Co 5th MI Inf; 61 to 64; Memphis PO
LETSINGER, John M., Ro-204-5; Pvt A Co 4th TN Cav; 25 Oct 62 to 12 Jul 65; Elverton PO
LETSINGER, William K-160-3; Ruth widow of; Pvt D Co 3rd TN; Mar 62 to Jan 65; Knoxville PO
LETT, Joseph, C-24-4(3); Pvt C Co 1st TN INf; 5-9-61 to __ 17-64; 1st Dist
LETT, Stenve, (sic) G-64-2; Bradford
LEUL, John Cl-52-1; Pvt E Co 8th TN Cav; 10-10-63 to 9-11-65; Quarter PO
LEURHENANIA?, Henry, Sh-171-1; Quarter master E Co MO Cav Vol; 8-8-61 to 10-22-64; Memphis PO
LEURY?, Andy J., De-22-2; Drummer C Co 152nd NY Inf; 1 Jan 64 to 10 Jun 65; Clifton PO
LEUWELLING, Alford M., He-57-1; Pvt G Co 6th TN Inf; 3-10-62 to 11-62; Law PO; CONF?
LEVAR, Joseph, see Jimison, Joseph
LEVAY?, Patrick, Wy-173-4; Roda F. Ponder formerly widow of; Pvt 14th IL Cav; Victory PO; discharge at Washington
LEVEE?, Wm., K-167-3; Sarah widow of; Pvt 1st___ Col; 63 to 65; Knoxville PO
LEVEL?, Monroe, O-135-1; Pvt A Co 16th TN Inf; 10 Dec 62 to 10 May 65; Troy PO
LEVELL, Benjamin, Ro-211-3; Pvt H Co 16th TN Inf; 62 to 65; Harriman PO; acute rheumatism, doesn't know dates
LEVI, Arthur H., H-50-5; Pvt F Co 6th R TN Mtd Inf; 9-12-64 to 6-30-65; Soddy PO
LEVI, James N., H-51-6; Nicie widow of; Pvt I Co 2nd TN Inf; 2-15-62 to died in prison; Albion View PO
LEVI, Peter, H-60-3; Cpl C Co 19th US Inf; 10-20-62 to 10-20-65; Chattanooga PO
LEVICE?, D. K-167-1, Mary widow of; Pvt 1st Hvy TN; 62 to 65; Knoxville PO
LEVICK, Jesse, Mc-110-1; Pvt B Co 2nd Hvy Art; 6-20-63 to 8-23-65; Fiketon PO
LEVINGOOD, Levi, Se-227-3; Pvt H Co 51st OH Inf; 10 Sep 61 to 5 Oct 64; Trundles X Roads PO; shot in left leg
LEVISTER, James J., We-225-2(1); Pvt K Co 6th TN Cav; Aug 7 62 to Jul 26 65; Dresden PO

LEVY, Missouri, O-141-3; no PO
LEVY, Wattenbarger, Mc-112-2; Jincy widow of; Pvt A Co 7th TN Mtd Inf; 63 to 65; Athens PO; wounded in left lung, no papers to get exact dates
LEWALLEN, Campbell, S-213-3; Pvt I Co 12th KY Inf; 10 Nov 61 to 65; Glenmary PO; rheumatism, loss of hearing
LEWALLEN, John, A-13-3; Pvt B Co 1st TN Inf; 6-1-63 to 8-65; Prosise PO; diarrhea
LEWALLEN, John, S-216-1; Pvt B Co 1st TN Vol; 1 Aug 61 to 5 Aug 65; Huntsvill PO; blind
LEWALLEN, William, K-167-5; Pvt I Co 9th TN Cav; 62 to 65; Knoxville PO; weak mind
LEWALLEN, William, S-213-1; Pvt A Co 1st TN Inf; Jun 61 to 65; Huntsville PO; head & lungs, from measels in arm y
LEWELLING, John W., O-138-3; Susan widow of; Pvt; Sep 64 to 10 Apr 65; Glass PO; CONF
LEWIS, Aaron, Ro-210-10; Tolah widow of; Pvt; Rockwood PO; CONF
LEWIS, Adlate, see Jones, George, Ro-210-4
LEWIS, Alexander, Sh-191-2; Memphis PO; records not seen
LEWIS, Alexander, Sh-191-3; Memphis PO
LEWIS, Alexander, Hd-54-3; Pvt E Co 6th TN Cav; Jan 16 64 to Jul 26 65; Ruth PO; scurvy, applied for pension
LEWIS, Alonzo, Hd-56-1; Pvt F Co 16th US Reg; 1-1-66 to 1-1-69; Adamsville PO
LEWIS, Bayles, W.H., R-162-1; H Co 10th TN Cav;___ to 8-65 (2 yrs); Dayton PO
LEWIS, Benjeman, Sh-190-1; Mary Richard widow of; Goerfield Alley, Memphis PO; cannot obtain particulars
LEWIS, Boston, K-161-4; Pvt A Co 131st VA Inf; Knoxville PO
LEWIS, Calvin, Mr-99-3; Pvt I Co 10th TN Inf; 7-4-63 to 7-17-75; Jasper PO
LEWIS, Carter, Hu-106-1; Pvt H Co 14th US C T; May 63 to 65; Waverly PO
LEWIS, Charles W., D-92-1; Pvt G Co 3rd OH Inf; Apr 61 to __; West Nashville PO
LEWIS, Charley, Sq-165-3; Julia A. widow of; Pvt K Co 4th TN Cav; 6-64 to 1-11-65; Dunlap PO received an honorable disc.
LEWIS, David M., Mc-117-2; 2nd Sgt E Co 7th TN Mtd Inf; 9-16-64 to 7-27-65; Mt. Vernon PO
LEWIS, Docter, K-165-2; F Co 7th Tn Inf; 8 Nov 64 to 27 Jul 65; Knoxville PO
LEWIS, Dread, Sh-146-4; US Sol; 3rd Civ Dis
LEWIS, Elija P., see Person, Elija
LEWIS, Elijah, Wh-181-1; Pvt G Co 6th TN Mtd Inf; Solon PO; suffers from relapse of measles
LEWIS, Ephraim, Ct-43-2; Pvt F Co 13th TN Cav; 9-21-63 to 6-15-65; Carter Furnace PO
LEWIS, Frank (see Frank Looney)
LEWIS, Frederick, Gi-132-1; Nicy Buford formerly widow of; Pvt H Co 111th USCV; Feb 17 64 to May 6 66; DeRay PO; husband died in prison
LEWIS, Frederk J., Ct-40-2; Pvt B Co 13th TN Cav; 9-22-63 to 9-5-65; Elizabethton PO; chronic rheumatism
LEWIS, George, F-44-2; Pvt A Co 59th __; May 62 to May 65; no PO
LEWIS, George Ge-95-1; Mariah widow of; Pvt E Co; Home PO
LEWIS, George W., Ja-86-2; Cpl Bat B 1st TN Art; 11-27-62 to 7-25-65; Long Savannah PO; chronic diarhea
LEWIS, Gideon, CT-43-2; Pvt A Co 13th TN Cav; 9-22-63 to 9-6-65; Carter Furnace PO
LEWIS, Griffith L., A-2-4; 1st Sgt L Co 9th TN Cav; 10-16-63 to 3-24-65; Hynds Creek PO; gun shot wound right thigh
LEWIS, Hampton H., Ct-37-2; Pvt F Co 8th TN Cav; 6-63 to deserted 1865; Ripshin PO; lung trouble
LEWIS, Henderson, Co-67-3; Martha widow of; Pvt B Co 10th MI Cav; Cosby PO; killed in service
LEWIS, Henry J., Je-141-1; Cpl A Co 3rd TN Inf; 10 Feb 62 to 23 Feb 65; New Market PO
LEWIS, Isaac, H-50-5; Pvt A Co 6th TN Mtd Inf; Soddy PO
LEWIS, Isaac J., H-54-1; Pvt B Co 1st WV Inf; Pvt G Co 13th WV Inf; 12-10-63 to 7-22-65; Sherman Heights PO; bronchitis in 1865; general debility

LEWIS, Jack, Ct-41-3; Elizabeth widow of; Pvt A Co 13th Tn Cav; Keenesburgh PO
LEWIS, James, Mu-209-6; Pvt A Co 48th TN; 61 to 63; Columbia PO; prisoner 7 months, Johnson Island; CONF
LEWIS, James A., Cf-40-2; Pvt A Co 32nd OH Inf; 4 Mar 64 to 20 Jun 65; Tullahoma PO; invalid from disease contracted in Andersonville & Florence Prisons
LEWIS, James C., H-49-5; 3rd Sgt A Co 6th TN Mtd Inf; 8-2-64 to 6-30-65; Daisy PO
LEWIS, James F. M., Ct-43-1; Pvt F Co 13th TN Cav; 9-22-63 to 9-5-65; Carter Furnace PO; wounded in battle at Morristown, TN; 11-13-64 run over by a horse
LEWIS, James P., Wh-185-1; Pvt G Co US Inf; 10-18-64 to 11-29-65; Cassville PO; loss of voice
LEWIS, James P., Di-36-2; 61 to 65; Bellsburgh PO; hospital Greensboro, AL 1 mo; CONF
LEWIS, Jesse, K-175-2; 1st Sgt E Co 11th TN Cav; 30 Jul 62 to 24 Mar 65; Snoterly PO
LEWIS, Jime, Sh-157-2; Pvt B Co 23rd IN; 63 to 65; Dist 13
LEWIS, John, D-98-1; Catharine widow of; Cpl F Co 101st US Col; Aug 16 64 to Jan 3 66; 19th Civ Dist
LEWIS, John Hd-55-1; Callie D. widow of; Pvt H Co 14th MI Inf; 5 Dec 62 to __ (2 yrs); Whitton PO; wounded in foot?, wasn't able to get back to his command and wasn't discharged
LEWIS, John He-62-1; Pvt 2nd GA Bat (S Sh)?; Sep 61 to Apr 65; Darden PO; CONF
LEWIS, John, Co-66-3(1); Pvt A Co 15th TN Cav; 30 Jan 61 to 18 Apr 65; English PO; CONF
LEWIS, John, Cu-16-2; Pvt G Co 6th TN Inf; 2-20-65 to 6-20-65; Solon PO, White Co
LEWIS, John D., Gi-127-2; Pvt D Co 39th IN Inf; __ to Jun 65 (3 yrs); Pulaski PO, was discharged from Co F 25th IN, was clerk at Col? Hdqtrs in 39th IN Cav
LEWIS, John L., Mo-120-1; Pvt A Co 5th TN Inf; 2-25-62 to 4-7-65; Glenloch PO; chronic diarhea, rheumatism, he is helpless
LEWIS, John R., Ch-13-2; Pvt C Co 6th TN Vol; 12-7-63 to 7-26-65; Henderson PO; rheumatism, stickendown at time severely
LEWIS, John S., K-177-2; US Sol; no PO
LEWIS, Joseph, Ca-22-2; Pvt E Co 5th TN Cav; 2-22-62 to 6-16-64; Hollow Springs PO
LEWIS, Joseph, Lo-187-3; Pvt I Co 5th TN Inf; 1 Jul 63 to 20 Jun 65; Loudon PO; lost use of both legs from wounds in hips
LEWIS, Joshua, Pu-147-2; Martha L. widow of; Pvt; Byrne PO
LEWIS, Leonard L., H-50-2(1); Cpl I Co 2nd R TN Inf; 11-11-61 to 6-30-65; Bunch PO; liver and kidney disease chronic
LEWIS, Madison, D-91-1; alias Rath; Pvt D Co 16th TN Inf; 17 Feb 65 to 16 Feb 66; Nashville Lumber Co., Nashville PO
LEWIS, Maria, Sh-184-2; widow US Sol; 78 Hill, Memphis PO
LEWIS, Moses, D-47-1; Pvt A Co 14th TN Col Inf; 5-1-62 to 1-24-65; Jackson nr. Park St, Nashville PO; now has right leg cut off
LEWIS, Moses, Sh-184-1; Pvt B Co 59th US Cav; 4-1-64 to 4-25-65; Memphis? PO
LEWIS, Moses, Ro-210-10; Pvt; Rockwood PO; CONF
LEWIS, Owen, Be-5-1; Pvt H Co 13th TN Inf; 5 May 65 to 10 Jan 66; Camden PO; ruptured
LEWIS, Richard, H-68-2; Pvt B Co 1st TN Col Art; 63 to 65; Chattanooga PO; dropsey, not able to work much
LEWIS, Robert, Sq-165-3; Pvt E Co 6th TN Mtd Inf; 9-11-64 to 6-12-65; Dunlap PO; received an honorable disc.
LEWIS, S. J., Gi-122-5; 5th Sgt H Co 9th AL Cav; Dec 62 to Jun 63; Prospect Sta. PO; CONF
LEWIS, Sallie, Sh-204-2; Walker Ave, Memphis PO
LEWIS, Sam Sr., Tr-267-1; Pvt; no PO
LEWIS, Samuel, P-156-1; Martha widow of; Pvt 48th TN Inf; 61 to 65; Lobelville PO; shot in left hand; CONF
LEWIS, Samuel B., Ct-43-2; Sgt L Co 13th TN Cav; 9-22-63 to 9-5-65; Carter Furnace PO; catarrh and neuralgia of head

LEWIS, Simeon, Sh-189-6; Sol US; Ga. St, Memphis PO
LEWIS, Solomon, Ct-35-4; Ann widow of; Pvt A Co 13th TN Cav; 9-22-63 to __; Lineback PO; no discharge date of death not known
LEWIS, Thomas D., K-169-1; Pvt I Co 82nd Vol Inf; 8 Aug 62 to 12 Jan 63; Knoxville PO; disabled in right groin
LEWIS, Thomas J. Mr-99-3; Pvt C Co 5th TN Inf; 9-7-64 to 6-30-65; Jasper PO
LEWIS, Thomas L., H-49-3; Pvt H Co 3rd E TN Inf; 3-14-62 to 3-14-65; Lake Side PO; hurt in left breast by a mule
LEWIS, Wilking, Sh-147-1; Pvt F Co 113th AR Inf; 15 Sep 62 to Apr 10 65; Ramsey PO
LEWIS, William, D-93-1; Pvt D Co 40th TN Inf; 5 Mar 64 to 25 Apr 66; Newsoms Sta.PO
LEWIS, William H. H., H-49-8; Pvt D Co 1st TN Lt Art; 10-9-62 to 7-25-65; Daisy PO; incurred gravel
LEWIS, William R., Wl-298-1; Sgt K Co 5th TN Cav; 22 Feb 63 to 14 Aug 65; Round Top PO; rheumatism, exposure while in the service
LEWIS, Winney, Cu-15-2; Pvt B Co 86th NY Inf; 9-7-61 to 12-26-62; Northville PO; shot throug left arm near elbo, kidney disease 26 (yrs?) total disability
LEWIS, Zackoriah, Ro-210-5; Eliza J. widow of; Pvt; Rockwood PO
LEWS, Peter, D-57-1; Pvt E Co 44th US Inf; 62 to Sep 65; No PO, 8th Ward
LEYSHON, Thomas, A-13-3; Margaret widow of; Pvt F Co 48th PA Vol; 8-22-61 to 11-22-62; Briceville PO; discharged in hospital
LIFORD, Dreff C., Cl-55-1; Pvt G Co 1st TN Cav; 7-1-62 to 5-27-65; Haynes Union Co PO; prisoner Andersonville 6 mos, hard of hearing
LIGGETT, Rufus M., Ro-201-4(2); Sgt D Co 1st TN Hvy Art; 27 Feb 64 to 31 Mar 66; Kingston PO
LIGGIN, Alfred, Sh-200-2; Roberta Dolley formerly widow of; Pvt; rear of 21 Polk St., Memphis PO
LIGHT, Samual, Hw-121-5(4); Pvt K? Co 29th TN Inf; 15 Jul 61 to 15 Apr 65; Chimney Top PO; CONF
LIGHT, Thomas, Su-240-1; Pvt B Co 4th US Cav; 63 to 65; Kindricks Creek PO; ruptured, fall from horse
LIGON, Cebron, Hy-76-2; US Sol; Stanton Depot PO
LIKINS, Sam, Cy-27-1; Pvt G Co 144th IN Mtd Inf; 1-31-65 to 8-5-65; Clementsville PO
LILES, Abner C., Mg-196-2; pvt; Apr 62 to 65; Coalfield PO; left eye out
LILES, Calvin M., Ro-207-1; Pvt E Co 1st TN Inf; 10 Aug 61 to Aug 64; Morris Gap PO; rheumatism, lung and piles
LILES, David A., La-108-1; Pvt G Co 10th TN Inf; 7-20-62 to 7-3-65; no PO
LILES, David H., Hn-75-1; Pvt A Co 1st TN Cav; 15 Nov 64 to 1 May 65; Manlyville PO
LILES, Jesse, Se-230-1; Pvt; 62 to 65; Richison's Cove PO; palsy
LILES, Joseph, Ro-211-2; Pvt H Co 3rd TN Inf; 10 Feb 62 to 23 Feb 65; Webster PO; wounded by gun shot
LILES, Major L., Mg-196-2; Pvt E Co 1st TN Inf; Aug 61 to Sep 64; Coalfield PO
LILES, Newton, Ro-201-2; Martha J. widow of; Cpl F Co 5th TN Inf; 25 Feb 62 to 29 Mar 65; Kingston PO
LILES, W. W., De-25-1; Cpl G Co 6th TN Cav; 18 Sep 62 to 26 Jul 65; Decaturville PO
LILES, William C., Ro-207-3; Providence B. widow of; Pvt A Co 2nd E TN Inf; 10 Aug 61 to died in army; Mossy Gap PO; measles
LILLARD, Abraham, Po-148-2; Cpl I Co 5th TN Mtd Inf; 9-8-64 to 6-26-65; Benton PO
LILLARD, Albert, Ca-20-2; Pvt C Co 5th TN Cav; 3-3-62 to 64; Woodbury PO
LILLARD, Calvin A., Co-67-1; Pvt C Co 26th TN Inf; May 62 to 9 May 65; Bison PO; CONF
LILLARD, Darrell, Po-148-3; Pvt I Co 5th TN Mtd Inf; 9-9-64 to 6-26-65; Benton PO; now about blind
LILLARD, Joseph B., Mo-121-1; Pvt D Co 11th TN Cav; 8-1-63 to 6-20-65; Eve Mi-ls PO; died in service (error here?); pensioner
LILLARD, Luther, Po-148-2; Cpl I Co 5th TN Mtd Inf; 9-8-64 to 6-26-65; Benton PO

LILLBURN, Maton, Me-89-1; Matilda E. widow of; 62 to 64; Big Spring PO
LILLEY, Thomas B., Hm-103-3; Pvt A Co 2nd IN Cav; Morristown PO
LILLY, Marvin B., Hn-70-1; Pvt B Co 1st MI Art; 25 Dec 63 to 8 Jul 65; Paris PO; shell wound right side of back; gunshot wound left arm joint
LIMANE, Thomas M., Mu-210-5; Pvt F Co 3rd TN Inf; 5-18-61 to 10-9-62; Spring Hill PO; CONF
LIMBAUGH, Lihew, Hw-121-5(4); Elizabeth widow of; Pvt H Co 8th TN Inf; Lucas PO
LIMBURGH, Hanse L., Ro-202-4; Pvt B Co 34d TN Inf; 5 Aug 63 to 3 Aug 65; Cave Creek PO; Lungs and paralysis, enlisted at 19 yrs
LINCH, George W., J-83-1; Pvt C Co 8th TN; 65 to 65; Flynns Lick PO
LINCH, Linas?, T-211-1; Pvt I Co 16th NY Art; Nov 29 63 to 21 Aug 65; Tipton PO; cronick case piles
LINCOLN, Eligah, Gi-122-2; Pvt A Co 16th AL Inf; Sep 20 62 to Jul 65; Prospect Sta. PO
LINCOLN, Isaac A., Ms-167-1; Pvt F Co 5th TN Cav; Sep 8 62 to Jun 25 65; Gas, Giles Co. PO
LINCOLN, John C., Li-142-1; Pvt F Co 5th TN Cav; 9-8-62 to 6-25-65; Moline PO; shot through left lung
LINCOLN, William A., Wi-270-1; Pvt G Co 21st IN (Ger? 3); (sic) 15 May? 62 to 20 Sep 64; South Harpeth PO
LIND, Strovads, W-189-2; Pvt E Co 73rd NY Inf--7-17-61 to 11-17-62; Pvt H Co 1st Bat. 12th US Inf--11-17-62 to 7-4-64; Capt E Co 100th US Col Inf--7-4-64 to 12-6-65; McMinnville PO
LINDELL, Samuel W., R-158-2; Pvt & Capt 9th TN Cav; 8-14-63 to 7-27-65; Spring City PO
LINDER, George, Cu-15-3; Pvt I Co 4th TN Cav; 2-62 to 65; Woody PO; kidney disease 20 yrs; CONF
LINDSAY, Archibald, C-25-1; Sgt F Co 6th TN Inf; 3-10-62 to 3-24-65; Whitman PO; shot through left thigh
LINDSAY, Goan, Gi-138-1; Pvt G Co 110th __; 63 to 66; Valesville PO
LINDSAY, William, St-163-1; US Sol; Dover PO
LINDSEY, Andrew J., Je-147-2; Pvt E Co 9th TN Cav; 1 Oct 63 to 11 Sep 65; Shady Grove PO
LINDSEY, Grove B., He-62-1; Wincy? A. widow of; Pvt C A 7th Ridgment TN Cav; 62 to __ (8 mos); Lexington PO; killed in service
LINDSEY, Henry, H-69-5; Pvt; Chattanooga PO
LINDSEY, Hiram E., Wy-177-1; Cpl 2nd TN Inf; 10-14-63 to 10-14-64; Moon PO
LINDSEY, Isaac, Mo-130-2; Sgt H Co 3rd TN Mtd Inf; 8-7-64 to 12-15-64; Ballplay PO
LINDSEY, Jackson, Sh-204-1; Jennette Ave, Memphis PO
LINDSEY, John L., Je-147-1; Pvt F Co 9th TN Cav; 2 Aug 63 to 15 Feb 64; Shady Grove PO
LINDSEY, John P., Wy-173-3; Pvt E Co 8th TN Mtd Inf; 3-1-65 to 9-1-65; Houston PO
LINDSEY, Stephen, Ha-117-1; Pvt C Co 2nd TN Cav; 61 60 62 (8 mos); Kyle's Ford PO; fever
LINDSEY, William, Je-147-1; Pvt M Co 2nd TN Cav; 8 Nov 62 to 14 Jun 65; Shady Grove PO
LINDSEY, William, He-60-2; Pvt A Co 7th TN Cav; Sep 62 to Feb 64; Alberton PO
LINDSEY, William H., H-68-2; America widow of; Pvt; 4 yrs; Chattanooga PO
LINE, Charles, D-92-1; Nashville PO
LINE, Henry (see Henry Lyons)
LINE, Joseph E. (see Joseph Lyons)
LINEBACK, Henery, Ct-35-4; Cpl C Co 13th TN Cav; 9-22-63 to 9-5-65; Lineback PO; in the 208 army
LINEBARGER, Alfred F., Se-225-4; Pvt B Co 8th TN Inf; 10 Apr 64 to 30 Jun 65; Cotlettsburg PQ head and eyes injured
LINEBARGER, John H., Se-227-2; Pvt 6th TN Inf; no PO
LINEBAUGH, Henry, Ge-87-3; Nancy widow of; Pvt; Almeda PO; chronic diabetus
LINEBAUGH, Jacob, Ge-92-2; Pvt F Co 4th TN Inf; 1 Jun 63 to __; Laurel Gap PO
LINEBAUGH, John, Ge-92-3; Pvt F Co 4th TN Inf; 15 Apr 63 to 18 May 65; Laurel Gap PO; chronic diarrhea & deafness

LINGAR, Robert, Cl-49-2; Pvt A Co 2nd TN Cav; 8-1-62 to 7-6-65; Zeb PO; general disability
LINGEFELT, Solomon S., Me-93-1; Saddler G Co 10th TN Cav; 2-20-64 to 8-1-65; Sewee PO; injury to lungs
LINGENFELTER, Henry T., Lo-192-1; Quartermaster Sgt I Co 3rd TN; Oct 63 to Jun 65; Coytee PO; deaf in 1 ear, cripled in hip
LINGENFELTER, Thomas, Bo-13-3(1); Pvt A Co 3rd TN Cav; 11-10-62 to 6-10-65; Miser PO
LINGHUE, Abner B., Di-36-2; Pvt F Co 45th TN Inf; 61 to 63; Bellsburgh PO; CONF
LINGO, Martha J., A-7-2; widow of?; Robertsville PO
LINGO, Thomas M., Cu-18-1; Elizabeth widow of; Pvt E Co 11th TN Cav; 7-8-62 to 3-24-64; Manning PO; died in Maryland 3-24-64
LINK, Lewis, Di-34-2; Pvt G Co 14th US Col Inf; 11-63 to 3-26-66; Dickson PO
LINKONS, Barnabous, Hw-126-1; Mary widow of; Sgt E Co 1st TN Cav; 1 Apr 62 to 11 Apr 65; Fishers Creek PO
LINKONS, David B., Hw-119-4(1); Pvt Inf; Alum Well PO
LINKONS, John W., Hw-119-4(1); Pvt D Co 1st US Inf; 4 Feb 64 to 28 Nov 65; Alum Well PO; scurvy & rheumatism
LINN, Andrew, Wy-171-1; Pvt A Co 2nd TN Cav; Oct 2 63 to Oct 14 64; Waynesboro PO; rib broken
LINN, Jesse A., Ro-205-1; Pvt K Co 12th TN Cav; 63 to 65; Kingston PO; boath legs bin brokins, 3 roes cut off at the time
LINN, John C., Wy-171-1; Pvt F Co 6th TN Cav; 9-1-62 to 7-26-65; no PO
LINN, Mansyard C., Wi-276-2; Pvt C Co 2nd IN Art; 62 to 65; Beechvile PO
LINN, William B., T-216-2; 14th Civil Dist.
LINN, William H., Mo-131-1; Pvt A Co 71st Mtd Inf; 1-8-65 to 8-65; Joe PO; hurt in left side & piles, shot through right leg
LINNEBERRY, Ransom, H-56-3; St. Elmo PO
LINNIER, George N., Wl-299-1; Pvt E Co 4th TN Inf; 1 Sep 63 to 25 Aug 64; Statesville PO
LINNSTEN, Fredric, Mg-198-3; Margarett J. Widdow of Pvt E Co 1st TN Inf; 19 Aug 61 to Jul 62; Rockwood PO
LINSAY, Carter, Ha-117-1; Pvt H Co 2nd TN Inf; 15 Feb 62 to 24 Feb 65; Kyle's Ford PO; measles
LINSDSY (sic), W. J., G-65-1; Pvt F Co 7th TN Cav; Jul 18 62 to Apr 15 63; Milan PO; lungs troble
LINSY, Isaac, Co-68-3; Sgt K Co 8th TN Cav; 63 to 65; Sutton PO; piles, diarrhaea & rheumtis
LINSY, Lige, Ru-241-4; Pvt TN Inf; Murfreesboro PQ shot in leg
LINT, Henry W., M-10-32; Pvt E Co 1st TN Inf; 11-63 to 2-65; Lafayette PO
LINTON, John, D-93-1; US Sol; 14th Civ Dist
LINTZ, John J., F-47=1; Pvt C Co 107th IL Inf; Aug 62 to Mar 64; Williston PO
LINVILLE, Ann, Wh-187-3; widow of sol; 9th Civil Dist
LINVILLE, George H., Ct-38-2; Pvt N Co 8th TN Cav; 5-31-63 to 9-11-65; Okolona PO; rheumatism
LINVILLE, ___, K-154-1; Margarett E. Huffaker, widow of; Knoxville PO
LIONS, Samul, Ja-84-3; Pvt G Co 5th TN Inf; 2-27-62 to 5-15-65; Normans Store PO; canceras arisypelas
LIPPS, George K., Su-242-2; Pvt C Co 13th TN Cav; 27 Jan 64 to 5 Sep 65; Bluff City PO; diarrhea and result diseas of rectum, is honest, hardworking man
LIPPS, Nelson, Ct-45-2; Pvt F Co 13th TN Cav; 9-22-63 to 7-22-65; Carter Furnace PO; shot in right kneww Morristown 1864, prisoner Danville VA 3 mos 9 days
LIPPS, William, H-53-5; Pvt 129th IN Inf; __ to 65 (2 yrs); Ridgedale PO
LIPSCOMB, James, Ru-236-1; Pvt D Co 111th TN Inf; 63 to __; Murfreesboro PO
LIPSCOMB, Samuel, Mu-196-2; Columbia PO
LIPTON, Jacob, U-247-3; Anna widow of; Pvt K Co 29th KY Cav; Aug 64 to 65; Erwin PO; lung disease, result of typhoid & brain fever
LISENBY, James, He-57-2; Pvt A Co 7th TN Cav; 5-12-63 to 5-12-6 __ (2 yrs); Speim PO; prisoner Andersonvill 11 mos
LISENLY, Peter, Su-240-3; Lt 8th TN Cav; Kindrick Creek PO; reumatism, not at home and failed

to find discharge
LISK, Ezra R., Cu-17-1; 1st Lt C Co 1st WI Hvy Art; 10-9-62 to 9-14-__ (1 yr 11 mos 5 days); Crossville PO; enlarged liver & spleen, unable for work
LISSANDA, Odom, Wa-261-1; Brownsboro PO; piles & hart diseas
LISTER, H. W., Sh-158-6(4); Sgt L Co 2nd US Art Hvy; 17 Jan 65 to 20 Apr 66; Memphis PO; discharged at close of war with discharge papers
LITLE, Absher, Sn-261-2(1); Mahala widow of; Sgt H Co 123rd IL Inf; no PO; cronic diareah; refer to #243, 731 Pension Bureau (duplicate)
LITTER, William L., We-231-1; Pvt D Co 13th IL Inf; 25 Jan 64 to Aug 31 65; 13th Dist
LITTLE, Asher, Sn-261-1; Sgt H Co 128th IL Inf; New Roe, Allen Co, KY PO; refer to #243, 731 Pension Bureau
LITTLE, Bettie, see Hibler.
LITTLE, Charles J., G-67-2; Pvt M Co 6th TN Cav; 1 Aug 62 to 15 Aug 65; Bradford PO; eyesight damaged
LITTLE, Charley, H-73-3; Mariah widow of; Pvt; Chattanooga PO
LITTLE, Franklin A., K-174-5; Pvt G Co 2nd TN Cav; 1 Oct 62 to 6 Jul 65; House Mountain PO; rheumatism
LITTLE, John H., Ov-136-1; Commisary Sgt A Co 11th TN Cav; 4-23-63 to 9-11-65; Livington PO; rheumatism & fever
LITTLE, John R., U-247-2; Pvt H Co 8th TN Cav; 15 Sep 63 to 11 Sep 65; Erwin PO; rheumatism & heart, lame arm
LITTLE, John W., O-132-1; US Sol; Dist 3
LITTLE, Martin V., Di-34-2; Sgt G Co 1st OH Cav; 8-12-61 to 9-30=65; Dickson PO; reenlisted veteran
LITTLE, Samuel, U-247-2; Pvt A Co 3rd NC Mtd Inf; Sep 64 to 16 Aug 65; Erwin PO; epilepsy
LITTLE, William B., Dy-28-1; Sgt M Co 6th TN Cav; Aug 6 62 to Jul 20 65; Finley PO; bone scurvy, drawing pension of $8 per month
LITTLEJOHN, Lawyer, Sh-162-1; Pvt Peter No 5; Feb 10 63 to 64; Bengs Town PO; right arm dislocated, shot in ride, was discharged off Red Rover? at Cairo, paymasters name Landy Ball
LITTLETON, George, Ro-202-4; Capt I Co 1st TN Inf; 9 Aug 61 to 10 May 62; Cave Creek PO; irritation of bladder, was not no whole yr but discharged so
LITTLETON, George P., Lo-195-2(1); Pvt I Co 1st TN Inf; 61 to __; Oral Roane Co PO
LITTLETON, Jesse M., Ro-202-4; Capt I Co 1st TN Inf; 9 Aug 61 to 17 Sep 64; Gray's Hill PO; scurvy, scorbatic?
LITZ, Ebenezar I., H-63-4; 403 W. 9th, Chattanooga PO
LIVELEY, Jordan A., A-6-3(1); Pvt F Co 5th TN Inf; 2-20-62 to 6-30-65; Olivers PO
LIVELY, John W., Ja-84-2; Pvt TN Inf; Harrison PO; has no discharge, cant tell no dates
LIVELY, Robert, A-6-5(3); Pvt F Co 5th TN Inf; 2-20-62 to 6-30-65; no PO
LIVELY, Wiley, A-6-5(3); Pvt F Co 5th TN Inf; 3-62 to 7-65; no PO
LIVESEY, Joseph, K-160-3; Capt 18th Inf; Knoxville PO
LIVINER, William C., Gu-48-1; Flora B. widow of; Capt K Co 49th OH Inf--9-3-61 to 1-31-63; Lt Col A Co 177th OH Inf--8-16-64 to 7-65; Tracy City PO
LIVINGSTON, George, Ct-45-1; Chief Bugler 13th TN Cab; 4-7-64 to 9-5-65; Stony Creek PO; horse fell with him, Love Creek, Knox County, 1864
LIVINGSTON, Jessy G., De-26-2; E Co 27th TN; Aug 12 61 to Feb 14 62; Northford PO; CONF
LIVINGSTON, Joe R., M-103-2; Pvt E Co 1st TN Inf; 11-25-63 to 1-22-65; Lafayette PO
LIVINGSTON, John, Ct-40-1; Pvt L Co 13th TN Cav; 1-1-64 to 9-5-65; Elizabethton PO; rheumatism
LIVINGSTON, Murry, Ct-38-1; Cpl L Co 13th TN Cav; 10-3-64 to 9-5-65; Milligan PO
LIVINGSTON, Samuel B., Ct-38-1; Pvt L Co 13th TN Cav; 10-5-64 to 9-8-65; Milligan PO
LIVINGSTON, W.C., H-66-1; Pvt 6th Grant Battery? GA; 8-21-61 to 11-13-61; Chattanooga PO

LIVINGSTONE, Henry, G-51-1; US Sol; 3rd Civil Division
LIVIS, Thomas S., Mo-128-1; Pvt A Co 22nd KY Inf; to 12-9-62; Bell Town PO
LIVSAY, Wilem D., Ha-117-2; 1st D Sgt E Co 8th TN Cav; 23 Sep 63 to 11 Sep 65; Kyle's Ford PO; lung desease, chronic rheumatism
LLEWELLYN, William, K-161-2; Pvt I Co 9th TN Cav; __ to 65; Knoxville PO; wounded in back
LLOYD, David, Hr-94-1; Pvt E Co 59th TN Inf; 63 to to __; N. Bett or Saulsbury PO; chronic diarhea, gunshot right hand, he draws a pension
LLOYD, Edward, D-45-2; Pvt B Co 8th OH Inf; 6-5-62 to 9-25-62; Nashville PO
LLOYD, Edward, D-45-3; Pvt B Co 54th OH Inf; 3-64 to 65; Nashville PO
LLOYD, James M., H-63-3; Pvt F Co 75th OH Inf; 9-11-61 to 9-64; cor 9th & Braod, Chattanooga PO, diseased testacles
LLOYD, John E., H-51-1; Pvt I Co 2nd R WI Vol; 5-13-61 to 1-3-63; Soddy PO; wounded in thigh
LLOYD, Johnson, S-215-2; Pvt; Norma PO
LLOYD, Joseph, Hw-133-3; Cpl C Co 1st TN Lt Art; 1 Apr 64 to 1 Aug 65; Burem's Store PO; catarh & chronic diereah
LOBACH, John, K-160-1; Pvt K Co 2nd PA; Knoxville PO
LOBBINS, Henry, Sh-158-3; Maria (commonly called Zucker?) widow of; Pvt; 1 yr; Memphis PO; husband killed in battle Fort Pillow; the widow has no papers but no doubt her husband was a soldier
LOCHART, John, K-172-3; Elizabeth J. widow of; Pvt D Co 5th IL Inf; 15 Mar 62 to 18 Apr 65; 14th Dist South Knoxville PO
LOCK, Isaac, D-64-3; Mary widow of; Pvt 110th __; Nashville PO
LOCK, James R., He-67-2; Pvt I Co 2nd TN Mtd Inf; Mar 29 64 to Mar 29 65; Sardis PO; chronic rheumatism 15 years, defect in hearing
LOCK, Mrs. Marie J., Sh-167-3; widow; 61 Exchange St., Memphis PO
LOCK, Ranson, D-66-2; Highland St., Nashville PO
LOCK, Robert H. Mn-121-2; Cpl A Co 6th TN Cav; 9-3-63 to 7-26-65; Rose Creek PO
LOCK, Wm., Wi-282-1; Sgt D Co 24th US Reg; Dec 27 75 to Dec 27 80; Peytonville PO
LOCKARD, Elija, Wl-303-1; Pvt A Co 4th TN Mtd Inf; Nov 62 to Ju 64; no PO; shot through thumb on right hand
LOCKARD, William T., L-101-1; Pvt C Co 2nd Del Inf; Dec 15 61 to Dec 15 64; Henning PO; shot 1 leg, r eye inflamation
LOCKE, Charles L., Sh-167-3; Pvt 15th AR, 6-9th TN; 27 Apr 61 to 13 May 65; no PO; one arm, in hospital several months; CONF
LOCKE, James, R-158-1; Charlotte widow of; Rhea Springs PO; widow does not know proper dates
LOCKE, William B., K-159-3; Pvt B Co 9th TN Cav; 63 to 65; Knoxville PO
LOCKET, William, Ma-116-1; Pvt B Co 38th GA Inf; 1 Sep 63 to 25 Apr 65; Hatchie PO
LOCKETT, Mary, Ro-204-5; widow US Sol; no PO
LOCKETT, Thomas F., K-156-5; Pvt A Co 1st TN Inf; 61 to 64; 5 W. Cumberland St, Knoxville PO
LOCKEY, John, T-207-1; Emma widow of; Pvt? H Co 21st IL; Apr 61 to Oct 65; Covington PO
LOCKHART, Francis, S-218-2; Pvt A Co 61st __; Aug 61 to 18 Sep 64; Hughett PO; chronick rheumatism
LOCKHART, J. W., G-57-2; Pvt E Co 9th TN Cav; 62 to 65; Yorkville PO; CONF
LOCKHART, James H., Mn-99-2; Pvt F Co 46th PA Inf; 8-62 to __; Jasper PO
LOCKHEART, Robert H., Sq-164-4(1); Sgt E Co 6th TN Mtd Inf; 8-11-64 to 6-30-65; Dunlap PO
LOCKMAN, Oliver B., Be-7-1; E Co; 4 years 4 months 12 days; Big Sandy PO; cronic diaroer
LOCKRIDGE, Porter T., Mu-209-3; Martha A. widow of; Pvt I Co 11th Inf; 62 to 65; Columbia PO; prisoner 8 months, cant tell where
LOCKRIDGE, Thos. P., Mu-209-4; Martha A. widow of; Pvt I Co 111th Inf; 62 to 65; Columbia PO; prisoner 8 months; CONF
LOCKWOOD, Thomas P. Sh-202-1; Pvt Forest Cap Cav; 9 Sep 61 to 65; Memphis PO; CONF

LODGIN, Jef, Ge-94-2(1); alias McDowell, Jessie; Pvt K Co 40th TN Col Inf; Mar 63 to May 64; Ham PO; dropsy in leg
LOFTICE, John, Mo-123-1; Pvt E Co 7th TN Mtd Inf; 9-16-64 to 7-27-65; Jalapa PO
LOFTICE, Joseph, Mo-123-1; Pvt E Co 7th TN Mtd Inf; 1-22-65 6o 7-27-65; Jalapa PO
LOFTIN, James J., Mu-209-7; Columbia PO; CONF
LOFTIN, John W., Mu-209-6; Pvt G Co 9th TN Cav; 62 to 63; Columbia PO; CONF
LOFTIN, Lovick, Mu-209-7; Sgt G Co 5th MO Cav; 6-3-61 to 6-16-65; Columbia PO; CONF
LOFTIN, William, Mu-209-6; Sallie A. widow of; Pvt C Co 48th TN Cav; 12-1-63 to 12-1-64; Columbia PO
LOFTIS, Fredrick S., K-167-6; Pvt E Co 3rd NC Mtd Inf; Oct 64 to Aug 65; Knoxville PO
LOFTIS, William J., Br-14-1; Pvt 5th TN Vol Inf; McDonald PO; left leg off below knee
LOFTIS, William M., J-79-1; Pvt J Co 9th KY Cav; 65 to 63; Whitleyville PO
LOFTUS, John X?, Hm-105-2; 5th Dist
LOGAN, Bunington, Bo-13-2; Pvt F Co 98th OH Inf; 8-62 to 3-29-63; New Concord, Muskingum Co, OH; wounded in left thigh
LOGAN, Henry, R-162-2; Pvt 44th Col GA Inf; Dayton PO
LOGAN, James, Ja-84-1; Susan widow of; Pvt F Co 6th TN Mtd Inf; Harrison PO
LOGAN, John A., Mc-117-3; Pvt E Co 9th TN Cav; 9-8-63 to 9-8-65; Cog Hill PO kidney & back
LOGAN, L. D., Gi-122-6; Pvt E Co 17th TN Inf; Mar 61 to Jul 65; Prospect Sta. PO; prison 3 months, Point Lookout, MD; CONF
LOGAN, Mary E., see Cole, Charles H.
LOGAN, Mary G., O-139-2; widow; Union City PO
LOGAN, Robbert, Ov-137-1; Louiza widow of; Pvt; no PO; I could do no better as to information
LOGAN, Sally (see William Stuard)
LOGAN, T. P., G-57-2; Pvt F Co 4th TN Cav; 5-1-61 to 4-1-65; Yorkville PO; CONF
LOINS, Berton, Hm-103-3; Emlie mother of; Pvt C Co 1st TN Hvy Art; 13 Mar 62 to 13 Mar 65; Morristown PO
LOLAR, Felix G., D-57-2; Pvt 56th KY Cap US Vol; 61 to Apr 65; Nashville PO; contract rheumatism
LOLLAR, Cabeam, Mu-210-3; Mary F.widow of; Pvt Cav; 61 to 62; Carters Creek PO; discharged on account of bad health; CONF
LOLLIS, William, Ro-204-3; Pvt K Co 1st TN Inf; 9 Aug 61 to 17 Sep 64; Elverton PO; rheumatism
LOMAN, John, Sm-170-2; Pvt A Co 1st TN Mtd Inf; 1-17-64 to 1-30-65; Maggart PO; chronic disorder of liver & kidneys
LOMAX, James F., P-151-3; Pvt F Co 2nd TN Mtd Inf; 64 to 65; Linden PO; electric shock
LOMMARD, Frank, D-64-3; Pvt F Co 13th TN Reg; Nashville PO
LONAS, Jacob K., K-155-1; Sherriff, Knox Co TN; Pvt C Co 1st TN Cav; 1 Apr 62 to 1 Apr 65; Knoxville PO
LONDON, Biter, Ms-181-1; Pvt B Co 11th TN Inf; 6-30-63 to 4-12-65; Cochran PO; in a bad condition, government should help
LONDON, Wm. W., Sh-201-2; Pvt H Co 87th PA Inf; 10 Aug 63 to 14 Aug 65; Memphis PO
LONE, Specks, Fr-115-1; Pvt D Co 177th OH Inf; Cowan PO
LONES, Samuel R., K-180-3; Pvt D Co 6th TN Inf; 18 Apr 62 to 27 Apr 65; Bearden PO; piles, rheumatism, lung trouble
LONES, William B., K-171-2; Sgt E Co 12th TN Cav; Oct 62 to Apr 65; Knoxville PO; CONF
LONG, Abner, K-184-2; Pvt D Co 3rd TN Cav; Dec 63 to Jan 65; Thorn Grove PO
LONG, Alexander, H-73-4(2); Chattanooga PO
LONG, Alexander R., Bo-15-3; Pvt G Co 6th TN Cav; 10-1-62 to 6-30-65; Maryville PO
LONG, Almeda (see Alexander McCamey)
LONG, Andrew, Sh-145-2; Pvt B Co 8th KY Cav; 15 Feb 62 to 4 Sep 64; Kerrville PO
LONG, Caesar, Mu-199-1; Hester widow of; Pvt E Co 46th US CI; Columbia PO

LONG, George, D-50-2; Liddia Hubbard former wife of; Pvt A Co 111th US Inf; Sep 62 to __; 318 Line,Nashville PO; died on battlefield
LONG, George C., J-78-1; Pvt K Co 1st TN Inf; 11-30-64 to 7-22-65; Haydensburg PO; eyes, bowels, and so on caused from small pox
LONG George W., Sn-262-2(1); Pvt 13th IN Lt Art; 19 Jan 64 to 10 Jul 65; Buck Lodge PO; disease contracted in the head
LONG, Gideon B., Cy-27-5(3); Pvt E Co 1st TN Mtd Inf; 10-63 to 1-65; Clementsville PO; tumor on left leg
LONG, Hanible, see Chester, Hanible
LONG, Henry, Wy-172-1; Pvt F Co; 62 to 62; Waynesboro PO
LONG, Isham, Mc-114-7; Pvt A Co 29th TN Inf; 6-12-62 to 6-1-63; Calhoun PO; CONF
LONG, J. O. B-9-1; Pvt H Co 9th __; 61 to 65; Midland PO
LONG, Jackson, Sh-155-1; Pvt B Co 46th AR Inf; 1 Apr 63 to 15 Jan 66; Germantown PO
LONG, Jame, H-76-2; Mary A. widow to; Pvt B Co 15th IN Vol; Chattanooga PO
LONG, James E., Hw-132-4; Pvt B Co 3rd TN Cav; 30 Jun 64 to 25 Oct 64; Otes PO; mounted cavalry
LONG, James M. WE-231-1; Latham PO; not able give facts
LONG, John, Sh-158-5(1); Pvt B Co 63rd US Col Inf; 27 Oct 63 to 9 Jan 66; Memphis PO; discharged at close of war with a discharge paper
LONG, John, Sq-165-1; Pvt G Co 6th TN Cav; 3-18-62 to 5-65; Delphi PO; shot through left thigh, received an honorable disc.; CONF?
LONG, John, Se-226-6; Rhoda C. widow of; Pvt D Co 3rd TN Cav; 2 Dec 62 to died Apr 65; Straw Plains, Jefferson Co PO
LONG, John D., Mc-112-9; Pvt A Co 4th TN Cav; 3-24-63 to __; Athens PO
LONG, John N., Ge-88-2; Pvt C Co 4th TN Inf; 62 to 65; Bulls Gap PO; sun stroke
LONG, Joseph, Po-151-1; Pvt 11th TN Cav; Servilla PO
LONG, Marry (see John Morton)
LONG, Melvin B., Mc-112-8; Pvt F Co 3rd TN Cav; 3-1-63 to 6-12-65; Athens PO; gunshot wound & heart disease
LONG, Miller, Po-152-3(1); Pvt I Co 60th OH Inf; 8-12-62 to 11-10-62; Ducktown PO; chronic diarrhoea, taken prisoner and parrolled
LONG, Milly A., see Howard, William
LONG, Mosses, Je-145-2; Chloa widow of; Pvt; Dumplin PO
LONG, Nathan P., L-110-1; Dist 12, Hansford PO
LONG, Rily R., Mc-11209; Pvt H Co 5th US Col Art; 3-24-64 to 5-1-65; Athens PO
LONG, Robert, He-64-2; Lt A Co 27th TN Cav; 1 May 62 to 1 Jun 65; Center Point PO;CONF
LONG, Robert, Hw-122-2; 5th Dist
LONG, Sampson, J-78-2; Mary C. widow of; Pvt; Rough Point PO
LONG, Samuel, K-180-1; Pvt D Co 3rd TN Inf; 10 Feb 62 to Feb 65; Bearden PO; scurvy
LONG, Samuel, HW-127-2; Pvt D Co 8th TN Inf; 15 Mar 63 to Jul 65; Austin Mill PO; gunshot wound & ch. diarrhea & piles
LONG, Thomas Bo-13-3(1); Pvt H Co 13th TN Cav; 10-63 to 3-64; Concord, Knox Co PO
LONG, Thomas, K-186-2; Pvt A Co 3rd TN Cav; 10 Nov 62 to 30 Jun 65; Knoxville PO; heart trouble
LONG, Thomas A., Ge-89-1; Cpl D Co 8th TN Inf; 15 Mar 63 to 30 Jun 65; Romeo PO
LONG, Thomas P., Ha-115-2; Pvt B Co 1st TN Art; Apr 63 to 13 Jul 65; Alanthers Hills PO; kidney troubled incurred
LONG Dr. William F., Rb-221-2; Surgeon K Co 1st KY; May 1 61 to May 1 62; Adams Stations PO; CONF
LONG, William L., J-78-2; Capt B Co 5th __; 64 to 65; Rough Point PO
LONG, William L., Gr-71-2; Pvt B Co 4th KY Inf; Tate Spring PO; discharge misplaced
LONGLY, John, C-33-4; Pvt D Co 3rd NH; 10-63 to 4-?-65; Jellico PO
LONGMIRE, James O., C-28-2(1); Pvt H Co 9th TN Cav; 9-20-63 to 9-11-65; Big Creek Gap PO; hepatitis

LONGMIRE, James S., Sh-159-4; Pvt B Co MS Mtd Inf; May 62 to 65; Memphis PO; captured and wounded; CONF
LONGSTON, Thomas F., Ms-178-1; Pvt F Co 1st TN & AL & 4th TN Mtd Inf; 9-1-63 to 6-1-64; South Berlin PO; rheumatism, neuralgia, ircipelus incured while in prison 1864 & 1865
LONIS, Sasseene, H-69-3; Maria widow of; Pvt 16th Col Reg Inf; Chattanooga PO
LONTZ, Isac, D-74-1; Sgt H Co 11th IN Z (sic); Apr 61 to Apr 64; 202 Fatherland, Nashville PO
LOOMIS, Julius F., H-67-3; Pvt G Co 8th PA Vol; 4-61 to 7-61; Chattanooga PO
LOONEY, Frank, Sh-174-4; Frank Lewis alias; Pvt A Co 18th AL Inf; 22 Hadden Ave, Memphis PO
LOONEY, Joel H., Mr-96-1; Pvt C Co 6th TN Mtd Inf; 9-12-64 to 6-14-65; Whitwell PO
LOONEY, John, Hr-89-1; Pvt B Co 29th IL; 62 to 65; Whiteville PO
LOONEY, Samuel, Hw-125-1; Pvt A Co 12th TN Bat; 62 to 65; Surgoinsville PO
LOONIS, Samuel P., H-51-5; Pvt E Co 2nd IL Cav; 7-8-61 to 11-13-61; Hill City PO
LOONY, Wm., Hw-125-1; Pvt C Co 59th TN Inf; 62 to May 65; Surgoinsville PO; CONF
LORANSOND, William A., Mc-114-5; Pvt D Co 5th TN Mtd Inf; 8-65 to 6-65 (sic); Santfordville PO; rheumatism & heart disease
LORD, Jim, Hy-76-1; alias Loyd, Jim M.; Pvt H Co 101st Col Inf; 28 Aug 64 to 24 Jan 66; Stanton Depot PO
LORD, Moses S., Sh-186-1; Lt 59th IL; Memphis PO; his wife did not no company
LORD, Oliver, K-172-1; Sarah widow of; Pvt I Co 10th MI Cav; Knoxville PO
LORD, Richard, Hd-50-3; Pvt; Lowryville PO
LORING, George, Mo-119-3; Pvt E Co 2nd IA Cav; Sweetwater PO
LORNOX, William A., P-150-2; US Sol; 1st Dist
LORY, James W., Sn-254-1; Pvt F Co 15th MO Inf; 9-19-64 to 7-16-65; Hendersonville PO
LOTHROPE, George B., H-52-2; dont know; Lookout Mt. PO
LOTTY, J. H., Hu-103-3; Pvt A Co 10th GA Inf; 29 May 62 to 20 Jul 64; PO omitted; marked through, probably CONF
LOTTY, T. L., Hu-103-3; Pvt E Co 11th TN Inf; 62 to 64; PO omitted; crossed through, probably CONF
LOTZ, Galen, Sh-195-1; Pvt E Co 51st Reg; __ to 8-2-65; Memphis PO
LOUDD, Patrick, D-99-1; Pvt A Co 1st TN Hvy Art; 15 Aug 62 to 1 Aug 65; Nashville PO; feeble minded; poorhouse
LOUDEBACK, James F., Hw-132-2; Pvt G Co 5th TN Cav; 20 Mar 62 to May 65; Persia PO; CONF
LOUDEBACK, Layfayette, Hw-132-5; Pvt E Co 2nd TN Cav; Jul 62 to Apr 65; Persia PO; CONF
LOUDEBACK, William, Hw-132-5; Mary widow of; Pvt TN Cav; __ to Apr 65; Persia PO; could not learn anymore; CONF
LOUDERBACK, Elias, K-161-2; Nancy widow of; Knoxville PO
LOUDERMILK, James, Ct-39-2; Pvt H Co 13th TN Cav; 9-63 to 9-65; Johnson City PO; frost bites & rheumatism
LOUDERMILK, John, C-34-1; Pvt A Co 4th TN Cav; 64 to 65 (1 yr 3 mos); Stanfill PO; contracted rheumatism
LOUIS, Adsel, Cl-48-1; Pvt; Old Town PO
LOUIS, Bennit, Ge-92-4; Misy widow of; Pvt F Co 3rd TN Inf; Laurel Gap PO; cant lern
LOUIS, Sam, Mn-121-1; Marteeca? widow of; Cpl? A Co 6th TN Cav; 12 Aug 62 to Jun 65; Rose Creek PO
LOUPOSSEY, William, K-172-5(1); Pvt A Co 6th TN Inf; 8 Mar 62 to 27 Apr 65; Sooke PO; shot through the thigh
LOUTHAM, George W., Sn-259-1; Pvt H Co 79th __; 11-12-61 to 6-21-65; Bethpage PO
LOUTHEN, David N., Ha-115-3; Sgt G Co 8th TN Cav; 12 Aug 63 to 11 Sep 65; Mulberry Gap PO; typhoid fever left lungs affected, pensioner
LOUTHEN, Thomas, Ha-115-3; Pvt G Co 8th TN Cav; 12 Aug 63 to 11 Sep 65; Mulberry Gap PO; typhoid fever left chest disease, pensioner

LOV, John, Je-144-1; Sarah A. widow of; Pvt 8th TN Cav; 2 yrs 7 mos; Vally Home PO; heart diseas and spinal affecion, in prison at Norhill?
LOVE, Albert, Ro-210-2; Pvt I Co 1st TN Inf; 3 Mar 62 to 6 Mar 65; Rockwood PO; hearing and leg
LOVE?, Ben, R-161-2; Pvt A Co 138th PA Inf; Dayton PO; discharge at Washington
LOVE, David H., Ha-114-1; Pvt D Co 9th TN Cav; 3 May 62 to 13 May 64; Xenophon PO
LOVE, John R., G-70-1; Martha C. widow of; Pvt K Co 12th IL; Dyer PO; killed
LOVE, Joseph N., Ro-201-2; Pvt D Co 5th TN Inf; 25 Feb 62 to 7 Apr 65; Kingston PO
LOVE, Lewis, G-68-1; US Sol; PO omitted
LOVE, Littleton P., Hn-71-1; or L. P. Barker (army name); Pvt A Co 59th TN Col Inf; Aug 64 to Jan 3 66; PO omitted
LOVE, Malinda, Sh-178-2; rear 251 Monroe St, Memphis PO
LOVE, Peter, Ru-232-1; Pvt B Co TN Inf; Mar 64 to Aug 64; 3rd Civil Dist
LOVE, Preston B., K-156-3; Pvt B Co 31st TN Inf; 61 to 66; 9 Temperance St, Knoxville PO; CONF
LOVE, Richard, Gi-123-2; Cpl B Co 12th TN Col Inf; Oncaster? PO; wounded in left leg, gun shot
LOVE, Richard, Rb-226-2; Pvt; Dist 12
LOVE, Robert A., Dk-39-6(2); Pvt L Co 5th TN Cav; 8-19-63 to 8-14-65; Laurel Hill PO
LOVE, Samuel, Hn-72-1; Cpl C Co 55th US Col; discharge at Washington, cannot remember dates; Paris PO; sunstroke
LOVE, Thomas, Wa-263-1; Pvt 64th VA Inf; Jonesboro PO; CONF
LOVE, William, Ge-85-1; Pvt E Co 3rd TN Cav; Cavey Branch PO
LOVE, William M., Po-148-2; Pvt A Co 6th TN Inf; 4-17-62 to 4-27-65; Benton PO
LOVEALL, William H., We-221-6(2); Pvt G Co 8th AR Cav; Feb 62 to 28 Jun 65; Martin PO; none but exposure; CONF
LOVEDAY, Edward, Se-221-3; Pvt M Co 2nd TN Cav; 8 Nov 62 to 6 Jul 65; East Fork PO
LOVEDAY, James, Se-226-3; Martha formerly widow of; Pvt; Sinking Springs PO; never returned home
LOVEJOY, Thomas (Col), H-56-4; GA; St. Elmo PO
LOVEL, Lindoff, He-61-3; Pvt G Co 7th TN Cav; 5 Aug 62 to 14 Oct 63; 15th Civil Dist
LOVEL, Rachel, Sn-264-2; widow; Portland PO
LOVELACE, Ira, K-154-3; Alice D. widow of; Cpl 6th TN Inf; 21 Sep 62 to 65; Knoxville PO
LOVELACE, John, Ct-42-1; Pvt A Co 13th TN Cav; Watauga PO
LOVELACE, John, Ro-210-9; Pvt; Rockwood PO; CONF
LOVELACE, John L., K-178-1; Pvt D Co 3rd TN Inf; 10 Feb 62 to 23 Feb 65; Vancouver PO; lost left eye
LOVELACE, Simon, Cr-8-1; Nancy (widow?); 1 yr; Gates PO; left leg shot off
LOVELACE, Zacharias T., D-104-1; Sgt E Co 7th KY Cav; 9 Jul 62 to 10 Jul 65; Whites Bend PO; hearing affected
LOVELADY, Aaron, Sn-261-1; Pvt D Co 52nd KY Inf (Mtd); 8-15-63 to 1-17-65; Rapids, Simpson Co. KY PO; came home on discharge 1-17-65 (duplicate on Sn-261-3(2))
LOVELADY, George W., H-49-6; Pvt K Co 5th TN Vol; 4-1-63 to 7-8-65; Daisy PO; wounded in left leg
LOVELADY, James, H-49-10; Pvt A Co 6th TN Mtd Inf; 8-2-64 to 6-30-65; Daisy PO
LOVELADY, William, H-58-5; Pvt A Co 6th TN Mtd Inf; 8-2-64 to 6-30-65; Retro PO
LOVELESS, James, U-247-2; Lt C Co 2nd TN Cav; Jul 62 to Jul 65; Erwin PO; piles, rheumatism & malarial
LOVELL, John, Co-62-3; Pvt D Co 4th TN Inf; 1 Jan 65 to 7 Aug 65; Bybee PO
LOVELL, John J., H-70-4(1); Pvt; Chattanooga PO
LOVELL, Mary H., Hm-109-5; widow US S; PO omitted
LOVELL, Richard M., H-53-6; Sgt Musician 97th PA Inf; 10-24-61 to 8-31-65; Sgt G Co 20th PA Cav; 7-9-63 to 7-6-64; Ridgedale PO; reenlisted
LOVELL, William, D-49-4; Nashville PO; a bugus pension agent taken all papers away & he dont remember dates

LOVELY, David, Mo-127-2; Pvt D Co 11th TN Cav; Notchy PO
LOVELY, John, A-9-3(1); Pvt C Co 11th TN Cav; 8-17-63 to __; Dutch Valley PO; was never discharged, was born (sic) upon rolls as a deserter
LOVERT, Seymore, Sn-254-2; Saundersville PO
LOVETTE, Jesse, K-168-3; Adair's Creek PO
LOVEYEAR, George, D-64-5; Nashville PO
LOVLACE, Curtis D., Hn-73-1; Sgt Co I 6th TN; 62 to 65; Como PO; rheumatism, broken rib, honable discharge
LOVVETT, John D., Ge-102-3; Pvt I Co 1st TN Cav; __ to 65 (3 yrs 5 mos); Woolsey College PO
LOW, Alexander, S-215-2; Pvt I Co 7th TN Inf; 8 Nov 64 to 27 Jul 65; High House PO
LOW, Frank, Ge-92-2; Pvt A Co 1st TN Lt Art; 12 Oct 63 to 3 Aug 65; Laurel Gap PO
LOW, Henry, Ge-100-1; Pvt A Co 12th TN Cav; 12 Aug 63 to 7 Oct 65; Midway PO
LOW, John, A-9-3; Pvt Mabry Lt Art TN; 3-4-62 to 1-4-63; Olivers Springs PO; no disability, discharged because of being under 16 yrs of age; CONF
LOW, John, S-215-2; Pvt G Co 7th TN Inf; 8 Nov 64 to 27 Jul 65; High House PO
LOW, Joseph, A-9-3; Hannah widow of; Pvt G Co 2nd TN Inf; 3-62 to 3-65; Olivers Springs PO
LOW, Michael, A-6-3(1); Pvt G Co 2nd TN Inf; 1-8-62 to 1-8-65; Olivers PO; shot through the right shoulder
LOW, Phillip, S-215-2; Pvt G Co 2nd TN Inf; 4 Mar 62 to 9 Mar 65; High House PO; struck in head, hand mashed, ruptured by prisoners
LOWE, Andrew J., Ge-89-2; Pvt; Mosheim PO
LOWE, Andrew R., Cu-16-2; Pvt C Co 32nd KY Inf; 11-4-62 to 8-12-63; Big Lick PO; piles
LOWE, Elizabeth (see Kerby, Wood)
LOWE, Elizabeth, Wh-184-1; she says he was in the US army but can tell nothing; Pollard PO; she said she never heard from him and can tell nothing
LOWE, George J., Ct-43-2; Pvt F Co 13th TN Cav; 9-22-63 to 9-5-65; Carter Furnace PO; chilblain and hip dislocated
LOWE?, Henry, Hd-48-2; Pvt F Co 14th Mish; Sep 63 to Aug 65; Savannah PO
LOWE, Henry C., Sh-186-1; Sgt A Co 144th IL; Memphis PO
LOWE, Isaac, Ja-85-1; Cpl A Co 4th TN Cav; 10-15-62 to 7-12-65; Thatchers Landing PO; weakness of back
LOWE, Jacob, Jo-153-2; Pvt D Co 13th TN Cav; 24 Sep 63 to 5 Sep 65; Pandora PO; diarrhoea, lund disease
LOWE, James B., Jo-153-2; Nancy C. widow of; Pvt D Co 13th TN Cav; 24 Sep 63 to 5 Sep 65; Pandora PO
LOWE, John, K-176-3; Pvt I Co 2nd TN Inf; 14 May 61 to 25 Sep 65; Halls X Roads PO
LOWE, John A., Ct-43-2; Martha W. widow of; Pvt F Co 13th TN Cav; 9-1-64 to 9-5-65; Carter Furnace PO
LOWE, John E., Jo-153-2; Pvt D Co 13th TN Cav; 2 Feb 64 to 5 Apr 65; Little Doe PO; diarrhoea, piles, spinal affection
LOWE, John G., Tr-269-1; Major 23rd TN Inf; 1 May 61 to 1 Jun 65; Hartsville PO; prisoner at Ft. Delaware, shot through the thigh
LOWE, John J., A-2-3; Pvt C Co 2nd TN Inf; 6-18-63 to 6-30-65; Lamontville PO; in prison 11 mos
LOWERY, David L., Se-226-5; Nancy E. Douglass formerly widow of; Pvt D Co 9th TN Cav; 14 Sep 62 to 18 Sep 65; Henrys X Roads PO
LOWERY, Elijah, D-50-3; Pvt B Co 122nd KY Inf; Sep 63 to Jan 66; Nashville PO
LOWERY, Frank, H-56-2; Pvt 9th GA Inf; 9-1-63 to 65 (2 yrs); East End PO
LOWERY, Henry, Sh-191-2; Elizabeth widow of; Pvt K Co 61st IN; 63 to 66 (2 yrs 6 mos); Memphis PO
LOWERY, James A., Ge-90-2; Pvt D Co 4th TN Inf; 30 Jan 63 to 18 Aug 65; Greenville PO; information of the eyes, exsposier camp life
LOWERY, William P., Ro-201-4(2); Chap 2nd TN Inf; 28 Sep 61 to 30 Sep 63; Kingston PO

LOWERY, ____, K-177-3; PO omitted; CONF
LOWHORN, McKiger, Fe-44-1; Pvt C Co 1st KY Cav; 8-20-63 to 9-30-65; Armathwaite PO; chronic diarhea
LOWNDES, Caesar D., H-70-4(1); Pvt; Chattanooga PO
LOWRANCE, Henderson, Wa-267-3; Pvt; Johnson City PO
LOWRY, Alexander, H-73-3; Pvt; Chattanooga PO
LOWRY, Benjamin, Sn-252-3; Mary widow of; Pvt 110th US Inf; Gallatin PO
LOWRY, Henry, Bo-15-3; 1st Cpl E Co 3rd TN Mtd Inf; 7-15-64 to 11-30-64; Blockhouse PO
LOWRY, Henry, R-157-2; Sol; 12th Dist, Grandview PO
LOWRY, James, Je-135-2; Pvt E Co 9th TN Cav; 24 Sep 63 to 11 Sep 65; Piedmont PO; consumption
LOWRY, James C., Mc-110-3(1); Maria F. widow of; Pvt D Co 4th TN Cav; 12-10-62 to 7-12-65; Mouse Creek PO
LOWRY, John M., Bo-22-1; Pvt D Co 2nd TN Cav; 9-1-62 to 7-6-65; Notime PO; hearing & rheumatism
LOWRY, Robert, Je-145-1; Pvt C Co 8th TN Cav; May 63 to 11 Sep 65; Cynthiana PO
LOWRY, Robert W., Cr-4-2; Almira widow of; Pvt; Bells Depot PO; CONF
LOWRY, W. W., Mc-115-1; Pvt D Co 5th TN Mtd Inf; 8-31-64 to 7-1-65; Riceville PO; yellow jaundice & fever
LOWS, Adam, Ge-100-2; Pvt A Co 12th TN Cav; 29 Mar 63 to 7 Oct 65; Midway PO
LOWSON, George W., Wy-173-1; Pvt F Co 6th TN Cav; 9-21-62 to 7-26-65; Lutts PO
LOWSON, James M., Lo-194-2; PVtt G Co 1st TN Inf; 11 Aug 61 to Oct 64; Lenoir PO
LOWSON, John M., Wy-173-1; Pvt F Co 6th TN Cav; 7-1-63 to 7-26-65; Lutts PO
LOWSON, Thomas J., Wy-173-1; Pvt B Co 2nd TN Mtd Inf; 10-15-63 to 10-17-64; Lutts PO
LOY, William, Un-259-2; Pvt L Co 11th TN Cav; 21 Sep 63 to 21 Apr 64; Lost Creek PO
LOY, William, C-24-4(3); Pvt I Co 7th TN Mtd Inf; 64 to 7-2-65; Forkvale PO; lungs and rheumatism
LOYD, George, We-222-1; Pvt A Co 54th Hills TN; Sep 61 to Jan 62; Gardner PO; CONF
LOYD, James, G-51-2; US Sol; 3rd Civil Dist
LOYD, James H., Ha-50-1; Pvt F Co 10th TN Inf; May 6 62 to Dec 19 63; Savannah PO
LOYD, Jim M. (see Lord, Jim)
LOYD, John, T-226-2; Pvt E Co 2nd MO Inf; Jan 63 to Jun 65; Leighs Chappel PO
LOYD, John, Wa-263-6; Pvt; May Day PO
LOYD, Robert, Ge-98-4; Orderly Sgt F Co 8th TN Cav; 3 May 63 to 11 Sep 65; PO omitted, piles & rheumatism 25 yrs
LOYD, Robert, Wa-263-6; Pvt; May Day PO
LOYD, Tennessee, Jo-153-1; Pvt B Co 4th TN Inf; 1 Apr 64 to 17 Jul 65; Little Doe PO; rheumatism
LOYD, Thomas, U-244-1; Pvt 3rd NC Inf; __ to 8 Aug 65; Cruestville PO
LOYD, Thomas, Ge-101-3; Nancy A. wife of; Pvt D Co 8th TN Inf; 15 Mar 64 to 30 Jun 65; Locust Sp. PO; died Jun 7, 1889
LOYD, William H., La-113-2; Pvt A Co 1st WI Inf; 8 Oct 61 to 13 Dec 64; Lawrenceburgh PO; in prison, Andersonville
LUALLEN, James W., C-24-2; Pvt I Co 9th TN Cav; Agee PO; lung __ affects of mumps
LUCAS, Fed, H-70-3(1); Pvt H Co 1st US Col Hvy Art; 6-12-64 to 3-12-66; Chattanooga PO
LUCAS, George W., Hw-121-5(4); Pvt Robersin's Battallion; Lucas PO; CONF
LUCAS, John M., Ha-115-3; Pvt; Mulberry Gap PO; CONF
LUCAS, William, D-50-1; Fannie A. widow of; Pvt; 606 N. High, Nashville PO; has no record or recollection
LUCE, Hiram M., R-161-1; Pvt F Co 4th MN Inf; 9-61 to 12-62; Dayton PO; from meningitis, hosp 1t 9th IA Cav; 63 to 2-66
LUCK, James M., Wl-297-1; Pvt D Co 4th TN Mtd Inf; 10-19-64 to 8-25-65; Water Town PO; lung disease by relaps of measel
LUCKEY, Paralee J. (see Yeargin, John B.)
LUFFMAN, Bengerman N., Di-42-1; Pvt C Co 7th TN Inf; 65 to 7-65; Tenn City PO; army
LUINICK, Wm. P., Sn-250-1; Sgt E Co 3rth __; 63 to 65; Castalian Springs PO

LUKE, D. D., Wa-268-2; Johnson City PO
LUKER, Clayton B., La-113-2; Sgt A Co 2nd TN Mtd Inf; 9-15-63 to 10-14-64; Lawrenceburgh PO; spinel damage
LUKER, William J., Wy-177-1; Martha E. widow of; Pvt B Co 2nd TN Mtd Inf; 10-15-63 to __ (7 mos 25 days); Moon PO; died at Clifton TN, 6-9-64
LUMBLEY, Nathin M., Hm-33-1(103); Cpl G Co 1st AL Cav; 1-1-63 to 1-64; Dyersburg PO; hemeridge of lungs
LUMER, John A., Ct-40-1; Pvt G Co 13th TN Cav; 9-24-63 to 9-5-65; Elizabethton PO; rheumatism
LUMER, Leander, Ct-40-2; Ruth widow of; Pvt G Co 13th TN Cav; 9-24-63 to __-8-65 (1 yr 11 mos); Elizabethton PO
LUMEY, Henry, Sh-157-7; 62 to __; Memphis PO
LUMPKINS, James M., La-111-2; Pvt D Co TN Cav; PO omitted; CONF
LUMPKINS, Joseph, C-30-1; Phebee widow of; Pvt 2nd TN Inf; 61 to __; Well Spring PO; died during service
LUMPKINS, Millie A. (see Miller, Thomas)
LUMPLINS, Henry, Sn-252-1; Pvt E Co 50th IL Inf; 6-15-63 to 1-10-66; Gallatin PO
LUNA, Hue V., Ms-169-1; Narley A. widow of; Pvt E Co 11th IN Inf; 3-15-62 to 4-10-65; Petersburg PO; wounded in left hip; discharged at expiration of service
LUNARD?, Joseph, D-57-3; also on same line the name Wright; Nashville PO; CONF
LUNCEFORD, James E., Ct-35-3; Pvt E Co 13th TN Cav; 9-24-63 to 9-5-65; Elk Mills PO; in US Army (disability)
LUNNEY, L., D-63-2; Frances widow of; Pvt G Co 17th US Col; 63 to 66; Nashville PO
LUNSFORD, Daron, Se-219-3; Anie widow of; Pvt 9th TN Cav; Jones Cave PO
LUNSFORD, Henry, Se-220-3; US Sol; Emerts Cave PO
LUNT, Alex., Ro-202-4; Elizabeth Smith widow of; Pvt I Co 1st TN Inf; 8-6-61 to 8-1-63; Paw Paw Ford PO; rheumatism
LUPPER, Hoabs, K-177-1; Pvt D Co 10th TN Inf; 5-20-62 to 4-14-65; Dante PO; CONF
LURBOW, Calvin J., P-151-4; Dist 6
LURKE, Adam, Sn-199-1; Pvt; __ to 65; 12 Moore Ave, Memphis PO
LUSBY, Scott W., K-183-3; Pvt Batt; Riverdale PO; CONF
LUSH, N. Joseph P., Br-8-3(1); Pvt A Co 7th TN Inf; 5-31-62 to 10-31-62; (by promotion); 1st Lt L Co 1st TN Cav; 11-1-62 to 6-15-65; Cleo PO; general loss of health
LUSK, George W., Mr-98-1; Pvt I Co TN Inf; 65 to 65 (7 mos); Stanley PO
LUSK, James M., H-49-1; 3rd Cpl M Co 5th TN Cav; 9-14-63 to 8-14-65; Brown's Chapel PO
LUSK, Landon H. P., Wa-268-1; 1st Lt H Co 4th TN Inf; 3-24-63 to 8-11-65; Johnson City PO
LUSK, Monroe R., H-49-1; Pvt M Co 5th TN Cav; 9-14-63 to 8-14-65; Redbank PO
LUSK, Samuel J., Br-8-4(2); Pvt B Co 1st TN Lt Art; 1-2-62 to 1-23-65; Cleo PO; deafness
LUSTER, Edward, Pi-155-1; Pvt H Co 12th KY Inf; e yrs; Otto PO; neuralgia
LUSTER, Hambleton, Hw-121-4(3); Pvt; 9-3-62 to 3-3-65; New Hope PO; feaver
LUSTER, James, Ge-101-1; Cpl A Co 4th TN Inf; 4-6-63 to 8-2-65; Ottway PO; Nashville--in service, diareia cronic
LUSTER, ___, R-161-2; Mahaley widow of; Dayton PO
LUTHER, Alfred G., Sh-180-1; Capt G Co 95th OH Inf; 4-17-61 to 5-7-64; 416 Orlean St, Memphis PO
LUTHER, David R., Se-230-3; Pvt C Co 25th NC Inf; 3-63 to 63 (6 mos); Richison's Cove PO; shot --left hand; CONF
LUTHER, William R., Se-230-1; Pvt G Co 1st M_ Cav; 5-61 to __ (4 yrs); Pokeberry PO; CONF
LUTON, Robert G?, K-179-4; Pvt A Co 5th TN Inf; 2-25-62 to 4-7-65; PO omitted
LUTRELL, Robert, Ge-87-2; Phebe widow of; Pvt 8th TN Inf; Little Chucky PO
LUTRELL, William H., K-164-2; Lettie W. widow of; Cpl G Co 2nd TN Vol; 9-1-62 to 7-6-65; PO omitted (Knoxville?)
LUTS?, Collumbus, Hi-85-1; Pvt C Co 48th TN Inf; 9-1-61 to 3-10-64; Spensers Mill PO; shot in right arm
LUTTERAL, Austin, Ro-210-4; Pvt; Rockwood PO
LUTTON, Corneliaus, La-108-1; US Sol; 1st Civil Dist
LUTTREL, George W., Wa-262-1; Pvt & Lt; I & M Cos, 1st & 13th KY Cav; 12-1-62 to 1-11-65; Washington College PO; piles & rheumatism
LUTTRELL, Jacob, Hm-103-2; Pvt E Co 8th TN Inf; 10-1-63 to 6-14-65; Morristown PO; rheumatism
LUTTRELL, Mark L., T-208-1; Pvt D Co 52nd IN; 63 to 65; Burleson PO
LUTTRELL, Noah F., K-183-1; Pvt B Co 6th TN Inf; 1-1-64 to 6-30-65; Riverdale PO
LUTTRELL, Richard, K-183-3; Pvt B Co 34th TN Cav; 10-12-62 to 9-15-65; High Point PO
LUTTRELL, Richard H., Jo-149-3; Mary C. widow of; Capt D Co 13th TN Cav; 9-24-63 to died 1-20-64; Mountain City PO
LUTTRELL, Samuel S., Wa-274-3; Jonesboro PO
LUTTRELL, Silas, T-208-1; Mary Crowder widow of; Pvt D Co 52nd IN; 63 to 65; Burleson PO
LUTTS, Jacob S., Hd-50-5; 1st Sgt E Co 8th TN Mtd Inf; 2-2-65 to 9-1-65; Nixon PO; gun shot wound on theogh and arm
LUTTS, Joseph W., La-112-1; Pvt H Co 2nd TN Mtd Inf; 1-13-64 to 4-17-65; Abner PO
LUTY, Fanny (see McGill, Henry)
LUTZ, William M., Mn-126-1; Pvt H Co 29th OH Inf; 8-2-62 to 6-14-65; Purdy PO; gunshot in right breast also by a falling tree
LYELL, John W., Ma-121-1; Pvt D Co 51st IN Inf; 61 to 65; Medina PO (Gibson Co.); Mr. John W. Lyell is a worthy man but needs help, contract rheumatism, is a diseased man but cant tell what all is the matter with him
LYHUGH, John, Sh-150-1; Jackson, John (same man); Cpl H Co 57th US Inf; 20 Jun __ to 66; Bartlett PO; shot in right arm and leg
LYISCOMB, Moses, D-67-1; Amlenda? widow of; Pvt I Co 17th Col Inf; Nashville PO
LYLE, Amos, Jo-152-2; Pvt A Co 10th TN Cav; 63 to 65; Doeville PO; wound left leg, was sent off sick, never received discharge
LYLE, James N., Je-136-3; Eliza L. widow of; Surgeon; PO omitted
LYLE, Thomas, Je-145-2; Pvt K Co 2nd TN Cav; 1 Dec 62 to 6 Jul 65; Dumplin PO
LYLE, W. B., U-246-1; Martha J. widow of; Pvt D Co 13th TN Cav; 24 Sep 63 to 5 Sep 65; Erwin PO
LYLE, William, Mu-205-2; Pvt C Co 11th TN Inf; 63 to 65; Williamsport PO; 3rd finger wound, papers lost
LYLES, Alexander, Br-12-6; McPherson PO
LYLES, Ambros, Hw-133-3; Susanna A. widow of; Pvt 16th NC Inf; 3 yrs; Burem's Store PO; CONF
LYLES, John H., Dk-36-1; Cpl B Co 1st TN Mtd Inf; 3-64 to 5-65; Smithville PO
LYLES, William B., Mo-130-2; Pvt F Co 2nd TN Cav; 10-10-62 to 6-65; Ballplay PO
LYMAN, Thomas, Mc-174-6; Pvt; Santfordville PO
LYMONS, Simon, F-42-1(3); Edith widow of; Elba PO; cant tell anything about husband's soldiering
LYNCH, Catherine, Cl-54-2; widow of US Soldier; PO omitted
LYNCH, David, Hi-91-1; Pvt C Co 4th Col US Inf; 64 to 65; Pleasantville PO
LYNCH, Eugene, Mg-199-2; Cpl H Co 1st TN Inf; Sep 61 to 64; Sunbright PO; ruptured at Marietta, TX
LYNCH, Hatfield, Cl-46-3(1); Pvt 9th TN Inf; 63 to 64; Jacket PO
LYNCH, Henry, Mu-210-1; Harriet widow of; I Co 44th Inf; 3 yrs; Spring Hill PO; wounded in left hip
LYNCH, John A., Cl-58-1; Pvt A Co 47th KY Mtd Inf; 7-10-63 to 64; Davo PO; affected heart & eyes
LYNCH, John A., Ge-86-2; Pvt D Co 4th TN Inf; 1 Mar 63 to 2 Aug 65; Thula PO; blood poison & lungs injured
LYNCH, Samuel, Mr-97-2; Pvt; Jarman? PO
LYNCH, Steven, D-64-5; Pvt; Nashville PO
LYNCH, William B., B-2-1; Pvt E Co 24th TN Inf; 10-61 to 10-63; Fairfield PO; eye shot out; CONF
LYNCH, William S., B-11-2(1); Pvt C Co 4th TN Mtd Inf; 12-20-64 to 8-25-65; PO omitted

LYNCH, William W., Jr., C-8-2; Pvt L Co 9th TN Cav; 9-1-63 to 9-11-65; Fincastle PO; bone of left leg affected by horse running over him, receives $49 per year
LYNN, Isaac, Lo-189-1; PO omitted
LYNN, Lemul, Un-255-2; Pvt G Co 7th TN Inf; 10 Dec 64 to 27 Ju 65; Warwick X Roads PO
LYNN, Mycajah, Gr-73-1; Pvt F Co 1st TN Cav; 1 Jan 63 to 25 May 65; Westerville PO; misseray in limbs, contracted in US service
LYNN, Nathan, H-54-5; Pvt G Co 98th OH Inf; 8-11-62 to 6-9-65; Sherman Heights PO; contract diarrhea, fistula & piles in the army and not now able to do but little work
LYNN, Newton, Ro-205-3; Pvt A Co 2nd TN Inf; 10 Aug 61 to 8 Feb 65; Knott PO; rheumatism &c
LYNN, William H., W-193-2; Martha J. widow of; Pvt G Co 5th TN Cav; 9-10-62 to was killed while in the service of the goverment in 1863
LYON, F. Marion, Ha-111-4(1); Pvt D Co 1st TN Art; 63 to May 65; Upper Clinch PO; CONF
LYON, Landon A., Su-242-1; Cpl H Co 13th TN Cav; Aug 64 to 5 Sep65; Bluff City PO; rupture (privates), horse jumping fence, Bulls Gap fight, discharge was sent to Washington City to obtain back pay and has not been returned
LYON, Landon E., O-138-4; Pvt; 9th Civil Dist
LYONS, Abram, Hw-127-3; Pvt M Co 1st US (Col) Hvy Art; 10 Oct 64 to 31 Mar 66; Rogersville PO; rheumatism
LYONS, C. G., Hw-125-2; Cpl A Co 12th TN Cav; Aug 62 to 65; Surgoinsville PO; shot in left hip
LYONS, Edward F., K-156-4; Albertain, widow of; Pvt 1st TN Inf; 61 to 64; 25 Pine St, Knoxville PO; CONF
LYONS, George, Gr-78-2; Pvt B Co 8th TN Cav; 1 Oct 63 to 11 Sep 65; Spring House PO
LYONS, Henry, Hm-104-4(2); alias Henry Line; Pvt D Co 9th TN Cav; Sep 63 to __ (9 mos); Morristown PO; typhoid fever located right leg, no discharge
LYONS, Joseph, Hm-104-3(1); alias Joseph E. Line; Pvt E Co 9th TN Cav; 28 Nov 64 to 11 Sep 65; Alpha PO; lungs affected, enlisted as Joseph Lyons
LYONS, Joseph, Ct-39-3; Pvt H Co TN Cav; 63 to 65; Gap Run PO
LYONS, Katy, Hw-125-2; Pvt TN Cav; 61 to 65; Stony Point PO
LYONS, Martha, Ct-41-3; widow?; 8th Dist
LYONS, Martin, Mg-198-2; Sgt F Co 1st TN Inf; 17 Aug 61 to 17 Sep 64; Kismet PO; rheumatism affected eyes
LYONS, Oston, Wi-270-1; Pvt C Co 142nd IN INF; 15 Oct 64 to 14 Jul 65; Gingo PO
LYONS, Samuell, Rb-206-1; Capt D Co; Greenbrier PO; is now in the Revenew at Distilery
LYONS, Thomas Sr., Fe-41-2; 2nd Civil Dist
LYONS, William, D-45-4; F Co 11th NY Inf; 64 to 65; Nashville PO
LYPE, Thomas, Hw-119-3(1); Pvt; Alum Well PO
LYPE, Wyley, Hw-127-2; Pvt K Co 13th TN Cav; 1 Oct 64 to 5 Sep 65; Rogersville PO; wounded in breast & saber cut on head
LYTLE, Gardner, Cr-7-1; 9th Dist
LYTLE, John, D-77-1; Pvt F Co 111th US Inf; Jun 63 to May 65; Nashville PO
LYTON, William, D-60-2; 222 Hardie St, Nashville PO
LYTTLE, Simon, Sh-146-4; US Sol; 3rd Civil Dist
MABE, George, Hw-130-2; Pvt F Co 2nd TN Inf; 20 Jul 62 to 15 Jun 65; Lee Valley PO
MABE, Samuel, Ro-206-3; Pvt C Co 3rd TN Inf; 64 to 65; Kingston PO
MABE, Samuel N., Cl-52-2; Pvt K Co 3rd TN Cav; 6-1-63 to 3-1-65; Quarter PO
MABERRY, Logan H., J-77-1; Pvt K Co 1st TN Cav; Gainesboro PO; acute chronic sore eyes
MABERRY, William, Di-36-2; Sarah Mitchel formerly widow of; Pvt 64th TN Inf; 12-10-61 to 11-30-64; Bellsburgh PO; CONF
MABRY, James P., La-111-1; Cpl I Co 1st AL Cav; 7-21-62 to 6-20-65; Pleasant Point PO; black scurvy caused as prisoner at Andersonville 17 mos
MABURY, James, Hy-75-1; Pvt; Stanton PO
MacDONALD, George W. D., Mo-128-1; Pvt K Co 12th TN Cav; 3-1-64 to 10-7-65; Tellico Plains PO
MACK, Alexander, Mu-190-2; June Moore daughter of; Culleoka PO; she does not know command of her husband?
MACK, John, H-53-1; Cpl B Co 14th WI Inf; 9-21-61 to 10-9-65; Chattanooga PO; reenlisted 12-11-63
MACKERY, Jas. B., Sn-262-1; Pvt F Co 2nd TN Cav; 11-1-61 to 2-63; Fountain Head PO; CONF
MACKEY, Bery, Gr-81-3(1); Pvt C Co 3rd TN Inf; 12 Feb 62 to 23 Mar 65; Clear Spring PO; I have though my expirer disabled me
MACKEY, Eric, Gr-82-1; Catharine widow of; Pvt A Co 12th TN Cav; 63 to 65 (1 yr); Ambro PO
MACKLIN, George E., Hy-84-3(5); Pvt A Co; Sep 64 to Mar 65; Woodville PO; rhumatism, discharge lost or misplaced
MACKLIN, Joseph, F-38-1; Pvt B Co 7th TN Cav; Oct 62 to Apr 65; Braden PO; CONF
MACLIN, Jerry, F-38-1; Pvt A Co 39th TN Inf; May 62 to May 65; Mason PO
MACON, Eliza, Wl-297-2; widow; Dist No 12
MACON, James M., Hm-106-1; Pvt A Co 2nd TN Cav; 1 Aug 62 to 1 Aug 65 (2 yrs 6 mos); Chestnut Bloom PO
MADAN, Andrew, Mc-114-3; Pvt D Co 5th TN Inf; 8-31-64 to 6-26-65; Raht PO
MADDEN, John C., Ja-84-2; Cpl C Co 5th TN Inf; 2-25-62 to 4-4-65; Norman's Store PO; wounded in ___ affected eyes
MADDEN, Michael, Ch-13-2; Landsman, no vessel, TN Vol Navy ___ brook; 64 to 3-65 (1 yr 4 mos); Wild Goose PO; lump on back supposed to have incured, first in West Gulf squadron and was transferred to MS squadron
MADDOCK, John, H-71-1; Lizzie Garrette wife of; Pvt C Co 9th l? Art; 62 to 65; Chattanooga PO
MADDOR, Lawson, Co-68-1; Hospital Stuart D Co 13th TN Cav; 62 to 65; Costner PO
MADE, William, H-49-1; Pvt H Co 1st US Eng; 62 to 65; Falling Water PO
MADISON, George, Hu-99-1; George Sutler, alias?; Pvt I Co 13th US Col Inf; 11 Jun 64 to 10 Jun 66; Johnsonville PO
MADISON, James, Sh-196-1; Pvt I Co 4th US Hvy Art; 64 to 2-24-66; 120 Dunlap St, Memphis PO
MADISON, John, A-4-3; Pvt D Co 125th PA Inf; 7-26-62 to 5-18-63; Coal Creek PO; spinal injury
MADISON, King S., Sh-161-1; US Sol; 16th Dist
MADISON, Manly, Se-228-3; Sol; 10th Dist
MADISON, Wesley, Sh-161-2; US Sol; 16th Dist
MADRON, George W., Jo-150-2; Pvt D Co 13th TN Cav; 22 Sep 63 to 5 Sep 65; Key Station PO
MADRON, Robbert, C-25-2; Pvt E Co 134th IN Inf; 5-5-64 to 9-2-64; Hatmaker PO
MAGEE, David A., Dy-25-2; Ordley K Co 53rd TN Inf; Dec 61 to May 63; Newbern PO; shot in hand, broken fingers; CONF
MAGGART, John A., Sm-170-3; 6th Cpl C Co 8th TN Mtd Inf; 1-27-64 to 8-17-65; Maggart PO; inflamatory rumatism
MAGGART, William P., Sn-260-5; Cpl A Co 1st TN Mtd Inf; 12-20-63 to 2-7-65; A.B.C. PO
MAGILL, James M., Ro-203-5(1); Pvt K Co 1st TN Inf; 9 Aug 61 to 17 Sep 64; Wheat PO; gunshot in arm
MAGILL, Robert M., Ro-203-5(1); Pvt C Co 7th TN Inf; 20 Aug 64 to 27 Jun 65; Wheat PO; asthma & neuralgia
MAGRUDER, Michel, Sh-188-1; Pvt Battery I 61st Regt Art; 3-64 to 1-10-65; 274 Saffron St, Memphis PO
MAGURES, James F., D-90-1; Pvt C Co 4th TN Mtd Inf; ___ to Aug 30 65 (8 or 9 mos); Nashville PO; strains & hemorhoids, he forgets exact dates
MAGVEE, Alford?, K-167-3; Mary widow of; Pvt D Co 1st TN Hvy; 20 May 64 to 10 Mar 66; Knoxville PO
MAHAFFY, John, H-66-2; Pvt D Co 7th KY Vol; 8-19-61 to 10-5-64; Chattanooga PO
MAHAN, Elcanah, Ja-86-2; Jane D. widow of; Pvt; 61 to __; Snowhill PO; died Nashville TN
MAHAN, William P., Hw-131-4; Cpl B Co 1st TN Cav; 13 Mar 62 to __; Otes PO; imprisoned and payrolled
MAHON, James, Mu-209-4; Pvt E Co 9th TN Cav; Jun 1 63 to Mar 1 65; Columbia PO; CONF

MAHONE, William, Gi-135-1; alias William Alexander; Pvt E Co 111th TN Inf; 62 to 66; Lynnville PO
MAHONEY, Josiah, Wa-274-2; 2nd Lt D Co 8th TN Cav; 3 Jun 63 to 11 Sep 65; Jonesboro PO; chronic diarrhoea
MAHONEY, Mahlew, Wa-272-1; Sgt D Co 8th TN Cav; 28 Sep 63 to 26 May 65; Locust Mount PO; chronic rheumatism, deaf in left ear, injury to right hip, scrotal hernia, injury to collar bone
MAHONEY, Nathan H., Wa-264-1; Elizabeth widow of; Pvt D Co 4th TN Cav; Jul 22 63 to Feb 11 64; Jonesboro PO; killed while doing picket duty
MAHONEY, Mrs. Wanda (see Vinston, H. L.)
MAHONEY, William, Ro-209-4; Glen Alice PO; CONF
MAHONEY, William, Ge-96-4; Pvt B Co 4th TN Cav; 5 Nov 62 to 12 Jul 65; Chuckey City PO; lung & heart dibility &c
MAILER, William H., Pu-144-3; Pvt G Co 6th KY Inf; 61 to ___; Ai PO; chronic dirhea
MAIN, Calvin, Jo-150-2; Pvt I Co 13th TN Cav; 22 Sep 63 to 5 Sep 65; Key Station PO
MAIN, Calvin, Jo-151-3; Rachel widow of; US Cav; Shown's & Roads PO; died in 1889
MAIN, Sidney, Jo-151-3; Pvt I Co 13th TN Cav; 22 Sep 63 to 5 Sep 65; Shown's & Roads PO; disease of eyes, ruptured
MAINE, Atwood W., Hw-127-3; Pvt B Co 1st NY Inf; 5 Sep 64 to 10 Jun 65; Rogersville PO
MAINE, Lemuel, C-33-3; Sgt G Co 2nd TN Inf; 8-1-63 to 8-3-65; Newcomb PO
MAINES, Nancy B., K-181-4(1); widow; Pvt B Co 2nd TN Cav; Fleniken PO; rheumatic 25 yrs
MAIRRIETT, James, St-5-41-1; Pvt D Co 8th? TN Cav; 6-21-63 to 9-11-65; Elizabethton PO; chronick rhumatism
MAJOR, Frank, Ru-241-4; Allen widow of; Pvt TN Inf; Murfreesboro PO; killed at Murfreesboro PO
MAJOR, John W., H-73-4(2); Chattanooga PO
MAJOR, Prince, Ru-238-1; Pvt L Co 1st USC Inf; 63 to Apr 65; Murfreesboro PO
MAJORS, John, Ro-209-3; Pvt; Glen Alice PO; CONF
MAJORS, John H., Ca-20-2; Pvt C Co 5th TN Cav; 1-1-61 to 64; Woodbury PO
MAJORS, Susan (see Johnson, Millo)
MAJORS, Thomas, K-168-4; Pvt G Co 1st TN Inf; Adair's Creek PO
MALACHI, James, D-69-2; US Sol, discharge lost; 25 Robinson St, Nashville PO
MALBAY, Reubin, Hw-131-2; Elisabeth J.; Pvt L Co 8th TN Cav; 1 Oct 63 to 2 Jun 65; Bulls Gap PO
MALCOM, William? B., Je-144-2; Pvt B Co 1st TN Cav; 63 to 65; Talbotts PO; lunge trouble
MALICOAT, John, Gr-81-4(2); Mary widow of; Pvt A Co 12th TN Cav; 63 to 65 (1 yr); Shelton's Ford PO; sore eyes, died January 13, 1888
MALITON, John J., Hw-133-3; Sgt K Co 16th NC Inf; 61 to Apr 65; Sigornsville PO; lung disease; CONF
MALLARD, Aarchie, D-87-1; Pvt TN; Nashville PO
MALLARD, John R., Mu-210-6; Pvt A Co 4th TN Cav; 17 Jun 61 to 24 May 65; Mallard PO; shot through thigh; CONF
MALLARD, Joseph W., Mr-102-3; Pvt F Co 5th TN Cav; 9-8-62 to 6-25-65; Dorans Cove, AL, PO
MALLECOAT, Milton, C-24-1; Pvt C Co 4th TN Cav; 5-1-62 to 6-12-65; Boy PO; cr. dirhea & kidney desease
MALLICAT, Joel, Gr-71-1; Pvt F Co 9th TN Cav; 14 Oct 63 to 11 Sep 65; Bean Station PO
MALLICOAT, Calvin, C-28-2(1); Pvt E Co 25th IL Inf; 7-31-63 to ___ (4 mos 10 days); Big Creek Gap PO; rheumatism
MALLICOAT, William S., Gr-79-2; Cpl A Co 9th TN Cav; 10 Sep 63 to 11 Sep 65; Thorn Hill PO
MALLICOT, Fayette, Gr-79-2; Mirie Dalton formerly widow of; Ball Point PO; CONF
MALLORY, Charles H., Sh-145-2; alias Godwin, Charles M.; Coxswaim US Sabine US Waschesatts; Mar 65 to 69; Millington PO; chronic diarhea & piles, rectum, first Michigan USM Capt Roe then US Sabine Capt R. G. Lowery
MALLORY, George, Mt-136-1; Pvt F Co 15th TN; Nov 7 64 to Apr 15 66; Port Royal PO
MALLORY, Jack, D-77-2; Nashville PO
MALLORY, William, Hw-128-1; Tempa widow of; Pvt K Co 13th TN Cav; Choptack PO; died in time of war

MALLORY, William, Col, D-46-1; Pvt E Co 16th Col Inf; 4-61 to 4-64; Nashville PO
MALLORY, William M., Ma-116-1; Pvt C Co 6th TN Cav; 64 to 65; Hatchie PO
MALLOY, Mary (see Phillips, Anderson)
MALO, John, Pi-155-2; Pvt B Co 13th KY Cav; 8-63 to 1-65; Byrdstown PO; none that is known
MALON, William, Wa-271-1; Pvt B Co 12th TN Cav; 14 Jun 63 to 25 Oct 65; Boones Creek PO
MALONE, Andrew J., Ge-97-1; Pvt A Co 4th Inf; 26 Dec 63 to 2 Aug 65; Maltsberger PO; chronic diarrha
MALONE, Autnil, Gi-135-2; Pvt E Co 110th TN Inf; 63 to 66; Lynnville PO
MALONE, D. E., Gi-122-3; Pvt A Co 53rd TN Inf; Dec 61 to May 65; Prospect Sta. PO; prison 18 mos; CONF
MALONE, Daniel, Fe-41-2; 2nd Civil Dist
MALONE, David, S-214-2; Pvt H Co 13th KY Cav; 19 Sep 61 to 10 Jan 65; Glenmary PO
MALONE, George, Ru-236-1; Pvt C Co 110th TN Inf; Pulaski PO; 62 to 65; Murfreesboro PO; suffering from piles & fistulow, they forget date of enlistment & discharge
MALONE, Jackson, Dk-35-1; Pvt A Co; Temperance Hall PO
MALONE, James, Sn-259-2; Pvt C Co 14th ___; 10-1-62 to 4-1-65; Bransford PO
MALONE, James (Bunk Alin), Dk-32-3; Pvt D Co 1st TN Mtd Inf; 10-20-64 to 8-25-65; Temperance Hall PO
MALONE, James B., Sm-173-1; Pvt G Co 1st TN Mtd Inf; 3-5-64-1 to 4-25-65; Sykes PO
MALONE, James L., Dk-35-2; Pvt G Co 1st TN Mtd Inf; Temperance Hall PO
MALONE, John, Ge-92-4; Pvt K Co 1st TN Cav; 12 Jul 62 to 5 Jun 65; Laurel Gap PO; rheumatism & purture
MALONE, John, Hw-121-4(3); Pvt A Co 4th TN Inf; Van Hill PO
MALONE, John H., Ge-97-4; Sol US; 20th Civil Dist
MALONE, John M., Ge-101-1; Pvt K Co 1st TN Cav; 16 Apr 63 to 19 Jun 65; Locust Sp. PO; Murfresborough hospitle
MALONE, Mary P. (see Baker, Clement)
MALONE?, Monroe, Dk-32-2; Pvt A Co 5th TN Cav; 11-23-63 to 5-14-65; Alexandria PO; defective in mind from fever
MALONE, Preston, Ru-238-1; Sgt A Co 14th USC Inf; 1 Oct 63 to 26 Mar 66; Murfreesboro PO
MALONE, Rebecca (see Foster, Isaac B.)
MALONE, Sanders, Ru-238-1; Pvt B Co 111th USC Inf; 22 Dec 63 to 31 Apr 66; Murfreesboro PO
MALONE, Thomas B., Ge-91-2; Pvt K Co 1st TN Cav; 12 Jul 62 to 12 Jun 65 (8 yrs 1 mo); Greeneville PO; diahhrea & wounded in left thigh
MALONE, Thomas D., Ge-92-5; Pvt B Co 3rd TN Mtd Inf; Romeo PO
MALONE, William, Wi-278-1; Pvt C Co 4th TN Mtd Inf; Nov 11 64 to Aug 10 65; Franklin PO; ruptured & mashed leg
MALONE, William A., Gi-127-3; Scout Pvt 9th & 10th IN Vols; May 62 to 64; Pulaski PO; was scout under Genl. Stockweather
MALONE, William J., Ge-92-3; Pvt D Co 8th TN Inf; 62 to 6 Jun 65; Greeneville PO
MALONEY, George L., K-169-1; 1st Lt C Co 52nd TN Inf; 18 Apr 62 to 28 Apr 65; Knoxville PO
MALONEY, James S., Ge-91-1; Pvt B Co 1st TN Cav; Aug 12 62 to Jun 9 65; Greeneville PO; rheumatism
MALTSBERGER, John, Ge-97-2; Pvt M Co 1st TN Cav; 25 Nov 62 to 19 Jun 65; Maltsberger PO; diareah
MAMGRUM, Louiza (see Berry, Robert H.)
MAN, Andrew J., Ge-99-2; Pvt M Co 13th TN Cav; May 64 to Jul 65; Limestone Springs PO; couldn't get exact dates
MANAGER, Leslie, Hy-81-1; Brownsville PO
MANARD, Ezekel, Sh-188-1; Pvt D Co 20th KY Inf; 8-61 to 5-61 (sic); 274 Saffron St, Memphis PO
MANEESE, Isaac, Rb-223-1; Pvt F Co 15th TN Inf; 63 to 65; Springfield PO
MANES, Dallas, Cl-53-2; Pvt L Co 8th TN Cav; 9-17-63 to 9-11-65; Springdale PO; lassap? sit
MANES, Duke, Gr-79-4; Pvt E Co 9th TN Cav; Thorn Hill PO; hearing
MANES, James A., Se-230-3; Richison's Cove PO

MANES, John, Se-230-3; Pvt E Co 48th TN Inf; 2 yrs 5 mos; Richison's Cove PO; CONF
MANES, Preston, C1-53-2; Pvt L Co 8th TN Cav; 9-18-63 to 5-14-65; Springdale PO
MANES, William D., Br-8-4(2); Pvt B Co 5th TN Mtd Inf; 8-26-64 to 7-19-65; Cleo PO
MANESS, Howard, Ha-113-1; Pvt G Co 1st TN Cav; 20 Jun 62 to 5 Jun 65; Sneedville PO
MANESS, James, De-22-3; Pvt A Co 51st TN Inf; 1 Sep 61 to 15 Oct 62; Dunbar PO; CONF
MANEY, John (see Riggs, John)
MANEYMAKER, Elizebeth, K-176-3; widow of Sol US; Pvt G Co 6th TN Inf; 16 Apr 62 to 17 May 65; Smithwood PO
MANFORD, William, Dk-32-4; Beck widow of; Pvt A Co 5th TN Cav; 8-14-62 to 6-25-65; Liberty PO
MANGER, Henry, Ro-202-3(1); Sgt G Co 3rd TN Cav; Jul 63 to Aug 65; Paw Paw Ford PO; rheumatism
MANGOLD, William, Wa-276-2; Pvt D Co 8th TN Cav; Nov 1 64 to Sep 11 65; Leesburg PO; hernia
MANGRUN, James N., Mu-209-5; Pvt A Co 9th TN Cav; Oct 1 62 to Jul 1 63; Columbia PO; CONF
MANGUM, James A., We-225-4(3); 1st Lt M Co 6th TN Cav; 62 to Aug 6 65; Dresden PO; rheumatism & deafness
MANIEL, James R., Mn-125-1; US Sol; Ninth Dist
MANING, Joe, Hy-82-1; Pvt B Co 5th MS Inf; 62 to 66; Rudolph PO
MANING, John, A-7-3; Pvt D Co 4th __; 10-27-64 to 7-20-65; Robertsville PO
MANIS, Danial, Hw-121-3(2); Pvt A Co 50th VA Inf; 7 Jun __ to 30 Jun 65;(4 yrs); Segonsville PO; CONF
MANIS, Henry J., Hw-119-3(1); Pvt E Co 1st TN Cav; 1 Nov 62 to __ (1 yr 16 mos); Alum Well PO; measles & mumps, spinal affec.
MANIS, James R., Mr-102-2; Cpl A Co 7th TN Mtd Inf; 9-19-64 to 7-7-65; South Pittsburg PO; shot in right leg in the war
MANIS, John, Pi-153-1; Pvt K Co 4th TN Inf; 2-15-65 to 8-15-65; Chanute PO
MANIS, Lucinda (see Dyer, Lawson)
MANIS, Thomas D., Je-138-2; Cpl B Co 9th TN Cav; 28 Sep 63 to 11 Sep 65; Kansas PO
MANIS, William, Hw-121-3(2); Marry J. widow of; Pvt F Co 1st TN Cav; 1 Mar 62 to 30 Mar 65; New Hope PO
MANKER, John J., H-54-3; Pvt B Co 34th OH Inf--9-2-61 to 8-16-62; Capt B Co 50th OH Inf--8-16-62 to 3-26-64; Sherman Heights PO; wounded left thigh at Princton, WV
MANLEY, Alec, Cr-14-1; Pvt; Clarksburg PO; heavy artilary
MANLEY, Ancel W., Ro-203-1; Ethel PO; CONF
MANLEY, Andrew, Wi-276-2; Pvt D Co 10th TN Cav; 4 May 62 to May 65; Beechville PO; CONF
MANLEY, William H., Gr-75-2; Pvt I Co 155th IL Inf; 20 Feb 65 to 4 Sep 65; Doyal PO; constipation
MANLY, David F., Je-145-2; 1st Lt B Co 1st TN Lt Art; 1 Apr 63 to 20 Jul 65; Dumplin PO
MANLY, W. J., He-57-2; Pvt B Co 3rd TN Cav; 8-5-63 to 10-16-64; Juno PO; prisoner Danvill 8 mos
MANN, Allen, K-156-4; Pvt R Co 1st OH Vol Hvy Art; 3 Oct 62 to 1 May 65; 98 Crozier St, Knoxville PO
MANN, Danil, Sn-264-2; Pvt A Co; Feb 63 to 65; Mittchellsville PO; this man cripled from exposur in the army, his papers lost; Capt Hull, Col Cox, Gen Hatch, Atlanta discharged
MANN, Dave, Hy-85-1; Cpl A Co 61st TN; 62 to 62 (2 yrs 7 mos); Caralina PO
MANN, David, Sh-159-6; Pvt A Co 55th AL; 10 May 61 to 65; Memphis PO
MANN, George W., Su-239-2; Pvt H Co 8th TN Cav; 15 Mar 65 to 19 Sep 65; Rotherwood PO
MANN, Gus, Hy-84-3(5); Woodville PO
MANN, J. F., Je-135-1(3); Pvt B Co 2nd TX Cav; 3 Apr 61 to 11 Sep 65; PO omitted; CONF
MANN, Loudon, L-101-1; alias London Shepard; Pvt B Co 2nd TN C Inf; Mar 62 to Sep 65; Henning PO; dont know exact dates of E & D
MANN, Samuel, Cf-42-1; Pvt L Co 10th MI Inf; 2-2-65 to 11-11-65; Hickerson PO
MANNERS, Alex, Wl-291-1; S US; Lagnordo PO
MANNERS, Christopher C., Sm-169-1; Pvt E Co 4th TN Mtd Inf; 8-11-64 to 8-25-65; Maggart PO; lungs affected
MANNERS, Michael, Sm-172-1; Pvt G Co 1st TN Inf; 9-64 to 8-65; Lancaster PO; jaundice
MANNING, Alfred, Sh-162-2(1); US Sol; Ramsey PO
MANNING, Benjamin, Se-225-1; Pvt G Co 5th TN Inf; 22 Nov 47 to 20 Jul 48; Allensville PO
MANNING, Charley H., H-51-4; Pvt K Co 2nd OH Inf; 7-24-62 to 6-4-65; Hill City PO
MANNING, Christopher C., K-166-3; Pvt D Co 9th TN Cav; 2 Sep 63 to __; Knoxville PO; chronic rheumatism
MANNING, Marion, Di-34-2; Pvt A Co 8th US Col Hvy Art; 2-1-64 to 7-10-66; Dickson PO
MANNING, Matthew, Gu-48-2; Pvt B Co 44th AL Col Inf; 61 to 64; Tracy City PO; shot in hip; lost record of discharge
MANNING, Samuel W., Cu-16-2; Pvt F Co 5th TN Inf; 62 to 65; Litton PO; disease of bowels
MANNING, Thomas F., Sh-204-1; Mississippi Ave, Memphis PO
MANNING, William, Cu-18-1; Pvt D Co 2nd TN Inf; 12-1-61 to 8-3-65; Glen Alice PO; lost one eye
MANNING, William J., H-58-5; Georgia A. widow of; Pvt C Co 5th TN Inf; Soddy PO
MANNUS, Jackson, D-43-2; Sol; Hothned St, Nashville PO
MANSFIELD, James, Sq-164-3(1); Pvt E Co 6th TN Mtd Inf; 8-11-64 to 6-30-65; Dunlap PO
MANSFIELD, William E., Je-146-2; Pvt D Co 3rd TN Cav; 1 Dec 62 to 10 Jan 65; White Pine PO; catarrh and deafness
MANSON, Andrew, K-161-3; Knoxville PO; contracted asthma
MANSON, Johnson, Hy-75-1; Pvt; May 63 to Aug 65; Dancyville PO; says his wound hurts him, wounded Lovejoy, Aug 12 64
MANSON, Martin C., Col?, Wl-295-1; Martin Clark; Cpl G Co 14th TN Inf; Feb 26 64 to Sep 1 66; Lebanon PO
MANSON, William, Ru-13-2; Pvt; 1 yr 6 mos; PO omitted
MANSON, William, Gr-75-1; Pvt K Co 12th KY Hvy Art; 28 Sep 64 to 24 Apr 66; Tampico PO; lung trouble & piles
MANTING, Isac, Sh-183-2; Memphis PO; papers lost
MANTLO, Franklin, Rb-220-2; Pvt C Co 49th TN Inf; M 10 62 to No 10 63; Springfield PO
MANUEL, Alexander H., Dy-31-1; Pvt D Co 7th TN Cav; Aug 62 to 26 Oct 63; PO omitted
MANUEL, Hoyl, Mc-112-3; Louisa Wilds former widow of; Cpl A Co 1st TN Col Hvy Art; 61 to 3-64; Athens PO
MANUS, Richard L., Ch-17-2; Pvt C Co 7th TN Cav; 9-1-63 to 8-4-65; Masseyville PO; bone disease
MAPELS, George, Se-222-3; Pvt M Co 2nd TN Cav; 8 Nov 62 to 6 Jul 65; 4th Dist
MAPELS, Guilford R., Se-222-1; Pvt E Co 2nd TN Cav; 8 Dec 62 to 26 May 65; Harrisburg PO
MAPELS, William, C1-53-2; Pvt A Co 49th KY Inf; 12-27-63 to 9-26-64; Springdale PO
MAPES, Samuel G., Hy-79-1; Musician F Co 50th NY Vol; Jun 61 to Jun 65; Brownsville PO; supposed to have contracted confection (sic) of liver, discharge papers at ____ KY
MAPLES, Anderson J., Br-10-1; Pvt I Co 11th TN Cav; 9-27-62 to 10-9-65; Cleveland PO
MAPLES, David C., Je-143-3; Pvt E Co 2nd TN Cav; 22 Sep 62 to 20 Aug 65; Mossy Creek PO; total blindness
MAPLES, George W., Se-229-1; Pvt I Co 2nd TN Cav; 22 Sep 62 to 7 Dec 63; Banner PO; rheumatism
MAPLES, James, Se-220-3; Pvt I Co 2nd TN Cav; 16 Sep 62 to 5 Jul 65; Emerts Cave PO
MAPLES, James F., K-177-5; Pvt K Co 3rd TN Inf; 62 to Mar 65; Powells Station PO; gun shot wound right thigh
MAPLES, John, Je-140-1; Mary A. P. widow of; Pvt K Co 3rd TN Inf; PO omitted
MAPLES, McCajah R., Wa-261-2; Pvt; 62 to 65; Conkling PO; CONF
MAPLES, Mitchel, Se-225-3; Pvt M Co 2nd TN Cav; 8 Nov 62 to 1 Apr 63; Cotlettsburg PO; diarrhoea and piles 25 yrs
MAPLES, P. (see McCarter, Joseph)

MAPLES, Reedmon, Se-222-2; Pvt M Co 2nd TN Cav; 22 Sep 62 to 14 Jul 65; Harrisburg PO; rumatism & results
MAPLES, Samuel, Se-229-1; Bugular I Co 2nd TN Cav; 22 Sep 62 to 6 Jul 65; Banner PO; kidney & testicals affected
MAPLES, William, Se-219-1; Pvt M Co 2nd TN Cav; 1 Jan 64 to 8 Jun 65; East Fork PO; chronic diarhoe, deafness
MAPLES, William D., Se-220-2; Pvt E Co 9th TN Cav; 1 Oct 63 to 11 Sep 65; Emerts Cave PO
MAPS, R. F., Gi-122-4; Pvt K Co 1st TN Cav; Oct. 64 to 65; Prospect Sta. PO; CONF
MARABLE, Joel, Mt-149-1; Pvt K Co 8th KY Hvy Art; 3-62 to 3-65; Palmyra PO; 2 fingers broken knee dislocated, 2 ribbs broken
MARABLE, Montgomery, Mt-148-1; Louisa widow of; Orgains X Roads PO; this widow can not give any satisfactory information
MARANVILLE, R. P., Bo-19-2; Pvt E Co 112th IL Mtd Inf; 8-12-62 to 5-30-65; South Rockford PO
MARBURY, Isack F., Be-5-1; Lule E. widow of; Pvt 7th TN Cav; 12 Feb 63 to 9 Aug 65; Bilbrey PO (Call. Co.); come home & died, widow draws pension
MARCH, John, D-66-1; Cpl I Co 12th US Col Inf; Aug 63 to 16 Jan 66; Nashville PO; 534 S Cherry PO
MARCH, John W., Col, Li-1521; Pvt C Co 44th OH; 62 to 65; Blakeville PO; shot 7 times--3 times seriously
MARCH, Lewis, D-94-1; Jane G. widow; Pvt G Co 48th IL Inf; 63 to 64; c/o E R Campbell, Nashville PO; contracted consumtpion, black woman in need
MARCH, Sinore, Fr-115-1; Nails B Co 4th MD Cav; Cowan PO; he cannot recollect
MARCH, Somers, Fr-115-1; Therey widow of; Cpl E Co 44th US Inf; 5-28-64 to 4-30-66; Cowan PO
MARCHBANKS, Elijah, De-26-2; H Co 9th TN; 62 to 65; Parkers Ld?; CONF
MARCHBANKS, Sam, Ms-183-1; Mary widow of; 17th Civil Dist; rheumatism 20 yrs
MARCUM, Arthur, C-33-3; Pvt H Co 2nd TN; 11-14-61 to 10-64; Newcomb PO
MARCUM, Rubin, S-212-1; Pvt TN; 14 Sep 62 to __; Onida PO; shot threw right arm
MARCUM, Simeon, S-215-1; Cpl C Co 32nd KY Inf; 3 Nov 62 to 12 Aug 63; Jeffers PO
MARCUM, Squire H., S-178-1; Pvt B Co 1st TN Inf; 9 Aug 61 to 17 Sep 65?; Hardin Valley PO
MARGAN, James H., We-220-1; Pvt I Co 6th TN Cav; 16 Mar 62 to 26 Jul 65; Catham PO; ruptured of testcel
MARGE, John, Ge-91-4; Pvt F Co 23rd IN Reg; 1 Jan 61 to 31 Aug 65; Greeneville PO; rheumatism
MARGERUM, George J., H-74-1; Pvt; Whiteside PO
MARHALL, Edmond, Ru-231-1; Pvt H Co 110th TN Inf; 3 yrs; Lavergne PO; bayonet wount
MARINE, George W., Se-225-3; Pvt A Co 6th TN Inf; Sevierville PO; rheumatism, ruptured 25 yrs
MARING, David W., K-174-1(1); Pvt D Co 2nd TN Cav; 1 Oct 62 to 25 Jul 65; Snoderly PO; leg broak sance the ware
MARION, Alexander, Un-252-2; Pvt B Co 49th KY Inf; 1 Jun 63 to 1 Dec 64; Simcoe PO
MARK, John, Wa-260-2; US Sol; 1st Civil Dist
MARKLAND, James, Ct-45-2; Pvt B Co 13th TN Cav; 8-15-64 to 9-5-65; Carter Furnace PO; typhoid fever Knoxville 1865; transferred to 13th TN Cav 8-64, served in 4th TN Inf 14 mos
MARKLAND, Neson J., Ct-35-1; Pvt F Co 13th TN Cav; 9-22-63 to 7-22-65; Hampton PO; in line of duty US Army
MARKLAND, Phillip, Ct-45-2; Evaline widow of; Carter Furnace PO; no record of enlistment or discharge
MARKLAND, Wesley G., H-54-5; Capt F Co 37th IN Inf; 10-11-61 to 64; Kings Point PO; suffering piles contracted in the army
MARKLAND, William B., Ct-45-2; Pvt B Co 13th TN Cav; 9-20-63 to 9-5-65; Carter Furnace PO; small pox Nashville TN 1864
MARKO, Mack, Li-149-2; Pvt K Co 110th US Col Inf; 1-13-64 to 12-15-66; Fayetteville PO
MARKS, Guff, Gi-131-2; Cook E Co 7th IA Inf; 16 Nov 63 to 23 Dec 64; Bass PO; was never discharged

MARKS, Jonas, Gi-127-4; Pvt G Co 111th TN Col Inf; 1-27-64 to 4-30-66; Pulaski PO
MARKS, Samuel N., Dy-25-7(3); Pvt AR Gurbers? Battry; May 61 to Apr 65; Newbern PO; Goribors? Battry, First MO; CONF
MARKUM, Edward, Sh-168-1; Pvt C Co 132nd IN Inf; 65 to 66; 129 Poplar St, Memphis PO
MARKWOOD, D. D., Wa-264-1; Capt H Co 8th TN Cav; 27 Sep 63 to 11 Sep 65; Jonesboro PO; chronic rheumatism
MARKWOOD, Lewis A., Wa-264-1; 2nd Lt H Co 8th TN Cav; 27 Sep 63 to 11 Sep 65; Jonesboro PO; wounded gun shot
MARLER, David, Ct-40-2; Pvt F Co 40th US Col Inf; Elizabethton PO
MARLER, George W., Br-13-2; Sgt E Co 4th TN Cav; 11-11-61 to 7-12-65; Georgetown PO; chronic bronchitis caused by measles
MARLER, William D., Ru-241-3; Pvt H Co 8th TN Cav; Feb 65 to May 65; Murfreesboro PO; duble hernia
MARLIN, Ethan C., Sh-177-1; Memphis? PO
MARLIN, Robert, Mu-209-7; Pvt; Columbia PO: CONF
MARLOW, Benjamin, A-9-1; Pvt G Co 7th TN Mtd Inf; 11-8-64 to 7-27-65; Ligias PO
MARLOW, Rubin, C-26-2; Pvt A Co 7th TN Inf; 4-6-62 to 4-20-65; Hy House PO
MARLOW, Thomas, C-27-2; Pvt A Co 1st TN Inf; 8-2-61 to 9-17-64; Caryville PO
MARMON, James R., Sm-169-3(5); Pvt A Co 8th TN Inf; 1-10-65 to 8-14-65; Defeated PO
MARNEY, David V., Lo-187-4; Pvt H Co 5th TN Inf; 7 Mar 62 to 16 May 65; Philadelphia PO; cripled in left hip
MARNEY, John, Ro-201-3(1); Sgt F Co 1st TN Inf; 9 Aug 61 to 3 Feb 63; Kingston PO
MARNEY, Robert, Me-94-1; Pvt C Co 42nd Inf; Euchee PO; claims discharge lost--prisoner 3 mos
MARNEY, Samuel, Ro-208-1; Pvt H Co 5th TN Inf; 7 Mar 62 to 16 May 65; Erie PO
MARQUIS, John, K-161-1; Julia widow of; Knoxville PO
MARR, James, Br-12-5, Pvt B Co 1st TN Art; 6-10-63 to 7-20-65; Sydneyton PO; enlargement of side
MARR, Nathan C., O-142-1; Pvt E Co 48th KY? Inf; 8 Jul 63 to 15 Dec 64; Obion PO; bronchitis, discharged at Bowling Green, KY
MARRS, John I., P-156-1; Pvt F Co 53rd TN Inf; 12-25-61 to 7-28-63; Lobelville PO; wnt home without discharge on above date; CONF
MARS, John R., D-76-1; Pvt H Co 1st MO Inf; 16 May 61 to 5 May 64; Nashville PO
MARSH, Calvin, Hw-123-1; Mary widow of; Pvt 8th TN Cav; Rotherwood PO
MARSH, Charles, Hw-124-1; Pvt H Co 8th TN Cav; 1 Sep 62 to 5 Jun 65; Opossum PO
MARSH, David, Di-34-1; Pvt H Co; 11-6? to __; Dickson PO; discharge in pension office & no record to report
MARSH, Ephram, Mg-200-3; Pvt H Co 104th OH Inf; 2 Aug 62 to 17 Jun 65; Tinah? (Tinch?) PO
MARSH, Geo. W., Sn-252-2; Cpl C Co 12th US Inf; 8-12-63 to 1-18-66; Gallatin PO
MARSH, Hosea J., H-61-5; Sgt G Co 64th Inf; 4-63 to 4-9-65; Chattanooga PO; wounded in left arm, use of it lost; CONF
MARSH, Isaac N., M-108-4; Pvt A Co 5th KY Inf; 9-15-61 to 11-16-64; Lafayette PO; disease of heart, plurysy & spleen
MARSH, James B., H-55-2; Pvt K Co 10th TN Cav; 4-63 to 65; Chickamauga PO; prisoner at Nashville 5 mos?
MARSH, Loan J., La-115-3; Pvt F Co 30th WI Vol Inf; 15 Aug 62 to 15 Sep 65; Summertown PO
MARSH, Simon, Sh-202-1; Pvt B Co Cav; 9 Sep 63 to 63 (1 yr); Memphis PO
MARSH, ____, Hw-125-2; Mary J. widow of; Pvt TN Cav; 62 to Dec 62 (2 mos); Yellow Stone PO; took sick & died
MARSHAL, Andrew J., Ge-84-2; Mary A. widow of; Sgt D Co 8th TN Cav; Jul __ to __; Greenville PO; got no discharge in hand
MARSHAL, David, Ro-210-7; Jane widow of; Pvt; Rockwood PO; shot through the leg

MARSHAL, James R., Hw-128-2; Pvt H Co 2nd US Inf; 13 Oct 64 to 7 Nov 65; Walnut Hill PO
MARSHALL, Nuton, F-43-1; Pvt M Co 4th IL US; Apr 63 to Apr 65; Rossville PO
MARSHALL, Thomas, Hy-74-1; Pvt M Co 4th TN Cav; 64 to 65; Eurekaton PO
MARSHALL, Wade, Hm-108-2(1); Pvt D Co 1st TN Cav; Apr 62 to 65; Springvale PO; rheumatism
MARSHALL, Houston, Hw-122-1; Pvt D Co 4th TN Inf; 13 Oct 62 to 2 Aug 65; New Canton PO; disease of left testicle
MARSHALL, John, K-169-2; away from home; Knoxville PO
MARSHALL, John D., Ge-84-1; Cpl E Co 2nd NC Inf; 1 Sep 63 to 16 Aug 65; Wolsey College PO; diseas of heart & liver
MARSHALL, Lewis O., Mu-190-1; Capt D Co 30th WI Inf; 8-18-62 to 9-21-65; Orderly Sgt F Co 1st WI Inf; 8-28-61 to 62; Culleoka PO
MARSHALL, Peter W., Gu-48-4(1); Pvt C Co 11th TN Col Inf; 64 to 66; PO omitted
MARSHALL?, Samuel, Ro-208-2; Pvt E Co 2nd NC Inf; 1 Sep 63 to 16 Aug 65; Morris Gap PO
MARSHALL, Samuel Thomas, Sh-184-2; Fireman Exchange (a vessel?); 9-64 to 8-4-64; 74 Hill St., Memphis PO; wounded by explosion of "Miama"
MARSHALL, Thomas P., Mr-98-1; Capt H Co 13th IA Inf; 11-2-61 to 4-6-65; Major H Co 13th IA Inf; 7-29-64 to 4-6-65; Kelly's Ferry PO; chronic diarhea & hearing injured by firing of artillery
MARSHALL, Tipton, Hm-109-1; Pvt D Co 4th TN Inf; 14 Apr 62 to 9 Jul 65; Three Springs PO
MARSHALL, William, Fr-114-1; Pvt F Co 143rd IN Inf; 63 to 12-64 (8 mos); Alto PO
MARSHALL, William S., H-66-1; Major 5th IA Reg; 7-15-61 to 2-65; Chattanooga PO
MARSIE, Joseph T., Cl-46-4(2); Susa L. widow of; Pvt K Co 49th KY Inf; 7-24-63 to 12-26-64; Ibex PO; backset from measles, wants pension
MARSTIN, Richard, Hm-108-2(1); Pvt D Co 30th VA Inf; Mar 61 to 9 Apr 65; Morristown PO; CONF
MARSTON, Alfred H., H-62-3; Pvt 2nd MI Cav; 408 Pine, Chattanoooga PO
MARTAIN, John, A-9-3(1); Martha W. widow of; Pvt; Briceville PO; was prisnor of war & discharged as a prisnor at close of war
MARTAIN, Patric., D-72-2; Pvt B Co 29th GA; 21 Jun 61 to 19 Jul 65; Nashville PO; wounded in hip, leg & sholder; CONF
MARTAIN, Sien, Hi-92-1; Elizebeth widow of; Aetna PO; coulden remember company and dates
MARTANS?, Thomas, Bo-15-2; Pvt D Co 1st TN Lt Art; 9-63 to ___; Maryville PO
MARTEND, Henry, Hm-108-4(3); Pvt F Co 45th VA Inf; May 61 to Apr 65; Russellville PO; rheumatism & heart disease
MARTHER, Dee, D-64-4; Nashville PO; shot in leg
MARTIES, Jesse M., Be-1-1; "yes"; 13th Dist
MARTIN, Aaron, Hr-87-1; Pvt; PO omitted
MARTIN, Alexander, M-103-2; Pvt K Co 16th US Inf; 6-6-58 to 6-17-63; Lafayette PO; shot in breast, in prison Richmond 2 months
MARTIN, Ammon A., Pu-145-2; Pvt L Co 1st Mtd Inf; 12-6-63 to 4-14-65; Fancher's Mills PO
MARTIN, Andrew C., Ha-115-2; Pvt A Co 25th VA Cav; 1 Oct 61 to 10 May 65; Fenton PO; prisoner at Camp Morton 18 months, reenlisted veteran; CONF
MARTIN, Andrew J., Mg-197-5; Pvt B Co 2nd TN Inf; 10 Aug 61 to ___; Wartburg PO; rupture, not discharged
MARTIN, Anthony, Gi-136-2; (mistake) sol; 16th Dist
MARTIN, Benjaniman, La-112-2; Pvt A Co 2nd TN Mtd Inf; 10-2-63 to 10-14-64; Pvt E Co 8th TN Mtd Inf; 3-9-65 to 9-1-65; Chisem PO
MARTIN, Benjamin, Ro-205-4; Pvt H Co 1st Blackenney? Art; 2 yrs 6 mos; Postoak Springs PO; general disability
MARTIN, Benjamin, Wy-173-4; Pvt B Co 2nd TN Mtd Inf; 10-15-63 to 10-17-64; Victory PO
MARTIN?, Charley, D-91-4; Teamster Pvt Davidson PO
MARTIN, Christain G., Ro-202-4; Pvt I Co 1st TN Inf; 9 Aug 61 to 12 Aug 64; Cave Creed PO; deafness, lung & throat trouble

MARTIN, Christopher C., Ch-14-1; Teamster A Co 22nd AR Cav; 11-12-64 to 3-16-65; Wild Goose PO; CONF
MARTIN, Clay, Je-142-2; Pvt B Co 1st US C A Hvy; New Market PO; hernia, discharge carried off by pension agt
MARTIN, David, Gr-73-2; Pvt F Co 9th TN Cav; 13 Sep 63 to 13 Sep 65; Turley's Mills PO
MARTIN, Edith C., (see Cline, David A.)
MARTIN, Edward, We-221-7; Dist 2
MARTIN, Ephraim P., Ov-135-2; Jane widow of; Sgt K Co 9th TN Cav; 1-30-63 to 9-11-65; Oakley PO
MARTIN, Epp, H-55-2; Pvt F Co 6th TN Mtd Inf; 9-12-64 to 6-30-65; Chickamauga PO
MARTIN, Franklin C., Br-9-2; Elizabeth widow of; Pvt; Cleveland PO; no discharge, died in service
MARTIN, Geor W., Lo-188-1; Martha L. widow of; Pvt F Co 4th TN Cav; 6 May 63 to 12 Jul 65; Erie PO
MARTIN, George W., B-7-1; Pvt H Co 5th TN Cav; 5-5-63 to 6-25-65; Shelbyville PO
MARTIN, George W., Dk-343-; Pvt F Co 4th TN Inf; 9-24-64 to 8-25-65; Dowelltown PO
MARTIN, Harvey, Mu-199-1; Pvt A Co 13th TN Inf; 12 Aug 63 to 10 Jan 66; Ettaton PO
MARTIN, Henry, Sh-200-2; refused to answer questions; 19 Polk St., Memphis PO
MARTIN, Henry, Rb-223-3(5); 9th Dist
MARTIN, Isaac, P-150-1; Pvt E Co 8th KY Inf; Apr 63 to Mar 65; 1st Dist
MARTIN, Isaac, U-246-2; Dist 4
MARTIN, Isaac A., R-163-1; Pvt B Co 6th TN Mtd Inf; 8-15-64 to 6-30-65; Graysville PO
MARTIN, Ivey?, S-216-2; Pvt 12th KY Inf; Capusiene PO; cripeld in right hand, now discharged
MARTIN, James, Ro-209-4; Pvt A Co 16th TN Cav; 63 to 64; Kings Creek PO; CONF
MARTIN, James G., Lo-189-3(1); Cpl & Capt D Co 62nd TN Inf; Jul 62 to released Mar 64; Philadelphia PO; taken prisoner & released at Knoxville TN; CONF
MARTIN, James H., Bo-14-4; Pvt L Co 2nd TN Cav; 9-8-63 to 7-6-65; Mint PO
MARTIN, James H., Wy-173-4; Pvt B Co 2nd TN Mtd Inf; 10-15-63 to 10-17-64; Victory PO
MARTIN, James L., Mr-102-1; Pvt A Co 34th KY Inf; South Pittsburg PO; shot in left ancle
MARTIN, James M., Wa-271-1; Sgt I Co 8th TN Cav; 20 Mar 64 to 11 Sep 65; Jonesboro PO; gunshot wound in left knee & rumatism
MARTIN, James P., La-117-3; Pvt M Co 15th MO Cav; Mar 62 to 65; 15th Dist; CONF
MARTIN, Jefferson A., Ro-201-5(3); Sgt K Co 94th OH Inf; 10 Aug 62 to 5 Jun 65; Kingston PO
MARTIN, Jennie N., (see King, Amos C.)
MARTIN, Joel F., Dk-35-1; Caroline widow of; Pvt; Temperance Hall PO
MARTIN, John, K-154-5(2); Knoxville PO: rheumatism 26 yrs
MARTIN, John, Dk-34-4; Pvt G Co 1st TN Inf; 3-1-64 to 4-21-65; Dowelltown PO
MARTIN, John, Br-13-4; Pvt L Co 1st TN Cav; 9-1-63 to 6-19-65; Cleveland PO; chronic catarrh
MARTIN, John, J-77-2; Gainesboro PO; chronic diarhea
MARTIN, John, Sh-153-1; Pvt B Co 61st TN Inf; 5 Apr 65 to 10 Feb 66; Bailey Sta. PO
MARTIN, John, Ma-114-1; Sgt E Co 2nd TN M?; 4 Jan 62 to 16 Apr 63; Pinson PO; wounded 5 times; CONF
MARTIN, John, Gi-135-2; Julia widow of; Pvt; Lynnville PO
MARTIN, John, Cf-35-3; Jane widow of; Pvt A Co 44th TN Inf; 6 Nov 61 to May 65; Gould PO; CONF
MARTIN, John, (see Countiss, John M.)
MARTIN, John H., Ha-115-3; Elizabeth widow of; Mulberry Gap PO; CONF
MARTIN, John M., Dy-25-2; Pvt I Co 11th WI Inf; 14 Oct 61 to 28 Sep 65; Newbern PO; deafness right ear, reenlisted veteran
MARTIN, Jno. R., Sh-163-1; "found while examining work"; PO omitted
MARTIN, Louis H., We-229-1; Pvt K Co 5th TN Cav; 22 Feb 63 to 14 Aug 65; Gleason PO; shot in the head

MARTIN, Louis H., La-110-1(2); Mary W. widow of; Pvt D Co 1st AL Inf; 64 to 10-18-65; Appleton PO
MARTIN, M. M., Hd-48-2; Pvt D Co 6th TN Cav; 24 Oct 62 to 13 Aug 65; Savannah PO; rheumatism
MARTIN, Major, H-56-3; B Co TN; 3-3-61 to 5-24-65; St. Elmo PO
MARTIN, Marcellus, Ja-85-2; Pvt E Co 5th TN Inf; 3-2-62 to 4-4-65; Birchwood PO
MARTIN, Margaret, (see Rogers, Ephraim)
MARTIN, Margaret I., (see Hoge, Joel W.)
MARTIN, Mary A., Cf-38-1; widow; 10th Civil Dist
MARTIN, Matison, Hw-123-2; Pvt A Co 5th TN Cav; 11 Jun 63 to 9 Nov 63; Rotherwood PO
MARTIN, Mitchell P., Sm-175-2(1); Pvt A Co TN Inf; 64 to 65; Bluff Creek PO
MARTIN, Ned, Wl-307-1; Elyza widow; Pvt; Partlow PO
MARTIN, Peter, Hy-75-2; Matilda widow of; Dancyville PO; lost the papers
MARTIN, Peter, D-63-1; Patsy widow of; Sgt A Co 17th TN Inf; Jul 65 to 5 Apr 66; Nashville PO
MARTIN, Richard, H-69-5; Pvt; 64 to 65; Chattanooga PO
MARTIN, Robert, Mu-209-3; Pvt; Columbia
MARTIN, Ruben E., Dk-34-3; Pvt F Co 4th TN Inf; 9-24-64 to __; Dowelltown PO; eyes affected
MARTIN, Samuel J., Mo-121-1; 1st Lt D Co 11th TN Cav; 8-15-63 to 2-20-64; 4th Civil Dist
MARTIN, Samuel L., Br-12-2; Pvt I Co 10th TN Cav; 4-4-63 to 7-3-65; Charleston PO
MARTIN, Samuel L., Ru-246-1; 18th Civil Dist
MARTIN, Stephen A., Ro-210-12; Pvt; Cardiff PO
MARTIN, Warrn, W-189-4; Pvt 99th OH Inf; McMinnville PO; discharge lost
MARTIN, Washington, Gi-136-1; Cpl B Co 110th TN Inf; 12-1-63 to 2-1-66; Buford Station PO
MARTIN, Wiey J., Dk-33-1; Pvt F Co 4th TN Inf; 9-24-64 to 8-25-65; Dowelltown PO; rheumatism & sight
MARTIN, William, K-174-2(1); Cpl G Co 2nd TN Cav; 1 Oct 62 to 6 Jul 65; Graveston PO; Egyptian? ophthalmi, he will probly go bline
MARTIN, William, Di-34-1; Pvt H Co 2nd Bttn Pa Inf; 6-16-63 to 7-21-64; Pvt E Co 57th PA Inf; 3-11-64 to 7-10-65; Dickson PO; reenlisted veteran
MARTIN, William, Ru-241-5; Pvt TN Inf; 63 to 66; Murfreesboro PO
MARTIN, William C., B-7-1; Cpl H Co 5th TN Cav; 11-10-62 to 6-15-65; Shelbyville PO
MARTIN, William L., G-67-1; Pvt M Co 6th TN Cav; 11 Aug 62 to 26 Apr 65; Bradford PO
MARTIN, Wm. P., C-34-2; Pvt H Co 1st KY Cav; 8-61 to 2-65; Buckeye PO; union man conscripted, deserted first chance (believe this comment refers to another veteran)
MARTIN, William T., Wy-175-1; Pvt A Co 2nd TN Mtd Inf; 9-15-63 to 10-14-64; Whittens Stand PO; wears glasses
MARTINDALE, Frank G., H-51-4; Major 1st NY Cav; 1-16-61 to 5-28-65; Hill City PO
MARTINE, Alfred H., K-166-4(2); Ensign, ship Sagamore; 3 Jan 65 to 30 Jul 65; Knoxville PO; catarrh, rheumatism
MARTON, Gilbert, R-161-6; Pvt H Co 5th TN Inf; 3-2-62 to 5-16-65; Dayton PO; lost right eye
MARTON, Robert, Mc-118-1; Ann widow of; Pvt A Co; 4-1-64 to 2-15-64; Cogshill PO
MARX, Dominic, Sh-191-2; Sgt 1st Col; 64 to 66; Memphis PO
MARY, Calvin, K-186-4; Pvt; Balls Camp PO
MARYAN, John, Mg-198-3; Pvt E Co 1st TN Inf; 20 Aug 61 to 17 Sep 64; Hunnicutt PO; affected eyes
MASANGALE, Annie, D-71-1; widow (US); Nashville PO
MASGROVE, William L., Mr-96-3(2); US Sol; 3rd Dist
MASINGALL, Juden, A-7-1; Robertsville PO
MASLEY, William, Cf-35-5(1); 5th Dist
MASON, Anthony, Sh-161-1; US Sol; 16th Dist
MASON, Arthur, D-92-2; US Sol; W. Nashville PO
MASON, Benjamin, Gi-122-8; Pvt K Co 110th TN Inf; 3 Mar 63 to 3 Mar 65; Prospect Sta PO; wounded by artilery wagon
MASON, David T., Wl-293-2; Pvt E? Co 7th TN; 19 Oct 61 to 17 Ju 62; Lockport PO; CONF
MASON, Fransis M., Mo-127-1; Pvt K Co 9th TN Cav; 5-7-63 to 9-11-65; Notchy PO

MASON, Henry, Sh-196-1; Pvt F Co 29th IL Inf; 1-62 to 65; 120 Dunlap St., Memphis PO; discharge lost
MASON, Henry, K-155-1; Pvt A Co 1st Col Art; Dec 62 to Jun 65; Knoxville PO; right testicle
MASON, Henry F., Mg-199-2; Pvt G Co 7th IN Inf; 61 to __; Sunbright PO
MASON, James, Cl-48-2; Pvt K Co 49th KY; 8-63 to 12-29-65; Old Town PO
MASON, James, T-219-1; alias James Westmolden; Pvt G Co 61st TN Inf; 62 to 65; Phelan PO; his discharge is not in his possession, hence no dates
MASON, John, Ro-210-11; Pvt E Co 1st TN Inf; Rockwood PO
MASON, John W., C-27-3; Pvt L Co 9th MI Cav; 62 to 64; Jacksboro PO
MASON, Lee H., Cr-4-5; Pvt C Co 20th TN Inf; 5-20-61 to 12-64; Bells Depot PO; wounded arm & leg; CONF
MASON, Louis, Sh-190-2; Sarah M. widow of; Pvt F Co 59th Col Inf; 5-12-63 to 1-31-66; Cor Broadway & Kentucky Ave., Memphis PO
MASON, Mary (see McCaney, Rolla)
MASON, Phillip T., K-166-4(2); Pvt E Co PA Inf; Jun 62 to Aug 65; Knoxville PO
MASON, Robert, Gi-127-2; Pulaski PO
MASON, Robert S., R-162-4; Sgt A Co 3rd TN Cav; 2-1-63 to 8-3-65; Dayton PO
MASON, Rufus M., Mo-125-1; Pvt D Co 3rd TN Mtd Inf; 7-25-64 to 11-30-64; Gudger PO
MASON, Squire, D-64-4; Cpl B Co 12th TN Inf; 31 Jul 65 to Jan 66; Nashville PO; heart disease
MASON, Thio L., D-77-3; Pvt H Co 5th MA Inf; 20 Sep 62 to 2 Jul 63; Nashville PO; rheumatism
MASON, Thomas, D-58-2; Pvt; Nashville PO
MASON, William, Je-139-1; Malinda widow of; Trion PO
MASON, Willis, Gi-127-4; Arie widow of; Pvt Co 110th TN C Inf; Pulaski PO; died in service, Arie Mason is pensioner
MASONER, Andrew S., Wa-262-1; Mary Jane widow of; Pvt K Co 13th TN Cav; __ to 65 (2 yrs 4 mos); Matilda PO
MASONER, Samuel, Col, Me-89-1; Pvt E Co 42nd US Inf; 7-65-1-66; Big Spring PO
MASSA, Andy, Pu-140-2; 1st Civil Dist
MASSA, Steven T., Pu-141-1; Pvt I Co 1st TN Inf; 8-20-64 to 7-20-65; Cookville PO; at home on sick furlough when reg. disch.
MASSANGILL, Anderson, Je-143-3; Pvt F Co 1st US Col Hvy Art; __ to 31 Mar 66; Mossy Creek PO; catarrh of head
MASSENGILL, David, A-2-4; Co E 34d TN Inf; Coal Creek PO; rheumatism, this solier not at home today and discharge locked up, hence a full record cant be made
MASSENGILL, Isaac J., Ch-14-1; Pvt C Co 52nd TN Inf; 12-19-61 to 12-19-63; Sweet Lips PO; shot through right leg, out of service 9 mos; CONF
MASSENGILL, James W., Hw-125-2; Cpl; 62 to 65; Stony Point PO; CONF
MASSENGILL, Sidney M., Ch-14-1; Pvt C Co 52nd TN Cav; 7-4-63 to 9-29-6? (2 mos 25 days); Wild Goose PO; hit with __ after captured; CONF
MASSEY, Andrew J., M-106-1; Pvt A Co 9th KY Vol Inf; 11-28-61 to 11-65; Dixons Springs PO; measles settled on left, pensioner
MASSEY, Baily P., Sm-170-2; Pvt L Co 5th TN Cav; 9-19-63 to 8-14-65; Maggart PO; chronic diarrhea, his bowels pains him severely
MASSEY, David, K-170-3; US Sol; Dist 12
MASSEY, George, Col, We-220-2; Pvt A Co TN Inf; 10 Dec 63 to 10 Feb 65; PO omitted
MASSEY, Horace, St-162-1; Fireman, St. Clare No. 19; May 63 to May 66; Cumberland City PO; eyes & head affected, papers lost
MASSEY, Isaac, Hu-103-4; R. A. widow of; Pvt E Co 10th TN Inf; 14 May 64 to 11 Sep 65; PO omitted
MASSEY, James, S-212-1; Pvt B Co 5th TN; 15 May 61 to 8 Nov 64; Onida PO; piles & rheumatism;CONF
MASSEY, James R., H-68-1; Pvt F Co 4th E TN; 5-7-63 to 7-18-65; Chattanooga PO; chronic diarhoea, at times not able to work
MASSEY, John, J-79-2; Pvt K Co 9th KY Inf; 11-30-61 to 1-6-65; North Springs PO; shell wound in left side

MASSEY, Wiley B., Dy-25-8(4); Martha widow of; Newbern PO; enlistment date unknown; CONF
MASSEY, William, Pu-144-4; Hudgins PO
MASSINGALE, Calvin, Pi-156-1; Pvt C Co 11th TN Cav; 63 to 9-65; Permelia PO; transferred to the 9th Co I TN
MASSINGALE, John, S-215-2; Pearl Louisa for. widow of; Pvt; Pioneer PO
MASSINGALE, Louis, Cy-28-1; Emily Lackey former widow of; Pvt D Co 12th KY Inf; 3-12-61 to 2-15-64; Celina PO
MASSINGILL, John, Ro-204-1; Pvt B Co 1st TN Inf; 1 Aug 61 to 17 Oct 64; Oliver Springs PO
MASSON, James, Ge-89-2; Sgt M Co 1st TN Cav; 15 Nov 62 to 5 Jun 65; Albany PO
MASSY, Pressly, D-77-2; Pvt B Co 110th US Col Inf; 63 to May 66; Nashville PO
MASTER, Wesley L., (see Wright, Percy)
MASTERS, Abraham, U-247-3; Nancy A. widow of; Pvt F Co 3rd NC Mtd Inf; 64 to 65; Erwin PO; died before discharge
MASTERS, Alexander, U-248-2; Pvt M Co 8th TN Cav; 31 May 63 to 11 Sep 65; Erwin PO
MASTERS, Thomas D., Ov-134-1; Cpl A Co South C Bat; 1-23-65 to 10-23-65; Hilham PO; had chills and fever
MASTERS, Wilkerson, U-248-2; Pvt M Co 8th TN Cav; 31 May 63 to 11 Sep 65; Erwin PO
MASTERSON, Monroe, H-49-9; Capt C Co 5th TN Inf; 2-25-62 to 4-13-63; Igon's Ferry PO; general debility, discharged on this account
MASTERSON, Richard, K-181-4(1); 1st Sgt C Co 6th TN Inf; 18 Apr 62 to 27 Apr 65; Knoxville PO
MASTERSON, Willoughby A., Dy-25-3; Pvt A Co 4th IN Inf; May 61 to Aug 65; Newbern PO; wounded
MASTON, Elizabeth, Mo-124-1; widow; Pvt B Co 3rd KY Inf; 3 yrs; Brakebille PO; blowed up on steam boat
MASTON, George H., Ct-38-1; Pvt F Co 8th TN Cav; 6-11-63 to 9-11-65; Milligan PO; chronic rheumatism
MATHAS, James, K-169-2; failed to see; Knoxville PO
MATHENA, John R., Hd-44-1; Pvt G Co 10th TN Inf; 5-2-62 to 6-28-65; Clifton PO (Wayne Co)
MATHENSON, Daniel G., Bo-12-2(1); Pvt B Co 4th TN Inf; 12-8-62 to 6-2-65; Rasor PO
MATHENY, Charlie, Hn-75-1; Pvt G Co 2nd IA Inf; 25 Oct 63 to 4 Feb 65; Springville PO
MATHENY, Isaiah, Ma-126-1; Pvt E Co 18th IN Inf; Nov 62 to Nov 64; Jackson PO; don't remember exact days of month
MATHER, George W., Cl-47-4; Pvt C Co 6th TN Inf; 62 to 5-65; Cappford PO; back & kidneys 1862; gone from home
MATHER, John, Ho-96-1; Pvt C Co 2nd IL Lt Art; 2 Dec 62 to 3 Aug 65; Erin PO
MATHER, S. D., Fr-110-1; Capt H Co 19th IL; 11 May 61 to 9 Nov 64; Belvidere PO
MATHERLY, Alexander, Ct-40-3; Jane widow of; Pvt A Co 13th TN Cav; 9-22-63 to 9-5-65; Elizabethton PO
MATHERLY, James, Jo-152-1; Ferby R. widow of; Pvt A Co 13th TN Cav; 22 Sep 63 to 5 Sep 65; High Health PO
MATHERLY, William, Wa-271-1; Sarah widow of; Flourville PO
MATHES, Allen, We-225-3(2); Pvt C Co 4th KY Hvy Art; 31 May 65 to 14 Apr 66; Dresden PO; small pox & measels settled in my eyes
MATHES, David, Gi-139-1; Pvt A Co 110th TN Inf; 5-15-61 to 65; Barcheers PO; shot in left arm & left leg
MATHES, Henry C., Ct-36-1; Pvt A Co 3rd NC Mtd Inf; 1 yr 6 mos; Shell Creek PO
MATHES, Willis, Hy-82-1; Pvt E Co 59th TN Inf; Mar 64 to 66; Brownsville PO
MATHESON, Daniel M., Jo-151-2; Pvt F Co 3rd NC Inf; 1 Sep 64 to 8 Aug 65; Bakers Gap PO; asthma of emphysema, Russian? left foot
MATHEWS, Ben, D-60-3; Malinda S. widow of; Pvt in Cav Co; 1303 Hynes St., Nashville PO; now the wife of Pepper, Patrick, colored
MATHEWS, Ben, Martha McCormack formerly widow of; Sm-168-1; Pvt TN Inf; 62 to 63; Bagdad PO; died Mar 64 to 66
MATHEWS, Chas. E., Sh-201-1; Pvt B Co US Col Reg Hvy Art; 10-15-63 to 9-12-65; Memphis PO

MATHEWS, Edmund F., Ma-129-1; Pvt B Co 48th IL; Dec 62 to Aug 65; Pinson PO; bronchitis
MATHEWS, Frank, T-216-2; 14th Civil Dist
MATHEWS, J. H., Hu-103-3; Pvt E Co 10th TN Inf; 1 Jan 61 to 1 Jan 65; PO omitted
MATHEWS, James, Mu-193-1; Caroline widow of; Pvt; 63 to 65; Columbia PO
MATHEWS, James, Pi-156-2; Pvt C Co 2nd KY Cav; 11-12-63 to 7-19-65; Travisville PO; rheumatism, now not able to do good work
MATHEWS, Laura, Sh-199-2; 309 Miss. St., Memphis PO
MATHEWS, Milley, D-103-2; widow US Sol; 24th Dist
MATHEWS, Nelson, Un-252-2; Pvt K Co 14th KY Inf; Dec 64 to Apr 65; Haynes PO
MATHEWS, Obediah, J-80-2; Parisee widow of; Pvt; Granville PO; piles, discharged destroyed & no dates given
MATHEWS, William, Br-9-5; Pvt I Co 123rd IL Inf; Cleveland PO
MATHEWS, William H., Mt-138-1; US Sol; Dist 7, New Providence PO
MATHIAS, Mary A., Jo-151-4; widow of soldier; PO omitted
MATHIS, Anderson, Ha-114-2; Pvt H Co 1st TN Inf; 10 Oct 64 to 20 Nov 65; Sneedville PO
MATHIS, Andrew J., Hw-121-1; Pvt K Co 9th TN Cav; 20 Sep 63 to 11 Sep 65; New Hope PO; none in wars
MATHIS, Bleuford, Dk-33-2; Pvt K Co 5th TN Cav; 3-5-63 to 8-14-65; Halesville PO
MATHIS, Cullen J., Me-88-3; Martha J. widow of; Pvt E Co 5th TN Inf; 3-2-62 to 4-4-65; Brittsville PO
MATHIS, George, Hn-69-1; Pvt H Co 4th C Hvy Art; May 64 to Mar 65; Paris PO; discharge lost
MATHIS, James, Mu-200-1; Pvt F Co 13th TN Cav; 63 to 65; Summertown PO; ankle & shoulder dislocated in service, made proof in 1888, recd. no pay
MATHIS, James, Wl-308-2; Pvt F Co 28th TN; 1 Sep 61 to 1 Sep 64; Rural Hill PO; captured; CONF
MATHIS, Jessee, Cl-58-1; Casander widow of; Pvt; 3 years; Minkton PO; killed in Handcock Co, TN in skirmish on 11 Dec? 1865, ignerant, cant tell much
MATHIS, Joe, D-49-3; Pvt G Co 13th __; 3 yrs; knows he was in service 3 years and that is all he knows
MATHIS, John C., Ha-113-2; Sgt B Co 1st TN Cav; 10 Apr 62 to 10 Apr 65; Sneedville PO
MATHIS, Kinchen, Di-34-3; Sgt G Co 12th TN Cav; 10-63 to 1-9-65; Colesburg PO; discharged wound in mouth
MATHIS, Lee, Bl-3-5; Pvt K Co 4th TN Cav; 2-64 to 6-1-65; Tanbark PO
MATHIS, Richard N., Dk-33-3; Pvt M Co 5th TN Cav; 2-19-64 to 8-14-65; Halesville PO; back & kidneys contracted in service
MATHIS, Sam, G-50-1; 2nd Civil Dist
MATHIS, Thomas B., Cf-40-3; Pvt G Co 4th TN Vol; 1 Dec 64 to 25 Aug 65; Tullahoma PO; gun shot on face, chronic rheumatism
MATHIS, William, Pi-155-2; Pvt C Co 5th TN Cav; 11-63 to 64; Byrdstown PO; fever & settled in shoulder
MATHIS, William H., Dk-33-3; Pvt M Co 5th TN Cav; 2-19-64 to 8-14-65; Halesville PO; broken ribs durring war by horse
MATIN, Edward P., St-160-2; 2nd Lt E Co 10th TN Cav; Oct 62 to Apr 65; Big Rock PO; CONF
MATIN, Fuller, We-221-7; Virginia M. Gordon widow of; Pvt AL Inf; 61 to __; Martin PO; lost his health? and died at home; CONF
MATLOCK, Charles, Mo-121-1; Sgt L Co 1st US Col Hvy Art; 8-19-64 to 3-31-66; Philadelphia PO; rheumatism, pensioner
MATLOCK, Clark, Mc-112-10; Pvt C Co 1st __; Mount Verd PO
MATLOCK, David, Ha-111-1; Pvt A Co 43rd TN Cav; 63 to 65 (about 1 yr 6 mos); PO omitted; CONF
MATLOCK, James P., Lo-195-1; Ord Sgt K Co 5th TN Inf; 1 Oct 62 to 30 Jun 65; Eaton's X Roads PO; rheumatism & heart disease
MATLOCK, John, K-171-6(5); Pvt 5th TN; PO omitted
MATLOCK, John W., Mc-110-2(1); Sgt D Co 5th TN Inf; Mouse Creek PO; discharge lost

MATLOCK, Lewis, Mc-114-5; Pvt F Co 2nd OH Inf;
 4-1-64 to no discharge (5 mos); Santfordville
 PO; in hospital
MATLOCK, Reuben, Lo-193-1; Pvt A Co 1st Col Art;
 1 Feb 64 to 31 Mar 66; Unitia PO
MATLOCK, Sandy, H-49-7; Daisy PO
MATLOCK, William, K-161-4; Knoxville PO; shot in
 side
MATNEY, John W., Wy-177-2; Pvt A Co 10th TN Inf;
 4-13-62 to 5-25-65; Waynesboro PO; overheat,
 rheumatism
MATTHEW, Martin, Ru-241-5; Cpl E Co 123rd KY Inf;
 63 to 66; Murfreesboro PO
MATTHEWS, Erwin, H., Mc-112-8; 1st Lt RAM 9th TN
 Cav; 8-18-63 to 9-11-64; Athens PO
MATTHEWS, George W., Ja-85-4; Pvt G Co 5th TN Inf;
 4-1-62 to 6-6-63; Georgetown PO; 2nd Lt F Co
 4th TN Cav; 6-6-63 to 4-6-64
MATTHEWS, Isham, Ru-239-1; Teamster 2nd MN? Inf;
 2 yrs; Patterson PO
MATTHEWS, James S., F-20-2; Pvt B Co 13th TN Inf;
 1 May 61 to 20 Jun 65; Hickory Withe PO; CONF
MATTHEWS, John T., Ja-85-4; Pvt F Co 4th TN Cav;
 4-1-63 to 6-12-65; Georgetown PO
MATTHEWS, Madison F., Sh-195-2; US Sol; Memphis PO
MATTHEWS, Martin, Mn-199-1; Pvt E Co 110th TN Inf;
 Mt. Pleasant PO
MATTHEWS, Thomas B., Fe-40-1; Cpl D Co 1st TN Mtd
 Inf; 10-10-63 to 4-25-65; Little Crabb PO;
 rheumatism & ruptured
MATTINGLY, Barnard, Je-143-3; 1st Lt H Co 1st Cap
 K. Gavils?; 1 Jul 64 to 12 Feb 65; Mossy
 Creek PO; wrean back
MATTISON, Andrew, H-50-5; Pvt E Co 41st R OH Inf;
 9-12-61 to 5-31-62; Soddy PO; shot in the knee
MATTOCK, Alford, Lo-187-4; Pvt K Co 1st US Col Hvy
 Art; Jul 64 to 31 Mar 66; Adolphus PO;
 rheumatism
MATTOCKS, Farmer N., Cl-48-3; Pvt 6th TN Inf; 3
 yrs; Compensation PO; wounded on chin by shell,
 not at home, can't get date of enlistment &
 discharge
MAUER, Alex, (see Tucker, Alex)
MAUL?, Isac, C-27-1; Pvt F Co 29th TN Inf; 7-61 to
 64 (2 yrs 8 mos); Jacksboro PO; CONF
MAULDIN, William, Ja-84-1; Malinda widow of; Cpl L
 Co 4th TN Cav; 1-63 to __; Harrison PO;
 killed on Mississippi raid
MAULEY, Alex L., Gr-70-1; Pvt H Co 1st TN Cal; 8
 Apr 62 to 8 Apr 65; Rutledge PO
MAUPIN, Ayers, C-30-2; Surgeon 6th TN Inf; 4-62
 to 5-65; Well Spring PO
MAUPIN, Henry, C-25-1; Pvt D Co 2nd TN Cav; 4-10-63
 to __ (8 mos); Jacksborough PO; never dis-
 charged
MAUPIN, John T., Ro-207-1; Pvt Com Off C Co 1st TN
 Inf; 9 Sep 61 to 17 Sep 64; Erie PO (Loudon
 Co.); wound in right leg
MAUPIN, Robert C., B-3-2; Sgt F Co 5th TN Cav;
 9-7-62 to 6-25-65; Wartrace PO
MAUPIN, William C., C-30-1; Pvt C Co 1st TN Inf;
 8-9-61 to 9-17-64; Well Spring PO
MAUPIN, ___, C-29-2; Sarah widow of; Fincastle PO
MAUTHEW, Charles J., D-50-3; Mus G Co 12th ME? Inf;
 23 Feb 65 to 3 Mar 66; 1014 N. Cherry,
 Nashville PO
MAVIM?, George, Me-89-2; Pvt A Co 1st TN Cav;
 2-8-63 to 2-23-64; Dayton PO; CONF
MAVIS, Edward, Ha-110-2; Pvt E Co 1st TN Cav;
 1 Apr 62 to 11 Apr 65; Treadway PO
MAXEY, Gabrel, Ha-116-2; US Sol; Dist No. 10
MAXEY, Marion J., Bo-19-3; Pvt C Co 6th TN Inf;
 5-62 to 4-65; Rockford PO
MAXEY, William D., M-106-1; Susan widow of; Pvt A
 Co 9th KY Vol Inf; 9-61 to __; Union Camp PO;
 gunshot in right arm, died in service,
 pensioner
MAXFIELD, John, Wl-295-1; Pvt G Co 4th TN Mtd Inf;
 64 to 65; Lebanon PO
MAXFIELD, Matilda, (see Peycke, Amandus)
MAXFIELD, Moses M., Cf-40-1; Pvt C Co 79th OH Vol;
 2 Aug 62 to 9 Jun 65; Tullahoma PO
MAXWELL, Betha, Wl-297-1; widow US Sol; Pvt G Co
 5th TN Cav; Watertown PO
MAXWELL, Byrd C., Pu-144-3; Pvt B Co 1st TN Mtd Inf;
 3-3-64 to 4-14-65; Cookeville PO; pneumonia &
 typhoid fever

MAXWELL, Charles, Gl-132-2; Elizabeth Reynolds
 formerly widow of; Pvt D Co 110th US C V;
 Dec 63 to died in the service (1 yr 3 mos 15
 days); Pulaski PO
MAXWELL, Clark, Gl-127-7; Pvt F Co 111th TN Col Inf;
 22 Dec 64 to 30 Apr 66; Pulaski PO
MAXWELL, David D., D-63-3; 638 Witmore, Nashville PO
MAXWELL, Henry C., K-180-4; Pvt D Co 6th TN Inf;
 18 Apr 62 to 30 Jun 65; Ebenezer PO; loss of
 sight in one eyes & indijestion
MAXWELL, Henry W., Hd-47-2; Savannah PO
MAXWELL, Isaac, D-49-4; Pvt H Co 15th __; 16 Jul 64
 to 16 Apr 66; Nashville PO
MAXWELL, Isaacs, Gl-135-1; Pollie widow of; Pvt B
 Co 110th TN Inf; 62 to 66; Lynnville PO
MAXWELL, James H., He-61-1; Cpl G Co 7th TN Cav;
 5 Aug 62 to 25 Oct 63; Pvt G Co 2nd TN Mtd Inf;
 30 Nov 63 to 28 Dec 64; Moores Hill PO
MAXWELL, James J. C., Mn-122-1; Sgt B Co 6th TN Cav;
 8-25-62 to 7-26-65; McNairy PO
MAXWELL, James S., Pu-145-5(6); Pvt C Co 1st Mtd
 Inf; 10-21-63 to 12-13-64; PO omitted
MAXWELL, John S., Wl-295-2; Lebanon PO
MAXWELL, Mary A., De-26-3; widow of Sol US;
 Poplar Springs PO
MAXWELL, Maston Y., Dy-25-8(4); Pvt D Co 5th TN Inf;
 5-20-61 to 7-4-64; Newbern PO; captured
 7-4-64; CONF
MAXWELL, Mitchell, Gl-132-2; alias Dougherty,
 Mitchell; Pvt K Co 5th US C Cav; __ to 65;
 Pulaski PO; cant find out date enlisted or
 discharged
MAXWELL, Robert, Sh-193-1; Pvt; Memphis PO
MAXWELL, Saml., D-60-2; in alley back of McCrairy,
 Nashville PO; colored
MAXWELL, Samuel H., Pu-144-2; Pvt L Co 5th TN Cav;
 7-63 to 6-10-65; Bloomington PO
MAXWELL, W. H., Hd-47-2; Seaman Gunboat "Robb";
 10 Aug 63 to 10 Aug 64; Savannah PO
MAXWELL, William, Sh-157-5; Sgt D Co 61st C Inf;
 63 to 66; PO omitted; I were shot in the right
 breast at White House landing at Miss side of
 the river
MAXWELL, William, D-45-4; Pvt L Co 5th TN Cav;
 8-25-63 to 8-26-65; Nashville PO; shot in
 right shoulder
MAXWELL, William H., J-80-2; Pvt L Co 5th TN Cav;
 63 to 65; Granville PO; overstrain of nerves
 in service & hydrosell in right testicle--
 lumbago, discharge is lost
MAXWELL, William T., Mc-111-2; Pvt A Co 7th TN Mtd
 Inf; __ to 7-3-65; Athens PO
MAY, Abraham, Ro-204-4; Pvt K Co 1st TN Inf; 9 Aug
 61 to 17 Sep 64; Kreis PO; disease of eyes & c
MAY, Alfred, H-72-2(1); Pvt H Co 14th KY Art;
 5-5-65 to 11-5-65; Chattanooga PO
MAY, Benjamin R., H-58-4; Pvt I Co 4th TN Cav;
 10-14-63 to 7-12-65; Sale Creek PO; neck,
 lungs & fistula on ano (anus?)
MAY, Berry, Br-9-1; Pvt E Co 5th TN Cav; Cleveland
 PO
MAY, Brown, (see Brown, John)
MAY, Edwin F., K-156-2; Sallie K. widow of; Pvt M
 Co 3rd GA Inf; 10 May 61 to 23 May 65; 14 Pine
 St., Knoxville PO; CONF
MAY, George A., Wa-263-6; May Day, 4th Dist PO
MAY, George W., Jo-150-1; Pvt I Co 13th TN Cav;
 15 Jan 64 to 3 May 65; Rheas Forge PO
MAY, Henry, Hu-103-3; Pvt E Co 10th TN Inf; 1 Jan
 62 to 23 Dec 64; PO omitted
MAY, Henry S., Mn-129-2; Sol US; PO omitted
MAY, Isaac, Wa-267-1; Pvt Inf; 64 to May 65;
 Jonesboro PO
MAY, J. F., Gl-139-2; Pvt D Co 9th TN Cav;
 12-8-62 to 5-10-65; Campbellsville PO; CONF
MAY, Jefferson, Jo-150-3; Pvt I Co 13th TN Cav;
 22 Sep 63 to 5 Sep 65; Trade PO
MAY, Jefferson A., Pu-144-2; Double Springs PO
MAY, Jno., Sh-190-1; Rachel widow of; Pvt C Co 3rd
 Col Art; 1-20-65 to 4-30-66; 74 Florida Ave.,
 Memphis PO; could obtain no particulars
MAY, John, D-75-3; Pvt A Co; Stewarts Ferry PO
MAY, John C., Wl-308-2; Pvt C Co 44th TN; 1 May 61
 to 1 May 65; Dodoburgh PO; CONF
MAY, John H., T-213-1; Pvt B Co 55th US Inf; __ to
 4 Jul 65 (4 yrs); Brighton PO; internal
 injuries, wears truss

MAY, Mary A., K-177-3; widow Sol US; PO omitted
MAY, Richard, H-73-3; Lucy widow of; Pvt B Co 1st TN Art; 186? to 3-65 (1 yr 6 mos); Chattanooga PO
MAY, Samuel, Fr-114-1; Pvt E Co 5th TN Mtd Inf; 9-5-64 to 1-26-65; Alto PO; old and froose
MAY, William, Br-7-2; Pvt G Co 1st TN Inf; 2-8-6? to ___; Coahulla PO
MAY, William W., O-138-2; Pvt H Co 45th TN; 15 Dec 61 to 15 May 65; Elbridge PO; CONF
MAYBERRY, John E., H-75-1; Chattanooga PO
MAYBERRY, John T., H-54-5; Alice Henry (widow?); Pvt G Co 16th US Inf; 3-64 to 3-65; Sherman Heights PO
MAYEN, P. D., Cl-53-1; Clariss Stone former widow of; Lt D Co 8th TN Cav; 7-1-61 to 7-1-63; Springdale PO
MAYER, Frederick, H-53-4; Rebecca widow of; Sgt Pvt; 2 yrs; Ridgedale PO; shot in leg and chin
MAYERS, William, Ge-94-1; Pvt G Co 8th TN Inf; 1 Jul 63 to 1 May 65; Home PO
MAYERS, William R., R-161-6; Pvt B Co 6th TN Mtd Inf; 8-18-64 to 6-30-65; Dayton PO
MAYES, Charles, D-64-4; Savanah McCarthy former widow of; Nashville PO
MAYES, James G., Gr-75-2; Pvt C Co 4th TN Cav; 1 Jan 63 to 12 Jul 65; Doyal PO; malarial poisin resulting in partial defness, heart trouble and rhumatism & dislocated thumb
MAYES, James P., H-57-1; Pvt 15th TN Inf; 63 to 65; Chattanooga PO
MAYES, James P., Hm-105-1; Pvt H Co 1st TN Cav; ___ to 63; Turley Mill PO
MAYES, Joel F., Sn-261-3(2); Pvt I Co 30th TN Inf; 12-23-61 to 9-7-62; Rapids PO (Simpson Co.); prison Camp Butler 7 mos 20 days, discharge 9-7-62 Camp Butler
MAYES, Sidney, Mu-195-2; Nannie widow of; A Co 13th TN; Columbia PO
MAYFIELD, General, Gi-125-2; Pvt E Co 14th US Col Inf; 1 Nov 63 to 28 Mar 66; Bodenham PO
MAYFIELD, James W., We-229-1; Pvt I Co 11th IL Cav; 30 Aug 62 to 9 Jun 65; McKinzie PO (Carrol Co); thrown from horse
MAYFIELD, William, Sh-146-1; Pvt B Co 11th IN; 63 to 65; Lucey PO
MAYHO, William, Sh-155-1; Pvt K Co 61st TN Inf; 15 Aug 63 to 15 Feb 65; Germantown PO
MAYHONNEY, Bob, Sh-157-6, Insely's Farm PO
MAYNARD, Andrew, Pu-145-1; Pvt I Co 5th Cav Vol; 11-24-62 to 8-14-65; Burton PO
MAYNARD, Ezekiel, Dk-39-1; Pvt C Co 1st TN Mtd Inf; 10-21-63 to 12-13-64; Bozarth PO; hemorrhoids & kicked by a horse leg & small of backside
MAYNARD, Gibson, Dk-36-2; Lt F Co 4th TN Mtd Inf; 64 to 8-65; Smithville PO
MAYNARD, Henry, D-90-1; Pvt A Co 111th TN Inf; ___ to Sep 65 (1 yr 6 mos); Nashville PO; discharge lost--4 yrs
MAYNARD, James, Pu-145-3(4); Elizabeth widow of; Pvt L Co 5th Cav Vol; 8-13-63 to 8-14-65; Silver Point PO
MAYNARD, James C., Gi-132-3; Pvt I Co 5th TN Cav; 25 Oct 62 to Aug 65; Wales PO; shot in shoulder
MAYNARD, John H., Dk-39-4(2); Pvt F Co 5th TN Cav; 9-62 to 6-65; Dekalb PO; spinal & kidney troubles
MAYNARD, Samuel L., Ro-204-2; Miller, Frank M. alias; Pvt E Co 2nd TN Cav; 63 to 65; Oliver Springs PO; has no discharge
MAYNARD, William, Dk-39-2; Pvt C Co 1st TN Mtd Inf; 10-24-63 to 12-20-64; Bozarth PO; chronic rheumatism, hemorrhoids, deafness and many other complaints so says the deponent
MAYNARD, William, Dy-23-1; Landsman Str. Warland, Str. Powhatan; 23 Jan 64 to 19 Aug 65; Dyersburg PO
MAYNER, Aham E., Mo-124-1; Pvt G Co 8th TN Cav; 63 to 65; Brakebille PO; failure in sight, his discharge not at home
MAYNOR, Samuel, Wh-181-1; Pvt; River Hill PO; only knows he was in the army
MAYO, Blackmore H., Mo-121-1; Pvt H Co 5th TN Inf; 4-6-62 to 5-16-65; Glenlock PO; rheumatism & lung disease
MAYO, George, D., We-223-1; Pvt A Co 20th TN Inf; cant give dates; Palmersville PO; CONF

MAYS, Andrew J., K-170-1; Pvt G Co 8th TN Cav; 15 May 63 to 11 Sep 65; Knoxville PO; gun shot in thigh
MAYS, Cornelius, Ge-98-5; Nancy widow of; Pvt G Co 8th TN Inf; Jeroldstown PO; rheumatism and disease of heart
MAYS, Jerreal D., Cl-58-3; Pvt C Co, 1st TN Lt Art; 1 Sep 63 to 8-1-65; Davo PO; chronic hemmorhibs resulting in general debilaty, quite feeble, hernia & e
MAYS, Jesse, Ge-98-5; Lydia widow of; Pvt; Jeroldstown PO
MAYS, John W., Ma-114-1; Cpl C Co 6th TN; 15 May 61 to 29 May 65; Pinson PO; CONF
MAYS, Rollin, Ha-113-2; Pvt B Co 1st TN Cav; 1 Apr 62 to 5 Apr 65; Sneedville PO
MAYS, Stephen, Wi-275-1; alias Davis, Stephen; Pvt F Co 12th TN Inf; 25 May 64 to 16 Jan 66; Forest Home PO
MAYS, Stephen, G-52-1; Pvt C Co 4th Col Hvy Art; 5-31-65 to 2-25-66; Humbolt PO
MAYS, Stewart, De-22-2; Pvt C Co 10th TN Cav; 10 Dec 62 to 5 Aug 65; Clifton PO
MAYS, William, D-49-3; Pvt; his papers were lost & he dont remember; Nashville PO
MAYS, William T., Cr-10-1; Cpl A Co 6th US Inf; 16 Mar 65 to 16 Oct 66; Stokes PO (Dyer Co)
MAYTON, William H., Ro-202-1; Pvt I Co 1st TN Inf; 9 Aug 61 to 17 Sep 64; Paw Paw Ford PO; rheumatism
MAYUPPY, James, Mg-198-3; Pvt F Co 1st AR Inf; 1 Mar 63 to 10 Aug 65; Rockwood PO; measles 2 mos
MAYWARD, Benjamin, K-155-2(1); Pvt; 138 Hill St., Knoxville PO; rheum. since war
MAZE, William H., Hm-103-3; Pvt D Co 1st TN Cav; 29 Nov 62 to 19 Jun 65; Morristown PO
McABSLAN, John A., Ro-209-4; Pvt I Co 26th TN Inf; 3 Aug 63 to 3 Aug 65; Rockwood PO
McADAMS, John W., Cf-40-4; Pvt G? Co 10th TN Cav; 20 May 62 to 3 Jul 65; Tullahoma PO
McADAMS, Samuel B., Wa-268-2; Johnson City PO; rheumatism
McADAMS, William, D-91-2; Harriet widow of; Pvt B Co 15th; Station C, Nashville PO
McADOO, Samuel, Mc-110-1; Pvt K Co 2nd IL Inf; 10-30-64 to 11-7-65; Rock Creek PO; chronic diarrhea
McAFEE, Samuel, A-10-1; Sabina (widow?); Pvt E Co 96th PA Inf; Briceville PO
McAFEE, William W., Hd-51-1; Gide & Scout for Hodge & Stevens; 63 to 64; Hamburgh PO
McALEXANDER, James R., Cr-8-1; Pvt C Co 1st KY Vol; 12 May 64 to 28 Feb 65; Pvt C Co Green River Battalion; 28 Feb 65 to 23 Aug 65; Lavinia PO
McALINSTER, Samuel, K-154-6(3); Knoxville PO; arm & leg broken 1 yr
McALLISTER, Alexander J., Br-11-2; Cpl I Co 10th TN Cav; 3-4-64 to 8-6-65; Chatata PO
McALLISTER, Charles L., La-113-3; Cpl C Co 13th OH Inf; 31 Aug 64 to 26 Jun 65; Ethridge PO
McALLISTER, James M., Br-6-3; Pvt I Co 10th TN Cav; Charleston PO; rheumatism and neuralgia
McALLISTER, William A., Co-67-2; Pvt I Co 9th TN Cav; 1 Sep 63 to 11 Sep 65; Cosby PO
McALPIN, Joshua A., Cy-26-1; Pvt H Co 5th KY Cav; 12-61 to 5-65; Moss PO
McAMIE, Hugh A., Ge-98-5; Pvt 8th TN Inf; New Port PO (Cocke Co) no report
McAMIS, Archable, K-167-3; Pvt K Co 7th TN Cav; 7 Jun 63 to ___ (1 yr); Locust Sp PO; shot through right sholder, never got back in service
McAMIS, David, K-164-3; Pvt; PO omitted (Knoxville)
McAMIS, James, Mo-122-1; Pvt Inf; ___ to 8-65; Dancing Branch PO; McAmis being temporarily away from home no further dates could be ascertained; CONF
McAMIS, Samuel M., Me-89-2; Pvt; 11-2-62 to 63; Maloney PO
McANALLY, Doctor, Hi-88-1; Pinewood PO
McANALLY, Richard M., Gr-71-2; Pvt I Co 8th TN Inf; 2 Jun 63 to 30 Jun 65; Jarmine PO
McANNA?, Mike, S-214-4; Pvt H Co 5th US Lt Art; 21 Aug 61 to 21 Aug 64; Robbins PO; asthma, rheumatism & piles

McANTIRE, William, Mn-121-1; Pvt A Co 6th TN Cav; Supose 10 Sep 62 to __ (3 mos); Rose Creek PO; Lupus PO; was captured 3 mos atr. enlistmt & peroled

McARDLE, John, Lk-112-2; 3rd Sgt D Co 59th IL Inf; Jul 61 to Dec 65; Tiptonville PO; loss of hearing of left ear, has asked for pension

McARTER, David C., Se-222-1; Pvt I Co 3rd TN Cav; 24 Oct 63 to 20 Jan 65; Harrisburg PO

McATPIN, David J., Cy-26-2; Pvt B Co 5th KY Cav; 10-10-61 to 5-3-65; Moss PO

McAULEY, James C., We-226-1; Pvt C Co 6th TN Cav; Jul 63 to __; Sharon PO

McBATH, James R., K-178-2; Lt H Co 1st TN Inf; 9 Aug 61 to 10 Oct 62; Ball Camp PO

McBEE, Emanuel, Je-146-4; Polly widow of; Pvt C Co 1st Cav Bat; White Pine PO; no discharge & widow don't know dates

McBEE, Thomas B., Mg-196-2; Pvt G Co 2nd TN Inf; 7 Jan 62 to Jan 65; Oliver Springs PO; injured in back & side

McBRIANT, Daniel, Br-12-6; Rhat PO; CONF

McBRIDE, Isaac R., He-67-2; Sgt F Co 10th TN Inf; 20 May 62 to 20 Jun 65; Sardis PO; chronic rheumatism 25 years

McBRIDE, James, D-76-1; Cpl I Co 111th USC Inf; 1 Feb 64 to 30 Apr 66; Nashville PO

McBRIDE, James E., R-161-2; Pvt A Co 10th OH Cav; 10-63 to 8-64; Dayton PO

McBRIDE, Pleasant H., Hd-54-2; 1st Lt H Co 7th TN Inf; 15 Apr 63 to 1 Sep 63; Saltillo PO; discharge taken by rebels

McBRIDE, Thomas G., He-67-2; Cpl C Co 6th TN Cav; 20 Jan 64 to 26 Jul 65; Sardis PO; chronic rheumatism 25yrs, contracted in war

McBRIENT, Sallie, (see Edwards, Jacob)

McBROOM, A. J., R-106-1; Pvt A Co 7th TN; 63 to __ (11 mos); 5th Civil Dist

McBROOM, George W., Pu-144-1; Pvt I Co 1st TN; 6-2-64 to 7-22-65; Double Springs PO

McBROOM, James, Pu-144-1; Mary E widow of; Pvt I Co 1st TN; 6-2-64 to 7-22-65; Double Springs PO

McBROOM, James A., Mc-111-3; Sarah M. widow of; Sgt E Co 7th TN Mtd Inf; 9-10-64 to 7-27-65; Mortimer PO

McBROOM, Marion F., Dk-39-6(2); Pvt H Co 4th TN Mtd Inf; 3-3-64 to 5-23-65; Laurel Hill PO

McBROOM, William, Mc-112-6; Cpl A Co 7th TN Inf; 8-16-64 to 7-29-65; Athens PO; rheumatism & piles

McBRYANT, John, Se-224-2; Cpl D Co 2nd TN Cav; 1 Sep 62 to 6 Jul 65; Wears Valley PO; bonchitis & catarrh

McCABE, Alex, Ge-94-3; Pvt I Co 7th NY Reg; 3 yrs; Ham PO; gunshot in thigh during war

McCABE, Peter, Su-236-1; Elizabeth widow of; Pvt 13th IN Inf; Arcadia PO; discharge lost

McCADDEN, Will, D-49-4; samuel; his wife knew he was a soldier but his papers in Washington; Nashville PO

McCAHN, George W., L-103-1; Pvt L Co MI Cav; Sep 61 to Jun 64; Golddust PO; wounded on brest, papers at Washington

McCAIN, Andrew J., K-186-1; Pvt D Co 7th TN Inf; 15 Jul 62 to __; Wilsons PO; ruptured

McCAIN, Daniell G., Hd-49-1; Pvt A Co 2nd TN Inf; 11 Oct 63 to 14 Oct 64; Martin Mills PO; mash foot, shoulder, hart, brest, bone break

McCAIN, Henry, O-132-1; Pvt G Co 26th KY Inf; 3 Dec 61 to 25 Jul 65; Dist 3

McCAIN, Rufus H., Sh-159-4; Lt; Memphis PO

McCALEB, A. M., G-57-1; 62 to 64; Yorkville PO; CONF

McCALEB, James M., Sm-172-3(1); Sgt K Co 1st TN Inf; 11-5-64 to 7-22-65; Gordonsville PO

McCALEB, Jerimah T. C., Ge-96-4; Lt I Co 8th TN Inf; 15 Dec 62 to 30 Jun 65; Chucky City PO; liver & kidny trouble

McCALEB, John A., Sm-172-3(1); Sarah P. widow of; Pvt K Co 1st TN Inf; 11-62 to __; Gordonsville PO; sicken & died while in service

McCALEB, Samuel M., Pu-144-3; Capt K Co 1st TN Mtd Inf; 1-1-64 to 7-22-65; Ditty PO; disease of eyes

McCALEB, William A., Pu-144-3; Pvt H Co 1st TN Mtd Inf; 2-9-64 to 5-23-65; Hudgins PO; falling of fever in right leg

McCALISTER, J. P., Gi-139-2; Pvt K Co 53rd TN Inf; 11-62 to 5-65; Campbellsville PO; partially deaf & blind; CONF

McCALL, Alexandria, Wa-263-4; Pvt; Alfred PO; consriped; CONF

McCALL, Berryman, Tr-265-1; Pvt F Co 101st US Inf; 14 Oct 64 to 26 Jan 66; Hartsville PO

McCALL, Daniel, Wl-294-1; Pvt F Co 101st TN Inf; Oct 63 to 15 Aug 65; Rome PO; no disability incurred, able to work

McCALL, Joe W., Cr-16-3; Surgeon A Co 7th TN Cav; 15 Sep 62 to 15 Mar 66; Huntingdon PO

McCALL, Robert H., Mo-122-3(1); Pvt A Co 3rd TN Inf; 2-10-62 to 9-4-63; Madisonville PO; CONF

McCALL, Samuel, Bo-12-1; Mary J. widow; Pvt A Co 3rd TN Inf; 62 to 8-2-65; Houk PO; killed Motly ford 1865

McCALL, Samuel A., Sh-201-4; Cpl D Co 1st NC Reg; 10 Jan 62 to 15 Nov 65; Memphis PO; CONF

McCALL, Vernetta, Dk-32-1; Sarah widow of; Pvt L Co 5th TN Cav; 2-22-63 to 12-9-64; Capt E Co 4th TN Mtd Inf; 12-9-64 to 8-26-65; Liberty PO

McCALL, W. W., Bo-11-7; Pvt A Co 3rd TN Inf; 2-10-62 to 2-23-65; Big Gulley PO

McCALLIE, Archibald L., Ja-85-1; Cpl E Co 5th TN Inf; 3-2-62 to 4-4-65; Birchwood PO; shot through left foot

McCALLIE, John, Ja-85-1; Sgt E Co 5th TN Inf; 3-2-62 to 4-4-65; Birchwood PO

McCALLISTER, John H., Sh-196-2; Sgt D Co 3rd US Cav; 11-10-63 to 1-26-66; Cover's Plans Mill; Memphis PO; joined under Capt. Starr

McCALLY, James, H-53-7; Pvt A Co 20th IL Inf; 6-15-61 to 8-10-64; Chattanooga PO; reenlisted

McCALLY, Viner, Sh-155-1; Pvt G Co 11th US Inf; 12 Jan 64 to 18 Jan 66; Germantown PO

McCAMBELL, Buster, Bo-21-2; Pvt A Co 1st TN Art; 10-30-62 to 4-4-65; Veeba PO; CONF

McCAMEY, Alexander, A-13-2; Almeda Long as widow; Pvt A Co TN Hvy Art; Briceville PO

McCAMEY, Andrew J., Ro-205-4; Pvt E Co 1st TN Inf; Postoak Springs PO; kidney trouble

McCAMIS, William C., Br-12-3; Pvt H Co 8th TN Inf; 10-20-62 to 6-65; Raht PO; granulated sore eyes

McCAMISH, Charles A., Ja-84-3; Pvt A Co 4th Cav; 10-25-62 to 7-12-65; Normans Store PO

McCAMMEL, Samuel, Hm-107-3; Pvt H Co 1st US Inf; 12 Jun 64 to 26 Jun 65; Witts Foundry PO; diarrhea 26 years

McCAMMON, O. P., Bo-14-4; Capt L Co 3rd TN Cav; 8-10-62 to 6-26-65; Clover Hill PO

McCAMMON, Thomas, K-181-2; Pvt E Co 3rd TN Cav; 1 Feb 63 to 3 Aug 65; French PO

McCAMMON, William C., K-181-3; 2nd Lt C Co 3rd TN Cav; 19 Nov 62 to 27 May 64; French PO

McCAMPBELL, Cornelius, Je-145-1; Pvt; 1 Nov 61 to 15 Apr 64; Cynthiana PO

McCAMPBELL, Samuel, Je-145-1; Lt of Linch Batter; 1 Nov 61 to 15 Apr 64; Cynthiana PO; CONF

McCAMPBELL, William L., K-166-2; Pvt G Co 6th TN Inf; 14 Apr 62 to 17 May 65; Knoxville PO; wounded in thigh, drawing pension

McCAMY, James, Bo-20-2; Pvt D Co 2nd TN Cav; 9-1-62 to 7-6-65; Bank PO

McCANEY, Rolla, Sh-174-4; Mary Mason formerly widow of; 40 Hadden Ave, Memphis PO; enlisted in Jackson TN

McCANN, Ephrem D., Ge-97-2; Pvt K Co 1st TN Cav; Aug 63 to 8 Jul 65; Newmanville PO; varicose veins, hert truble

McCANN, William W., Jo-148-1; Sgt G Co 13th TN Cav; 24 Sep 63 to 8 Aug 65; Head of Laurel PO

McCANNY, William, Co-68-1; Pvt B Co 2nd NC Inf; 64 to 65; Costner PO

McCARMEL, Edmund, Mu-190-2; alias Edmund Alexius?; Pvt G Co 110th Col Inf; 10-63 to 2-65; Culleoka PO; this man says was mustered in at Kingston GA and mustered out at Huntsville AL

McCARREL, Christopher C., Ro-206-2; Melissie widow of; Pvt I Co 5th TN Inf; 1 Nov 62 to 23 Aug 65; Emory Gap PO

McCARREL, James W., Ro-206-1; Pvt H Co 5th TN Inf; 21 May 62 to 16 May 65; Emory Gap PO

McCARRELL, Joseph C., K-181-6(3); Pvt C Co 6th TN Inf; 18 Apr 62 to 27 Apr 65; Knoxville PO

McCARROLL, Albert, Lo-187-4; Pvt A Co 5th TN Inf; 25 Feb 62 to 4 Apr 65; Loudon PO; weakness of eyes

McCARROLL (alias Boyd), Gilbert, Mu-196-2; Sgt E Co 17th OH; Mar 63 till musted out, 3 yrs 2 mos; Columbia PO

McCARROLL, Hamilton, Ro-210-3; Nancy widow of; Pvt 8th TN Cav; Nov 62 to 8 Apr 65; Rockwood PO; CONF

McCARROLL, James, K-180-2; Pvt C Co 6th TN Inf; 15 Feb 63 to 13 Jun 65; Bearden PO; neuralgia

McCARROLL, John, Lo-18704; Cornelia widow of; Pvt A Co 5th TN Inf; Loudon PO

McCARROLL, John A., Ru-13-2; Pvt M Co TN Cav; 11 Sep 63 to 24 Aug 65; PO omitted

McCARROLL, William S., Ro-210-10; Pvt; Rockwood PO; CONF

McCARRON, William? F., Mc-112-7; Pvt I Co 12th IA Inf; 8-61 to __; Athens PO; mustered out 1st Lt Co G 8th IA Cav

McCARTER, James, Cy-27-5(30); Cpl B Co 8th TN Mtd Inf; 1-15-65 to 8-17-65; Red Springs PO (Macon Co.)

McCARTER, Joseph, Se-230-2; Pvt M Co 9th TN Cav; 3 yrs; Pokeberry PO; chron. diarrhoea & feeblemind, P. Maples of Sevierville, TN, is his guardian

McCARTER, Lafayett, Se-229-2; Pvt E Co 9th TN Cav; 1 Oct 63 to 11 Sep 65; Gatlinburg PO; rheumatism & diarea

McCARTHY, Savanah (see Mayes, Charles)

McCARTHY, Timothy J., Sh-178-3; US Sol; 414 Beall, Memphis PO

McCARTT, Henry A., Mg-200-1; Pvt B Co 2nd TN Inf; 10 Aug 61 to 6 Oct 64; PO omitted

McCARTT, John H., Mg-199-3; 1st Sgt B Co 2nd TN Inf; 10 Aug 61 to 6 Oct 64; Emory PO; rheumatism, varicose veins & c

McCARTY, George, C1-47-1; Pvt C Co 1st TN Inf; 8-14-62 to 65 (3 yrs); St. Elmo PO; wounded right thigh

McCARTY, Herburt, Hn-71-1; 93rd IN; Paris PO; Mr. McCarty left Dist before I could get full particulars--his home is Paducah, KY

McCARTY, James, C1-47-1; Pvt C Co 1st TN Inf; 8-9-61 to 9-17-64; Speedwell PO

McCARTY, William, C-8-1; Dica M. widow of; Pvt H Co 9th TN Cav; 7-12-63 to 9-11-65; Well Spring PO; horse fell on him and injurys cause death

McCARTY, Wm. A., K-167-4; Pvt I Co 2nd __; 63 to 22 Dec 65; Knoxville PO; lame leg from gun shot, he draws a pension

McCARTY, Wm. A., K-167-2; Pvt 6th TN; 62 to 65; Knoxville PO

McCARTY, William S., Gr-78-1; Pvt C Co 1st TN Cav; 1 Jan 62 to 19 May 65; Larkeyton PO; rheumatis & piles, caused from "the service"

McCARVER, Felix T., O-142-1; Pvt G Co 1st AL Cav; 1 Jan 63 to 1 Jan 64; Obion PO; palpitation heart, neuralgia head, ruptured, discharged at Memphis TN

McCASLIN, Leonidas, D-101-1; Sgt A Co 10th TN Inf; 15 Jul 63 to 3 Jul 65; 22nd Civ Dist

McCASSON, James, K-171-6(5); Rachel M. widow of; Pvt; PO omitted; CONF

McCAULEY, James, K-166-1; Sgt A Co 25th IN Inf; Aug 61 to 8 Oct 65; Knoxville PO; loss of right arm

McCAULEY, James, Bo-23-2; Pvt A Co 3rd TN Cav; 9-18-62 to 8-3-65; PO omitted (Cades Cove?)

McCAULEY, Margaret Scales, Sh-183-2; widow of; Cpl C Co 11th US Inf; Memphis PO; died 5-1-62

McCAULEY, Seth H., Sh-182-1; Pvt F Co 11th TN; 4-64 to 12-66; 205 Poplar St., Memphis PO

McCAVE, Thos., Sh-178-3; US So; Cor Dunlap & Union Ave, Memphis PO

McCAY, Nancy A., Su-234-1; widow of US Soldier; 8th Civil Dist

McCAY, P., U-249-1; Lue S. Hensley formerly widow of; Pvt 5th NC Mtd Inf; 64 to 65; Flag Pond PO; now dead

McCEVY, Calvin, Ja-84-1; Nancy J. widow of; Pvt L Co 9th TN Cav; 9-18-63 to 9-11-65; Harrison PO; chronic diarhea, Verginner cant tell no names?

McCHRISTIAN, John L., Mc-109-5; Pvt D Co 3rd TN Inf; 2-10-62 to 2-23-65; Sweetwater PO (Monroe Co); hernia

McCHURCHUN, Allie, Sh-178-2; rear 251 Monroe St., Memphis PO

McCINEY, Jackson, C-32-2; Pvt J Co 2nd TN Inf; 6-3-61 to __ to 10-64 (3 yrs 5 mos); Jilicoe

McCINLEY, ____, Mg-198-1; Mary widow of; Pvt 4th TN; Lavender PO

McCINLLY?, Widow?, Ro-210-10; Pvt 2nd TN Cav; Jul 61 to __; Rockwood PO; CONF

McCLACHY, Mollie, Mc-114-6; widow of; Pvt A Co 42nd TN Inf; 3-61 to 1-31-64; Santfordville PO

McCLACHY, Nancy, Mc-114-7; widow of US Sol; 16th Civil Dist

McCLACHY, William H., Mc-114-7; Pvt; Santfordville PO; CONF?

McCLAIN, Abraham, K_171-1; Sarah A. widow; Pvt D Co 6th TN Inf; Apr 62 to 27 Apr 65; Knoxville PO

McCLAIN, Andrew C., K-164-2; Cpl H Co 1st TN Vol; 9 Aug 61 to 20 Sep 64; PO omitted (Knoxville?)

McCLAIN, Benjamin, Wy-177-2; Dulcenie widow of; Pvt A Co 2nd TN Mtd Inf; Chislem PO; died since war

McCLAIN, Benjamin M., D-89-1; Pvt G Co 118th K; Aug 62 to 65; Buchville or Nashville PO

McCLAIN, Bob, O-141-2; Union City PO

McCLAIN, Henry V., K-171-4(3); Pvt; Knoxville PO; ruptured

McCLAIN, Hiram, Je-141-3; Pvt; Mill Springs PO; discharge at Washington

McCLAIN, James H., Je-141-4; Pvt C Co 2nd TN Inf; 10 Aug 61 to 7 May 65; Mill Springs PO

McCLAIN, John, C-30-2; Hester A. widow of; Pvt C Co 1st TN Inf; 8-9-61 to 9-17-64; Well Springs PO

McCLAIN, Lewis, W1-290-1; Mona widow of; Pvt K Co 27th OH; 1 May 64 to 1 Aug 65; Lebanon PO; discharged

McCLAIN, Linard, Hw-121-4(3); Pvt K Co 1st TN Cav; 12 Jul 62 to 5 Jun 65; Van Hill PO; chronic direah

McCLAIN, Zion, Lo-195-1; Pvt D Co 6th TN Inf; 18 Apr 62 to 27 Apr 65; Vancouver PO; bronchitas of the lungs, sight

McCLANAHAN, David, Bo-21-3; Pvt B Co 3rd TN Cav; 7-12-62 to 6-10-65; Ellijay PO

McCLANAHAN, James F., Me-88-2; Pvt E Co 5th TN Inf; 3-3-63 to 7-4-65; Brillsville PO

McCLANAHAN, James R. Sr., Cr-4-1; Bugler G Co 46th TN Cav; 1 Nov 61 to 2 Nov 63; Bells Depot PO; CONF

McClANAHAN, John, Me-88-1; Pvt B Co 3rd TN Inf; 2-10-62 to 2-23-65; Birchwood PO

McCLANAHAN, Mason, Ja-85-3; Pvt E Co 5th TN Inf; 3-2-62 to 4-4-65; Birchwood PO

McCLANAHAN, Thomas A., Tr-265-1; Pvt A Co 2nd KS Inf; 1 Mar 63 to 1 Apr 64; Dixon's Springs PO

McCLANE, Francis M., Su-240-3; Pvt C Co 3rd NC Inf; 15 Sep 64 to 8 Nov 65; Slaughter PO; chronic piles

McCLANNAHAN, Benj. F., Mu-209-7; Malinda widow of; Pvt C Co 1st TN Cav; 6-1-61 to 6-65; Columbia PO

McCLANNAHAN, John W., Br-8-4(2); Pvt A Co 3rd TN Vol Cav; 8-25-63 to 9-11-65; Cleo PO; wounded in knee

McCLANNAHAN, Pinkney M., De-22-3; Pvt D? Co 27th TN Inf; 1 Aug 61 to 1 Oct 63; Dunbar PO; CONF

McCLANNAHAN, William C., Co-63-4; Pvt D Co 1st TN Cav; Newport PO

McCLARAN, Peter, D-57-2; Pvt C Co 106th US Inf; 22 Apr 64 to __; Nashville PO; shot in leg

McCLARDY, Thomas, W1-276-1; Pvt D Co 10th TN Cav; Oct 62 to Oct 62 (10 days); Beechville PO; CONF

McCLARIN, Lemul, D-51-2; Mary widow of; Pvt A Co 111th KY C Inf; Jul 62 to __; 319 Line St., Nashville PO

McCLARIN, Wm., D-43-1; Sgt C Co; Nashville PO

McCLARY, George, F-46-2; Biddie widow of; Pvt 59th TN; 63 to 64; LaGrange PO; died in 1864

McCLATCY, William M., H-65-1; Pvt B Co 2nd KY Cav; 4-61 to 4-65; Chattanooga PO; CONF

McCLEAN, John, We-233-1(2); Luv widow of; Pvt; Martin PO; left no record of service

McCLEANNELL, John C., G-61-1; Pvt D Co 13th TN Cav; 12 Dec 63 to furloid 64 (3 mos); 12th Civil Dist

McCLEARY, David, Sh-200-1; Mary widow of; Cpl A Co 3rd IA Inf; 71 Polk St, Memphis PO; right arm & shoulder badly ___

McCLELLAN, Iridell, Hw-133-1; 2nd Lt C Co 3rd TN Inf; Aug 61 to 13 May 65; Slide PO; CONF

McCLELLAN, James (Samuel), Wl-297-2; Pvt C Co 7th PA? Cav; Jul 62 to 17 Jun 65; Linwood PO

McCLELLAN, John, F-35-2(5); Pvt C Co 61st; 25 Jun 63 to 30 Dec 65; Brinkley PO; rheumatism

McCLELLAN, Neil, K-160-3; Cpl D Co 1st TN; Apr 62 to Apr 65; Knoxville PO

McCLELLAN, Reuben, Sh-197-1; Sgt H Co 11th Col Inf; __ to 65; Memphis PO; chronic diorrhea ¢ rheumatism

McCLELLAN, William A., Dk-34-2; Pvt I Co 5th TN Cav; 11-4-63 to 8-25-65; Dowelltown PO; lung trouble & eye sight; gun shot wound in left P & heart disease

McCLELLAND, Calvin, alias Gabriel Lane, Sh-174-3; Pvt I Co 111th US Inf; 4-13-63 to 2-15-66; 216 Linden St, Memphis PO; shot in left arm

McCLELLEN, James, K-176-2; Pvt D Co 6th TN Inf; 18 Apr 62 to Apr 65; Halls X Roads PO

McCLELLEN, Jane, (see Young, Louis)

McCLENAN, Harett A. (see Moss, Ben)

McCLENDAL, Isaac, Ro-210-6; Cpl B Co 6th TN Mtd Inf; 15 Sep 64 to 3 Jun 65; Rockwood PO

McCLENDEN, Jessie, Dy-27-1; Pvt 11th TN Cav; 61 to 65; Ro Ellen PO; CONF

McCLENNAHAN, William F., He-63-1; Alcy A. widow of; Scotts Hill PO

McCLERON, Alexander, Ge-88-1; Pvt A Co 34th KY Inf; 62 to 63; Marvin PO; lungs & pneoumeni

McCLERREY, ___, Se-222-2; Eliza A. widow of; Sevierville PO

McCLINTON, Saunders, R-157-1; 3rd Sgt V 6th Mtd Inf E TN; 2-10-62 to 6-30-65; Spring City PO; chr. rheumatism & kidney affection, enlist Co H 3rd Inf E.T.V. & transferred to 6th Mtd Inf (ETV)

McCLOCHY, Richard, Mc-114-5; Pvt K Co 1st TN Art; 7-5-64 to 3-21-65; Santfordville PO

McCLONCH, William D., Mo-129-1; Pvt F Co 2nd TN Cav; Povo PO

McCLONICK?, William B., Cl-56-2(1); Rachel M. Goines formerly widow of; 1st Lt C Co 1st TN Lt Art; 5-16-65 to 1-8-65; Head of Barren PO; died of chronic diarhea

McCLORE, Marcus D., Mc-112-6; Pvt F Co 3rd TN Cav; 11-1-62 to 6-10-65; Athens PO; chronic piles

McCLORG, John C., H-55-3; Pvt D Co 3rd TN Cav; 9-18-62 to 8-3-65; Kings Point PO

McCLOUD, Daniel, Sn-262-2(1); Pvt E Co 8th TN Cav; 63 to 65; Fountain Head PO; rheumatism, cant day of dis. & enlist.

McCLOUD, James, Ct-35-2; Mary widow of; Pvt I Co 13th TN Cav; 9-22-63 to 9-5-65; Butler PO (Johnson Co); in US Army

McCLOUD, James H., Sh-158-2; Capt of After-guards, US Str. Essex; 14 Sep 61 to 28 Sep 65; Memphis PO; "Essex" 1st Iron-clad in US Navy

McCLOUD, Jerry, Rb-221-3; Pvt 25th OH; Adams Station PO

McCLOUD, Tennessee, Jo-152-3; Pvt I Co 13th TN Cav; 23 Sep 63 to 5 Sep 65; Butler PO; saddle injure, cannot give day of enlist or discharge

McCLUNG, John C., Lo-191-2; Pvt G Co 3rd TN Vol Inf; 10 Feb 62 to 23 Feb 65; Greenback PO

McCLURE, Charles, Ms-183-1; Cpl I Co 111th US Col Inf; Comenville PO; consumption, body disease during service

McCLURE, Clemment, Ru-238-2; Pvt D Co 15th USC Inf; Murfreesboro PO

McCLURE, Frank, Ru-236-1; Pvt I Co 124th IN Inf; Murfreesboro PO; sun stroke, 8th June 64, Kenesaw Mountain

McCLURE, James, Ru-236-1; Pvt I Co 125 IN Inf; Murfreesboro PO

McCLURE, John, M-107-6; Pvt K Co 4th E TN Cav; 9-63 to ___ (1 yr 3 mos); North Springs PO (Jackson Co)

McCLURE, John, Br-7-2; Pvt E Co 6th TN Inf; 4-10-62 to 4-27-65; Felker PO; rheumatism

McCLURE, Thomas J., Se-223-2; Pvt B Co 2nd TN Cav; 15 Aug 62 to 6 Jul 65; Henderson Springs PO; spinal affec. & disease of legs

McCLURE, W. C., Mn-129-1; Pvt B Co 6th TN Cav; 7-22-63 to 7-26-65; Stantonville PO; shot through right leg & right arm

McCOIY, John, Je-139-2; Trion PO; piles, chronic diaro

McCOLLEN, Rye, T-218-1; Pvt K Co 56th TN Inf; Feb 63 to Sep 65; Tabernacle PO; back injured from a fall ___ in a battle

McCOLLISTER, David, Ja-86-1; Cpl G Co 81st OH Inf; 7-11-62 to 7-13-65; Oottewah PO; diarhea--chronic

McCOLLUM, Joseph B., Lo-191-1; Morganton PO: CONF

McCOLLUM, Samiel, Ge-92-4; 4th Sgt F Co 3rd TN Mtd Inf; 64 to 64 (3 mos); Laurel Gap PO

McCOLLUM, Thomas J., G-71-2; Pvt G Co 20th TN Inf; 11 Jun 61 to 11 Oct 62; Rutherford PO; shot in hip, crippled; CONF

McCOLLUM, ___, H-57-1; Frances widow of; Pvt US Col; 63 to 65; Orchard Knob PO

McCOMBS, Robert J., We-221-2; Fannie F. widow of; Pvt Cav; 63 to 65; Martin PO; CONF

McCOMEY, Samuel A., Br-14-1; Pvt B Co 1st TN Lt Art; McDonald PO; catarrh, bronchitis & rheumatism

McCONLEY, Terrence, Sh-159-1; Memphis PO; CONF

McCONLY, William, D-69-2; US Sol, no record of service; PO omitted (Nashville?)

McCONNEL, Stephen, D-89-1; Buchville PO; papers in the hands of an agent

McCONNELL, Cornelius (Col), H-56-4; Pvt 37th GA Cav; St. Elmo PO

McCONNELL, J. C., Bo-11-1; Pvt B Co 4th TN Inf; 4-5-63 to 8-2-65; Cloids Creek PO

McCONNELL, J. N., Bo-11-4; Pvt E Co 3rd TN Inf; 7-14-64 to 11-30-64; Brick Mill PO

McCONNELL, John R., R-161-4; Pvt K Co 34th KY; 8-18-62 to 5-25-63; Dayton PO

McCONNELL, Joseph, H-67-3; Sol US; Chattanooga PO

McCONNELL, Joseph R., Lo-192-1; Pvt G Co 3rd TN; 1 Dec 63 to Aug 65; Coytee PO; fever settled in 1 side

McCONNELL, Samuel B., Ro-203-3; Pvt 23rd TN Inf; Jul 61 to ___; Ethel PO; parolled May the 12, 1865

McCORCLE, George C., Me-69-2(1); Pvt D Co 5th TN Mtd Inf; 11-16-64 to 7-14-65; Meigs PO

McCORD, Robert J. S., Ms-182-1; Pvt A Co 5th TN Cav; 8-13-63 to 7-15-64; Venna PO; defection left shoulder, labors part of time on farm

McCORE, Anthony, D-58-2; Pvt D Co; Nashville PO; shot in right ankle

McCORKLE, Amanuel, Ch-13-2; Pvt I Co 11th IL Vol; 8-62 to ___ (2 yrs 2 mos); Jacks Creed PO

McCORKLE, Finas A., Dy-25-8(4); Pvt; Newbern PO; CONF

McCORKLE, Franklin B., Cr-23-2; Pvt G Co 27th TN Inf; Jun 61 to Sep 65; PO omitted; CONF

McCORKLE, John E.?, Dy-29-2; 2nd Lt D Co 13th TN Reg; May ___ to Oct ___; Newbern PO; CONF

McCORKLE, John J., Ct-41-2; Pvt J Co 1st US; 9-23-63 to 4-6-66; Elizabethton PO; piles, left hip and thy

McCORKLE, Moses, De-23-2; Pvt E Co 4th TN Cav; Mar 61 to Aug 65; Bath Springs PO; wounded left hip

McCORMACK, Martha (see Mathews, Ben)

McCORMICK?, Frank, M-105-1; Pvt E Co 1st TN Inf; 12-20-63 to 1-22-64; Hillsdale PO

McCORMICK, Hiram, H-56-3; Pvt; 61 to 65; St. Elmo PO

McCORMICK, Hiram, H-56-3; Sol US; St. Elmo PO

McCORMICK, Lewis N., R-163-4; Pvt I Co 86th IL Inf; 8-7-62 to 6-5-65; Ogden PO

McCORMICK, Patrick, H-58-5; Minnie widow of; Pvt F Co 2nd TN Inf; Retro PO; discharge misplaced

McCORRY, Louis, Sh-189-6; Mary widow of; Pvt C Co 55th US Col Inf; Spring 63 to can't get other information; Georgia Ave, Memphis PO

McCORTEY, Mike C., Mt-145-1; Pvt C Co 2nd KY Cav; 1 Jun 61 to 12 Aug 65; Palmyra PO

McCORY, John R., Wa-226-1; Margaret Brandon formerly widow of; Pvt B Co 4th TN Cav; Sep 62 to Jun 64; Fall Branch PO

McCORY, Malcome, Je-137-3; Pvt E Co 1st KY Cav; 29 Feb 64 to 1 Aug 65; Chestnut Hill PO

McCOVEY?, William, Ro-209-4; Glen Alice PO; CONF

McCOWN, Aaron M., Se-223-3; Pvt E Co 1st TN Bat; 2 Dec 63 to 2 Aug 65; Sevierville PO

McCOWN, Sanco?, Se-223-4; Pvt I Co 1st TN Bat; 10 Jul 64 to 31 Mar 66; Sevierville PO

McCOY, Alexander, Mr-97-2; Talithay widow of; Pvt I Co 11th TN Inf; 62 to 65; Jarman? PO

McCOY, Amanda, Ms-170-1; 4th Dist

McCOY, Andrew, G-65-1; "found while examining"; PO omitted

McCOY, Hiram H., Jo-149-1; Martha widow of; Pvt E Co 13th TN Cav; 1 Oct 64 to 5 Sep 65; Mountain City PO; chronic diarrhea

McCOY, Jacob E., Sh-201-3; Pvt A Co 27th OH Inf; 15 May 63 to 10 Jul 65; Memphis PO

McCOY, James, Un-255-1; Pvt M Co 9th TN Cav; 21 Sep 63 to 11 Sep $\overline{PO}$ (1 yr 11 mos 10 days); Warwicks X Roads PO; dispepesey & diap.

McCOY, James A., A-6-4(2); Margaret widow of; Pvt E Co 3rd TN Inf; 2-20-62 to 2-23-65; Fairview PO

McCOY, James W., Ge-102-1; Pvt E Co 4th TN Inf; 15 Nov 61 to 8 Aug 65; Camp Creek PO; rheumatism

McCOY, Thomas, Cu-15-2; Pvt G Co 2nd TN Inf; 1-7-62 to 1-9-65; Genesis PO

McCOY, William A., Fr-120-1; Pvt C Co 2nd TN Cav; Aug 62 to 8 Jun 65; Sewanee PO

McCOY, William L., Mr-97-2; Pvt C Co 2nd TN Cav; 8-22-63 to 7-6-65; Jarman? PO

McCRACKEN, James, Wa-274-2; Pvt B Co 4th US Vol; 15 Oct 64 to 4 May 65; Jonesboro PO; rheumatism & disease of heart

McCRACKEN, James, Mo-120-1; Cathorine M. widow of; Pvt Inf; Glenlock PO

McCRACKIN, Jas. E., La-117-4; Emily J. widow of; 15th Dist; CONF

McCRACKIN, John, Wa-267-2; Pvt G Co 3rd NC Inf; 1 Feb 65 to 8 Aug 65; Febuary PO

McCRACKIN, John B., Br-6-2; Fanney M. widow? of; Pvt A Co 8th TN Cav; 6-11-63 to 64 (died, date unknown); Chatala PO

McCRACKIN, Joseph, Cr-16-4; Pvt E Co 7th TN Cav; Dec 62 to ___; Huntington PO

McCRACKING, James M., Wa-261-2; Pvt I Co 1st TN Cav; 21 Sep 62 to 5 Jun 63; Conkling PO

McCRADY, John R., Mu-210-6; Pvt K Co 1st TN Cav; Jun 62 to 63; Spring Hill PO; CONF

McCRAIF, William M., Bo-12-4; Sol US; 17th Dist

McCRARY, Andrew, J-83-1; Pvt A Co 1st TN; 1-8-64 to 8-17-65; Flynns Lick PO

McCRARY, Arron B., Sm-170-3; 1st Lt A Co 1st TN Mtd Inf; 1-21-64 to 1-30-65; Maggart PO; sore eyes

McCRARY, Joseph, Ja-84-3; Pvt B Co 1st TN Lt Art; 4-18-63 to 7-20-65; Thatchers Landing PO; cold on lungs

McCRARY, Mallis, (see Williford, James)

McCRARY, Robert, Sm-170-1; Pvt A Co 1st TN Mtd Inf; 1-15-64 to 1-15-65; Maggart PO

McCRATH, John W., H-56-6; Capt B Co; 7-61 to 7-22-65 St. Elmo PO

McCRAVENRY, Peter, Sh-148-1; G Co 61st Col Inf; 21 Dec 63 to 30 ___ 65; (at Baton Route); Memphis PO

McCRAW, Samuel, F-39-1; Pvt Inf; 3 yrs; Braden PO; says he lost discharge

McCREARY, Thomas F., Di-34-2; Capt G Co 145th PA Inf; 5-22-62 to 9-13-63; Dickson PO; wounded in left leg (also 4-27-61 to 8-27-61)

McCREERY, William A., D-72-6; Pvt E Co 31st MO Inf; 63 to 65; Nashville PO; gun shot wound left leg, discharge ____general disability

McCRORY, George W., K-185-4; Pvt H Co 5th TN Cav; 62 to ___; Balls Camp PO; CONF

McCROSKEY, Alexander, Br-9-2; Pvt D Co 1st TN Hvy Art; Cleveland PO

McCROSKEY, James N., Se-231-2; Pvt K Co 2nd TN Inf; 9 Jan 62 to 9 Jan 65; Arther PO; varicosela 25 yrs

McCROSKEY, John, K-167-2; Easter widow of; Pvt 1st Hvy TN; 62 to 65; Knoxville PO

McCROSKEY, Pinkey, Mc-118-2; Sarah A. widow of; Pvt 7th TN Mtd Inf; Joshua PO

McCROY, Jesse, H-52-1; Mary W. widow of; Pvt F Co 6th TN Inf; 9-12-62 to 6-30-65; St. Elmo PO

McCRURY, James O., Wa-271-2; Pvt K Co 3rd NC Mtd Inf; 1 Mar 65 to 8 Aug 65; Jonesboro PO; rumatism

McCRUTCHEN, King, Gi-128-1; Pvt G Co 111th TN Inf; 63 to 65; 8th Civil Dist

McCUCHEON, James, D-67-1; Annie widow of; Pvt Col Inf; Nashville PO

McCUIN, James P., H-64-2; Pvt K Co 85th PA; Chattanooga PO

McCULEE, Wm. H., K-167-3; Mariah Cannon widow of; Pvt C Co 1st TN Hvy; ___ to died 64; Knoxville PO

McCULLAH, Thomas J., Bo-12-1; Pvt F Co 2nd TN Cav; 8-1-62 to 7-6-65; Houk PO; tranchined scull

McCULLEY, Andrew J., Bo-23-2; Pvt D Co 2nd TN Cav; 9-1-62 to 5-29-65; Cades Cove PO; g(un) shot in left foot, now has chronic diarea

McCULLEY, J. S., F-44-3; Pvt F Co 42nd MS __; 62 to 65; PO omitted; CONF

McCULLEY, James H., Pu-140-1; Margaret A. widow of; Sgt K Co 13th E TN Cav; Cookeville PO; rheumatism, served about 3 yrs

McCULLEY, James K., Br-8-1; Pvt B Co 5th TN Mtd Inf; 8-13-64 to 7-13-65; Blue Springs Station PO; rheumatism

McCULLEY, Louisa, Sn-257-1; widow of soldier; 9th Civil Dist

McCULLOCH, John A., Bo-21-2; Martha widow of; Pvt A Co 3rd TN Cav; 12-22-62 to 6-22-63?; Ellijay PO

McCULLOCH, John S., K-170-3; Chaplin 77th IL Inf; 5 Apr 64 to 22 Jul 65; Knoxville PO

McCULLOUGH, Ben, D-49-3; Pvt B Co 44th TN; 7 Apr 64 to 30 Apr 66; Nashville PO

McCULLOUGH, James, Cu-17-3; Pvt I Co TN Inf; 2-10-62 to 4-65; Grassy Cove PO; wounded

McCULLOUGH, John M., H-56-5; Pvt G Co 5th TN Inf; 61 to 65; St. Elmo PO; CONF

McCULLOUGH, Thomas, Cu-17-4; Pvt I Co 3rd E TN Inf; 2-10-62 to 2-22-63; Crab Orchard PO

McCULLUM, James P., K-158-1; Capt B Co 63rd TN Inf; May 61 to May 65; 28 Mabry St, Knoxville PO; CONF

McCULLY, William, C-29-1; Pvt I Co 9th TN Cav; 62 to 65; Fincastle PO; neuralgia, partial insanity incured

McCULLY, William, R-157-1; Pvt C Co 4th E TN Cav; 7-4-62 to ___ (2 yrs 11 mos 24 days); Lorraine PO; left ranks without furlough

McCULOUGH, William, Br-14-1; Julian Anne widow of; Pvt 8th TN Mtd Inf; 63 to ___; McDonald PO; died in the service

McCURRY, Duncan M., Ge-92-4; Sarah H. widow of; Pvt K Co 1st TN Cav; 12 Jul 62 to 5 Jun 65; Laurel Gap PO

McCURRY, John, Ge-97-1; Pvt H Co 8th TN Inf; 1 Oct 63 to Jun 65; Locust Springs PO; bronchitis et al

McCURRY, Martin, R., Wa-261-2; Pvt I Co TN Cav Firs?; 21 Sep 62 to 27 May 65; Brownsboro PO

McCUTCHEN, Robert P., Wi-276-2; Pvt D Co 10th TN Cav; May 62 to Oct 65; Beechville PO; CONF

McCUTCHER, J. C., Gi-139-2; Pvt K Co 53rd TN Inf; 11-62 to 63; Campbellsville PO; partially deaf

McDANEL, James H., Ro-209-4; Pvt A Co; 63 to 64; Rockwood PO; CONF

McDANEL, James N., Ro-205-2; Pvt; PO omitted

McDANIEL, C. C., Hr-96-1; Scout; 63 to 65; Pinetop PO; CONF

McDANIEL, Geo. C., G-71-2; Pvt C Co 22nd TN Inf; 5 Aug 61 to 5 Apr 62; Edmonds PO; CONF

McDANIEL, Geo. E., G-71-2; Pvt A Co 54th TN Cav; 26 Nov 64 to 6 Mar 65; Rutherford PO; CONF

McDANIEL, Green, Bl-3-1; Tanbone PO; Conf

McDANIEL, James, Mo-123-1; Pvt H Co 7th TN Mtd Inf; 3-20-65 to 7-27-65; Jalapa PO

McDANIEL, James, (see Troop, James)

McDANIEL, James T., Mo-123-1; Pvt H Co 7th TN Mtd Inf; 3-20-65 to 7-27-65; Jalapa PO

McDANIEL, Jane (see Parrott, George)

McDANIEL, Marcus L., Mc-111-1; Sgt E Co 1st TN Lt Art; 9-25-63 to 8-1-65; Gudger PO (Monroe Co)

McDANIEL, Mathias, Gr-75-1; Pvt F-M Co, 1st TN Cav; 12 May 63 to 19 Jun 65; Tampico PO; rheumatism & heart and liver affection

McDANIEL, Nelson, Ru-238-1; Jane widow of; Pvt C Co 111th USC Inf; 21 Mar 64 to 30 Apr 66; Murfreesboro PO

McDANIEL, Samuel, Wa-166-3; Emma C. widow of; Pvt 2nd TN Inf; chronic inflammatory rheumatism

McDANIEL, William L., D-72-3; Pvt C Co 74th OH Inf; 9 Dec 61 to 15 Mar 65; Nashville PO; wounded in left side

McDANIELS, Jasper, Ro-210-8; Pvt A Co 16th Batallion; 62 to 64; Rockwood PO; CONF
McDANILL, John, Bl-3-5; Margret E. widow of; Pvt 26th TN Inf; Tanbark PO; consumption
McDANILL, William, Bl-3-3; Pvt F Co 3rd TN Inf; 4-16-61 to 5-19-65; Billingsly PO
McDANNEL, Benton, K-179-5; US Sol; Concord PO
McDEARMON, Clement C., We-224-3(1); Pvt G Co 5th TN Cav; 15 Nov 61 to ___ (1 yr); Gleson Station PO; surrendered at Tiptonville, TN, no discharge; CONF
McDELLAN?, Albert, Ov-138-1; Sgt D Co 52nd KY Inf; 8-7-63 to 1-17-64; 10th Civil Dist
McDERMOTT, Howard, Mc-112-9; Pvt B Co 44th TN Inf; 3-4-64 to 4-65; Athens PO
McDERMOTT, Thomas, Mc-117-4; Pvt A Co 42nd TN Inf; 3- to ___ (2 yrs 2 mos); Carlock PO; piles
McDONALD, Alen, Li-149-1; Sgt K Co 110th US Col Inf; 1-13-64 to 12-15-66; Fayetteville PO
McDONALD, Amos, R-161-4; Nancy widow of; Pvt G Co 2nd TN Inf; 10-61 to ___ (1 yr 5 mos); Dayton PO; discharge on disability (lost)
McDONALD, Andy, Sm-166-3(1); Pvt; Monoville PO
McDONALD, Edger S., Su-243-1; Master Mart? Mait? Mendota; 23 Apr 64 to 12 Dec 65; Bristol PO; wounded
McDONALD, Frank, Li-149-1; Caroline widow of; Pvt K Co 110th US Col Inf; 1-13-64 to 12-15-66; Fayetteville PO
McDONALD, George W., Pi-153-3; Pvt H Co 3rd KY Inf; 11-62 to 1-64; West Fork PO
McDONALD, Isaac, F-47-2; US Sol; 14th Civil Dist
McDONALD, James, Ge-89-2; Pvt C Co 8th Cav; 11 Jun 63 to 11 Sep 65; Mosheim PO
McDONALD, John A., Pi-154-1; Pvt D Co 1st TN Mtd Inf; 7-64 to 7-65; Spurrier PO
McDONALD, John R., M-103-6; Cpl H Co 5th KY Cav; 12-4-61 to ___; Union Camp PO; not discharged on account of not being able to return to regiment
McDONALD, John W., Ge-100-2; Pvt 1st TN Cav; 9 Nov 61 to ___; Mohawk PO; imprison before join company
McDONALD, Miles, Hr-86-1; Pvt F Co 61st TN; Jan 63 to 66; Grand Junction PO; powder burnt, eyes badly effected
McDONALD, Peter, Tr-268-1; Pvt; Hartsville PO
McDONALD, Robert, Li-149-1; Blacksmith 8th OH Cav; Fayetteville PO; lost discharge
McDONALD, Sidney S., Sm-169-1; Pvt E Co 28th TN Inf; 10-18-62 to 1-14-65; Carthage PO; CONF
McDONALD, Sterlin B., Sm-174-1; Pvt G Co 4th TN Inf; 11-1-64 to 8-25-65; New Middleton PO
McDONALD, Thomas, M-103-5; Pvt B Co 37th KY Inf; 8-15-63 to 12-27-64; Lafayette PO
McDONALD, Toliver, Mc-115-2; Pvt D Co 5th TN; Riceville PO; hurt in should & head, dont know dates
McDONALD, Van B., Lo-192-1; Pvt K Co 5th TN; Oct 62 to Jun 65; Coytee PO; chronic rheumatism
McDONALD, William, H-56-2; 61 to 65; East End PO
McDONALD, William, Gi-132-3; Pvt K Co 15th USCV; Pulaski PO
McDONALD, William, H-65-1; A Co 13th US Inf; 61 to 64; Chattanooga PO
McDONALL, James, K-160-3; Knoxville PO
McDONIEL, George, Bl-4-2; Pvt H Co 4th TN Cav; 7-22-63 to 7-26-65; Morgan Springs PO (Rhea Co.)
McDONNALD, James M., M-103-2; Sarah T. widow of; Sgt B Co 5th TN Cav; 8-25-62 to 6-25-65; Lafayette PO
McDONNELL, John, Lo-194-2; Pvt C Co 1st TN Art; ___ to 30 Jul 65 (2 yrs 6 mos); Muddy Creek PO
McDONOUGH, John W., Hi-88-1; Sgt G Co 12th TN Cav; 2-15-64 to 7-3-65; Pinewood PO; catarrh of head, not able to work any
McDOUGLE, John, D-43-1; Pvt A Co; Nashville PO
McDOWAL, Robert, Sh-159-3; Pvt L Co 3rd US Art; 9 Dec 63 to 1 May 66; Memphis PO
McDOWEL, Charles E., S-214-2; Mabell Connor former widow of; Pvt KY Inf; 61 to ___; Glenmary PO; does not know any dates &c
McDOWEL, Phillis, Sh-149-2; widow; Nov 64 to Dec 66; Frazer PO
McDOWELL, Henry, F-47-1; Pvt C Co 59th TN Inf; 3-18-64 to 1-31-66; Willison PO

McDOWELL, Jessie (see Lodgin, Jef)
McDOWELL, Lewis, F-47-1; Pvt E Co 1st TN Art; 64 to Jan 31 66; Williston PO
McDOWELL, Malcolm, Mu-209-1; Pvt; Columbia PO
McDOWELL, William, Ca-25-1; Pvt L Co 5th TN Cav; to 5-65 (2 yrs 4 mos); Shoat? Mountain PO
McDOWELL, William, B-7-2; Mary E. widow of; 1st Lt A Co 4th TN Mtd Inf; 8-64 to 65 (1 yr 8 mos); Shelbyville PO; killed on steamer explosion April 1865
McDUFFEE, George W., M-106-1; Martha J. widow of; Pvt K Co 9th KY Vol Inf--11-7-61 to 7-6-63; Lt B Co 9th KY Vol Inf--3-10-65 to 8-17-65; Union Camp PO
McDUFFEE, Major B., Rb-218-1; Lt K Co 9th KY Inf; 1 Dec 61 to 15 Dec 64; Cross Plains PO; chronic diarrhea
McELHINEY, John, Di-42-1; Pvt D Co 2nd VA Cav; 9-1-61 to 12-31-63; Tenn City PO; vettern 12-31-65, discharged 1865
McELHINEY, William G., Di-42-1; Cpl G Co 78th PA Inf; 10-12-61 to 11-4-64; Tenn City PO; rheumatism army from exposier in army
McELMORE, Thomas B., K-186-2; Cpl B Co 6th TN Inf; 16 Apr 62 to 27 Apr 65; Ball's Camp PO; kidney trouble
McELROY, James, K-175-1; Pvt D Co 5th Sant? Cav; 13 May 62 to 1 Aug 64; Pedigo PO
McELYEA, George W., Jo-148-1; Pvt F Co 13th TN Cav; 13 Sep 63 to 13 Sep 65; Silver Lake PO; rheumatis
McELYEA, John, Jo-151-3; Pvt F Co 13th TN Cav; 22 Sep 63 to 5 Sep 65; Vaughtsville PO; brain fever resulting in lung disease, died in 1884
McELYEA, Landon, Jo-152-3; Pvt F Co 13th TN Cav; 22 Sep 63 to 5 Sep 65; Butler PO; contracted disease head, eyes & breast
McELYIN, Robert D., We-225-4(3); Pvt F Co 7th TN Cav; Pvt F Co 13th TN Cav; 62 to 65; bursted? up at Ft. Pillow; PO omitted
McENACKIN, Robert W., Wa-261-1; Pvt I Co TN Cav; 24 Sep 62 to 5 Jun 65; Brownsboro PO
McENROE, James D., Hu-98-1; Pvt E Co 8th TN Cav; 4 Oct 64 to 5 Sep 65; Waverley PO; thrown from horse, head injured and deafness
McENTOSH, Fielding A., Ct-44-1; Adaline widow of; Pvt C Co 2nd TN Cav; Hampton PO; discharge in Washington DC
McENTURFF, Samuel M., Ja-84-1; Mira A. widow of; Pvt I Co 2nd E TN Mtd Inf; 11-11-61 to 11-26-64; Harrison PO; loss of left leg
McEWEN, Alexander, H-58-3; Pvt K Co 8th TN Cav; 11-11-61 to 1-16-65; Sale Creek PO
McEWEN, John C., Jo-150-4; 1st Sgt M Co 13th TN Cav; 2 Feb 64 to 5 Sep 65; Osborn PO
McEWEN, William M., Rb-221-1; Pvt C Co 5th TN; May 15 63 to Sep 1 64; Adams Station PO
McFADDIN, Peter, L-102-1; Pvt G Co 8th KY; 64 to Jun 66; Fort Pillow PO; white swelling
McFALL, George W., Se-229-1; Pvt B Co 2nd TN Cav; 15 Sep 62 to 24 May 65; Pigeon Forge PO; chronic rheumatism
McFALL, James M., Wy-174-1; Pvt H Co 2nd TN; 1-8-64 to 4-7-65; Stout PO
McFALL, Moses, D-60-1; 116 Stonewall St, Nashville PO; colored
McFALLS, D. N., Hd-48-1; Pvt H Co 2nd TN Mtd Inf; Jan 11 64 to Apr 17 65; Savannah PO
McFALLS, J. M., Hd-48-1; Pvt 2nd TN Mtd Inf; Dec 17 63 to Apr 17 65; Savannah PO
McFALLS, James, Se-228-2(3); Mary A. widow of; Pvt B Co 2nd TN Cav; 16 Oct 62 to 63; Cox PO; was killed in battle
McFALLS, Joel, Po-152-1; Eliza widow of; Pvt I Co 10th TN Cav; 12-64 to 65; Ducktown PO; died in hospital at Nashville
McFARLAND, Elbert, Mr-96-2; Pvt B Co 7th PA Cav; 62 to 65; Whitwell PO; sun stroke
McFARLAND, Frank, D-91-3; Pvt 70th IN Inf; Zucklers Grocery, Nashville PO
McFARLAND, Isac, Hy-76-1; Stanton Depot PO
McFARLAND, J. L. (see Rowden, Shadrach)
McFARLAND, James B., La-113-3; Pvt A Co 110th OH Inf; 11 Aug 62 to 25 Jun 65; Ethridge PO
McFARLAND, John, H-59-2; Rebecca Jones widow of; Lt OH Cav; 62 to 65; Chattanooga PO

McFARLAND, Thomas, C-29-1; Pvt C Co 4th TN Cav; 7-26-62 to 6-22-65; Fincastle PO; liver & kidney complaint
McFARLAND, Warren, D-52-1; Pvt G Co 129th IL Inf; 8 Feb 62 to Aug 65; Nashville PO; four gun shot wounds, right & left leg & left side
McFARLING, James C., Ro-203-5(1); Pvt G Co 8th TN Inf; 1 Mar 63 to 30 Jun 65; Burns Mills PO; gunshot wound in shoulder
McFEE, Tom, Ja-84-1; alias Robert Waid?; Ainry widow of; Pvt Cav; Harrison PO
McFEETERS, James S., L-104-1; Charlotte R. widow of; Pvt A Co 6th IN Vol; Apr 23 61 to Aug 2 61; Curve PO
McFERRIN, James P. (see Cooper, James K. P.)
McFERRIN, Thomas, D-79-3; Pvt 14th MS Col T; about 3 yrs; Nashville, 23 Lisckey PO; shot in head, arm & leg
McFETERS, Alford, R-161-6; Dayton PO; could not get facts
McFLETCHER, Sol W., D-51-2; Pvt K Co 15th US C Inf; 63 to 65; 500 N College, Nashville PO
McGAHA, John, Co-68-2; Elisey widow of; Pvt E Co 2nd TN Cav; 62 to 65; Sutton PO; diabetus
McGAHA, Robert, Co-67-2; Pvt A Co 2nd TN Cav; 1 Nov 64 to 24 Aug 65; Cosby PO; hemhorage of lung
McGAHA, Samuel, Se-220-2; Pvt I Co 2nd TN Cav; 1 Nov 62 to 6 Jul 65; Emerts Cave PO
McGAHA, Solomon, Co-67-4; Cattie Waddle widow of; Pvt E Co 1st TN Art; 19 Sep 63 to ___; Naillon PO; died with smallpox June 25 1864
McGAHA, William R., Co-68-2; Cpl E Co 2nd TN Cav; 62 to 65; Cashy PO
McGAMAR, Thomas, A-6-1; Pvt B Co 4th VA Inf; 3-64 to 1-65; Olivers PO
McGARY, J. J., D-78-2; Pvt 74th OH Inf; Jan 62 to Feb 63; Nashville PO
McGAUGHEY, Edwin W., H-70-2(1); Pvt 20th IN Art--1 yr; Master Mate Steamer U. S. Grant--8 mos; Chattanooga PO
McGAUGHEY, John, Mc-112-3; Martha widow of; Martial? 7th TN Mtd Inf; 64 to died 2-65; Athens PO; killed
McGAUGHEY, William S., Mc-112-7; Lt B Co 7th TN Mtd Inf; Athens PO
McGEE, Bertie (see Hedge?, Hiram)
McGEE, Daniel K., La-112-1; Mary J. widow of; Pvt A Co 4th? TN Mtd Inf; 10-2-63 to ___; Lawrenceburg PO; killed in battle
McGEE, David, K-171-6(5); Rebecca G. widow of; Pvt; PO omitted; CONF
McGEE, Francis M., Wy-197-2; Emma widow of; Pvt G Co 10th TN Inf; 4-62 to 5-65; Moon PO; died since war
McGEE, James W., Ca-25-2; Pvt A Co 5th TN Cav; 7-29-62 to 7-27-65; Gassoway PO; rheumatism & thrown by mule
McGEE, John, Mc-112-2; Susan J. widow of; Pvt; Athens PO; died in service of fever, no papers at hand to get dates
McGEE, Jonas (black), Hu-105-1; Pvt F Co 101st Col Inf; 28 Sep 64 to 22 Jan 65; McEwen PO
McGEE, M. C., Gi-133-2; 2nd Cpl C Co 9th TN; 62 to 65; Bufords PO; CONF
McGEE, Patton F., Co-66-1; Pvt F Co 25th NC Inf; 10 Feb 64 to 1 ___ 65; Bison PO; CONF
McGEE, Sampson, C-27-2; Pvt B Co 8th TN Cav; 8-20-62 to ___ (4 mos); Caryville PO
McGEE, William H., Sm-172-4; Pvt H Co 12th TN Cav; 2-29-64 to 10-7-65; Gordonsville PO; shot through the back
McGEEHEE, Make, Le-137-1; Pvt E Co 1st TN Lt Art; 63 to 65; Hickory Ridge PO
McGEHEE, John, Sh-196-1; John Potter alias; Pvt I Co 61st TN Inf; 63 to 65 (1 yr 6 mos); 127 Exchange St, Memphis PO; discharged on surgeon's certificate, lost papers
McGEHEE, John S., We-223-3; did not get to see Mr. Mcgehee, therefore can not tell anything about record; Palmersville PO
McGEHEE, William T., Sh-159-1; Memphis PO; CONF
McGHEE, Alexander, C-27-3; Pvt A Co 1st TN Inf; 3-62 to 10-1-65; Caryville PO
McGHEE, Charles, Mo-124-1; Cpl L Co 1st US Hvy (Art?); 2 yrs; 4 Mile Branch PO
McGHEE, James, Mo-124-1; Pvt E Co 1st TN Hvy (Art?); 4 Mile Branch PO; went twice to his house, did not see him
McGHEE, Jerry, K-158-2; Melinda widow of; Pvt L Co 1st TN Inf; 62 to died in service; Knoxville, 208 Mabry PO
McGHEE, John, Bo-14-3; Pvt A Co 3rd TN Inf; 5-9-63 to 8-10-65; Huffstetler Store PO; rheumatism, loss hearing
McGHEE, Noah, Hy-75-2; Pvt E Co 55th C TN; 63 to ___; Dancyville PO; Baily Capt., Alexander, Col.
McGHEE, Robert, Bo-14-2(1); Pvt A Co 3rd TN Inf; 2-11-62 to 6-27-65; Huffstetlers Store PO
McGHEE, William, Ge-91-1; Sgt H Co 83rd SC Inf; Oct 63 to Nov 9 65; Greeneville PO; rheumatism & other disease
McGHEE, William, Bo-14-2(1); Pvt H Co 2nd TN Cav; 4-10-62 to 7-6-65; Huffstetlers Store PO
McGHEE, Wm. R., Hd-54-1; Angeline Jones wife of; Pvt; Saltillo PO; no data, was killed
McGILL, Henry, K-164-2; Fanny Luty widow of; Pvt E Co Col Art; 31 Mar ___ to 31 Mar 66; PO omitted (Knoxville?)
McGILL, James H., Se-224-3; Pvt H Co 9th TN Cav; 1 Oct 63 to ___ (11 mos); Wears Valley PO
McGILL, John H., H-64-2; Pvt E Co; Chattanooga PO
McGILL, Nappier, Je-141-4; US Sol; 4th Dist
McGILL, Richard, We-227-1; PVt I Co 4th TN Cav; 63 to 64; Greenfield PO
McGILL, Robert, Se-224-2; Pvt H Co 9th TN Cav; 1 Oct 63 to 65; Wears Valley PO; diarrhea & bronchitis, captured & starved 9 days
McGILL, Robin, Col, Ru-244-1; Pvt D Co Shafter; 2-15-63 to 4-15-65; Milton PO; by shell, struck at Nashville
McGILL, Thomas, Bo-12-3(1); Pvt D Co 2nd TN Cav; 9-1-62 to 7-6-65; Millers Cove PO
McGILL, William, Se-224-3; Rebecca widow of; Pvt E Co 9th TN Cav; 1 Oct 63 to 11 Sep 65; Wears Valley PO
McGILL, William, Se-227-3; Mary widow of; Pvt H Co 9th TN Cav; 63 to 4 May 64; Trundles X Roads PO
McGILL, William C., Mg-196-3; Pvt F Co 1st TN Inf; 9 Aug 61 to 17 Sep 64; Hunnicutt PO
McGILL, William M., H-58-6; Pvt K Co 5th TN Inf; 8-13-63 to 6-30-65; Retro PO; gravel
McGINLEY, William, Bo-22-3; 14th Dist
McGINNIS, James M., Ha-110-2; Martha J. widow of; Pvt I Co 8th TN Inf; Treadway PO; died in the service
McGIPPIN, Benjamin, St-164-1; Pvt K Co 36th OH Inf; 61 to 64; Stribling PO; gun shot wound in knee
McGLAUGHLIN, John A., Be-8-1; Pvt B Co 7th TN Cav; 7 Jul 62 to ___; Lavinia PO; lost from command, then transfered and captured before reaching command
McGLENN, Andrew, L-103-1; Pvt, Cpl G Co 5th US? (WI?) Inf; May 30 60 to Jul 25 67; Island 26 PO; no great disability, not in great distress
McGLOFFIN, William, Ov-135-1; Cpl M Co 8th TN Cav; 62 to 65; Oakley PO; sent his discharge to Washington, could not recollect dates
McGLOTHLIN, James, C-26-2; Pvt H Co 2nd TN Inf; 12-19-61 to 12-19-64; Jacksboro PO
McGOLDRICK, Thomas J., Gr-72-1; Pvt A Co 9th TN Cav; to 11 Sep 65; Noeton PO; Danville Prison 4 mos; imprisoned without fire, few clothes and little food
McGOWIN, Jaben (John?) W., We-221-6(2); Pvt TN Inf; 62 to 65; Martin PO; CONF
McGOY, Chris, D-64-1; Carrie widow of; Nashville PO
McGRAW, Franklin, C-8-1; Pvt H Co 9th TN Cav & B Co 11th TN Cav; 7-18-63 to 9-11-65; Well Spring PO
McGREGOR, George W., Cy-28-1; Capt F Co 66th OH Inf; 12-1-61 to 5-10-65; Celina PO
McGREGORY, Eylie, Sh-173-2; Monroe St, Memphis PO
McGREW, Berry M., B-3-2; 3rd Civil Dist
McGREW, John H., Mc-116-1; Pvt L Co 1st TN Cav; 9-1-62 to 6-5-65; Longs Mills PO; rheumatism
McGREW, William T., Mc-116-1; Pvt L Co 1st TN Cav; 9-1-62 to 8-27-63; Longs Mills PO; disease of lungs

McGUFFEY, Jessee, Dk-39-5(1); Catharine widow of; Laurel Hill PO
McGUFFEY, John, Sm-173-1; Pvt H Co 1st TN Mtd Inf; 3-20-64 to 5-23-65; Sykes PO
McGUIRE, John, Jo-152-1; Pvt M Co 13th TN Cav; Sep 64 to Sep 65; Doeville PO; thins eyes were affect, don't rember day enlisted
McGUIRE, Thomas A., Je-138-1; Eglantine J. widow of; Capt K Co 5th TN Cav; 63 to 64; Oak Grove PO
McGUYER, Marion, D-57-2; Pvt D Co 40th US Inf; Nashville PO; contracted pneumonia
McGUYES, Sarah, Be-6-2; widow of US Soldier; Pvt; 8th Dist
McHANE, John, Un-251-1; Pvt D Co 1st TN Inf; 29 Aug 61 to 17 Sep 64; Effie PO; lumbo rheumatism
McHENRY, Allen, D-82-1; Sol US; 4th Dist
McHENRY, Henry, Mt-137-2; in government employ; 62 to 65; no papers; St. Bethlehem PO
McHENRY, Robert, Ge-87-1; Pvt; Timberridge PO; hand cripled, wife says so, I dont know
McHORN, Pliant, Dy-27-2; Pvt K Co 38th VA Inf; 1 May 61 to Apr 65; Tatemville PO; imprisoned 2 yrs; CONF
McHORRIS, J. C., Ge-87-3; Pvt K Co 30th OH Mtd Inf; 6 Sep 62 to 18 Oct 64; Timberridge PO; gunshot wounds
McINTERFF, Laban W., Ge-91-1; Capt B Co 3rd NC Inf; Sep 1 63 to Aug 8 65; Greeneville PO; hemrhoids, fistula _____? & rheumatism
McINTOSH, James, Su-240-1; Pvt B Co 4th US Cav; 1 Jan 63 to 9 Jun 65; Clover Bottom PO; shot in right left sholder
McINTOSH, Joseph J., D-61-1; Pvt US; May 10 64 to Aug 10 64; Nashville PO
McINTURF, Christopher, Ge-96-3; Mahaley widow of; Pvt D Co 13th TN Cav; 62 to ___; Rheatown PO; died at Knoxville, cant get dates
McINTURFF, David J., U-246-1; Pvt B Co 8th TN Cav; 23 Jul 63 to 11 Sep 65; Limonite PO
McINTURFF, John, U-247-1; Pvt B Co 12th TN Cav; 14 Jul 63 to 24 Oct 65; Erwin PO; injury to eyes
McINTURFF, Nathaniel K., U-246-1; Pvt D Co 13th TN Cav; 5 Mar 64 to 5 Sep 65; Limonite PO
McINTURFF, Samuel, U-246-1; Pvt B Co 8th TN Cav; 23 Jul 63 to 11 Sep 65; Limonite PO
McINTURFF, Wesley, U-245-1; Pvt 12th TN Cav; 22 Jul 63 to 11 Aug 64; Marbleton PO; in the US service, I left on ny lief of absanc, get no discharg
McINTURFF, William, U-247-1; Pvt F Co 3rd NC Mtd Inf; ___ to 8 Aug 65; Erwin PO; heart disease, kidney, bronchitis & rheumatism, date of enlistment not known
McINTYRE, Augustine, H-53-1; Kate D. widow of; Capt H Co 114th USCI Inf; 1854 to 1877, entire length of Civil War; Chattanooga PO; killed in service in 1877, enlisted in Reg. army & served till his death in 1877
McINTYRE, D. Stewart, K-160-1; Pvt H Co 12th IN; 14th Aug 62 to 22 M 65; Knoxville PO; partial loss of hearing
McINTYRE, Vance, Dk-35-3(1); Annie widow of; Capling PO; died with small pox
McJUNKINS, Loranza, R-161-3; Dayton PO; is now blind in one eye
McKAIN, Houston, Dy-27-1; Lt H Co TN Cav; 12-63 to 8-64; Newbern PO; discharge by Dr.
McKAMEY, Andrew, C-26-2; Pvt J Co 7th TN Inf; 11-8-64 to 3-1-65; Caryville PO
McKAMEY, Andy, Ro-210-7; Pvt C Co 11th TN Cav; 11 Jul 63 to 11 Sep 65; Cardiff PO
McKAMEY, James M., A-4-6(2); Sgt J Co 7th TN Mtd Inf; 11-8-64 to 7-27-65; Coal Creek PO; injured back, side etc.
McKAMEY, Robert C., Ro-204-2; Pvt G Co 3rd TN; Oliver Springs PO; dis. sent to atty. at Wash, DC
McKAMEY, Samuel, A-6-3(1); Pvt E Co 3rd TN Inf; 2-12-62 to 9-17-62; Olivers PO
McKAMEY, William J., A-7-1; Robertsville PO
McKAY, Abraham, Co-61-2(1); Sgt H Co 60th NC Inf; Givens PO; CONF
McKAY, James A., Mu-210-4; Cpl E Co 1st TN Cav; 61 to 4-65; Carters Creek PO
McKEAN, Samuel, Hw-127-1; Pvt E Co 8th NH Cav; 26 Oct 61 to 17 Jan 65; Rogersville PO
McKEE, Andrew D., Dy-23-1; Pvt I Co 5th TN Inf; Nov 62 to ___ (3 yrs); Dyersburg PO
McKEE, Hawk, Hd-50-2; Pvt F Co 2nd TN Mtd Inf Vol; Dec 24 63 to Feb 1 65; Walnut Grove PO; chronic direa of bowell in camp
McKEE, Patrick, D-60-1; 309 Morgan St, Nashville PO; white
McKEE, Phedora L. (see Stepp, William)
McKEE, Thomas, H-56-5; PA; East End PO
McKEEHAN, George W., Mc-110-2(1); Nancy J. widow of; Pvt C Co 8th TN Cav; Mouse Creek PO; died in camps
McKEEHAN, John, Ge-96-3; Pvt H Co 40th OH Inf; 18 Oct 61 to 8 Dec 65; Rheatown PO; good soldier in 2 wars
McKEEHEN, Elbert G., Me-91-1; Pvt B Co 7th TN Mtd Inf; 10-7-64 to 7-27-65; Decatur PO
McKEEHEN, James L., Me-92-4(1); Pvt B Co 7th TN Mtd Inf; 10-17--4 to 7-31-65; Hester Mills PO; night-sweats and cough
McKEEL?, Henry W., Ja-84-2; Pvt I Co 4th TN Cav; 10-14-65 to 7-12-65; Harrison PO; cold on lungs by measels
McKEEVER, Daniel, St-164-2; Pvt H Co 56th OH Inf; Nov 15 61 to 66; Stribling PO; eyes affected, reenlisted vetteran
McKEITHAN, Elna? H., Mg-199-2; Cpl F Co 1st TN Cav; 1 Mar 62 to 30 Mar 62; Sunbright PO; piles
McKELDEN, Mary A., Bo-12-3(1); widow of Sol US; 17th Dist
McKELVEY, John W., Cr-9-1; Pvt Black Hawk; Jan 65 to Aug 65; Friendship PO
McKELVEY, Mathew G., Mu-188-1; Lt D Co 1st AR Inf; 7-20-62 to 1-6-63; Bryants Station PO; ankle throne out of place
McKELVEY, W. P., He-62-1; Tennessee widow of; Pvt; Mar 62 to Jan 63; Lone Elm PO; hemorage of lungs and scurvey; CONF
McKENZIE, Hess, G-64-2; Soldier; Bradford PO
McKENZIE, James, G-71-1; Pvt G Co 4th TN Cav; 15 Oct 61 to 24 Oct 62; Bradford PO; CONF
McKENZIE, James P., Me-91-1; 4th Civil Dist
McKENZIE, William, Sh-191-7(3); Memphis PO; records not seen
McKEY, James H., La-108-1; US Sol; 1st Civil Dist
McKEY, Nelson, Sh-202-2(1); Memphis PO
McKILDRY?, John, Se-223-1; Blacksmith B Co 2nd TN Cav; 15 Sep 62 to 6 Jul 65; Pigeon Forge PO
McKIMEY, Wilson, Ct-39-3; Gap Run PO; spinal affection loc off 3rd. loc, heart disease
McKINEY, George W., Hm-107-4; Pvt G Co 4th TN Cav; ___ to 65; Chestnut Bloom PO; Morristown PO; eyes, sholder &c
McKINEY, John G., G-71-3; Pvt F Co 39th GA Inf; 1 Apr 61 to 2 Apr 65; PO omitted; CONF
McKINEY, Law P., Cl-46-1; Pvt E Co 2nd TN; 8-16-61 10-10-64; Clairfield PO; bowls and lungs
McKINEY, Samuel C., K-185-1; Pvt C Co 1st TN Art; 1 Dec 63 to 1 Aug 65; Y. Z. PO
McKINEY, Thomas, Mc-118-2; Pvt D Co 10th TN Cav; 3-64 to 8-65; Cogshill PO; defect in bouth eyes 25 yrs
McKINGEE, D. A., Mc-114-1; Pvt C Co 10th TN Cav; 6-10-64 to 8-65; Magellan PO
McKINIS, George, M-103-4; Pvt A Co 8th TN Mtd Inf; 2-10-65 to 8-17-65; Lafayette PO
McKINIS, George, M-103-3; 1st Sgt I Co 9th KY Inf; 9-15-61 to 12-15-64; Lafayette PO
McKINLEY, Aaron G., Sh-178-3; US Sol; Cor Dunlap & Union Ave, Memphis PO
McKINLEY, Andrew, S-214-4; Pvt G Co 3rd TN Inf; 15 Mar 62 to ___; Robbins PO; was never discharged
McKINLEY, Rufus, Sm-166-2; Pvt B Co 1st TN Mtd Inf; 3-64 to 3-65; Carthage PO
McKINLEY, Thomas, Lo-192-1; Pvt C Co 1st TN; May 63 to Aug 65; Coytee PO
McKINN, George W., La-113-1; Sgt A Co 172nd OH ___; 16 Apr 61 to 18 Aug 61; Lawrenceburg PO; re-enlisted
McKINNEY, Abraham, Li-147-1; 6th Civil Dist
McKINNEY, Abram, Col, St-160-1; Pvt C Co 13th KY Inf; 10-5-62 to 65?; Legate PO; wond in leg, deficincy in walking
McKINNEY, Annanias, Ro-203-3; Pvt H Co 3rd TN Inf; 10 Feb 62 to 23 Feb 65; Ethel PO; chronic rheumatism

McKINNEY, Benj., Sh-178-4; US Sol; 286 Union, Memphis PO
McKINNEY, Charley P., Hm-103-1; Pvt G Co 4th TN Cav; 62 to 65; Morristown PO
McKINNEY, George, Sh-146-3; Pvt; Millington PO
McKINNEY, George W., Hm-104-4(2); Pvt D Co 9th TN Cav; 20 Sep 63 to 11 Sep 65; Morristown PO
McKINNEY, James, Sm-170-2; 1st Lt H Co 1st TN Mtd Inf; 1-16-64 to 5-1-66; Chestnut Mound PO; rheumatism
McKINNEY, John A., Me-89-2; Pvt A Co 5th TN Inf; 64 to 7-65; Maloney PO
McKINNEY, John F., Sm-171-1; Pvt A Co 1st TN Mtd Inf; 12-25-64 to 6-30-65; Chestnut Mound PO; sun stroke
McKINNEY, Joseph P., Ct-40-2; Pvt A Co 13th TN Cav; 9-22-63 to 9-5-65; Elizabethton PO
McKINNEY, Mack, Ro-210-2; Pvt; Rockwood PO
McKINNEY, Pleasant, Mg-199-1; Pvt H Co 4th TN Inf; 63 to 65; Sunbright PO; gravel
McKINNEY, Rankin, Mg-199-1; Pvt H Co 4th TN Inf; 63 to 65; Sunbright PO; hurting in breast
McKINNEY, Saml., Ct-37-2; Pvt D Co 8th TN Cav; 6-63 to deserted 1865; Ripshin PO; gun wound left side
McKINNEY, Umphery, D-72-3; Pvt K Co 15th TN Inf; Jul 4 61 to Sep 16 65; Nashville PO
McKINNEY, William, D-68-3; Rivert St, Nashville PO; discharge papers not at home
McKINNEY, William, Ct-37-1; Pvt H Co 4th TN Inf; 7-10-64 to 7-10-65; Ripshin PO; breast complaint, suffering 25 yrs
McKINNEY, William, D-49-4; Pvt B Co; 8 Jan 64 to 30 Apr 66; Nashville PO
McKINNIE, Abe, F-46-1; Tener widow of; 3 yrs; LaGrange PO; shot through right hip
McKINNIE, Henry, D-69-1; Sgt C Co 180th IL Inf; 8 Aug 62 to 25 Aug 65; Nashville PO
McKINNY, Boas, Hm-103-1; Pvt G Co 4th TN Cav; 62 to 65; Morristown PO
McKINOTT, Richard, Ch-118-1; Sgt E Co 51st TN Cav; 10 Oct 62 to 10 Apr 65; PO omitted; CONF
McKINSTRY, Alexandrew, D-47-1; Pvt B Co 10th TN Inf; 4-62 to 65; Jefferson St, Nashville PO
McKINSTRY, Ozias, Bl-5-2; Cpl B Co 34th IN Inf; 2-15-64 to 2-3-66; Brayton PO
McKISSACK, Alany, Mu-210-7; Sgt F Co 3rd TN Inf; May 61 to May 65; Spring Hill PO; CONF
McKISSACK, George, Gi-126-1; Cpl B Co 110th Col Inf; 8 Dec 63 to 6 Feb 66; Pulaski PO
McKISSACK, Orville W., Mu-210-2; Pvt in Gen Forest's Escort; __ to 65; Spring Hill PO; wounded in left leg; CONF
McKISSICK, Augustus (see Coleman, James M.)
McKISSICK, Levi, Mu-210-1; Harriet widow of; Pvt G Co 110th TN Inf; __ to 65 (3 yrs); Spring Hill PO
McKISSICK, Peter, Gi-127-8; Pvt D Co 110th TN Col Inf; Dec 22 64 to Apr 30 66; Pulaski PO
McKIVIN, Oliver, Mu-209-3; Sulphur Springs PO
McKIZZICK, Robert, Hm-57-4; US Sol; 10th Civil Dist
McKNABB, J. H., Bo-11-4; Pvt G Co 3rd TN Inf; 9-15-63 to 7-5-65; Greenback PO; 1 leg shot off
McKNIGHT, David A., Gi-133-1; Pvt C Co 3rd TN; Jun 61 to May 65; Bufords PO; CONF
McKNIGHT, H. K., Hd-46-1; Seaman Robb; Sep 15 63 to Sep 15 64; Savannah PO
McKNIGHT, John, Di-34-1; Cpl D Co 1st OH Hvy Art; 8-2-62 to 6-20-65; Dickson PO; hemorrhoids
McKNIGHT, Moses, D-61-2; Cpl A Co 44th TN; Sep 64 to Dec 65; Ament St, Nashville PO
McKNIGHT, Sarah F. (see Enochs, Robert)
McKNIGHT, T. W., Gi-122-2; Pvt G Co 53rd TN Inf; Dec 4 62 to 27 May 65; Prospect Sta. PO; prison 17 mos; CONF
McKNIGHT, Thomas M., Mc-118-5; Pvt E Co 5th TN Inf; 3-2-62 to 4-4-65; Calhoun PO; breast disease 26 yrs
McLAIN, Byron W., Mc-112-8; Athens PO; this man is gone & no dates known
McLAIN, George W., K-177-1; Pvt D Co 6th TN Inf; 18 Apr 62 to 28 Apr 65; Chumlea PO; prisoner Resaca GA 24 hours, now blind
McLAIN, Henry M., H-52-1; Pvt A Co 3rd TN Cav; 8-10-62 to 8-7-65; Lookout Mt. PO
McLAIN, J. P., He-57-2; Pvt I Co 4th TN Cav; 5-1-61 to 5-1-65; Law PO; CONF

McLAIN, John H., Hw-121-4(3); Pvt I Co 10th TN Inf; 16 Aug 63 to 23 Jun 65; New Hope PO; blind, piles
McLAIN, Joseph, Hw-121-1; Lusanner widow of; Pvt K Co 1st TN Cav; 12 Jul 62 to 5 Jun 65; Van Hill PO
McLAIN, Lewis, Hm-103-3; Pvt K Co 40th TN Inf; 29 Apr 65 to 25 Apr 66; Morristown PO
McLAIN, Mary, B-9-1; PO omitted
McLAIN, Shadrick V., Hw-121-4(3); Pvt K Co 1st TN Cav; 30 Jul 63 to 15 Aug 65; New Hope PO; thrown from hors, crippled
McLAIN, Stephen H., K-177-1; Pvt D Co 6th TN Inf; 18 Apr 62 to 27 Apr 65; Chumlea PO
McLAIN, William A., We-221-1(4); Pvt M Co 2nd IL Cav; 14 Apr 62 to 14 Apr 65; Martin PO
McLAIN, Wyatt, La-112-1; Martha A. widow of; Lawrenceburg PO
McLANEY, Patrick, Su-238-1; Cpl H Co 13th TN Cav; 24 Sep 63 to 5 Sep 65; Piney Flats PO; gun shot in right foot and trouble in spineal holum?
McLARON, ____ (see Easly, Harrison)
McLASKEY, James, H-76-2; Pvt A Co 49th PA Vol; 8-15-61 to 8-31-64; Chattanooga PO
McLAUGHLIN, Nelson, U-247-2; Capt M Co 8th TN Cav; 25 Sep 62 to 20 Jun 65; Erwin PO; chronic diarrhoea, hemorrhoids, rheumatism & heart disease
McLAUGHLON, Isral, Col, T-212-1; Cpl F Co 3rd US Hvy Art; 17 Mar 64 to 13 Apr 66; Tipton PO
McLAURINE, Anthony D., Gi-127-3; Easter Bell formerly widow of; Pvt 111th TN Col Inf; Pulaski PO; died in the service
McLELLAND, James, Je-143-1; Nancy E. wife of; 2nd Lt B Co 1st TN Inf; 16 Aug 61 to Feb 62; Mount Horeb PO; chronic diarea
McLEMON, John, K-183-1; Pvt B Co 6th TN Inf; 18 Jan 63 to 30 Jun 65; Riverdale PO
McLEMORE, E. J., He-57-1; Pvt D Co 56th TN Cav; 11-15-62 to 5-15-65; Law PO; wound in shoulder; CONF
McLEMORE, Henry (see Sledge, Henry)
McLEOD, Norman H., Cr-19-1; Pvt F Co 7th TN Cav; 9-24-62 to 10-25-62; Huntingdon PO
McLERRAN, Benagy, Cy-26-2; Pvt C Co 37th KY Inf; 8-11-63 to 6-22-65; Moss PO; in prison at Andersonville & Florence 7 mos
McLIN, Ann (see Vasser, Thomas)
McLINDON, Burton, Sh-152-2; Pvt B Co 38th GA Inf; 63 to 66; Dexter PO; broken knee, back injury, never has gotten a pension
McLOUD, James D., Se-221-2; Sarah C. widow of; Pvt K Co 2nd TN Cav; 10 Apr 64 to 6 Jul 65; Fair Garden PO
McLUR, H. F., Bo-11-2; Blacksmith F Co 2nd TN Cav; 8-1-62 to 7-6-65; Houk PO
McMAHAN, George M., D-79-2; Pvt F Co 11th TN Zouaves; Jun 62 to Aug 65; Nashville, 301 Foster PO; stricture of bowels
McMAHAN, Henderson H., Co-68-2; Pvt E Co 2nd TN Cav; 16 Sep 62 to 5 Jul 65; Cashy PO; wound by all in thigh at Athens, AL, Sep 2, 186?
McMAHAN, Henry, Mc-114-2; Pvt E Co 1st TN Inf; 3-64 to 4-66; Magellan PO
McMAHAN, Henry, K-161-6; alias Henry Toomey; Pvt G Co 15th TN Inf; Knoxville PO
McMAHAN, James, Co-67-1; Pvt F Co 5th TN Cav; Oct 62 to 12 May 65; Bison PO; CONF
McMAHAN, John, K-161-5(6); Knoxville PO
McMAHAN, Levi, Mc-114-2; Pvt M Co 2nd TN Cav; 8 Nov 62 to 6 Jul 65; Richison's Cove PO; piles, liver trouble &c
McMAHAN, Mack, C-27-2; Pvt C Co 102nd OH Inf; 5-14-62 to 6-1-65; Caryville PO
McMAHAN, Marion, Se-230-2; Pvt E Co 2nd TN Cav; 1 Dec 62 to 5 Jul 65; Pokeberry PO; chron. diarrhoea & lung
McMAHAN, Micel, Hm-108-4(3); Pvt C Co 56th NY Inf; 61 to 65; Russellville PO; heart disease, eyes & lungs
McMAHAN, Sanders, Se-219-3; 2nd Lt E Co 2nd TN Cav; 16 Sep 62 to 5 Jul 65; Jones Cave PO; injury to left foot
McMAHAN, William R., Se-230-3; Pvt H Co 29th TN Inf; Nov 62 to __ (1 yr 6 mos); Richison's Cove PO

McMAHON, James, Co-63-3; Pvt E Co 2nd TN Cav; 16 Sep 62 to 5 Jul 65; Newport PO
McMANIS, N., G-57-6; Pvt C Co 9th TN Cav; 1 Feb 64 to 1 May 64; Yorkville PO
McMELLAM, John J., K-183-2; Pvt B Co 6th TN Inf; 62 to 30 Jun 65; Riverdale PO
McMICHEAL, Joseph, We-224-3(1); Pvt A Co 5th TN Inf; 29 May 61 to 16 Jun 65; Como PO (Henry Co.); bronchitus contracted, discharge from prison at Point Lookout; CONF
McMILLAN, Andrew, Se-228-3; Pvt; Shiloh Church PO
McMILLAN, Daniel, K-160-2; Pvt T Co 9th TN Vol; 16 Oct 63 to 13 Sep 65; Knoxville PO; rheumatism
McMILLAN, Henry C., D-92-1; Pvt I Co 5th TN Inf; __ to 65; Nashville PO
McMILLAN, James H., K-158-1; Pvt 2nd TN Cav; May 61 to May 64; Knoxville PO; 181 State St, Knoxville PO; measles, paralysis from exposure
McMILLAN, John C., Lo-191-2; Candace widow of; Morganton PO; soldier died in army and have no records of regt or co
McMILLAN, Oscar, K-183-2; Pvt H Co 12th TN Reg; 6 Sep 64 to 24 Apr 66; Riverdale PO
McMILLAN, William H., Co-65-2; 8th Dist
McMILLAN, William H., St-162-3(1); Pvt A Co 76th TN Inf; 26 Aug 61 to Sep 15 64; Cumberland City PO; wounded in left foot
McMILLEN, Geo. W., Hw-132-2; Pvt A Co 1st TN Art; 63 to 65; Strahl PO
McMILLEN, James, Dk-31-3; Pvt K Co 5th TN Cav; 2-22-63 to 4-3-65; Alexandria PO; discharged surgeons certificate, totally disabled from work
McMILLEN, Samuel, Dk-31-3; Cpl I Co 5th TN Cav; 2-17-63 to 8-14-65; Alexandria PO; shot in right arm, right arm almost useless
McMILLEN, Samuel, Bo-13-3(1); Pvt I Co 100th OH Inf; 8-9-62 to 6-19-65; Millers Cove PO
McMILLIAN, Abraham, Ha-111-2; Pvt B Co 49th KY Inf; 26 Jun 63 to 26 Dec 64; Kyle's Ford PO
McMILLIN, Francis M., R-161-3; Pvt B Co 1st TN Inf; 10-1-63 to 8-3-65; Dayton PO
McMILLIN, J. W., Bo-11-3; Cpl F Co 2nd TN Cav; 8-1-62 to 7-6-65; Hout PO
McMILLIN, Silas, Bo-11-4; Pvt L Co 2nd TN Cav; 9-8-63 to 4-65; Brick Mill PO
McMILLION, George W., Hw-120-1; Pvt G Co 1st TN Cav; 1 Jul 62 to 5 Jun 65; War Gap PO; rheumatism & heart
McMILON, Anderson, Wi-270-2; Pvt F Co 2nd TN Cav; Dec 62 to Aug 65; Fern Vale PO; discharg in Washington
McMOYERS, James, Hm-107-3; Pvt A Co 7th IN Cav; 22 Aug 63 to 11 Aug 65; Witts Foundry PO; diarrhea
McMUREY, David M., Sh-188-1; Pvt B Co 7th PA Inf; 6-61 to 9-66; 75 Ohio Ave, Memphis PO
McMURRAY, Bart R., Bo-21-1; Pvt F Co 3rd TN Cav; 6-15-63 to 6-20-65; Veeba PO
McMURRAY, Henry, Sn-252-1; Teamster; Gallatin PO
McMURRY, Jackson D., H-50-5; Pvt B Co 1st R US VVE; 8-15-62 to 6-30-65; Soddy PO
McMURRY, Joseph C., Bo-21-1; Cpl F Co 3rd TN Cav; 6-15-63 to 6-20-65; Veeba PO
McMURRY, Simon, Je-135-3; Mary A. widow of; Pvt D Co 9th TN Cav; Sep 63 to __; Piedmont PO; died in the service
McMUSRY, Richard, Sn-250-2; Dist 1 and 2
McNAB, John, Sh-201-3; Pvt K Co 1st AL Cav; 11 Jul 63 to 10 Sep 65; Memphis PO
McNAB, Richard, Ro-202-1; Pvt F Co 3rd TN Inf; 1 Jan 63 to 17 May 65; Union X Roads PO; spinal affliction 27 yrs
McNABB, Alexander, H-73-5(3); Pvt; Chattanooga PO
McNABB, Alexander, Co-59-2; US Sol; 1st Dist
McNABB, Alexander J., Bo-14-5; Pvt 21st OH Lt Art; Clover Hill PO; lost discharge, cant give dates of enlistment & discharge
McNABB, Baptist, Co-67-1; Lydia E. widow of; Pvt C Co 26th TN Inf; Jun 61 to Feb 62; Bison PO; CONF
McNABB, Campbell, Co-65-1; Pvt K Co 8th TN Cav; 2 Feb 64 to 11 Sep 65; Wilton Springs PO; gun shot wound in right leg, not pensioned
McNABB, Henry C., Mc-117-2; Pvt E Co 9th TN Cav; 10-2-63 to 9-11-65; Mortimer PO
McNABB, James Jr., H-70-1; Capt G Co 11th MD Inf; Chattanooga PO; wounded by shell in knee
McNABB, James C., Pvt C Co 26th TN Inf; 10 Oct 62 to 21 Apr 63; Rankin PO; shot in both leg on 3th Jan 63; CONF
McNABB, James P., U-247-3; US Sol; 5th Civil Dist
McNABB, Johnathan H., U-245-1; Pvt A Co 17th AL Inf; 20 Jan 63 to 19 May 64; Mosehill PO; conscrip in Conf army; CONF
McNABB, Latimer B., R-159-1; Pvt; Spring City PO; chronic dioriah, cant work much
McNABB, Manuel, Ge-92-5; Pvt B Co 8th TN Cav; Romeo PO
McNABB, Silas, Mr-98-1; Sgt G Co 4th TN Cav; 4-6-63 to 7-12-65; Kelley's Ferry PO
McNABB, William, Un-251-2; Pvt D Co 1st TN Inf; 9 Aug 61 to 17 Sep 64; Esco PO; heart disease
McNABB, William, Mr-98-1; Pvt I Co 10th TN Inf; 4-13-63 to 6-23-65; Kelly's Ferry PO
McNAIL, R. H., G-57-2; 1st Lt F Co 12th TN Inf; 5-28-61 to 5-28-62; Yorkville PO
McNARY, Edward, Sh-147-1; Cpl A Co 59th TN Inf; 10 Jul 64 to 28 Apr 65; Cuba PO
McNARY, Emerline, Gi-128-2; widow of Soldier US; 8th Civil Dist
McNARY, John, Gi-128-2; 8th Civil Dist
McNARY, Mias, Gi-128-2; Ord Sgt E Co 12th TN Inf; Dec 63 to Jan 16 66; Pulaski PO
McNATT, Paschal B., Ch-12-2; Pvt H Co 21st TN Cav; 7-9-62 to 5-65; Custer Point PO; CONF
McNEAL, Clinton P., Cu-15-1; Pvt E Co 1st TN Inf; 8-20-61 to 9-17-64; Hebbertsburg PO; sun stroke at camp Dick Robinson, not able for dury for 2 m. after
McNEAL, Elizabeth (see Shelley, John)
McNEAL, Isham, T-219-1; Pvt A Co 59th TN Inf; Phelan PO; gun shot in right thigh, has no discharge, hence no dates
McNEAL, John, C-29-1; Pvt G Co 27th VA Cav; 62 to 66; Fincastle PO; surrendered at Cumberland Gap
McNEAL, Thomas T., H-73-3; Pvt; Chattanooga PO
McNEECE, F. H., Gi-139-3; Pvt B Co 10th IL Cav; 6-10-64 to 9-7-65; Wales Sta. PO; shot in right hand; CONF
McNEECE, James B., He-60-2; Pvt C Co 4th TN Inf; Apr 6 63 to Aug 2 65; Lexington PO; caused him to be deaf
McNEELEY, James P., C-8-1; Pvt F Co 6th TN Inf; Well Spring PO; has no discharge & can't get correct dates
McNEELY, Fannie, F-40-3; Oakland PO
McNEELY, Godfred D., C-29-1; Matilda A. widow of; Pvt B Co 11th TN Cav; Fincastle PO; partial blindness
McNEES, Elisha, Br-12-6; Pvt M Co 1st TN Cav; 11-25-62 to 12-4-63; McPherson PO; affected side
McNEES, Jacob, Ge-97-3; Pvt M Co 1st TN Cav; 29 Nov 62 to 28 Jul 65; Newmanville PO; bone scurvy
McNEESE, David M., Je-141-3; Pvt F Co 7th IN Cav; 28 Aug 63 to 27 May 65; Mill Springs PO
McNEESE, Elihu, Ge-97-3; Pvt M Co 1st TN Cav; 25 Nov 62 to 28 Jul 65; Rheatown PO; lung disease
McNEESE, Lucy, Gr-72-2; widow; 3rd Civil Dist
McNEIL, Washington, F-47-1; 3rd Sgt C Co 59th TN Inf; Feb 1 64 to Jan 31 66; Williston PO
McNELLY, John, H-54-5; Pvt D Co 4th US Cav; 4-27-61 to 4-27-65; Sherman Heights PO; wounded at Wilson's Creek, MO
McNEW, David, C-24-3; Pvt B Co 1st TN Inf; 7-20-63 to 8-3-65; Fork Vale PO; affects of the eye & genral disability
McNEW, James, C-24-3; Pvt B Co 1st TN Inf; 7-20-63 to 8-3-65; Fork Vale PO; epeleptic fitts
McNEW, John, C-30-2; Pvt B Co 8th TN Cav; 6-10-63 to 9-11-65; Well Spring PO
McNEW, W. R., Ge-87-1; Pvt A Co 2nd NC Inf; 15 Sep 62 to 5 Aug 65; Timberridge PO; liver disease
McNIECE, William R., H-55-1; Pvt M Co 1st TN Cav; 11-25-62 to 6-8-65; Tyner PO; thrown from cart, bursted creek? bone
McNUTT, William A., K-168-1; Sgt I Co 3rd TN Cav; 20 Sep 62 to 3 Aug 65; Knoxville PO; finger shot off

McNUTT, William M., Mn-126-2; Pvt G Co 6th TN Cav; 10-62 to 12-63; Purdy PO
McONIELL, John K. B., Bo-15-3; 3rd Sgt H Co 2nd TN Cav; 10-10-62 to 5-31-65; Maryville PO
McOVELSID?, L. H., Dk-32-2; Hattie widow of; Pvt E Co 4th TN Mtd Inf; 9-12-64 to 8-25-65; Liberty PO
McPEAK, Levi, Wa-273-2; Paulina widow of; Pvt I Co 8th TN Cav; 23 Sep 63 to 14 Feb 65; Keeblers X Roads PO; died of measles
McPEEK, Ephraim, Mc-111-2; Pvt B Co 185th OH Inf; 2-23-65 to 10-65; Nonaburg PO
McPETERS, Inman, Mg-197-1; Mary A. Wilson formerly widow of; Pvt B Co 2nd TN Inf; 2nd Dist (civil I presume) (sic)
McPHAIL, Byrd N., Mc-109-2; Pvt C Co 3rd TN Cav; 11-25-62 to 6-10-65; Ziegler PO; partial deafness, geneal weakness
McPHAIL, William D., Mc-109-2; Pvt B Co 7th TN Inf; 9-12-64 to 7-27-65; Sewee PO (Meigs Co.)
McPHERREN, Rufus, Br-12-3; Pvt A Co 8th TN Inf; 10-20-62 to 6-65; McPherren PO
McPHERRIN, Henry, Br-12-6; Lt A Co 8th TN Inf; McPherson PO; CONF
McPHERRON, Henry, Ro-209-2; Pvt E Co 1st TN Inf; Jul 63 to Sep 65; Rockwood PO
McPHERSON, Daniel L., Se-228-1(2); Pvt G Co 3rd TN Inf; 21 Dec 61 to 24 Feb 65; New Knob Creek PO; wounded in breast and leg
McPHERSON, George, Wa-274-2; Capt D Co 8th TN Cav; 5 Dec 63 to 11 Sep 65; Jonesboro PO; loss of right testicle & piles
McPHERSON, John, Se-228-2(3); Tennessee widow of; Pvt A Co 3rd TN Cav; 18 Sep 62 to 27 Apr 65; Cusick's X Roads PO
McPHERSON, John, Mu-190-1; Pvt B Co 111th Col Inf; Fountain Creek PO; dont know where he was enlisted but was mustered out at Chattanooga
McPHERSON, Jno. F., R-163-5; Ogden PO
McPHERSON, Richard F., K-166-3; Knoxville PO; not home, family did not know regiment
McQUARY, William, Cy-28-2; Pvt L Co 13th KY Cav; 1-27-63 to 1-9-64; Butlers Landing PO
McQUEEN, Alex H., Wa-271-1; Pvt G Co 13th TN Cav; Flourville PO
McQUEEN, Noah (Noah Dodson on same line without explanation--an alias?); Li-148-1; Pvt E Co 101st Col Inf; 4-25-61 to 1-21-62; Renegar PO; honorable discharge
McQUEEN, Sameul E., Jo-148-2; Sgt E Co 13th TN Cav; 23 Sep 63 to 8 Sep 65; Head of Laurel PO; affliction of right testicle by means of mumps
McQUISTER, Henry, Ho-96-2; Sgt K Co 31st IL Inf; Oct 1 61 to Jul 31 65; Erin PO; gun shot wound left foot, drawing pension
McRAE, William H., Ro-207-2; Pvt G Co 1st NC Inf; Jan 62 to 11 Jun 65; 17th Dist
McREE, Moses B., H-50-3(1); Pvt A Co 6th R TN Mtd Inf; 8-17-64 to 8-30-65; Soddy PO
McREE, R. A., F-44-2; Pvt B Co 8th TN; May 62 to 65; PO omitted
McREYNOLDS, Fayett, Esker N. alias, Mr-99-2; Pvt H Co 13th Col TN; 11-63 to 65 (3 yrs 2 mos); Jasper PO; wounded in the rist; slight
McREYNOLDS, James W., Wh-180-1; Pvt B Co 56th KY Cav; Sparta PO; no disease
McREYNOLDS, Jerry, Mr-96-2; Pvt E Co 19th OH Inf; 9-62 to 11-22-65; Whitwell PO; wounded in arm
McREYNOLDS, Martin, Col, W-189-3(2); Pvt A Co 19th OH Inf; 8-6? to ___; McMinnville PO; claims to have been home on furlough when regt. was discharged, and has no discharge
McREYNOLDS, Robert, K-179-4; Pvt F Co 4th OH Cav; PO omitted
McREYNOLDS, Samuel P., Pu-147-2; Pvt I Co 1st TN Mtd Inf; 1-22-64 to 7-22-65; Byrne PO; lung disease result of measles
McREYNOLDS, William W., Ru-235-1; Pvt I Co 34th OH Inf; 64 to 65; Smyrna PO
McROBERTS, Philip, H-67-1; Pvt L Co 1st US Col Hvy Art; 9-26-64 to 3-31-66; Chattanooga PO
McROBERTS, William C., Mu-193-2; Pvt A Co 66th OH Inf; 10-11-61 to 7-11-62; Columbia PO
McSEAVOR, Henry, Co-63-2; Pvt F Co 40th TN Inf; 3 Apr 63 to 25 Apr 66; Newport PO
McSINK, G. B., A-1-2; Pvt M Co 9th TN Inf; 10-2-63 to 9-11-65; Andersonville PO

McSPADDEN, Arnold, Mo-127-1; Pvt D Co 3rd TN Cav; 8-1-64 to 12-7-64; Notchy PO
McSPADDEN, Marshal W., Je-147-1; 1st Sgt C Co 9th TN Cav; 12 Jun 63 to 24 Mar 65; Shady Grove PO
McSPADDEN, Rufus, Je-147-2; Ellen S. Solomon formerly widow of; 1st Lt C Co 9th TN Cav; Shady Grove PO
McSPADDEN, Wm., Je-141-2; Pvt C Co 9th TN Cav; 12 Jun 63 to 11 Sep 65; New Market PO
McSPADDEN, Henry, Mo-130-1; Margaret A. widow of; Pvt A Co 3rd TN Inf; 2-10-62 to 7-23-65; Acorn PO
McSPADIN, Hannibal M., Mo-128-1; Pvt D Co 3rd TN Mtd Inf; 7-25-64 to 11-30-64; Belltown PO
McTEER, Andrew B., Bo-21-2; Nancy widow of; 1st Lt A Co 3rd TN Cav; 9-18-62 to 9-26-64; Ellijay PO
McTEER, Siliman B., Bo-14-1; Sgt F Co 2nd TN Cav; 8-1-62 to 7-6-65; Brick Mill PO; rheumatism & piles
McTHERISON, John A., Hw-131-2; Malassie mother of; Pvt D Co 8th TN Inf; 15 Mar 63 to 30 Jun 65; White Horn PO
MCULLEY, Harve, C-27-3; Pvt; Caryville PO
McUPTON, William, H-72-2(1); Harriet formerly widow of; Pvt K Co 1st US Hvy Art; Chattanooga PO
McVEAGH, John F., O-138-4; Pvt; 14th Civil Dist
McVEY, Jane (see Kegley, James)
McVIX, Robert, Fr-116-1(2); Cpl I Co 10th TN Inf; 7-23-62 to 6-23-65; Sherwood PO; sunstroke in service & rheumatism
McWHATES?, Francis L., We-223-2; Sgt J Co 33rd TN Inf; Jun 61 to Sep 61; Pamersville PO; all ok now; CONF
McWHEELEN?, George D., We-223-2; Pvt was under Gen. Forest; Palmersville PO; CONF
McWHERTER, Robert, We-223-5; Pvt H Co 33rd TN Inf; Sep 61 to May 62; Palmersville PO; right leg lost at knee, uses peg leg; CONF
McWHIRTER, William L., P-156-3; Pvt B Co 27th TN Inf; 7-4-61 to 2-27-65; Lobelville PO; shot in left leg; CONF
McWILLIAMS, Andrew J., Wy-173-3; Sgt F Co 6th TN Cav; 9-21-62 to 7-26-65; Sims PO
McWILLIAMS, Daniel, Bl5-1; Capt D Co 6th TN Mtd Inf; 10-26-64 to 6-30-65; Retro PO (Hamilton Co.)
McWILLIAMS, Henry, Hu-99-2; Sgt US Hvy Col Art; 1 May 64 to 31 Mar 66; Johnsonville PO; rheumatics
McWILLIAMS, James A., Wy-173-3; P t F Co 6th TN Cav; 9-21-62 to 7-26-65; Sims PO
MEACHUM, Jesse M., L-109-1; Pvt F Co 7th IN Cav; 22 Sep 63 to 26 May 65; Ripley PO; partially blind
MEAD, Samuel M., Ro-204-1; Pvt G Co 1st TN Inf; 9 Aug 61 to 17 Sep 64; Oliver Springs PO; ulcer stomache
MEADER, Isam, B-6-1; Pvt F Co 10th TN Inf; 7-11-63 to ___; Shelbyville PO
MEADLOCK, Burt, Hw-119-3(1); Elizabeth widow of; Pvt C Co TN Inf; Alum Well PO; died Mar 12 63; Newton MS
MEADOR, J. A., M-108-4; Pvt D Co 8th TN Mtd Inf; 2-10-65 to 8-31-65; Lafayette PO; mased by falling horse, crippled in back & arm
MEADOR, Silus B., M-108-2(2); Cpl & Pvt E Co 1st TN Mtd Inf; 10-21-63 to 1-22-65; Hamilton PO; lung trouble, gunshot wound in head
MEADOR, William T., Hd-54-1; Pvt G Co 10th TN Inf; 10 Jun 62 to 24 Jun 65; Saltillo PO; sight; he is seriously affected with kidney
MEADOW, Pleasant H., Ma-103-3; Pvt A Co 9th NY Inf; 9-25-61 to 6-14-65; Lafayette PO
MEADOWS, Albert A., Sm-169-4(6); Pvt I Co 9th KY Inf; 9-15-61 to 11-25-64; Donoho PO; relapse of measles, heart disease, transferred to veteran reserve corpse
MEADOWS, John H., Se-224-3; Pvt A Co 20th TN Inf; ___ to 3 Jul 65; Wears Valley PO; sight & deafness
MEADOWS, Jonas, He-66-2; Pvt C Co 6th TN Cav; Middlefork PO; dislocated shoulder, could no tell withot his discharge and that was in pension agents hands

MEADOWS, Moses A., Sm-169-4(6); Sgt I Co 9th KY Inf; 9-15-61 to 12-15-64; Donoho PO; rheumatism & chronic diareah
MEADOWS, R. S., Hu-103-3; Pvt I Co 21st TN Inf; 10 Aug 12 to 10 Jul 15; PO omitted
MEADOWS, Thomas, D-51-1; Pvt B Co 40th US Col Inf; 25 Apr 62 to 65; 438 North Market, Nashville PO; right arm sprain
MEADOWS, William D., Mu-210-1; Spring Hill PO; hired a substitute; CONF
MEAFORD, Jacob, Hm-109-3; Pvt C Co 8th TN Cav; Mar 63 to 65; Russellville PO
MEAFORD, Joseph, Hm-109-1; Pvt C Co 8th TN Cav; 18 May 63 to 11 Sep 65; Russellville PO; leg broken
MEAGHER, Patrack (son of), Sh-187-1(5); Sgt A Co & F Co 1st MO Inf; 7-16-61 to 5-12-65; 62 Safran St., Chelsy, Memphis PO; chills & fever
MEAKS, Frank, Mu-197-1; Dansey widow of; Pvt C Co 63 to 65; Columbia PO
MEALER, B. F., R-162-5 Pvt I Co 52nd GA Inf; 3-62 to __; Dayton PO; was not discharged but was paroled
MEALEY, George W., Dk-39-2; Pvt I Co 1st TN Mtd Inf; 8-1-64 to 7-22-65; Bozarth PO; chronic diarrhea
MEALPIN, Calvin A., Mn-121-2; Pvt E Co 6th TN Cav; 15 Oct 62 to 12 Mar 63; Rose Creek PO; on March 63 got substitute in his place, William Broun
MEANS, James, Hn-81-1; Gillie PO; could not find him; CONF?
MEANS, James, Hn-81-1; US Sol; Elkhorn PO
MEANS, Louis, T-209-2; Cpl M Co 3rd TN Art; 64 to 65; Munford PO
MEARIDIL, Harvil, Gr-79-1; Rebecca wife of; Inft; 5 Jan 62 to 13 Mar 63; Ball Point PO; poisened or yellow janders; CONF
MEBANE, Baker, F-40-1; Pvt E Co 3rd TN Inf; 15 May 62 to 15 Apr 65; Oakland PO
MECHAM, Richard (see Michell, Richard)
MECOULA, Eleis L., Gi-138-1; Pvt F Co 14th __; 9-26-63 to 3-26-66; Valesville PO
MECULUNK, King, Gi-138-2; Pvt D Co 110th Cav; 63 to 66; Valesville PO
MEDARIS, Joel B., Cr-17-1; Mary H. widow of; Pvt E Co 7th TN Cav Reg; 7-6? to 61; Buena Vista PO
MEDCALF, Renseller, L-102-1; Pvt F Co 1st IA; 29 Dec 62 to 16 Feb 66; Dist 13
MEDDIN, Mary F., G-61-1; widow of Pvt E Co 6th TN Cav; 8 Mar to 26 Jul 65; 12th Civil Dist
MEDLEN, John H., Dk-39-3(1); Pvt B Co 1st TN Mtd Inf; 1-1-64 to 4-20-65; Dekalb PO
MEDLEN, Thomas F., Bo-19-1; Pvt 18th N (NC?) Inf; 64 to 65; Rockford PO
MEDLEY, Aaron, Mt-138-2; US Sol; Dist No. 7, N. Providence PO
MEDLIN, Henry, Ha-110-1; Pvt E Co 3rd NC Inf; Oct 63 to Mar 65; Ball Point PO (Grainger Co)
MEDLIN, Samuel L., Pu-146-2; Pvt B Co 1st TN Mtd Inf Vol; 12-22-63 to 4-14-65; Ai PO; shoulder dislocated
MEDLIN, William J., K-171-5(4); Pvt C Co 3rd TN Inf; Jul 64 to 64 (3 mos); Bearden PO
MEDOWS, John O., Di-36-1; Pvt 24th TN Inf; 7-61 to 1-64; Bellsburgh PO; CONF
MEE, John, Hw-125-6; Pvt D Co 63rd TN Inf; 63 to 65; Yellow Stone PO; imprisoned at different places; shown twice
MEE, Richard, Hw-125-6; Pvt; Blevins PO; imprisoned at Vicksburg; CONF
MEE, Simon, Br-6-3; Pvt D Co 42nd US Col; Chatala PO; disease of lungs & Heurnie
MEE, Wiley, Br-12-1; Pvt I Co 1st TN Hvy Art; Charleston PO; rheumatism, catarrh & eyes
MEEK, Alice E., Gr-72-2; widow; 3rd Civil Dist
MEEK, Henry, Sh-185-1; Sgt B Co 11th US Col Inf; 7-11-63 to 1-12-66; 147 Ross Ave., Memphis PO
MEEK, William M., K-177-3; Pvt G Co 31st TN Inf; 1 Dec 62 to 4 Jul 64; PO omitted; CONF
MEEKER, Helber, Hi-87-1; Pvt E Co PA Vol; 8-19-61 to 11-30-64; Bonaqua PO
MEEKLES, J. Samuel, K-171-4(2); Pvt C Co 12th TN Cav; 62 to 65; PO omitted; CONF
MEEKS, Daniel, Sh-189-4; Sgt F Co 11th US Col Inf; Fall 63 to Spring 65; Alley off Carolina St., Memphis PO

MEEKS, David, Hw-122-2; Pvt A Co 3rd US Inf; 64 to 65; Margaret PO; disease of left testicle, could not find discharge
MEEKS, Peter, Gr-71-1; Pvt I Co 8th TN Inf; 1 Jun 62 to 15 Apr 64; Jarmine PO; neither enlosed or mustered out ser., enlargment of feet from force march
MEELER, Bergin, Po-152-5(1); Ducktown PO
MEGHER, Thomas, C-33-5; Cpl A Co 41th PA Rgt; 1-63 to 7-63; Newcomb PO
MEINLICKER, M. C. M., Gi-138-2; 18th Dist
MELER, Meridith A., Wi-173-1; Pvt K Co 10th TN Inf; 5 Mar 64 to 8 Apr 65; Boston PO
MELFORD, Alfered, Hw-118-2; Pvt; St. Clair PO
MELLON, William H., H-69-3; Cpl I Co 14th Col Reg Inf; 63 to 65; Chattanooga PO
MELSON, John M., Wy-173-2; Pvt D Co 2nd TN Mtd Inf; 9-15-63 to 2-1-65; Houston PO
MELSON, William, Lo-193-1; Pvt A Co 3rd TN Inf; 1 Feb 62 to 27 Feb 65; Unitia PO; wounded in left leg
MELSON, William, Br-7-4; Paulina F. widow of; Pvt L Co 1st TN Cav; 11-61 to __; Ocoee Po
MELSON, William R., Wy-173-2; Pvt A Co 2nd TN Mtd Inf; 10-15-63 to 10-17-64; Houston PO
MELTABARGER, Elijah, Un-256-1; Pvt D Co 1st TN Inf; 9 Aug 61 to 17 Sep 64; Rule PO; momps
MELTIBARGER, Archibald, Un-254-3; Pvt A Co 1st TN Inf; 1 Apr 63 to 3 Aug 65; Gravestown PO
MELTON, Aaron G., Hi-85-1; Sgt C Co 9th TN Cav; 2-1-63 to 3-1-65; Spencers Mill PO
MELTON, Alexander, Ro-202-4; Pvt K Co 42nd NC Inf; 26 Jan 64 to 26 Apr 65; Cave Creek PO; chronic diarrhea, 27 yrs afflicted; CONF
MELTON, Alexander J., G-71-2; Mary E. widow of; Pvt G Co 20th TN Cav; 21 May 61 to 21 Aug 65; Edmonds PO; CONF
MELTON, Columbus, F-35-1; Drum A Co 110th TN Reg; May 64 to 12 Jan 66; New Castle PO (Harde. Co) wound in hip, by guard in camp
MELTON, Frain, Ca-24-1; Pvt G Co 5th TN Cav; 8-28-62 to 8-14-65; Prater PO; neuralgia in eyes, 9 years after discharged
MELTON, Howard, A-1-2; Pvt F Co 6th TN Inf; 3-10-62 to 3-15-65; Andersonville PO
MELTON, James F., We-221-4; Cpl G Co 12th KY Cav; 1 May 61 to Jun 65; Martin PO; CONF
MELTON, James F., Me-90-1; Jane C. widow of; Pvt H Co 5th TN Inf; 3-27-62 to __; Goodfield PO; died at Nashville TN 3-63
MELTON, James M., B-7-2; Lt Col 2nd TN Inf; 8-10-61 to 10-10-64; PO omitted
MELTON, James P., Mc-114-2; Pvt D Co 5th TN Inf; 8-31-64 to 6-26-65; Magellan PO
MELTON, John, Ro-203-6; Pvt G Co 1st TN Inf; 10 Mar 62 to 25 Mar 65; Burns' Mills PO; chronic rheumatism
MELTON, John, Mc-112-9; Pvt A Co 7th TN Mtd Inf; 9-12-64 to 7-27-65; Athens PO
MELTON, John L., Ov-135-1; Nancy A. widow of; Pvt F Co 1st KY Cav; Oakley PO; discharge with pention agent forgot dates
MELTON, Louis, Ge-87-2; Cpl E Co 3rd NC Inf; Timberridge PO; lungs affected
MELTON, Marion, G-64-1; widow of; Pvt; 61 to 63; Bradford PO
MELTON, Melesia, Wl-297-1; widow of Pvt C Co 4th TN Mtd Inf; 12 Nov 64 to 25 Aug 65; Jennings PO
MELTON, Merit, Be-6-1; Pvt D Co 7th TN Cav; 15 Jan 64 to 9 Aug 65; Big Sandy PO
MELTON, Orval, Hw-128-2; Pvt G Co 1st TN Cav; 4 Jul 62 to 5 Jun 65; Lee Valley PO; rheumatism & eyesight
MELTON, Peter L., Hy-74-1; Nancy E. widow of; discharge lost or misland; discharged 11 Sep 65 at Knoxville; PO omitted
MELTON, Uriah, Br-12-3; Pvt H Co 5th TN Inf; 3-20-62 to 5-19-62; Raht PO
MELTON, William, Pi-154-2; Pvt 5th KY Cav; 62 to 65; Susonett PO; came home & no discharge
MELVIN, William, L-102-1; Pvt E Co 1st IN; 62 to 65; Dist 13
MENDEROW, James, K-175-1; Pvt C Co 1st TN Inf; 8 Aug 62 to 8 Mar 64; Snoterly PO
MENEER, Charles, Wl-295-2; Ord Sgt A Co 14th Reg Inf; 15 Jy 63 to 15 Sep 65; Lebanon PO

MENEER, David A., Col. Rb-228-1; Pvt F Co 15th __;
   1 yr 7 mos; Crunk PO
MENER, Hiram H., Sq-165-2; Pvt; 63 to 4-65; Delphi
   PO; received an honorable disc
MENEY, Patt, Sh-167-2; PO omitted
MENTLON, James A., Sn-250-2; 1st Lt C Co 2nd __;
   10-16-62 to __; Gallatin PO: CONF
MERACLE, John D., G-51-1; Pvt 36th VA Cav; 8-61-61
   to 8-12-62; Humboldt PO
MERCER, David H., H-54-1; Pvt C Co 97th OH Inf;
   8-4-62 to 6-17-65; Chattanooga PO; wounded
   gun shot right leg near Atlanta
MERCER, David W., Ge-90-1; Sgt A Co 4th TN Inf;
   27 Jun 63 to 7 Aug 65; Greeneville PO
MERCER, Joseph F., Ge-102-2; Pvt D Co 8th TN Cav; Sarah C. widow of;
   Camp Creek PO; rheumatism
MERCER, Peter, B1-4-1; Pvt G Co 8th TN Cav; 6-23-63
   to 9-20-65; Pikeville PO
MERCER, Robert T., Ge-96-2; Pvt D Co 8th TN Cav;
   Sep 63 to Aug 65; Jockey PO; spinal affection,
   discharge in Washington DC
MERCER, Thomas L., Ge-97-2; Pvt A Co 4th TN Inf;
   12 Aug 62 to 2 Aug 65; Upchurch PO; liver
   disease
MERCHANT, Joseph, Po-152-1; Pvt K Co 10th OH Cav;
   63 to 65; Ducktown PO; deafness
MEREDITH, John, Wa-267-4; Pvt C Co 13th TN Cav;
   24 Sep 63 to 5 Sep 65; PO omitted
MERIAM, Charles W., W-196-2; Pvt A Co 6th MI Inf;
   11-62 to 7-65; McMinnville PO
MERIDETH, Ezekel W., K-186-1; Pvt A Co 9th TN Inf;
   8 Jul 63 to 11 Sep 65; Chumlea PO; rheumatism
MERIDETH, John M., K-177-4; Pvt G Co 6th TN Inf;
   18 Apr 62 to 9 Jul 65; Knoxville PO
MERIDETH, William A., Ct-40-4; Pvt C Co 2nd TN Cav;
   Elizabethton PO
MERIDITH, James T., Fe-42-3; Pvt I Co 30th KY;
   1-29-64 to 4-18-65; Jamestown PO
MERILL, Nelson, Un-251-1; Pvt D Co 11th TN Cav;
   Effie PO; struck in breast by horse,
   discharged from sickness
MERIT, Edgecomb, Ct-39-2; Pvt F Co 8th TN Cav;
   5-63 to 9-65; Gap Run PO; doorhoea, piles &
   heart disease
MERIT, Henry J., Cr-16-2; Pvt M Co 6th TN Cav;
   18 Jul 62 to 26 Jul 65; Huntingdon PO;
   chronic rheumatism
MERITT, Miles, Mr-95-2; July widow of; Pvt I Co
   10th TN Inf; 4-13-63 to 6-23-65; Victoria PO
MERONEY, James, D-47-1; Sgt E Co 12th TN Cav;
   11-62 to 3-65; Jackson St., Nashville PO
MERONEY, Samuel N., H-49-11; Pvt B Co 1st TN Art;
   7-17-64 to 7-20-65; Daisy PO
MERRELL, James, D-64-4; Pvt; Nashville PO
MERRETT, John Q., Un-250-2; Nancy widow of; Pvt G
   Co 2nd TN Cav; 1 Oct 62 to died; Maynardville
   PO
MERRIAM, Isaac B., H-61-2; Sgt I Co 122nd NY Inf;
   8-1-62 to 7-1-64; Chattanooga PO; resection
   of r. elbow joint carried away by shell
MERRICK, Adam R., Lo-187-3; Pvt A Co McLaughlins
   squad OH Cav; 22 Aug 62 to 12 May 65; Loudon
   PO; rheumatism & heart disease
MERRICK, Robert, Ro-207-2; Pvt F Co OH Inf; 23 Jan
   65 to 20 Jan 66; Paint Rock PO; acute
   rheumatism
MERRILL, S. O., D-62-1; Pvt H Co 6th MA; 16 Jul 64
   to 27 Oct 64; Nashville PO, 1310 McGavock
MERRILLE, Joal J., R-161-4; Pvt H Co 2nd MO Cav;
   9-9-62 to 9-10-65; Dayton PO
MERRIMAN, Arthur C., K-154-1; Knoxville PO
MERRIT, Lucius, Hu-102-1; Pvt A Co 9th TN Cav; 13
   Jul 63 to 11 Sep 65; Cuba Ldg PO; inguinal
   hernia, injured about 2 yrs ago
MERRIT, Presley, Ca-24-1; Elizabeth widow of; Pvt
   H Co 5th TN Cav; 62 to 65; Prater PO; widow
   in destitute condition
MERRITT, Ephraim S., Ma-125-1; Pvt H Co 55th KY Inf;
   16 Feb 65 to __; Luttrell PO; piles
MERRITT, John, Un-253-2; Pvt C Co 7th TN Cav; 7 Apr
   62 to 7 Apr 65; Luttrell PO; piles
MERRITT, Leonard B., Ct-40-6; US Sol; 7th Civil Dist
MERRITT, Leonard B., Ct-40-3; Pvt 2nd TN Mtd Inf;
   Elizabethton PO
MERRITT, Leroy, Gr-81-1; Sgt A Co 2nd TN Cav; 1 Aug
   62 to 7 Jul 65; Clear Spring PO: effects of
   jaundice, partly disabled

MERRITT, Thomas, Ct-40-3; Rebecca widow of; this
   entry crossed out but not indicated as CONF
   --possibly entered in error; Elizabethton PO
MERRITT, Thomas J., R-157-2; 12th Dist, Grandview
   PO
MERRITTS, Louiza, Gr-82-2; 14th Dist
MERRIWEATHER, Horace, Sh-189-4; Pvt F Co 3rd US
   Col Hvy Art; 6-5-63 to 4-30-66; Carolina St,
   Memphis PO
MERRIWEATHER, Horace, Sh-192-1; US Unit; Memphis PO
MERRIWEATHER, Isaac, Sh-190-2; Pvt B Co 59th US Inf;
   63 to 65 (2 yrs 6 mos); Memphis PO
MERRIWEATHER, Squire, Sh-189-1; Pvt B Co 138th C Inf;
   15 Mar 62 to 12 Jan 65; Henning PO; shot right
   hip, reinlisted 8 Jul 65 to 9 Dec, 11 Apr 68
MERRUT, William, K-181-3; Flenniken PO: CONF
MERRY, W. W., Cr-16-3; Pvt F Co 2nd W TN Cav; 22
   Sep 62 to 20 Dec 63; 1st Lt I Co 7th TN Cav;
   20 Dec 63 to May 65; Huntington PO; mustd as
   1st Lt by order, deportment to dat, 20th Dec
   1863
MERSER, Elbert F., Ge-90-2; Pvt B Co 8th TN Cav;
   23 Jul 63 to 11 Sep 65; Greeneville PO
MERVILLE, George D., Hu-106-2; Quartermaster Sgt E
   Co 8th NY Hvy Art; 8-11-62 to 1-5-65; Waverly
   PO
MERVIN, Charles, F-47-3; Sgt C Co 97th OH Inf;
   8-22-62 to 6-15-65; Medina PO
MESSAMORE, Thomas H., A-5-2; Pvt F Co 7th TN Inf;
   11-8-64 to 7-27-65; Dossett PO
MESSEMORE, George D., A-3-4; Pvt E Co 12th TN Cav;
   62 to __; Clinch River PO
MESSER, David, Co-67-3; Lucinda widow of; Pvt NC;
   Nov 63 to __; Cosby PO; captured and died at
   Cumberland Gap, TN: CONF
MESSER, George W., Se-220-1; Pvt K Co 9th TN Cav;
   10 Sep 63 to 11 Sep 65; Emurts Cave PO; shot
   through left leg
MESSER, Samuel, Se-230-4; Sarah E. Hill formerly
   widow of (see Hannah, Harvey) Richison's Cove
   PO her present husband, sol (con) is still
   living but not with her
MESSER, William T., Ch-12-1; Pvt B Co 21th TN Inf;
   1-30-61 to 11-65; Custer Point PO; CONF
METCALF, John, U-249-2; Pvt G Co 3rd NC Mtd Inf;
   to 65 (1 yr); Flag Pond PO; rheumatis
METCALF, Whitfield, Mt-137-1; Civ, in government
   employ; 62 to 65; papers lost; St. Bethlehem PO
METERT, Lewis, Cf-42-1; Pvt G Co 11th MI Inf;
   8-24-61 to 11-3-64; Hickerson PO
METZGER, Philip, H-70-2(1); Philip I. Evesine alias;
   Pvt A Co 12th IN Inf--4-19-61 to 7-62; Pvt A
   Co 69th TN Inf--8-2-62 to 7-5-65; Chattanooga
   PO; double rupture
MEVON?, Samuel, G-55-1; alias Dodson; Pvt F Co 55th
   Col Inf; 62 to 65; Trenton PO; lost discharge
   and dont recollect dates
MEWBORN, James R., Wy-173-4; Cpl A Co 10th TN Inf;
   4-16-62 to 5-25-66; Victory PO
MEYER, Charles H., H-59-3; Capt and Stewart Gunboat
   J. P. Jackson; 8-62 to 64 (2 yrs);
   Chattanooga PO
MEYERS, Jacob M., Ge-93-2; 1st Lt? I Co TN Cav;
   1 Aug 62 to 8 Jun 65; Greeneville PO
MEYERS, Louis, (see Dunmeyer, Louis L.)
MEYERS, Moses M., Cr-20-3; US Sol; Hollow Rock PO
MEYERS, Vincen, C1-56-1; Capt C Co 1st TN Inf;
   7-1-62 to 8-1-65; PO omitted
MICHAEL, T. V., G-64-2; Sol; Bradford PO
MICHAM, George, F-38-1; alias Charly Thompson;
   Pvt I Co 61st US Inf; Jun 64 to Feb 66;
   St. Louis, MO PO
MICHEL, Henderson, A-3-3; Elizabeth widow of; Pvt
   D Co 1st TN Art; 11-30-63 to 7-20-66;
   Beveridg PO (Knox Co); lung disease
MICHELL, Mary E., He-66-1; 5th Dist
MICHELL, Richard, F-38-2; alias Mecham, Richard;
   Sgt F Co 61st US Inf; Lambert PO
MICHELL, Robert W., Dy-29-5; Pvt; Jan 63 to Feb 63;
   PO omitted; CONF
MICHOLS, Marry E., K-181-2; widow of US Sol; Nast PO
MICHOLSON, Zachriah, Br-14-1; Pvt F Co 4th TN Cav;
   5-25-63 to 7-12-65; Cleveland PO; deafness in
   one ear
MIDKIFF, George W., We-225-2(1); Amanda M. widow of;
   Dresden PO

MIDKIFF, Henry, He-67-1; Pvt F Co 10th TN Inf; 2 May 62 to 29 Jun 65; Sardis PO; shoulder & head from small pox & dimness of vision
MIDDLETON, Adolphus A., Ch-12-2; Pvt F Co 9th TN Cav; 10-16-61 to 5-65; Custer Point PO; CONF
MIDDLETON, B. F., Ge-97-3; Pvt B Co 8th TN Cav; 22 Jul 63 to 11 Sep 65; Newmanville PO; liver & kidny & diarrhea
MIDDLETON, Edward, Sh-199-1; Pvt; 553 Georgia St., Memphis PO
MIDDLETON, George, C-33-1; Pvt 12th Hvy Art; 12-64 to 4-64; Newcomb PO
MIDDLETON, James A., Ge-98-3; Cpl K Co 1st TN Cav; 11 Aug 62 to Jun 65; Jeroldstown PO; disease of kidney and rheumatism
MIDDLETON, Joseph, De-22-2; Pvt I Co 9th TN Cav; 1 Nov 62 to 1 Dec 65; New Era PO: Conf
MIDDLETON, T. A., Wa-264-1; Mary B. widow of; 1st Lt B Co 4th TN Inf; 18 Feb 64 to 27 Sep 64; Jonesboro PO; chronic rheumatism
MIDDLTON (sic), Alfand W., He-63-1; Cpl C Co 7th TN; 29 May 63 to 9 Aug 65; Long PO; in Andersonville Prison 8 mos
MIDLETON, James, G-64-1; Nancie Pearce widow of; Capt; 61 to 63; Brandford PO
MIES, William A., Un-259-2; Pvt B Co 1st TN Inf; 1 Aug 61 to 17 Sep 64; Rhodelia PO; bowels, cold in army
MIETT, John M., Sm-168-2; Pvt A Co 1st TN Inf; 64 to 65; Pleasant Shade PO; chronic disease of the bowels
MIKLES, James C., H-50-1; Pvt E Co 6th R TN Mtd Inf; 9-11-64 to 6-20-65; Daisy PO; gravel
MIKLES, William S., K-172-4; Hariet J. widow of; Pvt A Co 6th TN Inf; 17 Apr 62 to 27 Apr 62; PO omitted
MILAM, George, Hn-72-1; Pvt B Co 4th TN Inf; May 65 to 4 Mar 66; Paris PO
MILAN, Gladen S., Dy-27-2; Pvt 27th TN Inf; Jun 61 to Nov 63; Tatemville PO: CONF
MILAND, George, K-170-3; Pvt F Co 131st OH Inf; 2 May 64 to 25 Aug 64; Knoxville PO
MILBANKS, W. M., G-57-7(4); Pvt F Co; 1 yr; Yorkville PO: CONF
MILBUR, William E. F., Ge-91-2; Sgt B Co 12th TN Cav; 20 Nov 62 to 19 Oct 65; Greeneville PO; cronic diarrhea
MILER, William R., Rb-221-3; Pvt F Co 11th TN; 1 May 61 to 1 May 65; Cedar Hill PO; flesh wound; CONF
MILES, Ashley, Je-145-1; Pvt E Co 9th TN Cav; 19 Sep 63 to 11 Sep 65; Dumplin PO
MILES, Harrison, Sh-188-3; US Col; 181½ Anetron St, Memphis PO
MILES, John, Sh-189-4; Hester widow of; enlisted at Helena, AR--no other record; Ark. Ave, Memphis PO
MILES, John, Di-37-1; Pvt F Co 12th TN Inf; 8-12-63 to 1-16-66; Cumberland Furnace PO
MILES, John E., Ro-201-2; Pvt C Co 7th TN Inf; Oct 62 to Feb 63; Kingston PO
MILES, John J., Cy-27-5(3); Pvt A Co 1st KY Cap Guard; 5-20-64 to 1-65; Miles Cross Roads PO
MILES, Milo, Gi-127-1; alias Johnson, Moses; Pvt B Co 15th TN USC Inf; Dec 63 to 30 Apr 66; Pulaski PO; rheumatism
MILES, P. P., Gi-133-2; Cpl E Co 4th TN; 62 to 64; Bufords PO; CONF
MILES, Randall H., K-173-1; Pvt H Co 8th TN Cav; 62 to 64; McMillen PO; rheumatism; CONF
MILES, Samuel D., Ro-202-4; Pvt E Co 2nd TN Inf; 22 Jun 62 to Aug 64; Cave Creek PO; rheumatism & lungs 27 yrs afflicted
MILES, Silas, Sh-157-8; Pvt I Co 61st; 63 to 65; Dist 13
MILES, Thomas, Hw-129-1; Pvt B Co 1st US (Col?) Art; 22 Jan 64 to 31 Mar 66; Dellmonell PO; rheumatism
MILES, William, H-51-7; Pvt I Co 3rd TN Inf; 2-10-62 to 2-23-64; 16th Dist
MILEY, Isaac, Cl-52-1; Louiza widow of; Pvt N Co 58th IN Inf; 4-1-61 to 65; Quarter PO
MILIACEN, Calvin, Bl-3-1; Sgt 4th TN Inf; 61 to 7-4-63; Patten PO; CONF
MILLAN, William A., Je-144-1; Pvt B Co 3rd TN Inf; May 62 to 65; Talbotts PO; rheumatism from exposure in ware?

MILLAR, John H., D-92-2; US Sol; W. Nashville PO
MILLARD, Elkana, H-49-7; Pvt G Co 3rd TN Cav; 8-13-63 to 6-10-65; Daisy PO; hurt in shoulder on way to prison and contracted sore eyes in prison was on the Sultana
MILLBANKS, Jos. W., Sh-201-2; Mary E. widow of; Memphis PO; papers misplaced; CONF
MILLER, Abe, Mu-193-1; Orderly A Co; 1-15-63 to 1-1-65; Columbia PO
MILLER, Albert, Sh-161-1; US Sol; 16th Dist
MILLER, Alexander, B-11-2(1); Pvt A Co 17th US Col; 63 to 6-66; Poplins X Roads PO
MILLER, Alfred, Gi-125-2; Mariah Johnson widow of; Pvt; Wales PO; dies in army, could not get command
MILLER, Alfred C., K-166-1; Louisa widow of; Cpl C Co 1st TN Cav; 1 Apr 62 to 1 Apr 65; Knoxville PO
MILLER, Ambrose E., H-53-5; A Co 24th OH Inf; 4-22-61 to 6-65; Ridgedale PO; ruptured
MILLER, Andrew, Sh-191-2; Catharine widow of; Pvt L Co Lt Art; Memphis PO
MILLER, Andrew, Co-69-7(3); Pvt A Co 16th TN Cav; 15 Jan 63 to 15 May 65; Lead PO; CONF
MILLER, Andrew J., Lo-188-3; Pvt A Co 5th TN Inf; Stockton PO
MILLER, Andrew J., Gr-73-1; Pvt K-L Cox 1st TN Cav; 1 Mar 62 to 7 Apr 65; Turleys Mills PO; exposure in US service, acts in head
MILLER, Asahel L., H-61-2; Or(derly?) Sgt B Co 27th IL Inf; 8-28-61 to 5-62; Chattanooga PO; ruptured
MILLER, Auther, Un-256-3; Pvt D Co 7th TN Inf; 9 Aug 61 to 17 Sep 64; Loy's X Roads PO; deafness & stomache trobble
MILLER, Burris R., Sh-203-1; Pvt F Co 2nd TN Reg; May 61 to 19 Jun 65; Memphis PO; CONF
MILLER, Charles, Di-34-1; 2nd Lt B Co 42nd MO Inf; to 6-28-65; Dickson PO; rheumatism
MILLER, Charles G., R-159-1; Capt GVA 6th OH Cav; 61 to __; Spring City PO; deaf in one ear
MILLER, Charles H., St-159-1; Tammy E. widow of; Pvt; 2 yrs 4 mos; Legate PO
MILLER, Christian C., Mc-112-6; Sgt E Co 15th MI Vol Inf; 11-1-61 to 3-9-63; Athens PO
MILLER, Christian E., Ro-211-2; Sgt E Co 15th MI Inf; Oct 61 to Nov 62; Harriman PO; wounded in hip, discharged by surgeons certificate
MILLER, Christopher, Je-137-1; Pvt F Co 9th TN Cav; 24 Jul 63 to 15 Sep 65; Hickory Ridge PO
MILLER, Clabron, Je-139-2; Pvt I Co 2nd TN Cav; 22 Sep 62 to 20 Jul 65; Trion PO; rhumatism
MILLER, Creed F., Un-250-1; Pvt L Co 1st TN Cav; 1 Jan 64 to 19 Jun 65; Maynardville PO; diseas of back & kidneys; incured while in service
MILLER, Daniel P., Ms-174-1; Pvt H Co 13th US Inf; 22 Oct 63 to 10 Jan 66; Chapel Hill PO; partially deaf, discharge in Washington City
MILLER, David, K-164-3; 83 McGhee St, Knoxville PO
MILLER, David B., Bo-14-4; Pvt A Co 3rd TN Inf;
MILLER, De-Wolf, Hw-125-2; Pvt E Co 2nd TN Cav; 63 to 65; Yellow Stone PO; afflicted with rheumatism
MILLER, Eli, Un-257-2; Pvt B Co 2nd TN Cav; Oct 61 to Apr 65; Sharps Chapel PO; CONF
MILLER, Elias, K-168-2; Pvt; Beverly PO; received injurious blow on head
MILLER, Esaw, A-13-2; Pvt F Co 6th TN Inf; 3-10-62 to 3-24-65; Briceville PO; crippled in right hip & knee
MILLER, Francis M., Ct-36-3; Pvt A Co 6th IN Cav; 8-63 to 11-65; PO omitted
MILLER, Frank M., (see Maynard, Samuel L.)
MILLER, Franklin M., Jo-153-2; Pvt D Co 13th TN Cav; 24 Sep 63 to 5 Sep 65; Shady PO; rheumatism, gun shot
MILLER, George, Ho-96-2; PO omitted
MILLER, George, C-24-1; Pvt P & C Co 9th Cav; 1863 to 65; Boy PO
MILLER, George W., D-79-1; Cpl B Co TN Mtd Inf; 9 Jan 64 to 14 Apr 65; Nashville PO; asthma caused by exposure

MILLER, Green, Sm-168-1; Pvt TN Inf; 62 to 65; Bagdad PO
MILLER, Harpus, Sn-252-1; Pvt K Co 14th TN Inf; 11-16-63 to 3-29-66; Gallatin PO
MILLER, Harvey, C-29-2; Pvt E Co 9th TN Cav; 10-1-63 to 9-11-65; Fincastle PO; piles & catarrh
MILLER, Henry, K-168-2; Pvt I Co 1st Col Hvy Art; 8 Jul 64 to 31 Mar 66; Beverly PO
MILLER, Henry, Wa-263-2; Pvt H Co 8th TN Cav; 63 to 63; Garber Mills PO; rejected on act. of being a cripple
MILLER, Henry (Col), Fr-115-1; Teamster 10th OH Cav; 10-61 to 6-65; Cowan PO; Henry contracted dots vigonel, therefor he has estimad receipt therefor her husband's discharge
MILLER, Henry, T-216-2; 14th Civil Dist
MILLER, Isaac, Gr-72-2; Pvt A Co 9th TN Cav; 29 Oct 64 to 11 Sep 65; Beans Station PO; exposure in service
MILLER, Isaac, Mr-102-2; Pvt C Co 1st TN Cav; 1-1-62 to __-1-65; South Pittsburg PO
MILLER, J. K., Fr-118-1; Pvt D Co; 62 to __ (8 mos); Winchester PO; CONF
MILLER, Jack, Sh-198-1; America widow of; Cpl A Co 61st Col Inf; Memphis PO; she has claim agent's receipt for her husband's discharge
MILLER, Jacob, H-54-1; Pvt I Co 4th TN Cav; 8-7-63 to 7-5-65; Sherman Heights PO; chronic diarrhoea, prisoner 7 month in Andersonville, GA
MILLER, James, Cu-16-1; Pvt G Co 6th TN Mtd Inf; 2-25-65 to 6-30-65; Wine Sap PO; diarrhea
MILLER, James, C-27-1; Pvt A Co 27th OH Inf; 9-64 to __ (6 mos); Jacksboro PO
MILLER, James, C-27-3; Marthia widow of; Pvt 6th KY; 3 yrs; Jacksboro PO
MILLER, James, Ct-37-1; Pvt C Co 13th TN Cav; 9-24-63 to 9-24-65; Hopson PO; heart disease, cause unknown
MILLER, James, Je-137-2; Catherine widow of; Pvt F Co 9th TN Cav; Sep 63 to 65; Hickory Ridge PO
MILLER, James, Gr-72-1; Pvt A Co 9th TN Cav; 29 Oct 64 to 11 Sep 65; Noelon PO; extreme riding
MILLER, James A., H-49-9; Sarah A. widow of; Pvt F Co 4th TN Cav; 4-18-63 to 7-12-65; Daisy PO
MILLER, James D., Hm-106-2; Sgt C Co 37th TN Inf; Dec 61 to 65; Morristown PO; CONF
MILLER, James R., We-230-3; Mary N. widow of; Pvt K Co 21st TN Reg; McKinzie PO; CONF
MILLER, Jeremiah B., Ct-40-2; 1st Lt H Co 13th TN Cav; 10-28-63 to 4-7-65; Elizabethton PO
MILLER, John, U-246-1; Pvt A Co 3rd NC Mtd Inf; __ to 8 Aug __ (1 yr); Erwin PO
MILLER, John, Sh-169-1; Pvt A Co IL Inf; 61 to 64; Memphis PO
MILLER, John, Cf-42-1; Pvt H Co 81st OH Inf; 2-17-62 to 7-13-65; PO omitted; gun shot
MILLER, John C., Dy-29-2; Pvt 11th TN Cav; Apr 64 to Apr 64 (5 days); Newbern PO; CONF
MILLER, John G., Mu-210-3; Pvt A Co 10th TN Inf; 11-14-64 to 4-9-66; Spring Hill PO; shot in left leg
MILLER, John H., Lo-188-2; Sgt A Co 5th TN Inf; 25 Feb 62 to 4 Apr 65; Stockton PO
MILLER, John K., Mr-97-2; Pvt C Co 6th TN Inf; 9-17-64 to 6-30-65; Victoria PO; side affected from relapse of measles & mumps
MILLER, John P., H-54-6; Pvt G Co 5th TN Mtd Inf; 11-1-64 to 6-26-65; Sherman Heights PO; ruined health--enlargement of the heart, chronic rheumatism--eyes impaired, broken down, unable to work, neuralgia
MILLER, John S., Hm-103-2; Pvt M Co 5th IN Cav; 26 Aug 62 to Apr 65; Morristown PO; deseas of rectum
MILLER, John T., Lo-194-2; Cpl H Co 4th TN Inf; 6 Dec 63 to 2 Aug 65; Muddy Creek PO
MILLER, John W., K-166-2; Pvt A Co 1st TN Inf; 2 Aug 61 to 17 Sep 64; Knoxville PO; ruptured, drawing pension
MILLER, John W., Un-254-1; Pvt C Co 1st TN Cav; 1 Apr 62 to 21 Apr 65; Paulett PO; hearing effected by gun shot
MILLER, Jonathan, Un-256-1; Pvt; Rule PO
MILLER, Jonathan, Wa-273-1; Pvt I Co 8th TN Cav; 13 Sep 63 to 11 Sep 65; Keebler's X Roads PO; rheumatism
MILLER, Joseph, Bo-21-2; Cpl K Co 2nd TN Cav; 9-1-62 to 7-16-65; Ellijay PO

MILLER, Joseph K., Lo-188-1; Pvt C Co 7th TN Mtd Inf; 20 Aug 64 to 27 Jun 65; Stockton PO
MILLER, Lapolin, D-51-1 (Black); Rachiel widow of; Pvt 14th TN Inf; 450 N Cherry St, Nashville PO; cant furnish date or year
MILLER, Lawrenc K., Cr-20-1; Pvt I Co 7th TN Cav; 12-15-63 to 8-9-65; Bibbny PO; heart disease
MILLER, Lewis, C-24-2; Pvt B & H Co 11th & 9th Reg; 7-18-63 to 9-11-65; Boy PO; liver, lungs & piles
MILLER, Louis, K-166-5; US Sol, army; 16 N Walnut St, Knoxville PO
MILLER, Marklas T., Ct-41-2; Pvt G Co 13th TN Cav; 9-24-63 to 9-5-65; Keensburg PO; rheumatism, pluracy
MILLER, Martin V., Un-254-2; Pvt C Co 4th TN Cav; 11 Oct 63 to 11 Sep 65; Bartheney PO; shot in right side
MILLER, Mattison, Sn-252-3; Gallatin PO
MILLER, Mike, C-26-2; Pvt A Co 7th TN Inf; 8-2-61 to 7-9-65; Caryville PO
MILLER, Moses, Je-139-1; Pvt F Co 9th TN Cav; 24 Jul 63 to 11 Sep 65; Trion PO
MILLER, Moses, Wa-274-1; Pvt H Co 8th TN Cav; 15 Sep 63 to 11 Sep 65; Jonesboro PO; wounded in right arm
MILLER, Moses D., H-49-8; Mary widow of; Pvt; Daisy PO
MILLER, Nancy M., Me-88-4; widow; Brittsville PO
MILLER, Newel W., Ro-207-4; Sgt C Co 7th TN Mtd Inf; 20 Aug 64 to 27 Jun 65; Patties Gap PO; neralgia & rheumatism
MILLER, Olaver, Je-140-2; Sarah widow of; Pvt 1st TN Cav; Strawberry Plains PO; killed by train running over him
MILLER, Peter, D-87-1; Pvt TN; Nashville PO
MILLER, Philip, Sh-188-3; US white; 103 High St, Memphis PO
MILLER, Philip M., Hw-133-1; Pvt 1st TN Mtd Inf; __ to 65; Slide PO; wounded
MILLER, Planest M., We-223-4; Pvt G Co 7th TN Cav; 62 to 63; Elm Tree PO; CONF
MILLER, Plum, Sn-252-1; Narcis widow of; Cpl D Co 14th TN Inf; 10-63 to __; Gallatin PO
MILLER, R. C., Ms-177-1; Pvt F Co 2nd US Inf; 10-15-63 to 12-16-64; Lillards Mills PO
MILLER, R. J., Ce-20-2; alias James R. Johnson; H Co 30th KY Mtd Inf; 4-10-63 to 3-10-65; Marrowbone PO
MILLER, Richard, H-54-2; Pvt A Co; Sherman Heights PO; wounded in right leg and right arm--Ft. Donelson
MILLER, Richard, Cu-17-3; Pvt D Co 9th IN Inf; 4-3-62 to 4-3-65; Grassy Cove PO; wounded
MILLER, Richmond, Ru-13-3; Pvt 2nd __; Murfreesboro PO
MILLER, Robert S., Ge-91-1; Lt 16th US Inf; Greenville PO; chronic diarhea also insane
MILLER, Robert B., Sh-167-1; Pvt F Co Mon Dryfos; 12 May 61 to 6 Jun 62; PO omitted; CONF
MILLER, Robert B., Bo-14-4; Pvt A Co 3rd TN Inf; 2-10-62 to 3-10-65; Mint PO
MILLER, Samuel, Co-69-6(1); Pvt F Co 1st TN Inf; 1 Mar 62 to 20 May 65; Driskill PO; chronic dirhea, a pensioner
MILLER, Samuel, V-178-1; Pvt C Co 5th TN Cav; 3-63 to 10-63; Seals, Bledsoe Co PO; disabled by gun shot wound, after receiving wound, has got no discharge, was not with company any more
MILLER, Samuel, Mc-117-1; Matinda J. widow of; Pvt A Co 7th TN Mtd Inf; Mecca PO
MILLER, Samuel D., H-55-2; Pvt G Co 9th TN Inf; 64 to 6-21-65; Tyner PO
MILLER, Samuel M., C-27-2; Pvt D Co 13th 10SC? Cav; 15 Dec 63 to 6 Apr 64; Hornbeak PO
MILLER, Sarah E. (see Peeler, George)
MILLER, Sarah E. (see Parker, __)
MILLER, Sebastian, D-76-1; Pvt I Co 16th IL Inf; 27 May 61 to 10 Dec 62; Nashville PO
MILLER, Solomon, U-247-3; Pvt H Co 13th TN Cav; 27 Jan 63 to 5 Sep 65; Erwin PO; chronic diarrhoea & rheumatism
MILLER, Sterling, C-27-2; Pvt F Co 7th TN Inf; 11-8-64 to 7-27-65; Caryville PO
MILLER, T. J., Bo-11-2; Pvt A Co 8th TN Inf; 2-10-62 to 2-23-65; Brick Mill PO; neuralgia

MILLER, Thomas, Ge-83-3; Margett widow; Pvt I Co 1st TN Inf; Painters PO
MILLER, Thomas, C-30-1; Millie A. Lumpkins formerly widow of; Pvt 2nd TN Inf; 61 to __; Well Spring PO; reenlisted veteran
MILLER, Thomas, D-91-3; Pvt; Station C, Nashville PO
MILLER, Thomas, Me-88-3; Eliza widow of; 2nd Lt E Co 5th TN Inf; 3-2-62 to 4-4-65; Brittsville PO
MILLER, Thomas, Mt-139-2; Pvt A Co 14th TN; 1 yr; Carbondale PO
MILLER, Thomas J., Ro-207-1; A Co 5th TN Inf; 26 Feb 62 to 10 Apr 65; Patties Gap PO; disese of hips & bowels, claimed to be result of sea fever
MILLER, Thomas J., Ro-201-2; Pvt I Co 1st TN Inf; 9 Aug 61 to 17 Sep 64; Kingston PO
MILLER, Thomas M., De-26-2; A Co 51st TN; Feb 62 to __ (11 mos); Genette PO; CONF
MILLER, Ussy, Hy-75-1; widow; Dancyville PO; dount know much about it
MILLER, W. G., Li-161-2; Pvt C Co 4th OH Inf; 14 Sep 61 to 15 Nov 64; Lincoln PO
MILLER, W. L., Rb-218-1; Monteray widow; Pvt 17th KY Cav; Sep 63 to Aug 65; Mitchell PO; chronic diahhroea, papers in hand of agt
MILLER, William, H-66-2; Pvt H Co 35th IN Vol Inf; 61 to 65 (4 yrs 5 mos); Chattanooga PO
MILLER, William, Co-68-1; Pvt K Co 8th TN Cav; Costner PO
MILLER, William, Hw-128-2; Pvt E Co 8th TN Cav; 1 Jan 64 to 11 Sep 65; Choptack PO; chronic rheumatism
MILLER, William, Je-136-1; Non Com Officer C Co 9th TN Hvy Art; 12 Jun 63 to 11 Sep 65; Dandridge PO
MILLER, William, (see Blakemore, William)
MILLER, William, Ct-37-2; Pvt C Co 13th TN Cav; 9-24-63 to 9-5-65; Ripshin PO; rheumatism
MILLER, William, Fr-118-1; Pvt I Co 41st TN Inf; Jan 61 to Mar 64; Winchester PO
MILLER, William H., K-173-2; Pvt E Co 3rd TN Cav; 28 Nov 62 to 21 Aug 65; Troutman PO
MILLER, William H., C-32-2; Pvt C Co 9th TN Cav; 8-1-62 to 9-11-65; Well Spring PO; chronic dyree, liver & kidney 26 yrs
MILLER, William M., Lo-194-1; Pvt C Co 8th TN Cav; 1 yr 1 mo; Muddy Creek PO
MILLER, Williarm R., U-247-3; US Sol; 5th Civil Dist
MILLER, William Y., Mn-126-2; Pvt G Co 64 to __; Bethel Springs PO; has forgotten all about his record
MILLER, Willis W., We-223-4; Pvt G Co 7th TN Cav; Oct 63 to Mar 65; Elm Tree PO; CONF
MILLER, Winfield S., D-59-1; 1612 Church St., Nashville PO
MILLER, ___, Se-221-2; Martha J. widow of; Fox PO; could not get any information
MILLICAN, Moses T., Ro-210-3; Pvt E Co 1st TN Inf; 11 Aug 61 to 1 Oct 64; Rockwood PO
MILLICAN, William, H-49-10; Polina widow of; Pvt B Co KS Art; 9-5-64 to 7-10-65; Daisy PO
MILLIGAN, Jerry M., Gr-77-1; Pvt F Co 1st __; 29 Apr 64 to 30 Nov 64; Lea Spring PO; bone skirvey
MILLIGAN, Nelson, Sh-157-2; Pvt B Co 63rd US Col; 27 Oct 63 to 9 Jan 66; Dist 12
MILLIGAN, Samuel, K-180-2; Pvt D Co 9th TN Cav; 1 Oct 63 to 11 Sep 65; Bearden PO; lung trouble and injury from lightning
MILLIGAN, Thomas P., Mo-128-1; Pvt D Co 3rd TN Mtd Inf; 7-25-64 to 11-30-64; Belltown PO
MILLIGAN, Wm. B., Mo-130-2; Capt D Co 3rd TN Cav-Inf; 7-15-64 to 11-30-64; Ballplay PO
MILLIGAN, William H., La-108-1; Pvt H Co 1st AL Cav; 11-1-64 to 10-64; PO omitted
MILLIM?, Burrel, P-156-3; Pvt TN Cav; 7-61 to 8-64; Buffalo PO (Humphreys Co); went home without discharge on above date; CONF
MILLINER, Martain V. B., A-9-4(2); Ama. A. widow of; Pvt; Marlow PO; small pox & lung disease; was not discharged; CONF
MILLINGTON, Augustus O., H-64-2; Col 18th US Cav?; 4-17-61 to 3-15-66; Chattanooga PO

MILLOR, John A., Je-144-2; Pvt A Co 9th TN Cav; 2 Oct 63 to 11 Sep 65; Valleyhome PO; injur in back & righ leg; discharge at close ware
MILLS, Alcey, Ch-14-2; Pvt E Co 52nd TN Cav; 10-1-63 to 5-22-65; PO omitted; CONF
MILLS, Benj., De-25-1; Cpl A Co 48th IL Inf; 24 Mar 62 to 15 Aug 65; Decaturville PO
MILLS, Benjamin, Sh-193-2; Pvt; Memphis PO
MILLS, David, Bo-13-1; Pvt C Co 5th TN Inf; 2-62 to __ (3 mos); Freindsville PO; injured in ankle
MILLS, Delila, Mo-130-3; widow of US Sol; 16th Civil Dist
MILLS, Elijah, Cf-37-1; Pvt Ship Onward; 30 Jan 61 to 14 May 65; Hillsboro PO
MILLS, Frank, Je-142-2; Parthenia widow of; Pvt; New Market PO
MILLS, H. J., Wl-308-2; Pvt A Co 4th TN Cav; 1 Nov 61 to Apr 65; Mount Juliet PO; captured; CONF
MILLS, J. B., Mn-129-2; Pvt TN Scouts under Genl. Dodge; 7-14-63 to __; Adamsville PO; scout, no regular soldier
MILLS, John F., Ge-99-2; Pvt G Co 3rd NC Mtd Inf; 14 Oct 64 to 11 Aug 65; Limestone Springs PO; measles
MILLS, Jonethan, L-100-1; Pvt E Co 3rd AL Cav; 5 M 63 to 5 Mar 64; Ripley PO; wounded in right shoulder, hip and testicle and back
MILLS, Newton, Su-239-1; Pvt; Horace PO
MILLS, Robbert, Je-146-2; Pvt C Co 9th TN Cav; Jul 63 to 11 Sep 65; White Pine PO; old & feeble
MILLS, Robbert W., Je-146-2; Pvt C Co 9th TN Cav; 1 Jul 63 to 14 Sep 65; White Pine PO; blindness & rheumatism, the old man is badly used up
MILLS, Robert, Sh-179-3(1); Pvt B Co 46th US Inf; 4-11-63 to 1-30-66; Memphis PO
MILLS, Stephen A., H-51-3; Pvt; 61 to 64; Hill City PO
MILLS, W. L., D-65-1; Pvt H Co 6th O? Cav; Aug 63 to 17 Aug 65; Nashville PO; captured at Denwitty courthouse for 3 days
MILLSAP, Jason, Lo-189-2; Pvt; 64 to 65; Philadelphia PO; CONF
MILLSAPS, James, Bo-22-2; Cpl B Co 3rd TN Cav; 9-21-62 to 6-10-65; Gamble's Store PO
MILLSAPS, Jasper N., H-50-1; Pvt C Co 5th R TN Inf; 2-25-62 to 4-4-65; Daisy PO
MILLUAM, Thomas, Wl-293-1; L Co TN Inf; Nov 64 to 65; Austin PO
MILNER, Eliga, Mu-197-2; Pvt F Co 138th __; May 63 to 65; Columbia PO; shot in right arm in left side
MILNER?, William J., Ct-40-3; Pvt; Elizabethton PO; CONF
MILSTEAD, C. T., Hr-96-2; 2 yrs; Dorris PO; CONF
MILTIN, Math, Co-63-1; Pvt A Co 1st TN Art; 10 Jun 63 to __ (8 mos); Newport PO; deserted
MINCEY, Jno. W., K-160-2; Leathee J. widow of; Pvt G Co 8th TN Cav; 18 Aug 61 to 3 Sep 63; Knoxville PO
MINCEY, Robert, Lo-187-3; Pvt C Co 5th TN Inf; Feb 62 to 15 Jul 65; Loudon PO
MINCY, Albert M., K-171-3(2); Pvt; Knoxville PO; wounded right fore finger stiff
MINCY, David, Lo-189-3(1); Pvt B Co 5th TN Inf; Philadelphia PO; hips injured in RR wreck
MINCY, Henry, Un-257-2; Mary A. widow of; Pvt L Co 9th TN Cav; 61 to 63; Little Barren PO; died in army US, can't tell date in months and days
MINCY, R. S., B-10-1; Pvt H Co 5th TN Cav; 9-63 to 7-65; PO omitted
MINER, Eli B., K-159-2; Sgt 96th OH Inf; Jul 62 to __; Knoxville PO; chronic diareah, discharged surgeons certificate
MINGES, Esrom, Cu-18-1; Pvt J Co 12th TN Cav; 12-25-63 to 11-10-65; Manning PO
MINGLE, George W., Bo-15-2; Pvt H Co 2nd TN Cav; 10-10--2 to 7-6-65; Blockhouse PO
MINICK, John O., M-108-5; Mary K. widow of; Pvt A Co 9th KY Inf; 61 to __; Godfrey, KY PO; died of consumtpion during war, discharge lost
MINK, Abraham H., Ge-83-3; Pvt E Co 4th TN Inf; Nov 63 to Jun 64; Painters PO; cansor on foot
MINK, Amos W., Cl-56-2(1); Pvt H Co 2nd TN Inf; 3-1-62 to 3-4-63; Head of Barren PO; 12? mos & 10 days in prison

MINK, James E., C1-49-1; Pvt H Co 2nd TN Inf; 3-1-62 to 3-1-65; Cumberland Gap PO; nervous rhumatis
MINNICK, George R., O-138-3; Cpl G & D Cos 133rd & 156th IN; Minnick Box PO
MINNIS, John B., K-157-1; Lt Col 3rd TN Cav; Knoxville PO
MINOR, Alfred, Ha-111-3; Pvt E Co 8th TN Cav; 10 Oct 63 to 11 Sep 65; Milan PO
MINOR, Henry C., Su-243-1; Capt M Co 3rd OH Cav; 8 Oct 61 to 22 Nov 64; Bristor PO; re-enlisted
MINOR, Minnie, D-99-2; widow of Sol; Davidson Co. Poor House PO
MINTON, Bufice, Ct-41-2; Cpl L Co 13th TN Cav; 9-10-65 to 9-5-65; Elizabethton PO; rhumatism left leg mashted
MINTON, James M., K-171-1; Pvt C Co 7th TN Mtd Inf; Nov 64 to Apr 65; Knoxville PO
MINYARD, Jefferson, Mo-130-3; 16th Civil Dist
MINX, William, Fe-42-2; alias William Hill; Pvt I Co 6th KY Col; 63 to 65; Jamestown PO
MINYARD, Nancy (see Jackson, Andrew, H-49-6)
MIR, Britten, Sh-190-2; 106 Ky. Ave, Memphis PO
MIRANDY, Cyrus, Gi-129-1; Cpl M Co 16th IL Cav; __ to 65; Conway PO
MIRES, George W., Wh-186-2; Pvt H Co 4th TN Cav; 8-1-63 to 7-6-65; Bakers Cross Roads PO
MIRES, Reuben, Hw-121-6(1); Pvt B Co 8th TN Inf; 15 Dec 62 to 16 Jun 65; Strahl PO; none in ware
MIRES, William, Wa-271-2; Minerva widow of; Pvt 1st US Vols; Jonesboro PO
MISE, Henry J., Je-141-1; Cpl B Co 1st TN Inf; 1 Aug 61 to 17 Sep 64; New Market PO
MISE, Jesse S., C1-48-3; Pvt B Co 37th VA Inf; 4-1-61 to 7-1-65; Pleasant PO; wounded in right shoulder with shell; CONF
MISER, George M. D., Bo-13-3(1); Pvt G Co 3rd TN Inf; 2-10-62 to 2-23-65; Miser PO; injured in back
MITCAFF, John, Hd-46-1; Sarah J. widow of; Pvt D Co 2nd TN Mtd Inf; Cerro Gordo PO
MITCHAM, John, Sh-174-3; Pvt D Co 59th US Col Inf; 8-64 to __; 20 Turley St, Memphis PO
MITCHEL, Albert S., Di-36-2; Pvt G Co 50th TN Inf; 62 to 65; Bellsburgh PO; CONF
MITCHEL, Charly, Sh-167-2; PO omitted; CONF
MITCHEL, Henry, Gi-128-1; Pvt B Co 1st NC? Inf; 63 to 65; 8th Civil Dist
MITCHEL, Henry, Mc-109-6; Pvt 16th OH Inf; Prigmore PO; gun shot wound, prisoner at Brandon, MS, no discharge
MITHCEL, John, F-46-1; Wiley Mitchel alias; H Co 63rd TN; 19 mos; LaGrange PO
MITCHEL, Joseph, Col, H-56-5; Pvt F Co; East End PO
MITCHEL, Robt. R., T-206-1; Pvt A Co 77th OH Inf; Jul 13 62 to Jul 9 65; Covington PO
MITCHEL, Sarah (see Maberry, William)
MITCHEL, Walter T., D-92-2; US Sol; PO omitted
MITCHEL, William H., Mu-209-1; Pvt B Co 3rd TN Cav; Columbia PO
MITCHELL, Aleck, Mu-200-1; Adaline wife of; Cpl E Co 111th USC Inf; 10 Feb 64 to 30 Apr 66; Mt. Pleasant PO
MITCHELL, Alfred, Hw-127-2; Sgt F Co 1st US Hvy Art; 64 to 1 Mar 66; Rogersville PO; rheumatism
MITCHELL, Andrew J., K-154-3; Knoxville PO; CONF
MITCHELL, Andrew J., Ge-89-3; Sgt A Co 3rd TN Mtd Inf; 30 Jun 64 to 30 Dec 65; Albany PO
MITCHELL, Charles D., H-63-4; Pvt 7th OH Cav; 4-62 to 7-65; 28 Magazine St, Chattanooga PO
MITCHELL, Charles M., Rb-221-2; Pvt A Co 7th TN; May 1 63 to May 1 64; Adams Station PO; CONF
MITCHELL, Ephram, Sh-157-4; Pvt 11th US; 63 to 65; PO omitted
MITCHELL, Frances F., We-234-1; Pvt E Co 15th Cav; 12-1-65 to 10-66; Greenfield PO
MITCHELL, Henry, Sh-199-2; Pvt; 50 St. Paul St, Memphis PO
MITCHELL, Jack S., M-107-3; Pvt A Co 1st TN Mtd Inf; 12-18-63 to 1-13-65; Pvt D Co 8th TN Mtd Inf; 3-22-65 to 8-21-65; Walnut Shade PO
MITCHELL, James, Cr-1-1; Gadsden PO; forgotten regt
MITCHELL, James, Su-237-1; Pvt E Co US Steamer Yantic; Sep 61 to 26 May 65; Sac PO; shot through leg, could not give very much information concerning his service, he was perhaps as seaman, he was on the US Steamer Yantic
MITCHELL, James, Ru-235-1; Pvt K Co 44th Col US Inf; Florene Station PO
MITCHELL, James A., Hy-84-1; Artif. Lt Art Seldons Bat; Sep 62 to Apr 5 66; Forked Deer PO; CONF
MITCHELL, James H., G-63-1; US Sol; Milan PO
MITCHELL, James R., We-230-2; Sgt E Co 5th TN Reg; May 1 60 to May 1 62; PO omitted; CONF
MITCHELL, James W., Cu-15-1; Pvt A Co 4th TN Cav; 10-15-62 to 7-12-65; Hebbertsburg PO; relaps of measels effect lungs
MITCHELL, Joe, T-216-3; Pvt D Co 1st GA Inf; Feb 63 to 65; 14th Civil Dist
MITCHELL, John C., R-162-2; Pvt D Co 5th TN Mtd Inf; 8-31-64 to 6-26-65; Dayton PO
MITCHELL, John D., Ha-113-3; Lt D Co 19th KY Inf; 16 Oct 61 to 23 Apr 63; Sneedville PO
MITCHELL, John G., Cr-14-4; US Sol; 13th Civil Dist
MITCHELL, John M., Wa-272-1; Pvt D Co 8th TN Cav; 28 Sep 63 to 19 Jun 65; Locust Mount PO; disease of heart
MITCHELL, Joseph, Wa-267-2; Pvt I Co 8th TN Cav; 13 Oct 63 to 65; Johnson City PO
MITCHELL, Martin L., Cu-17-1; Pvt E Co 27th KY Inf; 9-61 to 11-62; Crossville PO; hernia and rheumatism
MITCHELL, Monroe, Sh-200-1; Pvt G Co 59th __ Inf; Dixon St, Memphis PO
MITCHELL, Richard P., Hw-127-1; Sgt 1st TN Lt Art; Rogersville PO
MITCHELL, Robert, Hw-133-3; Dulcina widow of; Pvt; 63 to __ (10 mos); Fry PO; CONF
MITCHELL, Rufus W., Li-146-1; Sgt F Co 14th US Inf; 2-28-64 to 3-28-66; Mulberry PO
MITCHELL, Sarah, F-44-4; widow US Sol; PO omitted
MITCHELL, Terry C., Ja-86-3; Pvt E Co 4th TN Cav; 11-61 to 7-65; Oottewah PO
MITCHELL, Thomas, Sh-188-2; Saffaron St. rear, Woodlawn Park, Memphis PO
MITCHELL, Wesley, Sh-179-3(1); Memphis PO
MITCHELL, William, We-230-3; Pvt A Co 5th TN Reg; Apr 1 61 to Jun 1 65; Greenfield PO; CONF
MITCHELL, William A., Gr-76-1; Pvt L Co 13th TN Cav; 4 Mar 64 to Sep 1 65; Indian Ridge PO
MITCHELL, William T., Ge-91-1; Comsary E Co 4th TN Inf; Oct 12 63 to Aug 7 65; Greeneville PO; dyspepsia
MITCHELL, William T., Mu-209-6; 1st Lt B Co 33rd TN; 5-61 to 5-65; Columbia PO; CONF
MITCHELL, William W., We-233-1(2); Pvt K Co 6th TN Cav; 7-20-62 to 9-26-65; Ralston PO
MITCHELL, Young, Sh-160-1; Rose Johnston widow of; Pvt H Co 6th MI Inf; Apr 1 to __; Memphis, Poplar St (126 to 130) PO; died in hospital camp fever 1863 (Rose also widow of Rembert, Zack)
MITCHELL, __, H-59-2; Pvt IL Inf; Chattanooga PO
MITTS, John, B1-3-1; Pvt F Co 2nd TN Cav; 61 to 63; Tanbone PO; CONF
MIXON, Charles, Hr-86-1; Charlotte wife of; dont know, only he died in the service; Grand Junction PO
MIZE, Ezaris W., K-166-2; Pvt B Co 112th OH Inf; 64 to 65; Knoxville PO
MIZE, George M. D., Un-250-3(1); Pvt B Co 1st TN Inf; 18 Aug 62 to 21 Jun 65; Maynardville PO; neuralgia of bowels & piles
MIZE, John, Rn-160-1; Pvt E Co 2nd VA; 12-1-62 to 8-20-65; 6th Civil Dist
MIZE, John, Un-250-1; Martha A. widow of; Pvt D Co 1st TN Inf; Aug 61 to Oct 64; Maynardville PO; dead
MIZE, Robert, Se-223-3; Pvt G Co 3rd TN Inf; 10 Feb 62 to 23 Feb 65; Sevierville PO
MIZE, Rufus L., Se-222-1; Sgt K Co 2nd TN Cav; 16 Oct 62 to 6 Jul 65; Pigeon Forge PO; chronic diarea
MIZE, William A., Se-230-1; Sgt K Co 2nd TN Cav; 16 Oct 62 to 12 Jul 64; Pigeon Forge PO; says he was discharged on account of inability
MIZELL, A. J., Cr-20-1; Sarah J. widow of; Pvt B Co 7th TN Cav; 64 to 65; Proffit PO
MIZER, James M., Br-14-2; Pvt E Co 5th TN Mtd Inf; 9-18-64 to 6-65; McDonald PO
MIZER, Wilson, Ha-117-3; Pvt E Co 2nd TN Inf; Sneedville PO

MLIFORD (sic), John, Sh-173-2; Wellington St, Memphis PO
MLIFORD (sic), Lawrence, Sh-173-2; Gayose St, Memphis PO
MOE?, Seth B., H-60-2; Lt A Co 14th OH Inf; 4-22-61 to 8-62; Chattanooga PO
MOFFEIT, Better, K-167-1; Pvt 1st Hvy TN; Mar 62 to May 65; Knoxville PO
MOFFEIT, Thos., K-167-6; Pvt A Co 6th TN Inf; Apr 62 to May 65; Knoxville PO
MOFFET, Patrick H., Mu-195-1; Sol, wife don't know; Columbia PO
MOGE, Edmond S., Sn-261-2(1); Pvt E Co 30th TN Inf; 9-1-61 to 5-9-65; Perdue PO; shot through left elbow (disabled in past); discharged from Sec. of War; CONF
MOGE, Henry W., Sn-261-2(1); Pvt E Co 30th TN Inf; 9-1-61 to 5-9-65; Perdue PO; prison Camp Butler, Louisville KY & Nashville 12 mos; CONF
MOHARE, Joseph J., Hd-53-3; Pvt F Co 13th IL Cav; 22 Dec 63 to 31 Aug 65; Seaman, Tyler--9 Feb 62 to 14 Jul 63; Coffee Landing PO; reinlisted in 13th IL Cav
MOHON, Robert, Un-250-2; Sarah widow of; Pvt E Co 4th TN Cav; Maynardville PO
MOINETTE, Peter, Fr-107-1; Cpl I Co 64th OH Inf; Oct 11 61 to Dec 10 64; Winchester PO; heart disease
MOLAN, Charles, Hy-84-3(5); Pvt 11th Inf; Jun 63 to 63; Woodville PO; discharge misplaced
MOLEDER, Samuel C., Ms-182-1; Pvt E Co 10th TN Inf; 12-26-62 to 6-22-65; Venna PO; rheumatism, able to perform a day's labor
MOLES, Henry, R-161-5; Pvt K Co 30th KY Mtd Inf; 2-28-64 to 4-18-65; Dayton PO
MOLES, Josiah, Ha-113-2; Melvina widow of; Pvt B Co 1st TN Cav; 9 Apr 62 to 5 Apr 65; Sneedville PO
MOLETT, Mariah, T-216-2; 14th Civil Dist
MOLONY, John Q., Ge-89-2; Pvt A Co 8th TN Inf; 20 Jun 63 to 2 Aug 65; Albany PO
MOLTZ, Henry A., H-76-1; Chattanooga PO
MOMAN, George W., Gi-139-2; Pvt C Co 100th TN Inf; 5-62 to 12-65; Campbellsville PO
MONCIER, George B., Ge-102-3; Pvt G Co 4th TN Inf; 15 Nov 62 to 19 Jun 65; Henshaw PO; rheumatism
MONDAY, Barzella T., Cu-16-2; Pvt A Co 6th TN Inf; 3-8-62 to 4-27-65; Big Lick PO; disease of back and eyes
MONDAY, W. T., K-182-1; Cpl G Co 9th TN Cav; Sep 63 to 65; Shooks PO; disabled in 1863; rheumatism and heart disease
MONDAY, William, Cl-48-2; Pvt A Co 12th TN Cav; 7-61 to 64; Pleasant PO; only enlisted for 1 yr but with army 4; CONF
MONDY, James, K-172-5(1); Pvt A Co 6th TN Inf; 62 to 65; 14th Dist
MONDY, James N., K-172-2; Pvt A Co 6th TN Inf; 8 Mar 62 to 27 Apr 65; Knoxville PO
MONDY, Joshua C., K-172-2; Pvt 13th TN Cav; ___ to Sep 65; 14th Dist
MONES?, Jack, Col, Mt-139-1; Pvt I Co 101th US; 64 to 66 (1 yr 6 mos); New Providence PO
MONEY, J. J., Fr-118-1; Pvt A Co 4th Conf Inf; Aug 61 to 62; Winchester PO; CONF
MONEY, Jake, F-38-2; alias Roman, Jocke; Sgt F Co 61st US Inf; 63 to Aug 65; Mason PO
MONEY, N. A., Fr-118-1; Pvt A Co 4th Conf Inf; Aug 61 to Nov 62; Winchester PO; CONF
MONEY MAKER, James, A-8-1; Pvt D Co 6th TN Inf; 4-18-62 to 5-5-65; Ledom PO
MONEYMAKER, William, K-178-1; Martha widow of; Pvt D Co 6th TN Inf; 24 Aug 63 to 20 Jun 65; Ball Campe PO; wounded in back
MONGOMERY, Joseph, Dy-22-1; Ord Sgt C Co 124th OH Inf; Sep 64 to Jul 10 65; Dyersburg PO
MONROE, Allen, Sh-185-1; US Sol; 274 Ross Ave, Memphis PO
MONROE, Amza R., We-231-1; PO omitted
MONROE, Augustus, L-101-1; Pvt C Co 11th C Inf; Oct 62 to dont know; Henning PO; discharge in hands of atty
MONROE, Elisha, Mc-112-4; widow of; Cpl D Co 3rd TN Inf; 2-10-61 to 2-22-65; Athens PO
MONROE, Elisha, Ro-211-3; Cpl D Co 3rd TN Inf; 10 Feb 62 to 23 Feb 64; Dayton PO; fever settled in back and kidneys
MONROE, George, Mc-116-4; Margret widow of; Pvt C Co 3rd TN Cav; 62 to ___; Athens PO; died while in service and exact dates cant be given
MONROE, George O., K-171-1; 2nd Lt B Co 6th TN Mtd Inf; 26 Oct 64 to 30 Jun 65; Knoxville PO
MONROE, Joyce, Mu-198-1; 10th Dist
MONROE, Mark, K-166-3; Quartermaster Sgt G Co 2nd TN Cav; 1 Oct 62 to 6 Jul 65; Knoxville PO; asthma, dyspepsia, pensioner
MONROE, Matison J., Hw-123-1; Pvt H Co 8th TN Cav; 63 to 65; New Canton PO
MONROE, Nathan, Gr-80-1; Sgt Co G 2nd TN Cav; 11 Oct 62 to 6 Jul 65; Thorn Hill PO
MONROE, William L., Hw-123-1; Pvt C Co 8th TN Cav; Rotherwood PO; slightly wounded, twice, afflicted with liver disease
MONTAGUE, Langdon T. (Dwight), H-66-1; Cpl A Co 144th OH; 4-64 to 64 (4 mos); Chattanooga PO
MONTAGUE, Theodore G., H-59-1; Lt 140th OH Inf; 63 to 63 (11 mos); Chattanooga PO
MONTGOMERY, A. N., C-24-2; Pvt F Co 6th TN Inf; 62 to 65 (3 yrs 1 mo 4 days); Girlton PO; dirhea & dropsin
MONTGOMERY, Albert A., We-230-4; Pvt K Co 10th TN Inf; May 1 62 to May 1 64; McKinzie PO; CONF
MONTGOMERY, Alexander, Hi-85-1; Elizabeth widow of; Pvt H Co TN Inf; 63 to 65; Lick Creek PO; shot in left leg
MONTGOMERY, Charley (see Wilson, Charley)
MONTGOMERY, David, Ro-209-1; Mary widow of; Pvt 1st TN Cav; Jul 61? to Aug 66; Rockwood PO
MONTGOMERY, David C., R-162-1; Sgt C Co 124th IN Inf; 62 to 6-27-65; Dayton PO; rheumatic trouble
MONTGOMERY, Francis, Ro-207-3; Pvt C Co 7th TN Mtd Inf; 20 Aug 64 to 27 Jun 65; Fossil PO; rheumatism
MONTGOMERY, George W., Wh-187-3; Pvt H Co 8th TN Inf; 3-24-63 to 10-16-65; Newark PO; contracted rheumatism, also shot in head
MONTGOMERY, James, Se-223-2; Martha E. Davis formerly widow of; Capt K Co 2nd TN Cav; Pigeon Forge PO; lung disease, discharge lost
MONTGOMERY, James G., De-22-3; Pvt C Co 2nd TN Inf; 1 Apr 64 to 5 May 65; Dunbar PO; shot in left foot
MONTGOMERY, James R., H-69-4; Pvt 3rd AL Inf; 61 to 65; Chattanooga PO; CONF
MONTGOMERY, Jefferson H., O-138-1; Lt B Co 75th IN Inf; 17 Apr 61 to 30 Jun 63; Troy PO
MONTGOMERY, John M., Ro-209-4; Glen Alice PO; CONF
MONTGOMERY, John W., Gr-70-4; Pvt B Co 1st TN Guard; 65 to 65; Rutledge PO; piles & sore eyes, exact dates unknown
MONTGOMERY, Mary (see Bowen, Lee)
MONTGOMERY, Randall, H-69-1; Pvt F Co 40th GA Inf; 62 to 65; Chattanooga PO
MONTGOMERY, Robert A., Se-223-4; Capt M Co 2nd TN Cav; 8 Nov 62 to 19 May 63; Hendersons Springs PO; lung disease, discharged on surgeon's certificate
MONTGOMERY, Rufus, Sh-196-1; Pvt C Co 1st US Col Hvy Art; 2-18-64 to 3-31-66; 182 Poplar St, Memphis PO; right ankle injured from a forced march
MONTGOMERY, S. B., Bo-11-3; Pvt H Co 3rd MD Cav; 9-18-63 to 9-13-65; Largonia? PO
MONTGOMERY, S. J., Gr-19-1; Pvt F Co 7th TN Cav; 8-5-62 to 10-25-63; Leach PO
MONTGOMERY, Samuel W., Ct-35-3; Pvt F Co 8th TN Cav; 6-11-62 to 9-6-65; Elk Mills PO; in US Army
MONTGOMERY, Thadeus L., Wy-178-1; Cpl A Co 10th TN Inf; 4-12-62 to 5-25-65; Cypress Inn PO
MONTGOMERY, Thomas J., H-63-3; Clerk Commissary, 62 to 64; 610 Pine, Chattanooga PO
MONTGOMERY, Wesley, K-162-1; Pvt A Co 1st C NY Cav; 62 to 65; Knoxville PO
MONTGOMERY, Willey, Ro-210-6; Pvt; Rockwood PO; hurn in back
MONTGOMERY, William, K-156-5; US Sol; 15 Kennedy St, Knoxville PO
MONTGOMERY, William H., H-53-8; Pvt; 2 yrs; Chattanooga PO; chronic diarrhoea

MONTGOMERY, William W., Se-223-2; Susan K. widow of; Capt K Co 2nd TN Cav; 15 Aug 62 to __; Henderson Springs PO; diarrhea
MONTGUMRY, Elexander, Ha-116-1; US Sol (widow); 13th Dist
MOODY, Charlie H., F-40-1; Pvt 18th NC Inf; Dec 63 to 15 May 65; Eads PO (Shelby Co.); CONF
MOODY, Ely A., Dy-25-9(1); Pvt E Co 2nd TN Cav; 7-62 to 9-64; Newbern PO
MOODY, Felix G., D-54-3; Martha widow of; Pvt H? Co 13th US Col Inf; Nashville PO
MOODY, George B., Rb-221-2; Sgt H Co 14th TN; May 20 61 to May 29 65; Adams Station PO; flesh wound, twice; CONF
MOODY, Isaiah, Li-142-1; Pvt F Co 111th Col Inf; was in the service about 7 mos and was captured at Sulphur Trestle, AL, L & N RR by Forrest during Hoods raid into TN in 12-63 & was never discharged
MOODY, James M., Gr-74-1; Pvt C Co 4th TN Cav; 1 Jan 63 to 12 Jul 65; May Spring PO
MOODY, John, Fe-40-2(1); Pvt Capt D. Beaty's Company of Indpt. Scouts of TN; 4-62 to 6-25-65; Moodyville PO; injured lungs from cold & exposure, captured by Capt. Scott Bledson
MOODY, Jones, Mu-209-5; Columbia PO; prisoner 3 mos at Murfresboro; CONF
MOODY, Martin, Cl-58-1; Pvt C Co 1st TN Art; 4-1-63 to 8-1-65; Davo PO; mustered in private, m. out 1st Lt
MOODY, Peter, Pi-156-2; Pvt David Beaty Independent Scouts; Travisville PO
MOODY, Samuel, Ho-96-2; US Sol; PO omitted
MOODY, William, Ge-96-3; Elizabeth widow of; Pvt H Co 4th TN Cav; 29 Jul 63 to 12 Jul 65; Rheatown PO
MOODY, William, Sh-193-1; Pvt E Co 11th Inf; __ to 10-8-63; Memphis PO; one leg broken, no other information
MOODY, William W., Je-143-3; 2nd Lt E Batallion; 25 Jul 61 to 24 Jun 62; Mossy Creek PO
MOON, Jeremiah, Hn-75-1; Pvt C Co 4th MN Inf; 27 May 64 to Jul 65; Springville PO
MOON, John, Bo-22-1; Celia E. wife of; Pvt A Co 3rd TN Cav; 11-62 to 63; Seaton PO; heart disease
MOON, Mack, Sh-145-3; Pvt A Co 43rd US Col Inf; Aug 63 to Jan 66; Millington PO; Capt. Simmons
MOON, William, Ch-12-2; Pvt A Co 2nd AR Inf; 5-8-61 to 65; Custer Point PO; CONF
MOON, William M., Se-225-1; Cpl I Co 2nd TN Cav; 21 Sep 62 to 15 Jul 66; Allensville PO; catarrh of lungs and heart disease 25 yrs and genl. disability
MOONAHAN, Owen B., Bl-2-1; Pvt K Co 1st AL Cav; 3-29-64 to 10-20-65; Glade Creek PO; shot in right shoulder and each arm, can do moderate labor
MOONEY, David, Hy-76-2; alias Mooring, David; Pvt D Co 11th US Col Inf; 27 Nov 63 to 12 Jul 65; Stanton Depot PO
MOONEY, George, Hw-128-2; Pvt F Co 8th TN Cav; 5 Apr 62 to 11 Sep 65; St. Clair PO; rheumatism resulting in disease of eyes
MOONEY, John, He-64-2; Pvt C Co 6th TN Cav; 1 Apr 62 to 20 Apr 65; Reagan PO
MOONEY, Nelson, Hy-76-2; alias Mooring, Nelson; Pvt C Co 11th US Col Inf; 27 Nov 63 to 12 Jan 65; Stanton PO
MOONEY, William, Wi-287-1; Pvt Cav; 2 yrs; Civ Dist 18
MOONEY, William, Hm-109-5; Pvt; Three Springs PO
MOONEYHAM, James, Co-59-1; Pvt Co D 2nd NC Inf; Sep 63 to Jun 65; Del Rio PO; rhumatism
MOONEYHAM, Calvin, Bl-2-1; Pvt F Co 5th TN Inf; 2-62 to 3-65; Pikeville PO
MOONINGHAM, James H., Mu-188-1; Pvt K Co 115th OH Inf; 64 to __; Parks Station PO; taken prisoner, paroled
MOONINGHAM, Ransom, Je-135-2; Pvt M Co 9th TN Cav; 2 Oct 63 to 11 Sep 65; Flat Gap PO; lost two toes, captured Jan 8 1865
MOONY, Orderly, Hm-118-2; Pvt; PO omitted
MOONZ, Daniel, Sh-169-1; Pvt D Co 4th MO Inf; 61 to Nov 64; Memphis PO
MOOR, Anna, Wy-174-1; widow US Sol; 9th Civil Dist

MOOR, George, A-6-5(3); Pvt; 62 to 65; PO omitted
MOOR, George M., Co-62-2; Cpl D Co 4th TN Inf; 18 Jan 63 to 2 Aug 65; Rankins PO; rheumatism
MOOR, John, Ct-37-1; Pvt E Co 3rd NC Inf; Ripshin PO; livery? disease, suffering 25 yrs
MOOR, John, Co-62-2; Pvt D Co 8th TN Inf; 24 Mar 63 to 1 Jul 65; Rankins PO; hart trouble
MOOR, Lissee B., Di-30-1; Cpl I Co 142nd PA Inf; Aug 62 to May 65; Dickson PO
MOOR, William, Co-62-2; Cpl D Co 4th TN Inf; 18 Jan 63 to 2 Aug 65; Rankins PO; rheumatism
MOOR, William, Co-62-2; 1st Lt C Co 8th TN Inf; 1 Dec 62 to 26 Oct 63; Help PO; diarrhara, piles & hart troble
MOORE, Abraham, D-45-2; Mary widow of; Pvt I Co 10th TN Inf; 9-8-63 to 7-2-64; Nashville PO
MOORE, Abraham, Di-34-2; Dickson PO
MOORE, Albert, Br-12-6; Rhat PO; CONF
MOORE, Albert A., Se-226-6; Quartermaster Sgt C Co 9th TN Cav; 12 Jan 63 to 24 Mar 65; Henrys X Roads PO; diarrhoea & rheumatism
MOORE, Alford, Hw-131-2; Susan widow of; Pvt B Co 8th TN Inf, Cav; 1 Dec 62 to 30 Jun 65; Bulls Gap PO
MOORE, Alfred, G-71-1; Pvt C Co 55th TN Inf; 3 Sep 61 to 26 Apr 65; Rutherford PO; CONF
MOORE, Alfred, H-59-2; Pvt TN Inf; Chattanooga PO
MOORE, Alonzo L., Po-152-1; Cpl F Co 5th Mtd Inf; Ducktown PO; liver and lung disease
MOORE, Andrew J., Ca-25-1; Pvt K Co 13th TN Cav; 9-22-63 to 9-65; Shoat? Mountain PO; feet frost bitten
MOORE, Andrew N., Je-137-2; Pvt F Co 9th TN Cav; 63 to Aug 25 65; Hickory Ridge PO
MOORE, Bayless, K-176-2; Halls X Roads PO; CONF
MOORE, Benjamin F., Hw-131-1; Pvt E Co 1st TN Cav; 1 Apr 62 to 11 Apr 65; Bulls Gap PO
MOORE, Benjamin H., H-53-3; Capt 36th OH Inf; 61 to 6-65; Chattanooga PO; staff officer
MOORE, Brazelton, Wa-266-2; Pvt B Co 4th TN Cav; 2 Dec 62 to 12 Jul 65; Fall Branch PO
MOORE, Calvin S., We-223-2; 2nd Sgt K Co 10th TN Cav; 18 Sep 63 to 15 Nov 64; Palmersville PO; CONF
MOORE, Charles N., Cr-4-1; Pvt L Co 7th TN Cav; Feb 62 to Apr 65; Bells Depot PO; CONF
MOORE, Cilvester L., Pu-143-1; Pvt C Co 8th TN Inf; 2-7-65 to 8-24-65; Irby PO; rheumatism
MOORE, Columbus, La-117-4; Pvt; 15th Dist; CONF
MOORE, Daniel, D-50-1; Pvt B Co 13th US Inf; Sum. 62 to 65; 612 N. High, Nashville PO
MOORE, Dempsy, Co-62-1; Pvt C Co 8th TN Inf; 20 Jan 62 to 30 Jun 65; Help PO
MOORE, Doctor T., A-2-2; Hannah E. Brooks formerly widow of; 1st Lt C Co 2nd TN Inf; 8-7-61 to 65; Hinds Creek PO; lung disease, died 2-24-74; captured 11-6-63; returned 1865
MOORE, Edward R., Lk-112-1; Rachel widow of; Lt D Co 77th OH Inf; Oct 61 to Aug 1 63; Tiptonville PO
MOORE, Elijah, A-4-4; Pvt J Co 7th TN Mtd Inf; 11-8-64 to 7-27-65; Coal Creek PO
MOORE, Elvise, Bo-11-2; widow of US Soldier; 1st Civil Dist
MOORE, Ephram, Col, Mt-139-1; Pvt H Co 16th (& 42nd?) US; 2 yrs 1 mo; New Providence PO; had rumatics, was transfered Co H 16th to Co G 42nd
MOORE, Felix, O-141-1; Pvt Co F 12th IN Vol; Jun 5 62 to Jun 4 65; Union City PO
MOORE, G. W., Mc-114-4; Texas A. widow of; Pvt; Calhoun PO
MOORE, George, Ge-83-2; PO omitted
MOORE, George D., Ge-92-4; 2nd Lt D Co 8th TN Inf; 15 Sep 62 to 15 Feb 65; Ottway PO
MOORE, Gilbert, Me-92-1; Sewee PO; did not get satisfactory answers
MOORE, Haywood, Ma-116-1; Pvt H Co 61st TN Inf; 1 Feb 63 to 30 Dec 65; Mercer PO
MOORE, Henry C., Mn-121-4; Pvt A Co 6th TN Cav; 9-1-62 to 7-26-65; Bethel Springs PO
MOORE, Isaac, Co-69-7(3); Pvt L Co 1st TN Art; 20 Sep 64 to 31 Mar 66; Rankin PO; loung trouble at Knoxvill TN, no pension yet
MOORE, Isaac F., Co-59-2; Pvt Co I 4th TN Inf; 1-25-65 to 7-14-65; Del Rio PO

MOORE, James, Sh-163-1; Rachel widow of; Pvt K Co 63rd Col; 63 to Jan 8 65; Memphis PO; died March 13, 1890, pneumonia
MOORE, James, Wi-280-1; Pvt I Co 111th Col Inf; Feb 1 64 to Apr 30 66; Thompson Sta. PO; suffering from rheumatism, incurred in army
MOORE, James, Sm-172-1; Pvt B Co 9th KY Inf; 9-61 to 9-63; Lancaster PO; prisoner at Andersonville 65 days
MOORE, James, C-34-3; Bettie A. widow of; Pvt 18th KY Inf; 10-8-63 to 12-19-63; died at Louisville, KY; Buckeye PO; draws pension
MOORE, James B., K-181-6(3); Pvt A Co 6th TN Inf; 21 Sep 62 to 13 Jun 65; Knoxville PO
MOORE, James F., Wa-264-1; Pvt I Co 8th TN Cav; 8 Sep 63 to 11 Sep 65; Telford PO; chronic diarrhea
MOORE, James H., Wa-263-2; Pvt B Co 8th TN Cav; Jul 23 63 to Sep 11 65; May Day PO
MOORE, James J., He-62-2; Pvt C Co 7th TN Cav; 62 to 63; Lexington PO
MOORE, James L., Dy-25-5(1); Pvt L Co 7th TN Cav; 62 to 65; Hornbeak PO (Obion Co.); CONF
MOORE, James N., Hd-52-2; Pvt E Co 26th MD? Inf; Sep 62 to Oct 65; Hamburg PO; wounded
MOORE, James R., P-150-2; US Sol; 1st Dist
MOORE, James R., A-2-2; Sgt D Co 1st TN Lt Art; 63 to ___; Hinds Creek PO; chronic diarrhea, piles and lung ___, discharge burned
MOORE, James W., Je-142-2; Pvt B Co 2nd TN Cav; Lucilla PO; bronchitis
MOORE, Jarret L., P-150-2; US Sol; 1st Dist
MOORE, Jerry C., Mc-116-2; Pvt C Co 32nd KY Inf; 11-14-62 to 8-15-63; Longs Mills PO; sun stroke in KY
MOORE, Jessie, Ru-241-4; Pvt K Co 111th TN Inf; 63 to 66; PO omitted
MOORE, Jim, Su-232-1; Pvt H Co 4th TN Inf; Ruthton PO
MOORE, John, Sh-152-2; Susan widow of; Dexter PO
MOORE, John, K-163-1; Sol 1st TN Reg; 61 to 65; Knoxville PO
MOORE, John A., F-40-2; Pvt F Co 6th NC Inf; Jun 61 to Apr 65; Hickory Withe PO; prisoner at Point Lookout 16 mos; CONF
MOORE, John C., Cr-14-3; Pvt H Co 18th IA? Inf; 15 Jul 63 to 20 Jul 65; Crider PO
MOORE, John J., Hd-53-1; Pvt I Co 136th IL Inf; 10 Sep 63 to 20 Jul 65; Sibley PO; gun shot wound
MOORE, John L., Ge-94-1; Cpl E Co 4th TN Inf; 15 Mar 63 to 2 Aug 65; Tusculum PO; plurisy and lung trouble
MOORE, John N., Hw-131-2; Cpl A Co 12th TN Cav; 28 Mar 63 to 7 Oct 65; Bulls Gap PO
MOORE, John R., Wa-263-2; Hannah M. widow of; Pvt NC; Garbers Mills PO; can not find out any particulars
MOORE, John R., Ge-89-4; Sgt A Co 12th TN Cav; 19 Mar 63 to 11 Jul 65; Romeo PO; cron. diarhea, hips wound
MOORE, John R., Hw-131-2; Cpl B Co 3rd TN Mtd Inf; 30 Jun 64 to 1 Nov 64; Bulls Gap PO
MOORE, John T., P-151-2; Pvt D Co 7th TN Vol Cav; 15 Sep 62 to 20 May 63; Parkers Ldg PO; chronic diarrihoea
MOORE, John W., Mc-112-9; Pvt B Co 2nd VA Inf; 5-20-61 to 5-22-65; Athens PO
MOORE, John W., Ch-13-2; Mary A. widow of; Pvt C Co 7th TN Vol; 5-63 to 4-65; Wild Goose PO; the discharge is not at home & will show exact time of service
MOORE, Johnathan B. (see Davis, Jonathan B.)
MOORE, Joseph B., D-104-1; Emily C. Herring formerly widow of; Sgt 25th TN Cav; Sep 62 to Sep 64; Whites Bend PO; killed in Sep 6, 1864
MOORE, Josephus, Col, Rb-219-1; Pvt C Co TN Reg; Feb 63to __ (1 yr 3 mos); Orlinda PO; shot through the thigh
MOORE, Lewis S., Hw-131-4; Rebecca Moore family widow of; Pvt B Co 8th TN Inf; PO omitted
MOORE, Lindle? H., Ch-17-2; Pvt G Co 6th TN Cav; 3-6-63 to 8-65; Masseyville PO
MOORE, Mark, K-180-3; Pvt D Co 6th TN Inf; 18 Apr 62 to 27 Apr 65; Bearden PO; chronic diarrhoea and loss of eye

MOORE, Marragret, Ge-93-2; widow US Sol; Pvt F Co 4th TN Inf; Greeneville PO
MOORE, Midleton L., Ce-30-1; Major 10th TN Inf; May 62 to Jun 64; Kingston Springs PO
MOORE, Murrell, Wa-266-2; Pvt B Co 4th TN Cav; 2 Dec 62 to 12 Jul 65; Fall Branch PO
MOORE, Nancy, Ro-211-4; widow of US Sol; 16th Civil Dist
MOORE, Nancy A., Wy-175-2; Pvt; 10th Civil Dist
MOORE, Nelson M., G-71-2; Pvt I Co 7th TN Cav; Oct 62 to Nov 63; Edmonds PO
MOORE, Newton, J-77-2; Pvt B Co 4th KY Cav; 9-63 to 9-65; Gainesboro PO
MOORE, Oliver, Sh-200-2; Pvt I Co 46th AR? Inf; 7-30-63 to 1-30-66; 508 Orleans St, Memphis PO
MOORE, Paschal E., P-151-1; Isabel E. widow of; Pvt F Co 2nd TN Mtd Inf; 8 Nov 63 to 19 Jan 64; Mousetail PO; died in the service
MOORE, Pheby, O-140-1; Union City PO
MOORE, R. W., Hd-48-2; Pvt A Co 2nd TN Mtd Inf; Oct 2 63 to Oct 14 64; Savannah PO; breaking out from small pox
MOORE, Ransome, H-72-2(1); Cpl G Co 1st US Inf; 63 to 4-30-66; Chattanooga PO
MOORE, Richard, Sh-191-1; Memphis PO
MOORE, Richard G., D-57-3; Pvt A Co 1st TN Cav; Jun 61 to Apr 63; Nashville PO; CONF
MOORE, Robert, H-53-6; Pvt A Co 17th IA Inf; 4-17-62 to ___; Ridgedale PO; wounded in left knee, cut off from command and has never received discharge
MOORE, Robert, H-51-7; Hill City PO
MOORE, Robert P., Su-233-1; Pvt B Co 13th TN Cav; Sep 63 to 65; Holston Vally PO; chronic diarher, partly disabled
MOORE, Samuel, U-249-2; Pvt H Co 3rd NC Mtd Inf; 1 Oct 64 to 8 Aug 65; Flag Pond PO; rheumites
MOORE, Samuel, Ma-116-1; US Sol; 4th Civil Dist
MOORE, Samuel, D-99-1; Pvt G Co 13th TN Inf; Oct 10 63 to Jan 20 64; Bakers PO
MOORE, Samuel A., Cy-27-3(1); Sgt D Co 9th KY Inf; 9-61 to 3-65; Moss PO; gun shot in right hip
MOORE, Samuel D., A-4-4; Pvt; 64 to 65; Coal Creek PO; CONF
MOORE, Samuel J., Ro-206-2; Pvt B Co 5th TN Inf; 4 Sep 62 to 26 May 65; Emory Gap PO
MOORE, Samuel L., Hw-131-2; 2nd Lt A Co 12th TN Cav; 29 Mar 63 to 24 Apr 64; Bulls Gap PO
MOORE, Seifir, D-99-1; Pvt G Co 13th TN Inf; Oct 10 63 to Jan 10 66; Goodlettsville PO
MOORE, Shepherd, Mt-137-1; Civ, Cook in US Army; Mar 62 to Apr 65; papers lost; St. Bethlehem PO
MOORE, Shipurd, Mt-137-1; Civ. employed as cook; Mar 62, dischgd. 1865; papers lost, St. Bethlehem PO
MOORE, Simon, D-64-3; Jane widow of; Nashville PO; wounded
MOORE, Thomas E., He-62-1; Pvt Co B 3rd NC; Aug 63 to Sep 64; Darden PO; deficiany in left knee and in right side of neck
MOORE, Thomas J., Hd-50-1; Pvt D Co 2nd TN Mtd Inf; Dec 29 63 to Feb 1 65; Savannah PO; gun shot wound in head? (hand?)
MOORE, Thomas J., Ge-83-1; Pvt D Co 61st TN Inf; 15 Jul 62 to 1 Apr 65; Chucky City PO
MOORE, Thomas S., Su-243-1; Mary E. widow of; Bristol PO
MOORE, Thomas R., F-40-2; Pvt A Co 5th NC Cav; 7 Apr 64 to 25 Mar 65; Hickory Withe PO; CONF
MOORE, W. C., St-161-1; Cpl A Co Min Col Vol; Jan 11 63 to Jan 25 66; Linton KY PO
MOORE, Wallace, Sh-199-2; Teamster; 1542 Georgia St, Memphis PO
MOORE, William, D-87-1; Pvt G Co 17th TN Inf; 30 Nov 60 to Apr 26 63; Nashville PO
MOORE, William, D-87-1; Pvt Col Inf; Nashville PO
MOORE, Wm., Br-6-3; Pvt A Co 11th TN Cav; Chatala PO; nervous prostration and desfness
MOORE, William A., Je-137-2; Pvt D Co 3rd TN Cav; 1 Dec 62 to 3 Aug 65; Dandridge PO; shot in left leg
MOORE, William C., Sh-158-2; Sgt G Co 1st MI Eng & Mach; 13 Dec 63 to 22 Sep 65; Memphis PO
MOORE, William E., We-221-2; Pvt E Co 18th MS Cav; Nov 62 to Apr 65; Martin PO; flesh wound; CONF

MOORE, William J., Mg-196-3; Cpl H Co 24th KY Inf; 1 Nov 62 to 25 Sep 65; Hunnicutt PO
MOORE, William P., Co-67-5; Pvt H Co 60th NC Inf; Naillon PO; CONF
MOORE, William R., Ge-92-1; Pvt A Co 3rd NC Inf; Laurel Gap PO
MOOREHEAD, Edward N., Mt-139-2; enlisted John N. Moorehead; Pvt B Co 5th US Regt; 4-21-65 to 10-10-66; Dist 21
MOORELAND, Ransom, H-55-1; Pvt C Co 12th TN Cav; 10-64 to 9-65; Tyner PO; asthma
MOORING, David (see Mooney, David)
MOORING, Nelson (see Mooney, Nelson)
MOORLOCK, Marion, Je-136-2; Pvt B Co 3rd TN Inf; PO omitted
MOOSE?, Frank, He-62-2; 16th Dist
MOOTY, Moses, La-113-2; Rhabeca A. widow of; Pvt G Co 10th TN Inf; 14 Jun 62 to 24 Jun 65; Lawrenceburgh PO; shot through bowells
MORAN, Austin, Hn-81-1; Sol US; Elkhorn PO
MORAN, Austin, Hn-81-1; Gillie PO; went to his house twice and failed to see him; CONF
MORAN, James, Mr-102-2; Eliza J. widow of; Pvt; South Pittsburg PO; discharge papers lost
MORE, Andrew J., Fe-42-1; Pvt H Co 30th KY; 10-63 to 4-18-65; Jamestown PO
MORE, Eliza J. (see Hartman, George)
MORE, Hayes, D-63-2; Pvt US Col; Nashville PO
MORE, Henry, Lo-188-1; Cpl K Co 1st TN Art; 24 Jul 64 to 31 Mar 66; Stockton PO
MORE, Hubbard, Ha-114-2; Sgt H Co 12th KY Cav; can not give dates; Xerxes PO
MORE, James, Hm-109-5; USS; PO omitted
MORE, William, Sh-157-6; Dist 13
MOREFIELD, Hamilton, Wa-268-4; discharge away from home; Johnson City PO; piles
MOREFIELD, John W., Jo-148-1; Pvt H Co 4th TN Inf; 9 Apr 65 to 7 Aug 55; Head of Laurel PO
MOREFIELD, Wm. A., Wa-267-1; Pvt G Co 4th TN Inf; 15 Aug 62 to 7 Jul 65; Johnson City PO; hernia
MOREHEAD, Abraham, Cf-41-1; Teal PO; absent, could not obtain co. & regt.
MORELAND, John A., K-174-2(1); Pvt C Co 3rd TN Cav; 1 Nov 62 to 63; Graveston PO; defective of hearing, discharged on surgan certificate
MORELAND, William, Jo-152-3; Dicy widow of; Pvt L Co 13th TN Cav; Mouth of Doe PO; died in service
MORELAND, William H., Lo-195-2(1); Pvt D Co 5th TN Inf; 20 Aug 61 to 30 Mar 65; Lenoir PO; rupture
MORELEY, Joe, Col, O-139-1; Pvt C Co 10th TN Col Inf; 63 to 65; Protemus PO
MORELOCK, Nathanial B., Hm-106-1; Pvt G Co 43rd TN Inf; Morristown PO; cant give dates, no discharge
MORETTE, Isaac, J-79-1; Pvt; 5-9-64 to 6-5-65; Whitleyville PO; flesh wound in right leg
MORFIELD, Alexander, Jo-151-2; Pvt F Co 13th TN Cav; 22 Sep 63 to ___; Bakers Gap PO; wounded accidentally, shot through knee, deserted after 11 mos service
MORFIELD, Daniel, Jo-152-1; Annie widow of; Pvt F Co 13th TN Cav; 22 Sep 63 to ___; Bakers Gap PO; fever-weak back, breast, deserted after 11 mos service
MORFORD, Daniel B., Sh-191-5(1); Pvt 83rd OH; Memphis PO; records not seen
MORGAIN, Samuel, Wa-262-1; Pvt I Co 1st TN Cav; 1 Aug 62 to 15 Jun 65; Telfords PO; chronic diarahea
MORGAN, Abel, Mc-114-3; Pvt G Co 12th IN Cav; 7-62 to 7-12-65; Calhoun PO
MORGAN, Adeline, H-76-2; widow?; Chattanooga PO
MORGAN, Alexander, Mg-197-4; Pvt E Co 3rd TN Inf; Jan 61 to ___; Wartburg PO; not discharged
MORGAN, Alexander, Je-143-2; Orderly K Co 3rd TN Inf; 10 Feb 62 to 23 Feb 65; Mossy Creek PO; diareah, rheumatism & piles
MORGAN, Andrew A., Me-90-2(1); Pvt A Co 3rd TN Mtd Inf; 8-64 to 12-24-64; Pine Land PO
MORGAN, Andrew J., H-55-2; Pvt H Co 2nd VA? Inf; 10-13-64 to 11-17-65; Tyner PO
MORGAN, Benjamin, We-231-1; Fulton, KY, PO; not able to give facts
MORGAN, Chesley, Gr-70-1; Pvt; Rutledge PO
MORGAN, E. Wash., D-99-3; Pvt K Co 23rd OH Inf; Jul 64 to Jun 65; State Penitentiary PO
MORGAN, Edward, Cr-21-1; Pvt F Co 7th TN Cav; Aug 27 62 to Oct 25 63; Huntingdon PO
MORGAN, Epram, C-33-3; Pvt G Co 49th KY Inf; 10-1-63 to 12-26-64; Newcomb PO
MORGAN, Francis M., Hd-52-2; Pvt A Co 7th TN Cav; Aug 14 63 to Aug 9 65; Pittsburg PO
MORGAN, George, H-56-4; Pvt A Co 85th NY Inf; 9-5-64 to 7-15-65; St. Elmo PO
MORGAN, Henry, G-57-1; Yorkville PO; CONF
MORGAN, Henry Clay, Sh-149-1; Pvt B Co 3rd US Inf; Feb 63 to 6 Jan 66; National Cemetery PO; papers in hand of claim agents
MORGAN, Isaac W., Hn-82-1; Pvt K Co 2nd TN Mtd Inf; 2-4-64 to 4-20-65; Buchanan PO; chronic diareah & lung affection
MORGAN, J. A., Wa-276-1; Pvt L Co 11th TN Cav; Jun 1 63 to ___; Limestone PO; no discharge
MORGAN, James, We-220-1; Pvt I Co 6th TN Cav; Mar 17 62 to ___ (1 yr); Catham PO; deserted and has no discharge
MORGAN, James, Sh-188-2; Pvt US Col Inf; 272 High St, Memphis PO
MORGAN, James, Ja-85-5; Leudemie widow of; Pvt G Co 5th TN Inf; 62 to ___ (e yrs 5 days); Long Savannah PO
MORGAN, James, A-4-1; Margarrettt A. widow of; Pvt; 9-6-61 to 11-6-62; Coal Creek PO
MORGAN, James A., Mc-113-1; Pvt C Co 10th TN Cav; 2-16-63 to 9-1-63; Rock Creek PO; no disability
MORGAN, James C., Hi-92-1; 1st Sgt C Co 14th Col Inf of TN; 62 to 65; Aetna PO; cant remember dates
MORGAN, James L., Lo-191-3; Pvt F Co 4th IN Cav--Feb 63 to May 64; Pvt B Co 5th US Vet Vols; Trigonia PO; ruptured
MORGAN, James W., De-25-1; 2nd Lt E Co 7th TN Cav; 28 Jul 62 to 11 Aug 65; Decaturville PO; leg & foot mashed
MORGAN, John (see Archie, John)
MORGAN, John, Ch-17-1; Wagoner 31st TN Cav; 9-12-61 to 4-65; Henderson PO; CONF
MORGAN, John, A-4-5; Pvt K Co 142nd PA Inf; 8-12-62 to 6-22-63; Coal Creek PO; leg lost
MORGAN, John, Hm-108-2(1); Pvt D Co 4th TN Inf; Feb 63 to 2 Aug 65; Chestnut Bloom PO; varicose veins
MORGAN, John, C-33-3; Pvt G Co 49th KY Inf; 10-1-63 to 12-24-64; Newcomb PO
MORGAN, John A., Cr-21-1; Pvt I Co 7th TN Cav; Feb 65 to 9 Aug 65; Huntingdon PO
MORGAN, John D., R-161-2; Sgt B Co 6th TN Mtd Inf; 8-15-64 to 6-30-66; Dayton PO; elbow broken & to broken
MORGAN, John G., We-229-1; Pvt I Co 7th TN Cav; 1 Jun 61 to 30 Jul 65; Gleason PO; partially incurd
MORGAN, John L., M-103-3; Pvt K Co 5th KY Cav; 12-2-61 to 5-3-65; Lafayette PO; gunshot in left ankle
MORGAN, John W., H-58-3; Pvt F Co 5th TN Inf; 2-25-62 to 65; Sale Creek PO; rheumatism
MORGAN, John W., De-22-2; Pvt E Co 10th TN Cav; 20 Aug 62 to 17 Jun 65; Bob PO; CONF
MORGAN, Joseph B., Po-152-2; Pvt F Co 10th TN Cav; 11-64 to 8-1-63; Ducktown PO; rupture
MORGAN, Juy J., Cr-21-1; Lavina J. wife; I Co 2nd M Inf; Dec 27 63 to Dec 25 64; Huntingdon PO
MORGAN, Lewis, H-58-3; Pvt L Co 12th TN Cav; Dayton PO
MORGAN, Lot, Mu-192-1; 8th Civil Dist
MORGAN, Marcus L., O-134-1; Pvt B Co 27th 10SC? Inf; Aug 10 61 to Aug 10 63; Hornbeak PO; shot in rite arm, shell wound; CONF
MORGAN, Milton, K-168-3; Smithwood PO
MORGAN, Morse, Co-68-3; Sarah E. widow of; Pvt B Co 8th TN; 63 to ___; Sutton PO
MORGAN, Perry, Cy-28-1; Pvt H Co 12th KY Inf; 10-12-61 to 10-12-63; Celina PO
MORGAN, Plesent, Hw-120-2; Pvt E Co 1st KY Art; 29 Nov 64 to 25 Jan 65; Eidson PO
MORGAN, Rob. M., Dy-21-1; Pvt C Co 9th AL Reg; 2 Mar 63 to Mar 2 65; Chestnut Bluff PO; CONF
MORGAN, Rufus, Mu-195-2; Sol C Co 57th IL Vol; 3 yrs; Columbia PO; wounded at Corinth, can't get about at times

MORGAN, Sallie, Mc-114-7; widow of US Sol; 16th Civil Dist
MORGAN, Samuel H., Mc-113-1; Pvt F Co 6th TN Mtd Inf; 9-12-64 to 6-30-65; Rock Creek PO; rheumatism
MORGAN, Silas S., Mc-113-2; Pvt E Co 6th TN Inf; 8-15-64 to 6-30-65; Riceville PO
MORGAN, Simon P., Br-13-4; Cpl I Co 10th TN Cav; 2-2-64 to 7-5-65; Cleveland PO; chronic diarrhoea & liver disease rectum
MORGAN, Thomas C., Bl-4-2; Pvt B Co 6th TN Mtd Inf; 8-15-64 to 6-30-65; Morgan Springs PO; (Rhea Co.)
MORGAN, William, R-106-1; Pvt A Co NW Vol Inf; 4-15-61 to 4-15-63; 7th Civil Dist
MORGAN, William, D-54-3; Duderick New Lane, Nashville PO
MORGAN, William, K-183-3; US Sol; PO omitted
MORGAN, Wm. B., Ha-117-2; Elisabeth A. Goins formerly widow of; Pvt; Kyle's Ford PO
MORGAN, Wm. B., R-163-4; Cpl B Co 6th TN Mtd Inf; 8-15-64 to 6-30-65; Morgans Springs PO
MORGAN, Wm. F., R-163-4; Capt C Co 6th TN Mtd Inf; 8-15-64 to 6-30-65; Dayton PO; contracted disease of heart
MORGAN, Wm. H., R-163-1; Pvt K Co 1st TN Inf; 12-26-62 to 8-6-65; Graysville PO; concussion of the brain, since almost blind
MORGAN, William L., Gr-74-2; Pvt B Co 8th TN Cav; 10 Jun 63 to 11 Sep 65; Rutledge PO
MORGAN, William R., Hm-106-1; Mary A. widow of; Pvt H Co 1st TN Cav; 15 Jul 62 to 15 Jan 65; Chestnut Bloom PO
MORGAN, William T., K-168-3; Pvt E Co 1st KY Lt Art; 29 Nov 63 to 25 Jan 65; Adair's Creek PO
MORLART, Dan, Sh-157-2; Cpl F Co 6th MI Inf; May 61 to 64; White Haven PO; shot in the breast, minney ball spent the small finger of the left hand
MORIS, Jessey, Mc-118-1; Pvt E Co 42nd TN Inf; 8-1-64 to 2-15-66; Cogshill PO; side pleurisy & rupture 25 yrs
MORISON, Jacob, Hw-121-5(4); Pvt G Co 31st TN Inf; 1 Mar 61 to 4 Apr 65; Chimney Top PO; CONF
MORISON, Jesse, Bo-11-2; Soldier; 1st Civil Dist
MORISSON, John M., Hm-108-2(1); Pvt E Co 62nd NC Con Vol; 1 Mar 64 to 1 Mar 65; Springvale PO; CONF
MORISSON, Richardson, Cl-54-1; Pvt H Co 8th TN Inf; 7-25-63 to 6-30-65; Bacchus PO; wonded in back & right hand
MORLEY, David J., Ct-35-2; Pvt K Co 13th TN Cav; 10-64 to 9-5-65; Fish Spring PO; dischard not at home
MORLEY, Hiram P., Hm-106-2; Lt A Co 4th OH; 62 to 64; Morristown PO
MORONEY, Jane, Sh-178-4; widow; 5 Charleston Hill, Memphis PO
MORPHIS, Fleet J., Mn-120-1; Pvt G Co 1st AL Cav; ___ to Jan 4 64 (1 yr); Falcon PO
MORRAR, John, Ge-94-2(2); Pvt A Co 4th TN Inf; 1 Apr 63 to 2 Aug 65; Greeneville PO; during the Civil War
MORRELL, Albert, Gi-132-2; Martha Phillips formerly widow of; Pvt K Co 110th US CV; Dec 16 63 to ___; DeRay PO; husband died in the service
MORRELL, Chrisley, Ct-42-2; Alzenia widow of; Pvt A Co 13th TN Cav; Watauga PO
MORRELL, Amanda A. (see Carlton, Goodwin)
MORRELL, J. O., U-245-1; Cpl D Co 63rd TN Inf; 23 Nov 62 to 8 May 65; Okolona PO (Carter Co.); CONF
MORRELL, Jonathan M., Gr-76-1; Pvt; 7th Dist; piles 25 yrs; CONF
MORRELL, Marshal, Su-242-1; Cpl A Co 13th TN Cav; 24 Sep 63 to 5 Sep 65; Bluff City PO; wound in head and left hip, rupture and diarrhea, general health not good
MORRELL, William R., Ct-42-2; Pvt A Co 13th TN Cav; Watauga PO
MORRIDY, Richard, Ge-100-2; Pvt A Co 8th KY Inf; 1 Sep 61 to 1 Apr 65; Midway PO
MORRIS, Albert M., J-82-1; Pvt B Co 6th TN Mtd Inf; 9-15-64 to 6-30-65; Mayfield PO; heart and lungs
MORRIS, Allen, Sh-157-7; Pvt E Co 3rd US Cav; Salm Bapt. Church, Memphis PO

MORRIS, Andrew J., D-46-1; Emily E. widow of; Pvt G Co 10th TN Inf; Nashville PO; papers lost
MORRIS, Arthum A., Gi-124-1; Pvt I? Co 4th TN Inf; Sep 26 62 to 25 Aug 65; Merritt PO
MORRIS, Baz, Ms-175-1; Pvt D Co 17th ___; 63 to ___ (2 yrs 4 mos); Lunns Store PO; shot in knee at Battle of Nashville
MORRIS, C. T., Jr, Fr-118-1; Pvt I Co 41st TN Inf; Feb 61 to Mar 62; Nashville PO; CONF
MORRIS, Cherlie, D-69-2; US Sol; Nashville PO
MORRIS, Elijah, Mn-126-1; Nancy E. widow of; Pvt C Co 6th TN Cav; Adamsville PO
MORRIS, Elisha T., Sm-166-1; Sgt A Co 5th TN Cav; 8-62 to 4-64; Carthage PO
MORRIS, F. W., Cr-15-1; Pvt C Co 7th TN Cav; 24 Apr 63 to 9 Aug 65; Poplar Springs PO; rumatism (legs & hips); served 8 mos in Andersonville
MORRIS, George, R-157-2; Sol; 12th Dist
MORRIS, George W., Ce-31-2; Bettie widow of; Pvt A Co 18th TN Inf; 1 Jun 61 to Apr 65; Ashland City PO; CONF
MORRIS, Isaac, H-70-3(1); Addie widow of; Chattanooga PO; jammd by cannon ball, widow destroyed his papers, not knowing what they were
MORRIS, Isiah, Cr-19-1; Pvt M Co 12th TN Cav; 8-7-64 to 10-12-65; Buxter PO
MORRIS, J. H., G-57-1; Pvt; 1 yr; Yorkville PO; CONF
MORRIS, J. M., D-76-1; Pvt I Co 10th MO Cav; Aug 30 62 to Jul 26 65; Nashville PO
MORRIS, Jas., Sh-145-4; Kerrville PO
MORRIS, James, Pi-156-1; Pvt K Co 4th TN Inf; 3-10-65 to 8-25-65; Permelia PO; ruptured, fall from horse, deaf left ear
MORRIS, James H., Co-61-6(2); Mary A. widow of; Capt; Bridgeport PO; CONF
MORRIS, John, Lo-188-1; May widow of; Pvt F Co 2nd TN Inf; May 62 to 7 May 63; Stockton PO
MORRIS, John H., Gi-127-3; Pvt IN; 64 to 65; Pulaski PO; forgotten dates
MORRIS, John R., La-114-1; Pvt A Co 17th R Cav; 25 Aug 62 to 16 Jun 65; Lawrenceburg PO; rheumatism & hart trouble
MORRIS, John S., Ch-14-1; Pvt A Co 22nd TN Cav; 5-1-62 to 65; Sweet Lips PO; CONF
MORRIS, Joseph, Hw-124-1; Pvt B Co 4th TN Cav; 1 Jul 63 to 1 Jul 65; Opossum PO
MORRIS, Joseph, K-167-3; Pvt C Co 69th OH Inf; 61 to 62; Knoxville PO
MORRIS, Joseph, Ce-31-2; Pvt A Co 18th TN Inf; 1 Jun 61 to Apr 65; Ashland City PO; shot in head; CONF
MORRIS, Joseph S., Mg-199-3; Cpl F Co 1st TN Inf; 18 Aug 61 to 63; Sunbright PO; lung disease & rheumatism
MORRIS, Larkin, Co-69-1; Cathrin widow of; Pvt; Driskill PO; killed in the (Conf) Army; CONF
MORRIS, Mary (see Elliot, Wesley)
MORRIS, Matt, Col, Ms-172-1; Pvt A Co 1st IL Bat; 6 Jan 63 to 6 Jan 65; Farmington PO; Morris cant tell dates, dont think he was ever ___ in, think he was employed as cook
MORRIS, Monroe, T-218-1; Pvt G Co 61st; 63 to 65; Covington PO; shot through, bowels hit
MORRIS, Mort G., Ch-14-1; Pvt C Co 52nd TN Inf; 11-28-61 to 1-15-65; Sweet Lips PO; CONF
MORRIS, Robert, Cy-28-1; Pvt F Co 8th TN Cav; 10-15-63 to 7-1-65; Celina PO
MORRIS, Samuel B., Ce-20-2; Pvt D Co 4th TN Mtd Inf; 64 to 65; Ashland City PO; rheumatism
MORRIS, Tandy G., We-221-3; Pvt G Co 5th TN; 61 to 65; Martin PO; explosion of a cannon ball, injuries his hearing; CONF
MORRIS, Thomas A., Sm-174-1; Cpl B Co 5th TN Cav; ___ to 65; Grant PO
MORRIS, Thomas J., Ct-40-4; 3 yrs; Elizabethton PO; CONF
MORRIS, William, Sh-162-1; Eliza Jones widow of; Bings Town PO
MORRIS, William, F-40-2; Pvt I Co 61st TN Inf; 21 Mar 63 to 20 May 65; Hickory Withe PO
MORRIS, Wm. B., C-34-3; Cpl H Co 1st TN Inf; 8-20-61 to 8-20-64; Pioneer PO; served term out
MORRIS, Wm. C., Rb-220-1; Engr. H Co 17th MO? Vol; 9 May 61 to Jun 21 65; Adairsville, KY, PO; CONF

MORRIS, William C., Wa-261-2; Pvt F Co NC Inf; 25 Mar 62 to 20 Apr 65; Nola Chuckey PO; CONF
MORRIS, William G., Sn-260-5; Pvt A Co 20th KY Inf; 62 to 63; A.B.C. PO; contracted neuralgia in service; CONF
MORRISETT, William R., Hu-100-1; Pvt E Co 48th US Inf; Sep 20 63 to Sep 10 64; Hustburg PO; CONF
MORRISON, Alfred, F-40-1; Cpl H Co 9th VA Cav; 10 Jun 61 to 21 Apr 65; Canadaville PO; shot through the thigh; CONF
MORRISON, Amazon, Me-92-1; Pvt B Co 7th TN Mtd Inf; Hester Mills PO
MORRISON, Benjamin F., Hw-127-4; Pvt; Amis PO
MORRISON, Ellen, Hw-118-3; widow US Sol; St. Clair PO
MORRISON, Fildan, Ge-101-2; Rutha widow of; Pvt K Co TN Cav; 63 to ___; Locust Sp. PO
MORRISON, J. J., F-48-1; Pvt G Co; 3-25-62 to 5-2-65; New Castle PO; CONF
MORRISON, James, K-158-2; Col 5th OH Inf; 61 to May 65; Knoxville PO
MORRISON, John M., Ge-93-2; Pvt I Co 1st TN Cav; Greeneville PO
MORRISON, Joseph, P-156-1; Pvt 42nd TN Inf; 63 to 64; Lobelville PO; sent home on account bad health; CONF
MORRISON, Lenore, Ge-94-3; Mary A. widow of; Pvt M Co 1st TN Cav; Nov 62 to 2 May 63; Ham PO; died during war in 1863
MORRISON, Marglin? L., Ro-210-3; Pvt I Co 26th TN Inf; 8 Apr 61 to 8 Apr 65; Rockwood PO; CONF
MORRISON, Thomas A. F., La-114-1; Pvt D Co 67th OH Inf Vol; Nov 1 64 to Aug 24 65; Summertown PO; ruptured
MORRISON, Thomas D., Hw-132-3(1); Pvt D Co 31st TN Inf; Mar 62 to Apr 65; Romeo PO (Greene Co.); CONF
MORRISON, William A., K-178-1; Pvt C Co 1st TN Lt Art; 17 Sep 63 to 1 Aug 65; Vancouver PO
MORRISON, Zacarryor, Mr-95-1; Pvt C Co 6th TN Cav; 9-2-64 to 7-11-65; Whitwell PO
MORRITZ, Carl, Gu-45-1; Capt; Altamont PO; rheumatism & heart disease
MORROW, Adam, Ge-94-2(1); Margaret A. widow of; Pvt A Co 3rd TN Vol Mtd Inf; 30 Jun 64 to 30 Nov 64; Greeneville PO
MORROW, Elbert G., U-244-1; Pvt A Co 1st Estess Forester; Jan 64 to Nov 65; Loganton PO; piles
MORROW, George, K-170-2; Pvt D Co 6th TN Cav; 18 Mar 62 to 27 May 65; Knoxville PO; weak eyes, 25 yrs
MORROW, James W., Co-59-1; Pvt Co H 1st TN Cav; 7-15-62 to 6-5-65; Del Rio PO
MORROW, Jerry, Ru-240-1; Rutherford PO
MORROW, Lewis W., Po-152-2; Pvt I Co 7th TN Mtd Inf; 1-1-65 to 6-15-65; Ducktown PO; relapse of measles and diarrhoea
MORROW, Newton, G-59-1; US Sol; 10th Civil Dist
MORROW, Robt. M., Mc-115-1; Pvt Ahls IN Bat; 7-15-63 to 5-25-65; Riceville PO; bronchitis
MORROW, Samuel, Wy-172-1; Nancy widow of; Sgt H Co 5th TN Vol Cav; 7-15-62 to 8-14-65; Waynesboro PO; ruptured & heart disease
MORROW, Thoms J., Ge-94-1; Eliza J. widow of; Pvt I Co (A?) 4th TN Inf; 1 Feb 64 to 2 Aug 65; Greeneville PO
MORROW, William H., Cy-28-2; 1st Lt D Co 9th KY Inf; 9-15-61 to 12-15-64; Celina PO
MORSBULL, Benjamin L., Ge-88-2; Pvt D Co 1st TN Cav; 2 Jan 63 to 19 Jun 65; Mohawk PO; rheumatism
MORSE, Alexander, O-137-1; Pvt E Co 3rd KY Cav; 1 Oct 64 to 18 Feb 65; Kenton PO; detail out of order on this sched.
MORSE, Ephram, C-137-1; Pvt I Co 7th TN Cav; Sep 63 to 15 Jun 65; Kenton PO; detail out of order on this sched.
MORSETT, Enic, Hw-132-5; Lucinda widow of; Pvt H Co 8th TN Inf; 23 Jul 63 to 16 Jun 65; Otes PO; rheumatism & diarrhea
MORSON, Alvin H., M-103-6; Pvt I Co 9th KY Mtd Inf; 9-26-61 to 12-23-65; Red Boiling Spring PO
MORSON, Thomas G., F-48-1; Pvt D Co 61st ___; 1-64 to 64; Brinkley PO
MORTIN, Isaac, Dk-34-4; Elizabeth widow of; Cpl F Co 4th TN Inf; 9-20-64 to ___; Dowelltown PO

MORTON, Charles, Wi-287-1; Pvt F Co 105th KY Inf; to 7 Mar ___ (2 yrs); Civ Dist No 18
MORTON, David M., Ct-37-1; Pvt B Co 13th TN Cav; 9-24-63 to 9-5-64; Ripshin PO; chronic rheumatism, suffering 25 yrs
MORTON, David N., Cy-27-5(3); Pvt F Co 21st KY Inf; 10-1-61 to 1-4-64; Spivey PO; gun shot in left shoulder, reenlisted veteran
MORTON, David R., A-2-3; Pvt C Co 1st TN Inf; 7-20-63 to 8-3-65; Hinds Creek PO; chronic diarrhea, piles and side pleurisy
MORTON, Elaxailder, Ct-44-2; Nancy E. widow of; Pvt A Co 13th TN Cav; 9-23-63 to 9-5-65; Hampton PO
MORTON, Howard, L-109-1; Driver in Wagon Train; 62 to 65; Glimpville PO
MORTON, John, Bo-15-3; Marry Long widow of; Pvt; Maryville PO
MORTON, John, Sh-174-3; Emily widow of; Pvt I Co 3rd US Hvy Art; ___ to 66; rear 152 De Soto St, Memphis PO
MORTON, John H., Bo-22-1; Capt B Co 3rd TN Cav; 11-5-62 to 8-3-65; Notime PO; shot in left shoulder
MORTON, Ransom, Ms-173-1; Pvt I Co 25th IN Inf; Rich Creek PO
MORTON, William A., C-24-4(3); Lt H Co 9th TN Cav; 7-12-63 to 9-11-65; Forkvale PO; chronic diarrhea
MORTON, Wm. L., P-151-4; Linden PO
MOSBY, James, Sh-191-4; Mary Ann Gray widow of; Memphis PO; records not seen
MOSELEY, John, Col, B-4-1; Pvt C Co 15th Reg US Col; 12-64 to 4-7-66; Bell Buckle PO; right leg mashed on forage boat, eyes affected by small pox
MOSELEY, Samuel S., Mu-209-5; Capt 1st TN Cav; Apr 61 to Apr 62; Columbia PO; CONF
MOSELY, Edmond, Sh-174-4; Major's Sgt 93rd IL; 196½ DeSoto St, Memphis PO; shot in left breast at Altoona, GA, in hospital 2 mos; ordered into battle by Capt. commanding--discharged on acct of disabilities
MOSELY, George, Ja-86-3; Pvt C Co 1st TN Cav; 8-62 to 12-65; Oottewah PO; smallpox & eraisypalis
MOSELY, Mose, G-71-3; Martha widow of; Pvt G Co 15th TN Inf; 12 May 61 to 20 Jun 64; PO omitted; CONF
MOSELY, Sameul, K-155-2(1); Pvt; Knoxville PO
MOSELY, William, Ru-239-1; Pvt A Co 7th TN Cav; 63 to ___ (11 mos); Patterson PO; home on furlough & stayed
MOSER, Andrew J., Mo-122-3(1); Pvt D Co 62nd TN Inf; 10-62 to 1-27-63; Hiwassee College PO; blind; CONF
MOSER, James P., Sn-252-4; Pvt G Co 10th TN Inf; 6-1-62 to 7-4-65; Pleasant View PO
MOSER, Theodore, Ma-121-1; Pvt K Co 7th KS Cav; Sep 15 63 to Sep 29 65; Carroll PO; liver & kidney afflicition
MOSES, James, Mc-117-4; Pvt K Co 12th TN Cav; Cog Hill PO
MOSES, Lee A., D-72-1; Pvt C Co 65th TN Inf; Oct 13 61 to Oct 12 62; Nashville PO; CONF
MOSES, William M., We-222-2; Pvt 45th TN; Nov 61 to Nov 62; Gardner PO; CONF
MOSHER, Harvey G., Cf-39-1; Pvt I Co 7th MS Inf; 14 Aug 62 to 17 Jul 65; Prairie Plains PO
MOSIER, Jacob, Hd-53-3; Pvt G Co 6th TN Cav; 15 Sep 62 to 26 Jul 65; Milledyeville PO; rheumatism
MOSIER, James M., Ro-203-8; Pvt I Co 1st TN Inf; 9 Aug 61 to 17 Sep 64; Burns' Mills PO; gunshot wound in leg, chronic rheumatism
MOSIER, William F., He-58-1; Pvt G Co 5th TN Cav; 8-25-62 to 8-1-64; PO omitted
MOSIN, Lewis H., Mg-199-2; Lt F Co 1stTN Inf; 19 Aug 61 to 62; Sunbright PO; piles
MOSLEY, Charles S., Gu-48-4(1); Pvt B Co 51st LA Inf; 4-63 to 6-65; 45 Turley St, Memphis PO
MOSLEY, Squire, Ru-13-3; Pvt K Co 111th Reg Inf; 3 yrs 3 mos; Murfreesboro PO
MOSLEY, William, Wa-266-1; Pvt B Co 4th TN Cav; 8 Sep 62 to 17 Jun 65; Fall Branch PO
MOSLEY, William, D-63-3; Pvt US Col; Nashville PO
MOSLEY, Wyly B., Su-239-1; Pvt C Co 4th TN Inf; 1 Feb 64 to 2 Aug 65; Edens Ridge PO

MOSMAN, Judson A., H-56-7; Pvt E Co MA Cav; 1-29-63 to 7-20-65; St. Elmo PO
MOSS, Andrew J., Cy-27-3(1); Pvt B Co 9th KY Inf; 9-24-61 to 12-15-64; Exeda PO; gunshot on right hand
MOSS, Bartlett, Hr-87-1; Pvt A Co 7th TN Lt (Art?); 9-20-64 to 7-30-65; Hickory Valley PO
MOSS, Ben, Ch-14-1; Harett A. McClenan widow of; Sweet Lips PO; CONF
MOSS, Clayburn, Sh-199-1; 120 Larose St, Memphis PO
MOSS, George N., Cr-4-2; Pvt F Co 7th TN Cav; 62 to 65; Bells Depot PO; CONF
MOSS, George W., Ch-13-3; Louiza widow of; Pvt B Co 6th TN Vol; 62 to died 1864; Wild Goose PO; this is the widow of an old soldier who was murdered while at home by rebels
MOSS, James, He-57-2; Pvt I Co 8th Colmer Inf; 3-1-63 to 5-1-65; Law PO; wonded in thigh, join? Lookout 3 mos; CONF?
MOSS, John C., Me-94-1; Sarah A. widow of; Pvt A Co 2nd TN Inf; Euchee PO; died in prison
MOSS, Joseph, Br-14-2; Pvt; McDonald PO; rheumatism
MOSS, Sarah (see Shote, Henderson)
MOSS, William, H-61-3; Mary K. Kinman former widow of; Chattanooga PO
MOSS, William A., Dk-39-5(1); Pvt G Co 4th TN Mtd Inf; 1-1-65 to 9-15-65; Laurel Hill PO
MOSSELL, Harrison, K-159-1; Minerva Cogswell widow of; Knoxville PO
MOT, Lander I., R-160-1; Pvt A Co 7th TN; 5th Civil Dist
MOTON?, Alferd, Ch-17-2; Pvt A Co TN Inf; 62 to 65; Masseyville PO
MOTT, George W., O-134-1; Capt F Co 2nd MO Cav; May 15 62 to May 25 65; Hornbeak PO; gun shot in rite arm, injured in the left side, falling horse; CONF
MOTTI?, Clarance M., K-167-4; Mollie Carnie widow of; Pvt US __; 62 to 66; Knoxville PO
MOULDEN, Francis A., K-179-5; Pvt A Co 1st USC Art Hvy; 23 Jan 64 to 31 Mar 66; Concord PO
MOULDEN, George W., Se-226-6; Civilian E. US; 12th Dist
MOULDEN, Jere, Ro-210-6; Sophia widow of; Pvt; Rockwood PO; CONF
MOULDEN, Reese, H-57-3; Pvt E Co 15th US Inf; 63 to 65; Orchard Knob PO
MOULTER, Earesno W., D-69-2; US Sol; Nashville PO
MOULTON, Andrew J., D-59-1; 1st Lt 124th OH; 1704 Church St, Nashville PO
MOUND, W. W., Ms-172-1; Capt I Co 10th TN Inf; 19 Jun 62 to 19 Jun 65; Farmington PO
MOUNDULY, Isaac N., Sm-174-1; Pvt G Co 4th TN Inf; 11-1-64 to 8-25-65; New Middleton PO
MOUNGER, Isaac L., Lo-195-2(1); Pvt F Co 3rd TN Inf; 11 Feb 62 to 23 Feb 65; Oral PO (Roane Co.); rheumatism-left leg
MOUNT, Napoleon B., Se-226-3; Teamster K Co 2nd TN Mtd Inf; Jul 62 to __; Henrys X Roads PO
MOUNT, Thos. H., Je-135-4; Nancy E. widow of; Pvt D Co 4th TN Cav; 10 Mar 63 to died in service; Piedmont PO; burned out
MOURLOCK, George, Hw-121-5(4); Pvt G Co 31st TN Inf; 1 Mar 61 to 4 Apr 65; Chimney Top PO
MOURLOCK, Samuel, Hw-121-5(4); Pvt G Co 31st TN Cav; Sep 64 to 65; Chimney Top PO; CONF
MOWDY, William, Su-240-1; G Co 8th TN Cav Pvt?; 22 Aug 63 to Sep 65; PO omitted
MOWENY, Adam M., We-226-1; Pvt L Co 6th TN Cav; 7 Aug 62 to __; Sharon PO; marked on roll, deserter
MOWER, George W., L-104-1; Sgt A Co 123rd IN Vol; Nov 18 63 to Aug 25 65; Curve PO; he is drawing a pension, resides in Indiana
MOWERY, Samuel M., Br-14-3; Pvt C Co 4th TN Cav; 12-5-62 to 7-12-65; Cleveland PO; ruptured
MOWLIN, Jacob, H-51-5; Pvt E Co 5th TN Inf; 9-12-64 to 9-22-65; Hill City PO
MOWREY, Lewis L., Br-13-1; Pvt D Co 10th TN Inf; 4-20-62 to 6-10-65; Cleveland PO
MOWREY, Peter W., Br-13-2; Pvt A Co 8th TN Inf; 2-62 to 7-65; Cleveland PO; chronic dirrhoea
MOWREY, William S., Br-13-3; Sgt E Co 4th TN Cav; 12-5-62 to 7-12-65; Cleveland PO; chronic dirrhoea & dyspepsia
MOWRY, Chas. E., R-163-4; Pvt H Co 28th MI Inf; 10-7-64 to 6-12-65; Ogden PO
MOWRY, James R., H-63-4; 1st Lt F Co 20th MI Inf; 8-62 to 4-65; cor. Chestnut & Broad, Chattanooga PO
MOXLEY, Alexander, Wl-288-1; Pvt B Co 45th TN; Jul 63 to 65; Laguards PO; didnt know exact date of enlistment
MOXLEY, Wesley, Col, D-(numbers omitted); Pvt I Co 123rd US C Inf; 1 yr 2 mos; First & Watson, Nashville PO
MOYER, Adolphus T., Sh-153-1; Pvt B Co 59th OH Inf; Oct 61 to Nov 64; Bailey Sta. PO
MOYER, Danial H., R-159-1; Pvt D Co 34th OH Inf; 12-20-63 to 7-65; Spring City PO
MOYERS, James L., Cl-47-3; Pvt E Co 6th __ Inf; 4-25-62 to 5-25-65; Cappford PO; rheumatism & frozen feet & legs 63 to 64
MOYERS, John A., Ge-88-3; Pvt C Co 8th TN Inf; 1 Mar 63 to 31 May 65; Bulls Gap PO; throat & lungs & piles & side
MOYERS, John E., Hm-107-2(1); Pvt C Co 9th TN Cav; 28 Jul 63 to 13 Sep 65; White Pine PO; chronic diarhoea
MUHLAR, Frank, Sh-202-1; Cpt WR Inf; 6 Jan 61 to 62; Memphis PO; right arm shot off
MUICEY, William, Gr-77-1; Pvt B Co 8th TN Inf; 10 Jan 62 to 19 Sep 65; Hargus PO; gun shot
MUICHE, Joseph A., Ro-201-5(3); Pvt I Co 1st TN Inf; 2 Nov 61 to 6 Nov 64; Kingston PO
MULDER, T. L., Mn-126-1; Pvt A Co 4th AR Cav; 64 to __; Purdy PO
MULENIX, John R., Wa-266-2; Pvt B Co 4th TN Cav; Fall Branch PO
MULKEY, Jacob B., H-51-1; Cpl H Co 7th R TN Mtd Inf; 3-2-65 to 7-27-65; Soddy PO; rupture and heart disease
MULKEY, Johnathon D., R-106-2(3); Pvt A Co GA Regt; 7th Civil Dist
MULL, Saml., Sh-159-2; Alexander, Rhoda widow of; Memphis PO
MULL, Samuel, H-61-1; Margaret H. Davis formerly widow of; Sgt F Co 177th NY Inf; fall 62 to fall 63; Chattanooga PO; health undermined by exposure
MULLANEY, Danial J., H-71-1; Pvt C Co 55th OH Inf; 62 to 65; Chattanooga PO
MULLEN, Almon, Pu-145-2; Pvt B Co 1st Mtd Inf; 3-5-64 to 4-14-65; Fancher's Mills PO
MULLEN, George W., Di-41-1; Pvt A Co 10th TN Inf; 2-12-63 to 7-3-65; White Bluff PO
MULLEN, James, D-48-1; Pvt? 16th US Inf; 16 __ 61 to 16 Jun 65; Nashville PO
MULLEN, Reuben, Mu-213-1; Cook; Glenns Store PO; pressed in the service as cook
MULLENNIX, Amos K., Su-241-1; Dist No 5
MULLENS, Andrew J., Me-92-4(1); Pvt H Co 3rd TN Mtd Inf; 64 to __; Pin Hook PO; crippled, ankle hurt
MULLENS, James, H-53-8; Pvt E Co 5th TN Mtd Inf; 9-3-64 to 5-26-65; Chattanooga PO; shot twice in jaw and neck
MULLENS, John M., Ro-204-3; Pvt B Co 5th TN Inf; 25 Feb 62 to 7 Apr 65; Elverton PO; rheumatism
MULLENS, William J., Ja-87-2; Pvt D Co 1st TN Cav; Apison PO; discharge lost
MULLER, Charles F., H-64-2; Capt B Co 29th PA Inf; 4-18-61 to 7-25-65; Chattanooga PO
MULLER, Lewis, D-67-1; OS A Co 12th Col Inf; Jul 12 65 to 66; Nashville PO
MULLICAN, Johnathan, W-194-1; Pvt K Co 5th TN Cav; 6-25-63 to 8-14-65; Clearmont PO
MULLIGAN, Burton, D-60-1; 118 Stonewall St, Nashville PO; mulatto
MULLIN, James M., B-3-1; Sgt A Co 3rd FL Cav; 5-10-63 to 7-15-64; Shelbyville PO
MULLIN, John, D-72-1; Pvt D Co 16th IL Inf; Apr 18 61 to Jun 19 64; Nashville PO
MULLIN, Peter, Col, S-214-2; Pvt G Co 119th US Inf; Glenmary PO
MULLINAX, Samuel W., Pi-155-3; Pvt D Co 1st TN Mtd Inf; 1-25-64 to 4-25-65; Byrdstown PO; eyes effected caused fever
MULLINS, Aaron S., Jo-153-2; Cpl G Co 4th TN Inf; Little Doe PO; injury to the breast
MULLINS, Archibal, Me-93-2; Pvt I Co 5th TN Cav; 6-8-64 to 6-20-65; Sewee PO

MULLINS, Christifer, Ha-116-1; US Sol; 13th Dist
MULLINS, Francis M., Ja-86-4; Cpl D Co 4th TN Cav; 11-13-62 to 7-12-65; Apison PO
MULLINS, Henry, Pi-153-2; Cpl G Co 5th KY Cav; 12-21-61 to 5-3-65; Chanute PO
MULLINS, Hesekiah, Ha-112-1; Pvt I Co 1st US Inf; 28 May 64 to 20 Jun 65; Datura PO
MULLINS, Jacob, D-80-1; 2nd Civil Dist
MULLINS, Jake, G-71-1; Pvt __ 14th TN Inf; 15 Jan 61 to 5 Mar 65; Rutherford PO
MULLINS, Jerry A., Hi-74-1?-3; Pvt B Co 50th VA Inf; 3 Aug 62 to 9 Apr 65; Sneedville PO; disease eyes 2 mos
MULLINS, Joe, D-51-1; Col; Pallace widow of; 415 N Cherry, Nashville PO; cant furnish any direct information
MULLINS, John C., D-72-1; Pvt C Co 3rd TN Inf; Jul 22 62 to Oct 23 64; Nashville PO; CONF
MULLINS, John H., Ca-24-1; Pvt A Co 1st TN Inf; 4-8-63 to 7-28-63; Prater PO; rheumatism, totaly disabled for any business, goes on crutches
MULLINS, John M., Ro-217-4; Sol US; 16th Dist
MULLINS, John W., Ov-135-2; Pvt H Co 5th KY Cav; 12-4-61 to 3-3-65; Monroe PO; rheumatism
MULLINS, Joseph S., Ro-208-2; Pvt A Co 5th TN Inf; 13 Nov 62 to 30 Jan 65; Morris Gap PO; chronic direa
MULLINS, Mathew S., B-7-1; Pvt C Co 5th TN Cav; 5-18-63 to 8-14-65; Shelbyville PO
MULLINS, Milton, Me-93-1; Pvt I Co 5th TN Cav; 8-1-64 to 7-8-65; Ten Mile Stand PO; injury to right shoulder
MULLINS, Robert C., He-60-1; Pvt A Co 7th TN Cav; 9-62 to about 4-63; Lexington PO
MULLINS, Samuel, Hw-122-1; Rachel M. widow of; Pvt I Co 8th TN Cav; Sep 63 to Sep 65; Blossom PO; gun shot and disease of stomach
MULLINS, Solomon, Hm-105-1; Pvt A Co Tri. Batl.; Turley Mill PO; ruptured
MULLINS, William, Pi-155-1; Pvt H Co 3rd KY Inf; 12-21-61 to 1-14-65; Byrdstown PO; wounded in left thigh
MULLINS, William C., Hd-53-3; Pvt Harrison Scouts and Gen. Doddy; Morris Chapel PO; effects of small pox, Andersonvill Prison 13 mos
MULLINS, William R., He-66-1; Pvt A Co 74th TN Cav; Aug 16 62 to Aug 21 65; Life PO
MULVANEY, Alen P., K-184-1; Pvt B Co 6th TN Inf; 18 Jan 62 to 30 Jun 65; Riverdale PO
MULVIHILL, Jeremiah, D-49-2; Cpl H Co 11th IL Cav; 23 Aug 62 to 11 Jun 65; 914 Gay St, Nashville PO; broken arm by horse falling with him while soldier
MUMFORD, Samuel, Sh-174-2; Pvt A Co 29th IL Inf (Col); about 12-64 to 12-65; Memphis PO
MUNCY, John, H-61-4; Pvt K Co 1st US Hvy Art; 62 to 4-9-65; Chattanooga, Burk's Hill PO; caught small pox in army
MUNCY, Peter, Gr-82-2; Tempy widow of; Pvt A Co 1st TN Cav; 18 Apr 62 to Feb 63; PO omitted; marked through, probably CONF
MUNDY, Jacob J., Ha-115-1; Pvt A Co 1st TN Inf; 5 Apr 62 to 5 Apr 65; Alanthers Hill PO; bone scurvy, yet living, not a pensioner
MUNGER, Joseph, Ja-85-3; Pvt G Co 3rd TN Cav; 7-12-63 to 8-3-65; Birchwood PO
MUNLEY, Gordon, A-1-2; Pvt H Co 2nd TN Cav; 7-4-63 to 9-11-65; Andersonville PO
MUNROE, James, Sh-189-3; Drummer 4th US Col Hvy Art; Spring 63 to 2-25-65; alley off Carolina St, Memphis PO
MUNS, Daniel B., Mg-198-4; Catharine widow of; Pvt E Co 1st TN Inf; 20 Aug 61 to __; Rockwood PO
MUNSEY, Peter, Un-252-2; Tempy C. widow of; Pvt A Co 1st TN Cav; 18 Jul 62 to Feb 63; Haynes PO
MUNY, William M., K-160-3; Capt H Co 2nd TN; Aug 61 to Aug 65; Knoxville PO
MUNYMAKER, Mathew, K-179-3; Pvt D Co 6th TN Inf; 26 Aug 63 to 10 Jul 65; Virtue PO
MUPHY, Cebant, Ge-83-1; Cpl G Co 4th TN Inf; 4 May 63 to __; Hanshaw PO
MURCER, Joseph, Hw-121-4(3); Pvt B Co 3rd TN Mtd Inf; 4 Jul 64 to 4 Nov 64; Segonsville PO
MURCER, William H., Ru-241-4; Pvt B Co 6th IN Cav; 61 to 11-13-65; Murfreesboro PO
MURE, John, Bo-15-1; Elen E. Potter widow of; Pvt A Co 3rd TN Inf; 2-11-62 to 8-1-63; Blockhouse PO

MURICEY, Laffaette, D-66-1; Pvt F Co 4th W VA Inf; 5 Jul 61 to 3 Feb 64; 2nd enlistment Pvt C Co 2nd W VA Inf—24 Jan 64 to 18 Jul 65; Nashville, 621 S Market PO; served two enlistments the second was in 2nd W VA Inf Co C
MURLEY, William M., B-7-2; Pvt F Co 89th IL Inf; 8-12-62 to 1-4-65; PO omitted
MURPH, Jethro A., Gr-74-1; Pvt H Co 8th NC Inf; 4 May 64 to 28 Apr 65; May Spring PO; left arm shot; CONF
MURPHA, James, Hn-74-1; 3rd Sgt I Co 33rd Mis Inf; 12 Aug 62 to 10 Aug 65; McKenzie PO
MURPHARY, J. B., F-44-3; Pvt B Co Forest; Mar 7 62 to 65; PO omitted; CONF
MURPHY, Arthur E., Se-222-2; Elisabeth widow of; Lt; 10 May 62 to 1 Jul 65; Sevierville PO
MURPHY, Daniel F., Se-224-1; Martha widow of; Pvt E Co 9th TN Cav; 1 Oct 63 to 11 Sep 65; Waldens Creek PO; imprisoned & killed
MURPHY, David, S-217-1; Pvt C Co 32nd KY Inf; 62 to 63; Winfield PO
MURPHY, David H., Br-9-1; Sgt A Co 6th IN Cav; 8-18-63 to 9-15-65; Cleveland PO
MURPHY, Ed, H-64-1; Pvt A Co 5th KY; 7-5-62 to 9-14-64; Chattanooga PO; leg hurt
MURPHY, Edward, Br-12-4; Pvt H Co 8th TN Inf; 5-6-63 to 6-16-65; Etola PO; shot in arm
MURPHY, Mrs. Elizio J., La-111-2; widow of sol?; Pvt H Co 2nd TN Inf; 12-9-63 to 6-21-65; Pleasant Point PO
MURPHY, George, K-161-6; Knoxville PO
MURPHY, Hariet, F-35-1; widow; 2nd Dist
MURPHY, Hue, Br-8-1; Margaret C. widow of; Pvt E Co 8th TN Vol Cav; 9-1-62 to 1-5-65; Cleveland PO
MURPHY, Jame, Hw-133-2; Pvt B Co 28th TN Inf; 28 Feb 62 to 28 Feb 63; Slide PO; CONF
MURPHY, James C., Br-12-2; Pvt D Co 2nd TN Cav; 9-1-62 to 7-65; Charleston PO; affected kidneys
MURPHY, James M., We-229-1; Cpl K Co 6th TN Cav; 3 Oct 62 to 17 Jul 65; McKinzie PO (Carroll Co.); deficient in sight
MURPHY, John, Mt-145-1; Eliza widow of; she dont know co and reg; Palmyra PO
MURPHY, John, D-78-2; Nashville PO
MURPHY, John, K-154-3; Knoxville PO
MURPHY, John, Hm-103-2; 1st Lt B Co 4th TN Inf; 1 Jan 63 to 10 May 64; Morristown PO; chronic rheumatism
MURPHY, John S., Tr-269-1; Pvt B Co 2nd KY Inf; 25 Sep 61 to 20 Apr 65; John PO
MURPHY, John W. H., Fr-105-1; Muc. 20th OH V Inf; 62 to 64; Winchester PO
MURPHY, John W. K., Fr-119-1; Musician 20th OH?; Estill Springs PO
MURPHY, Joseph, Sh-148-1; Pvt C Co 61st Col Inf; Memphis PO
MURPHY, Kemp, Jo-149-2; Pvt B Co 4th TN Inf; 25 Aug 62 to 7 Jul 65; Mountain City PO
MURPHY, Martin, Sh-177-1; A Co 1st NY Cav; 3-14-61 to 9-20-65; 57 Vance St, Memphis PO
MURPHY, Melvill W., K-182-1; Pvt H Co 6th TN Inf; 10 Aug 62 to Sep 65; Shooks PO; disabled 1864, shot in left hand
MURPHY, Mitchell J., Ho-96-2; Pvt B Co 4th PA Inf; Jun 10 61 to Jul 65; Erin PO; saber wound right leg; CONF
MURPHY, Patrick Sfinigs?, Mc-112-3; P-t C Co 42nd US Col Inf; 6-8-64 to 1-31-66; Athens PO
MURPHY, Robert, B-2-1; Pvt F Co 41st TN Inf; 11-1-61 to 4-15-65; Wartrace PO
MURPHY, Robert R., H-69-5; Ruthie R. widow of; Lt; Chattanooga PO
MURPHY, Silvester, Wy-173-2; Pvt A Co 2nd TN Cav; Marins Mills PO; discharge not at hand
MURPHY, Stephen, Jo-153-2; Mary widow of; Pvt; Little Doe PO
MURPHY, Thomas J., Je-138-1; Pvt B Co 2nd NC Inf; 15 Sep 63 to __ (2 yrs 3 mos); Oak Grove PO; chronic diarrhea, has no discharge
MURPHY, Wm., C-34-1; Pvt F Co 14th NC Inf; 5-3-61 to 4-65; Stanfill PO
MURPHY, William, Hw-131-3; Sallie widow of; B? 3/4 Bat. Stew_ Troops; 10 Sep 64 to 17 Jul 65; Otes PO
MURPHY, William B., Ge-94-1; Jun 62 to __; Tusculum PO; rupture

MURPHY, Wiliam C., L-109-1; Pvt E Co 8th MO Inf; 1 Apr 61 to 15 Apr 65; Lightfoot PO; shot between shoulders
MURPHY, William F., La-114-1; Pvt A Co 32nd OH Inf; Jan 1 64 to Jul 28 65; Elmira PO; inf. of lungs, chron. diareah
MURPHY, William F., Col, De-22-2; Pvt A Co 16th TN Inf; 1 Mar 63 to 1 Jun 64; Clifton PO
MURPHY, William Fulton, Mt-145-1; Pvt A Co 32nd OH Inf; 10 Feb 65 to 20 Jul 65; Palmyra PO
MURPHY, William M., Co-59-1; Pvt Co G 5th US Inf; 4-4-65 to 10-11-66; Del Rio PO
MURR, Andy H., Mo-129-2; Pvt; Loco PO
MURR, Rhoda (see Husky, Welcom, or William)
MURR, Westly, Co-66-2(1); Pvt A Co 9th TN Cav; 1 Nov 62 to Jul 65; English PO; shot through the shoulders; CONF
MURRAY, Alec, C-33-5; Tabitha widow of; Pvt B Co 6th TN Inf; 61 to 64; Newcomb PO
MURRAY, George, Cy-27-6(4); US Sol; 4th Civil Dist
MURRAY, Hugh B., Wl-295-1; Cpl C Co 6th MD Inf; Aug 20 61 to 20 Sep 64; Lebanon PO
MURRAY, Jacob, A-13-2; Pvt G Co 7th TN Inf; 11-8-64 to 7-27-65; Briceville PO; affected lungs & head caused from measles
MURRAY, James, C-32-1; Sarah widow of; Pvt I Co 9th TN Cav; 63 to __; Pine Mountain PO; widow
MURRAY, Jiles, Lo-195-2(1); Pvt I Co 1st TN Inf; 63 to __ (3 yrs) Eatson's X Roads PO; diarhea, exact dates not remembered
MURRAY, John, U-245-1; Pvt B Co 12th TN Cav; 9 Jul 63 to 25 Oct 65; Marbleton PO; cronic rheumatism
MURRAY, John, Li-165-1; Margaret A. Pylant formerly widow of; Elora PO
MURRAY, John A., Cy-27-5(3); Pvt K Co 5th KY Cav; 61 to 5-65 (3 yrs 6 mos); Clementsville PO
MURRAY, John L., He-60-1; Cpl F Co 10th IL Cav; 2-23-63 to 1-6-66; Lexington PO
MURRAY, Levander, H-60-5(2); Elizabeth widow of; Pvt A Co 2nd TN Cav; 61 to 6-65; Chattanooga PO; rheumatism
MURRAY, Peter J., Ma-126-1; belonged to Telegraph Corpse all the war, telegrapher; Jackson PO
MURRAY, Stephen, Je-135-1(3); Pvt B Co 9th TN Cav; 10 Aug 65 PO omitted
MURRAY, Theodore, H-66-2; Pvt B Co 148th NY Vol Inf; 8-62 to 3-17-64; Chattanooga PO
MURRAY, Wm., Sh-172-1; Sgt A Co 152nd NY Inf; 9-3-62 to 7-13-65; 419 Shelby St, Memphis PO
MURRAY, William K., C-32-2; Nancy widow of; Pvt J Co 49th KY Inf; 9-8-63 to 64; Big Creek Gap PO
MURRELL, A. R., F-44-2; Pvt B Co 13th TN; May 62 to May 65; PO omitted; CONF
MURRELL, Harriett, D-59-1; Murrell, Byrum or Byrum Stone; widow of; Pvt C Co 4th US Cav; 1708 Patterson St, Nashville PO; Byrum Stone is the true name
MURRELL, Harvey, Hw-130-2; Pvt L Co 8th TN Cav; 17 Sep 63 to 11 Sep 65; Lee Valley PO
MURRELL, Huston, F-20-3; Pvt D Co 11th TN Inf; Aug 63 to Sep 65; Hickory Withe PO
MURRELL, James, Hw-130-2; Pvt L Co 8th TN Cav; 17 Sep 63 to 11 Sep 65; Lee Valley PO
MURRELL, Mary, Co-66-3(1); widow of US Sol; 1st Dist
MURRELL, Newton J., Hw-119-2(1); Pvt K Co 4th KY Cav; 3 yrs 6 mos; Lee Valley PO; spinal affection, died June 18, 1890
MURREY, Thomas C., Hd-58-1; Pvt; Nixon PO
MURRILL, Richard W., We-221-5(2); Pvt; Martin PO; foot mashed at Humbolt, TN; CONF
MURRIN, Alfred, Bo-21-3; Pvt A Co 6th TN Inf; 3-8-62 to 4-27-65; Ellijay PO
MURRY, Alferd, D-58-1; alias Davis, Jim; with Capt. Baker Supply Train; Nashville PO
MURRY, Clayburn, Gi-139-1; Pvt H Co 110th TN Inf; 10-63 to 2-6-64; Wales PO
MURRY, Edwin, F-40-1; Pvt C Co 11th TN Inf; 15 Mar 63 to 15 May 65; Oakland PO
MURRY, James L., Co-69-6(1); Elizabeth A. widow of; Pvt D Co 8th TN Inf; 24 Dec 62 to 6 Jul 63; Help PO; Campelson KY & died with tifoid fever
MURRY, John, Mc-118-5; Pvt C Co 8th NY Cav; 9-10-61 to 12-64; Joshua PO; cancer on breast & rheumatism 18 yrs
MURRY, Lewis, Hr-91-1; Lt Mot(?) E Co 3rd Art; 7-63 to 8-65; PO omitted; contracted present disease, an issue of matter from a gill to a pint every 48 hrs
MURRY, Rufus K., Sh-195-2; Pvt 34th US Col Inf; 3-9-65 to 2-28-66; Memphis PO; got his foot mashed by moving cannon & shells
MURRY, Silas, Wy-173-4; Pvt A Co 6th TN Inf; 8-2-61 to 9-17-64; Victory PO
MURRY, Sinda (see Barker, Jack)
MURRY, William, Lo-192-2; Pvt A Co 3rd TN; 10 Feb 62 to 20 Mar 65; Morganton PO; bronchitis & cattarrah of lungs
MURRY, William Sr., C-25-2; Pvt A Co 1st TN Inf; 6-13-63 to 8-3-65; Coal Creek PO (Anderson Co.); rheumatism
MURRY, William M., K-157-1; Capt 2nd TN Inf; Knoxville PO
MURTA, Joseph S., F-45-1; Major 8th WI; 61 to 65; Moscow PO; Sgt 8th Reg WI Inf
MUSE, Bowling & James, C-34-2; Emily widow of; both pvts (no detail); Bowling killed in Army & Muse (James?) died since war
MUSE, Calab, Ch-17-2; Pvt C Co 7th TN Cav; 9-1-63 to 8-7-65; Masseyville PO
MUSE, Jason C., B-5-1; Pvt M Co 5th TN Cav; 9-30-63 to 8-14-65; Shelbyville PO
MUSELY, James L., Cu-16-1; Pvt F Co TN Inf; 62 to 65; Ornies? Store PO (Bledsoe Co.); partial loss sight
MUSGROV, Henry C., D-45-5; Ophelia St, Nashville PO
MUSGROVE, Lewis, Br-7-3; Pvt; Cleveland PO; rheumatism
MUSGROVE, William, Hy-79-2; Pvt; Civil Dist No 6
MUSGROVE, William G., Jo-150-2; Pvt I Co 13th TN Cav; 22 Sep 63 to 5 Sep 65; Trade PO
MUSGROVES, Hampton, L-99-1; Cook D Co 178th NY US Inf; Mar 63 to Apr 66; Durhamville PO; hemorrhage of bowels, caused from exposure
MUSNAM, J. W., Hy-76-1; Capt; Stanton Depot PO
MUSTIN, Ward, Hw-128-2; Catharine widow of; Pvt A Co 1st TN Lt Art; 63 to __; Walnut Hill PO; died before discharged
MYARS, Fritts N., Lo-188-1; Pvt I Co 12th PA Inf; 18 Mar 63 to 14 May 65; Adolphus PO
MYARS, Gabrial, Ca-23-1; Pvt A Co 9th TN Cav; 10-18-62 to 8-65; Leoni PO; wounded in limbs
MYATT, Eldredge, Pu-145-2; Sgt C Co 1st Mtd Inf; 10-21-63 to 12-13-64; Burton PO
MYATT, George W., Pu-145-2; Sgt C Co 1st Mtd Inf; 10-21-63 to 12-13-64; Burton PO
MYATT, James T., Di-30-1; Pvt A Co 40th TN Inf; 11-62 to 65; Dickson PO; CONF
MYATT, John E., Cu-15-2; Pvt A Co 22nd TN Inf; served over 1 yr; Genesis PO; right shoulder dis-located, was in CONF pris 355 days?; CONF
MYERS, Allen T. C., Co-61-6(2); Pvt; Bridgeport PO; Bright diseas
MYERS, Asel J., Gu-48-4(1); Pvt C Co 15th IN Inf; 4-15-61 to 6-21-64; PO omitted
MYERS, Charles, D-46-1; Lucy widow of; Pvt K Co 10thTN Inf; 4-62 to 8-65; Nashville PO; cannot give the day of month & has snet his discharge away
MYERS, Charles, Gu-48-5(2); Pvt G Co 4th NJ Inf; 10-19-63 to 7-65; New York, NY, PO
MYERS, F. L., F-38-1; Pvt Ashton Vessel; 28 Feb 65 to Jun 65; Lambert PO
MYERS, Francis J., Mc-118-5; Pvt C Co 10th TN Cav; 1-14-64 to 8-1-65; Calhoun PO; cripled in back 26 yrs
MYERS, G. W. (see Owen, Joseph N.)
MYERS, Isham, Cl-58-2; 1st Lt C Co 1st TN Lt Art; 3-2-63 to 9-18-64; Minkton PO; eyesight injured by shell
MYERS, Jacob, Gr-79-3; Pvt I Co 8th TN Inf; Jul 62 to Jul 64; Thorn Hill PO; measles fell in brain
MYERS, John, Gu-45-1; Bettie widow of; Pvt E Co 1st TN Cav Vidette; 63 to 64 (8 mos); Altamont PO
MYERS, John A., Ge-88-1; Sgt D & I Co 1st TN Cav; 12 Aug 62 to 5 Jun 65; Marvin PO; chronic diarareah & dysenter? or indigestion?

MYERS, John N., Gr-79-1; Co I 26th TN Inf; 15 Aug 61 to Furlough 65; Ball Point PO; not disabled: CONF
MYERS, Joseph, Wi-278-1; Pvt I Co 57th IN Inf; 8 Oct 61 to 4 Feb 65; Franklin PO; loss of eye
MYERS, Lawson F., Un-251-2; Pvt F Co 7th TN Inf; Oct 64 to Aug 65; Effie PO; heart disease & stomach
MYERS, Lesley, R-163-3; Mary widow of; Pvt B Co 6th TN Mtd Inf; 8-15-64 to 6-30-65; Graysville PO; contracted lung trouble
MYERS, Loranzo, B-2-1; Pvt Byrne Art; Wartrace PO; CONF
MYERS, Moses, Hm-109-8; Whitesburg PO
MYERS, Mychael C., Ge-90-1; Pvt I Co 1st TN Cav; 1 Aug 62 to 5 Jun 65; Greeneville PO; heart trubble, exsposure in the army with measles
MYERS, Peter V., Gi-132-3; Pvt East Guf Squadron; Pursuls? & others?; 22 Jan 64 to 10 Jun 65; DeRay PO
MYERS, Pink, Gi-132-1; on same line, Emmons, Pink; 111th USCV; DeRay PO; rheumatism
MYERS, Samuel A., Sh-174-1; 1st Lt B Co 24th NY Vol; Spring 61 to 62 or 63; Memphis PO
MYERS, Thos. J., B-2-1; Sgt Maj F Co 41st TN; 10-10-61 to 5-5-65; Wartrace PO; CONF
MYERS, Wm. A., Gr-79-1; Viney widow of; I Co 26th TN Cav; 62 to 65; Ball Point PO; breast complaint, now dead
MYERS, William H., Ge-90-1; Pvt I Co 1st TN Cav; 7 Aug 62 to 5 Jun 65; Greeneville PO
MYMS, Joseph, H-54-6; Pvt US Col; Kings Point PO
MYNATT, Anna, K-176-2; widow of Sol US; Halls X Roads PO
MYNATT, Charles, K-161-3; Knoxville PO; shot in side
MYNATT, Gain C., Gr-78-2; Pvt B Co 1st TN Cav; 28 Mar 63 to 24 Apr 65; Spring House PO; this was marked out, might be CONF
MYNATT, Martin J. S., K-174-3; Sgt D Co 1st TN Inf; 5 Mar 62 to 9 Mar 65; Floyd PO
MYNATT, Prior L., K-176-3; Cpl D Co 9th TN Cav; May 63 to Mar 65; Mynott PO
MYNATT, Spencer, Un-254-3; Sara J. Ray formerly widow of; Pvt A Co; Meltibarger PO
MYNATT, Spencer C., K-176-3; Pvt B Co 9th TN Cav; 20 Jul 63 to 11 Sep 65; Mynott PO
MYNATT, William H., Ct-71-2; Pvt C Co 9th TN Cav; 13 Oct 63 to __; Larkeyton PO; lung disease taken while in army
MYNOTT, Oliver C., K-176-2; Pvt F Co 32nd KY Inf; 13 Dec 62 to 13 Aug 63; Halls X Roads PO; shot in the leg
MYNOTT, Sarah, K-176-1; widow of US Sol; Pvt G Co 2nd TN Cav; 15 Jun 61 to 14 May 65; Halls X Roads PO
MYRACK, John W., We-225-1; Pvt L Co 6th TN Cav; 28 Jun 62 to 26 Aug 65; Dresden PO; ulcer of the rectum 25 yrs
MYRACLE, Harry W., De-25-1; Pvt E Co 81st IL Inf; 15 Aug 62 to 1 Sep 65; Decaturville PO
MYRES, Archible, C-28-1; Capt F Co 6th TN Inf; 3-10-62 to 3-24-65; Fincastle PO; deafness in right ear
MYRES, Charles, Hn-69-1; Pvt L Co 12th KY Cav; 1 May 63 to 1 May 65; Paris PO; discharge lost
MYRES, Jacob, Mc-112-10; Pvt C Co 3rd TN Cav; 11-1-62 to 6-10-65; Athens PO
MYRES, James C., W-192-1; Pvt A Co; 6-17-63 to 65; Steppsville PO
MYRES, John, Cl-52-2; Pvt I Co 8th TN Inf; 7-1-63 to 6-1-65; Hypratia PO; killed in battle (believ this notation is an error)
MYRES, John A., Se-224-2; Pvt F Co 9th TN Cav; 24 Jul 63 to 11 Sep 65; Wears Valley PO; rheumatism
MYSINGER, Grange M., Ge-84-3; Mary J. widow of; Pvt M Co 1st TN Cav; 12 Nov 61 to 11 Nov 65 (3 yrs 4 mos 2 days); Bird Bridge PO; dis. with diarrea & cholory
MYSINGER, John K., Ge-90-2; Mary E. widow of; Pvt 1st TN Cav; Jun 63 to Aug 65; Greeneville PO; eye weakness
MYZEE, Henry, Wa-274-3; Pvt F Co 1st US Col Hvy Art; 23 Apr 64 to 31 Mar 66; Jonesboro PO; rheumatism and rupture
NABORS, Gus, Sh-146-3; US Sol; 3rd Civ Dist

NABORS, Warner, Sh-146-3; US Sol; 3rd Civ Dist
NABLES (sic), William, Je-136-1; Pvt B Co 1st US Hvy Art; 1 yr; Dandridge PO
NAGLE, ___, Sh-191-2; Margaret widow of: Memphis PO; records not seen
NAIL, William R., G-70-1; Sarah J. widow of; Pvt E Co 13th TN Cav; Dyer PO; killed
NAILER, Sarah, Sh-104-1; widow; Walker Ave, Memphis PO
NAILL, James B., K-183-2; Pvt Battery; Riverdale PO; CONF
NALL, John W., H-51-2(1); Pvt K Co 11th TN Inf; 8-21-61 to 7-15-65; Hill City PO
NANCE, Alexander, C-26-2; Pvt F Co 6th TN Inf; 3-10-62 to 4-7-65; Jacksboro PO
NANCE, Eliza, Mt-138-1; widow US Sol; Dist 7, New Providence PO
NANCE, Henry T., Je-141-1; Pvt K Co 34d TN Inf; 1 Feb 62 to Aug 65; New Market PO
NANCE, Joseph, G-51-1; US Sol; 3rd Civil Division
NANCE, Richard, K-171-2; Pvt B Co 1st US Col Art; Knoxville PO
NANCE, Sterling, colored, Gr-76-1; Hanna E. widow of; Cpl E Co 1st TN Cav; 2 Apr 61 to 31 Mar 66; Indian Ridge PO; cough and consumption, died Aug 3, 1866
NANCE, Wm. C., D-99-3; Pvt C Co 9th TN Cav; 63 to 10 Jul 65; State Penitentiary PO
NANCE, William P., Hw-132-1; Capt 1st TN Cav; 61 to Apr 65; Strahl PO; wounded in the leg
NARD, Henry, Fr-115-1; Cpl A Co 45th US Inf; __ to 65 (2 yrs 8 mos); Cowan PO
NARE, Isaac N., Ct-42-1; Pvt A Co 13th TN Cav; Watauga PO; neuralgia
NARMORE, N. H., Ro-208-3; Mary widow of; US Sol; 9th Civ Dist
NARRAMOD, Christopher C., Sq-164-1; Pvt E Co 6th TN Mtd Inf; 8-11-64 to 6-30-65; Dunlap PO
NARRAMORE, John F., H-51-2(1); Pvt D Co 2nd TN Inf; 2-18-62 to 8-9-65; Hill City PO
NASH, Allin D., Di-36-1; Pvt K Co 16th TN Inf; 62 to 10-27-64; Bellsburgh PO; CONF
NASH, Andrew J., Gr-74-2; Susan widow of; Pvt; May Spring 63; CONF
NASH, Edmon, Pu-144-3; Pvt D Co 8th TN Mtd Inf; 2-1-65 to 8-31-65; Hudgins PO; measles & fever fell in hips
NASH, George B., Mg-200-3; Sailor; Rugly 12 Dist
NASH, Jackson, C-29-1; Pvt E Co 9th TN Cav; 6-62 to 2-65; Fincastle PO; breast bursted by horse
NASH, James M., R-161-3; Nancy C. Brumagim former widow of; Cpl F Co 5th TN Inf; Dayton PO; shot at Resaca GA 5-14-64, died 7-7-__; Greenfield Hosp.
NASH, Joseph P., H-61-5; Pvt F Co 4th GA Cav; 7-23-63 to 4-9-65; Chattanooga PO; CONF
NASH, William J., Un-253-2; Pvt B Co 1st US Inf; 28 Jul 62 to 28 Jul 65; Sharps Chapel; stomach & liver disease, chills & fever
NATHAN, Zachery, Ru-241-2(1); America A. widow of; Pvt 24th TN Inf; 3 yrs; Murfreesboro PO
NATIONS, Doctor S., Se-230-1; Pvt G Co 6th TN Cav; 10 May 62 to 10 May 65; Pigeon Forge PO; chronic diarrhoea
NATIONS, Joseph M., Ov-135-2; 7th Civil Dist
NATIONS, William M., Mc-112-5; Pvt B Co 2nd TN Cav; 8-14-62 to 7-65; Athens PO; swelling limbs
NAVE, Abraham, Ct-43-3; Sgt A Co 13th TN Cav; 9-22-63 to 9-5-65; Carter Furnace PO; rheumatism and heart trouble
NAVE, Daniel S., Ct-42-3; 1st Lt A Co 13th TN Cav; 9-22-63 to 9-5-65; Watauga PO; lung disease
NAVE, Henry T., Wa-268-4; Johnson City PO
NAVE, John, H-56-7; Pvt F Co 6th TN Cav; 63 to 65; St. Elmo PO
NAVE, Mack, Ct-43-3; Pvt A Co 13th TN Cav; 9-22-63 to 9-5-65; Watauga PO; shot through right foot in battle
NAVE, Pleasant G., Ct-43-1; Pvt A Co 13th TN Cav; 9-22-63 to 9-5-65; Carter Furnace PO; broken arm by horse falling
NAVE, Richard L., Hw-131-1; Cpl D Co 13th TN Cav; 24 Sep 63 to 5 Sep 65; Bulls Gap PO
NAYLOR, Theodore F., O-130-1; Pvt A Co 1st KY Cav; May 63 to Nov 63; Union City PO

NEAL, Charles B., Li-165-1; Mary C. Damron formerly widow of; Pvt E Co 1st AL Cav; 3 Mar 63 to 14 Jun 63; Elora PO; died in hospital, Corinth, MS
NEAL, Edward, Sh-196-2; Edward Jordan alias, Pvt F Co 122nd KY Inf; 10-64 to 10-65; 454 Poplar St, Memphis PO
NEAL, Emanuel, Ge-89-4; Pvt B Co 1st TN Inf; 1 Apr 62 to 12 Oct 64; PO omitted
NEAL, Henry, D-57-4; Charity widow of; Flagbear. F Co 13th Reg Cav; Nashville PO; killed in battle
NEAL?, Hiram, K-183-3; Pvt B Co 8th TN Cav; High Point PO
NEAL, James, K-165-2; Darthula widow of; Pvt B Co. 6th TN Inf; Nov 63 to __; 72 Elucid Av, Knoxville PO
NEAL, James O., Pi-154-2; Pvt C Co 8th TN Cav; 5-63 to 5-65; Otto PO
NEAL, John, Pi-155-1; Pvt H Co 30th KY Mtd Inf; 11-20-63 to 4-18-65; Otto PO; hearing injured caused by measles
NEAL, John, Dk-32-4; Cpl A Co 5th TN Cav; 7-28-62 to 6-25-65; Liberty PO
NEAL, John T., O-139-2; US Sol; Civil Dist 12
NEAL, John T., Sr., O-139-1; Martha A. widow of; Pvt E Co 6th TN Cav; 13 Sep 65 to 26 Jul 65 (6 mos 17 days); Protemus PO
NEAL, John W., G-71-3; Pvt D Co 17th SC Inf; 12 Jun 62 to Apr 65; PO omitted; CONF
NEAL, Joshua, Dk-32-2; Pvt F Co 1st TN Mtd Inf; 2-27-64 to 3-20-65; Donelton PO
NEAL, Levi N., Dk-32-4; Pvt L Co 5th TN Cav; Liberty PO
NEAL, Link W., Dk-32-2; Temperance Hall PO
NEAL, Lowery L., Mo-124-2; Pvt C Co 1st Hvy Inf; 1-22-64 to 4-65; 4 Mile Branch PO; rheumatic affection & breast, disabled one half the time
NEAL, Rubin, Hm-107-3; Pvt B Co 8th TN Inf; 14 Feb 63 to Jun 65; Witts Foundry PO; gunshot wound in knee
NEAL, Sophia W., B-20-1; widow; Shelbyville PO
NEAL, Dr. (W. W.), La-117-4; Pvt I Co 3rd TN Inf; May 61 to Jul 65; 15th Dist
NEAL, William, Lk-113-1; Pvt G Co 148th IN Inf; 3 Feb 65 to 5 Sep 65; Dist No 6
NEALY, Jack, St-163-1; Pvt D Co 111th US Inf; 10 Jan 63 to 4 Apr 65; Covert PO
NEAS, Adam, Ge-85-3; Pvt F Co 4th TN Inf; 15 Apr 63 to 7 Jun 65; Syren Burg PO; hemmorrhoids & chronic dysentery 28 yrs
NEAS, Andrew, Ge-85-3; Pvt G Co 4th TN Inf; 15 May 63 to 2 Jun 65; Cavey Branch PO; hemorage of lungs
NEAS, John, Co-60-2; Pvt B Co 8th TN Inf; 7-26-63 to 6-30-65; Salem PO; rheumatism
NEAS, John S., Co-61-3(1); Pvt B Co 8th TN Inf; 14 Feb 63 to 30 Jun 65; Givens PO
NEAS, John T., Ge-85-2; Pvt G Co 4th TN Inf; Siren Burg PO; cronic rheumatism
NEAS, Powell, Ge-85-3; Pvt B Co 8th TN Inf; 20 Jun 63 to 30 Jun 65; Syren Burg PO; running tumor of head
NEAS, Ruben, Ge-85-3; Pvt F Co 4th TN Inf; 15 Apr 63 to 3 Aug 65; Syren Burg PO; heart disease & pain in rt. side & liver disease
NEEDHAM, Frank C., Cu-17-1; Pvt A Co 1st KY Drag (Dragoons?); 8-7-62 to 7-18-65; Crossville PO
NEEDHAM, Henry, L-101-2; alias Henry Ivey; 1st Boy (colored soldier) 43rd MO?; 13 Sep 63 to 29 May 65; Henning PO; disable at present, fell from his horse, total fracture of knee?
NEEDHAM, John, Dy-32-1; US Sol; Trimble PO
NEEL, Benjamin, F-44-4; Pvt B Co 59th __; 63 to 64; 11th Civil Dist
NEEL, J. V., F-44-4; Sarah R. widow of; Pvt B Co 13th TN; May 62 to May 65; 11th Civil Dist; CONF
NEELEY, Henery, Sh-155-1; Pvt C Co 3rd TN Inf; 3 yrs; Germantown PO
NEELEY, James P., O-134-2; Pvt E Co 6th 10SC Cav; 18 Oct 64 to 27 Aug 65; Hornbeak PO
NEELEY, Thomas A., Me-88-3; Sgt G Co 3rd TN Cav; 7-12-63 to 8-8-65; Brittsville PO; vacination
NEELY, J. Mat., Ca-16-1; 1st Lt C Co 7th TN Cav; 6 Jul 63 to 9 Aug 65; Huntington PO; thrown from horse, paralyzed, 1st enlisted 16 Feb 62
NEELY, James W., B-12-1; Cpl F Co 1st AL Vidette Cav; 3-21-64 to 6-16-64; Bedford PO
NEELY, John, Sh-149-2; Pvt T Co (sic) 61st US Inf; Aug 63 to Dec 65; Memphis PO
NEELY, John H., B-12-1; Pvt C Co 4th TN Mtd Inf; 9-64 to 8-25-65; Bedford PO; hearing affected, date of enlistment was blotted out on discharge
NEELY, Samuell, Gi-122-7; Frances widow of; Sgt H Co 13th TN Inf; 10 Dec 62 to Jul 64; Prospect Sta PO; sickened and died in prison at Mobile AL
NEELY, William, Jo-184-1; Sarah J. widow of; Pvt E Co 13th TN Cav; Nov 62 to 65; Laurel Bloomery PO; bronchitis
NEES, Wm. J., D-78-1; 2nd Lt H Co 86th IA Inf; Sep 62 to Jul 63; Nashville PO
NEESE, Alford, Hn-82-1; Sgt K Co 2nd TN Mtd Inf; 2-14-64 to 6-27-65; Buchanan PO; hart disease & rheumatism
NEGLEY, Jacob C. P., Sh-145-3; 1st Lt A Co IN Cav-- 15 Jun 62 to Nov 63; 1st Lt E Co 2nd Reg US Vets Bat--Nov 63 to 20 May 64; Millington PO; camp diahhea & bronchitus, 1st Capt Stretch, Col Morgan 2B VR C
NEIGHBORS, James A., Mc-111-2; alias James A. Hutson; Cpl C Co 10th TN Cav; 1-8-64 to 8-1-65; Mortimer PO
NEIGHBORS, William B., Pu-146-2; Pvt B Co 1st TN Mtd Inf Vol; Pine Fork PO
NEIL, George W., Mg-200-3; Pvt was not at home, could not get record; Stowers PO
NEILL, Chauncy, E. L., Mc-112-1; Mary A. E. former widow of; Orderly Sgt F Co 4th TN Cav; 4-61 to died 4-15-65; Athens PO; died in service 4-15-65
NEILL, Mary J., col, Ms-172-1; widow of Pvt Corps 24 Capt Stam; 12 Jan 64 to 7 Mar 65; Farmington PO
NEILLS, James, K-156-3; Pvt A Co 42nd US Inf; 27 Patterson St, Knoxville PO
NEILZ, David, B-5-1; Pvt D Co 12th US Col Inf; 9-8-63 to 1-16-66; Fosterville PO; wound in finger, afflicted with rheumatism
NEISLER, Thomas J., He-64-1; Mary widow of; Pvt E Co 11th IL; 15 Mar 62 to 14 Mar 65; PO omitted
NELISON, John J., Sh-183-1; Pvt C Co IL; __ to 65; Memphis PO; lost left eye & frost bite
NELLUM, William, Sh-158-5(1); Pvt G Co 11th US Hvy Art; 11 Feb 63 to 12 Jan 66; Memphis PO; discharge at close of the war with discharge
NELMS, J. D., Cl-54-3(1); Pvt; __ to 65; Tazewell PO; CONF
NELMS, John W., Hm-106-2; Pvt F Co 61st TN Inf; 61 to __; Morristown PO: CONF
NELMS, Stephen J., F-40-1; Pvt B Co 16th VA Inf; 4 Mar 62 to 9 Apr 65; Hickory Wythe PO; CONF
NELSEN, John, Wa-263-5; Frances E. widow of; May Day PO
NELSON, Adam, Me-93-2; Pvt B Co 11th TN Cav; 7-15-63 to 9-11-65; Pin Hook Ldg PO; rheumatism, injury to eyes
NELSON, Alexander, Gu-45-2; Pvt J Co 7th OH Cav; 62 to 65 (3 yrs 7 mos); Beersheba Springs PO
NELSON, Alexander M., Bo-12-1; Mary C widow of; Pvt L Co 2nd TN Cav; Houk PO; for further information cant get
NELSON, Anderson, Gi-123-1; Pvt F Co 110th TN Col Inf; 62 to 65; Bethel PO
NELSON, Ben, Gi-127-1; Ada widow of; Sgt B Co 110th TN USC Inf; Pulaski PO
NELSON, Carl, H-76-1; Mary widow of; Pvt A Co 8th OH Cav; Chattanooga PO
NELSON, Charles, U-246-2; Barbara E. widow of; Pvt B Co 12th TN Cav; 30 Nov 62 to 24 Oct 65; Limonite PO
NELSON, Coalman, K-154-3; Knoxville PO
NELSON, Damuel, Gi-122-3; Pvt K Co 110th TN Inf; 61 to 63; Prospect Sta. PO; prison 8 months; CONF
NELSON, Daniel, Un-256-1; Pvt D Co 1st TN Inf; 8 Aug 61 to 17 Sep 64; Starkvale PO
NELSON, Daniell F., Dy-27-1; Pvt D Co 21st TN Cav; 4-14-62 to 4-20-64; Ro Ellen PO; ruptured on saddle, work--disagreeable
NELSON, David M., K-166-1; Sue H. widow of; Capt A Co 10th TN Cav; 62 to Jul 65; Knoxville PO

NELSON, Franklin, We-225-3(2); Pvt A Co 15th TN Inf; 62 to 65; Dresden PO; shot in arm
NELSON, G. W., Me-93-2; Pvt D Co 7th TN Mtd Inf; 10-9-64 to 7-27-65; 7th Civil Dist; scout 4 yrs service
NELSON, G. W., K-186-1; Pvt; Jun 62 to 13 Jun 65; Chumlea PO
NELSON, Gabriel, Un-259-1; Pvt D Co 1st TN Inf; 9 Aug 61 to 17 Sep 64; Rhodelia PO; lung & bronchitis, measles
NELSON, Geo. W., H-60-1; Pvt C Co 76th IL Inf; 8-7-62 to 8-7-65; Chattanooga PO
NELSON, Green, Sh-158-3; alias Green, Nelson; Pvt G Co 49th Col Inf; Jan 63 to May 65; Memphis PO
NELSON, Henderson L., Un-258-3; Pvt C Co 1st US? Vol; 9 Aug 61 to 17 Sep 64; Longhollow PO
NELSON, Henry F., Ge-83-2; Pvt E Co 4th TN Inf; Apr 63 to 2 Aug 65; Henshaw PO; side & eyes
NELSON, Hermen, Ma-125-1; Adoline Brown widow; Pvt K Co 18th IL Inf; Aug 62 to 65; Jackson PO; died in army
NELSON, Hezekiah M., La-113-2; Pvt C Co 14th IA Inf; 20 Sep 64 to 13 May 65; Lawrenceburg PO
NELSON, Hiram?, D-54-1; Henrietta widow of; Pvt H Co 12th US Col Inf; 12 Aug 63 to 16 Aug 66; Nashville PO
NELSON, Ira G., Ge-87-3; Pvt G Co 4th TN Inf; 1 Mar 65 to 1 Aug 65; Little Chucky PO; respiratory organs
NELSON, Isaac, K-178-2; Rhody C. widow of; Pvt G Co 1st Hvy Art; 21 May 64 to 31 Nov 65; Scarbrough PO
NELSON, J. V., Gi-122-7; 2nd Sgt G Co 9th Al Cav; Sep 61 to 4 May 65; Pettisville, AL; CONF
NELSON, James, Un-256-1; Pvt C Co 1st TN Inf; 9 Aug 61 to 17 Sep 64; Starkvale PO; disease of eyes & scurvy
NELSON, James, Hm-103-3; Pvt I Co 40th KY Hvy Art; 13 Mar 62 to 13 Mar 65; Morristown PO
NELSON, James F., Mu-211-1; Scout for 24th Army Corpse; 17 Dec 62 to Aug 63; Lava? PO
NELSON, Jennie, K-156-5; widow; 94 Kennedy St, Knoxville
NELSON, Jim, Gi-123-2; Pvt D Co TN Inf (Col); Aspen Hill PO; wounded in uper lip & jaw, gun shot
NELSON, John, Black, Lk-113-1; Pvt B Co 11th Inf MO; 62 to 65; 4th Civil Dist
NELSON, John, K-166-3; Pvt M Co 8th TN Cav; 25 Jan 64 to 11 Sep 65; Knoxville PO
NELSON, John C., R-162-1; Capt I Co 11th TN Cav; 10-63 to 10-1-64; Dayton PO; rheumatism and neuralgia
NELSON, John H., A-6-6(4); Pvt G Co 1st TN Inf; 8-9-61 to 9-17-64; Olivers PO
NELSON, John R., K-156-3; 3rd Sgt 1st TN Fielding Art; Burmis Battery; 25 Jun 61 to 15 Dec 62; 119 E. Cumberland St, Knoxville PO; CONF
NELSON, John S., Ro-206-3; Pvt I Co; 64 to 65; Emory Gap PO
NELSON, John S., Su-240-1; Pvt K Co 2nd US Inf; 13 Oct 64 to 7 Nov 65; Carnes Bottom PO; diarea & piles
NELSON, John W., K-165-1; Pvt 10th TN; Knoxville PO
NELSON, Jones, Cf-35-1; Pvt A Co 1st TN Inf; Tullahoma PO; CONF
NELSON, Joseph M., K-180-2; Margarett E. widow of; Pvt; Bearden PO
NELSON, Lee, K-176-3; Pvt G Co 7th TN Inf; 25 May 62 to 14 Sep 65; Halls X Roads PO
NELSON, Louis, D-77-1; Pvt F Co 111th US Inf; Dec 63 to __; Nashville PO; captured by Forrest, and imprisoned 6 mos at Mobile
NELSON, Luke, Sh-204-2; Idlett Ave, Memphis PO
NELSON, Martin, Un-256-1; Pvt C Co 1st TN Inf; 9 Aug 61 to 17 Sep 64; Starkvale PO; neuragia in head and neck and smotheren at heart
NELSON, Prior L., K-175-2; Pvt D Co 1st TN Inf; 22 Dec 61 to 22 Dec 64; Snoterly PO
NELSON, Robbert C., K-184-1; Pvt I Co 7th TN Inf; 8 Nov 64 to 19 Jun 65; Riverdale PO
NELSON, Robert, La-111-2; Pvt D Co 9th TN Cav; 2-62 to 11-62; PO omitted; CONF
NELSON, Samuel, Sh-145-4; US Sol; 3rd Civ Dist
NELSON, Thomas A., Sn-225-1; Goodlettsville PO (Davidson Co); failed to see him and no

NELSON, Thomas A., Sn-255-1; Goodlettsville PO (Davidson Co); failed to see him and no information cold be had of him as a soldier
NELSON, William, A-2-3; alias Joseph Whalen; Mary A. Beets formerly widow of; 1st TN Inf; Hinds Creek PO; deserted by first husband, last named, now deceased
NELSON, William H., Ct-37-1; Capt L Co 5th TN Cav; 6-2-62 to 8-14-65; Hopson PO; cripple, suffering 25 yrs
NELSON, William W., Cl-47-1; Pvt C Co 47th KY Inf; 8-14-63 to 12-26-64; Speedwell PO
NELSOR, Linda, (see Hopper, James)
NESBETT, Lee A., D-43-2; Sol widow; McGavach St, Nashville PO
NESBIT, William L., Hm-106-2; Sgt D Co 28th TN Inf; Sep 62 to Aug 63; Morristown PO
NESBITT, Curtis, Cr-20-2; Lucky widow of; Pvt; Hollow Rock PO
NESBITT, Mathew J. P., H-57-3; Pvt E Co 44th US Inf; 62 to 65; Orchard Knob PO
NESBITT, William A. J., Di-40-2; widow of; Pvt H Co 3rd US; 7-17-63 to 64; Omega PO (Houston Co)
NESBY, Sarah (see O'Keef, John)
NETHERLAND, Joseph, Hw-123-2; Cpl F Co US Cav; 4 May 63 to 31 Mar 66; Rotherwood PO
NETHERLY, Jordan, Jo-151-2; Mary widow of; Pvt E Co 13th TN Cav; 22 Sep 63 to 5 Sep 65; Vaughtsville PO; brain fever
NETHERTON, Elijah, J-77-2; Martha widow of; Pvt C Co; Gainesboro PO; measles
NETHERTON, George, Co-61-5(2); Martha widow of; Pvt; Bridgeport PO; wounded, shot in back; CONF
NEUCRUM, George W., O-140-2; 13th Civil Dist
NEUTON, Peter J., Co-69-6(1); Pvt H Co 1st DC Inf; 61 to Jun 65 (5 yrs); Rankin PO; none, dont remember dates, conscripted & was captured
NEVELS, Ike, Sh-146-2; Pvt D Co 59th __; Woodstock PO
NEVES, Godfrey, Gu-48-4(1); Pvt H Co 10th TN Cav; 63 to 64; Chattanooga PO
NEVIL, Virgil, L-101-1; Pvt D Co 1st TN C Inf; 64 to 65; Henning PO; shot left leg & buttox, discharge lost
NEVILL, Chas., (see Shelton, Charles)
NEVINS, James, D-96-1; Pvt B Co 40th US Col Inf; 29 Apr 64 to 25 Apr 66; Nashville PO; invalid with sore eyes, his sight is very bad
NEW, John, Dk-39-6(2); Blacksmith B Co 5th TN Cav; 12-21-64 to 8-24-65; Laurel Hill PO
NEWBERN, George T., D-72-2; Sarah widow of; Pvt B Co 19th TN; 25 Apr 61 to 21 Jun 63; Nashville PO; CONF
NEWBERN, William W., F-40-2; Maj TN Cav; Mar 62 to 20 May 65; Oakland PO; CONF
NEWBERRY, John, K-179-2; Ruth M. widow of; Pvt A Co 3rd TN Inf; 10 Feb 62 to 23 Feb 65; Virtue PO
NEWBERRY, Philip C., Mc-112-6; Pvt A Co 5th TN Cav; 6-9-61 to 8-1-65; Athens PO
NEWBERRY, Philip H., Hw-133-1; PO omitted; CONF
NEWBERY, Silas, Ge-84-4; Sarah widow of; Pvt 4th TN Inf; Greenville PO; dis. eyes and piles
NEWBILL, William G., Cr-21-1; Pvt I Co 7th TN Cav; 1 Dec 64 to 15 Dec 65; Huntingdon PO
NEWBILLE, William, Gi-128-2; Pvt K Co 110th TN Inf; 63 to 65; this Wm. N. is a US Sold; Pulaski PO
NEWBORN, James C., F-44-3; Pvt B Co 13th TN; 28 May 61 to Jun 61; PO omitted; CONF
NEWBURRY, Devid C., Se-222-1; Cpl I Co 2nd TN Cav; 22 Sep 62 to 14 Jul 65; Harrisburg PO; rumatism, resulting heart diseas
NEWBURRY, Richard, Lo-192-2; Pvt; Morganton PO
NEWBURRY, Stephen, Lo-192-2; Sarrah M. widow of; Pvt A Co 3rd TN; Feb 62 to Feb 65; Cloyds Creek PO; rheumatism & neuralgia
NEWBURY, Isaac N., Ge-102-2; Pvt B Co 13th TN Cav; 25 Sep 63 to 5 Sep 65; Whip PO; fever, now catarrh and rheumatism
NEWBURY, Louis C. S., Ov-137-2; Pvt G Co 5th KY Cav; 12-12-61 to 6-27-64; West Fork PO; lung, kidney & bladder & biles; Sgt F Co 7th V.R.C.; 6-20-64 to 11-15-65; reenlisted veteran
NEWBY, Elisha, R-159-2; Pvt G Co 6th TN Mtd Inf; 2-20-65 to 6-30-65; Spring City PO
NEWCOM, James L., K-165-2; Pvt B Co 6th TN Inf; 18 Apr 62 to May 65; 22 Washington St, Knoxville PO

NEWCOMB, Elliott L., Ro-202-6; Sgt I Co 2nd TN Cav; 22 Sep 62 to 14 Jun 65; Kingston PO; dyspepsia & piles
NEWELL, Gilbert M., Cf-39-1; Pvt C Co 101st OH Inf; 7 Aug 62 to 12 Jun 65; Prairie Plains PO; shott once in right hip & twice in left thigh (drawing $8.00 per month pension)
NEWELL, James G., Me-88-2; Pvt A Co 8th TN Inf; 3-1-62 to 3-5-65; Georgetown PO; prisner 1 day
NEWELL, John B., Hm-109-8; Pvt D Co 1st TN Art; 63 to 65; PO omitted
NEWELL, John H., Sh-200-1; 1-1-65 to 1-1-68; 296 Trent St, Memphis PO
NEWELL, Wesley, Col, Mt-139-1; Pvt 16th US; Woodlawn PO
NEWHOUSE, Geo. H., Ho-95-1; Cpl D Co 10th TN Inf; 10 Apr 62 to 16 Jun 65; Danvill PO; discharged as surgeon
NEWLAND, Cannon, Jo-148-1; Pvt G Co 13th TN Cav; 24 Sep 63 to 12 Jun 65; Head of Laurel PO; heart disease & rheumatis
NEWMAN, B. S., De-22-3; Capt B Co 51st TN Inf; 1 Sep 61 to 1 Sep 64; Dunbar PO; shot in right foot; CONF
NEWMAN, Ferdinand, Rb-226-1; Pvt K Co 192nd OH Inf; 21 Feb 65 to 1 Sep 65; Greenbrier PO
NEWMAN, Gibeon, Je-143-1; Mary A. wife of; Mount Horeb PO; discharge not obtainable
NEWMAN, Hue, K-184-3; Sarah wife of; Pvt K Co 2nd TN Inf; 13 Dec 61 to 15 Dec 64; Thorn Grove PO
NEWMAN, Jacob A., Se-226-6; Pvt H Co 68th __; 44th IN Inf; Jan 63 to Jun 65; Straw Plains PO (Jefferson Co)
NEWMAN, James, Je-144-1; Catheran widow of; Pvt; Talbotts PO
NEWMAN, John M., K-156-2; Pvt B Co 10th TN Cav; 7 Lithgoe St, Knoxville PO; CONF
NEWMAN, John N., K-156-6; B Co 9th TN; Knoxville PO
NEWMAN, Joseph, Wy-174-1; Pvt B Co OH; 12-17-64 to 11-9-65; Stout PO
NEWMAN, Larkin C., Mo-125-1; Pvt G Co 3rd TN Mtd Inf; 8-9-64 to 11-30-64; Mt. Vernon PO
NEWMAN, Moses S., Di-32-1; Pvt G Co 3rd MI Inf; 1-5-64 to 7-5-65; Spencers Mill PO
NEWMAN, Robert E., Je-143-3; 2nd Lt C Co 9th TN Cav; 10 Aug 63 to 11 Sep 65; Mossy Creek PO; hip & back crippled caused by horse falling
NEWMAN, Samuel H., H-50-4; Pvt C Co 5th R TN Inf; 2-25-61 to 4-8-65; Soddy PO; sore eyes
NEWMAN, Samuel T., Hd-52-1; Mandy C. widow of; Pvt E Co 6th TN; 10 Jan 62 to 5 Jan 64; Adamsville PO; measles proved fatal
NEWMAN, Taylor, Mc-109-2; Pvt B Co 7th TN Inf; 10-12-64 to 7-27-65; Sewee PO (Meigs Co)
NEWMAN, William, Je-137-1; Pvt F Co 9th TN Cav; 2 Sep 63 to 13 Sep 65; Hickory Ridge PO
NEWPORT, Ezekiel, S-213-1; Pvt C Co 7th TN Inf; Jul 62 to __; PO omitted; chronic diarrhea & rheumatism, not mustered out, left behind sick
NEWPORT, Fealing, S-218-1; Pvt H Co 9th TN Cav; 62 to 65; Huntsville PO; died from shott of brest, mem. 7th TN Inf Co E
NEWPORT, Jas. M., S-218-3; Pvt H Co 12th KY Inf; 3 Oct 61 to Jul 65; Huntsville PO; diseases of respitory organs & complication
NEWPORT, Phenix, S-214-2; Pvt F Co 7th TN Inf; Glenmary PO; cant tell date of disch.
NEWPORT, Richard, S-214-4; Anna widow of; Pvt; Robbins PO
NEWPORT, William Sr., S-218-1; Pvt H Co 9th IN Cav; 30 Jul 62 to 5 Jul 65; Huntsville PO; chronick dirhea & liver
NEWPORT, William A., S-213-1; Cpl E Co 11th TN Cav; 6 Apr 65 to 6 Apr 65; Huntsville PO; piles & rheumatism
NEWSOM, Alfred K., G-71-2; Flag bearer D Co 3rd NC Inf; 27 May 61 to 27 May 65; Edmonds PO; crippled by shot in foot; CONF
NEWSOM, Hubbard, D-86-1; Pvt I Co US Col Inf; 12 Sep 63 to 28 Feb 66; PO omitted
NEWSOM, Jefferson, D-93-1; Pvt C Co 12th TN Inf; 16 Jan 64 to 16 Jan 66; Belleview PO
NEWSOM, Jerry, Hy-76-1; 3rd Artilery G Co Batery Run?; 2 yrs 8 mos; Stanton Depot PO
NEWSOM, John W., F-40-1; Pvt B Co 15th TN Inf; 20 Jul 63 to 10 May 65; Oakland PO; CONF

NEWSOM, Joseph, De-25-1; Pvt E Co 6th TN Cav; 18 Sep 62 to 7 Sep 64; Decaturville PO
NEWSOME, J., D-63-1; Helen widow; Nashville PO
NEWSON, Eliza, Ru-241-1; widow; Murfreesboro PO
NEWSON, Louiza, (see Abston, Byrd)
NEWSON, Frank, Ro-210-7; Pvt H Co 12th OH Cav; 5 Nov 63 to 22 Nov 65; Rockwood PO
NEWSON, Til, Sq-164-4(1); Pvt; Brock PO
NEWTON, Henry, Bo-11-1; Pvt L Co 1st US Heavy Istil?; 9-4-65 to 3-31-66; Geen Back PO
NEWTON, Isaac B., Br-13-4; Sgt E Co 4th TN Cav-- 10-10-62 to 10-11-64; 1st Lt B Co 5th TN Mtd Inf--9-23-64 to 7-13-65; Cleveland PO
NEWTON, John, F-37-1; Violet widow of; Pvt; Somerville PO; papers in care of Shaw, Somerville, TN
NEWTON, John, Sn-253-1; Pvt H Co 4th IA Cav; 8-19-62 to 6-29-65; PO omitted
NEWTON, William H., La-111-1; Pvt; Pleasant Point PO; CONF
NEWTON, William T., We-231-1; Clarinda widow of; Pvt D Co 8th IL Inf; PO omitted
NICE, John, Ge-96-4; Pvt A Co 3rd NC Inf; 62 to 65 (1 yr 11 mos); Chucky City PO; dispepsia & mumps
NICELY, Anderson, Gr-82-2; Sarah widow of; Pvt H Co 8th TN Cav; 62 to __; PO omitted; CONF
NICELY, Jacob J., K-185-2; Lt B Co 3rd TN Cav; 63 to 65; Mascott PO; deafness
NICELY, James R., Hw-132-1; Pvt D Co 31th TN Cav; Feb 62 to 28 Aug 65; Strahl PO; CONF
NICELY, John W., Un-257-2; Pvt I Co 1st TN Cav; 62 to 65; Little Barren PO; gun shot & lung disease; CONF
NICHASON, William, Sh-146-4; US Sol; 3rd Civil Dist
NICHELSON, J. W., W-194-1; Lt D Co 4th TN Cav; 12-17-62 to 12-25-63; Davenport PO
NICHOL, Alexander M., Ro-204-3; Pvt F Co 152nd IL Inf; Feb 65 to Sep 65; Elverton PO; piles
NICHOL, John G., Wi-278-1; Pvt 3rd Col Cav; 5 mos; Franklin PO; ankle broken, papers destroyed by fire, does not know date of muster & c
NICHOLAS, James, Fe-42-1; Pvt H Co 60th NY (inf?); 9-10-61 to 7-31-65; Jamestown PO
NICHOLAS, Joseph G., B-6-1; Pvt C Co 5th TN Cav; 7-20-62 to 1-27-65; Havan PO
NICHOLAS, Pinkney G., De-22-2; Pvt C Co 6th TN Cav; 1 Sep 65 to 1 Apr 65; Dunbar PO; CONF
NICHOLAS, Sallie, Hn-77-1; Pvt K Co IN Inf; Po omitted
NICHOLAS, Vanide?, K-165-4; Pvt F Co 118th OH Inf; 12 Aug 62 to 24 Jun 65; Knoxville PO
NICHOLAS, Bennett A., Mu-210-4; Sgt C Co 9th TN Cav; 62 to 65; Carters Creek PO; CONF
NICHOLAS, Cristopher C., Br-11-1; Pvt C Co 5th TN US; 64 to 65; Chatala PO
NICHOLS, George W., Br-6-4; Sol US; not mustered; 1st Civil Dist
NICHOLS, Hiram, Se-228-2(3); Mary A. widow of; Pvt B Co 6th TN Inf; 8 Mar 62 to __ (3 yrs); Cusick's X Roads; made a good soldier
NICHOLS, Isaac, Wy-173-2; Pvt A Co 1st AL Cav; Houston PO; discharge lost
NICHOLS, James B., K-173-3; Caswell PO
NICHOLS, James R., Hn-78-1; Cpl K Co 6th US Inf; 3-65 to 10-11-66; Cottage Grove PO
NICHOLS, Jesse P., Ha-117-2; 2nd D Sgt C Co 8th TN Inf; Dec 62 to Aug 65; Kyle's Ford PO; brochitis & c
NICHOLS, John, Ha-117-1; Pvt E Co 8th TN Cav; 23 Sep 64 to 11 Sep 65; Kyle's Ford PO; measles
NICHOLS, John C., Br-10-2; Pvt I Co 4th MI Cav; 8-7-62 to 7-4-65; Cleveland PO
NICHOLS, John H., Mg-196-1; Pvt K Co 1st TN Inf; 9 Aug 61 to 17 Sep 65; Oliver Springs PO; ruptured
NICHOLS, Josiah, Ha-117-2; Cpl A Co 1st TN Cav; 20 Mar 62 to 4 Apr 65; Kyle's Ford PO; bronchitis, rheumatism, deafness & eyes
NICHOLS, Mary A., Se-228-5; widow Sol; 10th Dist
NICHOLS, Robert W., Ro-202-5; Pvt I & B? 1st TN Inf; 11 Jul 63 to 3 Aug 64; Cave Creek PO; chronic bronchitis & heart trouble
NICHOLS, Thomas, Sn-255-1; Worsham PO; failed to see him and no information could had of him as a soldier

235

NICHOLS, William B., Hw-119-1; Pvt G Co 4th TN Inf; 19 Jan 63 to 19 May 65; Lee Valley PO; shot
NICHOLSON, Isaac, Po-148-1; Sgt A Co 5th TN Mtd Inf; 9-10-64 to 6-20-65; Cog Hill PO
NICHOLSON, John, Sh-201-2; Narcissa N. widow of; Pvt I Co 55th US Col Vol; 10 Aug 63 to 10 Sep 65; Memphis PO
NICHOLSON, Leander N., Po-152-1; 1st Sgt A Co 5th TN Mtd Inf; 9-1-64 to 6-26-65; Ducktown PO
NICHOLSON, Samuel M., Po-152-1; Pvt A Co 5th TN Mtd Inf; 9-1-64 to 6-26-65; Ducktown PO
NICK, James, K-165-3; Pvt I Co 2nd TN Inf; 13 Feb 62 to 13 Feb 65; 9 Chamberlin St, Knoxville PO
NICKELS, Elizabeth F. (see Correll, George)
NICKELS, Joel M., Wa-274-2; Joseph M. Church alias; Pvt M Co 8th TN Cav; 15 Sep 63 to 11 Sep 65; Jonesboro PO
NICKELS, John W., Ge-83-2; Pvt M Co 8th TN Cav; 62 to Aug 66; Henshaw PO; sinal pas
NICKLE, William H., K-171-4(3); Cpl D Co 6th TN Inf; 18 Apr 62 to 27 Apr 65; Craigville PO; bronchitis & rheumatism
NICKLES, Dora (see Davis, Anten)
NICKLES, Norman, Bo-21-3; Pvt A Co 3rd TN Inf; 2-10-62 to 2-22-65; Ellijay PO
NICKLES, William, Wa-274-4; Rachel Brown formerly widow of; Jonesboro PO
NICKLESON, Hunter, K-171-3(2); Maj Adjt Gen Burfort Div; Apr 61 to 4 May 65; Knoxville PO; CONF
NICKLIN, John B., H-62-1; Pvt K Co 12th PA Inf & 100th PA Inf; 2-26-64 to 7-24-66; 516 Poplar, Chattanooga PO
NICKOLS, Alfred, Hw-132-4; Pvt D Co 1st TN Cav; 15 Apr 62 to 15 Apr 65; Otes PO; liver complaint
NICKS, George (see Towell, John)
NIECE, John, Cf-39-1; Pvt M Co 2nd PA Cav; 3 Oct 61 to 13 Jul 65; Tullahoma PO; rheumatis & chronic diarrhoea
NIECE, William, Ro-201-3(1); Charity widow of; Pvt F Co 1st TN Inf; 9 Aug 61 to 17 Sep 64; Kingston PO
NIGHT, Peater, L-100-2; Pvt B Co 59th US Col Inf; 62 to 64; Ripley PO; rumatism & phthisic
NIGHT, Susan, Hm-109-5; widow USS; PO omitted
NILLIONS, Peter, Fr-115-1; Pvt G Co 2nd US Inf; 7-18-64 to 9-27-65; Decherd PO
NILSON, Smith, Tr-269-2; Pvt G Co 16th TN Inf; Jan 63 to Nov 65; Caruthers PO
NIMBY, Alexander, Gu-45-2; Elisabeth widow of; Pvt E Co 1st TN Cav Vidette; 63 to 64 (8 mos); Altamont PO
NIPPER, Ambrose, D-45-3; Malissa widow of; Pvt H Co 6th TN Cav; 9-8-62 to 7-26-65; Nashville PO
NIPPER, James, H-50-4; Pvt I Co 1st R TN Mtd Inf; 11-10-64 to 7-22-65; Soddy PO
NIPPER, William P., Ro-207-2; Martha widow of; Pvt C Co 3rd TN Cav; 11 Jun 63 to 3 Aug 65; Patties Gap PO; hurt by a horse running over him
NISH, James, Sh-158-4; Pvt D Co 10th TN Inf; Apr 62 to Jun 65; Memphis PO; shot in left leg, in 1864, discharge papers in hands of Movers & Deadrick
NISLEY, Alfred, Co-63-4; Lt D Co 9th TN Cav; 11 Oct 63 to 11 Jun 65; Newport PO; chronic diareah
NITZSCHKE, Lewis F., Mg-200-1; Emily; Sgt F Co 1st TN Inf; 10 Aug 61 to 24 May 64; Kismet PO; his right arm shot off
NIX, John W., G-54-1; Pvt E Co 10th TN Inf; 62 to 65; Trenton PO
NIX, John W., G-56-1; Trenton PO
NIXON, Edward S., H-53-1; Capt F Co 14th MI Inf; 11-23-61 to 1-14-65; Chattanooga PO
NIXON, George, Sm-166-1; Pvt; 63 to 65; Carthage PO
NIXON, Wallace, L-108-1; Pvt I Co 3rd US Art; 63 to 64; Glimpville PO
NIXON, William, Mc-112-9; Pvt K Co 3rd OH Inf; 4-61 to 6-64; Athens PO
NIXON, William, H-51-6; Pvt B Co 4th US Cav; 11-28-63 to 11-28-66; Albion View PO
NOALS, William, Sh-179-1(2); Mary Sanders widow of; Pvt A Co 11th US Inf; 6-12-63 to 1-12-66; Memphis PO

NOBLE, Charles B., H-53-4; Martha A. widow of; Pvt 12th IL Inf; 63 to 6-65; Ridgedale PO
NOBLES, Peter, Ma-128-2; Cook; 2 yrs 9 mos; Jackson PO; did not know name of Co
NOBLIN, William, Ms-172-1; Pvt 5th TN Cav; 63 to 64; Farmington PO
NOE, David C., Sh-153-2; Pvt A Co 9th TN Cav; 1 Sep 63 to 11 Sep 65; Forest Hill PO
NOE, Eli, Gr-78-2; Pvt F Co 11th NC Inf; 10 May 62 to 10 Feb 65; Spring House PO (this was marked out, might be CONF)
NOE, Joseph A., Gr-75-2; Pvt H Co 1st TN Cav; Apr 62 to 8 Apr 65; Tampico PO; lungs, bronchitis of throat, heart trouble and sight and hearing
NOE, Thomas, Gr-74-1; Pvt H Co 1st TN; Nov 20 62 to Jn 15 65 (2 yrs 7 mos); McEwen PO; piles
NOEL, James K. R., Wa-276-1; Cpl H Co 12th KY Cav; Aug 24 63 to Nov 24 64; Limestone PO
NOKES, Thomas, Ca-25-1; US Sol; 10th Dist
NOLAN, James N., Hu-106-2; 2nd Lt 1st KS Batt; Mar 62 to Mar 65; Waverly PO
NOLAN, Jessie, Hu-103-2; Pvt C Co 10th TN Inf; 10 Aug 63 to 30 May 64; PO omitted
NOLEN, Allen T., Ch-12-1; Cpl C Co 6th TN Cav; 9-18-62 to 7-26-65; Wild Goose PO
NOLEN, Henry W., Wh-185-1; Pvt L Co 4th TN Mtd Inf; 2-15-65 to 8-25-65; Cassville PO
NOLEN, James K., St-164-1; Cpl C Co 14th KY Inf; Jul 4 63 to Sep 25 65; Moltke PO
NOLEN, Preston, St-164-1; Cpl M Co 6th KY Cav; Aug 18 62 to Jul 14 65; Moltke PO
NOLEN, Thomas, Col, Mo-123-2; Pvt A Co 42nd Col Inf; 3-10-64 to 2-23-66; Jalapa PO
NOLIN, Bedford, Ms-181-1; Pvt B Co 11th TN Inf; 6-30-63 to 4-12-65; Lewisburg PO
NOLIN, Benjamin, Co-66-3(1); Pvt C Co 8th TN Inf; 20 Dec 62 to 26 May 65; Newport PO
NOLLEN, Benjamin, Sm-172-4; Pvt C Co 5th TN Cav; 1-24-62 to ___; Hickman PO; now has but one leg
NOLLEN, James, Sm-172-3(1); Pvt G Co 4th TN Inf; 11-1-64 to 8-15-65; Gordonsville PO
NOLLEN, Thomas B., Sm-172-3(1); Pvt G Co 4th TN Inf; 11-1-64 to 8-15-65; Gordonsville PO
NOLLEY, Henry M., La-111-4; Sol US; 4th Civil Dist
NOLLING, James, Ms-170-1; Pvt G Co 4th TN Inf; Nov 1 64 to Nov 2 65; 4th Dist
NOLTA, Fredrick, Ge-84-1; Mary A. widow of; Pvt E Co 1st TN Art; 24 Dec 62 to 1 Aug 66 (2 yrs 8 mos 5 days); Wolsey College PO; diseas of ulcer of stomach
NORCUTT, Zachariah, Hd-53-2; Catharine widow of; 1st Lt D Co 6th TN Cav; 24 Oct 62 to died 20 Mar 63; Morris Chapel PO; remarried to J. W. Crouch
NORETUM, Adam R., Je-141-3; Pvt K Co 3rd TN Inf; 10 Feb 62 to 23 Feb 65; Mill Springs PO
NORETUN?, Francis, Je-141-2; Pvt F & M Cos 1st TN Cav; 1 Nov 62 to 25 May 65; New Market PO
NORFLEET, Gunnel W. (see Forfleet, Henry)
NORFLET, Steve, Sh-152-3; Pvt I Co 61st US Inf; 63 to 66; Collierville PO
NORIS?, Callaway, Un-259-3; Phoebe A. widow of; Pvt G Co 1st TN Inf; 12 Aug 61 to 12 Aug 64; Sharps Chapel PO
NORMAN, Allen, Ru-246-1; Pvt A Co 7th PA Cav; 63 to 5-65; Murfreesboro PO; rheumatism
NORMAN, Allen, Sh-146-2; who served as Corcoran, Allen, colored; Pvt Cpl F Co 44th Inf; Jun 63 to 65; Pearley PO; Col Johnson (Capt Edmonson)
NORMAN, Anthony, A-8-2; Sarah J. widow of; Pvt H Co 1st TN Inf; 8-9-61 to 8-10-63; Scarborough PO
NORMAN, Coleman, D-63-2; Pvt G Co Bat 9 US Col; 62 to 65; Nashville PO
NORMAN, Jefferson T., Ja-84-3; Pvt H Co 4th TN Cav; 7-17-63 to 6-16-65; Normans Store PO; inflamatory rheumatism
NORMAN, John, Mr-96-1; Pvt G Co 1st OH?; 12-1-61 to 1-3-63; Whitwell PO; wounded
NORMAN, Robert, Sh-157-3; Mattie widow of; Dist 13
NORMAN, Rufus M., K-186-1; Pvt H Co 1st TN Inf; 9 Aug 61 to 17 Sep 64; Beaver Ridge PO; piles, rheumatism

NORMAN, Tomas J., Su-232-1; Pvt E Co 1st TN Lt Art; 4 Sep 63 to 1 Aug 65; Bristol PO; desease of lungs
NORMAN, William, H-69-1; Hanah, widow of; Pvt 14th TN Inf; Chattanooga PO
NORMENT, N., F-42-2(4); Susan Williams widow of; Collierville PO; husband died in army; CONF
NORMON, Jorden, A-3-2; Pvt H Co 1st TN Inf; 8-16-61 to 7-27-65; Wilson PO; ryphoid fever, janders
NORMORE, Mike, H-49-2; Lydia A. formerly widow of; Pvt; Falling Water PO
NORRIS, Christopher C., U-245-1; Rache E. widow of; Pvt D Co 8th TN Cav; Apr 64 to 10 Jul 64; Marbleton PO; died with dipthery
NORRIS, David, Cu-16-2; Pvt I Co 89th KY Inf; 1-10-64 to 9-15-65; Big Lick PO; rheumatism
NORRIS, F. M., Un-250-1; Anna widow of; Pvt D Co 1st TN Inf; 9 Aug 61 to 17 Sep 64; Maynardville PO
NORRIS, Fraklin, Jo-152-1; Pvt E Co 13th TN Cav; 22 Sep 63 to 4 Aug 65; Doeville PO; contracted earysipalis & rheumatism
NORRIS, Hinman C., Br-8-4(2); Cleo PO; wounded; US & CONF
NORRIS, J. P., U-245-2; Pvt D Co 13th TN Cav; 6 Mar 64 to 5 Sep 65; Limestone Cove PO; Galleton, TN, 1864
NORRIS, Jacob H., Jo-149-1; Lorettea L. widow of; Capt E Co 13th TN Cav; 24 Sep 63 to 5 Sep 64; Mountain City PO
NORRIS, Jas., T-209-1; Pvt F Co 25th National Gards; 3 yrs; Randolph PO; claims to have been in the marine service, regular army
NORRIS, John, Cu-16-2; Pvt D Co 2nd TN Inf; 9-1-61 to 4-18-65; Big Lick PO; pleurisy, reenlisted veteran
NORRIS, Patrick H., Cu-16-1; Pvt B Co 2nd TN Inf; 8-14-61 to 10-6-64; Crossville PO
NORRIS, Thomas J., Ov-136-1; Pvt D Co 1st TN Inf; 10-10-63 to 4-25-65; Livingston PO; fever
NORRIS, Washington F., Ct-38-2; Cpl H Co 8th TN Cav; 9-15-63 to 6-24-65; Okolona PO; rheumatism & piles
NORRIS, William R., K-180-1; Pvt D Co 2nd TN Inf; 1 Sep 61 to 6 Oct 64; Ebenezer PO; broken wrist, gun shot wound
NORROD, Alexander, Ov-139-2; Pvt D Co 1st TN Inf; 10-10-63 to 4-25-65; Hanging Limb PO
NORROD, Benjamin F., Ov-139-2; Pvt D Co 1st TN Inf; 10-10-63 to 4-25-65; Hanging Limb PO
NORROD, Louis S., Ov-139-2; Pvt D Co 1st TN Inf; 10-10-63 to 4-25-65; Hanging Limb PO
NORROD, William J., Ov-137-3; 2nd Lt D Co 1st Mtd Inf; 10-10-63 to 8-25-65; Monroe PO; kidney disease
NORTEN, John, U-249-1; Pvt G Co 3rd NC Mtd Inf; 17 Sep 64 to 8 Aug 65; Briggs PO
NORTH, Edward, D-61-2; 1 yr; Hancock Cor Saffron, Nashville PO; could get no further information
NORTH, Ira Jr., La-113-2; Sgt A Co 10th TN Inf; 6 Apr 62 to 2 Jun 65; Ethridge PO
NORTH, Mose, Mo-119-2; Pvt A Co 42nd TN Inf; 4-61 to __ (1 yr 11 mos); Sweetwater PO; shot in right arm
NORTH, Richard (Dick), Col, Ru-247-1; Pvt C Co 111th TN Inf; 61 to 64; Murfreesboro PO
NORTHCUT, Jefferson M., Hd-49-1; Pvt B Co 2nd TN Mtd Inf; Oct 11 63 to Oct 14 64; Olive Hill PO; heart disease & lungs effection
NORTHCUTT, Henry, W-192-1; Cook I Co 4th OH; 10-23-63 to 3-5-65; Irving College PO
NORTHERN, George, Sn-254-2; Hendersonville PO
NORTHERN, Thomas S., Je-142-2; 2nd Lt B Co 9th TN Cav; 10 Feb 62 to 11 Sep 65; PO omitted
NORTHINGTON, Dudley, Mt-136-1; Pvt B Co 14th OH; 5-64 to 65; Omar PO
NORTHINGTON, Isac, Mt-136-1; Pvt A Co 15th __; 63 to 4-65; Omar PO
NORTHRUP, Hiram T., Fe-44-1; Pvt B Co 6th NY Hvy Art; 62 to __ (3 yrs); Allardt PO; asthma and rheumatism
NORTON, Benjamin A., H-54-3; Pvt A Co 4th TN Cav; 10-25-62 to 7-26-65; Sherman Heights PO; eye sight badly injured, contracted rheumatism
NORTON, Henry J., Ma-125-1; Irene? widow; Sgt B Co 11th? (4th?) WI Inf; Jackson PO

NORTON, Hirom, Un-255-1; Pvt H Co 9th TN; 25 Sep 63 to 11 Sep 65; Warwicks X Roads PO
NORTON, Irene, Ma-125-2; widow Soldier; Main St, Jackson PO
NORTON, Mary E., Cr-16-4; widow US Sol; PO omitted
NORTON, Preston, D-87-2; Pvt B Co 101st US C Inf; Jan 14 64 to Jan 21 66; Nashville PO; toes amputated of left foot
NORTON, Samuel, Lo-189-2; Pvt SC Inf; Philadelphia PO; CONF
NORTON, Steven A., Tr-269-1; Pvt G Co 2nd TN Cav; Dec 61 to 64; John PO
NORVELL, Clinton Y., Mc-111-2; Mary M. widow of; 2nd Lt F Co 3rd TN Cav; 8-31-63 to 3-65; Athens PO
NORVELLE, Thomas E., T-206-2; Dist, not Tipton Co., TN PO
NORVILL, William H., Cr-11-1; Pvt G Co 12th KY Cav; 10 Nov 63 to 20 May 65; Johnson Grove PO; CONF
NORVILLE, Elijah A., B-7-1; Cpl F Co 5th TN Cav; 9-25-62 to 6-25-65; Shelbyville PO
NORWOOD, Chas. W., H-60-2; Sgt G Co 31st KY Inf; 10-1-61 to 7-63; Lt 40th KY Inf--7-63 to 9-63; Chattanooga PO
NORWOOD, George, Gi-138-2; Cpl H Co 13th TN Cav; 2-19-64 to __-25-65; Shones PO
NORWOOD, Hannah (see Bird, Benjamin)
NORWOOD, James, Lo-191-4; Pvt C Co 42nd US Col Inf; 17 Sep 64 to 31 Jan 66; Trigonia PO
NORWOOD, James A. W., Ms-169-1; Pvt C Co 53rd IN Inf; 29 Sep 64 to 31 May 65; Petersburg PO; spinal affection incurred, discharged at close of war
NORWOOD, John H., Lo-191-3; Pvt E Co 3rd TN Inf; Aug 64 to __; Trigonia PO
NORWOOD, John R., Co-59-1; Pvt Co G 3rd NC Inf; 8-25-64 to 8-8-65; Del Rio PO
NORWOOD, Thomas J., Cr-17-1; Pvt E Co 7th TN Cav; 10-10-62 to 8-25-65; Buena Vista PO
NOST?, Syrenus, Je-147-2; Sarah C. widow of; 1st Lt F Co 9th TN Cav; 17 Oct 63 to 11 Sep 65; Shady Grove PO
NOTT, Joseph A., Co-62-4; USS; 4th Dist
NOWEL, Lucinda E., Sh-175-2; R 48 Echols St, Memphis PO
NOWELL, John A., Wi-270-1; Pvt H Co 6th IL Cav; 27 Dec 61 to 17 Jun 65; Naomi PO
NOWLEN, Martha A. (see Kirklin, William)
NUBBY, George, Sn-253-1; Pvt G Co 8th KY Hvy Art; 61 to 4-3-64; No. One PO; rheumatism
NUBY, Henry, Wl-302-3(5); Pvt K Co 14th TN Inf; Baird's Mills PO; wounded three times
NUE, Benjamin, F-46-1; G Co 4th TN; May 65 to Feb 66; LaGrange PO
NUN, Martin B., Mg-196-3; Pvt C Co 1st TN Inf; 9 Aug 61 to 17 Sep 64; Hunnicutt PO
NUNLEY, Jesse, Gu-48-2; Jane widow of; Pvt E Co 1st AL Indpt Vidette Cav; 10-10-63 to 6-16-64; Tracy City PO
NUNLY, General, W-196-1; Pvt M Co 5th TN Cav; 11-16-63 to 8-14-65; Horse Shoe Falls PO; mule fell and hurt right side
NUNLY, Henry, Sh-150-2; James Henry Cole; Pvt E Co 61st US Inf; 3 yrs; Mullins Station PO
NUNLY, John, W-191-1; Pvt H Co 5th TN Cav; 5-62 to 3-65; Safley PO; shot through right thigh
NUNLY, Willis, W-193-1; Pvt E Co TN Cav; 10-10-63 to __; Smartt PO; has not discharge
NUNN, J. H., Dy-21-1; Marry J. widow of; Chestnut Bluff PO; did not known the desired question; CONF
NUNN, John H., Ro-202-1; Pvt I Co 1st TN Inf; 26 Feb 62 to 14 Mar 63; Oral PO; lung disease
NURSE, Charles, De-22-1; Cook H Co 17th IA? Inf; 1 May 61 to 1 May 65; Clifton PO; CONF
NUTSON, Thomas, Sh-148-1; or Stephen Cratton; 3rd Cpl G Co 61st Col Inf; __ to Jun 63; Memphis PO
OAFF, John T., Ru-13-1; Pvt A Co 1st OH Inf; Jan 64 to 17 Jul 65; Murfreesboro PO; right eye defective, cause of eye injured small pox
OAKLEY, Berry, Dk-35-2; Pvt A Co OH Mtd Inf; 8-27-61 to 9-26-65; Temperance Hall PO
OAKLEY, Bove V., Dk-34-5(4); Sgt E Co 4th TN Cav; 9-28-64 to 8-25-65; Close PO

OAKLEY, Doss, Dk-32-3; Pvt E Co 4th TN Mtd Inf; 9-24-64 to 8-25-65; Temperance Hall PO; disabled from mumps
OAKLEY, James, Dk-32-2; Pvt E Co 4th TN Mtd Inf; 10-18-64 to 8-25-65; Liberty PO
OAKLEY, John, Dk-35-2; Pvt E Co 4th TN Mtd Inf; 9-27-64 to 8-25-65; Temperance Hall PO; back and breast trouble
OAKLEY, Joseph, Dk-32-3; Pvt E Co 4th TN Mtd Inf; 10-21-64 to 8-25-65; Alexandria PO
oakley, S. W., G-57-6; Pvt A Co 51st TN Inf; 1 Mar 62 to 1 Mar 64; Yorkville PO; CONF
OAKLEY, Thomas B., Wl-300-1; Pvt 4th TN Cav; 64 to 65; Cherry Valley PO
OAKLEY, Thomas D., Dk-34-5(4); Pvt K Co 5th TN Cav; 5-6-63 to 8-14-65; Temperance Hall PO
OAKLY, John, Wl-297-1; Martha O. widow of; Pvt B Co 5th TN Cav; 5 Sep 62 to 25 Jun 65; Watertown PO
OAKS, Isaac, Un-254-1; Mariah widow of; Pvt E Co 1st TN Art; Paulett PO
OAKS, Margaret A. (see Cox, Joseph)
OAR, Joseph T., Hu-106-1; Pvt E Co 111th USCI; 63 to 65; Waverly PO
OATIS, Pooler, H-64-3; Pvt L Co 1st WI Cav; 1-1-64 to 7-17-65; Chattanooga PO
OATTEN?, James, D-87-1; Lizzie Pratt widow of; Pvt TN; 2 Jul 61 to 65; Nashville PO
O'BANNON, A., Sh-184-1; Patsey widow of; Pvt C Co 88th TN Inf; 1-9-63 to 4-5-65; 237 Carroll Ave, Memphis PO
OBAUGH, Henry A., Ge-96-3; Sgt K Co 4th TN Cav; Apr 64 to 19 Jun 65; Rheatown PO; affected head, hemorage lungs
OBERFIELD, B. F., Be-5-2; Pvt F Co 31st OH Inf; Sep 13 61 to Sep 12 64; Big Sandy PO; shot through the foot
OBRIEN, John, Sh-188-1; US white; 50 Peyton Ave, Memphis PO
O'BRINE (sic), William H., U-245-2; Pvt G Co 4th TN Cav; Oct 62 to 64; Limestone Cove PO; captured 1 Jan 1863, reported to my command 1864
O'CALLIHAN, William, D-63-1; Capt I Co 116th PA Inf; Aug 15 62 to Feb 15 65; Nashville PO
O'CAUGHLIN, Patrick, Wl-294-1; Pvt F Co IL Inf; Aug 13 62 to May 12 65; Tuckers X Roads PO; wife reported lame arm & partially deaf
OCHS, Julius, H-62-2; Bertha widow of; Capt 52nd OH Vol Inf; 61 to 1-9-62; 415 West Fifth, Chattanooga PO
OCONERS, John, Hi-92-1; 21st IN Batry; Aetna PO; couldnt find out anything about enlistment and so on
O'CONNOR, Thos., Sh-146-2; Cpl C Co 50th __; Oct 25 61 to 64; Woodstock PO
OCONOR, John C., Pu-141-2; Cpl B Co 121st OH Inf; 63 to 65; Dry Valley PO; discharged at close of war
ODELL, Bethel, Cf-38-2; Pct; 10th Civil Dist
ODELL, Claton, Sn-262-2(1); Pvt H Co 5th TN Cav; 9-14-62 to 8-14-65; Buck Lodge PO; dropsy
ODELL, Delos, K-177-2; PO omitted
ODELL, Henry, Co-61-5(2); Cpl I Co 26th TN Inf; Bridgeport PO; CONF
ODELL, James P., A-13-2; Pvt G Co 2nd TN Cav; 3-7-62 to 8-27-65; Briceville
ODELL, Joseph B., Gr-81-1; Sgt A Co 12th TN Cav; 8 Jul 63 to 11 Jul 65; Clear Spring PO; rheu. & result in heart trubles, totly disabled
ODELL, Marshal L., Cl-57-2; Cpl E Co 6th Reg TN; Kecks Chappel PO; catarrh in head, lung affection, soldier has a sickly appearance
ODELL, Tilmon, Gr-81-3(1); Pvt A Co 12th TN Cav; 22 Nov 63 to 7 Oct 65; Clear Spring PO; fever & measels, partly disabled
ODELL, William, Mu-209-5; Capt B Co 1st KY Cav; Apr 61 to Apr 64; Columbia PO
ODELL, William A. J., Mu-209-3; Sarah E. widow of; Cpt B Co 1st KY Cav; Apr 61 to Apr 64; Columbia PO
ODEWAY, W. H., Hu-103-4; Pvt; Mar 61 to 65; PO omitted
ODIL, John C., Mu-210-6; Pvt C Co 9th TN Cav; 14 Feb 63 to 12 May 65; Mallard PO; CONF
ODLE, James L., Wh-182-1; Sol; 3rd Dist
ODOM, Jessie, Br-8-4(2); Pvt D Co 1st TN Lt Art; 3-23-64 to 6-65; Cleo PO
ODOM, John, Ha-110-3; Catherine widow of; Sgt G Co 8th TN Inf; Treadway PO
ODOM, Thomas, Black, Sn-264-1; Pvt D Co 40th __; Oct 62 to Apr 65; Mitchellsville PO; this man has forgot dates, his discharge paper burned up. He is now an invalid, infantry joined at Gallatin TN, Col Wade & Reeder
O'DONALSON, Patrick, D-99-1; Pvt H Co 10th NY Cav; Jan 30 64 to Aug 8 65; Goodlettsville PO; chronic rheumatism, sunstroke at battle of Weldermire?
ODONIEL, John, D-57-1; Pvt __ TN; 61 to 61; 8th Ward, PO omitted; CONF
ODUM, John L., Pu-140-1; Pvt I Co 5th TN Cav; 3-29-64 to 7-65; Cookeville PO
OEMAN, Wm. A., Be-1-1; "yes"; 13th Dist
OFFICER, Jefferon, Br-12-3; Pvt E Co 5th TN Inf; 9-26-64 to 6-26-65; McPherren PO
OGAN, John, Ha-116-1; Pvt I Co 8th TN Inf; 24 Jul 63 to 5 Jun 65; Bray's PO; cronic diareah
OGDEN, Charles H., K-159-1; Pvt C Co 176th OH Inf; 2 Jun 64 to 4 Jun 65; Knoxville PO
OGDEN, J. T., K-169-1; 2nd Lt 23rd OH Inf; 61 to Apr 65; Knoxville PO
OGDEN, James R., K-159-1; Pvt H Co 2nd OH Cav; 9 Sep 61 to 25 Sep 64; Knoxville PO
OGDEN, John J., M-107-3; Pvt C Co 37th KY Mtd Inf; 1-4-63 to 12-29-64; Walnut Shade PO; disease of kidneys
OGDON, Rutha E., Ha-110-2; widow; Blackwater PO
OGILVIE, Elijah, Mu-209-6; Pvt; Columbia PO; CONF
OGILVIE, George W., Ms-176-1; Col; Pvt C Co 31st WI; 11-4-63 to 7-1-65; Caney Springs (crossed out, no reason given)
OGLE, Aaron, Se-229-2; Pvt E Co 9th TN Cav; 1 Oct 63 to 26 Aug 65; Gatlinburg PO; cattarrh of head, leg fracture
OGLE, Bradford, Se-229-2; Pvt E Co 9th TN Cav; 1 Oct 63 to 11 Sep 65; Gatlinburg PO; rheumatism
OGLE, Calvin R., Sh-145-2; Pvt D Co 22nd IN Inf; 10 Jul 61 to 15 Aug 65; Kerrville PO; prisoner at Libby Prison 1 month, at Andersonville 2 mos; reenlisted veteran at Blevins; X Roads, 23 Dec 63, East TN
OGLE, Caswell T., Se-223-3; Cpl E Co 9th TN Cav; 1 Oct 63 to 11 Sep 65; Hendersons Springs PO
OGLE, Clewson, Se-230-2; Inf; Pokeberry PO; palsy, could not learn but little except of my own personal knowledge
OGLE, Eleson, K-161-1; Julia widow of; Knoxville PO
OGLE, H. B., A-1-3; Sgt R Co 2nd TN Inf; 10-16-62 to 5-31-63; Andersonville PO; general debility
OGLE, Henry, Se-229-2; Pvt E Co 9th TN Cav; 1 Oct 63 to 11 Sep 65; Gatlinburg PO; diarea, piles, hearing
OGLE, John, Sm-174-1; Pvt G Co 4th TN Inf; 12-1-64 to 8-25-65; Grant PO
OGLE, John, Se-230-1; Eliza M. widow of; Pvt M Co 2nd TN Cav; 62 to __ (2 days--sic); Pokeberry PO
OGLE, John H., Me-92-1; Sarah L. widow of; Cate PO
OGLE, Noah, Se-229-2; Pvt E Co 2nd TN Cav; 6 Sep 62 to 6 Jul 65; Gatlinburg PO; diarrhoea, heart & rheumatism
OGLE, Rebecca, Se-229-1; soldiers widow; PO omitted
OGLE, Wesley, Se-229-3; Pvt H Co 2nd TN Inf; Feb __ to __; Jones Cave PO; chronic diarhoe & liver
OGLESBY, Francis M., K-154-3; Pvt G Co 7th TN Mtd Inf; __ to 8 Nov 64; Knoxville PO
OGLESBY, Jerra, Sn-253-1; Pvt H Co TN Inf; 6 mos; no PO
OGLESBY, Jessie H., Dy-25-2; Pvt; 3 yrs; Newbern PO; CONF
OGLESBY, Richard, D-72-2; Pvt E Co 17th? TN Inf; Jan 7 64 to Apr 25 66; Nashville PO
OGLESBY, Wiley C., K-183-3; US Sol; 16th Dist
OGWIN, William H., Rb-219-1; Pvt H Co 30th TN Reg; Nov 62 to May 4 65; Orlinda PO; shot through the arm, prison C. Douglas 7 mos; CONF
O'HERN, Michael, Sh-169-2; Pvt B Co 10th TN Inf; 61 to 64; Memphis PO
OHOLLAND, Dennis, Tr-266-1(2); Pvt; 4 yrs 5 mos; Hartsville PO; CONF
O'KEEF, John, D-50-3; Sarah Nesby former wife of; 215 Jackson, Nashville PO

OLDER, Geo. D., H-63-1; Sgt D Co 108th Col Inf; 63 to 65 (1 yr 6 mos); 621 Cypress, Chattanooga PO
OLDFIELDS, John C., Cf-35-1; Pvt I Co 4th TN Cav; Tullahoma PO; CONF
OLDHAM, George, We-225-1; Pvt; 1 yr 6 mos; Dresden PO; wounded in foot
OLDHAM, Jerry, Sm-168-2; Pvt E Co 92nd OH Inf; 63 to 65; Pleasant Shade PO; small pox and shot in leg
OLDHAM, Peyton, T-210-1; Pvt A Co 11th US; Feb 11 65 to Jan 15 66; Quito PO
OLDHAM, Thomas, We-221-2; Pvt D Co KY Inf; Dec 64 to Apr 65; Martin PO; CONF
OLDHAM, William H., J-77-2; Pvt H Co 8th TN Cav; 10-64 to 8-17-65; Gainesboro PO; rupture
OLDHAM, William J., K-165-2; Sgt B Co 1st TN Cav; Jun 61 to __; Knoxville PO; paroled out; CONF
OLDHAM, Willis, L-99-2; Pvt I Co 2nd US Col Art; 65 to 66; Durhamville PO; small pox, date of enlistment and discharge as near as could be found
OLDS, George, Li-165-1; Francis widow of; Elora PO
OLDS, Gid. J., L-106-1; US Sol; 8th Dist
OLDS, Harry, Gi-132-3; Pvt A Co 2nd USCV; Feb 20 64 to Feb 18 66; Pulaski PO
OLER, John C., Ge-92-3; Pvt H Co 8th TN Inf; Jul 62 to 64 (2 yrs); Laurel Gap PO; diarrhea and hard of hearing
OLETON, Frederic, H-76-1; Chattanooga PO
OLINGER, Daniel, Bl-4-3; Pvt 5th TN Inf; 3-1-62 to 5-14-65; Pikeville PO
OLINGER, John, R-163-4; Cpl G Co 5th TN Cav; 10-22-63 to 8-14-65; Dayton PO
OLIVER, Alvey A., A-8-2; Susan E. formerly widow of; Pvt K Co 1st TN Inf; 8-9-61 to 11-26-61; Scarborough PO
OLIVER, Daniel M., La-111-1; Pvt 23rd TN Inf; 62 to 63; Pleasant Point PO; shot through the head in battle of Shilo; CONF
OLIVER, Edward (see Taylor, Edward)
OLIVER, Elijah D., Ct-42-1; Pvt H Co 4th TN Inf; Watauga PO
OLIVER, George, Ct-35-1; Pane widow of; Pvt A Co 13th TN Cav; __ to 9-5-65; Hampton PO; discharge at Washington
OLIVER, George W., H-53-8; Pvt D Co 22nd IN Inf; 2 yrs; Chattanooga PO; diarrhoea & disease of rectum
OLIVER, Henry, Se-226-5; Nancy A. widow of; 2nd Lt D Co 3rdTN Cav; 1 Dec 62 to Jul 65; Shady Grove PO (Jefferson Co.)
OLIVER, James, Ct-42-1; Pvt A Co 13th TN Cav; Watauga PO
OLIVER, James A., Ja-84-1; Sarah E. widow of; Pvt A Co 10th TN Cav; 7-27-63 to 8-1-65; Harrison PO; kidney disease
OLIVER, James T., D-72-4; Pvt G Co 7th TN Inf; May 18 61 to May 20 65; Nashville PO; CONF
OLIVER, John, P-151-2; Pvt F Co 17th US Cav; 63 to 65; Perryville PO
OLIVER, Jno., R-163-1; alias Jno. Bailey; Pvt M Co 5th TN Cav; 9-16-63 to 8-65; Graysville PO; discharge lost
OLIVER, John M., Sn-261-4(3); Cpl F Co 9th KY Inf; 11-15-61 to 64; Perdue PO; disease of chest or lung
OLIVER, John T., Gr-80-1; Pvt F Co 32nd KY Inf; 9 mos; Thorn Hill PO; disabled from yellow janders, cannot recollect dates omitted
OLIVER, Louis, Sh-193-2; Pvt; Memphis PO
OLIVER, Madison, F-43-1; Pvt 21st US Reg; 63 to 65; New Kent PO; is colored, can neither read nor write, does not know Col, Capt or any particulers
OLIVER, Thomas, Sh-147-2; Sgt F Co 10th DC Inf; 10 Jul 61 to 20 Apr 65; Cuba PO
OLIVER, Thomas, Jo-150-3; Francis widow of; Pvt; Trade PO
OLIVER, William D., Ct-42-1; Pvt A Co 13th TN Cav; Watauga PO
OLIVER, William H. (see Lester, Henry)
OLLIS, Thomas, Ro-204-2; Pvt E Co 1st TN Inf; Aug 61 to 64; Oliver Springs PO; no discharge found
OLLIVE, Jerry, Hn-77-1; Pvt D Co 3rd TN Inf; 1 Jan 63 to 1 Jan 65; PO omitted

OLLIVER, John, Ct-41-1; Pvt H Co 13th TN Cav; 9-24-63 to 9-5-65; South Wattauga PO; rhumatism and dylought
OLLIVER, John M., Sn-261-1; Cpl F Co 9th KY Inf; 11-15-61 to __; Perdue PO
OMALLEY, M. J. D. C., Cr-16-3; Pvt A Co 9th MI Inf; Apr 15 62 to Jun 66; Huntingdon PO; slightly ruptured, was Lt Quartermaster, changed
OMOHUNDRO, Orville C., D-61-1; Stuarts Cavalry; May 10 61 to May 20 65; Nashville PO; CONF
ONE, William (see Scott, William)
ONEAL, Alfred, Ms-171-1; Horseler (sic) I Co 2nd TN Cav; 64 to 65; Broadway, Memphis PO
ONEAL, James H., Lo-193-2; Pvt E Co 3rd TN Mtd Inf; 15 Jul 64 to 30 Nov 64; Unitia PO
ONEAL, John, Lo-193-1; Pvt H Co 3rd TN Inf; 3 Feb 62 to 14 Nov 65; Unitia PO
O'NEAL, John H., Wl-303-1; Pvt K Co 203rd IL Vol; 14 Aug 62 to Sep 65; PO omitted; rheumatism in right side
O'NEAL, Michael, Sh-189-2; Pvt D Co 40th NY Inf; 6-3-61 to 6-64; Broadway, Memphis PO
ONEAL, Olliver, Co-62-3; Hospital Stuart 1st TN Cav; 15 Apr 62 to 17 Apr 65; Bybee PO; fistula
ONEAL, Patrick H., Mr-102-2; Pvt A Co 10th OH Inf; 61 to 64; South Pittsburg PO
ONEAL, Phillip S., H-55-2; Pvt B Co TN Lt Art; 5-16-62 to 5-2-65; Jersey PO
ONEAL, Richard, A-6-5(3); Pvt; PO omitted
ONEAL, Rentan, H-68-1; Pvt A Co 5th TN Inf; 2-25-62 to 6-12-65; Chattanooga PO; chronic diarrhoea, not able to do anything
ONEAL, Walter A., Dy-27-3; Pvt A Co 1st TN Art; 61 to 65; Newbern PO; CONF
ONEAL, William, Gi-133-1; Pvt E Co 9th TN; Sep 62 to 65; Bufords PO; CONF
ONEAL, William, Gi-133-2; Pvt; 62 to 65; Bufords PO; CONF
O'NEILL, James, Gu-48-3; Pvt H Co 198th OH Mtd Inf; 3-65 to 6-65; Tracy City PO; record of discharge lost
ONESBY, Sick, Co-66-2(1); Genetie Gildon Farmley widow of; Pvt E Co 8th TN Cav; 10 Oct 63 to 11 Sep 65; Birdsville PO
ONIAL, Elvin, Bo-13-1; Pvt E Co 3rd TN Mtd Inf; 64 to __ (4 mos); Freindsville PO
ONKS, Josiah, Wa-263-2; Pvt; Johnson City PO; rheumatism
ONKST, Martha A. (see Hise, Robt. E.)
ONSLEY, Jacob M., Un-259-3; Pvt F Co 2nd TN Inf; 12 Aug 62 to 12 Aug 64; Sharps Chapel PO; piles in bowel
OPHLARITY, Mary J., Ct-39-1; widow?; Johnson City PO
ORBOLD, M. Eugene, Sh-167-1; Mattee widow of; Pvt; Sep 63 to 14 May 66; Memphis PO (61 Washington St.); CONF; has no papers
ORDWAY, James, D-78-2; Nashville PO
ORE, Pleas., Je-137-3; Dorcus M. widow of; Pvt; Chestnut Hill PO
ORE, Wilson, Je-141-2; Pvt B Co 9th TN Cav; 6 May 63 to 11 Sep 65; Mill Spring PO
OREN, Nancy, Ct-39-1; widow; Johnson City PO
ORENBY, John, K-170-3; US Sol; Dist 12
ORIC, Benjamin, Ha-114-3; US Sol; 7th Civil Dist
ORICK, John, C-28-1; Pvt C Co 9th TN Cav; 5-11-64 to 7-11-65; Fincastle PO
ORIE, James, Mc-109-5; Sweetwater PO (Monroe Co.); diarrhea
ORMAN, Robbert L., Mu-210-2; Pvt F Co 3rd TN Inf; 4-61 to 65; Spring Hill PO; CONF
ORMES, William, Co-66-1; Pvt K Co 26th TN Inf; 22 Apr 61 to 28 Mar 62; Bison PO; CONF
ORNDORFF, Miltin L., D-79-1; Pvt H Co 12th US Col Inf; Aug 12 63 to Jan 16 66; Nashville, Indiana Lumber Co. PO; constant pain in side
ORR, Caleb, Wa-269-1; Pvt B Co 2nd NC Mtd Inf; 15 Sep 63 to 25 Apr 65; Johnson City PO; sabre cut, shot in neck
ORR, Calib, Wa-268-4; Johnson City PO
ORR, Carson R., Gi-122-3; Pvt H Co 3rd TN Inf; 22 Jul 61 to 22 Feb 65; Prospect Sta. PO; CONF
ORR, John, Cr-19-1; Pvt F Co 7th TN Cav; 8-12-63 to 12-25-63; Crider PO
ORR, Joseph, B-11-2(1); Pvt A Co 4th TN Mtd Inf; 8-27-64 to 8-25-65; Poplins X Roads PO
ORR, Robert, Bo-13-2; Pvt L Co 2nd TN Cav; 10-15-63 to 7-6-65; Miser PO

ORRAN, Nash L., F-42-1(3); Pvt H Co 8th AR Vol; Spring 61 to Jun 65; Eads PO (Shelby Co.); CONF
ORRENCE, Lewis, Ct-39-1; Bugler O Co 3rd PA Cav; 63 to 65; Happy Valley PO; wounds inflicted during war
ORSBORN, C. C., K-183-3; Pvt; Thorn Grove PO
ORTEL, George, H-72-1; Pvt D Co 16th US Col Cav; 10-19-64 to 4-30-66; Chattanooga PO
ORTEN, Lerren, Wa-263-2; Pvt; Garbers Mills PO; CONF
ORTON, C. V., Mc-115-2; Pvt L Co 1st TN Cav; 10-1-62 to 5-12-65; Riceville PO; shot in neck & blow in head
ORTON, John, Mc-115-1; Pvt B Co 7th TN; 9-27-64 to 7-27-65; Riceville PO; ribs broken
ORTON, John Jr., Mc-115-1; Pvt L Co 1st TN Cav; 11-1-62 to 6-22-65; Riceville PO; measels & frost bite
ORWOOD, Samuel, Hm-108-4(3); Pvt D Co 4th TN Inf; 2 Jan 63 to 2 Aug 65; Russellville PO; rheumatism
OSBORN, Charls E., Wa-268-2; Pvt B Co 13th KY Inf; 23 Apr 61 to 6 Aug 61; Johnson City PO; kidney disease
OSBORN, Robert, K-186-3; Pvt F Co 7th TN Mtd Inf; Nov 64 to Jul 65; Chumlea PO
OSBORN, Washington, Ro-207-2; Pvt L Co 1st US Hvy Inf; 19 Sep 64 to 31 Mary 66; Patties Gap PO; kidney affection
OSBORNE, James M., Ce-31-1; Pvt F Co 45th NC Inf; Feb 63 to 10 May 65; Petway PO; CONF
OSBORNE, Samuel, K-158-2; Pvt G Co 12th KY Inf; Feb 63 to May 65; Knoxville, E. Clinch St. PO
OSBURN, Aleck, H-61-3; Angeline Center formerly widow of; Chattanooga PO
O'SHEA, William, D-77-2; Drummer B Co 10th TN Inf; 14 Apr 62 to 25 Jun 65; Nashville PO
OSMENT, J. P., Wl-308-3; Pvt F Co 45th TN; Dec 1 62 to Nov 1 63; Mount Juliet PO; CONF
OSMENT, R. G., Wl-308-2; Pvt TN; Apr 62 to Apr 64; Mount Juliet PO; captured; CONF
OSTANDER, Theodore F., K-159-2; Sgt 8th? 58th PA Inf; 3 Oct 61 to 19 Sep 65; Knoxville PO; neuralgia fistula, discharge by spcl. order
OSTEAN, James W., B-11-3(2); Pvt F Co 1st IN Vidette; Cav; 9-63 to 6-16-64; Unionville PO; sent home sick
OSTER, John, R-161-1; Pvt C Co 39th IA Inf; 8-2-62 to 65; Dayton PO; stomache trouble from dyspep; prisner Lantna or Mellon, has dropsey, unable to work
OSTIS, Henry B., Mu-210-2; Mary N. widow of; Lt 11th MS Inf; 4-61 to 4-10-65; Spring Hill PO; wounded in leg
OSTNANDEN, Alexander A., Di-31-1; Pvt E Co 21st MI Cav; 4-23-64 to 3-10-66; Hazel Ridge PO; shot in left jaw by pistol
OTES, William (see Butler, Oliver)
O'TOOLE, Peter, Sh-174-3; Saddler's Sgt McClellands Army; 149 Hernando St, Memphis PO
OTT, Charls, K-181-2; Capt F Co 3rd TN Cav; 10 Jun 63 to 10 Jul 65; Bank PO (Blunt Co.); ruptured rit grin, 30 yrs
OTT, John A., S-214-1; Pvt B Co 5th US Lt Art; Nov 59 to Nov 64; Robbins PO; loss right testicle, cause mumps
OTTER, James, Hm-107-2(1); Sgt C Co 1st TN Lt Art; 15 Nov 63 to 1 Aug 65; Witts Foundry PO; rheumatism
OTTINGER, Adam, Ge-85-2; Pvt B Co 8th TN Inf; 20 Sep 63 to 30 Jun 65; Cavey Branch PO; by the concussion of bomb while in battle at Columbia TN has injured my hearing
OTTINGER, Calvin, Ge-85-1; Pvt H Co 1st TN Cav; 30 Dec 62 to 29 Jun 65; Ottinger PO; spinal affection, suforing from kidneys
OTTINGER, Christopher, Ge-85-2; Erhla? widow of; Sgt B Co 8th TN Inf; Cavey Branch PO
OTTINGER, David C., Co-61-3(1); Pvt E Co 8th TN Inf; 1 May 63 to 30 Jun 65; Parrottsville PO; shot in thigh
OTTINGER, Dugless C., Br-13-1; Cpl B Co 5th TN Inf; 8-20-64 to 7-13-65; Cleveland PO
OTTINGER, Haskin? B., Ge-85-1; Sgt K Co 8th TN Inf; Cavey Branch PO; rheumatism and epilepsy
OTTINGER, Jacob Y., Co-60-1; B Co 8th TN Inf; Syrensburg PO; broken arm (right)
OTTINGER, John A., Ge-85-1; Pvt E Co 1st TN Cav; 3 Jul 62 to 5 Jun 65; Cavey Branch PO; rheumatism, eyes
OTTINGER, Jonas, Co-60-2; C Co 4th TN Inf; 4-6-63 to 8-2-65; Salem PO; rheumatism & diarhea
OTTINGER, Jonathan, Co-60-2; G Co 4th TN Inf; 5-4-63 to 8-2-65; Salem PO; rheumatism
OTTINGER, Michael, Co-60-2; C Co 4th TN Inf; 4-6-63 to 8-2-65; Salem PO; rheumatism & diarhea
OTTINGER, Peter, Co-61-3(1); Pvt A Co 4th TN Inf; Parrottsville PO
OUTAN, Thomas L., We-225-2(1); Pvt A Co South Cumberland Batt. KY; Jan 20 65 to Oct 23 65; Dresden PO
OUTEN, Evaline (see Billups, Jerry)
OUTLAW, Hays, St-160-1; Col; Judice A. widow of; Legate PO; died in US army
OUTLAW, Henry, C), Mt-140-1; Pvt A Co 16th TN Reg; 9-63 to 5-66; Sailors Risk PO
OVERALL, George, Hu-99-2; Pvt C Co 13th US Col Inf; Johnsonville PO
OVERALL, Jacob, Ru-241-4; Mary widow of; Pvt TN Inf; 1 yr 6 mos; Murfreesboro PO
OVERALL, James H., Dk-32-2; Sgt K Co 5th TN Cav; 6-22-63 to 8-14-65; Liberty PO
OVERALL, R. A., G-57-6; Pvt; Yorkville PO; CONF
OVERBEY, Herod, Cl-47-1; Pvt E Co 2nd TN Inf; 10-6-61 to 2-3-63; Speedwell PO
OVERBEY, Joab, Su-241-1; Blacksmith K Co 4th TN Cav; 13 May 64 to 12 Jul 65; Blairs Gap PO; exposure, bad water
OVERBY, Thomas, Col, O-141-3; Cpl C Co 8th Reg Hvy Art US Vol; Aug 15 64 to Feb 10 66; Union City PO
OVERBY, Thomas C., H-63-2; Pvt 10th KY Cav; 61 to 65; 625 Poplar, Chattanooga PO
OVERCAST, William B., B-7-2; Sgt C Co 5th TN Cav; 8-4-62 to 1-9-65; PO omitted
OVERHOLT, James W., Co-69-1; Pvt L Co 4th TN Inf; 3 Jan 63 to 2 Aug 65; Driskill PO; chronic deseas of the liver 27 yrs, a pensioner
OVERHOLT, Nicholas, W-196-1; Sgt D Co 6th IA Cav; 9-30-62 to 10-18-65; Dibril PO; rheumatism, heart dis.
OVERHULSTER, John M., Ge-84-3; Stuw, Hospital B Co 12th TN Cav; Oct 63 to Oct 65; Wolsey College PO; chronid of dis. of spain
OVERMAN, Nathan, He-63-2; Pvt C Co 7th TN Cav; Jul 1 63 to Aug 9 65; PO omitted
OVERMAN, Thomas J., Fr-112-2; Cpl K Co 12th IN Inf; 6-20-61 to 7-4-64; Tullahoma PO
OVERSTREET, William A., Cy-28-1; Pvt A Co 11th TN Cav; 4-17-63 to 9-11-65; Celina PO
OVERSTREET, William C., Mg-199-2; 1st KY Cav; Sunbright PO
OVERTON, Abner B., K-177-5; Pvt E Co 3rd TN Inf; 23 Feb 62 to 23 Feb 65; Powells Station PO
OVERTON, Charles, Sh-188-2; Pvt US Col; rear 214 Mill, Memphis PO
OVERTON, Jessee, Di-37-1; Ordlery Sgt G Co 12th TN Inf; 8-12-63 to 1-16-66; Cumberland Furnace PO
OVERTON, John Jr., Sh-159-7; Col; Memphis PO; CONF
OVERTON, John J., Lo-195-1; Pvt I Co 1st TN Cav; 9 Aug 61 to 17 Sep 64; Vancouver PO; lung trouble
OVERTON, Lee, Tr-268-1; Pvt F Co 13th TN Inf; Apr 64 to Jan 66; Hartsville PO
OVERTON, Lewis, Gi-126-1; Pvt D Co 110th Col Inf; 8 Dec 63 to 6 Feb 66; Pulaski PO
OVERTON, Robert R., Ha-115-2; 2nd Lt G Co 8th TN Cav; 13 Jun 63 to 11 Sep 65; Mulberry Gap PO; rupture bowels, reenlisted veteran
OVERTON, Robert W., Ro-201-6; Pvt I Co 1st TN Inf; 9 Aug 61 to 17 Sep 64; Kingston PO
OVERTON, Sevill, A-2-1; Sgt J Co 7th TN Inf; 11-8-64 to 7-27-65; Hynds Creek PO; chronic dierrhea, discharge mislaid
OVERTON, William E., Hy-78-1; Pvt O Co 52nd IN Inf; 25 Sep 63 to 23 Sep 65; Catalpa PO (Madison Co.)
OVERTURF, Henry, Gu-46-2(1); Pvt A Co 2nd IL Inf; 10-3-64 to 11-7-65; Tatesville PO
OWANS, William J., Pvt; Moresburg PO
OWEN, Anzil D., A-2-3; Persillor Capps formerly widow of; Pvt C Co 2nd NC Inf; Andersonville PO; captured and died at Camp Vance, NC

OWEN, Christian, H-74-1; Pvt D Battery 31st OH; 10-61 to 11-64; 1011 Fairview Ave, Chattanooga PO
OWEN, George W., Hw-134-1; Pvt E Co 1st TN Cav; 62 to 65; Rogersville PO; disease of lungs
OWEN, Grovier, M-107-3; Pvt A Co 9th KY Inf; Walnut Shade PO
OWEN, Jesse F., Mo-119-3; Lt F Co 10th TN Cav; 10-20-63 to 8-4-65; Sweetwater PO
OWEN, John M., Dy-25-3; Pvt E Co 10th TN Inf; 23 Ma 63 to 23 Jun 65; Newbern PO; chronic diarrhoea
OWEN, John R., Hm-107-5; Pvt C Co 8th TN Cav; 4 May 63 to 11 Sep 65; Witts Foundry PO; rheumatism
OWEN, Joseph N., D-91-2; Cpl C Co 21st KY Inf; 18 Mar 64 to 9 Dec 64; G. W. Myers, West Cedar St, Nashville PO; wounded in arm and stomach left leg paralyzed from hip to foot
OWEN, Nat, H-73-2(1); Pvt; Chattanooga PO
OWEN, Nickolus, Gr-70-3; Pvt G Co 2nd TN Cav; Oct 62 to Jun 65; Rutledge PO; mashed by horse, exact dates unk
OWEN, P. C., Hy-79-1; Pvt H Co 8th TN Reg; Sep 8 63 to Sep 11 65; Brownsville PO
OWEN, Presley (see Hammond, Presly)
OWEN, Richard, Hy-79-1; Pvt H Co 8th TN Reg; Brownsville PO
OWEN, Richard B., T-217-1(39); 1st Lt C Co 48th MO? Inf; 29 Jun 64 to 29 Jun 65; Covington PO
OWEN, Robert, D-69-1; Eliza Work wife of; D Co NY; Nashville PO
OWEN, Thomas, Fe-42-2; Pvt 13th KY; Allerdt PO
OWEN, Thomas, Sn-174-2; Pvt D Co 4th TN Inf; 10-2-64 to 8-25-65; Grant PO
OWEN, William A., Hw-132-2; Pvt A Co 1st TN Inf; 1 Sep 63 to 8 Aug 65; Persia PO
OWENS, Alex, D-72-3; Pvt A Co 16th TN Inf; Sep 1 64 to 65; Nashville PO; wounded in right leg
OWENS, Andrew J., Lo-188-3; Elizabeth widow of; Pvt C Co 3rd TN Cav; 1 Nov 62 to 3 Aug 65; Erie PO
OWENS, Bettie, Dy-29-4; widow of Conf Sol; Newbern PO; CONF
OWENS, Durnval, Su-240-3; Pvt K Co 8th TN Cav; 10 Sep 63 to 11 Sep 65; Kindricks Creek PO; no discharge; CONF
OWENS, Geo., Hw-125-1; Pvt A Co 43rd GA; 63 to 64; no PO; CONF
OWENS, George W. D., Gr-74-1; Lina A. widow of; Pvt B Co 8th TN Cav; Rutledge TN PO; sight
OWENS, J. B., G-57-2; Pvt H Co 23rd TN Inf; 7-28-61 to 5-2-65; Yorkville PO; CONF
OWENS, Jackson, K-170-1; Pvt M Co 1st US Art; 5 Sep 63 to 30 Mar 65; Knoxville PO; rheumatism 25 yrs
OWENS, James, Co-63-2; Pvt B Co 58th IL Inf; 20 Jul 63 to 1 Apr 66; Newport PO; ribs broken & spine injured
OWENS, James, H-57-2; Pvt B Co 104th OH Inf; 62 to 65 (2 yrs 9 mos); Orchard Knob PO
OWENS, James B., Ha-115-1; Pvt A Co 1st TN Cav; 5 Apr 62 to 5 Apr 65; Alanthers Hill PO; lung consumption, yet living, pensioner
OWENS, John, C-33-1; Pvt K Co 55th KY Inf; 3-65 to 9-65; Newcomb PO
OWENS, John, Ge-87-1; Pvt B Co 58th IL Inf; 62 to 1 Apr 66; Timberridge PO; chronic diarrhea & eryripelas
OWENS, John, K-161-5(6); Pvt C Co 1st US Hvy Art; Knoxville PO
OWENS, Reden S., He-60-1; Pvt C Co 7th TN Cav; 10-62 to 8-9-65; Lexington PO; slight wound in left shoulder; I was in Andersonvill prison 107 months (sic)
OWENS, Richard, Cr-16-2; Pvt I Co 3rdUS Art; 63 to 66; Huntingdon PO; shoulder hurt on duty, fails to remember date of discharge
OWENS, Thomas, Ha-117-2; Pvt C Co 25th VA Inf; 62 to 65; Kyle's Ford PO; rheumatism and sivetting? limbs; CONF
OWENS, Thomas A., Ce-23-1; Pvt A Co 49th TN; Sep 17 61 to Aug 11 64; Thomasville PO; CONF
OWENS, W. R., Gi-139-3; Pvt A Co 1st TN Art; 5-10-61 to 5-6-65; Campbellsville PO; CONF
OWENS, Wallace, Ru-235-1; Pvt B Co 1st TN Art; Smyrna PO
OWENS, Wesley C., S-216-2; Sol; 6th Dist
OWENS, William, Wa-263-2; Pvt H Co 10th TN Cav; Mar 1 64 to Aug 1 65; Garbers Mills PO; sore leg & rheumatism
OWENS, William, Gr-75-1; Pvt B Co 8th TN Cav; 11 Jun 63 to 22 Jul 65; Tampico PO; chronic diarrhrea & injury to right elbow
OWENS, William, Ha-115-1; Pvt A Co 1st TN Cav; 5 Apr 62 to 5 Apr 65; Alanthers Hill PO; not disabled, yet living
OWENS, William A., Gi-134-1; Dist 14
OWENS, William M., Lo-194-1; Pvt F Co 43rd TN; 15 Apr 62 to __ (3 yrs 15 days); Muddy Creek PO; CONF
OWENSBY, James F., Co-67-1; Pvt D Co 9th TN Cav; 15 Oct 63 to 22 Aug 65; Cosby PO
OWIN?, John, Hw-125-2; Jane widow of; Inf; 62 to 65; Surgoinsville PO
OWINGS, Marion M., Ro-210-7; Pvt A Co 1st TN Cav; 61 to __; Rockwood PO
OWINS, Samuel, Je-145-2; Pvt F Co 8th TN Cav; 28 May 62 to 11 Sep 63; Dumplin PO
OWNBY, Marian, Se-219-2; Pvt TN; Jones Cave PO
OWNBY, Thomas N., Se-229-2; Pvt A Co 5th TN Inf; Trentville PO; diarea & heart trouble
OWNES, Jacob, Cl-47-2; Pvt I Co 8th TN Inf; 3-1-63 to 6-30-65; Speedwell PO; gun shot left hip 1864
OWNEYS, Albert M., Ro-210-2; Pvt I Co 8th TN Cav; 1 Jul 63 to 11 Sep 65; Rockwood PO
OWNINGS, James C., Ro-210-11; Matilda widow of; Pvt E Co 1st TN Inf; Post Oak Springs PO
OWSLEY, John Q., Sn-254-1; Major 5th KY Cav; 11-1-61 to 8-20-63; Hendersonville PO; rheumatism, resulting in dropsy
OXENDINE, Archer, Un-252-2; Emily widow of; Pvt; Nave Hill PO; nothing to show where he belonged
OXFORD, Mary J., Fe-42-3; widow of US Sol; 3rd Civil Dist
OZIER, Levi, Cr-17-2; Pvt; Martha E. widow of; Pvt A Det 7th TN Cav; 8-13-62 to 8-9-65; Buena Vista PO
OZMENT, Branson, We-221-6(2); Pvt L Co 6th TN Cav; 2 Jul 62 to 27 Aug 64; Martin PO; CONF
OZMENT, John, O-141-1; Pvt L Co 12th KY Reg Vol Cav; 14 Dec 63 to Aug 20 65; PO omitted
OZMENT, Lacy, Mn-122-2; 3rd Civil Dist
OZMUN, Andrew, La-115-2; Pvt G Co 64th OH Vol; 19 Oct 61 to 19 Oct 64; Summertown PO; shot right foot
PACE, Carrol, Dy-29-5; Rebecca widow of; Newbern PO; CONF
PACE, William, Se-228-1(2); Pvt E Co 3rd TN Inf; Aug 64 to 30 Nov 64; New Knob Creek PO; variocele, dont know anything about him
PACE, William T., Dy-29-4; Pvt D Co 47th TN Inf; 22 Nov 61 to 11 May 65; Newbern PO; CONF
PACK, Archy B., Dk-36-1; Pvt F Co 4th TN Mtd Inf; 9-26-64 to 8-25-65; Smithville PO
PACK, John G., Po-152-3(1); Pvt E Co 7th TN Mtd Inf; 10-28-64 to 7-27-65; Ducktown PO; heart disease
PACK, Joseph N., Dk-39-1; Pvt F Co 4th TN Mtd Inf; Bozarth PO; hemorrhoids and disease of the testicles
PACK, William, Co-69-7(3); Pvt; Rankin PO; not at home, his wife knoes nothing the dates; CONF
PACKET, James, Lo-187-1; Millie widow of; Pvt I Co 5th TN Inf; Loudon PO
PADGES, William, Cl-53-2; Pvt L Co 9th TN Cav; Springdale PO
PADGET, Albert J., Co-69-7(12); Pvt B Co 22nd NC Inf; 1 May 61 to 16 Jun 65; Bibee PO; CONF
PADGET, F. M., Pi-153-3; Pvt D Co 12th TN Inf; 61 to 4-26-65; Spurnier PO
PADGETT, Benjamin W., Ja-86-3; 1st Lt L Co 4th TN Cav; 10-20-62 to 7-12-65; Oottewah PO; chronic diarhea
PADGETT, John, S-214-4; Pvt D Co 2nd TN Inf; Aug 61 to Nov 64; Robbins PO; chronic diarrhoea & piles
PADGETT, John N., Po-152-2; Emily A. widow of; Pvt; Ducktown PO; died in hospital Nashville
PADGETT, William S., Mu-209-7; Pvt C Co 1st TN Inf; 62 to 65; Columbia PO; CONF
PAGE, Archie, H-73-2(1); Pvt VA Inf; Chattanooga PO
PAGE, Barney B., Dk-36-2; Pvt B Co 4th TN Mtd Inf; 9-25-64; Smithville PO

PAGE, Charlie, Sm-166-1; Pvt; Carthage PO
PAGE, Ella (see Williams, John)
PAGE, George H., Rb-220-1; Capt H Co 8th KY; Jul 4 61 to May 18 65; Barrenplains PO; CONF
PAGE, James, Hu-103-3; Pvt A Co 6th GA Inf; 9 Feb 65 to 12 Aug 65; PO omitted; marked through, probably CONF
PAGE, John, G-68-1; alias John Felor Reece; Pvt F Co 13th GA; Apr 64 to 65; Gibson PO
PAGE, John, Col, Me-89-1; Pvt I Co 122nd OH Reg; 9-64 to 4-65; Big Spring PO
PATE, John, H-69-3; Pvt; Chattanooga PO
PAGE, Lucretia, Sh-200-3; widow of US Sol; Pvt; 514 Orleans St, Memphis PO; tumor 10 yrs
PAGE, R. Wine, Dk-35-4(2); Pvt F Co 4th TN Mtd Inf; 10-2-64 to 8-25-65; Hicks PO
PAGE, Robert, D-70-1; Sol; Nashville PO
PAGE, Thomas, Wl-295-1; Pvt D Co 14th TN Inf; Oct 22 64 to Mar 26 66; Lebanon PO
PAGE, W. H., Hu-103-3; Pvt A Co 6th GA Inf; 10 Sep 61 to 10 Jul 64; PO omitted; marked through, probably CONF
PAIN, George M., Ro-207-1; Pvt G Co 32nd KY Inf-- 15 Nov 62 to 12 Aug 63; 1st Hvy Art--6 Aug 64 to 7 Jun 65; Patties Gap PO; reenlisted in 1st OH Hvy Art
PAIN, James, Wl-305-1; Celia A. widow of; Pvt A Co 5th Stoker; Mar 6 62 to Aug 14 65; Partlow PO
PAINE, Ross W., Sh-201-1; Pvt I Co 61st US Col Inf; 5-15-63 to 6-1-65; Memphis PO
PAINE, Smyth F., Se-230-2; Sgt C Co 64th NC Inf; 15 Aug 63 to ___ (2 yrs); Pokeberry PO; this man came to the union side and served 8 mos after that time; CONF
PAINE, Thomas C., Sh-191-4; Memphis PO; records not seen
PAINTER, James H., Ge-94-3; Pvt H Co 8th TN Cav; 28 Sep 63 to Mar 65; Greeneville PO; chronic diarhea in 1863
PAINTER?, Jeremiah, Wa-272-2; Pvt H Co 8th TN Inf; Apr 64 to 65; Harmony PO; chronic rheumatism 24 yrs (he should be pensioned)
PAINTER, Jesse, Wa-260-1; Pvt B Co 12th Reg Cav; Oct 2 63 to May 18 65; Broyersville PO (Green Co.); rheumatism
PAINTER, Thomas, Ge-83-4; Pvt; Painters PO; liver & kidney disease
PAIR, Joseph D., Br-11-1; Pvt B Co 1st TN Lt Art; 7-22-62 to 65; Cleveland PO; chronic diarrhea
PAIR, Samuel A., Ro-201-5(3); Cpl B Co 1st TN Lt Art; 2 Jul 62 to 20 Jul 65; Kingston PO
PALAMORE, Clark P. (see Arronder, Clark P.)
PALE, Jack, Sh-160-2; Pvt; 15th Dist
PALM, Peter, Sh-149-2; Pvt F Co 3rd US Hvy Art; Nov 63 to 30 Jun 66; Raleigh PO
PALMAR, Nathan, Br-9-5; Cleveland PO; discharge in hand of agent
PALMER, Elizabeth, R-157-2; widow sol; 14th Dist
PALMER, Esaw W., Un-257-2; Sgt E Co 2nd TN Inf; Mar 1 63 to 9 Aug 65; Little Barren PO; broken right shoulder, injure spine
PALMER, Francis, Sh-178-4; US Sol; 337 Union, Memphis PO
PALMER, Frank, Wl-292-1; Lebanon PO
PALMER, George W., Hm-106-2; Pvt B Co 6th MI Hvy Art; 17 Aug 61 to 17 Aug 64; Morristown PO
PALMER, Henry, Cu-17-1; Pvt H Co 136th NY Inf; 5-63 to 2-4-65; Crossville PO; knee cut by bayonet
PALMER, John, Wl-297-2; Dist No 12
PALMER, Lucinda, Mr-96-3(2); widow US Sol; 3rd Dist
PALMER, Syrus B., Sh-201-2; Mary A. widow of; Memphis PO; papers misplaced
PALMER, Thomas M., Hn-73-1; Pvt Co I 6th TN; 62 to 65; Como PO; rheumatism; old and afflicted, needs help
PALMER, William N., Co-61-2(1); Pvt E Co 8th TN Inf; 1 Mar 63 to 12 May 65; Givens PO
PALMER, William S., Dk-31-1; Cpl G Co 1st TN Mtd Inf; 54-64 to 4-21-65; Alexandria PO
PALMORE, Fredric W., Wi-270-2; Pvt H Co 10th TN Inf; 15 Jun 63 to 24 Jun 65; Gingo PO
PALMORE, Robert T., Wi-270-1; Sgt H Co 10th TN Inf; 15 Jun 63 to 24 Jan 65; Gingo PO
PANCHER, John H., Ce-27-1; Pvt F Co 39th OH Rich?; 63 to 65; Terbine, Mont. Co., PO; sunstroke
PANCOAST, Joseph, Sh-184-1; Pvt B Co 39th OH Inf; 7-20-61 to 7-9-65; 15 Robeson, Memphis PO
PANE, George, Ge-90-3; Pvt B Co 8th TN Cav; 16 Jun 63 to 18 Apr 65; Greeneville PO; shot in arm & leg at Bulls Gat & VA Saltwork
PANE, James, K-169-1; Pvt; Knoxville PO
PANGLE, Fredrick, Hw-129-1; Cpl D Co 1st TN Cav; 15 Apr 62 to 15 Apr 65; Galbrath Springs PO; rheumatism & broncial affected
PANGLE, Isaac N., Hm-109-3; Pvt; 63 to 64; Whitesburg PO
PANGLE, William S., Hm-109-2; Pvt C Co 8th TN Cav; 1 Jun 62 to 18 Sep 65; Whitesburg PO
PANLIN, Avery, We-233-2; 18th Dist
PARCHMAN, Isaac, St-162-1; Waiter B Co WI; Cumberland City PO; sight affected, papers lost
PARCHMAN, Thomas (see Scott, Thomas)
PARDER, Hubbard, Di-31-1; Dorindy widow of; Pvt; Dickson PO; cant find out anything about this soldier
PARDNER, Albert E., Di-36-1; Pvt I Co 2nd TN Inf; 4-1-61 to 5-2-65; Bellsburg PO; CONF
PARETT, Henry, F-44-4; Pvt; PO omitted
PARHAM, Charlie, F-46-2; Eugene widow of; 59th TN; LaGrange PO; widow do not know dates
PARHAM, Henry Clay, K-180-4; US Sol; 11th Dist
PARHAM, John, Rb-229-1; Pvt TN Inf; 63 to 65; Sadlersville PO
PARHAM, Sarah F. (see Pounds, Danal W.)
PARHAM, Thomas (see Harris, Abrim)
PARISH, Arthur A., Gi-134-2; Dist 14
PARISH, Elizabeth, Cr-15-2; widow US Sol; Maple Creek PO
PARISH, Jacob, Col, Mt-139-1; Sgt I Co 111th US Col Inf; 64 to 66 (1 yr 6 mos); New Providence PO
PARISH, Samuel, Cr-15-1; Pvt D Co 7th TN Cav; Oct 20 62 to Apr 20 64; Maple Creek PO
PARISH, Siver?, Cr-15-1; Pvt D Co 7th TN Cav; 14 Aug 62 to 25 Oct 63; PO omitted
PARK, Alex J., H-66-1; 4th OH Inf; Co C?; 10-15-62 to 5-29-65; Chattanooga PO
PARK, James, Cr-17-2; Emily widow of; Pvt E Co 7th TN Cav; 62 to ___; Buena Vista PO; James Park died in prison, has no discharge
PARK, John, Dk-36-2; Pvt B Co 4th TN Mtd Inf; 9-64 to 8-64(5?); Smithville PO
PARK?, Joshua L., Gi-133-2; Bufords PO; CONF
PARK, Madison G., Hr-98-1; Pvt C Co 1st AL Cav; 5 Mar 63 to 3 Jan 64; U. Bet PO
PARK, Madison G., Hr-98-1; Pvt C Co 11th IL Cav; 25 Apr 64 to 13 Sep 65; U-Bet PO
PARK, Robert W., Cr-20-3; Martha J. widow of; Pvt I Co 7th TN Cav; Jan 5 62 to Aug 9 65; Hollow Rock PO
PARKER, Aaron, Bl-2-3; Pvt A Co 5th TN Inf; 2-25-62 to 4-4-65; Orme's Store PO; stunned by shell exploding & chronic diarhea, able to do moderate labor
PARKER, Abraham, Sn-259-1; Pvt C Co 14th ___; 10-1-63 to 3-1-65; Bransford PO
PARKER, Alvin, S-213-3; Rhoda A. widow of; Pvt K Co 30th KY Mtd Inf; 1 Feb 64 to 18 Apr 64; Hellenwood PO
PARKER, Andrew, Wh-187-3; Pvt K Co 4th TN Cav; 11-1-64 to 8-25-65; Key PO; ribs broken
PARKER, Anthoney, L-101-1; Pvt D Co 51st TN C Inf; 62 to 65; Ripley PO; hernia r. side, discharge in hand of atty
PARKER, Benjamin, Cl-56-1; Elisabeth widow of; Pvt 8th KY Inf; Big Barren PO
PARKER, Calvin, Jo-148-1; Mary J. Arnold late widow of; Pvt D Co 13th TN Cav; Oct 61 to Feb 62; Laurel Bloomery PO; died with smallpox while in service
PARKER, Cass, D-43-1; Pvt C Co 7th IL Cav; 61 to ___; Nashville PO
PARKER, Charles I., Sn-262-2(1); Pvt H Co 3rd MS Cav; 12-30-63 to 9-25-65; Fountain Head PO; diarrhea
PARKER, Dannel W., Tr-266-1; Sgt U Pvt H Co 5th KY Cav; Mar 62 to 65; Hartsville PO
PARKER, David H., Rb-228-2; Pvt; 61 (6 mos); Crunk PO; CONF
PARKER, Dick, Hy-81-1; Cpl F Co 4th US Col Art Hvy; 63 to 65; this entry crossed through, PO omitted
PARKER, Elbert, Se-227-1; Cpl K Co 2nd TN Inf; 15 Dec 62 to ___ (3 yrs); Trundles X Roads PO; piles

PARKER, Elizabeth, M-105-1; widow; Pvt F Co 25th KY Inf; 12-2-61 to 1-8-65; Echo PO
PARKER, Elvin, Un-253-3; Pvt G Co 4th TN Inf; 15 Dec 63 to 2 Aug 65; PO omitted
PARKER, Emberson, S-214-2; Elizabeth widow of; Pvt K Co 30th KY Inf; Glenmary PO
PARKER, Frank, C1-47-2; Polly widow of; Pvt B Co 49th KY Inf; 7-15-63 to 65; Compensation PO; has been gone 13 yrs & is supposed to be dead
PARKER, Frank, K-155-1; Pvt A Co 5th Col Inf; 63 to 66; Knoxville PO
PARKER, George W., Mr-98-2(5); P-t D Co 10th TN Inf; 4-10-62 to 5-29-65; Whiteside PO
PARKER, George W., Dy-29-2; Pvt; 61 to 64; Newbern PO; CONF
PARKER, George W., Dy-25-6; Pvt; Newbern PO; CONF
PARKER, George W., C-8-2; Pvt C Co 1st TN Cav; 9-63 to 8-65; Powells River PO; has no discharge
PARKER, George W., Hw-132-2; Pvt H Co 8th TN Inf; Jul 63 to __; Slide PO; heart disease, was not discharged on account of sickness
PARKER, Henry O., We-228-1(9); Pvt G Co 2nd TN Cav; Aug 62 to Dec 63; Gleason PO
PARKER, Henry B., Hu-106-2; Pvt C Co 1st MI Cav; Waverly PO
PARKER, Jacob, Ro-208-3; Pvt B Co 1st TN Inf; 6 Oct 62 to 3 Aug 65; Welker Mines PO
PARKER, James, A-4-2; Pvt B Co 11th TN Inf; 4-14-63 to 10-14-65; Coal Creek PO; rheumatism, discharge burned up
PARKER, James C., S-213-2; Sgt I Co 30th KY Inf; 25 Jun 64 to 18 Apr 65; Hellenwood PO
PARKER, James E., Ca-22-2; Pvt A Co 18th IL Cav; 9-1-64 to 12-1-65; Burgen PO
PARKER, James F., We-221-3; Pvt K Co 5th TN Inf; May 61 to 64; Martin PO; CONF
PARKER, James H., We-221-6(2); Pvt A Co 31st TN Inf; 17 Aug 61 to 19 May 64; Martin PO; CONF
PARKER, James M., Gi-139-1; Pvt A Co 11th TN Cav; 12-15-63 to 10-15-64; Barcheers PO; CONF
PARKER, James R., He-62-2; Pvt A Co 3rd TN Cav; Jun 63 to Jun 64; Alexander's Mill PO; cripled in left ancle
PARKER, Jesse H., K-174-2(1); Pvt B Co 3rd TN Inf; 28 Feb 62 to 23 Feb 65; Graveston PO; shot through neck, total disable from work
PARKER, John, Wh-187-3; Orderly Sgt K Co 4th TN Inf; 9-64 to 8-25-65; Key PO; contracted deafness
PARKER, John, H-49-5; Pvt E Co 5th TN Mtd Inf; 8-20-64 to 6-26-65; Daisy PO; hurt in a train wreck
PARKER, John A., Hw-133-2; Pvt A Co 8th TN Cav; 14 Mar 64 to 11 Sep 65; Slide PO; chronic diarhea
PARKER, John A., We-232-1; Eliz. C. widow of; Pvt A Co 1st PA Cav; 61 to __; Sharon PO; wounded in back, died from wound
PARKER, John B., Pu-145(6); Pvt K Co 5th Cav Vol; 4-25-63 to 8-14-65; Buffalo Valley PO
PARKER, John D., Cl-46-3(1); Pvt C Co 1st TN Art; 9-1-63 to 8-1-65; Ibex PO; draws pension
PARKER, John P., D-92-2; US Sol; W. Nashville PO
PARKER, Joseph, Ge-83-1; Emaline widow of; E Co TN Cav; Feb 7 64 to __ (1 yr); Pilat Hill PO
PARKER, Louis R., Br-8-3(1); Cleo PO; chronic liver & kidney affection
PARKER, Manuel, Gi-127-8; Pvt; 9th Dist
PARKER, Margarette (see Thomasson, Josephus)
PARKER, Martin, S-214-3; Pvt I Co 30th KY Inf; 4 Feb 64 to 18 Apr 65; New River PO
PARKER, Michael H., Je-135-1(3); Pvt B Co 9th TN Cav; 11 Jun 62 to 11 Sep 65; Piedmont PO; rheumatism
PARKER, Nasey, L-101-2; Pvt; Henning PO; cant tell what co & reg member of
PARKER, Nimrod E., K-156-2; Margaret C. Champ widow of; 1st Sgt K Co 2nd Reg TN Inf; 28 Dec 61 to 28 Dec 64; 89 Pine St, Knoxville PO
PARKER, Oliver, Sm-166-3(1); Pvt A Co 14th OH Inf; 10-61 to 3-64; Monoville PO
PARKER, Richard T., Jo-153-2; Pvt B Co 12th TN Cav; 28 Jul 63 to 24 Oct 65; Shady PO; diarrhoea, piles
PARKER, Samuel W., Sh-159-7; Sgt; 62 to 65; Memphis PO; CONF

PARKER, Sarah (see Smither, Jonathan)
PARKER, Thomas, Su-239-3; Pvt G Co 8th TN Cav; 12 Aug 63 to 11 Sep 65; Kingsport PO; old and feble
PARKER, William, Po-149-4(2); Sgt F Co 5th TN Mtd Inf; 9-26-64 to 6-26-65; Fetzerton PO
PARKER, William, Hw-123-2; Pvt F Co; Jul 63 to Oct 63; Rotherwood PO
PARKER, William, Sh-178-1; Pvt C Co 46th Art? Cans?; 62 to __ (2 yrs 20 mos); rear 400 Beale, Memphis PO; does not know date of enlistment
PARKER, William J., Hd-45-2; Josie E. widow; C Co 6th TN Cav; __ to 65; Cerro Gordo PO; discharg loose, hence deficiency in date abov
PARKER, William M., G-67-2; 17th Civil Dist
PARKER, William S., Dk-35-1; Pvt A Co 5th TN Cav; 8-9-62 to __; Temperance Hall PO; prisoner at Sparta
PARKER, William T., M-103-5; Pvt H Co 65th IL; Lafayette PO; lost hearing
PARKER, Willis T., Su-236-1; Pvt B Co TN Inf; 63 to Oct 64; Morell's Mill PO
PARKER, ____, Me-92-4(1); Sarah E. Miller formerly widow of; 7th TN Mtd Inf; Pin Hook PO
PARKER, ____, H-54-1; Delila widow of; Chattanooga PO
PARKES, Richard, Mr-95-2; Pvt C Co 5th TN Inf; 2-25-62 to 4-4-65; Victoria PO
PARKEY, Isaac, Ha-114-2; Pvt K Co 14th VA Cav; 11 May 62 to 16 Jun 64; George PO; CONF
PARKHILL, Luthur M., Hn-72-1; Quartermaster Sgt A Co 1st AL Cav; 8 Sep 62 to 16 Sep 63; Paris PO; neuralgia
PARKHURST, Simeon L., H-69-4; Cpl I Co 2nd VT Inf; 12-21-63 to 7-15-65; Chattanooga PO
PARKIN, Richard L., Sh-192-1; Sgt B Co 14th US Inf; 7-26-61 to 11-21-62; Memphis PO
PARKINSON, Elizabeth, Dy-32-1; widow US Sol; Trimble PO
PARKINSON, John A., MD, Mc-112-5; Asst Surgeon 5th TN Mtd Inf; 9-4-64 to 7-19-65; Athens PO
PARKINSON, Oliver, Dk-32-2; Sarah widow of; Pvt G Co 1st TN Mtd Inf; 3-22-64 to 4-__; Temperance Hall PO; died in hospital
PARKINSON, Page J., Ja-86-3; Pvt A Co 5th TN Inf; 2-62 to 4-65; Oottewah PO
PARKISON, James A., Mc-110-2(1); Lt E Co 10th TN Cav; 8-12-63 to 8-1-65; Mouse Creek PO
PARKS, Andrew, Dy-29-4; Bettie Pitman widow of; Newbern PO; CONF
PARKS, Calvin, Bo-13-3(1); Pvt A Co 3rd TN Inf; 2-10-62 to 2-23-65; Disco PO; wounded in left thigh
PARKS, Carrol, W-192-1; Pvt A Co; 6-17-63 to 65; Irving College PO; sore leg
PARKS, David, R-158-3; Lucy P. widow of; Pvt 5th TN Inf; Rhea Springs PO; died in service, widow draws pension
PARKS, Ephram, G-53-1(4); Pvt D Co 11th IL Cav; 63 to 63 (5 mos); Brazil PO
PARKS, George A., Pu-145-1; Pvt K Co 1st Mtd Inf; 10-17-64 to 7-22-65; Burton PO
PARKS, Henry J., Br-9-4; Pvt F Co 4th TN Cav; 5-25-63 to 7-12-65; Cleveland PO
PARKS, Hiram, Br-14-1; Pvt D Co 4th TN Cav; 1-9-62 to 7-12-65; McDonald PO; salivated by colomel in veins
PARKS, James, H-51-1; Pvt B Co 1st R TN Art; 10-17-62 to 9-20-65; Soddy PO; sore eyes and shot
PARKS, James, Ro-210-7; Pvt; Cardiff PO
PARKS, Martha, Sh-149-4; widow US Sol; 6th Civil Dist
PARKS, Milus, Mu-213-1; Blacksmith OH Cav; Feb 61 to Mar 64; Rally Hill PO; cut on arm by horse
PARKS, Paul, Po-150-1; 5th Civil Dist
PARKS, Samuel, H-55-1; Pvt B Co 1st TN Inf; 1 Aug 61 to 17 Sep 64; Alanthers Hill PO
PARKS, Tennessee M., Un-252-2; Ollie widow of; Pvt; Nave Hill PO; nothing to show where he belonged
PARKS, William F., Je-136-2; Pvt F Co 4th TN Inf; 6 Mar 63 to 11 Aug 65; PO omitted
PARKS, William F., H-50-5; Pvt A Co 6th R TN Mtd Inf; 8-17-64 to 6-30-65; Soddy PO; bronchitis
PARKS, William M., H-55-2; Musician B Co 5th TN Mtd Inf; 9-5-64 to 7-13-65; Tyner PO

PARKS, Williamson, H-55-2; Pvt GQ 3rd TN Cav; 2-8-64 to 3-22-64; Tyner PO; discharged on surgeons certificate
PARLISH, Martin, He-61-1; Pvt G Co 2nd TN Mtd Inf; 29 Jan 64 to 1 Feb 65; Spellings PO; rheumatism
PARMER, David, Ja-86-3; Ann widow of; Pvt; Oottewah PO
PARMER, Simon, Li-152-1; Pvt A Co; 64 to 65; Petersburg PO; Col
ΡARNALL, Clate, Hd-51-1; Pvt F Co 4th AL Inf; 20 Jun 62 to 65; Pickens PO; CONF
PARNELL?, Bart M., Hd-51-1; Pvt H Co 4th TN Cav; 15 Jul 61 to 62; Pickens PO; CONF
PARNIN, Isaac, Hw-125-2; Cpl F Co 16th TN Bat; 62 to 5 Sep 63 (1 yr); Surgoinsville PO
PARR, Marcus D.?, Ch-18-1; Pvt C Co 31st TN Inf; 21 Sep 61 to 14 Apr 65; PO omitted; CONF
PARRENT, Richard H., H-60-2; Pvt E Co 9th KY Cav; 8-62 to 5-63; Chattanooga PO
PARRETT, Anderson, Hm-103-1; Sallie widow of; Teamster Cav; Morristown PO
PARRIS, Henry S., G-65-1; Alcy widow of; Pvt K Co 7th TN Cav; Mar 63 to died Sep 64; Bradford PO; died in Andersonville
PARRIS, James, Ge-88-1; Pvt; PO omitted; dropsy; CONF
PARRIS, Lewis, Col, Pi-154-2; Los widow of; Pvt 13th US Col; found no papers or discharge; Hull PO
PARRISH, David B., Rb-228-1; Pvt; Oct 61 to ___ (4 mos); Crunk PO; CONF
PARRISH, Fanny, Hu-100-1; widow; 3rd Civil Dist
PARRISH, Turner, Mt-138-2; Blk US Sol; Dist 7, New Providence PO
PARROT, David F., Sh-187-1(5); Pvt K Co 118th OH Cav; 10-8-62 to 1-13-65; 43 Fifth St, Chelsy, Memphis PO; disabled, chills
PARROTT, Daniel, Hw-120-2; Elizabeth widow of; Pvt K Co 13th TN Cav; 1 Oct 64 to 5 Sep 65; Eidson PO
PARROTT, Elbert S., Co-61-1; Pvt K Co; Parrottsville PO
PARROTT, George, Ja-86-2; Jane McDaniel widow of; Pvt C Co 5th TN Inf; Oottewah PO; died at Cumberland Gap, prisoner
PARROTT, Henry, A-2-3; Pvt H Co 8th TN Cav; 7-25-63 to 6-30-65; Hinds Creek PO; measles and its sequences
PARROTT, Lewis G., We-225-3(2); Susan E. widow of; Pvt K Co 6th TN Cav; Aug 9 62 to Jul 26 65; Dresdin PO; typhoid fever
PARROTT, Monroe, H-49-7; Pvt C Co 5th TN Inf; 2-25-62 to 4-4-65; Ign's Ferry PO
PARSLEY, William, D-49-1; Cpl D Co 110th Inf; 2 yrs; Nashville PO; dont remember dates
PARSLEY, William N., Hm-104-1; Pvt C Co 3rd IL Cav; 1 May 63 to Jul 65; Mossy Creek PO
PARSON, John, Ro-205-1; Pvt C Co 24th KY Inf; 1 Jul 62 to 1 Jul 65; Kings Creek PO; piles & eye sight affectted 25 yrs
PARSONS, George W., Br-7-4; Cpl I Co 10th TN Cav; 2-2-64 to 8-1-65; Cleveland PO
PARSONS, John E., H-57-4; US Sol; 10th Civil Dist
PARSONS, Marshal M., H-62-3; Musician E Co 4th NY Hvy Art; 8-9-62 to 5-13-65; 314 Cedar, Chattanooga PO; suffering from chronic diarrhoea, in hospital 1 yr
PARSONS, Prince, Mn-125-1; Pvt D Co 44th US Col Inf; Oct 64 to May 66; Corinth, MS, PO
PARSONS, Robert, Pr-8-1; Pvt 16th IL Inf; 6-8-___ to 12 (11 mos); Cleveland PO
PARSONS, William R., Ov-139-1; Pvt I Co 1st AL Cav; 1-1-64 to 6-30-64; Lovejoy PO
PARTEE, George, Sh-196-3; Cpl C Co 61st US Inf; 1-63 to 5-65; Memphis PO; lost 3rd, 4th, 5th toes of right foot, pensioner
PARTEE, Nancy, L-105-1; widow Pvt; 7th Civil Dist
PARTIAN, John L., We-222-2; 2nd Sgt I & F Cos 7th & 45th TN Inf; 16 Jun 61 to May 65; Gardner PO; CONF
PARTIN, Benjamin C., Se-220-2; Pvt K Co 11th TN Cav; 11 Sep 63 to Sep 65; Emerts Cave PO; cramp in legs
PARTIN, Catharine, Se-220-3; widow US Sol; Emerts Cave PO
PARTIN, Huston, Se-220-3; US Sol; Emerts Cave PO

PARTIN, James B., Mc-117-1; 1st Lt E Co 49th KY Inf; 7-24-62 to 9-15-65; Mecca PO
PARTIN, John N., Dy-29-3; Conf & US; Pvt B Co 10th TN Cav; Dec 62 to Aug 64; Newbern PO; diseas of lungs, thinks one lung is perished
PARTLOW, Jack, Sh-150-2; Andrew Jackson; Pvt B Co US Hvy Art; 10 mos; Bartlett PO
PARTON, William A., Fr-112-3; Pvt D Co 17th TN Inf; 5-20-61 to 10-20-61; Estill Springs PO; CONF
PARTON, Wilson H., H-53-8; Pvt; 2 yrs; Chattanooga PO; mules ran away with him & crippled him
PARTRIDGE, Joseph G., Sh-196-3; Pvt 6th NY Lt Art; 8-61 to 63; Memphis PO; papers lost
PARX, Barry G., Sh-145-4; Pvt A Co 125th IL Inf; 7 Jun 65; Cuba PO; enlisted as private and then was regmtal com sgt, blind in r. eye, caused by bomb shell at Kenesaw Mountain 27 Jun 1864, Col ___ Hunean?
PASCHAL, John R., Ce-23-1; Louisa Basford former widow of; US Sol G Co 3rd Aft; 51 to Jan 9 63 (sic--12 yrs); Thomasville PO
PASCHAL, Richard, Hn-78-1; Nancy Johnson Paschal widow of; Pvt Hvy Art; Cottage Grove PO; this old lady could not give any information as to co or time of service. She was on the pension list for a while from the death of her soldier husband until she married the 2nd time. She is a widow now as you will see from family schedule.
PASCHAL, Rolly B., Ce-23-1; Cpl 97th; Jul 62 to ___ (5 mos); Thomasville PO; died while in army
PASCHALL, Osborne, D-57-2; Pvt F Co 15th US Cav; Feb 1 64 to Apr 7 66; PO omitted, 8th Ward
PASMIR, Sam, Sn-250-1; Pvt B Co 39th ___; 11-15-62 to 64; Castalian Springs PO
PASS, Herman B., Sh-149-3; US Sol; 6th Civil Dist
PASS, N. E., Me-89-2; Pvt B Co 6th TN Inf; 7-64 to 6-65; Big Spring PO
PASS, Nathan G., Ro-210-9; Pvt; Rockwood PO
PASSONS, William D., Wh-180-1; Sparta PO; discharge lost, can't remember
PAT, John A., Ge-92-3; Mary C. widow of; Pvt E Co 8th TN Cav; Laurel Gap PO
PATE, Anthonney, K-181-6(3); Pvt C Co 6th TN Inf; 18 Apr 62 to 27 Apr 65; Knoxville PO; diaria ruptur piles
PATE, Geor R., K-156-1; Pvt A Co 1st E TN; 21 Mar 64 to Mar 66; Pine 33, Knoxville PO
PATE, George W., K-178-2; Pvt V Co 1st ___; 9 Jun 64 to 31 Mar 66; Ball Camp PO
PATE, Ira J., Cl-54-3(1); Pvt G Co 22nd VA Cav; 8-17-62 to 65; Tazewell PO; CONF
PATE, John H., Se-223-4; Pvt I Co 1st TN Bat; 10 Jul 64 to 31 Mar 66; Sevierville PO
PATE, Stephen S., We-230-3; Pvt K Co 21st TN Reg; May 2 62 to May 2 64; McKinzie PO; CONF
PATE, Thomas, Wi-278-1; Pvt C Co 7th TN Cav; Dec 20 63 to Jan 1 65; Franklin PO; Andersonville PO
PATE, William N., Cr-4-2; Mary S. widow of; Pvt 22nd TN Inf; 61 to 61 (6 mos); Bells Depot PO; mortally wounded, died from wound; CONF
PATE, William T., Bo-22-2; Pvt J Co 1st US Art; 6-64 to 3-31-66; Hebronville PO
PATEN?, Robert A., K-165-4; Pvt C Co 12th CT Inf; 22 Aug 62 to 4 Jul 65; Knoxville PO
PATER, James W., Dy-25-6(2); Pvt; Newbern PO; wounded, dates all forgotten; CONF
PATERSON, Isah, He-63-2; Pvt C Co 7th TN Cav; May 25 63 to Aug 9 65; PO omitted
PATERSON, John Belle, Wl-307-1; Margaret E. widow of; Pvt C Co 136; 21 May 64 to 22 Oct 64; Leeville PO
PATES, John, Ge-90-2; Pvt L Co 1st TN Cav; 1 Apr 63 to 19 Jun 65; Greenville PO; heart disiase & piles, tifoid fever the caus
PATILLER, Otter, Hm-103-1; Pvt K Co 40th TN Inf; 1 yr 6 mos (___ to 65); Morristown PO
PATON, Angeline, Mu-197-2; Macedonia PO
PATRICK, Bryant, Se-224-2; Pvt F Co 7th KY Inf; 10 Aug 62 to 18 Jul 65; Wears Valley PO; came home on sick furlow
PATRICK, Hamilton G., Sn-260-5; Pvt D Co 3rd KY Inf; 11-61 to 11-62; Westmoreland PO; contracted measles settled in bowels & loungs
PATRICK, John, C-33-3; Pvt C Co 9th OH Cav; 5-4-63 to 7-20-65; Newcomb PO

PATRICK, John C., Ov-135-2; 7th Civil Dist
PATRICK, Mrs. Martha, La-111-2; Pvt I Co 1st AL Cav; 62 to 63 (8 mos); Pleasant Point PO; died with measles
PATRICK, Nathan, L-99-1; Pvt G Co 4th US Hvy Art; Oct 26 63 to Mar 30 66; Durhamville PO; small pox
PATRICK, Powm?, H-65-1; Pvt A Co 20th GA Vol; 5-61 to 64; Chattanooga PO; CONF
PATRICK, Rowel (see Fitzpatrick, Rolly)
PATRICK, Silas, Je-143-1; Pvt A Co 10th TN Cav--28 Nov 64 to 1 Aug 65; A Co 3rd TN Inf--30 Jun 64 to 30 Nov 64; Mossy Creek PO; spinal affection & catarrh
PATRICK, Thos. J., D-99-3; Pvt D Co 8th TN Cav; 26 Sep 63 to 11 Sep 65; State Penitentiary PO; saber cut in right cheek
PATRICK, William, Gi-127-6; Pvt D Co 110th US Col Inf; 1-2-64 to 4-3-66; Pulaski PO
PATRICK, William, Cr-8-2; Pvt H Co 26th AL; 1 Aug 61 to 1 Aug 63; Maury City PO; CONF
PATTAN, William T., Li-164-1; Pvt C Co 2nd KY Mtd Inf; 64 to 65; Kelso PO; disable in the arm
PATTEN, Anderson, Gi-138-2; Pvt D Co 110th __; 1-7-63 to 66; Shones PO
PATTEN, Ben, Wi-287-1; Pvt G Co 54th MA? Inf; Mar 63 to 65; Civ Dist No 18
PATTEN, Julian F., Fe-42-1; Pvt; Jamestown PO
PATTEN, Z. C., H-56-1; Pvt H Co 149th NY Inf; 8-62 to 7-64; St. Elm(o) PO
PATTER, James L., Gr-74-1; Pvt A Co 59th TN Inf; 1 May 62 to __ (4 mos); May Spring PO; left on account of dyspepsia; CONF
PATTERBERY, Augustus M., Ca-25-2; Pvt A Co 5th TN Cav; 8-9-61 to 7-10-64; Gassoway PO; gun shot left arm
PATTERSON, Alex, D-64-5; Mary widow of; Nashville PO
PATTERSON, Alexander, A-9-1; Pvt G Co 7th TN Mtd Inf; 2-25-65 to 7-27-65; Ligias PO
PATTERSON, Amous, Sh-147-1; Pvt D Co 3rd TN Art; 8 May 63 to 30 May 65; Cuba PO
PATTERSON, Charles, Sh-158-2; Seaman Curlew No. 12; 1 yr; Memphis PO; fell or thrown on hot boiler while in action and back badly hur, a very ignorant man, says his discharge papers sent to Washington
PATTERSON, Charles, Sh-190-2; alias Hawkins; gunboat US Nat?; 6th & Broadway, Memphis PO
PATTERSON, Clark, A-9-1; Jane widow of; Pvt H Co 2nd TN Inf; 8-61 to __; Ligias PO; discharge in hands of pension attorney
PATTERSON, David A., M-108-4; Pvt B Co 5th KY Cav; 63 to 6-65; Lafayette PO; hearing damaged, discharge not at hand--lost
PATTERSON, David W., Hd-45-2; Pvt E Co 6th TN Cav; 18 Sep 62 to 27 Jul 65; Swallow Bluff PO; back & piles, disabilities caus from horse falling on him in a ditch
PATTERSON, Edley A., Hw-122-1; Pvt D Co 4th TN Inf; 12 Oct 63 to 10 Aug 65; New Canton PO; disease of lungs, partially disabled
PATTERSON, Edmund, A-5-1; Pvt M Co 2nd TN Cav; 11-8-62 to 2-14-65; Clinton PO
PATTERSON, Edward M., H-51-3; Pvt K Co 41st TN Inf; 3-14-61 to 10-14-63; Hill City PO
PATTERSON, Fielding, Br-8-2; 1st Lt A Co 5th NY Cav; 4-6-61 to __; Cleveland PO; gangrene, scurvy, chronic diarrhea, festula ano?, in all the prisons of the South (also 1st Lt E Co 6th NY); lung trouble, too weak to give all the information
PATTERSON, Finley, A-9-2; Pvt I Co 9th TN Cav; 7-18-63 to 9-11-65; Podopholine PO; rheumatism incurred while a prisoner on Bells Island
PATTERSON, G. W., Ru-236-1; Pvt D Co 50th IL (Col?); Feb 64 to 27 Oct 65; Murfreesboro PO
PATTERSON, George W., Wl-300-2; Pvt H Co 4th TN Inf; 20 Oct 64 to 25 Aug 65; Watertown PO
PATTERSON, I. M., De-22-3; Pvt C Co 7th TN Cav; 1 Jan 65 to 8 Aug 65; Dunbar PO
PATTERSON, James, Sh-152-3; Pvt F Co 1st AL Cav; Oct 63 to 64; Dexter PO; wounded in hip and knee, unable to make support, never has received bounty or pension
PATTERSON, James, Sm-168-2; Pvt A Co 1st TN Inf; 2-64 to 2-65; Pleasant Shade PO; lost hearing and piles
PATTERSON, James, D-91-1; Pvt; Jackson's Grocery, Cedar St, Nashville PO
PATTERSON, James, A-9-2; Pvt I Co 7th TN Mtd Inf; 11-8-64 to 7-27-65; Podopholine PO; ruptur
PATTERSON, James A., Ms-176-1; Pvt A Co 42nd TN; 3-15-64 to 2-5-64; Caney Springs PO
PATTERSON, Jesse H., Hd-49-1; Pvt D Co 2nd TN Inf; Sep 1 63 to Feb 1 65; Olive Hill PO; rupture
PATTERSON, John, Sn-252-1; Millie widow of; Pvt E Co 14th US Inf; 11-16-63 to 3-29-66; Gallatin PO
PATTERSON, Jos. H., T-209-2; Randolph PO; not at home, information obtained from wife
PATTERSON, Josiah, Sh-159-6; Col; Memphis PO; CONF
PATTERSON, Levi N., Ch-17-1; Pvt C Co 31st TN Inf; 11-15-62 to 6-10-63; Henderson PO; CONF
PATTERSON, Lewis, Gi-127-5; Josie widow of; Pvt H Co 11th US Col T; 6-10-64 to 4-30-66; Pulaski PO
PATTERSON, Mansfild M. J., Ch-17-1; Pvt C Co 31st TN Inf; 2-14-62 to 10-64; Henderson PO; CONF
PATTERSON, Marton L., R-161-3; Emily L. widow of; Pvt K Co 65th IN Inf; 8-20-62 to __; Dayton PO; killed 3-3-64
PATTERSON, McCajah, Se-221-3; Pvt C Co 9th TN Cav; 12 Jun 63 to 15 Sep 65; Fair Garden PO
PATTERSON, Michael L., K-159-2; Lt Col 4th TN Inf; 9 Sep 64 to __; Knoxville PO
PATTERSON, Mose, Ru-238-1; Pvt A Co 14th USC Inf; 1 Oct 63 to 26 Mar 66; Murfreesboro PO
PATTERSON, Moses, Gi-127-7; Pvt B Co 13th US Col Inf; Sep 5 62 to Jun 3 66; Pulaski PO
PATTERSON, Reuben, Po-152-5(1); Pvt H Co 12th TN Cav; 1-26-64 to 10-7-65; Ducktown PO; gun shot wound of back
PATTERSON, Riley, Hd-49-1; Pvt B Co 2nd TN Mtd Inf; Oct 11 63 to Oct 17 64; Olive Hill PO
PATTERSON, Robbert, A-6-5(3); Cpl J Co 9th TN Cav; 7-18-63 to 9-11-65; PO omitted
PATTERSON, Robert, Li-158-1; Pvt K Co 106th US Col; Sep 62 to Jul 65; Blanche PO; in prison 8 mos
PATTERSON, Robert, Di-37-1; Pvt I Co 13th WI Inf; 8-24-63 to 7-25-65; Cumberland Furnace PO; discharged from hospital, in both CONF & US service
PATTERSON, Robert E., A-9-3; Pvt; 8-61 to __; Podopholine PO; killed during term of service
PATTERSON, Robert F., Sh-199-2; Col; Memphis PO
PATTERSON, Robert H., De-23-1; Pvt G Co 7th TN; Sep 62 to Aug 65; Thurman PO
PATTERSON, Rufus, Se-223-4; Pvt; Sevierville PO
PATTERSON, Rufus, Se-225-3; Pvt I Co 2nd TN Cav; 22 Sep 62 to 11 Jul 65; Sevierville PO; claims to be disabled 25 yrs
PATTERSON, Samuel, Mc-111-2; Pvt A Co 7th TN Mtd Inf; 9-20-64 to 7-27-65; Athens PO
PATTERSON, Samuel H., Wl-300-2; Pvt E Co 4th TN Cav; 64 to 65; Cherry Valley PO
PATTERSON, Sanford W., Ce-27-1; Pvt B Co 49th TN; Nov 61 to Aug 63; South Side PO
PATTERSON, Silas J., M-107-4; Pvt H Co 5th KY Cav; 12-4-61 to 5-65; Gibb's Cross Roads PO; disease of lungs--result of measles
PATTERSON, Smith J., Ch-17-1; Capt B Co 49th IN Vol; 64 to 5-25-65; Henderson PO
PATTERSON, Thomas, Mu-200-2; Terry PO; can tell nothing of service
PATTERSON, Thomas M., Sh-161-1; PO omitted
PATTERSON, Thomas M., K-159-2; 1st Lt E Co 10th OH Inf; 3 Jun 61 to 17 Jun 64; Knoxville PO; lost right fore arm at Perryville, enlisted vet reserve corps Aug 8/64 Co G 9th Vet 1st Lt discharge Jul 1/66
PATTERSON, Vines, A-8-2; Pvt K Co 1st IL Art; 6-6-64 to 7-15-65; Scarborough PO
PATTERSON, Watson, Gi-127-3; Julia widow of; Pulaski PO
PATTERSON, West., D-70-1; Pvt G Co 4th PA Cav; 61 to 64; Nashville PO
PATTERSON, William, Wl-299-1; Pvt H Co 4th TN Inf; 1 Dec 63 to 25 Aug 64; Statesville PO
PATTERSON, William, A-9-2; Pvt C Co 11th TN Cav; 7-18-63 to __; Podopholine PO
PATTERSON, William A., Hd-49-1; Sgt B Co 2nd TN Mtd Inf; Oct 11 63 to Oct 17 64; Olive Hill PO; rheumatism 24 yrs standing

PATTERSON, Wm. C., Sn-250-1; 2nd Lt C Co 2nd __;
-16-62 to 64; Castalian Springs PO; CONF
PATTERSON, William H., J-77-1; Pvt H Co 13th KY
Cav; 11-27-63 to 1-10-65; Gainesboro PO;
neuralgia of head & eyes
PATTERSON, Wm. R., Cl-48-2; Pvt K Co 3rd KY Inf;
9-61 to 61 (2 mos); Pleasant PO
PATTISON, David B., Ge-88-1; Pvt B Co 8th TN Inf;
15 Dec 62 to 5 Apr 65; Bulls Gap PO; spine,
liver & sun stroke
PATTON, David C., Pu-145-1; Pvt A Co 5th Cav Vol;
8-14-62 to 7-14-65; Ai PO
PATTON, Foster, Mu-193-2; 62 to 65; PO omitted
PATTON, George W., H-56-1; Pvt I Co 3rd IL Inf;
St. Elm(o) PO
PATTON, Haywood, K-168-2; Pvt I Co US Col Inf; 26
Apr 65 to 25 Apr 66; Knoxville PO
PATTON, Henry, Je-143-2; Pvt 40th NC Inf; Mossy
CreekPO; shot in left leg; discharge and other
papers got burned
PATTON, John, Sn-257-1; Pvt B Co 10th TN Cav; 8-17-
63 to 12-3-64; Gallatin PO; shot in right
elbow; pensioner
PATTON, John, Wl-299-2; 15th Civil Dist
PATTON, John, Bl-3-1; Sgt A Co 28th TN Inf; 8-8-61
to __; Patten PO; CONF
PATTON, John D., Wi-287-1; Sgt A Co 9th MS? Cav;
fall 62 to Jul 65; Civ Dist o 18
PATTON, Plesant, D-68-2; Mollie widow of; 101st
USC Inf; Hamler St, Nashville PO; gun shot in
left foot
PATTON, Samuel, D-50-3; Pvt I Co 12th US Inf; 63
to 65; 1015 N Cherry, Nashville PO
PATTON, Samuel B., Mr-99-2; Jasper PO; could not
get co & reg and dates
PATTON, Thomas W., Pu-144-2; Margaret F. widow of;
Pvt L Co 5th TN; 7-29-63 to 8-14-65; Double
Springs PO
PATTON, William, Pi-156-1; Pvt K Co 30th KY Inf;
3-64 to 4-65; Permelia PO; crippled knee,
now __ a crippled hand
PATTY, Francis E. S., Mc-111-1; Pvt A Co 7th TN
Mtd Inf; 9-8-64 to 7-27-65; Nonaburg PO
PATY, James P., Wl-302-1; Capt G Co 4th TN Mtd Inf
--2 Feb 65 to 25 Aug 65; Pvt B Co 5th TN Cav
--1 Aug 62 to 5 Dec 64; 1st Lt G Co 4th TN
Mtd Inf--Dec 64 to 1 Feb 65; PO omitted
PAUGLE, George N., H-75-1; Chattanooga PO; has 5
bullet holes in him, transferred from 3rd OH
Inf to 4th E TN Cav Co A
PAUL, Catherine, Wh-187-1; widow Sol; Pvt; Sparta
PO; husband killed
PAUL, George W., P-97-2; Pvt A Co 156th IN Inf;
7-61 to 65 (3 yrs 9 mos), 506 W 6th, Chatta-
nooga PO
PAUL, Joseph, Cl-57-2; Pvt B Co 2nd Bat TN; 4-1-
63 to 10-24-64; Goin PO; lungs, dispepsey
PAUL, Martin L., Mg-199-3; Pvt C Co 11th TN Cav;
63 to 65; Sunbright PO
PAUL, Squire, C-27-1; Pvt C Co 4th TN Cav; 8-8-62
to 7-12-65; Jacksboro PO
PAUL, Walker B., Mg-199-2; Pvt K Co 11th TN Cav;
13 Jul 63 to 17 Sep 65; Sunbright PO; rheumatism
PAULEY, Posy, G-57-4(1); Pvt C Co 63rd GA Inf; 11-
1-62 to 5-1-64; Yorkville PO; right 3rd
finger shot off; CONF
PAUREL, Isaac, Mc-127-1; Pvt D Co; 5-10-63 to 12-
25-64; Hopewell Springs PO
PAVIS, Joseph R., W-189-1; Cpl G Co 1st TN Mtd
Inf; 4-4-64 to 7-22-65; McMinnville PO
PAYGER?, Bluford, F-44-1; Pvt; Apr 1 64 to Jun 3
65; PO omitted
PAYMER, George T., We-221-2; Cpl C Co 5th TN Inf;
21 May 61 to Oct 64; Martin PO; one half of
left foot shot off; CONF
PAYNE, Allin, Col'd, We-223-1; Pvt L Co 8th US
Col Hvy; 63 to 65; Palmersville PO
PAYNE, Audy, B1-3-2; Croleti widow of; Lt G Co 6th
TN Inf; 2-20-63 to 6-13-63; Billingsly PO;
piles
PAYNE, David W., Se-231-2; Pvt K Co 2nd TN Inf; 9
Jan 62 to 4 Apr 65; Boyds Creek PO; psoriasis
24 yrs, defected in site 26 yrs
PAYNE, Elijah G., Hw-119-4(1); Pvt G Co 1st US Inf;
24 Jan 64 to 22 May 66; Alum Well PO; piles
& chronic constipation

PAYNE, Elisabeth (see Burdine, L. P.)
PAYNE, Flail W., Dy-25-6(2); Pvt A Co Inf; May 61
to Dec 61; Newbern PO; in general army, en-
listed as state gard, done no; CONF
PAYNE, George B., Dy-27-2; Pvt B Co 37th GA Inf;
3 Jul 62 to Apr 65; Newbern PO; CONF
PAYNE, George M., Jo-153-2; Pvt E Co 13th TN Cav;
24 Sep 63 to 5 Sep 65; Little Doe PO; rheuma-
tism, gun shot
PAYNE, George W., Sh-191-2; Cpl F Co 11th Col Inf;
1-12-64 to 1-12-66; Memphis PO
PAYNE, Henry, D-50-4; Mary widow of; Pvt; 3 yrs;
209 Jackson, Nashville PO; has no record
PAYNE, Jacob P., K-184-3; Sgt K Co 2nd TN Inf; 13
Dec 61 to 15 Dec 64; Thorn Grove PO
PAYNE, James A. W., Mo-128-1; Pvt D Co 3rd Mtd Inf;
7-25-64 to 64; Sink PO
PAYNE, James H., Ro-210-12; Pvt I Co 5th TN Inf;
Rockwood PO
PAYNE, James K., Cr-4-2; Pvt F Co 101st TN Inf; 61
to 64; Bells Depot PO; wound, right leg
PAYNE, Joel J., Mo-128-1; R. O. D Co 2nd NC Mtd Inf;
11-63 to __; Belltown PO
PAYNE, John, Mt-137-1; alias Ladd (Todd?); Civ
Nurse in Hosp at Indianapolis; papers lost;
St. Bethlehem PO
PAYNE, John, H-49-10; Mary A. widow of; Pvt F Co
2nd TN Inf; Daisy PO
PAYNE, John, H-56-6; 63 to 65; St. Elmo PO; CONF
PAYNE, John K., K-170-3; US Sol; Dist 12
PAYNE, John M., Jo-150-5; Sgt E Co 13th TN Cav; 22
Sep 63 to 5 Sep 65; Osborn PO
PAYNE, Lindsay, H-65-1; Pvt C Co 3rd MS Inf; 5-62
to 4-26-65; Chattanooga PO; CONF
PAYNE, Sam T., Dy-25-8(4); Newbern PO; CONF
PAYNE, Samuel M., Cl-52-1; Pvt E Co 8th TN Cav;
Quarter PO; leg mashed
PAYNE, Samuel, Ru-238-1; Sgt C Co 13th US C Inf;
62 to 65; Jefferson PO; lost leg eye from
small pox
PAYNE, Thomas, H-76-1; Chattanooga PO
PAYNE, Thomas, H-64-1; Rachel Harrison widow of;
Cpl B Co 1st US Hvy Art; 2-1-64 to 66;
Chattanooga PO; married Harrison & he died
PAYNE, Thomas C., Hd-50-5; Pvt F Co 1st AL Cav;
Nixon PO; disease of the lungs
PAYNE, Wade G., D-67-2; Pvt; Nashville PO; CONF
PAYNE, Wm. L., Hw-128-1; Pvt F Co 3rd TN Inf; 1 Jul
64 to 30 Nov 64; Choptack PO
PAYNE, Zebuland, Jo-150-5; Charity widow of; Pvt E
Co 13th TN Cav; 24 Sep 63 to 5 Sep 65; Osborn
PO
PAYNE, ___, D-54-1; Belle widow of; Pvt C Co 1st
US Col Inf; Nashville PO
PAYTON, Robert, Le-119-1; Pvt F Co 2nd TN Mtd Inf;
20 Feb 64 to 4 Mar 65; Strathmore PO; bronchi-
tis
PEACE, Frank P., K-165-3; Capt K Co 11th TN Cav;
61 Adkin St, Knoxville PO
PEACE, Silas H., Mo-125-1; Bettie M. widow of; Pvt
D Co 11th TN Cav; 3-63 to 2-64; Madisonville
PO
PEACH, Mat, Wl-308-2; Pvt H Co 45th TN; Nov 4 62 to
Sep 1 64; Rural Hill PO; captured; CONF
PEACOCK, Alexander, Ms-174-1; alias Alexander
Dwigins; Pvt D Co 17th US Inf; Wilhoit PO; no
discharge
PEACOCK, James, Sn-252-2; Pvt A Co 4th OH Inf (3
mos); Pvt K Co 59th NY Inf--9-61 to 9-64; Gal-
latin PO
PEAK, Albert, A-6-4(2); Pvt A Co 11th US Col Inf;
11-27-63 to 4-25-66; Olivers PO; small pox
PEAK, Jesse, Lo-187-3; Harriet widow of; Pvt B Co
10 TN Cav; Loudon PO
PEAK, John, Br-13-1; Cpl I Co 5th TN Inf; 11-1-62
to 6-30-65; Cleveland PO; homicidal insanity
PEAK, Spencer, Ro-210-7; Pvt L Co 1st TN Inf; Rock-
wood PO
PEAK (Peck?), William, A-6-6(4); Pvt A Co 26th TN
Inf; 8-16-62 to 5-65; Oliver PO; CONF
PEAKS, Eli, Ct-41-2; Pvt H Co 13th TN Cav; 9-24-63
to 9-5-65; Keensburg PO; chronick dyaryear
PEAL, Edward C., Ma-125-1; Pvt K Co 17th W VA Inf;
64 to 13 Jun 65; Jackson PO
PEARCE, Hamelton, Mc-116-1; Carline widow of; Pvt
K Co 9th TN Inf; 10-29-63 to 7-65; Riceville
PO; fever & rheumatism

PEARCE, James D., Co-61-5(2); Cpl H Co 4th TN Inf; 1 Nov 64 to 6 Aug 65; Bridgeport PO; in prison 16 mos
PEARCE, John, D-49-2; Cpl B Co 14th TN Inf; Dec 63 to Dec 66; Nashville PO; have no papers to refer to
PEARCE, Nancie (see Middleton, James)
PEARCE, Robt, Mc-115-1; Pvt A Co 10th TN Cav; 8-12-63 to 8-1-65; Riceville PO; heart trouble
PEARCE, Robert H., Wr-276-1; Pvt D Co 10th TN Cav; Oct 62 to Oct 65; Beechville PO; shot through left arm; CONF
PEARCE, Samuel D., Ct-43-3; Sarah E. widow of; Pvt H Co 4th TN Inf; 4-12-64 to 8-2-65; Watauga PO
PEARCE, William E., Ge-88-2; Serephine widow of; Pvt G Co 8th TN Cav; 12 Sep 63 to 11 Sep 65; Bulls Gap PO; ulceration of stomach
PEARCELY, Albert, Gu-48-5(2); Albert Gallian alias; Sgt D Co 13th TN Inf; 63 to 65; Nashville PO
PEARL, Louisa (see Massingale, John)
PEARMAN, James, Mc-109-6; US Sol; 2nd Civil Dist
PEARNAL, George, D-45-4; Julia widow of; Nashville PO
PEARSON, Amanda, He-58-2; widow of Sol; 8th Civil Dist
PEARSON, Charles G., Pu-142-2; Pvt B Co 40th IL Inf; 7-15-61 to 8-4-65; Clark Range? PO; chronic catarrh stomach & ___
PEARSON, G. R., D-77-3; Sailor, Alexandria VA from receiving ship, reenlisted in 1863 and was sent to N. Carolina; Nashville PO
PEARSON, Henry C., Sn-262-2(1); Pvt F Co 52nd KY Cav; 8 Dec 63 to 18 Jan 65; South Tunnell PO
PEARSON, J. L., Mo-130-2; Mary J. widow of; Capt D Co 3rd TN Mtd Inf; 7-12-64 to __; Ballplay PO
PEARSON, John, Gr-77-1; Pvt D Co 4th TN Inf; 1 Feb 62 to 8 Aug 65; Y.Z. PO; heart disease
PEARSON, John M., Rb-220-1; Pvt E Co 67th IN; Aug 12 61 to Aug 5 64; Adairsville KY PO
PEARSON, R. G., D-77-2; Sailor Congress US Navy; Jun 61 to Jun 63; Nashville PO
PEARSON, Thomas M., De-24-1; Pvt F Co 5th TN Cav; 62 to Jul 64; Decaturville PO; discharge lost
PEARSON, William, Cl-52-1; Pvt G Co 9th TN Cav; 12-31-64 to 9-13-65; Quarter PO
PEARSON, William J., H-49-1; Pvt F Co 5th TN Inf; 2-25-62 to 6-15-65; Falling Water PO
PEAS, Robert, Sh-202-1; Pvt A Co Inf; 12 Apr 61 to 65; Memphis PO
PEAS, Thomas, Hw-129-2; Pvt C Co 7th TN Mtd Inf; 64 to 65; Mooresburg PO; lost one lege from a wound in survis, rheumitism, def in, 1 yr diarrhea
PEAVYHOUSE, Elihough, P-151-3; Mrs. E.; Pvt; Linden PO
PEAVYHOUSE, George W., Fe-41-2; Pvt D Co 1st TN Inf; 64 to 65; Pall Mall PO
PEAY, Z. T., Ru-236-1; Pvt TN Cav; 63 to 65; Murfreesboro PO; wounded in leg, Lavergne, TN; he served until discharged
PECK, Benjamine F., Cf-40-3; Pvt 10th OH Bat; 11 Feb 62 to 23 Nov 63; Tullahoma PO; discharged by surgeons certificate of disability
PECK, Canada, Cl-54-2; Pvt I Co 3rd TN Inf; 2-10-62 to __; Tazewell PO; diareah, cant get the day of his discharge
PECK, Henry W., Sh-186-1; Pvt 22nd OH; Memphis PO; his wife did not no co
PECK, Joseph F., We-234-1; Capt C Co 13th KY Cav; 12-1-63 to 10-64; Greenfield PO; rumatism; KY state gard
PECK, Silas, Je-143-2; Pvt D Co 1st KY Hvy Art; 4 Mar 64 to 31 Mar 66; Mossy Creek PO
PECKHAM, Alphonse E., H-53-6; Pvt E Co 1st MI; 12-2-63 to 10-1-65; Ridgedale PO; injured sight & hernia
PECOE?, Madison H., Je-143-2; 1st Lt K Co 3rd TN Cav; 15 Feb 62 to 1 Apr 63; Mossy Creek PO; bronchitas, scurvy & kidney trouble
PEDAN, John W., Sn-261-3(2); Pvt I Co 30th TN Inf; 10-22-61 to 9-62; Rapids PO (Simpson Co., KY); prison Camp Butler 17 mos, taken the oath & came home 9-62; CONF
PEDIGO, Adonriam, K-186-5; Pvt A Co 6th TN Inf; 1 Sep 62 to 12 Jun 65; Balls Camp PO; eyes & liver

PEDIGO, Green B., Dk-38-2; Pvt K Co 5th TN Cav; 5-22-63 to 8-14-65; Crawfordton PO
PEDIGO, Green B., Dk-38-2; Pvt K Co 5th TN Cav; 5-22-63 to 65; Crawfordton PO
PEDIGO, Jesse A., Cy-27-4(2); Pvt I Co 1st TN Mtd Inf; 1-12-64 to 5-2-65; Sprivey PO
PEDIGO, Robert E., Dk-36-3; 1st Lt I Co 5th TN Cav; 9-14-64 to 65; Smithville PO
PEDIGO, Zacariah, Cy-27-4(2); Pvt E Co 1st TN Mtd Inf; 10-28-63 to 1-22-64; SpiveyPO
PEEBLES, William J., U-245-1; 1st Sgt F Co 34th VA Cav; Jun 62 to May 65; Marbleton PO; CONF
PEELER, George D., We-224-1; Miller, Sarah E. formerly widow of; Pvt; Como PO (Henry Co.); escaped from service at Island No 20, MS
PEELER, William D., H-68-2; Pvt F Co 3rd TN Cav; 3-1-63 to 6-27-65; Chattanooga PO; lungs weak, not able to do much
PEERMAN, William, Cl-48-3; Pvt; 3 yrs; Pleasant PO; CONF
PEETE, Elias, T-215-2; Pvt A Co; 3 yrs; Coving PO
PEETER, ___, S-212-1; Pvt C Co 4th TN; 11 Jul 63 to 14 Sep 65; Hellenwood PO; rheumatism
PEGG, Joel A., La-115-1; Pvt C Co 8th MI Inf; 13 Aug 61 to 22 Jul 63; Henryville PO; gun shot right leg
PEGRAM, Lenard, D-93-1; Pvt; Newsome Sta. PO
PEGRAM, William J., Ho-96-1; Com Sgt L Co 12th TN Cav; Mar 24 64 to Oct 15 64; Erin PO
PELEGRAM, Joseph, Sh-202-1; Pvt Inf; 12 Aug 64 to 64 (1 yr 8 mos 12 days); Memphis PO; shot in left leg
PELFNER, James, R-106-1; Pvt I Co TN; 5th Civil Dist
PELTIER, Anthony C., Su-239-2; Pvt K Co 13th TN Cav; 15 Sep 63 to 5 Sep 65; Kingsport PO
PEMBERTON, Andy J., Hu-103-1; Pvt H Co 10th TN Inf; 12 Jul 63 to 10 Nov 64; PO omitted
PEMBERTON, Daniel, A-13-4; Pvt C Co 2nd TN Inf; 8-7-61 to 2-8-65; Thomas Mill PO; chronic diarrhea and scurvy, imprisoned at Andersonville 14 (mos?)
PEMBERTON, David, A-13-4; Pvt C Co 2nd TN Inf; 61 to 65; Thomas Mill PO; rheumatism, 2nd Co in 2nd TN
PEMBERTON, Thomas, Gr-73-2; Pvt D Co 4th TN Inf; 1 Aug 63 to 2 Aug 65; Turley's Mills PO
PEMBERTON, Welcom A., Gr-73-2; Cpl D Co 4th TN Inf; 15 Apr 62 to 7 Jul 65; Turley's Mills PO
PENDAGRASS, John W., He-58-2; Sol; 8th Civil Dist
PENDARVIS, Joseph A., Sm-167-2; Hospital Steward A Co 1st TN Inf; 1-24-64 to 1-24-65; Dixon Springs PO
PENDER, Charles, Hu-100-1; Pvt F Co 7th US Cav; Oct 62 to Jan 65; Johnsonville PO
PENDER, Edward, Hy-79-1; Pvt; Brownsville PO
PENDERGRASS, Caterin, L-103-1; widow of Walker, W. T., died 184_); Pvt E Co 31st IL; Aug 15 62 to Aug 6 65; Island 26 PO
PENDERGRASS, Tom, Sh-160-2; Pvt I Co 16th WI Inf; 62 to Aug 65; Memphis PO; shot in head, has heart disease from injury
PENELTON, Thomas, Sh-159-7; Pvt E Co 16th TN; Memphis (Providence Chapple) PO; contracted cold, rheumatism
PENFIELD, Benjamin B., D-67-2; 1st Lt Aj I Co 6th CT Vol; Aug 30 62 to Aug 30 66; Nashville PO
PENGUS, Jessie, Sh-191-4; Memphis PO; records not seen
PENIC, W. H., F-44-2; Pvt F Co 12th TN; Aug 63 to Jun 65; PO omitted; CONF
PENLAN, James W., Mo-120-1; Pvt B Co 1st KY Cav; 4-62 to 6-65; Glenloch PO
PENN, John, Sn-252-2; Pvt C Co 40th TN Inf; 8-20-63 to 4-25-66; Gallatin PO
PENN, William, Ja-86-3; Pvt E Co 4th TN Cav; 12-62 to 7-29-65; Oottewah PO
PENNEY, George W., H-50-2(1); Cpl C Co 5th R TN Inf; 2-25-62 to 5-14-65; Igon's Ferry PO; rupture and wounded in left hip
PENNEY, Miles P., H-50-4; Sarah widow of; Cpl F Co 6th R TN Mtd Cav; 9-12-64 to 6-30-65; Soddy PO; chronic rheumatism
PENNEY, Thomas, Fr-114-1; Cpl A Co 5th OH Cav; 61 to 11-22-64; Alto PO
PENNINGTON, David W., Cy-27-1; P-t K Co 5th KY Cav; 10-61 to 8-64; Clementsville PO

PENNINGTON, Ephrahm J., O-138-1; Pvt F Co 2nd AR; 15 Jul 61 to 15 Sep 62; Lane PO; CONF
PENNINGTON, Harry, Rb-221-2; Viny widow of; Pvt; Adams Station PO
PENNINGTON, Isaiah C., Cy-27-2; Pvt; Clementsville PO
PENNY, Andrew J., H-49-9; Pvt C Co 5th TN Inf; 2-25-62 to 4-4-65; Igon's Ferry PO; wounded in stomach & thigh
PENNY, Ann, Mt-132-1; widow of sol; PO omitted
PENSOM, Thomas, D-69-3; US Sol; Nashville PO
PENTECOST, Andrew J., We-223-3; Pvt K Co 10th TN Cav; 18 Sep 62 to Aug 65; Palmersville PO; wounded in breste, well & hearty now; CONF
PENTECOST, Jefferson, We-223-3; Marthy widow of; cant give anything about record; CONF
PENTTE, Francy, F-36-1; Fayette Cormer PO
PEOPLE, Edward, Hi-87-1; US Sol; Civil Dist 5
PEOPLES, David, Wa-267-1; Tabitha widow of; Pvt F Co 4th TN Inf; 1 Dec 64 to 2 Aug 65; Jonesboro PO; rheumatism & dis of eye
PEOPLES, Jake, Be-1-1; Pvt K Co 38th IN; Oct 31 64 to Jul 23 65; Coxburg PO
PEPE, Thomas, Rb-223-1; Pvt I Co 15th TN Inf; Oct 62 to 65; Springfield PO
PEPPER, Daniel, St-163-1; Pvt G Co 3rd IL Inf; Mar 10 61 to Mar 8 64; Dover PO
PEPPER, Patrick (see Mathews, Ben)
PEPPER, Patrick, D-60-2; Pvt in Cav; 1309 Hines St, Nashville PO; Black
PEPPER, Richard, Gi-122-6; Pvt C Co 49th TN Inf; Dec 61 to Mar 62; Prospect Sta. PO; CONF
PERCIFULL, William, Hy-84-1; Elizabeth B. widow of; Pvt; 63 to 64; PO omitted; CONF
PERDEN, Jessie, M-103-3; Pvt E Co 1st TN Inf; Lafayette PO; paralysis
PERDUE, Eli G., Sn-261-1; Pvt F Co 52nd KY Cav; 5-14-63 to 12-27-64; Brachentown PO; discharge 12-27-64 (duplicate on Sn-261-2(1))
PERDUE, Fredric M., Sn-261-2(1); Pvt E Co 30th TN Inf; 6-27-61 to 9-1-63; New Roe, KY, PO; wounded in hip and imprisoned 18 mos at Ft. Delaware, surrendered by Lee 4-9-65; CONF
PERDUE, Harrison E., Cy-26-2; Pvt 14th KY Inf; 64 to 65; Ascot PO; dont remember co date of enlistment nor date of discharge
PERDUE, John D., Sn-261-5(4); Pvt I Co 30th TN Inf; 10-19-61 to 10-19-62; Perdue PO; prison at Springfield 7 mos; CONF
PERINE, Charles W., Sh-197-2; W(hite?); Memphis PO; not at home
PERINE, William H., Mo-123-1; Pvt G Co 12th OH Inf; 7-1-62 to 9-1-64; Jalapa PO
PERKINS, Andrew J., Su-239-1; Pvt F Co 3rd TN Cav; 1 Jul 64 to Nov 64; Peltier PO
PERKINS, Austin, D-61-1; Pvt; 61 to 65; Hawkins St, Nashville PO; shot in foot; claims to have papers
PERKINS, Brainard P., R-159-1; Pvt C Co 4th VT Inf; 6-19-64 to 8-20-65; Spring City PO; lung trouble, wounded four times
PERKINS, George, Wi-287-1; Teamster; 1 yr 5 mos 15 days; Civ Dist No. 18
PERKINS, Henry E., F-7-2; Sgt C Co 7th VT Inf; 16 Jan 62 to 25 Nov 65; Nashville PO; left leg lost in US Service
PERKINS, J. W., Gi-122-6; Pvt A Co 10th GA Inf; Mar 61 to Apr 65; Veto, AL, PO; CONF
PERKINS, Jacob F., Wa-262-1; Pvt G Co 13th TN Cav; 24 Sep 63 to 5 Sep 65; Telfords PO; chronic liver disease
PERKINS, James, L-109-1; Pvt K Co 1st US Hvy Art; 1 Apr 64 to 1 Mar 65; Ripley PO; right arm broken while on duty, now partially blind
PERKINS, James, Ro-202-1; Pvt A Co 118th OH Inf; 21 Apr 64 to 17 Jul 65; Kinston PO; rheumatism & lung disease
PERKINS, James C., Hy-84-2; Pvt B Co 48th GA; Mar 8 62 to May 15 65; Forkeddeer PO; CONF
PERKINS, James D., Mc-118-1; Cpl I Co 10th TN Cav; 1-64 to 8-65; Cogshill PO; rheumatism left shoulder stove up 24 yrs
PERKINS, James R., He-67-2; Pvt C Co 6th TN Cav; Jul 62 to deserted? 63; Sardis PO; diabetus & torpor of liver 20 yrs
PERKINS, Jerden, H-72-2(1); Pvt L Co 14th US Col Inf; Chattanooga PO

PERKINS, Joh, Col, D-45-1; Nashville PO
PERKINS, Lewis, C-33-6; US Sol; 11th Civil Dist
PERKINS, Peter, H-7-21; Pvt H Co 44th US Col Inf; 8-1-64 to 4-30-66; Chattanooga PO
PERKINS, Peter, C-33-2; Pvt G Co 7th KY Inf; 4-61 to 10-64; Jellico PO
PERKINS, Samuel, B-5-1; Jane Frazier formerly widow of; Pvt B Co 111th US Col Inf; 12-18-63 to 4-31-66; Fosterville PO
PERKINS, Thomas J., J-77-2; Pvt K Co 5th TN Cav; 1-64 to 8-65; Gainesboro PO; totally blind & in the county almshouse
PERKINS, Wm. J., Pu-140-1; Pvt A Co 1st TN Inf; 1-7-63 to 2-1-64; Cookeville PO; now has rheumatism
PERKINSON, Joel, R-158-1; D Co 5th TN Mtd Inf; 8-31-64 to 6-29-65; Rhea Springs PO
PERKISON, Wright, R-161-6; Dayton PO; discharge lost
PERREN, W. J., Gi-139-2; Sgt A Co 16th TN Cav; 5-16-62 to 5-65; Campbellsville PO
PERRIGO, James H., M-103-1; Pvt F Co 1st TN Inf; 2-23-64 to 5-29-65; Lafayette PO
PERRY, Alferd, D-58-2; Viney widow of; Pvt 13th US Col Inf; 1 yr 6 mos; Nashville PO
PERRY, Andrew T., Bo-22-2; Sgt B Co 3rd TN Cav; 11-25-62 to 6-10-65; Hebronville PO
PERRY, Antony, Gi-135-2; Pvt; Lynnville PO
PERRY, Calvin, Gi-135-2; Pvt A Co 13th TN Inf; 8-62 to 6-65; Lynnville PO
PERRY, Charles, Sh-153-1; Pvt A Co 59th USC Inf; 63 to 65; Collierville PO; wounded in hand
PERRY, Gale, J-81-3; 6th Civil Dist
PERRY, James, Gr-70-1; 1st Lt G Co 8th TN Cav; 10 Oct 63 to 15 Jun 64; Rutledge TN PO
PERRY, James, K-183-2; Pvt 2nd TN Cav; Mayo PO
PERRY, James A., K-182-2; Hospital Steward C Co 3rd NC Mtd Inf; Sep 64 to Aug 65; Shook PO; rheumatism and heart disease
PERRY, John, B-11-3(2); Winy L. widow of; Pvt E Co 17th US Col; 6-17-64 to 2-64 (sic); Unionville PO; died in the service
PERRY, John F., O-134-1; Pvt D Co 74th IN Inf; Aug 20 62 to Sep 10 64; Hornbeak PO
PERRY, John H., Wi-277-1; Pvt F Co 16th Com; Jul 27 62 to Jul 28 65; 8th Civil Dist
PERRY, Johnson, Mu-191-1; 7th Dist
PERRY, Joshua M., La-117-2; Pvt 53rd TN Inf; Jul 62 to Feb 65; 15th Dist; CONF
PERRY, Lewis, Ce-31-1; Pvt TN Inf; Nov 63 to Mar 64; Ashland City PO; CONF
PERRY, Mary L., Sh-162-1; widow Pvt; 7-25-63 to 64; Ramsey PO; paralyzed by jar of cannon
PERRY, Mary T. (see Waldunn, Francis)
PERRY, Noah, Me-90-5(2); Jane widow of; Pvt D Co 12th TN Cav; Meigs PO
PERRY, Oliver H., St-164-1; Pvt G Co 5th IL Cav; Oct 61 to 65; Moltke PO; eyes affected, re-enlisted veteran, no pention
PERRY, Samuel, A-6-4(2); Pvt; 62 to 65; Olive Springs? PO; CONF
PERRY, Simon, Cr-8-2; Cpl C Co 12th TN; 1 Jun 62 to 1 Jul 63; Maury City PO; CONF
PERRY, William J., Mc-114-1; Pvt D Co 5th TN Inf; 8-31-64 to 6-26-65; Riceville PO
PERRY, Absolem, Ms-173-1; Rich Creek PO
PERRYMAN, Jake P., G-69-1; Pvt A Co 1st TN Cav; 11 Feb 63 to 16 Jun 64; Rutherford PO
PERRYMAN, Jas. C., Sh-172-1; Pvt L Co 6th IL Cav; 9-7-61 to 12-26-64; Hotel St, Memphis PO
PERRYMAN, Samuel M., B-12-1; Pvt E Co 10th TN Inf; 7-5-62 to 6-23-65; Wheel PO; bronchitis
PERRYMAN, T. A., Se-222-2; Sgt M Co 2nd TN Cav; 8 Nov 62 to 6 Jul 65; Pigeon Forge PO; diareah and piles, disabled, hirt? & ankel
PERRYMAN, William G., B-12-2; Pvt E Co 10th TN Inf; 5-30-62 to 6-23-65; Wheel PO
PERSINGER, James E., Wa-274-3; Com Sgt H Co 13th TN Cav; 9-24-63 to 9-6-65; Jonesboro PO; disease of lungs, results of measles
PERSINGER, John H., Ct-38-1; CS Sgt A Co 8th TN Cav; 6-11-63 to 9-11-65; Milligan PO; gun shot wound in breast
PERSLEY, Thomas L., H-56-2; Pvt TN Inf; 62 to 65; East End PO

PERSON, Elija, Sh-158-1; Lewis, Elija P. (but while a slave); Pvt; 7-62 to __ (2 yrs); Memphis PO; very ignorant, says he was in Pioneer Corps all the time & never in ranks as soldier, after capture of Vicksburg brought to Memphis sick of ____, so tels after surrender in 65
PERSON, John, Sh-159-3; Pvt A Co TN; 1 yr 6 mos; Memphis PO
PERSON, Richard, Sh-157-5; Maj; 6-61 to 65; White Haven PO; CONF
PERSONS, William, K-177-5; Pvt K Co 64th VA Mtd Inf; 8-14-63 to 6-65; Povells Station PO; CONF
PERTEY, William, Bo-213-1; Pvt E Co 13th NC Inf; 9-17-64 to 8-8-66; Veeba PO
PERTLE, Elijah, M-103-1; Pvt H Co 5th KY Cav; 12-4-61 to 1-2-64; Lafayette PO
PESLEY, Samiel, Ge-92-1; Pvt D Co 8th TN Inf; 63 to __; Romeo PO
PETE, Joseph, T-215-2; Cpl I Co 4th Reg 26th; 11-63 to 2-25-66; Mason PO
PETERS, Andrew C., Co-60-1; C Co 4th TN Inf; 4-6-63 to 8-2-65; Syrensburg PO; chronic diarhea 20 yrs
PETERS, Benjamin H., Su-242-1; Sgt A Co 13th TN Cav; 9-22-63 to 9-5-65; Bluff City PO; hernia & diarrhea; prisoner 11 mos. at Knoxvill by rebels before enlistment
PETERS, David B., Ct-42-2; Pvt L Co 13th TN Cav; 11-18-63 to 9-5-65; Watauga PO
PETERS, E. P., Fe-21-1; Pvt K Co 13th TN; 3-9-62 to 3-9-65; Jamestown PO
PETERS, George, Sh-159-3; Pvt I Co 55th TN Inf; Memphis PO
PETERS, George W., K-166-4(2); Pvt F Co 3rd TN Inf; 2-20-62 to 2-23-65; Knoxville PO
PETERS, Hulda, A-7-2; widow of; Robertsville PO
PETERS, Jackson, Ct-43-3; Eveline E. Taylor, formerly widow of; Sgt L Co 13th TN Cav; 9-22-63 to __; Carter Furnace PO; killed by the enemy 12-31-64
PETERS, John, Un-253-3; Pvt F Co 3rd TN Inf; 2-10-62 to 2-23-65; Meltabarger PO; piles
PETERS, John, Ge-97-3; Pvt C Co 4th TN Inf; 4-6-63 to 8-2-65; Slate Mount PO; liver & chronic diareh
PETERS, John, Ge-85-2; Pvt G Co 4th TN Inf; 5-5-63 to 8-2-65; Cedar Creek PO; something like catarrh of head
PETERS, John M., Sh-159-4; IL; 3 yrs; Memphis PO
PETERS, Thomas H., Ct-44-2; Nancy widow of; Pvt A Co 13th TN Cav; 9-22-63 to 9-5-65; Hampton PO
PETERS, Tillman P., Ha-117-1; Pvt Rogers Batallion; 9-1-63 to 11-31-63; Kyle's Ford PO; the person on first line claims he was a Sol & had formed a Batalion & was endeavring to get to the Army to US to enlist
PETERS, Tobias, Ro-203-1; Pvt B Co 5th TN Inf; 2-25-62 to 3-1-65; Guenther PO
PETERS, Washington B., R-158-1; Mary E. widow of; Pvt G Co 1st Inf; 8-9-61 to 9-17-64; Darius PO
PETERS, William, Ct-42-2; Pvt L Co 13th TN Cav; 11-18-63 to 9-5-65; Watauga PO
PETERS, _____, Sh-179-1(2); Hannah widow of; Memphis PO
PETERSON, Charles P., H-53-4; Ridgedale PO
PETERSON, John D., Mc-112-1; 2nd Lt H Co 17th IN Foot; 5-23-61 to 9-23-63; Athens PO; ruptured
PETERSON, Robert L., Ro-206-2; Caroline widow of; Cpl B Co 5th TN Inf; 2-25-62 to __; killed in battle of Resacca GA
PETERSON, Samuel, Sh-161-2; US Sol; 16th Dist
PETITT, John B., Mg-197-2; Pvt K Co 114th? TN Cav; 8-20-63 to 9-6-65; Wartburg PO; diarrhea & ulcer on leg
PETTETT, Gustavus A., Mg-197-3; Malianor J. widow of; Pvt K Co 9th TN Cav; 8-18-63 to 9-11-65; Crooked Fork PO
PETTEY, James F., D-70-1; Pvt F Co 4th Mtd Inf; 9-26 64 go 8-25-65; Nashville PO
PETTEY, John S., Hm-103-2; 1st Lt Ast Sgt C Co 12th OH Inf; 9-11-62 to 7-31-65; Morristown PO; chronic diarr & partial deafness
PETTIBONE, William, H-49-2; Pvt & 2nd Lt; Chattanooga PO
PETTIE, Alexander, Dk-34-2; Pvt K Co 5th TN Cav; 5-3-63 to 8-14-65; Dowelltown PO; deafness; now very deaf
PETTIE, James A., Sh-174-1; ambulance driver at Camp Nelson KY; 62 to 63; Memphis PO
PETTIE, John O., Ch-14-2; Milded G. widow of; Pvt 51st TN Inf; 10-17-61 to 3-24-65; Henderson PO; in Camp Chase prison 3 mos; CONF
PETTIE, M., G-57-1; Mary widow of; 61 to 63; Yorkville PO; CONF
PETTIGREW, A., Cr-15-1; Pvt D Co 7th TN Cav; 8-22-62 to 10-25-63; Holaday PO; double hernia & heart & left
PETTILINE, Augustus H., Ge-91-5; Maj A Co 20th US Vol; 12-13-61 to 6-19-65; Greeneville PO; chronic liver complaint
PETTIS, Alex, D-98-1; Cpl H Co 17th Col US; 11-18-63 to 4-29-66; 19th Civil Dist
PETTUS, Henry, Ro-210-3; Pvt; 3 yrs; Rockwood PO
PETTWAY, John H., Tr-269-1; Pvt K Co 20th TN Inf; 6-8-61 to 4-20-62; John PO
PETTY, Alexander, O-141-1; Pvt E Co 17th Col US; 1-14-63 to 8-11-65; Union City PO
PETTY, Gilbert H., Di-30-2; Pvt A Co 42nd TN Inf; 2-61 to 12-64; Dickson PO; CONF
PETTY, Jackson, Mo-120-1; Pvt I Co 5th TN Cav; 12-2-62 to 6-30-65; Glenloch PO
PETTY, Joseph B., Hw-129-2; 2nd Sgt G Co 4th TN Cav; 4-13-63 to 7-12-65; Mooresburg PO; mashed ankle injuary
PETTY, Martian, Se-226-2; Pvt F Co 9th TN Cav; 8-12-63 to 9-11-65; Cynthiana PO (Jefferson Co.) diarrhoea
PETTY, Marvel M., O-138-3; Pvt G Co 6th OH; 12-5-64 to paroled 2-10-65; Elbridge PO; shot in head and hip
PETTY, Maning, Bo-19-3; Pvt F Co 9th TN Cav; 6-12-63 to 9-13-65; Rockford PO
PETTY, Mima (see Green, John)
PETTY, Neut J., Sm-169-3(5); Pvt; Defeated PO; CONF
PETTY, Rash P., Bo-14-2(1); Pvt A Co 10th TN Cav; 2-9-64 to 8-1-65; Huffstetlers Store PO; lungs & eyes injured
PETTY, Sarah (see Forester, John C.)
PETTY, Thomas W., Sm-169-2; Elmwood PO; CONF
PETWAY, Benjamin, D-97-1; Pvt D Co 2nd KY Cav; 62 to 65; Nashville PO; hand broken; CONF
PETWAY, Hinch, D-97-1; Pvt A Co 2nd TN Inf; 61 to 65; Nashville PO; shot in right leg; CONF
PETWAY, James, Wl-293-1; G Co 7th Cav; 10-63 to 64; Lockport PO; CONF
PETWAY, T. W., Ce-31-1; Pvt A Co 12th TN Cav; 2-2-62 to 8-20-64; Petway PO; CONF
PETWAY, William, Wl-293-1; F Co Inf; 61 to 65; Austin PO; CONF
PEW, Andrew, Cu-16-3; Lucinda widow of; Pvt B Co 2nd TN Inf; 62 to __ (2 mos); Big Lick PO; died 2 mos after enlisting
PEYCKE, Amandus, S-214-1; Matilda Maxfield formerly widow of; Sgt 4th OH Lt Art; 8-2-61 to 4-4-63; Robbins PO
PHAGAN, Joins N., Je-144-2; Pvt A Co 1st TN Art?; 9 Nov 62 to 8 Jul 65; Talbotts PO; chronic diarihea, discharged on set disability
PHARR, David W., Ct-42-3; Pvt A Co 13th TN Cav; Watauga PO
PHEEPS, Jerry, Gi-129-2; Sgt A Co 17th TN Inf; Nov 63 to Apr 66; Elkton PO
PHELPS, David R., Cr-4-5; Pvt I Co 12th TN Cav; 12-62 to 4-65; Bells Depot PO; CONF
PHELPS, Henry W., Ro-206-2; 3rd Sgt C Co 1st WI; 17 May 61 to 21 Aug 61; Nashville PO; served as millitary operator on telegraph ballance of war
PHELPS, John, K-181-1; Pvt A Co 3rd TN Cav; Jun 63 to Jun 65; French PO
PHELPS, N. S., Gi-139-3; Pvt K Co 1st TN Cav; 9-64 to 5-65; Wales Sta. PO
PHELPS, Samuel C., B-3-1; Pvt F Co 1st AL Cav; 3-21-63 to 6-18-64; Coldwell PO
PHELPS, Silas M., Sm-169-1; Cpl B Co 7th TN Inf; 5-10-61 to 62; Carthage PO; CONF
PHIBBS, Eli L., K-186-2; Pvt H Co 1st TN Inf; 9 Aug 61 to 1 Dec 62; Chumlea PO
PHIBBS, James, A-3-2; Sarah widow of; Pvt H Co 1st TN __; Beverridg PO (Knox Co.); died in service
PHIFER, Robert, Lo-188-2; Pvt A Co 5th TN Inf; 13 Nov 62 to 30 Jun 65; Stockton PO

PHILIPP, William W., Ch-12-1; Pvt C Co 6th TN Cav; 9-11-62 to 7-26-65; Milledgvill PO (McNairy Co.)
PHILIPS, Alan, Ro-206-1; Sarah widow of; Pvt; Emory Gap PO; CONF
PHILIPS, Jerry, Je-137-2; Annie widow of; Pvt I Co 2nd TN Cav; Hickory Ridge PO
PHILIPS, Lewis, A-3-2; Pvt H & A Cos 1st TN Inf; 7-3-62 to 8-8-65; Wilson PO; ankel, left hip, rhumatism; CONF
PHILIPS, Marth A., Mu-210-4; Carters Creek PO
PHILLIP, Abraham, S-214-3; Pvt 1st TN; Glenmary PO
PHILLIP, Brown B., Lo-194-1; Eliza L. widow of; Pvt; 3 yrs 2 mos; Muddy Creek PO
PHILLIPPS, ____, H-56-7; Catherine widow of; Pvt H Co 29th WI Inf; 12-13-63 to 10-9-65; St. Elmo PO
PHILLIPS, Abner L., He-67-2; Pvt K Co 7th TN Cav; May 27 63 to Jun 14 64; Sardis PO; chron. diabetus 25 yrs, contracted from effects of war and general disability
PHILLIPS, Albert, Gr-73-1; Sgt F Co 4th TN Inf; 1 Mar 63 to 2 Aug 65; Turley's Mills PO; catarrh in head, caused by measles
PHILLIPS, Alexander, Dk-36-1; Cpl B Co 1st TN Mtd Inf; 3-64 to 5-65; Smithville PO
PHILLIPS, Alvin, Ov-139-1; Pvt; 62 to 63; Beaver Hill PO
PHILLIPS, Anderson, D-50-3; Mary Malloy former wife of; Pvt US N; 831 N College, Nashville PO; killed at Vicksburg, rebels took papers from wife
PHILLIPS, Anderson, D-69-2; US Sol; 86 Mury St, Nashville PO
PHILLIPS, Andrew, Ru-241-3; Minta widow of; pvt TN Inf; Murfreesboro PO
PHILLIPS, Andrew, Sq-165-2; Pvt; Sunnyside PO
PHILLIPS, Brittan A., Mn-126-3; Pvt B Co 6th TN Cav; 8-22-62 to 7-65; Purdy PO
PHILLIPS, Cap, Wh-187-1; Asibee Cloid widow of; Capt; Yankeetown PO
PHILLIPS, Charley, C-27-2; Pvt H Co 2nd TN Inf; 61 to 7-64 (3 yrs); Careyville PO
PHILLIPS, Charley, D-91-2; Pvt; Station C, Nashville PO
PHILLIPS, David, H-53-4; Pvt A Co 42nd TN Inf; 63 to 65 (1 yr 10 mos); Chattanooga PO
PHILLIPS, David N., Ro-204-2; Ethel PO; has no discharge
PHILLIPS, Elias, Ro-204-4; Pvt B Co 1st TN Inf; 12 Mar 62 to 13 Mar 65; Elverton PO
PHILLIPS, Elija, Gi-132-3; Sgt D Co 12th USCV; Jul 63 to Jan 14 66; Wales PO
PHILLIPS, Ellers C., Mn-121-2; Pvt B Co 6th TN Cav; 8-1-62 to 5-28-63; Pocahontice PO; 5-63 sent home on disabela for survis
PHILLIPS, Forest, S-213-2; Pvt F Co 2nd TN Inf; 23 Sep 61 to 27 Apr 65; Hellenwood PO; rheumatism & gun shot wound
PHILLIPS, Frank, Ge-96-1; Pvt G Co 4th TN Inf; 6 Apr 63 to 20 Aug 65; Hascue PO; piles
PHILLIPS, G. L., U-247-3; Pvt E Co 3rd Reg Mtd NC; 25 Mar 64 to 8 Aug 65; Erwin PO; kidny disease, applicant for pension
PHILLIPS, George, Br-7-3; Pvt H Co 3rd TN Inf; 3-1-62 to 3-1-65; Cleveland PO; rheumatism
PHILLIPS, George W., H-53-2; Pvt B Co 8th TN Cav; 9-64 to 65 (1 yr); Chattanooga PO
PHILLIPS, George W., Hw-127-1; alias Cochreham, George W., Pvt H Co 1st TN Hvy Art; 27 May 64 to 31 Mar 65; Rogersville PO; measles settled in back
PHILLIPS, George W., Mg-198-1; Cpl D Co 1st OH Inf; 10 Jul 62 to 20 Jun 65; Deer Lodge PO; rheumatism, now deaf in right ear
PHILLIPS, Gilbert, Gi-132-1; Pvt F Co 110th USCV; Dec 6 63 to Feb 6 66; DeRay PO
PHILLIPS, Gorge W., Ge-96-2; Cpl? 8th TN Cav; __ to 65; Jockey PO; head hurt &c, discharge in Washington DC
PHILLIPS, Henderson P., U-246-1; Pvt A Co 8th TN Cav; 27 Nov 64 to 11 Sep 65; Limonite PO
PHILLIPS, Henry, D-94-1; Pvt B Co 15th TN Inf; 64 to 65; c/o E. R. Campbell, Nashville PO; shot in back, needy, helpless, pension applied for
PHILLIPS, Hubbrt F., We-221-1(4); Pvt D Co 10th TN Cav; Aug 63 to 14 May 65; Martin PO; hurt in right breast by a piece of bone; CONF
PHILLIPS, Isaiah, Ro-204-4; Pvt E Co 1st TN Inf; 20 Aug 61 to 17 Sep 64; Elverton PO; corns on feet
PHILLIPS, James, Cr-14-3; Pvt G Co 2nd TN Mtd Inf; 29 Dec 63 to 1 Feb 65; Cawthorn PO; reenlisted Co I 7th TN Cav
PHILLIPS, James, S-217-2; Pvt E Co 12th KY Inf; 29 Sep 61 to 14 Feb 65; Oneida PO
PHILLIPS, James E., Cr-8-1; Pvt D Co 57th TN? Maury City PO; CONF
PHILLIPS, James M., Me-92-2; Pvt C Co 9th TN Cav; 7-29-63 to 9-11-65; Hester Mills PO
PHILLIPS, James M., Ov-139-2; Pvt; 62 to 65; Beaver Hill PO; no discharge
PHILLIPS, James M., Sn-257-1; Bugler D Co 22nd PA Cav; 8-20-62 to 5-24-65; Gallatin PO
PHILLIPS, Jasper, Ov-139-1; Pvt D Co 1st TN Inf; Beaver Hill PO
PHILLIPS, Jehu, Ch-18-2; Pvt F Co 31st TN Inf; Sep 15 61 to 62; PO omitted; CONF
PHILLIPS, Jehue, S-213-3; US Scout; Huntsville PO
PHILLIPS, Jesse, Pi-154-2; 4th Civil Dist
PHILLIPS, Jesse, Ru-243-1(2); Pvt C Co 4th Reg Inf; Nov 20 62 to Aug 2 65; Cassi PO; rheumatism
PHILLIPS, Jessee, Gi-127-4; Cpl F Co 111th TN Inf; 1-6-64 to 4-30-66; Pulaski PO
PHILLIPS, John, Pi-154-2; Pvt F Co 5th KY Cav; 12-15-61 to 5-30-65; Susonett PO
PHILLIPS, John, Sh-146-3; US Sol; 3rd Civ Dist
PHILLIPS, John, A-9-2; Pvt H Co 2nd TN Inf; 8-61 to __; Podopholine PO; discharge in hands of pension attorney
PHILLIPS, John, Gr-73-1; Pvt F Co 4th TN Inf; 1 Jan 63 to 2 Aug 65; Turley's Mills PO; cattarrh of head, caused by fall of measles
PHILLIPS, John, Ro-204-1; Emily A. widow of; Pvt 5th TN Inf; 1 yr; Elverton PO
PHILLIPS, John C., We-233-1(2); Pvt G Co 2nd TN Mtd Inf; 8-62 to 12-28-64; Ralston PO
PHILLIPS, John E., Su-234-1; Cpl C Co 4th TN Inf; 6 Apr 63 to 64; Lella PO; McMinnvill, October 1863; yellow jaundice & in hospital
PHILLIPS, John F., C-24-3; Martha J. Stout formerly widow of; Lt B Co 1st TN Inf; 1-8-61 to 9-20-64; Fork Vale PO; gun shot wound in right hip
PHILLIPS, Marian, L-100-2; Sgt A Co 66th US Col Inf; Dec 63 to 20 Mar 65; Ripley PO; rumatism and defective eye
PHILLIPS, Martin V., Pi-154-2; Pvt F Co 6th KY Cav; 12-15-62 to 5-5-65; Otto PO; rheumatism
PHILLIPS, McCagia, A-9-1; Nancy E. widow of; Pvt C Co 2nd TN Inf; 8-61 to 10-64; Ligias PO; discharge in hands of pension attorney
PHILLIPS, Mitchel, Col, D-74-1; Buglar K Co 12th US Inf; Aug 22 63 to Nov 11 65; Firrt? & Watson PO; right arm broke at elbow, collar bone broken
PHILLIPS, Moses, A-9-1; Susan widow of; Pvt G Co 7th TN Mtd Inf; 11-8-64 to 7-27-65; Ligias PO
PHILLIPS, Moses, Ov-139-2; Pvt D Co 1st TN Inf; 1-25-64 to 4-25-65; Beaver Hill PO
PHILLIPS, Nathan, Ge-97-3; Cpl D Co 8th TN Cav; 11 Nov 63 to 11 Sep 65; Upchurch PO; stomach & kidney
PHILLIPS, Nicholas, Hd-56-1; Adamsville PO
PHILLIPS, Phillip H., H-51-4; Sgt A Co 33rd IL Inf; 1-1-64 to 11-25-65; Hill City PO
PHILLIPS, Reubin O., Br-7-2; Pvt E Co 5th TN Mtd Inf; 9-23-64 to 6-26-65; Cleveland PO
PHILLIPS, Riley, S-213-3; US Sol; Huntsville PO
PHILLIPS, Simon R., Pu-143-1; Pvt C Co 8th TN Inf; 3-13-65 to 8-17-65; Selby PO; fever
PHILLIPS, Thomas H. B. B., O-142-1; Pvt E Co 14th W VA Inf; 25 Jun 63 to 3 Jul 65; Obion PO; epilepsy with resulting diseases, 1st enlistment Dec 62, taken to Richmond VA, Co I 19th IN Inf, again taken prisoner Jun 17 64, Andersonville
PHILLIPS, Thos. J., Hd-54-3; Sarah widow of; Pvt C Co 6th TN Cav; Ruth PO; pulmonary phthisis
PHILLIPS, Wiley B., Cl-57-2; Pvt A Co 49th Reg Inf; 6-27-63 to 12-26-64; Cleveland PO
PHILLIPS, Wiley B., Cl-57-1; Pvt E Co 8th TN Inf; 8-9-61 to 2-25-63; Minkton PO; kidney, hearing 27 yrs

PHILLIPS, William, Mo-131-1; 17th Civil Dist
PHILLIPS, William (see Haywood, William)
PHILLIPS, William, S-213-1; Pvt G Co 9th TN Cav; 20 Jul 62 to 5 Jul 65; Huntsville PO; rheumatism
PHILLIPS, William, Co-63-3; Recruiting Office I Co 9th TN Cav; 10 Oct 63 to 65 (2 yrs); Newport PO; rheumatism
PHILLIPS, William R., Cr-10-1; Pvt 62 to 66; Friendship PO
PHILLUPS, Joseph, Sh-202-2(1); Memphis PO
PHILPOTT, Daniel E., We-221-4; Pvt L Co 6th TN Cav; 15 Jun 62 to 25 Jul 65; Martin PO; flesh weald (a ball struck buckle in left and injured side)
PHILPOTT, Ervine L., H-72-3(2); Pvt I Co 9th TN Cav; 3-20-64 to 4-11-65; Chattanooga PO
PHIPP, W. F., Hw-125-2; Pvt TN Inf; 62 to 65; Stony Point PO; CONF
PHIPPS, Richard (see Bradley, Richard)
PICKEL, John G., Lo-195-2; Pvt K Co 1st TN Inf; 23 Apr 63 to __; 1 yr 6 mos; PO omitted
PICKEL, W. H., Mc-117-4; Pvt D Co 10th TN Cav; 11-63 to __ (11 mos); Cog Hill PO; phthisic, command to be mustered out, was sick, not able to go back
PICKEL, William M., Lo-195-1; Pvt K Co 1st TN Inf; 23 Apr 63 to __ (1 yr 6 mos); Eatons X Roads PO
PICKELSIMER, Abraham, Po-152-5(1); Cpl L Co 9th TN Cav; 9-11-63 to 9-11-65; Ducktown PO; back, hips and left arm mashed, ought to have a pension
PICKENS, Richard, Hd-52-1; Pvt M Co 7th TN Cav; Jul 6 63 to Jul 23 65; Adamsville PO; bone scurvey, serious
PICKENS, Samuel, K-181-4(1); Pvt A Co 3rd TN Cav; 10 Sep 63 to 1 Jun 65; Fleniken PO; blind, was captered Sep 25th, 64; imprisoned 6 mos
PICKENS, Samuel W., Se-228-3; Pvt A Co 6th TN Inf; 24 Mar 62 to 15 Nov 62; Cap A Co 3rd TN Cav--15 Nov 62 to 4 Apr 64; Maj 3rd TN Cav--4 Apr 64 to 5 Aug 65; Cusick's X Roads PO
PICKENS, Thomas, Se-228-1(2); Sarah widow of; Lt B Co 3rd TN Cav; 17 Feb 63 to 26 Jan 64; Cox PO
PICKENS, William A., Su-240-2; Pvt C Co 70th TN; 1 Oct 62 to 4 Jul 65; Kindricks Creek PO; catar of head
PICKERELL, Marrie, Sh-167-3; widow US Sol; 32 Exchange St, Memphis PO
PICKERING, Ephraim, D-64-2; Matilda Fulqum widow of; Pvt 12th TN Col Inf; Nashville PO
PICKERING, John, Ge-97-1; Pvt C Co 4th TN Inf; Nov 61 to 65 (3 yrs 8 mos); Maltsberger PO; diarrhea, rhumatism, heart dis.
PICKERING, Joseph, Sh-186-1; Capt 34th KY; 8-61 to 5-64; Memphis PO
PICKERING, Levi, Ge-96-4; Capt E Co 4th TN Inf; 15 Feb 61 to 2 Aug 65; Chucky City PO; rheumatism, heart disease &c
PICKERING, William B., Sm-166-1; Sgt 3rd OH Inf; 4-17-61 to 9-25-65; Carthage PO
PICKETT, Edward, Sq-165-1; Pvt C Co 6th TN Mtd Inf; 9-2-64 to 6-13-65; Delphi PO; received an honorable disc.
PICKETT, George W., Mr-96-2; Pvt C Co 6th TN Inf; 9-64 to 6-65; Sunyside PO; direah
PICKETT, Isac, Sm-172-4; Pvt F Co 101st Patrol Inf; 9-28-64 to 1-21-66; Gordonsville PO
PICKETT, James, Sq-165-1; Pvt; Delphi PO; CONF
PICKETT, John, Mr-96-2; Pvt 6th TN Mtd Inf; Shirleyton PO
PICKETT, William, Mr-97-1; C Co TN Inf; 9-10-64 to 6-30-65; PO omitted
PICKETTE, John, H-52-1; Wauhatchie PO
PICKINS, Reuben, Hi-87-1; Sol US; Civil Dist 5
PICKLE, Calvin, Su-232-1; Sgt G Co 10th TN Cav; 29 Oct 63 to 12 Jul 65; Ruthton PO; palpatation of heart
PICKLE, George H., Ro-202-2; Pvt F Co 26th TN Inf; 12 Jul 61 to 30 Jan 65; Union X Roads PO; CONF
PICKLE, Henry H., K-171-6(5); Pvt I Co 1st TN Inf; Aug 61 to 63; PO omitted
PICKLE, Monroe, R-161-5; Pvt C Co 1st TN Inf; 10-11-64 to 3-31-66; Dayton PO

PICKLES, Jesse, Cr-17-2; Orderly Sgt B & A Co 7th TN Cav; 8-15-62 to 6-15-65; Buena Vista PO; enlargement of splene
PIEARCE, James, G-64-2; Pvt; 61 to 63; Bradford PO
PIERCE, Alexander, Ge-98-5; Pvt H Co 4th TN Cav; 3 Mar 63 to 12 Jul 65; Jeroldstown PO; chronic diarhea
PIERCE, Alexander H., Ge-98-2; 1st Sgt B Co 4th TN Cav; 10 Dec 62 to 12 Jul 65; Spinal disease result of small pox
PIERCE, Andrew, Ge-98-1; Manerva J. widow of; Pvt E Co 1st TN Lt Art Vol; PO omitted
PIERCE, Ansil, G-65-1; Pvt E Co 38th IL Inf; Aug 1 61 to Jun 1 63; Milan PO
PIERCE, Charly, Ru-236-1; Jane widow of; Pvt 14th Reg; __ to 65; Murfreesboro PO
PIERCE, Chirsty A. A., Wa-268-4; Johnson City PO
PIERCE, Clinton, C-30-2; Pvt B Co 8th TN Cav; 6-10-63 to 9-11-65; Well Spring PO
PIERCE, David, Me-94-1; Pvt F Co 13th TN Cav; 9-21-63 to 9-6-65; Euchee PO; fistulo result of diorhea, in prison 6 mos
PIERCE, Edward N., G-57-2; Catherine widow of; Pvt 47th TN Inf; 62 to 62 (6 mos); Yorkville PO; CONF
PIERCE, Elizabeth, K-186-5; widow; Beaver Ridge PO
PIERCE, George N., Fr-105-1; alias (Dock); Pvt E Co 43rd WI V Inf; 1 Aug 64 to 10 Jul 65; Winchester PO; scalp wound
PIERCE, Green, B-6-1; Pvt G Co 42nd US Col Inf; 11-17-64 to 1-31-66; Havan PO
PIERCE, Henery C., Ct-35-2; 1st Lt A Co 12th TN Cav; 9-22-65; Fish Spring PO; discharge not at home, date of discharge not known
PIERCE, Henry, Jo-153-2; Pvt B Co 13th TN Cav; 21 Sep 63 to 5 Sep 65; Pandora PO; heart and kidny disease
PIERCE, Humphrey, D-79-3; Sgt B Co 2nd MO Cav; May 25 61 to 29 Sep 65; Nashville, Custom House PO
PIERCE, J. P., Je-135-3; Pvt B Co 9th TN Cav; 24 Sep 63 to 11 Sep 65; Flat Gap PO; catarrh--head
PIERCE, Jacob S., Un-259-1; Pvt A Co 1st TN Inf; 6 Aug 61 to 27 Aug 65; New Prospect PO; no special disease
PIERCE, James, We-220-2; Pvt 1st KY Cav; 4th Civil Dist; discharge lost time of enlistment and discharge forgotten
PIERCE, James (see Cartright, Henry)
PIERCE, James L., Br-9-2; Sgt E Co 4th TN Cav; 12-25-62 to 7-24-65; Cleveland PO
PIERCE, James W., Gr-71-1; Sgt G Co 13th TN Cav; 24 Sep 63 to 5 Sep 65; Bean Station PO
PIERCE, John, He-64-3; Pvt B Co 10th TN Cav; 15 Sep 62 to 15 Sep 65; Reagan PO; CONF
PIERCE, John, Bl-5-1; Pvt A Co 6th TN Mtd Inf; 8-2-64 to 6-30-65; Graysville PO (Rhea Co.); injured while riding horse, injured by horse jumping or plunging
PIERCE, John, C-30-1; Pvt B Co 1st TN Inf; 8-12-61 to 9-17-64; Well Spring PO
PIERCE, John L., Po-149-1; Pvt A Co 4th TN Cav; Old Fort PO
PIERCE, John R., Mu-199-1; Eliza C. widow of; Pvt I Co 2nd TN Inf; Campbellsville PO
PIERCE, Julias D., Jo-152-3; Cpl E Co 2nd TN Mtd Inf; 1 Jun 63 to 5 Aug 65; Butler PO; rheumatism & bronchitis
PIERCE, Louis M., Ct-45-3; Pvt A Co 13th TN Cav; 9-23-63 to 9-5-65; Carter Furnace PO; neuralgia, Gallatin TN, 1864
PIERCE, Peter, C-30-1; Pvt B Co 8th TN Cav; 2-15-63 to 9-11-65; Well Spring PO
PIERCE, Robert V., Me-88-2; Pvt E Co 5th TN Inf; 3-2-62 to 4-4-65; Georgetown PO
PIERCE, Rufus H., K-164-2; Martha J. widow of; PO omitted (Knoxville?)
PIERCE, Samuel A., Fe-44-2; Pvt D Co 12th KY Inf; 10-10-61 to 2-3-65; Armathwaite PO; rheumatism 26 yrs
PIERCE, William, Un-256-3; Pvt C Co 9th TN Cav; Loy X Roads PO; neuralgea
PIERCE, William A., C-8-1; B Co 11th TN Cav; 7-15-63 to 9-11-65; Well Spring PO
PIERCE, William E., Ge-89-4; Pvt D Co 8th TN Cav; 62 to __; Romeo PO; dont remember dates

PIERCE, William K., Pi-155-2; Pvt B Co South C Belt KY Inf; 3-23-65 to 10-23-65; Byrdstown PO; shot in left thigh
PIERCE, Zadock, Ro-206-1; Pvt 8th MO Inf; Mar 62 to Apr 65; Emory Gap PO; CONF
PIERSAUL, Fredric, K-172-5(1); 14th Dist
PIERSON, James L., Gi-140-1; Pvt F Co 5th TN Cav; 9-12-62 to 6-25-65; PO omitted
PIERSON, Thomas, Gi-140-1; Pvt F Co 5th TN Cav; 9-11-62 to 6-25-65; Bunker Hill PO; left year shot off
PIG, Redford, K-185-2; Cpl G Co 9th TN Cav; 63 to 65; McMillans PO; hemoroids and chronic diarrhea
PIGG, Joseph, Ov-134-1; 1st Sgt C Co 8th TN Mtd Inf; 1-1-65 to 8-7-65; Hilham PO; throat affection & bronchitis contracted 7-65, still affected
PIGOTT, William, Mn-126-2; Orderly Sgt B Co 6th TN Cav; __ to 65; Bethel Springs PO
PIGRAM, George (see Catron, Rachel)
PIKE, Edith (see Hutchinson, John, A-2-3)
PIKE, George M., Un-256-3; Pvt F Co 6th TN Inf; 10 May 62 to 10 Apr 65; Loys X Roads PO; piles & deafness
PIKE, James, Rb-220-1; Pvt B Co 20th TN; Oct 15 61 to Aug 20 65; Barrenplains PO; gun shot left knee; CONF
PIKE, James M., Ch-13-2; Pvt A Co 3rd TN Vol; 8-26-63 to 64; Jack's Creek PO; right hip disabled, incidentally separated from
PILCHER, Charles, D-72-2; Pvt I Co 176th OH Inf; Oct 20 64 to Jun 30 65; Nashville PO
PILES, John, Un-256-3; Elzira widow of; Pvt F Co 6th TN Inf; 10 Mar 62 to __; Loys X Roads PO; died in army
PILES, Samuel W., D-52-1; Pvt A Co Independent Scouts; spring 62 to 65; Liberty, KY, PO; gunshot wound, left breast, shot twice in same place
PILES, William, A-1-2; Pvt F Co 6th TN Inf; 3-10-62 to 6-30-65; Custer PO
PILLOW, George, Mu-189-1; Pvt A Co 15th TN Inf; 4 mos; Columbia PO
PILLOW, John, K-177-4; Pvt G Co 6th TN Cav; 18 Apr 62 to 18 May 65; Knoxville PO
PILLOW, John L., Wa-261-1; Pvt K Co 8th Cav; Aug 63 to 11 Sep 65; Brownsboro PO
PILLOW, Jordan, Mu-195-2; Sol; wife don't know; Columbia PO
PILLOW, Sam, Mu-197-1; Cpl E Co 15th Col Reg; Apr 63 to __; Columbia PO
PILLOW, Thomas, Mu-193-2; Teamster 111th OH Cav; 3-15-62 to 3-15-65; PO omitted
PILLVEE, R. A., He-57-2; Pvt I Co 3rd TN Inf; 5-1-61 to 10-1-65; Law PO; wonded in right leg, Rock Island 11 mos; CONF?
PILTON, Geo. (see Wilson, Geo.)
PINCKLEY, Clark, Cr-14-2; Fannie A. widow of; Pvt G Co 7th TN Cav; 5 Aug 62 to 25 Oct 63; Clarksburg PO
PINCKLEY, Scott, Cr-14-1; 1st Sgt G Co 7th TN Cav; 5 Aug 62 to 25 Oct 63; Clarksburg PO; re-enlisted veteran, Hardies Batalian
PINCKLEY, Thomas F., Cr-14-1; Pvt C Co 2nd TN Mtd Inf; 29 Dec 63 to 1 Feb 65; Clarksburg PO
PINCKLY, Richard K., Cr-20-3; Pvt B Co 7th TN Cav; Aug 9 62 to Aug 15 65; Hollow Rock PO
PINDER, George, Mu-192-1; Pvt G Co IN Inf; 7-1-62 to 9-1-65; Bigbyville PO; foot shot
PINE, John, Hw-128-1; Pvt B Co 4th TN Inf; 18 Mar 63 to 2 Aug 65; Choptack PO; run over by wagon
PINEGAR, Martin, Di-31-1; Arzilla widow of; Pvt 12th TN Cav; 64 to __; Dickson PO; not discharged
PINEGAR, William J., Dk-38-1; Pvt I Co 18th IL Inf; 5-28-61 to 1-10-66; Pinegar PO
PINK, Ella, Sh-184-1; widow US Sol; 178 Carrol Ave, Memphis PO
PINKERMAN, Sam J., L-108-1; Pvt I Co 45th KY Inf; 63 to 64; Glimpville PO; rheumatism
PINKERTON, John C., P-156-1; Pvt F Co 42nd TN Inf; 11-62 to 7-64; Lobelville PO; shot in right leg, went home without discharge on above date
PINKES, John, U-247-3; Mariah widow of; Pvt 8th TN Cav; Erwin PO; died in service
PINKLY, William C., Cr-16-3; Pvt D Co 7th TN Cav; Aug 22 62 to Aug 9 65; Huntingdon PO; scurvy, was at Andersonville
PINKNEY, Nicholas G., De-22-2; Pvt C Co 6th TN Cav; 1 Sep 65 to 1 Apr 65; Dunbar PO; CONF
PINKNY, James (see Warren, James P.)
PINKSTON, Hamilton, G-67-3; Jane widow of; Pvt; Sep 64 to Feb 65; Bradford PO; two ribs broken
PINKSTON, Napolean B., Be-2-1; Pvt C Co 7th Reg?; Aug 64 to deserted; Divider PO
PINKSTON, William P., Cr-17-1; Pvt 21st KY Inf; 4-6-65 to 5-9-65; Family PO
PINSON, Joseph, Br-9-4; Pvt H Co 44th US Inf; Cleveland PO
PIPKIN, F. M., G-57-7(4); Pvt AR Bat; 11-61 to 4-1-62; Yorkville PO; CONF
PIPKIN, Ira M., M-108-3; PVt I Co 9th KY Inf; 10-25-61 to 12-15-64; Akersville PO; mumps & rheumatism
PIPKIN, Meredith H., M-103-5; Pvt E Co 1st TN Inf; 10-25-63 to 1-26-65; Lafayette PO
PIPKIN, W. C., M-108-2(1); Pvt A Co 9th KY Inf; 11-26-61 to 5-28-63; Salt Lick PO; loss of hearing
PIPPIN, Absolem, J-82-2; Pvt C Co 8th TN Mtd Inf; 3-30-65 to 8-17-65; Bloomington PO; result diarrhea & fever
PIPPIN, James P., J-82-2; Pvt H Co 1st TN Mtd Inf; 2-8-64 to 4-10-65; Mayfield PO
PIPPIN, Pinkney, J-82-2; Pvt K Co 13th TN Cav; 9-22-63 to 9-5-65; Bloomington PO; shot left shoulder & ankle
PIRKLE, Elijah, Br-10-2; 1st Orderly Sgt G Co 3rd TN Cav; 7-1-63 to 8-3-65; Cleveland PO
PIRKLE, Jesse M., Po-149-4(2); Cpl G Co 3rd TN Cav; 7-1-63 to 6-12-65; Ocoee PO; prisoner 7 mos 3 days at Cahaba, Macon & Andersonville
PIRTLE, James Y., He-64-3; Sol; 11th Civil Dist
PIRTLE, James Y., He-64-1; Pvt I Co; 7-26-63 to __ (3 mos); Shady Hill PO; flesh wound in left side, regiment captured, not mustered; CONF
PISANI, Francisco R. G., L-100-1; Seaman Vandalia; 59 to 2-4-64; Ripley PO; wounded in left sholder, causing lip? eye to be effected, cannot give dates
PISK?, Martin, Pu-143-1; 5th Cpl C Co 8th TN Inf; 1-1-65 to 8-17-65; Avolon PO
PISTOLE, Joseph, Dk-34-5(4); Pvt K Co 5th TN Cav; 6-9-63 to 8-14-65; Temperance Hall PO; sun stroke
PITMAN, David, Mr-96-2; Pvt E Co 10th TN Inf; 1-62 to 7-10-65; Whitewell PO; broken arm
PITMAN, Hamid, Mr-97-2; Pvt C Co 6th TN Inf; 9-17-64 to 6-30-65; Victoria PO
PITMAN, James E., Mn-123-2; Pvt H Co KS Cav; 62 to 65; Falcon PO; had lost discharge
PITNER, James, Se-228-2(3); Ellen widow of; Pvt E Co Lt TN Art; 9-23-63 to 8-1-65; New Knob Creek PO
PITNER, Robert M., Cr-4-4; Sgt K Co 10th MS Inf; 5-13-61 to 2-13-65; Bells Depot PO; CONF
PLANK, John, Mc-114-1; Pvt H Co 5th TN Inf; 3-25-62 to 5-16-65; Folger PO
PLANK, Wm. M., Mc-114-2; Sgt A Co 8th TN Inf; 10-25-62 to 6-30-65; Folger PO; hemorrhoids
PLATTENBURGH, John W., Fr-107-1; Pvt C Co 1st VA Inf; 9-5-61 to 7-19-65; Winchester PO; kidney blader & piles
PLATZ, John, D-72-6; Pvt E Co 49th MA Inf; 9-8-62 to 9-1-63; Nashville PO
PLEASANT, Charles T., F-44-3; Pvt C Co Rolentine; 5-6-62 to 5-6-65; PO omitted; CONF
PLEASANT, Frank, R-162-4; Pvt F Co 15th KY Cav; 9-61 to __; Dayton PO
PLEASANT, James M., Ct-45-2; Elizabeth widow of; Pvt F Co 13th TN Cav; 9-21-63 to 5-28-65; Carter Furnace PO
PLEASANT, Wm. H., Jo-152-1; Pvt B Co 4th TN Inf; 8-63 to 7-7-65; Doeville PO; bronchitis, piles & catarrh, don't remember day enlisted
PLEASNT (sic), Joseph G., Jo-153-2; Sgt F Co 13th TN Cav; 9-21-63 to 9-5-65; Little Doe PO; inflamation testicle, heart, head & back disease

PLEMINS, Thomas, Ro-208-2; Pvt A Co 3rd TN Cav; 11-10-62 to 6-10-65; Welker Mines PO; piles
PLESSAIR, Harison, Be-5-1; Pvt A Co 7th TN Inf?; 7-12-62 to 5-65; Camden PO
PLIQUE, Joseph, D-57-3; Pvt F Co; 4-10-65 to 11-29-65; PO omitted, 8th ward
PLOWMAN, Joshua, D-46-1; Pvt E Co 84th IL Inf; 6-8-62 to 6-8-65; Nashville PO
PLUMADORE, Joseph, A-6-5(3); Lt C Co 1st LA Cav; 61 to 63; CONF
PLUMLEE, Samuel N., Cy-26-1; Pvt B Co 37th KY Inf; 7-14-62 to 12-29-64; Moss PO
PLUMLEY, Anderson, R-161-2; Rosa Cummings widow of; Col; Dayton PO; killed, place unknown
PLUNK, Abraham, Hd-52-1; Pvt B Co 6th TN; 8-25-62 to 7-26-65; Adamsville PO
PLUNK, Alx., Mn-126-2; Hugh Pvt B Co 6th TN Cav; 8-26-62 to 7-26-65; Bethel Springs PO
PLUNK, Calvin, Hd-52-1; Pvt F Co 10th TN; 5-2-62 to 6-15-65; Adamsville PO
PLUNK, G. M., Hd-56-1; Pvt B Co 6th TN Cav; 8-25-62 to 7-26-64; Adamsville PO; rheumatism contracted in army
PLUNK, J. S., Hd-56-1; Pvt B Co 6th TN Cav; 9-15-62 to 7-26-64; Adamsville PO
PLUNK, John W., Mn-122-1; Cpl G Co 6th TN Cav; 9-15-62 to 7-26-65; McNairy PO
PLUNK, Miles, Mn-122-2; Pvt B Co 6th TN Regt Cav; 8-25-62 to 7-26-65; McNairy PO; chronic rheumatism, discharged GO No 12
PLYOFORD?, James, Di-37-1; Pvt F Co 2nd US Inf; 10-6-64 to 11-7-65; Cumberland Furnace PO; in both CONF and US Service
POAG, Laura S. (see Gibson, William)
POAG, Madison N., La-112-2; Mary T. formerly widow of; Pvt A Co 10th TN Inf; 4-21-62 to __ (3 yrs); Pickney PO; saber wound in right leg
POCK, Noah, Ge-100-2; Pvt E Co 8th TN Inf; 6-20-63 to 6-30-65; Midway PO
POE, Henry, Hw-121-6(1); Pvt F Co 34th TN Mtd Inf; 7-10-64 to 11-14-64; Strahl PO; chronic sore eyes 27 yrs
POE, James, Ge-88-3; Nannie widow of; Pvt M Co 1st TN Inf; 7-15-62 to 6-5-65; Mohawk PO; chronic diareah and bad eyes
POE, James C., Ja-87-2; Pvt D Co 6th KY Cav; 4-25-62 to 9-25-65; Ooltewah PO; frostbite, hernia, sight impaired, served about 25 days over time; discharge dates lost
POE, Jessee, Ge-88-2; Pvt B Co 13th TN Cav; __ to 65; Bulls Gap PO; rheumatism & wounded finger on right hand
POE, John L., Mc-114-7; US Sol; PO omitted
POE, Perry W., Hw-121-4(3); Pvt K Co 4th TN Cav; 9-4-63 to 7-12-65; Van Hill PO; defective in sight, rheumatism, deafness
POE, William, Jo-150-1; Pvt H Co 13th TN Cav; 4-15-65 to 8-2-65; Rheas Forge PO
POER, John J., De-22-1; Pvt G Co 23rd TN Reg; 7-10-61 to 4-17-65; Bath Springs PO; CONF
POGUE, William C., Cu-17-4; Pvt B Co 10th IN Inf; 9-18-61 to 9-17-64; Northville PO
POHL, ___, D-44-3; Cathrine widow of; Nashville PO; could get no better information
POINTER, Alex, D-64-1; Sallie widow of; Sgt 13th TN; Nashville PO
POINTER, Jessie, Sh-191-1; Pvt TN Inf; 64 to 65; Jackson's Grocery, Cedar St, Nashville
POINTER, Maurice, Sh-191-1; Memphis PO
POINTER, R. W., Pu-144-3; Mary A. Campbell formerly widow of; Pvt I Co 1st TN Mtd Inf; Hudgins PO
POLAND, William, Dy-29-5; Pvt; 61 to 65; PO omitted; CONF
POLARD, Isaac, Bl-3-3; Pvt I Co 8th TN Cav; 62 to 65; Billingsly PO
POLFREY, Thomas J., R-106-1; Sgt K Co 5th TN; 11-62 to 6-24-65; 5th Civil Dist
POLK, Bradley J., Ma-115-1; Pvt C Co; 7-63 to __; 2nd Civil Dist
POLK, Grandison, H-57-2; Pvt I Co 1st TN; 62 to 65; Orchard Knob PO
POLK, Henry, Mt-136-1; Pvt A Co 16th TN; 10-63 to 4-30-66; Port Royal PO
POLK, Henry P., D-45-5; Pvt A Co 129th IL Inf; 8-2-62 to 5-30-65; Nashville PO; part of finger shot off & was prisoner in Libby Prison

POLK, Isaac A., Sh-200-2; Cpl E Co 88th US Col Inf; 1-19-63 to 65; 31 Wilkerson St., Memphis PO
POLK, John, Sh-173-1; Rachael widow of; Pvt B Co 61st TN; 5-62 to 64 (2 yrs); Memphis PO
POLK, Manuel, D-49-2; Pvt G Co; 61 to 64; Nashville PO; only knows what is stated
POLK, Samuel, Mu-207-1; Theta PO; away from home & not seen, his family could tell nothing
POLK, Stanley G., R-157-2; Sol; 12th Dist, Grand View PO
POLLAND, James, Ro-205-1; Pvt B Co 5th TN Inf; 2-25-62 to 3-15-65; Kingston PO; rheumatism since 64
POLLARD, Edgar, Hd-50-4; Visa widow of; Pvt F Co 10th TN Inf; 5-62 to 65 (3 yrs); Nixon PO
POLLARD, George L., S-213-3; Pvt 5th TN; Glenmary PO
POLLARD, John W., H-51-2(1); Pvt F Co 2nd TN Cav; 8-15-61 to 4-26-65; Hill City PO; name crossed out, probably CONF
POLLARD, Samuel, Je-143-3; US Sol; Mt. Horeb PO
POLLER, William M., Gr-74-1; Pvt I Co 59th TN Cav; 12-16-62 to 5-8-65; May Spring PO; CONF
POLLORD, F. F., Gi-122-3; Pvt C Co 7th AL BLA?; 11-63 to 3-64; Prospect Sta. PO; CONF
POLSON, George W., J-77-2; Charlotte widow of; Pvt; Gainesboro PO
POLSON, Levi, Ov-137-3; Pvt F Co 13th KY Cav; 10-63 to 4-65; Monroe PO; lung disease
POLSTON, Elias, A-9-1; B Co 1st TN Inf; 8-3-61 to 10-17-64; Podopholine PO
POMEROY, Hanse, He-66-2; Susan E. widow of; Pvt K Co 7th TN Cav; 5-6-62 to __; Middlefork PO; died in prison, cant tell anything about it
POND, Kit (see Hodges, Willis)
POND, Theron C., Rb-223-3(5); Pvt F Co 2nd MS? Inf; Sep 61 to 25 Jul 65; 9th Dist
PONDER, Hartwell P., Dk-36-2; Pvt B Co 4th TN Mtd Inf; 9-25-64 to 8-25-65; Smithville PO
PONDER, Roda F. (see Levay?, Patrick)
PONDEXTER, Julious A., Hd-52-1; Pvt E Co 13th IN Cav; Nov 15 64 to Dec 10 64; Hurley PO; measles
PONTIUS, Johnathan, F-37-1; Pvt A Co 17th IN Mtd Inf; Sep 24 64 to Aug 65; Stanton PO
PONY, Robert J., Hm-106-3; Pvt; Morristown PO; CONF
POOL, Alexander, P-156-3; Roberta Ann formerly widow of; Pvt I Co 1st KY Cav; Lobelville PO; CONF
POOL, James M., Wy-174-1; Pvt C Co 27th AL Inf; 12-61 to 9-2-62; Stout PO; CONF
POOL, Josephus, Mg-199-2; Pvt F Co 1st OH Hvy Art; Jul 62 to 65; Sunbright PO
POOL, Wm. H., Ce-23-2; Pvt G Co; 61 to 64; Pleasant View PO; wounded at Franklin, TN, disabled 30 days
POOLL, William, H-69-2; Pvt A Co 9th VA Inf; 5-62 to 7-24-65; Chattanooga PO; CONF
POOR, Crofford, Un-256-2; Nancy widow of; Pvt F Co 6th TN Inf; 10 Ma 62 to __; Duk (sic) PO; died in service
POOR, Frank M., Gi-134-1; Dist 14
POOR, Henry, Cl-58-2; Pvt Co I 3rd TN Inf; 2-10-62 to 2-23-65; Davo PO; injured in spine, enemy trampled leg
POOR, Isaac W., Cl-58-2; Caroline widow of; Pvt I Co 3rdTN Inf; Davo PO
POOR, Thomas, Ct-36-2; Pvt C Co 13th TN Cav; 63 to 9-65 (1 yr 6 mos); Roan Mt. PO
POORE, Bradford, A-1-2; Pvt F Co 8th TN Inf; 4-30-62 to 6-30-65; Andersonville PO
POORE, Joseph, P-151-1; Pvt C Co 3rd KY Art; 63 to Jul 65; Pope PO; heart & kidneys (exposure)
POPE, Aausin P., D-48-1; Pvt B Co 101st Reg US Vols; 5-18-62 to 1-25-65; Nashville PO
POPE, Alexandrew, Ho-95-1; Pvt B Co 22nd WI Inf; Aug 15 62 to Jul 3 65; Stuart PO
POPE, J. D., Ro-208-3; Jane E. widow of; US Sol; 9th Civ Dist
POPE, J. K., Ru-236-1; Louisa widow of; Pvt C Co 5th TN Cav; Murfreesboro PO
POPE, James C., Ro-201-3(1); Sgt D Co 5th TN Inf; 26 Feb 62 to 28 Mar 65; Kingston PO
POPE, Lucy J. (see Giles, John)
POPE, Mary (see Burns, Robert J.)
POPE, Oscar, Mr-97-2; US Sol; Jarman? PO

POPE, William E., Ro-208-1; could not get anything more, discharge lost
POPE, William H., Dy-27-1; Pvt D Co 15th TN Cav; 5-10-63 to 11-1-64; Newbern PO
POPE, Wm. H., Rb-223-3(5); Pvt E Co 2nd MI Cav; 9 Aug 61 to 9 Jul 62; 9th Dist; contracted nasal catarrh
POPE, William R., Bl-4-2; Pvt A Co 8th TN Cav; 10-1-62 to 5-1-65; Pikeville PO; CONF
POPE, Wily M., Dy-29-4; Pvt A Co 27th TN Cav; 62 to 64; Newbern PO; CONF
POPEJOY, John H., Un-253-2; Pvt A Co 7th TN Inf; 7 Aug 62 to 21 Ju 65; Lorenaton PO; disease of lungs, spine
POPEJOY, John S., Un-253-1; Pvt F Co 24th MO Inf; Aug 20 61 to Dec 21 63; New Flat Creek PO
POPEJOY, John S., Un-253-1; Pvt A Co 21st MO Inf; Dec 21 63 to Apr 19 66; New Flat Creek PO; hearing, spinal, reenlisted veteran
POPLIN, Green T., Dy-25-8(4); Mattie E. widow of; Newbern PO; CONF
PORE, Cyrus, Hw-188-2; Pvt A Co 1st TN Art; 9-16-63 to 8-13-65; St. Clair PO; rheumatism
PORRELL, Lewis H., Mr-96-3(2); US Sol; 3rd Dist
PORSON, George M., Hr-87-1; Pvt D Co 5th TN Inf; 8-31-64 to 6-28-65; PO omitted
PORTER, Abraham, Bo-22-1; alias Abraham Johnson; Pvt G Co 1st US Art; 2-12-64 to 3-31-66; Gamble's Store PO; scrofulas sores on breast, can't get dates as he don't know them
PORTER, Allen, Mu-195-2; alias Carter, Allen; Sol A Co 15th TN Inf; Dec 2 63 to Apr 7 66; Columbia PO
PORTER, Bryant W., Rb-221-1; Pvt B Co 2nd KY; Nov 1 62 to May 1 65; Cedar Hill PO; prisoner Camp Duglas; CONF
PORTER, Charley, Hn-77-1; Pvt M Co 4th Hvy Art; May 65 to Mar 66; PO omitted
PORTER, Cyrus, La-115-2; Pvt 23rd IN Inf; 6 Dec 64 to May 65; Summertown PO
PORTER, Edward, Sm-167-2; Waggoner 6th TN Inf; Dixon Springs PO
PORTER, Henderson, Hn-77-1; Pvt E Co 19th KY Inf; 65 to 66; PO omitted
PORTER, Jacob, Wl-297-1; Pvt A Co 72nd TN Inf; Jan 62 to Dec 64; Bellwood PO; no disability incurred but sick for 12 mos after discharge
PORTER, Jacob, Hr-86-1; Grand Junction PO
PORTER, James D., Mc-118-1; Lt D Co 5th TN Mtd Inf; 9-1-64 to 6-26-65; Cogshill PO; rupture 28 yrs
PORTER, John, R-106-2(3); Pvt; 6th Civil Dist
PORTER, John, K-159-1; Pvt E Co 1st US Col Art; Knoxville PO
PORTER, John B., K-158-2; Pvt A Co 29th TN Inf; May 61 to May 65; Knoxville, 97 E Clinch PO; CONF
PORTER, Jno. C., Se-230-1; 1st Sgt B Co 2nd TN Cav; 15 Aug 62 to 6 Jul 65; Richison's Cove PO; bronchitis, kidney trouble & diarrhea
PORTER, John L., Mu-209-6; Pvt C Co 48th TN Cav; 12-1-61 to 6-1-65; Columbia PO; CONF
PORTER, John L., Mu-209-1; Pvt C Co 48th TN Inf; Dec 61 to Jan 65; Columbia PO; CONF
PORTER, John R., Cr-16-2; Pvt F Co 7th TN Cav--Aug 14 62 to Oct 25 63; Pvt I Co 7th TN Cav--Jan 6 65 to Aug 9 65; Huntingdon PO; rheumatism, result of exposure
PORTER, Manuel, Hn-75-1; 24th Civ Dist
PORTER, Martha (see Thompson, John)
PORTER, Morris, Sh-189-5; Pvt H Co 3rd US Col Hvy Art; 6-5-63 to 4-30-66; Ark Ave, Memphis PO
PORTER, Moses, Sh-204-2; Ellen widow of; Elmwood Ave, Memphis PO
PORTER, Nicholas C., Me-88-3; Melvina A. widow of; Pvt E Co 5th TN Inf; 3-2-62 to died 2-3-62; Birchwood PO
PORTER, S., H-51-4; Pvt C Co 1st US Vet Engineers; 8-64 to 9-25-65; Hill City PO
PORTER, Samuel T., Rb-228-2; Pvt; 61 to Feb 62 (5 mos); Crunk PO; CONF
PORTER, Sidney, G-57-5(3); Pvt; Yorkville PO; CONF
PORTER, Susan, Sh-204-1; widow; Orleans Extd., Memphis PO
PORTER, Thomas, Me-88-1; Pvt E Co 5th TN Inf; 3-2-62 to 4-4-65; Birchwood PO
PORTER, William, Sh-153-1; Pvt E Co 72nd USC Inf; Jan 64 to Dec 66; Collierville PO
PORTER, William, Sh-180-1; Sgt A Co 1st US Hvy Art; 2-21-63 to 3-31-65; 7 Kings Ave, Memphis PO
PORTERFIELD, Richard C., K-185-3; US Sol; River Dale PO
PORTERFIELD, Roofus M., Wl-299-1; Pvt H Co 4th TN Inf; 1 Dec 63 to 25 Aug 64; Statesville PO
PORTERFIELD, Samuel T., Wl-302-1; Pvt H Co 4th TN Mtd Inf; 5 Nov 64 to 25 Aug 65; Hendersons X Roads PO
PORTRESS, Milton, Gi-132-2; Cpl G Co 111th USCV; Ridell PO
PORTRUM, Samuel, Hw-132-1; Lt B Co 60th TN Inf; 61 to 65; Persia PO; CONF
PORTUM, Thomas W., Hw-118-1; Pvt D Co 1st TN Cav; 18 Nov 62 to 19 Dec 63; St. Clair PO; heart disease
PORTWOOD, McKajah, C-34-3; Pvt I Co 7th TN Inf; 11-8-64 to 7-28-65; Abbott PO; contracted piles
PORTWOOD, Micagh, A-3-; Pvt C Co 3rd TN Inf; 2-12-62 to 2-23-65; Clinton PO; chronic rumatism
POSEY, Benjamin, Gr-79-3; Pvt D Co 3rth TN; 27 Aug 61 to 16 Apr 65; Thorn Hill PO; shot in right arm; CONF
POSEY, Benjamin M., Cl-52-2; Pvt A Co 11th TN Cav; 10-10-63 to 9-14-65; Hypratia PO; injured by mumps
POSEY, Daniel, Lo-187-2; Pvt C Co 3rd TN Mtd Inf; 26 Jul 64 to 30 Nov 64; Loudon PO
POSEY, Frank, B-7-2; Pvt C Co 5th TN Cav; 9-17-63 to 8-14-65; PO omitted
POSEY, Hezikiah, Ja-84-3; Barbrey M. Brinnager formerly widow of; Normans Store PO; dropsey
POSEY, Juballe, Cl-52-3; Pvt G Co 9th TN Cav; 10-11-62 to 65; Hypatia PO; back injured
POSEY, Oliver N. Sr., H-49-5; Sarah V. widow of; Pvt H Co 7th TN Vol; Daisy PO
POSEY, William, B-7-2; Pvt C Co 4th TN Mtd Inf; 11-64 to 65 (9 mos); PO omitted
POSEY, William A., H-50-1; Pvt I Co 12th R TN Cav; 9-63 to 8-65; Bunch PO; catarrh
POSEY, William F., Gr-79-3; Pvt G Co 9th TN; __ to 65; Thorn Hill PO
POSEY, William M., Mc-116-3; Pvt H Co 13th KY Mtd Inf; 62 to 65; Williamsburg PO; disease of kidneys & breast, discharge misplaced, no dates as to service
POST, J. A., Sh-171-2; Pvt K Co 44th NY; 61 to 62 (1 yr 3 mos); 418 Madison St, Memphis PO
POST, Lansing, Ma-114-2; 1st Dist
POST, Peter, Sn-262-2(1); Pvt L Co 10th MO Cav; 10-28-62 to 5-30-65; Fountain Head PO; lost one eye & ulcer of bowels
POSTON, Jeremiah T., C-29-1; Pvt E Co 50th VA Inf; 5-12-61 to 4-65; Fincastle PO; neuralgia, surrendered at Saltville, VA
POSTON, Papalon, Su-240-1; Pvt F Co 3rd US Inf; 64 to 64 (1 yr); Butterfly PO; prisner of war
POSTON, Titus, Sh-193-2; Sledge Ave, Memphis PO
POSTON, Uris W., Po-150-1; Pvt H Co 5th TN Mtd Inf; 12-8-65 to 7-15-65; Syloo PO; rheumatism
POTETE, Frank, Sn-262-2(1); Pvt C Co 44th Inf; 4-3-64 to __; South Tunnell PO; consumption, dont know when discharged
POTTCOTTER, Barny, La-109-1; Pvt M Co 28th IN Cav; 10-15-62 to 7-15-63; St. Joseph PO; gun shot wound left hip, pensioner
POTTER, Andrew, Jo-150-4; Pvt H Co 4th TN Inf; 22 Aug 62 to __; Osborn PO
POTTER, Daniel B., Ct-36-1; Pvt H Co 3rd NC Inf; 10-63 to 8-65; Roan Mt. PO; right testicle mashed
POTTER, David R., K-179-1; Virtue PO
POTTER, Davis D., Bo-23-2; Pvt D Co 2nd TN Cav; 9-4-62 to 7-6-65; Cades Cove PO; contracted a cough, now coughing at times
POTTER, Ezra, Mu-200-1; Pvt D Co 110th TN Inf; 4 Dec 62 to 7 Feb 65; Terry PO
POTTER, Francis M., La-115-2; Pvt H Co 15th IN Inf; 8 May 61 to 8 Jul 61; Summertown PO
POTTER, Irvin, Hm-109-1; Pvt C Co 8th TN Cav; 10 May 63 to Oct 65; Russellville PO
POTTER, Jacob, Jo-150-5; Pvt I Co 13th TN Cav; 22 Sep 63 to 5 Sep 65; Osborn PO; dyspepsia
POTTER, James, Bo-15-2; Pvt B Co 3rd TN Cav; 9-26-62 to 8-3-65; Blockhouse PO
POTTER, John (see McGehee, John)

POTTER, John O., Jo-150-5; Pvt I Co 13th TN Cav; 22 Sep 63 to 5 Sep 65; Osborn PO; injury to breast
POTTER, Noah, Ct-35-4; Pvt 13th TN Cav; __ to 9-5-65; Ike Mills PO; in US Army, gone from home, discharge not found
POTTER, Paul, Hm-109-2; Isabel Y. widow of; Pvt; Brights PO
POTTER, Reubin, Jo-150-2; Pvt H Co 4th TN Inf; 16 Jun 64 to 20 Aug 65; Key Station PO
POTTER, Robert, Hm-109-1; Pvt A Co 1st TN Art; 6 Nov 63 to 10 Aug 65 (1 yr 5 mos 46 days); Whitesburg PO; diarrhoea for which is drawing pension
POTTER, Shadrick P., Jo-150-2; Pvt I Co 13th TN Cav; 22 Sep 63 to 5 Sep 65; Key Station PO
POTTER, Solomon, Cu-15-2; Pvt F Co 1st TN Inf; 8-9-61 to 9-17-64; Genesis PO; discharge lost
POTTER, Sylvester, Bo-13-2; Pvt A Co 31st IL Inf; 8-29-62 to 3-29-63; Freindsville PO; wounded in left shoulder, Tutt
POTTER, Thomas, Jo-150-4; Pvt I Co 13th TN Cav; 24 Sep 63 to 5 Sep 65; Rheas Forge PO
POTTER, William H., Ct-42-3; Sarah M. widow of; Pvt F Co 8th TN Cav; Elizabethton PO
POTTERS, James, H-69-3; Pvt; Chattanooga PO; CONF
POTTS, Isaac, Sh-196-1; Isaac Smith alias; Pvt I Co 61st TN Inf; 6-29-63 to 12-30-65; 450 Poplar St, Memphis PO
POTTS, John H., B-11-2(1); Sgt I Co 7th AL Vid; 2-28-63 to 6-16-64; Poplins X Roads PO
POTTS, John T., W-189-2; Pvt F Co 1st OH Lt Art; 8-20-61 to 7-29-65; McMinnville PO
POTTS, Joseph F., Sh-159-3; Anna widow of; Pvt; Memphis PO; CONF
POTTS, L. W., Gi-122-6; Pvt A Co 53rd TN Inf; Oct 62 to Dec 64; Aspen Hill PO; CONF
POTTS, Louis, Di-30-1; Adaline widow of; Pvt I Co 23rd TN Cav; 63 to 65; Dickson PO
POTTY, David W., Se-224-1; Pvt D Co 2nd TN Cav; 1 Sep 62 to 6 Jul 65; Hornett PO; stiffnes of & weak back
POUEL, Allen, G-67-3; Pvt G Co 2nd TN Mtd Inf; 30 Nov 63 to 19 Jan 65; Idlewild PO; one rib broken and shoulder hurt
POUEL, James W., G-67-3; Reckil E. widow of; Pvt M Co 6th TN Cav; Aug 62 to __; Idlewild PO
POUNDERS, Thomas R., Sh-149-2; Pvt B Co 1st AL Cav; 1 Feb 63 to 20 Oct 66; Raleigh PO
POUNDS, Danal W., We-223-2; Sarah F. Parham former widow of; Pvt A Co 5th TN Cav; have lost all papers and cant give co or regiment, died while in servises
POUNDS, John H., We-233-1(2); Pvt 6th TN Cav; 8-13-62 to 65; Ralston PO
POWAL, Robert (see Giles, Gilman)
POWEL, Charlesworth, Cu-17-3; 1st Lt 14th IL Inf; 4-61 to 5-25-64; Grassy Cove PO; wounded in right arm
POWEL, Garret, Mg-198-4; Pvt F Co 1st AR Inf; 1 Mar 63 to 10 Aug 65; Rockwood PO; flux
POWEL, James, Mo-123-1; Pvt D Co 3rd TN Mtd Inf; 7-25-64 to 11-30-64; Jalapa PO
POWEL, John, Col, Sh-146-2; Pvt E Co 59th Inf; Spring of 63 to May or Jun 65; Brunswick PO; Col Cowden, Capt Smock
POWEL, John, Sh-146-4; US Sol; 3rd Civ Dist
POWEL, Jo-eph, Mg-198-4; Pvt E Co 1st TN Inf; 20 Aug 61 to 17 Sep 64; Rockwood PO; two fingers shot off
POWEL, Madison, Hd-54-3; Pvt 6th TN Cav; 62 to 65; Sardis PO; could not obtain discharge for data
POWEL, Sal?, Su-240-2; Bichethal widow of; Wagon master TN Cav; 63 to Jul 65; Kindricks Creek PO; came out at the surrender
POWELL, Abraham, H-54-6; Pvt H Co 137th US Col Inf; 65 to __; Chattanooga PO; lost one left eye with small pox
POWELL, B. F., La-117-4; Pvt; 15th Dist; CONF
POWELL, Benjamin T., H-61-3; 2nd Sgt G Co 60th GA Inf; 7-1-61 to 4-9-65; Chattanooga PO; CONF
POWELL, Evan W., Dy-25-9(1); Pvt B Co 146th IN Inf; 2-1-64 to 8-21-65; Newbern PO; measels, eyes affected badly in sight
POWELL, Francis M., Mr-96-2; Pvt C Co 6th TN Mtd Inf; 9-64 to 65 (8 mos); Shirleyton PO; rheumatism

POWELL, Franklin B., Hd-50-5; Pvt D Co 2nd TN Mtd Inf; 63 to __; Nixon PO
POWELL, George W., Bo-23-2; Cpl B Co 6th TN Inf; 3-8-62 to 6-30-65; PO omitted (may be Cades Cove)
POWELL, Isaac, Mo-126-1; Pvt D Co 3rd TN Mtd Inf; 7-25-64 to 11-30-64; Hopewell Springs PO
POWELL, John, Lk-112-2; Sarah, separated; Tiptonville PO; John Powell in State Penn for murder no data obtainable
POWELL, John C., Ge-96-2; Sgt D Co 8th TN Cav; Sep 62 to 11 Sep 65; Jockey PO; piles &c &c
POWELL, John E., D-99-4; State Penitentiary PO
POWELL, John H., Jo-150-1; Pvt C Co 13th TN Cav; 24 Sep 63 to 5 Sep 65; Rheas Forge PO
POWELL, Jorden J., C-24-1; Pvt G Co 7th Inf; 11-8-64 to 7-27-65; Boy PO; frost bitten feet
POWELL, Lizzie (see Russel, Robert)
POWELL, M. M., La-110-1(2); Pvt E Co 2nd TN Inf; 11-63 to 5-18-65; Appleton PO; hydwealle
POWELL, Mich, Ru-243-1; Pvt F Co 10th TN Inf; 7-30-62 to 7-24-65; Fosterville PO; Andy Johnson bodyguard
POWELL, Nathan, G-52-1; Pvt A Co 162nd IL Inf; 10-62 to 3-65; Humboldt PO
POWELL, Smith, Jo-150-1; Pvt D Co 13th TN Cav; 24 Sep 63 to 5 Sep 65; Rheas Forge PO
POWELL, Thomas, D-45-2; Elizabeth widow of; Pvt F Co 2nd US Col; Nashville PO
POWELL, William, Ro-210-7; Pvt; Cardiff PO
POWELL, William H., Mr-96-1; Pvt D Co 6th TN Mtd Inf; 9-7-64 to 6-30-65; Whitwell PO; rheumatism
POWELL, William L., Ro-210-6; Elizabeth widow of; Pvt; Rockwood PO
POWERS, Christian S., Me-91-1; Pvt; Bonham PO; discharge on file in war dept.
POWERS, Henry M., He-63-1; Panilla widow of; Cpl H Co 7th TN; PO omitted
POWERS, Ira, He-63-1; Cpl A Co 7th TN Cav; Aug 18 62 to Aug 20 65; PO omitted
POWERS, James, D-64-5; Sarah widow of; Nashville PO
POWERS, John F., A-4-3; Pvt D Co 7th TN Mtd Inf; 11-19-63 to 8-9-65; Coal Creek PO
POWERS, John N., We-224-4; 6th Dist
POWERS, Josiah, Rb-228-2; Pvt A Co 3rd TN Inf; 10 Feb 62 to 10 Feb 65; Coopertown PO
POWERS, Mary A., P-150-2; widow US Sol; 1st Dist
POWERS, Nelson P., D-79-2; Lt G Co 25th IL Inf; Aug 8 61 to 1 Sep 64; Nashville, 251 Foster PO
POWERS, Noah, Ce-31-1; Pvt TN Inf; Oct 62 to Feb 63; Ashland City PO; CONF
POWERS, Pleasant D., We-225-2(1); Pvt A Co 1st TN Inf; Co 6th TN Cav; Jun 22 62 to Aug 65; Dresden PO; cronic diarrhea, have had no good health since
POWERS, Robt. H., Sh-201-4; Pvt D Co 29th IA Inf; 2 Jan 62 to 12 Mar 65; Memphis PO
POWERS, Rosa (see Charles, James)
POWERS, Stephen, He-63-2; Pvt A Co 7th TN Cav; Aug 18 62 to Aug 18 65; Long PO; in Andersonvill Prison 13 mos
POWERS, William, He-63-2; Pvt A Co 48th IL Inf; Mar 24 62 to Mar 24 65; Long PO; in Andersonvill Prison 13 mos
POWERS, Willis, St-161-1; Sallie A. E. widow of; Pvt G Co 61st IL Vol; 63 to 65; Bumpas Mills PO; is now in absolute poverty
POWLEN, Eli, Sm-172-1; Mary widow of; Lancaster PO
PRAIETT, George W., Po-148-2; Pvt C Co 13th TN Cav; fall 63 to fall 65; Chestewee Mills PO; ruptered, discharge filed at Washington
PRATER, Gabriel D., Ca-23-2; Pvt K Co 52nd KY Inf; 12-14-63 to 3-11-65; Leoni PO; back injured by horse, horse sprang while in battle
PRATER, James H., Ca-23-2; Pvt K Co 52nd KY Inf; 12-24-63 to 3-17-65; Leoni PO; health injured by cold
PRATER, John, Wh-187-2; Cpl K Co 52nd KY Inf; 11-14-65 to 3-11-65; Yankeetown PO; contracted rheumatism
PRATER, Thos., W-194-1; Lettie J. widow of; Pvt; 61 to 62; Leona PO; discharge lost
PRATHER, ____, Mc-112-10; Mrs. Margaret widow of; Athens PO
PRATOR, James, R-106-2(3); Pvt I Co 5th TN; 4-11-62 to 3-15-65; 7th Civil Dist

PRATOR, Joseph Jr., Un-256-1; Pvt K Co 4th TN Mtd Inf; 1 Dec 64 to 25 Aug 65; Rule PO; feaver
PRATT, Charles, K-183-2; Pvt B Co 6th TN Inf; 14 Apr 62 to 27 Apr 65; Riverdale PO
PRATT, Edgar J., K-166-4(2); Capt H Co 13th WI Inf; 30 Sep 61 to 7 Jul 65; Knoxville PO
PRATT, Elisiah, Cl-54-3(1); Pvt E Co 1st TN Cav; 60 to 64; Tazewell PO; horse fell on him, hurt hip
PRATT, Fredric J., L-100-1; Pvt 30th NY Lt Art; 62 to 65; Ripley PO; wounded and lost eye, cannot give dates
PRATT, George H., H-56-6; Pvt MA; 63 to 65; East End PO
PRATT, H., G-68-1; Pvt K Co 12th KS?; 60 to 65; Gibson PO
PRATT, James N., K-182-2; Pvt B Co 6th TN Inf; 18 Jan 63 to 18 Jul 65; Shooks PO; rheumatism, liver disease
PRATT, John, Ha-112-1; Pvt L Co 9th TN Cav; 15 Oct 63 to 11 Sep 65; Blackwater PO
PRATT, John H., De-26-2; F Co 27th TN __; Jun 61 to Jan 65; Northford PO; little finger shot off right hand; CONF
PRATT, Lizzie (see Oatten?, James)
PRATT, Richard, D-49-1; Pvt K Co 16th TN; Feb 62 to May 65; Nashville PO
PRATT, Robert, K-182-1; Pvt B Co 6th TN Inf; May 63 to Jun 65; PO omitted
PRATT, Silas R., Cf-37-1; Pvt C Co 5th TN Cav; 62 to 65; Stick PO
PRATT, Silas R., B-3-1; Pvt C Co 5th TN Cav; 11-5-62 to 7-25-65; Coldwell PO; wounded 11-62 by gunshot; still suffering from wound
PRATT, William J., Mu-193-2; Courier 12th TN Cav; 9-15-63 to 3-15-65; Columbia PO
PRATT, Willis V., Cr-4-3; Pvt K Co 9th KY Inf; 1 Apr 64 to 1 Apr 65; Bells Depot PO; CONF
PREATOR, Joseph Sr., Un-256-2; Martha widow of; Pvt K Co 4th TN Mtd Inf; 4 Apr 65 to 25 Aug 65; Rule PO
PRENTICE, Andrew J., H-59-2; Pvt D Co 21st MI Inf; 6-14-63 to 6-65; Chattanooga PO
PRENTICE, Robert, Pu-145-3(4); Adelaid widow of; Cpl C Co 1st Mtd Inf; 10-21-63 to 12-13-64; Silver Point PO
PRESCOT, Peter, Ge-95-2; Pvt C Co 6th NY Cav; __ to 65; Home PO; shot in right ankle, in prison at Richmond
PRESCOTT, William, Cr-6-1; G Co 4th IL Cav; 9-1-62 to 6-15-65; Cairo PO
PRESLEY, Greenberry, Hw-127-2; Pvt A Co 8th TN Cav; 11 Jun 63 to 11 Sep 65; Rogersville PO
PRESLEY, Jacob, Lo-190-1; Sarah A. widow of; Pvt I Co 5th TN Inf; Piney PO
PRESLEY, James P., Ro-210-3; Pvt; Rockwood PO; chronic diarea
PRESLEY, John, Tr-268-1; Mary Ann widow of; Pvt Inf; Hartsville PO; dropsy; dead & widow pensioned
PRESLEY, Simon P., Ge-99-2; Pvt E Co 2nd NC Mtd Inf; 1 Sep 63 to 16 Aug 65; Limestone Springs PO; spine, kidney & dyspepsia
PRESLY, John, Ro-205-3; Pvt G Co 52nd GA Ind; 12 Aug 61 to 12 Aug 64; Halfmoon Island, drops and indigestion of bowels
PRESLY, Josiah, Cl-57-2; Pvt E Co 6th TN Reg; 3-6-62 to __; Kecks Chappel PO; rheumatism, diarea, sol. looks broke down
PRESNAL, John, Hm-107-4; Pvt C Co 8th TN Mtd Inf; 63 to 65 (1 yr); Chestnut Bloom PO
PRESNEL, Isaac, Hm-107-4; Pvt A Co 8th NC Mtd Inf; 65 to __; Chestnut Bloom PO; chronic diarrhea, not discharged, lost all dates
PRESNELL, Isaac, K-177-5; Cpl 3rd TN Engineer Reg; 21 Mar 62 to Apr 65; Powells Station PO; CONF
PRESSLAR, Miles (see Hornback, Sarah)
PRESSLEY, Isaac, Mo-130-2; Pvt D Co 3rd TN Mtd Inf; 7-12-64 to 12-24-64; Ballplay PO
PRESSLEY, Washington, R-157-1; Pvt; Baptist PO; finger off; could not find him at home & secured this from a neighbor
PRESSLY, John, Hw-125-6; Pvt I Co; Blevins PO; CONF
PRESSLY, Thos., Mo-119-3; Pvt K Co 9th TN Cav; 8-3-63 to 9-4-65; Sweetwater PO
PRESSWOOD, Francis M., Po-151-1; Pvt B Co 1st TN Lt Art; 1-7-63 to 6-25-65; Servilla PO

PRESSWOOD, Samuel J., Mc-109-5; Pvt K Co 10th TN Cav; Erie PO (Loudon Co.)
PRESTON, Charles, D-43-1; Pvt C Co 64th IL; 62 to (3 yrs 4 mos); Nashville PO
PRESTON, George W., D-84-1; Cpl 18th OH Bat; 11 Aug 62 to 5 Jun 65; Antioch PO
PRESTON, James, Ca-24-1; Pvt G Co 5th TN Cav; 8-28-62 to 8-14-65; Talvine PO; rheumatism, neuralgia, effect cold taken in army
PRESTON, Taylor, D-54-1; Musician Inf; Nashville PO
PRESWELL, Wade, Cl-54-4(2); Pvt D Co 8th TN Inf; 2-28-62 to 5-5-65; Tazewell? PO; CONF
PRETTYMAN, Joseph, Mg-199-3; PA Cav; Sunbright PO
PREWET, Benjamin, Br-6-4; Sarah widow of; Pvt I Co 4th TN Cav; 10-14-63 to 7-12-65; Charleston PO
PREWETT, McKager, Ch-18-1; Cpl 2nd MS Inf; Feb 61 to 65; PO omitted; CONF
PREWETT, Vernal F., Ma-127-1; Pvt D Co 111th IL Inf; Aug 11 62 to Jun 28 65; Jackson PO
PREWIT, William A., Wl-288-1; Pvt C Co 13th KY Cav; Aug 63 to Aug 64; Sandersville PO
PREWITT, Derrick, De-137-1; Pvt 9th TN Cav; Sandy Ridge PO; rupture
PREWITT, George N., Hr-86-1; Pvt 13th TN; 64 to 65; Saulsbury PO; cronic diareah, enlisted under Maj. R. N. Thompson of 6th TN
PRICE, Andrew J., Me-90-2(1); Pvt D Co 12th TN Cav; 11-10-63 to 6-65; Meigs PO; shot in right foot
PRICE, Bery, Li-149-2; Cpl B Co 44th US Col Inf; 3-63 to 5-65; Fayetteville PO
PRICE, Betsey J., Ge-92-5; widow; 11th Dist
PRICE, Daniel (see Cobb, Daniel)
PRICE, David, Sh-150-1; Aurthor Price; Pvt I Co 61st Inf; Bonds PO; discharge stolen by a collecting agent
PRICE, Dorsey, Me-91-1; Pvt K Co 4th TN Cav; 4-25-64 to 6-26-65; Decatur PO
PRICE, Eliza, We-232-1; widow; Mt. Pelie PO
PRICE, Emmor?, H-60-2; Lt C Co 11th OH Inf; 6-20-61 to 6-21-64; Chattanooga PO; varicoule
PRICE, Frankling, U-245-2; Pvt D Co 13th TN Cav; Apr 64 to Sep 65; Marbleton (in 1865) PO; horse fell and dislocated left hip and ancle
PRICE, George, Hw-120-2; Pvt E Co 8th TN Cav; 10 Oct 63 to 11 Sep 65; Edison PO; gun shot
PRICE, George W., Wa-273-1; Pvt B Co 3rd NC Inf; 22 Jun 64 to 8 Aug 65; Morning Star PO; rheumatism and lung disease
PRICE, Gustavus, Sh-173-1; James Edds alias; Cpl A Co 55th US Inf; 5-13-63 to 12-31-65; Memphis PO
PRICE, Henry, H-51-4; Pvt A Co 1st TN Art; 1-18-64 to 3-31-65; Hill City PO
PRICE, Henry, H-51-5; Pvt; 61 to 65 (3 yrs 10 mos); Hill City PO
PRICE, Henry S., Wa-267-3; Sgt B Co 8th TN Cav; 23 Jul 63 to Sep 65; Johnson City PO; rheumatism, chrc.
PRICE, Isaiah, U-247-1; Pvt G Co 3rd NC Mtd Inf; 1 Sep 64 to 8 Aug 65; Erwin PO; rupture, kidneys & back, inlargment of testicles
PRICE, James, F-44-1; Pvt G Co 13th TN; Jan 28 61 to May 20 61; PO omitted; CONF
PRICE, James, Hw-128-1; Pvt E Co 8th TN Cav; 10 Oct 63 to 11 Sep 65; Choptack PO
PRICE, James, Fe-41-1; Pvt B Co 2nd TN Inf; 61 to 64; Jamestown PO
PRICE, James D., K-160-4; Knoxville, Morgan St. PO; no dates
PRICE, James H., Sh-152-2; alias Price, John; Cpl B Co Inf; 63 to __; Dexter PO; exposure while having measles, mr dr. says it gone to consumption
PRICE, James H., K-166-1; Pvt C Co 6th TN Inf; 18 Apr 62 to 27 Apr 65; Knoxville PO
PRICE, James L., Wa-267-2; Pvt I Co 6th IN Cav; 11 Jan 63 to 31 Aug 65; Febuary PO; asthma & rheumatism
PRICE, James P., Ct-38-2; Pvt D Co 13th TN Cav; 9-23-63 to 9-5-65; Johnson City PO; rheumatism, lesion of bowels & heart disease
PRICE, Jas. R., Wa-267-1; Sgt G Co 1st US Inf; 24 Mar 64 to 21 May 66; Jonesboro PO; rheumatism, chrc.
PRICE, James T., Co-67-4; Pvt K Co 8th TN Inf; 11 Sep 64 to 30 Jun 65; Naillon PO; gunshot in hips

PRICE, James V., K-177-3; PO omitted
PRICE, Jasper M., Ge-102-2; Pvt G Co 4th TN Inf; 5 May 62 to 10 Aug 65; Wolsey College PO; measels and diarear, now lung and hippe?
PRICE, Jerry, Sh-182-1; Driver wagon train 61st IL; 65 to Hawkinsville, GA, 1865; 294 Poplar St, Memphis PO; feble memory, cannot remember detachment
PRICE, John, K-161-5(6); Cynthia widow of; Pvt; Knoxville PO
PRICE, John A., Jo-153-2; Pvt D Co 13th TN Cav; 24 Sep 63 to 5 Sep 65; Shady PO; rheumatism, result of small pox
PRICE, Mark F., Je-141-3; Mary widow of; Pvt K Co 3rd TN Inf; Feb 62 to Feb 65; Mill Springs PO
PRICE, Nathaniel S., Br-12-1; 1st Sgt L Co 4th TN Cav; 12-22-62 to 7-12-65; Charleston PO; injury in hip & piles
PRICE, Oliver P., D-79-1; Pvt F Co 133rd OH Inf; May 6 64 to Aug 20 64; Nashville, No 225 Foster St. PO; rheumatism caused by swamp malaria
PRICE, Robert, Fr-112-2; Pvt F Co 9th TN Cav; 9-20-62 to 9-20-65; Tullahoma PO; pistol shot in left breast
PRICE, Robert I., La-117-1; Pvt A Co 48th TN Inf; Dec 3 63 to ___ (1 yr); 15th Dist; CONF
PRICE, Royal, Sh-149-2; Pvt C Co 3rd US Art; 24 Dec 63 to 30 Apr 66; Memphis PO
PRICE, Sampson, F-37-1; Pvt I Co 61st US Col Inf; May 1 65 to Dec 30 65; Somerville PO
PRICE, Saml., D-60-1; Daffy widow of; 228 Knowles St, Nashville PO; colored
PRICE, Samul, Mc-109-2; Pvt D Co 7th TN Inf; 10-1-64 to 7-27-65; Regret PO
PRICE, Solomon, Wl-290-1; 3rd Civil Dist
PRICE, Whittle P., K-164-1; Pvt D Co 6th TN Inf; 18 Apr 62 to Nov 63; PO omitted (Knoxville?)
PRICE, William, Cl-49-2; Pvt H Co 8th TN Inf; 7-22-63 to 6-26-65; Cumberland Gap PO; general disability
PRICE, William J., Hw-120-1; Pvt I Co 9th TN Cav; Jun 63 to Oct 65; War Gap PO; frost bitten feet
PRICE, William N., K-179-4; Pvt D Co 6th TN Inf; PO omitted
PRICE, Willis G., Mg-197-5; Pvt B Co 2nd TN Inf; 10 Aug 61 to 6 Oct 64; Wartburg PO; urinary organds diseased and rheumatism
PRICE, Willis J., We-220-2; Lieucind widow of; Pvt I Co 6th TN Cav; Mar 16 62 to Feb 16 63; Latham PO
PRICE, Wilson, K-167-2; 1st Hvy Cav; 62 to 65; Knoxville PO
PRICHARD, Alxr., Dk-36-2; Pvt B Co 4th TN Mtd Inf; 9-25-64 to 64(5?); Smithville PO
PRICHARD, Silas J., Dy-25-8(4); Pvt A Co 12th TN Inf; 5-61 to 5-62; Newbern PO; CONF
PRICHARD, Simon W., Pi-155-3; Pvt; 64 to ___ (6 mos); Byrdstown PO
PRICHARD, Stephen, Dk-39-6(2); Pvt I Co 1st TN Mtd Inf; 1-1-65 to 8-65; Laurel Hill PO
PRICHARD, William M., Mc-116-4; 11th Civil Dist
PRICHETT, J. E., Pi-153-1; Pvt D Co 1st TN Inf; 64 to 65; Byrdstown PO
PRICHETT, James, Dk-32-2; Pvt I Co 4th TN Mtd Inf; 11-1-64 to 8-25-65; Liberty PO
PRICHETT, Nathen C., Dy-28-1; Pvt A Co 7th TN Cav; Aug 8 62 to Aug 9 65; Finley PO; lung disease, contracted in Rebel Prison
PRIDDY, John, Ja-84-3; Pvt H Co 3rd TN Cav; 9-6-63 to 8-3-65; Thatchers Landing PO
PRIDE, Henry, Co., Lo-192-2; Pvt B Co 1st TN; Jun 64 to Mar 66; Greenback PO; rheumatism
PRIDEMORE, George W., Ha-117-1; Pvt C Co 8th TN Inf; 1 Dec 62 to 13 Jan 65; Kyle's Ford PO; gun shot r. shoulder, contracted lung disease
PRIDEMORE, Wiley, Ha-102-1; Cpl E Co 8th TN Cav; 23 Sep 63 to 11 Sep 65; Blackwater PO
PRIETO, Joseph A., O-141-1; Ast Sgt 13th US Mtd Inf; Jan 13 56 to Sep 15 65 (4 yrs 5 mos 2 days); Union City PO
PRIGMORE, Andrew, H-57-3; Pvt I Co 15th TN Inf; 63 to 65; Orchard Knob PO
PRIGMORE, Charles, Mc-109-6; Violet widow of; Pvt A Co 412th US Col Vol; Prigmore PO; died in service, no discharge to show dates

PRIGMORE, E. S., Mr-97-1; Pvt C Co TN Inf; 8-24-64 to 6-30-65; PO omitted
PRIGMORE, Robert, Me-92-1; Hester Mills PO; no satisfactory answers by family
PRIM, Jerry W., Ce-31-2; Pvt A Co 24th TN Cav; Feb 63 to 10 May 65; PO omitted; CONF
PRIME, Joseph, H-62-5; Hamilton House, Chattanooga PO; gone to New England City
PRIMM, Carol, Col, Tr-268-1; Rachel widow of; Pvt F Co 1st TN Inf; Hartsville PO; mustered out
PRIMM, Jerry W., Di-36-1; Pvt B Co TN Cav; 2-63 to 12-64; Bellsburgh PO; CONF
PRINCE, Calvin M., G-70-1; Mary A. widow of; Pvt; 1 Sep 62 to ___; Dyer PO; killed
PRINCE, Jesse W., Br-7-1; Lidia H. widow of; Pvt H Co 4th TN Cav; 10-14-63 to 7-12-65; Cleveland PO; chronic diarhea
PRINCE, John, Po-149-4(2); Pvt K Co 12th TN Cav; 3-20-64 to 10-7-65; Ocoee PO
PRINCE, John W., Li-147-1; Pvt C Co 4th TN Inf; 65 to ___ (5 mos); Bucksnort PO
PRINCE, Laborn P., Wy-177-2; Pvt K Co 46th OH Inf; 3-10-62 to 4-65; Moon PO
PRINCE, Martin V., Po-152-3(1); Sgt K Co 12th TN Cav; 3-20-64 to 10-7-65; Ducktown PO; rheumatism and liver disease
PRINCE, Matilda, O-141-3; Mother of a Soldier; Pvt B Co 12th IL Vol Inf; 62 to 65; Union City PO
PRINCE, William B., Ro-210-7; Pvt B Co 10th TN Cav; Cardiff PO
PRINCE, Young D., A-4-6(2); Cpl B Co 10th TN Cav; 9-15-63 to 6-11-65; Coal Creek PO; heart trouble, falling of horse
PRINCKLEY, Marcellen, Cr-14-4; US Sol; 13th Civil Dist
PRIOR, Shade C., Pi-153-1; Pvt D Co 1st TN Inf; 12-64 to 4-65; Chanute PO
PRIOR, Vinson, Je-146-5; Pvt B Co 3rd TN Cav; 10 Oct 63 to 11 Sep 65; White Pine PO; hurt in shoulder, a poor weak man
PRIOR, William M., Ke-22-2; Pvt D Co 3rd TN Col Cav; 22 Sep 62 to 20 Jun 65; Shooks PO; Cahamba? prison 6 mos, of survivor of the Sutana explosion
PRITCHARD, Sallie B., Cr-15-2; widow US Sol; Maple Creek PO
PRITCHARD, Vina E., Pi-156-3; widow of US Sol; 8th Civil Dist
PRITCHETT, Joseph, La-113-1; Pvt F Co 6th TN Inf; 3 Feb 63 to 26 Jul 65; Lawrenceburg PO
PRITCHETT, William, R-158-3; Pvt Capt Clark's 60th IL Inf; 5-20-64 to ___; Sheffield PO; chronic sore eyes, no discharge--sick and absent
PRITCHETT, William T., Wa-274-2; Sgt D Co 8th TN Cav; Jonesboro PO; disease of lungs and gun shot
PRIVATT, Isreal, Je-145-1; Pvt B Co 9th TN Cav; Cynthiana PO
PRIVETT, ___, Sh-191-2; Elizabeth widow of; Memphis PO
PRIVETTE, John W., K-186-3; Pvt; Beaver Ridge PO
PROFFITT, David, Se-220-1; Pvt E Co 2nd TN Cav; 15 Sep 62 to 5 Jul 65; Emurts Cave PO
PROFFITT, Fielding, Jo-151-3; Pvt M Co 13th TN Cav; 2 Feb 64 to 5 Sep 65; Vaughtsville PO; rheumatism
PROFFITT, Godfrey D., Jo-152-2; Pvt D Co 13th TN Cav; Sep 62 to Sep 65; Doeville PO; skull broken
PROFFITT, Ira H., Co-60-1; B Co 16th NC Inf; 4-17-61 to ___; Syrensburg PO
PROFFITT, John N., Jo-150-4; Sgt M Co 13th TN Cav; 2 Feb 64 to 5 Sep 65; Osborn PO
PROFITT, Cely, Se-219-4; widow of Sol, US; 1st Dist
PROPES, John H., Ro-203-6; Pvt D Co 3rd TN Inf; 20 Feb 62 to 20 Feb 65; PO omitted
PROPS, John, Ma-103-3; Marthy widow of; Lafayette PO; discharge at Washington
PROSISE, John A., A-13-3; PVt C Co 2nd TN Inf; 11-11-61 to 2-8-65; Prosise PO; prisoner Andersonville 13 mos, wounded in head
PROSSER, Abijah S., K-157-1; Maj 2nd TN Cav; Knoxville PO
PROSSER, James, K-167-1; 1st Hvy TN; 62 to 65; Knoxville PO; piles

PROTSMAN, Charles, Fr-117-1; Cpl C Co 54th IN Inf--5-27-62 to 9-11-62; Cpl I Co 117th IN Inf--8-6-63 to 2-24-64; PO omitted
PRUETT, Cylas, Sn-259-1; Pvt K Co 118th __; 9-26-64 to 10-18-65; Bransford PO
PRUETT, James H., Wl-297-2; Pvt C Co 58th IL Inf; 13 Dec 63 to 1 Aug 66; Linwood PO
PRUETT, Jiles M., Rb-230-1; Pvt A Co 1st TN Cav; May 63 to Jan 65; Springfield PO
PRUETT, John, Sn-257-1; Pvt F Co 13th US Inf; 9-29-63 to 1-10-66; Gallatin PO; pensioner
PRUETT, W. P., Hu-103-2; Pvt E Co 10th TN; 62 to 65; PO omitted
PRUETT, Willis, A-4-3; Angeline E. widow of; Pvt C Co 13th TN Cav; 9-24-63 to 9-5-65; Coal Creek PO
PRUIT, William, K-175-1; Pvt C Co 13th TN Cav; 18 Sep 62 to 18 Aug 65; Bullrun PO
PRUITT, Pat, Sn-250-2; Pvt C Co 2nd __; 10-16-62 to 65; Castalian Springs PO
PRYER, Thomas W., We-221-5(2); Sgt B Co 5th TN Inf; May 61 to Jul 64; Martin PO; imprisoned 2 mos; CONF
PRYER, William A., Mr-99-2; Pvt A Co 10th TN Cav; 8-12-63 to 8-1-65; Jasper PO
PRYOR, Chesley, Pi-154-1; Pvt D Co 3rd KY Inf; 12-61 to 5-65; Byrdstown PO; rheumatism, discharge lost by an attorney
PRYOR, Edward, Ov-137-2; Pvt; Monroe PO; lung disease, I failed to see this soldier
PRYOR, Harmon, R-161-5; Mary L. widow of; Pvt B Co; Dayton PO; no facts, in bad cond.
PRYOR, Jacob, Sn-252-3; Mickey L. widow of; Gallatin PO
PRYOR, James J., D-97-1; Pvt A Co Kings Batt GA Cav; Sep 1 63 to 65; Nashville PO; CONF
PRYOR, Jsoeph P., St-160-2; Big Rock PO
PRYOR, Mingo, Gi-127-4; Pvt B Co 12th Reg Col Inf; 8-4-63 to 8-23-65; Pulaski PO; shot in head, heart affection (hypertrophy of the hear), discharged on surgeons certificate--disability
PRYOR, Pleasant M., Mr-99-2; Pvt I Co 10th TN Inf; 6-62 to 10-62; Jasper PO
PRYOR, Richard S., Mr-99-3; Pvt I Co 10th TN Inf; 7-23-62 to 6-23-65; Jasper PO
PRYOR, Sampson, T-210-1; Cpl D Co 11th US; 63 to 66; Richardson Ldg. PO
PRYOR, Samuel, Bo-21-1; Pvt A Co 6th TN Inf; 4-24-62 to 4-27-65; Veeba PO
PRYOR, William, Mr-95-2; Capt C Co 4th TN Inf; 6-29-64 to 6-29-65; Victoria PO
PRYOR, William, Cy-29-1; Pvt H Co 2nd TN Inf; 12-19-61 to 12-19-64; Speck PO
PRYOR, William, D-99-1; Pvt; Nashville PO; poorhouse
PRYSOCK, William, Ge-83-1; Pvt G Co 3rd NC Inf; 11 Jul 64 to 8 Aug 65; Henshaw PO; lameness--wounded foot
PRYTER, Joshua, K-164-3; PO omitted (Knoxville)
PUCKETT, Charles, B-9-1; Pvt K Co 17th __; 64 to __; Fruit Valley PO
PUCKETT, Clinton, We-220-3; Pvt C Co State Troops; Oct 14 62 to Apr 14 62; 1st Civil Dist
PUCKETT, Jesse N., H-49-7; Pvt I Co 4th TN Cav; 10-14-63 to 7-12-65; Daisy PO; results of relapse from measles
PUCKETT, Orlena, Pu-140-2; widow; 1st Civil Dist, Cookeville PO
PUCKETT, Shimpman A., Je-141-1; Pvt B Co 9th TN Cav; 3 May 63 to 11 Sep 65; New Market PO
PUCKETT, William J., Mt-145-1; Pvt G Co 48th KY Mtd Inf; 8-1-63 to 1-1-65; Palmyra PO; foot broken wist? cannon
PUCKETT, William R., H-49-6; Cpl I Co 4th TN Cav; 10-14-63 to 7-12-65; Daisy? PO
PUGH, Allon, Col, Br-14-1; Pvt L Co 1st US Hvy Col Art; 9-14-64 to 3-31-66; McDonald PO; bad hearing & lung trouble
PUGH, Andrew J., Dk-33-2; Pvt K Co 5th TN Cav; 9-4-63 to 8-14-65; Liberty PO; hart disease
PUGH, Elisha, Ha-115-4; Capt of While Boat William T. Anderson; Oct 63 to May 65; Mulberry Gap PO
PUGH, Ephram, F-46-1; Pvt H Co 59th TN; 63 to 64; LaGrange PO
PUGH, G. W., Wl-308-2; Pvt 25th TN; Oct 1 63 to Mar 1 64; Rural Hill PO; CONF

PUGH, James, Mc-114-4; Pvt G Co 11th TN Cav; 9-28-63 to 5-23-65; Calhoun PO
PUGH, James N., Mu-200-1; Sara A. widow of; Pvt; Mt. Pleasant PO
PUGH, Jas. W., La-117-3; Pvt 48th TN Cav; Jun 3 63 to 65; 15th Dist; CONF
PUGH, Walter, Cr-16-4; PO omitted
PUGH, Wesley, Br-10-1; Pvt A Co 1st US Hvy Art; 1-26-64 to 3-31-66; Cleveland PO
PUGH, William, Sh-159-8; US Sol; Memphis PO
PUGH, Willis, F-35-2(5); Sgt H Co 59th; 63 to 65; Brinkley PO; rheumatism
PUGH, Zachariah, Ct-38-2; Pvt D Co 13th TN Cav; 9-23-63 to 9-5-65; Johnson City PO; rheumatism
PUIT, Martha, Cr-16-4; widow of US Sol; 23rd Civil Dist
PULIAM, Milton M., Wa-266-1; Pvt A Co 1st TN Cav; 1 Apr 62 to 4 Apr 65; Lovelace PO
PULLEN, Addison, Gi-127-6; Pvt C Co 11th US Col Inf; Dec 22 64 to Apr 30 66; Pulaski PO
PULLEN, Peter, Col, Gi-133-2; Cpl C Co 51st IL; 1 Mar 63 to 1 Jul 65; Bufords PO
PULLEN, William, Gi-127-7; Pulaski PO; papers misplaced
PULLEY, James J., Ma-122-1; Pvt C Co 2nd TN Mtd Inf; Jul 63 to Aug 64; Clay Brook PO; received no injury
PULLEY, John D., Hd-44-1; Pvt E Co 8th TN Mtd Inf; 64 to 65; Clifton PO (Wayne Co.)
PULLIAM, D. K., F-44-3; Pvt B Co 14th TN; May 62 to May 65; PO omitted; CONF
PULLIAM, Edward, Ge-91-3; Pvt; 1 May 67 to 1 May 70; Greeneville PO; eyes, neuralgia & other diseases
PULLIAM, John (see Jones, John, F-37-1)
PULLIAM, W. B., F-44-2; Surgan D Co 38th TN; Jan 61 to Jun 65; PO omitted; CONF
PULLIN, Acely, Sq-164-2(1); widow of Sol; 4th Civil Dist, Dunlap PO
PULLIN, Charlie, Dk-38-1; Eliza widow of; Pvt; 22nd Civil Dist
PULLING, Thomas, Sh-153-3; Parlee Watson widow; Sgt G Co 3rd Cav; Dec 63 to Jan 66; Collierville PO
PULLIUM, Joseph M., Dk-39-5(1); Palina E. Jarls? formerly widow of; Pvt I Co 5th TN Cav; Laurel Hill PO
PULLUM, Andrew J., Ge-98-2; Pvt B Co 4th TN Cav; 15 Nov 61 to 12 Jul 65; Lovelace PO; pleurisy
PULUM, Henry, Hw-121-5(4); Pvt G Co 13th TN Cav; 15 Jan 64 to 5 Sep.65; Blairs Gapp PO
PULUM, Samuel, Wa-266-1; Pvt B Co 4th TN Cav; 11 Aug 62 to 12 Jul 65; Fall Branch PO
PURCELL, Mathew T., Ha-11-4(1); Pvt F Co 16th TN Cav; 62 to 63; Upper Clinch PO; CONF
PURCELL, Thomas, K-182-2; Pvt A Co 2nd TN Cav; 61 to 65; Nast PO
PURDEE, Andy, Ms-171-2; Belfast PO
PURDY, Joseph, Lo-187-2; Pvt A Co 5th TN Inf; 25 Feb 62 to 4 Apr 65; Loudon PO; breast & ankle
PURDY, Lewis, Lk-112-1 (Col); Pvt C Co 64th MS Inf; Feb 63 to Mar 13 66; Tiptonville PO; loss of left eye, camp fever fell in eye
PURDY, William N., Ro-207-3; 5th TN Inf; 25 Feb 62 to 4 Apr 65; Pain Rock PO; deafness, result of bom shell
PURKEY, William, Mo-120-3(1); Mary J. widow of; Lt; SweetwaterPO
PURSELL?, James, Cl-49-2; Pvt I Co 3rd TN Inf; 7-62 to 63; Zeb PO
PURTLE, John C., Rb-223-1; Pvt H Co 125th IL Inf; 3 Aug 62 to 2 Jan? 65; Springfield PO
PUTMAN, James, Bl-3-2; Pvt B Co __ TN Inf; 2-12-62 to 2-23-65; Billingsly PO; piles
PUTMAN, John F., Mn-122-1; Sgt B Co 6th TN Cav; 8-25-62 to 7-26-65; McNairy PO; mustered out by Gen. order
PUTNAM, Lubim A., Mc-112-8; Sgt B Co 8th MI Cav; 8-8-64 to 10-19-65; Athens PO
PUTNAM, William C., K-165-4; Pvt A Co 53rd IL Cav; 62 to 64; Knoxville PO
PUTNUR, Junius M., Hu-99-1; Capt Commisery of Subristine?; 22 Feb 65 to 31 Dec 65; Jonsonville PO; served as clerk, subentins? Dept before being commissioned

PUTTMAN, Henry C., We-230-4; Capt F Co 7th KY Reg; May 15 63 to May 30 64; Greenfield PO; CONF
PYATT, Joel I., Mc-112-3; Pvt B Co 1st TN Inf; 2-1-63 to 5-11-65; Athens PO
PYLANT, Margaret A. (see Murray, John)
PYLE, Hugh M., O-135-1; Sgt A Co 13th TN Cav; 20 Oct 63 to 10 May 64; Troy PO; shot in right breast
PYLE, Wade H., O-125-1; Pvt D Co 8th IL Inf; 3 Oct 64 to 3 Oct 65; Troy PO
PYLES, Ithmar, La-115-1; Pvt E Co 92nd OH Foot Vol; 9 Aug 62 to 10 Jun 65; Blake Mills PO
PYLES, Robert, Sh-178-1; Cpl Gunner I Co; 63 to 65; rear 400 Beale, Memphis PO; 8 wks in hospital
PYOTT, Henry C., K-163-1; Pvt; 62 to 65; Knoxville PO; CONF
QUALL, Isaac, P-151-4; Dist 6
QUALLS, David C., Hd-50-2; Pvt A Co 5th TN Cav; Walnut Grove PO; ruptured in right bowels
QUALLS, Franklin, Hd-50-2; Pvt E Co 8th TN Mtd Inf; May-Jun 17 65 to Sep 1 65; Walnut Grove PO
QUALLS, George W., Ro-203-3; Cpl A Co 7th TN Inf; Nov 64 to ___; Ethel PO
QUALLS, James, Hd-50-3; Pvt A Co 2nd TN Mtd Inf; Oct 7 63 to Oct 14 64; Walnut Grove PO
QUALLS, Owen, Hd-50-5; Cpl F Co 6th TN Cav; 9-21-62 to 7-26-65; Nixon PO; heart and lung disease
QUALLS, Robert H. R., Hd-50-2; Pvt D Co 2nd TN Mtd Inf; Jan 1 64 to Feb 1 65; Savannah PO; Pvt E Co 8th TN Mtd Inf; May 17 65 to Sep 1 65
QUALLS, Thomas, Hd-50-3; Pvt D Co 6th IL Cav; 63 to 63; Walnut Grove PO
QUARLES, Andrew J., W-189-1; Elizabeth widow of; Pvt M Co 5th TN Cav; 10-63 to 8-65; McMinnville PO
QUARLES, Joham, Mr-99-2; Pvt 5th Co 7th Col; 1 yr; Jasper PO
QUARLES, Manuel, Hy-81-1; Pvt B Co 17th US Col Inf; Col Shafter; 7th Civil Dist
QUARLES, Marion I., Mr-99-2; 5th Co 7th Col; Jasper PO
QUARTERMAN, William A., Mu-195-3; Sol C Co 48th OH Vol; Oct 3 61 to Jun 20 65; Columbia PO
QUEEN, Lewis, Po-152-3(1); Margret E. widow of; Pvt; Ducktown PO; consumption
QUEENER, George R., C-27-4; Pvt M Co; 3 yrs; Jacksboro PO
QUEENER, Nelson, C-27-4; Pvt D Co 1st TN Inf; 3 yrs; Jacksboro PO
QUELLS, Phillips A., Po-148-2; Cpl D Co 7th TN Mtd Inf; 11-14-64 to 7-27-65; Benton PO
QUENER, Louis, Ro-205-2; Pvt H Co 1st C Hvy Art; Postoak Springs PO
QUICK, William, Mu-210-5; Pvt A Co 3rd IL Inf; 10-64 to 11-29-65; Carters Creek PO
QUILLEN, William M., La-108-1; Pvt D Co 3rd US Inf; 10-15-64 to 11-25-65; PO omitted
QUIMBY, Elipha, H-53-8; Pvt 3rd WI Lt Art; 61 to 10-64; Chattanooga PO
QUINE, Joe C., Rb-228-2; Pvt A Co 30th TN Inf; Sep 61 to Feb 62; Crunk PO; CONF
QUINN, Edward, Hm-107-1; Pvt G Co 4th TN Cav; 2 Jan 63 to Jun 65; Witts Foundry PO; did not get to see Quinn
QUINN, James M., Ov-135-1; Pvt 70th IN Inf; Oakley PO
QUINN, John M., De-26-2; A Co 3rd US Vol; 13 Oct 64 to 29 Nov 65; Bible Hill PO
QUINN, Peter, De-26-1; A Co 5th TN; 20 May 61 to ___ (3 yrs); Bible Hill PO; this name crossed out but marked US Sol
QUINN, Thomas, Sh-169-1; Pvt B Co 8th MO Inf; 61 to 64; Memphis PO
QUINN, William D., Co-62-3; USS; 4th Dist
QUINNS, William B., D-79-2; Pvt K Co 7th PA Inf; Apr 61 to Jul 61; Nashville, 2 Brown St. PO
QUINTON, John, Hm-105-1; Pvt M Co 9th TN Cav; Morristown PO; injured reuded?
RABB, Noah, Co-64-1; Pvt E Co 62nd NC Inf; 61 to 63; Philips PO; bronchitis; CONF
RABB, William J., Co-64-1; Pvt F Co 5th TN Cav; Sep 61 to 64 (2 yrs 6 mos); Newport PO; CONF
RABURN, John, G-52-1; Sgt G Co 1st AL Vol; 12-13-62 to 1-3-64; Humboldt PO
RABURN, John J., Mc-111-3; Pvt A Co 9th KY Cav; 2-62 to 65; Mortimer PO
RABY, Samuel, A-8-2; Cpl D Co 3rd TN Inf; 2-10-62 to 2-23-65; Scarborough PO; can now see very little
RABY, William, K-179-3; Nancy widow of; Pvt; Campbell PO; died of disease
RABY, William S., Ro-207-1; Pvt B Co 7th TN Mtd Inf; 8 Nov 64 to 3 Jul 65; Erie PO (Loudon Co.); chron. rheumatism
RACCARD, Thomas, K-182-3; Pvt K Co 2nd TN Vol Inf; 9 Jan 62 to 9 Nov 65; Gap Creek PO; horse fell on him, mashed brest
RACKLEY, Alexander, Cf-40-4; Tullahoma PO
RACKLEY, James, Ca-22-1; Mary widow of; Pvt; Hollow Springs PO
RADABAUGH, B. A., K-166-5; Pvt B Co 32nd OH Inf; 10 May 65 to 11 May 66; Knoxville PO
RADDEL, George, D-99-3; Pvt C Co 41st PA Inf; 63 to 15 Sep 65; State Penitentiary PO
RADER, Daniel, Ge-85-2; Susan E. widow of; Pvt B Co 8th TN Inf; 14 Feb 62 to ___ (2 yrs 5 mos 22 days); Cavey Branch PO
RADER, George H., Ge-88-3; Pvt F Co 4th TN Inf; 6 Apr 63 to 2 Aug 65; Mohawk PO; measles settled on lungs
RADER, Isaac F., Ge-85-2; Pvt F Co 4th TN Inf; 15 Apr 63 to 3 Aug 65; Cavey Branch PO; chronic diarhea & rheumatism
RADER, John A., Co-61-1; Pvt B Co 8th TN Inf; 1-5-63 to 6-30-65; Ottinger PO; kidney & liver disease, not able to work
RADER, Madison, Ge-87-1; Cpl A Co 3rd TN Mtd Inf; Jun 62 to 1 Apr 66; Timberridge PO; chronic rheumatism & heart trouble
RADER, Petter R., Ge-88-3; Kezih S. widow of; Pvt F Co 4th TN Inf; 6 Apr 63 to 2 Aug 65; Mohawk PO; chronic diarrhe & blader & kidney
RADER, Reuben, Ge-88-3; Cintha widow of; Bulls Gap PO; can't find out
RADFORD, Nelson, Mt-135-2; Sol US; 4th Dist
RADFORD, Phillip M., D-63-1; Nashville PO
RAE, Benj., Cl-58-3; Tazewell PO
RAFORD, Tom, Sh-160-1; Pvt 61st MI Cav; 61 to Apr 65; Memphis, Poplar St (126 to 130) PO; wounded right hand
RAGAINS, Gais, Lo-190-2; Capt H Co 5th TN Inf; 20 Mar 62 to 14 May 65; Loudon PO; shot in right hip
RAGAN, Alexander, Co-63-4; Pvt K Co 8th TN Inf; ___ Jul 63 to 18 May 65; Newport PO; rheumatism
RAGAN, Charles, Un-252-2; Nancy widow of; Pvt G Co 8th TN Cav; Haynes PO; dates not remembered
RAGAN, Daniel D., Co-61-4(1); 2nd Lt; Parrottsville PO
RAGAN, James, Un-252-1; Pvt B Co 9th TN Cav; 1 May 63 to Oct 65; Esco PO
RAGAN, Nelson, Mc-112-2; Susan widow of; Pvt H Co 1st US Col Art; 3-62 to 3-64; Athens PO; no papers to get exact dates
RAGIN, James E., Ge-100-1; Cpl I Co; Midway PO; failed to see
RAGLAND, Harvie H., M-103-3; Palistmie widow of; Pvt D Co 9th KY; Lafayette PO
RAGLAND, Rubin L., M-103-3; Pvt A Co 9th KY Inf; 9-25-61 to 1-5-63; Lafayette PO; shot in both legs
RAGLE, Alfred N., Ro-203-3; Elizabeth widow of; Capt K Co 5th TN Inf; Aug 61 to ___ (3 yrs 9 mos 13 days); Wheat PO; rheumatism, was discharged from hospital
RAGLIN, Hazie, Mc-112-10; Eliza A. widow of; Pvt L Co 1st Col Hvy Art; Athens PO; no papers to get dates
RAGON, Robert M., H-54-4; Cpl G Co 5th TN Inf; 3-2-62 to 5-15-65; Sherman Heights PO; wounded left hand--eye sight--body was impaired
RAGOR, Robert W., G-69-1; Pvt B Co 13th TN Cav; 20 Dec 62 to 20 Apr 63; Rutherford PO
RAGSDALE, Albert B., Rb-223-1; Springfield PO
RAGSDALE, Anderson, Mc-115-1; Pvt H Co 1st TN Hvy Art; 64 to 65; Riceville PO; feet frost bitten, dont know dates
RAGSDILL, William, Ge-97-2; Pvt A Co 4th Inf; 12 Aug 62 to 2 Aug 65; PO omitted

RAGSDILLE, John, Ge-97-2; Cpl A Co 4th TN Inf; 12 Aug 62 to 2 Aug 65; Newmanville PO; bronchitis, liver et al
RAIDER, John A., Hw-131-2; Pvt A Co 12th TN Cav; 19 Mar 63 to 19 Oct 65; Bulls Gap PO
RAINBOLT, John H., Jo-152-1; Matilda widow of; Sgt A Co 13th TN Cav; 26 Apr 64 to __ (2 mos); High Health PO; died while in service
RAINES, John P., H-55-2; Pvt F Co 5th TN Mtd Inf; 9-64 to 7-15-65; Chickamauga PO; lungs affected
RAINEY, John W., D-72-4; Pvt L Co 1st TN Inf; Jul 5 61 to 62; Nashville PO; CONF
RAINEY, Thomas, Mu-196-1; Celia widow of; Pvt A Co 100th __; Columbia PO
RAINEY, William, Gi-133-2; Bufords PO; CONF
RAINS, Alford, Se-230-2; Pvt C Co 8th TN Cav; PokeberryPO
RAINS, George, D-87-2; Sarah S. widow of; Gun Boat New Era; __ to 11 Jul 64; Nashville PO
RAINS, Isaac, Co-67-5; Cpl K Co 8th TN Cav; 27 Sep 63 to 11 Sep 65; Naillon PO
RAINS, James, Ja-86-2; Elvira widow of; Pvt; Long Savannah PO
RAINS, James E., Mo-130-1; Pvt D Co 3rd TN Mtd Inf; 7-12-64 to 9-30-64; Acorn PO; lung disease
RAINS, Jeff, Sh-157-3; Sgt K Co 15th AR Cav; 63 to __ (4 yrs); White Haven PO
RAINS, Moses M., C-24-2; Pvt E Co 11th TN Cav; 6-63 to 9-11-65; 1st Dist
RAINS, William, Ja-87-1; Pvt G Co 4th TN Cav; 4-1-63 to 7-12-65; Howardville PO; diarrhea; went home on leaf of absence, unable to read command, no discharge
RAINS, William R., Ro-201-5(3); Elizebeth widow of; Pvt B Co 5th TN Inf; 25 Feb 62 to 30 Mar 65; Kingston PO
RAINWATER, George A., Ro-210-1; Pvt E Co 1st TN Cav; 12 Dec 62 to 10 Jul 65; Rockwood PO; nasal catarrh & throat
RAINWATER, Harrison, Je-139-1; Sgt I Co 2nd TN Cav; 22 Sep 62 to 14 Jul 65; Trion PO; rheumatism & piles
RAINWATER, John W., Je-137-3; Pvt I Co 2nd TN Cav; 1 Jul 64 to Jul 65; Chestnut Hill PO
RALIFF, Silas, Su-240-1; Pvt F Co 3rd US Inf; Jul 64 to Oct 64; Kindricks Creek PO; mumps
RALSTON, Chas. I., Ho-96-1; Pvt 2nd KY Art; 63 to 64; Erin PO; was sick, did not get discharge
RALSTON, James A., Gi-122-2; Lt 2nd H Co 3rd TN Inf; Apr 61 to May 65; Lesters Sta. PO; prison 9 mos; CONF
RALSTON, James H., Ru-236-2; Pvt D Co 15th IN Inf; fall 62 to __; Murfreesboro PO; he has no regular home
RALSTON, Lusa?, Wl-293-2; Pvt D Co 7th TN; May 20 61 to Apr 65; Lockport PO; CONF
RALSTON, William C., Fr-105-1; Pvt D Co 102nd OH V Inf; 5 Aug 62 to 7 Jul 65; Winchester PO
RAMAGE, William J., K-159-3; Pvt C Co 19th IL Inf; 16 Jul 61 to 12 Jul 64; Knoxville PO
RAMBO, Alexander P., K-181-1; 1st Lt I Co 3rd TN Cav; 18 Aug 63 to 12 Aug 65; French PO
RAMBO, James T., Jo-152-1; Cpl F Co 4th TN Inf; 1 Aug 62 to 7 Jul 65; Doeville PO; spinal affection
RAMBO, William H., Jo-152-2; Pvt B Co 4th TN Inf; 1 Aug 62 to 7 Jul 65; Doeville PO; gun shot left arm
RAMBUGE, Manervie, R-161-6; widow of sol; Morgantown, 8th Civil Dist PO
RAMINS, Samuel, Co-68-3; Sarah widow of; 65 to 65; Sutton PO; diarrhaea
RAMSEY, Andrew J., Mr-99-2; Pvt B Co 6th TN Cav; 9-64 to 6-30-65; Jasper PO
RAMSEY, Chanson, Ov-138-1; Pvt; 10th Civil Dist
RAMSEY, Charles R., Ov-135-1; Pvt D Co 44th KY Inf; 7-5-63 to 3-30-64; Sgt I Co 7th KY Cav; 3-31-64 to 9-6-64; Oakley PO; wounded by mule
RAMSEY, D. A., G-57-4(1); Pvt C Co 13th TN Inf; 7-1-61 to 1-1-65; Yorkville PO
RAMSEY, David L., D-79-1; Pvt I Co 6th US Inf; Oct 9 67 to Oct 9 70; Nashville, 123 N 1st PO
RAMSEY, Edw., Sh-161-1; Cpl US F Co; 16th Dist
RAMSEY, George, D-51-1 (Black); Pvt 3rd KY Inf; 63 to 65; 456 N Cherry, Nashville PO
RAMSEY, Gui, Col, Mg-196-4; Pvt C Co 4th Col Inf; 61 to 65; Chattaway PO
RAMSEY, James, Br-8-1; Pvt 5th TN Inf; 63 to 65 (2 yrs 8 mos); Cleveland PO
RAMSEY, James G. M., K-156-2; Pvt Carnes Battery; 15 Mar 61 to 18 Apr 65; E Main 163, Knoxville PO; CONF
RAMSEY, Jas. T., La-117-1; Pvt K Co 53rd TN Inf; Nov 14 61 to __ (4 yrs); West Point PO; shot in left side; CONF
RAMSEY, Job, U-244-1; Sgt C Co 2nd NC Inf; Oct 63 to Aug 65; Flag Pond PO; paralysis
RAMSEY, Joel, K-168-2; Sarah Reed widow of; Pvt F Co 9th TN Cav; 30 Sep 63 to 11 Sep 65; Knoxville PO
RAMSEY, John B., Ms-172-1; Pvt D Co 12th IA Inf; 6 Dec 64 to 6 Dec 65; Farmington PO
RAMSEY, John J., Ja-84-2; Nancy widow of; Pvt G Co 4th E TN Inf; 2-27-62 to 3-17-65; Harrison PO; fever & paralasis
RAMSEY, John L., We-222-1; Pvt C Co 11th TN Cav; 6 Nov 62 to 8 May 65; Gardner PO; CONF
RAMSEY, John W., K-160-2; Pvt T Co 9th TN; 63 to 65; Knoxville PO
RAMSEY, John W., K-168-4; 2nd Dist
RAMSEY, Josiah, Ha-114-2; Pvt I Co 12th TN Inf; 1 Jun 63 to 15 Jul 64; Yellow Springs PO
RAMSEY, Kinsle? A., Br-8-1; Sgt 5th TN Inf; 63 to 65 (2 yrs 8 mos); Cleveland PO
RAMSEY, R. N., G-57-6; Pvt B Co 55th TN Inf; 1 Jun 61 to 1 Mar 65; Yorkville PO; CONF
RAMSEY, Samuel, Se-220-2; Pvt A Co 2nd TN Cav; 1 Nov 62 to 6 Jul 65; Emerts Cave PO
RAMSEY, W. D., G-57-4(1); Pvt; 4-1-62 to 4-1-64; Yorkville PO; CONF
RAMSEY, W. J., G-57-6; Lt K Co 4th TN Cav; Jun 61 to Jun 65; Yorkville PO; CONF
RAMSEY, William, Co-68-3; Pvt A Co 2nd TN Cav; Cashy PO; piles & rheumatism
RAMY, Daniel B., Ch-14-2; Pvt C Co 1st KY Cav; 8-14-64 to 2-14-65; PO omitted
RAMY, Henry, H-53-2; Cloe widow of; Pvt; 61 to __ (4 yrs); Chattanooga PO; colored hroops (sic) GA
RANDAL, Adolphus, La-117-4; E Co 80th OH Inf; Dec 18 61 to Dec 28 65; 15th Dist
RANDAL, James, T-216-1; Pvt D Co US Hvy Art; 31 Aug 63 to 13 May 66; Corona PO
RANDALL, Edwin L., Je-141-1; Pvt C Co 13th MI Inf; 2 Dec 61 to Aug 65; New Market PO
RANDALL, John S., T-207-1; Pvt B Co 66th IL Inf; Oct 20 61 to Jun 21 65; Covington PO
RANDALL, Robert S., O-139-2; Hornbeak PO
RANDALL, William E., Sh-159-1; Pvt VA Inf; 65 to 65 (3 mos); Memphis PO; CONF
RANDELL, I. H. (Randell, Henry), Hm-104-2; Cpl K Co 25th MI Inf; 18 Jul 62 to 24 Jun 65; Talbotts PO (Jefferson Co.)
RANDELS?, Samul W., K-165-2; Pvt E Co 24th NC? Inf; 25 Ja 70 to 75 (sic); 403 Asylum St, Knoxville PO
RANDLE, John, D-66-1; alias Payton Gress; Gustenar? Sgt A Co 2nd Legit? Col Art; 27 Jan 64 to 13 Jan 66; Nashville, 512 South Cherry PO; CONF
RANDLE, John E., Mr-99-3; Pvt C Co 5th TN Cav; 62 to 65; Jasper PO
RANDLES, Ballie, D-66-2; S Cherry St, Nashville PO
RANDLES, John B., Se-231-2; Pvt C Co 4th TN Inf; 14 FEb 63 to 2 Aug 65; Arther PO; shot in left leg 26 yrs
RANDOL, Noah C., Gi-126-1; Pvt I Co 2nd TN Inf; 16 Nov 63 to 21 Jan 65; Good Springs PO
RANDOLPH, Earl S., Br-7-4; Pvt L Co 1st TN Cav; 9-1-62 to 6-5-65; Cleveland PO; blind
RANDOLPH, Elijah C., Wh-182-1; Doyle's Sta. PO; no discharge
RANDOLPH, Harrison, Rb-219-1; Pvt B Co 30th TN Reg; Oct 61 to May 65; Black Jack PO; infantry service; CONF
RANDOLPH, James N., Mc-114-3; Pvt C Co 10th TN Cav; 1-14-64 to 8-65; Leamontville PO; disabled physically
RANDOLPH, James P., Ch-18-2; Capt C Co 31st TN; Sep 13 61 to __ (2 yrs); PO omitted; CONF
RANDOLPH, Jasper, Cu-18-2; 63 to 65; Big Lick PO
RANDOLPH, Jeptha, Mc-114-3; Pvt B Co 8th TN Inf; 64 to 8-17-65; Riceville PO

RANDOLPH, Martha, Mo-126-2; widow of Sol; 12th Civil Dist
RANDOLPH, Sonny, Gi-122-7; Pvt E Co 110th TN Inf; Oct 62 to May 66; Veto, AL, PO
RANDOLPH, Washington, Mt-138-1; Sgt I Co 16th Reg US C Inf; Feb 64 to 30 Apr 66; New Providence PO
RANES, Isham, C-32-2; Pvt J Co 16th KY Inf; 8-10-61 to 3-1-65; Clearfield PO
RANEY, Joseph, H-68-1; Pvt I Co; __ to 6-12-65; Chattanooga PO
RANEY, William, D-92-1; Pvt G Co 10th TN Inf; 6 May 62 to 25 Jun 65; Nashville PO
RANGE, John N., Wa-275-1; Pvt B Co 12th TN Cav; 22 Jul 63 to 8 Aug 65; Matuta PO
RANK, Amos, H-51-6; Pvt C Co Squirrel Hunter; 9-62 (3 mos); Fairmount PO
RANKANS, Martin, Mu-197-2; Pvt A Co 13th US; Aug 12 63 to Jan 66; Columbia PO; shot in the right foot
RANKIN, Alex P., Je-135-3; Pvt B Co 9th TN Cav; 12 Dec 63 to 11 Sep 65; Flat Gap PO; bronchitis
RANKIN, Dennis, H-73-2(1); Pvt GA Inf; 62 to 65; Chattanooga PO
RANKIN, Francis M., Mn-122-2; Pvt C Co 6th TN Cav; 8-25-62 to 7-26-65; McNairy PO; chronic rheumatism
RANKIN, Henry, H-58-6; Pvt L Co 7th PA Cav; Retro PO; discharge misplaced
RANKIN, James, Hm-109-2; Pvt D Co Inf; 62 to 65; Russellville PO
RANKIN, James H., Ro-210-12; Pvt A Co 4th TN Cav; 1 Dec 62 to 12 Jul 65; Cardiff PO
RANKIN, John C., Gr-74-2; Pvt H Co 4th TN Inf; 10 Feb 62 to 2 Aug 65; Dyers Ferry PO
RANKIN, John F., Je-135-3; Pvt C Co 4th TN Cav; 10 Dec 62 to 2 Jul 65; Mount Horeb PO; catarrh and deafness
RANKIN, John G., Je-143-1; Pvt D Co 9th TN Cav; 29 Feb 64 to 14 Apr 64; Mount Horeb PO; measles settled on lungs
RANKIN, John P., Je-143-1; Quartermaster Sgt B Co 9th TN Cav; 1 Aug 63 to 24 Mar 65; Mount Horeb PO; chronic catarrh throat and lungs
RANKIN, Joh- T., Jo-149-3; Pvt E Co 13th TN Cav; 24 Sep 63 to May 65; Mountain City PO; lungs & rheumatism
RANKIN, Oral (see Holden, Lewis)
RANKIN, Peter, H-58-6; Chany widow of; Pvt A Co 39th IN Inf; Retro PO; discharge lost
RANKIN, Sam, Col, Mr-99-3; Pvt A Co; 64 to 65; Jasper PO
RANKIN, Samuel E., Je-143-3; 1st Lt B Co 9th TN Cav; 27 Jul 63 to 13 Feb 66; Mossy Creek PO; catarrh & bronchitis
RANKIN, Thomas M., K-161-3; Knoxville PO
RANKIN, William T., Je-136-2; Emily Harris formerly widow of; Hesia? Surgeon; 1st TN Cav; Dec 62 to Feb 65; PO omitted
RANSIN, Edward, Mo-125-1; Bettie widow of; Pvt TN Cav; 63 to 65; Madisonville PO
RANSOM, Albert A., Gu-246-2(1); Pvt E Co 138th IN Inf; 4-64 to 9-64; Tatesville PO
RANSOM, Caleb C., C-139-1; Pvt F Co KY Cav; 1 Mar 65 to 20 Sep 65; Protemus PO
RANSOM, Richard, Gi-134-1; Lt A Co 24th TN Inf; Dec 24 61 to May 1 65; Murfreesboro PO; CONF
RANSOM, Thomas, H-75-2; Pvt; Chattanooga PO; papers lost
RANSOM, Wilbanks, Sh-163-1; Pvt A Co 13th MS Cav; Oct 10 63 to Feb 1 66; Memphis PO; wounded twice
RANSOM, Willis, D-46-1; Cpl A Co 17th US Col; 1-17-64 to 4-25-66; Nashville PO; pensioned at $4 per month
RANSON, Perry, D-54-2; Pvt A Co 54th IN Inf; Jul 62 to Oct 62; Nashville PO; away from home & could not give record
RANSUM, Charlie, F-40-1; Pvt C Co 9th VA Inf; 5 May 61 to 9 Apr 65; Hickory Wythe PO
RANSUM, Joseph, H-64-1; Pvt D Co 17th TN; Chattanooga PO; affection of brain
RANY, George W., Ro-211-1; Pvt H Co 2nd TN Inf; 20 Nov 61 to no discharge; Webster PO; rheumatism, also lame in foot
RAONNE, Prince, H-61-4; Pvt A Co 42nd US Col Inf; 3-4-64 to 1-31-66; Chattanooga PO
RAPER, Dismond?, Mo-122-1; Mary J. widow of; Pvt TN Inf; 61 to __; Madisonville PO; died in prison, dates coul- not be ascertained; CONF
RAPER, William F., Mo-122-1; Pvt C Co 7th TN Mtd Inf; 9-10-64 to 8-6-65; Dancing Branch PO; CONF
RAPHEART, Founten P., Di-36-1; 4th TN Inf; 9-64 to 65 (1 yr); Bellsburgh PO; CONF
RASBERRY, Francis A., Dy-29-3; widow US Sol; Newbern PO
RASH, Amos, Jo-152-2; Pvt B Co 13th TN Cav; Butler PO; rheumatism, piles, heart disease
RASLER, Jacob, Ja-85-2; Pvt G Co 3rd TN Cav; 8-21-63 to 6-8-65; Birchwood PO
RASOR, James H., Bo-14-2(1); Sgt G Co 8th TN Inf; 12-14-62 to 6-30-65; Yellow Sulphur PO; rheumatism
RATCLIFF, Jane, Wi-273-1; 4th Civil Dist
RATCLIFFE, Peter R., Wi-279-1; Pvt B Co 15th TN Inf; 63 to Apr 12 66; Carl PO
RATHBONE, William, Bo-23-1; Pvt C Co 2nd TN Inf; 62 to __; Tuckaleechee Cove PO; diareah & piles, now unable work at all
RATHCOTE, ____, H-60-5(2); Pvt USC (Col) Inf; Chattanooga PO
RATHER, Albert H., Rb-219-1; Pvt A Co 52nd KY Reg; Aug 17 63 to Jan 64; Orlinda PO; cavalry service
RATLEY, George W., Ca-25-2; Pvt A Co. 2nd TN Mtd Inf; 7-65 to 65; Gassoway PO
RATLIFF, Henry, Sh-191-1; Memphis PO; partially deaf, records not at hand
RATLIFF, James, Ge-98-3; 1st Lt I Co 8th TN Cav; 5 Sep 63 to 11 Sep 65; Jeroldstown PO; piles and lung affection
RATNEY, James, H-57-2; Clara widow of; Pvt 16th US Col; 63 to 65; Orchard Knob PO
RATTLE, Thos. J., H-75-1; Annie M. widow of; Sgt F Co 2nd OH Cav; 10-19-62 to __; Chattanooga PO; wife dont know when discharged
RAULSTON, William O., Se-226-1; Pvt L Co 2nd TN Cav; 8 Sep 63 to 6 Jul 65; Straw Plains PO; in service
RAULSTON, William S., H-49-6; Pvt C Co 5th TN Inf; 3-1-63 to 6-20-65; Daisy PO
RAUSIN, David D., Mo-121-2; Pvt H Co 5th TN Inf; 2-25-62 to 5-16-65; Philadelphia PO; pleurasy
RAUSIN, James H., Mo-121-1; Pvt H Co 5th TN Inf; 2-25-62 to 5-16-65; Philadelphia PO; rheumatism
RAWLEN, Thomas M., K-159-2; Pvt C Co 11th TN Cav; 15 May 63 to 11 Sep 65; Knoxville PO
RAWLING, Richard, Sh-149-3; Cpl C Co 3rd Hvy Art; 8 Mar 65 to 30 Apr 66; Raleigh PO
RAWLINS, Charles M., S-159-3; Pvt K Co 12th OH Inf; __ to 16 Jun 65; Knoxville PO
RAWLS, James T., Rb-228-2; Pvt A Co; 62 (6 mos); Crunk PO; failed
RAY, Addison G., D-79-2; Pvt H Co 18th NY Cav; Oct 3 64 to Oct 3 65; Nashville, Trentland St PO; shot in hip
RAY, Barnett, U-248-2; Pvt K Co 3rd NC Inf; 1 Mar 65 to 8 Aug 65; Erwin PO
RAY, David, C-30-2; Pvt C Co 1st TN Inf; 63 to __; Stockville PO; no discharge
RAY, Edmun, Gi-134-1; Dist 14
RAY, Edmund, B-3-1; Pvt E Co 14th US Col V Inf; 11-1-63 to 3-26-66; Shelbyville PO
RAY, G. C., La-117-3; Pvt 10th AL Cav; Mar 63 to 65; 15th Dist; CONF
RAY, Geo., O-133-1; US Sol; Rives PO
RAY, Govnor C., La-117-4; 15th Dist; CONF
RAY, Green, Un-257-3; Pvt I Co 8th TN Cav; 1 Oct 63 to 12 Oct __; New Prospect PO; palsy, rheumatism & kidney, he was captured & has no date of discharge
RAY, Jack, Gi-127-7; Pulaski PO; papers misplaced
RAY, James, Br-8-4(2); Jane A. widow of; Pvt D Co 18th IL Inf; 3-4-65 to __ (died) (16 days); Cleo PO; brain fever
RAY, James, Hm-108-5(4); Pvt B Co 12th TN Bat; Apr 63 to Apr 65; Russellville PO; diareah; CONF
RAY, James, Ro-202-6; Pvt F Co 26th TN Inf; __ to 65 (1 yr 2 mos); Kingston PO; eyes not good, rheumatism, lost his discharge

RAY, James A., H-55-3; Pvt TN Inf; 64 to 65; Harrison PO
RAY, James C., J-78-2; Pvt K Co 1st TN Inf; 11-30-64 to 7-22-65; Rough Point PO
RAY, James F., B-11-2(1); 1st Sgt A Co 4th TN Mtd Inf; 8-21-64 to 8-25-65; Poplins X Roads PO
RAY, James O., Ma-114-2; Lt B Co 14th TN Cav; Sep 13 61 to May 1 65; Pinson PO; CONF
RAY, James R., Cy-27-1; Pvt I Co 28th TN Inf; 9-61 to 11-62; Clementsville PO; (name crossed out on schedule without explanation, but probably a CONF)
RAY, John, H-64-3; US Sol; Hellen St, Chattanooga PO
RAY, John H., Sm-171-1; Pvt B Co 1st TN Mtd Inf; 1-31-64 to 4-20-65; Chestnut Mound PO
RAY, Joseph B., K-177-2; Sol US; PO omitted
RAY, Lafayette, Ho-97-1; Pvt H Co 1st TN Mtd Inf; 9 Jan 64 to 23 May 65; Erin PO; left thum of
RAY, Lawson, R-162-2; Dayton PO
RAY, Moses P., L-100-2; Pvt H Co 61st IL Inf; 7 Mar 65 to Sep 8 65; Ripley PO; rumatism, phthisic & blindness
RAY, O., Bo-11-2; Pvt I Co 5th TN Inf; 10-31-62 to 6-28-64; Big Gulley PO
RAY, Robert C., Br-13-4; Cpl E Co 4th TN Cav; 1-20-63 to 5-26-65; Cleveland PO; stomach & heart disease
RAY, Robt. F., G-67-1; Pvt; Oct 62 to 64; Bradford PO; wounded in the back
RAY, Sam, B-5-1; Annie R. widow of; Pvt Inf; 3 yrs; Bell Buckle PO; was discharged for disability, Widow Ray cannot find discharge
RAY, Samuel, Hr-96-2; Pinetop PO
RAY, Sara J. (See Mynatt, Spencer)
RAY, Stephen, Pu-140-2; 1st Civil Dist
RAY, Thomas A., Ja-86-2; Pvt A Co 98th IL Cav; 63 to ___; Snowhill PO
RAY, Tommas J., Wy-171-1; Pvt H Co 1st TN Mtd Inf; 1-20-64 to 4-17-65; Waynesboro PO
RAY, Thomas J., Ge-99-2; Pvt C Co 2nd NC Mtd Inf; 1 Mar 64 to 16 Aug 65; Limestone Springs PO; deafness caused by measles
RAY, Virgil, Wl-296-1; Cpl E Co 4th TN Cav; 20 Nov 64 to 23 Aug 65; Cherry Valley PO; rheumatism
RAY, William E., We-225-3(2); Pvt E Co 87th OH Inf; 1st OH Hvy Art; 62 to 65; Dresden PO
RAY, William J., We-225-1; Pvt B Co 7th TN Cav; 24 Nov 64 to 7 Aug 65; Dresden PO
RAY, William O., O-142-1; Pvt E Co 17th KY Inf; 13 Oct 61 to 23 Jan 65; Obion PO
RAYBURN, Esaw, Ro-202-3(1); Pvt H Co 3rd TN Inf; 3 Mar 61 to 3 Mar 64; Paw Paw Ford PO; head bursted
RAYBURN, James, Ro-202-3(1); Pvt B Co 16th TN Cav; 26 Apr 62 to May 64; Paw Paw Ford PO; CONF
RAYBURN, Waller, Mt-137-2; in government employ; 62 to 65; St. Bethlehem PO
RAYGON, Duke R., Ro-205-3; Pvt I Co 26th TN Inf; Oct 62 to 19 Jun 65; Deamond PO; rheumatism
RAYL, George W., Ja-86-3; Pvt; Snowhill PO
RAYL, James A., Su-236-1; Cpl G Co 9th MO Cav; Nov 62 to Apr 64; Bloomingdale PO
RAYL, Samuel J., Ja-87-1; Pvt C Co 5th TN Inf; 2-62 to ___; Howardville PO; piles
RAYMOND, William W., We-225-3(2); Pvt A Co Bat 1 TN Lt Art; 62 to Aug 65; Dresden PO; rheumatism, rheumatism has continued
RAYNER, Henry L., Ro-207-2; Sarah C. widow of; Pvt H Co 3rd E TN Cav; 20 Feb 62 to 18 Jul 63; 8th Cavl
RAYNES, Casuel, C-26-2; Pvt A Co 7th TN Inf; 2-23-62 to 2-23-65; Jacksboro PO
RAYNOLS, Simon, G-69-1; Rutherford PO
READ, Frank, Hm-109-4; Pvt D Co 1st TN Cav; 7 Jan 63 to 19 Jun 65; Three Springs PO
READ, Garrett, Hm-109-1; US Navy; 63 to 65; Russellville PO
READ, Solomon, Hy-81-1; Luddy or Laura widow of; Pvt inlisted at Greeneville, MS, discharge lost; 7th Civil Dist
READON, Dan, D-49-3; Pvt A Co 11th MO; 65 to 66; dont remember exact dates; Nashville PO
READWINE, Elihu S., Co-62-3; Pvt B Co 150th IL Inf; 25 Jan 65 to 16 Jan 66; Givens PO
READY, Aaron, D-45-5; Pvt D Co 4th TN Mtd Inf; 9-64 to 8-25-65; Nashville PO

REAGAN, Daniel W. S., Se-227-3; Pvt G Co 6th TN Inf; 10 May 62 to 17 May 65; Trundles X Roads PO; disease of the left eye
REAGAN, Ephraim, Se-229-2; Pvt G Co 6th TN Inf; 16 Sep 62 to 30 Jun 65; Trentville PO; rheumatism & hearing
REAGAN, George W., Ov-137-3; Cpl G Co 9th TN Cav; 8-7-62 to 9-9-65; Monroe PO; neuralgia
REAGAN, James D., Fe-40-1; Pvt A Co 11th TN Cav; 8-63 to 65 (1 yr); Little Crabb PO; chrc. dis. of rheumatism
REAGAN, James M., K-186-2; Pvt C Co 3rd TN Inf; 30 Dec 62 to 2 Aug 65; Balls Camp PO
REAGAN, Jessie F., Fe-40-1; Pvt G Co 9th TN Cav; 6-22-63 to 9-11-65; Little Crabb PO
REAGAN, Joel L., Fe-40-1; 2nd Sgt D Co 1st TN Mtd Inf; 9-63 to 4-25-65; Little Crabb PO; rupture of lower abdomen
REAGAN, John C., Pi-153-2; Rebecca widow of; Pvt D Co 2nd TN Inf; 5-63 to 3-3-65; Spurnier PO
REAGAN, Michael, D-77-2; Pvt B Co 10th TN Inf; 10 Jun 62 to 25 Jun 65; Nashville PO
REAGAN, Richard R., Se-229-2; C Sgt E Co 2nd TN Cav; 16 Sep 62 to 30 Jun 65; Trentville PO; piles & rheumatism
REAGAN, Thomas, Pi-156-2; Mary C. widow of; Pvt D Co 2nd TN Cav; Byrdtown PO
REAGAN, Thomas J., Fe-43-1; 62 to ___; Jamestown PO
REAGAN, William H., Pi-155-2; 1st Sgt A Co 11th TN Cav; 62 to 65; Byrdtown PO
REAGOR, Washington L., G-71-2; Pvt D Co 13th TN Cav; 21 Sec 63 to 9 Apr 64; Rutherford PO
REAL, Charles H., Bl-5-2; Pvt A Co 4th TN Cav; Brayton PO
REAL, Michael, Bl-5-2; Ann widow of; Pvt; Brayton PO
REAME?, Moses G., Cl-54-3(1); Pvt; 62 to 65; Tazewell PO; CONF
REANSON, John, Cl-53-1; Pvt A Co 12th TN Cav; 8-8-63 to 7-1-65; Springdale PO
REANSON, Milley (see Herrell, Drew P.)
REASON, Rolley, F-43-1; Pvt E Co 66th US Reg; 62 to May 65; New Kent PO
REASONOVER, Solomon, Sm-172-4; Pvt F Co 101st Patrol Inf; 9-28-64 to 1-21-66; Gordonsville PO
REAVES, G. H., Wy-174-1; Pvt E Co 8th TN; 3-1-64 to 65; Stout PO
REAVES, Jasper, Wy-171-3; Pvt 10th TN Inf; 4-16-62 to 5-25-65; Sorby PO
REAVES, John, Hy-76-2; Pvt I Co 18th IL Inf; 1 yr 6 mos; Stanton Depot PO
REAVES, John Thomas, Hd-45-2; Delila S? Wilson widow; Pvt A Co 6th TN Cav; Jun 62 to Dec 62; Cerro Gordo PO; James T. Reaves died Dec 62
REAVES, Willis H., H-52-1; Pvt 44th TN Cav; 64 to 65; Wauhatchie PO
REAVIS, David J., B-14-1; Pvt F Co 1st TN & AL Vidette Cav; 8-15-62 to 6-23-64; Wisener PO; lost his hearing
REAVIS, Eligah R., We-225-3(2); Pvt K Co 6th TN Cav; Aug 9 62 to Jul 26 65; Dresden PO; disease of eyes
REAVIS, George, Ms-173-1; Pvt G? Co 10th TN Inf; 13 Aug 62 to 26 Jun 65; Rich Creek PO
REAVIS, John J., B-14-1; Pvt C Co 4th TN Mtd Inf; 12-2-64 to 8-25-65; Wisener PO
REAVIS, Leonides W., We-225-3(2); Pvt K Co 6th TN Cav; Aug 9 62 to Jul 26 65; Dresden PO; weak eyes
REAVS, Franklin, Cy-27-4(2); Pvt E Co 1st TN Mtd Inf; 10-16-63 to 1-16-65; Spivey PO
REAVS, Luke M., Cy-27-4(2); Pvt I Co 1st TN Mtd Inf; 1-13-63 to 4-65; Spivey PO; gun shot in right leg
REBMAN, John J., K-157-1; Capt A Co 126th PA Inf; 2 Apr 62 to 3 Jun 65; Knoxville PO
RECHTIN, J. J., F-39-1; Pvt B Co 181st OH Vol Inf; 7 Sep 64 to 10 Jul 65; Galloway PO
RECORD, George A., Mc-112-5; Harriet widow of; Pvt F Co 2nd MN Cav; 12-22-63 to 12-2-65; Athens PO; dispepsia
RECORD, Leonard S., Mc-112-8; Cpl F Co 2nd MN Cav; 2-20-64 to 12-2-65; Athens PO
RECTER, James H., Ge-98-5; Pvt K Co 12th TN Cav; 15 Nov 62 to Jun 65; Jeroldstown PO; piles

RECTER, William R., Se-220-1; Pvt C Co 3rd NC Inf; 1 Mar 65 to Jul 65; Tudors Cave PO; discharge lost by US Agt
RECTOR, John, Ge-89-1; Pvt F Co 3rd TN Mtd Inf?; 1 Jul 64 to 30 Nov 64; Pilotknob PO
RECTOR, Jules A., Co-59-2; US Sol; 1st Dist
RECTOR, Juliss, Co-59-1; Pvt C Co 3rd NC Inf; 8-10-64 to 8-8-65; Del Rio PO
RED, Henry, Ro-208-2; Pvt F Co 119th KY Inf; had no discharge, knew no dates; Welker Mines PO; piles
REDD, John, K-154-3; Lt I Co 86th OH; __ to Apr 61; Knoxville PO
REDDEN, Levi, A-4-4; Ann B. widow of; Pvt J Co 6th TN Inf; Coal Creek PO; eye lost or put out, discharge not at home
REDDICK, Wesley, S-217-2; Pvt K Co 102nd IN Inf; 12 Aug 62 to 30 Jun 65; Winfield PO
REDDIN, John, H-50-1; Pvt D Co 10th R TN Cav; 1-16-64 to __; Soddy PO; wounded in hip
REDDING, Jason D., Mo-119-2; Pvt; Sweetwater PO
REDEN, Samul, K-175-1; Pvt C Co 1st TN Inf; 13 Sep 62 to 1 Aug 65; Pedigo PO
REDFIELD, Joseph H., Wi-278-1; Pvt E Co 128th OH Inf; Dec 19 63 to Jul 5 65; Franklin PO; deafness
REDMAN, David, Mt-137-2; in Government Employ; no papers; 62 to 65; St. Bethlehem PO
REDMAN, David, Mt-137-2; Civ. in Gov. Employ; papers lost; 62 to 65; St. Bethlehem PO
REDMAN, Jasper N., Me-93-1; Pvt D Co 7th TN Mtd Inf; 11-64 to 8-5-65; Regret PO (McMinn Co.)
REDMAN, Jerry A., Co-67-4; Pvt 1st KY Cav; Naillon PO; CONF
REDMAN, Marlin F., Mg-196-3; Sgt F Co 1st TN Inf, 14 Aug 62 to 21 Jun 65; Wartburg PO
REDNOURS, George, Ge-88-2; Longdonia PO; not at home & cant get facts
REDUS, Toliver, Col, Gi-133-2; Sgt I Co 110th AL; Dec 24 63 to Feb 6 66; Bufords PO
REDWINE, John W., Cu-17-4; Rebecca widow of; Pvt F Co 3rd E TN Inf; 2-10-62 to 2-16-65; Crab Orchard PO
REDWINE, Joseph N., Co-61-2(1); Pvt D Co 160th IL Inf; 15 Dec 64 to 31 Jan 66; Givens PO; blindness
REDWINE, Martha L. (see Carter, Jessie)
REDWINE, Robert W., Bo-15-3; Cpl D Co 2nd TN Cav; 9-1-62 to 7-6-65; Maryville PO
REECE, James, Jo-150-5; Pvt E Co 13th TN Cav; 22 Sep 63 to 5 Sep 65; Osborn PO; rheumatism
REECE, John Felor (see Page, John)
REECE, John J., Hm-104-4(2); Pvt M Co 9th TN Cav; 11 Feb 63 to 11 Sep 65; Alpha PO; tumor in groin, disable from labor
REECE, Joseph H., Sn-259-1; Pvt K Co 20th __; Bransford PO; leg broke
REECE, Ruben, Co-59-2; Pvt Co B 8th TN Inf; 1-5-63 to 6-30-65; Del Rio PO
REECE, Thomas, Co-62-1; Pvt D Co 8th TN Inf; 1 Jun 63 to 1 Jun 65; Warrensburg PO
REECE, William J., Sm-169-2; Pvt; Defeated PO; CONF
REECE, Wilson, Mu-210-2; Susan widow of; Pvt 12th TN Inf; 2 yrs; Spring Hill PO
REED, Abner, H-60-3; Pvt K Co 108th OH Inf; 2-8-65 to 9-20-65; Chattanooga PO
REED, Alison, Je-145-2; Margarett formly of; Pvt 12th KY Inf; Dumplin PO
REED, Allen, S-212-2; Pvt F Co 1st TN; 1 Oct 64 to 30 Jul 65; Porch Corn PO; shot in right thigh
REED, Birdwell, K-173-2; Lusinda widow of; Pvt G Co 10th MI Cav; 13 Oct 63 to 17 Ma 64; Caswell PO
REED, Caleb, Sm-167-1; Pvt A Co 8th TN Mtd Inf; 3-6-65 to 7-5-65; Riddleton PO
REED, Calvin, Sh-158-1; Pvt C Co 3rd Col Hvy Art; 5 Jun 63 to 30 Apr 66; Memphis PO
REED, Campbell C., S-217-2; Martha widow of; Pvt 2nd TN Inf; 61 to 65; Oneida PO
REED, Dickerson, D-57-4; Cpl B Co 110th TN Inf; 61 to 63; Nashville PO
REED, Edmond, Gi-128-2; Pvt F Co 110th TN Inf; 63 to 65; Pulaski PO
REED, Elishe B., B-11-3(2); Pvt E Co 10th TN Inf; 6-23-63 to 7-3-65; Unionville PO
REED, Emly B., Wi-281-2; 22nd Dist

REED, Enoch G., O-138-2; Pvt C Co 1st TN; 1 Sep 61 to 1 Mar 65; Elbridge PO; CONF
REED, Flemen, Mc-114-2; Pvt; Magellan PO
REED, G. W., Wl-308-2; Martha widow of; Pvt TN; Dec 61 to Dec 62; Mount Juliet PO
REED, Harrison, S-213-2; Pvt G Co 2nd TN Inf; 5 Dec 61 to 8 Dec 64; New River PO; rheumatism & piles, in Anderson & Bell 11 mos
REED, Hugh A., G-57-7(4); Yorkville PO; CONF
REED, Isaac, Di-42-1; Pvt I Co 62nd TN Cav; Tenn City PO
REED, Jack A., Bo-13-1; Pvt; 6-13-62 to __; Disco PO
REED, Jacob T., K-171-5(4); Pvt D Co 6th TN Inf; Apr 62 to Apr 65; Bearden PO
REED, James M., K-171-5(4); Pvt D Co 6th TN Inf; 18 Apr 62 to Apr 65; Bearden PO
REED, Jerry, Gi-128-2; Pvt F Co 110th TN Inf; 63 to 65; Pulaski PO
REED, John, Gi-129-2; Patsey widow; Conway PO
REED, John, Sm-172-1; Pvt G Co 1st TN Inf; 9-26-64 to 7-22-65; Lancaster PO; chronic sore eyes
REED, John, Cu-18-1; Pvt K Co 5th TN Inf; 3-18-62 to 3-30-65; Jewett PO; rheumatism & deafness
REED, John W., C-25-2; Pvt C Co 11th TN Cav; 5-7-62 to 4-4-65; Coal Creek PO (Anderson Co.); could not learn when enlisted or discharged
REED, Lewis W., K-181-1; 3rd Sgt C Co 6th TN; 18 Apr 62 to 27 Apr __ (3 yrs 5 days); Thaxter PO
REED, Loretta (see Aytse, A. C.)
REED, Louis, Cl-47-4; Sally mother of; Pvt 2nd TN Inf; 62 to __; Cappford PO; died 1864 at Louisville, KY
REED, Mary J. (see Turner, Taskem)
REED, Matthias, R-163-4; Ogden PO
REED, Orrin S., H-61-5; Cornelia A. widow of; Chattanooga PO
REED, Prissilla, D-78-2; widow US Sol; Nashville PO
REED, Robert, Ge-96-2; Pvt K Co 1st TN Cav; 5 Dec 62 to 10 Jun? 65; Jockey PO; chronic diareah
REED, Robert M., Hd-50-5; Pvt 1st AL Cav; 10-20-63 to 9-28-64; Nixon PO; partial paralysis
REED, Sirenious, He-62-3; Cpl Co A 7th TN Cav; Aug 5 62 to Aug 9 65; Lexington PO; bone scurvey, rheumatism and heart disease
REED, Starling, Sh-200-3; Winnie T. widow of; Pvt 61st US Col Inf; Walnut St, Memphis PO
REED, Washington C., Cr-14-3; Pvt K Co 2nd TN Mtd Inf; 1 Jun 64 to 27 Jun 65; Cawthorn PO; discharge lost, served about 3 yrs
REED, William E., H-54-4; Pvt G Co 10th TN Cav; East Chattanooga PO; wounded in right arm and right side by a gun shot, disabled his arm and side
REED, William M., Ro-203-5(1); Pvt K Co 1st TN Inf; 9 Aug 61 to 19 Sep 64; Wheat PO; leg fractured & gunshot in groin
REED, Willis, A-7-3; Cpl J Co 9th P; 3-3-63 to 9-11-65; Robertsville PO
REEDER, John, Pi-155-2; Pvt D Co 1st TN Mtd Inf; 8-63 to 4-65; Byrdstown PO; jaundice
REEDY, Jacob, Bl-5-3; Delila widow of; Pvt D Co 6th TN Mtd Inf; 9-12-64 to 6-30-65; Pitts X Roads PO
REEL, Peter, Bl-3-3; Pvt I Co 2nd TN Inf; 62 to 65; Pikeville PO; rheumatism, priner Andersonville
REELS, Isaac, Ov-134-1; Pvt 8th TN Cav; 2-65 to 65; Garrott PO; does not remember day of discharge or enlistment
REESE, Alfred, Co-59-1; Elisabeth widow of; Pvt Co G 4th TN Cav; 8-31-64 to 5-26-65 .
REESE, Frank F., Co-62-1; Help PO
REESE, Henry, Wi-274-1; Pvt K Co 12th TN Inf; 20 Aug 62 to Jan 66; Franklin PO
REESE, Henry H., Gi-122-5; Pvt I Co NC Inf; Jul 62 to May 65; Prospect Sta. PO; CONF
REESER, Anthony, Ov-137-2; Pvt H Co 3rd KY Inf; 12-20-61 to 5-10-65; Monroe PO; crippled in back as result has kidney disease
REESER, Arnold M., Wa-276-1; Pvt C Co 4th TN Inf; Apr 6 63 to Aug 2 65; Limestone PO; rheumatism & bronchial affection
REESER, William B., Ge-96-3; Sgt G Co 4th TN Inf; 26 Nov 62 to 2 Aug 65; Jockey PO; rheumatism, piles, heart
REEVES, Ben, F-46-1; Jane Sulavan widow of; LaGrance PO

REEVES, Dely F., He-62-1; Artillery man; 27th __;
  Jan 61 to Jan 62; Darden PO; CONF
REEVES, Evans, Wl-295-2; Pvt B Co 4th Reg Inf; Aug
  16 63 to Apr 18 65; Lebanon PO
REEVES, Henry, D-87-2; Pvt B Co 21st MS Cav; 12
  Jun 62 to May 64; Nashville PO
REEVES, James, Dk-38-1; Sarah J. Hayes formerly
  widow of; Sgt; Crawfordton PO
REEVES, John D., Ro-203-6; Pvt A Co 1st TN Inf; 28
  Mar 63 to 3 Aug 65; Union X Roads PO; blind-
  ness
REEVES, Moses, Mt-138-2; Pvt H Co 16th R USC Inf;
  23 Mar 64 to 30 Apr 66; New Providence PO
REEVES, Thomas A., Wl-298-1; Eva widow of; Pvt B
  Co 5th TN Cav; 4 Aug 62 to 22 Oct 63; Round
  Top PO
REEVES, Thomas H., Wa-274-2; Lt Col 4th TN Inf; 15
  Nov 61 to 2 Aug 65; Jonesboro PO
REGAN, Jesse, H-56-3; Pvt B Co 86th LA Inf; 64 to
  65; St. Elmo PO
REGESTER, James, R-159-1; Pvt K Co 16th PA Cav; 2-
  65 to 8-65; Spring City PO; crippled in knee,
  cant work much
REGISTER, William, R-157-1; Pvt C Co 16th PA Cav;
  3-7-61 to 8-11-66; Lorraine PO; chron. rheu-
  matism
REICH, Owen A., Wl-294-1; Pvt E Co 11th OH Inf;
  Apr 17 61 to Nov 10 64; Lebanon PO; ruptured
  at Buzzard Roost, GA, not able to work
REICHMANN, Henry, Sh-191-5(1); Memphis PO; records
  not seen
REID, James, Ge-98-3; Pvt K Co 1st TN Cav; 22 Nov
  62 to 19 Jun 65; Milburnton PO; disease of
  eyes, kidneys &c
REID, James, K-185-3; Pvt; Mascott PO; CONF
REID, Jessee, Sh-186-1; Pvt C Co 138th Col; 5-65 to
  1-66; Memphis PO; died 1880, his wife Julia
  Reid
REID, John H., H-53-3; Augusta A. widow of; Capt
  C Co 86th OH Inf--7-3-63 to 1-64; 2 M Capt--
  5-6-64 to __ (100 days); Chattanooga PO; sun
  stroke, enlisted for 6 mos, cause paralysis,
  enlisted for 100 days
REID, Robert B., Wa-264-1; Pvt E Co 4th TN Inf; 25
  Apr 63 to 29 May 64; Telford PO; shot in
  right thigh
REID, Thomas J., D-61-1; Surgeon 32nd TN; Apr 1 61
  to May 1 65; Nashville PO; CONF
REILLY, Joseph M., Gu-48-1; Sgt E Co 99th PA Inf;
  8-22-61 to 2-7-63; Tracy City PO
REINHART, Maggie (see Thomas, John)
REINHART, Marius, K-161-6; Pvt I Co 11th VA Inf;
  Knoxville PO
RELIFORD, Jennie, Sh-173-1; Pvt B Co 61st TN Inf;
  3 yrs 6 mos; Memphis PO
REMBERT, Zack (see Young, Mitchell)
REMBERT, Zack, Sh-160-1; Rose Johnston widow of;
  Pvt TN Hvy Art; 62 to 65; Memphis, Poplar
  St (126 to 130); injured from small pox;
  (Rose also widow of Mitchell, Young)
REMINGTON, James D., Mg-200-1; Pvt I Co 73rd IL
  Inf; 10 Aug 62 to 26 Jun 65; PO omitted
RENALDS, Peter, Sh-149-3; Pvt C Co 55th TN Inf;
  Feb 63 to 23 Dec 66; Raleigh PO
RENEAU, John, Je-137-2; Margaret widow of; Hickory
  Ridge PO
RENEAU, John E., H-50-4; Pvt F Co 9th R TN Cav;
  9-12-63 to 9-11-65; Soddy PO; chronic rheu-
  matism, siege of Knoxville, loss of hearing
RENEAU, Nipolian, Je-147-1; Pvt M Co 2nd TN Cav; 8
  Nov 62 to 10 Aug 65; Shady Grove PO
RENEAU, Thomas J., H-50-3(1); Pvt F Co 9th TN R
  Cav; 8-2-63 to 9-9-65; Igon's Ferry PO; tumor
  of stomach, disabled at siege of Knoxville
RENEAU, Thomas S., H-50-3(1); Pvt F Co 9th R TN
  Cav; 8-11-63 to 9-11-65; Soddy PO; liver
  disease
RENEAU, William, Je-147-2; Cpl I Co 2nd TN Cav; 22
  Sep 62 to Jul 65; Allensville PO; shot in the
  heart and lungs
RENEAU, William B., Je-147-2; Cpl F Co 9th TN Cav;
  2 Aug 63 to 24 Mar 65; Shady Grove PO
RENEGAR, Siller, Li-148-1; PO omitted
RENELS, Dave, Ms-181-1; Pvt A Co 10th TN Inf; 6-10-
  63 to 4-12-65; Lewisburg PO
RENFRO, George W., Ro-206-2; Elizabeth C. widow of;
  Chapl 62nd TN Cav; Oct 61 to 64; Emory Gap
  PO; no correct dates; CONF
RENFRO, William W., K-161-1; Susana widow of; Pvt
  D Co 2nd TN Inf; 1 Sep 61 to 31 Jan 63;
  Knoxville PO; relapse of measles
RENFROE, James, Me-94-2; Pvt B Co 5th TN Inf; 2-25-
  62 to 3-26-65; Euchee PO; shot through left
  shoulder
RENFROE, Sire, He-62-1; Infantry Co D 38th IL; Jul
  62 to Dec 1 65; Darden PO; wounded in hip
RENFROW, Henry, Ct-41-4; Pvt B Co 1st NC Cav; 63 to
  __; Elizabethton PO; CONF
RENFROW, James, K-174-2(1); Sarah K. widow of; Pvt
  B Co 3rd TN Inf; 28 Feb 62 to 23 Feb 65;
  Graveston PO; paralyzed in left side and hips
RENFROW, Robert, Me-94-1; Rebecca widow of; Euchee
  PO
RENNABB, Allen S., M-107-1; Pvt A Co 8th TN Mtd Inf;
  1-17-65 to 8-17-65; Red Boiling Springs PO;
  injury to right arm
RENNER, Andrew, Ge-85-2; Pvt M Co 1st TN Cav; 15
  Jul 62 to 7 Jun 65; Cavey Branch PO; rupture
  & dislocated elbow
RENNER, David, Ge-85-2; Cpl B Co 8th TN Inf; 5 Jun
  63 to 30 Jun 65; Cavey Branch PO; piles &
  chronic dysentry
RENNER, David J., D-91-3; Pvt 139th OH Inf; 10 Sep
  64 to 13 Dec 64; F__ & Church Sts, Nashville
  PO
RENNER, John H., Ge-85-3; Pvt G Co 4th TN Inf;
  Syren Burg PO; has no discharge
RENNER, William, Ge-99-2; Pvt M Co 1st TN Cav; 18
  Jan 62 to __; Cedar Creek PO; finger mashed
  off, did not get any discharge
RENSHAW, James, Ro-211-2; Pvt G Co 2nd TN Inf; 28
  Sep 62 to 3 Feb 64; Webster PO
RENTFRO, John, K-177-5; Pvt G Co 6th TN Inf; 15
  Apr 62 to 9 Apr 65; Powells Station PO; rheu-
  matism & diaerhoe
RENTH, John, Sh-167-2; Sgt K Co 88th IL; 9 Aug 62
  to 9 Jun 65; PO omitted
REONAUGH, Thomas, L-103-1; Pvt; Island 26
RESE, James S., Hm-106-1; Pvt E Co 1st TN Art; 27
  Nov 63 to 1 Aug 65; Morristown PO
RESE, Orville A., Hw-119-3(1); Pvt E Co 29th TN
  Inf; Aug 62 to May 65; Alum Well PO; CONF
RESTOR, Jacob, Ge-87-2; Pvt __ 1st TN Cav; Timber-
  ridge PO; wound right arm
RETHERFORD, Thomas J., C-27-1; Pvt F Co 6th TN Inf;
  3-10-62 to 4-1-65; Jacksboro PO
REUBETT, John A., Sm-166-1; Chap(lain?) 27th PA
  Inf; 3-25-61 to 8-27-61; Carthage PO
REUFF, Claiborn, Gr-81-3(1); Pvt D Co 1st TN Inf;
  1 May 63 to 11 Aug 65; Clear Spring PO;
  cattarh & rupter, partly disabled
REUFF, Wm. S., Gr-81-1; Cpl D Co 1st TN Art; 21
  Sep 63 to 25 Jul 65; Clear Spring PO; rheuma-
  tis &c, partly disabled
REUL, James J., Wa-263-6; Pvt E Co 4th TN Inf; Apr
  63 to Jun 65; Conkling PO
REYER?, Lewis C., Sh-257-1; Pvt; PO omitted
REYNOLDS, Lewis, Gi-122-7; Pvt D Co 111th TN Inf;
  Dec 63 to Oct 65; Veto, AL PO
REYNOLD, William H., D-94-1; Cpl G Co 38th IL Inf;
  Oct 22 61 to 67; c/o E. N. Campbell, Nashville
  PO; rheumatism & liver disease, witness dead,
  pension applied for
REYNOLDS, Abe, H-63-1; Pvt E Co 44th Col Inf; 6-
  18-64 to 3-66; 701 Cypress, Chattanooga PO
REYNOLDS, Abraham, Gi-126-1; Pvt C Co 110th Col
  Inf; 10 Jan 64 to 6 Feb 66; Good Springs PO
REYNOLDS, Absalom, Gi-132-1; Pvt D Co 110th US
  Cav; about Sep 7 63 to Feb 7 66; DeRay PO
REYNOLDS, Alfred, Gi-135-3; Pvt A Co 110th TN Inf;
  64 to 64 (6 mos); Lynnville PO
REYNOLDS, Andy, K-177-4; Pvt I Co 14th TN Inf; 63
  to 65; Chumlea PO
REYNOLDS, Benjamin, Gi-132-2; Pvt B Co 110th USCV;
  Dec 63 to Feb 66; Ridell PO
REYNOLDS, Berry, H-58-3; Cpl E Co 5th TN Inf; 3-2-
  62 to 4-5-65; Sale Creek PO; crhonic
  diarrhoea, weak eyes
REYNOLDS, Burt M., Gu-48-4(1); Gen Wagon Master,
  B Co 1st MI __; 61 to 64; Union City PO
  (Obion Co.)
REYNOLDS, Calvin, Gi-127-6; Pvt B Co 110th US Col
  Inf; 11-20-63 to 2-6-66; Pulaski PO; eruption
  right groins, wears truss

REYNOLDS, Crawford, Ge-101-3; Mary A. widow of; Pvt TN Inf; Ottway PO; died in service
REYNOLDS, Edgar F., Cf-41-1; Pvt G Co 16th PA Cav; 15 Sep 62 to 15 Jun 65; Noah PO
REYNOLDS, Edward W., K-173-1; Pvt D Co 6th TN Inf; 18 Apr 62 to 11 May 65; McMillen PO; rheumatism
REYNOLDS, Elizabeth (see Maxwell, Charles)
REYNOLDS, Elizy J. (see Fleit, Gorge W.)
REYNOLDS, Felix, Gi-132-1; Pvt H Co 111th USCV; Feb 15 64 to May 6 66; DeRay PO
REYNOLDS, George W., Di-40-1; George Ann wife of; Pvt D Co 10th TN Cav; 8-1-62 to 65; Adinburgh PO; still living here & husband death
REYNOLDS, Gilmore, Gi-132-3; Pvt B Co 110th USCV; Dec 63 to Feb 7 66; DeRay PO
REYNOLDS, Gilmore, Gi-132-1; DeRay PO
REYNOLDS, Hannah (see Brown, George)
REYNOLDS, Henry, H-56-7; St. Elmo PO
REYNOLDS, Jack, Gi-125-2; Pvt A Co 14th US Col Inf; Nov 63 to 6 Mar 66; Wales PO
REYNOLDS, Jack, Gi-125-1; Pvt A Co 14th US Col Inf; Nov 62 to 6 Mar 66; Bodenham PO
REYNOLDS, Jacob, Ge-101-1; Pvt B Co 8th TN Cav; 63 to 64; Ottway PO; sent home--could not get back
REYNOLDS, James W., Dk-32-2; Pvt E Co 4th TN Mtd Inf; 10-18-64 to 8-25-65; Temperance Hall PO
REYNOLDS, Jefferson, Ov-137-2; Pvt K Co 4th TN Mtd Inf; 11-1-64 to 8-25-65; Eagle Creek PO
REYNOLDS, John, G-53-4; Pvt G Co 6th TN Cav; 8-62 to 8-1-65; Humboldt PO
REYNOLDS, John, D-67-2; Emma widow of; Pvt A Co 14th Col Inf; Nov 1 63 to Nov 26 66; Nashville PO
REYNOLDS, John, Wa-276-1; Pvt H Co 4th TN Cav; Aug 63 to May 65; Limestone PO; crippled hip and back & darrhea, discharge burned, cant say as to dates
REYNOLDS, John, Dk-34-4; Pvt G Co 1st TN Mtd Inf; 8-23-64 to 7-22-65; Dowelltown PO; mumps
REYNOLDS, Joseph, Gi-126-1; Pvt K Co 17th Col Inf; 21 Dec 63 to 27 Jul 65; Good Springs PO
REYNOLDS, Joseph, S-217-2; Nancy widow of; Pvt E Co 12th KY Inf; Dec 61 to __; Oneida PO
REYNOLDS, Joshua, Ge-101-1; Pvt A Co 4th TN Inf; 11 Aug 62 to 2 Aug 65; Ottway PO; No 4 Hospitle, Louisville KY, accute heart disease
REYNOLDS, Lamuel H., G-67-3; PVt 32nd IL Inf; 13 Mar 62 to 13 Mar 65; Bradford PO
REYNOLDS, Lee, Gi-132-1; Pvt B Co 12th USCV; __ to Mar 30 65; 3 yrs; DeRay PO
REYNOLDS, Louis H., Ro-211-3; Pvt B Co 7th OH Inf; 22 Apr 61 to 28 Aug 61; Sgt H Co 24th MS Inf --5 Oct 61 to 27 Sep 62; Harriman PO
REYNOLDS, Margaret, Sq-165-3; widow Sol; 3rd Civil Dist
REYNOLDS, Mary (see Buford, Peter)
REYNOLDS, Obediah, Gi-125-2; Pvt; Wales PO; failed to see him
REYNOLDS, Oscar, St-164-1; Pvt F Co 8th KY Inf; 63 to 65; Stribling PO
REYNOLDS, Pitts E., Cf-40-3; 2nd & 1st Lt G Co 6th TN Cav; Sep 62 to Sep 65; Tullahoma PO
REYNOLDS, Richard, Gi-__; Mary White formerly widow of; H Co 111th USC_; Pulaski PO; died in the service
REYNOLDS, Robert, Mc-117-4; Mary J. widow of; 2nd Lt E Co 9th TN Cav; 6-63 to 9-65; Carlock PO; chronic diareah, died 9-1-1881
REYNOLDS, Samuel A., Fr-119-1; Pvt C Co 4th TN Lt Art; Sep 64 to Aug 65; Estill Springs PO
REYNOLDS, Smith, Gi-132-1; Sgt D Co 111th USCV; DeRay PO; rheumatism & crippled knee
REYNOLDS, Thomas P., Lo-189-2; Pvt Co G 12th KY Cav; 20 Aug 62 to 26 Dec 64; Philadelphia PO
REYNOLDS, W. S., A-1-2; Sgt A Co 1st TN Inf; 8-1-61 to 9-7-64; Andersonville PO; gun shots
REYNOLDS, Wesley, K-177-4; Body Guard; Powells Station PO
REYNOLDS, William, Gi-125-2; Pvt D Co 111th US Col Inf; 25 Dec 63 to 6 Feb 66; Wales PO
REYNOLDS, William, Wl-298-1; Pvt K Co 10th TN Inf; 24 Oct 62 to 23 Jun 65; Alexandria PO; stomacke disease 15 yrs, not able to work but part of time
REYNOLDS, William, G-60-1; Kersey widow of; Pvt in 6th TN Cav; 9 Aug? 61 to 1 Jun 64; Bradford PO
REYNOLDS, William, Hw-132-2; Pvt D Co 31st TN Inf; 63 to 65; Persia PO; CONF
REYNOLDS, William, Dk-31-3; 13th Civil Dist
REYNOLDS, Wm. M., K-177-2; PO omitted
REYNOLDS, Willis, Mc-111-1; Cpl E Co 142nd US Col Inf; 9-23-64 to 1-31-66; Gudger PO (Monroe Co.)
REYNOLDS, Wyatt, Gi-132-4; PO omitted
REYNOLDS, Z. T., G-57-1; Pvt G Co 15th TN Cav; 62 to 65; Yorkville PO; CONF
REZER, Lewis, Sh-157-6; Insely's Farm PO
RHEA, Alfred F., Ge-98-3; Rebecca widow of; Sgt K Co 1st TN Cav; Jerroldstown? PO; measles
RHEA, Andrew J., Bo-21-2; Wagonmaster F Co 3rd TN Cav; 6-15-63 to 7-12-65; Ellijay PO
RHEA, David, Hm-109-3; Lt A Co 1st TN Art; 1 Nov 63 to 8 May 65; Whitesburg PO
RHEA, Francis A., Hd-47-1; Pvt E Co 3rd US Inf; 64 to 65; Savannah PO; piles
RHEA, James A., A-2-1; Allen Rhea alias; Pvt J Co 7th TN Mtd Inf; 11-8-64 to 7-27-65; Hynds Creek PO
RHEA, James M., Ge-101-2; Pvt K Co 1st TN Cav; 15 Nov 61 to 6 Apr 65; Locust Sp. PO
RHEA, Jessee, Gr-79-2; E Co 8th E TN Cav; 10 Oct 63 to Jan 64; Ball Point PO; not disabled
RHEA, John P., Ge-98-3; Pvt D Co 8th TN Inf; Mar 63 to 30 Jun 65; Jeroldstown PO; rheumatism and nervous prostration
RHEA, John W., A-4-2; Pvt D Co 1st TN Lt Art; 11-5-63 to 7-3-65; Offutts PO; chronic diarrhea
RHEA, Nancy J., Hm-109-5; widow USS; PO omitted
RHEA, Osias, Mo-126-1; Pvt D Co 3rd TN Mtd Inf; 7-25-64 to 11-13-64; Notchy PO; reinlisted veteran
RHEA, Osias, Mo-126-1; Pvt D Co 3rd TN Mtd Inf; 7-25-64 to 11-13-64; Notchy PO; reinlisted veteran
RHEA, Patterson, K-181-2; Sgt I Co 3rd TN Cav; 28 Sep 62 to 13 Jun 65; French PO; cronic rheumatism 25 yrs
RHEA, Sterlin, Ha-114-2; Pvt Co F 10th IN Cav; 4 Apr 62 to 20 Jun 64; Sneedville PO; CONF
RHEA, Thomas, Mo-126-1; Pvt I Co 2nd TN Inf; Notchy PO; discharge misplaced
RHEAY, Isaac, W-192-1; Pvt A Co; 6-17-63 to 65; Irving College PO
RHEGNESS, William E., G-56-1; Cpl 5th OH Batty; 2-1-64 to 7-31-65; Trenton PO; deafness in left ear
RHINEHEART, Joseph, Wh-187-1; Pvt C Co 3rd KY Inf; 61 to __ (2 yrs); Cherry Creek PO; ribs broken
RHOADS, William T. J., M-107-4; Sgt A Co 8th TN Mtd Inf; 11-22-64 to 8-17-65; Salt Lick PO; ulcerated sore eyes
RHODE, William, D-43-2; Sol; High St, Nashville PO
RHODES, Amercus, La-113-3; Pvt B Co 112th Col Inf; 62 to Aug 62; Ethridge PO; re-enlisted, shot left leg, discharge lost
RHODES, Benjamin J., Ch-17-1; Pvt H Co 21st TN Cav; 2-15-63 to 5-1-65; Henderson PO; CONF
RHODES, Edward H., Cr-16-1; Cpl F Co 7th TN Cav; Aug 62 to Nov 63; Huntingdon PO; CONF
RHODES, John M., He-58-1; Pvt A Co 7th TN Vol Cav; 7-22-62 to 1-4-65; PO omitted
RHODES, Mathew, A-5-6(2); Pvt K Co 13th TN Cav; 10-4-63 to 9-5-65; Coal Creek PO
RHODES, Miles, D-57-2; Lizzie widow of; Pvt C Co 15th US Inf; 63 to Dec 30 64; PO omitted, 8th Ward; kill at Springfield, Dec 30 64
RHODES, Victora, St-161-1; widow US Sol; PO omitted
RHOTON, Joseph H., Cf-35-4; Pvt K Co 24th TN Inf; 20 Jun 63 to 24 Jun 65; Normandy PO; CONF
RHYMER, Stephen, Hw-130-2; Cpl G Co 1st TN Cav; 20 Jul 62 to 15 Jun 65; PO omitted
RHYNE, E., Bo-11-7; Pvt A Co 8th TN Inf; 2-10-62 to 2-23-65; Big Gulley PO; wound on head
RICE, Edmund, Sh-158-2; PVt A & I Cos 3rd SC Cav; Oct 62 to Jul 65; Memphis PO; discharge papers lost, seems to be honest and ignorant
RICE, Frank, K-161-4; Pvt 1st US Hvy Art; Knoxville PO

RICE, George, Se-219-2; Pvt B Co 2nd TN Cav; 15 Aug 62 to 6 Jul 65; Jones Cave PO; liver & heart disease, diarhea
RICE, George, K-155-2(1); alias Georg Bramer; Pvt F Co 1st Col Art; 64 to __; Knoxville PO
RICE, George O., H-72-1; Cpl D Co 1st US Col Art; 7-14-64 to 3-31-66; Chattanooga PO
RICE, Isaac, Ge-99-1; PVt G Co 3rd NC Inf; 63 to 65; Limestone Springs PO; neuralgia, cant get the dates
RICE, Jacob, L-99-1; Pvt F Co 4th US Hvy Art; 63 to 66; Orysa PO; sight, date of months of enlistment & discharge unknown
RICE, James N., T-213-1; Pvt K Co 7th TN Cav; 29 May 61 to 23 Dec 63; Covington PO; CONF
RICE, James Y., Dy-29-2; Pvt & Ord Sgt B Co 12th TN Inf; 11 May 61 to 11 May 65; Newbern PO; CONF
RICE, Jasper N., Br-14-2; Pvt I Co 4th TN Cav; 2-64 to 7-12-65; McDonald PO; wounded in breast by horse
RICE, Jesse S., U-247-3; US Sol; 5th Civil Dist
RICE, John, H-51-7; Hill City PO
RICE, Joseph, Co-64-1; Capt H Co 29th TN Inf; 61 to 63 (3 yrs 10 mos); Newport PO; shot in left arm; CONF
RICE, Kizia, Cf-38-1; widow; 10th Civil Dist
RICE, Matilds, L-99-2; widow US Sol; Durhamville PO
RICE, Oliver T., De-26-2; E Co 27th TN; Aug 16 61 to Jan 10 63; Northford PO; right arm shot off; CONF
RICE, Robert M., Hw-126-1; Pvt L Co 12th TN Cav; 3 Aug 64 to 7 Oct 65; Starns PO; liver affected, dates given from memory
RICE, Sarah, Gr-82-2; 13th Dist
RICE, William, Cl-54-2; Soldier US; PO omitted
RICE, William J., U-249-1; Pvt K Co 13th TN Cav; 1 Oct 63 to 5 Sep 65; Flag Pond PO
RICE, William L., Mc-110-1; Pvt B Co 7th TN Inf; 9-21-64 to 7-27-65; Chuckaluck PO
RICH, Calvin, Pi-154-1; Pvt D Co 32nd KY Inf; 10-28-62 to 8-12-63; Byrdstown PO; rheumatism
RICH, Edmond, Sh-159-3; Sarah J. widow of; Surgeon IA; Memphis PO
RICH, Elisha, Cy-26-1; Pvt B Co 37th KY Inf; 7-17-63 to 12-29-64; Moss PO; first enlisted 65th IL Inf, captured at Harpers Ferry VA, parolled, joined 37th KY
RICH, Henry J., Sh-54-6; Pvt; Sherman Heights PO
RICH, Isic O., U-245-2; Sgt E Co 42nd NC Inf; 62 to 65; Marion, NC, McLowe Co. PO; surrendered with Johnson army, got no discharge; CONF
RICH, James D., Hd-46-1; Pvt A Co 2nd TN Mtd Inf; Oct 10 63 to Nov 13 64; Economy PO
RICH, James O., Ca-25-2; Pvt D Co 4th TN Mtd Inf; 10-19-64 to 8-25-65; Gassoway PO
RICH, John, Pi-156-2; Pvt I Co 30th KY Inf; 63 to 65; Travisville PO
RICH, John N., Sh-159-1; Marttee widow of; Pvt D Co PA Cav; 62 to 63; Memphis PO; CONF
RICH, Mollie, Sh-159-8; widow US Sol; Memphis PO
RICH, William, Dk-33-2; Pvt I Co 5th TN Cav; 11-22-62 to 8-14-65; Gasaway PO; sunstroke
RICH, William, Cy-26-1; Pvt B Co 37th KY Inf; 7-17-63 to 12-29-64; Moss PO
RICH, William F., Wy-175-2; Pvt A Co 10th TN Inf; 4-16-62 to 7-5-65; Whittens Stand PO; chronic diarrhea and rheumatism
RICHARD, Mary (see Lewis, Benjeman)
RICHARD, Preston?, F-38-1; Pvt 7th TN Cav; 63 to 64; Mason PO; CONF
RICHARD, William P., O-141-1; Pvt Co A KY Cav 8th Vol Reg; 6 Sep 62 to Jun 26 65; Union City PO
RICHARD, William S., Sm-166-1; Sgt A Co 1st TN Inf; 12-18-63 to 1-30-65; Carthage PO
RICHARDS, Andrew J., Hw-121-4(3); Nancy J. widow of; Pvt C Co 8th TN Cav; 4 May 64 to 22 Jul 65; Lucas PO; wound in the left leg, consumption
RICHARDS, James, K-159-1; Pvt H Co 4th TN Inf; __ to 4 Aug 65; Knoxville PO
RICHARDS, Lewis, W-189-2; Pvt; McMinnville PO; did not see Mr. Richards discharge and cannot give dates
RICHARDS, Martha, K-183-3; widow; Pvt B Co 9th TN Cav; PO omitted

RICHARDS, Newton, Hw-133-1; Sarah widow of; recruit 8th TN Cav; Beurams Store PO; crushed by horse
RICHARDS, Newton, Hm-105-1; Pvt A Co 1st TN Sh?; Sep 63 to 12 Aug 65; Morristown PO; health injured & other __?
RICHARDS, Richard, O-141-1; Cpl M Co 4th Hvy Art; 63 to 65; Union City PO
RICHARDSON, Calvin, P-150-2; US Sol; 1st Dist
RICHARDSON, Daniel, Cr-8-1; Pvt D Co 47th TN; Dec 16 61 to May 4 65; Chestnut Bluff PO; CONF
RICHARDSON, David, Ro-209-1; Pvt D Co; Rockwood PO
RICHARDSON, Doc W., Br-12-1; 1st Lt A Co 110th OH Inf; 8-12-62 to 7-1-65; Charleston PO; hemorrhoids
RICHARDSON, Elbridge G., O-138-2; Pvt A Co 9th TN; 1 Apr 61 to 65; Elbridge PO; CONF
RICHARDSON, Elijah, Hw-124-1; Pvt H Co 4th TN Inf; 28 Apr 63 to 2 Aug 65; New Canton PO
RICHARDSON, Elsberry, Ct-36-1; Malinda widow of; Pvt 13th TN Cav; Shell Creek PO
RICHARDSON, Francis M., Ca-22-2; Pvt E Co 10th TN Inf; 3-1-61 to 5-__; Hollow Springs PO
RICHARDSON, George (see King, George)
RICHARDSON, George, A-6-1; Annie widow of; Pvt; 62 to 65; Olivers PO
RICHARDSON, George W., Un-256-1; Pvt G Co 2nd IN Cav; 11 Oct 62 to 3 Ma 65; Rule PO
RICHARDSON, George W., Cl-58-2; Pvt Co E 2nd TN Inf; 8-9-61 to __; Davo PO; frerloed and did not return to comand, was not mustered out
RICHARDSON, Henry, G-50-1; Almoda J. Huges widow of; Teamster 6th IL; 8-62 to 1-65; Humboldt PO
RICHARDSON, Hiser V., Pu-144-4; Pvt A Co 5th TN Cav; 8-4-62 to 6-25-65; Pine Fork PO; shot through thigh
RICHARDSON, Jason?, J-79-1; Mary M. widow of; Pvt; Whitleyville PO; could no give dates but draws pension
RICHARDSON, John F., Mt-146-1; Pvt E Co 9th TN Cav; 63 to 15 Sep 65; Fredonia PO
RICHARDSON, John H., C-25-1; Cpl A Co 1st TN Inf; 8-2-61 to 9-17-64; Whitman PO; cattarh of head, testicles, reumatism
RICHARDSON, John R., D-54-2; Sgt K Co 2nd MI? Cav; Dec 61 to Nov 64; Nashville PO
RICHARDSON, Mary (see King, George)
RICHARDSON, N. C., Gi-122-3; Susan F. widow of; Maj A Co 53rd TN Inf; 61 to 28 Jul 64; Prospect Sta. PO; died of wound in service, prisoner 10 mos; CONF
RICHARDSON, Patrick, Col, G-73-1; Pvt A Co 1st US Inf; Aug 9 64 to Apr 14 65; Trenton PO
RICHARDSON, Peter, Ov-135-1; Pvt D Co 9th TN Cav; 10-20-64 to 9-11-65; Eagle Creek PO; say he was sick & got no discharge
RICHARDSON, Ream, Pu-146-2; Pvt C Co 1st TN Mtd Inf Vol; 10-21-63 to 12-13-64; Pine Fork PO; spine injured
RICHARDSON, Riley S., J-78-2; Pvt B Co 8th TN Inf; 1-15-65 to 8-17-65; Highland PO; kidneys
RICHARDSON, Samuel M., D-67-1; Allis widow of; Pvt E Co 17th Col Inf; 62 to 65; Nashville PO
RICHARDSON, Thos. J., Ro-208-1; Lt G Co 3rd MD Inf; 61 to 65; Barnardsville PO; kidney disease
RICHARDSON, Thomas L., La-113-2; Pvt I Co 4th TN Mtd Inf; 10 Oct 64 to 25 Aug 65; Lawrenceburgh PO
RICHARDSON, Watson, Ru-237-1; Pvt E Co 31st OH Inf; 1 Mar 62 to 15 Jul 64; Eagleville PO; shoulder fractured
RICHARDSON, Wiliam W., C-25-1; Pvt A Co 1st TN Inf; 8-2-61 to 9-17-64; Jacksborough PO; neuralgia, disease of hart, testicles disease
RICHARDSON, William H., C-28-1; Pvt A Co 1st TN Inf; 8-2-61 to 9-27-64; Big Cree Gap PO
RICHARDSON, William S., D-71-1; Matilda? widow of; US Sol; Nashville PO
RICHARDSON, __, P-150-2; Amanda L. widow of; US Sol; 1st Dist
RICHEE, Isiac, H-76-2; Pvt A Co 114th IL Inf; 8-11-62 to 6-18-65; Chattanooga PO
RICHESON, Samuel, Mc-109-2; Pvt H Co 2nd TN Inf; 8-12-63 to 8-5-65; Prigmore PO; small pox & results, in Belle Island Prison 5 mos

RICHEY, Henry J., Je-146-3; Pvt L Co 1st TN Cav; 1 Jul 63 to 23 May 65; White Pine PO; rheumatism and asthma, not able to work (but does)
RICHEY, William H., H-50-4; Pvt A Co 6th R TN Mtd Inf; 8-2-64 to 6-30-65; Soddy PO; chronic diarhea
RICHMAN, Lewis, Col, Tr-267-1; Pvt A Co 14th TN Cav; May 62 to May 65; Emon. College PO
RICHMOND, Crossley, Hw-120-1; Pvt K Co KY Cav; Jun 63 to Mar 65; War Gap PO
RICHMOND, Curtis, Gi-122-7; Pvt E Co 8th WI Inf; Jun 61 to Jul 65; Prospect Sta. PO
RICHMOND, John S., Sh-198-1; Sgt H Co 1st MI Lt Art; 6-17-62 to 6-17-65; Memphis PO; has his discharge
RICHMOND, Samuel M., Br-7-2; Pvt F Co 1st KY Cav; 3-22-62 to 6-9-65; Coahulla PO; wounded
RICHMOND, William C., Br-7-2; Matilda J. widow of; Pvt F Co 1st TN Cav; Coahulla PO
RICHTER, Oliver, La-113-2; Pvt E Co 17th OH Inf; Apr 61 to Aug 61; Lawrenceburgh PO
RICKARD, William P., Je-136-1; Pvt A Co 9th TN Cav; Dandridge PO
RICKER, J. P., Ge-87-2; Sarah E. widow of; Pvt E Co 8th TN Inf; 62 to 63; Little Chucky PO
RICKETS, Robert, Ca-22-3; Narcissas Gye widow of; Pvt; Burt PO; died in army, deceased left children
RICKETS, Stacey, Hd-46-1; Stacey (sic) widow of; Pvt C Co 6th TN Cav; Jul 26 65; Cerro Gordo PO
RICKETTS, B. M., Hu-106-2; Pvt 8th IL Inf--18 Apr 61 to 7-1-61; Pvt 73rd IL Inf--1 Jul 62 to 3-25-63; 1st Sgt & Adjt 13th US C T--25 Nov 63 to 16 Jan 66; Waverly PO
RICKETTS, Benjamin R., K-171-4(3); Pvt C Co 6th TN Inf; 18 Apr 62 to 18 Apr 65; Knoxville PO; chronic diarear & rheumatism
RICKETTS, Ruben R., Ch-12-2; Sgt H Co 21st TN Cav; 8-61 to 65; Custer Point PO; CONF
RICKETTS, Thomas T., H-53-7; Pvt C Co 39th OH Inf; 61 to 65; Chattanooga PO; wounded in left knee
RICKETTS, William M., Wl-300-2; Pvt H Co 4th TN Inf; 1 Jan 65 to 25 Aug 65; Cherry Valley PO
RICKEY, James W., Ge-84-2; Pvt A Co 3rd ___ Mtd Inf; 30 Jan 64 to 30 Nov 64; Greenville PO; chronic diarreas
RICKMAN, James G., Hn-70-1; Pvt H Co 12th KY Inf; 3 Oct 61 to 31 Dec 63; Paris PO; reenlisted veteran, now in feeble h.
RICKMAN, William I., Wi-281-1; Nancy Ann widow of; Capt H Co 5th TN; Sep 62 to Aug 65; Allisona PO; shocked by bomb shell
RICKS, Christopher C., Mc-113-2; Pvt M Co 5th TN Cav; 3-25-64 to 8-15-65; Riceville PO
RICKS, Mose, Mu-205-1; Linda widow of; Williamsport PO; papers lost
RICKS, Thomas, Te-216-3; Sgt I Co 17th US Inf; Aug 63 to 17 May 63; 14th Civil Dist
RIDDLE, Fountain R., Cy-30-1; Pvt H Co 13th KY Cav; 9-19-63 to 11-10-64; Mouth of Wolf PO; rheumatism
RIDDLE, James P. W., Me-94-1; Pvt H Co 7th TN Mtd Inf; Knott PO; house burned and discharge
RIDDLE, John, U-248-1; Sarah M. widow of; Pvt E Co 3rd NC Inf; 10 Oct 64 to 10 Aug 65; Clear Branch PO
RIDDLE, Milo S., R-161-4; Sarah E. widow of; Sgt F Co 5th TN; 2-25-62 to 3-29-65; Dayton PO
RIDDLE, Peter, Cl-52-3; Pvt D Co 9th TN Cav; 10-1-62 to 9-1-65; Hypatia PO; shot in nee and shoulder
RIDDLE, Pleasant F., Mc-109-3; Pvt B Co 7th TN Inf; 10-1-64 to 7-27-65; Regret PO; voice injured
RIDDLE, Thos., La-117-2; Rebecca widow of; Pvt Inf; 64 to ___ (4 yrs); 15th Dist; CONF
RIDDLE, William, Ja-87-1; Pvt D Co 1st TN Cav; 3-2-62 to 4-15-65; Howardville PO; gun shot wound lung disease
RIDELL, John, S-213-2; Pvt F Co 7th KY Inf; 61 to ___ PO omitted
RIDENOWER, John, Un-256-2; Pvt F Co 6th TN Inf; 10 Mar 62 to Apr 65; Duk PO; piles & resung? in head
RIDEOUT, Richard, Sh-178-3; US Sol; 308 Beall, Memphis PO
RIDEOUT, William, Sh-178-1; Sgt C Co 2nd FL;

4-1-65 to ___; 358 Beale, Memphis PO; CONF
RIDER, Spotswood, Mc-123-1; Pvt A Co 2nd US Col Inf; 3-26-64 to 1-31-66; Jalapa PO
RIDGE, D. H., Bo-11-4; Pvt G Co 8th TN Cav; 10-15-63 to 9-11-65; Brick Hill PO
RIDGE, David, Mr-96-1; Martha widow of; Lt 6th TN Vol; Shirleyton PO
RIDGE, George W., H-53-1; Staff Sheridan AL Scouts; entire length of Civil War; Chattanooga PO; information from wife
RIDGE, John, Bo-11-2; Pvt C Co 3rd TN Mtd Inf; 7-26-64 to 11-30-64; Big Gulley PO
RIDGLY, Enock G., Ca-16-1; Pvt F Co 48th IL Inf; Feb 1 64 to Aug 15 65; Huntingdon PO; wound in right arm; Conf deserter? Iowa corn dist?
RIDINGS, Robert W., Cr-19-1; Pvt G Co 2nd TN Cav; 11-11-63 to 12-28-64; Huntingdon PO
RIDINGS, William, Lo-191-1; Pvt D Co 2nd TN Cav; 1 Sep 62 to 16 May 65; Greenback PO
RIDLEY, Henry, D-100-1; alias Jake Bryant; Pvt; Nashville PO; does not know when he went in or when he came out
RIDLEY, Martin, Wi-286-2(1); Pvt H Co 4th ___; Nolinsville PO; flesh wound left temple, details forgotten
RIDLEY, Mary D., D-59-1; widow of; Engineer US Marine Service; 1813 Patterson St, Nashville PO
RIDLY, Alicandria, R-162-5; Pvt H Co 5th TN Mtd Inf; Dayton PO; chronic diarrhea during service & ruptured during service
RIDNER, John, Gi-133-1; Pvt E Co; Nov 64 to Jan 1 65; Bufords PO; CONF
RIDNOUR, Harvey G., C-24-4(3); Pvt C Co 9th TN Cav; 7-22-63 to 9-11-65; Agee PO; cattarr of head
RIGG, Jessie C. J., C-26-1; Pvt D Co 3rd TN Inf; 2-10-62 to 2-22-65; Coal Creek PO (also C-25-3)
RIGGES, Fulps?, Hm-106-2; Pvt; Morristown PO; dont know anything about it; CONF
RIGGLY, Sarah C., R-158-3; widow of US Sol; Pvt; 2nd Civil Dist
RIGGS, Edwin C., Hm-103-2; Mary B. widow of; Pvt C Co 1st TN Cav; no dates; Morristown PO
RIGGS, H. P., T-214-1; Pvt M Co 5th OH Cav; 25 Sep 62 to 17 Oct 64; Mason Depot PO
RIGGS, Irvin W., Gi-123-1; Pvt I Co 2nd Mtd Inf; Jan 63 to Jan 65; Bethel PO
RIGGS, James ___, De-26-1; C Co 2nd TN; Genett PO
RIGGS, John, Hw-127-2; John Maney alias; Pvt G Co 1st US Hvy Art; Rogersville PO; hurt in back
RIGGS, John P., Wa-267-1; Pvt E Co 3rd US Inf; 17 Oct 64 to 19 Nov 65; Jonesboro PO; kidney trouble; CONF (sic)
RIGGS, John T., Hn-75-1; Pvt B Co 6th TN Cav; 25 Aug 62 to 24 Jun 65; Springvale PO; discharge on acct sickness
RIGGS, Joseph, Ro-211-1; Pvt E Co 1st TN Inf; 20 Aug 61 to 17 Sep 64; Webster PO; throat, piles and chronic diar, also, lungs
RIGGS, Martha A., La-114-1; widow US Sol; PO omitted
RIGGS, Press., Col, Li-152-1; Pvt F Co 40th IL; 63 to 65; Blakeville PO; right shoulder sprained
RIGGS, Robert C., Gi-123-2; Pvt I Co 2nd Mtd Inf; Dec 63 to Feb 65; Heron PO
RIGGS, Samuel, C-28-1; Pvt C Co 9th TN Cav; ___ to 9-18-65; Fincastle PO
RIGGS, Samuel L., Mc-116-1; Pvt D Co 5th TN Mtd Inf; 8-31-64 to 6-26-65; Longs Mills PO; chronic rheumatism
RIGGS, Thomas, C-26-1; Pvt D Co 3rd TN Inf; 2-10-62 to 2-22-65; Coal Creek PO
RIGGS, Thomas, C-25-3; Pvt D Co 3rd TN Inf; 2-10-62 to 2-22-65; Coal Creek PO
RIGHT, James, Wy-173-4; Pvt E Co 8th TN Mtd Inf; 3-1-65 to 9-1-65; Victory PO
RIGHT, James M., Co-66-1; Pvt I Co 3rd NC Inf; 10 Mar 63 to 15 Aug 65; Birdsville PO
RIGHT, John, Cy-27-2; 2nd Lt B Co 5th KY Cav; 10-10-61 to 3-30-65; Clementsville PO
RIGHT, William, Hw-118-2; Pvt C Co 8th TN Cav; St. Clair PO; lung disease
RIGHTSELL, William C., Hm-107-2(1); Pvt D Co 4th TN Inf; 18 Jan 63 to 2 Aug 65; Witts Foundry PO; chronic diarrhea

RIGSBEY, James L., B1-4-1; Pvt C Co 43rd TN Inf; 12-20-62 to 6-20-63; Pikeville PO; CONF
RIGSBEY, John, B1-4-2; Ann widow of; Pvt I Co 8th TN Cav; 10-1-64 to 4-1-65; Pikeville PO; general debility, died June 1885
RIGSBY, Andrew, Dk-39-1; Pvt C Co 37th KY Mtd Inf; 6-20-63 to 12-29-64; Bozarth PO; lungs injured by measles
RIGSBY, John D., Dk-36-2; Pvt B Co 4th TN Mtd Inf; 9-25-64 to 8-25-65; Smithville PO
RIBSBY, Robert P., Ca-24-1; Pvt H Co 10th TN Inf; 5-21-63 to 7-3-65; Talvine PO; rheumatism, effect of cold in service
RIGSBY, William B., We-224-3(1); Cpl L Co 4th TN Inf; 17 Dec 61 to May 65; Dresden PO; under remarks it says something like "have a page, Robt."; CONF
RIKER, B. E. (see Kyker, Benjamin E.)
RIKER, Thomas H., H-68-3; 1st Lt D Co 6th IL Vol; 11-8-61 to 7-8-65; Chattanooga PO
RILES, James C., He-63-1; Eliza J. widow of; Pvt A Co 7th TN; PO omitted
RILEY, Allen, Hi-88-1; Pvt I Co 2nd TN Inf?; 11-16-63 to 6-21-65; Pinewood PO
RILEY, Andrew, Su-242-1; Pvt A Co 13th TN Cav; 1 Feb 64 to 21 Jun? 65; Bluff City PO; diahrhea, piles, prolapsus ani, nervous debility, irregularity of discharge is owing to confinement (65-6---sic) by sickness
RILEY, Annie, D-78-2; widow US Sol; Nashville PO
RILEY, Daniel, D-64-4; Nashville PO
RILEY, Frank, Sh-159-7; PO omitted
RILEY, Henry, Pu-144-1; Cpl E Co 52nd KY; 8-11-63 to __; Double Springs PO
RILEY, James, Mu-194-1; Cpl A Co 100th KY Inf; 5-22-64 to 1-1-66; Columbia PO
RILEY, Jas. L., R-163-1; Pvt B Co 23rd KY Inf; 11-15-61 to 3-12-63; Graysville PO; dropsy & heart disease, the above figures are guessed
RILEY, John A., L-108-2; Lou widow of; Pvt; PO omitted
RILEY, Richard, St-159-1; Pvt B Co 17th IL Inf; 61 to 64; Indian Mount PO
RILEY, Robert C., C-33-2; Pvt H Co 99th NY Inf; 5-28-61 to 2-65; Jellico PO; was a prisoner 9 mos 5 days confined in Richmond VA & Belle Isle & Andersonville GA, Florane SC
RILEY, William, Hm-108-4(3); Pvt D Co 71st IN Inf; Apr 64 to Dec 64; Russellville PO; rheumatism 25 yrs
RILEY, William C., H-64-1; Pvt K Co 1st MI Eng; 10-7-61 to 10-1-65; Chattanooga PO; general debillity
RILLS?, David N., Ct-41-4; Sgt C Co 4th TN Inf; 10-6-63 to 2-8-65; South Wattauga PO
RINEHART, Andy E., Mt-146-1; Pvt A Co 87th OH Inf; 61 to 61 (3 mos); Pvt E Co 82nd OH Hvy Art; Jun? 62 to 65; Fredonia PO
RINEHART, James H., Je-137-2; Pvt I Co 2nd TN Cav; 22 Sep 62 to Jul 65; Chestnut Hill PO
RINES, Jacob, Lo-190-3; Pvt K Co 9th TN Cav; 9 Apr 63 to 11 Sep 65; Piney PO; deafness, blindness and prisoner 2 mos
RING, Wiley, A-5-3; Cpl K Co 11th TN Cav; 6-63 to 9-11-65; Clinton PO
RINGER, Joab, Dy-25-6(2); Pvt I Co 14th VA Cav; Sep 62 to 65; Newbern PO; CONF
RINGROSE, Micheal, Sh-197-1; Hannah widow of; 10th Cav; Memphis PO; papers burned
RINIS?, Robert, Hi-71-2; Pvt B Co 13th KY Col Inf; 2 yrs 6 mos; Stanton Depot PO; frost bit
RINK, John, He-67-2; Mary A. widow of; Pvt K Co 46th OH Inf; May 63 to Aug 65; Sardis PO
RIORDAM, Eugene, H-70-3(1); Pvt H Co 177th NY Inf; 62 to 63; Chattanooga PO
RIPETOE, George W., Hm-108-5(4); Pvt B Co 8th TN Inf; 1 Oct 63 to 29 May 65; Langdonic PO; wounded 3 times
RIPLEY, Sylvester B., Ge-95-2; Pvt F Co 4th TN Inf; 13 Apr 63 to 2 Aug 65; Chucky City PO
RIPLEY, William P., Hw-133-2; Sgt E Co 1st TN Cav; 18 Mar 62 to 18 May 63; Fry PO; bronchitus
RIPPETOE, James M., Hm-109-2; Margarett A. widow of; Pvt C Co 3rd TN Cav; 62 to __; Whitesburg PO
RIPPETOE, William B., B-3-1; Pvt K Co 16th IN Regt --4-20-61 to 5-10-62; 1st Lt 18th IN Battery --7-13-62 to 7-3-65; Coldwell PO; 18th IN Battery was Lt Art
RIPPLE, William, Fr-105-1; Mu I Co 31st NJ V Inf; 3 Sep 62 to 24 Jun 63; Winchester PO
RIPPS, Ellis J., Je-146-1; Pvt A Co 9th TN Cav; 1 Jul 63 to 13 Sep 65; White Pine PO; gun shot right shoulder
RIPPY, Andrew, Sn-260-6; Pvt A Co TN Cav; 64 to 65 (11 mos); Pondville PO; CONF
RIPPY, Jesse (see Jones, King E.)
RISEDEN, Isaac, S-214-3; 1st Lt E Co 11th TN Cav; 4 Jul 62 to __; New River PO; was in prison
RISEDORF, Frank C., D-68-2; Pvt D Co 47th NY Inf; 6 May 61 to 20 Mar 64; 247 Fillmore St, Nashville PO
RISLEY, L. W., H-60-3; Sgt D Co 18th MD Inf; 6-11-61 1-23-63; Chattanooga PO
RITCHEE, James P., Ct-43-1; Sgt F Co 13th TN Cav; 9-22-63 to 15-7-65; Carter Furnace PO; chronic diarrhea & piles
RITCHEY, Adelbert L., D-58-2; Surgeon 10th IL; May 61 to May 65; Nashville PO; spine and hip wound by explosion of amuntion
RITCHEY, Joseph G., Ja-84-2; Jane A. widow of; 1st Lt L Co 4th TN Cav; Harrison PO
RITCHEY, Thomas H., Mr-98-1; Pvt C Co 6th TN Inf; 9-7-64 to 6-30-65; Stanley PO
RITCHIE, Alvin P., Ct-42-3; Martha widow of; Pvt U Co 13th TN Cav; Watauga PO
RITCHWILD, James R., Ct-41-4; Pvt Co K 26th TN Inf; 61 to 65; Keensburgh PO; lung trouble
RITER, Joseph H., Sh-158-1; Pvt E Co 11th MI Vol Cav; Oct or Nov 63 to __ (1 yr 6 mos); Memphis PO; left index finger shot off & hip injured by fall from horse while on patrol guard, discharge lost
RITTENBERRY, James B., B-12-2; Pvt A Co 5th TN Cav; Wheel PO; can not enumerate disabilities, claimed could not find discharge and could not give dates
RITTENBERRY, John L., Pu-146-1; Pvt H Co 1st TN Mtd Inf Vol W(hite?); 11-64 to 5-23-65; Buffalo Valley PO; shot in right foot, now suffering with eyes
RITTENBERY, Thomas A., B-7-2; Pvt F Co 1st Vidette Cav; 8-12-63 to 7-4-64; PO omitted
RITTER, H. C., Gr-81-4(2); Sgt A Co 12th TN Cav; 28 Jun 63 to 7 Oct 65; Shelton's Ford PO; heart failure, disabled
RIVERS, Alfred, Mu-195-2; Sol wife dont know; Columbia PO
RIVERS, Amos, F-47-1; Pvt D Co 43rd IL Inf; Feb 63 to Dec 65; Somerville PO
RIVERS, Henry, Gi-132-2; Pvt D Co 110th USCV; Dec 6 63 to Feb 6 66; DeRay PO
RIVERS, Jilce, Sh-151-1; Pvt B Co 88th TN Inf; Jan 17 64 to May 31 65; Arlington PO
RIVERS, Margaret (see Cardon, Nathan)
RIVERS, Martha, F-36-1; Corner PO
RIVERS, Virginia, Sh-178-2; widow US Sol; rear 253 Monroe St, Memphis PO
RIVERS, Wesley, Gi-127-4; Bettie widow of; Sgt K Co 110th TN C Inf; Dec 15 63 to Feb 6 66; Pulaski PO; was killed by dynimite explosion, April 1890
ROACH, A. A., De-22-3; Pvt B Co 31st TN Inf; 1 Sep 62 to 1 Jul 65; Dunbar PO; CONF
ROACH, Alfred M., Gr-76-2(1); Pvt F Co 1st TN Cav; 1 Mar 62 to 13 Mar 65; Spring House PO; accidental injury and piles
ROACH, Alya L., Je-141-3; Cpl F Co 1st TN Cav; 1 Mar 62 to 13 Mar 65; Mill Springs PO
ROACH, Anderson J., Gr-76-2(1); Pvt F Co 8th TN Cav; 19 Jul 63 to 11 Sep 65; Tampico PO; sciatic affection from exposure
ROACH, Benjamin F., C-24-2; Ruthee widow of; Pvt F Co 6th TN Inf; 3-62 to 4-27-65; Boy PO; murdered 1880
ROACH, Berry, Mg-197-2; Pvt I Co 9th TN Cav; 13 Sep 63 to 11 Sep 65; Wartburg PO; weak eyes
ROACH, George L., C-27-2; Pvt TN Inf; 3 mos; Caryville PO
ROACH, Harison, K-165-3; Pvt E Co 3rd TN Inf; 45 Hauer Ave, Knoxville PO
ROACH, John, C-28-2(1); Cpl C Co 9th TN Cav; 9-24-63 to 9-11-65; Big Creek Gap PO; rheumatism & neuralgia

ROACH, John C., Cr-13-1; Pvt B Co 1st W TN Inf; Jul 2 62 to captured and paroled 62; Atwood PO; none incured, captured Dec 20 and paroled
ROACH, Morgan, Mc-114-5; Pvt; Santfordville PO
ROACH, Moses, Ma-123-1; Pvt Co A 16th TN Inf; Jun 10 63 to Jul 66; Buch Bluff PO; came home sick with diarrhea without a discharge
ROACH, Simston, S-213-3; US Sol; 2nd Civil Dist
ROACH, Thomas M., Sh-201-3; Charity widow of; Pvt E Co 55th US Col Inf; 10 May 62 to 15 Jul 65; Memphis PO
ROACH, William, C-24-2; Pvt C Co 9th TN Cav; 8-7-63 to 9-11-65; Girlton PO; murder since the war (mistake here, probably refers to William Wrigt or Geroge Brown)
ROACH, William H., Mc-114-6; Pvt K Co 1st TN Inf; 9-62 to no discharge (3 yrs); Santfordville PO
ROADY, Preston D., K-159-3; Sgt G Co 8th TN Cav; 18 Aug 63 11 Sep 65; Knoxville PO
ROAN, W. H., Hd-47-1; Margaret A. widow of; Pvt I Co 21st MO (Md?) Inf; 64 to 65; Savannah PO
RAON, William M., Hn-78-1; Ordinary Seaman Ouichita; 10-16-64 to 10-16-65; Cottage Grove PO
ROARK, Asa W., M-108-3; Pvt A Co 9th KY Inf; 9-25-61 to 5-15-63; Lafayette PO; chronic dierhea
ROARK, Henry M., Cr-14-1; 2nd Duty Sgt G Co 7th TN Cav; 5 Aug 62 to 25 Oct 63; Clarksburg PO; deases lungs
ROARK, James, Ja-85-1; Pvt; Birchwood PO
ROARK, John B., Ja-85-2; Cpl E Co 5th TN Inf; 3-2-62 to 4-4-65; Birchwood PO
ROARK, John L., Ja-85-1; Pvt E Co 5th TN Inf; 3-2-62 to 4-4-65; Birchwood PO
ROARK, Solamon, Hw-133-4; Catharine widow of; Pvt E Co; Fry PO; killed; CONF
ROARK, Timothy, Jo-150-1; Pvt B Co 2nd VA Cav; 10 Jul 63 to 30 Jun 65; Rheas Forge PO
ROARKS, James, Cl-54-1; Mary A. widow of; Sgt I Co 3rd TN Inf; 2-4-62 to 2-23-65; Bacchus PO; expiration of time
ROARKS, John, Cl-54-1; Pvt I Co 3rd TN Inf; 2-10-62 to 3-9-65; Tazewell PO; injure of spine & testicles account of mumps
ROBARTS, Absolem, Gr-70-1; Pvt; Rutledge PO; company &c unknown
ROBB, John, D-49-1; Pauline widow of; Cpl G Co 12th TN; 2 yrs; soldier dead, widow dont know dates
ROBB, Rachel F., H-74-2; widow US Soldier; Chattanooga PO
ROBERTS, F. A., A-6-4(2); Pvt G Co 7th TN Inf; 11-8-64 to 7-27-65; Robertsville PO
ROBBES, Edward, Ro-209-2; Pvt E Co 1st TN Inf; 20 Aug 61 to 1 Mar 65; Rockwood PO
ROBBINS, George, Pi-153-2; Pvt C Co 12th KY Inf; 10-3-61 to 9-17-63; Spurnier PO; CONF
ROBBINS, Harrison, S-213-3; Pvt B Co 2nd TN Inf; Robbins PO; three ribs broken, wasn't discharged by furlow only
ROBBINS, James M., Ov-137-3; Tennessee widow of; Pvt 2nd TN Inf; Monroe PO; best widow could do
ROBBINS, William, S-218-2; Lucinda widow of; Capt; Hughett PO; hip & sid, the result of rheumatism during war of rebellion, cav 7th TN Co E, 11th TN H 9 TN Cav
ROBBINS, William B., A-9-6(4); 1st Lt I Co 9th TN Cav; 5-28-63 to 7-14-65; Dutch Valley PO; piles & kidney disease & disease of testicles in REble Prison 12 mos
ROBBINSON, W. V., Cr-15-1; Pvt D Co 7th TN Cav; 14 Aug 62 to Oct 16 63; Maple Creek PO; gun shot & sore eyes
ROBBINSON, William, Ge-91-3; Sgt B Co 14th US Inf; 1 Nov 63 to 28 Mar 66; Greeneville PO; paralasis & wounded in shoulder
ROBBS, Henry, H-67-2; Pvt H Co 14th TN US Col Inf; 3-64 to 3-66; Chattanooga PO; shot in right leg, now crippled
ROBERSON, Albert, Sh-160-2; Pvt; 15th Dist
ROBERSON, Andrew W., Sm-172-3(1); Sgt K Co 1st TN Inf; 7-14-64 to 7-22-65; Gordonsville PO; rheumatism & piles
ROBERSON, Angeline, K-154-4; widow Sol; Knoxville PO
ROBERSON, Charles, Fr-110-1; Pvt A Co; 4 mos; Belvidere PO; rheumatism

ROBERSON, Charles J., Ro-210-3; Pvt I Co 1st TN Inf; 9 Aug 61 to 1 Jul 62; Rockwood PO
ROBERSON, Eli (see Bell, Elial)
ROBERSON, Frank M., La-108-1; Pvt 6th TN Cav; 11-1-63 to 7-1-65; PO omitted
ROBERSON, Freeling S., Pu-142-1; Cpl K Co 25th TN Mtd Inf; 11-10-64 to 7-65; Shuyle PO (White Co.); liver complaint
ROBERSON, Garner, K-181-4(1); Salley Frank widow of; Cav; Knoxville PO
ROBERSON, George, Col, Wh-185-1; Pvt F Co 100th KY Inf; 8-1-64 to 12-10-65; Peeled Chestnut PO; abscesses, chronic rheumatism, disease of the spine
ROBERSON, H. C., Bl-4-1; Pvt I Co 8th TN Cav; 3-1-62 to 4-1-65; Pikeville PO; CONF
ROBERSON, Isaac, D-60-1; alley back of McCrairy PO (Nashville); colored
ROBERSON, Jack, Sh-144-2; Cpl G Co 55th Col Inf; 63 to 31 Dec 65; Arlington PO
ROBERSON, James, Mu-201-1; Mt. Pleasant PO
ROBERSON, James, Bl-4-1; Lt 4th TN Cav; 7-1-62 to 4-10-65; Pikeville PO; lay 2 yrs in Northern prisons; CONF
ROBERSON, James, Lo-187-3; Pvt A Co 5th TN Inf; 27 Feb 62 to 4 Apr 65; rheumatism
ROBERSON, John, Me-91-1; Pvt C Co 3rd TN Cav; Decatur PO
ROBERSON, John, K-154-5(2); Martha J. widow of; Pvt M Co 8th TN Inf; Knoxville PO
ROBERSON, John C., We-221-7; Pvt 33rd TN Inf; Nov 62 to Feb 64; Martin PO; CONF
ROBERSON, Joseph, La-117-2; Eliza widow of; Pvt A Co TN Cav; 61 to __ (2 yrs); 15th Dist; CONF
ROBERSON, Moses, Sh-149-2; P-t A Co 61st TN Inf; May 63 to Nov 66; Raleigh PO
ROBERSON, Moses P., Ct-40-5; Pvt H Co 13th TN Cav; 9-24-63 to 9-5-65; Elizabethton PO
ROBERSON, Nat, Tr-266-1(2); Pvt D Co 2nd TN Cav; Apr 61 to 65; Hartsville PO; CONF
ROBERSON, Reason, L-103-2; Pvt H Co 70th Inf; Jan 63 to 65; Plum Point PO; have applyed for help
ROBERSON, Samuel P., Ro-207-4; Sarah E. widow of; Pvt B Co 5th TN Inf; 25 Feb 62 to 31 Mar 65; Fossil PO; rheumatism & kidney
ROBERSON, William A., Ja-85-4; Sgt A Co 4th TN Cav; 10-25-62 to 7-12-65; Georgetown PO; shot through left side
ROBERSON, William W., Mn-121-1; Pvt B Co 4th TN Inf; 1 Jan 64 to 1 Jul 65; Rose Creek PO
ROBERSON, Wylie (see Askew, Wylie)
ROBERT, Jesse, Co-67-4; Pvt H Co 6th NC Inf; 61 to __; Naillon PO; CONF
ROBERTS, Benjamin F., Ro-203-1; Lt B Co 5th TN Inf; 28 Feb 62 to 30 Mar 65; Wheat PO; disease of liver & kidney
ROBERTS, C. S., D-76-1; Pvt C Co 2nd TN Cav; Sep 3 62 to Jan 5 65; Nashville PO; gun shot wd. left foot &c
ROBERTS, Chas., Sh-199-1; Sgt 1st IA Reg; 63 to 65; 46 Broadway St, Memphis PO
ROBERTS, Charles W., Ro-202-6; Pvt E Co 4th TN Inf; 11 Aug 61 to Aug 64; Kingston PO; rheumatism & heart disease
ROBERTS, David, Hw-122-2; Pvt K Co 8th TN Cav; 15 Aug 63 to never discharged; Clover Botton PO; chr. diarhea & chr. rheumatism, almost totally disabled
ROBERTS, David F., Ge-83-2; Pvt C Co 13th TN Cav; 24 Sep 63 to __; Horse Creek PO; hait through wright leg
ROBERTS, David R., Wl-298-1; Pvt I Co 4th TN Mtd Inf; 16 Feb 65 to 20 Aug 65; Round Top PO; kidney disease, by measles, exposure while in the service
ROBERTS, Edward C., Ro-211-1; 1st Lt H Co 3rd TN Inf; 10 Feb 62 to 23 Feb 65; Webster PO; wounded in left leg May 14th 1864
ROBERTS, Eli H., Se-225-2; Sgt M Co 2nd TN Cav?; 8 Nov 62 to 6 Jul 65; Millican PO; neuralgia and heart disease 25 yrs, system debilitated
ROBERTS, Elijah, De-25-1; Mahley widow of; Capt A Co 6th TN Cav; 18 Sep 62 to 15 Jan 65; Decaturville PO
ROBERTS, F. R., Cr-16-2; Cpl F Co 7th TN Cav; Sep 29 62 to __ (4 mos); Huntingdon PO; was captured, failed to get discharge

ROBERTS, George, Se-222-2; Ketiel? M. widow of; Sevierville PO
ROBERTS, George, Fe-41-1; Pvt D Co 1st TN Inf; 61 to 64; Jamestown PO
ROBERTS, George P., Ov-137-3; Pvt Batys Scouts; 1-62 to 65; Eagle Creek PO
ROBERTS, George R., Me-88-2; Sgt E Co 5th TN Inf; 3-2-62 to 4-4-65; Brittsville PO
ROBERTS, George W., Pu-143-1; Pvt C Co 8th TN Inf; 1-1-65 to 8-17-65; Avolon PO
ROBERTS, Houston, De-25-1; C Sgt E Co 6th TN Cav; 18 Sep 62 to 24 Jul 65; Decaturville PO
ROBERTS?, Isaac A., Ro-208-2; Pvt F Co 2nd OH 4? Cell?; 9 Aug 63 to 19 Aug 65; Welker Mines PO; shot in right hand and left leg
ROBERTS, James, Gr-73-1; Pvt D Co 4th TN Inf; __ to 2 Aug 65; Westerville PO
ROBERTS, James, H-54-2(3); Chattanooga PO
ROBERTS, James D., H-60-1; Drummer 53rd OH Inf; 5-10-61 to 9-10-65; Chattanooga PO
ROBERTS, James D., K-168-1; Pvt C Co; Knoxville PO
ROBERTS, James G., Ro-206-3; Capt G Co 1st TN Inf; 9 Aug 61 to 23 Feb 65; Kingston PO
ROBERTS, James M., Ro-207-2; Eliza J. widow of; Pvt A Co 5th TN Inf; 26 Feb 62 to 62; Paint Rock PO
ROBERTS, John, Se-223-1; Pvt E Co 9th TN Cav; 1 Oct 63 to 11 Sep 65; Pigeon Forge PO; bronchitis & diarrhea
ROBERTS, John, Sm-168-2; Pvt F Co 1st TN Inf; 2-64 to 5-65; Pleasant Shade PO; yellow janders and measles, result weak breast
ROBERTS, John, Me-94-2; Pvt D Co 7th TN Mtd Inf; Euchee PO: deserter (marked)
ROBERTS, John, Ct-45-3; Malvaly Grindstaff formerly widow of; Sgt F Co 13th TN Cav; 9-1-63 to __; Carter Furnace PO; killed at Marion VA 12-24-64
ROBERTS, John, Ct-40-4; Pvt H Co 2nd TN Inf; 7-22-62 to 1-5-65; Elizabethton PO; gunshot wounds
ROBERTS, John, K-154-2; Knoxville PO
ROBERTS, John, H-64-1; Anna Kelly widow of; Sgt 8th TN Inf; 63 to __; Chattanooga PO; lost in the war, John Roberts has never been heard of by his family since the war, can't get date of enlistment
ROBERTS, John A., K-160-1; Sgt D Co 3rd TN; 10 Feb 62 to 14 May 63; Knoxville PO; disease of lungs & rheumatism
ROBERTS, John H., Se-227-3; Pvt E Co 9th TN Cav; 63 to 65; Trundles X Roads PO; diarrhoea & piles
ROBERTS, John W., Je-146-2; White Pines PO; soldier not home, cant give dates
ROBERTS, Jonathan, Ro-203-5(1); Pvt D Co 1st TN Art; 30 Oct 63 to 22 Jul 65; Wheat PO; blindness
ROBERTS, Joseph, Ha-117-1; Nancy M. widow of; Pvt 62 to 65; Kyle's Ford PO; discharge lost and can't get dates
ROBERTS, Joseph D., Pu-145-3(4); Pvt I Co 5th Cav Vol; 11-24-62 to 8-14-65; Silver Point PO
ROBERTS, Levi S., Se-223-3; Blacksmith K Co 2nd TN Cav; 8 Nov 62 to 6 Jul 65; Hendersons Springs PO
ROBERTS, Lindsey A., A-5-4; Pvt C Co 19th USC __; 11-63 to 7-17-65; Clinton PO; right arm amputated
ROBERTS, Matilda, Se-227-2; widow of US Sol; 9th Dist
ROBERTS, Matlock J., Dk-31-2; Almarinda F. widow of; Sgt K Co 5th TN Cav; 5-63 to 8-14-65; Alexandria PO
ROBERTS, Nancy, Ha-116-1; widow US Sol; 13th Dist
ROBERTS, Rachel (black), R-157-1; Spring City PO
ROBERTS, Richard, D-72-5; Mary M. widow of; Capt F Co 49th TN Inf; Dec 14 62 to Feb 16 63; Nashville PO; in prison 7 mos, discharged on dr. certificate; CONF
ROBERTS, Ruben, H-56-2; Pvt F Co 6th TN Inf; 3-8-63 to 7-10-65; East End PO
ROBERTS, Ruben Z., K-169-2; 1st Lt G Co 53rd PA; 16 Oct 61 to 12 Jul 64; Knoxville PO
ROBERTS, Samantha, Mo-130-3; widow of US Sol; 16th Civil Dist
ROBERTS, Samuel, Ro-211-1; Pvt E Co 1st TN Inf; 20 Aug 61 to 17 Sep 64; Webster PO; rheumatism and heart disease
ROBERTS, Samuel H., A-10-1; Pvt J Co 9th TN Cav; 1-26-64 to 9-11-65; Briceville PO
ROBERTS, Sarah J. (see Swaggerty, Roley?)
ROBERTS, Squire L., M-108-1; Pvt D Co 8th TN Mtd Inf; 2-10-65 to 8-31-65; Salt Lick PO; rheumatism
ROBERTS, Spencer, We-231-1; #13 Weakley PO
ROBERTS, Thomas, Sh-145-1; Sgt I Co 12th TN Cav; Apr 63 to Nov 65; Millington PO
ROBERTS, Thomas, Mg-197-4; Chaplin 12th OH Cav; Jan 64 to Dec 65; Wartburg PO; kidney disease, time not known
ROBERTS, Thomas F., Jo-153-2; Landsman, Ship Sabion; 16 Jun 64 to 27 Jun 66; Little Doe PO; bronchitis
ROBERTS, Thomas J., Mg-200-2; Sgt Co B 1st TN Inf; 3 Mar 62 to May 65; Kismet PO
ROBERTS, Thomas L., Ro-201-1; Sgt 5th TN Inf; 25 Feb 62 to 4 Apr 65; Kingston PO; scared (sic) in face by shell
ROBERTS, W. M., Hu-103-3; Pvt H Co 6th GA Inf; 10 Sep 61 to 10 Jul 64; crossed through, probably CONF; PO omitted
ROBERTS, Watson, R-158-2; Pvt E Co 9th TN Cav; 10-63 to 5-65; Carp PO; bone scurvy, pensioner
ROBERTS, William, T-216-1; Pvt G Co 62nd IL Inf; Feb 63 to Mar 65; Corona PO
ROBERTS, William, Se-230-1; Pvt A Co 9th TN Cav; Richison's Cove PO; diarrhea; CONF
ROBERTS, William, Di-30-2; Pvt E Co 14th NC Inf; 61 to 65; Dickson PO; CONF
ROBERTS, William, Dy-29-2; Pvt; Trimble PO; crippled, could not learn much about him; CONF
ROBERTS, William, R-158-2; Pvt G Co 69th TN Mtd Inf; __ to 6-30-65; Pin Hook PO (Meigs Co.)
ROBERTS, William, Ct-45-3; Elizabethton PO; CONF
ROBERTS, William, Ge-90-3; Pvt D Co 6th IN Cav; 11 Jun 63 to 31 Aug 65; Greeneville PO; spinal defect, hurt by schewing a mule
ROBERTS, William, Hw-132-1; Pvt D Co 31st TN Cav; 62 to 65; Strahl PO; wounded by shot in the leg; CONF
ROBERTS, William, Ro-210-12; Pvt G Co 3rd TN Inf; 7 May 61 to 5 Aug 62; Cardiff PO; CONF
ROBERTS, William E., Je-136-1; 64 to 65; Dandridge PO
ROBERTS, William H., H-54-3; Pvt D Co 12th IN Vol; 10-18-64 to 7-7-65; Sherman Heights PO
ROBERTS, William H., K-160-2; 1st Lt Adj 3rd TN; 10 Feb 62 to 26 Feb 66; Knoxville PO; rheumatism
ROBERTS, William M., Ro-204-5; Pvt G Co 1st TN Inf; 11 Aug 61 to __; Elverton PO; loss of right eye, discharge not found
ROBERTS, William M., Se-225-2; 1st Sgt M Co 9th TN Cav?; 8 Nov 62 to 6 Jul 65; Trotters Store PO; rheumatism resulting in heart disease 25 yrs
ROBERTS, William S. P., Mc-112-10; Pvt A Co TN Scout and Guide; 9-15-63 to 2-20-64; Mount Verd PO
ROBERTS, Wright L., Ro-202-6; Pvt M Co 11th TN Cav; Nov 62 to 15 Sep 65; Kingston PO; rheumatism & heart disease
ROBERTSON, Alfred, D-90-1; alias Afred, Wiley; Pvt F Co 13th TN Col Inf; Sep 15 63 to Jan 10 66; Hobbs & Beer's McLemore & Cedart St., Nashville PO; shot in left hand, not disabled from work much
ROBERTSON, B. A., Ha-11-42; Cpl D Co 9th VA; Yellow Springs PO; CONF
ROBERTSON, Caleb, Se-223-2; Pvt M Co 2nd TN Cav; 8 Nov 62 to 6 Jul 65; Pigeon Forge PO; diarrhea, liver & kidney
ROBERTSON, Daniel G., Br-9-2; Pvt E Co 4th TN Cav; Cleveland PO
ROBERTSON, Dio C., Se-223-1; Pvt M Co 2nd TN Cav; 8 Nov 62 to 6 Jul 65; Pigeon Forge PO
ROBERTSON, George, D-54-3; Amand Hill widow of; Pvt 15th US Col Inf; Nashville PO
ROBERTSON, George L., H-54-3; Pvt D Co 50th IL; 61 to 62; Sherman Heights PO
ROBERTSON, James, Pi-153-1; Pvt C Co 1st KY Cav; 5-3-63 to 9-6-65; Chanute PO

ROBERTSON, James, H-64-3; Cpl D Co 114th KY Inf; 6-16-62 to __; Chattanooga PO; shot in left ankel
ROBERTSON, James C., Ct-41-2; Pvt C Co 4th TN Inf; 9-6-63 to 8-2-65; South Wattauga PO; kidney trouble
ROBERTSON, Jennie, Sh-149-4; Widow Sol; 6th Civil Dist
ROBERTSON, John B., Ce-28-1; Pvt B Co 1st AL Cav; 6 Feb 64 to 20 Oct 65; Lillamay PO; wounded in thigh
ROBERTSON, Mc., Le-118-1; Pvt G Co 16th IL Cav; 62 to 64; Rockdale PO; dates cannot be obtained
ROBERTSON, R. S., Ca-20-1; Pvt A Co 4th TN Cav; 12-15-62 to 12-24-64; Woodbury PO
ROBERTSON, Rebeckah (see Franklin, Jery)
ROBERTSON, Ritchard T., Cl-48-3; Pvt E Co 2nd TN Cav; 7-4-61 to 4-9-65; Old Town PO; health greatly impaired; CONF
ROBERTSON, Samuel S., La-112-1; Pvt; Ulnus PO
ROBERTSON, Spencer, D-99-1; Pvt A Co 15th VA Inf; May __ to Jul __; Nashville PO; wounded in both legs, in a bad fix, poorhouse
ROBERTSON, Thomas, K-165-1; Pvt H (N?) Co; 28 May 64 to 31 Mar 66; Knoxville PO
ROBERTSON, Thomas, F-47-1; Pvt D Co 13th TN Cav; 61 to 66; Williston PO
ROBERTSON, Tugner? G., Me-92-1; Nancy J. widow of; A Co 10th TN Cav; Hester Mills PO
ROBERTSON, Washington, K-165-1; Sgt N Co US Hvy? Cav; 28 May 64 to 31 Mar 66; Knoxville PO
ROBERTSON, Wm., Sn-250-1; Pvt C Co 2nd __; 10-16-62 to 10-4-65; Castalian Springs PO
ROBERTSON, William, Mt-138-1; (blk) US Sol; Dist 7, New Providence PO
ROBERTSON, William, Sm-169-2; Pvt; Elmwood PO
ROBERTSON, William, D-67-3; Pvt Col Inf; Nashville PO
ROBERTSON, Zedoc R., Mu-210-2; Pvt; 61 to 65; Garters Creek PO; enlisted at beginning and served during entire war
ROBESON, Green R., Mr-96-2; Pvt B Co 2nd NC Inf; 9-63 to 8-18-65; Cedar Spring PO; urinary trouble
ROBESON, Hiram, Mc-109-2; Pvt C Co 3rd TN Cav; 12-16-62 to 6-10-65; Ziegler PO; eyes weak, gunshot wound
ROBESON, Jerre, R-162-4; Pvt E Co 17th US Inf; 2 yrs; Dayton PO; captured by bushwackers & robbed of discharge
ROBESON, Malinda C., Mc-112-11; widow; 7th Dist
ROBINETT, Malinda (sic), Ha-114-1; Pvt E Co 11th VA Cav; 2 Dec 62 to 17 Jan 64; Xenophon PO
ROBINS, John H., Wy-173-1; Mary A. widow of; Pvt F Co 6th TN Cav; 9-21-62 to 6-10-65; Houston PO
ROBINS, Joseph A., He-63-2; Pvt C Co 7th TN Cav; 63 to Jun 7 65; PO omitted
ROBINS, Lewis W., Hd-54-3; US Sol; PO omitted
ROBINS, Mclur? M., Ma-114-2; Pvt C Co 31st TN Inf; Jul 61 to Mar 30 65; Pinson PO; CONF
ROBINS, Silvester, Ov-139-2; Mary R. widow of; Pvt 2nd TN Inf; 61 to 63; Hanging Limb PO
ROBINS, William, C-24-3; Pvt A Co 1st TN Inf; 8-2-61 to 9-17-64; Agee PO; chronic diarhea & disease of liver
ROBINSON, Alvin J., We-234-1; Sarah Langly former widow of; Pvt 6th TN Cav; 10-12-62 to died 1863 (1 yr 3 mos); Greenfield PO; dide at Bolivar TN, TN State Gard
ROBINSON, Andrew, W-196-2; Quartermaster Sgt G Co 7th WI Vol; 9-14-61 to 6-26-62; McMinnville PO; hernia
ROBINSON, Awdy A., Dk-34-6(5); Pvt A Co 5th TN Cav; 12-1-63 to __; Close PO; measles
ROBINSON, Benjamin, Sh-191-3; Pvt A Co Hvy Art; 6-4-63 to 4-66; Memphis PO; disabled is an invalid
ROBINSON, Charles N., P-150-2; US Sol; 2nd Dist
ROBINSON, Charls T., Mo-110-3(1); Pvt F Co 155th IL Inf; 2-25-65 to 9-4-65; Mouse Creek PO
ROBINSON, Columbus H., Dk-34-1; Christopher C. Robinson alias; Pvt I Co 4th TN Cav; __ to 8-25-65 (11 mos); Dowelltown PO; crippled in left ankle
ROBINSON, Daniel, G-55-1; Pvt B Co 60th Col Inf; 10-62 to 12-65; Trenton PO; lost discharge and does not know dates

ROBINSON, David, Mu-190-1; Pvt A Co 2nd TN Mtd Inf; 9-15-63 to not discharged; Culleoka PO; has not his papers & dont know date of enlistment or discharge
ROBINSON, David, O-141-2; Cpl C Co 60th Vol IN Inf; Mar 22 62 to Mar 22 65; Union City PO
ROBINSON, Elijah, Wl-298-2; 2nd Lt F Co 4th TN Mtd Inf; 29 Oct 64 to 25 Aug 65; Auburn PO; knee cap fractured, not able to work but little
ROBINSON, G. W., G-57-3; Pvt I Co 13th TN Cav; 63 to 65; Yorkville PO
ROBINSON, Gilmore, Gi-123-3; PO omitted
ROBINSON, Henry, F-37-2; Nannie Lennon formerly widow of; Cpl D Co 119th US Col Inf; Yum Yum PO; wounded
ROBINSON, Henry, Co-63-1; Teamster D Co 11th TN Cav; 2 yrs; Newport PO; prisiner taken to Richmond prison
ROBINSON, Hezekia, Fr-107-1; Pvt D Co 12th IN Cav; Dec 1 63 to Nov 10 65; Winchester PO; partely blind
ROBINSON, Houstin S., D-70-1; Sailor; 1022 Market St, Nashville PO
ROBINSON, Howell, Sh-200-2; Pvt C Co 59th US Col Inf; 6-1-63 to 1-31-66; 51 McKinley St, Memphis PO; chronic diarrhea
ROBINSON, James, Cl-53-1; Mary E. widow of; Pvt D Co 32nd KY Cav; 10-28-62 to 8-12-63; Springdale PO
ROBINSON, James, Dk-35-2; Pvt K Co 5th TN Cav; Temperance Hall PO
ROBINSON, James, Dk-39-3(1); Pvt K Co 1st TN Mtd Inf; 11-9-64 to 7-22-65; Dekalb PO; hemorrhoids and chronic diarrhea
ROBINSON, James, Dk-34-2; 3rd Sgt F Co 4th TN Mtd Inf; 9-4-64 to 8-25-65; Dowelltown PO; neuralgia
ROBINSON, James B., F-44-1; Pvt B Co 14th TN; Oct 62 to Apr 20 65; PO omitted; CONF
ROBINSON, James H., Mg-197-4; Wartburg PO
ROBINSON, James M., Ja-87-2; Pvt E Co 6th IN Cav; 1-11-63 to 9-15-65; Ooltewah PO
ROBINSON, James N., Mc-110-1; Cpl B Co 1st US Inf; 1-24-64 to 11-27-65; Rock Creek PO
ROBINSON, Jasper, Sh-178-2; Pvt I Co US __; 11-10-64 to 66; 396 Monroe St, Memphis PO
ROBINSON, John, Mc-110-2(1); Pvt B Co 7th TN Inf; 9-12-64 to 7-27-65; Mt. Vera PO
ROBINSON, John, D-91-1; Celia widow of (now married); Pvt D Co 12th Inf; 1 Aug 63 to 16 Jan 66; Primitive Baptist Chur., Broat St, Nashville PO
ROBINSON, John, K-154-4; Pvt M Co 1st TN? Hvy Art; __ to 31 May 66; Knoxville PO
ROBINSON, John, Fe-42-1; Pvt D Co 5th TN; 8-7-62 to 6-25-65; Jamestown PO
ROBINSON, John B., D-67-1; 5th TN Cav; 61 to 65; Nashville PO
ROBINSON, John E., Dk-35-2; Pvt F Co 5th TN Cav; Temperance Hall PO
ROBINSON, John W., Wl-298-1; Pvt K Co 10th TN Inf; 13 Oct 62 to 23 Jun 65; Round Top PO
ROBINSON, Joseph, D-92-1; Acklin, Joseph (on same line); Pvt E Co MI Lt Art; 1 Oct 63 to 30 Oct 65; Nashville PO; deaf partially
ROBINSON, Joseph D., Sh-191-1; Sgt H Co 59th Col Inf; 6-20-63 to 1-31-66; Memphis PO
ROBINSON, Karmon, Dk-39-3(1); Pvt K Co 1st TN Mtd Inf; 9-21-64 to 7-22-65; Dekalb PO; chronic rheumatism
ROBINSON, King, M-107-4; Pvt D Co 9th KY Inf; 10-25-61 to 12-17-64; Gibb's Cross Roads PO; gunshot wound left side & shoulder
ROBINSON, Lemuel A., D-97-1; Sgt G Co TN Cav; Mar 1 63 to Mar 1 64; Nashville PO; CONF
ROBINSON, Levi D., Dk-33-1; Pvt F Co 4th TN Inf; 10-2-64 to 8-25-65; 4th Civil Dist; hemerage of lungs
ROBINSON, Lilbern, Hw-127-4; Mary Vincent formerly widow of; Rogersville PO
ROBINSON, Loyd, T-214-1; Pvt I Co 41st US Inf; Dec 64 to Jun 65; Mason Depot PO; rheumatism
ROBINSON, Nelson, Sh-157-8; Pvt F? Co 3rd USB; 62 to 65; Ensley PO; invilid
ROBINSON, Richard, Lo-190-2; Pvt K Co 9th TN Cav; 20 Jun 63 to 11 Sep 65; Loudon PO; chronic diarrhoea

ROBINSON, Ritchard T., Cl-48-2; Pvt B Co 1st TN Lt Art; 4-1-63 to 7-20-65; Pleasant PO; general disbility
ROBINSON, Robert, Sh-179-1(2); Hattie Henderson widow of; Pvt; Memphis PO; doesn't remember
ROBINSON, Rufus, Un-259-2; Pvt E Co 2nd TN Cav; 15 Oct 62 to 15 Oct 63; Sharps Chapel PO; CONF
ROBINSON, Sampson C., Ct-45-3; Pvt E Co 3rd NC Cav; Carter Furnace PO; recruiting officer, sick, never returned to command, no discharge
ROBINSON, Samuel, Sm-166-1; Pvt A Co 1st TN Inf; 12-18-63 to 1-30-65; Carthage PO
ROBINSON, Samuel C., Lo-189-3(1); Pvt M Co 2nd OH Hvy Art; 12 Feb 64 to 29 Aug 65; 4th Civil Dist
ROBINSON, Solomon C., J-82-2; Pvt L Co 10th IN Cav; 12-30-63 to 8-31-65; Mayfield PO; disease lungs
ROBINSON, Tyre R., Pu-142-1; Pvt I Co 5th TN Vol Cav; 11-16-62 to 8-14-65; Verble PO; paralasis
ROBINSON, William, Mg-197-4; Clia widow of; Pvt B Co 5th TN Inf; Mar 62 to __; Wartburg PO
ROBINSON, William, K-161-3; Caroline widow of; Knoxville PO
ROBINSON, William, Mg-199-3; Celia widow of; Pvt B Co 5th TN Inf; Emory PO
ROBINSON, William C., K-165-3; Pvt G Co 1st TN Inf; 9 Aug 61 to 23 Feb 65; 16 Chamberlin St, Knoxville PO
ROBINSON, William F., H-68-3; Pvt G Co 33rd WI Inf; 3-20-65 to __; Chattanooga PO
ROBINSON, William M., Sh-159-4; Pvt A Co 1st MS Inf; Aug 61 to 65; Memphis, 52 Beale St, PO; captured; CONF
ROBINSON, Wilson, Wi-274-1; Pvt C Co 42nd TN Inf; 64 to Dec 65; Franklin PO
ROBINSON, Wingate T., Dk-34-1; 1st Lt K Co 5th TN Cav; 8-6-63 to 8-14-65; Dowelltown PO; throat, lungs & piles, served as scout from 3-4-63 to 8-6-63
ROBISON, Benj. W., K-179-1; Pvt G Co 1st TN Inf; 9 Aug 61 to 17 Sep 64; Rodelin PO
ROBISON, Charles, Sh-188-2; Pvt B Co 59th US Col; 63 to 64; Maxwell, Memphis PO
ROBISON, George W., Mn-121-1; Pvt A Co 6th TN Cav; 4 Oct 63 to 26 Jul 65; Bethel Springs PO
ROBISON, Isaac N. P., K-172-3; Pvt G Co 6th TN Inf; 62 to 65; 14th Dist, South Knoxville PO
ROBISON, James M., A-4-5; Pvt K Co 9th TN Cav; 2-4-64 to 9-11-65; Coal Creek PO
ROBISON, Jerry, K-158-1; Nance B. widow of; Pvt; not known to wife; 61 to 65; Knoxville, 9 E Clinch PO; shot in leg, bone broken
ROBISON, John, Jo-150-2; Pvt G Co 39th NJ Inf; Key Station PO; sight
ROBISON, Thomas L., Mn-121-1; Pvt A Co 6th TN Cav; 11 Aug 62 to 26 Jul 65; Bethel Springs PO
ROBISON, William, Sh-168-1; Pvt A Co 88th TN Inf; Feb 64 to Feb 20 65; 78 Washington St, Memphis PO
ROBISON, William M., Cr-17-2; Pvt C Co 7th TN Cav; 1-1-65 to 8-14-65; Family PO; evil, resulting from pneumonia and fever settling in legs
ROBNETT, James S., Wy-172-1; Pvt A Co 2nd TN Mtd Inf; 10-2-63 to 10-14-64; Waynesboro PO; festula & piles
ROBNETT, Joseph S., Wy-172-1; 3rd Sgt A Co 2nd TN Mtd Inf; 10-2-63 to 10-14-64; Waynesboro PO; piles
ROBTERS (sic), Lewis, Hd-51-1; Pvt D Co; 25 Dec 61 to 7 Apr 66; Pickens PO; CONF
ROBTS (sic), Leroy F., We-223-2; Pvt H Co 33rd TN Inf; Sep 62 to Dec 63; Palmersville PO; CONF
ROBY, William, H-73-2(1); Pvt 63rd AL Inf; 6-61 to 5-65; Chattanooga PO; poor sight since the war; CONF
ROCCO, Henry, Sh-191-2; 1st Sgt G Co IN; 62 to 65; Memphis PO
ROCHELL, Eli S., Gi-122-1; Pvt (4 yrs); Prospect Sta. PO; CONF
ROCHELL, Rufus, La-112-2; Pvt H Co 2nd TN Mtd Inf; 12-7-63 to 1-21-65; Chisem PO
ROCKAFELLOW, Theodore P., Lo-187-1; Pvt I Co 13th PA Cav; 23 Feb 64 to 14 Jul 65; Loudon PO; sunstroke followed by brain fever
ROCKHOLT, Franklin, Me-90-2(1); Pvt D Co 5th TN Mtd Inf; 8-30-64 to 6-20-65; Meigs PO

ROCKHOLT, Thomas, Me-90-2(1); Rachel C. widow of; Pvt D Co 5th TN Mtd Inf; Goodfield PO
ROCKNITZ, Charles, D-91-2; Pvt 13th IN Bat; Sep 62 to Jun 65; Market House, Nashville PO
ROCKWELL, Morgan, H-56-6; St. Elmo PO
RODDIE?, William H., Di-30-1; Lt I Co 142nd TN Inf; 8-4-62 to 5-65; Dickson PO
RODDY, Christopher C., Bo-20-1; Pvt C Co 6th TN Inf; 4-18-62 to 4-27-65; Bank PO
RODDY, Holston, Mu-210-5; Pvt C Co Ths. Ley Inf; 10-62 to 3-31-65; Carters Creek PO; CONF
RODDY, John, K-170-1; Pvt 6th TN Inf; 63 to 65; Knoxville PO
RODEHEAVER, J. J., C-33-5; Pvt E Co 6th WV Cav; 3-64 to 5-66; Newcomb PO
RODEHEAVER, T. H., C-33-5; Cpl H Co 6th WV Cav; 6-28-61 to 8-15-64; Newcomb PO; wound gunshot shot at Bull Run 28 Aug 62
RODERICK, Adolphus, Mc-113-2; Pvt H Co 3rd TN Cav; 10-1-63 to 8-3-65; Riceville PO
RODES, Alonzo, Gi-132-2; Sgt F Co 110th USCV; Dec 6 63 to Feb 6 66; Wales PO
RODES, Benjamin, Gi-132-2; Cpl G Co 12th USCV; Jul 22 63 to FEb 18 66; Ridell PO
RODES, Barbary (see Collier, Joseph)
RODES, Simon, Gi-127-1; Pvt F Co 111th TN C Inf; Jan 6 64 to Apr 30 66; Pulaski PO
RODES, Wm., Gi-132-4; PO omitted
RODGERS, Alexander, R-161-5; Mary A. Hutchison formerly widow of; Pvt F Co 5th TN Inf; 2-25-62 to __; Dayton PO
RODGERS, Austin, F-39-2(1); Pvt D Co 57th US Col Inf; 63 to 15 Apr 66; PO omitted
RODGERS, Canida H., C-8-1; Lt C Co 1st TN Inf; 8-9-61 to 9-17-64; PO omitted; chronic rheumatism
RODGERS, Eligh A., Dy-21-1; Pvt D Co 10th TN Cav; 4 Nov 63 to May 8 65; Fowlkes Sta. PO
RODGERS, Elijah, K-182-3; Riverdale PO
RODGERS, Henry, Mu-196-1; Pvt B Co 13th Reg; May 61 to 63?; Columbia PO; left arm shattered by bursting gun in the army
RODGERS, Henry N., Wa-263-3; Elizabeth Mary Shields widow of; Cpl B Co 4th TN Cav; May Day PO; killed in the war
RODGERS, J. C., La-117-1; Pvt C Co 28th MS Cav; Oct 62 to __ (2 yrs 11 mos); 15th Dist; CONF
RODGERS, James H., Un-259-3; Pvt C Co 8th TN Inf; 1 Feb 63 to 30 Jan 65; Sharps Chapel PO; piles in bowels
RODGERS, James M., Wa-260-1; Pvt F Co 8th Reg Cav; Nov 26 64 to Aug 8 65; Nola Chucky PO; lung & kidney disese
RODGERS, Jeremiah, Wa-260-1; Sgt L Co 1st Reg Cav; Sep 21 62 to 5 Jun 65; Nola Chucky PO; could not come at his discharge
RODGERS, John R., Mo-123-2; Pvt H Co 10th TN Cav; Mt. Vernon PO; I could not find out the dates
RODGERS, Jonathan N., Ro-202-2; Pvt C Co 1st TN Inf; 1 Feb 61 to 19 Jul 65; Union X Roads PO; lung disease
RODGERS, Joseph, Ro-209-3; Cpl E Co 11th TN Inf; 1 Oct 61 to 26 Sep 65; Glen Alice PO; CONF
RODGERS, Levi, Sm-173-2; Pvt H Co 5th TN Cav; 10-11-62 to 8-14-65; Brush Creek PO; prisoner at Andersonville 8 mos
RODGERS, Mose, Me-51-2; US Sol; 20th Civil Dist
RODGERS, Prinnen?, K-156-5; Pvt H Co 1st TN Art; 2 Jun 64 to 31 Mar 66; 96 E. Church St, Knoxville PO
RODGERS, Stephen, B-7-2; Pvt F Co 5th TN Cav; 9-25-62 to 6-25-65; PO omitted
RODGERS, Thomas J., Sm-173-2; Pvt B Co 5th TN Cav; 8-1-62 to 6-5-65; Brush Creek PO; rheumatism, prisoner at Andersonville 8 mos
RODGERS, Thomas L., R-162-2; Dayton PO
RODGERS, William A., K-174-3(2); Surgeon 3rd TN Inf; 31 Aug 61 to 10 Jul 64; Graveston PO; bronchitis and hemorrhage 26 yrs, partly disable
RODGERS, William R., R-161-6; Quartermaster Sgt L Co 3rd TN Cav; 6-10-64 to 6-10-65; Dayton PO
RODGERS, William W., Ro-203-6; Sgt F Co 5th TN Inf; 28 Feb 62 to Mar 65; PO omitted
RODGERS, Willis, H-69-2; Pvt E Co 15th Mis (MO or MS?) Inf; Chattanooga PO
RODOM, George, Col, Hd-45-1; Pvt 15th OH Inf; 63 to __; Whitton PO

ROE, Robert, K-179-1; Pvt D Co 3rd TN Inf; 10 Feb 62 to 23 Feb 65; Rodelin PO
ROE, Robert S., Hw-133-2; Orderly Sgt G Co 10th TN Cav; 29 Oct 63 to 26 Aug 65; Burem's Store PO; chronic diareah & rheumatism
ROE, Wesley, G-56-1; Pvt; Trenton PO
ROESCH, John W., D-45-3; alias John Williams; Pvt B Co 47th MS Inf; 63 to 63 (9 mos); Nashville PO
ROGAN, Ben, Sn-252-3; Pvt C Co 14th US Inf; 11-16-63 to __; Gallatin PO
ROGERS, A. A., De-26-2; Mary J. widow of; O Co 7th ; 14 Aug 62 to __ (1 yr); Poplar Springs PO (Henderson Co.)
ROGERS, A. L., Ha-113-3; Lt L Co 10th TN Cav; 17 Sep 63 to Mar 64; Sneedville PO
ROGERS, Andy, H-57-1; Pvt K Co 44th US Inf; 63 to 65; Orchard Knob PO
ROGERS, Barnabus, Me-88-1; Pvt B Co 7th TN Inf; 9-5-63 to 8-1-65; Birchwood PO
ROGERS, Charles C., Ro-211-3; Cpl C Co 98th NY Inf; Jan 61 to 65; Harriman PO; scrofula of liver
ROGERS, Chauncey P., Sh-149-1; Col 83rd PA Inf; Aug 8 61 to Jun 28 65; Memphis PO; gun shot in foot, knee, hip & shoulder
ROGERS, Coleman, Gi-133-3; Virginia Ami widow of; Pvt 1st TN; 61 to 62; Bufords PO
ROGERS, E. S., K-167-5; Pvt D Co 19th TN Cav; Aug 64 to Mar 65; Knoxville PO
ROGERS, Eliza (see Brooks, Archibald T.)
ROGERS, Ephraim, H-49-2; Margaret Martin formerly widow of; Pvt; Lake Side PO; shot through the thigh
ROGERS, Gilbert E., We-226-2; Pvt I Co 4th E TN Cav; Oct 63 to Jul 65; Sharon PO; lost papers, forgot days of month
ROGERS, Harbert S., Hw-119-2(1); Lt L Co 8th TN Cav--17 Sep 63 to __ (1 yr 5 mos 13 days); Capt--Mar 65 to 20 Sep 65; Lee Valley PO; disease back & left hip
ROGERS, Harrison H., Un-257-3; Pvt C Co 8th TN Inf; Aug 62 to 64; New Prospect PO
ROGERS, Henderson, Cl-47-1; Pvt C Co 1st TN Inf; 8-9-61 to 9-17-64; Speedwell PO
ROGERS, Huse, Ro-210-8; Lt E Co 11th TN Cav (Union?); 1 Mar 64 to __; Pvt P? Co 29th NC Inf, no dates (CONF) Rockwood PO
ROGERS, Jackson, Hm-107-4; Pvt D Co 4th TN Inf; 18 Jan 62 to 65; Springvale PO; heart disease, discharge burned, dates forgotten
ROGERS, James, F-44-1; Pvt D Co 48th TN; Dec 27 61 to Jun 17 65; PO omitted; CONF
ROGERS, James B., B-14-1; Pvt F Co 6th TN Cav; 9-6-62 to 6-25-65; Brandville PO; old and feeble
ROGERS, James C., H-58-5; Pvt A Co 6th TN Mtd Inf; 8-2-64 to 30-30-65; Retro PO
ROGERS, James F., Ca-16-1; Sgt D Co 7th TN Cav; Aug 14 62 to Nov 25 63; __ Musician G Co 2nd TN Mtd Inf; Dec 14 63 to Mar 27 65; Huntingdon PO; Jun 63 reenlisted Comp C 7th TN Cav, Jul 6th 63
ROGERS, James M., Hw-119-4(2); Sarah E. Thomas formerly widow of; Sgt A Co 1st TN Cav; 15 Apr 62 to 15 Apr 65; Alum Well PO; from measles, now deceased
ROGERS, Jessee, Hm-107-4; Pvt L Co 8th TN Cav; 1 Oct 63 to 11 Sep 65; Springvale PO; inflamation of stomach
ROGERS, Jessee N., Mc-116-1; Pvt D Co 5th TN Inf; 11-13-62 to 6-19-65; Longs Mills PO; diarhea & lung disease
ROGERS, Jessie, Hu-103-3; M. P. widow of; Pvt E Co 10th TN Inf; 10 Aug 61 to 20 Dec 64; PO omitted
ROGERS, John, Bl-5-3; Pvt D Co 6th TN Mtd Inf; 9-12-64 to 6-30-65; Pitts X Roads PO
ROGERS, John A., We-225-4(3); Sol; Dresden PO
ROGERS, John B., H-49-4; 3rd Sgt K Co 4th TN Cav; 5-14-64 to 7-16-65; Lake Side PO
ROGERS, John C., H-49-6; Pvt F Co 6th TN Mtd Inf; Daisy PO
ROGERS, John C., H-50-3(1); Sgt F Co 6th R TN Mtd Inf; 9-1-64 to 6-3-65; Daisy PO; caused defect in hearing
ROGERS, John H., H-49-4; Rebecca widow of; Pvt 5th TN Cav; Lake Side PO
ROGERS, John H., He-63-1; Cpl A Co 7th TN Cav; Aug 16 62 to Aug 6 65; PO omitted
ROGERS, Louis, Hw-129-2; Eliza widow of; Pvt; Mooresburg PO
ROGERS, Milton, D-50-2; Lizzie widow of; Lt 69th OH Inf; 4 yrs; Nashville PO
ROGERS, Paul M., H-49-7; Pvt F Co 6th TN Mtd Inf; 9-3-64 to 6-30-65; Daisy PO
ROGERS, Phil, D-70-1; Sol; 1020 Market St, Nashville PO
ROGERS, Pleasant C., H-49-4; Pvt I Co 2nd E TN Inf; 2-6-62 to 2-13-65; Lake Side PO
ROGERS, Pumas, K-156-6; Matilda Cox widow of; and widow of Andy Cox; E Clinth St, 186, Knoxville PO
ROGERS, Robert E., F-38-1; Pvt B Co 7th TN Cav; 19 May 61 to 19 May 65; Mason PO; CONF
ROGERS, Sam, Gi-139-2; Pvt Cav; 11-62 to 3-63; Wales Sta. PO; CONF
ROGERS, Squire, Su-233-1; Pvt 5th OH Cav; Mar 65 to 8 May 65; Shady Vally PO; deafness produced by artilery, able to do very little
ROGERS, Thomas H., Ha-115-3; Landsman USS Ossipee West Gulf Squadran; 15 Jan 64 to 21 Jul 65; Mulberry Gap PO; fracture of left leg by gun shot, pensioner
ROGERS, W. H., Hu-103-3; Pvt H Co 10th TN Inf; 10 Aug 61 to 26 Dec 64; PO omitted
ROGERS, Washington, St-160-2; Pvt F Co 14th TN Inf; May 61 to Aug 25 62; Big Rock PO; CONF
ROGERS, William, Br-12-4; Sarah widow of; Pvt G Co 3rd TN Cav; Georgetown PO
ROGERS, William, H-53-7; Carrie widow of; Quartermaster 13th TN Mtd Inf; 1 yr 8 mos; Chattanooga PO
ROGERS, William C., Wa-273-2; Sgt D Co 4th TN Inf; 17 Dec 62 to 2 Aug 65; Pettibone PO; lung disease
ROGERS, William H., Su-233-1; Pvt D Co 36th OH? Inf; 30 Jul 61 to 27 Aug 64; Holston Vally PO; week brest & rupture, almost entirely disabled
ROGERS, Wm. R., R-163-1; Sarah A. widow of; Pvt C Co 5th TN Inf; Graysville PO
ROGERSON, James H., Ro-206-1; Virginia widow of; Lt 10th IL Inf; Emory Gap PO
ROGGERS, James, Hm-106-2; Pvt F Co 9th TN Cav; 10 Jul 63 to 11 Sep 65; Morristown PO
ROGGERS, William, Bo-20-1; Cpl E Co 9th TN Cav; 2-4-62 to 8-10-65; Bank PO; chronic direa, exact dates, discharge at home
ROGIN, Granville, Fr-109-1; Pvt C Co 1st AL Cav; 64 to 65; Maxwell PO; ruptured by horse jumping
ROGINS, James, D-64-3; Pvt C Co 14th TN Inf; Nashville PO; wounded in back
ROHELIA, Andrew J., D-50-1; Pvt; 611 N. Summer, Nashville PO
ROHELIA, Martin, Cf-39-1; Roper, Caroline formerly widow of; Pvt 5th TN Cav; 64 to __; Prairie Plains PO
ROHLER, Jos., D-99-3; Pvt H Co 6th OH Inf; 17 Apr 61 to 23 Jun 64; State Penitentiary PO
ROKHOLT, James K., Me-90-2(1); Pvt D Co 5th TN Mtd Inf; 8-31-64 to 6-28-65; Meigs PO
ROLEN, James M., C-33-2; Sgt A Co 8th KY Cav; 8-61 to 10-62; Jellico PO
ROLEN, Mike, Bo-12-2(1); Cpl F Co 10th TN Cav; 1-10-63 to 81-65; Rasor PO
ROLIMON, James A., Mn-121-4; Pvt B Co 4th TN Mtd Inf; 1-1-64 to 6-18-65; Bethel Springs PO
ROLIN, James, Se-219-3; Martha widow of; Pvt D Co 9th TN Cav; Sep 63 to Mar 64; Jones Cave PO
ROLINS, Green R., Ge-89-3; 2nd Sgt A Co 2nd NC; 64 to 65; Mosheim PO
ROLL, Israel, H-51-3; Pvt G Co 1st Col Cav; 5-27-62 to 5-27-66; Hill City PO
ROLLAND, Jacob H., Ch-17-3; Margret widow of; Pvt TN Cav; Masseyvill PO; CONF
ROLLAND, Lewis, J-77-2; Pvt; Gainesboro PO; right eye out & left greatly impared
ROLLEN, John B., S-214-2; Pvt B Co 3rd NC Inf; Glenmary PO; loss right eye, cant tell date of enlistment
ROLLIN, Luke, Mo-119-3; Pvt C Co US Hvy Art; Sweetwater PO
ROLLINS, James M., Ge-99-2; Pvt K Co 13th TN Cav; 12 Oct 63 to 5 Sep 65; Woolsey College PO; spinal disease

ROLLINS, Jesse E., Be-8-1; Pvt A Co 7th TN Cav; 4 Jul 63 to 13 Jun 65; Lavinia PO
ROLLINS, Joe P., J-81-2; Pvt A Co 2nd TN; 8-11-61 to 5-28-65; Gainesboro PO; shot in thy May 63, shot in sholder & wrist May 65
ROLLINS, John C., Cr-8-1; Pvt C Co 3rd TN Cav; Jun 63 to __; Cedar Grove PO; taken prisoner and turned loose without discharge
ROLLINS, John F., Co-66-2(1); Pvt F Co 25th NC Inf; 9 Apr 62 to 9 Apr 64; Birdville PO; CONF
ROLLINS, Robert S., Co-67-1; Sgt A Co 3rd GA Inf; 11 May 61 to 12 May 65; Bison PO; CONF
ROLLINS, William J., Co-67-3; Jane Layman widow of; Pvt E Co 1st TN Art; 13 Sep 63 to __; Cosby PO
ROLSTON, William C., Fr-107-1; Pvt D Co 107th OH Inf; 5 Feb 62 to Jul 7 65; Belvedere PO
ROMAN, Jocke (see Money, Jake)
ROMINE, Isaac W., K-171-1; Pvt B Co 1st TN Art; Feb 62 to Feb 65; Bearden PO
ROMINE, William, Se-226-4; PVtt I Co 3rd TN Cav; 9 Sep 63 to 27 Jun 65; Sinking Springs PO; piles
ROMINES, Daniel C., Br-13-2; Pvt A Co 2nd TN Cav; 11-1-62 to 7-6-65; Cleveland PO; chronic bronchitis
ROMINES, David, Br-14-4; Pvt I Co 10th TN Cav; 2-5-62 to 8-1-65; McDonald PO; piles, deaf & blind partly
ROMINES, James, Br-12-3; Pvt A Co 8th TN Inf; 11-11-61 to 1-16-64; Georgetown PO; fever sores
ROMINES, Jonathan, Br-7-4; Sarah widow of; Pvt D Co 19th KY Inf; Stamper PO
ROMINES, Riley, Br-7-3; Pvt A Co 2nd TN Cav; Cleveland PO; blind
ROMINES, Zachariah, C-34-2; Leer widow of; Pvt A Co 1st TN Inf; 8-8-61 to 10-1-64; Elk Valley PO
ROMINGER, Franklin L., Ct-36-2; Pvt F Co 46th IL Inf; 2-17-63 to 6-2-65; Roan Mt. PO; wounded in leg
RONEY, Sam C., K-166-4(2); Lt A Co 20th PA Inf; Jun 63 to Oct 63; Knoxville PO
RONEY, Thos. J., O-139-2; US Sol; Civil Dist 12
RONY, John A., J-81-4; K Co 1st TN; 9-1-64 to 7-22-65; 8th Civil Dist
ROOKARD, James, C-34-2; Cpl or Pvt C Co 49th KY Inf; 7-63 to 12-26-64; Buckeye PO
ROOKARD, Lewies, C-32-1; Pvt C Co 49th KY Inf; 8-10-63 to 12-26-64; Pine Mountain? PO
ROOKS, Emery, We-221-4; Pvt Pvt 15th TN Cav; 28 Nov 63 to Mar 64; Martin PO; CONF
ROOP, Abner L., Wi-281-2; Sol; 12th Dist
ROOP, Alvin L., Wi-281-1; Capt E Co 82nd IN; Aug 62 to Dec 7 63; Bethesda PO; heart disease, nervous protration
ROOT, Jon M., Sh-186-1; Pvt C Co 3rd NY; 9-1-64 to 7-14-65; Memphis PO
ROPER, Caroline (see Rohelia, Martin)
ROPER, Charles W., Ge-94-2(1); 1st Lt C Co 4th TN Inf; 6 Apr 63 to 2 Aug 65; Tusculum PO; during Civil War, left side partially paralized
ROSE, Albert A., Hd-44-1; Pvt E Co 8th TN Mtd Inf; 3-14-65 to 9-1-65; Clifton PO (Wayne Co.)
ROSE, Alexander, A-2-1, Pvt D Co 8th TN Cav; Twinville PO (Knox Co.); deserter
ROSE, Anderson, Gi-127-5; Sophie widow of; 110th TN Inf; Pulaski PO; paper destroyed by fire
ROSE, Dempsey R., Rb-219-2; Pvt I Co MO Reg--Jul 62 to Dec 6l; Pvt MO Reg--May 62 to Aug 62; Pvt G Co 16th MO Reg--Aug 62 to May 65; Orlinda PO; a wound in left leg, 4th day of Jul 1863
ROSE, Elisha, Ro-204-4; Pvt A Co 5th TN Inf; 25 Feb 62 to 4 Apr 65; Elverton PO; rheumatism, also lung & kidney trouble
ROSE, G. C., Gi-139-1; Pvt; 10-64 to 6-65; Campbellsville PO; hurt in left hip
ROSE, Isaac, Hd-49-1; Pvt D Co 2nd TN Inf--Dec 21 63 to Feb 1 65; Pvt E Co 8th TN Mtd Inf--Mar 11 65 to Sep 1 65; Martins Mills PO; reumatism
ROSE, Jacob, Su-238-1; Pvt E Co 8th TN Inf; 1 Feb 64 to 27 Jun 65; White Store PO; shot in left hip
ROSE, James, C1-56-1; Pvt C Co 8th TN Cav; 6-11-63 to 9-11-65; Hagues PO
ROSE, James, Dy-29-5; Pvt B Co TN Inf; Oct 64 to May 65; Newbern PO; CONF
ROSE, James, D-77-3; 8th St, Nashville PO
ROSE, James E., Ro-208-2; Pvt D Co 5th TN Inf; 26 Feb 62 to 22 Apr 65; Morris Gap PO; rheumatism
ROSE, James R., Se-227-3; Pvt F Co 9th TN Cav; 17 Jul 63 to 11 Sep 65; Trundles X Roads PO; defect in eyes, this sol. never discharged
ROSE, Jessee, Wy-173-2; Pvt G Co 10th TN Inf; 6-20-62 to 6-24-65; Marins Mills PO
ROSE, John, Wy-171-1; Pvt F Co 6th TN; Sep 22 62 to 26 Jul 65; Waynesboro PO; catarrh & lung affection
ROSE, John, Mc-115-1; Pvt D Co 5th TN; Riceville PO; chronic diorhea, piles & rheumatism
ROSE, Joseph, R-163-3; Pvt B Co 6th TN Mtd Inf; 8-15-64 to 6-20-65; Graysville PO
ROSE, Joseph W., Lo-188-2; Rachel widow of; Pvt D Co 5th TN Inf; 25 Feb 62 to 22 Apr 65; Stockton PO
ROSE, Lewis, A-2-2; Cpl L Co 8th TN Cav; Hinds Creek PO; gun shot in leg
ROSE, McKinsie, Cu-17-4; Sgt B Co 5th TN Inf; 2-25-62 to 3-30-65; Crab Orchard PO
ROSE, Nicolas C., Rb-219-1; Pvt C Co 14th TN Reg; May 16 61 to Jul 1 63; Orlinda PO; wounded left leg; CONF
ROSE, Rice R., Dy-29-5; Pvt TN Cav; Apr 62 to Oct 64; Newbern PO; taken prisoner; CONF
ROSE, Tempa, Ma-123-1; widow; Pvt; 14th Dist
ROSE, Thomas, C1-55-1; Pvt E Co 6th TN Inf; 7-15-63 to 6-13-65; Haynes PO (Union Co.)
ROSE, William J. M., Mn-126-2; Pvt A Co 6th TN Cav; 62 to 8-6-65; Bethel Springs PO
ROSEBORROW, Aleck, Sh-162-1; Pvt F Co 117th IL Inf; 62 to 65; Bings Town PO; frost bitten, discharged at Springfield IL
ROSENBALM, Hamilton, C1-55-1; Pvt A Co 12th TN Cav; 12-22-63 to 10-17-65; Lone Mountain PO
ROSEOR, Alexander, D-57-3; Sgt 1st Reg VA Art; Apr 1 62 to Apr 9 65; Nashville PO; woundes at Lew Mills; CONF
ROSIER, D. H., C-33-3; Pvt G Co 7th TN Inf; 63 to 65; Newcomb PO
ROSIER, David C., C-24-1; Pvt F Co 6th TN Inf; 9-62 to 6-12-65; Fincastle PO; neuralgia & dececuse? of heart
ROSS, Alford, S-217-2; Honor widow of; Pvt G Co 2nd TN Inf; 62 to died in army; Winfield PO
ROSS, Amelia, Sh-190-2; widow of Sol; 74 Fla. Ave, Memphis PO
ROSS, Benjamin, Sh-200-2; Patient widow of; Cpl; 520 Orleans St, Memphis PO
ROSS, Beryman, B-6-1; Pvt 13th US Col Inf; Shelbyville PO
ROSS, Charles E., Mg-198-2; Pvt G Co 48th OH Inf; 29 May 62 to 20 Sep 62; Deer Lodge PO; pneumonia & abuninara; Pvt B Co 2nd Misso. Cav; 18 Nov 62 to 23 Jul 65
ROSS, Dugal W., He-64-2; Pvt K Co 7th TN Cav; 15 May 63 to 2 Oct 65; Middle Fork PO
ROSS, Frederic, K-161-6; Lucy widow of; Pvt 1st US Hvy Art; Knoxville PO
ROSS, George W., K-163-1; Lt A Co; 61 to 65; Knoxville PO; exposure of war
ROSS, Henry, Ms-183-1; Sgt C Co 111th US Col Inf; 12-15-63 to 4-30-66; Comenville PO; considerably ____, drawing small pension
ROSS, Isaac C., Hd-50-2; Pvt D Co 2nd TN Mtd Inf; Jan 9 64 to Feb 1 65; Savannah PO; gun shot wound in left leg, the leg has perished away working, a very bad cripple
ROSS, J. M., Hy-82-1; Pvt G Co 18th IL Inf; May 28 61 to 11 Jun 64; Tibbs PO
ROSS, James, Ms-183-1; Louise widow of; Cpl B Co 111th US Col Inf; 1-15-64 to died 3-64; Comenville PO; died in service, now drawing pension
ROSS, James, Br-12-1; Isabella widow of; Pvt A Co 8th TN Inf; 62 to 1-29-65; Charleston PO; died in hospital
ROSS, James A., Bl-4-2; Asst. Surgeon 16th TN Inf; 5-28-62 to 5-65; Pikeville PO; CONF
ROSS, James F., O-142-1; Pvt Brownlow Guards; 2 Mar 67 to Dec 67; Obion PO; under Capt. Stokes, disbanded, rec'd no discharge
ROSS, John, H-69-5; Silvany widow of; Pvt 47th KY Inf; 61 to 65; Chattanooga PO

ROSS, John J., Dk-34-6(5); Pvt K Co 5th TN Cav; 4-3-63 to 6-24-65; Copling PO; heart disease
ROSS, John M., Lk-113-3; Pvt 1st B 28 1st IN Inf; Nov 4 63 to Jun 22 65; 6th Civil Dist
ROSS, Marquis D., Cy-26-2; Sgt E Co 10th TN Cav; 1-16-63 to 7-15-65; Rocktown PO
ROSS, Robert, Sh-157-2; Lt A Co 3rd Art; May 62 to 65; Memphis PO
ROSS, Wiley C., We-220-1; Pvt C Co 1st KY Inf; May 20 64 to Feb 28 65; Latham PO
ROSS, William, Hy-76-1; alias Jeff Collier; Pvt E Co 53rd Col Inf; Mar 62 to Mar 64; Stanton Depot PO
ROSS, William T?, D-50-4; 1st Lt E Co 16th IL Inf; May 2 61 to Jul 14 65; N. College, Nashville PO; wounded 5 times
ROSSEN, William I., Cl-47-2; Pvt A Co 1st TN Inf; 7-2-62 to 8-3-65; Cappford PO; diareah 1864
ROSTON, Henderson, D-84-1; Maria widow of; Pvt B Co 15th Inf; Aug 62 to May 65; Wrencoe PO
ROSWELL, Seth, Hd-54-3; US Sol; PO omitted
OTH, Martha, Mu-201-1; widow of Sol; Mt. Pleasant PO
ROTHROCK, John, D-61-1; Pvt G Co 14th TN Vol; Dec 1 62 to May 1 65; Hawkins St, Nashville PO; lost finger
ROULLY, Pomp, Sh-157-7; Pvt D Co 59th USC; 62 to 65; Memphis, Beal St. 107 PO
ROULSTON, Samuel H., Mr-102-2; Pvt F Co 5th TN Cav; 9-8-62 to 6-25-65; South Pittsburg PO
ROUN, John C., Su-236-1; Cpl B Co 3rd NC Inf; Jun 63 to Aug 65; Morell's Mills PO
ROUND, Jos., Sh-201-1; Pvt Co. Gas; 15 Nov 62 to 15 Nov 65; Memphis PO; Co made up of gas works employees
ROUNDTREE, Albert, Mu-210-4; Mary widow of; Sgt C Co 13th TN Inf; 3 mos; Carters Creek PO; died of smallpox
ROUNS, John G., P-156-3; Pvt I Co 2nd KY Cav; __ to 11-12-65 (2 yrs); Lobelville PO; CONF
ROUSE, J. M., Hd-53-3; Pvt A Co 42nd IN Inf; 28 Jan 63 to 4 Aug 65; Morris Chapel PO
ROUSE, Pulser, Su-233-1; Pvt F Co 6th IN Cav; 11 Jun 63 to 15 Sep 65; Holston Vally PO; chronic rheumatism, almost entirely disabled
ROUSEY, George W., Mn-121-3; Falcon PO; discharged from being wonded, discharge & enlistment cant give dates of enlistment
ROUSUIN, Isaac C., Ch-17-3; Pvt A Co 6th TN Cav; 13 Dec 63 to 26 Jul 65; Masseyville PO
ROUTH, Kinzie L., Lo-189-2; Philadelphia PO; CONF
ROUTH, Sol, Gr-81-5(3); Jane widow of Sol US; PO omitted
ROW, Thomas A., Cy-29-1; Pvt F Co 5th KY Cav; 10-61 to 5-5-65; Willow Grove PO; vaction left arm
ROWAN, Alfred, Lo-187-3; Pvt E Co 1st US Col Hvy Art; 64 to 66; Loudon PO
ROWAN, Harry, Mo-119-1; Pvt D Co 1st US Col Hvy Art; 2-18-64 to 3-31-66; Sweetwater PO
ROWAN, Marselles, Bo-22-1; Pvt B Co 6th TN Inf; 3-10-62 to 4-8-65; Notime PO; rheumatism & thistles
ROWAN, William, Hw-133-1; Pvt Hewalls Batery Lt Art; 63 to furlough May 65 (3 mos); Slide PO; CONF
ROWDEN, Abednego, Me-91-1; 2nd Lt I Co 9th TN Cav; 5-15-63 to 9-11-65; Decatur PO; heart disease, prisoner in Libby & other prisons of the South 11 mos
ROWDEN, Shadrach, Me-94-1; Cpl D Co 5th TN Cav; 62 to 65; Euchee PO; discharge with J. L. McFarland
ROWDEN, Thomas M., H-59-2; Pvt A Co 2nd TN Inf; 8-10-61 to 10-6-64; Chattanooga PO
ROWE, Albert G., Wa-263-3; Pvt B Co 3rd NC Mtd Inf; Garbers Mills PO
ROWE, Daniel C., Co-59-2; US Sol; 1st Dist
ROWE, James W., Cr-17-2; Pvt C Co 7th TN Cav; 1-1-65 to 8-9-65; Family PO; lameness in hip & ankle, discharged as John W. Rowe
ROWE, John W., Ct-38-1; Pvt D Co 13th TN Cav; 8-18-64 to 9-5-65; PO omitted
ROWE, Thomas Y., Ct-38-2; Pvt B Co 4th TN Inf; 11-1-63 to 8-2-65; Dry Creek PO; diarrhea
ROWLAND, Carlos B., O-141-2; in as Pvt out as Lt, Drill master, Com Lt; Aug 8 61 to Jan 4 65; Union City PO

ROWLAND, Eben, Cr-20-2; Eliza A. wid. of; Pvt I Co 7th TN Cav; Aug 15 62 to Aug 9 65; Hollow Rock PO; died
ROWLAND, James A., Mc-117-1; Pvt A Co 7th TN Mtd Inf; 9-11-64 to 7-27-65; Mecca PO
ROWLAND, James D., Sm-172-4; Pvt I Co 5th TN Cav; 6-1-63 to 7-10-63; Gordonsville PO
ROWLAND, John M., S-215-1; Quartermaster B Co 8th KY Cav; 15 Oct 62 to 15 Oct 63; Pioneer PO
ROWLAND, William, Dk-39-5(2); Kariah widow of; Laurel Hill PO
ROWLET, Daniel, Sh-200-2; Charlotte Williams formerly widow of; Pvt A Co 59th US Col Inf; 6-27-63 to 66; 406 Georgia St, Memphis PO; shot in hip
ROWLETT, William T., Cl-50-2(1); Pvt G Co 1st TN Cav; 7-5-62 to 1-5-65; Sprowles PO
ROWLING, Thomas, Sn-262-1; Pvt B Co 3rd MI Inf; 5-1-61 to 6-10-65; Fountain Head PO; diarhea
ROY, Hector, K-156-1; Bettie widow of; Pvt B Co 42nd TN Inf; 12 Mar 64 to 20 May 65; 12 Pine St, Knoxville PO
ROY, James B., Ja-86-1; Pvt E Co 4th TN Cav; 4-4-63 to 7-12-65; Oottewah PO; general breakup of health
ROY, James H., C-33-4; Jellico PO
ROY, John W., Ja-86-3; Pvt E Co 4th TN Cav; 63 to 65; Snowhill PO; pistol shoot in left thigh
ROY, Joseph B., Ja-86-1; Pvt K Co 7th TN Inf; 2-63 to __; Oottewah PO; captured & never returned to army
ROYELS, William S., Sh-167-1; 4th Cpl GWA Co 7th AL; 63 to 25 May 65; Memphis, 141 Main St PO; dont know the dates of enlistment; CONF
ROYER, David M., Cf-40-3; Pvt D Co 12th KY Cav; 12 Aug 62 to 13 Aug 65; Tullahoma PO
ROYERS, Turner, He-63-1; Pvt H Co 7th TN Cav; PO omitted
ROYSDEN, George W., Se-226-5; Cynthia Farmer formerly widow of; Pvt; Straw. Plains PO; left sick by company and never mustered out
ROYSTER, Sylvester, Sm-166-3(1); Pvt K Co 92nd OH Inf; 5-27-63 to 7-3-65; Monoville PO
ROYSTON, Robert A., Ha-110-2; Pvt I Co 8th TN Inf; 1 Jul 63 to 30 Jun 65; Luther PO
ROYSTON, William, Mo-121-1; Pvt D Co 1st TN Lt Art; 9-20-62 to 7-20-65; Philadelphia PO; injury to breast bone
RUBENDITTS? (sic) ____, We-221-6(2); Pvt B Co 22nd TN Cav; 16 Sep 63 to 24 May 65; Martin PO; CONF
RUBLE, John, O-134-2; Pvt Scout Cav; Aug 16 61 to Jul 31 65; Hornbeak PO; CONF
RUCH, John, Fr-110-1; Pvt F Co 19th OH; S ep 7 61 to Nov 25 65; Belvidere PO
RUCKER, Austin, Un-257-3; Mary H. widow of; Pvt 1st TN Inf; 5 Aug 61 to 15 Apr 62; New Prospect PO; pneumonia fever, this is disease husband died with
RUCKER, David, D-83-1; Pvt K Co 111th US Inf; 2 Mar 62 to 65; Brooklyn PO
RUCKER, Eliza (see Young, Joseph)
RUCKER, Manerva (see Haynes, Napoleon B.)
RUCKER, Robert, Cr-8-2; Pvt I Co 17th TN; 2 May 62 to 2 May 63; Maury City PO; CONF
RUCKER, Thomas N., Ro-207-1; Pvt D Co 1st TN Inf; 19 Oct 64 to 16 Jun 65; Regrett PO (McMinn Co.); hemriag of lungs
RUCKER, William, Un-257-3; Pvt D Co 1st TN Lt Art; Sep 63 to Sep 65; New Prospect PO; hip injured
RUCKER, William E., Br-13-3; Cpl E Co 4th TN Cav; 12-1-62 to 7-12-65; Cleveland PO; chronic piles
RUCKETTS, Burch, Hm-104-3(1); Pvt H Co 2nd KY Inf; 20 Aug 61 to 5 Oct 64; Alpha PO
RUCKS, Henry, Wl-295-1; Pvt A Co 14th TN Inf; Oct 13 63 to Mar 65; Lebanon PO
RUD, William H., Mc-116-3; Pvt A Co 7th TN Mtd Inf; 8-13-64 to 7-27-65; Williamsburg PO
RUDD, Charity, W-196-2; Pvt C Co 42nd OH Vol; 9-10-61 to 2-27-64; McMinnville PO; wounded
RUDDER, Archabel A., K-181-6(3); Pvt C Co 18th TN Inf; 62 to 27 Apr 65; Knoxville PO
RUDDER, Johnson, Ge-89-2; Pvt A Co 12th TN Cav; 24 Mar 63 to 7 Oct 65; Mosheim PO
RUDDER, Robert P., K-180-1; Pvt C Co 6th TN Inf; 18 Apr 62 to 27 Apr 65; Bearden PO

RUDEN, Adam, W-189-2; Pvt I Co 31st IL Inf; 12-64 to 8-65; McMinnville PO; discharge lost
RUDER, Samuel, Je-140-1; Pvt A Co 12th TN Cav; Hodges? PO; no discharge
RUDINE, George W., J-81-4; B Co 1st TN; 7-13-64 to 4-13-65; 8th Civil Dist
RUDLIN, Codwell, F-39-1; Pvt B Co 110th AL Inf; 16 Apr 63 to 6 Feb 66; Galloway PO; CONF
RUDUS, Burle, B-3-1; Pvt I Co 110th US Col Inf; 12-30-63 to 2-6-66; Shelbyville PO; maimed by gunshot 11-64, prisoner at Mobile 9 mos
RUE, William H., Br-8-4(2); Pvt 10th TN Cav; 3 yrs 3 mos; Cleo PO; rupture
RUFF, Nelson (Black), Dy-28-1; Pvt H Co 88th TN Inf; Apr 1 64 to Jun 10 65; Finley PO
RUFF, Silas, Co-67-3; Eliza widow of; Pvt NC Inf; Cosby PO; killed at Cumberland Gap TN, CONF
RUFFNER, Christian, Mg-196-2; Sgt F Co 5th TN Inf; 25 Feb 62 to 5 Apr 65; Coalfield PO
RUFFNER, Peter, Mg-196-2; Cpl K Co 1st TN Inf; 9 Aug 61 to 27 Sep 6 ; Coalfield PO; collar bone broken
RUGGLES, Thomas C., K-183-2; Pvt A? Co 13th KY Cav; Mayo PO
RUHN, John, D-45-1; Pvt 4th US Art--10-10-61 to 9-15-63; 1st Lt M Co 15th US Col Inf--10-10-63 to 4-1-66; Nashville PO
RULE, Caleb, Se-228-2(3); Pvt K Co 3rd TN Cav; 25 Jul 63 to 10 Jun 65; New Knob Creek PO; diarrhoe
RULE, M. A., K-186-1; Beaver Ridge PO
RULE, Robert, Bo-19-2; Pvt A Co 3rd TN Cav; 11-62 to 6-10-65; Rockford? PO
RULER, Eyra, Hu-103-1; Pvt E Co Inf 10th TN; 10 Jul 62 to 10 Dec 65; PO omitted
RULLAND, Monroe, Sh-153-1; Pvt C Co 101st USC Inf; 2 yrs 6 mos; Collierville PO
RUMAGE, William C., Mc-117-3; Mary C. widow of; Pvt K Co 8th TN Inf; 62 to __ (6 mos); Carlock PO; application in for pension
RUMMEL, James, Cf-41-1; Pvt F Co 142nd OH Inf; Manchester PO
RUNABAUM, Henry, La-113-2; Pvt A Co 58th OH Inf; 8 Jan 62 to 6 Jan 65; Lawrenceburgh PO
RUNDLE, Johnathan, D-64-1; Pvt 2nd VA Reg; Jan 61 to Feb 62; Nashville PO; CONF
RUNION, James C., Cl-56-1; Pvt F Co 8th TN Cav; 4?-28-62 to 5-26-65; Big Barren PO
RUNIONS, George W., Po-150-1; 5th Civil Dist
RUNNALS, John S., Hr-94-1; Cpl A Co 4th NH Inf; 9-18-61 to 8-65; N. Bett PO; thumb, forefinger right hand off, dont know the date of discharge
RUNNALS, Moses J., K-156-3; Pvt I Co 2nd OH Art; 61 to Jun 65; 123 Crozier St, Knoxville PO
RUNNELS, James Allison, H-54-6; Pvt H Co 2nd NH Inf--12-6-62 to 10-9-63; Pvt C Co 150th York Negon (NY?) Inf--8-11-64 to 6-18-65; Kings Point PO
RUNNION, Berry O., U-248-1; Pvt 64th CN Inf; 11 Sep 62 to 20 Jul 64; PO omitted; CONF
RUNNIONS, James M., Po-152-3(1); Pvt B Co 10th TN Cav; 9-15-62 to 8-1-65; Ducktown PO; injury to head, back and side
RUNNIVER, Oliver P., K-184-3; Cpl K Co 2nd TN Inf; 13 Dec 61 to 15 Dec 64; Thorn Grove PO
RUNNYAN, John H., Se-223-3; Catharine Carns formerly widow of; Ordinary Seaman, US Str. Silver Lake; 8 Feb 64 to 11 Feb 65; Henderson Springs PO
RUNYAN, Thomas B., Lo-187-1; Pvt A Co 20th OH Inf; 8 Aug 62 to 30 Jul 63; Loudon PO; both eyes shot out
RUNYON, Simon P., Ja-85-4; Sgt; Georgetown PO
RUP, Solomon, Di-34-1; Pvt F Co 50th PA Inf; 9-20-64 to 6-2-65; Dickson PO
RUSAR, Daniel, Bo-14-3; Sarah widow of; Pvt L Co 2nd TN Cav; 9-63 to 7-6-65; Mountvale PO
RUSEL, John, Bl-3-3; Pvt; Billingsly PO; CONF
RUSH, George, D-45-5; Ophelia Ave, Nashville PO
RUSH, Isaac C., Cy-27-4(2); Pvt B Co 5th KY Cav; 10-10-61 to 5-9-65; Spivey PO
RUSH, James, H-62-1; Pvt 106th US Col Inf; 40th US Col Inf; alley bet. Cedar & Pleasant, Chattanooga PO
RUSH, James H., J-77-2; Pvt; Gainesboro PO
RUSH, Joseph, Br-6-1; Pvt C Co 10th TN Cav; 1-14-64 to 8-1-65; Chatala PO; nervous prostration
RUSH, William, Hw-118-1; Pvt H Co 12th TN Cav; St. Clair PO; breast & back
RUSH, William, Hw-118-2; Pvt D Co 1st TN Cav; 16 Apr 63 to __; St. Clair PO; rheumatism
RUSH, William P., J-77-2; Pvt; Gainesboro PO
RUSH, William R., Po-149-1; Pvt F Co 5th TN Inf; 9-26-64 to 6-26-65; Old Fort PO; Mtd Inf one year
RUSH, Wm. W., He-59-1; Sol US; PO omitted
RUSHING, Bengimon, Hn-77-1; Millie widow of; Pvt; PO omitted
RUSHING, Berry, H-56-5; B Co 8th IN; 10-62 to 65 (3 yrs); East End PO
RUSHING, Richard, He-60-1; Pvt G Co 6th TN Cav; 10-62 to 8-65; Lexington PO; catarrh incurred by being in service in war
RUSHMONT, D. E., H-64-2; Georgia A. widow of; Col PA; Chattanooga PO
RUSS, F. M., F-38-1; Pvt 7th TN Cav; Feb 62 to Apr 65; Mason PO; CONF
RUSS, James, Ja-85-4; Pvt E Co 4th TN Cav; 5-25-63 to 7-12-65; Long Savannah PO
RUSSEL, Aaron, Ro-202-1; Barbra widow of; Pvt 3rd TN Inf; Union X Roads PO; spinal affliction
RUSSEL, David C., Mo-126-2; Sol; 12th Civil Dist
RUSSEL, George, Hy-82-1; Pvt B Co 3rd US Hvy Art; 65 to 66; Rudolph PO
RUSSEL, Robert, H-61-3; Lizzie Powell formerly widow of; Pvt; Chattanooga PO
RUSSEL, Samuel, Mg-198-3; Martha F. widow of; Pvt F Co 5th TN Inf; 14 Feb 62 to 10 Nov 62; Rockwood PO
RUSSEL, Travis, H-56-6; Pvt E Co 60th OH Inf; St. Elmo PO
RUSSEL, William T., Se-224-3; Pvt D Co 2nd TN Cav; 1 Sep 62 to 6 Jul 65; Wears Valley PO; total blindness in one eye, had small pox & lost eyesight
RUSSELL, And. H., Li-147-1; 6th Civil Dist
RUSSELL, Barkly, Bo-11-3; Pvt; Largonia? PO; couldent get dates or R
RUSSELL, Bluford, Cf-42-1; Pvt 2nd Div Lucy (Lacy?) 1-64 to 7-5-65; Tullahoma PO; blindness
RUSSELL, Charles, Mc-110-1; Pvt B Co 7th TN Cav; 9-12-64 to 7-27-65; Chuckaluck PO
RUSSELL, Charley, Se-225-1; Pvt M Co 2nd TN Cav; 8 Nov 62 to 11 Sep 65; Allensville PO; chronic diarrhoea and rheumatism 25 yrs, disease of eyes and catarrh of head
RUSSELL, Ednan, Bo-15-2; Pvt B Co 8th TN Cav; Maryville PO
RUSSELL, Emeline, R-163-3; widow; Civil Dist 13
RUSSELL, Futher?, M-103-5; Pvt B Co 8th TN Inf; 2-5-65 to 8-17-65; Alton Hill PO
RUSSELL, George, Hw-132-3(1); Pvt M Co 13th TN Cav; Jan 62 to __; Strahl PO; could not obtain any information
RUSSELL, George, Bo-13-3(1); Cpl B Co 8th TN Cav; 5-10-63 to 6-17-65; Louisville PO; injured in left ankle
RUSSELL, George W., Ct-45-1; Pvt D Co 1st OH Hvy Art; 8-1-63 to 8-1-65; Stony Creek PO; diarrhea, rheumatism, Knoxville 1864
RUSSELL, Henry, Se-219-3; Pvt B Co 7th TN Cav; 26 Sep 63 to 11 Sep 65; Jones Cave PO
RUSSELL, Henry C., Un-258-1; Pvt 8th TN Inf; 12 Dist
RUSSELL, Henry M., Ro-210-11; Pvt B Co 1st AL Cav; Rockwood PO
RUSSELL, Hesiciah, Wa-263-4; Jane widow of; Pvt 10th TN Inf; May Day PO; died at Nashville, TN
RUSSELL, Hiram H., Wa-272-3; Pvt E Co 3rd NC Mtd Inf; 1 Oct 64 to 8 Aug 65; Free Hill PO; spinal disease, injury to eyes
RUSSELL, Isaac H., Bo-15-3; Pvt D Co 2nd TN Cav; 9-1-62 to 7-6-65; Maryville PO
RUSSELL, James, Ru-237-1; Pvt I Co 5th MS Inf; 20 Jul 62 to 20 Jul 64; Eagleville PO
RUSSELL, James, Un-257-3; Pvt I Co 8th TN Inf; Nov 1 63 to 30 Jun 65; New Prospect PO; catarrh of head
RUSSELL, James, De-25-2; Decaturville PO
RUSSELL, James, Ro-211-1; Pvt H Co 3rd TN Inf; 10 Feb 62 to no discharge; Webster PO

RUSSELL, James A., Gr-70-1; Pvt B Co 1st TN Cav; 9 Apr 61 to 9 Apr 64; Rutledge PO; kidney aff
RUSSELL, James B., Ro-204-2; Pvt I Co 7th TN Inf; 8 Nov 64 to 27 Jul 65; Oliver Springs PO
RUSSELL, James M., Sm-168-1; Pvt A Co 9th KY Inf; 9-61 to 12-64; Difficult PO; deafness, crippled back, is almost blind
RUSSELL, James W., Gi-122-6; Sgt A Co 53rd TN Inf; 6 Dec 61 to Jan 64; Prospect Sta PO; in prison 7 mos, Indianapolis, IN; CONF
RUSSELL, Jessie, F-20-3; Pvt B Co 22nd IN Inf; 18 Aug 61 to 25 May 65; Hickory Withe PO; shot through the right leg
RUSSELL, John, Sh-176-1; 97 Causert St, Memphis PO
RUSSELL, John, Ro-207-3; Pvt I Co 5th TN Inf; 1 Jan 64 to 30 Jun 65; Paint Rock PO; nervisnest
RUSSELL, John, Ct-45-3; Amy M. Campbell formerly widow of; Pvt; Carter Furnace PO; no record of enlistment or discharge
RUSSELL, John F., Ro-203-7; Pvt F Co 5th TN Cav; 1 Feb 62 to Mar 65; Wheat PO; right arm partially paralyzed
RUSSELL, John V., Hw-133-1; Pvt F Co 5th? GA Inf; 4 Mar 62 to 31 Dec 64; Slide PO; CONF
RUSSELL, Joseph T., Cl-57-2; Pvt F Co 7th TN Regt; 11-1-64 to 7-7-65; PO omitted; kidney disease 20 yrs, deaf 1 yr, sol. looks weekly
RUSSELL, Judda, Bo-19-3; Pvt; Rockford PO; ruptured
RUSSELL, Norman A., H-53-6; Pvt Engineers 1st MI Engineers; 62 to 64; Ridgedale PO
RUSSELL, O. Conley, Lo-187-2; Pvt C Co 3rd TN Cav; 4 Dec 62 to 10 Jun 65; Loudon PO; ruptured
RUSSELL, Rob. B., We-230-4; Ester E. widow of; Pvt K Co 16th TN Inf; May 1 62 to May 1 64; McKinzie PO; CONF
RUSSELL, Robert, Sh-199-1; 136 Larose St, Memphis PO
RUSSELL, Robert F., Cl-57-2; Sgt F Co 7th TN Regt; 11-1-64 to 7-7-65; Goin PO; piles
RUSSELL, S. H., Sh-153-1; Pvt K Co 1st IL Art; 2 Jan 64 to 15 Jul 65; Collierville PO
RUSSELL, Samuel M., Hm-33(103)-1; Pvt; Dyersburg PO
RUSSELL, Thomas, Lo-187-2; Sarah J. widow of; Pvt US Col Hvy Art; 64 to 66; Loudon PO
RUSSELL, Thomas J., Ro-203-3; Pvt I Co 3rd TN Inf; Apr 64 to __; Wheat PO
RUSSELL, William, Se-228-1(2); Pvt L Co 2nd TN Inf; 6 mos; Ellejoy PO
RUSSELL, William, A-6-4(2); Pvt K Co 5th TN Inf; 2-25-62 to 6-30-65; Robertsville PO
RUSSELL, William B., H-51-2(1); Pvt I Co 11th IN Cav; 10-16-63 to 4-18-65; Hill City PO
RUSSELL, William E., H-107-4; Amanda widow of; Pvt A Co 9th KY Inf; 61 to 63; Gibb's Cross Roads PO; consumption result of measles
RUSSELL, William J., Je-142-1; Sgt K Co 2nd TN Inf; 9 Jan 62 to 5 Jun 65; New Market PO
RUSSELL, William H., Ro-206-1; Pvt H Co 1st AL Cav; 64 to 65; Emory Gap PO
RUSSELL, William M., R-163-2; Pvt D Co 4th TN Cav; 4-27-63 to 7-12-65; Graysville PO; total disability--cronic diareah
RUSSUM, Asa, Mn-122-2; Sarah widow of; Pvt A Co 6th TN Cav; 8-11-62 to 1-16-64; Bethel PO; consumption
RUST, Ernest, H-64-2; Josephine widow of; Cpl E Co 182nd OH V; Chattanooga PO; cant give dates
RUST, John R., Cr-16-1; Pvt F Co 7th TN Cav--Aug 6 62 to Feb 1 63; Pvt I Co 7th TN Cav--Jan 6 65 to Aug 8 65; Huntingdon PO; reenlisted
RUSTIN, John R., Ge-92-5; Pvt I Co 1st TN Cav; 1 Aug 62 to 5 Jun 65; Romeo PO; catarrh of head & rheumatism
RUTH, Francis M., Br-7-3; Pvt; Cleveland PO
RUTH, Henry C., Hd-54-2; Pvt 2nd TN Mtd Inf; Oct 63 to Oct 64; Ruth PO
RUTHEFORD, Henry, C-33-5; Pvt A Co 49th KY; 62 to 62 (9 mos); Newcomb PO
RUTHERFORD, Ben, Sn-250-1; Cpl C Co 7th __; 5-20-61 to 5-20-65; Castalian Springs PO; CONF
RUTHERFORD, Carrick, K-168-4; Adair's Creek PO
RUTHERFORD, Elliot, Ge-89-4; Mary widow of; Pvt B Co 3rd TN Mtd Inf; 30 Jun 64 to 20 Oct 64; Pilot Knob PO
RUTHERFORD, Grandille, C-27-1; Pvt F Co 6th TN Inf; 3-10-62 to 3-24-65; Jacksboro PO
RUTHERFORD, H. S., A-1-3; Pvt F Co 6th TN Inf; 3-10-62 to 3-24-65; Andersonville PO
RUTHERFORD, Henary, Un-256-3; Pvt M Co 11th TN Cav; 63 to 65; Loyes X Roads PO; injury of head by rock
RUTHERFORD, Joseph, Je-139-2; Pvt E Co 2nd TN Cav; 16 Sep 62 to 3 Jul 65; Oak Grove PO
RUTHERFORD, Melv H., K-174-1; Cpl F Co 3rd TN Inf; 10 Feb 62 to 23 Feb 65; Floyd PO; desease of eyes
RUTHERFORD, Parris P., K-174-4(3); Pvt G Co 7th TN Inf; 12 Nov 64 to 27 Jul 65; Floyde PO; no disability
RUTHERFORD, Peter, Wl-290-1; Pvt K Co 27th OH; May 1 64 to Aug 1 65; Lebanon PO; discharged
RUTHERFORD, Preston, Ja-86-4; Ord Sgt D Co 4th TN Cav; 1-1-62 to 7-12-65; Apison PO; rupture
RUTHERFORD, R. T., Mc-117-3; Pvt E Co 7th TN Mtd Inf; 9-15-64 to 7-22-65; Cog Hill PO; accute rheumatism
RUTHERFORD, Squire, D-69-2; US Sol, no record; Nashville PO
RUTHERFORD, William A., R-162-1; Pvt B Co 5th TN Inf; 3-30-62 to 11-30-65; Dayton PO; shot in thigh, right hand crippled, __ on left leg
RUTHERFORD, William M., K-173-3; Pvt B Co 22nd IN Inf; 21 Sep 64 to 6 Jul 65; Troutman PO
RUTHERFORD, Zacheure, Un-256-2; Pvt 11th TN Cav; Loy X Roads PO
RUTHORD, Joshua, Un-255-2; Pvt F Co 6th TN Inf; 10 Ma 62 to 10 Apr 65; Lay's X Roads PO; rumatism & blind
RUTLAND, Dennis (see Clark, Dennis)
RUTLEDGE, Baxter S., K-177-3; Pvt K Co 29th TN Inf; 15 Aug 61 to 14 Apr 65; Dante PO; CONF
RUTLEDGE, Lee, Col, Ge-91-2; Pvt H Co 1st US Hvy Art?; Ma 62 to Ma 65; Greeneville PO
RUTLEDGE, William, Gi-135-1; Pvt E Co 110th TN Inf; 9-24-64 to 5-1-65; Lynnville PO
RUTLEDGE, William P., Sn-256-1; Pvt E Co 12th TN Reg; 11-63 to 11-65; Gallatin PO; discharge lost and cant say as to exact date of enlistment and discharge
RUTLEDGE, Z., D-101-1; Capt K Co 14th IA Inf; Apr 61 to Oct 65; 22nd Civ Dist
RUTLIAGE, Salmuel, K-177-1; Pvt A Co 12th TN Cav; 30 Aug 62 to 14 Apr 65; Dante PO; absess; CONF
RUTTARD?, James, Wl-308-2; Pvt A Co 20th TN; May 1 61 to May 1 64; Dodoburgh PO; CONF
RUY, William A., Wa-263-2; Cpl B Co 29th NC Inf; Aug 61 to Feb 20 62; Garbers Mills PO; CONF
RYAN, Dennis, Rb-223-1; Pvt 22nd IN; 17 Apr 61 to 20 May 65; Springfield PO
RYAN, George, Ct-40-5; Elizabeth widow of; Pvt B Co 4th TN Cav; Elizabethton PO
RYAN, James, St-164-2; Pvt A Co 5th KY Inf; Jul 9 61 to Dec 62; Stribling PO; camp diorhea, discharged on surgeons certificate
RYAN, James, Sh-178-3; US Sol; Monroe St, Memphis PO
RYAN, James R., H-53-6; Engineers; Ridgedale PO; Engineer corps
RYAN, Mary J. (see Terry, Joseph)
RYAN, Mike P., Sh-193-1; Pvt; Memphis PO; papers in claim agts hand
RYBARGER, Franklin, Ge-87-2; Sgt I Co 1st TN Cav; 1 Jun 62 to Jun 65; Timberridge PO; chronic diarrhes, diseased stomach
RYCKMAN, Benjiman, Hn-74-1; Sgt F Co 1st MI Inf; 25 Jan 63 to 22 Sep 65; Como PO; discharged special order
RYNE, Moses S., S-216-2; Pvt G Co 2nd TN Inf; 6 Oct 61 to 19 Aug 65; Gome Fork PO
RYNES, Wiliam, Mo-122-4(1); Pvt G Co 62nd TN Inf; 3-10-63 to 7-8-63; PO omitted; CONF
SADDLER, Alexander P., Sm-170-2; Cpl E Co 52nd KY Mtd Inf; 63 to 65; Maggart PO; blood poison from typhoid fever, settled in right thigh
SADDLER, Berry (black), Sm-171-1; Pvt L Co 5th TN Mtd Inf; 64 to 65; Chestnut Mound PO
SADDLER, Lewis, Sh-199-1; Pvt; 6 Simmons Ave, Memphis PO

SADDLER, William G., H-56-1; Jane widow of; Pvt 89th IL Inf; 62 to 6-6-65; St. Elm(o) PO
SADDLER, William T., Ce-31-1; Pvt G Co 13th KY Cav --1 Oct 63 to Jan 4 65; Cpl F Co 17th KY Cav --22 Feb 65 to 20 Sep 65; Ashland City PO; shot in right arm
SADLER, Jane, H-56-8; widow Sol US; St. Elmo PO
SADLER, Jos. K. P., D-90-1; Pvt G Co 10th TN Inf; Jun 61 to about May 65; Nashville PO
SADLER, Rufus C., Sn-260-5; Pvt F Co 17th KY Cav; 1-64 to 65; Westmoreland PO; shot in knee
SADON, Richmond Jr. (see Shumaker, J. W.)
SADRICK, Joseph H., C-27-1; Pvt L Co 9th TN Cav; 9-1-63 to 9-11-65; Jacksboro PO; small pox
SAFFELL, James T., Lo-191-3; 1st Lt G Co 3rd TN Inf; 10 Feb 62 to 20 Sep 63; Morganton PO
SAFFELS, Harl, Mg-197-1; Mary A. Bales formerly widow of; Lt 11th TN Cav; 4th Dist
SAFFER, Casper, H-59-2; Pvt OH Cav; 62 to 65; Chattanooga PO
SAFFILL, Lewis N., Se-226-6; Cpl B Co 1st US Col Hvy Art; __ to 31 Mar 65; Henrys X Roads PO; rheumatism & liver disorder
SAFFLES, Stephen D., R-160-1; Pvt D Co 3rd TN; 2-25-64 to 11-13-64; 7th Civil Dist
SAGAR, Peter, S-214-3; Sophia widow of; Pvt WI Inf; New River PO
SAILS, Bonned, Sh-158-5(1); Sgt A Co US AL Inf; 2 Apr 62 to 66; Memphis PO; discharge at close of the war, with discharge papers
SAIN, Andrew, Co-60-2; Mary widow of; Pvt B Co 58th IN; Parrotsville PO; died in service
SAINE, James W., Me-88-1; Cpl E Co 5th TN Inf; 3-2-62 to 4-4-65; Birchwood PO
ST. CLAIR, Benjamin, O-141-2; Pvt H Co 59th IL Vol Inf; Aug 21 61 to Sep 17 64; Union City PO
ST. CLAIR, John W., S-214-1; Pvt H Co 104th PA Inf; 61 to 64; Robbins PO
SALEN, Godfrey, Sh-171-1; Pvt A Co 1st TN Reg; 6-21-62 to 8-3-65; Memphis PO
SALSBERRY, William W., Ge-90-3; Pvt M Co 9th TN Cav; 1 Nov 64 to 11 Sep 65; Greeneville PO; spinal defect
SALTER, Jessie, Ch-17-2; Pvt A Co 11th TN Cav; 63 to 65; Masseyville PO
SALTER, Wm. M., D-49-3; Pvt I Co 5th US Cav; 16 Sep 63 to Sep 65; 612 Line, Nashville PO
SALTS, Alexander, Bo-15-4; Purreaty widow of; Pvt B Co 2nd TN Cav; Maryville PO
SALTS, William, Su-242-1; Emely Jenkins formerly widow of; Pvt F Co 13th TN Cav; 16 Sep 63 to died in prison; Bluff City PO; was captured by rebels Jan, 1864, and was exchanged for in May 64 to and died in pris., May 64
SAM, Thos., Li-157-1; Pvt A Co 111th TN; Jan 10 64 to May 66; Dellrose PO
SAMES, James, Co-66-1; Pvt B Co 2nd NC Inf; 15 Mar 64 to 1 Aug 64; Birdsville PO; palpitation of heart
SAMPLE, Harriet, D-77-4; #85 Georgia St, Nashville PO
SAMPLE, James A., Co-64-2; Pvt M Co 8th TN Cav; 8 Oct 63 to 11 Sep 65; Newport PO
SAMPLE, Major, Sh-145-1; Pvt F Co 59th US Col Inf; 10 Jun 63 to 31 Jan 66; Millington PO; Cap B. S. Chittenden, Co F
SAMPLER, Charles, D-79-1; Jennie Crawford widow; Pvt G Co 42nd US Col Inf; Oct 15 63 to Jan 31 66; Nashville, Rev. R. Vandever PO; injured in knee
SAMPLES, Reece B., Co-64-1; Pvt M Co 8th TN Cav; 8 Oct 63 to 11 Sep 65; Newport PO; loss of speech
SAMPLES, Timothy D., G-71-1; Pvt G Co 47th TN Inf; 5 Mar 61 to 2 Jun 64; Bradford PO; CONF
SAMPSEL, John P., Gr-71-1; Pvt E Co 13th TN Cav; 63 to 63; Tate Spring PO; no discharge from service
SAMPSON, Caloway, Hm-108-1; Rebeckah widow of; Pvt L Co 13th TN Cav; 20 Mar 64 to 5 Sep 65; Russellville PO; rheumatism
SAMPSON, George W., Sm-169-1; Pvt A Co 1st TN Mtd Inf; 12-18-63 to 1-31-65; Carthage PO
SAMPSON, Reuben E., H-51-4; Pvt F Co 4th TN Cav; 10-14-63 to 6-19-65; Hill City PO
SAMPSON, Richard S., Mc-112-2; Sgt H Co 5th TN Cav; 9-20-62 to 65; Athens PO; wife dont know dates

SAMPTER, James, Gi-136-2; Pvt B Co 110th TN Inf; 12-12-63 to 2-6-66; Odd Fellow Hill PO; wounded in head
SAMS, Abslun, Lk-113-1; Pvt B Co 13th; Mar 63 to Feb 66; 6th Civil Dist
SAMS, David H., Bo-14-3; 1st Lt 51st USC Inf; 7-61 to 65; Mountval PO
SAMS, Elijah, Hw-124-1; Pvt D Co 1st TN Art; Oct 63 to Sep 65; Opossum PO
SAMS, Marion, K-160-3; Margaret widow of; Pvt A Co 13th Caf (sic); Knoxville PO
SAMSEL, James A., Ro-204-2; Pvt K Co 5th TN Inf; 9 Aug 62 to 13 Jun 65; Oliver Springs PO
SAMSEL, Richard C., Gr-71-2; Bean Station PO
SAMTER, Marks, Sh-176-1; Pvt G Co 3rd Reg; 71 Beale St, Memphis PO
SAMUEL, Howard, H-60-1; Pvt L Co 1st US Inf; 63 to 65 (1 yr 6 mos); Chattanooga PO
SAMUEL, Isabel, Sh-145-3; Pvt C Co 3rd US Hvy Art; Oct 63 to Jan 66; Millington PO; 1st Cap Coe, 2nd Capt Mathula
SAMUEL, Norman, Mu-189-1; Pvt D Co 4th US Cav; 11-5-65 to 11-6-68; Columbia PO
SAMUEL, William H., Rb-219-2; Pvt E Co 9th KY Reg; Jul 64 to Apr 26 65 (11 mos); Black Jack PO; shot left shoulder breaking shoulder blade; CONF
SAMUELS, David R., K-164-2; Cpl H Co 1st TN Vol; 9 Aug 61 to 20 Sep 64; PO omitted (Knoxville?)
SANDEFORD, Robert, G-52-1; Pvt F Co 55th IN Col (or Cav?); 5-17-63 to 12-13-65; Gibson Wells PO
SANDER, Henry, F-37-2; Pvt C Co 59th US Col Inf; to Jan 31 66; Somerville PO
SANDERS, Abraham, C-25-1; Pvt M Co 9th TN Cav; 10-4-64 to 9-16-65; Agee PO; diareah & crippled in sholder by being thown from horse
SANDERS, Abraham, Ru-241-5; Cpl G Co 14th TN Inf; 63 to 65; Murfreesboro PO; shot in foot
SANDERS, Andrew J., Mo-126-2; Missima E. widow of; Pvt 2nd TN Inf; Tevis PO
SANDERS, Brewer, Ch-13-2; Jane B. widow of; Pvt C Co 1st AL Vol; Fall 62 to __ (2 yrs); Jacks Creek PO; was kill while army
SANDERS, Daniel, A-1-3; Pvt I Co 7th TN Inf; 11-8-64 to 7-28-65; Andersonville PO; disease of the lungs, only able to do half work
SANDERS, David, Mu-193-1; Pvt D Co 111th OH Cav; 5-2-63 to 9-6-63; Columbia PO
SANDERS, Dillo, Je-145-1; Emily widow of; Pvt C Co 9th TN Cav; 12 Jun 63 to 11 Sep 65; Dumplin PO
SANDERS, Drur. D., Mn-121-1; Pvt 4th TN Mtd Inf; 66 (sic) to Jun 65; Bethel Springs PO; old and cant git all the information
SANDERS, Eli, Un-256-3; US Sol; PO omitted
SANDERS, Forman C., Cr-16-1; Sgt D Co 7th TN Cav; Sep 24 62 to Oct 26 63; Huntingdon PO
SANDERS, George, Sh-179-1(2); Pvt C Co 58th US Inf; Memphis PO
SANDERS, Henry, Mu-193-1; Pvt; 1-1-63 to 3-15-65; Columbia PO
SANDERS, Henry C., D-85-1(2); Maj 4th TN Inf; Jan 1 63 to Aug 6 65; Paragon Mills PO
SANDERS, Cf-35-3; Pvt C Co 1st TN Inf; 27 Jul 61 to 3 Aug 62; Normandy PO; CONF
SANDERS, James A., Mu-210-6; Pvt G Co 1st TN Inf; 5-1-61 to 5-65; Kidian PO; shot through left leg; CONF
SANDERS, James D., Sm-169-1; Pvt A Co 4th TN Mtd Inf; 8-23-64 to 8-23-65; Carthage PO
SANDERS, James M., Gi-138-2; Pvt C Co 3rd IL; 10-64 to 65; Valesville PO
SANDERS, Jesse, He-60-2; Martha widow of; Pvt A Co 73rd IL Reg; 61 to 65 (about 4 yrs); Lexington PO; deafness & scurvy
SANDERS, Joel D., Mn-126-1; B Co; 9-62 to 5-22-65; Purdy PO
SANDERS, John, Un-258-3; Pvt C Co 1st TN Inf; 9 Aug 61 to 17 Sep 64; Longhollow PO
SANDERS, John L., A-10-1; Pvt I Co 1st TN Inf; 63 to 65; Briceville PO
SANDERS, John M., Cr-15-2; US Sol; Maple Creek PO
SANDERS, John R., Br-8-1; P-t A Co 4th TN Cav; 10-25-62 to 7-12-65; Blue Springs Stn. PO; sun stroke

SANDERS, Lavega A., M-105-1; 2nd Sgt? B Co 37th KY Mtd Inf; 1-1-63 to 12-29-64; Echo PO
SANDERS, Martha J., Ru-231-1; 2nd Dist
SANDERS, Micheal, Su-238-1; Mary widow of; Pvt M Co 13th TN Cav; 1 Aug 65 to 65 (9 mos); White Store PO; chronic diarhea, died in horspittal
SANDERS, Robt. W., Hu-103-1; Pvt E Co 10th TN Inf; 10 Jul 62 to 10 Dec 65; PO omitted
SANDERS, Thomas, Ro-206-1; Pvt D Co 1st TN Inf; 9 Aug 61 to 17 Sep 64; Emory Gap PO
SANDERS, Thos. J., Dy-27-3; Pvt C Co 47th TN Inf; Jan 62 to Apr 65; Tatemville PO; CONF
SANDERS, Wm., Cr-20-1; Tabitha J. widow of; Pvt; Profit PO
SANDERS, Willis C., Sh-144-1; Pvt C Co 1st KY Cav; Nov 64 to May 65; Tipton St, Memphis PO
SANDERSON, William R., Hd-49-1; Pvt C Co 6th TN Cav; Jun 6 63 to Aug 65; Olive Hill PO
SANDIDGE, Harvey, Br-7-1; Pvt L Co 1st TN Cav; 9-1-62 to 6-5-65; Felker PO
SANDLIN, Cornelius, Sh-175-1; Pvt D Co 3rd US Inf; 5-63 to 4-65; Memphis PO
SANDLIN, James M., Dk-32-3; Pvt C Co 5th TN Cav; 8-8-63 to 8-14-65; Alexandria PO
SANDLING, Orman, Cr-8-2; Pvt C Co 27th TN; 30 Jul 61 to 31 Jul 64; Maury City PO; shot through 4 leg; CONF
SANDRIGE, Perry S., Hw-125-5; Mtd Inf B Co 2nd KY Bat; 62 to Jan 65; Surgoinsville PO; CONF
SANDS, Jessee, K-174-2(1); Pvt D Co 9th TN Cav; 22 Jul 63 to 11 Sep 65; Church Grove PO
SANDS, John (see Walker, Joseph L.)
SANDS, John, Bo-23-2; Harriett L. widow of; Pvt D Co 6th TN Inf; 4-62 to 12-25-64; Cades Cove PO; rheumatism, now not able to work half time (error here; may refer to Joseph L. Walker)
SANDS, John, Cl-58-2; Sarah A. widow of; Pvt; Davo PO
SANDS, William A., K-171-5(4); Tennessee widow of; Pvt G Co 7th TN Mtd Inf; 19 Dec 64 to 27 Jul 65; Bearden PO
SANDUSKEY, Julias H., Gi-138-1; Pvt I Co 4th E(ng?); 10-1-64 to 8-20-65; Bodinham PO
SANDY, Thomas W., La-117-1; Pvt I Co 48th TN Inf; Oct 17 61 to __; Pinkereney PO; CONF
SANE, Jacob, Co-60-1; Annie widow of; Co B 8th TN; 1 yr; Parrattsville PO; died in service
SANFORD, Edward J., K-155-2(1); Pvt; 192 Hill St, Knoxville PO
SANFORD, Joseph L., Co-67-3; Pvt H Co 11th NC Inf; 15 Jan 63, captured & parrolled; Cosby PO; gun shot left leg; CONF
SANFORD, Robert, Dy-27-3; Mary E. wife of; Pvt TN Cav; Feb 63 to Apr 65; Tatemville PO; CONF
SAPP, John T., Wh-181-1; Pvt G Co 6th TN Mtd Inf; PO omitted
SARGENT, David F., Fe-41-4(2); Pvt G Co 1st WV Cav; 8-14-61 to 9-19-64; Boat Land PO; resulting dis. left lung, captured 2nd Bat Bull Run
SARGENT, John J., Un-256-2; Pvt C Co 9th TN Cav; Oct 63 to Sep 65; Rule PO; cronic diarhear
SARNCAR, Rebecca, Dy-29-1; widow US Sol; 9th Civil Dist
SARRETT, John, Ge-83-4; Pvt 26th VA Inf; 64 to 65; Horse Creek PO
SARRETT, Samuel H., Se-225-3; Martha A. widow of; Pvt B Co 6th TN Inf; 8 Mar 62 to Jul 65; Cotlettsburg PO; catarrh of head 25 yrs
SARRETT, William R., D-72-5; Pvt; 61 to 65; Nashville PO; in prison 2 yrs at F. Delaware; CONF
SARTEN, John W., Je-146-5; Pvt C Co 3rd TN Cav; 1 Aug 63 to 13 Sep 65; White Pine PO; dont know disease, I think he was shot
SARTIN, Alexander, Ro-210-10; Pvt I Co 6th TN Inf; 10 Jun 62 to 12 Jun 65; Rockwood PO
SARTIN, Alexander, Je-146-1; Pvt B Co 9th TN Cav; 29 Jul 63 to 11 Sep 65; White Pine PO; piles & heat disease, old man bad off
SARTIN, Cornelius, Sm-171-1; Mary widow of; Pvt H Co 5th TN Mtd Inf; 8-63 to 8-65; Chestnut Mount PO
SARTIN, David M., Je-146-2; Pvt C Co 9th TN Cav; 1 Aug 63 to 13 Sep 65; White Pines PO; I dont know disability, looks bad

SARTIN, Joseph, Ro-203-2; US Sol; Wheat PO
SARVER, Isaac, Sn-259-1; Pvt C Co 14th __; 6-2-62 to 7-2-65; Bethpage PO; ruptured
SARVER, Peter, Sn-262-3(2); Pvt; Fountain Head PO; lost his discharge and he is deaf, can not find out anything about him
SASSEEN, David R., Se-226-5; Cpl D Co 3rd TN Cav; 1 Dec 62 to 3 Aug 65; Shady Grove PO (Jefferson Co.); crippled l. hip, l. elbow & back
SASSEENE, Louis, H-69-5; Pvt; Chattanooga PO
SATERFIELD, Alex L., Gr-70-1; Pvt B Co 18th KY Inf; 15 Jul 63 to 15 Nov 65; Rutledge PO; rheumatism
SATON, S. J., H-52-1; Lookout Mt. PO
SATTERFIELD, Benjamin C., Je-146-5; Pvt A Co 9th TN Cav; 62 to 65; White Pine PO
SATTERFIELD, John, Mu-195-1; Sol wife dont know; Columbia PO
SATTERFIELD, John W., Gr-81-4(2); Pvt A Co 12th TN Cav; 8 Jun 63 to 28 Oct 65; Liberty Hill PO; chron dyrhie, no prostrate
SATTERFIELD, Levi, Gr-81-5(3); Sarah widow of; Pvt 2nd TN Inf; Shelton's Ford PO; died in service at Cumberland Gap
SAULESBURY, James M., Ge-100-1; Pvt M Co 9th TN Cav; 1 Jun 63 to 11 Sep 65; Midway PO; not curable
SAUME?, Isaac, Ru-249-1; Pvt A Co 29th OH; 9-15-64 to 5-17-65; Pinckard PO; skull fractured, right eye affected, criple in left leg
SAUNDERS, David, Se-226-6; Nancy Hickman formerly widow of; Pvt; Cynthiana PO (Jefferson Co.)
SAUNDERS, John, L-100-1; Pollie widow of; Pvt F Co 4th US Col Hvy Art; Ripley PO; cannot give dates
SAUNDERS, Michael F., Di-42-1; Pvt D Co 16th WI Inf; 2-6-62 to 5-11-63; Tenn City PO; also Pvt 13th Bat WI Art; 9-24-63 to 7-20-65
SAUNDERS, Milo, Fr-105-2; Pvt I Co 3rd VT V Inf; 1 Jun 61 to 27 Jul 64; Winchester PO
SAUXTER, Braxtan, D-73-1; Pvt; 3 yrs 6 mos; Nashville PO
SAVAGE, Charles (see Frasure, Carrel)
SAVAGE, John, Un-251-1; Pvt M Co 9th TN Cav; Sep 63 to Sep 65; Effie PO; diaresh
SAVAGE, Thos., Col, Sm-168-2; Pvt TN Inf; 62 to 4-65; Pleasant Shade PO; chronic disease of the bowels, ruptured
SAVAGE, William E., Un-259-1; Pvt D Co 1st TN Inf; 7 Aug 61 to 1 Nov 64; Rhodelia PO; lung & liver & heart 28 yrs, exposure & fever
SAVERS, William, K-174-2(1); Mary widow of; Pvt G Co 4th TN Inf; 15 Dec 63 to 7 Jun 65; Snoderly PO
SAWYER, Francis, Sh-204-2; Franklin Ave, Memphis PO
SAWYER, Horatio G., Sh-180-1; Lt I Co 8th NH Inf; 12-12-61 to 11-7-65; 449 Pontotoc St, Memphis PO
SAWYER, Isac, D-97-1; Pvt B Co 14th MS Inf; Oct 14 61 to 65; Nashville PO; CONF
SAWYER, J. M., Gr-70-1; Maj B Co 8th TN Cav; 15 Apr 62 to 11 Sep 65; Rutledge PO
SAWYER, John, Hn-75-1; Pvt I Co 136th IL Inf; 15 Apr 63 to 20 Oct 63; Big Sandy PO
SAWYER, John S., Moo-216-1; Cpl G Co 6th IL Cav; Sep 61 to 25 Jul 65; Lynchburg PO
SAWYERS, Eli L., R-158-2; Pvt C Co 5th TN Inf; 8-15-63 to 10-26-64; Adjutant 6th TN Mtd Inf; 10-26-64 to 5-26-65 (resigned); Rhea Springs PO
SAWYERS, James T., Jo-150-3; Pvt D Co 1st AL Cav; 24 Aug 63 to 28 Sep 64; Trade PO
SAXON, John M., Hd-50-4; Nancy widow of; Pvt; Nixon PO
SAXON, Nelson, Sh-160-1; Pvt TN Cav; Apr 61 to Oct 65; Memphis, Poplar Street (126 to 130) PO; consumption
SAXON, Robert L., Hd-50-4; Pvt H Co 6th TN Vol Cav (also 60th TN?); 12-1-62 to 7-26-65; Nixon PO; gun shot wound in ankle
SAYLES, Bonaparte, Sh-189-3; Dee Ave, Memphis PO
SAYLOR, Burtis W., Wh-186-2; Pvt K Co 1st TN Mtd Inf; 10-23-64 to 7-22-65; Bakers Cross Roads PO
SAYLOR, David, Wa-269-2; Johnson City PO; chronic diarhea, piles, soldier and discharge away from home

SAYLOR, Isaac, Wa-269-1; Mahulda C. widow; Cpl H Co 8th TN Cav; 15 Sep 63 to 11 Sep 65; Johnson City PO
SAYLOR, Thomas, Wa-267-3; 2nd Cpl G Co 8th TN Cav; 15 Sep 63 to 29 Oct 64; Jonesboro PO
SCALES, Alfred, Hd-51-2; US Sol; 10th Civil Dist
SCALES, Margaret (see McCauley, _____)
SCALES, Samuel H., Ru-13-2; Pvt Litter Forrest Art; 62 to 63; Murfreesboro PO; CONF
SCALES, Vigon, Sh-183-2; Margaret widow of; Cpl B Co 4th R Inf; 10-1-64 to 9-1-65; Memphis PO; died on 9-15-1870
SCALES, William, D-49-2; Jennie widow of; Pvt C Co 101st US Inf; Nashville PO; knows nothing more
SCALF, Isaac, Su-242-2; US Sol; 16th Civil Dist
SCALF, James, Ct-41-3; Marge A. widow of; Pvt H Co 13th TN Cav; 9-24-63 to 9-5-65; South Wattauga PO
SCALF, William J., Ct-41-2; Pvt H Co 13th TN Cav; 9-24-63 to 9-5-65; South Wattauga PO; masht knee and rhumatism
SCALS, Felix, Bl-3-6; Pvt G Co 6th TN Cav; 7-63 to 3-65; Tanbark PO; inflamation lungs
SCARBOORO, Robt. F., We-220-3; 1st Civil Dist
SCARBOROUGH, Thomas, R-159-2; Mace widow of; Pvt TN Inf; 3-61 to __; Rhea Springs PO; died in army
SCARBOROUGH, William V., A-8-2; Pvt K Co 5th TN Inf; 4-24-62 to 5-13-65; Scarborough PO
SCARBROUGH, Albert A., Ro-203-3; Pvt G Co 1st TN Inf; 9 Aug 61 to 17 Sep 64; Ethel PO; rheumatism
SCARBROUGH, James, D-47-1; Pvt H Co 13th TN Cav; 62 to 65; Hamilton St, Nashville PO
SCARBROUGH, James B., Ro-206-1; Pvt B Co 5th TN Inf; 27 Feb 62 to 28 May 65; Emory Gap PO
SCARBROUGH, John J., Ro-202-1; Cpl D Co 5th TN Inf; 22 Feb 62 to 30 Mar 65; Union X Roads PO; throat, lungs & heart
SCARBROUGH, Jonathan R., Ro-202-2; Pvt I Co 1st TN Inf; 11 Aug 61 to 1 Jul 62; Union X Roads PO; fever in legs
SCARBROUGH, William H., Mc-116-1; Sgt D Co 10th TN Cav; 1-1-64 to 8-1-65; Riceville PO; piles contracted in the war
SCARLET, John, Je-135-1(3); Pvt E Co 1st TN Cav; 20 Apr 62 to 21 Apr 65; Leonidas PO; discharged--time out
SCARLET, John C., Br-10-2; 6th Civil Dist
SCARLETT, Margarett, K-154-5(2); widow; Knoxville PO
SCARLETT, Moses, Pu-147-2; Permelia widow of; Pvt C Co 8th TN Mtd Inf; Byrne PO
SCARLETT, Stephen, Se-226-1; Wgn Master D Co 9th TN Cav; 11 Feb 63 to 11 Aug 65; Cynthiana PO (Jefferson Co.); pile of corn fell on him & ruptured him
SCATES, Green, He-61-1; Pvt C Co 7th TN Cav; 24 Apr 63 to 9 Aug 65; Alberton PO
SCHADE, John, La-113-1; Pvt E Co 58th OH Inf; 23 Feb 65 to 16 Sep 65; Lawrenceburgh PO
SCHAEFFER, John B., Sh-167-2; Pvt I Co 14th OH Inf; 2 May 64 to 24 Sep 64; PO omitted
SCHARF, Fanny, Sh-167-3; PO omitted
SCHAUFNER, David, C-28-2(1); Pvt B Co 8th TN Cav; _-15-63 to 9-11-65; Big Creek Gap PO; ribs broken
SCHERER, Charles J., Sh-167-3; PO omitted
SCHILL, August, R-162-1; Pvt M Co 4th TN Cav; 10-64 to 6-65; Dayton PO; left leg broken and disabled
SCHLEY, Elija E., Sh-183-1; don't know any more; Memphis PO
SCHLOSSHAN, Philip, C-30-1; Pvt 16th IL Inf; Well Spring PO
SCHMIDT, Elizabeth, D-66-1; widow, lost her papers; Pvt 47th NY Inf; Nashville PO; 604 S Chery PO
SCHMIDT, Frederick, Hd-52-1; Sgt D Co 107th NY; Mar 16 62 to Sep 16 66; Pittsburg PO; arm shot off
SCHMIDT, Robert, D-63-2; Rebecca widow of; Pvt I Co 9th OH Inf; Apr 22 61 to Jan 7 64; Nashville PO
SCHNABEL, Michael, Sh-184-2; 28th OH Art; 6-6-61 to 6-26-64; rear 98 Robeson St, Memphis PO; thrown from horse & wounded in grone causing rupture (duplicate)
SCHNABELL, Michael, Sh-184-1; Pvt A Co 28th OH Inf; 6-13-61 to 6-25-65; Memphis PO; wounded in groin (duplicate)
SCHNEIDER, Paul, Sh-176-1; Bugler 5th US Art; 12-1-62 to 11-30-65; 85 Mulberry St, Memphis PO; slightly wounded but entirely recovered
SCHNEIDER, William, Sh-197-1; Pvt A Co 1st White ?; 5-61 to 7-64; Memphis PO; papers at Washington
SCHNIETZLER, George, Li-160-1; Pvt C Co 7th NY; May 63 to Aug 65; Goshen PO
SCHOENE, August, Sh-158-1; Cpl G Co 5th MO Vol Cav; 16 Aug 61 to 1 Oct 62; Memphis PO
SCHRAMM, Louis, H-62-5; US Sol; 111 W Sixth St, Chattanooga PO
SCHRIMPF, Charles C., D-45-1; 3rd Sgt I Co 28th KY Inf; 8-7-62 to 6-14-65; Nashville PO
SCHRIMSHER, James E., Lo-189-2; Pvt 5th TN Inf; Philadelphia PO
SCHROEDER, C., Sn-264-1; Bugler C Co 3rd Art; Mar 29 __ to 66 (5 yrs); Portland PO; this man was a reenlisted man from Art to Cav, mustered in 1866 at Ft. Macon, NC, Hasting Capt. Emory, Col., both discharges lost
SCHROLL, John B., K-181-6(3); Pvt E Co 45th PA Vol; Jul 61 to __; Knoxville PO
SCHROM, John, Fr-105-1; Pvt H Co 28th OH V Inf; 11 Jul 62 to 6 Jul 65; Winchester PO; shot in lef arm
SCHROYER, Aaron V., D-79-2; PVt 3rd PA RVC, re-enlist H Co 188th PA Vol; Jul 11 61 to Jul 25 62 and May 7 63 to Dec 14 65; Nashville PO; rupture, caused by exposure
SCHROYER, Jno., La-117-2; Pvt C Co 34th OH Mtd Inf; Apr 21 61 to Jun 65; 15th Dist
SCHULER, Elias T., Sh-201-4; Fannie widow of; Memphis PO
SCHULLZ, George, Sh-157-1; Pvt; PO omitted
SCHULTZ, George S., Sh-157-6; Insely's Farm PO
SCHULTZ, Wm. M., H-60-1; Pvt B Co 12th TN Cav; 9-63 to 12-65; Chattanooga PO; right inguinal hernia
SCHULZE, Louis C., W-193-2; Pvt E Co 9th IN Cav; 8-31-63 to 2-3-66; Smartt PO
SCHWEDER, Louis, D-91-2; Sgt E Co 12th MO Inf; Aug 61 to Sep 64; Nashville PO; wounded in right elbow
SCIVALLEY, John W., Fr-110-1; Pvt B Co 29th MO; Aug 13 62 to Oct 5 64; Maxwell PO; shot through thigh and one finger off
SCOATT, William, K-176-3; Halls X Roads PO
SCOBEY, David J., Dy-29-3; Pvt D Co 13th TN Cav; Dec 63 to 14 Feb 64; Newbern PO
SCOBEY, Willie B., Dy-29-3; Pvt D Co 13th TN Cav; Dec 63 to 14 Feb 64; Newbern PO
SCOGGINS, James P., Br-12-4; Pvt; Georgetown PO; rheumatism
SCORBROUGH, Jonathan, A-6-5(3); Pvt D Co 1st TN Art; 11-1-63 to 6-1-65; PO omitted
SCOTT, Alexander, B-5-1; Pvt A Co 17th US Col Inf; 1-64 to 5-66; Shelbyville PO; wounded right hip
SCOTT, Aurther J., T-209-2; Sol; 4th Civil Dist
SCOTT, Celia, Mt-138-2; widow US Sol; Dist No 7, N. Providence PO
SCOTT, Charles, Sh-191-4; Elizabeth widow of; Memphis PO; records not seen
SCOTT, Daniel H., He-60-1; Pvt A Co 7th TN Cav; 9-62 to 8-65; Lexington PO; contract a case of reumatism, I was Andersonville prison 6 mos
SCOTT, Dock, Sh-150-3; Sgt A Co 1st TN Inf; 2 yrs 6 mos; Bartlett PO
SCOTT, Elisha L., Lo-195-3(1); Pvt G Co 3rd TN Mtd Inf; 5 Aug 62 to 30 Nov 64; Loudon PO; two ribs & right wrist broken, Pvt C Co 7th TN Mtd Inf--1 Dec 64 to 12 Jul 65
SCOTT, Francis, Hu-102-1; Sol; 4th Civil Dist; CONF
SCOTT, George, Li-148-1; PO omitted
SCOTT, George W., Sh-145-2; Pvt E Co 17th KY Inf; 15 Oct 61 to Mar 63; Millington PO; hernia left groin, draws a pension, Capt James W. Anthony, Col Jno. H. McHeny

SCOTT, Henry C., Cr-14-2; Pvt G Co 7th TN Cav; 5 Aug 62 to 25 Oct 63; Clarksburg PO; reenlisted
SCOTT, Henry J., Cr-8-1; Barbara A. widow of; Pvt I Co 7th TN Cav; Jul __ to __; Spring Creek PO; camp scurvy, died at Andersonville
SCOTT, Israel, Lo-188-2; Pvt A Co 5th TN Inf; 25 Feb 62 to 4 Apr 65; Stockton PO
SCOTT, J. T. H., Rb-220-1; Orderly B Co 30th TN; Mar 11 61 to Sep 9 64; Barrenplains PO; shot in left breast; CONF
SCOTT, James, W-193-1; Barbary A. widow of; Pvt K Co 100th Col Inf; Thaxton PO; discharge sent to Washington & not returned but bounty was paid
SCOTT, James H., R-162-3; Pvt E Co 3rd TN Mtd Inf; 7-20-64 to 11-13-64; Dayton PO; rheumatism and lungs diseased, caused from exposure in service
SCOTT, James J., He-59-1; Sol US; PO omitted
SCOTT, James M., Hd-44-1; Pvt 6th TN Cav; PO omitted
SCOTT, James M., Wa-263-5; Pvt B Co 12th TN Cav; 14 Jun 63 to Oct 65; Telford PO
SCOTT, James R., Lo-188-1; Pvt C Co 3rd TN Cav; 5 Dec 62 to 10 Jun 65; Adolphus PO
SCOTT, Jesse R., He-64-1; Pvt A Co 7th TN Cav; 24 Aug 62 to 26 Jun 65; Middle Fork PO
SCOTT, Jim, Ma-124-1; Betsie widow of; Jackson PO
SCOTT, Jim, G-57-3; Pvt H Co 1st TN Cav; 62 to 64; Yorkville PO; CONF
SCOTT, John, Hr-86-1; Navy; Grand Junction PO; flesh wound, was under Capt Letherbury
SCOTT, John Jr., Bo-15-1; Pvt E Co 3rd TN Mtd Inf; 4-2-64 to 11-20-64; Mountvale PO
SCOTT, John, Gu-45-1; Pvt E Co 1st TN Cav Vid(ette); 63 to 64 (8 mos); Altamont PO
SCOTT, John H., B-15-1; Pvt H Co 136th PA Inf; 8-62 to 5-63; Shelbyville PO
SCOTT, John H., 4-63-2; Pvt A Co 5th OH Cav; 10-64 to 6-65; 710 Cypress, Chattanooga PO
SCOTT, John R., Lo-188-2; Elizabeth widow of; Pvt; Adolphus PO; discharge lost
SCOTT, John W., Hd-50-3; Pvt F Co 6th TN Mtd? Cav?; Oct 1 62 to __; Stout PO
SCOTT, Joseph, A-4-4; Pvt C Co; Coal Creek PO; CONF
SCOTT, Joseph F., K-156-1; Pvt Hualls Batter 1st E TN; 23 Sep 62 to 11 Apr 63; 57 Pine, Knoxville PO; CONF
SCOTT, Joseph F., Gi-127-6; Pvt B Co 3rd TN Cav; 63 to 6-65; Pulaski PO; discharge lost
SCOTT, Joshua, Dk-32-3; Martha A. widow of; Pvt A Co 5th TN Cav; 7-28-62 to __ (2 mos 24 days); Liberty PO; died in hospital
SCOTT, Lenard M., Dk-32-3; Pvt E Co 4th TN Mtd Inf; 9-24-64 to 8-25-65; Liberty PO
SCOTT, Loranza D., U-247-2; Pvt H Co 13th TN Cav; 27 Jan 63 to 5 Sep 65; Erwin PO; rheumatism & heart disease
SCOTT, Manson B., Dk-35-1; Pvt E Co 4th TN Mtd Inf; 10-5-64 to 8-25-65; Temperance Hall PO; ruptured
SCOTT, Marcus L., Co-61-3(1); Pvt H Co 1st TN Cav; Givens PO; CONF
SCOTT, Nathan, F-37-2; Pvt C Co US Col Inf; 6 mos; Somerville PO; dismissed on account of sickness
SCOTT, Peter H., We-227-1; Pvt F Co 111th IL Inf; 27 Jun 63 to 14 Aug 65; Greenfield PO; shot in left foot
SCOTT, Richard, Hr-86-1; Pvt B Co 59th TN; 63 to 66; Grand Junction PO; flesh wound in leg
SCOTT, Robert, Sm-175-2(1); Pvt H Co 5th TN Cav; 5-63 to 8-65; Enoch PO
SCOTT, Samuel M., Ja-84-3; Pvt G Co 5th TN Inf; 12-62 to __; Normans Store PO; rupture
SCOTT, Samuel R., B-3-2; 3rd Civil Dist
SCOTT, Samuel T., Cr-14-3; Pvt G Co 2nd TN Mtd Inf; 29 Dec 63 to 1 Feb 65; Clarksburg PO; wound on head
SCOTT, Thomas, St-162-1; alias Thomas Parchman; Artilery D Co 8th US Hvy; Mar __ to __ (2 yrs 6 mos); Cumberland City PO; bleeding at lungs; papers all lost
SCOTT, Thomas, Lo-188-3; Pvt G Co 3rd TN Mtd Inf; 25 Aug 64 to 20 Nov 64; Stockton PO
SCOTT, William (William One), L-99-1; Pvt 152nd NY US Inf; 65 to 66; Henning PO; pneumonia, he went by name of William One
SCOTT, William, H-53-1; Queen widow of; Pvt B Co 78th PA Inf; 11-4-64 to 65 (8 mos); Chattanooga PO; scalp wound
SCOTT, William A., Di-36-1; Pvt K Co 25th TN Inf; 3-61 to 65; Bellsburgh PO; CONF
SCOTT, William B., H-49-10; Pvt A Co 6th TN Mtd Inf; 8-2-64 to 6-30-65; Daisy PO
SCOTT, William C., M-103-5; Cpl H Co 5th KY Cav; 12-4-61 to 5-30-65; Lafayette PO; relapse of measles
SCOTT, William C., Ge-95-2; Pvt K Co 8th TN Cav; 12 Oct 63 to 11 Sep 65; Rheatown PO; nasal catarrah
SCOTT, William H., Lo-188-2; Pvt G Co 3rd TN Mtd Inf; 25 Aug 64 to 30 Mar 64; Stockton PO
SCOTT, William J., Mg-197-5; Lt 3rd TN Inf; 21 May 62 to 29 May 64; Montgomery PO; rheumatism
SCOTT, William M., Sn-264-1; Pvt A Co 1st __; 5 Feb 64 to Apr 65; Portland PO; shot in left foot, still suffers from wound, this mans papers on file at Wash DC, Mtd Inf
SCOUT?, C. F., Hr-96-1; Pvt B Co 7th TN Cav; 63 to 65; Dorris PO; CONF
SCRIBNER, Charles, Rb-218-1; Pvt G Co 15th OH Inf; 61 to 64; Cross Plains PO
SCRIBNER, L. S., Gi-133-2; Pvt 1st TN; 64 to 65; Bufords PO; CONF
SCROTH, Charles, H-51-2(1); Pvt 9th OH Inf; 5-12-61 to 5-28-67; Hill City PO
SCRUDGINGTON, Alexander, Ge-92-3; Pvt A Co 4th TN Inf; Ottway PO
SCRUGGS, Armstead S., H-72-1; Musician D Co 44th US Col Inf; 5-20-64 to 4-30-66; Chattanooga PO; captured & held as waiter, 3 mos
SCRUGGS, Calvin, Ja-84-1; Celia A. widow of; Pvt D? Co 44th Reg TN Inf; Harrison PO
SCRUGGS, D. S., Mu-197-1; Pvt C Co 111th US Inf; 63 to __; Columbia PO
SCRUGGS, Henry, Sh-162-2(1); Pvt A Co 14th Col Inf; 63 to 65; Ramsey PO; discharged at Nashville
SCRUGGS, James C., A-5-3; Pvt C Co 2nd TN Inf; 8-7-61 to 5-1-65; Clinton PO
SCRUGGS, Jessey, Sh-150-3; Winnie widow of; Cpl I Co 59th US Inf; 1 Jan 63 to 3 Jan 66; Bartlett PO
SCRUGGS, John W., A-13-2; Pvt B Co 3rd TN Inf; 3-26-62 to 5-10-65; Briceville PO; priner 17 mos
SCRUGGS, Nathan, A-5-4; Jucy widow of; Pvt A Co 1st USC HA (Hvy Art); 1-21-64 to 3-31-66; Clinton PO
SCRUGGS, Thomas J., A-5-3; Pvt C Co 2nd TN Inf; 8-7-61 to 2-65; Clinton PO
SCRUGS, Jacob, Mc-111-1; Barbara widow of; Pvt C Co 42nd US Col Inf; 9-23-64 to 9-15-65; Gudger PO (Monroe Co.)
SCUDLER, David, Ru-241-3; Pvt A Co 5th TN Inf; 63 to 64; PO omitted
SCURLOCK, Jim, Sh-157-1; (alias?) Jones, Manuel; Pvt C Co 3rd US Col Lt Art; 63 to 65; Dist 13
SEA, David, Sh-145-3; 2nd Cpl H Co 15th US Col Inf; 2-63 to 3-66; Millington PO
SEA, Rufus R., Ge-88-3; Mairidee widow of; Pvt; Marvin PO; no discharge & dont tell dates
SEABORN, Benjamin F., D-75-2; Lt I Co 20th TN Inf; 6-1-61 to 5-25-65; Stewarts Ferry PO; reinlisted veteran; CONF
SEABORN, Isaac R., D-75-3; Margaret J. widow of; Pvt IU 20th TN Inf; Stewarts Ferry PO; CONF
SEABORN, John K., Br-13-1; 2nd Sgt G Co 5th TN Inf; 12-1-64 to 6-13-65; Cleveland PO
SEAGLE, James A., H-56-7; Mary C. widow of; Cpl D Co 4th TN Cav; 7-63 to 7-65; St. Elmo PO
SEAL, Alfred, Ha-113-2; Pvt E Co 8th TN Cav; 11-10-63 to 10-10-65; Sneedville PO
SEAL, Anderson, Ha-110-3; Pvt A Co 47th KY Inf; 7-3-63 to 12-26-64; Michburgh PO
SEAL, Champ M., Ha-116-3(1); Pvt B? Co 1st TN Cav; 3-11-62 to 4-10-65; Sneedville PO; kick by a horse, cronic direha
SEAL, Darkar, Ha-114-1; Pvt H Co 4th OH Cav; 7-12-64 to 6-10-65; Xenophon PO; arm shot off; CONF
SEAL, Enoch, Ha-114-2; Pvt C Co 9th TN Cav; 11-1-63 to 11-2-64; Xerxes PO
SEAL, Frederick, Ha-110-3; Pvt A Co 47th KY Inf; 7-3-63 to 12-26-64; Michburgh PO; rheumatism

SEAL, Ivin, Ha-116-3(1); Pvt (S) C Co 10th TN Cav; 9-23-63 to __ (1 yr); Clinch PO; lungs affect, prizend 6 mos at Richmond

SEAL, William, Ha-111-3; Matilda widow of; Maness, Scott Co., VA

SEALS, James Jr., Bl-2-2(1); Pvt TN?; Seals PO

SEALS, James W., Ca-24-1; Pvt D Co 3rd TN Inf; 10-15-64 to 11-29-65; Talvine PO; phthisic, effect of cold in service

SEALS, Nancy A. (see Simmons, Monroe)

SEAMAN, William, Sh-188-2; Pvt US Col Inf; 5-18-63 to 65; Haynes Alley, Memphis PO

SEAMANE, Fran G., K-154-2; Sgt; 7-6-61 to 9-14-63; Knoxville PO; during war incured

SEARCEY, Robert, B-2-1; Pvt Haddam's Battery; 4-61 to 4-64; Fairfield PO

SEARCY, Ephriham, D-64-1; Nashville PO

SEARCY, James, B-3-2; Pvt F Co 5th TN Cav; 9-7-62 to 6-25-65; Wartrace PO

SEARS, Houston, Sm-174-2; Pvt A Co 42nd US Col Inf; 9-2-64 to 1-31-66; Grant PO

SEARS, James L., Br-13-2; Pvt L Co 4th TN Cav; 12-25-63 to 7-24-65; Georgetown PO

SEAT, Anderson, D-85-1(2); Pvt C Co 29th IL Inf; 10-1-61 to 1-65; Paragon Mills PO; reinlisted vetran

SEAT, Cornelia, G-50-1; widow?; 2nd Civil Dist

SEATES, Zebalen B., We-230-1; Pvt K Co 6th TN Reg; 4-4-64 to 1-11-65; Greenfield PO; CONF

SEATON, Benjamin F., Ge-102-1; Pvt E Co 4th TN Inf; 11-15-61 to 7-7-65; Camp Creek PO

SEATON, Elisha, D-78-1; Pvt C Co 4th TN Mtd Inf; 9-64 to 4-65; Nashville PO

SEATON, James B., Bo-20-1; Pvt M Co 2nd TN Cav; 11-8-62 to 12-23-63; Bank PO; cronic cattarrh, resigned on disabilities

SEATON, James H., Se-222-2; Pvt M Co 2nd TN Cav; 11-8-62 to 7-6-65; Harrisburg PO; rumatism, mind, site, hearing

SEATON, N. G., Bo-22-3; Pvt E Co 9th TN Cav; 12-1-64 to 9-11-65; Seaton PO

SEATON, Pinckney P., Se-223-3; Lt E Co 9th TN Cav; 10-1-63 to 9-11-65; Henderson Springs PO

SEATON, Sarah (see Trotter, Lorenzey)

SEATON, William, Hd-50-6; Pvt D Co 2nd TN Mtd Inf; 3-8-64 to 5-13-65; Nixon PO

SEATON, William B., Bo-20-2; 1st Sgt E Co 9th TN Cav; 12-9-62 to 12-9-64; Maryville PO; chronic diarhea, sore eyes

SEATON, Wm. P., Ge-99-2; Sarah E. widow of; Pvt F Co 8th TN Cav; Cedar Creek PO; killed; couldn't get any of the dates

SEATS, Louis M., Sh-201-1; Pvt Memphis PO; discharge papers lost; CONF

SEATTLES, Jos., Mu-196-1; discharge is out of Seattles hands just now; Columbia PO; one eye shot out

SEAY, Charley, Wl-294-1; Pvt G Co 14th TN Inf; 1-63 to 4-65; Tuckers X Roads PO; hurt building stockade, eyes also defective

SEAY, George, D-91-3; Pvt Station C, Nashville PO

SEAY, Henry L., Hd-53-3; Cpl M Co 7th TN Cav; 7-6-63 to 6-23-65; Morris Chapel PO; chronic rheumatism, drawing pension

SEAY, John H., H-53-2; Pvt D Co 24th TN Inf; 6-61 to 63 (2 yrs); Chattanooga PO; chronic diarrhea, discharg could not be found

SEAY, John M., Hd-51-1; Pvt E Co 1st AL Inf; 8-29-63 to 12-6-64; Hamburg PO

SEAY, Page, Wl-294-1; Pvt G Co 14th TN Inf; 63 to 11-65; Tuckers X Roads PO; wounded erecting block house, almost disabled

SEAY, Rill, Wl-295-1; Pvt F Co 101st TN Inf; 62 to 65; Lebanon PO

SEAY, Wm., Ge-87-1; Pvt K Co 13th TN Cav; 10-62 to 65 (1 yr 6 mos); Timerridge PO

SEAY, William T., D-72-4; Pvt A Co 7th TN Cav; 9-5-61 to 4-30-63; Nashville PO; discharged on Dr. certificate; CONF

SEBOLT, Arch, Ha-115-1; Narcisa widow of; Pvt I Co 54th VA Cav; 10-12-62 to 4-1-65; not disabled, yet living; CONF

SEBREE, Dudley, Mt-137-1; Pvt E Co 6th US Col Cav; 11-19-62 to 4-15-66; St. Bethlehem PO; frost bitten

SECHRIST, Izeral B., Ge-102-3; Musician M Co 1st MD Cav; 2-64 to 8-65; Whig PO; rheumatism

SEELEY, Freeman H., Ch-13-2; Pvt I Co 24th IL Vol; 7-18-61 to 78; Jacks Creek PO; right hand crippled & deafness, left ear, thrown from baggage from wagon & injured

SEETON, John A., Se-222-1; Pvt M Co 2nd TN Cav; 11-8-62 to 7-6-65; Midel Creeke PO; diseas breast & lungs

SEGO, John J., He-62-2; Pvt Co A 55th TN; 12-16-61 to 7-25-62; Lexington PO; CONF

SEGRAVES, Jessie, Bl-3-1; Pvt I Co 8th TN Cav; 62 to 4-9-63; Patten PO; CONF

SEGRAVES, Moses, He-59-1; Fedral Sol; PO omitted

SEIBER, Fredrick, A-9-5(3); Pvt I Co 9th TN Cav; 8-28-63 to 9-11-65; Prosises PO; measles resulting in lung disease, prisoner 1 mo on Belle Isle

SEIBER, Jackson, S-218-1; Pvt G Co 7th TN ___; 62 to 63?; PO omitted

SEIBER, Jacob, A-9-5(3); Pvt Gibsons Gorillas; 6-63 to 9-63; Dutch Valley PO; came home sick in 9-62 & remained at home; CONF

SEIBER, James, Mg-196-4; Pvt I Co 7th TN Inf; 11-8-64 to 7-27-65; Oliver Springs PO

SEIBER, Mark, Ro-206-3; Elizabeth widow of; Pvt 11th TN Inf; Emory Gap PO; discharge lost

SEIDERS, Henry, H-53-1; Pvt A Co 110th OH Inf; 2-2-63 to 6-20-65; Chattanooga PO; sickness in army from which has not recovered, asthma, lame back etc.

SEIFARD, George W., Cl-50-1; Pvt B Co 7th TN Cav; 6-20-63 to 9-11-65; Cedarford PO; about 8-4-64

SEIFRIED, Theodore, D-91-2; Pvt F Co 22nd IA Inf; 8-11-62 to 7-65; 335 Cherry St, Nashville PO

SEITERS, William M., H-65-1; Pvt K Co 1st OH Art; 7-18-63 to 7-25-65; Chattanooga PO

SEIVERS, Clark B., A-6-4(2); Pvt J Co 9th TN Cav; 5-28-63 to 9-11-65; Fairview PO

SELCER, Absalom, Me-91-1; Pvt D Co 10th TN Cav; 1-1-64 to 8-3-65; Decatur PO; rheumatism, piles & nervousness

SELCER, Absolom, H-49-2; Arleria E. widow of; Capt A Co 6th TN Mtd Inf; 8-2-64 to __; Falling Water PO

SELCER, James M., H-55-1; Martha widow of; Pvt TN Cav; 62 to 65 (2 yrs 6 mos); Tyner PO

SELF, Joseph F., Ge-89-1; Sgt D Co 8th TN Inf; 3-15-63 to 3-26-65; Pilot Knob PO

SELF, Thomas F., Ge-89-2; Pvt C Co 8th TN Inf; 62 to )); Mosheim PO

SELF, William F., Ge-91-1; Com Sgt I Co 1st TN Cav; 11-62 to 6-65; Greeneville PO; catarrhal ophthalmy

SELF, William M., K-180-1; Avalene widow of; Pvt C Co 5th TN Mtd Inf; 9-23-64 to 7-16-65; Ebenezer PO

SELIVAN, Loid, Sh-157-5; Betsey widow of; Pvt 59th US Col?; 62 to ___; White Haven PO

SELLARS, Monroe, Su-288-1; Teamster 4th IN Vol Art; 17-63 to 6-64; Green Hill PO

SELLERS, Alfred, Ge-92-2; Pvt B Co 3rd TN Mtd Inf; 64 to __ (3 mos); Laurel Gap PO

SELLERS, Bob, Mu-210-5; Pvt A Co 13th TN Cav; 8-62 to 65; Mallard PO; shot through finger

SELLERS, Joseph C., Cr-14-3; Pvt; Crider PO

SELLERS, T. M., Je-135-2; Pvt B Co 9th TN Cav; 6-12-63 to 9-11-65; Piedmont PO

SELLERS, William, Mu-210-5; Pvt D Co 3rd TN Inf; 64 to deserted 65 (5 mos); Carters Creek PO

SELLERS, William B., Mc-109-6; Pvt C Co 3rd TN Cav; 12-5-62 to 6-10-65; Mouse Creek PO; chronic diarrhea & rheumatism

SELLERS, William J., Dy-25-1; Pvt Newbern PO; CONF

SELLS, Andrew, Su-237-1; Pvt A Co 13th TN Cav; 8-1-64 to __ (3 mos 12 days); Wahoo PO; hemorrhage of lungs, has never received a discharge, he has entered the service in 8-64 & was captured in 11 following

SELLS, David L., Ov-135-1; Cpl D Co 9th TN Cav; 1-30-63 to 9-11-65; Eagle Creek PO

SELLS, Jacob H., Pi-154-2; Pvt D Co 3rd KY Inf; 12-16-61 to 6-27-63; Byrdstown PO; kidney disease

SELLS, Kilory, Fe-41-1; Pvt D Co 5th TN Cav; 62 to 64; Jamestown PO

SELLS, Samuel, Pi-153-3; Charlottie widow of; Pvt D Co 2nd TN Inf; 12-9-61 to 3-16-64; West Fork PO; died 3-16-64

SELLS, Samuell, Ct-41-2; Scout D Co 3rd NC Inf; 8-2-64 to ___; Turkey Town PO; rhumatism
SELLS, Susa A. (see Threet, Jessie D.)
SELLS, Thos. L., Pi-153-2; Louesa widow of; Pvt D Co 2nd TN Inf; 9-12-61 to 3-4-62; West Fork PO
SELLS, Tilda J., Pi-156-3; Widow of US Sol; 8th Civil Dist
SELVIDGE, John C., H-70-2(1); Lt E Co 2nd TN Inf; 4-17-61 to 6-23-63; Chattanooga PO; also in Mexican War
SELVIDGE, Levi L., H-64-1; Wagon Master; 63 to 65; Chattanooga PO
SELVIDGE, William G., Un-252-1; Pvt L Co 11th TN Cav; 9-3-63 to 9-11-65; Esco PO; chronic liver disease
SELVY, John, K-185-3; Pvt L Co 8th TN Cav; 6-63 to 7-65; McMillans PO
SEMORE, Edward, Mo-120-3(1); Pvt A Co TN Inf; 64 to ___ (100 days); Sweetwater PO
SENNDER?, Isaac M., Pu-145-5(6); Pvt G Co 1st Mtd Inf; 2-23-64 to 4-21-65; Buffalo Valley PO
SENTELL, Gideon S., Ge-120-2; Lt B Co 8th TN Cav; 7-23-63 to 9-11-65; Henshaw PO; catarrh in head
SENTELL, William R., Ge-84-2; Pvt FH? Co 2nd NC Inf; Greenville PO; chronic dea. of heart
SERGEANT, James F., Ha-117-2; Pvt C Co 8th TN Inf; 12-1-62 to 8-65; Kyle's Ford PO; disease r hip, side & shoulder from fever & measles
SERGEANT, Stephen G., Ha-113-1; Cpl D Co 19th KY Inf; 11-1-61 to 3-11-66; Sneedville PO; reinlisted veteran
SETSER, Joel P., Hw-131-4; Pvt C Co 8th TN Cav; 4-17-63 to 9-11-65; White Horn PO; wounded by horse
SETT, Jacob, A-1-2; Pvt S Co 6th TN Cav; 10-11-63 to 4-11-64; Andersonville PO
SETTLE, Jno. T., T-209-1; Pvt; Randolph PO; shot in shoulder & head, not at home, information from wife
SETTLE, Noah, Lo-194-2; Pvt E Co 9th TN Cav; Muddy Creek PO
SETTLE, William, A-13-4; Pvt I Co 8th TN Cav; 9-5-63 to 9-11-65; Clinton PO; wounded in left hand
SETTLES, Aldridge, Un-256-1; Pvt M Co 11th TN Cav; 12-30-64 to 3-23-65; Starkvale PO; heart, kidney, rheumatism
SETTLES, Charles, H-58-6; Catharine widow of; Pvt I Co 2nd TN Inf; 2-12-62 to 3-20-65; Soddy PO
SETTLES, Joseph P., G-53-4; 5th Civil Dist
SETTLES, Robert, Sh-149-3; Jennie widow of; Cpl E Co 1st US Art; 63 to 66; Raleigh PO
SEVIER, Maree Elbert, Je-145-1; Altimire widow of; Cynthiana PO
SEWARD, Charles R., H-51-2(1); Pvt B Co 3rd PA Cav; 61 to 64; Hill City PO
SEWARD, Edward C., F-40-1; Pvt A Co 42nd TN Inf; 11-61 to 11-20-64; Eads PO (Shelby Co.); shot through the leg; CONF
SEWARD, John, Ro-210-10; Cloa widow of; Pvt; Rockwood PO
SEWARD, Sarah E., Sh-167-2; widow; PO omitted; CONF
SEWEL, Arch, Mc-117-3; Pvt A Co 5th TN Mtd Inf; 9-64 to 7-65; Cog Hill PO; piles
SEWEL, Clemon B., Dy-25-4; Pvt H Co; 61 to 64; Newbern PO; CONF
SEWELL, James K., J-83-1; Pvt L Co 5th TN; 6-63 to 8-65; Flynns Lick PO
SEWELL, Joseph, Lo-189-2; Pvt KY Lt Art; 10-20-61 to 11-28-64; Philadelphia PO
SEWELL, William M., Mc-114-2; Pvt K Co 1st TN Inf; 2-10-64 to 4-1-64; Leamontville PO
SEWENNEY, John, Ge-95-2; Pvt B Co 4th TN Inf; 6-3-63 to 8-2-65; Chucky City PO; rheumatism, hearing
SEWILL, Doss, Mu-205-1; Adelaide widow of; 15th TN Inf; Williamsport PO; papers lost
SEXTON, Aaron, S-213-1; Pvt 12th KY Inf; PO omitted
SEXTON, Christopher, S-213-2; Pvt F Co 12th KY Inf; 61 to ___; Hellenwood PO; gun shot wound in left leg
SEXTON, Elbert, Un-251-2; Pvt G Co 2nd TN Cav; 10-2-62 to 7-6-65; Esco PO; bilious colic
SEXTON, Elige E., K-156-2; Pvt K Co 13th TN Cav; 11-1-64 to 5-6-65; 105 Pine, Knoxville PO
SEXTON, George W., Ge-91-4; Pvt C Co 2nd NC Mtd Inf; Greeneville PO; ruptured & general disability
SEXTON, James, C-34-2; 60 days under Gen. Burnside; 11th Civil Dist
SEXTON, John, Un-251-2; G Co 2nd TN Cav; 10-2-62 to ___; Effie PO; died in hospital before discharge
SEXTON, Lewis K., K-154-5(2); Pvt L Co 8th TN Cav; 63 to 9-65; Knoxville PO
SEXTON, Pleasant W., K-154-5(2); Lt 9th TN Cav; Knoxville PO
SEXTON, Reuben H., K-156-2; Pvt K Co 8th TN Inf; 6-4-63 to 7-10-65; 18 Patterson St, Knoxville PO
SEXTON, Samuel M., Co-59-1; Pvt A Co 2nd NC Inf; 10-23-63 to 8-16-65; Del Rio PO; rumatism & hart deseas
SEXTON, Wm., R-163-2; Pvt L Co 9th TN Cav; 9-1-63 to 9-11-65; Graysville PO; bayonet through leg, since afflicted rheumatism
SEXTON, William, K-168-2; Pvt; Knoxville PO; rheumatism
SEXTON, William D., Ha-111-2; Pvt K Co 51st VA Inf; 12-64 to 6-22-65; Kyles Ford PO; CONF
SEXTON, William N., Un-251-1; Pvt G Co 2nd TN Cav; 10-1-62 to 7-6-65; Effie PO; indigestion, injury to breast
SEYERS, Samuel C., Hy-81-2; Pvt C Co 32nd MO; 63 to 64; 7th Civil Dist
SEYMOUR, Capten, G-63-1; Barbara A. widow of; H Co 45th IL Vol; 11-23-61 to 6-3-65; Milan PO; lung affection, died from the affects
SEYMOUR, Edward H., H-54-5; Laidser? Talapoosa Glaucus; 1-25-64 to 1-18-65; Sherman Heights PO; bowel disease, lung disease
SHAAN, Silas, Fr-116-1(2); Pvt I Co 10th TN Inf; 7-23-62 to 7-3-65; Sherwood PO
SHACK, James, Mu-192-1; Pvt A Co 1st TN Inf; 1-26-62 to 7-1-63; Bigbyville PO; not wounded
SHADDEN, Joseph A., Ro-210-8; Pvt E Co 1st TN Inf; 61 to 64; Rockwood PO
SHADDEN, William (see Lester, William)
SHADDENGER, Nathan, F-37-2; Pvt C Co 15th IN Inf; 4-13-61 to 5-10-65; Somerville PO; wounded in shoulder in Comp M, 7th US Hvy Art, 10 mos
SHADOWIN, John, Di-41-1; Pvt C Co 12th TN Cav; White Bluff PO; small pox
SHADRICK, Henry C., H-49-5; Pvt E Co 6th TN Mtd Inf; 9-19-64 to 6-30-65; Lakeside PO; thrown by horse & hurt
SHADRICK, John, Gu-48-3; Pvt E Co 6th TN Mtd Inf; 7-64 to 7-20-65; Tracy City PO; partial blindness, record of discharge sent to Washington
SHADRICK, Rufus, H-49-5; Pvt F Co 6th TN Mtd Inf; 9-12-64 to 6-30-65; Lakeside PO
SHADRICK, William, R-162-3; Elizabeth widow of; Pvt; Dayton PO
SHADWICK, Gilbert, Sq-164-5(1); Pvt B Co 6th TN Mtd Inf; 8-15-64 to 5-29-65; Brock PO
SHAEFFER, George W., La-112-2; Pvt H Co 14th IA Inf; 3-23-62 to 3-23-65; Chisem PO
SHAFFER, Emanuel, Je-138-2; Pvt D Co 9th TN Cav; Kansas PO; has no discharge
SHAHAN, Jasper L., Po-151-1; Pvt 9th TN Inf; 11-63 to 2-64; Servilla PO
SHAIVILES, Mikeal, H-52-1; Pvt; 6-61 to 63; Lookout Mt. PO
SHAMBERS, John, Fe-44-3(2); Pvt 32nd IN Inf; 61 to 64; Rugby PO; right arm & leg wounded
SHAMBLIN, Columbus C., Br-13-2; Lieuesa S. Smolling formerly widow of; Pvt E Co 5th TN Inf; 3-2-62 to ___; Ora PO
SHAHAN, George W., W-193-1; Pvt K Co 1st TN Cav; Thaxton PO; thrown from a horse & hurt duren the war
SHANE, Samuel, Ru-241-2(1); Minnie widow of; D Co 17th TN Inf; Murfreesboro PO
SHANK, C. M., Pu-146-2; Pvt C Co 1st TN Mtd Inf Vol; 10-13-63 to 11-28-64; Buffalo Valley PO
SHANKLE, John, We-230-1; Pvt K Co 16th TN Reg; 4-16-64 to 12-10-64; Greenfield PO; CONF
SHANKLES, H. C., Sh-146-2; Pvt E Cav; 64 to 65; Lucy PO
SHANKS, Christian, Hw-128-1; Sgt H Co 8th TN Inf; 9-10-63 to 6-13-65; Choptack PO; rheumatism

SHANKS, Elbert K., Ge-96-2; Pvt B Co 12th TN Cav; 7-22-63 to 10-27-65; Jockey PO; chronic diareah
SHANKS, Elbert S., Ge-89-2; Pvt F Co 3rd TN Cav; 6-64 to 12-64; Albany PO
SHANKS, Henry, Hw-127-1; Pvt K Co 1st US Inf; 6-13-64 to 11-27-65; Rogersville PO; bronchitis & neuralgia
SHANKS, Robert, Ge-95-2; Pvt M Co 1st TN Cav; 12-22-62 to 8-4-63; Home PO; chronic diarhear
SHANKS, William, Hw-134-1; Pvt K Co 1st US Inf; Ju 7 64 to 11-27-65; Rogersville PO; wound left foot, neuralgia head
SHANKS, Wm. H., Ha-111-1; Sarah L. Snapp formerly widow of; Upper Clinch PO
SHANN, Thoms, Lo-194-2; Pvt C Co 3rd TN Inf; 1-62 to 3-63; Lenoir PO
SHANNON, Nick, Sn-253-1; Pvt PA; 3 yrs; Gallatin PO; ruptured
SHANNON, Pleasant R., A-8-3; Cpl E Co 3rd TN Inf; 2-12-62 to 2-23-65; Scarborough PO
SHANNON, William R., Mg-199-2; Flag bearer H Co 9th TN Cav; 7-2-62 to 7-4-65; Emory PO; breast complaint & piles
SHANTON, Edward D., K-170-1; Pvt H Co 73rd IN Inf; 8-5-62 to 7-7-65; bloody piles
SHANYO, Merrill, Fr-112-1; Pvt B Co 3rd Ver Inf; 4-16-61 to 7-16-64; Tullahoma PO; shot through lef foot, contracted liver complaint
SHARA, Caroline E., Mc-114-7; widow of US Sol; 16th Civil Dist
SHAREK, Jeremiah, Sh-145-2; Pvt C Co 156th OH Nat. Grds.; 5-64 to 9-15-64; Millington? PO; under Cap Ephraim Shellis, Nat. Gds. 156th OH
SHARP, Allen, Un-259-1; Pvt F Co 3rd TN Inf; 2-1-62 to 7-30-62; Rhodelia PO; head jared by bomb shell, caused by bomb shell
SHARP, Alonzo G., H-62-3; Capt B Co 46th OH Inf; 4-61 to 63 (2 yrs); 427 Chestnut, Chattanooga PO
SHARP, Boyd A., K-181-1; Cpl A Co 3rd TN Cav; 11-29-62 to 6-20-65; French PO
SHARP, David, Col, Me-93-1; Pvt B Co 6th TN Inf; 64 to 65; Ten Mile Stand PO
SHARP, E., D-43-2; widow Sol; Wine St, Nashville PO
SHARP, Elie, C-24-4(3); Pvt B Co 13th KY Cav; 2-7-64 to 2-15-65; Agee PO; bronchitus & heart disease
SHARP, Elvinton, A-1-2; Mary widow of; Pvt F Co 6th TN Inf; 3-6-62 to 65?; died in prison; Andersonville PO
SHARP, Elyhue M., Un-258-3; Pvt C Co 1st TN YZ?; 9-18-63 to 5-31-65; Longhollow PO; ruptured
SHARP, G. W., S-215-1; Kesiah widow of; Pvt G Co 8th TN Cav; Norma PO; killed Aug 6 1864 at Atlanta GA
SHARP, Green, Un-257-2; QMS C Co 1st TN Lt Art; 9-1-62 to 7-64; Sharps Chapel PO; shot in right hand
SHARP, Henry, A-1-2; Catharine widow of; Pvt F Co 11th TN Inf; 3-10-62 to 3-15-65; Andersonville PO
SHARP, Henry, Un-259-2; Cpl K Co 2nd TN Cav; 8-15-62 to 7-14-65; Rhodelia PO; sun frain? in head, measles & sun frain?
SHARP, Isaac, Un-254-2; Pvt F Co 3rd TN Inf; 2-20-62 to 2-23-65; Bartheney PO; fore finger shot off
SHARP, J. W., Bl-3-5; Pvt C Co 1st?; 8-20-64 to 1-23-65; Letton PO; piles
SHARP, Jacob, Un-250-1; 1st Lt D Co 1st TN Inf; 8-9-61 to 9-17-64; Miltabarger PO; hydrocill, 23 yrs standing incured while in service
SHARP, James, K-171-4(3); Pvt G Co 12th Hvy Art Col; 5-24-64 to 3-31-66; PO omitted
SHARP, James B., Hm-106-2; Capt F Co 9th TN Cav; 6-8-62 to 10-7-65; Morristown PO
SHARP, John, Un-250-2; Elizabeth E. widow of; Capt; Maynardville PO
SHARP, John, Ge-94-3; Vilet C. widow of; Pvt M Co 1st US Cav Hvy Art; 64 to 66 (1 yr 6 mos); Tusculum PO; chronic diarhea
SHARP, John C., C-25-2; Pvt G Co 7th TN Inf; 11-8-64 to 7-27-65; Hatmaker PO; heart disease, chronic diereah
SHARP, John E., Un-259-1; Sgt D Co 1st TN Inf; 8-9-61 to 9-17-64; Rhodelia PO; pile, hardships in war
SHARP, John F., Un-256-3; Pvt A Co 1st TN Inf; 8-1-61 to 9-17-64; Loy's X Roads PO; measels, fever & jondice
SHARP, Levi C., G-51-1; Cpl F Co 132nd IN Inf; 5-5-64 to 9-15-64; Humboldt PO
SHARP, Nelson S., A-1-2; Pvt C Co 7th TN Inf; 8-7-61 to 10-6-64; Andersonville PO; hurt by fall of a horse
SHARP, Newton, Bo-13-3(1); Pvt C Co 3rd TN Cav; 12-62 to 7-65; Concord PO (Knox Co.); injured in back
SHARP, Nicholas, A-4-6(2); Pvt F Co 6th TN Inf; 3-10-62 to 3-24-65; Coal Creek PO
SHARP, Pleasant, A-4-6(2); Cpl A Co 1st TN Inf; 8-2-61 to 9-17-64; Coal Creek PO
SHARP, Robert, C-34-2; Pvt G Co 7th TN Inf; 11-8-64 to 7-27-65; Buckeye PO
SHARP, Shields, Un-253-2; Pvt F Co 3rd TN Inf; 2-10-62 to 2-23-65; Meltabarger PO
SHARP, Simon, Me-88-2; Jane C. widow of; Pvt E Co 5th TN Inf; 3-2-62 to __; Georgetown PO
SHARP, Tillman, S-215-1; Qtr. Mst B Co 7th KY Cav; 3-7-63 to 2-6-65; Pioneer PO; shot in thigh, able to work
SHARP, William A., Ro-207-2; Pvt K Co 10th TN Cav; 3-3-64 to 8-1-65; Fossel PO; piles
SHARP, William D., K-171-1; Pvt F Co 7th TN Mtd Inf; 11-8-__ to 7-27-__; Knoxville PO
SHARP, William M., H-70-2(1); Pvt 16th TN Inf; about 3 yrs; Chattanooga PO; shot thro' the abdomen
SHARP, William S., Un-254-3; Pvt F Co 3rd TN Inf; 2-20-62 to 2-23-65; Meltabarger PO
SHARPE, James L., D-66-2; Pvt H Co 10th MI Inf; 10-62 to 64; 35 Fellonore St, Nashville PO; sent to hospital in Nashville from Chat. & reported from hospital as dead & never mustered out of service
SHATTEY, W. M., G-54-1; Martha widow of; Pvt B Co 1st TN Lt Art; Eaton PO
SHATTUCK, Abbot S., D-69-1; Cap? B Co 6th MO Inf; 4-13-61 to 8-2-61; Nashville PO; left knee & side
SHAUB, James K., Sn-264-1; Pvt D Co 52nd KY Inf; 10-10-63 to 1-17-65; Portland PO; this mans papers all right in DC
SHAUGHNESSY, Michael, Sh-160-1; Pvt Ind Inf; 4-61 to 4-65; Memphis, Poplar St (126-130); right hand lost 3 fingers
SHAVER, Aaron A., Gr-70-3; Sarah widow of; Pvt 4th TN Inf; Spring House PO; co & dates unknown
SHAVER, Alex A., Se-227-3; Pvt C Co 3rd TN Cav; 8 Feb 63 to 23 Jun 65; Trundles X Roads PO; injury to right shoulder, was a prisoner
SHAVER, George W., Gr-75-1; Pvt D Co 4th TN Inf; 1 Feb 63 to 2 Aug 65; Doyal PO
SHAVER, Michael, Mg-198-2; Pvt F Co 1st TN Cav; 1 Mar 62 to 1 Sep 65; Kismet PO; sunstroke, rheumatism
SHAVERS, Jack, Wl-290-1; Manerva widow of; Pvt K Co 27th OH; May 1 64 to Aug 1 65; Lebanon PO; discharged
SHAVOE, Jess, Wh-185-1; Sindy widow of (Col); Walkers? Cross Roads PO; no papers
SHAW, Booker, Sh-192-1; US unit; Memphis PO
SHAW, Candace (see Exum, Matthew)
SHAW, Charles, O-141-2; Sgt A Co 52nd Col Inf Vol; Jun 3 63 to Dec 30 65; Union City PO
SHAW, Clem, H-57-2; Pvt 16th US Col; 63 to 65; Orchard Knob PO
SHAW, Craig N., Dy-27-2; Pvt E Co 9th TN Cav; 1 Jan 62 to 24 Dec 63; Tatemville PO; left eye shot out; CONF
SHAW, David A., Hd-45-2; Pvt C Co 4th TN Mtd Inf; 1 Jan 65 to 25 Aug 65; Saltillo PO; piles &c
SHAW, Elisha, Ge-87-2; Susan widow of; Pvt M Co 9th TN Cav; 63 to 65; Timberridge PO
SHAW, Francis L., Po-151-1; Pvt F Co 49th TN; Sep 61 to Dec 62; Pleasant View PO; rheumatism
SHAW, James, Mc-114-3; Pvt A Co 5th TN Inf; Calhoun PO; sight injured
SHAW, James M., Ge-87-2; Cpl A Co 12th TN Cav; 29 Mar 63 to 7 Oct 65; Timberridge PO; rheumatism & heart disease

SHAW, John P., Lk-112-1; 1st Sgt I Co 7th TN Cav; 18 Jul 62 to Aug 26 65; Tiptonville PO; scurvy in mouth, able to do full work
SHAW, Jonathan, Cf-38-1; Pvt E Co 135th OH Inf; 2 May 64 to 1 Sep 64; Croton PO; chronic diarhea and heart, Tr?
SHAW, Joseph, Sh-149-4; US Sol; 6th Civil Dist
SHAW, Louis, Wa-274-1; Rachel widow of; Pvt E Co 8th TN Vol; Jonesboro PO
SHAW, Peter R., Gi-135-2; Pvt A Co 17th TN Inf; 2-24-64 to 4-25-66; Lynnville PO
SHAW, Taylor, Sh-146-4; 3rd Civil Dist
SHAW, Thomas G., Ge-102-1; Pvt E Co 4th TN Inf; 1 Sep 63 to 2 Aug 65; Henshaw PO; loss of an eye, now unable to do good work
SHAW, W. Dublin, L-99-1; Cpl L Co 4th US Col Hvy Art; Mar 14 64 to Feb 24 66; Orysa PO; consumption, caused from exposure
SHAW, Walter C., Ro-211-3; Pvt 2nd IN Lt Art; 14 Oct 64 to 3 Jul 65; Harriman PO
SHAWL, Levi, Di-34-2; Pvt B Co 139th PA Inf; 9-1-62 to 6-28-65; Dickson PO; wounded in right shoulder
SHAWLEN, Juda, Se-219-4; Widow US Sol; 1st Dist
SHAY, John O., Gi-125-1; Sgt B Co 1st US AL Cav; 22 Feb 64 to 13 Oct 65; Bodenham PO
SHEA, Patrick, He-67-1; Pvt K Co 8th NH Inf; fall of 61 to Jan 65; Sardis PO; gun shot wound right shoulder & injury of right elbow
SHEAF, Charles A., Ru-241-1; Cap I Co 59th OH Inf; Oct 61 to 65; PO omitted
SHEAR, Abe, Sh-189-4; Pvt F Co 3rd US Col Cav; 6-63 to fall 65; Ark Ave, Memphis PO
SHEARER, William, Mc-116-2; Pvt B Co 7th TN Mtd Inf; 10-21-64 to 7-27-65; Williamsburg PO; disease of the lungs contracted while in the service
SHEARER, William A., Ro-203-5(1); Pvt; Burns Mills PO
SHEARL, John, Lo-190-2; Pvt I Co 5th TN Inf; 1 Nov 62 to 30 Jun 65; Loudon PO; shot in left arm
SHECKELS, Timothy, Un-255-1; Pvt G Co 1st TN; 1 Oct 62 to 6 Jun 65; Warwicks X Roads PO; stum
SHEDDAN, William E., Mu-202-1; Nancy J. widow of; Hospital Steward B Co 4th TN Inf; Apr 1 63 to Aug 2 65; 14th Civ Dist
SHEDDEW, John E., Bo-13-1; Pvt E Co 98th IL Mtd Inf; 6-12-62 to 6-12-65; Freindaville PO
SHEEN, Jame O., Hm-107-2(1); Cpl C Co 1st TN Cav; 1 Apr 62 to 1 Apr 65; Witts Foundry PO; gun shot
SHEEN, William G., Su-243-1; Maj D Co 39th MA Inf; 62 to 64; Bristol PO; re-enlisted
SHEFFIELD, William S., Hw-120-2; Sgt M Co 13th TN Cav; 2 Feb 63 to 5 Sep 65; Eidson PO
SHEGAY, Anderson, Mu-191-1; Pvt A Co 12th TN Vol; Bigbyville PO
SHEHAN, Aaron, U-248-1; Pvt M Co 8th TN Cav; 16 Sep 63 to 11 Sep 65; Ernestville PO
SHEHAN, Buiens?, Se-219-4; US Sol; 1st Dist
SHEHAN, Neeld (Nedd), Ge-90-3; Pvt C Co 16th TN Inf; 61 to 65; Greeneville PO; shot in right side at Columbia SC
SHEHAN, Patrick, Ov-133-1; Pvt A Co 27th KY Inf; 5-15-61 to 4-10-65; Netherland PO; general disabilities
SHEHAN, William, Ja-85-3; Georgtown PO
SHEHINE, Isaac, Dk-33-3; Pvt F Co 4th TN Inf; 10-16-64 to 8-25-65; Halesville PO; back & kidneys
SHELBERN, Joseph, Wi-280-1; Pvt D Co 17th Col Inf; Aug 62 to 65; Thompson Sta. PO
SHELBY, James, Un-258-3; Cpl A Co 2nd TN Cav; 1 Aug 62 to 24 May 65; Longhollow PO
SHELBY, John L., Un-256-1; Pvt A Co 2nd TN Cav; 1 Aug 62 to 17 Jul 65; Rule PO; diarhear, resulting in piles & fits
SHELBY, Ruphus J., Un-258-3; Pvt G Co 2nd TN Cav; 1 Oct 62 to 6 Jul 65; Longhollow PO
SHELBY, W. A., T-216-3; Pvt C Co TN Inf; Apr 61 to May 65; 14th Civil Dist; CONF
SHELL, Albert, Ha-114-3; Pvt L Co 4th NC Inf; 9 May 64 to 14 Sep 65; Sneedville PO
SHELL, Andrew J., P-151-4; Pvt B Co 5th TN Mtd Inf; 9-13-64 to 6-19-65; Sherman Heights PO; wounded in left--horse fell on him, disable right leg and side
SHELL, Elkaney, Wa-269-1; Pvt H Co 13th TN Cav; 24 Sep 63 to 5 Sep 65; Johnson City PO; rheumatism, heart disease
SHELL, James W., Ct-36-2; Pvt F Co 10th MI Cav; 4-63 to 6-65; Roan Mt. PO
SHELL, John G., Ct-40-2; Susan F. widow of; Cpl G Co 13th TN Cav; 9-24-63 to 9-5-65; Elizabethton PO
SHELL, Malon, Ct-36-2; Pvt G Co 146th IL Inf; __ to 6-16-65; Shell Creek PO
SHELL, Parris M., K-173-2; Pvt I Co 115th IN Inf; 6 Jul 63 to 25 Feb 64; Union Church PO
SHELL, Robert P., Ct-41-3; Pvt H Co 13th TN Cav; South Wattauga PO; piles & hearing
SHELL, Samuel, Ct-40-6; Pvt B Co 4th TN Inf; 11-1-62 to 8-2-65; Elizabethton PO
SHELL, William W., Ct-40-2; Pvt; 12-62 to __; Elizabethton PO; CONF
SHELLEY, John, Se-228-2(3); Pvt H Co 3rd TN Cav; 15 Aug 62 to 12 Jun 65; Cusick's X Roads PO; prisoner at Andersonville 7 mos
SHELLEY, John, T-216-1; Elizabeth McNeal widow of; Pvt; Corona PO
SHELLY, James T., Ro-210-1; Maj 1st TN Inf; 31 Aug 61 to 14 Jul 64; Col 5th Reg Inf--62 to 65; Col 7th Reg Mtd Inf--65 to 65; Rockwood PO
SHELOX, William, Cl-47-3; Cappford PO
SHELTON, Baxter, Ge-102-2; Pvt M Co 1st TN Cav; 25 Nov 62 to 19 Jun 65; Camp Creek PO; frozen feet, now neuralgy
SHELTON, Charles, Lk-112-1; alias Chas. Nevill; Pvt C Co 64th LA Inf; 63 to 65; Tiptonville PO; has forgotten dates
SHELTON, Chrisley, Cl-52-2; Pvt D Co 9th TN Cav; 62 to 65; Hypratia PO
SHELTON, Daniel, U-249-1; Elisabeth widow of; Pvt E Co 2nd NC Inf; Flag Pond PO; shot and kiled July 64 at Cold Springs TN
SHELTON, David, Ge-99-1; Pvt G Co 3rd NC Inf; 1 Jun 64 to 8 Aug 65; Limestone Springs PO; mule fell on him & crippled in hip, knee & ankle
SHELTON, David, Ge-99-2; Pvt F Co 10th TN Cav; Jan 64 to 12 Jul 65; Limestone Springs PO; chronic diarrhea, couldnt day moth enlisted
SHELTON, David L., Wy-177-1; Pvt I Co 1st AL Cav; 10-17-63 to 7-19-65; Waynesboro PO; hurt in neck from being struck with gun in battle
SHELTON, Elaphus, U-249-1; Pvt G Co 3rd NC MTd Inf; 1 Aug 63 to 8 Aug 65; Briggs PO
SHELTON, Esaw M., U-249-2; Pvt A Co 13th KY Cav; 5 Apr 63 to 10 Jan 65; Briggs PO; shot threw right leg, fracturd left ankle
SHELTON, Flavinius J., P-151-4; Dist 6
SHELTON, George W., Je-137-3; Pvt I Co 2nd TN Cav; 22 Sep 62 to Jul 65; Chestnut Hill PO
SHELTON, Henry F., A-3-1; Pvt H Co 9th TN; 9-1-63 to 9-11-65; Wilson PO
SHELTON, James, Co-67-4; Duty Sgt E Co 2nd NC Inf; 14 Oct 65 to __; Naillon PO; gunshot in hips
SHELTON, Jas. F., La-117-3; Pvt 20th TN Inf; Dec to __; 15th Dist; CONF
SHELTON, James M., Mc-114-2; Pvt K Co 1st TN Inf; 2-10-67 to 4-1-67; Leamontville PO
SHELTON, James P., Cf-35-4; Pvt D Co 1st TN Inf; 27 Apr 61 to 20 Jun 62; Gould PO; CONF
SHELTON, John, Ge-99-1; 1st Lt E Co 2nd NC Inf; 1 Sep 63 to 16 Aug 65; Limestone Springs PO; rheumatism, physically broke down
SHELTON, John, Sh-159-5; PO omitted
SHELTON, Johnathan J., Ov-139-1; Pvt B Co 25th TN Inf; 10 to 65; France PO
SHELTON, Joseph, C-33-1; Pvt C Co 7th KY Art?; 10-27-61 to 2-65; Newcomb PO
SHELTON, Kittie, Sn-254-2; C Co 14th US Col Inf; Saundersville PO
SHELTON, Mack, Gi-138-1; Pvt 54th __; 61 to 63; Fullrin PO
SHELTON, Mark, Gr-81-5(3); Pvt H Co 1st TN Cav; 15 Jul 62 to 5 Jun 65; Oleot PO; thrown from horse, disabled
SHELTON, Olynthus, P-151-4; Pvt E Co 6th TN Cav; 9-18-62 to 7-10-65; Dist 6
SHELTON, Robert, He-66-1; Middlefork PO; chronic sore on leg
SHELTON, S. A., P-151-3; Linden PO
SHELTON, Solamon? W., Cf-40-2; Pvt A Co KY Bat Vol; 20 Jan 65 to 23 Oct 65; Tullahoma PO

SHELTON, Thomas, Sh-147-1; Pvt B Co 61st TN Inf; 10 Jun 63 to 30 Apr 65; Cuba PO
SHELTON, Thomas, He-58-2; Sol; 8th Civil Dist
SHELTON, Thomas G., Rb-220-1; Pvt A Co 30th TN; Oct 16 62 to May 1 65; Barrenplains PO
SHELTON, W. C., Mc-117-3; Capt A Co 8th TN Inf; 11-11-61 to 43signed 1864 (3 yrs 8 mos); Carlock PO; rheumatism
SHELTON, William B., Lo-188-3; Pvt B Co 1st TN Inf; 3 Dec 62 to 3 Aug 65; Erie PO
SHEPARD, Lewis, P-156-2; Blacksmith A Co 10th TN Cav; 11-62 to 1-65; Lobelville PO; CONF
SHEPAD, London (see Mann, London)
SHEPARD, Wm. H., Sh-149-4; widow; 6th Civil Dist
SHEPERD, John, Mu-197-1; Pvt; 63 to 65; Columbia PO
SHEPHERD, George M., C-8-2; Lt G Co 13th VA Inf; 4-1-64 to 4-1-65; Well Spring PO; catarrh in head & poor chits?; CONF
SHEPHERD, Granville, S-217-2; 4th Sgt K Co 12th KY Inf; Oneida PO; left shoulder broken
SHEPHERD, James W., Se-219-3; Pvt E Co 2nd TN Cav; 16 Sep 62 to 5 Jul 65; Jones Cove PO; chronic diarhoea, rumatism
SHEPHERD, Thos., Sh-179-1(2); Pvt A Co 12th US Inf; Memphis PO
SHEPHERD, William, S-217-2; Louisa widow of; Pvt G Co 7th KY Inf; Oneida PO
SHEPPARD, Thomas, Po-152-1; Pvt A Co 6th IL Cav; 6-30-63 to 8-20-64; Ducktown PO; gun shot wound of hand
SHEPPARD, Thos. T., Sm-168-2; Pvt B Co 37th KY Cav; 5-1-63 to 8-65; Pleasant Shade PO; mumps and disease of the testacles
SHEPPARD, William M., Po-152-3(1); Pvt A Co 7th TN Mtd Inf; 9-1-64 to 7-27-65; Ducktown PO; rupture and loss of left eye
SHEPPHEARD, Alfred R., Mu-199-2; Pvt E Co 14th MI Inf; Mt. Pleasant PO
SHERALD, Mariah, Mu-197-2; Macedonia PO
SHERFEY, David, Wa-270-2; Pvt C Co 13th TN Cav; Nov 63 to 65; Johnson City PO; injury left leg
SHERFY, Andrew, Wa-273-2; Pvt I Co 8th TN Cav; 25 Sep 63 to 20 Sep 65; Keeblers X Roads PO; frost bit
SHERIDAN, Daniel T., Mr-102-2; Pvt A Co 60th NY Inf; 8-6-62 to 8-4-62; South Pittsburg PO
SHERK, John H., T-206-2; 2nd Lt K Co 9th IN Inf; May 61 to Oct 23 63; Leighs Chappel PO
SHERLEY, Isaac N., R-163-3; Pvt E Co 6th TN Mtd Inf; 11-13-64 to 6-30-65; Dayton PO; horse fell on leg and mashed it, since caused a chronic sore
SHERLEY, James, Lo-190-3; Pvt I Co 5th TN Inf; 10 Aug 63 to 30 Jun 65; Piney PO; frozen feet & ercyphlas
SHERLEY, James C., R-163-3; Sarah J. widow of; Pvt F Co 5th TN Vol; 2-25-62 to 3-29-65; Dayton PO; shot in hip & small of back, died of blood poison from wound
SHERMAN, Edmon, Mc-112-7; Pvt C Co 1st US Hvy Art; Athens PO
SHERMAN, Emanuel, Lo-188-2; Cpl C Co 1st US Art; 18 Feb 63 to 31 Mar 66; Erie PO
SHERMAN, George, Mc-112-2; Pvt A Co 44th US Col Inf; 3-64 to 4-30-66; Athens PO
SHERMAN, Henny, Wl-297-1; Pvt F Co 10th Reg Inf; 26 May 62 to 1 Sep 62; Commerce PO; rheumatism
SHERMAN, John A., Dy-23-1; Seaman Str. Independence; Dec 64 to 22 May 66; Dyersburg PO
SHERMAN, Winston, H-76-2; Chattanooga PO
SHERRELL, Llewellen, Ch-18-1; Pvt C Co TN Cav; 10 Oct 62 to 15 May 65; PO omitted; CONF
SHERRELL, Richard, Gi-129-1; Cpl A Co 106th TN Inf; Feb 63 to Nov 65; Conway PO
SHERRILL, Phillip, Gi-127-5; E Co 12th US Col Inf; Pulaski PO; papers lost
SHERROD, F., G-57-2; Pvt F Co 11th AL Cav; 5-18-64 to 5-18-65; Yorkville PO; CONF
SHERROD, James, Sh-153-2; alias Sherrod, Abram; Pvt C Co 64th USC Inf; 63 to 65; Collierville PO
SHERROD, Will., Col, Rb-222-1; Pvt I Co 15th US Inf; 64 to 65; Cedar Hill PO; frost bitten, discharged on surgeons certificate

SHERROD, William N., Cr-4-3; Pvt H Co 27th TN Cav; 6-15-63 to 3-64; Bells Depot PO; CONF
SHERRY, Henry C., Ma-127-1; Pvt A Co 3rd WI Inf; Jul 14 61 to Feb 24 65; Jackson PO; chronic diarhea
SHEWALTER, James, Hw-123-2; Pvt H Co 181st OH Inf; Sep 64 to Jul 65; Rotherwood PO
SHIELDS, Alford, Sh-150-2; Wyatt, Alford; Pvt C Co 88th US Inf; 8 mos; Mullins Station PO
SHIELDS, Bazzel, La-115-1; Pvt K Co 2nd MS Inf; 1 May 61 to 1 Mar 63; Henryville PO; left arm off; CONF
SHIELDS, Elenor J., O-141-2; Ordley Sgt A Co 11th KY Vol Inf; Sep 17 61 to May 30 62; Union City PO
SHIELDS, Elizabeth Mary (see Rodgers, Henry N.)
SHIELDS, G. P., Gi-122-6; Pvt A Co 53rd TN Inf; Jul 62 to Aug 63; Prospect Sta. PO; 7 mos in prison at Camp Morton, IN; CONF
SHIELDS, Irvin, Hw-125-5; Pvt A Co 12th TN Cav; 62 to 65; Yellow Stone PO; CONF
SHIELDS, Jesse W., Se-230-2; Mary A. widow of; Pvt M Co 2nd TN Cav; Pokeberry PO; she draws on account of her husband being in the Mexican War
SHIELDS, John, D-91-1; Pvt; Harris Bros., Line St, Nashville PO
SHIELDS, John J., Ro-205-3; Pvt A Co 2nd TN Inf; 10 Aug 61 to 19 Aug 63; Deamond PO; lung and kidney trouble 9 yrs
SHIELDS, Joseph, K-161-5(6); Pvt E Co 1st US Hvy Art; 10 Apr 64 to 31 Mar 66; Knoxville PO
SHIELDS, Joseph T., Ge-90-3; Pvt F Co 8th TN Cav; 11 Jun 63 to 11 Sep 65; Greeneville PO; chronic hemorage of lungs
SHIELDS, Joshua C., H-51-2(1); Pvt C Co 4th Col Cav; 9-20-61 to 10-11-64; Hill City PO
SHIELDS, Lecar K., Se-222-1; Rebecca widow of; Pvt E Co 2nd KY? Cav; Midel Creeke PO; diereah, rumatism, site, heering and speach 1864
SHIELDS, Lonnie, F-43-1; Clara widow of; 5th TN Hvy Art; 63 to 64; New Kent PO; colored and cannot give much particulars
SHIELDS, William, K-161-1; Cpl F Co 1st TN Hvy Art; Knoxville PO
SHILCUT, James, F-43-2; alias James Kimble; Pvt C Co 3rd US Col Cav; Jan 64 to May 65; Piperton PO
SHILLINGS, William K., Ro-205-2; Pvt Scouts; 63 to 1 Jun 65; Kings Creek PO; gun shot, rheumatism 25 yrs
SHINAULT, Walter, Sh-193-2; Mariah widow of; Pvt A Co 46th Reg Inf (US); __ to 3-5-64; Memphis PO
SHINLEVER, Henry, A-4-5; Milley J. widow of; Pvt D Co 1st TN Hvy Art; 12-25-64 to 4-8-66; Coal Creek PO; rupture, discharge not at home
SHINLIVER, Charles L., K-179-2; Pvt F Co 4th TN Inf; 10 Feb 64 to 2 Aug 65; Virtue PO
SHINN, Andrew G., Jo-153-1; Vinie L. widow of; Pvt L Co 13th TN Cav; 2 Feb 64 to 5 Sep 65; Little Doe PO
SHIPE, Jackson, K-173-2; Pvt G Co 7th TN Cav; 10 Dec 64 to 27 Jul 65; McMillen PO
SHIPE, John L., A-5-3; Sgt Major C Co 3rd TN Inf; 2-62 to 3-65; Clinton PO
SHIPLEY, A. C. E., Cl-54-3(1); Pvt; Tazewell PO
SHIPLEY, Adam, Wa-272-1; Sgt B Co 4th TN Cav; 20 Nov 62 to 12 Jul 65; Locust Mount PO; double inguinal hernia
SHIPLEY, Austin L., H-58-1; Pvt F Co 1st TN Inf; 11-11-61 to 11-15-64; Sale Creek PO
SHIPLEY, Betsee (see Brown, Thomas)
SHIPLEY, David W., Hm-33(103)-1; US; Civil Dist 17
SHIPLEY, Elbert, M.D. (see Walden, Thomas)
SHIPLEY, Elijah E., Wa-272-1; Pvt B Co 4th TN Cav; 20 Nov 62 to 21 Jun 63; Locust Mount PO; varicose veins left leg, disease of kidneys, liver and mouth, loss of teeth results of scurvy
SHIPLEY, Enoch, Br-12-5; Lt I Co 4th TN Cav; 12-4-62 to 6-64; Georgetown PO; disease of eyes
SHIPLEY, James, Wa-270-2; Pvt D Co 8th TN Cav; 21 Sep 63 to 21 Sep 65; Johnson City PO; rheumatism
SHIPLEY, Jesse P., H-58-3; Pvt A Co 6th TN Inf; 8-2-64 to 6-30-65; Sale Creek PO

SHIPLEY, McLun, Cl-52-3; Jane widow of; Pvt A Co 11th TN Cav; 62 to 65; Hypatia PO
SHIPLEY, Nathan, Wa-274-2; 1st Sgt I Co 8th TN Cav; 5 Sep 63 to 12 Sep 65; Jonesboro PO; chronic rheumatism & bronchitis &c
SHIPLEY, Pattan H., Hm-33(103)-1; Pvt D Co 5th TN Cav; Nov 10 47 to Jul 20 43; Mexican War; Dyersburg PO
SHIPLEY, Wesley, H-58-4; Pvt 6th TN Mtd Inf; Sale Creek PO; did not see discharge
SHIPLEY, Wm., Cl-48-2; Margaret widow of; Pvt Cav; to 65 (2 yrs); Pleasant PO
SHIPLEY, William M., H-58-6; Pvt C Co 5th TN Inf; 2-25-62 to 4-4-65; Retro PO
SHIPLY, John T., Lo-188-2; Pvt C Co 133rd IL Inf; 9 May 64 to 24 Sep 64; Erie PO
SHIPMAN, John S., Ge-86-1; Pvt A Co 2nd NC Inf; 24 Dec 63 to 6 Sep 65; Warrensburgh PO; wounded in thigh
SHIPMAN, Martha E., Wy-171-3; widow of US Sol; 5th Civil Dist
SHIPMAN, Nelson, K-163-1; Pvt E Co; 62 to 65; Knoxville qO
SHIPP, Preston, Hy-79-1; Sgt G Co 100th KY Col Inf; May 31 64 to Dec 26 65; Brownsville PO
SHIPWASH, Michael, Lo-192-2; Pvt K Co 5th TN; Feb 62 to Jul 65; Greenback PO; cripled in left ankle
SHIRK, John W., Mc-110-1; Pvt K Co 1st KY Cav; 7-20-63 to 6-20-65; Piketon PO
SHIRLEY, George A., Gr-70-3; Pvt F Co 1st TN Cav; 1 Mar 62 to 30 Mar 65; Lulaville PO
SHIRLY, _____, Mn-126-1; Elizabeth widow of; Purdy PO
SHITE, Martha, A-6-2; widow?; Olive Springs, Lookout Ave, PO
SHIVER, Christian, O-138-2; Pvt B Co 24th TN; 28 Jun 61 to 20 Apr 65; Elbridge PO; CONF
SHOCK, Leander D., De-23-2; Pvt Art; Jun 61 to Jun 64; Swallow Bluff PO; CONF
SHOCKLEY, Winright, Gr-79-1; Pvt; 62 to __ (3 mos); Thorn Hill PO; CONF
SHOEMAKE, James M., Sm-169-1; Cpl A Co 1st TN Mtd Inf; 11-28-63 to 1-31-65; Elmwood PO; gun shot
SHOEMAKE, Patrick A., Sm-169-1; TN unit; Chestnut Mount PO; 3 gun shot wounds, reenlisted; CONF
SHOEMAKE, Thomas R. S., K-156-1; Patton 64, Knoxville PO; CONF
SHOEMAKE, William, Sm-171-1; Pvt H Co 1st TN Mtd Inf; 6-30-64 to 5-30-65; Chestnut Mound PO
SHOEMAKER, Adam J., Bl-4-2; Pvt E Co 11th MI Inf; 2-27-64 to 10-1-65; Morgan Springs PO (Rhea Co.); scurvy and varicose veins of leg, unable at times to labor
SHOEMAKER, Calvin, Mc-118-1; Pvt A Co 5th TN Mtd Inf; 9-1-64 to 6-26-65; Longs Mills PO; strangelation 25 yrs
SHOEMAKER, David, Co-63-3; Pvt E Co 2nd TN Cav; 16 Sep 62 to 5 Jul 65; Newport PO
SHOEMAKER, Isaac M., S-213-2; Pvt K Co 30th KY Mtd Inf; Feb 64 to Apr 65; Hellenwood PO; lumbago & hooping cough
SHOEMAKER, John, Br-12-6; 9th Dist
SHOEMAKER, Noah, Me-92-4(1); volunteered but captured before he got to the army; Pin Hook PO; rheumatism & chronic diarrheoa while in prison at Knoxville & Vicksburg, not able to work ½ of the time
SHOENS, John W., Ja-87-1; Pvt H Co 17th MI Inf; 8-7-62 to 6-65; Howardville PO; rheumatism, discharge mislaid
SHOFER, Columbus, A-7-1; Robertsville PO
SHOFFNER, Berry, Un-257-2; Pvt B Co 8th TN Cav; Jun 63 to 65; New Prospect PO
SHOFFNER, John, D-49-3; Pvt K Co 12th TN Inf; 62 to 65; Nashville PO; all he knows
SHOFFNER, Mike R., O-141-3; Pvt A Co 4th TN Vols Mtd Inf; Aug 63 to Aug 65; Union City PO
SHOFFRON, Jefferson H., Cr-20-1; Sgt K Co 15th TN Inf; 9-63 to 1-12-66; Hollow Rock PO; rheumatism in
SHOFNER, Daniel E., Sh-201-2; Jane S. widow of; Memphis PO; papers misplaced; CONF
SHOFNER, John, Cf-35-5(1); Pvt; PO omitted
SHOFNER, John, Cf-35-1; Pvt; Tullahoma PO; CONF
SHOFNER, Plummer W., B-3-1; Pvt F Co 5th TN Cav; 9-7-62 to 2-20-64; Wartrace PO; chronic diarrhea, discharged on account of disability
SHOMKEN, Sidney S., Sm-170-3; Pvt L Co 5th TN Cav; 8-19-63 to 8-14-65; Maggart PO; rheumatism
SHORT, Aaron, Gi-127-5; Eliza widow of; Pvt D Co 110th TN Inf; Pulaski PO; discharge & dates lost
SHORT, Calb W., J-79-1; Pvt B Co 9th KY Inf; Whitleyville PO
SHORT, Cuford, Hy-75-1; Pvt 62 to 62 (few days); Dancyville PO; doubt very much if ever enlisted
SHORT, Edom B., Ro-205-4; Pvt B Co 5th TN Inf; 25 Feb 62 to 31 Mar 65; Hoods Landing PO; heart disease & rheumatism
SHORT, Edwin P., J-79-1; Pvt F Co 1st TN Mtd Inf; 6-11-64 to 7-5-65; Whitleyville PO
SHORT, Eldridge, Hw-132-4; Pvt B Co 8th TN Cav; __ to 65 (2 yrs); Otes PO; rheumatism, could not get further information
SHORT, Henry, Hy-75-1; Pvt; 63 to __ (4 mos); Enrickaton? PO; deserted
SHORT, James M., Wa-273-2; Barbara A. widow of; Pvt I Co 8th TN Cav; Jul 64 to Jul 65 (1 day); Bashors Mill PO; killed same day sworn in
SHORT, Robert P., R-162-1; Pvt E Co 1st TN Inf; 8-62 to __; Dayton PO
SHORT, Samuel, Hw-131-3; Pvt D Co 1st TN Cav; 15 Apr 62 to 28 May 65; St. Clair PO
SHORT, Thomas S., G-71-3; Mary A. widow of; Pvt G Co 5th TN Inf; 5 Apr 61 to 15 Sep 62; PO omitted; CONF
SHORT, Washington, Gi-126-1; Pvt F Co 111th Col Inf; 6 Jan 64 to 30 Apr 66; Pulaski PO
SHORT, William, Ha-110-3; Pvt L Co 8th TN Inf; 1 Jan 65 to 11 Sep 65; Treadway PO
SHORT, William, Gi-127-3; Cook G Co 110th TN Col Inf; Pulaski PO; health considerably impaired
SHORTER, Isaac, W1-295-2; 10th Dist
SHOTE, Samuel, K-179-1; Rodelin PO
SHOTE, Henderson, Mo-119-1; Sarah Moss widow of; Pvt H Co Inf; Sweetwater PO; killed in a skirmish
SHOTTLE, Sandy (see Shotwell, Sandy)
SHOTWELL, Sandy, Sh-152-2; alias Shottle, Sandy; Pvt B Co 54th US Inf; 27 Aug 63 to 27 Aug 65; Dexter PO
SHOULDER, Augustus V., H-62-2; Pvt G Co 20th OH Inf--4-61 to 8-61; Pvt K Co 115th OH Mtd Inf; 8-15-62 to 6-22-65; 308 West Fifth, Chattanooga PO
SHOWN, David F., C-25-1; Pvt D Co 13th TN Cav; 9-24-63 to 9-5-65; Jacksborough PO; chronic dierie, pains in sholder & back
SHOWN, Elihu A., Jo-153-2; Pvt D Co 13th TN Cav; 24 Sep 63 to 5 Sep 65; Pandora PO; umbilical hernia
SHOWN, Isaac A., Jo-153-2; Pvt D Co 13th TN Cav; 24 Sep 63 to 5 Sep 65; Pandora PO; rheumatism & crippled in feet
SHRADER, Christopher C., Je-137-2; Pvt F Co 9th TN Cav; 13 Sep 63 to 13 Sep 65; Sandy Ridge PO
SHRADER, Geo. W., Je-135-3; Pvt I Co 9th TN Cav; 14 Sep 63 to 11 Sep 65; Flat Gap PO
SHRADER, Samuel, Je-136-1; Pvt F Co 9th TN Cav; 13 Sep 63 to 10 Sep 65; Dandridge PO
SHRADER, Sidney J. (see Ferguson, Robert)
SHRADER, William, Se-221-2; Louisa Walker former widow of; Pvt I Co 2nd TN Cav; 1 Jan 64 to 4 Apr 64; Fair Garden PO; died April 4, 1865
SHRADER, William D. A., Se-221-2; Cpl E Co 1st TN Cav; 8 Jul 62 to 5 Jun 65; Fox PO
SHROPSHIRE, John D., Ja-86-2; Pvt F Co 6th TN Mtd Inf; 64 to 65; Oottewah PO
SHROPSHIRE, Zebedee B., Ja-86-2; Pvt Bat B 1st TN Lt Art; 62 to 65; Oottewah PO; lost 1 eye
SHRUM, Samuls?, H-71-1; Pvt H Co 95th OH Inf; 8-62 to 65; Chattanooga PO
SHUBERT, Caswell, Lo-187-4; Pvt 7th TN Inf; Adolphus PO
SHUBERT, Henry M., Ro-208-3; Nancy A. widow of; 9th Civ Dist
SHUBERT, Henry M., Ro-208-2; Pvt I Co 1st TN Inf; Oct 62 to Aug 65; Welker Miles PO; effects of smallpox
SHUFF, Samuel, We-224-1; Pvt A Co 15th TN Inf; 61 to 65; Como PO (Henry Co.); CONF

SHUFFIELD, John C., Ct-35-3; Pvt G Co 13th TN Cav; 9-24-63 to 9-5-65; Lineback PO; in US Army
SHUFFIELD, William E., Ct-35-3; Pvt G Co 13th TN Cav; 9-24-63 to 9-5-65; Lineback PO; in US Army
SHULER, John, H-56-3; Pvt C Co 19th IN Inf; 63 to __ (1 yr 6 mos); St. Elmo PO
SHULL, Andrew J., Cf-44-1; Teamster K Co 14th KY Cav; 6-63 to 6-64; Hampton PO
SHULL, Franklin T., Ro-210-1; Lt A Co 2nd TN Cav; 10 Aug 61 to 8 Apr 65; Rockwood PO; left legg shot; CONF
SHULL, Giles, Hd-50-5; Sarah widow of; Pvt F Co 10th TN Inf; 5-62 to __; Nixon PO
SHULL, John H., Fr-115-2; Jenni widow of; Capt K Co 6th TN Mtd Inf; 5-61 to 6-26-64; Cowan PO
SHULL, William H., Ct-44-1; Lucinda E. widow of; Blacksmith L Co 13th TN Cav; 9-26-63 to 9-5-65; Hampton PO
SHULTS, George, Co-67-2; Quartermasters Dept C Co; 4 Nov 64 to 28 Mar 65; Cosby PO; gunshot wound in hand
SHULTS, Jacob W., Je-143-3; Pvt K Co 11th TN Cav; Mossy Creek PO; fever settled in breast
SHULTS, John R., Co-63-4; 1st Lt K Co 8th TN Cav; 26 Jun 63 to 27 Mar 65; Newport PO; injury of spine, piles, rheumatism, leg injured
SHULTS, John S., Se-220-2; Harrett widow of; Pvt E Co 2nd TN Cav; 15 Sep 62 to 6 Jul 65; Emerts Cave PO
SHULTS, John W., Co-67-2; Pvt E Co 2nd TN Cav; 13 Sep 62 to 5 Jul 65; Cosby PO
SHULTS, Martin, Se-219-4; US Sol; 1st Dist
SHULTS, Martin B. K., Se-220-2; Eliza widow of; Pvt K Co 9th TN Cav; Emerts Cave PO
SHULTS, Mitchel, Se-219-2; Pvt K Co 9th TN Cav; 20 Sep 63 to 11 Sep 65; Costner PO
SHULTS, Sargent W., We-221-5(2); Pvt H Co 21st TN Cav; Dec 64 to Apr 65; Martin PO; CONF
SHULTZ, Alexander P., Gr-74-2; Sgt E Co 2nd TN Cav; 16 Sep 62 to 5 Jul 65; Dyers Ferry PO
SHULTZ, Daniel, U-245-2; Pvt K Co 9th TN Cav; 20 Sep 63 to 11 Sep 65; Limestone Cove PO; Knoxville TN 1863
SHULTZ, Eli, Hm-104-1; William alias; Pvt H Co 2nd TN Cav; 1 Jan 65 to 65 (8 mos); Talbotts PO (Jefferson Co.)
SHUMACKE, D. Sampson, B-2-2; Martha widow of; Pvt C Co 5th TN Cav; Haley PO
SHUMAKE, Morris, Mr-95-1; Pvt E Co 6th TN Inf; 9-2-64 to 7-11-65; Victoria PO
SHUMAKER, J. W., R-106-1; also on same line, Richmond Sadon Jr; Ordinary Seaman; 6-60 to 8-63; 6th Civil Dist
SHUPE, Andrew J., Wa-263-1; Pvt I Co 8th TN Cav; Sep 21 64 to Sep 11 65; Garbers Mills PO; rheumatism & bronchitis
SHUPE, Danil D., Jo-153-2; Pvt K Co 9th TN Cav; 25 Jun 63 to 5 Sep 65; Little Doe PO; bronchitis
SHURTZ, Wesley, K-173-2; Pvt G Co 6th TN Inf; 30 Nov 62 to 30 Jun 65; Union Church PO; rhumatism
SHUTE, Andrew, Sn-254-2; Hendersonville PO
SHUTT, Martha, Hd-46-2; Third Civil Dist
SHUVE?, William I., Ro-211-3; Pvt H Co 110th? OH Inf; May 64 to Sep 64; Harriman PO
SIBLY, George, L-99-2; Pvt 14th US Inf; 65 to 66; Durhamville PO; wounded in r leg, r arm, 1 arm and side
SIDWELL, William T., Ov-135-1; Pvt D Co 12th KY Inf; 11-19-62 to 7-11-65; Hillham PO; lung diseas, hearing
SIEBER, Nancy T., A-7-2; widow; Robertsville PO
SIEFRIED, Martin, D-45-2; Pvt K Co 9th OH Inf; 4-16-61 to 6-20-64; Nashville PO
SIGGLER, George W., Me-90-1; Pvt E Co 10th TN Cav; 2-20-64 to 7-10-65; Magellan PO; shot on left arm, now receiving pension
SIGLEY, Charles H., H-54-2(3); Pvt A Co 1st PA Inf --61 to 61 (3 mos); Pvt C Co 46th PA Inf-- __ to 65; Chattanooga PO; discharge lost
SIGMAN, Logan H., Su-242-2; US Sol; 16th Civil Dist
SIKES, J. L., M-108-3; Pvt K Co 5th KY Cav; 11-10-61 to __; Akersville PO (KY); received no discharge
SIKES, James M., Hm-106-1; Cpl C Co 8th TN Cav; 28 Jul 63 to 11 Sep 65; Russellville PO
SIKES, Martin, Sh-174-2; Martin Gibbs alias; Cpl K Co 11th US Col Inf; 3-1-64 to 1-12-66; 141 Beal St, Memphis PO
SILCOX, Emry B., Mg-197-4; Pvt B Co 2nd TN Inf; 61 to __; Wartburg PO; rheumatism, received no discharge
SILCOX, Levi M., S-215-1; Pvt H Co 9th TN Cav; 3 Aug 62 to 5 Jul 65; Jeffers PO; pris. at Bell Is.
SILCOX, Stephen, S-215-2; Pvt H Co 9th TN Cav; 5 Jun 63 to 14 Sep 65; Jeffers PO; sight affected and catarrh in head 26 yrs
SILER, Calway, C-32-2; Pvt C Co 49th KY Inf; 63 to 64; Jilicoe PO
SILER, Jacob, Cl-46-1; Pvt A Co 8th KY; 9-8-61 to 12-20-64; Clairfield PO; lunge disis
SILER, John, La-111-2; Pvt G Co 10th TN Inf; 8-1-62 to 4-1-65; Pleasant Point PO
SILER, W. (see Brint, Henry)
SILES, David, Je-140-1; Pvt G Co 148th Ilias? Inf; Lucilla PO
SILLARD, Isaac, K-157-1; Pvt; Knoxville PO
SILLAWAY, James, W-196-2; Pvt C Co 116th NY Vol; 8-62 to 5-63; Seeds PO; typhoid fever
SILVEY, Celia A., Ro-204-5; widow US Sol; PO omitted
SILVEY, Peter, Ro-203-1; Marinda widow of; Pvt K Co 5th TN Inf; 4 Apr 62 to __; Ethel PO
SILVEY, Samuel, Ro-204-4; Alpha widow of; Pvt I Co 9th TN Cav; 25 Sep 63 to 11 Sep 65; Kreis PO
SILVEY, Thomas, Ro-211-4; Elizabeth widow of; Kingston PO
SILVEY, Wesley, Ro-203-1; Pvt K Co 5th TN Inf; Apr 62 to May 65; Guenther PO
SILVEY, William, Ro-204-4; Angeline widow of; Elverton PO; no disc., killed during war
SILVINUS, Moses, Je-138-1; Pvt E Co 1st TN Cav; 15 Apr 62 to 14 Apr 65; Oak Grove PO
SIMER, Littleton L., Me-88-1; Cpl H Co 12th TN Cav; 2-1-64 to 12-14-65; Birchwood PO
SIMERLEY, Abraham, Bo-15-3; Cpl H Co 2nd TN Cav; 10-10-62 to 7-6-65; Marville PO; mashed up in hips
SIMERLEY, Adam, Bo-15-2; Pvt H Co 2nd TN Cav; 10-10-62 to 7-6-65; Blockhouse PO
SIMERLEY, James, Bo-15-2; Pvt H Co 2nd TN Cav; 10-10-62 to 7-6-65; Blockhouse PO
SIMERLEY, James A., Bo-15-2; Pvt H Co 2nd TN Cav; 10-10-62 to 7-6-65; Blockhouse PO
SIMERLEY, John, Bo-15-3; Nanca W. Willbern widow of; Pvt D Co 1st TN Lt Art; 9-1-63 to 7-20-65
SIMERLY, George, Ct-40-4; Pvt A Co 13th TN Cav; 9-22-63 to 9-5-65; Hampton PO; hearing
SIMERLY, Henry, Bo-15-4; Margaret M. Whitehead widow of; Pvt H Co 2nd TN Cav; 10-10-62 to 7-6-65; Blockhouse PO
SIMMON, Albert, Cl-58-1; Pvt B Co 1st TN Lt Art; 4-1-63 to 7-__ (2 yrs 7 mos); Minkton PO; injured kindys & liver, rupture
SIMMONS, Andrew A., We-223-2; Pvt H Co 33rd TN Inf; Sep 62 to __; Palmersville PO; captured and imprisoned, dont know where was __; CONF
SIMMONS, Benjaman, M-103-2; Pvt F Co 42nd US Col Inf; 11-15-63 to 6-1-66; Lafayette PO
SIMMONS, Britton L., Wa-224-1; Pvt TN Cav; Dec 61 to 16 Jun 62; Dresden PO; hernia from concussion of cannon shot, all papers in the hands of pension agt. at Dresden TN; CONF
SIMMONS, Dollie, Hw-126-1; widow; New Canton PO
SIMMONS, Elkanah, Ge-97-1; Nancy widow of; Pvt F Co 3rd TN Mtd Inf; 100 days; Milberton PO
SIMMONS, George W., V-178-1; Pvt M Co 5th TN Cav; 3-64 to 65; River Hill PO; meases, small pox & pneumonia
SIMMONS, Isham C., Br-6-2; Pvt A Co 4th TN Cav; 5-24-63 to 7-12-65; Chatala PO; atrophy liver, diarrhoea & heart, use of sight some destroyed
SIMMONS, Jackson C., Wa-266-1; Pvt F Co 3rd TN Mtd Inf; Meadow Brook PO
SIMMONS, James, Ge-97-1; Pvt F Co 3rd TN Mtd Inf; 100 days; Milberton PO; right leg shot
SIMMONS, James M., K-154-3; Knoxville PO; CONF
SIMMONS, Jane (see Taylor, Ben)
SIMMONS, John, Bl-2-2(1); Clarasa widow of; Pvt D Co KY State Vol; 3-29-65 to 10-23-65; Pearson PO

SIMMONS, John J., Br-6-3; Pvt I Co 10th TN Cav; 2-2-64 to 8-1-65; Grief PO; diarhoea & piles
SIMMONS, Joseph, K-164-2; Cpl E Co 2nd TN Inf; 9 Aug 61 to 6 Oct 64; PO omitted (Knoxville?)
SIMMONS, Mary A., O-142-2; widow US Sol; 15th Dist
SIMMONS, Monroe, B1-2-1; Nancy A. Seals formerly widow of; Pvt I Co 4th TN Cav, 6-62 to 64 (2 yrs); Seals PO; died in hospital, Louisville KY
SIMMONS, R. T., Cr-23-2; Pvt; 63? to 63 (1 yr); PO omitted; Mexican & CONF
SIMMONS, Raphael, Sh-191-3; Memphis PO; records not seen
SIMMONS, Robert, Un-255-1; Pvt E Co 2nd TN; 18 Nov 62 to 28 Nov 64; Warwicks PO; left lung & hit (sic) dishese
SIMMONS, Robert N., Hy-78-1; Pvt F Co 2nd US Inf; 6 Oct 64 to 6 Nov 65; Brownsville PO
SIMMONS, Samuel, Hm-105-2; Pvt B Co 3rd NC Art?; Sep 64 to 28 Jul 65; Morristown PO; gunshot in the thigh
SIMMONS, Sarah, Wy-178-1; widow US Sol; 13th Civil Dist
SIMMONS, W. P., O-136-1; Pvt L Co 6th TN Cav; Aug 1 62 to Jul 26 65; Limbs PO
SIMMONS, William, Sh-159-3; alias Cuningham, William; Pvt E Co 55th MS Inf; Memphis PO
SIMMONS, William T., B1-2-1; Pvt I Co 4th TN Cav; 8-15-63 to 1-11-65; Pikeville PO; kidney disease & deafness, can do moderate labor
SIMMS, Allen, Fr-105-2; Pvt C Co 106th US V Inf; Winchester PO; did not know when enlisted or discharged
SIMMS, Elis, Wl-293-1; Pvt I Co 42nd __; Oct 18 64 to Ju 7 65; Lockport PO
SIMMS, Ephraim, Sq-164-5(1); Pvt K Co 4th TN Cav; 8-14-63 to 1-65; Brock PO
SIMMS, George W., Me-92-2; Pvt 7th TN Mtd Inf; 64 to __; Sewee PO; no discharge
SIMMS, Jefferson, B-12-1; Eliza widow of; Pvt; Bedford PO; attorney got discharge and could tell nothing
SIMMS, Thomas, Sq-164-1; PVt K Co 4th TN Cav; __ to 65; Fillmore PO
SIMONDS, Henry A., A-5-5; Pvt 2nd MN Lt Art; 2-26-62 to 3-30-65; Clinton PO
SIMONDS, Nicholas, D-45-1; Pvt Baty 13th IN Vol; 9-17-63 to 7-10-65; Nashville PO; lost one eye
SIMONS, David C., G-61-1; Pvt 1st KY Inf; Jul 62 to 62 (3 mos); 12th Civil Dist
SIMONS, Green B., Fr-107-1; Pvt Col; 63 to 65; Winchester PO; lost discharge, was at Ft. Pillow
SIMONS, Mary L., Hd-50-6; widow of US Sol; 8th Civil Dist
SIMONS, William H. H., Mc-112-6; Pvt M Co 1st TN Cav; 10-29-64 to 7-12-65; Athens PO; rheumatism
SIMPKINS, Pitt, Di-41-1; Pvt F Co 13th US Col Inf; 29-63 to 1-6-66; White Bluff PO
SIMPKINS, Thomas, Je-141-2; Susan widow of; Pvt; Mill Spring PO
SIMPKINS, William G., La-111-1; Pvt D Co 9th TN Cav; 62 to 65 (2 yrs 6 mos); Pleasant Point PO; CONF
SIMPSON, Alfred, Rb-223-1; Springfield PO
SIMPSON, Charly W., We-230-4; Bugler C Co 16th TN Reg; Oct 15 62 to Nov 1 63; McKinzie PO; CONF
SIMPSON, Cornealous, D-45-2; Nashville PO
SIMPSON, Daniel, Ge-92-4; 2nd Lt A Co 3rd TN Mtd Inf; 1 Jul 64 to 30 Nov 64; Ottway PO; diseas of liver
SIMPSON, David A., W-193-1; Smartt PO; trying for a pension, his discharge is at Washington
SIMPSON, Elihu B., C-34-3; PVt F Co 62nd TN Inf; 9-62 to 5-16-63, deserted at Black River; Buckeye PO; conscripted in CONF
SIMPSON, Elisha H., Mc-118-2; Pvt K Co 4th TN Cav; 2-14-64 to 5-16-65; Cogshill PO; disease of back & lungs & heart 25 yrs
SIMPSON, George, Col, Ha-110-1; Pvt H Co MA Inf; 63 to 65 (1 yr); Treadway PO
SIMPSON, James, Gi-126-1; Pvt Col Inf; Pulaski PO
SIMPSON, James H., St-159-1; Pvt F Co 48th KY Cav; 8-62 to 12-64; Legate PO

SIMPSON, James M., Mc-116-4; Pvt F Co 4th TN Cav; 12-4-62 to 5-30-65; Athens PO; injure to eyes & kidney disease contracted while in service
SIMPSON, John, Je-136-1; Pvt B Co 1st US Hvy Art; 3 yrs; Dandridge PO
SIMPSON, John, S-217-1; Pvt C Co 47th KY Inf; Jul 63 to 25 Dec 64; Winfield PO; piles
SIMPSON, John, H-50-2(1); Pvt M Co 4th R US A(rt?); 12-13-62 to 12-13-65; Soddy PO; chronic liver disease
SIMPSON, John C., A-6-5(3); Perlina widow of; Pvt F Co 2nd TN Inf; 12-6-61 to 12-6-64
SIMPSON, John H., Lo-191-1; Pvt D Co 5th TN Inf; 1 Feb 62 to 10 Mar 65; Morganton PO; disease of lung and eyes
SIMPSON, John H., K-161-6(3); Pvt I Co 3rd TN Cav; 14 Oct 63 to 10 Jun 65; Knoxville PO
SIMPSON, Joe T., K-160-2; Knoxville PO
SIMPSON, Lewis, Gi-128-1; Pvt K Co 110th TN Inf; 18 Feb 63 to 15 65; 8th Dist
SIMPSON, Maiquis L., Hd-44-2; Elisebeth widow of; Pvt A Co 1st VT Inf; __ to 12-1-65 (1 yr 6 mos); PO omitted
SIMPSON, Nathan B., Su-239-1; Pvt I Co 8th TN Cav; 20 Nov 63 to Sep 29 65; Peltier PO; Dec 1864
SIMPSON, Dr. Samuel P., We-221-3; Surgeon 11th KY Inf; Dec 11 61 to Mar 66; Martin PO
SIMPSON, Thomas, Cf-41-1; Mary A. M. widow of; Pvt A Co 10th TN Inf; 63 to 65; Holly PO
SIMPSON, Thomas J., K-166-3; Mary J. widow of; 5th TN Inf; Knoxville PO; chronic diarrhea
SIMPSON, William, Cr-14-3; Pvt G Co 2nd TN Mtd Inf; 29 Dec 63 to 1 Feb 65; Clarksburg PO
SIMPSON, William A.?, Sh-200-1; Pvt I Co 11th OH Inf; 9-5-62 to 7-1-65; 20 Phelan St, Memphis PO
SIMPSON, William E., Hd-55-1; Pvt H Co 2nd TN Inf; Feb 63 to Apr 65; Olive Hill PO; measels settled on lungs, now suffering with lung disease
SIMPSON, Willis, Sm-173-2; Pvt C Co 44th US Col Inf; 3-64 to 4-66; Brush Creek PO
SIMPSON, Zuritha C., Wl-301-1; 17th Dist
SIMS, Andrew J., Wh-180-1; Cpl G Co 12th OH Inf; 4-21-61 to 7-21-64; Sparta PO; kidney disease contracted
SIMS, Chesley, Se-225-3; Pvt E Co 9th TN Cav; 1 Sep 63 to 11 Sep 65; Cotlettsburg PO; rheumatism, heart dis. 25 yrs
SIMS, Elijah, Mc-111-3; Pvt A Co 7th TN Mtd Inf; 8-64 to 7-65; Mortimer PO
SIMS, Greenbery D., Wh-180-1; Sparta PO; gone from house--no information
SIMS, Harvey M., Fe-44-1; Pvt F Co 3rd TN Cav; 8-1-63 to 8-3-65; Allardt PO; piles from chronic diarrhea
SIMS, Henry, Ct-39-3; Gap Run PO; right arm broken & rib broken, piles & frost bites
SIMS, James H., Se-222-2; Sevierville PO; dierea, reumatism & hearing defected
SIMS, John, Cy-26-2; Pvt B Co 5th KY Cav; 10-10-61 to 5-8-64; Moss PO
SIMS, Joseph, Ja-85-2; Sarah A. widow of; Pvt E Co 5th TN Inf; 3-2-62 to __; Birchwood PO
SIMS, Lewis, Sh-158-3; Pvt A Co Col Inf; 63 to __ (2 yrs); Memphis PO; rheumatis, Sims wife satisfied me he was a soldier by papers etc, but cant not be definite as to dates, etc.
SIMS, M., G-57-5(3); 62 to 65; Yorkville PO; CONF
SIMS, Peter, D-54-2; Lt I Co 14th US Col Inf; Nashville PO
SIMS, Ranson, Ct-39-3; widow; Gap Run PO
SIMS, Ransom F., Se-229-2; Pvt B Co 2nd TN Cav; 1 Feb 64 to 6 Jul 65; Gatlinburg PO; hearing affected
SIMS, Robert H. C., Wy-173-4; Pvt H Co 2nd TN Mtd Inf; 1-16-64 to 4-17-65; Sims PO
SIMS, Samuel, Ru-238-1; PVt B Co 16th US C Inf; 13 Apr 62 to 65; Walter Hill PO; shot in left wrist
SIMS, Samuel, Wh-187-1; Pvt TN Inf; 61 to 65; Cherry Creek PO
SIMS, Shields, Wy-173-3; Sgt H Co 2nd TN Mtd Inf; 12-15-63 to 1-19-65; Sims PO
SIMS, Thomas J., S-214-2; Glenmary PO; piles
SIMS, Tony, B-20-1; Bedford PO

SIMS, Westley B., Se-223-1; Pvt B Co 2nd TN Cav; Pigeon Forge PO
SIMS, William T., K-181-4(1); Pvt C Co 9th TN Cav; 22 Sep 63 to 11 Sep 65; Knoxville PO
SINANEY, Baley P., Sn-250-2; Pvt K Co 2nd __; 5-3-61 to 62; Castalian Springs PO; CONF
SINARD, William D., Je-146-3; Pvt 1st TN Cav; White Pine PO; spinal affection of back, old & feeble
SINERT, Adam, Hw-125-2; PVt D Co 4th VA Bat; 8-62 to 4-8-65; Stony Point PO; CONF
SINGLETON, Hugh T., Bo-19-1; widow of; Pvt E Co 3rd TN Inf; 9-61 to 4-65; Rockford PO; CONF
SINGLETON, James P., De-23-1; Pvt K Co 7th TN; 9-1-62 to 9?-16-65; Thurman PO; contracted piles & privets trouble also chronic diarhea
SINGLETON, James T., Hd-45-1; Cpl A Co 6th TN Cav; 8-11-62 to 7-26-65; Cerro Gordo PO; rheumatism
SINGLETON, Jane, Bo-19-1; widow of Sol; Pvt; Rockford PO; CONF
SINGLETON, Jerry, Gr-79-2; Liney widow of; Pvt I Co 26th TN; __ to 64; Ball Point PO; killed; CONF
SINGLETON, John, H-76-2; Pvt E Co 16th Col TN Inf; Chattanooga PO
SINGLETON, John W., He-58-2; Sol; 8th Civil Dist
SINGLETON, Robbert, Hm-105-2; Pvt A Co 3rd TN Lt Art; 9-61 to 5?-65; Morristown PO; heering & sight injured
SINGLETON, Robert, Gr-79-4; Pvt; Bull Point PO; CONF
SINGLETON, Robert, Bo-19-1; Pvt L Co; Rockford PO; CONF
SINGLETON, William G., W-189-1; Charlotte widow of; Pvt C Co 5th TN Cav; Smartt PO
SINGLETON, William L., Ru-234-1; Pvt H Co 4th TN Mtd Inf; 9-1-64 to 8-5-65; Jefferson PO; wounded & feet frosted
SINKS, William A., Mt-149-1; Pvt D Co 12th TN Cav; 1-6-64 to 6-16-65; Palmyra PO
SIPE, John C., Wa-270-2; Pvt H Co TN Inf; 4-1-62 to 4-65; Austin's Springs PO; rheumatism
SIPES, Abraham, Hd-56-1; Lucinda widow of; Pvt B Co 6th TN Cav; 8-25-62 to 7-26-65; Adamsville PO; died in 1880, affects US service
SIRVALLY, George R., Moo-215-1; Pvt D Co 3rd USV; 10-15-64 to 11-29-65; Sirvally PO; rheumatism & piles, he is not to work
SISK, Charles, Col, Wh-185-1; Pvt B Co 41st TN Inf; 3-25-63 to 2-8-65; Cassville PO; chronic rheumatism
SISK, John H., Gi-128-2; Pvt I Co 12th TN Cav; 2-10-64 to 5-28-65; Pulaski PO
SISK, John W., Br-13-4; Pvt C Co 14th Pl-O-Neer Army Corps; Cleveland PO; chronic bronchitis
SISK, Miles, C-86-4; Pvt B Co 5th TN Inf; 8-9-64 to 7-13-65; Naillon PO
SISK, William, Se-219-2; Pvt C Co 14th TN Inf; Jones Fork PO; fever & chills
SISKS, Houston, Co-66-1; Pvt I Co 26th TN Inf; 9-1-62 to 4-6-63; Bison PO; CONF
SISON, John, Le-118-1; Pvt K Co 173rd OH Inf; 8-64 to 7-65; Aetna PO; CONF
SISSINNY, Stephen, D-89-1; Nashville PO; discharge in the hands of claim agt.
SISSOM, Isaah, Ca-22-1; Pvt F Co 5th TN Cav; 61 to 62; Hollow Springs PO
SISSON, Joseph, Hd-50-4; Mary widow of; Pvt 1st AL; Nixon PO
SITZ, William J., Gu-48-1; Pvt K Co 13th TN Cav; 10-62 to 63; Tracy City PO; while home recruiting was closed, never got his discharge papers
SITZLAR, Jasper, Ro-207-3; Pvt H Co 143rd IN Inf; 1-23-65 to 10-17-65; Paint Rock PO; indigestion & heart palpitation result of smallpox
SIVELS, Solomon W., Ro-210-6; Mahala widow of; Pvt I Co 2nd TN Inf; 8-10-61 to 4-1-63; Rockwood PO; died
SIVILS, Timothy G., Cl-48-1; Pvt B Co 1st TN Lt Art; 8-20-63 to 6-21-65; Old Town PO
SIZEMORE, Edward D., Hw-119-2(1); Pvt E Co 8th TN Cav; 63 to __ (4 mos); Alum Well PO; spinal affection
SIZEMORE, George W., Ct-36-1; Pvt C Co 13th TN Cav; 9-63 to 9-65; Shell Creek PO

SIZEMORE, Owen, Ha-117-3; Elizabeth widow of; Pvt 24th KY Inf; Sneedville PO; died in service
SIZEMORE, Solomon S., Ha-117-4; US Sol; 12th Dist
SIZEMORE, William O., K-179-2, Susana widow of; Lt 8th TN Cav; Virtue PO
SIZMORE, James, Sh-162-2(1); Pvt D Co 5th Art; 1-4-64 to 5-20-66; Ramsey PO
SKAGGS, Benjamin F., Un-253-1; Pvt B Co 7th TN Inf; 8-7-61 to 9-17-64; Lorenaton PO; neuralgia, head
SKEEN, Chesly, Je-144-1; Pvt C Co 1st TN Cav; 4-1-62 to 4-1-65; White Pine PO; subject to typhoid fever
SKEEN, Columbus H., Je-146-1; Cpl C Co 1st TN Cav; 4-16-62 to 4-1-65; Kansas PO; kidney & piles
SKEEN, Crocket, K-167-5; Pvt C Co 1st TN Cav; 4-1-62 to 4-1-64; Knoxville PO; pension
SKEENS?, Lafayette, Ro-210-5; Pvt; Rockwood PO
SKELTON, John F., H-51-7; Hill City PO
SKELTON, Robert, Sh-159-6; Memphis PO
SKILES, Ephraim, Bl-5-2; Pvt D Co 6th TN Mtd Inf; 8-7-64 to 6-30-65; Brayton PO; chronic rheumatism
SKILES, George, Bl-5-2; Sgt D Co 6th TN Mtd Inf; 8-7-64 to 6-30-65; Brayton PO
SKILES, Henry, H-58-5; Pvt I Co 2nd TN Inf; 11-11-61 to 2-5-63; Retro PO; broncetes & heart disease, mustered out by reason of disability on surgeon's certificate
SKILES, John, Bl-5-1; Pvt I Co 2nd TN Mtd Inf; 61 to __ (no discharge); Brayton PO; absent without leave but later returned to duty in 64 but not recorded
SKILES, William C., H-50-2(1); Pvt A Co 9th R TN Cav; 9-1-63 to 9-11-65; Daisy PO; chronic diorreah
SKILLERN, Napolean B., La-112-1; Sgt H Co 2nd TN Mtd Inf; 12-15-63 to 1-1-65; Abner PO
SKINNER, George W., Dy-25-5(1); Pvt K Co 43 MS Inf; 4-62 to __ (3 yrs); Newbern PO; never discharged, taken at Vicksburg & paroled; CONF
SKINNER, William J., Wi-281-1; Pvt H Co 5th TN; 12-25-63 to 8-65; Allisona PO
SKULLEY, Micheil, Wl-290-1; 3rd Civil Dist.
SKURLOCK, Zachariah, Wh-182-1; Doyle's Sta. PO; no discharge
SKYLES, John W., Ge-83-3; Pvt C Co 4th TN Inf; 11-12-62 to 5-2-65; Painters PO; wound in head, diseas of lungs?
SLADE, Isaac N., D-64-3; 1st Lt 23 KY Inf; 62 to 64; Nashville PO
SLAGLE, David E., Wa-267-3; Pvt B Co 8th TN Cav; 7-23-63 to 9-11-65; Johnson City PO; chrc. rheumatism
SLAGLE, Henry, Ge-98-4; Pvt G Co 8th TN Inf; 62 to 65; no PO; relapse of measels
SLAGLE, Henry C., S-215-1; Pvt E Co 4th KY Inf; 1-20-62 to 4-14-65; Pioneer PO; hip mashed; I don't like rebels
SLAGLE, Henry M., Wa-271-1; Sgt B Co 8th TN Cav; 7-23-63 to 9-11-65; Jonesboro PO; rumatism
SLAGLE, John P., Wa-269-1; Pvt F Co 7th IN Cav; 8-22-63 to 8-25-65; Johnson City PO; heart & kidneys
SLAGLE, William, Cf-42-1; Pvt F Co 47th MI Inf; 8-14-62 to 7-11-65; Hickerson PO; gun shot wound
SLAGLE, William H., Pu-141-1; Pvt F Co 3rd TN Inf; 9-15-64 to 2-20-65; Cookville PO; chronic rheumatism, discharged at expiration of time
SLAGS, Thomas M., Sh-201-2; Sarah J. widow of; Pvt H Co 11th IA Inf; 11-5-62 to 11-10-65; Memphis PO; CONF(?)
SLATEN, Richard, S-212-1; Pvt K Co 30th KY; 2-2-64 to 4-18-65; Porch Corn PO; feet frost bit
SLATER, James T., Bl-5-1; Pvt I Co 1st NJ Inf; 2-26-64 to 6-29-65; Pvt F Co 21st NJ Inf; 8-25-62 to 6-19-63; Brayton PO; re-enlisted
SLATON, John T., Je-139-2; Pvt C Co 9th TN Cav; 7-12-63 to 9-11-65; Oak Grove PO
SLATTERY, Alexander P., K-181-3; Capt D Co 3rd TN Cav; 12-1-62 to Apr 65; Nast PO
SLATTON, Nade? H., Mr-96-2; Pvt C Co 1st IN Cav; 3-15-64 to 6-16-64; Shirleyton PO; relapse measels

SLAUGHTER, George, Hu-104-1(2); Pvt B Co 156th India(sic); 64 to __(1 yr); McEwen PO
SLAUGHTER, George W., A-9-4(2); Pvt I Co 7th TN Mtd Inf; 11-8-64 to 6-12-65; Lowe Sulphur Springs PO; measles resulting in lung & head disease, discharged from genl hospital Knoxville TN
SLAUGHTER, Gilbert L., Hr-89-1; Pvt L Co 10th TN; 11-63 to 65; Cidar Chappell PO
SLAUGHTER, James, Hu-104-1(2); Pvt C Co 156th Brit. (sic); 64 to 65; McEwen PO
SLAUGHTER, Lenton S., Hn-68-1; 1st Sgt A Co 1st US CI; 8-22-64 to 2-10-66; Paris PO
SLAVER, Polly, S-212-2; widow; 12th Dist.
SLAYTON, Wm. M., H-60-3; Pvt F Co 13th MI inf; 10-63 to 11-65; Chattanooga PO
SLEDGE, Henry, Sh-197-1; alias Henry McLemore; Sgt K Co 63rd Col Inf; Memphis PO; papers at Washington
SLIANE, Isaac, D-103-1; Pvt E Co 10th IL Cav; 9-20-61 to 10-12-62; Joelton PO; chron diarhea, draws pension
SLIGER, Andrew R., Pu-141-1; Pvt K Co 4th TN Inf; 11-1-64 to 8-12-65; Cookville PO; discharged at expiration of time
SLIGER, Peter, K-167-4; Pvt C Co 1st TN H; 62 to 65; Knoxville PO; rheumatism, gets pension
SLIMP, David J., Ho-151-2; Pvt M Co 13th TN Cav; 2-2-64 to 9-5-65; Bakers Gap PO; rheumatism, frost bitten feet
SLIMP?, Frederick, Jo-149-1; Capt F Co 13th TN Cav; Mountain City PO; chronic dirrhea, disease rectum & skin
SLIMP, Thomas M., K-184-1; Pvt F Co 1st TN Inf; 61 to 10-17-64; Asbury PO
SLIMP, William H., Jo-152-3; Pvt G Co 13th TN Cav; 9-23-63 to 9-5-65; Mouth of Doe PO; gun shot, nasal catarrh
SLIYER, Will, Ge-88-4; Margett widow of; Bulls Gap PO
SLOAN, Alexander H., H-54-5; Pvt B Co 98th OH Inf; 7-6-62 to 1-1-65; Sherman Heights PO; bronchitis contracted from measles in 1-63
SLOAN, Clifford, Bo-22-3; Pvt B Co 13th TN Cav; 4-15-63 to 9-5-65; Gamble's Store PO
SLOAN, Elisha B., Sm-168-2; Pvt A Co 1st TN Inf; 5-1-64 to 7-5-65; Pleasant Shade PO; disease of head and breast
SLOAN, George W., Mo-127-1; Pvt D Co 3rd TN Cav; 8-1-64 to 12-25-64; Notchy PO
SLOAN, Jabus B., Se-224-3; Pvt E Co 3rd NC Mtd Inf; 3-21-64 to 8-8-65; Wears Valley PO; wond in the hip, I was guarding a wagon & got shot
SLOAN, James A., D-72-5; Capt A Co 4th GA Cav; 2-62 to __; Nashvile PO; CONF
SLOAN, James R., Mo-127-1; Pvt D Co 3rd TN Cav; 8-1-64 to 12-25-64; Notchy PO
SLOAN, John A., Hd-54-2; Cpl G Co 10th TN Inf; 6-1-62 to 6-24-65; Ruth PO
SLOAN, John A., Mo-127-2; Sgt K Co 11th TN Cav; Notchy PO
SLOAN, John M., M-107-5; 1st Sgt A Co 1st TN Mtd Inf; 5-1-64 to 7-5-65; Gibbs Cross Roads PO
SLOAN, Levi, Sh-168-1; Pvt D Co 88th TN Inf; 1-23-65 to 4-13-66; 130 Exchange St., Memphis PO
SLOAN, Madison J. C., Mo-127-1; Pvt D Co 3rd TN Cav; 8-1-64 to 12-7-64; Notchy PO
SLOAN, William, K-177-4; Pvt A Co 9th OH Cav; 10-62 to __; Powells Station PO; ruptured
SLOAN, William H., Mo-127-1; 1st Lt A Co 3rd TN Cav; 8-1-62 to 65; Notchy PO
SLOTHARD, Anne, D-54-2; widow; Nashville PO; away from city & no one could give information
SLOVER, Henry C., A-5-5; Pvt C Co 2nd TN Inf; 1-1-63 to 5-27-65; Clinton PO; Andersonville prison month
SLOVER, John C., A-4-6(2); Capt C Co 2nd TN Inf; 8-12-61 to 3-31-65; Coal Creek PO; piles & erysepelas
SLOVER, Pleasant A., A-4-2; Pvt E Co 3rd TN Inf; 3-13-62 to __; Offutts PO; chronic diarrhea, no discharge been given
SLOVER, Samuel M., A-10-1; Pvt F Co 7th TN Inf; 11-8-64 to 7-27-65; Briceville PO

SLOVER, William H., A-4-2; Pvt F Co 7th TN Mtd Inf; 11-8-64 to 7-27-65; Coal Creek PO; liver complaint
SLUVEN, Jefferson, S-217-2; Pvt I Co 30th KY Inf; 2-64 to 4-65; Winfield PO
SLYAN, Ollie, Ct-37-2; Pvt D Co 8th TN Cav; 6-63 to deserted 65; Ripshin PO; frost bite & bruse for horse falling
SMALL, Albert G., Mc-112-2; Mary P. widow of; Major 11th TN Cav; 9-26-62 to __; Athens PO; No discharge to show dates.
SMALL, Augustus, Ch-12-3; Lt B Co 21st TN Cav; 11-4-63 to 11-64; Wild Goose PO; CONF
SMALL, Burl, Li-147-1; Susan widow of; Sgt I Co 15th US Inf; __ to 65 (18 mos); Norris Creek PO; consumption
SMALL, James A., Ge-95-1; Sgt C Co 8th TN Cav; Home PO
SMALL, James W., Mc-109-5; Pvt F Co 4th TN Cav; 11-21-63 to 7-12-65; Mouse Creek PO; gun shot wound in left hip
SMALL, Jasper, S-213-1; Pvt C Co 42nd IN Inf; 10-64 to 65; New River PO
SMALL, Peter (see Hull, Peter)
SMALL, Thomas H., Mc-109-5; Pvt F Co 4th TN Cav; 5-6-63 to 6-30-65; Sweetwater, Monroe Co. PO rheumatism & piles 26 yrs
SMALLEN, Elkana, K-180-3; Jane widow of; Pvt L Co 2nd TN Cav; Ebenezer PO; died in army
SMALLEY, Alexander, Be-6-1; Pvt C Co 13th TN Inf; 7-29-65 to 1-10-66; Big Sandy PO
SMALLWOOD, George, Mn-129-1; Pvt B Co 6th TN Cav; 63 to 65; Stantonville PO; I can not find when he was discharged
SMALLWOOD, William, Mn-129-1; Pvt G Co 6th TN Cav; 12-28-63 to 65; Purdy PO; no discharge
SMALZREID, George, Sh-159-5; no PO
SMART, Benjamon, Col, Me-89-1; Pvt K Co; Big Spring PO
SMART, C. H., D-62-1; Pvt C Co 10th US; 11-1-61 to 2-13-67; 1508 Laurel St., Nashville PO
SMART, Henry, Me-90-1; Pvt K Co 1st TN Hvy Art; Big Spring PO
SMART, Joseph, Co-67-5; Pvt H Co 2nd NC Inf; 8-61 to __; Naillon PO; gunshot right shoulder, captured & put in prison; CONF
SMARTT, Alfred, H-63-3; Jennie Weaver formerly wife of; Pvt TN Cav; 63 to 65; 613 Broad st., Chattanooga PO
SMARTT, Jonothan B., Sm-173-1; Pvt G Co 4th TN Mtd Inf; 11-1-64 to 8-25-65; Brush Creek PO; piles
SMARTT, Reuben, Gu-45-1; Pvt E Co 1st TN Cav Vidette; 63 to 64 (8 mos); Altamont PO
SMARTT, William, Gu-45-2; Esther widow of; Pvt E Co 1st TN Cav vidette; 63 to 64 (8 mos); Altamont PO
SMARTT, William, Gu-45-2; 4th Dist
SMATTINS?, Jacob, Ct-41-4; Pvt A Co 8th VA Cav; 8-14-61 to __; Elizabethton PO; rhumatism; CONF
SMEABAUGH, Lemuel C., Sn-253-1; Sgt H Co 46th PA Inf; 8-24-61 to 9-13-64; No. One PO
SMEDLEY, George W., R-161-6; Blacksmith L Co 1st TN Cav; 9-1-62 to 6-5-65; Dayton PO
SMELCER, Ephraim, Se-219-2; Pvt E Co 2nd TN Cav; 9-16-62 to 3-19-65; Richerson Cave PO; small pox
SMELCER, Newton F., Ge-87-3; Pvt E Co 1st TN Cav; 7-62 to 6-5-65; Almeda PO; gunshot wound
SMELLAGE, Hartwell J., We-221-3; Lt K Co 4th TN Cav; 12-3-62 to 8-25-66; Martin PO; hernia by horse falling
SMELSER, Henry A., Ge-87-2; Pvt A Co 12th TN Cav; Timberridge PO; hernia right side
SMELSER, Henry J., Ge-89-2; June widow of; Pvt A Co 4th TN inf; 6-2-64 to 8-2-65; Mosheim PO
SMIDDY, James, A-13-2; Mary widow of; Pvt F Co 7th TN Inf; 11-8-64 to 7-27-65; Briceville PO
SMIDDY, James F., C-27-2; Pvt F Co 6th TN Inf; no dates (3 yrs); Caryville PO
SMIDDY, John, C-27-2; Cpl K Co 2nd TN Cav; 8-17-62 to 7-6-65; Caryville PO
SMIDDY, Rubin, C-32-1; Easter widow of; Pvt B Co 1st TN Inf; no dates; New Comb PO; widow
SMIFF, George (see Isbell, George)

SMILEY, Richard, Ms-171-1; Teamster A Co 4th TN Inf; 8-64 to 9-65; Belfast PO
SMILEY, William G., B-3-1; Pvt A Co 5th TN Cav; 9-2-62 to 6-25-65; Shelbyville PO; hernia 10-64
SMIRES, John, Cy-26-1; Pvt I Co 9th TN Cav; 9-21-61 to 10-26-61(4?) (3 yrs 1 mo 5 days); Moss PO; wounds from gun shot
SMITH, Aaron, Cf-38-1; pvt; Trousdale PO, Warren Co.
SMITH, Abraham, A-6-1; Pvt H Co; 1862 to 1865; Olivers PO
SMITH, Abram, Hy-75-1; Pvt E Co 59th C TN; Apr 63 to __; Dancyville PO; says wounds hurting him; wounded at Fort Pillow
SMITH, Adelima B., Cf-42-1; pvt I Co 140th MO Inf; 15 Oct 64 to 11 Jul 65; Bellmont PO; gun shot in neck
SMITH, Aden, Co-61-3(1); Lucindia widow of; Pvt D Co 8th TN Inf; 28 Mar 63 to 30 Jun 63; Parrottsville PO; diah-ear
SMITH, Alanson, Hi-84-1; Pvt H Co 33rd IN Inf; Jun 63 to 24 Aug 65; Graytown PO
SMITH, Alen P., K-184-4; Pvt K Co 2nd TN Inf; 10 Dec 61 to 15 Dec 64; Thorn Grove PO
SMITH, Alexander, Ge-98-3; Pvt K Co 1st TN Cav; 12 Jul 62 to 5 Jun 65; Jeroldstown PO; rheumatism and chronic diarhea
SMITH, Alexander, Ge-98-5; Mary widow of; Pvt; Jeroldstown PO
SMITH, Alexander, Ge-96-2; Pvt B Co 1st TN Art; 21 Jan 65 to 21 Jul 65; Jockey PO
SMITH, Alexander, Ge-97-1; Pvt C Co 1st TN Mtd Inf; Apr 63 to 2 Aug 65; Maltsberger PO; chronic diarrhea, eye lost?
SMITH, Alexander, Je-146-3; Pvt C Co 8th TN Cav; 63 to Dec 65; Leadvale PO; old man looks bad
SMITH, Alexander, F-37-2; Pvt G Co 55th US Col Inf; Feb 63 to Jan 66; Yum Yum PO
SMITH, Alexander E., Co-69-2; Pvt D Co 3rd TN Inf; 27 Oct 62 to 10 May 65; Rankin PO; don't remember dates; CONF
SMITH, Alexander G., S-213-1; Sgt G Co 7th TN Inf; 25 Nov 61 to 3 Feb 65; Huntsville PO
SMITH, Alexander P., H-51-4; Pvt A Co 6th TN Inf; 2 Jul 64 to 15 Jul 65; Hill City PO
SMITH, Alx M., K-179-1; Pvt D Co 3rd TN Inf; 10 Feb 62 to 23 Feb 65; Virtue PO
SMITH, Allen, Mo-122-3(1); Pvt K Co 2nd TN Cav; 1861 to 1865; Hiwassee College PO; loss of one eye; CONF
SMITH, Andrew, Cu-15-3; 6th Civil District
SMITH, Andrew, D-89-2; 11th Civil District
SMITH, Andrew, Col, Me-92-4(1); Pin Hook PO; frost bit feet; did not get to see him
SMITH, Andrew, Sh-146-2; Catherin, orphan (Kate); Pvt F Co 55th Col Inf; 20 May 63 to 29 May 63; Pearley PO
SMITH, Andrew, Wl-293-2; Pvt G Co; 63 to 64; Austin PO
SMITH, Andrew J., Ge-98-6; US Sol; 11th District
SMITH, Andrew T., A-6-4(2); Sgt J Co 11th TN Cav; 23 Aug 63 to 11 Sep 65; Olivers PO
SMITH, Andy J., H-49-7; Pvt C Co 5th TN Inf; 23 Aug 64 to 4 Apr 65; Daisy PO; lost a finger
SMITH, Anna, Sh-191-7(3); rear of Clay St., Memphis PO
SMITH, Asa, Fe-41-3(1); Pvt Cupt Beaty Co Independent TN Scouts; 1862 to 1865; Boat Land PO
SMITH, Bailey P., S-213-3; Pvt I Co 1st KY Cav; 1 Aug 63 to 30 Sep 65; Huntsville PO; gunshot in left ankle
SMITH, Barney W., K-186-1; Sarah E. widow of; Pvt B Co 3rd TN Inf; 63 to 64; Beaver Ridge PO
SMITH, Barton, Pi-153-2; Nancy widow of; Pvt C Co 32nd KY Inf; 2 Jun 62 to 12 Aug 62; Spurnier PO; CONF
SMITH, Benjamin F., Cu-18-1; Pvt C Co 2nd TN Inf; 5-61 to 8-64; Glen Alice PO
SMITH, Benjamin P., Ro-201-1; Pvt I Co 1st TN Inf; 9 Aug 61 to 17 Sep 64; Kingston PO
SMITH, Benjamin P., Hm-107-1; Pvt C Co 9th TN Cav; 12 Aug 63 to 11 Sep 65; Witts Foundry

PO; liver stomach & heart trouble; over look when enumerated
SMITH, Berry, Wl-292-1; alias William Berry Smith; 1st Sgt H Co 40th USCI; 17 Sep 64 to 25 Apr 66; Lebanan PO
SMITH, Bery, Li-149-1; Pvt K Co 110th US Col Inf; Jan 64 to 15 Dec 66; Fayetteville PO
SMITH, Britton, He-63-1; Amey widow of; Cpl C Co 7th TN; Scotts Hill PO; in Andersonville Prison 13 months 4 days
SMITH, Burton, Mc-112-6; Sarah J. widow of; Major K Co 1st TN Cav; 1861 to Apr 65; Athens PO; rupture & rheumatism
SMITH, C., L-106-1; Jamima widow of; Pvt I Co 12th TN Cav; 6 Jul 61 to 11 Sep 65; Naukapoo PO; hip stifen by a stab
SMITH, Caleb A., U-247-3; Jane widow of; Pvt 4th TN Inf; Erwin PO; died since discharged
SMITH, Cassander, widow Sol US; H-49-11; 2nd Civil Dist.
SMITH, Charles, K-157-1; Cpl H Co 1st Col Art; __ to 65; Knoxville PO
SMITH, Charles, Mg-198-2; Pvt A Co 2nd US Inf; 64 to 65; Kismet PO
SMITH, Charles, Hn-70-1; Pvt G Co 9th Mis Inf; Paris PO; time of service unknown
SMITH, Charles, Li-152-1; alias Charles Edmiston; Pvt E Co 40th Inf; 1863 to 1865; Petersburg PO; Col
SMITH, Charles, Sh-172-2; US Sol; 382 Main St., Memphis PO
SMITH, Charles A., Sh-174-2; Agnes widow of; 157 Beale St., Memphis PO; discharge lost
SMITH, Charles G., Mn-122-1; Pvt H Co 3rd MI Cav; 26 Jan 64 to 12 Feb 66; McNairy PO; disch. at close of hostilities
SMITH, Charles H., Un-254-1; Pvt B Co 1st KY Cav; 62 to 65; Gravestown PO; CONF
SMITH, Charls W., A-8-1; Pvt K Co 5th TN Inf; 19 Apr 62 to 19 May 65; Scarborough PO; peritrflesh? right foot 8-63
SMITH, Claiborne, R-158-3; alias Claiborne Baldwin; Pvt C Co 17th US Col Inf; 10 Jan 64 to 1 Oct 64; Pvt 101st US Col Inf 1 Oct 64 to 5 Feb 66; Rhea Springs PO; lung disease; draws pension
SMITH, Clark, Col, Cr-14-3; Pvt I Co 3rd US Hvy Art; Cawthorn PO
SMITH, Coleman P., We-220-2; Pvt I Co 6th TN Cav; 16 Jun 62 to 26 Jul 65; 4th Civil Dist.
SMITH, Cornelius, Ge-97-4; Sol US; 16th Civil Dist.
SMITH, Couvad F., G-56-1; Capt C Co 27th WI Inf; 8-1-62 to 9-26-65; Trenton PO
SMITH, Danial, Gi-125-1; Pvt C Co 110th US Col Inf; 23 Dec 63 to 6 Feb 66; Weakly PO
SMITH, Daniel, H-56-7; Pvt A Co 10th TN Cav; 11-22-63 to 4-65; St. Elmo PO
SMITH, Daniel, Fe-42-1; Pvt C Co 7th TN; 8-3-62 to ?; Jamestown PO
SMITH, Daniel, Un-250-2; G Co 2nd TN Cav; 62 to __; Maynardville PO
SMITH, Daniel, T-206-2; Pvt I Co TN Inf; Brummel? Covington PO
SMITH, Daniel, Gi-131-1; Lucinda Ingram was wife of; Pvt 111th Col Inf; 63 to 65; Young PO; died in Army
SMITH, Daniel F., Un-250-1; Pvt D Co 1st TN Inf; 9 Aug 61 to 17 Sep 64; Maynardville PO; chronic diarrhea & lung disease; incurred while in service
SMITH, David, H-74-1; Pvt C Co 14th TN; 10-63 to 3-66; 614 Tenth St., Chattanooga PO
SMITH, David, S-212-2; Pvt D Co 30th KY; 15 Nov 63 to 18 Apr 65; Porch Corn PO; toe fros rigt off
SMITH, David L., K-166-1; Pvt 101st PA Inf; 8 Mar 65 to 25 Jun 65; Knoxville PO
SMITH, Dru, C-33-4; Pvt; 90 days; Jellico PO
SMITH, Edward, K-156-3; Pvt O Co 13th Col E TN Art; 23 Feb 64 to Mar 65; 27 Mill St., Knoxville PO
SMITH, Edward, D-58-1; Pvt A Co 40th US Col Inf; Jan 64 to Apr 66; Nashville PO; ruptured
SMITH, Edward, Sh-196-1; Maria Coffin former widow of; Cpl B Co 61st TN Inf; Providence Chapel, Memphis PO; died with small pox in

hospital at Memphis, served Capt. Kelly
SMITH, Edward, Sh-161-2; US Sol; 16th Dist.
SMITH, Edward H., Cr-14-3; pvt G Co 7th TN Cav; 5 Aug 62 to 25 Oct 63; Crider PO
SMITH, Elihu, Ro-202-2; Barbra widow of; Pvt L Co 1st TN Cav; 1 Feb 63 to 19 Jun 65; Union X Roads PO; chronic rheumatism
SMITH, Elihu F., Mr-99-2; Mary A. widow of; Jasper PO
SMITH, Elijah, K-179-3; Pvt D Co 3rd TN Inf; 1 Jan 63 to 8 Aug 65; Campbell PO
SMITH, Elijah, La-111-1; Pvt AR Inf; 4-62 to 1865; Snob Creek PO; CONF
SMITH, Elisha K., H-51-7; Pvt A Co 6th TN Inf; 8-2-64 to 6-30-65; 16th Dist.
SMITH, Dliza, P-150-2; widow US Sol; 2nd Dist.
SMITH, Elizabeth (see Kenady, Samuel)
SMITH, Elizabeth (see Lunt, Alex)
SMITH, Emerson, Hw-132-3(1); Pvt C Co 63rd TN Inf; __ to 65; Strahl PO; could not get other information; CONF
SMITH, Estel, R-157-2; Sol; 12th Dist.; Grand View PO
SMITH, Fenton, T-209-2; alias Clark Fenton; Pvt I Co 4th TN Art; 62 to 65; Getedg PO
SMITH, Fethias, Ge-98-3; Pvt K Co 1st TN Cav; 11 Aug 62 to 19 Jun 65; Swancey PO; injury to shoulder thrown from horse
SMITH, Findley, Ct-40-5; Lorina Angel formerly widow of; Elizabethton PO
SMITH, Fletcher, Dy-27-2; Pvt C Co 15th TN Cav; 5-63 to 5-65; Ro Ellen PO: CONF
SMITH, Frances (see Gibson, Lanney)
SMITH, Francis M., Ct-42-2; Pvt 13th TN Cav; Watauga PO
SMITH, Francis M., Co-61-3(1); Pvt D Co 8th TN Inf; 28 Mar 63 to 30 Jun 65; Parrottsville PO; diarraha
SMITH, Francis M., Pi-155-3; Pvt D Co 1st TN Mtd Inf; 2-10-63 to 4-25-65; Byrdstown PO; hearing injured by artillery
SMITH, Frank, Sh-146-2; alias Frank Cook; Pvt 3rd Hvy Art; Woodstock PO
SMITH, Frederic, Un-254-1; pvt D Co 1st TN Inf; 9 Aug 61 to 17 Sep 64; Paulett PO; rheumatis; paralized can't walk
SMITH, G. W., Gi-139-3; Pvt TN Inf; Wales Sta. PO; CONF
SMITH, George, Co-61-2(1); Pvt D Co 8th TN Inf; 9 Feb 63 to 30 Jun 65; Parrottsville PO
SMITH, George, Sh-191-7(3); Memphis PO; records not seen
SMITH, George, Rb-223-3(5); 9th Dist.
SMITH, George, D-50-3; Callie Ewin for, wife of; 901 N. College, Nashville PO; shot in leg; wid. has no record
SMITH, George, Mu-200-2; 12th Dist.
SMITH, George B., Se-226-4; Pvt K Co 3rd TN Inf; 10 Feb 62 to 23 Feb 65; Dumplin PO, Jefferson Co.; rhumatism & heart trouble
SMITH, George M., Se-226-4; Francis E. widow of; Pvt E Co 9th TN Cav; Dumplin PO, Jefferson Co.
SMITH, George T., Sh-162-1; Pvt A Co 6th TN Cav; Aug 11, 62 to Aug 12, 65; 134 Poplar St., Memphis PO; shot in left leg; discharged at Nashville TN
SMITH, George W., Fe-41-4(2); Pvt Capt Beaty's Co. Indpt TN Scouts; 12-62 to 4-65; Boat Land PO; captured by Col. Hughes
SMITH, George W., Lo-187-3; Pvt A Co 12th IN Cav; 30 Nov 63 to __; Loudon PO; lungs & indigestion
SMITH, George W., Hw-121-1; Pvt G Co 4th TN Inf; 1 Nov 62 to 2 Aug 65; Lucas PO; cidney spinal back
SMITH, George W., C-27-1; Pvt A Co 1st TN?; 8-61 to ?(1 yr 9 mos); Jacksboro PO
SMITH, George W., Hm-106-2; Pvt F Co 61st TN Inf; Morristown PO; CONF
SMITH, George W., F-20-3; Pvt I Co 38th TN Inf; Mar 62 to May 65; Hickory Withe PO; CONF
SMITH, George W., Hd-52-2; Pvt E Co 2nd TN; Oct 63 to May 65; Hurley PO
SMITH, George Washington, K-184-3; Pvt K Co 2nd TN Inf; 13 Dec 61 to 15 Dec 64; cronic dirie; Thorn Grove PO

SMITH, Gilbert C., Je-137-2; Pvt F Co 9th TN Cav; 13 Jul 63 to __; Fox PO
SMITH, Gilbert M., K-156-3; 1st Sgt A Co 25th IN Inf; Apr 61 to Dec 65; 56 E. Clinch St., Nashville PO; gunshot wounds in right thigh causing chronic disease
SMITH, Gorg, S-212-1; Pvt I Co 12th KY; 10 Oct 61 to __; Porchcorn PO; feet frost bit
SMITH, Grace, D-66-1; 416 S. Cherry, Nashville PO; his wife could not find his papers
SMITH, Green B., Cl-47-3; Pvt B Co 1st ? J.T.; 4-1-63 to 7-20-65; Cappford PO; rupture 1864
SMITH, Greenberry T., Cf-42-2; Pvt Navy; 1862 to 1865; Manchester PO; papers in hands of pension attorney
SMITH, Harkless, K-178-2; Pvt K Co 1st TN Hvy Art; 21 Jul 64 to 31 Mar 66; Hardin Valley PO
SMITH, Harrison, Wh-181-1; Martha E. widow of; Pvt; Perila PO; this woman badly needs a pension
SMITH, Harvey (Thos.), Ro-202-3(1); Pvt H Co 3rd TN Inf; 10 Feb 62 to 23 Mar 65; Gray's Hill PO; gun shot wound; 57 years old
SMITH, Harwell M., Pi-156-2; Pvt H Co 3rd KY Inf; 11-21-61 to 1-14-65; Byrdtown PO; piles; now disabled from work
SMITH, Henderson, Wl-302-3(5); Pvt B Co 5th TN Cav; Lebanon PO
SMITH, Henry, Ge-91-3; Sgt G Co 1st US Col?; 9 May 64 to 31 Mar 66; Greeneville PO
SMITH, Henry, K-161-5; Pvt A Co 5th OH Cav; St. Clair PO
SMITH, Henry, H-56-7; St. Elmo PO
SMITH, Henry, K-161-6; C Co 1st US Hvy Art; Knoxville PO; wound in leg
SMITH, Henry, Se-226-2; Pvt K Co 2nd TN Mtd Inf; 4 Mar 62 to 4 Mar 65; Sinking Springs PO; scurvy, Andersonville
SMITH, Henry, D-87-1; Pvt 17th Inf; Nashville PO
SMITH, Henry, Hy-85-1; Watchman, Gunboat Cairo; 62 to 65; Nut Bush PO
SMITH, Henry, D-69-2; US Sol, no record; Nashville PO
SMITH, Henry (see Clark, William)
SMITH, Henry, Sn-252-1; Pvt E Co 50th IL inf; Gallatin PO; shot in left breast
SMITH, Henry C., Dk-33-3; Pvt H Co 4th TN Cav; 10-15-62 to 8-14-65; Cathage Home PO; meassels settled in bowels & lungs
SMITH, Henry C., Mo-120-1; Pvt D Co 92nd OH Inf; 7-26-62 to 6-10-65; Glenloch PO; wounded at Mission Ridge
SMITH, Henry D., D-77-2; Cpl B Co 17th US Inf; Apr 64 to May 66; Nashville PO
SMITH, Hogan, Sh-191-3; Louisa widow of; Pvt H Co Hvy Art; 1863 to 1865; Memphis PO; records not seen
SMITH, Huston, Je-146-4; Pvt; White Pine PO; diseased & very intemperate; got name from neighbors, no dates
SMITH, Irvin W., Ru-241-5; Pvt B Co TN Inf; 1863 to 1866; Murfreesboro PO
SMITH, Irwin W., We-222-1; Pvt B Co Bradfords US Vol TN; 1 Oct 63 to 65; Gardner PO
SMITH, Isaac, H-50-4; Pvt D Co 6th R TN Inf; 8-16-64 to 6-30-65; Soddy PO
SMITH, Isaac, B-3-2; Wartrace PO
SMITH, Isaac (see Potts, Isaac)
SMITH, Isaac A., K-161-4; Martha A. widow of; Pvt B Co 2nd TN Inf; Knoxville PO; died in service
SMITH, Isaac N., Bl-1-1; Pvt L Co 3rd TN Cav; 1-15-64 to 6-14-65; Pikeville PO; chronic diarrhea and deafness
SMITH, Isaac W., Cl-47-3; Pvt E Co 6th TN Inf; 3-6-62 to 4-27-65; Cappford PO; rheumatism bowel troubles 1864
SMITH, Isam, O-130-1; Pvt K Co 4th KY Hvy Art; Dec 63 to 65; Harris PO
SMITH, Isreal O., K-168-4; Sgt G Co 6th TN Inf; 17 Apr 62 to 17 May 65; Smithwood PO; chronic diarrhea
SMITH, J. M., A-1-1; Pvt E Co 2nd TN Inf; 12-18-61 to 11-15-65; Andersonville PO; heart disease; a county pauper
SMITH, J. M., Mn-129-1; Pvt G Co 137th IN Inf; 5-15-64 to 9-21-64; Stantonville PO

SMITH, J. T., Cr-7-1; Pvt I Co 13th VA Inf; 10-63 to 6-22-65; Crockett Mills PO
SMITH, Jaby, Gr-78-1; Pvt B Co 8th TN Cav; 11 Jun 63 to 1 Aug 65; Spring House PO; heart & liver; not able to do manual labor
SMITH, Jackson, Hw-132-2; Pvt C Co 8th TN Cav; Jun 63 to 65; Strahl PO; chronic diarhea & piles
SMITH, Jackson I., H-51-4; Susan J. widow of; Pvt I Co 4th TN Cav; 10-14-63 to 6-19-65; Hill City PO
SMITH, Jacob, Ge-92-3; Pvt K Co 1st TN Cav; 12 Jul 62 to 5 Jun 65; Ottway PO; gun shot wound of hip
SMITH, Jacob, Ge-96-3; Nancy widow of; Pvt 8th TN Inf; 63 to __; Rheatown PO; discharge in Washington DC; cant get dates
SMITH, Jacob, Je-139-1; Pvt F Co 1st TN Inf; Trion PO
SMITH, Jacob, Pi-153-2; Pvt 30th KY Cav; 1864 to 65; Byrdstown PO; CONF
SMITH, Jacob, Li-149-1; Pvt K Co 110th US Col; 1-13-64 to 12-66; Fayetteville PO
SMITH, Jacob F., O-138-2; Lt K Co 10th SC; 2 Sep 61 to 15 Apr 65; Elbridge PO; CONF
SMITH, James, Ge-92-1; Cpl K Co 1st TN Cav; 15 Nov 61 to 5 Apr 65; Romeo PO; hert of back & rheumatism
SMITH, James, C-29-1; Nancy widow of; Pvt A Co 1st TN Inf; 7-1-63 to 8-3-65; Fincastle PO; bronchitis, caused death
SMITH, James, Hw-132-5; Pvt E Co 3rd TN Inf; 24 Jan 61 to 3 May 65; Strahl PO; CONF
SMITH, James, Co-61-1; Wagner; Parrottsville PO
SMITH, James, H-57-2; Sharp Shooter C Co 15th TN Col; 63 to 65; Orchard Knob PO
SMITH, James, Ge-96-3; Pvt K Co 13th TN Cav; Aug 62 to 65; Jeroldstown PO; chronic diarhea
SMITH, James, H-69-2; Pvt F Co 49th TN Inf (evidently Col); 62 to 7-5-65; Chattanooga PO
SMITH, James, Hw-127-3; Pvt I Co 8th TN Cav; 25 Sep 63 to 11 Sep 65; Rogersville PO; bronchitis
SMITH, James, K-186-2; Rachael widow of; Pvt 3rd TN Inf; Balls Camp PO
SMITH, James, Ha-111-1; Polly widow of; Upper Clinch PO
SMITH, James, Ro-210-11; Seaman Merrimack; 61 to 65; Rockwood PO
SMITH, James, Ov-139-1; Pvt I Co 1st TN Inf; 8-64 to 7-65; Beaver Hill PO
SMITH, James, Col, Rb-261-6(2); Pvt Battery; 63 to 65; Springfield PO; scalp wound and flesh wound in leg; Collard US
SMITH, James, Mu-209-4; Pvt; Columbia PO; CONF
SMITH, James, Col, Ru-247-1; Pvt C Co 111th TN Inf; dates not know (2 yrs 6 mos); Murfreesboro PO
SMITH, James A., Un-258-1; Pvt E Co 2nd TN Inf; Nov 61 to Nov 64; Newprospect PO
SMITH, James A., H-49-10; 1st Sgt A Co 6th TN Mtd Inf; 8-2-64 to 6-30-65; Daisy PO
SMITH, James A., Co-67-3; Pvt A Co 8th TN Cav; 63 to __; Cosby PO
SMITH, James C., O-134-1; Pvt E Co 48th TN; Oct 15, 61 to 15 Jul 65; Hornbeak PO
SMITH, James D., Hm-109-3; Pvt A Co 2nd TN Inf; 62 to 65; Whitesburg PO
SMITH, James E., C-30-2; Pvt E Co 6th TN Inf; 3-6-62 to 6-65; Well Spring PO; shot through left hand
SMITH, James F., Co-61-6(2); Pvt; Bridgeport PO; CONF
SMITH, James F., Jo-152-3; Pvt G Co 13th TN Cav; Nov 64 to 5 Sep 65; Mouth of Doe PO; gun shot & liver disease
SMITH, James G., Br-6-1; Pvt A Co 4th TN Cav; 5-24-63 to 7-12-65; Chatala PO; rheumatism
SMITH, James H., W-189-3(2); US Sol; McMinnville PO
SMITH, James H., Se-220-1; Pvt I Co 3rd TN Inf; 2 Jun 62 to __; Emurts Cave PO; left shoulder mashed, discharge lost
SMITH, James H., K-168-3; Smithwood PO
SMITH, James H., Ha-115-4; Pvt A Co 1st TN Cav; 19 Jun 62 to 25 May 65; Mulberry Gap PO; shot through arm & shoulder
SMITH, James J., Mn-120-1; Chaplain A Co 6th TN Cav; Sep 25, 62 to Jul 26, 65; Falcon PO; chronic diarrhea

SMITH, James M., O-138-2; Pvt K Co 28th TN; 28 Dec 61 to 25 Apr 65; Elbridge PO; CONF
SMITH, James M., Ov-137-1; Pvt M? Co 3rd KY Inf; 9-12-61 to 1-14-65; Nettle Carrier PO; lung disease
SMITH, James M., Di-36-1; Pvt G Co 50th TN Inf; 61 to 64; Bellsburgh PO; CONF
SMITH, James M., A-5-2; Pvt F Co 13th KY Cav; 10-63 to 1-10-65; Dossett PO; typhoid fever settled in legs, reenlisted
SMITH, James M., Ct-42-3; Elizabeth widow of; Pvt 13th TN Cav; Watauga PO
SMITH, James R., C-33-4; Pvt A Co 21st PA Cav; 2-10-65 to 7-8-65; Jellico PO
SMITH, James S., Su-242-1; Cpl B Co 6th US Inf; Apr 65 to Oct 67; Bluff City PO; loss of right eye 1866, Alkali Lake, hit by explosion of a cartridge, injury to right testicle 1865, Camp Wardwill sol. by a horse falling
SMITH, James T., Dy-25-2; Pvt K Co 4th TN Inf; Apr 61 to Apr 63; Newbern PO; CONF
SMITH, James W., H-70-4(1); Pvt B Co 6th TN Inf; 3-4-62 to 6-8-65; Chattanooga PO
SMITH, Jane, K-154-5(2); widow; Knoxville PO
SMITH, Jefferson, Cf-38-2; Pvt; 9th Civil Dist
SMITH, Jefferson R., L-103-1; Pvt, Bugler B Co 6th US Cav; 1 Apr 62 to Jan 65; Golddust PO; afflicted sore eyes and neuralgia, disability caused exposure with measles
SMITH, Jeptha M., Se-220-2; Pvt B Co 2nd TN Cav; 15 Sep 62 to 6 Jul 65; Emerts Cave PO
SMITH, Jerry, Dk-35-4(2); Pvt A Co 11th OH Cav; 6-6-63 to 6-10-66; Capling PO
SMITH, Jerry, Sh-163-1; PO omitted
SMITH, Jessey, H-71-1; 62 to 65; Chattanooga PO
SMITH, Joel, D-79-2; Pvt 15th IN Bat; Jun 4, 62 to Jun 30, 65; 309 Foster PO (Nashville)
SMITH, Joel M., H-63-3; Quarter master commissary; 62 to 65; 608 Pine, Chattanooga PO
SMITH, John Jr., John C. Smith alias, Fe-41-4(2); Pvt Capt Beaty's Co Indpt TN Scouts; 9-62 to 4-65; Boat Land PO; chr. dis. of dispepsy; captured by Col Hughes & parolled
SMITH, John, J-81-3; Pvt C Co 1st TN; 2-63 to 2-64; Bloomington PO; measles 4 mos; CONF
SMITH, John, Bl-2-2(1); Pvt G Co 6th TN Mtd Inf; 64 to 65; Farmingdale PO
SMITH, John, K-184-4; Elisbeth wife of; Pvt B Co 6th TN Inf; Thorn Grove PO
SMITH, John, Hd-45-2; Pvt 6th TN Cav; Cerro Gordo PO
SMITH, John, L-103-2; 3rd Sgt K Co 41st PA Inf; Dec 64 to Dec 65; Plum Point PO; infantry & navy, 1 yr each
SMITH, John, D-72-5; Jennie widow of; Pvt 5th TN Inf; 63 to 66; Nashville PO
SMITH, John, Ja-87-2; Pvt C Co 3rd NC Inf; 1-1-65 to 8-8-65; Apison PO
SMITH, John, D-63-1; Pvt A Co 10th TN Cav; __ to Oct 16, 66; Nashville PO
SMITH, John, D-69-2; US Sol, has no record; Nashville PO
SMITH, John, D-67-2; Pvt 2nd Col Inf; Nashville PO
SMITH, John, Su-242-1; Nancy A. widow of; volunteered in 13th TN Cav under Alex Fouger but was acting as pilot was captured and killed by the rebels Jan 12, 1865 before muster; Bluff City PO; he lost life by running the river recruiting for the 13th Cav. He made 3 trips, 25 Knox and one to Chattanooga. Some efforts have been made for the relief of this widow but so far to no effect. She is needy
SMITH, John, M-107-5; Pvt D Co 9th KY Inf; 61 to 64; Willette PO; disease of testicles--result of mumps
SMITH, John, Sh-192-1; Pvt H Co 128th US Inf; Stevens Ave, Memphis PO
SMITH, John, We-230-3; Sgt C Co 16th TN Inf; May 1, 62 to May 1, 63; McKinzie PO; CONF
SMITH, John, B-20-1; Bedford PO
SMITH, John, T-214-1; alias John Blakemore; Pvt B Co 61st US Inf; 63 to 65; Dist 9
SMITH, John A., Pi-153-3; Pvt D Co 1st TN Inf; 8-25-63 to 4-25-65; Byrdstown PO

SMITH, John A., Sm-174-1; Sgt F Co 101st Inf Vol; 9-28-64 to 1-31-66; New Middleton PO
SMITH, John A., Ov-137-2; Charlotte widow of; Pvt H Co 3rd KY Inf; 2-61 to __; Nettle Carrier PO; best information I could get
SMITH, John B., Hw-121-5(4); Pvt G Co 39th TN Cav; __ to 65; Lucas PO; wound in left arm; CONF
SMITH, John C., Wh-180-1; Pvt K Co 4th TN Inf; Sparta PO; no disease; refused to answer
SMITH, John C., La-114-1; Pvt 5th WI Art; 1 Oct 61 to 1 Oct 64; Lawrenceburg PO; disability, lungs & eyes
SMITH, John C., Ov-137-2; Isabell widow of; Pvt H Co 3rd KY Inf; Eagle Creek PO
SMITH, John C., Ct-40-5; Pvt F Co 2nd TN Inf; 7-22-63 to 7-19-65; Elizabethtown PO
SMITH, John C., Gu-45-2; Pvt; Beersheba PO; eye out by small pox; discharge at Washington, reenlisted
SMITH, John D., La-111-1; Pvt D Co 9th TN Cav; 64 to 65; Pleasant Point PO
SMITH, John E., K-174-4(3); Elizabeth widow of; Pvt G Co 2nd TN Cav; about 1 Oct 62 to about 6 Jul 65; House Mountain PO
SMITH, John F., Ha-111-4(1); Sgt A Co 1st TN Cav; 19 Jun 62 to 8 Jun 65
SMITH, John G. (see Goldsmith, John)
SMITH, John G., Un-250-1; Pvt F Co 6th TN Inf; 10 Mar 62 to 10 Mar 65; Maynardville PO
SMITH, John G., Hw-49-9; 1st Cpl G Co 3rd TN Cav; 7-6-63 to 5-19-65; Daisy PO; thrown from horse & hurt
SMITH, John H., Ro-210-12; Pvt; Post Oak Springs PO
SMITH, John H., Cr-4-5; Pvt E Co 6th TN Cav; 1-7-64 to 6-20-65; Bells Depot PO
SMITH, John H., Ch-16-1; Pvt A Co 6th TN Cav; 9-62 to 7-65; Henderson PO
SMITH, John H., Ja-85-5; Sgt G Co 5th TN Cav; 9-6-62 to 8-14-65; Georgetown PO
SMITH, John H., Cl-52-2; Elvenia Fugate formerly widow of; Sgt A Co 11th TN Cav; 10-1-63 to 12-30-64; Hypratia PO
SMITH, John J., We-226-1; Courier F Co 32nd OH Inf; Limbs PO; lost his discharge, forgot dates
SMITH, John M., A-4-5; Pvt; Coal Creek PO; CONF
SMITH, John M., C-29-2; Pvt C Co 9th TN Cav; 7-10-63 to 9-11-65; Stockville PO; disease of head, throat & rectum
SMITH, John M., Co-61-2(1); Pvt A Co 3rd TN M Inf; Parrottsville PO; gun shot wound in shoulder
SMITH, John P., Sh-159-2; 4 yrs; Memphis PO; CONF
SMITH, John P., Wa-274-3; 2nd Lt B Co 4th TN Inf; 3 Jun 63 to 2 Aug 65; Jonesboro PO
SMITH, John S., Mc-110-3(1); Pvt F Co 4th TN Cav; 4-4-64 to 7-7-65; Mouse Creek PO
SMITH, John T., L-105-1; Martha J. widow of; Curve PO; papers mislayed
SMITH, John W., Ja-85-6; Pvt G Co 5th TN Cav; 4-2-62 to 7-29-63; Capt G Co 5th TN Cav; 7-29-63 to 5-4-65; Georgetown PO
SMITH, John W., Ja-85-4; Capt G Co 4th TN Cav; Georgetown PO; CONF
SMITH, John W., We-225-1; Pvt 6th TN Cav; __ to 26 Jul 65; Dresden PO; rheumatism 25 yrs
SMITH, John H. (see Hemppail, John W.)
SMITH, Johnathan, Ja-85-2; Louisa widow of; Pvt E Co 5th TN Inf; 3-2-62 to 4-4-65; Birchwood PO; chronic diarrhoea
SMITH, Johnithon M., Ce-25-1; Pvt C Co 128th IL; Mar 63 to __ (1 yr); Henrietta PO; "Mr. Johnithan M. Smith informed me that he had lost his discharge consequently he could give me but little information"
SMITH, Joseph, K-182-3; Pvt K Co 2nd TN Vol Inf; 13 Dec 61 to 15 Dec 64; Arthur PO (Sevier Co.); right foot mashed
SMITH, Joseph, Po-151-1; Nancy M. widow of; Pvt; Servilla PO
SMITH, Joseph C., Br-10-2; 6th Civil Dist; US Sol
SMITH, Joseph H., H-69-1; Pvt A Co GA Inf; 62 to 63 (10 mos); Chattanooga PO; CONF
SMITH, Joseph P., M-107-3; Pvt H Co 5th KY Cav; Spiva PO (Clay Co.)
SMITH, Joseph S., Col, Lo-192-3; Pvt L Co 1st TN; Mar 64 to 65; Morganton PO; rheumatism & eyes affected

SMITH?, Josiah, Ge-98-2; Rebecca widow of; Pvt C Co 4th TN Inf; Jeroldstown PO; chronic diarhea
SMITH, Josiah J., Hd-50-4; Pvt F Co 6th TN Vol 2-3-63 to 7-26-65; Nixon PO; disease of the spine
SMITH, Jule A., We-222-2; Sgt B Co 12th TN Inf; May 61 to May 63; Gardner PO; rheumatism; CONF
SMITH, Julius W., Wl-295-2; Pvt G Co 10th Reg TN Cav; Feb 15, 64 to Aug 5, 65; Lebanon PO
SMITH, Junius S., Mg-200-2; Cpl H Co 22nd MI Inf; 11 May 62 to 11 Jun 65; Skene PO
SMITH, L. H., Li-158-1; Pvt; 17th Dist
SMITH, Lafayette J., Cy-28-1; Pvt B Co 1st KY Cav; 3-4-62 to 4-11-64; Celina PO
SMITH, Levi, Sh-191-5(1); Memphis PO; unk; records not seen
SMITH, Louis, Sh-174-3; Susan widow of; 62 to __; 82 Hadden Ave, Memphis PO; whot in right shoulder and thigh, in hospital 3 or 4 mos; discharged on acct. of disabilities, died 6 mos after discharge
SMITH, Lydia, D-64-6; widow; 216 S. Sumner, Nashville PO
SMITH, M. L., K-183-2; Pvt B Co 6th TN Inf; 8 Mar 62 to 27 Apr 65; High Point PO
SMITH, Malkin D., B-11-3(2); Cpl A Co 5th TN Cav; 8-5-63 to 6-16-65; Fall Creek PO
SMITH, Manuel, B-4-1; Cpl A Co 42nd Reg US Col; __ to 1-66 (2 yrs); Bell Buckle PO
SMITH, Marion, Gi-131-1; Cook H Co 7th IA Inf; Dec 63 to __ (1 yr); was not discharged
SMITH, Mary B., We-220-3; 1st Civil Dist
SMITH, Mary E., K-177-3; PO omitted
SMITH, McDaniel, D-75-3; Pvt F Co 30th TN Inf; 15 Apr 62 to 1 Jan 64; Stewarts Ferry PO; shot in arm; prisoner 8 mos, Lomesville
SMITH, McKinney, Bl-1-2; in US service all dates lost & forgotten; Palo PO; chronic sore eyes, in Gowans Regiment
SMITH, Mike, H-54-2(3); Pvt; Chattanooga PO
SMITH, Moore, Gi-123-1; Pvt Col Troops; Bethel PO
SMITH, Moses, H-49-7; 2nd Sgt A Co 6th TN Mtd Inf; 8-2-64 to 05-8-65; Daisy PO
SMITH, Nancy (see Brown, Reuben J.)
SMITH, Nathan J., Ge-83-2; Sgt H Co 4th TN Inf; 18 Apr 63 to Jul 65; Horse Creek; rheumatism
SMITH, Nathan W., Hn-75-1; Pvt F Co 5th MI Cav; 15 Aug 62 to 3 Jul 65; Manlyville PO; blind, piles
SMITH, Nathan W., H-62-2; Pvt; 404 Cedar, Chattanooga PO
SMITH, Nathanial, R-161-3; Sarah Cross formerly widow of; Sgt B Co 4th TN Inf; 3 yrs 6 mos; Dayton PO; other facts not known
SMITH, Nathaniel J., Ct-35-1; Cpl G Co 13th TN Cav; 9-23-63 to 9-5-65; Fish Spring PO; in US Army (disability)
SMITH, Nehemiah H., Jo-153-1; Pvt B Co 4th TN Inf; 1 May 63 to 2 Aug 65; Little Doe PO; rheumatism
SMITH, Neil S., Sn-254-1; Pvt B Co 8th TN Mtd Inf; 4-7-65 to 8-18-65; Hendersonville PO
SMITH, Nelson, Ds-254-2; Pvt C Co 13th US Col Inf; Hendersonville PO
SMITH, Nelson E., Sm-171-1; Pvt C Co 8th TN Mtd Inf; 2-10-65 to 8-17-65; Chestnut Mound PO
SMITH, Nevel H., We-222-1; Pvt F Co Col Nitans TN Reg; 11-63 to Jun 65; Gardner PO; CONF
SMITH, P. T., Hm-107-2(1); Pvt D Co 1st TN Cav; 1 Jan 63 to 1 Jun 65; Witts Foundry PO; cattarrh of head--eyes
SMITH, Peter, Ge-92-1; Pvt K Co 1st TN Cav; 12 Jul 62 to 5 Jun 65; Romeo PO
SMITH, Peter, H-73-1; Pvt 1st US Art; no dates; Chattanooga PO
SMITH, Peter, H-73-3; Pvt 16th OH; Chattanooga PO
SMITH, Peter, Sh-188-2; Pvt Marine Gunboat Marora #2; 6-16-63 to 9-28-64; 72 Ohio St, Memphis PO
SMITH, Phillip P., T-216-3; 14th Civil Dist
SMITH, Plesant, Hm-105-1; Lt C Co 4th TN Cav; 1 Jan 63 to 12 Jul 65; Jarnagan PO; poils (sic) & chronic dyare
SMITH, Pompy, K-167-4; Pvt 1st Hvy; Aug 62 to May 65; Knoxville PO; rheumatism, on crutches 2 yrs
SMITH, Quincy, Ru-236-2; 7th Dist

SMITH, Rank R., Hm-108-2(1); Pvt F Co 1st TN Vol; 61 to 65; Chestnut Bloom PO; rheumatism
SMITH, Ransom, Mr-96-1; Lt I Co 10th TN Inf; 7-62 to 62; Whitwell PO; dropsy of chest
SMITH, Richard, Ca-20-1; Fannie widow of; Pvt A Co 4th TN Cav; 5-25-63 to 5-64; Woodbury PO; killed
SMITH, Richard, H-74-1; Pvt A Co 1st GA Vol; 7-29-64 to 7-29-65; 100 Fairview Ave, Chattanooga PO
SMITH, Richard, H-64-2; Martha widow of; Col; Pvt; Chattanooga PO
SMITH, Richard, Hd-45-1; Pvt H Co 6th TN Cav; 12-8-62 to 7-26-65; Cerro Gordo PO; fistula
SMITH, Richard, Hr-96-2; PO omitted
SMITH, Richard E., Hu-104-1(2); Cpl L Co 17th KY Cav; Sep 14, 64 to Sep 20, 65; McEwen PO
SMITH, Robbert, Mu-210-1; Pvt A Co 7th GA Inf; 9-21-61 to Lee's surrender 1865; Spring Hill PO; CONF
SMITH, Robert, Ge-89-4; Pvt B Co 3rd TN Mtd Inf; 30 Jun 64 to 30 Nov 64; Romeo PO; hips wound & lung
SMITH, Robert, Hw-132-4; Julia widow of; Pvt D Co TN Cav; 61 to 65; Persia P_; was killed about the close of the war; CONF
SMITH, Robert, Mg-200-1; Pvt B Co 34th OH Inf; PO omitted
SMITH, Robert, Hr-89-1; Pvt H Co 54th MA; 2-62 to 64; Whiteville PO
SMITH, Robt., Sh-152-2; Pvt K Co 59th US Inf; Apr 63 to Jun 65; Dexter PO
SMITH, Robt., B-12-1; Rachel J. widow of; Pvt; 64 to ___; Wheel PO; husband left her and died 9 yrs ago
SMITH, Robert A., Dk-33-3; Pvt A Co 5th TN Cav; 8-9-62 to 6-25-65; Liberty PO; hurt by hose (horse?) in action with Wheeler near Liberty
SMITH, Robt. B., M-103-2; Pvt F Co 117th US Col Cav; 12-13-63 to 4-25-66; Lafayette PO
SMITH, Robert K., Ja-85-6; Jennie widow of; Pvt D Co 4th TN Cav; 10-25-62 to 7-12-65; Long Savannah PO
SMITH, Robert L., Ct-35-1; Sgt A Co 13th TN Cav; 9-24-63 to 9-5-65; Fish Springs PO; in US Army (disability)
SMITH, Rufus M., Un-250-1; Agga D. widow of; Pvt D Co 1st TN Inf; 9 Aug 61 to 17 Sep 64; Maynardville PO
SMITH, S. B., Hm-107-2(1); Pvt D Co 1st TN Cav; 1 Jan 63 to ___; Witts Foundry PO
SMITH, S. L., Gi-138-2; Pvt I Co 2nd TN; __ to 65; Bodinham PO
SMITH, Sam, S-212-2; Pvt K Co 30th KY; 2 Feb 64 to 18 Apr 65; Porch Corn PO; feet froze, rheumatism
SMITH, Sam, Hy-82-1; Pvt C Co 61st TN Inf; 61 to 64; Rudolph PO
SMITH, Sam, Li-148-1; PO omitted
SMITH, Samuel, Ro-210-2; Pvt; Rockwood PO
SMITH, Samuel, K-185-1; Emily wife of; Pvt; Mascott PO
SMITH, Saml., W-194-1; Pvt B Co 1st TN Inf; 1-7-63 to 7-20-65; Daylight PO
SMITH, Samuel A., Ja-85-2; Pvt E Co 5th TN Inf; 3-2-62 to 4-4-65; Birchwood PO
SMITH, Samuel K., Co-60-2; L Co 8th TN Cav; 9-15-63 to 9-11-65; Parrattsville PO; pneumonia fever 2 mos
SMITH, Samuel Y., Hm-107-4; Pvt C Co 4th TN Cav; 1 Dec 62 to 15 Mar 65; Witts Foundry PO; disease of lungs & left side
SMITH, Sarah, Bd-64-6; widow; 204 S. Sumner, Nashville PO
SMITH, Sarah, Mt-135-2; widow US Sol; PO omitted
SMITH, Sarah C. (see Downing, John A.)
SMITH, Sarah L. (see Walker, Robert H.)
SMITH, Sidney J., H-53-4; Musician B Co 4th IA Inf; 7-10-61 to 1-23-62; Chattanooga PO; asthma & rupture
SMITH, Silas, D-64-6; 301 S. Sumner, Nashville PO
SMITH, Silas G., D-103-1; Pvt K Co 95th PA Inf; Oct 26, 61 to Sep 9, 62; Whites Creek PO; gun shot right arm, draws pension
SMITH, Silas G., D-103-2; 24th Dist
SMITH, Simon, K-161-5(6); Pvt 1st US Hvy Art; Knoxville PO

SMITH, Stephen, K-185-2; Elizabeth wife of; Pvt; McMillans PO; CONF
SMITH, Stephen, S-213-1; Pvt A Co 1st Cav; Sep 62 to ___; Huntsville PO; gun shot in left hand
SMITH, T. J., Cr-16-4; Sgt B Co 2nd KY? Cav; Aug 10, 63 to 22 Jun 65; Huntingdon PO; scurvey
SMITH, T. M., He-57-2; Pvt H Co 27th TN Inf; 8-1-62 to 4-20-64; Speim PO; CONF
SMITH, Theodore, Hm-107-3; Sgt G Co 4th TN Cav; 2 Jan 63 to 12 Jul 65; Witts Foundry PO; hearing and sight
SMITH, Thomas, K-178-2; Pvt D Co 3rd TN Inf; 23 Feb 62 to 25 Mar 65; Ball Camp PO
SMITH, Thomas, Co-61-3(1); Pvt D Co 8th TN Inf; 28 Mar 63 to 30 Jun 65; Parrottsville PO
SMITH, Thomas, Dk-35-3(1); Pvt L Co 5th TN Cav; Hicks PO; back hurt
SMITH, Thomas, Hm-106-1; Pvt D Co 9th TN Cav; 1 Jan 64 to 11 Sep 65; Morristown PO; cant give dates, no discharge
SMITH, Thomas, Bl-3-2; Cpl D Co 7th TN Inf; 10-9-64 to 7-27-65; Orones Store PO; weak lungs
SMITH, Thomas, Mc-112-7; Sarah widow of; Pvt C Co 1st US Hvy Art; ___ to 3-66; Athens PO
SMITH, Thomas, D-77-2; Pvt C Co 111th US Inf; Apr 64 to May 66; Nashville PO
SMITH, Thomas, Pi-154-1; Mary widow of; Pvt H Co 3rd KY Inf; 12-61 to 62; Olympus PO; died in hospital in 1862
SMITH, Thomas, Se-226-4; Pvt K Co 2nd TN Inf; 31 Dec 61 to 3 Feb 65; Sinking Springs PO; injured eyes, scurvey & bronchitis
SMITH, Thomas, D-87-2; Pvt TN Inf; Nashville PO
SMITH, Thomas, D-67-2; alias Cox; Nancy Smith widow of; Pvt Col Inf; Nashville PO
SMITH, Thomas A., He-60-1; Major 7th TN Cav; 8-62 to 12-64; Lexington PO; rupture & brights disease of kidney; I was in Charleston prison 8 mos 10 days
SMITH, Thomas H., K-184-4; Lt B Co 6th TN Inf; Mar 63 to May 65?; Riverdale PO
SMITH, Thomas J., K-165-3; Pvt B Co 27th OH Inf; 23 Feb 64 to 11 Jul 65; 24 Oak St, Knoxville PO
SMITH, Thomas N., Dk-31-2; Cpl L Co 5th TN Cav; 8-12-63 to 8-14-65; Alexandria PO; eyes in bad fix
SMITH, Viny (see Dykes, Levy)
SMITH, W. A., Ov-134-1; Pvt A Co 63rd IN Inf; 12-3-63 to 3-11-64; Hilham PO; had diorhea and was 7 mos in hospital and is still affected
SMITH, W. C., Pi-153-3; Matilda widow of; Pvt D Co 2nd TN Inf; 9-1-61 to 1-8-64; West Fork PO; killed Jan 8, 64
SMITH, W. M., Hu-103-1; Pvt C Co 10th TN Inf; 10 Jul 62 to 10 Dec 65; PO omitted
SMITH, Wade, Mu-195-2; Sol; Columbia PO
SMITH, Wade H., Je-143-1; Pvt K Co 1st US Col Art; Oct 64 to 14 Mar 66; Mossy Creek PO; rheumatism & lung trouble
SMITH, Walker, Col, Ru-234-1; Pvt I Co 8th KY Bat; Apr 63 to Apr 65; Jefferson PO; eyes damaged by gun bursting
SMITH, Warren, Hd-49-3; US Sol; 4th Civil Dist
SMITH, Washington, Ru-241-3; Pvt C Co 44th TN Inf; 10 Apr 64 to 30 Apr 66; Murfreesboro PO
SMITH, Washington, Sm-174-1; Pvt F Co 101st Inf Vol; 9-28-64 to 1-31-66; New Middleton PO
SMITH, Washington, St-159-1; Pvt A Co 16th TN Inf; 63 to 5-___; Indian Mound PO
SMITH, William, Gr-77-1; Nancy widow of; Pvt; 62 to 65; Strawberry Plains PO; soldier died of consumption after war
SMITH, William, H-72-3(2); Georgia formerly widow of; Chattanooga PO
SMITH, Wiliam, Co-68-1; Pvt A Co 2nd TN Cav; 61 to ___; Costner PO
SMITH, William, Fe-42-1; Elzira widow of; Pvt 13th KY; Jamestown PO; in maut?
SMITH, William, Gu-46-2(1); Pvt A Co 4th TN Cav; Tatesville PO; as William Smith was absent, I could not get any information from his wife
SMITH, William, Hm-103-1; Pvt A Co 1st TN Lt Art; 10 Oct 63 to 3 Aug 65; Morristown PO; injury of left shoulder
SMITH, William, H-66-1; reenlisted; Orderly Sgt M Co 10th KY Cav; 10-1-62 to 9-11-63; Pvt C Co 16th AL Inf; 10-1-62 to 9-17-63; Chattanooga

SMITH, William, Gr-74-2; Anna E. widow of; Pvt E Co 4th TN Cav; May Spring PO
SMITH, William, Co-67-5; Pvt C Co 8th TN Inf; 1 Dec 62 to ___; Naillon PO
SMITH, William, H-51-4; Sgt A Co 5th kTN Inf; 3-21-62 to 5-16-65; Hill City PO
SMITH, William, Je-143-2; 1st Asst Surgon 8th TN Cav; 10 Aug 63 to Feb 64; Mossy Creek PO
SMITH, William, Ro-210-12; Pvt; Rockwood PO; CONF
SMITH, William, K-164-2; Pvt F Co 24th OH Inf; 61 to 64; PO omitted (Knoxville?)
SMITH, William, C-33-3; Jellico PO
SMITH, William, K-184-4; Rachel wife of; Pvt B Co 6th TN Inf; Thorn Grove PO
SMITH, William, K-184-3; Didama wife of; Pvt B Co 6th TN Inf; 8 Jan 63 to 30 Jan 65; Thorn Grove PO
SMITH, William, L-100-1; Pvt F Co 2nd US Reg Lt Art; Ripley PO; cannot give dates
SMITH, William, O-141-2; Union City PO; Negros and couldn't tell
SMITH, William, Sh-148-2; Memphis PO
SMITH, William, Ja-85-3; Pvt E Co 5th TN inf; 3-2-62 to 4-4-65; Birchwood PO
SMITH, William, Se-227-2; Nancy widow of; Pvt B Co 3rd TN Cav; 10 Feb 62 to 23 Feb 65; Trundles X Roads PO
SMITH, William, Se-221-1; Hannah widow of; Pvt G Co 6th TN Inf; Allensville PO; can't get any correct dates
SMITH, William, Bl-5-2; Sgt D Co 4th KY Cav; 6-16-62 to 6-28-65; Brayton PO; gunshot wound in right hip
SMITH, William, Sh-161-2; US Sol; 16th Dist.
SMITH, William, Sh-161-2; US Sol; 16th Dist
SMITH, William A., Gi-138-2; 18th Dist.
SMITH, William B., S-212-1; Pvt K Co 19th KY; 13 Sep 62 to 15 Oct 65; Porchcorn PO
SMITH, William B. C., Ct-40-6; Sgt G Co 13th TN Cav; 9-24-63 to 9-5-65; Elizabethton PO
SMITH, William Berry (see Berry Smith)
SMITH, William H., H-67-1; Pvt G Co 4th TN Cav; 6-26-63 to 7-18-65; Chattanooga PO
SMITH, William H., M-103-5; Pvt B Co 37th KY Inf; 7-1-63 to 12-1-64; Hillsdale PO; rupture of bowels
SMITH, William H., Ho-96-1; Pvt 1st OH Bat; Jul 21, 61 to Jun 23, 65; Erin PO; colored does not know dates of enlistment
SMITH, William H., Hu-104-1(2); Pvt A Co 34th OH; Jun 62 to 65; McEwen PO
SMITH, William H., W-195-1; Pvt TN Cav; 1863 to 1864; Daylight PO; discharge is not at home; Pvt C Co TN Cav; 1864 to 1865
SMITH, William H., Cf-40-2; Pvt G Co 28th WI Inf; 18 Aug 62 to 23 Aug 65; Tullahoma PO
SMITH, William J., Mt-135-1; Pvt C Co 16th TN Inf; 3-1-62 to 1863; Oakwood PO
SMITH, William J., Ov-137-3; Pvt L Co 13th KY Cav; 9-15-63 to 1-10-65; Monroe PO; rheumatism and hearing impaired
SMITH, William J., We-222-1; PO omitted; CONF
SMITH, William J., Sh-176-1; Brig. Gen. 6th TN Cav; 8-16-62 to 8-16-65; 82 Linden St., Memphis PO
SMITH, William J., We-221-1(4); Pvt D Co 13th TN Cav; 63 to Mar 64; Martin PO; Constitution ruined
SMITH, William K., Ge-96-2; Pvt B Co 1st TN Art; 5 Feb 65 to 20 Jul 65; Hascue PO; diareah & rheumatism
SMITH, William M., Br-14-1; Pvt D Co 4th TN Cav; 6-11-62 to 7-12-65; McDonald PO; right ankle sprained
SMITH, Wm. M., Cr-17-2; Pvt I Co 7th TN Cav; 9-15-63 to 8-9-65; Buena Vista PO; rheumatism & piles; has never been pentioned
SMITH, William M., Hd-44-1; Pvt H Co 6th TN Cav; 12-10-62 to 7-26-65; Clifton PO, Wayne Co.
SMITH, Wm. M., Sh-201-3; Julia J. widow of; Memphis PO; CONF
SMITH, William S., K-180-4; Pvt; Ebenezer PO
SMITH, Wm. T., Hm-107-2(1); Pvt C Co 9th TN Cav; 1 Jan 65 to 13 Sep 65; Witts Foundry PO; heart disease
SMITH, Willis J., A-5-1; Pvt G Co 19th TN Cav; 12-63 to 65; Clinton PO; rheumatism

SMITH, Young B., Ge-89-4; Elizabeth widow of; Pvt B Co 8th TN Inf; Romeo PO; dates at Washington
SMITH, Z., G-64-1; Lincy Jones widow of; Bradford PO
SMITH, Zachariah T., Hd-44-1; PO omitted
SMITH, ___, Agnes P. widow of, J-77-1; Gainesboro PO
SMITH, ___, H-58-4; Elizabeth widow of; Retro PO; could not learn what service; discharge in hand of other parties
SMITH, ___, Mc-112-7; Narcis widow of; Athens PO; no papers
SMITHAM?, Thomas, Ro-209-1; Pvt A Co 50th AL Inf; 61 to 65; Glen Alice PO; CONF
SMITHE, Charles, F-44-2; Pvt 1st Miss Cav; 63 to May 65; PO omitted
SMITHEN, Reubin, Fe-42-1; Martha widow of; Pvt 7th TN; Jamestown PO
SMITHER, Jesse, S-217-2; Pvt H Co 1st AL Cav; 62 to 63; Winfield PO
SMITHER, Jonathan, S-214-2; Sarah Parker formerly widow of; Pvt F Co 1st TN Inf; 61 to ___; Robbins PO; husband died while in the service
SMITHER, Reuben, S-214-1; Pvt F Co 1st TN Inf; 10 Aug 61 to ___; Robbins PO; discharged since war
SMITHERS, Isaac S., Cr-19-2; 12th Civil Dist.
SMITHERS, Seborn S., Cr-19-1; Pvt E Co 7th TN Cav; 6-28-62 to 6-22-65; Buxter PO
SMITHNECK, Leonadus, Wl-293-3; Inf; 61 to 65; Lockport PO; CONF
SMITHSON, H. P., La-117-3; Pvt A Co 48th TN Cav; Dec 63 to Apr 65; 15th Dist.; CONF
SMITHSON, James, Ca-25-2; Pvt A Co 5th TN Cav; 11-20-62 to 8-10-65; Gassoway PO; struck by lightning
SMITHSON, John T., Ca-25-2; Pvt F Co 4th TN Mtd Inf; 9-64 to 8-65; Gassoway PO
SMITHSON, William H., Ms-174-1; Pvt H Co 5th TN Cav; 25 Apr 63 to 14 Aug 65; Holts Corner PO
SMITHSON, William L., Su-243-2; Pvt G Co 13th TN Cav; Oct 64 to May 65; Bristul PO
SMOLLING, Benjamin L., Br-13-2; Pvt E Co 5th TN Inf; 3-2-62 to 4-26-65; Ora PO
SMOLLING, Lieuesa S. (see Shamblin, Columbus C.)
SMOTHERS, Francis J., Be-2-2; Pvt K Co 2nd TN Mtd Inf; Aug 20, 64 to Jun 27, 65; Holladay PO
SMOTHERS, James F., Be-2-2; Pvt C Co 7th TN Cav; Jun 28, 62 to Aug 15, 65; Holladay PO
SMOTHERS, Pinkney L., P-151-4; Linden PO
SMOTHERS, Wily, De-26-3; 2nd Sgt C Co 12th TN; no dates (4 yrs); Poplar Springs PO
SNAPP, J. V., Hw-125-4; Pvt F Co 3rd TN P?; 63 to 63 (8 mos); Stony Point PO
SNAPP, John W., Mo-120-1; Pvt I Co 36th OH Inf; 5-1-61 to 10-65; Sweetwater PO; wounded in Hunter's Raid; his eye sight is impaired
SNAPP, Minerva J. (see Fockner, John)
SNAPP, Sarah (see Shanks, Wm. H.)
SNEAD, John S., Cl-51-1; 2nd Sgt B Co 48th VA Cav Vol; 7-13-61 to 4-62; Ritchie PO; CONF
SNEED, Alfred, Mo-119-1; Mary J. widow of; Pvt D Co 1st US Col Hvy Art; Sweetwater PO; lost little toe of right foot and fever settled in foot
SNEED, Andrew J., Se-220-2; Pvt A Co 2nd TN Cav; 1 Aug 62 to 6 Jul 65; Emerts Cave PO
SNEED?, Henry J., D-72-1; Pvt F Co 4th TN Cav; Jul 11, 61 to Jan 16, 65; Nashville PO; CONF
SNEED, James, Gi-125-1; Pvt A Co 10th TN Inf; Nov 63 to 3 Jul 65; Bodenham PO
SNEED, James H., Wi-276-1; Pvt 9th TN Cav; Aug 62 to Jun 65; Beechville PO; CONF
SNEED, Lee, Se-226-6; Vickey widow of; Pvt G Co 1st US Col Hvy Art; Sinking Springs PO
SNEED, William, H-50-2(1); Pvt C Co 3rd R NC Inf; 11-5-64 to 8-8-65; Daisy PO; chronic diorreah, measles, mumps and rheumatism
SNEED, William, Mc-113-2; Pvt D Co 5th TN Inf; 1864 to 1865 (11 mos); Rock Creek PO; could not give exact dates
SNEED, William A., Mc-113-1; Pvt C Co 10th TN Cav; 1864 to 1865; Rock Creek PO
SNEED, Wilson, Mo-119-1; Sgt D Co 1st US Col Hvy Art; 2-18-64 to 3-31-66; Sweetwater PO; ribs broken and not set right

SNELL, Cesar, Ru-241-4; Pvt B Co 69th OH Inf; 5-62 to 65; Murfreesboro PO; shot in arm
SNELL, James T., B-18-1; Pvt F Co 5th TN Cav; 9-10-62 to 6-26-65; Flat Creek PO
SNELL, Please, H-69-1; Pvt; Chattanooga PO
SNELLBAKER, David,H-59-3; Sgt B Co 181st OH Inf; 9-64 to 6-65; Chattanooga PO
SNELLING, Patten A., B-3-2; Pvt H Co 5th TN Cav; 9-3-62 to 9-3-65; Wartrace PO
SNELSON, William R., Bo-13-3(1); Sgt I Co 3rd NC Mtd Inf?; 1-1-65 to 8-8-65; Miser PO
SNIBUSTER?, James, Mr-96-2; Pvt D Co 1st TN Art; 3-17-64 to 3-31-66; Sunyside PO
SNIDER, Andrew J., Jo-150-2; Pvt E Co 13th TN Cav; 22 Sep 63 to 5 Sep 65; Key Station PO
SNIDER, Benonia, We-225-3(2); Pvt 31st IL Inf; Aug 31, 61 to Jan 65; Dresden PO; sun stroak
SNIDER, Daniel C., K-170-2; Pvt K Co 13th TN Cav; 1 Mar 65 to 5 Sep 65; Knoxville PO; consumption 25 yrs
SNIDER, G. T., Bo-19-2; Cpl B Co 1st US Art; 2-2-64 to 3-66; Rockford PO; ruptured
SNIDER, George, H-54-3; Sgt G Co 9th TN Cav; Sherman Heights PO
SNIDER, Jessee, Jo-150-4; Pvt I Co 13th TN Cav; 24 Sep 63 to 5 Sep 65; Rheas Forge PO
SNIDER, John H., Mo-120-1; Pvt H Co 5th TN Inf; 2-62 to 5-65; Glenloch PO; ruptured in service
SNIDER, John R., Jo-151-1; Pvt M Co 13th TN Cav; 64 to 5 Sep 65; Casper PO; rheumatism
SNIDER, Peter, Li-161-1; Emaline Askins formerly widow of; 63 to __ (6 mos); Moline PO; Peter went off with the army, was not a soldier
SNIDER, Robert, Hw-130-1; Pvt A Co 1st TN Inf; 6 Jul 62 to 14 Jan 63; Lee Valley PO; chronic bronchitis; imprisoned and received no discharge
SNIDER, Samuel V., Bo-12-2(1); Pvt I Co 5th TN Inf; 11-1-62 to 6-30-65; Mountainville PO on Chilhowee; wounded right thigh and knee; Rasacca Georgia (place where wounded)
SNIDER, William, D-66-1; 1st Duty Sgt I Co 13th Col TN?; 63 to 65; 816 S. Cherry, Nashville PO; wounded twice in left leg; his papers in Washington
SNIPES, Allen, Hy-78-1; Pvt G Co 54th AR Inf; 63 to 66; Rein PO
SNODERLEY, George, A-13-2; Pvt A Co 130th IN Inf; 1-4-64 to 12-2-65; Briceville PO; injury of the testicles
SNODERLY, Alvis A., Un-250-2; 1st Lt G Co 2nd TN Cav; Maynardville PO; chronic diarhea & herney, received while in service
SNODERLY, John, Un-254-2; Eliza A. widow of; Pvt C Co 2nd TN Inf; Aug 61 to __; Paulett PO
SNODGRASS, Charles, Wh-180-2; Sparta PO; can't remember
SNODGRASS, Wm., H-60-2; Pvt E Co 81st OH Inf; 9-11-61 to 9-64; Pvt C Co 43rd OH Inf; 2-22-65 to 7-13-65; wounded in back, also chronic diarrhoea
SNODLEY, John, Un-255-2; Pvt H Co 8?th TN Cav; no dates (2 mos); Gale? PO; rumatism
SNODLEY, Louis, Un-255-2; Pvt F Co 6th TN Cav; 10 M 62 to 20 Apr 65; PO omitted
SNODY, Thomas D., Cf-35-4; Pvt I Co 4th TN Inf; Nov 61 to Apr 65; Normandy PO; CONF
SNOW, A., Sm-169-2; Elmwood PO; CONF
SNOW, Andrew J., Lo-188-1; Pvt A Co 2nd TN Cav; 10 Aug 61 to 8 Feb 65; Stockton PO
SNOW, Ebeneazer, Dk-33-1; Pvt F Co 4th TN Cav; 9-24-64 to 8-25-65; 4th Civil Dist; disease of kidneys
SNOW, Fletcher J., Ma-126-1; Pvt C Co 7th IL Inf; 18 Apr 61 to 25 Jul 61; Sgt A Co 36th IL Inf; 2 Aug 61 to 25 Aug 64; Jackson PO; gunshot wound & deafness; bomb bursted over head at Corrinth, MS
SNOW, Green S., Sh-183-1; Memphis PO
SNOW, Henry, D-63-3; Capt K Co 11th MA Inf; May 61 to Jun 65; Nashville PO
SNOW, John, Dy-25-9(1); Newbern PO; wounded head & hand; is now dead, dates unknown
SNOWDEN, Charles, Sh-145-4; Janee Williams widow of; Millington PO; was killed; Capt Hutch__?
SNOWDEN, Robert B., Sh-159-6; Col TN; 60 to 65; Memphis PO; CONF
SNYDER, Adram (sic), A-7-2; Robertsville PO
SNYDER, Alexander M., Jo-149-1; Sgt I Co 13th TN Cav; 24 Sep 63 to 29 Jun 65; Mountain City PO; injury to heart & right hand; rheumatism result hert
SNYDER, George W., H-54-5; Pvt D Co 21st IL Inf; 6-14-61 to 7-5-64; East Chattanooga PO
SNYDER, Jacob B., K-170-2; Cpl I Co 3rd TN Inf; 20 Mar 62 to 28 Mar 65; Knoxville PO
SNYDER, Jacob W., Jo-152-3; Pvt M Co 13th TN Cav; 2 Feb 64 to 5 Sep 65; Mouth of Doe PO
SNYDER, Joseph, W-189-1; Pvt 22nd WI Inf; 2-28-65 to 5-17-65; McMinnville PO
SNYDER, Lucinda (see Aabny, Henri)
SNYDER, Truncia J., K-160-2; Pvt G Co 111th OH; 1 Aug 62 to 27 Jun 65; Knoxville PO
SNYDER, William H., D-103-1; Mrs. Nancy widow of; Sgt M Co 5th IN Cav; 61 to __; RidgePost PO; chron. diarhea, draws pension
SNYDER, William R., Po-149-3(2); Cpl E Co 4th TN Cav; 15-62 to 7-12-65; Ocoee PO
SODDARD, William, Bo-15-4; Pvt H Co 2nd TN Cav; 10-10-62 to 7-6-65; Corn PO; piece of cap in eye
SOILER?, Monroe, D-69-1; Emma Williamson widow of; on Perduc?; Nashville PO
SOLMON, John W., Ge-93-2; Pvt A Co 4th TN Inf; 27 Jan 63 to 2 Aug 65; Albany PO
SOLOMAN, Andrew, Bl-4-1; Pvt A Co 144th IN Inf; ..1-1-65 to 7-1-65; Pikeville PO
SOLOMON, Adam, W-193-2; Charlota widow of; Pvt; Thaxton PO; this is a colored man & his discharge is in Washington
SOLOMON, Balden H., Co-69-5; Pvt A Co 8th TN Inf; 63 to 64; Driskill PO; longl? fever; dont no date of inlistment nor death
SOLOMON, Baulden, Co-69-5; Catrin J. Fowler formerly widow of; Pvt TN Inf; 63 to Aug 64 (11 mos); Driskill PO; not known for sirtan; died on his march to Knoxvill TN
SOLOMON, Bengeman F., Hm-109-3; Pvt B Co 4th TN Cav; Mar 62 to 65; Russelville PO
SOLOMON, Bird, Hw-131-1; Pvt A Co 1st TN Lt Art; 18 Nov 63 to 7 Aug 65; Bulls Gap PO; catarrh of the head, discharged
SOLOMON, Calvin L., Co-69-1; Pvt Co D 4th TN Inf; 15 Ma 63 to 1 Jul 63; Driskill PO; conscriped but a union man
SOLOMON, Ellen S. (see McSpadden, Rufus)
SOLOMON, Henry, Gr-73-1; Pvt 15th KY Inf; Turley's Mills PO; re-enlisted
SOLOMON, Isaac N., Hw-131-1; Saddler D Co 1st TN Cav; 15 Apr 62 to 15 Apr 65; PO omitted; cripled by horse falling; pension claim filed
SOLOMON, Jerry M., Ge-87-1; Pvt A Co 4th TN Inf; 11 Feb 63 to Aug 65; Midway PO
SOLOMON, Jesse, Ro-211-2; Pvt E Co 1st TN Inf; 18 Dec 61 to 20 Dec 64; Webster PO; rheumatism, heart disease; also, neuralgia and function of throat
SOLOMON, Overton, Hm-107-5; Elizabeth widow of; Pvt 1st TN Cav; Springvale PO; chronic deairhea; discharge at Washington DC
SOLOMON, Richard N., Hw-131-1; Pvt L Co 8th TN Cav; 20 Nov 63 to 11 Sep 65; PO omitted; bowel trouble
SOLOMON, William, Hw-131-1; Pvt G Co 8th TN Inf; 15 Mar 63 to 30 Jun 65; Bulls Gap PO; gun shot lower jaw; pensioned, 8
SOLOMON, William P., Me-88-3; Pvt G Co 5th TN Inf; 3-27-62 to 5-15-65; Brittsville PO
SOMMERS, James, Sh-159-2; Pvt G Co 26th NY; 62 to 65; Memphis PO
SONGER, Gordon T., Ct-40-1; Pvt H Co 46th VA Inf; 6-61 to 4-9-65; Elizabethton PO; CONF
SOONEY, William, Ge-102-3; Pvt E Co 2nd NC Inf; 4 Sep 63 to 10 Aug 65; Whig PO
SORRICK, Franklin H., Fr-107-1; Pvt B Co 64th OH Inf; Oct 19 __ to Dec 11, 64 (3 yrs 1 mo 10 days); Winchester PO
SOTHERD, Kate G., R-161-6; widow of soldier; Morgantown PO; 8th Civil Dist
SOURING, Henry, A-1-1; Catherine widow of; Pvt G Co 7th TN Inf; 1-10-62 to (killed in war, date unknown); Andersonville PO
SOUSONG, William, Se-226-2; Pvt 8th TN Cav; Thorn Grove PO

SOUTHALL, Mary (see Carlock, William H.)
SOUTHALL, Wesley, Col, St-160-1; Pvt D Co 101st TN Inf; 7-1-64 to 1-21-66; Big Rock PO; catarh contracted
SOUTHARD, Spencer, Po-152-1; Eliza widow of; Pvt 5th Mtd Inf; Ducktown PO
SOUTHARD, William, Hr-94-1; Cpl D Co 55th AL Inf; May 62 to __ (3 yrs); Saulsbury PO
SOUTHERLAND, Elbert, Ge-85-3; Pvt G Co 4th TN Inf; 15 Nov 61 to 7 Jul 65; Syren Burg PO; rheumatism
SOUTHERLAND, Mary E., Wi-280-1; Dist #11
SOUTHERLAND, Nathaniel, Ge-85-3; Pvt G Co 4th TN Inf; 18 Nov 61 to 7 Jul 65; Syren Burg PO; rheumatism, now blind in right eye and has hemorrhoids
SOUTHERLAND, William, U-249-1; Pvt I Co 6th US Inf; 1 Mar 65 to 9 Oct 66; Briggs PO
SOUTHERLINED, Ely, Bl-3-3; Cpl E Co TN Cav; 9-64 to 65; Billingsly PO
SOUTHWORTH, Walter H., Dy-23-1; Pvt B Co 3rd Bat Lt Art; 21 Sep 63 to 15 Jun 65; Dyersburg PO
SOWARDS, Henry, Ro-202-3(1); Pvt F Co 3rd TN Inf; Jun 62 to 17 May 65; Union X Roads PO; no disability
SOWDERS, William H., Cl-46-4(2); Cpl K Co 49th KY Inf; 7-62 to 8-63; Ibex PO; health injured; wants pension
SOWELL, James A., Mu-209-7; Pvt E Co 9th TN Cav; 5-62 to 5-65; Columbia PO; CONF
SOWELL, Thomas C., Mu-210-5; Pvt B Co 27th TN Inf; 8-18-61 to 4-26-65; Mallard PO; CONF
SOWELS, William M., Ca-23-1; Pvt C Co 4th KY Cav; 7-3-62 to 7-19-65; Leoni PO; wounded in leg and arm
SOWER, Frank, D-71-2; Nashville PO
SPAIN, Calvin G., G-57-6; P-t; no dates (2 yrs); Yorkville PO; CONF
SPAIN, Eli A., Wy-178-1; Pvt I Co 2nd US Vol Inf; 10-13-64 to 11-7-65; Pleasant Valley PO
SPAIN, R., D-72-2; Pvt M Co 23rd TN Cav; Oct 20, 64 to Nov 30, 65; Nashville PO; CONF
SPAIN, Wilburn, He-64-2; Pvt K Co 7th TN Cav; 20 Jun 62 to 20 Aug 65; Center Point PO
SPANGLE, Solomon, Hm-103-3; Pvt B Co 35th IN Inf; 28 Sep 64 to 24 Jun 65; Morristown PO; chronic diarrhea
SPANGLER, Catherine (see Dunn, John)
SPANGLER, David, Un-258-3; Elizabeth A. widow of; Pvt C Co 5th KY; May 62 to Jun 65; Longhollow PO
SPANGLER, Silvester S., C-30-1; Pvt B Co 11th TN Cav; 7-63 to 9-14-65; Well Spring PO
SPARKES, Wm. E., Dy-21-1; Pvt C Co 55th AL Reg; 1 Jun 61 to 64; Fowlkes Sta. PO; CONF
SPARKS, Benjamin W., W-189-3(2); Surgeon 154th IL Inf; 8-64 to 65; McMinnville PO
SPARKS, Calvin, Cl-47-3; Pvt B Co 1st TN Lt Art; 4-63 to 7-20-65; Compensation PO; apoplexy injured by wagon 64
SPARKS, Charles, H-56-6; Pvt B Co ? TN Inf; 4-3-6? to 8-24-65; St. Elmo PO; lost a leg
SPARKS, Danuel G. W., Hu-103-3; Pvt E Co 10th TN Inf; 10 Aug 61 to 28 Dec 64; PO omitted
SPARKS, David C., Ro-207-2; Capt D Co 5th TN Inf; 26 Feb 62 to 30 Mar 65; 17th Dist
SPARKS, James A., Cl-47-1; Pvt 49th KY Inf; 10-15-63 to 12-65; Speedwell PO
SPARKS, James W., K-154-3; Knoxville PO; CONF
SPARKS, Josuiah, Fr-114-1; Capt E Co 101st IN Inf; 62 to 65; Dechard PO
SPARKS, Lamuel J., Lo-189-1; Pvt K Co 2nd TN Cav; Feb 62 to 20 May 65; Philadelphia PO; CONF
SPARKS, Mathew, D-57-2; Pvt H Co 23rd TN; Jun 61 to __; Nashville PO; lost finger shot in should.; CONF
SPARKS, Silas S., U-244-1; Pvt 3rd NC Inf; __ to Aug 65; Flag Pond PO
SPEAK, Abraham, D-64-5; 5th MI Reg; Nashville PO
SPEAK, John T., Sh-192-1; US Unit; Memphis PO
SPEAKMAN, Robert, J-78-1; Pvt B Co 9th KY Inf; 9-26-61 to 1-12-65; Haydensburg PO; blindness, cant see much a tall
SPEAR, James D., G-69-1; Pvt K Co 7th TN Cav; 25 Dec 63 to 9 Aug 65; Rutherford PO
SPEAR, John A., Jo-153-2; Pvt B Co 4th TN Inf; 22 Aug 62 to 17 Jul 65; Little Doe PO; bronchitis

SPEAR, John W., Cr-13-1; Nancy A. widow of; Pvt C Co 7th TN Cav; Atwood PO; can't find out, cannot learn dates of enlistment
SPEARRS, James, Ge-83-4; US Sol; Chickey City PO
SPEARS, Ashley L., Mr-99-3; Pvt D Co 5th TN Inf; 2-25-62 to 4-14-65; Jasper PO
SPEARS, Daniel, A-4-6(2); Soldier; Coal Creek PO
SPEARS, Jefferson C., Wh-186-2; Pvt K Co 1st TN Mtd Inf; 3-4-64 to 4-14-65; Newark PO; rheumatism
SPEARS, John T., Bo-19-3; Pvt A Co 3rd TN Inf; Rockford PO; broken arm
SPEARS, William A., Hw-121-5(4); Pvt B Co 3rd TN Mtd Inf; 25 Oct 63 to no discharge; Van Hill PO
SPEER, George W., Sh-168-1; Pvt F Co 193rd OH Inf; Feb 20, 65 to 20 Aug 65; 109 Exchange St, Memphis PO
SPEIGHT, Wesly, Di-36-1; Pvt G Co 50th TN Inf; 11-61 to 5-6? (3 yrs 6 mos); Bellsburgh PO; CONF
SPELLINGS, John, Cr-17-2; 1st Sgt A Co 7th TN Cav; 8-15-62 to 6-30-65; Buena Vista PO; weakness of eyes resulting from chronic diarrhea
SPELLMAN, William, Sh-191-6(2); Pvt A Co 25th IN; Memphis PO
SPENABLE, Edward E., K-156-4; Pvt A Co 95th IL Inf; 13 Aug 62 to 28 Aug 65; 203 Gay St, Knoxville PO
SPENCE, Carter D., Cl-52-1; Pvt A Co 7th NC Cav; 9-14-64 to 5-1-65; Quarter PO; injured by horse
SPENCE, Henderson, Ru-241-2(1); Pvt C Co 101st TN Inf; 16 Feb 64 to 1 Jan 66; Murfreesboro PO
SPENCE, John F., K-159-2; Chapl. 48th OH Vols & 2nd OH Hvy Art; 62 to 65; Knoxville PO
SPENCE, Joseph S., Cr-8-1; Pvt C Co 9th TN; 7-13-61 to 5-14-65; Chestnut Bluff PO; CONF
SPENCE, Robbert, Mu-210-1; Mariah widow of; Pvt; Spring Hill PO
SPENCE, Robert, Bo-23-1; Pvt B Co 1st AL Inf; 5-4-63 to 6-22-65; PO omitted
SPENCE, William, D-62-1; Mary widow of; Pvt MI; 3 yrs; West Demontrem St, Nashville PO
SPENCER, Allerton?, A-3-4; Nancy widow of; Pvt C Co 4th TN Inf; 11-26-64 to 8-7-65; Clinch River PO
SPENCER, Edward, D-77-1; Pvt F Co 111th US Inf; Jun 63 to May 65; Nashville PO
SPENCER, James K. P., Mu-199-1; Pvt H Co 5th TN Cav; 15 Jul 62 to 14 Aug 65; Mt. Pleasant PO
SPENCER, John, Hd-50-6; Sol US; 6th Civil Dist
SPENCER, John A., G-58-1; Rutherford PO
SPENCER, John C., Gr-76-1; Pvt F Co 1st TN Cav; 1 Mar 62 to 30 Mar 65; Tampico PO; pneumonia & rheumatism
SPENCER, Joseph H., P-156-2; Pvt K Co 42nd TN Inf; 9-62 to 5-6-63; Lovelville PO; CONF
SPENCER, Morris, Pi-156-2; Pvt H Co 1st KY Cav; 10-12-61 to 12-31-64; Travisville PO; now has a crippled hand
SPENCER, Nathan, Gr-70-3; Pvt F Co 1st TN Cav; 1 Mar 62 to 30 Mar 65; Spring House PO; diarhea
SPENCER, Stepen M., Ge-95-2; Pvt E Co 4th TN Inf; 6 May 63 to 2 Aug 65; Home PO; rheumatism, diarrhea
SPENCER, William, Hd-46-1; Pvt C Co 6th TN Cav; Sep 10, 62 to 26 Dec 62; Cerro Gordo PO
SPERGEON, John, Co-66-2(1); Pvt F Co 5th TN Inf; Harrett, widow of; 6 Jun 63 to 15 Jun 65; Birdville PO
SPERMAN, Benjamin S., Po-148-1; Pvt D Co 5th TN Mtd Inf; 8-31-64 to 6-20-65; Chestewee Mills PO; now consumptive
SPERMAN, John A., B-2-1; Lt D Co 23rd TN Inf; 7-1-61 to 4-10-65; Wartrace PO CONF
SPICKARD, Jacob, Hm-104-3(1); Blacksmith A Co 9th TN Inf; 63 to Nov 65; Morristown PO; spinal from service as blk smith; papers lost on retreat from Bulls Sp.
SPICKARD, John M., Je-146-4; Pvt L Co 8th TN Cav; 1 Oct 63 to 11 Sep 65; White Pine PO; not at home, wife don't know
SPIERS?, John, Be-5-1; Susan A. widow; Pvt 7th TN Cav; 63 to May 65; Camden PO; died with cronik D.; widow draws pension
SPIKER, William H., O-138-1; Pvt D Co 53rd IL; 15 Nov 61 to 10 Apr 63; Lanes PO; this entry crossed out

SPILLER, Henry, Gi-129-1; Pvt B Co 17th TN Inf; Elkton PO
SPINKS, J. H., Cr-8-1; Artilry B Co 9th TN; 17 Apr 61 to 9 Apr 63; Chestnut Bluff PO; CONF
SPINTZER, William, K-160-3; Margaret widow of; Pvt C Co 8th TN Inf; Knoxville PO
SPIRA, James, Gr-70-1; Pvt H Co 1st TN Cav; 10 Jun 62 to 10 Jun 65; Rutledge PO; piles
SPIRE, W. (Ira?), W1-290-1; Pvt E Co 6th MA; Sep 1 62 to 1 Nov 64; Lebanon PO; discharged
SPIRES, John C., Gr-71-1; Rebecca widow of; Pvt B Co 23rd MO Inf; 20 Jun 63 to 18 Jul 65; Bean Station PO
SPITSER, George W., Hw-127-2; Margaret widow of; Pvt H Co 8th TN Inf; Rogersville PO; chron. diarrhea & cold on lungs; died from effects of same
SPITTLER, David A., H-57-3; Pvt B Co US Reg; 64 to 68; Orchard Knob PO
SPITZER, James, K-176-1; Recruit G Co 7th TN Cav; 14 Jan 62 to 14 Jul 65; Halls X Roads PO
SPITZER, William D., K-174-2(1); Pvt C Co 8th TN Inf; 1 Mar 63 to 30 Jun 65; Church Grove PO
SPIVEY?, Isaac, Hy-83-1; Pvt I Co 59th TN Cav; Brownsville PO; rheumatism, old age; lost discharge
SPIVEY, William W., Cy-28-1; Pvt K Co 13th TN; Butlers Landing PO; cannot give dates
SPIVY, Joseph, Hw-124-1; Pvt B Co 11th TN Inf; 63 to 64; Opossum PO
SPOON, John, Gr-74-1; Pvt C Co 4th TN Cav; 24 Nov 62 to 12 Jul 65; May Spring PO; hearing, piles
SPOON, Joseph E., Hm-103-3; Pvt C Co 1st TN Cav; 1 Jan 63 to 19 Jun 65; Morristown PO; desias of kidnys, rectum 26 yrs
SPOON, Peter, Hr-89-1; Jane widow of; Pvt H Co 9th TN; 62 to 65; Whiteville PO
SPOONS, Lewis, Gr-72-1; Pvt A Co 9th TN Cav; 1 Oct 64 to 11 Sep 63; Noelon PO; head wound; struck with gun
SPORE, Washington, L-103-1; Sgt 2nd Batery IN Art; Feb 22 62 to 22 Feb 65; Ashport PO; no great disability, surrendered to Lee in VA
SPRADLIN, Jacob, K-171-4(3); Cinthia widow of; Pvt 8th TN Inf; Craigville PO
SPRADLING, Melvin, Bo-11-7; Carline widow of; Pvt C Co 3rd TN Mtd Inf; 8-5-64 to 11-30-64; Big Gulley PO
SPRAKER, Alexander, Ro-202-2; Pvt B Co 45th GA Inf; Mar 62 to Jul 62; Union X Roads PO; dropsy; CONF
SPRATT, Amanda, Wi-281-2; 12th Dist
SPREWER, Antrey, H-73-2(1); Julia widow of; Pvt; Chattanooga PO
SPRIGGS, George A., Br-13-3; Pvt I Co 42nd TN Col Inf; __ to 3-65; Cleveland PO
SPRIGGS, Isaac, Br-11-2; Pvt D Co 42nd US Col Inf; 8-64 to 3-66; Chatata PO; chronic rheumatism 25 yrs; lef hip & ankle
SPRING, Charles C., H-58-5; Pvt A Co 14th TN Inf; Retro PO; discharge misplaced
SPRINGER, Aaron F., La-111-1; Pvt D Co 9th TN Cav; 12-3-62 to 5-10-65; Pleasant Point PO; prisoner Rock Island, IL 4 mos; CONF
SPRINGER, Benj B., Cr-14-1; 1st Sgt G Co 7th TN Cav; 5 Aug 62 to 25 Oct 63; Clarksburg PO
SPRINGER, George, De-22-1; Pvt B Co 50th TN Inf; 1 May 62 to 2 Jun 65; Bath Springs PO; shot in left hip
SPRINGER, Hosea, Cr-14-2; 4th Sgt G Co 7th TN Cav; 5 Aug 62 to 25 Oct 63; Clarksburg PO
SPRINGER, Robert, La-117-3; Pvt B Co 23rd TN Inf; Jul 9 61 to __; 15th Dist; CONF
SPRINGFIELD, Henry B., H-49-7; May A. widow of; Daisy PO
SPRINGFIELD, Hiram J., H-49-10; Capt US Scout Guides, 11th IN Cav; 63 to 64; Daisy PO
SPRINGFIELD, Milton, H-49-9; Pvt 1st AL Vidette Cav; Daisy PO
SPRINGS, Joe, T-216-2; 11th Civil Dist
SPRINGS, William, W1-297-1; Pvt H Co 4th TN Inf; 20 Oct 64 to 25 Aug 65; Commerce PO; broken leg
SPRINKEL, Micajah, Wy-172-1; Pvt A Co 10th TN Inf; 4-5-62 to __ (6 mos); Leap Year PO; at home on furlo, got sick and did not return
SPRINKLE, George W., Wa-264-1; Pvt G Co 4th TN Inf; May 5 62 to __; Jonesboro PO; disease of lungs, date of discharge unknown
SPROUSE, Davidson, Co-61-5(2); Pvt K Co 8th TN Cav; 10 Sep 63 to 19 Jun 65; Bridgeport; in prison 71 days
SPRY, George W., Ca-22-2; Pvt F Co 1st IN Videt; 8-27-63 to 6-16-64; Hollow Springs PO
SPUCEY, John T., St-206-1; Pvt G Co 52nd IN Vol; 14 Oct 61 to Jul 65; Covington PO; scurvey from imprisonment; A B Webb, Washington has discharge
SPURGEN, James W., K-184-2; Pvt C Co 8th TN Cav; 63 to __ (1 yr 6 mos); Thorn Grove PO
SPURLING, Lewis, Pi-154-2; Pvt G Co 3rd TN Inf; 7-5-64 to 11-30-64; 4th Civil Dist
SPURLING, Nathan A., Se-227-1; Pvt A Co 7th TN Inf; 10 Aug 64 to 27 Jul 65; Trundles X Roads PO; chronic diarrhoea
SPURLING, William A., Mg-200-2; Pvt H Co 10th TN Inf; 8 Jul 63 to 4 Jul 65; Skene PO; gunshot right shoulder, disease of lungs and chest, result of measles
SPURLOCK, Joseph, W-195-1; Irby widow of; Pvt TN Inf; 62 to 64; 13th Dist
SPURLOCK, Thomas, Ha-115-2; Pvt A Co 4th KY Inf; 12 May 64 to 17 Aug 65; Alanthers Hill PO; no wounds, not a pensioner
SQUIBB, Joseph M., Ge-96-4; Pvt G Co 4th TN Inf; 20 Feb 62 to 1 Oct 63; Rheatown PO; dispepsia piles &c; cant get dates
SQUIBB, Uriah H., Wa-273-3; Pvt D Co 8th TN Cav; 25 Oct 63 to 11 Sep 65; Morning Star PO; rheumatism, diarrhoea and lung disease
SQUIRE, Homer C., H-60-1; Antoinette widow of; Pvt D Co 2nd OH Cav; 8-22-61 to 2-19-63; PO omitted (probably Chattanooga); dead
SRAD, Parazella, M-107-6; 7th Civil Dist
SREE, James S., B-11-2(1); Sgt C Co 4th TN Mtd Inf; 8-24-64 to 8-5-65; Fall Creek PO
STACK, John W., Ce-23-1; Pvt A Co 49th TN; May 61 to May 65; Thomasville PO; CONF
STACKPALER, Thomas R., Mc-112-8; Capt; Athens PO
STACKPOLE, T. R., Mc-112-10; Cpl; Athens PO; gone from home, no dates
STACY, John F., Dk-39-6(2); Pvt L Co 5th TN Cav; 7-6-63 to 8-14-65; Laurel Hill PO
STACY, William J., Ca-22-2; Pvt F Co 6th Videt Cav; 8-27-63 to 6-16-64; Burgen PO
STADDON, Georg W., Sh-167-2; Pvt K Co 142nd OH? Inf; Apr 64 to Sep 64; PO omitted
STAFFORD, Acey A., O-138-1; Cav B Co 7th TN; 10 Sep 61 to 10 May 62; Elbridge PO; CONF
STAFFORD, Anderson C., J-77-2; Pvt B Co 8th TN Cav; 12-26-64 to 8-17-65; Gainesboro PO; chronic rheumatism
STAFFORD, James M., Se-227-2; Cpl H Co 3rd TN Cav; PO omitted
STAFFORD, James N., We-234-1; US Sol; PO omitted
STAFFORD, James R., F-40-2; Pvt A Co 13th TN Cav; May 62 to Jul 64; Hickory Withe PO; CONF
STAFFORD, James W., J-77-1; Pvt D Co 1st TN Cav; 3-27-64 to 5-23-65; Gainesboro PO; in right lung
STAFFORD, John H., J-77-1; Pvt H Co 1st TN Cav; 4-15-62 to 5-23-65; Gainesborough PO
STAFFORD, Pleasant, Se-223-5(1); Ellen J. widow of; Pvt G Co 6th TN Inf; 10 May 62 to 17 May 65; Sevierville PO
STAFFORD, Raus N. M., J-77-1; Pvt C Co 37th KY Cav; 10-13-62 to 12-64; Gainsboro PO; in US service (injured there?)
STAFFORD, William J., We-225-2(1); Nancy C. widow of; Pvt K Co 6th TN Cav; __ to Jul 26 65; Dresden PO; hurt by horse falling; now dead 6 yrs
STAGGS, Early B. (or D.), Wy-172-1; Pvt H Co 2nd TN Mtd Inf; 1-10-64 to 1-21-65; Waynesboro PO
STAGGS, George B., Mu-200-1; Susan C. widow of; Sgt H? Co TN; 64 to 17 Apr 65; Terry PO; shot through left foot; on pension roll, No. 159232, date 26 Apr 1879
STAGGS, James N., Le-119-1; Pvt H Co 5th TN Mtd Inf; 20 Feb 64 to 4 Mar 65; Strathmore PO
STAGGS, Joseph, La-113-3; Mary A. widow of; Pvt A Co 10th TN Inf; Apr 62 to __; Ethridge PO; died in the service

STAGGS, Willis D., Le-119-1; Pvt A Co 2nd TN Mtd Inf; 2 Oct 63 to 14 Oct 64; Strathmore PO, bronchitis and spinnatorrhoea; discharged by Comdy Colonel
STAINBACK, Lewis, Sh-193-1; Pvt; Memphis PO; papers in claim agts hand
STAISLY, William, Gi-136-1; Pvt B Co 64th AR Inf; 11-4-63 to 2-4-65; Odd Fellow Hall PO
STALEN, Mansfield, Mc-118-1; Pvt D Co 10th TN Cav; 8-15-64 to ?; Longs Mills PO; pils 24 yrs
STALEY, William B., K-169-2; very sick not able to give instruction; Knoxville PO
STALLARD, Walter W., B-5-1; Eliza M widow of; Pvt E Co 10th TN Inf; 6-62 to ?; Bell Buckle PO; was killed or captured & killed
STALLEY, Marion, Hd-50-6; US Sol, 6th Civil Dist.
STALLING, Samuel, H-59-2; Pvt TN Inf; Chattanooga PO
STALLINGS, Frank P., K-185-2; Pvt; McMillans PO
STALLINGS, Thomas, Se-226-1; Pvt A Co 12th TN Cav; Jul 62 to __; Straw Plains PO; left service without discharge
STALLINGS, Vinson W., K-185-2; Pvt C Co 2nd TN Cav; 27 Jul 62 to 6 Jul 65; McMillans PO
STALLS, Samul, Ch-15-1; Color Bearer L Co 4th US Cav; 2-15-60 to 4-15-66; Henderson PO; wounded in leg Bat. Shilo
STALNAKER, Lemuel E., W-189-4; Pvt A Co 38th ? Inf; 10-64 to 7-65; McMinnville PO
STAMBAUGH, Samuel R., H-62-2; Pvt K Co 65th PA Inf; 8-1-61 to 8-1-64; 524 Poplar, Chattanooga PO
STAMFORD, Rubin, Cl-52-1; Pvt B Co 2nd TN Art; 8-1-64 to 10-1-65; Quarter PO
STAMMES, Anderson, B-11-3(2); Malissy M. widow of; Pvt; 1863 to 1864; Unionville PO; died from hurt in hip; discharge lost
STAMPER, Dewitt C., Fr-112-3; Pvt D Co 17th TN Inf; 11-1-62 to 5-5-65; Elk River PO; physically disabled; CONF
STAMPS, J. T., Cr-7-1; Pvt E Co 6th TN Cav; 2-5-64 to 7-26-65; Crockett Mills PO
STAMPS, Joseph L., Sn-259-1; Pvt C Co 52nd ?; 8-27-63 to 1-17-65; Bransford PO; injured in back
STAMPS, Thomas, Wh-187-3; Mary J. widow of; Pvt 12th TN Cav; Key PO; died in service
STANBERRY, John W., Ge-88-2; Pvt D Co 1st TN Cav; 12 Aug 62 to 5 Jun 65; Thula PO; piles for 26 years
STANBERY, Ezekiel, Hw-120-2; Delana widow of; Pvt D Co 8th TN; Edison PO
STAND, Stephen, Cl-54-4(2); pvt D Co 63rd TN Inf; 3-61 to 1865; Tazewell? PO; CONF
STANDEFER, George W., Mc-112-6; Capt 1st TN Cav; 9-15-62 to 1-1-65; Athens PO; measles & smallpox
STANDFIELD, John D., Ch-12-3; Pvt B Co 21st TN Cav; 8-1-62 to 5-65; Custer Point PO; deafness
STANDFIELD, Samuel P., Ge-95-2; Levenia Chapatin formerly widow of; 1st Sgt E Co 4th TN Inf; 3 Ma 63 to 2 Aug 65; Home PO
STANDIFER, Jobe, Cl-53-2; Amanda widow of; Pvt B Co; Springdale PO
STANDIFT, Elias, D-89-1; 1st Sgt G Co 50th OH; Aug 13, 62 to Jun 65; Brentwood PO; general debility
STANDSBURY, Harrison R., K-177-1; Pvt D Co 3rd TN Inf; 10 Apr 62 to 10 Feb 64; Chumlea PO; ruptured; discharged on surgeon cert.
STANFIELD, John M., Hd-45-1; 2nd Sgt A Co 2nd TN Mtd Inf; 21 Oct 63 to 14 Oct 64; Cerro Gordo PO; piles & cronic diarhoea
STANFIELD, Joseph, Br-12-4; Pvt E Co 5th TN Inf; 3-2-62 to 1-1-65; Georgetown PO; lung trouble
STANFIELD, Lizzie, D-67-2; widow of Pvt Col Inf; Nashville PO
STANFIELD, William J., D-99-1; Pvt E Co 10th TN Cav; Jul 63 to 65; Bakers PO; leg hurt by being thrown from horse
STANFILL, Rily T., He-67-1; Pvt F Co 145th IL inf; May 20, 64 to Sep 23, 64; Sardis PO; hemorhoids, diarhea chron.; he now also consumption
STANFORD, Isam, H-63-2; Pvt C Co 44th TN Inf; 9-25-63 to 3-15-66; 409 W. 9th, Chattanooga PO; kidney disease
STANLEY, A., Dk-34-2; Telitha widow of; Pvt K Co 5th TN Cav; 7-26-63 to 8-14-65; Dowelltown PO
STANLEY, Andrew J., Hy-84-1; Pvt E Co 38th TN; 62 to __(1 yr 3 mos); Woodville PO; CONF
STANLEY, H. M., Gi-122-5; S. J. widow of; Pvt A Co 3rd TN Inf; 63 to 66; Prospect Sta. PO; CONF
STANLEY, Hittie, Rb-226-2; widow; District 12
STANLEY, James, Sh-185-1; alias James Andrews; Pvt C Co 3rd US Col Hvy Art; 6-5-63 to 4-30-66; 271 Dunlap St., Memphis PO; prisoner in stockade (15 days) Ft. Pickering, Memphis
STANLEY, John, D-51-1 (Black); Lizzie Dozier widow; Pvt; Capital Ave., Nashville PO; cant furnish any direct information
STANLEY, John S., R-161-6; Mary widow of; Cpl L Co 9th TN Cav; 9-1-63 to 9-11-65; Dayton PO
STANLEY, N. J., Lk-112-1; Pvt F Co 1st MO Cav; 4 Apr 63 to 1 Sep 65; Tiptonville PO
STANLEY, Rhods, S-216-1; Pvt H Co 16th KY Vol; 21 Nov 64 to 15 Jul 65; Windfield PO; cronick rheumatism
STANLEY, William, Ru-246-1; Pvt C Co 40th US Col Inf; 1864 to 1866; Murfreesboro PO; feet badly mashed by cannon
STANLY, William, Ge-97-1; Margaret widow of; Pvt L Co 1st TN Cav; May? 62 to Jan 65 (2-7-18); Maltsberger? PO
STANSBERRY, Thomas G., A-4-3; Pvt __ TN Inf; Coal Creek PO; neuralgia & rheumatism; discharge lost
STANSBEY, Andrew H., Mr-99-2; Pvt H Co 1st Reg TN; Il-1-61 to 11-5-64; Jasper PO
STANSBERY, Prior L., K-182-2; Pvt F Co 9th TN Vol Cav; 12 Sep 63 to 14 Sep 65; Gapcreek PO; kidney desease, jaundice
STANSBURY, Jackson, Gr-70-1; Pvt A Co 9th OH Cav; 10 May 62 to 2 Aug 65; Rutledge PO; fever settled in leg & Hips
STANSBURY, James S., Me-88-3; Cpl E Co 6th KS Cav; 7-1-62 to 6-27-?(2 yrs 11 mos 26 days); Birchwood PO; ruptured thown from horse
STANSELL, John T., Ch-14-3; Pvt E Co 7th W TN Cav; 9-17-63 to 12-16-64; Henderson PO; in prison Atlanta 10 mos, Andersonville 3 mos; Florence SC 12 mos; scurvy ulcerated on leg
STANTON, George S., Wa-261-2; Nola Chuckey PO
STANTON, Robert, Wa-261-2; Pvt I Co 1st TN Cav; 21 Sep 62 to 5 Jun 65; Nola Chuckey PO
STANTON, William, Jo-151-1; Ediny M. widow of; Pvt E Co 13th TN Cav; 22 Sep 63 to __; Casper PO; measles--relapse, died in service
STANZEBURY, William F., C-26-1; __ Co H 13th TN Cav; 10-1-63 to 9-5-65; Coal Creek PO
STAPLES, Benjamin T., Mg-199-1; Millia widow of; Adj. 11th TN Cav; Sunbright PO
STAPLES, James W., Mg-196-1; Cpl C Co 1st TN Art; 15 Jul 64 to 31 Mar 66; Oliver Springs PO
STAPLES, Michel, Ro-210-1; Elizabeth C. widow of; Pvt E Co 1st TN Inf; Aug 61 to Sep 64; Rockwood PO
STAPLETON, John, He-119-1; Pvt L Co 8th TN Cav; Oct 63 to Sep 65; Lee Valley PO; thrown from horse, back hurt
STAPLETON, Larkin, Hw-120-2; Pvt C Co 8th TN Cav; 11 Jun 63 to 11 Sep 65; Eidson PO
STAPLETON, Nelson, Hw-119-1; Blacksmith L Co 8th TN Cav; Jul 63 to Sep 65; Eidson PO; spinal affection
STAPLETON, William S., Hw-120-1; Cpl L Co 8th TN Cav; 17 Sep 63 to 11 Sep 65; War Gap PO; lung trouble
STAR, James, A-5-1; Pvt C Co 3rd TN Inf; 2-62 to 3-65; Clinton PO; soar eyes; blind, almost
STARBUCK, William, P-151-1; Pvt E Co 2nd TN Mtd Inf; Mar 64 to 65; Pope PO; hemorrhoids & rheumatism
STARK, Little, Sh-189-3; Pvt B Co; no record could be had; Dee Ave., Memphis PO
STARK, Moses A., Dk-34-1; Sgt I Co 5th TN Cav; 11-30-62 to 8-14-65; Dowelltown PO; piles
STARK, Thomas H., Dk-32-1; Pvt L Co 5th TN Cav; 8-13-63 to 8-14-65; Liberty PO
STARKEY, Harrison, Sn-262-3(2); Elizabeth A. widow of; Cpl E Co 195th OH inf; 25 Feb 64 to 18 Dec 65; Fountain Head PO; heart trouble; has two enlistments & two discharges; "I put both together"

STARKS, Isam, Mt-135-1; Cpl D Co 63rd TN Inf; 1863 to 1865; Oakwood PO
STARKS, Sam (see Woods, Sam)
STARKY, Cassander, Cf-38-1; widow; 10th Civil Dist
STARNES, Berquet F., Pu-144-1; Pvt I Co 5th TN; 10-12-64 to 8-14-65; Double Springs PO; right shoulder & arm hurt
STARNES, Daniel W., La-113-2; Pvt B Co 10th IN Inf; 18 Oct 61 to 18 Oct 64; Lawrenceburgh PO; rheumatic & head affected
STARNES, Elisha, Wa-263-1; Pvt H Co 4th TN Cav; Aug 4, 62 to Jul 16, 65; Garbers Mills PO
STARNES, Jackson J., Hw-134-1; US Sol; 20th Civil Dist.
STARNES, Leonard S., Ge-101-1; Pvt, Cpl D Co 8th TN Inf; 1 Aug 63 to 16 Jun 65; Locust Sp. PO; shot in right leg
STARNES, Pleasant H., Hw-119-2(1); Capt A Co 10th TN Cav; 17 Sep 63 to __; Lee Valley PO; diarrhea
STARNES, William, Wa-265-1; Pvt I Co 11th TN Cav; 1 Aug 63 to 11 Sep 65; Trump PO; rheumatism, kidny?
STARNS, Christian M., Hw-126-1; Cpl L Co 8th TN Cav; 63 to 65; Starns PO; rheumatism; dates not known
STARNS, John A., Ge-97-1; Jane widow of; Pvt C Co 4th TN Inf; 2 Jan 63 to 2 Apr 65; Locust Spring PO; nervious rheumatism & hart?
STARNS, John F., Ge-91-3; Sgt D Co 6th TN Inf; 28 Apr 62 to 27 Apr 65; Greeneville PO; blood pois. wounded & others
STARNS, William A., Ct-44-2; Pvt C Co 1st US Inf; 3-64 to 12-65; Hampton PO; chronic dysentery; discharge lost
STARR, John J. W., La-113-1; Lt C Co 48th US Col Inf; 8-22-62 to 1-4-65; Lawrenceburg PO; all the information could get
STARR, Junenis L., Br-11-2; Pvt D Co 7th TN Lt Art; 3-64 to 7-65; Chatata PO; bleeding piles 25 yrs
STARR, Leon, D-67-2; Pvt; Nashville PO
STATON, Jackson, Cr-14-2; Pvt I Co 88th US Col Inf; 6 Apr 64 to 10 Jan 65; Clarksburg PO
STATT, Abdill, Se-222-1; Mary A. widow of; Pvt G Co 7th AL Cav; 10 Jan 64 to 16 Jan 64; Midel Creeke PO; discharged disability erasiplas
STATTON, John, Mr-96-3(2); Pvt; Whitwell PO
STEADMAN, George, Su-241-2; Pvt C Co 6th IN Cav; 15 Jul 63 to 12 Jul 65; Clover Bottom PO; dyreah--weak eyes
STEAGALD, Albert, De-24-1; Catherine widow of; Pvt D Co 2nd TN Mtd Inf; 63 to 64; Decaturville PO; cant get any information
STEAGER, David, D-99-1; Poorhouse; Pvt A Co 17th TN Inf; 64 to 66; Nashville PO; old
STEARNS, Samuel E., D-45-1; Pvt G Co 6th Mass Inf; 8-12-62 to 6-3-63; Cpl G Co 6th Mass Inf; 7-7-64 to 10-27-64; Nashville PO
STEAVENS, James, Jn K-184-3; Jane wife of; Pvt I Co 6th TN Cav; Thorn Grove PO
STEBBINS, Asa D., H-61-5; Pvt I Co 4th MI Cav; 6-18-63 to 6-29-65; Chattanooga PO; hernia, partial paralysis
STEEL, Jackson, Sh-189-1; Pvt 14th TN Inf; fall 62 to spring 66; mustered in at Gallatin; Ark. Ave., Memphis PO
STEEL, James, Bo-19-2; Pvt J Co 1st TN Cav; 1862 to ?; Rockford PO; CONF
STEEL, John H., M-108-5; Pvt K Co 1st TN Mtd Inf; 1864 to 1865; Akersville KY PO; lung & kidney disease; discharge not at hand
STEEL, Samuel Y.?, Hn-74-1; Duty Sgt I Co 6th TN Cav; 5 Jun 62 to 26 Jul 65; McKenzie PO; discharged on special order
STEEL, ___, Hi-88-1; Rachal widow of; 6th Dist
STEELE, Mary N., Hi-88-1; (widow?); 6th District
STEELE, Nelson, D-44-2(1); Lucinda widow of; Sgt D Co 13th TN Inf; 12-3-63 to 1865; Nashville PO; wounded hip & hand
STEELE, Walter O., H-72-3(2); Alma S. widow of; 2nd Co Sharpshooters 22nd Mar (MD or MA?) Inf; Chattanooga PO
STEGALL, Samuel A., Ro-208-3; US Sol; 10th Civil Dist.
STELLE, Wm. A., R-163-2; Sgt E Co 18th IL Inf; 5-28-61 to 12-16-65; Graysville PO; flesh wound in head; re-enlisted veteran
STEP, Pery, Bl-3-3; Pvt TN Cav; Pikeville PO; CONF
STEPHANS, Thos., K-167-5; Capt D Co 2nd TN Cav; 13 Jul 62 to May 64; Knoxville PO; resigned, got hurt by horse
STEPHEN, Monroe, Hd-54-3; US Sol; PO omitted
STEPHENS, Andrew J., Fe-42-3; Charlotte widow of; Pvt Capt David Beaty's Co TN Ind Scouts; Boatland PO
STEPHENS, Benjamin, Mu-191-1; 7th Dist.
STEPHENS, Burton, Fe-42-2; Pvt Capt David Beaty's Co TN Ind Scouts; Jamestown PO
STEPHENS, Danal F., Sh-188-2; Pvt G Co 179th OH Inf; 1861 to 1865; 62 Peyton Ave., Memphis PO
STEPHENS, Dannel P., Mo-130-1; Cpl D Co 3rd TN Mtd Inf; 7-12-64 to 9-30-64; Acorn PO
STEPHENS, David Y., Mn-121-2; Susanah R. A. Tranium widow of; Pvt I Co 11th IL Cav; 8-18-62 to 9-18-64; Ralston PO
STEPHENS, George, We-233-1(2); Catharen widow of; Pvt VA; no dates (2 yrs); Ralston PO
STEPHENS, George W., Fe-42-2; Pvt Capt David Beaty's Co TN Ind Scouts; Jamestown PO
STEPHENS, Henry W., H-73-1; Pvt 2nd SC Inf; 1861 to 5-65; Chattanooga PO; skull cracked by shell; can't endure heat now
STEPHENS, Horace, Sh-159-2; S Gunboat; Memphi PO; shot in the body
STEPHENS, Isaah, Fe-43-1; Pvt TN Scouts; 1861 to 1864; Jamestown PO
STEPHENS, Ellenger J. (see Beaty, James)
STEPHENS, James E., La-115-2; Pvt E Co 75th IN Vol; 1 Aug 62 to 8 Jul 65; Henryville PO; sore on right leg
STEPHENS, James M., H-68-2; Seaman U.S.S. Bertau?; 9-3-64 to 8-22-65; Chattanooga PO; ruptured
STEPHENS, James N., Ro-203-1; Ellage wife of; Wheat PO; CONF
STEPHENS, Jerry, Wi-275-1; Addison Jackson alias; Pvt F Co 12th TN Inf; Nov 64 to Dec 65; Franklin PO; shell wound in leg, shot in head & arm; papers out of possession
STEPHENS, Jessee, D-57-1; Susan widow of; Pvt; Jan 31, 61 to Mar 28, 65; 8th Ward, Nashville PO?
STEPHENS, John, Sh-153-2; alias Steven Johns; Sgt C Co 61st USC Inf; Apr 62 to Dec 65; Bailey Sta. PO
STEPHENS, John R., Cu-17-2; Pvt G Co 6th TN Mtd Inf; 3-25-65 to 6-30-65; Crossville PO
STEPHENS, Jordan, Lo-193-1; Cherry wife of; Pvt H Co 1st TN Hvy Art; 1 Jun 62 to 1 Jul 62; Unitia PO
STEPHENS, Joseph, H-65-1; US Sol; 140 Cowart St., Chattanooga PO
STEPHENS, Joseph C., T-209-1; alias Side Dicarson; Cpl A Co 10th ___; Nov 62 to Nov 65; Randolph PO
STEPHENS, Joshua, D-60-1; alley back of McCrairy, Nashville PO; colored
STEPHENS, Marshall, Mg-197-3; Maj 4th TN Cav; 10 Aug 61 to 12 Jul 65; Crooked Fork PO; chronic rheumatism
STEPHENS, Noah, Mo-120-2; Adeline Black formerly widow of; Pvt B Co 7th TN Inf; 11-1-64 to 7-27-65; Glenloch PO
STEPHENS, Peter R., K-161-2; Sgt B Co 3rd TN Inf; 3 Aug 61 to 17 Sep 64; Knoxville PO
STEPHENS, Royal, Co-61-6(2); Pvt; Bridgeport PO; consumption
STEPHENS, Sampson, Fe-41-3(1); Pvt D Co 2nd E TN Mtd Inf; 12-15-61 to 3-11-65; Little Crabb PO; dis. of heart & lost lung; chnc. rheumatism resulting; in prison on Bell's Island
STEPHENS, Thomas, Je-143-3; Pvt A Co 6th KY Cav; 20 Sep 61 to Oct 65; Mossy Creek PO; two horses fell on subject on the march to Cumberland Gap
STEPHENS, Warren, T-219-1; Pvt G Co 55th TN Inf; 14 Sep 63 to 31 Dec 65; Phelan PO
STEPHENS, William M., J-77-1; Pvt G Co 3rd KY Inf; 8-61 to 10-64; Gainesboro PO; sun stroke
STEPHENS, William R., Lo-188-4; US Sol; 3rd Civil Dist.
STEPHENSON, Elizabeth, Hd-51-2; widow US Sol; PO omitted

STEPHENSON, Freeman, D-103-2; Pvt I Co OH Inf; Jul 1, 61 to Jan 23, 63; Ridge Post PO; lost papers
STEPHENSON, George, Sh-169-1; Pvt G Co Kanser Cav; Nov 2, 61 to Nov 16, 64; Memphis PO
STEPHENSON, Grant, Mu-198-2; 10th Dist.
STEPHENSON, John C., Mc-112-6; Pvt A Co 5th TN Mtd Inf; 9-1-64 to 6-24-65; Athens PO; injury to sight & chronic diarrhea
STEPHENSON, John J., Mc-116-2; Cyntha E. widow of; Pvt D Co 5th TN Mtd Inf; 10-1-64 to 6-25-65; Athens PO; killed by locomotive engine
STEPHENSON, John Jackson, Mu-211-1; Pvt F Co 113th OH Vol; Mar 63 to Jun 65; Britton PO; diseas of side
STEPHENSON, John Q. A., Hw-124-1; Cpl Clk? B Co 4th TN Cav; 12 Oct 62 to 12 Jul 65; Opossum PO
STEPHENSON, William, Gi-135-2; Pvt F Co 13th TN Inf; 1863 to 1866; Lynnville PO
STEPHENSON, William A., Dy-27-1; Pvt A Co 4th AL reg.; 11-15-62 to 5-65; Ro Ellen PO; CONF
STEPHENSON, William H., B-12-5; Pvt C Co 4th TN Mtd Inf; ? to 8-25-65; Wheel PO; discharge lost could not give dates
STEPHUS, John, Fe-42-3; Pvt Capt David Beaty's Co TN Ind Scouts; Boatland PO
STEPHUS, Russul, Fe-42-3; Pvt Capt David Beaty's Co TN Ind Scouts; Boatland PO
STEPP, Nathan L., Gr-74-2; Pvt A Co 20th VA Bat.; Jul 61 to 23 Jul 65; Dayal PO; partially deaf; pneumonia fever cause; CONF
STEPP, Stephen, C-29-1; Sgt D Co 60th NC Cav; 7-62 to 6-13-65; Fincastle PO; bloodshotten
STEPP, William--McKEE, Phedora L., Wa-261-1; (both these names on same line, other data opposite Stepp); Pvt I Co TN Cav; 23 Sep 62 to Jun 65; Cankling PO
STEPP, William, Fe-40-2(1); Pvt D Co 2nd TN Inf; 9-1-61 to 1-2-65; Moodyville PO; both right & left foot frozen; in Richmond, Bells Island prison
STEPPENS, Frank, Dy-28-1; Pvt H Co 14th PA Cav; Jun 62 to Jul 21, 65; Finley PO; wound in leg by gun shot; no pension yet
STERCHI, John L. H., K-177-4; Sgt 4th TN Cav; Sep 62 to 14 Apr 65; Dante PO; CONF
STERLING, Calton, F-37-2; Pvt G Co 61st US Col Inf; Jun ___ to Dec 30, 65; Somerville PO
STERLING, John K., Je-135-3; Pvt C Co 1st TN Cav; 1 Apr 62 to 1 Apr 65; Mount Horeb PO; catarrh & lung trouble
STEVANS, James, Br-10-1; Pvt B Co 5th WI Inf; 8-13-62 to 7-3-65; Cleveland PO
STEVELY, Clayburn, K-158-2; Pvt E Co 6th PA Inf; Apr 61 to May 65; Knoxville PO; 105 Patton St.; chronic rheumatism from exposure; right side useless
STEVENS, Allen, K-171-2; US Sol; 12th Civil Dist.
STEVENS, Calvin, Bo-22-1; Pvt H Co 2nd TN Cav; 10-62 to 5-65; Notime PO; lug disease; can't get the day of E & D
STEVENS, Goodlow W., Sm-174-2(1); Pvt D Co 4th TN Inf; 9-64 to 8-20-65; Enoch PO
STEVENS, James D., O-134-2; Pvt E Co 4th TN Inf; Jun 15, 61 to Mar 15, 65; Hornbeak PO; CONF
STEVENS, James W., Sm-173-1; Pvt A Co 6th US Vol; 3-16-65 to 10-16-66; Temperance Hall PO, DeKalb Co
STEVENS, Joseph, Cu-15-2; Pvt B Co 1st NJ Cav; 12-30-63 to 7-24-65; Genesis PO; partial deafness; cold contracted & exposure
STEVENS, Vaden S., Ce-30-1; Pvt E Co 10th TN Inf; May 62 to Jun 65; Craggie Hope PO; rheumatism
STEVENS, Wm. J., Cr-3-1; Pvt E Co 6th TN R; Nov 65 to Jun 65; Gadsden PO
STEVENS, ____, H-49-7; Caroline widow of; Daisy PO
STEVENSON, James H., Hn-71-1; Pvt C Co 2nd TN Cav; 62 to 4 Jul 65; Osage PO; Mr. Stevenson claims that his health was injured by exposure and fall from horse while in service
STEVENSON, Joe, Sm-168-1; Pvt TN Inf; 1861 to 1864; Kempville PO
STEVENSON, Judith (see Fatis, James)

STEVENSON, Nias, Gi-129-2; Pvt A Co 111th TN Inf; 15 Jun 64 to 30 Apr 66; Bryson PO
STEVENSON, Richard, Gi-129-2; Pvt A Co 111th TN Inf; 15 Jun 64 to 30 Apr 66; Bryson PO
STEVENSON, Thomas, D-79-2; Pvt I Co 2nd NY Vet Cav; 62 to 65; 235 Trentland, Nashville PO; shot in left leg, near ankle
STEVENSON, Wm., Mo-119-1; Pvt L Co 5th IN Cav; 8-5-62 to 10-15-65; Sweetwater PO
STEVENSON, Wm., D-91-1; Katie widow of; Pvt F Co 44th Inf; 2 yrs 9 mos; Harris Bro Line St., Nashville PO
STEVINS, Andrew J., Ge-91-1; Lt E Co 2nd NC Inf; Sep 1, 63 to Aug 16, 65; Greeneville PO; diarrhea
STEVINS, John, Ct-37-2; Pvt D Co 8th TN Cav; 6-63 to 1865 (2 yrs); Ripshin PO; lung trouble
STEVINS, Mikiel S., Ct-37-1; Capt H Co 4th TN Inf; 1-1-64 to 8-1-65; Roar Mtn. PO
STEWARD, Claiton, Ge-64-1; Pvt A Co 6th TN; 62 to 65; Bradford PO
STEWARD, Dock, P-156-3; Pvt 10th TN Inf; Lobelville PO; CONF
STEWARD, Fannie, Hy-75-1; widow; Dancyville PO; doesnt know anything
STEWARD, James D., G-55-1; Pvt G Co 2nd TN Inf; 12-2-63 to 12-28-64; Trenton PO
STEWARD, James H., Wi-270-1; Pvt H Co 101st OH Inf; Sep 62 to Oct 64; Gingo PO; ingury of back by shell
STEWARD, Louis, Ro-201-4(1); Sgt C Co 1st TN Hvy Art; 12 Jan 64 to 30 Apr 66; Kingston PO
STEWARD, Newton, Mc-118-2; Tillie widow of; Pvt; Joshua PO
STEWART, Alford M., He-64-2; Pvt E Co 11th IL Inf; 15 Mar 62 to 14 Mar 65; Reagan PO
STEWART, Alfred, Col, D-45-1; Pvt C Co 111th US Col Inf; 2-19-64 to 4-30-66; Nashville PO
STEWART, Andrew W., Ce-23-1; Pvt, Lt, Capt, Gid & Lowe 18th Reg; 61 to 65; Thomasville PO
STEWART, Carly, Mc-109-2; Pvt K Co 1st MN Hvy Art; 2-14-65 to 9-20-65; Ziegler PO
STEWART, Charles, D-65-1; Nashville PO (actually reads Sleuart)
STEWART, Charles S., Mu-209-6; Pvt A Co 9th TN; 61 to 65; Columbia PO; CONF
STEWART, Charles T., H-63-2; Clerk Quarter Master; 1862 to 1865 (2 yrs 9 ms); 416 W. 6th, Chattanooga PO; hearing
STEWART, Demetrius M., H-56-1; Pvt I Co 11th OH Inf; 1861 to 1864; Chattanooga PO
STEWART, Edward Harrison, J-81-3; Pvt 1st TN; 7-1-64 to 7-1-65; Gurnesboro PO
STEWART, Felix R., Sh-176-1; US Sol; 466 Maine St. Memphis PO
STEWART, George, Ro-210-11; Pvt; Rockwood PO
STEWART, George W., D-58-2; Sol; Walnut St., Nashville PO
STEWART, George W., We-224-2; Pvt F Co 46th TN Inf; Oct 61 to May 65; PO omitted
STEWART, J. A., Bo-11-4; Cpl B Co 4th TN Inf; 3-27-63 to 8-2-65; Brick Mill PO; neuralgia
STEWART, Jacob M., Dk-32-4; Pvt G Co 1st TN Mtd Inf; 12-30-64 to 7-22-65; Doneltown PO
STEWART, James K. P., Ov-137-3; Cpl B Co 1st TN Mtd Inf; 2-1-64 to 4-14-65; Monroe PO
STEWART, James P., Cf-40-1; Cpl C Co 34th OH Inf; 2 Sep 61 to 8 Sep 64; Tullahoma PO; gun shot wound in ankle
STEWART, James R., He-66-1; Pvt K Co 7th TN Cav; Aug 8, 63 to ___; Huron PO
STEWART, James T., K-179-3; Pvt F Co 41st IN 2 Cav; 2 Sep 61 to 4 Oct 64; Concord PO
STEWART, Jerimiah, Pu-146-2; Pvt I Co 1st TN Mtd Inf; 10-15-64 to 7-22-65; Silver Point PO; lung & kidney disease & frostbite; still suffering
STEWART, John, Bl-5-2; Sgt D Co 6th TN Mtd Inf; 8-16-64 to 6-30-65; Retro PO, Hamilton Co; had measles and mumps; caught cold been affected ever since
STEWART, John S., H-64-2; Pvt; Chattanooga PO
STEWART, Jno. W., K-160-2; Surgeon T Co 1st AL Cav; 1 Aug 64 to 1 Oct 65; Knoxville PO; hand broken
STEWART, Joseph, Le-118-1; Pvt A Co 46th MO Inf; Oct 62 to Nov 64; Isams Store PO

STEWART, Joseph O., La-113-1; Pvt F Co 3rd NC Mtd Inf; 16 Oct 64 to 16 Aug 65; Lawrenceburg PO
STEWART, Peter, Sh-159-2; Sgt; no dates (4 mos); Memphis PO
STEWART, Robert, Bl-5-1; Pvt D Co 6th TN Mtd Inf; 8-16-64 to 6-30-65; Stevens Chapel PO
STEWART, Robt. B., R-163-4; Pvt K Co 1st IA V Inf; 4-19-61 to 8-19-61; Sgt F Co 24th IA V Inf; 8-6-62 to 8-3-65; Dayton PO; shot through right shoulder
STEWART, Sam S., J-81-3; Pvt I Co 11th KY; 9-1-63 to 9-1-65; Gurnesboro PO; sick 18 months kidneys
STEWART, Theodore F., H-62-4; Pvt C Co 39th OH Inf; 7-22-61 to 7-15-65; 403 West Sixth, Chattanooga PO
STEWART, William, Fr-118-1; Zibah widow of; Pvt I Co 17th TN Inf; 62 to Sep 63; Winchester PO: CONF
STEWART, William, D-49-1; Pvt C Co 41st PA; 64 to 65 (1 yr 6 mos); Nashville PO; his best recollection of dates
STEWART, William, Fr-109-1; Pvt E Co 184th OH Inf; 26 Jan 65 to 29 Sep __(8 mos 3 days); Huntland PO
STEWART, William F., Cf-42-1; Pvt G Co 5th IA Inf; 7-61 to 7-65; Tullahoma PO; shot in hand
STEWART, William G., Dk-53-3(1); Pvt F Co 4th TN Cav; Hicks PO
STEWART, William R., He-64-3; Cpl E Co 11th IL Inf; 15 Mar 62 to 14 Mar 65; Reagan PO
STEWART, William W., H-54-5; Sarah W. widow of; Pvt I Co 7th TN Inf; 3-16-6? to 7-4-6?; Sherman Heights PO; died of chronic diarrhea 7-30-72
STEWERT, Joe S., Cy-27-1; Pvt D Co 3rd KY Cav; 6-64 to 7-65; Clementsville PO
STEWERT, John W., G-61-1; Pvt G Co 2nd __ Mtd Inf; Oct 63 to Jan 65; 12th Civil Dist
STHETHS, Kenner, La-117-1; Pvt B Co 2nd TN Mtd Inf, Cav; Oct 15, 63 to Oct 17 64; Pinkerney PO
STIDHAM, Edward D., Hi-92-1; Pvt D Co 150th OH Inf; Feb 7 65 to 16 Jan 66; Aetna PO
STIDMAN, James, Su-240-1; Pvt G Co 8th US Cav; 12 Sep 63 to 11 Sep 65; Butterfly PO; mashed up by train, thigh broke angle & __; disabled
STIEN, Eli W., K-162-1; Sgt E Co 91st OH Inf; 8 Aug 62 to 7 Sep 63; Knoxville PO; right lung contracted disease
STIER, Ada B. (see Campbell, Geo. P.)
STIKE, Cather, Jo-148-1; Elkana Stike alias; Pvt B Co 3rd NC Inf; 1 Apr 64 to 8 Aug 65; Malney PO; disease of the lungs
STILES, George B., Ov-136-1; Sgt E Co 77th IL Inf; 5-12-62 to 4-15-63; Livingston PO; severe deafness
STILES, James C., K-167-1; Pvt B Co 31st IN Inf; May 63 to May 65; Knoxville PO; in state? troops
STILES, Philip, Co-68-2; Pvt E Co 2nd TN Cav; 62 to 65; Sutton PO; fever & ague
STILES, Samuel, W-189-2; Pvt K Co 13th TN Cav; 7-1-64 to 9-5-65; McMinnville PO
STILL, Andrew J., Hw-193(1); Pvt A Co 12th TN Cav; Apr 62 to Mar 64; Alum Well PO; CONF
STILL, James O. A., Mc-112-2; Pvt E Co 5th TN Mtd Inf; 9-24-64 to 6-26-65; Athens PO
STILL, Joseph L., Br-8-1; Pvt E Co 5th TN Mtd Inf; 9-64 to 7-1-65; Cleveland PO; rupture
STILL, ___, Br-8-4(2); Letha widow of; Blue Springs Station PO
STILLWELL, Susan (widow of soldier), Br-8-2; 5th Civil Dist.; rheumatism
STILS, William D., Ge-84-2; Pvt G Co 3rd VA Mtd Inf; 12 Sep 64 to 8 Aug 65; Greenville PO; chronic dis. lungs
STILWELL, James W., G-57-4(1); Pvt C Co 11th TN Cav; 9-1-62 to 1-1-65; Yorkville PO
STILZMAN?, Joshuay, K-185-1; Pvt; Mar 62 to Dec 65; Mascott PO; shot in hand; CONF
STIMET, Thomas E., D-45-5; Fillmore Ave., Nashville PO
STIMKE, Albert, R-159-1; Pvt B Co 73rd OH Inf; 10-27-62 to 6-63; Spring City PO; typhoid fever; brought on by exposure

STINE, Chas. L., Cr-4-2; Pvt C Co 197th OH Inf; 15 Mar 65 to 31 Jul 65; Bells Depot PO
STINE, George A., O-142-2; US Sol; Obion PO
STINE?, Rufus J., T-208-1; pvt A Co 3rd AR; 63 to 65; Fulton PO; crippled
STINER, James, Un-257-1; Pvt E Co 2nd TN Inf; Jul 63 to 64; New Prospect PO
STINERS, Charles E., H-51-6; 1st Lt I Co 18th OH Inf; 11-29-62 to 9-5-65; Red Bank PO
STINET, John, Bl-3-5; Pvt B Co 62nd TN Inf; 12-25-62 to 1863; Tanbark PO; hip fracture; CONF
STINNETT, Damuel, Gi-122-3; Pvt A Co 111th TN Inf; Jan 63 to May 65; Prospect Sta. PO
STINNETT, David, Se-223-2; Pvt B Co 9th TN Cav; 15 Sep 63 to 11 Sep 65; Pigeon Forge PO; came home on sick furlow, could not back
STINNETT, James L., Lo-189-1; Sgt D Co 18th MS Inf; 61 to 65; Philadelphia PO; CONF
STINNETT, Jno., K-183-1; Pvt A? Co 1st TN Inf; 11 Jul 63 to 3 Aug 65; River Dale PO
STINNETT, John R., K-184-1; Pvt C Co 1st TN Cav; 8 Aug 61 to 11 Sep 64; Riverdale PO; defect of the eyes
STINNETT, Mason, Gi-128-1; Sgt K Co 110th TN Inf; Feb 63 to Apr 15, 65; 8th Dist.
STINNETT, Wm., Wi-271-1; Pvt K Co 10th TN Inf; 19 Nov 62 to 8 Apr 65; Boston PO
STINSON, John T., Be-1-1; Lucretia widow of; Pvt M Co 12th TN Cav; Aug 12, 64 to Aug 17, 65; Sugar Tree PO
STINSON, Samuel, Co-59-2; US Sol; 1st Dist.
STINSON, William B., Wi-270-2; Pvt A Co 9th TN Cav; 12 Aug 63 to 27 Jun 64; Union Valley PO
STOCKARD, Henry, D-69-3; 54 Lewis St., Nashville
STOCKTON, Allen, J-80-2; Pvt 13th KY Inf; Granville PO
STOCKTON, Robert G., Dy-29-3; Pvt F Co 1st AL Cav; 4 Apr 63 to 27 Apr 64; Trimble PO; bronchitis
STOCKWELL, Charls A., La-115-3; Pvt K Co 83rd IL Inf; 1 Aug 63 to 3 Jul 65; Summertown PO
STOCKWELL, Joshua W., S-218-2; Pvt B Co 1st WI Art? 62 to Aug 65; PO omitted; eyes defect sunstroke
STOFFORD, William R., Ma-114-2; US Sol; Pinson PO; piles & deafness
STOKELY, Benjamin, L-101-1; Pvt A Co 40th TN C Inf; 64 to 65; Henning PO; lost discharge
STOKELY, Henry, L-108-1; Pvt K Co 55th US Inf; 20 May 62 to May 65; Glimpville PO
STOKELY, Mary A. (see Davis, John P.)
STOKER, William B., Dk-31-1; Col 5th TN Cav; 4-25-62 to 5-65 (3 yrs 15 days); Alexandria PO; shot in left side; now almost helpless
STOKER, William J., We-223-2; Susan E. widow of; Pvt I Co 6th TN Cav; __ to Aug 65; Palmersville PO; died 1 March 1871
STOKES, Alexander A., Br-10-1; Pvt I Co 124th IL Vol; 2-23-64 to 9-2-65; Cleveland PO
STOKES, David S., H-53-5; B Co 1st TN Art; 1862 to 8-65; Ridgedale PO
STOKES, John, Mr-97-2; US Sol; Jarman? PO
STOKES, William J., Rb-228-1; Pvt C Co 1st TN Cav; Aug 61 to __(4 yrs); Crunk PO; CONF
STONE, Alexander, H-51-3; Pvt E Co; 62 to __; Hill City PO
STONE, Allen W., P-25-7(3); Pvt; 5 yrs; Newbern PO; shot twice, dates unknown
STONE, Byrum (see Murrell, Harriett)
STONE, Clarissa (see Mayen, P. D.)
STONE, Clarke, F-42-2(4); 1st Lt K Co 15th TN Cav; 62 to 65; Rossville PO; CONF
STONE, Columbus P., Mo-122-1; Pvt H Co 2nd TN Cav; 10-10-62 to 7-6-65; Dancing Branch PO; cronic diarrhea & sight
STONE, David Crockett, Sh-162-1; Mary J. widow of; Lt 27th IN Cav; 61 to 65; 152 Front St, Memphis PO; chronic dysentery; enlisted at Evansville
STONE, Elihu P., Wh-183-1; Pvt G Co 53rd IN Inf; 9-22-64 to 5-31-65; Quebeck PO; no disability incurred
STONE, Enoch H., Wh-183-1; Lt I Co 5th TN Cav; 7-22-62 to 9-10-64; Quebeck PO; no disability incurred
STONE, James L., Pi-155-1; Pvt D Co 32nd KY Inf; 11-4-62 to 8-12-63; Otto PO; pulmonary hemorage lungs

STONE, James M., Ct-40-1; Pvt F Co 13th TN Cav; 9-22-63 to 9-5-65; Elizabethton PO; injury left knee and side
STONE, Jeremire, Cy-26-2; Pvt G Co 23rd MO Inf; 1862 to 1865 (2 yrs 11 mos 19 days); Rocktown PO
STONE, John R., Ce-20-2; Cpl G Co 10th TN Inf; 4-20-63 to 6-5-65; Marrowbone PO
STONE, M., B-2-2; Pvt F Co 5th TN Cav; Haley PO
STONE, Nathan, Hd-47-1; Pvt H Co 25th US Inf; 68 to 71; Savannah PO
STONE, Noble, He-67-2; Pvt H Co 25th US Inf; May 20, 62 to Jun 20, 65; Sardis PO; ruptured in privates during war
STONE, Patrick L., Bl-2-2(1); Pvt G Co 6th TN Mtd Inf; 3-25-65 to 6-30-65; Grape Vine PO
STONE, Reece B., Wa-273-2; 1st Sgt A Co 13th TN Cav; 22 Sep 63 to 5 Sep 65; Jonesboro PO; chronic diarrhoea, disease of breast and rheu.
STONE, Rolan J., Pi-156-1; Pvt C Co 1st TN Inf; 1862 to 1864; Permelia PO; crippled by a horse; now troubled with piles
STONE, Samuel, K-180-3; Pvt; Bearden PO
STONE, Samuel, Sn-261-5(4); Jane widow of; Pvt; Perdue PO; CONF
STONE, Thadeus L., He-67-2; Pvt H Co 25th US Inf; Dec 1, 68 to 71; Sardis PO; two ribs broken in left side; in the army US, 26 years
STONE, Thomas, Ro-207-3; pvt G Co; Paint Rock PO; rheumatism & piles
STONE, Thomas W., Cl-58-1; Emaline widow of; Pvt H Co 2nd TN Inf; Mar 62 to 1865; Minkton PO; captured Rogersville TN Oct 63; prisoner at Bells Island
STONE, Thomas W., Cl-54-2; Sgt A Co 12th TN Cav; 2-15-64 to 10-27-65; Tazewell PO
STONE, W. A., Fr-115-1; Pvt M Co 6th OH Cav; 12-30-63 to 8-17-66; Cowan PO
STONE, William, Fe-40-1; Anna widow of; 2nd Lt D Co 11th TN Vol; 8-63 to 10-64; Little Crabb PO; wounded and in Richmond prison; died immediately after release
STONE, William B., Gu-48-4(1); pvt A Co 10th KS Inf; 4-9-63 to 3-65; Oceona PO; Mississippi Co., AR
STONE, William F., Mg-198-2; Pvt C Co 16th KY Inf; 5 Sep 61 to Mar 62; Deer Lodge PO; measles, cattarh; Capt F Co 16th KY Inf; 5 Mar 62 to 15 Jun 65
STONEBRAKER, Isreal, Li-149-1; Louvenia widow of; Pvt K Co 110th US Col Inf; 1-13-64 to 12-15-66; Fayetteville PO
STONECIPHER, Absalom, Br-7-2; Pvt D Co 183rd OH Inf; 10-1-63 to 7-17-65; Cleveland PO
STONECIPHER, Abslom, K-175-1; Bullrun PO
STONECIPHER, Curtis, Mg-200-1; Pvt B Co 2nd TN Inf; 10 Aug 61 to 6 Nov 64; PO omitted
STONECIPHER, Ezra, Mg-196-1; Sgt K Co 1st TN Inf; 21 Aug 61 to 17 Sep 64; Coalfield PO
STONECIPHER, Joseph, S-213-3; Pvt Detcht. 2nd TN Inf; 13 Jun 63 to 3 Aug 65; Robbins PO; chronic diarrhea
STONECIPHER, Martin, Mg-197-3; Pvt K Co 9th TN Cav; 9 Aug 64 to 11 Sep 65; Crooked Fork PO; chronic bronchitus & rheumatism 2½ yrs
STONECYPHER, Jacob B., Ge-96-3; Pvt E Co 4th TN Inf; 17 Jan 63 to 2 Aug 65; Chucky City PO; nervousness
STONES, Henry P., C-27-3; Pvt A Co 1st MD Cav; 9-62 to 10-65; Caryville PO
STOOKESBURY, Robert, Wy-173-4; Jane widow of; Pvt F Co 6th TN Inf; 3-10-62 to 5-25-65; Sims PO
STOOPS, Andrew J., H-52-2; Pvt K Co 6th OH Inf; 1861 to 1861; Lookout Mt. PO
STORE, James W., T-216-3; Cpl H Co 8th KY Art; 64 to __ (2 yrs); 14th Civil Dist.
STORIC, Eli, Fe-40-1; Mary A. widow of; Pvt C Co 1st KY Cav; 1861 to 1864; Little Crabb PO
STORRIS, Elias, D-89-1; Pvt P Co 1st R; Aug 64 to __; Nashville PO; will get discharge papers sometime 1890
STORRY, Crisp C., K-165-1; 64 to 65; Knoxville PO; I was in the recuts
STORY, Beraman, Hw-132-1; Pvt C Co 1st TN Cav; Jul 61 to 11 Apr 65; Otes PO; rheumatism; heart diesease &c

STORY, Eli, Wa-267-2; Pvt H Co 8th TN Cav; 8 Sep 63 to 11 Sep 65; Febuary PO; wound in left thigh
STORY, George, Wa-263-4; Pvt H Co 8th TN Cav; Sep 63 to Sep 65; Garbers Mills PO
STORY, Jesse, Wa-263-1; Pvt M Co 8th TN Cav; 15 Sep 63 to 11 Sep __ (1-11-28); Garbers Mills PO; claims dis. of chronic bronchitis, rheumatism
STORY, Oliver, Wa-263-2; Pvt M Co 8th TN Cav; Sep 63 to Sep 19, 65; Garbers Mills PO; rheumatism
STORY, Thomas J., Wa-263-2; Pvt M Co 8th TN Cav; Sep 63 to 65; Garbers Mills PO; bronchitis
STORY, W. T., Hd-48-1; Seaman Gunboat Mound? Citty; Feb 23, 63 to 23 Feb 65; Svannah PO; rheumatism
STORY, William, Pi-155-1; Pvt H Co 3rd KY Inf; 12-21-61 to 1-14-65; Byrdstown PO; fevers & theumatism, 3 ribs broken
STOSIA, Stephen A., Hd-45-1; Seaman Stewart Robb; 9-6-63 to 9-26-64; Cerro Gordo PO
STOUT, Alferd A., Jo-153-2; Pvt M Co 13th TN Cav; 2 Feb 64 to 5 Sep __; Little Doe PO; rheumatism
STOUT, Andrew T., Ct-36-1; Pvt 13th TN Cav; Shell Creek PO; chronic diarrhea
STOUT, Daniel, Jo-151-2; Pvt M Co 13th TN Cav; __ to 5 Sep 65 (1 yr); Bakers Gap PO; deafness-right ear-breast disease
STOUT, David, Ct-36-1; Laurane widow of; Pvt F Co 2nd TN Inf; 62 to __; Shell Creek PO; died in prison, Andersonville GA
STOUT, Elijah, De-25-1; Pvt E Co 8th US Col Hvy Art; 1 Apr 64 to 10 Feb 66; Decaturville PO
STOUT, Frank A., Mo-119-2; Lizzie B. widow of; Sgt; Sweetwater PO
STOUT, George W., J-83-1; Pvt B Co 8th TN; 1-28-65 to 8-17-65; Nameless PO
STOUT, Granville W., Ct-35-4; Pvt G Co 13th TN Cav; 9-22-63 to 9-5-65; Elkmills PO; in the 23 Army (disability)
STOUT, Isaac, Ro-201-4(2); Pvt B Co 6th TN Inf; 25 Feb 62 to 30 Mar 65; Kingston PO
STOUT, Jacob N., Jo-151-2; Pvt M Co 13th TN Cav; 2 Feb 64 to 5 Sep 65; Bakers Gap PO; diarrhoia, rheumatism
STOUT, James M., D-45-5; Leovel St, Nashville PO
STOUT, James R., Ct-35-3; PVt F Co 3rd NC Inf; __ to __; Elk Mills PO; in US Army (disability); discharge not at home, dates not known
STOUT, John B., Ct-41-2; Pvt K Co 26th TN Inf; 61 to 65; Keensburgh PO; rhumatism and hart trouble; CONF
STOUT, Lawson E., Jo-151-2; Pvt F Co 13th TN Cav; 22 Sep 63 to 5 Sep 65; Bakers Gap PO; rheumatism-bronchitis
STOUT, Martha J. (see Phillips, John F.)
STOUT, Mary P., Sh-162-2; widow; Ramsey PO
STOUT, Wiley, D-51-2; Nellie A. widow of; Sgt I Co 15th TN C Inf; Nashville PO
STOUT, William, Pu-147-1; Pvt B Co 8th TN Mtd Inf; 1-15-65 to 8-17-65; Gabatha PO (Jackson Co.)
STOVALL, Ann, D-77-3; Foster St, Nashville PO
STOVALL, Daniel, G-56-1; Pvt B Co 4th US Col; 4-3-64 to 7-5-__ (1 yr 3 mos 2 days); Trenton PO
STOVALL, George A., Sh-176-1; 19 Linden St, Memphis PO
STOVEALL, S. G., Gi-122-8; Pvt H Co 43rd TN Inf; 61 to 65; Prospect Sta. PO; shot in hip, walked on crutches 3 yrs; CONF
STOVER, Abraham I., R-106-1; Pvt I Co 34th OH; 8-14-62 to 6-12-65; 5th Civil Dist
STOVER, George, We-230-2; Pvt F Co 18th KY Inf; Jan 15 63 to 15 Feb 65; PO omitted
STOVER, Jerry E., Br-13-1; Pvt G Co 5th TN Inf; 62 to 65; McDonalds PO; contracted heart disease
STOVER, John, H-58-3; Pvt G Co 5th TN Inf; 2-27-62 to 5-15-65; Sale Creek PO; back hurt by bursting shell
STOVER, Nelson, Ct-40-4; Pvt 13th TN Cav; Elizabethton PO
STOW, Cas., Hm-103-3; Carline widow of; Pvt A Co 40th Inf; 4 May 65 to 24 Apr 66; Morristown PO

STOW, William R., K-172-1; Pvt H Co 49th E TN? Mtd Inf; 9 Aug 62 to Feb 65; Knoxville PO
STOWE, B. M., We-220-1; Pvt I Co 6th TN Cav; Jun 5, 62 to __; Catham PO; dysease of liver, rheumatism; now not able to work
STOWE, Isaac C., We-220-2; Pvt A Co 1st TN Inf; Jan 15, 62 to __; PO omitted; furlowed and remained at home
STRADER, Godfrey D., K-166-2; Knoxville PO; man from home, women could not tell what regiment
STRADER, James F., A-5-4; Pvt F Co 7th TN Inf; 11-18-64 to 7-27-65; Clinton PO
STRAIN, Charles T., O-138-2; Pvt G Co 18th TN Cav; 1 Apr 63 to 1 Aug 64; Elbridge PO; CONF
STRALEY, Godlet W., Dy-25-9(1); Pvt; Newbern PO; dates of enlistment not know at present
STRANGE, John R., Cl-48-3; Orderly Sgt & Lt D Co 51st VA Inf; 6-28-61 to 4-5-65; Pleasant PO
STRANGE, John W., K-166-2; Pvt C Co 8th TN Cav; 2 Oct 63 to 11 Sep 65; Knoxville PO
STRANGE, Thomas, K-160-3; Nancy widow of; Pvt D Co 3rd TN; Mar 62 to Mar 65; Knoxville PO
STRANGE, William H., Co-69-3; Pvt C Co 8th TN Cav; 1 Jan 62 to 15 Apr 65; Rankin PO
STRANY, Rev. David, Li-161-2; Sgt B Co 100th PA Inf; 14 Aug 62 to 31 May 65; Lincoln PO; right hip shot
STRATMAN, Anthony H., Sh-191-7(3); Pvt 6th TN Cav; Memphis PO
STRATTON, Albert, D-87-1; Lucresus widow of; Pvt TN; Nashville PO
STRATTON, Benj. H., Mn-120-1; Sailor; PO omitted
STRATTON, John, Sh-184-1; Sol US; 90 Alabama, Memphis PO
STRATTON, John M., He-66-1; Pvt M Co 7th TN Cav; Jul 6 63 to 30 Jun 65; Lexington PO
STRATTON, Peter L., Mu-196-1; Pvt A Co 14th Reg; Aug 62 to 63 to 66; Columbia PO; eye shot out (right eye)
STRATTON, Richard R., Mo-131-1; Pvt K Co 12th TN Cav; 3-5-64 to 10-8-65; Corringer PO
STRATTON, Sidney E., Mo-130-1; Cpl K Co 9th MO Cav; 11-15-62 to 7-5-65; Acorn PO
STRATTON, Watking, Mu-198-1; 10th Dist
STRAYHORN, Jiessie L., Sh-145-3; 2nd Cpl D Co 3rd US Inf; 10 Oct 64 to 11 Dec 65; Kerrville PO; Capt Rehwinkle 1st Lt Wm. Taylor
STRAYHORN, Phillip, Mu-205-1; Pvt E Co 11th MS Inf; 63 to May 65; Williamsport PO; middle finger of right hand wounded
STREATER, Thomas, H-59-1; Pvt TN Inf; 10-64 to 6-65; Chattanooga PO
STREET, David R., Di-30-2; Pvt 10th TN Art?; 9-62 to 12-64; Dickson PO; CONF
STREET, James H., Pu-144-2; Pvt 1st KY; 9-20-61 to __; Double Springs PO
STREET, Lucinda, Cf-38-1; widow; 10th Civil Dist
STREET, Robert F., St-160-2; Pvt E Co 11th TN Cav; __ to May 5, 65 (2 yrs); Big Rock PO; wounded in leg; difficulty in walking; CONF
STREET, Samel, Ct-37-2; Pvt D Co 8th TN Cav; 6-63 to deserted 65; Ripshin PO; bruised by horse kick
STREET, Thomas, U-245-2; Mary formerly widow of; Cpl B Co 13th TN Cav; 11 May 64 to Apr 65; Limestone Cove PO; smallpox, died in April 1864 (sic)
STREET, William, H-68-2; Pvt F Co 78th PA Inf; 9-10-61 to 11-4-64; Chattanooga PO; chronic dysentery
STREETER, Henry, B-3-2; Cpl C Co 17th Regt Col Inf; 1-23-63 to 4-25-66; Wartrace PO
STRIBS, Isaac, F-44-2; Sinnie widow of; Pvt; PO omitted
STRICKLAND, Joseph, Ro-210-11; Pvt E Co 1st TN Inf; 9 Aug 61 to 17 Sep 64; Rockwood PO
STRICKLAND, William, Wa-268-2; Johnson City PO; rheumatism
STRICKLIN, Samuel H., Wy-177-2; Pvt B Co 2nd TN Mtd Inf; 10-15-63 to 10-17-64; Moon PO; overheat
STRICTLIN, Peter O., He-67-3; Pvt H Co 6th TN Cav; Sep 18, 62 to 26 Jul 65; Scotts Hill PO; chronic diabetus 26 yrs
STRINGER, Jordan, Ro-204-3; Elizabeth widow of; Elverton PO
STROCK, Jacob, P-150-1; Pvt I Co 26th OH Inf; Jul 23, 61 to Sep 65; Dist 1
STROE, Jessie, Ov-135-2; Cpl K Co 4th TN Mtd Inf; 9-1-64 to 8-25-65; Monroe PO
STRONG, Israel, T-212-1; "found while examing work" no address
STRONG, Isral, T-212-1; Col; alias Williams, Ben; Pvt C Co 61st US Inf; no dates; Atoka PO
STRONG, John, A-4-1; Sgt A Co 14th KY Mtd Cav; 12-24-63 to 7-20-65; Coal Creek PO; rheumatism and ruptured
STRONG, William, Cy-27-4(2); Pvt B Co 9th KY Inf; 9-61 to 3-63; Spivey PO
STRONG, William D., Ge-91-1; Pvt H Co 8th TN Inf; Jul 23 63 to Jun 65; Greeneville PO; diarhea resulting diseas rectum, rheumatism
STROSIER, George, L-105-1; Pvt I Co 136th GA Inf; Jul 63 to Dec 66; Halls PO; no ailments, discharg lost
STROUD, Anderson, Li-158-1; PVt F Co 1st TN; May 62 to Jan 63; Roperton PO; loss of eye sight, nearly blind, no pension
STROUD, James H., Ge-86-2; Pvt C Co 3rd TN Cav; 3 Dec 62 to 10 Jun 65; Thula PO; asthma, in prison six mos
STROUD, James S., Ge-88-2; Pvt C Co 3rd TN Cav; 2 Dec 62 to 19 Jun 65; Thula PO; heart & enlargement of left leg
STUARD, William, Hw-132-1; Sally Logan formerly widow of; Pvt TN; 27 Jan 63 to died 63 (9 Apr?); Persia PO; died from heart disease at Vicksburg, MS
STUART, Alexander M., Wa-274-3; Pvt I Co 8th TN Cav; 5 Sep 63 to 13 Jun 65; Jonesboro PO; feet frost bitten
STUART, Charles K., Po-152-1; 1st Lt C Co 5th TN Mtd Inf; 9-23-64 to 7-16-65; Ducktown PO; hepitiatus and bronchitis
STUART, Iley, Po-152-1; Margret A. widow of; Pvt 11th TN Cav; 64 to __; Ducktown PO; killed while at home on furlough
STUART, Jacob, Mc-117-2; Tenny widow of; Pvt H Co 7th TN Mtd Inf; 13th Civil Dist
STUART, James J., Po-152-3(1); Pvt; Ducktown PO; small pox and measles
STUART, Rufus, Sm-166-1; Pvt E Co 5th TN Inf; 11-22-64 to 4-25-65; Carthage PO; wounded in leg; badly from a gun shot
STUART, William S., We-223-2; Pvt C Co TN Inf; 62 to 62 (4 mos); Palmersville PO
STUBBLEFIELD, Allex, Ha-114-3; Pvt H Co 1st TN Cav; 25 May 62 to 2 Jun 63; Sneedville PO
STUBBLEFIELD, Dallis, Ho-95-1; Pvt B Co 7th TN Inf; Feb 1 63 to Aug 30 65; McKinnon PO
STUBBLEFIELD, George, W-192-1; Pvt A Co; 6-17-63 to 65; Irving College PO
STUBBLEFIELD, John, Ha-113-2; Malissa widow of; Pvt B Co 1st TN Cav; 10 Apr 62 to __; died in service; Sneedville PO
STUBBLEFIELD, P. B., We-221-2; Mrs. Sina C. widow; Lt G Co 9th TN Inf; 62 to 65; Martin PO; CONF
STUBLEFIELD, Nancie (see Crider, Labern)
STUBLEFIELD, Samuel, D-92-1; Sgt D Co 13th US Col Inf; 17 Jul 64 to 25 Apr 66; Nashville PO
STUBLETON, Nelson, Gr-79-3; Sarah A. widow of; Lt 1st TN; __ to Oct 64; Ball Point PO; killed
STUERT, James, Co-66-1; Pvt C Co 26th TN Inf; 16 Oct 62 to 1 Apr 64; Bison PO; CONF
STUFFLESTREET, George, Jo-151-1; alias Fritts; Pvt F Co 13th TN Cav; 22 Sep 63 to 5 Sep 65; Bakers Gap PO; weak back--result of mumps
STUFFLESTREET, John M., Ct-35-2; Viney widow of; Pvt J Co 13th TN Cav; __ to 9-5-65; Fish Spring PO; in US Army (disability); discharge not seen, do not know the date of enrollment
STULL, Horatio, Br-9-2; Pvt A Co 43rd OH Inf; 9-23-64 to 6-4-65; Cleveland PO
STULTS, Lonzo D., Mu-205-1; Pvt F Co 40th OH Inf; Apr 61 to May 65; Water Valley PO; detached locomitive engineer
STULTZ, Chas., H-68-2; Sallie Howard formerly widow of; Pvt; Chattanooga PO
STUMP, Christian H., Se-223-5(1); Pvt K Co 17th IN Inf; 3 Apr 61 to 14 Apr 65; Sevierville PO
STURART, George G. (see Bailey, Henry F.)

STURART, George G., Wa-261-2; on same line with Bailey, Henry F.; Pvt G Co 63rd TN Inf; 63 to 30 Jul 65; Nola Chuckey PO; this data must belong to one of the two men; CONF
STURDIVANT, Henry M., Dy-25-1; Newbern PO; CONF
STURDIVANT, Thomas J., Ma-116-1; Pvt C Co 6th TN Cav; 25 Jun 63 to 29 Jul 65; Mercer PO
STURDIVANT, Herburt A., D-82-1; Martha A. widow of; Pvt E Co 1st TN Inf; May 1 62 to 65; Hermitage PO
STURGES, Columbus L., Ro-201-3(1); Pvt I Co 1st TN Inf; 9 Aug 61 to 22 Sep 65; Kingston PO
STURT, Arcebel A., K-165-2; Pvt B Co 8th TN Cav; 12 May 63 to 11 Aug? 65; 281 Asylum St, Knoxville PO
STYNES?, George N., C-33-5; Cpl C Co 2nd NC; 9-26-63 to 8-10-65; Newcomb PO; reumatism on march to NC
STYPS?, Richard, K-183-2; Pvt Battery; Mayo PO; CONF
SUDARDS, Isaac, Co-63-3; Pvt I Co 1st OH Hvy Inf; 1 yr; Newport PO; rheumatism, no discharge, was in prison
SUDDATH, Jackson, Ro-211-3; Pvt H Co 1st US Inf; 4 Jun 64 to 31 Mar 66; Kingston PO; weak eyes from measles
SUDDATH, John, Ro-211-4; Anne widow of; Pvt H Co 1st US Cav; 28 May 64 to 31 Mar 66; Kingston PO; lingering diarrhea
SUESS, John, Ct-40-3; Pvt A Co 41st NY Inf; Pvt C Co 112th NY Inf; Pvt K Co 115th NY Inf; 5-61 to 8-30-65; defective eyesight & hemeroids; Elizabethton PO
SUFFERAGE, Charles, C1-58-2; Nancy widdow of; Pvt 6th TN Inf; Old Town PO; killed in battle, Marietta GA; can't recolect dates
SUGG, James B., Rb-221-2; Mary C. widow of; Qtr Master 60th TN; May 1 61 to May 1 65; Adams Station PO; CONF
SUGG, John D., Di-30-2; Sgt D Co 49th TN Inf; 12-61 to 7-27-63; Dickson PO; CONF
SUGGS, John, Wy-171-1; Sgt H Co 2nd TN Mtd Inf; 1-16-64 to 1-21-65; Waynesboro PO
SUGGS, Prince, Gi-127-2; Pvt D Co 12th Reg US; Sep 27 64 to 16 Jan 66; Pulaski PO
SUGGS, Washington, Gi-127-2; PVt D Co 14th TN Col Inf; Oct 63 to ___; Pulaski PO; feet frost bitten, was captured Dec 1864
SULAVAN, Jane (see Reeves, Ben)
SULFRAGE, William L., Un-254-2; Pvt F Co 8th TN Inf; 15 Jul 63 to 24 Jul 65; Paulett PO
SULFRIDGE, Andrew, C1-51-1; Margrett widow of; Pvt B Co 1st TN US Lt Art; 1-1-63 to 7-20-65; Ritchie PO
SULFRIDGE, Clinton, C1-51-2; US Soldier; 6th Civil Dist
SULIVAN, John L., Sm-172-1; Sgt D Co 136th IL Inf; 4-5-62 to 12-1-64; Buffalo Valley PO
SULIVAN, W. H., Wl-308-2; Pvt G Co 7th TN; May 1 61 to May 1 63; Rural Hill PO; captured
SULLAVAN, James, D-92-2; Nashville PO
SULLAVAN, James, D-92-2; US Sol; Davidson Co.
SULLINS, Alexander, Mr-99-2; Pvt; Jasper PO; discharge lost
SULLINS, Samuel, Ca-25-3; Pvt G Co 1st TN Mtd Inf; 8-24-64 to 7-22-65; Gassoway PO; contracted rheumatism
SULLIVAN, James, Hi-88-1; Cpl G Co 12th TN Col; 2-15-64 to 10-65; Pinewood PO
SULLIVAN, James, Cy-29-1; PVt F Co 2nd KY Cav; 7-8-61 to 10-12-64; Willow Grove PO; defective eye sight 3 yrs
SULLIVAN, James A., G-71-2; Pvt G Co 5th TN Cav; 5 Apr 61 to 5 Apr 63; Rutherford PO; CONF
SULLIVAN, James B., We-221-2; Pvt TN Inf; Martin PO; constitution broken; CONF
SULLIVAN, John, H-60-4; Pvt A Co 10th OH Inf; 5-14-61 to 2-65; Chattanooga PO; gunshot wound left leg
SULLIVAN, John, Sh-191-7(3); Pvt A Co 5th OH Inf; 5-61 to 6-20-64; 1101 W. Sixth St, Cincinnati OH; diarohea
SULLIVAN, John H., Sq-164-5(1); Lt TN Inf; 9-28-61 to ___; Brock PO
SULLIVAN, Patrick, K-161-3; Knoxville PO; shot in leg
SULLIVAN, William, St-164-2; Seaman, NanKee?; 62 to 65; Stribling PO; rheumatism
SULLIVAN, William M., Wl-299-2; 15th Civil Dist
SULTAN, James, B-6-1; Pvt I Co 5th Regt US Col Inf; Fall Creek PO; gun shott wound
SUMACE, James M., J-83-1; Pvt C Co 37th KY; 6-20-63 to 9-18?-65; Flynns Lick PO
SUMACE, Mike, J-83-1; Pvt A Co 1st TN; 12-63 to 1-65; Flynns Lick PO
SUMMERS, Jacob W., H-53-4; Cpl I Co 102nd OH Inf; Chattanooga PO
SUMMERS, James M., We-230-4; Pvt E Co 22nd TN Reg; Apr 1 61 to 1 May 63; McKinzie PO; CONF
SUMMERS, Josire, Hw-121-1; Pvt K Co 29th TN Inf; 1 Jun 62 to 1 May 65; Van Hill PO; CONF
SUMMERS, Lorenzo, C-34-3; Pvt; Buckeye PO; 2nd vist, absent from home
SUMMERS, Martin, Sh-189-2; Musician Pvt 59th US Col Inf; Alley off Carolina St, Memphis PO
SUMMERS, Nathaniel, Gr-76-1; Pvt C Co 9th TN Cav; 16 Sep 63 to 15 Sep 65; Tampico PO; rheumatism
SUMMERS, Walter, B-2-1; Syrena widow of; Fairfield PO; CONF
SUMMERS, William, Un-255-2; Pvt I Co 7th TN; 28 Dec 64 to 28 Ju 65; PO omitted
SUMNER, Watson, D-69-2; US Sol; no record of service; Nashville PO
SUMPTER, Abner, Je-136-2; Pvt I Co 3rd TN Cav; Dec 63 to ___; PO omitted
SUNONS, John, Sh-187-1(5); Sol; Memphis PO
SURBER, Alfred, Ha-115-1; Mary widow of; Pvt A Co 63rd TN Inf; Apr 62 to ___; Alanthers Hill PO; died of pleurisy while on duty; CONF
SURRATT, Abe, Sh-145-4; Judee Harris widow of; Pvt H Co 55th US Col Inf; Aug 63 to Feb 65; Millington PO; said to be killed on duty
SURTIN, Calvin, Co-65-1; Pvt C Co 3rd TN Cav; no dates (discharge lost); Wilton Springs PO; discharge burned in house
SUTHERLAND, Jahugh, Wi-270-2; Williamson Co.; not give exact time of service
SUTHERLAND, James K., Hw-133-3; Pvt 22nd VA Inf; 1 Dec 64 to 1 Apr 65; Burem's Store PO; CONF
SUTHERLAND, Joe Anna, O-141-2; Landsman, Naval Service; Union City PO; dates unknown
SUTLER, George (see George Madison)
SUTTLE, Anderson, Gi-128-2; Pvt H Co 44th GA Inf; 63 to 65; Pulaski PO
SUTTLE, Henry F., Sn-260-6; Pvt B Co 8th KY Mtd Inf; 8-64 to 4-18-65; A.B.C. PO; CONF
SUTTLE, Marten, Un-258-3; Pvt M Co 9th TN Cav; 15 Jan 64 to 15 Sep 65; Longhollow PO
SUTTLES, Phillip S., R-162-3; Pvt E Co 5th TN Inf; Dayton PO
SUTTON, Alford, B-5-1; Cpl M Co 5th TN Cav; 9-30-63 to 8-14-65; Fosterville PO
SUTTON, Buck, H-49-1; Pvt A Co 6th TN Mtd Inf; 1864 to 1865; Falling Water PO
SUTTON, Carter, Co-68-2; Pvt E Co 9th TN Cav; 65 to 65; Sutton PO; lungs & back effected
SUTTON, Dallas, Gi-125-2; Pvt A Co 44th US Col Inf; 63 to 64; Wales PO
SUTTON, Francis, Sh-198-1; Cpl D Co US Col Inf; June or July 1864 to May 66; Memphis PO; had his discharge, but gave it to a claim agent
SUTTON, Henry H., C-28-1; Capt H Co 34th KY Inf; 10-3-61 to 7-2-65; Fincastle PO; hepatitis & Laryngitis
SUTTON, James M., Co-68-3; Cpl E Co 1st TN Bat; 63 to 65; Sutton PO
SUTTON, James W., Pu-146-1; Cpl L Co 6th TN Cav W(hite?); 2-11-64 to 8-14-65; Buffalo Valley PO; rheumatism
SUTTON, John B., Lo-191-2; Pvt D Co 3rd TN Mtd Inf; 25 Jul 64 to 30 Nov 64; Morganton PO
SUTTON, John M., C1-50-1; Pvt A Co 27th TN Inf; 5-10-62 to 12-24-63; Hoot PO; CONF?
SUTTON, Joseph, Wl-299-2; 15th Civil Dist.
SUTTON, Lawson, Se-230-3; Mary widow of; Pvt; Richison's Cove PO
SUTTON, Norbourn E., K-156-1; 1st Lt E Co 11th TX Cav; 10 May 61 to 26 Apr 65; 48 Ellinet, Knoxville PO; CONF
SUTTON, Roe, Fr-112-2; Pvt 15th MI Inf; 4-65 to ?; Tullahoma PO; never received a discharge
SWABE, Charley, Se-228-1(2); Pvt Sevierville PO; CONF

SWAFFORD, Henry, H-59-1; Pvt TN Inf; 1864 to 1865 (9 mos); Chattanooga PO
SWAFFORD, Henry Harrison, H-58-6; Pvt A Co 39th IN Inf; Retro PO; discharge misplaced
SWAFFORD, Samuel, Bl-2-3; 1st Lt D Co 7th TN Mtd Inf; 10-10-64 to 8-1-65; Orme's Store PO; hearing affected in left ear
SWAFFORD, William B., B1-2-2(1); Pvt D Co 7th TN Mtd Inf; 10-9-64 to 8-11-65; Orme's Store PO
SWAGERD, Edney, Rb-226-1; widow; District 12
SWAGERTY, Claburn N., Bo-19-1; Pvt C Co 6th TN Inf; 4-21-62 to 1865 (3 yrs 3 mo); Rockford PO; disease of lungs
SWAGERTY, George, K-17-2; Pvt E Co 1st US Art; 17 Apr 64 to 31 Mar 66; Knoxville PO; chronic diarreah 25 yrs; hearing badly injured
SWAGERTY, Harrison, Co-63-2; Pvt I Co 40th NC Inf; Apr 64 to Apr 65 (1 yr); Newport PO; rheumatism
SWAGERTY, Henry, Co-63-2; Pvt; Newport PO
SWAGERTY, J. M., Bo-19-3; Pvt C Co 6th TN Inf; 4-18-62 to 4-18-65; Rockford PO
SWAGERTY, Soney, Co-63-3; Teamster; 14th TN Cav; 1863 to 1865 (2 yr 5 mos); Newport PO
SWAGERTY, William S., Se-227-2; Mary A. widow of; Pvt B Co 3rd TN Cav; Oct 62 to Jun 65; Cynthiana, Jefferson Co. PO
SWAGGERTY, James M., Se-227-2; US Sol; 9th Dist.
SWAGGERTY, John, Mc-114-4; Charlottie widow of; Pvt D Co 1st TN Inf; 12-62 to 7-4-65; Santford PO; small pox
SWAGGERTY, Roley?, K-182-3; Sarah J. Roberts widow of; Pvt L Co 9th TN Vol Cav; 63 to 65; Gap Creek PO
SWAGGERTY, Willis, K-182-3; Pvt E Co 3rd TN Vol Cav; Feb 63 to Aug 65; Gapcreek PO; sore eyes
SWAIN, Elijah, La-113-2; Pvt I Co 7th OH Inf; 5 Dec 61 to 15 Jan 65; Lawrenceburgh PO
SWAIN, Harriet, D-43-2; Sol widow; Vine St., Nashville PO
SWAIN, Joseph J., Mn-122-1; Pvt A Co 6th TN Cav; 3-1-64 to 7-26-65; Bethel Springs PO; spinal iritation; disch. by GO no. 12
SWALLOWS, Dee, Ov-139-1; Pvt B Co 25th TN Inf; 1-14-65 to 1865; Lovejoy PO
SWALLOWS, Isaac R., J-79-1; Elisebeth widow of; 3rd Sgt G Co 93rd IN inf; 8-28-62 to 8-10-65; Whitleyville PO
SWALLOWS, James R., Pu-143-1; Cpl I Co 1st TN Inf; 12-4-64 to 7-29-65; Jeremiah PO; thigh broken
SWAMNER, Amon P., K-178-2; Sgt G Co 8th TN Cav; 3 Jul 63 to 11 Sep 65; Hardin Valley PO
SWAN, Robert C., Cu-17-3; 1st Lt D Co 2nd TN Inf; 9-1-61 to 12-26-61; Grassy Cove PO; catarrh lungs & bowel trouble & sciatica; resigned on account of disability
SWAN, Samuel O., Juda A. widow of; Pu-144-2; Pvt G Co 6th TN Mtd Inf; 3-26-65 to 6-30-65; Bloomington PO
SWAN, William, Sh-171-1; Pvt E Co 42nd OH Vol; 1861 to 1863; Memphis PO
SWANER, Jacob, H-50-4; Pvt D Co 6th R TN Mtd Inf; 8-16-64 to 6-30-65; Soddy PO; reumatism
SWANEY, George W., Lo-191-3; Pvt M Co 13th TN Cav; May 64 to __; Trigonia PO
SWANEY, Isaac M., Lo-191-3; Sgt K Co 1st TN Cav; 12 Jul 62 to 5 Jun 65; Trigonia PO; loss of hearing, right ear caused by concussion of bomb
SWANEY, L. C., Bo-11-7; Pvt C Co 3rd TN Mtd Inf; 7-26-64 to 11-30-64; Houk PO; bunions on feet; now in very poor circumstances
SWANGER, George W., Ct-38-2; Pvt I Co 6th US Vol Inf; Okolona PO; rheumatism & resulting disease of heart, discharge lost
SWANN, Huston, H-73-3; Pvt; Chattanooga PO; injury of left eye, now blind in left eye
SWANN, Isaac, H-73-3; Malinda widow of; Pvt; Chattanooga PO
SWANNEE, J. R., K-183-3; Pvt A Co 13th TN Cav; Lyonton PO
SWANSON, Ben, Wi-274-1; PVt F Co 12th TN Inf; Southall PO; dont know dates

SWANSON, Warren, D-60-2; 1111 Cedor St, Nashville PO; Colored
SWARRINGER, John W., Lk-112-1; Pvt H Co 46th; 61 to 65; Tiptonville PO; CONF
SWARTZ, ____, H-70-3(1); Chattanooga PO; tried to get at hime but failed; couldn't find anyone to tell me his name
SWATZEL, Samuel, Co-61-3(1); Ord Lay? K Co 8th TN Inf; 1 Jul 63 to 30 Jun 65; Givens PO; effects of fever & diarhea
SWATZEL, Thomas, Co-61-3(1); Pvt A Co 3rd TN M Inf; Aug 63 to __; Givens PO
SWAFORD, Thomas, R-182-3; Pvt K Co 5th TN Inf; 8-63 to __: Dayton PO
SWEAT, George, Bl-2-2(1); Pvt A Co 13th TN Cav; 4-63 to 65; Orme's Store PO; hearing lost
SWEAT, John M., L-101-1; Pvt C Co 1st AL Cav; Mar 18 63 to 20 Oct 65; Henning PO; hernia r side chronic neurilgia & rheumatism
SWEENEY, Frank G., D-74-1; Prentice Boy Lay Ship Hartford; 63 to May 65; 229 Shelby Ave, Nashville PO
SWEENEY, W. G., Wl-20803; 2nd Lt D Co 30th TN; Nov 1 61 to May 65; Hermitage PO; captured; CONF
SWEET, Frank P., Wa-268-3; Johnson City PO
SWEET, Martha, Sh-178-3; widow US; 352 Beall, Memphis PO
SWEET, Samuel, H-54-1; Pvt A Co 39th OH Inf; 2-1-63 to 7-22-65; Sherman Heights PO
SWEETLAND, Ovis B., La-116-1; Pvt G Co 6th MI Inf; Aug 20 61 to 20 Aug 65; Henryville PO
SWICK, Henry F., Fr-112-1; Pvt G Co 18th US Inf; Feb 12 62 to 12 Feb 65; Tullahoma PO; shot through right thigh; contracted chronic diarrhea
SWIFT, Edwin E., M. D., Lk-112-1; Pvt A Co 114th IL Inf; 30 Aug 64 to 14 Jul 65; Tiptonville PO; discharge lost; dont recolect as to dates
SWIFT, John, Ru-238-1; Pvt D Co 111th USC Inf; 1 Jan 64 to 30 Apr 66; Murfreesboro PO
SWIFT, John, F-44-2; Pvt D Co 59th; 63 to 65; PO omitted
SWIFT, Randol, Sh-160-2; Pvt TN Inf; 61 to 62; Memphis PO; rheumatism from exposure
SWIFT, Toney, Gi-122-7; Pvt D Co 111th TN Inf; Dec 63 to Oct 65; Prospect Sta. PO; in prison Mobile, AL
SWILLEA?, Howell, Gi-129-2; Cpl I Co 110th TN Inf; 30 Dec 63 to 6 Feb 66; Elkton PO
SWINDLE, Antony N., M-103-5; Pvt H Co 5th KY Cav; 12-4-61 to 5-3-65; Lafayette PO
SWINDLE, Jesse H., M-103-5; Mary widow of; Pvt H Co 5th KY Cav; Lafayette PO
SWINDLE, John J., Sm-166-1; Pvt H Co 5th KY Cav; 11-61 to 7-65; Carthage PO; leg & breast badly hurt from horse falling
SWINEY, John, Ja-87-2; Pvt I Co 1st TN Cav; Apison PO; gunshot piles & rheumatism, discharge away from home
SWINGER, Henry H., Gi-130-1; Pvt A Co 14th TN Col Inf; 62 to 65; Bradshaw PO
SWINNA, Joel, Mo-120-4(2); Lydia widow of; Pvt B Co 5th TN Mtd Inf; 2-63 to __; Sweetwater PO; died in service
SWINNEA, James H., Hd-53-1; Seaman Tyler; 9 Feb 62 to 13 Feb 65; Sibley PO
SWINNEY, Peter, T-216-1; Pvt A Co 32nd MS Inf; Corona PO; CONF
SWINNEY, William, Hd-56-1; Pvt E Co 17th IL Cav; 26 Dec 63 to 19 Dec 64; Coffee Ledg PO; loss of arm from gun shot
SWINNY, George, Rb-223-3(5); 9th Dist
SWINSON, Andrew, B1-3-3; Pvt K Co 5th TN Inf; 10-18-62 to 6-30-65; Billingsly PO; rheumatism
SWINSON, James, B1-3-3; Pvt F Co 5th TN Inf; 10-14-62 to 7-31-63; Billingsly PO; bowell trouble
SWOFFORD, Aaron P., Br-13-2; Mary A. Howell formerly widow of; Sgt E Co 4th TN Cav; 62 to __; Cleveland PO
SWOFFORD, GEo. W., H-49-3; Pvt F Co 4th TN Cav; 62 to 7-12-65; Sherman Heights PO; effect of relapse of measles

SWOFFORD, John, Bl-3-3; Pvt E Co 6th TN Inf; 9-22-64 to 7-13-65; Billingsly PO; sight affected
SWOFFORD, John, Bl-3-1; Pvt I Co __ TN Cav; 10-62 to 3-63; Babtis PO; CONF
SWOFORD, Frank, Col, Me-88-3; Pvt G Co; Brittsville PO
SWOPE, W. W., Ro-210-2; Pvt; Rockwood PO
SYKES, Columbus, Gi-127-1; Pulaski PO
SYKES, William, Sh-157-5; Cpl M Co 3rd USC; 63 to 66; Memphis PO
SYLVESTESTER, Charls W., La-114-1; Pvt H Co 9th MI Inf; Sep 30 64 to 20 Jun 65; Ethridge PO
TAB, Elisha, Cr-16-1; Pvt I Co 7th TN Cav; Jan 6 65 to 20 Aug 65; Huntingdon PO
TAB?, Jessie M., Ca-16-1; 1st Cpl I Co 7th TN Cav; Jan 6 65 to 2 Jul 65; Huntingdon PO; back hurt by horse
TABER, Harrison, D-45-3; Pvt D Co 13th OH Inf; 4-21-61 to 7-21-61; Pvt H Co 26th OH Inf; 7-21-61 to 1-20-64; Pvt H Co 26th OH Inf; 1-20-65 to 11-1-65; Nashville PO
TABLER, Ephrin, K-174-3(2); Pvt K Co 3rd TN Inf; 10 Feb 62 to 23 Feb 65; Graveston PO; gun shout in left side
TABOR, Bluford A., Ru-245-1; Pvt D Co 20th KY Inf; 10-7-61 to 8-4-63; Halls Hill PO; rheumatism & heart disease
TACKET, Thomas, Hd-48-1; Seaman Tyler; Feb 9 62 to Jan 26 63; Savannah PO
TAGGART, Charles, H-51-3; Pvt D Co 2nd IN Cav; 7-16-62 to 7-21-65; Hill City PO
TAILOR, Granville, Cr-13-2; Pvt G Co 15th TN Inf; Jan 63 to Apr 65; Milan PO (Gibson Co.); yes; dont know exact dates of enlistment or discharge
TALBOT, Frank, T-218-1; Pvt A Co 12th TN Inf; 16 Jul 64 to Feb 66; Tabernacle PO
TALBOT, John B., D-97-1; Lt H Co 7th TN; May 20, 61 to 65; Nashville PO; CONF
TALBOTT, Paul, Col, Hm-104-1; Pvt C Co 27th OH Inf; 3 Feb 64 to 25 Sep 65; Talbotts PO (Jefferson Co.)
TALENT, Benjamin, K-154-4; Margarett A. widow of; Pvt 13th TN Cav; Knoxville PO
TALENT, Cyrus H., Mo-131-1; 20th Civil Dist
TALENT, Lemeul, Cl-53-1; Cpl F Co 2nd TN Cav; 7-2-62 to 7-1-65; Lone Mountain PO; lung disease
TALIAFERRO, Archie, Hy-81-2; 7th Civil Dist
TALIAFERRO, Elbeck H., D-72-5; Mus A Co 9th VA Cav; Apr 61 to Sep 63; Nashville PO; imprisoned at White Oak 3 weeks; CONF
TALIAFERRO, Harden, Ja-86-2; Martha widow of; Pvt IN Bat; 3-64 to __ (1 yr); Snowhill PO; died Nashville TN
TALIAFERRO, James E., G-71-2; Pvt D Co 13th TN Cav; 12 May 61 to 21 Aug 65; Edmonds PO
TALIAFORE, William, Hy-79-1; Pvt; Civil Dist No 6
TALL, James, Hd-53-2; Pvt G Co 25th US Col TN Inf; 14 Feb 64 to Dec 65; Sibley PO
TALLANT, Thomas A., Pu-144-4; Pvt B Co 1st TN Mtd Inf; 2-19-64 to 4-65; Pine Fork PO; back hurt
TALLENT, Japten?, Br-10-2; 1st Cpl B Co 5th TN Mtd Inf; 8-13-64 to 7-19-65; Cleveland PO
TALLENT, John, Mc-110-2(1); Talitha Large widow of; Pvt; Mt. Vera PO; had no record
TALLENT, Jonathan, R-163-2; Pvt I Co 7th TN Mtd Inf; 11-25-64 to 7-14-65; Graysville PO; served as Cpl about ½ time
TALLENT, Lemuel, Mo-120-3(1); Pvt; Madisonville PO; his wife could not answer these questions
TALLENT, Louis, H-53-6; Nancy widow of; Pvt D Co 4th TN Cav; 6-62 to 6-65; Ridgedale PO; chronic diarrhoea
TALLENT, William J., Pu-146-3; Pvt B Co 1st Mtd Inf Vol; 1-14-64 to 4-14-66; Boma PO
TALLEY, Bradley W., Co-69-6; Ordley I Co 62nd TN Inf; 8 Apr 62 to 8 May 65; Driskill PO; non; CONF
TALLEY, Carter B., Co-69-1; Pvt E Co 8th TN; 1 Mar 63 to 16 Jun 65; Driskill PO; catarrh & rheumaties; pensioner
TALLEY, Crawford H., Cf-40-2; Matilda widow of; Pvt A Co 10th TN Cav; 12 Aug 63 to 13 May 65; Tullahoma PO
TALLEY, Dudley H., Br-11-5; Sgt B Co 1st TN Lt Art; 10-18-62 to 7-20-65; Cleveland PO; chronic rheumatism 25 yrs

TALLEY, Foster D., Sh-159-1; Memphis PO; CONF
TALLEY, George T. H., Co-69-1; Pvt C Co 8th TN Cav; 5 Ma 63 to 10 Jun 65; Driskill PO; spinal of the back & kindneys
TALLEY, James, Sm-172-3(1); Pvt B Co 5th TN Cav; 8-14-62 to 6-28-65; Hickman PO
TALLEY, Joel A., Ja-85-1; Sarah E. widow of; Pvt G Co 5th TN Inf; 3-2-62 to __; Birchwood PO; died before discharged
TALLEY, John, Hw-118-2; Pvt A Co; St. Clair PO; rupture
TALLEY, Samuel A., Gr-75-1; Rhoda widow of; Pvt K & H Co 4th TN Inf; 6 Feb 64 to 2 Aug 65; Tampico PO; shot through heel
TALLEY, William B., Co-69-6(1); Pvt F Co 4th TN Inf; 23 Jan 65 to 2 Aug 65; Driskill PO; measels setled on longs; a pensioner
TALLING, Johnathan, Lo-195-3(1); Mary A. widow of; Pvt H Co 5th TN Inf; Loudon PO; dates not remembered
TALLITT, William W., Cr-20-1; Sarah S. widow of; Pvt; Profit PO
TALLY, Dock, H-57-3; Pvt I Co 1st TN Inf; 62 to 65; Orchard Knob PO
TALLY, Ely, D-54-1; Sallie widow of; Pvt US Col Inf; Nashville PO
TALLY, John, Je-138-2; Pvt E Co 1st US Col Art; 18 Mar 64 to 31 Mar 66; Dandridge PO
TALLY, Joseph, Hm-109-3; Pvt A Co 12th TN Cav; 20 Nov 62 to 7 Oct 65; Russelville PO; heornea
TALLY, Joseph A., Wa-268-1; Pvt D Co 4th TN Inf; 20 Jan 63 to 11 Jul 65; Johnson City PO; kidney disease
TALMAN, Jesse L., M-108-2(1); Lt H Co 5th IN Cav; 9-16-63 to __; A Co 6th IN Inf; 4-10-61 to 9-16-65; Salt Lick PO; gunshot wound in heel; (soldier wrote census bureau later to explain he was a bugler, not a lt, in Co H 5th IN Cav & Co H 6th IN Cav)
TALMAN, William, We-221-1(4); Pvt Inf; Martin PO; CONF
TALOR, William W., Un-258-1; Pvt C Co 9th TN Cav; 15 Sep 63 to 13 Sep 65; Phebe PO
TANDY, James, Bl-5-2; Pvt C Co 5th TN Inf; 11-10-61 to 12-22-64; Brayton PO
TANER, Nathaniel, Mu-188-1; Pvt K Co 5th TN Inf; 3-26-62 to 6-65; Grovelin PO; shot in left leg
TANEY, James E., Sm-168-2; Pvt A Co 1st TN Inf; 12-63 to 1-31-65; Pleasant Shade PO; chronic diarhea
TANEY, Walter L., Sm-168-2; Pvt A Co 1st TN Inf; 1-64 to 1-65; Pleasant Shade PO; lung disease (an invalid with hemorage of lungs)
TANKERSLEY, M., Hu-103-3; Pvt A Co 6th GA Inf; 10 Sep 61 to 10 Aug 64; PO omitted; crossed out, probably CONF
TANKERSLEY, W. R., Fr-118-1; Pvt H Co 42nd TN Inf; 1 Oct 61 to 25 Dec 64; Winchester PO; CONF
TANNANT, Tennie C. (see Tarnwell, John G.)
TANNER, James K., Mu-195-1; Sol wife dont know; Columbia PO
TANNER, William T., Mt-149-1; PVt E Co 10th TN Cav; 16 Feb 64 to 1 Aug 65; Riggins PO; rupture & rheumatism
TANNOR, James, Hd-52-1; Darthuly widow of; Pvt E Co 6th IL Inf; Feb 3 63 to 11 Jul 65; Adamsville PO; chronic consumption; proved fatal
TAPLEY, Henry C., H-72-2(1); 1st Sgt G Co 111th US Col Inf; 1-15-64 to 4-30-64; Chattanooga PO
TAPLEY, John, Wh-185-1; Pvt H Co 37th KY Inf; 6-29-63 to 12-29-66; Peeled Chestnut PO; chronic rheumatism, hands drawn up
TAPP, Benjamin F., K-173-1; Pvt C Co 52nd IN Inf; 21 Aug 64 to 10 Sep 65; McMillen PO; rheumatism
TAPP, Jacob, U-247-2; Pvt A Co 3rd NC Mtd Inf; 1 Jan 65 to 8 Aug 65; Erwin PO; rheumatism & heart
TAPP, Louis, K-167-5; Sgt C Co 13th TN Cav; 61 to 13 Sep 65; Knoxville PO
TAPP, Vincent, U-246-1; Pvt A Co 3rd NC Inf Mtd; 1 Jan 65 to 8 Aug 65; Erwin PO
TARKINGTON, William H., O-139-1; Pvt B Co 15th KY Cav; 1 Sep 62 to 13 Oct 63 Protemus PO

TARLINGER, Andrew M., B-7-1; 1st Lt E Co 10th TN Inf; 5-16-62 to 7-3-65; Shelbyville PO
TARLINGER, Henry M., B-7-1; Musician E Co 10th TN Inf; 5-17-62 to 7-3-65; Shelbyville PO
TARLINGER, John W., B-7-2; Pvt A Co 4th TN Mtd Inf; 8-64 to 65 (10 mos); PO omitted
TARLTON, Wilson, Dy-27-3; Susan wife of; Pvt TN Cav; 63 to 65; Tatemville PO; killed at close, first husband; CONF
TARNWELL, John G., W-189-2; Tennie C. Tannatt widow of; Capt; McMinnville PO
TARPENNEY, James M., Cu-17-4; Pvt D Co 12th IA Inf; 10-8-61 to 12-5-62; Cpl C Co 47th IA Inf; 5-1-64 to 9-27-64; Northville PO; chronic diarrhea
TARPLEY, Austin, Gi-125-2; Pvt G Co 110th US Col Inf; 23 Dec 63 to 6 Feb 66; Weakly PO
TARPLEY, Wesly, Gi-125-1; Lucinda J. widow of; Cpl G Co 110th US Col Inf; 23 Dec 63 to 6 Feb 66; Weakly PO
TARRY, N. M., F-44-3; Pvt A Co 1st AL; Jun 63 to Dec 23 63; PO omitted
TARVER, Samuel J., K-174-5; Lt G Co 2nd TN Cav; 1 Oct 62 to 6 May 65; House Mountain PO
TARWATER, Clark, K-154-6(3); Knoxville PO; crippled leg
TARWATER, HEnry C., Mc-112-1; Sgt C Co 6th E TN Inf; 12-18-62 to 5-17-65; Athens PO; lost left leg
TARWATER, James F., Ro-210-1; Pvt F Co 9th TN Cav; 28 Sep 63 to 13 Oct __; Rockwood PO
TATAM, William, Di-30-2; Pvt A Co 11th TN Inf; 9-61 to 5-64; Dickson PO; CONF
TATE, Alfred, Col, Gr-70-1; Pvt F Co 1st TN Hvy; Mar 64 to May 64; Rutledge PO; rheumatism, days of enlistment unknown
TATE, Allen S., Gr-70-1; Pvt H Co 1st TN Cav; 8 Apr 62 to 8 Apr 65; Rutledge PO
TATE (Coe), Andrew, Ct-38-1; Sgt B Co 1st TN Hvy Art; 2 yrs 6 mos; Johnson City PO
TATE, Andrew, P-151-1; Pvt E Co 2nd TN Mtd Inf; 62 to 65; Aldon PO; rheumatism from exposure
TATE, Ed O., Hm-103-2; Pvt H Co 1st TN Cav; 1 Apr 62 to 1 Apr 65; Morristown PO; cervites of spine; was in prison Madison GA
TATE, Elisha, Sq-165-1; Sgt D Co; 7-24-61 to 6-30-65; Delphi PO; received an honorable disc.
TATE, Henry H., W-193-1; Pvt K Co 71st IN Inf; 7-28-62 to 1-7-62; Vernilla PO; was wounded; he is drawing a pension
TATE, James, Gu-48-1; Pvt TN Vidette Cav; 62 to 63; Tracey City PO; record of discharge lost; Pvt I Co 16th KY Inf; 64 to 65
TATE, Jazeal, Mr-95-2; Cpl D Co 2nd TN Cav; 6-25-63 to 7-1-64; Tracy City PO
TATE, Jefferson, Ro-207-4; Pvt C Co 7th TN Mtd Inf; 20 Aug 64 to 27 Jun 66; Morris Gap PO; hemrage of lungs
TATE, John J., Gu-45-2; 4th Dist
TATE, John K., O-134-1; Sgt D Co 13th (105C) Cav; Dec 15 63 to Apr 6 64; Hornbeak PO
TATE, Marion, Mn-123-1; Pvt B Co 61st TN Inf; Caffey PO; lost hearing; have forgotten time of enlistment, kidney disease
TATE, Pleasant H., Sq-165-2; Pvt D Co 1st TN Cav; 7-31-63 to 6-16-64; Delphi PO; received an honorable disc.
TATE, Robert, Mo-123-1; Pvt D Co 3rd TN Mtd Inf; 7-25-64 to 11-23-64; Tellico Plains PO
TATE, Samuel, P-151-1; Pvt Vol 2nd TN Mtd Inf; Jun 64 to Dec 65; Mousetail PO
TATE, William, Mo-130-1; Pvt D Co 3rd TN Mtd Inf; 7-12-64 to 12-23-64; Povo PO; lung disease
TATE, William S., We-233-1(2); Sariah U. widow of; Pvt B Co 13th TN Cav; 1-64 to __ (8 yrs); Ralston PO; died in Andersonville prison
TATOM, James H., Di-30-1; Pvt K Co 11th TN Inf; 12-2-62 to 1-2-63; Dickson PO; CONF
TATON, Marian C., F-40-2; Pvt B Co 15th TN Cav; Apr 64 to May 65; Hickory Withe PO; CONF
TATTY, John, Hi-85-1; Pvt G Co 12th TN Inf; 2-14-64 to 10-7-65; Tatty's Bend PO
TATTY, Jonathan N., Hi-86-1; Pvt G Co 12th TN; 63 to 64; Tatty's Bend PO; fall of bale hay (Jonathan N. Tatty wonded by bale of hay falling on him while loading wagon)
TATUM, James A., Gi-139-1; Pvt A Co 10th AL Cav; 64 to 5-65 (10 mos); Campbellville PO

TAVERD, John, Co-60-1; M Co 1st TN Cav; 3-15-61 to 5-12-65; Syrensburg PO; rheumatism 24 yrs
TAYLER, Ryle, Ru-236-1; Pvt D Co 44th Inf; 63 to 65; Murfreesboro PO
TAYLER, William P., Pi-154-2; Pvt; 65 to 65; Eagle Creek PO; home guard
TAYLER, William H., We-225-1; Pvt K Co 6th TN Cav; 15 Aug 62 to 26 Jul 65; Dresden PO
TAYLER, A. H., Bo-11-2; Pvt E Co 3rd TN Inf; 7-15-64 to 11-30-64; Big Gulley PO
TAYLER, Abraham, Sh-188-2; Capt KY; Kerr St, Memphis PO
TAYLOR, Absalom P., Sh-198-2; Pvt E Co 45th KY Mtd Inf; 9-62 to 1-65; Memphis PO; has his discharge
TAYLOR, Aburn B., Un-250-1; Pvt A Co 14th TN Cav; 3-61 to 5-14-65; Miltabarger PO; dead
TAYLOR, Adam, Col, Lo-187-2; Lucinda widow of; Pvt E Co Col Reg from VA; Loudon PO
TAYLOR, Addaline (see Blevins, John)
TAYLOR, Albert, Sh-199-1; Pvt L Co 11th US Reg; 61 to 65; 44 Stewart Ave, Memphis PO
TAYLOR, Alexander L., S-217-1; Recruit Off 2nd TN; 11-1-61 to __; Isham PO; wound in right elbow
TAYLOR, Alfred D., Hm-109-1; Pvt H Co 13th TN Cav; 9-13-63 to 9-25-65; Three Springs PO; gunshot in wound, fell from horse
TAYLOR, Alvin, Ct-45-3; Pvt B Co 13th TN Cav; 9-22-63 to 9-5-65; Carter Furnace PO; prisoner Richmond VA
TAYLOR, Andrew J., K-154-2; Surgeon 3rd TN Cav; Knoxville PO; during war
TAYLOR, Arville, A-2-2; Pvt C Co 2nd TN Inf; 8-7-61 to 2-9-65; Clinton PO; disease of stomach & eyes, Andersonville prison 13 mos 5 days
TAYLOR, Barney B., Dk-34-2; Pvt E Co 4th TN Inf; 11-20-64 to 8-25-65; Dowelltown PO; injury to left side & hip & left testicle & spermatic cord
TAYLOR, Bazelia, Dk-35-3(1); Pvt F Co 4th TN Cav; 9-5-64 to 8-)); Capling PO
TAYLOR, Ben, Li-165-1; Jane Simmons widow of; Elora PO; slight wound in leg
TAYLOR, Benjamin, Bo-14-3; Nancy widow of; Pvt H Co 30th MO Inf; 8-20-62 to 2-18-63; Huffstetler Store PO
TAYLOR, Benjamin F., K-167-3; Pvt 47th KY Inf; 12-63 to 5-65; Knoxville PO
TAYLOR, Berry, D-64-2; Nashville PO
TAYLOR, Beverley, Sh-151-1; Brunswick PO
TAYLOR, Bill, Gi-134-1; Pvt D Co 12th TN Inf; 9-1-62 to 9-1-65; Campbellsville PO
TAYLOR, Bromley F., Sh-186-2; Pvt A Co 36th __; 7-17-61 to 12-64; Pvt A Co 7th IL?; 4-17-61 to 7-17-61; Memphis PO; enlisted for 3 mos & then for 3 yrs; latter part of service was on Gen. Granger's staff
TAYLOR, Charles D., M-106-3(2); Pvt D Co 14th IL Inf; 3-27-64 to 5-30-65; Lafayette PO; chronic rheumatism, applied for pension
TAYLOR, Chesley, Dk-35-4(2); Pvt F Co 4th TN Mtd Inf; 10-20-64 to 8-25-65; Capling PO
TAYLOR, Clinton, Sh-158-3; Amanda formerly widow of; Bugler 3rd Col Cav; 64 to 66; Memphis PO rec'd bounty? discharge papers with agent, died in 1878
TAYLOR, David, Ge-98-3; Pvt H? Co 4th TN Cav; 8-3-63 to 7-12-65; Jeroldstown PO; rheumatism resulting in disease of heart, frost bit feet
TAYLOR, David, A-9-4(2); Sgt C Co 3rd TN Inf; 2-22-62 to 2-22-65; Marlow PO
TAYLOR, David A., Ct-40-5; Pvt B Co 4th TN Inf; 4-14-63 to __; Elizabethton PO
TAYLOR, David B., Ma-114-1; Pvt D Co 24th NC; 10-25-61 to 4-9-65; Pinson PO; paralasys; CONF
TAYLOR, David C., A-2-2; Pvt Battery D 1st TN Art; to __; Andersonville PO; rheumatism, catarrh result of small pox, discharge burned in a house
TAYLOR, David H., Cr-9-1; Pvt B Co 13th TN Cav; 2-12-64 to 11-17-64; Cairo PO; gun shot wound right jaw, abdomen, left thigh
TAYLOR, David W., Ct-39-2; Pvt H Co 13th TN Cav; 9-63 to 10-65; Gap Run PO; cold settled on lungs
TAYLOR, Duncan, Sh-144-2; US Sol; First Dist

TAYLOR, Edward, Sh-196-1; Pvt A Co 11th US Hvy
Art; 12-21-63 to 8-65; 120 Dunlap St.,
Memphis PO; served under Capt. Canfield
TAYLOR, Edward, Sh-174-2; Mary widow of; Pvt;
rear 148 De Soto St., Memphis PO; overheated
in July or August 1865, died in a few hours
TAYLOR, Edward, Sh-196-2; Edward Oliver alias;
Pvt I Co 59th TN Inf; 7-63 to 6-65; 120
Dunlap St., Memphis PO; cut off at Guntown
Raid
TAYLOR, Eli C., Ct-35-3; Pvt G Co 18th TN Cav;
9-24-63 to 9-5-64; Lineback PO; in US Army
(disability)
TAYLOR, Eveline E. (see Peters, Jackson)
TAYLOR, Ezekiel W., Wl-307-1; Pvt F Co 4th TN
Inf; 9-12-64 to 8-25-65; Beckwith PO
TAYLOR, Francis M., Pi-152-2; Pvt J Co 1st KY
Cav; 3-10-63 to 5-25-65; Eagle Creek PO;
rheumatism, slight deafness
TAYLOR, Franklin, T-219-1; alias Franklin Jetts;
Pvt A Co 59th TN Inf; 5-6-63 to 6-31-66;
Philan PO
TAYLOR, Garrett, Cr-17-1; Pvt B Co 2nd TN Cav;
8-17-62 to 10-3-63; Family PO
TAYLOR, Georg M., C-34-1; Jane Cox former widow
of; Sgt F Co 6th TN Inf; 3-10-62 to 3-24-65;
Elk Valley PO
TAYLOR, George W. (white); Ru-247-1; Pvt H Co
10th TN Inf; 9-63 to 6-65; Sharperville PO
TAYLOR, George W., Sh-190-1; Pvt E Co 46th US
Inf; 64 to __ (12 mos); Gilfield Alley,
Memphis PO
TAYLOR, George W., T-216-1; Pvt A Co 55th US Inf;
5-63 to 65; Corona PO
TAYLOR, Grandison, G-56-1; Pvt; Trenton PO
TAYLOR, Henry, Sh-174-2; 32 Echols St., Memphis
TAYLOR, Henry, Ro-205-4; Pvt H Co 13th TN Inf;
8-12-61 to 10-12-64; Kingston PO; lung
trouble 15 yrs
TAYLOR, Henry, D-77-4; #44 Seventh St.,
Nashville
TAYLOR, Henry, Di-41-1; Pvt F Co 10th TN Inf;
2-2-64 to 6-29-65; White Bluff PO
TAYLOR, Henry R., Dk-35-4(2); Pvt F Co 4th TN
Mtd Inf; 9-30-64 to 8-25-65; Hicks PO
TAYLOR, Isaac C., Ct-38-2; Pvt N Co 8th TN Cav;
1-6-64 to 9-13-65; Okolona PO; disease of
the lungs
TAYLOR, J. B., G-57-2; Yorkville PO; CONF
TAYLOR, Jack, Mt-137-2; In Government Employ; no
papers 62 to 66; St. Bethlehem PO
TAYLOR, Jackson General, Ct-45-2; Pvt B Co 13th
TN Cav; 9-21-63 to 9-5-65; Carter Furnace
PO; discharged on surgeon certificate
TAYLOR, Jacob, Jo-149-2; Rachel widow of; 2nd Lt
F Co 13th TN Cav; __ to 8-65; Mountain City
PO
TAYLOR, James, Bo-19-2; Pvt F Co 63rd TN Inf;
9-8-62 to 3-1-63; South Rockford PO; CONF
TAYLOR, James, Sh-157-3; __ to 65; Ensley PO
TAYLOR, James, D-68-2; Sgt C Co 44th USC Inf;
3-26-64 to 4-30-66; 203 Fillmore St. Nash-
ville; been troubled with piles & sore eyes
since 4-66
TAYLOR, James, Cr-20-2; Pvt I Co 7th TN Cav;
1-20-64 to 8-9-65; Profit PO; rhumatism 25
yrs, con in the service
TAYLOR, James, Se-228-2(3); Pvt K Co 11th TN Inf;
Cusick's X Roads PO
TAYLOR, James, Dk-34-3; Pvt G Co 1st TN Inf;
64 to 7-25-6? (1 yr); Dowellton PO;
deafness
TAYLOR, James E., Sn-264-1; Pvt F Co 4th Mtd Inf;
9-30-64 to 8-25-65; Mitchellville PO; This
man is crippled with rheumatism. His papers
all right. I have examined this man is bad
off in distress, can't work, a helpless
family, his legs frozen on Pickett, he has
a good name. Capt. W. L. Hathaway, discharged at Nashville
TAYLOR, James F., Cr-20-2; Pvt B Co 7th TN Cav;
8-15-62 to 8-9-65; Hollow Rock PO
TAYLOR, James H., Lo-195-1; Pvt C Co 5th TN Inf;
4-4-62 to 5-4-63; Eatons X Roads PO
TAYLOR, James J., Wa-272-2; Harmony PO; rheumatism
injury to eyes

TAYLOR, James M., Ct-38-2; Sgt B Co 4th TN Inf;
12-8-62 to 8-2-65; Okolona PO; ruptured
TAYLOR, James M., U-244-1; Pvt A Co 2nd NC Inf;
9-15-63 to 8-16-65; Logantown PO; piles
TAYLOR, James N., Cr-9-1; Pvt A Co 13th TN Cav;
2-4-64 to 64; Friendship PO; gun shot wound
of right hip
TAYLOR, James P., Mg-196-4; Elizabeth widow of;
Pvt; Hunnicutt PO
TAYLOR, James W., Un-257-3; 1st Sgt C Co 4th TN
Cav; 8-2-62 to 7-12-65; New Prospect PO;
rheumatism
TAYLOR, James Z., Cu-17-1; Pvt B Co 8th TN Cav;
6-64 to 9-65; Crossville PO
TAYLOR, Jeremiah, Ro-205-4; Pvt K Co 13th TN Cav;
11-1-62 to 6-1-65; Kingston PO; rheumatism
& gun shot
TAYLOR, Jerr, Hy-84-3(5); Pvt A Co 61st Inf;
6-20-63 to 12-30-65; Nutbush PO; rheumatism
TAYLOR, Joe C., Wl-293-2; Pvt A Co 14th; 63 to
M-26-66; Lockport PO
TAYLOR, Joel, Gr-81-4(2); Pvt A Co 12th TN Cav;
12-63 to 5-28-65; Shelton's Ford PO;
rupture, disabled
TAYLOR, John, K-185-1; Pvt D Co 3rd TN Cav;
12-1-62 to 6-10-65; Mascott PO; right
shoulder maimed, A survivor of the Sultana
TAYLOR, John, Cl-47-1; Susan widow of; Pvt E Co 2nd
TN Inf; 6-61 to 65; Speedwell PO
TAYLOR, John, Ro-210-11; Pvt B Co 11th TN Cav;
Rockwood PO
TAYLOR, John, Dk-34-6(5); Lucind widow of; Pvt K
Co 5th TN Cav; 7-26-63 to 8-14-65; Close PO
TAYLOR, John, Col, H-56-4; Pvt GA Inf; St Elmo PO
TAYLOR, John, D-79-3; Ellen widow of; Pvt G Co
79th OH Inf; 6-61 to 66; 17 Arrington,
Nashville PO
TAYLOR, John B., D-100-1; Pvt F Co 5th W TN Cav;
9-25-62 to 6-25-65; E. L. Wingroves Store,
North 1st St., East Nashville PO; asthma
from cold taken while in the army, also
rheumatism
TAYLOR, John F., Po-148-2; Sgt F Co 4th TN Cav;
4-24-63 to 5-31-65; Benton PO; prisoner
2 weeks
TAYLOR, John F., H-54-2(3); Pvt 14th NY; Sherman
Heights PO; hearing damaged, rheumatism
TAYLOR, John H., Ro-205-4; Pvt; Postook Springs
PO; rheumatism 25 yrs
TAYLOR, John L., K-186-2; Pvt D Co 1st TN Art;
9-14-63 to 7-20-65; Chumlea PO; piles,
dispepsia
TAYLOR, John M., He-64-2; Pvt H Co 27th TN Inf;
11-1-64 to 2-1-65; Reagan PO; CONF
TAYLOR, John P., Wa-272-2; Pvt I Co 8th TN Cav;
10-30-63 to 12-24-64; Clover Bottom PO;
disease of heart, injury to eyes
TAYLOR, John W., Dy-29-2; Pvt D Co; 62 to __ (4 mos)
Newbern PO; deserter; CONF
TAYLOR, John W., Gi-122-2; Pvt A Co 3rd TN Inf;
12-20-63 to 2-3-65; Prospect Sta. PO;
shot in left shoulder; CONF
TAYLOR, John W., P-151-3; Capt F Co 2nd TN Mtd
Inf; (1 yr 3 mos); PO omitted
TAYLOR, John W., Ct-43-2; Pvt B Co 13th TN Cav;
9-22-63 to 9-5-65; Carter Furnace PO;
shot through left foot Salsbury, NC
TAYLOR, Joseph, H-73-2(1); Pvt; Chattanooga PO
TAYLOR, Joseph, Br-6-1; Pvt K Co 5th TN Mtd Inf;
12-1-64 to 7-20-65; Chatala PO; disease of
the eyes
TAYLOR, Leroy, Mo-102-2; Pvt 2nd TN Cav; 2-63 to
5-6-65; Madisonville PO; full dates not
known; CONF
TAYLOR, Levi, Mr-97-1; Pvt E Co TN Inf; 6-25-62
to 6-22-65; PO omitted
TAYLOR, Louis, F-48-1; Pvt K Co 100th ?; 8-1-64
to 1-1-66; Brinkly PO
TAYLOR, Marian D., Ge-94-2(1); Pvt I Co 1st TN
Cav; 11-15-61 to 4-7-65; Tusculum PO;
during the late war
TAYLOR, Micheal, Ct-43-3; Sarah A. widow of; Pvt
B Co 13th TN Cav; 9-22-63 to 9-5-65; Carter
Furnace PO; chronic dierhea, died of
chronic dierhea 1879

TAYLOR, Mose, Sh-159-2; Pvt 7th OH; 65 to 65 (5 mos); Memphis PO
TAYLOR, Moses, Hr-91-1; Pvt E Co 3rd IL Cav; 7-62 to 7-10-63; Bolivar PO; wound & lungs affected from war
TAYLOR, P., Gi-133-2; Pvt D Co 3rd TN; 61 to 64; Buford PO; CONF
TAYLOR, Perry, Li-166-1; Mary A. widow of; Pvt; 63 to ___; Civil Dist no. 25
TAYLOR, Peter, Col, D-103-1; Pvt G Co 13th TN Inf; 10-10-63 to 1-10-66; Joelton PO; rectal disease, draws pension
TAYLOR, Peter, Sh-152-1; alias Peter Forde; Pvt K Co 59th US Troops; 63 to 66; Collierville PO
TAYLOR, R. T., O-137-1; Pvt I Co 7th TN Mtd Inf; 11-64 to 65; Kenton PO; detail our of order on this sched.
TAYLOR, Robert, Sh-161-2; Sgt in US A; 16th Dist.
TAYLOR, Robert, Sh-178-1; Pvt Cav. K Co 3rd US; 9-9-64 to 5-9-66; rear 108 Wellington, Memphis
TAYLOR, Robert, Sh-158-6(4); Pvt C Co 2nd Dist Sh Cty, Col Vol Inf; 5-64 to 12-66; Memphis PO; discharged at Washing. City--at close of war with discharge papers
TAYLOR, Robert, L-101-1; Pvt G Co 4th Hvy Art; 11-73 to 3-16-66; Henning PO
TAYLOR, Robert C., K-178-1; Pvt K Co 1st TN Inf; 11-2-61 to 10-4-63; Scarborough PO
TAYLOR, Robert H., We-226-2; Mary A. widow of; Sgt K Co 6th TN Cav; 8-13-62 to 9-6-63; Sharon PO
TAYLOR, Robert H., Jo-150-4; Rachel E. widow of; Osborn PO; no record found
TAYLOR, Rufus, Co-64-1; Pvt H Co 4th TN Cav; 3-14-62 to 7-12-65; no PO
TAYLOR, Samuel, Cu-15-2; Matilda widow of; Pvt A Co 2nd KY; 3-18-65 to 10-23-61; Crossville PO; general disability caused from exposure
TAYLOR, Samuel, Ct-45-3; Pvt H Co 4th TN Inf; Carter Furnace PO; prisoner Richmond VA from 8-64 to 5-65, no discharge
TAYLOR, Stephen, Hu-103-4; Pvt; 64 to 66; no PO
TAYLOR, Steven, D-64-3; alias Thomas Jefferson; Pvt D Co 3rd Art; Nashville PO
TAYLOR, Thomas, Sh-189-1; Ella widow of; died 1-31-1890; widow dont know his record; La. Ave., Memphis PO
TAYLOR, Thomas, Ro-202-6; Sarah H., widow of; Pvt I Co 5th TN Inf; 2-25-62 to 6-14-65; Paw Paw Ford PO; rupture
TAYLOR, Thomas D., H-73-1; Pvt A Co 6th NC; 11-16-62 to 5-25-65; Chattanooga PO
Taylor, Thomas F., Ct-43-1; Margret widow of; Pvt F Co 13th TN Cav; 9-22-63 to 9-5-65; Carter Furnace PO; heart trouble, died 10-82
TAYLOR, Thomas J., Br-13-2; Cpl A Co 8th TN inf; 7-6-62 to 6-30-65; Cleveland PO; left shoulder shot
TAYLOR, Thomas L., Cr-15-2; US Sol; Maple Creek PO
TAYLOR, Thorne?, K-173-2; Pvt D Co 2nd TN Cav; 9-8-62 to 7-6-65; Troutman PO
TAYLOR, W. M., Bo-11-4; Cpl E Co 3rd TN Inf; 7-26-64 to 11-30-64; Greenback PO
TAYLOR, Washington, H-64-1; Malina widow of; Chattanooga PO; died on vessell
TAYLOR, Washington, A-9-2; Rachel widow of; Pvt C Co 2nd TN inf; 3-62 to ___; Oliver Springs PO; died while in Bell Island Prison
TAYLOR, Wesley, Mu-190-2; Pvt E Co 110th Col Inf; 11-63 to ___; Culleoka PO; deserted
TAYLOR, Wiley P1, Bo-12-1; Pvt B Co 24th KY Inf; 10-1-61 to ?-62; reenlisted as Sgt G Co 14th KY Cav; 10-1-62 to 3-24-64; Chilhowee PO
TAYLOR, William, Ms-174-1; Pvt C Co 17th US Inf; 2 yrs 6 days; Beasly PO; discharge lost
TAYLOR, William, Ro-211-1; Pvt G Co 3rd KY Cav; 4-20-62 to 7-23-65; Webster PO; wounded in right thigh, reenlisted
TAYLOR, William, A-6-5(3); Pvt 5th TN Inf; 3-62 to 2-63; PO omitted

TAYLOR, William, Cl-46-1; Pvt C Co 1st TN; 8-16-62 to 9-17-64; Clairfield PO; liver dirie
TAYLOR, William, Ct-40-2; Pvt H Co 13th TN Cav; 10-1-64 to 9-5-65; Elizabethton PO
TAYLOR, William, D-99-1; Pvt A Co 13th AL Inf; 6-63 to 65; Nashville PO; wounded badly in mouth, paralyzed from wound
TAYLOR, William, P-151-3; F Co 2nd TN Mtd Inf; Linden PO
TAYLOR, William B., Br-8-3(1); Pvt G Co 5th TN Mtd Inf; 1-1-65 to 7-13-65; Blue Springs PO; rheumatism
TAYLOR, William B., A-9-4(2); Pvt E Co 3rd TN Inf; 2-22-62 to 2-22-65; Marlow PO; head affected by exploding shell
TAYLOR, William B., Ct-41-2; Pvt H Co 13th TN Cav; 9-24-63 to 9-5-65; South Wattauga PO; varicocets rhumatism
TAYLOR, William D., Mt-135-1; Capt MO Inf; 6-1-61 to 4-14-65; Woodlawn PO; prisoner 4 mos at IL shot in the right leg; CONF
TAYLOR, William D., Hn-73-1; Pvt Co A 18th IL; 61 to 64; Como; contracted piles while in service
TAYLOR, William J., We-226-1; Pvt K Co 6th TN Cav; 2-1-64 to 7-26-65; Sharon PO
TAYLOR, William M., Ge-98-2; Pvt B Co 4th TN Cav; 9-8-62 to ___; Lovelace PO; disease of eyes
TAYLOR, William R., C-27-4; Sgt C Co 4th TN Cav; 8-2-62 to 6-2-65; Jacksboro PO
TAYLOR, William V., K-178-1; Cpl H Co 1st TN Inf; 8-9-61 to 9-17-64; Hardin Valley PO
TAYLOR, Wm. W., Rb-220-2; Pvt B Co 30th TN Inf; 1-23-62 to 12-18-64; PO omitted
TEAG, Josua, Cl-48-2; Pvt A Co 9th TN Cav; 63 to 65 (2 yrs 6 mos); Pleasant PO; lost hearing in left ear; got no discharge
TEAGUE, David, H-54-5; Pvt L Co 4th TN Cav; 3-64 to 7-65; Sherman Heights PO; chronic diarrhea, fever settle in the left side & leg; shortness of breath & lung trouble very cose viens in back legs
TEAGUE, David B., H-54-4; Cpl B Co 44th OH Inf; 9-10-61 to 9-23-65; Chattanooga PO; parorasin of lef arm
TEAGUE, George R., Br-13-2; Pvt L Co 1st TN Cav; 9-1-62 to 6-4-65; Cleveland PO; chronic rheumatism
TEAGUE, Harrison H., Mo-130-1; Pvt A Co 3rd TN Mtd Inf; 7-1-63 to 12-24-65; Acorn PO; liver & lungs
TEAGUE, Henry H., Mo-123-1; Pvt D Co 3rd TN Mtd Inf; 7-25-64 to 11-30-64; Jalapa PO
TEAGUE, James A., He-60-1; Cpl A Co 7th TN Cav; 9-8-62 to 8-9-65; Lexington PO; I was in Andersonvill prison 10 mos 18 days
TEAGUE, John N., Ma-126-1; Pvt Batery E 1st TN Lt Art; 12-15-63 to 8-5-65; Jackson PO; dispepsia & malarial poison
TEAGUE, John W., Mc-117-1; Sarah A. Johnson widow of; Pvt; Mecca PO
TEAGUE, Leander A., He-60-2; Sgt A Co 7th TN Reg; 8-11-62 to 8-9-65; Lexington PO
TEAGUE, Logan, Ct-37-2; Pvt F Co 26th NC Inf; 61 to 62 (1 yr); Hopson PO; breast complaint; CONF
TEAGUE, Nathan A., Ct-37-1; Pvt K Co 1st US Inf; 7-12-64 to 11-15-65; Hopson PO; breast, suffering 25 yrs
TEAGUE, Samuel M., Br-13-3; Pvt I Co 4th TN Cav; 2-21-64 to 7-24-65; Cleveland PO; ruptured
TEAGUE, William M., Ge-94-3; Pvt L Co 13th TN Cav; 9-24-63 to 9-5-65; Ham PO; injured in side during war 1864
TEAS, Joseph W., La-111-4; US Sol; 5th Civil Dist
TEASE, R. W., Hu-103-2; M. I. widow of; Pvt E. Co; 62 to 62 (6 mos); PO omitted
TEASLEY, John, H-59-3; Caroline widow of; Pvt TN Inf; ___ to 1865; Chattanooga PO; killed
TEDDEN, John E., Ca-19-1; Pvt D Co 4th TN Cav; 10-11-64 to 8-23-65; Auburn PO
TEETERS, John J., Bl-4-1; Pvt E Co 6th TN Inf; 9-12-64 to 6-13-65; Pikeville PO
TEFFETALLER, J. A., Bo-22-1; Pvt; 63 to 65; Seaton PO
TEINE, James C., B-7-1; Sgt E Co 10th TN Inf; 6-1-62 to 7-3-65; PO omitted

TELL, William, Sh-174-3; Pvt 11th Regular Hvy Art; 63 to 66 (2 yrs 10 mos); rear 152 DeSoto St., Memphis; chronic dysentery; scurvy
TELLOCK, Smith R., Ge-91-4; Pvt I Co 1st TN Cav; 8-1-62 to 6-5-65; Greeneville PO; wounded in a charge
TELLON, Luther M., D-62-1; Pvt F Co 3rd WI; 61 to Aug or Sep 64; Nashville PO, West Demontrem St.
TELSON, Lathosia, Cr-14-4; widow US Sol; Clarksburg PO
TEMPLE, Benjamin W., K-171-4(3); Pvt G Co 1st TN Inf; 6-61 to 10-64; PO omitted
TEMPLE, Matthias, Wi-274-1; Pvt F Co 16th IN Inf; 5-7-61 to 5-7-62; Franklin PO; disabled from fever
TEMPLER, William, Hw-118-2; Pvt F Co 6th IN Cav; 6-63 to 9-22-65; St. Clair PO
TEMPLETON, Aron A., Hw-120-1; Cpl C Co 2nd TN Cav; 7-27-62 to 7-6-65; War Gap PO; rheumatism & heart
TEMPLETON, George E., Sn-255-1; Cpl D Co 10th TN Inf; 4-14-62 to 6-10-65; Goodlettsville PO, Davidson Co; deafness in right ear, cause—soldier pouring hot coffee in his ear, contracted rheumatism in the war
TEMPLETON, James, Fe-43-1; Clark Range PO
TEMPLETON, James A., Sn-255-1; Pvt A Co 10th TN Cav; 8-12-63 to 9-28-65; Goodlettsville PO, Davidson Co.; went through unhurt
TEMPLETON, John, Hw-120-1; Catherine widow of; Sgt 1st TN __; War Gap PO
TEMPLETON, William B., H-50-3(1); Pvt H Co 12th R TN Cav; 1-4-64 to 65; Soddy; fall back of measles
TEMPLIN, David, Co-66-2(1); Sgt F Co 62nd TN Inf; 11-1-62 to 7-4-63; Birdsville PO; CONF
TENASS, Fred, D-67-2; Pvt Col Inf; Nashville PO
TENBROECK, Swict?, Ca-25-1; Maggie M. widow of; Col I Co(?) 2nd MN Vet Vol; Mechanicsville PO; gun shot through abdomen
TENERSON, Braford, F-44-3; Pvt A Co 12th __; 8-62 to 5-65; PO omitted
TENEUR, Henry, K-182-3; Pvt Watteree; 9-22-63 to 4-27-66; Riverdale PO
TENNELL, Green, Hu-99-1; Cpl G Co 14th US Col Inf; 12-2-63 to 3-26-66; Johnsonville PO
TENNIS, Alfred K., Cf-40-3; Pvt E Co 10th KY Cav; 9-24-62 to 9-63; Tullahoma PO
TENNY, Lewis, Ch-12-2; Pvt C Co 21st TN Cav; 8-62 to 65; Custer Point PO
TENRY, Ruffus, T-215-2; Pvt; Mason PO
TENY, Washington, Sn-252-1; Pvt K Co 14th TN Inf; 1-1-64 to 3-29-66; Gallatin PO; shot in right thigh
TEREY, Lewis, Sh-188-1; Pvt A Co 1st MO Inf; 12-24-62 to 5-65; 72 Peyton St., Memphis PO
TERHUNE, Jno., Sh-187-1(5); Sol; Memphis PO
TERRELL, Alexander F., Sh-159-5; Pvt; PO omitted; CONF
TERRELL, Alfred T., He-64-3; Cpl A Co 7th TN Cav; 8-8-62 to 8-8-65; Reagan PO
TERRELL, James, Dy-27-1; Pvt G Co 47th TN Reg; 3-62 to 3-64; Ro Ellen PO
TERRELL, Wm. H., D-57-1; Pvt; 63 to 65; PO omitted but 8th Ward, Nashville; CONF
TERRIL, James, Hw-130-2; Pvt; Lee Vally PO; War of Mexico Sol.
TERRILL, George W., G-57-4(1); Pvt C Co 12th TN Inf; 7-12-61 to 4-1-63; Yorkville PO; CONF
TERRY, Adrain, K-159-3; Maj Inspector Dept of VA; 9-13-61 to 5-11-66; Knoxville PO; promoted to Maj for gallantry at Ft. Fisher
TERRY, Calvin G., Ch-14-2; Pvt C Co 1st TN Cav; 4-20-61 to 6-15-65; PO omitted;CONF
TERRY, Eligah, S-216-1; Pvt E Co 12th KY Inf; 9-29-61 to 7-11-65; Huntsville PO; rheumatism 20 yrs, cripeld, than in army(sic)
TERRY, Elisha, Hd-50-6; Sol MS; 8th Civil Dist.
TERRY, Isam, H-53-3; Pvt 34th NY Inf; __ to 65; Chattanooga PO; in prison, information from mother
TERRY, Joseph, Rb-223-2; Mary J.widow of; Pvt G Co 10th MI Inf; 5-18-61 to 5-15-64; Mian St., Springfield PO
TERRY, Joseph M., Se-221-1; Margery widow of; Pvt I Co 3rd TN Cav; 9-10-63 to 8-15-64; Allensville PO; died Aug 15, 1864

TERRY, L. L., D-67-3; Pvt D Co 101st OH Inf; 8-12-62 to 6-65; Nashville PO
TERRY, Marion, C-34-1; Pvt G Co 7th TN Inf; 11-8-64 to 7-28-65; Stanfil- PO; served in 2 rgts
TERRY, Susanah (see Keeney, Wiley)
TERRY, Willey C., K-184-1; Pvt L Co 3rd TN Cav; __ to 6-18-65; Riverdale PO
TERRY, Wilson, D-61-2; Bilbo Ave., Nashville PO; shot in side, could give no other information
TESTER, Henry R., Jo-151-3; Pvt D Co 13th TN Cav; 9-22-63 to 9-5-65; Vaughtsville PO; spinal affection
TESTER, Richard R., Jo-151-1; Cpl F Co 13th TN; 9-22-63 to 9-5-65; Casper PO; chronic diarrhoea
TESTER, Robert D., Jo-151-3; Pvt D Co 13th TN Cav; 9-22-63 to 9-5-65; Vaughtsville PO; chronic diarrhoa, died in 1885
TESTERMAN, William P., Ha-112-1; Capt E Co 8th TN Cav; 9-23-63 to 9-11-65; Datura PO
TETER, Henrietta M., Sh-184-1; widow US Sol; 85 Hill, Memphis PO
THACKER, James R., Gu-48-2; Mary E. widow of; Cpl B Co 6th TN Cav; Tracy City PO; died in hospital at Loudon, TN
THACKER?, Simon, We-231-1; Pvt B Co 7th TN Cav; 9-10-64 to 3-65; PO omitted
THACKER, Thos. A., Mo-119-3; Cpl K Co 47th KY Cav; 10-62 to 3-65; Sweetwater PO; shot in right leg & stuck with bayonet
THACKER, William, Lo-187-1; Pvt I Co 5th TN Inf; 3-1-63 to 6-13-65; Loudon PO; back injured in RR wreck
THACKER, William, Cl-51-1; Pvt E Co 1st TN Lt Art; 1-15-64 to 7-15-65; Ritchie PO; leg off
THACKER, William, Hd-45-1; Pvt C Co 2nd TN Mtd Inf; 2-16-64 to 5-6-66; Whiton PO
THACKSTON?, Black B., Sm-170-1; Sgt B Co 2nd TN Inf; 5-20-61 to 4-20-65; Maggart PO; shot twice 1 in right leg 1 in body; CONF
THARP, Peter, Un-254-1; Pvt F Co 3rd TN Inf; 2-20-62 to 1-23-65; Paulett PO
THARPE, Allonzo, Hn-69-1; Pvt I Co 13th C Inf; 5-1-64 to about 6-8-65; Paris PO; discharge lost
THARPE, George, Hn-69-1; Pvt K Co 4th C HA; 5-64 to 3-65; Paris PO; lost one eye in service, discharge lost
THATCH, John H., Br-14-1; Pvt B Co 9th MI V I; 4-19-62 to 9-8-62; Sgt I Co 5th TN V I; 11-1-62 to 5-27-65; McDonald PO; rupture & chronic dierrhoa; (John H. Thatch was discharged by general order 36 for rupture. This order discharged all unable for duty in army. Discharged on said certificate 36. Mr. Thatch also contracted a chronic dioerrhoe during his service in the army. He also contracted throat & bronchial trouble & rheumatic trouble in the war.)
THATCH, Robert, W-189-2; Pvt I Co 4th TN Mtd Inf; 9-64 to 8-65; McMinnville PO; discharge lost
THAYER, Robert, A-6-5(3); PO omitted
THEAD, John T., Mu-108-1; Pvt J Co 4th TN Inf; 2-11-65 to 8-25-65; Bryants Station PO; rib broke
THEIRY, John W., H-51-6; Pvt E Co 130th OH Inf; 5-1-64 to 9-28-66; Red Bank PO
THERMAN, Robert A., Cy-28-1; Pvt C Co 10th TN Cav; 12-1-63 to 8-6-65; Celina PO
THETFORD, Joseph R., Cr-14-2; 3rd Sgt M Co 6th TN Cav; 8-25-62 to 7-26-65; Clarksburg PO; chronic
THETFORD, Kin W., O-138-3; Drummer G Co 7th TN Inf; 4-1-62 to 7-1-63; Minnick Box PO; CONF
THETFORD, King W., O-138-4; Pvt; 9th Civil Dist
THEURER, Lewis P., D-50-3; Pvt F Co 74th IL Inf; 4-22-61 to 11-22-66; Nashville PO
THOGMORTIN, Andy, Cr-16-2; Pvt C Co 13th TN Inf; 64 to 65; Huntingdon PO; dint know when inlisted
THOM, George W., Gi-123-1; Pvt E Co 64th IL Inf; Mar 62 to 11 Jul 65; Bethel PO
THOMAS, Absolum H., Po-152-3(1); Pvt 9th TN Mtd Inf; 8 mos; Ducktown PO; rheumatism, deserted
THOMAS, Adam S., K-173-2; Pvt D Co 6th TN Inf; 18 Apr 62 to 27 Apr 65; Troutman PO; lame back

THOMAS, Albert, D-49-3; he is away and his wife only knows he was a soldier; PO omitted
THOMAS, Alfred, K-156-5; Marth Banyon widow of; 141 Pine St, Knoxville PO
THOMAS, Almon, Wl-300-1; Pvt K Co 2nd TN Inf; 17 Oct 64 to 65; Watertown PO
THOMAS, Andrew J., Hm-107-4; Pvt L Co 8th TN Cav; Witts Foundry PO; ruptered
THOMAS, Andrew J., Hw-119-3(1); Cpl E Co 1st TN Cav; 1 Apr 63 to 10 Apr 65; Alum Well PO; chronic rheumatism
THOMAS, Asbury, Pu-145-1; Pvt C Co 1st Mtd Inf; 10-21-63 to 12-13-64; Burton PO
THOMAS, Benjamine F., Sm-174-1; Pvt G Co 4th TN Inf; 11-1-64 to 8-25-65; New Middleton PO
THOMAS, Bird, H-50-5; Rosannah widow of; Lt 6th R TN Mtd Inf; ___ to 6-30-65; Soddy PO; piles
THOMAS, Caleb, Di-34-3; Pvt D Co 15th US Col Inf; 7-6-64 to 4-7-66; Dickson PO
THOMAS, Carroll, Se-221-1; Pvt M Co 2nd TN Cav; 8 Nov 61 to 3 Jun 63; Shrader PO; died Jun 3, 63
THOMAS, Charles, Hy-82-1; Pvt B Co 3rd TN Hvy Art; 65 to 66; Rudolph PO
THOMAS, Charles, Ru-13-2; Capt C Co 9th MI Inf; Aug 61 to Oct 65; Murfreesboro PO; wounded in shoulder
THOMAS, Crosier S., Mo-122-1; Pvt B Co TN Inf; 3-10-63 to 9-8-63; Dancing Branch PO; CONF
THOMAS, Cyrus H., H-56-2; OH;; 63 to 65; East End PO
THOMAS, David, H-58-3; Pvt I Co 4th TN Cav; 10-17-63 to 7-12-65; Sale Creek PO; chronic diarrhoea & weak eyes
THOMAS, Davis F., Ch-18-2; Pvt F Co 54th TN Inf; Dec 62 to May 65; PO omitted; CONF
THOMAS, Doc, L-108-1; Pvt G Co; 5 yrs; PO omitted
THOMAS, Eliga, Cl-49-2; Pvt A Co 2nd TN Cav; 8-1-62 to 7-6-65; Zeb PO
THOMAS, Elizabeth, D-58-2; widow US Sol; Cedar St, Nashville PO
THOMAS, Frank G., Sh-203-2; Pvt A Co 11th TN Reg; 62 to 65; Memphis PO; CONF
THOMAS, Fred?, Mo-122-1; Pvt B Co TN Inf; 1-26-63 to 7-26-63; Gudger PO; CONF
THOMAS, George, Sh-153-3; Lulu, widow; Collierville PO
THOMAS, George C., We-221-4; Capt TN Inf; 62 to 65; Martin PO; wounded in right arm, he has died 3 Jun 90, cannot get details full; CONF
THOMAS, George S., Ro-209-3; Pvt A Co 64th VA Inf; Jul 62 to Feb 65; Rockwood PO; CONF
THOMAS, George W., Mc-112-5; Pvt F Co 3rd TN Cav; 5-63 to 11-65; Athens PO; gun shot wound; first in CONF army 7 mo 12 days
THOMAS, George W., He-64-1; Pvt A Co 7th TN Cav; 7 Jul 63 to ___ (9 mos); Middle Fork PO; regiment captured, not mustered
THOMAS, George W., Se-219-1; Marry widow of; Pvt C Co 8th TN Cav; Oct 62 to Sep 65; East Fork PO; generall disability
THOMAS, George W., H-58-2; Pvt A Co 6th TN Mtd Inf; ___ to 6-30-65; Sale Creek PO; chronic diarrhoea
THOMAS, Harm, Cl-46-1; Thursey widow of; PO omitted
THOMAS, Henderson D., Pu-145-1; Pvt D Co 1st Mtd Inf; 12-18-63 to 4-25-65; Burton PO
THOMAS, Henry, Un-252-2; Sidney E. widow of; Pvt C Co 1st TN Inf; Aug 62 to Oct 65; Simcoe PO
THOMAS, Henry, Sh-157-7; Pvt B Co 31st TN Inf; 62 to 65; Memphis PO; hand, ankel, thigh, groins
THOMAS, Henry, Rb-223-1; Pvt C Co 15th TN Inf; 12 Jan 64 to Apr 65; Springfield PO; shot in the hand; can use only two fingers
THOMAS, Henry, Sh-161-2; US Sol; 16th Dist
THOMAS, Henry, Sh-158-6(4); Pvt A Co 3rd US Hvy Art; 63 to 65; Memphis PO; discharged at close of war with discharge papers
THOMAS, Henry Clay, Col, Sh-145-1; Pvt G Co 23rd US Col Inf; May 64 to Nov 65; Millington PO; enlisted under Capt Street--discharged under Cap Scott
THOMAS, Isaac L., Ha-115-3; 3rd Lt B Co 25th VA Cav; 15 Dec 62 to 21 Apr 65; Mulberry Gap PO; CONF
THOMAS, Isham, Mu-191-3; 7th Dist

THOMAS, J. T., Wl-300-2; Emma J. widow of; Lt H Co 4th TN Cav; 4 Oct 64 to 25 Aug 65; Cherry Valley PO
THOMAS, James, Sh-173-1; 95 De Soto St, Memphis PO
THOMAS, James B., C-24-3; Pvt B Co 1st TN Inf; 8-1-61 to 9-17-64; Fork Vale PO; affects of hips & sciatica heart kidney & liver & neuralgia
THOMAS, James H., He-60-2; Pvt A Co 7th TN Reg; Aug 20 62 to Aug 9 65; Lexington PO; caused scurvy, I was in Andersonvill prison 8 mos
THOMAS, James M., Co-69-5; Pvt D Co 12th TN Cav; Apr 63 to 63 (1 mo 15 das); Help PO; sunstroke, dont remember dates discharge; has not
THOMAS, James W., Ov-135-2; Cpl K Co 9th TN Cav; 1-3-63 to 9-11-65; Monroe PO; ruptured
THOMAS, Jeff, O-133-1; US Sol; Rives PO
THOMAS, Jefferson B., H-58-1; Sgt F Co 5th TN Inf; 2-25-62 to 3-29-65; Sale Creek PO; scurvy
THOMAS, Jeremiah, St-164-2; Pvt A Co 44th Inf; Mar 7 64 to 30 Apr 66; Stribling PO
THOMAS, Joe G., G-59-1; Pvt B Co 6th TN Cav; 15 Sep 63 to 15 Aug 65; Kenton PO
THOMAS, Joel, Ca-23-1; Pvt G Co 52nd KY Inf; 11-18-63 to 1-19-65; Leoni PO; no injuries
THOMAS, Joel W., Br-11-2; Cpl G Co 5th TN Inf; 4-11-62 to 5-16-65; Chatata PO
THOMAS, John, D-64-1; Pvt A Co 13th TN Inf; Aug 12 63 to Oct 63; Nashville PO
THOMAS, John, C-33-1; Pvt H Co 15th US Col; 2-64 to 4-66; Newcomb PO
THOMAS, John, Gu-47-1; Pvt? TN; 63 to 64 (2 yrs); Pelham PO; had a discharge, disabled
THOMAS, John, K-161-6; alias John Warren; Maggie Reinhart widow of; Knoxville PO; shot in thigh and died from effects after being discharged
THOMAS, John, Lo-190-2; Caroline widow of; Pvt; Loudon PO
THOMAS, John, Ce-29-1; 2nd Sgt I Co 12th TN Cav; Feb 63 to 65; Kingston Springs PO
THOMAS, John A., Br-8-1; Pvt H Co; 62 to 65 (2 yrs 11 mos 25 days); Cleveland & Blue Springs PO
THOMAS, Jno. F., W-194-1; Pvt? G Co 50th IL Inf; 10-12-61 to 4-12-62; Morrison PO
THOMAS, John F., Sh-175-1; Pvt F Co 6th LA Inf; 4-63 to 65; Memphis PO
THOMAS, John H., Se-225-1; Pvt F Co 9th TN Cav; 11 Sep 63 to 11 Sep 65; Allensville PO; rheumatism and hart disease; 25 yrs gen. disability
THOMAS, John M., Cl-58-1; Pvt D Co 6th TN Inf; 9-19-62 to 6-13-65; Davo PO
THOMAS, John M., Li-147-1; 1st Sgt I Co 15th TN Inf; 2-18-65 to ___ (8 mos); Norris Creek PO
THOMAS, John W., Pu-144-3; Sgt A Co 5th TN Cav; 8-1-62 to 6-20-65; Pine Fork PO; injury of spine & hips
THOMAS, John W., D-70-2; 9 Lindsley Ave, Nashville PO
THOMAS, Joseph, Sh-191-1; Memphis PO
THOMAS, Joseph C., Cl-48-2; Pvt G Co 25th VA Cav; 63 to 4-65; Pleasant PO; CONF
THOMAS, Joseph M., Sm-174-1; Pvt G Co 4th TN Inf; 11-1-64 to 8-25-65; New Middleton PO
THOMAS, Marion, Bo-19-2; Pvt E Co 3rd TN Cav; 12-63 to 6-11-65; Rockford PO
THOMAS, Martha (see Caswell, Solomon)
THOMAS, Mary (see Walker, Joseph C.)
THOMAS, Nehemiah, Mg-196-1; Pvt F Co 195th PA Inf; 14 Feb 65 to Feb 66; Oliver Springs PO
THOMAS, Nellie, widow; Sh-159-7; Memphis PO
THOMAS, Noah, Mo-130-2; Marth G. widow of; Pvt A Co 3rd TN Cav; 9-18-62 to 6-10-65; Ballplay PO
THOMAS, Noah L., Hw-121-6(1); Pvt B Co 3rd TN Mtd Inf; 30 Jun 64 to 30 Nov 64; Strahl PO; rheumatism and heart deas
THOMAS, Orval B., Hm-107-4; Pvt D Co 4th TN Inf; 6 Jan 63 to 2 Aug 65; Chestnut Bloom PO; loss of eye & rheumatism
THOMAS, Owen, T-214-1; Pvt I Co 55th US Inf; 62 to 65; Dist 9
THOMAS, Peter, Sh-150-3; Pvt I Co 9th Hvy Art; no dates (2 yrs); Dexter PO

THOMAS, Ples, Sh-195-1; Cpl K Co 11th Col Inf; Memphis PO
THOMAS, Prisilla A., D-66-2; S. Chery St, Nashville PO
THOMAS, Randle, D-69-2; US Sol, no record; Nashville PO
THOMAS, Richard, Rb-226-1; Collared; Pvt 16th TN Inf; 63 to 63; Chanury? PO
THOMAS, Richard, Mu-205-1; Pvt A Co 101st TN US Inf; Aug 63 to Jan 65; Water Valley PO; papers lost
THOMAS, Samuel, Su-234-1; PVt C Co 13th TN Cav; 28 Feb 64 to Jul 64; Vances Tank? PO; Camp Nelson KY to Nashville 64; discharged on account of disability
THOMAS, Sarah E. (see Rogers, James M.)
THOMAS, Seth, De-26-1; G Co 27th TN; Aug 61 to ___ (9 mos); Genett PO; piles & bowels complaint; CONF
THOMAS, Thomas, Mc-114-4; Pvt; Calhoun PO; hemorrhoid
THOMAS, Thomas W., A-4-2; Pvt K Co 43rd PA Inf; 7-3-63 to 6-22-65; Coal Creek PO; discharge not at home
THOMAS, Veranda, M-107-6; widow of US Sol; 7th Civil Dist
THOMAS, Webster, R-162-1; Capt E Co 47th OH Inf; 7-16-61 to 9-64; Dayton PO; left hip disabled; also C.S.V. with rank above
THOMAS, Wesley, Cr-10-1; Cook; Mar 61 to Jun 10 64; Stokes PO (Dyer Co.)
THOMAS, William, Se-219-1; Pvt I Co 2nd TN Cav; 1 Aug 63 to Jul 65; East York PO; asma & rumetism
THOMAS, William, K-183-3; Pvt E Co 1st TN Lt Art; River Dale PO
THOMAS, William, Cl-47-1; Pvt C Co 1st TN Inf; 8-1-61 to 9-17-64; Speedwell PO
THOMAS, William (see Vinson, William)
THOMAS, William B., Dk-35-4(4); Pvt F Co 4th TN Mtd Inf; 9-29-64 to 8-25-65; Capling PO
THOMAS, William C., M-107-6; Pvt 8th TN Mtd Inf; 2-25-65 to 8-17-65; Gibbs Cross Roads PO; general debility result mumps & fever
THOMAS, William H., K-169-2; gone from home, Knoxville PO
THOMAS, William I., H-49-7; Cpl A Co 6th TN Mtd Inf; 8-2-64 to 6-30-65; Daisy PO
THOMAS, William L., Hm-107-3; Sgt D Co 25th MI Inf; 7 Aug 62 to 26 Jun 65; Witts Foundry PO; gunshot wound 26 yrs
THOMAS, Wm. M., Sh-201-3; Pvt G Co 2nd IL Lt Art; 1 Aug 62 to 1 Aug 65; Memphis PO
THOMAS, William M., Mg-199-3; Cpl C Co 1st KY Cav; 62 to 65; Sunbright PO
THOMAS, William P., Me-94-2; Pvt C Co 5th TN Cav; 8-19-62 to 6-25-65; Pin Hook PO
THOMASON, Alvis H., Dk-35-4(2); Pvt D Co 4th TN Mtd Inf; 9-17-64 to 8-27-65; Temperance Hall PO
THOMASON, George, O-141-3; Cpl A Co 4th Hvy Art; Feb 63 to Feb 22 66; Union City PO
THOMASON, Israel, D-63-3; Overt St, Nashville PO
THOMASON, James, Hm-108-3(2); Sarah K.? widow of; Pvt; Russellville PO; CONF
THOMASON, Joel, K-177-5; Pvt War Conf; 62 to 9 A. 65; Powells Station PO; CONF
THOMASON, Joel, K-177-6; Pvt I Co 2nd TN Cav; 62 to May 65; Powells Station PO; CONF
THOMASON, Josephus, M-106-3(2); Margarette Parker formerly widow of; Pvt D Co 8th TN Mtd Inf; 12-10-64 to 8-31-65; Hillsdale PO
THOMASON, Logun, Hw-132-4; Pvt; Otes PO; 1 leg off, could not get full particulars; CONF
THOMASON, William, Sn-261-4(3); Pvt; Brackentown PO; CONF
THOMASON, William M., O-136-1; Pvt L Co 6th TN Cav; Jul 20 62 to 26 Jul 65; Terrill PO
THOMASON, William R., Sh-167-1; Pvt A Co 2nd MSM? Cav; 20 Jan 64 to 12 Jul 65; PO omitted
THOMASSON, Walker, Sh-174-4; Pvt F Co 46th US Col Inf; 11-63 to 4-65; 44 Hadden Ave, Memphis PO; chronic diarrhoea
THOMERSON, David T., Sm-173-2; Sgt H Co 4th TN Mtd Inf; 11-1-64 to 8-25-65; Brush Creek PO
THOMMAS, Elijah R., Se-231-1; Pvt E Co 1st TN Art; 23 Sep 63 to 1 Aug 65; Boyds Creek PO; acute rheumatis, 3 mos

THOMPSON, A. P., Ro-209-2; Sgt E Co 1st TN Inf; 20 Aug 61 to 17 Sep 64; Glen Alice PO
THOMPSON, A. W., Wl-308-3; Pvt F Co 4th TN; Nov 1 61 to May 1, 65; Mount Juliet PO; CONF
THOMPSON, Abraham J., Dy-20-1; US Sol; Dist 1
THOMPSON, Alex S., K-182-1; 1st Lt E Co 114th OH Vol Inf; 8 Sep 62 to Mar 64; PO omitted
THOMPSON, Alfred, Hr-87-1; Pvt I Co 3rd MS Cav; Hickory Valley PO; discharge special order
THOMPSON, Andrew, D-72-3; Pvt I Co 111th TN Inf; Feb 1 64 to 13 Apr 65; Nashville PO; rheumatism
THOMPSON, Andrew J., Wl-302-1; Pvt H Co 4th TN Mtd Inf; 5 Nov 64 to 25 Aug 65; Cherry Valley PO; formerly Andrew wannisac
THOMPSON, Ascar, Ro-209-2; Pvt C Co 7th TN Inf; 12 Aug 61 to 16 Jun 65; Glen Alice PO
THOMPSON, Berry, Lo-188-2; Nan J. widow of; Pvt A Co 2nd TN Inf; 11 Aug 61 to ___; Stockton PO
THOMPSON, Cal?, St-164-1; Pvt I Co 14th TN Inf; 62 to 64; Stribling PO
THOMPSON, Calvin, H-64-1; Margarett widow of; Pvt 1st Hvy Art; 62 to 65; Chattanooga PO; cant give letter nor date
THOMPSON, Calvin L., Cr-13-2; Pvt M Co 7th TN Cav; Mar 1 62 to May 66; Milan PO; yes; cannot find discharge
THOMPSON, Charles, Col, Sh-(numbers omitted by transcriber); Mary widow of; 64 to 65; widow could not remember anything more; Millington PO
THOMPSON, Charly (see Micham, George)
THOMPSON, Danl., Ca-20-2; Pvt C Co 5th TN Cav; 4-15-62 to 6-15-63; Woodbury PO; this name crossed off schedule--no reason given
THOMPSON, Daniel G., Hm-102-1; Pvt K Co 12th TN Cav; ___ to 65 (1 yr 7 mos); Morristown PO; chronic diarrhea
THOMPSON, David, D-72-3; Sgt F Co 13th TN Inf; Feb 24 61 to 24 Feb 65; Nashville PO
THOMPSON, David, Sh-191-8(4); 14 Rayburn St, Memphis PO
THOMPSON, Edmund, Mu-196-1; Pvt K Co 12th Reg; ___ to 66 (2 yrs 6 mos); Columbia PO
THOMPSON, Enos, Ge-97-1; Sarah widow of; Pvt; Maltsberger PO
THOMPSON, Ephraim, Sh-139-3; Pvt F Co 3rd US Art; 20 Nov 64 to 30 Apr 66; Raleigh PO
THOMPSON, Esau, S-213-1; PO omitted
THOMPSON, Ezra, Ca-22-1; Sara Fletcher former widow of; Pvt; Hollow Springs PO
THOMPSON, Francis D., Mc-112-5; Pvt G Co 13th OH Vol Cav; 6-18-62 to 9-24-65; Athens PO; gunshot wound
THOMPSON, Franklin C., G-71-1; Pvt I Co ___ Inf; 5 Nov 64 to 4 Mar 65; Rutherford PO; CONF
THOMPSON, G., Di-41-1; Amy C. widow of; Pvt A Co 12th ___; White Bluff PO; she dont know anything about it
THOMPSON, George, Je-140-2; Pvt Art; Strawberry Plains PO; deserter
THOMPSON, George, Bo-15-1; Pvt A Co 3rd TN Inf; 2-10-62 to 8-1-63; Corn PO; rhumatism
THOMPSON, George W., H-73-1; Pvt B Co 8th GA Brit; 9-10-61 to 4-26-65; Chattanooga PO
THOMPSON, Harrison (see Cannon, J. Harrison)
THOMPSON, Harry R., H-68-3; 400 Whiteside St, Chattanooga PO
THOMPSON, Henry, Mr-102-1; Ord Sgt E Co 14th US Col Inf; 11-16-63 to 3-25-66; South Pittsburg PO
THOMPSON, Henry A., Pi-155-1; Pvt G Co 18th US Inf; 3-6-66 to 3-6-69; Otto PO; feet badly froze
THOMPSON, Henry M., Ha-115-2; Pvt; Alanthers Hill PO; CONF
THOMPSON, Horace E., Mu-210-2; Emma widow of; Sailor; 4 yrs; Spring Hill PO
THOMPSON, J., G-57-1; Sgt H Co 47th TN Inf; 61 to 65; Yorkville PO; CONF
THOMPSON, J. R., Bo-11-1; 5th Sgt G Co 3rd TN Inf; 2-10-62 to 3-65; Cloids Creek PO; chronic diarhoea & resulting disease, cant give dates of discharge
THOMPSON, James, Ge-101-2; Pvt D Co 1st TN Cav; 12 Aug 62 to Jul 65; Locust Sp. PO
THOMPSON, James A., Ca-20-2; Pvt C Co 5th TN Cav; 8-1-62 to 8-15-63; Woodbury PO
THOMPSON, James D., Cr-16-2; Pvt F Co 52nd IN Inf; Jun 5 62 to 5 Jun65; Huntington PO

THOMPSON, James F., Ha-115-3; Pvt A Co 1st TN Cav; 18 Oct 61 to 3 Jul 65; Mulberry Gap PO; CONF
THOMPSON, James K. P., Pu-147-2; Pvt H Co 1st TN Mtd Inf; 4-1-64 to 5-23-65; Byrne PO
THOMPSON, James O., Mt-132-1; Pvt D Co 8th TN Inf; 2-7-65 to 8-26-65; 1st Civil Dist
THOMPSON, James P., Ge-89-2; Pvt B Co 4th TN Inf; 26 Dec 62 to 2 Aug 65; Mosheim PO
THOMPSON, James R., Ro-206-2; Capt B Co 5th TN Inf; 25 Feb 62 to 30 Mar 65; Emory Gap PO
THOMPSON, James T. S., Mu-210-7; Leanora W. of; Lt; Spring Hill PO; CONF
THOMPSON, Jessie K., Cy-29-2; heart disease, 8th Civil Dist
THOMPSON, John, D-72-6; Sol; Nashville PO
THOMPSON, John, D-72-6; Martha Porter former widow of; Pvt A Co 13th SC Inf; Nashville PO
THOMPSON, John, Hr-96-1; Pvt B Co 7th TN Cav; 61 to 64; Crainsville PO; CONF
THOMPSON, John, Dy-29-5; Pvt 22nd TN Inf; 61 to 63; PO omitted
THOMPSON, John, A-5-4; Pvt C Co 7th TN Inf; 8-7-61 to 3-65; Clinton PO; chronic diarrhea
THOMPSON, John B., Wl-299-2; 15th Civil Dist
THOMPSON, John H., Bo-15-1; Pvt H Co 2nd TN Cav; 10-10-62 to 7-6-65; Mountvale PO; rhumatism and diarea
THOMPSON, John L., Br-13-1; Pvt E Co 4th TN Cav; 1-9-63 to 7-12-65; Georgetown PO
THOMPSON, John R., K-167-4; Pvt C Co 188th __; 63 to 22 Dec 65; Knoxville PO; no pension
THOMPSON, John R., Wl-302-2; Oakpoint PO; absent when ennumerated
THOMPSON, John R., Gi-136-1; Pvt H Co 5th TN Cav; 8-62 to 8-65; Odd Fellow Hall PO
THOMPSON, John W., K-171-5(4); Pvt D Co 6th TN Inf; 18 Apr 62 to May 65; Knoxville PO; rhumatism
RHOMPSON, Joseph, Hm-103-1; Pvt B Co 2nd OH Inf; 31 Aug 61 to 10 Oct 64; Morristown PO
THOMPSON, Joseph R., Wl-307-1; Pvt H Co 10th __; 1 Oct 62 to 65; Leeville PO
THOMPSON, Jos. W., Sh-189-1; Sgt E Co 44th MS Inf; 4-27-61 to 3-15-65; Memphis PO; CONF
THOMPSON, Leander, G-57-7(4); Pvt F Co 9th TN Cav; 1 Sep 61 to 1 Apr 65; Yorkville PO; shot through right shoulder; CONF
THOMPSON, Lee B., R-161-2; Sgt B Co 1st TN Lt Art; 12-7-62 to 7-20-65; Dayton PO
THOMPSON, Levi, Gi-124-1; Or Sgt F Co 6th TN Cav; 21 Sep 62 to 26 Jul 65; Minor Hill PO
THOMPSON, Lorenzo W., Lo-191-1; Pvt; Greenback PO; rheumatism, heart disease, right arm partially useless; CONF
THOMPSON, Martha, D-48-1; widow; Sgt G Co 12th US Vols; 8-12-63 to 1-16-66; Nashville PO
THOMPSON, Mathew A., K-171-1; Pvt D Co 6th TN Inf; 18 Apr 62 to 27 Apr 65; Bearden PO
THOMPSON, Nelson, Wi-287-1; Lt? C Co 11th TN Inf; 5 May 62 to 6 May 64; Trinne PO
THOMPSON, R. M., Cl-54-4(2); Pvt C Co 29th TN Inf; 7-30-63 to 3-65; Tazewell PO; CONF
THOMPSON, Rebeca A. J. (see Baily, John)
THOMPSON, Richard, Br-9-5; Pvt E Co 4th TN Cav; 2-13-63 to 7-24-65; Cleveland PO
THOMPSON, Robert, H-73-2(1); Cliza widow of; Pvt; Chattanooga PO
THOMPSON, Robert H., Lo-191-2; Greenback PO; CONF
THOMPSON, Samuel J., Ch-12-2; Pvt H Co 21st TN Cav; 9-63 to 5-65; Custer Point PO; CONF
THOMPSON, Samuel M., Bo-13-2; Pvt F Co 2nd TN Cav; 8-1-62 to 7-6-65; Miser PO; left arm stiffened by vacination
THOMPSON, Samuell, Ct-41-1; Pvt H Co 13th TN Cav; 9-24-63 to 9-5-65; South Wattauga PO; rhumatism of ? and finger eff.; wright elbow
THOMPSON, Stephen, D-47-1; Pvt A Co 39th US Inf; 3-63 to 12-65; Station B, Nashville PO; burn on neck and back; is ruptured from strain on r. side
THOMPSON, Susie E., D-72-6; widow; Nashville PO
THOMPSON, Thomas, Br-12-6; Rhat PO
THOMPSON, Thomas, Ge-98-1; Hannah widow of; Pvt A Co 9th TN Cav; PO omitted
THOMPSON, Thomas J., Ca-24-1; Rebecca widow of; Pvt G Co 5th TN Cav; 8-28-62 to 8-28-65; Talvine PO; phthisic dead; died from phthisic contracted in the army

THOMPSON, Wesley, Br-12-4; Pvt K Co 1st TN Inf; Sydneyton PO
THOMPSON, Wesly, F-43-1; Pvt C Co 59th Col TN Inf; 62 to __; PO omitted
THOMPSON, William A., We-223-1; Pvt E Co 5th TN Inf; 61 to 64; Palmersville PO; wounded in head; CONF
THOMPSON, William H., Cl-51-1; Pvt E Co 48th IN V Inf; 9-20-63 to 5-12-65; Hoop PO; ruptured in rick(?) on train in Washington DC 5-10-65
THOMPSON, William H. C., Mc-111-2; 2nd Lt E Co 7th TN Mtd Inf; 1-1-65 to 7-27-65; Nonaburg PO
THOMPSON, William V., G-71-1; Pvt I Co 18th TN Inf; 7 May 61 to 7 Sep 65; Edmonds PO; CONF
THOMPSON, William W., G-71-2; Pvt C Co 4th TN Cav; 14 Sep 61 to 20 Oct 62; Edmonds PO; leg broken & hearing dulled; CONF
THOMPSON, Wilson, Wl-296-1; Pvt H Co 4th TN Inf; 65 to 65; Shop Spring PO
THOMPTSON, James M., Me-88-2; Pvt H Co 5th TN Inf; 1-4-65 to 7-15-65; Birchwood PO
THOMSON, George W., Mc-118-1; Pvt B Co 11th KY Cav; 63 to __; Cogshill PO; chronic catarrh 15 yrs
THOMSON, Henry, H-67-3; Capt Clara Dunning; 1862 to 1866; Chattanooga PO
THOMSON, Jacob C., Ge-83-2; Pvt A Co 62nd TN Inf; Sep 63 to 64; Painters PO
THOMSON, Sarah J., O-141-3; Pvt D Co 13th TN Vol Cav; Dec 4 63 to 11 May 64; Union City PO
THOMSON, Thomas, Bo-14-3; Pvt L Co 2nd TN Cav; 9-8-63 to 7-6-65; Huffstetlers Store PO
THOMSON, Thomas J., Bo-14-3; Pvt A Co 3rd TN Inf; to 2-23-65; Huffstetlers Store PO
THOMSON, Wm. H., D-78-2; Pvt E Co 9th MN Inf; Aug 19 62 to 20 Jan 64; Nashville PO; was discharged on account of chronic bronchitis
THORN, JAmes T., La-114-1; Pvt E Co 6th IL Cav; 17 Dec 61 to 1 Dec 64; Marsella Falls PO; chron. diareah, piles, bronchitis
THORNBERG, Jacob M., K-169-2; gone to Washinton DC; Knoxville PO
THORNBURG, D. G., K-158-2; Col 3rd TN Cav; 62 to Oct 64; 84 Mabry St, Knoxville PO; chronic rheumatism from exposure
THORNBURG, Daniel, Lo-190-2; Pvt E Co 1st TN Cav; Oct 63 to 65; Loudon PO; small pox
THORNBURG, William, Ge-87-2; Cpl A Co 3rd TN Mtd Inf; 64 to 65 (1 yr 9 mos); Timberridge PO; deafness
THORNBURGH, Franklin, Lo-187-1; Charlotta widow of; Pvt E Co 3rd TN Mtd Inf; 26 Jul 64 to 23 Dec 64; Loudon PO
THORNBURGH, Lowery, Se-226-3; Mary Cate formerly widow of; Pvt K Co 3rd TN Cav; Henrys X Roads PO
THORNBURGH, Noah E., Ge-98-5; Cpl B Co 4th TN Cav; 16 Nov 62 to 12 Jul 65; Jeroldstown PO; chronic diarhea and knee joint
THORNBURGH, Patrick, Lo-187-4; Pvt E Co 3rd TN Mtd Inf; 26 Jul 64 to 23 Dec 64; Loudon PO
THORNBURY, Russell, Je-141-1; Maj 1st TN Cav; 21 Nov 62 to 19 Jun 65; New Market PO
THORNHILL, Thomas, Hm-104-3(1); Pvt C Co 1st TN Cav; 25 Jan 63 to 19 Jun 65; Alpha PO; prolapsus
THORNTON, Albert G., Wi-279-1; Pvt G Co 84th OH; Oct 64 to 65; Carl PO
THORNTON, George, D-73-1; Pvt H Co 13th TN Inf; 64 to 65; Olympic St, Nashville PO
THORNTON, James, Gi-127-1; Narcis widow of; Pvt G Co 111th TN Col Inf; Pulaski PO
THORNTON, John, G-67-1; Pvt F Co 62nd IL Inf; 22 Oct 62 to 1 Nov 65; Bradford PO; diarrhea
THORNTON, L. D., La-117-3; Pvt K Co 1st TN Cav; Jan 61 to 65; 15th Dist; CONF
THORNTON, Lee, L-99-2; US Sol; Durhamville PO
THORNTON, M., Hd-51-1; Lt D Co; Jun 62 to __; Pickens PO; CONF
THORNTON, William, Sh-200-3; Pvt; Polk Alley, Memphis PO
THORNTON, William, H-63-1; Margaret widow of; 2nd Lt Gunboat; 61 to 62; 17 Magazine, Chattanooga PO; dead; CONF
THORNTON, William, Mr-99-2; Pvt C Co 5th TN Inf; 3-31-62 to 6-13-65; Jasper PO; disabled in right arm; caused by being bled

THORP, Henry, We-223-4; Pvt I Co 13th TN Inf; 63 to 65; Elm Tree PO
THORPE, Benjamin, G-64-2; Bradford PO
THORSTON, Edward H., Mc-112-5; Pvt E Co 128th OH Inf; 12-62 to 7-65; Athens PO
THRAILKILL, James K., Ro-211-2; Pvt H Co 3rd TN Inf; 8 May 62 to no discharge (6 mos); Webster PO
THREAT, George, Fe-42-3; Margret widow of; Pvt Capt David Beaty's Co TN Ind Scouts; Boatland PO
THREAT, W. C., Fe-42-2; Pvt Capt David Beat's TN Ind Scouts; Jamestown PO
THREET, James, Ov-138-1; Pvt; 10th Civil Dist.
THREET, Jessee D., Fe-41-3(1); Susa A. Sells formerly widow of; Pvt Capt Beaty's Indpt Scouts of TN; 1861 to 1865; Boat Land PO; killed in service
THRESHER, Hardy, Cy-30-1; Catharine widow of; Pvt A Co Bristoe's Battalion; 2-64 to 10-23-65; Willow Grove PO
THRONEBERRY, Levi, Cf-35-3; Pvt A Co 4th TN Inf; 61 to May 65; Gould PO; CONF
THRUSTON, Gates P., D-54-1; Cpl C Co 1st OH Inf; Aug 61 to __; Nashville PO
THURMAN, Benjamin, Hw-125-3; Pvt E Co 1st TN Cav; 17 Mar 62 to 17 Apr 65; Yellow Stone PO
THURMAN, Calvin, R-161-3; Quartermaster? Dept; 1-64 to 1864; Dayton PO; discharge lost
THURMAN, Chas., B1-3-5; Armanda widow of; Pvt; 3-62 to 1862; Letton PO; scull fracture; CONF
THURMAN, Elisabeth (see Allen, William L.)
THURMAN, Henry, Sq-165-1; Pvt 12th TN Cav; 10-1-64 to 10-14-65; Delphi PO; received an honorable disc.
THURMAN, Isaac N., B1-2-3; Pvt G Co 6th TN Mtd Inf; 2-20-65 to 6-30-65; Orme's Store PO; bronchitis; troubled with bronchitis & rheumatism
THURMAN, John G., Hw-125-6; E Co 1st TN Cav; 17 Mar 64 to Mar 64; Yellow Stone PO
THURMAN, Lucinda, K-181-7(4); widow US Sol; Flenniken PO
THURMAN, Monroe R., H-53-3; Capt C Co 4th TN Inf; 10-22-62 to 1865 (3 yrs 5 mos); Chattanooga PO; broken ankle
THURMAN, Thomas, H-61-4; Pvt; 5-61 to 8-61; Chattanooga PO; CONF
THURMAN, William A., B1-5-3; Pvt D Co 6th TN Mtd Inf; 8-16-64 to 5-31-65; Sequachee College PO; falling back of measles in 1865 which resulted in disease of right lungs
TIBBITS, George, Sh-188-1; Pvt A Co 1st MI Inf; 12-7-61 to 9-22-65; 22 Peyton St., Memphis
TIBBS, Daniel A., A-10-1; 1861 to 1865; Briceville PO; commissary major was not mustered; CONF
TIBBS, Pleasant H., D-68-1; 2nd Lt G Co 10th TN Inf; 10 May 62 to 24 Jun 65; Fillmore, Nashville PO; partial deafness caused by pneumonia and typhoid fever while in the US Service, Nov 1862
TICE, Steven J., We-226-1; Susan E. widow of; Pvt B Co 7th TN Cav; __ to 21 Jun 64; Sharon PO; died on date, under discharge
TIDEWELL, William M., H-56-5; Pvt B Co 1st TN Cav; 8-62 to 1865; St. Elmo PO; CONF
TIDROE, Alfred Y., Pi-155-1; Pvt F Co 13th KY Cav; 10-62 to 1-64; Otto PO; direa & piles
TIDROE, Frederick B., Pi-155-1; Polly A. widow of; Pvt F Co 13th KY Inf; __ to 1865 (1 yr 2 mos); Otto PO
TIDWELL, Francis M., H-49-2; Pvt K Co 5th US Vol; 4-65 to 12-66; Falling Water PO
TIDWELL, James, Mu-193-1; Susan widow of; Pvt; no dates (2 yrs); Columbia PO
TIDWELL, William B., Mu-209-5; Pvt A Co 35th AL Inf; Apr 62 to 65; Columbia PO; prisoner 4 months New Orleans; CONF
TIERSON, George, Mu-198-2; 10th Dist.
TIERSON, Monroe, Mu-198-2; 10th Dist.
TIGNOR, Mary (see Wooton, Robert)
TILL, Bridger D., Dy-25-6(2); Newbern PO; CONF
TILLER, Benjamin F., B-12-1; Mariah E. widow of; Cpl M Co 5th TN Cav; 9-6-63 to 8-14-65; Wheel PO

TILLERY, John, K-166-1; Pvt G Co 6th TN Inf; 18 Apr 62 to 17 May 65; Knoxville PO; rheumatism, heart disease
TILLERY, Samuel, A-3-1; Pvt C Co 3rd TN Inf; 2-12-62 to 2-13-65; Wilson PO; dierrea, gun shot
TILLERY, William K., Me-92-1; Pvt D Co 7th TN Mtd Inf; 12-13-64 to 7-27-65; Cate PO; wounded by legthing(?)
TILLETT, George H., K-184-3; Capt C Co TN Cav; 18 Sep 62 to 15 Sep 65; Thorn Grove PO
TILLETT, Kate (see Fry, Daniel)
TILLEY, Samuel H., K-165-3; Pvt B Co 4th TN Inf; 9 Aug 62 to 19 Jul 65; 76 Meger St., Knoxville PO
TILLEY, William C., Jo-152-2; Pvt B Co 4th TN Inf; 1 Aug 62 to 7 Jul 65; Doeville PO; back & hips
TILLMAN, B. M., Ch-17-1; Capt C Co 52nd TN Inf; 9-61 to 6-65; Henderson PO; CONF
TILLMAN, Henry, Sh-191-3; Sarah widow of; Pvt; Memphis PO; records not seen
TILMAN, James, H-72-1; Pvt C Co 16th US Col Inf; 3-18-64 to 4-30-66; Chattanooga PO
TILSON, Elizabeth, U-244-2; 9th Civil Dist. MO
TILSON, Joshua E., U-249-1; Pvt H Co 8th TN Cav; 1 Feb 64 to 11 Sep 65; Flag Pond PO
TILTON, Albert (see Johnson, Albert)
TIMANS, John, L-99-2; US Sol; Durhamville PO
TIMMINS, James, Di-34-3; Cpl G Co 12th TN Cav; 10-63 to 9-1-65; Colesburg PO
TIMMONS, Daniel, Mc-115-1; Pvt K Co 1st TN Inf; 8-9-61 to 10-17-64; Riceville PO; cripled or diseased leg
TIMS, Elisabeth, W1-302-2; widow; PO omitted
TINCH, George A., 7-78-1; Pvt K Co 4th TN Inf; 11-1-64 to 8-24-65; Rough Point PO; scroffolo & lungs; and now is not to work much
TINDELL, Charles M., Je-138-2; Pvt C Co 1st TN Cav; Mar 63 to __ (3 yrs); Kansas PO; has no discharge
TINGLEY, Henry S., Di-34-3; Pvt C Co 83rd PA Inf; 3-1-64 to 6-28-65; Dickson PO
TINKER, Eli, Co-67-2; Rebecca widow of; Birdsville PO
TINKER, Robert L., U-246-1; Levisa E. widow of; Lt M Co 8th TN Cav; Erwin PO
TINKER, Sidney, H-54-1; 1st Lt D Co 93rd IN Inf; 8-2-62 to 8-16-65; Chattanooga PO; shell wound on left hip; was prisoner at _____ Charleston &
TINNEL, James, Ro-202-3(1); Pvt 1st TN Inf; Aug 62 to __ no disch. (15 mos); Grays Hill PO; lung trouble thru, 65 years old
TINNEL, Jesse, Ro-202-5; Pvt I Co 1st TN Inf; 11 Jul 63 to 3 Aug 64; Cave Creek PO; chronic diarrhea
TINSLEY, Evaline, K-154-5(2); widow; Knoxville PO
TINSLEY, James, G-56-1; Pvt; Trenton PO
TINSLEY, Manse, Sn-254-1; Pvt F Co 101st US Col Inf; 9-1-64 to 1-12-66; Hendersonville PO
TINSLY, Joseph S., La-113-3; Pvt C Co 154th IN Inf; 21 Mar 65 to 4 Aug 65; Ethridge PO
TIPETT, Houston, W1-297-2; Dist. No. 12
TIPFORD, Lewis D., Jo-150-1; Pvt G Co 13th TN Cav; 1 Feb 64 to 5 Sep 65; Rheas Forge PO
TIPPS, James, K-174-1; US Sol; 5th Dist.
TIPTAM, Bubiner?, J., Bo-15-2; Pvt F Co MO Mtd Inf; 1863 to 1865; Blockhouse PO
TIPTON, Benjamin, Wa-272-1; Clarissa widow; Pvt D Co 8th TN Cav; 16 Jun 63 to 24 Jul 63 (died); Locust Mount PO
TIPTON, C. T., Bo-11-1; St Sgt I Co 5th TN Inf; 10-1-63 to 6-30-65; Brick Mill PO
TIPTON, Charles C., Je-143-2; Pvt A Co 3rd NC Mtd Inf; 25 Jun 64 to 8 Aug 65; Mossy Creek PO; Frost bit feet & rheumatism
TIPTON, Caswell C., Se-227-2; Pvt B Co 6th TN Inf; 21 Sep 62 to 12 Jun 65; Trundles X Roads PO
TIPTON, David M., Ct-36-1; Pvt D Co 3rd NC Inf; 6-4-64 to 8-8-65; Shell Creek PO; run over by horses
TIPTON, Gilbert H., Lo-190-3; Lt I Co 5th TN Inf; 25 Feb 62 to 30 Jun 65; Piney PO
TIPTON, Isaac N., K-179-1; Pvt C Co 6th TN Inf; 18 Apr 62 to May 65; Rodelin PO

TIPTON, Jacob, K-181-1; Pvt A Co 1st TN Inf;
  1 Nov 62 to 5 Jul 65; French PO
TIPTON, Lyddia, Co-65-2; widow US Sol; Pvt; 15th
  District
TIPTON, Rufus M., Ha-115-2; Pvt H Co 37th VA Inf;
  Mar 62 to 10 May 64; Alanthers Hill PO; shot
  through leg; CONF
TIPTON, Stephen P., Gu-45-2; Louisa E. widow of;
  2nd Lt E Co 1st TN Cav Vidette; 1862 to 1864;
  Altamont PO; killed by the enemy in 1864
TIPTON, Volentine, U-248-1; Pvt G Co 34d NC Inf;
  10 Oct 64 to 10 Aug 65; Clear Branch PO
TIPTON, William C., Fe-42-2; Pvt Capt David Beaty's
  Co TN Ind Scouts; Jamestown PO
TISON, Frances, L-105-1; widow; Pvt; 7th Civil
  Dist.
TISON, Henry, K-185-3; US Sol; River Dale PO
TISON, James H., Dk-34-1; Pvt A Co 4th TN Cav;
  9-64 to 8-25-65; Dowelltown PO; disease of
  throat & lungs
TITE, Henry M., Dk-34-3; Sgt E Co 4th TN Inf;
  11-26-64 to 8-25-65; Dowelltown PO; rheum-
  atism & weak eyes
TITTLE, Ephrain, U-248-1; Catherin widow of; pvt
  M Co 4th TN Cav; 16 Sep 63 to 15 Sep 65;
  PO omitted
TITTLE, Gorge W., Ct-41-1; Pvt H Co 13th TN Cav;
  9-24-63 to 9-5-65; South Wattauga PO;
  dispolytane in head
TITTLE, John, U-244-1; Pvt C Co 10th VA Cav;
  Oct 63 to __; Loganton PO; asthma
TITTLETON, William C., Tr-265-1; Pvt F Co 1st TN
  Mtd Inf; 1 Jan 64 to 6 May 65; Hartsville
  PO; contracted piles
TITTSWORTH, James O., Je-135-3; Martha M. widow
  of; Cpl K Co 3rd TN inf; 10 Feb 62 to
  9 May 63; Mount Horeb PO
TITTSWORTH, Richard, Dk-38-1; Pvt; Holmes Creek PO
TIVAL, J. J., Mn-129-1; Pvt D Co 1st AL Cav;
  6-64 to 7-65; Stantonville PO
TIVERDY, George W., D-67-1; Pvt Col Inf; 64 to 65;
  Nashville PO
TIVLEY, Ransom H., H-70-3(1); 1st Lt TN Inf;
  Chattanooga PO
TIWATER, Charley T., He-66-1; Pvt C Co 4th TN Cav;
  Dec 2, 64 to Aug 25, 65; Life PO; rheumatism
TOBES, Albert B., Je-143-3; 1st Duty Sgt A Co 15th
  PA Cav; 7 Aug 62 to __ (2 yr 5 mo); Mossy
  Creek PO; horse shot & fell & mashed his leg
TOBINS, Hall, D-54-3; Nashville PO; away &
  landlady couldnt give record
TOBLER, George, K-171-6(5); Hos. Stwt. D Co 6th
  TN inf; Apr 62 to Apr 65; PO omitted
TOBY, Johnathan, Co-62-4; USS; 4th Dist. Cock Co.;
  lameness--from a child
TOD, Rufus, Sh-149-4; US Sol; 6th Civil Dist.
TOD, Thomas, K-168-3; Pvt; Knoxville PO
TODD, Ben, He-59-1; Sol US; PO omitted
TODD, George W., S-214-4; Pvt G Co 2nd TN Inf;
  1 Aug 63 to 3 Aug 65; Glenmary PO; rheum-
  atism disease eye & scurvy
TODD, Granville, Ca-22-2; Mary A. Howland former
  widow of; Pvt; 3-13-62 to 6-16-64; Burt PO;
  widow and children have lately drawn pension
TODD, John, We-233-1(2); Pvt K Co TN Inf; 1862 to
  ?; Dresden PO
TODD, Lafayette, L-102-1; Pvt C Co 51st US C Inf;
  61 to 64; Dist 4
TODD, Noah, Li-149-1; Pvt K Co 15th US Col Inf;
  3-64 to 3-66; Fayetteville PO
TODD, Samuel S., Wy-177-1; Pvt H Co 14th IA Inf;
  3-26-62 to 3-26-65; Moon PO
TODD, Stephen J., K-159-1; Cpl E Co 2nd OH Cav;
  1 Aug 61 to 16 Sep 64; Knoxville PO
TODD, William, We-230-3; Pvt K Co 21st TN Reg;
  May 10, 63 to May 12, 64; Greenfield PO;
  CONF
TODD, William T., We-220-1; Pvt I Co 6th TN Cav;
  Jun 5, 62 to Jul 26, 65; Catham PO
TOLAND, John, Cf-42-1; Pvt C Co 150th MI Inf;
  2-14-65 to 8-5-65; Hickerson PO; shot in
  hand
TOLAND, R. G., Hu-103-4; R. G. widow of; Pvt E
  Co 10th TN Inf; 10 Aug 64 to 12 May 65;
  PO omitted
TOLBERT, Wm. F., Wi-275-1; Pvt A Co 25th OH Inf;
  61 to 62; Bingham PO; rheumatism contracted;
  papers burned or lost

TOLBOT, Jacob, K-170-2; Elizabeth widow of; Pvt
  B Co 1st US Art; 2 Feb 64 to 1 Mar 66;
  Knoxville PO; blind?
TOLIAFERRO, Wilson, Ja-85-4; Georgetown PO
TOLIVER, Milton, D-90-1; Pvt C Co 100th KY Inf;
  63 to __ (3 yrs 9 mos); Nashville PO; knee
  slightly injured; sear? on neck; discharge
  papers lost long ago
TOLLE, James H., Wy-171-3; Pvt A Co 2nd TN Mtd Inf;
  10-2-63 to 10-14-65; Sorby PO; curvature of
  spine total disability
TOLLET, George, Wa-268-2; Johnson City PO
TOLLEY, Arter, De-24-1; Pvt G Co 6th TN Cav;
  18 Sep 62 to 26 Jul 65; Decaturville PO
TOLLEY, Grover K., D-94-1; Pvt D Co 10th MI Inf;
  Nov 9, 61 to Feb 6, 65; c/o E. R. Campbell,
  Nashville PO; skurvy & disease of liver;
  pension applied for; widow __ dead
TOLLEY, William, Co-61-3(1); Lydia widow of; Pvt;
  Parrottsville PO
TOLLISON, James, Wh-185-1; Pvt B Co 1st TN Inf;
  1-14-64 to 4-14-65; Walkers? Cross Roads PO;
  inflammatory rheumatism & rupture right
  side; loss of speech
TOLLISON, Madison, Wh-185-1; Pvt B Co 1st TN Inf;
  10-1-63 to 8-14-65; Walkers? Cross Roads PO;
  chronic rheumatism, shot in head and left
  hip; loss hearing
TOLLIVER, Lafayette, Rb-223-1; Springfield PO
TOMAS, John W., D-75-2; Pvt I Co 20th TN Inf;
  7 Jun 61 to 27 Aug 62; Stewarts Ferry PO;
  shot through left lung; discharged on
  surgeons certificate; CONF
TOMKIN, William, Sh-153-3; Collierville PO
TOMLINSON, David M., Wi-280-1; Bettis? Goode?
  formerly widow of; Pvt G Co 12th TN Cav;
  Feb 15, 64 to Oct 7, 65; Harpeth PO
TOMLINSON, John D., Dy-32-1; US Sol; Trimble PO
TOMPKINS, Alfred S., R-159-1; Sgt H Co 4th IN Cav;
  8-8-62 to 6-13-65; Spring City PO; wounded
  4 times; wounded in lungs & arm
TOMPKINS, John B., U-244-2; Pvt
  F Co 2nd TN Inf; 16 May 63 t __; Loganton PO
TOMPKINS, Stephens, Co-69-1; Pvt B Co 2nd TN Mtd
  Inf; 1 Jun 65 to 8 Aug 65; Help PO; liver,
  rheumaties; not a pensioner
TOMPSON, Henry B., Jo-149-3; Margret J. widow of;
  Pvt E Co 13th TN Cav; 24 Sep 63 to 5 Sep 65;
  Mountain City PO
TONCNEY?, William J., Ct-40-5; D Sgt E Co 2nd TN
  Mtd Inf; 5-14-62 to 5-14-65; Elizabethton PO
TONEY, George R., H-60-2; Pvt K Co 19th NY V Cav;
  7-62 to 7-65; Chattanooga PO; gun shot
  wound left knee
TONEY, Jesse J., U-247-2; Pvt D Co 13th TN Cav;
  3 Sep 63 to 5 Sep 65; Erwin PO; rheumatism,
  heart & paralysis
TONEY, Samuel W., U-247-1; Pvt F Co 2nd TN Inf;
  22 Jul 62 to 19 Jun 65; Erwin PO; rheumatism
  bronchitis uralysis
TOOLE, Robert H., Ct-35-2; Sgt & 2nd Lt A Co 6th
  NY Inf; 3-24-61 to 6-14-66; Butler PO,
  Johnson CO; no disability claimed; no dis-
  charge producer unacquainted just moved
  from VA to TN
TOOMEY, Henry (see McMahan, Henry)
TOOMEY, Patrick, S-214-2; Marget widow of; 26th
  KY Inf; Glenmary PO; does not know dates
TOOPS, Samuel, Hi-87-4; Sarah widow of; Pvt E Co
  14th OH Rgt of Vol; 8-21-61 to 1-12-65;
  Bonaqua PO
TOOTEN, Joseph, Lo-188-3; Catharine widow of; Pvt
  A Co 5th TN Inf; Stockton PO
TORENCE, James T., F-44-1; Pvt B Co 13th TN Inf; Oct
  20 61 to 18 May 65; PO omitted; CONF
TORROTT, Nothlet, Dy-25-1; Ellen F. Conner widow
  of; Pvt; Newbern PO; died in hospitals; CONF
TORY, William, K-175-2; Pvt D Co 13th NC? Inf; 28
  Dec 62 to 28 Dec 65; Pedigo PO
TOSELAND, John, Ms-172-1; Pvt 9th OH Bat; 26 Aug
  63 to 25 Jul 65; Farmington PO
TOSH, John G., Cr-14-2; Francie P. widow of; Pvt
  M Co 6th TN Cav; 25 Aug 62 to 26 Jul 65;
  Clarksburg PO
TOSH, Layfaette M., Cr-14-2; Pvt G Co 7th TN Cav;
  5 Aug 62 to 25 Oct 63; Clarksburg PO; re-
  enlisted

318

TOTE, Harriett, De-24-1; widow US Sol; Decaturville PO
TOTHACER, Chas. L., D-78-2; Nashville PO
TOTTY, F. L., Hu-103-4; Pvt E Co 10th TN Inf; 10 Aug 64 to 12 May 65; PO omitted
TOULER, G. W., Hu-103-4; Pvt E Co 10th TN Inf; 10 Aug 64 to 12 May 65; PO omitted
TOVLER, David L., Mn-125-1; Sol Federa; PO omitted
TOW, Shade M., K-179-1; Pvt 3rd NC Inf; Rodelin PO
TOWE, Elmina, K-154-5(2); Knoxville PO
TOWELL, John, D-90-1; alias Nicks, George; Pvt 12th TN Inf; Nashville PO; one finger crippled; did not see him, his wife gave me all I have put down
TOWER, Herbert B., H-61-4; Pvt K Co 105th OH Inf; 6-4-64 to 7-12-65; Chattanooga PO
TOWER, William C., M-106-2(1); Piercy A. Devreese formerly widow of; Pvt 5th TN Cav; 12-62 to ___ (1 yr); Hillsdale PO; died of typhoid fever 2-20-64; not or never drew a pension
TOWNES, Justin D., Gi-127-4; Samantha widow of; Capt; Pulaski PO
TOWNEY, John S., Ge-84-1; Pvt D Co 11th TN Cav; 7 Oct 63 to 5 Sep 65; Bird Bridge PO; diarrehea and hart deas
TOWNS, R. R., Ru-231-1; Pvt E Co 10th IN Cav; 30 Nov 63 to 31 Aug 65; Lamar PO
TOWNS, Shon, Be-5-1; Marthey Hoskins widow of; Pvt E Co 7th TN Cav; Jul 62 to Aug 65; PO omitted
TOWNSAND, Fountain, Li-144-1; Rittie widow of; (Col); Flintville PO; right knee broke & abcess in breast; an invalid for 40 yrs (sic)
TOWNSAND, Nathaniel, Cr-17-1; Pvt E and C Co 7th TN Cav; 6-2-62 to 8-9-65; Buena Vista PO
TOWNSEND, Albert M., G-71-1; Sgt G Co 47th TN Inf; 10 Jun 61 to 20 Feb 64; Rutherford PO; CONF
TOWNSEND, Daniel A., Fr-105-1; 1st Sgt I Co 15th TN Col V Inf; Feb 63 to Apr 66; Winchester PO
TOWNSEND, George, Wa-263-4; Luphina widow of; Pvt; Alfred PO; died with measels; CONF
TOWNSEND, George W., Gu-48-4(1); Pvt C Co 7th TN Cav; 5-6-62 to 12-65; Flintville PO (Lincoln Co.); small pox
TOWNSEND, Henry, L-101-1; Pvt D Co 55th C Inf; Henning PO; flesh wound l. breast; discharge in hands of atty.
TOWNSEND, Isiah, D-67-2; Pvt B Co 101st Col Inf; Feb 24 64 to 21 Jul 66; Nashville PO
TOWNSEND, James, Se-230-1; Mary E. widow of; Pvt 5th TN Cav; 62 to ___ (1 yr); Pokeberry PO; cant learn much of him; CONF
TOWNSEND, Lysander E., R-162-3; Quartermaster Sgt G Co 4th US Art; 5-11-61 to 5-11-65; Dayton PO; contracted rheumatism
TOWNSEND, Stafford, B-5-1; alias Jackson; Pvt I Co 15th TN Inf; 2-24-64 to 4-7-66; Fosterville PO; afflicted with rheumatism
TOWNSLEY, Thomas, Gr-76-1; Pvt H Co 1st TN Cav; 20 Dec 62 to 19 Jun 65; Indian Ridge PO; diarrhea and piles
TOWNSON, Calep, Mo-129-2; Pvt G Co; Lomotley PO
TOWNSON, Henry, L-99-2; Pvt 149th US Col Inf; 62 to 66; Durhamville PO; leg broken; date of enlistment and no. of reg. uncertain
TOWRISTER, William M., Mo-127-1; Pvt M Co 13th TN Cav; 13-15-62 to 9-1-64; Notchy PO
TOWSON, Hearty, Sn-252-2; Cpl J Co 14th US Inf; Gallatin PO
TOY, Joseph, Hi-85-1; Emily widow of; Pvt H Co PA Inf; 61 to 65; Lick Creek PO
TOZER, Samuel, Hr-96-2; Ordly C Co 6th TN Inf; Mar 61 to home 64; Norris PO; CONF
TRACY, Henry, Ro-211-3; Pvt C Co 10th OH Inf; 18 May 63 to 65; Harriman PO
TRACY, John J., Cu-17-1; Pvt D Co 4th VT Inf; 9-64 to 7-18-65; Crossville PO
TRAFFORD, George, Sh-158-3; Pvt G Co 10th TN Inf; Apr 62 to Jun 65; Memphis PO; no disability, discharge papers at Nashville
TRAFFORD, George W., Cr-9-1; Cpl G Co 10th TN Inf; May 12 62 to 24 Jun 65; Chestnutt Bluff PO; neuralgia from exposure
TRAINOR, Owen W., Sh-201-3; Memphis PO; CONF
TRAITOR, Henry, D-51-2; Pvt C Co 109th KY C Inf; 504 North Cherry, Nashville PO; this man discharge out in Texas, 1886

TRAMEL, William H., Dk-35-3(1); Louisa E. widow of; Pvt K Co 5th TN Cav; Capling PO
TRAMELL, Merida, Ge-99-1; Pvt C Co 4th TN Inf; 16 Nov 61 to 7 Jul 65; Limestone PO; diarrhia & piles
TRAMMEL, John M., Dk-35-3(1); Pvt E Co 4th TN Mtd Inf; 11-26-64 to 8-25-65; Capling PO
TRAMMEL, Shadrach, Dk-35-3(1); Pvt G Co 44th IN Inf; 2-1-65 to 6-7-65; Capling PO
TRAMMELL, Davina, S-216-2; widow; Huntsville PO
TRANBARGER, James, Ov-135-2; Pvt D Co 3rd KY Inf; 11-5-61 to 1-10-65; Monroe PO; wounded in hand
TRANNE?, David, Wa-270-1; Pvt C Co 56th VA In;f 61 to 65; Johnson City PO
TRANTHAM, Thomas, Co-61-1; Pvt A Co 4th TN Inf; 12-13-63 to 8-2-65; Salem PO
TRAUNICHT, Henry, D-45-4; Catherine wife of; Cpl E Co 2nd MO; 8-1-61 to 12-14-62; Nashville PO
TRAVELSTEAD, Solomon, Sn-261-5(4); Pvt E Co 15th IL Cav; 61 to ___; Brackentown PO; enlarge of splene 25 yrs
TRAVER, John J., Ct-45-2; Cpl D Co 6th MD Inf; 8-22-62 to 6-22-65; Carter Furnace PO; lungs, Petersburg, January 1865
TRAVILLION, Thomas, Hd-54-2; Pvt B Co 46th OH Inf; 11 Mar 62 to 31 Mar 66; Ruth PO; wounded in right shoulder
TRAVIS, B. B., R-160-1; Pvt G Co 3rd TN Cav; 9-15-63 to 6-10-65; 6th Civil Dist
TRAVIS, Gilbert, Hn-75-1; Pvt I Co 13th TN Inf; Aug 64 to May 65; Manlyville PO
TRAVIS, Jacob, Mu-205-2; Pvt E Co 98th OH Inf; 24 Jul 61 to 30 Sep 65; Williamsport PO; gunshot wound in left knee
TRAVIS, James C., Hn-77-3(1); Pvt I Co 48th Mtd Inf; 20 Aug 63 to 20 Dec 64; Paris PO
TRAVIS, Sidney, Ge-100-1; Pvt A Co 2nd NY Cav; Feb 65 to ___; Midway PO; never discharged
TRAVIS, Thomas, Sh-149-1; Pvt E Co 26th KY Inf; 27 Aug 63 to 25 Mar 64; Frazar PO
TRAYSER, Paul, Sh-175-2; 152 Hadden Ave, Memphis PO
TRAYWICK, Henry A., Cr-16-4; Pvt K Co 2nd TN Mtd Inf; Jun 1 64 to Jun 29 65; Huntingdon PO
TREADWAY, Richman, L-99-1; Pvt E Co 3rd US Hvy Art; Apr 63 to May 66; Orysa PO
TREADWAY, William H., Ct-38-2; Pvt H Co 13th TN Cav; 9-24-63 to 10-23-65; Dry Creek PO; left foot cut off
TREDWELL, Darling M., La-117-3; Pvt; no dates; 15th Dist; CONF
TREDWELL, Henry, Sh-157-2; Pvt G Co 11th US Inf; 64 to 66; No. 65 Clay St., Memphis PO
TREECE, Jessee, Cl-48-1; Pvt C Co 1st TN Inf; 8-9-61 to 8-17-64; Old Town PO; gun shot in right arm
TREECE, John, Cl-48-3; Charity widow of; Pvt C Co 1st TN Inf; 61 to ___; Old Town PO; mumps was not able for duty any more, widow dont know date of enlistment and discharged, had no disc.
TREECE, Square, Cl-48-1; Pvt C Co 1st TN Inf; 8-9-61 to 9-6-65; Old Town PO
TREN, John J., Me-92-5(2); Pvt D Co 5th TN Inf; 2-26-62 to 3-30-65; Pin Hook PO; rheumatism & rupture; has not been able to work for 6 mos
TRENT, Curren M., Hw-130-2; Cpl M Co 1st TN Cav; 1 Feb 63 to 19 Jun 65; Lee Valley PO
TRENT, Dannel G., Ha-116-2; US Sol; Dist No 10
TRENT, David, Ha-116-1; US Sol; 13th Dist
TRENT, Flemming, H-62-4; 226 Chestnut, Chattanooga PO
TRENT, James G., Ha-112-1; Nancy widow of; Pvt B Co 1st TN Cav; Datura PO; gunshot through lungs
TRENT, Joel, Hw-120-2; Nancy widow of; Pvt H Co 1st TN Cav; 9 Mar 62 to 5 Sep 65; Eidson PO
TRENT, John, Cl-52-1; Pvt D Co 1st TN Cav; 3-11-62 to 4-28-65; Quarter PO; lungs injured by cold
TRENT, John C., Ha-116-3(1); Pvt D Co; 30 Feb 62 to 8 Oct 63; Clinch PO
TRENT, John H., Hm-106-3; Capt A Co 1st TN Cav; 26 Nov 62 to 26 Sep 63; Morristown PO
TRENT, Madison, Ha-110-2; Black Water PO
TRENT, Robbert, Cl-55-1; Mary E. widow of; Pvt G Co 2nd TN; 10-62 to ___; Lone Mountain PO; died in hospital Louisville, KY

TRENT, Robert A., Ha-116-3(1); Sgt B Co 1st TN Cav; 11 Mar 62 to 29 May 65; Mitchburgh PO
TRENT, Wiley R., Ha-110-3; Pvt G Co 9th TN Cav; 4 Aug 64 to 11 Sep 65; Luther PO
TRENT, William R., Ha-110-3; Pvt B Co 1st TN Cav; 11 Mar 62 to 10 Apr 65; Michburgh PO
TRENT, William X., Ha-112-1; Pvt A Co 1st TN Lt Art; 1 Mar 64 to 3 Aug 65; Datura PO
TRENT, Zeackariah G., K-181-2; Sgt A Co 1st TN Cav; 6 Mar 62to 11 Apr 65; Nast PO; varicose vains
TRENTHAM, Caleb L., Se-229-2; Pvt C Co 1st TN Art; 1 Apr 64 to 1 Aug 65; Trentville PO; rheumatism & hearing
TRESSLEY, John, Bo-19-2; Pvt A Co 8th TN Cav; 61 to 65; Rockford PO
TREW, Barnett M., Me-94-2; Cpl L Co 12th TN Cav; 64 to 65; Pin Hook PO; discharge lost
TREWHITT, Daniel C., H-51-7; Hill City PO
TREWHITT, Thomas L., H-54-1; Sgt Maj 6th TN Inf; 11-1-61 to 3-8-65; Chattanooga PO; 7 mos a prisoner at Tuscalossa & Mobile AL; suffering from neuralgia and rheumatism contracted in prison
TRIBBLE, Joel W., We-221-5(2); Pvt E Co 5th TN Inf; 25 Aug 61 to 6 May 65; Martin PO; two flesh waulds in left thigh; CONF
TRICE, John, Ch-13-2; Pvt I Co 2nd TN Vol; 9-63 to 5-65; Jacks Creek PO; supposed rheumatism, pension agent kept discharge
TRICE, Toney, Mt-138-1; (blk) US Sol; Dist 7, New Providence PO
TRICE, William, Sh-189-1; Pvt F Co 88th US Col Inf; 12-64 to 2-66; La. Ave, Memphis PO
TRICKARD, John W., Dy-25-1; Pvt C Co 47th TN Inf; Oct 15 61 to Jun 28 64; Newbern PO; lost left arm; CONF
TRICKE, Arnold Henry, D-78-1; Pvt 4th OH Art; Aug 2 61 to 27 Aug 64; Nashville PO
TRIGGS, Isaac, T-216-1; Mariah widow of; Pvt; Corona PO
TRIM, John V., We-226-1; Pvt L Co 6th TN Cav; 15 Aug 62 to __; Sharon PO; marked on roll, deserter
TRIMBLE, Marion, D-73-1; Mary widow of; Pvt; Vernon Ave, Nashville PO; widow lost papers
TRIMELEY, Henry C., Mt-141-1; H Co TN Vol; Dist 11
TRIMER, Andrew J., Cr-1-2(1); Marth A. widow of; Pvt NJ; Gadsden PO
TRINDLE, John, H-53-1; Pvt K Co 56th MA Inf; 2-64 to 8-22-65; Chattanooga PO; loss of left leg; served 2 yrs in Navy before enlistment in army
TRIOR, Henry N., Cl-51-2; 1st Lt F Co 8th TN Cav; 2-28-63 to 9-11-65; Ritchie PO
TRIPPLET, Hiram, Sh-163-1; "found examining work"; PO omitted
TRIPLETT, Jeremiah, Br-14-3; Narcissas widow of; G Co 5th TN Inf; 4-11-62 to 5-15-65; Black Fox PO; deafness in one ear
TRIPLETT, Joseph, Br-6-1; Pvt A Co 10th TN Cav; 8-12-63 to 8-1-65; Climer PO; diarrhoea etc.
TRISDELL, James, Cy-27-3(1); Sgt A Co 1st TN Cav; 63 to 65; Moss PO
TRITT, William, Co-68-2; Pvt A Co 2nd TN Cav; 63 to 65; Cashy PO; chronic diarrhea, rheumism, piles
TRITTEROW, William P., K-179-5; Pvt K Co 3rd TN Cav; 5th Oct 63 to 8 Aug 65; Concord PO
TROBAUGH, George A., Ge-90-2; Pvt A Co 8th TN Cav; 11 Jun 63 to 11 Sep 65; Myers PO; piles & rumatism
TROBAUGH, George M., Hm-108-2(1); Pvt D Co 1st TN Cav; 15 Apr 62 to 15 Apr 65; Bulah PO; lungs diseased
TROBAUGH, James, J-77-1; Pvt H Co 37th KY Cav; 7-1-63 to 10-29-64; Gainesboro PO; measles & kidney disease
TROLLINGER, Andy, Ms-173-1; Pvt C Co 5th TN Cav; 18 Aug 64 to 3 Jul 65; Rich Creek PO
TROOP, James, D-67-1; alias McDaniel; Pvt 17th Col Inf; 62 to 65; Nashville PO
TROOPE, John H., D-64-3; Katie Throope widow of; pilot & master; May Duke Charmer? Conistoga; 62 to 65; Nashville PO
TROTT, Mike, B-9-1; Pvt M Co 5th __; 63 to 65; Vannatta PO

TROTTER, James C., Se-223-1; Sarah widow of; Pvt B Co 2nd TN Cav; 15 Sep 62 to 6 Jul 65; Pigeon Forge PO; diarrhea
TROTTER, John M., Se-223-1; Tryphinia widow of; Pvt M Co 2nd TN Cav; 8 Nov 62 to 6 Jul 65; Pigeon Forge PO
TROTTER, Lorenzey D., Se-223-3; Sarah E. Seaton formerly widow of; Sgt M Co 2nd TN Cav; 8 Nov 62 to 14 Feb 63; Hendersons Springs PO
TROTTER, McMillan, Se-225-2; Pvt M Co 2nd TN Cav?; 9 Nov 62 to 30 Jun 65; Trotters Store PO; piles and chronic diarrhoea 25 yrs; originated in service
TROTTER, Pleasant H., Se-223-1; Malinda S. widow of; Pvt H Co 9th TN Cav; Pigeon Forge PO
TROTTER, William J., Se-223-1; Mary R. widow of; Capt E Co 9th TN Cav; 1 Oct 63 to 28 Jun 64; Pigeon Forge PO
TROUP, Jackson M., B-7-2; Cpl C Co 5th Reg TN Cav; 9-62 to 6-65; PO omitted
TROUT, Francis M., K-185-2; Pvt E Co 48th TN Inf; McMillans PO; CONF
TROUT, George W., K-185-1; Pvt C Co 1st TN Cav; Apr 62 to Apr 65; Scaggston PO; shot in left thigh
TROUT, Jerry, K-170-1; Pvt G Co 7th TN Inf; 8 Nov 64 to 27 Jul 65; Knoxville PO
TROUT, William, Be-1-1; Pvt; balance not known; Coxburg PO
TROUTMAN, Adam A., H-49-6; Pvt E Co 3rd TN Cav; 1-29-62 to 8-3-65; Daisy PO
TROUTMAN, Eliz. J., K-185-3; widow; River Dale PO
TROUTMAN, Jacob A., H-58-2; Cpl H Co 4th TN Inf; 11-15-64 to 8-2-65; Sale Creek PO; rheumatism & kidney disease
TROWER, John E., H-53-7; Chickamauga PO; shot in thumb
TROXDALE, Rebecca A. (see Welch, Gideon)
TRUE, D. H., La-117-3; Pvt K Co 20th TN Inf; Nov 61 to 65; 15th Dist; CONF
TRUELOVE, Benjamin J., Rb-228-2; Pvt A Co 1st GA Inf; Jul 62 to Apr 65; Coopertown PO; CONF
TRUELOVE, Hal, Hy-75-1; Pvt H Co Hvy Art; Jun 63 to May? 65; Stanton PO; Kepner Eve?
TRUETT, William, W1-298-2; Pvt H Co 5th TN Cav; 15 Oct 62 to 14 Aug 65; Auburn PO; shot in one foot; able to do half work
TRULL, Salathel, P-157-1; Pvt F Co 2nd TN Cav; 2-20-64 to 3-4-65; Linden PO
TRUMAN, Wm. T., Wa-267-2; Pvt G Co 13th TN Cav; Sep 63 to 5 Sep 65; Johnson City PO; catarrh of head & lung dis.
TRUNDLE, William H., Se-231-1; Pvt H Co 1st Hvy Art; 8 Jun 64 to 21 Mar 66; Boyds Creek PO
TRUNK, John, Br-9-1; Pvt E Co 2nd OH Hvy Art; 7-1-63 to 6-9-65; Cleveland PO
TRUSLEY, Henry, Hw-120-1; Pvt F Co 8th TN Cav; no dates (1 yr); War Gap PO; rheumatism & liver
TRUSTEY, James F., Hw-120-1; Pvt M Co 8th TN Cav; 15 Sep 63 to 11 Sep 65; War Gap PO; rheumatism & heart
TRUXAL, Benjamin F., H-63-3; Pvt 102nd PA Inf; 62 to 64; 217 W. 7th, Chattanooga PO; wounded left arm; 10 mos hospital
TRYER, Samuel, H-69-2; Pvt; Chattanooga PO
TSCHOPIK, Adolph, H-59-3; Capt PA Inf; Chattanooga PO
TUAK, David, Lo-193-1; Pvt I Co 5th TN Inf; 1 Jul 62 to 28 Jun 65; Unitia PO
TUBBS, Frances M., Ma-122-1; Sgt G Co 23rd IN Inf; 12 Jul 61 to 23 Jul 65; Spring Creek PO; injury of spine, done while in Andersonville prison
TUBBS?, James P., Dk-34-6(5); 13th Civil Dist
TUBBS, Lowerty, De-26-2; B Co 52nd TN; Dec 61 to (6 mos); Northford PO; CONF
TUCK, Ferdinand N., We-225-2(1); Pvt E Co 15th KY Cav; Feb 63 to Nov 15, 63; C pl M Co 2nd IL Cav; Nov 25 63 to May 27 65; Dresden PO; cronic diarrhea, not able to labor now
TUCK, George W., M-103-6; Pvt B Co 5th TN Cav; 8-24-62 to 6-25-65; Union Camp PO
TUCK, Moses, Bo-14-4; Pvt I Co 5th TN Inf; 12-3-63 to 6-30-65; Huffstetlers Store PO; chronic diarrhea
TUCK, Moses, A-8-1; Pvt B Co 7th TN; 11-1-64 to 7-27-65; Scarborough PO; rheumatism

TUCK, William, M-108-2(1); Loue F. widow of; Cpl
  & Pvt F Co 59th KY Cav; 8-24-63 to 1-18-65;
  Salt Lick PO
TUCKER, Alden T., Ge-92-5; Pvt F Co 1st TN Cav; 1
  Mar 62 to 30 Mar 65; Ottway PO; rheumatism,
  resulting disease of heart & lung disease
TUCKER, Alex, Hy-81-2; alias Alex Mauer; Pvt F Co
  4th US Col Cav; 63 to 66; 7th Civil Dist
TUCKER, Alexandria, R-162-2; Pvt 6th TN Cav; 61
  to __ (2 yrs); Dayton PO; Mr. Tucker during
  the service
TUCKER, Alix, De-23-1; Sgt G Co 27th TN Inf; Aug
  11 61 to 26 Apr 65; Bath Springs PO; CONF
TUCKER, Branch, Hw-133-4; Pvt G Co 31st TN Cav;
  Feb 62 to 8 Apr 65; rheumatism; Fry PO; CONF
TUCKER, Crawford, Sh-159-6; Jane widow of; Sgt
  59th TN; Memphis PO; died in the army
TUCKER, Edmond, Mc-110-2(1); Pvt A Co 3rd TN Inf;
  2-10-62 to 1-13-63; Fiketon PO
TUCKER, Edward, Sh-150-2; Pvt A Co; 2 yrs; Mullins
  Station PO
TUCKER, Elijah, K-161-5(6); Precilla Wells widow
  of; Knoxville PO
TUCKER, F. N., Wa-270-1; Pvt G Co 60th TN Inf; 16
  Oct 62 to Nov 65; Austin's Spring PO; pris-
  oner in Andersonville
TUCKER, George M., H-51-6; Bugler F Co 3rd MI Cav;
  1-19-64 to 2-12-66; Red Bank PO
TUCKER, George W., Ch-17-2; Pvt B Co 6th TN Cav; 8-
  62 to 7-65; Masseyville PO
TUCKER, Hettie, Mc-116-4; alms house, Athens PO
TUCKER, Horatio N., H-53-6; Lenora H. widow of; Pvt
  E Co 20th CT Inf; 6-13-62 to 6-13-65; Ridge-
  dale PO; chronic diarrhoea
TUCKER, Jacob, Ms-174-1; Pvt H Co 13th US Inf; 22
  Oct 63 to 10 Jan 66; Chapel Hill PO; rheuma-
  tism
TUCKER, James, Cr-8-2; Pvt K Co 9th TN; 1 May 61
  to 65; Maury City PO; CONF
TUCKER, James H., Dy-29-4; Pvt; 61 to 65; Newbern
  PO; CONF
TUCKER, James L., Hd-50-5; 1st Lt F Co 10th TN Inf;
  5-6-62 to 6-20-65; Nixon PO; right ankle
  wounded; totaly disabled for work
TUCKER, John, Hw-133-2; Pvt D Co 31st TN Cav; Mar
  64 to Sep 64; Fry PO; CONF
TUCKER, John C., K-186-3; Chumlea PO
TUCKER, John J., Mo-131-1; Pvt C Co 3rd TN Inf;
  8-15-63 to 12-24-63; Joe PO
TUCKER, John P., D-72-4; Pvt F Co 16th IL Inf; Jun
  6, 61 to 1 May 65; Nashville PO
TUCKER, John W., Wi-276-2; Pvt Batery Arillry; Aug
  61 to Feb 62; Beechville PO; both hands lost;
  CONF
TUCKER, Joseph, Me-88-3; Sarah J. widow of; Col;
  Pvt E Co; Birchwood PO
TUCKER, L. C., D-43-1; Orderly A Co 119th PA; 64
  to 65; Nashville PO
TUCKER, Lon (see Jones, Lon)
TUCKER, Margaret (see Graham, Andrew J.)
TUCKER, McGilbert, Sh-145-2; Pvt C Co 110th US Col
  Inf; 15 Apr 63 to 6 Feb 66; Millington PO;
  Cap McNelly, Col Kiddman; mustered out at
  Huntsville, AL
TUCKER, Monroe, Sh-181-6; Pvt F Co 111th USC Inf; 6
  Jan 64 to 30 Apr 66; Fillmore, Nashville PO;
  crippled in shoulder and one leg while a
  prisoner of war at Mobile, AL, in the year
  1865
TUCKER, Nathin B., Hw-121-3(2); Pvt F Co 1st TN
  Cav; 1 Mar 62 to 30 Mar 65; New Hope PO;
  chronic rheumatism
TUCKER, R. F., Hd-53-1; Pvt C Co 6th TN Cav; 10
  Jul 63 to 26 Jul 65; Saltillo PO; effect of
  mumps by being exposed on duty
TUCKER, Rubin H., De-22-1; Pvt D Co 19th TN Cav;
  8 Feb 63 to 1 May 65; Bath Springs PO; CONF
TUCKER, Silas, H-66-2; Pvt E Co 43rd Col Inf; 8-
  64 to 5-65; Chattanooga PO
TUCKER, Solomon, Gr-77-1; Nancey widow of; Y. Z.
  PO
TUCKER, Straly S., U-247-1; Pvt M Co 8th TN Cav;
  10 Sep 63 to 11 Sep 65; Erwin PO; rheumatism
  26 yrs
TUCKER, Thomas H., Br-13-3; Pvt E Co 4th TN Cav;
  8-5-62 to 7-12-65; Ora PO; chronic piles
TUCKER, William G., Bo-12-4; Sol US; 17th Dist

TUCKER, William H., Hw-133-4; Sgt G Co 31st TN Mtd
  Inf; 15 Oct 63 to 15 Apr 65; Fry PO; CONF
TUCKER, William N., Pu-145-5(6); Pvt 1st Mtd Inf;
  3-16-64 to 5-23-65; Buffalo Valley PO
TUCKER, Wilson M., Mu-210-6; Pvt G Co 1st TN Inf;
  6 Feb 63 to 64; Spring Hill PO; CONF
TUDER, James H., S-214-3; Pvt I Co 1st TN Inf; 9
  Aug 61 to 17 Oct 64; Robbins PO; rheumatism
  & heart disease
TUDER, JOhn W., Se-220-1; Pvt I Co 1st TN. Inf; 20
  Aug 61 to 12 Apr 65; Tudors Cave PO
TUGGLE, Adam G., K-170-3; US Sol; Dist 12
TUGGLE, Henry, Wl-297-1; Pvt D Co 4th TN Mtd Inf;
  29 Sep 64 to 25 Aug 65; Grant PO (Smith Co.)
TUGGLE, James, Mc-117-3; Pvt D Co 12th KY; 10-22-
  61 to 7-11-65; Kimbrough's Store PO; rheumatism
TUGGLE, Thomas, Wl-297-1; PVt H Co 4th TN Mtd Inf;
  1 Dec 64 to 25 Aug 65; Grant PO; paralsis,
  loss of mind?, cause by fall
TULEY, John M., D-96-1; Ordrly Sgt Cav 6th TN Reg;
  62 to 65; c/o S. B. Howlett, Nashville PO;
  invalid, husband not at home, information
  from wife
TULL, D. G., G-57-7(4); Asst Sur H Co 7th MS Cav;
  6 May 61 to 15 Apr 65; Yorkville PO; CONF
TULLOCH, J. C., Bo-11-3; Pvt A Co 3rd TN Inf; 2-
  10-62 to 2-23-65; Big Gulley PO
TULLOCH, William H., Bo-14-4; Pvt A Co 3rd TN Inf;
  2-10-62 to 4-29-65; Huffstetlers Store PO
TULLOO, James, R-162-3; Cook G Co 19th MI Inf;
  63 to __; Dayton PO; shot through ancl; taken
  prisoner during service
TULLUS, Littleton, D-80-1; Sgt A Co 101st Reg?; 63
  to 65; Donelson PO; left knee fractured
TULLY, Britton, Dy-27-2; Pvt I Co 12th TN Inf;
  Aug 61 to May 65; Newbern PO; CONF
TULTON, John R., K-160-1; Sgt A Co 22nd NJ Vol; 12
  Aug 61 to 30 Sep 62; Knoxville PO
TUMAN, John A., Pu-142-2; Pvt D Co 1st TN Inf;
  10-31-64 to 6-15-65; Binyon Hill PO; shot in
  left hip
TUMLIN, George H., Sm-171-2; Pvt C Co 8th TN Mtd
  Inf; 2-20-65 to 8-25-65; Chestnut Mount PO
TUMMINS, William H., Di-42-1; E Sgt G Co 12th TN
  Cav; 12-23-62 to 6-9-65; Tenn City PO
TUNE, Thomas K., B-5-1; Pvt E Co 10th TN Inf;
  1-7-62 to 1-23-65; Bell Buckle PO
TUNNAGE, Riley, Sh-162-1; Pvt F Co; no. dates
  (3 yrs); Bings Town PO
TUNNEL, James M., Po-148-1; Pvt I Co 5th TN Inf;
  10-23-62 to 1-30-65; Cog Hill PO
TUNNELL, James H., Hw-121-6(1); Lt B Co 34d TN Mtd
  Inf; 30 Jan 64 to 30 Nov 64; Strahl PO;
  dyspepsy 26 yr
TUNNELL, Thomas C., A-7-1; Robertsville PO
TUNNER, Harmon, K-184-1; Pvt F Co 1st TN Inf;
  61 to 17 Oct 64; Asbury PO
TUNVIL, John, U-245-2; Pvt D Co 13th TN Cav;
  10 Sep 63 to 5 Sep 65; Dry Creek PO, Carter
  Co.; in the service of US in year 1865;
  left my command on lief of absence
TURBEYVILLE, Harvey, K-166-4(2); Pvt D Co 9th TN
  Cav; 1 Sep 63 to 11 __ 65; Knoxville PO
TUREHEN, Dannel T., Ca-23-1; Pvt G Co 154th IL Inf;
  1864 to 1865 (8 mos); Leoni PO; no injuries
TURMS, Joseph, Mr-97-2; Pvt E Co 6th TN Inf;
  9-4-64 to 6-30-65; Jarman? PO
TURNAGE, David E., F-40-1; Mary widow of; Pvt C
  Co 13th TN Inf; 20 Mar 61 to May 65; Hickory
  Withe PO; CONF
TURNBILL, Richard, Ro-202-2; Pvt I Co 1st TN Inf;
  1 Oct 62 to Sep 63; Oral PO; bronchitis,
  loss of teeth
TURNBOW, Thomas, G-57-5(3); Pvt; Yorkville PO;
  CONF
TURNER, Albert, F-43-1; Pvt B Co 61st Col US Inf;
  __ to May 64; PO omitted; at home on furlow
  sick when Reg was mustered out
TURNER, Alexander, Ho-97-1; Pvt E Co 18th TN Inf;
  10 Mar 64 to 24 Aug 65; Medcalf PO; dis-
  charged on account of close of war
TURNER, Andrew J., Cu-15-2; Pvt Baitties Batt. TN;
  11-62 to 1865 (2 yrs 6 mos); Crossville PO;
  catarrh of head 8 years
TURNER, Archie, Sh-174-2; Pvt A Co 52nd US Col Inf;
  1863 to 5-6-66; 226 Pontotoc St., Memphis PO

TURNER, Ben F., Cr-3-1; Mins? G Co 111th US; 63 to 65; Gadsden PO
TURNER, Benjamon, De-23-1; Pvt C Co 6th TN Cav; Sep 62 to May 25, 65; Thurman PO; horse fell and broke leg; cant do any servace and has ?
TURNER, Berry, L-100-2; Leoman? Pvt; Monarch No. 2; Sep 64 to 14 Jan 65; Ripley PO; piles, rumatism & blindness
TURNER, Charles, Hr-94-1; Musician I Co 59th TN Inf; 1-1-63 to 1-31-66; Saulsbury PO; rheumatism
TURNER, David, Hu-98-1; Col; Pvt A Co 13th TN Inf; 6 Jul 64 to 6 Nov 64; Waverley PO; left army by sickness
TURNER, David, O-140-2; Pvt G Co 4th TN Inf; Oct 63 to 11 Mar 66; Rives PO
TURNER, David S., Un-259-1; Sgt K Co 2nd TN Cav; 15 Aug 62 to 14 Jul 65; Rhodelia PO; spinal iritation; caused by fever in 1862
TURNER, Edward D., Co-61-5(2); Pvt K Co 8th TN Inf; 10 Mar 63 to 20 Jun 65; Bridgeport PO
TURNER, Elijah L., Hm-104-3(1); (Turner, Elisha W.); Pvt D Co 1st TN Cav; 2 Dec 63 to 25 Oct 65; Vally Home PO; Scurvy
TURNER, Emanuel, F-47-1; Musician C Co 59th TN Inf; Feb 1, 64 to Jan 31, 66; Williston PO
TURNER, Evan S., Gr-74-2; Pvt C Co 4th TN Cav; 1 Jan 63 to 12 Jul 65; May Spring PO
TURNER, Francis M., K-180-2; Pvt D Co 6th TN Inf; 18 Apr 62 to 27 Apr 65; Ebenezer PO; piles result of fever in leg
TURNER, Francis M., Ha-113-1; Lt E Co 8th TN Cav; 10 Oct 63 to 22 Sep 65; Sneedville PO
TURNER, Gabrel G., Un-256-3; Pvt D Co 1st TN Inf; 9 Aug 61 to 17 Sep 64; Loy's X Roads PO; diarhear
TURNER, George, Ru-235-1; Teamster A Co 17th IN Cav; Smyrna PO
TURNER, George M., Sm-173-2; Pvt G Co 5th TN Cav; 9-27-62 to 8-14-65; Brush Creek PO
TURNER, Green, D-57-2; Cpl A Co 2nd US Art; Nov 65 to 67; Nashville PO, 8th Ward
TURNER, Harry, C-8-1; Pvt B Co 11th TN Cav; Well Spring PO; could not get dates of discharge
TURNER, J. S., M-108-5; Pvt A Co 5th KY Inf; 11-28-61 to 6-26-65; Lafayette PO; hearing slightly damaged
TURNER, Jack E., Ce-23-2; Lt (Conf) A Co 47th TN Jan 61 to Nov 63; Thomasville PO; wounded with shell at Ft. D.; paralyzed 4 years
TURNER, Jackson, K-167-3; Pvt A Co 1st TN Hvy; 63 to Oct 65; Knoxville PO
TURNER, Jake, Sh-193-1; Pvt; Memphis PO; shot in one foot
TURNER, James, Wa-263-1; Pvt H Co 13th TN Cav; 26 Sep 63 to 7 Mary 65; Garbers Mills PO; claims disease of neuralgia & heart dis., lungs, deafness
TURNER, James, Sh-147-2; Bugler D Co 4th US Art; 1 Jul 63 to 25 Feb 66; Cuba PO
TURNER, James, We-221-2; Pvt L Co 6th TN Cav; 6 Jul 62 to 7 Aug 65; Martin PO; thrown from a horse at LaGrange TN
TURNER, James L., K-159-2; 1st Lt D Co 6th TN Inf; 18 Apr 62 to 27 Apr 65; Knoxville PO
TURNER, James W., Sm-174-2; New Middleton PO
TURNER, Jessie, Hd-45-2; Sarah A. widow of; Pvt; Swift PO
TURNER, JOhn, Fe-41-3(1); Pvt Capt Beaty's Co. Indept. Scouts of TN; 9-61 to Spring 1865; Boat Land PO; blindness, mumps, mealels, fever & yellow jaundice; _____ in military service
TURNER, John, H-62-3; 303 Pine, Chattanooga PO
TURNER, John B., Cr-4-3; Virginia N. widow of; Pvt L Co 1st TN Inf; 8 Oct 62 to 8 Oct 63; Bells Depot PO; CONF
TURNER, John J., D-80-1; Pvt H Co 27th MI Inf; Oct 29 62 to 30 Oct 65; Una PO; rheumatism
TURNER, Joseph, Dk-34-1; Pvt D Co 4th TN Inf; 9-5-64 to 8-25-65; Dowelltown PO; rheumatism & eye sight
TURNER, Joseph D., Lo-188-3; Sgt? D Co 5th TN Inf; 10 Aug 61 to 22 Feb 64; Erie PO
TURNER, Liker?, Mr-95-1; Dicy widow of; Pvt 9th TN; 7-15-63 to 8-11-65; Whitwell PO
TURNER, Louis, H-62-3; 316 Chestnut, Chattanooga PO

TURNER, Mary J. (see Clark, Ben)
TURNER, Mary J. (see Cummings, Peter)
TURNER, Peter M., Sm-173-2; Pvt D Co 4th TN Mtd Inf; 10-2-64 to 8-25-65; Brush Creek PO
TURNER, Ranson B., Di-36-1; Pvt A Co 16th TN Cav; 61 to 63; Bellsburgh PO; COND
TURNER, Robert, K-184-4; Jane wife of; Pvt 8th TN Inf; Thorn Grove PO
TURNER, Robert, Sh-161-2; US Sol; 16th Dist
TURNER, Robert T., Gr-73-2; Pvt 4th TN Cav; 63 to 65; Turley's Mills PO
TURNER, Solomon, Bl-2-1; Pvt B Co 6th TN Inf; 9-12-64 to 6-30-65; Glade Creek PO; rheumatism & piles & catarrh; not able to do much work
TURNER, Steven, D-64-3; alias Steven Jackson; Pvt G Co 12th TN Inf; Nashville PO
TURNER, Taskem, Co-69-6(12); Mary J. Reed widow of; Pvt D Co 8th TN Inf; Mar 62 to 64; Driskill P PO; died; dont no eny dates correct
TURNER, Thomas, Cf-35-3; Pvt B Co 16th TN Inf; 15 Jun ___ to 23 Jan 64; Manchester PO; CONF
TURNER, Thomas, Ru-241-3; Pvt A Co 34th TN Inf; 6-63 to 5-28-66; PO omitted
TURNER, Thos. J., Jo-148-2; Pvt B Co 4th TN Inf; 64 to 65; Laurel Bloomery PO; eyes afflicted from exposure
TURNER, W. M., Un-255-1; Sgt B Co 8th TN; 11 Ju 63 to 11 Sep 65; Warwicks X Roads PO; rumatism
TURNER, William, F-46-2; Pvt H Co 36th NC; 63 to 66; LaGrange PO; mashed by seagt. gun
TURNER, William, F-47-1; US Sol; 14th Civil Dist
TURNER, William, Ge-100-2; Pvt D Co 1st TN Cav; 12 Aug 62 to 5 Jan 65; Mohawk PO
TURNER, William, Ha-113-1; Pvt E Co 8th TN Cav; 15 Nov 63 to 15 May 64; Sneedville PO
TURNER, William, Ru-241-2(1); Cpl C Co 17th TN Inf; 20 Apr 63 to 24 May 66; Murfreesboro PO; shot in the head
TURNER, William C., Ro-210-11; Pvt E Co 1st? TN Inf; Post Oak Springs PO
TURNER, William F., Dk-31-1; Sgt B Co 5th TN Cav; 8-1-62 to 6-25-65; Alexandria PO; suffering with rheumatism; debility & partial loss of sight
TURNER, William M., K-164-1; Pvt H Co 8th TN Vol; 23 Jul 63 to 22 Jul 65; Knoxville PO; measles settled in side; claims to not be in good health
TURNER, William N., Cr-4-1; Pvt C Co 19th TN Cav; 4 Aug 62 to 2 Jun 64; Bells Depot PO; CONF
TURNER, William W., Dy-23-1; Pvt Bat B Chicago Art; 61 to 64 (discharge burnt); Dyersburg PO
TURNER, Wyatt, L-100-1; Pvt I Co 88th Col Inf; 63 to 65; Ripley PO; cannot give dates
TURP, Nancy (see Duncan, Elijah)
TURPIN, David, Ge-96-1; Cpl K Co 5th TN Inf; 1 Jul 62 to 11 Jun 65; Hascue PO; paralisis
TURPIN, George W., Ro-203-6; Pvt C Co 7th TN Mtd Inf; 64 to ___; Wheat PO
TURPIN, Isaac, A-8-3; Catherine widow of; Pvt K Co 1st TN Inf; 8-9-61 to ___; Ledom PO
TURPIN, Martin, Ro-203-2; US Sol; Wheat PO
TUSTON, Thomas, Sh-188-2; US White; 42 Peyton Ave, Memphis PO
TUTTERS, Harmon, Wh-187-1; Pvt K Co 49th KY Inf; 64 to ___ (1 yr 6 mos); Bon Air PO
TUTTLE, Josiah M., A-4-4; Pvt G Co 2nd TN Inf; 12-25-61 to 7-5-65; Coal Creek PO; bronchitis, enlistment dated back from above
TUTTLE, William R., K-155-2(1); Pvt 105th OH Inf; 62 to 65; Knoxville PO
TWIGGS, Frank, D-79-1; Feriman, Marine, Reindeer; about Nov 1, 63 to Autumn 64; 123 N. 1st, Nashville PO; shot in thigh
TWINE, William, Sh-189-2; Pvt L Co 5th MA Cav; Fall 63 to Fall 65; Broadway, Memphis PO
TYERS, William, Hy-76-2; US Sol; Stanton Depot PO
TYLER, Byron, Sh-204-1; McLeMore Ave, Memphis PO
TYLER, Dolphus, Cf-35-5(1); Pvt A Co 92nd IL Inf; 9 Aug 62 to 1 Nov 64; Tullahoma PO
TYLER, Dolphus, Cf-35-1; Pvt A Cl 92nd IL Inf; 9 Aug 62 to 1 Nov 64; Tullahoma PO
TYLER, Francis V., H-64-2; Chattanooga PO
TYLER, Jasper F., Mu-190-1; Pvt D Co 1st AL Cav; 2-22-63 to 7-1-63; Culleoka PO; chronic diorrhoea, chorn. bronchitis

TYLER, Jasper M., Cf-35-1; Pvt F Co 23rd Inf; 9 Feb 63 to 10 Jul 63; Tullahoma PO; CONF
TYLER, John, Ov-139-1; Pvt D Co 11th IL Inf; 62 to 7-65; Beaver Hill PO
TYLER, Joseph X?, D-69-1; Pvt B Co 5th TN Cav; 24 Aug 62 to 25 Jun 65; Nashville PO
TYLER, Levinus A., R-162-5; Pvt B Co 2nd NY Inf; 4-14-61 to 2-22-63; Dayton PO; heart disease contracted while in service
TYLOR, Emily, Sh-187-1(5); widow of Sol; Memphis PO
TYRA, James, C-33-5; Pvt D Co 34th KY Inf; 7-62 to 65 (2 yrs 10 mos); Newcomb PO
TYREE, David A., J-80-1; Pvt A Co 1st TN Inf; 12-18-63 to 1-13-65; Bagdad PO; double hernia & astropia of testicles
TYREE, William, Su-243-2; Pvt I Co 13th TN Cav; Oct 63 to 5 Dec 65; Bristul PO; wound
TYSON, Jacob, Se-226-1; Capt A Co; 1 Nov 64 to __; Straw Plains PO
UDELL, Dewitt C., O-142-1; Qtr Mas. depty under Col Grimes; Raleigh, MO?; forgotten exact dates, 63 to 65; Obion PO
ULREY, David, Mc-112-2; 1st Lt I & H Cos 51st IN Inf; 5-61 to 2-64; Athens PO; chronic diarrhea, discharge burned--dates unknown
UMBARGER, James A., K-181-7(4); Pvt A Co; Knoxville PO; CONF
UMSTEAD, Louisa J., Cr-15-2; widow US Sol; Maple Creek PO
UNDERDOWN, Gilbert W., K-184-2; 1st Lt K Co 2nd TN Inf; 13 Dec 61 to 15 Dec 64; Thorn Grove PO; despepsy & bronkites
UNDERDOWN, Joseph D., Se-226-3; Cap K Co 2nd TN Inf; 29 Dec 61 to 65; Sinking Springs PO; r. leg & l. thigh shot in service; permanently crippled
UNDERHILL, Elden R., H-53-3; no detail on unit or dates (3 yrs); Chattanooga PO; injury from cart falling on him
UNDERWOOD, Benj. F., Ro-202-4; A & B Co's 11-9th TN Cav; 4 Apr 63 to 31 Aug 65; Cave Creek PO; no disease, not damaged
UNDERWOOD, Ephrim J., Se-226-2; Pvt K Co 2nd TN Inf; 29 Dec 61 to 29 Dec 64; Sinking Springs PO; bronchitis of lungs & piles
UNDERWOOD, F. M., Mc-113-2; Pvt C Co 6th TN Cav; 1-14-64 to 8-1-65; Riceville PO
UNDERWOOD, Georg R., Mg-200-3; C Co 3rd OH Cav; 3 Sep 61 to 6 Dec 62; Glade PO; injury to testicles result from horse falling
UNDERWOOD, George, Un-254-3; Pvt B Co 4th TN Inf; 18 Mar 63 to 2 Aug 65; Gravestown PO
UNDERWOOD, George A., H-561-1; Pvt; 63 to 65; St. Elm (St. Elmo PO, now part of Chattanooga)
UNDERWOOD, George W., Mg-199-2; Pvt A Co 11th TN Cav; 8 Jun 63 to Sep 63; Sunbright PO
UNDERWOOD, George W., Cl-48-1; Pvt A Co 26th NC Inf; 62 to 64; Old Town PO; shot in left hip and heel; don't remember date of enlistment; CONF
UNDERWOOD, James, Ro-209-3; Pvt E Co 1st TN Inf; Jul 63 to 65; Rockwood PO
UNDERWOOD, James, K-184-3; Pvt K Co 2nd TN Inf; 13 Dec 61 to 15 Dec 64; Thorn Grove PO
UNDERWOOD, James J., Mu-209-4; Pvt A Co 48th TN Inf; Dec 61 to May 65; Columbia PO; prison, Camp Douglas; skull fractured; CONF
UNDERWOOD, James P., Ro-210-10; Pvt Rockwood PO
UNDERWOOD, Jasper W., Mc-112-5; Pvt C Co 10th TN Cav; 1-14-64 to 8-1-65; Athens PO; left hip injured
UNDERWOOD, Joe H., K-171-1; Pvt G Co 3rd TN Inf; 10 Feb 62 to 13 Feb 65; PO omitted
UNDERWOOD, John P., Mc-113-1; Pvt D Co 5th TN Mtd Inf; 8-31-64 to 6-20-65; Riceville PO; kidney affection
UNDERWOOD, John W., Mu-210-6; Pvt B Co 2nd TN Cav; 10-15-62 to 5-10-65; Mallard PO
UNDERWOOD, Marace, Ro-209-1; Pvt B Co 1st TN Inf; Jul 61 to 10 Aug 65; Rockwood PO
UNDERWOOD, Mary A., Mn-123-2; widow Sol US; 4th Dist
UNDERWOOD, Reuben R., Ge-98-2; Pvt E Co 13th TN Cav; 1 Dec 64 to 5 Sep 65; Lovelace PO; hips and back
UNDERWOOD, Robert J., Mc-93-1; Pvt H Co 7th TN Mtd Inf; 1-22-65 to 7-27-65; Sewee PO; injury to eyes from measles

UNDERWOOD, Samuel G., Wl-293-2; 61 to 64; Buhler PO; CONF
UNDERWOOD, Sandero J., D-61-1; Wagon Master US; __ to May 65; Nashville PO
UNDERWOOD, William, Rb-219-2; Pvt K Co 30th TN Reg; May 15 66? to May 65 (4 yrs); Black Jack PO; left arm shot off; infantry; CONF
UNDERWOOD, William, Me-92-2; Cpl K Co 10th TN Cav; 2-15-64 to 8-1-65; Chuckaluck PO; lung disease
UNDERWOOD, William T., K-182-4; Cpl F Co 9th TN Cav; 18 Aug 63 to 11 Sep 65; Arthur PO (Sevier Co.)
UNDERWOOD, William T., Se-226-4; Pvt K Co 2nd TN Inf; Sinking Springs PO
UPCHURCH, Henderson, Fe-41-2; Pvt J Co 30th KY Inf; 1-1-64 to 4-18-65; Travisville PO
UPCHURCH, Richard, Lo-191-2; Pvt F Co 26th NC Vols; 1 Jul 61 to 18 Jun 65; Morganton PO; gunshot in head, abdomen and right foot; CONF
UPCHURCH, William H., Gi-122-5; H Pvt Co 5th AL Cav; Nov 61 to 17 Apr 65; Prospect Sta. PO; CONF
UPSHAW, Jasper, Gi-127-5; Emelina widow of; Pvt 111th TN Col Inf; Pulaski PO; draws pension but does not know dates
UPSHAW, JOseph, Sh-157-7; Insley Farm PO
UPTON, Daniel M., O-138-2; 1st Lt C Co 1st TN; 18 May 61 to 5 Jun 65; Elbridge PO; CONF
UPTON, Edward H., Lk-113-3; Pvt K Co 12th OH Inf?; __ to Jan 15 65; PO omitted
UPTON, James, Li-164-1; Pvt F Co 5th TN; Oct 63 to 65; Kelso PO
UPTON, Marshall, Mc-109-6; US Sol; 1st Civil Dist
UPTON, Robert, Lo-188-3; Pvt D Co 1st US Art; Sweetwater PO
URIGHT, Markham G., K-156-3; Pvt; 21 Patterson St, Knoxville PO
URMSTON, Stephen L., Fr-112-1; Pvt G Co 120th IL Inf; Mar 1 65 to 10 Sep 65; Tullahoma PO
USAM, Barbary B. (see Walker, John)
USELTON, Alford, Cf-35-4; PVt A Co 44th TN Inf; 61 to Apr 65; Normandy PO; CONF
USELTON, John W., Cf-35-3; Pvt A Co 44th TN Inf; 61 to May 65; Gould PO; CONF
USERY, Daniel, Gi-136-1; Julia widow of; Pvt E Co 110th ?; Lynnville PO
USERY, Garrison, Ro-204-2; Cynthia widow of; Oliver Springs PO; died in army
USSELTON, William, Cf-42-2; Sallie C. widow of; Pvt 31st IL Inf; 63 to 7-65; Noah PO
VALENTINE, David, Se-230-3; Pvt E Co 1st TN Art; Richison's Cove PO; chron. diarrhoea
VALENTINE, Edward, D-91-2; Pvt 12th TN Inf; Johnny Winns Grocery, Nashville PO
VALENTINE, Felix, Gi-136-1; Pvt H Co 111th TN Inf; 2-64 to 4-65; Odd Fellow Hall PO; shot in left eye
VALENTINE, Henry, Co-67-2; PVt I Co 2nd TN Cav; 20 Sep 62 to Jul 65; Cosby PO
VALENTINE, Matin V., We-221-3; Cpl D Co 45th TN Inf; Nov 29, 61 to Feb 65; Martin PO; CONF
VALENTINE, Reuben, Hr-86-2; Pvt F Co 18th OH Inf; 62 to 63; Grand Junction PO
VALENTINE, Robert, Co-68-3; Pvt I Co 2nd TN Cav; 62 to 65; Casby PO
VALENTINE, William, Se-230-3; PO omitted
VALENTINE, William, Co-68-1; Pvt A Co 4th TN Cav; 62 to 65; Costner PO
VALES, Henry H., Di-40-1; Mary E. widow of; Pvt G Co 32nd KY Cav; 62 to 65; Adinburgh PO; discharge lost, killed at work on an ore washer 5 yrs ago
VALLABY, James, A-4-4; PVt C Co 5th TN Inf; __ to __; Coal Creek PO; finger shot off, discharge not at home
VAN, John W., D-48-1; PVt G Co 7th TN Cav; 8-21-61 to 2-12-62; Nashville PO
VAN BUREN, Martin, H-73-1; Pvt E Co 8th GA Inf; 1-15-61 to 5-65; Chattanooga PO
VANCE, Brisco, Hw-131-1; Pvt M Co 1st US Col Art; 14 Oct 64 to 31 Mar 66; Whites Burg PO; chronic rheumatism heart disease, pensioned $8 (Col)
VANCE, Clinton, Gi-122-5; Lucinda Hatchett widow of; Pvt K Co 110th TN Inf; 62 to 66; Prospect Sta. PO; 3 mos in prison
VANCE, Ephram, Gi-127-8; Pvt G Co 111th TN Inf; Dec 22 64 to 30 Apr 66; Pulaski PO

VANCE, Hugh, Su-238-1; Pvt C Co 13th TN Cav; Sep 63 to Sep 65; Piney Flats PO; rheumatism, small pox settled on lungs
VANCE, James Sr., Gi-127-2; Paralee Estes formerly widow of; Pvt I Co 110th TN Col Inf; Nov 63 to Feb 66; Pulaski PO; was castrated from mumps; has been dead 17 yrs
VANCE, James, Gi-127-3; Pvt I Co 110th TN Col Inf; 13 Dec 63 to 6 Feb 66; Pulaski PO; was hot in top of head
VANCE, John, D-72-2; Carrie widow of; Pvt TN Inf; Nashville PO; CONF
VANCE, John H., Jo-149-3; Pvt C Co 13th TN Cav; 24 Sep 63 to 5 Sep 65; Mountain City PO
VANCE, John M., Sm-169-3(5); Pvt A Co 1st TN Mtd Inf; 11-63 to 1-13-65; Kempville PO; disease of lungs; reenlisted veteran
VANCE, Joseph C., H-63-1; Pvt 66th OH Inf; 10-61 to 11-62; 212 Prospect St, Chattanooga PO; chronic diarrhoea
VANCE, Samuel, Je-140-1; Sgt D Co 9th TN Cav; 8 Nov 63 to 11 Sep 65; Hodges PO; scurvy
VANCE, Thomas W., Je-136-3; 2nd Dist
VANDAGRIFF, Jacob, Mr-96-2; Pvt A Co 6th TN Inf; 8-2-64 to 1-30-65; Sherleyton PO
VANDAGRIFF, James, K-175-2; Pvt C Co 1st TN Cav; Apr 62 to Aug 65; Bayliss PO
VANDAGRIFF, William, Dk-34-3; Pvt D Co 4th TN Inf; 9-24-64 to 8-25-65; Dowelltown PO; nervous debility
VANDEGRIFF, Alfred, H-49-2; Hily widow of; Pvt A Co 6th TN Mtd Inf; 8-2-64 to 2-14-65 (died); Brown's Chapel PO
VANDEGRIFF, William, Mr-96-2; Pvt A Co 6th TN Mtd Inf; 8-2-64 to 6-30-65; Falling Water PO
VANDEGRIFF, William J., Ru-13-2; Pvt I Co 18th Reg; Oct 62 to May 2, 65; Murfreesboro PO; wounded in shoulder; CONF
VANDEGRIFF, Maron F., Ca-25-2; Susan widow of; Pvt I Co 5th TN Cav; 62 to __; Gassoway PO; get shot & killed in war; the widow is drawing a pension
VANDEGRIFF, William J., Ca-25-3; Blacksmith I Co 5th TN Cav; 11-19-62 to 8-19-65; Gassoway PO; finger shot off & hip hurt by mule
VAN DEMAY, Joseph H., H-62-3; Capt 66th OH Inf; 10-11-61 to 12-18-62; Capt 10th OH Inf; 12-18-62 to 5-18-64; 440 Pine, Chattanooga PO; in Libby Prison 4 mos
VANDENBERGER, John A., Fe-44-1; Pvt H Co 187th OH Inf; 2-65 to 1-66; Rugby PO; cronic diarrhea
VANDERGRIFF, Gilbert, H-56-7; Pvt A Co 6th TN Inf; 7-64 to 7-65; St. Elmo PO
VANDERGRIFF, Jacob, H-51-6; Cpl I Co 3rd TN Inf; 2-10-62 to 2-23-65; Fairmount PO
VANDERGRIFF, John F., Sq-55-3; Pvt I Co 3rd TN Inf; 2-62 to 4-65; Sunnyside PO; received an honorable disc.
VANDERGRIFF, William, H-66-1; Pvt I Co 2nd TN Inf; 11-11-61 to 65 (4 yrs 9 mos); Chattanooga PO
VANDERGRIFF, Wm. T., H-60-3; Pvt A Co 6th TN Mtd Inf; 8-2-64 to 6-31 (sic)-65; Chattanooga PO; eyes and hearing injured from measles
VANDERS, James, Sn-252-2; Pvt G Co 1st US Art; Gallatin PO
VANDEVER, George A., Cu-16-2; Pvt D Co 4th TN Mtd Inf; 3-23-65 to 9-25-65; Crossville PO
VANDEVER, Nicholas D., Cu-16-2; Pvt I Co 89th KY Inf; 63 to 9-23-65 (2 yrs); Crossville PO; fever settled in leg
VANDIGRIFF, Linsey, Un-254-1; Pvt E Co; Paulett PO
VANDIKE, Dunkin, He-67-1; Martha J. widow; Pvt C Co 6th TN Cav; 62 to 65; Sardis PO; hemerhoids 25 yrs; the fam. reports discharge at Washington
VANDINE, Michael, He-61-2; Sol; 18th Civil Dist
VANDIVER, George S., Hd-50-3; Pvt H Co IL Vol Inf; Jul 12, 62 to 6 Nov 65; Stout PO
VANDOGRIFF, George W., Mr-96-2; Pvt; Sunyside PO
VAN DRESSER, Alfred P., Sh-159-5; Capt C Co NY 104th; Nov 61 to 65; PO omitted
VANDYKE, Angus M., He-64-2; Pvt I Co 13th TN Reg; Apr 61 to __ (3 yrs 9 mos); Center Point PO; flesh wound in left shoulder; CONF
VAN DYKE, Joseph D., Ch-12-1; Sgt B Co 1st TN Inf; 5-1-61 to 5-3-65; Custer Point PO; CONF
VANER, William (see Debro, Sam)

VAN HORN, John, Sh-163-1; Pvt 2nd KS? Cav; Aug 62 to May 65; Memphis PO; badly ruptured
VANHOY, Anderson, Ct-41-4; Pvt B Co 10th NC Inf; 4-64 to __; Elizabethton PO; rhumatism; CONF
VANHOY, Norman H., Ct-41-4; Pvt B Co 1st NC Cav; 2-23-63 to 2-23-65; Elizabethton PO; CONF
VANHUSS, Daniel S., Ct-42-3; Cpl B Co 4th TN Inf; 6-1-63 to 7-7-65; Watauga PO; disease of liver
VANHUSS, John, Hm-106-3; Pvt F Co 4th TN Inf; 15 Nov 61 to 7 Jul 65; Morristown PO
VANHUSS, William, Hm-106-3; Sgt F Co 4th TN Inf; 15 Nov 61 to 7 Jul 65; Morristown PO
VANLEER, Edmond, Mt-148-1; Patsey widow of; Pvt I Co 12th Col Vol TN; Orgains X Roads PO
VANLEER, Edward, Di-37-1; Susan widow of; Pvt F Co 16th TN Inf; 12-24-63 to 4-30-66; Cumberland Furnace PO; chronic diarrea
VANLEER, Fin, Di-37-1; Pvt K Co 12th TN Inf; 8-12-63 to 1-16-66; Cumberland Furnace PO
VANLEER, Reuben, Mu-194-1; Pvt F Co 16th US Col Inf 1-1-64 to 7-1-66; Columbia PO; shot in right shoulder and left hip; transferred to 101st Col Inf
VANN, Daniel, A-7-2; Robertsville PO
VANN, Edward, A-6-6(4); Pvt C Co 9th TN Cav; 5-1-62 to 7-9-65; Olivers PO; prisoner at Richmond VA
VANN, Japer (Jasper?), A-6-5(3); pvt G Co 1st TN Inf; 8-9-61 to 9-17-64
VANN, Martin V., Ro-203-6; Juletta J. formerly widow of; Pvt G Co 1st TN Inf; 9 Aug 61 to 17 Jul 65; Burns' Mills PO
VANNATTA, Samuel, Dk-33-1; pvt D Co 4th TN Inf; 9-24-64 to 8-25-65; Dowellton PO
VAN NESS, Cornelius, Fr-112-1; Pvt H Co 36th IL Inf; Aug 14, 61 to Nov 20, 64; Tullahoma PO; gun shot wound in right arm
VANORDSTRAND, Jn. F., Sh-168-1; widow; 106½ Fourth St., Memphis PO
VANOVER, Cintha, Jo-150-3; widow; Osborn PO
VANOY, Crockett, Li-149-1; Pvt H Co 15th US Col Inf; 4-63 to 12-65; Fayetteville PO
VAN PELT, Samuel, Sh-146-1; Clarissa widow of; Woodstock PO; this man died at Woodstock 6 years ago
VAN WAGNER, Charles, H-53-2; Pvt F Co 7th NY Inf; 10-61 to 12-64; Chattanooga PO; chronic diarrhea
VARNELL, Albert, K-181B-3; Cpl I Co 3rd TN Cav; 25 Mar 63 to 19 Jun 65; Flenekin PO; CONF
VARNELL, Albert, K-181-4(1); Cpl I Co 3rd TN Cav; 25 Sep 63 to 12 Jun 65; Fleniken PO
VARNELL, Glass W., H-55-3; 2nd Lt F Co 6th TN Mtd Inf; 3-1-65 to 6-30-65; Tyner PO
VARNELL, Isaac, Br-6-1; Pvt A Co 4th TN Cav; 10-25-62 to 7-12-65; Cleveland PO; tonsilletis & injury to the shoulder
VARNELL, John R., Je-135-3; Pvt K Co 3rd TN Cav; 8 Feb 63 to 20 Jun 65; Flat Gap PO; discharge with pension attorney
VARNER, Allen, H-50-2(1); pvt A Co 6th R TN Mtd Inf; 8-17-64 to 6-30-65; Bunch PO; chronic diorreah
VARNER, David, Sq-164-2(1); Elizabeth A. widow of; Pvt D Co 6th TN Mtd Inf; 9-12-64 to 6-30-__ (9 mos 18 days); Dunlap PO
VARNER, George, K-176-3; Pvt; PO omitted
VARNER, George, H-50-2(1); Pvt I Co 2nd R TN Cav; 11-11-61 to 11-26-64; Bunch PO; wounded in arm and shoulder
VARNER, Thomas M., H-49-6; Pvt F Co 2nd E TN Mtd Inf; 2-14-62 to 2-14-65; Trewhitt PO
VARNEY, Stephen H., R-159-1; Lt E Co 116th IL Inf; 1862 to 1864; Spring City PO; diseamed in body
VARRAMORE, Newton, Sq-165-3; Pvt E Co 6th TN Mtd Inf; 9-11-64 to 6-12-65; Dunlap PO; shot in right leg; received an honorable disc.
VASSER, Alex, F-40-2; Pvt L Co 3rd TN Cav; Feb 62 to Apr 65; Hickory Withe PO
VASSER, Thomas, Gi-129-2; Ann McLin widow of; Pvt 110th TN Inf; Conway PO
VAUGH, John, Ge-97-2; Pvt 1st KY Art Bat?; 8 Nov 62 to 29 May 65; Lost Mountain PO
VAUGH, Wm., Hw-125-3; B Co 8th TN Inf; Blevins PO
VAUGHAN, Alfred, Wl-290-1; Sol US; 3rd Civil Dist.
VAUGHAN, Calvin, Mu-189-1; Pvt F Co 1st TN Inf; no dates (2 yrs 4 mos); PO omitted

VAUGHAN, Daniel, W1-295-2; Sgt C Co 14th Reg Inf; Oct 63 to Mar 66; Lebanon PO
VAUGHAN, George E., H-59-2; Pvt NY Inf; Chattanooga PO
VAUGHAN, George W., Ha-111-1; Pvt E Co 13th TN Cav; Sep 62 to Apr 65; Upper Clinch PO; CONF
VAUGHAN, H. A., G-57-7(4); Pvt; 1st TN Inf; 61 to 65; Yorkville PO
VAUGHAN, J. P., Hr-96-1; Pvt B Co 7th TN Cav; 63 to 65; Bolivar PO; CONF
VAUGHAN, John, Ha-111-4(1); Pvt C Co 1st TN Cav; Sep 62 to Apr 65; Upper Clinch PO; I did not get any discharge; CONF
VAUGHAN, Peter, Cpl I Co 101st US Col; 1 Oct 62 to 21 Jan 66; St. Bethlehem PO
VAUGHAN, William, Cr-8-2; 10th Dist.
VAUGHAN, William C., R-162-5; 2nd Lt B Co 167th OH Vol Inf; 5-7-64 to 9-8-64; Dayton PO
VAUGHN, Abraham, D-64-5; Pvt; Nashville PO
VAUGHN, Abram, D-50-2; Maria widow of; Pvt Miss?; 310 Line, Nashville PO
VAUGHN, Alfred, Fr-112-1; Mary A. E. widow of; Pvt 4th TN Cav; 62 to 65; Tullahoma PO; gun shot in left leg; papers in hand of pension agt.; unable to give dates
VAUGHN, Alvin P., Ov-138-1; Pvt F Co 31st KY Inf; 10-6-63 to 12-29-64; 10th Civil Dist.
VAUGHN, Amos, Pu-146-2; Pvt C Co 1st TN Mtd Inf Vol; 10-64 to 1-65; Boma PO
VAUGHN, Eli, Wa-274-1; Pvt E Co 3rd NC Mtd Inf; 16 Aug 64 to 8 Aug 65; Jonesboro PO
VAUGHN, George, Sm-167-2; Pvt 6th TN Inf; Dixon Springs PO; rheumatism
VAUGHN, George, D-91-3; Pvt I Co 13th TN Inf; 14 Mar 63 to 22 Aug 65; Station C, Nashville
VAUGHN, Hardie M. D., D-102-1; Pvt E Co 5th KY Cav; 4 Oct 61 to 3 May 65; Jordonia PO
VAUGHN, Hicks J., Mc-112-10; Pvt I Co 13th TN Vol; 1-26-64 to ___; Athens PO; nervousness
VAUGHN, Jane (widow?), Dk-36-3; 9th Civil Dist.
VAUGHN, John, K-162-1; Martha E. widow of; Pvt 8th TN Cav; ___ to 65; died in Andersonville Prison
VAUGHN, John, Mn-121-2; Nancy widow of; Pvt A Co 6th TN Cav; 16 Jun 62 to 26 Jul 65; Rose Creek PO
VAUGHN, John J., Po-152-5(1); Pvt D Co 10th TN Cav; 1-23-64 to 8-1-65; Ducktown PO; rheumatism, diarrhoea and loss of eye
VAUGHN, John T., Dy-25-1; Pvt; no dates (4 yrs); Newbern PO; enlistment dates unknown; CONF
VAUGHN, Joshua, Hw-125-4; Sylvia widow of; Pvt E Co 1st KY Lt Art; Nov 63 to Jan 65; Surgoinsville PO; died small pox
VAUGHN, Leroy A., Pu-146-2; Pvt C Co 1st TN Mtd Inf Vol; 1863 to 1865; Bloomington PO; eyes and lungs
VAUGHN, Perry W., Ro-206-2; Margret L. widow of; Pvt B Co 1st US Art; 15 Feb 63 to 17 Jun 65; Emory Gap PO
VAUGHN, William, Mc-112-5; Martha J. widow of; Pvt A Co 7th TN Mtd Inf; 9-9-64 to 7-19-65; Athens PO; spinal affection & rupture; no discharge at hand to get dates
VAUGHN, William H., M-107-4; Pvt A Co 8th TN Mtd Inf; 3-20-65 to 8-17-65; Salt Lick PO; diareah resulting in heart rheumatism
VAUGHN, Zachariah, Cy-30-1; Pvt 1st KY Lt Art; 9-63 to ___ (6 mos); Mouth of Wolf PO; shot through thigh; no discharge have
VAUGHT, Isaac N., Ru-245-1; Pvt H Co 4th TN Mtd Inf; 10-5-64 to 8-30-65; Milton PO; rheumatism
VAUGHT, Joseph L., Jo-151-4; Com Sgt M Co 13th TN Cav; 2 Feb 64 to 5 Sep 65; Vaughtsville PO; effects of mumps, chronic diarrhoia
VAUGHT, William, Ct-35-2; Amanda E. widow of; Pvt 13th TN Cav; ___ to ___; Butler PO, Johnson Co.; died in US Army; widow had no discharge and does not know E & D dates
VAUGHT, William J., Ru-245-1; Pvt H Co 4th TN Mtd Inf; 10-5-64 to 8-20-65; Milton PO; rheumatism
VAUGN, James E., Se-225-3; Cpl K Co 13th TN Cav; 22 Sep 63 to 5 Sep 65; Boyds Creek PO
VAUSS, Geo., T-209-2; Sol; 4th Civil Dist.
VAWL, W. J., We-233-1(2); Pvt K Co 6th TN Cav; 7-18-62 to 7-26-65; Ralston PO; defect eyes

VAWN, James W., We-230-4; Pvt F Co 7th KY Inf; Sep 1, 61 to Sep 15, 61; McKinzie PO; CONF
VEAL, Henry, De-25-1; Pvt; 11 Aug 62 to 15 Sep 62; Decaturville PO
VEAZLY, Herman W., Ro-211-3; Pvt A Co 11th NH Inf; 28 Aug 62 to 28 Jun 65; Harriman PO; gunshot wound; shot in left thigh
VENABLE, James W., Ro-210-10; Pvt G Co 8th VA Cav; Rockwood PO; wounded; CONF
VENABLE, William L., Jo-148-2; Pvt D Co 13th TN Cav; 24 Sep 63 to 8 Sep 65; Head of Laurel PO; rheumatism contracted
VENERABLE, John T., Hw-13-3(1); Nancy widow of; Pvt H Co 8th TN Inf; 15 Apr 64 to 30 Jun 65; Strahl PO; rheumatism; could not get full particulars
VENTIS, James W., K-180-2; 2nd Lt F Co 6th TN Inf; 10 Mar 62 to 24 Mar 65; Bearden PO; chronic diarrhea & results
ventrici, Robert, D-50-3; Jennie Irvin former wife of; Nashville PO; wounded
VERMILLION, Frank, We-230-2; Pvt F Co 15th KY Inf Nov 1, 63 to May 1, 65; Greenfield PO
VERNON, J. W., Sh-171-1; Sgt K Co 4th IA Vol; 11-61 to 12-64; Memphis PO
VERNON, James B., Ch-12-1; Pvt B Co 21st TN Cav; 1863 to 5-65; Custer Point PO; CONF
VESER, Sarah, Gr-73-2; widow of US Sol; Tp. 4
VIALS, Richard, Su-239-3; Pvt K Co 13th TN Cav; 15 Sep 63 to 5 Sep 65; Kingsport PO; hepless with rumatism
VIAR, S. H., O-137-1; Bug E Co 6th TN Cav; 15 Dec 63 to 26 Jul 65; Trimble? PO; detail out of order on this sched.
VIARS, John, Ch-12-1; Sarah C. widow of; Pvt B Co 6th TN Cav; 8-25-62 to 7-26-65; Wild Goose PO
VICARS, Jonathan, Gu-45-1; Pvt M Co; Tarlton PO; discharge at Nashville TN
VICARS, Uliska, Gu-45-2; 4th Dist.
VICK, Morsitos? C., Dk-32-1; Lt E Co 4th TN Mtd Inf; 12-4-64 to 8-25-65; Liberty PO
VICK, Thomas, C-33-2; Mary widow of; Pvt B Co 1st TN Cav; 4-9-62 to 4-10-65; Jellico PO
VICKERS, Elizza, G-61-1; 12th Civil Dist.
VICKERS, Geo. W., Cr-16-1; Pvt M Co 12th TN Cav; Aug 23, 64 to Sep 7, 65; Huntingdon PO; chronic rhumatism; partially disabled since 63
VICKERS, James C., Dk-39-2; Mary E. widow of; Pvt A Co 5th TN Cav; 8-4-62 to 6-25-65; Bozarth PO
VICKERS, Linsey, Pu-144-4; Betsy widow of; Pvt I Co 5th TN Cav; Pine Fork PO; killed
VICKERS, Thomas J., G-60-1; Pvt F Co 7th TN Cav; 8 Aug 62 to 25 Oct 63; Dyer PO; reenlisted, Sgt in 12th TN Cav; 25 Aug 64 to 7 Oct 65
VICKERS, William P., Pu-146-2; Pvt C Co 1st TN Mtd Inf Vol; 10-13-63 to 11-28-64; Byrne PO; lung disease
VICKERY, John A., D-72-3; Pvt B Co 1st TN Art; Dec 28 62 to 20 Jul 65; Nashville PO; wounded in left leg; CONF
VICORY, Henry, D-63-2; Pvt H Co 4th TN Inf; 62 to 66; Nashville PO
VIDSON, James, Hw-125-5; Pvt C Co 63rd TN Inf; Apr 63 to Aug 63; Surgoinsville PO; CONF
VIETS, Elijah, La-115-1; Phebia G. widow of; Pvt I Co 152nd OH; 7 Jul 63 to 15 Dec 64; Henryville PO
VILES, James H., A-5-4; Louvie widow of; Pvt; Clinton PO; died a prisoner; never returned home
VILES, Levi, Ha-116-1; US Sol; 13th Dist
VILES, Ransom, Gi-135-3; Pvt F Co 1st TN Inf; 9-62 to 9-65; Lynnville PO
VINCENT, Jocephus, We-220-3; Pvt C Co State Troops; Oct 14 64 to 14 Apr 65; PO omitted
VINCENT, Mary (see Robinson, Lilbern)
VINCENT, Thomas, We-220-3; Pvt C Co State Troops; Oct 14 64 to 14 Apr 65; PO omitted
VINCENT, Wallace, G-57-2; Yorkville PO
VINES, Calvin F., Wa-263-1; Eliza J. widow of; Pvt 6th IN Cav; Garbers Mills PO
VINEYARD, Young, Tr-268-1; Amanda widow of; Pvt C Co 31st IL Vol; 61 to ___; Hartsville PO
VINING, Jno. W., D-78-1; Pvt G Co 21st KY; May 23, 62 to 19 May 66; Nashville PO

VINSON, James, D-91-1; Pvt GA Inf; 3 yrs; Johny? Winns Grocery, Cedar St, Nashville PO; CONF
VINSON, John W., Co-69-7(3); Pvt K Co 1st TN Inf; 64 to 65; Rankin PO; rheumatism, Knoxvall TN; dont no dates
VINSON, Stewart H., Cy-27-4(2); Pvt F Co 1st TN Mtd Inf; 1-64 to 5-65; Spivey PO; blind
VINSON, Thomas, Pu-145-2; Elizabeth widow of; Pvt A Co 5th Cav Vol; 10-15-63 to 8-14-65; Fancher's Mills PO
VINSON, William, Sh-144-1; alias William Thomas; Pvt C Co 4th Hvy Art; May 63 to 66 (discharge lost); Brunswick PO
VINSTON, H. L., Ro-209-4; Mrs. Manda Mahoney widow of; Lt I Co 46th TN Inf; Glen Alice PO
VINYARD, John, Lo-192-1; Pvt D Co 2nd TN; Sep 62 to Jul 65; Coytee PO
VINYARD, Jonah? H., K-185-1; Pvt E Co TN Cav; 61 to __; Scaggston PO; CONF
VINYARD, Joshua, K-171-3(2); Pvt H Co 1st US Col Hvy Art; 62 to 65; PO omitted
VINYARD, Morgan H., Di-30-1; Pvt K Co 11th TN Inf; 10-9-62 to 5-6-65; Dickson PO; CONF
VINYARD, Nicholis, K-181-2; Cpl C Co 6th TN Inf; Apr 62 to May 65; French PO
VINYARD, William T., Bo-21-1; Pvt F Co 8th TN Cav; 6-30-61 to 9-30-63; Bank PO
VIRE, Thomas, Dk-33-4; Pvt D Co 4th TN Inf; 9-22-64 to 8-25-64; Youngblood PO; sight
VIRES, William, Mn-126-1; Purdy PO
VIRRETT, W. B., Wl-308-3; Ord Sgt F Co 45th TN; Dec 1, 62 to Aug 1, 63; Stewarts Ferry PO; captured; CONF
VITTETOE, Thomas, Gr-81-3(1); Pvt D Co 1st TN Inf; Nov 62 to 64; Clear Spring PO; chills & fever; partly disabled
VITTITOE, Abner, Gr-81-1; Pvt F Co 7th TN Inf; 1 Dec 64 to 22 Aug 65; Clear Spring PO; relaps of measels; partly disabled
VOGEL, Charles H., US Sol; Sh-185-1; 300 Manassas St., Memphis PO
VOGEL, Levi, K-161-2; Knoxville PO; ruptural hernia
VOILES, James C., Ro-205-4; Pvt E Co 1st TN Inf; 10 Aug 61 to 10 Nov 64; Cardiff PO; chronic diarrihea
VOMER, Hezekiah, H-51-1; Pvt F Co 6th R TN Mtd Inf; 9-12-64 to 6-30-65; Soddy PO
VON, Henry, D-73-1; Pvt E Co 17th USC Inf; Mar 8, 65 to Mar 19, 66; Mt. Vernon Ave., Nashville PO
VONLEER, Ransom, Di-37-1; Pvt F Co 16th TN Inf; 12-24-63 to ?; Cumberland Furnace PO; deserted
VOORHEIS, William M., Mu-209-5; Col 48th TN; Jul 61 to Aug 65; Columbia PO; CONF
VOORHIES, Thomasas, D-68-3; alias Henderson, Thomas; Pvt D Co 13th USC Inf; 10 Sep 63 to 10 Jan 66; 12 S. Sycamore St., Nashville PO; gun shot wound right leg and hearing and eyes injured in the army
VOREIS, Mary, D-99-2; widow of Sol; Davidson Co. Poorhouse
VORNER, Madison, Sh-191-1; Memphis PO
VOUX, Hamilton, L-100-2; Ripley PO; US Sol
VOWEL, Francis C., A-13-3; Pvt H Co 1st TN Inf; 8-9-61 to 8-27-62; Briceville PO; chronic diarrhea
VOWELL, Aaron, A-9-6(4); Margaret A. widow of; Pvt I Co 7th TN Mtd Inf; 11-8-64 to 7-27-65; Dutch Valley PO; measles resulting in disease of back or spine
VOWELL, Granderson D., A-4-2; Mary E. widow of; Cpl J Co 9th TN Cav; 8-1-63 to 9-11-65; Coal Creek PO; chronic diarrhea
VOWELL, John S., A-5-6(2); Lt C Co 11th TN Cav; Coal Creek PO; chronic piles; has no discharge
WACKER, Archibald B., Fe-40-2(1); Pvt G Co 5th KY Cav; 12-12-61 to 12-14-62; Moodyville PO; received blow with gun on right leg; right leg now reduced very much from natural size
WACKER, Thomas, Ge-93-1; Pvt A Co 4th TN Inf; 15 Mar 63 to 2 Aug 65; Greeneville PO
WADDELL, Ben M., Ge-85-3; Pvt M Co 1st TN Cav; 16 Nov 62 to 19 Jun 65; Cavey Branch PO; chronic dysentery
WADDEY, John R., G-61-1; Pvt; 12th Civil Dist.

WADDLE, Benjamin F., K-164-1; Sgt E Co 4th TN Vol; 15 Jun 61 to 8 Jul 65; Knoxville? PO; wounded in right arm and right leg and left wrist, was wounded at Cumberland Mt. TN
WADDLE, Benjamin H., Cy-29-1; Pvt B Co 9th KY Inf; 9-61 to 12-17-64; Fox Springs PO
WADDLE, Cattie (see McGaha, William)
WADDLE, James S., Mu-210-4; Pvt A Co 1st TN Cav; 5-61 to 65; Carters Creek PO
WADDLE, Johnathan, Ge-102-1; Pvt F Co 4th TN Inf; 15 Nov 61 to 8 Jul 65; Camp Creek PO; spinel affection
WADDLE, Martin, Ge-99-1; Pvt G Co 4th TN Cav; 14 Sep 63 to 2 Aug 65; Limestone Springs PO; ankle throwed out of place
WADDLE, Matison G., Ge-91-5; Sgt G Co 4th TN Inf; 18 Nov 62 to 2 Aug 65; Greeneville PO; sore eyes
WADDLE, Rhebecca(sic), Ha-114-1; Cpl C Co 7th TN Inf; 28 May 64 to 29 Aug 64; Xenophon PO
WADE, Chas., T-209-1; Pvt; 62 to 65; Randolph PO; lost discharge, don't know dates
WADE, Chas. F., Sh-201-3; Annie widow of; Pvt I Co 61st US Col Inf; 23 Aug 63 to 30 Dec 65; Memphis PO
WADE, Christopher C., Wl-299-1; Pvt H Co 4th TN Inf; 1 Jan 65 to 25 Aug 65; Statesville PO
WADE, G. Jackson, Gr-78-2; Pvt F Co 3rd TN Inf; 16 Mar 64 to 16 Feb 65; Larkeyton PO
WADE, George A., Se-226-4; Pvt 4th Co 52nd TN Cav; 62 to 65; Sinking Springs PO; discharge stolen from me by burglar
WADE, George N., K-156-4; 1st Sgt B Co 3rd TN Cav; 5 Nov 62 to 3 Aug 65; 33 E Cumberland St, Knoxville PO
WADE, Gisell, Mn-125-1; US Sol; 5th Dist
WADE, James M., Se-227-1; Lt K Co 3rd TN Cav; 15 Jun 63 to 21 Jan 65; Trundle's X Roads PO; rheumtism & heart trouble, in prison, Interprice? MS
WADE, Jerry J., Se-231-1; 1st Lt B Co 3rd TN Cav; 5 Nov 62 to 21 Jun 65; Boyd's Creek PO; varicocela, hydrocela 24 yrs
WADE, John, Fr-120-1; Pvt B Co 1st DC Vols; Sep 63 to Jun 65; Sewanee PO
WADE, John, P-151-4; Pvt; Linden PO
WADE, John M., Un-252-2; Susan widow of; Pvt F Co 3rd __; 17 Oct 64 to 15 Oct 65; Nave Hill PO
WADE, Leo, Sh-200-2; Margaret widow of; Pvt; corner Polk & Orleans, Memphis PO
WADE, Osias H., Cr-4-3; Lt G Co 12th TN Cav; 64 to Sep 64; Pvt G Co 47th TN Inf; 62 to 64; Bells Depot PO; wounded, left foot; CONF
WADE, Paul, Wi-274-1; Teamster; Apr 61 to Aug 64; Franklin PO; enlisted & discharged, dont know dates
WADE, Ransome? C., We-221-5(2); Pvt F Co 7th TN Cav; 15 Sep 61 to 20 May 65; Martin PO; flesh in left leg; CONF
WADE, Rufus D., P-151-1; Pvt F Co 6th TN Cav; 5 Aug 63 to 5 Aug 65; Aldon PO; affected in mind, small pox
WADE, Silas M., Mc-110-1; Cpl C Co 3rd TN Cav; 11-1-62 to 6-10-65; Chuckaluck PO; rheumatism & deafness, prison at Cahubee 6 mos
WADE, Sylvester, H-60-5(2); Pvt I Co 37th US Col Inf; 8-13-64 to 2-11-67; Chattanooga PO
WADE, Blaney W., Gi-122-4; Pvt F Co 1st TN Cav; 1 Oct 62 to 13 Mar 66; Lesters Sta. PO; 22 mos in prison; CONF
WADE, William, Hd-47-2; Savannah PO
WADE, William A., P-151-3; Pvt F Co 2nd TN Mtd Inf; Nov 20 66 to 19 Jan 65; Linden PO
WADE, William D., A-5-3; Pvt C Co 2nd TN Inf; 5-62 to 8-65; Clinton PO
WADE, William D., Mc-112-1; Louisa widow of; Pvt C Co 3rd TN Cav; 11-1-62 to 6-10-65; Athens PO; measles
WADE, William H., We-221-3; Solom J. widow of; Sgt TN Art?; 61 to Apr 65; Martin PO; constitution broken; CONF
WADE, William M., Be-7-1; Pvt E Co 6th TN Cav; 16 Sep 62 to 8 Jul 65; Dist 9
WADE, William W., Dk-36-1; Cpl F Co 4th TN Mtd Inf; 9-25-64 to 8-25-65; Smithville PO
WADKINS, Andrew, Cy-27-1; Pvt B Co 5th KY Cav; 10-10-62 to 5-28-65; Clementsville PO

WADKINS, Modisa?, Je-144-1; Pvt A Co 9th TN Cav; 20 Sep 63 to 11 Sep 65; Vallyhome PO; piles by exposure in war
WADKINS, Dr. Thomas A., Sh-159-5; Sgt D Co TN 6th Inf; May 61 to 4 Jun 65; Buntyn PO; shot in right leg and face; CONF
WADKINS, William, K-180-2; Pvt M Co 13th TN Cav; 2 Feb 64 to 5 Sep 65; Bearden PO
WADLEY, Thomas M., Ma-129-1; Pvt K Co 7th TN Cav; Feb 1 64 to Aug 65; Pinson PO; palpitation heart
WADSWORTH, James, Hy-75-1; Pvt I Co 61st Col Inf; Apr 63 to 65; Dancyville PO; mustered out at Baton Rouge
WADSWORTH, William R., H-61-2; Pvt G Co 1st MS Lt Art; 3-64 to 4-9-65; Chattanooga PO; CONF
WAGGENER, John R., We-232-1; Sgt L Co 6th TN Cav; 8-16-62 to 7-26-65; Martin PO
WAGGONER, James K., Un-252-1; Pvt K Co 8th TN Cav; 11 Aug 63 to 11 Sep 65; Esco PO
WAGGONER, John, D-80-1; Pvt B Co 5th TN; 62 to 65; Una PO
WAGGONER, Samuel, Un-252-1; Cpl F Co 16th KY Inf; 1 Nov 62 to 28 Jul 65; Esco PO; blind
WAGGONER, Thomis B., We-221-6(2); Lt L Co 6th TN Cav; 2 Jul 62 to 27 Aug 64; Martin PO; a fall from a horse caused special irritation
WAGNER, John, Li-152-1; Pvt A Co; 64 to 64 (7 mos); Howell PO; Col
WAGNER, Joseph H., Jo-149-3; Maj E Co 13th TN Cav; 2 Jan 64 to 27 Mar 65; Mountain City PO
WAGNER, Joseph L., Ct-35-1; Pvt G Co 13th TN Cav; 9-24-63 to 9-5-65; Fish Springs PO; in servis of US Army
WAGNER, McChesney, Wa-262-1; Pvt C Co 4th TN Inf; 6 Apr 63 to 2 Aug 65; Limestone PO; chronic diarahea
WAGNER, Noah, Jo-149-1; Pvt M Co 13th TN Cav; 2 Feb 64 to 5 Sep 65; Shoures & Roads PO; deafness head & eyes
WAGNER, William, Gu-48-5(2); Pvt I Co 63rd LA Inf; ___ to 65; Memphis PO; shot in right arm
WAGNER, Zelora, Sh-191-7(3); Pvt H Co 11th OH; 61 to 65; Memphis PO
WAGONER, George, Br-12-6; McPherson PO; rheumatism
WAGONER, Lad, D-45-5; Scott, TN (or Scott St., Nashville?); CONF?
WAGONER, Pritchard, Cl-48-1; Pvt L Co 1st TN Cav; Old Town PO; CONF
WAGSTER, R. A., G-57-1; Pvt K Co 4th TN Inf; 5-13-61 to 65; Yorkville PO
WAID, Jarrel, Ma-114-7; Pvt D Co 5th TN Cav; 10-62 to no discharge; Calhoun PO; CONF?
WAID?, Robert (see Mcfee, Tom)
WAID, Robert, Ja-84-1; Pvt Cav; Harrison PO; kicked by mule ___ an ___ on leg
WAINSCOTT, Isaac C., We-226-1; Cpl L Co 6th TN Cav; 5 Jun 62 to 26 Jul 65; Limbs PO
WAINSCOTT, John W., We-226-1; Pvt L Co 6th TN Cav; 24 Jul 62 to ___; Limbs PO; marked on roll, deserter
WAITE, Charlotte H., Sh-199-1; Cav; 326 Miss. Ave, Memphis PO
WAITES, Allen, Ge-92-1; Pvt B Co 8th TN Inf; Feb 63 to 30 Jun 65; Laurel Gap PO
WAITS, James W., A-3-2; Pvt A Co 4th GA Inf; 62 to 63; Wilson PO; dierea; CONF
WAKEFIELD, Gilbert H., M-107-5; Pvt B Co 9th KY Inf; 12-6-61 to 12-6-64; Willette PO; gunshot wound right knee, heart disease, also left varicocile
WAKEFIELD, Isaac N., M-103-6; Pvt E Co 1st TN Inf; 10-21-63 to 1-22-65; Lafayette PO
WAKEFIELD, James N., M-107-4; Pvt F Co 1st TN Mtd Inf; 2-1-64 to 5-3-65; Gibb's Cross Roads PO; disease of lungs result of measles
WAKER, James H., St-160-2; Pvt D Co 14th TN Inf; Apr 1 61 to Aug 63; Big Rock PO; wonded in shoulder blade; CONF
WAKER, James M., H-51-5; Pvt C Co 37th IN Inf; 6-25-62 to 12-31-62; Hill City PO
WAKER, Wm. H., Hw-125-3; Pvt L Co; 62 to 65; Yellow Stone PO; shot in back; CONF
WALACE, Anderson, Bo-19-1; Sgt H Co 1st Col Art; 6-4-64 to 3-9-66; South Rockford PO
WALACE, Johnson, C-25-2; Milley A. Hatmaker widow of; Pvt H Co 2nd TN Inf; 12-15-61 to 12-19-64; Hatmaker PO; chronic diareah
WALBACH, Abriham K., Br-13-4; 1st Lt C Co 3rd OH Inf; 6-17-61 to 3-11-65; Cleveland PO; piles
WALDEN, David C., Co-65-1; Pvt H Co 4th TN Cav; 22 Jul 63 to 12 Jul 65; Newport PO; gun shot wound in right shoulder, not pensioned
WALDEN, Giles J., Cy-28-1; Pvt E Co 13th KY Cav; 8-13-63 to 1-10-65; Celine PO
WALDEN, J. B., St-162-1; Musician C Co 32nd KY Inf--Dec 62 to Oct 63; F Co 37th KY Inf--Nov 63 to 64; Cumberland City PO; lungs affected; E Co 55th KY Cav--Jan 64 to Sep 65
WALDEN, James, C-32-1; Pvt K Co 18th KY Inf; Newcomb PO; spinel diseas 25 yrs
WALDEN, James T., C-32-1; Pvt D Co 49th KY Inf; 8-11-63 to 12-20-64; Pine Mountain PO; unerina origans 25 yrs
WALDEN, John F., H-76-2; Chattanooga PO
WALDEN, Thomas, Me-94-1; Elisabeth M. widow of; Knott PO; refers to Elbert Shipley MS, Athens
WALDIN, Jerome, K-177-1; Pvt A Co 2nd NJ Inf; 22 May 61 to 27 Nov 62; Chumlea PO
WALDREN, Isaac, Hm-106-3; Pvt; 63 to 65; Morristown PO; CONF
WALDRIP, John, He-60-1; Cpl E Co 2nd TN Mtd Inf; 5-62 to 7-3-65; Lexington PO
WALDRON, Jas. S., Sh-172-1; Malinda A. widow of; Pvt A Co 1st MS Cav; 12-22-63 to 6-26-65; 4 Howard Row, Memphis PO; died from rupture, worthy of consideration, has applied for pension but failed
WALDRON, Thomas S., Gi-129-3; Pvt I Co 110th OH Inf; 4 Oct 62 to Jun 65; Elkton PO; prisoner at Libby 3 mos
WALDROP, Amos W., Ge-84-1; Pvt G Co 10th IN Cav; 11 Nov 63 to ___; Wolsey College PO; dis. rupture and mumps
WALDRUP, William, Hd-50-2; Cpl F Co 6th TN Cav; Sep 21 62 to 26 Jul 65; Savannah PO
WALDUNN, Francis, Ce-31-1; Mary T. Perry former widow of; Pvt 31st KY Inf--Feb 61 to Mar 64; Pvt KY Cav--Apr 64 to 5 May 65; Ashland City PO; re-enlisted veteran
WALEN, William W., D-70-1; Pvt K Co 11th MI Inf; 62 to 65; Nashville PO
WALKER, Abner L., Jo-153-1; Pvt B Co 4th TN Inf; 3 Aug 62 to 2 Aug 65; Pandora PO
WALKER, Alexander C., Cl-57-1; Pvt F Co 3rd TN Inf; 2-20-62 to 2-20-65; Kecks Chappel PO; gun shot wound left thigh
WALKER, Allen, Sh-155-1; Pvt D Co 11th US Inf; Nov 63 to 8 Jan 66; Germantown PO
WALKER, Alvin, Gr-70-1; Pvt B Co 14th IL Cav; 62 to 65; Rutledge TN PO; small pox affected eyes, exact dates unknown
WALKER, Anderson, F-43-1; Pvt 2nd ___; Mar 63 to May 64; Rossville PO; Col and cannot give much information
WALKER?, Anderson W., Ge-91-2; Ellen C. widow of; Capt 3rdTN ___; Greeneville PO; dont know dates
WALKER, Austin, Di-34-2; Pvt E Co 8th US Col Hvy Art; 64 to ___; Dickson PO; discharge lost
WALKER, Bennet, D-71-1; 917 Summer, Nashville PO
WALKER, Berry, C-33-6; US Soldier; PO omitted
WALKER, Beverly, Gu-48-5(2); Pvt D Co 24th TN Inf; Rogersville PO
WALKER, Calvin, Mu-193-2; Pvt D Co 111th OH Cav; 1-15-63 to 3-15-65; PO omitted
WALKER, Calvin, K-174-4(3); Sarah E. widow of; Pvt F Co 3rd TN Inf; 1 Apr 62 to ___; died of deseas Jul 3 1863
WALKER, Chas., D-99-3; Pvt G Co 13th TN Cav; May 63 to Jun 65; State Penitentiary PO; shot wound in thigh
WALKER, Daniel B., Mc-116-1; Mary J. widow of; Pvt G Co 1st TN Cav; 9-1-62 to 8-27-63; Athens PO; killed on the Sultana boat
WALKER, David C., Bo-14-1; Pvt F Co 25th IA Inf; 1-15-64 to 7-24-65; Cliff PO
WALKER, David H., Bl-2-2(1); Sgt D Co 2nd TN Inf; 6-19-62 to 6-19-65; Farmingdale PO; ruptured by strain, now unable to do much work
WALKER, Edmond H., Mg-199-1; Pvt A Co 11th TN Cav; 28 May 63 to 31 Jul 65; Sunbright PO; catarrh of the head

WALKER, Edmund C., Dk-35-4(2); Pvt E Co 4th TN Mtd Inf; 11-26-64 to 8-23-65; Hicks PO; kicked by horse
WALKER, Edwin, Be-1-1; 13th Dist
walker, Elizabeth A., Gi-134-1; widow US Sol; Dist 14
WALKER, Elkanah W., Wa-274-1; Sgt Blacksmith B Co 12th TN Cav; 1 Oct 63 to 1 Oct 65; Jonesboro PO; stomach disease
WALKER, F. M., Mc-109-1 (Frank M. Wofford alias); Pvt G Co 10th TN Cav; 2-15-64 to 8-1-65; Chuckaluck PO; sciatica and rheumatism
WALKER, F. M., Wa-270-1; Pvt H Co 4th TN Cav; Dec 62 to 65; Johnson City PO
WALKER, Gale, Hw-131-3; Pvt D Co 8th TN Inf; 9 Apr 63 to 26 Jun 65; White Horn PO; piles
WALKER, George, Sh-201-4; Pvt A Co 61st US Col Inf; 16 May 63 to 30 Dec 65; Memphis PO
WALKER, George, Bl-3-2; Mary C. widow of; Pvt I Co 2nd TN Inf; 7-9-62 to 7-28-65; Orones Store PO; rupture
WALKER, George W., K-172-1; Pvt A Co 6th TN Inf; 28 Apr 62 to 27 Apr 65; Knoxville PO; in prison 12 mos 4 das
WALKER, George W., De-22-1; Pvt; Clifton PO; CONF
WALKER, Gus A., Mo-122-2; Pvt D Co 62nd Mtd Inf; 8-15-61 to 6-15-65; Sweetwater PO
WALKER, Harriett, Dy-32-1; widow US Sol; 15th Civil Dist
WALKER, Harris, Sh-163-1; PO omitted
WALKER, Harry, Sn-252-2; Pvt E Co 110th TN Inf; 10-63 to 8-66; Gallatin PO
WALKER, Harvey, Mu-192-1; Celia widow of; PO omitted; papers lost, widow drawing pension
WALKER, Henry (of John), Wa-273-1; 1st Lt K Co 13th TN Cav; 15 Aug 63 to 4 Sep 65; Morning Star PO; rheumatism and piles
WALKER, Henry D., Be-1-2; Hockletown PO
WALKER, Henry H., Sq-164-2(1); Pvt; Dunlap PO
WALKER, Henry M. (of Andrew), Wa-273-1; Pvt I Co 8th TN Cav; 25 Sep 63 to 25 May 65; Locust Mt. PO; lung disease
WALKER, Howard, Bl-2-2(1); Elizabeth widow of; Recruiting Officer; Orme's Store PO; killed March 1865
WALKER, Israiel, Hy-76-2; US Sol; Stanton Depot PO
WALKER, J. H., Bo-11-3; Sgt F Co 2nd TN Cav; 8-1-62 to 7-6-65; Brick Mill PO
WALKER, James, Je-142-1; Pvt M Co 8th KY Cav; 13 Jan 63 to 17 Sep 63; Lucilla PO
WALKER, James A., Sm-173-2; Cpl I Co 4th TN Mtd Inf; 2-16-65 to 8-5-65; Alexandria PO (Dekalb Co.)
WALKER, James H., Bo-19-2; Capt F Co 2nd TN Cav; 8-1-62 to 8-1-65; Rockford PO
WALKER, James H., Po-152-2; 1st Sgt D Co 10th TN Cav; 1-1-64 to 8-1-65; Ducktown PO; rheumatism and heart disease
WALKER, Jeff, C-27-1; Pvt F Co 6th TN Inf; 7-61 to 64; Jacksboro PO
WALKER, Jerry, K-171-3(2); Pvt 1st Col US Hvy Art; 64 to 66; Knoxville PO
WALKER, Joe, K-73-4(2); Chattanooga PO
WALKER, John, K-174-4(3); Elizabeth widow of; Pvt F Co 3rd TN Inf; 1 Apr 62 to __; died of disease Feb 12, 1864
WALKER, John, D-67-1; Pvt Col Inf; Nashville PO
WALKER, John, Su-235-1; Cpl I Co 15th KY Cav; 4 Mar 63 to 15 Apr 65; Bristol PO; gunshot
WALKER, John, Gr-81-3(1); Pvt C Co 59th OH Inf; 5 Jan 63 to 16 Jul 65; Clear Spring PO; rheumatism, partly disabled
WALKER, John, H-58-1; Barbary B. Usam formerly widow of; Pvt A Co 4th TN Cav; Sale Creek PO; discharge misplaced
WALKER, John, Hw-131-3; 1st Lt D Co 8th TN Inf; 1 Nov 63 to 15 May 65; St. Clair PO
WALKER, John, Jo-152-2; Doeville PO
WALKER, John, Wl-293-2; Pvt B Co 4th __; Oct 61 to 63; Lockport PO; CONF
WALKER, John A., Hw-131-2; Pvt B Co 8th TN Inf; 15 Sep 62 to 30 Jun 65; White Horn PO
WALKER, John B., Se-223-3; Sgt F Co 4th TN Cav; 10 Apr 63 to 7 Jul 65; Hendersons Springs PO
WALKER, John B., D-49-1; Pvt M Co 3rd OH; 10 Jul 62 to 25 Mar 65; 427 Spruce St, Nashville PO; gun shot wound
WALKER, John L., H-59-1; Pvt F Co 10th IA Inf; 5-62 to 9-65; Chattanooga PO
WALKER, John M., Dk-31-3; Sgt I Co 5th TN Cav; 12-24-63 to 8-14-65; Alexandria PO; catarrh stomach 8 yrs
WALKER, John N., Se-224-3; PVt E Co 1st TN Lt Art; 9 Oct 63 to 1 Aug 65; Wears Valley PO; mumps & diarrhea, got rheumatism, cant walk good
WALKER, John P., R-161-5; Sarah widow of; Pvt F Co 5th TN Inf--2-25-62 to 10-25-64; Dayton PO; Capt B Co 6th TN Mtd Inf--10-26-64 to 10-26-65; Walker, Jos., T-209-1; alias Jos. Lavalley; Sgt G Co 4th IL; 61 to 65; Randolph PO
WALKER, Joseph, Bo-21-2; Sgt D Co 2nd TN Cav; 9-1-62 to 7-16-65; Ellijay PO
WALKER, Joseph, Sh-146-4; 3rd Civ Dist
WALKER, Joseph, Bo-23-1; S widow of; Pvt D Co 2nd TN Cav; 9-15-63 to 3-18-65; Tuckaleechee Cove PO; at home on furlow & got no discharge
WALKER, Joseph C., L-99-1; Mary Thomas formerly widow of; Cpl C Co 29th US Col Troops; Jan 22 64 to Nov 6 65; Durhamville PO; wounded in right leg
WALKER, Joseph D., Sarah widow of; H-50-4; Soddy PO
WALKER, Joseph L., Bo-23-3; Pvt D Co 2nd TN Cav; 9-1-62 to 7-7-65; Cades Cove PO; small pox; widow does not know date of enlistment (believe this data refers to John Sands)
WALKER, Josiah C., Su-242-1; Mary A. widow of; Blacksmith G Co 8th TN Cav; 6 Jul 63 to 11 Sep 65; Bluff City PO; rheumatism, married March 11 67 and parted Sep 12 70, also Mar.13, 84, no cause is assigned for his cours (sic), died Tuskigee
WALKER, Lilburn H., C-28-2(1); Pvt F Co 6th TN Inf; 3-10-62 to 3-24-65; Big Creek Gap PO; broken veins
WALKER, Louisa (see Shrader, William)
WALKER, Louise, D-66-2; Nashville, 2 Tillmore Ave, PO
WALKER, Marion, Hw-131-4; Phenelissy Walker family widow of; 2nd Lt D Co 8th TN Inf; 15 Dec 62 to __; PO omitted
WALKER, Marshal A., K-72-2; Pvt A Co 6th TN Inf; 17 Apr 62 to 27 Apr 65; Knoxville PO
WALKER, Martin, Fr-116-1(2); Pvt Co 36th OH Vol; 8-12-61 to 7-31-62; Sherwood PO; rupture
WALKER, Mathew M., Ro-207-1; Claris E. widow of; Sgt F Co 10th TN Cav; 20 Oct 63 to died in service; Erie PO (Loudon Co.); chron. dirhrae
WALKER, Matthew, Gi-127-6; Pvt A Co 110th US Col Inf; Jan 2 64 to Apr 3 66; Pulaski PO
WALKER, Mode, Mc-109-5; Sinthia J. widow of; Pvt 5th TN Inf; Sweetwater PO (Monroe Co.); soldier dead, discharge misplaced
WALKER, Nancy J. (see Harmon, John B.)
WALKER, Patsy (see Ezell, Caye)
WALKER, Peter E., Se-223-5(1); Lt A Co 9th TN Cav; 4 Aug 63 to 11 Sep 65; Sevierville PO; rheumatism, enlisted privated, discharged 2nd Lt
WALKER, Peter J., Je-141-3; Pvt D Co 4th TN Inf; 1 Nov 63 to 2 Aug 65; Mill Springs PO
WALKER, Philip, Dy-24-1; Pvt 5th TN Inf; 61 to 65; Dyersburgh PO; unhurt; CONF
WALKER, Preston, Hm-109-1; Pvt H Co 8th TN Inf; 15 Jul 63 to 20 Jun 65; Three Springs PO; rheumatism
WALKER, Preston C., Hw-131-3; Pvt B Co 3rd TN Inf; 15 Mar 63 to 3May 65; Otes PO; wounded gun shot
WALKER, Raphael A., H-72-3(2); Susan widow of; 1st Sgt G Co 5th TN Mtd Inf; 10-5-64 to 7-13-65; Chattanooga PO
WALKER, Richard E., K-182-3; Caroline B. widow of; Pvt A Co 6th TN Vol Inf; 61 to 64; Knoxville PO

WALKER, Robert H., R-161-1; Sarah L. Smith formerly widow of; Blacksmith M Co 1st AL Inf; 62 to 65; Dayton PO; discharge lost
WALKER, Rufus, D-68-1; Mary widow of; 166½ Fillmore, Nashville PO; discharge papers lost
WALKER, Sal, Sh-144-1; alias William Walker; Pvt K Co 7th US Col Inf; Ma 63 to 65; Brunswick PO; criple in arm; has a discharge in LA
WALKER, Samuel, Mc-114-3; Catherine widow of; Pvt F Co; 3-1-63 to 7-6-65; Raht PO
WALKER, Samuel D., Dy-25-3; Mary F. widow of; Pvt Inf; May 61 to __ (6 mos); Newbern PO; wounded, CONF
WALKER, W., Di-34-1; Pvt H Co 4th Col US Hvy Art; 10-26-63 to 2-25-66; Dickson PO
WALKER, Stephen, Cu-16-1; Pvt D Co 2nd TN Inf; 6-3-62 to 6-19-65; Wine Sap PO
WALKER, Thomas, K-182-2; Pvt A Co 6th TN Vol Inf; 27 Apr 62 to 27 Apr 65; Gapcreek PO
WALKER, Thomas, Je-137-2; Hickory Ridge PO
WALKER, Thomas J., Sh-183-2; Ann M. widow of; Capt D Co 48th R Inf; 12-10-62 to 3-3-65; Memphis PO; wonded
WALKER, Tom, Wl-291-1; F Co 72nd IN; __ to 64; Lebanon PO
WALKER, W. T. (see Pendergrass, Caterin)
WALKER, Walter, H-62-1; Jane widow of; Pvt; Alley bet. Cedar & Pleasant, Chattanooga PO
WALKER, William, Bl-2-3; Rutha E. widow of; 6th KY Cav; 3-62 to 63 (1 yr); Orme's Store PO; died in the service 1863
WALKER, William H., Dy-25-7(3); Pvt F Co 9th KY Inf; May 62 to May 65; Newbern PO; CONF
WALKER, William T., R-161-6; Pvt B Co 6th TN Mtd Inf; 8-18-64 to 8-30-65; Dayton PO
WALKER, William W., A-13-3; Pvt C Co 11th MI Cav; 12-2-62 to 1-3-65; Briceville PO
WALKER, Wilson, C-28-1; Sgt H Co 9th TN Cav; 7-1-63 to 9-11-65; Big Cree Gap PO
WALKINS, Edward, Sh-157-7; Pvt M Co 3rd US Cav; 64 to Jan 26 66; Memphis PO; injured in left leg and knee
WALKINS, Henry, Mu-197-2; Dollie widow of; Pvt 12th __; 63 to 65; Columbia PO
WALL, J. T., Gi-139-2; Pvt K Co 33rd TN Inf; 10-61 to 5-65; Bercheers PO
WALL, John, H-49-5; Pvt C Co 5th TN Inf; 4-1-63 to 7-14-6_; Daisy PO; kidney & liver disease
WALL, John O., Cr-14-1; Pvt G Co 2nd TN Mtd Inf; 29 Dec 63 to 1 Feb 65; Clarksburg PO
WALL, Robert B., Ro-211-3; Pvt G Co 16th WI Inf; Nov 61 to 64; Harriman PO; ruptured
WALL, William, H-53-1; Fannie widow of; Chattanooga PO; particulars unknown
WALL, William H., Cr-14-2; Pvt G Co 2nd TN Mtd Inf; 29 Dec 63 to 1 Feb 65; Clarksburg PO
WALLACE, A. L., Ro-210-2; Pvt; Rockwood PO
WALLACE, Ambrose, Ho-96-1; Pvt K Co 20th IL Inf; Apr 4 61 to Apr 20 62; Erin PO
WALLACE, Andrew J., Ch-12-1; Gunsmith I Co 11th IL Cav; 10-1-62 to 6-16-65; Wild Goose PO; eraciples & loss of sight
WALLACE, Charles, Ha-63-3; Louisa widow of; Pvt Inf; 63 to 65; 809 Pine, Chattanooga PO
WALLACE, Chas. T., Br-10-1; Pvt H Co 86th IL Inf; 8-27-62 to 6-6-65; Cleveland PO
WALLACE, David, Ca-20-1; Pvt E Co 1st MO Inf; 5-10-62 to 5-15-64; Braxton PO
WALLACE, Elkanah, Jo-150-2; Pvt I Co 13th TN Cav; 22 Sep 63 to 5 Sep 65; Key Station PO
WALLACE, Elvis, A-5-4; Rebeckie widow of; Pvt C Co 2nd TN Mtd Inf; 8-61 to 9-64; Clinton PO
WALLACE, Francis L., Gi-122-4; 2nd Sgt G Co 50th NC Inf; 6 Apr 62 to 25 Apr 65; Prospect Sta. PO; CONF
WALLACE, Fred S., H-56-2; Pvt 82nd OH Inf; 61 to 65; East End PO
WALLACE, George W., Jo-150-2; Pvt I Co 13th TN Cav; 22 Sep 62 to __; Key Station PO
WALLACE, Howell E., Po-148-2; Pvt A Co 5th TN Mtd Inf; 9-1-64 to 6-26-65; Cog Hill PO
WALLACE, Isaac, Ro-208-2; Pvt A Co 5th TN Inf; 25 Feb 62? to 27 May 63; Welker Mines PO
WALLACE, James H., Ov-137-2; Pvt H Co 3rd KY Inf; 3-25-63 to 8-65; Monroe PO; rheumatism in body and limbs and sunstroke, recd. 3 gunshot wounds and was struck with piece of shell in service

WALLACE, John, Sh-162-2; US Sol; Ramsey PO
WALLACE, Landon, Bo-14-4; Pvt H Co 2nd TN Cav; 10-10-62 to 7-6-65; Maryville PO
WALLACE, Martin A., M-107-5; Pvt H Co 4th TN Mtd Inf; 11-1-64 to 8-21-65; Gibbs Cross Roads PO; disease of lungs
WALLACE, Mary (see Johnson, Daniel)
WALLACE, Mary A. (see Brewer, William T.)
WALLACE, Millus D., A-5-2; Pvt C Co 11th TN Cav; 8-1-63 to 9-16-65; Clinton PO
WALLACE, Pharoah C., A-2-2; 1st Lt C Co 2nd TN Inf; 8-7-61 to 1-8-62; Hinds Creek PO; liver & kidney disease
WALLACE, Riley, Un-254-3; Pvt D Co 1st TN Cav; 8 Jul 62 to __; Meltibarger PO
WALLACE, Robert R., He-64-2; Pvt K Co 7th TN Cav; 20 Apr 63 to 16 Jun 65; Center Point PO; eye lost in prisson
WALLACE, Samuel R., A-2-3; Pvt C Co 114th US Col Inf; 6-10-64 to 4-2-67; Clinton PO; pensioner
WALLACE, Theophilus T., Bo-15-1; Cpl H Co 2nd TN Cav; 10-10-62 to 7-6-65; Blockhouse PO; rhumatism
WALLACE, Thomas, Hw-132-4; Pvt B Co TN Inf; Feb 65 to Apr 65; Otes PO; rheumatism, could not tell any more; CONF
WALLACE, William, Ro-210-10; Pvt I Co 4th TN Cav; Rockwood PO; CONF
WALLACE, William C., Wh-181-1; 1st Sgt G Co 4th AR Cav; 2-6-64 to 7-26-65; Green Tree PO
WALLACE, William H., A-10-1; Pvt D Co 1st TN Lt Art; 4-25-64 to 6-28-65; Briceville PO; hearing
WALLAS, Andrew J., Hu-104-1(2); Pvt G Co 12th TN Cav; Dec 29 63 to May 26 65; McEwen PO; ruptured by fall and piles
WALLEN, Alfred, Ha-111-3; Pvt C Co 8th TN Inf; 1 Dec 62 to 30 Jun 65
WALLEN, Aron V., Hw-120-2; Pvt L Co 8th TN Cav; 1 Oct 63 to 25 Sep 65; Kyles Ford PO; desease of eyes
WALLEN, Ivin, Ha-111-3; Mary A. widow of; PO omitted
WALLEN, James R., Ha-117-1; Jane widow of; Pvt 11th TN Cav; 63 to __; Kyle's Ford PO; discharged from service from disability, can't find causes
WALLEN, Joseph, Ha-111-3; 1st D Sgt L Co 8th TN Cav; 1 Oct 63 to 11 Sep 65; PO omitted
WALLEN, Juda (see Fields?, ____)
WALLEN, Robt. B., Ha-117-1; Pvt G Co 1st TN Cav; 1 Jul 62 to 12 Jun 65; Kyle's Ford PO; kidney disease, chronic diarrhea
WALLER, Calvin, Ro-210-5; Pvt; Rockwood PO
WALLER, George, Ro-202-3(1); Pvt I Co 2nd TN Inf; Sep 64 to May 65; Union X Roads PO; CONF
WALLER, George P., Ro-202-1; Pvt B Co 63rd TN Inf; 9 Sep 62 to 9 Apr 65; Union X Roads PO; no disability; CONF
WALLER, Henry, Ro-202-3(1); Pvt I Co 2nd TN Inf; Sep 64 to May 65; Union X Roads PO; CONF
WALLER, Jacob L., Ro-202-1; Capt E Co 19th TN Inf; 11 Jun 61 to Apr 65; Union X Roads PO; wound in left leg; CONF
WALLER, John, Ro-205-2; Pvt; Postoak Springs PO
WALLER, Preston J., We-223-2; Pvt Carter Batry Art?; Jun 61 to 25 Apr 65; Palmersville PO; all ik now; CONF
WALLER, Richard B., Pu-144-2; Pvt K Co 5th TN Cav; 5-63 to 8-13-65; Pine Fork PO; piles
WALLER, Thomas, Sh-197-1; Cpl I Co 3rd Col Art; 8-31-63 to 4-30-66; Memphis PO
WALLER, Wallis, F-44-4; Emily Hunter widow of; Pvt B Co 59th __; 63 to 65; PO omitted
WALLER, William, Wa-276-2; Pvt D Co 3rd TN Cav; Jul 10 64 to Nov 30 64; Leesburg PO; gen. disability & disease of chest & lungs
WALLER, William, Ro-202-3(1); Pvt B Co 63rd TN Inf; 18 Apr 62 to 9 Apr 65; Philadelphia PO; shot through left hand & leg; CONF
WALLER, William M., Sh-196-3; Memphis PO
WALLICE, George, Ru-236-1; Cpl H Co 13th W S; 16 Oct 63 to 12 Jan 65; Murfreesboro PO; been sufering from reumatic pain in ankle, he is able to work
WALLICE, William, Col, H-56-4; Pvt GA Inf; St. Elmo PO

WALLS, Alexander, K-186-2; Pvt 2nd TN Cav; Balls Camp PO
WALLS, John, Ca-20-2; Ann widow of; Pvt C Co 5th TN Cav; 62 to 63; Talvine PO; (this name crossed out--no reason given)
WALLS, Robert A., Mg-196-3; Pvt K Co 1st TN Inf; 9 Aug 61 to 17 Sep 64; Elverton PO; catarrh; prisoner at Libey(sic)
WALLS, Zachariah, Gi-133-2; Pvt K Co 53rd TN; Dec 61 to 65; Bufords PO; CONF
WALLSMITH, William, G-68-1 Pvt C Co 79th IN; Aug 8, 62 to Jun 10, 65; Gibson PO; loss of health
WALPOOLE, Benjamin F., Cr-13-2; Pvt F Co 7th TN Cav; Jun 1, 62 to Dec 20, 62; Atwood PO
WALSH, James, D-60-2; Cpl C Co 124th OH Vol; Sep 20, 62 to Aug 1, 65; 1203 Cedor St., Nashville PO; gunshot wound; white, bland with scheds.
WALSH, T. J., He-57-2; Pvt C Co 1st KY Inf; 6-10-61 to 6-10-64; Juno PO
WALSH, William H., Br-9-1; Lt D Co 10th TN Cav; Cleveland PO; discharge at Washington
WALTER, George W., Wa-260-2; Sgt G Co 4th TN Inf; Nov 5, 62 to Jun 19, 65; Pilot Hill PO; by reason of order of War Dept A.C.U.
WALTER, Philipias, Cf-41-1; Elizabeth widow of; Pvt; Teal PO; could not learn the command
WALTERS, John, La-117-3; US Sol; 15th Dist.
WALTERS, William M., K-173-2; Pvt D Co; McMillen PO; CONF
WALTON, Horace, Mt-137-1; Civ at work on Forts; 62 to 65; papers lost; St. Bethlehem PO
WALTON, John, Sh-178-1; Fifer H Co 11th US Inf; 63 to 65; 289 Union St. Memphis PO
WALTON, Junine, Sh-192-1; Ord Sgt G Co 40th US Col Inf; 4-65 to 66; Memphis PO
WALTON, Polk, St-159-1; Pvt E Co 16th TN Inf; 1-63 to 65; Indian Mount PO
WALTON, R. J., Wl-293-2; 61 to 64; Lockport PO; CONF
WALTON, Reuben R? H., Be-2-1; Pvt E Co 7th TN Cav; Dec 14, 63 to Aug 25, 65; Holladay PO; chronic scurvy
WALTON, Samuel, Ma-128-1; Jackson PO; wife could give no information
WALTON, Slone B., O-134-2; Pvt C Co 34th MS; May 15, 62 to Oct 15, 65; Hornbeak PO; CONF
WALTON, Stokly, D-51-1 (Black); Pvt 14th TN Inf; 62 to 65; 228 Capital Ave., Nashville PO
WALTON, Tyre H., Dy-29-4; Elizabeth F. widow of; Newbern PO; CONF
WALTON, William, D-64-2; Pvt 16th TN Reg; Back 213 S. Summer St., Nashville PO; shot in head & back & hand
WALTON, William B., D-56-1; Capt H Co 1st TN Vol Inf; 30 May 46 to May 47; Mexican War; Nashville PO
WAMACK, Jas. S., Ca-20-2; Pvt C Co 5th TN Cav; 1-1-63 to 2-64; Talvine PO
WAMPLER, Isaac, Ge-100-1; Wagner B Co 8th TN Inf; 17 Dec 62 to Jun 65; Midway PO; disable (not cureul)
WAMPLER, James S., Ge-94-2(1); Sgt A Co 8th TN Cav; 11 Jun 63 to 11 Sep 65; Greeneville PO; smallpox in 1864
WAMPLER, Joseph A., Ge-87-3; Pvt A Co 12th TN Cav; 1 Apr 62 to 65; Timberridge PO; wounded side
WANDEY?, Alexander, Cu-15-2; Woody PO; CONF
WANNEMAKER, James, Hu-100-2; Pvt I Co 10th TN Inf; 62 to 65; Waverly PO
WARD, Burgess, Bo-14-1; Elizabeth widow of; Cpl L Co 2nd TN Cav; Clover Hill PO; captured & died in prison
WARD, Clark, St-159-1; Pvt; 2 Yrs 5 mos; Legate PO
WARD, Duke, C-26-1; Pvt I Co 7th TN Inf; 11-8-64 to 7-27-65; Jacksboro PO
WARD, Enoch, Je-146-4; Julia widow of; Pvt H Co 23rd US Inf; White Pine PO
WARD, Ephiram, Hw-131-1; Pvt B Co TN Mtd Inf; 3 Jun 64 to 25 Oct 64; Bulls Gap PO; paralysis by shot
WARD, George W., Sn-254-1; Pvt B Co 4th US Inf; 6-1-64 to 6-24-65; Hendersonville PO
WARD, Harry M., Br-12-1; Pvt AL Inf; Charleston PO; chronic diarhea

WARD, Henry B., Wh-182-1; Pvt C Co 137th OH Na. G., 5-2-64 to 8-19-65; Pvt I Co 177th OH Inf, 9-12-64 to 6-24-65; Doyle's Sta. PO
WARD, Henry P., Se-225-1; Cpl C Co 8th TN Cav; 11 Jun 63 to 11 Sep 65; Allensbille PO; one testacle mashed by a horse
WARD, Isaac, Je-144-1; Pvt D Co 9th TN Cav; 63 to 65; White Pine PO; rheumatism
WARD, James A., He-66-1; Pvt K Co 7th TN Cav; Sep 11, 63 to Sep 15, 65; Lexington PO; liver disease
WARD, Jerry, D-69-3; 57 Claborn St., Nashville PO
WARD, John, Sh-190-1 (& Sh-190-2); Memphis, 196 Georgia St. PO
WARD, John J., O-140-1; Pvt Mar 62 to Mar 62 (7 days); Union City PO; discharge lost and question not known
WARD, John M., Ro-208-2; Pvt A Co 2nd TN Inf; 12 Aug 61 to 6 Oct 64; Morris Gap PO; rheumatism
WARD, Johnathan S., Bl-2-1; Sgt D Co 25th OH Inf; 6-25-61 to 6-28-64; Sampson PO; shot in left hip & thigh
WARD, Jonathan, Se-221-2; East Fork PO; had gone to NC, no one could give information
WARD, Josua, Dy-29-4; Mary E. widow of; Newbern PO; CONF
WARD, Julia, (see Boulen, Daniel)
WARD, Robert M., Dy-27-2; Pvt A Co 12th TN Inf; May 61 to May 65; Ro Ellen PO; CONF
WARD, Tapley M., Ct-35-1; Keron widow of; Pvt F Co 13th TN Cav; Fish Spring PO; died in US Army, no discharge
WARD, Thomas, Hw-124-2(1); 7th Civil Dist
WARD, Thomas Alen?, Be-5-1; Marthy J. widow; Pvt; Camden PO; died in Andersonvill prison; widow drawes pension
WARD, Thomas H., Ch-18-3(5); Pvt B Co 6th TN Cav; Aug 25, 64 to Aug 8, 65; Montezuma PO; gun shot in left shoulder; "atrophied" has made application for pension
WARD, Thomas H., Ch-18-1; Pvt B Co 6th TN Cav; 25 Aug 62 to 8 Aug 65; Montezuma PO; gun shot in left shoulder (atrophy)
WARD, William, Sh-150-2; Pvt B Co US Hvy Art; 3 yrs; Bartlett PO
WARD, William, C-26-2; Pvt J Co 7th TN Inf; 11-8-64 to 7-27-65; Caryville PO
WARD, William, Cl-52-2; Pvt A Co 12th TN Cav; 6-24-63 to 10-7-65; Hypratia PO
WARD, William C., Ct-35-4; Pvt F Co 13th TN Cav; 9-27-63 to 9-5-65; Lineback PO; in the US Army
WARD, William G., Ro 207-1; Pvt A Co 2nd E TN Inf; 10-Aug 61 to 6 Oct 64; Patties Gap PO; cron. dirhea & desease of lungs
WARD, Wilson, D-78-2; Pvt A Co 30th LA Inf; 62 to Apr 65; Nashville PO
WARDELL, Daniel G., K-171-5(4); Pvt D Co 6th TN Inf; 62 to 65; Bearden PO
WARDELL, Joseph D., Se-231-1; Pvt D Co 6th TN Inf; 11 May 63 to 30 Jun 6t;Boyds Creek PO; frost bit feete 25 years
WARDELL, Michael, Se-227-1; Pvt D Co 6th TN Inf; 15 Feb 63 to 2 Jun 65; Trundles X Roads PO; injury to left hip
WARDEN, Aquilla A., D-57-1; Mary C. widow of; Pvt H Co 12th US Reg Inf; 63 to __ (5 yrs); PO omitted (but in 8th Ward, Nashville)
WARDEN, Elijah D., Ct-43-2; Lydia widow of; Pvt B Co 13th TN Cav; 9-22-63 to 9-5-65; Carter Furnace PO; rheumatism, died of rheumatism 1881
WARDEN, Isaac C., Gr-73-1; Pvt C Co 91st OH Inf; 26 Sep 64 to 24 Jun 65; Turley's Mills PO
WARDEN, Joseph, We-220-3; Dresden PO
WARDER, James A., H-64-2; Capt C Co 2nd KY Cav; Chattanooga PO
WARE, George, H-60-3; Julia Brown formerly widow of; Or Sgt A Co 44th TN Inf; Chattanooga PO; wounded in side by shell
WARE, Green, S-213-2; Pvt C Co 19th KY Inf; 16 Oct 61 to 26 Jun 65; Hellenwood PO; chronic sore eyes contracted in army
WARE, Hartford, Hy-76-2; Pvt G Co 3rd GA Inf; 2 yrs; Stanton Depot PO
WARE, James, Br-8-2; Capt E Co 10th TN Cav; 10-7?-63 to 3-22-65; Cleveland PO

WARE, William, Sh-193-2; Pvt; Memphis PO; papers have been lost
WARETON, William C., H-51-1; Pvt D Co 42nd R IA? Inf; 9-15-61 to 10-24-64; Soddy PO; rheumatism & sore eyes
WARFIELD, Feline, Rb-221-3; Pvt G Co 16th TN; 1 Jan 64 to 1 Mar 65; Adams Station PO
WARFIELD, Smith, St-162-2; Pvt H Co 2nd TN Mtd Inf; 64 to 65; Dover PO; discharge lost
WARICK, William L., Ro-208-2; Pvt A Co 2nd TN Inf; 14 Aug 61 to 3 Jun 6t; Morris Gap PO; chronic kidny disease
warix, Jasper, O-137-1; Pvt H Co 12th KY Inf; 8 Sep 63 to Mar 65; Kenton PO; detail out of order on this sched.
WARN?, James M., F-42-2(4); Pvt 13th __; 61 to 65; Rossville PO; CONF
WARNER, Abigah G., Mc-116-3; Pvt F Co 58th IL Inf; 1-1-62 to 5-15-63; Mortimer PO; disease of right eye
WARNER, Adonijah, K-161-6; Knoxville PO
WARNER, Anderson, B-11-2(1); Pvt G Co 14th US Col; 7-20-64 to 3-1-66; Poplins X Roads PO; eye hurt
WARNER, David A., R-106-1; Pvt A Co 1st NY Guard? US Richinal?; 2-21-64 to 6-65; 5th Civil Dist
WARNER, Phillip H., Lo-189-2; Pvt G Co 97th PA Inf; 4 Mar 65 to 28 Aug 65; shot through right ankle, discharged on surgeons ctf.
WARNER, Richard, O-130-1; Pvt I Co 43rd OH V Inf; 25 Dec 63 to 13 Jul 65; Fulton PO, KY
WARNER, Thomas C., H-62-3; Pvt C Co 4th OH Inf; 4-61 to 63 (2 yrs); 411 Chestnut, Chattanooga PO
WARNICK, Gipson, K-174-4(3); Pvt F Co 3rd TN Inf; 20 Feb 62 to 12 May 63; Graveston PO; deseas of lungs and bronchitis 26 yrs
WARREN, Campbell E., Su-233-1; Quartermaster Sgt C Co 13th TN Cav; Jan 64 to Sep 65; Bristol PO; chronic dierher & blindness, disabled for labor
WARREN, Charles A., H-64-1; Lue widow of; Petty Officer Gunboat Ft. Henry; 3-9-62 to 3-19-63; Chattanooga PO
WARREN, Columbus, A-13-4; Briceville PO
WARREN, Cornelius, Jo-150-2; Pvt I Co 13th TN Cav; 15 Jan 64 to 5 Sep 65; Trade PO
WARREN, Dennis, K-180-1; Pvt C Co 44th TN Col Inf; 17 Nov 64 to 30 Apr 66; Ebenezer PO
WARREN, Doc R., K-171-5(4); Ordely M Co 1st US Hvy Art Col; Oct 63 to Jul 64; Knoxville PO
WARREN, George, Sh-190-1; Pvt E Co 64th TN Inf; 12-63 to 5-66; 227 Virginia, Memphis PO; hearing
WARREN, Henry, Sh-182-1; Pvt E Co 55th TN; 11-63 to 12-65; 205 Poplar St. Memphis PO; shot in head-rheumatism contracted during war
WARREN, James, K-182-3; Pvt F Co 6th IN Vol Cav; 18 Aug 63 to 15 Sep 65; Arthur PO, Sevier Co.; right leg broke
WARREN, James P., F-43-2; alias? James Pinkny; Pvt D Co 12th IL; Apr 1 64 to Jul 10 65; Piperton PO
WARREN, Jasper, G-51-2; US Sol; Humboldt PO
WARREN, John (see Thomas, John)
WARREN, John B., Gi-124-1; Cpl I Co 2nd TN Cav; 4 Nov 63 to 19 Jan 65; Marbuts PO
WARREN, John E., Se-231-2; Black S(mith?) F Co 6th IN Cav; 18 Aug 63 to 15 Sep 65; Boyds Creek PO; fustalum ennis 26 yrs
WARREN, John M., D-72-4; Pvt M Co 13th IL Cav; Dec 31, 63 to Aug 31, 65; Nashville PO
WARREN, John R., Ge-99-1; Pvt M Co 9th TN Cav; 15 Nov 64 to 11 Sep 65; Limestone Springs PO; lost an eye
WARREN, Joseph, D-72-4; Sgt B Co 42nd TN Inf; Mar 27, 63 to 65; Nashville PO
WARREN, Joseph A., P-156-1; Musician K Co 42nd TN Inf; 11-61 to 8-11-64; Lobelville PO; piles; CONF
WARREN, Meneda? C., K-174-3(2); Pvt I Co 3rd TN Inf; 10 Feb 62 to 2 Aug 65; Snoderly PO
WARREN, Moses, F-39-2(1); Pvt E Co 106th US Cav; Jul 63 to 3 Jan 66; PO omitted; discharge in Washington
WARREN, Reuben, Mr-99-4; Sol US; Jasper PO

WARREN, Robert M., K-179-2; Pvt G Co 1st TN Inf; 9 Aug 61 to 11 Sep 65; Virtue PO; transferred to 11th TN Cav
WARREN, Samuel, Mu-196-2; Pvt C Co 42nd Reg; Jul 63 to Oct 65; Columbia PO; struck by lightning while in service, now paralyzed and can not walk scarcely without sticks
WARREN, Samuel M., Su-238-1; Sgt H Co 4th TN Inf; 20 Apr 64 to 2 Aug 65; Piney Flats PO; wound in head, jaundice & diarhea
WARREN, Steve, Cr-16-2; Pvt I Co 3rd US Inf; 63 to 66; Huntingdon PO; lost discharge
WARREN, Thoma V., Wl-305-1; Pvt B Co 77th __; 14 Aug 62 to 3 Jun 65; Bairds Hill PO; diseased
WARREN, Thomas E., Sn-251-1; Cpl A Co 143rd IL Inf; 5-20-64 to 10-64; Gallatin PO
WARREN, William, P-157-1; Pvt F Co 2nd TN Cav; 2-20-64 to 3-4-65; Linden PO
WARRICK, William K., K-174-3(2); Pvt F Co 3rd TN Inf; 11 Feb 62 to 23 Feb 65; Graveston PO; deseas of liver
WARWICK, Charles H., D-99-5; Pvt; Central Hos. for Insane PO
WARWICK, John, K-175-2; Pvt E Co 3rd KY Cav; 3 Dec 64 to 3 Dec 65; Bayless PO
WARWICK, John, K-156-1; 3rd Sgt F Co 26th SC Inf; 9 Jan 61 to 11 Apr 63; 123 Cunbulerd St., Knoxville PO; CONF
WARWICK, William H., K-171-4(3); Pvt D Co 2nd TN Cav; 62 to 65; PO omitted; CONF
WASHBURN, James, La-115-3; Pvt H Co 21st MI Inf; 12 Aug 62 to 8 Jun 65; Summertown PO
WASHBURNE, Francis, H-70-2(1); Annie I. widow of; Lt US Meminac; Chattanooga PO
WASHINGTON, Alex, K-154-5(2); Knoxville
WASHINGTON, Alferd, Sh-157-4; Cpl D Co 113th Inf; 63 to 65; White Haven PO; three shots, 2 in the head, one shoulder, the shot in the shoulder effects ver much
WASHINGTON, Boyd, H-57-3; Pvt I Co 15th US Reg; 62 to 65; Orchard Knob PO
WASHINGTON, Charles (see Gilmore, Charles)
WASHINGTON, Datson, Hr-86-1; Pvt B Co 63rd LA; 63 to 65; Grand Junction PO; no disability incurred, came home when the war was over
WASHINGTON, Deme?, Rb-223-1; Pvt; Springfield PO; CONF
WASHINGTON, Denie (see Hught, William)
WASHINGTON, Frank, Rb-230-1; Pvt B Co 41st TN Inf; Jan 62 to Jan 65; Springfield PO
WASHINGTON, George, Mg-196-4; US Sol; 10th Dist
WASHINGTON, George, H-66-2; Pvt G Co 44th Col Inf; 62 to 65; Chattanooga PO
WASHINGTON, George, Sh-152-1; alias Cuningham, George; Pvt K Co 55th MS Inf; May 63 to 8 Jan 65; Collierville PO
WASHINGTON, George, F-40-3; Pvt L Co 3rd TN Inf; Sep 62 to May 65; Hickory Withe PO
WASHINGTON, George, Sh-201-4; Pvt G Co 18th MO Inf; 12 Aug 62 to 12 Aug 65; Memphis PO
WASHINGTON, George, Sh-174-2; Pvt H Co Corps De Afrique 20th NY Inf; 12-12-63 to 10-7-65; 24½ Turley St., Memphis PO
WASHINGTON, George L., Sh-150-1; George Bunn; Pvt D Co 57th TN Hvy Art; 3 yrs; Bartlett PO
WASHINGTON, Henry, Sh-157-8; Pvt Co B 3rd US Lt Art; Ensley PO
WASHINGTON, Henry, O-140-1; Pvt C Co 25th TN Inf; Jan 62 to Nov 63; Union City PO; suffers some from exposure
WASHINGTON, Henry, Sh-191-7(3); Cpl F Co 37th GA Inf; 63 to 66; Memphis PO
WASHINGTON, Jacob, Wl-306-1; Pvt B Co 40th TN Inf; 61 to 65; Partlow PO; disease contracted by exposure in army, not able to do good labor
WASHINGTON, James, Sh-148-1; Pvt B Co 45th __; Jun 12, 63 to Jan, 65; Memphis PO
WASHINGTON, John (see Cole, John)
WASHINGTON, Larkin?, Hm-106-3; Drum(mer?) F Co 62nd NC Inf; 21 Aug 62 to 22 Jul 65; Morristown PO
WASHINGTON, Logan, Mc-115-1; Pvt D Co 25th TN; 12-7-63 to 65; Riceville PO; struck in side with shell, dont know date of discharge
WASHINGTON, Louis, Mu-196-1; Susan widow of; Pvt A Co Lt Art; 2 yrs 11 mos; Columbia PO

WASHINGTON, Mason, Sh-150-2; Pvt K Co 2nd __; 3 yrs; Mullins Station PO
WASHINGTON, Monrow, T-215-2; US Sol; Mason PO
WASHINGTON, Moses, D-68-1; Parilee Turner formerly widow of; Pvt K Co 44th US C Inf; 84 Fain St, Nashville PO; discharge papers lost
WASHINGTON, Robert, Wi-287-1; Pvt B Co 14th TN Inf; 15 Nov 62 to 16 Mar 65; Civ Dist 18
WASHINGTON, Sam, Rb-222-1; US Sol; 8th Dist
WASHINGTON, Squire, D-87-2; Pvt B Co 15th TN Inf; 62 to May 65; Nashville PO
WASHINGTON, Stephen, Sh-191-5(1); Memphis PO; records not seen
WASHINGTON, Thomas, B-3-1; Pvt I Co 15th US Col Inf; 2-7-64 to 4-27-66; Shelbyville PO; 3 wounds 1864-5; pleural con., chron. diar. 1865; discharged from hospital
WASON, Clyde, Se-224-3; George W. Derby alias; Pvt E Co 41st OH Inf; 15 Nov 62 to Nov 65; Wears Valley PO; wonds, shot in leg & hip
WASSON, Alexander S., Me-92-1; Ruth A. widow of; Pvt 6th TN Inf; Sewee PO
WASSON, John, R-158-1; Pvt C Co 1st US Hvy Art Col; Rhea Springs PO; lost left eye from sore eyes, draws pension
WASSON, William J., Hy-84-3(5); Pvt E Co 23rd MS; Sep 61 to 63; Woodville PO; CONF
WATERFORD, Wm., Sh-173-2; 149 Monroe St, Memphis PO
WATERHOUSE, Adam, H-72-1; Pvt A Co US Col Inf; Chattanooga PO
WATERHOUSE, Charley, Col, Br-10-2; Pvt B Co 44th Col TN Inf; Cleveland PO
WATERHOUSE, Isaac, Br-8-1; Pvt __ Inf; Cleveland PO
WATERS, Elijah, Fe-42-2; Pvt K Co 1st KY; Jamestown PO
WATERS, Frank M., Po-152-5(1); Ducktown PO
WATERS, James I., Co-63-4; Pvt E Co 2nd East TN Cav; 16 Sep 62 to 5 Jul 65; Newport PO; mashed up by horse falling on him
WATERS, Jere, D-87-1; Cpl F Co 12th TN Inf; 12 Aug 62 to Jan 65; Nashville PO
WATERS, John A., Be-6-1; Pvt D Co 6th TN Cav; 2 Dec 63 to 26 Jul 65; Big Sandy PO
WATERS, Joseph H.., R-158-2; PVt F Co 1st OH Cav; 8-15-61 to 12-65; Rhea Springs PO; rheumatism
WATERS, Mary, widow of Sanders, Hm-104-1; Mossy Creek PO (Jefferson Co.)
WATERS, Thos., Rb-224-1; LC B Co 4th TN Mtd Inf; Dec 64 to Aug 65; Springfield PO
WATKIN, Rufus, Wa-272-1; Pvt K Co 8th TN Cav; Jun 64 to 11 Sep 65; Harmony PO; rheumatism
WATKINS, Anderson, D-58-2; Pvt F Co 13th US Col Inf; Aug 64 to Jan 66; Nashville PO; drum of ears busted supporting Artilly (or Anderson W. Atkins?)
WATKINS, Andrew, Wl-288-1; Pvt; 61 to 65; Beckwith PO; shot in left arm, not disabled from work
WATKINS, Arther, Mt-147-1; Pvt C Co 16th US Col Cav TN; Feb 64 to 66; McCalisters Cross Roads PO; discharge sent to Washington
WATKINS, Calvin, Sh-189-1; Pvt A Co 3rd US Col Hvy Art; 6-5-63 to 4-30-66; La. Ave, Memphis PO
WATKINS, Daniel, Ru-238-1; Pvt G Co 12th USC Inf; Murfreesboro PO; injured at Fort Negly by fall
WATKINS, Daniel, Mu-198-1; Pvt A Co 13th Col TN Reg; Aug 25 63 to Jan 25 64; Canaan PO; side, shoulder & leg caused by the falling of a log while building breastworks
WATKINS, Eli, Sn-181-1; Pvt D Co 4th TN Cav; Gallatin PO
WATKINS, Eliza, K-156-6; widow; Pine 153, Knoxville PO
WATKINS, Fredrick, Mt-132-1; Pvt H Co 101st TN Inf; 10-3-64 to 2-10-66; 1st Civil Dist
WATKINS, Gilbert, Ru-13-3; Pvt F Co 23rd KY; 62 to 65; Murfreesboro PO
WATKINS, Henry, Ru-232-1; Pvt C Co 40th TN Inf; 63 to Aug 66; Smyrna PO
WATKINS, Henry, Sn-252-2; Pvt B Co 36th IN Bat; 1-1-61 to 1-3-64; Gallatin PO
WATKINS, Isaish, Dy-24-1; S-class Seaman West Department; 63 to 64; Newburn PO; unhurt, discharged
WATKINS, James, H-54-1; Pvt D Co 4th TN Cav; 12-3-62 to 7-12-65; Sherman Heights PO; contracted rheumatism, heart disease, indigestion
WATKINS, James T., Je-141-4; Pvt A Co 8th KY Inf; 7 Jan 63 to 10 Aug 65; Mill Springs PO
WATKINS, John F., H-52-1; 19th Dist
WATKINS, John P., D-57-3; Pvt H Co 55th TN Inf; Oct 61 to Apr 9 65; Nashville PO; relisted con soldare; CONF
WATKINS, John S., D-54-2; Nashville PO; failed to get record
WATKINS, John W., Ja-84-2; Capt I Co 4th TN Cav; 12-3-62 to 5-4-64; Harrison PO; rheumatism & service diarhea
WATKINS, Lony B., D-62-1; Col; Nashville, West McGavock St, PO
WATKINS, Vina, Sh-162-2; widow; Ramsey PO
WATKINS, William, Ja-84-1; Cpl D Co 4th TN Cav; 12-3-62 to 7-12-65; Harrison PO; chronic diarhe & sore eyes
WATKINS, William D., Lo-190-3; 1st Sgt I Co 4th TN Cav; 10 Dec 62 to 17 May 65; Pines PO; rheumatism & sore legs result of fever
WATKINS, William R., Po-149-3(2); Pvt C Co 5th TN Mtd Inf; 9-64 to 7-65; Fetzerton PO; mashed in hips and back by horse, dates unknown
WATLEY, George W., Mr-99-3; Pvt I Co 2nd KY Cav; 7-16-63 to 7-16-__ (2 yrs); Jasper PO
WATS, Thomas, Ce-23-2; Pvt A Co 30th TN; Oct 20 61 to 16 Apr 65; Pleasant View PO
WATSON, Abraham S., Fe-40-1; Pvt A Co 1st Bat KY State Troops; 2-10-65 to 10-23-65; Little Crabb PO; lay in hospital
WATSON, Alfred G., Ro-211-1; Pvt I Co 1st TN Inf; 24 Jun 62 to 27 Jan 65; Webster PO; wounded in left hip
WATSON, Anderson, Su-238-1; Pvt M Co 13th TN Cav; 2 Feb 64 to 5 Sep 65; Boring PO; lung desease
WATSON, Andrew M., Wi-281-1; Pvt I Co 2nd IL; Oct 64 to Oct 65; Allisona PO
WATSON, Bird H., O-130-1; Mary F. widow of; Pvt G Co 2nd TN Inf; 63 to Jan 65; Florence, AL PO; bronchial affection, suffered from disease til death
WATSON, Clara, D-46-2; widow of Sol; Nashville PO
WATSON, David C., Se-230-2; Pvt E Co 9th TN Cav; 1 Oct 63 to 11 Sep 65; Pokeberry PO; chron. diarrhoea
WATSON, Dock, Ms-181-1; A Co 10th TN Inf; 6-10-63 to 4-12-65; Lewisburg PO
WATSON, Edman, Wl-293-1; G Co Inf; 63 to 64; Lockport PO; CONF
WATSON, Elbert, Cu-15-1; Louisa C. widow of; Pvt E Co 1st TN Inf; 8-20-61 to 9-17-64; Hebbertsburg PO; cause of disability feever, died 4-16-1887
WATSON, Eliza, O-141-1; Union City PO; infirmation unknown
WATSON, George S., Se-230-2; Pvt E Co 2nd TN Cav; Sep 16 62 to __; Pokeberry PO; lung trouble
WATSON, Giles, Fe-42-1; Pvt D Co 30th KY; 10-63 to __ (6 mos); Jamestown PO
WATSON, Goodden, Gi-139-1; Pvt D Co 4th TN Inf; 5-62 to 65; Rodinham PO; wounded in chin & right leg
WATSON, Henry, Cl-57-2; Goin PO; fitts 40 years; CONF
WATSON, Henry F., Se-230-1; Pvt E Co 2nd TN Cav; 2 yrs 8 mos; Pokeberry PO; horse fell on him
WATSON, Isaac H., Cu-15-1; Sgt B Co 6th TN Inf; 3-8-62 to 4-27-65; Hebbertsburg PO; relaps of measels effect lungs
WATSON, James, Sh-175-1; Sgt A Co __ Inf; 62 to 65; Memphis PO
WATSON, James E., Wh-180-1; Pvt K Co 4th TN Inf; 3-1-62 to 8-14-65; Methodist PO; lost left eye
WATSON, James H., Cf-39-1; Pvt I Co 5th TN Cav; 14 Feb 62 to 14 Aug 65; Prairie Plains PO; loss or right eyesight & hearing on r ear
WATSON, James W., Li-143-1; Pvt G Co 79th IL Inf; 62 to 65; Rowell PO
WATSON, James W., Gr-70-1; Pvt; Rutledge PO
WATSON, John D., Gr-71-2; Pvt I Co 8th TN Inf; Tate Spring PO
WATSON, JohnL., Gr-70-3; Pvt D Co 1st TN Cav; 12 Mar 62 to 64; Spring House PO; wounded, other dates unknown
WATSON, John W., Se-230-2; Pvt E Co 2nd TN Cav; 16 Sep __ to 3 Jul 65 (2 yrs 8 mos 17 days); Pokeberry PO

WATSON, Joseph D., Hd-50-1; PUSN; Jan 1, 64 to Jan 29, 65; Savannah PO
WATSON, Louisa C., (see Barnes, Chupley)
WATSON, M. S., Gi-123-2; Pvt A Co 1st MS Cav; Jul 5, 64 to Jul 65; Bethel PO
WATSON, Milton, Jo-150-2; Pvt B Co 1st US Vol; 24 Jan 64 to 11 Nov 65; Key Station PO; hearing & bronchitis
WATSON, Mosses, Mt-132-1; Pvt F Co 15th TN Inf; 3-9-64 to 4-6-65; 1st Civil Dist
WATSON, Parlee (see Pulling, Thomas)
WATSON, S. P., Lk-112-1; Pvt C & H Cos, 7th TN Cav; 3 to Aug 9, 65; Tiptonville PO; erysipelas, chronic, scrofulous nature
WATSON, Simmons, Rb-218-1; alias Watson, Spencer; Cpl B Co 115th US Col Inf; 7 Aug 63 to Mar 65; Mitchell PO; papers lost
WATSON, Small, Ru-241-4; Pvt A Co 26th OH Inf; 63 to 66 (3 yrs 6 mos); Murfreesboro PO
WATSON, Thomas, Gr-72-1; Pvt C Co 4th TN Cav; 10 Dec 62 to 12 Jul 65; Noelon PO; Missionary Ridge Battle
WATSON, Tilmon, Cl-48-2; Pvt D Co 1st US Inf; 1-24-63 to 11-28-65; Pleasant PO; relapse on measels
WATSON, Wm., Gr-70-1; Pvt 8th TN Inf; Spring House PO; head injured
WATSON, William, Jo-151-1; Susan widow of; Stump Knob PO; measles--death
WATSON, William A., Un-259-2; Pvt H Co 22nd NC Inf; 22 Mar 62 to 22 Jun 65; Lost Creek PO; bowels & lungs 18 mos, caused by cold & hardship; CONF
WATSON, William H., Cf-40-3; Pvt F Co 107th IN Inf; 23 Jun 62 to 65; Tullahoma PO
WATSON, William J., Tr-265-1; Pvt F Co 5th TN Cav; 25 Jul 62 to 25 Jun 65; Dixons Springs PO
WATSON, William J., Ro-203-6; Pvt I Co 1st TN Inf; 9 Aug 61 to 17 Sep 64; Burns' Mills PO; was captured--never discharged
WATSON, William W., O-133-1; Duty Sgt K Co 1st MI? Cav; 19 Dec 63 to 4 Jul 65; Rives PO; discharge lost
WATSON, William W., De-22-2; Pvt E Co 17th TN Inf; 1 Aug 61 to 5 Aug 65; Peters Landing PO; CONF
WATSON, Wood, Sh-198-1; Pvt A Co 55th Col Inf; Summer 62 to Fall 65; Memphis PO; discharge burned in his mother's house
WATTENBARGER, Ananias, Mc-109-1; Pvt B Co 7th TN Inf; 10-20-64 to 7-27-65; Chuckaluck PO; piles and hernia in right side
WATTENBARGER, Enoch B., Ge-92-1; Margaret J. widow of; Pvt F Co 1st TN Cav; 1 Mar 62 to 30 Mar 65; Laurel Gap PO
WATTENBARGER, William C., Me-93-1; Pvt I Co 9th TN Cav; 12-29-63 to 9-11-65; Regret PO, McMinn Co.; injury to lungs
WATTENBARGER, Wilson, Br-7-4; US Sol; 3rd Civil Dist
WATTENBURGER, Adam, Ro-210-3; Pvt E Co 36th TN Inf; 62 to __; Rockwood PO; CONF
WATTENBARGER, James, Wa-262-1; Pvt B Co 12th TN Cav; 2 Oct 63 to 65; Telfords PO; chro. rheumatism, gun shot
WATTERS, Adam F., Bo-12-3(1); Sgt B Co 6th TN Inf; 3-7-62 to 6-12-63; Waters PO
WATTINGBARGER, Wigley, Me-88-3; 3rd Sgt F Co 1st TN Cav; 3-1-62 to 3-30-65; Brittsville PO
WATTISON, Bell, Se-230-4; widow Conf; Richison's Cove PO; her husband was Colored Sol (con) and she cannot give particulars
WATTS, Alexander, Hy-79-1; alias Young, Augustus; Sgt D Co 3rd Col Hvy Inf; Jul 3, 63 to Apr 30, 66; Brownsville PO
WATTS, Eliza F., K-176-3; widow of Sol Conf; Pvt F Co 2nd TN Cav; 62 to 63; Smithwood PO; CONF
WATTS, Horton, Gi-122-1; Betsey Hedgpath widow of; Pvt; Prospect Sta. PO; CONF
WATTS, James M., Se-230-3; 2nd? Sgt C Co 3rd NC Mtd Inf; 63 to Jun 65; Richison's Cove PO; shot in left shoulder
WATTS, John, Hm-108-4(3); Pvt E Co 1st TN Cav; Apr 63 to Apr 65; Russellville PO
WATTS, John M., Sm-174-1; Pvt G Co 4th TN Inf; 11-1-64 to 8-25-65; New Middleton PO

WATTS, Pleasant, Hm-109-2; Pvt E Co 1st TN Cav; 62 to 2 Apr 65; Russellville PO
WATTS, Warner, Mt-138-2; (blk) US Sol; Dist No. 7, N. Providence PO
WATTS, William, U-248-1; Pvt K Co 13th TN Cav; 20 Sep 63 to 5 Sep 65; Brownlow PO
WATTS, William M., H-76-2; Pvt C Co 16th US Col Inf; 12-12-63 to 4-30-66; Chattanooga PO
WAUGH, James Willis, Cr-21-1; Pvt I Co 7th TN Cav; Oct 64 to __ (12 mos); Huntingdon PO
WAULKER, Daniel, S-218-2; Pvt H Co 9th TN Cav; 62 to Jul 65; Hughett PO; piles & deseased breast
WAY, Margaret, Ho-96-2; widow of US Sol; no PO
WAY, Wm., Hw-125-5; Pvt C Co TN Inf; 65 to 65 (1 mo 12 days); Yellow Stone PO; CONF
WAYES, Dave, K-167-1; Pvt G Co 3rd IN; Mar 62 to 65; Knoxville PO; hurt by a mule in breast
WAYMAN, William T., Mo-129-1; Pvt E Co 3rd TN Inf; 10-62 to 11-13-64; Four Mile Branch PO
WAYMIRES, Charles, Co-69-7(3); Pvt; Rankin PO; nearley deaf, dont no dates nor time
WEAKLEY, Richard W., D-99-5; Pvt K Co 4th TN Col Cav; Apr 61 to May 26 65; Nashville PO; central hosp. for insane; CONF
WEAKS, Charles, K-161-4; Pvt B Co 3rd US Hvy Art; Knoxville PO
WEATHERFORD, Ceasar, Sh-159-5; PO omitted; CONF
WEATHERFORD, Thomas, Wa-268-2; Pvt C Co 9th TN Cav; 19 Aug 63 to 9 Dec 64; Johnson City PO
WEATHERFORD, William T., Ro-211-3; Sgt H Co 9th TN Cav; 1 Aug 63 to 11 Sep 65; Webster PO; lost sight in right eye
WEATHERINGTON, Thomas B., Ch-14-1; Pvt H Co 2nd MS Inf; 4-1-62 to 6-1-64; Sweet Lips PO; shot 4 times right leg & left jaw, lay over 5 & 6 mos; CONF
WEATHERLY, George, Col, Ma-125-1; Pvt H Co 55th AL Inf; 15 Jun 63 to Jul 66; Jackson PO; good health, dont know much about his service
WEATHERLY, Samuel, Be-5-1; Lt A Co 8th TN Inf; 11 Nov 61 to 27 Aug 64; Eggville PO; very corse in right leg
WEAVER, Andrew, K-177-4; Pvt C Co 2nd TN Cav; 15 Nov 62 to 65; Chumlea PO
WEAVER, Andrew J., K-172-3; 2nd Lt C Co 39th GA Inf; 63 to 65; PO omitted; CONF
WEAVER, Antney, Mc-118-2; Pvt 10th TN Cav; 64 to __; Cogshill PO; disease of liver & legs 25 yrs
WEAVER, C. M., A-1-3; Pvt I Co 9th TN Inf; 6-21-63 to 7-24-65; Andersonville PO; rheumatism
WEAVER, Charles, A-13-2; Pvt G Co 5th KY Cav; 9-9-64 to 3-16-66; Briceville PO; feble in health
WEAVER, David B., Di-40-1; Amanda M. wife of; Pvt G Co 10th TN Inf; 5-6-62 to 6-24-65; Danielsville PO; right eye out, caused by small pox, draws a pention
WEAVER, David H., K-164-1; Pvt G Co Vet PA Corps; 11 Aug 62 to 29 Jun 65; Knoxville PO; shot in both hands, one finger off, draws pension
WEAVER, George, Sh-175-1; Pvt E Co 59th Inf; 63 to 65; Memphis PO
WEAVER, George W., Cu-15-2; Pvt C Co 7th TN Inf; 8-20-64 to 6-27-65; Crossville PO; slight wound in foot in battle at Perryville, KY
WEAVER, Henry, Wy-173-5(1); US Sol; 8th Civil Dist
WEAVER, Henry, B-6-1; Pvt C Co 1st AL Col; 1-1-65 to 10-15-65; Shelbyville PO
WEAVER, Henry, A-1-2; Pvt A Co 1st TN Inf; 2-20-62 to 2-14-65; Andersonville PO; rheumatism
WEAVER, Isaac W., Ch-17-2; Ordley G Co 49th IL Inf; 21 Jul 62 to 22 Jul __ (3 yrs 21 days); McNairy PO
WEAVER, J. J., La-117-3; Pvt H Co 6th TN Cav; Jan 62 to Jan 65; 15th Dist
WEAVER, James, Wl-297-2; Sgt H Co 4th TN Mtd Inf; 1 Nov 64 to 28 Aug 65; Commerce PO
WEAVER, Jennie (see Smartt, Alfred)
WEAVER, John, D-92-1; Pvt E Co 192nd OH Inf; 22 Feb 64 to 4 Dec 64; West Nashville PO; piles, chronic diareah
WEAVER, John, K-173-3; Pvt G Co 7th TN Inf; 9 Jan 64 to 12 Aug 65; Troutman PO

WEAVER, John W., Ro-203-3; Pvt H Co 1st TN Inf; 9 Aug 61 to 17 Sep 64; Ethel PO
WEAVER, Newton, Dy-27-1; Manda widow of; Pvt 27th TN Reg; 5-1-61 to 6-63; Ro Ellen PO; CONF
WEAVER, Robbert, K-176-3; Pvt G Co 2nd TN Inf; 14 Jun 62 to 15 Oct 65; Halls X Roads PO
WEAVER, Samuel G., Br-7-1; Pvt G Co 10th TN Cav; 2-15-64 to 8-1-65; Felker PO; rupture
WEAVER, Thomas, K-186-2; Pvt C Co 2nd TN Cav; 5 Nov 62 to 6 Jul 65; Balls Camp PO
WEAVER, Timothy W., A-2-4; Pvt C Co 2nd TN Inf; 2-12-62 to 2-23-65; Andersonville PO; piles
WEAVER, Valentine W., A-9-5(3); Pvt M Co 9th TN Cav; 4-3-63 to 9-11-65; Dutch Valley PO; diarrhea resulting constipation & piles
WEAVER, Wesley, K-170-1; Pvt G Co 7th TN Inf; 8 Nov 64 to 27 Jul 65; Knoxville PO
WEAVER, William, Un-255-2; Mick wife of; Pvt F Co 7th TN Inf; 8 Nov 64 to 27 Ju 65; Gale PO; rupure
WEAVER, William, He-67-2; Pvt A Co 7th TN Cav; Aug 28 62 to Jul 11 65; Centre Point PO (Chester Co.); chronic bronchitus contracted in Andersonville 25 yrs
WEAVER, William R., K-154-4; Pvt D Co 9th TN Cav; 62 to 65; Knoxville PO
WEAVER, William S., Hd-49-2; Pvt A Co 10th TN Inf; Apr 14 62 to May 65; Gillis Mills PO; sore eyes & rheumatism
WEAVER, William T., Co-67-2; A Co 2nd TN Cav; Sep 62 to Sep 63; Bison PO
WEAVER, William W., A-2-4; 1st Sgt, 2nd Lt C Co 2nd TN Inf; 8-7-61 to 6-62; Hinds Creek PO; varicose veins right leg and resigned about Jan 1864, commissioned chaplain 2nd E TN Cav 12-10-62
WEAVER, Woodson, H-60-4; Sgt G Co US CI; Chattanooga PO; hearing affected
WEB, Mose, Ru-238-1; Pvt Peioneer Corp; Murfreesboro PO
WEBB, Abel I., L-103-1; Elizabeth A. widow of; Pvt; Nov 11 61 to ___ (4 yrs); Golddust PO; CONF
WEBB, Benjamin, K-181-2; Pvt B Co 2nd TN Cav; 15 Aug 62 to 6 Jul 65; Nast PO; defect eye for 25 yrs, gravel 25 yrs
WEBB, Benjamin, Sh-204-2; Pvt H Co Hvy Art; 63 to 65; Walker PO, Memphis PO
WEBB, Bery, Bo-11-2; Pvt; Big Gulley PO; canot give any information as to service
WEBB, Crisly, Co-68-2; Lyddia A. widow of; Pvt K Co 2nd TN Cav; 62 to ___; Cashy PO
WEBB, D. C., Bo-23-2; Pvt C Co 3rd TN Inf; 7-26-64 to 11-30-64; Tuckaleechee Cove PO; spinal affection, now suffering with piles
WEBB, Dr. D. S., Hr-96-2; Surgeon B Co 7th TN; 61 to 64; Pinetop PO; CONF
WEBB, Daniel S., Lo-187-1; Eliza widow of; Pvt; Loudon PO; died in prison
WEBB, Elijah N., Mo-126-1; Sgt C Co 1st US Vol Inf; 1-25-64 to 12-65; Tevis PO; discharge misplaced
WEBB, Elisha, R-161-3; Pvt D Co 3rd TN Inf; 7-25-64 to 6-65; Dayton PO
WEBB, Frank, Wl-295-1; Pvt D Co 14th Reg Inf; Apr 28 61 to 65; Lebanon PO; in jail--his former PO Partlow, TN
WEBB, Frederic, Mo-109-5; Pvt C Co 148th NY Inf; 8-26-62 to 6-22-65; Sweetwater PO (Monroe Co.)
WEBB, Georg, S-216-1; Pvt H Co 1st TN Inf; 9 Aug 61 to 17 Sep 64; Huntsville PO; chronick numona 20 yrs
WEBB, George, Se-221-3; Martha Blazer former widow of; Pvt M Co 2nd TN Cav; 8 Nov 62 to 63; Fair Garden PO; could not get date of death
WEBB, George W., A-4-3; Pvt H Co 2nd TN Inf; 3-62 to 9-62; Coal Creek PO
WEBB, George W., Br-14-2; Pvt B Co 5th TN Mtd Inf; 9-64 to 6-65; McDonald PO
WEBB, Henry, Cr-15-2; Pvt D Co 7th TN Cav; 20 Oct 63 to 20 Oct 65; Maple Creek PO
WEBB, Henry, D-50-3; Sgt C Co 11th US Inf; Mar 1 61 to Apr 29 65; Nashville PO; wounded
WEBB, Henry, Sh-179-1(2); Mary widow of; Pvt; Memphis PO; doesn't remember
WEBB, Isaac C., Mc-114-6; Pvt L Co 9th TN Cav; 9-17-63 to 9-11-65; Lamontville PO
WEBB, James, Co-68-1; Cpl E Co 2nd TN Cav; 62 to 65; Cosby PO; rheumatism
WEBB, James A., K-171-3(2); Pvt F Co 9th TN Cav; 28 Jul 63 to Sep 65; Knoxville PO
WEBB, James B., J-78-1; Clarissia Ann widow of; Pvt K Co 81st IL Inf; Gainesboro PO; the time served couldn't be known
WEBB, James H., Ms-180-1; Pvt I Co 128th IL Inf; 10-6-61 to 11-6-65; Globe PO; tarpia liver and lungs, large family and homeless
WEBB, James M., W-189-1; Sgt M Co 5th TN Cav; 10-20-63 to 8-14-65; McMinnville PO; right hand disabled by wound
WEBB, James P., Je-135-4; Sarah C. widow of; Pvt; 13 Apr 63 to died 30 May 63; Mt. Horeb PO; died in service
WEBB, James P., Je-143-1; Sarah C. wife of; 2nd TN Cav; 14 Apr 63 to ___ (1 yr 1 mo 17 days); Mount Horeb PO; typhoid fever
WEBB, James R., C-25-3; Sgt B Co 7th TN Cav; 8-1-61 to 9-17-64; Coal Creek PO (also C-26-1)
WEBB, James W., Sm-174-1; Pvt G Co 4th Inf Vol; 11-1-64 to 8-25-65; New Middleton PO
WEBB, Jeremiah, W-195-1; Pvt 46th Talahatchee; 1-16-64 to 6-15-65; 12th Dist
WEBB, Jessey, Co-68-1; Pvt E Co 2nd TN Cav; 62 to 65; Cosby PO; mashed by horse
WEBB, John, Je-139-1; Sgt B Co 1st AL Cav; Trion PO
WEBB, John, K-171-3(2); Pvt G Co 9th TN Cav; 28 Jul 63 to 14 Sep 65; Knoxville PO
WEBB, Jno. E., Dy-27-1; Pvt A Co 4th TN Cav; 4-12-61 to 4-16-65; Ro Ellen PO; CONF
WEBB, John R., Cr-20-1; Pvt E Co 7th TN Cav; 1-28-62 to 8-9-65; Roxie PO; piles accute, contracted in the service
WEBB, Lewis, Me-92-2; Pvt B Co 7th TN Mtd Inf; 10-12-64 to 7-27-65; Sewee PO
WEBB, Linch, Bo-21-2; Pvt B Co 2nd TN Cav; 9-15-62 to 3-24-66; Veeba PO; F. M. Webb served in his father's place over 2 yrs
WEBB, M. Calvin, T-206-1; Cpl A Co 133rd IL Inf; May 5 64 to Sep 2 64; Covington PO
WEBB, Neuton L., Sh-147-1; Pvt A Co 55th TN Inf; 15 Aug 62 to 6 Apr 65; Cuba PO
WEBB, Newton, Mc-116-4; Pvt D Co 3rd TN Mtd Inf; 8-5-64 to 11-30-65; Williamsburg PO; rheumatism & heart disease contracted while in service
WEBB, Olivia C., D-77-4; 52 Bass St, Nashville PO
WEBB, Perry, Se-219-1; Pvt TN Cav; East York PO
WEBB, Riley, Mg-197-1; Anna Husky formerly widow of; B Co 2nd TN Inf; PO omitted
WEBB, Robert, D-78-1; Pvt F Co 9th KY; Sep 61 to Dec 64; Nashville PO
WEBB, Theopolus, Cr-15-1; Pvt E Co 7th TN Cav; Hiliday PO; scurvey, served 12 mos in Andersonville
WEBB, Thomas L., Ma-125-2; US Sol; Jackson St, Jackson PO
WEBB, Warren D., Gi-122-1; Pvt AL Inf; 62 to 64; Prospect Sta. PO; CONF
WEBB, Welcom, Mg-199-3; Pvt B Co 2nd TN Inf; 3 Jul 61 to 5 Dec 62; Emory PO; kidney disease
WEBB, William M., Cu-16-2; Pvt G Co 6th TN Inf; 2-20-65 to 6-30-65; Litton PO (Bledsoe Co.); falling of mumps, afflicted with scrofula
WEBB, William R., Ro-203-3; Sarah widow of; Pvt K Co 1st TN Inf; Aug ___ to ___; Ethel PO; was killed
WEBB, Willie K?, Cr-4-2; Lt C Co 12th TN Cav; 4 Dec 61 to 12 May 65; Bells Depot PO; CONF
WEBB, Willis, S-214-3; Pvt B Co 7th TN Inf; 11 Jul 61 to Dec 62; Glenmary PO
WEBBER, Jacob (see Hawkins, George)
WEBBER, Joseph, D-72-1; Pvt G Co 39th OH Inf; Jul 27 61 to Jul 19 65; Nashville PO; two bone? finger and ribs broken, rheumatism
WEBER?, William M., K-160-2; 1st Lt 15th IN Inf; 1 May 61 to 1 Jul 64; Knoxville PO
WEBSDALE, William, Sh-190-1; Pvt E Co 42nd OH; 10-61 to 11-15-64; 809 Main St, Memphis PO
WEBSTER, Adison, D-71-1; US; Nashville PO
WEBSTER, Alfred, Un-253-3; Cpl C Co 7th TN Inf; Oct 64 to 18 Aug 65; Lorenaton PO; discharge lost and dates not none
WEBSTER, Arthur, Je-136-3; Pvt C Co 30th MI Inf; 26 Nov 64 to 17 Jun 65; PO omitted

WEBSTER, Benjamin, Hw-131-3; Susan widow of; Otes PO; CONF
WEBSTER, Charles G., Ro-204-3; Cpl G Co 1st TN Inf; 18 Dec 61 to 20 Dec 64; Elverton PO; rheumatism & piles
WEBSTER, Charles H., Bo-15-3; Marry C. widow of; Pvt I Co 3rd TN Cav; 63 to 65; Maryville PO
WEBSTER, Dan E., Sh-175-2; 299 Wilmington St, Memphis PO
WEBSTER, Daniel, D-68-2; Cpl K Co 17th USC Inf; 6 Jan 64 to 25 Apr 66; 97 Wharf Ave, Nashville PO
WEBSTER, George W., K-159-2; Pvt C Co 9th TN Cav; 8 Aug 63 to 11 Sep 65; Knoxville PO
WEBSTER, Glee?, D-90-1; Pvt G Co 15th TN Col Inf; 2 yrs; Nashville PO; 2? fingers shot--crippled wife's testimony, he was absent
WEBSTER, James, Hw-133-2; Pvt D Co 31st TN Cav; 15 May 62 to 25 Apr 65; Burem's Store PO; CONF
WEBSTER, John H., Ro-204-3; Pvt G Co 1st TN Inf; 2 Apr 62 to 18 Apr 65; Elverton PO
WEBSTER, Lea, D-89-1; Pvt D? Co 13th TN; Aug 63 to Jan 66; Nashville PO; two fingers on left hand disabled
WEBSTER, Martin, Mu-196-1; Cpl B Co 13th Reg; 2 yrs 9 mos; Columbia PO
WEBSTER, William, Se-227-1; Trundle's X Roads PO; injury of head
WEBSTER, William B., K-173-2; Pvt K Co 4th TN Inf; 10 Jan 64 to 2 Aug 65; Union Church PO
WEBSTER, William R., A-9-5(3); Celia widow of; Pvt G Co 1st TN Inf; 8-9-61 to 9-17-64; Dutch Valley PO; lung disease resulting in his death 1-7-86
WEDDINGTON, George, Fr-107-1; Franklin Co. PO
WEDDLE, John B., Cr-4-2; Pvt 20th TN Cav; Oct 63 to Apr 65; Bells Depot PO; CONF
WEDELSTEDT, Charles, Be-6-1; Pvt E Co 52nd NY Inf; Aug 61 to 1 Jan 66; Big Sandy PO; wounded in head at Fiar Oaks, VA
WEECE?, William J., Ro-208-2; Pvt G? Co 5th TN Inf; Feb 61 to Apr 65; PO omitted
WEED, Martin V., Br-9-1; Mary E. widow of; Capt J Co 60th IL Inf; 2-12-62 to 1-31-65; Cleveland PO
WEEDEN, John, Ja-86-1; Pvt E Co 4th TN Cav; 7-63 to 7-12-65; Oottewah PO; shot in neck
WEEMES, Elbert S., Ge-92-3; Pvt A Co 12th TN Cav; Laurel Gap PO; hurt in shoulder & brest
WEEMES, John A., Ge-92-4; Pvt A Co 4th TN Inf; ___ to 65; Ottway PO
WEEMES, Nancy A. (see Brown, Gotham)
WEEMS, Abriham, Hw-121-4(3); Pvt B Co 8th TN Inf; 1 Mar 64 to 25 Jul 65; Van Hill PO; lung, spinal of back
WEEMS, George J., Ge-88-1; Pvt D Co 8th TN Inf; 1 Mar 63 to 12 Jun 65; Mohawk PO; gun shot in right hip
WEEMS, James C., Ge-101-2; Catherine widow of; Lt H Co 8th TN Inf; Jul 63 to Nov 64; Locust Sp. PO; bone scurvey, Atlanta GA, died Aug 3, 1880
WEEMS, Robert M., Ge-102-3; Pvt B Co 3rd TN Mtd Inf; Jul 64 to ___; Whig PO; hurt in back, now kidney disease
WEESE, William C., H-69-3; Cpl F Co; Chattanooga PO
WEGHT, Elberson, H-56-5; Pvt C Co 34th NY Inf; East End PO
WEIDENBACKER, Andrew F., D-62-1; Mary E. widow of; 2nd Lt E Co 32nd OH; 61 to ___; Nashville PO
WEIDNER, John B., Fr-105-1; Sgt B Co 47th IN V Inf; 5 Oct 61 to 3 Nov 65; Winchester PO
WEILAND, George, K-170-3; US Sol; Dist 12
WEIMER, Charles B., D-44-3; Sgt F Co 14th TN Inf; 4-22-67 to 4-2-75; Nashville PO; wounded in left arm
WEIMERS, J., D-63-2; Aleda widow of; Pvt 49th KY Inf; 63 to ___; Nashville PO
WEIR, Nathan, Mc-114-2; Melvina widow of; Pvt; Magellan PO
WEISE, Frank, D-44-2(1); Pvt 45th NY Vol Inf; 9-9-61 to 7-3-65; Nashville PO
WEITREL, Philip, H-70-1; 1st Lt A Co 54th OH Inf; Chattanooga PO
WELBURN, John R., Wa-273-3; 1st Lt I Co 4th NC Inf;

Mar 63 to Aug 65; Jonesboro PO; sight and hearing, discharge lost in moving to TN
WELCH, Charlie, Sn-253-1; Pvt H Co 14th TN Inf; 1-15-62 to 3-1-64; No. One PO; chronic dirhea
WELCH, Cornealous, Po-149-1; Pvt F Co 5th TN Inf; 10-20-64 to 7-17-65; Old Fort PO; Mtd Inf--one yr
WELCH, Creed N., Je-143-3; 2nd Lt H Co 7th TN Mtd Inf; 10 Feb 65 to 22 Mar 65; Mossy Creek PO; chronic diareah
WELCH, Geo. K., La-117-3; Sgt B Co 23rd TN Inf; Jul 9 61 to Apr 9 65; 15th Dist; CONF
WELCH, George T., O-141-1; Pvt Co K 6th TN Vol Cav; Jan 14 63 to Aug 11 65; Union City PO
WELCH, Geo. W., La-117-2; Lt B Co 23rd TN Inf; Jul 961 to May 3 65; 15th Dist; CONF
WELCH, George W., Su-240-2; Pvt K Co 51st VA Inf; 20 Apr 62 to Apr 65; Kindricks Creek PO; bronchitis; CONF
WELCH, Gideon, Mr-102-1; Rebecca A. Troxdale formerly widow of; Pvt C Co 188th PA Vol; 6-28-63 to 6-23-65; South Pittsburg PO
WELCH, Hugh E., H-49-1; Cpl I Co 136th IL Vol; 5-64 to 10-28-64; Lake Side PO
WELCH, Hugh E., H-49-3; Pvt 9th E TN Vol; 8-62 to ___; Pvt Col Cliff's (regiment?); 6-1-62 to 8-62; Chattanooga PO
WELCH, James B., Cu-18-1; Pvt A Co 1st MD Cav; 1-11-63 to 6-15-65; Manning PO; shot in leg
WELCH, James H., Co-64-1; Pvt K Co 102nd NC Inf; 1 Aug 61 to Apr 65; Philips PO; frost bite in boath feet; CONF
WELCH, James W., Hd-49-3; US Sol; 4th Civil Dist
WELCH, John, Su-239-2; Lucinda widow of; Horace PO
WELCH, Dr. Jno. W., La-117-2; Lt B Co 23rd TN Inf; Jul 9 61 to May 3 65; 15th Dist; CONF
WELCH, Robbert M., Li-161-2; Pvt L Co 142nd OH Inf; May 64 to Sep 64; Lincoln PO
WELCH, Roberd A., Cy-27-3(1); Pvt 5th KY Cav; 9-61 to 4-65; Moss PO
WELCH, W. Green, Un-257-1; Pvt F Co 7th TN Inf; 8 Nov 64 to 3 Aug 65; Sharps Chapel PO
WELCH, William J., Cl-51-1; Pvt J Co 8th TN Cav; 1-64 to 9-11-65; PO omitted
WELDON, William C., La-111-4; US Sol; 5th Civil Dist
WELKS, John J., We-221-3; Pvt B Co 24th Mis Cav; 63 to Apr 65; Martin PO; CONF
WELLER, John, Mu-190-1; Pvt H Co 106th OH Inf; 10-3-64 to 7-17-65; Culleoka PO
WELLER, William, H-53-1; Chattanooga PO; rupture from fall of horse, defective sight from exposure, chief scout for Sheridan and Rosecrans
WELLS, Caleb D., Di-30-2; Pvt B Co 42nd TN Inf; 62 to 6-15-64; Dickson PO; CONF
WELLS, Eli T., Sn-262-2(1); Pvt E Co 103rd OH Inf; 8-24-61 to 6-14-65; Fountain Head PO; rheumatism
WELLS, Ellison, Se-228-2(3); Melinda Bauer widow of; Pvt; New Knob Creek PO
WELLS, Frank, O-142-2; US Sol; 15th Dist
WELLS, George W., K-165-1; Pvt Co 6th TN Inf; 11 Dec 62 to 30 J 65; Knoxville PO
WELLS, Henry A., Je-143-2; Pvt H Co 1st TN Cav; Mossy Creek PO; rupture & breast trouble, transferred from Co H to Invalid Corps
WELLS, Henry H., Je-137-2; Pvt F Co 9th TN Cav; 1 Oct 64 to 11 Sep 65; Fox PO; shot in neck
WELLS, James B., Br-13-1; Pvt I Co 4th TN Cav; 7-18-63 to 7-12-65; Cleveland PO; sciatic rheumatism
WELLS, James M., K-178-2; Sgt G Co 1st TN Inf; 10 Nov 61 to 10 Nov 64; Hardin Valley PO
WELLS, Jesse J., K-181-4(1); 3rd Cpl C Co 3rd TN Inf; 18 Apr 62 to 30 May 65; Fleniken PO
WELLS, Jesse J., K-181-3; Cpl C Co 6th TN Inf; 18 Apr 62 to 30 May 65; Knoxville PO; CONF
WELLS, John, Hd-50-2; Pvt M Co 7th TN Cav; Apr 24 63 to Jun 27 65; Savannah PO
WELLS, John, Cl-56-1; Pvt B Co 9th E TN Cav; 6-5-63 to ___ (1 yr 6 mos 13 days); Big Barren PO; disabled leg from typhoid pneumonia
WELLS, John A., Lo-195-3(1); Cpl D Co 5th TN Inf; 7 Mar 62 to 28 Mar 65; Loudon PO; gun shot wound--both hips

WELLS, Mack, Hy-82-1; Pvt F Co 4th MS Hvy Art; Aug 63 to 66; Rudolph PO
WELLS, Mary (see Branson, Henry)
WELLS, Precilla (see Tucker, Elijah)
WELLS, Tim, Hw-125-3; Yellow Stone PO
WELLS, William, La-111-1; Sgt H Co 9th NY Cav; 9-23-61 to 5-23-62; Pleasant Point PO; general debility (also La-111-3)
WELLS, William H., K-177-5; Pvt D Co 5th TN Inf; 25 Mar 62 to 27 Jun 65; Chumlea PO; gunshot wound right lung & right foot & left hand
WELLS, William J., Lo-195-2(1); Sgt I Co 1st TN Inf; 9 Aug 61 to __; Loudon PO; gunshot wound--left leg
WELLS, William S., H-53-5; Pvt E Co 24th OH Inf--5-19-61 to 5-19-64; Pvt K Co 23rd OH Inf--7-19-64 to 7-26-65; Ridgedale PO; ruptured
WELSH, James H., O-139-1; Pvt B Co 7th TN Cav; 16 Jan 64 to 10 Aug 65; Protemus PO
WELSH, Levi J., T-208-1; Pvt A Co 3rd AR; 63 to 65; Fulton PO
WELSH, Samuel D., H-54-3; Capt 15th OH Inf; Sherman Heights PO; contracted piles
WENTZELL, Henry, Sh-189-4; could not get his record; Penn Ave, Memphis PO
WERNER, John G., V-178-1; Pvt G Co 20th OH Inf; 10-10-62 to 7-4-63; Seals PO (Bledsoe Co.); rheumatism right side
WESCOAT, Joseph W., We-223-1; Capt C Co 6th TN Hvy Cav; cant give dates; Palmersville PO
WESCOTT, Lorenza, H-69-2; 1st Lt A Co 34th IL Inf; 8-25-61 to 4-64; Chattanooga PO
WESLER, George B., Su-240-3; Pvt K Co 1st IN Cav; 3 Oct 64 to 3 Oct 65; Kindricks Creek PO; cronic dirrhea
WESLEY, Casper, Ov-136-1; Pvt; Livingston PO
WESLEY, Daniel, K-176-1; Pvt G Co 7th TN Cav; Mynott PO
WESLEY, George, K-171-2; Pvt A Co 1st US Hvy Art Col; Knoxville PO
WESLEY, John, K-171-2; Pvt B Co (A?) 1st US Hvy Art Col; PO omitted
WESSEL, Annie E. (see Leffering, Herman)
WESSEL, Geo. (see Leffering, Herman)
WESSENBERG, __, H-62-1; Harriet R. widow of; 60 Pleasant St, Chattanooga PO
WESSON, Henry A., H-68-1; Pvt E Co 51st MA Vol; 8-63 to 7-65; Chattanooga PO
WEST, Abraham, Hw-132-3(1); Sarah widow of; Pvt; Romeo PO (Greene Co.); was never discharged
WEST, Calvin M., Gr-75-2; Pvt F Co 1st TN Cav; 1 Mar 62 to 1 Mar 65; Doyal PO; sight, diarhea, injury of rectom, back, liver & heart disease
WEST, Charles H., A-9-2; Pvt H Co 9th TN Cav; 8-12-62 to 7-5-65; Podopholine PO; loss of ball of right thumb
WEST, Curtis, Tr-265-1; Pvt F Co 3rd US Inf; 17 Oct 64 to 15 Nov 65; Hartsville PO
WEST, Elijah J., Me-94-2; 8th Civil Dist
WEST, Glaspy, A-3-1; Pvt L Co 2nd TN Inf; 9-8-62 to 7-8-65; Willson PO
WEST, Hamilton, M-108-2(1); Pvt H Co 5th KY Cav; 12-4-61 to 5-3-65; Salt Lick PO; gunshot wound in head
WEST, Henry W., Gr-80-2; Pvt A Co 11th TN Cav; Jun or Jul 64 to __; Shelton's Ford PO; dyspepsa, canot recollect date of enlistment, never discharged--was separated from com. and got with them anymore
WEST, Isaac D., Sm-169-2; Pvt; Defeated PO; CONF
WEST, Isaac W., Sn-261-3(2); 2nd Orderly Sgt F Co 16th TN Inf; 6-5-61 to 4-9-65; Portland PO; middle finger shot off; prisoner at Louisville KY 3 mos, came home on discharge 4-9-65; CONF
WEST, Jackson, Lo-195-2(1); Mary E. widow of; 2nd Lt I Co 1st TN Inf; 61 to __; Oral PO (Roane Co.)
WEST, James, Hw-132-1; Sarah widow of; Pvt C Co 1st TN Cav; Jul 61 to 11 Apr 65; Otes PO
WEST, James H., R-161-5; Pvt 2nd TN Col Art; 8-61 to __; Dayton PO; gunshot in left leg, now very old
WEST, Jesse, M-103-6; Pvt H Co 5th KY Cav; 12-4-61 to 5-3-65; Union Camp PO
WEST, John, Po-151-1; Pvt 5th TN Inf; Servilla PO
WEST, John, S-217-1; Pvt H Co 2nd TN Inf; 5 Feb 62 to 5 Aug 65; Winfield PO; rheumatism

335

WEST, John, Hw-131-3; Viney widow of; Otes PO; CONF
WEST, John, Cf-35-3; Mary C. widow of; Pvt I Co 4th TN Inf; 6 Nov 61 to __; Manchester PO; CONF
WEST, John, Ru-236-1; alias John DeJarnett; Pvt H Co 14th TN Inf; FAll 63 to Mar 65; Murfreesboro PO
WEST, John, Gi-139-3; 2nd Lt K Co 53rd TN Inf; 61 to __; Campbellsville PO; killed at Nashville, M. C. West wife of West
WEST, John N., Gr-75-2; Sgt D Co 4th TN Inf; 1 Feb 63 to 2 Aug 65; Doyal PO; rupture sciatic rheumatism, heart disease and food? poison
WEST, Joseph A., Gr-79-3; Pvt A Co 11th TN; Hipati PO; varicos vains
WEST, Manual, He-62-3; Pvt Co I 7th TN Cav; 62 to 63; Lexington PO; cripled in right leg
WEST, Martin, Sh-189-2; Broadway, Memphis PO
WEST, Mary, D-99-2; Poorhouse (Nashville?) PO; widow of Sol
WEST, Miles, M-108-2(1); Sgt H Co 5th KY Cav; 12-4-61 to 5-3-65; Salt Lick PO; lung trouble
WEST, Nathaniel B., K-168-4; Pvt C Co 6th TN Inf; 24 Apr 62 to 10 May 65; Smithwood PO; spinal injuries
WEST, Phesily, S-213-3; widow US Sol; 2nd Civil Dist
WEST, Phillip A., Fr-112-3; Pvt D Co 3rd MI Inf; 9-1-64 to 7-3-65; Tullahoma PO (Coffee Co.)
WEST, PLeasant W., S-217-2; Pvt G Co 7th TN Inf; 17 Jul 62 to 63; Oneida PO; shot in right arm
WEST, Reason, S-214-1; Pvt A Co 1st TN Inf; 18 Jul 62 to Jun 65; Robbins PO
WEST, Ridley, Sm-169-2; Pvt; Defeated PO; CONF
WEST, Ruben, Hy-79-2; Pvt; Civil Dist No 6
WEST, Shelby, Sn-259-1; Sgt C Co 14th __; 10-1-63 to 3-26-66; Bethpage PO; shot through ankle
WEST, Thomas L., Rb-219-2; Pvt B Co 30th TN Inf; Sep 61 to Aug 63; Black Jack PO; shot through the back part of neck, the wound was a severe one; CONF
WEST, Wade, Rb-219-2; Pvt G Co 8th KY Reg; Aug 11 62 to Sep 23 63; Franklin KY PO; hurt in back, thrown from horse, cavalry service
WEST, William, R-162-5; Mary A. widow of; Pvt D Co 7th TN Inf; __ to 8-5-65; Dayton PO
WEST, Wm., M-105-4; Cpl TN Cav; 63 to 65; Surgoinsville PO
WEST, William, Hw-131-3; Pvt B Co 3rd TN Mtd Inf; 30 Jun 64 to __; Otes PO
WEST, William D., K-171-5(4); Pvt C Co 6th TN Inf; 18 Dec 63 to 13 Jun 65; Bearden PO
WEST, William J., Ca-23-2; Pvt K Co 5th TN Inf; 7-64 to 6-65; Leoni PO; hurt by unloading wagon
WEST, William R., M-108-2(1); Pvt H Co 5th KY Cav; 12-4-61 to 3-3-65; Salt Lick PO; hearing damaged
WESTBROOK, Rufus M., D-50-4; Pvt F Co 4th TN Cav; 64 to 65; 111 Jefferson PO; shot in forehead, injured eyes, served in Mexican War
WESTBROOKS, Jackson, Sh-15-21; alias Westbrooks, Samuel; Pvt TN Vol; Oct 63 to deserted Jan 64; Collierville PO
WESTBROOKS, James A., P-157-1; Pvt F Co 6th TN Inf; 12-20-64 to 3-4-65; Theodore PO
WESTBROOKS, Katharine F. (see Carter, Louis)
WESTCOAT, Samuel E., We-222-2; Pvt G Co Capt Edwards 9th TN; Feb 61 to May 62; Gardner PO; 2 bones broken, left leg below knee; CONF
WESTER, Daniel C., Cl-48-3; Pvt D Co 4th TN Inf; 11-28-62 to 8-2-65; Old Town PO
WESTER, Henry, Ro-201-5(3); Cpl C Co 1st TN Hvy Art; 17 Feb 64 to 31 Mar 66; Kingston PO
WESTER, John M., Ro-201-2; 2nd Lt Col G Co 1st TN Inf; Aug 61 to Oct 63; Kingston PO
WESTER, Louis M., Ro-201-1; Capt G Co 1st TN Inf; 9 Aug 61 to 9 Nov 62; Kingston PO
WESTERN, Tolbert E., D-82-1; Sol US; 4th Dist
WESTFIELD, Gilbert, Hu-99-1; Pvt 40th Col US Inf; Johnsonville PO
WESTMOLDEN, James (see Mason, James)
WESTMORELAND, Henry J., Br-8-2; 4th Civil Dist
WESTMORELAND, John F., Gi-122-3; Steward A Co 53rd TN Inf; Nov 62 to 24 Oct 64; Prospect Sta. PO; CONF

WESTMORELAND, Joseph, Gi-122-5; H Pvt D Co 111th TN Inf; 1 Jan 64 to 13 Apr 66; Prospect Sta. PO; prison 9 mos
WESTON, Abner R., Ha-117-2; Jane widow of; Pvt; Kyle's Ford PO; died of measles, no record kept of his date of enlistment &c
WESTON, David, De-23-1; Pvt; Apr 63 to Apr 64; Bath Springs PO; CONF
WESTON, David, Sh-191-6(2); Pvt C Co 4th Col Inf; 64 to 66; Memphis PO
WESTON, Richd., Sh-189-5; Mary Ann Booth widow of; Sgt H Co 3rd US Col Hvy Art; 6-5-63 to 4-30-66; Penn. Ave, Memphis PO
WETHERELL, Ephraim H., D-92-1; Sgt D Co 5th MI Inf; 25 Aug 62 to 31 May 65; West Nashville. PO; sciatic rheumatism
WETZELL, Henry B., K-169-1; Cpl H Co 51st PA; 18 Aug 62 to 18 May 65; Knoxville PO
WHALEN, Joseph (see Nelson, William)
WHALEY, Calvin, Wa-263-1; Catherine widow of; Pvt 13th TN Inf; Apr 64 to __; Garbers Mills PO; Calvin Whaley died in Conf Prison
WHALEY, George W., Wa-263-1; Pvt H Co 8th TN Cav; Sep 28 63 to 11 Sep 65; Garbers Mills PO; rheumatism & lungs
WHALEY, Isaac T., A-8-1; Pvt C Co 7th TN Mtd Inf; 9-10-64 to 6-27-65; Scarborough PO; spinal affection of back
WHALEY, Jacob, U-247-2; Pvt H Co 8th TN Cav; 16 Sep 63 to 11 Sep 65; Erwin PO; lungs heart & erycipilus
WHALEY, John, Mc-117-4; Mary E. widow of; Pvt; Carlock PO; cant give any dates
WHALEY, John W., Mc-109-2; Cpl A Co 5th TN Inf; 3-5-62 to 3-5-65; Sewee PO (Meigs Co.); lumbago, in hospital about 12 mos
WHALEY, West O., Se-223-2; Mary King formerly widow of; Hendersons Springs PO; diarrhea, died March 26 63, Murfreesboro
WHALEY, William B., A-8-2; Pvt A Co 5th TN Inf; 7-12-63 to 9-16-65; Scarborough PO; now totally blind
WHALIN, John W., Ro-203-6; Pvt K Co 1st TN Inf; 9 Aug 61 to __; Wheat PO; rheumatism & throat disease
WHEANER, J. P., Sh-174-1; alias James Price; Musician G Co 49th IN Vol; B Co 7th Vet R Corps; about 7-62 to about 7-65; 182 De Soto St, Memphis PO; chronic diarrhaea & typh. fever, 6 mos in hospital, eyes permanently injured
WHEATLY, Daniel W., Mu-209-4; Cpl A Co 48th TN Inf; Oct 1 61 to 1 Jul 64; Columbia PO; prisoner at Ft. Donaldson, 2 mos; CONF
WHEATLY, Thomas W., Sh-183-1; Sgt; Memphis PO
WHEATLY, William H., Jo-150-4; Pvt H Co 8th TN Cav; 4 Mar 64 to __; Osborn PO
WHEELER, Anderson, Gi-123-3; PO omitted
WHEELER, Christopher C., Wa-274-3; Pvt A Co 75th IL Inf; 8 Jul 62 to 13 May 64; Asst Sur 8th TN Cav; 13 May 64 to 11 Sep 65; bayonet wound and rheumatism
WHEELER, Ephraim C., C-27-3; Pvt A Co 1st TN Inf; 7-4-63 to 9-25-65; Jacksboro PO
WHEELER, Hen, H-66-2; Sgt G Co 67th OH Inf; 10-26-61 to 6-30-62; reenlisted Cap I Co 129th OH Inf; 1-1-63 to 3-8-64; Chattanooga PO
WHEELER, James F., C-27-2; Pvt A Co 1st TN Inf; 8-1-61 to 9-17-64; Caryville PO
WHEELER, James T., B1-2-1; Pvt GA Inf; 63 to __ (4 mos); Glade Creek PO; tubusculous from exposure, unable to perform labor
WHEELER, Jasper, Bo-19-3; Cpl C Co 6th TN Inf; 4-62 to 4-65; Rockford PO
WHEELER, Jerry, Gi-123-3; PO omitted
WHEELER, John, Col, Mt-139-1; Pvt G Co 13th US Col Inf; 63 to 65 (2 yrs 4 mos); Woodlawn PO
WHEELER, John O., D-58-1; Pvt K Co 50th US C Inf; Sep 63 to Dec 66; Nashville PO; health lost by exposure in the army
WHEELER, Marcus D., C-27-2; Pvt A Co 1st TN Inf; 7-6-63 to 7-22-65; Caryville PO
WHEELER, Dr. Obed., We-221-3; Surgeon; 62 to 65; Martin PO
WHEELER, William, Ma-127-1; Ord Sgt D Co 8th MO Inf; Jun 14 61 to Jul 3 64; Jackson PO
WHEELER, William R., Hm-108-5(4); Quartermaster Sgt B Co 51st VA Inf; 20 Jun 61 to 8 Apr 65; Russellville PO

WHELAND, George W., H-56-3; Pvt G Co 118th OH Inf; 8-22-62 to 6-5-65; St. Elmo PO
WHERRY, Isham, D-61-2; 4 yrs 6 mos; Ament cor. Hancock, Nashville PO
WHETSELL, William L., Bo-15-3; Pvt H Co 2nd TN Cav; __ to 7-6-65; Maryville PO
WHETSTONE, Jerrie M., J-81-2; Pvt H Co 105th OH; 8-11-62 to 6-3-65; Gainesboro PO; shot in left hip 10-8-62
WHETSTONE, John S., Sm-172-1; Pvt F Co 7th IL Cav; 9-16-62 to 1-27-65; Buffalo Valley PO (Putnam Co.); left ankle dislocated
WHETZEL, Martin M., H-54-1; Pvt F Co 9th WV Inf; 2-62 to 2-65; Sherman Heights PO; wounded in right hand, accidnet, chronic diorrhoea in 1865, hernia on left side
WHIGHT, Jacob H., Ge-83-2; Pvt M Co 1st TN Cav; 5 Nov 62 to 25 May 65; Henshaw PO; chronic diarrhea
WHIGHT, Lemuel, Wl-208-1; M. E. widow of; Pvt F Co 45th TN; Dec 2 61 to Jan 28 63; Dodoburgh PO
WHIPPLE, Charles, Mg-198-2; Pvt; Apr 61 to May 61; Deer Lodge PO; sunstroke, Pvt H Co 25th MS Inf, 2 Aug 62 to 11 Jan 65
WHIPPLE, Rubert, H-56-6; Pvt E Co 84th IN Inf; 6-13-61 to 7-25-65; St. Elmo PO
WHIRTMUELLER, Robert, D-45-1; Catherine wife of (widow?); Capt D Co 10th TN Inf; 62 to 62; Nashville PO
WHITACRE, John S., R-162-5; Pvt F Co 146th OH Inf; 5-2-64 to 9-64; Dayton PO
WHITAKER, Etull?, Je-140-1; Pvt D Co 8th TN Cav; 28 Sep 63 to 11 Sep 65; Lucilla PO; diharea chronic, frostbitten feet
WHITAKER, Henry C., Je-141-4; Pvt M Co 7th NY Cav; 18 Aug 62 to 5 Jun 65; New Market PO
WHITAKER, Hugh, K-186-3; Pvt; 18 Apr 62 to 16 Jun 65; Knoxville PO
WHITAKER, Jesse, Ge-98-3; Pvt C Co 4th TN Inf; 5 Apr 62 to 2 Aug 65; Milbernton PO; dropsey of the chest
WHITAKER, John, Pu-141-2; Pvt K Co 4th TN Inf; 64 to 8-65; Void PO; discharged at close of war
WHITAKER, Joseph, Cl-51-1; Pvt L Co 63rd TN Inf; 5-15-63 to 9-1-63; PO omitted; CONF
WHITAKER, Samuel, Li-149-1; Margarett widow of; Pvt G Co 101st US Col Inf; Fayetteville PO; date of enlistment & discharge not known
WHITAKER, William, J-77-2; Pvt C Co 9th KS Cav; 10-16-62 to 7-17-65; Gainesboro PO
WHITAKY, Richard, Wa-272-2; Pvt D Co 8th TN Cav; Pettibone PO; chronic diarrhoea and rheumatism
WHITAT, Timothy, Cl-54-3(1); Pvt I Co 3rd TN Inf; 3-61 to 64; Tazewell PO; measles
WHITE, Abraham, U-247-2; Pvt M Co 8th TN Cav; 15 Sep 63 to 11 Sep 65; Erwin PO; rheumatism, heart & kidney
WHITE, Alex, D-60-3; Rillar Butler former widow of; Pvt; #312 McCrony St, Nashville PO
WHITE, Alford, Hm-107-5; Pvt D Co 4th TN Inf; 17 Dec 63 to 2 Aug 65; Chestnut Bloom PO; druggs of measles
WHITE, Allen W., Mo-129-1; Pvt D Co 11th TN Cav; 63 to 9-65; Huling PO
WHITE, Amandy (see Wills, Ferdinand)
WHITE, Archable, Ge-101-1; Pvt B Co 3rd TN Cav; 30 Jun 64 to 30 Nov 64; Locust Sp. PO; Knoxville TN Camps
WHITE, Arher B., Mo-129-1; Pvt D Co 11th TN Cav; 63 to 9-65; Huling PO
WHITE, Benjamin, He-60-2; Pvt I Co 3rd US Art Hvy; Sep 62 to Apr 65; Lexington PO
WHITE, Benj., Mu-198-1; 10th Dist
WHITE, Chas., Gi-123-2; Pvt F Co 110th TN Col Inf; 63 to 66; Stella PO
WHITE, Christifor H., De-23-2; Pvt G Co 27th TN Inf; Aug 61 to Apr 65; Bath Springs PO; shot in wright foot; CONF
WHITE, Christopher C., Sm-189-1; Pvt A Co 1st TN Cav; 11-28-63 to __-30-65; Maggart PO; wound & hearing
WHITE, Claborn E., Sm-170-2; Pvt C Co 8th TN Mtd Inf; 3-15-65 to 8-15-65; Maggart PO
WHITE, D. A., Hw-118-2; Cpl A Co 1st TN Art; 6 Oct 63 to 8 Aug 65; St. Clair PO; rupture

WHITE, Daniel, Un-259-1; Pvt M Co 9th TN Cav; 20 Oct 64 to 11 Sep 65; Rhodelia PO; vericoes vain, hard march
WHITE, David, A-9-2; Pvt I Co 9th TN Cav; 5-18-64 to 9-11-65; Podopholine PO; recieved injury to chest
WHITE, David, Je-146-3; Pvt D Co 4th TN Inf; 1 Aug 63 to 2 Aug 65; Leadvale PO; rheumatism
WHITE, David C., H-73-4(2); Sgt B Co 72nd KY Inf; 1-10-65 to 11-16-66; Chattanooga PO
WHITE, David W., Ct-35-2; Pvt G Co 13th TN Cav; 9-22-63 to 9-5-65; Butler, Johnson Co. PO; in US Army
WHITE, Dock H., M-103-4; Pvt D Co 8th TN Inf; 12-20-64 to 8-21-65; Alton Hill PO
WHITE, Eanesa, (see Hargrave, Spencer)
WHITE, Elie H., Sm-170-2; Pvt A Co 1st TN Mtd Inf; 4-22-64 to 4-18-65; Maggart PO; chronic diarea
WHITE, Eligia, A-9-4(2); Pvt A Co 1st KY Cav; 2-5-65 to 7-15-65; Lowe Sulphur Springs PO; gunshot wound in right foot
WHITE, Emanuel, Sh-191-4; Memphis PO; records not seen
WHITE, Erastus, Hr-89-1; alias Owen Evrett; Pvt D Co 138th GA; 65 to 66; Whitesville PO
WHITE, Frances M., Ge-102-3; Pvt M Co 1st TN Cav; Nov 62 to 19 Jun 65; Henshaw PO
WHITE, Francis M., Hw-119-4(1); Jane widow of; Gillenwater PO
WHITE, Frank, Ma-123-1; Pvt Co D 3rd Hvy Art; Jun 10 63 to 8 May 66; Jackson PO; got wounded since the war but not during the war
WHITE, Franklin M., Cf-43-1; Pvt L Co 13th TN Cav; 9-22-63 to 9-5-65; Carter Furnace PO; heart trouble, rheumatism
WHITE, Garrett, Ms-174-1; Pvt A Co 17th US Inf; 14 Dec 63 to 30 Apr 66; Chapel Hill PO
WHITE, George, Sh-192-1; Pvt US; Memphis PO
WHITE, George, H-62-1; Pvt; alley bet. Cedar & Pleasant, Chattanooga PO
WHITE, George H., Wy-173-3; Nancy A. widow of; Pvt A Co 2nd TN Mtd Inf; 10-2-63 to 10-14-64; Houston PO
WHITE, George S., Mo-126-1; Pvt H Co 3rd TN Mtd Inf; 10-1-64 to 11-30-64; Hopewell Springs PO
WHITE, George T., Dy-25-6(2); Sgt D Co 50th MO Cav; Nov 64 to May 65; Newbern PO
WHITE, George W., Ct-43-3; Pvt L Co 13th TN Cav; 2-65 to 9-5-65; Carter Furnace PO
WHITE, George W., Mo-127-1; Madisonville PO
WHITE, Harison, Cy-29-1; Pvt C Co 6th IN Inf; 7-15-62 to 7-15-65; Batesvible PO; diseas of lungs? & piles
WHITE, Henry, Sh-173-1; 76 Hernando St, Memphis PO
WHITE, Henry, D-49-3; Pvt H Co 17th TN Inf; 61 to 64; this is all he claims to know
WHITE, Henry, Sh-159-6; Pvt A Co 53rd OH; Memphis PO; arms broken or deformed
WHITE, Henry, Sh-157-8; Dist 13
WHITE, Henry, Sh-157-3; Pvt G Co 11th Inf; 63 to 65; Ensly PO
WHITE, Henry W., M-103-2; Pvt C Co 1st TN Vol Inf; 10-21-63 to 1-14-65; Lafayette PO
WHITE, Isaac, K-166-4(2); Capt A Co 10th IN Inf; Knoxville PO
WHITE, Isaac E., Bl-4-1; Sgt I Co 6th TN Cav; 10-8-62 to 8-1-63; Pikeville PO; CONF
WHITE, Isaac H., A-13-2; Pvt H Co 1st TN Inf; 8-8-61 to 9-17-64; Briceville PO; rheumatism
WHITE, Isaac N., D-75-2; Stewarts Ferry PO
WHITE, Jacob, Gi-135-2; Pvt D Co 1st MD Inf; 12-10-63 to 7-18-65; Lynnville PO
WHITE, Jacob, Di-37-2; Pvt K Co 12th TN Inf; 8-12-63 to 1-16-66; Cumberland Furnace PO
WHITE, James, Ro-209-2; Maggie widow of; Lt; Glen Alice PO; CONF
WHITE, James, K-175-2; Pvt E Co 6th TN Inf; 6 Mar 62 to 3 Mar 65; Bullrun PO
WHITE, James, Br-11-2; Pvt B Co 18th IL Inf; 62 to 65; Chatata PO
WHITE, James, A-11-1; Pvt E Co 3rd TN Inf; 2-14-62 to 3-22-65; Clinton PO
WHITE, James, Me-92-1; Cpl D Co 7th TN Mtd Inf; 10-9-64 to 7-27-65; Sewee PO; horse fell and hurt hip & stomach
WHITE, James, Sh-153-2; Pvt I Co 42nd USC Inf; Baily Sta. PO

WHITE, James A., Hd-50-4; Pvt D Co 2nd TN Mtd Inf; 63 to 64; Pybyms Bluff PO; foot broken by horse falling
WHITE, James A., Bl-4-2; Pvt I Co 8th TN Cav; 10-15-62 to 1-1-63; Pikeville PO; wounded in face & right arm, arm broken
WHITE, James C., Mo-126-1; Pvt; Hopewell Springs PO
WHITE, Jas. D., Wa-271-1; Flourville PO
WHITE, James E., Mo-126-2; Cpl G Co 9th TN Cav; 5-7-63 to 7-22-65; Tevis PO; scalls & bruises in explosion of Sultana boat, also scurvy contracted in prison, Andersonville prison 1 yr 1 mo 1 day
WHITE, James F., Je-145-1; Pvt B Co 9th TN Cav; 20 Sep 63 to 11 Sep 65; Cynthiana PO
WHITE, James H., Dk-34-1; Nancy P. widow of; 1st Lt F Co 4th TN Cav; Dowelltown PO; hurt in hips by horse falling
WHITE, James H., Gr-78-1; Pvt E Co 9th TN Cav; 13 Oct 63 to 11 Sep 65; Larkeyton PO; heart disease
WHITE, James H., J-78-2; Pvt B Co 8th TN Inf; 3-17-65 to 8-17-65; Rough Point PO; sprannia back piles
WHITE, James H. R., M-103-3; 1st Sgt E Co 1st TN Mtd Inf; 10-6-63 to 1-22-65; Lafayette PO
WHITE, James J., Wa-263-4; Pvt H Co 8th TN Cav; Sep 15 63 to 12 Sep 65; Garbers Mills PO; prison at Danville & Richmond
WHITE, James L., Je-146-3; Pvt G Co 13th TN Cav; 63 to 8 Sep 65; White Pine PO; rheumatism
WHITE, James L., Ct-43-2; Julia A. Ferguson formerly widow of; Pvt L Co 13th TN Cav; 11-6-63 to __; Carter Furnace PO; killed in battle Marrion VA Dec 24 1864
WHITE, James M., Gi-123-1; Pvt Guide & Scout; Jan 65 to Aug 65; Bethel PO
WHITE, Jethro Z., Sh-174-1; Sgt C Co 11th TN Inf; 1-28-64 to 1-12-66; 236 Pontotac St, Memphis PO
WHITE, Joel, Cy-26-1; Pvt B Co 37th KY Inf; 8-11-63 to 12-29-64; Moss PO
WHITE, John, Sn-259-1; Eliza widow of; Pvt; 61 to 64; Bransford PO
WHITE, John, Mu-203-1; alias White, Scott; Pvt I Co 14th TN Inf; 10 Dec 63 to 20 Dec 65; Hampshire PO
WHITE, John, Sh-158-5(1); Pvt D Co 3rd US Cav; Feb 64 to Jun 66; Memphis PO; discharged at close of the war with discharge paper
WHITE, John, Gr-77-2; USS; Strawberry Plains PO
WHITE, John, H-76-2; Pvt E Co 5th TN Inf Vol; Chattanooga PO
WHITE, John, Hd-55-1; Pvt A Co 2nd TN Mtd Inf; 2 Oct 64 to 2 Oct 65; Cerro Gordo PO; rheumatism and neuralgia, now suffering with eyes
WHITE, John, Lk-112-1; Pvt H Co 5th IL Inf; Apr 65 to Spring 65 (2 yrs); Tiptonville PO
WHITE, John, Hd-46-1; Pvt B Co 2nd TN Mtd Inf; Sep 3 64 to Sep 3 65; Savannah PO
WHITE, John, O-134-2; Pvt B Co 10th MO Cav; Jun 1 63 to May 11 65; Hornbeak PO; CONF
WHITE, John, Wa-263-4; Mary wife of; Comisary Sgt H Co 8th TN Cav; Oct 63 to Sep 12 65; Garbers Mills PO
WHITE, John, Wa-267-2; Susan widow of; Pvt H Co 8th TN Cav; 28 Sep 63 to 4 May 65; Febuary PO; epilepsy
WHITE, John B., A-13-3; Pvt C Co 2nd TN Inf; 8-7-61 to 10-6-64; Briceville PO; rheumatism
WHITE, John C., U-246-2; Pvt M Co 8th TN Cav; 27 Sep 63 to 15 May 65; Erwin PO
WHITE, John E., A-13-3; Elizabeth widow of; Pvt H Co 2nd TN Inf; 12-19-61 to 12-19-64; Briceville PO
WHITE, John H., D-58-2; Sol Mexican War; Bostic Ave, Nashville PO
WHITE, John H., Hd-53-3; Pvt F Co 10th TN Inf; 12 Sep 62 to 3 Jul 65; Adamsville PO; scabra wound on shoulder
WHITE, John H., Wl-293-2; Pvt F Co 28th TN Inf?; May 61 to 62; Austin PO; CONF
WHITE, John K., Wa-265-1; Pvt H Co 8th TN Cav; 15 Sep 62 to 11 Sep 65; Trump PO; disease of eyes

WHITE, John M., Ge-88-2; Marcy C. widow of; Clerk H Co 8th TN Inf; Oct 63 to 65; Bulls Gap PO; can't get facts at all
WHITE, John W., Gr-79-3; Pvt E Co 9th TN Cav; 18 Oct 64 to 15 Sep 65; Ball Point PO; thy broken
WHITE, John W., M-103-1; Pvt D Co 8th TN; Lafayette PO; sun stroke
WHITE, Jonathan, H-58-2; Pvt A Co 7th TN Inf; 6-3-62 to __; Coulterville PO; piles, transferred to Battery B TN
WHITE, Joseph, Hw-121-4(3); Pvt H Co 8th TN Inf; 25 Jul 63 to 30 Jun 65; New Hope PO; cronic dirhear, rumatism
WHITE, Joseph, Hy-76-1; B Co 33rd MS Inf?; 2 yrs; Stanton Depot PO
WHITE, Joseph, M-103-6; Pvt H Co 5th KY Cav; 12-4-61 to 5-3-65; Lafayette PO
WHITE, Joseph A., B-2-2; Pvt A Co 4th TN Inf; 7-30-64 to 8-25-65; Haley PO
WHITE, Joseph E., H-51-7; Hill City PO
WHITE, Joseph J., Mc-117-1; Pvt E Co 7th TN Mtd Inf; Mecca PO
WHITE, Joseph M., Ge-83-1; Eliza widow of; Pvt G Co 4th TN Inf; 22 Jul 63 to 2 Aug 65; Hanshaw PO; chronic diarrhear
WHITE, Landon, Wa-270-2; Pvt H Co Inf; 62 to 65; Austins Springs PO
WHITE, Lawson, Ct-39-2; Pvt C Co 2nd NC Cav; Happy Valley PO; chronic diorhoea
WHITE, Leander A., U-247-3; Pvt B Co 3rd NC Mtd Inf; 10 Jul 64 to 8 Aug 65; Erwin PO; diarrhoea & rheumatism
WHITE, Lemiel C., Dy-25-2; Pvt G Co TN Cav; 64 to 65; Newbern PO; CONF
WHITE, Levi, Hm-107 2(1); Pvt D Co 4th TN Inf; 17 Dec 63 to 2 Aug 65; Witts Foundry PO; rheumatism
WHITE, Lizzie, Sh-173-1; 76 Hernando St., Memphis
WHITE, Logan J., M-103-4; Sarah widow of; Pvt B Co 37th KY Inf; 8-5-63 to 12-29-64; Alton Hill PO
WHITE, Louis, Hy-76-1; alias Denis Cook; Stanton Depot PO; cooked for Lt
WHITE, Lucy E. (see Campbell, James M.)
WHITE, Madison, D-46-1; Cpl K Co 12th Col Inf; 8-12-63 to 2-3-66; L & N RR Freight Office; Nashville PO; wounded in right hip
WHITE, Mary (see Reynolds, Richard)
WHITE, Mida W., Di-34-3; alias Richard White; Sarah C. widow of; Colesburg PO
WHITE, Moses, H-70-4(1); Pvt 85th OH Inf; 1 yr; Chattanooga PO
WHITE, P. W., Wi-271-1; Sgt D Co 10th TN Inf; 30 Apr 62 to 18 Mar 65; Boston PO; phthisic (exposure on battlefield) at Murfreesboro TN
WHITE, Peter, Ms-173-1; Rich Creek PO
WHITE, Peter H., Gr-79-3; Pvt E Co 9th TN Cav; 18 Oct 64 to 15 Sep 65; Ball Point PO; piles and rheumatism
WHITE, Pollard, D-79-2; Cpl D Co 83rd OH Vol Inf; Aug 12, 62 to Aug 12, 65; Nashville PO, 310 Trentland St; deaf, concussion of shell
WHITE, Richard, A-10-1; Pvt I Co 9th TN Cav; 64 to 65; Briceville PO; hemoredge of lung, discharge stolen
WHITE, Richard, Sh-157-5; Pvt B Co 4th TN; 62 to __ (8 mos); Dist 13
WHITE, Robt., D-49-1; Sallie former widow of; Nashville PO
WHITE, Robert Hagerty, Sh-157-7; Pvt; Memphis PO, 55 Union St.
WHITE, Robt. K., Cr-7-1; Crockett Mills PO
WHITE, Robert N., Mr-96-2; Pvt E Co 6th TN Mtd Inf; 10-1-64 to 6-30-65; Shirleyton PO; vicors & garter
WHITE, Russell, Me-94-1; Cpl K Co 10th TN Cav; 2-15-64 to 8-1-65; Knott PO; disease of lungs from measels
WHITE, S. S., Je-135-1(3); Christiny widow of; Pvt B Co 1st TN Inf; 24 Jan 64 to 27 Nov 65; PO omitted
WHITE, Samuel, Ro-207-1; Pvt D Co 5th TN Inf; 26 Feb 62 to 30 Mar 65; Patties Gap PO; catarrh of head, affection of lungs, claimed to be result of smallpox
WHITE, Samuel, Ge-86-1; Susan M. widow of; Pvt C Co 8th TN Inf; 4 Jul 63 to 2 Aug 65; no PO

WHITE, Samuel, Wy-173-2; Pvt B Co 2nd TN Mtd Inf; 10-15-63 to 10-17-64; Houston PO
WHITE, Samuel G., Sm-169-1; Cpl A Co 1st TN Mtd Inf; 12-18-63 to 1-31-65; Elmwood PO; bronchitis, reenlisted
WHITE, Samuel W., L-99-1; Pvt 8th US Cav (TN); 63 to 65; Orysa PO; heart disease, caused from exposure
WHITE, Seth, D-92-2; US Sol; W. Nashville PO
WHITE, Spencer, Ro-241-3; Rosa widow of; Pvt NT Inf; 63 to 66; Murfreesboro PO
WHITE, Stephen F., M-103-4; Pvt B Co 37th KY Inf; 6-1-63 to 12-29-64; Pvt D Co 8th TN Inf; 11-1-64 to 8-31-65(sic); Lafayette PO
WHITE, Thadius, D-54-1; Sgt A Co 13th US Col Inf; 63 to __ (10 mos); Nashville PO; gives record from memory
WHITE, Thomas, Hm-106-2; Pvt G Co 4th TN Cav; 2 Jan? 63 to 12 Jan? 65; Morristown PO
WHITE, Thomas, Wa-268-1; Pvt C Co 3rd US Art; Johnson City PO; sight
WHITE, Thomas C., Ct-35-2; Mary A widow of; 1st Lt G Co 13th TN Cav; 9-22-63 to 9-5-65; Fish Spring PO; in US Army
WHITE, Thomas S., Mg-198-1; Cpl F Co 1st TN Inf; 19 Aug 61 to 17 Sep 64; Island Ford PO; measles
WHITE, William, Sn-257-1; Pvt H Co 14th US Col Inf; __ to 3-26-66; Gallatin PO
WHITE, William, T-207-1; Cor Ullman Lt Art; Oct 9, 61 to Mar 8, 62; Covington PO
WHITE, William, Mo-129-1; Pvt TN; Huling PO
WHITE, William A., Sh-149-1; Pvt A Co 34th IL Inf; 24 Aug 63 to 24 Aug 65; Frazer PO
WHITE, William B., We-227-1; Pvt I Co 50th OH Inf; 21 Aug 62 to 1 Jul 65; Greenfield PO; shot in right jaw and broke
WHITE, William F., We-221-2; Pvt K Co 40th MS Inf; 27 Aug 64 to 18 Jul 65; Martin PO; had measles and ruined lungs
WHITE, William G., He-67-2; Ordinary Seaman, Pvt Hospital Ship Red Rover; Nov 15, 63 to Jun 15, 65; Pipkin PO; deaf in right ear, blind right eye, spinal paralysis caused by strain in Naval Service 1864
WHITE, William H., De-24-2; US Sol; 3rd Dist
WHITE, William H., Ch-12-2; Pvt 53rd TN Inf; 9-62 to 5-65; Custer Point PO; CONF
WHITE, William M., Ja-85-6; Georgetown PO
WHITE, William N., Ge-83-3; Pvt B Co 3rd NC Inf; 25 Mar 64 to 8 Aug 65; Painters PO; ingery to brest, diseas of hart?
WHITE, William O., K-166-4(2); Capt I Co 4th TN Cav; 22 Dec 62 to 12 Jul 65; Knoxville PO
WHITE, William R., We-221-3; Martha L. Griffeth widow of; Pvt; __ to 64; Martin PO; CONF
WHITE, William S., Bl-1-1; Pvt E Co 6th TN Mtd Inf; 9-4-64 to 6-30-65; Sampson PO; chronic rheumatism
WHITE, Zillman, Sh-174-4; Hannah widow of; 63 to __; 40 Hadden Ave, Memphis PO; discharge lost
WHITED, John A., Fe-41-3(1); Pvt Capt Beaty's Co. Indept. Scouts of TN; 4-62 to 11-65; West Fork PO (Overton Co.); consumption, hemorage of lungs
WHITEFIELD, Pearce, Sh-159-5; Cpl G Co 61st US Inf; 27 Feb 64 to 30 Dec 65; Memphis PO; served until the end
WHITEHEAD, Andrew J., Bo-12-3(1); Sol US; 3rd Dist
WHITEHEAD, David A., Ct-37-1; Pvt C Co 13th TN Cav; 9-24-63 to 9-5-65; Hopson PO; frost bite, suffering 25 yrs
WHITEHEAD, Granvill, Ct-35-4; Martha J. widow of; Pvt G Co 13th TN Cav; 9-22-63 to 9-5-65; Lineback PO; death date not known, no discharge
WHITEHEAD, J. J., Bo-22-1; Pvt C Co 1st TN Cav; 11-1-62 to 5-25-65; Seaton PO; loss of use both legs
WHITEHEAD, James, Co-67-1; Pvt C Co 8th TN Cav; 26 Sep 63 to 25 Aug 65; Cosby PO; gunshot wound in shoulder
WHITEHEAD, James K., Bo-12-2(1); Taheney or Danny widow; Pvt F Co 6? 2nd Mtd Inf; 63 to 9-65; Rasor PO
WHITEHEAD, John G., Bo-12-4; Sol US; 3rd Dist

WHITEHEAD, John W., Se-221-1; Margaret widow of; Pvt G Co 1st TN Cav; 1 Jul 62 to 5 Jun 65; Allensville PO
WHITEHEAD, Mathias, Bo-12-2(1); Pvt B Co 8th TN Inf; 12-14-62 to6-30-65; Rasor PO
WHITEHEAD, Susannah (see Inman, Joseph)
WHITEHEAD, Thos., Ct-37-1; Pvt C Co 13th TN Cav; 9-24-63 to 9-5-65; Hopson PO; chronic direah, suffering 25 yrs
WHITEHEAD, William H., Rb-221-3; Pvt F Co 49th TN; Dec 14 61 to May 5 65; Adams Station PO; slightly wounded 60 days hospital; CONF
WHITEHURST, Alford F., Mn-121-1; Pvt D Co 6th TN Cav; 12 Sep 62 to 26 Jul 65; Bethel Springs PO; sciatica and lung? truble
WHITESIDE, Thos., Gr-79-1; Emily Holt formerly widow of; Cpl I Co; 61 to 65; Ball Point PO; CONF
WHITESIDES, Forstin?, Hm-106-4; Morristown PO; refuse to answer; CONF
WHITESIDES, William B., Wa-268-3; Johnson City PO
WHITFIED, Morris, Gi-122-5; Pvt D Co 111th TN Inf; 1 Jan 64 to 4 May 66; Prospect Sta. PO; CONF
WHITFIED, William S., Gi-122-2; Pvt A Co 3rd TN Inf; May 10 61 to May 64; Prospect Sta. PO; prison 7 mos; CONF
WHITFIELD, Charlie C., O-140-1; ___ to 64 (4 yrs); Union City PO; rib broken, discharge lost & little known
WHITFIELD, Daniel, Sh-160-2; Pvt B Co 11th TN Inf; 61 to 65; Memphis PO
WHITFIELD, James, Sh-152-1; Collierville PO
WHITFIELD, Josiah, H-67-1; Pvt K Co US Col Inf; 2-15-65 to 2-14-66; Chattanooga PO
WHITFIELD, Thomas, Gi-132-4; Pvt A Co 7th IA Inf; Wales PO; deserted
WHITHURST, Moses H., G-69-1; Pvt K Co 7th TN Cav; 17 Nov 63 to 18 Feb 65; Rutherford PO
WHITICAR, Joseph, Co-61-6(2); Sarah E. widow of; Pvt; Bridgeport PO; CONF
WHITING, Phillip F., Hm-103-2; Pvt K Co 1st NY Drag; 12 Aug 62 to 13 Jun 65; Morristown PO
WHITLER, Conrand, Mg-200-1; Pvt F Co 15th IL Inf; 23 Apr 61 to Sep 64; Skene PO; chronic bronchitis
WHITLEY, Billy, T-215-2; Pvt; Mason PO
WHITLEY, Elijah, G-57-5(3); Pvt; 61 to 63; Yorkville PO; CONF
WHITLEY, Horace, Sh-149-1; Emma widow; Sgt B Co 39th US Inf; 17 May 63 to 31 Jan 66; National Cemetery PO
WHITLEY, James M., M-107-2; Alcey M. widow of; Pvt D Co 9th KY Inf; 10-1-61 to 12-15-64; Red Boiling Springs PO
WHITLEY, Jefferson, M-107-2; Cpl D Co 9th KY Inf --9-15-61 to 11-7-63; 2nd Sgt A Co 8th TN Mtd Inf--11-27-64 to 8-17-65; Red Boiling Springs PO; gunshot wound & result of mumps
WHITLEY, Jordan W., Gi-139-1; Pvt A Co 53rd TN Inf; 11-61 to 1-65; Barcheers PO; CONF
WHITLEY, Kinchen, M-107-2; Lucinda widow of; Pvt D Co 9th KY Inf; 9-61 to 12-64; Red Boiling Springs PO; rheumatism
WHITLEY, Noah B., M-107-2; Pvt D Co 9th KY Inf; 11-26-61 to 12-10-64; Red Boiling Springs PO; paralysis as result of typhoid fever
WHITLEY, Noah B., M-107-2; Pvt D Co 9th KY Inf; 11-26-61 to 12-10-64; Red Boiling Springs PO; paralysis as result of typhoid fever
WHITLEY, Wiley A., M-107-1; 1st Lt D Co 9th KY Inf--9-61 to 4-19-62; Pvt A Co 8th TN Mtd Inf--11-22-64 to 8-18-65; Red Boiling Springs PO; lumbago & lung disease
WHITLEY, William, Sh-200-1; Pvt F Co 11th US Col Inf; 1-11-64 to 1-12-66; Corner Tale & McKinley Sts, Memphis PO
WHITLOCK, Jacob W., Wa-276-2; Pvt; Jan 1 62 to Jun 5 65; Leesburg PO; crippled knee by runaway team, discharge in Wash City DC
WHITLOCK, James S., Wa-272-2; Cpl B Co 8th TN Cav; 20 Jul 63 to 11 Sep ___ (2 yrs 2 mos 18 days); Morning Star PO; disease of lungs
WHITLOCK, Michael K., Hw-122-2; Sgt F Co 8th TN Cav; 5 Apr 63 to 11 Sep 65; Van Hill PO; chronic rheumatism, partially disabled
WHITLOCK, Preston, L-188-2; Pvt A Co 5th TN Inf; 25 Aug 62 to 13 May 65; Adolphus PO
WHITLOCK, Smith B., Sm-173-3; 1st Lt G Co 4th TN Mtd Inf; 2-4-65 to 8-25-65; Brush Creek PO; reenlisted from 5th TN Cav
WHITLOCK, Thomas C., Ro-205-2; Pvt A Co 5th TN Inf; 25 Feb 62 to 4 Apr 65; Hatch PO; discharged on account of disability
WHITLOCK, William, Cu-15-1; 1st Lt A Co 5th TN Inf; 2-25-62 to 4-21-65; Hebbertsburg PO; diabetes, and small pox, results from which broken constitution
WHITLOW, Ganerella H., Hd-45-1; Cpl C Co 2nd TN Mtd Inf; 2-16-64 to 5-6-65; Whitton PO
WHITMAN, Fidellar S., Ch-15-1; Henderson PO
WHITMAN, John, Gu-45-1; Pvt E Co 1st TN Vid Cav; 63 to 64; Tarlton PO
WHITMAN, Peach A., H-72-1; Pvt H Co 9th PA Cav; 12-62 to 8-10-65; Chattanooga PO
WHITMON, Buoy, Hr-86-2; Pvt B Co 69th TN Inf; 1-10-64 to 11-29-66; Grand Junction PO
WHITMORE, Edwin, F-38-1; Pvt C Co 7th TN Cav; 10 Jun 61 to Jun 62; Mason PO; CONF
WHITMORE, James, Cl-58-1; Mary widow of; Pvt F Co 12th MI Art; ___ to 65; Davo PO; coneris, mustered at Detroit, MI
WHITNEY, Ferice L., Hm-33(103)-1; US; Civil Dist 17
WHITSIT, John A., D-72-6; Lt I Co 26th IN Inf; Jul 30 61 to Feb 66; Nashville PO
WHITSITT, John C., We-221-2; Pvt A Co 15th TN Cav; Sep 63 to Apr 65; Martin PO; CONF
WHITSON, Isaac, Ro-211-2; Sarah C. widow of; Pvt H Co 3rd TN Inf; 10 Feb 62 to 23 Feb 65; Webster PO; fever settled on lung
WHITSON, James, K-176-3; Pvt I Co 8th TN Inf; 13 Jun 61 to 14 Sep 65; Halls X Roads PO
WHITSON, William, Co-67-1; Pvt A Co 16th TN Cav; 62 to May 65 (2 yrs); Bison PO; CONF
WHITT, Elizabeth M. (see Dyke, Robt. J.)
WHITTAKER, Charlie, Lo-194-2; Muddy Creek PO
WHITTAKER, George, Wa-272-3; Pvt I Co 9th TN Cav; Clara PO
WHITTAKER, Harriet, G-51-1; widow US Sol; Humboldt PO
WHITTED, John D., Sh-176-1; Pvt 27th IN Reg; 63 to 66; 65 Linden St, Memphis PO
WHITTED, Vard, Se-220-2; Pvt E Co 1st TN Art; 19 Sep 63 to 1 Aug 65; Emerts Cave PO
WHITTENBURG, Daniel J., Ja-87-2; Pvt D Co 4th TN Cav; Ooltewah PO; rheumatism, heart disease, eyes?, discharge lost
WHITTENBURG, Joseph, Ja-87-2; Pvt K Co 5th TN Inf; 10-11-62 to 1-30-65; Ooltewah PO
WHITTINGTON, William K., Wa-263-5; Pvt K Co 53rd NC Inf; May 61 to May ___; May Day PO; prisoner Point Lookout
WHITTLE, George M., H-53-7; Pvt F Co 6th TN Mtd Inf; 10-4-64 to 7-11-65; Chattanooga PO; rheumatism in feet
WHITTLE, James M., Se-227-2; Pvt F Co 2nd TN Cav; 62 to 65; Shiloh Church PO
WHITTON, James, Br-7-3; Pvt G Co 11th TN Cav; 10-20-63 to 9-11-65; Coahulla PO; chronic diarhea
WHITTON, Joseph, Ja-84-1; Pvt; Harrison PO; shot in hip
WHITTON, Thomas, Ja-86-2; Caroline widow of; Pvt; Snowhill PO
WHITTON, W. W., A-1-2; Cpl F Co 6th TN Inf; 3-10-62 to 6-30-64; Custer PO; rheumatism
WHITUS, James M., Gi-122-4; Pvt D Co 44th TN Inf; 1 Jan 62 to 1 Jan 64; Prospect Sta. PO; wound in wrist; CONF
WHITWELL, J. A., G-57-6; Pvt; 62 to 65; Yorkville PO; CONF
WHITWORTH, Nicholas, Sn-254-2; PO omitted
WHITWORTH, Wm. H., Ce-23-1; Pvt I Co 49th TN; Oct 61 to May 65; Thomasville PO; shot 1 oz ball through thigh, disabled 2 mos
WHORT?, John, Hw-129-2; Cpl H Co 2nd KY Inf; 1 Nov 61 to 9 Jan 65; Mooresburg PO; rheumatism, infusion? of eyes
WICE, Wesley, Hm-107-4; Pvt M Co 9th TN Cav; Jun 63 to Sep 65; Chestnut Bloom PO; rheumatism, exact dates not known
WICKER, Jasper, Hd-52-1; Pvt C Co 6th TN Cav; Feb 5 63 to 26 Jul 65; Adamsville PO; crippled by being ron oper by horse, serious

WICKERSHAM, David C., Cu-16-3; Pvt 5th WI Bat Lt Lt Art; 9-5-61 to 9-30-64; Pleasant Hill PO; bronchial troubles, independent battery
WICKHAM, Robert L., Mt-149-1; Pvt; 63 to 65; Palmyra PO
WICOX, Thomas, Cu-15-3; Pvt D Co 45th IL Inf; 10-5-64 to 7-12-66; Clark Range PO; Fentress Co.
WIDENER, Eli, Wa-268-2; Johnson.City PO; CONF
WIDNER, James, K-182-3; Pvt 9th TN Cav; Sep 62 to 63; Gap Creek PO
WIDNER, Russell, Br-12-2; Emeline widow of; Pvt E Co 1st TN Lt Art; PO omitted
WIEHL, Fred F., H-60-1; Pvt & Sgt H Co 78th PA Inf; 9-17-61 to 11-64; Chattanooga PO
WIEL, John L., Hm-109-3; Pvt M Co 3rd TN Cav; 22 Jul 63 to 5 Dec 65; Whitesburg PO; diarhoea & piles
WIESGARBER, Charles, K-165-3; Pvt C Co 9th TN Cav; 24 Oct 63 to 11 Sep 65; Knoxville PO
WIGGINS, Ben, Fr-115-2; Cowan PO
WIGGINS, Chas. W., Sh-193-1; Pvt; Memphis PO
WIGGINS, Frank L., Ro-210-5; Pvt G Co 8th TN Cav; 63 to 65; Rockwood PO; lungs affected
WIGGINS, Henry, Ct-39-3; Bugler B Co 13th TN Cav; 62 to 64?; Dry Creek PO; sabre wound of right const?, gun shot left shoulder
WIGGINS, James L., Mo-129-1; Pvt D Co 11th TN Cav; 3-27-63 to 9-11-65; Four Mile Branch PO
WIGHT, Eli, H-70-1; Millicent M. widow of; Surgeon 5th ME Inf--5-5-61 to 7-15-61; Lt B Co 23rd ME Inf--8-10-62 to 3-63; Ass. Surgeon 1st US Col Hvy Art--2-9-65 to 3-8-66; Chattanooga PO; hemorrhage of lungs
WILAS, Jacob H., Co-59-2; US Sol; 1st Dist.
WILBERLY, Noah W., H-52-1; Lookout MT. PO
WILBERN, Leander, Jo-153-1; Pvt; Little Doe PO
WILBOURN, Stephen, Ha-113-2; Pvt G Co 8th TN Cav; 1 Mar 63 to 26 Sep 63; Sneedville PO
WILBUR, William S., D-72-5; Pvt D Co 16th IL Inf; Jul 15, 62 to 65; Nashville PO
WILBURN, Gentery, C-32-2; Pvt F Co 6th IN Cav; 9-1-62 to 6-10-65; Newcomb PO; rupture 26 yrs
WILBURN, James, C-32-1; Pvt F Co 6th TN Inf; 3-10-62 to 4-15-65; New Comb PO; cripel in hip & back, very ___
WILBURN, Philip A., Mo-126-2; Pvt B Co 6th TN Inf; 3-8-62 to ___; Madisonville PO; gunshot wound, heart disease, discharge missplaced
WILBURN, Stanston, Mo-130-3; Pvt; Ballpray PO
WILCOX, David P., Ct-40-6; 1st LT H Co 2nd TN Inf; 7-22-62 to 6-24-64; Elizabethton PO; gunshot wound
WILCOX, John M., Ct-40-5; 2nd Lt G Co 13th TN Cav; 9-24-63 to 9-5-65; Elizabethton PO
WILCOX, Lewis, Dy-27-1; Pvt B Co 12th TN Cav; 8-63 to 4-65; Ro Ellen PO; CONF
WILCOX, Orion, Cu-17-1; Pvt H Co 142nd NY Inf; 8-62 to 6-65; Crossville PO; deafness and chronic diarrhea, deafness increasing
WILCOX, William W., Lo-189-1; Pvt D Co 19th OH Inf; 10 Sep 61 to 31 Dec 63; Philadelphia PO; pleuro pneumonia, reenlisted in same co.
WILCOXEN, Samuel, Ro-203-7; Pvt A Co 1st TN Cav; Mar 63 to ___; Wheat PO
WILCOXON, David, Po-152-4(2); Pvt F Co 10th TN Cav; 11-27-63 to 8-1-65; Ducktown PO; lung disease
WILDER, Garele G., Co-69-6(1); Pvt C Co 8th TN Inf; 1 Mar 63 to 15 Apr 64; Driskill PO; rheumatism & fever, not a pensioner
WILDER, John T., Wa-268-3; Johnson City PO
WILDON, Tillery E., A-4-3; Pvt F Co 7th TN Mtd Inf; 11-8-64 to 7-27-65; Coal Creek PO
WILDS, John, K-171-4(3); Pvt C Co 12th TN Cav; 62 to 65; PO omitted; CONF
WILDS, Louisa (see Manuel, Hoyl)
WILER, Nathan, D-48-1; Capt D Co Eng ___; 8-13-61 to 1-31-64; Nashville PO
WILES, Franklin, Su-242-2; Pvt E Co 160th OH NG; 2 May 64 to 7 Sep 64; Bluff City PO; also listed as Wiles, Francis M. (S), Pvt G? Co 191st OH Inf; 28 Feb 65 to 28 Aug 65; holds discharge as regular
WILES, William B., Ms-177-1; Pvt F Co 1st TN Inf; 9-4-63 to 11-19-65; Lillards Mills PO

WILEY, Andrew P., Cf-35-4; Pvt D Co 24th TN Inf; 20 Jun 63 to 24 Jun 65; Gould PO (dupl)
WILEY, Andrew P., Cf-35-5(1); Pvt R Co 24th TN Inf; 20 Jun 63 to 24 Jun 65; PO omitted
WILEY, Ben, Mu-190-2; alias Ben Abernathy; Pvt D Co 110th Col Inf; 62 to 65; Culleoka PO; this man has lost discharge papers & does not recollect date of enlistment or discharge
WILEY, Caleb T., P-150-2; US Sol; 1st Dist
WILEY, Edwin A., Cu-16-1; Pvt US Gunboat Osceola; 1-64 to 12-64; Crossville PO; paralysis
WILEY, Edwin H., K-169-2; Capt 5th TN Inf; 25 Feb 62 to 13 Apr 65; Knoxville PO
WILEY, Green, Sh-157-6; Insely's Farm PO
WILEY, Green, Sh-157-1; Pvt 61st; White H Township PO
WILEY, John E., Mu-213-1; Mary J. widow of; Lt; ___ to 65; Glenns Store PO
WILEY, William, A-6-1; Pvt F Co 5th TN Inf; 2-62 to 4-5-65; Oliver PO
WILEY, William, Co-61-6(2); Pvt K Co 8th TN Inf; Bridgeport PO
WILHITE, J. W., La-110-1(2); Pvt Transporting Dept; 9-64 to 6-65; Appleton PO
WILHITE, William H., Wh-187-1; Sarah widow of; Orderly Sgt B Co 1st TN Inf; 2-26-64 to 4-14-65; Cherry Creek PO; contracted cold, reenlisted veteran
WILHOIT, Isaac, Ge-84-3; Pvt E Co 8th TN Cav; 13 Oct 63 to 11 Sep 65; Bird Bridge PO; mo. diar. given(?)
WILHOIT, J. S. Z., Ge-83-1; Cpl L Co 13th TN Cav; Sep 63 to 5 Sep 65; Henshaw PO; trouble of lung, measles
WILHOIT, Jery, Ge-83-2; Elizabeth widow of; Pvt E Co 4th TN Inf; ___ to Jun 65; Henshaw PO
WILHOIT, Lous, Ge-83-1; Pvt F Co 4th TN Inf; Apr 63 to 1 Aug 65; Hanshaw PO; paralysis
WILHOIT, Thomas J., D-45-4; Pvt B Co 1st TN Cav; Nashville PO; shot three times--breast, side and leg
WILKERSON, Andrew J., Gu-48-2; Pvt B Co 6th TN Inf; 1-64 to 5-65; Tracy City PO; no discharge record
WILKERSON, Argails A., Cy-27-2; Mary widow of; Pvt; Clementsville PO
WILKERSON, Austin, Gi-125-1; Martha widow of; Pvt G Co 110th US Col Inf; 23 Dec 63 to died 4 Jan 64; Weakly PO
WILKERSON, Ceasar, Sh-188-2; US Col; 242 Saffron St., Memphis PO
WILKERSON, Dock, Sm-174-1; Pvt G Co 4th TN Inf; 11-1-64 to 8-25-65; New Middleton PO
WILKERSON, Doctor, Gi-135-1; Mary J. Carpenter formerly widow of; Pvt D Co 110th TN Inf; 63 to 65; Lynnville PO
WILKERSON, Hall S., Un-254-2; Sarah J. widow of; Pvt A Co 2nd TN Inf; Paulett PO
WILKERSON, John, A-1-1; Pvt J Co 8th TN Cav; 10-20-63 to 9-11-65; Andersonville PO
WILKERSON, John B., Gi-125-2; Cpl C Co; Bodenham PO; could not get command
WILKERSON, Joseph, D-57-4; Pvt A Co 1st AL Cav; 61 to 63; Nashville PO
WILKERSON, Richard L., G-71-3; Pvt A Co 5th TN Inf; 15 Jan 62 to 15 Jun 63; PO omitted; CONF
WILKERSON, Richard T., Ge-86-2; Pvt C Co (8th TN Inf?); 1 Jan 63 to 30 Jun 65; Thula PO; rheumatism & diarrhera
WILKERSON, Richard T., La-109-1; Pvt H Co 11th OH Inf--6-1-61 & 2-13-64; Pvt C Co 31st OH Inf --2-13-64 to 7-12-65; Loretto PO; bad sore leg scurvy, reenlisted vet, 6 lb cannon ball scalped shoulder, captured, parrolled
WILKERSON, Robert E., A-3-3; Pvt H Co 1st TN Inf; 8-12-61 to 9-16-64; Bud PO; blindness
WILKERSON, Samuel, D-50-2; Nettie widow of; Pvt; Nashville PO
WILKERSON, William D., Sh-159-5; Com TN; Memphis PO
WILKERSON, William N., J-80-2; Pvt I Co 5th KY Cav; 10-1-61 to 5-3-65; Granville PO; gun shot wound in right lung & fistula innano?
WILKERSON, William W., Su-234-1; 2nd Lt D Co 13th TN Cav; 16 Nov 63 to 16 Mar 65; Blountville PO

341

WILKERSON, Willis, La-113-3; Pvt A Co 14th TN Inf; Nov 62 to 30 Mar 65; Ethridge PO; discharge lost
WILKES, G. W., Cr-19-1; Margaret A. widow of; Pvt F Co 7th TN Cav; 8-5-62 to 10-26-63; Huntingdon PO
WILKEY, Calvin V., Ro-201-4(2); Sgt B Co 6th TN Inf; 25 Feb 62 to 30 Mar 65; Kingston PO
WILKEY, Cam, R-162-2; Pvt; Dayton PO
WILKEY, Richard, R-162-3; Pvt F Co 1st TN Inf; Dayton PO
WILKIE, Emory O., Sh-201-3; Pvt G Co 2nd IL Lt Art; 15 Aug 61 to 4 Sep 65; Memphis PO
WILKINS, Frank (Black), K-164-2; Ann widow of; US Sol; Knoxville? PO
WILKINS, William, Sh-190-1; Pvt K Co 61st Inf; to 66 (3 yrs); Goerfield Alley, Memphis PO; piles
WILKINSON, Arnell, Wy-173-5(1); Manda Anderson widow of; Pvt 10th TN Inf; Houston PO
WILKINSON, George M., Gi-138-1; Sgt I Co 2nd TN; 10-1-63 to 10-1-64; Bodinham PO
WILKINSON, James, K-168-2; Mary M. widow of; Pvt D Co 65th IN; Adair's Creek PO
WILKISON, W. W., D-79-1; Pvt H Co 2nd IN Cav; about Sep 61 to Oct 2, 64; 329 N. Cherry, Nashville PO
WILKS, Ashley, Sn-250-1; Sarah widow of; Pvt C Co 2nd __; 10-16-62 to __(7 mos); Castalian Springs PO; CONF
WILKS, Dr. John L., Sn-250-2; Pvt K Co 2nd __; 5-3-61 to 63; Castalian Springs PO
WILLARD, Jesse, Br-12-5; Cpl G Co 3rd TN Cav; 8-14-63 to 6-10-65; Georgetown PO; neuralgia of had(sic), now blind
WILLARD, William A., H-52-2; Mary E. widow of; Drummer K Co 19th MI Inf; 8-3-62 to 5-63; Lookout Mt. PO
WILLBANKS, Barnett, O-135-1; Pvt I Co 12th KY Cav; Aug 61 to __; PO omitted
WILLBERN, John H., Bo-15-3; Pvt F Co 2nd TN Cav; 1-1-63 to 7-6-65; Maryville PO
WILLBERN, Nanca V. (see Simerley, John)
WILLDER, Horace M., Wa-268-4; Pvt I Co 17th IN Mtd Inf; 20 Oct 63 to 8 Aug 65; Johnson City PO; dierrhea
WILLEFORD, Charles H., Gi-130-1; Pvt C Co 12th TN Cav; 19 Jul 64 to 7 Oct 65; Bradshaw PO; right shoulder broke, now disabled from manual labor
WILLET, Ambros, Co-69-2; Pvt I Co 62nd TN Inf; 20 Aug 62 to 20 Apr 65; Newport PO; CONF
WILLET, John W., Pu-143-1; Jeremiah PO
WILLETT, Jacob, Ge-90-1; Sgt K Co 13th TN Cav; 62 to 65; Greeneville PO; rupture
WILLEY, Thomas W., He-60-2; Pvt K Co 7th TN Reg; Aug 63 to about Aug 65; Lexington PO; caused bad health by being exposed
WILLHELEMS, James, Un-255-2; Pvt G Co 7th TN Inf; 8 Nov 64 to 21 Ju 65; Lays X Roads PO
WILLHELMANS, Jack R., Be-5-1; Marthey J. widow of; Pvt; Camden PO; died after war, widow draws pension
WILLHITE, David, C-28-2(1); Emily S. widow of; Pvt G Co 7th TN Mtd Inf; 11-8-64 to 7-27-65; Big Creek Gap PO
WILLHITE, James, Hu-103-1; Pvt E Co Inf; 63 to 65; PO omitted
WILLHITE, James H., Wh-180-1; Pvt K Co 4th TN Inf; 2-1-64 to 8-26-65; Sparta PO; unable to give any information
WILLHITE, John W., S-216-2; Sol; 6th Dist
WILLHITE, William M., H-75-1; Chattanooga PO
WILLHOIT, Adam J., Ge-84-3; Pvt M Co 1st TN Cav; 10 Nov 61 to __; Bird Bridge PO; has not bin must(ered?)
WILLHOIT, John, H-50-3(1); Sgt E Co 8th R TN Cav; 10-10-63 to 10-6-66; Soddy PO
WILLHOIT, Samuel L., Ge-84-3; Pvt D Co 12th TN Cav; 16 Sep 63 to 11 Sep 65; Bird Bridge PO; dis. wound and rheumatis
WILLHOUR, Joshua, D-77-1; Nancy Bunting widow of; Pvt 16th US Col Inf; Nashville PO
WILLIAM, Allen, Co-65-1; Sgt K Co 8th TN Cav; Jun 11, 63 to Sep 11, 65; Edwina PO; piles, rheumatism & hart diseas, not pensioned
WILLIAM, Dennis (see Cannon, Dennis)

WILLIAM, Ellen, Sh-183-2; widow of James William; Memphis PO; papers lost
WILLIAM, Fredrick, Cr-14-2; Pvt B Co 11th NY Cav; 29 Dec 63 to 30 Sep 65; Clarksburg PO
WILLIAM, Goodly D., Ro-201-1; Pvt K Co 5th TN Inf; 18 Oct 62 to 30 Jun 65; Kingston PO
WILLIAM, Hammock, Un-257-2; Cpl D Co 1st TN Inf; 9 Aug 61 to 17 Sep 64; New Prospect PO; hydergeal (sic)
WILLIAM, Hardy W., Pi-156-3; Capt David Beaty's Independent Scouts; Mt. Pisgah PO, Wayne Co KY
WILLIAM, Henry, Hr-87-1; or Mason, Ideman; Pvt; PO omitted
WILLIAM, Jesse, Hu-99-1; Pvt F Co 38th Col US Inf; 3 Mar 62 to 3 Mar 66; Johnsonville PO; name was Wray
WILLIAM, Robbert, Ge-91-4; Pvt E Co 3rd TN Inf; Greeneville PO
WILLIAM, Thomas J., Gi-138-1; Cpl I Co 2nd TN; 4-15-64 to 4-15-65; Fullrin PO
WILLIAM, Winkel, Hw-121-6(1); Pvt M Co 10th KY Cav; 1 Dec 62 to 25 Mar 63; New Hope PO; catarrh, hearing
WILLIAM, ____; Sh-153-3; Julia widow of; Collierville PO
WILLIAMS, A. A., Wl-308-1; Pvt G Co 4th TN; Mar 1 62 to Oct 1 62; Rural Hill PO; CONF
WILLIAMS, Abel P., Wl-302-1; Pvt H Co 4th TN Mtd Inf; 17 Jan 65 to 25 Aug 65; Hendersons X Roads PO
WILLIAMS, Adolph, Su-243-1; Sgt A Co 6th IL Inf; 61 to 64; Bristol PO; shot through leg
WILLIAMS, Albert, H-73-3; Pvt I Co 10th Cav; Chattanooga PO
WILLIAMS, Alexander, Ct-40-3; Pvt A Co 13th TN Cav; 9-22-63 to 9-5-65; Elizabethton PO
WILLIAMS, Alexander C., Mn-121-4; Pvt A Co 1st AL Cav; 1-1-64 to 10-20-65; Rose Creek PO
WILLIAMS, Alexander M., Lo-189-3(1); Pvt H Co 3rd TN Inf; 20 Apr 61 to 20 Dec 62; Philadelphia PO; discharged on surg. certificate; CONF
WILLIAMS, Alfred, K-179-2; Pvt D Co 3rd TN Inf; 10 Feb 62 to 2 Aug 65; Virtue PO; transferred to 4th TN Inf
WILLIAMS, Alonzo S., Sh-158-1; Pvt B Co 2nd IL Lt Art; Dec 63 to Aug 65; Memphis PO; hearing of left ear injured at bat. Guntown, MS, now disabled by consumption
WILLIAMS, Allen (see Anderson, Allen)
WILLIAMS, Andrew, Sh-173-1; Pvt D Co 3rd Hvy Art; 1-63 to 11-64; Memphis PO
WILLIAMS, Archie, F-37-1; Nancy Dickinson formerly widow of; Pvt D Co 58th US Inf; Somerville PO; died of smallpox at Bayou Fasha, New Orleans LA
WILLIAMS, Asbury T., A-2-1; Cpl H Co 1st TN Inf; 8-9-61 to 9-17-64; Hynds Creek PO; rheumatism, shoulder hurt by horse falling on him
WILLIAMS, Authur A., Ct-42-1; Pvt A Co 13th TN Cav; 9-2-63 to 9-5-65; Watauga PO
WILLIAMS, Ben (see Strong, Isral)
WILLIAMS, Benjaman, D-97-1; Pvt B Co 2nd KY Cav; Jul 1, 61 to 63; Nashville PO; CONF
WILLIAMS, Benjaman, Sh-188-1; Pvt G Co 42nd US Inf; 7-13-64 to 1-31-66; rear 104 ____, Memphis PO
WILLIAMS, Benjamin, Ca-22-1; Pvt G Co 5th TN Cav; 9-6-62 to 8-14-65; Hollow Springs PO; in Libby prison 5 mos
WILLIAMS, Billie, Hr-86-1; Pvt H Co 10th TN; 62 to 64; Grand Junction PO; shot in head & leg, was in hospital at Nashville
WILLIAMS, Borden W., Sq-164-1; Pvt H Co 6th TN Cav; 63 to __; Fillmore PO
WILLIAMS, Calaway, Ha-114-3; Cpl K Co 13th KY Cav; 9 Dec 62 to 14 Feb 63; Sneedville PO
WILLIAMS, Callisine, Cl-46-2; Soldier's widow; PO omitted
WILLIAMS, Chas., Gr-70-1; Pvt D Co 1st TN Inf; 61 to 64; Rutledge PO
WILLIAMS, Charles, Sh-144-2; Pvt B Co 55th Col Inf; May 18, 63 to Dec 31, 65; Arlington PO
WILLIAMS, Charles, Wi-273-1; Pvt 110th TN Inf; Spring Hill, Maury Co. PO; could give no further information
WILLIAMS, Charles, Sh-196-2; Charles Hayes alias; Cpl H Co 110th AL Inf; 12-63 to 1-65; 139 Jeff St., Memphis PO

WILLIAMS, Charley, Mn-122-2; Pvt C Co 17th Col Inf; 4-16-64 to 4-25-66; McNairy PO
WILLIAMS, Charlotte (see Rowlet, Daniel)
WILLIAMS, Chriley, G-64-2; Clany widow of; Bradford PO; CONF
WILLIAMS, Curinton J., Rb-228-1; 62 to __ (4 yrs 8 mos); Ridge Port PO
WILLIAMS, Danel, Ru-241-2(1); Pvt A Co 19th IL Inf; 63 to 64; Murfreesboro PO
WILLIAMS, David, Br-14-3; Marine Sabogra; 1-10-64 to 9-10-65; Black Fox PO
WILLIAMS, David, Ca-22-1; Mary E. widow of; Pvt G Co 5th TN Cav; 9-6-62 to 8-14-65; Hollow Springs PO
WILLIAMS, David, A-6-1; Pvt F Co 5th TN Inf; 3-10-62 to 10-17-64; Olivers PO; shot in the neck
WILLIAMS, David, Hd-49-2; Pvt A Co 2nd TN Mtd Inf; Oct 2 63 to Oct 14 64; Stouts PO; rheumatism
WILLIAMS, David, Ch-18-1; Pvt; PO omitted; CONF
WILLIAMS, David, T-216-1; Pvt K Co 3rd Hvy Art; 28 Aug 64 to 12 Apr 66; Corona PO
WILLIAMS, David R., Sh-186-1; Airbell widow of; 1st Sgt 4th Vet Res; 8-25-61 to 9-6-64; Memphis PO
WILLIAMS, David W., Cl-46-3(1); Pvt E Co 6th TN Inf; 3-2-62 to 4-27-65; Ibex PO; wounded, draws pension
WILLIAMS, David W., Sq-164-1; Caroline widow of; 1st Lt D Co 6th TN Cav; Fillmore PO
WILLIAMS, Dorn, Sh-157-6; Sallie widow of; PO omitted
WILLIAMS, Drury M., He-64-2; Musician G Co 17th AL Reg; Aug 61 to 65; Reagin PO; CONF
WILLIAMS, Edmon J., Hm-57-1; M. E. widow of; Pvt G Co 7th TN Inf; 3-10-61 to 5-1-63; Law PO
WILLIAMS, Edward, Hr-87-1; Pvt A Co 3rd TN Hvy Art; 9-63 to 8-65; Hickory Valley PO; discharge special order
WILLIAMS, Elisha K., Ge-99-2; Pvt E Co 3rd NC Inf; Jan 64 to Mar 65; Woolsey College PO; couldnt get dates
WILLIAMS, Ely, Co-68-3; Pvt E Co 1st TN Bat; 63 to 65; Cashy PO; measles
WILLIAMS, Esrick?, H-72-2(1); Pvt; Chattanooga PO
WILLIAMS, Eward, Wl-300-2; Pvt 10th __; Apr 63 to 14 Aug 65; Cherry Valley PO; back hurt, went insane
WILLIAMS, Ezekiel, Hm-106-1; Cpl C Co 4th TN Cav; 29 Nov 62 to 12 Jun 65; Morristown PO; discharge lost & dates unknown
WILLIAMS, Ezekiel H., Je-136-2; Pvt E Co 8th TN Inf; PO omitted
WILLIAMS, Frances, D-86-1; widow; Brentwood PO
WILLIAMS, Frank, D-45-4; Pvt I Co 69th OH Inf; 63 to __; Nashville PO
WILLIAMS, Fred (see Aldworth, Fred)
WILLIAMS, George, H-57-1; Pvt B Co 104th OH Inf; 62 to 65 (2 yrs 8 mos); Orchard Knob PO
WILLIAMS, George, D-87-2; Pvt Artillery; Sep 14 63 to __ (3 yrs); Nashville PO; taken the rheumatism in the army, died from rheumatism
WILLIAMS, George, Hy-83-1; Brownsville PO
WILLIAMS, George, Sh-191-5(1); Memphis PO; records not seen
WILLIAMS, George L., O-140-1; Pvt, Cpl & Sgt D Co 52nd IL Inf; 10 Sep 61 to 12 Jul 65; Union City PO; rheumatism, suffers much with rheum. & lungs
WILLIAMS, George P., Sn-262-3(2); Pvt 3rd MI Cav; 18 Dec 63 to Jan 65; Fountain Head PO; diarrhea, malarial poison, information rec'd from brother
WILLIAMS, George W., Lo-188-3; Pvt; Sweetwater PO
WILLIAMS, George W., Sm-175-1; Pvt G Co 4th TN Inf; 11-64 to 8-65; Rome PO; loung trouble
WILLIAMS, George W., Cr-17-1; Pvt A Co 7th TN Cav; 8-25-62 to 8-9-65; Buena Vista PO
WILLIAMS, George W., Un-257-1; Pvt; New Prospect PO
WILLIAMS, George W., Se-230-2; Pvt E Co 1st TN Art; Pokeberry PO; rheum., neuralgia, heart trouble & piles &c &c
WILLIAMS, George W., Wl-307-1; Samatha J. widow of; Pvt H Co 4th __; 1 Oct 64 to 25 Aug 65; Leeville PO
WILLIAMS, Green, Sh-191-2; Sgt 88th Col Inf; 64 to 65; Memphis PO
WILLIAMS, Gustavus A., We-221-3; 2nd Lt A Co 11th TN Cav; Sep 62 to May 13 65; Martin PO; imprisoned 6 mos; CONF
WILLIAMS, Hardin, Mu-194-1; Musician G Co 14th US Inf; 11-1-63 to 3-26-66; Columbia PO
WILLIAMS, Harrison G., H-57-4; US Sol; 10th Civil Dist
WILLIAMS, Harvey, Sh-195-1; Amanda Win formerly widow of; Pvt; Memphis PO
WILLIAMS, Henderson, D-89-1; Nashville PO; papers in hand claim agent
WILLIAMS, Henry, H-62-4; 108 Third, Chattanooga PO
WILLIAMS, Henry, Sh-157-8; Pvt; 3 yrs; Ensley PO
WILLIAMS, Henry, D-91-3; Pvt; Nashville PO
WILLIAMS, HEnry, L-108-2; Pvt K Co MD; 17 Jun __ to 11 May __ (2 yrs 6 mos); McIntyre PO
WILLIAMS, Henry, Sh-174-3; Pvt D Co 59th US Inf; about 12-1-62 to 5-31-66; rear 150 Hernando St, Memphis PO; first joint of forefinger of left hand shot off, shot in left breast, captured at Tupelo, MS, and reported dead, recaptured 6 mos later and returned to company
WILLIAMS, Henry F., D-44-3; Permelia J. Johnson formerly widow of; KY Inf; Nashville PO; Capt. M. C. Nolan's company
WILLIAMS, Hezekah, Hm-103-2; Sgt C Co 4th TN Cav; 8 Feb 63 to 12 Jul 65; Morristown PO; chronic bronchitis
WILLIAMS, Houston, Mo-129-1; Pvt I Co 1st TN Inf; 63 to 64; Loco PO
WILLIAMS, Houston L., Hm-107-3; Pvt C Co 4th TN Cav; 1 Dec 62 to 12 Jul 65; Witts Foundry PO
WILLIAMS, Isaac J., H-68-1; Ensign; __ to 6-12-65; Chattanooga PO
WILLIAMS, Isaac N., Wa-276-1; Pvt B Co 4th TN Inf; 24 Nov 62 to Aug 2 65; Mill Brook PO
WILLIAMS, J. N., Gi-133-1; Pvt F Co 28th AL; 61 to 61 (6 mos); Buford PO; CONF
WILLIAMS, Jackson, Sh-191-1; Memphis PO; records not seen
WILLIAMS, Jacob, Lo-194-1; Pvt D Co 3rd TN Inf; 10 Feb 62 to 2 Aug 65; Muddy Creek PO
WILLIAMS, James, H-56-1; Pvt M Co 4th TN Cav; 63 to 65; St. Elmo PO
WILLIAMS, James, Co-63-2; Pvt E Co 2nd NC Mtd Inf; 64 to 16 Aug 65 (1 yr); Newport PO; feet frost bitten & rheumatism
WILLIAMS, James, Su-242-1; Martha Feathers formerly widow of; Pvt; 62 to __; Bluff City PO; died of wound in rebel prison at Vicksburg, MS, arm and side, the woman cannot give co or regt nor anything definite
WILLIAMS, James, Se-219-2; Pvt A Co 9th TN Cav; 16 Oct 63 to 11 Sep 65; Costner PO
WILLIAMS, James, Se-219-4; Sol US; 1st Dist
WILLIAMS, James, Ce-28-1; Eliza widow of; Pvt H Co 1st TN Inf; widow's PO, Junkston; discharge papers at pension office
WILLIAMS, James, T-209-2; Sol; Randolph PO
WILLIAMS, James H., Dk-34-5(4); Amanda P. widow of; 2nd Lt E Co 4th TN Inf; 12-9-64 to __; Close PO; hurt by horse falling on him
WILLIAMS, James M., Hw-128-2; Adeline widow of; Cpl H Co 8th TN Inf; 25 Jul 63 to 30 Jun 65; Choptack PO; shot in right hip
WILLIAMS, James N., Hm-108-3(2); Sgt B Co 4th VA Inf; 14 Apr 61 to 28 Mar 65; Russellville PO; CONF
WILLIAMS, James R., H-68-2; Pvt F Co 8th Reg __ Res Corps; 8-31-62 to 11-16-65; Chattanooga PO
WILLIAMS, James W., Lo-194-1; Pvt D Co 3rd TN Inf; 10 Feb 62 to 2 Aug 65; Muddy Creek PO
WILLIAMS, Janee (see Snowden, Charles)
WILLIAMS, Jennie (see Folwell, Frank)
WILLIAMS, Jerry, Fr-120-1; Pvt H Co 59th Col Inf; May 63 to Apr 65; Sewanee PO
WILLIAMS, Joel H., Lo-194-2; Lt 13th TN Cav; Oct 63 to 13 Jan 65; Muddy Creek PO
WILLIAMS, John, H-71-1; Ella Page wife of; 62 to 65; Chattanooga PO
WILLIAMS, John, C-24-4(3); Pvt; Forkvale PO
WILLIAMS, John, W-189-2; Pvt H Co 126th OH Home Svce Inf; 5-65 to 9-65; McMinnville PO

WILLIAMS, John, D-72-1; Callie D. widow of; Sgt B Co 17th TN Inf; 63 to Feb 3 64; Nashville PO
WILLIAMS, John, D-73-2; Vernon St, Nashville PO
WILLIAMS, John, Sh-157-1; Dist 13
WILLIAMS, John (see Roesch, John W.)
WILLIAMS, John, F-38-2; US Sol; Civil Dist No 5
WILLIAMS, John, G-67-3; Pvt G Co 2nd TN Mtd Inf; 30 Nov 63 to 10 Feb 65; Idlewild PO
WILLIAMS, John, G-57-5(3); Pvt A Co 9th TN Cav; Jul 64 to 65; Yorkville PO; CONF
WILLIAMS, John, Sh-157-1; Cpl B Co 26th NY Inf; Jan 63 to Dec 65; Dist 13
WILLIAMS, John, Sh-162-2(1); Pvt C Co 8th KY Inf; 63 to 65; Ramsey PO
WILLIAMS, John, Rb-230-1; alias John Anderson; Pvt E Co 15th TN Inf; Nov 62 to Jan 65; Springfield PO
WILLIAMS, John, Ru-237-1; Pvt H Co 13th TN Inf; 29 Sep 63 to 10 Jan 66; Eagleville PO; hip fractured
WILLIAMS, John A., Ro-209-1; Pvt B Co 1st TN Inf; Jul 61 to 65; Glen Alice PO
WILLIAMS, John B., Ct-35-1; Cpl A Co 13th TN Cav; 9-24-63 to 9-5-65; Fish Spring PO; in US Army
WILLIAMS, John B., De-24-2; US Sol; crossed out with remark "on 4th page recorded by error"; 3rd Dist
WILLIAMS, John D., K-166-1; Pvt A Co 6th TN Inf; Knoxville PO; wounded in foot
WILLIAMS, John D., G-64-2; Sol; Bradford PO
WILLIAMS, John F., Ro-206-1; Pvt B Co 1st TN Inf; 9 Aug 63 to 9 Aug 65; Emory Gap PO
WILLIAMS, John F., Be-2-1; Pvt F & I Cos 7th TN; Sep 28 62 to 9 Aug 65; Holladay PO
WILLIAMS, John G., Mc-116-1; Pvt D Co 10th TN Cav; 1-1-64 to 8-1-65; Athens PO; injure of right leg
WILLIAMS, John L., Hm-106-3; Pvt B Co 1st SC Cav; 61 to 65; Morristown PO
WILLIAMS, John T., F-44-3; Pvt B Co 31st __; 61 to 65; PO omitted; CONF
WILLIAMS, John W., A-3-1; Pvt H Co 1st TN Inf; 8-13-61 to 9-8-64; Wilson PO; chills and fever, dierea
WILLIAMS, John W., Me-89-1; Sarah L. widow of; Sgt H Co 3rd TN Cav; 9-26-63 to 8-3-65; Big Spring PO
WILLIAMS, John W., Cr-4-2; Pvt B Co 44th TN Inf; 62 to 64; Bells Depot PO
WILLIAMS, John W., Ce-20-2; Pvt G Co 15th IN Inf; 6-13-61 to 7-25-64; Ashland City PO
WILLIAMS, Johnathan, Ru-236-1; Pvt A Co 9th TN Cav; Jul 63 to Aug 65; Murfreesboro PO; wounded in leg, he can not see good
WILLIAMS, Jordan, H-70-3(1); Jordan Lucas alias; Pvt E Co 1st US Col Hvy Art; 3-24-64 to 3-31-66; Chattanooga PO
WILLIAMS, Joseph, Mg-196-4; Col; Pvt; __ to 65; Memphis PO
WILLIAMS, Joseph, Dk-39-1; Pvt C Co 8th TN Mtd Inf; 1-1-65 to 8-17-65; Bozarth PO; chronic rheumatism
WILLIAMS, Joseph, D-77-3; Crooked St, Nashville PO
WILLIAMS, Joseph, Sh-147-2; Teamster A Co 1st IN Inf; 15 Apr 62 to 6 Apr 64; Cuba PO
WILLIAMS, Joseph, St-160-2; Millie A. widow of; Pvt; Big Rock PO
WILLIAMS, Joseph, Col, Ma-128-1; Cook & Private; Jackson PO; papers destroyed, could give no information
WILLIAMS, Joseph J. N. B., Mn-121-4; Pvt A Co 1st AL Cav; 1-1-64 to 10-20-65; Bethel Springs PO
WILLIAMS, Joseph P., K-154-6(3); Knoxville PO; crippled all over
WILLIAMS, Joseph R., Mo-126-1; Pvt G Co 6th TN Inf; 12-18-63 to 6-30-65; Hopewell Springs PO; sunstroke
WILLIAMS, Julia A. (see Brown, Jordan)
WILLIAMS, Julia M., K-154-2; Knoxville PO
WILLIAMS, Landon D., U-246-1; Pvt F Co 7th IN Cav; Limonite PO
WILLIAMS, Layton, Sm-168-1; Pvt Cav; 63 to 65; Kempville PO; kidney disease, broken down in health
WILLIAMS, Leghu, H-76-1; Chattanooga PO
WILLIAMS, Lewis, K-180-3; Pvt H Co 13th TN Cav; 1 Oct 63 to 5 Sep 65; Wilson PO (Anderson Co.); gun shot wound, blood poison
WILLIAMS, Loranza D., Ct-43-3; Pvt F Co 13th TN Cav; 9-22-63 to 9-5-65; Watauga PO; liver, dropsy, malsaral poison, 3 mos in Danville prison
WILLIAMS, Louis M., Dy-25-7(3); Capt K Co 22nd TN Inf; 2 Dec 61 to 5 Jul 62; Newbern PO; camp feavor; CONF
WILLIAMS, Marinda, Sh-197-2; Memphis PO
WILLIAMS, Marner, D-60-1; Mebry A. widow of; 202 Knowles St, Nashville PO; colored
WILLIAMS, Marth A., K-181-7(4); widow of Conf Sol; Knoxville PO; CONF
WILLIAMS, Mary A., K-186-3; 2nd Lt; Balls Camp PO
WILLIAMS, May, K-155-2(1); Knoxville PO
WILLIAMS, McKindry C., Ge-99-1; S M (staff sgt?) D Co 1st TN Cav; 15 Apr 62 to 15 Apr 65; Limestone Springs PO; disease of spine & lung
WILLIAMS, Miles W., O-139-1; Pvt B Co 31st IL; 10 Aug 61 to 19 Jul 65; Protemus PO
WILLIAMS, Miles W., O-139-1; no PO (this entry crossed out)
WILLIAMS, Milliam M., Mg-197-3; Mary D. widow of; Pvt B Co 2nd TN Inf; Crooked Fork PO
WILLIAMS, Mitchell, Sh-158-3; alias Michael Williams; Pvt M Co 3rd US Col'd Cav; 24 Feb 64 to 26 Jan 66; Memphis PO; rheumatism in right hip and thigh from exposure so that he walks with diffuculty with walking stick, and unable to ride, discharge papers in good order, this is a worthy man
WILLIAMS, Nathan H., A-3-2; Pvt H Co 7th? TN Inf; 8-13-61 to 7-64; Wilson PO; loss of teeth
WILLIAMS, Nathon, Col, Br-10-2; Pvt A Co 16th NC Inf; 62 to 65; Cleveland PO
WILLIAMS, Obediah, C-33-5; Pvt G Co 151st OH Inf; 61 to 65; Newcomb PO; spinal metigitis Jun 64; French Derussey DC
WILLIAMS, Oliver F., Dk-31-1; Pvt D Co 4th TN Mtd Inf; 9-23-64 to 8-25-65; Alexandria PO; nervous system suffering
WILLIAMS, P. A., Di-36-2; 1st Lt H Co 22nd AL Inf; 4-1-61 to 5-13-65; Bellsburgh PO
WILLIAMS, Perry, G-67-3; Pvt G Co 2nd TN Mtd Inf; 30 Nov 63 to 25 Feb 65; Idlewild PO; eyes damaged and diarrhea
WILLIAMS, Perry, K-185-2; Pvt D Co 3rd NC Inf; Sep 63 to __; Scaggston PO
WILLIAMS, Peter, Sh-153-1; Pvt A Co 67th TN Inf; 12 mos; Collierville PO
WILLIAMS, Philip, Hw-127-2; Pvt A Co 1st US Hvy Art; 22 Jan 64 to 31 Jan 66; Rogersville PO; rheumatism
WILLIAMS, Pleas, P-156-2; Pvt A Co 42nd TN Inf; 62 to 63 (7 mos); Lobelville PO; went home on above date without discharge
WILLIAMS, Pleasant, Ct-43-3; Capt A Co 13th TN Cav; 9-22-63 to 5-65; Watauga PO; chronic diarrhea & dropsy, died June 15, 1890
WILLIAMS, Pleasant C., Gr-81-4(2); Pvt A? Co 12th TN Cav; 24 Jun 63 to 28 Oct 65; Clear Spring PO; in sight totley blind
WILLIAMS, Pleasant M., Cf-39-3; Happy Valley PO
WILLIAMS, Pleasant M., Co-60-2; Sarah widow of; Pvt L Co 8th TN Cav; Parrottsville PO; chronic diarrhea
WILLIAMS, R. L., Cr-7-1; Officer Sgt E Co 13th TN Vol Cav; 2-4-64 to 7-26-65; Stokes PO (Dyer Co.); abscess of lung--internal piles
WILLIAMS, Rachel (see Furguson, James)
WILLIAMS, Rancellaer J., Mc-112-4; Pvt F Co 110th OH Inf; 10-1-61 to 5-5-62 & 12-20-63 to 6-25-65; Athens PO; derangement of the rectum
WILLIAMS, Richd., L-108-1; Pvt I Co 14th US; Nov 63 to Mar 65; PO omitted
WILLIAMS, Richard, Col, G-73-1; Pvt C Co 1st US Inf; Inf; Apr 10 63 to Apr 10 665; Trenton PO; shot in hip
WILLIAMS, Richard T., Sh-201-2; Pvt; Memphis PO
WILLIAMS, Robert, Hm-109-1; Catharine widow of; Pvt F Co 1st TN Art; 14 Jul 62 to __; Three Springs PO; died of smallpox 8 Mar 64
WILLIAMS, Robert, Sh-186-2; Pvt 109th KY; 6-63 to 3-66; Memphis PO
WILLIAMS, Robert, Se-219-2; Pvt E Co 2nd TN Cav; 19 Sep 62 to 5 Jul 65; Jones Cave PO; yellow janders & gravail

WILLIAMS, Robt., Sh-190-1; Gilfield Alley, Memphis PO; cripled in leg
WILLIAMS, Robert M., Ro-203-7; Pvt K Co 5th TN Inf; 18 Oct 62 to 30 Jun 65; Eatons X Roads PO; injury from mumps & jaundice
WILLIAMS, Robet H., Ca-22-2; Pvt G Co 5th TN Cav; 9-6-62 to 8-14-65; Hollow Springs PO; weakness of lungs
WILLIAMS, S. N., Cr-16-3; Pvt G Co 2nd TN Cav; Aug 6 62 to 25 Oct 63; Huntingdon PO
WILLIAMS, Sallie, Sn-250-1; Castalian Springs PO
WILLIAMS, Sam, Mt-136-1; Pvt E Co 15th TN Inf; 11-64 to 4-66; Port Royal PO; wound in little finger left hand
WILLIAMS, Sam, Sh-144-2; US Sol; First Dist
WILLIAMS, Samuel, Sh-152-3; Rebecca widow; Dexter PO
WILLIAMS, Samuel, Wi-287-1; Civ. Dist No 18
WILLIAMS, Samuel B., K-156-4; Chaplain 1st E TN Mtd Inf; 10 Apr 61 to 11 Apr 65; 50 Temperance St, Knoxville PO
WILLIAMS, Samuel D., Lk-112-2; Pvt I Co 1st IN? Art; 62 to 65; Redfoot PO; weak limbs from small pox and measles
WILLIAMS, Samuel M., Lo-195-1; Chaplin 1st TN Cav; Aug 61 to 64; Eaton's X Roads PO
WILLIAMS, Samuel W., Sq-164-1; Pvt D Co 5th TN Mtd Inf; 5-16-64 to 6-13-65; Fillmore PO
WILLIAMS, Sandy, Gi-125-2; Pvt; Bodenham PO; could not give command
WILLIAMS, Senel?, Dk-32-3; Carline widow of; Pvt G Co 1st TN Mtd Inf; 2-24-64 to 3-21-65; Temperance Hall PO; injured in left hip
WILLIAMS, Shadric, Cl-51-2; Pvt C Co 1st TN Inf; 9-4-61 to 2-4-63; Cedar Fork PO
WILLIAMS, Sherwood, Pu-144-2; Pvt 42nd OH; Double Springs PO
WILLIAMS, Sibus H., Cl-54-2; Sgt F Co 8th TN Cav; 4-28-63 to 9-11-65; Bacchus PO; rhieumatism & jeanoh?
WILLIAMS, Silvester, P-156-1; Pvt A Co 16th TN; 61 to 64; Lobelville PO; CONF
WILLIAMS, Solomon, Se-230-3; Richison's Cove PO
WILLIAMS, Solomon, Se-219-2; Pvt B Co 9th TN Cav; 11 Oct 63 to 11 Sep 65; Jones Cave PO
WILLIAMS, Solomon G., Cr-9-1; Cpl C Co 6th TN Cav; Jan 28 64 to Jul 26 65; Chestnutt Bluff PO; chronic diareah and piles
WILLIAMS, Squire L., Sn-262-2(1); Pvt; Fountain Head PO; could not find any papers
WILLIAMS, Stephen, O-136-1; Pvt G Co 1st TN Cav; Mar 1 63 to Oct 1 65; Gardner Sta? PO
WILLIAMS, Susan (see Norment, N.)
WILLIAMS, Thomas, Sh-146-4; US Sol; 3rd Civ Dist
WILLIAMS, Thomas, Sh-172-2; 403 Second St, Memphis PO
WILLIAMS, Thomas B., Ru-235-1; Smyrna PO
WILLIAMS, Thomas M., K-184-2; Pvt B Co 4th TN Cav; 8 Sep 62 to 12 Jun 65; Riverdale PO; rupture of the bowls
WILLIAMS, Tolton F., G-54-1; Pvt; Eaton PO
WILLIAMS, Wash, F-40-3; Pvt C Co 61st TN Inf; Jun 63 to Sep 65; Hickory Withe PO
WILLIAMS, Wiley, G-53-1(4); Pvt A Co 22nd IL Inf; 10-10-63 to ___ (6 mos); Brazil PO
WILLIAMS, Willaby, Sh-147-2; Pvt C Co 3rd TN Inf; 20 Jul 62 to 5 Apr 65; Cuba PO
WILLIAMS, William, K-181-4(1); 5th Sgt C Co 6th TN Inf; 18 Apr 62 to 27 Apr 65; Knoxville PO
WILLIAMS, William, Lo-190-1; Sarah widow of; Pvt G Co 24th OH Inf; Piney PO
WILLIAMS, William, Hw-121-3(2); Pvt C Co 1st TN Art; 7 Sep 63 to 1 Aug 65; Segonsville PO; bronchitus, rheumatism 27 yrs
WILLIAMS, William, Co-66-2(1); Pvt A Co 9th TN Cav; 10 Oct 63 to 11 Sep 65; Bison PO
WILLIAMS, William, Ge-84-2; Sgt B Co 42nd VA Inf; 24 Ma 63 to 21 Ma 65; Greenville PO; dis. diarriare, piles, rhumatis
WILLIAMS, William, Ge-96-2; Sarah A. widow of; Chef 8th TN Cav; 24 Sep 64 to 65 (1 yr 8 mos 5 days); Hascue PO; cant assertain dates
WILLIAMS, William, Ct-42-2; Pvt D Co 13th TN Cav; Watauga PO; shot four times
WILLIAMS, William, Sm-176-1; Pvt C Co TN Inf; 4-30-64 to 4-7-65; Rome PO
WILLIAMS, William, Sh-149-2; Pvt F Co 14th Col Inf; 64 to 66; Raleigh PO
WILLIAMS, William B., We-224-3(1); Pvt I and B? Co's 7th TN Inf; Aug 62 to 22 Nov 63; Como PO (Henry Co.); times of service out, came home without no discharge
WILLIAMS, William E., R-158-1; Dorcas PO; away from home--no information
WILLIAMS, Wm. H., Sh-161-2; US Sol; 16th Dist
WILLIAMS, William H., D-75-1; 2nd Sgt H Co 38th TN Inf; 25 Oct 61 to 15 Oct 64; Stewarts Ferry PO; CONF
WILLIAMS, William H., Mg-197-3; Pvt K Co 13th TN Cav; 30 Jul 64 to 5 Sep 65; 2nd Dist
WILLIAMS, William L., La-117-2; Pvt K Co 1st MO Inf; Jan 27 61 to ___ (4 yrs); 15th Dist, shot through nose; CONF
WILLIAMS, William M., Ct-39-3; Pvt A Co 13th Cav; Gap Run PO; liver disease rupture right side
WILLIAMS, Williams, Se-219-2; Pvt E Co 1st TN Lt Art; 17 Sep 63 to 1 Aug 65; Costner PO; diarhoea & rumatism & piles
WILLIAMS, Willy, Gr-71-2; 1st Lt C Co 4th TN Cav; 17 Nov 62 to 1 Apr 65; Jarmine PO; gunshot wound in right thigh, transfer from C to G, same rgt.
WILLIAMS, Wiloughoby, Sh-145-3; Pvt C Co 3rd US Col Hvy Art; Aug 63 to Jan 64; Millington PO
WILLIAMS, Zackery, Ru-231-1; Pvt A Co 12th TN Cav; Oct 63 to 15 Feb 64; May Ella PO
WILLIAMS, ___, Me-92-1; Charity Jones formerly widow of; Hesters Mills PO; no satisfactory answers
WILLIAMSON, Charles, C-24-2; Pvt C Co 49th KY Cav; 7-63 to 12-26-64; Girlton PO
WILLIAMSON, Emma (see Soiler?, Monroe)
WILLIAMSON, Geo. W., Hd-53-2; Pvt H Co 7th TN Cav; Aug 62 to 27 Jun 65; Sibley PO; in back, in Andersonville Pris. 13 mos
WILLIAMSON, Ike, G-58-1; Pvt C Co IL Inf; 10 Mar 61 to 10 May 64; Rutherford
WILLIAMSON, James, D-77-3; Nashville PO, Foster St.
WILLIAMSON, James, Bo-11-1; M. E. widow of; Pvt G Co 8th TN Cav; 63 to 65; Cloids Creek PO; heart disease
WILLIAMSON, James K., D-57-1; Pvt C Co 1st TN Inf; Apr 27, 61 to Nov 29, 65; PO omitted (but 8th Ward, Nashville)
WILLIAMSON, James P., Se-220-2; Pvt E Co 1st TN Art; 19 Sep 63 to 1 Aug 65; Emerts Cave PO; prisner at Danville 4 mos
WILLIAMSON, Joseph, Gi-127-4; Pvt 111th IL Mtd Inf; about 4-64 to 64; Pulaski PO
WILLIAMSON, Joseph, Co-68-3; Pvt E Co 1st TN Bat; 62 to 65; Sutton PO; run over by wagon
WILLIAMSON, Kindrick, Bo-11-2; Leidy A. widow of; Pvt; canot give dates very liable; Houk PO
WILLIAMSON, Milton T., Sh-148-2; Memphis PO
WILLIAMSON, Peter J., D-61-2; Adj Genl 1st Cav WI; 62 to 66; Ament St., Nashville PO; shot in leg, badly disabled now
WILLIAMSON, Samuel S., Gi-122-7; Pvt TN Cav; 62 to 65; Prospect Sta. PO; CONF
WILLIENS, Calvin, C-33-2; Pvt B Co 1st Inf; 61 to 64; Jellico PO
WILLIFORD, Fielden L., Lo-187-2; Pvt A Co 9th TN Cav; 9 Jan 64 to 11 Sep 65; Loudon PO; rheumatism
WILLIFORD, Jacob, Je-138-1; Pvt K Co 9th TN Cav; 24 Oct 63 to 11 Sep 65; Oak Grove PO; shot in arm and hip
WILLIFORD, James W., Lo-187-4; Pvt F Co 13th TN Cav; 26 Sep 63 to 8 Sep 65; Loudon PO
WILLIFORD, Simean, Hm-109-3; Pvt K Co 9th TN Cav; 62? to 65; Russelville PO
WILLIM, W. J., Sh-158-6(4); Drummer B Co 63rd US Inf; Apr 65 to 9 Jan 66; Memphis PO; discharged at close of war with discharge papers
WILLIN, Thomas, Jo-150-5; Pvt E Co 13th TN Cav; 22 Sep 63 to 5 Sep 65; Osborn PO; white swelling
WILLINGHAM, Robert B., Hy-83-1; Pvt US Col Co; 63 to 64; Brownsville PO; lost discharge
WILLINGHAM, William A., H-61-4; Pvt 3rd SC Cav; Spring 62 to Fall 62 (6 mos); Chattanooga PO CONF
WILLIS, David, Ha-117-3; Pvt G Co 1st TN Cav; 15 Apr 62 to 14 Apr 65; Kyle*s Ford PO; rheumatism & heart disease

WILLIS, David E., U-248-1; Pvt M Co 8th TN Cav; 16 Sep 63 to 10 Jul 65; Clear Branch PO
WILLIS, David V., Dy-25-4; Pvt 5th TN Inf; 61 to 64; Newbern PO; CONF
WILLIS, F. M., Mc-114-1; Harriet widow of; Pvt H Co 5th KY Inf; 3-2-62 to 5-16-65; Folger PO; wounded in his side, caused by falling from train
WILLIS, George W., K-171-4(3); Pvt 1st Hvy Art Col; PO omitted
WILLIS, Henry, Sn-252-3; Gallatin PO
WILLIS, John A., U-249-2; Pvt H Co 5th NC Mtd Inf; 1 Oct 64 to 8 Aug 65; Flag Pond PO; lost right testicle, cause mumps
WILLIS, Jno. M., La-117-2; Pvt I Co 9th AL Inf; May 2, 61 to __(2 yrs 3 mos); 15th Dist, in prison 9 mos; CONF
WILLIS, John R., Sn-261-1; Pvt A Co 9th KY Inf; 9-25-61 to 12-15-64; Pondville PO; camp fever fell in right hip & leg, came home on discharge 12-15-64 (duplicate on Sn-261-3(2)
WILLIS, Leonard, Ha-111-3; Pvt G Co 1st TN Cav; 15 Apr 62 to Feb 65; PO omitted
WILLIS, Mathew, Ha-114-2; Pvt; can not get further information; Xerxes PO
WILLIS, Mc., R-158-1; Pvt G Co 44th TN Inf; 6-15-64 to __(about 11 mos)
WILLIS, Morgan, D-77-2; Pvt A Co 11th US Inf; 63 to May 66; Nashville PO; rheumatism
WILLIS, Richmond, O-142-1; Pvt H Co 1st IA Col Inf; 10 Sep 63 to Apr 65; Obion PO; neuralgia, blind in left eye & soon will be in right eye, should have a pension, changed to Pvt H Co 60th Col Inf, discharge lost
WILLIS, Solomon, Sh-179-1(2); Pvt; Memphis PO
WILLIS, Thomas, Ha-111-3; Pvt G Co 1st TN Cav; 15 Apr 62 to 14 Apr 65; PO omitted
WILLIS, Wilson W., Hw-119-1; Maj 8th TN Cav; Aug 63 to Jun 64; Lee Valley PO; bronchitis
WILLMOTH, Rufus Y.?, Ov-133-2(1); Cpl H Co 1st TN Inf; 2-7-64 to 5-23-65; Oak Hill PO; disabled by exposures
WILLOBY, Arbama (see Buttram, Joel)
WILLOUGHBEY, John, C-24-1; Pvt B Co 1st Inf; 8-1-61 to 10-1-64; Boy PO; affected of measels & fever
WILLOUGHBY, James B., A-4-2; Pvt B Co 1st TN Inf; 7-1-63 to 8-3-65; Coal Creek PO; chronic rheumatism
WILLOUGHBY, James L., K-181-6(3); 1st Sgt K Co 13th KY Cav; Sep 63 to 10 Jan 65; Knoxville PO
WILLOUGHBY, John W. C., Wa-262-1; Cpl K Co 13th KY Cav; 25 Nov 63 to 20 Jan 65; Washington College PO; liver disease
WILLOUGHBY, William, Ge-88-1; Candacy J. widow of; Capt C Co 1st TN Cav; Bulls Gap PO
WILLROY, Charles, Sh-167-2; Pvt 44th MS; Jan 62 to Jul 63; PO omitted; CONF
WILLS, Albert B., Jo-149-3; Sgt D Co 13th TN Cav; 24 Sep 63 to 2 Jun 65; Mountain City PO; rheumatism, lung, liver
WILLS, Ferdinand, Gi-127-4; Amandy White formerly widow of; Cpl G Co 111th TN Col Inf; Pulaski PO
WILLS, John, Gi-127-5; Pvt G Co 111th TN Col Inf; Pulaski PO; dates forgotten
WILLS, Macon R., Jo-149-1; Pvt B Co 2nd WV Cav; 6 Aug 63 to 13 Jun 65; Shouris & Roads PO; cartreage shot wound in leg
WILLS, Manual, D-72-3; Sgt G Co 17th TN Inf; Nov 16, 63 to Apr 1, 65; Nashville PO
WILLS, Mary E., Hi-88-1; widow?; 6th Dist
WILLSAN, Rollis F., We-221-1(4); Pvt K Co 6th TN Cav; 26 Jul 62 to 26 Jul 65; Martin PO
WILLSON, Alexander B., Ge-91-1; Lt F Co 4th TN Inf; Apr 3, 63 to Aug 2, 65; Greeneville PO; incurred several, dont know names
WILLSON, Charles R., Ge-91-4; Pvt I Co 13th TN Cav; 7-27-62 to 7-6-65; Dayton PO; concussion from art.
WILLSON, Danniel C., Ge-91-4; Pvt I Co 13th TN Cav; 26 Sep 63 to 13 Jun 64; Greeneville PO; heart trouble
WILLSON, James, Ha-114-1; Pvt F Co 3rd TN Cav; 1 Jun 64 to 24 Jun 65; Xenophon PO; CONF
WILLSON, Jesse, Sh-195-2; US Sol; Memphis PO

WILLSON, John R., Mn-122-1; Pvt A Co 6th TN Cav; 9-15-62 to 7-26-65; McNairy PO
WILLSON, June, K-165-2; widow; Pvt G Co 9th TN Cav; 29 Mar 63 to 25 Jan 65; 13 Cuither St., Knoxville PO
WILLSON, Thomas, C-26-1; Pvt F Co 6th TN Inf; 3-10-62 to 3-24-65; Jacksboro PO
WILLSON, William K., K-172-5(1); Lucy A. widow of; Pvt A Co 6th TN Inf; 62 to __; died in prison; 14th Dist, South Knoxville PO
WILLSON, William L., R-161-2; Pvt C Co 2nd TN Cav; 7-27-62 to 7-6-65; Dayton PO
WILLUMS, Richard, D-63-1; OH; Nashville PO
WILSFONER, William J., Gi-133-3; Pvt D Co 3rd TN; 61 to 8-21-65; Bufords PO
WILSON, Abriham, Jo-149-2; Pvt D Co 13th TN Cav; 24 Sep 63 to 65; Mountain City PO; rheumatism
WILSON, Adam, Col, Ct-160-2; Driver? 101st TN Inf; 62 to 65; Big Rock PO
WILSON, Alexander, Jo-150-4; Elizabeth widow of; Pvt I Co 13th TN Cav; 1 Mar 64 to __; Rheas Forge PO
WILSON, Alexander, Bo-14-4; Pvt L Co 1st US Col; Maryvill PO
WILSON, Alexander P., Ct-45-2; Pvt H Co 4th TN Inf; 6-63 to 8-2-65; Stony Creek PO; Kingston TN 1864; diarrhea
WILSON, Allen T., Wa-263-2; Pvt A Co 14th IL Cav; Oct 20 63 to May 28 65; Garbers Mills PO; ruptured in the Shortman? raid in GA
WILSON, Amasa J. T., We-225-1; Pvt K Co 6th TN Cav; 1 Feb 64 to 26 Jul 65; Dresden PO; sight
WILSON, Andrew J., Jo-149-2; Pvt D Co 13th TN Cav; 24 Sep 63 to 5 Sep 65; Mountain City PO; bronkitis, rheumatism & liver
WILSON, Andrew L., A-5-4; Pvt B Co 2nd TN Inf; 8-3-61 to 10-6-64; Clinton PO; consumption
WILSON, Andrew S., Jo-153-1; Pvt D Co 4th TN Inf; 25 Aug 62 to 17 Jul 65; Little Doe PO; bronchitis, rheumatism
WILSON, Andy, Ov-133-1; Pvt G Co 19th KY Inf; 8-15-62 to 10-15-65; Netherland PO
WILSON, Ben F., Ce-23-2; Pvt G Co 49th TN; Sep 61 to May 15, 65; Thomasville PO; CONF
WILSON, Cashelton B. D., Hw-119-4(1); Pvt C Co 5th TN Cav; 19 Aug 62 to 25 Jun 65; Gillenwater PO
WILSON, Charles, Sh-150-2; Pvt K Co 2nd Inf; 3 yrs; Bartlett PO
WILSON, Charles, D-63-2; Maria widow of; Pvt A Co 17th US Col; Nov 16 63 to 25 Apr 66; Nashville PO
WILSON, Charles M., Cr-21-1; Pvt F Co 6th TN Cav; Sep 62 to Oct 63; Huntingdon PO
WILSON, Charley, Br-9-3; Charley Montgomery alias; Pvt K Co 1st US __; 8-5-64 to 3-31-66; Cleveland PO
WILSON, Columbus, Cr-16-2; Pvt I Co 7th TN Cav; Oct 10 64 to 9 Aug 65; Huntingdon PO; hurt back
WILSON, Cyrus C., O-141-2; Maj F Co 26th KY Vol Inf; Dec 15, 62 to 17 Jun 65; Union City PO
WILSON, Daniel, Gi-123-2; Pvt K Co 4th TN Col Inf; Dec 62 to Jan? 65 Heron PO; wounded in back & nose
WILSON, Daniel, Ha-117-1; Pvt K Co 8th TN Cav; Apr 63 to 19 Sep 65; Kyle's Ford PO; disease r. shoulder & l. eye
WILSON, David N., Mc-117-5; brigade wagoner; Carlock PO; chronic diareah, brigade wagon master; service under Chamberlain as
WILSON, Delila S.? (see Reaves, John Thomas)
WILSON, Ed, K-167-3; Sgt H Co 1st Col TN Inf; 63 to May 65; Knoxville PO
WILSON, Elexander, Hm-109-8; Mahaly widow of; Pvt D Co 1st TN Cav; Three Springs PO
WILSON, Elijah, Ct-42-2; Christina widow of; Pvt 13th TN Cav; Watauga PO; gunshot wound; nose sawed off since war
WILSON, Elijah, Jo-153-1; Saraphine widow of; Pvt; Little Doe PO
WILSON, Emanuel E., Su-234-1; Ellen E. widow of; Bugler U Co 9th TN Cav; 2 yrs 20 mos; Bluff City PO; Gallatin April 1864; discharged on account of disability
WILSON, Ephraim, Ro-210-5; Rosie widow of; Pvt; Rockwood PO

WILSON, F. A., He-57-2; Sgt C Co 7th TN Cav; 5-1-63 to 8-5-65; Juno PO; prisoner Andersonville 6 mos
WILSON, Fisher, Sh-157-7; Inesly Farm PO
WILSON, Franklin, Wi-279-1; Pvt G Co 140th IN Inf; Sep 64 to 65; Franklin PO
WILSON, G. W., Ov-139-1; Pvt; Lovejoy PO
WILSON, George, Sh-179-2; 316 Linden St, Memphis PO
WILSON, Geo., Sh-179-1(2); alias Geo. Pilton; Pvt A Co 50th US Inf; 5-1-65 to 3-20-66; Memphis PO (this entry crossed out for some unknown reason)
WILSON, George, H-49-1; Pvt F Co 30th NJ Inf; 4-62 to 6-63; Daisy Falling Water PO
WILSON, George, Ca-20-1; Sarah B. widow of; Pvt; 5-11-62 to 12-25-64; Burk PO; killed; now drawing a pension from U.S. The company etc of George Wilson is unknown and cant be found out
WILSON, George, Hy-81-1; alias George Eason; Pvt C Co 12th TN Inf; 7th Civil Dist
WILSON, George, Pi-156-2; Sarah widow of; Pvt; Byrdtown PO
WILSON, George A., Mc-116-2; Pvt K Co 1st US Art; 7-24-64 to 3-31-65; Athens PO; injure in right hip
WILSON, George D., Jo-149-3; Pvt D Co 13th TN Cav; 1 Mar 65 to 9 Sep 65; Mountain City PO
WILSON, George W., We-225-3(2); Harriett widow of; 1st Lt D Co 7th TN Inf; Aug 62 to Jul 63; Dresden PO
WILSON, George W., Ct-42-2; Pvt F Co 13th TN Cav; Watauga PO
WILSON, George W., Ge-87-3; Sgt A Co 1st TN Lt Art; Sep 63 to Aug 65; Pates Hill PO; chronic diarrhea &c
WILSON, H. K., Mn-129-1; Pvt D Co 6th TN; 62 to 8-65; Adamsville PO
WILSON, Hack, Mt-141-1; alias Hack Craze; A Co 101st Col Vol; Dist 11
WILSON, Harry, Col, Sh-146-2; Sgt M Co WI; 62 to 65; Pearly PO; wounded upper post? left arm at Vicksburg, MS, Jul 4, 1863
WILSON, Hawood R., Cy-27-4(2); Pvt G Co 6th KY Cav; 12-15-61 to 62 (3 mos); Spivey PO
WILSON, Henry (see Faraby, Henry)
WILSON, Henry, Mg-196-4; Sgt B Co 14th TN Inf; 16 Jun 61 to 65; Big Mountain PO
WILSON, Henry, K-161-6; Knoxville PO
WILSON, Henry, D-99-3; Pvt H Co 136th MO Cav; 62 to 4 Jul 65; State Penitentiary PO; shot in left foot
WILSON, Henry, Hy-78-1; Pvt E Co 13th US Inf; 3 yrs 6 mos; Bells PO (Crockett Co.)
WILSON, Henry D., Po-152-1; Pvt F Co 5th TN Mtd Inf; 11-21-64 to 10-1-65; rheumatism; Ducktown PO
WILSON, Henry M., Hn-70-1; Pvt I Co 27th MS Inf; 21 Aug 62 to 21 Sep 65; Paris PO; discharge by Gen. Order War Dept.
WILSON, Henry T., Pi-156-3; Pvt C Co 49th KY Inf; 5-27-63 to 12-26-64; Mt. Pisgah PO, Wayne Co, KY
WILSON, Isaac, Mc-112-3; Margaret widow of; Pvt 1st US Col Art; 63 to 4-66; Athens PO; consumption; no papers to get dates
WILSON, Iseral, C-33-2; Cpl F Co 6th TN Inf; 3-26-62 to 3-25-65; Jellico PO
WILSON, J. M., Un-256-1; 1st Sgt A Co 2nd TN Cav; 1 Aug 62 to 17 Jul 65; Starkvale PO; lungs, testicals, eyes, ears
WILSON, Jack, D-73-2; Black A Co 17th TN Cav; 62 to 65; Vernon Ave, Nashville PO
WILSON, Jackson, Mc-116-2; Pvt L Co 1st Col Regt; 9-25-64 to 3-31-66; Athens PO; injure in left side; contracted in service
WILSON, Jacop, T-218-1; Pvt A Co Art; 15 Jul 61 to 4 May 65; Mason PO; shot in the back of the head
WILSON, James, Sh-198-1; Pvt M Co US Hvy Art; 12-63 to 5-66; Memphis PO; lost his discharge
WILSON, James, S-214-1; Robbins PO; this man was give to me and the proprietor of the house where he boarded
WILSON, James, Ro-206-3; Caroline widow of; Pvt 5th TN Inf; Aug 61 to 65; Emory Gap PO

WILSON, James, H-50-2(1); Pvt C Co 2nd R TN Cav; 12-8-63 to 7-6-65; Bunch PO; crippled in hip by train
WILSON, James, Ct-35-2; Pvt G Co 13th TN Cav; 9-5-63 to 9-5-65; Hampton PO; in US Army (disability)
WILSON, James, Ct-42-2; Pvt L Co 13th TN Cav; Watauga PO; measles fellow lungs
WILSON, James, Col, Sh-145-1; Pvt K Co 1st Col MS Cav US; 10 Apr 64 to 31 Oct 65; Kerrville PO; under Col. Orsborne & Major Clark and was discharged at Memphis
WILSON, James, Se-224-1; Sgt D Co 18th PA Cav; Sep 62 to Aug 65; Hornett PO; wond on the right wrist
WILSON, James C., W-189-2; Pvt M Co 5th TN Cav; 11-2-63 to 8-14-65; McMinnville PO; lungs affected
WILSON, James C., Cf-35-1; Pvt F Co 16th TN Inf; 29 Dec 63 to 30 Dec 64; Tullahoma PO; CONF
WILSON?, James H., Hw-119-4(1); Pvt B Co 60th TN Inf; Nov 62 to 4 Jul 63; Gillenwater PO; CONF
WILSON, James J., Sh-203-1; Sgt A Co Forrest Reg; May 61 to May 65; Memphis PO; wounded in shin; CONF
WILSON, James M., Mr-102-1; Pvt G Co 5th TN Cav; 1-62 to 5-65; South Pittsburg PO; shot in hand, ruptured in side & contracted deafness
WILSON, James R., C-25-1; Pvt B Co 11th TN Cav; 7-1-63 to 9-11-65; Whitman PO; heart disease, piles, schurvy 25 yrs; was wounded in leg
WILSON, James W., We-225-2(1); Marthy E. widow of; Pvt L Co 6th TN Cav; Jul 15, 63 to died Oct 3, 63; Dresden PO
WILSON, James W., D-79-2; Pvt I Co 5th CT Inf; Jun 63 to about May 65; 307 Berns, Nashville PO
WILSON, Jefferson, J-78-1; Pvt B Co 8th TN Inf; 1-15-65 to 8-17-65; Rough Point PO; hart dease & rumatism; not able to work any
WILSON, Jerry, Se-230-3; I Co; Feb 64 to Apr 65; Richison's Cove PO; Black man, cant tell much
WILSON, Jesse, J-78-2; Sgt G Co 5th KY Cav; 12-20-61 to 3-3-65; Haydensburg PO; rumatis
WILSON, Jesse, A-4-1; Pvt F Co 6th TN Inf; 3-10-62 to 3-25-65; Coal Creek PO; eye put out
WILSON, Jessee, Mc-112-7; Rachel M. widow of; Pvt D Co 10th TN Cav; 1-1-64 to 9-65; Athens PO
WILSON, Jhew, D-68-1; Fillmore, Nashville PO
WILSON, John, Ro-201-1; Pvt B Co 5th TN Inf; 25 Feb 62 to 30 Mar 65; Kingston PO
WILSON, John, H-62-3; Seaman Niagara before the war; 61 to 7-20-62; Sgt Act.? Engineers Ind PA Vol; 7-28-62 to 6-20-65; 313 Poplar, Chattanooga PO
WILSON, John, K-183-2; Pvt D Co 9th TN Cav; 1 Nov 63 to 11 Sep 65; Mayo PO
WILSON, John, D-75-2; Annie widow of; Pvt G Co 2nd TN Inf; 15 Feb 63 to 15 Dec 64; Stewarts Ferry PO; died Clarksville PO
WILSON, John, Un-251-2; Capt L Co 11th TN Cav; M Co 9th TN Cav; 29 Mar 64 to 6 Jun 65; Esco PO; liver, lung & heart disease
WILSON, John, Hd-45-2; Pvt I Co 21st Mosou (sic) Inf; Aug 61 to Dec 64; Cerro Gordo PO; left leg perishing away
WILSON, John A., Sh-202-2(1); Pvt C Co 13th Inf; 13 Sep 61 to 13 Sep 64; Memphis PO; term? expired
WILSON, John B., Ca-25-1; Pvt M Co 5th TN Cav; 12-1-62 to 8-14-65; Shoat? Mountain PO; rheumatism
WILSON, John H., Lo-192-1; Pvt G Co 1st TN; 62 to 65; Griffitts PO; liver disease; CONF
WILSON, John L., H-66-2; Pvt B Co 50th NY V Inf; 3-17-64 to 6-19-65; Pvt A Co 2nd OH V Inf; 1-63 to 8-30-63; Chattanooga PO
WILSON, John L., Mu-194-1; Sallie E. widow of; Major K Co 21st IL Inf; Columbia PO; cant find out when enlisted or discharged
WILSON, John M., Wi-276-1; Pvt I Co 44th TN Inf; Sep 62 to May 65; Beechville PO; CONF
WILSON, John M., F-20-3; Pvt B Co 38th TN Inf; Mar 62 to 1 Jun 62; Hickory Withe PO; CONF
WILSON, Johnathan B., J-79-2; 1st Sgt B Co 9th KY Inf; 9-24-61 to 12-15-64; North Springs PO; shot in left shoulder
WILSON, Joseph, Br-9-4; Cleveland PO

347

WILSON, Joseph, Ro-203-7; Pvt A Co 5th TN Inf; Wheat PO; gunshot wound in right side
WILSON, Jos., Ro-209-4; Mary J. McDanel widow of; Rockwood PO; CONF
WILSON, Joseph, H-53-7; Pvt; no dates (2 yrs); Chickamauga PO; shot in right leg
WILSON, Joseph B., Ge-96-3; Cpl I Co 13th TN Cav; 22 Sep 63 to 5 Sep 65; Rheatown PO
WILSON, Joseph W., Cr-13-2; Holmes PO; havent got any discharge
WILSON, Josephus, Gi-127-1; Lucy widow of; Pvt H Co 13th TN USC Inf; Jul 62 to Jul 64; Pulaski PO
WILSON, Josiah, D-64-3; Patsy Willson widow of; Nashville PO
WILSON, Lenard, Sh-157-4; Dist 13
WILSON, Levi, C-25-1; Pvt H Co 11th TN Cav; 6-63 to 9-63; Whitman PO; kidney affection, has no discharge, does not remember date
WILSON, Lewis, C-27-4; Pvt F Co 6th TN Inf; 3-63 to 7-5-65; Jacksboro PO
WILSON, Lewis C., Se-226-4; Pvt A Co 3rd NC Mtd Inf; 2 yrs 6 mos; Sinking Springs PO; measles settled in chest
WILSON, Margaret (see Kelly, Timethy)
WILSON, Marion, Sh-144-1; Pvt D Co 15th US Col Inf; Dec 18 64 to 7 Apr 66; Brunswick PO
WILSON, Marshal, Co-63-2; Sgt B Co 2nd TN Cav; 15 Sep 62 to 6 Jul 65; Newport PO; side hurt by hors stepping on him
WILSON, Mary A. (see McPeters, Inmon)
WILSON, Matison T., Jo-149-3; Pvt H Co 4th? TN Inf; 7 May 64 to 2 Aug 65; Mountain City PO; chronic rheumatism, jaundice, hart
WILSON, Moses, Sh-157-1; Harriet widow of; Pvt F Co 61st Inf; Jun 62 to ___; PO omitted
WILSON, Nathan, D-50-4; Pvt G Co 13th US Inf; Oct 5 63 to 13 Jan 66; 209 Jackson, Nashville PO
WILSON, Oscar, Bl-5-2; Pvt C Co 4th OH Cav; 7-14-63 to 2-22-64; Brayton PO
WILSON, Percival C., H-70-1; Lt C Co 2nd OH Hvy Art; 63 to 65; Chattanooga PO
WILSON, Phillipp, Ro-205-1; Pvt A Co 5th TN Inf; 12 Dec 62 to 25 Aug 65; Kingston PO; piles, 1865; gunshot in arm
WILSON, Richard L., Jo-151-2; 1st Lt R.Q.M. 12th TN Cav; 1 Sep 63 to 5 Sep 65; Bakers Gap PO; single right side hernia, injury to left leg
WILSON, Robert, Sn-255-1; Pvt I Co 5th TN Inf; 4-1-63 to 7-1-65; Goodlettsville PO (Davidson Co.); struck on head by butt of gun, shot through left hip, not disabled from work
WILSON, Rufus, Lo-187-4; Pvt D Co 5th TN Inf; 62 to ___; Adolphus PO
WILSON, Samuel D., Dy-25-7(3); Newbern PO; dates of enlistment unknown; CONF
WILSON, Samuel M., Ro-207-2; 1st Lt I Co 11th TN Cav; Sep 63 to Sep 64; Paint Rock PO; rheumatism & stomache affection
WILSON, Sarah, Mn-122-2; 3rd Civil Dist
WILSON, Taylor, L-99-1; Pvt B Co 149th IN Inf; Jan 65 to Apr 65; Orysa PO; flux, caused from exposure
WILSON, Thomas, Ms-172-1; Rebecca L. widow of; Orderly Sgt I Co 10th TN Inf; 63 to ___; Farmington PO
WILSON, Thomas H., Jo-152-2; Pvt B Co 13th TN Cav; 23 Sep 63 to 5 Sep 65; Doeville PO; rheumatism
WILSON, Ulish, Gi-127-5; Pvt D Co 110th IL Col Inf; Pulaski PO; cant tell what co. nor dates
WILSON, W. A., G-57-2; Sgt G Co 44th TN Inf; 12-13-62 to 12-13-64; Yorkville PO; CONF
WILSON, W. A. J., P-151-2; Pvt F Co 48th KY Inf; 20 Jul 63 to 23 Dec 64; Mousetail PO; paralisis
WILSON, Wiley, Ro-208-2; Pvt A Co 5th TN Inf; 25 Feb 62 to 7 Apr 65; Welker Mines PO
WILSON, William, H-61-4; Martha widow of; Pvt Lookout Art; 8-63 to 4-9-65; Chattanooga PO; CONF
WILSON, William, Sh-145-1; Pvt A Co 59th US Col Inf; 1 Apr 63 to 31 Jan 66; Millington PO
WILSON, William, Se-230-2; Pvt H Co 9th TN Inf; Oct 62 to ___ (2 yrs); Pokeberry PO; incurred no desease; CONF
WILSON, William A., O-134-1; Lt B Co 27th IOSC?

5 Jul 61 to 5 Jul 65; Hornbeak PO; shot in knee; CONF
WILSON, William D., Ct-36-1; Pvt C Co 2nd TN Cav; 7-62 to 7-65; Shell Creek PO; died at Nashville TN
WILSON, Wm. E., Je-135-2; Pvt H Co 3rd TN Cav; 20 Mar 65 to 3 Aug 65; Piedmont PO; shot in leg
WILSON, William H., Pu-142-1; Pvt L Co 13th KY Cav; 10-63 to 3-11-65; Void PO; ruptured & nuralgia
WILSON, Wm. M., K-155-2(1); Pvt; 109 W. Main St., Knoxville PO; deaf in left ear
WILSON, William N., Mu-195-2; C Co 124th IN Vol; 11-10-63 to 6-12-65; Columbia PO
WILSON, William T., Ro-211-2; Masouri widow of; Pvt B Co 12th KY Inf; 31 Oct 61 to Jun 62; Webster PO; discharged on physicians certificate
WILSON, William W., Wi-276-1; Pvt A Co 8th TN Cav; Oct 62 to 16 Jun 63; Beechville PO; right leg lost, Feb 1863; CONF
WIMBERLY, Harrison, Mt-137-1; Civilian, employed on R R No 62 to 65; papers lost; St. Bethlehem PO
WIMPEE, Mathew M., Ja-87-1; Pvt; Apison PO; discharge away from home
WIN, Amanda (see Williams, Harvey)
WIN?, William P., B-11-1; Pvt F Co 5th TN Cav; 9-63 to 8-20-65; Healey PO
WINBURN, Frank, Col, Ma-119-1; Pvt I Co 61st Col US; Aug 63 to Nov 65; Jackson PO
WINCHESLY, James, W-195-2; Pvt G Co 5th TN Cav; 8-15-64 to 8-14-65; Mangrum PO
WINCHESTER, Henry, Sh-189-5; Amanda widow of; Sgt B Co—no other record to be had; La. Ave, Memphis PO
WINCHESTER, John F., Pu-146-1; Pvt H Co 1st Mtd Inf Vol W(hite?); 11-22-64 to 5-23-65; Buffalo Valley PO
WINCHESTER, John T., A-8-4; Pvt K Co 1st TN Inf; 9-15-61 to 9-14-64; Scarborough PO
WINCHESTER, Matilda, Ma-115-1; widow; PO omitted
WINDER, Alexander, Mo-120-1; Pvt H Co 7th TN Inf; 2-10-65 to 7-27-65; Glenloch PO
WINDOM, George M., Mo-120-4(2); Mary A. widow of; Pvt OH Cav; 62 to 65; Sweetwater PO; deserted his wife
WINEMAN, Albert G., T-212-1; "found while examing work"; no address
WINER, William, T-216-2; 11th Civil Dist
WINFREY, James, Pu-147-1; Pvt F Co 101st TN Inf; 9-28-64 to 1-21-66; Enigma PO (Smith Co.)
WINFREY, Lemuel M., Pu-146-1; Pvt G Co 1st TN Cav Vol W(hite?); Buffalo Valley PO
WINFREY, William R., Dk-35-2; Cpl I Co 5th TN Cav; 2-9-64 to 8-22-65; Temperance Hall PO; shot through hand
WINGFIELD, Albert, Mu-196-1; Fifer H Co 13th Reg; 21 Sep 63 to 10 Jan 66; Columbia PO; flesh wound in groin
WINGLAN, James C., Cl-56-1; 11th Dist
WINGO, Andrew J., Mc-116-1; Pvt D Co 5th TN Inf; 8-31-64 to 6-26-65; Riceville PO; paralyzed since the war; right eye injured in the war
WINGO, Benjamin, White, Li-154-1; Pvt A Co 12th MO Cav; 4-14-63 to 3-12-66; Clardy Ville PO; has a honorable discharge at his son
WINGO, William H., Mc-116-2; Pvt E Co 10th TN Cav; 1-1-64 to 8-1-65; Longs Mills; injure in left side; contracted while in service
WINGWOOD, Elias, Ct-38-1; Ellen widow of; Pvt J Co 2nd TN Cav; Milligan PO; died of diarrhea
WINIGER, William, Hw-125-1; Pvt A Co 5th TN Cav; 5 Sep 62 to 5 Jun 65; Opossum PO
WINKFURD, Obidah, D-57-2; Pvt D Co LA Cav; Apr 61 to May 65; 8th Ward, Nashville PO; CONF
WINKLE, Joseph, K-182-2; Pvt E Co 3rd TN Cav; 62 to 65; Shooks PO
WINKLES, Almarine, Gr-72-1; Pvt I Co 8th TN Inf; 6 Jan 63 to 6 Aug 65; Noeton PO; Bell Island prison 3 mos
WINN, John, T-206-1; Pvt G Co 4th KY Hvy Art; Covington PO
WINN, Levin A., Ru-239-1; Pvt G Co 10th TN Inf; Jun 30 63 to 5 May 65; Rockvale PO; eye put out by forced march
WINN, ____, B-11-2(1); Margret C. widow of; Pvt 5th TN Cav; 9-62 to ___; Farmington PO; died

WINNETTE, Calvin, Ca-23-1; Pvt B Co 5th TN Cav; 8-27-62 to 6-25-65; Woodbury PO; injured by fall of horse
WINNETTE, James G., Ca-23-1; Pvt B Co 5th TN Cav; 8-28-62 to 6-25-65; Leoni PO; no injuries
WINNETTE, Norman, Ca-23-1; Pvt B Co 5th TN Cav; 8-27-62 to 6-5-65; Leoni PO; rheumatism caused cold
WINNIGHAN, Solomon W., Ov-137-3; Pvt C Co 12th KY Inf; 10-61 to 7-65; Monroe PO; sorcomas
WINNINGHAM, Henry A., Fe-42-2; Martha widow of; Pvt A Co 2nd TN; 8-6-61 to __; Jamestown PO
WINNINGHAM, John E., Fe-41-3(1); Pvt Capt Beaty's Co. Indept. TN Scouts; 62 to 65; Boat Land PO; afflicted eyes, exposed to bad weather in 62 and 63, with result of sore eyes to present
WINNINGHAM, Richard A., Fe-41-3(1); Pvt B Co 2nd E TN Mtd Inf; 7-2-61 to 10-6-64; Little Crabb PO; inflamed eyes from measels; Madison Saulsbury prison 12 mos
WINNINGHAM, Seth, Pi-153-2; Pvt D Co 2nd TN Inf; 8-61 to 4-19-65; Spurnier PO
WINNS, Johny (see Harvey, Joe)
WINSETT, William R., Bl-4-2; Pvt D Co 1st TN Cav; 10-1-61 to 4-1-65; Pikeville PO; wounded in shoulder, injured partially; CONF
WINSHIP, George, H-60-6; Lookout St, Chattanooga PO
WINSLOW, Ewing, D-51-2; Elizabeth widow of; Cpl B Co 13th TN C Inf; May 64 to Jun 65; N. College, Nashville PO
WINSLOW, Samuel B., Ge-96-2; Cpl B Co 4th TN Cav; 5 Nov 62 to 25 Jul 65; Jockey PO
WINSTEAD, John, Hw-130-1; Pvt L Co 10th TN Cav; Aug 63 to __; Lee Valley PO
WINSTEAD, ____, Hw-134-2; Evaline widow of; 20th Civil Dist
WINSTED, George P., Hw-119-2(1); Pvt D Co 9th TN Cav; 18 Sep 63 to __ (18 mos); Alum Well PO
WINSTED, James G., Hw-119-2(1); Pvt C Co 64th TN Inf; Oct 62 to __ (15 mos); Alum Well PO
WINSTED, Richard, Hw-133-2; Pvt K Co 1st TN Inf; 14 Jun 61 to 27 Nov 65; Slide PO
WINSTON, Chas., Sh-187-1(5); Sol; Memphis PO
WINSTON?, Houstin?, D-69-1; Pvt E Co 44th Del Rg.; 33 Perkins St, Nashville PO
WINSTON, James, D-64-5; Julia widow of; Pvt; Nashville PO
WINSTON, John, Mu-196-1; Pvt I Co 12th Reg.; 3 yrs 6 mos; Columbia PO; eye sight weakened from small pox; caught in army
WINSTON, Marshal, Sh-150-3; Pvt H Co TN Inf; no dates (6 mos); Bartlett PO
WINSTON, Robert, D-81-1; Pvt; 62 to 65; Sigler St., Nashville PO; shot in ankle
WINSTON, William, T-213-1; Pvt K Co 17th US Inf; 64 to 65; Mason PO
WINSTREAD, Mack, Ha-110-3; Pvt L Co 8th TN Cav; 26 Dec 64 to 11 Sep 65; Lee Valley PO, Hawkins Co.
WINTER, James, H-49-8; Pvt A Co 6th TN Mtd Inf; 8-2-64 to 6-30-65; Daisy PO; lost right ear in hearing
WINTERS, Jacob, Co-69-1; Mary widow of; Cpl 8th TN Inf; Driskill PO; jellow janders; not a pensioner
WINTON, Alfred, K-170-1; Pvt M Co 1st US Art; 5 Sep 63 to 30 Mar 65; Knoxville PO; blind, piles 25 yrs
WINTON, John A., Ro-209-4; Lt I Co 46th; Glen Allice PO; CONF
WIRT, John H., F-44-1; Pvt B Co 6th __; May 8, 61 to Sep 1, 63; PO omitted; CONF
WISDOM, Jas. W., La-117-1; Joannea wid. of; pvt; __ to 61 (8 mos); 15th Dist; CONF
WISE, Anderson, Co-69-7(12); Pvt O Co 5th TN Inf; 62 to Apr 65 (2 yr 6 mos); Bibee PO; shot in thigh, conscriped; CONF
WISE, Heenny P., Je-144-1; Pvt 8th TN Inf; Oct 63 to __(1 yr 8 mos); Valleyhome PO; got no discharge
WISE, James, Co-62-3; Pvt D Co 4th TN Inf; 1 Jan 63 to 5 Aug 65; Bybee PO; piles & disably rheumatism
WISE, John, He-58-1; Pvt A Co 7th TN Vol Cav; 8-1-62 to 6-26-65; PO omitted

WISE, Martha A., T-216-2; 11th Civil Dist
WISE, Nelson, Co-63-1; Pvt K Co 8th TN Inf; Aug 63 to __(1 yr); Newport PO; rheumatism; no discharge--was at home sick
WISE, Simon, Co-69-5; Pvt D Co 4th TN Inf; Feb 62 to Aug 65; Driskill PO; no pension yet but applicant
WISECARVER, John, Ge-86-2; 2nd Lt C Co 3d TN Cal (Col or Cav?); 3 Nov 62 to 3 Aug 65; Warrensburgh PO
WISEMAN, Jacob C., Mo-122-3(1); Pvt C Co 10th TN Cav; 1863 to 1865; Glenloch PO; general debility
WISEMAN, James W., Mo-122-3(1); Pvt C Co 10th TN Cav; 1-63 to 1865; Glenloch PO
WISER, John D., Cf-35-3; Pvt B Co 16th TN Inf; 61 to 65; Manchester PO; CONF
WISER, John W., Cf-35-3; Pvt K Co 24th TN Inf; 20 Jun 63 to 24 Jun 65; Manchester PO; CONF
WISSON, Henry A., H-56-4; Pvt E Co 81st MA Inf; 1863 to 7-65; East End PO
WISTERALL, Thomas W., D-67-3; Pvt; Nashville PO
WITCHER, James L., M-107-2; Pvt F Co 52nd Reg. Mtd Inf; 9-20-63 to 1-18-65; Red Boiling Springs PO; piles
WITT, D.A., Sm-168-1; Pvt TN Cav; 1861 to 1864; Difficult PO
WITT, Daniel T., Hm-107-3; Cpl G Co 4th TN Cav; 13 Apr 63 to 19 Jun 65; Witts Foundry PO; lungs, liver, throat 25 years
WITT, Edmon, Un-256-2; Lucinda widow of; 2nd Lt D Co 1st TN Inf; 9 Aug 61 to 17 Sep 62; Rule PO; killed by rebbels after his return home
WITT, J. E., Un-256-2; C Sgt A Co 2nd TN Cav; 1 Aug 62 to 17 Sep 65; Rule PO; diarhear & deafness
WITT, John, Un-259-2; Pvt I Co 7th TN Inf; 8 Nov 64 to 18 Jul 65; Lost Creek PO; no special disease
WITT, Joseph __, Ja-85-5; Capt G Co 3rd TN Cav; 7-5-63 to 5-26-64; Georgetown PO; discharged on surgeon certificate
WITT, Nat, R-159-1; Lt E Co 5th TN Inf; 3-2-62 to 5-15-65; Spring City PO; diseased in legs; cant work much
WITT, Noah, Co-62-1; Pvt G Co 8th TN Cal(cav?); 10 Oct 63 to 65 (2 yrs); Warrensburg PO; chronic disease
WITT, Noah D., Hm-107-3; Lucinda A. widow of; Cpl L Co 8th TN Cav; 15 Nov 63 died Jan 64; Witts Foundry PO; typhoid fever cause of death
WITT, Plasent, Wa-261-2; Pvt H Co 5th TN Cav; 5 Dec 61 to 19 Apr 65; Conkling PO; CONF
WITT, Porter J., Hm-107-2(1); Pvt G Co 4th TN Cav; 2 Jan 63 to 12 Jul 65; Witts Foundry PO; chronic diarhea
WITT, Richard M., Hm-109-8; Pvt D Co 1st TN Cav; Russelville PO
WITTINBARGER, Drury W., Se-227-3; Pvt E Co 3rd TN Cav; 13 Dec 62 to 10 Jun 65; Trundles X Roads PO; weak lungs; was a prisoner
WITZGAN, John, Cr-8-2; Pvt D Co 56th GA; 61 to 65; McBride PO; shot through L leg & L foot?; CONF
WIX, Tolliver, H-60-3; Pvt 10th TN Cav; __ to 1865; Chattanooga PO
WIYET, Charles, Mc-113-2; Pvt A Co 7th TN Inf; 10-16-62 to 4-18-63; Athens PO
WODDLE, Benjamin A., Ge-83-1; Pvt E Co 4th TN Inf; Aug 63 to Aug 65; Henshaw PO; hart & lunges
WODINE?, David A., H-76-1; Pvt 63rd OH Cav; 10-4-61 to 5-31-62; Chattanooga PO
woeller, Louis (dead), husband of Mary E. D. Woeller, Sh-189-5; Lt 68th NY Inf; resigned 5-16-63; La. Ave., Memphis PO
WOLEY, Andrew J., Lo-190-2; Pvt F Co 52nd GA Inf; Sep 62 to __; Piney PO; CONF
WOLF, Campbell C., K-172-3; Cpl F Co 9th TN Cav; 13 Sep 63 to 15 Sep 65; 14th Dist South Knoxville PO
WOLF, Henry, Mn-126-3; Pvt G Co 6th TN Cav; 8-62 to 1865; Bethel Springs PO
WOLF, Jacob P., Mn-126-3; Pvt E Co 6th TN Cav; 8-62 to 9-26-62; Bethel Springs PO
WOLF, James F., Bo-20-1; Pvt E Co 3rd TN Cav; 3-20-63 to 8-3-65; Bank PO

WOLF, Jerramiah M., Ja-86-3; Cpl D Co 4th TN Cav; 62 to 7-65; Oottewah PO; measles & smallpox
WOLF, Josias, Bo-22-1; Pvt; 62 to __; Seaton PO; rheumatism; can't get the dates at all
WOLF, Meredith, H-60-4; Pvt B Co 5th TN Mtd Inf; 9-22-64 to 7-13-65; Chattanooga PO; broken arm
WOLFE, Adam, Gr-79-2; Rebecca Dalton formerly widow of; Pvt 1st TN; Thorn Hill PO; died in the army; CONF
WOLFE, Calvin, Ha-115-2; Pvt B Co 1st TN Cav; 9 Apr 62 to 9 Apr 65; Alanthers Hill PO; shot through ankle, pensioner
WOLFE, Elijah, Ha-115-2; Pvt C Co 29th TN Inf; 5 Aug 61 to 14 Aug 64; Jap? VA; prisoner at Louisville
WOLFE, Greene B., Ha-110-1; Pvt I Co 8th TN Inf; 62 to 65; Treadway PO
WOLFE, Jacob W., D-64-4; Pvt B Co 16th IL Inf; 24 May 61 to 12 Jun 64; Nashville PO; sickness from war
WOLFE, John, Br-14-1; Cpl G Co 4th TN Cav; 5-25-63 to 7-12-65; McDonald PO; badly hurt in side on a raid
WOLFE, John, Gr-79-2; Pvt I Co 8th TN Inf; 63 to 65; Thorn Hill PO; not disabled
WOLFE, John J., Hw-127-2; Lt A Co 1st TN Cav; 9 Mar 62 to 4 Apr 65; Rogersville PO; wounded in leg
WOLFE, Melvin C., Jo-152-3; Cpl E Co 13th TN Cav; 24 Sep 63 to 5 Sep 65; Butler PO
WOLFE, Nathaniel, Ha-110-1; Pvt I Co 8th TN Inf; 1 Jul 63 to 30 Jun 65; Bray's PO; stiffness of hips
WOLFE, Wiley, Ha-110-1; Pvt I Co 8th TN Inf; 62 to 65; Treadway PO
WOLFE, William, Hw-122-2; Elizabeth widow of; Pvt; Margaret PO; died of measles; never discharged
WOLFENBARGER, George, Ha-115-2; Martha widow of; Pvt C Co 29th TN Inf; 5 Aug 61 to 10 Oct 62; Fenton PO; died while on duty at Chattanooga TN; CONF
WOLFENBARGER, Jacob T., Ha-115-3; Mary widow of; Pvt C Co 29th TN Inf; 10 Sep 61 to 20 Aug 64; Fenton PO; killed by bushwhackers while at home on furlough; CONF
WOLFENBARGER, William D., Hm-104-3(1); Pvt A Co 12th TN Cav; 2 Dec 63 to 25 Oct 65; Vally Home PO; rhumatism
WOLFENBARGER, Geo. W., Gr-82-2; Sol; 13th Dist
WOLFINBARGER, James, Gr-83-5(3); Pvt A Co 12th TN Cav; 28 Jun 63 to 7 Oct 65; Liberty Hill PO; disabled by horse falling on him
WOLFINBARGER, John, Sr., Gr-80-2; Sgt A Co 12th TN Cav; 8 Jul 63 to June or Jul 65; Shelton's Ford PO; ruptured
WOLFINBARGER, T. F., Gr-81-1; Pvt A Co 9th TN Cav; Sep 63 to Nov 63; Clear Spring PO
WOLFINBARGER, William, Gr-81-3(1); Pvt R Co 12th TN Cav; May 63 to Oct 65; Clear Spring PO; maimed in right hand with ax; disabled
WOLFINBURGER, Peter, Gr-81-3(1); Pvt A Co 12th TN Cav; 8 Jun 63 to Jul 65; Clear Spring PO; chron dyeree; partly disabled
WOLFINBURGER, Peter Jr., Gr-81-3(1); Sgt E Co 47th KY Inf; 20 Jun 63 to 26 Dec 64; Clear Spring PO; chron dyerhea, partly disabled
WOLIVER, Alexander, Je-146-3; Pvt K Co 1st IL Lt Art; 22 Jul 63 to Aug 65; White Pine PO; lungs & rheumatism
WOMAC, Riley B., Po-148-1; Pvt D Co 5th TN Mtd Inf; 8-31-64 to 2-20-65; Cog Hill PO
WOMACK, Peyton, Moo-217-1; Pvt E Co 5th US; Apr 65 to Oct 66; County Line PO
WOMBLE, John, H-59-1; Lovinda widow of; Pvt OH Inf; 63 to 65; Chattanooga PO
WOMPLER, Catharine, R-206-2(3); widow; 7th Civil Dist
WONNBER, Henry, R-106-2(3); Pvt B Co TN; PO omitted; discharge not at hand
WOOD, Alexander, Sh-167-2; Pvt D Co 2nd MI Inf; 18 Sep 61 to 10 Apr 65; PO omitted
WOOD, Andrew, Je-146-3; Pvt E Co 17th KY Cav; Leadvale PO; can't give dates
WOOD, Aurelius T., H-61-2; Josephine widow of; Sgt I Co 137th IN Inf; 5-10-64 to 9-21-65; Chattanooga PO

WOOD, David J., H-49-10; Pvt B Co 10th TN Cav; 10-5-63 to 8-1-64; Daisy PO; lung disease from pneumonia
WOOD, Dick (see Woodland, Dick)
WOOD, Elijah, A-7-1; Robertsville PO
WOOD, Francis, Sn-254-1; Cpl D Co 8th TN Inf; 12-10-64 to 8-30-65; Hendersonville PO
WOOD, Francis J., Cr-4-2; Capt G Co 27th TN Inf; 20 May 61 to 20 Apr 65; Bells Depot PO; CONF
WOOD, George H., He-60-2; Pvt C Co 7th TN Cav; Aug 62 to Jun 23 65; Chesterfield PO; caused pyles & scurvy; 13 mos in Andersonville Prison
WOOD, Gustroons? A., H-73-5(3); Col 15th IN; 6-14-61 to 7-1-64; Chattanooga PO
WOOD, Henderson, Ms-175-1; Pvt Staflers; 64 (3 mos); Chapel Hill PO; lame ankle
WOOD, Henry, Ru-231-1; 1st Dist
WOOD, James A., R-158-2; Pvt K Co 9th TN Cav; 63 to 65; Carp PO
WOOD, James M., H-49-9; Pvt C Co 10th TN Cav; 10-3-63 to 6-8-65; Daisy PO; horse fell on him
WOOD, James M., Ro-211-2; Sgt F Co 8th TN Cav; 19 Aug 63 to 11 Sep 65; Webster PO
WOOD, Jephtha, Co-62-3; Pvt D Co 4th TN Inf; 29 Jan 63 to 2 Aug 65; Givens PO
WOOD, Jesse B., K-175-2; Sarah E. widow of; Pvt H Co 6th TN Cav; 18 Apr 62 to 18 Aug 65; Snoterly PO
WOOD, Jesse M., Ha-50-2; Seaman, Key West; Aug 27 63 to 18 Sep 64; Walnut Grove PO; measles settled on lungs; he has been in bad helth by same
WOOD, Jessy L., He-62-3; Pvt Co A 7th TN Cav; Aug 13 62 to Feb 64; Darden PO; rheumatism
WOOD, John R., La-113-2; Sgt E Co 14th MI Inf; 1 Dec 63 to 3 Jul 65; Lawrenceburgh PO
WOOD, John W., Su-243-1; Pvt KY Inf; 61 to __ (1 yr); Bristol PO
WOOD, Joseph, Co-62-3; Susan A. widow of; Pvt C Co 8th TN Inf; 61 to Jun 65 (3 yrs 6 mos); Bybee PO; chronic direah
WOOD, Marth M., K-177-2; widow Sol US; PO omitted
WOOD, Nathaniel, A-13-3; Pvt F Co 6th TN Inf; 3-10-62 to 3-25-65; Briceville PO; shot in left knee
WOOD, Neil, Gi-124-1; Pvt C Co 10th KY? Cav; 20 Nov 63 to 25 Oct 65; Marbuts PO
WOOD, Palles L., Dk-31-1; Cpl H Co 61st IL Vet Inf; 2-8-64 to 9-8-65; Alexandria PO; shot through left hand, suffering with rheumatism
WOOD, Pleasant, J-78-2; Pvt B Co 8th TN Inf; dates illegible; Highland PO; cillart? of the head
WOOD, Robert L., K-166-3; Cpl B Co 8th TN Cav; 11 Jun 63 to 11 Sep 65; Knoxville PO; diarrhea, injured in head
WOOD, Rufis K., Hw-121-1; Pvt H Co 1st TN Cav; 15 Nov 61 to 19 Jun 65; Van Hill PO; rheumatism, imprisoned 9 mos
WOOD, Simeon, Un-259-1; Pvt A Co 1st TN Inf; 2 Aug 61 to 17 Sep 64; Rhodelia PO; heart disease, hardships in war
WOOD, Steven, C-34-3; Nancy widow of; Pvt; Buckeye PO; drawing pension
WOOD, William, Wl-300-1; Sgt B Co 5th TN Cav; 28 Jul 62 to 25 Jan 65; Watertown PO
WOOD, William H., He-58-1; Pvt A Co 7th TN Vol Cav; 8-5-62 to 7-1-64; PO omitted
WOOD, Wm. W., Fe-41-4(2); Elisabeth J. formerly widow of, now widow of Anderson Young, Hogue OH; Pvt M Co 1st AL Cav; 9-10-63 to 10-20-65; 5th Sgt M Co 1st AL Cav--11-1-63 to 10-20-65; Pvt Co F 1st TN Inf; 8-61 to 12-61; Boat Land PO; resulting dis. of lungs, died in hospital; died 7-1-1887 with dropsy, piles & lung trouble, at Crab Orchard KY
WOODALL, Ewin M., D-83-1; 1st AL Cav Co K; 22 Aug 62 to 19 Jul 65; Antioch PO; shot through right arm
WOODARD, John, D-73-1; Harret widow of; Pvt G Co; No. 1 Noel? Black, Nashville PO
WOODARD, John, Bo-12-4; Sol US; 17th Dist
WOODARD, Joseph, D-79-1; Nashville PO; not able to get the facts as to this case
WOODARD, Lee C., L-110-1; Pvt K Co 16th MO Inf; Jun 6 62 to Apr 65; Halls PO
WOODARD, Stephen A., Br-7-1; Pvt G Co 10th TN Cav; 2-15-64 to 8-31-65; Felker PO; feeblemindedness

WOODARD, Thomas L., Gi-133-3; Sarah J. widow of;
 Pvt D Co 3rd TN; 63 to 65; Bufords PO
WOODBY, Heziechiah, U-245-2; Pvt B Co 13th TN Cav;
 23 Sep 63 to 5 Sep 65; Limestone Cove PO;
 cronic rheumatism for 26 yrs
WOODBY, Jourry?, Ct-37-2; Pvt B Co 13th TN Cav; 9-
 23-63 to 9-5-65; Hopson PO; rheumatism
WOODBY, Luis, Se-222-2; Nancey widow of; Pvt 13th
 TN Cav; Pigeon Forge PO; diereah, deceased
 1882
WOODCOCK, Nathan, M-103-3; Pvt C Co 9th KY Inf; 11-
 26-61 to 12-15-64; Lafayette PO
WOODCOCK, William, D-74-1; 1st Lt B Co 9th KY Inf;
 Sep 24, 61 to 15 Dec 64; Cumberland Ironworks
 Nashville PO
WOODCOCK, William E., M-103-1; Pvt F Co 1st TN Inf;
 2-18-64 to 5-3-65; Lafayette PO
WOODEN, James, Br-13-2; Cpl B Co 5th TN Inf; 8-23-
 64 to 7-18-65; Georgetown PO
WOODLAND, Dick, Hy-76-2; alias Wood, Dick; Pvt G
 Co 61st TN Inf; 6 mos; Stanton Depot PO
WOODRUFF, Marcellus, We-225-3(2); Pvt K Co 6th TN
 Cav; Aug 8 62 to Aug 65; Dresden PO; rheuma-
 tism; never been well since
WOODRUFF, William W., K-169-1; Capt I Co 82nd Vol
 Inf; 8 Aug 62 to 12 Jan 63; Knoxville PO
WOODRUFF, William W., Wa-263-5; Pvt B Co 8th TN
 Cav; 11 Jun 63 to 11 Sep 65; Conkling PO
WOODRUM, George W., S-217-1; Pvt C Co 27th KY;
 Isham PO; defect of eye & shot in right leg
WOODS, Allen, Mg-168-2; Pvt B Co 11th TN Cav; 19
 Jul 63 to __; Coalfield PO
WOODS, Benjamin Sr., Ca-23-2; 8th Civil Dist
WOODS, Dick, Wl-296-1; Pvt 15th TN Inf; 61 to 64;
 Linwood PO; shot through shoulder; lost all
 his papers
WOODS, Doc, Gu-48-2; Pvt D Co 1st IL Col Inf; 8-61
 to 9-64; Tracy City PO
WOODS, Edward, D-45-5; don't know anything; Nash-
 ville PO
WOODS, Edward, D-45-5; Madison St, Nashville PO
WOODS, Elija, Je-137-2; Pvt F Co 9th TN Cav; 63 to
 65; Hickory Ridge PO
WOODS, Foster, Ms-183-1; Martha widow of; Pvt I Co
 111th US Col Inf; 64 to __; Comenville PO;
 died in service; drawing a pension
WOODS, George, Sh-191-1; Hallie widow of; Memphis
 PO; records destroyed
WOODS, George W., Ja-85-4; Pvt K Co 1st TN Col Hvy
 Art; 7-24-64 to 3-21-66; Georgetown PO
WOODS, George W. M. D., Ca-24-1; Pvt I Co 5th TN
 Cav; 2-8-63 to 8-14-65; Talvine PO; injury
 right hip & back; from jerk of horse when in
 army
WOODS, Gilbert H., H-53-1; Pvt A Co 2nd OH Art; 7-
 16-63 to 5-25-65; Chattanooga PO; chronic
 diarrhea, shot in face
WOODS, Hector, Co-62-3; USS; 5th Dist; sight
WOODS, Hency C., Ms-177-1; Dist #11
WOODS, Henry, Sh-149-1; Pvt B Co 114th IL Hvy Art;
 6 Mar 63 to 6 Jan 66; National Cemetery PO;
 lost his papers
WOODS, James, Mc-114-5; Pvt; Santfordville PO
WOODS, James, D-93-1; Pvt G Co 11th TN Cav; 62 to
 65; Newsoms Sta. PO
WOODS, James, Cl-48-2; Pvt C Co 114th KY; Old Town
 PO; he lost his discharge, cant tell date of
 enlistment & discharge
WOODS, James, Hm-107-3; Pvt A Co 13th TN Cav; 22
 Sep 63 to 21 Sep 65; Witts Foundry PO; epileptic fits 25 yrs
WOODS, James H., A-4-1; Pvt D Co 1st TN Lt Art;
 11-2-63 to 7-20-65; Coal Creek PO; rheumatism
 in shoulder
WOODS, James K. P., Ca-23-1; Pvt I Co 5th TN Cav;
 2-12-63 to 8-14-65; Leoni PO; eyes injured by
 exposure
WOODS, James M., Dy-25-7(3); Cpl I Co 7th TN Cav;
 1 Aug 64 to 9 Aug 65; Newbern PO; rupture on
 duty by horse falling
WOODS, Jeff, Sh-158-5(1); Pvt C Co 59th US Col Inf;
 2 Oct 63 to 7 Aug 65; Memphis PO; discharged
 at the close of war with discharge papers
WOODS, John, L-100-1; Pvt I Co 17th US Col Inf; 20
 Dec 63 to 65; Ripley PO; wounded at Nashville,
 cannot give date of discharge
WOODS, John, Mn-122-1; Pvt A Co 6th TN Cav;
 9-25-62 to 7-26-65; McNairy PO
WOODS, John F., D-74-1; 203 Fatherland St, Nash-
 ville PO
WOODS, John W., M-106-1; Pvt F Co 52nd KY Inf;
 Dixons Springs PO; discharge misplaced
WOODS, John W., Lo-191-1; Farr. L Co 6th KY Cav;
 20 Aug 62 to 14 Jul 65; Morganton PO
WOODS, Joseph, Sh-149-3; US Sol; 6th Civil Dist
WOODS, Losson, He-60-2; Pvt C Co 7th TN Cav; 62 to
 Aug 65; Chesterfield PO; scurvy, imprisoned
WOODS, Mathew, Hn-77-1; Pvt A Co 4th Hvy Art; Jan
 63 to Mar 66; PO omitted
WOODS, N. B., Bo-11-7; E. E. widow of; Cpl E Co
 3rd __ Home Guard; 61 to 65; Houk PO; ruptured
WOODS, Sam, Hy-76-2; alias Starks, Sam; Cpl F Co
 59th US Col Inf; 23 Jan 63 to 31 Jun 66;
 Stanton Depot PO
WOODS, Samuel C., Be-2-1; Pvt K Co 2nd TN Mtd Inf;
 62 to 64; Holladay PO; chronic piles
WOODS, Samul, Br-6-4; Pvt F Co 5th TN Mtd Inf; 10-
 5-64 to __; Charleston PO; rheumatism,
 deserted
WOODS, Thomas, Lk-113-1; Pvt L Co 3rd KY Cav; Dec
 1, 61 to 25 Jan 64; 5th Civil Dist
WOODS, Thomas G., Ca-23-1; Pvt K Co 5th TN Cav; 2-
 63 to 5-63; Leoni PO; no injuries
WOODS, Wade, M-106-1; Francis widow of; Pvt E Co
 1st TN Vol Inf; 1-12-64 to __; Union Camp PO;
 husband killed
WOODS, William, Sh-146-3; US Sol; 3rd Civ Dist
WOODS, William C., Mc-112-3; Pvt K Co 59th OH Inf;
 7-62 to 7-65; Athens PO; transferred from H
 Co to K Co
WOODS, William T., He-61-3; Pvt A Co 7th TN Cav;
 Jan 64 to 9 Aug 65; 15th Civil Dist
WOODSIDE, James K., Cf-37-1; Pvt G Co 1st TN Mtd
 Inf; Mar 5 64 to Apr 21, 65; Hillsboro PO
WOODSIDE, L. N., Dk-32-1; Sgt A Co 5th TN Cav; 7-
 29-62 to 3-20-64; Liberty PO; cartarrh, lung
 trouble; 1st Lt G Co 1st TN Mtd Inf; 3-21-64
 to 3-18-65
WOODSIDE, William H., W-193-2; Sgt A Co 5th TN Cav;
 9-6-63 to 8-14-65; Viala PO
WOODSON, Alfred, Sn-259-1; Pvt C Co 14th __; 10-1-
 63 to 3-26-66; Bethpage PO
WOODSON, George, Cl-52-1; P Wag; 63 to __; Quarter
 PO; shot thrue nee
WOODSON, Henry M., Sh-159-2; Memphis PO; CONF
WOODSON, James B., H-64-3; Chattanooga PO; general
 debility; pensioned
WOODSON, Julia A., Li-155-1; widow; Pvt US Art; 64
 to 66; Boon's Hill PO; camp diarhear; died
 soon after got home from camp as chronic
 diarhea contracted
WOODSON, Silas, C-30-1; 2nd Lt I Co 9th TN Cav; 6-
 63 to 6-6-65; Well Spring PO
WOODWARD, Cornelius, Ca-20-2; Pvt C Co 5th TN Cav;
 8-1-62 to 8-1-64; Woodbury PO; shot through
 hip
WOODWARD, Henry D., Ch-14-1; Pvt C Co 10th NC Art;
 4-1-62 to 4-26-65; Wild Goose PO; CONF
WOODWARD, Richard H., H-61-1; Pvt F Co 1st Reg
 forces for local defense around Richmond; 63
 to 4-15-65; Chattanooga PO; CONF?
WOODWORTH, George B., H-60-2; Pvt H Co 12th PA Inf;
 4-21-61 to none (4 mos); Chattanooga PO
WOODY, Hezekiah, Ro-206-2; Martha A. widow of;
 Pvt E Co 1st TN Inf; 20 Aug 61 to 17 Sep 64;
 Emory Gap PO
WOODY, Joshua A., De-23-2; Pvt G Co; Aug 63 to Apr
 65; Swallow Bluff PO
WOODY, Julia A., De-24-1; widow US Sol; Decatur-
 ville PO
WOODY, Richard, H-72-2(1); Pvt D Co 1st US Col Art;
 3-15-64 to 3-21-66; Chattanooga PO
WOODY, William, Me-90-2(1); Goodfield PO; CONF
WOODY, William D., Po-151-1; Pvt H Co 5th TN Inf;
 Servilla PO
WOODY, William M., Ro-211-2; Sgt H Co 3rd TN Inf;
 10 Feb 62 to 23 Feb 65; Webster PO; wounded
 by shell
WOOLART, John, Je-141-2; Elizabeth Howard widow of;
 New Market PO
WOOLDRIDGE, John, D-51-1; Pvt D Co 171st OH Inf;
 Apr 1, 64 to Aug 64; Commercial Hotel, Cedar
 St, Nashville PO
WOOLDUGE, Scion B., Mt-141-1; 13th KY Cal (Col or
 Cav?); Dist 11

WOOLFORT, Melvina, widow, Sh-193-2; Memphis PO
WOOLIVER, George, K-169-1; Pvt A Co 2nd TN Cav; 20 Oct 63 to 11 Sep 65; Knoxville PO
WOOLSBERG?, Edward, Sh-200-1; Pvt MO unit; Corner McKinley & Dixon St., Memphis PO
WOOLSEY, Fithias, Ge-98-3; Recruiting Officer; 5 Nov 61 to __; Milburnton PO; eyripelas
WOOLSEY, James, Ge-98-3; Frances E. widow of; Pvt H Co 1st TN Cav; 62 to 63; Jeroldstown PO; rheumatism & crippled shoulder
WOOLSEY, Samuel, Ro-206-1; Pvt B Co 5th TN Cav; Apr 62 to Apr 65; Emory Gap PO; CONF
WOOLSON, William A., H-54-3; Pvt G Co 148th OH Inf; 5-11-64 to 1864; Sherman Heights PO
WOOSLEY, Mel C., Rb-229-1; Synthia A. widow of; Pvt 3rd KY Cav; 64 to 65; Sadlersville PO
WOOSLEY, Mosses W., Mt-132-1; Pvt A Co 3rd KY Cav; 10-15-61 to 1-11-65; 1st Civil Dist.
WOOTEN, Daniel B., D-57-3; Pvt Joe Thompson; Oct 63 to 65; Nashville PO; CONF
WOOTEN, Thomas L., M-108-3; Mahala J. widow of; Pvt A Co 9th KY Inf; 9-23-61 to __; Lafayette PO; discharge not at hand
WOOTEN, William, Br-12-6; Rhat PO
WOOTON, Robert, Ha-111-4(1); Mary Tignor formerly widow of; Upper Clinch PO
WOOTTON, John S., M-103-6; Pvt B Co 37th KY Mtd Inf; 1-11-63 to 12-28-64; Pvt I Co 8th TN Inf; 4-25-65 to 8-31-65; Lafayette PO
WOOTTON, William P., M-107-2; Pvt D Co 9th KY Inf; 10-1-61 to 12-15-64; Red Boiling Springs PO; injury to back & arm
WORD, Eliza Ann (see Cuthbert, B.)
WORD, Anthony, T-209-1; Pvt I Co 16th KY Inf; 63 to 65; Randolph PO; Negro & very ignorant
WORD, William, Ge-88-1; Bulls Gap PO; somethink lik heart dis., not at home and cant get facts
WORDS, Hartwell, B-6-1; Pvt B Co 14th US Col Inf; 11-1-63 to 1866; Fall Creek PO
WORICK, Haron, Gr-82-2; Sol.; 13th Dist
WORK, Eliza (see Owen, Robert)
WORKMAN, John C., We-220-2; Pvt C Co TN State Troop; Oct 14, 64 to Apr 14, 65; PO omitted
WORLEY, Charles W., H-50-3(1); Pvt C Co 6th R TN Mtd Inf; 9-7-64 to 6-30-65; Soddy PO; lung disease
WORLEY, Hascue, Jo-148-1; Pvt D Co 13th TN Cav; 63 to 5 Sep 65; Laurel Bloomery PO; frost bite
WORLEY, Hurman G., Ov-137-2; Pvt E Co 117th IN Inf; 7-5-63 to 12-25-63; Monroe PO; diruscis
WORLEY, John, Sh-153-2; Pvt F Co; 65 to 65; Bailey Sta. PO
WORLEY, John N., Ov-137-3; Pvt 117th IN Inf; 7-63 to 3-64; Monroe PO; disease of stomach and piles and lung disease
WORLEY, Saml. A. H-60-3; Pvt B Co 5th IN Cav; 6-19-63 to 1-26-64; Pvt B Co 13th OH Cav; 12-25-63 to 7-4-65; Chattanooga PO; wounded in back, also chronic diarrhoea
WORLEY, Thomas C., D-72-4; Pvt C Co 11th TN Inf; Nov 31, 63 to Apr 16, 65; Nashville PO; CONF
WORLEY, William P., Mc-114-4; Pvt A Co 5th TN Inf; 10-10-64 to 7-14-65; Calhoun PO
WORLEY, William R., Mr-96-1; Pvt A Co 4th TN Cav; Whitwell PO
WORLY, Daniel, Hd-50-6; Pvt C Co 3rd KY Inf; 10-3-64 to 2-14-65; Nixon PO
WORLY, David, Hd-50-6; Pvt D Co 2nd TN Mtd Inf; 12-21-63 to 2-1-65; Nixon PO
WORTHAM, Thomas J., Hw-131-2; Pvt D Co 8th TN Cav; 28 Sep 63 to 11 Sep 65; White Horn PO
WORTHAM, St-160-1; Lafayette PO; Christian Co. KY; CONF
WORTHINGTON, Cristopher, Bl-3-1; Pvt I Co 3rd TN Cav; 1864 to 5-9-65; Patten PO; crn(chronic?) rheumatism; CONF
WORTHINGTON, David, Bl-3-1; Pvt G Co 6th Mtd Inf; 4-21-65 to 1-30-65(sic); Billingsly PO; inflammation back
WORTHINGTON, Francis H., Sh-150-3; sea captain; no dates (32 years); Barl bt PO
WORTHINGTON, James, Bl-3-2; Pvt F Co 2nd TN Cav 5-61 to 3-21-65; Orones Store PO; rupture; CONF
WORTHINGTON, James, Bl-3-1; Pvt F Co __ TN Cav; 7-61 to 1865; Patten PO; CONF

WORTHINGTON, James M., Cf-35-3; Pvt A Co 51st TN Inf; 18 Aug 61 to 16 Jun 65; Gould PO; CONF
WORTHINGTON, Jessie, Bl-3-2; Pvt F Co 3rd TN Cav; 7-2-61 to 12-64; Orones Store PO; finger off; CONF
WORTHINGTON, John, K-168-4; Smithwood PO
WORTHINGTON, John J., Mg-197-4; __ to 22 Aug 65; Wartburg PO; rheumatism; Great Western Navy
WORTHINGTON, Samuel, Bl-3-5; Pvt F Co 2nd TN Cav; 7-9-61 to 25-65; Tanbark PO; CONF
WORTHINGTON, Thomas A., D-98-1; Pvt A Co 12th IL; Sep 12, 61 to Jul 10, 65; 19th Civ. Dist.
WORTHINGTON, William L., K-166-3; 1st Lt D Co 8th TN Inf; 2 Dec 62 to 18 Oct 63; Knoxville PO; deaf, rheumatism, heart disease; pensioner
WOSKEY, James M., Di-41-1; Cpl H Co 5th MN Inf; 2-1-62 to 2-5-63; Cragihope PO; Ft. Snelen
WOY, Joseph, H-66-2; Pvt L Co 3rd TN Cav; 2-64 to 10-31-65; Chattanooga PO
WRAY, Antony, D-100-1; Cpl F Co 12th TN Inf; Aug 12, 63 to Jan 16, 66; Nashville PO; says he has his discharge
WRAY, George W., Mn-120-1; Sgt G Co 1st AL Cav; 62 to Jan 4, 64; Pocahontas PO
WRAY, J. L., Wi-276-2; widow of; Pvt D Co 10th TN Cav; Oct 62 to Oct 65; Beechville PO; CONF
WRAY, Jesse? (see William, Jesse)
WRAY, Lewis W., A-9-5(3); Dutch Valley PO; measles resulting in partial deafness in left ear; CONF
WRAY, Monroe, Hr-91-1; Pvt G Co 1st AL Cav; 3-3-63 to __; 1st TN Bat. & Lt Art; 3-29-64 to 8-11-65; Bolivar PO; weak lungs; typhoid pneumonia, cancer
WRAY, William E., Cr-4-5; Pvt A Co 35th GA Inf; 2-9-62 to 4-19-65; Bells Depot PO; wounded shoulder, CONF
WREN, Samuel J., Je-146-2; Pvt C Co 8th TN Cav; 16 Jul 63 to 11 Sep 65; White Pine PO; rheumatism & sore eyes; eyes look very bad
WRIGHT, Aaron S., Hw-132-3(1); Pvt D Co 31st TN Inf; Feb 62 to May 64; Strahl PO; CONF
WRIGHT, Alferd, D-48-1; Sgt I Co Nashville PO
WRIGHT, Charles C., H-69-2; Pvt 1st AL? Water's esear?; 1863 to 1865; Chattanooga PO; CONF
WRIGHT, Charly, H-73-1; Pvt H Co 1st US Col Cav; Chattanooga PO
WRIGHT, D. W., Wl-308-3; Pvt 45th TN; Jun 61 to Jun 64; Mount Juliet PO; captured; CONF
WRIGHT, Edmund, Sh-200-1; Mary widow of; Cpl G Co 11th US Col Inf; 1-11-64 to 1-12-66; Cone St., Memphis PO; died of dysentery
WRIGHT, Edmund, Fr-116-1(2); Orderly Sgt I Co 44th IA; 2-65 to 6-28-65; Sherwood PO
WRIGHT, Eldridge, We-221-5(2); Pvt I Co 31st TN Inf; Sep 61 to Apr 65; Martin PO; CONF
WRIGHT, Elizabeth (see Gusbee, John)
WRIGHT, Emsbry, Hn-77-2; Pvt E Co NC Inc; May 62 to 63; PO omitted
WRIGHT, Francis M., Gi-134-1; Pvt E Co 8th TN Inf; 3-5-65 to 9-1-65; Yokley PO
WRIGHT, Frank A., Dk-35-1; Cpl E Co 4th TN Mtd Inf; 11-28-64 to 8-25-65; Temperance Hall PO; thrown from horse
WRIGHT, George, Wl-308-2; Pvt 46th TN; May 61 to May 64; Mount Juliet PO; captured; CONF
WRIGHT, George, D-75-2; Pvt A Co Whartons? Cav; 15 Jun 63 to 15 Aug 63; Stewarts Ferry PO; paroled at Nashville; CONF
WRIGHT, George P., Co-138-4; Pvt; 14th Civil Dist.
WRIGHT, George W., Ro-203-3; Pvt F Co 32nd KY Inf; 62 to __; Ethel PO; came home on furlough and never returned
WRIGHT, Henry, Lo-188-1; Pvt L Co 1st TN Art; Adolphus PO
WRIGHT, Henry, Co-65-1; Eller widow of; Pvt; Wilton Springs PO
WRIGHT, Horance, A-6-5(3); Pvt B Co 2nd TN Inf; 8-10-61 to 10-6-64
WRIGHT, Hughes, Hm-109-2; Pvt A Co 1st TN Art; 24 Jul 62 to 5 Aug 65; Russelville PO
WRIGHT, Isaac G., Mc-113-1; Pvt A Co TN Inf; 5-64 to 12-64; Goodfield PO
WRIGHT, Isreal E., Ro-202-1; Elizabeth widow of; pvt F Co 1st TN Inf; 9 Aug 61 to 17 Sep 64; Paw Paw Ford PO; rheumatism
WRIGHT, J. David, Je-141-3; Margret widow of; Mill Springs PO

WRIGHT, J. R., A-1-1; Pvt G Co 7th TN Inf; 12-1-64 to 7-27-65; Andersonville PO
WRIGHT, Jack, Ro-207-3; Pvt 22nd IL Inf; discharge lost; Paint Rock PO; ruptured
WRIGHT, Jackson, H-67-1; Pvt A Co 110th US Col Inf; 12-64 to 2-6-66; Chattanooga PO; camp measles effected head & eyes
WRIGHT, Jacob, Dy-25-3; Pvt 22nd TN Inf; Dec 62 to (4 mos); Newbern PO; CONF
WRIGHT, James, A-7-2; Robertsville PO
WRIGHT, James, Gr-71-2; Pvt G Co 8th TN Inf; 1 Mar 63 to 30 Jun 6t; Jarmine PO
WRIGHT, James, K-163-1; Pvt 3rd TN Reg; 62 to 65; Knoxville PO; CONF
WRIGHT, James K., Rb-218-1; Pvt B Co 1st KY Inf; M 64 to Jan 65 (8 mos); Handleyton PO; deaf in right ear
WRIGHT, Jas. L., Wl-308-1; Lt G Co 4th TN Cav; Jul 1, 61 to May 21, 65; PO omitted; CONF
WRIGHT, Jas. S., Wl-308-1; Pvt H Co 4th TN; May 1, 63 to Apr 1, 65; Dodoburgh PO; CONF
WRIGHT, James W., He-64-2; Pvt G Co 32nd TN Inf; 1 May 61 to 15 Feb 62; Center Point PO; discharged for sickness; CONF
WRIGHT, James W., Pu-140-1; Sgt D Co 1st TN Mtd Inf; 9-63 to 1864; Cookeville PO; Maj D Co 1st TN Mtd Inf; 1864 to 1865
WRIGHT, Jefferson, Sh-175-2; 16 Avery St., Memphis
WRIGHT, John, Sh-157-2; Pvt C Co 13th TN H; May 16, 61 to 64; Dist 13
WRIGHT, John, Mo-122-2; Pvt G Co 43rd TN Inf; 11-61 to 8-20-63; Dancing Branch PO; CONF
WRIGHT, John, D-70-3; Pvt E Co 17th __; Apr 25, 64 to Apr 25, 66; Trimbles School, Nashville PO; rheumatism, largeness of stem blader, back & eye ache
WRIGHT, John, Bl-2-2(1), Nancy A. widow of; Pvt K Co 4th TN Cav; Farmingdale PO
WRIGHT, John, Ge-86-2; Sgt G Co 9th TN Cav; 17 May 63 to 13 Sep 65; Thula PO
WRIGHT, John B., Dy-29-2; Pvt A Co 15th TN Cav; 62 to 65; Yorkville PO; CONF
WRIGHT, John C., Fe-41-1; Pvt D Co 11th TN Cav; 9-10-63 to 9-11-65; Pall Mall PO
WRIG(T), John E., Wy-173-3; Martha E. Hicks formerly widow of; Pvt A Co 10th TN Inf; 4-12-62 to 5-25-65; Sims PO
WRIGHT, John E., D-75-2; Pvt F Co 30th TN Inf; 1 Nov 61 to 13 Sep 62; Stewarts Ferry PO; prisoner Camp Butler IL 7 mos; CONF
WRIGHT, John W., Sh-145-4; Pvt H Co 76th NY Inf; 27 Sep 62 to 13 Feb 65; Millington PO
WRIGHT, John W., Ct-37-1; Pvt B Co 13th TN Cav; 9-23-63 to 9-5-65; Hopson PO; lung trouble
WRIGHT, Joseph? (see Lunard?, Joseph)
WRIGHT, Joseph, Hw-127-1; Pvt C Co 9th TN Cav; 11 Aug 63 to 11 Sep 65; Rogersville PO; rheumatism, partially deaf
WRIGHT, Louis, Ro-201-6; Pvt D Co 1st TN Hvy Art; 8 Mar 64 to 31 Mar 66; Kingston PO
WRIGHT, Luke, Cl-48-1; Pvt G Co 4th KY Mtd Inf; 1864 to 8-65 (11 mos); Old Town PO
WRIGHT, Madison G., Mo-122-2; Pvt F Co 3rd TN Cav; 4-26-63 to 8-3-65; Dancing Branch PO
WRIGHT, Mary B., widow US Sol, G-51-2; Humboldt PO
WRIGHT, Mitchell, Fe-42-2; Amanda widow of; Cpl E Co 37th KY; 8-17-63 to 12-29-64; Jamestown PO
WRIGHT, Morgan, Un-258-1; Pvt 8th TN Inf; May 62 to Jul 64; Speedwell PO, Claiborne Co.
WRIGHT, Moses, Hw-123-1; Jane widow of; Pvt H Co 8th TN Inf; New Canton PO
WRIGHT, Moses M., K-154-4; Pvt B Co; 63 to 65; Knoxville PO
WRIGHT Mosses W., Wl-308-3; Pvt I Co 20th TN; May 10, 61 to Apr 4, 65; Mount Juliet PO; CONF
WRIGHT, Nancy J. (see Casteel, James H.)
WRIGHT, Perry, H-67-1; Wesley L. Master alias; pvt F Co 110th US Col Inf; 3-63 to 1866 (2 yrs 9 mos); Chattanooga PO
WRIGHT, Pleasant, Pu-142-1; Charity widow of; Pvt; Neversare PO
WRIGHT, Richard F., K-154-6(3); Knoxville PO
WRIGHT, Robert, Hm-109-3; Penelope widow of; Pvt TN Cav; Russelville? PO; gunshot in thigh
WRIGHT, Samuel, (Col?), Ro-202-5; Sgt M Co 1st TN Inf; 18 Aug 64 to Mar 66; Adolphus PO; diarrhea and swelling cramp

WRIGHT, Samuel Z., K-163-1; Sol E Co 31st TN Reg; 62 to 64; Knoxville PO; CONF
WRIGHT, Sparrl? B., K-172-3; 2nd Lt H Co 11th VA Inf; 15 May 61 to Apr 65; PO omitted; CONF
WRIGHT, Thomas, D-89-1; Pvt B Co 1st NC; Sep 25, 63 to Aug 16, 65; Nashville PO
WRIGHT, Thomas C., Ro-203-1; Cpl; 62 to __; Ehtel PO; CONF
WRIGHT, Veyix(sic), G-65-1; Pvt A Co 4th TN Mtd Inf; Apr 62 to 63; Gann PO
WRIGHT, Wade H., D-75-2; Pvt F Co 30th TN Inf; 1 May 61 to 1 May 65; Stewarts Ferry PO; prisoner Chicago IL 4 mos; CONF
WRIGHT, William, Sh-189-3; no record could be had; Va. Ave., Memphis PO
WRIGHT, William, Gi-122-6; Pvt E Co 1st TN Bat; 8 Aug 61 to Feb 65; Lesters Sta. PO; CONF
WRIGHT, William, D-91-3; Pvt K Co 8th TN Inf; 63 to 66; 500 N. College St., Nashville PO
WRIGHT, William (see Roach, William)
WRIGHT, William, C-24-2; Sarah Baily formerly widow of; Pvt 1st TN Inf; died Flat Lick KY; Boy PO; disease of back loins & kidneys; neuralgia & rheumatism
WRIGHT, William, A-6-3(1); Pvt B Co TN Cav; 1861 to 1865; Olivers PO
WRIGHT, William, Ro-201-4(1); Pvt B Co 2nd TN Inf; 1 Oct 62 to 19 Jun 65; Kingston PO
WRIGHT, William A., Ro-207-1; Pvt F & B Cos. 1st TN Inf; 10 Aug 63 to 3 Aug 65; Erie PO, Loudon Co.; catarrh & hemrage of lungs
WRIGHT, William B., De-23-1; Pvt E Co 6th TN Cav; Sep 18, 62 to Aug 6, 65; Bath Springs PO
WRIGHT, Wm. G., Se-227-2; Pvt B Co 6th TN Inf; 8 Mar 62 to 30 Jun 65; Trundles X Roads PO; louseness in back
WRIGHT, William G. B., A-8-1; Pvt G Co 8th TN Cav; 8-3-62 to 9-65; Scarborough PO
WRIGHT, William T., D-75-2; Pvt I Co 20th TN Inf; 1 Jun 61 to Jun 65; Stewarts Ferry PO; pris. at Camp Butler 7 mos
WRIGHT, William T., Fr-119-1; Cpl F Co 40th IN; Dectal? 1863 (1 yr 8 mos); Dochert PO; heart disease; struck by a ball or c__?
WRIGHT, Willis R., Fe-44-3(2); Pvt F Co 7th E TN Inf; 6-62 to __(18 mos); Armathwaite PO; lung disease
WRIGHT, Young, Sn-261-2(1); gunner B Co 3rd TN Cav; 11-9-61 to __ (4 yrs about); PO omitted; prisoner Gallatin Louisville 27 months; exchanged; CONF
WRINKLE, George T., K-182-4; Cpl C Co 1st TN Lt Art; 18 Sep 63 to 3 Mar 65; Gap Creek PO; lost eyesight
WRINKLE, Wiley, R-158-3; Eliza widow of; Pvt 9th TN Cav; 1863 to died 1864; Washington PO; husb. died in army; widow draws pension
WRINKLE, Wyley M., Ja-85-3; Pvt I Co 4th TN Cav; 9-15-63 to 7-12-65; Birchwood PO
WRINN, Michael, Lo-189-2; Pvt D Co 3rd TN Inf; 10 Feb 62 to 28 Feb 65; Philadelphia PO; ankle broken; pensioned
WUERTZ, Joachem, Gu-46-1; Pvt K Co 4th MO Inf; 8-20-61 to 2-1-63; Genetter PO
WYAN, Williams, Ge-97-2; Pvt F Co 3rd TN N.T.?; 1 Mar 64 to Apr 65; Maltsberger PO; diareh heart dis
WYATT, Alford (see Shields, Alford)
WYATT, Alfred (see Buckner, Alfred)
WYATT, Benjamin, Cl-57-2; Pvt H Co 49th Reg KY; 7-4-63 to 12-26-64; Goin PO; right eye out & deared off
WYATT, Eli C., Gi-122-4; Pvt G Co 63rd VA Inf; 1 Feb 62 to 1 Apr 65; Prospect Sta. PO; 10 mos in prison
WYATT, Fransis M., Cl-58-2; Pvt 11th TN Cav; Davo PO; injered from horse, can't get much information
WYATT, Henry D., H-62-2; 1st Lt B Co 15th NH Inf; 10-10-62 to 8-63; Surgeon 1st US Hvy Art; 5-8-65 to 4-31(sic)-66; 527 Chestnut, Chattanooga PO
WYATT, Hiram, Dy-23-1; Pvt B Co 120th OH Inf; 10 May 62 to 64; Dyersburg PO
WYATT, James, Sm-171-2; Ann widow of; Pvt C Co 8th TN Mtd Inf; 2-20-64 to 8-17-65; Chestnut Mound PO

WYATT, James E., Mo-125-1; Pvt A Co 7th TN Mtd Inf; 8-27-61 to 7-27-65; Gudger PO
WYATT, Jess, De-22-3; Pvt G Co 51st TN Inf; 15 Jan 61 to 1 May 61; Dunbar PO; CONF
WYATT, Joseph, Ro-203-6; Pvt K Co 5th TN Inf; 25 Mar 62 to 65; Burns' Mills PO; foot broken
WYATT, Joseph H., Se-221-3; Clarissa widow of; Cpl F Co 9th TN Cav; 1 Oct 63 to 7 Jul 64; Fox PO; died Jul 7, 1864
WYATT, Josia N., Dy-25-1; Capt C Co 12th TN Inf; May 61 to May 65; Newbern PO; CONF
WYATT, Samuel A., Ro-201-1; Pvt C Co 7th TN Inf; 1 Aug 64 to 1 Jul 65; Kingston PO
WYATT, Sarrah A. (see Croslin, William)
WYATT, Thomas R., Me-88-3; 1st Lt G Co 5th TN Cav; 11-24-64 to 7-13-65; Brittsville PO
WYATT, Turner, Gi-127-5; Teamster C Co; Pulaski PO; papers burnt & does not remember
WYATT, W. A., G-57-3; Pvt E Co; 4 mos; Yorkville PO
WYATT, William, De-22-3; Pvt G Co 27th TN Inf; 1 Dec 61 to 29 May 65; Dunbar PO; shot in left arm
WYATT, William B., Cr-20-3; Pvt C Co 7th TN Cav; Jan 28 62 to Aug 9 65; Hollow Rock PO
WYATT, William B., Sm-171-2; Pvt C Co 8th TN Mtd Inf; 2-20-65 to 8-25-65; Chestnut Mound PO
WYATT, William F., Sm-171-2; Pvt I Co 1st TN Mtd Inf; 10-15-64 to 7-22-65; Chestnut Mound PO
WYERMAN, James, Cl-58-2; Pvt Co E 2nd TN Inf; 8-9-61 to 10-6-64; Davo PO; can't get more information
WYKLE, James, Ge-90-3; Mary E. widow of; Sgt F Co 4th TN Inf; 63 to 65; Greeneville PO
WYLEY, Cornelius, D-77-3; Sgt C Co 14th US Inf; Nashville PO
WYLEY, Dotson, M-103-5; Pvt D Co 8th TN Inf; 3-1-65 to 8-31-65; Red Boiling Springs PO
WYLIE, Nickson, G-61-1; Pvt 1st AL; 12th Civil Dist
WYLIE, William B., Cl-54-1; Pvt C Co 9th TN Cav; 8-7-63 to 9-11-65; Bacchus PO; expiration of time
WYMAN, John, Hw-127-2; Pvt A Co 1st TN Lt Art; 10 Oct 63 to 3 Aug 65; Rogersville PO; disease of eyes, back, side &c &c
WYNN, Andy, Mn-126-1; Purdy PO
WYNN, Ezkariah M., Se-225-3; Capt M Co 2nd TN Cav; Sevierville PO
WYNN, Henry V. C., Dy-25-3; Pvt C Co TN Cav; 62 to 64; Newbern PO; wounded in hand & a cripple; CONF
WYRICK, Alexander, K-174-5; could not find out; House Mountain PO
WYRICK, F. C., Cl-54-3(1); Pvt A Co; 5-63 to __; Tazewell? PO; CONF
WYRICK, George M., Un-251-2; Pvt E Co 6th TN Inf; 15 Apr 62 to 27 Apr 65; Effie PO
WYRICK, James H., Le-118-1; Pvt G Co 5th TN Cav; 4 Sep 62 to 14 Aug 65; Rockdate PO
WYRREK?, Landes, Me-89-2; Pvt K Co 13th TN Cav; 63 to 65; Dayton PO; ruptured
YANCY, Columbus A., Hy-84-1; Pvt F Co 31st Inf; 11-1-62 to 5-1-63; Woodville PO
YANKEE, Michael, Hw-122-2; Pvt F Co 8th TN Cav; 6-16-63 to 9-11-65; Blairs Gap PO; chr. rheumatism result of gun shot, partially disabled
YARBERRY, Elisha, Se-219-2; Anahap widow of; Pvt E Co 1st TN Bat; Jones Cave PO
YARBERRY, William, Se-219-1; Pvt C Co 8th TN Cav; 9-28-63 to 6-18-65; East Fork PO; chronic diarhoe
YARBO, Alen C., De-24-1; Pvt I Co 3rd TN Inf; 8-18-63 to 4-30-66; Decaturville PO
YARBOR, Jasper, Mc-112-9; Pvt E Co 1st KY Lt Art; 2-29-64 to 9-5-65; Athens PO
YARBRO, Mary A., De-24-2; widow US Sol; 3rd Dist
YARBROUGH, Miles, St-160-2; H? Pvt G Co 50th TN Inf; 11-1-61 to 4-26-63; Big Rock PO; prison 7 mos; CONF
YARBROUGH, Nathan E., St-160-2; Pvt I Co 14th TN Inf; 2-10-61 to 12-63; Big Rock PO; CONF
YARBROUGH, Wilkins, Wi-285-1; Phillis widow of; Pvt B Co 12th __ Inf; 1-63 to 1-65; Wrencoe PO; died in hospital
YARNELL, Harrison J., A-8-3; Pvt G Co 6th TN Inf; 4-18-62 to 5-18-65; Scarborough PO

353

YARNELL, James M., K-178-2; Reas Sgt 2nd TN Cav; 11-4-62 to 7-6-65; Ball Camp PO
YARNELL, James S., K-177-4; Pvt G Co 6th TN Inf; 4-18-62 to 5-18-65; Powells Station PO; rheumatism & hearing
YARNELL, John G., K-186-4; Rachel M. widow of; Pvt E Co 3rd TN Inf; 3-62 to __; Balls Camp PO
YARNELL, Joseph, K-186-4; Pvt C Co 2nd TN Cav; 11-11-? to 7-65; Balls Camp PO; piles
YARNELL, Laura O., K-186-5; widow of; Beaver Ridge PO
YATES, Benjamin, Gr-75-1; Pvt K Co 3rd TN Inf; 2-10-62 to 2-10-65; Tampico PO; hearing & diahea
YATES, Clifford P., Mo-130-1; Pvt B Co GA Inf; 8-10-64 to ?; Povo PO
YATES, David, Gr-73-1; Pvt K Co 3rd TN Inf; 2-62 to 3-65; Rutledge PO; rheumatism in limbs, exposure in US Service
YATES, Hilliard G., Be-1-1; Pvt M Co 12th KY Cav; 2-64 to 8-65; Sugar Tree PO; discharge lost
YATES, Houston A., Rb-221-2; Pvt; Adams Station PO
YATES, Isham, Di-30-2; Pvt C Co 100th KY Inf; 63 to 5-9-65; Dickson PO
YATES, James, Gr-76-1; Pvt K Co 3rd TN Inf; 2-10-62 to 2-23-65; PO omitted
YATES, James M., Dy-29-2; Pvt B Co 5th TN Inf & Cal; 3-62 to 12-63; Newbern PO; reenlisted in 63 & served 1 yr; CONF
YATES, James W., Hw-133-2; Pvt A Co 12th TN Cav; 5-1-63 to 3-10-65; Burem's Store PO; CONF
YATES, John W., He-67-1; Sgt G Co 10th TN Inf; 6-19-62 to 6-24-65; Sardis PO; no disability
YATES, Mathew, G-71-2; Pvt F Co 12th TN Inf; 1-10-61 to 4-30-63; Rutherford PO
YATES, Ralph H., H-70-2(1); Pvt A Co 6th OH Inf; 4-19-61 to 6-24-64; Chattanooga PO
YATES, Robert H., Lo-191-2; Pvt H Co 21st VA Vols; 7-3-61 to 4-9-65; Morganton PO; gunshot through right arm
YATES, Samuel, Mo-127-2; Pvt; Notchy PO
YATES, William, Wl-307-1; Pvt K Co 3rd TN Inf; 2-10-62 to 2-10-65; Beckwith PO
YEAGER, Bruce F., Wa-276-1; Pvt B Co 12th TN Cav; 11-20-63 to 11-9-64; Limeston PO; rheumatism, lungs & kidneys
YEARGIN, John B., D-46-1; Paralee J. Luckey formerly widow of; Pvt A Co 5th TN Cav; 8-18-62 to 6-25-65; West Jefferson St, Nashville PO; scrofula & deafness
YEAROUT, Murry, Bo-23-2; Pvt B Co 2nd TN Cav; 8-6-62 to 7-13-65; Tuckaleechee Cove PO; rheumatism, now suffering mainely from so__
YEARWOOD, Richard, Mc-112-3; Amanda widow of; Pvt; Athens PO; pain in side, thes widow knows he was a sol but no dates
YEARWOOD, William A., Ru-246-1; Pvt G Co 3rd US Inf; 10-15-64 to 11-29-65; Murfreesboro PO
YEATMAN, Peter, Sn-254-1; Pvt B Co 14th US Col Inf; 6-1-64 to ?; Hendersonville PO
YELL, James C., B-2-2; Sgt C Co 5th TN Vol; 8-1-62 to 7-1-65; Haley PO
YERBY, Culnan, Sh-175-2; 268 Eliot St, Memphis PO
YERGEN, Jim, Wi-287-1; Cook E Co 38th OH Inf; 3-8-63 to 7-22-65; Civil Dist No 18
YERGIN?, John H., Dk-32-4; Pvt D Co 4th TN Mtd Inf; 9-23-64 to 8-25-65; Liberty PO; lung, kidney & liver trouble
YODER, William, R-162-5; Pvt D Co 1st TN Art; 62 to __; Dayton PO; had measles affected left lung & lost hearing in left ear
YOES, George T., Ms-174-1; Pvt A Co 1st AL Cav; 2-21-63 to 6-16-64; Chapel Hill PO
YOKELY, Charissa A. M., Mu-191-3; 7th Dist
YOKELY, John, Ge-91-4; Pvt F Co 8th TN Cav; 10-63 to 9-65; Greeneville PO; lungs affected
YOKELY, Malichy, Hw-121-4(3); Pvt K Co 8th TN Inf; 11-15-62 to 11-15-65; New Hope PO; rheumatism
YOKELY, Scott, Gi-132-2; Ellen Green formerly widow of; Pvt US CV; DeRay PO; former husbnad killed in battle
YOKEY, Jonas, Mg-198-2; Seaman, Chastain; 12-1-63 to 12-1-64; Deer Lodge PO
YORK, Amos, Mg-200-2; Pvt; 8-63 to 7-64; Rugby PO
YORK, David, S-218-1; Marget widow of; Pvt E Co 11th TN Cav; 5-19-63 to __ (10 mos); Huntsville PO; diseas of right hip

YORK, George W., Fe-42-3; Pvt Capt David Beaty's Co TN Ind Scouts; Boatland PO
YORK, Hulet W., M-107-3; Pvt A Co 8th TN Mtd Inf; 3-20-65 to 8-17-65; Walnut Shade PO
YORK, James, C-34-3; Jane Keethley former widow of; Pvt 2nd TN Inf; 3-7-62 to __; Abbott PO; couldn't get information
YORK, Jessey, S-218-2; Luesy widow of; 1st __ D Co 5th KY Cav; 1-8-62 to 1-64; Hughett PO; died of gunshot wound
YORK, Mack C., Co-66-2(1); Pvt K Co 2nd TN Inf; 6-6-63 to 6-18-65; English PO
YORK, Marlin F., M-107-3; Elisabeth E. widow of; Pvt F Co 1st TN Mtd Inf; 64 to 65; Gamaliel PO (Monroe Co., KY)
YORK, Merida, La-117-4; Pvt 15th Dist; CONF
YORK, Merrida, Cy-27-4(2); Pvt E Co 1st TN Cav; 63 to 65; Spivey PO
YORK, Nathan A., K-177-1; Pvt C Co 1st TN Cav; 3-1-62 to 6-5-65; Dante PO; cronic diarea; CONF
YORK, Simon, K-164-1; Pvt; PO omitted (Knoxville?)
YORK, Thomas G., M-107-3; Pvt F Co 4th KY Cav; 10-11-62 to 7-11-65; Salt Lick PO; relapse of measles
YORK, William, C-28-1; Pvt C Co 9th TN Cav; 9-15-63 to 9-11-65; Fincastle PO; neuralgia
YORK, William, K-176-1; Pvt I Co TN Inf; 2-13-63 to 6-12-65; Halls X Roads PO
YORK, William, M-107-4; Cpl 8th TN Mtd Inf; Red Boiling Spring PO
YORK, William A., J-79-1; Pvt F Co 1st TN Mtd Inf; 4-14-64 to 5-16-65; Whitleyville PO
YORK, William M., Fe-41-3(1); Pvt K Co 13th KY Cav; 9-12-63 to 1-10-65; Boat Land PO; bronchial troubles
YORKLEY, Amos, Gi-134-1; Dist 14
YOTHER?, George W., H-49-10; Elisabeth widow of; Pvt A Co 6th TN Mtd Inf; 8-2-64 to __; Daisy PO
YOTHER, William W., H-50-1; Malissa widow of; Pvt C Co 5th R TN Inf; 2-25-61 to 4-8-65; Bunch PO; chronic diarreah, measles
YOUGHT, Hugh L., Mg-199-2; Pvt A Co 6th US Cav; Sunbright PO; camp diarrhoea
YOUNCE, Elizabeth C., Mo-121-2; widow; 4th Civil Dist
YOUNG, Paul, Sh-145-4; Musician, Pvt 113th US Col Inf; 9-63 to 1-65; Kerrville PO; Cap Barker/Col Whooper of Minnesota
YOUNG, Adam, Gi-127-7; Pulaski PO; papers lost
YOUNG, Alexander, H-53-7; Pvt D Co; 1 yr; Chattanooga PO
YOUNG, Alfred, Wa-268-2; Johnson City PO; rheumatism
YOUNG, Anderson (see Wood, Wm. W.)
YOUNG, Andrew, C-34-2; Pvt D Co 1st SC Cav; 5-6-61 to 5-6-65; Buckeye PO; shot collarbone, knee foot & hand; CONF
YOUNG, Andy, Mo-129-1; Elisabeth widow of; Pvt; PO omitted
YOUNG, Augustus (see Watts, Alexander)
YOUNG, Bengeman I., Ch-14-2; Nancy E. widow of; Pvt; PO omitted; CONF
YOUNG, C., K-163-1; Margaret C. widow of; I Co Cav; 8-61 to 65; Knoxville PO
YOUNG, Calvin, Gi-128-1; Pvt G Co 111th TN Inf; 63 to 65; 8th Civil Dist
YOUNG, Daniel, Ho-96-2; US Sol; PO omitted
YOUNG, David K., A-5-2; Capt D Co 1st TN Lt Arty; 11-63 to 9-2-64; Clinton PO
YOUNG, David P., Hw-129-2; Pvt C Co 8th TN Mtd Inf; 62 to __; Mooresburg PO; ruptured by horse falling when taking Cumberland Gap
YOUNG, Edward B., Bo-14-4; Pvt A Co 3rd TN Cav; 11-10-62 to 7-6-65; Maryville PO
YOUNG, Elie, G-64-1; Haret Yount widow of; Pvt; 2 yrs; Bradford PO
YOUNG, Ewin E., Ro-201-4(2); Pvt B Co 5th TN Inf; 2-25-62 to 3-20-65; Kingston PO
YOUNG, Free M., Ro-201-6; Lt Col 5th TN Inf; 2-28-62 to 10-26-63; Kingston PO
YOUNG, George W., K-171-6(5); Pvt G Co 29th TN Inf; 10-62 to 65; PO omitted; CONF
YOUNG, Henry, H-59-2; Mary widow of; Pvt TN Inf; __ to 65; Chattanooga PO
YOUNG, Henry, Br-7-1; Pvt C Co 5th TN Inf; 10-64 to 7-16-65; Felker PO; rheumatism

YOUNG, Henry, Hu-99-1; Pvt 8th Ioway 13th US Inf; Johnsonville PO
YOUNG, Isaac P., Hu-103-2; Capt B Co 10th TN Inf; 5-10-61 to 12-23-65; PO omitted
YOUNG, James, Ja-86-1; Martha J. widow of; Pvt I Co 2nd TN Inf; 61 to died 5-64; Oottewah PO
YOUNG, James M., Gr-79-3; Minerva widow of; recruiting officer; Ball Point PO; killed
YOUNG, James M., Dk-39-3(1); Pvt; Dekalb PO
YOUNG, John, Di-34-3; Pvt C Co 8th TN Mtd Inf; 3-7-65 to __; Dickson PO; at home on furlough when Co. was discharged
YOUNG, John, Sh-145-3; Pvt I Co 56th US Col Cav; 10-64 to 1-66; Memphis PO; shot right ancle & head
YOUNG, John C., Ch-14-2; Pvt C Co 52nd TN Inf; 12-19-61 to 5-22-65; PO omitted; CONF
YOUNG, John J., Hw-129-1; Pvt A Co 26th TN Lt Art; 6-__ to __; Galbrath Springs PO; wounded in legg, gun shot, no discharge, deserter
YOUNG, John P., Sh-159-7; Pvt A Co 7th TN; 10-64 to 5-65; Memphis PO; CONF
YOUNG, Joseph, Gi-132-4; Eliza Rucker formerly widow of; Pvt 12th USCV; Wales PO; husband never herad from
YOUNG, Joseph, Br-13-3; Pvt G Co 5th TN Inf; 4-11-62 to 5-15-65; Cleveland PO; chronic pintegition
YOUNG, King, D-46-2; Manerva widow of; Pvt G Co 15th Col Inf; 1-24-64 to 4-7-66; Nashville PO
YOUNG, Lewis, Mu-196-2; Minerva Jestis formerly widow of; 111th US Inf; Columbia PO
YOUNG, Lonnie (see Bennett, George)
YOUNG, Louis, Hy-84-3(5); Pvt 11th US Inf; 63 to 65; Woodville PO; asthma, discharge lost
YOUNG, Louis, Col, Dk-31-1; Jane McClellan formerly widow of; H Co 17th US Col Inf; Alexandria PO; now a widow alone
YOUNG, Manuel, Ru-240-1; 2nd Sgt I Co 17th TN; 63 to 65; Rucker PO
YOUNG, Minerva, Je-141-4; widow US Sol; 4th Dist (Newmarket)
YOUNG, Mitchell, Sh-163-1; Pvt K Co 11th MS Inf; 10-4-64 to 1-12-66; Buntyn Station PO
YOUNG, Monroe, Sh-157-3; Cpl K Co 61st US Hvy; White Haven PO; wounded eye & fingers
YOUNG, Moody, Cr-7-1; Pvt 6th TN Inf; 5-28-61 to 12-64; Stokes PO; CONF
YOUNG, Phillip, H-56-1; Pvt E Co 43rd OH Inf; 12-7-61 to 3-17-65; St. Elm(o) PO
YOUNG, Ples L., Hm-103-3; Pvt A Co 1st TN Lt Art; 9-11-63 to 8-3-65; Morristown PO; heart diseas 25 yrs
YOUNG, Preston, Gr-70-1; Pvt A Co 17th TN Inf; 61 to 2; Rutledge PO
YOUNG, Richard, Hw-125-5; A Co 80th __; 61 to 65; Yellow Stone PO
YOUNG, Robert, Cu-18-1; Cpl H Co 3rd IN Cav; 9-20-62 to 1-8-65; Manning PO
YOUNG, Robert A., Sr., Dy-25-5(1); 1 yr; Newbern PO; shot in face, my position was wagon master; CONF
YOUNG, Robert M., Wa-263-3; Pvt; Garbers Mills PO; this name was crossed out
YOUNG, Rufus T., R-159-2; Pvt H Co 3rd TN Mtd Inf; 9-20-64 to 11-30-64; Spring City PO; hearing, speech
YOUNG, Samuel Jones, Sh-179-3(1); Pvt; Memphis PO
YOUNG, Samuel M., Sh-149-2; Pvt F Co 15th TN Inf; 2-3-64 to 4-7-66; Memphis PO
YOUNG, Shelley C., Mr-98-2(5); Pvt C Co 1st AL Cav; 9-19-63 to 6-16-64; Whiteside PO
YOUNG, Simeon, Mg-198-4; Capt B Co 10th KY Cav; 9-6-62 to 8-10-65; Rockwood PO
YOUNG, Simon, Mu-193-1; Pvt; 1-63 to 3-14-65; Columbia PO
YOUNG, Solomon, S-214-4; Pvt E Co 11th TN Cav; 8-61 to 10-12-64; Glenmary PO; kidney & bladder disease
YOUNG, Steve, G-65-1; Pvt E Co 15th MS Inf; 3-63 to 10-15-66; Gann PO
YOUNG, Thomas, Hy-75-2; Pvt B Co 15th IA Inf; 9-64 to __; Koko PO; parplysis, drawing 30 per month pension
YOUNG, Thomas J., D-86-1; Cpl D Co 17th TN Inf; 2-4-63 to 6-4-63; PO omitted
YOUNG, Tony, Sh-144-2; US Sol; First Dist

YOUNG, William, Sh-198-1; Pvt Col Inf; 7-63 to 6-65; Memphis PO; lost his discharge
YOUNG, William, Sh-189-3; Drummer F Co 5th US Col Hvy Art; Spring 63 to 4-66; Va. Ave, Memphis PO
YOUNG, William D., D-63-2; Pvt C Co 10th IN Cav; 61 to 65; Nashville PO
YOUNG, William J., Me-88-2; Pacas E. widow of; Pvt; Brittsville PO
YOUNG, William N., White, Li-144-1; Pvt G Co 42nd TN Inf; 4-62 to 6-28-65; Flintville PO
YOUNGBLOOD, Archie, Ca-23-1; Pvt G Co 25th MO Inf; 11-62 to 5-63; Leoni PO; no injuries
YOUNGBLOOD, Artur, Wh-187-1; Pvt; Amanda PO
YOUNGBLOOD, Charles F., K-154-1; Knoxville PO; rank & regiment not found; CONF
YOUNGBLOOD, James F., Dk-32-5; Soldier; Liberty PO
YOUNGBLOOD, Thomas M., Ro-210-9; Pvt; Rockwood PO
YOUNGER, Nathan M., K-180-1; Pvt B Co; 61 to 65; Ebenezer PO
YOUNGER, William, M-107-5; Pvt H Co 4th TN Mtd Inf; 1-1-65 to 8-25-65; Gibb's Cross Roads PO; neuralgia
YOUNT, Allen, G-64-1; Pvt M Co 6th TN; 2-1-63 to 65; Bradford PO
YOUNT, Haret (see Young, Elie)
YOUNT, John F., Cf-42-1; Pvt B Co 1st TN Inf; 6-63 to 8-65; Bellmont PO; deafness--right ear
YOUNT, Robert E., Br-7-3; Pvt F Co 7th TN Mtd Inf; 11-8-64 to 7-25-65; Old Fort PO (Polk Co.); paralysis & blind
YOUNT, Samuel, R-159-1; Pvt A Co 8th OH? Cav; 1-20-63 to 7-31-65; Spring City PO; wounded in leg; not lame enough to be noticed
YOURIE, Thomas J., Dy-25-6(2); Lt D Co 2nd TN Cav; 61 to 5-65 (3 yrs 10 mos); Newbern PO; CONF
YUNG, Rhodia, Ma-124-1; Pvt; Jackson PO
ZACHARY, Branch M., K-174-5; Pvt F Co 3rd TN Inf; 2-12-62 to 2-23-65; Hargus PO; disability of spine of back, not dangersly bad
ZACHARY, Gilbert, K-174-4(3); Pvt F Co 3rd TN Inf; 2-10-62 to 2-28-65; Floyd PO; frost bite of foot, clames one of his feet injured from frost bite
ZACHARY, Milton, Pi-155-2; Pvt B Co 1st KY Cav; 5-20-63 to 9-30-65; Byrdstown PO; lung disease
ZACHARY, Peter A., Pi-155-2; Emiline widow of; Pvt; Byrdstown PO
ZACHERY, Pleasant J., Ov-135-1; Pvt C Co 1st KY Cav; 7-6-61 to 12-31-64; Oakley PO; family could not give co. or dates (?)
ZACHRY, J. K. P., Pi-153-1; Pvt D Co 1st TN Inf; 8-10-63 to 4-28-65; Chanute PO
ZACHRY, Jackson, Pi-153-2; Pvt D Co 32nd KY Inf; 5-1-62 to 4-9-65; Chanute PO
ZACHRY, William, Gr-82-1; Nancy widow of; Sgt G Co 2nd TN Cav; 10-1-63 to 7-6-65; Powder Spring PO
ZACKERY, Charles, K-164-1; 1st Sgt F Co 3rd TN Vol; 2-10-62 to 2-10-65; Knoxville PO
ZANDER, Leopold, D-44-2(1); Katheran widow of; Surgeon 39th NY Inf; 8-11-61 to __; Nashville PO; see pension records
ZIEGLER, Jacob, Me-88-1; Manucia T. widow of; Capt E Co 5th TN Inf; 3-2-62 to __; Birchwood PO
ZIEGLER, Jacob, Mc-109-2; 2nd Lt A Co 4th TN Cav; 8-14-62 to 7-12-65; Ziegler PO; malaria & results 26 yrs
ZIEGLER, William, Bl-4-2; Pvt E Co 5th TN Inf; 3-5-62 to 4-11-65; Pikeville PO
ZIEGLER, William B., Me-90-2(1); Pvt E Co 5th TN Inf; 3-20-62 to 4-24-65; Pine Land PO
ZIEGLER, William L., Me-90-2(1); Pvt E Co 5th TN Inf; 3-20-62 to 4-24-65; Pine Land PO
ZIMMER, John R., Wl-299-2; 15th Civil Dist
ZIMMERLE, Henry, He-64-1; Sgt G Co 10th TN Inf; 6-13-62 to 6-26-65; Lexington PO; rheumatism
ZIMMERMAN, Isaac, Su-239-3; Sol; Pettier PO
ZINCK, Allan, Ce-28-1; Pvt A Co 168th OH Inf; 5-4-64 to 9-9-64; Junkstown PO; varicose in both limbs, had varicose both limbs, forced march
ZORBRO, Rebecca, De-25-2; widow; Decaturville PO
ZUCKER, Simon, Sh-167-2; Sgt K Co 10th US; 3-1-58 to 3-1-63; PO omitted
CHA___, Hugh, Me-90-1; Pvt E Co 5th TN Inf; 3-2-62 to __; Tabor PO
___, Cebrem W., Di-30-2; Pvt I Co 11th TN Inf; 2-63 to 63 (4 mos); Dickson PO

www.ingramcontent.com/pod-product-compliance
Lightning Source LLC
Chambersburg PA
CBHW032000220426
43664CB00005B/83